ST/ESA/STAT/SER.R/48

Department of Economic and Social Affairs
Département des affaires économiques et sociales

2018
Demographic Yearbook
Annuaire démographique

Sixty-ninth issue/Soixante-neuvième édition

United Nations
New York, 2019

Department of Economic and Social Affairs
Département des affaires économiques et sociales

The Department of Economic and Social Affairs of the United Nations is a vital interface between global policies in the economic, social and environmental spheres and national action. The Department works in three main interlinked areas: (i) it compiles, generates and analyses a wide range of economic, social and environmental data and information on which United Nations Member States draw to review common problems and to take stock of policy options; (ii) it facilitates the negotiations of Member States in many intergovernmental bodies on joint courses of action to address ongoing or emerging global challenges; and (iii) it advises interested Governments on the ways and means of translating policy frameworks developed in United Nations conferences and summits into programmes at the country level and, through technical assistance, helps build national capacities.

Le Département des affaires économiques et sociales des Nations Unies assure un rôle essentiel de liaison entre les politiques mondiales en matière économique, sociale et environnementale et les initiatives engagées au niveau national. Le Département articule son action autour de trois grands axes qui se recoupent : i) il compile, génère et analyse un large éventail de données et informations économiques, sociales et environnementales dont se servent les États Membres de l'Organisation pour examiner les problèmes communs et évaluer les diverses options possibles; ii) il facilite les négociations entre les États Membres au sein de nombreux organes intergouvernementaux sur les mesures communes à prendre pour trouver une solution aux problèmes mondiaux, en cours ou émergents; et iii) il donne aux gouvernements intéressés des avis sur les moyens utilisables pour traduire en programmes nationaux les cadres politiques élaborés lors des conférences et des sommets des Nations Unies et, à travers l'assistance technique, il contribue à renforcer les capacités nationales.

NOTE

NOTE

ST/ESA/STAT/SER.R/48

UNITED NATIONS PUBLICATION
Sales number: B.20.XIII.1 H

PUBLICATION DES NATIONS UNIES
Numéro de vente: B.20.XIII.1 H

ISBN 978-92-1-148320-8
eISBN 978-92-1-004366-3
Print ISSN: 0082-8041
Online ISSN: 2412-0006

Topics of the Demographic Yearbook series: 1948 - 2018

Sujets des diverses éditions de l'Annuaire démographique : 1948 - 2018

Year Année	Sales No. - Numéro de vente	Issue - Edition	Special topic - Sujet spécial
1948	49.XIII.1	First-Première	General demography-Démographie générale
1949-50	51.XIII.1	Second-Deuxième	Natality statistics-Statistiques de la natalité
1951	52.XIII.1	Third-Trosième	Mortality statistics-Statistiques de la mortalité
1952	53.XIII.1	Fourth-Quatrième	Population distribution-Répartition de la population
1953	54.XIII.1	Fifth-Cinquième	General demography-Démographie générale
1954	55.XIII.1	Sixth-Sixième	Natality statistics -Statistiques de la natalité
1955	56.XIII.1	Seventh-Septième	Population censuses-Recensement de population
1956	57.XIII.1	Eighth-Huitième	Ethnic and economic characteristics of population-Caractéristiques ethniques et économiques de la population
1957	58.XIII.1	Ninth-Neuvième	Mortality statistics- Statistiques de la mortalité
1958	59.XIII.1	Tenth-Dixième	Marriage and divorce statistics- Statistiques de la nuptialité et de la divortialité
1959	60.XIII.1	Eleventh-Onzième	Natality statistics- Statistiques de la natalité
1960	61.XIII.1	Twelfth-Douzième	Population trends- l' évolution de la population
1961	62.XIII.1	Thirteenth-Treizième	Mortality Statistics- Statistiques de la mortalité
1962	63.XIII.1	Fourteenth-Quatorzième	Population census statistics I- Statistiques des recensements de population I
1963	64.XIII.1	Fifteenth-Quinzième	Population census statistics II- Statistiques des recensements de population II
1964	65.XIII.1	Sixteenth-Seizième	Population census statistics III- Statistiques des recensements de population III
1965	66.XIII.1	Seventeenth-Dix-septième	Natality statistics- Statistiques de la natalité
1966	67.XIII.1	Eighteenth-Dix-huitième	Mortality statistics I- Statistiques de la mortalité I
1967	E/F.68.XIII.1	Nineteenth-Dix-neuvième	Mortality statistics II - Statistiques de la mortalité II
1968	E/F.69.XIII.1	Twentieth-Vingtième	Marriage and divorce statistics-Statistiques de la nuptialité et de la divortialité
1969	E/F.70.XIII.1	Twenty-first-Vingt et unième	Natality statistics-Statistiques de la natalité
1970	E/F.71.XIII.1	Twenty-second-Vingt-deuxième	Population trends-l' évolution de la population
1971	E/F.72.XIII.1	Twenty-third-Vingt-troisième	Population census statistics I- Statistiques de recensements de population I
1972	E/F.73.XIII.1	Twenty-fourth-Vingt-quatrième	Population census statistics II- Statistiques des recensements de population II
1973	E/F.74.XIII.1	Twenty-fifth-Vingt-cinquième	Population census statistics III- Statistiques des recensements de population III
1974	E/F.75.XIII.1	Twenty-sixth-Vingt-sixième	Mortality statistics - Statistiques de la mortalité
1975	E/F.76.XIII.1	Twenty-seventh-Vingt-septième	Natality statistics- Statistiques de la natalité
1976	E/F.77.XIII.1	Twenty-eighth-Vingt-huitième	Marriage and divorce statistics- Statistiques de la nuptialité et de la divortialité
1977	E/F.78.XIII.1	Twenty-ninth-Vingt-neuvième	International Migration Statistics- internationales
1978	E/F.79.XIII.1	Thirtieth-Trentième	General tables- Tableaux de caractère général
1978	E/F.79.XIII.8	Special issue-Edition spéciale	Historical supplement-Supplément rétrospectif
1979	E/F.80.XIII.1	Thirty-first-Trente et unième	Population census statistics-Statistiques des recensements de population
1980	E/F.81.XIII.1	Thirty-second-Trente-deuxième	Mortality statistics- Statistiques de la mortalité
1981	E/F.82.XIII.1	Thirty-third-Trente-troisième	Natality statistics-Statistiques de la natalité
1982	E/F.83.XIII.1	Thirty-fourth-Trente-quatrième	Marriage and divorce statistics-Statistiques de la nuptialité et de la divortialité
1983	E/F.84.XIII.1	Thirty fifth-Trente-cinquième	Population census statistics I-Statistiques des recensements de population I
1984	E/F.85.XIII.1	Thirty-sixth-	Population census statistics II-

Topics of the Demographic Yearbook series: 1948 - 2018

Sujets des diverses éditions de l'Annuaire démographique : 1948 - 2018

Year Année	Sales No. - Numéro de vente	Issue - Edition	Special topic - Sujet spécial
		Trente-sixième	Statistiques des recensements de population II
1985	E/F.86.XIII.1	Thirty-seventh- Trente-septième	Mortality statistics- Statistiques de la mortalité
1986	E/F.87.XIII.1	Thirty-eighth- Trente-huitième	Natality statistics- Statistiques de la natalité
1987	E/F.88.XIII.1	Thirty-ninth- Trente-neuvième	Household composition- Les éléments du ménage
1988	E/F.89.XIII.1	Fortieth- Quarantième	Population census statistics- Statistiques des recensements de population
1989	E/F.90.XIII.1	Forty-first- Quarante-et-unième	International Migration Statistics- Statistiques des migration internationales
1990	E/F.91.XIII.1	Forty-second- Quarante-deuxième	Marriage and divorce statistics- Statistiques de la nuptialité et de la divortialité
1991	E/F.92.XIII.1	Forty-third- Quarante-troisième	General tables- Tableaux de caractère général
1991	E/F.92.XIII.9	Special Issue	Population Ageing and the Situation of Elderly Persons Vieillissement de la population et situation des personnes âgées
1992	E/F.94.XIII.1	Forty-fourth- Quarante-quatrième	Fertility and mortality statistics- Statistiques de la fecondité et de la mortalité
1993	E/F.95.XIII.1	Forty-fifth- Quarante-cinquième	Population census statistics I- Statistiques des recensements de population I
1994	E/F.96.XIII.1	Forty-sixth- Quarante-sixième	Population census statistics II- Statistiques des recensements de population II
1995	E/F.97.XIII.1	Forty-seventh- Quarante-septième	Household composition-Les éléments du ménage
1996	E/F.98.XIII.1	Forty-eighth- Quarante-huitième	Mortality statistics- Statistiques de la mortalité
1997	E/F.99.XIII.1	Forty-ninth- Quarante-neuvième	General tables- Tableaux de caractère général
1997	E/F.99.XIII.12	Special issue- Edition spéciale (CD)	Historical supplement- Supplément rétrospectif
1998	E/F.00.XIII.1	Fiftieth- Cinquantième	General tables- Tableaux de caractère général
1999	E/F.01.XIII.1	Fifty-first- Cinquante-et-unième	General tables- Tableaux de caractère général
1999	E/F.02.XIII.6	Special issue- Edition spéciale (CD)	Natality Statistics- Statistiques de la natalité
2000	E/F.02.XIII.1	Fifty-second- Cinquante-deuxième	General tables- Tableaux de caractère général
2001	E/F.03.XIII.1	Fifty-third- Cinquante- troisième	General tables- Tableaux de caractère général
2002	E/F.05.XIII.1	Fifty-fourth- Cinquante-quatrième	General tables- Tableaux de caractère général
2003	E/F.06.XIII.1	Fifty-fifth- Cinquante-cinquième	General tables- Tableaux de caractère général
2004	E/F.07.XIII.1	Fifty-sixth- Cinquante-sixième	General tables- Tableaux de caractère général
2005	E/F.08.XIII.1	Fifty-seventh- Cinquante-septième	General tables- Tableaux de caractère général
2006	E/F.09.XIII.1	Fifty-eighth- Cinquante-huitième	General tables- Tableaux de caractère général
2007	E/F.10.XIII.1	Fifty-ninth- Cinquante-neuvième	General tables- Tableaux de caractère général
2008	E/F.11.XIII.1	Sixtieth- Soixantième	General tables- Tableaux de caractère général
2009 - 2010	B.12.XIII.1 H	Sixty-first Soixante-et-unième	General tables- Tableaux de caractère général
2011	B.13.XIII.1 H	Sixty-second Soixante- deuxième	General tables- Tableaux de caractère général
2012	B.14.XIII.1 H	Sixty-third Soixante- troisième	General tables- Tableaux de caractère général

Topics of the Demographic Yearbook series: 1948 - 2018

Sujets des diverses éditions de l'Annuaire démographique : 1948 - 2018

Year Année	Sales No. - Numéro de vente	Issue - Edition	Special topic - Sujet spécial
2013	B.15.XIII.1 H	Sixty-fourth Soixante- quatrième	General tables- Tableaux de caractère général
2014	B.16.XIII.1 H	Sixty-fifth Soixante- cinquième	General tables and Whipple's Index, censuses,1985-2014 - Tableaux de caractère général et l'indice de Whipple, recensements, 1985-2014
2015	B.17.XIII.1 H	Sixty-sixth Soixante- sixième	General tables and Whipple's Index, censuses,1985-2015 - Tableaux de caractère général et l'indice de Whipple, recensements, 1985-2015
2016	B.18.XIII.1 H	Sixty-seventh Soixante- septième	General tables and Whipple's Index, censuses,1985-2016 - Tableaux de caractère général et l'indice de Whipple, recensements, 1985-2016
2017	B.19.XIII.1 H	Sixty-eighth Soixante- huitième	General tables and Whipple's Index, censuses,1985-2017 - Tableaux de caractère général et l'indice de Whipple, recensements, 1985-2017
2018	B.20.XIII.1 H	Sixty-ninth Soixante- neuvième	General tables and Whipple's Index, censuses,1985-2018 - Tableaux de caractère général et l'indice de Whipple, recensements, 1985-2018

CONTENTS - TABLE DES MATIERES

Explanations of symbols ix   Explication des signes ix

TEXT	**TEXTE**

INTRODUCTION 1   INTRODUCTION 14

TECHNICAL NOTES ON THE STATISTICAL TABLES   NOTES TECHNIQUES SUR LES TABLEAUX STATISTIQUES

1. General remarks 2   1. Remarques d'ordre général 15

2. Geographical aspects 2   2. Considérations géographiques 16

3. Population 4   3. Population 17

4. Vital statistics 6   4. Statistiques de l'état civil 20

TABLES	**TABLEAUX**

Table	Page	Tableau	Page

A. Demographic Yearbook 2018 synoptic table 30   A. Tableau synoptique de l'Annuaire démographique 2018 30

WORLD SUMMARY   **APERCU MONDIAL**

1. Population, rate of increase, birth and death rates, surface area and density for the world, major areas and regions: selected years 40

1. Population, taux d'accroissement, taux de natalité et taux de mortalité, superficie et densité pour l'ensemble du monde, les grandes régions et les régions géographiques : diverses années 43

2. Estimates of population and its percentage distribution, by age and sex and sex ratio for all ages for the world, major areas and regions: 2018 47

2. Estimations de la population et pourcentage de répartition selon l'âge et le sexe et rapport de masculinité pour l'ensemble du monde, les grandes régions et les régions géographiques : 2018 48

3. Population by sex, annual rate of population change, surface area and density 51

3. Population selon le sexe, taux de changement annuel de la population, superficie et densité 53

3a. Whipple's Index by sex and urban/rural residence 1985 - 2018 69

3a. L'indice de Whipple par le sexe et la résidence urbaine/rurale 1985 - 2018 70

4. Vital statistics summary and life expectancy at birth: 2014 - 2018 85

4. Aperçu des statistiques de l'état civil et de l'espérance de vie à la naissance : 2014 - 2018 87

POPULATION   **POPULATION**

5. Estimations of mid-year population: 2009 - 2018 110

5. Estimations de la population au milieu de l'année : 2009 - 2018 111

6. Total and urban population by sex: 2009 - 2018 120

6. Population totale et population urbaine selon le sexe : 2009 - 2018 126

7. Population by age, sex and urban/rural residence: latest available year, 2009 - 2018 176

7. Population selon l'âge, le sexe et la résidence, urbaine/rurale : dernière année disponible, 2009 - 2018 178

8. Population of capital cities and cities of 100 000 or more inhabitants: latest available year, 1999 - 2018 289

FERTILITY

9. Live births and crude birth rates, by urban/rural residence: 2014 - 2018 362

10. Live births by age of mother and sex of child, general and age-specific fertility rates: latest available year, 2009 - 2018 377

11. Live births and live birth rates by age of father: latest available year, 2009 - 2018 400

FOETAL MORTALITY

12. Late foetal deaths and late foetal death ratios, by urban/rural residence: 2014 - 2018 415

13. Legally induced abortions: 2009 - 2018 425

14. Legally induced abortions by age and number of previous live births of woman: latest available year, 2009 - 2018 430

INFANT AND MATERNAL MORTALITY

15. Infant deaths and infant mortality rates, by urban/rural residence: 2014 - 2018 443

16. Infant deaths and infant mortality rates by age and sex: latest available year, 2009 - 2018 457

17. Maternal deaths and maternal mortality ratios: 2007 - 2016 492

GENERAL MORTALITY

18. Deaths and crude death rates, by urban/rural residence: 2014 - 2018 503

19. Deaths by age and sex and age-specific death rates by sex: latest available year, 2009 - 2018 517

20. Probability of dying in the five year interval following specified age ($_5q_x$), by sex: latest available year, 2004 - 2018 581

21. Life expectancy at specified ages for each sex: latest available year, 1999 - 2018 589

8. Population des capitales et des villes de 100 000 habitants ou plus : dernière année disponible, 1999 - 2018 291

NATALITÉ

9. Naissances vivantes et taux bruts de natalité selon la résidence urbaine/rurale : 2014 - 2018..................... 364

10. Naissances vivantes selon l'âge de la mère et le sexe de l'enfant, taux de fécondité et taux de fécondité par âge : dernière année disponible, 2009 - 2018 379

11. Naissances vivantes et taux de natalité selon l'âge du père : dernière année disponible, 2009 - 2018 402

MORTALITÉ FŒTALES

12. Morts fœtales tardives et rapport de mortinatalité selon la résidence urbaine/rurale : 2014 - 2018 417

13. Avortements provoqués légalement : 2009 - 2018 426

14. Avortements provoqués légalement selon l'âge de la femme et selon le nombre des naissances vivantes précédentes : dernière année disponible, 2009 - 2018............ 431

MORTALITÉ INFANTILE ET MORTALITÉ LIÉE À LA MATERNITÉ

15. Décès d'enfants de moins d'un an et taux de mortalité infantile, selon la résidence urbaine/rurale : 2014 - 2018 445

16. Décès d'enfants de moins d'un an et taux de mortalité infantile selon l'âge et le sexe : dernière année disponible, 2009 - 2018 459

17. Mortalité liée à la maternité, nombre de décès et taux : 2007 - 2016 494

MORTALITÉ GÉNÉRALE

18. Décès et taux bruts de mortalité, selon la résidence urbaine/rurale : 2014 - 2018.......................................505

19. Décès et taux de mortalité selon l'âge, le sexe : dernière année disponible, 2009 - 2018 519

20. Probabilité de décès dans l'intervalle de cinq ans qui suit un âge donné ($_5q_x$), par sexe : dernière année disponible, 2004 - 2018 582

21. Espérance de vie à un âge donnée pour chaque sexe : dernière année disponible, 1999 - 2018 590

NUPTIALITY

22. Marriages and crude marriages rates, by urban/rural residence: 2014 - 2018 608

23. Marriages by age of groom and by age of bride: latest available year, 2009 - 2018 622

DIVORCE

24. Divorces and crude divorce rates by urban/rural residence: 2014 - 2018 666

25. Divorces and percentage distribution by duration of marriage, latest available year: 2009 - 2018 678

ANNEX

I: Annual mid-year population, United Nations estimates: 2009 - 2018 691

II: Vital statistics summary, United Nations medium variant projections: 2015 - 2020 696

INDEX

Historical index 700

Supplemental index of datasets published online.....803

NUPTIALITÉ

22. Mariages et taux bruts de nuptialité, selon la résidence, urbaine/rurale : 2014 - 2018 610

23. Mariages selon l'âge de l'époux et selon l'âge de l'épouse : dernière année disponible, 2009 - 2018 629

DIVORTIALITÉ

24. Divorces et taux bruts de divortialité, selon la résidence, urbaine/rurale : 2014 - 2018 668

25. Divorces et répartition des pourcentages selon la durée du mariage, dernière année disponible : 2009 - 2018 679

ANNEX

I: Population au milieu de l'année, estimations des Nations Unies : 2009 - 2018 691

II: Aperçu des statistiques de l'état civil, variante moyenne, projections des Nations Unies : 2015 - 2020 696

INDEX

Index historique 751

EXPLANATIONS OF SYMBOLS

Category not applicable	..
Data not available..	...
Magnitude zero or less than half of unit employed	-
Provisional	*
Data tabulated by year of registration rather than occurrence	+
Based on less than specified minimum	◆
Relatively reliable data	Roman type
Data of lesser reliability	*Italics*

EXPLICATION DES SIGNES

Sans objet	..
Données non disponibles	...
Néant ou chiffre inférieur à la moitié de l'unité employée	-
Données provisoires	*
Donnée exploitées selon l'année de l'enregistrement et non l'année de l'événement	+
Rapport fondé sur un nombre inférieur à celui spécifié..	◆
Données relativement sûres...	Caractères romains
Données dont l'exactitude est moindre	*Italiques*

INTRODUCTION

The *Demographic Yearbook* is an international compendium of national demographic statistics provided by national statistical authorities to the Statistics Division of the United Nations Department of Economic and Social Affairs. The *Demographic Yearbook* is part of the set of coordinated and interrelated publications issued by the United Nations and its specialized agencies, designed to supply statistical data for such users as demographers, economists, public-health workers and sociologists. Through the co-operation of national statistical services, available official demographic statistics are compiled in the *Demographic Yearbook* for more than 230 countries or areas throughout the world.

The *Demographic Yearbook 2018* is the sixty-ninth issue in a series published by the United Nations since 1948. It contains tables on a wide range of demographic statistics, including a world summary of selected demographic statistics, statistics on the size, distribution and trends in national populations, fertility, foetal mortality, infant and maternal mortality, general mortality, nuptiality and divorce. Data are shown by urban/rural residence, as available. The volume provides Technical Notes, a synoptic table, a historical index and a listing of the issues of the *Demographic Yearbook* published to date. This issue of *Demographic Yearbook* contains data as available including reference year 2018.

This edition of the *Demographic Yearbook* features also table 3a with Whipple's index by sex and urban/rural residence for the population censuses conducted worldwide since 1985. Whipple's index is an index of age preference in age reporting and can therefore serve to highlight some of the problems related to age distribution.

The Technical Notes on the Statistical Tables are provided to assist the reader in using the tables. Table A, the synoptic table, provides an overview of the completeness of data coverage of the current *Demographic Yearbook*. The cumulative historical index is a guide on content and coverage of all sixty-nine issues, and indicates, for each of the topics that have been published, the issues in which they are presented and the years covered. It also contains a list of tables published online through UNdata[1] (http://data.un.org/Explorer.aspx?d=POP). A list of the *Demographic Yearbook* issues, with their corresponding sales numbers and the special topics featured in each issue are shown on pages iii, iv and v. Additionally, all issues of the *Demographic Yearbook* are available online at the Statistics Division's website: https://unstats.un.org/unsd/demographic-social/products/dyb/index.cshtml.

Until the forty-eighth issue (1996), each issue consisted of two parts, the general tables and special topic tables, published in the same volume[2]. Beginning with the forty-ninth issue (1997), the special topic tables were being disseminated in digital format as supplements to the regular issues. Two CD-ROMs have been issued: the *Demographic Yearbook Historical Supplement*, which presents a wide panorama of basic demographic statistics for the period 1948 to 1997, and the *Demographic Yearbook: Natality Statistics*, which contains a series of detailed tables dedicated to natality and covering the period from 1980 to 1998. Later on, three volumes of *Demographic Yearbook* Special Census Topics for the 2000 round of censuses, covering the period from 1995 to 2004, were published on-line at http://unstats.un.org/unsd/demographic/products/dyb/dybcens.htm. Current *Demographic Yearbook* population and housing censuses data for the 2000, 2010 and 2020 rounds (1995 to the present) are presented at https://unstats.un.org/unsd/demographic-social/products/dyb/index.cshtml#censusdatasets. These datasets cover basic population characteristics, educational, household, ethnocultural and economic characteristics, and also foreign-born and foreign population. Special tabulations on household and economic characteristics with data based on population censuses since 1995 are available respectively at https://unstats.un.org/unsd/demographic-social/products/dyb/dyb_household/ and https://unstats.un.org/unsd/demographic-social/products/dyb/dyb_eco/.

Population statistics are not available for all countries or areas, for a variety of reasons. In an effort to provide estimates of mid-year population and of selected vital statistics for all countries and areas, two annexes are presented. Annex I presents United Nations population estimates for the period 2009-2018 and Annex II presents the medium variant estimates of crude birth and death rates, infant mortality and total fertility rates, as well as life expectancy at birth over the period 2015-2020. These data were produced by the United Nations Population Division and are published in the *2019 Revision of World Population Prospects*[3].

Demographic statistics shown in this issue of the *Demographic Yearbook* are available online at the *Demographic Yearbook* website https://unstats.un.org/unsd/demographic-social/products/dyb/index.cshtml#overview.

Information about the Statistics Division's data collection and dissemination programme is also available on the same website. Additional information can be made available by contacting the Statistics Division of the United Nations Department of Economic and Social Affairs at demostat@un.org.

TECHNICAL NOTES ON THE STATISTICAL TABLES

1. GENERAL REMARKS

1.1 Arrangement of Technical Notes

These Technical Notes are designed to provide the reader with relevant information related to the statistical tables. Information pertaining to the *Demographic Yearbook* in general is presented in the sections dealing with geographical aspects, population and vital statistics. In addition, preceding each table are notes describing the variables, remarks on the reliability and limitation of the data, countries and areas covered, and information on the presentation of earlier data. When appropriate, details on computation of rates, ratios or percentages are presented.

1.2 Arrangement of tables

The numbering of tables from one issue of *Demographic Yearbook* to the next is preserved to the extent possible. However, since for some of the tables the numbering may not correspond exactly to those in previous issues, the reader is advised to use the historical index that appears at the end of this book to find the reference to data in earlier issues.

1.3 Source of data

The statistics presented in the *Demographic Yearbook* are national data provided by official statistical authorities unless otherwise indicated. The primary source of data for the *Demographic Yearbook* is a set of questionnaires sent annually by the United Nations Statistics Division to over 230 national statistical services. Data reported on these questionnaires are supplemented, to the extent possible, with data taken from official national publications, official websites and through correspondence with national statistical services. In the interest of comparability, rates, ratios and percentages have been calculated by the Statistics Division of the United Nations, except for the life table functions, the total fertility rate, and also crude birth rate and crude death rate for some countries or areas as appropriately noted. The methods used by the Statistics Division to calculate these rates and ratios are described in the Technical Notes for each table. The population figures used for these computations are those pertaining to the corresponding years published in this or previous issues of the *Demographic Yearbook*.

In cases when data in this issue of the *Demographic Yearbook* differ from those published in earlier issues or related publications, statistics in this issue may be assumed to reflect revisions to the data received by June 2019.

2. GEOGRAPHICAL ASPECTS

2.1 Coverage

Data are shown for all individual countries or areas that provided information. Table 3 is the most comprehensive in geographical coverage, presenting data on population and surface area for all countries or areas with a population of at least 50 persons. Not all of these countries or areas appear in subsequent tables. In many cases the data required for a particular table are not available. In general, the more detailed the data required for a table, the fewer the number of countries or areas that can provide them.

In addition, rates and ratios are presented only for countries or areas reporting at least a minimum number of relevant events. The minimums are stated in the Technical Notes to individual tables.

Except for summary data shown for the world and by major areas and regions in tables 1 and 2 and data shown for capital cities and cities with a population of 100 000 or more in table 8, all data are presented at the national level. The number of countries or areas shown in each table is provided in table A, the synoptic table.

2.2 Territorial composition

To the extent possible, all data, including time series data, relate to the territory within 2018 boundaries. Exceptions are footnoted in individual tables. Relevant clarifications are specified below.

Data relating to **Denmark** exclude Faeroe Islands and Greenland, which are shown separately.

Data relating to **Finland** include Åland Islands, unless otherwise indicated by a footnote.

Data relating to **France** exclude Overseas Departments, which are shown separately, unless otherwise indicated by a footnote.

Data relating to **United Kingdom of Great Britain and Northern Ireland** exclude Guernsey, Isle of Man and Jersey which are shown separately.

Data relating to **Western Sahara** comprise the Northern Region (former Saguia el Hamra) and Southern Region (former Rio de Oro).

2.3 Nomenclature

Because of space limitations, the country or area names listed in the tables are generally the commonly employed short titles currently in use[4] in the United Nations, the full titles being used only when a short form is not available. The latest version of the *Standard Country or Area Codes for Statistics Use* can be accessed at https://unstats.un.org/unsd/methodology/m49/.

2.3.1 Order of presentation

Countries or areas are listed in English alphabetical order within the following continents: Africa, North America, South America, Asia, Europe and Oceania.

The designations and presentation of the material in this publication were adopted solely for the purpose of providing a convenient geographical basis for the accompanying statistical series. The same qualification applies to all notes and explanations concerning the geographical units for which data are presented.

2.4 Surface area data

Surface area data shown in table 1 represent the land area, whereas in table 3 the total surface area unless otherwise indicated. The total surface area comprises land area and inland waters (assumed to consist of major rivers and lakes) and excluding only Polar Regions and uninhabited islands. The surface area given is the most recent estimate available. They are presented in square kilometres; a conversion factor of 2.589988 having been applied to surface areas originally reported in square miles.

2.4.1 Comparability over time

Comparability over time in surface area estimates for any given country or area may be affected by changes in the surface area estimation procedures, increases in actual land surface by reclamation, boundary changes, changes in the concept of "land surface area" used or a change in the unit of measurement used. In most cases it was possible to ascertain the reason for a revision; otherwise, the latest figures have generally been accepted as correct.

2.4.2 International comparability

Lack of international comparability between surface area estimates arises primarily from differences in definition. In particular, there is considerable variation in the treatment of coastal bays, inlets and gulfs, rivers and lakes. International comparability is also impaired by the variation in methods employed to estimate surface area. These range from surveys based on modern scientific methods to conjectures based on diverse types of information. Some estimates are recent while others may not be. Since neither the exact method of determining the surface area nor the precise definition of its composition and time reference is known for all countries or areas, the estimates in table 3 should not be considered strictly comparable from one country or area to another.

3. POPULATION

Population statistics, that is, those pertaining to the size, geographical distribution and demographic characteristics of the population, are presented in a number of tables of the *Demographic Yearbook*.

Summary estimates of the mid-year population of the world, major areas and regions for selected years and of its age and sex distribution in 2018 are set forth in tables 1 and 2, respectively.

Data for countries or areas include population census figures, estimates based on results of sample surveys (in the absence of a census), postcensal or intercensal estimates and those derived from continuous population registers. In the present issue of the *Demographic Yearbook*, the latest available census figure of the total population of each country or area and mid-year estimates for 2010 and 2018 are presented in table 3. Mid-year estimates of total population for ten years (2009-2018) are shown in table 5 and mid-year estimates of urban and total population by sex for ten years (2009-2018) are shown in table 6. The latest available data on population by age, sex and urban/rural residence are given in table 7. The latest available figures on the population of capital cities and of cities or urban agglomerations of 100 000 or more inhabitants are presented in table 8.

The statistics on total population, population by age, sex, or urban/rural distribution are used for the calculation of rates in the *Demographic Yearbook*. Vital rates by residence (urban/rural), age or sex were calculated using data presented in tables 6 or 7 in this issue or the corresponding tables of previous issues of the *Demographic Yearbook*.

3.1 Sources of variation of data

The comparability of data is affected by several factors, including (1) the definition of total population; (2) the definition used to classify the population into its urban/rural components; (3) the accuracy of age reporting; (4) the extent of over-enumeration or under-enumeration in the most recent census or other source of benchmark population statistics; and (5) the quality of population estimates. These five factors will be discussed in some detail in sections 3.1.1 to 3.1.3 below. Other relevant problems are discussed in the technical notes to the individual tables. Readers interested in more detail, relating in particular to the basic concepts of population size, distribution and characteristics as elaborated by the United Nations, should consult the *Principles and Recommendations for Population and Housing Censuses, Revision 3*[5].

3.1.1 Total population

The most important impediment to comparability of total populations is the difference between the concept of a *de facto* and *de jure* population. A *de facto* population includes all persons physically present in the country or area at the reference date. The *de jure* population, by contrast, includes all usual residents of the given country or area, whether or not they were physically present in the area at the reference date. By definition, therefore, a *de facto* total and a *de jure* total are not entirely comparable.

Comparability of even two *de facto* or *de jure* totals is often affected by the fact that strict conformity to either of these concepts is rare. For example, some so-called *de facto* counts do not include foreign military, naval and diplomatic personnel present in the country or area on official duty, and their accompanying family and household members; some do not include foreign visitors in transit through the country or area or transients on ships in harbours. On the other hand, they may include such persons as merchant seamen and fishermen who are temporarily out of the country or area working at their trade.

The *de jure* population figure presents even greater variations in comparability, in part because it depends in the first place on the concept of "usual residence", which varies from one country or area to another and is difficult to apply consistently in a census or survey enumeration. For example, non-national civilians temporarily in a country or area as short-term workers may officially be considered residents after a stay of a specified period of time or they may be considered as non-residents throughout the duration of their stay; at the same time, these individuals may be officially considered as residents or non-residents of the country or area from which they came, depending on the duration and/or purpose of their absence. Furthermore, regardless of the official treatment, individual respondents may apply their own interpretation of residence in responding to the inquiry. In addition, there may be considerable differences in the accuracy with which countries or areas are informed about the number of their residents temporarily out of the country or area.

The population statistics presented in the tables of the *Demographic Yearbook* refer to the *de facto* population or to the *de jure* population. In an effort to overcome, to the extent possible, the effect of the lack of strict conformity to either the *de facto* or the *de jure* concept given above, significant exceptions with respect to inclusions and exclusions of specific population groups, are footnoted when they are known.

A possible source of variation within the statistics of a single country or area may arise from the fact that some countries or areas collect information on both the *de facto* and the *de jure* population in, for example, a census, but prepare detailed tabulations for only the *de jure* population. Hence, even though the total population shown in table 3 is de facto, the figures shown in the tables presenting various characteristics of the population, for example, urban/rural distribution, age and sex distribution, may be on the *de jure* concept.

3.1.2 Urban/rural classification

International comparability of urban/rural distributions is seriously impaired by the wide variation among national definitions of the concept of "urban". The definitions used by individual countries or areas and their implications are shown at the end of technical notes for table 6.

3.1.3 Age distribution

The classification of population by age is a core element of most analyses, estimation and projection of population statistics. Unfortunately, age data are subject to a number of sources of error and non-comparability. Accordingly, the reliability of age data should be of concern to users of these statistics.

3.1.3.1 Collection and compilation of age data

Age is the estimated or calculated interval of time between the date of birth and the date of the census or survey, expressed in completed solar years[6]. There are two methods of collecting information on age. The first is to obtain the date of birth for each member of the population in a census or survey and then to calculate the completed age of the individual by subtracting the date of birth from the date of enumeration[7]. The second method is to record the individual's completed age at the time of the census or survey, that is to say, age at last birthday.

The recommended method is to calculate age at last birthday by subtracting the exact date of birth from the date of the census. Some practices, however, do not use this method but instead calculate the difference between the year of birth and the year of the census. Classifications of this type are footnoted whenever possible. They can be identified to a certain extent by a smaller than expected population under one year of age. However, an irregular number of births from one year to the next or age selective omission of infants may also obscure the expected population under one year of age.

3.1.3.2 *Errors in age data*

Errors in age data may be due to a variety of causes, including ignorance of the correct age; reporting years of age in terms of a calendar concept other than completed solar years since birth[8]; carelessness in reporting and recording age; a general tendency to state age in figures ending in certain digits (such as zero, two, five and eight); a tendency to exaggerate length of life at advanced ages; a subconscious aversion to certain numbers; and wilful misrepresentations.

These reasons for errors in reported age data are common to most investigations of age and to most countries or areas, and they may significantly impair comparability of the data.

As a result of the above-mentioned difficulties, the age-sex distribution of population in many countries or areas shows irregularities which may be summarized as follows: (1) a deficiency in the number of infants and young children; (2) a concentration at ages ending with zero and five (that is, 5, 10, 15, 20, ...); (3) heaping at even ages (for example, 10, 12, 14, ...) relative to odd ages (for example, 11, 13, 15, ...); (4) unexpectedly large differences between the frequency of males and females at certain ages; and (5) unaccountably large differences between the frequencies in adjacent age groups. Comparing of identical age-sex cohorts from successive censuses, as well as studying the age-sex composition of each census, may reveal these and other inconsistencies, some of which in varying degree are characteristic of even the most modern censuses.

This edition of the *Demographic Yearbook* features a tabulation (table 3a) with Whipple's index by sex and urban/ rural residence for the population censuses conducted worldwide since 1985. Whipple's index is an index of age preference in age reporting and can therefore serve to highlight some of the problems related to age distribution.

4. VITAL STATISTICS

For purposes of the *Demographic Yearbook*, vital statistics of concern are those of live birth, death, foetal death, marriage and divorce.

This volume of the *Demographic Yearbook* presents tables on fertility, nuptiality and divorce as well as tables on mortality referring to foetal mortality, infant and maternal mortality and general mortality.

4.1 Sources of variation of data

Most of the vital statistics data published in this *Demographic Yearbook* are sourced from national civil registration systems. The completeness and the accuracy of the data that these systems produce vary from one country or area to another.

National civil registration systems may not exist in all countries, and in some cases, the registration system covers only certain vital events. For example, in some countries or areas only births and deaths are registered. There are also differences in the effectiveness with which national laws pertaining to civil registration operate in the various countries or areas. The manner in which the law is implemented and the degree to which the public complies with the legislation determine the reliability of vital statistics obtained from the civil registers.

It should be noted that some statistics on marriage and divorce are obtained from sources other than civil registers. For example, in some countries or areas, the only source for data on marriages is church registers. Divorce statistics, on the other hand, are obtained from court records and/or civil registers according to national practice. The actual compilation of these statistics may be the responsibility of the civil registrar, the national statistical office or other government offices.

Other factors affecting international comparability of vital statistics are much the same as those that must be considered in evaluating the variations in other population statistics. Differences in statistical definitions of vital events, differences in geographical and ethnic coverage of the data and diverse tabulation procedures may also influence comparability.

In addition to vital statistics from civil registers, some vital statistics published in the *Demographic Yearbook* are official estimates. These estimates are frequently from population censuses and sample surveys. As such, their comparability may be affected by the national completeness of reporting in population censuses and household surveys, whether a *de facto* or *de jure* based census, non-sampling and sampling errors and other sources of bias.

Readers interested in more detailed information on standards for vital statistics should consult the *Principles and Recommendations for a Vital Statistics System Revision 3*[9]; *Guidelines on the Legislative Framework for Civil Registration, Vital Statistics and Identity Management*[10]; *Handbook on Civil Registration and Vital Statistics Systems: Management, Operation and Maintenance, Revision 1*[11]; *Handbook on civil registration, vital statistics and identity management systems: Communication for development*[12]; *Handbook on Civil Registration and Vital Statistics Systems: Policies and Protocols for the Release and Archiving of Individual Records*[13]; and *Handbook on Civil Registration and Vital Statistics Systems: Computerization*[14]. The *Handbook on the Collection of Fertility and Mortality Data*[15] provides information in collection and evaluation of data on fertility and mortality collected in population censuses and household surveys. These publications are also available on the website at https://unstats.un.org/unsd/demographic-social/Standards-and-Methods/index.cshtml.

4.1.1 Statistical definition of events

An important source of variation lies in the statistical definition of each vital event. The *Demographic Yearbook* attempts to collect data on vital events, using the standard definitions put forth in Chapter I of *Principles and Recommendations for a Vital Statistics System Revision 3*. These definitions are as follows:

LIVE BIRTH is the complete expulsion or extraction from its mother of a product of conception, irrespective of the duration of pregnancy, which after such separation breathes or shows any other evidence of life such as beating of the heart, pulsation of the umbilical cord, or definite movement of voluntary muscles, whether or not the umbilical cord has been cut or the placenta is attached; each product of such a birth is considered live-born.

DEATH is the permanent disappearance of all evidence of life at any time after the occurrence of live birth, i.e., the postnatal cessation of vital functions without capability of resuscitation. This definition excludes foetal deaths.

FOETAL DEATH is death prior to the complete expulsion or extraction from its mother of a product of conception, irrespective of the duration of the period of gestation. Death is indicated by the fact that after such separation, the foetus does not breathe or show any other evidence of life, such as beating of the heart, pulsation of the umbilical cord, or definite movement of voluntary muscles.

MARRIAGE is an act, ceremony or process by which the legal relationship of spouses is constituted. The legality of the union may be established by civil, religious or other means as recognized by the laws of each country. Countries may wish to expand the definition to cover civil unions if they are registered. In that case, registered partnership usually refers to a legal construct, entailing registration with the public authorities according to the laws of each country, that becomes the basis for legal conjugal obligations between two persons.

DIVORCE is a final legal dissolution of a marriage, that is, the separation of spouses that confers on the parties the right to remarriage under civil, religious and/or other provisions, according to the laws of each country. In the case where a country recognizes registered partnerships, a legal dissolution of a registered partnership constitutes the legal final dissolution of such a partnership, according to national laws, which confers on the parties the right to enter into another partnership or marriage.

In addition to these internationally recommended definitions, the *Demographic Yearbook* collects and presents data on abortions, defined as:

ABORTION is defined, with reference to the woman, as any interruption of pregnancy before 28 weeks of gestation with a dead foetus. There are two major categories of abortion: spontaneous and induced. Induced abortions are those initiated by deliberate action undertaken with the intention of terminating pregnancy; all other abortions are considered spontaneous.

4.1.2 Problems relating to standard definitions

A basic problem affecting international comparability of vital statistics is deviations from the standard definitions of vital events. An example of this can be seen in the cases of live births and foetal deaths. In some countries or areas, an infant must survive for at least 24 hours, to be inscribed in the live-birth register. Infants who die before the expiration of the 24-hour period are classified as late foetal deaths and, barring special tabulation procedures, they would not be counted either as live births or as deaths. Similarly, in several other countries or areas, those infants who are born alive but die before registration of their birth, are also considered late foetal deaths.

Unless special tabulation procedures are adopted in such cases, the live-birth and death statistics will both be deficient by the number of these infants, while the incidence of late foetal deaths will be increased by the same amount. Hence the infant mortality rate is underestimated. Although both components (infant deaths and live births) are deficient by the same absolute amount, the deficiency is proportionately greater in relation to the infant deaths, causing greater errors in the infant mortality rate than in the birth rate.

Moreover, the practice exaggerates the late foetal death ratios. Some countries or areas make provision for correcting this deficiency (at least in the total frequencies) at the tabulation stage. Data for which the correction has not been made are indicated by a footnote whenever possible.

The definitions used for marriage and divorce also present problems for international comparability. Unlike birth and death, which are biological events, marriage and divorce are defined only in terms of law and custom and as such are less amenable to universally applicable statistical definitions. They have therefore been defined for statistical purposes in general terms referring to the laws of individual countries or areas. Laws pertaining to marriage and particularly to divorce, vary from one country or area to another. With respect to marriage, the most widespread requirement relates to the minimum age at which persons may marry but frequently other requirements are specified.

When known the minimum legal age of men and women at which marriage can occur with or without parental consent is presented in table 23-1. Laws and regulations relating to the dissolution of marriage by divorce range from total prohibition, through a wide range of grounds upon which divorces may be granted, to the granting of divorce in response to a simple statement of desire or intention by spouses.

4.1.3 Fragmentary geographical or ethnic coverage

As per the international standards, vital statistics for any given country or area should cover the entire geographical area and include all ethnic groups. Fragmentary coverage is, however, not uncommon. In some countries or areas, registration is compulsory for only a small part of the population, limited to certain ethnic groups, for example. In other places there is no national provision for compulsory registration, but only municipal or state ordinances that do not cover the entire geographical area. Still others have developed a registration area that comprises only a part of the country or area, the remainder being excluded because of inaccessibility or for economic and cultural considerations that make regular registration practically impossible.

4.1.4 Tabulation procedures

4.1.4.1 By place of occurrence

Vital statistics presented at the national level relate to the de facto, that is, the present-in-area population. Thus, unless otherwise noted, vital statistics for a given country or area cover all the events that occur within its present boundaries and among all segments of the population therein. They may be presumed to include events among nomadic tribes and indigenous peoples, and among nationals and foreigners. When known, deviations from the de facto concept are footnoted.

Urban/rural differentials in vital rates for some countries may vary considerably depending on whether the relevant vital events were tabulated on the basis of place of occurrence or place of usual residence. For example, if a substantial number of women residing in rural areas near major urban centres travel to hospitals or maternity homes located in a city to give birth, urban fertility and neo-natal and infant mortality rates will usually be higher (and the corresponding rural rates will usually be lower) if the events are tabulated on the basis of place of occurrence rather than on the basis of place of usual residence. A similar process will affect general mortality differentials if substantial numbers of persons residing in rural areas use urban health facilities when seriously ill.

4.1.4.2 By date of occurrence versus by date of registration

To the extent possible, the vital statistics presented in the *Demographic Yearbook* refer to events that occurred during the specified year, rather than to those that were registered during that period. However, a considerable number of countries or areas tabulate their vital statistics not by date of occurrence, but by date of registration. Because such statistics can be misleading, the countries or areas known to tabulate vital statistics by date of registration are identified in the tables by a plus sign "+". Since information on the method of tabulating vital statistics is not available for all countries and areas, tabulation by date of registration may be more prevalent than the symbols on the vital statistics tables would indicate.

Because quality of data is inextricably related to the timeliness of registration, this must always be considered in conjunction with the quality code description in section 4.2.1 below. If registration of births is complete and timely (code "C"), the ill effects of tabulating by date of registration are, for all practical purposes, nullified. Similarly, with respect to death statistics, the effect of tabulating events by date of registration may be minimized in many countries or areas in which the sanitary code requires that a death must be registered before a burial permit can be issued, and this regulation tends to make registration prompt. With respect to foetal death, registration is usually done right away or not at all. Therefore, if registration is prompt, the difference between statistics tabulated by date of occurrence and those tabulated by date of registration may be negligible. In many cases, the length of the statutory time period allowed for registering various vital events plays an important part in determining the effects of tabulation by date of registration on the comparability of data.

With respect to marriage and divorce, the practice of tabulating data by date of registration does not generally pose serious problems. In many countries or areas marriage is a civil legal contract which, to establish its legality, must be celebrated before a civil officer. It follows that for these countries or areas registration would tend to be almost automatic at the time of, or immediately following, the marriage ceremony. Because the registration of a divorce in many countries or areas is the responsibility solely of the court or the authority which granted it, and since the registration record in such cases is part of the records of the court proceedings, it follows that divorces are likely to be registered soon after the decree is granted.

On the other hand, if registration is not prompt, vital statistics by date of registration will not produce internationally comparable data. Under the best circumstances, statistics by date of registration will include primarily events that occurred in the immediately preceding year; in countries or areas with less developed systems, tabulations will include some events that occurred many years in the past. Examination of available information reveals that delays of many years are not uncommon for birth registration, though the majority is recorded between two to four years after birth.

As long as registration is not prompt, statistics by date of registration will not be internationally comparable either among themselves or with statistics by date of occurrence.

It should also be mentioned that lack of international comparability is not the only limitation introduced by date-of-registration tabulation. Even within the same country or area, comparability over time may be lost by the practice of counting registrations rather than occurrences. If the number of events registered from year to year fluctuates because of *ad hoc* incentives to stimulate registration, or to the sudden need, for example, for proof of (unregistered) birth or death to meet certain requirements, vital statistics tabulated by date of registration are not useful in measuring and analyzing demographic levels and trends. All they can give is an indication of the fluctuations in the need for a birth, death or marriage certificate and the work-load of the registrars. Therefore, statistics tabulated by date of registration may be of very limited use for either national or international studies.

4.2 Quality of published vital statistics

The quality of vital statistics can be assessed in terms of a number of factors. Most fundamental is the completeness of the civil registration system on which these statistics are based.

4.2.1 Quality code for vital statistics from registers.

In the *Demographic Yearbook* annual "Questionnaire on Vital Statistics" national statistical offices are asked to provide their own estimates of the completeness of the births, deaths, late foetal deaths, marriages and divorces recorded in their civil registers.

On the basis of information from the questionnaires, from direct correspondence and from relevant official publications, it has been possible to classify current national statistics from civil registers of birth, death, infant death, late foetal death, marriage and divorce into three broad quality categories, as follows:

C: Data estimated to be virtually complete, that is, representing at least 90 per cent of the events occurring each year.

U: Data estimated to be incomplete, that is representing less than 90 per cent of the events occurring each year.

|: Data not derived from civil registration systems but considered reliable, such as estimates derived from population and housing censuses.

...: Data for which no specific information is available regarding completeness.

These quality codes appear in the first column of the tables which show total frequencies and crude rates (or ratios) over a period of years for all tables on live births, late foetal deaths, infant deaths, deaths, marriages, and divorces. Reliability of maternal mortality statistics is provided by the World Health Organisation.

The classification of countries and areas in terms of these quality codes may not be uniform. Nevertheless, it was felt that national statistical offices were in the best position to judge the quality of their data. It was considered that even the very broad categories that could be established on the basis of the available information would provide useful indicators of the quality of the vital statistics presented in the *Demographic Yearbook.*

Among the countries or areas indicating that the registration of live births was estimated to be 90 per cent or more complete (and hence classified as "C" or "+C" in table 9), the following countries or areas provided information on the method used to evaluate the completeness estimate:

(a) Demographic analysis – Argentina, Australia, Austria, Brazil, Bulgaria, Chile, China - Hong Kong SAR, Croatia, Dominican Republic, Egypt, Estonia, Italy, Kazakhstan, Kenya. Latvia, Luxemburg, Lithuania, Malaysia, Malta, Mauritius, New Zealand, Panama, Peru, Romania, Republic of Moldova, San Marino, Saudi Arabia, Seychelles, South Africa, State of Palestine and Venezuela (Bolivarian Republic of).

(b) Dual record check – Australia, Austria, Belgium, Brazil, Cuba, Cyprus, Estonia, Faeroe Islands, Greenland, Hungary, Israel, Italy, Latvia, Malaysia, Mongolia, Montserrat, New Zealand, Norway, Oman, Qatar, Republic of Korea, Romania, Saint Vincent and the Grenadines, Uruguay and Venezuela (Bolivarian Republic of).

(c) Other specified methods – Armenia, Aruba, Australia, Bahrain, Bolivia (Plurinational State of), Botswana, Brazil, Curaçao, Denmark, France, Germany, Guatemala, Guinea, India, Ireland, Jordan, Kyrgyzstan, Lebanon, Liechtenstein, Malaysia, Poland, Puerto Rico, Russian Federation, Singapore, Slovenia, Spain, Sweden, Tajikistan, Uzbekistan and Venezuela (Bolivarian Republic of).

Among the countries or areas indicating that the registration of late foetal-deaths was estimated to be 90 per cent or more complete (and hence classified as "C" or "+C" in table 12), the following countries or areas provided information on the method used to evaluate the completeness estimate:

(a) Demographic analysis – Argentina, Armenia, Austria, Bulgaria, Croatia, Egypt, Estonia, Italy, Kazakhstan, Latvia, Lithuania, Luxemburg, Malta, Mauritius, Oman, Republic of Korea, Romania, San Marino, Saudi Arabia and Venezuela (Bolivarian Republic of).

(b) Dual record check – Austria, Belgium, Cuba, Estonia, Greenland, Hungary, Israel, Italy, Latvia, Lithuania, Montserrat, New Zealand, Norway and Romania.

(c) Other specified methods – Bahrain, Denmark, France, Germany, Kyrgyzstan, Poland, Puerto Rico, Slovenia, Spain, Sweden, Russian Federation and Uzbekistan.

Among the countries or areas indicating that the registration of infant deaths was estimated to be 90 per cent or more complete (and hence classified as "C" or "+C" in table 15), the following countries or areas provided information on the method used to evaluate the completeness estimate:

(a) Demographic analysis – Argentina, Armenia, Australia, Austria, Brazil, Bulgaria, Chile, China - Hong Kong SAR, Croatia, Egypt, Estonia, Israel, Italy, Kazakhstan, Kenya, Latvia, Lithuania, Luxemburg, Malta, Mauritius, New Zealand, Oman, Panama, Republic of Korea, Republic of Moldova, Romania, San Marino, Saudi Arabia and Seychelles.

(b) Dual record check – Austria, Belgium, Brazil, Cuba, Cyprus, Estonia, Faeroe Islands, Greenland, Hungary, Ireland, Israel, Italy, Latvia, Lithuania, Mongolia, Montserrat, New Zealand, Norway, Qatar, Romania and Saint Vincent and the Grenadines.

(c) Other specified methods – Aruba, Bahrain, Brazil, Curaçao, Cayman Islands, Denmark, France, Germany, Guinea, Kyrgyzstan, Lebanon, Liechtenstein, Poland, Puerto Rico, Russian Federation, Singapore, Slovenia, Spain, Sweden, Tajikistan and Uzbekistan.

Among the countries or areas indicating that the registration of deaths was estimated to be 90 per cent or more complete (and hence classified as "C" or "+C" in table 18), the following countries or areas provided information on the method used to evaluate the completeness estimate:

(a) Demographic analysis – Argentina, Australia, Austria, Brazil, Bulgaria, Chile, China - Hong Kong SAR, Croatia, Dominican Republic, Egypt, Estonia, Israel, Italy, Kazakhstan, Latvia, Lithuania, Luxemburg, Malaysia, Malta, Mauritius, New Zealand, Oman, Panama, Peru, Republic of Korea, Republic of Moldova, Romania, San Marino, Saudi Arabia, Seychelles, South Africa, State of Palestine, United States of America and Venezuela (Bolivarian Republic of).

(b) Dual record check – Austria, Belgium, Brazil, Cuba, Cyprus, Estonia, Faeroe Islands, Greenland, Hungary, Israel, Italy, Latvia, Lithuania, Malaysia, Mongolia, Montserrat, New Zealand, Norway, Qatar, Romania, Saint Vincent and the Grenadines and Venezuela (Bolivarian Republic of).

(c) Other specified methods – Armenia, Aruba, Bahrain, Botswana, Brazil, Curaçao, Denmark, France, Germany, Guinea, India, Kyrgyzstan, Liechtenstein, Poland, Puerto Rico, Russian Federation, Singapore, Slovenia, Spain, Sweden, United States of America and Uzbekistan.

Among the countries or areas indicating that the registration of marriages was estimated to be 90 per cent or more complete (and hence classified as "C" or "+C" in table22), the following countries or areas provided information on the method used to evaluate the completeness estimate:

(a) Demographic analysis – Argentina, Australia, Austria, Bulgaria, Chile, China - Hong Kong SAR, Croatia, Egypt, Estonia, Italy, Latvia, Lithuania, Luxemburg, Malta, Mauritius, Republic of Moldova, Romania, San Marino, Saudi Arabia, Seychelles and Venezuela (Bolivarian Republic of).

(b) Dual record check – Austria, Belgium, Cuba, Estonia, Faeroe Islands, Hungary, Italy, Kazakhstan, Latvia, New Zealand, Norway, Oman, Qatar, Republic of Korea, Romania and State of Palestine.

(c) Other specified methods – Aruba, Curaçao, Denmark, France, Germany, Jordan, Kyrgyzstan, Lebanon, Liechtenstein, Poland, Puerto Rico, Russian Federation, Slovenia, Spain, Sweden, Tajikistan and Uzbekistan.

Among the countries or areas indicating that the registration of divorces was estimated to be 90 per cent or more complete (and hence classified as "C" or "+C" in table 24), the following countries or areas provided information on the method used to evaluate the completeness estimate:

(a) Demographic analysis – Australia, Austria, Bulgaria, Croatia, Egypt, Estonia, Italy, Latvia, Lithuania, Luxemburg, Republic of Moldova, Romania, San Marino, Saudi Arabia, Seychelles and Venezuela (Bolivarian Republic of).

(b) Dual record check – Austria, Belgium, Cuba, Estonia, Faeroe Islands, Hungary, Italy, Kazakhstan, Latvia, New Zealand, Norway, Oman, Qatar, Republic of Korea, Romania and State of Palestine.

(c) Other specified methods – Aruba, Curaçao, Denmark, Germany, Jordan, Kyrgyzstan, Lebanon, Liechtenstein, Mauritius, Poland, Puerto Rico, Russian Federation Slovenia, Sweden, Tajikistan and Uzbekistan.

4.2.2 Treatment of vital statistics from registers

On the basis of the quality code described above, the vital statistics shown in all tables of the *Demographic Yearbook* are treated as either reliable or unreliable. Data coded "C" are considered reliable and appear in roman type. Data coded "U" or "..." are considered unreliable and appear in *italics*.

It should be noted that the indications of reliability used for infant mortality rates, maternal mortality ratios and late foetal death ratios (all of which are calculated using the number of live births in the denominator) are determined on the basis of the quality codes for infant deaths, deaths and late foetal deaths respectively. To evaluate these rates and ratios more precisely, one would have to take into account the quality of the live-birth data used in the denominator of these rates and ratios. The quality codes for live births are shown in table 9 and described more fully in the text of the technical notes for that table.

4.2.3 Treatment of estimated vital statistics

In addition to data from vital registration systems, estimated frequencies and rates of the events, usually *ad hoc* official estimates that have been derived either from the results of a population census or sample survey or by demographic analyses, also appear in the *Demographic Yearbook*. Estimated frequencies and rates have been included in the tables because it is assumed that they provide information that is more accurate than that from existing civil registration systems. By implication, they are assumed to be reliable and as such they are set in roman type.

Estimated data are denoted by the symbol "|".

4.3 Cause of death

World Health Organization (WHO) Member States are bound by the International Nomenclature Regulations to provide the Organization with cause of death data coded in accordance with the current revision of the International Statistical Classification of Diseases and Related Health Problems (ICD). In order to promote international comparability of cause of death statistics, the World Health Organization organizes and conducts an international conference for the revision of the ICD on a regular basis in order to ensure that the Classification is kept current with the most recent clinical and statistical concepts. The data are now usually submitted to WHO at the full four-character level of detail provided by the ICD and are compiled and stored in the WHO Mortality Database at the level of detail as provided by the country. Data from the WHO Mortality Database are available in electronic format at http://www3.who.int/whosis/menu.cfm.

Although revisions provide an up-to-date version of the ICD, such revisions create several problems related to the comparability of cause of death statistics. The first is the lack of comparability over time that inevitably accompanies the use of a new classification. The second problem affects comparability between countries and areas because they may adopt a new classification at different times. The more refined the classification becomes the greater is the need for expert clinical diagnosis of cause of death. In many countries or areas, few of the deaths occur in the presence of an attendant who is medically trained, i.e., most deaths are certified by a non-medically trained attendant. Because the ICD contains many diagnoses that cannot be identified by a non-medically trained person, the ICD is not always accurately or precisely used, which affects international comparability particularly between countries and areas where the level of medical services differs widely.

The chapters of the tenth revision[16], consist of an alphanumeric coding scheme of one letter followed by three numbers at the four-character level. Chapter one contains infectious and parasitic diseases, chapter two refers to all neoplasms, chapter three to disorders of the immune mechanism including diseases of the blood and blood-forming organs; and chapter four to endocrine, nutritional and metabolic diseases. The remaining chapters group diseases according to the anatomical site affected, except for chapters that refer to mental disorders; complications of pregnancy, childbirth and the puerperium; congenital malformations; and conditions originating in the perinatal period. Finally, an entire chapter is devoted to symptoms, signs, and abnormal findings. The eleventh revision is released in 2018 and is available online at https://www.who.int/classifications/icd/en/.

4.3.1 Maternal mortality

According to the tenth revision of the ICD, "Maternal death" is defined as the death of a woman while pregnant or within 42 days of termination of pregnancy, irrespective of the duration and the site of the pregnancy, from any cause related to or aggravated by the pregnancy or its management but not from accidental or incidental causes.

"Maternal deaths" should be subdivided into direct and indirect obstetric deaths. Direct obstetric deaths are those resulting from obstetric complications of the pregnant state (pregnancy, labour and puerperium), from interventions, omissions, incorrect treatment, or from a chain of events resulting from any of the above. Indirect obstetric deaths are those resulting from previous existing disease or disease that developed during pregnancy and which was not due to direct obstetric causes, but which was aggravated by physiologic effects of pregnancy.

While the denominator for the maternal mortality ratio theoretically should be the number of pregnant women, it is impossible to determine the number of pregnant women. A further recommendation by the tenth revision is therefore that maternal mortality ratios be expressed per 100,000 live births or per 100,000 total births (live births and foetal deaths). The maternal mortality ratio calculated here is expressed per 100,000 live births. Although live births do not represent an unbiased estimate of pregnant women, this figure is more reliable than other estimates. In particular, live births are more accurately registered than live births plus foetal deaths.

---

[1] UNdata is an Internet based data service maintained by the Statistics Division of the United Nations Department of Economic and Social Affairs.

[2] There are two exceptions – the 1978 and 1991 issues, which were disseminated in separate volumes from the respective regular issues.

[3] United Nations, Department of Economic and Social Affairs, Population Division (2019), *2019 Revision of World Population Prospects* (https://population.un.org/wpp/).

[4] ST/ESA/STAT/SER.M/49/Rev.4/WWW; https://unstats.un.org/unsd/methodology/m49/; see also Standard Country or Area Codes for Statistical Use, Sales No. M.98.XVII.9, United Nations, New York, 1999.

[5] Sales No. E.15.XVII.10, United Nations, New York, 2015.

[6] Ibid, para. 4.151.

[7] Alternatively, if a population register is used, completed ages are calculated by subtracting the date of birth of individuals listed in the register from a reference date to which the age data pertain.

[8] A source of non-comparability may result from differences in the method of reckoning age, for example, the Western versus the Eastern or, as it is usually known, the English versus the Chinese system. By the latter, a child is considered one year old at birth and advances an additional year at each Chinese New Year. The effect of this system is most obvious at the beginning of the age span, where the frequencies in the under-one-year category are markedly understated. The effect on higher age groups is not so apparent. Distributions constructed on this basis are often adjusted before publication, but the possibility of such aberrations should not be excluded when census data by age are compared.

[9] Sales No. E.13.XVII.10, United Nations, New York, 2014.

[10] https://unstats.un.org/unsd/demographic-social/Standards-and-Methods/files/Handbooks/crvs/CRVS_GOLF_Final_Draft-E.pdf United Nations, New York, 2019.

[11] https://unstats.un.org/unsd/demographic-social/Standards-and-Methods/files/Handbooks/crvs/crvs-mgt-E.pdf United Nations, New York, 2018.

[12] https://unstats.un.org/unsd/demographic-social/Standards-and-Methods/files/Handbooks/crvs/CRVS-IdM-E.pdf United Nations, New York, 2019.

[13] Sales No. E.98.XVII.6, United Nations, New York, 1998.

[14] Sales No. E.98.XVII.10, United Nations, New York, 1998.

[15] Sales No. E.03.XVII.11, United Nations, New York, 2004.

[16] *International Statistical Classification of Diseases and Related Health Problems*, Tenth Revision, Volume 2, World Health Organization, Geneva, 1992.

INTRODUCTION

L'Annuaire démographique est un recueil de statistiques démographiques internationales qui est établi par la Division de statistique du Département des affaires économiques et sociales de l'Organisation des Nations Unies. Il fait partie d'un ensemble de publications complémentaires publiées par l'Organisation des Nations Unies et les institutions spécialisées, qui ont pour objet de fournir des statistiques aux démographes, aux économistes, aux spécialistes de la santé publique et aux sociologues. Grâce à la coopération des services nationaux de statistique, il a été possible de faire figurer dans la présente édition de *l'Annuaire démographique* les statistiques officielles disponibles pour plus de 230 pays ou zones du monde entier.

L'Annuaire démographique 2018 est la soixante-neuvième édition d'une série que publie l'ONU depuis 1948. Le présent volume comprend un aperçu mondial des statistiques démographiques de base et des tableaux qui regroupent des statistiques sur la dimension, la répartition et les tendances de la population, la natalité, la mortalité fœtale, la mortalité infantile et la mortalité liée à la maternité, la mortalité générale, la nuptialité et la divortialité. Des données classées selon le lieu de résidence (zone urbaine ou rurale) sont présentées dans un grand nombre de tableaux. *L'Annuaire démographique* contient des notes techniques, un tableau synoptique, un index historique et une liste des éditions de *l'Annuaire démographique* publiées jusqu'à présent. Cette édition de l'*Annuaire démographique* contient les données disponibles couvrant les années de référence jusqu'à 2018.

La présente édition de l'*Annuaire démographique* comprend aussi le tableau 3a avec l'indice de Whipple selon le sexe et la résidence urbaine/rurale pour les recensements de la population effectués dans le monde entier depuis 1985. L'indice de Whipple est un indice de préférence pour certains âges dans la déclaration de l'âge et peut donc servir à mettre en évidence certaines des difficultés liées à la répartition par âge.

Les notes techniques sur les tableaux statistiques sont destinées à aider le lecteur. Le tableau A, qui correspond au tableau synoptique, donne un aperçu de l''exhaustivité des données publiées dans la présente édition de l'*Annuaire démographique*. Un index cumulatif donne des renseignements sur les matières traitées dans chacune des 69 éditions et sur les années sur lesquelles portent les données. L'index contient aussi une liste des tableaux publiés en ligne à travers le portail UNdata[1] (http://data.un.org/Explorer.aspx?d=POP). Les numéros de vente des éditions antérieures et une liste des sujets spéciaux traités dans les différentes éditions sont indiqués aux pages iii, iv, et v. En plus, toutes les éditions de l'*Annuaire démographique* sont disponibles en ligne sur le site web de la Division des Statistiques : https://unstats.un.org/unsd/demographic-social/products/dyb/index.cshtml

Jusqu'à la quarante-huitième édition (1996), chaque édition se composait de deux parties : les tableaux de caractère général et ceux sur des sujets spéciaux, publiés dans le même volume[2]. À partir de quarante-neuvième édition (1997), les tableaux sur les sujets spéciaux ont été publiés dans un format numérique en tant que suppléments à l'*Annuaire démographique*. Deux CD-ROM ont été produits : l'*Annuaire démographique : Supplément historique*, qui présente un grand nombre de statistiques démographiques pour la période allant de 1948 à 1997, et l'*Annuaire démographique : Statistiques de la natalité*, qui contient des tableaux détaillés sur la natalité pour la période allant de 1980 à 1998. Par la suite, trois volumes concernant l'*Annuaire démographique* consacrés à des thèmes de recensement spéciaux pour le cycle de recensements de 2000 ont été publiés en ligne à l'adresse suivante : http://unstats.un.org/unsd/demographic/products/dyb/dybcens.htm. Les données actuelles sur les thèmes du recensement de l'*Annuaire démographique* pour les années de référence entre 1995 et aujourd'hui, lorsqu'elles sont disponibles, sont présentées sur https://unstats.un.org/unsd/demographic-social/products/dyb/index.cshtml#censusdatasets. Ils comprennent des données sur la population selon les principales caractéristiques démographiques, scolaires, ethnoculturelles et économiques, les caractéristiques des ménages ainsi que des données sur les étrangers dans le pays ou les personnes nées à l'étranger. Particulièrement, on a présenté sous forme de table aux adresses suivantes, les données des recensements pour les années de référence entre 1995 et aujourd'hui, qui portent sur les thèmes des caractéristiques des ménages et des caractéristiques économiques : https://unstats.un.org/unsd/demographic-social/products/dyb/dyb_household/ et https://unstats.un.org/unsd/demographic-social/products/dyb/dyb_eco/.

Les statistiques sur la population ne sont pas disponibles pour tous les pays et zones pour plusieurs raisons. Deux annexes sont présentées afin d'offrir des estimations sur la population en milieu d'année et un aperçu des statistiques de l'état civil pour chaque pays ou zone. La première porte sur des estimations concernant la population pour la période 2009-2018. La seconde présente les estimations des variantes moyennes concernant les taux bruts de natalité et de mortalité, la mortalité infantile, les indicateurs synthétiques de fécondité et l'espérance de vie à la naissance pour la période 2015-2020. Ces données ont été établies par la Division de la population de l'ONU et publiées dans les *Perspectives de la population mondiale : La révision de 2019*[3].

Les statistiques démographiques figurant dans la présente édition de l'*Annuaire démographique* sont disponibles en ligne sur les pages Web consacrées à *l'Annuaire démographique* : https://unstats.un.org/unsd/demographic-social/products/dyb/index.cshtml#overview. On trouvera également des renseignements sur le programme de collecte et de diffusion des données de la Division de statistique sur le même site. Il est possible de se procurer d'autres données en contactant la Division de statistique du Département des affaires économiques et sociales de l'Organisation des Nations Unies à l'adresse suivante : demostat@un.org.

NOTES TECHNIQUES SUR LES TABLEAUX STATISTIQUES

1. REMARQUES D'ORDRE GÉNÉRAL

1.1 Notes techniques

Les notes techniques ont pour but de donner au lecteur des informations pertinentes en lien avec les tableaux statistiques. Les renseignements qui concernent l'*Annuaire démographique* en général sont présentés dans des sections portant sur diverses considérations géographiques, sur la population et sur les statistiques de natalité et de mortalité. Les tableaux sont ensuite commentés séparément et l'on trouvera pour chacun une description des variables et des observations sur la fiabilité et les lacunes des données ainsi que sur les pays et zones visés et sur les données publiées antérieurement. Des détails sont également donnés, le cas échéant, sur le mode de calcul des taux, quotients et pourcentages.

1.2 Tableaux

Dans la mesure du possible, la numérotation des tableaux dans les éditions successives de *l'Annuaire démographique* est préservée. Comme la numérotation des tableaux ne correspond pas exactement à celle des éditions précédentes, il est recommandé de se reporter à l'index qui figure à la fin du présent ouvrage pour trouver les données publiées dans les précédentes éditions.

1.3 Origine des données

Sauf indication contraire, les statistiques présentées dans *l'Annuaire démographique* sont des données nationales fournies par les organismes de statistique officiels. Elles sont recueillies essentiellement au moyen de questionnaires qui sont envoyés tous les ans à plus de 230 services nationaux de statistique. Les données communiquées en réponse à ces questionnaires sont complétées, dans toute la mesure possible, par des données tirées de publications nationales officielles et des sites web d'organismes officiels et des renseignements communiqués par les services nationaux de statistique à la demande de l'ONU. Pour que les données soient comparables, les taux, rapports et pourcentages ont été calculés par la Division de statistique de l'ONU, à l'exception des paramètres des tables de mortalité et des indicateurs synthétiques de fécondité ainsi que des taux bruts de natalité et de mortalité pour certains pays et zones, qui ont été dûment signalés en note. Les méthodes suivies par la Division pour le calcul des taux et rapports sont décrites dans les notes techniques relatives à chaque tableau. Les chiffres de population utilisés pour ces calculs sont ceux qui figurent dans la présente édition de *l'Annuaire démographique* ou qui ont paru dans des éditions antérieures.

Chaque fois que l'on constatera des différences entre les données du présent volume et celles des éditions antérieures de *l'Annuaire démographique*, ou de certaines publications apparentées, on pourra en conclure que les statistiques publiées cette année sont des chiffres révisés communiqués à la Division de statistique avant juin 2019.

2. CONSIDÉRATIONS GÉOGRAPHIQUES

2.1 Portée

Des données sont présentées sur tous les pays ou zones qui en ont communiquées. Le tableau 3, le plus complet, contient des données sur la population et la superficie de chaque pays ou zone ayant une population d'au moins 50 habitants. Ces pays ou zones ne figurent pas tous dans les tableaux qui suivent. Dans bien des cas, les données requises pour un tableau particulier n'étaient pas disponibles. En général, les pays ou zones qui peuvent fournir des données sont d'autant moins nombreux que les données demandées sont plus détaillées.

De plus, les taux et rapports ne sont présentés que pour les pays ou zones ayant communiqué des chiffres correspondant à un nombre minimal de faits considérés. Les minimums sont indiqués dans les notes techniques relatives à chacun des tableaux.

À l'exception des données récapitulatives présentées dans les tableaux 1 et 2 pour l'ensemble du monde et les grandes zones et régions et des données relatives aux capitales et aux villes de 100 000 habitants ou plus dans le tableau 8, toutes les données se rapportent aux pays. Le nombre de pays sur lequel porte chacun des tableaux est indiqué dans le tableau A.

2.2 Composition territoriale

Autant que possible, toutes les données, y compris les séries chronologiques, se rapportent au territoire de 2018. Les exceptions à cette règle sont signalées en note à la fin des tableaux. Des clarifications importantes sont présentées ci-dessous.

Les données relatives au **Danemark** ne comprennent pas les Îles Féroé et le Groenland, qui font l'objet de rubriques distinctes.

Les données relatives à la **Finlande** comprennent les Îles d'Åland, sauf indication contraire en note de bas de page.

Les données relatives à la **France** ne comprennent pas les départements d'outre-mer, qui font l'objet de rubriques distinctes, sauf indication contraire en note de bas de page.

Les données relatives au **Royaume-Uni de Grande-Bretagne et d'Irlande du Nord** ne comprennent pas la Guernesey, l'île de Man et Jersey, qui font l'objet de rubriques distinctes.

Les données relatives au **Sahara Occidental** comprennent la région septentrionale (ancien Saguia-el-Hamra) et la région méridionale (ancien Rio de Oro).

2.3 Nomenclature

En règle générale, pour gagner de la place, on a jugé commode de désigner dans les tableaux les pays ou zones par les noms abrégés couramment utilisés par l'Organisation des Nations Unies[4], les désignations complètes n'étant utilisées que lorsqu'il n'existait pas de forme abrégée. La liste des désignations des pays ou zones est disponible à l'adresse suivante : https://unstats.un.org/unsd/methodology/m49/ .

2.3.1 Ordre de présentation

Les pays ou zones sont classés dans l'ordre alphabétique anglais et regroupés par continent comme ci-après : Afrique, Amérique du Nord, Amérique du Sud, Asie, Europe et Océanie.

Les appellations employées dans la présente édition et la présentation des données qui y figurent n'ont d'autre objet que de donner un cadre géographique commode aux séries statistiques. La même observation vaut pour toutes les notes et précisions concernant les unités géographiques pour lesquelles des données sont présentées.

2.4 Superficie

Les données relatives à la superficie qui figurent dans le tableaux 1 représentent la superficie des terres alors que les données relatives à la superficie qui figurent dans le tableaux 3 représentent la superficie totale, sauf indication contraire par une note. La superficie totale englobe les terres émergées (la superficie des terres) et les eaux intérieures qui sont censées comprendre les principaux lacs et cours d'eau, mais excluent les régions polaires et les îles inhabitées. Les données relatives à la superficie correspondent aux chiffres estimatifs les plus récents. Les superficies sont toutes exprimées en kilomètres carrés ; les chiffres qui avaient été communiqués en miles carrés ont été convertis au moyen d'un coefficient de 2,589988.

2.4.1 Comparabilité dans le temps

La révision des estimations antérieures de la superficie, des augmentations effectives de la superficie terrestre due par exemple à des travaux d'assèchement, à des rectifications de frontières, à des changements d'interprétation du concept de « terres émergées » ou à l'utilisation de nouvelles unités de mesure peut avoir des incidences sur la comparabilité dans le temps des estimations relatives à la superficie d'un pays ou d'une zone donnés. Dans la plupart des cas, il a été possible de déterminer la raison de ces révisions ; toutefois, même lorsque la raison n'était pas connue, on a généralement admis que ces derniers sont exacts.

2.4.2 Comparabilité internationale

Le manque de comparabilité internationale entre les données relatives à la superficie est dû principalement à des différences de définition. En particulier, la définition des golfes, baies et criques, lacs et cours d'eau varie sensiblement d'un pays à l'autre. La diversité des méthodes employées pour estimer les superficies nuit elle aussi à la comparabilité internationale. Certaines données proviennent de levés effectués selon des méthodes scientifiques modernes ; d'autres ne représentent que des conjectures reposant sur diverses catégories de renseignements. Certains chiffres sont récents, d'autres pas. Étant donné que ni la méthode de calcul de la superficie ni la composition du territoire et la date à laquelle se rapportent les données ne sont connues avec précision pour tous les pays ou zones, les estimations figurant dans le tableau 3 ne doivent pas être considérées comme rigoureusement comparables d'un pays ou d'une zone à une autre.

3. POPULATION

Les statistiques de la population, c'est-à-dire celles qui se rapportent à la dimension, à la répartition géographique et aux caractéristiques démographiques de la population, sont présentées dans un certain nombre de tableaux de *l'Annuaire démographique*.

Les tableaux 1 et 2 présentent respectivement des estimations récapitulatives de milieu d'année de la population du monde, des grandes zones et régions, pour certaines années présélectionnées, ainsi que de sa répartition selon l'âge et le sexe pour l'année 2018.

Les données concernant les pays ou les zones représentent les résultats de recensements de population, des estimations fondées sur les résultats d'enquêtes par sondage (s'il n'y a pas eu recensement), des estimations postcensitaires ou intercensitaires, ou des estimations établies à partir de données provenant des registres permanents de population. Dans la présente édition, le tableau 3 indique pour chaque pays ou zone le chiffre le plus récent de la population totale issu du dernier recensement et des estimations établies au milieu de l'année 2010 et de l'année 2018. Le tableau 5 contient des estimations de la population totale au milieu de chaque année pendant 10 ans (2009-2018), et le tableau 6 des estimations de la population urbaine et de la population totale, par sexe, au milieu de chaque année pendant 10 ans (2009-2018). Les dernières données disponibles sur la répartition de la population selon l'âge, le sexe et le lieu de résidence (zone urbaine ou rurale) sont présentées dans le tableau 7. Les derniers chiffres disponibles sur la population des capitales et des villes de 100 000 habitants ou plus sont regroupés dans le tableau 8.

On a utilisé pour le calcul des taux les statistiques de la population totale et de la population répartie selon l'âge, le sexe ou le lieu de résidence (zone urbaine ou rurale). Les taux démographiques selon la résidence (urbaine/rurale), l'âge ou le sexe ont été calculés à partir des données présentées dans les tableaux 6 ou 7 de la présente édition ou dans les tableaux correspondants d'éditions précédentes de *l'Annuaire démographique*.

3.1 Sources de variation des données

Plusieurs facteurs influent sur la comparabilité des données : 1) la définition de la population totale ; 2) les définitions utilisées pour faire la distinction entre population urbaine et population rurale ; 3) les difficultés liées aux déclarations d'âge ; 4) l'étendue du surdénombrement ou du sous-dénombrement dans le recensement le plus récent ou dans une autre source de statistiques de référence sur la population ; 5) la qualité des estimations relatives à la population. Ces cinq facteurs sont analysés en détail aux sections 3.1.1 à 3.1.3 ci-après. D'autres questions seront traitées dans les notes techniques relatives à chaque tableau. Pour plus de précisions concernant, notamment, les notions fondamentales de dimension, de répartition et de caractéristiques de la population qui ont été élaborées par l'Organisation des Nations Unies, le lecteur est invité à se reporter aux *Principes et recommandations concernant les recensements de la population et de l'habitat, Révision 3*[5].

3.1.1 Population totale

Le principal obstacle à la comparabilité des données relatives à la population totale est la différence qui existe entre population de fait et population de droit. La population de fait comprend toutes les personnes présentes dans le pays ou la zone à la date de référence, tandis que la population de droit comprend toutes celles qui résident habituellement dans le pays ou la zone, qu'elles y aient été ou non présentes à la date de référence. Par définition, la population totale de fait et la population totale de droit ne sont donc pas rigoureusement comparables entre elles.

Même lorsque l'on veut comparer deux totaux qui se rapportent à des populations de fait ou deux totaux qui se rapportent à des populations de droit, on risque souvent de faire des erreurs pour cette raison qu'il est rare que l'une et l'autre notions soient appliquées strictement. Pour citer quelques exemples, certains chiffres qui sont censés porter sur la population de fait ne tiennent pas compte du personnel militaire, naval et diplomatique étranger en fonction dans le pays ou la zone, ni des membres de leurs familles et de leurs ménages ; d'autres ne comprennent pas les visiteurs étrangers de passage dans le pays ou la zone ni les personnes à bord de navires ancrés dans des ports. En revanche, il arrive que l'on compte des personnes, inscrits maritimes et marins pêcheurs par exemple, qui, en raison de leur activité professionnelle, se trouvent hors du pays ou de la zone de recensement.

Les risques de disparités sont encore plus grands quand il s'agit de comparer des populations de droit, car les comparaisons dépendent au premier chef de la définition que l'on donne à l'expression « lieu de résidence habituel », qui varie d'un pays ou d'une zone à l'autre et qu'il est, de toute façon, difficile d'appliquer uniformément pour le dénombrement lors d'un recensement ou d'une enquête. Par exemple, les civils étrangers qui se trouvent temporairement dans un pays ou une zone comme travailleurs à court terme peuvent officiellement être considérés comme résidents après un séjour d'une durée déterminée, mais ils peuvent aussi être considérés comme non-résidents pendant toute la durée de leur séjour ; ailleurs, ces mêmes personnes peuvent être considérées officiellement comme résidents ou comme non-résidents du pays ou de la zone d'où elles viennent, selon la durée et, éventuellement, la raison de leur absence. En plus, quel que soit son statut officiel, chacun des recensés peut, au moment de l'enquête, interpréter à sa façon la notion de résidence. De plus, les autorités nationales ou les entités responsables des zones ne savent pas toutes avec la même précision combien de leurs résidents se trouvent temporairement à l'étranger.

Les chiffres de population présentés dans les tableaux de *l'Annuaire démographique* représentent la population de fait ou la population de droit. Lorsque l'on savait que les données avaient été recueillies selon une définition de la population de fait ou de la population de droit qui s'écartait sensiblement de celle exposée plus haut, on l'a signalé en note, de manière à compenser dans toute la mesure possible les conséquences des divergences.

Il peut y avoir hétérogénéité dans les statistiques d'un même pays ou d'une même zone dans le cas des pays ou zones qui ne font une exploitation statistique détaillée des données que pour la population de droit alors qu'ils recueillent des données sur la population de droit et sur la population de fait à l'occasion d'un recensement, par exemple. Ainsi, tandis que les chiffres relatifs à la population totale qui figurent au tableau 3 se rapportent à la population de fait, ceux des tableaux qui présentent des données sur diverses caractéristiques de la population, par exemple le lieu de résidence (zone urbaine ou rurale), l'âge et le sexe, peuvent être basés sur le concept de la population de droit.

3.1.2 Lieu de résidence (zone urbaine ou rurale)

L'hétérogénéité des définitions nationales du terme « urbain » nuit considérablement à la comparabilité internationale des données concernant la répartition selon le lieu de résidence. Les définitions utilisées par les différents pays ou zones et leurs implications sont exposées à la fin des notes techniques correspondant au tableau 6.

3.1.3 Répartition par âge

La répartition de la population selon l'âge est un paramètre fondamental de la plupart des analyses, estimations et projections relatives aux statistiques de la population. Malheureusement, ces données sont sujettes à un certain nombre d'erreurs et difficilement comparables. C'est pourquoi pratiquement tous les utilisateurs de ces statistiques doivent considérer ces répartitions avec la plus grande circonspection.

3.1.3.1 Collecte et exploitation des données sur l'âge

L'âge est l'intervalle de temps déterminé par calcul ou par estimation qui sépare la date de naissance de la date du recensement et qui est exprimé en années solaires révolues[6]. Les données sur l'âge peuvent être recueillies selon deux méthodes : la première consiste à obtenir la date de naissance de chaque personne à l'occasion d'un recensement ou d'un sondage, puis à calculer l'âge en années révolues en soustrayant la date de naissance de celle du dénombrement[7]. La seconde consiste à enregistrer l'âge en années révolues au moment du recensement, c'est-à-dire l'âge au dernier anniversaire.

La méthode recommandée consiste à calculer l'âge au dernier anniversaire en soustrayant la date exacte de la naissance de la date du recensement. Toutefois, on n'a pas toujours recours à cette méthode ; certains pays ou zones calculent l'âge en faisant la différence entre l'année du recensement et l'année de la naissance. Lorsque les données sur l'âge ont été établies de cette façon, on l'a signalé chaque fois que possible par une note. On peut d'ailleurs s'en rendre compte dans une certaine mesure, car les chiffres dans la catégorie des moins d'un an sont plus faibles qu'ils ne devraient l'être. Cependant, un nombre irrégulier de naissances d'une année à l'autre ou l'omission de certains âges parmi les moins d'un an peut aussi fausser les chiffres de la population de moins d'un an.

3.1.3.2 Erreurs dans les données sur l'âge

Les causes d'erreurs dans les données sur l'âge sont diverses : on peut citer notamment l'ignorance de l'âge exact, la déclaration d'années d'âge correspondant à un calendrier différent de celui des années solaires révolues depuis la naissance[8], la négligence dans les déclarations et dans la façon dont elles sont consignées, la tendance générale à déclarer des âges se terminant par certains chiffres tels que 0, 2, 5 ou 8, la tendance pour les personnes âgées à exagérer leur âge, une aversion subconsciente pour certains nombres, et les fausses déclarations faites délibérément.

Les causes d'erreurs mentionnées ci-dessus, communes à la plupart des enquêtes sur l'âge et à la plupart des pays ou zones, peuvent nuire sensiblement à la comparabilité.

À cause des difficultés indiquées ci-dessus, les répartitions par âge et par sexe de la population d'un grand nombre de pays ou de zones font apparaître les irrégularités suivantes : 1) sous-estimation des groupes d'âge correspondant aux enfants de moins d'un an et aux jeunes enfants ; 2) polarisation des déclarations sur les âges se terminant par les chiffres 0 ou 5 (c'est-à-dire 5, 10,15, 20...) ; 3) prépondérance des âges pairs (par exemple 10, 12, 14...) au détriment des âges impairs (par exemple 11, 13, 15...) ; 4) écart considérable et surprenant entre le rapport masculin/féminin à certains âges ; 5) différences importantes et difficilement explicables entre les données concernant des groupes d'âge voisins. En comparant les statistiques provenant de recensements successifs pour des cohortes identiques sur le plan de l'âge et de la répartition par sexe et en étudiant la répartition par âge et par sexe de la population à chaque recensement, on peut déceler l'existence de ces incohérences et de quelques autres, un certain nombre d'entre elles se retrouvant à des degrés divers même dans les recensements les plus modernes.

La présente édition de l'*Annuaire démographique* comprend le tableau 3a avec l'indice de Whipple selon le sexe et la résidence urbaine/rurale pour les recensements de la population effectués dans le monde entier depuis 1985. L'indice de Whipple est un indice de préférence pour certains âges dans la déclaration de l'âge et peut donc servir à mettre en évidence certaines des difficultés liées à la répartition par âge.

4. STATISTIQUES DE L'ÉTAT CIVIL

Aux fins de *l'Annuaire démographique*, on entend par statistiques de l'état civil les statistiques des naissances vivantes, des décès, des morts fœtales, des mariages et des divorces.

Dans le présent volume de l'*Annuaire démographique*, on a présenté des tableaux sur la natalité, la mortalité, la nuptialité et la divortialité. Les tableaux consacrés à la mortalité sont groupés sous les rubriques suivantes : mortalité fœtale, mortalité infantile, mortalité liée à la maternité et mortalité générale.

4.1 Sources de variations des données

La plupart des statistiques de l'état civil publiées dans le présent volume de l'*Annuaire démographique* émanent des systèmes nationaux d'enregistrement des faits d'état civil. Le degré d'exhaustivité et d'exactitude de ces données varie d'un pays ou d'une zone à l'autre.

Il n'existe pas partout de système national d'enregistrement des faits d'état civil et, dans quelques cas, seuls certains faits sont enregistrés. Par exemple, dans certains pays ou zones, seuls les naissances et les décès sont enregistrés. Il existe également des différences quant au degré d'efficacité avec lequel les lois relatives à l'enregistrement des faits d'état civil sont appliquées dans les divers pays ou zones. La fiabilité des statistiques provenant des registres d'état civil dépend des modalités d'application de la loi et de la mesure dans laquelle le public s'y soumet.

Il est à signaler que dans certains cas les statistiques de la nuptialité et de la divortialité sont tirées d'autres sources que les registres d'état civil. Dans certains pays ou zones, par exemple, les seules données disponibles sur la nuptialité proviennent des registres des églises. Selon la pratique suivie par chaque pays, les statistiques de la divortialité sont tirées des actes des tribunaux et/ou des registres d'état civil. L'officier de l'état civil, le service national de statistique ou d'autres services administratifs peuvent être chargés d'établir ces statistiques.

Les autres facteurs qui influent sur la comparabilité internationale des statistiques de l'état civil sont à peu près les mêmes que ceux qu'il convient de prendre en considération pour interpréter les variations observées dans les statistiques de la population. La définition des faits d'état civil aux fins de statistique, la portée des données du point de vue géographique et ethnique ainsi que les méthodes d'exploitation des données sont autant d'éléments qui peuvent influer sur la comparabilité.

En plus des statistiques tirées des registres d'état civil, l'*Annuaire démographique* présente des statistiques de l'état civil qui sont des estimations officielles nationales, fondées souvent sur les résultats de sondages ou des recensements de la population. Aussi leur comparabilité varie-t-elle en fonction du degré d'exhaustivité des déclarations recueillies lors des recensements de la population ou d'enquêtes sur les ménages, des erreurs d'échantillonnage ou autres, et des distorsions d'origines diverses.

Pour plus de détails sur les normes d'établissement des statistiques d'état civil, le lecteur pourra se reporter aux : *Principes et recommandations pour un système de statistiques de l'état civil, troisième révision*[9] ; *Guidelines on the Legislative Framework for Civil Registration, Vital Statistics and Identity Management*[10] ; *Manuel des systèmes d'enregistrement des faits d'état civil et de statistiques de l'état civil : Gestion, fonctionnement et tenue, Révision 1*[11]; *Handbook on civil registration, vital statistics and identity management systems: Communication for development*[12]; *Manuel des systèmes d'enregistrement des faits d'état civil et de statistiques de l'état civil : Principes et protocoles concernant la communication et l'archivage des documents individuels*[13]; *Manuel des systèmes d'enregistrement des faits d'état civil et de statistiques de l'état civil : Informatisation*[14]. Le *Manuel de collecte de données sur la fécondité et la mortalité*[15] fournit des informations ayant trait à la collecte et à l'évaluation des données sur la fécondité, sur la mortalité et sur d'autres faits d'état civil, qui ont été recueillies au cours des enquêtes sur les ménages. Ces publications sont également disponibles sur le Web à partir des adresses suivantes : https://unstats.un.org/unsd/demographic-social/Standards-and-Methods/index.cshtml

4.1.1 Définition des faits d'état civil aux fins de la statistique

Une cause importante d'hétérogénéité dans les données est le manque d'uniformité des définitions des différents faits d'état civil. Aux fins de *l'Annuaire démographique*, il est recommandé de recueillir les données relatives aux faits d'état civil en utilisant les définitions établies au Chapitre I des *Principes et recommandations pour un système de statistiques de l'état civil, troisième révision*. Ces définitions sont les suivantes :

La NAISSANCE VIVANTE est l'expulsion ou l'extraction complète du corps de la mère, indépendamment de la durée de la gestation, d'un produit de la conception qui, après cette séparation, respire ou manifeste tout autre signe de vie, tel que battement de cœur, pulsation du cordon ombilical ou contraction effective d'un muscle soumis à l'action de la volonté, que le cordon ombilical ait été coupé ou non et que le placenta soit ou non demeuré attaché ; tout produit d'une telle naissance est considéré comme « enfant né vivant ».

Le DÉCÈS est la disparition permanente de tout signe de vie à un moment quelconque postérieur à la naissance vivante (cessation des fonctions vitales après la naissance sans possibilité de réanimation). Cette définition ne comprend pas les morts fœtales.

La MORT FŒTALE est le décès d'un produit de la conception lorsque ce décès est survenu avant l'expulsion ou l'extraction complète du corps de la mère, indépendamment de la durée de la gestation. Le décès est indiqué par le fait qu'après cette séparation le fœtus ne respire ni ne manifeste aucun signe de vie, tel que battement de cœur, pulsation du cordon ombilical ou contraction effective d'un muscle soumis à l'action de la volonté.

Le MARIAGE est l'acte, la cérémonie ou la procédure qui établit un rapport légal entre les époux. L'union peut être rendue légale par une procédure civile ou religieuse, ou par toute autre procédure, conformément à la législation du pays.

Le DIVORCE est la dissolution légale et définitive des liens du mariage, c'est-à-dire la séparation des époux qui confère aux parties le droit de se remarier civilement ou religieusement, ou selon toute autre procédure, conformément à la législation du pays.

En plus de ces notions définies internationalement, l'*Annuaire démographique* recueille et met à disposition ces données sur les avortements :

Par référence à la femme, l'AVORTEMENT se définit comme toute interruption de grossesse qui est survenue avant 28 semaines de gestation et dont le produit est un fœtus mort. Il existe deux grandes catégories d'avortement : l'avortement spontané et l'avortement provoqué. L'avortement provoqué a pour origine une action délibérée entreprise en vue d'interrompre une grossesse. Tout autre avortement est considéré comme spontané.

4.1.2 Problèmes posés par les définitions établies

Les variations par rapport aux définitions établies des faits d'état civil sont le principal obstacle à la comparabilité internationale des statistiques de l'état civil. Un exemple en est fourni par le cas des naissances vivantes et celui des morts fœtales. Dans certains pays ou zones, il faut que le nouveau-né ait vécu 24 heures pour pouvoir être inscrit sur le registre des naissances vivantes. Les décès d'enfants qui surviennent avant l'expiration du délai de 24 heures sont classés parmi les morts fœtales tardives et, en l'absence de méthodes spéciales d'exploitation des données, ne sont comptés ni dans les naissances vivantes ni dans les décès. De même, dans plusieurs autres pays ou zones, les décès d'enfants nés vivants et décédés avant l'enregistrement de leur naissance sont également comptés parmi les morts fœtales tardives.

À moins que des méthodes spéciales n'aient été adoptées pour l'exploitation de ces données, les statistiques des naissances vivantes et des décès ne tiendront pas compte de ces cas, qui viendront en revanche accroître d'autant le nombre des morts fœtales tardives. Le taux de mortalité infantile sera donc sous-estimé. Bien que les éléments constitutifs du taux (décès d'enfants de moins d'un an et naissances vivantes) accusent exactement la même insuffisance en valeur absolue, les lacunes sont proportionnellement plus fortes pour les décès de moins d'un an, ce qui cause des erreurs plus importantes dans les taux de mortalité infantile.

De plus, cette pratique augmente les rapports de mortinatalité. Quelques pays ou zones effectuent les ajustements nécessaires pour corriger cette anomalie (du moins dans les fréquences totales) au moment de l'établissement des tableaux. Si aucun ajustement n'a été effectué, cela est indiqué dans les notes chaque fois que possible.

Les définitions du mariage et du divorce posent aussi un problème du point de vue de la comparabilité internationale. Contrairement à la naissance et au décès, qui sont des faits biologiques, le mariage et le divorce sont uniquement déterminés par la législation et la coutume et, de ce fait, il est moins facile d'en donner une définition statistique qui ait une application universelle. À des fins statistiques, ces notions ont donc été définies de manière générale par référence à la législation de chaque pays ou zone. La législation relative au mariage et plus particulièrement au divorce varie d'un pays ou d'une zone à l'autre. En ce qui concerne le mariage, l'âge de nubilité est la condition la plus fréquemment requise, mais il arrive souvent que d'autres conditions soient exigées.

Lorsqu'il est connu, l'âge minimum auquel le mariage peut avoir lieu avec le consentement des parents (et dans certains cas sans le consentement des parents) est indiqué au tableau 23-1. Les lois et règlements relatifs à la dissolution du mariage par le divorce vont de l'interdiction absolue, en passant par diverses conditions requises pour l'obtention du divorce, jusqu'à la simple déclaration, par l'épouse, de son désir ou de son intention de divorcer.

4.1.3 Couverture géographique ou ethnique fragmentaire

Selon les standards internationaux, les statistiques de l'état civil devraient s'étendre à l'ensemble du pays ou de la zone auxquels elles se rapportent et englober tous les groupes ethniques. En fait, il n'est pas rare que les données soient fragmentaires. Dans certains pays ou zones, l'enregistrement n'est obligatoire que pour une petite partie de la population, par exemple pour certains groupes ethniques. Dans d'autres, il n'existe pas de disposition qui prescrive l'enregistrement obligatoire sur le plan national, mais seulement des règlements ou décrets des municipalités ou des États, qui ne s'appliquent pas à l'ensemble du territoire. Il en est encore autrement dans d'autres pays ou zones où les autorités ont institué une zone d'enregistrement comprenant seulement une partie du territoire, le reste étant exclu en raison des difficultés d'accès ou parce qu'il est pratiquement impossible, pour des raisons d'ordre économique ou culturel, d'y procéder à un enregistrement régulier.

4.1.4 Méthodes de présentation des données

4.1.4.1 Selon le lieu de l'événement

Les statistiques de l'état civil qui sont présentées pour l'ensemble du territoire national se rapportent à la population de fait ou la population présente. En conséquence, sauf indication contraire, les statistiques de l'état civil relatives à une zone ou à un pays donné portent sur tous les faits survenus dans l'ensemble de la population, à l'intérieur des frontières actuelles de la zone ou du pays considéré. On peut donc estimer qu'elles englobent les faits d'état civil survenus dans les tribus nomades et parmi les populations autochtones ainsi que parmi les ressortissants du pays et les étrangers. Des notes signalent les exceptions lorsque celles-ci sont connues.

Pour certains pays, les écarts entre les taux démographiques pour les zones urbaines et pour les zones rurales peuvent varier notablement selon que les faits d'état civil ont été exploités sur la base du lieu de l'événement ou du lieu de résidence habituel. Par exemple, si un nombre appréciable de femmes résidant dans des zones rurales proches de grands centres urbains accouchent dans les hôpitaux ou maternités d'une ville, les taux de fécondité ainsi que les taux de mortalité néo-natale et infantile seront généralement plus élevés dans les zones urbaines (et par conséquent plus faibles dans les zones rurales) si les faits sont exploités en se fondant sur le lieu de l'événement et non sur le lieu de résidence habituel. Le phénomène sera le même dans le cas de la mortalité générale si un bon nombre de personnes résidant dans des zones rurales font appel aux services de santé des villes lorsqu'elles sont gravement malades.

4.1.4.2 Selon la date de l'événement ou la date de l'enregistrement

Autant que possible, les statistiques de l'état civil figurant dans l'Annuaire démographique se rapportent aux faits survenus pendant l'année considérée et non aux faits enregistrés au cours de ladite année. Bon nombre de pays ou zones, toutefois, exploitent leurs statistiques de l'état civil selon la date de l'enregistrement et non selon la date de l'événement. Comme ces statistiques risquent d'induire en erreur, les pays ou zones dont on sait qu'ils établissent leurs statistiques d'après la date de l'enregistrement sont signalés dans les tableaux par un signe plus « + ». On ne dispose toutefois pas pour tous les pays ou zones de renseignements complets sur la méthode d'exploitation des statistiques de l'état civil et les données sont peut-être exploitées selon la date de l'enregistrement plus souvent que ne le laisserait supposer l'emploi des signes.

Étant donné que la qualité des données est inextricablement liée aux retards dans l'enregistrement, il faudra toujours considérer en même temps le code de qualité qui est décrit à la section 4.2.1 ci-après. Évidemment, si l'enregistrement des naissances est complet et effectué en temps voulu (code « C »), les effets perturbateurs de la méthode consistant à exploiter les données selon la date de l'enregistrement seront pratiquement annulés. De même, s'agissant des statistiques des décès, les effets pourront bien souvent être réduits au minimum dans les pays ou zones où le code sanitaire subordonne la délivrance du permis d'inhumer à l'enregistrement du décès, ce qui tend à hâter l'enregistrement. Quant aux morts fœtales, elles sont généralement déclarées immédiatement ou ne sont pas déclarées du tout. En conséquence, si l'enregistrement se fait dans un délai très court, la différence entre les statistiques établies selon la date de l'événement et celles qui sont établies selon la date de l'enregistrement peut être négligeable. Dans bien des cas, la durée des délais légaux accordés pour l'enregistrement des faits d'état civil est un facteur dont dépend dans une large mesure l'incidence sur la comparabilité de l'exploitation des données selon la date de l'enregistrement.

En ce qui concerne le mariage et le divorce, la pratique consistant à exploiter les statistiques selon la date de l'enregistrement ne pose généralement pas de graves problèmes. Le mariage étant, dans de nombreux pays ou zones, un contrat juridique civil qui, pour être légal, doit être conclu devant un officier de l'état civil, il s'ensuit que dans ces pays ou zones l'enregistrement a lieu presque systématiquement au moment de la cérémonie ou immédiatement après. De même, dans de nombreux pays ou zones, le tribunal ou l'autorité qui a prononcé le divorce est le seul habilité à enregistrer cet acte, et comme l'acte d'enregistrement figure alors sur les registres du tribunal l'enregistrement suit généralement de peu le jugement.

En revanche, si l'enregistrement n'a lieu qu'avec un certain retard, les statistiques de l'état civil établies selon la date de l'enregistrement ne sont pas comparables sur le plan international. Au mieux, les statistiques par date de l'enregistrement prendront surtout en considération des faits survenus au cours de l'année précédente ; dans les pays ou zones où le système d'enregistrement n'est pas très développé, il y entrera des faits datant de plusieurs années. Il ressort des documents dont on dispose que des retards de plusieurs années dans l'enregistrement des naissances ne sont pas rares, encore que, dans la majorité des cas, les retards ne dépassent pas deux à quatre ans.

Tant que l'enregistrement se fera avec retard, les statistiques fondées sur la date d'enregistrement ne seront comparables sur le plan international ni entre elles ni avec les statistiques établies selon la date de fait d'état civil.

Il convient également de noter que l'exploitation des données selon la date de l'enregistrement ne nuit pas seulement à la comparabilité internationale des statistiques. Même à l'intérieur d'un pays ou d'une zone, le procédé qui consiste à compter les enregistrements et non les faits peut compromettre la comparabilité des chiffres sur une longue période. Si le nombre des faits d'état civil enregistrés varie d'une année à l'autre (par suite de l'application de mesures visant tout particulièrement à encourager l'enregistrement ou parce qu'il est subitement devenu nécessaire de produire le certificat d'une naissance ou d'un décès non enregistré pour l'accomplissement de certaines formalités), les statistiques de l'état civil établies d'après la date de l'enregistrement ne permettent pas de quantifier ni d'analyser l'état et l'évolution de la population. Tout au plus peuvent-elles révéler l'évolution des conditions d'exigibilité de l'acte de naissance, de décès ou de mariage et les fluctuations du volume de travail des bureaux d'état civil. Les statistiques établies selon la date de l'enregistrement peuvent donc ne présenter qu'une utilité très réduite pour des études nationales ou internationales.

4.2 La qualité des statistiques de l'état civil qui sont publiées

La qualité des statistiques de l'état civil peut être évaluée en se fondant sur plusieurs facteurs. Le facteur essentiel est la complétude du système d'enregistrement des faits d'état civil d'après lequel ces statistiques sont établies.

4.2.1 Codage qualitatif des statistiques provenant des registres de l'état civil

Dans le questionnaire relatif au mouvement de la population qui leur est envoyé chaque année dans le cadre de l'établissement de *l'Annuaire démographique*, les services nationaux de statistique sont invités à donner leur propre évaluation du degré de complétude des données sur les naissances, les décès, les décès d'enfants de moins d'un an, les morts fœtales tardives, les mariages et les divorces figurant dans leurs registres d'état civil.

D'après les renseignements directement communiqués par les gouvernements ou extraits des questionnaires ou de publications officielles pertinentes, il a été possible de classer les statistiques de l'enregistrement des faits d'état civil (naissances, décès, décès d'enfants de moins d'un an, morts fœtales tardives, mariages et divorces) en trois grandes catégories, selon leur qualité :

C : Données jugées pratiquement complètes, c'est-à-dire représentant au moins 90 % des faits d'état civil survenant chaque année.

U : Données jugées incomplètes, c'est-à-dire représentant moins de 90 % des faits survenant chaque année.

| : Données ne provenant pas des systèmes nationaux d'enregistrement des faits d'état civil, mais jugées fiables, telles que les estimations dérivées des recensements de population ou du logement.

... : Données dont le degré de complétude ne fait pas l'objet de renseignements précis.

Ces codes de qualité figurent dans la première colonne des tableaux qui présentent, pour un nombre d'années déterminé les chiffres absolus et les taux (ou rapports) bruts concernant les naissances vivantes, les morts fœtales tardives, les décès d'enfants de moins d'un an, les décès, les mariages et les divorces. Les niveaux de fiabilité des statistiques de mortalité maternelle sont transmis par l'Organisation mondiale de la santé.

La classification des pays ou zones selon ces codes de qualité peut ne pas être uniforme. On a estimé néanmoins que les services nationaux de statistique étaient les mieux placés pour juger de la qualité de leurs données. On a pensé que les catégories que l'on pouvait distinguer sur la base des renseignements disponibles, bien que très larges, permettaient cependant de se faire une idée de la qualité des statistiques de l'état civil publiées dans l'*Annuaire démographique*.

Sur les pays ou zones qui ont estimé à 90 % ou plus le degré d'exhaustivité de leur enregistrement des naissances vivantes (classé « C » ou « +C » dans le tableau 9), les pays ou zones suivants ont communiqué des renseignements concernant les bases sur lesquelles leur estimation reposait :

a) Analyse démographique : Afrique du Sud, Arabie saoudite, Argentine, Australie, Autriche, Brésil, Bulgarie, Chili, Chine - Hong Kong RAS, Croatie, Égypte, Estonie, État de Palestine, Italie, Kazakhstan, Kenya, Lettonie, Lituanie, Luxemburg, Malaisie, Malte, Maurice, Nouvelle-Zélande, Panama, Pérou, République de Moldova, République dominicaine, Roumanie, Saint-Marin, Seychelles, et Venezuela (République bolivarienne du).

b) Double contrôle des registres : Australie, Autriche, Belgique, Brésil, Chypre, Cuba, Estonie, Groenland, Hongrie, Îles Féroé, Israël, Italie, Lettonie, Malaisie, Mongolie, Montserrat, Norvège, Nouvelle-Zélande, Oman, Qatar, République de Corée, Roumanie, Saint Vincent et les Grenadines, Uruguay et Venezuela (République bolivarienne du).

c) Autre méthode : Allemagne, Arménie, Aruba, Australie, Bahreïn, Bolivie (État plurinational de), Botswana, Brésil, Curaçao, Danemark, Espagne, Fédération de Russie, France, Guatemala, Guinée, Inde, Irlande, Jordanie, Kirghizstan, Liban, Liechtenstein, Malaisie, Mexique, Ouzbékistan, Pologne, Porto Rico, Singapour, Slovénie, Suède, Tadjikistan et Venezuela (République bolivarienne du).

Sur les pays ou zones qui ont estimé à 90 % ou plus le degré d'exhaustivité de leur enregistrement des morts fœtales tardives (classé « C » ou « +C » dans le tableau 12), les pays ou zones suivants ont communiqué des renseignements concernant les bases sur lesquelles leur estimation reposait :

a) Analyse démographique : Arabie saoudite, Argentine, Arménie, Autriche, Bulgarie, Croatie, Égypte, Estonie, Italie, Kazakhstan, Lettonie, Lituanie, Luxemburg, Malte, Maurice, Mexique, Oman, République de Corée, Roumanie, Saint-Marin et Venezuela (République bolivarienne du).

b) Double contrôle des registres : Autriche, Belgique, Cuba, Estonie, Groenland, Hongrie, Israël, Italie, Lettonie, Lituanie, Montserrat, Norvège, Nouvelle-Zélande et Roumanie,

c) Autre méthode : Allemagne, Bahreïn, Danemark, Espagne, Fédération de Russie, France, Kirghizstan, Ouzbékistan, Pologne, Porto Rico, Slovénie et Suède.

Sur les pays ou zones qui ont estimé à 90 % ou plus le degré d'exhaustivité de leur enregistrement des décès à moins d'un an (classé « C » ou « +C » dans le tableau 15), les pays ou zones suivants ont donné des indications touchant la base de cette estimation :

a) Analyse démographique : Arabie saoudite, Argentine, Australie, Arménie, Autriche, Brésil, Bulgarie, Chili, Chine - Hong Kong RAS, Croatie, Égypte, Estonie, État de Palestine, Israël, Kazakhstan, Kenya, Italie, Lettonie, Lituanie, Luxemburg, Malte, Maurice, Nouvelle-Zélande, Oman, Panama, République de Corée, République de Moldova, Roumanie, Saint-Marin et Seychelles.

b) Double contrôle des registres : Autriche, Belgique, Brésil, Cuba, Chypre, Estonie, Groenland, Hongrie, Îles Féroé, Irlande, Israël, Italie, Lettonie, Lituanie, Mongolie, Montserrat, Norvège, Nouvelle-Zélande, Qatar, Roumanie et Saint-Vincent-et-les-Grenadines.

c) Autre méthode : Allemagne, Aruba, Bahreïn, Brésil, Curaçao, Danemark, Espagne, Fédération de Russie, France, Guinée, Îles Caïmans, Kirghizstan, Liban, Liechtenstein, Ouzbékistan, Pologne, Porto Rico, Singapour, Slovénie, Suède et Tadjikistan.

Sur les pays ou zones qui ont estimé à 90 % ou plus le degré d'exhaustivité de leur enregistrement des décès (classé « C » ou « +C » dans le tableau 18), les pays ou zones suivants ont donné des indications touchant la base de cette estimation :

a) Analyse démographique : Arabie saoudite, Afrique du Sud, Argentine, Australie, Autriche, Brésil, Bulgarie, Chili, Chine - Hong Kong RAS, Croatie, Égypte, Estonie, États-Unis d'Amérique, Israël, Italie, Kazakhstan, Lettonie, Lituanie, Luxemburg, Malaisie, Malte, Maurice, Nouvelle-Zélande, Oman, Panama, Pérou, République de Corée, République de Moldova, République dominicaine, Roumanie, Saint-Marin, Seychelles, et Venezuela (République bolivarienne du).

b) Double contrôle des registres : Autriche, Belgique, Brésil, Cuba, Chypre, Estonie, Groenland, Hongrie, Îles Féroé, Israël, Italie, Lettonie, Lituanie, Malaisie, Mongolie, Montserrat, Norvège, Nouvelle-Zélande, Qatar, Roumanie, Saint Vincent et les Grenadines et Venezuela (République bolivarienne du).

c) Autre méthode : Allemagne, Arménie, Aruba, Bahreïn, Botswana, Brésil, Curaçao, Danemark, Espagne, États-Unis d'Amérique, Fédération de Russie, France, Guinée, Inde, Kirghizstan, Liechtenstein, Ouzbékistan, Pologne, Porto Rico, Singapour, Slovénie et Suède.

Sur les pays ou zones qui ont estimé à 90 % ou plus le degré d'exhaustivité de leur enregistrement des mariages (classé « C » ou « +C «» dans le tableau 22), les pays ou zones suivants ont communiqué des renseignements concernant les bases sur lesquelles leur estimation reposait :

a) Analyse démographique : Arabie saoudite, Argentine, Australie, Autriche, Bulgarie, Chili, Chine - Hong Kong RAS, Croatie, Égypte, Estonie, Italie, Lettonie, Lituanie, Luxemburg, Malte, Maurice, République de Moldova, Roumanie, Saint-Marin, Seychelles et Venezuela (République bolivarienne du).

b) Double contrôle des registres : Autriche, Belgique, Cuba, Estonie, État de Palestine, Hongrie, Îles Féroé, Italie, Kazakhstan, Lettonie, Norvège, Nouvelle-Zélande, Oman, Qatar, République de Corée et Roumanie.

c) Autre méthode : Allemagne, Aruba, Curaçao, Danemark, Espagne, Fédération de Russie, France, Kirghizstan, Jordanie, Liban, Liechtenstein, Ouzbékistan, Pologne, Porto Rico, Roumanie, Slovénie, Suède et Tadjikistan.

Sur les pays ou zones qui ont estimé à 90 % ou plus le degré d'exhaustivité de leur enregistrement des divorces (classé « C » ou « +C » dans le tableau 24), les pays ou zones suivants ont communiqué des renseignements concernant les bases sur lesquelles leur estimation reposait :

a) Analyse démographique : Arabie saoudite, Australie, Autriche, Bulgarie, Croatie, Égypte, Estonie, Italie, Lettonie, Lituanie, Luxemburg, République de Moldova, Roumanie, Saint-Marin, Seychelles, Suède et Venezuela (République bolivarienne du).

b) Double contrôle des registres : Autriche, Belgique, Cuba, Estonie, État de Palestine, Hongrie, Îles Féroé, Italie, Kazakhstan, Lettonie, Norvège, Nouvelle-Zélande, Oman, Qatar, République de Corée et Roumanie.

c) Autre méthode : Allemagne, Aruba, Curaçao, Danemark, Fédération de Russie, Jordanie, Kirghizstan, Liban, Liechtenstein, Maurice, Ouzbékistan, Pologne, Porto Rico, Slovénie et Tadjikistan.

4.2.2 Traitement des statistiques tirées des registres d'état civil

Dans tous les tableaux de l'*Annuaire démographique*, on a indiqué le degré de fiabilité des statistiques de l'état civil en se fondant sur le codage qualitatif décrit ci-dessus. Les statistiques codées « C », jugées sûres, sont imprimées en caractères romains. Celles qui sont codées « U » ou « ... », jugées douteuses, sont reproduites en *italique*.

Il convient de noter que, pour les taux de mortalité infantile, les taux de mortalité maternelle et les rapports de morts fœtales tardives (calculées en utilisant au dénominateur le nombre de naissances vivantes), les indications relatives à la fiabilité sont déterminées sur la base des codes de qualité utilisés pour les décès d'enfants de moins d'un an, les décès totaux et les morts fœtales tardives, respectivement. Pour évaluer ces taux et rapports de façon plus précise, il faudrait tenir compte de la qualité des données relatives aux naissances vivantes, utilisées au dénominateur dans leur calcul. Les codes de qualité pour les naissances vivantes figurent au tableau 9 et sont décrits plus en détail dans les notes techniques se rapportant à ce tableau.

4.2.3 Traitement des estimations fondées sur les statistiques de l'état civil

En plus des données provenant des systèmes d'enregistrement des faits d'état civil, *l'Annuaire démographique* contient aussi des estimations relatives aux fréquences et aux taux. Il s'agit d'estimations officielles, généralement calculées à partir des résultats d'un recensement de la population ou d'un sondage ou par analyse démographique. Si des estimations concernant les fréquences et les taux figurent dans les tableaux, c'est parce que l'on considère qu'elles fournissent des renseignements plus exacts que les systèmes existants d'enregistrement des faits d'état civil. En conséquence, elles sont également jugées sûres et sont donc imprimées en caractères romains.

Les données estimatives sont dénotées par le «|».

4.3 Causes de décès

Les États membres de l'Organisation mondiale de la santé (OMS) sont tenus de communiquer à celle-ci les données sur les causes de décès codifiées selon la révision en vigueur de la Classification internationale des maladies et des problèmes de santé connexes (CIM). Pour assurer la comparabilité internationale des statistiques des causes de décès, l'OMS organise régulièrement des conférences internationales de révision de la Classification internationale des maladies afin de suivre, au fur et à mesure, les progrès les plus récents de la médecine clinique et de la statistique. Les données sont généralement présentées à l'OMS selon le degré de détail à tous les quatre caractères requis par la CIM et sont compilées et archivées dans la Base de données sur la mortalité de l'OMS au degré de détail présenté par le pays. Les données de la Base de données sur la mortalité de l'OMS sont disponibles sur le site Internet suivant : http://www3.who.int/whosis/menu.cfm.

Les révisions de la CIM permettent certes de disposer d'une version actualisée, mais elles posent plusieurs problèmes de comparabilité des statistiques des causes de décès. Le premier tient au manque de comparabilité dans le temps, qui accompagne inévitablement la mise en œuvre d'une classification nouvelle. Le deuxième est celui de la comparabilité entre pays ou zones, car les différents pays peuvent adopter la nouvelle classification à des époques différentes. Établir la cause des décès exige des compétences de plus en plus poussées à mesure que la classification devient plus précise. Or, dans beaucoup de pays ou zones, il est rare que les décès se produisent en présence d'un témoin possédant une formation médicale et le certificat de décès est le plus souvent établi par quelqu'un qui n'est pas qualifié sur le plan médical. Étant donné que la CIM répertorie de nombreux diagnostics qu'il est impossible d'établir si l'on n'a pas de formation en médecine, la CIM n'est pas toujours exactement ou précisément utilisée ce qui affecte la comparabilité internationale, notamment entre pays ou zones où la qualité des services médicaux est très disparate.

Les chapitres de la dixième révision[16] se fondent sur un système de codification alphanumérique à une lettre suivie de trois chiffres pour les catégories à quatre caractères. Le chapitre 1 concerne les maladies infectieuses et parasitaires et le chapitre 2 l'ensemble des néoplasmes. Le chapitre 3 a trait aux troubles du système immunitaire, aux maladies du sang et aux organes hématopoïétiques. Le chapitre 4 porte sur les maladies du système endocrinien, de la nutrition et du métabolisme. Les autres chapitres groupent les maladies selon leur site anatomique, à l'exception de ceux qui concernent les affections mentales, les complications de la grossesse, de l'accouchement et des suites de couches, les malformations congénitales et les affections de la période périnatale. Enfin, un chapitre entier est consacré aux symptômes, manifestations et résultats anormaux. La onzième révision a été lancée en 2018 et est disponible en ligne : https://www.who.int/classifications/icd/en/.

4.3.1 Mortalité liée à la maternité

D'après la dixième révision de la CIM, la « mortalité liée à la maternité » est définie comme le décès d'une femme survenu au cours de la grossesse ou dans un délai de 42 jours après sa terminaison, quelle qu'en soit la durée et la localisation, pour une cause quelconque déterminée ou aggravée par la grossesse ou les soins qu'elle a motivés, mais ni accidentelle ni fortuite.

Les « décès liés à la maternité » doivent se répartir en décès par cause obstétricale directe et indirecte. Les décès par cause obstétricale directe sont ceux qui résultent de complications obstétricales de l'état de grossesse (grossesse, travail et suites de couches), d'interventions, d'omissions, d'un traitement incorrect ou d'un enchaînement d'événements de l'un quelconque des facteurs ci-dessus. Les décès par cause obstétricale indirecte sont ceux qui résultent d'une maladie préexistante ou d'une affection apparue au cours de la grossesse, sans qu'elle soit due à des causes obstétricales directes, mais qui a été aggravée par les effets physiologiques de la grossesse.

En théorie, le nombre de femmes enceintes aurait dû être pris comme dénominateur pour le taux de mortalité maternelle, mais il est impossible de déterminer ce nombre. En conséquence, il est en outre recommandé dans la dixième révision d'exprimer les taux de mortalité maternelle sur la base de 100 000 naissances vivantes ou 100 000 naissances totales (naissances vivantes et morts fœtales). Le taux de mortalité maternelle est ici calculé par 100 000 naissances vivantes. Bien que les naissances vivantes ne permettent pas d'évaluer sans distorsion le nombre des femmes enceintes, leur nombre est plus fiable que d'autres estimations car le nombre des naissances vivantes est plus exactement enregistré que celui des naissances vivantes et des morts fœtales.

---

[1] UNdata est un service de données en ligne géré par la Division de statistique du Département des affaires économiques et sociales de l'Organisation des Nations Unies.

[2] Les éditions de 1978 et de 1991 font exception à la règle, puisque les tableaux sur des sujets spéciaux ont été publiés séparément.

[3] Organisation des Nations Unies, Département des affaires économiques et sociales, Division de la population (2019). Perspectives de la population mondiale : La révision de 2019 (https://population.un.org/wpp/).

[4] ST/ESA/STAT/SER.M/49/Rev.4/WWW ; https://unstats.un.org/unsd/methodology/m49/ ; voir également Code standard des pays et des zones à usage statistique, numéro de vente : M.98.XVII.9, Nations Unies, New York, 1999.

[5] Numéro de vente : E.15.XVII.10, Nations Unies, New York, 2015.

[6] Ibid., par. 4.151.

[7] Lorsque l'on utilise un registre de la population, on peut également calculer l'âge en années révolues en soustrayant la date de naissance de chaque personne inscrite sur le registre de la date de référence à laquelle se rapportent les données sur l'âge.

[8] L'emploi de méthodes différentes de calcul de l'âge, par exemple la méthode occidentale et la méthode orientale, ou, comme on les désigne plus communément, la méthode anglaise et la méthode chinoise, représente une cause de non-comparabilité. Selon la méthode chinoise, on considère que l'enfant est âgé d'un an à sa naissance et qu'il avance d'un an à chaque nouvelle année chinoise. Les répercussions de cette méthode sont particulièrement apparentes dans les données pour le premier âge : les données concernant les enfants de moins d'un an sont nettement inférieures à la réalité. Les effets sur les chiffres relatifs aux groupes d'âge suivants sont moins visibles. Les séries ainsi établies sont souvent ajustées avant d'être publiées, mais il ne faut pas exclure la possibilité d'aberrations de ce genre lorsque l'on compare des données censitaires sur l'âge.

[9] Numéro de vente : E.13.XVII.10, publication des Nations Unies, New York, 2014.

[10] https://unstats.un.org/unsd/demographic-social/Standards-and-Methods/files/Handbooks/crvs/CRVS_GOLF_Final_Draft-E.pdf
United Nations, New York, 2019.

[11] https://unstats.un.org/unsd/demographic-social/Standards-and-Methods/files/Handbooks/crvs/crvs-mgt-E.pdf
United Nations, New York, 2018.

[12] https://unstats.un.org/unsd/demographic-social/Standards-and-Methods/files/Handbooks/crvs/CRVS-IdM-E.pdf
United Nations, New York, 2019

[13] Numéro de vente : F.98.XVII.6, publication des Nations Unies, New York, 1998.

[14] Numéro de vente : F.98.XVII.10, publication des Nations Unies, New York, 1998.

[15] Numéro de vente : F.03.XVII.11, United Nations, New York, 2004.

[16] Organisation mondiale de la santé, Classification statistique internationale des maladies et problèmes de santé connexes, dixième révision, vol. 2, Genève, 1992.

Table A. Demographic Yearbook 2018 synoptic table: Availability of data by country/area, table and sex, where applicable
Tableau A. Tableau synoptique de l'Annuaire démographique 2018 : Disponibilité des données par pays ou zone, tableau et le sexe, si disponible

General topic and table number - Sujet général et numéro de tableau

Continent and country or area — Continent et pays ou zone	Table totals	Summary - Aperçu 3 Total	3 M/F	4	5	Population 6 Total¹	6 M/F	7 Total	7 M/F	8 Total	8 M/F	Fertility - Natalité 9	10 Total	10 M/F	11	Foetal mortality - Mortalité foetale 12	13	14
Total number of countries or areas - Total des pays ou zones	..	240	225	188	225	231	231	221	216	209	168	171	157	129	88	90	62	51
AFRICA - AFRIQUE																		
Algeria - Algérie	18	•	•	•	•	•	•	•	•	•	…	•	…	…	…	•	…	…
Angola	14	•	•	•	•	•	•	•	•	•	…	•	…	…	…	…	…	…
Benin - Bénin	10	•	•	…	•	•	•	•	•	•	…	…	…	…	…	…	…	…
Botswana	22	•	•	•	•	•	•	•	•	•	•	•	•	•	•	…	…	…
Burkina Faso	10	•	•	…	•	•	•	•	•	•	…	•	…	…	…	…	…	…
Burundi	13	•	•	•	•	•	•	•	•	•	…	•	…	…	…	•	…	…
Cabo Verde	12	•	•	…	•	•	•	•	•	•	…	…	…	…	…	…	…	…
Cameroon - Cameroun	10	•	•	•	•	•	•	•	•	•	…	…	…	…	…	…	…	…
Central African Republic - République centrafricaine	2	•	•	…	…	…	…	…	…	…	…	…	…	…	…	…	…	…
Chad - Tchad	7	•	•	…	…	…	…	•	…	…	…	…	…	…	…	…	…	…
Comoros - Comores	2	•	•	…	…	…	…	…	…	…	…	…	…	…	…	…	…	…
Congo	18	•	•	•	•	•	•	•	•	•	•	•	•	•	•	…	…	…
Côte d'Ivoire	18	•	•	•	•	•	•	•	•	•	•	•	•	•	•	…	…	…
Democratic Republic of the Congo - République démocratique du Congo	2	•	•	…	…	…	…	…	…	…	…	…	…	…	…	…	…	…
Djibouti	9	•	•	…	•	•	•	•	•	•	…	…	…	…	…	…	…	…
Egypt - Égypte	25	•	•	•	•	•	•	•	•	•	•	•	•	•	•	•	…	…
Equatorial Guinea - Guinée équatoriale	8	•	•	…	•	•	•	•	•	•	…	…	…	…	…	…	…	…
Eritrea - Érythrée	9	•	•	…	•	•	•	•	•	•	…	…	…	…	…	…	…	…
Eswatini	9	•	•	…	•	•	•	•	•	•	…	…	…	…	…	…	…	…
Ethiopia - Éthiopie	9	•	•	…	•	•	•	•	•	•	…	…	…	…	…	…	…	…
Gabon	6	•	•	…	…	•	•	•	•	…	…	…	…	…	…	…	…	…
Gambia - Gambie	7	•	•	…	•	•	•	…	…	…	…	…	…	…	…	…	…	…
Ghana	14	•	•	•	•	•	•	•	•	•	…	•	…	•	…	…	…	…
Guinea - Guinée	18	•	•	•	•	•	•	•	•	•	•	•	•	•	•	…	…	…
Guinea-Bissau - Guinée-Bissau	10	•	•	…	•	•	•	•	•	•	…	…	…	…	…	…	…	…
Kenya	18	•	•	•	•	•	•	•	•	•	•	•	•	•	…	…	…	…
Lesotho	20	•	•	•	•	•	•	•	•	•	•	•	•	•	•	…	…	…
Liberia - Libéria	8	•	•	•	•	•	…	•	…	…	•	…	…	…	…	…	…	…
Libya - Libye	8	•	•	•	•	•	…	•	…	…	…	…	…	…	…	…	…	…
Madagascar	8	•	•	…	…	•	…	•	…	…	…	…	…	…	…	…	…	…
Malawi	16	•	•	•	•	•	•	•	•	•	•	•	…	…	…	…	…	…
Mali	13	•	•	•	•	•	•	•	•	•	…	•	…	…	…	…	…	…
Mauritania - Mauritanie	9	•	…	…	•	•	•	•	•	•	…	…	…	…	…	…	…	…
Mauritius - Maurice	27	•	•	•	•	•	•	•	•	•	•	•	•	•	•	•	•	…
Mayotte	18	•	•	•	•	•	•	•	•	•	…	•	…	…	…	…	…	…
Morocco - Maroc	9	•	…	…	•	•	•	•	•	•	…	…	…	…	…	…	…	…
Mozambique	12	•	•	•	•	•	•	•	•	•	…	•	…	…	…	…	…	…
Namibia - Namibie	14	•	•	•	•	•	•	•	•	•	…	•	…	•	…	…	…	…
Niger	11	•	•	…	•	•	•	•	•	•	…	…	…	…	…	…	…	…
Nigeria - Nigéria	6	•	•	…	•	•	•	…	…	…	…	…	…	…	…	…	…	…
Republic of South Sudan - République de Soudan du Sud	11	•	•	…	•	•	•	•	•	•	…	…	…	…	…	…	…	…
Reunion - Réunion	21	•	•	•	•	•	•	•	•	•	…	•	…	…	…	…	•	…
Rwanda	11	•	•	…	•	•	•	•	•	•	…	…	…	…	…	…	…	…
Saint Helena ex. dep. - Sainte-Hélène sans dép.	23	•	…	•	•	•	•	•	•	•	•	•	•	•	•	…	…	…
Saint Helena: Ascension - Sainte-Hélène: Ascension	1	•	…	…	…	…	…	…	…	…	…	…	…	…	…	…	…	…
Saint Helena: Tristan da Cunha - Sainte-Hélène: Tristan da Cunha	4	•	…	…	•	•	•	…	…	…	…	…	…	…	…	…	…	…
Sao Tome and Principe - Sao Tomé-et-Principe	16	•	•	•	•	•	•	•	•	•	…	•	…	…	…	…	…	…
Senegal - Sénégal	11	•	•	…	•	•	•	•	•	•	…	…	…	…	…	…	…	…
Seychelles	24	•	•	•	•	•	•	•	•	•	•	•	•	•	•	…	•	•
Sierra Leone	13	•	•	•	•	•	•	•	•	•	…	•	…	…	…	…	…	…
Somalia - Somalie	3	•	•	…	…	•	…	…	…	…	…	…	…	…	…	…	…	…
South Africa - Afrique du Sud	27	•	•	•	•	•	•	•	•	•	•	•	•	•	•	…	…	…
Sudan - Soudan	10	•	•	…	•	•	•	•	•	•	…	…	…	…	…	…	…	…
Togo	8	•	•	…	•	•	•	•	•	…	…	…	…	…	…	…	…	…
Tunisia - Tunisie	19	•	•	•	•	•	•	•	•	•	•	•	•	…	…	…	…	…

Table A. Demographic Yearbook 2018 synoptic table: Availability of data by country/area, table and sex, where applicable
Tableau A. Tableau synoptique de l'Annuaire démographique 2018 : Disponibilité des données par pays ou zone, tableau et le sexe, si disponible

Continent and country or area / Continent et pays ou zone	General topic and table number - Sujet général et numéro de tableau												
	Infant and maternal mortality - Mortalité infantile et mortalité liée à la maternité				General mortality - Mortalité générale					Nuptiality and divorces - Nuptialité et divortialité			
	15	16 Total	16 M/F	17	18	19 Total	19 M/F	20	21	22	23	24	25
Total number of countries or areas - Total des pays ou zones	141	106	104	129	170	156	155	71	189	143	106	117	85

AFRICA - AFRIQUE

Country	15	16 Total	16 M/F	17	18	19 Total	19 M/F	20	21	22	23	24	25
Algeria - Algérie	•	…	…	…	•	•	…	…	•	•	…	…	…
Angola	•	…	…	…	•	…	…	…	•	…	…	…	…
Benin - Bénin	…	…	…	…	…	…	…	…	•	…	…	…	…
Botswana	•	•	•	…	•	•	•	…	•	•	•	•	…
Burkina Faso	…	…	…	…	…	…	…	…	•	…	…	…	…
Burundi	…	…	…	…	…	…	…	…	•	…	…	…	…
Cabo Verde	…	…	…	•	…	…	…	…	•	…	…	…	…
Cameroon - Cameroun	…	…	…	…	…	…	…	…	…	…	…	…	…
Central African Republic - République centrafricaine	…	…	…	…	…	…	…	…	…	…	…	…	…
Chad - Tchad	…	…	…	…	…	…	…	…	…	…	…	…	…
Comoros - Comores	…	…	…	…	…	…	…	…	•	…	…	…	…
Congo	•	…	…	…	•	…	…	…	•	…	…	…	…
Côte d'Ivoire	•	…	…	…	•	…	…	…	•	…	•	…	…
Democratic Republic of the Congo - République démocratique du Congo	…	…	…	…	…	…	…	…	…	…	…	…	…
Djibouti	…	…	…	…	…	…	…	…	…	…	…	…	…
Egypt - Égypte	•	•	…	•	•	•	…	…	•	•	…	…	•
Equatorial Guinea - Guinée équatoriale	…	…	…	…	…	…	…	…	•	…	…	…	…
Eritrea - Érythrée	…	…	…	…	…	…	…	…	•	…	…	…	…
Eswatini	…	…	…	…	…	…	…	…	•	…	…	…	…
Ethiopia - Éthiopie	…	…	…	…	…	…	…	…	…	…	…	…	…
Gabon	…	…	…	…	…	…	…	…	…	…	…	…	…
Gambia - Gambie	…	…	…	…	…	…	…	…	…	…	…	…	…
Ghana	…	…	…	…	…	•	…	•	…	…	…	…	…
Guinea - Guinée	•	…	…	…	•	…	…	…	•	…	…	…	…
Guinea-Bissau - Guinée-Bissau	•	…	…	…	…	…	…	…	…	…	…	…	…
Kenya	•	…	…	…	•	…	…	…	•	…	…	…	•
Lesotho	•	…	…	…	•	…	…	…	•	…	…	…	•
Liberia - Libéria	…	…	…	…	…	…	…	…	…	…	…	…	…
Libya - Libye	…	…	…	…	…	…	…	…	…	…	…	…	…
Madagascar	…	…	…	…	…	…	…	…	•	…	…	…	…
Malawi	…	…	…	…	…	•	…	…	…	…	…	…	…
Mali	…	…	…	…	…	•	…	…	…	…	…	…	…
Mauritania - Mauritanie	…	…	…	…	…	…	…	…	•	…	…	…	…
Mauritius - Maurice	•	•	•	…	•	•	•	…	•	•	•	•	•
Mayotte	•	…	…	…	…	…	…	…	…	…	…	…	…
Morocco - Maroc	…	…	…	•	…	…	…	…	•	…	…	…	…
Mozambique	…	…	…	…	…	…	…	…	…	…	…	…	…
Namibia - Namibie	…	…	…	…	…	…	…	…	…	…	…	…	…
Niger	…	…	…	…	…	…	…	…	…	…	…	…	…
Nigeria - Nigéria	…	…	…	…	…	…	…	…	…	…	…	…	…
Republic of South Sudan - République de Soudan du Sud	…	…	…	…	…	•	…	•	…	…	…	…	…
Reunion - Réunion	•	…	…	•	…	…	…	…	•	…	…	•	…
Rwanda	…	…	…	…	…	…	…	…	…	…	…	…	…
Saint Helena ex. dep. - Sainte-Hélène sans dép.	•	•	•	…	•	•	…	…	•	…	…	…	…
Saint Helena: Ascension - Sainte-Hélène: Ascension	…	…	…	…	…	…	…	…	…	…	…	…	…
Saint Helena: Tristan da Cunha - Sainte-Hélène: Tristan da Cunha	…	…	…	…	…	…	…	…	…	…	…	…	…
Sao Tome and Principe - Sao Tomé-et-Principe	…	…	…	…	…	•	…	…	…	…	…	…	…
Senegal - Sénégal	…	…	…	…	…	…	…	…	…	…	…	…	…
Seychelles	•	…	…	…	•	…	…	…	•	•	•	•	…
Sierra Leone	…	…	…	…	…	•	…	…	…	…	…	…	…
Somalia - Somalie	…	…	…	…	…	…	…	…	…	…	…	…	…
South Africa - Afrique du Sud	…	…	…	…	…	…	…	…	•	…	•	•	…
Sudan - Soudan	…	…	…	…	…	…	…	…	•	…	…	•	…
Togo	…	…	…	…	…	…	…	…	•	…	…	•	…
Tunisia - Tunisie	…	…	…	•	…	…	…	…	•	•	•	•	…

31

Table A. Demographic Yearbook 2018 synoptic table: Availability of data by country/area, table and sex, where applicable
Tableau A. Tableau synoptique de l'Annuaire démographique 2018 : Disponibilité des données par pays ou zone, tableau et le sexe, si disponible (continued - suite)

General topic and table number - Sujet général et numéro de tableau

Continent and country or area / Continent et pays ou zone	Table totals	Summary - Apercu 3 Total	3 M/F	4	5	Population 6 Total[1]	6 M/F	7 Total	7 M/F	8 Total	8 M/F	9	Fertility - Natalité 10 Total	10 M/F	11	Foetal mortality - Mortalité foetale 12	13	14

AFRICA - AFRIQUE

Country	Table totals
Uganda - Ouganda	10
United Republic of Tanzania - République Unie de Tanzanie	10
Western Sahara - Sahara occidental	3
Zambia - Zambie	13
Zimbabwe	10

AMERICA, NORTH - AMÉRIQUE DU NORD

Country	Table totals
Anguilla	17
Antigua and Barbuda - Antigua-et-Barbuda	14
Aruba	25
Bahamas	24
Barbados - Barbade	13
Belize	20
Bermuda - Bermudes	28
British Virgin Islands - Îles Vierges britanniques	19
Canada	24
Cayman Islands - Îles Caïmanes	18
Costa Rica	29
Cuba	29
Curaçao	23
Dominica - Dominique	13
Dominican Republic - République dominicaine	29
El Salvador	24
Greenland - Groenland	20
Grenada - Grenade	24
Guadeloupe	20
Guatemala	26
Haiti - Haïti	9
Honduras	11
Jamaica - Jamaïque	22
Martinique	21
Mexico - Mexique	30
Montserrat	21
Nicaragua	19
Panama	28
Puerto Rico - Porto Rico	27
Saint Kitts and Nevis - Saint-Kitts-et-Nevis	9
Saint Lucia - Sainte-Lucie	17
Saint Pierre and Miquelon - Saint Pierre-et-Miquelon	19
Saint Vincent and the Grenadines - Saint-Vincent-et-les Grenadines	22
Saint-Barthélemy	16
Saint-Martin (French part) - Saint-Martin (partie française)	16
Sint Maarten (Dutch part) - Saint-Martin (partie néerlandaise)	13
Trinidad and Tobago - Trinité-et-Tobago	21
Turks and Caicos Islands - Îles Turques et Caïques	21
United States of America - États-Unis d'Amérique	25
United States Virgin Islands - Îles Vierges américaines	9

Table A. Demographic Yearbook 2018 synoptic table: Availability of data by country/area, table and sex, where applicable
Tableau A. Tableau synoptique de l'Annuaire démographique 2018 : Disponibilité des données par pays ou zone, tableau et le sexe, si disponible (continued - suite)

General topic and table number - Sujet général et numéro de tableau

Continent and country or area / Continent et pays ou zone	Infant and maternal mortality - Mortalité infantile et mortalité liée à la maternité				General mortality - Mortalité générale					Nuptiality and divorces - Nuptialité et divortialité			
	15	16 Total	16 M/F	17	18	19 Total	19 M/F	20	21	22	23	24	25
AFRICA - AFRIQUE													
Uganda - Ouganda	...	...	...	...	...	...	•	...	...	...	•	...	...
United Republic of Tanzania - République Unie de Tanzanie	...	...	...	...	...	...	•	...	...	...	•	...	...
Western Sahara - Sahara occidental	...	...	...	...	...	...	•	...	...	...	•	...	...
Zambia - Zambie	...	...	...	•	•	...	...	...	...	...	•	...	...
Zimbabwe	...	...	...	...	...	...	•	...	...	...	•	...	...
AMERICA, NORTH - AMÉRIQUE DU NORD													
Anguilla	...	...	...	•	•	•	...	...	...	•	...	•	...
Antigua and Barbuda - Antigua-et-Barbuda	•	...	...	•	•	•	...	...	...	•	...	•	...
Aruba	•	•	•	•	•	•	•	...	•	•	•	•	•
Bahamas	•	•	•	•	•	•	•	...	•	•	•	•	•
Barbados - Barbade	•	•	•	•	•	•	•	•	•	•	•	•	•
Belize	•	•	•	•	•	•	•	•	•	•	•	•	•
Bermuda - Bermudes	•	•	•	•	•	•	•	...	•	•	•	•	•
British Virgin Islands - Îles Vierges britanniques	•	...	...	•	•	•	...	...	...	•	•	•	•
Canada	•	•	•	•	•	•	•	•	...	•	•	...	...
Cayman Islands - Îles Caïmanes	...	•	...	•	•	•	...	...	...	•	•	•	•
Costa Rica	•	•	•	•	•	•	•	•	•	•	•	•	•
Cuba	•	•	•	•	•	•	•	•	•	•	•	•	•
Curaçao	•	•	•	...	•	•	•	...	•	•	•	•	•
Dominica - Dominique	...	•	...	...	•	•	...	...	...	•	•	•	•
Dominican Republic - République dominicaine	•	•	•	•	•	•	•	•	•	•	•	•	•
El Salvador	•	•	•	•	•	•	•	•	•	•	•	...	•
Greenland - Groenland	•	•	•	...	•	•	•	•	•	•	•	•	•
Grenada - Grenade	•	•	•	•	•	•	•	...	•	•	•	•	•
Guadeloupe	•	•	•	•	•	•	•	•	•	•	•	•	•
Guatemala	•	•	•	•	•	•	•	•	•	•	•	•	•
Haiti - Haïti	...	...	...	...	...	...	...	...	...	...	...	...	...
Honduras	•	•	•	•	•	•	•	•	•	•	•	•	•
Jamaica - Jamaïque	•	•	•	•	•	•	•	...	•	•	•	•	•
Martinique	•	•	•	•	•	•	•	•	•	•	•	•	•
Mexico - Mexique	•	•	•	•	•	•	•	•	•	•	•	•	•
Montserrat	•	•	•	•	•	•	•	...	•	•	•	•	•
Nicaragua	•	•	•	•	•	•	•	•	•	•	•	•	•
Panama	•	•	•	•	•	•	•	•	•	•	•	•	•
Puerto Rico - Porto Rico	•	•	•	•	•	•	•	•	•	•	•	•	...
Saint Kitts and Nevis - Saint-Kitts-et-Nevis	...	•	...	•	•	...	...	...	...	...	...	•	...
Saint Lucia - Sainte-Lucie	•	•	•	•	•	•	•	•	•	...	•	•	•
Saint Pierre and Miquelon - Saint Pierre-et-Miquelon	...	...	...	...	...	•	...	...	...	•	...	...	...
Saint Vincent and the Grenadines - Saint-Vincent-et-les Grenadines	•	•	•	•	•	•	...	...	...	•	•	•	•
Saint-Barthélemy	...	...	...	...	...	...	...	...	...	...	...	...	...
Saint-Martin (French part) - Saint-Martin (partie française)	•	...	...	...	•	•	...	...	...	...	•	...	...
Sint Maarten (Dutch part) - Saint-Martin (partie néerlandaise)	...	...	...	...	...	...	•	...	...	•	•	•	•
Trinidad and Tobago - Trinité-et-Tobago	...	•	...	...	•	•	•	•	...	•	...	...	•
Turks and Caicos Islands - Îles Turques et Caïques	•	•	•	•	•	•	•	...	•	•	•	...	•
United States of America - États-Unis d'Amérique	•	•	•	•	•	•	•	•	•	•	...	•	...
United States Virgin Islands - Îles Vierges américaines	...	...	...	•	...	...	...	...	...	...	•	...	...

Table A. Demographic Yearbook 2018 synoptic table: Availability of data by country/area, table and sex, where applicable
Tableau A. Tableau synoptique de l'Annuaire démographique 2018 : Disponibilité des données par pays ou zone, tableau et le sexe, si disponible (continued - suite)

General topic and table number - Sujet général et numéro de tableau

Continent and country or area / Continent et pays ou zone	Table totals	Summary - Apercu 3 Total	M/F	4	5	Population 6 Total[1]	M/F	7 Total	M/F	8 Total	M/F	9	Fertility - Natalité 10 Total	M/F	11	Foetal mortality - Mortalité foetale 12	13	14

AMERICA, SOUTH - AMÉRIQUE DU SUD

Argentina - Argentine	22	•	•	•	•	•	•	•	•	•	•		•	•	...	...	...	...
Bolivia (Plurinational State of) - Bolivie (État plurinational de)	17	•	•	•	•	•	•	•	•	•	•		•	...	...	...	...	•
Brazil - Brésil	26	•	•	•	•	•	•	•	•	•	•	...	•	...	•	•	•	
Chile - Chili	27	•	•	•	•	•	•	•	•	•	•		•	•	•	•	•	
Colombia - Colombie	25	•	•	•	•	•	•	•	•	•	•		•	•	•	•	•	
Ecuador - Équateur	29	•	•	•	•	•	•	•	•	•	•		•	•	•	•	•	
Falkland Islands (Malvinas) - Îles Falkland (Malvinas)	8	•	•	...	...	•	•	•	•	•	•		•	...	•	•	...	
French Guiana - Guyane française	20	•	•	•	•	•	•	•	•	•	•		•	•	•	•	•	
Guyana	13	•	•	•	•	•	•	•	•	•	•	...	•	...	•	•	•	
Paraguay	21	•	•	•	•	•	•	•	•	•	•		•	•	•	•	•	
Peru - Pérou	24	•	•	•	•	•	•	•	•	•	•		•	•	•	•	•	
Suriname	22	•	•	•	•	•	•	•	•	•	•		•	•	•	•	•	
Uruguay	25	•	•	•	•	•	•	•	•	•	•		•	•	•	•	•	
Venezuela (Bolivarian Republic of) - Venezuela (République bolivarienne du)	26	•	•	•	•	•	•	•	•	•	•	...	•	...	•	•	•	

ASIA - ASIE

Afghanistan	10	•	•	...	•	•	•	•	•	•	•		...	...	...	...	•	
Armenia - Arménie	29	•	•	•	•	•	•	•	•	•	•		...	•	•	•	•	•
Azerbaijan - Azerbaïdjan	30	•	•	•	•	•	•	•	•	•	•		•	•	•	•	•	•
Bahrain - Bahreïn	28	•	•	•	•	•	•	•	•	•	•		•	•	•	•	•	
Bangladesh	19	•	•	•	•	•	•	•	•	•	•		...	•	•	...	...	
Bhutan - Bhoutan	13	•	•	•	•	•	•	•	•	•	•		...	•	•	•	•	
Brunei Darussalam - Brunéi Darussalam	24	•	•	•	•	•	•	•	•	•	•		•	•	•	•	•	
Cambodia - Cambodge	9	•	•	...	...	•	•	•	•	•	•		•	...	...	...	...	
China - Chine[2]	14	•	•	•	•	•	•	•	•	•	•		•	...	•	•	•	
China, Hong Kong SAR - Chine, Hong Kong RAS	29	•	•	•	•	•	•	•	•	•	•		•	•	•	•	•	
China, Macao SAR - Chine, Macao RAS	27	•	•	•	•	•	•	•	•	•	•		•	•	•	•	...	
Cyprus - Chypre	25	•	•	•	•	•	•	•	•	•	•	...	•	•	•	•	•	
Democratic People's Republic of Korea - République populaire démocratique de Corée	5	•	•	...	...	•	•	•	•	•	•		•	...	...	...	...	
Georgia - Géorgie	28	•	•	•	•	•	•	•	•	•	•		•	•	•	•	•	•
India - Inde[3]	14	•	•	•	•	•	•	•	•	•	•		...	•	•	...	...	
Indonesia - Indonésie	16	•	•	•	•	•	•	•	•	•	•		...	•	•	...	...	
Iran (Islamic Republic of) - Iran (République islamique d')	23	•	•	•	•	•	•	•	•	•	•		•	...	•	•	•	
Iraq	10	•	•	...	•	•	•	•	•	•	•		•	...	...	...	...	
Israel - Israël[4]	30	•	•	•	•	•	•	•	•	•	•		•	•	•	•	•	•
Japan - Japon	30	•	•	•	•	•	•	•	•	•	•		•	•	•	•	•	•
Jordan - Jordanie	17	•	•	•	•	•	•	•	•	•	•		...	•	•	...	...	
Kazakhstan	29	•	•	•	•	•	•	•	•	•	•		•	•	•	•	•	•
Kuwait - Koweït	26	•	•	•	•	•	•	•	•	•	•		•	•	•	•	•	
Kyrgyzstan - Kirghizstan	30	•	•	•	•	•	•	•	•	•	•		•	•	•	•	•	•
Lao People's Democratic Republic - République démocratique populaire lao	11	•	•	•	•	•	•	•	•	•	•		•	...	...	...	...	
Lebanon - Liban	11	•	•	...	•	•	•	...	•	•	•		...	•	...	...	...	
Malaysia - Malaisie	21	•	•	•	•	•	•	•	•	•	•	...	•	...	•	•	•	
Maldives	25	•	•	•	•	•	•	•	•	•	•		•	•	•	•	•	
Mongolia - Mongolie	29	•	•	•	•	•	•	•	•	•	•		•	•	•	•	•	•
Myanmar	21	•	•	•	•	•	•	•	•	•	•		•	•	•	...	...	
Nepal - Népal	10	•	•	...	•	•	•	•	•	•	•		•	...	...	...	...	
Oman	25	•	•	•	•	•	•	•	•	•	•		•	•	•	•	•	
Pakistan[5]	8	•	•	•	•	•	•	•	•	...	...		...	...	...	...	...	
Philippines	24	•	•	•	•	•	•	•	•	•	•	...	•	...	•	•	•	
Qatar	27	•	•	•	•	•	•	•	•	•	•		•	•	•	•	...	
Republic of Korea - République de Corée	28	•	•	•	•	•	•	•	•	•	•		•	•	•	•	•	
Saudi Arabia - Arabie saoudite	19	•	•	•	•	•	•	•	•	•	•		•	•	•	•	•	
Singapore - Singapour	29	•	•	•	•	•	•	•	•	•	•	...	•	•	•	•	•	

Continent and country or area Continent et pays ou zone	15	16 Total	16 M/F	17	18	19 Total	19 M/F	20	21	22	23	24	25
AMERICA, SOUTH - AMÉRIQUE DU SUD													
Argentina - Argentine	•	...	...	•	...	...	•	...	...	•	...	...	...
Bolivia (Plurinational State of) - Bolivie (État plurinational de)	...	...	...	...	...	...	•	...	•	...	•	...	...
Brazil - Brésil	...	•	•	...	...	•	•	...	•	•	•	•	•
Chile - Chili	•	•	•	•	...	•	•	•	•	•	•	...	•
Colombia - Colombie	•	•	•	•	...	•	•	...	•	...	•	•	•
Ecuador - Équateur	•	•	•	•	...	•	•	•	•	•	•	•	•
Falkland Islands (Malvinas) - Îles Falkland (Malvinas)	...	...	...	...	...	...	...	...	...	...	...	...	...
French Guiana - Guyane française	...	...	...	...	•	•	•	•	•	•	•	...	•
Guyana	...	...	...	...	•	•	•	•	•	•	•	...	...
Paraguay	...	...	...	...	...	•	•	...	•	•	•	...	...
Peru - Pérou	•	•	•	•	...	•	•	...	•	•	•	...	•
Suriname	•	...	...	•	...	•	•	•	•	•	•	...	...
Uruguay	•	•	•	•	...	•	•	...	•	•	•	...	•
Venezuela (Bolivarian Republic of) - Venezuela (République bolivarienne du)	•	•	•	•	...	•	•	•	•	•	•	•	•
ASIA - ASIE													
Afghanistan	...	...	...	...	...	...	...	•	...	...	...	...	...
Armenia - Arménie	•	•	•	•	•	•	•	•	•	•	•	•	•
Azerbaijan - Azerbaïdjan	•	•	•	•	•	•	•	•	•	•	•	•	•
Bahrain - Bahreïn	•	•	•	•	...	•	•	•	•	•	•	•	•
Bangladesh	•	•	•	•	...	...	...	•	...	•	•	...	...
Bhutan - Bhoutan	...	...	...	...	...	•	•	•	•	...	...	...	...
Brunei Darussalam - Brunéi Darussalam	•	...	...	•	•	•	•	•	•	...	...	...	...
Cambodia - Cambodge	...	...	...	...	...	...	...	•	...	...	...	...	...
China - Chine[2]	...	...	...	...	...	•	•	•	•	...	...	...	...
China, Hong Kong SAR - Chine, Hong Kong RAS	•	•	•	•	...	•	•	•	•	•	•	...	•
China, Macao SAR - Chine, Macao RAS	•	•	•	...	...	•	•	•	•	•	•	•	•
Cyprus - Chypre	•	•	•	•	•	•	•	•	•	•	•	•	•
Democratic People's Republic of Korea - République populaire démocratique de Corée	...	...	...	...	...	...	...	•	...	...	...	...	...
Georgia - Géorgie	•	•	•	•	•	•	•	•	•	•	•	•	•
India - Inde[3]	•	...	...	•	...	...	...	•	...	•	•	...	...
Indonesia - Indonésie	...	...	...	...	...	...	...	•	...	...	...	...	...
Iran (Islamic Republic of) - Iran (République islamique d')	•	...	...	•	...	...	•	...	•	•	•	...	•
Iraq	...	...	...	•	...	...	•	...	•	...	...	...	...
Israel - Israël[4]	•	•	•	•	•	•	•	•	•	•	•	•	•
Japan - Japon	•	•	•	•	•	•	•	•	•	•	•	•	•
Jordan - Jordanie	...	•	•	•	...	•	•	•	•	•	•	•	•
Kazakhstan	•	•	•	•	•	•	•	•	•	•	•	•	•
Kuwait - Koweït	•	•	•	•	...	•	•	•	•	•	•	•	•
Kyrgyzstan - Kirghizstan	•	•	•	•	•	•	•	•	•	•	•	•	•
Lao People's Democratic Republic - République démocratique populaire lao	...	...	...	...	...	...	...	•	...	...	...	...	...
Lebanon - Liban	...	...	...	...	...	...	...	•	...	...	...	•	...
Malaysia - Malaisie	•	•	•	•	...	•	•	•	•	•	•	...	•
Maldives	•	•	•	•	...	•	•	•	•	•	•	...	•
Mongolia - Mongolie	•	•	•	•	...	•	•	•	•	•	•	•	•
Myanmar	...	...	...	...	...	...	...	•	...	...	...	...	...
Nepal - Népal	...	...	...	...	...	...	...	•	...	...	...	...	...
Oman	...	...	...	...	...	...	...	•	...	...	...	...	...
Pakistan[5]	...	...	...	...	...	...	...	•	...	...	...	...	...
Philippines	•	•	•	•	...	•	•	•	•	...	...	...	...
Qatar	•	•	•	•	...	•	•	•	•	•	•	•	•
Republic of Korea - République de Corée	•	•	•	•	...	•	•	•	•	•	•	•	•
Saudi Arabia - Arabie saoudite	...	...	...	...	...	...	...	•	...	...	•	•	•
Singapore - Singapour	•	•	•	•	...	•	•	•	•	•	•	•	•

General topic and table number - Sujet général et numéro de tableau

Continent and country or area / Continent et pays ou zone	Table totals	Summary - Aperçu 3 Total	M/F	4	5	Population 6 Total[1]	M/F	7 Total	M/F	8 Total	M/F	9	Fertility - Natalité 10 Total	M/F	11	Foetal mortality - Mortalité foetale 12	13	14

ASIA - ASIE

Sri Lanka	23	•	•	•	•	•	•	•	•	•	•	•	•	•	...			
State of Palestine - État de Palestine	19	•	•	•	•	•	•	•	...	•	...	...		...				
Syrian Arab Republic - République arabe syrienne	10	•	...	•	•	•	•	•	•	...	...	•	•	•	...			
Tajikistan - Tadjikistan	28	•	•	•	•	•	•	•	•	•	•	•	•	...	•	•		
Thailand - Thaïlande	23	•	•	•	•	•	•	•	•	•	•	•	•	...		•		
Timor-Leste	13	•	•	•	•	•	•	•	•	...	...	•	•					
Turkey - Turquie	27	•	•	•	•	•	•	•	•	•	•	•	•	•	•			
Turkmenistan - Turkménistan	3	•	...	...	...	•	•	...	...	...	...	•						
United Arab Emirates - Émirats arabes unis	22	•	•	•	•	•	•	•	•	...	...	•	•		•			
Uzbekistan - Ouzbékistan	29	•	•	•	•	•	•	•	•	•	•	•	•	•				
Viet Nam	9	•	•	•	•	•	•	•	•	•	...	...	...	•				
Yemen - Yémen	12	•	•	•	•	•	•	•	•	•	...	...	...					

EUROPE

Åland Islands - Îles d'Åland	27	•	•	•	•	•	•	•	•	•	•	•	•	•				
Albania - Albanie	27	•	•	•	•	•	•	•	•	•	•	•	•	•			•	
Andorra - Andorre	24	•	•	•	•	•	•	•	•	•	•	•	•	•			...	
Austria - Autriche	28	•	•	•	•	•	•	•	•	•	•	•	•	•			...	
Belarus - Bélarus	29	•	•	•	•	•	•	•	•	•	•	•	•	...				
Belgium - Belgique	30	•	•	•	•	•	•	•	•	•	•	•	•	•			•	
Bosnia and Herzegovina - Bosnie-Herzégovine	24	•	•	•	•	•	•	•	•	...	•	•	•	•		•	...	
Bulgaria - Bulgarie	30	•	•	•	•	•	•	•	•	•	•	•	•	•			•	
Croatia - Croatie	29	•	•	•	•	•	•	•	•	•	•	•	•	•			•	
Czechia - Tchéquie	30	•	•	•	•	•	•	•	•	•	•	•	•	•			•	
Denmark - Danemark	30	•	•	•	•	•	•	•	•	•	•	•	•	•			•	
Estonia - Estonie	30	•	•	•	•	•	•	•	•	•	•	•	•	•			•	
Faeroe Islands - Îles Féroé	29	•	•	•	•	•	•	•	•	•	•	•	•	•			•	
Finland - Finlande	30	•	•	•	•	•	•	•	•	•	•	•	•	•			•	
France	29	•	•	•	•	•	•	•	•	•	•	•	•	•			•	
Germany - Allemagne	30	•	•	•	•	•	•	•	•	•	•	•	•	•			•	
Gibraltar	17	•	•	•	•	•	•	•	•	•	•	•	•	...			...	
Greece - Grèce	28	•	•	•	•	•	•	•	•	•	•	•	•	•			•	
Guernsey - Guernesey	11	•	•	•	•	•	•	•	•	...	...	•	•					
Holy See - Saint-Siège	6	•	•	...	•	•	•	•	•	...	...	...	...					
Hungary - Hongrie	30	•	•	•	•	•	•	•	•	•	•	•	•	•			•	
Iceland - Islande	28	•	•	•	•	•	•	•	•	•	•	•	•	•			•	
Ireland - Irlande	26	•	•	•	•	•	•	•	•	•	...	•	•	•			...	
Isle of Man - Île de Man	16	•	...	•	•	•	•	•	•	•	•	•	•			•		
Italy - Italie	30	•	•	•	•	•	•	•	•	•	•	•	•	•			•	
Jersey	13	•	•	•	•	•	•	•	•	•	...	•	•					
Latvia - Lettonie	30	•	•	•	•	•	•	•	•	•	•	•	•	•			•	
Liechtenstein	22	•	...	•	•	•	•	•	•	•	•	•	•			•		
Lithuania - Lituanie	30	•	•	•	•	•	•	•	•	•	•	•	•	•			•	
Luxembourg	28	•	•	•	•	•	•	•	•	•	•	•	•	•			•	
Malta - Malte	28	•	•	•	•	•	•	•	•	•	•	•	•	•			•	
Monaco	14	•	•	•	•	•	•	•	•	...	...	•	•			•		
Montenegro - Monténégro	26	•	•	•	•	•	•	•	•	•	•	•	•	•			•	
Netherlands - Pays-Bas	28	•	•	•	•	•	•	•	•	•	•	•	•	•			•	
North Macedonia - Macédoine du Nord	28	•	•	•	•	•	•	•	•	•	•	•	•	•			•	
Norway - Norvège	29	•	•	•	•	•	•	•	•	•	•	•	•	•			•	
Poland - Pologne	30	•	•	•	•	•	•	•	•	•	•	•	•	•			•	
Portugal	30	•	•	•	•	•	•	•	•	•	•	•	•	•			•	
Republic of Moldova - République de Moldova	29	•	•	•	•	•	•	•	•	•	•	•	•	...			•	
Romania - Roumanie	30	•	•	•	•	•	•	•	•	•	•	•	•	•			•	
Russian Federation - Fédération de Russie	23	•	•	...	•	•	•	•	•	•	•	•	•	•			•	
San Marino - Saint-Marin	28	•	•	•	•	•	•	•	•	•	•	•	•	...			...	
Serbia - Serbie	30	•	•	•	•	•	•	•	•	•	•	•	•	•			•	
Slovakia - Slovaquie	30	•	•	•	•	•	•	•	•	•	•	•	•	•			•	
Slovenia - Slovénie	30	•	•	•	•	•	•	•	•	•	•	•	•	•			•	
Spain - Espagne	30	•	•	•	•	•	•	•	•	•	•	•	•	•			•	

Table A. Demographic Yearbook 2018 synoptic table: Availability of data by country/area, table and sex, where applicable
Tableau A. Tableau synoptique de l'Annuaire démographique 2018 : Disponibilité des données par pays ou zone, tableau et le sexe, si disponible (continued - suite)

General topic and table number - Sujet général et numéro de tableau

Continent and country or area / Continent et pays ou zone	15	16 Total	16 M/F	17	18	19 Total	19 M/F	20	21	22	23	24	25
ASIA - ASIE													
Sri Lanka	•	•	•	...	•	•	•	•	•	•	•	•	...
State of Palestine - État de Palestine	•	...	...	...	•	•	•	•	•	•	•	•	...
Syrian Arab Republic - République arabe syrienne	...	...	...	•	•	•	•	•	•	•	•	•	•
Tajikistan - Tadjikistan	•	•	•	•	•	•	•	•	•	•	•	•	•
Thailand - Thaïlande	•	•	•	•	•	•	•	•	•	•	...	•	•
Timor-Leste	...	...	...	•	•	...	...	•	•	•	•	•	•
Turkey - Turquie	•	•	•	•	•	•	•	•	•	•	•	•	•
Turkmenistan - Turkménistan	...	...	...	•	...	...	...	•	•	•	•	•	•
United Arab Emirates - Émirats arabes unis	•	•	•	•	•	•	•	•	•	•	•	•	•
Uzbekistan - Ouzbékistan	•	•	•	•	•	•	•	•	•	•	•	•	•
Viet Nam	...	...	...	...	•	...	...	•	•	•	•	•	...
Yemen - Yémen	...	...	...	...	•	...	...	•	...	•	•	•	...
EUROPE													
Åland Islands - Îles d'Åland	•	•	•	•	•	•	•	•	•	•	•	•	•
Albania - Albanie	•	•	•	...	•	•	•	•	•	•	•	•	...
Andorra - Andorre	•	•	•	•	•	•	•	•	•	...	•	•	•
Austria - Autriche	•	•	•	•	•	•	•	•	•	•	•	•	•
Belarus - Bélarus	•	•	•	•	•	•	•	•	•	•	•	•	•
Belgium - Belgique	•	•	•	•	•	•	•	•	•	•	•	•	•
Bosnia and Herzegovina - Bosnie-Herzégovine	•	•	•	•	•	•	•	...	•	•	•	•	•
Bulgaria - Bulgarie	•	•	•	•	•	•	•	•	•	•	•	•	•
Croatia - Croatie	•	•	•	•	•	•	•	•	•	•	•	•	•
Czechia - Tchéquie	•	•	•	•	•	•	•	•	•	•	•	•	•
Denmark - Danemark	•	•	•	•	•	•	•	•	•	•	•	•	•
Estonia - Estonie	•	•	•	•	•	•	•	•	•	•	•	•	•
Faeroe Islands - Îles Féroé	•	•	•	...	•	•	•	•	•	•	•	•	•
Finland - Finlande	•	•	•	•	•	•	•	•	•	•	•	•	•
France	•	•	•	•	•	•	•	•	•	•	•	•	•
Germany - Allemagne	•	•	•	•	•	•	•	•	•	•	•	•	•
Gibraltar	...	...	...	...	•	•	•	•	•	•	•	•	•
Greece - Grèce	•	•	•	•	•	•	•	•	•	•	•	•	•
Guernsey - Guernesey	...	...	...	...	•	•	•	•	...	...	...	...	...
Holy See - Saint-Siège													
Hungary - Hongrie	•	•	•	•	•	•	•	•	•	•	•	•	•
Iceland - Islande	•	•	•	•	•	•	•	•	•	...	•	•	•
Ireland - Irlande	•	•	•	•	•	•	•	•	•	•	•	•	•
Isle of Man - Île de Man	•	...	...	...	•	•	•	•	•	•	•	•	...
Italy - Italie	•	•	•	•	•	•	•	•	•	•	•	•	•
Jersey	...	...	...	...	•	•	•	•	•	...	...	...	...
Latvia - Lettonie	•	•	•	•	•	•	•	•	•	•	•	•	•
Liechtenstein	•	•	•	•	•	•	•	•	•	•	•	•	•
Lithuania - Lituanie	•	•	•	•	•	•	•	•	•	•	•	•	•
Luxembourg	•	•	•	•	•	•	•	•	•	•	•	•	•
Malta - Malte	•	•	•	•	•	•	•	•	•	•	•	•	•
Monaco	•	•	•	•	•	•	•	•	•	...	•	•	•
Montenegro - Monténégro	•	•	•	•	•	•	•	•	•	•	•	•	•
Netherlands - Pays-Bas	•	•	•	•	•	•	•	•	•	•	•	•	•
North Macedonia - Macédoine du Nord	•	•	...	•	•	•	•	•	•	•	•	•	•
Norway - Norvège	•	•	•	•	•	•	•	•	•	•	•	•	•
Poland - Pologne	•	•	•	•	•	•	•	•	•	•	•	•	•
Portugal	•	•	•	•	•	•	•	•	•	•	•	•	•
Republic of Moldova - République de Moldova	•	•	•	•	•	•	•	•	•	•	•	•	•
Romania - Roumanie	•	•	•	•	•	•	•	•	•	•	•	•	•
Russian Federation - Fédération de Russie	...	•	•	•	•	•	...	•	•	•	...	...	•
San Marino - Saint-Marin	•	•	•	•	•	•	•	•	•	•	•	•	•
Serbia - Serbie	•	•	•	•	•	•	•	•	•	•	•	•	•
Slovakia - Slovaquie	•	•	•	•	•	•	•	•	•	•	•	•	•
Slovenia - Slovénie	•	•	•	•	•	•	•	•	•	•	•	•	•
Spain - Espagne	•	•	•	•	•	•	•	•	•	•	•	•	•

Continent and country or area — Continent et pays ou zone	Table totals	General topic and table number - Sujet général et numéro de tableau															
		Summary - Aperçu				Population						Fertility - Natalité			Foetal mortality - Mortalité foetale		
		3		4	5	6		7		8		9	10		11	12	13	14
		Total	M/F			Total[1]	M/F	Total	M/F	Total	M/F		Total	M/F				

EUROPE

Svalbard and Jan Mayen Islands - Îles Svalbard et Jan Mayen	2	•	•	...	...	...	...	...	...	...	...	...	...	...	...	...	...	...
Sweden - Suède	30	•	•	•	•	•	•	•	•	•	•	•	•	•	•	•	•	•
Switzerland - Suisse	30	•	•	•	•	•	•	•	•	•	•	•	•	•	•	•	•	•
Ukraine	29	•	•	•	•	•	•	•	•	•	•	•	•	•	...	•	•	•
United Kingdom of Great Britain and Northern Ireland - Royaume-Uni de Grande-Bretagne et d'Irlande du Nord	30	•	•	•	•	•	•	•	•	•	•	•	•	•	•	•	•	•

OCEANIA - OCÉANIE

American Samoa - Samoas américaines	19	•	•	•	•	•	•	•	•	•	•	•	•	•	...	...	...	...
Australia - Australie	28	•	•	•	•	•	•	•	•	•	•	•	•	•	•	•	...	...
Cook Islands - Îles Cook	18	•	•	•	•	•	•	•	•	•	•	•	•	...	•	...	...	...
Fiji - Fidji	16	•	•	•	•	•	•	•	•	•	•	...	...	...	...	...	...	...
French Polynesia - Polynésie française	15	•	...	•	•	•	•	•	•	•	•	•	•	...	...	...	...	...
Guam	25	•	•	•	•	•	•	•	•	•	•	•	•	•	...	...	...	...
Kiribati	12	•	•	...	•	•	•	•	•	•	•	...	...	...	...	...	...	...
Marshall Islands - Îles Marshall	9	•	•	...	•	•	•	•	•	...	...	...	...	...	...	...	...	...
Micronesia (Federated States of) - Micronésie (États fédérés de)	9	•	•	...	•	•	•	•	•	...	...	...	...	...	...	...	...	...
Nauru	15	•	•	•	•	•	•	•	•	...	...	...	...	...	...	...	...	...
New Caledonia - Nouvelle-Calédonie	22	•	•	•	•	•	•	•	•	...	•	•	•	...	...	...	...	...
New Zealand - Nouvelle-Zélande	30	•	•	•	•	•	•	•	•	•	•	•	•	•	•	...	...	...
Niue - Nioué	16	•	...	•	•	•	•	•	•	•	•	•	•	...	...	...	...	...
Norfolk Island - Île Norfolk	9	•	•	•	...	•	•	•	•	...	...	...	...	...	...	...	...	...
Northern Mariana Islands - Îles Mariannes septentrionales	14	•	•	•	•	•	•	•	•	•	•	...	...	...	...	...	...	...
Palau - Palaos	18	•	•	•	•	•	•	•	•	•	•	•	•	...	•	•	...	...
Papua New Guinea - Papouasie-Nouvelle-Guinée	9	•	•	...	•	•	•	...	•	•	•	...	...	...	...	...	...	...
Pitcairn	7	•	...	...	...	•	•	•	•	•	•	...	...	...	...	...	...	...
Samoa	19	•	•	•	•	•	•	•	•	•	•	•	•	...	...	...	...	...
Solomon Islands - Îles Salomon	9	•	•	•	•	•	•	•	•	...	...	...	...	...	...	...	...	...
Tokelau - Tokélaou	8	•	•	•	•	•	•	•	•	...	...	•	...	...	...	...	...	...
Tonga	8	•	•	•	•	•	•	•	•	•	...	...	...	...	...	...	...	...
Tuvalu	13	•	...	•	•	•	•	•	•	•	•	...	•	...	...	...	...	...
Vanuatu	15	•	•	•	•	•	•	•	•	•	•	•	•	...	...	...	...	...
Wallis and Futuna Islands - Îles Wallis et Futuna	8	•	...	...	•	•	•	•	•	•	•	...	...	...	...	...	...	...

Table A. Demographic Yearbook 2018 synoptic table: Availability of data by country/area, table and sex, where applicable
Tableau A. Tableau synoptique de l'Annuaire démographique 2018 : Disponibilité des données par pays ou zone, tableau et le sexe, si disponible (continued - suite)

Continent and country or area / Continent et pays ou zone	Infant and maternal mortality - Mortalité infantile et mortalité liée à la maternité				General mortality - Mortalité générale					Nuptiality and divorces - Nuptialité et divortialité			
	15	16 Total	16 M/F	17	18	19 Total	19 M/F	20	21	22	23	24	25
EUROPE													
Svalbard and Jan Mayen Islands - Îles Svalbard et Jan Mayen	…	…	…	…	…	…	…	…	…	…	…	…	…
Sweden - Suède	•	•	•	•	•	•	•	•	•	•	•	•	•
Switzerland - Suisse	•	•	•	•	•	•	•	•	•	•	•	•	•
Ukraine	•	•	•	•	•	•	•	•	•	•	•	•	•
United Kingdom of Great Britain and Northern Ireland - Royaume-Uni de Grande-Bretagne et d'Irlande du Nord	•	•	•	•	•	•	•	•	•	•	•	•	•
OCEANIA - OCÉANIE													
American Samoa - Samoas américaines	•	…	…	…	•	…	…	•	…	…	…	…	…
Australia - Australie	•	•	•	•	•	•	•	•	•	•	•	•	•
Cook Islands - Îles Cook	•	•	•	•	•	•	•	•	…	•	•	•	•
Fiji - Fidji	•	•	•	•	•	•	•	•	…	•	•	•	•
French Polynesia - Polynésie française	•	•	•	•	•	•	•	•	•	•	•	•	•
Guam	•	•	•	•	•	•	•	•	…	•	•	•	•
Kiribati	…	…	…	•	•	•	•	•	…	…	…	…	…
Marshall Islands - Îles Marshall	…	…	…	•	•	•	•	•	…	•	…	…	…
Micronesia (Federated States of) - Micronésie (États fédérés de)	…	…	…	…	•	…	…	…	…	…	…	…	…
Nauru	…	…	…	•	•	•	•	•	…	…	…	…	…
New Caledonia - Nouvelle-Calédonie	•	•	•	•	•	•	•	•	…	•	•	•	•
New Zealand - Nouvelle-Zélande	•	•	•	•	•	•	•	•	•	•	•	•	•
Niue - Nioué	…	…	…	…	•	…	…	•	…	…	…	…	…
Norfolk Island - Île Norfolk	…	…	…	…	•	•	•	•	…	…	…	…	…
Northern Mariana Islands - Îles Mariannes septentrionales	•	•	•	•	•	•	•	•	…	•	…	…	…
Palau - Palaos	•	•	•	•	•	•	•	•	…	…	…	…	…
Papua New Guinea - Papouasie-Nouvelle-Guinée	…	…	…	…	•	…	…	…	…	…	…	…	…
Pitcairn	…	…	…	…	•	…	…	…	…	…	…	…	…
Samoa	•	…	…	•	•	•	•	•	…	•	•	•	•
Solomon Islands - Îles Salomon	•	…	…	•	•	…	…	•	…	…	…	…	…
Tokelau - Tokélaou	…	…	…	…	•	…	…	…	…	…	…	…	…
Tonga	…	…	…	…	•	•	•	•	…	…	…	…	…
Tuvalu	…	…	…	…	•	•	•	•	…	…	…	…	…
Vanuatu	•	…	…	•	•	•	•	•	…	…	…	…	…
Wallis and Futuna Islands - Îles Wallis et Futuna	…	…	…	…	•	…	…	•	…	…	…	…	…

FOOTNOTES - NOTES

• Data presented in the table. - Les données présentées dans le tableau.

… Data not available. - Données non disponibles.

[1] Including countries with data on total population by sex but without data on urban population. - Y compris les pays avec des données sur la population totale selon le sexe mais pas sur la population urbaine.

[2] For statistical purposes, the data for China do not include those for the Hong Kong Special Administrative Region (Hong Kong SAR), Macao special Administrative Region (Macao SAR) and Taiwan province of China. - Pour la présentation des statistiques, les données pour Chine ne comprennent pas la Région Administrative Spéciale de Hong Kong (Hong Kong RAS), la Région Administrative Spéciale de Macao (Macao RAS) et Taïwan province de Chine.

[3] Including data for the Indian-held part of Jammu and Kashmir, the final status of which has not yet been determined. - Y compris les données pour la partie du Jammu et du Cachemire occupée par l'Inde dont le statut définitif n'a pas encore été déterminé.

[4] Including data for East Jerusalem and Israeli residents in certain other territories under occupation by Israeli military forces since June 1967. - Y compris les données pour Jérusalem-Est et les résidents israéliens dans certains autres territoires occupés depuis 1967 par les forces armées israéliennes.

[5] Excluding data for the Pakistan-held part of Jammu and Kashmir, the final status of which has not yet been determined. - Non compris les données concernant la partie du Jammu et Cachemire occupée par le Pakistan dont le statut définitif n'a pas été déterminé.

Table 1 – *Demographic Yearbook 2018*

Table 1 presents for the world and major areas and regions estimates of the order of magnitude of population size, rates of population increase, crude birth and death rates, land area as well as population density.

Description of variables: Estimates of world population by major areas and by regions are presented for 1960, 1970, 1980, 1990, 2000, 2010 and 2018. Average annual percentage rates of population growth, crude birth and crude death rates are shown for the period from 2015 to 2020. Land area in square kilometers and population density estimates relate to 2018.

All population estimates and rates presented in this table were prepared by the Population Division of the United Nations Department of Economic and Social Affairs, and have been published in the *2019 Revision of World Population Prospects*[1].

The scheme of regionalization used for these estimates is described below. Although some continental totals are given, this table presents six major areas that are so drawn as to obtain greater homogeneity in sizes of population, types of demographic circumstances and accuracy of demographic statistics. Five of the major areas are subdivided into a total of 20 regions, which are arranged within the major areas; these regions together with Northern America, which is not subdivided, make a total of 21 regions.

The major areas of Northern America and Latin America and the Caribbean are distinguished, rather than the conventional continents of North America and South America, because population trends in the middle American mainland and the Caribbean region more closely resemble those of South America than those of America north of Mexico. Data for the traditional continents of North and South America can be obtained by adding Central America and Caribbean region to Northern America and deducting from Latin America. Latin America, as defined here, has somewhat wider limits than it would be if defined only to include the Spanish-speaking, French-speaking and Portuguese-speaking countries.

The average annual percentage rates of population growth are calculated by the Population Division of the United Nations using an exponential rate of increase.

Crude birth and crude death rates are expressed in terms of the average annual number of births and deaths, respectively, per 1 000 mid-year population. These rates are estimated.

The land areas of regions are estimated by the Population Division of the United Nations.

Computation: Density, calculated by the Statistics Division of the United Nations, is the number of persons in the total population of 2018 per square kilometer of the respective land area.

Reliability of data: With the exception of land area, all data are set in *italic* type to indicate their conjectural quality.

Limitations: The estimated orders of magnitude of population and land area are subject to all the basic limitations set forth in connection with table 3, and to the same qualifications set forth for population and surface area statistics in sections 3 and 2.4 of the Technical Notes, respectively.

Likewise, rates of population increase and population density are affected by the limitations of the original figures. However, it may be noted that, in compiling data for regional and major areas totals, errors in the components may tend to compensate each other and the resulting aggregates may be more reliable than the quality of the individual components would imply.

Because of their estimated character, many of the birth and death rates shown should also be considered only as orders of magnitude, and not as measures of the true level of fertility or mortality.

In interpreting the population densities, one should consider that some of the regions include large segments of land that are uninhabitable or barely habitable, and density values calculated as described make no allowance for this, nor for differences in patterns of land settlement.

Composition of major areas and regions

AFRICA

Eastern Africa
Burundi
Comoros
Djibouti
Eritrea
Ethiopia
Kenya
Madagascar
Malawi
Mauritius
Mayotte
Mozambique
Réunion
Rwanda
Seychelles
Somalia
South Sudan
Uganda
United Republic of Tanzania
Zambia
Zimbabwe

Middle Africa
Angola
Cameroon
Central African Republic
Chad
Congo
Democratic Republic of the
  Congo
Equatorial Guinea
Gabon
Sao Tome and Principe

Northern Africa
Algeria
Egypt
Libyan Arab Jamahiriya
Morocco
Sudan
Tunisia
Western Sahara

Southern Africa
Botswana
Eswatini
Lesotho
Namibia
South Africa

Western Africa
Benin
Burkina Faso
Cabo Verde
Côte d'Ivoire

Gambia
Ghana
Guinea
Guinea-Bissau
Liberia
Mali
Mauritania
Niger
Nigeria
Saint Helena
Senegal
Sierra Leone
Togo

ASIA

Eastern Asia
China
China, Hong Kong SAR
China, Macao SAR
Democratic People's
  Republic of Korea
Japan
Mongolia
Republic of Korea

South-Central Asia
Afghanistan
Bangladesh
Bhutan
India
Iran (Islamic Republic of)
Kazakhstan
Kyrgyzstan
Maldives
Nepal
Pakistan
Sri Lanka
Tajikistan
Turkmenistan
Uzbekistan

South-Eastern Asia
Brunei Darussalam
Cambodia
Indonesia
Lao People's Democratic
  Republic
Malaysia
Myanmar
Philippines
Singapore
Thailand
Timor Leste
Viet Nam

Western Asia
Armenia
Azerbaijan
Bahrain
Cyprus
Georgia
Iraq
Israel
Jordan
Kuwait
Lebanon
Oman
Qatar
Saudi Arabia
State of Palestine
Syrian Arab Republic
Turkey
United Arab Emirates
Yemen

EUROPE

Eastern Europe
Belarus
Bulgaria
Czech Republic
Hungary
Poland
Republic of Moldova
Romania
Russian Federation
Slovakia
Ukraine

Northern Europe
Åland Islands
Denmark
Estonia
Faeroe Islands
Finland
Guernsey
Iceland
Ireland
Isle of Man
Jersey
Latvia
Lithuania
Norway
Sweden
United Kingdom of Great Britain
  and Northern Ireland

Southern Europe
Albania
Andorra
Bosnia and Herzegovina

Croatia
Gibraltar
Greece
Holy See
Italy
Malta
Montenegro
North Macedonia
Portugal
San Marino
Serbia
Slovenia
Spain

Western Europe
Austria
Belgium
France
Germany
Liechtenstein
Luxembourg
Monaco
Netherlands
Switzerland

LATIN AMERICA and the CARIBBEAN

Caribbean
Anguilla
Antigua and Barbuda
Aruba
Bahamas
Barbados
Bonaire, Saba and Sint Eustatius
British Virgin Islands
Cayman Islands
Cuba
Curaçao
Dominica
Dominican Republic
Grenada
Guadaloupe

Haiti
Jamaica
Martinique
Montserrat
Puerto Rico
Saint Kitts and Nevis
Saint Lucia
Saint Vincent and the
  Grenadines
Sint Maarten (Dutch part)
Trinidad and Tobago
Turks and Caicos Islands
United States Virgin
  Islands

Central America
Belize
Costa Rica
El Salvador
Guatemala
Honduras
Mexico
Nicaragua
Panama

South America
Argentina
Bolivia (Plurinational State of)
Brazil
Chile
Colombia
Ecuador
Falkland Islands (Malvinas)
French Guiana
Guyana
Paraguay
Peru
Suriname
Uruguay
Venezuela (Bolivarian Republic of)

NORTHERN AMERICA
Bermuda
Canada
Greenland
Saint Pierre and Miquelon
United States of America

OCEANIA

Australia and New Zealand
Australia
New Zealand
Norfolk Island

Melanesia
Fiji
New Caledonia
Papua New Guinea
Solomon Islands
Vanuatu

Micronesia
Guam
Kiribati
Marshall Islands
Micronesia (Federated States of)
Nauru
Northern Mariana Islands
Palau

Polynesia
American Samoa
Cook Islands
French Polynesia
Niue
Pitcairn
Samoa
Tokelau
Tonga
Tuvalu
Wallis and Futuna Islands

---

[1] United Nations, Department of Economic and Social Affairs, Population Division (2019). World Population Prospects: The 2019 Revision (https://population.un.org/wpp/

Tableau 1 – *Annuaire démographique 2018*

Le tableau 1 présente, pour l'ensemble du monde et les grandes zones et régions, des estimations concernant l'ordre de grandeur de la population, les taux d'accroissement démographique, les taux bruts de natalité et de mortalité, la superficie des terres et la densité de peuplement.

Description des variables : des estimations de la population mondiale par grandes zones et régions sont présentées pour 1960, 1970, 1980, 1990, 2000 et 2010 ainsi que pour 2018. Les taux annuels moyens d'accroissement de la population et les taux bruts de natalité et de mortalité portent sur la période allant de 2015 à 2020. Les indications concernant la superficie des terres exprimée en kilomètres carrés et les estimations de la densité de population se rapportent à 2018.

Toutes les estimations de population et les taux de natalité, taux de mortalité et taux annuels d'accroissement de la population qui sont présentés dans le tableau 1 ont été établis par la Division de la population du Département des affaires économiques et sociales de l'Organisation des Nations Unies, et ont été publiés dans les *Perspectives de la population mondiale : La révision de 2019*[1].

Bien que l'on ait donné certains totaux pour les continents (tous les autres pouvant être calculés), on a réparti le monde en six grandes zones qui ont été découpées de manière à obtenir une plus grande homogénéité du point de vue des dimensions de population, des types de situations démographiques et de l'exactitude des statistiques démographiques. Cinq de ces six grandes zones ont été subdivisées en 20 régions. Avec l'Amérique septentrionale, qui n'est pas subdivisée, on arrive à un total de 21 régions.

Au lieu de faire la distinction classique entre l'Amérique du Nord et l'Amérique du Sud, on a choisi d'opérer une comparaison entre l'Amérique septentrionale et l'Amérique latine et Caraïbes, parce que les tendances démographiques dans la partie continentale de l'Amérique centrale et dans la région des Caraïbes se rapprochent davantage de celles de l'Amérique du Sud que de celles de l'Amérique au nord du Mexique. On obtient les données pour les continents traditionnels de l'Amérique du Nord et de l'Amérique du Sud en extrayant les données concernant l'Amérique centrale et les Caraïbes de celles relatives à l'Amérique latine et en les regroupant avec celles relatives à l'Amérique septentrionale. L'Amérique latine ainsi définie a par conséquent des limites plus larges que celles des pays ou zones de langues espagnole, portugaise et française qui constituent l'Amérique latine au sens le plus strict du terme.

Les taux annuels moyens d'accroissement de la population sont calculés par la Division de la population de l'Organisation des Nations Unies en appliquant un taux d'accroissement exponentiel.

Les taux bruts de natalité et de mortalité représentent respectivement le nombre annuel moyen de naissances et de décès par millier d'habitants en milieu d'année. Ces taux sont estimatifs.

La superficie des terres pour les régions a été estimée par la Division de la population de l'Organisation des Nations Unies.

Calculs : la densité, calculée par la Division de statistique de l'Organisation des Nations Unies, est égale au rapport entre l'effectif total de la population en 2018 et la superficie des terres exprimée en kilomètres carrés.

Fiabilité des données : á l'exception des données concernant la superficie des terres, toutes les données sont reproduites en *italique* pour en faire ressortir le caractère conjectural.

Insuffisance des données : les estimations concernant l'ordre de grandeur de la population et la superficie des terres reposent en partie sur les données du tableau 3 ; elles appellent donc toutes les réserves fondamentales formulées à propos de ce tableau, et celles qui ont été respectivement formulées aux sections 3 et 2.4 des Notes techniques en ce qui concerne les statistiques relatives à la population et à la superficie.

Les taux d'accroissement et les indices de densité de la population se ressentent eux aussi des insuffisances inhérentes aux données de base. Toutefois, il est à noter que, lorsque l'on additionne des données par territoire pour obtenir des totaux régionaux et par grandes zones, les erreurs qu'elles comportent arrivent parfois à s'équilibrer, de sorte que les agrégats obtenus peuvent être un peu plus exacts que chacun des éléments dont on est parti.

Vu leur caractère estimatif, nombre des taux de natalité et de mortalité du tableau 1 doivent être considérés uniquement comme des ordres de grandeur et ne sont pas censés mesurer exactement le niveau de la natalité ou de la mortalité.

Pour interpréter les valeurs de la densité de population, on se souviendra qu'il existe dans certaines des régions de vastes étendues de terres inhabitables ou à peine habitables et que les chiffres calculés selon la méthode indiquée ne tiennent compte ni de ce fait ni des différences de dispersion de la population selon le mode d'habitat.

Composition des grandes zones et régions

AFRIQUE

Afrique orientale
Burundi
Comores
Djibouti
Érythrée
Éthiopie
Kenya
Madagascar
Malawi
Maurice
Mayotte
Mozambique
Ouganda
République-Unie de Tanzanie
Réunion
Rwanda
Seychelles
Somalie
Soudan du Sud
Zambie
Zimbabwe

Afrique centrale
Angola
Cameroun
Congo
Gabon
Guinée équatoriale
République centrafricaine
République démocratique du Congo
Sao Tomé-et-Principe
Tchad

Afrique septentrionale
Algérie
Égypte
Jamahiriya arabe libyenne
Maroc
Sahara occidental
Soudan
Tunisie

Afrique australe
Afrique du Sud
Botswana
Eswatini
Lesotho
Namibie

Afrique occidentale
Bénin
Burkina Faso
Cabo Verde

Côte d'Ivoire
Gambie
Ghana
Guinée
Guinée-Bissau
Libéria
Mali
Mauritanie
Niger
Nigéria
Sainte-Hélène
Sénégal
Sierra Leone
Togo

AMÉRIQUE LATINE ET CARAÏBES

Caraïbes
Anguilla
Antigua-et-Barbuda
Aruba
Bahamas
Barbade
Bonaire, Saint-Eustache et Saba
Cuba
Curaçao
Dominique
Grenade
Guadeloupe
Haïti
Îles Caïmanes
Îles Turques et Caïques
Îles Vierges américaines
Îles Vierges britanniques
Jamaïque
Martinique
Montserrat
Porto Rico
République dominicaine
Saint-Kitts-et-Nevis
Sainte-Lucie
Saint-Martin (partie néerlandaise)
Saint-Vincent-et-les Grenadines
Trinité-et-Tobago

Amérique centrale
Belize
Costa Rica
El Salvador
Guatemala
Honduras

Mexique
Nicaragua
Panama

Amérique du Sud
Argentine
Bolivie (État plurinational de)
Brésil
Chili
Colombie
Équateur
Guyana
Guyane française
Îles Falkland (Malvinas)
Paraguay
Pérou
Suriname
Uruguay
Venezuela (République bolivarienne du)

AMÉRIQUE SEPTENTRIONALE
Bermudes
Canada
États-Unis d'Amérique
Groenland
Saint-Pierre-et-Miquelon

ASIE

Asie orientale
Chine
Chine, Région administrative spéciale de Hong Kong
Chine, Région administrative spéciale de Macao
Japon
Mongolie
République de Corée
République populaire démocratique de Corée

Asie centrale et Asie du Sud
Afghanistan
Bangladesh
Bhoutan
Inde
Iran (République Islamique d')
Kazakhstan
Kirghizistan
Maldives
Népal
Ouzbékistan

44

Pakistan
Sri Lanka
Tadjikistan
Turkménistan

Asie du Sud-Est
Brunéi Darussalam
Cambodge
Indonésie
Malaisie
Myanmar
Philippines
République démocratique populaire lao
Singapour
Thaïlande
Timor-Leste
Viet Nam

Asie occidentale
Arabie saoudite
Arménie
Azerbaïdjan
Bahreïn
Chypre
Émirats arabes unis
État de Palestine
Géorgie
Iraq
Israël
Jordanie
Koweït
Liban
Oman
Qatar
République arabe syrienne
Turquie
Yémen

EUROPE

Europe orientale
Bélarus
Bulgarie
Fédération de Russie
Hongrie

Pologne
République de Moldova
République tchèque
Roumanie
Slovaquie
Ukraine

Europe septentrionale
Danemark
Estonie
Finlande
Guernesey
Île de Man
Îles d'Åland
Îles Féroé
Îles Svalbard et Jan Mayen
Irlande
Islande
Jersey
Lettonie
Lituanie
Norvège
Royaume-Uni de Grande-
    Bretagne et d'Irlande du
    Nord
Suède

Europe méridionale
Albanie
Andorre
Bosnie-Herzégovine
Croatie
Espagne
Gibraltar
Grèce
Italie
Macédoine du Nord
Malte
Monténégro
Portugal
Saint-Marin
Saint-Siège
Serbie
Slovénie

Europe occidentale
Allemagne
Autriche
Belgique
France
Liechtenstein
Luxembourg
Monaco
Pays-Bas
Suisse

OCÉANIE

Australie et Nouvelle-Zélande
Australie
Île Norfolk
Nouvelle-Zélande

Mélanésie
Fidji
Îles Salomon
Nouvelle-Calédonie
Papouasie-Nouvelle-Guinée
Vanuatu

Micronésie
Guam
Îles Mariannes septentrionales
Îles Marshall
Kiribati
Micronésie (États fédérés de)
Nauru
Palaos

Polynésie
Îles Cook
Îles Wallis et Futuna
Nioué
Pitcairn
Polynésie française
Samoa
Samoa américaines
Tokélaou
Tonga
Tuvalu

---

[1] *Organisation des Nations Unies, Département des affaires économiques et sociales, Division de la population (2019). Perspectives de la population mondiale : La révision de 2019* (https://population.un.org/wpp/)

1. Population, rate of increase, birth and death rates, land area and density for the world, major areas and regions: selected years

Population, taux d'accroissement, taux de natalité et taux de mortalité, superficie des terres et densité pour l'ensemble du monde, les régions macro géographiques et les composantes géographiques : diverses années

Major areas and regions / Régions macro géographiques et composantes	Mid-year population estimates - Estimations de population au milieu de l'année (millions)							Annual rate of increase - Taux d'accroissement annuel (%)	Crude birth rate - Taux bruts de natalité	Crude death rate - Taux bruts de mortalité	Land area (km2) - Superficie des terres (km2) (000s)	Density - Densité[1]
	1960	1970	1980	1990	2000	2010	2018	2015-2020			2018	
WORLD TOTAL - ENSEMBLE DU MONDE	3 034.9	3 700.4	4 458.0	5 327.2	6 143.5	6 956.8	7 631.1	1.1	18	8	130 094	59
AFRICA - AFRIQUE	283.4	363.4	476.4	630.3	811.0	1 039.3	1 275.9	2.5	34	8	29 648	43
Eastern Africa - Afrique orientale	83.6	109.7	146.5	197.2	257.4	339.3	422.6	2.7	34	7	6 667	63
Middle Africa - Afrique centrale	32.2	40.2	52.9	70.9	96.1	131.6	169.1	3.0	40	10	6 497	26
Northern Africa - Afrique septentrionale	63.2	82.5	106.8	139.7	171.3	202.9	237.3	1.9	25	6	7 769	31
Southern Africa - Afrique méridionale	19.4	25.0	32.4	42.0	51.4	58.4	65.7	1.4	21	9	2 651	25
Western Africa - Afrique occidentale	84.9	106.1	137.8	180.5	234.7	307.0	381.2	2.7	37	10	6 064	63
LATIN AMERICA AND CARIBBEAN - AMÉRIQUE LATIN ET CARAÏBES	220.5	286.7	361.3	442.8	521.8	591.4	642.2	0.9	17	6	20 139	32
Caribbean - Caraïbes	20.7	25.2	29.6	34.1	38.1	41.2	43.2	0.4	17	8	226	191
Central America - Amérique centrale	51.1	69.4	91.1	113.4	135.3	157.6	175.5	1.2	19	6	2 452	72
South America - Amérique méridionale	148.7	192.1	240.5	295.4	348.4	392.5	423.6	0.9	16	6	17 461	24
NORTHERN AMERICA - AMÉRIQUE SEPTENTRIONALE	204.6	231.0	254.0	279.8	312.4	343.3	364.3	0.7	12	9	18 652	20
ASIA - ASIE	1 705.0	2 142.5	2 649.6	3 226.1	3 741.3	4 209.6	4 560.7	0.9	16	7	31 033	147
Eastern Asia - Asie orientale	805.9	999.4	1 198.1	1 393.3	1 519.8	1 604.9	1 666.5	0.4	11	7	11 560	144
South Central Asia - Asie centrale méridionale	619.1	775.4	980.4	1 240.0	1 511.9	1 775.4	1 967.9	1.2	20	7	10 327	191
South Eastern Asia - Asie méridionale orientale	214.0	281.4	357.6	444.5	525.0	596.9	655.3	1.1	18	6	4 341	151
Western Asia - Asie occidentale	66.1	86.2	113.5	148.3	184.6	232.4	271.0	1.6	21	5	4 805	56
EUROPE	605.4	656.9	693.6	720.9	725.6	736.4	746.4	0.1	10	11	22 135	34
Eastern Europe - Europe orientale	253.5	276.2	294.7	309.8	303.9	294.9	293.8	-0.1	11	13	18 053	16
Northern Europe - Europe septentrionale	81.7	87.3	89.8	92.0	94.5	100.4	105.2	0.5	11	9	1 702	62
Southern Europe - Europe méridionale	117.8	127.5	138.6	143.5	144.8	153.0	152.6	-0.1	8	10	1 295	118
Western Europe - Europe occidentale	152.4	166.0	170.5	175.5	182.3	188.1	194.8	0.4	10	10	1 085	180
OCEANIA - OCÉANIA	16.0	19.9	23.2	27.3	31.4	36.9	41.6	1.4	17	7	8 486	5
Australia and New Zealand - Australie et Nouvelle Zélande	12.6	15.6	17.7	20.4	22.9	26.5	29.6	1.2	13	7	7 946	4
Melanesia - Melanésie	2.9	3.7	4.7	6.0	7.5	9.2	10.7	1.9	27	7	530	20
Micronesia	0.2	0.2	0.3	0.4	0.5	0.5	0.5	1.0	21	6	3	170
Polynesia - Polynésie	0.3	0.4	0.5	0.5	0.6	0.7	0.7	0.5	20	6	8	84

FOOTNOTES - NOTES

[1] Population per square kilometre of land area. Figures are estimates of population divided by land area and are not to be considered as either reflecting density in the urban sense or as indicating the supporting power of a territory's land and resources. - Habitants par kilomètre carré. Il s'agit simplement du quotient calculé en divisant la population par la superficie des terres et n'est par considéré comme indiquant la densité au sens urbain du terme ni l'effectif de population que les terres et les ressources du territoire sont capables de nourrir.

Table 2 - *Demographic Yearbook 2018*

Table 2 presents estimates of population and the percentage distribution by age group and sex as well as the sex ratio for all ages; data are presented for the world, the six major areas and the twenty regions for 2018.

Description of variables: All population estimates presented in this table are prepared by the Population Division of the United Nations Department of Economic and Social Affairs. These estimates are published (using more detailed age groups) in the *2019 Revision of World Population Prospects*[1].

The scheme of regionalization used for these estimates is discussed in detail in the technical notes for table 1. Age groups presented in this table are: 0-14 years, 15-64 years, and 65 years or over. Sex ratio refers to the number of males per 100 females of all ages.

The percentage distributions and the sex ratios that appear in this table were calculated by the Statistics Division of the United Nations Department of Economic and Social Affairs using the estimates prepared by the Population Division of the United Nations Department of Economic and Social Affairs.

Reliability of data: All data are set in *italic* type to indicate their conjectural quality.

Limitations: The data presented in this table are from the same series of estimates, prepared by the Population Division of the United Nations, presented in table 1. The estimated orders of magnitude of population are subject to all the basic limitations set forth for population statistics in section 3 of the Technical Notes. In brief, because they are estimates, these distributions by broad age groups and sex should be considered only as orders of magnitude. However, in compiling data for regional and major areas' totals, errors in the components tend to compensate each other and the resulting aggregates may be somewhat more reliable than the quality of the individual components would imply.

In addition, data in this table are limited by factors affecting data by age. These factors are described in the technical notes for table 7. Because the age groups presented in this table are broad, these problems are minimized.

---

[1] *United Nations, Department of Economic and Social Affairs, Population Division (2019). World Population Prospects: The 2019 Revision* (https://population.un.org/wpp/)

Tableau 2 – *Annuaire démographique 2018*

Le tableau 2 présente, pour l'ensemble du monde, les six grandes zones et les vingt régions, des estimations concernant la population en 2018 ainsi que sa répartition en pourcentage selon des tranches d'âge et le sexe, et le rapport de masculinité pour tous les âges.

Description des variables : toutes les données figurant dans le tableau 2 ont été établies par la Division de la population du Département des affaires économiques et sociales de l'Organisation des Nations Unies, et ont été publiés dans les *Perspectives de la population mondiale : La révision de 2019*[1].

La classification géographique utilisée pour établir ces estimations est exposée en détail dans les notes techniques relatives au tableau 1. Les groupes d'âge présentés dans ce tableau sont définis comme suit : de 0 à 14 ans, de 15 à 64 ans et 65 ans ou plus. Le rapport de masculinité correspond au nombre d'individus de sexe masculin pour 100 individus de sexe féminin sans considération d'âge.

Les pourcentages et les rapports de masculinité qui sont présentés dans le tableau 2 ont été calculés par la Division de statistique du Département des affaires économiques et sociales de l'Organisation des Nations Unies à partir des estimations établies par la Division de la population de l'Organisation des Nations Unies.

Fiabilité des données : toutes les données figurant dans ce tableau sont reproduites en *italique* pour en faire ressortir le caractère conjectural.

Insuffisance des données : les données de ce tableau appartiennent à la même série d'estimations, établie par la Division de la population de l'Organisation des Nations Unies, que celles qui figurent au tableau 1. Les estimations concernant l'ordre de grandeur de la population appellent donc toutes les réserves fondamentales qui ont été formulées à la section 3 des Notes techniques à propos des statistiques relatives à la population. Sans entrer dans le détail, il convient de préciser que les données relatives à la répartition par grand groupe d'âge et par sexe doivent être considérées uniquement comme des ordres de grandeur en raison de leur caractère estimatif. Toutefois, il est à noter que, lorsque l'on additionne des données par territoire pour obtenir des totaux régionaux et par grandes zones, les erreurs qu'elles comportent arrivent parfois à s'équilibrer, de sorte que les agrégats obtenus peuvent être un peu plus exacts que chacun des éléments dont on est parti.

En outre, les donnés figurant dans le tableau 2 comportent certaines imprécisions en raison des facteurs influant sur les données par âge (voir à ce propos les notes techniques relatives au tableau 7). Ces imprécisions sont cependant atténuées du fait de l'étendue des groupes d'âge présentés dans le tableau 2.

---

[1] *Organisation des Nations Unies, Département des affaires économiques et sociales, Division de la population (2019). Perspectives de la population mondiale : La révision de 2019* (https://population.un.org/wpp/)

2. Estimates of population and its percentage distribution by age group and sex, and sex ratio, for the world, major areas and regions: 2018

Estimations de la population et pourcentage de répartition selon les tranches d'âge et le sexe, et le rapport de masculinité, pour l'ensemble du monde, les grandes régions et les régions géographiques : 2018

Major areas and regions / Grandes régions et régions	Population (millions)												Sex ratio - Rapport de masculinité[1]
	Both sexes - Les deux sexes				Male - Masculin				Female - Féminin				
	All ages - Tous âges	0-14	15-64	65+	All ages - Tous âges	0-14	15-64	65+	All ages - Tous âges	0-14	15-64	65+	
WORLD TOTAL - ENSEMBLE DU MONDE													
Number - Nombre	7 631	1 965	4 988	678	3 847	1 015	2 528	304	3 784	950	2 459	374	
Percent - Pourcentage	100.0	25.8	65.4	8.9	100.0	26.4	65.7	7.9	100.0	25.1	65.0	9.9	101.7
AFRICA - AFRIQUE													
Number - Nombre	1 276	520	712	44	637	264	354	20	639	256	358	24	
Percent - Pourcentage	100.0	40.7	55.8	3.4	100.0	41.4	55.6	3.1	100.0	40.1	56.0	3.8	99.8
Eastern Africa - Afrique orientale													
Number - Nombre	423	180	231	12	210	91	114	5	213	89	117	7	
Percent - Pourcentage	100.0	42.6	54.6	2.9	100.0	43.3	54.2	2.5	100.0	41.8	54.9	3.2	98.4
Middle Africa - Afrique centrale													
Number - Nombre	169	77	88	5	84	39	44	2	85	38	44	3	
Percent - Pourcentage	100.0	45.5	51.8	2.8	100.0	45.9	51.6	2.5	100.0	45.0	51.9	3.0	99.5
Northern Africa - Afrique septentrionale													
Number - Nombre	237	78	147	13	119	40	73	6	118	38	73	7	
Percent - Pourcentage	100.0	32.7	61.8	5.5	100.0	33.3	61.6	5.1	100.0	32.0	62.0	6.0	101.0
Southern Africa - Afrique méridionale													
Number - Nombre	66	20	43	3	32	10	21	1	33	10	22	2	
Percent - Pourcentage	100.0	29.8	65.0	5.2	100.0	30.6	65.3	4.2	100.0	29.1	64.8	6.2	97.0
Western Africa - Afrique occidentale													
Number - Nombre	381	166	204	11	192	85	102	5	189	82	102	6	
Percent - Pourcentage	100.0	43.6	53.6	2.8	100.0	44.1	53.4	2.6	100.0	43.0	53.9	3.0	101.3
LATIN AMERICA AND CARIBBEAN - AMÉRIQUE LATIN ET CARAÏBES													
Number - Nombre	642	158	430	54	316	80	212	24	326	77	219	30	
Percent - Pourcentage	100.0	24.5	67.0	8.4	100.0	25.5	67.0	7.5	100.0	23.7	67.0	9.3	96.8
Caribbean - Caraïbes													
Number - Nombre	43	11	28	4	21	5	14	2	22	5	14	2	
Percent - Pourcentage	100.0	24.4	65.5	10.1	100.0	25.2	65.5	9.3	100.0	23.6	65.4	11.0	97.6
Central America - Amérique centrale													
Number - Nombre	175	49	115	12	86	25	56	5	89	24	59	7	
Percent - Pourcentage	100.0	27.6	65.5	6.9	100.0	28.8	64.9	6.3	100.0	26.5	66.0	7.5	96.1
South America - Amérique méridionale													
Number - Nombre	424	99	287	38	209	50	142	16	215	48	145	21	
Percent - Pourcentage	100.0	23.3	67.8	8.9	100.0	24.1	68.0	7.9	100.0	22.5	67.6	9.9	97.1
NORTHERN AMERICA - AMÉRIQUE SEPTENTRIONALE													
Number - Nombre	364	67	239	58	180	34	120	26	184	33	119	32	
Percent - Pourcentage	100.0	18.4	65.6	16.0	100.0	19.0	66.5	14.4	100.0	17.8	64.7	17.4	98.0
ASIA - ASIE													
Number - Nombre	4 561	1 091	3 091	379	2 333	570	1 587	176	2 228	521	1 504	203	
Percent - Pourcentage	100.0	23.9	67.8	8.3	100.0	24.4	68.0	7.5	100.0	23.4	67.5	9.1	104.7
Eastern Asia - Asie orientale													
Number - Nombre	1 666	288	1 173	206	850	153	602	95	816	135	571	111	
Percent - Pourcentage	100.0	17.3	70.4	12.3	100.0	18.1	70.8	11.2	100.0	16.5	69.9	13.6	104.1
South Central Asia - Asie centrale méridionale													
Number - Nombre	1 968	557	1 296	115	1 014	291	668	55	954	267	628	59	
Percent - Pourcentage	100.0	28.3	65.9	5.8	100.0	28.7	65.9	5.5	100.0	28.0	65.8	6.2	106.3
South Eastern Asia - Asie méridionale orientale													
Number - Nombre	655	168	443	43	327	87	222	19	328	82	221	25	
Percent - Pourcentage	100.0	25.7	67.7	6.6	100.0	26.4	67.8	5.7	100.0	25.0	67.5	7.5	99.8
Western Asia - Asie occidentale													
Number - Nombre	271	78	178	15	142	40	95	7	129	38	83	8	
Percent - Pourcentage	100.0	28.6	65.8	5.6	100.0	28.0	67.3	4.7	100.0	29.2	64.3	6.5	109.7
EUROPE													
Number - Nombre	746	119	489	138	360	61	242	57	386	58	247	81	
Percent - Pourcentage	100.0	16.0	65.5	18.5	100.0	17.0	67.3	15.7	100.0	15.0	63.9	21.1	93.3
Eastern Europe - Europe orientale													
Number - Nombre	294	49	198	47	138	25	96	17	156	24	101	30	
Percent - Pourcentage	100.0	16.7	67.3	16.0	100.0	18.2	69.7	12.0	100.0	15.3	65.2	19.5	88.8
Northern Europe - Europe septentrionale													
Number - Nombre	105	18	67	20	52	9	34	9	53	9	34	11	
Percent - Pourcentage	100.0	17.6	63.8	18.6	100.0	18.2	64.8	17.0	100.0	16.9	62.9	20.2	97.4
Southern Europe - Europe méridionale													
Number - Nombre	153	22	99	32	75	11	50	14	78	10	50	18	
Percent - Pourcentage	100.0	14.2	65.1	20.8	100.0	15.0	66.6	18.4	100.0	13.4	63.6	23.0	95.4

2. Estimates of population and its percentage distribution by age group and sex, and sex ratio, for the world, major areas and regions: 2018

Estimations de la population et pourcentage de répartition selon les tranches d'âge et le sexe, et le rapport de masculinité, pour l'ensemble du monde, les grandes régions et les régions géographiques : 2018 (continued - suite)

Major areas and regions Grandes régions et régions	Population (millions)												Sex ratio - Rapport de masculinité[1]
	Both sexes - Les deux sexes				Male - Masculin				Female - Féminin				
	All ages - Tous âges	0-14	15-64	65+	All ages - Tous âges	0-14	15-64	65+	All ages - Tous âges	0-14	15-64	65+	
Western Europe - Europe occidentale													
Number - Nombre	195	30	125	40	96	16	63	17	99	15	62	22	
Percent - Pourcentage	100.0	15.6	64.0	20.4	100.0	16.3	65.5	18.1	100.0	14.9	62.6	22.5	96.4
OCEANIA - OCÉANIA													
Number - Nombre	41.57	9.86	26.59	5.13	20.81	5.07	13.33	2.40	20.76	4.79	13.25	2.72	
Percent - Pourcentage	100.0	23.7	64.0	12.3	100.0	24.4	64.1	11.5	100.0	23.0	63.8	13.1	100.2
Australia and New Zealand - Australie et Nouvelle Zélande													
Number - Nombre	29.64	5.71	19.29	4.64	14.73	2.93	9.62	2.18	14.91	2.78	9.67	2.46	
Percent - Pourcentage	100.0	19.3	65.1	15.7	100.0	19.9	65.3	14.8	100.0	18.6	64.8	16.5	98.8
Melanesia - Melanésie													
Number - Nombre	10.72	3.78	6.53	0.40	5.46	1.95	3.32	0.19	5.25	1.83	3.21	0.22	
Percent - Pourcentage	100.0	35.3	60.9	3.8	100.0	35.8	60.8	3.5	100.0	34.8	61.1	4.1	104.0
Micronesia													
Number - Nombre	0.54	0.16	0.34	0.03	0.27	0.08	0.17	0.02	0.27	0.08	0.17	0.02	
Percent - Pourcentage	100.0	29.8	63.9	6.3	100.0	30.3	64.0	5.6	100.0	29.2	63.7	7.1	102.2
Polynesia - Polynésie													
Number - Nombre	0.68	0.20	0.43	0.05	0.34	0.10	0.22	0.02	0.33	0.10	0.21	0.02	
Percent - Pourcentage	100.0	30.0	63.2	6.8	100.0	30.6	63.1	6.4	100.0	29.4	63.3	7.3	102.9

FOOTNOTES - NOTES

[1] Males per 100 females of all ages - Hommes pour 100 femmes de tous âges

Table 3 - *Demographic Yearbook 2018*

Table 3 presents for each country or area of the world the total, male and female population enumerated at the latest population census, estimates of the mid-year total population for 2010 and 2018, the average annual exponential rate of population increase (or decrease) for the period 2010 to 2018, the surface area and the population density for 2018.

Description of variables: The total, male and female population is the population enumerated at the most recent census for which data are available. The date of this census is given. Population census data are usually the results of a nation-wide gathering of individual information through full field enumeration. Alternatively, other approaches for generating reliable statistics on population and housing can be used by countries, such as the use of population registers. Data that are the result of such an alternative approach are also coded as census and are footnoted accordingly. Also, the results of sample surveys, essentially national in character, may be presented showing the appropriate code.

Mid-year population estimates refer to the population on 1 July. Otherwise, a footnote is appended. Mid-year estimates of the total population are those provided by national statistical offices.

Surface area, expressed in square kilometres, refers to the total surface area, comprising land area and inland waters (assumed to consist of major rivers and lakes) and excluding polar regions as well as uninhabited islands. Exceptions to this are noted. Surface areas, originally reported in square miles by the country or area, have been converted to square kilometres using a conversion factor of 2.589988.

Computation: The annual rate of population increase is the average annual exponential rate of population growth between 2010 and 2018, computed by the Statistics Division of the United Nations Department of Economic and Social Affairs using the unrounded mid-year estimates of 2010 and 2018. This rate is expressed as percentage.

Density is the number of persons in the 2018 total population per square kilometre of total surface area.

Reliability of data: Reliable mid-year population estimates are those that are based on a complete census (or a sample survey) and have been adjusted by a continuous population register or on the basis of the calculated balance of births, deaths and migration. Mid-year estimates of this type are considered reliable and appear in roman type. Mid-year estimates not calculated on this basis are considered less reliable and are shown in italics.

Census data and sample survey results are considered reliable and, therefore, appear in roman type.

Rates of population increase that were calculated using population estimates considered less reliable, as described above, are set in italics rather than roman type.

All surface area data are assumed to be reliable and therefore appear in roman type.

Population density data, however, are considered reliable or less reliable on the basis of the reliability of the 2018 population estimates used as the numerator.

Limitations: Statistics on the total population enumerated at the time of the census, surface area data and estimates of the mid-year total population are subject to the same qualifications as have been set forth for surface area and population data in sections 2.4 and 3 of the Technical Notes, respectively.

Regarding the limitations of census data, it should be noted that although census data are considered reliable, and therefore appear in roman type, the actual quality of census data varies widely from one country or area to another. When known, an estimate of the extent of over-enumeration or under-enumeration is given in footnotes.

Rates of population increase are subject to all the qualifications of the population estimates mentioned above. In some cases, they simply reflect the rate calculated or assumed in constructing the estimates themselves when adequate measures of natural increase and net migration were not available. Despite their shortcomings, these rates provide a useful index for studying population change and can be also useful in evaluating the accuracy of vital and migration statistics.

Population density data as shown in this table give only an indication of actual population density as they do not take account of the dispersion or concentration of population within countries or areas nor the proportion of habitable land. They should not be interpreted as reflecting density in the urban sense or as indicating the supporting power of a territory's land and resources.

Tableau 3 – *Annuaire démographique 2018*

Le tableau 3 indique pour chaque pays ou zone du monde la population totale selon le sexe d'après les derniers recensements effectués, les estimations concernant la population totale au milieu de l'année 2010 et de l'année 2018, le taux moyen d'accroissement annuel exponentiel positif ou négatif de la population pour la période allant de 2010 à 2018, ainsi que la superficie et la densité de population en 2018.

Description des variables : la population masculine et féminine totale est, la population enregistrée lors du recensement le plus récent sur lequel on dispose de données. La date de ce recensement est indiquée. Les données des recensements de la population sont habituellement le résultat d'un collecte à l'échelle nationale des données individuelles obtenues au moyen d'un dénombrement complet. Les pays peuvent recourir à d'autres moyens pour établir des statistiques fiables sur la population et le logement, tels que des registres de la population. Les données obtenues par ce moyen sont présentées comme celles d'un recensement et sont annotées en conséquence. Par ailleurs, les résultats des enquêtes par sondage, réalisées habituellement à l'échelle nationale, peuvent être présentés à l'aide du code correspondant.
Les estimations de la population en milieu d'année sont celles de la population au 1er juillet. Lorsque la date est différente, cela est signalé par une note. Les estimations de la population totale en milieu d'année sont celles qui ont été communiquées par les services nationaux de statistique.

La superficie - exprimée en kilomètres carrés - représente la superficie totale, c'est-à-dire qu'elle englobe les terres émergées et les eaux intérieures (qui sont censées comprendre les principaux lacs et cours d'eau) mais exclut les régions polaires et certaines îles inhabitées. Les exceptions à cette règle sont signalées en note. Les superficies initialement exprimées en miles carrés par les pays ou les zones ont été transformées en kilomètres carrés au moyen d'un coefficient de conversion de 2,589988.

Calculs : le taux d'accroissement annuel est le taux exponentiel annuel moyen de variation (en pourcentage) de la population entre 2010 et 2018, calculé par la Division de statistique du Département des affaires économiques et sociales de l'Organisation des Nations Unies à partir des estimations en milieu d'année non arrondies pour les années 2010 et 2018.

La densité est égale au rapport de l'effectif total de la population en 2018 à la superficie totale, exprimée en kilomètres carrés.

Fiabilité des données : les estimations en milieu d'année qui sont considérées sûres sont fondées sur un recensement complet (ou sur une enquête par sondage) et ont été ajustées en fonction des données provenant d'un registre permanent de population ou en fonction de la balance établie par le calcul des naissances, des décès et des migrations. Les estimations de ce type sont considérées comme sûres et apparaissent en caractères romains. Les estimations en milieu d'année dont le calcul n'a pas été effectué sur cette base sont considérées comme moins sûres et apparaissent en italique.

Les données de recensements ou les résultats d'enquêtes par sondage sont considérés comme sûrs et apparaissent par conséquent en caractères romains.

Les taux d'accroissement de la population, calculés à partir d'estimations jugées moins sûres d'après les normes décrites ci-dessus, sont indiqués en italique plutôt qu'en caractères romains.

Toutes les données de superficie sont présumées sûres et apparaissent par conséquent en caractères romains. En revanche, les données relatives à la densité de la population sont considérées plus ou moins sûres en fonction de la fiabilité des estimations de la population en 2018 ayant servi de numérateur.

Insuffisance des données : les statistiques portant sur la population totale dénombrée lors d'un recensement, les données de superficie et les estimations de la population totale en milieu d'année appellent les mêmes réserves que celles formulées aux sections 2.4 et 3 des Notes techniques à propos des statistiques relatives à la superficie et à la population.

S'agissant de l'insuffisance des données obtenues par recensement, il convient d'indiquer que, bien que ces données soient considérées comme sûres et apparaissent par conséquent en caractères romains, leur qualité réelle varie considérablement d'un pays ou d'une région à l'autre. Lorsque l'on possédait les renseignements voulus, on a donné une estimation du degré de sur-dénombrement ou de sous-dénombrement.
Les taux d'accroissement appellent toutes les réserves formulées plus haut à propos des estimations concernant la population. Dans certains cas, ils représentent seulement le taux calculé ou que l'on a pris

pour base pour établir les estimations elles-mêmes lorsque l'on ne disposait pas de mesures appropriées de l'accroissement naturel et des migrations nettes. Malgré leurs imperfections, ces taux fournissent des indications intéressantes pour l'étude du mouvement de la population et, utilisés avec les précautions nécessaires, ils peuvent également servir à évaluer l'exactitude des statistiques de l'état civil et des migrations.

Les données relatives à la densité de population figurant dans le tableau 3 n'ont qu'une valeur indicative en ce qui concerne la densité de population effective, car elles ne tiennent compte ni de la dispersion ou de la concentration de la population à l'intérieur des pays ou zones, ni de la proportion du territoire qui est habitable. Il ne faut donc y voir d'indication ni de la densité au sens urbain du terme ni du nombre d'habitants qui pourraient vivre sur les terres et avec les ressources naturelles du territoire considéré.

54

3. Population by sex, annual rate of population change, surface area and density
Population selon le sexe, taux de changement annuel de la population, superficie et densité

Continent, country or area and census date / Continent, pays ou zone et date du recensement	Census type[a]	Population at the latest available census / Population d'après le dernier recensement disponible (in units — en unités) Both sexes / Les deux sexes	Male Masculin	Female Feminin	Estimate type[a]	Mid-year estimates / Estimations au milieu de l'année (in thousands — en milliers) 2010	2018	Annual rate of change Taux de changement annuel 2010-18	Surface area Superficie (km²) 2018	Density Densité 2018[b]
AFRICA - AFRIQUE										
Algeria - Algérie										
16 IV 2008	DF	34 452 759[1]	17 428 500[1]	17 024 259[1]	DJ	35 978	...	...	2 381 741	...
Angola										
16 V 2014	DF	25 789 024	12 499 041	13 289 983	DF	17 430[2]	29 250[3]	6.5	1 246 700	23
Benin - Bénin										
11 V 2013	DF	10 008 749	4 887 820	5 120 929	DF	8 779[4]	11 496[5]	3.4	114 763	100
Botswana										
9 VIII 2011	DF	2 024 904	988 957	1 035 947	DJ	1 823	2 303[6]	2.9	582 000	4
Burkina Faso										
9 XII 2006	DF	14 196 259	6 842 560	7 353 699	DJ	15 731[4]	...	...	272 967	...
Burundi										
16 VIII 2008	DF	7 877 728	3 838 045	4 039 683	DF	9 461	11 772	2.7	27 834	423
Cabo Verde										
16 VI 2010	DJ	491 683	243 403	248 280	DJ	494[4]	544[4]	1.2	4 033	135
Cameroon - Cameroun										
11 XI 2005	DF	17 052 134	8 408 495	8 643 639	DJ	20 127[7]	24 863[7]	2.6	475 650	52
Central African Republic - République centrafricaine										
8 XII 2003	DF	3 151 072	1 569 446	1 581 626		...	...	...	622 984	...
Chad - Tchad										
20 V 2009	DJ	11 039 873	5 452 483	5 587 390	DJ	11 470	15 162	3.5	1 284 000	12
Comoros - Comores										
1 IX 2003	DF	575 660[8]	285 590[8]	290 070[8]		...	...	...	2 235	...
Congo										
28 IV 2007	DF	3 697 490	1 821 357	1 876 133	DJ	4 119	5 203	2.9	342 000	15
Côte d'Ivoire										
15 V 2014	DF	22 224 509	11 441 896	10 782 613	DF	20 845[9]	25 196[10]	2.4	322 462	78
Democratic Republic of the Congo - République démocratique du Congo										
1 VII 1984	DF	29 916 800	14 543 800	15 373 000		...	...	...	2 344 858	...
Djibouti										
29 V 2009	DF	818 159	440 067	378 092	DF	841[11]	...	...	23 200	...
Egypt - Égypte										
18 IV 2017	DF	94 798 827	48 891 518	45 907 309	DF	78 685	97 147	2.6	1 002 000	97
Equatorial Guinea - Guinée équatoriale										
20 VI 2015	DF	*1 222 442	*651 820	*570 622	DF	1 622[12]	*1 358[13]	-2.2	28 051	48
Eritrea - Érythrée										
9 V 1984	DF	2 621 566[14]	1 309 736[14]	1 311 830[14]	DF	2 691[15]	3 295[15]	2.5	121 144	27
Eswatini										
29 IV 2017	DJ	*1 093 238	*531 111	*562 127	DJ	1 056[16]	1 159[16]	1.2	17 363	67
Ethiopia - Éthiopie										
29 V 2007	DF	73 750 932	37 217 130	36 533 802	DF	79 634[17]	96 503[17]	2.4	1 104 300	87
Gabon										
22 V 2013	DF	1 811 079	934 072	877 007		...	...	...	267 668	...
Gambia - Gambie										
15 IV 2013	DF	*1 882 450	*930 699	*951 751	DF	1 731	2 148	2.7	11 295	190
Ghana										
26 IX 2010	DF	24 658 823	12 024 845	12 633 978	DF	...	29 614[18]	...	238 537	124
Guinea - Guinée										
15 III 2014	DJ	10 523 261	5 084 306	5 438 955	DJ	9 557[19]	11 884[20]	2.7	245 836	48
Guinea-Bissau - Guinée-Bissau										
15 III 2009	DF	1 497 859	725 956	771 903	DF	1 460[4]	1 585[4]	1.0	36 125	44
Kenya										
24 VIII 2009	DF	38 610 097	19 192 458	19 417 639	DF	38 474[21]	47 849[21]	2.7	591 958	81
Lesotho										
10 IV 2016	DJ	2 007 201	982 133	1 025 068	DF	1 892[22]	...	...	30 355	...
Liberia - Libéria										
21 III 2008	DF	3 476 608	1 739 945	1 736 663	DF	3 627	...	...	111 369	...
Libya - Libye										
15 IV 2006	DF	*5 298 152[23]	*2 687 513[23]	*2 610 639[23]	DF	5 689[23]	...	...	1 676 198	...

3. Population by sex, annual rate of population change, surface area and density
Population selon le sexe, taux de changement annuel de la population, superficie et densité (continued - suite)

Continent, country or area and census date / Continent, pays ou zone et date du recensement	Census type[a]	Population at the latest available census / Population d'après le dernier recensement disponible (in units — en unités)			Estimate type[a]	Mid-year estimates / Estimations au milieu de l'année (in thousands — en milliers)		Annual rate of change / Taux de changement annuel 2010-18	Surface area / Superficie (km²) 2018	Density / Densité 2018[b]
		Both sexes / Les deux sexes	Male / Masculin	Female / Feminin		2010	2018			
AFRICA - AFRIQUE										
Madagascar										
1 VIII 1993	DF	12 238 914	6 088 116	6 150 798	DF	20 142[24]	24 934[24]	2.7	587 041	42
Malawi										
3 IX 2018	DJ	17 563 749	8 521 460	9 042 289	DF	13 948[4]	...	...	117 726	...
Mali										
1 IV 2009	DF	14 528 662	7 204 990	7 323 672	DF	15 370[25]	...	...	1 240 192	...
Mauritania - Mauritanie										
24 III 2013	DF	3 460 388[26]	...	...	DF	3 341[4]	...	...	1 030 700	...
Mauritius - Maurice[27]										
4 VII 2011	DF	1 237 000	611 053	625 947	DJ	1 281[28]	1 265[29]	-0.2	1 979	639
Mayotte										
21 VIII 2012	DJ	212 645	103 173	109 471	DJ	...	*265[30]	...	368	721
Morocco - Maroc										
1 IX 2014	DJ	33 848 242	...	...	...	31 894[31]	35 220[32]	...	446 550	79
Mozambique										
1 VIII 2017	DF	*28 861 863	*13 800 857	*15 061 006	DF	22 417[16]	...	...	799 380	...
Namibia - Namibie										
28 VIII 2011	DF	2 113 077	1 021 912	1 091 165	DF	2 143[4]	2 414[33]	1.5	824 116	3
Niger										
10 XII 2012	DF	16 734 935	8 183 513	8 551 422	DJ	15 204[4]	...	...	1 267 000	...
Nigeria - Nigéria										
21 III 2006	DF	140 431 790	71 345 488	69 086 302	DF	159 608[22]	...	...	923 768	...
Republic of South Sudan - République de Soudan du Sud										
21 IV 2008	DF	8 260 490	4 287 300	3 973 190	DF	9 005[34]	12 323[34]	3.9	658 841	19
Reunion - Réunion										
1 I 2015	DJ	850 727	411 435	439 292	DJ	821[35]	*864[30]	0.6	2 510	344
Rwanda										
15 VIII 2012	DF	10 393 542	4 981 197	5 412 345	DF	10 413[4]	12 090[36]	1.9	26 338	459
Saint Helena ex. dep. - Sainte-Hélène sans dép.										
7 II 2016	DF	4 802	...	...	DF	4	5	1.0	123[37]	37
Saint Helena: Ascension - Sainte-Hélène: Ascension										
7 II 2016	DF	556[38]	...	...	...	...	...	...	88	...
Saint Helena: Tristan da Cunha - Sainte-Hélène: Tristan da Cunha										
9 II 2016	DJ	271[38]	...	...	...	...	...	...	98	...
Sao Tome and Principe - Sao Tomé-et-Principe										
13 V 2012	DJ	178 739	88 867	89 872	...	164	202[39]	...	964	209
Senegal - Sénégal										
19 XI 2013	DF	13 357 492	6 658 089	6 699 403	DJ	12 509[40]	15 726[4]	2.9	196 712[41]	80
Seychelles										
26 VIII 2010	DF	90 945	46 912	44 033	DF	90	97	0.9	457	212
Sierra Leone										
5 XII 2015	DF	7 092 113	3 490 978	3 601 135	DF	5 747	...	...	72 300	...
Somalia - Somalie										
15 II 1987	DF	7 114 431	3 741 664	3 372 767		...	...	...	637 657	...
South Africa - Afrique du Sud										
10 X 2011	DF	51 770 560	25 188 791	26 581 769	DF	50 724[42]	57 726[3]	1.6	1 221 037	47
Sudan - Soudan										
21 IV 2008	DF	30 894 000	15 786 677	15 107 323	DF	32 962	...	...	...	...
Togo										
6 XI 2010	DJ	6 191 155	3 009 095	3 182 060	DJ	6 191[4]	7 440[3]	2.3	56 785	131
Tunisia - Tunisie										
23 IV 2014	DF	10 982 754	5 472 338	5 510 416	DF	10 566	11 552	1.1	163 610	71
Uganda - Ouganda										
27 VIII 2014	DF	34 634 650	16 897 849	17 736 801	DF	31 785	39 059[10]	2.6	241 550	162

3. Population by sex, annual rate of population change, surface area and density
Population selon le sexe, taux de changement annuel de la population, superficie et densité (continued - suite)

Continent, country or area and census date / Continent, pays ou zone et date du recensement	Census type[a]	Population at the latest available census / Population d'après le dernier recensement disponible (in units — en unités)			Estimate type[a]	Mid-year estimates / Estimations au milieu de l'année (in thousands — en milliers)		Annual rate of change / Taux de changement annuel 2010-18	Surface area / Superficie (km²) 2018	Density / Densité 2018[b]
		Both sexes / Les deux sexes	Male / Masculin	Female / Feminin		2010	2018			
AFRICA - AFRIQUE										
United Republic of Tanzania - République Unie de Tanzanie										
26 VIII 2012	DF	44 928 923[43]	21 869 990[43]	23 058 933[43]	DF	43 188[44]	54 199[36]	2.8	947 303	57
Western Sahara - Sahara occidental[45]										
31 XII 1970	DF	76 425	43 981	32 444		...	...	...	266 000	...
Zambia - Zambie										
16 X 2010	DF	12 526 314	6 117 253	6 409 061	DJ	...	16 888[46]	...	752 612	22
Zimbabwe										
17 VIII 2012	DF	13 061 239	6 280 539	6 780 700	DF	...	14 849[39]	...	390 757	38
AMERICA, NORTH - AMÉRIQUE DU NORD										
Anguilla										
11 V 2011	DF	13 572	6 707	6 865	DF	16	...	...	91	...
Antigua and Barbuda - Antigua-et-Barbuda										
27 V 2011	DF	88 566	...	...	...	91	95[33]	...	442	215
Aruba										
29 IX 2010	DJ	101 484	48 241	53 243	DJ	102	111	1.1	180	619
Bahamas										
3 V 2010	DJ	351 461	170 257	181 204	DJ	352[46]	381[46]	1.0	13 940	27
Barbados - Barbade										
1 V 2010	DJ	277 821[47]	133 018[47]	144 803[47]	DJ	278	...	...	431	...
Belize										
12 V 2010	DJ	322 453	161 227	161 226	DJ	324	398	2.6	22 966	17
Bermuda - Bermudes										
20 V 2016	DJ	63 779[48]	30 690[48]	33 089[48]	DJ	64[49]	64[50]	0.0	54	1 185
British Virgin Islands - Îles Vierges britanniques										
12 VII 2010	DF	28 054	13 820	14 234	DF	28	...	...	151	...
Canada										
10 V 2016	DJ	35 151 730[51]	17 264 200[51]	17 887 530[51]	DJ	34 005[52]	*37 059[53]	1.1	9 984 670	4
Cayman Islands - Îles Caïmanes										
10 X 2010	DJ	55 036[54]	27 218[54]	27 818[54]	DJ	56	66[40]	2.1	264	249
Costa Rica										
30 V 2011	DJ	4 301 712	2 106 063	2 195 649	DJ	4 538[55]	5 004[56]	1.2	51 100	98
Cuba										
14 IX 2012	DJ	11 167 325	5 570 825	5 596 500	DJ	11 171	*11 215	0.0	109 884	102
Curaçao										
26 III 2011	DJ	150 563	68 848	81 715	DJ	149[42]	160[3]	0.9	444	360
Dominica - Dominique										
14 V 2011	DF	68 913	34 973	33 940	DF	71	...	...	750	...
Dominican Republic - République dominicaine										
1 XII 2010	DJ	9 445 281	4 739 038	4 706 243	DJ	9 479[4]	10 266[4]	1.0	48 671	211
El Salvador										
12 V 2007	DJ	5 744 113	2 719 371	3 024 742	DJ	6 183[57]	6 643[57]	0.9	21 041	316
Greenland - Groenland										
1 I 2008	DJ	56 462[58]	29 885[58]	26 577[58]	DJ	57[58]	56[58]	-0.1	2 166 086	0
Grenada - Grenade										
12 V 2011	DF	106 667	53 898	52 769	DF	105	...	...	345	...
Guadeloupe										
1 I 2015	DJ	397 990[59]	183 479[59]	214 511[59]	DJ	404[59]	422[60]	0.6	1 639	258
Guatemala										
24 XI 2002	DJ	11 237 196	5 496 839	5 740 357	DJ	14 362[44]	17 311[44]	2.3	108 889	159
Haiti - Haïti										
11 I 2003	DJ	8 373 750	4 039 272	4 334 478	DJ	10 085[61]	11 412[61]	1.5	27 750	411
Honduras										
10 VIII 2013	DF	8 303 771	4 052 316	4 251 456	DF	8 046[62]	9 012[5]	1.4	112 492	80

Continent, country or area and census date / Continent, pays ou zone et date du recensement	Census type[a]	Population at the latest available census / Population d'après le dernier recensement disponible (in units — en unités)			Estimate type[a]	Mid-year estimates / Estimations au milieu de l'année (in thousands — en milliers)		Annual rate of change / Taux de changement annuel 2010-18	Surface area / Superficie (km²) 2018	Density / Densité 2018[b]
		Both sexes / Les deux sexes	Male / Masculin	Female / Feminin		2010	2018			
AMERICA, NORTH - AMÉRIQUE DU NORD										
Jamaica - Jamaïque										
4 IV 2011	DJ	2 697 983[63]	1 334 533[63]	1 363 450[63]	DJ	2 702	*2 728	0.1	10 991	248
Martinique										
1 I 2015	DJ	380 877	176 328	204 549	DJ	394[35]	369[35]	-0.8	1 090	338
Mexico - Mexique										
12 VI 2010	DF	112 336 538[64]	54 855 231[64]	57 481 307[64]	DJ	*113 749*[65]	*125 328*[66]	1.2	1 964 375	64
Montserrat										
12 V 2011	DJ	4 922	2 546	2 376	DF	5	...	...	103	...
Nicaragua										
4 VI 2005	DJ	5 142 098	2 534 491	2 607 607	DJ	*5 816*	*6 460*	1.3	130 373	*50*
Panama										
16 V 2010	DF	3 405 813	1 712 584	1 693 229	DF	*3 662*[18]	4 159[18]	1.6	75 320	55
Puerto Rico - Porto Rico										
1 IV 2010	DJ	3 725 789[67]	1 785 171[67]	1 940 618[67]	DJ	3 721[68]	3 195[69]	-1.9	8 868	360
Saint Kitts and Nevis - Saint-Kitts-et-Nevis										
15 V 2011	DF	*46 398	*22 846	*23 552	DF	*53	...	...	261	...
Saint Lucia - Sainte-Lucie										
10 V 2010	DJ	165 770	82 268	83 502	DF	...	179	...	539[70]	332
Saint Pierre and Miquelon - Saint Pierre-et-Miquelon										
1 I 2015	DJ	6 021	2 940	3 081		...	...	...	242	...
Saint Vincent and the Grenadines - Saint-Vincent-et-les Grenadines										
12 VI 2012	DJ	109 991	56 419	53 572	DJ	110	111	0.1	389	284
Saint-Barthélemy										
1 I 2015	DJ	9 625	5 117	4 508		...	...	...	22	...
Saint-Martin (French part) - Saint-Martin (partie française)										
1 I 2015	DJ	35 684	16 884	18 800	DJ	...	35	...	53	669
Sint Maarten (Dutch part) - Saint-Martin (partie néerlandaise)										
9 IV 2011	DF	33 609	15 868	17 741	DF	36	41[35]	1.7	34	1 195
Trinidad and Tobago - Trinité-et-Tobago										
9 I 2011	DF	1 332 901	...	...	DF	1 318[28]	1 359[29]	0.4	5 127	265
Turks and Caicos Islands - Îles Turques et Caïques										
25 I 2012	DJ	*31 458[71]	*16 037[71]	*15 421[71]	DJ	35	*41	2.3	948[72]	44
United States of America - États-Unis d'Amérique										
1 IV 2010	DJ	308 745 538	151 781 326	156 964 212	DJ	309 348[73]	327 167[73]	0.7	9 833 517	33
United States Virgin Islands - Îles Vierges américaines										
1 IV 2010	DJ	106 405[67]	50 854[67]	55 551[67]	DJ	106[74]	...	...	347	...
AMERICA, SOUTH - AMÉRIQUE DU SUD										
Argentina - Argentine										
27 X 2010	DF	40 117 096	19 523 766	20 593 330	DF	40 788[46]	44 495[46]	1.1	2 796 427[75]	16
Bolivia (Plurinational State of) - Bolivie (État plurinational de)										
21 XI 2012	DF	10 059 856	5 019 447	5 040 409	DF	10 031	11 307	1.5	1 098 581[76]	10
Brazil - Brésil										
31 VII 2010	DJ	190 755 799	93 406 990	97 348 809	DJ	*195 498*[77]	*208 495*[77]	0.8	8 515 767	24

Continent, country or area and census date / Continent, pays ou zone et date du recensement	Census type[a]	Population at the latest available census / Population d'après le dernier recensement disponible (in units — en unités)			Estimate type[a]	Mid-year estimates / Estimations au milieu de l'année (in thousands — en milliers)		Annual rate of change / Taux de changement annuel 2010-18	Surface area / Superficie (km²) 2018	Density / Densité 2018[b]
		Both sexes / Les deux sexes	Male / Masculin	Female / Feminin		2010	2018			
AMERICA, SOUTH - AMÉRIQUE DU SUD										
Chile - Chili										
24 IV 2002 ...... DF		15 116 435	7 447 695	7 668 740	DF	17 066	18 552	1.0	756 102	25
Colombia - Colombie										
22 V 2005 ...... DF		41 468 384	20 336 117	21 132 267	DJ	45 510[78]	49 834[78]	1.1	1 141 748	44
Ecuador - Équateur										
28 XI 2010 ...... DF		14 483 499	7 177 683	7 305 816	DF	15 012[79]	17 023[79]	1.6	257 217[80]	66
Falkland Islands (Malvinas) - Îles Falkland (Malvinas)[81]										
15 IV 2012 ...... DF		2 840[82]	1 491[82]	1 349[82]		...	...	...	12 173	...
French Guiana - Guyane française										
1 I 2015 ...... DJ		259 865	128 973	130 892	DJ	229[35]	282[35]	2.6	83 534	3
Guyana										
15 IX 2012 ...... DF		746 955	371 805	375 150	DF	752	...	...	214 969	...
Paraguay										
28 VIII 2002 ...... DF		5 163 198	2 603 242	2 559 956	DF	6 266[83]	7 053[83]	1.5	406 752	17
Peru - Pérou										
22 VIII 2017 ...... DF		29 381 884[84]	14 450 757[84]	14 931 127[84]	DF	29 462[85]	32 162[85]	1.1	1 285 216	25
Suriname										
13 VIII 2012 ...... DJ		541 638	270 629	271 009	DJ	531	...	...	163 820	...
Uruguay										
4 X 2011 ...... DJ		3 286 314	1 577 725[86]	1 708 481[86]	DJ	3 397	3 506[4]	0.4	173 626	20
Venezuela (Bolivarian Republic of) - Venezuela (République bolivarienne du)										
1 IX 2011 ...... DJ		27 227 930	13 549 752	13 678 178	DF	28 396[87]	31 671	1.4	929 690	34
ASIA - ASIE										
Afghanistan										
23 VI 1979 ...... DF		13 051 358[88]	6 712 377[88]	6 338 981[88]	DF	24 486[89]	30 075[89]	2.6	652 864	46
Armenia - Arménie										
12 X 2011 ...... DF		2 871 771	1 346 729	1 525 042	DJ	3 045	2 973[35]	-0.3	29 743	100
Azerbaijan - Azerbaïdjan										
13 IV 2009 ...... DJ		8 922 447	4 414 398	4 508 049	DJ	9 054	9 936	1.2	86 600	115
Bahrain - Bahreïn										
27 IV 2010 ...... DJ		1 234 571	768 414	466 157	DJ	1 229	1 503	2.5	778	1 931
Bangladesh										
15 III 2011 ...... DF		144 043 697	72 109 796	71 933 901	DF	148 620	164 600	1.3	147 570	1 115
Bhutan - Bhoutan										
30 V 2017 ...... DF		727 145	380 453	346 692	DF	696[90]	...	...	38 394	...
Brunei Darussalam - Brunéi Darussalam										
20 VI 2011 ...... DJ		393 372	203 144	190 228	...	387[42]	442	...	5 765	77
Cambodia - Cambodge										
3 III 2008 ...... DF		13 395 682[91]	6 516 054[91]	6 879 628[91]	DF	14 303[92]	...	...	181 035	...
China - Chine										
1 XI 2010 ...... DJ		1 339 724 852[93]	686 852 572[93]	652 872 280[93]	DF	1 337 700[94]	1 392 730[94]	0.5	9 600 000	145
China, Hong Kong SAR - Chine, Hong Kong RAS										
30 VI 2016 ...... DJ		7 336 585[95]	3 375 362[95]	3 961 223[95]	DJ	7 024	7 451	0.7	1 107	6 731
China, Macao SAR - Chine, Macao RAS										
12 VIII 2011 ...... DF		625 674	305 398	320 276	DJ	537	*667	2.7	30[96]	22 247
Cyprus - Chypre										
1 X 2011 ...... DJ		840 407[97]	408 780[97]	431 627[97]	DJ	829[98]	864[99]	0.5	9 251	93
Democratic People's Republic of Korea - République populaire démocratique de Corée										
1 X 2008 ...... DJ		24 052 231	11 721 838	12 330 393		...	...	...	120 538	...

3. Population by sex, annual rate of population change, surface area and density
Population selon le sexe, taux de changement annuel de la population, superficie et densité (continued - suite)

Continent, country or area and census date / Continent, pays ou zone et date du recensement	Census type[a]	Population at the latest available census / Population d'après le dernier recensement disponible (in units — en unités)			Estimate type[a]	Mid-year estimates Estimations au milieu de l'année (in thousands — en milliers)		Annual rate of change Taux de changement annuel 2010-18	Surface area Superficie (km²) 2018	Density Densité 2018[b]
		Both sexes Les deux sexes	Male Masculin	Female Feminin		2010	2018			
ASIA - ASIE										
Georgia - Géorgie										
5 XI 2014	DJ	3 713 804	1 772 864	1 940 940	...	4 453	3 730[100]	...	69 700	54
India - Inde										
9 II 2011	DF	1 210 854 977[101]	623 270 258[101]	587 584 719[101]	DF	1 176 742[102]	1 298 041[102]	1.2	3 287 263	395
Indonesia - Indonésie										
1 V 2010	DJ	237 641 326	119 630 913	118 010 413	DJ	238 519[103]	264 162[104]	1.3	1 910 931	138
Iran (Islamic Republic of) - Iran (République islamique d')										
24 IX 2016	DJ	79 926 270	40 498 442	39 427 828	DJ	74 340[105]	82 084[105]	1.2	1 628 762	50
Iraq										
16 X 1997	DF	19 184 543[106]	9 536 570[106]	9 647 973[106]	DF	32 211	*37 842	2.0	435 052	87
Israel - Israël										
27 XII 2008	DF	7 412 180[107]	3 663 910[107]	3 748 270[107]	DJ	7 624[108]	*8 884[108]	1.9	22 072	402
Japan - Japon										
1 X 2015	DJ	127 094 745[109]	61 841 738[109]	65 253 007[109]	DJ	128 070[109]	126 529[110]	-0.2	377 930[111]	335
Jordan - Jordanie										
30 XI 2015	DF	9 531 712[112]	5 046 824[112]	4 484 888[112]	DF	6 699[113]	10 309[113]	5.4	89 318	115
Kazakhstan										
25 II 2009	DF	16 009 597	7 712 224	8 297 373	DF	16 322[114]	18 276[115]	1.4	2 724 902	7
Kuwait - Koweït										
21 IV 2011	DF	3 065 850	1 738 372	1 327 478	DF	2 933	4 125	4.3	17 818	231
Kyrgyzstan - Kirghizstan										
24 III 2009	DJ	5 362 793	2 645 921	2 716 872	DJ	5 448[30]	6 323[30]	1.9	199 949	32
Lao People's Democratic Republic - République démocratique populaire lao										
1 III 2015	DJ	6 492 228	3 254 770	3 237 458	DJ	6 230[13]	7 013[13]	1.5	236 800	30
Lebanon - Liban										
1 X 2011	SDF	3 779 859[116]	1 840 940[116]	1 938 919[116]		...	...	...	10 452	...
Malaysia - Malaisie										
6 VII 2010	DJ	28 334 135[117]	14 562 638[117]	13 771 497[117]	DJ	28 589[118]	32 385[118]	1.6	330 621	98
Maldives										
20 IX 2014	DF	402 071[119]	227 749[119]	174 322[119]	DF	320	512[120]	5.9	300	1 707
Mongolia - Mongolie										
11 XI 2010	DF	2 647 199	1 314 246	1 332 953	DF	2 739	3 208	2.0	1 564 116	2
Myanmar										
29 III 2014	DF	51 486 253[121]	24 824 586[121]	26 661 667[121]	DF	59 780[122]	53 863[123]	-1.3	676 577	80
Nepal - Népal										
22 VI 2011	DJ	26 494 504	12 849 041	13 645 463	DJ	28 044	29 219[33]	0.5	147 181	199
Oman										
12 XII 2010	DF	2 773 479	1 612 408	1 161 071	DF	...	4 602[124]	...	309 500	15
Pakistan										
15 III 2017	DF	*207 774 520[125]	*106 449 322[126]	*101 314 780[126]	DF	173 510[125]	...	...	796 095	...
Philippines										
1 VIII 2015	DJ	100 979 303[127]	51 069 962[127]	49 909 341[127]	DJ	93 135[18]	106 599[18]	1.7	300 000	355
Qatar										
20 IV 2015	DF	2 404 776	1 816 981	587 795	DF	1 715	2 760	5.9	11 627	237
Republic of Korea - République de Corée										
1 XI 2015	DJ	51 069 375	25 608 502	25 460 873	DJ	49 554	51 607	0.5	100 339	514
Saudi Arabia - Arabie saoudite										
27 IV 2010	DF	27 236 156	15 531 471	11 704 685	DF	27 411	33 414	2.5	2 206 714	15
Singapore - Singapour										
30 VI 2010	DJ	3 771 721[128]	1 861 133[128]	1 910 588[128]	DJ	5 077[129]	5 639[129]	1.3	723[130]	7 804
Sri Lanka										
20 III 2012	DJ	20 359 439	9 856 634	10 502 805	...	20 675	*21 670	...	65 610	330
State of Palestine - État de Palestine										
1 XII 2017	DF	4 705 855	2 394 359	2 311 496	DF	4 023	4 854	2.3	6 025	806
Syrian Arab Republic - République arabe syrienne										
22 IX 2004	DF	*17 921 000[131]	*9 161 000[131]	*8 760 000[131]	DF	20 619[131]	...	...	185 180	...

3. Population by sex, annual rate of population change, surface area and density
Population selon le sexe, taux de changement annuel de la population, superficie et densité (continued - suite)

Continent, country or area and census date / Continent, pays ou zone et date du recensement	Census type[a]	Population at the latest available census / Population d'après le dernier recensement disponible (in units — en unités)			Estimate type[a]	Mid-year estimates / Estimations au milieu de l'année (in thousands — en milliers)		Annual rate of change / Taux de changement annuel 2010-18	Surface area / Superficie (km²) 2018	Density / Densité 2018[b]
		Both sexes / Les deux sexes	Male / Masculin	Female / Feminin		2010	2018			
ASIA - ASIE										
Tajikistan - Tadjikistan										
21 IX 2010	DF	7 564 502	3 817 004	3 747 498	DF	7 519	8 931[35]	2.2	142 600	63
Thailand - Thaïlande										
1 IX 2010	DJ	65 981 659	32 355 032	33 626 627	DJ	63 878	65 700[4]	0.4	513 140	128
Timor-Leste										
11 VII 2015	DF	1 183 643	601 112	582 531	DF	1 089[4]	1 261[4]	1.8	14 919	85
Turkey - Turquie										
3 X 2011	DJ	74 526 000[132]	37 431 000[132]	37 095 000[132]	DJ	73 723[133]	81 339[134]	1.2	783 562	104
Turkmenistan - Turkménistan										
10 I 1995	DF	4 483 251	2 225 331	2 257 920		...	...	...	488 100	...
United Arab Emirates - Émirats arabes unis										
5 XII 2005	DF	4 106 427[135]	2 806 141[135]	1 300 286[135]	DF	8 264[135]	...	...	71 024[136]	...
Uzbekistan - Ouzbékistan										
12 I 1989	DJ	19 810 077	9 784 156	10 025 921	DJ	28 562[115]	32 657[137]	1.7	448 969	73
Viet Nam										
1 IV 2009	DJ	85 846 997	42 413 143	43 433 854	DJ	86 947[138]	*94 666[138]	1.1	331 236	286
Yemen - Yémen										
16 XII 2004	DF	19 685 161	10 036 953	9 648 208	DJ	23 154[4]	...	...	527 968	...
EUROPE										
Åland Islands - Îles d'Åland										
31 XII 2000	DJ	25 776[139]	12 700[139]	13 076[139]	DJ	28[58]	30[58]	0.8	1 583	19
Albania - Albanie										
1 X 2011	DJ	2 800 138	1 403 059	1 397 079	...	2 913	2 870[35]	...	28 748	100
Andorra - Andorre										
31 XII 2011	DJ	69 758[58]	35 147[58]	34 611[58]	DJ	70[140]	75[141]	0.8	468	160
Austria - Autriche										
31 X 2011	DJ	8 401 940	4 093 938	4 308 002	DJ	8 361	8 822[35]	0.7	83 878	105
Belarus - Bélarus										
14 X 2009	DJ	9 503 807	4 420 039	5 083 768	DJ	9 491	9 492[35]	0.0	207 600	46
Belgium - Belgique										
1 I 2011	DJ	11 000 638	5 401 718	5 598 920	DJ	10 896	11 399[35]	0.6	30 528	373
Bosnia and Herzegovina - Bosnie-Herzégovine										
30 IX 2013	DJ	3 531 159	1 732 270	1 798 889	DF	3 843	...	...	51 209	...
Bulgaria - Bulgarie										
1 II 2011	DJ	7 364 570	3 586 571	3 777 999	DJ	7 534	7 050[35]	-0.8	110 372	64
Croatia - Croatie										
1 IV 2011	DJ	4 284 889	2 066 335	2 218 554	DJ	4 295	4 105[35]	-0.6	56 594	73
Czechia - Tchéquie										
25 III 2011	DJ	10 436 560	5 109 766	5 326 794	DJ	10 474	10 610[35]	0.2	78 870	135
Denmark - Danemark[142]										
1 I 2011	DJ	5 560 628[58]	2 756 582[58]	2 804 046[58]	DJ	5 545[58]	5 790[58]	0.5	42 933	135
Estonia - Estonie										
31 XII 2011	DJ	1 294 455	600 526	693 929	DJ	1 331	1 319[35]	-0.1	45 227	29
Faeroe Islands - Îles Féroé										
11 XI 2011	DJ	48 346	25 125	23 221	DJ	49	51	0.6	1 396	37
Finland - Finlande										
31 XII 2010	DJ	5 375 276	2 638 416	2 736 860	DJ	5 335[143]	5 513[141]	0.4	336 869[144]	16
France										
1 I 2015	DJ	64 300 821	31 138 550	33 162 271	DJ	62 918[145]	*64 769[145]	0.4	551 500	117
Germany - Allemagne										
9 V 2011	DJ	80 219 695	39 145 941	41 073 754	DJ	81 757	82 792[146]	0.2	357 582	232
Gibraltar										
12 XI 2012	DJ	32 194[147]	16 061[147]	16 133[147]	DF	31[148]	...	...	6	...
Greece - Grèce										
9 V 2011	DF	10 816 286	5 303 223	5 513 063	DF	11 121	10 741[35]	-0.4	131 957	81
Guernsey - Guernesey										
31 III 2015	DJ	62 234	30 819	31 415	DJ	62[149]	62[149]	0.0	64	974

3. Population by sex, annual rate of population change, surface area and density
Population selon le sexe, taux de changement annuel de la population, superficie et densité (continued - suite)

Continent, country or area and census date / Continent, pays ou zone et date du recensement	Census type[a]	Population at the latest available census / Population d'après le dernier recensement disponible (in units — en unités) Both sexes Les deux sexes	Male Masculin	Female Feminin	Estimate type[a]	Mid-year estimates Estimations au milieu de l'année (in thousands — en milliers) 2010	2018	Annual rate of change Taux de changement annuel 2010-18	Surface area Superficie (km²) 2018	Density Densité 2018[b]
EUROPE										
Holy See - Saint-Siège[150]										
1 VII 2009 .... DF		466[151]	320	146	DF	0[152]	...	...	0[153]	...
Hungary - Hongrie										
1 X 2011 .... DF		9 937 628	4 718 479	5 219 149	DJ	10 000	9 778[154]	-0.3	93 023	105
Iceland - Islande										
31 XII 2011 .... DJ		315 556[155]	158 151[155]	157 405[155]	DJ	318[155]	348[156]	1.1	103 000	3
Ireland - Irlande										
24 IV 2016 .... DJ		4 761 865	2 354 428	2 407 437	DF	4 560	4 830[154]	0.7	69 825	69
Isle of Man - Île de Man										
24 IV 2016 .... DF		78 560	...	...	DJ	83[157]	...	...	572	
Italy - Italie										
9 X 2011 .... DJ		59 433 744	28 745 507	30 688 237	DJ	59 277	60 484[35]	0.3	302 069	200
Jersey										
27 III 2011 .... DJ		97 857	48 296	49 561	DJ	97[35]	107[35]	1.2	116	921
Latvia - Lettonie										
1 III 2011 .... DJ		2 070 371	946 102	1 124 269	DJ	2 098	1 934[35]	-1.0	64 573	30
Liechtenstein										
31 XII 2015 .... DJ		37 622	...	...	DJ	36	38	0.7	160	239
Lithuania - Lituanie										
1 III 2011 .... DJ		3 043 429	1 402 604	1 640 825	DJ	3 097	2 809[154]	-1.2	65 286	43
Luxembourg										
1 II 2011 .... DJ		512 353	254 967	257 386	DJ	507	602[35]	2.1	2 586	233
Malta - Malte										
20 XI 2011 .... DF		417 432	207 625	209 807	DJ	415[158]	476[159]	1.7	315	1 510
Monaco										
7 VI 2016 .... DJ		37 308[160]	18 240[160]	19 068[160]	DJ	36[160]	38[161]	0.9	2	19 150
Montenegro - Monténégro										
1 IV 2011 .... DJ		620 029	306 236	313 793	DJ	619	622[162]	0.1	13 812	45
Netherlands - Pays-Bas										
1 I 2011 .... DJ		16 655 799	8 243 482	8 412 317	DJ	16 615	17 181[35]	0.4	41 543	414
North Macedonia - Macédoine du Nord										
31 X 2002 .... DJ		2 022 547	1 015 377	1 007 170	DJ	2 055	2 075[35]	0.1	25 713	81
Norway - Norvège										
19 XI 2011 .... DJ		4 979 955[163]	2 495 777[163]	2 484 178[163]	DJ	4 889[162]	5 296[154]	1.0	323 772	16
Poland - Pologne										
31 III 2011 .... DJ		38 044 565	18 420 389	19 624 176	DJ	38 042[162]	37 977[154]	0.0	312 679	121
Portugal										
21 III 2011 .... DF		10 282 306	4 868 755	5 413 551	DJ	10 573	10 291[35]	-0.3	92 226	112
Republic of Moldova - République de Moldova										
12 V 2014 .... DF		2 805 194[164]	1 352 353[164]	1 452 841[164]	DJ	3 562[165]	2 706[166]	-3.4	33 846	80
Romania - Roumanie										
20 X 2011 .... DF		20 039 141	9 736 342	10 302 799	...	20 247[162]	19 531[35]	...	238 391	82
Russian Federation - Fédération de Russie										
14 X 2010 .... DF		143 436 145	66 457 074	76 979 071	DJ	142 849	...	...	17 098 246	...
San Marino - Saint-Marin										
7 XI 2010 .... DF		*30 652	*14 791[167]	*15 818[167]	...	33[58]	35[58]	...	61	566
Serbia - Serbie										
1 X 2011 .... DJ		7 186 862[168]	3 499 176[168]	3 687 686[168]	DJ	7 291[168]	7 001[169]	-0.5	88 444	79
Slovakia - Slovaquie										
21 V 2011 .... DJ		5 397 036	2 627 772	2 769 264	DJ	5 431	5 443[35]	0.0	49 035	111
Slovenia - Slovénie										
1 I 2015 .... DJ		2 062 874	1 022 229	1 040 645	DJ	2 049	2 067[35]	0.1	20 273	102
Spain - Espagne										
1 XI 2011 .... DJ		46 815 915	23 104 350	23 711 560	DJ	46 562	46 658[156]	0.0	505 987	92
Svalbard and Jan Mayen Islands - Îles Svalbard et Jan Mayen										
1 XI 1960 .... DF		3 431[170]	2 545[170]	886[170]		...	...	...	62 422	...
Sweden - Suède										
31 XII 2011 .... DJ		9 482 855[58]	4 726 834[58]	4 756 021[58]	DJ	9 378[58]	10 120[171]	1.0	438 574	23

3. Population by sex, annual rate of population change, surface area and density
Population selon le sexe, taux de changement annuel de la population, superficie et densité (continued - suite)

| Continent, country or area and census date — Continent, pays ou zone et date du recensement | Census type[a] | Population at the latest available census — Population d'après le dernier recensement disponible (in units — en unités) | | | Estimate type[a] | Mid-year estimates — Estimations au milieu de l'année (in thousands — en milliers) | | Annual rate of change — Taux de changement annuel 2010-18 | Surface area — Superficie (km²) 2018 | Density — Densité 2018[b] |
		Both sexes — Les deux sexes	Male — Masculin	Female — Feminin		2010	2018			
EUROPE										
Switzerland - Suisse										
31 XII 2011	DF	8 035 391	3 973 280	4 062 111	DJ	7 825	8 484[172]	1.0	41 291	205
Ukraine										
5 XII 2001	DF	48 240 902	22 316 317	25 924 585	DF	45 871	42 386[173]	-1.0	603 500	70
United Kingdom of Great Britain and Northern Ireland - Royaume-Uni de Grande-Bretagne et d'Irlande du Nord[174]										
27 III 2011	DF	63 379 787	31 126 054	32 253 733	DJ	62 759	66 274[154]	0.7	242 495	273
OCEANIA - OCÉANIE										
American Samoa - Samoas américaines										
1 IV 2010	DJ	55 519[67]	28 164[67]	27 355[67]	DJ	67[67]	...	...	199	...
Australia - Australie										
9 VIII 2016	DF	23 717 421[175]	11 686 665[175]	12 030 751[175]	DJ	22 032[176]	24 993[176]	1.6	7 692 024	3
Cook Islands - Îles Cook[177]										
1 XII 2016	DF	*17 459	*8 597	*8 862	DF	24	...	...	236	...
Fiji - Fidji										
17 IX 2017	DF	884 887	448 595	436 292	DF	857	...	...	18 272	...
French Polynesia - Polynésie française										
17 VIII 2017	DF	281 674	...	...	DF	265[30]	276[35]	0.5	4 000	69
Guam										
1 IV 2010	DJ	159 358	81 552	77 806	DJ	...	168[67]	...	549	306
Kiribati										
7 XI 2015	DF	110 136	54 096	56 040		...	...	...	726[178]	...
Marshall Islands - Îles Marshall										
3 IV 2011	DF	53 158	27 243	25 915	DF	54[179]	...	...	181	...
Micronesia (Federated States of) - Micronésie (États fédérés de)										
1 IV 2010	DJ	102 843	52 193	50 650	DJ	108[4]	104[180]	-0.4	702	149
Nauru										
31 X 2011	DF	10 084	5 105	4 979		...	...	...	21	...
New Caledonia - Nouvelle-Calédonie										
26 VIII 2014	DF	268 767	135 542	133 225	DF	250	...	...	19 100	...
New Zealand - Nouvelle-Zélande										
5 III 2013	DF	4 353 198[181]	2 119 464[181]	2 233 734[181]	DJ	4 351[182]	4 886[183]	1.4	268 107	18
Niue - Nioué										
9 III 2017	DF	*1 719	...	...	DJ	1	...	...	260	...
Norfolk Island - Île Norfolk										
9 VIII 2011	DF	2 302	1 082	1 220		...	...	...	36	...
Northern Mariana Islands - Îles Mariannes septentrionales										
1 IV 2010	DF	53 883	27 746	26 137	DF	48	...	...	457	...
Palau - Palaos										
13 IV 2015	DJ	17 661	9 433	8 228	DJ	21	18	-1.5	459	40
Papua New Guinea - Papouasie-Nouvelle-Guinée										
10 VII 2011	DF	7 275 324	3 772 864	3 502 460		...	...	...	462 840	...
Pitcairn										
21 IX 2019	DJ	44	...	...		...	...	...	5	...
Samoa										
7 XI 2016	DF	195 979	100 892	95 087	DF	186	199[184]	0.8	2 842	70

Continent, country or area and census date / Continent, pays ou zone et date du recensement	Census type[a]	Population at the latest available census / Population d'après le dernier recensement disponible (in units — en unités)			Estimate type[a]	Mid-year estimates / Estimations au milieu de l'année (in thousands — en milliers)		Annual rate of change / Taux de changement annuel 2010-18	Surface area / Superficie (km²) 2018	Density / Densité 2018[b]
		Both sexes / Les deux sexes	Male / Masculin	Female / Feminin		2010	2018			

OCEANIA - OCÉANIE

Solomon Islands - Îles Salomon										
22 XI 2009 .... DF	DF	515 870[185]	264 455[185]	251 415[185]	DF	*555*[186]	*667*[186]	2.3	28 896	23
Tokelau - Tokélaou										
18 X 2016 .... DF	DF	1 285	652	633	...	...	...	...	12	...
Tonga										
30 XI 2016 .... DF	DF	100 266	...	...	...	...	...	...	747	...
Tuvalu										
4 XI 2012 .... DF	DF	10 782	...	...	...	...	...	...	26	...
Vanuatu										
7 XI 2016 .... DF	DF	272 459	138 265	134 194	DF	*239*	...	...	12 189	...
Wallis and Futuna Islands - Îles Wallis et Futuna										
23 VII 2018 .... DF	DF	11 562	...	...	...	...	...	...	142	...

FOOTNOTES - NOTES

Italics: estimates which are less reliable. - Italiques : estimations moins sûres.

* Provisional. - Données provisoires.

[a] 'Code' indicates the source of data, as follows:
DF - De facto
DJ - De jure
SDF - Sample survey, de facto
SDJ - Sample survey, de jure

Le 'Code' indique la source des données, comme suit :
DF - Population de fait
DJ - Population de droit
SDF - Enquête par sondage, population de fait
SDJ - Enquête par sondage, Population de droit

[b] Population per square kilometre of surface area. Figures are estimates of population divided by surface area and are not to be considered either as reflecting density in the urban sense or as indicating the supporting power of a territory's land and resources. - Nombre d'habitants au kilomètre carré. Il s'agit simplement d'estimations de la population divisé par celui de la superficie: il ne faut pas y voir d'indication de la densité au sens urbain du terme ni de l'effectif de population que les terres et les ressources du territoire sont capables de nourrir.

[1] Total resident population including common and collective households of nomadic population, and population counted separately. - Population résidente totale y compris les ménages ordinaires et collectifs de la population nomade, et la population comptée à part.

[2] Unrevised data that do not take into account the results of the 2014 population census. - Ces données n'ont pas été revisées et elles ne prennent pas en compte les résultats du recensement de la population de 2014.

[3] Postcensal estimates. - Estimations post censitaires.

[4] Data refer to national projections. - Les données se réfèrent aux projections nationales.

[5] Projections based on the 2013 Population Census. - Projections fondées sur le recensement de la population de 2013.

[6] Data based on the 2011 Census. - Données fondées sur le recensement de 2011.

[7] Source: Population projections and estimates of priority targets for the various health programs and interventions, National Institute of Statistics (2016). - Source : Projections démographiques et estimations des cibles prioritaires des différents programmes et interventions de sante, Institut National de la Statistique (2016).

[8] Excluding Mayotte. - Non compris Mayotte.

[9] Estimates based on the 2014 Population Census. - Estimations fondées sur le recensement de la population de 2014.

[10] Projections based on the 2014 Population Census. - Projections fondées sur le recensement de la population de 2014.

[11] Data are calculated from the results of the Population and Housing Census of 2009. - Les données sont calculées à partir des résultats du recensement de la population et de l'habitat de 2009.

[12] Data refer to projections based on the 1983 Population Census. - Les données se réfèrent aux projections basées sur le recensement de la population de 1983.

[13] Estimates based on the results of 2015 population census. - Estimations fondées sur les résultats du recensement de la population de 2015.

[14] Source: The 1984 Population and Housing Census of Ethiopia (Analytical Report at National Level). - Source : Recensement de la population et des logements de l'Éthiopie en 1984 (rapport analytique au niveau national).

[15] Projections based on the 2000 quick population count results and 1995, 2002 and 2010 Eritrea Demographic and Health Surveys. - Projections fondées sur le dénombrement rapide de la population de 2000 et sur les enquêtes érythréennes de la démographie et de la santé de 1995, 2002 et 2010.

[16] Data refer to national projections based on 2007 census. - Les données sont des projections nationales d'après les résultats du recensement de la population de 2007.

[17] Estimates considering also the results of the 2007 Population Census. - Estimations en prennant en considération les résultats du recensement de la population de 2007.

[18] Data based on the 2010 Population Census. - Les données sont fondées sur le recensement de la population de 2010.

[19] Intercensal estimates. Population in households only. - Estimations inter-censitaires. Population dans les ménages seulement.

[20] Population in households only. Postcensal estimates. - Population dans les ménages seulement. Estimations post censitaires.

[21] Post-censal estimates based on the 2009 Population Census. - Les estimations post-censitaire fondées sur le recensement de la population de 2009.

[22] Data are projections based on the 2006 Population Census. - Projections fondées sur le recensement de la population de 2006.

[23] Data refer to Libyan nationals only. - Les données se raportent aux nationaux libyens seulement.

[24] Data refer to projections based on the 1993 Population Census. - Les données se réfèrent aux projections basées sur le recensement de la population de 1993.

[25] Projections considering also the results of the 2009 Population Census. - Projections en prennant en considération les résultats du recensement de la population de 2009.

[26] Including nomadic population. - Y compris la population nomade.

[27] Excludes the islands of St. Brandon and Agalega. - Non compris les îles St. Brandon et Agalega.

[28] Based on the results of the 2000 Population Census. - Basé sur les résultats du recencement de la population de 2000.

[29] Based on the results of the 2011 Population Census. - Basé sur les résultats du recencement de la population de 2011.

[30] Data refer to annual average population. - Les données correspondent à la population annuelle moyenne.

[31] Based on the results of the 2004 Population Census. - D'après des résultats du recensement de la population de 2004.

[32] Projections based on the results of national survey on population and health conducted between 2010 and 2011, and especially population and housing census 2014. - Des projections de la population fondées sur les résultats de l'enquête nationale de la population et de la santé réalisée entre 2010 et 2011 et, surtout, du recensement général de la population et de l'habitat de 2014.

[33] Data refer to projections based on the 2011 Population Census. - Les données se réfèrent aux projections basées sur le recensement de la population de 2011.

[34] Data are projections based on the 2008 Population and Housing Census. - Projection basée sur le recensement 2008 de la population et des logements.

[35] Data refer to 1 January. - Données se raportent au 1 janvier.

[36] Projections based on the 2012 Population and Housing Census. - Projections fondées sur le recensement 2012 de la population et des logements.

[37] St. Helena Island has no substantial natural inland waters however there are 15 reservoirs and similar open water storage features on island. - L'île de Sainte-Hélène ne dispose d'aucune grande étendue d'eau intérieure naturelle, mais on y trouve 15 réservoirs et autres installations similaires.

[38] Data refer to Saint Helenian resident population. - Pour la population résidante de Sainte-Hélène.

[39] Projections based on the 2012 Population Census. - Projections fondées sur le recensement de la population de 2012.

[40] Data refer to 31 December. - Données se raportent au 31 décembre.

[41] Surface area is based on the 2002 population and housing census. - La superficie est fondée sur les données provenant du recensement de la population et du logement de 2002.

[42] Intercensal estimates. - Estimations inter-censitaires.

[43] Data have not been adjusted for underenumeration, estimated at 7 per cent. - Les données n'ont pas été ajustées pour compenser les lacunes du dénombrement, estimées à 7 p. 100.

[44] Projections based on the 2002 Population Census. - Projections fondées sur le recensement de la population de 2002.

[45] Comprising the Northern Region (former Saguia el Hamra) and Southern Region (former Rio de Oro). - Comprend la région septentrionale (ancien Saguia-el-Hamra) et la région méridionale (ancien Rio de Oro).

[46] Projections based on the 2010 Population and Housing Census. - Projections fondées sur le recensement 2010 de la population et des logements.

[47] Data refers to resident population adjusted for the undercount of 18 per cent and including the institutional population. - Les données concernent la population résidente, y compris la population des institutions, et ont été ajustées pour tenir compte du sous-dénombrement estimé à 18 p. 100.

[48] Bermuda is 100 per cent urban. - 100 pour cent de la population des Bermudes est urbaine.

[49] Bermuda is 100 per cent urban. Data based on the 2010 Population Census. - 100 pour cent de la population des Bermudes est urbaine. Les données sont fondées sur le recensement de la population de 2010.

[50] Bermuda is 100 per cent urban. Data refer to projections based on the 2016 Population Census. - 100 pour cent de la population des Bermudes est urbaine. Les données se réfèrent aux projections basées sur le recensement de la population de 2016.

[51] To ensure confidentiality, the values, including totals are randomly rounded either up or down to a multiple of '5' or '10.' As a result, when these data are summed or grouped, the total value may not match the individual values since totals and sub-totals are independently rounded. Similarly, percentages, which are calculated on rounded data, may not necessarily add up to 100%. - À des fins de confidentialité, les chiffres, y compris les totaux, sont aléatoirement arrondis au multiple de 5 ou de 10 inférieur ou supérieur. Par conséquent, lorsque ces chiffres sont additionnés, le total peut ne pas correspondre à la somme des valeurs individuelles, dans la mesure où les totaux et les totaux partiels sont arrondis indépendamment. De même, la somme des pourcentages, qui sont calculés à partir des données arrondies, peut ne pas correspondre à 100 %.

[52] Adjusted for census net undercoverage (including adjustment for incompletely enumerated Indian reserves). Final intercensal estimates. - Ajusté pour la sous-estimation du recensement (y compris les réservations en Inde incomplètement énumérées). Estimations inter-censitaires definitives.

[53] Preliminary postcensal estimates. Adjusted for census net undercoverage (including adjustment for incompletely enumerated Indian reserves). - Estimations post censitaires préliminaires. Ajusté pour la sous-estimation du recensement (y compris les réservations en Inde incomplètement énumérées).

[54] Excluding the institutional population. - Non compris la population dans les institutions.

[55] Based on the national household surveys 2010-2014 and the 2011 population census. - D'après les données de l'enquête nationale des ménages 2010-2014 et les résultats du recensement de la population de 2011.

[56] Based on the national household survey of 2018. - D'après l'enquête nationale auprès des ménages de 2018.

[57] Estimates or projections based on the 2007 Population Census. - Estimations ou projections fondées sur le recensement de la population de 2007.

[58] Population statistics are compiled from registers. - Les statistiques de la population sont compilées à partir des registres.

[59] Excluding data for Saint Barthélémy and Saint Martin. - Non compris les données pour Saint Barthélémy et Saint Martin.

[60] Excluding data for Saint Barthélémy and Saint Martin. Data refer to 1 January. - Non compris les données pour Saint Barthélémy et Saint Martin. Données se raportent au 1 janvier.

[61] Projections produced by l'Institut Haïtien de Statistique et d'Informatique (IHSI) and the Latin American and Caribbean Demographic Centre (CELADE) - Population Division of ECLAC. - Les données sont projections produits par l'Institut Haïtien de Statistique et d'Informatique (IHSI) et le centre démographique de l'Amérique latine et les Caraïbes - Division de la population de la CEPALC.

[62] Data refer to projections based on the 2001 Population Census. - Les données se réfèrent aux projections basées sur le recensement de la population de 2001.

[63] The figures represent the census counts adjusted for under-coverage. Adjustments are done by applying weights calculated (to 4 decimal places) for each sex and age group to the enumerated population when the tabulations are produced. Minor discrepancies between totals and the sum of the component parts of a table and minor discrepancies between the totals across tables are due to rounding after weights are applied. - Les chiffres représentent le dénombrement résultant du recensement ajusté pour tenir compte du sous-dénombrement. Les ajustements sont effectués en appliquant un coefficient de pondération calculé (à la quatrième décimale) pour chaque sexe et groupe d'âges de la population dénombrée lors de l'établissement des tableaux. Les écarts mineurs entre les totaux et la somme des éléments constitutifs d'un tableau ainsi qu'entre les totaux figurant dans différents tableaux sont dus au fait que les chiffres sont arrondis après la pondération.

[64] Including an estimation of 1 334 585 persons corresponding to 448 195 housing units without information of the occupants. - Y compris une estimation de 1 334 585 personnes correspondant aux 448 195 unités d'habitation sans information sur les occupants.

[65] Data revised by CONAPO (National Population Council). - Données révisées par CONAPO (Conseil national de la population).

[66] The population projections of CONAPO (National Population Council). - Les projections démographiques de la CONAPO (Conseil national de la population).

[67] Including armed forces stationed in the area. - Y compris les militaires en garnison sur le territoire.

[68] Including armed forces stationed in the area. Based on the results of the 2010 Population Census. - Y compris les militaires en garnison sur le territoire. D'après le résultats du recensement de la population de 2010.

[69] Including armed forces stationed in the area. Postcensal estimates. - Y compris les militaires en garnison sur le territoire. Estimations post censitaires.

[70] Refers to habitable area. Excludes St. Lucia's Forest Reserve. - S'applique à la zone habitable. Exclut la réserve forestière de Sainte-Lucie.

[71] Excluding residents of institutions. - À l'exclusion de personnes en établissements de soins.

[72] Including low water level for all islands (area to shoreline). - Incluent le niveau de basses eaux pour toutes les îles.

[73] Excluding U.S. Armed Forces overseas and civilian U.S. citizens whose usual place of residence is outside the United States. Postcensal estimates. - Non compris les militaires américains à l'étranger et les civils américains dont le lieu de résidence habituel est en dehors des États-Unis. Estimations post censitaires.

[74] Source: U.S. National Center for Health Statistics, National Vital Statistics Reports (NVSR). Including armed forces stationed in the area. - Source : US National Center for Health Statistics, National Vital Statistics Reports (NVSR). Y compris les militaires en garnison sur le territoire.

[75] The total area includes continental areas and islands, and excludes Antarctic area. - La superficie totale comprend les zones continentales et les îles, mais n'inclut pas la région de l'Antarctique.

[76] Data updated according to "Superintendencia Agraria". Interior waters correspond to natural or artificial bodies of water or snow. - Données actualisées d'après la « Superintendencia Agraria ». Les eaux intérieures correspondent aux étendues d'eau naturelles ou artificielles et aux étendues neigeuses.

[77] Data include persons in remote areas, military personnel outside the country, merchant seamen at sea, civilian seasonal workers outside the country, and other civilians outside the country, and exclude nomads, foreign military, civilian aliens temporarily in the country, transients on ships and Indian jungle population. Data refer to national projections. - Y compris les personnes vivant dans des régions éloignées, le personel militaire en dehors du pays, les marins marchands, les ouvriers saisonniers en dehors du pays, et autres civils en dehors du pays, et non

compris les nomades, les militaires étrangers, les étrangers civils temporairement dans le pays, les transiteurs sur des bateaux et les Indiens de la jungle. Les données se réfèrent aux projections nationales.

[78] Data are revised projections taking into consideration also the results of the 2005 census. - Les données sont des projections révisées tenant compte également des résultats du recensement de 2005.

[79] Data based on the 2010 Population Census. Excludes nomadic Indian tribes. - Les données sont fondées sur le recensement de la population de 2010. Non compris les tribus d'Indiens nomades.

[80] Excludes nomadic Indian tribes. - Non compris les tribus d'Indiens nomades.

[81] A dispute exists between the governments of Argentina and the United Kingdom of Great Britain and Northern Ireland concerning sovereignty over the Falkland Islands (Malvinas). - La souveraineté sur les îles Falkland (Malvinas) fait l'objet d'un différend entre le Gouvernement argentin et le Gouvernement du Royaume-Uni de Grande-Bretagne et d'Irlande du Nord.

[82] Excluding military personnel and their families, visitors and transients. - Non compris les militaires et leur familles, ni les visiteurs et transients.

[83] Estimates or projections considering also the results of the 2012 Population Census. - Estimations ou projections en prennant en considération les résultats du recensement de la population de 2012.

[84] Data have not been adjusted for underenumeration and exclude an estimated population of 1,855,501. - Les données n'ont pas été ajustées pour compenser les lacunes du dénombrement. Les données excluent un nombre de personnes estimé à 1,855,501.

[85] Data refer to 30 June. - Données se raportent au 30 juin.

[86] Figures for male and female population do not add up to the figure for total population, because they exclude 108 homeless people of unknown sex. - Les chiffres relatifs à la population masculine et féminine ne correspondent pas au chiffre de la population totale, parce que l'on en a exclu 108 personnes sans toit dont le sexe n'est pas connu.

[87] Revised data. - Données révisées.

[88] Data refer to the settled population based on the 1979 Population Census and the latest household prelisting. The refugees of Afghanistan in Iran, Pakistan, and an estimated 1.5 million nomads, are not included. Excluding nomad population. - Les données se rapportent à la population stationnaire sur la base du recensement de 1979 et du recensement préliminaire des logements le plus récent. Sont exclus les réfugiés d'Afghanistan en Iran et au Pakistan et les nomades estimés à 1,5 million. Non compris les nomades.

[89] Data refer to the settled population based on the 1979 Population Census and the latest household prelisting. The refugees of Afghanistan in Iran, Pakistan, and an estimated 1.5 million nomads, are not included. - Les données se rapportent à la population stationnaire sur la base du recensement de 1979 et du recensement préliminaire des logements le plus récent. Sont exclus les réfugiés d'Afghanistan en Iran et au Pakistan et les nomades estimés à 1,5 million.

[90] Data refer to projected figures based on the Population and Housing Census 2005 (district projection). - Les données se réfèrent aux projections basées sur le recensement de la population et de l'habitat de 2005 (projections locales).

[91] Excluding foreign diplomatic personnel and their dependants. - Non compris le personnel diplomatique étranger et les membres de leur famille les accompagnant.

[92] Excluding foreign diplomatic personnel and their dependants. Data based on the 2008 Population Census. - Non compris le personnel diplomatique étranger et les membres de leur famille les accompagnant. Données fondées sur le recensement de population de 2008.

[93] For statistical purposes, the data for China do not include those for the Hong Kong Special Administrative Region (Hong Kong SAR), Macao Special Administrative Region (Macao SAR) and Taiwan province of China. Data are from Communique of the National Bureau of Statistics of the People's Republic of China on Major Figures of the 2010 Population Census (No.1). - Pour la présentation des statistiques, les données pour la Chine ne comprennent pas la Région Administrative Spéciale de Hong Kong (Hong Kong RAS), la Région Administrative Spéciale de Macao (Macao RAS) et Taïwan province de Chine. Données issues du communiqué du Bureau national de la statistique de la République populaire de Chine sur les chiffres importants du recensement de 2010 (n° 1).

[94] For statistical purposes, the data for China do not include those for the Hong Kong Special Administrative Region (Hong Kong SAR), Macao Special Administrative Region (Macao SAR) and Taiwan province of China. Data have been estimated on the basis of the annual National Sample Survey on Population Changes. - Pour la présentation des statistiques, les données pour la Chine ne comprennent pas la Région Administrative Spéciale de Hong Kong (Hong Kong RAS), la Région Administrative Spéciale de Macao (Macao RAS) et Taïwan province de Chine. Les données ont été estimées sur la base de l'enquête annuelle "National Sample Survey on Population Changes".

[95] Data refer to Hong Kong resident population at the census moment, which covers usual residents and mobile residents. Usual residents refer to two categories of people: (1) Hong Kong permanent residents who had stayed in

Hong Kong for at least three months during the six months before or for at least three months during the six months after the census moment, regardless of whether they were in Hong Kong or not at the census moment; and (2) Hong Kong non-permanent residents who were in Hong Kong at the census moment. Mobile Residents, they are Hong Kong permanent residents who had stayed in Hong Kong for at least one month but less than three months during the six months after the census moment, regardless of whether they were in Hong Kong or not at the census moment. Data are estimates from sample enquiry. - Les données se rapportent à la population résidente à Hong Kong au moment du recensement. Cette population est composée des résidants habituels et des résidants mobiles. La population résidente est partagée en deux catégories: (1) les résidents permanents qui ont habité à Hong Kong au moins trois mois pendant les six mois précédents ou les six mois suivants le recensement; (2) les habitants non-permanents de Hong Kong qui étaient à Hong Kong au moment du recensement. La population mobile se rapporte aux résidents permanents de Hong Kong qui ont habité à Hong Kong pendant les six mois après le recensement pour une période comprise entre un mois et trois mois, indépendamment du fait qu'ils étaient à Hong Kong au moment du recensement au pays. Les données sont des chiffres estimatifs dérivés d'une enquête par sondage.

[96] Inland waters include the reservoirs. - Les eaux intérieures comprennent les réservoirs.

[97] Data refer to government controlled areas. - Les données se rapportent aux zones contrôlées par le Gouvernement.

[98] Data refer to government controlled areas. Data refer to annual average population. - Les données se rapportent aux zones contrôlées par le Gouvernement. Les données correspondent à la population annuelle moyenne.

[99] Data refer to government controlled areas. Data refer to 1 January. - Les données se rapportent aux zones contrôlées par le Gouvernement. Données se raportent au 1 janvier.

[100] Data refer to 1 January. Based on the results of the 2014 Population Census. - Données se raportent au 1 janvier. D'après les résultats du recensement de la population de 2014.

[101] Includes data for the Indian-held part of Jammu and Kashmir, the final status of which has not yet been determined. - Y compris les données pour la partie du Jammu et du Cachemire occupée par l'Inde dont le statut définitif n'a pas encore été déterminé.

[102] Includes data for the Indian-held part of Jammu and Kashmir, the final status of which has not yet been determined. Data refer to 1 March. Data refer to projections based on the 2001 Population Census. - Y compris les données pour la partie du Jammu et du Cachemire occupée par l'Inde dont le statut définitif n'a pas encore été déterminé. Données se raportent au 1 mars. Les données se réfèrent aux projections basées sur le recensement de la population de 2001.

[103] Data are based on the publication: "Indonesia Population Projection 2010-2035" - Les données sont basées sur la publication : << Indonesia Population Projection 2010-2035 >>

[104] Data are based on the publication: "Indonesia Population Projection 2015-2045" - Les données sont basées sur la publication : << Indonesia Population Projection 2015-2045 >>

[105] Data refer to the Iranian Year which begins on 21 March and ends on 20 March of the following year. - Les données concernent l'année iranienne, qui commence le 21 mars et se termine le 20 mars de l'année suivante.

[106] Excluding the population in three autonomous provinces in the north of the country. - La population des trois provinces autonomes dans le nord du pays est exclue.

[107] Data are rounded for confidentiality reasons. Includes data for East Jerusalem and Israeli residents in certain other territories under occupation by Israeli military forces since June 1967. - Chiffres arrondis pour des raisons de confidentialité. Y compris les données pour Jérusalem-Est et les résidents israéliens dans certains autres territoires occupés depuis 1967 par les forces armées israéliennes.

[108] Includes data for East Jerusalem and Israeli residents in certain other territories under occupation by Israeli military forces since June 1967. Data refer to Israeli citizens and permanent residents who are listed in the Population Register. - Y compris les données pour Jérusalem-Est et les résidents israéliens dans certains autres territoires occupés depuis 1967 par les forces armées israéliennes. Les données se rapportent aux citoyens israéliens et aux résidents permanents qui sont répertoriés dans le registre de la population.

[109] Excluding diplomatic personnel outside the country and foreign military and civilian personnel and their dependants stationed in the area. - Non compris le personnel diplomatique hors du pays ni les militaires et agents civils étrangers en poste sur le territoire et les membres de leur famille les accompagnant.

[110] Excluding diplomatic personnel outside the country and foreign military and civilian personnel and their dependants stationed in the area. Because of rounding, totals are not in all cases the sum of the respective components. Estimates based on the complete counts of the 2015 Population Census. - Non

compris le personnel diplomatique hors du pays ni les militaires et agents civils étrangers en poste sur le territoire et les membres de leur famille les accompagnant. Les chiffres étant arrondis, les totaux ne correspondent pas toujours rigoureusement à la somme des composants respectifs. Estimations basées sur le dénombrement complet du recensement de la population de 2015.

[111] Data refer to 1 October 2007. - Les données se réfèrent au 1er octobre 2007.

[112] Excluding data for Jordanian territory under occupation since June 1967 by Israeli military forces. - Non compris les données pour le territoire jordanien occupé depuis juin 1967 par les forces armées israéliennes.

[113] Excluding data for Jordanian territory under occupation since June 1967 by Israeli military forces. Data refer to 31 December. - Non compris les données pour le territoire jordanien occupé depuis juin 1967 par les forces armées israéliennes. Données se raportent au 31 décembre.

[114] Data refer to resident population. Recalculated population estimates taking into account late registration of births and deaths until May 2017. - Les données concernent la population résidente. Réestimation du nombre d'habitants compte tenu de l'enregistrement tardif des naissances et des décès jusqu'en mai 2017.

[115] Data refer to resident population. - Les données concernent la population résidente.

[116] Source: Living conditions of household survey, October 2011 to September 2012. - Source: Enquête sur les conditions de vie des ménages, octobre 2011 à septembre 2012.

[117] Data have been adjusted for underenumeration. - Les données ont été ajustées pour compenser les lacunes du dénombrement.

[118] Estimates based on the adjusted results of the Population and Housing Census of 2010. - Les estimations sont fondée sur les résultats ajustées du recensement de la population et de l'habitat de 2010.

[119] Data refer to resident population which includes resident Maldivians and resident foreigners. - Les données concernent la population résidente, qui comprend les Maldiviens et les étrangers.

[120] Data refer to resident population which includes resident Maldivians and resident foreigners. Estimates based on the 2014 Population Census. - Les données concernent la population résidente, qui comprend les Maldiviens et les étrangers. Estimations fondées sur le recensement de la population de 2014.

[121] The total for the whole country includes 1,206,353 persons estimated not to have been counted in parts of States of Rakhine, Kachin and Kayin. - Le total pour l'ensemble du pays s'élève à 1 206 353 personnes qui ne vivraient pas dans les États rakhine, kachin et kayin.

[122] Data refer to 1 October. - Données se raportent au 1 octobre.

[123] Data refer to 1 October. Based on the results of the 2014 Population Census. - Données se raportent au 1 octobre. D'après les résultats du recensement de la population de 2014.

[124] Data refer to registered population data from Royal Oman Police. - Les données portent sur la population enregistrée par la police royale de l'Oman.

[125] Excluding data for the Pakistan-held part of Jammu and Kashmir, the final status of which has not yet been determined. - Non compris les données concernant la partie du Jammu et Cachemire occupée par le Pakistan dont le statut définitif n'a pas été déterminé.

[126] Excluding data for the Pakistan-held part of Jammu and Kashmir, the final status of which has not yet been determined. Figures for male and female may not add up to the total, since they do not include the category "Unknown". - Non compris les données concernant la partie du Jammu et Cachemire occupée par le Pakistan dont le statut définitif n'a pas été déterminé. La somme des chiffres indiqués pour les sexes masculin et féminin peut n'être pas égale au total parce qu'elle n'inclut pas la catégorie " inconnue ".

[127] Excluding 2134 Filipinos in Philippine Embassies, Consulates and Missions Abroad. - Excepté 2134 Philippins travaillant dans les ambassades, les consulats et les missions des Philippines à l'étranger.

[128] Urban and rural breakdown not applicable as Singapore is a city-state. Data are based on the latest register-based population estimates for 2010. Data refer to resident population which comprises Singapore citizens and permanent residents. - La ventilation entre zones urbaines et zones rurales ne s'applique pas à Singapour, puisqu'il s'agit d'une ville État. Données basées sur les estimations démographiques les plus récentes fondées sur les registres de 2010. Les données se rapportent à la population résidente composé des citoyens de Singapour et des résidents permanents.

[129] Data refer to total population, which comprises Singapore residents and non-residents. Data refer to 30 June. Data exclude residents who have been away from Singapore for a continuous period of 12 months or longer as at the reference date. - Les données se rapportent à la population totale composé des résidents de Singapour et les non résidents. Données se raportent au 30 juin. Non compris les résidents hors de Singapour pour une période ininterrompue de 12 mois ou plus avant la date de référence.

[130] The land area of Singapore comprises the mainland and other islands. - La superficie terrestre de Singapour comprend l'île principale et les autres îles.

[131] Including Palestinian refugees. - Y compris les réfugiés de Palestine.

[132] Based on a sample taken at the time of census. Because of rounding, totals are not in all cases the sum of the respective components. - D'après un échantillon obtenu au moment du recensement. Les chiffres étant arrondis, les totaux ne correspondent pas toujours rigoureusement à la somme des composants respectifs.

[133] Data refer to 31 December. Data based on Address Based Population Registration System. - Données se raportent au 31 décembre. Les données sont basées sur le registre national de la population basé sur l'adresse.

[134] Data based on address-based population registration system. - Les données sont basées sur le registre national de la population basé sur l'adresse.

[135] Data include non-national population. - Les données comprennent les non-nationaux.

[136] Land area only. - La superficie des terres seulement.

[137] Data refer to 1 January. Data refer to resident population. - Données se raportent au 1 janvier. Les données concernent la population résidente.

[138] Data are adjusted according to the results of the 2009 census and 2014 intercensus. - Les données ont été ajustées à partir des résultats du recensement de la population de 2009 et des données intercensitaires de 2014.

[139] Statistics are compiled from registers. - Les statistiques sont compilées à partir des registres.

[140] Decrease in population due to revision in administrative registers. Population statistics are compiled from registers. Data refer to 1 January. - Diminution de la population due à la révision des registres administratifs. Les statistiques de la population sont compilées à partir des registres. Données se raportent au 1 janvier.

[141] Data refer to 1 January. Population statistics are compiled from registers. - Données se raportent au 1 janvier. Les statistiques de la population sont compilées à partir des registres.

[142] Excluding Faeroe Islands and Greenland shown separately, if available. - Non compris les Iles Féroé et le Groenland, qui font l'objet de rubriques distinctes, si disponible.

[143] Population statistics are compiled from registers. Excluding Åland Islands. - Les statistiques de la population sont compilées à partir des registres. Non compris les Îles d'Åland.

[144] Excluding Åland Islands. - Non compris les Îles d'Åland.

[145] Excluding diplomatic personnel outside the country and including members of alien armed forces not living in military camps and foreign diplomatic personnel not living in embassies or consulates. - Non compris le personnel diplomatique hors du pays et y compris les militaires étrangers ne vivant pas dans des camps militaires et le personnel diplomatique étranger ne vivant pas dans les ambassades ou les consulats.

[146] Data refer to 1 January. Data based on the 2011 Census. - Données se raportent au 1 janvier. Données fondées sur le recensement de 2011.

[147] Excluding military personnel, visitors and transients. - Non compris les militaires, ni les visiteurs et transients.

[148] Excluding military personnel, visitors and transients. Data refer to 31 December. - Non compris les militaires, ni les visiteurs et transients. Données se raportent au 31 décembre.

[149] Data refer to 31 March. - Données se raportent au 31 mars.

[150] Data refer to the Vatican City State. - Les données se rapportent à l'Etat de la Cité du Vatican.

[151] The population figure is 466 persons. - La population est égale à 466 personnes.

[152] The population figure is 466 persons. Data refer to 6 December. - La population est égale à 466 personnes. Données se raportent au 6 décembre.

[153] Surface area is 0.44 km². - Superficie: 0,44 km².

[154] Data refer to 1 January. Data refer to usually resident population. - Données se raportent au 1 janvier. Les données concernent la population habituellement résidente.

[155] Data refer to registered resident population. - Les données concernent la population enregistrée résidente.

[156] Data refer to registered resident population. Data refer to 1 January. - Les données concernent la population enregistrée résidente. Données se raportent au 1 janvier.

[157] Data refer to 30 April. - Données se raportent au 30 avril.

[158] Including civilian nationals temporarily outside the country. - Y compris les civils nationaux temporairement hors du pays.

[159] Including civilian nationals temporarily outside the country. Data refer to 1 January. - Y compris les civils nationaux temporairement hors du pays. Données se raportent au 1 janvier.

[160] Data refer to resident population only. - Pour la population résidante seulement.

[161] Data refer to resident population only. Data refer to 1 January. - Pour la population résidante seulement. Données se raportent au 1 janvier.

[162] Data refer to usually resident population. - Les données concernent la population habituellement résidente.

163 Including residents temporarily outside the country. Population statistics are compiled from registers. - Y compris les résidents se trouvant temporairement hors du pays. Les statistiques de la population sont compilées à partir des registres.

164 Tiraspol, Bender, Slobozia, Ribnita, Camenca Yrigoricpol/Grigoriopol are districts from Transnistria where the census was not conducted. - Tiraspol, Bender, Slobozia, Ribnita, Camenca, Yrigoricpol/Grigoriopol sont des districts de la Transnistrie où le recensement n'a pas eu lieu.

165 Excluding Transnistria and the municipality of Bender. - Les données ne tiennent pas compte de l'information sur la Transnistria et la municipalité de Bender.

166 Excluding Transnistria and the municipality of Bender. Data refer to usual resident population based on the 2014 Census. Tiraspol, Bender, Slobozia, Ribnita, Camenca Yrigoricpol/Grigoriopol are districts from Transnistria where the 2014 census was not conducted. - Les données ne tiennent pas compte de l'information sur la Transnistria et la municipalité de Bender. Les données se rapportent à la population habituellement résidente et sont fondées sur le recensement de 2014. Tiraspol, Bender, Slobozia, Ribnita, Camenca, Yrigoricpol/Grigoriopol sont des districts de la Transnistrie où le recensement n'a pas eu lieu.

167 Figures for male and female may not add up to the total, since they do not include the category "Unknown". - La somme des chiffres indiqués pour les sexes masculin et féminin peut n'être pas égale au total parce qu'elle n'inclut pas la catégorie " inconnue ".

168 Excludes data for Kosovo and Metohia. - Sans les données pour le Kosovo et Metohie.

169 Excludes data for Kosovo and Metohia. Data refer to 1 January. Based on the results of the 2011 Population Census. - Sans les données pour le Kosovo et Metohie. Données se raportent au 1 janvier. Basé sur les résultats du recencement de la population de 2011.

170 Inhabited only during the winter season. The Norwegian population of these islands is included also in the de jure population of Norway. - N'est habitée que pendant la saison d'hiver. La population norvégienne de ces îles est comprise également dans la population de droit de la Norvège.

171 Data refer to 1 January. Population statistics are compiled from registers. Data refer to registered resident population. - Données se rapportent au 1 janvier. Les statistiques de la population sont compilées à partir des registres. Les données concernent la population enregistrée résidente.

172 Data refer to legal resident population. Data refer to 1 January. - Les données concernent la population légalement résidente. Données se rapportent au 1 janvier.

173 Data refer to 1 January. The Government of Ukraine has informed the United Nations that it is not in a position to provide statistical data concerning the Autonomous Republic of Crimea and the city of Sevastopol. - Données se raportent au 1 janvier. Le gouvernement Ukrainien a informé l'ONU qu'il n'est pas en mesure de fournir des données statistiques concernant la République autonome de Crimée et la ville de Sébastopol.

174 Excluding Channel Islands (Guernsey and Jersey) and Isle of Man, shown separately, if available. - Non compris les îles Anglo-Normandes (Guernesey et Jersey) et l'île de Man, qui font l'objet de rubriques distinctes, si disponible.

175 These data have been randomly rounded to protect confidentiality. Individual figures may not add up to totals, and values for the same data may vary in different tables. Including population in off-shore, migratory and shipping. - Ces données ont été arrondies de façon aléatoire afin d'en préserver la confidentialité. La somme de certains chiffres peut ne pas correspondre aux totaux indiqués et les valeurs des mêmes données peuvent varier d'un tableau à un autre. Y compris les populations extraterritoriales, les populations nomades et les populations maritimes.

176 Based on the results of the 2016 Population Census. - Basé sur les résultats du recencement de la population de 2016.

177 Excluding Niue, shown separately, which is part of Cook Islands, but because of remoteness is administered separately. - Non compris Nioué, qui fait l'objet d'une rubrique distincte et qui fait partie des îles Cook, mais qui, en raison de son éloignement, est administrée séparément.

178 Land area only. Excluding 84 square km of uninhabited islands. - La superficie des terres seulement. Exclut les îles inhabitées d'une superficie de 84 kilomètres carrés.

179 Projections are prepared by the Secretariat of the Pacific Community based on the 1999 census of population and housing. - Les projections sont preparées par le Secrétariat de la Communauté du Pacifique à partir des résultats du recensement de la population et de l'habitat de 1999.

180 Based on the 2010 Population and Housing Census and 2013/2014 Household Income and Expenditure Survey. - Données fondées sur les résultat du recensement de la population et de l'habitat de 2010, et ceux de l'enquête auprès des ménages sur des revenus et des dépenses de 2013/2014.

181 Data include overseas visitors in New Zealand on census night. These data have been randomly rounded to protect confidentiality. Individual figures may not add up to totals, and values for the same data may vary in different tables. - Y compris les visiteurs étrangers qui se trouvaient en Nouvelle-Zélande le soir du recensement. Ces données ont été arrondies de façon aléatoire afin d'en préserver la confidentialité. La somme de certains chiffres peut ne pas correspondre aux totaux indiqués et les valeurs des mêmes données peuvent varier d'un tableau à un autre.

182 Because of rounding, totals are not in all cases the sum of the respective components. - Les chiffres étant arrondis, les totaux ne correspondent pas toujours rigoureusement à la somme des composants respectifs.

183 Because of rounding, totals are not in all cases the sum of the respective components. Intercensal estimates. - Les chiffres étant arrondis, les totaux ne correspondent pas toujours rigoureusement à la somme des composants respectifs. Estimations inter-censitaires.

184 Estimates based on the 2016 Population Census. - Estimations basées sur le recensement de la population de 2016.

185 Data have not been adjusted for underenumeration. - Les données n'ont pas été ajustées pour compenser les lacunes du dénombrement.

186 Projections based on adjusted 2009 census counts. - Projections fondées à partir des comptes rajustés du recensement de 2009.

Table 3a – *Demographic Yearbook 2018*

Table 3a presents the values of the Whipple's index by sex, urban or rural residence, for total area and both sexes combined, according to the availability of the underlying data in the *Demographic Yearbook* database.

The data used to compile these indices are the datasets of population by single years of age, sex, and urban or rural residence, of the population censuses conducted worldwide since 1985. These datasets have been reported by the National Statistical Offices to the United Nations Statistics Division via the *Demographic Yearbook* questionnaires.

The footnotes that appear at the end of this table are notes that refer to the respective dataset of population by single years of age, sex, and urban or rural residence.

Whipple's index is an index of age preference in age reporting. The way it is calculated for this table, it is meant to indicate preference or avoidance of ages ending in digits "0" (zero) or "5" (five) during age reporting for a population census.

The formula used to calculate the values of the Whipple's index for this table is:

$$\frac{P25+P30+P35+P40+P45+P50+P55+P60}{\frac{1}{5}(P23+P24+P25+\cdots+P58+P59+P60+P61+P62)} *100$$

where Px refers to the number of persons of age x in completed years. The sum in brackets in the denominator is the sum of the number of persons of every single age from 23 to 62.

The values of the Whipple's index generally vary between 100, indicating no preference for "0" or "5" (in other words no heaping in ages ending in "0" or "5"), and 500, indicating that age reporting was entirely concentrated in ages ending in digits "0" or "5". The higher than 100 the value of the index, the higher is the heaping of age reporting in ages ending in "0" or "5".

For more information about the measurement of age and digit preference, please refer to *The Methods and Materials of Demography, Second Edition* (2004), Edited by Jacob S. Siegel and David A. Swanson.

Tableau 3a – *Annuaire démographique 2018*

Le tableau 3a présente les valeurs de l'indice de Whipple par sexe, résidence urbaine ou rurale, pour la superficie totale et les sexes combinés, selon la disponibilité des données sous-jacentes dans la base de données de l'*Annuaire démographique*.

Les données utilisées pour établir ces indices sont les séries de données de la population par âge simple, sexe et résidence urbaine ou rurale, pour les recensements de la population effectués dans le monde entier depuis 1985. Ces séries de données sont communiquées par les services nationaux de statistique à la Division de statistique de l'Organisation des Nations Unies par le biais des questionnaires de l'*Annuaire démographique*.

Les notes qui figurent à la fin de ce tableau sont des notes renvoyant aux différentes séries de données de la population par âge simple, sexe et résidence urbaine ou rurale.

L'indice de Whipple est un indice de préférence de certains âges dans les déclarations de l'âge. La manière dont il est calculé pour ce tableau permet d'indiquer l'attraction ou la répulsion pour des âges se terminant par les chiffres « 0 » (zéro) ou « 5 » (cinq) lors de la déclaration de l'âge effectuée dans le cadre d'un recensement de population.

La formule utilisée pour calculer les valeurs de l'indice de Whipple pour ce tableau est la suivante:

$$\frac{P25+P30+P35+P40+P45+P50+P55+P60}{\frac{1}{5}(P23+P24+P25+\cdots+P58+P59+P60+P61+P62)} *100$$

Px étant le nombre de personnes d'âge x en années révolues. La somme entre parenthèses en dénominateur est la somme du nombre de personnes selon l'âge simple de 23 à 62 ans.

Les valeurs de l'indice de Whipple varient généralement entre 100, indication d'absence de préférence pour « 0 » ou « 5 » (en d'autres termes pas de prépondérance des âges se terminant par « 0 » ou « 5 »), et 500, indiquant que les déclarations de l'âge étaient entièrement polarisées sur les âges se terminant par les chiffres « 0 » ou « 5 ». Plus la valeur de l'indice est supérieure à 100, plus les déclarations de l'âge sont polarisées sur les âges se terminant par « 0 » ou « 5 ».

Pour en savoir plus sur la mesure de l'âge et la préférence pour les chiffres, prière de consulter l'ouvrage intitulé *The Methods and Materials of Demography, Second Edition (2004)*, publié sous la direction de Jacob S. Siegel et David A. Swanson.

Continent, country or area, date and code[a] Continent, pays ou zone, date et code[a]	Total			Urban - Urbaine			Rural - Rurale		
	Both sexes Les deux sexes	Male Masculin	Female Féminin	Both sexes Les deux sexes	Male Masculin	Female Féminin	Both sexes Les deux sexes	Male Masculin	Female Féminin
AFRICA - AFRIQUE									
Algeria - Algérie[1]									
16 IV 2008 (CDJC)	100.7	100.5	100.9	100.7	100.5	100.9	100.7	100.6	100.8
Angola									
16 V 2014 (CDFC)	106.1	105.3	106.8	104.9	104.5	105.4	108.2	107.1	109.1
Benin - Bénin									
15 II 1992 (CDFC)	216.1	205.6	224.6	185.4	171.6	197.9	234.6	228	239.6
11 II 2002 (CDJC)	229.1	218.9	237.8	190.4	180.1	200	257.5	250	263.5
Botswana									
21 VIII 1991 (CDFC)	104.8	106.6	103.3	102.4	103.6	101.4	107.7	110.8	105.3
17 VIII 2001 (CDFC)	100.9	101.8	100.2	...	...	...	...	...	...
9 VIII 2011 (CDFC)	100.8	101.3	100.3	101.7	101.8	101.6	99	100.5	97.5
Burkina Faso									
10 XII 1985 (CDJC)	193	173.8	208.4	153.1	140.9	166.7	198.6	179.4	213.2
10 XII 1996 (CDJC)	162.6[2]	144[2]	177.5[2]	99.5[3]	99.6[3]	99.5[3]	99.6[3]	99.7[3]	99.5[3]
9 XII 2006 (CDJC)	145.1	133.8	154.5	131.1	130.5	131.8	150.2	135.3	161.5
Burundi									
16 VIII 1990 (CDJC)	152.9	141.7	163	...	...	...	...	...	...
16 VIII 2008 (CDJC)	156.8	149.4	164.4	137.2	136.5	138.3	159.4	151.5	167.1
Cabo Verde									
23 VI 1990 (CDFC)	111.9	110.7	112.8	108	107.7	108.3	115.3	113.7	116.4
16 VI 2010 (CDJC)	105.8	105.7	105.9	105.3	105.1	105.6	106.7	106.8	106.5
Cameroon - Cameroun									
11 XI 2005 (CDJC)	173.5	165.1	181.4	...	...	...	...	...	...
Central African Republic - République centrafricaine									
8 XII 1988 (CDFC)....................	139.4	132	146.1	129.9	125.2	134.3	144.5	135.8	152.3
Chad - Tchad									
20 V 2009 (CDJC)	231.3	216.3	245.2	...	...	...	...	...	...
Congo									
1 I 1985 (CDJC)	107.3	107.5	107.1	...	...	...	...	...	...
28 IV 2007 (CDFC)	103.5	103.1	103.8	...	...	...	...	...	...
Côte d'Ivoire									
1 III 1988 (CDFC)	126.3	117.3	136.2	116.4	112.7	121	132.7	120.5	145
15 V 2014 (CDJC)	116.5	114.3	118.9	112.3	111.8	112.9	121.2	117.1	125.6
Egypt - Égypte									
21 XI 2006 (CDFC)	196.5	175.3	218.2	177.1	162.7	191.9	213.5	186.4	241.4
Eswatini									
25 VIII 1986 (CDFC)	125.9	125.4	126.3	118.3	118.2	118.5	129.3	130.1	128.8
11 V 1997 (CDFC)	120.6	121.5	119.7	116.9	117.9	115.8	122.3	123.7	121.2
11 V 2007 (CDJC)	99.8	101.2	98.6	99	100.7	97.4	100.1	101.5	99.1
Ethiopia - Éthiopie									
11 X 1994 (CDFC)	272.3	258.9	285	248.7	232.6	264	276.5	263.7	288.7
29 V 2007 (CDJC)....................	252.1	241	262.9	232.3	222.5	242.4	256.7	245.4	267.5
Gabon									
31 VII 1993 (CDFC)	116.6	115.9	117.4	...	...	...	...	...	...
Gambia - Gambie									
15 IV 1993 (CDFC)	229.8	215.2	244.5	191.2	183.2	201.2	256.2	241.6	268.9
Ghana									
26 III 2000 (CDFC)	184	175.8	191.6	159.7	154.7	164.5	205.6	195.2	215.3
26 IX 2010 (CDFC)	159.1	155.2	162.5	138.3	136.6	139.8	184.7	178.2	190.6
Guinea - Guinée									
15 III 2014 (CDJC)	200.7	185	214	166.2	160.8	171.9	221.1	202.1	235.4
Guinea-Bissau - Guinée-Bissau[4]									
15 III 2009 (CDJC)	137.8	128.9	145.7	...	...	...	...	...	...
Kenya									
24 VIII 1989 (CDJC)	147.8	142.6	152.8	144.1	140.8	149.4	148.9	143.3	153.5
24 VIII 1999 (CDFC)	148.3	143.2	153.2	...	...	...	...	...	...
24 VIII 2009 (CDFC)	146.4	144.6	148.2	141.1	141.1	141.2	149.8	147.1	152.2
Lesotho									
13 IV 2006 (CDJC)	105.3	105.8	104.9	...	...	...	...	...	...
Liberia - Libéria									
21 III 2008 (CDFC)	142.2	136.3	148.1	...	...	...	...	...	...
Malawi									
1 IX 1987 (CDFC)	138.5	137.9	139.1	...	...	...	...	...	...
1 IX 1998 (CDFC)	147.7	149.2	146.4	142.6	146.5	137.3	148.7	149.7	147.7
8 VI 2008 (CDFC)	120.6	121	120.2	113	114.7	111	122.2	122.5	121.9
3 IX 2018 (CDJC)	106.2	105.7	106.6	104.7	104.6	104.8	106.5	106	107

Continent, country or area, date and code[a] Continent, pays ou zone, date et code[a]	Total			Urban - Urbaine			Rural - Rurale		
	Both sexes Les deux sexes	Male Masculin	Female Féminin	Both sexes Les deux sexes	Male Masculin	Female Féminin	Both sexes Les deux sexes	Male Masculin	Female Féminin
AFRICA - AFRIQUE									
Mali									
1 IV 1987 (CDJC)	184.5	171.4	195.9	163.7	154.1	173	190.4	176.7	202
1 IV 1998 (CDJC)	180.1	166.8	192.3	166.5	158	175.2	185.6	170.7	198.6
1 IV 2009 (CDFC)	156.5	145.7	166.6	142.7	139.1	146.8	161.1	148.2	172.5
Mauritius - Maurice[5]									
1 VII 1990 (CDFC)	103.4	102.4	104.3	...	...	...	...	...	...
2 VII 2000 (CDJC)	102.4	102.1	102.7	102.3	102	102.7	102.5	102.2	102.7
4 VII 2011 (CDJC)	100.6	101	100.3	100.8	101.2	100.3	100.5	100.9	100.2
Mayotte									
31 VII 2007 (CDJC)	124.4	126.9	122.3	...	...	...	...	...	...
21 VIII 2012 (CDJC)	101.1	102.9	99.6	...	...	...	...	...	...
Morocco - Maroc									
1 IX 2004 (CDFC)	113.4	108.4	118	110.1	107.5	112.5	118.2	109.8	126.2
Mozambique									
1 VIII 1997 (CDJC)	118.6	117.9	119.3	111.7	110.9	112.4	121.5	121	121.9
1 VIII 2007 (CDFC)	126	126.2	125.9	...	...	...	...	...	...
Namibia - Namibie									
21 X 1991 (CDFC)	105.8	104.9	106.5	103.5	102.9	104.2	107.1	106.4	107.6
27 VIII 2001 (CDFC)	103.9	103.2	104.5	103.6	102.9	104.4	104.1	103.5	104.6
28 VIII 2011 (CDFC)	103.9	103.8	104	104.3	103.6	105	103.4	104.1	102.9
Niger									
20 V 2001 (CDJC)	270.1	254.7	285.2	...	...	...	...	...	...
10 XII 2012 (CDJC)	105.1	104.7	105.4	...	...	...	...	...	...
Nigeria - Nigéria									
26 XI 1991 (CDFC)	293.5	279.8	307.1	...	...	...	...	...	...
Republic of South Sudan - République de Soudan du Sud									
21 IV 2008 (CDFC)	183.1	178.4	187.9	...	...	...	...	...	...
Reunion - Réunion									
15 III 1990 (CDFC)	99.9	99.8	100.1	...	...	...	...	...	...
8 III 1999 (CDJC)	100	100.3	99.7	...	...	...	...	...	...
1 I 2015 (CDJC)	99.2	98.7	99.6	99.1	98.6	99.6	104.3	103.4	105.1
Rwanda									
16 VIII 2002 (CDJC)	106.3	106.6	106.1	107.4	108.3	106.2	106	106	106.1
15 VIII 2012 (CDJC)	110.2	110.4	109.9	108.3	109.3	107.1	110.6	110.7	110.5
Saint Helena ex. dep. - Sainte-Hélène sans dép.									
8 III 1998 (CDJC)	101	98.8	103.3	...	...	...	...	...	...
10 II 2008 (CDJC)[6]	98.8	99.9	97.8	...	...	...	...	...	...
7 II 2016 (CDJC)[7]	103.9	99.4	109	...	...	...	...	...	...
Saint Helena: Ascension - Sainte-Hélène: Ascension									
8 III 1998 (CDJC)	117.5	111	130.7	...	...	...	...	...	...
Saint Helena: Tristan da Cunha - Sainte-Hélène: Tristan da Cunha									
22 II 1987 (CDFC)	55.2	48.6	61	...	...	...	...	...	...
Sao Tome and Principe - Sao Tomé-et-Principe									
4 VIII 1991 (CDFC)	102.7	101.5	103.8	...	...	...	...	...	...
25 VIII 2001 (CDJC)	105.7	106.2	105.3	...	...	...	...	...	...
13 V 2012 (CDJC)	104.1	103.2	105	...	...	...	...	...	...
Seychelles									
17 VIII 1987 (CDFC)	100.9	102.8	99	...	...	...	...	...	...
26 VIII 1994 (CDFC)	100.9	99.9	102	...	...	...	...	...	...
29 VIII 1997 (CDFC)	101.6	100.8	102.5	...	...	...	...	...	...
26 VIII 2002 (CDJC)	100.8	99.2	102.5	...	...	...	...	...	...
26 VIII 2010 (CDFC)	101.3	101.7	101	...	...	...	...	...	...
South Africa - Afrique du Sud									
5 III 1985 (CDFC)	124.3	120.9	127.7	...	...	...	...	...	...
7 III 1991 (CDFC)	113.1	111.5	114.7	...	...	...	...	...	...
10 X 1996 (CDFC)[8]	100.5	100.3	100.7	99.3	99.5	99.1	102.5	101.7	103.1
10 X 2001 (CDFC)	97.1	97	97.2	...	...	...	...	...	...
10 X 2011 (CDFC)	97.6	97.8	97.4	...	...	...	...	...	...
Tunisia - Tunisie									
20 IV 1994 (CDFC)	102.4	102.4	102.4	102.4	102.4	102.4	102.4	102.3	102.4
Uganda - Ouganda									
12 I 1991 (CDFC)	168	154.8	180.5	158.6	150.8	167.3	169.4	155.5	182.2

Continent, country or area, date and code[a] / Continent, pays ou zone, date et code[a]	Total			Urban - Urbaine			Rural - Rurale		
	Both sexes Les deux sexes	Male Masculin	Female Féminin	Both sexes Les deux sexes	Male Masculin	Female Féminin	Both sexes Les deux sexes	Male Masculin	Female Féminin
AFRICA - AFRIQUE									
12 IX 2002 (CDFC)	134.2	129.6	138.4	128.2	128.5	128	135.2	129.7	140
27 VIII 2014 (CDFC)	131.5	129	133.7	130.6	132.2	129	131.8	127.7	135.4
United Republic of Tanzania - République Unie de Tanzanie									
28 VIII 1988 (CDFC)	189.2	175.1	201.8	173.7	167.3	180.7	193.3	177.4	206.7
26 VIII 2012 (CDFC)	154.4	152.6	156.1	139.5	141.5	137.7	162.3	158.8	165.5
Zambia - Zambie									
20 VIII 1990 (CDFC)	120.7	121.9	119.6	117.2	119.8	114.2	123.1	123.5	122.7
25 X 2000 (CDFC)	127.6	128.9	126.3	123.9	125.3	122.4	129.9	131.4	128.5
16 X 2010 (CDJC)	123.8	126.8	120.7	122.3	125.2	119.3	124.9	128.2	121.8
Zimbabwe									
18 VIII 1992 (CDFC)	120.6	122.2	119.2	115.9	119.5	111.4	123.7	124.6	123
17 VIII 2002 (CDFC)	115.1	115.2	115	109.7	110.9	108.4	119	119	119.1
17 VIII 2012 (CDFC)	110.8	110.8	110.8	...	...	...	...	...	...
AMERICA, NORTH - AMÉRIQUE DU NORD									
Anguilla									
13 IV 1992 (CDFC)	104.8	109	100.4	...	...	...	...	...	...
9 V 2001 (CDFC)	104.4	105.6	103.2	...	...	...	...	...	...
Antigua and Barbuda - Antigua-et-Barbuda									
28 V 2001 (CDJC)	104.3	103.1	105.4	...	...	...	...	...	...
Aruba									
6 X 1991 (CDJC)	99.3	99.4	99.3	...	...	...	...	...	...
14 X 2000 (CDJC)	103.9[9]	103.3	104.5	...	...	...	...	...	...
29 IX 2010 (CDJC)[9]	103.4	103.6	103.3	...	...	...	...	...	...
Bahamas									
1 V 1990 (CDFC)	103.4	102.3	104.5	...	...	...	...	...	...
1 V 2000 (CDFC)	101.5	100.4	102.5	...	...	...	...	...	...
3 V 2010 (CDJC)	101.3	101.6	101.1	...	...	...	...	...	...
Barbados - Barbade									
1 V 2000 (CDFC)	103.8	104.4	103.3	...	...	...	...	...	...
Belize									
12 V 1991 (CDFC)	103.5	103.2	103.8	...	...	...	...	...	...
12 V 2010 (CDJC)	104.2	103.9	104.5	...	...	...	...	...	...
Bermuda - Bermudes									
20 V 1991 (CDJC)	99	97.9	100	...	...	...	...	...	...
20 V 2000 (CDJC)[10]	100.2	100	100.3	...	...	...	...	...	...
20 V 2010 (CDJC)[11]	100.9	101.1	100.8	100.9	101.1	100.8	...	...	...
20 V 2016 (CDJC)[11]	101.2	100.5	101.8	...	...	...	...	...	...
British Virgin Islands - Îles Vierges britanniques									
12 V 1991 (CDJC)	102.6	104.5	100.5	...	...	...	...	...	...
Canada									
4 VI 1991 (CDJC)	99.6	99.6	99.6	99.6	99.6	99.7	99.6	99.6	99.5
14 V 1996 (CDJC)	99.7	99.7	99.7	...	...	...	...	...	...
15 V 2001 (CDJC)	99.7	99.7	99.8	99.8	99.8	99.8	99.6	99.5	99.8
16 V 2006 (CDJC)[9]	99.9	100	99.9	100	100	100	99.6	99.6	99.7
2 V 2011 (CDJC)	100.8	101	100.7	100.9	101.1	100.8	100.4	100.6	100.3
10 V 2016 (CDJC)[12]	100.8	101	100.7	100.9	101	100.7	100.7	100.7	100.7
Cayman Islands - Îles Caïmanes									
15 X 1989 (CDFC)	104.1	102.7	105.5	...	...	...	...	...	...
10 X 2010 (CDJC)[10]	102.3	102.8	101.8	102.3	102.8	101.8	...	...	...
Costa Rica									
26 VI 2000 (CDJC)	109.1	109.8	108.4	108.6	108.9	108.3	109.9	111.1	108.6
30 V 2011 (CDJC)	104	104.2	103.9	103.8	103.8	103.9	104.6	105.2	103.9
Cuba									
7 IX 2002 (CDJC)	102.2	102.5	101.9	102.5	102.7	102.2	101.5	102	100.9
14 IX 2012 (CDJC)	101.5	101.6	101.3	...	...	...	...	...	...
Dominican Republic - République dominicaine									
24 IX 1993 (CDJC)	116.5	114.9	118	111.5	109.9	113	123.5	121.4	125.5
18 X 2002 (CDJC)	108	108.9	107.1	105.8	106.3	105.4	112.1	113.5	110.7
1 XII 2010 (CDJC)	111.5	113.8	109.2	109.9	111.9	108.1	116.5	119.3	113.1

Continent, country or area, date and code[a] / Continent, pays ou zone, date et code[a]	Total			Urban - Urbaine			Rural - Rurale		
	Both sexes Les deux sexes	Male Masculin	Female Féminin	Both sexes Les deux sexes	Male Masculin	Female Féminin	Both sexes Les deux sexes	Male Masculin	Female Féminin
AMERICA, NORTH - AMÉRIQUE DU NORD									
El Salvador									
27 IX 1992 (CDFC)............	126	127.5	124.6	119.9	119.7	120	133.5	136.6	130.7
12 V 2007 (CDJC)............	105.9	107.1	105	105.3	106.3	104.5	107.3	108.7	106.2
Guadeloupe									
8 III 1999 (CDJC)............	100.5	100.5	100.4	...	...	...	...	...	...
1 I 2015 (CDJC)[13]............	100.2	99.8	100.4	100.2	99.8	100.5	99.3	102.4	96.2
Honduras									
11 V 1988 (CDFC)............	104.1	104.5	103.6	102.4	102.5	102.3	105.3	105.9	104.8
28 VII 2001 (CDJC)............	121.8	123.3	120.4	118.5	118.8	118.3	125.1	127.5	122.7
10 VIII 2013 (CDFC)............	119.7	121.6	118.1	120	120.9	119.1	119.4	122.4	116.6
Jamaica - Jamaïque									
7 IV 1991 (CDJC)............	107.6	108.8	106.5	...	...	...	...	...	...
10 IX 2001 (CDJC)[14]............	107.4	108.7	106.1	106.9	107.5	106.4	107.9	110	105.7
4 IV 2011 (CDJC)............	103.3	103.4	103.1	103.6	103.6	103.6	102.8	103.2	102.5
Martinique									
15 III 1990 (CDJC)............	104.4	104.1	104.6	...	...	...	...	...	...
1 I 2015 (CDJC)	99.4	100.7	98.4	99.5	100.7	98.5	97.1	100	94.5
Mexico - Mexique									
12 III 1990 (CDJC)............	125.2	123.5	126.8	...	...	...	...	...	...
14 II 2000 (CDJC)............	116.7	116.5	116.9	114.8	114.3	115.3	123.4	124.3	122.7
17 X 2005 (CDJC)............	118.8	118.7	118.9	117.5	117	117.9	123.8	124.8	122.8
12 VI 2010 (CDFC)[15]............	114	114.1	113.9	113.7	113.6	113.9	115.1	116.2	114.1
Montserrat									
12 V 2011 (CDJC)............	101.9	95.9	108.4	...	...	...	...	...	...
Nicaragua									
4 VI 2005 (CDJC)............	111.6	112.8	110.5	108.5	109.2	107.8	116.4	117.8	115.1
Panama									
13 V 1990 (CDFC)............	109.3	109.2	109.3	104.6	104.5	104.8	115.6	115	116.3
14 V 2000 (CDFC)............	103.2	103.3	103.2	...	...	...	...	...	...
Puerto Rico - Porto Rico									
1 IV 1990 (CDJC)............	105.6	106.1	105.1	...	...	...	...	...	...
1 IV 2000 (CDJC)............	101.7	102	101.6	...	...	...	...	...	...
1 IV 2010 (CDJC)[16]............	102	102	102	...	...	...	...	...	...
Saint Lucia - Sainte-Lucie									
12 V 1991 (CDFC)............	110.5	110.5	110.4	...	...	...	...	...	...
22 V 2001 (CDFC)............	105.5	105.8	105.2	104	100.5	107.3	106.2	108	104.4
Saint Pierre and Miquelon - Saint Pierre-et-Miquelon									
8 III 1999 (CDFC)............	100.5	104.6	96.1	...	...	...	...	...	...
1 I 2015 (CDJC)............	100	96.6	103.5	...	...	...	...	...	...
Saint Vincent and the Grenadines - Saint-Vincent-et-les Grenadines									
12 V 1991 (CDFC)............	106.6	105.2	107.9	...	...	...	...	...	...
12 VI 2001 (CDFC)............	105.3	105.3	105.3	105.6	106.8	104.4	105.1	104.1	106.1
Saint-Barthélemy									
1 I 2015 (CDJC)	102.3	99.3	105.8	...	...	...	...	...	...
Saint-Martin (French part) - Saint-Martin (partie française)									
1 I 2015 (CDJC)............	97.3	102.2	93.5	...	...	...	...	...	...
Sint Maarten (Dutch part) - Saint-Martin (partie néerlandaise)									
9 IV 2011 (CDFC)............	100.7	100.2	101.2	...	...	...	...	...	...
Trinidad and Tobago - Trinité-et-Tobago									
9 I 2011 (CDJC)............	106.6	107.2	105.9	...	...	...	...	...	...
Turks and Caicos Islands - Îles Turques et Caïques									
10 IX 2001 (CDFC)............	104.2	100.1	108.6	...	...	...	...	...	...
United States of America - États-Unis d'Amérique									
1 IV 1990 (CDJC)............	104.5	104.8	104.2	...	...	...	...	...	...
1 IV 2000 (CDJC)[17]............	101.8	102.1	101.5	102.1	102.4	101.7	100.8	101	100.5
1 IV 2010 (CDJC)............	102.2	102.5	102	102.4	102.7	102.2	101.5	101.7	101.2

Continent, country or area, date and code[a] Continent, pays ou zone, date et code[a]	Total			Urban - Urbaine			Rural - Rurale		
	Both sexes Les deux sexes	Male Masculin	Female Féminin	Both sexes Les deux sexes	Male Masculin	Female Féminin	Both sexes Les deux sexes	Male Masculin	Female Féminin
AMERICA, SOUTH - AMÉRIQUE DU SUD									
Argentina - Argentine									
15 V 1991 (CDFC)	104.2	103.3	105.2	...	...	...	...	...	...
18 XI 2001 (CDFC)	102.4	101.8	103	...	...	...	...	...	...
27 X 2010 (CDFC)	102.6	102.5	102.7	102.6	102.5	102.7	102.5	102.9	102
Bolivia (Plurinational State of) - Bolivie (État plurinational de)									
3 VI 1992 (CDFC)	125.4	121.1	129.5	111.4	108	114.4	146.1	139.4	152.7
5 IX 2001 (CDFC)	114.6	113.1	116	109.1	108	110.2	124.6	121.9	127.6
21 XI 2012 (CDFC)	110.4	110.5	110.3	108	108.1	108	115.7	115.4	116.1
Brazil - Brésil									
1 IX 1991 (CDJC)[18]	103.3	103.3	103.3	102.3	102.3	102.2	107.2	106.9	107.4
1 VIII 2000 (CDJC)[18]	104.2	104.3	104	103.6	103.7	103.5	107.1	107.3	107
31 VII 2010 (CDJC)	104.8	105.6	104.1	104.7	105.4	104	105.6	106.6	104.4
Chile - Chili									
22 IV 1992 (CDFC)	100.3	98.9	101.7	100.2	98.6	101.7	101	100.2	101.9
24 IV 2002 (CDFC)	99.5	98.5	100.5	99.4	98.2	100.5	100.2	100	100.4
Colombia - Colombie									
15 X 1985 (CDFC)	147.9	146.5	149.2	139.8	136.8	142.4	166.9	166.5	167.3
24 X 1993 (CDFC)	118.9	117.7	120	111.7	108.9	114.1	139.6	139.9	139.4
22 V 2005 (CDFC)	103.5	104.2	102.9	102.1	102.4	101.8	108.6	109.8	107.3
22 V 2005 (CDJC)	103.5	104.2	102.9	102.1	102.4	101.8	108.7	109.9	107.3
Ecuador - Équateur									
25 XI 1990 (CDFC)[19]	132.5	131.2	133.8	122.9	121	124.7	146.6	145.4	147.9
25 XI 2001 (CDFC)[19]	112.1	111.8	112.4	107.9	107	108.7	119.9	120.4	119.4
28 XI 2010 (CDFC)	103.7	104.1	103.3	103	103.4	102.7	104.9	105.4	104.4
French Guiana - Guyane française									
15 III 1990 (CDJC)	106.2	105.7	106.7	...	...	...	...	...	...
8 III 1999 (CDJC)	101.1	100.9	101.3	...	...	...	...	...	...
1 I 2015 (CDJC)	101.6	101.5	101.6	102.2	102.5	102	97	95.9	98.5
Paraguay									
26 VIII 1992 (CDFC)	108.6	107.9	109.3	105.7	104.3	107	112	111.8	112.3
28 VIII 2002 (CDFC)	104.8	104.3	105.2	103.2	102.6	103.7	107.1	106.5	107.8
Peru - Pérou									
21 X 2007 (CDFC)[20]	109.4	109.1	109.6	106.9	106.5	107.3	118.8	118.5	119.1
22 VIII 2017 (CDFC)[21]	101.3	101.2	101.5	101.4	101.3	101.6	100.9	100.8	101
Suriname									
2 VIII 2004 (CDJC)	101.1	100.4	102	102.4[22]	101.4[22]	103.5[22]	98.3[22]	98.2[22]	98.4[22]
13 VIII 2012 (CDJC)	101.7	101.8	101.7	...	...	...	...	...	...
Uruguay									
23 X 1985 (CDFC)	106.2	104.9	107.4	106.2	104.7	107.5	106.3	106.1	106.5
22 V 1996 (CDFC)	103.3	102.8	103.8	103.2	102.5	103.8	104	104.5	103.3
1 VI 2004 (CDFC)[23]	106	105.9	106.2	106.1	105.9	106.3	105.4	105.7	105
4 X 2011 (CDJC)	101.8	101.9	101.7	101.8	101.9	101.7	101.8	101.6	102
Venezuela (Bolivarian Republic of) - Venezuela (République bolivarienne du)									
20 X 1990 (CDFC)[24]	106.4	106.5	106.3	105	104.8	105.3	114.9	116.1	113.4
1 IX 2011 (CDJC)	101.3	101.6	101	101.3[25]	101.6[25]	101[25]	101.4[25]	102[25]	100.7[25]
ASIA - ASIE									
Armenia - Arménie									
10 X 2001 (CDJC)	103	102.8	103.3	103.7	103.7	103.8	101.6	101.1	102.1
12 X 2011 (CDJC)	101.8	101.5	102	102.4	102.3	102.6	100.6	100.2	101
Azerbaijan - Azerbaïdjan									
27 I 1999 (CDJC)	100.4	99.8	101	100.3	99.8	100.8	100.5	99.7	101.2
13 IV 2009 (CDJC)	100.4	100.1	100.7	100.8	100.3	101.3	99.9	99.7	100.1
Bahrain - Bahreïn									
16 XI 1991 (CDFC)	96.6	98.3	93.6	...	...	...	...	...	...
7 IV 2001 (CDJC)	100.2	99.9	100.9	...	...	...	...	...	...
27 IV 2010 (CDJC)	100.2	99.3	101.9	...	...	...	...	...	...
Bangladesh[26]									
22 I 2001 (CDFC)	299.5	295.8	303.4	283.1	277.9	289.8	305	302.6	307.4
Bhutan - Bhoutan									
30 V 2005 (CDFC)	116.4	117.7	114.9	118.7	119.6	117.4	115.4	116.8	113.9

Continent, country or area, date and code[a] Continent, pays ou zone, date et code[a]	Total			Urban - Urbaine			Rural - Rurale		
	Both sexes Les deux sexes	Male Masculin	Female Féminin	Both sexes Les deux sexes	Male Masculin	Female Féminin	Both sexes Les deux sexes	Male Masculin	Female Féminin
ASIA - ASIE									
30 V 2017 (CDFC)...............	108.1	110.4	105.4	...	...	...	...	...	...
Brunei Darussalam - Brunéi Darussalam									
7 VIII 1991 (CDFC)............	98.8	98.7	98.8	...	...	...	...	...	...
20 VI 2011 (CDJC)............	100.9	101.6	100.2	100.6	101.3	99.8	102	102.3	101.6
Cambodia - Cambodge									
3 III 1998 (CDFC)............	118.1	116.2	119.6	119.8	117.6	121.8	117.6	115.9	119.1
3 III 2008 (CDFC)[27].........	109.9	108.2	111.3	109.7	108.5	110.8	109.9	108.1	111.5
China - Chine									
1 VII 1990 (CDFC)............	101	101.1	100.9	101.9	102	101.8	100.6	100.7	100.5
1 XI 2000 (CDJC)............	101.7	101.7	101.6	101.6	101.8	101.4	101.7	101.7	101.7
1 XI 2010 (CDJC)[28].........	98.8	98.9	98.8	98.7	98.9	98.6	98.9	98.9	99
China, Hong Kong SAR - Chine, Hong Kong RAS									
11 III 1986 (CDFC)............	101.7	101.4	102.1	101.7	101.3	102.1	102.1	102.5	101.7
15 III 1996 (CDJC)............	99.7	99.8	99.7	...	...	...	...	...	...
14 III 2001 (CDJC)[29].........	100.2	100.3	100.1	...	...	...	...	...	...
14 VII 2006 (CDJC)[30].........	98.3	98.4	98.3	...	...	...	...	...	...
30 VI 2011 (CDJC)[29].........	99.4	100	98.9	...	...	...	...	...	...
30 VI 2016 (CDJC)[30].........	99.9	99.9	99.8	...	...	...	...	...	...
China, Macao SAR - Chine, Macao RAS									
30 VIII 1991 (CDJC).........	100.8	101.4	100.3	...	...	...	...	...	...
23 VIII 2001 (CDJC).........	95.5	94.7	96.2	...	...	...	...	...	...
12 VIII 2011 (CDJC).........	98.9	97.6	100	...	...	...	...	...	...
Cyprus - Chypre									
1 X 1992 (CDJC)............	98.7	98.3	99	98.8	98.4	99.3	98.4	98.3	98.5
1 X 2001 (CDJC)[31].........	100.7	100.7	100.6	100.9	101.4	100.4	100.1	99.1	101.1
1 X 2011 (CDJC)[31].........	105.4	106.6	104.4	...	...	...	...	...	...
Democratic People's Republic of Korea - République populaire démocratique de Corée									
31 XII 1993 (CDJC).........	105	105.2	104.7	104.4	104.6	104.2	105.8	106.2	105.5
1 X 2008 (CDJC)............	101	100.6	101.3	...	...	...	...	...	...
Georgia - Géorgie									
17 I 2002 (CDJC)............	101.4	101.7	101.1	101.6	102	101.3	101.1	101.4	100.8
5 XI 2014 (CDJC)............	99.9	99.9	99.8	99.8	99.6	99.9	100	100.4	99.7
India - Inde									
1 III 1991 (CDFC)[32].........	290.3	292.6	287.9	258.7	253.8	264.3	302.1	307.7	296.2
1 III 2001 (CDFC)[33].........	230	241	218.4	217.2	216.8	217.8	235.5	252	218.7
9 II 2011 (CDFC)[34].........	171	174.6	167.4	152.9	151	154.9	180.5	187.1	173.8
Indonesia - Indonésie									
31 X 1990 (CDFC)............	163.3	160.2	166.3	139.7	135.8	143.7	174.2	171.7	176.5
30 VI 2000 (CDJC)[35].........	152.2	151.3	153.1	136.8	136.4	137.2	164.2	163.1	165.2
1 V 2010 (CDJC)............	114.5	114.2	114.9	110.2	110.2	110.2	119	118.4	119.7
Iran (Islamic Republic of) - Iran (République islamique d')									
22 IX 1986 (CDFC)............	122.6	121.1	124.1	114.4	113.4	115.5	133.1	131.3	134.8
11 IX 1991 (CDJC)............	128.7	127	130.4	122.5	121.3	123.9	138.5	136.4	140.6
11 IX 1994 (CDJC)............	107.4	106.8	108.1	107.1	108	106.2	107.8	104.5	111.2
23 X 1996 (CDJC)............	108.8	108.6	109	105.7	105.6	105.8	114.1	114	114.3
28 X 2006 (CDJC)[36].........	111.6	110.4	112.8	109.3	108.5	110.1	117.2	115.2	119.2
24 X 2011 (CDJC)............	103.7	103.8	103.5	103.6	103.8	103.5	103.7[37]	103.8[37]	103.6[37]
24 IX 2016 (CDJC)............	104.1	104.2	104	104[36]	104.1[36]	103.9[36]	104.5[36]	104.6[36]	104.3[36]
Iraq									
16 X 1997 (CDFC)............	106.2	105.6	106.8	105.5	104.9	106.1	108	107.6	108.5
Israel - Israël									
4 XI 1995 (CDFC)[38].........	101.4	101.8	101	101.3	101.8	100.9	101.9	101.5	102.3
4 XI 1995 (CDJC)............	101.1	101.1	101.1	101	101	101	101.5	101.6	101.4
27 XII 2008 (CDFC)[39].........	98.9	99	98.9	99	99.1	98.9	98.6	98.3	99
Japan - Japon									
1 X 1985 (CDFC)............	98.4	98.4	98.3	98.3	98.4	98.2	98.7	98.5	98.8
1 X 1990 (CDFC)............	98.9	98.9	98.8	98.9	99	98.8	98.8	98.6	99
1 X 1995 (CDJC)............	99	99	99	99	99.1	99	98.8	98.6	98.9
1 X 2000 (CDJC)............	99.1	99.1	99	99.1	99.2	99	99	98.8	99.2
1 X 2005 (CDJC)[40].........	99.1	99.2	99.1	99.2	99.2	99.1	99	98.8	99.1
1 X 2010 (CDJC)[40].........	100.9	100.9	100.9	100.9	100.9	100.8	101	100.9	101.1

Continent, country or area, date and code[a] Continent, pays ou zone, date et code[a]	Total			Urban - Urbaine			Rural - Rurale		
	Both sexes Les deux sexes	Male Masculin	Female Féminin	Both sexes Les deux sexes	Male Masculin	Female Féminin	Both sexes Les deux sexes	Male Masculin	Female Féminin
ASIA - ASIE									
1 X 2015 (CDJC)[40]	100.8	100.7	100.8	100.8	100.7	100.8	100.8	100.7	100.9
Jordan - Jordanie									
1 X 2004 (CDFC)[41]	100.8	100.4	101.3	...	...	...	...	...	...
30 XI 2015 (CDFC)[42]	111.4	112.3	110.3	...	...	...	...	...	...
Kazakhstan									
12 I 1989 (CDFC)	98.9	98.8	99	98.7	98.6	98.8	99.2	99	99.4
26 II 1999 (CDJC)[43]	99.9	99.8	99.9	100.1	100	100.2	99.5	99.5	99.4
Kuwait - Koweït									
20 IV 1985 (CDFC)	139.5	142.6	133.9	...	...	...	...	...	...
21 IV 2011 (CDFC)	102.2	102.6	101.7	102.2	102.6	101.7	...	...	...
Kyrgyzstan - Kirghizstan									
12 I 1989 (CDJC)	99.3	99.1	99.5	98.4	98	98.8	99.9	99.8	100.1
24 III 1999 (CDJC)	99.4	99.2	99.6	99.2	98.9	99.5	99.5	99.3	99.7
24 III 2009 (CDJC)	100.6	100.5	100.8	...	...	...	...	...	...
Lao People's Democratic Republic - République démocratique populaire lao									
1 III 2005 (CDJC)	138.3	136.4	140.2	120.8[44]	120.9[44]	120.6[44]	146[44]	143.3[44]	148.5[44]
1 III 2015 (CDJC)	129.3	128.4	130.2	...	...	...	...	...	...
Malaysia - Malaisie									
14 VIII 1991 (CDFC)	114.2	113.8	114.6	110.3	110.2	110.3	118.8	117.9	119.7
6 VII 2010 (CDJC)	120.4	120.7	120	120.6	120.7	120.5	119.7	120.6	118.7
6 VII 2010 (CDJC)[45]	120.7	121.1	120.3	...	...	...	...	...	...
Maldives									
25 III 1985 (CDFC)	176.7	175.3	178.4	166.3	170.9	159.4	180.7	177.2	184.2
8 III 1990 (CDFC)	156.4	159.9	152.7	149.3	154.5	142.6	159.2	162.4	156.1
25 III 1995 (CDFC)	143.1	144.5	141.7	137.3	137.9	136.7	145.5	147.5	143.5
31 III 2000 (CDFC)	106.9	109.5	104.3	...	...	...	...	...	...
21 III 2006 (CDFC)[46]	103.8	104.9	102.8	104	105.5	102.5	103.7	104.5	102.9
20 IX 2014 (CDFC)[47]	105.4	109.8	99.1	106.1	110.5	100.1	105	109.4	98.3
Mongolia - Mongolie									
5 I 2000 (CDFC)	99.9	99.6	100.2	99.9	99.7	100.1	99.9	99.5	100.2
11 XI 2010 (CDJC)	101.6	101.3	101.9	101.7	101.4	102	101.5	101.3	101.7
Myanmar[48]									
29 III 2014 (CDFC)	123.3	124	122.6	115.8	116	115.6	126.7	127.6	125.8
Nepal - Népal									
22 VI 1991 (CDJC)	202.4	195.6	209	186.2	179.2	193.9	204.2	197.6	210.5
22 VI 2001 (CDJC)	206.1	205.7	206.6	...	...	...	...	...	...
22 VI 2011 (CDJC)	188.6	191.3	186.2	169.9	167.8	172	193.1	197.5	189.3
Oman									
7 XII 2003 (CDFC)	158.5	165.6	146.9	154.9	163.1	141.1	170.2	174.1	164.4
Philippines									
1 IX 1995 (CDJC)	115.7	116.5	114.9	...	...	...	...	...	...
1 V 2000 (CDJC)	110.8	111.6	110	...	...	...	...	...	...
1 VIII 2007 (CDJC)	104.8	104.9	104.7	...	...	...	...	...	...
1 V 2010 (CDJC)[49]	108.5	109.1	107.9	...	...	...	...	...	...
1 VIII 2015 (CDJC)[50]	106.8	107.2	106.3	107.5	108	107	105.9	106.4	105.4
Qatar									
16 III 1986 (CDFC)	149.1	151.9	140.2	...	...	...	...	...	...
Republic of Korea - République de Corée									
1 XI 1985 (CDFC)	99.4	98.9	99.8	99.6	99.4	99.8	98.8	97.9	99.6
1 XI 1990 (CDFC)	99.5	99.2	99.8	99.6	99.4	99.8	99.1	98.5	99.7
1 XI 1995 (CDJC)	99.9	99.7	100.1	100	99.8	100.2	99.4	99.2	99.6
1 XI 2000 (CDJC)[51]	100	99.8	100.2	100.2	100	100.4	99.2	98.9	99.4
1 XI 2005 (CDJC)[51]	100.4	100.2	100.6	100.6	100.4	100.8	99.4	99.2	99.7
1 XI 2015 (CDJC)	101.8	101.3	102.3	101.8	101.3	102.2	101.8	101.2	102.5
Singapore - Singapour									
30 VI 2000 (CDJC)	98.2	98.1	98.3	...	...	...	...	...	...
30 VI 2010 (CDJC)[52]	99.7	99.7	99.7	...	...	...	...	...	...
Sri Lanka									
17 VII 2001 (CDFC)[53]	97	97.5	96.4	98.2	98.5	97.8	96.8[54]	97.3[54]	96.2[54]
20 III 2012 (CDJC)	100.2	100.3	100	100.3	100.7	100	100.1	100.2	100.1
State of Palestine - État de Palestine									
9 XII 1997 (CDFC)[55]	109.1	103	115.3	...	...	...	...	...	...
1 XII 2007 (CDFC)[35]	103.8	102.6	104.9	104.4[56]	103.2[56]	105.7[56]	100.8	100	101.6

3a. Whipple's Index by sex and urban/rural residence, 1985 - 2018
L'indice de Whipple par le sexe et la résidence urbaine/rurale, 1985 - 2018 (continued - suite)

Continent, country or area, date and code[a] Continent, pays ou zone, date et code[a]	Total			Urban - Urbaine			Rural - Rurale		
	Both sexes Les deux sexes	Male Masculin	Female Féminin	Both sexes Les deux sexes	Male Masculin	Female Féminin	Both sexes Les deux sexes	Male Masculin	Female Féminin
ASIA - ASIE									
Syrian Arab Republic - République arabe syrienne[57]									
3 IX 1994 (CDFC)	111.8	109.9	113.8	111.9	110.4	113.5	111.7	109.2	114.1
Tajikistan - Tadjikistan									
12 I 1989 (CDJC)	99	98.9	99.1	97.6	97.1	98	99.9	100	99.9
20 I 2000 (CDFC)	99.3	99.2	99.4	100.1	100	100.1	99	98.9	99.1
21 IX 2010 (CDFC)	103.6	103.9	103.4	105.8	106.6	105	102.8	102.9	102.7
Thailand - Thaïlande									
1 IV 2000 (CDJC)[58]	104.7	104.7	104.8	108.1	108.1	108.1	103	103	103
1 IX 2010 (CDJC)	110.6	111.1	110.1	115.6	116.2	115	106.3	106.8	105.8
Timor-Leste									
11 VII 2010 (CDFC)	130.3	128.9	131.7	126	125.6	126.5	132.3	130.6	134
11 VII 2015 (CDFC)	125	125.1	125	119.4	119.3	119.5	127.8	128.1	127.5
Turkey - Turquie									
20 X 1985 (CDFC)	149.4	133.8	165.3	...	...	...	...	...	...
21 X 1990 (CDFC)	139.7	128.9	150.8	...	...	...	...	...	...
22 X 2000 (CDFC)	125.7	123.2	128.3	122.7	121.3	124.2	131.7	127.2	136.4
3 X 2011 (CDJC)[59]	101.2	101.7	100.8	101.4	101.7	101.1	100.8	101.5	99.9
Viet Nam									
1 IV 1989	98.5	98.1	98.8	98.3	97.8	98.8	98.4	98	98.7
1 IV 1999 (CDJC)	99.2	98.8	99.6	99.1	98.6	99.6	99.3	98.8	99.7
1 IV 2009 (CDJC)	100.4	99.8	100.9	100.6	100	101.1	100.3	99.8	100.8
Yemen - Yémen									
16 XII 1994 (CDFC)	293.9	282.6	304.9	245	229.6	265	311.7	305.8	316.8
EUROPE									
Åland Islands - Îles d'Åland[60]									
31 XII 2000 (CDJC)	100.7	101.5	99.8	102.9	101.9	103.8	99	101.2	96.7
Austria - Autriche									
15 V 1991 (CDJC)	97.9	97.9	97.9	97.8	97.9	97.7	98.2	98.1	98.2
15 V 2001 (CDJC)	97.4	97.5	97.3	97.3	97.5	97.2	97.5	97.3	97.6
31 X 2011 (CDJC)	100	100.1	100	100.2	100.2	100.2	99.7	99.8	99.7
Belarus - Bélarus									
12 I 1989 (CDJC)	99.4	99.3	99.5	98.9	98.8	99.1	100.3	100.3	100.2
16 II 1999 (CDJC)	99.6	99.4	99.8	99.7	99.6	99.9	99.2	98.9	99.5
14 X 2009 (CDJC)	101.5	101.6	101.5	101.7	101.6	101.7	101	101.3	100.7
Belgium - Belgique									
1 X 2001 (CDJC)	99.5	99.4	99.7	99.5	99.4	99.7	99.2	98.9	99.4
1 I 2011 (CDJC)	100	99.9	100.1	100	99.9	100.1	100.3	99.1	101.6
Bosnia and Herzegovina - Bosnie-Herzégovine									
31 III 1991 (CDJC)	100.4	100.5	100.2	...	...	...	...	...	...
30 IX 2013 (CDJC)	100.1	99.8	100.3	...	...	...	...	...	...
Bulgaria - Bulgarie									
1 II 2011 (CDJC)	101.2	101	101.4	101.1	100.9	101.3	101.4	101.4	101.4
Croatia - Croatie									
31 III 1991 (CDFC)	99.1	99.2	99.1	99	99.3	98.8	99.2	99.1	99.4
31 III 2001 (CDJC)	98.2	98.4	98.1	98.3	98.6	98.1	98.1	98.1	98.2
1 IV 2011 (CDJC)	100.3	100.5	100.2	100.3	100.4	100.2	100.4	100.5	100.2
Czechia - Tchéquie									
3 III 1991 (CDJC)	99	98.8	99.1	...	...	...	...	...	...
1 III 2001 (CDJC)	99.2	99.1	99.3	99	98.9	99.1	99.8	99.8	99.9
25 III 2011 (CDJC)	99.6	99.6	99.7	99.5	99.4	99.6	99.9	100.1	99.8
Denmark - Danemark[61]									
1 I 1991 (CDJC)	100.5	100.6	100.5	...	...	...	...	...	...
Estonia - Estonie									
31 III 2000 (CDJC)	100	99.7	100.3	100.2	100	100.4	99.7	99.1	100.2
31 XII 2011 (CDJC)	100	100	100.1	100.1	100	100.1	100	99.9	100.2
Finland - Finlande									
17 XI 1985 (CDJC)	99.8	99.9	99.6	...	...	...	...	...	...
31 XII 1990 (CDJC)	99.5	99.6	99.5	...	...	...	...	...	...
31 XII 2000 (CDJC)	99.5	99.6	99.4	99.9	100.1	99.7	98.9	98.9	98.8
31 XII 2010 (CDJC)	100.1	100.1	100	100	100.1	99.8	100.3	100	100.5
France									
5 III 1990 (CDJC)	99.2	99	99.3	99.5	99.4	99.6	98.2	98.1	98.4

Continent, country or area, date and code[a] / Continent, pays ou zone, date et code[a]	Total			Urban - Urbaine			Rural - Rurale		
	Both sexes Les deux sexes	Male Masculin	Female Féminin	Both sexes Les deux sexes	Male Masculin	Female Féminin	Both sexes Les deux sexes	Male Masculin	Female Féminin
EUROPE									
8 III 1999 (CDJC)[62]	100.5	100.5	100.5	100.5	100.5	100.5	100.8	100.7	100.8
1 I 2015 (CDJC)	100	100	100.1	100	100	100.1	100	100.1	99.9
Germany - Allemagne									
9 V 2011 (CDJC)	100	100	100.1	100	100	100.1	100.1	100.1	100.1
Gibraltar									
14 X 1991 (CDFC)	105.7	104.9	106.6	...	...	...	...	...	...
12 XI 2001 (CDFC)[63]	98	98.6	97.5	...	...	...	...	...	...
12 XI 2012 (CDJC)[64]	99.5	100.3	98.7	...	...	...	...	...	...
Greece - Grèce									
17 III 1991 (CDFC)	108.8	107.4	110.1	108.5	107.3	109.7	109.1	107.6	110.7
18 III 2001 (CDJC)[65]	105	104.9	105.1	104.8	104.6	104.9	105.8	105.7	106
9 V 2011 (CDFC)	101.4	101.8	101.1	101.3	101.6	101.1	101.8	102.3	101.2
Guernsey - Guernesey									
23 III 1986 (CDJC)	96.1	96.1	96	...	...	...	...	...	...
13 III 1996 (CDJC)	97.5	98.5	96.6	...	...	...	...	...	...
29 IV 2001 (CDJC)	97.2	97.4	96.9	...	...	...	...	...	...
31 III 2015 (CDJC)[43]	101.4	102.4	100.3	...	...	...	...	...	...
Hungary - Hongrie									
1 I 1990 (CDFC)	102.1	102.5	101.8	102.4	102.8	102	101.7	101.9	101.5
1 II 2001 (CDFC)	101.6	101.8	101.5	101.9	102.2	101.6	101.2	101.2	101.2
1 X 2011 (CDFC)	100.2	100.2	100.2	100.1	100.2	100.1	100.4	100.3	100.5
Ireland - Irlande									
21 IV 1991 (CDFC)	100.5	100.5	100.4	...	...	...	...	...	...
28 IV 1996 (CDFC)	100.2	100.2	100.1	100.3	100.5	100.2	99.9	99.7	100
28 IV 2002 (CDFC)	99.5	99.8	99.2	99.7	99.9	99.4	99.3	99.5	99
23 IV 2006 (CDFC)	100.9	101	100.8	101	101.2	100.8	100.8	100.7	100.8
10 IV 2011 (CDFC)	100.7	101	100.5	100.9	101.2	100.5	100.5	100.5	100.4
Isle of Man - Île de Man									
6 IV 1986 (CDJC)	99.2	98.6	99.8	...	...	...	...	...	...
14 IV 1991 (CDJC)	97.7	98.1	97.3	...	...	...	...	...	...
14 IV 1996 (CDJC)	97.9	98.9	97	...	...	...	...	...	...
29 IV 2001 (CDJC)	97.8	98	97.5	...	...	...	...	...	...
23 IV 2006 (CDJC)	98.3	98.4	98.3	...	...	...	...	...	...
27 III 2011 (CDJC)	99.3	100.4	98.2	...	...	...	...	...	...
24 IV 2016 (CDJC)	99	99.3	98.7	...	...	...	...	...	...
Italy - Italie									
21 X 2001 (CDJC)	101.1	101	101.1	...	...	...	...	...	...
9 X 2011 (CDJC)	99.8	99.8	99.8	...	...	...	...	...	...
Jersey									
23 III 1986 (CDFC)	98	98	98	...	...	...	...	...	...
10 III 1991 (CDJC)	99.2	100.6	97.8	...	...	...	...	...	...
10 III 1996 (CDJC)	99.4	100.7	98.1	...	...	...	...	...	...
11 III 2001 (CDJC)	98.9	99.6	98.3	...	...	...	...	...	...
27 III 2011 (CDJC)	100	100.7	99.3	...	...	...	...	...	...
Latvia - Lettonie									
31 III 2000 (CDJC)[66]	100.5	100.2	100.7	100.4	100.4	100.4	100.6	99.8	101.5
1 III 2011 (CDJC)	99.4	99.6	99.3	99.5	99.7	99.3	99.3	99.3	99.4
Liechtenstein									
31 XII 2010 (CDJC)	100.5	102.1	99	...	...	...	...	...	...
Lithuania - Lituanie									
12 I 1989 (CDJC)	100.6	100.5	100.7	100.7	100.6	100.8	100.3	100.2	100.4
6 IV 2001 (CDJC)	99.8	99.7	99.9	99.4	99	99.7	100.8	101.1	100.5
1 III 2011 (CDJC)	100	100.1	99.9	100	100.2	99.8	100	99.9	100
Luxembourg									
15 II 2001 (CDJC)	99.2	98.9	99.6	...	...	...	...	...	...
1 II 2011 (CDJC)	99.7	99	100.4	...	...	...	...	...	...
Malta - Malte									
26 XI 1995 (CDJC)	101.2	101.2	101.2	101.2	101.2	101.2	125.7	107.6	138.4
27 XI 2005 (CDJC)	101.3	101.9	100.6	101.2	102	100.5	114.3	100	127.3
20 XI 2011 (CDFC)	99.4	100	98.9	99.4	99.9	98.9	100.3	102.3	98.1
Monaco									
21 VI 2000 (CDJC)	100.9	99.9	101.9	...	...	...	...	...	...
Montenegro - Monténégro									
31 X 2003 (CDJC)	100.2	99.9	100.5	100.2	99.6	100.8	100.2	100.3	100
1 IV 2011 (CDJC)	100	99.7	100.3	99.9	99.3	100.5	100.1	100.2	99.9
Netherlands - Pays-Bas									
1 I 2002 (CDJC)	101.2	101.3	101	101.3	101.5	101.1	101	101.1	101

3a. Whipple's Index by sex and urban/rural residence, 1985 - 2018
L'indice de Whipple par le sexe et la résidence urbaine/rurale, 1985 - 2018 (continued - suite)

Continent, country or area, date and code[a] Continent, pays ou zone, date et code[a]	Total			Urban - Urbaine			Rural - Rurale		
	Both sexes Les deux sexes	Male Masculin	Female Féminin	Both sexes Les deux sexes	Male Masculin	Female Féminin	Both sexes Les deux sexes	Male Masculin	Female Féminin
EUROPE									
1 I 2011 (CDJC)...............	100.2	100.2	100.2	...	...	...	...	...	...
North Macedonia - Macédoine du Nord									
20 VI 1994 (CDJC)...............	100.2	100.2	100.2	100	100.1	99.8	100.6	100.5	100.8
31 X 2002 (CDJC)...............	100.3	100.3	100.3	...	...	...	...	...	...
Norway - Norvège									
3 XI 1990 (CDJC)...............	99.9	99.9	99.9	99.9	99.9	100	99.9	100	99.8
3 XI 2001 (CDJC)[67]...............	100.1	100.1	100.1	100.1	100.1	100.2	99.7	99.9	99.6
19 XI 2011 (CDJC)[67]...............	99.8	99.8	99.7	99.7[68]	99.6[68]	99.7[68]	100.1[68]	100.4[68]	99.8[68]
Poland - Pologne									
6 XII 1988 (CDFC)...............	100.5	100.6	100.4	100.5	100.6	100.4	100.5	100.6	100.5
20 V 2002 (CDJC)[69]...............	100.7	100.7	100.7	100.9	100.8	100.9	100.4	100.5	100.2
31 III 2011 (CDJC)...............	100.1	100.1	100.1	100.1	100.1	100.1	100.1	100.1	100
Portugal									
15 IV 1991 (CDFC)...............	101.4	101.7	101.1	101.4	101.7	101.2	101.3	101.6	101.1
21 III 2011 (CDJC)...............	100.7	100.8	100.5	100.8	101	100.7	100.4	100.4	100.3
Republic of Moldova - République de Moldova									
12 I 1989 (CDJC)...............	100.5	100.4	100.5	100.2	99.9	100.4	100.7	100.8	100.6
5 X 2004 (CDFC)[70]...............	103.2	103.3	103.2	102.9	102.9	102.9	103.5	103.5	103.5
12 V 2014 (CDFC)[71]...............	100.5	100.3	100.6	100.3	100	100.7	100.5	100.4	100.6
Romania - Roumanie									
7 I 1992 (CDJC)...............	96.2	96.2	96.2	95.6	95.8	95.4	97.1	96.8	97.4
18 III 2002 (CDJC)...............	95.8	95.9	95.8	95.3	95.5	95.2	96.5	96.3	96.7
20 X 2011 (CDJC)...............	96.6	96.6	96.6	96.4	96.5	96.3	96.8	96.7	96.9
Russian Federation - Fédération de Russie									
12 I 1989 (CDJC)...............	97.8	97.7	97.9	97.7	97.6	97.7	98.3	98.2	98.4
14 X 2010 (CDJC)...............	103	103	103	103.5	103.5	103.5	101.7	101.6	101.7
Serbia - Serbie[72]									
31 III 2002 (CDJC)...............	99.9	99.9	100	100.4	100.4	100.5	99.2	99.3	99.2
1 X 2011 (CDJC)...............	99.4	99.2	99.5	99.7	99.3	100	98.9	99.1	98.7
Slovakia - Slovaquie									
3 III 1991 (CDJC)...............	100	99.8	100.2	...	...	...	...	...	...
25 V 2001 (CDJC)...............	99.5	99.5	99.6	99.7	99.6	99.8	99.3	99.3	99.3
21 V 2011 (CDJC)...............	100.2	100.2	100.3	100.3	100.2	100.4	100.2	100.2	100.1
Slovenia - Slovénie									
31 III 1991 (CDJC)...............	99	99.1	98.9	99.7	99.7	99.6	98.4	98.6	98.1
31 III 2002 (CDJC)...............	101.9	102.1	101.8	102.2	102.3	102.2	101.6	101.9	101.3
1 I 2011 (CDJC)...............	100.6	100.1	101.3	100.7	100.1	101.3	100.6	100	101.3
1 I 2015 (CDJC)...............	99.3	99.5	99	99.3	99.6	99.1	99.2	99.4	99
Spain - Espagne									
1 III 1991 (CDJC)...............	102.4	102.4	102.3	...	...	...	...	...	...
1 XI 2001 (CDFC)[73]...............	99	99	99	99	99	98.9	99.1	99	99.1
1 XI 2011 (CDJC)...............	98.3	98.6	98.1	...	...	...	...	...	...
Sweden - Suède									
1 XI 1990 (CDJC)...............	99.7	99.8	99.6	...	...	...	...	...	...
31 XII 2003 (CDJC)...............	100	100	100.1	...	...	...	...	...	...
31 XII 2011 (CDJC)...............	99.7	99.8	99.6	...	...	...	...	...	...
Switzerland - Suisse									
4 XII 1990 (CDJC)...............	100.6	100.9	100.2	100.7	100.9	100.5	100.2	100.7	99.7
5 XII 2000 (CDFC)...............	99.7	99.9	99.5	99.7	99.9	99.6	99.5	99.9	99.1
31 XII 2011 (CDJC)...............	99.9	99.9	99.9	99.9	99.9	99.8	100	99.9	100.1
Ukraine									
5 XII 2001 (CDFC)...............	102.7	102.7	102.7	103.1	103.1	103.2	101.7	101.8	101.5
United Kingdom of Great Britain and Northern Ireland - Royaume-Uni de Grande-Bretagne et d'Irlande du Nord[74]									
21 IV 1991 (CDFC)[75]...............	98	98	98	...	...	...	...	...	...
29 IV 2001 (CDFC)[76]...............	98.1	98	98.1	98.2	98.2	98.2	97.6	97.5	97.7
27 III 2011 (CDJC)...............	100.2	100.3	100.2	100.3	100.3	100.3	99.8	99.8	99.8

Continent, country or area, date and code[a] Continent, pays ou zone, date et code[a]	Total			Urban - Urbaine			Rural - Rurale		
	Both sexes Les deux sexes	Male Masculin	Female Féminin	Both sexes Les deux sexes	Male Masculin	Female Féminin	Both sexes Les deux sexes	Male Masculin	Female Féminin
OCEANIA - OCÉANIE									
Australia - Australie									
30 VI 1986 (CDFC).........................	101.6	101.7	101.5	101.6	101.6	101.5	101.8	102	101.6
6 VIII 1991 (CDFC).........................	101.7	101.4	102.1	...	...	...	...	...	...
9 VIII 1996 (CDFC).........................	101.6	101.5	101.7	...	...	...	...	...	...
7 VIII 2001 (CDJC).........................	101.4	101.3	101.5	101.4	101.3	101.5	101.3	101.4	101.3
8 VIII 2006 (CDJC)[77].....................	100.2[78]	100.3[78]	100.2[78]	100.2	100.2	100.1	100.4	100.5	100.3
9 VIII 2011 (CDJC)[77].....................	100.8[78]	100.8[78]	100.7[78]	100.7	100.7	100.7	101.3	101.3	101.3
9 VIII 2016 (CDJC)[77].....................	101.1[78]	101.1[78]	101[78]	101	101	101	101.8	102	101.6
Cook Islands - Îles Cook[79]									
1 XII 1996 (CDJC).........................	99.1	97.2	101.1	...	...	...	...	...	...
Fiji - Fidji									
31 VIII 1986 (CDFC).......................	105.4	105	105.7	...	...	...	...	...	...
25 VIII 1996 (CDFC).......................	100.2	100.6	99.8	99.8	99.9	99.7	100.6	101.3	99.9
French Polynesia - Polynésie française									
3 IX 1996 (CDFC).........................	98.6	97.8	99.5	...	...	...	...	...	...
20 VIII 2007 (CDFC).......................	102.8	103.2	102.4	...	...	...	...	...	...
Guam									
1 IV 1990 (CDJC).........................	107.1	106.2	108.2	107	105.5	108.7	107.2	106.6	107.8
1 IV 2000 (CDJC)[16].......................	100.3	100.4	100.3	...	...	...	...	...	...
Kiribati									
10 X 2010 (CDFC).........................	104.7	103.3	105.9	106	106	106.1	103.3	100.7	105.7
7 XI 2015 (CDFC).........................	105.8	107.1	104.5	107.5	110.9	104.5	103.9	103.1	104.6
Marshall Islands - Îles Marshall									
13 XI 1988 (CDFC).........................	101.2	103.3	98.9	...	...	...	...	...	...
1 VI 1999 (CDFC).........................	104	106.2	101.7	...	...	...	...	...	...
3 IV 2011 (CDFC).........................	103.7	102	105.3	103.1	102.9	103.3	105.4	99.4	111.9
Micronesia (Federated States of) - Micronésie (États fédérés de) -									
1 IV 2010 (CDJC).........................	102.5	102.3	102.7	...	...	...	...	...	...
New Caledonia - Nouvelle-Calédonie									
4 IV 1989 (CDFC).........................	99.5	99.4	99.6	...	...	...	...	...	...
New Zealand - Nouvelle-Zélande									
4 III 1986 (CDJC).........................	100.7	100.6	100.7	100.7	100.7	100.8	100.2	99.9	100.6
5 III 1991 (CDJC).........................	100.3	100.4	100.3	100.5	100.6	100.4	99.7	99.3	100
5 III 1996 (CDJC).........................	100	100	100	100.1	100.1	100.1	99.5	99.5	99.5
6 III 2001 (CDJC)[77].......................	100	99.9	100	100.2	100.1	100.2	99	99	99.1
7 III 2006 (CDFC)[77].......................	99.7	...	...	...	...	...	...	...	...
7 III 2006 (CDJC)[77].......................	99.6	99.7	99.6	99.7	99.8	99.7	99.1	99.3	98.9
5 III 2013 (CDJC)[77].......................	100.3	100	100.5	100.3	100.1	100.5	100.2	100	100.4
Niue - Nioué									
29 IX 1986 (CDFC).........................	105.8	106	105.6	...	...	...	...	...	...
7 IX 2001 (CDFC).........................	98.5	93.8	103.4	...	...	...	...	...	...
Northern Mariana Islands - Îles Mariannes septentrionales									
1 IV 1990 (CDFC).........................	108	108.4	107.4	111.7	111.2	112.1	106.6	107.5	105.3
Palau - Palaos									
15 IV 2000 (CDJC).........................	103.4	105.5	100.5	...	...	...	...	...	...
Papua New Guinea - Papouasie-Nouvelle-Guinée									
11 VII 1990 (CDFC).........................	139	140.1	137.7	...	...	...	...	...	...
9 VII 2000 (CDFC).........................	134	134.2	133.8	131	133.4	128	134.5	134.4	134.7
Pitcairn									
31 XII 1991 (CDFC).........................	96.2	90.9	100	...	...	...	...	...	...
Samoa									
5 XI 2001 (CDFC).........................	96.4	95.9	97	...	...	...	...	...	...
7 XI 2011 (CDFC).........................	97.5	96	99.1	...	...	...	...	...	...
7 XI 2016 (CDFC).........................	97.5	96.6	98.4	97.5	97.2	97.9	97.5	96.5	98.6
Tokelau - Tokélaou									
18 X 2011 (CDFC).........................	102.7	104.3	101.2	...	...	...	...	...	...
18 X 2011 (CDJC)[80].......................	105.7	109.6	102	...	...	...	...	...	...
Tonga									
28 XI 1986 (CDJC).........................	98.2	99	97.4	...	...	...	...	...	...
30 XI 1996 (CDFC)[81].....................	100.7	101.7	99.6	...	...	...	...	...	...
30 XI 2006 (CDJC).........................	98.6	97.8	99.4	95.2	93.3	97.2	99.7	99.3	100.1
30 XI 2016 (CDJC).........................	99.6	99.7	99.4	96	97.1	95	100.7	100.6	100.9

Continent, country or area, date and code[a] / Continent, pays ou zone, date et code[a]	Total			Urban - Urbaine			Rural - Rurale		
	Both sexes Les deux sexes	Male Masculin	Female Féminin	Both sexes Les deux sexes	Male Masculin	Female Féminin	Both sexes Les deux sexes	Male Masculin	Female Féminin
OCEANIA - OCÉANIE									
Tuvalu									
1 XI 2002 (CDFC)...............	98.5	100.8	96.4	...	...	...	...	...	...
Vanuatu									
16 V 1989 (CDJC)...............	106.9	104.8	109	102.4	98.1	107.8	108.1	106.8	109.3
16 XI 2009 (CDFC)...............	110.5	111.3	109.7	...	...	...	...	...	...
7 XI 2016 (CDFC)...............	112.2	112.9	111.6	...	...	...	...	...	...
Wallis and Futuna Islands - Îles Wallis et Futuna									
3 X 1996 (CDFC)...............	96	97.8	94.3	...	...	...	...	...	...

FOOTNOTES - NOTES

Italics: estimates which are less reliable. - Italiques : estimations moins sûres.

* Provisional. - Données provisoires.

[a] 'Code' indicates the source of data, as follows:
CDFC - Census, de facto, complete tabulation
CDJC - Census, de jure, complete tabulation

Le 'Code' indique la source des données, comme suit :
CDFC - Recensement, population de fait, tabulation complète
CDJC - Recensement, population de droit, tabulation complète

[1] Data refer to population in housing units and collective living quarters only. - Correspond aux personnes qui vivent dans des unités d'habitation et dans des logements collectifs seulement.

[2] Data for urban and rural do not add up to the total; reason for discrepancy not ascertained. - La somme des données pour la résidence urbaine et rurale n'est pas égale au total; on ne sait pas comment s'explique la divergence.

[3] Urban and rural data were reported in different years and do not add up to the total. - Les données concernant la population urbaine et la population rurale portent sur des années différentes et leur somme ne correspond pas au total cité.

[4] Excludes collective living quarters. - Exclut les logements collectifs.

[5] Excludes the islands of St. Brandon and Agalega. - Non compris les îles St. Brandon et Agalega.

[6] Data refer to Saint Helenian resident population. - Pour la population résidante de Sainte-Hélène.

[7] Data refer to total resident population, Saint Helenian and other nationalities. - Les données concernent la population résidente totale, originaire de Sainte-Hélène ou possédant une autre nationalité.

[8] Data have been adjusted for underenumeration, estimated at 10.69 per cent. - Les données ont été ajustées pour compenser les lacunes du dénombrement estimées à 10,69 p. 100.

[9] Because of rounding, totals are not in all cases the sum of the respective components. - Les chiffres étant arrondis, les totaux ne correspondent pas toujours rigoureusement à la somme des composants respectifs.

[10] Excluding the institutional population. - Non compris la population dans les institutions.

[11] Bermuda is 100 per cent urban. - 100 pour cent de la population des Bermudes est urbaine.

[12] To ensure confidentiality, the values, including totals are randomly rounded either up or down to a multiple of '5' or '10.' As a result, when these data are summed or grouped, the total value may not match the individual values since totals and sub-totals are independently rounded. Similarly, percentages, which are calculated on rounded data, may not necessarily add up to 100%. - À des fins de confidentialité, les chiffres, y compris les totaux, sont aléatoirement arrondis au multiple de 5 ou de 10 inférieur ou supérieur. Par conséquent, lorsque ces chiffres sont additionnés, le total peut ne pas correspondre à la somme des valeurs individuelles, dans la mesure où les totaux et les totaux partiels sont arrondis indépendamment. De même, la somme des pourcentages, qui sont calculés à partir des données arrondies, peut ne pas correspondre à 100 %.

[13] Excluding data for Saint Barthélémy and Saint Martin. - Non compris les données pour Saint Barthélémy et Saint Martin.

[14] Total represents population in private dwellings, the non-institutional population and persons found on the streets between the hours of 5am and 7am on September 26, 2001; the figures represent the census counts adjusted for under-coverage. - Le total représente la population vivant dans des logements privés et les personnes trouvées dans la rue entre 5 et 7 heures du matin le 26 septembre 2001, mais ne tient pas compte des personnes vivant dans des établissements; les chiffres sont ceux du recensement corrigés pour tenir compte du sous-dénombrement.

[15] Including an estimation of 1 334 585 persons corresponding to 448 195 housing units without information of the occupants. - Y compris une estimation de 1 334 585 personnes correspondant aux 448 195 unités d'habitation sans information sur les occupants.

[16] Including armed forces stationed in the area. - Y compris les militaires en garnison sur le territoire.

[17] Excluding U.S. Armed Forces overseas and civilian U.S. citizens whose usual place of residence is outside the United States. - Non compris les militaires américains à l'étranger et les civils américains dont le lieu de résidence habituel est en dehors des États-Unis.

[18] Data include persons in remote areas, military personnel outside the country, merchant seamen at sea, civilian seasonal workers outside the country, and other civilians outside the country, and exclude nomads, foreign military, civilian aliens temporarily in the country, transients on ships and Indian jungle population. - Y compris les personnes vivant dans des régions éloignées, le personel militaire en dehors du pays, les marins marchands, les ouvriers saisonniers en dehors du pays, et autres civils en dehors du pays, et non compris les nomades, les militaires étrangers, les étrangers civils temporairement dans le pays, les transiteurs sur les bateaux et les Indiens de la jungle.

[19] Excludes nomadic Indian tribes. - Non compris les tribus d'Indiens nomades.

[20] Excluding population in the Carmen Alto district, Huamanga province and Ayacucho department. - À l'exclusion de la population du district de Carmen Alto, de la province de Huamanga et du département d'Ayacucho.

[21] Data have not been adjusted for underenumeration and exclude an estimated population of 1,855,501. - Les données n'ont pas été ajustées pour compenser les lacunes du dénombrement. Les données excluent un nombre de personnes estimé à 1,855,501.

[22] The districts of Paramaribo and Wanica are considered urban areas, whereas all other districts are considered more or less rural areas. - Les districts de Paramaribo et de Wanica sont considérés comme des zones urbaines, les autres districts étant considérés comme des zones rurales à divers degrés.

[23] Unrevised data. Data refer to resident population in Uruguay according to Census Phase 1, carried out between the months of June and July 2004. - Les données n'ont pas été révisées. Les données se rapportent à la population résidente en Uruguay d'après la phase 1 du recensement, qui a eu lieu entre juin et juillet 2004.

[24] Excluding Indian jungle population. - Non compris les Indiens de la jungle.

[25] For operational purposes, population centers with 2,500 and more inhabitants are considered as urban area and less than 2,500 are considered as rural area. - À des fins opérationnelles, les centres de population comptant 2 500 habitants ou plus sont considérés comme zones urbaines, ceux qui en comptent moins de 2 500 comme zones rurales.

[26] Data have not been adjusted for underenumeration, estimated at 4.96 per cent. - Les données n'ont pas été ajustées pour compenser les lacunes du dénombrement, estimées à 4,96 p.100.

[27] Excluding foreign diplomatic personnel and their dependants. - Non compris le personnel diplomatique étranger et les membres de leur famille les accompagnant.

28 For statistical purposes, the data for China do not include those for the Hong Kong Special Administrative Region (Hong Kong SAR), Macao Special Administrative Region (Macao SAR) and Taiwan province of China. Data exclude 2.3 million servicemen, 4.65 million persons with permanent resident status difficult to define, and 0.12 per cent undercount based on the post enumeration survey. - Pour la présentation des statistiques, les données pour la Chine ne comprennent pas la Région Administrative Spéciale de Hong Kong (Hong Kong RAS), la Région Administrative Spéciale de Macao (Macao RAS) et Taïwan province de Chine. Les données ne comprennent pas 2,3 millions de militaires, 4,65 millions de personnes ayant le statut de résident permanent mais difficiles à définir, et des lacunes estimées à 0,12 pour cent sur la base de l'enquête de vérification du recensement.

29 Data refer to Hong Kong resident population at the census moment, which covers usual residents and mobile residents. Usual residents refer to two categories of people: (1) Hong Kong permanent residents who had stayed in Hong Kong for at least three months during the six months before or for at least three months during the six months after the census moment, regardless of whether they were in Hong Kong or not at the census moment; and (2) Hong Kong non-permanent residents who were in Hong Kong at the census moment. Mobile Residents, they are Hong Kong permanent residents who had stayed in Hong Kong for at least one month but less than three months during the six months before or for at least one month but less than three months during the six months after the census moment, regardless of whether they were in Hong Kong or not at the census moment. - Les données se rapportent à la population résidente à Hong Kong au moment du recensement. Cette population est composée des résidants habituels et des résidants mobiles. La population résidente est partagée en deux catégories: (1) les résidents permanents qui ont habité à Hong Kong au moins trois mois pendant les six mois précédents ou les six mois suivants le recensement; (2) les habitants non-permanents de Hong Kong qui étaient à Hong Kong au moment du recensement. La population mobile se rapporte aux résidents permanents de Hong Kong qui ont habité à Hong Kong pendant les six mois après le recensement pour une période comprise entre un mois et trois mois, indépendamment du fait qu'ils étaient à Hong Kong au moment du recensement au pays.

30 Data refer to Hong Kong resident population at the census moment, which covers usual residents and mobile residents. Usual residents refer to two categories of people: (1) Hong Kong permanent residents who had stayed in Hong Kong for at least three months during the six months before or for at least three months during the six months after the census moment, regardless of whether they were in Hong Kong or not at the census moment; and (2) Hong Kong non-permanent residents who were in Hong Kong at the census moment. Mobile Residents, they are Hong Kong permanent residents who had stayed in Hong Kong for at least one month but less than three months during the six months before or for at least one month but less than three months during the six months after the census moment, regardless of whether they were in Hong Kong or not at the census moment. Data are estimates from sample enquiry. - Les données se rapportent à la population résidente à Hong Kong au moment du recensement. Cette population est composée des résidants habituels et des résidants mobiles. La population résidente est partagée en deux catégories: (1) les résidents permanents qui ont habité à Hong Kong au moins trois mois pendant les six mois précédents ou les six mois suivants le recensement; (2) les habitants non-permanents de Hong Kong qui étaient à Hong Kong au moment du recensement. La population mobile se rapporte aux résidents permanents de Hong Kong qui ont habité à Hong Kong pendant les six mois après le recensement pour une période comprise entre un mois et trois mois, indépendamment du fait qu'ils étaient à Hong Kong au moment du recensement au pays. Les données sont des chiffres estimatifs dérivés d'une enquête par sondage.

31 Data refer to government controlled areas. - Les données se rapportent aux zones contrôlées par le Gouvernement.

32 Excluding data for Jammu and Kashmir. - Non compris les données concernant la partie du Jammu et Cachemire.

33 Includes data for the Indian-held part of Jammu and Kashmir, the final status of which has not yet been determined. Excluding Mao-Maram, Paomata and Purul sub-divisions of Senapati district of Manipur. The population of Manipur including the estimated population of the three sub-divisions of Senapati district is 2,291,125 (Males 1,161,173 and females 1,129,952). - Y compris les données pour la partie du Jammu et du Cachemire occupée par l'Inde dont le statut définitif n'a pas été déterminé. Non compris les subdivisions Mao-Maram Paomata et Purul du district de Senapati dans l'État du Manipur. Cet État compte 2 291 125 habitants (1 161 173 hommes et 1 129 952 femmes), y compris la population estimative des trois subdivisions du district de Senapati.

34 Includes data for the Indian-held part of Jammu and Kashmir, the final status of which has not yet been determined. - Y compris les données pour la partie du Jammu et du Cachemire occupée par l'Inde dont le statut définitif n'a pas encore été déterminé.

35 Data have not been adjusted for underenumeration. - Les données n'ont pas été ajustées pour compenser les lacunes du dénombrement.

36 Differences between the total figures and sum of urban and rural areas are due to the inclusion of unsettled population. - Les différences entre les chiffres pour l'ensemble du pays et la somme des zones urbaines et rurales s'expliquent par l'inclusion de la population non sédentaire.

37 Including unsettled population. - Y compris la population non sédentaire.

38 The data is from the census sample. - Données extraites de l'échantillon de recensement.

39 Because of rounding, totals are not in all cases the sum of the respective components. Includes data for East Jerusalem and Israeli residents in certain other territories under occupation by Israeli military forces since June 1967. Data are rounded for confidentiality reasons. - Les chiffres étant arrondis, les totaux ne correspondent pas toujours rigoureusement à la somme des composants respectifs. Y compris les données pour Jérusalem-Est et les résidents israéliens dans certains autres territoires occupés depuis 1967 par les forces armées israéliennes. Chiffres arrondis pour des raisons de confidentialité.

40 Excluding diplomatic personnel outside the country and foreign military and civilian personnel and their dependants stationed in the area. - Non compris le personnel diplomatique hors du pays ni les militaires et agents civils étrangers en poste sur le territoire et les membres de leur famille les accompagnant.

41 Excluding data for Jordanian territory under occupation since June 1967 by Israeli military forces. Including registered Palestinian refugees and Jordanians abroad. - Non compris les données pour le territoire jordanien occupé depuis juin 1967 par les forces armées israéliennes. Y compris les réfugiés palestiniens enregistrés et les Jordaniens à l'étranger.

42 Excluding data for Jordanian territory under occupation since June 1967 by Israeli military forces. - Non compris les données pour le territoire jordanien occupé depuis juin 1967 par les forces armées israéliennes.

43 Unrevised data. - Les données n'ont pas été révisées.

44 Excluding usual residents not in the country at the time of census. - À l'exclusion des résidents habituels qui ne sont pas dans le pays au moment du recensement.

45 Data have been adjusted for underenumeration. - Les données ont été ajustées pour compenser les lacunes du dénombrement.

46 Total population is taken as de facto and de jure together. - Population totale considérée comme de fait et de droit.

47 Data refer to resident population which includes resident Maldivians and resident foreigners. - Les données concernent la population résidente, qui comprend les Maldiviens et les étrangers.

48 Data refer to enumerated population. The total for the whole country excludes 1,206,353 persons estimated not to have been counted in parts of States of Rakhine, Kachin and Kayin. - Les données se rapportent à la population dénombrée. L' effectif de la population pour le pays ne comprend pas les personnes qui ne sont pas dénombrées dans certaines régions des États de Rakhine, Kachin et Kayin estimées à un chiffre de 1 206 353 personnes.

49 Excluding 2739 Filipinos in Philippine Embassies, Consulates and Missions Abroad. - Excepté 2739 Philippins travaillant dans les ambassades, les consulats et les missions des Philippines à l'étranger.

50 Excluding 2134 Filipinos in Philippine Embassies, Consulates and Missions Abroad. - Excepté 2134 Philippins travaillant dans les ambassades, les consulats et les missions des Philippines à l'étranger.

51 Excluding foreigners. - Non compris les étrangers.

52 Data are based on the latest register-based population estimates for 2010. Data refer to resident population which comprises Singapore citizens and permanent residents. - Données basées sur les estimations démographiques les plus récentes fondées sur les registres de 2010. Les données se rapportent à la population résidente composé des citoyens de Singapour et des résidents permanents.

53 The Population and Housing Census 2001 did not cover the whole area of the country due to the security problems; data refer to the 18 districts for which the census was completed only (in three districts it was not possible to conduct the census at all and in four districts it was partially conducted). Unrevised data. - Le recensement de la population et du logement de 2001 n'a pas été réalisé sur la superficie totale du pays à cause de problèmes de sécurité; les données ne concernent que les 18 districts entièrement recensés (3 districts n'ont pas été recensés du tout, et 4 ont été recensés en partie). Les données n'ont pas été révisées.

54 Data for rural areas include data of estate sectors consisting of all plantations which are 20 acres or more in extent and with ten or more resident labourers. - Les données pour les zones rurales comprennent celles pour les domaines, dont l'ensemble des plantations de plus de 10 hectares comptant au moins 10 travailleurs résidents.

55 Total population does not include Palestinian population living in those parts of Jerusalem governorate which were annexed by Israel in 1967, amounting to 210 209 persons. Likewise, the results does not include the estimates of not enumerated population based on the findings of the post enumeration study, i.e

83 805 persons. - Les données relatives à la population totale ne comprennent pas la population palestinienne -équivalent à 210 209 personnes - habitant dans les territoires du gouvernorat de Jérusalem qui ont été annexés par Israël en 1967. Egalement, les données ne tiennent pas compte des estimations de la population calculée sur la base des résultats de l'enquête postcensitaire, équivalent à 83 805 personnes.

56 Data for urban include population in refugee camps. - Les données pour la population urbaine comprennent la population dans les camps réfugiés.

57 Including Palestinian refugees. - Y compris les réfugiés de Palestine.

58 All persons falling within the scope of the census were enumerated on a de jure basis, except students who were enumerated on a de facto basis. - Toutes les personnes englobées dans le recensement ont été dénombrées comme population de droit, à l'exception des étudiants qui ont été dénombrés comme population de fait.

59 Based on a sample taken at the time of census. Because of rounding, totals are not in all cases the sum of the respective components. The figures are calculated by dividing and rounding to thousand. Therefore, "0" may indicate value of less than 500. - D'après un échantillon obtenu au moment du recensement. Les chiffres étant arrondis, les totaux ne correspondent pas toujours rigoureusement à la somme des composants respectifs. Les chiffres ont été calculés en divisant et en arrondissant au millier. Par conséquent, "0" peut indiquer une valeur inférieure à 500.

60 Statistics are compiled from registers. - Les statistiques sont compilées à partir des registres.

61 Excluding Faeroe Islands and Greenland shown separately, if available. - Non compris les Iles Féroé et le Groenland, qui font l'objet de rubriques distinctes, si disponible.

62 Data include Overseas Departments. - Y compris les données des départements d'outre-mer.

63 Excluding families of military personnel, visitors and transients. - Non compris les familles des militaires, ni les visiteurs et transients.

64 Excluding military personnel, visitors and transients. - Non compris les militaires, ni les visiteurs et transients.

65 Including armed forces stationed outside the country and alien forces in the area. - Y compris les militaires nationaux hors du pays et les militaires étrangers en garnison sur le territoire.

66 Age classification is based on the difference between the year of birth and the year of the census, rather than on completed years of age. - La classification par âge est fondée sur la différence entre l'année de naissance et l'année de recensement,et non sur l'âge en années révolues.

67 Including residents temporarily outside the country. Population statistics are compiled from registers. - Y compris les résidents se trouvant temporairement hors du pays. Les statistiques de la population sont compilées à partir des registres.

68 The total number may include 'Unknown residence', but the categories urban and rural do not. - Le nombre total peut inclure les personnes dont la résidence n'est pas connue, à l'inverse des catégories de population urbaine et rurale.

69 Excluding civilian aliens within the country, but including civilian nationals temporarily outside the country. - Non compris les civils étrangers dans le pays, mais y compris les civils nationaux temporairement hors du pays.

70 Excluding Transnistria and the municipality of Bender. Excluding non-residents present in country at time of census. - Les données ne tiennent pas compte de l'information sur la Transnistria et la municipalité de Bender. Non compris les non-résidents présents dans le pays au moment du recensement.

71 Excludes non-residents present in country at time of census (visitors, foreigners temporarily residing in country, etc.). Tiraspol, Bender, Slobozia, Ribnita, Camenca Yrigoricpol/Grigoriopol are districts from Transnistria where the census was not conducted. - Exclue les non-résidents présents dans le pays au moment du recensement (visiteurs, étrangers résidant temporairement dans le pays, etc.). Tiraspol, Bender, Slobozia, Ribnita, Camenca, Yrigoricpol/Grigoriopol sont les districts de la Transnistrie où le recensement n'a pas eu lieu.

72 Excludes data for Kosovo and Metohia. - Sans les données pour le Kosovo et Metohia.

73 Excluding transients visitors. - Non compris les visiteurs en transit.

74 Excluding Channel Islands (Guernsey and Jersey) and Isle of Man, shown separately, if available. - Non compris les îles Anglo-Normandes (Guernesey et Jersey) et l'île de Man, qui font l'objet de rubriques distinctes, si disponible.

75 Counts for the 1991 Census are taken from 'Key Statistics for Urban and Rural Areas: Great Britain 1991' published volume based on the usually resident population. - Les chiffres du recensement de 1991 sont extraits de l'ouvrage « Key Statistics for Urban Areas: Great Britain 1991 » et sont fondés sur la notion de résidence habituelle.

76 Counts for the 2001 Census are taken from 'Key Statistics table 1 for the Urban/Rural classification: England and Wales' available on CD based on the usually resident population. - Les chiffres du recensement de 2001 proviennent du tableau intitulé « Key Statistics table 1 for the Urban/Rural classification:

England and Wales » disponible sur CD-ROM et sont fondés sur la notion de résidence habituelle.

77 These data have been randomly rounded to protect confidentiality. Individual figures may not add up to totals, and values for the same data may vary in different tables. - Ces données ont été arrondies de façon aléatoire afin d'en préserver la confidentialité. La somme de certains chiffres peut ne pas correspondre aux totaux indiqués et les valeurs des mêmes données peuvent varier d'un tableau à un autre.

78 Including population in off-shore, migratory and shipping. - Y compris les populations extraterritoriales, les populations nomades et les populations maritimes.

79 Excluding Niue, shown separately, which is part of Cook Islands, but because of remoteness is administered separately. - Non compris Nioué, qui fait l'objet d'une rubrique distincte et qui fait partie des îles Cook, mais qui, en raison de son éloignement, est administrée séparément.

80 Data includes Tokelaun Public Service employees and their immediate families based in Apia but excludes non-residents present at the time of census. - Les données comprennent les agents de la fonction publique des Tokélaou et leur famille directe basés à Apia mais excluent les non-résidents présents au moment du recensement.

81 Data refer to Tongans and part-Tongans only. - Les données ne concernent que la population tongane et partie-Tongans seulement.

84

Table 4 - *Demographic Yearbook 2018*

Table 4 presents, for each country or area of the world, basic vital statistics for the period 2014 - 2018: live births, crude birth rate, deaths, crude death rate, rate of natural increase, infant deaths, infant mortality rate, life expectancy at birth by sex and total fertility rate.

Description of variables: The vital events and rates shown in this table are defined as follows[1]:

Live birth is the complete expulsion or extraction from its mother of a product of conception, irrespective of the duration of pregnancy, which after such separation breathes or shows any other evidence of life such as beating of the heart, pulsation of the umbilical cord, definite movement of voluntary muscles, whether or not the umbilical cord has been cut or the placenta is attached; each product of such a birth is considered live born.

Death is the permanent disappearance of all evidence of life at any time after live birth has taken place (post-natal cessation of vital functions without capability of resuscitation).

Infant deaths are deaths of live born infants under one year of age.

Life expectancy at birth is defined as the average number of years of life for males and females if they continued to be subject to the same mortality experienced in the year(s) to which these life expectancies refer.

The total fertility rate is the average number of children that would be born alive to a hypothetical cohort of women if, throughout their reproductive years, the age-specific fertility rates remained unchanged. The standard method of calculating the total fertility rate is the sum of the age-specific fertility rates.

Crude birth rates and crude death rates presented in this table are calculated using the number of live births and the number of deaths obtained from civil registers. These civil registration data are used only if they are considered reliable (estimated completeness of 90 per cent or more).

Similarly, infant mortality rates presented in this table are calculated using the number of live births and the number of infant deaths obtained from civil registers. If, however, the registration of births or infant deaths for any given country or area is estimated to be less than 90 per cent complete, the rates are not calculated.

For some countries, the data and rates presented in this table are based on vital statistics data sourced from censuses or demographic surveys.

Rate computation: The crude birth and death rates are the annual number of each of these vital events per 1 000 mid-year population. Infant mortality rate is the annual number of deaths of infants under one year of age per 1 000 live births in the same year.

Rates of natural increase are the difference between the crude birth rate and the crude death rate. It should be noted that the rates of natural increase presented here may differ from the population growth rates presented in table 3 as rates of natural increase do not take net international migration into account while the population growth rates do.

Crude birth rates, crude death rates and infant mortality rates that appear in this table have been calculated by the United Nations Statistics Division, unless otherwise noted. Exceptions include official estimated rates for India, which were based on the sample registration system. Rates calculated by the United Nations Statistics Division presented in this table have been limited to those countries or areas having a minimum number of 30 events (for live births, deaths or infant deaths) in a given year.

Reliability of data: Rates calculated on the basis of registered vital statistics which are considered unreliable (estimated to be less than 90 per cent complete) are not calculated. Estimated rates, prepared by individual countries or areas, are presented whenever applicable.

The designation of vital statistics as being either reliable or unreliable is discussed in general in section 4.2 of the Technical Notes. The technical notes for tables 9, 15 and 18 provide specific information on reliability of statistics on live births, infant deaths, and deaths, respectively.

The values shown for life expectancy in this table come from official life tables. It is assumed that, if necessary, the basic data (population and deaths classified by age and sex) have been adjusted for deficiencies before their use in constructing the life tables.

Limitations: Statistics on births, deaths and infant deaths are subject to the same qualifications as have been set forth for vital statistics, in general, in section 4 of the Technical Notes and in the technical notes for individual tables presenting detailed data on these events (table 9, live births; table 15, infant deaths; table 18, deaths).

In assessing comparability, it is important to take into account the reliability of the data used to calculate the rates, as discussed above.

The problem of obtaining precise correspondence between numerator (births and deaths) and denominator (population for crude birth and death rates) as regards the inclusion or exclusion of armed forces, refugees, displaced persons and other special groups is particularly difficult where vital rates are concerned.

It should also be noted that crude rates are particularly affected by the age-sex structure of the population. Infant mortality rates, and to a much lesser extent crude birth rates and crude death rates, are affected by the variation in the definition of a live birth and tabulation procedures.

NOTES

[1] *Principles and Recommendations for a Vital Statistics System Revision 3,* Sales No. E.13.XVII.10, United Nations, New York, 2014.

Tableau 4 – *Annuaire démographique 2018*

Le tableau 4 présente, pour chaque pays ou zone du monde, des statistiques de base de l'état civil pour les années 2014 – 2018 : les naissances vivantes, le taux brut de natalité, les décès, le taux brut de mortalité et le taux d'accroissement naturel de la population, les décès d'enfants de moins d'un an et le taux de mortalité infantile, l'espérance de vie à la naissance par sexe et l'indice synthétique de fécondité.

Description des variables : les faits d'état civil utilisés aux fins du calcul des taux présentés dans le tableau 4 sont définis comme suit[1] :

La naissance vivante est l'expulsion ou l'extraction complète du corps de la mère, indépendamment de la duré de la gestation, d'un produit de la conception qui après cette séparation, respire ou manifeste tout autre signe de vie, tel que battement de cœur, pulsation du cordon ombilical ou contraction effective d'un muscle soumis à l'action de la volonté, que le cordon ombilical ait été coupé ou non et que le placenta soit ou non demeuré attaché ; tout produit d'une telle naissance est considéré comme « enfant né vivant ».

Le décès est la disparition permanente de tout signe de vie à un moment quelconque postérieur à la naissance vivante (cessation des fonctions vitales après la naissance sans possibilité de réanimation).

Il convient de préciser que les chiffres relatifs aux décès d'enfants de moins d'un an se rapportent aux naissances vivantes.

L'espérance de vie à la naissance est le nombre moyen d'années que vivraient les individus de sexe masculin et de sexe féminin s'ils continuaient d'être soumis aux mêmes conditions de mortalité que celles qui existaient pendant les années auxquelles se rapportent les valeurs indiquées.

L'indice synthétique de fécondité représente le nombre moyen d'enfants que mettrait au monde une cohorte hypothétique de femmes qui seraient soumises, tout au long de leur vie, aux mêmes conditions de fécondité par âge que celles auxquelles sont soumises les femmes, dans chaque groupe d'âge, au cours d'une année ou d'une période donnée. La méthode standard pour calculer l'indice synthétique de fécondité consiste à additionner les taux de fécondité par âge simple.

Les taux bruts de natalité et de mortalité ont été établis sur la base du nombre de naissances vivantes et du nombre de décès inscrits sur les registres de l'état civil. Ces données n'ont été utilisées que lorsqu'elles étaient considérées comme sûres (degré estimatif de complétude égal ou supérieur à 90 p. 100).

De même, les taux de mortalité infantile présentés dans le tableau 4 ont été établis à partir du nombre de naissances vivantes et du nombre de décès d'enfants de moins d'un an, inscrits sur les registres de l'état civil. Toutefois, lorsque les données relatives aux naissances ou aux décès d'enfants de moins d'un an pour un pays ou zone quelconque n'étaient pas considérées complètes à 90 p. 100 au moins, les indices n'ont pas été calculés.

Pour quelques pays, les données et les taux présentés dans ce tableau ont été extraites des recensements de la population ou des enquêtes démographiques.

Calcul des taux : les taux bruts de natalité et de mortalité, représentent le nombre annuel de chacun de ces faits d'état civil pour 1 000 habitants au milieu de l'année considérée. Les taux de mortalité infantile correspondent au nombre annuel de décès d'enfants de moins d'un an pour 1 000 naissances vivantes survenues pendant la même année.

Le taux d'accroissement naturel est égal à la différence entre le taux brut de natalité et le taux brut de mortalité. Il y a lieu de noter que les taux d'accroissement naturel indiqués dans le tableau 4 peuvent différer des taux d'accroissement de la population figurant dans le tableau 3, les taux d'accroissement naturel ne tenant pas compte des taux nets de migration internationale, alors que ceux-ci sont inclus dans les taux d'accroissement de la population.

Sauf indication contraire, les taux bruts de natalité et de mortalité, et les taux de mortalité infantile figurant dans le tableau 4, ont été calculés par la Division des statistiques de l'Organisation des Nations Unies. Les exceptions comprennent l'Inde, pour laquelle les taux estimatifs officiels ont été fournis sur la base d'un système d'enregistrement par échantillonnage. Les taux calculés par la Division des statistiques de l'Organisation des Nations Unies qui sont présentés dans le tableau 4 se rapportent aux pays ou zones où l'on a enregistré au moins 30 événements (pour les naissances vivantes, les décès ou pour les décès d'enfants de moins d'un an) au cours d'une année donnée.

Fiabilité des données : les taux n'ont pas été calculés lorsque les statistiques de l'état civil issues de systèmes d'enregistrement d'état civil étaient jugées douteuses (degré estimatif de complétude inférieur à 90 p.100) et des taux estimatifs, calculés par les pays ou zones, ont été présentés lorsqu'ils étaient disponibles.

On trouve à la section 4.2 des Notes techniques des explications générales concernant la façon dont les statistiques de l'état civil ont été classées selon leur degré de fiabilité. Les notes techniques relatives aux tableaux 9, 15 et 18 ont trait respectivement à la fiabilité des statistiques des naissances vivantes, des décès d'enfants de moins d'un an et des décès.

Les valeurs relatives à l'espérance de vie figurant dans le tableau 4 proviennent de tables officielles de mortalité. On présume que les données de base (la population et les décès par sexe et âge) ont été rectifiées d'éventuelles insuffisances avant d'être utilisées pour construire les tables de mortalité.

Insuffisance des données : les statistiques des naissances, décès et décès d'enfants de moins d'un an appellent toutes les réserves qui ont été formulées à propos des statistiques de l'état civil en général à la section 4 des Notes techniques et dans les notes techniques relatives aux différents tableaux présentant des données détaillées sur ces événements [tableau 9 (naissances vivantes), tableau 15 (décès d'enfants de moins d'un an) et tableau 18 (décès)].

Pour évaluer la comparabilité des divers taux, il importe de tenir compte de la fiabilité des données utilisées pour calculer ces taux, comme il a été indiqué précédemment.

Le calcul des taux est particulièrement affecté par la difficulté à obtenir une correspondance parfaite entre le numérateur (naissances et décès) et le dénominateur (population, pour les taux bruts de natalité et de mortalité) en raison de l'inclusion ou non dans la population des forces armées, des réfugiés, des personnes déplacées ou d'autres groupes sociaux.

Il y a lieu de noter que la structure par âge et par sexe de la population influe de façon particulière sur les taux bruts. Le manque d'uniformité dans la définition des naissances vivantes et dans les procédures de mise en tableaux a une incidence sur les taux de mortalité infantile et, à un moindre degré, sur les taux bruts de natalité et les taux bruts de mortalité.

NOTE

[1] *Principles and Recommendations for a Vital Statistics System Revision 3,* Sales No. E.13.XVII.10, United Nations, New York, 2014

Continent, country or area and year / Continent, pays ou zone et année	Live births / Naissances vivantes Code[a]	Number Nombre	Crude birth rate Taux brut de natalité	Deaths / Décès Code[a]	Number Nombre	Crude death rate Taux brut de mortalité	Rate of natural increase Taux d'accroissement naturel	Infant deaths / Décès d'enfants de moins d'un an Code[a]	Number Nombre	Rate (per 1000 births) Taux (par 1000 naissances)	Life expectancy at birth / Espérance de vie à la naissance Male[b] Masculin[b]	Female[b] Féminin[b]	Total fertility rate L'indice synthétique de fécondité
AFRICA - AFRIQUE													
Algeria - Algérie													
2014	C	1 014 248[1]	25.9	U	173 781[1]	...	...	U	22 282[1]	...	76.6[2]	77.8[2]	3.030
2015	C	1 040 285[1]	26.0	U	182 570[1]	...	...	U	23 150[1]	...	76.4[2]	77.8[2]	3.100
2016	C	1 066 823[1]	26.1	U	180 404[1]	...	...	U	22 271[1]	...	77.1[2]	78.2[2]	3.100
2017		...	...		...	...	...		...	...	76.9[2]	78.2[2]	...
Angola													
2014	I	1 152 490[3]	44.5	I	239 252[3]	9.2	35.3	I	45 627[3]	39.6	...	...	...
2018		...	...		...	...	...		...	...	60.6	63.4	...
Botswana													
2014	U	41 741[4]	...	U	12 177[4]	...	...	U	1 045[4]	...	...	...	...
2015	U	46 765[4]	...	U	13 030[4]	...	...	U	1 012[4]	...	...	...	...
2016	U	49 984[4]	...	U	12 825[4]	...	...	U	1 041[4]	...	64.9[5]	65.9[5]	2.300[5]
2017	C	43 290[4]	19.1	U	12 386[4]	...	...	U	985[4]	...	...	...	...
Burundi													
2014	+U	253 698[6]	...		...	...	...		...	...	56.5	60.6	6.140
2015	+U	266 820[6]	...		...	...	...		...	...	...	...	5.700
2016		...	...		...	...	...		...	...	56.3	60.5	5.500[7]
2017		...	...		...	...	...		...	...	56.9	61.3	4.340
Cabo Verde[8]													
2014		...	...		...	...	...		...	...	71.1	79.7	...
2015		...	...		...	...	...		...	...	71.5	79.9	...
2016		...	...		...	...	...		...	...	71.8	80.0	...
2017		...	...		...	...	...		...	...	72.2	80.2	...
2018		...	...		...	...	...		...	...	72.6	80.4	...
Cameroon - Cameroun													
2014		...	...		...	...	...		...	...	...	...	4.900[9]
2018		...	...		...	...	...		...	...	...	...	4.800[10]
Congo													
2014	+U	111 360[11]	...	+U	13 413	...	...	+U	2 240[11]	...	...	...	4.400
Côte d'Ivoire													
2014	+U	631 804	...	+U	45 023[12]	...	...	I	44 530[3]	52.9	...	...	4.790
2015	+U	626 783	...	+U	47 065[12]	...	...		...	...	...	...	...
2016	+U	659 247	...	+U	45 995[12]	...	...		...	...	54.9	57.5	...
2017	+U	619 181	...	+U	44 813[12]	...	...		...	...	...	...	...
2018	+U	635 924	...	+U	46 385[12]	...	...		...	...	...	...	...
Egypt - Égypte													
2014	+C	2 720 495	31.3	C	531 864	6.1	25.2	C	39 679	14.6	...	...	3.500
2015	+C	2 685 276	30.2	C	573 879	6.5	23.7	C	42 050	15.7	...	...	3.500
2016	+C	2 600 173	28.6	C	556 148	6.1	22.5	C	39 301	15.1	70.5	73.3	3.500
2017	+C	2 557 440	26.9	C	547 208	5.7	21.1	C	38 685	15.1	70.8	73.6	...
2018		...	...		...	...	...		...	...	71.2	74.0	...
Eswatini													
2014		...	...		...	...	...		...	...	...	...	3.600
2015		...	...		...	...	...		...	...	...	...	3.500
2018		...	...		...	...	...		...	...	44.1[13]	48.1[13]	...
Guinea - Guinée													
2014	I	440 340[14]	41.5	I	119 969[15]	11.3	30.2	I	33 762[16]	76.7	57.4[17]	60.4[17]	5.200[18]
2015		...	...		...	...	...		...	...	...	...	5.000[18]
2016		...	...		...	...	...		...	...	...	...	4.800[18]
2017		...	...		...	...	...		...	...	58.4	61.4	4.745[18]
2018		...	...		...	...	...		...	...	...	...	4.690[18]
Guinea-Bissau - Guinée-Bissau													
2014		...	...		...	...	...		...	...	51.2	53.6	...
Kenya													
2014	+U	954 254	...	+U	198 611	...	...	+U	22 986	...	...	...	3.900[19]
2015	+U	950 224	...	+U	200 205	...	...	+U	23 123	...	...	...	3.900[19]
2016	+U	948 351	...	+U	189 930	...	...	+U	21 475	...	...	...	3.900[19]

Continent, country or area and year / Continent, pays ou zone et année	Live births Naissances vivantes			Deaths Décès			Rate of natural increase Taux d'accroissement naturel	Infant deaths Décès d'enfants de moins d'un an			Life expectancy at birth Espérance de vie à la naissance		Total fertility rate L'indice synthétique de fécondité
	Code[a]	Number Nombre	Crude birth rate Taux brut de natalité	Code[a]	Number Nombre	Crude death rate Taux brut de mortalité		Code[a]	Number Nombre	Rate (per 1000 births) Taux (par 1000 naissances)	Male[b] Masculin[b]	Female[b] Féminin[b]	
AFRICA - AFRIQUE													
Kenya													
2017	+U	923 487	...	+U	190 877	...	...	+U	19 895	...	...	...	3.900[19]
2018	+U	1 148 352	...	+U	192 019	...	...	+U	20 350	...	...	...	3.900[19]
Lesotho													
2015	+U	10 800	...	+U	17 929	...	...	+U	218	...	...	...	
2016	+U	9 655	...	+U	13 768	...	...	+U	17	...	51.7[20]	59.6[20]	
2017	+U	9 463	...	+U	13 671	...	...	+U	158	...	...	...	
Liberia - Libéria													
2014		...			...				...	...	...	...	4.600
Madagascar[21]													
2018		...	...		...	...	...		...	...	63.3	65.2	...
Malawi[22]													
2018	I	576 525	32.8	I	110 776	6.3	26.5		...	...	...	...	...
Mauritius - Maurice[23]													
2014	+C	13 283	10.5	+C	9 682	7.7	2.9	+C	194	14.6	III71.0	77.6	1.424
2015	+C	12 640	10.0	+C	9 747	7.7	2.3	+C	173	13.7	III71.1	77.8	1.362
2016	+C	12 948	10.2	+C	10 174	8.1	2.2	+C	154	11.9	III71.2	77.8	1.399
2017	+C	13 385	10.6	+C	10 140	8.0	2.6	+C	164	12.3	III71.3	77.9	1.449
2018	+C	12 980	10.3	+C	10 787	8.5	1.7	+C	181	13.9	III71.3	77.7	1.407
Mayotte													
2014	C	7 306	32.0	C	590	2.6	29.5	C	70	9.6	74.7	77.9	4.120
2015	C	8 997	38.3	C	636	2.7	35.6	C	71	7.9	75.3	77.2	4.880
2016	C	9 496	38.9	C	705	2.9	36.0	C	96	10.1	...	...	4.950
2017	C	9 762	38.2	C	735	2.9	35.3	C	86	8.8	75.4	76.0	4.910
Mozambique													
2014	U	794 718[24]	...		...	...	...		...	...	50.2	55.4	...
2015		...	...		...	...	...		...	...	51.7	55.9	...
2016		...	...		...	...	...		...	...	52.0	56.2	...
Reunion - Réunion													
2014	C	14 095[25]	16.6	C	4 355	5.1	11.5	C	94	6.7	77.1	83.7	2.440
2015	C	14 011[25]	16.4	C	4 531	5.3	11.1	C	93	6.6	77.1	83.6	2.460
2016	C	13 742[25]	16.0	C	4 689	5.5	10.5	C	98	7.1	77.5	84.2	2.440
2017	C	13 708[25]	15.9	C	4 673	5.4	10.5	C	87	6.3	78.1	84.5	2.460
Rwanda													
2014		...	...		...	...	...		...	...	63.3	67.1	...
2015		...	...		...	...	...		...	...	63.7	67.5	...
2017		...	...		...	...	...		...	...	64.6	68.4	...
Saint Helena ex. dep. - Sainte-Hélène sans dép.													
2014	C	48	10.9	C	61	13.9	-3.0	C	1	...	...	...	...
2015	C	40	8.9	C	55	12.3	-3.4	C	1	...	...	...	...
2016	C	35	7.5	C	45	9.7	-2.1	C	1	...	...	...	...
2017	C	36	7.9	C	58	12.7	-4.8	C	-	...	...	...	...
2018	C	26	...	C	52	11.3	...	C	-	...	X74.3[26]	80.4[26]	...
Sao Tome and Principe - Sao Tomé-et-Principe													
2014	C	4 939	26.6	C	1 243	6.7	19.9		...	...	62.8	69.2	...
2015	C	5 022	26.5	C	1 226	6.5	20.0		...	...	63.2	69.7	...
2016	C	5 105	26.4	C	1 212	6.3	20.1		...	...	63.6	70.1	...
2017	C	5 190	26.3	C	1 202	6.1	20.2		...	...	64.0	70.5	...
Senegal - Sénégal[5]													
2014		...	...		...	...	...		...	...	...	...	5.000
2015		...	...		...	...	...		...	...	...	...	4.900
2016		...	...		...	...	...		...	...	...	...	4.700
2017		...	...		...	...	...		...	...	...	...	4.600
Seychelles													
2014	+C	1 557	17.0	+C	725	7.9	9.1	+C	17	...	68.4	78.3	2.340
2015	+C	1 592	17.0	+C	703	7.5	9.5	+C	17	...	...	...	...
2016	+C	1 645	17.4	+C	747	7.9	9.5		...	...	...	...	...

Continent, country or area and year / Continent, pays ou zone et année	Live births — Naissances vivantes			Deaths — Décès			Rate of natural increase Taux d'accroissement naturel	Infant deaths — Décès d'enfants de moins d'un an			Life expectancy at birth — Espérance de vie à la naissance		Total fertility rate L'indice synthétique de fécondité
	Code[a]	Number Nombre	Crude birth rate Taux brut de natalité	Code[a]	Number Nombre	Crude death rate Taux brut de mortalité		Code[a]	Number Nombre	Rate (per 1000 births) Taux (par 1000 naissances)	Male[b] Masculin[b]	Female[b] Féminin[b]	
AFRICA - AFRIQUE													
Seychelles													
2017	+C	1 651	17.2	+C	748	7.8	9.4	+C	18	...	70.3	78.5	...
2018	+C	1 650	17.1	+C	818	8.5	8.6		...	...	68.5	77.4	...
Sierra Leone[27]													
2015		...	...		...	...	...		...	...	48.3	50.8	...
South Africa - Afrique du Sud													
2014	U	1 019 495	...	U	476 891	...	...	U	26 785	...	59.1	63.1	2.500
2015	U	966 162	...	U	473 266	...	...	U	24 994	...	...	...	2.470
2016	C	906 375	16.2	U	456 612	...	...	U	20 649	...	...	...	2.450
2017	C	913 499	16.1		...	...	...		...	...	...	...	2.420
2018		...	...		...	...	...		...	...	...	...	2.400
Tunisia - Tunisie													
2014	C	225 887	20.5	U	62 785	...	...		...	...	...	...	2.415
2015	C	222 534	20.0	U	65 743	...	...		...	...	74.5	77.8	2.302
2016	C	219 441	19.4	U	62 601	...	...		...	...	74.5	78.1	2.314
2017	C	209 236	18.3	U	67 447	...	...		...	...	...	...	...
Uganda - Ouganda[28]													
2014		...	...		...	...	...		...	...	62.2	64.2	...
United Republic of Tanzania - République Unie de Tanzanie[29]													
2014		...	...		...	...	...		...	...	...	...	5.300
2015		...	...		...	...	...		...	...	...	...	5.200
2016		...	...		...	...	...		...	...	...	...	5.200
2017		...	...		...	...	...		...	...	...	...	5.100
AMERICA, NORTH - AMÉRIQUE DU NORD													
Anguilla													
2014	+C	151	10.6	+C	59[30]	4.1	6.5		...	...	...	...	...
2015	+C	165	11.2	+C	61[30]	4.1	7.1		...	...	...	...	...
2016	+C	135	9.0	+C*	83[30]	5.5	3.4		...	...	...	...	...
2017	+C	145	...		...	...	...		...	...	...	...	...
Antigua and Barbuda - Antigua-et-Barbuda													
2014	+C	1 100	12.3	+C	590	6.6	5.7	+C	13	...	72.3	79.4	...
2015	+C	1 159	12.8	+C	527	5.8	7.0	+C	10	...	80.5	75.2	...
2016	+C	1 063	11.5	+C	542	5.9	5.7	+C	13	...	80.1	75.2	...
2017	+C	1 108	11.8	+C	599	6.4	5.4		...	...	74.4	80.5	...
2018	+C	1 015	10.7	+C	581	6.1	4.6		...	...	...	...	...
Aruba													
2014	C	1 376	12.8	C	643	6.0	6.8	+C	5	...	...	...	2.041
2015	C	1 244	11.4	C	679	6.2	5.2	+C	6	...	...	...	1.821
2016	C	1 259	11.4	C	781	7.1	4.3	+C	5	...	...	...	1.821
2017	C	1 202	10.8	C	707	6.4	4.5	+C	6	...	...	...	1.746
2018	C*	1 028	9.2	C*	717	6.4	2.8		...	...	...	...	...
Bahamas													
2014	+U*	4 365	...	+C*	2 132	5.9	...	+C*	85	...	...	...	1.475*
2015	+U*	4 253	...	+C*	2 243	6.1	...	+C*	82	...	...	...	...
2016	+U*	4 093	...	+C*	2 288	6.1	...	+C*	70	...	...	...	...
2017	+U*	4 017	...	+C*	2 372	6.3	...	+C*	72	...	...	...	...
Barbados - Barbade													
2014	+C	2 902	10.5	+C	2 580	9.3	1.2		...	...	...	...	...
Belize													
2014	U	7 319	...	U	1 620	...	...	U	91	...	...	...	2.353
2015	U	7 459	...	U	1 772	...	...	U	127	...	...	...	2.347
2016	U	7 226	...	U	1 805	...	...	U	100	...	...	...	2.195

4. Vital statistics summary and life expectancy at birth: 2014 - 2018
Aperçu des statistiques de l'état civil et de l'espérance de vie à la naissance : 2014 - 2018 (continued - suite)

Continent, country or area and year / Continent, pays ou zone et année	Code[a]	Live births Number Nombre	Crude birth rate Taux brut de natalité	Code[a]	Deaths Number Nombre	Crude death rate Taux brut de mortalité	Rate of natural increase Taux d'accroissement naturel	Code[a]	Infant deaths Number Nombre	Rate (per 1000 births) Taux (par 1000 naissances)	Male[b] Masculin[b]	Female[b] Féminin[b]	Total fertility rate L'indice synthétique de fécondité
AMERICA, NORTH - AMÉRIQUE DU NORD													
Belize													
2017	U	7 252	...	U	1 872	...	...	U	104	...	...	...	...
2018	U	7 775	...	U	1 886	...	...	U	98	...	...	...	...
Bermuda - Bermudes													
2014	C	574[31]	9.3	C	480[31]	7.8	1.5	C	2[32]	...	77.1	84.7	1.420
2015	C	583[31]	9.4	C	478[31]	7.7	1.7	C	2[32]	...	77.3	84.9	1.443
2016	C	591[31]	9.3	C	492[31]	7.7	1.6	C	2[32]	...	77.5	85.1	1.435
2017	C	576[31]	9.0	C	481[31]	7.5	1.5	C	_[32]	...	77.7	85.4	1.400
2018	C	527[31]	8.2		...	...	...		...	...	79.5	85.7	...
British Virgin Islands - Îles Vierges britanniques													
2014	C	280	...	C	111	...	...	C	5	...	...	...	...
2015	C	266	9.1	C	136	4.7	4.5	C	4	...	...	...	...
2016	C	269	...	C	120	...	...	C	4	...	...	...	...
2017	C	248	...	C	155	...	...	C	7	...	...	...	...
Canada													
2014	C	384 100[33]	10.8	C	258 821[33]	7.3	3.5	C	1 794[33]	4.7	...	...	1.582
2015	C	382 392[33]	10.7	C	264 333[33]	7.4	3.3	C	1 737[33]	4.5	[III]79.9	84.0	1.563
2016	C	383 102[33]	10.6	C	267 213[33]	7.4	3.2	C	1 742[33]	4.5	[III]80.0	84.1	1.543
2017	C	376 291[33]	10.3	C	276 689[33]	7.6	2.7	C	1 700[33]	4.5	...	...	1.496
Cayman Islands - Îles Caïmanes													
2014	C	711	12.5	C	163[34]	2.9	9.6		...	...	...	...	...
2015	C	649	11.0	C	170[34]	2.9	8.1		...	...	...	...	...
2016	C	660	10.8	C	193[34]	3.2	7.7		...	...	...	...	...
2017	C	625	9.9	C	216[34]	3.4	6.4		...	...	...	...	...
2018	C	640	9.7	C	214[34]	3.3	6.5		...	...	...	...	...
Costa Rica													
2014	C	71 793[35]	15.0	C	20 553	4.3	10.7	C	575	8.0	77.2	82.3	1.860
2015	C	71 819	14.9	C	21 039	4.4	10.5	C	557	7.8	77.4	82.4	1.750
2016	C	70 004	14.3	C	22 603	4.6	9.7	C	555	7.9	...	...	1.700*
2017	C	68 816	13.9	C	23 251	4.7	9.2	C	548	8.0	77.6	82.7	1.671*
2018	C*	68 479	13.7	C*	23 786	4.8	8.9	C*	573	8.4	77.8	82.9	1.662*
Cuba													
2014	C	122 643	10.9	C	96 330	8.6	2.3	C	514	4.2	...	...	1.681
2015	C	125 064	11.1	C	99 691	8.9	2.3	C	535	4.3	...	...	1.721
2016	C	116 872	10.4	C	99 388	8.8	1.6	C	497	4.3	...	...	1.626
2017	C	114 971	10.2	C	106 949	9.5	0.7	C	465	4.0	...	...	1.610
2018	C*	116 333	10.4	C*	106 201	9.5	0.9	C*	461	4.0	...	...	...
Curaçao													
2014	C	1 963	12.6	C	1 370	8.8	3.8	C	24	...	[IV]74.0	81.2	2.000
2015	C	1 877	11.9	C	1 398	8.8	3.0	C	20	...	...	...	1.900
2016	C	1 789	11.2	C	1 482	9.3	1.9	C	20	...	74.9	81.0	1.700
2017	C	1 548	9.7	C	1 420	8.9	0.8	C	16	...	[III]74.7	81.5	1.500
2018	C	1 727	10.8	C	1 399	8.8	2.1	C	14	...	...	...	1.700
Dominica - Dominique													
2014	+C	858	12.0	+C	590	8.2	3.7		...	...	...	...	...
Dominican Republic - République dominicaine													
2014	U	165 783	...	U	40 697	...	...	U	848	...	...	...	2.364
2015	U	161 622	...	U	41 234	...	...	U	935	...	[VI]70.0	74.8	2.336
2016	U	152 370	...	U	43 382	...	...	U	810	...	...	...	2.310
2017	U	148 061	...	U	41 152	...	...	U	674	...	...	...	2.286
2018		...	...		...	...	...		...	...	...	...	2.263
El Salvador													
2014	C	108 903[36]	17.2	C	37 461	5.9	11.3	C	876[37]	8.0	...	...	...
2015	C	109 617[36]	17.0		...	...	...		...	...	...	...	...

4. Vital statistics summary and life expectancy at birth: 2014 - 2018
Aperçu des statistiques de l'état civil et de l'espérance de vie à la naissance : 2014 - 2018 (continued - suite)

Continent, country or area and year / Continent, pays ou zone et année	Live births Naissances vivantes Code[a]	Number Nombre	Crude birth rate Taux brut de natalité	Deaths Décès Code[a]	Number Nombre	Crude death rate Taux brut de mortalité	Rate of natural increase Taux d'accroissement naturel	Infant deaths Décès d'enfants de moins d'un an Code[a]	Number Nombre	Rate (per 1000 births) Taux (par 1000 naissances)	Life expectancy at birth Espérance de vie à la naissance Male[b] Masculin[b]	Female[b] Féminin[b]	Total fertility rate L'indice synthétique de fécondité
AMERICA, NORTH - AMÉRIQUE DU NORD													
Greenland - Groenland													
2014	C	805	14.3	C	461	8.2	6.1	C	6	...	[V]69.1	73.7	1.991
2015	C	854	15.2	C	472	8.4	6.8	C	9	...	...	...	2.112
2016	C	830	14.8	C	487	8.7	6.1	C	6	...	...	...	2.047
2017	C	853	15.2	C	499	8.9	6.3	C	6	...	...	...	2.096
2018	C	819	14.6	C	487	8.7	5.9	C	5	...	[II]69.4	72.5	1.997
Grenada - Grenade													
2014	+C	1 750	16.0	+C	958	8.8	7.2	+C	33	18.9	...	...	...
2015	+C	1 694	15.4	+C	869	7.9	7.5	+C	28	...	...	...	...
2016	+C	1 577	14.2	+C	898	8.1	6.1	+C	31	19.7	...	...	...
2017	+C	1 398	12.5	+C	885	7.9	4.6	+C	34	24.3	...	...	...
Guadeloupe													
2014	C	5 683[25]	14.2	C	3 451[25]	8.6	5.6	C	41[25]	7.2	76.1	83.4	2.270
2015	C	5 368[25]	13.5	C	3 052[25]	7.7	5.8	C	43[25]	8.0	77.0	84.8	2.180
2016	C	5 276[25]	13.4	C	3 383[25]	8.6	4.8	C	41[25]	7.8	...	...	2.200
2017	C	4 626[25]	11.8	C	3 273[25]	8.3	3.5	C	40[25]	8.6	...	...	1.980
Guatemala													
2014	C	386 195	24.4	C	77 807	4.9	19.5	C	7 342	19.0	...	...	...
2015	C	391 425	24.2	C	80 876	5.0	19.2	C	8 202	21.0	[VI]67.9	75.0	...
2016	C	390 382	23.6	C	82 565	5.0	18.6	C	8 366	21.4	...	...	...
2017	C	381 664	22.5	C	81 726	4.8	17.7	C	7 626	20.0	...	...	...
Jamaica - Jamaïque													
2014	C	36 996	13.6	U	18 320	...	...	...	...	...	...	...	...
2015	C	37 900	13.9	U	19 249	...	...	...	...	...	...	...	...
2016	C	36 160	13.3	U	19 761	...	...	...	...	...	...	...	...
2017	C	34 169	12.5	U	18 879	...	...	...	...	...	...	...	...
2018	C*	33 092	12.1	U	18 859	...	...	...	...	...	...	...	...
Martinique													
2014	C	4 367[25]	11.4	C	3 319[25]	8.7	2.7		...	...	78.1	83.9	...
2015	C	3 972[25]	10.5	C	3 058[25]	8.1	2.4		...	...	79.4	84.7	...
2016	C	3 782[25]	10.0	C	3 284[25]	8.7	1.3		...	...	...	...	...
2017	C	3 640[25]	9.8	C	3 217[25]	8.7	1.1	C	40	11.0	...	...	...
Mexico - Mexique													
2014	C	2 129 825[38]	17.8	+C	632 587[39]	5.3	12.5	+C	26 385[39]	12.4	72.1	77.6	...
2015	C	2 096 274[38]	17.3	+C	654 593[39]	5.4	11.9	+C	26 045[39]	12.4	72.3	77.7	...
2016	C	2 028 358[38]	16.5	+C	684 437[39]	5.6	11.0	+C	24 722[39]	12.2	...	...	...
2017	C*	2 234 039	18.0	+C	693 848[39]	5.6	12.4	+C	25 180[39]	11.3	...	...	...
2018		...	...		...	...	...		...	...	72.2	77.9	...
Montserrat													
2014	C	50	10.0	C	32	6.4	3.6	C	-	...	...	...	...
2015	C	48	9.6	C	49	9.8	-0.2	C	3	...	...	...	...
2016	C	46	9.1	C	43	8.5	0.6	C	-	...	...	...	...
Nicaragua													
2016	+U	137 772	...	+U	23 205	...	...		...	...	...	...	...
Panama													
2014	C	75 183	19.2	C	18 171	4.6	14.6	C	1 036	13.8	74.6[40]	80.7[40]	2.400
2015	C*	75 901	19.1	C	18 182	4.6	14.5	C	935	12.3	74.8[40]	80.9[40]	2.400
2016	C*	75 184	18.6	C*	18 882	4.7	13.9	C*	1 046	13.9	75.0[40]	81.1[40]	2.400
2017	C*	76 166	18.6	C*	19 482	4.8	13.8	C*	1 063	14.0	75.2[40]	81.2[40]	2.400
2018	C*	74 518	17.9	C*	18 478	4.4	13.5		...	...	...	...	...
Puerto Rico - Porto Rico													
2014	C	34 503	9.8	C	30 333	8.6	1.2	C	242	7.0	...	...	1.434
2015	C	31 241	9.0	C	28 409	8.2	0.8	C	222	7.1	[III]76.4	84.0	1.339
2016	C	28 344	8.3	C	29 649	8.7	-0.4	C	222	7.8	[III]76.6	84.1	1.246
2017	C	24 395	7.3	C	31 140	9.3	-2.0	C	172	7.1	[III]76.6	84.4	1.104
2018	C	21 467	6.7	C	29 060	9.1	-2.4	C	142	6.6	[III]76.5	84.7	...

4. Vital statistics summary and life expectancy at birth: 2014 - 2018
Aperçu des statistiques de l'état civil et de l'espérance de vie à la naissance : 2014 - 2018 (continued - suite)

Continent, country or area and year — Continent, pays ou zone et année	Code[a]	Live births — Naissances vivantes Number Nombre	Crude birth rate Taux brut de natalité	Code[a]	Deaths — Décès Number Nombre	Crude death rate Taux brut de mortalité	Rate of natural increase Taux d'accrois-sement naturel	Code[a]	Infant deaths — Décès d'enfants de moins d'un an Number Nombre	Rate (per 1000 births) Taux (par 1000 naiss-ances)	Life expectancy at birth — Espérance de vie à la naissance Male[b] Masculin[b]	Female[b] Féminin[b]	Total fertility rate L'indice synthétique de fécondité
AMERICA, NORTH - AMÉRIQUE DU NORD													
Saint Kitts and Nevis - Saint-Kitts-et-Nevis													
2014	+C	641	...	+C	411	...	...		...	...	...	...	...
Saint Lucia - Sainte-Lucie													
2014	+C	2 026	11.7	+C	1 358	7.9	3.9	+C	29	...	...	...	...
Saint Pierre and Miquelon - Saint Pierre-et-Miquelon													
2014	C	61	...	C	50	...	...	C	-	...	...	...	...
2017	C	30	...	C	65	...	...	C	-	...	...	...	...
Saint Vincent and the Grenadines - Saint-Vincent-et-les Grenadines													
2014	C	1 841	16.7	C	1 006	9.1	7.6	C	29	...	68.4	74.6	2.211
2015	C	1 813	16.4	C	885	8.0	8.4	C	26	...	...	...	2.188
2016	C	1 729	15.7	C	930	8.4	7.2	C	25	...	71.0	75.2	2.102
2017	C*	1 540	13.9		...	...	...		...	...	...	...	1.900
Saint-Barthélemy													
2014		96	10.0	C	53	5.5	4.5		...	...	...	...	...
2017	C	72	...	C	40	...	...	C	-	...	...	...	...
Saint-Martin (French part) - Saint-Martin (partie française)													
2014	C	693	19.6	C	161	4.5	15.0	C	5	...	...	...	...
2017	C	500	14.0	C	152	4.3	9.8	C	5	...	...	...	...
Sint Maarten (Dutch part) - Saint-Martin (partie néerlandaise)													
2014	+C	532	14.3	+C	169	4.6	9.8		...	...	...	...	...
2015	+C	500	13.1	+C	197	5.2	7.9		...	...	[III]73.8	80.5	...
2016	+C	458	11.6	+C	160	4.1	7.6		...	...	[III]74.0	80.6	...
2017	+C	363	9.0	+C	172	4.2	4.7		...	...	[III]74.0	82.8	...
Trinidad and Tobago - Trinité-et-Tobago													
2014	C*	18 729	13.9	C*	11 461	8.5	5.4		...	...	...	...	...
2015	C*	18 062	13.4	C*	11 240	8.3	5.1		...	...	...	...	...
Turks and Caicos Islands - Îles Turques et Caïques													
2014	C	437	12.4	C	76[41]	2.2	10.3	C	1	...	...	...	...
2015	C	437	11.9	C	97[41]	2.6	9.3	C	1	...	...	...	...
2016	C	518	13.7	C	89[41]	2.3	11.3		...	...	...	...	...
2017	C	555	13.9	C	122[41]	3.1	10.9	C	3	...	...	...	...
2018	C*	454	11.0	C*	103[41]	2.5	8.5	C*	-	...	...	...	...
United States of America - États-Unis d'Amérique													
2014	C	3 988 076	12.5	C	2 626 418	8.2	4.3	C	23 215	5.8	76.4	81.2	1.863
2015	C	3 978 497	12.4	C	2 712 630	8.5	3.9	C	23 455	5.9	76.3	81.2	1.844
AMERICA, SOUTH - AMÉRIQUE DU SUD													
Argentina - Argentine													
2014	C	777 012	18.2	C	325 539	7.6	10.6	C	8 202	10.6	...	...	2.357
2015	C	770 040	17.9	C	333 407	7.7	10.1	C	7 445	9.7	73.7[8]	80.3[8]	2.321
2016	C	728 035	16.7	C	352 992	8.1	8.6	C	7 093	9.7	...	...	2.183
2017	C	704 609	16.0	C	341 688	7.8	8.2	C	6 579	9.3	...	...	2.100

Continent, country or area and year / Continent, pays ou zone et année	Live births / Naissances vivantes Co-de[a]	Number Nombre	Crude birth rate Taux brut de natalité	Deaths / Décès Co-de[a]	Number Nombre	Crude death rate Taux brut de mortalité	Rate of natural increase Taux d'accroissement naturel	Infant deaths / Décès d'enfants de moins d'un an Co-de[a]	Number Nombre	Rate (per 1000 births) Taux (par 1000 naissances)	Life expectancy at birth / Espérance de vie à la naissance Male[b] Masculin[b]	Female[b] Féminin[b]	Total fertility rate L'indice synthétique de fécondité
AMERICA, SOUTH - AMÉRIQUE DU SUD													
Bolivia (Plurinational State of) - Bolivie (État plurinational de)													
2014	U	153 016	...		...	...	...		...	...			...
2015	+U	277 498	...		...	...	...		...	...	VI65.0	69.4	...
2016		...	...		...	...	...		...	...	II68.6[42]	75.3[42]	...
2017		...	...		...	...	...		...	...	II69.1[43]	75.9[43]	...
Brazil - Brésil													
2014	U	2 913 121[44]	...	+C	1 194 164[45]	5.9	...	U	31 679[46]	...	71.6[40]	78.8[40]	1.742[47]
2015	C	3 058 783	15.0	+C	1 231 400[45]	6.0	8.9	+C	31 238	10.2	71.9	79.1	1.716[47]
2016	C	2 903 933	14.1	+C	1 274 630[45]	6.2	7.9	+C	30 541	10.5	...	...	1.692[47]
2017	C	2 962 815	14.3	+C	1 277 579[45]	6.2	8.1	+C	30 636	10.3	...	...	...
Chile - Chili													
2014	C	250 997	14.1	C	101 960	5.7	8.4	C	1 825	7.3	76.8	82.5	1.850
2015	C	244 670	13.6	C	103 327	5.7	7.8	C	1 683	6.9	77.1	82.7	1.790
2016	C	231 749	12.7	C	104 026	5.7	7.0	C	1 629	7.0	76.7	81.8	1.690
2017	C*	219 186	11.9	C*	106 344	5.8	6.1	C*	1 559	7.1	...	...	...
Colombia - Colombie													
2014	U	669 137	...	U	210 051	...	...	U	7 589	...	...	...	...
2015	U	660 999	...	U	219 472	...	...	U	7 244	...	VI72.1	78.5	...
2016	U	647 521	...	U	223 078	...	...	U	7 220	...	...	...	...
2017	U	656 704	...	U	227 624	...	...	U	7 044	...	...	...	2.289[48]
Ecuador - Équateur[49]													
2014	U	278 460	...	U	63 788	...	...	U	2 862	...	73.2[5]	78.6[5]	2.587[50]
2015	U	283 313	...	U	65 391	...	...	U	3 011	...	VI73.2[50]	78.8[50]	2.542[50]
2016	U	272 090	...	U	68 304	...	...	U	3 078	...	73.7[50]	79.3[50]	2.499[50]
2017	U*	288 123	...	U	69 247	...	...	U	3 252	...	73.9[50]	79.5[50]	2.459[50]
2018		...	...		...	...	...		...	...	74.1[50]	79.7[50]	2.421[50]
French Guiana - Guyane française													
2014	C	6 591[25]	26.1	C	786[25]	3.1	23.0		...	...	76.7	83.1	...
2015	C	6 806[25]	26.7	C	834[25]	3.3	23.5		...	...	76.4	82.0	...
2016	C	7 270[25]	27.7	C	901[25]	3.4	24.3		...	...	...	...	...
2017	C	8 057[25]	29.4	C	964[25]	3.5	25.9		...	...	...	...	...
Guyana													
2014		...	...	+C	5 268	7.1	...		...	...	...	...	...
2015		...	...	+C	4 922	6.6	...		...	...	...	...	...
2016		...	...	+C	5 109	6.9	...		...	...	...	...	...
2017		...	...	+C	4 909	6.6	...		...	...	...	...	...
Paraguay													
2014	+U	116 592	...	+U	22 625	...	...	+U	468	...	...	...	...
2015	+U	132 241	...	+U	24 885	...	...		...	...	...	...	...
2016	+U	128 117	...	+U	27 243	...	...	+U	485	...	...	...	...
2017	+U	129 903	...	+U	26 404	...	...		...	...	...	...	...
2018	+U	123 187	...	+U	29 139	...	...	+U	490	...	71.4	77.2	...
Peru - Pérou													
2014	+U	492 008[51]	...	+U	96 460[51]	...	...	+U	4 243[51]	...	...	...	2.328[5]
2015	+U	529 029[51]	...	+U	96 240[51]	...	...	+U	3 852[51]	...	VI71.5	76.8	2.294[5]
2016	+U	522 269[51]	...	+U	97 241[51]	...	...	+U	3 756[51]	...	...	...	2.263[5]
2017	+U*	511 867[51]	...	+U*	121 024[51]	...	...	+U*	5 224[51]	...	...	...	2.233[5]
2018	+U*	494 034[52]	...		...	...	...		...	...	...	...	2.204[5]
Suriname													
2014	C	10 407	18.6	C	3 738	6.7	11.9	C	163	15.7	...	...	2.370
2015	C	10 148	17.9	C	3 663	6.5	11.4	C	149	14.7	III70.1	75.3	2.330
2016	C	9 910	17.2	C	3 591	6.2	11.0	C	170	17.2	...	...	2.230
2017	C	9 785	16.8	C	3 508	6.0	10.8	C	199	20.3	...	...	2.119

Continent, country or area and year Continent, pays ou zone et année	Code[a]	Live births Naissances vivantes Number Nombre	Crude birth rate Taux brut de natalité	Code[a]	Deaths Décès Number Nombre	Crude death rate Taux brut de mortalité	Rate of natural increase Taux d'accroissement naturel	Code[a]	Infant deaths Décès d'enfants de moins d'un an Number Nombre	Rate (per 1000 births) Taux (par 1000 naissances)	Life expectancy at birth Espérance de vie à la naissance Male[b] Masculin[b]	Female[b] Féminin[b]	Total fertility rate L'indice synthétique de fécondité
AMERICA, SOUTH - AMÉRIQUE DU SUD													
Uruguay													
2014	C	48 368	14.0	C	32 122	9.3	4.7	C	376	7.8	...	...	1.936
2015	C	48 926	14.1	C	32 967	9.5	4.6	C	367	7.5	...	...	...
2016	C	47 058	13.5	C	34 273	9.8	3.7	C	376	8.0	73.8	80.6	...
2017	C	43 036	12.3	C	33 173	9.5	2.8	C	280	6.5	...	...	...
Venezuela (Bolivarian Republic of) - Venezuela (République bolivarienne du)													
2014	U	597 773	...	C	159 239	5.3	...	C	8 396	...	...	...	2.410[53]
2015	U	600 875	...	C	163 712	5.4	...	C	9 276	...	...	...	...
2016	U	642 644	...	C	188 725	6.1	...	C	11 783	...	72.3[54]	78.4[54]	...
2017	U	579 349	...	C	190 236	6.1	...	C	11 671	...	72.4[54]	78.5[54]	...
2018		...	...		...	...	...		...	...	72.6[54]	78.7[54]	...
ASIA - ASIE													
Armenia - Arménie													
2014	C	43 031	14.3	C	27 714[55]	9.2	5.1	C	376[55]	8.7	...	...	1.700
2015	C	41 763	13.9	C	27 878[55]	9.3	4.6	C	370[55]	8.9	‖71.7	78.2	1.600
2016	C	40 592	13.6	C	28 226[55]	9.4	4.1	C	352[55]	8.7	‖71.6	78.3	...
2017	C	37 700	12.7	C	27 157[55]	9.1	3.5	C	311[55]	8.2	‖71.9	78.7	...
Azerbaijan - Azerbaïdjan													
2014	+C	170 503[55]	17.9	+C	55 648[55]	5.8	12.0	+C	1 655[55]	9.7	72.2	77.3	2.200
2015	+C	166 210[55]	17.2	+C	54 697[55]	5.7	11.6	+C	2 033[55]	12.2	72.7	77.6	2.100
2016	+C	159 464[55]	16.3	+C	56 648[55]	5.8	10.5	+C	1 666[55]	10.4	72.8	77.5	2.000
2017	+C	144 041[55]	14.6	+C	57 109[55]	5.8	8.8	+C	1 700[55]	11.8	73.1	77.8	...
Bahrain - Bahreïn													
2014	C	20 931[56]	15.9	C	2 805[56]	2.1	13.8	C	218[57]	10.4	...	...	2.108
2015	C	20 983[56]	15.3	C	2 787[56]	2.0	13.3	C	156[57]	7.4	ⅵ75.8	77.4	2.093
2016	C	20 714[56]	14.5	C	2 858[56]	2.0	12.5	C	109[57]	5.3	...	...	1.984
2017	C	20 581[56]	13.7	C	2 902[56]	1.9	11.8	C	133[57]	6.5	...	...	1.945
Bangladesh													
2014	U	2 963 520	...	U	815 360	...	...	U	88 906	...	...	...	2.110
2015	U	2 987 320	...	U	810 390	...	...	U	86 632	...	...	...	2.100
2016	U	3 006 960	...	U	820 080	...	...	U	84 195	...	70.3[58]	72.9[58]	2.100
2017	U	3 009 950	...	U	829 770	...	...	U	72 239	...	70.6	73.5	2.050
Bhutan - Bhoutan[3]													
2017	I	11 239	15.5	I	4 894	6.7	8.7		...	...	...	...	...
Brunei Darussalam - Brunéi Darussalam													
2014	+C	6 891	16.9	+C	1 470	3.6	13.3	+C	51	7.4	75.8	78.5	1.900
2015	+C	6 699	16.2	+C	1 547	3.8	12.5	+C	58	8.7	...	...	1.900
2016	+C	6 437	15.4	+C	1 632	3.9	11.5	+C	52	8.1	76.9	78.7	1.900
2017	+C	6 452	15.0	+C	1 696	3.9	11.1	+C	60	9.3	76.3	78.3	...
China - Chine[59]													
2014	I	16 870 000	12.4	I	9 770 000	7.2	5.2		...	...	...	...	...
2015	I	16 550 000	12.1	I	9 750 000	7.1	5.0		...	...	...	...	...
2016	I	17 860 000	13.0	I	9 770 000	7.1	5.9		...	...	...	...	...
2017	I	17 230 000	12.4	I	9 860 000	7.1	5.3		...	...	...	...	...
2018	I	15 230 000	10.9	I	9 930 000	7.1	3.8		...	...	...	...	...
China, Hong Kong SAR - Chine, Hong Kong RAS													
2014	C	62 305	8.6	C	45 087	6.2	2.4	C	103	1.7	81.2	86.9	1.235[60]
2015	C	59 878	8.2	C	46 108	6.3	1.9	C	85	1.4	81.4	87.3	1.196[60]
2016	C	60 856	8.3	C	46 905	6.4	1.9	C	109	1.8	81.3	87.3	1.205[60]

4. Vital statistics summary and life expectancy at birth: 2014 - 2018
Aperçu des statistiques de l'état civil et de l'espérance de vie à la naissance : 2014 - 2018 (continued - suite)

Continent, country or area and year / Continent, pays ou zone et année	Live births - Naissances vivantes			Deaths - Décès			Rate of natural increase - Taux d'accrois-sement naturel	Infant deaths - Décès d'enfants de moins d'un an			Life expectancy at birth - Espérance de vie à la naissance		Total fertility rate - L'indice synthétique de fécondité
	Code[a]	Number Nombre	Crude birth rate Taux brut de natalité	Code[a]	Number Nombre	Crude death rate Taux brut de mortalité		Code[a]	Number Nombre	Rate (per 1000 births) Taux (par 1000 naiss-ances)	Male[b] Masculin[b]	Female[b] Féminin[b]	
ASIA - ASIE													
China, Hong Kong SAR - Chine, Hong Kong RAS													
2017	C	56 548	7.7	C	46 829	6.3	1.3	C	97	1.7	81.9	87.6	1.125[60]
2018	C	53 716	7.2	C	47 400	6.4	0.8	C	80	1.5	82.3	87.7	1.072[60]
China, Macao SAR - Chine, Macao RAS													
2014	C	7 360	11.8	C	1 939	3.1	8.7	C	15	...	IV79.6	86.0	1.224
2015	C	7 055	11.0	C	2 002	3.1	7.9	C	11	...	IV79.9	86.3	1.142
2016	C	7 146	11.1	C	2 248	3.5	7.6	I	12[61]	...	IV80.2	86.4	...
2017	C	6 529	10.0	C	2 120	3.2	6.8		...	...	IV80.3	86.4	...
2018	C*	5 925	8.9	C*	2 069	3.1	5.8		...	...	IV80.6	86.6	...
Cyprus - Chypre[62]													
2014	C	9 258	10.9	C	5 424[63]	6.4	4.5	C	19	...	80.2	84.2	1.310
2015	C	9 170	10.8	C	5 859[63]	6.9	3.9	C	25	...	79.8	83.5	1.320
2016	C	9 455	11.1	C	5 471[63]	6.4	4.7	C	25	...	80.3	84.7	...
2017	C	9 229	10.7	C	5 996[63]	7.0	3.8		...	...	80.0	84.1	...
Georgia - Géorgie													
2014	C	60 635	16.3	C	49 087[55]	13.2	3.1	C	578[55]	9.5	...	...	2.200
2015	C	59 249	15.9	C	49 121[55]	13.2	2.7	C	507[55]	8.6	68.6	77.2	2.300
2016	C	56 569	15.2	C	50 771[55]	13.7	1.6	C	507[55]	9.0	68.2	77.1	2.200
2017	C	53 293	14.3	C	47 822[55]	12.8	1.5	C	512[55]	9.6	...	...	...
2018	C*	51 138	13.7	C*	46 524[55]	12.5	1.2		...	...	...	...	...
India - Inde[64]													
2014	I	...	21.0 [65]	I	...	6.7 [65]	...	I	...	39.0 [65]	...	...	2.300
2015	I	...	20.8 [65]	I	...	6.5 [65]	...	I	...	37.0 [65]	...	...	2.300
2016	I	...	20.4 [65]	I	...	6.4 [65]	...	I	...	34.0 [65]	V67.4	70.2	2.300
2017	I	...	20.2 [65]	I	...	6.3 [65]	...	I	...	33.0 [65]	...	...	2.200
Indonesia - Indonésie													
2015		...	...		...	...	...		...	...	...	...	2.170[66]
2016		...	...		...	...	...		...	...	...	...	2.156[66]
2017		...	...		...	...	...		...	...	...	...	2.142[66]
2018		...	...		...	...	...		...	...	69.3	73.2	2.128[66]
Iran (Islamic Republic of) - Iran (République islamique d')													
2014	+C	1 534 362[67]	19.7	+C	446 333[67]	5.7	14.0	+C	7 430[67]	4.8	...	...	...
2015	+C	1 570 219[67]	19.9	+C	374 827[67]	4.8	15.2		...	...	...	...	...
2016	+C	1 528 053[67]	19.1	+C	369 751[67]	4.6	14.5	+C	8 261[67]	5.4	72.5[67]	75.5[67]	2.113
2017	+C	1 487 913[67]	18.4	+C	376 678[67]	4.6	13.7	+C	8 304[67]	5.6	...	...	...
2018	+C*	1 388 249[67]	16.9	+C*	376 839[67]	4.6	12.3		...	...	...	...	...
Israel - Israël[68]													
2014	C	176 427	21.5	C	42 457[69]	5.2	16.3	C	548[69]	3.1	80.3	84.1	3.085
2015	C	178 723	21.3	C	44 507[69]	5.3	16.0	C	563[69]	3.2	80.1	84.1	3.093
2016	C	181 405	21.2	C	44 244[69]	5.2	16.0	C	570[69]	3.1	80.7	84.2	3.108
2017	C	183 648	21.1	C	44 867[69]	5.1	15.9	C	564[69]	3.1	80.6	84.6	3.112
2018	C*	184 135	20.7	C	44 434[69]	5.0	15.7	C	543[69]	2.9	...	...	...
Japan - Japon[70]													
2014	C	1 003 539[71]	7.9	C	1 273 004[71]	10.0	-2.1	C	2 080[71]	2.1	80.5	86.8	1.422[72]
2015	C	1 005 677[71]	7.9	C	1 290 444[71]	10.1	-2.2	C	1 916[71]	1.9	80.8	87.1	1.450[72]
2016	C	976 978[71]	7.7	C	1 307 748[71]	10.3	-2.6	C	1 928[71]	2.0	81.0	87.1	1.441[72]
2017	C	946 065[71]	7.5	C	1 340 397[71]	10.6	-3.1	C	1 761[71]	1.9	81.1	87.3	1.428[72]
2018	C*	918 397	7.3	C*	1 362 482	10.8	-3.5		...	...	...	...	...
Jordan - Jordanie[73]													
2014	C	188 902	21.5	U	25 782	...	...		...	...	...	...	...
2015	C	198 018	20.7	U	26 640	...	...		...	...	...	...	...
2016	C	197 789	20.2	U	27 608	...	...		...	...	72.8	74.2	3.380
2017	C	211 441	21.0	U	27 516	...	...		...	...	72.4	74.6	...

Continent, country or area and year / Continent, pays ou zone et année	Live births / Naissances vivantes Code[a]	Number Nombre	Crude birth rate Taux brut de natalité	Deaths / Décès Code[a]	Number Nombre	Crude death rate Taux brut de mortalité	Rate of natural increase Taux d'accrois-sement naturel	Infant deaths / Décès d'enfants de moins d'un an Code[a]	Number Nombre	Rate (per 1000 births) Taux (par 1000 naiss-ances)	Life expectancy at birth / Espérance de vie à la naissance Male[b] Masculin[b]	Female[b] Féminin[b]	Total fertility rate L'indice synthétique de fécondité
ASIA - ASIE													
Kazakhstan													
2014	C	399 309	23.1	U	132 287	...	...	C	3 907	9.8	66.9	75.8	2.730
2015	C	398 458	22.7	U	130 811	...	...	C	3 751	9.4	67.5	76.3	2.739
2016	C	400 694	22.5	U	131 231	...	...	C	3 438	8.6	68.0	76.6	2.775
2017	C	390 262	21.6	U	129 009	...	...	C	3 109	8.0	68.7	76.9	2.732
2018	C	397 799	21.8	U	130 448	...	...	C	3 184	8.0	68.9	77.2	2.837
Kuwait - Koweït													
2014	C	61 313	16.3	C	6 031	1.6	14.7	C	456	7.4	78.7	80.2	1.900
2015	C	59 271	14.9	C	6 481	1.6	13.3	C	456	7.7	79.1	80.0	...
2016	C	58 797	14.4	C	6 338	1.6	12.9	C	448	7.6	81.0	80.5	...
2017	C	59 172	14.7	C	6 679	1.7	13.1	C	413	7.0	79.7	82.7	...
Kyrgyzstan - Kirghizstan													
2014	C	161 813	27.7	C	35 564	6.1	21.6	C	3 268	20.2	66.5	74.5	3.186
2015	C	163 452	27.4	C	34 808	5.8	21.6	C	2 945	18.0	66.8	74.8	3.189
2016	C	158 160	26.0	C	33 475	5.5	20.5	C	2 621	16.6	67.0	75.1	3.059
2017	C	153 620	24.8	C	33 166	5.4	19.4	C	2 401	15.6	67.2	75.4	2.953
2018	C	171 149	27.1	C	32 989	5.2	21.8		...	...	67.4	75.6	3.280
Lao People's Democratic Republic - République démocratique populaire lao													
2014		...	...		...	...	...		...	...	...	...	3.060
2015		...	...		...	...	...		...	...	61.8[74]	65.2[74]	3.200
2016		...	...		...	...	...		...	...	63.0[74]	67.0[74]	...
2017		...	...		...	...	...		...	...	64.0[74]	67.0[74]	...
2018		...	...		...	...	...		...	...	64.0[74]	68.0[74]	...
Lebanon - Liban													
2014	C	104 872	...	C	27 020	...	...		...	...	...	...	...
Malaysia - Malaisie													
2014	C	528 612	17.2	C	150 318	4.9	12.3	C	3 543	6.7	...	...	2.072
2015	C	521 136	16.7	C	155 786	5.0	11.7	C	3 582	6.9	...	...	2.002
2016	C	508 203	16.1	C	162 201	5.1	10.9	C	3 390	6.7	72.6	77.2	1.918
2017	C	508 685	15.9	C	168 168	5.3	10.6	C	3 496	6.9	72.7	77.4	1.890
2018		...	...		...	...	...		...	...	72.7	77.6	...
Maldives													
2014	C	7 245[75]	21.2	C	1 143[75]	3.3	17.9	C	59[75]	8.1	73.1	74.8	2.460
2015	C	6 986[75]	20.3	C	1 130[75]	3.3	17.0	C	63[75]	9.0	73.1	74.6	...
2016	C	6 756[75]	19.3	C	1 226[75]	3.5	15.8	C	53[75]	7.8	73.0	74.7	...
2017	C	6 723[75]	18.8	C	1 241[75]	3.5	15.4	C	64[75]	9.5	...	...	...
Mongolia - Mongolie													
2014	+C	82 839	28.0	+C	16 521	5.6	22.4	+C	1 251	15.1	65.9	75.5	3.100
2015	+C	82 130	27.1	+C	17 620	5.8	21.3	+C	1 234	15.0	x65.3	74.8	3.100
2016	+C	79 920	25.9	+C	17 763	5.8	20.1	+C	1 315	16.5	...	...	3.000
2017	+C	75 321	23.9	+C	17 357	5.5	18.4	+C	1 009	13.4	65.9	75.4	2.800
2018	+C	78 444	24.5	+C	17 864	5.6	18.9	+C	1 037	13.2	66.1	75.8	3.000
Myanmar													
2014	+U	736 369[76]	...	+U	213 085[76]	...	...	+U	9 386[76]	...	61.0[77]	68.6[77]	2.505
2015	+U	739 152[76]	...	+U	225 526[76]	...	...	+U	9 849[76]	...	59.7[77]	69.3[77]	2.483
2016	+U	765 844[76]	...	+U	213 187[76]	...	...	+U	9 476[76]	...	60.3[77]	69.8[77]	2.459
Oman													
2014	U	82 981[78]	...	U	7 819[78]	...	...	U	645[78]	...	74.8	78.5	2.900
2015	U	86 286[78]	...	U	8 167[78]	...	...	U	818[78]	...	74.2[79]	78.8[79]	2.900
2016	U	88 346[78]	...	U	8 196[78]	...	...	U	816[78]	...	...	...	2.900
2017	C	90 371	19.8	U	8 861	...	...	C	850	9.4	74.8[79]	79.2[79]	2.896
2018	C	89 071	19.4	U	8 979	...	...	C	762	8.6	75.0[79]	79.1[79]	2.858
Pakistan													
2014		...	...		...	...	...		...	...	...	...	3.900[80]
2018		...	...		...	...	...		...	...	...	...	3.600[81]

4. Vital statistics summary and life expectancy at birth: 2014 - 2018
Aperçu des statistiques de l'état civil et de l'espérance de vie à la naissance : 2014 - 2018 (continued - suite)

Continent, country or area and year / Continent, pays ou zone et année	Live births / Naissances vivantes Code[a]	Number Nombre	Crude birth rate Taux brut de natalité	Deaths / Décès Code[a]	Number Nombre	Crude death rate Taux brut de mortalité	Rate of natural increase Taux d'accroissement naturel	Infant deaths / Décès d'enfants de moins d'un an Code[a]	Number Nombre	Rate (per 1000 births) Taux (par 1000 naissances)	Life expectancy at birth / Espérance de vie à la naissance Male[b] Masculin[b]	Female[b] Féminin[b]	Total fertility rate L'indice synthétique de fécondité
ASIA - ASIE													
Philippines													
2014	C	1 748 857	17.5	C	551 716	5.5	12.0	C	21 572	12.3	...	...	...
2015	C	1 744 767	17.2	C	560 605	5.5	11.7	C	20 750	11.9	...	...	...
2016	C	1 731 289	16.8	C	582 183	5.6	11.1	C	21 874	12.6	...	...	...
2017	C	1 700 618	16.2	C*	579 262	5.5	10.7		...	...	...	...	...
Qatar													
2014	C	25 443	11.5	C	2 366	1.1	10.4	C	168	6.6	...	...	2.000
2015	C	26 622	10.9	C	2 317	1.0	10.0	C	197	7.4	77.5	82.1	2.000
2016	C	26 816	10.2	C	2 347	0.9	9.3	C	161	6.0	78.9	82.3	1.850
2017	C	27 906	10.2	C	2 294	0.8	9.4	C	151	5.4	79.0	82.5	1.833
2018	C*	25 513	9.2	C*	2 320	0.8	8.4		...	...			
Republic of Korea - République de Corée													
2014	C	435 435[82]	8.6	C	267 692[83]	5.3	3.3	C	1 305[83]	3.0	78.6	85.0	1.205[83]
2015	C	438 420[82]	8.6	C	275 895[83]	5.4	3.2	C	1 190[83]	2.7	79.0	85.2	1.239[83]
2016	C	406 243[82]	7.9	C	280 827[83]	5.5	2.5	C	1 154[83]	2.8	79.3	85.4	1.172[83]
2017	C	357 771[82]	7.0	C	285 534[83]	5.6	1.4	C	1 000[83]	2.8	79.7	85.7	1.052[83]
Saudi Arabia - Arabie saoudite													
2014	I	514 325[84]	17.0		...	...	...		...	...	...	...	2.750[8]
2015	I	449 149[84]	14.5	I	69 206[85]	2.2	12.2		...	...	73.1[8]	75.7[8]	2.690[8]
2016	I	447 040[84]	14.1	I	58 097[85]	1.8	12.2	I	5 084[84]	11.4	73.5[86]	74.8[86]	2.360[84]
2017	I	488 130[87]	15.0	I	58 915[84]	1.8	13.2	I	6 608[87]	13.5	...	...	2.535[87]
2018		...	...		...	...	...		...	...	73.7[86]	76.4[86]	...
Singapore - Singapour													
2014	C	42 232	10.9	+C	19 393	5.0	5.9	+C	83	2.0	80.3[88]	84.8[88]	1.250[89]
2015	C	42 185	10.8	+C	19 862	5.1	5.7	+C	84	2.0	80.5[88]	85.1[88]	1.240[89]
2016	C	41 251	10.5	+C	20 017	5.1	5.4	+C	101	2.4	80.7[88]	85.1[88]	1.200[89]
2017	C	39 615	10.0	+C	20 905	5.3	4.7	+C	94	2.4	80.7[90]	85.2[90]	1.160[89]
2018		...	...		...	...	...		...	...	81.0[90]	85.4[90]	...
Sri Lanka													
2014	+C	349 744	16.8	+C	128 185	6.2	10.7	+C	2 662	7.6	...	...	...
2015	+C	336 097	16.0	+C*	131 614	6.3	9.8	+C*	2 845	8.5	...	...	...
2016	+C*	331 073	15.6	+C*	130 765	6.2	9.4		...	...	...	...	...
2017	+C*	326 052	15.2	+C*	139 822	6.5	8.7		...	...	...	...	...
2018	+C*	328 112	15.1	+C*	139 498	6.4	8.7		...	...	...	...	...
State of Palestine - État de Palestine													
2014	U	128 073[91]	...	U	13 390[91]	...	...	U	800[91]	...	71.8	74.7	...
2015	U	133 185[91]	...	U	12 075[91]	...	...	U	871[91]	...	72.0	75.0	...
2016	U	138 238[91]	...	U	12 202[91]	...	...	U	880[91]	...	72.1	75.2	...
2017	U	140 441[91]	...	U	11 778[91]	...	...	U	821[91]	...	72.8	75.1	...
Tajikistan - Tadjikistan													
2014	U	229 460[92]	...	U	32 879[55]	...	...	U	3 273[55]	...	71.6	75.4	2.980
2015	U	237 541[92]	...	U	33 563[55]	...	...	U	3 082[55]	...	...	...	3.064
2016	U	230 044[92]	...	U	34 134[55]	...	...	U	2 725[55]	...	71.9	75.7	2.930
2017	U	224 057[92]	...	U	32 027[55]	...	...	U	2 405[55]	...	73.0	76.9	2.830
Thailand - Thaïlande													
2014	+U	776 370	...	+U	435 624	...	...	+U	4 615	...	71.3	78.2	...
2015	+U	738 930	...	+U	445 964	...	...	+U	4 221	...	71.6	78.4	...
2016	+U	666 207	...	+U	469 085	...	...	+U	4 233	...	71.8	78.6	...
2017	+U	656 570	...	+U	458 010	...	...	+U	3 861	...	72.0	78.8	...
2018		...	...		...	...	...		...	...	72.2	78.9	...
Timor-Leste													
2014		...	...		...	...	...		...	...	...	...	5.526[5]
2015	I	36 202[93]	30.2	I	9 209[93]	7.7	22.5		...	...	...	...	4.290[5]
2016		...	...		...	...	...		...	...	...	...	4.090[5]
2017		...	...		...	...	...		...	...	...	...	3.900[5]
2018		...	...		...	...	...		...	...	66.3[5]	68.8[5]	3.703[5]

Continent, country or area and year / Continent, pays ou zone et année	Code[a]	Live births Naissances vivantes Number Nombre	Crude birth rate Taux brut de natalité	Code[a]	Deaths Décès Number Nombre	Crude death rate Taux brut de mortalité	Rate of natural increase Taux d'accroissement naturel	Code[a]	Infant deaths Décès d'enfants de moins d'un an Number Nombre	Rate (per 1000 births) Taux (par 1000 naissances)	Life expectancy Male[b] Masculin[b]	Life expectancy Female[b] Féminin[b]	Total fertility rate L'indice synthétique de fécondité
ASIA - ASIE													
Turkey - Turquie													
2014	C	1 349 467	17.4	C	391 091[94]	5.0	12.3	C	14 951[94]	11.1	75.3	80.7	2.182
2015	C	1 334 465	16.9	C	405 365[94]	5.1	11.8	C	13 666[94]	10.2	III75.3	80.7	2.151
2016	C	1 311 895	16.4	C	422 726[94]	5.3	11.1	C	13 006[94]	9.9	III75.3	80.7	2.105
2017	C	1 291 055	16.1	C	425 781[94]	5.3	10.8	C	11 849[94]	9.2	III75.3	80.8	...
2018	C*	1 248 847	15.4	C*	426 106[94]	5.2	10.1		...	...	...	...	...
United Arab Emirates - Émirats arabes unis													
2014	...	95 860[95]	...	...	8 265[95]	...	...	...	652[95]	...	...	...	...
2015	...	97 328[95]	...	...	8 755[95]	...	...	...	640[95]	...	...	...	...
2016	...	98 299[95]	...	...	8 988[95]	...	...	...	597[95]	...	...	...	...
2017	C	97 738	10.5	C	8 826	0.9	9.6	C	607	6.2	...	...	...
Uzbekistan - Ouzbékistan													
2014	+C	718 036	23.3	+C	149 761[55]	4.9	18.5	+C	7 688[55]	10.7	71.1	75.8	2.457
2015	+C	734 141	23.5	+C	152 035[55]	4.9	18.6	+C	8 320[55]	11.3	71.2	76.0	2.491
2016	+C	726 170	22.8	+C	154 791[55]	4.9	17.9	+C	7 764[55]	10.7	71.4	76.2	2.455
2017	+C	715 519	22.1	+C	160 723[55]	5.0	17.1	+C	8 235[55]	11.5	71.3	76.1	2.419
2018	+C*	768 520	23.5	+C*	154 913[55]	4.7	18.8		...	...	...	...	...
Viet Nam													
2014		...	...		...	...	...		...	...	70.6	76.0	2.090
2015		...	...		...	...	...		...	...	70.7	76.1	2.100
2016		...	...		...	...	...		...	...	70.8	76.1	2.090
2017		...	...		...	...	...		...	...	...	...	2.041
2018		...	...		...	...	...		...	...	70.9	76.2	2.050
Yemen - Yémen													
2014	U	476 570[96]	...	U	32 140[97]	...	...		...	...	...	...	...
2016	U	575 556[96]	...	U	25 927[97]	...	...		...	...	...	...	...
2017	U	645 833[96]	...	U	31 999[97]	...	...		...	...	...	...	...
EUROPE													
Åland Islands - Îles d'Åland													
2014	C	282	9.8	C	251	8.7	1.1	C	-	...	80.9	84.3	1.783
2015	C	275	9.5	C	285	9.8	-0.3	C	-	...	80.6	84.0	1.689
2016	C	293	10.1	C	297	10.2	-0.1	C	1	...	78.5	83.6	1.792
2017	C	279	9.5	C	235	8.0	1.5	C	-	...	81.2	85.9	1.684
2018	C*	280	9.4	C	272	9.2	0.3	C	-	...	...	...	...
Albania - Albanie													
2014	C	35 760	12.4	C	20 656	7.1	5.2	C	281	7.9	...	...	...
2015	C	32 715	11.4	C	22 418	7.8	3.6	C	233	7.1	...	...	...
2016	C	31 733	11.0	C	21 388	7.4	3.6	C	277	8.7	77.0	80.1	...
2017	C	30 869	10.7	C	22 232	7.7	3.0	C	248	8.0	77.1	80.0	...
2018	C	28 934	10.1	C	21 804	7.6	2.5		...	...	...	...	...
Andorra - Andorre													
2014	C	639	9.1	C	276	3.9	5.2	C	2	...	...	...	...
2015	C	659	9.3	C	282	4.0	5.3	C	-	...	...	...	...
2016	C	634	8.8	C	310	4.3	4.5		...	...	...	...	...
2017	C	588	8.0	C	323	4.4	3.6		...	...	...	...	...
2018	C	543	7.3	C	335	4.5	2.8		...	...	...	...	...
Austria - Autriche													
2014	C	81 722	9.6	C	78 252[98]	9.2	0.4	C	249	3.0	79.1	84.0	1.465
2015	C	84 381[99]	9.8	C	83 073[98]	9.6	0.2	C	259	3.1	78.6	83.6	1.494
2016	C	87 675[99]	10.0	C	80 669[98]	9.2	0.8	C	269	3.1	79.1	84.0	1.529
2017	C	87 633[99]	10.0	C	83 270[98]	9.5	0.5	C	256	2.9	79.3	83.9	...
2018	C*	85 535[99]	9.7	C	83 975[98]	9.5	0.2	C	231	2.7	...	...	...
Belarus - Bélarus													
2014	C	118 534	12.5	C	121 542	12.8	-0.3	C	409	3.5	67.8	78.6	1.696
2015	C	119 028	12.5	C	120 026	12.6	-0.1	C	352	3.0	68.6	78.9	...

4. Vital statistics summary and life expectancy at birth: 2014 - 2018
Aperçu des statistiques de l'état civil et de l'espérance de vie à la naissance : 2014 - 2018 (continued - suite)

Continent, country or area and year / Continent, pays ou zone et année	Live births — Naissances vivantes			Deaths — Décès			Rate of natural increase — Taux d'accrois-sement naturel	Infant deaths — Décès d'enfants de moins d'un an			Life expectancy at birth — Espérance de vie à la naissance		Total fertility rate — L'indice synthétique de fécondité
	Code[a]	Number Nombre	Crude birth rate Taux brut de natalité	Code[a]	Number Nombre	Crude death rate Taux brut de mortalité		Code[a]	Number Nombre	Rate (per 1000 births) Taux (par 1000 naiss-ances)	Male[b] Masculin[b]	Female[b] Féminin[b]	
EUROPE													
Belarus - Bélarus													
2016	C	117 779	12.4	C	119 379	12.6	-0.2	C	373	3.2	68.9	79.0	...
2017	C	102 556	10.8	C	119 311	12.6	-1.8	C	332	3.2	69.3	79.2	...
Belgium - Belgique													
2014	C	125 014[100]	11.1	C	104 755[100]	9.3	1.8	C	423[100]	3.4	78.6	83.5	...
2015	C	122 274[100]	10.8	C	110 541[100]	9.8	1.0	C	400[100]	3.3	78.5[101]	83.1[101]	...
2016	C	121 896[100]	10.8	C	108 097[100]	9.5	1.2	C	387[100]	3.2	...	...	...
2017	C	119 690[100]	10.5	C	109 666[100]	9.6	0.9	C	429[100]	3.6	...	...	...
2018	C*	118 319[100]	10.4	C	110 645[100]	9.7	0.7		...	...	79.2	83.7	...
Bosnia and Herzegovina - Bosnie-Herzégovine													
2014	C	29 247	8.3	C	34 824	9.9	-1.6	C	140	4.8	...	...	...
2015	C	28 906	8.2	C	37 070	10.5	-2.3	C	174	6.0	...	...	...
2016	C	29 276	8.3	C	35 530	10.1	-1.8	C	152	5.2	...	...	...
2017	C	29 158	8.3	C	36 336	10.4	-2.0	C	183	6.3	...	...	...
Bulgaria - Bulgarie													
2014	C	67 585	9.4	C	108 952	15.1	-5.7	C	517	7.6	71.1	78.0	1.523
2015	C	65 950	9.2	C	110 117	15.3	-6.2	C	434	6.6	III71.1	78.0	1.529
2016	C	64 984	9.1	C	107 580	15.1	-6.0	C	423	6.5	III71.2	78.2	1.542
2017	C	63 955	9.0	C	109 791	15.5	-6.5	C	408	6.4	III71.3	78.4	...
2018		...	...	C	108 526	15.4	...	C	358	...	...	...	...
Croatia - Croatie													
2014	C	39 566	9.3	C	50 839	12.0	-2.7	C	199	5.0	74.7	81.0	...
2015	C	37 503	8.9	C	54 205	12.9	-4.0	C	154	4.1	...	...	...
2016	C	37 537	9.0	C	51 542	12.3	-3.4	C	161	4.3	...	...	...
2017	C	36 556	8.9	C	53 477	13.0	-4.1	C	148	4.0	74.9	81.0	...
2018	C*	36 945	9.0	C*	52 706	12.8	-3.8		...	...	...	...	...
Czechia - Tchéquie													
2014	C	109 860	10.4	C	105 665	10.0	0.4	C	263	2.4	75.8	81.7	1.528
2015	C	110 764	10.5	C	111 173	10.5	0.0	C	272	2.5	75.8	81.4	1.570
2016	C	112 663	10.7	C	107 750	10.2	0.5	C	317	2.8	76.2	82.1	1.630
2017	C	114 405	10.8	C	111 443	10.5	0.3	C	304	2.7	76.0	81.8	...
2018	C*	114 036	10.7	C*	112 920	10.6	0.1		...	...	...	...	...
Denmark - Danemark[102]													
2014	C	56 870	10.1	C	51 340	9.1	1.0	C	229	4.0	78.5	82.7	1.691
2015	C	58 205	10.3	C	52 555	9.3	1.0	C	216	3.7	II78.6	82.5	1.714
2016	C	61 614	10.8	C	52 824	9.2	1.5	C	194	3.1	II78.8	82.8	1.785
2017	C	61 397	10.7	C	53 261	9.2	1.4	C	231	3.8	II79.0	82.9	...
2018		...	...	C	55 232	9.5	...	C	226		...	...	...
Estonia - Estonie													
2014	C	13 551	10.3	C	15 484	11.8	-1.5	C	36	2.7	72.3	81.5	1.540
2015	C	13 907	10.6	C	15 243	11.6	-1.0	C	35	2.5	73.1	81.8	1.580
2016	C	14 053	10.7	C	15 392	11.7	-1.0	C	33	2.3	73.2	81.9	1.600
2017	C	13 784	10.5	C	15 543	11.8	-1.3	C	32	2.3	73.7	82.3	...
2018	C*	14 270	10.8	C	15 751	11.9	-1.1		...	...	...	...	...
Faeroe Islands - Îles Féroé													
2014	C	636	13.1	C	394	8.1	5.0	C	4	...	...	...	2.563
2015	C	605	12.4	C	377	7.7	4.7	C	-	...	II78.3	84.5	2.427
2016	C	675	13.6	C	379	7.7	6.0	C	3	...	...	...	2.624
2017	C	656	13.1	C	447	8.9	4.2	C	6	...	II80.9	83.7	2.470
2018	C	684	13.4	C	392	7.7	5.7	C	-	...	II80.1	84.8	...
Finland - Finlande													
2014	C	56 950[103]	10.5	C	51 935[103]	9.6	0.9	C	124[103]	2.2	78.2[103]	83.9[103]	1.710
2015	C	55 197[103]	10.1	C	52 207[103]	9.6	0.5	C	97[103]	1.8	78.5[103]	84.1[103]	1.650
2016	C	52 521[103]	9.6	C	53 626[103]	9.8	-0.2	C	99[103]	1.9	78.4[103]	84.1[103]	1.570
2017	C	50 042[103]	9.1	C	53 487[103]	9.8	-0.6	C	102[103]	2.0	78.7[103]	84.2[103]	...
2018	C*	47 307	8.6	C	54 255[103]	9.8	-1.3	C	101[103]	2.1	...	...	...
France													
2014	C	806 101	12.6	C	545 021	8.5	4.1	C	2 598	3.2	III78.9[101]	85.1[101]	1.974[101]
2015	C	760 421	11.8	C	581 770	9.0	2.8	C	2 655	3.5	IV79.1[101]	85.1[101]	1.924[101]

Continent, country or area and year / Continent, pays ou zone et année	Code[a]	Live births / Naissances vivantes Number / Nombre	Crude birth rate Taux brut de natalité	Code[a]	Deaths / Décès Number / Nombre	Crude death rate Taux brut de mortalité	Rate of natural increase Taux d'accroissement naturel	Code[a]	Infant deaths / Décès d'enfants de moins d'un an Number / Nombre	Rate (per 1000 births) Taux (par 1000 naissances)	Life expectancy at birth / Espérance de vie à la naissance Male[b] Masculin[b]	Female[b] Féminin[b]	Total fertility rate L'indice synthétique de fécondité
EUROPE													
France													
2016	C	744 697	11.5	C	581 073	9.0	2.5	C	2 577	3.5	[III]79.2	85.3	1.894[101]
2017	C	730 242	11.3	C	593 606	9.2	2.1	C	2 639	3.6	...	...	...
2018	C	719 737	11.1	C*	595 500	9.2	1.9		...	...	...	...	...
Germany - Allemagne													
2014	C	714 927	8.8	C	868 356	10.7	-1.9	C	2 284	3.2	78.7	83.6	1.470
2015	C	737 575	9.0	C	925 200	11.3	-2.3	C	2 405	3.3	[III]78.2	83.1	1.500
2016	C	792 137	9.6	C	910 902	11.1	-1.4	C	2 700	3.4	...	...	...
2017	C	784 901	9.5	C	932 272	11.3	-1.8	C	2 571	3.3	78.7	83.4	...
2018	C*	787 523	9.5	C	954 874	11.5	-2.0	C	2 505	3.2	...	...	...
Gibraltar													
2014	+C	488[104]	14.7	+C	248[105]	7.5	7.2		...	...	...	...	...
2015	+C	492[104]	14.7	+C	235[105]	7.0	7.7		...	...	...	...	...
2016	+C	424[104]	12.5	+C	249[105]	7.3	5.1		...	...	...	...	...
Greece - Grèce													
2014	C	92 149	8.5	C	113 740	10.4	-2.0	C	346	3.8	78.5	83.5	...
2015	C	91 847	8.5	C	121 183	11.2	-2.7	C	364	4.0	78.1	83.2	...
2016	C	92 898	8.6	C	118 785	11.0	-2.4	C	387	4.2	78.4	83.4	...
2017	C	88 553	8.2	C	124 501	11.6	-3.3	C	306	3.5	78.8	83.9	...
2018	C	86 440	8.0	C	120 297	11.2	-3.2	C	300	3.5	...	...	...
Guernsey - Guernesey													
2014	C	628	10.1	C	526	8.4	1.6		...	...	...	...	...
2015	C	580	9.3	C	557	9.0	0.4		...	...	...	...	...
2016	C	595	9.6	C	536	8.6	0.9		...	...	...	...	...
2017	C	571	9.2	C	586	9.4	-0.2		...	...	...	...	...
2018	C	543	8.7	C	575	9.2	-0.5		...	...	...	...	...
Hungary - Hongrie													
2014	C	93 281[106]	9.5	C	126 294[107]	12.8	-3.3	C	418[108]	4.5	72.1	78.9	1.410
2015	C	92 135[106]	9.4	C	131 575[107]	13.4	-4.0	C	383[108]	4.2	72.1	78.6	1.440
2016	C	95 361[106]	9.7	C	127 098[107]	13.0	-3.2	C	368[108]	3.9	72.4	79.2	1.490
2017	C	94 646[106]	9.7	C	131 877[107]	13.5	-3.8	C	328[108]	3.5	72.4	79.0	1.490
2018	C*	89 522	9.2	C	131 045[107]	13.4	-4.2	C	304[108]	3.4	...	...	1.490
Iceland - Islande													
2014	C	4 375	13.4	C	2 049	6.3	7.1	C	9	...	[II]80.6	83.6	1.932
2015	C	4 129	12.5	C	2 178	6.6	5.9	C	9	...	[II]81.0	83.6	1.805
2016	C	4 034	12.0	C	2 309	6.9	5.1	C	3	...	[II]80.7	83.7	1.745
2017	C	4 071	11.9	C	2 238	6.5	5.3	C	11	...	[II]80.6	83.9	...
2018	C	4 228	12.1	C	2 254	6.5	5.7	C	7	...	...	...	...
Ireland - Irlande													
2014	+C	67 285	14.4	+C	29 188	6.3	8.2	+C	224	3.3	79.3[101]	83.5[101]	1.950
2015	+C	65 537	13.9	+C	30 064	6.4	7.5	+C	225	3.4	...	...	1.940
2016	+C	63 836	13.4	+C	30 390	6.4	7.0	+C	208	3.3	...	...	...
2017	+C	61 824	12.9	+C	30 317	6.3	6.6	+C	174	2.8	80.4	84.0	...
2018	+C*	61 016	12.6	+C*	31 116	6.4	6.2	+C	187	3.1	...	...	...
Isle of Man - Île de Man													
2014	+C	805	9.3	+C	787	9.1	0.2		...	...	...	...	...
2015	+C	785	9.0		...	...	...		...	...	...	...	...
2016	+C	758	8.9	+C	852	10.0	-1.1	I	2[20]	...	...	...	1.683
2017	+C	753	9.0	+C	837	10.0	-1.0		...	...	...	...	...
2018	+C	717	...	+C	903	...	...		...	...	...	...	...
Italy - Italie													
2014	C	502 596	8.3	C	598 364	9.8	-1.6	C	1 523	3.0	80.3	85.0	1.370
2015	C	485 780	8.0	C	647 571	10.7	-2.7	C	1 398	2.9	...	...	1.350
2016	C	473 438	7.8	C	615 261	10.1	-2.3	C	1 427	3.0	80.6	85.0	...
2017	C	458 151	7.6	C	649 061	10.7	-3.2	C	1 251	2.7	80.6	84.9	...
Jersey													
2014	+C	985[38]	9.8	+C	704	7.0	2.8		...	...	...	...	...
2015	+C	1 021[38]	9.9	+C	762	7.4	2.5		...	...	...	...	...
2016	+C	1 020[38]	9.8	+C	831	8.0	1.8		...	...	...	...	...

Continent, country or area and year / Continent, pays ou zone et année	Live births — Naissances vivantes			Deaths — Décès			Rate of natural increase Taux d'accroissement naturel	Infant deaths — Décès d'enfants de moins d'un an			Life expectancy at birth — Espérance de vie à la naissance		Total fertility rate L'indice synthétique de fécondité
	Code[a]	Number Nombre	Crude birth rate Taux brut de natalité	Code[a]	Number Nombre	Crude death rate Taux brut de mortalité		Code[a]	Number Nombre	Rate (per 1000 births) Taux (par 1000 naissances)	Male[b] Masculin[b]	Female[b] Féminin[b]	
EUROPE													
Jersey													
2017	+C	954[38]	9.0	+C	803	7.6	1.4		...	...	...	...	...
2018	+C	942[38]	8.8	+C	...	...	...		...	...	...	...	...
Latvia - Lettonie													
2014	C	21 746	10.9	C	28 466	14.3	-3.4	C	83	3.8	69.3	79.5	1.654
2015	C	21 979	11.1	C	28 478	14.4	-3.3	C	90	4.1	69.7	79.3	1.707
2016	C	21 968	11.2	C	28 580	14.6	-3.4	C	81	3.7	69.8	79.4	1.743
2017	C	20 828	10.7	C	28 757	14.8	-4.1	C	86	4.1	69.8	79.6	...
2018	C	19 314	10.0	C	28 820	14.9	-4.9		...	...	...	...	...
Liechtenstein													
2014	C	372	10.0	C	268	7.2	2.8	C	1	...	...	...	...
2015	C	325	8.7	C	252	6.7	1.9	C	2	...	...	...	...
2016	C	378	10.0	C	271	7.2	2.8	C	1	...	...	...	1.610
2017	C	338	8.9	C	249	6.6	2.3	C	-	...	...	...	...
Lithuania - Lituanie													
2014	C	30 369	10.4	C	40 252	13.7	-3.4	C	118	3.9	69.1	79.9	...
2015	C	31 475	10.8	C	41 776	14.4	-3.5	C	132	4.2	69.1	79.6	...
2016	C	30 623	10.7	C	41 106	14.3	-3.7	C	139	4.5	69.5	80.0	...
2017	C	28 696	10.1	C	40 142	14.2	-4.0	C	85	3.0	70.7	80.4	...
2018	C*	28 517	10.2	C	39 574	14.2	-4.0	C	96	3.4	...	...	...
Luxembourg													
2014	C	6 070	10.9	C	3 841	6.9	4.0	C	17	...	[III]79.3	84.0	...
2015	C	6 115	10.7	C	3 983	7.0	3.7	C	17	...	...	...	...
2016	C	6 050	10.4	C	3 967	6.8	3.6	C	23	...	[III]80.7	85.4	...
2017	C	6 174	10.4	C	4 263	7.1	3.2	C	20	...	[III]79.9	84.4	1.390
2018	C	6 274	10.4	C	4 318	7.2	3.2	C	27	...	...	...	1.380
Malta - Malte													
2014	C	4 191	9.6	C	3 270	7.5	2.1	C	21	...	79.8	84.3	1.380
2015	C	4 325	9.7	C	3 442	7.7	2.0	C	25	...	79.7	84.0	1.370
2016	C	4 476	9.8	C	3 342	7.3	2.5	C	33	7.4	80.6	84.4	1.370
2017	C	4 319	9.2	C	3 571	7.6	1.6	C	30	6.9	80.2	84.6	1.260
2018	C	4 444	9.3	C	3 688	7.8	1.6	C	25	...	...	...	1.230
Monaco													
2014	C	974[109]	26.4	C	524[110]	14.2	12.2		...	...	...	...	...
2015	C	1 067[109]	28.4	C	595[110]	15.8	12.6		...	...	...	...	...
2016	C	938[109]	24.6	C	503[111]	13.2	11.4		...	...	...	...	...
2017	C	958[109]	25.5	C	490[110]	13.0	12.5		...	...	...	...	...
2018	C	983[109]	25.7	C	528[110]	13.8	11.9		...	...	...	...	...
Montenegro - Monténégro													
2014	C	7 529	12.1	C	6 014	9.7	2.4	C	37	4.9	...	...	...
2015	C	7 386	11.9	C	6 329	10.2	1.7	C	16	...	...	...	...
2016	C	7 569	12.2	C	6 464	10.4	1.8	C	26	...	...	...	...
2017	C	7 432	11.9	C	6 523	10.5	1.5	C	10	...	...	...	...
2018	C	7 264	11.7	C	6 504	10.5	1.2	C	12	...	...	...	...
Netherlands - Pays-Bas													
2014	C	175 181[112]	10.4	C	139 223[112]	8.3	2.1	C	630[112]	3.6	80.0	83.5	...
2015	C	170 510[112]	10.1	C	147 134[112]	8.7	1.4	C	561[112]	3.3	...	...	...
2016	C	172 520[112]	10.1	C	148 997[112]	8.7	1.4	C	597[112]	3.5	...	...	...
2017	C	169 836[112]	9.9	C	150 214[112]	8.8	1.1	C	607[112]	3.6	80.2	83.4	...
2018	C	168 525[112]	9.8	C	153 363[112]	8.9	0.9		...	...	...	...	...
North Macedonia - Macédoine du Nord													
2014	C	23 596	11.4	C	19 718	9.5	1.9	C	233	9.9	73.5	77.4	1.500
2015	C	23 075	11.1	C	20 461	9.9	1.3	C	198	8.6	73.4	77.4	1.500
2016	C	23 002	11.1	C	20 417	9.9	1.2	C	273	11.9	73.7	77.5	1.500
2017	C	21 754	10.5	C	20 318	9.8	0.7	C	201	9.2	...	...	...
2018	C	21 333	10.3	C	19 727	9.5	0.8	C	122	5.7	...	...	...
Norway - Norvège													
2014	C	58 976	11.5	C	40 369[113]	7.9	3.6	C	139[113]	2.4	80.1	84.2	1.760
2015	C	58 815	11.3	C	40 676[113]	7.8	3.5	C	133[113]	2.3	...	...	1.730

Continent, country or area and year / Continent, pays ou zone et année	Co-de[a]	Live births / Naissances vivantes Number Nombre	Crude birth rate Taux brut de natalité	Co-de[a]	Deaths / Décès Number Nombre	Crude death rate Taux brut de mortalité	Rate of natural increase Taux d'accrois-sement naturel	Co-de[a]	Infant deaths / Décès d'enfants de moins d'un an Number Nombre	Rate (per 1000 births) Taux (par 1000 naiss-ances)	Life expectancy at birth / Espérance de vie à la naissance Male[b] Masculin[b]	Female[b] Féminin[b]	Total fertility rate L'indice synthétique de fécondité
EUROPE													
Norway - Norvège													
2016	C	58 890	11.3	C	40 726[113]	7.8	3.5	C	128[113]	2.2	...	...	1.710
2017	C	56 633	10.7	C	40 774[113]	7.7	3.0	C	130[113]	2.3	...	...	1.620
2018	C	55 120	10.4	C	40 840[113]	7.7	2.7	C	129[113]	2.3	81.0	84.5	1.560
Poland - Pologne													
2014	C	375 160	9.9	C	376 467	9.9	0.0	C	1 583	4.2	73.7	81.7	1.290
2015	C	369 308	9.7	C	394 921	10.4	-0.7	C	1 476	4.0	73.6	81.6	1.289
2016	C	382 257	10.1	C	388 009	10.2	-0.2	C	1 522	4.0	73.9	81.9	1.357
2017	C	401 982	10.6	C	402 852	10.6	0.0	C	1 604	4.0	74.0	81.8	...
2018	C	388 178	10.2	C	414 200	10.9	-0.7	C	1 494	3.8	73.9	81.7	...
Portugal													
2014	C	82 367[38]	7.9	C	104 843[114]	10.1	-2.2	C	236[114]	2.9	III77.2	83.0	1.230
2015	C	85 500[38]	8.3	C	108 539[114]	10.5	-2.2	C	250[114]	2.9	III77.4	83.2	1.300
2016	C	87 126[38]	8.4	C	110 573[114]	10.7	-2.3	C	282[114]	3.2	III77.6	83.3	1.360
2017	C	86 154[38]	8.4	C	109 758[114]	10.7	-2.3	C	229[114]	2.7	III77.7	83.4	...
2018	C	87 020[38]	8.5	C	113 000[114]	11.0	-2.5	C	...	...	77.8	83.4	...
Republic of Moldova - République de Moldova[115]													
2014	C	38 616	13.5	C	39 494	13.8	-0.3	C	372	9.6	67.5	75.4	1.280
2015	C	38 610	13.6	C	39 906	14.1	-0.5	C	375	9.7	67.5	75.5	1.300
2016	C	37 394	13.3	C	38 489	13.7	-0.4	C	353	9.4	68.1	76.2	1.280
2017	C	34 060	12.4	C	36 768	13.3	-1.0	C	330	9.7	69.4	77.0	1.190
2018	C	32 606	12.0	C	37 200	13.7	-1.7	C	326	10.0	...	...	1.166
Romania - Roumanie													
2014	C	198 740	10.0	C	254 965	12.8	-2.8	C	1 632	8.2	III72.0	78.9	...
2015	C	197 491	10.0	C	261 294	13.2	-3.2	C	1 500	7.6	III71.9	78.9	...
2016	C	200 009	10.1	C	257 215	13.1	-2.9	C	1 398	7.0	...	...	...
2017	C	202 151	10.3	C	261 402	13.3	-3.0	C	1 364	6.7	III72.3	79.2	...
2018	C*	186 450	9.5	C*	262 987	13.5	-3.9	...	...	...	...	...	...
San Marino - Saint-Marin													
2014	C	296	8.8	C	252	7.5	1.3	C	1	...	...	...	...
2015	C	269	8.0	C	235	6.9	1.0	C	-	...	...	...	...
2016	C	262	7.7	C	253	7.4	0.3	C	1	...	...	...	...
2017	C	228	6.6	C	278	8.1	-1.5	C	-	...	82.7	86.8	...
2018	C	235	6.8	C	244	7.1	-0.3	C	1	...	...	...	...
Serbia - Serbie[116]													
2014	+C	66 461	9.3	+C	101 247	14.2	-4.9	+C	381	5.7	72.6	77.7	1.465
2015	+C	65 657	9.3	+C	103 678	14.6	-5.4	+C	346	5.3	72.6	77.7	1.464
2016	+C	64 734	9.2	+C	100 834	14.3	-5.1	+C	348	5.4	72.7	77.8	1.460
2017	+C	64 894	9.2	+C	103 722	14.8	-5.5	+C	305	4.7	73.0	77.9	...
2018	+C*	63 543	9.1	+C*	103 091	14.7	-5.6	...	...	...	...	...	...
Slovakia - Slovaquie													
2014	C	55 033	10.2	C	51 346	9.5	0.7	C	318	5.8	73.2	80.0	1.367
2015	C	55 602	10.3	C	53 826	9.9	0.3	C	285	5.1	73.0	79.7	1.400
2016	C	57 557	10.6	C	52 351	9.6	1.0	C	311	5.4	73.7	80.4	...
2017	C	57 969	10.7	C	53 914	9.9	0.7	C	263	4.5	73.8	80.3	...
2018		...	...	C	54 293	10.0	...	C	288	...	73.7	80.4	...
Slovenia - Slovénie													
2014	C	21 165	10.3	C	18 886	9.2	1.1	C	39	1.8	78.0	83.7	1.580
2015	C	20 641	10.0	C	19 834	9.6	0.4	C	33	1.6	...	...	1.570
2016	C	20 345	9.9	C	19 689	9.5	0.3	C	41	2.0	II77.6	83.5	...
2017	C	20 241	9.8	C	20 509	9.9	-0.1	C	42	2.1	78.1	83.7	1.620
2018	C	19 585	9.5	C	20 485	9.9	-0.4	C	33	1.7	78.3	84.0	1.610
Spain - Espagne													
2014	C	426 076	9.2	C	393 734	8.5	0.7	C	1 202	2.8	80.4	86.2	1.320
2015	C	418 432	9.0	C	420 408	9.1	0.0	C	1 117	2.7	...	...	1.330
2016	C	408 734	8.8	C	408 231	8.8	0.0	C	1 097	2.7	80.3	85.8	1.330
2017	C	391 265	8.4	C	422 037	9.1	-0.7	C	1 064	2.7	80.4	85.7	...
2018	C*	367 374	7.9	C*	423 636	9.1	-1.2	...	...	...	...	...	...

4. Vital statistics summary and life expectancy at birth: 2014 - 2018
Aperçu des statistiques de l'état civil et de l'espérance de vie à la naissance : 2014 - 2018 (continued - suite)

Continent, country or area and year / Continent, pays ou zone et année	Code[a]	Live births - Naissances vivantes Number Nombre	Crude birth rate Taux brut de natalité	Code[a]	Deaths - Décès Number Nombre	Crude death rate Taux brut de mortalité	Rate of natural increase Taux d'accroissement naturel	Code[a]	Infant deaths - Décès d'enfants de moins d'un an Number Nombre	Rate (per 1000 births) Taux (par 1000 naissances)	Life expectancy at birth - Espérance de vie à la naissance Male[b] Masculin[b]	Female[b] Féminin[b]	Total fertility rate L'indice synthétique de fécondité
EUROPE													
Sweden - Suède													
2014	C	114 907	11.9	C	88 976	9.2	2.7	C	251	2.2	80.4	84.2	1.880
2015	C	114 870	11.7	C	90 907	9.3	2.4	C	282	2.5	...	...	1.850
2016	C	117 425	11.8	C	90 982	9.2	2.7	C	292	2.5	...	...	1.850
2017	C	115 416	11.5	C	91 972	9.1	2.3	C	278	2.4	80.8	84.1	...
2018	C*	115 832	11.4	C*	92 185	9.1	2.3		...	...	...	...	...
Switzerland - Suisse													
2014	C	85 287	10.4	C	63 938	7.8	2.6	C	331	3.9	II80.7	84.9	1.540
2015	C	86 559	10.5	C	67 606	8.2	2.3	C	340	3.9	II80.8	85.0	1.540
2016	C	87 883	10.5	C	64 964	7.8	2.7	C	316	3.6	II81.1	85.0	1.550
2017	C	87 381	10.3	C	66 971	7.9	2.4	C	310	3.5	II81.4	85.3	...
2018	C	87 851	10.4	C	67 088	7.9	2.4		...	...	81.7	85.4	...
Ukraine[117]													
2014	+C	465 882[118]	10.8	+C	632 296[119]	14.7	-3.9	+C	3 656[119]	7.8	...	...	...
2015	+C	411 781[118]	9.6	+C	594 796[119]	13.9	-4.3	+C	3 318[119]	8.1	...	...	...
2016	+C	397 037[118]	9.2	+C	583 631[119]	13.7	-4.4	+C	2 955[119]	7.4	66.7	76.5	...
2017	+C	363 987[118]	8.6	+C	574 123[119]	13.5	-4.9	+C	2 786[119]	7.7	67.0	76.8	...
2018	+C*	335 874[118]	7.9	+C*	587 665[119]	13.9	-6.0	+C	2 397[119]	7.1	...	...	...
United Kingdom of Great Britain and Northern Ireland - Royaume-Uni de Grande-Bretagne et d'Irlande du Nord[120]													
2014	C	775 908[121]	12.0	+C	568 840	8.8	3.2	+C	2 990	3.9	...	...	1.820
2015	C	776 746[121]	11.9	+C	601 272	9.2	2.7	+C	3 004	3.9	...	...	...
2016	C	774 386[121]	11.8	+C	595 655	9.1	2.7	+C	2 976	3.8	III79.2	82.9	...
2017	C	754 754[121]	11.4	+C	605 748	9.2	2.3	+C	2 947	3.9	III79.2	82.9	...
OCEANIA - OCÉANIE													
American Samoa - Samoas américaines													
2014	C	1 084	17.5	C	259	4.2	13.3	C	9	...	...	...	...
2015	C	1 096	18.0	C	314	5.2	12.8	C	11	...	...	...	...
2016	C	1 013	16.8	C	280	4.7	12.2	C	14	...	...	...	...
2017	C	1 001	16.6	C	310	5.1	11.5	C	14	...	...	...	...
Australia - Australie													
2014	C	299 697	12.8	C	153 580	6.5	6.2	C	1 012	3.4	III80.3	84.4	1.795
2015	C	305 377	12.8	C	159 052	6.7	6.1	C	991	3.2	III80.4	84.5	1.796
2016	C	311 104	12.9	C	158 504	6.6	6.3	C	970	3.1	III80.5	84.6	1.792
2017	C	309 142	12.6	C	160 909	6.5	6.0	C	1 019	3.3	III80.5	84.6	1.741
2018		...	...	C	158 493	6.3	...		...	...	...	...	...
Cook Islands - Îles Cook[122]													
2014	+C	204	11.0	+C	113	6.1	4.9	+C	-	...	...	...	...
2015	+C*	205	11.0	+C*	102	5.5	5.5	+C	-	...	...	...	...
Fiji - Fidji													
2014	+C	18 251	21.1	+C	5 801	6.7	14.4	+C	141	7.7	...	...	...
French Polynesia - Polynésie française													
2014	C	4 151	15.3	C	1 441	5.3	10.0	C	27	...	73.8	78.0	1.960
2015	C	3 888	14.2	C	1 405	5.1	9.1	C	24	...	74.4	78.1	...
2016	C	3 969	14.5	C	1 390	5.1	9.4	C	21	...	74.5	78.6	...
2017	C	3 820	13.9	C	1 581	5.7	8.1	C	29	...	74.0	77.7	...
Guam													
2014	C	3 396[123]	21.1	C	952[123]	5.9	15.2	C	28[123]	...	75.8	82.1	2.380
2015	C	3 367[123]	20.8	C	1 009[123]	6.2	14.6	C	47[123]	14.0	75.9	82.2	...
2016	C	3 433[123]	21.1	C	1 022[123]	6.3	14.8	C	37[123]	10.8	...	...	...

Continent, country or area and year / Continent, pays ou zone et année	Live births / Naissances vivantes			Deaths / Décès			Rate of natural increase / Taux d'accroissement naturel	Infant deaths / Décès d'enfants de moins d'un an			Life expectancy at birth / Espérance de vie à la naissance		Total fertility rate / L'indice synthétique de fécondité
	Code[a]	Number / Nombre	Crude birth rate / Taux brut de natalité	Code[a]	Number / Nombre	Crude death rate / Taux brut de mortalité		Code[a]	Number / Nombre	Rate (per 1000 births) / Taux (par 1000 naissances)	Male[b] / Masculin[b]	Female[b] / Féminin[b]	
OCEANIA - OCÉANIE													
Guam													
2017	C	3 292[123]	20.1	C	1 008[123]	6.2	13.9	C	28[123]	...	73.6	78.6	2.800
2018	C	3 175[123]	18.9	C	1 056[123]	6.3	12.6	C	37[123]	11.7	...	...	2.678
Nauru													
2015	C	360	31.9	C	90	8.0	23.9		...	...	...	...	...
2016	C	358	32.5	C	100	9.1	23.4		...	...	...	...	...
2017	C	304	...	C	94				...	...	...	...	...
New Caledonia - Nouvelle-Calédonie													
2014	C	4 370	16.3	C	1 406	5.2	11.1	C	23	...	...	...	...
2015	C	4 191	15.4	C	1 465	5.4	10.0	C	25	...	...	...	...
2016	C	4 271	15.6	C	1 569	5.7	9.8	C	16	...	...	...	...
2017	C	4 059	14.6	C	1 529	5.5	9.1	C	20	...	75.1	80.1	...
New Zealand - Nouvelle-Zélande													
2014	+C	57 243[124]	12.7	+C	31 065[124]	6.9	5.8	+C	327[124]	5.7	[III]79.6	83.3	1.924
2015	+C	61 038[124]	13.3	+C	31 608[124]	6.9	6.4	+C	249[124]	4.1	...	...	1.994
2016	+C	59 427[125]	12.7	+C	31 179[126]	6.6	6.0	+C	213[126]	3.6	...	...	1.875
2017	+C	59 610[125]	12.4	+C	33 339[126]	7.0	5.5	+C	228[126]	3.8	...	...	1.811
2018	+C	58 020[125]	11.9	+C	33 222[126]	6.8	5.1	+C	222[126]	3.8	...	...	1.710*
Niue - Nioué													
2014	C	20	...	C	5	...	...		...	...	...	...	...
2015	C	26	...	C	16	...	...		...	...	...	...	...
2016	C	27	...	C	7	...	...		...	...	...	...	...
Norfolk Island - Île Norfolk[127]													
2014		...	...	+C	13	...	...		...	...	...	...	...
2015		...	...	+C	11	...	...		...	...	...	...	...
Northern Mariana Islands - Îles Mariannes septentrionales													
2014	U	1 057[128]	...	U	220[128]	...	...	U	7[129]	...	...	...	...
Palau - Palaos													
2014	C	241	13.7	C	167	9.5	4.2	C	3	...	...	...	...
2015	C	242	13.7	C	136	7.7	6.0	C	4	...	...	...	...
2016	C	213	12.0	C	175	9.9	2.1	C	-	...	...	...	...
2017	C	221	12.4	C	183	10.3	2.1	C	5	...	...	...	...
2018	C	256	14.0	C	143	7.8	6.2	C	3	...	...	...	...
Samoa													
2014	+U	8 521[130]	...	+U	882[130]	...	...		...	...	...	...	4.400
2015	+U	8 206[130]	...	+U	1 112[130]	...	...		...	...	...	...	...
2016	+U	9 378[130]	...	+U	2 020[130]	...	...		...	...	...	...	...
2017	+U	9 277[130]	...	+U	1 037[130]	...	...		...	...	...	...	...
2018	+U	13 234[131]	...	+U	1 114[130]	...	...		...	...	...	...	...
Tuvalu													
2014	+U	261	...	+U	85	...	...		...	...	...	...	...
2015	+U	208	...	+U	66	...	...		...	...	...	...	...
2016	+U	210	...	+U	90	...	...		...	...	...	...	...
Vanuatu													
2014	+U	6 774	...	+U	614	...	...	+U	86	...	...	...	...

FOOTNOTES - NOTES

Italics: data from civil registers which are incomplete or of unknown completeness. - Italiques : données incomplètes ou dont le degré d'exactitude n'est pas connu, provenant des registres de l'état civil.

* Provisional. - Données provisoires.

[a] 'Code' indicates the source of data, as follows:
C - Civil registration, estimated over 90% complete
U - Civil registration, estimated less than 90% complete
| - Other source, estimated reliable
+ - Data tabulated by date of registration rather than occurence
... - Information not available

Le 'Code' indique la source des données, comme suit :
C - Registres de l'état civil considérés complets à 90 p. 100 au moins

U - Registres de l'état civil qui ne sont pas considérés complets à 90 p. 100 au moins

| - Autre source, considérée fiable

+ - Données exploitées selon la date de l'enregistrement et non la date de l'événement

... - Information non disponible

[b] A Roman number in front of the data for males specifies the range of the reference period of life expectancy for males and females presented on the row. For example, a reference year of 2005 and a range of V years means that the reference period for the life expectancy is 2001 - 2005. The absence of a Roman number means the reference period is one year and the reference period therefore coincides with the reference year. - Un chiffre romain devant la donnée relative aux hommes indique l'étendue de la période de référence concernant l'espérance de vie des hommes et des femmes présentée dans la ligne. Par exemple, une année de référence 2005 et une étendue de V signifie que la période de référence pour l'espérance de vie est 2001-2005. L'absence de chiffre romain signifie que la période de référence est d'un an et donc coïncide avec l'année de référence.

[1] Excluding live-born infants who died before their birth was registered. Data refer to Algerian population only. - Non compris les enfants nés vivants décédés avant l'enregistrement de leur naissance. Les données ne concernent que la population algérienne.

[2] Data refer to Algerian population only. - Les données ne concernent que la population algérienne.

[3] Data refer to the 12 months preceding the census in May. - Les données se rapportent aux 12 mois précédant le recensement de mai.

[4] Source: Vital Statistics Report. - Source: Vital Statistics Report.

[5] Data refer to national projections. - Les données se réfèrent aux projections nationales.

[6] Data refer only to events recorded in hospitals and health centres. - Ces données ne concernent que les faits d'état civil enregistrés dans les hôpitaux et les centres de santé uniquement.

[7] The calculation of the total fertility rate is based on the number of live births during the three year period prior to the survey. - L' indice synthétique de fécondité a été calculé sur bases des enfants nés sur la période des trois années précédant l'enquête.

[8] Projections based on the 2010 Population and Housing Census. - Projections fondées sur le recensement 2010 de la population et des logements.

[9] Source: Demographic and Health Survey (DHS) and Multiple Indicator Cluster Survey (MICS) 2014. - Source : Enquête Démographique et de Santé (EDS) et L'Enquête par Grappes à Indicateurs Multiples (MICS) 2014.

[10] Source: Demographic and Health Survey (ESDC-V) 2018. - Source : Enquête Démographique et de Santé (EDSC-V) 2018.

[11] Urban area here is composed of six communes: Brazzaville, Pointe-Noire, Dolisie, N'kayi, Mossendjo and Ouesso. The data on rural area are the result of the difference between total and urban area. - Le milieu urbain ici est constitué des six communes: Brazzaville, Pointe-Noire, Dolisie, N'kayi, Mossendjo et Ouesso. Les informations sur la zone rurale ont été déduites en celles de l'ensemble et du milieu urbain.

[12] The rate of registration of deaths is less than 20 per cent at the national level. - Le taux d'enregistrement des décès est inférieur à 20 p. 100 au niveau national.

[13] Data refer to projections based on the 2007 Population Census. - Les données se réfèrent aux projections basées sur le recensement de la population de 2007.

[14] Adjusted number of births in households referring to the 12 months preceding the census in March. - Le nombre ajusté de naissances vivantes des ménages ordinaires se rapportent aux 12 mois précédant le recensement de mars.

[15] Adjusted number of deaths in households referring to the 12 months preceding the census in March. - Le nombre ajusté de décès des ménages ordinaires se rapportent aux 12 mois précédant le recensement de mars.

[16] Adjusted number of infant deaths in households referring to the 12 months preceding the census in March. - Le nombre ajusté de décès d'enfants des ménages ordinaires se rapportent aux 12 mois précédant le recensement de mars.

[17] Based on underlying data of the Population and Housing Census 2014. - Données fondées sur le recensement de la population de 2014.

[18] Based on underlying data of the Population and Housing Census 2014 and Multiple Indicator Cluster Survey 2016. - Estimations basées sur le Récensement Général de la Population et de l'Habitation 2014 et Enquête par Grappes à Indicateurs Multiples 2016.

[19] Source: Kenya Demographic and Health Survey data. - Source: Données de l'enquête du Kenya sur la démographie et la santé.

[20] Data refer to the 12 months preceding the census in April. - Les données se rapportent aux douze mois précédant le recensement d'avril.

[21] Data refer to projections based on the 1993 Population Census. - Les données se réfèrent aux projections basées sur le recensement de la population de 1993.

[22] Data refer to the 12 months preceding the census in September. - Les données se rapportent aux 12 mois précédant le recensement de septembre.

[23] Excludes the islands of St. Brandon and Agalega. - Non compris les îles St. Brandon et Agalega.

[24] Source: Ministry of Health, National Directorate of Planning and Cooperation. - Source : Ministère de la santé, Direction nationale de la planification et de la coopération.

[25] Excluding live-born infants who died before their birth was registered. - Non compris les enfants nés vivants décédés avant l'enregistrement de leur naissance.

[26] Data refer to Saint Helenian resident population. - Pour la population résidante de Sainte-Hélène.

[27] Data refer to the 12 months preceding the census in December. - Les données se rapportent aux 12 mois précédant le recensement de décembre.

[28] Provisional data. Based on the results of the 2014 Population Census. - Données provisoires. D'après les résultats du recensement de la population de 2014.

[29] Source: Demographic and Health Survey. - Source : Demographic and Health Survey (enquête démographique et sanitaire).

[30] Excluding visitors. - Ne comprend pas les visiteurs.

[31] Bermuda is 100 per cent urban. Excluding non-residents and foreign service personnel and their dependants. - 100 pour cent de la population des Bermudes est urbaine. À l'exclusion des non-résidents et du personnel diplomatique et de leurs charges de famille.

[32] Bermuda is 100 per cent urban. - 100 pour cent de la population des Bermudes est urbaine.

[33] Including Canadian residents temporarily in the United States, but excluding United States residents temporarily in Canada. - Y compris les résidents canadiens se trouvant temporairement aux Etats-Unis, mais ne comprenant pas les résidents des Etats-Unis se trouvant temporairement au Canada.

[34] Including resident deaths outside of the islands but buried in the islands. - Y compris les décès de résidents hors des îles mais inhumés dans les îles.

[35] Definition of urban and rural distribution changed from the year 2014. - La définition de la répartition urbaine et rurale a changé depuis 2014.

[36] Excluding children born in the country of non-resident mothers. - Exceptés les enfants nés dans le pays des mères non-résidentes.

[37] Excluding infant deaths to mothers living abroad. - Exception faite des décès d'enfants en bas âge survenus lorsque la mère résidait à l'étranger.

[38] Data refer to births to resident mothers. - Ces données concernent les enfants nés de mères résidentes.

[39] Data refer to resident population only. - Pour la population résidante seulement.

[40] Excluding Indian jungle population. - Non compris les Indiens de la jungle.

[41] Excluding deaths of persons living abroad. - Exception faite des personnes décédées à l'étranger.

[42] Data refer to the 12 months from 30 June 2015 to 30 June 2016. - Les données font référence aux douze mois de 30 juin 2015 à 30 juin 2016.

[43] Data refer to the 12 months from 30 June 2016 to 30 June 2017. - Les données font référence aux douze mois de 30 juin 2016 à 30 juin 2017.

[44] Including births abroad and births of unknown residence of mother. - Y compris les naissances à l'étranger et les naissances pour lesquelles le lieu de résidence de la mère est inconnu.

[45] Including deaths abroad and deaths of unknown place of residence. - Y compris décès à l'étranger et décès dont le lieu de résidence n'est pas connu.

[46] Including deaths abroad and deaths of unknown residence of mother. - Y compris décès à l'étranger et décès de nourrissons nés de mères dont le lieu de résidence n'est pas connu.

[47] Projected value based on the results of 2000 and 2010 censuses, statistics from civil registration and reporting of live births in the ministry of health system. - Projection basée sur les résultats des recensements de 2000 et 2010, des statistiques d'état civil et les registres des naissances vivantes du Ministère de la santé.

[48] Estimate for 2015 – 2020. - Estimation pour la période 2015-2020.

[49] Excludes nomadic Indian tribes. - Non compris les tribus d'Indiens nomades.

[50] Data based on the 2010 Population Census. - Les données sont fondées sur le recensement de la population de 2010.

[51] Source: Reports of the Ministry of Health. - Source : Rapports du Ministère de la Santé.

[52] Data extracted from online system representing only 86.8 per cent of estimated births. - Données extraites du système en ligne, qui ne représentent que 86,8 % du nombre total estimé de naissances.

[53] Indicators based on projected or estimated fertility from the 2001 Population Census. - Les indicateurs sont fondés sur la fécondité projetée ou estimée à partir du recensement de population de 2001.

54 Based on the results of the 2011 Population Census. - Basé sur les résultats du recencement de la population de 2011.

55 Excluding infants born alive of less than 28 weeks' gestation, of less than 1 000 g in weight and 35 cm in length, who die within seven days of birth. - Non compris les enfants nés vivants après moins de 28 semaines de gestations, pesant moins de 1 000 g, mesurant moins de 35 cm et décédés dans les sept jours qui ont suivi leur naissance.

56 Sources: Births and Deaths National Registration System database, and medical records of government hospitals. - Les sources: Les bases de données des << Births and Deaths National Registration System >> et les dossiers médicaux des hôpitaux du gouvernement.

57 Deaths include deaths among some visitors. Sources: Births and Deaths National Registration System database, and medical records of government hospitals. - Les décès comprennent des décès parmi certains visiteurs. Les sources: Les bases de données des << Births and Deaths National Registration System >> et les dossiers médicaux des hôpitaux du gouvernement.

58 Source: Sample vital registration system of Bangladesh - Source : << Sample Vital Registration System >> du Bangladesh.

59 For statistical purposes, the data for China do not include those for the Hong Kong Special Administrative Region (Hong Kong SAR), Macao Special Administrative Region (Macao SAR) and Taiwan province of China. Data have been estimated on the basis of the annual National Sample Survey on Population Changes. - Pour la présentation des statistiques, les données pour la Chine ne comprennent pas la Région Administrative Spéciale de Hong Kong (Hong Kong RAS), la Région Administrative Spéciale de Macao (Macao RAS) et Taïwan province de Chine. Les données ont été estimées sur la base de l'enquête annuelle "National Sample Survey on Population Changes".

60 The fertility rates have been compiled using a population denominator which has excluded female foreign domestic helpers. - Les taux de fécondité ont été compilés pour une population (en dénominateur) ne comprenant pas les domestiques étrangères.

61 Data refer to the 12 months preceding the census in August. - Les données se rapportent aux 12 mois précédant le recensement d'août.

62 Data refer to government controlled areas. - Les données se rapportent aux zones contrôlées par le Gouvernement.

63 Data refer to deaths of residents only. - Les données renvoient aux décès de résidents uniquement.

64 Includes data for the Indian-held part of Jammu and Kashmir, the final status of which has not yet been determined. - Y compris les données pour la partie du Jammu et du Cachemire occupée par l'Inde dont le statut définitif n'a pas encore été déterminé.

65 Rates were obtained by the Sample Registration System of India, which is a large demographic survey. - Les taux ont été obtenus par le Système de l'enregistrement par échantillon de l'Inde qui est une large enquête démographique.

66 Data are based on the publication: "Indonesia Population Projection 2015-2045". - Les données sont basées sur la publication : << Indonesia Population Projection 2015-2045 >>

67 Data refer to the Iranian Year which begins on 21 March and ends on 20 March of the following year. - Les données concernent l'année iranienne, qui commence le 21 mars et se termine le 20 mars de l'année suivante.

68 Includes data for East Jerusalem and Israeli residents in certain other territories under occupation by Israeli military forces since June 1967. - Y compris les données pour Jérusalem-Est et les résidents israéliens dans certains autres territoires occupés depuis 1967 par les forces armées israéliennes.

69 Including deaths abroad of Israeli residents who were out of the country for less than a year. - Y compris les décès à l'étranger de résidents israéliens qui ont quitté le pays depuis moins d'un an.

70 Data refer to Japanese nationals in Japan only. - Les données se raportent aux nationaux japonais au Japon seulement.

71 The total number may include 'Unknown residence', but the categories urban and rural do not. - Le nombre total peut inclure les personnes dont la résidence n'est pas connue, à l'inverse des catégories de population urbaine et rurale.

72 Total fertility rate computed as the sum of the age-specific fertility rates from age 15 to 49 years old. - Le taux de fécondité cumulé est calculé comme somme des taux de fécondité par âge de 15 à 49 ans.

73 Excluding data for Jordanian territory under occupation since June 1967 by Israeli military forces. Excluding foreigners, including registered Palestinian refugees. - Non compris les données pour le territoire jordanien occupé depuis juin 1967 par les forces armées israéliennes. Non compris les étrangers, mais y compris les réfugiés de Palestine enregistrés.

74 Based on underlying data of the 2015 census. - Données fondées sur celles extraites du recensement de 2015.

75 Data do not include foreigners. - Les données sur les etrangers ne sont pas inclus.

76 Data are from Vital Registration System (VRS). - Les données proviennent du système d'enregistrement des faits d'état civil.

77 Based on Vital Registration System (VRS). - Système d'enregistrement des faits d'état civil.

78 Data from Births and Deaths Notification System (Ministry of Health and all health care providers). - Les données proviennent du système de notification des naissances et des décès (Ministère de la santé et tous prestataires de soins de santé).

79 Data refer to Omani citizen only. - Les données concernent les citoyens d'Oman uniquement.

80 Based on the results of the Pakistan Social and Living Standards Measurement survey (PSLM). - D'après les résultats de l'étude sur la mesure des normes sociales et des niveaux de vie au Pakistan.

81 Based on the results of the Pakistan Demographic and Health Survey (PDHS). - D'après les résultats de l'étude sur la santé et la démographie du Pakistan.

82 Data refer to residence of child. Excluding alien armed forces, civilian aliens employed by armed forces, and foreign diplomatic personnel and their dependants. - Les données correspondent à la résidence de l'enfant. Non compris les militaires étrangers, les civils étrangers employés par les forces armées ni le personnel diplomatique étranger et les membres de leur famille les accompagnant.

83 Excluding alien armed forces, civilian aliens employed by armed forces, and foreign diplomatic personnel and their dependants. - Non compris les militaires étrangers, les civils étrangers employés par les forces armées ni le personnel diplomatique étranger et les membres de leur famille les accompagnant.

84 Survey based estimates. Data refer to Saudi Arabian nationals only. - Estimations basées sur des enquêtes. Les données ne concernent que les ressortissants saoudiens.

85 Data refer to Saudi Arabian nationals only. Based on 2010 population census and 2016 demographic survey. - Les données ne concernent que les ressortissants saoudiens. D'après le recensement de la population de 2010 et l'enquête démographique de 2016.

86 Data refer to Saudi Arabian nationals only. - Les données ne concernent que les ressortissants saoudiens.

87 Survey based estimates. - Estimations basées sur des enquêtes.

88 Data refer to resident population which comprises Singapore citizens and permanent residents. - Les données se rapportent à la population résidente composé des citoyens de Singapour et des résidents permanents.

89 Data refer to resident total fertility rate. - Les données se rapportent aux indices synthétique de fécondité de la population résidante.

90 Data refer to resident population which comprises Singapore citizens and permanent residents. Provisional data. - Les données se rapportent à la population résidente composé des citoyens de Singapour et des résidents permanents. Données provisoires.

91 Source: Palestinian Central Bureau of Statistics, Population Register, updated version 2018. Data exclude Jerusalem ID holders. - Source: Bureau central de statistique palestinien, registre de la population, version actualisée jusqu'au 2018. Les données ne tiennent pas compte des détenteurs de carte d'identité de Jérusalem.

92 Data have been adjusted for under-registration. Excluding infants born alive of less than 28 weeks' gestation, of less than 1 000 g in weight and 35 cm in length, who die within seven days of birth. - Y compris un ajustement pour sous-enregistrement. Non compris les enfants nés vivants après moins de 28 semaines de gestations, pesant moins de 1 000 g, mesurant moins de 35 cm et décédés dans les sept jours qui ont suivi leur naissance.

93 Data refer to the 12 months preceding the census in July. - Les données se rapportent aux 12 mois précédant le recensement de juillet.

94 Data from MERNIS (Central Population Administrative System). - Données de MERNIS (Système central de données démographiques).

95 The registration of births and deaths is conducted by the Ministry of Health. An estimate of completeness is not provided. - L'enregistrement des naissances et des décès est mené par le Ministère de la Santé. Le degré estimatif de complétude n'est pas fourni.

96 Including Non-Yemeni births. - Y compris les naissances non-yéménites.

97 Including Non-Yemeni deaths. - Y compris les décès non-yéménites.

98 Including deaths of nationals abroad. - Y compris les décès des nationaux survenus à l'étranger.

99 Including births occurring abroad of mothers with residence in Austria. - Y compris les naissances survenues à l'étranger des mères avec résidence en Autriche.

100 Including armed forces stationed outside the country, but excluding alien armed forces stationed in the area. - Y compris les militaires nationaux hors du pays, mais non compris les militaires étrangers en garnison sur le territoire.

101 Provisional data. - Données provisoires.

102 Excluding Faeroe Islands and Greenland shown separately, if available. - Non compris les Îles Féroé et le Groenland, qui font l'objet de rubriques distinctes, si disponible.

103 Excluding Åland Islands. - Non compris les Îles d'Åland.

[104] Including live births by military personnel and their dependants. - Y compris les naissances vivantes parmi les membres du personnel militaire et leurs personnes à charge.

[105] Excluding armed forces. - Non compris les militaires en garnison.

[106] Data include the live births of women with unknown residence and homeless. Data include the live births of women with Hungarian usual residence regardless of whether the live birth occurred in Hungary or in a foreign country, and do not include the live births of women with foreign country usual residence. - Les données incluent les enfants nés vivants de femmes dont la résidence n'est pas connue et de femmes sans domicile fixe. Les données concernent les enfants nés vivants de femmes dont la résidence habituelle est en Hongrie, que la naissance vivante ait eu lieu en Hongrie ou dans un pays étranger, et ne comprennent pas les enfants nés vivants de femmes dont la résidence habituelle est dans un pays étranger.

[107] Data include the deceased persons with Hungarian usual residence regardless of whether the death occurred in Hungary or in a foreign country, and do not include the deceased persons with foreign country usual residence. - Les données comprennent tous les décès survenus alors que leur résidence habituelle était en Hongrie, que le décès ait eu lieu en Hongrie ou dans un pays étranger, et ne comprennent pas les décès des personnes dont la résidence habituelle était dans un pays étranger.

[108] Data include the deceased infants with Hungarian usual residence regardless of whether the death occurred in Hungary or in a foreign country, and do not include the deceased infants with foreign country usual residence. - Les données comprennent les nourrissons décédés alors que leur résidence habituelle était en Hongrie, que le décès ait eu lieu en Hongrie ou dans un pays étranger, et ne comprennent pas les nourrissons décédés dont la residence habituelle était dans un pays étranger.

[109] Source: City Hall, Civil Status Registry Office, resident and non-resident births. - Source : La mairie, Bureau de l'État Civil, toutes les naissances.

[110] Source: City Hall, Civil Status Registry Office, resident and non-resident deaths. - Source : La mairie, Bureau de l'État Civil, toutes les décès.

[111] Source: City Hall, Civil Status Registry Office, resident and non-resident deaths. Including still births. - Source : La mairie, Bureau de l'État Civil, toutes les décès. Les données comprennent les mortinaissances.

[112] Including residents outside the country if listed in a Netherlands population register. - Englobe les résidents se trouvant à l'étranger à condition qu'ils soient inscrits sur le registre de population des Pays-Bas.

[113] Including residents temporarily outside the country. - Y compris les résidents se trouvant temporairement hors du pays.

[114] Data refer to usually resident population. - Les données concernent la population habituellement résidente.

[115] Excluding Transnistria and the municipality of Bender. - Les données ne tiennent pas compte de l'information sur la Transnistria et la municipalité de Bender.

[116] Excludes data for Kosovo and Metohia. - Sans les données pour le Kosovo et Metohie.

[117] The Government of Ukraine has informed the United Nations that it is not in a position to provide statistical data concerning the Autonomous Republic of Crimea and the city of Sevastopol. - Le gouvernement Ukrainien a informé l'ONU qu'il n'est pas en mesure de fournir des données statistiques concernant la République autonome de Crimée et la ville de Sébastopol.

[118] Data refer to births with weight 500g and more (if weight is unknown - with length 25 centimeters and more, or with gestation during 22 weeks or more). - Données concernant les nouveau-nés de 500 grammes ou plus (si le poids est inconnu – de 25 centimètres de long ou plus, ou après une grossesse de 22 semaines ou plus).

[119] Data includes deaths resulting from births with weight 500 g and more (if weight is unknown - with length 25 cm and more, or with gestation during 22 weeks or more). - Y compris les décès de nouveau-nés de 500 g ou plus (si le poids est inconnu – de 25 cm de long ou plus, ou après une grossesse de 22 semaines ou plus).

[120] Excluding Channel Islands (Guernsey and Jersey) and Isle of Man, shown separately, if available. - Non compris les îles Anglo-Normandes (Guernesey et Jersey) et l'île de Man, qui font l'objet de rubriques distinctes, si disponible.

[121] Data tabulated by date of occurrence for England and Wales, and by date of registration for Northern Ireland and Scotland. - Données exploitées selon la date de l'événement pour l'Angleterre et le pays de Galles, et selon la date de l'enregistrement pour l'Irlande du Nord et l'Ecosse.

[122] Excluding Niue, shown separately, which is part of Cook Islands, but because of remoteness is administered separately. - Non compris Nioué, qui fait l'objet d'une rubrique distincte et qui fait partie des îles Cook, mais qui, en raison de son éloignement, est administrée séparément.

[123] Including United States military personnel, their dependants and contract employees. - Y compris les militaires des Etats-Unis, les membres de leur famille les accompagnant et les agents contractuels des Etats-Unis.

[124] Random rounding to base 3 is applied in this table as a confidentiality measure. - Les chiffres sont arrondis à la base 3 de manière aléatoire, pour des raisons de confidentialité.

[125] Random rounding to base 3 is applied in this table as a confidentiality measure. Data refers to births registered in the country to mothers resident in the country. - Les chiffres sont arrondis à la base 3 de manière aléatoire, pour des raisons de confidentialité. Les données se rapportent aux naissances enregistrées dans le pays pour lesquelles la mère réside dans le pays.

[126] Random rounding to base 3 is applied in this table as a confidentiality measure. Data refer to deaths of residents only. - Les chiffres sont arrondis à la base 3 de manière aléatoire, pour des raisons de confidentialité. Les données renvoient aux décès de résidents uniquement.

[127] Data cover the period from 1 July of the previous year to 30 June of the present year. - Pour la période allant du 1er juillet de l'année précédente au 30 juin de l'année en cours.

[128] Source: Commonwealth Health Center - Vital Statistics Office - Source : Centre de Santé du Commonwealth - Bureau des statistiques d'État civil

[129] Source: U.S. National Center for Health Statistics, National Vital Statistics Reports (NVSR). - Source : US National Center for Health Statistics, National Vital Statistics Reports (NVSR).

[130] Source: Births, Deaths, and Marriages Registration Division, Samoa Bureau of Statistics. - Source : Division de l'enregistrement des naissances, des décès et des mariages du Bureau de statistique du Samoa.

[131] Source: Births, Deaths, and Marriages Registration Division, Samoa Bureau of Statistics. The huge increase in 2018 is due to late registrations of all unregistered persons regardless of their age conducted mid-February to June. - Source : Division de l'enregistrement des naissances, des décès et des mariages du Bureau de statistique du Samoa. La forte augmentation constatée en 2018 s'explique par l'organisation, de la mi-février au mois de juin, d'une campagne de déclaration tardive pour toutes les personnes qui n'étaient pas encore déclarées, quel que soit leur âge.

Table 5 - *Demographic Yearbook 2018*

Table 5 presents national estimates of mid-year population for all available years between 2009 and 2018.

Description of variables: Mid-year estimates of the total population are those provided by national statistical offices. They refer to the *de facto* or *de jure* population on 1 July of the reference year. Exceptions to this are footnoted accordingly. The data are presented in thousands, rounded by the Statistics Division of the United Nations Department of Economic and Social Affairs.

For some countries or areas the figures presented in this table and the figures used to calculate rates in subsequent tables are not the same, as these countries have provided a reference population for vital events that is different than the total population.

Unless otherwise indicated, all estimates relate to the population within present geographical boundaries. Major exceptions to this principle are explained in footnotes.

Reliability of data: Reliable mid-year population estimates are those that are based on a complete census (or on a sample survey) and have been adjusted on a basis of a continuous population register or on the balance of births, deaths and migration. Reliable mid-year estimates appear in roman type. Mid-year estimates that are not calculated on this basis are considered less reliable and are shown in *italics*.

Limitations: Statistics on estimates of the mid-year total population are subject to the same qualifications as have been set forth for population statistics in general in section 3 of the Technical Notes.

International comparability of mid-year population estimates is also affected by the fact that some of these estimates refer to the *de jure*, and not the *de facto*, population. These are indicated in the column titled "Code". The difference between the *de facto* and the *de jure* population is discussed in section 3.1.1 of the Technical Notes.

Earlier data: Estimates of mid-year population have been shown in previous issues of the *Demographic Yearbook*. Information on the years and specific topics covered is presented in the Historical Index.

Tableau 5 – *Annuaire démographique 2018*

Le tableau 5 présente des estimations nationales de la population en milieu d'année pour le plus grand nombre possible d'années entre 2009 et 2018.

Description des variables : les estimations de la population totale en milieu d'année sont celles qui ont été communiquées par les services nationaux de statistique. Elles correspondent à la population de fait ou se réfèrent à la population de droit, au 1er juillet de l'année de référence. Lorsque la date est différente, cela est signalé par une note. Sauf indication contraire, tous les chiffres sont exprimés en milliers. Les données ont été arrondies par la Division de statistique du Département des affaires économiques et sociales de l'Organisation des Nations Unies.

Pour certains pays ou territoires, les données présentées dans ce tableau sont différentes des données utilisées pour calculer les taux dans les tableaux suivants, parce que ces pays ont fourni une population de référence pour les événements démographiques différente de la population totale.

Sauf indication contraire, toutes les estimations se rapportent à la population présente sur le territoire actuel des pays ou zones considérés. Les principales exceptions à cette règle sont expliquées en note.

Fiabilité des données : les estimations de la population en milieu d'année sont considérées sûres quand elles sont fondées sur un recensement complet (ou sur une enquête par sondage) et ont été ajustées en fonction des données provenant d'un registre permanent de population ou en fonction des naissances, décès et mouvements migratoires qui ont eu lieu pendant la période. Les estimations considérées comme sûres apparaissent en caractères romains. Les estimations dont le calcul n'a pas été effectué sur cette base sont considérées comme moins sûres et apparaissent en italique.

Insuffisance des données : les statistiques concernant les estimations de la population totale en milieu d'année appellent toutes les réserves qui ont été formulées à la section 3 des Notes techniques à propos des statistiques de la population en général.

Le fait que certaines des estimations concernant la population en milieu d'année se réfèrent à la population de droit et non à la population de fait influe sur la comparabilité internationale. Ces cas ont été signalés dans la colonne « Code ». La différence entre la population de fait et la population de droit est expliquée à la section 3.1.1 des Notes techniques.

Données publiées antérieurement : des estimations de la population en milieu d'année ont été publiées dans des éditions antérieures de l'*Annuaire démographique*. Pour plus de précisions concernant les années et les sujets pour lesquels des données ont été publiées, se reporter à l'index.

5. Estimates of mid-year population: 2009 - 2018
Estimations de la population au milieu de l'année : 2009 - 2018

Continent and country or area / Continent et pays ou zone	Code[a]	Population estimates (in thousands) - Estimations (en milliers)									
		2009	2010	2011	2012	2013	2014	2015	2016	2017	2018
AFRICA - AFRIQUE											
Algeria - Algérie	DJ	35 268	35 978	36 717	37 495	38 297	39 114	39 963	40 836	41 696	...
Angola	DF	16 889[1]	17 430[1]	17 992[1]	18 577[1]	19 184[1]	25 901[2]	26 682[2]	27 504[2]	28 360[2]	29 250[2]
Benin - Bénin	DF	8 498[3]	8 779[3]	9 067[3]	9 365[3]	...	10 293[4]	10 585[4]	10 883[4]	11 187[4]	11 496[4]
Botswana	DJ	1 776	1 823	1 850	2 071[5]	2 115[5]	2 156[5]	2 195[5]	2 231[5]	2 267[5]	2 303[5]
Burkina Faso[3]	DJ	15 225	15 731	16 249	16 779	17 323	17 880	18 450	19 034	19 632	...
Burundi	DF	...	9 461	9 771	10 073	10 367	10 654	10 933	11 215	11 495	11 772
Cabo Verde	DF	509	...								
	DJ		494[3]	500[3]	506[3]	512[3]	518[3]	525[3]	531[3]	538[3]	544[3]
Cameroon - Cameroun[6]	DJ	19 571	20 127	20 710	21 277	21 848	22 454	23 050	23 642	24 254	24 863
Chad - Tchad	DJ	...	11 470	11 881	12 307	12 747	13 201	13 670	14 152	14 649	15 162
Congo	DF	3 838	...	...	...	4 278	...	...	...	4 709	...
	DJ		4 119	4 257	4 394		4 666	4 802	4 934		5 203
Côte d'Ivoire	DF	20 389[7]	20 845[7]	21 302[7]	21 758[7]	22 215[7]	22 723[8]	23 334[8]	23 950[8]	24 571[8]	25 196[8]
Djibouti[9]	DF	...	841	865	...						
Egypt - Égypte	DF	76 925	78 685	80 530	82 550	84 629	86 811	88 958	91 023	95 203	97 147
Equatorial Guinea - Guinée équatoriale	DF	1 566[10]	1 622[10]					1 268[11]	1 312[11]	*1 358[11]	
Eritrea - Érythrée[12]	DF	2 627	2 691	2 759	2 829	2 901	2 976	3 052	3 131	3 212	3 295
Eswatini[13]	DJ	1 044	1 056	1 068	1 080	1 093	1 106	1 119	1 133	1 146	1 159
Ethiopia - Éthiopie[14]	DF	77 651	79 634	81 668	83 741	85 837	87 952	90 075	92 205	94 352	96 503
Gambia - Gambie	DF	1 674	1 731	1 790	1 850	1 857	1 898	1 959	2 020	2 083	2 148
Ghana	DF	23 417	...	25 235[15]	25 825[15]	26 428[15]	27 043[15]	27 670[15]	28 308[15]	28 957[15]	29 614[15]
Guinea - Guinée	DJ	9 306[16]	9 557[16]	9 812[16]	10 071[16]	10 334[16]	10 600[2]	10 918[17]	11 233[17]	11 555[17]	11 884[17]
Guinea-Bissau - Guinée-Bissau[3]	DF	...	1 460	1 472	1 485	1 499	1 514	1 531	1 548	1 566	1 585
Kenya[18]	DF	37 725	38 474	39 545	40 657	41 788	42 961	44 157	45 389	46 595	47 849
Lesotho[19]	DF	1 887	1 892	1 897	1 903	1 909	1 917	1 924	...	...	...
Liberia - Libéria	DF	3 551	3 627	3 705	3 784	3 865	3 946		...	...	...
Libya - Libye[20]	DF	5 589	5 689	5 791	5 892	5 994	6 096	6 162	...	...	...
Madagascar[21]	DF	19 601	20 142	20 696	21 263	21 842	22 434	23 040	23 658	24 290	24 934
Malawi[3]	DF	13 520	13 948	14 389	14 845	15 317	15 805	16 310	16 833	...	...
	DJ									17 373	
Mali[22]	DF	14 671	15 370	15 843	16 312	16 808	17 319	17 819	18 341	...	...
Mauritania - Mauritanie[3]	DF	3 251	3 341	3 297	3 378	3 537	3 637	3 720	3 783	...	...
Mauritius - Maurice[23]	DJ	1 275[24]	1 281[24]	1 252[25]	1 256[25]	1 259[25]	1 261[25]	1 263[25]	1 263[25]	1 265[25]	1 265[25]
Mayotte	DJ	...	...	...	...	...	228[26]	230[27]	*244[26]	*256[26]	*265[26]
Morocco - Maroc	DF	31 543[28]	31 894[28]	32 245[28]	32 597[28]	32 950[28]	...				
	DJ						33 770[29]	34 125[29]	34 487[29]	34 852[29]	35 220[29]
Mozambique[13]	DF	21 803	22 417	23 050	23 701	24 366	25 042	25 728	26 424	27 129	...
Namibia - Namibie	DF	2 104[3]	2 143[3]	2 116[30]	2 155[30]	2 196[30]	2 238[30]	2 281[30]	2 324[30]	2 369[30]	2 414[30]
Niger	DJ	14 693[3]	15 204[3]	15 731[3]	16 994[31]	17 680[31]	18 389[31]	19 125[31]	19 865[31]	...	...
Nigeria - Nigéria[19]	DF	154 582	159 608	164 798	170 157	175 690	181 403	187 302	193 393	...	...
Republic of South Sudan - République de Soudan du Sud[32]	DF	8 685	9 005	9 389	9 783	10 182	10 585	11 000	11 425	11 868	12 323
Reunion - Réunion	DJ	816[27]	821[27]	829[27]	834[27]	839[26]	847[26]	851[27]	*858[26]	*860[26]	*864[26]
Rwanda	DF	10 117[3]	10 413[3]	10 718[3]	10 483[31]	10 737[31]	10 997[31]	11 263[31]	11 533[31]	11 809[31]	12 090[31]
Saint Helena ex. dep. - Sainte-Hélène sans dép.	DF	4	4	4	4	4[33]	4	4	5	5	5
Saint Helena: Tristan da Cunha - Sainte-Hélène: Tristan da Cunha[34]	DF	0	...	...	...	...	...	...	...	...	...
Sao Tome and Principe - Sao Tomé-et-Principe	DF	161	164	167	...						
	DJ	...	...	...	...	182[35]	186[35]	190[35]	194[35]	198[35]	202[35]
Senegal - Sénégal	DJ	12 171[33]	12 509[33]	12 842[33]	13 208[33]	13 509[3]	13 926[3]	14 357[3]	14 800[3]	15 256[3]	15 726[3]
Seychelles	DF	87	90	87	88	90	91	93	95	96	97
Sierra Leone	DF	5 608	5 747	5 890	6 038	...					
South Africa - Afrique du Sud	DF	49 928[36]	50 724[36]	51 551[36]	52 410[2]	53 282[2]	54 167[2]	55 056[2]	55 947[2]	56 837[2]	57 726[2]
Sudan - Soudan	DF	31 957	32 962	33 998	35 064	36 163	37 292	38 454	39 648	...	...
Togo	DF	5 731	...								
	DJ		6 191[3]	6 278[2]	6 431[2]	6 589[2]	6 752[2]	6 921[2]	7 092[2]	7 265[2]	7 440[2]
Tunisia - Tunisie	DF	10 458	10 566	10 674	10 784	10 895	11 007	11 154	11 304	11 446	11 552
Uganda - Ouganda	DF	30 661	31 785	32 940	34 131	...	34 141[8]	35 502[8]	36 653[8]	37 839[8]	39 059[8]
United Republic of Tanzania - République Unie de Tanzanie	DF	41 916[37]	43 188[37]	44 485[37]	45 798[37]	46 356[31]	47 831[31]	49 359[31]	50 942[31]	52 555[31]	54 199[31]
Zambia - Zambie	DF	12 897[3]	...								
	DJ		...	13 719[38]	14 145[38]	14 580[38]	15 023[38]	15 474[38]	15 934[38]	16 405[38]	16 888[38]
Zimbabwe	DF	13 668[37]	...	...	...	13 369[35]	13 652[35]	13 943[35]	14 240[35]	14 542[35]	14 849[35]

5. Estimates of mid-year population: 2009 - 2018
Estimations de la population au milieu de l'année : 2009 - 2018 (continued - suite)

Continent and country or area / Continent et pays ou zone	Code[a]	Population estimates (in thousands) - Estimations (en milliers)									
		2009	2010	2011	2012	2013	2014	2015	2016	2017	2018
AMERICA, NORTH - AMÉRIQUE DU NORD											
Anguilla	DF	16	16	...	14	14	14	15	15	...	...
Antigua and Barbuda - Antigua-et-Barbuda	DF	89	91	...	...	...	...	...	...	...	...
	DJ	...	...	86[30]	87[30]	88[30]	89[30]	91[30]	92[30]	94[30]	95[30]
Aruba	DJ	102	102	103	105	106	108	109	110	111	111
Bahamas	DF	342[39]	...	...	...	...	...	...	...	...	...
	DJ	...	352[38]	355[38]	359[38]	362[38]	366[38]	370[38]	373[38]	377[38]	381[38]
Barbados - Barbade	DF	275	...	...	...	...	...	...	...	...	...
	DJ	...	278	278	278	277	277	275	...	...	...
Belize	DF	315	...	...	...	...	...	...	...	...	...
	DJ	...	324	332	341	350	359	368	378	388	398
Bermuda - Bermudes	DJ	64[39]	64[40]	63[40]	62[40]	62[40]	62[40]	62[40]	64[41]	64[41]	64[41]
British Virgin Islands - Îles Vierges britanniques	DF	28	28	28	28	29	29	29	...	...	...
Canada[42]	DJ	33 629[43]	34 005[43]	34 339[43]	34 714[43]	35 083[43]	35 437[43]	35 703[43]	36 109[44]	36 540[45]	*37 059[46]
Cayman Islands - Îles Caïmanes	DJ	57	56	55	56	56	57	59	61	63[33]	66[33]
Costa Rica	DJ	4 620[47]	4 538[48]	4 592[48]	4 651[48]	4 712[48]	4 772[48]	4 834[49]	4 890[50]	4 947[51]	5 004[52]
Cuba	DJ	11 174	11 171	11 172	11 174	11 192	11 224	11 239	11 239	11 230	*11 215
Curaçao	DJ	147[36]	149[36]	151[36]	152[2]	154[2]	156[2]	158[2]	160[2]	160[2]	160[2]
Dominica - Dominique	DF	71	71	71	71	71	72	...	...	...	...
Dominican Republic - République dominicaine[3]	DJ	9 380	9 479	9 580	9 681	9 785	9 883	9 980	10 075	10 169	10 266
El Salvador[53]	DJ	6 153	6 183	6 216	6 251	6 289	6 328	6 460	6 521	6 582	6 643
Greenland - Groenland[54]	DJ	56	57	57	57	56	56	56	56	56	56
Grenada - Grenade	DF	105	105	...	108	109	109	110	111	111	...
Guadeloupe[55]	DJ	402	404	404	403	401	399	397	395	429[27]	422[27]
Guatemala[37]	DJ	14 017	14 362	14 714	15 073	15 438	15 807	16 183	16 556	16 932	17 311
Haiti - Haïti[56]	DJ	9 923	10 085	10 248	10 413	10 579	10 746	10 912	11 078	11 245	11 412
Honduras	DF	7 877[67]	8 046[67]	8 215[57]	8 385[57]	...	8 432[4]	8 577[4]	8 721[4]	8 866[4]	9 012[4]
Jamaica - Jamaïque	DJ	2 696	2 702	2 700	2 708	2 715	2 721	2 725	2 728	2 729	*2 728
Martinique	DJ	396[27]	394[27]	392[27]	388[27]	386[27]	382	378[27]	377[27]	375[27]	369[27]
Mexico - Mexique	DJ	112 095[58]	113 749[58]	115 367[58]	116 936[58]	118 454[58]	119 936[58]	121 348[58]	122 715[59]	124 042[59]	125 328[59]
Montserrat	DF	5	5	...	...	...	...	...	...	...	...
	DJ	...	...	5	5	5	5	5	5	...	...
Nicaragua	DJ	5 742	5 816	5 997	6 071	6 134	6 198	6 263	6 328	6 394	6 460
Panama	DF	3 600[60]	3 662[15]	3 724[15]	3 788[15]	3 851[15]	3 913[15]	3 975[15]	4 037[15]	4 098[15]	4 159[15]
Puerto Rico - Porto Rico[61]	DJ	3 740[36]	3 721[62]	3 679[2]	3 634[2]	3 593[2]	3 535[2]	3 473[2]	3 407[2]	3 337[2]	3 195[2]
Saint Kitts and Nevis - Saint-Kitts-et-Nevis	DF	*52	*53	...	...	...	...	...	...	...	...
Saint Lucia - Sainte-Lucie	DF	165	...	167	169	171	173	174	176	177	179
Saint Pierre and Miquelon - Saint Pierre-et-Miquelon	DJ	...	...	6[27]	6[27]	...	...	6	...	...	...
Saint Vincent and the Grenadines - Saint-Vincent-et-les Grenadines	DJ	110	110	110	...	110	110	110	110	110	111
Saint-Barthélemy[27]	DJ	...	...	...	...	...	9	10	...	...	...
Saint-Martin (French part) - Saint-Martin (partie française)	DJ	...	...	...	...	...	35	...	...	36	35
Sint Maarten (Dutch part) - Saint-Martin (partie néerlandaise)	DF	39	36	33	35	37	37[27]	38[27]	39[27]	41[27]	41[27]
Trinidad and Tobago - Trinité-et-Tobago	DF	1 310[24]	1 318[24]	...	1 335[25]	1 341[25]	1 345[25]	1 350[25]	1 354[25]	1 357[25]	1 359[25]
Turks and Caicos Islands - Îles Turques et Caïques	DJ	36	35	34	32	34	35	37	38	40	*41
United States of America - États-Unis d'Amérique[63]	DJ	306 772[36]	309 348[2]	311 663[2]	313 998[2]	316 205[2]	318 563[2]	320 897[2]	323 128[2]	325 147[2]	327 167[2]
United States Virgin Islands - Îles Vierges américaines[64]	DJ	110	106	106	105	105	104	...	...	...	...

Continent and country or area / Continent et pays ou zone	Code[a]	Population estimates (in thousands) - Estimations (en milliers)									
		2009	**2010**	**2011**	**2012**	**2013**	**2014**	**2015**	**2016**	**2017**	**2018**
AMERICA, SOUTH - AMÉRIQUE DU SUD											
Argentina - Argentine	DF	40 134	40 788[38]	41 261[38]	41 733[38]	42 203[38]	42 670[38]	43 132[38]	43 590[38]	44 045[38]	44 495[38]
Bolivia (Plurinational State of) - Bolivie (État plurinational de)	DF	9 870	10 031	10 191	10 351	10 508	10 666	10 825	10 985	11 146	11 307
Brazil - Brésil[65]	DJ	193 544	195 498	197 397	199 242	201 033	202 769	204 451	206 081	207 661	208 495
Chile - Chili	DF	16 877	17 066	17 256	17 445	17 632	17 819	18 006	18 192	18 374	18 552
Colombia - Colombie[66]	DJ	44 979	45 510	46 045	46 582	47 121	47 662	48 203	48 748	49 292	49 834
Ecuador - Équateur[67]	DF	14 738	15 012	15 266	15 521	15 775	16 027	16 279	16 529	16 777	17 023
French Guiana - Guyane française[27]	DJ	224	229	238	240	244	252	255	263	274	282
Guyana	DF	753	752	751	747	746	746	745	743	741	...
Paraguay[68]	DF	6 169	6 266	6 363	6 461	6 559	6 657	6 756	6 855	6 954	7 053
Peru - Pérou[69]	DF	29 132	29 462	29 798	30 136	30 475	30 814	31 152	31 489	31 826	32 162
Suriname	DJ	524	531	540	...	550	559	567	576	583	...
Uruguay	DJ	3 378	3 397	3 413	3 426[3]	3 440[3]	3 454[3]	3 467[3]	3 480[3]	3 493[3]	3 506[3]
Venezuela (Bolivarian Republic of) - Venezuela (République bolivarienne du)	DF	27 980[70]	28 396[70]	28 811	29 231	29 650	30 070	30 489	30 883	31 277	31 671
ASIA - ASIE											
Afghanistan[71]	DF	23 994	24 486	24 988	25 500	26 023	26 557	27 101	27 657	28 224	30 075
Armenia - Arménie	DJ	3 066	3 045	3 028	3 024	3 022	3 014	3 005	2 992	2 979	2 973[27]
Azerbaijan - Azerbaïdjan	DJ	8 947	9 054	9 173	9 296	9 417	9 535	9 649	9 758	9 854	9 936
Bahrain - Bahreïn	DJ	1 178	1 229	1 195	1 209	1 253	1 315	1 370	1 424	1 501	1 503
Bangladesh	DF	146 600	148 620	150 611	152 700	154 790	156 880	158 900	160 800	162 700	164 600
Bhutan - Bhoutan[72]	DF	683	696	708	721	733	745	757	769	...	...
Brunei Darussalam - Brunéi Darussalam	DF	380[36]	387[36]	...	...	...	...	...	...	...	...
	DJ	...	...	...	399	403	408	412	417[73]	430	442
Cambodia - Cambodge[74]	DF	14 085	14 303	14 521	14 741	14 963	15 184	15 405	...	...	...
China - Chine[75]	DF	1 331 300[76]	1 337 700[76]	1 344 100[77]	1 350 695[77]	1 357 380[76]	1 364 270[76]	1 371 220[76]	1 378 665[76]	1 386 395[76]	1 392 730[76]
China, Hong Kong SAR - Chine, Hong Kong RAS	DJ	6 973	7 024	7 072	7 150	7 179	7 230	7 291	7 337	7 392	7 451
China, Macao SAR - Chine, Macao RAS	DJ	535	537	550	568	592	622	643	*645	*653	*667
Cyprus - Chypre[78]	DJ	808[26]	829[26]	851[26]	864[26]	862[26]	853[26]	848[26]	852[26]	860[26]	864[27]
Georgia - Géorgie	DF	4 411	4 453	4 483	4 491	4 487					
	DJ	...	...	...	...	...	3 727[79]	3 711[79]	3 719[79]	3 724[80]	3 730[81]
India - Inde[82]	DF	1 160 813	1 176 742	1 192 506	1 208 116	1 223 581	1 238 887	1 254 019	1 268 961	1 283 600	1 298 041
Indonesia - Indonésie	DJ	231 370[83]	238 519[84]	241 991[84]	245 425[84]	248 818[84]	252 165[84]	255 588[85]	258 497[85]	261 355[85]	264 162[85]
Iran (Islamic Republic of) - Iran (République islamique d')[86]	DJ	73 202	74 340	...	76 038	76 942	77 856	78 773	80 038	81 070	82 084
Iraq	DF	31 393	32 211	33 052	33 913	34 794	35 736	36 659	...	...	*37 842
Israel - Israël[87]	DJ	7 486	7 624	7 766	7 911	8 059	8 216	8 380	8 546	8 713	*8 884
Japan - Japon[88]	DJ	128 047	128 070	127 833[89]	127 629[89]	127 445[89]	127 276[89]	127 141[90]	126 995[90]	126 786[89]	126 529[90]
Jordan - Jordanie[91]	DF	6 490	6 699	6 993	7 427	8 114	8 804	9 559	9 798	10 053	10 309
Kazakhstan[92]	DF	16 093[93]	16 322[93]	16 557[93]	16 792[93]	17 036[93]	17 288[93]	17 543[93]	17 794[93]	18 038[93]	18 276
Kuwait - Koweït	DF	2 778	2 933	3 107	3 247	3 428	3 767	3 971	4 079	4 022	4 125
Kyrgyzstan - Kirghizstan[26]	DJ	5 383	5 448	5 515	5 608	5 720	5 836	5 957	6 080	6 198	6 323
Lao People's Democratic Republic - République démocratique populaire lao[11]	DJ	6 111	6 230	6 349	6 466	6 581	6 693	6 672	6 787	6 901	7 013
Malaysia - Malaisie	DJ	28 081[94]	28 589[95]	29 062[95]	29 510[95]	30 214[95]	30 709[95]	31 186[95]	31 634[95]	32 023[95]	32 385[95]
Maldives	DF	315	320	325	331	336	438[96]	454[96]	472[96]	492[96]	512[96]
Mongolia - Mongolie	DF	2 691	2 739	2 786	2 840	2 899	2 963	3 027	3 089	3 149	3 208
Myanmar	DF	59 130[97]	59 780[97]	50 149[98]	50 667[98]	51 184[98]	51 991[98]	52 451[98]	52 799[79]	53 388[98]	53 863[98]
Nepal - Népal	DJ	27 504	28 044	28 585	26 873[30]	27 257[30]	27 646[30]	28 038[30]	28 431[30]	28 826[30]	29 219[30]
Oman	DF	3 174	...	3 295[99]	3 623[99]	3 855[99]	3 993[99]	4 159[99]	4 414[99]	4 560[99]	4 602[99]
Pakistan[100]	DF	169 940	173 510	177 100	...	184 350	188 020	191 710	...	...	...
Philippines	DJ	92 227[39]	93 135[15]	94 824[15]	96 511[15]	98 197[15]	99 880[15]	101 562[15]	103 243[15]	104 921[15]	106 599[15]
Qatar	DF	1 639	1 715	1 733	1 833	2 004	2 216	2 438	2 618	2 725	2 760
Republic of Korea - République de Corée	DJ	49 308	49 554	49 937	50 200	50 429	50 747	51 015	51 218	51 362	51 607
Saudi Arabia - Arabie saoudite	DF	26 576	27 411	28 173	28 897	29 613	30 340	31 062	31 788	32 613	33 414
Singapore - Singapour[101]	DJ	4 988	5 077	5 184	5 312	5 399	5 470	5 535	5 607	5 612	5 639

Continent and country or area Continent et pays ou zone	Co-de[a]	Population estimates (in thousands) - Estimations (en milliers)									
		2009	2010	2011	2012	2013	2014	2015	2016	2017	2018
ASIA - ASIE											
Sri Lanka	DF	20 476	20 675	20 892	...	...	...	...	...	...	...
	DJ	...	...	...	20 425	20 585	20 778	20 970	*21 203	*21 444	*21 670
State of Palestine - État de Palestine	DF	3 922	4 023	4 125	4 226	4 328	4 429	4 530	4 632	4 733	4 854
Syrian Arab Republic - République arabe syrienne[102]	DF	20 125	20 619	21 124							
Tajikistan - Tadjikistan	DF	7 334	7 519	7 714	7 897	8 074	8 257	8 452	8 647	8 837	8 931[27]
Thailand - Thaïlande	DJ	63 525	63 878	64 076	64 266	64 621	64 955	65 027	65 013	65 522	65 700[3]
Timor-Leste[3]	DF	1 115	1 089	1 120	1 152	1 180	1 212	1 200	1 221	1 242	1 261
Turkey - Turquie	DJ	72 561[103]	73 723[103]	74 724[103]	75 627[103]	76 668[103]	77 696[103]	78 741[103]	79 815[103]	80 313[104]	81 339[104]
United Arab Emirates - Émirats arabes unis[105]	DF	8 200[33]	8 264	...	...	...	...	...	9 121[33]	9 304[33]	...
Uzbekistan - Ouzbékistan[92]	DJ	27 767	28 562	29 339	29 774	30 243	30 758	31 299	31 848	32 389	32 657[27]
Viet Nam[106]	DJ	86 025	86 947	87 860	88 809	89 760	90 729	91 710	92 695	*93 678	*94 666
Yemen - Yémen[3]	DJ	22 492	23 154	23 833	24 527	25 235	25 956	26 687	27 426	28 170	...
EUROPE											
Åland Islands - Îles d'Åland[54]	DJ	28	28	28	28	29	29	29	29	29	30
Albania - Albanie	DF	2 928	2 913	...	...	...	...	...	...	...	...
	DJ	...	...	2 905	2 900	2 895	2 889	2 881	2 876	2 873	2 870[27]
Andorra - Andorre[54]	DJ	85	70[107]	70[27]	70[27]	70	70	71	72	73[27]	75[27]
Austria - Autriche	DJ	8 341	8 361	8 389	8 426	8 477	8 544	8 629	8 740	8 795	8 822[27]
Belarus - Bélarus	DJ	9 507	9 491	9 473	9 464	9 466	9 475	9 490	9 502[26]	9 498[26]	9 492[27]
Belgium - Belgique	DJ	10 796	10 896	11 044	11 128	11 183	11 231	11 285[26]	11 331[26]	11 375[26]	11 399[27]
Bosnia and Herzegovina - Bosnie-Herzégovine	DF	3 843	3 843	3 841	3 837	...	...	...	...	...	...
	DJ	...	...	...	...	3 531	3 526	3 518	3 511	*3 510[27]	...
Bulgaria - Bulgarie	DJ	7 585	7 534	7 348	7 306	7 264	7 224	7 178	7 128[26]	7 076[26]	7 050[27]
Croatia - Croatie	DJ	4 305	4 295	4 281	4 268	4 256	4 238	4 204	4 174	4 125	4 105[27]
Czechia - Tchéquie	DJ	10 444	10 474	10 496	10 511	10 511	10 525	10 543	10 565	10 590	10 610[27]
Denmark - Danemark[108]	DJ	5 519	5 545	5 567	5 587	5 609	5 640	5 678	5 724	5 761	5 790
Estonia - Estonie	DJ	1 335	1 331	1 327	1 323	1 318	1 315	1 315	1 316[26]	1 317	1 319[27]
Faeroe Islands - Îles Féroé	DJ	49	49	49	48	48	48	49	49	50	51
Finland - Finlande[54]	DJ	5 311[109]	5 335[109]	5 360[109]	5 386[109]	5 410[109]	5 433[109]	5 451[109]	5 466[109]	5 479[109]	5 513[27]
France[110]	DJ	62 615	62 918	63 223	63 537	63 863	64 164	64 385	*64 544	*64 672	*64 769
Germany - Allemagne	DJ	81 875	81 757	80 275[5]	80 426[5]	80 646[5]	80 983[5]	81 687[5]	82 349[111]	82 657[111]	82 792[112]
Gibraltar[113]	DF	31	31	32	33	33	33	34	34	...	...
Greece - Grèce	DF	11 107	11 121	11 105	11 045	10 965	10 892	10 821	10 776	10 761	10 741[27]
Guernsey - Guernesey[114]	DJ	62	62	63	63	63	62	62	62	62	62
Holy See - Saint-Siège[115]	DF	...	0[116]	...	0[117]	...	...	...	...	...	...
Hungary - Hongrie	DJ	10 023	10 000	9 972	9 920	9 893	9 866[118]	9 843[118]	9 814[118]	9 788[118]	9 778[119]
Iceland - Islande[120]	DJ	319	318	319	321	324	327	331	335	343	348[27]
Ireland - Irlande	DF	4 459	4 560	4 580	4 600	4 624	4 658	4 702	4 755	4 807	4 830[119]
Isle of Man - Île de Man[121]	DJ	82	83	...	85	86	86	87	86	84	...
Italy - Italie	DJ	59 095	59 277	59 379	59 540	60 234	60 789	60 731	60 627	60 537	60 484[27]
Jersey[27]	DJ	96	97	98	99	100	101	103	104	106	107
Latvia - Lettonie	DJ	2 142	2 098	2 060	2 034	2 013	1 994	1 978	1 960	1 942	1 934[27]
Liechtenstein	DJ	36	36	36	37	37	37	37	38	38	38
Lithuania - Lituanie	DJ	3 163	3 097	3 028	2 988	2 958	2 932[118]	2 905[118]	2 868[118]	2 828[118]	2 809[119]
Luxembourg	DJ	498	507	518	531	543	556	570	583	596	602[27]
Malta - Malte	DJ	413[122]	415[122]	416[122]	420	426	435	445	455	468[122]	476[123]
Monaco[124]	DJ	35	36	36	36	37	37[27]	38[27]	38[27]	38[27]	38[27]
Montenegro - Monténégro	DJ	632	619	620	621	621	622[118]	622[118]	622[118]	622[118]	622[118]
Netherlands - Pays-Bas	DJ	16 530	16 615	16 693	16 755	16 804	16 865	16 940	17 030	17 100	17 181[27]
North Macedonia - Macédoine du Nord	DJ	2 051	2 055	2 059	2 061	2 064	2 067	2 070	2 072	2 075	2 075[27]
Norway - Norvège[118]	DJ	4 829	4 889	4 953	5 019	5 080	5 137	5 189	5 235[26]	5 277[26]	5 296[27]
Poland - Pologne	DJ	38 153[125]	38 042[118]	38 051[118]	38 059[118]	38 032[118]	38 006[118]	37 982[118]	37 957[118]	37 962[118]	37 977[119]
Portugal	DJ	10 568	10 573	10 558	10 515	10 457	10 401	10 358	10 325	10 300	10 291[27]
Republic of Moldova - République de Moldova[126]	DJ	3 566	3 562	3 560	3 560	3 559	2 857[127]	2 835[127]	2 802[127]	2 755[127]	2 706[127]
Romania - Roumanie	DF						19 916	19 822	19 707	19 592	19 531[27]
	DJ	20 367[118]	20 247[118]	20 148[118]	20 060[118]	19 989[118]	...	...	...	...	...
Russian Federation - Fédération de Russie	DJ	142 785	142 849	142 961	143 202	143 507	...	...	...	...	...

Continent and country or area / Continent et pays ou zone	Code[a]	Population estimates (in thousands) - Estimations (en milliers)									
		2009	2010	2011	2012	2013	2014	2015	2016	2017	2018

EUROPE

Continent and country or area / Continent et pays ou zone	Code[a]	2009	2010	2011	2012	2013	2014	2015	2016	2017	2018
San Marino - Saint-Marin[54]	DF	33	33	33	34	33	34	34[27]	34[27]	34[27]	...
	DJ	...	...	...	...	...	...	...	...	...	35
Serbia - Serbie[128]	DJ	7 321	7 291	7 237[25]	7 201[25]	7 167[25]	7 132[25]	7 095[25]	7 058[25]	7 021[25]	7 001[129]
Slovakia - Slovaquie	DJ	5 418	5 431	5 398	5 408	5 413	5 419	5 424	5 431	5 439	5 443[27]
Slovenia - Slovénie	DJ	2 042	2 049	2 052	2 056	2 059	2 062	2 063	2 064	2 066	2 067[27]
Spain - Espagne	DJ	46 368	46 562	46 736	46 766	46 593	46 481[120]	46 448[120]	46 450[120]	46 533[120]	46 658[130]
Sweden - Suède[54]	DJ	9 299	9 378	9 449	9 519	9 600[120]	9 696[120]	9 799[120]	9 923[131]	10 058[131]	10 120[130]
Switzerland - Suisse	DJ	7 744	7 825	7 912	7 997	8 089	8 189[132]	8 282[132]	8 373[132]	8 452[133]	8 484[134]
Ukraine	DF	46 053	45 871	45 706	45 593	45 553[27]	45 426[27]	42 845[135]	42 673[135]	42 485[135]	42 386[136]
United Kingdom of Great Britain and Northern Ireland - Royaume-Uni de Grande-Bretagne et d'Irlande du Nord[137]	DJ	62 260	62 759	63 285	63 705	64 106[118]	64 597[118]	65 110[118]	65 648[118]	66 041[138]	66 274[119]

OCEANIA - OCÉANIE

Continent and country or area / Continent et pays ou zone	Code[a]	2009	2010	2011	2012	2013	2014	2015	2016	2017	2018
American Samoa - Samoas américaines[61]	DJ	70	67	64	64	63	62	61	60	60	...
Australia - Australie[139]	DJ	21 692	22 032	22 340	22 733	23 128	23 476	23 816	24 191	24 598	24 993
Cook Islands - Îles Cook[140]	DF	23	24	19	20	*19	*19	*19	*20	...	...
Fiji - Fidji	DF	843	857	854	858	862	866	867[141]	871	...	...
French Polynesia - Polynésie française	DF	263[26]	265[26]	267[26]	268[26]	270[26]	271[26]	273[26]	275[26]	276[26]	276[27]
Guam[61]	DJ	159	...	160	160	160	161	162	163	164	168
Kiribati[141]	DF	...	...	...	...	109	...	...	...	...	...
Marshall Islands - Îles Marshall	DF	54[142]	54[142]	...	...	54[141]	...	...	...	...	...
Micronesia (Federated States of) - Micronésie (États fédérés de)	DJ	108[3]	108[3]	103[143]	103[143]	103[143]	104[143]	104[143]	104[143]	104[143]	104[143]
Nauru	DF	...	...	...	10[3]	...	...	11[3]	11	...	...
New Caledonia - Nouvelle-Calédonie	DF	246	250	254	259	264	268	272	275[27]	279[27]	...
New Zealand - Nouvelle-Zélande[144]	DJ	4 303	4 351	4 384	4 408	4 442	4 510	4 596	4 693	4 794	4 886[36]
Niue - Nioué	DJ	2	1	1	1[145]	2[145]	2[145]	2[145]	2[145]	...	...
Northern Mariana Islands - Îles Mariannes septentrionales	DF	51	48	46	51[146]	51[146]	51[146]	...	...	...	...
Palau - Palaos	DJ	21	21	21	21	18	18	...	18	18	18
Papua New Guinea - Papouasie-Nouvelle-Guinée[147]	DF	...	...	...	...	...	...	...	8 151	...	...
Samoa	DF	185	186	185	189[148]	191[148]	192[148]	193[148]	...	198[149]	199[149]
Solomon Islands - Îles Salomon	DF	518[3]	555[150]	570[150]	584[150]	598[150]	612[150]	625[150]	639[150]	653[150]	667[150]
Tokelau - Tokélaou[151]	DF	...	...	...	...	1	...	...	...	...	...
Tuvalu	DF	...	...	11	11	11	11	11	11	...	...
Vanuatu	DF	...	239	245	250	265	271	...	...	...	...
Wallis and Futuna Islands - Îles Wallis et Futuna[147]	DF	...	...	...	...	...	...	...	12	...	...

FOOTNOTES - NOTES

Italics: estimates which are less reliable. - Italiques : estimations moins sûres.

* Provisional. - Données provisoires.

[a] 'Code' indicates source of data, as follows: - Le 'Code' indique la source des données, comme suit :
DF: Population de facto - Population de fait
DJ : Population de jure - Population de droit

[1] Unrevised data that do not take into account the results of the 2014 population census. - Ces données n'ont pas été revisées et elles ne prennent pas en compte les résultats du recensement de la population de 2014.

[2] Postcensal estimates. - Estimations post censitaires.

[3] Data refer to national projections. - Les données se réfèrent aux projections nationales.

[4] Projections based on the 2013 Population Census. - Projections fondées sur le recensement de la population de 2013.

[5] Data based on the 2011 Census. - Données fondées sur le recensement de 2011.

[6] Source: Population projections and estimates of priority targets for the various health programs and interventions, National Institute of Statistics (2016). - Source : Projections démographiques et estimations des cibles prioritaires des différents programmes et interventions de sante, Institut National de la Statistique (2016).

[7] Estimates based on the 2014 Population Census. - Estimations fondées sur le recensement de la population de 2014.

[8] Projections based on the 2014 Population Census. - Projections fondées sur le recensement de la population de 2014.

9 Data are calculated from the results of the Population and Housing Census of 2009. - Les données sont calculées à partir des résultats du recensement de la population et de l'habitat de 2009.

10 Data refer to projections based on the 1983 Population Census. - Les données se réfèrent aux projections basées sur le recensement de la population de 1983.

11 Estimates based on the results of 2015 population census. - Estimations fondées sur les résultats du recensement de la population de 2015.

12 Projections based on the 2000 quick population count results and 1995, 2002 and 2010 Eritrea Demographic and Health Surveys. - Projections fondées sur le dénombrement rapide de la population de 2000 et sur les enquêtes érythréennes de la démographie et de la santé de 1995, 2002 et 2010.

13 Data refer to national projections based on 2007 census. - Les données sont des projections nationales d'après les résultats du recensement de la population de 2007.

14 Estimates considering also the results of the 2007 Population Census. - Estimations en prennant en considération les résultats du recensement de la population de 2007.

15 Data based on the 2010 Population Census. - Les données sont fondées sur le recensement de la population de 2010.

16 Population in households only. Intercensal estimates. - Population dans les ménages seulement. Estimations inter-censitaires.

17 Population in households only. Postcensal estimates. - Population dans les ménages seulement. Estimations post censitaires.

18 Post-censal estimates based on the 2009 Population Census. - Les estimations post-censitaire fondées sur le recensement de la population de 2009.

19 Data are projections based on the 2006 Population Census. - Projections fondées sur le recensement de la population de 2006.

20 Data refer to Libyan nationals only. - Les données se raportent aux nationaux libyens seulement.

21 Data refer to projections based on the 1993 Population Census. - Les données se réfèrent aux projections basées sur le recensement de la population de 1993.

22 Projections considering also the results of the 2009 Population Census. - Projections en prennant en considération les résultats du recensement de la population de 2009.

23 Excludes the islands of St. Brandon and Agalega. - Non compris les îles St. Brandon et Agalega.

24 Based on the results of the 2000 Population Census. - Basé sur les résultats du recencement de la population de 2000.

25 Based on the results of the 2011 Population Census. - Basé sur les résultats du recencement de la population de 2011.

26 Data refer to annual average population. - Les données correspondent à la population annuelle moyenne.

27 Data refer to 1 January. - Données se raportent au 1 janvier.

28 Based on the results of the 2004 Population Census. - D'après des résultats du recensement de la population de 2004.

29 Projections based on the results of national survey on population and health conducted between 2010 and 2011, and especially population and housing census 2014. - Des projections de la population fondées sur les résultats de l'enquête nationale de la population et de la santé réalisée entre 2010 et 2011 et, surtout, du recensement général de la population et de l'habitat de 2014.

30 Data refer to projections based on the 2011 Population Census. - Les données se réfèrent aux projections basées sur le recensement de la population de 2011.

31 Projections based on the 2012 Population and Housing Census. - Projections fondées sur le recensement 2012 de la population et des logements.

32 Data are projections based on the 2008 Population and Housing Census. - Projection basée sur le recensement 2008 de la population et des logements.

33 Data refer to 31 December. - Données se raportent au 31 décembre.

34 Data refer to 31 December. Based on the results of a population count. The population figures are 264, 263 and 262 persons for 2007, 2008 and 2009 respectively. - Données se raportent au 31 décembre. D'après les résultats d'un comptage de la population. La population est respectivement égale à 264, 263 et 262 personnes pour les années 2007, 2008 et 2009.

35 Projections based on the 2012 Population Census. - Projections fondées sur le recensement de la population de 2012.

36 Intercensal estimates. - Estimations inter-censitaires.

37 Projections based on the 2002 Population Census. - Projections fondées sur le recensement de la population de 2002.

38 Projections based on the 2010 Population and Housing Census. - Projections fondées sur le recensement 2010 de la population et des logements.

39 Data refer to projections based on the 2000 Population Census. - Les données se réfèrent aux projections basées sur le recensement de la population de 2000.

40 Data based on the 2010 Population Census. Bermuda is 100 per cent urban. - Les données sont fondées sur le recensement de la population de 2010. 100 pour cent de la population des Bermudes est urbaine.

41 Bermuda is 100 per cent urban. Data refer to projections based on the 2016 Population Census. - 100 pour cent de la population des Bermudes est urbaine. Les données se réfèrent aux projections basées sur le recensement de la population de 2016.

42 Adjusted for census net undercoverage (including adjustment for incompletely enumerated Indian reserves). - Ajusté pour la sous-estimation du recensement (y compris les réservations en Inde incomplètement énumérées).

43 Final intercensal estimates. - Estimations inter-censitaires definitives.

44 Final postcensal estimates. - Estimations postcensitaires definitives.

45 Updated postcensal estimates. - Estimations post censitaires mises à jour.

46 Preliminary postcensal estimates. - Estimations post censitaires préliminaires.

47 The source of data is the national household survey. - La source des données est l'enquête nationale des ménages.

48 Based on the national household surveys 2010-2014 and the 2011 population census. - D'après les données de l'enquête nationale des ménages 2010-2014 et les résultats du recensement de la population de 2011.

49 Based on the national household survey of 2015. - Basée sur l' enquête nationale auprès des ménages de 2015.

50 Based on the national household survey of 2016. - D'après l'enquête nationale auprès des ménages de 2016.

51 Based on the national household survey of 2017. - D'après l'enquête nationale auprès des ménages de 2017.

52 Based on the national household survey of 2018. - D'après l'enquête nationale auprès des ménages de 2018.

53 Estimates or projections based on the 2007 Population Census. - Estimations ou projections fondées sur le recensement de la population de 2007.

54 Population statistics are compiled from registers. - Les statistiques de la population sont compilées à partir des registres.

55 Excluding data for Saint Barthélémy and Saint Martin. - Non compris les données pour Saint Barthélémy et Saint Martin.

56 Projections produced by l'Institut Haïtien de Statistique et d'Informatique (IHSI) and the Latin American and Caribbean Demographic Centre (CELADE) - Population Division of ECLAC. - Les données sont projections produits par l'Institut Haïtien de Statistique et d'Informatique (IHSI) et le centre démographique de l'Amérique latine et les Caraïbes - Division de la population de la CEPALC.

57 Data refer to projections based on the 2001 Population Census. - Les données se réfèrent aux projections basées sur le recensement de la population de 2001.

58 Data revised by CONAPO (National Population Council). - Données révisées par CONAPO (Conseil national de la population).

59 The population projections of CONAPO (National Population Council). - Les projections démographiques de la CONAPO (Conseil national de la population).

60 Estimates based on the 2010 Population Census. - Estimations basées sur le recensement de la population de 2010.

61 Including armed forces stationed in the area. - Y compris les militaires en garnison sur le territoire.

62 Based on the results of the 2010 Population Census. - D'après le résultats du recensement de la population de 2010.

63 Excluding U.S. Armed Forces overseas and civilian U.S. citizens whose usual place of residence is outside the United States. - Non compris les militaires américains à l'étranger et les civils américains dont le lieu de résidence habituel est en dehors des États-Unis.

64 Including armed forces stationed in the area. Source: U.S. National Center for Health Statistics, National Vital Statistics Reports (NVSR). - Y compris les militaires en garnison sur le territoire. Source : US National Center for Health Statistics, National Vital Statistics Reports (NVSR).

65 Data include persons in remote areas, military personnel outside the country, merchant seamen at sea, civilian seasonal workers outside the country, and other civilians outside the country, and exclude nomads, foreign military, civilian aliens temporarily in the country, transients on ships and Indian jungle population. Data refer to national projections. - Y compris les personnes vivant dans des régions éloignées, le personel militaire en dehors du pays, les marins marchands, les ouvriers saisonniers en dehors du pays, et autres civils en dehors du pays, et non compris les nomades, les militaires étrangers, les étrangers civils temporairement dans le pays, les transiteurs sur des bateaux et les Indiens de la jungle. Les données se réfèrent aux projections nationales.

66 Data are revised projections taking into consideration also the results of the 2005 census. - Les données sont des projections révisées tenant compte également des résultats du recensement de 2005.

67 Excludes nomadic Indian tribes. Data based on the 2010 Population Census. - Non compris les tribus d'Indiens nomades. Les données sont fondées sur le recensement de la population de 2010.

68 Estimates or projections considering also the results of the 2012 Population Census. - Estimations ou projections en prennant en considération les résultats du recensement de la population de 2012.

69 Data refer to 30 June. - Données se raportent au 30 juin.

70 Revised data. - Données révisées.

71 Data refer to the settled population based on the 1979 Population Census and the latest household prelisting. The refugees of Afghanistan in Iran, Pakistan, and an estimated 1.5 million nomads, are not included. - Les données se rapportent à la population stationnaire sur la base du recensement de 1979 et du recensement préliminaire des logements le plus récent. Sont exclus les réfugiés d'Afghanistan en Iran et au Pakistan et les nomades estimés à 1,5 million.

72 Data refer to projected figures based on the Population and Housing Census 2005 (district projection). - Les données se réfèrent aux projections basées sur le recensement de la population et de l'habitat de 2005 (projections locales).

73 Source: 2016 Population and Housing Census Update. - Source : Révision des chiffres du recensement de la population et des logements de 2016.

74 Excluding foreign diplomatic personnel and their dependants. Data based on the 2008 Population Census. - Non compris le personnel diplomatique étranger et les membres de leur famille les accompagnant. Données fondées sur le recensement de population de 2008.

75 For statistical purposes, the data for China do not include those for the Hong Kong Special Administrative Region (Hong Kong SAR), Macao Special Administrative Region (Macao SAR) and Taiwan province of China. - Pour la présentation des statistiques, les données pour la Chine ne comprennent pas la Région Administrative Spéciale de Hong Kong (Hong Kong RAS), la Région Administrative Spéciale de Macao (Macao RAS) et Taïwan province de Chine.

76 Data have been estimated on the basis of the annual National Sample Survey on Population Changes. - Les données ont été estimées sur la base de l'enquête annuelle "National Sample Survey on Population Changes".

77 Data have been adjusted on the basis of the Population Census of 2010. - Les données ont été ajustées à partir des résultats du recensement de la population de 2010.

78 Data refer to government controlled areas. - Les données se rapportent aux zones contrôlées par le Gouvernement.

79 Based on the results of the 2014 Population Census. - D'après les résultats du recensement de la population de 2014.

80 Data refer to annual average population. Based on the results of the 2014 Population Census. - Les données correspondent à la population annuelle moyenne. D'après les résultats du recensement de la population de 2014.

81 Data refer to 1 January. Based on the results of the 2014 Population Census. - Données se raportent au 1 janvier. D'après les résultats du recensement de la population de 2014.

82 Data refer to 1 March. Includes data for the Indian-held part of Jammu and Kashmir, the final status of which has not yet been determined. Data refer to projections based on the 2001 Population Census. - Données se rapportent au 1 mars. Y compris les données pour la partie du Jammu et du Cachemire occupée par l'Inde dont le statut définitif n'a pas encore été déterminé. Les données se réfèrent aux projections basées sur le recensement de la population de 2001.

83 Data are based on the publication: "Indonesia Population Projection 2005-2015" - Les données sont basées sur la publication : << Indonesia Population Projection 2005-2015 >>

84 Data are based on the publication: "Indonesia Population Projection 2010-2035" - Les données sont basées sur la publication : << Indonesia Population Projection 2010-2035 >>

85 Data are based on the publication: "Indonesia Population Projection 2015-2045" - Les données sont basées sur la publication : << Indonesia Population Projection 2015-2045 >>

86 Data refer to the Iranian Year which begins on 21 March and ends on 20 March of the following year. - Les données concernent l'année iranienne, qui commence le 21 mars et se termine le 20 mars de l'année suivante.

87 Includes data for East Jerusalem and Israeli residents in certain other territories under occupation by Israeli military forces since June 1967. Data refer to Israeli citizens and permanent residents who are listed in the Population Register. - Y compris les données pour Jérusalem-Est et les résidents israéliens dans certains autres territoires occupés depuis 1967 par les forces armées israéliennes. Les données se rapportent aux citoyens israéliens et aux résidents permanents qui sont répertoriés dans le registre de la population.

88 Excluding diplomatic personnel outside the country and foreign military and civilian personnel and their dependants stationed in the area. - Non compris le personnel diplomatique hors du pays ni les militaires et agents civils étrangers en poste sur le territoire et les membres de leur famille les accompagnant.

89 Estimates based on the complete counts of the 2015 Population Census. - Estimations basées sur le dénombrement complet du recensement de la population de 2015.

90 Because of rounding, totals are not in all cases the sum of the respective components. Estimates based on the complete counts of the 2015 Population Census. - Les chiffres étant arrondis, les totaux ne correspondent pas toujours

rigoureusement à la somme des composants respectifs. Estimations basées sur le dénombrement complet du recensement de la population de 2015.

91 Data refer to 31 December. Excluding data for Jordanian territory under occupation since June 1967 by Israeli military forces. - Données se raportent au 31 décembre. Non compris les données pour le territoire jordanien occupé depuis juin 1967 par les forces armées israéliennes.

92 Data refer to resident population. - Les données concernent la population résidente.

93 Recalculated population estimates taking into account late registration of births and deaths until May 2017. - Réestimation du nombre d'habitants compte tenu de l'enregistrement tardif des naissances et des décès jusqu'en mai 2017.

94 Intercensal Mid-Year Population Estimates based on the adjusted Population and Housing Census of 2000 and 2010. - Les estimations inter-censitaires au millieu de l'année sont fondée sur les résultats ajustées des recensements de la population et de l'habitat de 2000 et 2010.

95 Estimates based on the adjusted results of the Population and Housing Census of 2010. - Les estimations sont fondée sur les résultats ajustés du recensement de la population et de l'habitat de 2010.

96 Data refer to resident population which includes resident Maldivians and resident foreigners. Estimates based on the 2014 Population Census. - Les données concernent la population résidente, qui comprend les Maldiviens et les étrangers. Estimations fondées sur le recensement de la population de 2014.

97 Data refer to 1 October. - Données se raportent au 1 octobre.

98 Data refer to 1 October. Based on the results of the 2014 Population Census. - Données se raportent au 1 octobre. D'après les résultats du recensement de la population de 2014.

99 Data refer to registered population data from Royal Oman Police. - Les données portent sur la population enregistrée par la police royale de l'Oman.

100 Excluding data for the Pakistan-held part of Jammu and Kashmir, the final status of which has not yet been determined. - Non compris les données concernant la partie du Jammu et Cachemire occupée par le Pakistan dont le statut définitif n'a pas été déterminé.

101 Data refer to 30 June. Data refer to total population, which comprises Singapore residents and non-residents. Data exclude residents who have been away from Singapore for a continuous period of 12 months or longer as at the reference date. - Données se raportent au 30 juin. Les données se rapportent à la population totale composé des résidents de Singapour et les non résidents. Non compris les résidents hors de Singapour pour une période ininterrompue de 12 mois ou plus avant de la date de référence.

102 Including Palestinian refugees. - Y compris les réfugiés de Palestine.

103 Data refer to 31 December. Data based on Address Based Population Registration System. - Données se raportent au 31 décembre. Les données sont basées sur le registre national de la population basé sur l'adresse.

104 Data based on address-based population registration system. - Les données sont basées sur le registre national de la population basé sur l'adresse.

105 Data include non-national population. - Les données comprennent les non-nationaux.

106 Data are adjusted according to the results of the 2009 census and 2014 intercensus. - Les données ont été ajustées à partir des résultats du recensement de la population de 2009 et des données intercensitaires de 2014.

107 Data refer to 1 January. Decrease in population due to revision in administrative registers. - Données se raportent au 1 janvier. Diminution de la population due à la révision des registres administratifs.

108 Excluding Faeroe Islands and Greenland shown separately, if available. Population statistics are compiled from registers. - Non compris les Iles Féroé et le Groenland, qui font l'objet de rubriques distinctes, si disponible. Les statistiques de la population sont compilées à partir des registres.

109 Excluding Åland Islands. - Non compris les Îles d'Åland.

110 Excluding diplomatic personnel outside the country and including members of alien armed forces not living in military camps and foreign diplomatic personnel not living in embassies or consulates. - Non compris le personnel diplomatique hors du pays et y compris les militaires étrangers ne vivant pas dans des camps militaires et le personnel diplomatique étranger ne vivant pas dans les ambassades ou les consulats.

111 Data refer to annual average population. Data based on the 2011 Census. - Les données correspondent à la population annuelle moyenne. Données fondées sur le recensement de 2011.

112 Data refer to 1 January. Data based on the 2011 Census. - Données se raportent au 1 janvier. Données fondées sur le recensement de 2011.

113 Data refer to 31 December. Excluding military personnel, visitors and transients. - Données se raportent au 31 décembre. Non compris les militaires, ni les visiteurs et transients.

114 Data refer to 31 March. - Données se raportent au 31 mars.

115 Data refer to the Vatican City State. - Les données se rapportent à l'Etat de la Cité du Vatican.

116 Data refer to 26 February. The population figure is 460 persons. - Données se raportent au 26 février. La population est égale à 460 personnes.

117 Data refer to 21 June. The population figure is 451 persons. - Données se raportent au 21 juin. La population est égale à 451 personnes.

118 Data refer to usually resident population. - Les données concernent la population habituellement résidente.

119 Data refer to 1 January. Data refer to usually resident population. - Données se raportent au 1 janvier. Les données concernent la population habituellement résidente.

120 Data refer to registered resident population. - Les données concernent la population enregistrée résidente.

121 Data refer to 30 April. - Données se raportent au 30 avril.

122 Including civilian nationals temporarily outside the country. - Y compris les civils nationaux temporairement hors du pays.

123 Data refer to 1 January. Including civilian nationals temporarily outside the country. - Données se raportent au 1 janvier. Y compris les civils nationaux temporairement hors du pays.

124 Data refer to resident population only. - Pour la population résidante seulement.

125 Excluding civilian aliens within the country, but including civilian nationals temporarily outside the country. - Non compris les civils étrangers dans le pays, mais y compris les civils nationaux temporairement hors du pays.

126 Excluding Transnistria and the municipality of Bender. - Les données ne tiennent pas compte de l'information sur la Transnistria et la municipalité de Bender.

127 Data refer to usual resident population based on the 2014 Census. Tiraspol, Bender, Slobozia, Ribnita, Camenca Yrigoricpol/Grigoriopol are districts from Transnistria where the 2014 census was not conducted. - Les données se rapportent à la population habituellement résidente et sont fondées sur le recensement de 2014. Tiraspol, Bender, Slobozia, Ribnita, Camenca, Yrigoricpol/Grigoriopol sont des districts de la Transnistrie où le recensement n'a pas eu lieu.

128 Excludes data for Kosovo and Metohia. - Sans les données pour le Kosovo et Metohie.

129 Data refer to 1 January. Based on the results of the 2011 Population Census. - Données se rapportent au 1 janvier. Basé sur les résultats du recencement de la population de 2011.

130 Data refer to 1 January. Data refer to registered resident population. - Données se raportent au 1 janvier. Les données concernent la population enregistrée résidente.

131 Data refer to annual average population. Data refer to registered resident population. - Les données correspondent à la population annuelle moyenne. Les données concernent la population enregistrée résidente.

132 Data refer to legal resident population. - Les données concernent la population légalement résidente.

133 Data refer to annual average population. Data refer to legal resident population. - Les données correspondent à la population annuelle moyenne. Les données concernent la population légalement résidente.

134 Data refer to 1 January. Data refer to legal resident population. - Données se raportent au 1 janvier. Les données concernent la population légalement résidente.

135 Data refer to annual average population. The Government of Ukraine has informed the United Nations that it is not in a position to provide statistical data concerning the Autonomous Republic of Crimea and the city of Sevastopol. - Les données correspondent à la population annuelle moyenne. Le gouvernement Ukrainien a informé l'ONU qu'il n'est pas en mesure de fournir des données statistiques concernant la République autonome de Crimée et la ville de Sébastopol.

136 Data refer to 1 January. The Government of Ukraine has informed the United Nations that it is not in a position to provide statistical data concerning the Autonomous Republic of Crimea and the city of Sevastopol. - Données se raportent au 1 janvier. Le gouvernement Ukrainien a informé l'ONU qu'il n'est pas en mesure de fournir des données statistiques concernant la République autonome de Crimée et la ville de Sébastopol.

137 Excluding Channel Islands (Guernsey and Jersey) and Isle of Man, shown separately, if available. - Non compris les îles Anglo-Normandes (Guernesey et Jersey) et l'île de Man, qui font l'objet de rubriques distinctes, si disponible.

138 Data refer to annual average population. Data refer to usually resident population. - Les données correspondent à la population annuelle moyenne. Les données concernent la population habituellement résidente.

139 Based on the results of the 2016 Population Census. - Basé sur les résultats du recencement de la population de 2016.

140 Excluding Niue, shown separately, which is part of Cook Islands, but because of remoteness is administered separately. - Non compris Nioué, qui fait l'objet d'une rubrique distincte et qui fait partie des îles Cook, mais qui, en raison de son éloignement, est administrée séparément.

141 Projections are prepared by the Secretariat of the Pacific Community based on the 2011 census of population and housing. - Les projections sont preparées par le Secrétariat de la Communauté du Pacifique à partir des résultats du recensement de la population et de l'habitat de 2011.

142 Projections are prepared by the Secretariat of the Pacific Community based on the 1999 census of population and housing. - Les projections sont preparées par le Secrétariat de la Communauté du Pacifique à partir des résultats du recensement de la population et de l'habitat de 1999.

143 Based on the 2010 Population and Housing Census and 2013/2014 Household Income and Expenditure Survey. - Données fondées sur les résultat du recensement de la population et de l'habitat de 2010, et ceux de l'enquête auprès des ménages sur des revenus et des dépenses de 2013/2014.

144 Because of rounding, totals are not in all cases the sum of the respective components. - Les chiffres étant arrondis, les totaux ne correspondent pas toujours rigoureusement à la somme des composants respectifs.

145 Intercensal estimates. Data refer to usually resident population. - Estimations inter-censitaires. Les données concernent la population habituellement résidente.

146 Source: U.S. National Center for Health Statistics, National Vital Statistics Reports (NVSR). - Source : US National Center for Health Statistics, National Vital Statistics Reports (NVSR).

147 Estimates are prepared by the Secretariat of the Pacific Community based on the last population and housing census. - Les estimations sont preparées par le Secrétariat de la Communauté du Pacifique à partir des résultats du dernier recensement de la population et de l'habitat.

148 Estimates based on the 2011 Population Census. - Estimations basées sur le recensement de la population de 2011.

149 Estimates based on the 2016 Population Census. - Estimations basées sur le recensement de la population de 2016.

150 Projections based on adjusted 2009 census counts. - Projections fondées à partir des comptes rajustés du recensement de 2009.

151 Data refer to 1 December. - Données se raportent au 1 décembre.

Table 6 - *Demographic Yearbook 2018*

Table 6 presents total population by sex for as many years as possible between 2009 and 2018, as well as urban population as available.

Description of variables: Data are from nation-wide population censuses or are estimates, some of which are based on sample surveys of population carried out among all segments of the population. This characteristic of the data is indicated in the column "Code". The codes used are explained at the end of the table.

Urban is defined according to the national census definition. The definitions for each country, as available, are provided as part of this technical note.

Percentage computation: Urban percentages are the number of persons residing in an area defined as "urban" per 100 total population. They are calculated by the Statistics Division of the United Nations Department of Economic and Social Affairs. In very few cases the data for total population have been revised whereas the data for the urban and rural population have not been revised. These data are footnoted accordingly. In these cases, particular caution should be used in interpreting the figures for the percentages urban.

Reliability of data: Estimates that are believed to be less reliable are set in *italics* rather than in roman type. Classification in terms of reliability is based on the method of construction of the total population estimate discussed in the technical notes for table 3.

Limitations: Statistics on urban population by sex are subject to the same qualifications as have been set forth for population statistics in general, as discussed in section 3 of the Technical Notes.

The basic limitations imposed by variations in the definition of the total population and in the degree of under-enumeration are perhaps more important in relation to urban/rural than to any other distributions. The classification by urban and rural is affected by variations in defining usual residence for purposes of sub-national tabulations. Likewise, the geographical differentials in the degree of under-enumeration in censuses affect the comparability of these categories throughout the table. The distinction between *de facto* and *de jure* population is also very important with respect to urban/rural distributions. The difference between the *de facto* and the *de jure* population is discussed at length in section 3.1.1 of the Technical Notes.

A most important and specific limitation, however, lies in the national differences in the definition of urban. Because the distinction between urban and rural areas is made in so many different ways, the definitions have been included at the end of this table. The definitions are necessarily brief and, where the classification of urban involves administrative civil divisions, they are often given in the terminology of the particular country or area. As a result of variations in terminology, it may appear that differences between countries or areas are greater than they actually are. On the other hand, similar or identical terms (for example, town, village, district) as used in different countries or areas may have quite different meanings.

The definition of urban/rural areas is based on both qualitative and quantitative criteria that may include any combination of the following: size of population, population density, distance between built-up areas, predominant type of economic activity, conformity to legal or administrative status and urban characteristics such as specific services and facilities[1]. Although statistics classified by urban/rural areas are widely available, no international standard definition appears to be possible at this time since the meaning differs from one country or area to another. The urban/rural classification of population used here is reported according to the national definition.

Earlier data: Urban and total population by sex have been shown in previous issues of the Demographic Yearbook. For information on specific years covered, readers should consult the Historical Index.

DEFINITION OF "URBAN"

AFRICA

Algeria: The urban/rural delimitation is performed after the census operation based on the classification of built-up areas. Groupings of 100 or more constructions, distant less than 200 metres from one another are considered urban.
Botswana: Agglomeration of 5 000 or more inhabitants where 75 per cent of the economic activity is non-agricultural.

Burkina Faso: All administrative centres of provinces (total of 45) plus 4 medium-sized towns are considered as urban areas.

Burundi: Commune of Bujumbura.

Comoros: Every locality or administrative centre of an island, region or prefecture that has the following facilities: asphalted roads, electricity, a medical centre, telephone services, etc.

Egypt: Governorates of Cairo, Alexandria, Port Said, Ismailia, Suez, frontier governorates and capitals of other governorates, as well as district capitals (Markaz). The definition of urban areas for the 2006 Census is "shiakha", a part of a district.

Equatorial Guinea: District centres and localities with 300 dwellings and/or 1 500 inhabitants or more.

Ethiopia: Localities of 2 000 or more inhabitants.

Eswatini: A geographical area constituting of a city or town, characterized by higher population density and vast human features in comparison to areas surrounding it.

Guinea: Administrative centres of prefectures and the capital city (Conakry).

Kenya: Areas having a population of 2 000 or more inhabitants that have transport systems, build-up areas, industrial/manufacturing structures and other developed structures.

Lesotho: All administrative headquarters and settlements of rapid growth.

Liberia: Localities of 2 000 or more inhabitants.

Malawi: All townships and town planning areas and all district centres.

Mauritius: The five Municipal Council Areas which are subdivided into twenty Municipal Wards defined according to proclaimed boundaries.

Namibia: Proclaimed urban areas for which cadastral data is available and other unplanned squatter areas.

Niger: Capital city, capitals of the departments and districts.

Reunion: A commune or a group of communes with more than 2,000 inhabitants in a continuous building area (no more than 200 meters between two buildings).

Rwanda: All administrative areas recognized as urban by the law. These are all administrative centres of provinces, and the cities of Kigali, Nyanza, Ruhango and Rwamagana.

Senegal: Agglomerations of 10 000 or more inhabitants.

South Africa: Places with some form of local authority.

Sudan: Localities of administrative and/or commercial importance or with population of 5 000 or more inhabitants.

Tunisia: Population living in communes.

Uganda: Gazettes, cities, municipalities and towns.

United Republic of Tanzania: Areas legally recognized (gazetted) as urban and all areas recognized by local government authorities as urban.

Zambia: Localities of 5 000 or more inhabitants, the majority of whom all depend on non-agricultural activities.

AMERICA, NORTH

Bermuda: The country is considered 100 per cent urban.

Canada: Areas with 1 000 or more inhabitants and a population density of 400 or more persons per square kilometre, based on population counts from the recent population census.

Costa Rica: Administrative centres of cantons.

Cuba: Localities with 2 000 or more inhabitants; or localities with more than 1 000 inhabitants having half or more of economically active population engaged in non-agricultural activities.

Dominican Republic: Administrative centres of municipalities and municipal districts, some of which include suburban zones of rural character.

El Salvador: Administrative centres of municipalities.

Greenland: Localities of 200 or more inhabitants.

Guadeloupe: A commune or a group of communes with more than 2,000 inhabitants in a continuous building area (no more than 200 meters between two buildings).

Guatemala: Municipality of Guatemala Department and officially recognized centres of other departments and municipalities.

Haiti: Administrative centres of communes.

Honduras: Localities of 2 000 or more inhabitants, having essentially urban characteristics.

Jamaica: Localities of 2 000 or more inhabitants, having urban characteristics.

Martinique: A commune or a group of communes with more than 2 000 inhabitants in a continuous building area (no more than 200 meters between two buildings).

Mexico: Localities of 2 500 or more inhabitants.

Nicaragua: Administrative centres of municipalities and localities of 1 000 or more inhabitants or with more than 150 dwellings, with streets, electric light, water service, school and health centre.

Panama: Localities of 1 500 or more inhabitants having essentially urban characteristics. Beginning 1970, localities of 1 500 or more inhabitants with such urban characteristics as streets, water supply systems, sewerage systems and electric light.

Puerto Rico: Agglomerations of 2 500 or more inhabitants, generally having population densities of 1 000 persons per square mile or more. Two types of urban areas: urbanized areas of 50 000 or more inhabitants and urban clusters of at least 2 500 and less than 50 000 inhabitants.

Saint-Barthélemy: A commune or a group of communes with more than 2 000 inhabitants in a continuous building area (no more than 200 meters between two buildings).

Saint-Martin (French part): A commune or a group of communes with more than 2 000 inhabitants in a continuous building area (no more than 200 meters between two buildings).

Saint Pierre and Miquelon: A commune or a group of communes with more than 2 000 inhabitants in a continuous building area (no more than 200 meters between two buildings).

United States of America: Agglomerations of 2 500 or more inhabitants, generally having population densities of 1 000 persons per square mile or more. Two types of urban areas: urbanized areas of 50 000 or more inhabitants and urban clusters of at least 2 500 and less than 50 000 inhabitants.

United States Virgin Islands: Agglomerations of 2 500 or more inhabitants, generally having population densities of 1 000 persons per square mile or more. Two types of urban areas: urbanized areas of 50 000 or more inhabitants and urban clusters of at least 2 500 and less than 50 000 inhabitants. (As of the 2000 Census, no urbanized areas are identified in the United States Virgin Islands.)

AMERICA, SOUTH

Argentina: Populated centres with 2 000 or more inhabitants.

Bolivia: Localities of 2 000 or more inhabitants.

Brazil: Area inside the urban perimeter of a city or town, defined by municipal law.

Chile: Areas of concentrated housing units with more than 2 000 inhabitants, or between 1 001 and 2 000 inhabitants having 50 per cent or more of its economically active population doing secondary or tertiary activities. As an exception, centres of tourism and recreation with more than 250 housing units that do not satisfy the population requirement are nevertheless considered urban.

Colombia: Urban census area, defined by Departamento Administrativo Nacional de Estadistica (DANE) for statistical purposes, corresponding to the areas delimited by the census perimeter.

Ecuador: Capitals of provinces and cantons.

Falkland Islands (Malvinas): Town of Stanley.

French Guiana: A commune or a group of communes with more than 2 000 inhabitants in a continuous building area (no more than 200 meters between two buildings).

Paraguay: Cities, towns and administrative centres of departments and districts.

Peru: Populated centres with more than 5 000 inhabitants, which have public services, educational institutions and health facilities.

Suriname: The districts of Paramaribo and Wanica.

Uruguay: Cities, villages, towns and other populated areas as defined by the Law of Population Centers.

Venezuela (Bolivarian Republic of): Centres with a population of 2 500 or more inhabitants.

ASIA

Armenia: Cities and urban-type localities, officially designated as such, usually according to the criteria of number of inhabitants and predominance of agricultural, or number of non-agricultural workers and their families.

Azerbaijan: An administrative division which covers more than 15 000 population, engaging mainly in industrial and other economic and social activities and which include administrative and cultural centers.

Bahrain: Communes or villages of 2 500 or more inhabitants.

Brunei Darussalam: Municipality areas of Bandar Seri Begawan, Kuala Belait, Seria, Pekan Tutong and Pekan Bangar; and heavily populated areas with urban characteristics.

Cambodia: Areas at the commune level satisfying the following three conditions: (1) Population Density exceeding 200 per square Km, (2) Percentage of male employed in agriculture below 50 per cent, (3) Total population of the commune exceeds 2 000 inhabitants.

China: According to the Regulation on the Classification of Urban/Rural Residence for Statistical Purposes.

Cyprus: As determined by the Department of Town Planning and Housing of the Ministry of Interior.

Georgia: Cities and urban-type localities, officially designated as such, usually according to the criteria of number of inhabitants and predominance of agricultural, or number of non-agricultural workers and their families.

India: Towns (places with municipal corporation, municipal area committee, town committee, notified area committee or cantonment board); also, all places having 5 000 or more inhabitants, a density of not less than 1 000 persons per square mile or 400 per square kilometre, pronounced urban characteristics and at least three fourths of the adult male population employed in pursuits other than agriculture.

Indonesia: Area which satisfies certain criteria in terms of population density, percentage of agricultural households, access to urban facilities, existence of additional facilities, and percentage of built up area not for housing.

Iran (Islamic Republic of): Every district with a municipality.

Israel: Localities with 2 000 or more residents.

Japan: City (shi) having 50 000 or more inhabitants with 60 per cent or more of the houses located in the main built-up areas and 60 per cent or more of the population (including their dependants) engaged in manufacturing, trade or other urban type of business.

Jordan: Localities of 5 000 or more inhabitants.

Kazakhstan: Cities of Republican status (population centres of special national importance or with a population of usually more than one million), Oblast status (population centres that are major economic and cultural centres with developed industrial and social infrastructure and a population of more than 50,000, the country has 40 Oblast status cities), Raion status and settlements located under their administrative jurisdiction.

Kuwait: All localities in Kuwait are urban.

Kyrgyzstan: Cities and urban-type localities, officially designated as such, usually according to the criteria of number of inhabitants and predominance of agricultural, or number of non-agricultural workers and their families.

Lao People's Democratic Republic: Areas or villages that satisfy at least three of the following five conditions: located in metropolitan areas of district or province, there is access to road in dry and rainy seasons, more than 70 per cent of the population has access to piped water, more than 70 per cent of the population has access to public electricity, there is a permanent market operating every day.

Malaysia: Gazetted areas with their adjoining built-up areas which have a combined population of 10 000 or more. Built-up areas are defined as areas contiguous to a gazetted area and have at least 60 per cent of their population (aged 15 years and over) engaged in non-agricultural activities. The definition of urban areas also takes into account the special development area which is not gazetted and can be indentified and separated from the gazetted area or built-up area of more than 5km and a population of at least 10 000 with 60 per cent of the population (aged 15 years and over) engaged in non-agricultural activities.

Maldives: Malé, the capital.

Mongolia: Capital (Ulaanbaatar), provincial centers and towns.

Myanmar: Areas classified by the General Administration Department as wards. Generally, these areas have an increased density of building structures, population and better infrastructure development.

Nepal: As declared by the government municipalities.

Pakistan: Places with metropolitan corporation, municipal corporation, municipal committee, town committee or cantonment at the time of the census.

Philippines:
Areas (barangays) with more than 5 000 inhabitants, at least one establishment with a minimum of 100 employees, or five or more small establishments with 10 to 99 employees and five or more facilities within the two-kilometre radius from the barangay hall, as per *Philippine Statistics Authority (PSA) Board Resolution No. 01, Series of 2017-098 – Adoption of the Operational Definition of Urban Areas in the Philippines*. In addition, all barangays in the National Capital Region are automatically classified as urban.

Republic of Korea: For estimates: Localities with 50 000 or more inhabitants. For census: the figures are composed in the basis of the minor administrative divisions such as Dongs (mostly urban areas) and Eups or Myeons (rural areas).

Saudi Arabia: Localities with more than 5 000 inhabitants.

Singapore: Singapore is a city-state.

Sri Lanka: All areas administered by municipal and urban councils.

State of Palestine: Any locality where the population amounts to 10 000 persons or more. This applies to all governorates/districts regardless of their size, and to all localities whose populations vary from 4 000 to 9 999 persons provided they have at least four of the following elements: public electricity network, public water network, post office, health center with a full time physician and a school offering a general secondary education certificate.

Syrian Arab Republic: Cities, Mohafaza centres and Mantika centres, and communities with 20 000 or more inhabitants.

Tajikistan: Cities and urban-type localities, officially designated as such, usually according to the criteria of number of inhabitants and predominance of agricultural, or number of non-agricultural workers and their families.

Thailand: Municipal areas.

Turkey: Localities with 20 000 inhabitants or more.

Turkmenistan: Cities and urban-type localities, officially designated as such, usually according to the criteria of number of inhabitants and predominance of agricultural, or number of non-agricultural workers and their families.

Uzbekistan: Cities and urban-type localities, officially designated as such, usually according to the criteria of number of inhabitants and predominance of agricultural, or number of non-agricultural workers and their families.

Viet Nam: Urban areas include inside urban districts of cities, urban quarters and towns. All other local administrative units (communes) belong to rural areas.

EUROPE

Albania: Towns and other industrial centres of more than 400 inhabitants.

Austria: Urban areas are localities with 2 000 or more inhabitants. The delineation of localities goes back to 1991.

Belarus: Urban settlements are settlements authorized under the law as towns, urban-type settlements, workers settlements and health resort areas.

Belgium: All the communes which are not part of the list of rural communes are considered as urban communes. There are 33 communes which are considered rural: Alveringem, Amblève, Bertogne, Bièvre, Bullange, Burg-Reuland, Clavier, Erezée, Fauvillers, Frasnes-lez-Anvaing, Froidchapelle, Gedinne, Gouvy, Havelange, Herstappe, Heuvelland, Houffalize, Houyet, Langemark-Poelkapelle, Léglise, Lierneux, Lo-Reninge, Manhay, Momignies, Ravels, Sainte-Ode, Sint-Laureins, Sivry-Rance, Stoumont, Tenneville, Vaux-sur-Sûre, Vleteren and Vresse-sur-Semois.

Bulgaria: All towns and cities according to the Territorial and Administrative-Territorial Division of the country.

Czech Republic: Localities with 2 000 or more inhabitants.

Estonia: Urban settlements include cities, cities without municipal status and towns.

Finland: Urban communes including those municipalities in which at least 90 per cent of the population lives in urban settlements or in which the population of the largest urban settlement is at least 15 000.

France: A commune or a group of communes with more than 2 000 inhabitants in a continuous building area (no more than 200 meters between two buildings).

Greece: Urban is considered every municipal or communal department of which the largest locality has 2 000 inhabitants and over.

Hungary: Localities recognized by the President of the Republic with the title of town, on the basis of specific (economic, commercial, institutional, cultural etc.) criteria.

Iceland: Localities of 200 or more inhabitants.

Ireland: Cities and towns including suburbs of 1 500 or more inhabitants.

Latvia: Cities and urban-type localities, officially designated as such, usually according to the criteria of number of inhabitants and predominance of agricultural, or number of non-agricultural workers and their families.

Lithuania: Urban population refers to persons who live in cities and towns, i.e., the population areas with closely built permanent dwellings and with the resident population of more than 3 000 of which 2/3 of employees work in industry, social infrastructure and business. In a number of towns the population may be less than 3 000 since these areas had already the status of "town" before the law was enforced (July 1994).

Malta: Grid cells of 1 square km with a density of at least 300 inhabitants per square km and a minimum population of 5 000, and densely populated areas (i.e. areas with a density superior to 500 inhabitants per square km).

Montenegro: According to the current law of territorial division of Montenegro, which conveys to each local community the obligation to decide which settlements are urban and which are rural.

Netherlands: Urban: Municipalities with a population of 2 000 and more inhabitants. Semi-urban: Municipalities with a population of less than 2 000 but with not more than 20 per cent of their economically active male population engaged in agriculture, and specific residential municipalities of commuters.

Norway: A hub of buildings inhabited by at least 200 people and where the distance between the buildings does not exceed 50 metres. The boundaries are dynamic and may be changed due to developments and population changes.

North Macedonia: A city is a populated place that has more than 3000 inhabitants, has a developed industrial and social infrastructure, and over 51% of employees work outside the primary activities.

Poland: All areas which have town rights or the status of a town with provisions of separate laws.

Portugal: Localities with 2 000 or more inhabitants.

Republic of Moldova: Cities and urban-type localities, officially designated as such, usually according to the criteria of number of inhabitants and predominance of agricultural, or number of non-agricultural workers and their families.

Romania: Localities in which the majority of the resources are employed in non-agricultural activities with a diversified level of endowment, having a constant and significant socio-economic influence on the whole area.

Russian Federation: Cities and urban-type localities, officially designated as such, usually according to the criteria of number of inhabitants and predominance of agricultural, or number of non-agricultural workers and their families.

Serbia: Municipalities, cities and the city of Belgrade.

Slovakia: Municipalities with the status of towns, according to the following criteria: 1) it is an economic, administrative, cultural or tourism centre; 2) provides services for other municipalities; 3) has urban character (at least partly); and 4) has 5 000 inhabitants or more.

Slovenia: Settlements of 3 000 or more inhabitants, settlements that serve as seats of municipalities with at least 1 400 inhabitants, and sub-urban areas that are being gradually integrated with an urban settlement of 5 000 or more inhabitants

Switzerland: Agglomerations and isolated towns (towns not attached to a cluster with at least 10,000 inhabitants) are the urban space.

Ukraine: Cities and urban-type localities officially designated as such, usually according to the criteria of number of inhabitants and predominance of agricultural, or number of non-agricultural workers and their families.

United Kingdom of Great Britain and Northern Ireland: For England and Wales, the built-up areas of 10 000 or more inhabitants; for Scotland, the settlements of 3 000 or more inhabitants; and for Northern Ireland, the settlements of 5 000 or more inhabitants.

OCEANIA

Australia: Areas of concentrated urban development with populations of 200 people or more, primarily identified using objective dwelling and population density criteria using data from the 2016 Census.

American Samoa: Agglomerations of 2 500 or more inhabitants, generally having population densities of 1 000 persons per square mile or more. Two types of urban areas: urbanized areas of 50 000 or more inhabitants and urban clusters of at least 2 500 and less than 50 000 inhabitants. (As of Census 2000, no urbanized areas are identified in American Samoa.)

Cook Islands: Raratonga, the most populous island.

Guam: Agglomerations of 2 500 or more inhabitants, generally having population densities of 1 000 persons per square mile or more, referred to as "urban clusters".

New Caledonia: Nouméa and communes of Païta, Nouvel Dumbéa and Mont-Dore.

New Zealand: All cities, plus boroughs, town districts, townships and country towns with a population of 1 000 or more usual residents.

Northern Mariana Islands: Agglomerations of 2 500 or more inhabitants, generally having population densities of 1 000 persons per square mile or more. Two types of urban areas: urbanized areas of 50 000 or more inhabitants and urban clusters of at least 2 500 and less than 50 000 inhabitants.

Palau: States with 2 500 inhabitants or more (the only state which satisfies this condition is Koror state).

Samoa: Only Apia Urban Area (AUA) region.

Tokelau: All of Tokelau's population is considered to be rural.

Tonga: Nuku'alofa.

Vanuatu: Luganville centre and Port Vila.

_____

NOTES

[1] For further information, see *Social and Demographic Statistics: Classifications of Size and Type of Locality and Urban/Rural Areas.* E/CN.3/551, United Nations, New York, 1980.

Tableau 6 – *Annuaire démographique 2018*

Le tableau 6 présente des données sur la population totale selon le sexe pour le plus grand nombre possible d'années entre 2009 et 2018, ainsi que la population urbaine si disponible.

Description des variables : les données proviennent de recensements de la population ou sont des estimations fondées, dans certains cas, sur des enquêtes par sondage portant sur toute la population. Le code qui figure dans la colonne « Code » du tableau indique comment les données ont été obtenues. Les codes utilisés sont expliqués à la fin du tableau.

Le sens donné au terme « urbain » est conforme aux définitions utilisées dans les recensements nationaux. Les définitions pour chaque pays, si disponible, font partie de ce note technique.

Calcul des pourcentages : les pourcentages de la population urbaine sont calculés par la Division de statistique du Département des affaires économiques et sociales de l'Organisation des Nations Unies et représentent le nombre de personnes qui vivent dans des régions considérées comme urbaines pour 100 personnes de la population totale. Dans de très rares cas, les données pour la population totale ont été révisées mais les données pour la population urbaine et la population rurale ne l'ont pas été. Ces données sont indiquées en note. Dans ces cas, les proportions de population urbaine ou rurale sont à interpréter avec précaution.

Fiabilité des données : les estimations considérées comme moins sûres sont indiquées en italique plutôt qu'en caractères romains. Le classement du point de vue de la fiabilité est fondé sur la méthode utilisée pour établir l'estimation de la population totale qui figure au tableau 3 (voir les explications dans les notes techniques relatives à ce même tableau).

Insuffisance des données : les statistiques de la population urbaine selon le sexe appellent toutes les réserves qui ont été formulées à la section 3 des Notes techniques à propos des statistiques de la population en général.

Les limitations fondamentales imposées par les variations de la définition de la population totale et par les lacunes du recensement se font peut-être sentir davantage dans la répartition de la population en population urbaine et population rurale que dans sa répartition suivant toute autre caractéristique. De fait, des différences dans la définition du lieu de résidence habituel utilisée pour l'exploitation des données à l'échelon sous-national influent sur la classification en population urbaine et en population rurale. De même, les différences de degré de sous-dénombrement suivant la zone, à l'occasion des recensements, ont une incidence sur la comparabilité de ces deux catégories dans l'ensemble du tableau. La distinction entre population de fait et population de droit est également très importante du point de vue de la répartition de la population en population urbaine et en population rurale. Cette distinction est expliquée en détail à la section 3.1.1 des Notes techniques.

Toutefois, la difficulté la plus importante tient aux différences de définition du terme « urbain » selon le pays. Les distinctions faites entre « zone urbaine » et « zone rurale » varient tellement que les définitions utilisées ont été reproduites à la fin de ces notes techniques. Les définitions sont forcément brèves et, lorsque le classement en « zone urbaine » repose sur des divisions administratives, on a souvent désigné celles-ci par le nom qu'elles portent dans la zone ou le pays considéré. Par suite des variations dans la terminologie, les différences entre pays ou zones peuvent sembler plus grandes qu'elles ne le sont réellement. Il se peut aussi que des termes similaires ou identiques, tels que ville, village ou district, aient des significations très différentes selon les pays ou zones.

La distinction entre « zone urbaine » et « zone rurale » repose sur une série de critères qualitatifs aussi bien que quantitatifs, notamment l'effectif de la population, la densité de peuplement, la distance entre îlots d'habitations, le type prédominant d'activité économique, le statut juridique ou administratif, et les caractéristiques d'une agglomération urbaine, c'est-à-dire l'existence de services publics et d'équipements collectifs[1]. Bien que les statistiques différenciant les zones urbaines des zones rurales soient très répandues, il ne paraît pas possible pour le moment d'adopter une classification internationale type de ces zones, vu la diversité des interprétations nationales. La classification de la population en population urbaine et population rurale retenue ici est celle qui correspond aux définitions nationales.

Données publiées antérieurement : des statistiques concernant la population urbaine et la population totale selon le sexe ont été publiées dans des éditions antérieures de l'*Annuaire démographique*. Pour plus de précisions concernant les années pour lesquelles ces données ont été publiées, se reporter à l'index historique.

DÉFINITIONS DU TERME « URBAIN »

AFRIQUE

Algérie : La délimitation des zones urbaines et rurales se font après l'opération du recensement sur la base de la classification des agglomérations. Regroupement de 100 constructions ou plus distantes l'une à l'autre de moins de 200m ont été considérées comme zones urbaines.

Afrique du Sud : Zones dotées d'une administration locale.

Botswana : Agglomération de 5 000 habitants ou plus dont 75 p. 100 de l'activité économique n'est pas de type agricole.

Burkina Faso : Tous les chefs-lieux de province (45 au total) plus 4 villes moyennes ont été considérées comme zones urbaines.

Burundi : Commune de Bujumbura.

Comores : Toute localité ou chef-lieu d'une île, région/préfecture disposant des infrastructures suivantes : route bitumée, électricité, centre hospitalier, téléphone, etc.

Égypte : Chefs-lieux des gouvernorats du Caire, d'Alexandrie, de Port Saïd, d'Ismaïlia, de Suez ; chefs-lieux des gouvernorats frontaliers, autres chefs-lieux de gouvernorat et chefs-lieux de district (Markaz). La définition des zones urbaines pour le recensement de 2006 est celle de « shiakha », une partie d'un district.

Éthiopie : Localités de 2 000 habitants ou plus.

Eswatini : Zone géographique qui constitue une ville et se caractérise par une densité de population et de constructions humaines plus élevée que dans les zones qui l'entourent.**Guinée :** Centres administratifs des préfectures et la ville capitale (Conakry).

Guinée équatoriale : Chefs-lieux de district et localités comprenant 300 habitations et/ou 1 500 habitants ou plus.

Kenya : Zone ayant une population de 2 000 habitants ou plus qui dispose de réseaux de transport, comporte des zones bâties, des structures industrielles ou manufacturières et d'autres équipements modernes.

Lesotho : Tous les chefs-lieux administratifs et établissements en forte croissance.

Libéria : Localités de 2 000 habitants ou plus.

Malawi : Toutes les villes et zones urbanisées et tous les chefs-lieux de district.

Maurice : Les cinq circonscriptions municipales, divisées en vingt arrondissements municipaux dont les limites ont été officiellement définies.

Namibie : Zones urbaines déclarées pour lesquelles il existe des données cadastrales et autres zones d'habitat non planifié.

Niger : Ville capital, villes capitales de départements ou de districts.

Ouganda : « Gazettes », villes, municipalités et bourgs.

République-Unie de Tanzanie : Toutes les zones érigées en communes et les zones reconnues par les autorités gouvernementales comme urbaines.

Réunion : Une commune ou un ensemble de communes présentant une zone de bâti continu (pas de coupure de plus de 200 mètres entre deux constructions) qui compte au moins 2 000 habitants.

Rwanda : Toutes les zones administratives reconnues comme urbaines par la loi. Il s'agit de tous les chefs - lieux des provinces, de la ville de Kigali ainsi que des villes de Nyanza, Ruhango et Rwamagana.

Sénégal : Agglomérations de 10 000 habitants ou plus.

Soudan : Centres administratifs et/ou commerciaux ou localités ayant une population de 5 000 habitants ou plus.

Tunisie : Population vivant dans les communes.

Zambie : Localités de 5 000 habitants ou plus dont l'activité économique prédominante n'est pas de type agricole.

AMÉRIQUE DU NORD

Bermudes : Le pays est considéré entièrement urbain.

Canada : Agglomérations de 1 000 habitants ou plus ayant une densité de population d'au moins 400 habitants au kilomètre carré, basé sur les chiffres de population du dernier recensement de la population.

Costa Rica : Chefs-lieux de canton.

Cuba : Localités ayant une population supérieure à 2 000 habitants ; ou une population supérieure à 1 000 habitants dont la moitié de la population économiquement active s'occupe des activités non-agricoles.

El Salvador : Chefs-lieux des municipalités.

États-Unis d'Amérique : Agglomérations de 2 500 habitants ou plus ayant généralement une densité de population d'au moins 1 000 habitants au mile carré. Deux types de zones urbaines : zones urbanisées de 50 000 habitants ou plus et groupements urbains comptant au moins 2 500 habitants mais moins de 50 000.

Groenland : Localités d'au moins 200 habitants.

Guadeloupe : Une commune ou un ensemble de communes présentant une zone de bâti continu (pas de coupure de plus de 200 mètres entre deux constructions) qui compte au moins 2 000 habitants.

Guatemala : Municipalité du département de Guatemala et centres administratifs officiels d'autres départements et municipalités.

Haïti : Chefs-lieux de communes.

Honduras : Localités d'au moins 2 000 habitants ayant des caractéristiques essentiellement urbaines.

Îles Vierges américaines : Agglomérations de 2 500 habitants ou plus ayant généralement une densité de population d'au moins 1 000 habitants au mile carré. Deux types de zones urbaines : zones urbanisées de 50 000 habitants ou plus et groupements urbains comptant au moins 2 500 habitants mais moins de 50 000. (D'après les résultats du recensement de 2 000, les Îles Vierges américaines ne comptent aucune zone urbanisée.)

Jamaïque : Localités de 2 000 habitants ou plus ayant des caractéristiques urbaines.

Martinique : Une commune ou un ensemble de communes présentant une zone de bâti continu (pas de coupure de plus de 200 mètres entre deux constructions) qui compte au moins 2 000 habitants.

Mexique : Localités d'au moins 2 500 habitants.

Nicaragua : Centres administratifs des municipalités et localités d'au moins 1 000 habitants ou d'au moins 150 logements, possédant des rues, un éclairage électrique, un réseau de distribution d'eau, une école et un dispensaire.

Panama : Localités d'au moins 1 500 habitants ayant des caractéristiques essentiellement urbaines. À partir de 1970, localités de 1 500 habitants ou plus présentant des caractéristiques urbaines, telles que rues, éclairage électrique, systèmes d'approvisionnement en eau et réseaux d'égouts.

Porto Rico : Agglomérations de 2 500 habitants ou plus ayant généralement une densité de population d'au moins 1 000 habitants au mile carré. Deux types de zones urbaines : zones urbanisées de 50 000 habitants ou plus et groupements urbains comptant au moins 2 500 habitants mais moins de 50 000.

République dominicaine : Chefs-lieux des municipalités et districts municipaux, dont certains comprennent des zones suburbaines ayant des caractéristiques rurales.

Saint-Barthélemy : Une commune ou un ensemble de communes présentant une zone de bâti continu (pas de coupure de plus de 200 mètres entre deux constructions) qui compte au moins 2 000 habitants.

Saint-Martin (Partie française) : Une commune ou un ensemble de communes présentant une zone de bâti continu (pas de coupure de plus de 200 mètres entre deux constructions) qui compte au moins 2 000 habitants.

Saint-Pierre-et-Miquelon : Une commune ou un ensemble de communes présentant une zone de bâti continu (pas de coupure de plus de 200 mètres entre deux constructions) qui compte au moins 2 000 habitants.

AMÉRIQUE DU SUD

Argentine : Centres comptant au moins 2 000 habitants.

Bolivie : Localités de 2 000 habitants ou plus.

Brésil : Zone à l'intérieur du périmètre urbain d'une ville, définie par la législation municipale.

Chili : Zones d'habitat concentré comptant 2 000 habitants ou plus, ou comptant entre 1 001 et 2 000 habitants dont 50 pour cent au moins de la population active s'occupe d'une activité secondaire ou tertiaire. Par dérogation, les centres qui ont une fonction touristique ou récréative et plus de 250 unités de logement mais n'atteignent pas le critère de population sont néanmoins considérés comme zones urbaines.

Colombie : Zone urbaine de recensement, définie par le Département administratif national d'État (DANE) à des fins statistiques, correspondant aux zones délimitées par le périmètre de recensement.

Équateur : Capitales des provinces et chefs-lieux de canton.

Guinée française : Une commune ou un ensemble de communes présentant une zone de bâti continu (pas de coupure de plus de 200 mètres entre deux constructions) qui compte au moins 2 000 habitants.

Îles Falkland (Malvinas) : Ville de Stanley.

Paraguay : Grandes villes, villes et chefs-lieux des départements et des districts.

Pérou : Centres peuplés de plus de 5 000 habitants, dotés de services publics, d'établissements d'enseignement et d'établissements de santé.

Suriname : Les districts de Paramaribo et de Wanica.

Uruguay : Les villes, villages et autres zones habitées répondant aux définitions de la loi sur les agglomérations.

Venezuela (République bolivarienne du) : Centres de 2 500 habitants ou plus.

ASIE

Arabie saoudite : Localités de plus de 5 000 habitants.

Arménie : Grandes villes et localités de type urbain, officiellement désignées comme telles, généralement sur la base du nombre d'habitants et de la prédominance des travailleurs agricoles ou non agricoles avec leur famille.

Azerbaïdjan : Division administrative regroupant plus de 15 000 habitants se livrant principalement à des activités industrielles et autres activités économiques et sociales et comprennant des centres administratifs et culturels.

Bahreïn : Communes ou villages comptant au moins 2 500 habitants.

Brunéi Darussalam : Les communes de Bandar, Seri Begawan, Kuala Belait, Seria, Pekan Tutong and Pekan Bangar; et les zones densement peuplé qui possèdent des caractéristiques urbaines.

Cambodge : Zones au niveau de la commune répondant aux trois conditions suivantes : 1) Densité démographique supérieure à 200 habitants au km carré, 2) pourcentage d'hommes travaillant dans l'agriculture inférieur à 50 pour cent, 3) population totale de la commune supérieure à 2 000 habitants.

Chine : Suivant la Réglementation sur la classification de la résidence urbaine/rurale à des fins de statistiques.

Chypre : Selon la définition du Département de l'urbanisme et du logement du Ministère de l'intérieur.

État de Palestine : Localités peuplées de plus de 10 000 personnes. L'expression désigne tous les gouvernorats (districts), quelle qu'en soit la taille, ainsi que toutes les villes dont la population est comprise entre 4 000 et 9 999 personnes qui disposent d'au moins quatre des éléments suivants : réseau public de distribution d'électricité, réseau public de distribution d'eau, bureau de poste, centre médical doté d'un médecin à temps plein et école préparant les élèves au certificat général de l'enseignement secondaire.

Géorgie : Grandes villes et localités de type urbain, officiellement désignées comme telles, généralement sur la base du nombre d'habitants et de la prédominance des travailleurs agricoles ou non agricoles avec leur famille.

Inde : Villes [localités dotées d'une charte municipale, d'un comité de zone municipale, d'un comité de zone déclarée urbaine ou d'un comité de zone de regroupement (cantonnement)] ; également toutes les localités qui ont une population de 5 000 habitants au moins, une densité de population d'au moins 1 000 habitants au mile carré ou 400 au kilomètre carré, des caractéristiques urbaines prononcées et où les trois quarts au moins des adultes de sexe masculin ont une occupation non agricole.

Indonésie : Les zones urbaines sont celles qui répondent à certains critères : densité de population, pourcentage de ménages agricoles, accès aux équipements urbains, existence d'équipements supplémentaires, et pourcentage de superficie bâtie à usage autre que l'habitation.

Iran (République islamique d') : Tous les districts comptant une municipalité.

Israël : Tous les lieux comptant au moins 2 000 résidents.

Japon : Villes (shi), comptant au moins 50 000 habitants, où 60 p. 100 au moins des logements sont situés dans les principales zones bâties, et dont 60 p. 100 au moins de population (y compris les personnes à charge) exercent un métier dans l'industrie, le commerce et d'autres branches d'activités essentiellement urbaines.

Jordanie : Localités comptant 5 000 habitants ou plus.

Kazakhstan : Villes ayant statut républicain (centres de population présentant une importance nationale spéciale ou comptant une population généralement de plus d'un million d'habitants), statut régional (Oblast') (centres de population qui sont de grands centres économiques et culturels, dotés d'une infrastructure industrielle et sociale développée et comptant une population de plus 50 000 habitants, le pays compte 40 villes ayant statut régional), statut départemental, et agglomérations relevant de leur juridiction administrative.

Kirghizistan : Grandes villes et localités de type urbain, officiellement désignées comme telles, généralement sur la base du nombre d'habitants et de la prédominance des travailleurs agricoles ou non agricoles avec leur famille.

Koweït : Toutes les localités sont urbaines au Koweït.

Malaisie : Zone ayant le statut de centre urbain et dont la population totale dépasse 10 000 habitants. On nomme périphérie toute zone contiguë à un centre urbain dont au moins 60 % de la population (âgée de 15 ans et plus) a une activité non agricole. La définition des zones urbaines couvre également les zones spéciales de développement qui n'ont pas officiellement le statut de centre urbain, se trouvent à 5 kilomètres ou plus d'un tel centre ou de sa périphérie et comptent au moins 10 000 habitants dont 60 % (parmi les plus de 15 ans) ont une activité non agricole.

Maldives : Malé (la capitale).

Mongolie : Ulaanbaatar (la capitale), les chefs-lieux des provinces et les villes.

Myanmar : Les zones reconnues par les autorités gouvernementales comme urbaines. Ces zones se caractérisent par une densité de population et de constructions humaines plus élevée et disposent de meilleures infrastructures.

Népal : Zones déclarées telles par les municipalités.

Ouzbékistan : Grandes villes et localités de type urbain, officiellement désignées comme telles, généralement sur la base du nombre d'habitants et de la prédominance des travailleurs agricoles ou non agricoles avec leur famille.

Pakistan : Lieux avec une corporation métropolitaine, une corporation municipale, un comité municipal, un comité municipal ou un cantonnement au moment du recensement.

Philippines : Zones (barangays) de plus de 5 000 habitants, au moins un établissement d'au moins 100 employés, ou au moins cinq petits établissements comptant de 10 à 99 employés et cinq installations ou plus dans un rayon de deux kilomètres du barangay, comme Résolution no. 01 du Conseil de la Philippine Statistics Authority (PSA), série du 2017-098 - Adoption de la définition opérationnelle des zones urbaines aux Philippines. En outre, tous les barangays de la région de la capitale nationale sont automatiquement classés en zones urbaines.

République arabe syrienne : Villes, chefs-lieux de district (Mohafaza) et chefs-lieux de sous district (Mantika), et communes d'au moins 20 000 habitants.

République de Corée : Pour les estimations : localités de 50 000 habitants ou plus. Pour recensements, les données sont établies sont la base des divisions administratives mineures comme les Dongs (principalement en zone urbaines) et des Eups ou Myeons (en zones rurales).

République démocratique populaire lao : Zones ou villages répondant à au moins trois des cinq conditions suivantes: situés dans l'aire métropolitaine du district ou de la province, accessibles par la route en toute saison, plus de 70 pour cent de la population ayant accès à de l'eau distribuée par canalisation, plus de 70 pour cent de la population ayant accès au réseau d'électricité et existence d'un marché ouvert tous les jours.

Singapour : Le pays consiste seulement d'une ville.

Sri Lanka : Toutes les zones administrées par les conseils municipaux et urbains.

Tadjikistan : Grandes villes et localités de type urbain, officiellement désignées comme telles, généralement sur la base du nombre d'habitants et de la prédominance des travailleurs agricoles ou non agricoles avec leur famille.

Thaïlande : Zones municipales.

Turkménistan : Grandes villes et localités de type urbain, officiellement désignées comme telles, généralement sur la base du nombre d'habitants et de la prédominance des travailleurs agricoles ou non agricoles avec leur famille.

Turquie : Localités comptant 20 000 habitants ou plus.

Viet Nam : Zones urbaines comprises à l'intérieur des districts urbains des villes ainsi que des quartiers urbains et des localités. Toutes les autres unités administratives locales (communes) sont considérées comme zones rurales.

EUROPE

Albanie : Villes et autres centres industriels de plus de 400 habitants.

Autriche : Les zones urbaines sont les localités comptant 2 000 habitants ou plus. Leur délimitation remonte à 1991.

Bélarus : Les établissements urbains sont des établissements autorisés en vertu de la loi comme les villes, les agglomérations de type urbain, les cités ouvrières et les zones de villégiature de santé.

Belgique : Toutes les communes qui ne sont pas dans la liste des communes rurales sont considérées comme des communes urbaines. Il y a 33 communes qui sont considérées comme rurales: Alveringem, Amblève, Bertogne, Bièvre, Bullange, Burg-Reuland, Clavier, Erezée, Fauvillers, Frasnes-lez-Anvaing, Froidchapelle, Gedinne, Gouvy, Havelange, Herstappe, Heuvelland, Houffalize, Houyet, Langemark-Poelkapelle, Léglise, Lierneux, Lo-Reninge, Manhay, Momignies, Ravels, Sainte-Ode, Sint-Laureins, Sivry-Rance, Stoumont, Tenneville, Vaux-sur-Sûre, Vleteren et Vresse-sur-Semois.

Bulgarie : Toutes les zones considérées comme villes et bourgs selon la Division territoriale et administrative du pays.

Estonie : Les établissements urbains comprennent les villes et les agglomérations n'ayant pas de statut municipal.

Fédération de Russie : Grandes villes et localités de type urbain, officiellement désignées comme telles, généralement sur la base du nombre d'habitants et de la prédominance des travailleurs agricoles ou non agricoles avec leur famille.

Finlande : Communes urbaines (communes où au moins 90 % de la population vit en milieu urbain ou dont le plus grand centre urbain compte au moins 15 000 habitants).

France : Une commune ou un ensemble de communes présentant une zone de bâti continu (pas de coupure de plus de 200 mètres entre deux constructions) qui compte au moins 2 000 habitants.

Grèce : Est considérée comme zone urbaine toute municipalité ou commune dont la plus grande localité compte 2 000 habitants ou plus.

Hongrie : Localités dont le statut de ville a été reconnu par le Président de la République compte tenu de critères spécifiques (économiques, commerciaux, institutionnels, culturels, etc.).

Irlande : Localités, y compris leur banlieues, comptant 1 500 habitants ou plus.

Islande : Localités de 200 habitants ou plus.

Lettonie : Grandes villes et localités de type urbain, officiellement désignées comme telles, généralement sur la base du nombre d'habitants et de la prédominance des travailleurs agricoles ou non agricoles avec leur famille.

Lituanie : Par population urbaine, on entend les personnes qui vivent dans des villes ou des localités, à savoir les zones habitées comportant des logements permanents proches les uns des autres et dont la population est d'au moins 3 000 habitants, les deux tiers desquels étant employés dans le secteur industriel, l'infrastructure sociale ou le commerce. Un certain nombre de villes peuvent compter moins de 3 000 habitants dans la mesure où elles avaient acquis le statut de ville avant l'entrée en vigueur de la nouvelle loi en juillet 1994.

Macédoine du Nord : Villes sont les localités comptant au moins 3 000 habitants, dotés d'une infrastructure industrielle et sociale développée, dont plus de 51 pour cent de la population active s'occupe des activités qui ne sont pas primaires.

Malte : Zones de 1 kilomètre carré avec une densité minimum de 300 au kilomètre carré et un minimum de 5 000 habitants, et zones à forte densité de population (supérieure à 500 habitants au kilomètre carré).

Monténégro : D'après la législation actuelle relative à l'organisation territoriale du Monténégro, qui oblige chaque collectivité à déterminer quelles sont ses zones urbaines et rurales.

Norvège : Ensemble construit habité par au moins 200 personnes, où les bâtiments ne sont pas éloignés de plus de 50 mètres les uns des autres. Les limites en sont évolutives et peuvent être redéfinies pour tenir compte de l'urbanisation et de l'évolution de la population.

Pays Bas : Zones urbaines : municipalités comptant au moins 2 000 habitants. Zones semi-urbaines : municipalités comptant moins de 2 000 habitants, mais où 20 p. 100 au maximum de la population active de sexe masculin pratiquent l'agriculture, et certaines municipalités de caractère résidentiel dont les habitants travaillent ailleurs.

Pologne : Toutes les zones qui ont les droits d'une ville ou le statut d'une ville avec dispositions de lois distinctes.

Portugal : Localités comptant 2 000 habitants ou davantage.

République de Moldova : Grandes villes et localités de type urbain, officiellement désignées comme telles, généralement sur la base du nombre d'habitants et de la prédominance des travailleurs agricoles ou non agricoles avec leur famille.

République tchèque : Localités d'au moins 2 000 habitants.

Roumanie : Localités où la majorité des ressources en main-d'œuvre est employée dans des activités non agricoles avec un niveau diversifié de ressources, exerçant une influence socioéconomique constante et importante sur l'ensemble de la zone.

Royaume-Uni de Grande-Bretagne et d'Irlande du Nord : Pour l'Angleterre et le Pays de Galles, les zones bâties comptant 10 000 habitants ou plus ; pour l'Écosse, les établissements humains comptant 3 000 habitants ou davantage et pour l'Irlande du Nord, les établissements comptant 5 000 habitants.

Serbie : Municipalités, villes et Belgrade.

Slovaquie : Municipalités avec statut de ville, conformément aux critères : 1) est un centre économique, administratif, culturel ou touristique ; 2) fournit des services pour d'autres municipalités ; 3) a un caractère urbain, au moins en partie ; et 4) compte 5 000 habitants ou plus.

Slovénie : Établissements de 3 000 habitants ou plus, chefs-lieux de municipalités comptant au moins 1 400 habitants, et quartiers suburbains qui s'intègrent progressivement dans une ville de 5 000 habitants ou plus.

Suisse : L'espace urbain comprend les agglomérations et les villes isolées (n'appartenant pas à une agglomération et comptant au moins 10 000 habitants à elles seules).

Ukraine : Grandes villes et localités de type urbain, officiellement désignées comme telles, généralement sur la base du nombre d'habitants et de la prédominance des travailleurs agricoles ou non agricoles avec leur famille.

OCÉANIE

Australie : Zones de développement urbain concentré comptant 200 habitants ou plus, identifiées principalement à l'aide de critères objectifs en matière de logement et de densité de population, à l'aide des données du recensement de 2016.

Guam : Agglomérations de 2 500 habitants ou plus ayant généralement une densité de population d'au moins 1 000 habitants au mile carré et considérées comme étant des groupements urbains.

Îles Cook : Rarotonga, île la plus peuplée.

Îles Mariannes septentrionales : Agglomérations de 2 500 habitants ou plus ayant généralement une densité de population d'au moins 1 000 habitants au mile carré. Deux types de zones urbaines : zones urbanisées de 50 000 habitants ou plus et groupements urbains comptant au moins 2 500 habitants mais moins de 50 000.

Nouvelle-Calédonie : Nouméa et communes de Païta, Dumbéa et Mont-Dore.

Nouvelle-Zélande : Toutes les villes et les quartiers, districts et bourgs ayant 1 000 habitants permanents ou plus.

Palaos : États comptant 2 500 habitants ou plus (le seul État qui remplit cette condition est l'État de Koror).

Samoa : Seule la région urbaine d'Apia (AUA).

Samoa américaines : Agglomérations de 2 500 habitants ou plus ayant généralement une densité de population d'au moins 1 000 habitants au mile carré. Deux types de zones urbaines : zones urbanisées de 50 000 habitants ou plus et groupements urbains comptant au moins 2 500 habitants mais moins de 50 000. (D'après les résultats du recensement de 2000, les Samoa américaines ne comptent aucune zone urbanisée.)

Tokélaou : L'ensemble de la population est considéré comme vivant en milieu rural.

Tonga : Nuku'alofa.

Vanuatu : Centre de Luganville et Port-Vila.

NOTES

[1] Pour plus de précisions, voir *Social and Demographic Statistics : Classifications of Size and Type of Locality and Urban/Rural Areas*, E/CN.3/551, publication des Nations Unies, New York, 1980.

6. Total and urban population by sex: 2009 - 2018
Population totale et population urbaine selon le sexe : 2009 - 2018

Continent, country or area, and date / Continent, pays ou zone et date	Code[a]	Both sexes - Les deux sexes Total	Urban - Urbaine Number Nombre	Urban - Urbaine Percent P.100	Male - Masculin Total	Urban - Urbaine Number Nombre	Urban - Urbaine Percent P.100	Female - Féminin Total	Urban - Urbaine Number Nombre	Urban - Urbaine Percent P.100
AFRICA - AFRIQUE										
Algeria - Algérie										
1 VII 2009	ESDJ	35 268 000	...	...	17 846 000	...	...	17 422 000	...	...
1 VII 2010	ESDJ	35 978 000	...	...	18 205 000	...	...	17 773 000	...	...
1 VII 2011	ESDJ	36 717 000	...	...	18 579 000	...	...	18 138 000	...	...
1 VII 2012	ESDJ	37 495 000	...	...	18 976 000	...	...	18 519 000	...	...
1 VII 2013	ESDJ	38 297 000	...	...	19 383 000	...	...	18 914 000	...	...
1 VII 2014	ESDJ	39 114 275	...	...	19 801 163	...	...	19 313 112	...	...
1 VII 2015	ESDJ	39 963 249	...	...	20 235 204	...	...	19 728 045	...	...
1 VII 2016	ESDJ	40 835 602	...	...	20 680 271	...	...	20 155 331	...	...
1 VII 2017	ESDJ	41 695 626	...	...	21 118 894	...	...	20 576 732	...	...
Angola										
1 VII 2009[1]	ESDF	16 888 858	...	...	8 158 550			8 730 308		
1 VII 2010[1]	ESDF	17 429 637	...	...	8 427 802	...	...	9 001 835		
1 VII 2011[1]	ESDF	17 992 033	...	...	8 707 868	...	...	9 284 165	...	...
1 VII 2012[1]	ESDF	18 576 568	...	...	8 999 074	...	...	9 577 494	...	...
1 VII 2013[1]	ESDF	19 183 590	...	...	9 301 632			9 881 958		
16 V 2014[2]	CDFC	25 789 024	16 153 987	62.6	12 499 041	7 860 614	62.9	13 289 983	8 293 373	62.4
1 VII 2014[2]	ESDF	25 901 182	16 235 542	62.7	12 553 707	7 900 523	62.9	13 347 475	8 335 019	62.4
1 VII 2015[2]	ESDF	26 681 590	16 761 094	62.8	12 943 812	8 165 438	63.1	13 737 778	8 595 656	62.6
1 VII 2016[2]	ESDF	27 503 526	17 310 474	62.9	13 355 101	8 442 190	63.2	14 148 425	8 868 284	62.7
1 VII 2017[2]	ESDF	28 359 634	17 881 283	63.1	13 783 460	8 729 543	63.3	14 576 174	9 151 740	62.8
1 VII 2018[2]	ESDF	29 250 009	18 473 609	63.2	14 228 926	9 027 566	63.4	15 021 083	9 446 043	62.9
Benin - Bénin										
1 VII 2009[3]	ESDF	8 497 827	3 682 496	43.3	4 159 291	1 808 057	43.5	4 338 536	1 874 439	43.2
1 VII 2010[3]	ESDF	8 778 648	3 873 462	44.1	4 301 224	1 903 683	44.3	4 477 424	1 969 779	44.0
1 VII 2011[3]	ESDF	9 067 076	4 072 574	44.9	4 446 877	2 003 366	45.1	4 620 199	2 069 208	44.8
1 VII 2012[3]	ESDF	9 364 619	4 280 693	45.7	4 597 122	...	...	4 767 497	...	...
11 V 2013	CDFC	10 008 749	4 460 503	44.6	4 887 820	...	...	5 120 929	...	...
1 VII 2014[4]	ESDF	10 293 235	...	...	5 033 372	...	...	5 259 863	...	...
1 VII 2015[4]	ESDF	10 584 935	...	...	5 182 478	...	...	5 402 457	...	...
1 VII 2016[4]	ESDF	10 882 953	...	...	5 334 603	...	...	5 548 350	...	...
1 VII 2017[4]	ESDF	11 186 785	...	...	5 489 507	...	...	5 697 278	...	...
1 VII 2018[4]	ESDF	11 496 140	...	...	5 647 059	...	...	5 849 081	...	...
Botswana										
1 VII 2009	ESDJ	1 776 494	...	...	871 964	...	...	904 530	...	...
1 VII 2010	ESDJ	1 822 859	...	...	895 007	...	...	927 852	...	...
1 VII 2011	ESDJ	1 849 692	...	...	910 404	...	...	939 288	...	...
9 VIII 2011	CDFC	2 024 904	1 297 287	64.1	988 957	619 472	62.6	1 035 947	677 815	65.4
1 VII 2012[5]	ESDJ	2 070 984	1 361 699	65.8	1 010 236	664 243	65.8	1 060 748	697 456	65.8
1 VII 2013[5]	ESDJ	2 114 890	1 411 436	66.7	1 031 654	688 505	66.7	1 083 236	722 931	66.7
1 VII 2014[5]	ESDJ	2 156 366	1 460 383	67.7	1 051 886	712 382	67.7	1 104 480	748 001	67.7
1 VII 2015[5]	ESDJ	2 195 134	1 508 277	68.7	1 070 797	735 745	68.7	1 124 337	772 532	68.7
1 VII 2016[5]	ESDJ	2 230 905	1 554 836	69.7	1 088 246	758 457	69.7	1 142 659	796 379	69.7
1 VII 2017[5]	ESDJ	2 266 857	1 602 216	70.7	1 110 760	785 086	70.7	1 156 097	817 130	70.7
1 VII 2018[5]	ESDJ	2 302 878	...	...	1 134 505	...	...	1 168 373	...	...
Burkina Faso[3]										
1 VII 2009	ESDJ	15 224 780	...	...	7 346 835	...	...	7 877 945	...	...
1 VII 2010	ESDJ	15 730 977	...	...	7 590 133	...	...	8 140 844	...	...
1 VII 2011	ESDJ	16 248 558	...	...	7 839 350	...	...	8 409 208	...	...
1 VII 2012	ESDJ	16 779 206	...	...	8 095 324	...	...	8 683 882	...	...
1 VII 2013	ESDJ	17 322 796	...	...	8 357 967	...	...	8 964 829	...	...
1 VII 2014	ESDJ	17 880 386	...	...	8 627 830	...	...	9 252 556	...	...
1 VII 2015	ESDJ	18 450 494	...	...	8 904 256	...	...	9 546 238	...	...
1 VII 2016	ESDJ	19 034 397	...	...	9 187 904	...	...	9 846 493	...	...
1 VII 2017	ESDJ	19 632 147	...	...	9 478 805	...	...	10 153 342	...	...
Burundi										
1 VII 2010	ESDF	9 461 117	...	...	4 667 414	...	...	4 793 703	...	...
1 VII 2011	ESDF	9 770 966	...	...	4 821 919	...	...	4 949 047	...	...
1 VII 2012	ESDF	10 072 586	...	...	4 972 342	...	...	5 100 244	...	...
1 VII 2013	ESDF	10 367 166	...	...	5 119 077	...	...	5 248 090	...	...
1 VII 2014	ESDF	10 654 129	...	...	5 261 796	...	...	5 392 333	...	...
1 VII 2015	ESDF	10 933 352	...	...	5 400 270	...	...	5 533 083	...	...
1 VII 2016	ESDF	11 215 024	...	...	5 539 816	...	...	5 675 209	...	...
1 VII 2017	ESDF	11 495 438	...	...	5 678 570	...	...	5 816 869	...	...
1 VII 2018	ESDF	11 772 322	...	...	5 815 408	...	...	5 956 914	...	...

Continent, country or area, and date / Continent, pays ou zone et date	Code[a]	Both sexes - Les deux sexes			Male - Masculin			Female - Féminin		
		Total	Urban - Urbaine		Total	Urban - Urbaine		Total	Urban - Urbaine	
			Number Nombre	Percent P.100		Number Nombre	Percent P.100		Number Nombre	Percent P.100
AFRICA - AFRIQUE										
Cabo Verde										
1 VII 2009 ....ESDF		508 633	310 958	61.1	246 219	...	...	262 414	...	...
16 VI 2010 ....CDJC		491 683	303 673	61.8	243 403	151 219	62.1	248 280	152 454	61.4
1 VII 2010[3] ....ESDJ		494 040	...	...	244 338	...	...	249 702	...	...
1 VII 2011[3] ....ESDJ		499 929	...	...	247 814	...	...	252 115	...	...
1 VII 2012[3] ....ESDJ		505 983	...	...	251 384	...	...	254 599	...	...
1 VII 2013[3] ....ESDJ		512 173	...	...	255 033	...	...	257 140	...	...
1 VII 2014[3] ....ESDJ		518 467	...	...	258 744	...	...	259 723	...	...
1 VII 2015[3] ....ESDJ		524 833	...	...	262 501	...	...	262 331	...	...
1 VII 2016[3] ....ESDJ		531 239	...	...	266 287	...	...	264 951	...	...
1 VII 2017[3] ....ESDJ		537 661	...	...	270 091	...	...	267 570	...	...
1 VII 2018[3] ....ESDJ		544 081	...	...	273 904	...	...	270 177	...	...
Cameroon - Cameroun[6]										
1 VII 2009 ....ESDJ		19 570 989	...	...	9 708 607	...	...	9 862 382	...	...
1 VII 2010 ....ESDJ		20 127 358	...	...	9 975 947	...	...	10 151 411	...	...
1 VII 2011 ....ESDJ		20 709 658	...	...	10 271 305	...	...	10 438 353	...	...
1 VII 2012 ....ESDJ		21 277 400	...	...	10 548 982	...	...	10 728 418	...	...
1 VII 2013 ....ESDJ		21 848 088	...	...	10 825 833	...	...	11 022 255	...	...
1 VII 2014 ....ESDJ		22 454 094	...	...	11 134 230	...	...	11 319 864	...	...
1 VII 2015 ....ESDJ		23 050 282	...	...	11 417 323	...	...	11 632 959	...	...
1 VII 2016 ....ESDJ		23 642 400	...	...	11 706 438	...	...	11 935 962	...	...
1 VII 2017 ....ESDJ		24 253 757	...	...	12 008 210	...	...	12 245 547	...	...
1 VII 2018 ....ESDJ		24 863 335	...	...	12 302 528	...	...	12 560 807	...	...
Chad - Tchad										
20 V 2009 ....CDJC		11 039 873	2 404 145	21.8	5 452 483	1 240 663	22.8	5 587 390	1 163 482	20.8
1 VII 2010 ....ESDJ		11 469 500	2 542 406	22.2	5 668 049	1 256 418	22.2	5 801 451	1 285 988	22.2
1 VII 2011 ....ESDJ		11 880 614	2 665 217	22.4	5 876 234	1 318 235	22.4	6 004 379	1 346 982	22.4
1 VII 2012 ....ESDJ		12 306 561	2 793 589	22.7	6 092 153	1 382 919	22.7	6 214 408	1 410 671	22.7
1 VII 2013 ....ESDJ		12 746 650	2 927 481	23.0	6 315 618	1 450 487	23.0	6 431 033	1 476 994	23.0
1 VII 2014 ....ESDJ		13 200 844	3 066 996	23.2	6 546 755	1 521 029	23.2	6 654 089	1 545 966	23.2
1 VII 2015 ....ESDJ		13 670 084	3 212 470	23.5	6 786 021	1 594 715	23.5	6 884 063	1 617 755	23.5
1 VII 2016 ....ESDJ		14 152 314	3 363 534	23.8	7 032 311	1 671 346	23.8	7 120 003	1 692 188	23.8
1 VII 2017 ....ESDJ		14 649 076	3 520 661	24.0	7 286 344	1 751 151	24.0	7 362 731	1 769 510	24.0
1 VII 2018 ....ESDJ		15 162 044	3 684 377	24.3	7 548 902	1 834 383	24.3	7 613 141	1 849 993	24.3
Congo										
1 VII 2009 ....ESDF		3 838 238	...	...	1 891 558	...	...	1 946 680	...	...
1 VII 2010 ....ESDJ		4 118 775	2 299 393	55.8	2 025 613	1 134 755	56.0	2 093 162	1 164 638	55.6
1 VII 2011 ....ESDJ		4 257 195	2 383 630	56.0	2 102 229	1 176 896	56.0	2 154 966	1 206 734	56.0
1 VII 2012 ....ESDJ		4 394 327	2 460 535	56.0	2 170 749	1 215 331	56.0	2 223 578	1 245 204	56.0
1 VII 2013 ....ESDJ		4 530 366	2 537 004	56.0	2 238 395	1 253 501	56.0	2 291 971	1 283 503	56.0
1 VII 2014 ....ESDJ		4 666 379	2 613 169	56.0	2 306 196	1 291 468	56.0	2 360 183	1 321 701	56.0
1 VII 2015 ....ESDJ		4 801 684	2 688 943	56.0	2 373 559	1 329 192	56.0	2 428 125	1 359 751	56.0
1 VII 2016 ....ESDJ		4 934 312	2 764 263	56.0	2 438 566	1 366 645	56.0	2 495 746	1 397 618	56.0
1 VII 2017 ....ESDJ		5 069 800	2 839 087	56.0	2 506 780	1 403 795	56.0	2 563 020	1 435 292	56.0
1 VII 2018 ....ESDJ		5 203 073	2 913 720	56.0	2 572 865	1 440 803	56.0	2 630 208	1 472 917	56.0
Côte d'Ivoire										
1 VII 2009[7] ....ESDF		20 388 627	...	...	10 500 861	...	...	9 887 766	...	...
1 VII 2010[7] ....ESDF		20 845 167	...	...	10 742 336	...	...	10 102 831	...	...
1 VII 2011[7] ....ESDF		21 301 704	...	...	10 983 811	...	...	10 317 893	...	...
1 VII 2012[7] ....ESDF		21 758 244	...	...	11 225 286	...	...	10 532 958	...	...
1 VII 2013[7] ....ESDF		22 214 787	...	...	11 466 762	...	...	10 748 025	...	...
15 V 2014 ....CDFC		22 224 509	10 881 387	49.0	11 441 896	5 495 438	48.0	10 782 613	5 385 949	50.0
1 VII 2014[8] ....ESDF		22 723 460	11 444 572	50.4	11 734 076	5 834 493	49.7	10 989 384	5 610 079	51.0
1 VII 2015[8] ....ESDF		23 334 439	11 830 560	50.7	12 036 040	6 102 272	50.7	11 298 398	5 728 288	50.7
1 VII 2016[8] ....ESDF		23 950 475	12 262 643	51.2	12 340 861	6 318 521	51.2	11 609 614	5 944 122	51.2
1 VII 2017[8] ....ESDF		24 571 044	12 678 659	51.6	12 648 124	6 526 432	51.6	11 922 920	6 152 227	51.6
Djibouti										
29 V 2009 ....CDFC		818 159	577 933	70.6	440 067	322 796	73.4	378 092	255 137	67.5
Egypt - Égypte										
1 VII 2009 ....ESDF		76 925 139	33 082 770	43.0	39 327 098	16 887 176	42.9	37 598 041	16 195 594	43.1
1 VII 2010 ....ESDF		78 684 622	33 804 181	43.0	40 228 119	17 255 735	42.9	38 456 503	16 548 446	43.0
1 VII 2011 ....ESDF		80 529 566	34 495 468	42.8	41 152 525	17 596 284	42.8	39 377 041	16 899 184	42.9
1 VII 2012 ....ESDF		82 549 976	35 372 982	42.9	42 167 660	18 031 407	42.8	40 382 316	17 341 575	42.9
1 VII 2013 ....ESDF		84 628 982	36 213 473	42.8	43 217 105	18 470 748	42.7	41 411 877	17 742 725	42.8
1 VII 2014 ....ESDF		86 811 192	37 098 131	42.7	44 300 565	18 894 134	42.6	42 510 627	18 203 997	42.8

Continent, country or area, and date / Continent, pays ou zone et date	Code[a]	Both sexes - Les deux sexes			Male - Masculin			Female - Féminin		
		Total	Urban - Urbaine Number Nombre	Urban - Urbaine Percent P.100	Total	Urban - Urbaine Number Nombre	Urban - Urbaine Percent P.100	Total	Urban - Urbaine Number Nombre	Urban - Urbaine Percent P.100
AFRICA - AFRIQUE										
Egypt - Égypte										
1 VII 2015	ESDF	88 957 833	37 999 018	42.7	45 378 728	19 347 041	42.6	43 579 105	18 651 977	42.8
1 VII 2016	ESDF	91 023 393	38 895 815	42.7	46 413 993	19 787 083	42.6	44 609 400	19 108 732	42.8
18 IV 2017	CDFC	94 798 827	...	...	48 891 518	...	...	45 907 309	...	...
1 VII 2017	ESDF	95 202 532	40 432 110	42.5	49 095 021	20 818 309	42.4	46 107 511	19 613 801	42.5
1 VII 2018	ESDF	97 147 368	41 398 653	42.6	50 070 213	21 293 773	42.5	47 077 155	20 104 880	42.7
Equatorial Guinea - Guinée équatoriale										
20 VI 2015*	CDFC	1 222 442	863 313	70.6	651 820	...	...	570 622	...	...
Eritrea - Érythrée[9]										
1 VII 2009	ESDF	2 626 931	934 510	35.6	1 297 153	447 525	34.5	1 329 778	486 984	36.6
1 VII 2010	ESDF	2 691 414	959 076	35.6	1 328 220	458 920	34.6	1 363 194	500 156	36.7
1 VII 2011	ESDF	2 758 710	984 049	35.7	1 360 721	470 508	34.6	1 397 989	513 542	36.7
1 VII 2012	ESDF	2 828 680	1 009 342	35.7	1 394 589	482 248	34.6	1 434 091	527 093	36.8
1 VII 2013	ESDF	2 901 138	1 034 874	35.7	1 429 730	494 104	34.6	1 471 407	540 771	36.8
1 VII 2014	ESDF	2 975 851	1 060 585	35.6	1 466 026	506 044	34.5	1 509 825	554 541	36.7
1 VII 2015	ESDF	3 052 498	1 086 415	35.6	1 503 313	518 040	34.5	1 549 185	568 375	36.7
1 VII 2016	ESDF	3 131 148	1 112 354	35.5	1 541 625	530 088	34.4	1 589 523	582 266	36.6
1 VII 2017	ESDF	3 211 946	1 138 401	35.4	1 581 036	542 187	34.3	1 630 910	596 213	36.6
1 VII 2018	ESDF	3 294 680	1 164 508	35.3	1 621 437	554 316	34.2	1 673 242	610 192	36.5
Eswatini										
1 VII 2009[10]	ESDJ	1 043 509	233 504	22.4	494 061	111 704	22.6	549 448	121 800	22.2
1 VII 2010[10]	ESDJ	1 055 506	237 641	22.5	500 070	113 554	22.7	555 436	124 087	22.3
1 VII 2011[10]	ESDJ	1 067 773	241 947	22.7	506 186	115 493	22.8	561 587	126 454	22.5
1 VII 2012[10]	ESDJ	1 080 337	246 441	22.8	512 432	117 528	22.9	567 905	128 913	22.7
1 VII 2013[10]	ESDJ	1 093 158	251 122	23.0	518 788	119 658	23.1	574 370	131 464	22.9
1 VII 2014[10]	ESDJ	1 106 189	255 986	23.1	525 232	121 881	23.2	580 957	134 105	23.1
1 VII 2015[10]	ESDJ	1 119 375	261 028	23.3	531 737	124 195	23.4	587 638	136 833	23.3
1 VII 2016[10]	ESDJ	1 132 657	266 230	23.5	538 274	126 593	23.5	594 383	139 637	23.5
29 IV 2017*	CDJC	1 093 238	...	...	531 111	...	...	562 127	...	...
1 VII 2017[10]	ESDJ	1 145 970	271 573	23.7	544 811	129 068	23.7	601 159	142 505	23.7
1 VII 2018[10]	ESDJ	1 159 250	277 042	23.9	551 317	131 612	23.9	607 933	145 430	23.9
Ethiopia - Éthiopie[11]										
1 VII 2009	ESDF	77 651 000	13 318 000	17.2	39 155 000	6 649 000	17.0	38 496 000	6 669 000	17.3
1 VII 2010	ESDF	79 634 000	13 931 000	17.5	40 123 000	6 950 000	17.3	39 511 000	6 981 000	17.7
1 VII 2011	ESDF	81 668 000	14 589 000	17.9	41 119 000	7 274 000	17.7	40 549 000	7 315 000	18.0
1 VII 2012	ESDF	83 741 000	15 246 000	18.2	42 135 000	7 598 000	18.0	41 606 000	7 648 000	18.4
1 VII 2013	ESDF	85 837 000	15 979 000	18.6	43 164 000	7 960 000	18.4	42 673 000	8 019 000	18.8
1 VII 2014	ESDF	87 952 000	16 734 000	19.0	44 204 000	8 332 000	18.8	43 748 000	8 402 000	19.2
1 VII 2015	ESDF	90 075 000	17 521 000	19.5	45 250 000	8 721 000	19.3	44 825 000	8 800 000	19.6
1 VII 2016	ESDF	92 205 000	18 327 000	19.9	46 303 000	9 120 000	19.7	45 902 000	9 207 000	20.1
1 VII 2017	ESDF	94 352 138	19 161 490	20.3	47 364 992	9 534 811	20.1	46 987 146	9 626 679	20.5
1 VII 2018	ESDF	96 503 000	20 057 000	20.8	48 430 000	9 977 000	20.6	48 073 000	10 080 000	21.0
Gabon										
22 V 2013	CDFC	1 811 079	1 577 646	87.1	934 072	813 098	87.0	877 007	764 548	87.2
Gambia - Gambie										
15 IV 2013*	CDFC	1 882 450	...	...	930 699	...	...	951 751	...	...
31 XII 2015[12]	SSDF	1 922 950	1 057 467	55.0	915 357	503 304	55.0	1 007 593	554 163	55.0
Ghana										
1 VII 2009	ESDF	23 416 518	10 243 312	43.7	11 600 326	5 006 198	43.2	11 816 192	5 237 114	44.3
26 IX 2010	CDFC	24 658 823	12 545 229	50.9	12 024 845	6 016 059	50.0	12 633 978	6 529 170	51.7
1 VII 2011[13]	ESDF	25 235 268	12 844 745	50.9	12 319 770	6 270 758	50.9	12 915 498	6 573 987	50.9
1 VII 2012[13]	ESDF	25 824 920	13 144 879	50.9	12 621 125	6 424 150	50.9	13 203 795	6 720 729	50.9
1 VII 2013[13]	ESDF	26 427 760	13 451 714	50.9	12 928 916	6 580 808	50.9	13 498 844	6 870 906	50.9
1 VII 2014[13]	ESDF	27 043 093	13 764 931	50.9	13 242 709	6 740 539	50.9	13 800 384	7 024 392	50.9
1 VII 2015[13]	ESDF	27 670 174	13 817 894	49.9	13 562 093	6 903 107	50.9	14 108 081	6 914 787	49.0
1 VII 2016[13]	ESDF	28 308 301	...	...	13 886 734	...	...	14 421 567	...	...
1 VII 2017[13]	ESDF	28 956 587	...	...	14 216 288	...	...	14 740 299	...	...
1 VII 2018[13]	ESDF	29 614 337	...	...	14 550 431	...	...	15 063 906	...	...
Guinea - Guinée										
1 VII 2009[14]	ESDJ	9 305 872	...	...	4 490 907	...	...	4 814 965	...	...
1 VII 2010[14]	ESDJ	9 557 125	...	...	4 612 159	...	...	4 944 966	...	...
1 VII 2011[14]	ESDJ	9 812 181	...	...	4 735 246	...	...	5 076 935	...	...
1 VII 2012[14]	ESDJ	10 071 008	...	...	4 860 153	...	...	5 210 855	...	...
1 VII 2013[14]	ESDJ	10 333 576	...	...	4 986 865	...	...	5 346 711	...	...

Continent, country or area, and date / Continent, pays ou zone et date	Code[a]	Both sexes - Les deux sexes			Male - Masculin			Female - Féminin		
		Total	Urban - Urbaine Number Nombre	Urban - Urbaine Percent P.100	Total	Urban - Urbaine Number Nombre	Urban - Urbaine Percent P.100	Total	Urban - Urbaine Number Nombre	Urban - Urbaine Percent P.100
AFRICA - AFRIQUE										
Guinea - Guinée										
15 III 2014	CDJC	10 523 261	3 657 122	34.8	5 084 306	1 821 369	35.8	5 438 955	1 835 753	33.8
1 VII 2014[2]	ESDJ	10 599 848	3 684 996	34.8	5 115 365	1 832 976	35.8	5 484 483	1 852 020	33.8
1 VII 2015[15]	ESDJ	10 917 711	3 825 273	35.0	5 273 425	1 847 667	35.0	5 644 286	1 977 606	35.0
1 VII 2016[15]	ESDJ	11 233 038	3 966 389	35.3	5 430 371	1 917 466	35.3	5 802 667	2 048 923	35.3
1 VII 2017[15]	ESDJ	11 555 062	4 111 607	35.6	5 590 797	1 989 359	35.6	5 964 265	2 122 248	35.6
1 VII 2018[15]	ESDJ	11 883 517	4 260 887	35.9	5 754 536	2 063 314	35.9	6 128 981	2 197 573	35.9
Guinea-Bissau - Guinée-Bissau										
15 III 2009	CDFC	1 497 859	...	...	725 956	...	...	771 903	...	...
1 VII 2010[3]	ESDF	1 460 221	584 228	40.0	709 482	283 859	40.0	750 739	300 369	40.0
1 VII 2011[3]	ESDF	1 472 233	595 358	40.4	716 622	289 796	40.4	755 611	305 562	40.4
1 VII 2012[3]	ESDF	1 485 189	606 976	40.9	724 208	295 974	40.9	760 981	311 002	40.9
1 VII 2013[3]	ESDF	1 499 277	619 166	41.3	732 337	302 438	41.3	766 940	316 728	41.3
1 VII 2014[3]	ESDF	1 514 451	631 938	41.7	740 981	309 191	41.7	773 470	322 747	41.7
1 VII 2015[3]	ESDF	1 530 673	645 283	42.2	750 119	316 226	42.2	780 554	329 057	42.2
1 VII 2016[3]	ESDF	1 547 777	659 138	42.6	759 666	323 512	42.6	788 111	335 626	42.6
1 VII 2017[3]	ESDF	1 565 842	673 556	43.0	769 659	331 072	43.0	796 183	342 484	43.0
1 VII 2018[3]	ESDF	1 584 791	688 511	43.4	780 070	338 902	43.4	804 721	349 609	43.4
Kenya										
1 VII 2009[16]	ESDF	37 724 850	12 200 486	32.3	18 674 184	6 109 258	32.7	19 050 666	6 091 229	32.0
24 VIII 2009	CDFC	38 610 097	12 487 375	32.3	19 192 458	6 278 811	32.7	19 417 639	6 208 564	32.0
1 VII 2010[16]	ESDF	38 473 893	...	...	19 047 448	...	...	19 426 445	...	...
1 VII 2011[16]	ESDF	39 545 118	...	...	19 583 833	...	...	19 961 285	...	...
1 VII 2012[16]	ESDF	40 656 572	...	...	20 137 201	...	...	20 519 371	...	...
1 VII 2013[16]	ESDF	41 787 735	...	...	20 707 136	...	...	21 080 599	...	...
1 VII 2014[16]	ESDF	42 961 187	...	...	21 289 752	...	...	21 671 435	...	...
1 VII 2015[16]	ESDF	44 156 577	14 280 766	32.3	21 886 677	7 160 225	32.7	22 269 900	7 120 541	32.0
1 VII 2016[16]	ESDF	45 389 112	14 679 464	32.3	22 508 628	7 363 696	32.7	22 880 484	7 315 769	32.0
1 VII 2017[16]	ESDF	46 595 199	15 069 937	32.3	23 117 881	...	...	23 477 319	...	...
1 VII 2018[16]	ESDF	47 848 953	15 475 429	32.3	23 750 828	...	...	24 098 124	...	...
Lesotho										
1 VII 2009[17]	ESDF	1 887 479	...	...	912 760	...	...	974 719	...	...
1 VII 2010[17]	ESDF	1 891 830	...	...	913 030	...	...	978 800	...	...
1 VII 2011[17]	ESDF	1 896 833	...	...	913 701	...	...	983 132	...	...
1 VII 2012[17]	ESDF	1 902 707	...	...	914 954	...	...	987 753	...	...
1 VII 2013[17]	ESDF	1 909 321	...	...	916 722	...	...	992 599	...	...
1 VII 2014[17]	ESDF	1 916 573	...	...	918 944	...	...	997 629	...	...
1 VII 2015[17]	ESDF	1 924 381	...	...	921 565	...	...	1 002 816	...	...
10 IV 2016	CDJC	2 007 201	685 938	34.2	982 133	...	...	1 025 068	...	...
Liberia - Libéria										
1 VII 2009	ESDF	3 551 078	1 682 364	47.4	1 776 406	823 978	46.4	1 774 672	858 386	48.4
1 VII 2010	ESDF	3 627 144	1 732 457	47.8	1 813 631	846 461	46.7	1 813 513	885 996	48.9
1 VII 2011	ESDF	3 704 838	1 784 042	48.2	1 851 636	869 557	47.0	1 853 202	914 485	49.3
1 VII 2012	ESDF	3 784 197	1 837 163	48.5	1 890 438	893 283	47.3	1 893 759	943 880	49.8
1 VII 2013	ESDF	3 865 256	1 891 865	48.9	1 930 053	917 657	47.5	1 935 203	974 208	50.3
1 VII 2014	ESDF	3 946 311	1 946 567	49.3	1 969 668	942 031	47.8	1 976 643	1 004 536	50.8
Libya - Libye[18]										
1 VII 2009	ESDF	5 589 289	4 926 097	88.1	2 833 691	2 500 626	88.2	2 755 598	2 425 471	88.0
1 VII 2010	ESDF	5 689 419	5 013 386	88.1	2 883 880	2 544 388	88.2	2 805 538	2 468 998	88.0
1 VII 2011	ESDF	5 790 518	5 101 275	88.1	2 934 512	2 588 402	88.2	2 856 006	2 512 874	88.0
1 VII 2012	ESDF	5 892 239	5 189 460	88.1	2 985 408	2 632 510	88.2	2 906 831	2 556 950	88.0
1 VII 2013	ESDF	5 994 241	5 277 638	88.0	3 036 393	2 676 558	88.1	2 957 849	2 601 081	87.9
1 VII 2014	ESDF	6 096 208	5 365 529	88.0	3 087 301	2 720 398	88.1	3 008 907	2 645 131	87.9
1 VII 2015	ESDF	6 162 356	5 411 529	87.8	3 129 260	2 707 215	86.5	3 033 156	2 704 314	89.2
Madagascar[19]										
1 VII 2009	ESDF	19 601 026	...	...	9 704 252	...	...	9 896 774	...	...
1 VII 2010	ESDF	20 142 015	...	...	9 972 090	...	...	10 169 925	...	...
1 VII 2011	ESDF	20 696 070	...	...	10 246 397	...	...	10 449 673	...	...
1 VII 2012	ESDF	21 263 403	...	...	10 527 277	...	...	10 736 126	...	...
1 VII 2013	ESDF	21 842 167	...	...	10 813 817	...	...	11 028 350	...	...
1 VII 2014	ESDF	22 434 363	...	...	11 107 006	...	...	11 327 357	...	...
1 VII 2015	ESDF	23 040 065	...	...	11 406 883	...	...	11 633 182	...	...
1 VII 2016	ESDF	23 657 964	...	...	11 712 798	...	...	11 945 166	...	...

Continent, country or area, and date / Continent, pays ou zone et date	Code[a]	Both sexes - Les deux sexes			Male - Masculin			Female - Féminin		
		Total	Urban - Urbaine		Total	Urban - Urbaine		Total	Urban - Urbaine	
			Number Nombre	Percent P.100		Number Nombre	Percent P.100		Number Nombre	Percent P.100

AFRICA - AFRIQUE

Madagascar[19]

1 VII 2017	ESDF	24 289 542	...	...	12 025 485	...	...	12 264 057	...	...
1 VII 2018	ESDF	24 933 879	...	...	12 344 489	...	...	12 589 390	...	...

Malawi

1 VII 2009[3]	ESDF	13 520 098	...	...	6 585 786	...	...	6 934 312	...	...
1 VII 2010[3]	ESDF	13 947 592	...	...	6 804 310	...	...	7 143 282	...	...
1 VII 2011[3]	ESDF	14 388 550	...	...	7 029 149	...	...	7 359 401	...	...
1 VII 2012[3]	ESDF	14 844 822	...	...	7 261 499	...	...	7 583 323	...	...
1 VII 2013[3]	ESDF	15 316 860	...	...	7 501 653	...	...	7 815 207	...	...
1 VII 2014[3]	ESDF	15 805 239	...	...	7 749 963	...	...	8 055 276	...	...
1 VII 2015[3]	ESDF	16 310 431	...	...	8 006 715	...	...	8 303 716	...	...
1 VII 2016[3]	ESDF	16 832 910	...	...	8 272 152	...	...	8 560 758	...	...
1 VII 2017[3]	ESDJ	17 373 200	...	...	8 546 500	...	...	8 826 700	...	...
3 IX 2018	CDJC	17 563 749	2 816 492	16.0	8 521 460	1 401 373	16.4	9 042 289	1 415 119	15.7

Mali

1 IV 2009	CDFC	14 528 662	3 274 727	22.5	7 204 990	1 643 671	22.8	7 323 672	1 631 056	22.3
1 VII 2010[20]	ESDF	15 370 000	...	...	7 679 000	...	...	7 691 000	...	...
1 VII 2011[20]	ESDF	15 843 000	...	...	7 919 000	...	...	7 924 000	...	...
1 VII 2012[20]	ESDF	16 312 000	...	...	8 159 000	...	...	8 153 000	...	...
1 VII 2013[20]	ESDF	16 808 000	...	...	8 411 000	...	...	8 397 000	...	...
1 VII 2014[20]	ESDF	17 319 000	...	...	8 671 000	...	...	8 648 000	...	...
1 VII 2015[20]	ESDF	17 819 000	...	...	8 838 000	...	...	8 981 000	...	...
1 VII 2016[20]	ESDF	18 341 000	...	...	9 244 000	...	...	9 097 000	...	...

Mauritania - Mauritanie

1 VII 2010[3]	ESDF	3 340 627	...	...	1 678 324	...	...	1 662 303	...	...
1 VII 2011[3]	ESDF	3 296 958	...	...	1 644 572	...	...	1 652 386	...	...
24 III 2013	CDFC	3 460 388[21]	1 697 792	49.1	...	...	...	...	...	...
1 VII 2013[3]	ESDF	3 537 368	...	...	1 743 074	...	...	1 794 294	...	...
1 VII 2015[3]	ESDF	3 720 125	...	...	1 834 735	...	...	1 885 390	...	...
1 VII 2016[3]	ESDF	3 782 701	...	...	1 864 664	...	...	1 918 037	...	...

Mauritius - Maurice[22]

1 VII 2009[23]	ESDJ	1 275 032	532 591	41.8	629 157	261 041	41.5	645 875	271 550	42.0
1 VII 2010[23]	ESDJ	1 280 924	533 771	41.7	631 692	261 489	41.4	649 232	272 282	41.9
1 VII 2011[24]	ESDJ	1 252 404	509 229	40.7	619 591	249 439	40.3	632 813	259 790	41.1
4 VII 2011	CDFC	1 237 000	496 841	40.2	611 053	243 629	39.9	625 947	253 212	40.5
1 VII 2012[24]	ESDJ	1 255 882	509 177	40.5	621 297	249 422	40.1	634 585	259 755	40.9
1 VII 2013[24]	ESDJ	1 258 653	519 306	41.3	622 861	254 605	40.9	635 792	264 701	41.6
1 VII 2014[24]	ESDJ	1 260 934	518 370	41.1	624 002	254 204	40.7	636 932	264 166	41.5
1 VII 2015[24]	ESDJ	1 262 605	517 482	41.0	624 769	253 796	40.6	637 836	263 686	41.3
1 VII 2016[24]	ESDJ	1 263 473	516 160	40.9	625 206	253 181	40.5	638 267	262 979	41.2
1 VII 2017[24]	ESDJ	1 264 613	514 937	40.7	625 727	252 588	40.4	638 886	262 349	41.1
1 VII 2018[24]	ESDJ	1 265 303	513 556	40.6	626 030	251 972	40.2	639 273	261 584	40.9

Mayotte

21 VIII 2012	CDJC	212 645			103 173			109 471		
1 VII 2014[25]	ESDJ	227 961	...	...	109 603	...	...	118 358	...	...
1 I 2015	ESDJ	230 315	...	...	111 736	...	...	118 579	...	...
1 VII 2016*[25]	ESDJ	244 343	...	...	118 536	...	...	125 807	...	...
1 VII 2017*[25]	ESDJ	255 535	...	...	121 795	...	...	133 740	...	...
1 VII 2018*[25]	ESDJ	265 425	...	...	126 521	...	...	138 904	...	...

Morocco - Maroc

1 VII 2009[26]	ESDF	31 543 000	18 097 000	57.4	15 657 000	8 891 000	56.8	15 886 000	9 205 000	57.9
1 VII 2010[26]	ESDF	31 894 046	18 446 241	57.8	15 831 463	9 051 145	57.2	16 062 583	9 395 096	58.5
1 VII 2011[26]	ESDF	32 245 120	18 802 208	58.3	16 010 979	9 212 763	57.5	16 234 141	9 589 444	59.1
1 VII 2012[26]	ESDF	32 596 997	19 157 539	58.8	16 190 815	9 373 546	57.9	16 406 182	9 783 993	59.6
1 VII 2013[26]	ESDF	32 950 445	19 512 904	59.2	16 371 475	9 533 742	58.2	16 578 971	9 979 162	60.2
1 VII 2014[27]	ESDJ	33 769 512	20 352 799	60.3	16 825 793	10 068 187	59.8	16 943 719	10 284 612	60.7
1 IX 2014	CDJC	33 848 242	20 432 439	60.4	...	...	...	...	...	...
1 VII 2015[27]	ESDJ	34 124 870	20 751 800	60.8	17 001 717	10 255 722	60.3	17 123 153	10 496 078	61.3
1 VII 2016[27]	ESDJ	34 486 536	21 154 782	61.3	17 180 879	10 445 229	60.8	17 305 657	10 709 553	61.9
1 VII 2017[27]	ESDJ	34 852 121	21 560 585	61.9	17 361 992	10 636 101	61.3	17 490 129	10 924 484	62.5
1 VII 2018[27]	ESDJ	35 219 547	21 968 101	62.4	17 544 027	10 827 825	61.7	17 675 520	11 140 276	63.0

Mozambique

1 VII 2009[10]	ESDF	21 802 866	6 685 108	30.7	10 499 954	3 277 805	31.2	11 302 912	3 407 303	30.1
1 VII 2010[10]	ESDF	22 416 881	6 908 291	30.8	10 799 284	3 384 605	31.3	11 617 597	3 523 686	30.3

Continent, country or area, and date / Continent, pays ou zone et date	Code[a]	Both sexes - Les deux sexes Total	Urban - Urbaine Number Nombre	Urban - Urbaine Percent P.100	Male - Masculin Total	Urban - Urbaine Number Nombre	Urban - Urbaine Percent P.100	Female - Féminin Total	Urban - Urbaine Number Nombre	Urban - Urbaine Percent P.100
AFRICA - AFRIQUE										
Mozambique										
1 VII 2011[10] ...... ESDF	ESDF	23 049 621	7 141 715	31.0	11 108 128	3 496 582	31.5	11 941 493	3 645 133	30.5
1 VII 2012[10] ...... ESDF	ESDF	23 700 715	7 385 294	31.2	11 426 321	3 613 684	31.6	12 274 394	3 771 610	30.7
1 VII 2013[10] ...... ESDF	ESDF	24 366 112	7 639 557	31.4	11 751 849	3 736 166	31.8	12 614 263	3 903 391	30.9
1 VII 2014[10] ...... ESDF	ESDF	25 041 922	7 905 004	31.6	12 082 782	3 864 267	32.0	12 959 140	4 040 737	31.2
1 VII 2015[10] ...... ESDF	ESDF	25 727 911	8 181 475	31.8	12 419 014	3 997 895	32.2	13 308 897	4 183 580	31.4
1 VII 2016[10] ...... ESDF	ESDF	26 423 623	8 468 799	32.1	12 760 324	4 136 950	32.4	13 663 299	4 331 849	31.7
1 VII 2017[10] ...... ESDF	ESDF	27 128 530	8 766 777	32.3	13 106 447	4 281 319	32.7	14 022 083	4 485 458	32.0
1 VIII 2017* ...... CDFC	CDFC	28 861 863	...	...	13 800 857	...	...	15 061 006	...	...
Namibia - Namibie										
1 VII 2009[3] ...... ESDF	ESDF	2 103 761	...	...	1 027 736	...	...	1 076 025	...	...
1 VII 2010[3] ...... ESDF	ESDF	2 143 410	...	...	1 047 900	...	...	1 095 510	...	...
1 VII 2011[28] ...... ESDF	ESDF	2 116 077	900 163	42.5	1 026 911	439 993	42.8	1 089 166	460 170	42.2
28 VIII 2011 ...... CDFC	CDFC	2 113 077	903 434	42.8	1 021 912	440 334	43.1	1 091 165	463 100	42.4
1 VII 2012[28] ...... ESDF	ESDF	2 155 440	940 825	43.6	1 046 434	459 668	43.9	1 109 006	481 157	43.4
1 VII 2013[28] ...... ESDF	ESDF	2 196 086	982 519	44.7	1 066 541	479 844	45.0	1 129 545	502 675	44.5
1 VII 2014[28] ...... ESDF	ESDF	2 237 894	1 025 147	45.8	1 087 178	500 469	46.0	1 150 716	524 678	45.6
1 VII 2015[28] ...... ESDF	ESDF	2 280 716	1 068 625	46.9	1 108 276	521 496	47.1	1 172 440	547 129	46.7
1 VII 2016[28] ...... ESDF	ESDF	2 324 388	1 112 868	47.9	1 129 754	542 893	48.1	1 194 634	569 975	47.7
1 VII 2017[28] ...... ESDF	ESDF	2 368 747	1 157 806	48.9	1 151 533	564 615	49.0	1 217 214	593 191	48.7
1 VII 2018[28] ...... ESDF	ESDF	2 413 643	1 203 340	49.9	1 173 540	586 616	50.0	1 240 103	616 724	49.7
Niger										
1 VII 2009[3] ...... ESDJ	ESDJ	14 693 113	2 911 006	19.8	7 337 909	1 457 958	19.9	7 355 203	1 453 048	19.8
1 VII 2010[3] ...... ESDJ	ESDJ	15 203 820	3 104 574	20.4	7 594 624	1 555 201	20.5	7 609 198	1 549 372	20.4
1 VII 2011[3] ...... ESDJ	ESDJ	15 730 756	3 309 954	21.0	7 859 534	1 658 395	21.1	7 871 221	1 651 559	21.0
1 VII 2012[29] ...... ESDJ	ESDJ	16 993 563	2 750 279	16.2	8 446 540	1 366 889	16.2	8 547 023	1 383 390	16.2
10 XII 2012 ...... CDFC	CDFC	16 734 935	...	...	8 183 513	...	...	8 551 422	...	...
1 VII 2013[29] ...... ESDJ	ESDJ	17 679 758	2 899 523	16.4	8 792 478	1 441 063	16.4	8 887 281	1 458 460	16.4
1 VII 2014[29] ...... ESDJ	ESDJ	18 389 162	3 010 567	16.4	9 150 266	1 496 252	16.4	9 238 897	1 514 315	16.4
1 VII 2015[29] ...... ESDJ	ESDJ	19 124 882	3 125 234	16.3	9 521 427	1 553 241	16.3	9 603 456	1 571 993	16.4
1 VII 2016[29] ...... ESDJ	ESDJ	19 865 066	3 242 161	16.3	9 898 628	1 611 354	16.3	9 966 438	1 630 807	16.4
Nigeria - Nigéria[17]										
1 VII 2009 ...... ESDF	ESDF	154 581 566	...	...	78 836 599	...	...	75 744 967	...	...
1 VII 2010 ...... ESDF	ESDF	159 608 173	...	...	81 400 168	...	...	78 208 005	...	...
1 VII 2011 ...... ESDF	ESDF	164 798 232	...	...	84 047 098	...	...	80 751 134	...	...
1 VII 2012 ...... ESDF	ESDF	170 157 060	...	...	86 780 100	...	...	83 376 959	...	...
1 VII 2013 ...... ESDF	ESDF	175 690 143	...	...	89 601 973	...	...	86 088 170	...	...
1 VII 2014 ...... ESDF	ESDF	181 403 148	...	...	92 515 605	...	...	88 887 542	...	...
1 VII 2015 ...... ESDF	ESDF	187 301 926	...	...	95 523 982	...	...	91 777 944	...	...
1 VII 2016 ...... ESDF	ESDF	193 392 517	...	...	98 630 184	...	...	94 762 333	...	...
Republic of South Sudan - République de Soudan du Sud[30]										
1 VII 2009 ...... ESDF	ESDF	8 684 963	...	...	4 495 511	...	...	4 189 452	...	...
1 VII 2010 ...... ESDF	ESDF	9 005 261	...	...	4 652 459	...	...	4 352 803	...	...
1 VII 2011 ...... ESDF	ESDF	9 389 376	...	...	4 844 597	...	...	4 544 780	...	...
1 VII 2012 ...... ESDF	ESDF	9 782 927	...	...	5 041 284	...	...	4 741 642	...	...
1 VII 2013 ...... ESDF	ESDF	10 182 291	...	...	5 240 881	...	...	4 941 410	...	...
1 VII 2014 ...... ESDF	ESDF	10 585 044	...	...	5 442 151	...	...	5 142 892	...	...
1 VII 2015 ...... ESDF	ESDF	11 000 128	...	...	5 649 689	...	...	5 350 439	...	...
1 VII 2016 ...... ESDF	ESDF	11 425 377	...	...	5 862 347	...	...	5 563 030	...	...
1 VII 2017 ...... ESDF	ESDF	11 868 209	...	...	6 083 876	...	...	5 784 333	...	...
1 VII 2018 ...... ESDF	ESDF	12 323 419	...	...	6 311 618	...	...	6 011 801	...	...
Reunion - Réunion										
1 I 2009 ...... ESDJ	ESDJ	816 364	...	...	395 688	...	...	420 676	...	...
1 I 2010 ...... CDJC	CDJC	821 136	808 540	98.5	398 006	391 623	98.4	423 130	416 917	98.5
1 I 2010 ...... ESDJ	ESDJ	821 136	...	...	397 953	...	...	423 183	...	...
1 I 2011 ...... ESDJ	ESDJ	828 581	...	...	401 139	...	...	427 442	...	...
1 I 2012 ...... ESDJ	ESDJ	833 944	...	...	403 504	...	...	430 440	...	...
1 VII 2013[25] ...... ESDJ	ESDJ	838 935	...	...	405 519	...	...	433 416	...	...
1 VII 2014[25] ...... ESDJ	ESDJ	846 747	816 334	96.4	409 549	394 281	96.3	437 198	422 052	96.5
1 I 2015 ...... CDJC	CDJC	850 727	838 228	98.5	411 435	405 123	98.5	439 292	433 105	98.6
1 I 2015 ...... ESDJ	ESDJ	850 727	...	...	410 762	...	...	439 965	...	...
1 VII 2016*[25] ...... ESDJ	ESDJ	858 404	...	...	413 922	...	...	444 482	...	...

Continent, country or area, and date / Continent, pays ou zone et date	Code[a]	Both sexes - Les deux sexes			Male - Masculin			Female - Féminin		
		Total	Urban - Urbaine		Total	Urban - Urbaine		Total	Urban - Urbaine	
			Number Nombre	Percent P.100		Number Nombre	Percent P.100		Number Nombre	Percent P.100
AFRICA - AFRIQUE										
Reunion - Réunion										
1 VII 2017*[25]	ESDJ	860 110	...	...	412 960	...	...	447 150	...	...
1 VII 2018*[25]	ESDJ	864 459	...	...	414 304	...	...	450 155	...	...
Rwanda										
1 VII 2009[3]	ESDF	10 117 029	...	...	4 880 233	...	...	5 236 796	...	...
1 VII 2010[3]	ESDF	10 412 820	1 541 097	14.8	5 029 450	...	...	5 383 371	...	...
1 VII 2011[3]	ESDF	10 718 379	1 564 883	14.6	5 183 505	...	...	5 534 874	...	...
1 VII 2012[29]	ESDF	10 482 641	1 732 175	16.5	5 049 164	889 118	17.6	5 433 477	843 057	15.5
15 VIII 2012	CDFC	10 393 542	1 760 994	16.9	4 981 197	902 501	18.1	5 412 345	858 493	15.9
1 VII 2013[29]	ESDF	10 736 771	1 844 040	17.2	5 178 354	889 382	17.2	5 558 417	954 658	17.2
1 VII 2014[29]	ESDF	10 996 891	1 962 945	17.8	5 310 430	947 912	17.9	5 686 461	1 015 033	17.8
1 VII 2015[29]	ESDF	11 262 564	2 086 390	18.5	5 445 206	1 008 724	18.5	5 817 359	1 077 666	18.5
1 VII 2016[29]	ESDF	11 533 445	2 214 421	19.2	5 582 519	1 071 844	19.2	5 950 925	1 142 578	19.2
1 VII 2017[29]	ESDF	11 809 300	2 347 098	19.9	5 722 258	1 137 299	19.9	6 087 041	1 209 799	19.9
1 VII 2018[29]	ESDF	12 089 721	2 484 438	20.6	5 864 287	1 205 111	20.6	6 225 434	1 279 327	20.6
Saint Helena ex. dep. - Sainte-Hélène sans dép.										
1 VII 2012	ESDF	4 123	...	...	2 094	...	...	2 029	...	...
31 XII 2013	ESDF	4 211	...	...	2 139	...	...	2 072	...	...
7 II 2016[31]	CDJC	4 534	...	...	2 396	...	...	2 138	...	...
Saint Helena: Tristan da Cunha - Sainte-Hélène: Tristan da Cunha[32]										
31 XII 2009	ESDF	262[33]	...	...	123	...	...	139	...	...
Sao Tome and Principe - Sao Tomé-et-Principe										
1 VII 2009	ESDF	160 820	...	...	79 027	...	...	81 794	...	...
1 VII 2010	ESDF	163 783	...	...	80 409	...	...	83 375	...	...
1 VII 2011	ESDF	166 728	...	...	81 783	...	...	84 945	...	...
13 V 2012	CDJC	178 739	119 781	67.0	88 867	58 710	66.1	89 872	61 071	68.0
1 VII 2013[34]	ESDJ	182 328	122 398	67.1	90 577	60 805	67.1	91 751	61 593	67.1
1 VII 2014[34]	ESDJ	186 024	125 121	67.3	92 347	62 113	67.3	93 677	63 008	67.3
1 VII 2015[34]	ESDJ	189 819	127 922	67.4	94 173	63 464	67.4	95 646	64 457	67.4
1 VII 2016[34]	ESDJ	193 712	130 798	67.5	96 053	64 857	67.5	97 659	65 941	67.5
1 VII 2017[34]	ESDJ	197 700	133 748	67.7	97 988	66 291	67.7	99 712	67 457	67.7
1 VII 2018[34]	ESDJ	201 784	136 775	67.8	99 978	...	...	101 806	...	...
Senegal - Sénégal										
31 XII 2009	ESDJ	12 171 264	4 949 461	40.7	5 991 214	2 453 764	41.0	6 180 050	2 495 697	40.4
31 XII 2010	ESDJ	12 509 434	5 086 978	40.7	6 157 675	2 521 940	41.0	6 351 759	2 565 038	40.4
31 XII 2011	ESDJ	12 841 702	6 086 966	47.4	6 350 673	3 010 218	47.4	6 491 029	3 076 748	47.4
1 VII 2013[3]	ESDJ	13 508 715	...	...	6 735 420	...	...	6 773 295	...	...
19 XI 2013	CDFC	13 357 492	...	...	6 658 089	...	...	6 699 403	...	...
1 VII 2014[3]	ESDJ	13 926 253	...	...	6 941 357	...	...	6 961 847	...	...
1 VII 2015[3]	ESDJ	14 356 575	...	...	7 153 656	...	...	7 202 919	...	...
1 VII 2016[3]	ESDJ	14 799 859	...	...	7 372 487	...	...	7 427 372	...	...
1 VII 2017[3]	ESDJ	15 256 346	...	...	7 597 938	...	...	7 658 408	...	...
1 VII 2018[3]	ESDJ	15 726 037	...	...	7 829 997	...	...	7 896 040	...	...
Seychelles										
1 VII 2009	ESDF	87 298	...	...	45 022	...	...	42 276	...	...
1 VII 2010	ESDF	89 770	...	...	45 907	...	...	43 863	...	...
26 VIII 2010	CDFC	90 945	...	...	46 912	...	...	44 033	...	...
1 VII 2011	ESDF	87 441	...	...	43 127	...	...	44 314	...	...
1 VII 2012	ESDF	88 303	...	...	43 313	...	...	44 990	...	...
1 VII 2013	ESDF	89 949	...	...	44 735	...	...	45 214	...	...
1 VII 2014	ESDF	91 359	...	...	45 278	...	...	46 081	...	...
1 VII 2015	ESDF	93 419	...	...	46 322	...	...	47 097	...	...
1 VII 2016	ESDF	94 677	...	...	47 343	...	...	47 334	...	...
1 VII 2017	ESDF	95 843	...	...	48 793	...	...	47 050	...	...
1 VII 2018	ESDF	96 762	...	...	49 259	...	...	47 503	...	...
Sierra Leone										
1 VII 2009	ESDF	5 607 930	2 221 331	39.6	2 719 034	1 097 256	40.4	2 888 896	1 124 075	38.9
1 VII 2010	ESDF	5 746 800	2 304 955	40.1	2 786 797	1 138 563	40.9	2 960 003	1 166 392	39.4
1 VII 2011	ESDF	5 890 080	2 394 041	40.6	2 856 755	1 182 568	41.4	3 033 325	1 211 473	39.9

Continent, country or area, and date / Continent, pays ou zone et date	Code[a]	Both sexes - Les deux sexes			Male - Masculin			Female - Féminin		
		Total	Urban - Urbaine		Total	Urban - Urbaine		Total	Urban - Urbaine	
			Number Nombre	Percent P.100		Number Nombre	Percent P.100		Number Nombre	Percent P.100
AFRICA - AFRIQUE										
Sierra Leone										
1 VII 2012	ESDF	6 037 660	2 489 123	41.2	2 928 862	1 229 535	42.0	3 108 798	1 259 588	40.5
5 XII 2015	CDFC	7 092 113	2 905 097	41.0	3 490 978	1 438 591	41.2	3 601 135	1 466 506	40.7
South Africa - Afrique du Sud										
1 VII 2009[35]	ESDF	49 928 233	...	...	24 252 209	...	...	25 676 024	...	...
1 VII 2010[35]	ESDF	50 724 112	...	...	24 661 209	...	...	26 062 903	...	...
1 VII 2011[35]	ESDF	51 550 684	...	...	25 084 701	...	...	26 465 983	...	...
10 X 2011	CDFC	51 770 560	32 559 331	62.9	25 188 791	...	...	26 581 769	...	...
1 VII 2012[2]	ESDF	52 409 724	...	...	25 516 359	...	...	26 893 365	...	...
1 VII 2013[2]		53 282 289	...	...	25 954 314	...	...	27 327 975	...	...
1 VII 2014[2]	ESDF	54 166 787	...	...	26 397 906	...	...	27 768 881	...	...
1 VII 2015[2]	ESDF	55 055 626	...	...	26 843 180	...	...	28 212 446	...	...
1 VII 2016[2]	ESDF	55 946 872	...	...	27 289 661	...	...	28 657 211	...	...
1 VII 2017[2]	ESDF	56 837 474	...	...	27 736 884	...	...	29 100 590	...	...
1 VII 2018[2]	ESDF	57 725 606	...	...	28 180 101	...	...	29 545 505	...	...
Sudan - Soudan										
1 VII 2009	ESDF	31 956 791	10 860 950	34.0	16 275 239	5 531 361	34.0	15 681 552	5 329 589	34.0
1 VII 2010	ESDF	32 961 966	11 296 966	34.3	16 774 288	5 749 007	34.3	16 187 678	5 547 959	34.3
1 VII 2011	ESDF	33 997 538	11 749 240	34.6	17 289 105	5 974 957	34.6	16 708 434	5 774 283	34.6
1 VII 2012	ESDF	35 064 299	12 218 313	34.8	17 820 009	6 209 462	34.8	17 244 290	6 008 851	34.8
1 VII 2013	ESDF	36 162 516	12 704 550	35.1	18 367 086	6 452 691	35.1	17 795 430	6 251 858	35.1
1 VII 2014	ESDF	37 292 376	13 208 281	35.4	18 930 385	6 704 798	35.4	18 361 991	6 503 483	35.4
1 VII 2015	ESDF	38 454 040	13 729 842	35.7	19 509 961	6 965 944	35.7	18 944 080	6 763 898	35.7
1 VII 2016	ESDF	39 647 621	14 269 540	36.0	20 105 842	7 236 276	36.0	19 541 779	7 033 264	36.0
Togo										
6 XI 2010	CDJC	6 191 155	2 334 495	37.7	3 009 095	1 131 533	37.6	3 182 060	1 202 962	37.8
1 VII 2011[2]	ESDJ	6 277 718	2 498 763[36]	39.8	3 051 882	1 219 982[36]	40.0	3 225 836	1 278 782[36]	39.6
1 VII 2012[2]	ESDJ	6 430 825	2 580 788[36]	40.1	3 127 501	1 257 830[36]	40.2	3 303 324	1 322 958[36]	40.0
1 VII 2013[2]	ESDJ	6 589 095	2 663 899[36]	40.4	3 205 772	1 296 177[36]	40.4	3 383 324	1 367 722[36]	40.4
1 VII 2014[2]	ESDJ	6 752 334	2 748 039[36]	40.7	3 286 603	1 335 012[36]	40.6	3 465 731	1 413 028[36]	40.8
1 VII 2015[2]	ESDJ	6 920 514	2 833 093[36]	40.9	3 369 994	1 374 280[36]	40.8	3 550 520	1 458 814[36]	41.1
1 VII 2016[2]	ESDJ	7 092 022	2 918 932[36]	41.2	3 455 135	1 413 914[36]	40.9	3 636 888	1 505 018[36]	41.4
1 VII 2017[2]	ESDJ	7 265 286	3 005 419[36]	41.4	3 541 238	1 453 848[36]	41.1	3 724 048	1 551 572[36]	41.7
1 VII 2018[2]	ESDJ	7 440 364	3 092 420[36]	41.6	3 628 345	1 494 021[36]	41.2	3 812 019	1 598 399[36]	41.9
Tunisia - Tunisie										
1 VII 2009	ESDF	10 458 095	6 937 505	66.3	5 224 946	...	...	5 233 149	...	...
1 VII 2010	ESDF	10 565 704	7 039 718	66.6	5 275 893	...	...	5 289 811	...	...
1 VII 2011	ESDF	10 674 420	7 084 742	66.4	5 327 337	...	...	5 347 083	...	...
1 VII 2012	ESDF	10 784 255	7 248 086	67.2	5 379 282	...	...	5 404 972	...	...
1 VII 2013	ESDF	10 895 219	7 354 268	67.5	5 431 735	...	...	5 463 485	...	...
23 IV 2014	CDFC	10 982 754	7 437 671	67.7	5 472 338	3 713 527	67.9	5 510 416	3 724 144	67.6
1 VII 2014	ESDF	11 007 326	7 461 796	67.8	5 484 581	...	...	5 522 745	...	...
1 VII 2015	ESDF	11 154 372	7 574 564	67.9	5 557 966	...	...	5 596 404	...	...
1 VII 2016	ESDF	11 304 482	7 671 696[37]	67.9	5 620 629	...	...	5 683 853	...	...
1 VII 2017	ESDF	11 446 316	7 797 248	68.1	...	...	...	...	...	...
Uganda - Ouganda										
1 VII 2009	ESDF	30 661 300	4 524 900	14.8	14 933 900	2 171 400	14.5	15 727 400	2 353 500	15.0
1 VII 2010	ESDF	31 784 600	...	...	15 516 600	...	...	16 268 000	...	...
1 VII 2011	ESDF	32 939 800	...	...	16 118 600	...	...	16 821 200	...	...
1 VII 2012	ESDF	34 131 400	...	...	16 741 400	...	...	17 390 000	...	...
1 VII 2014[8]	ESDF	34 141 299	...	...	16 594 490	...	...	17 546 809	...	...
27 VIII 2014	CDFC	34 634 650	8 438 009	24.4	16 897 849	4 042 324	23.9	17 736 801	4 395 685	24.8
1 VII 2015[8]	ESDF	35 502 100	...	...	17 344 000	...	...	18 158 100	...	...
1 VII 2016[8]	ESDF	36 652 700	...	...	17 926 900	...	...	18 725 800	...	...
1 VII 2017[8]	ESDF	37 838 900	...	...	18 527 900	...	...	19 311 000	...	...
1 VII 2018[8]	ESDF	39 059 000	...	...	19 146 800	...	...	19 912 200	...	...
United Republic of Tanzania - République Unie de Tanzanie										
1 VII 2009[38]	ESDF	41 915 880	10 892 350	26.0	20 604 730	5 375 260	26.1	21 311 150	5 517 090	25.9
1 VII 2010[38]	ESDF	43 187 823	11 378 015	26.3	21 252 423	5 618 133	26.4	21 935 400	5 759 882	26.3
1 VII 2011[38]	ESDF	44 484 857	11 875 395	26.7	21 914 229	5 867 287	26.8	22 570 628	6 008 108	26.6
1 VII 2012[38]	ESDF	45 798 475	12 386 841	27.0	22 585 634	6 123 839	27.1	23 212 841	6 263 002	27.0
26 VIII 2012[39]	CDFC	44 928 923	13 305 004	29.6	21 869 990	6 407 396	29.3	23 058 933	6 897 608	29.9

Continent, country or area, and date / Continent, pays ou zone et date	Code[a]	Both sexes - Les deux sexes			Male - Masculin			Female - Féminin		
		Total	Urban - Urbaine		Total	Urban - Urbaine		Total	Urban - Urbaine	
			Number Nombre	Percent P.100		Number Nombre	Percent P.100		Number Nombre	Percent P.100
AFRICA - AFRIQUE										
United Republic of Tanzania - République Unie de Tanzanie										
1 VII 2013[29] .... ESDF		46 356 279	...	...	22 585 059	...	...	23 771 220	...	...
1 VII 2014[29] .... ESDF		47 831 361	...	...	23 323 466	...	...	24 507 895	...	...
1 VII 2015[29] .... ESDF		49 359 408	...	...	24 088 086	...	...	25 271 322	...	...
1 VII 2016[29] .... ESDF		50 941 672	...	...	24 879 894	...	...	26 061 778	...	...
1 VII 2017[29] .... ESDF		52 554 628	...	...	25 687 154	...	...	26 867 474	...	...
1 VII 2018[29] .... ESDF		54 199 163	...	...	26 510 095	...	...	27 689 068	...	...
Zambia - Zambie										
16 X 2010 .... CDFC		12 526 314	5 021 022	40.1	6 117 253	2 452 904	40.1	6 409 061	2 568 118	40.1
1 VII 2011[40] .... ESDJ		13 718 722	5 563 212	40.6	6 786 799	2 757 061	40.6	6 931 923	2 806 151	40.5
1 VII 2012[40] .... ESDJ		14 145 327	5 780 936	40.9	6 997 492	2 863 581	40.9	7 147 835	2 917 355	40.8
1 VII 2013[40] .... ESDJ		14 580 290	6 005 218	41.2	7 212 648	2 973 485	41.2	7 367 642	3 031 733	41.1
1 VII 2014[40] .... ESDJ		15 023 315	6 235 786	41.5	7 432 123	3 086 651	41.5	7 591 192	3 149 135	41.5
1 VII 2015[40] .... ESDJ		15 473 905	6 472 258	41.8	7 655 669	3 202 882	41.8	7 818 236	3 269 376	41.8
1 VII 2016[40] .... ESDJ		15 933 883	6 715 149	42.1	7 884 009	3 322 364	42.1	8 049 874	3 392 785	42.1
1 VII 2017[40] .... ESDJ		16 405 229	6 964 965	42.5	8 117 939	3 445 261	42.4	8 287 290	3 519 704	42.5
1 VII 2018[40] .... ESDJ		16 887 720	7 221 318	42.8	8 357 340	3 571 368	42.7	8 530 380	3 649 950	42.8
Zimbabwe										
1 VII 2009[38] .... ESDF		13 667 894	...	...	6 642 551	...	...	7 025 344	...	...
17 VIII 2012 .... CDFC		13 061 239	4 284 145	32.8	6 280 539	2 039 224	32.5	6 780 700	2 244 921	33.1
1 VII 2013[34] .... ESDF		13 368 620	4 424 783[37]	33.1	6 428 233	2 108 204[37]	32.8	6 940 389	2 316 578[37]	33.4
1 VII 2014[34] .... ESDF		13 652 297	4 535 793[37]	33.2	6 564 085	2 162 369[37]	32.9	7 088 214	2 373 427[37]	33.5
1 VII 2015[34] .... ESDF		13 943 242	4 648 970[37]	33.3	6 703 559	2 217 591[37]	33.1	7 239 681	2 431 379[37]	33.6
1 VII 2016[34] .... ESDF		14 240 168	4 763 408[37]	33.5	6 846 020	2 273 413[37]	33.2	7 394 149	2 489 990[37]	33.7
1 VII 2017[34] .... ESDF		14 542 235	4 878 395[37]	33.5	6 991 066	2 329 497[37]	33.3	7 551 172	2 548 898[37]	33.8
1 VII 2018[34] .... ESDF		14 848 905	4 993 375[37]	33.6	7 138 445	2 385 567[37]	33.4	7 710 459	2 607 811[37]	33.8
AMERICA, NORTH - AMÉRIQUE DU NORD										
Anguilla										
11 V 2011 .... CDFC		13 572	...	...	6 707	...	...	6 865	...	...
Antigua and Barbuda - Antigua-et-Barbuda										
27 V 2011 .... CDJC		85 567	...	...	40 986	...	...	44 581	...	...
1 VII 2011[28] .... ESDJ		85 567	...	...	40 988	...	...	44 579	...	...
1 VII 2012[28] .... ESDJ		86 793	...	...	41 572	...	...	45 221	...	...
1 VII 2013[28] .... ESDJ		88 069	...	...	42 180	...	...	45 889	...	...
1 VII 2014[28] .... ESDJ		89 391	...	...	42 810	...	...	46 581	...	...
1 VII 2015[28] .... ESDJ		90 755	...	...	43 460	...	...	47 295	...	...
1 VII 2016[28] .... ESDJ		92 157	...	...	44 129	...	...	48 028	...	...
1 VII 2017[28] .... ESDJ		93 581	...	...	44 809	...	...	48 772	...	...
1 VII 2018[28] .... ESDJ		95 014	...	...	45 493	...	...	49 521	...	...
Aruba										
1 VII 2009 .... ESDJ		101 604	...	...	48 291	...	...	53 312	...	...
1 VII 2010 .... ESDJ		101 873	...	...	48 419	...	...	53 454	...	...
29 IX 2010 .... CDJC		101 484	...	...	48 241	...	...	53 243	...	...
1 VII 2011 .... ESDJ		102 809	...	...	48 801	...	...	54 008	...	...
1 VII 2012 .... ESDJ		104 577	...	...	49 557	...	...	55 020	...	...
1 VII 2013 .... ESDJ		106 383	...	...	50 329	...	...	56 054	...	...
1 VII 2014 .... ESDJ		107 823	...	...	50 990	...	...	56 833	...	...
1 VII 2015 .... ESDJ		109 225	...	...	51 681	...	...	57 544	...	...
1 VII 2016 .... ESDJ		110 352	...	...	52 251	...	...	58 101	...	...
1 VII 2017 .... ESDJ		110 848	...	...	52 544	...	...	58 304	...	...
1 VII 2018 .... ESDJ		111 466	...	...	52 798	...	...	58 668	...	...
Bahamas										
1 VII 2009[41] .... ESDF		342 400	...	...	166 800	...	...	175 600	...	...
3 V 2010 .... CDJC		351 461	...	...	170 257	...	...	181 204	...	...
1 VII 2010[40] .... ESDJ		351 500	...	...	170 200	...	...	181 300	...	...
1 VII 2011[40] .... ESDJ		355 020	...	...	171 810	...	...	183 210	...	...
1 VII 2012[40] .... ESDJ		358 600	...	...	173 460	...	...	185 140	...	...

Continent, country or area, and date / Continent, pays ou zone et date	Code[a]	Both sexes - Les deux sexes			Male - Masculin			Female - Féminin		
		Total	Urban - Urbaine		Total	Urban - Urbaine		Total	Urban - Urbaine	
			Number Nombre	Percent P.100		Number Nombre	Percent P.100		Number Nombre	Percent P.100
AMERICA, NORTH - AMÉRIQUE DU NORD										
Bahamas										
1 VII 2013[40] .... ESDJ		362 230	...	...	175 120	...	...	187 110	...	...
1 VII 2014[40] .... ESDJ		365 920	...	...	176 810	...	...	189 110	...	...
1 VII 2015[40] .... ESDJ		369 670	...	...	178 530	...	...	191 140	...	...
1 VII 2016[40] .... ESDJ		373 480	...	...	180 280	...	...	193 200	...	...
1 VII 2017[40] .... ESDJ		377 360	...	...	182 300	...	...	195 060	...	...
1 VII 2018[40] .... ESDJ		381 320	...	...	184 380	...	...	196 940	...	...
Barbados - Barbade										
1 VII 2009 .... ESDF		275 441	...	...	133 133	...	...	142 308	...	...
1 V 2010[42] .... CDJC		277 821	...	...	133 018	...	...	144 803	...	...
1 VII 2010 .... ESDJ		277 758	...	...	133 018	...	...	144 740	...	...
1 VII 2011 .... ESDJ		277 622	...	...	133 119	...	...	144 503	...	...
1 VII 2012 .... ESDJ		277 668	...	...	133 355	...	...	144 313	...	...
1 VII 2013 .... ESDJ		277 492	...	...	133 369	...	...	144 123	...	...
1 VII 2014 .... ESDJ		277 199	...	...	133 343	...	...	143 856	...	...
1 VII 2015 .... ESDJ		274 633	...	...	131 146	...	...	143 487	...	...
Belize										
1 VII 2009 .... ESDF		315 082	142 447	45.2	157 622	69 450	44.1	157 460	72 997	46.4
12 V 2010 .... CDJC		322 453	145 832	45.2	161 227	71 087	44.1	161 226	74 745	46.4
1 VII 2010 .... ESDJ		323 598	146 323	45.2	161 800	71 328	44.1	161 798	74 995	46.4
1 VII 2011 .... ESDJ		332 084	149 955	45.2	166 043	73 110	44.0	166 041	76 845	46.3
1 VII 2012 .... ESDJ		340 792	153 683	45.1	170 397	74 938	44.0	170 395	78 745	46.2
1 VII 2013 .... ESDJ		349 728	157 508	45.0	174 865	76 815	43.9	174 863	80 693	46.1
1 VII 2014 .... ESDJ		358 899	161 434	45.0	179 451	78 740	43.9	179 448	82 694	46.1
1 VII 2015 .... ESDJ		368 310	165 463	44.9	184 157	80 717	43.8	184 153	84 746	46.0
1 VII 2016 .... ESDJ		377 968	169 598	44.9	188 986	82 746	43.8	188 982	86 852	46.0
1 VII 2017 .... ESDJ		387 879	173 841	44.8	193 942	84 827	43.7	193 937	89 014	45.9
1 VII 2018 .... ESDJ		398 050	178 195	44.8	199 028	...	...	199 022	...	...
Bermuda - Bermudes										
1 VII 2009[41] .... ESDJ		64 395	...	...	30 704	...	...	33 691	...	...
20 V 2010[43] .... CDJC		64 237	64 237	100.0	30 858	30 858	100.0	33 379	33 379	100.0
1 VII 2010[44] .... ESDJ		64 129	...	...	30 792	...	...	33 337	...	...
1 VII 2011[44] .... ESDJ		63 193	...	...	30 218	...	...	32 975	...	...
1 VII 2012[44] .... ESDJ		62 408	...	...	29 819	...	...	32 589	...	...
1 VII 2013[44] .... ESDJ		61 954	...	...	29 587	...	...	32 367	...	...
1 VII 2014[44] .... ESDJ		61 777	...	...	29 499	...	...	32 278	...	...
1 VII 2015[44] .... ESDJ		61 735	...	...	29 480	...	...	32 255	...	...
20 V 2016[43] .... CDJC		63 779	...	...	30 690	...	...	33 089	...	...
1 VII 2016[45] .... ESDJ		63 791	...	...	30 695	...	...	33 096	...	...
1 VII 2017[45] .... ESDJ		63 892	...	...	30 737	...	...	33 155	...	...
1 VII 2018[45] .... ESDJ		63 973	...	...	30 768	...	...	33 205	...	...
British Virgin Islands - Îles Vierges britanniques										
12 VII 2010 .... CDFC		28 054	...	...	13 820	...	...	14 234	...	...
Canada										
1 VII 2009[46] .... ESDJ		33 628 895	...	...	16 663 413	...	...	16 965 482	...	...
1 VII 2010[46] .... ESDJ		34 004 889	...	...	16 847 823	...	...	17 157 066	...	...
2 V 2011 .... CDJC		33 476 690	27 147 190	81.1	16 414 225	13 190 225	80.4	17 062 455	13 956 960	81.8
1 VII 2011[46] .... ESDJ		34 339 328	...	...	17 014 528	...	...	17 324 800	...	...
1 VII 2012[46] .... ESDJ		34 714 222	...	...	17 209 900	...	...	17 504 322	...	...
1 VII 2013[46] .... ESDJ		35 082 954	...	...	17 401 165	...	...	17 681 789	...	...
1 VII 2014[46] .... ESDJ		35 437 435	...	...	17 581 697	...	...	17 855 738	...	...
1 VII 2015[46] .... ESDJ		35 702 908	...	...	17 712 801	...	...	17 990 107	...	...
10 V 2016[47] .... CDJC		35 151 730	28 575 665	81.3	17 264 200	13 912 045	80.6	17 887 530	14 663 615	82.0
1 VII 2016[48] .... ESDJ		36 109 487	...	...	17 916 496	...	...	18 192 991	...	...
1 VII 2017[49] .... ESDJ		36 540 268	...	...	18 133 380	...	...	18 406 888	...	...
1 VII 2018*[50] .... ESDJ		37 058 856	...	...	18 403 310	...	...	18 655 546	...	...
Cayman Islands - Îles Caïmanes										
31 XII 2009 .... ESDJ		56 005	56 005	100.0	27 840	27 840	100.0	28 165	28 165	100.0
10 X 2010[51] .... CDJC		55 036	55 036	100.0	27 218	27 218	100.0	27 818	27 818	100.0
31 XII 2010 .... ESDJ		55 036	55 036	100.0	27 219	27 219	100.0	27 817	27 817	100.0
31 XII 2011 .... ESDJ		55 517	55 517	100.0	27 454	27 454	100.0	28 063	28 063	100.0

Continent, country or area, and date / Continent, pays ou zone et date	Code[a]	Both sexes - Les deux sexes			Male - Masculin			Female - Féminin		
		Total	Urban - Urbaine		Total	Urban - Urbaine		Total	Urban - Urbaine	
			Number Nombre	Percent P.100		Number Nombre	Percent P.100		Number Nombre	Percent P.100
AMERICA, NORTH - AMÉRIQUE DU NORD										
Cayman Islands - Îles Caïmanes										
31 XII 2012	ESDJ	56 732	56 732	100.0	27 753	27 753	100.0	28 979	28 979	100.0
31 XII 2013	ESDJ	55 747	55 747	100.0	27 133	27 133	100.0	28 614	28 614	100.0
31 XII 2014	ESDJ	58 238	58 238	100.0	28 322	28 322	100.0	29 916	29 916	100.0
31 XII 2015	ESDJ	60 413	60 413	100.0	30 264	30 264	100.0	30 149	30 149	100.0
31 XII 2016	ESDJ	61 361	61 361	100.0	29 422	29 422	100.0	31 939	31 939	100.0
31 XII 2017	ESDJ	63 415	63 415	100.0	32 212	32 212	100.0	31 203	31 203	100.0
31 XII 2018	ESDJ	65 813	65 813	100.0	31 875	31 875	100.0	33 938	33 938	100.0
Costa Rica										
1 VII 2009[52]	ESDJ	4 620 482	2 722 273	58.9	2 291 886	1 325 468	57.8	2 328 596	1 396 805	60.0
1 VII 2010[53]	ESDJ	4 538 307	3 304 248[54]	72.8	2 206 526	1 579 816[54]	71.6	2 331 781	1 724 432[54]	74.0
30 V 2011	CDJC	4 301 712	3 130 871	72.8	2 106 063	1 509 161	71.7	2 195 649	1 621 710	73.9
1 VII 2011[53]	ESDJ	4 592 346	3 343 241	72.8	2 238 615	1 603 354	71.6	2 353 731	1 739 887	73.9
1 VII 2012[53]	ESDJ	4 651 166	3 384 925	72.8	2 266 220	1 621 617	71.6	2 384 946	1 763 308	73.9
1 VII 2013[53]	ESDJ	4 711 986	3 427 548	72.7	2 276 708	1 624 941	71.4	2 435 278	1 802 607	74.0
1 VII 2014[53]	ESDJ	4 772 098	3 469 802	72.7	2 325 438	1 662 288	71.5	2 446 660	1 807 514	73.9
1 VII 2015[55]	ESDJ	4 833 752	3 512 683	72.7	2 350 223	1 683 770	71.6	2 483 529	1 828 913	73.6
1 VII 2016[56]	ESDJ	4 889 762	3 551 728	72.6	2 373 531	1 703 473	71.8	2 516 231	1 848 255	73.5
1 VII 2017[57]	ESDJ	4 946 700	3 592 070	72.6	2 405 636	1 722 499	71.6	2 541 064	1 869 571	73.6
1 VII 2018[58]	ESDJ	5 003 673	3 630 938	72.6	2 431 983	1 742 776	71.7	2 571 690	1 888 162	73.4
Cuba										
1 VII 2009	ESDJ	11 174 474	8 420 630	75.4	5 594 504	4 145 111	74.1	5 579 971	4 275 519	76.6
1 VII 2010	ESDJ	11 171 443	8 416 524	75.3	5 592 729	4 143 388	74.1	5 578 714	4 273 136	76.6
1 VII 2011	ESDJ	11 171 679	8 409 543	75.3	5 592 332	4 140 377	74.0	5 579 347	4 269 166	76.5
1 VII 2012	ESDJ	11 174 287	8 494 128	76.0	5 583 306	4 159 342	74.5	5 590 981	4 334 786	77.5
14 IX 2012	CDJC	11 167 325	8 575 189	76.8	5 570 825	4 177 485	75.0	5 596 500	4 397 704	78.6
1 VII 2013	ESDJ	11 191 608	8 596 991	76.8	5 580 810	4 186 436	75.0	5 610 798	4 410 555	78.6
1 VII 2014	ESDJ	11 224 190	8 625 144	76.8	5 595 379	4 199 578	75.1	5 628 811	4 425 566	78.6
1 VII 2015	ESDJ	11 238 661	8 639 191	76.9	5 600 904	4 205 871	75.1	5 637 757	4 433 320	78.6
1 VII 2016	ESDJ	11 239 114	8 644 181	76.9	5 599 279	4 207 382	75.1	5 639 835	4 436 798	78.7
1 VII 2017	ESDJ	11 230 142	8 642 754	77.0	5 591 525	4 204 316	75.2	5 638 617	4 438 438	78.7
1 VII 2018*	ESDJ	11 215 344	8 637 568	77.0	5 580 437	4 199 163	75.2	5 634 908	4 438 406	78.8
Curaçao										
1 VII 2009[35]	ESDJ	146 833	...	...	67 237	...	...	79 596	...	...
1 VII 2010[35]	ESDJ	148 703	...	...	68 065	...	...	80 639	...	...
26 III 2011	CDJC	150 563	...	...	68 848	...	...	81 715	...	...
1 VII 2011[35]	ESDJ	150 831	...	...	68 910	...	...	81 921	...	...
1 VII 2012[2]	ESDJ	152 088	...	...	69 490	...	...	82 598	...	...
1 VII 2013[2]	ESDJ	153 822	...	...	70 342	...	...	83 480	...	...
1 VII 2014[2]	ESDJ	155 909	...	...	71 269	...	...	84 640	...	...
1 VII 2015[2]	ESDJ	157 980	...	...	72 187	...	...	85 794	...	...
1 VII 2016[2]	ESDJ	159 663	...	...	72 990	...	...	86 674	...	...
1 VII 2017[2]	ESDJ	160 175	...	...	73 246	...	...	86 929	...	...
1 I 2018[2]	ESDJ	160 012	...	...	73 172	...	...	86 840	...	...
Dominica - Dominique										
1 VII 2009	ESDF	70 747	...	...	35 811	...	...	34 936	...	...
1 VII 2010	ESDF	70 730	...	...	35 604	...	...	35 126	...	...
14 V 2011	CDFC	68 913	...	...	34 973	...	...	33 940	...	...
1 VII 2011	ESDF	70 755	...	...	35 762	...	...	34 992	...	...
1 VII 2012	ESDF	71 042	...	...	36 053	...	...	34 989	...	...
1 VII 2013	ESDF	71 221	...	...	36 144	...	...	35 077	...	...
1 VII 2014	ESDF	71 575	...	...	36 324	...	...	35 251	...	...
Dominican Republic - République dominicaine										
1 VII 2009[3]	ESDJ	9 380 152	6 788 782	72.4	4 699 042	3 331 179	70.9	4 681 110	3 457 603	73.9
1 VII 2010[3]	ESDJ	9 478 612	6 992 189	73.8	4 747 103	3 431 480	72.3	4 731 509	3 560 709	75.3
1 XII 2010	CDJC	9 445 281	7 013 575	74.3	4 739 038	3 449 122	72.8	4 706 243	3 564 453	75.7
1 VII 2011[3]	ESDJ	9 580 139	7 172 502	74.9	4 796 628	3 520 702	73.4	4 783 511	3 651 800	76.3
1 VII 2012[3]	ESDJ	9 680 963	7 348 975	75.9	4 845 755	3 608 025	74.5	4 835 208	3 740 950	77.4
1 VII 2013[3]	ESDJ	9 784 680	7 524 149	76.9	4 896 319	3 694 713	75.5	4 888 361	3 829 436	78.3
1 VII 2014[3]	ESDJ	9 883 486	7 691 885	77.8	4 944 386	3 777 718	76.4	4 939 100	3 914 167	79.2
1 VII 2015[3]	ESDJ	9 980 243	7 854 203	78.7	4 991 398	3 858 029	77.3	4 988 845	3 996 174	80.1

Continent, country or area, and date / Continent, pays ou zone et date	Code[a]	Both sexes - Les deux sexes Total	Urban - Urbaine Number Nombre	Urban - Urbaine Percent P.100	Male - Masculin Total	Urban - Urbaine Number Nombre	Urban - Urbaine Percent P.100	Female - Féminin Total	Urban - Urbaine Number Nombre	Urban - Urbaine Percent P.100
AMERICA, NORTH - AMÉRIQUE DU NORD										
Dominican Republic - République dominicaine										
1 VII 2016[3]	ESDJ	10 075 045	8 011 084	79.5	5 037 329	3 935 569	78.1	5 037 716	4 075 515	80.9
1 VII 2017[3]	ESDJ	10 169 172	8 163 504	80.3	5 082 876	4 010 852	78.9	5 086 296	4 152 652	81.6
1 VII 2018[3]	ESDJ	10 266 149	8 314 335	81.0	5 129 824	4 085 301	79.6	5 136 325	4 229 034	82.3
El Salvador[59]										
1 VII 2009	ESDJ	6 152 558	3 890 523	63.2	2 903 737	1 806 310	62.2	3 248 821	2 084 213	64.2
1 VII 2010	ESDJ	6 183 002	3 954 803	64.0	2 913 743	1 834 400	63.0	3 269 259	2 120 404	64.9
1 VII 2011	ESDJ	6 216 143	4 019 742	64.7	2 925 284	1 862 924	63.7	3 290 858	2 156 818	65.5
1 VII 2012	ESDJ	6 251 495	4 086 880	65.4	2 938 123	1 892 642	64.4	3 313 372	2 194 238	66.2
1 VII 2013	ESDJ	6 288 899	4 156 007	66.1	2 952 174	1 923 447	65.2	3 336 726	2 232 560	66.9
1 VII 2014	ESDJ	6 328 196	...	...	2 967 351	...	...	3 360 845	...	...
1 VII 2015	ESDJ	6 460 271	4 502 693	69.7	3 042 036	2 119 867	69.7	3 418 235	2 382 826	69.7
1 VII 2016	ESDJ	6 520 675	4 590 491	70.4	3 070 065	2 161 168	70.4	3 450 610	2 429 323	70.4
1 VII 2017	ESDJ	6 581 940	4 678 816	71.1	3 098 633	2 202 778	71.1	3 483 307	2 476 038	71.1
Greenland - Groenland[60]										
1 VII 2009	ESDJ	56 323	47 230	83.9	29 873	24 865	83.2	26 451	22 366	84.6
1 VII 2010	ESDJ	56 534	47 646	84.3	29 939	25 045	83.7	26 595	22 601	85.0
1 VII 2011	ESDJ	56 682	48 045	84.8	29 992	25 233	84.1	26 690	22 812	85.5
1 VII 2012	ESDJ	56 810	48 224	84.9	30 105	25 331	84.1	26 705	22 893	85.7
1 VII 2013	ESDJ	56 483	48 221	85.4	29 867	25 333	84.8	26 616	22 888	86.0
1 VII 2014	ESDJ	56 295	48 232	85.7	29 742	25 320	85.1	26 553	22 912	86.3
1 VII 2015	ESDJ	56 114	48 284	86.0	29 634	25 329	85.5	26 480	22 955	86.7
1 VII 2016	ESDJ	56 186	48 447	86.2	29 701	25 436	85.6	26 485	23 011	86.9
1 VII 2017	ESDJ	56 171	48 527	86.4	29 651	25 435	85.8	26 520	23 092	87.1
1 VII 2018	ESDJ	56 025	48 568	86.7	29 538	25 448	86.2	26 487	23 120	87.3
Grenada - Grenade										
1 VII 2009	ESDF	105 175	...	...	52 720	...	...	52 455	...	...
1 VII 2010	ESDF	105 038	...	...	52 788	...	...	52 250	...	...
12 V 2011	CDFC	106 667	...	...	53 898	...	...	52 769	...	...
1 VII 2012	ESDF	107 599	...	...	54 435	...	...	53 164	...	...
1 VII 2013	ESDF	108 580	...	...	54 926	...	...	53 654	...	...
1 VII 2014	ESDF	109 374	...	...	55 185	...	...	54 189	...	...
1 VII 2015	ESDF	110 096	...	...	55 543	...	...	54 553	...	...
1 VII 2016	ESDF	110 910	...	...	55 955	...	...	54 955	...	...
1 VII 2017	ESDF	111 467	...	...	56 222	...	...	55 245	...	...
Guadeloupe[61]										
1 VII 2009	ESDJ	402 455	...	...	187 890	...	...	214 565	...	...
1 I 2010	CDJC	403 355	397 070	98.4	187 932	184 752	98.3	215 423	212 318	98.6
1 VII 2010	ESDJ	403 995	...	...	187 847	...	...	216 148	...	...
1 VII 2011	ESDJ	403 975	...	...	187 410	...	...	216 565	...	...
1 VII 2012	ESDJ	402 717	...	...	186 558	...	...	216 159	...	...
1 VII 2013	ESDJ	401 153	...	...	185 375	...	...	215 778	...	...
1 VII 2014	ESDJ	399 102	...	...	184 152	...	...	214 950	...	...
1 I 2015	CDJC	397 990	391 984	98.5	183 479	180 438	98.3	214 511	211 546	98.6
1 VII 2015	ESDJ	397 001	...	...	182 561	...	...	214 440	...	...
1 VII 2016	ESDJ	394 826	...	...	181 161	...	...	213 666	...	...
1 I 2017	ESDJ	429 085	...	...	197 571	...	...	231 514	...	...
1 I 2018	ESDJ	422 290	...	...	194 321	...	...	227 969	...	...
Guatemala[38]										
1 VII 2009	ESDJ	14 017 057	...	...	6 836 849	...	...	7 180 208	...	...
1 VII 2010	ESDJ	14 361 666	...	...	7 003 337	...	...	7 358 328	...	...
1 VII 2011	ESDJ	14 713 763	...	...	7 173 966	...	...	7 539 797	...	...
1 VII 2012	ESDJ	15 073 375	...	...	7 352 869	...	...	7 720 506	...	...
1 VII 2013	ESDJ	15 438 384	...	...	7 903 145	...	...	7 535 238	...	...
1 VII 2014	ESDJ	15 806 675	...	...	8 087 279	...	...	7 719 396	...	...
1 VII 2015	ESDJ	16 182 732	...	...	7 906 856	...	...	8 275 876	...	...
1 VII 2016	ESDJ	16 555 556	...	...	8 092 768	...	...	8 462 788	...	...
1 VII 2017	ESDJ	16 932 440	...	...	8 281 066	...	...	8 651 374	...	...
1 VII 2018	ESDJ	17 311 086	...	...	8 469 989	...	...	8 841 097	...	...
Haiti - Haïti[62]										
1 VII 2009	ESDJ	9 923 243	...	...	4 912 515	...	...	5 010 728	...	...
1 VII 2010	ESDJ	10 085 214	4 817 666	47.8	4 993 731	2 321 608	46.5	5 091 483	2 496 059	49.0

Continent, country or area, and date / Continent, pays ou zone et date	Code[a]	Both sexes - Les deux sexes Total	Urban - Urbaine Number Nombre	Urban - Urbaine Percent P.100	Male - Masculin Total	Urban - Urbaine Number Nombre	Urban - Urbaine Percent P.100	Female - Féminin Total	Urban - Urbaine Number Nombre	Urban - Urbaine Percent P.100
AMERICA, NORTH - AMÉRIQUE DU NORD										
Haiti - Haïti[62]										
1 VII 2011	ESDJ	10 248 306	...	...	5 075 517	...	...	5 172 789	...	...
1 VII 2012	ESDJ	10 413 211	5 154 940	49.5	5 158 254	2 495 108	48.4	5 254 957	2 659 832	50.6
1 VII 2013	ESDJ	10 579 230	...	...	5 241 572	...	...	5 337 658	...	...
1 VII 2014	ESDJ	10 745 665	...	...	5 325 099	...	...	5 420 566	...	...
1 VII 2015	ESDJ	10 911 819	...	...	5 408 465	...	...	5 503 354	...	...
1 VII 2016	ESDJ	11 078 033	...	...	5 491 848	...	...	5 586 185	...	...
1 VII 2017	ESDJ	11 244 774	...	...	5 575 496	...	...	5 669 278	...	...
1 VII 2018	ESDJ	11 411 527	...	...	5 659 140	...	...	5 752 387	...	...
Honduras										
1 VII 2009[63]	ESDF	7 876 662	...	...	3 882 957	...	...	3 993 705	...	...
1 VII 2010[63]	ESDF	8 045 990	...	...	3 965 430	...	...	4 080 560	...	...
10 VIII 2013	CDFC	8 303 771	4 480 746	54.0	4 052 316	2 116 113	52.2	4 251 456	2 364 633	55.6
1 VII 2014[4]	ESDF	8 432 153	...	...	4 113 061	...	...	4 319 092	...	...
1 VII 2015[4]	ESDF	8 576 532	...	...	4 181 657	...	...	4 394 875	...	...
1 VII 2016[4]	ESDF	8 721 014	...	...	4 250 392	...	...	4 470 622	...	...
1 VII 2017[4]	ESDF	8 866 351	...	...	4 319 664	...	...	4 546 687	...	...
1 VII 2018[4]	ESDF	9 012 229	...	...	4 389 313	...	...	4 622 916	...	...
Jamaica - Jamaïque										
1 VII 2009	ESDJ	2 695 583	...	...	1 328 124	...	...	1 367 460	...	...
1 VII 2010	ESDJ	2 702 314	...	...	1 324 134	...	...	1 378 180	...	...
4 IV 2011[64]	CDJC	2 697 983	1 454 153	53.9	1 334 533	700 957	52.5	1 363 450	753 196	55.2
1 VII 2011	ESDJ	2 699 838	...	...	1 335 466	...	...	1 364 372	...	...
1 VII 2012	ESDJ	2 707 805	...	...	1 339 740	...	...	1 368 065	...	...
1 VII 2013	ESDJ	2 714 669	...	...	1 343 798	...	...	1 370 871	...	...
1 VII 2014	ESDJ	2 720 554	...	...	1 346 711	...	...	1 373 843	...	...
1 VII 2015	ESDJ	2 725 288	...	...	1 349 294	...	...	1 375 994	...	...
1 VII 2016	ESDJ	2 728 151	...	...	1 350 950	...	...	1 377 201	...	...
1 VII 2017	ESDJ	2 728 915	...	...	1 351 375	...	...	1 377 540	...	...
Martinique										
1 I 2009	ESDJ	396 404	...	...	183 655	...	...	212 749	...	...
1 I 2010	CDJC	394 173	380 973	96.7	182 073	175 573	96.4	212 100	205 400	96.8
1 I 2010	ESDJ	394 173	...	...	182 110	...	...	212 063	...	...
1 I 2011	ESDJ	392 291	...	...	180 676	...	...	211 615	...	...
1 I 2012	ESDJ	388 364	...	...	178 824	...	...	209 540	...	...
1 I 2013	ESDJ	385 551	...	...	177 955	...	...	207 596	...	...
1 VII 2014	ESDJ	382 392	316 323	82.7	177 001	145 508	82.2	205 391	170 815	83.2
1 I 2015	CDJC	380 877	367 749	96.6	176 328	169 911	96.4	204 549	197 838	96.7
1 I 2015	ESDJ	378 243	...	...	174 193	...	...	204 050	...	...
1 I 2016	ESDJ	376 847	...	...	174 200	...	...	202 647	...	...
1 I 2017	ESDJ	374 780	...	...	173 293	...	...	201 487	...	...
1 I 2018	ESDJ	368 640	...	...	169 594	...	...	199 046	...	...
Mexico - Mexique										
1 VII 2009[65]	ESDJ	112 095 388	...	...	54 851 391	...	...	57 243 997	...	...
12 VI 2010[66]	CDFC	112 336 538	86 287 410[67]	76.8	54 855 231	41 946 540[67]	76.5	57 481 307	44 340 870[67]	77.1
1 VII 2010	ESDJ	113 748 671[65]	82 629 456[67]	72.6	55 671 595[65]	...	...	58 077 076[65]	...	...
1 VII 2011	ESDJ	115 367 452[65]	83 726 767[67]	72.6	56 472 858[65]	...	...	58 894 594[65]	...	...
1 VII 2012	ESDJ	116 935 670[65]	84 776 446[67]	72.5	57 246 931[65]	...	...	59 688 739[65]	...	...
1 VII 2013	ESDJ	118 453 929[65]	85 792 843[67]	72.4	57 992 814[65]	...	...	60 461 115[65]	...	...
1 VII 2014	ESDJ	119 936 411[65]	86 782 031[67]	72.4	58 721 525[65]	...	...	61 214 886[65]	...	...
1 VII 2015	ESDJ	121 347 800[65]	87 743 091[67]	72.3	59 416 305[65]	...	...	61 931 495[65]	...	...
1 VII 2016	ESDJ	122 715 165[68]	88 677 252[67]	72.3	60 090 244[68]	...	...	62 624 921[68]	...	...
1 VII 2017	ESDJ	124 041 731[68]	89 586 802[67]	72.2	60 740 740[68]	...	...	63 300 991[68]	...	...
1 VII 2018	ESDJ	125 327 797[68]	92 297 621[67]	73.6	61 368 864[68]	...	...	63 958 933[68]	...	...
Montserrat										
12 V 2011	CDJC	4 922	...	...	2 546	...	...	2 376	...	...
1 VII 2016	ESDJ	5 045	...	...	2 596	...	...	2 449	...	...
Nicaragua										
1 VII 2009	ESDJ	5 742 316	3 259 955	56.8	2 844 244	1 569 555	55.2	2 898 072	1 690 400	58.3
1 VII 2010	ESDJ	5 815 524	...	...	2 878 523	...	...	2 937 001	...	...
1 VII 2011	ESDJ	5 996 619	...	...	2 966 111	...	...	3 030 508	...	...
1 VII 2012	ESDJ	6 071 045	...	...	3 000 778	...	...	3 070 267	...	...
1 VII 2013	ESDJ	6 134 270	...	...	3 029 990	...	...	3 104 280	...	...
1 VII 2014	ESDJ	6 198 154	...	...	3 059 810	...	...	3 138 344	...	...

Continent, country or area, and date / Continent, pays ou zone et date	Code[a]	Both sexes - Les deux sexes			Male - Masculin			Female - Féminin		
		Total	Urban - Urbaine		Total	Urban - Urbaine		Total	Urban - Urbaine	
			Number Nombre	Percent P.100		Number Nombre	Percent P.100		Number Nombre	Percent P.100
AMERICA, NORTH - AMÉRIQUE DU NORD										
Nicaragua										
1 VII 2015	ESDJ	6 262 703	3 630 420	58.0	3 090 448	1 755 776	56.8	3 172 255	1 874 644	59.1
1 VII 2016	ESDJ	6 327 927	3 676 119	58.1	3 122 048	1 776 327	56.9	3 205 879	1 899 792	59.3
1 VII 2017	ESDJ	6 393 824	3 722 549	58.2	3 154 465	1 797 179	57.0	3 239 359	1 925 370	59.4
Panama										
1 VII 2009[69]	ESDF	3 600 000	...	...	1 810 794	...	...	1 789 206	...	...
16 V 2010	CDFC	3 405 813	...	...	1 712 584	...	...	1 693 229	...	...
1 VII 2010[13]	ESDF	3 661 835	2 385 445	65.1	1 841 305	1 171 489	63.6	1 820 530	1 213 956	66.7
1 VII 2011[13]	ESDF	3 723 821	2 449 917	65.8	1 871 749	1 203 430	64.3	1 852 072	1 246 487	67.3
1 VII 2012[13]	ESDF	3 787 511	2 514 402	66.4	1 903 085	1 235 377	64.9	1 884 426	1 279 025	67.9
1 VII 2013[13]	ESDF	3 850 735	2 578 868	67.0	1 934 264	1 267 319	65.5	1 916 471	1 311 549	68.4
1 VII 2014[13]	ESDF	3 913 275	2 643 353	67.5	1 965 087	1 299 262	66.1	1 948 188	1 344 091	69.0
1 VII 2015[13]	ESDF	3 975 404	2 707 838	68.1	1 995 695	1 331 207	66.7	1 979 709	1 376 631	69.5
1 VII 2016[13]	ESDF	4 037 043	2 772 324	68.7	2 026 044	1 363 153	67.3	2 010 999	1 409 171	70.1
1 VII 2017[13]	ESDF	4 098 135	2 836 794	69.2	2 056 085	1 395 090	67.9	2 042 050	1 441 704	70.6
1 VII 2018[13]	ESDF	4 158 783	2 901 275	69.8	2 085 950	1 427 378	68.4	2 072 833	1 473 897	71.1
Puerto Rico - Porto Rico[70]										
1 VII 2009[35]	ESDJ	3 740 410	...	...	1 793 049	...	...	1 947 361	...	...
1 IV 2010	CDJC	3 725 789	3 493 256	93.8	1 785 171	...	...	1 940 618	...	...
1 VII 2010[71]	ESDJ	3 721 208	...	...	1 782 619	...	...	1 938 589	...	...
1 VII 2011[2]	ESDJ	3 678 732	...	...	1 763 441	...	...	1 915 291	...	...
1 VII 2012[2]	ESDJ	3 634 488	...	...	1 739 072	...	...	1 895 416	...	...
1 VII 2013[2]	ESDJ	3 593 077	...	...	1 720 280	...	...	1 872 797	...	...
1 VII 2014[2]	ESDJ	3 534 874	...	...	1 688 886	...	...	1 845 988	...	...
1 VII 2015[2]	ESDJ	3 473 177	...	...	1 656 336	...	...	1 816 841	...	...
1 VII 2016[2]	ESDJ	3 406 520	...	...	1 620 193	...	...	1 786 327	...	...
1 VII 2017[2]	ESDJ	3 337 177	...	...	1 582 703	...	...	1 754 474	...	...
Saint Kitts and Nevis - Saint-Kitts-et-Nevis										
1 VII 2009*	ESDF	51 970	...	...	25 415	...	...	26 555	...	...
1 VII 2010*	ESDF	52 650	...	...	25 750	...	...	26 900	...	...
15 V 2011*	CDFC	46 398	...	...	22 846	...	...	23 552	...	...
Saint Lucia - Sainte-Lucie										
1 VII 2009	ESDF	164 726	...	...	81 795	...	...	82 931	...	...
10 V 2010	CDJC	165 770	...	...	82 268	...	...	83 502	...	...
1 VII 2011	ESDF	167 366	...	...	82 925	...	...	84 441	...	...
1 VII 2012	ESDF	169 115	...	...	83 669	...	...	85 446	...	...
1 VII 2013	ESDF	170 745	...	...	84 368	...	...	86 377	...	...
1 VII 2014	ESDF	172 623	...	...	85 639	...	...	86 984	...	...
1 VII 2015	ESDF	174 257	...	...	86 472	...	...	87 786	...	...
1 VII 2016	ESDF	175 819	...	...	87 261	...	...	88 558	...	...
1 VII 2017	ESDF	177 301	...	...	88 003	...	...	89 298	...	...
1 VII 2018	ESDF	178 696	...	...	88 693	...	...	90 002	...	...
Saint Pierre and Miquelon - Saint Pierre-et-Miquelon										
1 I 2015	CDJC	6 021	...	...	2 940	...	...	3 081	...	...
1 VII 2015	ESDJ	6 021	...	...	2 940	...	...	3 081	...	...
Saint Vincent and the Grenadines - Saint-Vincent-et-les Grenadines										
1 VII 2009	ESDJ	109 727	49 911	45.5	55 814	...	...	53 912	...	...
1 VII 2010	ESDJ	109 815	49 951	45.5	55 859	...	...	53 956	...	...
1 VII 2011	ESDJ	109 903	49 991	45.5	55 904	...	...	53 999	...	...
12 VI 2012	CDJC	109 991	50 926	46.3	56 419	...	...	53 572	...	...
1 VII 2013	ESDJ	110 079	50 967	46.3	56 464	...	...	53 615	...	...
1 VII 2014	ESDJ	110 167	51 008	46.3	56 509	...	...	53 658	...	...
1 VII 2015	ESDJ	110 255	51 048	46.3	56 555	...	...	53 701	...	...
1 VII 2016	ESDJ	110 343	...	...	56 600	...	...	53 744	...	...
1 VII 2017	ESDJ	110 431	...	...	56 645	...	...	53 787	...	...
1 VII 2018	ESDJ	110 520	...	...	56 690	...	...	53 829	...	...

Continent, country or area, and date — Continent, pays ou zone et date	Code[a]	Both sexes - Les deux sexes			Male - Masculin			Female - Féminin		
		Total	Urban - Urbaine		Total	Urban - Urbaine		Total	Urban - Urbaine	
			Number Nombre	Percent P.100		Number Nombre	Percent P.100		Number Nombre	Percent P.100
AMERICA, NORTH - AMÉRIQUE DU NORD										
Saint-Barthélemy										
1 I 2015	CDJC	9 625	...	...	5 117	...	...	4 508	...	...
Saint-Martin (French part) - Saint-Martin (partie française)										
1 VII 2014	ESDJ	35 405	...	...	17 144	...	...	18 261	...	...
1 I 2015	CDJC	35 684	...	...	16 884	...	...	18 800	...	...
1 VII 2017	ESDJ	35 640	...	...	17 244	...	...	18 396	...	...
1 VII 2018	ESDJ	35 457	...	...	17 151	...	...	18 306	...	...
Sint Maarten (Dutch part) - Saint-Martin (partie néerlandaise)										
1 VII 2009	ESDF	39 172	...	...	18 918	...	...	20 254	...	...
1 VII 2010	ESDF	35 526	...	...	16 927	...	...	18 600	...	...
9 IV 2011	CDFC	33 609	...	...	15 868	...	...	17 741	...	...
1 VII 2011	ESDF	33 436	...	...	15 772	...	...	17 656	...	...
1 VII 2012	ESDF	34 670	...	...	16 656	...	...	18 005	...	...
1 VII 2013	ESDF	36 611	...	...	17 910	...	...	18 701	...	...
1 I 2014	ESDF	37 132	...	...	18 159	...	...	18 973	...	...
1 I 2015	ESDF	38 247	...	...	18 694	...	...	19 553	...	...
1 I 2016	ESDF	39 410	...	...	19 256	...	...	20 155	...	...
1 I 2017	ESDF	40 535	...	...	19 769	...	...	20 766	...	...
1 I 2018	ESDF	40 614	...	...	19 759	...	...	20 855	...	...
Trinidad and Tobago - Trinité-et-Tobago										
1 VII 2009[23]	ESDF	1 310 106	...	...	657 018	...	...	653 088	...	...
1 VII 2010[23]	ESDF	1 317 714	...	...	660 822	...	...	656 892	...	...
9 I 2011	CDJC	1 328 019	...	...	666 305	...	...	661 714	...	...
1 I 2012[24]	ESDF	1 335 194	...	...	669 905	...	...	665 289	...	...
1 VII 2013[24]	ESDF	1 340 557	...	...	672 596	...	...	667 961	...	...
1 VII 2014[24]	ESDF	1 345 343	...	...	674 997	...	...	670 346	...	...
1 VII 2015[24]	ESDF	1 349 667	...	...	677 166	...	...	672 501	...	...
1 VII 2016[24]	ESDF	1 353 895	...	...	679 288	...	...	674 607	...	...
1 VII 2017[24]	ESDF	1 356 633	...	...	680 661	...	...	675 972	...	...
1 VII 2018[24]	ESDF	1 359 193	...	...	681 946	...	...	677 247	...	...
Turks and Caicos Islands - Îles Turques et Caïques										
1 VII 2009	ESDJ	36 000	...	...	18 810	...	...	17 190	...	...
1 VII 2010	ESDJ	34 500	...	...	17 810	...	...	16 690	...	...
1 VII 2011	ESDJ	33 500	...	...	17 160	...	...	16 340	...	...
25 I 2012*[72]	CDJC	31 458	...	...	16 037	...	...	15 421	...	...
1 VII 2012	ESDJ	32 199	...	...	16 365	...	...	15 834	...	...
1 VII 2013	ESDJ	33 677	...	...	17 132	...	...	16 545	...	...
1 VII 2014	ESDJ	35 168	...	...	17 907	...	...	17 261	...	...
1 VII 2015	ESDJ	36 689	...	...	18 689	...	...	18 000	...	...
1 VII 2016	ESDJ	37 910	...	...	19 169	...	...	18 741	...	...
1 VII 2017	ESDJ	39 790	...	...	20 296	...	...	19 494	...	...
1 VII 2018*	ESDJ	41 360	...	...	21 104	...	...	20 256	...	...
United States of America - États-Unis d'Amérique										
1 VII 2009[73]	ESDJ	306 771 529	...	...	150 807 454	...	...	155 964 075	...	...
1 IV 2010	CDJC	308 745 538	249 253 271	80.7	151 781 326	121 698 595	80.2	156 964 212	127 554 676	81.3
1 VII 2010[74]	ESDJ	309 348 193	...	...	152 088 743	...	...	157 259 450	...	...
1 VII 2011[74]	ESDJ	311 663 358	...	...	153 263 360	...	...	158 399 998	...	...
1 VII 2012[74]	ESDJ	313 998 379	...	...	154 467 180	...	...	159 531 199	...	...
1 VII 2013[74]	ESDJ	316 204 908	...	...	155 589 564	...	...	160 615 344	...	...
1 VII 2014[74]	ESDJ	318 563 456	...	...	156 780 062	...	...	161 783 394	...	...
1 VII 2015[74]	ESDJ	320 896 618	...	...	157 960 035	...	...	162 936 583	...	...
1 VII 2016[74]	ESDJ	323 127 513	...	...	159 078 923	...	...	164 048 590	...	...
1 VII 2017[74]	ESDJ	325 147 121	...	...	160 125 630	...	...	165 021 491	...	...
1 VII 2018[74]	ESDJ	327 167 434	...	...	161 128 679	...	...	166 038 755	...	...

Continent, country or area, and date / Continent, pays ou zone et date	Code[a]	Both sexes - Les deux sexes			Male - Masculin			Female - Féminin		
		Total	Urban - Urbaine		Total	Urban - Urbaine		Total	Urban - Urbaine	
			Number Nombre	Percent P.100		Number Nombre	Percent P.100		Number Nombre	Percent P.100
AMERICA, NORTH - AMÉRIQUE DU NORD										
United States Virgin Islands - Îles Vierges américaines[70]										
1 IV 2010 .... CDJC		106 405	...	...	50 854	...	...	55 551	...	...
AMERICA, SOUTH - AMÉRIQUE DU SUD										
Argentina - Argentine										
1 VII 2009 .... ESDF		40 134 425	36 553 965	91.1	19 657 086	17 810 843	90.6	20 477 339	18 743 122	91.5
1 VII 2010[40] .... ESDF		40 788 453	37 126 653	91.0	19 940 704	17 996 224	90.2	20 847 749	19 130 429	91.8
27 X 2010 .... CDFC		40 117 096	36 467 245	90.9	19 523 766	17 596 022	90.1	20 593 330	18 871 223	91.6
1 VII 2011[40] .... ESDF		41 261 490	37 600 508	91.1	20 180 791	18 236 611	90.4	21 080 699	19 363 897	91.9
1 VII 2012[40] .... ESDF		41 733 271	38 073 305	91.2	20 420 391	18 476 577	90.5	21 312 880	19 596 728	91.9
1 VII 2013[40] .... ESDF		42 202 935	38 544 203	91.3	20 659 037	18 715 667	90.6	21 543 898	19 828 536	92.0
1 VII 2014[40] .... ESDF		42 669 500	39 021 268	91.5	20 896 203	18 958 322	90.7	21 773 297	20 062 946	92.1
1 VII 2015[40] .... ESDF		43 131 966	39 487 935	91.6	21 131 346	19 195 446	90.8	22 000 620	20 292 489	92.2
1 VII 2016[40] .... ESDF		43 590 368	39 951 022	91.7	21 364 470	19 430 772	90.9	22 225 898	20 520 250	92.3
1 VII 2017[40] .... ESDF		44 044 811	40 410 715	91.7	21 595 623	19 664 392	91.1	22 449 188	20 746 323	92.4
1 VII 2018[40] .... ESDF		44 494 502	40 866 408	91.8	21 824 372	19 895 973	91.2	22 670 130	20 970 435	92.5
Bolivia (Plurinational State of) - Bolivie (État plurinational de)										
1 VII 2009 .... ESDF		*9 870 229*		...	*4 973 094*	...	...	*4 897 135*		...
1 VII 2010 .... ESDF		*10 030 501*		...	*5 056 056*	...	...	*4 974 445*		...
1 VII 2011 .... ESDF		*10 190 775*		...	*5 138 206*	...	...	*5 052 569*		...
1 VII 2012 .... ESDF		*10 351 118*	*6 965 568*	*67.3*	*5 219 006*	*3 437 451*	*65.9*	*5 132 112*	*3 528 117*	*68.7*
21 XI 2012 .... CDFC		*10 059 856*	*6 788 962*	*67.5*	*5 019 447*	*3 314 824*	*66.0*	*5 040 409*	*3 474 138*	*68.9*
1 VII 2013 .... ESDF		*10 507 789*	*7 110 575*	*67.7*	*5 297 727*	*3 511 796*	*66.3*	*5 210 062*	*3 598 779*	*69.1*
1 VII 2014 .... ESDF		*10 665 841*	*7 256 749*	*68.0*	*5 376 880*	*3 586 449*	*66.7*	*5 288 961*	*3 670 300*	*69.4*
1 VII 2015 .... ESDF		*10 825 013*	*7 403 841*	*68.4*	*5 456 332*	*3 661 290*	*67.1*	*5 368 681*	*3 742 551*	*69.7*
1 VII 2016 .... ESDF		*10 985 059*	*7 551 625*	*68.7*	*5 535 975*	*3 736 216*	*67.5*	*5 449 084*	*3 815 409*	*70.0*
1 VII 2017 .... ESDF		*11 145 770*	*7 699 908*	*69.1*	*5 615 713*	*3 811 135*	*67.9*	*5 530 057*	*3 888 773*	*70.3*
1 VII 2018 .... ESDF		*11 307 314*	*7 848 776*	*69.4*	*5 695 665*	*3 886 115*	*68.2*	*5 611 649*	*3 962 661*	*70.6*
Brazil - Brésil										
1 VII 2009[75] .... ESDJ		*193 543 969*	*162 670 274*	*84.0*	*95 776 055*	...	...	*97 767 914*	...	...
1 VII 2010[75] .... ESDJ		*195 497 797*	*164 920 459*	*84.4*	*96 706 703*	...	...	*98 791 094*	...	...
31 VII 2010 .... CDJC		*190 755 799*	*160 925 804*	*84.4*	*93 406 990*	*77 710 179*	*83.2*	*97 348 809*	*83 215 625*	*85.5*
1 VII 2011[75] .... ESDJ		*197 397 018*	*167 096 245*	*84.6*	*97 610 297*		...	*99 786 721*	...	...
1 VII 2012[75] .... ESDJ		*199 242 462*	*169 230 105*	*84.9*	*98 487 258*		...	*100 755 204*	...	...
1 VII 2013[75] .... ESDJ		*201 032 714*	*171 317 079*	*85.2*	*99 336 858*		...	*101 695 856*	...	...
1 VII 2014[75] .... ESDJ		*202 768 562*	*173 358 764*	*85.5*	*100 159 507*		...	*102 609 055*	...	...
1 VII 2015[75] .... ESDJ		*204 450 649*	*175 355 103*	*85.8*	*100 955 522*		...	*103 495 127*	...	...
1 VII 2016[75] .... ESDJ		*206 081 432*	*177 309 126*	*86.0*	*101 726 102*		...	*104 355 330*	...	...
1 VII 2017[75] .... ESDJ		*207 660 929*	*179 217 279*	*86.3*	*102 471 274*		...	*105 189 655*	...	...
1 VII 2018[75] .... ESDJ		*208 494 900*	...	...	*101 971 173*		...	*106 523 727*	...	...
Chile - Chili										
1 VII 2009 .... ESDF		16 876 767	14 677 912	87.0	8 354 788	7 187 042	86.0	8 521 979	7 490 870	87.9
1 VII 2010 .... ESDF		17 066 142	14 855 979	87.0	8 447 879	7 275 736	86.1	8 618 263	7 580 243	88.0
1 VII 2011 .... ESDF		17 255 527	15 034 027	87.1	8 541 374	7 364 669	86.2	8 714 153	7 669 358	88.0
1 VII 2012 .... ESDF		17 444 799	15 211 974	87.2	8 635 093	7 453 791	86.3	8 809 706	7 758 183	88.1
1 VII 2013 .... ESDF		17 631 579	15 386 310	87.3	8 727 358	7 541 225	86.4	8 904 221	7 845 085	88.1
1 VII 2014 .... ESDF		17 819 054	15 559 039	87.3	8 819 725	7 628 149	86.5	8 999 329	7 930 890	88.1
1 VII 2015 .... ESDF		18 006 407	15 729 803	87.4	8 911 940	7 714 356	86.6	9 094 467	8 015 447	88.1
1 VII 2016 .... ESDF		18 191 884	15 898 145	87.4	9 003 254	7 799 463	86.6	9 188 630	8 098 682	88.1
1 VII 2017 .... ESDF		18 373 917	16 063 564	87.4	9 092 950	7 883 072	86.7	9 280 967	8 180 492	88.1
1 VII 2018 .... ESDF		18 552 218	16 225 850	87.5	9 180 864	7 965 073	86.8	9 371 354	8 260 777	88.1
Colombia - Colombie[76]										
1 VII 2009 .... ESDJ		*44 978 832*	*33 892 634*	*75.4*	*22 203 708*	*16 343 820*	*73.6*	*22 775 124*	*17 548 814*	*77.1*
1 VII 2010 .... ESDJ		*45 509 584*	*34 388 013*	*75.6*	*22 466 660*	*16 587 100*	*73.8*	*23 042 924*	*17 800 913*	*77.3*
1 VII 2011 .... ESDJ		*46 044 601*	*34 883 399*	*75.8*	*22 731 299*	*16 830 795*	*74.0*	*23 313 302*	*18 052 604*	*77.4*
1 VII 2012 .... ESDJ		*46 581 823*	*35 377 138*	*75.9*	*22 997 087*	*17 073 806*	*74.2*	*23 584 736*	*18 303 332*	*77.6*
1 VII 2013 .... ESDJ		*47 121 089*	*35 869 246*	*76.1*	*23 264 039*	*17 315 981*	*74.4*	*23 857 050*	*18 553 265*	*77.8*

Continent, country or area, and date / Continent, pays ou zone et date	Code[a]	Both sexes - Les deux sexes			Male - Masculin			Female - Féminin		
		Total	Urban - Urbaine Number Nombre	Urban - Urbaine Percent P.100	Total	Urban - Urbaine Number Nombre	Urban - Urbaine Percent P.100	Total	Urban - Urbaine Number Nombre	Urban - Urbaine Percent P.100
AMERICA, SOUTH - AMÉRIQUE DU SUD										
Colombia - Colombie[76]										
1 VII 2014	ESDJ	47 661 787	36 359 268	76.3	23 531 670	17 556 826	74.6	24 130 117	18 802 442	77.9
1 VII 2015	ESDJ	48 203 405	36 846 935	76.4	23 799 679	17 796 724	74.8	24 403 726	19 050 211	78.1
1 VII 2016	ESDJ	48 747 708	37 332 955	76.6	24 069 035	18 035 960	74.9	24 678 673	19 296 995	78.2
1 VII 2017	ESDJ	49 291 609	37 816 051	76.7	24 337 747	18 273 530	75.1	24 953 862	19 542 521	78.3
1 VII 2018	ESDJ	49 834 240	38 295 351	76.8	24 605 796	18 509 148	75.2	25 228 444	19 786 203	78.4
Ecuador - Équateur										
1 VII 2009[77]	ESDF	14 738 472	9 236 112	62.7	7 316 020	4 528 987	61.9	7 422 452	4 707 125	63.4
1 VII 2010[77]	ESDF	15 012 228	9 412 612	62.7	7 443 875	4 611 039	61.9	7 568 353	4 801 573	63.4
28 XI 2010	CDFC	14 483 499	9 090 786	62.8	7 177 683	4 451 434	62.0	7 305 816	4 639 352	63.5
1 VII 2011[77]	ESDF	15 266 431	9 596 628	62.9	7 567 676	4 700 620	62.1	7 698 755	4 896 008	63.6
1 VII 2012[77]	ESDF	15 520 973	9 780 650	63.0	7 691 912	4 790 437	62.3	7 829 061	4 990 213	63.7
1 VII 2013[77]	ESDF	15 774 749	9 963 884	63.2	7 815 935	4 880 045	62.4	7 958 814	5 083 839	63.9
1 VII 2014[77]	ESDF	16 027 466	10 145 875	63.3	7 939 552	4 969 197	62.6	8 087 914	5 176 678	64.0
1 VII 2015[77]	ESDF	16 278 844	10 326 384	63.4	8 062 610	5 057 750	62.7	8 216 234	5 268 634	64.1
1 VII 2016[77]	ESDF	16 528 730	10 505 180	63.6	8 184 970	5 145 594	62.9	8 343 760	5 359 586	64.2
1 VII 2017[77]	ESDF	16 776 977	10 682 148	63.7	8 306 557	5 232 565	63.0	8 470 420	5 449 583	64.3
1 VII 2018[77]	ESDF	17 023 408	10 857 208	63.8	8 427 261	5 318 564	63.1	8 596 147	5 538 644	64.4
Falkland Islands (Malvinas) - Îles Falkland (Malvinas)[78]										
15 IV 2012	CDFC	2 840	...	...	1 491	...	...	1 349	...	...
French Guiana - Guyane française										
1 I 2009	ESDJ	224 469	...	...	111 201	...	...	113 268	...	...
1 I 2010	CDJC	229 040	201 042	87.8	113 599	98 933	87.1	115 441	102 109	88.5
1 I 2010	ESDJ	229 040	201 042	87.8	113 599	98 933	87.1	115 441	102 109	88.5
1 I 2011	ESDJ	237 549	...	...	117 732	...	...	119 817	...	...
1 I 2012	ESDJ	239 648	...	...	119 538	...	...	120 110	...	...
1 I 2013	CDJC	244 118	...	...	121 653	...	...	122 465	...	...
1 I 2013	ESDJ	244 118	...	...	121 653	...	...	122 465	...	...
1 I 2014	ESDJ	252 338	...	...	125 189	...	...	127 149	...	...
1 I 2015	CDJC	259 865	224 631	86.4	128 973	110 366	85.6	130 892	114 265	87.3
1 I 2015	ESDJ	254 541	...	...	127 237	...	...	127 304	...	...
1 I 2016	ESDJ	262 527	...	...	130 596	...	...	131 931	...	...
1 I 2017	ESDJ	274 153	...	...	136 093	...	...	138 060	...	...
1 I 2018	ESDJ	281 612	...	...	139 842	...	...	141 770	...	...
Guyana										
1 VII 2009	ESDF	753 227	...	...	377 759	...	...	375 468	...	...
1 VII 2010	ESDF	752 113	...	...	377 267	...	...	374 846	...	...
1 VII 2011	ESDF	750 663	...	...	376 596	...	...	374 067	...	...
1 VII 2012	ESDF	746 724	...	...	371 731	...	...	374 993	...	...
15 IX 2012	CDFC	746 955	...	...	371 805	...	...	375 150	...	...
1 VII 2013	ESDF	746 263	...	...	371 609	...	...	374 654	...	...
1 VII 2014	ESDF	745 873	...	...	371 519	...	...	374 355	...	...
1 VII 2015	ESDF	744 945	...	...	371 149	...	...	373 796	...	...
1 VII 2016	ESDF	743 458	...	...	370 491	...	...	372 967	...	...
1 VII 2017	ESDF	741 365	...	...	369 520	...	...	371 845	...	...
Paraguay[79]										
1 VII 2009	ESDF	6 168 757	3 569 718	57.9	3 116 847	1 744 890	56.0	3 051 910	1 824 828	59.8
1 VII 2010	ESDF	6 265 877	3 652 713	58.3	3 165 316	1 785 556	56.4	3 100 561	1 867 157	60.2
1 VII 2011	ESDF	6 363 276	3 738 905	58.8	3 213 839	1 827 856	56.9	3 149 438	1 911 049	60.7
1 VII 2012	ESDF	6 461 041	3 825 311	59.2	3 262 466	1 870 215	57.3	3 198 575	1 955 096	61.1
1 VII 2013	ESDF	6 559 027	3 911 850	59.6	3 311 123	1 912 591	57.8	3 247 904	1 999 259	61.6
1 VII 2014	ESDF	6 657 232	3 998 524	60.1	3 359 806	1 954 982	58.2	3 297 426	2 043 541	62.0
1 VII 2015	ESDF	6 755 756	4 085 396	60.5	3 408 566	1 997 419	58.6	3 347 190	2 087 977	62.4
1 VII 2016	ESDF	6 854 536	4 174 834	60.9	3 457 365	2 041 139	59.0	3 397 170	2 133 695	62.8
1 VII 2017	ESDF	6 953 646	4 264 473	61.3	3 506 242	2 084 904	59.5	3 447 404	2 179 568	63.2
Peru - Pérou										
30 VI 2009	ESDF	29 132 013	21 398 222	73.5	14 605 206	10 584 348	72.5	14 526 807	10 813 874	74.4
30 VI 2010	ESDF	29 461 933	21 805 837	74.0	14 768 901	10 784 345	73.0	14 693 032	11 021 492	75.0
30 VI 2011	ESDF	29 797 694	22 219 201	74.6	14 935 396	10 987 090	73.6	14 862 298	11 232 111	75.6
30 VI 2012	ESDF	30 135 875	22 635 742	75.1	15 103 003	11 191 332	74.1	15 032 872	11 444 410	76.1
30 VI 2013	ESDF	30 475 144	23 054 394	75.6	15 271 062	11 396 589	74.6	15 204 082	11 657 805	76.7

Continent, country or area, and date / Continent, pays ou zone et date	Code[a]	Both sexes - Les deux sexes Total	Urban - Urbaine Number Nombre	Urban - Urbaine Percent P.100	Male - Masculin Total	Urban - Urbaine Number Nombre	Urban - Urbaine Percent P.100	Female - Féminin Total	Urban - Urbaine Number Nombre	Urban - Urbaine Percent P.100
AMERICA, SOUTH - AMÉRIQUE DU SUD										
Peru - Pérou										
30 VI 2014	ESDF	30 814 175	23 474 069	76.2	15 438 887	11 602 321	75.1	15 375 288	11 871 748	77.2
30 VI 2015	ESDF	31 151 643	23 893 654	76.7	15 605 814	11 808 006	75.7	15 545 829	12 085 648	77.7
30 VI 2016	ESDF	31 488 625	24 313 862	77.2	15 772 385	12 013 953	76.2	15 716 240	12 299 909	78.3
30 VI 2017	ESDF	31 826 018	24 735 295	77.7	15 939 059	12 220 551	76.7	15 886 959	12 514 744	78.8
22 VIII 2017[80]	CDFC	29 381 884	23 311 893	79.3	14 450 757	11 377 486	78.7	14 931 127	11 934 407	79.9
30 VI 2018	ESDF	32 162 184	25 156 589	78.2	16 105 008	12 427 084	77.2	16 057 176	12 729 505	79.3
Suriname										
13 VIII 2012	CDJC	541 638	359 146	66.3	270 629	177 215	65.5	271 009	181 931	67.1
1 VII 2013	ESDJ	550 222	...	...	274 859	...	...	275 363	...	...
1 VII 2014	ESDJ	558 773	...	...	279 071	...	...	279 702	...	...
1 VII 2015	ESDJ	567 291	...	...	283 259	...	...	284 032	...	...
1 VII 2016	ESDJ	575 763	...	...	287 422	...	...	288 341	...	...
1 VII 2017	ESDJ	583 200	386 500	66.3	290 800	190 700	65.6	292 400	195 800	67.0
Uruguay										
1 VII 2009	ESDJ	3 378 083	3 191 384	94.5	1 632 052	1 527 146	93.6	1 746 031	1 664 238	95.3
1 VII 2010	ESDJ	3 396 706	3 216 519	94.7	1 640 886	1 539 959	93.8	1 755 820	1 676 560	95.5
1 VII 2011	ESDJ	3 412 636	3 238 644	94.9	1 648 466	1 551 366	94.1	1 764 170	1 687 279	95.6
4 X 2011	CDJC	3 286 314	3 110 701	94.7	1 577 725[81]	1 478 967[81]	93.7	1 708 481[81]	1 631 626[81]	95.5
1 VII 2012[3]	ESDJ	3 426 466	3 253 370	94.9	1 655 693	1 559 292	94.2	1 770 774	1 694 078	95.7
1 VII 2013[3]	ESDJ	3 440 157	3 268 281	95.0	1 662 884	1 567 325	94.3	1 777 273	1 700 956	95.7
1 VII 2014[3]	ESDJ	3 453 691	3 283 177	95.1	1 670 026	1 575 363	94.3	1 783 665	1 707 813	95.7
1 VII 2015[3]	ESDJ	3 467 054	3 297 948	95.1	1 677 118	1 583 363	94.4	1 789 936	1 714 585	95.8
1 VII 2016[3]	ESDJ	3 480 222	3 312 523	95.2	1 684 140	1 591 280	94.5	1 796 082	1 721 243	95.8
1 VII 2017[3]	ESDJ	3 493 205	3 326 886	95.2	1 691 102	1 599 115	94.6	1 802 103	1 727 772	95.9
1 VII 2018[3]	ESDJ	3 505 985	3 341 003	95.3	1 697 985	1 606 843	94.6	1 808 000	1 734 160	95.9
Venezuela (Bolivarian Republic of) - Venezuela (République bolivarienne du)										
1 VII 2011	ESDF	28 810 899	...	...	14 443 172	...	...	14 367 727	...	...
1 IX 2011	CDJC	27 227 930	24 182 998[82]	88.8	13 549 752	11 902 155[82]	87.8	13 678 178	12 280 843[82]	89.8
1 VII 2012	ESDF	29 230 592	...	...	14 654 181	...	...	14 576 411	...	...
1 VII 2013	ESDF	29 650 188	...	...	14 865 265	...	...	14 784 923	...	...
1 VII 2014	ESDF	30 069 829	...	...	15 075 999	...	...	14 993 830	...	...
1 VII 2015	ESDF	30 489 354	...	...	15 283 762	...	...	15 205 592	...	...
1 VII 2016	ESDF	30 883 254	...	...	15 488 512	...	...	15 394 742	...	...
1 VII 2017	ESDF	31 277 130	...	...	15 690 386	...	...	15 586 744	...	...
1 VII 2018	ESDF	31 670 952	...	...	15 889 454	...	...	15 781 498	...	...
ASIA - ASIE										
Afghanistan[83]										
1 VII 2009	ESDF	23 993 500	5 507 300	23.0	12 272 900	2 835 900	23.1	11 720 600	2 671 400	22.8
1 VII 2010	ESDF	24 485 600	5 690 300	23.2	12 524 700	2 929 900	23.4	11 960 900	2 760 400	23.1
1 VII 2011	ESDF	24 987 700	5 879 200	23.5	12 782 000	3 027 400	23.7	12 205 700	2 851 800	23.4
1 VII 2012	ESDF	25 500 100	6 074 200	23.8	13 044 400	3 127 700	24.0	12 455 700	2 946 500	23.7
1 VII 2013	ESDF	26 023 100	6 275 600	24.1	13 312 400	3 231 600	24.3	12 710 700	3 044 000	23.9
1 VII 2014	ESDF	26 556 754	6 483 434	24.4	13 585 933	3 338 764	24.6	12 970 821	3 144 670	24.2
1 VII 2015	ESDF	27 101 365	6 698 033	24.7	13 865 015	3 449 379	24.9	13 236 350	3 248 654	24.5
1 VII 2016	ESDF	27 657 145	6 919 560	25.0	14 149 838	3 563 570	25.2	13 507 307	3 355 990	24.8
1 VII 2017	ESDF	28 224 323	7 148 224	25.3	14 438 456	3 631 353	25.2	13 785 867	3 516 871	25.5
1 VII 2018	ESDF	30 075 018	7 507 953	25.0	15 312 423	3 792 857	24.8	14 762 595	3 715 096	25.2
Armenia - Arménie										
1 VII 2009	ESDJ	3 066 045	1 950 215	63.6	1 471 121	915 610	62.2	1 594 924	1 034 605	64.9
1 VII 2010	ESDJ	3 044 868	1 933 144	63.5	1 460 773	906 766	62.1	1 584 095	1 026 378	64.8
1 VII 2011	ESDJ	3 027 938	1 918 721	63.4	1 452 588	899 253	61.9	1 575 350	1 019 468	64.7
12 X 2011	CDFC	2 871 771	1 847 124	64.3	1 346 729	851 475	63.2	1 525 042	995 649	65.3
1 VII 2012	ESDJ	3 024 127	1 915 060	63.3	1 450 560	897 133	61.8	1 573 567	1 017 927	64.7
1 VII 2013	ESDJ	3 021 979	1 915 758	63.4	1 447 572	896 463	61.9	1 574 407	1 019 295	64.7
1 VII 2014	ESDJ	3 013 839	1 913 481	63.5	1 441 323	894 594	62.1	1 572 516	1 018 887	64.8
1 VII 2015	ESDJ	3 004 588	1 909 960	63.6	1 434 095	891 769	62.2	1 570 493	1 018 191	64.8
1 VII 2016	ESDJ	2 992 364	1 904 230	63.6	1 423 906	886 581	62.3	1 568 458	1 017 649	64.9

Continent, country or area, and date / Continent, pays ou zone et date	Code[a]	Both sexes - Les deux sexes			Male - Masculin			Female - Féminin		
		Total	Urban - Urbaine		Total	Urban - Urbaine		Total	Urban - Urbaine	
			Number Nombre	Percent P.100		Number Nombre	Percent P.100		Number Nombre	Percent P.100
ASIA - ASIE										
Armenia - Arménie										
1 VII 2017	ESDJ	2 979 442	1 898 630	63.7	1 413 485	881 506	62.4	1 565 957	1 017 124	65.0
1 I 2018	ESDJ	2 972 732	...	...	1 408 199	...	...	1 564 533	...	...
Azerbaijan - Azerbaïdjan										
13 IV 2009	CDJC	8 922 447	4 739 123	53.1	4 414 398	2 330 527	52.8	4 508 049	2 408 596	53.4
1 VII 2009	ESDJ	8 947 300	4 751 400	53.1	4 427 900	2 337 100	52.8	4 519 400	2 414 300	53.4
1 VII 2010	ESDJ	9 054 300	4 802 200	53.0	4 486 300	2 364 400	52.7	4 568 000	2 437 800	53.4
1 VII 2011	ESDJ	9 173 100	4 859 100	53.0	4 550 300	2 394 700	52.6	4 622 800	2 464 400	53.3
1 VII 2012	ESDJ	9 295 800	4 936 900	53.1	4 616 200	2 435 200	52.8	4 679 600	2 501 700	53.5
1 VII 2013	ESDJ	9 416 800	5 016 000	53.3	4 681 200	2 476 300	52.9	4 735 600	2 539 700	53.6
1 VII 2014	ESDJ	9 535 100	5 072 100	53.2	4 744 700	2 505 700	52.8	4 790 400	2 566 400	53.6
1 VII 2015	ESDJ	9 649 300	5 126 300	53.1	4 805 700	2 534 000	52.7	4 843 600	2 592 300	53.5
1 VII 2016	ESDJ	9 757 800	5 175 700	53.0	4 863 400	2 559 600	52.6	4 894 400	2 616 100	53.5
1 VII 2017	ESDJ	9 854 000	5 218 400	53.0	4 914 600	2 581 600	52.5	4 939 400	2 636 800	53.4
1 VII 2018	ESDJ	9 936 100	5 261 900	53.0	4 955 500	2 603 100	52.5	4 980 600	2 658 800	53.4
Bahrain - Bahreïn										
1 VII 2009	ESDJ	1 178 415	...	...	731 997	...	...	446 418	...	...
27 IV 2010	CDJC	1 234 571	1 234 571	100.0	768 414	768 414	100.0	466 157	466 157	100.0
1 VII 2010	ESDJ	1 228 543	...	...	764 357	...	...	464 186	...	...
1 VII 2011	ESDJ	1 195 020	...	...	741 483	...	...	453 537	...	...
1 VII 2012	ESDJ	1 208 964	...	...	760 449	...	...	448 515	...	...
1 VII 2013	ESDJ	1 253 191	...	...	788 381	...	...	464 810	...	...
1 VII 2014	ESDJ	1 314 562	...	...	806 487	...	...	508 075	...	...
1 VII 2015	ESDJ	1 370 322	...	...	846 365	...	...	523 957	...	...
1 VII 2016	ESDJ	1 423 726	...	...	888 389	...	...	535 337	...	...
1 VII 2017	ESDJ	1 501 116	...	...	951 312	...	...	549 804	...	...
1 VII 2018	ESDJ	1 503 091	...	...	946 864	...	...	556 227	...	...
Bangladesh										
1 VII 2010	ESDF	148 620 000	38 540 000	25.9	76 120 000	20 427 000	26.8	72 500 000	18 113 000	25.0
15 III 2011[84]	CDFC	149 772 364	...	...	74 980 386	...	...	74 791 978	...	...
1 VII 2011	ESDF	150 611 000	39 000 000	25.9	77 101 062	20 560 587	26.7	73 509 938	18 439 413	25.1
1 VII 2012	ESDF	152 700 000	41 100 000	26.9	78 200 000	...	...	74 500 000	...	...
1 VII 2013	ESDF	154 790 000	42 580 000	27.5	77 510 000	...	...	77 280 000	...	...
1 VII 2014	ESDF	156 880 000	44 110 000	28.1	78 560 000	...	...	78 320 000	...	...
1 VII 2015	ESDF	158 900 000	45 700 000	28.8	79 600 000	...	...	79 300 000	...	...
1 VII 2016	ESDF	160 800 000	47 400 000	29.5	80 500 000	...	...	80 300 000	...	...
1 VII 2017	ESDF	162 700 000	49 216 750	30.3	81 400 000	24 623 500	30.3	81 300 000	24 593 250	30.3
Bhutan - Bhoutan										
1 VII 2009[85]	ESDF	683 407	232 232	34.0	357 305	124 246	34.8	326 102	107 986	33.1
1 VII 2010[85]	ESDF	695 823	242 001	34.8	363 384	129 298	35.6	332 439	112 703	33.9
1 VII 2011[85]	ESDF	708 265	252 038	35.6	369 476	134 484	36.4	338 789	117 554	34.7
1 VII 2012[85]	ESDF	720 679	262 325	36.4	375 554	139 798	37.2	345 125	122 530	35.5
1 VII 2013[85]	ESDF	733 004	272 839	37.2	381 582	145 219	38.1	351 421	127 619	36.3
1 VII 2014[85]	ESDF	745 153	283 543	38.1	387 520	150 737	38.9	357 633	132 806	37.1
1 VII 2015[85]	ESDF	757 042	294 402	38.9	393 324	156 328	39.7	363 718	138 074	38.0
1 VII 2016[85]	ESDF	768 577	...	...	398 948	...	...	369 629	...	...
30 V 2017	CDFC	727 145	274 316	37.7	380 453	143 313	37.7	346 692	131 003	37.8
Brunei Darussalam - Brunéi Darussalam										
1 VII 2009[35]	ESDF	380 100	...	...	196 300	...	...	183 800	...	...
1 VII 2010[35]	ESDF	386 800	...	...	199 800	...	...	187 000	...	...
20 VI 2011	CDJC	393 372	296 257	75.3	203 144	151 663	74.7	190 228	144 594	76.0
1 VII 2012	ESDJ	398 700	...	...	205 800	...	...	192 900	...	...
1 VII 2013	ESDJ	403 300	...	...	207 900	...	...	195 400	...	...
1 VII 2014	ESDJ	407 600	...	...	209 700	...	...	197 900	...	...
1 VII 2015	ESDJ	412 400	...	...	211 900	...	...	200 500	...	...
1 VII 2016[86]	ESDJ	417 256	312 448	74.9	214 104	160 061	74.8	203 152	152 387	75.0
1 VII 2017	ESDJ	429 500	...	...	223 400	...	...	206 100	...	...
1 VII 2018	ESDJ	442 400	...	...	233 400	...	...	209 000	...	...
Cambodia - Cambodge										
1 VII 2009[87]	ESDF	14 085 324	2 814 943	20.0	6 859 756	1 351 939	19.7	7 225 568	1 463 004	20.2
1 VII 2010[87]	ESDF	14 302 779	2 926 810	20.5	6 973 994	1 406 183	20.2	7 328 785	1 520 627	20.7
1 VII 2011[87]	ESDF	14 521 275	3 042 794	21.0	7 088 691	1 462 518	20.6	7 432 584	1 580 276	21.3
1 VII 2012[87]	ESDF	14 741 414	3 165 683	21.5	7 204 166	1 520 722	21.1	7 537 248	1 644 961	21.8
3 III 2013[88]	SSDF	14 676 591	3 146 212	21.4	7 121 508	1 527 479	21.4	7 555 083	1 618 734	21.4

6. Total and urban population by sex: 2009 - 2018
Population totale et population urbaine selon le sexe : 2009 - 2018 (continued - suite)

Continent, country or area, and date / Continent, pays ou zone et date	Code[a]	Both sexes - Les deux sexes Total	Urban - Urbaine Number Nombre	Urban - Urbaine Percent P.100	Male - Masculin Total	Urban - Urbaine Number Nombre	Urban - Urbaine Percent P.100	Female - Féminin Total	Urban - Urbaine Number Nombre	Urban - Urbaine Percent P.100
ASIA - ASIE										
Cambodia - Cambodge										
1 VII 2013[87]	ESDF	14 962 591	3 285 951	22.0	7 320 112	1 580 866	21.6	7 642 479	1 705 085	22.3
1 VII 2014[87]	ESDF	15 184 116	3 412 183	22.5	7 436 178	1 642 397	22.1	7 747 938	1 769 786	22.8
1 VII 2015[87]	ESDF	15 405 157	3 540 575	23.0	7 551 944	1 705 018	22.6	7 853 213	1 835 557	23.4
China - Chine[89]										
1 VII 2009[90]	ESDF	1 331 300 000	645 120 000[92]	48.5	686 470 000[91]	...	...	648 030 000[91]	...	...
1 VII 2010[90]	ESDF	1 337 700 000	669 780 000[92]	50.1	687 480 000[91]	...	...	653 430 000[91]	...	...
1 XI 2010[93]	CDJC	1 339 724 852	665 575 306	49.7	686 852 572	...	...	652 872 280	...	...
1 VII 2011[94]	ESDF	1 344 100 000	691 000 000[92]	51.4	691 000 000[91]	...	...	657 000 000[91]	...	...
1 VII 2012[94]	ESDF	1 350 695 000	701 305 000[95]	51.9	692 315 000	...	...	658 380 000	...	...
1 VII 2013[90]	ESDF	1 357 380 000	721 465 000[95]	53.2	695 615 000	...	...	661 765 000	...	...
1 VII 2014[90]	ESDF	1 364 270 000	740 135 000[95]	54.3	699 035 000	...	...	665 235 000	...	...
1 VII 2015[90]	ESDF	1 371 220 000	760 160 000[95]	55.4	702 465 000	...	...	668 755 000	...	...
1 VII 2016[90]	ESDF	1 378 665 000	782 070 000[95]	56.7	706 145 000	...	...	672 520 000	...	...
1 VII 2017[90]	ESDF	1 386 395 000	803 225 000[95]	57.9	709 760 000	...	...	676 635 000	...	...
1 VII 2018[90]	ESDF	1 392 730 000	822 420 000[95]	59.1	712 440 000	...	...	680 290 000	...	...
China, Hong Kong SAR - Chine, Hong Kong RAS										
1 VII 2009	ESDJ	6 972 800	...	...	3 284 800	...	...	3 688 000	...	...
1 VII 2010	ESDJ	7 024 200	...	...	3 294 300	...	...	3 729 900	...	...
30 VI 2011[96]	CDJC	7 071 576	...	...	3 303 015	...	...	3 768 561	...	...
1 VII 2011	ESDJ	7 071 600	...	...	3 303 000	...	...	3 768 600	...	...
1 VII 2012	ESDJ	7 150 100	...	...	3 327 300	...	...	3 822 800	...	...
1 VII 2013	ESDJ	7 178 900	...	...	3 329 900	...	...	3 849 000	...	...
1 VII 2014	ESDJ	7 229 500	...	...	3 344 500	...	...	3 885 000	...	...
1 VII 2015	ESDJ	7 291 300	...	...	3 365 600	...	...	3 925 700	...	...
30 VI 2016[97]	CDJC	7 336 585	...	...	3 375 362	...	...	3 961 223	...	...
1 VII 2016	ESDJ	7 336 600	...	...	3 375 400	...	...	3 961 200	...	...
1 VII 2017	ESDJ	7 391 700	...	...	3 392 500	...	...	3 999 200	...	...
1 VII 2018	ESDJ	7 451 000	...	...	3 410 300	...	...	4 040 700	...	...
China, Macao SAR - Chine, Macao RAS										
1 VII 2009	ESDJ	535 000	...	...	257 900[91]	...	...	277 200[91]	...	...
1 VII 2010	ESDJ	537 000	...	...	257 200[91]	...	...	279 700[91]	...	...
1 VII 2011	ESDJ	549 600	...	...	263 500	...	...	286 100	...	...
12 VIII 2011	CDFC	625 674	...	...	305 398	...	...	320 276	...	...
1 VII 2012	ESDJ	567 900	...	...	274 300	...	...	293 600	...	...
1 VII 2013	ESDJ	591 900	...	...	285 700	...	...	306 200	...	...
1 VII 2014	ESDJ	621 700	...	...	305 500	...	...	316 200	...	...
1 VII 2015	ESDJ	642 900	...	...	317 500	...	...	325 400	...	...
7 VIII 2016[98]	SSDJ	650 834	...	...	314 018	...	...	336 816	...	...
Cyprus - Chypre[99]										
1 VII 2009[25]	ESDJ	808 035	...	...	394 766	...	...	413 270	...	...
1 VII 2010[25]	ESDJ	829 446	...	...	404 182	...	...	425 264	...	...
1 VII 2011[25]	ESDJ	850 881	...	...	413 876	...	...	437 006	...	...
1 X 2011	CDJC	840 407	566 191	67.4	408 780	273 065	66.8	431 627	293 126	67.9
1 VII 2012[25]	ESDJ	863 945	...	...	420 015	...	...	443 930	...	...
1 VII 2013[25]	ESDJ	861 930	...	...	419 183	...	...	442 747	...	...
1 VII 2014[25]	ESDJ	852 504	...	...	414 682	...	...	437 823	...	...
1 VII 2015[25]	ESDJ	847 700	...	...	412 300	...	...	435 400	...	...
1 VII 2016[25]	ESDJ	851 600	...	...	414 700	...	...	436 900	...	...
1 VII 2017[25]	ESDJ	859 519	...	...	419 086	...	...	440 434	...	...
1 I 2018	ESDJ	864 236	...	...	421 508	...	...	442 728	...	...
Georgia - Géorgie										
1 VII 2009	ESDF	4 410 900	2 332 700	52.9	2 094 800	...	...	2 316 100	...	...
1 VII 2010	ESDF	4 452 800	2 360 900	53.0	2 118 100	...	...	2 334 700	...	...
1 VII 2011	ESDF	4 483 400	2 381 500	53.1	2 135 600	...	...	2 347 800	...	...
1 VII 2012	ESDF	4 490 700	...	...	2 141 300	...	...	2 349 400	...	...
1 VII 2013	ESDF	4 487 150	...	...	2 140 100	...	...	2 347 050	...	...
5 XI 2014	CDJC	3 713 804	2 122 623	57.2	1 772 864	980 985	55.3	1 940 940	1 141 638	58.8
1 VII 2015[100]	ESDJ	3 717 100	2 125 700	57.2	1 776 300	...	...	1 940 800	...	...
1 VII 2016[100]	ESDJ	3 719 300	2 128 500	57.2	1 780 500	...	...	1 938 800	...	...
1 VII 2017[101]	ESDJ	3 723 917	...	...	1 786 530	...	...	1 937 387	...	...
1 I 2018[100]	ESDJ	3 729 633	...	...	1 791 559	...	...	1 938 074	...	...

Continent, country or area, and date / Continent, pays ou zone et date	Code[a]	Both sexes - Les deux sexes			Male - Masculin			Female - Féminin		
		Total	Urban - Urbaine		Total	Urban - Urbaine		Total	Urban - Urbaine	
			Number Nombre	Percent P.100		Number Nombre	Percent P.100		Number Nombre	Percent P.100
ASIA - ASIE										
India - Inde[102]										
1 III 2009[103] .... ESDF		1 160 813 000	...	...	600 816 000	...	...	889 997 000	...	...
1 III 2010[103] .... ESDF		1 176 742 000	...	...	609 107 000	...	...	567 634 000	...	...
9 II 2011 .... CDFC		1 210 854 977	377 106 125	31.1	623 270 258	195 489 200	31.4	587 584 719	181 616 925	30.9
1 III 2011[103] .... ESDF		1 192 506 000	...	...	617 316 000	...	...	575 191 000	...	...
1 III 2012[103] .... ESDF		1 208 116 000	...	...	625 446 000	...	...	582 670 000	...	...
1 III 2013[103] .... ESDF		1 223 581 000	...	...	633 505 000	...	...	590 076 000	...	...
1 III 2014[103] .... ESDF		1 238 887 000	...	...	641 484 000	...	...	597 403 000	...	...
1 III 2015[103] .... ESDF		1 254 019 000	...	...	649 374 000	...	...	604 644 000	...	...
1 III 2016[103] .... ESDF		1 268 961 000	...	...	657 168 000	...	...	611 793 000	...	...
1 III 2017[103] .... ESDF		1 283 600 000	...	...	664 802 000	...	...	618 799 000	...	...
1 III 2018[103] .... ESDF		1 298 041 000	...	...	672 334 000	...	...	625 707 000	...	...
Indonesia - Indonésie										
1 VII 2009[104] .... ESDJ		231 369 500	...	...	115 817 900	...	...	115 551 600	...	...
1 V 2010 .... CDJC		237 641 326	118 320 256	49.8	119 630 913	59 559 622	49.8	118 010 413	58 760 634	49.8
1 VII 2010[105] .... ESDJ		238 518 787	118 803 981	49.8	119 852 718	59 698 817	49.8	118 666 069	59 105 164	49.8
1 VII 2011[105] .... ESDJ		241 990 736	122 164 186	50.5	121 602 475	61 382 741	50.5	120 388 261	60 781 445	50.5
1 VII 2012[105] .... ESDJ		245 425 244	125 558 071	51.2	123 331 006	63 081 616	51.1	122 094 238	62 476 455	51.2
1 VII 2013[105] .... ESDJ		248 818 090	128 964 283	51.8	125 036 002	64 785 519	51.8	123 782 088	64 178 764	51.8
1 VII 2014[105] .... ESDJ		252 164 786	132 387 038	52.5	126 715 188	66 493 813	52.5	125 449 598	65 893 225	52.5
1 VII 2015[106] .... ESDJ		255 587 921	135 901 402	53.2	128 483 450	68 279 703	53.1	127 104 471	67 621 699	53.2
1 VII 2016[106] .... ESDJ		258 496 505	139 103 578	53.8	129 910 159	69 868 278	53.8	128 586 346	69 235 300	53.8
1 VII 2017[106] .... ESDJ		261 355 475	142 318 766	54.5	131 310 606	71 462 134	54.4	130 044 869	70 856 632	54.5
1 VII 2018[106] .... ESDJ		264 161 642	145 541 658	55.1	132 682 955	73 058 747	55.1	131 478 687	72 482 911	55.1
Iran (Islamic Republic of) - Iran (République islamique d')										
1 VII 2009[107] .... ESDJ		73 202 096	50 365 184	68.8	37 198 776	25 660 500	69.0	36 003 320	24 704 684	68.6
1 VII 2010[107] .... ESDJ		74 339 576	51 242 546	68.9	37 767 220	26 114 342	69.1	36 572 356	25 128 204	68.7
24 X 2011 .... CDJC		75 149 669	53 646 661	71.4	37 905 669	27 023 638	71.3	37 244 000	26 623 023	71.5
1 VII 2012[107] .... ESDJ		76 037 535	54 611 776[108]	71.8	38 336 983	27 547 622[108]	71.9	37 700 552	27 064 154[108]	71.8
1 VII 2013[107] .... ESDJ		76 942 276	55 506 192[108]	72.1	38 777 566	27 988 342[108]	72.2	38 164 710	27 517 850[108]	72.1
1 VII 2014[107] .... ESDJ		77 856 411	56 412 837	72.5	39 224 036	28 435 933	72.5	38 632 375	27 976 904	72.4
1 VII 2015[107] .... ESDJ		78 773 093	57 326 841	72.8	39 672 171	28 887 379	72.8	39 100 922	28 439 462	72.7
1 VII 2016[107] .... ESDJ		80 038 166	59 226 231	74.0	40 551 419	29 880 878	73.7	39 486 747	29 345 353	74.3
24 IX 2016 .... CDJC		79 926 270	59 146 847[109]	74.0	40 498 442	29 841 414[109]	73.7	39 427 828	29 305 433[109]	74.3
1 VII 2017[107] .... ESDJ		81 070 480	60 281 499	74.4	41 048 740	30 517 645	74.3	40 021 740	29 763 854	74.4
1 VII 2018[107] .... ESDJ		82 083 918	61 329 440	74.7	41 538 139	31 030 645	74.7	40 545 779	30 298 795	74.7
Iraq										
1 VII 2009 .... ESDF		31 392 903	...	...	16 010 232	...	...	15 382 671	...	...
1 VII 2010 .... ESDF		32 210 813	...	...	16 418 691	...	...	15 792 122	...	...
1 VII 2011 .... ESDF		33 051 526	...	...	16 839 048	...	...	16 212 479	...	...
1 VII 2012 .... ESDF		33 913 305	23 475 543	69.2	17 270 036	11 954 703	69.2	16 643 269	11 520 840	69.2
1 VII 2013 .... ESDF		34 794 194	24 162 634	69.4	17 710 750	12 299 131	69.4	17 083 444	11 863 502	69.4
1 VII 2014 .... ESDF		35 736 260	24 896 261	69.7	18 182 503	12 667 144	69.7	17 553 757	12 229 117	69.7
1 VII 2015 .... ESDF		36 658 503	25 631 821	69.9	18 520 532	12 935 587	69.8	18 137 971	12 696 234	70.0
Israel - Israël[110]										
1 VII 2009 .... ESDJ		7 485 565	6 864 957[91]	91.7	3 701 159	3 384 295[91]	91.4	3 784 406	3 480 662[91]	92.0
1 VII 2010 .... ESDJ		7 623 561	6 987 615[91]	91.7	3 771 020	3 446 730[91]	91.4	3 852 541	3 540 885[91]	91.9
1 VII 2011 .... ESDJ		7 765 832	7 111 015[91]	91.6	3 843 068	3 509 308[91]	91.3	3 922 764	3 601 706[91]	91.8
1 VII 2012 .... ESDJ		7 910 525	7 235 231[91]	91.5	3 916 125	3 572 531[91]	91.2	3 994 400	3 662 700[91]	91.7
1 VII 2013 .... ESDJ		8 059 456	7 369 053[91]	91.4	3 991 347	3 640 471[91]	91.2	4 068 109	3 728 581[91]	91.7
1 VII 2014 .... ESDJ		8 215 668	7 502 325[91]	91.3	4 070 269	3 707 183[91]	91.1	4 145 398	3 795 142[91]	91.6
1 VII 2015 .... ESDJ		8 380 149	7 643 990[91]	91.2	4 153 233	3 778 276[91]	91.0	4 226 916	3 865 714[91]	91.5
1 VII 2016 .... ESDJ		8 546 009	7 795 761[91]	91.2	4 237 229	3 855 306[91]	91.0	4 308 780	3 940 455[91]	91.5
1 VII 2017 .... ESDJ		8 713 268	7 950 920[91]	91.3	4 321 810	3 933 949[91]	91.0	4 391 458	4 016 970[91]	91.5
Japan - Japon[111]										
1 VII 2009 .... ESDJ		128 047 000	...	...	62 354 000	...	...	65 693 000	...	...
1 VII 2010 .... ESDJ		128 070 000	...	...	62 330 000	...	...	65 740 000	...	...
1 X 2010 .... CDJC		128 057 352	116 156 631	90.7	62 327 737	56 569 051	90.8	65 729 615	59 587 580	90.7
1 VII 2011[112] .... ESDJ		127 833 000	...	...	62 202 000	...	...	65 631 000	...	...
1 VII 2012[112] .... ESDJ		127 629 000	...	...	62 085 000	...	...	65 544 000	...	...
1 VII 2013[112] .... ESDJ		127 445 000	...	...	61 987 000	...	...	65 458 000	...	...
1 VII 2014[112] .... ESDJ		127 276 000	...	...	61 906 000	...	...	65 370 000	...	...

Continent, country or area, and date / Continent, pays ou zone et date	Code[a]	Both sexes - Les deux sexes Total	Urban - Urbaine Number Nombre	Urban - Urbaine Percent P.100	Male - Masculin Total	Urban - Urbaine Number Nombre	Urban - Urbaine Percent P.100	Female - Féminin Total	Urban - Urbaine Number Nombre	Urban - Urbaine Percent P.100
ASIA - ASIE										
Japan - Japon[111]										
1 VII 2015[113] .... ESDJ		127 141 000	...	...	61 848 000	...	...	65 294 000	...	...
1 X 2015 .... CDJC		127 094 745	116 137 232	91.4	61 841 738	56 532 149	91.4	65 253 007	59 605 083	91.3
1 VII 2016[113] .... ESDJ		126 995 000	...	...	61 781 000	...	...	65 213 000	...	...
1 VII 2017[112] .... ESDJ		126 786 000	...	...	61 681 000	...	...	65 105 000	...	...
1 VII 2018[113] .... ESDJ		126 529 000	...	...	61 558 000	...	...	64 972 000	...	...
Jordan - Jordanie[114]										
31 XII 2009 .... ESDF		6 490 000	5 863 000	90.3	3 340 000	...	...	3 150 000	...	...
31 XII 2010 .... ESDF		6 699 000	6 051 000	90.3	3 448 000	...	...	3 250 000	...	...
31 XII 2011 .... ESDF		6 993 000	6 318 000	90.3	3 704 852	...	...	3 288 148	...	...
31 XII 2012 .... ESDF		7 427 000	6 710 000	90.3	3 934 783	...	...	3 492 217	...	...
31 XII 2013 .... ESDF		8 114 000	7 331 000	90.4	4 298 752	...	...	3 815 248	...	...
31 XII 2014 .... ESDF		8 804 000	7 954 000	90.3	4 664 310	...	...	4 139 690	...	...
30 XI 2015 .... CDFC		9 531 712	8 611 323	90.3	5 046 824	4 561 944	90.4	4 484 888	4 049 379	90.3
31 XII 2015 .... ESDF		9 559 000	8 636 000	90.3	5 061 000	...	...	4 498 000	...	...
31 XII 2016 .... ESDF		9 798 000	8 852 000	90.3	5 188 000	...	...	4 610 000	...	...
31 XII 2017 .... ESDF		10 053 000	9 082 000	90.3	5 323 000	...	...	4 730 000	...	...
31 XII 2018 .... ESDF		10 309 000	9 313 600	90.3	5 458 000	...	...	4 851 000	...	...
Kazakhstan										
25 II 2009 .... CDFC		16 009 597	8 662 432	54.1	7 712 224	4 055 341	52.6	8 297 373	4 607 091	55.5
1 VII 2009[115] .... ESDF		16 092 822	8 741 269	54.3	7 753 418	4 092 781	52.8	8 339 404	4 648 488	55.7
1 VII 2010[115] .... ESDF		16 321 872	8 896 771	54.5	7 866 461	4 165 677	53.0	8 455 411	4 731 094	56.0
1 VII 2011[115] .... ESDF		16 557 201	9 050 732	54.7	7 983 365	4 237 915	53.1	8 573 836	4 812 817	56.1
1 VII 2012[115] .... ESDF		16 792 089	9 202 707	54.8	8 100 335	4 309 949	53.2	8 691 754	4 892 758	56.3
1 VII 2013[115] .... ESDF		17 035 550	9 355 723	54.9	8 221 757	4 383 901	53.3	8 813 793	4 971 822	56.4
1 VII 2014[115] .... ESDF		17 288 285	9 635 300	55.7	8 348 857	4 523 126	54.2	8 939 428	5 112 174	57.2
1 VII 2015[115] .... ESDF		17 542 806	9 936 301	56.6	8 477 451	4 672 945	55.1	9 065 355	5 263 356	58.1
1 VII 2016[115] .... ESDF		17 794 055	10 142 840	57.0	8 605 139	4 774 020	55.5	9 188 916	5 368 820	58.4
1 VII 2017[115] .... ESDF		18 037 776	10 336 836	57.3	8 729 888	4 868 292	55.8	9 307 888	5 468 544	58.8
1 VII 2018[116] .... ESDF		18 276 452	10 604 004	58.0	8 852 247	4 998 115	56.5	9 424 205	5 605 890	59.5
Kuwait - Koweït										
1 VII 2009 .... ESDF		2 777 861	...	...	1 597 843	...	...	1 180 018	...	...
1 VII 2010 .... ESDF		2 933 268	...	...	1 674 156	...	...	1 259 112	...	...
21 IV 2011 .... CDFC		3 065 850	3 065 850	100.0	1 738 372	1 738 372	100.0	1 327 478	1 327 478	100.0
1 VII 2011 .... ESDF		3 106 676	...	...	1 767 685	...	...	1 338 991	...	...
1 VII 2012 .... ESDF		3 246 622	...	...	1 856 265	...	...	1 390 357	...	...
1 VII 2013 .... ESDF		3 427 595	...	...	1 968 382	...	...	1 459 213	...	...
1 VII 2014 .... ESDF		3 767 415	...	...	2 161 594	...	...	1 605 821	...	...
1 I 2015 .... ESDF		3 743 660	...	...	2 185 298	...	...	1 558 362	...	...
1 VII 2016 .... ESDF		4 079 305	...	...	2 505 012	...	...	1 574 293	...	...
1 VII 2017 .... ESDF		4 022 255	...	...	2 428 774	...	...	1 593 481	...	...
1 VII 2018 .... ESDF		4 124 606	...	...	2 548 919	...	...	1 575 687	...	...
Kyrgyzstan - Kirghizstan										
24 III 2009 .... CDJC		5 362 793	1 827 136	34.1	2 645 921	863 002	32.6	2 716 872	964 134	35.5
1 VII 2009[25] .... ESDJ		5 383 277	1 835 028	34.1	2 656 660	866 718	32.6	2 726 617	968 310	35.5
1 VII 2010[25] .... ESDJ		5 447 960	1 854 245	34.0	2 689 231	876 120	32.6	2 758 729	978 125	35.5
1 VII 2011[25] .... ESDJ		5 514 754	1 873 047	34.0	2 722 714	885 117	32.5	2 792 040	987 930	35.4
1 VII 2012[25] .... ESDJ		5 607 511	1 878 643	33.5	2 770 269	887 727	32.0	2 837 242	990 916	34.9
1 VII 2013[25] .... ESDJ		5 719 852	1 921 936	33.6	2 827 672	909 216	32.2	2 892 180	1 012 720	35.0
1 VII 2014[25] .... ESDJ		5 835 816	1 965 159	33.7	2 886 758	930 751	32.2	2 949 058	1 034 408	35.1
1 VII 2015[25] .... ESDJ		5 957 271	2 008 148	33.7	2 948 932	952 329	32.3	3 008 339	1 055 819	35.1
1 VII 2016[25] .... ESDJ		6 079 840	2 051 748	33.7	3 011 702	973 955	32.3	3 068 138	1 077 793	35.1
1 VII 2017[25] .... ESDJ		6 198 465	2 097 487	33.8	3 072 164	996 210	32.4	3 126 301	1 101 277	35.2
1 VII 2018[25] .... ESDJ		6 323 115	...	...	3 135 726	...	...	3 187 390	...	...
Lao People's Democratic Republic - République démocratique populaire lao										
1 VII 2009[117] .... ESDJ		6 110 600	...	...	3 046 400	...	...	3 064 200	...	...
1 VII 2010[117] .... ESDJ		6 230 200	...	...	3 106 600	...	...	3 123 700	...	...
1 VII 2011[117] .... ESDJ		6 348 800	...	...	3 166 300	...	...	3 182 500	...	...
1 VII 2012[117] .... ESDJ		6 465 800	...	...	3 225 200	...	...	3 240 600	...	...
1 VII 2013[117] .... ESDJ		6 580 800	...	...	3 283 200	...	...	3 297 600	...	...
1 VII 2014[117] .... ESDJ		6 693 300	...	...	3 339 800	...	...	3 353 400	...	...
1 III 2015 .... CDJC		6 492 228	2 137 831	32.9	3 254 770	1 076 928	33.1	3 237 458	1 060 903	32.8

Continent, country or area, and date / Continent, pays ou zone et date	Code[a]	Both sexes - Les deux sexes			Male - Masculin			Female - Féminin		
		Total	Urban - Urbaine		Total	Urban - Urbaine		Total	Urban - Urbaine	
			Number Nombre	Percent P.100		Number Nombre	Percent P.100		Number Nombre	Percent P.100
ASIA - ASIE										
Lao People's Democratic Republic - République démocratique populaire lao										
1 VII 2015[117] ...... ESDJ		6 671 680	...	...	3 342 462	...	...	3 329 218	...	...
1 VII 2016[117] ...... ESDJ		6 787 007	...	...	3 400 453	...	...	3 386 554	...	...
1 VII 2017[117] ...... ESDJ		6 900 846	...	...	3 457 542	...	...	3 443 304	...	...
1 VII 2018[117] ...... ESDJ		7 012 994	...	...	3 513 775	...	...	3 499 219	...	...
Lebanon - Liban[118]										
1 X 2011 ...... SSDF		3 779 859	...	...	1 840 940	...	...	1 938 919	...	...
Malaysia - Malaisie										
1 VII 2009[119] ...... ESDJ		28 081 497	19 675 872	70.1	14 456 940	10 085 459	69.8	13 624 557	9 590 413	70.4
1 VII 2010[120] ...... ESDJ		28 588 637	20 290 864	71.0	14 730 542	10 404 757	70.6	13 858 095	9 886 107	71.3
6 VII 2010[84] ...... CDJC		28 334 135	20 124 970	71.0	14 562 638	10 298 698	70.7	13 771 497	9 826 272	71.4
1 VII 2011[120] ...... ESDJ		29 062 036	20 826 580	71.7	14 980 010	10 684 359	71.3	14 082 026	10 142 221	72.0
1 VII 2012[120] ...... ESDJ		29 510 022	21 355 255	72.4	15 215 309	10 965 006	72.1	14 294 713	10 390 249	72.7
1 VII 2013[120] ...... ESDJ		30 213 664	22 041 500	73.0	15 604 813	11 330 984	72.6	14 608 851	10 710 516	73.3
1 VII 2014[120] ...... ESDJ		30 708 527	22 597 286	73.6	15 867 796	11 624 061	73.3	14 840 731	10 973 225	73.9
1 VII 2015[120] ...... ESDJ		31 186 135	23 173 701	74.3	16 112 125	11 925 089	74.0	15 074 010	11 248 612	74.6
1 VII 2016[120] ...... ESDJ		31 633 518	23 677 030	74.8	16 346 281	12 186 777	74.6	15 287 237	11 490 253	75.2
1 VII 2017[120] ...... ESDJ		32 022 575	24 080 382	75.2	16 542 746	12 392 317	74.9	15 479 829	11 688 065	75.5
1 VII 2018[120] ...... ESDJ		32 384 982	24 496 667	75.6	16 721 618	12 603 976	75.4	15 663 364	11 892 691	75.9
Maldives										
1 VII 2009 ...... ESDF		314 542	...	...	159 159	...	...	155 383	...	...
1 VII 2010 ...... ESDF		319 738	...	...	161 708	...	...	158 030	...	...
1 VII 2011 ...... ESDF		325 135	...	...	164 349	...	...	160 786	...	...
1 VII 2012 ...... ESDF		330 655	...	...	167 058	...	...	163 597	...	...
1 VII 2013 ...... ESDF		336 224	...	...	169 800	...	...	166 424	...	...
1 VII 2014[121] ...... ESDF		437 535	171 165	39.1	261 709	101 744	38.9	175 826	69 422	39.5
20 IX 2014[122] ...... CDFC		402 071	153 904	38.3	227 749	85 438	37.5	174 322	68 466	39.3
1 VII 2015[121] ...... ESDF		454 434	180 019	39.6	274 607	107 894	39.3	179 827	72 125	40.1
1 VII 2016[121] ...... ESDF		472 426	189 458	40.1	288 502	114 514	39.7	183 924	74 944	40.7
1 VII 2017[121] ...... ESDF		491 589	199 523	40.6	303 478	121 647	40.1	188 111	77 876	41.4
1 VII 2018[121] ...... ESDF		512 038	210 248	41.1	319 663	129 334	40.5	192 375	80 914	42.1
Mongolia - Mongolie										
1 VII 2009 ...... ESDF		2 691 115	1 743 008	64.8	1 314 729	840 520	63.9	1 376 386	902 488	65.6
1 VII 2010 ...... ESDF		2 738 622	1 799 648	65.7	1 335 111	863 536	64.7	1 403 511	936 112	66.7
11 XI 2010 ...... CDFC		2 647 199	1 797 338	67.9	1 314 246	869 827	66.2	1 332 953	927 511	69.6
1 VII 2011 ...... ESDF		2 786 322	1 856 224	66.6	1 354 472	886 139	65.4	1 431 850	970 085	67.8
1 VII 2012 ...... ESDF		2 839 711	1 911 462	67.3	1 379 091	910 746	66.0	1 460 620	1 000 716	68.5
1 VII 2013 ...... ESDF		2 899 011	1 961 169	67.6	1 409 648	936 682	66.4	1 489 363	1 024 487	68.8
1 VII 2014 ...... ESDF		2 963 113	1 993 017	67.3	1 446 149	955 833	66.1	1 516 964	1 037 184	68.4
1 VII 2015 ...... ESDF		3 026 864	2 043 251	67.5	1 485 034	985 919	66.4	1 541 830	1 057 332	68.6
1 VII 2016 ...... ESDF		3 088 856	2 122 131	68.7	1 518 797	1 027 311	67.6	1 570 059	1 094 820	69.7
1 VII 2017 ...... ESDF		3 148 917	2 139 269	67.9	1 548 177	1 034 384	66.8	1 600 740	1 104 885	69.0
1 VII 2018 ...... ESDF		3 208 189	2 172 343	67.7	1 577 109	1 049 578	66.6	1 631 080	1 122 765	68.8
Myanmar										
1 X 2009 ...... ESDF		59 129 900	18 133 654	30.7	29 399 744	8 888 838	30.2	29 730 156	9 244 816	31.1
1 X 2010 ...... ESDF		59 780 329	18 342 824	30.7	29 723 184	8 992 226	30.3	30 057 145	9 350 598	31.1
1 X 2011[100] ...... ESDF		50 149 496	14 650 579	29.2	24 185 705	7 009 280	29.0	25 963 791	7 641 299	29.4
1 X 2012[100] ...... ESDF		50 666 887	14 824 863	29.3	24 435 871	7 092 798	29.0	26 231 016	7 732 085	29.5
1 X 2013[100] ...... ESDF		51 184 273	14 999 184	29.3	24 686 034	7 176 313	29.1	26 498 239	7 822 871	29.5
29 III 2014[123] ...... CDFC		50 279 900	14 877 943	29.6	24 228 714	7 114 224	29.4	26 051 186	7 763 719	29.8
1 X 2014[100] ...... ESDF		51 991 031	15 173 838	29.2	25 066 439	7 256 002	28.9	26 924 592	7 917 836	29.4
1 X 2015[100] ...... ESDF		52 450 516	15 363 901	29.3	25 256 187	7 331 696	29.0	27 194 329	8 032 205	29.5
1 VII 2016[100] ...... ESDF		52 799 191	15 510 836	29.4	25 401 382	7 391 103	29.1	27 397 809	8 119 733	29.6
1 X 2017[100] ...... ESDF		53 387 948	15 762 776	29.5	25 647 847	7 494 003	29.2	27 740 101	8 268 773	29.8
1 X 2018[100] ...... ESDF		53 862 731	15 970 715	29.7	25 847 922	7 580 078	29.3	28 014 809	8 390 637	30.0
Nepal - Népal										
1 VII 2009 ...... ESDJ		27 504 280	...	...	13 790 836	...	...	13 713 444	...	...
1 VII 2010 ...... ESDJ		28 043 744	...	...	14 066 638	...	...	13 977 106	...	...
22 VI 2011 ...... CDJC		26 494 504	4 523 820	17.1	12 849 041	2 306 049	17.9	13 645 463	2 217 771	16.3
1 VII 2011 ...... ESDJ		28 584 975	...	...	14 343 343	...	...	14 241 632	...	...
1 VII 2012[28] ...... ESDJ		26 873 066	...	...	13 030 795	...	...	13 842 271	...	...
1 VII 2013[28] ...... ESDJ		27 257 347	...	...	13 215 791	...	...	14 041 556	...	...

6. Total and urban population by sex: 2009 - 2018
Population totale et population urbaine selon le sexe : 2009 - 2018 (continued - suite)

Continent, country or area, and date / Continent, pays ou zone et date	Code[a]	Both sexes - Les deux sexes Total	Urban - Urbaine Number Nombre	Urban - Urbaine Percent P.100	Male - Masculin Total	Urban - Urbaine Number Nombre	Urban - Urbaine Percent P.100	Female - Féminin Total	Urban - Urbaine Number Nombre	Urban - Urbaine Percent P.100
ASIA - ASIE										
Nepal - Népal										
1 VII 2014[28]	ESDJ	27 646 053	...	...	13 403 432	...	...	14 242 621	...	...
1 VII 2015[28]	ESDJ	28 037 904	...	...	13 593 069	...	...	14 444 835	...	...
1 VII 2016[28]	ESDJ	28 431 494	5 552 712	19.5	13 784 009	2 825 721	20.5	14 647 486	2 726 992	18.6
1 VII 2017[28]	ESDJ	28 825 709	...	...	13 975 678	...	...	14 850 032	...	...
1 VII 2018[28]	ESDJ	29 218 867	...	...	14 167 241	...	...	15 051 626	...	...
Oman										
1 VII 2009	ESDF	3 173 917	2 314 865	72.9	1 971 115	1 457 197	73.9	1 202 802	857 668	71.3
12 XII 2010	CDFC	2 773 479	2 091 320	75.4	1 612 408	1 227 680	76.1	1 161 071	863 640	74.4
1 VII 2011	ESDF	3 295 298[124]	2 484 794[125]	75.4	2 090 883[124]	1 591 989[125]	76.1	1 204 415[124]	895 881[125]	74.4
1 VII 2012	ESDF	3 623 001[124]	2 731 895[125]	75.4	2 332 687[124]	1 776 097[125]	76.1	1 290 314[124]	959 775[125]	74.4
1 VII 2013	ESDF	3 855 206[124]	2 906 988[125]	75.4	2 502 235[124]	1 905 190[125]	76.1	1 352 971[124]	1 006 381[125]	74.4
1 VII 2014	ESDF	3 992 893[124]	3 010 810[125]	75.4	2 579 811[124]	1 964 256[125]	76.1	1 413 082[124]	1 051 093[125]	74.4
1 VII 2015	ESDF	4 159 102[124]	3 136 138[125]	75.4	2 684 844[124]	2 044 228[125]	76.1	1 474 258[124]	1 096 598[125]	74.4
1 VII 2016	ESDF	4 414 051[124]	3 432 019[126]	77.8	2 886 083[124]	2 296 140[126]	79.6	1 527 968[124]	1 133 279[126]	74.2
1 VII 2017	ESDF	4 559 963[124]	3 542 940[126]	77.7	2 984 404[124]	2 374 363[126]	79.6	1 575 559[124]	1 168 577[126]	74.2
1 VII 2018[124]	ESDF	4 601 706	...	...	2 990 103	...	...	1 611 603	...	...
Pakistan[127]										
1 VII 2009	ESDF	169 940 000	...	...	87 940 000	...	...	82 010 000	...	...
1 VII 2010	ESDF	173 510 000	...	...	89 760 000	...	...	83 750 000	...	...
1 VII 2011	ESDF	177 100 000	...	...	91 590 000	...	...	85 510 000	...	...
15 III 2017*	CDFC	207 774 520	75 584 989	36.4	106 449 322[128]	39 149 151[128]	36.8	101 314 780[128]	36 428 187[128]	36.0
Philippines										
1 VII 2009[41]	ESDJ	92 226 600	...	...	46 368 900	...	...	45 857 700	...	...
1 V 2010[129]	CDJC	92 335 113	41 855 571	45.3	46 634 257	20 840 798	44.7	45 700 856	21 014 773	46.0
1 VII 2010[13]	ESDJ	93 135 100	...	...	46 980 200	...	...	46 154 900	...	...
1 VII 2011[13]	ESDJ	94 823 800	...	...	47 832 400	...	...	46 991 400	...	...
1 VII 2012[13]	ESDJ	96 510 900	...	...	48 684 200	...	...	47 826 700	...	...
1 VII 2013[13]	ESDJ	98 196 500	...	...	49 535 100	...	...	48 661 400	...	...
1 VII 2014[13]	ESDJ	99 880 300	...	...	50 385 100	...	...	49 495 200	...	...
1 VII 2015[13]	ESDJ	101 562 300	...	...	51 234 200	...	...	50 328 100	...	...
1 VIII 2015[130]	CDJC	100 979 303	51 728 697	51.2	51 069 962	25 884 921	50.7	49 909 341	25 843 776	51.8
1 VII 2016[13]	ESDJ	103 242 900	...	...	52 081 400	...	...	51 161 500	...	...
1 VII 2017[13]	ESDJ	104 921 400	...	...	52 927 400	...	...	51 994 000	...	...
1 VII 2018[13]	ESDJ	106 598 600	...	...	53 772 800	...	...	52 825 800	...	...
Qatar										
1 VII 2009	ESDF	1 638 626	1 638 626	100.0	1 265 146	1 265 146	100.0	373 480	373 480	100.0
21 IV 2010	CDFC	1 699 435	...	...	1 284 739	...	...	414 696	...	...
1 VII 2010	ESDF	1 715 098	1 715 098	100.0	1 296 110	1 296 110	100.0	418 988	418 988	100.0
1 VII 2011	ESDF	1 732 717	1 732 717	100.0	1 288 590	1 288 590	100.0	444 127	444 127	100.0
1 VII 2012	ESDF	1 832 903	1 832 903	100.0	1 355 199	1 355 199	100.0	477 704	477 704	100.0
1 VII 2013	ESDF	2 003 700	2 003 700	100.0	1 477 632	1 477 632	100.0	526 068	526 068	100.0
1 VII 2014	ESDF	2 216 180	2 216 180	100.0	1 652 037	1 652 037	100.0	564 143	564 143	100.0
20 IV 2015	CDFC	2 404 776	...	...	1 816 981	...	...	587 795	...	...
1 VII 2015	ESDF	2 437 790	2 437 790	100.0	1 840 643	1 840 643	100.0	597 147	597 147	100.0
1 VII 2016	ESDF	2 617 634	2 617 634	100.0	1 975 536	1 975 536	100.0	642 098	642 098	100.0
1 VII 2017	ESDF	2 724 606	2 724 606	100.0	2 046 047	2 046 047	100.0	678 559	678 559	100.0
1 VII 2018	ESDF	2 760 170	2 760 170	100.0	2 048 206	2 048 206	100.0	711 964	711 964	100.0
Republic of Korea - République de Corée										
1 VII 2009	ESDJ	49 307 835	...	...	24 774 341	...	...	24 533 494	...	...
1 VII 2010	ESDJ	49 554 112	...	...	24 881 114	...	...	24 672 998	...	...
1 XI 2010[131]	CDJC	48 580 293	39 822 647	82.0	24 167 098	19 798 739	81.9	24 413 195	20 023 908	82.0
1 VII 2011	ESDJ	49 936 638	...	...	25 069 867	...	...	24 866 771	...	...
1 VII 2012	ESDJ	50 199 853	...	...	25 187 380	...	...	25 012 473	...	...
1 VII 2013	ESDJ	50 428 893	...	...	25 285 319	...	...	25 143 574	...	...
1 VII 2014	ESDJ	50 746 659	...	...	25 445 077	...	...	25 301 582	...	...
1 VII 2015	ESDJ	51 014 947	...	...	25 585 894	...	...	25 429 053	...	...
1 XI 2015	CDJC	51 069 375	41 677 695	81.6	25 608 502	20 791 896	81.2	25 460 873	20 885 799	82.0
1 VII 2016	ESDJ	51 217 803	...	...	25 670 949	...	...	25 546 854	...	...
1 VII 2017	ESDJ	51 361 911	...	...	25 736 793	...	...	25 625 118	...	...
1 VII 2018	ESDJ	51 606 633	...	...	25 863 502	...	...	25 743 131	...	...

Continent, country or area, and date / Continent, pays ou zone et date	Code[a]	Both sexes - Les deux sexes			Male - Masculin			Female - Féminin		
		Total	Urban - Urbaine		Total	Urban - Urbaine		Total	Urban - Urbaine	
			Number Nombre	Percent P.100		Number Nombre	Percent P.100		Number Nombre	Percent P.100
ASIA - ASIE										
Saudi Arabia - Arabie saoudite										
1 VII 2009	ESDF	26 576 321	...	...	15 074 067	...	...	11 502 254	...	...
27 IV 2010	CDFC	27 236 156	...	...	15 531 471	...	...	11 704 685	...	...
1 VII 2010	ESDF	27 410 508	...	...	15 643 804	...	...	11 766 704	...	...
1 VII 2011	ESDF	28 173 195	...	...	16 124 760	...	...	12 048 435	...	...
1 VII 2012	ESDF	28 896 840	...	...	16 566 096	...	...	12 330 744	...	...
1 VII 2013	ESDF	29 613 064	...	...	16 974 234	...	...	12 638 830	...	...
1 VII 2014	ESDF	30 339 795	...	...	17 393 435	...	...	12 946 360	...	...
1 VII 2015	ESDF	31 062 069	...	...	17 818 656	...	...	13 243 413	...	...
1 VII 2016	ESDF	31 787 580	...	...	18 259 719	...	...	13 527 861	...	...
1 VII 2017	ESDF	32 612 846	...	...	18 746 422	...	...	13 866 424	...	...
1 VII 2018	ESDF	33 413 660	...	...	19 240 956	...	...	14 172 704	...	...
Singapore - Singapour										
30 VI 2009[132]	ESDJ	4 987 573	...	...	2 602 010	...	...	2 385 563	...	...
30 VI 2010[133]	CDJC	3 771 721	...	...	1 861 133	...	...	1 910 588	...	...
30 VI 2010[132]	ESDJ	5 076 732	...	...	2 641 339	...	...	2 435 393	...	...
30 VI 2011[132]	ESDJ	5 183 688	...	...	2 690 534	...	...	2 493 154	...	...
30 VI 2012[132]	ESDJ	5 312 437	...	...	2 765 614	...	...	2 546 823	...	...
30 VI 2013[132]	ESDJ	5 399 162	...	...	2 824 655	...	...	2 574 507	...	...
30 VI 2014[132]	ESDJ	5 469 724	...	...	2 864 408	...	...	2 605 316	...	...
30 VI 2015[132]	ESDJ	5 535 002	...	...	2 891 101	...	...	2 643 901	...	...
30 VI 2016[132]	ESDJ	5 607 283	...	...	2 920 951	...	...	2 686 332	...	...
30 VI 2017[132]	ESDJ	5 612 253	...	...	2 897 264	...	...	2 714 989	...	...
30 VI 2018[132]	ESDJ	5 638 676	...	...	2 893 284	...	...	2 745 392	...	...
Sri Lanka										
1 VII 2009	ESDF	20 476 000	...	...	10 174 000	...	...	10 302 000	...	...
1 VII 2010	ESDF	20 675 000	...	...	10 273 000	...	...	10 402 000	...	...
1 VII 2011	ESDF	20 892 000	...	...	10 381 000	...	...	10 511 000	...	...
20 III 2012	CDJC	20 359 439	3 704 470	18.2	9 856 634	1 800 327	18.3	10 502 805	1 904 143	18.1
1 VII 2012	ESDJ	20 425 000	...	...	9 888 000	...	...	10 537 000	...	...
1 VII 2013	ESDJ	20 585 000	...	...	9 966 000	...	...	10 619 000	...	...
1 VII 2014	ESDJ	20 778 000	...	...	10 059 000	...	...	10 719 000	...	...
1 VII 2015	ESDJ	20 970 000	...	...	10 153 000	...	...	10 817 000	...	...
1 VII 2016*	ESDJ	21 203 000	...	...	10 265 460	...	...	10 937 540	...	...
1 VII 2017*	ESDJ	21 444 350	...	...	10 382 372	...	...	11 061 978	...	...
1 VII 2018*	ESDJ	21 670 000	...	...	10 492 000	...	...	11 178 000	...	...
State of Palestine - État de Palestine										
1 VII 2009	ESDF	3 922 130	...	...	1 991 828	...	...	1 930 302	...	...
1 VII 2010	ESDF	4 023 462	...	...	2 043 857	...	...	1 979 605	...	...
1 VII 2011	ESDF	4 124 795	...	...	2 095 887	...	...	2 028 908	...	...
1 VII 2012	ESDF	4 226 410	...	...	2 148 060	...	...	2 078 350	...	...
1 VII 2013	ESDF	4 327 751	...	...	2 200 092	...	...	2 127 659	...	...
1 VII 2014	ESDF	4 429 084	...	...	2 252 122	...	...	2 176 962	...	...
1 VII 2015	ESDF	4 530 416	...	...	2 304 151	...	...	2 226 265	...	...
1 VII 2016	ESDF	4 632 025	...	...	2 356 322	...	...	2 275 703	...	...
1 VII 2017	ESDF	4 733 357	...	...	2 408 351	...	...	2 325 006	...	...
1 XII 2017	CDFC	4 705 855	4 018 942[134]	85.4	2 394 359	2 043 943[134]	85.4	2 311 496	1 974 999[134]	85.4
1 VII 2018	ESDF	4 854 013	...	...	2 469 162	...	...	2 384 851	...	...
Syrian Arab Republic - République arabe syrienne[135]										
1 VII 2009	ESDF	20 125 000	10 769 000	53.5	10 287 000	5 526 000	53.7	9 838 000	5 243 000	53.3
1 VII 2010	ESDF	20 619 000	11 033 000	53.5	10 539 000	5 661 000	53.7	10 080 000	5 372 000	53.3
1 VII 2011	ESDF	21 124 000	11 297 000	53.5	10 794 000	5 795 000	53.7	10 330 000	5 502 000	53.3
Tajikistan - Tadjikistan										
1 VII 2009	ESDF	7 334 083	1 944 038	26.5	3 699 641	979 510	26.5	3 634 442	964 528	26.5
1 VII 2010	ESDF	7 519 280	1 996 961	26.6	3 794 467	1 007 796	26.6	3 724 813	989 165	26.6
21 IX 2010	CDFC	7 564 502	2 006 605	26.5	3 817 004	1 012 642	26.5	3 747 498	993 963	26.5
1 VII 2011	ESDF	7 714 198	2 042 660	26.5	3 893 798	1 032 106	26.5	3 820 401	1 010 554	26.5
1 VII 2012	ESDF	7 897 313	2 085 698	26.4	3 987 517	1 054 904	26.5	3 909 796	1 030 794	26.4
1 VII 2013	ESDF	8 074 266	2 138 737	26.5	4 078 857	1 083 119	26.6	3 995 409	1 055 618	26.4
1 VII 2014	ESDF	8 256 572	2 193 224	26.6	4 174 269	1 112 352	26.6	4 082 303	1 080 873	26.5
1 VII 2015	ESDF	8 451 630	2 237 893	26.5	4 276 777	1 136 493	26.6	4 174 854	1 101 401	26.4

Continent, country or area, and date / Continent, pays ou zone et date	Code[a]	Both sexes - Les deux sexes Total	Urban - Urbaine Number Nombre	Urban - Urbaine Percent P.100	Male - Masculin Total	Urban - Urbaine Number Nombre	Urban - Urbaine Percent P.100	Female - Féminin Total	Urban - Urbaine Number Nombre	Urban - Urbaine Percent P.100
ASIA - ASIE										
Tajikistan - Tadjikistan										
1 VII 2016	ESDF	8 646 973	2 280 367	26.4	4 379 342	1 159 476	26.5	4 267 631	1 120 891	26.3
1 VII 2017	ESDF	8 837 002	2 321 759	26.3	4 479 048	1 182 016	26.4	4 357 954	1 139 743	26.2
Thailand - Thaïlande										
1 VII 2009	ESDJ	63 525 062	...	...	31 293 096	...	...	32 231 966	...	...
1 VII 2010	ESDJ	63 878 267	...	...	31 451 801	...	...	32 426 466	...	...
1 IX 2010	CDJC	65 981 659	29 133 829	44.2	32 355 032	14 120 842	43.6	33 626 627	15 012 987	44.6
1 VII 2011	ESDJ	64 076 033	...	...	31 529 148	...	...	32 546 885	...	...
1 VII 2012	ESDJ	64 266 365	...	...	31 614 938	...	...	32 651 427	...	...
1 VII 2013	ESDJ	64 621 302	...	...	31 773 349	...	...	32 847 953	...	...
1 VII 2014	ESDJ	64 955 313	...	...	31 922 490	...	...	33 032 823	...	...
1 VII 2015	ESDJ	65 027 401	...	...	31 932 092	...	...	33 095 309	...	...
1 VII 2016	ESDJ	65 013 495	...	...	31 894 480	...	...	33 119 015	...	...
1 VII 2017	ESDJ	65 521 660	32 257 097	49.2	31 807 391	15 626 525	49.1	33 714 269	16 630 572	49.3
1 VII 2018[3]	ESDJ	65 700 000	...	...	31 877 000	...	...	33 823 000	...	...
Timor-Leste										
11 VII 2010	CDFC	1 066 409	316 086	29.6	544 198	166 163	30.5	522 211	149 923	28.7
1 VII 2013[3]	ESDF	1 180 069	...	...	602 526	...	...	577 544	...	...
1 VII 2014[3]	ESDF	1 212 107	...	...	618 789	...	...	593 318	...	...
1 VII 2015[3]	ESDF	1 200 379	...	...	613 386	...	...	586 993	...	...
11 VII 2015	CDFC	1 183 643	349 208	29.5	601 112	179 565	29.9	582 531	169 643	29.1
1 VII 2016[3]	ESDF	1 221 133	...	...	623 430	...	...	597 703	...	...
1 VII 2017[3]	ESDF	1 241 506	...	...	633 197	...	...	608 309	...	...
1 VII 2018[3]	ESDF	1 261 407	...	...	642 639	...	...	618 768	...	...
Turkey - Turquie										
31 XII 2009[136]	ESDJ	72 561 312	50 872 734	70.1	36 462 470	25 607 137	70.2	36 098 842	25 265 597	70.0
31 XII 2010[136]	ESDJ	73 722 988	52 340 830	71.0	37 043 182	26 348 394	71.1	36 679 806	25 992 436	70.9
3 X 2011[137]	CDJC	74 526 000	53 321 000	71.5	37 431 000	26 777 000	71.5	37 095 000	26 544 000	71.6
31 XII 2011[136]	ESDJ	74 724 269	53 630 845	71.8	37 532 954	26 947 983	71.8	37 191 315	26 682 862	71.7
31 XII 2012[136]	ESDJ	75 627 384	54 705 188	72.3	37 956 168	27 442 260	72.3	37 671 216	27 262 928	72.4
31 XII 2013[136]	ESDJ	76 667 864	66 488 105[138]	86.7	38 473 360	33 344 846[138]	86.7	38 194 504	33 143 259[138]	86.8
31 XII 2014[136]	ESDJ	77 695 904	67 720 318	87.2	38 984 302	33 954 681	87.1	38 711 602	33 765 637	87.2
31 XII 2015[136]	ESDJ	78 741 053	69 004 143	87.6	39 511 191	34 598 184	87.6	39 229 862	34 405 959	87.7
31 XII 2016[136]	ESDJ	79 814 871	70 165 359	87.9	40 043 650	35 162 317	87.8	39 771 221	35 003 042	88.0
31 XII 2017[136]	ESDJ	80 810 525	71 253 963	88.2	40 535 135	35 693 468	88.1	40 275 390	35 560 495	88.3
United Arab Emirates - Émirats arabes unis[139]										
31 XII 2009	ESDF	8 199 996	...	...	6 120 885	...	...	2 079 111	...	...
1 VII 2010	ESDF	8 264 070	...	...	6 161 820	...	...	2 102 250	...	...
31 XII 2016	ESDF	9 121 167	...	...	6 298 294	...	...	2 822 873	...	...
31 XII 2017	ESDF	9 304 277	...	...	6 415 942	...	...	2 888 335	...	...
Uzbekistan - Ouzbékistan[116]										
1 VII 2009	ESDJ	27 767 408	14 330 900	51.6	13 893 825	7 129 600	51.3	13 873 583	7 201 300	51.9
1 VII 2010	ESDJ	28 562 405	14 661 700	51.3	14 291 711	7 295 300	51.0	14 270 694	7 366 400	51.6
1 VII 2011	ESDJ	29 339 368	15 062 700	51.3	14 680 424	7 496 500	51.1	14 658 944	7 566 200	51.6
1 VII 2012	ESDJ	29 774 448	15 285 000	51.3	14 905 603	7 613 400	51.1	14 868 845	7 671 600	51.6
1 VII 2013	ESDJ	30 243 172	15 462 637	51.1	15 148 116	7 707 450	50.9	15 095 056	7 755 187	51.4
1 VII 2014	ESDJ	30 757 669	15 651 614	50.9	15 414 846	7 809 449	50.7	15 342 823	7 842 165	51.1
1 VII 2015	ESDJ	31 298 929	15 855 953	50.7	15 695 568	7 919 014	50.5	15 603 361	7 936 939	50.9
1 VII 2016	ESDJ	31 847 898	16 133 260	50.7	15 979 935	8 063 139	50.5	15 867 963	8 070 121	50.9
1 VII 2017	ESDJ	32 388 563	16 414 114	50.7	16 259 425	8 207 397	50.5	16 129 138	8 206 717	50.9
1 I 2018	ESDJ	32 656 700	16 532 700	50.6	...	...	...	...	...	...
Viet Nam										
1 IV 2009	CDJC	85 846 997	25 436 896	29.6	42 413 143	12 349 995	29.1	43 433 854	13 086 901	30.1
1 VII 2009[140]	ESDJ	86 024 979	25 584 740	29.7	42 523 416	...	...	43 501 563	...	...
1 VII 2010[140]	ESDJ	86 947 439	26 515 900	30.5	42 993 487	...	...	43 953 952	...	...
1 VII 2011[140]	ESDJ	87 860 387	27 719 300	31.5	43 446 781	...	...	44 413 606	...	...
1 VII 2012[140]	ESDJ	88 809 279	28 269 200	31.8	43 908 201	...	...	44 901 078	...	...
1 VII 2013[140]	ESDJ	89 759 538	28 874 900	32.2	44 364 894	...	...	45 394 644	...	...
1 VII 2014[140]	ESDJ	90 728 941	30 035 405	33.1	44 758 132	...	...	45 970 809	...	...
1 VII 2015[140]	ESDJ	91 709 825	31 067 492	33.9	45 224 031	...	...	46 485 794	...	...
1 VII 2016[140]	ESDJ	92 695 121	31 985 992	34.5	45 705 601	...	...	46 989 520	...	...
1 VII 2017*[140]	ESDJ	93 677 594	32 823 139	35.0	46 266 288	...	...	47 411 306	...	...
1 VII 2018*[140]	ESDJ	94 665 973	33 829 988	35.7	46 785 200	...	...	47 880 773	...	...

Continent, country or area, and date / Continent, pays ou zone et date	Code[a]	Both sexes - Les deux sexes			Male - Masculin			Female - Féminin		
		Total	Urban - Urbaine		Total	Urban - Urbaine		Total	Urban - Urbaine	
			Number Nombre	Percent P.100		Number Nombre	Percent P.100		Number Nombre	Percent P.100
ASIA - ASIE										
Yemen - Yémen[3]										
1 VII 2009	ESDJ	22 492 035	6 475 802	28.8	11 454 963	...	...	11 037 072	...	...
1 VII 2010	ESDJ	23 153 982	6 673 916	28.8	11 789 814	...	...	11 364 168	...	...
1 VII 2011	ESDJ	23 832 569	6 875 789	28.9	12 133 362	...	...	11 699 207	...	...
1 VII 2012	ESDJ	24 526 703	7 075 639	28.8	12 485 039	...	...	12 041 664	...	...
1 VII 2013	ESDJ	25 235 079	7 280 367	28.9	12 844 169	...	...	12 390 910	...	...
1 VII 2014	ESDJ	25 955 920	7 488 312	28.9	13 209 834	...	...	12 746 086	...	...
1 VII 2015	ESDJ	26 687 013	7 699 217	28.9	13 580 896	...	...	13 106 117	...	...
1 VII 2016	ESDJ	27 426 016	7 912 406	28.9	13 956 092	...	...	13 469 924	...	...
1 VII 2017	ESDJ	28 170 408	8 127 151	28.8	14 334 126	...	...	13 836 282	...	...
EUROPE										
Åland Islands - Îles d'Åland[60]										
1 VII 2009	ESDJ	27 595	11 064	40.1	13 724	5 264	38.4	13 871	5 800	41.8
1 VII 2010	ESDJ	27 871	11 157	40.0	13 880	5 327	38.4	13 991	5 830	41.7
1 VII 2011	ESDJ	28 181	11 227	39.8	14 045	5 364	38.2	14 137	5 863	41.5
1 VII 2012	ESDJ	28 429	11 305	39.8	14 172	5 408	38.2	14 257	5 897	41.4
1 VII 2013	ESDJ	28 585	11 370	39.8	14 255	5 445	38.2	14 330	5 925	41.3
1 VII 2014	ESDJ	28 792	11 437	39.7	14 375	5 490	38.2	14 417	5 947	41.2
1 VII 2015	ESDJ	28 950	11 471	39.6	14 466	5 521	38.2	14 484	5 950	41.1
1 VII 2016	ESDJ	29 099	11 513	39.6	14 526	5 538	38.1	14 573	5 975	41.0
1 VII 2017	ESDJ	29 352	11 621	39.6	14 644	5 583	38.1	14 708	6 038	41.1
1 VII 2018	ESDJ	29 638	11 709	39.5	14 795	5 621	38.0	14 843	6 088	41.0
Albania - Albanie										
1 VII 2009	ESDF	2 927 519	1 518 397	51.9	1 463 537	752 178	51.4	1 463 982	766 219	52.3
1 VII 2010	ESDF	2 913 021	1 541 310	52.9	1 457 661	763 780	52.4	1 455 360	777 530	53.4
1 VII 2011	ESDJ	2 904 780	1 564 139	53.8	1 455 074	775 313	53.3	1 449 706	788 826	54.4
1 X 2011	CDJC	2 800 138	1 498 508	53.5	1 403 059	742 671	52.9	1 397 079	755 837	54.1
1 VII 2012	ESDJ	2 900 401	...	...	1 459 681	...	...	1 440 720	...	...
1 VII 2013	ESDJ	2 895 092	...	...	1 461 076	...	...	1 434 016	...	...
1 VII 2014	ESDJ	2 889 104	...	...	1 461 389	...	...	1 427 715	...	...
1 VII 2015	ESDJ	2 880 703	...	...	1 459 831	...	...	1 420 872	...	...
1 VII 2016	ESDJ	2 876 101	...	...	1 456 000	...	...	1 420 101	...	...
1 VII 2017	ESDJ	2 873 457	...	...	1 446 071	...	...	1 427 386	...	...
1 I 2018	ESDJ	2 870 324	...	...	1 438 609	...	...	1 431 715	...	...
Andorra - Andorre[60]										
1 VII 2009	ESDJ	85 116	...	...	44 444	...	...	40 672	...	...
1 I 2010[141]	ESDJ	70 290	...	...	35 592	...	...	34 698	...	...
1 I 2011	ESDJ	69 772	...	...	35 204	...	...	34 568	...	...
31 XII 2011	CDJC	69 758	...	...	35 147	...	...	34 611	...	...
1 I 2012	ESDJ	69 758	...	...	35 147	...	...	34 611	...	...
1 VII 2013	ESDJ	69 929	...	...	35 206	...	...	34 723	...	...
1 VII 2014	ESDJ	70 155	...	...	35 364	...	...	34 791	...	...
1 VII 2015	ESDJ	70 901	...	...	35 741	...	...	35 160	...	...
1 VII 2016	ESDJ	72 358	...	...	36 590	...	...	35 768	...	...
1 I 2017	ESDJ	73 105	...	...	37 047	...	...	36 058	...	...
1 I 2018	ESDJ	74 794	...	...	38 031	...	...	36 763	...	...
Austria - Autriche										
1 VII 2009	ESDJ	8 341 483	...	...	4 061 195	...	...	4 280 288	...	...
1 VII 2010	ESDJ	8 361 069	...	...	4 071 773	...	...	4 289 296	...	...
1 VII 2011	ESDJ	8 388 534	...	...	4 087 188	...	...	4 301 346	...	...
31 X 2011	CDJC	8 401 940	5 643 239	67.2	4 093 938	2 713 930	66.3	4 308 002	2 929 309	68.0
1 VII 2012	ESDJ	8 426 311	...	...	4 109 431	...	...	4 316 880	...	...
1 VII 2013	ESDJ	8 477 230	...	...	4 138 693	...	...	4 338 537	...	...
1 VII 2014	ESDJ	8 543 975	...	...	4 176 554	...	...	4 367 421	...	...
1 VII 2015	ESDJ	8 629 496	...	...	4 229 064	...	...	4 400 432	...	...
1 VII 2016	ESDJ	8 739 806	...	...	4 295 164	...	...	4 444 642	...	...
1 VII 2017	ESDJ	8 795 073	...	...	4 324 737	...	...	4 470 336	...	...
1 I 2018	ESDJ	8 822 267	...	...	4 338 518	...	...	4 483 749	...	...
Belarus - Bélarus										
1 VII 2009	ESDJ	9 506 765	7 052 045	74.2	4 421 789	3 266 240	73.9	5 084 976	3 785 805	74.5
14 X 2009	CDJC	9 503 807	7 064 529	74.3	4 420 039	3 271 014	74.0	5 083 768	3 793 515	74.6

Continent, country or area, and date / Continent, pays ou zone et date	Code[a]	Both sexes - Les deux sexes			Male - Masculin			Female - Féminin		
		Total	Urban - Urbaine		Total	Urban - Urbaine		Total	Urban - Urbaine	
			Number Nombre	Percent P.100		Number Nombre	Percent P.100		Number Nombre	Percent P.100
EUROPE										
Belarus - Bélarus										
1 VII 2010 .... ESDJ		9 490 583	7 100 147	74.8	4 413 225	3 285 104	74.4	5 077 358	3 815 043	75.1
1 VII 2011 .... ESDJ		9 473 172	7 148 636	75.5	4 403 227	3 303 932	75.0	5 069 945	3 844 704	75.8
1 VII 2012 .... ESDJ		9 464 495	7 198 575	76.1	4 397 910	3 324 299	75.6	5 066 585	3 874 276	76.5
1 VII 2013 .... ESDJ		9 465 997	7 247 854	76.6	4 399 369	3 345 878	76.1	5 066 628	3 901 976	77.0
1 VII 2014 .... ESDJ		9 474 511	7 299 978	77.0	4 405 204	3 369 054	76.5	5 069 307	3 930 824	77.5
1 VII 2015 .... ESDJ		9 489 616	7 347 512	77.4	4 415 020	3 390 465	76.8	5 074 596	3 957 047	78.0
1 VII 2016[25] .... ESDJ		9 501 534	7 385 438	77.7	4 423 680	3 407 394	77.0	5 077 854	3 978 044	78.3
1 VII 2017[25] .... ESDJ		9 498 264	7 406 475	78.0	4 424 027	3 415 947	77.2	5 074 237	3 990 528	78.6
1 I 2018 .... ESDJ		9 491 823	7 412 118	78.1	4 421 534	3 417 894	77.3	5 070 289	3 994 224	78.8
Belgium - Belgique										
1 VII 2009 .... ESDJ		10 796 493	10 641 089	98.6	5 290 436	5 212 557	98.5	5 506 057	5 428 532	98.6
1 VII 2010 .... ESDJ		10 895 638	10 739 291	98.6	5 341 252	5 262 796	98.5	5 554 386	5 476 495	98.6
1 I 2011 .... CDJC		11 000 638	10 842 520	98.6	5 401 718	5 322 172	98.5	5 598 920	5 520 348	98.6
1 VII 2011 .... ESDJ		11 043 788	10 884 939	98.6	5 425 814	5 345 964	98.5	5 617 974	5 538 975	98.6
1 VII 2012 .... ESDJ		11 128 246	...	...	5 469 608	...	...	5 658 638	...	...
1 VII 2013 .... ESDJ		11 182 817	...	...	5 497 753	...	...	5 685 065	...	...
1 VII 2014 .... ESDJ		11 231 213	...	...	5 522 163	...	...	5 709 051	...	...
1 VII 2015[25] .... ESDJ		11 284 776	...	...	5 552 760	...	...	5 732 016	...	...
1 VII 2016[25] .... ESDJ		11 331 422	...	...	5 579 268	...	...	5 752 154	...	...
1 VII 2017[25] .... ESDJ		11 375 158	...	...	5 601 745	...	...	5 773 413	...	...
1 I 2018 .... ESDJ		11 398 589	...	...	5 614 218	...	...	5 784 371	...	...
Bosnia and Herzegovina - Bosnie-Herzégovine										
1 VII 2009 .... ESDF		3 842 566	...	...	1 877 312	...	...	1 965 254	...	...
1 VII 2010 .... ESDF		3 843 126	...	...	1 877 587	...	...	1 965 539	...	...
1 VII 2011 .... ESDF		3 841 224	...	...	1 876 546	...	...	1 964 678	...	...
1 VII 2012 .... ESDF		3 837 455	...	...	1 874 608	...	...	1 962 848	...	...
30 IX 2013 .... CDJC		3 531 159	...	...	1 732 270	...	...	1 798 889	...	...
Bulgaria - Bulgarie										
1 VII 2009 .... ESDJ		7 585 131	5 408 330	71.3	3 670 296	2 598 442	70.8	3 914 835	2 809 888	71.8
1 VII 2010 .... ESDJ		7 534 289	5 388 142	71.5	3 644 560	2 587 844	71.0	3 889 729	2 800 298	72.0
1 II 2011 .... CDJC		7 364 570	5 338 261	72.5	3 586 571	2 580 734	72.0	3 777 999	2 757 527	73.0
1 VII 2011 .... ESDJ		7 348 328	5 336 366	72.6	3 577 847	2 579 205	72.1	3 770 481	2 757 161	73.1
1 VII 2012 .... ESDJ		7 305 888	5 316 384	72.8	3 555 920	2 568 535	72.2	3 749 968	2 747 849	73.3
1 VII 2013 .... ESDJ		7 263 859	...	...	3 534 276	...	...	3 729 584	...	...
1 VII 2014 .... ESDJ		7 223 937	5 279 577	73.1	3 513 480	2 548 437	72.5	3 710 457	2 731 140	73.6
1 VII 2015 .... ESDJ		7 177 991	5 247 331	73.1	3 489 596	2 530 439	72.5	3 688 395	2 716 892	73.7
1 VII 2016[25] .... ESDJ		7 127 822	5 215 784	73.2	3 463 578	2 512 987	72.6	3 664 244	2 702 797	73.8
1 VII 2017[25] .... ESDJ		7 075 947	5 193 070	73.4	3 436 194	2 500 348	72.8	3 639 753	2 692 722	74.0
1 I 2018 .... ESDJ		7 050 034	5 181 755	73.5	3 422 409	2 494 068	72.9	3 627 625	2 687 687	74.1
Croatia - Croatie										
1 VII 2009 .... ESDJ		4 305 181	...	...	2 075 321	...	...	2 229 860	...	...
1 VII 2010 .... ESDJ		4 295 427	...	...	2 071 195	...	...	2 224 232	...	...
1 IV 2011 .... CDJC		4 284 889	2 368 506	55.3	2 066 335	1 121 328	54.3	2 218 554	1 247 178	56.2
1 VII 2011 .... ESDJ		4 280 622	...	...	2 064 314	...	...	2 216 308	...	...
1 VII 2012 .... ESDJ		4 267 558	...	...	2 058 701	...	...	2 208 857	...	...
1 VII 2013 .... ESDJ		4 255 689	...	...	2 053 788	...	...	2 201 901	...	...
1 VII 2014 .... ESDJ		4 238 389	...	...	2 045 801	...	...	2 192 588	...	...
1 VII 2015 .... ESDJ		4 203 604	...	...	2 028 640	...	...	2 174 964	...	...
1 VII 2016 .... ESDJ		4 174 349	...	...	2 014 837	...	...	2 159 512	...	...
1 VII 2017 .... ESDJ		4 124 531	...	...	1 990 341	...	...	2 134 190	...	...
1 I 2018 .... ESDJ		4 105 493	...	...	1 981 799	...	...	2 123 694	...	...
Czechia - Tchéquie										
1 VII 2009 .... ESDJ		10 443 936	...	...	5 126 422	...	...	5 317 514	...	...
1 VII 2010 .... ESDJ		10 474 410	...	...	5 141 699	...	...	5 332 711	...	...
25 III 2011 .... CDJC		10 436 560	7 650 450	73.3	5 109 766	3 712 348	72.7	5 326 794	3 938 102	73.9
1 VII 2011 .... ESDJ		10 496 088	...	...	5 152 721	...	...	5 343 368	...	...
1 VII 2012 .... ESDJ		10 510 786	...	...	5 161 280	...	...	5 349 506	...	...
1 VII 2013 .... ESDJ		10 510 719	7 683 793	73.1	5 161 617	3 740 790	72.5	5 349 102	3 943 003	73.7
1 VII 2014 .... ESDJ		10 524 783	7 693 352	73.1	5 169 146	3 744 873	72.4	5 355 637	3 948 479	73.7
1 VII 2015 .... ESDJ		10 542 942	7 702 624	73.1	5 180 242	3 749 901	72.4	5 362 700	3 952 723	73.7
1 VII 2016 .... ESDJ		10 565 284	7 725 090	73.1	5 193 012	3 761 862	72.4	5 372 272	3 963 228	73.8
1 VII 2017 .... ESDJ		10 589 526	7 742 524	73.1	5 207 575	3 772 123	72.4	5 381 951	3 970 401	73.8
1 I 2018 .... ESDJ		10 610 055	7 753 337	73.1	5 219 791	3 778 892	72.4	5 390 264	3 974 445	73.7

Continent, country or area, and date / Continent, pays ou zone et date	Code[a]	Both sexes - Les deux sexes			Male - Masculin			Female - Féminin		
		Total	Urban - Urbaine Number Nombre	Urban - Urbaine Percent P.100	Total	Urban - Urbaine Number Nombre	Urban - Urbaine Percent P.100	Total	Urban - Urbaine Number Nombre	Urban - Urbaine Percent P.100
EUROPE										
Denmark - Danemark[142]										
1 VII 2009	ESDJ	5 519 441	...	...	2 735 983	...	...	2 783 458	...	...
1 VII 2010	ESDJ	5 545 039	...	...	2 748 439	...	...	2 796 600	...	...
1 I 2011	CDJC	5 560 628	...	...	2 756 582	...	...	2 804 046	...	...
1 VII 2011	ESDJ	5 566 856	...	...	2 760 140	...	...	2 806 716	...	...
1 VII 2012	ESDJ	5 587 085	...	...	2 771 208	...	...	2 815 877	...	...
1 VII 2013	ESDJ	5 608 784	...	...	2 782 661	...	...	2 826 123	...	...
1 VII 2014	ESDJ	5 639 719	...	...	2 799 895	...	...	2 839 824	...	...
1 VII 2015	ESDJ	5 678 348	...	...	2 822 535	...	...	2 855 813	...	...
1 VII 2016	ESDJ	5 724 456	...	...	2 848 030	...	...	2 876 426	...	...
1 VII 2017	ESDJ	5 760 694	...	...	2 866 952	...	...	2 893 742	...	...
1 VII 2018	ESDJ	5 789 957	...	...	2 881 620	...	...	2 908 337	...	...
Estonia - Estonie										
1 VII 2009	ESDJ	1 334 515	907 675	68.0	621 060	410 130	66.0	713 455	497 545	69.7
1 VII 2010	ESDJ	1 331 475	904 365	67.9	620 250	408 720	65.9	711 225	495 645	69.7
1 VII 2011	ESDJ	1 327 439	903 066	68.0	618 919	408 988	66.1	708 520	494 078	69.7
31 XII 2011	CDJC	1 294 455	879 157	67.9	600 526	396 719	66.1	693 929	482 438	69.5
1 VII 2012	ESDJ	1 322 696	902 743	68.3	617 153	409 784	66.4	705 543	492 959	69.9
1 VII 2013	ESDJ	1 317 997	900 071	68.3	615 543	408 564	66.4	702 454	491 507	70.0
1 VII 2014	ESDJ	1 314 545	897 901	68.3	614 654	407 677	66.3	699 891	490 224	70.0
1 VII 2015	ESDJ	1 314 608	899 288[108]	68.4	615 549	406 894[108]	66.1	699 059	492 395[108]	70.4
1 VII 2016[25]	ESDJ	1 315 790	900 266[108]	68.4	617 123	406 142[108]	65.8	698 667	494 124[108]	70.7
1 VII 2017	ESDJ	1 317 384	912 157[108]	69.2	619 311	414 881[108]	67.0	698 073	497 277[108]	71.2
1 I 2018	ESDJ	1 319 133	914 850[108]	69.4	621 084	416 987[108]	67.1	698 049	497 863[108]	71.3
Faeroe Islands - Îles Féroé										
1 VII 2009	ESDJ	48 798	18 001	36.9	25 345	9 117	36.0	23 453	8 884	37.9
1 VII 2010	ESDJ	48 669	18 131	37.3	25 276	9 195	36.4	23 393	8 936	38.2
1 VII 2011	ESDJ	48 563	18 110	37.3	25 179	9 120	36.2	23 384	8 990	38.4
11 XI 2011	CDJC	48 346	...	...	25 125	...	...	23 221	...	...
1 VII 2012	ESDJ	48 319	18 033	37.3	25 074	9 072	36.2	23 245	8 961	38.6
1 VII 2013	ESDJ	48 286	18 220	37.7	25 014	9 147	36.6	23 272	9 073	39.0
1 VII 2014	ESDJ	48 462	18 373	37.9	25 048	9 207	36.8	23 414	9 166	39.1
1 VII 2015	ESDJ	48 929	18 663	38.1	25 312	9 381	37.1	23 617	9 282	39.3
1 VII 2016	ESDJ	49 497	18 964	38.3	25 546	9 514	37.2	23 951	9 450	39.5
1 VII 2017	ESDJ	50 204	19 241	38.3	25 881	9 667	37.4	24 323	9 574	39.4
1 VII 2018	ESDJ	51 040	19 600	38.4	26 352	9 873	37.5	24 688	9 727	39.4
Finland - Finlande										
1 VII 2009[143]	ESDJ	5 311 276	3 615 933	68.1	2 604 636	1 753 169	67.3	2 706 640	1 862 764	68.8
1 VII 2010[143]	ESDJ	5 335 481	3 643 170	68.3	2 617 862	1 767 855	67.5	2 717 620	1 875 315	69.0
31 XII 2010	CDJC	5 375 276	3 662 915	68.1	2 638 416	1 777 697	67.4	2 736 860	1 885 218	68.9
1 VII 2011[143]	ESDJ	5 360 091	3 671 777	68.5	2 631 431	1 783 058	67.8	2 728 660	1 888 719	69.2
1 VII 2012[143]	ESDJ	5 385 543	3 701 923	68.7	2 645 408	1 799 025	68.0	2 740 136	1 902 898	69.4
1 VII 2013[143]	ESDJ	5 410 389	3 732 928	69.0	2 659 239	1 815 818	68.3	2 751 150	1 917 110	69.7
1 VII 2014[143]	ESDJ	5 432 721	3 762 906	69.3	2 671 740	1 831 826	68.6	2 760 981	1 931 080	69.9
1 VII 2015[143]	ESDJ	5 450 581	3 849 116	70.6	2 682 211	1 875 949	69.9	2 768 370	1 973 167	71.3
1 VII 2016[143]	ESDJ	5 466 204	3 880 555	71.0	2 692 383	1 893 551	70.3	2 773 822	1 987 004	71.6
1 VII 2017[143]	ESDJ	5 478 862	3 904 835	71.3	2 701 086	1 907 533	70.6	2 777 777	1 997 303	71.9
1 I 2018[60]	ESDJ	5 513 130	...	...	2 719 131	...	...	2 793 999	...	...
France										
1 VII 2009[144]	ESDJ	62 615 472	...	...	30 322 692	...	...	32 292 780	...	...
1 I 2010[144]	CDJS	62 765 235	48 387 303	77.1	30 393 079	23 208 841	76.4	32 372 156	25 178 462	77.8
1 VII 2010[144]	ESDJ	62 917 790	...	...	30 475 789	...	...	32 442 001	...	...
1 VII 2011[144]	ESDJ	63 223 158	...	...	30 626 399	...	...	32 596 759	...	...
1 VII 2012[144]	ESDJ	63 536 918	...	...	30 782 589	...	...	32 754 329	...	...
1 VII 2013[144]	ESDJ	63 862 912	...	...	30 945 467	...	...	32 917 445	...	...
1 VII 2014[144]	ESDJ	64 164 390	...	...	31 086 155	...	...	33 078 235	...	...
1 I 2015	CDJC	64 300 821	49 781 175	77.4	31 138 550	23 891 441	76.7	33 162 271	25 889 734	78.1
1 VII 2015[144]	ESDJ	64 384 807	...	...	31 181 794	...	...	33 203 013	...	...
1 VII 2016*[144]	ESDJ	64 543 604	...	...	31 248 627	...	...	33 294 977	...	...
1 VII 2017*[144]	ESDJ	64 671 734	...	...	31 303 616	...	...	33 368 118	...	...
1 VII 2018*[144]	ESDJ	64 768 552	...	...	31 343 809	...	...	33 424 743	...	...
Germany - Allemagne										
1 VII 2009	ESDJ	81 874 770	...	...	40 133 270	...	...	41 741 500	...	...
1 VII 2010	ESDJ	81 757 471	...	...	40 099 871	...	...	41 657 600	...	...

Continent, country or area, and date / Continent, pays ou zone et date	Code[a]	Both sexes - Les deux sexes Total	Urban - Urbaine Number Nombre	Urban - Urbaine Percent P.100	Male - Masculin Total	Urban - Urbaine Number Nombre	Urban - Urbaine Percent P.100	Female - Féminin Total	Urban - Urbaine Number Nombre	Urban - Urbaine Percent P.100
EUROPE										
Germany - Allemagne										
9 V 2011	CDJC	80 219 695	64 444 232	80.3	39 145 941	31 227 832	79.8	41 073 754	33 216 400	80.9
1 VII 2011[5]	ESDJ	80 274 983	...	...	39 177 274	...	...	41 097 709	...	...
1 VII 2012[5]	ESDJ	80 425 823	...	...	39 305 462	...	...	41 120 362	...	...
1 VII 2013[5]	ESDJ	80 645 605	...	...	39 468 950	...	...	41 176 655	...	...
1 VII 2014[5]	ESDJ	80 982 500	...	...	39 696 190	...	...	41 286 310	...	...
1 VII 2015[5]	ESDJ	81 686 663	...	...	40 174 816	...	...	41 511 847	...	...
1 VII 2016[145]	ESDJ	82 348 669	...	...	40 605 621	...	...	41 743 048	...	...
1 VII 2017[145]	ESDJ	82 657 002	...	...	40 770 342	...	...	41 886 661	...	...
1 I 2018[5]	ESDJ	82 792 351	...	...	40 843 565	...	...	41 948 786	...	...
Gibraltar[146]										
31 XII 2009	ESDF	30 963	...	...	15 378	...	...	15 585	...	...
31 XII 2010	ESDF	31 465	...	...	15 666	...	...	15 799	...	...
31 XII 2011	ESDF	32 003	...	...	15 977	...	...	16 026	...	...
12 XI 2012	CDJC	32 194	...	...	16 061	...	...	16 133	...	...
31 XII 2012	ESDF	32 577	...	...	16 311	...	...	16 266	...	...
31 XII 2013	ESDF	32 734	...	...	16 460	...	...	16 274	...	...
31 XII 2014	ESDF	33 140	...	...	16 694	...	...	16 446	...	...
31 XII 2015	ESDF	33 573	...	...	16 938	...	...	16 635	...	...
31 XII 2016	ESDF	34 003	...	...	17 093	...	...	16 910	...	...
Greece - Grèce										
1 VII 2009	ESDF	11 107 024	...	...	5 458 449	...	...	5 648 575	...	...
1 VII 2010	ESDF	11 121 383	...	...	5 457 186	...	...	5 664 197	...	...
9 V 2011	CDFC	10 816 286	8 285 259	76.6	5 303 223	4 022 889	75.9	5 513 063	4 262 370	77.3
1 VII 2011	ESDF	11 104 995	...	...	5 438 712	...	...	5 666 283	...	...
1 VII 2012	ESDF	11 045 040	...	...	5 395 104	...	...	5 649 936	...	...
1 VII 2013	ESDF	10 965 241	...	...	5 339 750	...	...	5 625 491	...	...
1 VII 2014	ESDF	10 892 369	...	...	5 290 797	...	...	5 601 572	...	...
1 VII 2015	ESDF	10 820 964	...	...	5 246 345	...	...	5 574 619	...	...
1 VII 2016	ESDF	10 775 989	...	...	5 222 749	...	...	5 553 240	...	...
1 VII 2017	ESDF	10 761 447	...	...	5 218 481	...	...	5 542 966	...	...
1 I 2018	ESDF	10 741 165	...	...	5 210 040	...	...	5 531 125	...	...
Guernsey - Guernesey										
31 III 2009	ESDJ	62 274	...	...	30 777	...	...	31 497	...	...
31 III 2010	ESDJ	62 431	...	...	30 695	...	...	31 736	...	...
31 III 2011	ESDJ	62 915	...	...	31 025	...	...	31 890	...	...
31 III 2012	ESDJ	62 904	...	...	30 966	...	...	31 938	...	...
31 III 2013	ESDJ	62 732	...	...	31 081	...	...	31 651	...	...
31 III 2014	ESDJ	62 341	...	...	30 804	...	...	31 537	...	...
31 III 2015	CDJC	62 234	...	...	30 819	...	...	31 415	...	...
31 III 2015	ESDJ	62 234	...	...	30 819	...	...	31 415	...	...
31 III 2016	ESDJ	62 208	...	...	30 824	...	...	31 384	...	...
31 III 2017	ESDJ	62 065	...	...	30 731	...	...	31 334	...	...
31 III 2018	ESDJ	62 307	...	...	30 858	...	...	31 449	...	...
Holy See - Saint-Siège[147]										
1 VII 2009	CDFC	466[148]	...	...	320	...	...	146	...	...
Hungary - Hongrie										
1 VII 2009	ESDJ	10 022 650	6 861 432	68.5	4 759 975	3 215 749	67.6	5 262 675	3 645 683	69.3
1 VII 2010	ESDJ	10 000 023	6 953 071	69.5	4 750 401	3 260 344	68.6	5 249 623	3 692 727	70.3
1 VII 2011	ESDJ	9 971 727	6 945 873	69.7	4 737 813	3 256 796	68.7	5 233 914	3 689 077	70.5
1 X 2011	CDFC	9 937 628	6 903 858	69.5	4 718 479	3 241 911	68.7	5 219 149	3 661 947	70.2
1 VII 2012	ESDJ	9 920 362	6 877 231	69.3	4 720 310	3 234 447	68.5	5 200 052	3 642 785	70.1
1 VII 2013	ESDJ	9 893 082	6 864 757	69.4	4 709 672	3 229 480	68.6	5 183 410	3 635 277	70.1
1 VII 2014[149]	ESDJ	9 866 468	6 950 391	70.4	4 699 585	3 272 050	69.6	5 166 883	3 678 342	71.2
1 VII 2015[149]	ESDJ	9 843 028	6 937 836	70.5	4 692 149	3 267 756	69.6	5 150 879	3 670 081	71.3
1 VII 2016[149]	ESDJ	9 814 023	6 916 274	70.5	4 681 905	3 259 506	69.6	5 132 118	3 656 768	71.3
1 VII 2017[149]	ESDJ	9 787 966	6 896 039	70.5	4 673 447	3 252 609	69.6	5 114 520	3 643 431	71.2
1 I 2018[149]	ESDJ	9 778 371	...	...	4 671 602	...	...	5 106 769	...	...
Iceland - Islande[150]										
1 VII 2009	ESDJ	319 246	298 890	93.6	161 548	150 604	93.2	157 698	148 286	94.0
1 VII 2010	ESDJ	318 006	297 432	93.5	159 838	148 901	93.2	158 168	148 531	93.9
1 VII 2011	ESDJ	319 014	300 395	94.2	160 185	...	...	158 829	...	...
31 XII 2011	CDJC	315 556	295 874	93.8	158 151	147 681	93.4	157 405	148 193	94.1
1 VII 2012	ESDJ	320 716	300 237	93.6	160 901	150 074	93.3	159 815	150 163	94.0
1 VII 2013	ESDJ	323 764	303 136	93.6	162 378	151 471	93.3	161 386	151 665	94.0

Continent, country or area, and date / Continent, pays ou zone et date	Code[a]	Both sexes - Les deux sexes			Male - Masculin			Female - Féminin		
		Total	Urban - Urbaine		Total	Urban - Urbaine		Total	Urban - Urbaine	
			Number Nombre	Percent P.100		Number Nombre	Percent P.100		Number Nombre	Percent P.100
EUROPE										
Iceland - Islande[150]										
1 VII 2014 .... ESDJ		327 386	306 633	93.7	164 252	153 265	93.3	163 134	153 368	94.0
1 VII 2015 .... ESDJ		330 815	309 868	93.7	166 228	155 146	93.3	164 587	154 723	94.0
1 VII 2016 .... ESDJ		335 439	314 123	93.6	169 152	157 819	93.3	166 288	156 304	94.0
1 VII 2017 .... ESDJ		343 400	321 288	93.6	174 317	162 440	93.2	169 083	158 848	93.9
1 I 2018 .... ESDJ		348 450	...	...	177 600	...	...	170 850	...	...
Ireland - Irlande										
1 VII 2009 .... ESDF		4 458 942	...	...	2 215 646	...	...	2 243 297	...	...
1 VII 2010 .... ESDF		4 560 155	...	...	2 265 200	...	...	2 294 955	...	...
10 IV 2011 .... CDFC		4 588 252	2 846 882	62.0	2 272 699	1 389 160	61.1	2 315 553	1 457 722	63.0
1 VII 2011 .... ESDF		4 580 084	...	...	2 271 713	...	...	2 308 372	...	...
1 VII 2012 .... ESDF		4 599 533	...	...	2 278 731	...	...	2 320 803	...	...
1 VII 2013 .... ESDF		4 623 816	...	...	2 289 656	...	...	2 334 160	...	...
1 VII 2014 .... ESDF		4 657 740	...	...	2 304 596	...	...	2 353 144	...	...
1 VII 2015 .... ESDF		4 701 957	...	...	2 326 242	...	...	2 375 715	...	...
24 IV 2016 .... CDJC		4 761 865	...	...	2 354 428	...	...	2 407 437	...	...
1 VII 2016 .... ESDF		4 755 335	...	...	2 353 530	...	...	2 401 805	...	...
1 VII 2017 .... ESDF		4 807 388	...	...	2 380 071	...	...	2 427 317	...	...
1 I 2018[149] .... ESDF		4 830 392	...	...	2 392 223	...	...	2 438 169	...	...
Isle of Man - Île de Man										
30 IV 2009 .... ESDJ		82 371	...	...	40 849	...	...	41 522	...	...
30 IV 2010 .... ESDJ		82 691	...	...	41 053	...	...	41 638	...	...
27 III 2011 .... CDJC		84 497	...	...	41 971	...	...	42 526	...	...
30 IV 2012 .... ESDJ		85 047	...	...	42 273	...	...	42 775	...	...
30 IV 2013 .... ESDJ		85 682	...	...	42 622	...	...	43 060	...	...
30 IV 2014 .... ESDJ		86 322	...	...	42 971	...	...	43 352	...	...
30 IV 2015 .... ESDJ		86 963	...	...	43 319	...	...	43 644	...	...
24 IV 2016 .... CDJC		83 314	...	...	41 269	...	...	42 045	...	...
30 IV 2016 .... ESDJ		85 619	...	...	42 665	...	...	42 954	...	...
Italy - Italie										
1 VII 2009 .... ESDJ		59 095 365	...	...	28 609 696	...	...	30 485 669	...	...
1 VII 2010 .... ESDJ		59 277 417	...	...	28 682 321	...	...	30 595 096	...	...
1 VII 2011 .... ESDJ		59 379 449	...	...	28 720 928	...	...	30 658 521	...	...
9 X 2011 .... CDJC		59 433 744	...	...	28 745 507	...	...	30 688 237	...	...
1 VII 2012 .... ESDJ		59 539 717	...	...	28 808 098	...	...	30 731 619	...	...
1 VII 2013 .... ESDJ		60 233 948	...	...	29 187 081	...	...	31 046 867	...	...
1 VII 2014 .... ESDJ		60 789 140	...	...	29 493 077	...	...	31 296 063	...	...
1 VII 2015 .... ESDJ		60 730 582	...	...	29 478 956	...	...	31 251 626	...	...
1 VII 2016 .... ESDJ		60 627 498	...	...	29 451 031	...	...	31 176 467	...	...
1 VII 2017 .... ESDJ		60 536 709	...	...	29 436 674	...	...	31 100 035	...	...
1 I 2018 .... ESDJ		60 483 973	...	...	29 427 607	...	...	31 056 366	...	...
Jersey										
1 I 2010 .... ESDJ		97 108	...	...	47 822	...	...	49 286	...	...
1 I 2011 .... ESDJ		98 105	...	...	48 360	...	...	49 745	...	...
27 III 2011 .... CDJC		97 857	...	...	48 296	...	...	49 561	...	...
1 I 2012 .... ESDJ		98 999	...	...	48 837	...	...	50 162	...	...
1 I 2013 .... ESDJ		100 208	...	...	49 478	...	...	50 730	...	...
1 I 2014 .... ESDJ		101 007	...	...	49 900	...	...	51 107	...	...
1 I 2015 .... ESDJ		102 704	...	...	50 768	...	...	51 936	...	...
1 I 2016 .... ESDJ		104 190	...	...	51 636	...	...	52 554	...	...
1 I 2017 .... ESDJ		105 598	...	...	52 406	...	...	53 192	...	...
1 I 2018 .... ESDJ		106 800	...	...	53 061	...	...	53 739	...	...
Latvia - Lettonie										
1 VII 2009 .... ESDJ		2 141 669	1 453 570	67.9	981 789	650 486	66.3	1 159 880	803 084	69.2
1 VII 2010 .... ESDJ		2 097 555	1 422 675	67.8	959 435	634 393	66.1	1 138 120	788 282	69.3
1 III 2011 .... CDJC		2 070 371	1 404 251	67.8	946 102	625 150	66.1	1 124 269	779 101	69.3
1 VII 2011 .... ESDJ		2 059 709	1 394 429	67.7	941 375	620 484	65.9	1 118 334	773 945	69.2
1 VII 2012 .... ESDJ		2 034 319	1 374 215	67.6	930 696	611 604	65.7	1 103 623	762 611	69.1
1 VII 2013 .... ESDJ		2 012 647	1 362 004	67.7	921 813	606 624	65.8	1 090 834	755 380	69.2
1 VII 2014 .... ESDJ		1 993 782	1 353 269	67.9	914 126	603 112	66.0	1 079 656	750 157	69.5
1 VII 2015 .... ESDJ		1 977 527	1 344 291	68.0	907 753	599 629	66.1	1 069 774	744 662	69.6
1 VII 2016 .... ESDJ		1 959 537	1 336 137	68.2	899 991	596 307	66.3	1 059 546	739 830	69.8
1 VII 2017 .... ESDJ		1 942 248	...	...	892 662	...	...	1 049 586	...	...
1 I 2018 .... ESDJ		1 934 379	1 324 704	68.5	889 641	591 954	66.5	1 044 738	732 750	70.1

Continent, country or area, and date / Continent, pays ou zone et date	Code[a]	Both sexes - Les deux sexes			Male - Masculin			Female - Féminin		
		Total	Urban - Urbaine		Total	Urban - Urbaine		Total	Urban - Urbaine	
			Number Nombre	Percent P.100		Number Nombre	Percent P.100		Number Nombre	Percent P.100
EUROPE										
Liechtenstein										
1 VII 2009	ESDJ	35 789	...	...	17 716	...	...	18 073	...	...
1 VII 2010	ESDJ	36 010	...	...	17 817	...	...	18 193	...	...
31 XII 2010	CDJC	36 149	...	...	17 886	...	...	18 263	...	...
1 VII 2011	ESDJ	36 281	...	...	17 950	...	...	18 331	...	...
1 VII 2012	ESDJ	36 636	...	...	18 123	...	...	18 513	...	...
1 VII 2013	ESDJ	36 942	...	...	18 314	...	...	18 628	...	...
1 VII 2014	ESDJ	37 215	...	...	18 458	...	...	18 757	...	...
1 VII 2015	ESDJ	37 468	...	...	18 580	...	...	18 888	...	...
1 VII 2016	ESDJ	37 686	...	...	18 673	...	...	19 013	...	...
1 VII 2017	ESDJ	37 877	...	...	18 768	...	...	19 109	...	...
1 VII 2018	ESDJ	38 201	...	...	18 949	...	...	19 252	...	...
Lithuania - Lituanie										
1 VII 2009	ESDJ	3 162 916	2 112 248	66.8	1 461 776	953 885	65.3	1 701 140	1 158 363	68.1
1 VII 2010	ESDJ	3 097 282	2 068 095	66.8	1 428 711	931 128	65.2	1 668 571	1 136 967	68.1
1 III 2011	CDJC	3 043 429	2 031 211	66.7	1 402 604	912 943	65.1	1 640 825	1 118 268	68.2
1 VII 2011	ESDJ	3 028 115	2 021 365	66.8	1 395 367	907 995	65.1	1 632 748	1 113 370	68.2
1 VII 2012	ESDJ	2 987 773	1 997 436	66.9	1 376 201	896 102	65.1	1 611 572	1 101 334	68.3
1 VII 2013	ESDJ	2 957 689	1 981 924	67.0	1 362 443	888 578	65.2	1 595 246	1 093 346	68.5
1 VII 2014[149]	ESDJ	2 932 367	1 968 596	67.1	1 351 126	881 978	65.3	1 581 241	1 086 618	68.7
1 VII 2015[149]	ESDJ	2 904 910	1 952 920	67.2	1 337 932	873 571	65.3	1 566 978	1 079 349	68.9
1 VII 2016[149]	ESDJ	2 868 231	1 927 148	67.2	1 320 897	860 905	65.2	1 547 334	1 066 243	68.9
1 VII 2017[149]	ESDJ	2 828 403	1 897 895	67.1	1 304 740	848 512	65.0	1 523 663	1 049 383	68.9
1 I 2018[149]	ESDJ	2 808 901	...	...	1 297 293	...	...	1 511 608	...	...
Luxembourg										
1 VII 2009	ESDJ	497 782	...	...	247 120	...	...	250 662	...	...
1 VII 2010	ESDJ	506 953	...	...	252 013	...	...	254 941	...	...
1 II 2011	CDJC	512 353	...	...	254 967	...	...	257 386	...	...
1 VII 2011	ESDJ	518 347	...	...	258 220	...	...	260 127	...	...
1 VII 2012	ESDJ	530 946	...	...	265 116	...	...	265 830	...	...
1 VII 2013	ESDJ	543 360	...	...	271 765	...	...	271 595	...	...
1 VII 2014	ESDJ	556 319	...	...	278 544	...	...	277 775	...	...
1 VII 2015	ESDJ	569 604	...	...	285 583	...	...	284 021	...	...
1 VII 2016	ESDJ	583 458	...	...	292 917	...	...	290 541	...	...
1 VII 2017	ESDJ	596 336	...	...	299 611	...	...	296 726	...	...
1 I 2018	ESDJ	602 005	...	...	302 580	...	...	299 425	...	...
Malta - Malte										
1 VII 2009[151]	ESDJ	412 530	...	...	205 432	...	...	207 098	...	...
1 VII 2010[151]	ESDJ	414 562	...	...	206 333	...	...	208 229	...	...
1 VII 2011[151]	ESDJ	416 318	...	...	207 072	...	...	209 246	...	...
20 XI 2011	CDFC	417 432	400 557	96.0	207 625	199 151	95.9	209 807	201 406	96.0
1 VII 2012	ESDJ	420 082	...	...	209 066	...	...	211 016	...	...
1 VII 2013	ESDJ	426 019	...	...	212 482	...	...	213 537	...	...
1 VII 2014	ESDJ	434 606	...	...	217 537	...	...	217 069	...	...
1 VII 2015	ESDJ	445 105	...	...	223 467	...	...	221 638	...	...
1 VII 2016	ESDJ	455 410	...	...	229 058	...	...	226 352	...	...
1 VII 2017[151]	ESDJ	468 056	...	...	236 159	...	...	231 897	...	...
1 I 2018[151]	ESDJ	475 701	...	...	240 599	...	...	235 102	...	...
Monaco[152]										
7 VI 2016	CDJC	37 308	...	...	18 240	...	...	19 068	...	...
Montenegro - Monténégro										
1 VII 2009	ESDJ	631 532	400 928	63.5	311 258	195 088	62.7	320 278	205 840	64.3
1 VII 2010	ESDJ	619 426	...	...	305 674	...	...	313 752	...	...
1 IV 2011	CDJC	620 029	399 264	64.4	306 236	193 691	63.2	313 793	205 573	65.5
1 VII 2011	ESDJ	620 079	...	...	306 242	...	...	313 837	...	...
1 VII 2012	ESDJ	620 601	...	...	306 580	...	...	314 021	...	...
1 VII 2013	ESDJ	621 207	...	...	306 978	...	...	314 229	...	...
1 VII 2014[149]	ESDJ	621 810	...	...	307 339	...	...	314 471	...	...
1 VII 2015[149]	ESDJ	622 159	...	...	307 628	...	...	314 531	...	...
1 VII 2016[149]	ESDJ	622 303	...	...	307 743	...	...	314 560	...	...
1 I 2017[149]	ESDJ	622 387	...	...	307 752	...	...	314 635	...	...
1 I 2018	ESDJ	622 359	...	...	307 741	...	...	314 618	...	...

Continent, country or area, and date / Continent, pays ou zone et date	Code[a]	Both sexes - Les deux sexes			Male - Masculin			Female - Féminin		
		Total	Urban - Urbaine		Total	Urban - Urbaine		Total	Urban - Urbaine	
			Number Nombre	Percent P.100		Number Nombre	Percent P.100		Number Nombre	Percent P.100
EUROPE										
Netherlands - Pays-Bas										
1 VII 2009	ESDJ	16 530 388	10 938 780	66.2	8 179 936	5 383 776	65.8	8 350 452	5 555 004	66.5
1 VII 2010	ESDJ	16 615 394	11 096 288	66.8	8 223 479	5 464 083	66.4	8 391 915	5 632 205	67.1
1 I 2011	CDJC	16 655 799	11 124 721	66.8	8 243 482	5 478 213	66.5	8 412 317	5 646 508	67.1
1 VII 2011	ESDJ	16 693 074	...	...	8 263 177	...	...	8 429 897	...	...
1 VII 2012	ESDJ	16 754 962	...	...	8 295 105	...	...	8 459 857	...	...
1 VII 2013	ESDJ	16 804 432	...	...	8 320 862	...	...	8 483 570	...	...
1 VII 2014	ESDJ	16 865 007	...	...	8 353 621	...	...	8 511 386	...	...
1 VII 2015	ESDJ	16 939 923	...	...	8 394 997	...	...	8 544 926	...	...
1 VII 2016	ESDJ	17 030 314	...	...	8 445 119	...	...	8 585 195	...	...
1 I 2017	ESDJ	17 081 507	...	...	8 475 102	...	...	8 606 405	...	...
1 I 2018	ESDJ	17 181 084	...	...	8 527 041	...	...	8 654 043	...	...
North Macedonia - Macédoine du Nord										
1 VII 2009	ESDJ	2 050 671	...	...	1 027 810	...	...	1 022 861	...	...
1 VII 2010	ESDJ	2 055 004	...	...	1 029 848	...	...	1 025 156	...	...
1 VII 2011	ESDJ	2 058 539	...	...	1 031 403	...	...	1 027 136	...	...
1 VII 2012	ESDJ	2 061 044	...	...	1 032 532	...	...	1 028 512	...	...
1 VII 2013	ESDJ	2 064 032	...	...	1 033 990	...	...	1 030 042	...	...
1 VII 2014	ESDJ	2 067 471	...	...	1 035 680	...	...	1 031 791	...	...
1 VII 2015	ESDJ	2 070 225	...	...	1 037 060	...	...	1 033 166	...	...
1 VII 2016	ESDJ	2 072 490	...	...	1 038 107	...	...	1 034 383	...	...
1 VII 2017	ESDJ	2 074 502	...	...	1 038 948	...	...	1 035 554	...	...
1 I 2018	ESDJ	2 075 301	...	...	1 039 283	...	...	1 036 018	...	...
Norway - Norvège										
1 VII 2009[149]	ESDJ	4 828 726	...	...	2 410 903	...	...	2 417 823	...	...
1 VII 2010[149]	ESDJ	4 889 252	...	...	2 443 801	...	...	2 445 452	...	...
1 VII 2011[149]	ESDJ	4 953 088	...	...	2 479 860	...	...	2 473 228	...	...
19 XI 2011[153]	CDJC	4 979 955	3 951 427[108]	79.3	2 495 777	1 959 424[108]	78.5	2 484 178	1 992 003[108]	80.2
1 VII 2012[149]	ESDJ	5 018 573	...	...	2 517 390	...	...	2 501 183	...	...
1 VII 2013[149]	ESDJ	5 079 623	...	...	2 551 458	...	...	2 528 165	...	...
1 VII 2014[149]	ESDJ	5 137 232	...	...	2 583 105	...	...	2 554 127	...	...
1 VII 2015[149]	ESDJ	5 188 607	...	...	2 611 414	...	...	2 577 194	...	...
1 VII 2016[154]	ESDJ	5 234 519	...	...	2 636 378	...	...	2 598 142	...	...
1 VII 2017[154]	ESDJ	5 276 968	...	...	2 658 751	...	...	2 618 218	...	...
1 I 2018[149]	ESDJ	5 295 619	...	...	2 668 371	...	...	2 627 248	...	...
Poland - Pologne										
1 VII 2009[155]	ESDJ	38 153 389	23 293 906	61.1	18 423 343	11 032 562	59.9	19 730 046	12 261 344	62.1
1 VII 2010[149]	ESDJ	38 042 403	23 156 309	60.9	18 422 344	11 000 170	59.7	19 620 059	12 156 139	62.0
31 III 2011	CDJC	38 044 565	23 116 673	60.8	18 420 389	10 977 424	59.6	19 624 176	12 139 249	61.9
1 VII 2011[149]	ESDJ	38 051 032	23 111 377	60.7	18 422 837	10 973 937	59.6	19 628 195	12 137 440	61.8
1 VII 2012[149]	ESDJ	38 059 134	23 066 408	60.6	18 424 160	10 948 639	59.4	19 634 974	12 117 769	61.7
1 VII 2013[149]	ESDJ	38 031 632	23 000 324	60.5	18 411 126	10 915 023	59.3	19 620 506	12 085 301	61.6
1 VII 2014[149]	ESDJ	38 006 154	22 951 357	60.4	18 397 470	10 888 729	59.2	19 608 684	12 062 628	61.5
1 VII 2015[149]	ESDJ	37 981 588	22 916 634	60.3	18 384 771	10 869 587	59.1	19 596 817	12 047 047	61.5
1 VII 2016[149]	ESDJ	37 956 779	22 872 493	60.3	18 370 677	10 846 647	59.0	19 586 102	12 025 846	61.4
1 VII 2017[149]	ESDJ	37 962 318	22 859 045	60.2	18 373 411	10 839 076	59.0	19 588 907	12 019 969	61.4
1 I 2018[149]	ESDJ	37 976 687	...	...	18 380 299	...	...	19 596 388	...	...
Portugal										
1 VII 2009	ESDJ	10 568 247	...	...	5 064 992	...	...	5 503 255	...	...
1 VII 2010	ESDJ	10 573 100	...	...	5 058 644	...	...	5 514 456	...	...
21 III 2011	CDFC	10 282 306	6 286 712	61.1	4 868 755	2 949 862	60.6	5 413 551	3 336 850	61.6
1 VII 2011	ESDJ	10 557 560	...	...	5 041 990	...	...	5 515 570	...	...
1 VII 2012	ESDJ	10 514 844	...	...	5 013 067	...	...	5 501 777	...	...
1 VII 2013	ESDJ	10 457 295	...	...	4 976 859	...	...	5 480 437	...	...
1 VII 2014	ESDJ	10 401 062	...	...	4 940 843	...	...	5 460 219	...	...
1 VII 2015	ESDJ	10 358 076	...	...	4 912 588	...	...	5 445 489	...	...
1 VII 2016	ESDJ	10 325 452	...	...	4 891 983	...	...	5 433 469	...	...
1 VII 2017	ESDJ	10 300 300	...	...	4 875 074	...	...	5 425 226	...	...
1 I 2018	ESDJ	10 291 027	...	...	4 867 692	...	...	5 423 335	...	...
Republic of Moldova - République de Moldova										
1 VII 2009[156]	ESDJ	3 565 604	1 476 390	41.4	1 714 209	694 134	40.5	1 851 395	782 257	42.3
1 VII 2010[156]	ESDJ	3 562 045	1 479 196	41.5	1 712 783	695 603	40.6	1 849 262	783 593	42.4
1 VII 2011[156]	ESDJ	3 559 986	1 483 731	41.7	1 711 916	697 492	40.7	1 848 070	786 239	42.5

Continent, country or area, and date / Continent, pays ou zone et date	Code[a]	Both sexes - Les deux sexes			Male - Masculin			Female - Féminin		
		Total	Urban - Urbaine		Total	Urban - Urbaine		Total	Urban - Urbaine	
			Number Nombre	Percent P.100		Number Nombre	Percent P.100		Number Nombre	Percent P.100
EUROPE										
Republic of Moldova - République de Moldova										
1 VII 2012[156]	ESDJ	3 559 520	1 488 966	41.8	1 712 036	699 880	40.9	1 847 484	789 086	42.7
12 V 2014[157]	CDFC	2 805 194	951 226	33.9	1 352 353	446 554	33.0	1 452 841	504 672	34.7
1 VII 2014[158]	ESDJ	2 856 950	...	...	1 371 528	...	...	1 485 422	...	...
1 VII 2015[158]	ESDJ	2 834 530	...	...	1 363 262	...	...	1 471 269	...	...
1 VII 2016[158]	ESDJ	2 802 170	...	...	1 346 567	...	...	1 455 603	...	...
1 VII 2017[158]	ESDJ	2 755 158	...	...	1 319 613	...	...	1 435 546	...	...
1 VII 2018[158]	ESDJ	2 706 049	...	...	1 291 242	...	...	1 414 807	...	...
Romania - Roumanie										
1 VII 2009[149]	ESDJ	20 367 437	10 976 558	53.9	9 916 107	5 249 975	52.9	10 451 330	5 726 583	54.8
1 VII 2010[149]	ESDJ	20 246 798	10 922 169	53.9	9 856 669	5 223 471	53.0	10 390 129	5 698 698	54.8
1 VII 2011[149]	ESDJ	20 147 657	10 878 099	54.0	9 805 108	5 198 460	53.0	10 342 549	5 679 639	54.9
20 X 2011	CDFC	20 039 141	10 858 790	54.2	9 736 342	5 185 636	53.3	10 302 799	5 673 154	55.1
1 VII 2012[149]	ESDJ	20 060 182	10 823 218	54.0	9 770 353	5 170 875	52.9	10 289 829	5 652 343	54.9
1 VII 2013[149]	ESDJ	19 988 694	10 772 678	53.9	9 756 310	5 153 631	52.8	10 232 384	5 619 047	54.9
1 VII 2014	ESDF	19 916 451	10 728 929	53.9	9 730 258	5 134 314	52.8	10 186 193	5 594 615	54.9
1 VII 2015	ESDF	19 822 250	10 671 868	53.8	9 681 656	5 099 405	52.7	10 140 594	5 572 463	55.0
1 VII 2016	ESDF	19 706 529	10 585 664	53.7	9 628 271	5 053 625	52.5	10 078 258	5 532 039	54.9
1 VII 2017	ESDF	19 591 668	10 519 506	53.7	9 579 992	5 021 154	52.4	10 011 676	5 498 352	54.9
1 I 2018	ESDF	19 530 631	...	...	9 553 249	...	...	9 977 382	...	...
Russian Federation - Fédération de Russie										
1 VII 2009	ESDJ	142 785 349	104 988 448	73.5	65 988 356	47 969 474	72.7	76 796 993	57 018 974	74.2
1 VII 2010	ESDJ	142 849 468	105 241 319	73.7	66 033 070	48 081 267	72.8	76 816 398	57 160 052	74.4
14 X 2010	CDFC	143 436 145	...	...	66 457 074	...	...	76 979 071	...	...
1 VII 2011	ESDJ	142 960 908	105 581 615	73.9	66 113 269	48 243 019	73.0	76 847 639	57 338 596	74.6
1 VII 2012	ESDJ	143 201 730	105 930 122	74.0	66 264 910	48 419 208	73.1	76 936 820	57 510 914	74.8
San Marino - Saint-Marin										
1 VII 2009[60]	ESDF	33 066	...	...	16 088	...	...	16 978	...	...
1 VII 2010[60]	ESDF	33 270	...	...	16 171	...	...	17 099	...	...
7 XI 2010*	CDFC	30 652	...	...	14 791[128]	...	...	15 818[128]	...	...
1 VII 2011[60]	ESDF	33 389	...	...	16 221	...	...	17 169	...	...
1 VII 2012[60]	ESDF	33 518	...	...	16 296	...	...	17 222	...	...
1 VII 2013[60]	ESDF	33 469	...	...	16 280	...	...	17 189	...	...
1 VII 2014[60]	ESDF	33 648	...	...	16 396	...	...	17 252	...	...
1 I 2015[60]	ESDF	33 738	...	...	16 425	...	...	17 313	...	...
1 I 2016[60]	ESDF	34 006	...	...	16 560	...	...	17 446	...	...
1 I 2017[60]	ESDF	34 267	...	...	16 677	...	...	17 590	...	...
1 VII 2018[60]	ESDJ	34 536	34 536	100.0	16 835	16 835	100.0	17 701	17 701	100.0
Serbia - Serbie[159]										
1 VII 2009	ESDJ	7 320 807	4 279 035	58.5	3 560 048	2 039 934	57.3	3 760 759	2 239 101	59.5
1 VII 2010	ESDJ	7 291 436	4 283 985	58.8	3 546 374	2 041 949	57.6	3 745 062	2 242 010	59.9
1 VII 2011[24]	ESDJ	7 236 519	4 275 178	59.1	3 523 911	2 041 228	57.9	3 712 608	2 233 950	60.2
1 X 2011	CDJC	7 186 862	4 271 872	59.4	3 499 176	2 039 105	58.3	3 687 686	2 232 767	60.5
1 VII 2012[24]	ESDJ	7 201 497	4 273 861	59.3	3 506 947	2 039 649	58.2	3 694 550	2 234 212	60.5
1 VII 2013[24]	ESDJ	7 166 552	4 272 061	59.6	3 489 683	2 037 554	58.4	3 676 869	2 234 507	60.8
1 VII 2014[24]	ESDJ	7 131 787	4 270 367	59.9	3 472 746	2 035 772	58.6	3 659 041	2 234 595	61.1
1 VII 2015[24]	ESDJ	7 095 383	4 267 079	60.1	3 455 335	2 033 446	58.8	3 640 048	2 233 633	61.4
1 VII 2016[24]	ESDJ	7 058 322	4 262 256	60.4	3 437 630	2 030 532	59.1	3 620 692	2 231 724	61.6
1 VII 2017[24]	ESDJ	7 020 858	4 256 129	60.6	3 419 815	2 027 177	59.3	3 601 043	2 228 952	61.9
1 I 2018[24]	ESDJ	7 001 444	...	...	3 410 592	...	...	3 590 852	...	...
Slovakia - Slovaquie										
1 VII 2009	ESDJ	5 418 374	2 978 004	55.0	2 633 428	1 430 928	54.3	2 784 946	1 547 076	55.6
1 VII 2010	ESDJ	5 431 024	2 975 976	54.8	2 639 896	1 429 637	54.2	2 791 128	1 546 339	55.4
21 V 2011	CDJC	5 397 036	2 937 735	54.4	2 627 772	1 412 818	53.8	2 769 264	1 524 917	55.1
1 VII 2011	ESDJ	5 398 384	2 938 053	54.4	2 628 463	1 412 966	53.8	2 769 922	1 525 087	55.1
1 VII 2012	ESDJ	5 407 579	2 935 710	54.3	2 633 866	1 411 738	53.6	2 773 714	1 523 972	54.9
1 VII 2013	ESDJ	5 413 393	2 931 444	54.2	2 637 520	1 409 503	53.4	2 775 873	1 521 941	54.8
1 VII 2014	ESDJ	5 418 649	2 925 291	54.0	2 640 694	1 406 300	53.3	2 777 955	1 518 991	54.7
1 VII 2015	ESDJ	5 423 801	2 919 718	53.8	2 644 205	1 403 692	53.1	2 779 596	1 516 027	54.5
1 VII 2016	ESDJ	5 430 798	2 925 475	53.9	2 648 883	1 406 787	53.1	2 781 915	1 518 688	54.6
1 VII 2017	ESDJ	5 439 232	2 921 207	53.7	2 654 099	1 404 749	52.9	2 785 133	1 516 458	54.4
1 I 2018	ESDJ	5 443 120	...	...	2 656 514	...	...	2 786 606	...	...

Continent, country or area, and date / Continent, pays ou zone et date	Code[a]	Both sexes - Les deux sexes			Male - Masculin			Female - Féminin		
		Total	Urban - Urbaine		Total	Urban - Urbaine		Total	Urban - Urbaine	
			Number Nombre	Percent P.100		Number Nombre	Percent P.100		Number Nombre	Percent P.100

EUROPE

Slovenia - Slovénie

1 VII 2009 ....ESDJ		2 042 335	1 024 087	50.1	1 011 767	500 253	49.4	1 030 568	523 834	50.8
1 VII 2010 ....ESDJ		2 049 261	1 024 812	50.0	1 014 716	500 063	49.3	1 034 545	524 749	50.7
1 I 2011 ....CDFC		2 058 051	1 030 172	50.1	1 019 826	503 083	49.3	1 038 225	527 089	50.8
1 VII 2011 ....ESDJ		2 052 496	1 023 650	49.9	1 015 430	498 490	49.1	1 037 066	525 160	50.6
1 VII 2012 ....ESDJ		2 056 262	1 023 236	49.8	1 017 414	498 297	49.0	1 038 848	524 939	50.5
1 VII 2013 ....ESDJ		2 059 114	1 047 560	50.9	1 019 658	513 084	50.3	1 039 456	534 476	51.4
1 VII 2014 ....ESDJ		2 061 623	1 051 087	51.0	1 021 419	514 828	50.4	1 040 204	536 259	51.6
1 I 2015 ....CDJC		2 062 874	1 107 064	53.7	1 022 229	542 636	53.1	1 040 645	564 428	54.2
1 VII 2015 ....ESDJ		2 063 077	1 106 955	53.7	1 022 554	542 847	53.1	1 040 523	564 108	54.2
1 VII 2016 ....ESDJ		2 064 241	1 107 409	53.6	1 023 872	543 571	53.1	1 040 369	563 838	54.2
1 VII 2017 ....ESDJ		2 066 161	1 141 453	55.2	1 025 973	561 337	54.7	1 040 188	580 116	55.8
1 I 2018 ....ESDJ		2 066 880	...	...	1 027 041	...	...	1 039 839	...	...

Spain - Espagne

1 VII 2009 ....ESDJ		46 367 545	...	...	22 934 497	...	...	23 433 048	...	...
1 VII 2010 ....ESDJ		46 562 486	...	...	23 008 587	...	...	23 553 899	...	...
1 VII 2011 ....ESDJ		46 736 255	...	...	23 073 274	...	...	23 662 981	...	...
1 XI 2011 ....CDJC		46 815 915	...	...	23 104 350	...	...	23 711 560	...	...
1 VII 2012 ....ESDJ		46 766 399	...	...	23 055 715	...	...	23 710 684	...	...
1 VII 2013 ....ESDJ		46 593 236	...	...	22 933 751	...	...	23 659 485	...	...
1 VII 2014[150] ....ESDJ		46 480 882	...	...	22 852 004	...	...	23 628 879	...	...
1 VII 2015[150] ....ESDJ		46 447 697	...	...	22 817 983	...	...	23 629 714	...	...
1 VII 2016[150] ....ESDJ		46 450 439	...	...	22 805 443	...	...	23 644 996	...	...
1 VII 2017[150] ....ESDJ		46 532 869	...	...	22 829 748	...	...	23 703 121	...	...
1 I 2018[150] ....ESDJ		46 658 447	...	...	22 881 882	...	...	23 776 565	...	...

Sweden - Suède[60]

1 VII 2009 ....ESDJ		9 298 515	...	...	4 626 362	...	...	4 672 153	...	...
1 VII 2010 ....ESDJ		9 378 126	...	...	4 669 629	...	...	4 708 497	...	...
1 VII 2011 ....ESDJ		9 449 213	...	...	4 708 539	...	...	4 740 674	...	...
31 XII 2011 ....CDJC		9 482 855	...	...	4 726 834	...	...	4 756 021	...	...
1 VII 2012 ....ESDJ		9 519 375	...	...	4 746 370	...	...	4 773 005	...	...
1 VII 2013[150] ....ESDJ		9 600 379	...	...	4 790 131	...	...	4 810 248	...	...
1 VII 2014[150] ....ESDJ		9 696 110	...	...	4 843 299	...	...	4 852 811	...	...
1 VII 2015[150] ....ESDJ		9 799 186	...	...	4 901 603	...	...	4 897 583	...	...
1 VII 2016[160] ....ESDJ		9 923 085	...	...	4 972 157	...	...	4 950 929	...	...
1 VII 2017[160] ....ESDJ		10 057 698	...	...	5 048 005	...	...	5 009 693	...	...
1 I 2018[150] ....ESDJ		10 120 242	...	...	5 082 662	...	...	5 037 580	...	...

Switzerland - Suisse

1 VII 2009 ....ESDJ		7 743 832	5 699 003	73.6	3 808 621	2 786 186	73.2	3 935 211	2 912 817	74.0
1 VII 2010 ....ESDJ		7 824 909	...	...	3 851 028	...	...	3 973 882	...	...
1 VII 2011 ....ESDJ		7 912 398	5 823 816	73.6	3 899 840	2 853 440	73.2	4 012 559	2 970 376	74.0
31 XII 2011 ....CDFC		8 035 391	5 920 706	73.7	3 973 280	2 909 793	73.2	4 062 111	3 010 913	74.1
1 VII 2012 ....ESDJ		7 996 861	5 887 939	73.6	3 945 389	2 887 886	73.2	4 051 473	3 000 053	74.0
1 VII 2013 ....ESDJ		8 089 346	5 958 174	73.7	3 995 308	2 925 500	73.2	4 094 038	3 032 674	74.1
1 VII 2014[161] ....ESDJ		8 188 649	6 033 396[162]	73.7	4 047 986	2 964 948[162]	73.2	4 140 663	3 068 448[162]	74.1
1 VII 2015[161] ....ESDJ		8 282 396	6 997 929	84.5	4 097 676	3 451 374	84.2	4 184 721	3 546 555	84.8
1 VII 2016[161] ....ESDJ		8 373 338	7 078 247	84.5	4 147 454	3 494 909	84.3	4 225 884	3 583 339	84.8
1 VII 2017[163] ....ESDJ		8 451 840	...	...	4 189 936	...	...	4 261 905	...	...
1 I 2018[161] ....ESDJ		8 484 130	7 191 266	84.8	4 206 434	3 554 201	84.5	4 277 696	3 637 065	85.0

Ukraine

1 VII 2009 ....ESDF		46 053 307	31 556 002	68.5	...	...	...	...	...	...
1 VII 2010 ....ESDF		45 870 741	31 483 222	68.6	21 175 816	14 436 554	68.2	24 694 925	17 046 668	69.0
1 VII 2011 ....ESDF		45 706 086	31 411 262	68.7	21 110 638	14 401 999	68.2	24 595 448	17 009 263	69.2
1 VII 2012 ....ESDF		45 593 342	31 379 757	68.8	21 075 702	14 392 490	68.3	24 517 640	16 987 267	69.3
1 I 2013 ....ESDF		45 553 047	31 378 639	68.9	21 068 718	14 397 904	68.3	24 484 329	16 980 735	69.4
1 I 2014 ....ESDF		45 426 249	31 336 623	69.0	21 024 262	14 382 728	68.4	24 401 987	16 953 895	69.5
1 VII 2015[164] ....ESDF		42 844 907	29 629 033	69.2	19 851 984	13 612 229	68.6	22 992 924	16 016 804	69.7
1 VII 2016[164] ....ESDF		42 672 529	29 533 633	69.2	19 780 361	13 569 991	68.6	22 892 169	15 963 642	69.7
1 VII 2017[164] ....ESDF		42 485 473	29 426 654	69.3	19 700 510	13 520 068	68.6	22 784 963	15 906 587	69.8
1 I 2018[165] ....ESDF		42 386 403	29 370 995	69.3	19 657 310	13 492 648	68.6	22 729 093	15 878 347	69.9

Continent, country or area, and date / Continent, pays ou zone et date	Code[a]	Both sexes - Les deux sexes Total	Urban - Urbaine Number Nombre	Urban - Urbaine Percent P.100	Male - Masculin Total	Urban - Urbaine Number Nombre	Urban - Urbaine Percent P.100	Female - Féminin Total	Urban - Urbaine Number Nombre	Urban - Urbaine Percent P.100
EUROPE										
United Kingdom of Great Britain and Northern Ireland - Royaume-Uni de Grande-Bretagne et d'Irlande du Nord[166]										
1 VII 2009	ESDJ	62 260 486	...	...	30 532 211	...	...	31 728 275	...	...
1 VII 2010	ESDJ	62 759 456	...	...	30 805 490	...	...	31 953 966	...	...
27 III 2011	CDFC	63 379 787	51 399 714	81.1	31 126 054	25 214 631	81.0	32 253 733	26 185 083	81.2
1 VII 2011	ESDJ	63 285 145	...	...	31 097 259	...	...	32 187 886	...	...
1 VII 2012	ESDJ	63 705 030	...	...	31 315 222	...	...	32 389 808	...	...
1 VII 2013[149]	ESDJ	64 105 654	...	...	31 533 021	...	...	32 572 633	...	...
1 VII 2014[149]	ESDJ	64 596 752	...	...	31 793 752	...	...	32 803 000	...	...
1 VII 2015[149]	ESDJ	65 110 034	...	...	32 074 445	...	...	33 035 589	...	...
1 VII 2016[149]	ESDJ	65 648 054	...	...	32 377 674	...	...	33 270 380	...	...
1 VII 2017[154]	ESDJ	66 041 075	...	...	32 588 011	...	...	33 453 064	...	...
1 I 2018[149]	ESDJ	66 273 576	...	...	32 709 956	...	...	33 563 620	...	...
OCEANIA - OCÉANIE										
American Samoa - Samoas américaines[70]										
1 IV 2010	CDJC	55 519	...	...	28 164	...	...	27 355	...	...
1 VII 2016	ESDJ	60 200	...	...	29 597	...	...	30 603	...	...
Australia - Australie										
1 VII 2009[167]	ESDJ	21 691 653	18 574 681	85.6	10 800 797	9 201 882	85.2	10 890 856	9 372 799	86.1
1 VII 2010[167]	ESDJ	22 031 750	18 886 173	85.7	10 967 831	9 354 529	85.3	11 063 919	9 531 644	86.2
1 VII 2011[167]	ESDJ	22 340 024	19 172 952	85.8	11 118 234	9 494 673	85.4	11 221 790	9 678 279	86.2
9 VIII 2011[168]	CDFC	21 727 158[169]	19 312 642	88.9	10 737 148[169]	9 471 918	88.2	10 990 010[169]	9 840 724	89.5
1 VII 2012[167]	ESDJ	22 733 465	19 536 489	85.9	11 312 979	9 675 582	85.5	11 420 486	9 860 907	86.3
1 VII 2013[167]	ESDJ	23 128 129	19 903 669	86.1	11 506 165	9 856 019	85.7	11 621 964	10 047 650	86.5
1 VII 2014[167]	ESDJ	23 475 686	20 235 122	86.2	11 667 886	10 012 749	85.8	11 807 800	10 222 373	86.6
1 VII 2015[167]	ESDJ	23 815 995	20 565 241	86.4	11 827 652	10 170 404	86.0	11 988 343	10 394 837	86.7
1 VII 2016[167]	ESDJ	24 190 907	20 924 730	86.5	12 003 039	10 341 382	86.2	12 187 868	10 583 348	86.8
9 VIII 2016[168]	CDFC	23 717 421[169]	21 806 740	91.9	11 686 665[169]	10 676 368	91.4	12 030 751[169]	11 130 367	92.5
1 VII 2017[167]	ESDJ	24 597 528	21 314 066	86.7	12 201 837	10 531 804	86.3	12 395 691	10 782 262	87.0
1 VII 2018[167]	ESDJ	24 992 860	...	...	12 397 401	...	...	12 595 459	...	...
Cook Islands - Îles Cook[170]										
1 XII 2011	CDFC	17 794	...	...	8 815	...	...	8 979	...	...
1 XII 2016*	CDFC	17 459	...	...	8 597	...	...	8 862	...	...
Fiji - Fidji										
1 VII 2010	ESDF	857 000	446 000	52.0	...	...	...	...	...	...
17 IX 2017	CDFC	884 887	494 252	55.9	448 595	245 928	54.8	436 292	248 324	56.9
French Polynesia - Polynésie française										
1 I 2009	ESDF	264 000	...	...	135 200	...	...	128 800	...	...
1 I 2011	ESDF	269 989	...	...	138 127	...	...	131 862	...	...
22 VIII 2012	CDFC	268 207	...	...	136 996	...	...	131 211	...	...
1 I 2015	ESDF	271 796	...	...	138 447	...	...	133 349	...	...
Guam										
1 VII 2009[70]	ESDJ	159 323	...	...	81 010	...	...	78 313	...	...
1 IV 2010	CDJC	159 358	149 918	94.1	81 552	...	...	77 806	...	...
1 VII 2011[70]	ESDJ	159 600	...	...	81 053	...	...	78 547	...	...
1 VII 2012[70]	ESDJ	159 914	...	...	81 165	...	...	78 749	...	...
1 VII 2013[70]	ESDJ	160 378	...	...	81 354	...	...	79 024	...	...
1 VII 2014[70]	ESDJ	161 001	...	...	81 625	...	...	79 376	...	...
1 VII 2015[70]	ESDJ	161 785	...	...	81 978	...	...	79 807	...	...
1 VII 2016[70]	ESDJ	162 742	...	...	82 420	...	...	80 322	...	...
1 VII 2017[70]	ESDJ	163 875	...	...	82 951	...	...	80 924	...	...
1 VII 2018[70]	ESDJ	167 772	...	...	86 329	...	...	81 443	...	...
Kiribati										
10 X 2010	CDFC	103 058	...	...	50 796	...	...	52 262	...	...
7 XI 2015	CDFC	110 136	56 388	51.2	54 096	27 159	50.2	56 040	29 229	52.2

6. Total and urban population by sex: 2009 - 2018
Population totale et population urbaine selon le sexe : 2009 - 2018 (continued - suite)

Continent, country or area, and date / Continent, pays ou zone et date	Code[a]	Both sexes - Les deux sexes			Male - Masculin			Female - Féminin		
		Total	Urban - Urbaine		Total	Urban - Urbaine		Total	Urban - Urbaine	
			Number Nombre	Percent P.100		Number Nombre	Percent P.100		Number Nombre	Percent P.100
OCEANIA - OCÉANIE										
Marshall Islands - Îles Marshall										
1 VII 2009[171]	ESDF	53 763	...	...	27 567	...	...	26 196	...	...
1 VII 2010[171]	ESDF	54 305	...	...	27 843	...	...	26 462	...	...
3 IV 2011	CDFC	53 158	39 205	73.8	27 243	19 927	73.1	25 915	19 278	74.4
Micronesia (Federated States of) - Micronésie (États fédérés de)										
1 VII 2009[3]	ESDJ	107 973	...	...	54 275	...	...	53 698	...	...
1 IV 2010	CDJC	102 843	22 924	22.3	52 193	...	...	50 650	...	...
1 VII 2010[3]	ESDJ	107 839	...	...	54 158	...	...	53 681	...	...
1 VII 2011[172]	ESDJ	103 022	...	...	52 284	...	...	50 738	...	...
1 VII 2012[172]	ESDJ	103 202	...	...	52 375	...	...	50 827	...	...
1 VII 2013[172]	ESDJ	103 382	...	...	52 467	...	...	50 915	...	...
1 VII 2014[172]	ESDJ	103 562	...	...	52 558	...	...	51 004	...	...
1 VII 2015[172]	ESDJ	103 743	...	...	52 650	...	...	51 093	...	...
1 VII 2016[172]	ESDJ	103 923	...	...	52 741	...	...	51 182	...	...
1 VII 2017[172]	ESDJ	104 104	...	...	52 833	...	...	51 271	...	...
1 VII 2018[172]	ESDJ	104 286	...	...	52 925	...	...	51 361	...	...
Nauru										
31 X 2011	CDFC	10 084	...	...	5 105	...	...	4 979	...	...
1 VII 2012[3]	ESDF	10 376	...	...	5 126	...	...	5 250	...	...
1 VII 2015[3]	ESDF	11 288	...	...	5 701	...	...	5 587	...	...
1 VII 2016	ESDF	11 014	...	...	5 467	...	...	5 547	...	...
New Caledonia - Nouvelle-Calédonie										
26 VIII 2014	CDFC	268 767	...	...	135 542	...	...	133 225	...	...
1 I 2016	ESDF	274 579	...	...	138 197	...	...	136 382	...	...
1 I 2017	ESDF	278 495	...	...	140 000	...	...	138 495	...	...
New Zealand - Nouvelle-Zélande										
1 VII 2009[91]	ESDJ	4 302 600	3 703 800[173]	86.1	2 104 700	1 797 800[173]	85.4	2 197 900	1 906 000[173]	86.7
1 VII 2010[91]	ESDJ	4 350 700	3 743 300[173]	86.0	2 127 700	1 816 700[173]	85.4	2 222 900	1 926 600[173]	86.7
1 VII 2011[91]	ESDJ	4 384 000	3 765 400[173]	85.9	2 143 600	1 826 900[173]	85.2	2 240 400	1 938 500[173]	86.5
1 VII 2012[91]	ESDJ	4 408 100	3 784 600[173]	85.9	2 155 000	1 836 200[173]	85.2	2 253 100	1 948 500[173]	86.5
5 III 2013[174]	CDFC	4 353 198	3 732 537	85.7	2 119 464	1 801 341	85.0	2 233 734	1 931 199	86.5
1 VII 2013[91]	ESDJ	4 442 100	3 818 300[173]	86.0	2 172 200	1 853 100[173]	85.3	2 269 900	1 965 200[173]	86.6
1 VII 2014[91]	ESDJ	4 509 700	3 884 000[173]	86.1	2 209 600	1 889 100[173]	85.5	2 300 200	1 995 000[173]	86.7
1 VII 2015[91]	ESDJ	4 595 700	3 959 200[173]	86.2	2 257 200	1 931 800[173]	85.6	2 338 500	2 027 400[173]	86.7
1 VII 2016[91]	ESDJ	4 693 200	4 056 200[173]	86.4	2 309 100	1 983 600[173]	85.9	2 384 100	2 072 600[173]	86.9
1 VII 2017[91]	ESDJ	4 793 900	4 144 300[173]	86.4	2 361 100	2 029 700[173]	86.0	2 432 800	2 114 600[173]	86.9
1 VII 2018[175]	ESDJ	4 885 500	4 223 700	86.5	2 408 900	2 071 400	86.0	2 476 600	2 152 300	86.9
Niue - Nioué										
1 VII 2010	ESDJ	1 496	...	...	754	...	...	740	...	...
1 VII 2011	ESDJ	1 460	...	...	738	...	...	722	...	...
11 IX 2011	CDFC	1 611	...	...	802	...	...	809	...	...
1 VII 2012[176]	ESDJ	1 482	...	...	752	...	...	730	...	...
1 VII 2013[176]	ESDJ	1 503	...	...	767	...	...	736	...	...
1 VII 2014[176]	ESDJ	1 515	...	...	781	...	...	737	...	...
1 VII 2015[176]	ESDJ	1 541	...	...	797	...	...	744	...	...
1 VII 2016[176]	ESDJ	1 567	...	...	812	...	...	755	...	...
Norfolk Island - Île Norfolk										
9 VIII 2011	CDFC	2 302	...	...	1 082	...	...	1 220	...	...
Northern Mariana Islands - Îles Mariannes septentrionales										
1 VII 2009	ESDF	51 484	...	...	24 738	...	...	26 746	...	...
1 IV 2010	CDFC	53 883	...	...	27 746	...	...	26 137	...	...
1 VII 2010	ESDF	48 317	...	...	23 231	...	...	25 086	...	...
1 VII 2011	ESDF	46 050	...	...	22 153	...	...	23 897	...	...
Palau - Palaos										
1 XII 2012	CDJC	17 501	14 202	81.1	9 217	7 506	81.4	8 284	6 696	80.8
13 IV 2015	CDJC	17 661	14 209	80.5	9 433	7 620	80.8	8 228	6 589	80.1

6. Total and urban population by sex: 2009 - 2018
Population totale et population urbaine selon le sexe : 2009 - 2018 (continued - suite)

Continent, country or area, and date / Continent, pays ou zone et date	Code[a]	Both sexes - Les deux sexes Total	Urban - Urbaine Number Nombre	Urban - Urbaine Percent P.100	Male - Masculin Total	Urban - Urbaine Number Nombre	Urban - Urbaine Percent P.100	Female - Féminin Total	Urban - Urbaine Number Nombre	Urban - Urbaine Percent P.100
OCEANIA - OCÉANIE										
Papua New Guinea - Papouasie-Nouvelle-Guinée										
10 VII 2011 ....CDFC		7 275 324	...	...	3 772 864	...	...	3 502 460	...	...
1 VII 2016[177] ....ESDF		8 151 300	...	...	4 205 000	...	...	3 946 300	...	...
Pitcairn										
10 VIII 2012 ....CDJC		48	...	...	22	...	...	26		
31 XII 2013 ....CDJC		49	...	...	23	...	...	26		
Samoa										
1 VII 2009 ....ESDF		184 988	37 124	20.1	95 665	18 739	19.6	89 324	18 385	20.6
1 VII 2010 ....ESDF		186 404	36 930	19.8	96 327	18 612	19.3	90 077	18 318	20.3
1 VII 2011 ....ESDF		184 864	38 568	20.9	95 814	19 556	20.4	89 050	19 012	21.3
7 XI 2011 ....CDFC		187 820	36 735	19.6	96 990	18 485	19.1	90 830	18 250	20.1
1 VII 2012[178] ....ESDF		189 236	36 866	19.5	97 653	18 540	19.0	91 583	18 326	20.0
1 VII 2013[178] ....ESDF		190 652	36 997	19.4	98 315	18 595	18.9	92 336	18 402	19.9
1 VII 2014[178] ....ESDF		192 067	37 129	19.3	98 978	18 650	18.8	93 090	18 479	19.9
1 VII 2015[178] ....ESDF		193 483	37 260	19.3	99 640	18 705	18.8	93 843	18 555	19.8
7 XI 2016 ....CDFC		195 979	37 391	19.1	100 892	18 760	18.6	95 087	18 631	19.6
1 VII 2017[179] ....ESDF		197 611	37 522	19.0	101 672	18 815	18.5	95 938	18 707	19.5
1 VII 2018[179] ....ESDF		199 243	37 653	18.9	102 453	18 870	18.4	96 790	18 783	19.4
Solomon Islands - Îles Salomon										
1 VII 2009[3] ....ESDF		518 321	...	...	267 704	...	...	250 617	...	...
22 XI 2009[180] ....CDFC		515 870	102 030	19.8	264 455	53 596	20.3	251 415	48 434	19.3
1 VII 2010[181] ....ESDF		555 447	...	...	285 040	...	...	270 408	...	...
1 VII 2011[181] ....ESDF		569 600	...	...	292 105	...	...	277 495	...	...
1 VII 2012[181] ....ESDF		583 672	...	...	299 131	...	...	284 541	...	...
1 VII 2013[181] ....ESDF		597 653	...	...	306 112	...	...	291 541	...	...
1 VII 2014[181] ....ESDF		611 538	...	...	313 044	...	...	298 494	...	...
1 VII 2015[181] ....ESDF		625 374	...	...	319 954	...	...	305 420	...	...
1 VII 2016[181] ....ESDF		639 157	...	...	326 837	...	...	312 321	...	...
1 VII 2017[181] ....ESDF		652 886	...	...	333 693	...	...	319 193	...	...
1 VII 2018[181] ....ESDF		666 557	...	...	340 521	...	...	326 036	...	...
Tokelau - Tokélaou										
18 X 2011 ....CDFC		1 205	...	...	600	...	...	605	...	...
1 XII 2013 ....ESDF		1 383	...	...	683	...	...	700	...	...
18 X 2016 ....CDFC		1 285	...	...	652	...	...	633	...	...
Tonga										
30 XI 2011 ....CDJC		103 252	24 229	23.5	51 979	12 156	23.4	51 273	12 073	23.5
30 XI 2016 ....CDJC		100 651	23 221	23.1	50 255	...	...	50 396	...	...
Tuvalu										
1 VII 2011 ....ESDF		11 206	...	...	5 582	...	...	5 625	...	...
1 VII 2013 ....ESDF		10 730	...	...	5 600	...	...	5 400	...	...
1 VII 2016 ....ESDF		11 153	...	...	5 100[177]	...	...	5 000[177]	...	...
Vanuatu										
16 XI 2009 ....CDFC		234 023	57 195	24.4	119 091	29 618	24.9	114 932	27 577	24.0
1 VII 2010 ....ESDF		239 374	59 199	24.7	121 726	...	...	117 648	...	...
1 VII 2011 ....ESDF		244 847	61 277	25.0	124 420	...	...	120 427	...	...
1 VII 2012 ....ESDF		250 445	63 432	25.3	127 173	...	...	123 273	...	...
1 VII 2013 ....ESDF		264 652	...	...	135 170	...	...	129 483	...	...
1 VII 2014 ....ESDF		271 087	...	...	138 474	...	...	132 613	...	...
7 XI 2016 ....CDFC		272 459	67 749	24.9	138 265	34 506	25.0	134 194	33 243	24.8
Wallis and Futuna Islands - Îles Wallis et Futuna										
22 VII 2013 ....CDFC		12 197	...	...	5 927	...	...	6 270	...	...
1 VII 2016[177] ....ESDF		11 800	...	...	5 700	...	...	6 100	...	...

FOOTNOTES - NOTES

Italics: estimates which are less reliable. - Italiques : estimations moins sûres.

[*] Provisional. - Données provisoires.

[a] 'Code' indicates the source of data, as follows:
CDFC - Census, de facto, complete tabulation
CDFS - Census, de facto, sample tabulation
CDJC - Census, de jure, complete tabulation
CDJS - Census, de jure, sample tabulation
SSDF - Sample survey, de facto

SSDJ - Sample survey, de jure
ESDF - Estimates, de facto
ESDJ - Estimates, de jure

Le 'Code' indique la source des données, comme suit :
CDFC - Recensement, population de fait, tabulation complète
CDFS - Recensement, population de fait, tabulation par sondage
CDJC - Recensement, population de droit, tabulation complète
CDJS - Recensement, population de droit, tabulation par sondage
SSDF - Enquête par sondage, population de fait
SSDJ - Enquête par sondage, population de droit
ESDF - Estimations, population de fait
ESDJ - Estimations, population de droit

[1] Unrevised data that do not take into account the results of the 2014 population census. - Ces données n'ont pas été revisées et elles ne prennent pas en compte les résultats du recensement de la population de 2014.

[2] Postcensal estimates. - Estimations post censitaires.

[3] Data refer to national projections. - Les données se réfèrent aux projections nationales.

[4] Projections based on the 2013 Population Census. - Projections fondées sur le recensement de la population de 2013.

[5] Data based on the 2011 Census. - Données fondées sur le recensement de 2011.

[6] Source: Population projections and estimates of priority targets for the various health programs and interventions, National Institute of Statistics (2016). - Source : Projections démographiques et estimations des cibles prioritaires des différents programmes et interventions de santé, Institut National de la Statistique (2016).

[7] Estimates based on the 2014 Population Census. - Estimations fondées sur le recensement de la population de 2014.

[8] Projections based on the 2014 Population Census. - Projections fondées sur le recensement de la population de 2014.

[9] Projections based on the 2000 quick population count results and 1995, 2002 and 2010 Eritrea Demographic and Health Surveys. - Projections fondées sur le dénombrement rapide de la population de 2000 et sur les enquêtes érythréennes de la démographie et de la santé de 1995, 2002 et 2010.

[10] Data refer to national projections based on 2007 census. - Les données sont des projections nationales d'après les résultats du recensement de la population de 2007.

[11] Estimates considering also the results of the 2007 Population Census. - Estimations en prennant en considération les résultats du recensement de la population de 2007.

[12] Source: Integrated Household Survey (IHS) 2015/2016. - Source: Enquête intégrée auprès des ménages (IHS) 2015/2016.

[13] Data based on the 2010 Population Census. - Les données sont fondées sur le recensement de la population de 2010.

[14] Intercensal estimates. Population in households only. - Estimations inter-censitaires. Population dans les ménages seulement.

[15] Population in households only. Postcensal estimates. - Population dans les ménages seulement. Estimations post censitaires.

[16] Post-censal estimates based on the 2009 Population Census. - Les estimations post-censitaire fondées sur le recensement de la population de 2009.

[17] Data are projections based on the 2006 Population Census. - Projections fondées sur le recensement de la population de 2006.

[18] Data refer to Libyan nationals only. - Les données se raportent aux nationaux libyens seulement.

[19] Data refer to projections based on the 1993 Population Census. - Les données se réfèrent aux projections basées sur le recensement de la population de 1993.

[20] Projections considering also the results of the 2009 Population Census. - Projections en prennant en considération les résultats du recensement de la population de 2009.

[21] Including nomadic population. - Y compris la population nomade.

[22] Excludes the islands of St. Brandon and Agalega. - Non compris les îles St. Brandon et Agalega.

[23] Based on the results of the 2000 Population Census. - Basé sur les résultats du recencement de la population de 2000.

[24] Based on the results of the 2011 Population Census. - Basé sur les résultats du recencement de la population de 2011.

[25] Data refer to annual average population. - Les données correspondent à la population annuelle moyenne.

[26] Based on the results of the 2004 Population Census. - D'après des résultats du recencement de la population de 2004.

[27] Projections based on the results of national survey on population and health conducted between 2010 and 2011, and especially population and housing census 2014. - Des projections de la population fondées sur les résultats de l'enquête nationale de la population et de la santé réalisée entre 2010 et 2011 et, surtout, du recensement général de la population et de l'habitat de 2014.

[28] Data refer to projections based on the 2011 Population Census. - Les données se réfèrent aux projections basées sur le recensement de la population de 2011.

[29] Projections based on the 2012 Population and Housing Census. - Projections fondées sur le recensement 2012 de la population et des logements.

[30] Data are projections based on the 2008 Population and Housing Census. - Projection basée sur le recensement 2008 de la population et des logements.

[31] Data refer to total resident population, Saint Helenian and other nationalities. - Les données concernent la population résidente totale, originaire de Sainte-Hélène ou possédant une autre nationalité.

[32] Based on the results of a population count. - D'après les résultats d'un comptage de la population.

[33] The population figures are 264, 263 and 262 persons for 2007, 2008 and 2009 respectively. - La population est respectivement égale à 264, 263 et 262 personnes pour les années 2007, 2008 et 2009.

[34] Projections based on the 2012 Population Census. - Projections fondées sur le recensement de la population de 2012.

[35] Intercensal estimates. - Estimations inter-censitaires.

[36] The urban area is reconfigured by extending the urban agglomeration of Lomé to include all the prefecture of Golfe and the new prefecture of Agoènyvé. - L'espace urbaine a été reconstitué par l'extension de l'agglomération de Lomé à toute la préfecture du Golfe et à la nouvelle préfecture d'Agoènyvé.

[37] Data for urban and rural do not add up to the total; reason for discrepancy not ascertained. - La somme des données pour la résidence urbaine et rurale n'est pas égale au total; on ne sait pas comment s'explique la divergence.

[38] Projections based on the 2002 Population Census. - Projections fondées sur le recensement de la population de 2002.

[39] Data have not been adjusted for underenumeration, estimated at 7 per cent. - Les données n'ont pas été ajustées pour compenser les lacunes du dénombrement, estimées à 7 p. 100.

[40] Projections based on the 2010 Population and Housing Census. - Projections fondées sur le recensement 2010 de la population et des logements.

[41] Data refer to projections based on the 2000 Population Census. - Les données se réfèrent aux projections basées sur le recensement de la population de 2000.

[42] Data refers to resident population adjusted for the undercount of 18 per cent and including the institutional population. - Les données concernent la population résidente, y compris la population des institutions, et ont été ajustées pour tenir compte du sous-dénombrement estimé à 18 p. 100.

[43] Bermuda is 100 per cent urban. - 100 pour cent de la population des Bermudes est urbaine.

[44] Bermuda is 100 per cent urban. Data based on the 2010 Population Census. - 100 pour cent de la population des Bermudes est urbaine. Les données sont fondées sur le recensement de la population de 2010.

[45] Bermuda is 100 per cent urban. Data refer to projections based on the 2016 Population Census. - 100 pour cent de la population des Bermudes est urbaine. Les données se réfèrent aux projections basées sur le recensement de la population de 2016.

[46] Adjusted for census net undercoverage (including adjustment for incompletely enumerated Indian reserves). Final intercensal estimates. - Ajusté pour la sous-estimation du recensement (y compris les réservations en Inde incomplètement énumérées). Estimations inter-censitaires definitives.

[47] To ensure confidentiality, the values, including totals are randomly rounded either up or down to a multiple of '5' or '10.' As a result, when these data are summed or grouped, the total value may not match the individual values since totals and sub-totals are independently rounded. Similarly, percentages, which are calculated on rounded data, may not necessarily add up to 100%. - À des fins de confidentialité, les chiffres, y compris les totaux, sont aléatoirement arrondis au multiple de 5 ou de 10 inférieur ou supérieur. Par conséquent, lorsque ces chiffres sont additionnés, le total peut ne pas correspondre à la somme des valeurs individuelles, dans la mesure où les totaux et les totaux partiels sont arrondis indépendamment. De même, la somme des pourcentages, qui sont calculés à partir des données arrondies, peut ne pas correspondre à 100 %.

[48] Adjusted for census net undercoverage (including adjustment for incompletely enumerated Indian reserves). Final postcensal estimates. - Ajusté pour la sous-estimation du recensement (y compris les réservations en Inde incomplètement énumérées). Estimations postcensitaires definitives.

[49] Updated postcensal estimates. Adjusted for census net undercoverage (including adjustment for incompletely enumerated Indian reserves). - Estimations post censitaires mises à jour. Ajusté pour la sous-estimation du recensement (y compris les réservations en Inde incomplètement énumérées).

50 Adjusted for census net undercoverage (including adjustment for incompletely enumerated Indian reserves). Preliminary postcensal estimates. - Ajusté pour la sous-estimation du recensement (y compris les réservations en Inde incomplètement énumérées). Estimations post censitaires préliminaires.

51 Excluding the institutional population. - Non compris la population dans les institutions.

52 The source of data is the national household survey. - La source des données est l'enquête nationale des ménages.

53 Based on the national household surveys 2010-2014 and the 2011 population census. - D'après les données de l'enquête nationale des ménages 2010-2014 et les résultats du recensement de la population de 2011.

54 Definition of urban and rural distribution changed from the year 2010. - La définition des régions urbaines et rurales a changée depuis 2010.

55 Based on the national household survey of 2015. - Basée sur l' enquête nationale auprès des ménages de 2015.

56 Based on the national household survey of 2016. - D'après l'enquête nationale auprès des ménages de 2016.

57 Based on the national household survey of 2017. - D'après l'enquête nationale auprès des ménages de 2017.

58 Based on the national household survey of 2018. - D'après l'enquête nationale auprès des ménages de 2018.

59 Estimates or projections based on the 2007 Population Census. - Estimations ou projections fondées sur le recensement de la population de 2007.

60 Population statistics are compiled from registers. - Les statistiques de la population sont compilées à partir des registres.

61 Excluding data for Saint Barthélémy and Saint Martin. - Non compris les données pour Saint Barthélémy et Saint Martin.

62 Projections produced by l'Institut Haïtien de Statistique et d'Informatique (IHSI) and the Latin American and Caribbean Demographic Centre (CELADE) - Population Division of ECLAC. - Les données sont projections produits par l'Institut Haïtien de Statistique et d'Informatique (IHSI) et le centre démographique de l'Amérique latine et les Caraïbes - Division de la population de la CEPALC.

63 Data refer to projections based on the 2001 Population Census. - Les données se réfèrent aux projections basées sur le recensement de la population de 2001.

64 The figures represent the census counts adjusted for under-coverage. Adjustments are done by applying weights calculated (to 4 decimal places) for each sex and age group to the enumerated population when the tabulations are produced. Minor discrepancies between totals and the sum of the component parts of a table and minor discrepancies between the totals across tables are due to rounding after weights are applied. - Les chiffres représentent le dénombrement résultant du recensement ajusté pour tenir compte du sous-dénombrement. Les ajustements sont effectués en appliquant un coefficient de pondération calculé (à la quatrième décimale) pour chaque sexe et groupe d'âges de la population dénombrée lors de l'établissement des tableaux. Les écarts mineurs entre les totaux et la somme des éléments constitutifs d'un tableau ainsi qu'entre les totaux figurant dans différents tableaux sont dus au fait que les chiffres sont arrondis après la pondération.

65 Data revised by CONAPO (National Population Council). - Données révisées par CONAPO (Conseil national de la population).

66 Including an estimation of 1 334 585 persons corresponding to 448 195 housing units without information of the occupants. - Y compris une estimation de 1 334 585 personnes correspondant aux 448 195 unités d'habitation sans information sur les occupants.

67 Unrevised data. - Les données n'ont pas été révisées.

68 The population projections of CONAPO (National Population Council). - Les projections démographiques de la CONAPO (Conseil national de la population).

69 Estimates based on the 2010 Population Census. - Estimations basées sur le recensement de la population de 2010.

70 Including armed forces stationed in the area. - Y compris les militaires en garnison sur le territoire.

71 Based on the results of the 2010 Population Census. - D'après le résultats du recensement de la population de 2010.

72 Excluding residents of institutions. - À l'exclusion de personnes en établissements de soins.

73 Excluding U.S. Armed Forces overseas and civilian U.S. citizens whose usual place of residence is outside the United States. Intercensal estimates. - Non compris les militaires américains à l'étranger et les civils américains dont le lieu de résidence habituel est en dehors des États-Unis. Estimations inter-censitaires.

74 Postcensal estimates. Excluding U.S. Armed Forces overseas and civilian U.S. citizens whose usual place of residence is outside the United States. - Estimations post censitaires. Non compris les militaires américains à l'étranger et les civils américains dont le lieu de résidence habituel est en dehors des États-Unis.

75 Data include persons in remote areas, military personnel outside the country, merchant seamen at sea, civilian seasonal workers outside the country, and other civilians outside the country, and exclude nomads, foreign military, civilian aliens temporarily in the country, transients on ships and Indian jungle population. Data refer to national projections. - Y compris les personnes vivant dans des régions éloignées, le personel militaire en dehors du pays, les marins marchands, les ouvriers saisonniers en dehors du pays, et autres civils en dehors du pays, et non compris les nomades, les militaires étrangers, les étrangers civils temporairement dans le pays, les transiteurs sur des bateaux et les Indiens de la jungle. Les données se réfèrent aux projections nationales.

76 Data are revised projections taking into consideration also the results of the 2005 census. - Les données sont des projections révisées tenant compte également des résultats du recensement de 2005.

77 Data based on the 2010 Population Census. Excludes nomadic Indian tribes. - Les données sont fondées sur le recensement de la population de 2010. Non compris les tribus d'Indiens nomades.

78 A dispute exists between the governments of Argentina and the United Kingdom of Great Britain and Northern Ireland concerning sovereignty over the Falkland Islands (Malvinas). Excluding military personnel and their families, visitors and transients. - La souveraineté sur les îles Falkland (Malvinas) fait l'objet d'un différend entre le Gouvernement argentin et le Gouvernement du Royaume-Uni de Grande-Bretagne et d'Irlande du Nord. Non compris les militaires et leur familles, ni les visiteurs et transients.

79 Estimates or projections considering also the results of the 2012 Population Census. - Estimations ou projections en prennant en considération les résultats du recensement de la population de 2012.

80 Data have not been adjusted for underenumeration and exclude an estimated population of 1,855,501. - Les données n'ont pas été ajustées pour compenser les lacunes du dénombrement. Les données excluent un nombre de personnes estimé à 1,855,501.

81 Figures for male and female population do not add up to the figure for total population, because they exclude 108 homeless people of unknown sex. - Les chiffres relatifs à la population masculine et féminine ne correspondent pas au chiffre de la population totale, parce que l'on en a exclu 108 personnes sans toit dont le sexe n'est pas connu.

82 For operational purposes, population centers with 2,500 and more inhabitants are considered as urban area and less than 2,500 are considered as rural area. - À des fins opérationnelles, les centres de population comptant 2 500 habitants ou plus sont considérés comme zones urbaines, ceux qui en comptent moins de 2 500 comme zones rurales.

83 Data refer to the settled population based on the 1979 Population Census and the latest household prelisting. The refugees of Afghanistan in Iran, Pakistan, and an estimated 1.5 million nomads, are not included. - Les données se rapportent à la population stationnaire sur la base du recensement de 1979 et du recensement préliminaire des logements le plus récent. Sont exclus les réfugiés d'Afghanistan en Iran et au Pakistan et les nomades estimés à 1,5 million.

84 Data have been adjusted for underenumeration. - Les données ont été ajustées pour compenser les lacunes du dénombrement.

85 Data refer to projected figures based on the Population and Housing Census 2005 (district projection). - Les données se réfèrent aux projections basées sur le recensement de la population et de l'habitat de 2005 (projections locales).

86 Source: 2016 Population and Housing Census Update. - Source : Révision des chiffres du recensement de la population et des logements de 2016.

87 Data based on the 2008 Population Census. Excluding foreign diplomatic personnel and their dependants. - Données fondées sur le recensement de population de 2008. Non compris le personnel diplomatique étranger et les membres de leur famille les accompagnant.

88 Based on the results of the Cambodia Intercensal Population Survey. Data exclude foreign diplomatic personnel and their dependants. - Sur la base de l'enquête intercensitaire de la population de Cambodge. Non compris le personnel diplomatique étranger et les membres de leur famille les accompagnant.

89 For statistical purposes, the data for China do not include those for the Hong Kong Special Administrative Region (Hong Kong SAR), Macao Special Administrative Region (Macao SAR) and Taiwan province of China. - Pour la présentation des statistiques, les données pour la Chine ne comprennent pas la Région Administrative Spéciale de Hong Kong (Hong Kong RAS), la Région Administrative Spéciale de Macao (Macao RAS) et Taïwan province de Chine.

90 Data have been estimated on the basis of the annual National Sample Survey on Population Changes. - Les données ont été estimées sur la base de l'enquête annuelle "National Sample Survey on Population Changes".

91 Because of rounding, totals are not in all cases the sum of the respective components. - Les chiffres étant arrondis, les totaux ne correspondent pas toujours rigoureusement à la somme des composants respectifs.

92 Because of rounding, totals are not in all cases the sum of the respective components. The military personnel are classified as urban population. - Les chiffres étant arrondis, les totaux ne correspondent pas toujours rigoureusement

à la somme des composants respectifs. Le personnel militaire est classé dans la population urbaine.

93 Data are from Communique of the National Bureau of Statistics of the People's Republic of China on Major Figures of the 2010 Population Census (No.1). - Données issues du communiqué du Bureau national de la statistique de la République populaire de Chine sur les chiffres importants du recensement de 2010 (n° 1).

94 Data have been adjusted on the basis of the Population Census of 2010. - Les données ont été ajustées à partir des résultats du recensement de la population de 2010.

95 The military personnel are classified as urban population. - Le personnel militaire est classé dans la population urbaine.

96 Data refer to Hong Kong resident population at the census moment, which covers usual residents and mobile residents. Usual residents refer to two categories of people: (1) Hong Kong permanent residents who had stayed in Hong Kong for at least three months during the six months before or for at least three months during the six months after the census moment, regardless of whether they were in Hong Kong or not at the census moment; and (2) Hong Kong non-permanent residents who were in Hong Kong at the census moment. Mobile Residents, they are Hong Kong permanent residents who had stayed in Hong Kong for at least one month but less than three months during the six months before or for at least one month but less than three months during the six months after the census moment, regardless of whether they were in Hong Kong or not at the census moment. - Les données se rapportent à la population résidente à Hong Kong au moment du recensement. Cette population est composée des résidants habituels et des résidants mobiles. La population résidente est partagée en deux catégories: (1) les résidents permanents qui ont habité à Hong Kong au moins trois mois pendant les six mois précédents ou les six mois suivants le recensement; (2) les habitants non-permanents de Hong Kong qui étaient à Hong Kong au moment du recensement. La population mobile se rapporte aux résidents permanents de Hong Kong qui ont habité à Hong Kong pendant les six mois après le recensement pour une période comprise entre un mois et trois mois, indépendamment du fait qu'ils étaient à Hong Kong au moment du recensement au pays.

97 Data refer to Hong Kong resident population at the census moment, which covers usual residents and mobile residents. Usual residents refer to two categories of people: (1) Hong Kong permanent residents who had stayed in Hong Kong for at least three months during the six months before or for at least three months during the six months after the census moment, regardless of whether they were in Hong Kong or not at the census moment; and (2) Hong Kong non-permanent residents who were in Hong Kong at the census moment. Mobile Residents, they are Hong Kong permanent residents who had stayed in Hong Kong for at least one month but less than three months during the six months before or for at least one month but less than three months during the six months after the census moment, regardless of whether they were in Hong Kong or not at the census moment. Data are estimates from sample enquiry. - Les données se rapportent à la population résidente à Hong Kong au moment du recensement. Cette population est composée des résidants habituels et des résidants mobiles. La population résidente est partagée en deux catégories: (1) les résidents permanents qui ont habité à Hong Kong au moins trois mois pendant les six mois précédents ou les six mois suivants le recensement; (2) les habitants non-permanents de Hong Kong qui étaient à Hong Kong au moment du recensement. La population mobile se rapporte aux résidents permanents de Hong Kong qui ont habité à Hong Kong pendant les six mois après le recensement pour une période comprise entre un mois et trois mois, indépendamment du fait qu'ils étaient à Hong Kong au moment du recensement au pays. Les données sont des chiffres estimatifs dérivés d'une enquête par sondage.

98 Population by-census is conducted between two population censuses, adopting a sampling method to select 29,421 housing units in Macao for enumeration, with the unit of observation being the individuals residing in the selected housing units. - Aux fins du recensement partiel de la population, conduit entre deux recensements, la méthode d'échantillonnage adoptée a permis de sélectionner 29 421 unités d'habitation à Macao, l'unité d'observation étant les personnes qui y résident.

99 Data refer to government controlled areas. - Les données se rapportent aux zones contrôlées par le Gouvernement.

100 Based on the results of the 2014 Population Census. - D'après les résultats du recensement de la population de 2014.

101 Based on the results of the 2014 Population Census. Data refer to annual average population. - D'après les résultats du recensement de la population de 2014. Les données correspondent à la population annuelle moyenne.

102 Includes data for the Indian-held part of Jammu and Kashmir, the final status of which has not yet been determined. - Y compris les données pour la partie du Jammu et du Cachemire occupée par l'Inde dont le statut définitif n'a pas encore été déterminé.

103 Data refer to projections based on the 2001 Population Census. - Les données se réfèrent aux projections basées sur le recensement de la population de 2001.

104 Data are based on the publication: "Indonesia Population Projection 2005-2015" - Les données sont basées sur la publication : << Indonesia Population Projection 2005-2015 >>

105 Data are based on the publication: "Indonesia Population Projection 2010-2035" - Les données sont basées sur la publication : << Indonesia Population Projection 2010-2035 >>

106 Data are based on the publication: "Indonesia Population Projection 2015-2045" - Les données sont basées sur la publication : << Indonesia Population Projection 2015-2045 >>

107 Data refer to the Iranian Year which begins on 21 March and ends on 20 March of the following year. - Les données concernent l'année iranienne, qui commence le 21 mars et se termine le 20 mars de l'année suivante.

108 The total number may include 'Unknown residence', but the categories urban and rural do not. - Le nombre total peut inclure les personnes dont la résidence n'est pas connue, à l'inverse des catégories de population urbaine et rurale.

109 Differences between the total country figures and sum of urban and rural areas are due to the inclusion of unsettled population. - Les différences entre les chiffres pour l'ensemble du pays et la somme des zones urbaines et rurales s'expliquent par l'inclusion de la population non sédentaire.

110 Includes data for East Jerusalem and Israeli residents in certain other territories under occupation by Israeli military forces since June 1967. Data refer to Israeli citizens and permanent residents who are listed in the Population Register. - Y compris les données pour Jérusalem-Est et les résidents israéliens dans certains autres territoires occupés depuis 1967 par les forces armées israéliennes. Les données se rapportent aux citoyens israéliens et aux résidents permanents qui sont répertoriés dans le registre de la population.

111 Excluding diplomatic personnel outside the country and foreign military and civilian personnel and their dependants stationed in the area. - Non compris le personnel diplomatique hors du pays ni les militaires et agents civils étrangers en poste sur le territoire et les membres de leur famille les accompagnant.

112 Estimates based on the complete counts of the 2015 Population Census. - Estimations basées sur le dénombrement complet du recensement de la population de 2015.

113 Estimates based on the complete counts of the 2015 Population Census. Because of rounding, totals are not in all cases the sum of the respective components. - Estimations basées sur le dénombrement complet du recensement de la population de 2015. Les chiffres étant arrondis, les totaux ne correspondent pas toujours rigoureusement à la somme des composants respectifs.

114 Excluding data for Jordanian territory under occupation since June 1967 by Israeli military forces. - Non compris les données pour le territoire jordanien occupé depuis juin 1967 par les forces armées israéliennes.

115 Data refer to resident population. Recalculated population estimates taking into account late registration of births and deaths until May 2017. - Les données concernent la population résidente. Réestimation du nombre d'habitants compte tenu de l'enregistrement tardif des naissances et des décès jusqu'en mai 2017.

116 Data refer to resident population. - Les données concernent la population résidente.

117 Estimates based on the results of 2015 population census. - Estimations fondées sur les résultats du recensement de la population de 2015.

118 Source: Living conditions of household survey, October 2011 to September 2012. - Source: Enquête sur les conditions de vie des ménages, octobre 2011 à septembre 2012.

119 Intercensal Mid-Year Population Estimates based on the adjusted Population and Housing Census of 2000 and 2010. - Les estimations inter-censitaires au milieu de l'année sont fondée sur les résultats ajustées des recensements de la population et de l'habitat de 2000 et 2010.

120 Estimates based on the adjusted results of the Population and Housing Census of 2010. - Les estimations sont fondée sur les résultats ajustées du recensement de la population et de l'habitat de 2010.

121 Data refer to resident population which includes resident Maldivians and resident foreigners. Estimates based on the 2014 Population Census. - Les données concernent la population résidente, qui comprend les Maldiviens et les étrangers. Estimations fondées sur le recensement de la population de 2014.

122 Data refer to resident population which includes resident Maldivians and resident foreigners. - Les données concernent la population résidente, qui comprend les Maldiviens et les étrangers.

123 Data refer to enumerated population. The total for the whole country excludes 1,206,353 persons estimated not to have been counted in parts of States of Rakhine, Kachin and Kayin. - Les données se rapportent à la population dénombrée. L' effectif de la population pour le pays ne comprend pas les personnes qui ne sont pas dénombrées dans certaines régions des États de Rakhine, Kachin et Kayin estimées à un chiffre de 1 206 353 personnes.

124 Data refer to registered population data from Royal Oman Police. - Les données portent sur la population enregistrée par la police royale de l'Oman.

125 Data for the urban and rural population are based on the percentage distribution according to the 2010 census. - Les données de la population urbaine et rurale sont fondées sur la répartition des pourcentages d'après le recensement de 2010.

126 Data for the urban and rural population are based on percentage distribution according to the 2016 survey. - Les données de la population urbaine et rurale sont fondées sur la répartition des pourcentages d'après l'enquête de 2016.

127 Excluding data for the Pakistan-held part of Jammu and Kashmir, the final status of which has not yet been determined. - Non compris les données concernant la partie du Jammu et Cachemire occupée par le Pakistan dont le statut définitif n'a pas été déterminé.

128 Figures for male and female may not add up to the total, since they do not include the category "Unknown". - La somme des chiffres indiqués pour les sexes masculin et féminin peut n'être pas égale au total parce qu'elle n'inclut pas la catégorie " inconnue ".

129 Excluding 2739 Filipinos in Philippine Embassies, Consulates and Missions Abroad. - Excepté 2739 Philippins travaillant dans les ambassades, les consulats et les missions des Philippines à l'étranger.

130 Excluding 2134 Filipinos in Philippine Embassies, Consulates and Missions Abroad. - Excepté 2134 Philippins travaillant dans les ambassades, les consulats et les missions des Philippines à l'étranger.

131 Excluding usual residents not in the country at the time of census. - À l'exclusion des résidents habituels qui ne sont pas dans le pays au moment du recensement.

132 Data exclude residents who have been away from Singapore for a continuous period of 12 months or longer as at the reference date. Data refer to total population, which comprises Singapore residents and non-residents. - Non compris les résidents hors de Singapour pour une période ininterrompue de 12 mois ou plus avant de la date de référence. Les données se rapportent à la population totale composé des résidents de Singapour et les non résidents.

133 Data are based on the latest register-based population estimates for 2010. Data refer to resident population which comprises Singapore citizens and permanent residents. Urban and rural breakdown not applicable as Singapore is a city-state. - Données basées sur les estimations démographiques les plus récentes fondées sur les registres de 2010. Les données se rapportent à la population résidente composé des citoyens de Singapour et des résidents permanents. La ventilation entre zones urbaines et zones rurales ne s'applique pas à Singapour, puisqu'il s'agit d'une ville État.

134 Data for urban include population in refugee camps. - Les données pour la population urbaine comprennent la population dans les camps réfugiés.

135 Including Palestinian refugees. - Y compris les réfugiés de Palestine.

136 Data based on Address Based Population Registration System. - Les données sont basées sur le registre national de la population basé sur l'adresse.

137 Because of rounding, totals are not in all cases the sum of the respective components. Based on a sample taken at the time of census. - Les chiffres étant arrondis, les totaux ne correspondent pas toujours rigoureusement à la somme des composants respectifs. D'après un échantillon obtenu au moment du recensement.

138 The reason for the differences in the urban-rural population from the previous years is the changes in administrative attachment, legal entity and borders, regulated by related laws. - La raison des différences dans la population urbaine-rurale par rapport aux années précédentes est la modification de l'attachement administratif, de l'entité juridique et des frontières, réglementée par des lois connexes.

139 Data include non-national population. - Les données comprennent les non-nationaux.

140 Data are adjusted according to the results of the 2009 census and 2014 intercensus. - Les données ont été ajustées à partir des résultats du recensement de la population de 2009 et des données intercensitaires de 2014.

141 Decrease in population due to revision in administrative registers. - Diminution de la population due à la révision des registres administratifs.

142 Excluding Faeroe Islands and Greenland shown separately, if available. Population statistics are compiled from registers. - Non compris les Iles Féroé et le Groenland, qui font l'objet de rubriques distinctes, si disponible. Les statistiques de la population sont compilées à partir des registres.

143 Population statistics are compiled from registers. Excluding Åland Islands. - Les statistiques de la population sont compilées à partir des registres. Non compris les Îles d'Åland.

144 Excluding diplomatic personnel outside the country and including members of alien armed forces not living in military camps and foreign diplomatic personnel not living in embassies or consulates. - Non compris le personnel diplomatique hors du pays et y compris les militaires étrangers ne vivant pas dans des camps militaires et le personnel diplomatique étranger ne vivant pas dans les ambassades ou les consulats.

145 Data refer to annual average population. Data based on the 2011 Census. - Les données correspondent à la population annuelle moyenne. Données fondées sur le recensement de 2011.

146 Excluding military personnel, visitors and transients. - Non compris les militaires, ni les visiteurs et transients.

147 Data refer to the Vatican City State. - Les données se rapportent à l'Etat de la Cité du Vatican.

148 The population figure is 466 persons. - La population est égale à 466 personnes.

149 Data refer to usually resident population. - Les données concernent la population habituellement résidente.

150 Data refer to registered resident population. - Les données concernent la population enregistrée résidente.

151 Including civilian nationals temporarily outside the country. - Y compris les civils nationaux temporairement hors du pays.

152 Data refer to resident population only. - Pour la population résidante seulement.

153 Including residents temporarily outside the country. Population statistics are compiled from registers. - Y compris les résidents se trouvant temporairement hors du pays. Les statistiques de la population sont compilées à partir des registres.

154 Data refer to usually resident population. Data refer to annual average population. - Les données concernent la population habituellement résidente. Les données correspondent à la population annuelle moyenne.

155 Excluding civilian aliens within the country, but including civilian nationals temporarily outside the country. - Non compris les civils étrangers dans le pays, mais y compris les civils nationaux temporairement hors du pays.

156 Excluding Transnistria and the municipality of Bender. - Les données ne tiennent pas compte de l'information sur la Transnistria et la municipalité de Bender.

157 Tiraspol, Bender, Slobozia, Ribnita, Camenca Yrigoricpol/Grigoriopol are districts from Transnistria where the census was not conducted. - Tiraspol, Bender, Slobozia, Ribnita, Camenca, Yrigoricpol/Grigoriopol sont des districts de la Transnistrie où le recensement n'a pas eu lieu.

158 Data refer to usual resident population based on the 2014 Census. Tiraspol, Bender, Slobozia, Ribnita, Camenca Yrigoricpol/Grigoriopol are districts from Transnistria where the 2014 census was not conducted. Excluding Transnistria and the municipality of Bender. - Les données se rapportent à la population habituellement résidente et sont fondées sur le recensement de 2014. Tiraspol, Bender, Slobozia, Ribnita, Camenca, Yrigoricpol/Grigoriopol sont des districts de la Transnistrie où le recensement n'a pas eu lieu. Les données ne tiennent pas compte de l'information sur la Transnistria et la municipalité de Bender.

159 Excludes data for Kosovo and Metohia. - Sans les données pour le Kosovo et Metohie.

160 Data refer to annual average population. Data refer to registered resident population. - Les données correspondent à la population annuelle moyenne. Les données concernent la population enregistrée résidente.

161 Data refer to legal resident population. - Les données concernent la population légalement résidente.

162 From 2014, urban refers to urban centers and areas under the influence of urban centers. - A partir de 2014, le territoire urbain inclut l'espace des centres urbains ainsi que l'espace sous influence des centres urbains.

163 Data refer to legal resident population. Data refer to annual average population. - Les données concernent la population légalement résidente. Les données correspondent à la population annuelle moyenne.

164 Data refer to annual average population. The Government of Ukraine has informed the United Nations that it is not in a position to provide statistical data concerning the Autonomous Republic of Crimea and the city of Sevastopol. - Les données correspondent à la population annuelle moyenne. Le gouvernement Ukrainien a informé l'ONU qu'il n'est pas en mesure de fournir des données statistiques concernant la République autonome de Crimée et la ville de Sébastopol.

165 The Government of Ukraine has informed the United Nations that it is not in a position to provide statistical data concerning the Autonomous Republic of Crimea and the city of Sevastopol. - Le gouvernement Ukrainien a informé l'ONU qu'il n'est pas en mesure de fournir des données statistiques concernant la République autonome de Crimée et la ville de Sébastopol.

166 Excluding Channel Islands (Guernsey and Jersey) and Isle of Man, shown separately, if available. - Non compris les îles Anglo-Normandes (Guernesey et Jersey) et l'île de Man, qui font l'objet de rubriques distinctes, si disponible.

167 Based on the results of the 2016 Population Census. - Basé sur les résultats du recensement de la population de 2016.

168 These data have been randomly rounded to protect confidentiality. Individual figures may not add up to totals, and values for the same data may vary in different tables. - Ces données ont été arrondies de façon aléatoire afin d'en préserver la confidentialité. La somme de certains chiffres peut ne pas

correspondre aux totaux indiqués et les valeurs des mêmes données peuvent varier d'un tableau à un autre.

[169] Including population in off-shore, migratory and shipping. - Y compris les populations extraterritoriales, les populations nomades et les populations maritimes.

[170] Excluding Niue, shown separately, which is part of Cook Islands, but because of remoteness is administered separately. - Non compris Nioué, qui fait l'objet d'une rubrique distincte et qui fait partie des îles Cook, mais qui, en raison de son éloignement, est administrée séparément.

[171] Projections are prepared by the Secretariat of the Pacific Community based on the 1999 census of population and housing. - Les projections sont préparées par le Secrétariat de la Communauté du Pacifique à partir des résultats du recensement de la population et de l'habitat de 1999.

[172] Based on the 2010 Population and Housing Census and 2013/2014 Household Income and Expenditure Survey. - Données fondées sur les résultat du recensement de la population et de l'habitat de 2010, et ceux de l'enquête auprès des ménages sur des revenus et des dépenses de 2013/2014.

[173] Population estimates by urban/rural residence exclude inland waters and oceanic areas. - Les estimations de la population par lieu de résidence urbaine ou rurale excluent les eaux intérieures et les zones océaniques.

[174] These data have been randomly rounded to protect confidentiality. Individual figures may not add up to totals, and values for the same data may vary in different tables. Data include overseas visitors in New Zealand on census night. - Ces données ont été arrondies de façon aléatoire afin d'en préserver la confidentialité. La somme de certains chiffres peut ne pas correspondre aux totaux indiqués et les valeurs des mêmes données peuvent varier d'un tableau à un autre. Y compris les visiteurs étrangers qui se trouvaient en Nouvelle-Zélande le soir du recensement.

[175] Intercensal estimates. Because of rounding, totals are not in all cases the sum of the respective components. - Estimations inter-censitaires. Les chiffres étant arrondis, les totaux ne correspondent pas toujours rigoureusement à la somme des composants respectifs.

[176] Intercensal estimates. Data refer to usually resident population. - Estimations inter-censitaires. Les données concernent la population habituellement résidente.

[177] Estimates are prepared by the Secretariat of the Pacific Community based on the last population and housing census. - Les estimations sont préparées par le Secrétariat de la Communauté du Pacifique à partir des résultats du dernier recensement de la population et de l'habitat.

[178] Estimates based on the 2011 Population Census. - Estimations basées sur le recensement de la population de 2011.

[179] Estimates based on the 2016 Population Census. - Estimations basées sur le recensement de la population de 2016.

[180] Data have not been adjusted for underenumeration. - Les données n'ont pas été ajustées pour compenser les lacunes du dénombrement.

[181] Projections based on adjusted 2009 census counts. - Projections fondées à partir des comptes rajustés du recensement de 2009.

175

Table 7 - *Demographic Yearbook 2018*

Table 7 presents population by age, sex and urban/rural residence for the latest available year between 2009 and 2018.

Description of variables: Data in this table are either population census figures or estimates, some of which are based on sample surveys. The source of data is indicated by the 'code' explained at the end of the table.

The reference date of the census or estimate appears in the left-most column of the table. In general, the estimates refer to mid-year, i.e. 1 July.

Age is defined as age at last birthday, that is, the difference between the date of birth and the reference date of the age distribution expressed in completed solar years. The age classification used in this table is the following: under 1 year, 1-4 years, 5-year groups through 95-99 years, and 100 years or over.

Statistics are presented for one year, the most recent available. However, if more complete disaggregation is available for an earlier year, both are displayed.

The urban/rural classification of population is that provided by each country or area; it is presumed to be based on the national census definitions of urban population that have been set forth at the end of the technical notes to table 6.

Reliability of data: Estimates which are believed to be less reliable are set in *italics* rather than in roman type.

Limitations: Statistics on population by age and sex are subject to the same qualifications as have been set forth for population statistics in general and age distributions in particular, as discussed in sections 3 and 3.1.3, respectively, of the Technical Notes.

Comparability of population data classified by age and sex is limited by variations in the definition of total population, discussed in detail in section 3 of the Technical Notes, and by the accuracy of the original enumeration. Both factors are more important in relation to certain age groups than to others. For example, under-enumeration is known to be more prevalent among infants and young children than among older persons. Similarly, the exclusion from the total population of certain groups that tend to be of selected ages (such as the armed forces) can markedly affect the age structure and its comparability with that for other countries or areas. Consideration should be given to the implications of these basic limitations in using the data.

In addition to these general qualifications are the special problems of comparability that arise in relation to age statistics in particular. Age distributions of population are known to suffer from certain deficiencies that have their origin in irregularities in age reporting. Although some of the irregularities tend to be obscured or eliminated when data are tabulated in five-year age groups rather than by single years, precision still continues to be affected, though the degree of distortion is not always readily seen.

Another factor limiting comparability is the age classification employed by the various countries or areas. Age may be based on the year of birth rather than the age at last birthday, in other words, calculated using the day, month and year of birth. Distributions based only on the year of birth are footnoted when known.

The absence of data in the unknown age group does not necessarily indicate completely accurate reporting and tabulation of the age item. The unknowns may have been eliminated by assigning ages to them before tabulation, or by proportionately distributing the unknown category across the age groups after tabulation.

As noted in connection with table 5, intercensal estimates of total population are usually revised to accord with the results of a census of population if inexplicable discontinuities appear to exist. Intercensal age-sex distributions, however, are less likely to be revised in this way. When it is known that a total population estimate for a given year has been revised and the corresponding age distribution has not been revised, a note is provided. Distributions of this type should be used with caution when studying trends over a period of years, though their utility for studying age structure for the specified year is probably unimpaired.

The comparability of data by urban/rural residence is affected by the national definitions of urban and rural used in tabulating these data. When known, the definitions of urban used in national population censuses are presented at the end of the technical notes for table 6. As discussed in detail in the technical notes for table 6, these definitions vary considerably from one country or area to another.

Earlier data: Population by age, sex and urban/rural residence has been shown in previous issues of the *Demographic Yearbook*. For more information on specific topics, and years for which data are reported, readers should consult the Historical Index. In addition, population data by single years of age, sex and urban/rural residence, for censuses conducted since 1995, are shown in the *Demographic Yearbook* webpage https://unstats.un.org/unsd/demographic-social/products/dyb/index.cshtml#censusdatasets.

Tableau 7 – *Annuaire démographique 2018*

Le tableau 7 présente les données les plus récentes disponibles pour la période 2009-2018 sur la population selon l'âge, le sexe et le lieu de résidence (zone urbaine ou rurale).

Description des variables : les données de ce tableau proviennent de recensements de la population ou correspondent à des estimations, fondées dans certains cas, sur des enquêtes par sondage. Le 'code' indique comment les données ont été obtenues. Les codes utilisés sont expliqués à la fin du tableau.

La date du recensement ou de l'estimation figure dans la colonne de gauche du tableau. En général, les estimations se rapportent au milieu de l'année (1er juillet).

L'âge désigne l'âge au dernier anniversaire, c'est-à-dire la différence entre la date de naissance et la date de référence de la répartition par âge exprimée en années solaires révolues. La classification par âge utilisée dans ce tableau est la suivante : moins d'un an, 1 à 4 ans, groupes quinquennaux jusqu'à 95-99 ans et 100 ans ou plus.

Les statistiques portent sur une année, qui correspond à celle pour laquelle on dispose des statistiques les plus récentes. Toutefois, si l'on dispose de répartitions plus complètes pour des années antérieures, les statistiques sont alors présentées pour les deux années.

La classification par zones urbaines et rurales de la population est celle qui est communiquée par chaque pays ou zone ; on part du principe qu'elle repose sur les définitions de la population urbaine utilisées pour les recensements de la population nationaux telles qu'elles sont reproduites à la fin des notes techniques du tableau 6.

Fiabilité des données : les estimations considérées comme moins sûres sont indiquées en italique plutôt qu'en caractères romains.

Insuffisance des données : les statistiques de la population selon l'âge et le sexe appellent les mêmes réserves que celles qui ont été formulées aux sections 3 et 3.1.3 des Notes techniques à propos des statistiques de la population en général et des répartitions par âge en particulier.

La comparabilité des statistiques de la population selon l'âge et le sexe pâtit du manque d'uniformité dans la définition de la population totale (voir la section 3 des Notes techniques) et des lacunes des dénombrements. L'influence de ces deux facteurs varie selon les groupes d'âge. Ainsi, le dénombrement des enfants de moins d'un an et des jeunes enfants comporte souvent plus de lacunes que celui des personnes plus âgées. De même, le fait que certains groupes de personnes appartenant souvent à des groupes d'âge déterminés, par exemple les militaires, ne soient pas pris en compte dans la population totale peut influer sensiblement sur la structure par âge et sur la comparabilité des données avec celles d'autres pays ou zones. Il conviendra de tenir compte de ces facteurs fondamentaux lorsque l'on utilisera les données du tableau.

Outre ces difficultés d'ordre général, la comparabilité pose des problèmes particuliers lorsqu'il s'agit des données par âge. On sait que les répartitions de la population selon l'âge présentent certaines imperfections dues à l'inexactitude des déclarations d'âge. Certaines de ces anomalies ont tendance à s'estomper ou à disparaître lorsque l'on classe les données par groupes d'âge quinquennaux et non par années d'âge, mais une certaine imprécision subsiste, même s'il n'est pas toujours facile de voir à quel point il y a distorsion.

Le degré de comparabilité dépend également de la classification par âge employée dans les divers pays ou zones. L'âge retenu peut être défini par date exacte (jour, mois et année) de naissance ou par celle du dernier anniversaire. Lorsqu'elles étaient connues, les répartitions établies seulement d'après l'année de la naissance ont été signalées en note à la fin du tableau.

Si aucun nombre ne figure dans la rangée réservée aux âges inconnus, cela ne signifie pas nécessairement que les déclarations d'âge et l'exploitation des données par âge aient été tout à fait exactes. C'est souvent une indication que l'on a attribué un âge aux personnes d'âge inconnu avant l'exploitation des données ou qu'elles ont été réparties proportionnellement entre les différents groupes après cette opération.

Comme on l'a indiqué à propos du tableau 5, les estimations intercensitaires de la population totale sont d'ordinaire rectifiées d'après les résultats des recensements de population si l'on constate des discontinuités inexplicables. Les données intercensitaires concernant la répartition de la population par âge et par sexe ont toutefois moins de chance d'être rectifiées de cette manière. Lorsque l'on savait qu'une estimation de la population totale pour une année donnée avait été rectifiée sans qu'il en soit de même pour la répartition par âge correspondante, cela a été indiquée dans une note. Les répartitions de ce type doivent être utilisées avec prudence lorsque l'on étudie les tendances sur un certain nombre d'années, quoique leur utilité pour l'étude de la structure par âge de la population pour l'année visée reste probablement entière.

La comparabilité des données selon le lieu de résidence (zone urbaine ou rurale) peut être limitée par les définitions nationales des termes « urbain » et « rural » utilisées pour la mise en tableaux de ces données. Les définitions du terme « urbain » utilisées pour les recensements nationaux de population ont été présentées à la fin des notes techniques du tableau 6 lorsqu'elles étaient connues. Comme on l'a précisé dans les notes techniques relatives au tableau 6, ces définitions varient considérablement d'un pays ou d'une zone à l'autre.

Données publiées antérieurement : des statistiques concernant la population selon l'âge, le sexe et le lieu de résidence (zone urbaine ou rurale) ont été présentées dans des éditions antérieures de l'*Annuaire démographique*. Pour plus de précisions concernant les années et les sujets pour lesquels des données ont été publiées, se reporter à l'index historique. En plus, des statistiques disponibles concernant la « Population selon chaque année d'âge, le sexe et la résidence urbaine/rurale », pour les recensements depuis 1995, ont été présentées dans la page internet suivante de l'*Annuaire démographique* https://unstats.un.org/unsd/demographic-social/products/dyb/index.cshtml#censusdatasets.

Continent, country or area, date, code[a] and age (in years) / Continent, pays ou zone, date, code[a] et âge (en années)	Total			Urban - Urbaine			Rural - Rurale		
	Both sexes Les deux sexes	Male Masculin	Female Féminin	Both sexes Les deux sexes	Male Masculin	Female Féminin	Both sexes Les deux sexes	Male Masculin	Female Féminin
AFRICA - AFRIQUE									
Algeria - Algérie									
1 VII 2017 (ESDJ)									
Total	41 695 626	21 118 894	20 576 732	...	...	...	...	...	...
0	1 021 058	524 107	496 951	...	...	...	...	...	...
1 - 4	3 916 677	2 013 103	1 903 574	...	...	...	...	...	...
5 - 9	4 189 528	2 155 222	2 034 306	...	...	...	...	...	...
10 - 14	3 256 178	1 672 925	1 583 253	...	...	...	...	...	...
15 - 19	2 963 876	1 513 910	1 449 966	...	...	...	...	...	...
20 - 24	3 391 633	1 728 672	1 662 960	...	...	...	...	...	...
25 - 29	3 725 030	1 887 412	1 837 618	...	...	...	...	...	...
30 - 34	3 759 980	1 891 310	1 868 670	...	...	...	...	...	...
35 - 39	3 310 996	1 672 000	1 638 996	...	...	...	...	...	...
40 - 44	2 637 762	1 322 807	1 314 955	...	...	...	...	...	...
45 - 49	2 270 354	1 128 564	1 141 789	...	...	...	...	...	...
50 - 54	1 921 129	957 002	964 127	...	...	...	...	...	...
55 - 59	1 529 628	764 232	765 395	...	...	...	...	...	...
60 - 64	1 237 817	623 980	613 837	...	...	...	...	...	...
65 - 69	917 624	464 950	452 674	...	...	...	...	...	...
70 - 74	592 925	288 205	304 720	...	...	...	...	...	...
75 - 79	489 454	237 094	252 360	...	...	...	...	...	...
80 - 84	327 360	156 185	171 174	...	...	...	...	...	...
85 +	236 619	117 213	119 406	...	...	...	...	...	...
Angola[1]									
1 VII 2018 (ESDF)									
Total	29 250 009	14 228 926	15 021 083	18 473 609	9 027 566	9 446 043	10 776 400	5 201 360	5 575 040
0	1 023 470	512 432	511 038	654 226	328 150	326 076	369 244	184 282	184 962
1 - 4	3 865 148	1 925 108	1 940 040	2 413 869	1 209 511	1 204 358	1 451 279	715 597	735 682
5 - 9	4 868 159	2 416 082	2 452 077	2 886 759	1 430 960	1 455 799	1 981 400	985 122	996 278
10 - 14	3 869 021	1 913 727	1 955 294	2 388 882	1 169 737	1 219 145	1 480 139	743 990	736 149
15 - 19	3 067 047	1 501 376	1 565 671	1 974 049	957 885	1 016 164	1 092 998	543 491	549 507
20 - 24	2 514 086	1 220 352	1 293 734	1 669 833	806 537	863 296	844 253	413 815	430 438
25 - 29	2 085 591	998 917	1 086 674	1 420 296	682 360	737 936	665 295	316 557	348 738
30 - 34	1 750 668	831 729	918 939	1 198 069	574 976	623 093	552 599	256 753	295 846
35 - 39	1 472 519	695 906	776 613	997 578	481 264	516 314	474 941	214 642	260 299
40 - 44	1 219 572	576 944	642 628	811 666	394 530	417 136	407 906	182 414	225 492
45 - 49	981 841	467 839	514 002	630 420	310 706	319 714	351 421	157 133	194 288
50 - 54	782 208	371 352	410 856	485 278	239 430	245 848	296 930	131 922	165 008
55 - 59	594 650	279 576	315 074	350 057	171 668	178 389	244 593	107 908	136 685
60 - 64	440 871	204 340	236 531	247 654	119 559	128 095	193 217	84 781	108 436
65 - 69	299 894	135 569	164 325	157 806	73 487	84 319	142 088	62 082	80 006
70 - 74	198 608	87 644	110 964	97 132	43 209	53 923	101 476	44 435	57 041
75 - 79	116 181	49 681	66 500	50 365	20 348	30 017	65 816	29 333	36 483
80 +	100 475	40 352	60 123	39 670	13 249	26 421	60 805	27 103	33 702
Benin - Bénin									
1 VII 2011 (ESDF)[2]									
Total	9 067 076	4 446 877	4 620 199	4 072 574	2 003 366	2 069 208	4 994 502	2 443 511	2 550 991
0 - 4	1 629 512	828 064	801 448	633 629	321 667	311 962	995 883	506 397	489 486
0	350 292	178 565	171 727	...	...	...	...	...	...
1 - 4	1 279 220	649 499	629 721	...	...	...	...	...	...
5 - 9	1 335 166	675 912	659 254	511 822	251 283	260 539	823 344	424 629	398 715
10 - 14	1 137 068	572 756	564 312	517 373	244 437	272 936	619 695	328 319	291 376
15 - 19	1 081 199	553 241	527 958	550 694	279 420	271 274	530 505	273 821	256 684
20 - 24	767 946	398 920	369 026	406 496	224 092	182 404	361 450	174 828	186 622
25 - 29	609 489	291 598	317 891	303 896	153 731	150 165	305 593	137 867	167 726
30 - 34	537 893	227 400	310 493	264 521	117 596	146 925	273 372	109 804	163 568
35 - 39	494 619	213 385	281 234	236 804	106 800	130 004	257 815	106 585	151 230
40 - 44	378 111	175 956	202 155	178 115	86 225	91 890	199 996	89 731	110 265
45 - 49	308 866	142 056	166 810	145 334	68 351	76 983	163 532	73 705	89 827
50 - 54	232 650	110 074	122 576	101 866	48 831	53 035	130 784	61 243	69 541
55 - 59	171 970	82 190	89 780	77 819	37 319	40 500	94 151	44 871	49 280
60 - 64	135 768	64 968	70 800	52 261	24 642	27 619	83 507	40 326	43 181
65 - 69	75 534	35 915	39 619	31 238	14 546	16 692	44 296	21 369	22 927
70 - 74	82 740	36 511	46 229	30 032	12 558	17 474	52 708	23 953	28 755
75 - 79	36 453	15 591	20 862	14 064	5 573	8 491	22 389	10 018	12 371
80 +	52 092	22 340	29 752	16 610	6 295	10 315	35 482	16 045	19 437

180

7. Population by age, sex and urban/rural residence: latest available year, 2009 - 2018
Population selon l'âge, le sexe et la résidence, urbaine/rurale : dernière année disponible, 2009 - 2018 (continued - suite)

Continent, country or area, date, code[a] and age (in years) / Continent, pays ou zone, date, code[a] et âge (en années)	Total			Urban - Urbaine			Rural - Rurale		
	Both sexes Les deux sexes	Male Masculin	Female Féminin	Both sexes Les deux sexes	Male Masculin	Female Féminin	Both sexes Les deux sexes	Male Masculin	Female Féminin
AFRICA - AFRIQUE									
Benin - Bénin									
1 VII 2018 (ESDF)[3]									
Total	11 496 140	5 647 059	5 849 081	...	...	...	...	...	...
0 - 4	1 771 128	903 445	867 683	...	...	...	...	...	...
5 - 9	1 660 861	838 292	822 569	...	...	...	...	...	...
10 - 14	1 654 258	838 200	816 058	...	...	...	...	...	...
15 - 19	1 289 410	663 989	625 421	...	...	...	...	...	...
20 - 24	1 007 377	510 094	497 283	...	...	...	...	...	...
25 - 29	850 692	383 835	466 857	...	...	...	...	...	...
30 - 34	761 689	325 539	436 150	...	...	...	...	...	...
35 - 39	639 136	291 441	347 695	...	...	...	...	...	...
40 - 44	503 488	236 956	266 532	...	...	...	...	...	...
45 - 49	399 400	197 278	202 122	...	...	...	...	...	...
50 - 54	263 321	130 076	133 245	...	...	...	...	...	...
55 - 59	247 442	119 534	127 908	...	...	...	...	...	...
60 - 64	121 624	60 776	60 848	...	...	...	...	...	...
65 - 69	143 917	67 214	76 703	...	...	...	...	...	...
70 - 74	61 754	28 963	32 791	...	...	...	...	...	...
75 - 79	62 810	27 607	35 203	...	...	...	...	...	...
80 +	57 833	23 820	34 013	...	...	...	...	...	...
Botswana[4]									
1 VII 2017 (ESDJ)									
Total	2 266 990	1 107 191	1 159 799	1 452 383	693 532	758 851	814 607	413 658	400 948
0 - 4	61 940	31 397	30 544	37 124	18 879	18 245	24 816	12 518	12 298
5 - 9	203 745	102 949	100 797	116 405	58 772	57 632	87 341	44 176	43 164
10 - 14	240 886	121 521	119 365	141 315	70 695	70 619	99 571	50 826	48 745
15 - 19	232 077	116 903	115 174	140 422	69 995	70 428	91 655	46 908	44 746
20 - 24	235 942	117 349	118 592	161 551	77 071	84 479	74 391	40 278	34 113
25 - 29	224 303	108 876	115 427	158 279	74 123	84 156	66 023	34 752	31 271
30 - 34	232 702	113 292	119 409	165 346	77 884	87 462	67 356	35 408	31 948
35 - 39	190 931	94 619	96 312	136 536	65 716	70 821	54 395	28 904	25 491
40 - 44	151 385	76 617	74 768	105 606	51 881	53 725	45 779	24 735	21 043
45 - 49	111 168	54 597	56 571	75 396	36 406	38 991	35 772	18 192	17 580
50 - 54	92 096	42 410	49 686	59 159	27 007	32 152	32 936	15 403	17 533
55 - 59	74 296	33 298	40 998	45 078	20 249	24 828	29 218	13 048	16 170
60 - 64	60 511	27 281	33 229	34 113	15 217	18 896	26 398	12 064	14 334
65 - 69	42 077	19 418	22 660	21 535	9 303	12 231	20 543	10 114	10 429
70 - 74	31 064	13 707	17 358	15 223	6 191	9 031	15 842	7 516	8 326
75 - 79	24 922	10 595	14 327	11 975	4 485	7 490	12 948	6 111	6 837
80 - 84	20 031	7 801	12 230	9 604	3 262	6 341	10 428	4 539	5 889
85 - 89	14 799	5 458	9 342	6 843	2 171	4 672	7 957	3 287	4 670
90 - 94	9 233	3 163	6 070	4 418	1 362	3 055	4 815	1 800	3 015
95 - 99	4 390	1 542	2 848	2 062	669	1 393	2 328	872	1 455
100 +	8 492	4 400	4 092	4 394	2 192	2 202	4 098	2 208	1 890
1 VII 2018 (ESDJ)									
Total	2 302 878	1 134 505	1 168 373	...	...	...	...	...	...
0 - 4	237 605	119 929	117 676	...	...	...	...	...	...
5 - 9	251 537	127 110	124 427	...	...	...	...	...	...
10 - 14	221 177	111 626	109 551	...	...	...	...	...	...
15 - 19	208 951	105 421	103 530	...	...	...	...	...	...
20 - 24	209 631	105 164	104 467	...	...	...	...	...	...
25 - 29	202 809	99 747	103 062	...	...	...	...	...	...
30 - 34	206 384	100 719	105 665	...	...	...	...	...	...
35 - 39	186 229	91 970	94 259	...	...	...	...	...	...
40 - 44	146 981	74 104	72 877	...	...	...	...	...	...
45 - 49	109 824	54 949	54 875	...	...	...	...	...	...
50 - 54	85 463	40 199	45 264	...	...	...	...	...	...
55 - 59	69 954	31 270	38 684	...	...	...	...	...	...
60 - 64	56 342	24 977	31 365	...	...	...	...	...	...
65 - 69	40 341	18 166	22 175	...	...	...	...	...	...
70 - 74	27 031	11 915	15 116	...	...	...	...	...	...
75 - 79	19 989	8 335	11 654	...	...	...	...	...	...
80 +	22 630	8 904	13 726	...	...	...	...	...	...

Continent, country or area, date, code[a] and age (in years) / Continent, pays ou zone, date, code[a] et âge (en annèes)	Total			Urban - Urbaine			Rural - Rurale		
	Both sexes Les deux sexes	Male Masculin	Female Féminin	Both sexes Les deux sexes	Male Masculin	Female Féminin	Both sexes Les deux sexes	Male Masculin	Female Féminin
AFRICA - AFRIQUE									
Burkina Faso[2]									
1 VII 2017 (ESDJ)									
Total	19 632 147	9 478 805	10 153 342	...	...	...	...	...	...
0 - 4	3 525 706	1 801 439	1 724 267	...	...	...	...	...	...
5 - 9	3 087 852	1 579 270	1 508 582	...	...	...	...	...	...
10 - 14	2 632 326	1 362 875	1 269 451	...	...	...	...	...	...
15 - 19	2 189 799	1 103 007	1 086 792	...	...	...	...	...	...
20 - 24	1 717 098	819 089	898 009	...	...	...	...	...	...
25 - 29	1 354 144	602 864	751 280	...	...	...	...	...	...
30 - 34	1 101 379	446 597	654 782	...	...	...	...	...	...
35 - 39	940 308	394 465	545 843	...	...	...	...	...	...
40 - 44	738 498	321 898	416 600	...	...	...	...	...	...
45 - 49	607 436	266 800	340 636	...	...	...	...	...	...
50 - 54	491 293	216 418	274 875	...	...	...	...	...	...
55 - 59	386 018	170 086	215 932	...	...	...	...	...	...
60 - 64	292 493	131 763	160 730	...	...	...	...	...	...
65 - 69	221 482	102 575	118 907	...	...	...	...	...	...
70 - 74	160 000	73 416	86 584	...	...	...	...	...	...
75 - 79	96 701	45 723	50 978	...	...	...	...	...	...
80 +	89 614	40 520	49 094	...	...	...	...	...	...
Burundi									
1 VII 2015 (ESDF)[5]									
Total	9 823 828	4 822 838	5 000 990	1 473 574	723 426	750 148	8 350 254	4 099 412	4 250 842
0 - 4	1 712 483	856 714	855 769	220 830	99 976	120 854	1 491 653	756 738	734 915
5 - 9	1 379 000	679 740	699 260	172 229	76 843	95 386	1 206 771	602 897	603 874
10 - 14	1 234 086	604 457	629 629	154 449	67 431	87 018	1 079 637	537 026	542 611
15 - 19	1 021 915	496 353	525 562	161 685	74 964	86 721	860 230	421 389	438 841
20 - 24	974 645	467 123	507 522	176 946	89 742	87 204	797 699	377 381	420 318
25 - 29	843 366	397 323	446 043	174 840	90 183	84 657	668 526	307 140	361 386
30 - 34	659 106	321 348	337 758	140 254	76 414	63 840	518 852	244 934	273 918
35 - 39	466 561	236 115	230 446	82 657	46 719	35 938	383 904	189 396	194 508
40 - 44	366 466	182 701	183 765	57 283	33 163	24 120	309 183	149 538	159 645
45 - 49	310 594	153 796	156 798	40 803	22 094	18 709	269 791	131 702	138 089
50 - 54	265 180	134 933	130 247	30 364	16 749	13 615	234 816	118 184	116 632
55 - 59	225 278	113 470	111 808	25 692	13 147	12 545	199 586	100 323	99 263
60 - 64	145 211	74 556	70 655	14 954	7 579	7 375	130 257	66 977	63 280
65 - 69	90 785	44 744	46 041	9 023	4 024	4 999	81 762	40 720	41 042
70 - 74	54 548	25 722	28 826	4 874	2 027	2 847	49 674	23 695	25 979
75 - 79	36 220	16 056	20 164	3 504	1 175	2 329	32 716	14 881	17 835
80 +	38 384	17 687	20 697	3 187	1 196	1 991	35 197	16 491	18 706
1 VII 2018 (ESDF)									
Total	11 772 322	5 815 408	5 956 914	...	...	...	...	...	...
0	362 913	183 258	179 655	...	...	...	...	...	...
1 - 4	1 391 577	698 998	692 579	...	...	...	...	...	...
5 - 9	1 742 161	872 347	869 814	...	...	...	...	...	...
10 - 14	1 503 474	749 047	754 427	...	...	...	...	...	...
15 - 19	1 194 431	590 134	604 296	...	...	...	...	...	...
20 - 24	1 065 983	521 648	544 334	...	...	...	...	...	...
25 - 29	1 001 279	483 185	518 093	...	...	...	...	...	...
30 - 34	866 696	417 661	449 035	...	...	...	...	...	...
35 - 39	662 749	327 288	335 461	...	...	...	...	...	...
40 - 44	472 266	236 134	236 133	...	...	...	...	...	...
45 - 49	365 379	179 102	186 277	...	...	...	...	...	...
50 - 54	322 382	158 581	163 801	...	...	...	...	...	...
55 - 59	275 615	136 959	138 657	...	...	...	...	...	...
60 - 64	224 612	110 809	113 803	...	...	...	...	...	...
65 - 69	145 145	70 827	74 318	...	...	...	...	...	...
70 - 74	82 526	38 731	43 796	...	...	...	...	...	...
75 - 79	52 236	23 420	28 816	...	...	...	...	...	...
80 +	40 898	17 280	23 618	...	...	...	...	...	...
Cabo Verde									
16 VI 2010 (CDJC)									
Total	491 683	243 403	248 280	303 673	151 219	152 454	188 010	92 184	95 826
0 - 4	50 200	25 131	25 069	30 842	15 542	15 300	19 358	9 589	9 769
5 - 9	50 208	25 168	25 040	29 705	14 799	14 906	20 503	10 369	10 134

Continent, country or area, date, code[a] and age (in years) / Continent, pays ou zone, date, code[a] et âge (en années)	Total			Urban - Urbaine			Rural - Rurale		
	Both sexes Les deux sexes	Male Masculin	Female Féminin	Both sexes Les deux sexes	Male Masculin	Female Féminin	Both sexes Les deux sexes	Male Masculin	Female Féminin
AFRICA - AFRIQUE									
Cabo Verde									
16 VI 2010 (CDJC)									
10 - 14	55 225	27 864	27 361	30 408	15 260	15 148	24 817	12 604	12 213
15 - 19	59 060	29 655	29 405	33 772	16 678	17 094	25 288	12 977	12 311
20 - 24	52 905	27 327	25 578	34 402	17 504	16 898	18 503	9 823	8 680
25 - 29	44 341	23 336	21 005	30 990	16 055	14 935	13 351	7 281	6 070
30 - 34	34 504	18 165	16 339	24 684	13 012	11 672	9 820	5 153	4 667
35 - 39	27 236	14 106	13 130	18 641	9 726	8 915	8 595	4 380	4 215
40 - 44	26 291	12 988	13 303	17 086	8 680	8 406	9 205	4 308	4 897
45 - 49	23 512	11 347	12 165	15 227	7 625	7 602	8 285	3 722	4 563
50 - 54	18 161	8 162	9 999	11 243	5 392	5 851	6 918	2 770	4 148
55 - 59	12 143	4 947	7 196	7 183	3 229	3 954	4 960	1 718	3 242
60 - 64	6 193	2 613	3 580	3 656	1 663	1 993	2 537	950	1 587
65 - 69	6 215	2 499	3 716	3 420	1 411	2 009	2 795	1 088	1 707
70 - 74	8 666	3 437	5 229	4 237	1 656	2 581	4 429	1 781	2 648
75 - 79	7 433	2 980	4 453	3 602	1 377	2 225	3 831	1 603	2 228
80 - 84	5 277	2 092	3 185	2 485	891	1 594	2 792	1 201	1 591
85 - 89	2 185	827	1 358	1 058	331	727	1 127	496	631
90 - 94	1 073	377	696	520	171	349	553	206	347
95 +	497	172	325	248	65	183	249	107	142
Unknown - Inconnu	358	210	148	264	152	112	94	58	36
1 VII 2018 (ESDJ)[2]									
Total	544 081	273 904	270 177	...	...	...	...	...	...
0 - 4	52 364	26 786	25 579	...	...	...	...	...	...
5 - 9	49 954	25 305	24 649	...	...	...	...	...	...
10 - 14	51 519	25 695	25 825	...	...	...	...	...	...
15 - 19	48 100	24 333	23 766	...	...	...	...	...	...
20 - 24	50 019	25 504	24 514	...	...	...	...	...	...
25 - 29	54 901	28 693	26 208	...	...	...	...	...	...
30 - 34	50 340	26 851	23 489	...	...	...	...	...	...
35 - 39	40 370	22 000	18 370	...	...	...	...	...	...
40 - 44	31 192	16 625	14 567	...	...	...	...	...	...
45 - 49	26 153	13 384	12 769	...	...	...	...	...	...
50 - 54	24 926	12 086	12 839	...	...	...	...	...	...
55 - 59	20 260	9 449	10 811	...	...	...	...	...	...
60 - 64	13 938	5 707	8 230	...	...	...	...	...	...
65 - 69	8 151	3 239	4 912	...	...	...	...	...	...
70 - 74	5 319	2 109	3 210	...	...	...	...	...	...
75 - 79	4 911	1 860	3 052	...	...	...	...	...	...
80 - 84	5 615	2 103	3 512	...	...	...	...	...	...
85 - 89	3 843	1 476	2 367	...	...	...	...	...	...
90 - 94	1 596	563	1 033	...	...	...	...	...	...
95 +	612	136	475	...	...	...	...	...	...
Cameroon - Cameroun[6]									
1 VII 2018 (ESDJ)									
Total	24 863 335	12 302 528	12 560 807	...	...	...	...	...	...
0	827 513	402 465	425 048	...	...	...	...	...	...
1 - 4	3 008 365	1 487 421	1 520 944	...	...	...	...	...	...
5 - 9	3 397 608	1 677 370	1 720 238	...	...	...	...	...	...
10 - 14	3 038 816	1 552 521	1 486 295	...	...	...	...	...	...
15 - 19	2 656 944	1 346 838	1 310 106	...	...	...	...	...	...
20 - 24	2 248 154	1 147 555	1 100 599	...	...	...	...	...	...
25 - 29	2 023 157	1 028 762	994 395	...	...	...	...	...	...
30 - 34	1 788 960	850 913	938 047	...	...	...	...	...	...
35 - 39	1 427 074	660 412	766 662	...	...	...	...	...	...
40 - 44	1 179 667	563 517	616 150	...	...	...	...	...	...
45 - 49	869 151	428 111	441 040	...	...	...	...	...	...
50 - 54	722 235	343 391	378 844	...	...	...	...	...	...
55 - 59	548 838	271 771	277 067	...	...	...	...	...	...
60 - 64	452 609	216 498	236 111	...	...	...	...	...	...
65 - 69	277 573	140 753	136 820	...	...	...	...	...	...
70 - 74	206 850	98 273	108 577	...	...	...	...	...	...
75 - 79	107 058	50 165	56 893	...	...	...	...	...	...
80 +	82 763	35 792	46 971	...	...	...	...	...	...

Continent, country or area, date, code[a] and age (in years) / Continent, pays ou zone, date, code[a] et âge (en années)	Total			Urban - Urbaine			Rural - Rurale		
	Both sexes Les deux sexes	Male Masculin	Female Féminin	Both sexes Les deux sexes	Male Masculin	Female Féminin	Both sexes Les deux sexes	Male Masculin	Female Féminin
AFRICA - AFRIQUE									
Chad - Tchad									
20 V 2009 (CDJC)									
Total	11 039 873	5 452 483	5 587 390	2 404 145	1 240 663	1 163 482	8 635 728	4 211 820	4 423 908
0	408 173	205 993	202 180	84 121	42 693	41 428	324 098	163 340	160 758
1 - 4	1 822 506	923 700	898 805	343 168	175 080	168 088	1 479 846	748 959	730 886
5 - 9	1 999 768	1 012 471	987 297	378 090	190 980	187 110	1 622 222	821 871	800 350
10 - 14	1 350 648	700 015	650 633	294 766	151 248	143 518	1 055 889	548 845	507 044
15 - 19	1 060 388	502 894	557 494	263 941	130 975	132 967	796 138	371 760	424 378
20 - 24	864 890	382 122	482 768	228 865	115 325	113 540	635 635	266 522	369 113
25 - 29	753 685	320 063	433 622	181 866	89 987	91 879	571 640	229 911	341 729
30 - 34	612 724	277 322	335 402	149 238	77 290	71 948	463 330	199 895	263 435
35 - 39	502 485	241 971	260 515	117 072	62 807	54 265	385 338	179 089	206 249
40 - 44	430 068	215 887	214 181	100 595	56 420	44 175	329 406	159 397	170 009
45 - 49	303 308	163 952	139 357	70 456	41 151	29 305	232 813	122 763	110 050
50 - 54	280 744	147 725	133 019	60 886	34 220	26 666	219 862	113 499	106 363
55 - 59	147 755	84 938	62 817	33 694	20 537	13 158	114 049	64 389	49 659
60 - 64	177 720	92 696	85 024	36 142	19 479	16 663	141 603	73 233	68 371
65 - 69	85 452	48 054	37 398	17 221	9 623	7 598	68 245	38 444	29 802
70 - 74	105 348	56 059	49 289	19 504	9 792	9 711	85 878	46 295	39 583
75 - 79	41 518	24 148	17 371	7 680	4 299	3 381	33 852	19 860	13 992
80 - 84	46 433	24 947	21 486	8 002	3 832	4 169	38 451	21 132	17 319
85 - 89	14 919	9 086	5 833	2 580	1 454	1 126	12 345	7 638	4 708
90 - 94	12 317	6 852	5 465	2 134	1 075	1 059	10 188	5 782	4 407
95 - 99	8 722	5 113	3 609	1 586	836	749	7 136	4 279	2 857
100 +	2 523	1 323	1 200	466	205	260	2 062	1 120	942
Unknown - Inconnu	7 778	5 153	2 625	2 072	1 354	717	5 703	3 797	1 906
Congo									
1 VII 2009 (ESDF)									
Total	3 838 238	1 891 558	1 946 680	...	...	...	...	...	...
0 - 4	586 578	294 305	292 273	...	...	...	...	...	...
5 - 9	475 864	238 682	237 182	...	...	...	...	...	...
10 - 14	417 074	208 162	208 912	...	...	...	...	...	...
15 - 19	382 673	186 405	196 268	...	...	...	...	...	...
20 - 24	358 745	167 519	191 226	...	...	...	...	...	...
25 - 29	339 133	160 897	178 236	...	...	...	...	...	...
30 - 34	304 009	152 642	151 367	...	...	...	...	...	...
35 - 39	254 997	131 794	123 203	...	...	...	...	...	...
40 - 44	198 594	103 248	95 346	...	...	...	...	...	...
45 - 49	148 798	76 921	71 877	...	...	...	...	...	...
50 - 54	111 812	54 925	56 887	...	...	...	...	...	...
55 - 59	80 842	38 051	42 791	...	...	...	...	...	...
60 - 64	59 601	27 592	32 009	...	...	...	...	...	...
65 - 69	46 706	20 879	25 827	...	...	...	...	...	...
70 - 74	34 961	14 954	20 007	...	...	...	...	...	...
75 - 79	21 868	8 820	13 048	...	...	...	...	...	...
80 +	15 983	5 762	10 221	...	...	...	...	...	...
Côte d'Ivoire[7]									
1 VII 2017 (ESDF)									
Total	24 571 044	12 648 124	11 922 920	12 678 659	6 526 432	6 152 227	11 892 385	6 121 692	5 770 693
0	830 679	422 830	407 849	371 171	190 700	180 471	459 508	232 130	227 378
1 - 4	3 054 526	1 566 438	1 488 088	1 364 848	706 478	658 370	1 689 678	859 959	829 697
5 - 9	3 502 451	1 804 903	1 697 548	1 583 344	809 635	773 709	1 919 107	995 268	923 839
10 - 14	2 942 549	1 535 496	1 407 053	1 556 643	785 508	771 135	1 385 906	749 988	635 918
15 - 19	2 380 938	1 250 881	1 130 057	1 427 256	740 842	686 414	953 682	510 039	443 643
20 - 24	2 052 959	1 020 756	1 032 203	1 177 474	590 233	587 241	875 484	430 523	444 961
25 - 29	2 083 203	1 005 785	1 077 418	1 154 531	555 762	598 769	928 671	450 022	478 649
30 - 34	1 938 494	959 503	978 991	1 061 166	528 354	532 812	877 327	431 148	446 179
35 - 39	1 584 277	835 508	748 769	872 829	468 853	403 976	711 448	366 655	344 793
40 - 44	1 174 597	650 422	524 175	624 850	353 876	270 974	549 748	296 547	253 201
45 - 49	868 173	475 047	393 126	441 488	243 974	197 514	426 684	231 072	195 612
50 - 54	689 484	362 925	326 559	348 864	185 197	163 667	340 620	177 728	162 892
55 - 59	524 814	274 600	250 214	267 036	142 470	124 566	257 778	132 130	125 648
60 - 64	354 683	189 578	165 105	173 791	96 277	77 514	180 893	93 301	87 592
65 - 69	250 087	130 570	119 517	114 005	61 409	52 596	136 082	69 161	66 921
70 - 74	156 528	76 914	79 614	66 327	32 729	33 598	90 201	44 185	46 016

Continent, country or area, date, code[a] and age (in years) Continent, pays ou zone, date, code[a] et âge (en années)	Total			Urban - Urbaine			Rural - Rurale		
	Both sexes Les deux sexes	Male Masculin	Female Féminin	Both sexes Les deux sexes	Male Masculin	Female Féminin	Both sexes Les deux sexes	Male Masculin	Female Féminin
AFRICA - AFRIQUE									
Côte d'Ivoire[7]									
1 VII 2017 (ESDF)									
75 - 79	93 253	44 218	49 035	38 231	18 011	20 220	55 022	26 207	28 815
80 +	89 350	41 751	47 599	34 807	16 123	18 684	54 543	25 628	28 915
Djibouti									
29 V 2009 (CDFC)									
Total	818 159	440 066	378 093	577 933	322 796	255 137	240 226	117 270	122 956
0 - 4	91 132	49 863	41 269	59 318	34 064	25 254	31 814	15 799	16 014
5 - 9	101 271	56 117	45 154	66 864	38 619	28 246	34 406	17 498	16 909
10 - 14	85 472	48 135	37 337	61 462	35 788	25 674	24 010	12 347	11 663
15 - 19	85 634	46 351	39 283	63 948	35 848	28 100	21 685	10 502	11 183
20 - 24	84 058	43 786	40 272	64 412	34 919	29 493	19 646	8 867	10 779
25 - 29	82 217	40 222	41 995	60 526	31 105	29 421	21 690	9 117	12 574
30 - 34	69 555	35 558	33 997	49 815	26 329	23 486	19 740	9 229	10 511
35 - 39	56 074	29 563	26 512	40 283	22 133	18 150	15 792	7 430	8 362
40 - 44	44 981	25 247	19 734	32 223	18 741	13 482	12 758	6 506	6 252
45 - 49	34 926	19 470	15 456	25 042	14 447	10 595	9 885	5 023	4 861
50 - 54	28 841	16 363	12 479	19 611	11 537	8 074	9 230	4 826	4 404
55 - 59	18 185	10 325	7 860	12 779	7 612	5 167	5 406	2 714	2 692
60 - 64	15 172	8 495	6 677	9 472	5 331	4 141	5 700	3 163	2 537
65 +	20 641	10 572	10 069	12 177	6 323	5 854	8 464	4 248	4 216
Egypt - Égypte									
1 VII 2018 (ESDF)									
Total	97 147 368	50 070 213	47 077 155	41 398 653	21 293 773	20 104 880	55 748 715	28 776 440	26 972 275
0	2 658 783	1 368 026	1 290 757	957 984	485 509	472 475	1 700 799	882 517	818 282
1 - 4	10 564 944	5 386 205	5 178 739	3 966 493	2 009 164	1 957 329	6 598 451	3 377 041	3 221 410
5 - 9	10 776 815	5 596 177	5 180 638	4 144 629	2 156 134	1 988 495	6 632 186	3 440 043	3 192 143
10 - 14	9 255 844	4 821 179	4 434 665	3 675 362	1 911 282	1 764 080	5 580 482	2 909 897	2 670 585
15 - 19	9 231 529	4 791 188	4 440 341	3 824 678	1 978 063	1 846 615	5 406 851	2 813 125	2 593 726
20 - 24	8 437 449	4 338 842	4 098 607	3 693 287	1 890 684	1 802 603	4 744 162	2 448 158	2 296 004
25 - 29	8 370 330	4 132 410	4 237 920	3 620 282	1 787 135	1 833 147	4 750 048	2 345 275	2 404 773
30 - 34	7 524 727	3 855 156	3 669 571	3 336 873	1 693 221	1 643 652	4 187 854	2 161 935	2 025 919
35 - 39	6 645 161	3 417 387	3 227 774	2 969 056	1 527 673	1 441 383	3 676 105	1 889 714	1 786 391
40 - 44	5 278 799	2 721 411	2 557 388	2 451 967	1 240 623	1 211 344	2 826 832	1 480 788	1 346 044
45 - 49	4 500 010	2 339 623	2 160 387	2 092 000	1 086 246	1 005 754	2 408 010	1 253 377	1 154 633
50 - 54	4 095 879	2 099 684	1 996 195	1 944 691	997 897	946 794	2 151 188	1 101 787	1 049 401
55 - 59	3 340 192	1 755 327	1 584 865	1 610 878	842 829	768 049	1 729 314	912 498	816 816
60 - 64	2 714 395	1 450 387	1 264 008	1 355 106	729 497	625 609	1 359 289	720 890	638 399
65 - 69	1 762 281	965 085	797 196	860 788	480 177	380 611	901 493	484 908	416 585
70 - 74	1 040 945	543 787	497 158	489 176	261 890	227 286	551 769	281 897	269 872
75 +	949 285	488 339	460 946	405 403	215 749	189 654	543 882	272 590	271 292
Eritrea - Érythrée[8]									
1 VII 2018 (ESDF)									
Total	3 294 680	1 621 437	1 673 242	1 164 508	554 316	610 192	2 130 172	1 067 121	1 063 051
0	106 430	53 097	53 333	29 588	14 068	15 520	76 842	39 029	37 813
1 - 4	393 226	195 542	197 684	114 197	54 218	59 979	279 029	141 323	137 706
5 - 9	429 065	212 838	216 227	133 144	63 167	69 977	295 921	149 671	146 250
10 - 14	354 118	175 391	178 727	116 295	55 243	61 053	237 823	120 148	117 675
15 - 19	279 698	140 421	139 278	94 954	45 508	49 446	184 744	94 913	89 831
20 - 24	312 475	160 897	151 579	100 797	51 869	48 928	211 678	109 028	102 650
25 - 29	316 945	160 633	156 312	107 328	53 745	53 582	209 617	106 887	102 730
30 - 34	254 468	126 437	128 030	100 713	47 332	53 382	153 754	79 106	74 649
35 - 39	175 113	85 267	89 845	80 972	37 673	43 299	94 141	47 594	46 547
40 - 44	136 270	59 401	76 869	64 629	28 518	36 111	71 641	30 883	40 758
45 - 49	127 906	57 055	70 851	57 942	26 461	31 481	69 964	30 594	39 370
50 - 54	97 411	44 513	52 898	40 073	18 712	21 361	57 338	25 801	31 538
55 - 59	84 416	38 686	45 730	33 004	15 320	17 684	51 412	23 366	28 046
60 - 64	66 171	33 632	32 539	25 879	13 289	12 590	40 292	20 342	19 949
65 - 69	56 019	27 965	28 054	22 949	10 764	12 185	33 071	17 201	15 870
70 - 74	46 374	21 804	24 570	18 975	8 030	10 945	27 399	13 774	13 625
75 - 79	31 986	14 237	17 749	12 252	5 181	7 071	19 734	9 056	10 678
80 - 84	17 503	8 601	8 902	6 820	3 236	3 584	10 683	5 365	5 318
85 +	9 086	5 022	4 064	3 999	1 984	2 015	5 087	3 038	2 049

Continent, country or area, date, code[a] and age (in years) / Continent, pays ou zone, date, code[a] et âge (en années)	Total			Urban - Urbaine			Rural - Rurale		
	Both sexes Les deux sexes	Male Masculin	Female Féminin	Both sexes Les deux sexes	Male Masculin	Female Féminin	Both sexes Les deux sexes	Male Masculin	Female Féminin
AFRICA - AFRIQUE									
Eswatini[9]									
1 VII 2017 (ESDJ)									
Total	1 145 970	544 811	601 159	271 573	129 068	142 505	874 397	415 743	458 654
0 - 4	152 127	77 478	74 649	28 212	14 355	13 857	123 915	63 123	60 792
5 - 9	139 135	71 216	67 919	23 317	11 872	11 445	115 818	59 344	56 474
10 - 14	125 977	63 854	62 123	20 173	9 992	10 181	105 804	53 862	51 942
15 - 19	127 374	63 188	64 186	21 159	9 507	11 652	106 215	53 681	52 534
20 - 24	121 764	59 293	62 471	27 316	11 793	15 523	94 448	47 500	46 948
25 - 29	106 346	50 075	56 271	34 291	15 621	18 670	72 055	34 454	37 601
30 - 34	88 190	38 866	49 324	34 784	16 705	18 079	53 406	22 161	31 245
35 - 39	71 287	29 674	41 613	26 498	12 947	13 551	44 789	16 727	28 062
40 - 44	53 935	21 745	32 190	18 862	9 173	9 689	35 073	12 572	22 501
45 - 49	42 820	17 287	25 533	13 927	6 669	7 258	28 893	10 618	18 275
50 - 54	32 823	13 684	19 139	9 126	4 442	4 684	23 697	9 242	14 455
55 - 59	25 604	10 988	14 616	6 214	2 985	3 229	19 390	8 003	11 387
60 - 64	19 571	8 647	10 924	3 686	1 628	2 058	15 885	7 019	8 866
65 - 69	14 735	6 803	7 932	1 953	754	1 199	12 782	6 049	6 733
70 - 74	10 670	5 148	5 522	994	322	672	9 676	4 826	4 850
75 - 79	6 839	3 459	3 380	589	192	397	6 250	3 267	2 983
80 +	6 773	3 406	3 367	472	111	361	6 301	3 295	3 006
1 VII 2018 (ESDJ)									
Total	1 159 250	551 317	607 933	...	...	...	...	...	...
0 - 4	152 990	77 918	75 072	...	...	...	...	...	...
5 - 9	140 917	72 116	68 801	...	...	...	...	...	...
10 - 14	126 497	64 384	62 113	...	...	...	...	...	...
15 - 19	127 464	63 576	63 888	...	...	...	...	...	...
20 - 24	122 436	59 855	62 581	...	...	...	...	...	...
25 - 29	108 144	51 178	56 966	...	...	...	...	...	...
30 - 34	89 880	39 779	50 101	...	...	...	...	...	...
35 - 39	72 969	30 248	42 721	...	...	...	...	...	...
40 - 44	55 572	22 171	33 401	...	...	...	...	...	...
45 - 49	43 681	17 388	26 293	...	...	...	...	...	...
50 - 54	33 613	13 795	19 818	...	...	...	...	...	...
55 - 59	25 996	11 059	14 937	...	...	...	...	...	...
60 - 64	19 794	8 693	11 101	...	...	...	...	...	...
65 - 69	14 831	6 851	7 980	...	...	...	...	...	...
70 - 74	10 683	5 183	5 500	...	...	...	...	...	...
75 - 79	6 917	3 555	3 362	...	...	...	...	...	...
80 +	6 866	3 568	3 298	...	...	...	...	...	...
Ethiopia - Éthiopie[10]									
1 VII 2017 (ESDF)									
Total	94 352 138	47 364 992	46 987 146	19 161 490	9 534 811	9 626 679	75 190 648	37 830 181	37 360 467
0 - 4	13 528 590	6 876 421	6 652 169	1 811 130	916 366	894 764	11 717 460	5 960 055	5 757 405
5 - 9	12 448 401	6 301 867	6 146 534	1 997 393	994 561	1 002 832	10 451 008	5 307 306	5 143 702
10 - 14	11 359 359	5 747 959	5 611 400	2 116 099	1 045 113	1 070 986	9 243 260	4 702 846	4 540 414
15 - 19	10 500 705	5 336 198	5 164 507	2 205 114	1 094 367	1 110 747	8 295 591	4 241 831	4 053 760
20 - 24	9 322 415	4 725 170	4 597 245	2 201 754	1 099 832	1 101 922	7 120 661	3 625 338	3 495 323
25 - 29	8 110 849	4 047 502	4 063 347	2 114 464	1 035 202	1 079 262	5 996 385	3 012 300	2 984 085
30 - 34	6 687 272	3 281 910	3 405 362	1 754 863	878 820	876 043	4 932 409	2 403 090	2 529 319
35 - 39	5 518 185	2 692 328	2 825 857	1 422 837	722 152	700 685	4 095 348	1 970 176	2 125 172
40 - 44	4 257 426	2 070 519	2 186 907	977 335	503 594	473 741	3 280 091	1 566 925	1 713 166
45 - 49	3 413 015	1 658 680	1 754 335	746 608	379 131	367 477	2 666 407	1 279 549	1 386 858
50 - 54	2 660 564	1 320 044	1 340 520	535 794	271 036	264 758	2 124 770	1 049 008	1 075 762
55 - 59	2 093 237	1 042 645	1 050 592	414 152	201 275	212 877	1 679 085	841 370	837 715
60 - 64	1 569 090	786 289	782 801	309 257	143 766	165 491	1 259 833	642 523	617 310
65 - 69	1 152 886	582 858	570 028	218 632	100 563	118 069	934 254	482 295	451 959
70 - 74	804 281	409 104	395 177	156 165	70 226	85 939	648 116	338 878	309 238
75 - 79	500 836	256 264	244 572	99 355	44 448	54 907	401 481	211 816	189 665
80 +	425 027	229 234	195 793	80 538	34 359	46 179	344 489	194 875	149 614
Gambia - Gambie[11]									
31 XII 2015 (SSDF)									
Total	1 922 950	915 357	1 007 593	1 057 467	503 304	554 163	865 483	412 053	453 430
0 - 4	311 156	155 654	155 502	156 283	76 198	80 085	154 874	79 456	75 418
5 - 9	298 089	150 122	147 966	145 387	71 306	74 081	152 702	78 816	73 886
10 - 14	228 988	115 261	113 727	114 825	58 394	56 431	114 164	56 868	57 296

Continent, country or area, date, code[a] and age (in years) / Continent, pays ou zone, date, code[a] et âge (en années)	Total			Urban - Urbaine			Rural - Rurale		
	Both sexes Les deux sexes	Male Masculin	Female Féminin	Both sexes Les deux sexes	Male Masculin	Female Féminin	Both sexes Les deux sexes	Male Masculin	Female Féminin
AFRICA - AFRIQUE									
Gambia - Gambie[11]									
31 XII 2015 (SSDF)									
15 - 19	198 367	87 274	111 093	114 445	47 786	66 660	83 922	39 489	44 433
20 - 24	180 479	76 050	104 429	115 445	47 655	67 790	65 034	28 395	36 639
25 - 29	151 669	62 431	89 237	96 080	40 579	55 501	55 589	21 852	33 737
30 - 34	127 754	57 532	70 222	78 401	38 439	39 962	49 352	19 093	30 259
35 - 39	109 161	49 913	59 248	66 199	32 130	34 069	42 961	17 783	25 178
40 - 44	81 698	39 032	42 666	47 312	23 918	23 394	34 386	15 114	19 272
45 - 49	61 757	32 235	29 522	34 649	19 389	15 260	27 107	12 846	14 262
50 - 54	52 727	27 286	25 441	28 742	16 285	12 457	23 985	11 001	12 984
55 - 59	35 759	18 075	17 685	20 122	9 561	10 562	15 637	8 514	7 123
60 - 64	30 155	16 034	14 121	14 511	8 600	5 911	15 644	7 434	8 210
65 +	55 191	28 457	26 734	25 063	13 063	12 000	30 128	15 393	14 734
Ghana[12]									
1 VII 2015 (ESDF)									
Total	27 670 174	13 562 093	14 108 081	13 817 894	6 903 107	6 914 787	13 852 280	6 658 986	7 193 294
0	841 301	425 611	415 690	403 605	195 150	208 455	437 696	230 461	207 235
1 - 4	3 158 109	1 595 165	1 562 944	1 513 925	731 409	782 516	1 644 184	863 756	780 428
5 - 9	3 312 878	1 688 452	1 624 426	1 579 799	755 911	823 888	1 733 079	932 541	800 538
10 - 14	3 097 352	1 567 043	1 530 309	1 538 503	749 266	789 237	1 558 849	817 777	741 072
15 - 19	2 825 578	1 414 987	1 410 591	1 458 024	735 981	722 043	1 367 554	679 006	688 548
20 - 24	2 537 799	1 251 759	1 286 040	1 377 177	736 425	640 752	1 160 622	515 334	645 288
25 - 29	2 252 493	1 083 877	1 168 616	1 211 633	636 338	575 295	1 040 860	447 539	593 321
30 - 34	1 967 166	935 947	1 031 219	1 014 879	537 402	477 477	952 287	398 545	553 742
35 - 39	1 665 237	785 200	880 037	840 000	437 656	402 344	825 237	347 544	477 693
40 - 44	1 404 309	661 789	742 520	703 098	362 522	340 576	701 211	299 267	401 944
45 - 49	1 145 932	546 030	599 902	560 013	275 131	284 882	585 919	270 899	315 020
50 - 54	933 268	445 531	487 737	477 984	238 760	239 224	455 284	206 771	248 513
55 - 59	728 002	348 118	379 884	337 828	159 376	178 452	390 174	188 742	201 432
60 - 64	570 616	270 642	299 974	271 174	129 651	141 523	299 442	140 991	158 451
65 - 69	419 501	196 219	223 282	178 422	73 727	104 695	241 079	122 492	118 587
70 - 74	313 256	142 378	170 878	149 542	68 333	81 209	163 714	74 045	89 669
75 - 79	223 087	96 514	126 573	90 638	36 406	54 232	132 449	60 108	72 341
80 +	274 290	106 831	167 459	111 650	43 663	67 987	162 640	63 168	99 472
Guinea - Guinée[13]									
1 VII 2018 (ESDJ)									
Total	11 883 516	5 754 536	6 128 983	4 260 887	2 063 314	2 197 573	7 622 629	3 691 221	3 931 408
0	424 810	214 243	210 567	128 750	62 291	66 459	338 034	173 147	164 888
1 - 4	1 590 000	803 138	786 862	426 956	206 883	220 073	1 129 768	575 060	546 010
5 - 9	1 808 886	919 143	889 744	580 472	278 307	302 165	1 228 414	640 835	587 578
10 - 14	1 513 041	760 096	752 945	575 846	271 150	304 696	937 195	488 946	448 249
15 - 19	1 227 090	603 961	623 129	516 003	246 004	269 999	711 087	357 957	353 130
20 - 24	1 032 219	486 724	545 495	477 470	238 602	238 869	554 748	248 122	306 626
25 - 29	877 631	385 375	492 256	401 519	193 430	208 089	476 112	191 945	284 167
30 - 34	729 170	315 643	413 527	284 850	134 900	149 951	444 320	180 744	263 576
35 - 39	587 065	257 192	329 873	212 926	102 151	110 774	374 140	155 041	219 099
40 - 44	484 318	216 381	267 937	169 703	82 637	87 066	314 615	133 744	180 871
45 - 49	394 265	183 534	210 732	132 918	66 612	66 305	261 348	116 921	144 426
50 - 54	321 474	155 004	166 470	105 215	52 944	52 271	216 259	102 060	114 199
55 - 59	255 963	129 724	126 239	80 312	42 040	38 272	175 651	87 684	87 967
60 - 64	205 013	105 717	99 296	60 060	32 314	27 746	144 954	73 404	71 550
65 - 69	159 420	82 415	77 006	43 930	23 494	20 437	115 490	58 921	56 569
70 - 74	116 268	59 766	56 502	29 516	15 235	14 281	86 752	44 531	42 221
75 - 79	76 153	38 174	37 979	16 924	7 610	9 314	59 229	30 564	28 665
80 +	80 730	38 306	42 424	17 517	6 709	10 807	63 213	31 596	31 617
Guinea-Bissau - Guinée-Bissau[2]									
1 VII 2018 (ESDF)									
Total	1 584 791	780 070	804 721	688 511	338 902	349 609	896 280	441 168	455 112
0 - 4	268 980	137 696	131 284	97 048	48 174	48 874	171 932	89 522	82 410
5 - 9	233 885	119 545	114 340	87 950	42 220	45 730	145 935	77 325	68 610
10 - 14	184 685	92 720	91 965	80 931	37 686	43 245	103 754	55 034	48 720
15 - 19	167 827	84 488	83 339	83 013	40 899	42 114	84 814	43 589	41 225
20 - 24	143 206	72 162	71 044	75 415	39 403	36 012	67 791	32 759	35 032
25 - 29	136 172	66 645	69 527	67 818	35 171	32 647	68 354	31 474	36 880

187

Continent, country or area, date, code[a] and age (in years) / Continent, pays ou zone, date, code[a] et âge (en années)	Total			Urban - Urbaine			Rural - Rurale		
	Both sexes Les deux sexes	Male Masculin	Female Féminin	Both sexes Les deux sexes	Male Masculin	Female Féminin	Both sexes Les deux sexes	Male Masculin	Female Féminin
AFRICA - AFRIQUE									
Guinea-Bissau - Guinée-Bissau[2]									
1 VII 2018 (ESDF)									
30 - 34	114 766	54 034	60 732	56 775	28 316	28 459	57 991	25 718	32 273
35 - 39	97 573	44 816	52 757	44 118	21 434	22 684	53 455	23 382	30 073
40 - 44	62 680	29 153	33 527	28 904	14 320	14 584	33 776	14 833	18 943
45 - 49	54 005	24 534	29 471	23 480	11 324	12 156	30 525	13 210	17 315
50 - 54	36 934	16 951	19 983	15 386	7 651	7 735	21 548	9 300	12 248
55 - 59	32 878	14 838	18 040	12 558	5 839	6 719	20 320	8 999	11 321
60 - 64	19 804	8 833	10 971	6 503	2 974	3 529	13 301	5 859	7 442
65 - 69	13 506	6 578	6 928	4 116	1 932	2 184	9 390	4 646	4 744
70 - 74	8 935	3 825	5 110	2 456	976	1 480	6 479	2 849	3 630
75 - 79	4 756	1 843	2 913	1 161	369	792	3 595	1 474	2 121
80 +	4 199	1 409	2 790	879	214	665	3 320	1 195	2 125
Kenya									
24 VIII 2009 (CDFC)									
Total	38 610 097	19 192 458	19 417 639	12 487 375	6 278 811	6 208 564	26 122 722	12 913 647	13 209 075
0	1 221 937	616 843	605 094	388 883	195 861	193 022	833 054	420 982	412 072
1 - 4	4 717 369	2 383 596	2 333 773	1 350 368	679 969	670 399	3 367 001	1 703 627	1 663 374
5 - 9	5 597 716	2 832 669	2 765 047	1 484 285	742 473	741 812	4 113 431	2 090 196	2 023 235
10 - 14	5 034 855	2 565 313	2 469 542	1 312 671	650 438	662 233	3 722 184	1 914 875	1 807 309
15 - 19	4 169 543	2 123 653	2 045 890	1 244 054	587 384	656 670	2 925 489	1 536 269	1 389 220
20 - 24	3 775 103	1 754 105	2 020 998	1 572 026	708 458	863 568	2 203 077	1 045 647	1 157 430
25 - 29	3 201 226	1 529 116	1 672 110	1 442 798	715 957	726 841	1 758 428	813 159	945 269
30 - 34	2 519 506	1 257 035	1 262 471	1 056 483	568 615	487 868	1 463 023	688 420	774 603
35 - 39	2 008 632	1 004 361	1 004 271	785 390	431 054	354 336	1 223 242	573 307	649 935
40 - 44	1 476 169	743 594	732 575	533 174	297 202	235 972	942 995	446 392	496 603
45 - 49	1 272 745	635 276	637 469	422 941	235 467	187 474	849 804	399 809	449 995
50 - 54	956 206	478 346	477 860	286 074	159 814	126 260	670 132	318 532	351 600
55 - 59	711 953	359 466	352 497	187 793	103 563	84 230	524 160	255 903	268 257
60 - 64	593 778	295 197	298 581	139 271	73 800	65 471	454 507	221 397	233 110
65 - 69	390 763	183 151	207 612	83 728	41 299	42 429	307 035	141 852	165 183
70 - 74	339 301	160 301	179 000	68 868	32 691	36 177	270 433	127 610	142 823
75 - 79	218 508	99 833	118 675	42 247	19 276	22 971	176 261	80 557	95 704
80 +	383 701	159 125	224 576	77 003	30 335	46 668	306 698	128 790	177 908
Unknown - Inconnu	21 086	11 478	9 608	9 318	5 155	4 163	11 768	6 323	5 445
1 VII 2017 (ESDF)[14]									
Total	46 595 199	23 117 881	23 477 319	...	...	...	...	...	...
0	1 479 846	749 229	730 617	...	...	...	...	...	...
1 - 4	5 649 697	2 848 841	2 800 856	...	...	...	...	...	...
5 - 9	6 409 780	3 233 878	3 175 902	...	...	...	...	...	...
10 - 14	5 668 486	2 867 168	2 801 317	...	...	...	...	...	...
15 - 19	4 948 884	2 510 323	2 438 561	...	...	...	...	...	...
20 - 24	4 335 111	2 139 798	2 195 314	...	...	...	...	...	...
25 - 29	3 909 855	1 871 462	2 038 393	...	...	...	...	...	...
30 - 34	3 366 938	1 587 480	1 779 458	...	...	...	...	...	...
35 - 39	2 696 724	1 306 876	1 389 848	...	...	...	...	...	...
40 - 44	2 057 867	1 032 134	1 025 733	...	...	...	...	...	...
45 - 49	1 631 976	818 166	813 809	...	...	...	...	...	...
50 - 54	1 240 344	618 971	621 373	...	...	...	...	...	...
55 - 59	949 533	472 914	476 619	...	...	...	...	...	...
60 - 64	728 997	358 931	370 066	...	...	...	...	...	...
65 - 69	521 927	251 108	270 819	...	...	...	...	...	...
70 - 74	391 353	184 500	206 853	...	...	...	...	...	...
75 - 79	254 042	116 739	137 303	...	...	...	...	...	...
80 +	353 840	149 363	204 477	...	...	...	...	...	...
Lesotho									
10 IV 2016 (CDJC)									
Total	2 007 201	982 133	1 025 068	...	...	...	...	...	...
0 - 4	200 155	100 793	99 362	...	...	...	...	...	...
5 - 9	221 476	109 953	111 523	...	...	...	...	...	...
10 - 14	215 813	107 879	107 934	...	...	...	...	...	...
15 - 19	209 866	106 214	103 652	...	...	...	...	...	...
20 - 24	199 267	98 827	100 440	...	...	...	...	...	...
25 - 29	188 943	95 802	93 141	...	...	...	...	...	...

Continent, country or area, date, code[a] and age (in years) / Continent, pays ou zone, date, code[a] et âge (en années)	Total			Urban - Urbaine			Rural - Rurale		
	Both sexes Les deux sexes	Male Masculin	Female Féminin	Both sexes Les deux sexes	Male Masculin	Female Féminin	Both sexes Les deux sexes	Male Masculin	Female Féminin
AFRICA - AFRIQUE									
Lesotho									
10 IV 2016 (CDJC)									
30 - 34	168 145	86 956	81 189	...	...	...	...	...	...
35 - 39	130 381	68 246	62 135	...	...	...	...	...	...
40 - 44	96 295	48 665	47 630	...	...	...	...	...	...
45 - 49	74 887	36 425	38 462	...	...	...	...	...	...
50 - 54	70 359	31 785	38 574	...	...	...	...	...	...
55 - 59	59 817	25 759	34 058	...	...	...	...	...	...
60 - 64	49 221	20 770	28 451	...	...	...	...	...	...
65 - 69	37 358	15 311	22 047	...	...	...	...	...	...
70 - 74	30 808	12 017	18 791	...	...	...	...	...	...
75 - 79	24 174	8 467	15 707	...	...	...	...	...	...
80 - 84	18 621	5 424	13 197	...	...	...	...	...	...
85 - 89	7 074	1 873	5 201	...	...	...	...	...	...
90 - 94	2 789	662	2 127	...	...	...	...	...	...
95 +	1 752	305	1 447	...	...	...	...	...	...
Libya - Libye[15]									
1 VII 2015 (ESDF)									
Total	6 162 247	3 129 026	3 033 221	...	...	...	...	...	...
0 - 4	615 556	316 497	299 059	...	...	...	...	...	...
5 - 9	577 905	297 303	280 602	...	...	...	...	...	...
10 - 14	555 149	284 318	270 831	...	...	...	...	...	...
15 - 19	525 115	268 106	257 009	...	...	...	...	...	...
20 - 24	546 408	278 875	267 533	...	...	...	...	...	...
25 - 29	571 230	289 113	282 117	...	...	...	...	...	...
30 - 34	568 834	287 480	281 354	...	...	...	...	...	...
35 - 39	551 606	279 699	271 907	...	...	...	...	...	...
40 - 44	466 373	235 088	231 285	...	...	...	...	...	...
45 - 49	360 825	180 029	180 796	...	...	...	...	...	...
50 - 54	253 647	126 799	126 848	...	...	...	...	...	...
55 - 59	173 760	87 135	86 625	...	...	...	...	...	...
60 - 64	116 033	56 199	59 834	...	...	...	...	...	...
65 - 69	102 645	51 782	50 863	...	...	...	...	...	...
70 - 74	72 486	38 750	33 736	...	...	...	...	...	...
75 - 79	52 558	26 942	25 616	...	...	...	...	...	...
80 - 84	30 271	15 038	15 233	...	...	...	...	...	...
85 +	21 846	9 873	11 973	...	...	...	...	...	...
Malawi									
3 IX 2018 (CDJC)									
Total	17 563 749	8 521 460	9 042 289	2 816 492	1 401 373	1 415 119	14 747 257	7 120 087	7 627 170
0 - 4	2 552 406	1 265 971	1 286 435	363 248	180 649	182 599	2 189 158	1 085 322	1 103 836
5 - 9	2 632 878	1 298 962	1 333 916	356 343	175 089	181 254	2 276 535	1 123 873	1 152 662
10 - 14	2 533 303	1 247 212	1 286 091	357 385	170 863	186 522	2 175 918	1 076 349	1 099 569
15 - 19	2 035 945	1 004 780	1 031 165	326 916	158 140	168 776	1 709 029	846 640	862 389
20 - 24	1 651 576	777 577	873 999	325 879	154 120	171 759	1 325 697	623 457	702 240
25 - 29	1 229 411	582 866	646 545	262 278	127 606	134 672	967 133	455 260	511 873
30 - 34	1 107 226	516 505	590 721	235 218	115 871	119 347	872 008	400 634	471 374
35 - 39	968 998	468 188	500 810	198 212	103 760	94 452	770 786	364 428	406 358
40 - 44	729 600	367 171	362 429	136 555	76 737	59 818	593 045	290 434	302 611
45 - 49	535 868	273 749	262 119	84 480	48 491	35 989	451 388	225 258	226 130
50 - 54	387 812	188 400	199 412	56 344	30 748	25 596	331 468	157 652	173 816
55 - 59	306 921	144 046	162 875	38 354	20 244	18 110	268 567	123 802	144 765
60 - 64	234 918	107 820	127 098	27 551	14 907	12 644	207 367	92 913	114 454
65 - 69	240 551	107 911	132 640	20 628	10 951	9 677	219 923	96 960	122 963
70 - 74	144 788	63 805	80 983	11 580	6 113	5 467	133 208	57 692	75 516
75 - 79	124 718	51 598	73 120	7 750	3 808	3 942	116 968	47 790	69 178
80 - 84	63 675	24 130	39 545	3 732	1 649	2 083	59 943	22 481	37 462
85 - 89	54 754	20 751	34 003	2 642	1 104	1 538	52 112	19 647	32 465
90 - 94	15 130	5 245	9 885	785	290	495	14 345	4 955	9 390
95 +	13 271	4 773	8 498	612	233	379	12 659	4 540	8 119
Mali									
1 IV 2009 (CDFC)									
Total	14 528 662	7 204 990	7 323 672	3 274 727	1 643 671	1 631 056	11 253 935	5 561 319	5 692 616
0 - 4	2 623 385	1 328 871	1 294 514	501 628	253 735	247 893	2 121 757	1 075 136	1 046 621
5 - 9	2 357 823	1 202 875	1 154 948	438 784	220 467	218 317	1 919 039	982 408	936 631

Continent, country or area, date, code[a] and age (in years) / Continent, pays ou zone, date, code[a] et âge (en années)	Total			Urban - Urbaine			Rural - Rurale		
	Both sexes Les deux sexes	Male Masculin	Female Féminin	Both sexes Les deux sexes	Male Masculin	Female Féminin	Both sexes Les deux sexes	Male Masculin	Female Féminin
AFRICA - AFRIQUE									
Mali									
1 IV 2009 (CDFC)									
10 - 14	1 784 004	918 866	865 138	382 494	183 203	199 291	1 401 510	735 663	665 847
15 - 19	1 516 146	732 526	783 620	427 554	194 158	233 396	1 088 592	538 368	550 224
20 - 24	1 141 903	529 535	612 368	341 272	171 703	169 569	800 631	357 832	442 799
25 - 29	995 702	449 099	546 603	267 899	132 127	135 772	727 803	316 972	410 831
30 - 34	812 798	385 003	427 795	206 544	109 060	97 484	606 254	275 943	330 311
35 - 39	651 949	325 055	326 894	164 783	89 830	74 953	487 166	235 225	251 941
40 - 44	546 603	271 239	275 364	128 845	70 127	58 718	417 758	201 112	216 646
45 - 49	445 887	228 626	217 261	103 042	56 502	46 540	342 845	172 124	170 721
50 - 54	381 806	189 424	192 382	82 013	44 826	37 187	299 793	144 598	155 195
55 - 59	282 677	148 594	134 083	57 960	31 957	26 003	224 717	116 637	108 080
60 - 64	251 018	127 557	123 461	46 442	23 790	22 652	204 576	103 767	100 809
65 - 69	165 374	88 292	77 082	30 159	15 641	14 518	135 215	72 651	62 564
70 - 74	133 382	67 319	66 063	23 729	11 518	12 211	109 653	55 801	53 852
75 - 79	77 101	40 904	36 197	12 871	6 306	6 565	64 230	34 598	29 632
80 +	85 594	41 992	43 602	14 246	6 009	8 237	71 348	35 983	35 365
Unknown - Inconnu	275 510	129 213	146 297	44 462	22 712	21 750	231 048	106 501	124 547
1 VII 2016 (ESDF)[16]									
Total	18 341 000	9 244 000	9 097 000	...	...	...	...	...	...
0 - 4	3 475 000	1 751 000	1 724 000	...	...	...	...	...	...
5 - 9	2 821 000	1 422 000	1 399 000	...	...	...	...	...	...
10 - 14	2 353 000	1 186 000	1 167 000	...	...	...	...	...	...
15 - 19	1 957 000	986 000	971 000	...	...	...	...	...	...
20 - 24	1 661 000	837 000	824 000	...	...	...	...	...	...
25 - 29	1 411 000	711 000	700 000	...	...	...	...	...	...
30 - 34	1 159 000	584 000	575 000	...	...	...	...	...	...
35 - 39	917 000	462 000	455 000	...	...	...	...	...	...
40 - 44	693 000	349 000	344 000	...	...	...	...	...	...
45 - 49	516 000	260 000	256 000	...	...	...	...	...	...
50 - 54	403 000	203 000	200 000	...	...	...	...	...	...
55 - 59	329 000	166 000	163 000	...	...	...	...	...	...
60 - 64	244 000	123 000	121 000	...	...	...	...	...	...
65 - 69	196 000	99 000	97 000	...	...	...	...	...	...
70 - 74	115 000	58 000	57 000	...	...	...	...	...	...
75 - 79	61 000	31 000	30 000	...	...	...	...	...	...
80 +	30 000	15 000	15 000	...	...	...	...	...	...
Mauritania - Mauritanie[2]									
1 VII 2016 (ESDF)									
Total	3 782 701	...	...	...	...	...	...	...	...
0 - 4	579 832	...	...	...	...	...	...	...	...
5 - 9	567 643	...	...	...	...	...	...	...	...
10 - 14	478 293	...	...	...	...	...	...	...	...
15 - 19	396 650	...	...	...	...	...	...	...	...
20 - 24	333 473	...	...	...	...	...	...	...	...
25 - 29	280 531	...	...	...	...	...	...	...	...
30 - 34	236 864	...	...	...	...	...	...	...	...
35 - 39	196 168	...	...	...	...	...	...	...	...
40 - 44	164 707	...	...	...	...	...	...	...	...
45 - 49	137 439	...	...	...	...	...	...	...	...
50 - 54	111 936	...	...	...	...	...	...	...	...
55 - 59	90 008	...	...	...	...	...	...	...	...
60 - 64	68 836	...	...	...	...	...	...	...	...
65 - 69	50 266	...	...	...	...	...	...	...	...
70 - 74	36 188	...	...	...	...	...	...	...	...
75 - 79	24 540	...	...	...	...	...	...	...	...
80 +	29 328	...	...	...	...	...	...	...	...
Mauritius - Maurice[17]									
4 VII 2011 (CDJC)									
Total	1 236 817	610 848	625 969	499 349	244 688	254 661	737 468	366 160	371 308
0 - 4	73 078	36 702	36 376	26 297	13 220	13 077	46 781	23 482	23 299
5 - 9	89 015	44 947	44 068	32 036	16 177	15 859	56 979	28 770	28 209
10 - 14	93 639	47 302	46 337	35 028	17 523	17 505	58 611	29 779	28 832
15 - 19	101 008	50 715	50 293	39 403	19 725	19 678	61 605	30 990	30 615
20 - 24	92 671	46 871	45 800	37 224	18 836	18 388	55 447	28 035	27 412

Continent, country or area, date, code[a] and age (in years) / Continent, pays ou zone, date, code[a] et âge (en années)	Total			Urban - Urbaine			Rural - Rurale		
	Both sexes Les deux sexes	Male Masculin	Female Féminin	Both sexes Les deux sexes	Male Masculin	Female Féminin	Both sexes Les deux sexes	Male Masculin	Female Féminin
AFRICA - AFRIQUE									
Mauritius - Maurice[17]									
4 VII 2011 (CDJC)									
25 - 29	90 937	45 589	45 348	35 908	17 899	18 009	55 029	27 690	27 339
30 - 34	103 429	52 182	51 247	39 099	19 805	19 294	64 330	32 377	31 953
35 - 39	87 797	44 241	43 556	32 781	16 142	16 639	55 016	28 099	26 917
40 - 44	89 386	45 150	44 236	34 449	17 010	17 439	54 937	28 140	26 797
45 - 49	99 341	49 800	49 541	41 705	20 637	21 068	57 636	29 163	28 473
50 - 54	86 337	42 996	43 341	37 429	18 627	18 802	48 908	24 369	24 539
55 - 59	73 054	35 713	37 341	32 421	15 983	16 438	40 633	19 730	20 903
60 - 64	57 342	27 143	30 199	25 449	12 058	13 391	31 893	15 085	16 808
65 - 69	35 439	15 846	19 593	16 700	7 527	9 173	18 739	8 319	10 420
70 - 74	25 375	10 986	14 389	12 872	5 661	7 211	12 503	5 325	7 178
75 - 79	18 044	7 349	10 695	9 320	3 851	5 469	8 724	3 498	5 226
80 - 84	11 369	4 176	7 193	6 028	2 253	3 775	5 341	1 923	3 418
85 - 89	6 368	2 135	4 233	3 427	1 179	2 248	2 941	956	1 985
90 - 94	1 982	512	1 470	1 046	275	771	936	237	699
95 - 99	491	107	384	297	60	237	194	47	147
100 +	96	13	83	55	7	48	41	6	35
Unknown - Inconnu	619	373	246	375	233	142	244	140	104
1 VII 2018 (ESDJ)[18]									
Total	1 265 303	626 030	639 273	...	...	...	...	...	...
0	13 000	6 650	6 350	...	...	...	...	...	...
1 - 4	52 047	26 558	25 489	...	...	...	...	...	...
5 - 9	73 387	37 121	36 266	...	...	...	...	...	...
10 - 14	88 741	45 202	43 539	...	...	...	...	...	...
15 - 19	97 650	49 644	48 006	...	...	...	...	...	...
20 - 24	97 056	48 914	48 142	...	...	...	...	...	...
25 - 29	96 442	48 863	47 579	...	...	...	...	...	...
30 - 34	83 911	42 359	41 552	...	...	...	...	...	...
35 - 39	98 517	49 954	48 563	...	...	...	...	...	...
40 - 44	91 020	46 121	44 899	...	...	...	...	...	...
45 - 49	81 161	41 062	40 099	...	...	...	...	...	...
50 - 54	93 866	46 764	47 102	...	...	...	...	...	...
55 - 59	86 490	42 311	44 179	...	...	...	...	...	...
60 - 64	72 374	34 776	37 598	...	...	...	...	...	...
65 - 69	58 717	27 259	31 458	...	...	...	...	...	...
70 - 74	35 842	15 564	20 278	...	...	...	...	...	...
75 - 79	20 738	8 438	12 300	...	...	...	...	...	...
80 - 84	14 016	5 279	8 737	...	...	...	...	...	...
85 +	10 328	3 191	7 137	...	...	...	...	...	...
Mayotte									
1 I 2018* (ESDJ)									
Total	259 154	125 728	133 426	...	...	...	...	...	...
0 - 4	40 945	20 617	20 328	...	...	...	...	...	...
5 - 9	39 080	19 570	19 510	...	...	...	...	...	...
10 - 14	34 404	17 008	17 396	...	...	...	...	...	...
15 - 19	26 780	13 085	13 695	...	...	...	...	...	...
20 - 24	15 834	7 085	8 749	...	...	...	...	...	...
25 - 29	17 908	7 159	10 749	...	...	...	...	...	...
30 - 34	18 912	8 055	10 857	...	...	...	...	...	...
35 - 39	17 597	8 075	9 522	...	...	...	...	...	...
40 - 44	14 187	7 493	6 694	...	...	...	...	...	...
45 - 49	9 390	4 896	4 494	...	...	...	...	...	...
50 - 54	7 598	3 995	3 603	...	...	...	...	...	...
55 - 59	5 827	3 176	2 651	...	...	...	...	...	...
60 - 64	4 043	2 240	1 803	...	...	...	...	...	...
65 - 69	2 482	1 262	1 220	...	...	...	...	...	...
70 - 74	1 856	921	935	...	...	...	...	...	...
75 - 79	1 117	565	552	...	...	...	...	...	...
80 - 84	732	315	417	...	...	...	...	...	...
85 - 89	255	110	145	...	...	...	...	...	...
90 - 94	152	76	76	...	...	...	...	...	...
95 +	55	25	30	...	...	...	...	...	...

7. Population by age, sex and urban/rural residence: latest available year, 2009 - 2018
Population selon l'âge, le sexe et la résidence, urbaine/rurale : dernière année disponible, 2009 - 2018 (continued - suite)

Continent, country or area, date, code[a] and age (in years) / Continent, pays ou zone, date, code[a] et âge (en années)	Total			Urban - Urbaine			Rural - Rurale		
	Both sexes Les deux sexes	Male Masculin	Female Féminin	Both sexes Les deux sexes	Male Masculin	Female Féminin	Both sexes Les deux sexes	Male Masculin	Female Féminin
AFRICA - AFRIQUE									
Morocco - Maroc[19]									
1 VII 2018 (ESDJ)									
Total	35 219 547	17 544 027	17 675 520	21 968 101	10 827 825	11 140 276	13 251 446	6 716 202	6 535 244
0	590 049	301 599	288 450	352 660	180 239	172 421	237 389	121 360	116 029
1 - 4	2 478 550	1 266 057	1 212 493	1 446 220	738 375	707 845	1 032 330	527 682	504 648
5 - 9	3 302 333	1 688 195	1 614 138	1 878 016	959 688	918 328	1 424 317	728 507	695 810
10 - 14	3 011 292	1 536 104	1 475 188	1 706 549	869 705	836 844	1 304 743	666 399	638 344
15 - 19	3 028 020	1 542 834	1 485 186	1 741 045	881 135	859 910	1 286 975	661 699	625 276
20 - 24	2 974 479	1 487 061	1 487 418	1 830 245	899 088	931 157	1 144 234	587 973	556 261
25 - 29	2 987 341	1 475 780	1 511 561	1 946 493	936 987	1 009 506	1 040 848	538 793	502 055
30 - 34	2 731 359	1 339 915	1 391 444	1 792 081	863 290	928 791	939 278	476 625	462 653
35 - 39	2 557 288	1 248 599	1 308 689	1 681 123	808 111	873 012	876 165	440 488	435 677
40 - 44	2 294 500	1 112 372	1 182 128	1 510 842	716 333	794 509	783 658	396 039	387 619
45 - 49	2 072 067	1 011 501	1 060 566	1 388 915	667 848	721 067	683 152	343 653	339 499
50 - 54	1 790 935	870 585	920 350	1 213 200	582 957	630 243	577 735	287 628	290 107
55 - 59	1 706 866	844 350	862 516	1 144 259	567 293	576 966	562 607	277 057	285 550
60 - 64	1 280 397	658 918	621 479	851 502	440 398	411 104	428 895	218 520	210 375
65 - 69	992 848	501 648	491 200	631 251	324 223	307 028	361 597	177 425	184 172
70 - 74	550 449	264 153	286 296	336 718	160 540	176 178	213 731	103 613	110 118
75 - 79	451 649	205 185	246 464	269 935	121 869	148 066	181 714	83 316	98 398
80 +	419 125	189 171	229 954	247 047	109 746	137 301	172 078	79 425	92 653
Mozambique[9]									
1 VII 2017 (ESDF)									
Total	27 128 530	13 106 447	14 022 083	8 766 777	4 281 319	4 485 458	18 361 753	8 825 128	9 536 625
0 - 4	4 557 840	2 277 526	2 280 314	1 163 788	580 924	582 864	3 394 052	1 696 602	1 697 450
5 - 9	3 997 583	1 992 967	2 004 616	1 108 187	552 191	555 996	2 889 396	1 440 776	1 448 620
10 - 14	3 519 245	1 749 479	1 769 766	1 092 175	539 751	552 424	2 427 070	1 209 728	1 217 342
15 - 19	2 946 806	1 473 812	1 472 994	1 044 149	515 419	528 730	1 902 657	958 393	944 264
20 - 24	2 470 502	1 179 270	1 291 232	965 641	476 936	488 705	1 504 861	702 334	802 527
25 - 29	2 035 518	914 196	1 121 322	807 851	387 340	420 511	1 227 667	526 856	700 811
30 - 34	1 692 760	752 742	940 018	640 494	297 453	343 041	1 052 266	455 289	596 977
35 - 39	1 362 667	634 117	728 550	502 245	237 161	265 084	860 422	396 956	463 466
40 - 44	1 123 344	528 397	594 947	396 939	191 051	205 888	726 405	337 346	389 059
45 - 49	918 912	430 645	488 267	314 503	152 578	161 925	604 409	278 067	326 342
50 - 54	696 087	342 800	353 287	222 907	112 234	110 673	473 180	230 566	242 614
55 - 59	550 481	264 269	286 212	170 928	84 738	86 190	379 553	179 531	200 022
60 - 64	428 657	194 900	233 757	123 516	59 143	64 373	305 141	135 757	169 384
65 - 69	319 540	145 236	174 304	88 321	41 584	46 737	231 219	103 652	127 567
70 - 74	225 428	102 256	123 172	57 447	25 630	31 817	167 981	76 626	91 355
75 - 79	146 194	65 188	81 006	35 638	15 096	20 542	110 556	50 092	60 464
80 +	136 966	58 647	78 319	32 048	12 090	19 958	104 918	46 557	58 361
Namibia - Namibie[20]									
1 VII 2018 (ESDF)									
Total	2 413 643	1 173 540	1 240 103	1 203 340	586 616	616 724	1 210 303	586 924	623 379
0	67 673	34 260	33 413	34 659	17 543	17 116	33 014	16 717	16 297
1 - 4	260 809	131 823	128 986	127 579	64 472	63 107	133 230	67 351	65 879
5 - 9	301 878	152 237	149 641	...	...	...	...	...	...
10 - 14	251 316	126 503	124 813	...	...	...	...	...	...
15 - 19	238 928	118 994	119 934	...	...	...	...	...	...
20 - 24	238 148	116 964	121 184	...	...	...	...	...	...
25 - 29	218 476	106 957	111 519	...	...	...	...	...	...
30 - 34	181 356	88 221	93 135	...	...	...	...	...	...
35 - 39	146 942	70 976	75 966	...	...	...	...	...	...
40 - 44	122 948	58 889	64 059	...	...	...	...	...	...
45 - 49	97 642	45 706	51 936	...	...	...	...	...	...
50 - 54	78 100	35 469	42 631	...	...	...	...	...	...
55 - 59	60 987	26 349	34 638	...	...	...	...	...	...
60 - 64	45 011	18 892	26 119	...	...	...	...	...	...
65 - 69	35 826	15 380	20 446	...	...	...	...	...	...
70 - 74	26 750	11 021	15 729	...	...	...	...	...	...
75 - 79	17 496	6 873	10 623	...	...	...	...	...	...
80 +	23 357	8 026	15 331	...	...	...	...	...	...

Continent, country or area, date, code[a] and age (in years) / Continent, pays ou zone, date, code[a] et âge (en années)	Total			Urban - Urbaine			Rural - Rurale		
	Both sexes Les deux sexes	Male Masculin	Female Féminin	Both sexes Les deux sexes	Male Masculin	Female Féminin	Both sexes Les deux sexes	Male Masculin	Female Féminin
AFRICA - AFRIQUE									
Niger[21]									
1 VII 2016 (ESDJ)									
Total	19 865 067	9 898 628	9 966 439	3 242 161	1 617 882	1 624 278	16 622 906	8 280 747	8 342 160
0 - 4	3 966 109	2 009 845	1 956 264	560 061	281 015	279 046	3 406 048	1 728 830	1 677 218
5 - 9	3 533 085	1 810 213	1 722 872	514 367	259 802	254 565	3 018 718	1 550 412	1 468 306
10 - 14	2 790 727	1 418 659	1 372 068	450 479	223 341	227 137	2 340 248	1 195 317	1 144 931
15 - 19	2 021 025	1 010 216	1 010 809	344 569	173 980	170 589	1 676 456	836 236	840 220
20 - 24	1 619 917	777 760	842 157	316 826	159 697	157 130	1 303 090	618 063	685 027
25 - 29	1 236 640	592 643	643 996	220 452	107 039	113 413	1 016 188	485 605	530 583
30 - 34	1 013 696	493 232	520 464	186 768	91 960	94 808	826 927	401 271	425 656
35 - 39	845 916	404 801	441 115	153 624	74 733	78 891	692 293	330 068	362 225
40 - 44	679 710	326 886	352 824	123 978	61 940	62 037	555 732	264 946	290 786
45 - 49	544 473	267 053	277 420	98 818	50 233	48 585	445 656	216 820	228 836
50 - 54	460 236	223 786	236 450	81 307	40 036	41 271	378 929	183 750	195 179
55 - 59	351 487	174 412	177 075	62 257	30 864	31 393	289 230	143 548	145 681
60 - 64	264 109	129 848	134 261	45 097	22 523	22 574	219 012	107 324	111 687
65 - 69	192 038	94 284	97 754	31 661	15 974	15 688	160 376	78 310	82 066
70 - 74	145 168	69 830	75 338	22 937	11 136	11 801	122 231	58 694	63 537
75 - 79	99 975	48 349	51 626	15 105	7 379	7 725	84 870	40 970	43 900
80 +	100 757	46 811	53 946	13 855	6 229	7 626	86 902	40 582	46 320
Nigeria - Nigéria[22]									
1 VII 2016 (ESDF)									
Total	193 392 517	...	...	...	...	...	...	...	...
0 - 4	31 116 156	...	...	...	...	...	...	...	...
5 - 9	27 549 964	...	...	...	...	...	...	...	...
10 - 14	22 221 265	...	...	...	...	...	...	...	...
15 - 19	20 518 404	...	...	...	...	...	...	...	...
20 - 24	18 501 820	...	...	...	...	...	...	...	...
25 - 29	16 816 694	...	...	...	...	...	...	...	...
30 - 34	13 038 009	...	...	...	...	...	...	...	...
35 - 39	10 096 763	...	...	...	...	...	...	...	...
40 - 44	8 891 384	...	...	...	...	...	...	...	...
45 - 49	6 322 797	...	...	...	...	...	...	...	...
50 - 54	5 851 717	...	...	...	...	...	...	...	...
55 - 59	2 845 486	...	...	...	...	...	...	...	...
60 - 64	3 374 357	...	...	...	...	...	...	...	...
65 - 69	1 585 140	...	...	...	...	...	...	...	...
70 - 74	1 832 402	...	...	...	...	...	...	...	...
75 - 79	798 511	...	...	...	...	...	...	...	...
80 - 84	1 046 690	...	...	...	...	...	...	...	...
85 +	984 956	...	...	...	...	...	...	...	...
Republic of South Sudan - République de Soudan du Sud[23]									
1 VII 2018 (ESDF)									
Total	12 323 420	6 311 618	6 011 801	...	...	...	...	...	...
0 - 4	2 583 635	1 301 082	1 282 553	...	...	...	...	...	...
5 - 9	2 063 286	1 036 396	1 026 890	...	...	...	...	...	...
10 - 14	1 283 328	674 769	608 559	...	...	...	...	...	...
15 - 19	1 272 679	674 552	598 127	...	...	...	...	...	...
20 - 24	1 026 431	552 586	473 845	...	...	...	...	...	...
25 - 29	851 834	442 942	408 891	...	...	...	...	...	...
30 - 34	703 523	343 313	360 210	...	...	...	...	...	...
35 - 39	661 345	317 791	343 554	...	...	...	...	...	...
40 - 44	504 869	243 196	261 673	...	...	...	...	...	...
45 - 49	440 328	221 473	218 855	...	...	...	...	...	...
50 - 54	307 725	157 507	150 218	...	...	...	...	...	...
55 - 59	240 125	130 983	109 143	...	...	...	...	...	...
60 - 64	161 580	86 498	75 082	...	...	...	...	...	...
65 - 69	89 691	50 690	39 001	...	...	...	...	...	...
70 - 74	73 472	41 750	31 722	...	...	...	...	...	...
75 - 79	34 683	20 477	14 206	...	...	...	...	...	...
80 - 84	18 816	11 648	7 168	...	...	...	...	...	...
85 - 89	4 503	2 942	1 561	...	...	...	...	...	...

Continent, country or area, date, code[a] and age (in years) / Continent, pays ou zone, date, code[a] et âge (en années)	Total			Urban - Urbaine			Rural - Rurale		
	Both sexes Les deux sexes	Male Masculin	Female Féminin	Both sexes Les deux sexes	Male Masculin	Female Féminin	Both sexes Les deux sexes	Male Masculin	Female Féminin
AFRICA - AFRIQUE									
Republic of South Sudan - République de Soudan du Sud[23]									
1 VII 2018 (ESDF)									
90 - 94	1 483	965	518	...	...	...	...	...	...
95 +	83	57	26	...	...	...	...	...	...
Reunion - Réunion									
1 I 2015 (CDJC)									
Total	850 727	411 435	439 292	838 228	405 123	433 105	12 499	6 312	6 187
0 - 4	62 021	31 643	30 377	61 139	31 203	29 936	882	440	442
5 - 9	68 814	35 386	33 428	67 849	34 856	32 992	965	530	435
10 - 14	71 429	36 713	34 716	70 409	36 202	34 208	1 020	512	508
15 - 19	67 979	34 756	33 223	67 007	34 252	32 754	972	504	469
20 - 24	54 703	27 392	27 312	53 896	26 970	26 926	807	422	385
25 - 29	52 295	24 326	27 969	51 522	23 977	27 545	774	350	424
30 - 34	52 379	23 815	28 564	51 620	23 434	28 186	759	381	378
35 - 39	56 023	25 787	30 236	55 270	25 412	29 858	753	375	378
40 - 44	60 610	28 755	31 855	59 755	28 323	31 432	856	432	423
45 - 49	65 416	31 471	33 945	64 340	30 897	33 442	1 077	574	503
50 - 54	60 858	29 842	31 017	59 902	29 329	30 573	956	513	444
55 - 59	50 551	24 330	26 221	49 807	23 950	25 857	744	380	364
60 - 64	40 918	19 874	21 043	40 336	19 584	20 752	582	290	291
65 - 69	29 519	14 070	15 448	29 146	13 878	15 268	373	192	181
70 - 74	21 688	9 895	11 794	21 287	9 717	11 570	402	178	224
75 - 79	16 390	6 870	9 521	16 112	6 750	9 363	278	120	158
80 - 84	10 203	3 920	6 283	10 030	3 846	6 183	173	73	100
85 - 89	5 681	1 762	3 919	5 594	1 727	3 867	87	35	52
90 - 94	2 505	662	1 843	2 473	651	1 822	32	11	21
95 - 99	560	120	441	555	120	436	5	-	5
100 +	183	47	137	179	46	134	4	1	3
1 VII 2018* (ESDJ)[24]									
Total	864 459	414 304	450 155	...	...	...	...	...	...
0	12 020	6 108	5 912	...	...	...	...	...	...
1 - 4	49 168	24 710	24 458	...	...	...	...	...	...
5 - 9	66 395	33 472	32 923	...	...	...	...	...	...
10 - 14	70 777	36 560	34 217	...	...	...	...	...	...
15 - 19	68 810	35 094	33 716	...	...	...	...	...	...
20 - 24	50 697	25 176	25 521	...	...	...	...	...	...
25 - 29	49 675	23 208	26 467	...	...	...	...	...	...
30 - 34	51 330	22 954	28 376	...	...	...	...	...	...
35 - 39	54 042	24 308	29 734	...	...	...	...	...	...
40 - 44	57 267	26 283	30 984	...	...	...	...	...	...
45 - 49	61 778	29 517	32 261	...	...	...	...	...	...
50 - 54	65 915	32 022	33 893	...	...	...	...	...	...
55 - 59	56 573	27 483	29 090	...	...	...	...	...	...
60 - 64	47 596	22 725	24 871	...	...	...	...	...	...
65 - 69	36 113	17 031	19 082	...	...	...	...	...	...
70 - 74	24 729	11 527	13 202	...	...	...	...	...	...
75 - 79	18 565	8 090	10 475	...	...	...	...	...	...
80 - 84	12 807	4 830	7 977	...	...	...	...	...	...
85 - 89	6 465	2 184	4 281	...	...	...	...	...	...
90 - 94	2 835	839	1 996	...	...	...	...	...	...
95 +	902	183	719	...	...	...	...	...	...
Rwanda[21]									
1 VII 2018 (ESDF)									
Total	12 089 721	5 864 287	6 225 434	2 484 438	1 205 111	1 279 327	9 605 283	4 659 176	4 946 108
0 - 4	1 648 441	832 116	816 325	303 818	144 018	159 800	1 344 623	688 098	656 526
5 - 9	1 512 717	755 053	757 664	251 534	117 889	133 645	1 261 184	637 164	624 019
10 - 14	1 519 598	755 699	763 899	267 027	123 038	143 989	1 252 571	632 661	619 910
15 - 19	1 300 459	641 237	659 222	277 866	121 482	156 385	1 022 593	519 755	502 838
20 - 24	1 117 150	547 949	569 202	300 544	146 090	154 455	816 606	401 859	414 747
25 - 29	1 023 675	495 808	527 868	282 724	143 525	139 199	740 951	352 282	388 669
30 - 34	932 515	456 574	475 941	239 543	126 353	113 190	692 972	330 221	362 751
35 - 39	786 062	381 334	404 728	189 183	100 614	88 569	596 880	280 720	316 159
40 - 44	536 752	247 042	289 711	114 292	59 115	55 177	422 460	187 926	234 534

Continent, country or area, date, code[a] and age (in years) Continent, pays ou zone, date, code[a] et âge (en années)	Total			Urban - Urbaine			Rural - Rurale		
	Both sexes Les deux sexes	Male Masculin	Female Féminin	Both sexes Les deux sexes	Male Masculin	Female Féminin	Both sexes Les deux sexes	Male Masculin	Female Féminin
AFRICA - AFRIQUE									
Rwanda[21]									
1 VII 2018 (ESDF)									
45 - 49	415 822	189 639	226 183	76 421	39 309	37 113	339 400	150 330	189 070
50 - 54	334 996	152 403	182 593	51 475	26 156	25 319	283 521	126 248	157 273
55 - 59	324 215	144 622	179 593	45 478	22 228	23 249	278 737	122 393	156 344
60 - 64	240 689	105 583	135 106	32 276	15 161	17 115	208 413	90 422	117 991
65 - 69	166 859	71 693	95 166	22 520	9 798	12 723	144 338	61 895	82 443
70 - 74	92 467	36 347	56 120	11 746	4 498	7 248	80 721	31 849	48 872
75 - 79	67 821	25 135	42 685	8 916	3 056	5 860	58 905	22 079	36 826
80 +	69 482	26 054	43 427	9 075	2 782	6 293	60 407	23 272	37 135
Saint Helena ex. dep. - **Sainte-Hélène sans dép.[25]**									
7 II 2016 (CDJC)									
Total	4 534	2 396	2 138	...	...	...	...	...	...
0	50	24	26	...	...	...	...	...	...
1 - 4	163	83	80	...	...	...	...	...	...
5 - 9	209	116	93	...	...	...	...	...	...
10 - 14	191	98	93	...	...	...	...	...	...
15 - 19	236	123	113	...	...	...	...	...	...
20 - 24	203	122	81	...	...	...	...	...	...
25 - 29	235	128	107	...	...	...	...	...	...
30 - 34	288	141	147	...	...	...	...	...	...
35 - 39	249	130	119	...	...	...	...	...	...
40 - 44	334	184	150	...	...	...	...	...	...
45 - 49	403	222	181	...	...	...	...	...	...
50 - 54	357	182	175	...	...	...	...	...	...
55 - 59	365	188	177	...	...	...	...	...	...
60 - 64	314	176	138	...	...	...	...	...	...
65 - 69	343	178	165	...	...	...	...	...	...
70 - 74	269	159	110	...	...	...	...	...	...
75 - 79	152	74	78	...	...	...	...	...	...
80 - 84	102	52	50	...	...	...	...	...	...
85 - 89	44	12	32	...	...	...	...	...	...
90 - 94	23	4	19	...	...	...	...	...	...
95 - 99	3	-	3	...	...	...	...	...	...
100 +	1	-	1	...	...	...	...	...	...
Unknown - Inconnu	-	-	-	...	...	...	...	...	...
Sao Tome and Principe - **Sao Tomé-et-Principe[26]**									
1 VII 2017 (ESDJ)									
Total	197 700	97 988	99 712	133 748	66 291	67 457	63 952	31 697	32 255
0 - 4	24 133	12 031	12 102	16 249	8 217	8 032	7 883	3 814	4 070
5 - 9	27 500	13 833	13 667	18 273	9 375	8 898	9 227	4 458	4 769
10 - 14	25 390	12 677	12 714	17 054	8 509	8 546	8 336	4 168	4 168
15 - 19	21 345	10 673	10 672	14 430	7 149	7 281	6 915	3 524	3 391
20 - 24	18 341	9 278	9 062	12 555	6 298	6 257	5 786	2 981	2 805
25 - 29	15 841	7 895	7 946	11 026	5 460	5 566	4 815	2 435	2 380
30 - 34	14 665	7 276	7 389	10 078	4 984	5 094	4 587	2 292	2 295
35 - 39	12 358	6 105	6 252	8 237	4 046	4 191	4 120	2 059	2 061
40 - 44	9 546	4 762	4 784	6 404	3 155	3 249	3 142	1 607	1 535
45 - 49	7 654	3 831	3 822	5 256	2 618	2 638	2 398	1 214	1 184
50 - 54	6 033	2 880	3 153	4 200	2 000	2 200	1 833	881	953
55 - 59	5 004	2 384	2 620	3 518	1 690	1 827	1 486	694	792
60 - 64	3 431	1 573	1 858	2 326	1 054	1 272	1 105	519	586
65 - 69	2 249	1 076	1 173	1 477	689	787	772	386	385
70 - 74	1 500	665	835	932	400	532	568	265	303
75 - 79	1 313	535	777	796	320	477	516	216	301
80 +	1 400	514	886	938	329	609	463	185	277
Senegal - Sénégal[2]									
1 VII 2016 (ESDJ)									
Total	14 799 859	7 372 487	7 427 372	...	...	...	...	...	...
0 - 4	2 384 522	1 212 846	1 171 676	...	...	...	...	...	...
5 - 9	2 016 277	1 037 276	979 001	...	...	...	...	...	...
10 - 14	1 784 725	918 849	865 876	...	...	...	...	...	...
15 - 19	1 560 123	797 927	762 196	...	...	...	...	...	...

Continent, country or area, date, code[a] and age (in years) / Continent, pays ou zone, date, code[a] et âge (en années)	Total			Urban - Urbaine			Rural - Rurale		
	Both sexes Les deux sexes	Male Masculin	Female Féminin	Both sexes Les deux sexes	Male Masculin	Female Féminin	Both sexes Les deux sexes	Male Masculin	Female Féminin
AFRICA - AFRIQUE									
Senegal - Sénégal[2]									
1 VII 2016 (ESDJ)									
20 - 24	1 359 140	675 294	683 846	...	...	...	...	...	...
25 - 29	1 166 100	559 321	606 779	...	...	...	...	...	...
30 - 34	973 530	466 740	506 790	...	...	...	...	...	...
35 - 39	795 699	384 264	411 435	...	...	...	...	...	...
40 - 44	645 123	307 640	337 483	...	...	...	...	...	...
45 - 49	511 410	240 118	271 292	...	...	...	...	...	...
50 - 54	430 078	204 461	225 617	...	...	...	...	...	...
55 - 59	360 730	174 948	185 782	...	...	...	...	...	...
60 - 64	276 702	135 025	141 677	...	...	...	...	...	...
65 - 69	198 778	97 438	101 340	...	...	...	...	...	...
70 - 74	141 928	69 235	72 693	...	...	...	...	...	...
75 - 79	90 654	43 423	47 231	...	...	...	...	...	...
80 +	104 340	47 682	56 658	...	...	...	...	...	...
Seychelles									
1 VII 2017 (ESDF)									
Total	95 843	48 793	47 050	...	...	...	...	...	...
0 - 4	7 682	3 971	3 711	...	...	...	...	...	...
5 - 9	6 336	3 225	3 111	...	...	...	...	...	...
10 - 14	5 218	2 629	2 589	...	...	...	...	...	...
15 - 19	4 012	1 980	2 032	...	...	...	...	...	...
20 - 24	3 694	2 202	1 492	...	...	...	...	...	...
25 - 29	5 958	3 368	2 590	...	...	...	...	...	...
30 - 34	7 990	4 680	3 310	...	...	...	...	...	...
35 - 39	9 323	4 814	4 509	...	...	...	...	...	...
40 - 44	6 859	3 529	3 330	...	...	...	...	...	...
45 - 49	8 439	4 333	4 106	...	...	...	...	...	...
50 - 54	6 856	2 991	3 865	...	...	...	...	...	...
55 - 59	8 424	4 177	4 247	...	...	...	...	...	...
60 - 64	5 812	2 901	2 911	...	...	...	...	...	...
65 - 69	3 863	1 924	1 939	...	...	...	...	...	...
70 - 74	2 086	995	1 091	...	...	...	...	...	...
75 - 79	1 528	603	925	...	...	...	...	...	...
80 - 84	994	315	679	...	...	...	...	...	...
85 - 89	540	116	424	...	...	...	...	...	...
90 +	229	40	189	...	...	...	...	...	...
Sierra Leone									
1 VII 2010 (ESDF)									
Total	5 746 800	2 786 797	2 960 003	2 304 955	1 138 563	1 166 392	3 441 845	1 648 234	1 793 611
0 - 4	878 231	437 908	440 323	297 865	147 565	150 300	580 366	290 343	290 023
5 - 9	856 605	424 222	432 383	307 007	145 641	161 366	549 598	278 581	271 017
10 - 14	662 651	338 453	324 198	303 094	148 401	154 693	359 557	190 052	169 505
15 - 19	637 914	308 982	328 932	287 597	141 564	146 033	350 317	167 418	182 899
20 - 24	488 054	221 932	266 122	241 599	119 622	121 977	246 455	102 310	144 145
25 - 29	473 952	210 004	263 948	205 137	102 492	102 645	268 815	107 512	161 303
30 - 34	356 727	160 822	195 905	149 414	73 308	76 106	207 313	87 514	119 799
35 - 39	341 470	160 326	181 144	133 461	66 104	67 357	208 009	94 222	113 787
40 - 44	247 978	123 279	124 699	97 102	51 623	45 479	150 876	71 656	79 220
45 - 49	201 708	107 932	93 776	76 536	41 832	34 704	125 172	66 100	59 072
50 - 54	149 167	77 236	71 931	55 139	30 564	24 575	94 028	46 672	47 356
55 - 59	96 801	51 344	45 457	37 477	21 157	16 320	59 324	30 187	29 137
60 - 64	99 394	44 873	54 521	31 058	14 915	16 143	68 336	29 958	38 378
65 - 69	71 174	34 054	37 120	24 423	11 420	13 003	46 751	22 634	24 117
70 - 74	61 847	28 198	33 649	18 941	8 268	10 673	42 906	19 930	22 976
75 - 79	41 728	21 586	20 142	12 876	6 356	6 520	28 852	15 230	13 622
80 +	81 399	35 646	45 753	26 229	7 731	18 498	55 170	27 915	27 255
5 XII 2015 (CDFC)									
Total	7 092 113	3 490 978	3 601 135	...	...	...	...	...	...
0 - 4	938 453	469 092	469 361	...	...	...	...	...	...
5 - 9	1 108 715	555 292	553 423	...	...	...	...	...	...
10 - 14	847 292	431 588	415 704	...	...	...	...	...	...
15 - 19	873 620	430 792	442 828	...	...	...	...	...	...
20 - 24	662 819	308 135	354 684	...	...	...	...	...	...
25 - 29	607 983	277 618	330 365	...	...	...	...	...	...

Continent, country or area, date, code[a] and age (in years) / Continent, pays ou zone, date, code[a] et âge (en annèes)	Total			Urban - Urbaine			Rural - Rurale		
	Both sexes Les deux sexes	Male Masculin	Female Féminin	Both sexes Les deux sexes	Male Masculin	Female Féminin	Both sexes Les deux sexes	Male Masculin	Female Féminin
AFRICA - AFRIQUE									
Sierra Leone									
5 XII 2015 (CDFC)									
30 - 34	434 203	199 964	234 239	...	...	...	...	...	...
35 - 39	421 172	201 459	219 713	...	...	...	...	...	...
40 - 44	299 215	154 121	145 094	...	...	...	...	...	...
45 - 49	242 188	133 783	108 405	...	...	...	...	...	...
50 - 54	186 793	99 050	87 743	...	...	...	...	...	...
55 - 59	110 449	59 261	51 188	...	...	...	...	...	...
60 - 64	112 682	53 987	58 695	...	...	...	...	...	...
65 - 69	73 722	36 414	37 308	...	...	...	...	...	...
70 - 74	65 568	30 606	34 962	...	...	...	...	...	...
75 - 79	39 728	20 044	19 684	...	...	...	...	...	...
80 - 84	31 359	13 177	18 182	...	...	...	...	...	...
85 - 89	15 888	7 258	8 630	...	...	...	...	...	...
90 - 94	9 984	4 430	5 554	...	...	...	...	...	...
95 +	10 280	4 907	5 373	...	...	...	...	...	...
South Africa - Afrique du Sud[1]									
1 VII 2018 (ESDF)									
Total	57 725 606	28 180 101	29 545 505	...	...	...	...	...	...
0	1 178 916	592 110	586 807	...	...	...	...	...	...
1 - 4	4 750 035	2 378 193	2 371 842	...	...	...	...	...	...
5 - 9	5 862 081	2 941 029	2 921 052	...	...	...	...	...	...
10 - 14	5 252 485	2 623 611	2 628 874	...	...	...	...	...	...
15 - 19	4 733 790	2 360 947	2 372 843	...	...	...	...	...	...
20 - 24	5 019 161	2 490 594	2 528 566	...	...	...	...	...	...
25 - 29	5 486 952	2 756 645	2 730 307	...	...	...	...	...	...
30 - 34	5 345 242	2 709 109	2 636 133	...	...	...	...	...	...
35 - 39	4 381 136	2 226 629	2 154 507	...	...	...	...	...	...
40 - 44	3 449 186	1 739 843	1 709 343	...	...	...	...	...	...
45 - 49	2 892 370	1 402 166	1 490 204	...	...	...	...	...	...
50 - 54	2 422 581	1 084 700	1 337 881	...	...	...	...	...	...
55 - 59	2 062 367	919 710	1 142 656	...	...	...	...	...	...
60 - 64	1 665 090	724 416	940 674	...	...	...	...	...	...
65 - 69	1 253 626	526 610	727 015	...	...	...	...	...	...
70 - 74	853 963	338 535	515 429	...	...	...	...	...	...
75 - 79	553 023	201 946	351 076	...	...	...	...	...	...
80 +	563 604	163 309	400 295	...	...	...	...	...	...
Sudan - Soudan									
1 VII 2016 (ESDF)									
Total	39 647 621	20 105 842	19 541 779	14 269 540	7 236 276	7 033 264	25 378 082	12 869 567	12 508 515
0	1 495 606	762 197	733 409	454 208	223 675	230 524	1 041 398	538 523	502 885
1 - 4	5 388 576	2 744 131	2 644 444	1 636 483	805 294	831 198	3 752 093	1 938 838	1 813 247
5 - 9	5 479 254	2 801 266	2 677 988	1 758 182	874 065	884 117	3 721 072	1 927 201	1 793 872
10 - 14	4 522 096	2 325 624	2 196 472	1 542 867	777 406	765 461	2 979 229	1 548 218	1 431 011
15 - 19	4 025 611	2 073 006	1 952 605	1 447 819	739 848	707 970	2 577 793	1 333 158	1 244 635
20 - 24	3 537 491	1 816 041	1 721 450	1 363 235	711 648	651 587	2 174 256	1 104 393	1 069 863
25 - 29	3 067 006	1 547 613	1 519 393	1 222 270	635 394	586 876	1 844 735	912 219	932 517
30 - 34	2 625 594	1 295 965	1 329 629	1 066 750	549 164	517 585	1 558 844	746 801	812 043
35 - 39	2 221 636	1 085 101	1 136 535	908 234	463 534	444 700	1 313 401	621 567	691 835
40 - 44	1 840 327	891 195	949 131	741 484	371 028	370 456	1 098 843	520 167	578 675
45 - 49	1 494 962	732 711	762 251	600 105	301 816	298 289	894 857	430 895	463 963
50 - 54	1 175 703	589 400	586 304	472 806	241 174	231 632	702 897	348 225	354 672
55 - 59	899 359	458 118	441 240	358 957	184 543	174 414	540 402	273 575	266 827
60 - 64	654 915	340 396	314 518	256 819	133 591	123 228	398 096	206 805	191 290
65 - 69	474 001	248 570	225 431	181 190	93 976	87 214	292 812	154 595	138 217
70 - 74	322 506	170 069	152 437	118 162	60 482	57 680	204 344	109 588	94 757
75 - 79	206 936	109 224	97 712	70 332	34 777	35 555	136 604	74 447	62 157
80 +	216 042	115 214	100 828	69 638	34 862	34 776	146 405	80 353	66 052
Togo[1]									
1 VII 2018 (ESDJ)									
Total	7 440 364	3 628 345	3 812 019	3 092 420[27]	1 494 021[27]	1 598 399[27]	4 347 944	2 134 324	2 213 620
0	225 454	114 140	111 314	85 721[27]	43 355[27]	42 366[27]	139 733	70 785	68 948
1 - 4	849 981	426 726	423 255	322 827[27]	161 554[27]	161 273[27]	527 155	265 173	261 982
5 - 9	934 293	467 597	466 697	337 859[27]	168 114[27]	169 745[27]	596 435	299 483	296 952

7. Population by age, sex and urban/rural residence: latest available year, 2009 - 2018
Population selon l'âge, le sexe et la résidence, urbaine/rurale : dernière année disponible, 2009 - 2018 (continued - suite)

Continent, country or area, date, code[a] and age (in years) / Continent, pays ou zone, date, code[a] et âge (en années)	Total			Urban - Urbaine			Rural - Rurale		
	Both sexes Les deux sexes	Male Masculin	Female Féminin	Both sexes Les deux sexes	Male Masculin	Female Féminin	Both sexes Les deux sexes	Male Masculin	Female Féminin
AFRICA - AFRIQUE									
Togo[1]									
1 VII 2018 (ESDJ)									
10 - 14	927 836	465 997	461 839	306 503[27]	148 237[27]	158 266[27]	621 333	317 760	303 573
15 - 19	845 797	433 924	411 873	311 235[27]	143 163[27]	168 072[27]	534 563	290 761	243 802
20 - 24	659 308	342 483	316 826	313 850[27]	146 859[27]	166 991[27]	345 459	195 624	149 835
25 - 29	564 650	273 623	291 027	307 672[27]	149 120[27]	158 552[27]	256 979	124 503	132 476
30 - 34	517 598	226 751	290 847	271 371[27]	127 762[27]	143 609[27]	246 227	98 989	147 239
35 - 39	451 092	201 623	249 470	217 703[27]	103 293[27]	114 411[27]	233 389	98 330	135 059
40 - 44	369 073	174 450	194 624	167 310[27]	82 814[27]	84 497[27]	201 763	91 636	110 127
45 - 49	296 629	139 808	156 821	131 897[27]	65 196[27]	66 702[27]	164 732	74 613	90 120
50 - 54	232 911	111 867	121 045	102 045[27]	50 121[27]	51 924[27]	130 867	61 746	69 121
55 - 59	172 434	81 289	91 146	73 771[27]	34 692[27]	39 079[27]	98 663	46 597	52 067
60 - 64	118 428	53 647	64 781	54 895[27]	28 023[27]	26 872[27]	63 533	25 624	37 909
65 - 69	100 764	44 858	55 906	41 880[27]	23 881[27]	17 999[27]	58 884	20 977	37 907
70 - 74	71 571	29 743	41 829	22 827[27]	10 932[27]	11 895[27]	48 745	18 811	29 934
75 - 79	49 225	19 494	29 732	11 326[27]	3 618[27]	7 708[27]	37 900	15 876	22 024
80 +	53 322	20 330	32 992	11 733[27]	3 291[27]	8 442[27]	41 589	17 039	24 550
Tunisia - Tunisie									
1 VII 2016 (ESDF)									
Total	11 304 483	5 620 629	5 683 853	...	...	...	...	...	...
0 - 4	1 057 906	547 797	510 109	...	...	...	...	...	...
5 - 9	893 438	465 886	427 551	...	...	...	...	...	...
10 - 14	805 398	418 206	387 192	...	...	...	...	...	...
15 - 19	801 924	411 502	390 422	...	...	...	...	...	...
20 - 24	887 393	442 927	444 466	...	...	...	...	...	...
25 - 29	920 248	440 306	479 942	...	...	...	...	...	...
30 - 34	970 488	463 176	507 312	...	...	...	...	...	...
35 - 39	886 447	428 736	457 710	...	...	...	...	...	...
40 - 44	751 607	367 808	383 800	...	...	...	...	...	...
45 - 49	694 780	337 759	357 022	...	...	...	...	...	...
50 - 54	666 469	328 083	338 386	...	...	...	...	...	...
55 - 59	579 393	289 974	289 419	...	...	...	...	...	...
60 - 64	466 135	233 321	232 814	...	...	...	...	...	...
65 - 69	311 467	152 789	158 678	...	...	...	...	...	...
70 - 74	219 781	105 487	114 294	...	...	...	...	...	...
75 - 79	170 737	81 875	88 862	...	...	...	...	...	...
80 +	220 872	104 998	115 875	...	...	...	...	...	...
Uganda - Ouganda									
27 VIII 2014 (CDFC)									
Total	34 634 650	16 897 849	17 736 801	8 438 009	4 042 324	4 395 685	26 196 641	12 855 525	13 341 116
0 - 4	6 131 028	3 173 950	2 957 078	1 342 058	699 470	642 588	4 788 970	2 474 480	2 314 490
5 - 9	5 551 678	2 834 456	2 717 222	1 135 262	575 893	559 369	4 416 416	2 258 563	2 157 853
10 - 14	4 920 443	2 462 789	2 457 654	1 017 614	487 602	530 012	3 902 829	1 975 187	1 927 642
15 - 19	3 956 633	1 917 797	2 038 836	1 015 017	449 250	565 767	2 941 616	1 468 547	1 473 069
20 - 24	3 188 611	1 444 438	1 744 173	1 024 995	444 919	580 076	2 163 616	999 519	1 164 097
25 - 29	2 486 176	1 143 467	1 342 709	825 746	377 888	447 858	1 660 430	765 579	894 851
30 - 34	1 951 739	908 447	1 043 292	584 396	280 869	303 527	1 367 343	627 578	739 765
35 - 39	1 535 837	726 355	809 482	434 901	214 481	220 420	1 100 936	511 874	589 062
40 - 44	1 272 417	617 034	655 383	316 293	162 345	153 948	956 124	454 689	501 435
45 - 49	921 124	452 081	469 043	217 719	112 768	104 951	703 405	339 313	364 092
50 - 54	808 103	371 126	436 977	172 367	81 867	90 500	635 736	289 259	346 477
55 - 59	480 284	224 765	255 519	97 541	46 042	51 499	382 743	178 723	204 020
60 - 64	440 053	195 283	244 770	81 233	36 927	44 306	358 820	158 356	200 464
65 - 69	301 150	136 107	165 043	50 965	22 770	28 195	250 185	113 337	136 848
70 - 74	277 236	115 862	161 374	46 835	19 032	27 803	230 401	96 830	133 571
75 - 79	150 473	69 095	81 378	25 771	11 009	14 762	124 702	58 086	66 616
80 - 84	131 269	51 871	79 398	23 763	9 044	14 719	107 506	42 827	64 679
85 - 89	51 776	21 572	30 204	9 925	3 912	6 013	41 851	17 660	24 191
90 - 94	37 171	15 125	22 046	8 116	3 484	4 632	29 055	11 641	17 414
95 +	41 449	16 229	25 220	7 492	2 752	4 740	33 957	13 477	20 480
1 VII 2018 (ESDF)[7]									
Total	39 059 000	19 146 800	19 912 200	...	...	...	...	...	...
0	1 453 900	736 300	717 600	...	...	...	...	...	...
1 - 4	5 371 000	2 736 500	2 634 500	...	...	...	...	...	...

Continent, country or area, date, code[a] and age (in years) Continent, pays ou zone, date, code[a] et âge (en années)	Total			Urban - Urbaine			Rural - Rurale		
	Both sexes Les deux sexes	Male Masculin	Female Féminin	Both sexes Les deux sexes	Male Masculin	Female Féminin	Both sexes Les deux sexes	Male Masculin	Female Féminin
AFRICA - AFRIQUE									
Uganda - Ouganda 1 VII 2018 (ESDF)[7]									
5 - 9	5 831 300	3 011 200	2 820 100	...	...	...	...	...	...
10 - 14	5 355 400	2 724 600	2 630 800	...	...	...	...	...	...
15 - 19	4 673 800	2 327 000	2 346 800	...	...	...	...	...	...
20 - 24	3 714 800	1 775 300	1 939 500	...	...	...	...	...	...
25 - 29	2 976 200	1 339 400	1 636 800	...	...	...	...	...	...
30 - 34	2 305 700	1 062 900	1 242 800	...	...	...	...	...	...
35 - 39	1 801 900	838 200	963 700	...	...	...	...	...	...
40 - 44	1 423 600	673 600	750 000	...	...	...	...	...	...
45 - 49	1 154 300	559 800	594 500	...	...	...	...	...	...
50 - 54	843 600	407 300	436 300	...	...	...	...	...	...
55 - 59	709 500	322 000	387 500	...	...	...	...	...	...
60 - 64	419 900	193 800	226 100	...	...	...	...	...	...
65 - 69	376 100	164 700	211 400	...	...	...	...	...	...
70 - 74	246 000	108 700	137 300	...	...	...	...	...	...
75 - 79	201 000	82 400	118 600	...	...	...	...	...	...
80 +	201 000	83 100	117 900	...	...	...	...	...	...
United Republic of Tanzania - République Unie de Tanzanie 1 VII 2013 (ESDF)[28]									
Total	47 132 580	23 267 957	23 864 623	12 909 536	6 386 303	6 523 233	34 223 044	16 881 654	17 341 390
0	1 776 107	895 971	880 136	403 952	203 710	200 242	1 372 155	692 261	679 894
1 - 4	6 536 000	3 295 033	3 240 967	1 521 372	766 466	754 906	5 014 628	2 528 567	2 486 061
5 - 9	7 160 846	3 608 891	3 551 955	1 723 220	857 109	866 111	5 437 626	2 751 782	2 685 844
10 - 14	5 464 181	2 735 494	2 728 687	1 364 854	661 195	703 659	4 099 327	2 074 299	2 025 028
15 - 19	4 985 943	2 494 983	2 490 960	1 427 786	682 734	745 052	3 558 157	1 812 249	1 745 908
20 - 24	4 340 143	2 179 173	2 160 970	1 333 476	672 789	660 687	3 006 667	1 506 384	1 500 283
25 - 29	3 484 607	1 730 600	1 754 007	1 134 814	563 796	571 018	2 349 793	1 166 804	1 182 989
30 - 34	2 852 197	1 289 114	1 563 083	974 580	450 823	523 757	1 877 617	838 291	1 039 326
35 - 39	2 601 610	1 207 182	1 394 428	867 422	418 436	448 986	1 734 188	788 746	945 442
40 - 44	2 121 302	1 032 605	1 088 697	672 984	346 836	326 148	1 448 318	685 769	762 549
45 - 49	1 568 017	770 149	797 868	469 417	248 681	220 736	1 098 600	521 468	577 132
50 - 54	1 234 201	604 621	629 580	339 138	180 385	158 753	895 063	424 236	470 827
55 - 59	881 484	422 141	459 343	223 562	117 172	106 390	657 922	304 969	352 953
60 - 64	734 938	347 604	387 334	172 297	88 004	84 293	562 641	259 600	303 041
65 - 69	466 882	223 365	243 517	100 337	50 363	49 974	366 545	173 002	193 543
70 - 74	387 755	179 960	207 795	78 544	35 541	43 003	309 211	144 419	164 792
75 - 79	245 872	115 076	130 796	46 843	20 380	26 463	199 029	94 696	104 333
80 +	290 495	135 995	154 500	54 938	21 883	33 055	235 557	114 112	121 445
1 VII 2018 (ESDF)[21]									
Total	54 199 163	26 510 095	27 689 068	...	...	...	...	...	...
0	2 013 744	1 018 016	995 728	...	...	...	...	...	...
1 - 4	7 394 603	3 730 626	3 663 977	...	...	...	...	...	...
5 - 9	7 323 756	3 669 021	3 654 735	...	...	...	...	...	...
10 - 14	6 935 564	3 472 863	3 462 701	...	...	...	...	...	...
15 - 19	5 862 972	2 926 853	2 936 119	...	...	...	...	...	...
20 - 24	4 812 548	2 364 348	2 448 200	...	...	...	...	...	...
25 - 29	3 991 084	1 810 761	2 180 323	...	...	...	...	...	...
30 - 34	3 509 847	1 600 754	1 909 093	...	...	...	...	...	...
35 - 39	2 929 416	1 369 916	1 559 500	...	...	...	...	...	...
40 - 44	2 442 560	1 181 295	1 261 265	...	...	...	...	...	...
45 - 49	1 900 179	930 852	969 327	...	...	...	...	...	...
50 - 54	1 411 171	701 389	709 782	...	...	...	...	...	...
55 - 59	1 208 013	560 038	647 975	...	...	...	...	...	...
60 - 64	756 549	378 717	377 832	...	...	...	...	...	...
65 - 69	647 276	307 889	339 387	...	...	...	...	...	...
70 - 74	403 060	191 872	211 188	...	...	...	...	...	...
75 - 79	322 047	144 283	177 764	...	...	...	...	...	...
80 +	334 774	150 602	184 172	...	...	...	...	...	...
Zambia - Zambie[29] 1 VII 2018 (ESDJ)									
Total	16 887 720	8 357 340	8 530 380	7 221 318	3 571 368	3 649 950	9 666 402	4 785 972	4 880 430
0 - 4	3 007 844	1 516 294	1 491 550	1 189 301	601 804	587 497	1 818 543	914 490	904 053

Continent, country or area, date, code[a] and age (in years) / Continent, pays ou zone, date, code[a] et âge (en annèes)	Total			Urban - Urbaine			Rural - Rurale		
	Both sexes Les deux sexes	Male Masculin	Female Féminin	Both sexes Les deux sexes	Male Masculin	Female Féminin	Both sexes Les deux sexes	Male Masculin	Female Féminin
AFRICA - AFRIQUE									
Zambia - Zambie[29]									
1 VII 2018 (ESDJ)									
0	653 238	330 262	322 976	...	...	...	...	...	...
1 - 4	2 354 606	1 186 032	1 168 574	...	...	...	...	...	...
5 - 9	2 579 490	1 295 454	1 284 036	953 821	481 151	472 670	1 625 669	814 303	811 366
10 - 14	2 148 691	1 077 767	1 070 924	829 478	416 173	413 305	1 319 213	661 594	657 619
15 - 19	1 826 529	911 405	915 124	780 145	377 706	402 439	1 046 384	533 699	512 685
20 - 24	1 612 918	795 680	817 238	747 504	352 852	394 652	865 414	442 828	422 586
25 - 29	1 300 275	622 450	677 825	669 544	318 054	351 490	630 731	304 396	326 335
30 - 34	1 027 320	471 781	555 539	538 865	252 801	286 064	488 455	218 980	269 475
35 - 39	870 438	417 673	452 765	444 300	218 789	225 511	426 138	198 884	227 254
40 - 44	683 612	348 618	334 994	335 212	177 661	157 551	348 400	170 957	177 443
45 - 49	522 513	270 848	251 665	237 797	129 091	108 706	284 716	141 757	142 959
50 - 54	368 128	187 550	180 578	155 086	81 516	73 570	213 042	106 034	107 008
55 - 59	293 917	141 455	152 462	118 696	58 073	60 623	175 221	83 382	91 839
60 - 64	206 349	98 281	108 068	83 058	40 475	42 583	123 291	57 806	65 485
65 - 69	146 037	68 952	77 085	55 003	27 310	27 693	91 034	41 642	49 392
70 - 74	115 976	51 352	64 624	36 900	17 504	19 396	79 076	33 848	45 228
75 - 79	75 710	33 754	41 956	21 716	9 858	11 858	53 994	23 896	30 098
80 +	101 973	48 026	53 947	24 892	10 550	14 342	77 081	37 476	39 605
Zimbabwe[30]									
1 VII 2018 (ESDF)									
Total	14 848 905	7 138 445	7 710 459	4 993 375	2 385 567	2 607 811	9 962 261	4 807 069	5 155 192
0 - 4	1 963 868	966 005	997 863	687 394	340 453	346 941	1 364 514	669 253	695 261
5 - 9	1 934 432	956 182	978 249	627 296	310 872	316 423	1 338 620	661 051	677 569
10 - 14	1 727 760	856 473	871 287	473 070	231 798	241 272	1 252 155	623 360	628 795
15 - 19	1 691 926	844 770	847 155	428 885	205 227	223 658	1 261 502	638 707	622 795
20 - 24	1 451 054	721 161	729 892	453 105	195 769	257 335	996 840	524 726	472 114
25 - 29	1 200 413	550 136	650 277	479 725	206 106	273 619	720 207	343 862	376 345
30 - 34	1 126 462	510 135	616 328	486 672	220 697	265 976	639 550	289 519	350 031
35 - 39	941 990	446 973	495 017	401 633	195 373	206 261	540 120	251 694	288 426
40 - 44	752 871	366 411	386 461	303 749	155 521	148 228	448 816	210 926	237 890
45 - 49	547 802	277 546	270 256	218 810	117 838	100 973	328 758	159 743	169 015
50 - 54	352 521	167 479	185 042	134 948	68 547	66 401	217 375	98 919	118 456
55 - 59	329 014	129 708	199 307	102 558	47 226	55 332	225 611	82 368	143 243
60 - 64	272 265	112 185	160 079	78 721	37 759	40 963	193 065	74 235	118 830
65 - 69	207 322	86 591	120 731	50 387	23 853	26 535	156 132	62 394	93 738
70 - 74	142 023	59 727	82 296	30 127	13 485	16 641	110 916	45 802	65 114
75 - 79	101 041	43 579	57 462	18 997	8 111	10 886	80 950	34 911	46 039
80 +	106 141	43 384	62 757	17 298	6 932	10 367	87 130	35 599	51 531
AMERICA, NORTH - AMÉRIQUE DU NORD									
Anguilla									
11 V 2011 (CDFC)									
Total	13 572	6 707	6 865	...	...	...	...	...	...
0	245	130	115	...	...	...	...	...	...
1 - 4	813	416	397	...	...	...	...	...	...
5 - 9	1 056	529	527	...	...	...	...	...	...
10 - 14	1 069	530	539	...	...	...	...	...	...
15 - 19	916	466	450	...	...	...	...	...	...
20 - 24	917	466	451	...	...	...	...	...	...
25 - 29	1 120	533	587	...	...	...	...	...	...
30 - 34	1 016	480	536	...	...	...	...	...	...
35 - 39	1 145	569	576	...	...	...	...	...	...
40 - 44	1 138	567	571	...	...	...	...	...	...
45 - 49	1 089	538	551	...	...	...	...	...	...
50 - 54	878	425	453	...	...	...	...	...	...
55 - 59	694	347	347	...	...	...	...	...	...
60 - 64	453	228	225	...	...	...	...	...	...
65 - 69	323	161	162	...	...	...	...	...	...
70 - 74	250	118	132	...	...	...	...	...	...
75 +	450	204	246	...	...	...	...	...	...

Continent, country or area, date, code[a] and age (in years) / Continent, pays ou zone, date, code[a] et âge (en années)	Total			Urban - Urbaine			Rural - Rurale		
	Both sexes Les deux sexes	Male Masculin	Female Féminin	Both sexes Les deux sexes	Male Masculin	Female Féminin	Both sexes Les deux sexes	Male Masculin	Female Féminin
AMERICA, NORTH - AMÉRIQUE DU NORD									
Antigua and Barbuda - Antigua-et-Barbuda[20]									
1 VII 2018 (ESDJ)									
Total	95 014	45 493	49 521	...	...	...	...	...	...
0 - 4	6 798	3 432	3 366	...	...	...	...	...	...
5 - 9	6 903	3 486	3 417	...	...	...	...	...	...
10 - 14	6 796	3 459	3 337	...	...	...	...	...	...
15 - 19	7 299	3 680	3 619	...	...	...	...	...	...
20 - 24	7 710	3 869	3 841	...	...	...	...	...	...
25 - 29	7 287	3 567	3 720	...	...	...	...	...	...
30 - 34	7 030	3 319	3 711	...	...	...	...	...	...
35 - 39	6 947	3 253	3 694	...	...	...	...	...	...
40 - 44	6 943	3 170	3 773	...	...	...	...	...	...
45 - 49	6 912	3 169	3 743	...	...	...	...	...	...
50 - 54	6 528	3 017	3 511	...	...	...	...	...	...
55 - 59	5 543	2 569	2 974	...	...	...	...	...	...
60 - 64	4 050	1 886	2 164	...	...	...	...	...	...
65 - 69	2 981	1 365	1 616	...	...	...	...	...	...
70 - 74	2 204	992	1 212	...	...	...	...	...	...
75 - 79	1 362	597	765	...	...	...	...	...	...
80 - 84	748	311	437	...	...	...	...	...	...
85 - 89	629	241	388	...	...	...	...	...	...
90 - 94	240	81	159	...	...	...	...	...	...
95 +	104	30	74	...	...	...	...	...	...
Aruba									
1 VII 2018 (ESDJ)									
Total	111 466	52 798	58 668	...	...	...	...	...	...
0	1 127	578	549	...	...	...	...	...	...
1 - 4	5 336	2 781	2 555	...	...	...	...	...	...
5 - 9	6 692	3 364	3 327	...	...	...	...	...	...
10 - 14	7 124	3 669	3 456	...	...	...	...	...	...
15 - 19	7 183	3 633	3 550	...	...	...	...	...	...
20 - 24	6 433	3 288	3 145	...	...	...	...	...	...
25 - 29	6 759	3 359	3 400	...	...	...	...	...	...
30 - 34	6 809	3 249	3 560	...	...	...	...	...	...
35 - 39	7 278	3 326	3 952	...	...	...	...	...	...
40 - 44	7 482	3 432	4 050	...	...	...	...	...	...
45 - 49	8 622	3 971	4 650	...	...	...	...	...	...
50 - 54	8 884	4 073	4 811	...	...	...	...	...	...
55 - 59	9 010	4 183	4 827	...	...	...	...	...	...
60 - 64	7 456	3 387	4 069	...	...	...	...	...	...
65 - 69	5 689	2 615	3 074	...	...	...	...	...	...
70 - 74	3 964	1 690	2 274	...	...	...	...	...	...
75 - 79	2 680	1 161	1 518	...	...	...	...	...	...
80 - 84	1 685	611	1 073	...	...	...	...	...	...
85 - 89	880	323	557	...	...	...	...	...	...
90 - 94	284	82	202	...	...	...	...	...	...
95 - 99	78	20	58	...	...	...	...	...	...
100 +	3	2	1	...	...	...	...	...	...
Bahamas[31]									
1 VII 2018 (ESDJ)									
Total	381 320	184 380	196 940	...	...	...	...	...	...
0	5 750	2 960	2 790	...	...	...	...	...	...
1 - 4	22 780	11 600	11 180	...	...	...	...	...	...
5 - 9	29 010	14 530	14 480	...	...	...	...	...	...
10 - 14	31 920	15 770	16 150	...	...	...	...	...	...
15 - 19	32 060	15 860	16 200	...	...	...	...	...	...
20 - 24	31 670	15 830	15 840	...	...	...	...	...	...
25 - 29	29 070	14 550	14 520	...	...	...	...	...	...
30 - 34	26 450	12 790	13 660	...	...	...	...	...	...
35 - 39	27 400	12 990	14 410	...	...	...	...	...	...
40 - 44	28 580	13 660	14 920	...	...	...	...	...	...
45 - 49	28 030	13 350	14 680	...	...	...	...	...	...
50 - 54	25 030	11 950	13 080	...	...	...	...	...	...

Continent, country or area, date, code[a] and age (in years) / Continent, pays ou zone, date, code[a] et âge (en années)	Total			Urban - Urbaine			Rural - Rurale		
	Both sexes Les deux sexes	Male Masculin	Female Féminin	Both sexes Les deux sexes	Male Masculin	Female Féminin	Both sexes Les deux sexes	Male Masculin	Female Féminin
AMERICA, NORTH - AMÉRIQUE DU NORD									
Bahamas[31]									
1 VII 2018 (ESDJ)									
55 - 59	21 770	10 210	11 560	...	...	...	...	...	...
60 - 64	15 310	6 960	8 350	...	...	...	...	...	...
65 - 69	10 260	4 650	5 610	...	...	...	...	...	...
70 - 74	7 120	3 120	4 000	...	...	...	...	...	...
75 - 79	4 790	1 980	2 810	...	...	...	...	...	...
80 + ...	4 320	1 620	2 700	...	...	...	...	...	...
Barbados - Barbade[32]									
1 V 2010 (CDJC)									
Total................	277 821	133 018	144 803	...	...	...	...	...	...
0 - 4	17 352	8 873	8 479	...	...	...	...	...	...
5 - 9	18 838	9 683	9 155	...	...	...	...	...	...
10 - 14	18 567	9 445	9 122	...	...	...	...	...	...
15 - 19	18 870	9 452	9 418	...	...	...	...	...	...
20 - 24	18 169	9 061	9 108	...	...	...	...	...	...
25 - 29	19 088	9 313	9 775	...	...	...	...	...	...
30 - 34	18 785	9 150	9 635	...	...	...	...	...	...
35 - 39	20 516	9 884	10 632	...	...	...	...	...	...
40 - 44	20 113	9 663	10 450	...	...	...	...	...	...
45 - 49	21 365	10 062	11 303	...	...	...	...	...	...
50 - 54	20 050	9 411	10 639	...	...	...	...	...	...
55 - 59	16 653	7 871	8 782	...	...	...	...	...	...
60 - 64	13 486	6 326	7 160	...	...	...	...	...	...
65 - 69	10 151	4 511	5 640	...	...	...	...	...	...
70 - 74	8 680	3 804	4 876	...	...	...	...	...	...
75 - 79	6 937	2 863	4 074	...	...	...	...	...	...
80 - 84	5 153	1 986	3 167	...	...	...	...	...	...
85 + ...	5 048	1 660	3 388	...	...	...	...	...	...
Belize									
1 VII 2018 (ESDJ)									
Total................	398 050	199 028	199 022	...	...	...	...	...	...
0	9 147	4 659	4 488	...	...	...	...	...	...
1 - 4	37 551	19 163	18 388	...	...	...	...	...	...
5 - 9	48 432	24 394	24 038	...	...	...	...	...	...
10 - 14	46 541	23 288	23 253	...	...	...	...	...	...
15 - 19	42 774	21 397	21 377	...	...	...	...	...	...
20 - 24	37 704	18 519	19 185	...	...	...	...	...	...
25 - 29	32 722	15 832	16 890	...	...	...	...	...	...
30 - 34	28 192	13 684	14 508	...	...	...	...	...	...
35 - 39	25 528	12 463	13 065	...	...	...	...	...	...
40 - 44	21 409	10 638	10 771	...	...	...	...	...	...
45 - 49	18 460	9 428	9 032	...	...	...	...	...	...
50 - 54	14 472	7 340	7 132	...	...	...	...	...	...
55 - 59	10 664	5 558	5 106	...	...	...	...	...	...
60 - 64	7 681	4 061	3 620	...	...	...	...	...	...
65 - 69	5 427	2 888	2 539	...	...	...	...	...	...
70 - 74	4 314	2 288	2 026	...	...	...	...	...	...
75 - 79	3 163	1 605	1 558	...	...	...	...	...	...
80 + ...	3 869	1 823	2 046	...	...	...	...	...	...
Bermuda - Bermudes[33]									
20 V 2010 (CDJC)									
Total................	64 237	30 858	33 379	64 237	30 858	33 379	-	-	-
0	709	372	337	709	372	337	-	-	-
1 - 4	2 858	1 479	1 379	2 858	1 479	1 379	-	-	-
5 - 9	3 456	1 759	1 697	3 456	1 759	1 697	-	-	-
10 - 14	3 481	1 706	1 775	3 481	1 706	1 775	-	-	-
15 - 19	3 431	1 682	1 749	3 431	1 682	1 749	-	-	-
20 - 24	3 342	1 608	1 734	3 342	1 608	1 734	-	-	-
25 - 29	4 076	1 947	2 129	4 076	1 947	2 129	-	-	-
30 - 34	4 645	2 259	2 386	4 645	2 259	2 386	-	-	-
35 - 39	5 050	2 572	2 478	5 050	2 572	2 478	-	-	-
40 - 44	5 158	2 588	2 570	5 158	2 588	2 570	-	-	-
45 - 49	5 731	2 811	2 920	5 731	2 811	2 920	-	-	-

Continent, country or area, date, code[a] and age (in years) Continent, pays ou zone, date, code[a] et âge (en années)	Total			Urban - Urbaine			Rural - Rurale		
	Both sexes Les deux sexes	Male Masculin	Female Féminin	Both sexes Les deux sexes	Male Masculin	Female Féminin	Both sexes Les deux sexes	Male Masculin	Female Féminin
AMERICA, NORTH - AMÉRIQUE DU NORD									
Bermuda - Bermudes[33]									
20 V 2010 (CDJC)									
50 - 54	5 427	2 531	2 896	5 427	2 531	2 896	-	-	-
55 - 59	4 498	2 146	2 352	4 498	2 146	2 352	-	-	-
60 - 64	3 692	1 733	1 959	3 692	1 733	1 959	-	-	-
65 - 69	2 807	1 290	1 517	2 807	1 290	1 517	-	-	-
70 - 74	2 163	961	1 202	2 163	961	1 202	-	-	-
75 - 79	1 768	747	1 021	1 768	747	1 021	-	-	-
80 - 84	1 120	432	688	1 120	432	688	-	-	-
85 - 89	584	185	399	584	185	399	-	-	-
90 - 94	187	41	146	187	41	146	-	-	-
95 - 99	48	8	40	48	8	40	-	-	-
100 +	6	1	5	6	1	5	-	-	-
1 VII 2018 (ESDJ)[34]									
Total	63 973	30 768	33 205	...	...	...	...	...	...
0	568	285	283	...	...	...	...	...	...
1 - 4	2 343	1 178	1 165	...	...	...	...	...	...
5 - 9	3 241	1 630	1 611	...	...	...	...	...	...
10 - 14	3 227	1 662	1 565	...	...	...	...	...	...
15 - 19	3 207	1 571	1 636	...	...	...	...	...	...
20 - 24	2 959	1 470	1 489	...	...	...	...	...	...
25 - 29	3 201	1 547	1 654	...	...	...	...	...	...
30 - 34	4 015	1 934	2 081	...	...	...	...	...	...
35 - 39	4 603	2 211	2 392	...	...	...	...	...	...
40 - 44	4 596	2 339	2 257	...	...	...	...	...	...
45 - 49	4 982	2 537	2 445	...	...	...	...	...	...
50 - 54	5 186	2 608	2 578	...	...	...	...	...	...
55 - 59	5 499	2 620	2 879	...	...	...	...	...	...
60 - 64	4 728	2 176	2 552	...	...	...	...	...	...
65 - 69	3 717	1 721	1 996	...	...	...	...	...	...
70 - 74	2 942	1 304	1 638	...	...	...	...	...	...
75 - 79	2 064	894	1 170	...	...	...	...	...	...
80 - 84	1 525	641	884	...	...	...	...	...	...
85 +	1 370	440	930	...	...	...	...	...	...
British Virgin Islands - Îles Vierges britanniques									
12 VII 2010 (CDFC)									
Total	28 054	13 820	14 234	...	...	...	...	...	...
0 - 4	2 134	1 126	1 008	...	...	...	...	...	...
5 - 9	2 090	1 065	1 025	...	...	...	...	...	...
10 - 14	2 044	1 032	1 012	...	...	...	...	...	...
15 - 19	1 767	867	900	...	...	...	...	...	...
20 - 24	1 720	789	931	...	...	...	...	...	...
25 - 29	2 316	1 126	1 190	...	...	...	...	...	...
30 - 34	2 537	1 165	1 372	...	...	...	...	...	...
35 - 39	2 599	1 226	1 373	...	...	...	...	...	...
40 - 44	2 559	1 236	1 323	...	...	...	...	...	...
45 - 49	2 338	1 193	1 145	...	...	...	...	...	...
50 - 54	1 842	962	880	...	...	...	...	...	...
55 - 59	1 387	680	707	...	...	...	...	...	...
60 - 64	1 028	541	487	...	...	...	...	...	...
65 - 69	670	350	320	...	...	...	...	...	...
70 - 74	415	204	211	...	...	...	...	...	...
75 - 79	230	98	132	...	...	...	...	...	...
80 - 84	216	91	125	...	...	...	...	...	...
85 - 89	84	39	45	...	...	...	...	...	...
90 +	78	30	48	...	...	...	...	...	...
Canada									
10 V 2016 (CDJC)[35]									
Total	35 151 730	17 264 200	17 887 530	28 575 665	13 912 050	14 663 615	6 576 065	3 352 150	3 223 910
0	369 735	189 085	180 645	303 795	155 030	148 765	65 935	34 055	31 880
1 - 4	1 529 060	783 945	745 115	1 248 230	639 935	608 295	280 830	144 010	136 820
5 - 9	2 018 130	1 034 685	983 445	1 633 720	836 950	796 770	384 410	197 740	186 670
10 - 14	1 922 645	985 200	937 445	1 546 225	791 500	754 730	376 420	193 700	182 720

7. Population by age, sex and urban/rural residence: latest available year, 2009 - 2018

Population selon l'âge, le sexe et la résidence, urbaine/rurale : dernière année disponible, 2009 - 2018 (continued - suite)

Continent, country or area, date, code[a] and age (in years) Continent, pays ou zone, date, code[a] et âge (en années)	Total			Urban - Urbaine			Rural - Rurale		
	Both sexes Les deux sexes	Male Masculin	Female Féminin	Both sexes Les deux sexes	Male Masculin	Female Féminin	Both sexes Les deux sexes	Male Masculin	Female Féminin
AMERICA, NORTH - **AMÉRIQUE DU NORD**									
Canada									
10 V 2016 (CDJC)[35]									
15 - 19	2 026 160	1 039 215	986 940	1 641 330	839 980	801 345	384 830	199 235	185 595
20 - 24	2 242 695	1 144 495	1 098 200	1 907 165	967 775	939 390	335 525	176 715	158 805
25 - 29	2 285 990	1 144 475	1 141 515	1 976 755	986 505	990 255	309 235	157 970	151 265
30 - 34	2 329 400	1 148 290	1 181 105	1 989 865	978 690	1 011 170	339 535	169 605	169 935
35 - 39	2 288 365	1 118 635	1 169 730	1 924 280	935 630	988 645	364 085	183 000	181 085
40 - 44	2 255 135	1 104 445	1 150 690	1 871 860	910 205	961 655	383 280	194 240	189 035
45 - 49	2 359 965	1 157 755	1 202 205	1 925 635	939 350	986 290	434 325	218 410	215 915
50 - 54	2 678 070	1 318 755	1 359 320	2 120 605	1 038 360	1 082 250	557 465	280 395	277 070
55 - 59	2 620 240	1 285 190	1 335 050	2 029 030	986 135	1 042 895	591 210	299 055	292 155
60 - 64	2 290 510	1 114 880	1 175 630	1 745 665	835 295	910 375	544 850	279 585	265 260
65 - 69	1 972 475	953 070	1 019 405	1 506 495	710 615	795 875	465 985	242 455	223 535
70 - 74	1 420 875	677 975	742 900	1 097 395	507 680	589 710	323 480	170 290	153 190
75 - 79	1 021 850	469 550	552 305	817 520	363 230	454 285	204 335	106 315	98 020
80 - 84	749 645	325 760	423 885	622 775	262 700	360 075	126 875	63 065	63 810
85 - 89	482 525	185 535	296 985	413 945	155 020	258 925	68 575	30 510	38 065
90 - 94	223 505	68 675	154 835	196 075	58 750	137 325	27 435	9 920	17 510
95 - 99	56 525	13 245	43 280	49 945	11 535	38 410	6 585	1 705	4 870
100 +	8 230	1 340	6 895	7 355	1 175	6 180	875	160	710
1 VII 2018* (ESDJ)[36]									
Total	37 058 856	18 403 310	18 655 546	...	...	...	...	...	...
0	385 067	197 338	187 729	...	...	...	...	...	...
1 - 4	1 565 957	801 849	764 108	...	...	...	...	...	...
5 - 9	2 030 883	1 036 784	994 099	...	...	...	...	...	...
10 - 14	1 990 826	1 013 290	977 536	...	...	...	...	...	...
15 - 19	2 106 893	1 082 667	1 024 226	...	...	...	...	...	...
20 - 24	2 437 542	1 271 388	1 166 154	...	...	...	...	...	...
25 - 29	2 573 476	1 324 764	1 248 712	...	...	...	...	...	...
30 - 34	2 550 512	1 288 341	1 262 171	...	...	...	...	...	...
35 - 39	2 514 450	1 250 324	1 264 126	...	...	...	...	...	...
40 - 44	2 378 927	1 176 696	1 202 231	...	...	...	...	...	...
45 - 49	2 405 692	1 195 595	1 210 097	...	...	...	...	...	...
50 - 54	2 578 047	1 285 508	1 292 539	...	...	...	...	...	...
55 - 59	2 726 152	1 354 975	1 371 177	...	...	...	...	...	...
60 - 64	2 456 212	1 207 653	1 248 559	...	...	...	...	...	...
65 - 69	2 035 754	988 337	1 047 417	...	...	...	...	...	...
70 - 74	1 625 256	779 411	845 845	...	...	...	...	...	...
75 - 79	1 109 870	515 927	593 943	...	...	...	...	...	...
80 - 84	765 850	336 986	428 864	...	...	...	...	...	...
85 - 89	504 086	199 768	304 318	...	...	...	...	...	...
90 - 94	237 609	76 792	160 817	...	...	...	...	...	...
95 - 99	69 827	17 143	52 684	...	...	...	...	...	...
100 +	9 968	1 774	8 194	...	...	...	...	...	...
Cayman Islands - Îles Caïmanes									
31 XII 2017 (ESDJ)									
Total	63 414	32 212	31 203	63 414	32 212	31 203	...	...	...
0	278	162	116	278	162	116	...	...	...
1 - 4	3 024	1 601	1 423	3 024	1 601	1 423	...	...	...
5 - 9	3 620	2 019	1 601	3 620	2 019	1 601	...	...	...
10 - 14	3 721	1 963	1 758	3 721	1 963	1 758	...	...	...
15 - 19	3 231	1 940	1 290	3 231	1 940	1 290	...	...	...
20 - 24	2 692	1 392	1 300	2 692	1 392	1 300	...	...	...
25 - 29	5 292	2 812	2 481	5 292	2 812	2 481	...	...	...
30 - 34	5 766	2 994	2 772	5 766	2 994	2 772	...	...	...
35 - 39	6 041	2 944	3 097	6 041	2 944	3 097	...	...	...
40 - 44	6 596	3 322	3 275	6 596	3 322	3 275	...	...	...
45 - 49	6 680	3 459	3 221	6 680	3 459	3 221	...	...	...
50 - 54	5 168	2 283	2 885	5 168	2 283	2 885	...	...	...
55 - 59	3 687	1 879	1 807	3 687	1 879	1 807	...	...	...
60 - 64	2 316	1 066	1 250	2 316	1 066	1 250	...	...	...
65 - 69	2 097	991	1 106	2 097	991	1 106	...	...	...
70 - 74	1 221	507	714	1 221	507	714	...	...	...

Continent, country or area, date, code[a] and age (in years) Continent, pays ou zone, date, code[a] et âge (en années)	Total			Urban - Urbaine			Rural - Rurale		
	Both sexes Les deux sexes	Male Masculin	Female Féminin	Both sexes Les deux sexes	Male Masculin	Female Féminin	Both sexes Les deux sexes	Male Masculin	Female Féminin
AMERICA, NORTH - **AMÉRIQUE DU NORD**									
Cayman Islands - Îles Caïmanes									
31 XII 2017 (ESDJ)									
75 - 79	830	369	461	830	369	461	...	...	...
80 - 84	553	299	254	553	299	254	...	...	...
85 - 89	299	116	184	299	116	184	...	...	...
90 - 94	139	47	92	139	47	92	...	...	...
95 - 99	23	-	23	23	-	23	...	...	...
100 +	-	-	-	-	-	-	...	...	...
Unknown - Inconnu	140	47	93	140	47	93	...	...	...
Costa Rica[37]									
1 VII 2018 (ESDJ)									
Total	5 003 673	2 431 983	2 571 690	3 630 938	1 742 776	1 888 162	1 372 735	689 207	683 528
0 - 4	299 645	151 341	148 304	204 161	105 488	98 673	95 484	45 853	49 631
5 - 9	366 183	185 681	180 502	254 628	129 531	125 097	111 555	56 150	55 405
10 - 14	379 845	199 520	180 325	256 893	134 331	122 562	122 952	65 189	57 763
15 - 19	408 544	214 926	193 618	287 798	150 162	137 636	120 746	64 764	55 982
20 - 24	420 005	213 599	206 406	308 372	155 965	152 407	111 633	57 634	53 999
25 - 29	385 252	190 811	194 441	290 968	144 544	146 424	94 284	46 267	48 017
30 - 34	380 592	179 419	201 173	279 822	134 474	145 348	100 770	44 945	55 825
35 - 39	354 813	164 283	190 530	258 034	117 820	140 214	96 779	46 463	50 316
40 - 44	320 716	149 442	171 274	234 872	109 038	125 834	85 844	40 404	45 440
45 - 49	290 230	134 028	156 202	208 626	93 999	114 627	81 604	40 029	41 575
50 - 54	317 002	151 341	165 661	229 912	107 323	122 589	87 090	44 018	43 072
55 - 59	286 840	135 603	151 237	217 245	99 900	117 345	69 595	35 703	33 892
60 - 64	247 820	115 038	132 782	186 510	81 729	104 781	61 310	33 309	28 001
65 - 69	198 031	91 568	106 463	153 133	70 133	83 000	44 898	21 435	23 463
70 - 74	134 723	56 696	78 027	104 020	41 148	62 872	30 703	15 548	15 155
75 - 79	95 125	47 958	47 167	69 045	32 740	36 305	26 080	15 218	10 862
80 - 84	63 355	28 350	35 005	47 570	19 662	27 908	15 785	8 688	7 097
85 - 89	31 394	13 016	18 378	21 401	8 290	13 111	9 993	4 726	5 267
90 - 94	17 356	7 286	10 070	13 474	5 248	8 226	3 882	2 038	1 844
95 +	6 202	2 077	4 125	4 454	1 251	3 203	1 748	826	922
Cuba									
1 VII 2018* (ESDJ)									
Total	11 215 344	5 580 437	5 634 908	8 637 568	4 199 163	4 438 406	2 577 776	1 381 274	1 196 502
0	115 136	59 762	55 375	94 335	48 923	45 412	20 801	10 839	9 963
1 - 4	482 163	250 052	232 111	388 486	201 706	186 780	93 677	48 346	45 332
5 - 9	620 490	319 198	301 292	466 007	239 585	226 423	154 483	79 614	74 870
10 - 14	581 637	299 444	282 194	435 765	223 697	212 068	145 873	75 747	70 126
15 - 19	691 447	355 705	335 743	527 658	270 016	257 643	163 789	85 689	78 100
20 - 24	693 375	357 790	335 585	530 517	270 991	259 526	162 858	86 799	76 059
25 - 29	800 752	413 046	387 707	615 222	311 683	303 540	185 530	101 363	84 167
30 - 34	748 207	383 379	364 828	576 428	289 155	287 273	171 779	94 224	77 555
35 - 39	620 240	315 229	305 012	468 782	232 898	235 884	151 459	82 331	69 128
40 - 44	792 589	396 982	395 607	591 242	288 712	302 530	201 347	108 270	93 077
45 - 49	997 076	494 596	502 481	751 455	361 804	389 651	245 622	132 792	112 830
50 - 54	1 016 407	496 744	519 663	789 833	374 736	415 098	226 574	122 009	104 566
55 - 59	786 388	381 457	404 931	618 732	291 488	327 244	167 657	89 970	77 687
60 - 64	591 059	282 258	308 801	462 778	213 455	249 323	128 281	68 803	59 478
65 - 69	532 374	254 418	277 956	422 054	194 588	227 466	110 321	59 830	50 491
70 - 74	434 810	202 617	232 193	344 273	154 448	189 826	90 537	48 170	42 367
75 - 79	324 034	149 791	174 243	255 512	112 233	143 279	68 522	37 558	30 964
80 - 84	200 678	89 872	110 806	156 411	65 351	91 060	44 268	24 522	19 746
85 +	186 485	78 101	108 385	142 082	53 698	88 384	44 404	24 403	20 001
Curaçao[1]									
1 VII 2017 (ESDJ)									
Total	160 175	73 246	86 929	...	...	...	...	...	...
0	1 657	839	818	...	...	...	...	...	...
1 - 4	7 823	3 989	3 834	...	...	...	...	...	...
5 - 9	9 830	5 064	4 766	...	...	...	...	...	...
10 - 14	9 862	4 996	4 867	...	...	...	...	...	...
15 - 19	10 249	5 305	4 944	...	...	...	...	...	...
20 - 24	9 332	4 681	4 651	...	...	...	...	...	...

7. Population by age, sex and urban/rural residence: latest available year, 2009 - 2018
Population selon l'âge, le sexe et la résidence, urbaine/rurale : dernière année disponible, 2009 - 2018 (continued - suite)

Continent, country or area, date, code[a] and age (in years) / Continent, pays ou zone, date, code[a] et âge (en années)	Total			Urban - Urbaine			Rural - Rurale		
	Both sexes Les deux sexes	Male Masculin	Female Féminin	Both sexes Les deux sexes	Male Masculin	Female Féminin	Both sexes Les deux sexes	Male Masculin	Female Féminin
AMERICA, NORTH - AMÉRIQUE DU NORD									
Curaçao[1]									
1 VII 2017 (ESDJ)									
25 - 29	9 017	4 180	4 838	...	...	...	...	...	...
30 - 34	9 479	4 216	5 263	...	...	...	...	...	...
35 - 39	9 237	3 951	5 286	...	...	...	...	...	...
40 - 44	10 088	4 422	5 666	...	...	...	...	...	...
45 - 49	11 888	5 316	6 573	...	...	...	...	...	...
50 - 54	12 709	5 603	7 106	...	...	...	...	...	...
55 - 59	12 382	5 334	7 048	...	...	...	...	...	...
60 - 64	10 441	4 551	5 890	...	...	...	...	...	...
65 - 69	8 997	3 973	5 024	...	...	...	...	...	...
70 - 74	6 935	2 900	4 035	...	...	...	...	...	...
75 - 79	4 589	1 880	2 709	...	...	...	...	...	...
80 - 84	3 151	1 229	1 923	...	...	...	...	...	...
85 - 89	1 629	578	1 052	...	...	...	...	...	...
90 - 94	661	198	463	...	...	...	...	...	...
95 - 99	186	35	151	...	...	...	...	...	...
100 +	40	12	28	...	...	...	...	...	...
Dominica - Dominique									
14 V 2011 (CDFC)									
Total	68 913	34 973	33 940	...	...	...	...	...	...
0 - 4	6 380	3 240	3 140	...	...	...	...	...	...
5 - 9	5 096	2 601	2 495	...	...	...	...	...	...
10 - 14	5 822	2 946	2 876	...	...	...	...	...	...
15 - 19	6 297	3 237	3 060	...	...	...	...	...	...
20 - 24	5 258	2 691	2 567	...	...	...	...	...	...
25 - 29	4 861	2 389	2 472	...	...	...	...	...	...
30 - 34	4 029	2 118	1 911	...	...	...	...	...	...
35 - 39	4 507	2 271	2 236	...	...	...	...	...	...
40 - 44	4 953	2 544	2 409	...	...	...	...	...	...
45 - 49	4 472	2 337	2 135	...	...	...	...	...	...
50 - 54	3 946	2 162	1 784	...	...	...	...	...	...
55 - 59	3 093	1 682	1 411	...	...	...	...	...	...
60 - 64	2 493	1 281	1 212	...	...	...	...	...	...
65 - 69	2 159	1 054	1 105	...	...	...	...	...	...
70 - 74	1 867	884	983	...	...	...	...	...	...
75 - 79	1 587	724	863	...	...	...	...	...	...
80 - 84	1 102	467	635	...	...	...	...	...	...
85 - 89	599	212	387	...	...	...	...	...	...
90 - 94	274	101	173	...	...	...	...	...	...
95 +	118	32	86	...	...	...	...	...	...
Dominican Republic - République dominicaine									
1 VII 2018 (ESDJ)									
Total	10 266 149	5 129 824	5 136 325	8 314 335	4 085 301	4 229 034	1 951 814	1 044 523	907 291
0 - 4	961 511	490 753	470 758	781 698	396 848	384 850	179 813	93 905	85 908
0	191 686	98 064	93 622	...	...	...	...	...	...
1 - 4	769 825	392 689	377 136	...	...	...	...	...	...
5 - 9	966 913	492 690	474 223	779 986	394 883	385 103	186 927	97 807	89 120
10 - 14	963 553	489 128	474 425	774 452	389 283	385 169	189 101	99 845	89 256
15 - 19	952 608	480 685	471 923	768 216	381 770	386 446	184 392	98 915	85 477
20 - 24	909 074	455 533	453 541	739 906	363 527	376 379	169 168	92 006	77 162
25 - 29	851 132	424 547	426 585	698 031	341 356	356 675	153 101	83 191	69 910
30 - 34	772 876	383 093	389 783	633 737	308 511	325 226	139 139	74 582	64 557
35 - 39	699 538	346 017	353 521	572 269	278 223	294 046	127 269	67 794	59 475
40 - 44	629 778	311 134	318 644	513 818	249 424	264 394	115 960	61 710	54 250
45 - 49	566 751	279 693	287 058	462 278	223 472	238 806	104 473	56 221	48 252
50 - 54	504 188	249 345	254 843	410 723	198 537	212 186	93 465	50 808	42 657
55 - 59	429 475	212 370	217 105	347 631	167 607	180 024	81 844	44 763	37 081
60 - 64	342 649	168 638	174 011	274 081	131 247	142 834	68 568	37 391	31 177
65 - 69	258 947	126 529	132 418	203 977	96 791	107 186	54 970	29 738	25 232
70 - 74	184 550	90 002	94 548	143 406	67 740	75 666	41 144	22 262	18 882
75 - 79	128 296	61 894	66 402	99 022	46 022	53 000	29 274	15 872	13 402
80 +	144 310	67 773	76 537	111 104	50 060	61 044	33 206	17 713	15 493

Continent, country or area, date, code[a] and age (in years) / Continent, pays ou zone, date, code[a] et âge (en années)	Total			Urban - Urbaine			Rural - Rurale		
	Both sexes Les deux sexes	Male Masculin	Female Féminin	Both sexes Les deux sexes	Male Masculin	Female Féminin	Both sexes Les deux sexes	Male Masculin	Female Féminin
AMERICA, NORTH - AMÉRIQUE DU NORD									
El Salvador[38]									
1 VII 2017 (ESDJ)									
Total	6 581 940	3 098 633	3 483 307	...	...	...	...	...	...
0	111 299	56 941	54 358	...	...	...	...	...	...
1 - 4	446 740	228 345	218 395	...	...	...	...	...	...
5 - 9	567 307	289 964	277 343	...	...	...	...	...	...
10 - 14	614 163	314 135	300 028	...	...	...	...	...	...
15 - 19	682 932	347 360	335 572	...	...	...	...	...	...
20 - 24	703 384	351 669	351 715	...	...	...	...	...	...
25 - 29	597 142	284 515	312 627	...	...	...	...	...	...
30 - 34	474 137	210 535	263 602	...	...	...	...	...	...
35 - 39	406 945	173 276	233 669	...	...	...	...	...	...
40 - 44	376 093	159 892	216 201	...	...	...	...	...	...
45 - 49	340 258	145 527	194 731	...	...	...	...	...	...
50 - 54	291 141	124 103	167 038	...	...	...	...	...	...
55 - 59	242 500	103 228	139 272	...	...	...	...	...	...
60 - 64	203 360	87 005	116 355	...	...	...	...	...	...
65 - 69	167 862	71 983	95 879	...	...	...	...	...	...
70 - 74	132 816	56 878	75 938	...	...	...	...	...	...
75 - 79	100 621	42 776	57 845	...	...	...	...	...	...
80 - 84	67 398	28 096	39 302	...	...	...	...	...	...
85 +	55 842	22 405	33 437	...	...	...	...	...	...
Greenland - Groenland[39]									
1 VII 2018 (ESDJ)									
Total	56 025	29 538	26 487	48 568	25 448	23 120	7 457	4 090	3 367
0	808	421	387	701	363	338	107	58	49
1 - 4	3 201	1 661	1 540	2 750	1 418	1 332	451	243	208
5 - 9	3 900	2 030	1 870	3 360	1 754	1 606	540	276	264
10 - 14	3 795	1 936	1 859	3 232	1 648	1 584	563	288	275
15 - 19	3 700	1 874	1 826	3 168	1 604	1 564	532	270	262
20 - 24	4 276	2 179	2 097	3 683	1 885	1 798	593	294	299
25 - 29	4 643	2 368	2 275	4 071	2 079	1 992	572	289	283
30 - 34	4 255	2 170	2 085	3 797	1 908	1 889	458	262	196
35 - 39	3 673	1 927	1 746	3 223	1 670	1 553	450	257	193
40 - 44	2 947	1 618	1 329	2 601	1 420	1 181	346	198	148
45 - 49	3 459	1 871	1 588	2 982	1 611	1 371	477	260	217
50 - 54	5 145	2 763	2 382	4 444	2 365	2 079	701	398	303
55 - 59	4 370	2 394	1 976	3 801	2 057	1 744	569	337	232
60 - 64	3 196	1 812	1 384	2 720	1 517	1 203	476	295	181
65 - 69	1 923	1 096	827	1 659	939	720	264	157	107
70 - 74	1 331	776	555	1 153	663	490	178	113	65
75 - 79	839	410	429	733	352	381	106	58	48
80 - 84	371	163	208	314	136	178	57	27	30
85 - 89	156	55	101	140	46	94	16	9	7
90 - 94	34	11	23	33	10	23	1	1	-
95 +	3	3	-	3	3	-	-	-	-
Grenada - Grenade									
1 VII 2017 (ESDF)									
Total	111 467	56 222	55 245	...	...	...	...	...	...
0	1 375	735	640	...	...	...	...	...	...
1 - 4	6 779	3 547	3 232	...	...	...	...	...	...
5 - 9	7 427	3 793	3 634	...	...	...	...	...	...
10 - 14	8 668	4 392	4 276	...	...	...	...	...	...
15 - 19	9 687	4 869	4 818	...	...	...	...	...	...
20 - 24	9 824	5 027	4 797	...	...	...	...	...	...
25 - 29	9 480	4 758	4 722	...	...	...	...	...	...
30 - 34	7 110	3 596	3 514	...	...	...	...	...	...
35 - 39	6 554	3 424	3 130	...	...	...	...	...	...
40 - 44	6 024	3 120	2 904	...	...	...	...	...	...
45 - 49	6 614	3 416	3 198	...	...	...	...	...	...
50 - 54	6 374	3 179	3 195	...	...	...	...	...	...
55 - 59	4 686	2 455	2 231	...	...	...	...	...	...
60 - 64	3 571	1 806	1 765	...	...	...	...	...	...
65 - 69	2 758	1 261	1 497	...	...	...	...	...	...

Continent, country or area, date, code[a] and age (in years) / Continent, pays ou zone, date, code[a] et âge (en années)	Total			Urban - Urbaine			Rural - Rurale		
	Both sexes Les deux sexes	Male Masculin	Female Féminin	Both sexes Les deux sexes	Male Masculin	Female Féminin	Both sexes Les deux sexes	Male Masculin	Female Féminin
AMERICA, NORTH - AMÉRIQUE DU NORD									
Grenada - Grenade									
1 VII 2017 (ESDF)									
70 - 74	2 393	1 106	1 287	...	...	...	...	...	...
75 - 79	1 731	732	999	...	...	...	...	...	...
80 - 84	1 112	417	695	...	...	...	...	...	...
85 - 89	527	168	359	...	...	...	...	...	...
90 +	275	78	197	...	...	...	...	...	...
Guadeloupe[40]									
1 I 2015 (CDJC)									
Total	397 990	183 479	214 511	391 984	180 438	211 546	6 006	3 041	2 965
0	4 009	2 045	1 965	3 965	2 025	1 941	44	20	24
1 - 4	18 400	9 247	9 153	18 216	9 148	9 068	184	99	85
5 - 9	26 769	13 707	13 062	26 476	13 552	12 923	294	155	139
10 - 14	29 794	15 004	14 790	29 418	14 801	14 617	376	203	173
15 - 19	29 000	14 731	14 269	28 658	14 539	14 120	342	193	149
20 - 24	19 884	10 153	9 731	19 628	9 997	9 631	256	156	100
25 - 29	18 266	8 227	10 039	18 021	8 104	9 918	245	123	122
30 - 34	19 526	7 926	11 600	19 305	7 808	11 497	222	119	103
35 - 39	22 312	9 201	13 111	22 041	9 074	12 967	271	127	144
40 - 44	29 148	12 518	16 630	28 680	12 286	16 394	468	232	236
45 - 49	31 360	13 926	17 434	30 817	13 646	17 171	544	281	263
50 - 54	31 975	14 748	17 227	31 442	14 477	16 965	533	271	262
55 - 59	27 674	12 884	14 790	27 179	12 626	14 554	495	258	237
60 - 64	24 635	11 204	13 431	24 202	10 992	13 210	433	213	221
65 - 69	20 327	9 336	10 991	19 938	9 146	10 792	389	190	199
70 - 74	15 353	6 850	8 503	15 013	6 692	8 322	340	158	182
75 - 79	11 957	5 315	6 642	11 696	5 193	6 503	261	122	139
80 - 84	8 552	3 359	5 193	8 381	3 287	5 093	172	72	100
85 - 89	5 364	1 891	3 472	5 275	1 858	3 417	88	33	55
90 - 94	2 625	882	1 742	2 588	867	1 720	37	15	22
95 - 99	817	268	549	807	266	541	10	2	8
100 +	240	56	184	236	55	181	4	1	3
1 I 2018 (ESDJ)									
Total	422 290	194 321	227 969	...	...	...	...	...	...
0 - 4	22 562	11 424	11 138	...	...	...	...	...	...
5 - 9	26 544	13 520	13 024	...	...	...	...	...	...
10 - 14	30 261	15 223	15 038	...	...	...	...	...	...
15 - 19	28 783	14 731	14 052	...	...	...	...	...	...
20 - 24	20 013	10 025	9 988	...	...	...	...	...	...
25 - 29	20 104	9 293	10 811	...	...	...	...	...	...
30 - 34	20 025	8 365	11 660	...	...	...	...	...	...
35 - 39	22 090	9 060	13 030	...	...	...	...	...	...
40 - 44	27 554	11 619	15 935	...	...	...	...	...	...
45 - 49	31 981	14 069	17 912	...	...	...	...	...	...
50 - 54	33 590	15 213	18 377	...	...	...	...	...	...
55 - 59	32 162	15 100	17 062	...	...	...	...	...	...
60 - 64	28 369	13 094	15 275	...	...	...	...	...	...
65 - 69	24 777	11 371	13 406	...	...	...	...	...	...
70 - 74	19 125	8 700	10 425	...	...	...	...	...	...
75 - 79	13 415	5 828	7 587	...	...	...	...	...	...
80 - 84	10 306	4 048	6 258	...	...	...	...	...	...
85 - 89	6 245	2 244	4 001	...	...	...	...	...	...
90 - 94	3 198	1 026	2 172	...	...	...	...	...	...
95 - 99	1 057	338	719	...	...	...	...	...	...
100 +	129	30	99	...	...	...	...	...	...
Guatemala[28]									
1 VII 2018 (ESDJ)									
Total	17 311 086	8 469 989	8 841 097	...	...	...	...	...	...
0 - 4	2 304 007	1 174 848	1 129 159	...	...	...	...	...	...
5 - 9	2 209 740	1 125 844	1 083 896	...	...	...	...	...	...
10 - 14	2 085 169	1 059 860	1 025 310	...	...	...	...	...	...
15 - 19	1 889 494	954 428	935 065	...	...	...	...	...	...
20 - 24	1 686 608	843 100	843 508	...	...	...	...	...	...
25 - 29	1 413 323	693 436	719 886	...	...	...	...	...	...

Continent, country or area, date, code[a] and age (in years) / Continent, pays ou zone, date, code[a] et âge (en années)	Total			Urban - Urbaine			Rural - Rurale		
	Both sexes Les deux sexes	Male Masculin	Female Féminin	Both sexes Les deux sexes	Male Masculin	Female Féminin	Both sexes Les deux sexes	Male Masculin	Female Féminin
AMERICA, NORTH - AMÉRIQUE DU NORD									
Guatemala[28]									
1 VII 2018 (ESDJ)									
30 - 34	1 202 126	574 360	627 766	...	...	...	...	...	...
35 - 39	999 618	461 515	538 103	...	...	...	...	...	...
40 - 44	801 107	356 135	444 972	...	...	...	...	...	...
45 - 49	633 751	277 730	356 020	...	...	...	...	...	...
50 - 54	510 636	225 694	284 941	...	...	...	...	...	...
55 - 59	408 107	183 916	224 191	...	...	...	...	...	...
60 - 64	348 127	160 872	187 255	...	...	...	...	...	...
65 +	819 274	378 250	441 024	...	...	...	...	...	...
Haiti - Haïti[41]									
1 VII 2010 (ESDJ)									
Total	10 085 214	4 993 731	5 091 483	4 817 666	2 321 608	2 496 059	5 267 548	2 672 123	2 595 424
0 - 4	1 263 322	644 550	618 772	532 352	274 597	257 755	730 970	369 953	361 017
5 - 9	1 195 479	608 495	586 984	493 368	249 982	243 386	702 111	358 513	343 598
10 - 14	1 158 478	588 618	569 860	532 573	255 002	277 571	625 905	333 616	292 289
15 - 19	1 092 364	551 467	540 897	583 183	276 258	306 925	509 181	275 209	233 972
20 - 24	1 019 589	509 042	510 547	600 175	296 233	303 943	419 414	212 809	206 604
25 - 29	919 636	454 123	465 513	537 063	267 198	269 865	382 573	186 925	195 648
30 - 34	702 596	340 518	362 078	390 054	189 432	200 622	312 542	151 086	161 456
35 - 39	548 004	261 157	286 847	272 855	128 575	144 280	275 149	132 582	142 567
40 - 44	488 482	235 182	253 300	225 057	106 072	118 985	263 425	129 110	134 315
45 - 49	423 377	204 077	219 300	179 712	81 240	98 472	243 665	122 837	120 828
50 - 54	342 913	166 418	176 495	138 580	61 854	76 726	204 333	104 564	99 769
55 - 59	284 731	136 034	148 697	107 391	46 062	61 329	177 340	89 972	87 368
60 - 64	206 835	95 939	110 896	73 562	29 974	43 588	133 273	65 965	67 308
65 - 69	175 898	81 854	94 044	61 671	24 975	36 696	114 227	56 879	57 348
70 - 74	129 436	58 181	71 255	44 448	17 100	27 347	84 988	41 081	43 908
75 - 79	80 898	35 538	45 360	27 630	10 473	17 158	53 268	25 065	28 202
80 +	53 176	22 538	30 638	17 992	6 581	11 412	35 184	15 957	19 226
1 VII 2018 (ESDJ)									
Total	11 411 527	5 659 140	5 752 387	...	...	...	...	...	...
0 - 4	1 295 906	661 535	634 371	...	...	...	...	...	...
5 - 9	1 247 619	635 927	611 692	...	...	...	...	...	...
10 - 14	1 197 091	608 695	588 396	...	...	...	...	...	...
15 - 19	1 146 787	580 801	565 986	...	...	...	...	...	...
20 - 24	1 089 914	547 618	542 296	...	...	...	...	...	...
25 - 29	1 013 281	504 926	508 355	...	...	...	...	...	...
30 - 34	936 810	463 541	473 269	...	...	...	...	...	...
35 - 39	793 197	387 698	405 499	...	...	...	...	...	...
40 - 44	594 836	285 013	309 823	...	...	...	...	...	...
45 - 49	485 166	230 537	254 629	...	...	...	...	...	...
50 - 54	431 114	206 255	224 859	...	...	...	...	...	...
55 - 59	357 489	170 991	186 498	...	...	...	...	...	...
60 - 64	282 415	134 300	148 115	...	...	...	...	...	...
65 - 69	211 207	97 454	113 753	...	...	...	...	...	...
70 - 74	147 063	66 084	80 979	...	...	...	...	...	...
75 - 79	104 921	46 188	58 733	...	...	...	...	...	...
80 +	76 710	31 576	45 134	...	...	...	...	...	...
Honduras									
10 VIII 2013 (CDFC)									
Total	8 303 771	4 052 316	4 251 456	4 480 746	2 116 113	2 364 633	3 823 025	1 936 203	1 886 823
0 - 4	971 015	494 034	476 980	485 103	247 341	237 762	485 911	246 693	239 218
5 - 9	958 543	489 821	468 723	472 721	240 952	231 769	485 823	248 868	236 954
10 - 14	1 020 406	520 842	499 564	499 521	251 358	248 163	520 885	269 485	251 400
15 - 19	982 164	487 949	494 215	523 989	248 745	275 244	458 175	239 204	218 971
20 - 24	840 800	398 093	442 708	483 289	219 539	263 750	357 511	178 554	178 957
25 - 29	656 443	303 379	353 065	384 221	171 360	212 861	272 222	132 019	140 203
30 - 34	567 367	262 951	304 416	329 661	147 590	182 072	237 705	115 361	122 344
35 - 39	484 740	224 965	259 775	277 833	124 524	153 309	206 907	100 441	106 465
40 - 44	399 555	190 323	209 232	231 557	106 187	125 370	167 998	84 135	83 862
45 - 49	318 026	150 635	167 391	183 503	84 007	99 495	134 524	66 628	67 896
50 - 54	293 256	141 174	152 082	167 798	77 351	90 447	125 458	63 823	61 636
55 - 59	210 708	101 062	109 646	116 409	53 286	63 124	94 299	47 777	46 522

Continent, country or area, date, code[a] and age (in years) / Continent, pays ou zone, date, code[a] et âge (en années)	Total			Urban - Urbaine			Rural - Rurale		
	Both sexes Les deux sexes	Male Masculin	Female Féminin	Both sexes Les deux sexes	Male Masculin	Female Féminin	Both sexes Les deux sexes	Male Masculin	Female Féminin
AMERICA, NORTH - AMÉRIQUE DU NORD									
Honduras									
10 VIII 2013 (CDFC)									
60 - 64	189 636	91 291	98 345	103 821	47 002	56 819	85 815	44 290	41 526
65 - 69	135 709	64 441	71 267	72 921	32 263	40 657	62 788	32 178	30 610
70 - 74	106 566	51 803	54 762	57 407	25 756	31 650	49 159	26 047	23 112
75 - 79	78 407	38 419	39 988	41 388	18 486	22 902	37 019	19 933	17 086
80 - 84	48 965	22 977	25 988	26 407	11 230	15 177	22 558	11 748	10 810
85 - 89	29 532	13 681	15 851	16 153	6 682	9 471	13 380	7 000	6 380
90 - 94	8 241	3 162	5 079	4 867	1 717	3 150	3 374	1 445	1 929
95 +	3 692	1 313	2 379	2 177	738	1 439	1 515	575	940
1 VII 2018 (ESDF)[3]									
Total	9 012 229	4 389 313	4 622 916	...	...	...	...	...	...
0 - 4	964 030	490 840	473 190	...	...	...	...	...	...
5 - 9	972 839	495 115	477 724	...	...	...	...	...	...
10 - 14	983 394	494 153	489 241	...	...	...	...	...	...
15 - 19	947 363	465 978	481 385	...	...	...	...	...	...
20 - 24	878 739	425 714	453 025	...	...	...	...	...	...
25 - 29	803 646	385 503	418 143	...	...	...	...	...	...
30 - 34	703 644	335 305	368 339	...	...	...	...	...	...
35 - 39	571 892	270 718	301 174	...	...	...	...	...	...
40 - 44	478 711	225 854	252 857	...	...	...	...	...	...
45 - 49	393 229	185 343	207 886	...	...	...	...	...	...
50 - 54	327 013	154 061	172 952	...	...	...	...	...	...
55 - 59	268 761	126 874	141 887	...	...	...	...	...	...
60 - 64	218 094	102 626	115 468	...	...	...	...	...	...
65 - 69	172 196	80 365	91 831	...	...	...	...	...	...
70 - 74	127 317	59 120	68 197	...	...	...	...	...	...
75 - 79	92 591	42 820	49 771	...	...	...	...	...	...
80 +	108 771	48 925	59 846	...	...	...	...	...	...
Jamaica - Jamaïque									
4 IV 2011 (CDJC)									
Total	2 697 983	1 334 533	1 363 450	1 454 151	700 957	753 194	1 243 832	633 576	610 256
0 - 4	209 871	106 107	103 764	109 121	55 157	53 965	100 750	50 950	49 799
5 - 9	226 378	114 792	111 586	114 520	57 817	56 703	111 858	56 975	54 883
10 - 14	266 586	136 183	130 403	138 596	70 428	68 168	127 990	65 755	62 235
15 - 19	274 658	139 777	134 881	143 644	72 173	71 471	131 014	67 604	63 410
20 - 24	250 711	125 243	125 468	140 770	68 692	72 078	109 941	56 551	53 390
25 - 29	226 120	109 919	116 201	129 961	61 980	67 981	96 159	47 939	48 220
30 - 34	185 495	87 810	97 685	106 228	49 452	56 776	79 267	38 358	40 909
35 - 39	183 756	86 647	97 109	103 560	47 408	56 152	80 196	39 239	40 957
40 - 44	173 924	85 656	88 268	97 069	46 377	50 693	76 855	39 279	37 575
45 - 49	155 389	79 201	76 188	88 044	41 385	46 658	67 345	37 816	29 530
50 - 54	137 895	67 297	70 598	74 271	34 341	39 930	63 624	32 956	30 668
55 - 59	100 798	50 717	50 081	54 090	26 020	28 070	46 708	24 697	22 011
60 - 64	88 057	44 407	43 650	46 868	22 549	24 319	41 189	21 858	19 331
65 - 69	65 164	32 543	32 621	33 182	15 691	17 491	31 982	16 852	15 130
70 - 74	51 276	24 627	26 649	25 354	11 785	13 569	25 922	12 842	13 080
75 - 79	42 762	19 847	22 915	20 542	9 085	11 458	22 220	10 762	11 457
80 - 84	30 738	13 258	17 480	14 941	6 132	8 809	15 797	7 126	8 671
85 - 89	18 457	7 267	11 190	8 789	3 151	5 638	9 668	4 116	5 552
90 - 94	6 921	2 303	4 618	2 303	957	2 281	3 683	1 346	2 337
95 - 99	2 503	808	1 695	1 119	326	793	1 384	482	902
100 +	524	124	400	243	53	190	281	71	210
1 VII 2017 (ESDJ)									
Total	2 728 915	1 351 375	1 377 540	...	...	...	...	...	...
0 - 4	180 672	92 151	88 521	...	...	...	...	...	...
5 - 9	200 295	101 561	98 734	...	...	...	...	...	...
10 - 14	215 272	108 949	106 323	...	...	...	...	...	...
15 - 19	247 511	126 151	121 360	...	...	...	...	...	...
20 - 24	271 136	137 643	133 493	...	...	...	...	...	...
25 - 29	243 420	121 867	121 553	...	...	...	...	...	...
30 - 34	217 119	105 767	111 352	...	...	...	...	...	...
35 - 39	183 616	87 269	96 347	...	...	...	...	...	...
40 - 44	172 149	80 997	91 152	...	...	...	...	...	...

Continent, country or area, date, code[a] and age (in years) / Continent, pays ou zone, date, code[a] et âge (en années)	Total			Urban - Urbaine			Rural - Rurale		
	Both sexes Les deux sexes	Male Masculin	Female Féminin	Both sexes Les deux sexes	Male Masculin	Female Féminin	Both sexes Les deux sexes	Male Masculin	Female Féminin
AMERICA, NORTH - AMÉRIQUE DU NORD									
Jamaica - Jamaïque									
1 VII 2017 (ESDJ)									
45 - 49	171 811	82 738	89 073	...	...	...	...	...	...
50 - 54	153 454	77 004	76 450	...	...	...	...	...	...
55 - 59	133 003	66 170	66 833	...	...	...	...	...	...
60 - 64	99 197	49 379	49 818	...	...	...	...	...	...
65 - 69	80 133	40 443	39 690	...	...	...	...	...	...
70 - 74	59 150	29 002	30 148	...	...	...	...	...	...
75 +	100 977	44 284	56 693	...	...	...	...	...	...
Martinique									
1 I 2015 (CDJC)									
Total	380 877	176 328	204 549	367 749	169 911	197 838	13 128	6 417	6 711
0 - 4	19 514	9 968	9 545	18 927	9 661	9 267	586	308	279
5 - 9	23 179	11 841	11 338	22 465	11 480	10 985	713	361	353
10 - 14	24 846	12 616	12 229	24 010	12 176	11 834	835	440	395
15 - 19	25 065	12 913	12 152	24 241	12 506	11 736	824	408	416
20 - 24	18 914	9 758	9 157	18 354	9 455	8 899	561	303	258
25 - 29	17 978	8 092	9 886	17 471	7 846	9 625	507	246	261
30 - 34	17 884	7 651	10 233	17 393	7 444	9 948	491	207	284
35 - 39	19 983	8 508	11 474	19 389	8 247	11 142	594	262	332
40 - 44	26 375	11 391	14 984	25 498	10 985	14 512	877	405	472
45 - 49	31 052	13 979	17 073	30 020	13 471	16 549	1 032	508	524
50 - 54	32 777	14 886	17 891	31 588	14 274	17 314	1 188	611	577
55 - 59	28 564	13 462	15 101	27 524	12 915	14 609	1 040	547	492
60 - 64	24 838	11 229	13 609	23 903	10 764	13 139	935	465	470
65 - 69	20 492	9 408	11 084	19 679	9 002	10 677	814	406	407
70 - 74	15 786	7 148	8 638	15 119	6 850	8 269	667	298	369
75 - 79	13 601	6 019	7 582	13 027	5 737	7 291	573	282	291
80 - 84	9 800	4 090	5 710	9 346	3 897	5 449	454	193	261
85 - 89	6 010	2 174	3 836	5 747	2 066	3 681	263	108	154
90 - 94	2 962	895	2 067	2 840	851	1 989	123	44	78
95 - 99	971	241	731	932	228	704	39	12	27
100 +	287	59	228	275	57	218	12	2	10
1 I 2018 (ESDJ)									
Total	368 640	169 594	199 046	...	...	...	...	...	...
0 - 4	17 297	8 702	8 595	...	...	...	...	...	...
5 - 9	20 661	10 461	10 200	...	...	...	...	...	...
10 - 14	23 134	11 676	11 458	...	...	...	...	...	...
15 - 19	23 451	12 065	11 386	...	...	...	...	...	...
20 - 24	16 735	8 585	8 150	...	...	...	...	...	...
25 - 29	17 058	7 869	9 189	...	...	...	...	...	...
30 - 34	17 334	7 425	9 909	...	...	...	...	...	...
35 - 39	17 626	7 403	10 223	...	...	...	...	...	...
40 - 44	21 232	9 096	12 136	...	...	...	...	...	...
45 - 49	28 277	12 468	15 809	...	...	...	...	...	...
50 - 54	32 717	14 630	18 087	...	...	...	...	...	...
55 - 59	30 850	14 331	16 519	...	...	...	...	...	...
60 - 64	26 539	12 242	14 297	...	...	...	...	...	...
65 - 69	22 531	10 284	12 247	...	...	...	...	...	...
70 - 74	17 511	8 026	9 485	...	...	...	...	...	...
75 - 79	13 821	6 070	7 751	...	...	...	...	...	...
80 - 84	10 755	4 548	6 207	...	...	...	...	...	...
85 - 89	6 341	2 418	3 923	...	...	...	...	...	...
90 - 94	3 141	938	2 203	...	...	...	...	...	...
95 - 99	1 199	286	913	...	...	...	...	...	...
100 +	430	71	359	...	...	...	...	...	...
Mexico - Mexique									
12 VI 2010 (CDFC)[42]									
Total	112 336 538	54 855 231	57 481 307	86 287 410	41 946 540	44 340 870	26 049 128	12 908 691	13 140 437
0 - 4	10 528 322	5 346 943	5 181 379	7 766 149	3 945 636	3 820 513	2 762 173	1 401 307	1 360 866
5 - 9	11 047 537	5 604 175	5 443 362	8 124 337	4 124 524	3 999 813	2 923 200	1 479 651	1 443 549
10 - 14	10 939 937	5 547 613	5 392 324	7 974 649	4 041 649	3 933 000	2 965 288	1 505 964	1 459 324
15 - 19	11 026 112	5 520 121	5 505 991	8 191 229	4 097 876	4 093 353	2 834 883	1 422 245	1 412 638
20 - 24	9 892 271	4 813 204	5 079 067	7 725 598	3 775 245	3 950 353	2 166 673	1 037 959	1 128 714

Continent, country or area, date, code[a] and age (in years) / Continent, pays ou zone, date, code[a] et âge (en annèes)	Total			Urban - Urbaine			Rural - Rurale		
	Both sexes Les deux sexes	Male Masculin	Female Féminin	Both sexes Les deux sexes	Male Masculin	Female Féminin	Both sexes Les deux sexes	Male Masculin	Female Féminin
AMERICA, NORTH - AMÉRIQUE DU NORD									
Mexico - Mexique									
12 VI 2010 (CDFC)[42]									
25 - 29	8 788 177	4 205 975	4 582 202	6 985 279	3 354 569	3 630 710	1 802 898	851 406	951 492
30 - 34	8 470 798	4 026 031	4 444 767	6 719 047	3 188 789	3 530 258	1 751 751	837 242	914 509
35 - 39	8 292 987	3 964 738	4 328 249	6 642 253	3 160 713	3 481 540	1 650 734	804 025	846 709
40 - 44	7 009 226	3 350 322	3 658 904	5 633 205	2 676 230	2 956 975	1 376 021	674 092	701 929
45 - 49	5 928 730	2 824 364	3 104 366	4 739 911	2 241 753	2 498 158	1 188 819	582 611	606 208
50 - 54	5 064 291	2 402 451	2 661 840	4 051 487	1 904 317	2 147 170	1 012 804	498 134	514 670
55 - 59	3 895 365	1 869 537	2 025 828	3 043 924	1 443 868	1 600 056	851 441	425 669	425 772
60 - 64	3 116 466	1 476 667	1 639 799	2 403 645	1 119 077	1 284 568	712 821	357 590	355 231
65 - 69	2 317 265	1 095 273	1 221 992	1 719 078	794 137	924 941	598 187	301 136	297 051
70 - 74	1 873 934	873 893	1 000 041	1 338 906	603 945	734 961	535 028	269 948	265 080
75 - 79	1 245 483	579 689	665 794	892 237	399 026	493 211	353 246	180 663	172 583
80 - 84	798 936	355 277	443 659	576 855	244 082	332 773	222 081	111 195	110 886
85 - 89	454 164	197 461	256 703	322 844	132 826	190 018	131 320	64 635	66 685
90 - 94	164 924	68 130	96 794	116 950	45 123	71 827	47 974	23 007	24 967
95 - 99	65 732	25 920	39 812	44 084	16 122	27 962	21 648	9 798	11 850
100 +	18 475	7 228	11 247	10 451	3 753	6 698	8 024	3 475	4 549
Unknown - Inconnu	1 397 406	700 219	697 187	1 265 292	633 280	632 012	132 114	66 939	65 175
1 VII 2018 (ESDJ)[43]									
Total	125 327 797	61 368 864	63 958 933	...	...	...	...	...	...
0	2 169 955	1 104 787	1 065 168	...	...	...	...	...	...
1 - 4	8 792 330	4 473 907	4 318 423	...	...	...	...	...	...
5 - 9	11 088 816	5 643 658	5 445 158	...	...	...	...	...	...
10 - 14	11 169 666	5 684 589	5 485 077	...	...	...	...	...	...
15 - 19	11 046 851	5 600 601	5 446 250	...	...	...	...	...	...
20 - 24	10 886 913	5 485 727	5 401 186	...	...	...	...	...	...
25 - 29	10 485 837	5 207 498	5 278 339	...	...	...	...	...	...
30 - 34	9 603 156	4 637 981	4 965 175	...	...	...	...	...	...
35 - 39	8 740 590	4 116 400	4 624 190	...	...	...	...	...	...
40 - 44	8 249 368	3 881 085	4 368 283	...	...	...	...	...	...
45 - 49	7 592 336	3 616 151	3 976 185	...	...	...	...	...	...
50 - 54	6 557 785	3 134 022	3 423 763	...	...	...	...	...	...
55 - 59	5 514 767	2 626 559	2 888 208	...	...	...	...	...	...
60 - 64	4 347 698	2 054 113	2 293 585	...	...	...	...	...	...
65 - 69	3 218 842	1 500 998	1 717 844	...	...	...	...	...	...
70 - 74	2 330 842	1 068 188	1 262 654	...	...	...	...	...	...
75 - 79	1 614 583	721 761	892 822	...	...	...	...	...	...
80 - 84	1 023 832	443 160	580 672	...	...	...	...	...	...
85 - 89	567 338	237 348	329 990	...	...	...	...	...	...
90 - 94	242 724	97 901	144 823	...	...	...	...	...	...
95 - 99	71 241	27 742	43 499	...	...	...	...	...	...
100 +	12 327	4 688	7 639	...	...	...	...	...	...
Montserrat									
12 V 2011 (CDJC)									
Total	4 922	2 546	2 376	...	...	...	...	...	...
0 - 4	301	157	144	...	...	...	...	...	...
5 - 9	311	146	165	...	...	...	...	...	...
10 - 14	359	187	172	...	...	...	...	...	...
15 - 19	319	179	140	...	...	...	...	...	...
20 - 24	269	152	117	...	...	...	...	...	...
25 - 29	299	154	145	...	...	...	...	...	...
30 - 34	298	138	160	...	...	...	...	...	...
35 - 39	368	172	196	...	...	...	...	...	...
40 - 44	406	189	217	...	...	...	...	...	...
45 - 49	381	196	185	...	...	...	...	...	...
50 - 54	331	183	148	...	...	...	...	...	...
55 - 59	314	181	133	...	...	...	...	...	...
60 - 64	275	165	110	...	...	...	...	...	...
65 - 69	231	130	101	...	...	...	...	...	...
70 - 74	145	75	70	...	...	...	...	...	...
75 - 79	116	61	55	...	...	...	...	...	...
80 - 84	94	44	50	...	...	...	...	...	...
85 +	105	37	68	...	...	...	...	...	...

Continent, country or area, date, code[a] and age (in years) Continent, pays ou zone, date, code[a] et âge (en années)	Total			Urban - Urbaine			Rural - Rurale		
	Both sexes Les deux sexes	Male Masculin	Female Féminin	Both sexes Les deux sexes	Male Masculin	Female Féminin	Both sexes Les deux sexes	Male Masculin	Female Féminin
AMERICA, NORTH - **AMÉRIQUE DU NORD**									
Nicaragua 1 VII 2017 (ESDJ)									
Total	6 393 824	3 154 465	3 239 359	3 722 549	1 797 179	1 925 370	2 671 275	1 357 286	1 313 989
0 - 4	679 444	347 128	332 316	335 461	174 369	161 092	343 983	172 759	171 224
5 - 9	678 786	346 271	332 515	355 520	182 519	173 001	323 266	163 752	159 514
10 - 14	648 245	330 132	318 113	349 081	177 414	171 667	299 164	152 718	146 446
15 - 19	630 345	319 935	310 410	348 231	174 655	173 576	282 114	145 280	136 834
20 - 24	627 690	314 266	313 424	362 183	177 082	185 101	265 507	137 184	128 323
25 - 29	570 080	280 857	289 223	339 353	162 817	176 536	230 727	118 040	112 687
30 - 34	508 427	247 440	260 987	312 277	147 292	164 985	196 150	100 148	96 002
35 - 39	439 523	209 400	230 123	277 999	127 747	150 252	161 524	81 653	79 871
40 - 44	359 194	169 454	189 740	232 818	108 016	124 802	126 376	61 438	64 938
45 - 49	292 467	139 449	153 018	190 838	89 414	101 424	101 629	50 035	51 594
50 - 54	245 700	117 462	128 238	159 264	73 630	85 634	86 436	43 832	42 604
55 - 59	215 887	101 958	113 929	139 688	63 182	76 506	76 199	38 776	37 423
60 - 64	176 700	83 162	93 538	112 726	50 503	62 223	63 974	32 659	31 315
65 - 69	110 334	51 986	58 348	69 975	31 080	38 895	40 359	20 906	19 453
70 - 74	79 732	37 489	42 243	50 788	22 300	28 488	28 944	15 189	13 755
75 - 79	63 811	29 534	34 277	41 831	18 060	23 771	21 980	11 474	10 506
80 +	67 459	28 542	38 917	44 516	17 099	27 417	22 943	11 443	11 500
Panama[12] 1 VII 2018 (ESDF)									
Total	4 158 783	2 085 950	2 072 833	2 901 275	1 427 378	1 473 897	1 257 508	658 572	598 936
0	74 242	37 946	36 296	46 479	23 791	22 688	27 763	14 155	13 608
1 - 4	296 019	151 232	144 787	184 186	94 244	89 942	111 833	56 988	54 845
5 - 9	366 458	187 146	179 312	228 758	116 902	111 856	137 700	70 244	67 456
10 - 14	362 470	184 993	177 477	226 030	114 906	111 124	136 440	70 087	66 353
15 - 19	356 486	181 696	174 790	228 713	115 041	113 672	127 773	66 655	61 118
20 - 24	337 992	171 607	166 385	231 502	115 692	115 810	106 490	55 915	50 575
25 - 29	318 627	160 888	157 739	220 054	109 001	111 053	98 573	51 887	46 686
30 - 34	307 778	155 056	152 722	223 070	110 093	112 977	84 708	44 963	39 745
35 - 39	294 150	148 233	145 917	223 199	111 002	112 197	70 951	37 231	33 720
40 - 44	281 104	141 226	139 878	220 141	109 137	111 004	60 963	32 089	28 874
45 - 49	259 860	129 885	129 975	203 803	99 531	104 272	56 057	30 354	25 703
50 - 54	224 482	111 556	112 926	175 822	85 328	90 494	48 660	26 228	22 432
55 - 59	189 481	93 349	96 132	145 010	69 536	75 474	44 471	23 813	20 658
60 - 64	148 622	72 341	76 281	110 064	51 274	58 790	38 558	21 067	17 491
65 - 69	113 896	54 674	59 222	79 644	36 206	43 438	34 252	18 468	15 784
70 - 74	85 652	40 486	45 166	57 780	25 485	32 295	27 872	15 001	12 871
75 - 79	61 626	28 538	33 088	40 652	17 539	23 113	20 974	10 999	9 975
80 - 84	40 611	18 313	22 298	27 813	11 420	16 393	12 798	6 893	5 905
85 +	...	...	...	28 555	11 250	17 305	10 672	5 535	5 137
85 - 89	23 454	10 234	13 220	...	...	...	...	...	...
90 - 94	11 117	4 673	6 444	...	...	...	...	...	...
95 - 99	3 901	1 580	2 321	...	...	...	...	...	...
100 +	755	298	457	...	...	...	...	...	...
Puerto Rico - Porto Rico[44] 1 VII 2017 (ESDJ)									
Total	3 337 177	1 582 703	1 754 474	...	...	...	...	...	...
0	27 379	14 142	13 237	...	...	...	...	...	...
1 - 4	120 591	61 649	58 942	...	...	...	...	...	...
5 - 9	177 739	90 227	87 512	...	...	...	...	...	...
10 - 14	198 257	101 890	96 367	...	...	...	...	...	...
15 - 19	222 678	113 803	108 875	...	...	...	...	...	...
20 - 24	232 150	116 962	115 188	...	...	...	...	...	...
25 - 29	223 828	110 409	113 419	...	...	...	...	...	...
30 - 34	190 755	90 911	99 844	...	...	...	...	...	...
35 - 39	207 678	97 113	110 565	...	...	...	...	...	...
40 - 44	208 209	98 529	109 680	...	...	...	...	...	...
45 - 49	214 945	102 124	112 821	...	...	...	...	...	...
50 - 54	224 402	103 713	120 689	...	...	...	...	...	...
55 - 59	219 484	100 731	118 753	...	...	...	...	...	...
60 - 64	210 332	95 614	114 718	...	...	...	...	...	...
65 - 69	195 563	87 884	107 679	...	...	...	...	...	...

Continent, country or area, date, code[a] and age (in years) / Continent, pays ou zone, date, code[a] et âge (en années)	Total			Urban - Urbaine			Rural - Rurale		
	Both sexes Les deux sexes	Male Masculin	Female Féminin	Both sexes Les deux sexes	Male Masculin	Female Féminin	Both sexes Les deux sexes	Male Masculin	Female Féminin
AMERICA, NORTH - AMÉRIQUE DU NORD									
Puerto Rico - Porto Rico[44]									
1 VII 2017 (ESDJ)									
70 - 74	171 623	76 642	94 981	...	...	...	...	...	...
75 - 79	123 063	54 006	69 057	...	...	...	...	...	...
80 - 84	84 508	35 247	49 261	...	...	...	...	...	...
85 +	83 993	31 107	52 886	...	...	...	...	...	...
Saint Lucia - Sainte-Lucie									
1 VII 2018 (ESDF)									
Total	178 696	88 693	90 002	...	...	...	...	...	...
0 - 4	10 539	5 340	5 199	...	...	...	...	...	...
5 - 9	10 728	5 492	5 236	...	...	...	...	...	...
10 - 14	11 854	6 058	5 796	...	...	...	...	...	...
15 - 19	13 206	6 674	6 531	...	...	...	...	...	...
20 - 24	15 092	7 654	7 438	...	...	...	...	...	...
25 - 29	15 357	7 748	7 609	...	...	...	...	...	...
30 - 34	14 776	7 300	7 477	...	...	...	...	...	...
35 - 39	13 842	6 956	6 885	...	...	...	...	...	...
40 - 44	12 946	6 555	6 391	...	...	...	...	...	...
45 - 49	12 754	6 368	6 385	...	...	...	...	...	...
50 - 54	12 166	6 051	6 114	...	...	...	...	...	...
55 - 59	10 638	5 319	5 319	...	...	...	...	...	...
60 - 64	8 054	3 927	4 127	...	...	...	...	...	...
65 - 69	5 834	2 784	3 050	...	...	...	...	...	...
70 - 74	4 358	1 977	2 381	...	...	...	...	...	...
75 - 79	3 090	1 319	1 771	...	...	...	...	...	...
80 +	3 461	1 170	2 291	...	...	...	...	...	...
Saint Pierre and Miquelon - Saint Pierre-et-Miquelon									
1 I 2015 (CDJC)									
Total	6 021	2 940	3 081	...	...	...	...	...	...
0 - 4	315	142	172	...	...	...	...	...	...
5 - 9	392	200	191	...	...	...	...	...	...
10 - 14	392	197	194	...	...	...	...	...	...
15 - 19	335	174	160	...	...	...	...	...	...
20 - 24	205	117	88	...	...	...	...	...	...
25 - 29	271	140	131	...	...	...	...	...	...
30 - 34	378	172	205	...	...	...	...	...	...
35 - 39	390	188	201	...	...	...	...	...	...
40 - 44	452	219	233	...	...	...	...	...	...
45 - 49	567	281	286	...	...	...	...	...	...
50 - 54	531	273	258	...	...	...	...	...	...
55 - 59	450	233	217	...	...	...	...	...	...
60 - 64	377	198	179	...	...	...	...	...	...
65 - 69	301	138	163	...	...	...	...	...	...
70 - 74	214	101	112	...	...	...	...	...	...
75 - 79	195	92	102	...	...	...	...	...	...
80 - 84	134	38	96	...	...	...	...	...	...
85 - 89	78	24	54	...	...	...	...	...	...
90 - 94	32	8	25	...	...	...	...	...	...
95 - 99	11	3	8	...	...	...	...	...	...
100 +	1	-	1	...	...	...	...	...	...
Saint Vincent and the Grenadines - Saint-Vincent-et-les Grenadines									
1 VII 2018 (ESDJ)									
Total	110 520	56 690	53 829	...	...	...	...	...	...
0	1 584	799	785	...	...	...	...	...	...
1 - 4	7 165	3 603	3 562	...	...	...	...	...	...
5 - 9	8 623	4 396	4 227	...	...	...	...	...	...
10 - 14	9 880	5 145	4 735	...	...	...	...	...	...
15 - 19	10 033	5 157	4 876	...	...	...	...	...	...
20 - 24	8 712	4 443	4 268	...	...	...	...	...	...
25 - 29	8 418	4 315	4 104	...	...	...	...	...	...

Continent, country or area, date, code[a] and age (in years) / Continent, pays ou zone, date, code[a] et âge (en années)	Total			Urban - Urbaine			Rural - Rurale		
	Both sexes Les deux sexes	Male Masculin	Female Féminin	Both sexes Les deux sexes	Male Masculin	Female Féminin	Both sexes Les deux sexes	Male Masculin	Female Féminin
AMERICA, NORTH - AMÉRIQUE DU NORD									
Saint Vincent and the Grenadines - Saint-Vincent-et-les Grenadines									
1 VII 2018 (ESDJ)									
30 - 34	7 957	3 967	3 990						
35 - 39	7 645	3 918	3 727	...	...	...	...	...	...
40 - 44	7 244	3 849	3 395	...	...	...	...	...	...
45 - 49	7 558	3 940	3 618	...	...	...	...	...	...
50 - 54	6 630	3 506	3 123	...	...	...	...	...	...
55 - 59	5 094	2 696	2 398	...	...	...	...	...	...
60 - 64	3 868	2 010	1 858	...	...	...	...	...	...
65 - 69	2 876	1 487	1 389	...	...	...	...	...	...
70 - 74	2 567	1 308	1 258	...	...	...	...	...	...
75 - 79	2 001	983	1 019	...	...	...	...	...	...
80 - 84	1 459	677	783	...	...	...	...	...	...
85 +	1 204	490	715	...	...	...	...	...	...
Saint-Barthélemy									
1 I 2015 (CDJC)									
Total	9 625	5 117	4 508	...	...	...	...	...	...
0	91	46	44	...	...	...	...	...	...
1 - 4	409	215	195	...	...	...	...	...	...
5 - 9	500	270	230	...	...	...	...	...	...
10 - 14	462	241	221	...	...	...	...	...	...
15 - 19	346	177	169	...	...	...	...	...	...
20 - 24	624	309	316	...	...	...	...	...	...
25 - 29	929	505	424	...	...	...	...	...	...
30 - 34	866	467	399	...	...	...	...	...	...
35 - 39	830	430	400	...	...	...	...	...	...
40 - 44	803	425	378	...	...	...	...	...	...
45 - 49	949	563	386	...	...	...	...	...	...
50 - 54	814	459	356	...	...	...	...	...	...
55 - 59	684	384	300	...	...	...	...	...	...
60 - 64	419	219	201	...	...	...	...	...	...
65 - 69	299	152	147	...	...	...	...	...	...
70 - 74	242	116	125	...	...	...	...	...	...
75 - 79	160	67	93	...	...	...	...	...	...
80 - 84	118	43	75	...	...	...	...	...	...
85 - 89	48	18	30	...	...	...	...	...	...
90 - 94	26	11	15	...	...	...	...	...	...
95 - 99	5	-	5	...	...	...	...	...	...
100 +	-	-	-	...	...	...	...	...	...
Saint-Martin (French part) - Saint-Martin (partie française)									
1 VII 2018 (ESDJ)									
Total	35 457	17 151	18 306	...	...	...	...	...	...
0	377	193	184	...	...	...	...	...	...
1 - 4	1 600	816	784	...	...	...	...	...	...
5 - 9	2 178	1 114	1 064	...	...	...	...	...	...
10 - 14	2 200	1 125	1 075	...	...	...	...	...	...
15 - 19	2 184	1 119	1 065	...	...	...	...	...	...
20 - 24	1 979	1 000	979	...	...	...	...	...	...
25 - 29	2 029	1 003	1 026	...	...	...	...	...	...
30 - 34	2 144	1 045	1 099	...	...	...	...	...	...
35 - 39	2 240	1 095	1 145	...	...	...	...	...	...
40 - 44	2 203	1 087	1 116	...	...	...	...	...	...
45 - 49	2 415	1 194	1 221	...	...	...	...	...	...
50 - 54	2 384	1 170	1 214	...	...	...	...	...	...
55 - 59	2 294	1 112	1 182	...	...	...	...	...	...
60 - 64	2 166	1 033	1 133	...	...	...	...	...	...
65 - 69	2 093	988	1 105	...	...	...	...	...	...
70 - 74	1 677	778	899	...	...	...	...	...	...
75 - 79	1 151	510	641	...	...	...	...	...	...

Continent, country or area, date, code[a] and age (in years) / Continent, pays ou zone, date, code[a] et âge (en années)	Total			Urban - Urbaine			Rural - Rurale		
	Both sexes Les deux sexes	Male Masculin	Female Féminin	Both sexes Les deux sexes	Male Masculin	Female Féminin	Both sexes Les deux sexes	Male Masculin	Female Féminin
AMERICA, NORTH - AMÉRIQUE DU NORD									
Saint-Martin (French part) - Saint-Martin (partie française)									
1 VII 2018 (ESDJ)									
80 - 84	991	401	590	...	...	...	...	...	...
85 - 89	710	248	462	...	...	...	...	...	...
90 - 94	338	97	241	...	...	...	...	...	...
95 +	104	23	81	...	...	...	...	...	...
Sint Maarten (Dutch part) - Saint-Martin (partie néerlandaise)									
1 I 2018 (ESDF)									
Total	40 614	19 759	20 855	...	...	...	...	...	...
0 - 4	2 614	1 349	1 265	...	...	...	...	...	...
5 - 9	2 773	1 437	1 336	...	...	...	...	...	...
10 - 14	2 741	1 387	1 354	...	...	...	...	...	...
15 - 19	2 721	1 360	1 361	...	...	...	...	...	...
20 - 24	2 165	1 139	1 025	...	...	...	...	...	...
25 - 29	2 466	1 142	1 324	...	...	...	...	...	...
30 - 34	3 083	1 432	1 651	...	...	...	...	...	...
35 - 39	3 342	1 510	1 832	...	...	...	...	...	...
40 - 44	3 546	1 651	1 895	...	...	...	...	...	...
45 - 49	3 471	1 665	1 806	...	...	...	...	...	...
50 - 54	3 446	1 727	1 719	...	...	...	...	...	...
55 - 59	2 795	1 348	1 447	...	...	...	...	...	...
60 - 64	2 223	1 091	1 132	...	...	...	...	...	...
65 - 69	1 573	759	813	...	...	...	...	...	...
70 - 74	881	431	450	...	...	...	...	...	...
75 - 79	430	207	223	...	...	...	...	...	...
80 - 84	217	93	125	...	...	...	...	...	...
85 - 89	79	18	61	...	...	...	...	...	...
90 +	47	11	36	...	...	...	...	...	...
Trinidad and Tobago - Trinité-et-Tobago[18]									
1 VII 2018 (ESDF)									
Total	1 359 193	...	...	...	...	...	...	...	...
0 - 14	279 833	...	...	...	...	...	...	...	...
15 - 19	100 688	...	...	...	...	...	...	...	...
20 - 24	116 922	...	...	...	...	...	...	...	...
25 - 29	126 417	...	...	...	...	...	...	...	...
30 - 34	108 058	...	...	...	...	...	...	...	...
35 - 39	94 711	...	...	...	...	...	...	...	...
40 - 44	88 186	...	...	...	...	...	...	...	...
45 - 49	98 370	...	...	...	...	...	...	...	...
50 - 54	89 231	...	...	...	...	...	...	...	...
55 - 59	74 934	...	...	...	...	...	...	...	...
60 - 64	60 024	...	...	...	...	...	...	...	...
65 +	121 819	...	...	...	...	...	...	...	...
Turks and Caicos Islands - Îles Turques et Caïques									
1 VII 2017 (ESDJ)									
Total	39 792	20 296	19 496	...	...	...	...	...	...
0 - 4	2 824	1 426	1 398	...	...	...	...	...	...
5 - 9	2 499	1 270	1 229	...	...	...	...	...	...
10 - 14	2 303	1 146	1 157	...	...	...	...	...	...
15 - 19	2 266	1 111	1 155	...	...	...	...	...	...
20 - 24	2 671	1 306	1 365	...	...	...	...	...	...
25 - 29	3 232	1 582	1 650	...	...	...	...	...	...
30 - 34	3 774	1 889	1 885	...	...	...	...	...	...
35 - 39	4 388	2 248	2 140	...	...	...	...	...	...
40 - 44	4 172	2 162	2 010	...	...	...	...	...	...
45 - 49	3 718	1 948	1 770	...	...	...	...	...	...
50 - 54	2 949	1 553	1 396	...	...	...	...	...	...
55 - 59	1 983	1 050	933	...	...	...	...	...	...

Continent, country or area, date, code[a] and age (in years) / Continent, pays ou zone, date, code[a] et âge (en années)	Total			Urban - Urbaine			Rural - Rurale		
	Both sexes Les deux sexes	Male Masculin	Female Féminin	Both sexes Les deux sexes	Male Masculin	Female Féminin	Both sexes Les deux sexes	Male Masculin	Female Féminin
AMERICA, NORTH - AMÉRIQUE DU NORD									
Turks and Caicos Islands - Îles Turques et Caïques									
1 VII 2017 (ESDJ)									
60 - 64	*1 366*	*730*	*636*	...	...	...	...	...	...
65 - 69	*820*	*445*	*375*	...	...	...	...	...	...
70 - 74	*471*	*258*	*213*	...	...	...	...	...	...
75 - 79	*206*	*112*	*94*	...	...	...	...	...	...
80 +	*150*	*60*	*90*	...	...	...	...	...	...
United States of America - États-Unis d'Amérique									
1 IV 2010 (CDJC)									
Total	308 745 538	151 781 326	156 964 212	249 253 271	121 698 595	127 554 676	59 492 267	30 082 731	29 409 536
0 - 4	20 201 362	10 319 427	9 881 935	16 838 001	8 597 234	8 240 767	3 363 361	1 722 193	1 641 168
5 - 9	20 348 657	10 389 638	9 959 019	16 597 127	8 464 939	8 132 188	3 751 530	1 924 699	1 826 831
10 - 14	20 677 194	10 579 862	10 097 332	16 576 171	8 466 809	8 109 362	4 101 023	2 113 053	1 987 970
15 - 19	22 040 343	11 303 666	10 736 677	17 946 265	9 149 187	8 797 078	4 094 078	2 154 479	1 939 599
20 - 24	21 585 999	11 014 176	10 571 823	18 653 468	9 450 066	9 203 402	2 932 531	1 564 110	1 368 421
25 - 29	21 101 849	10 635 591	10 466 258	18 163 244	9 110 029	9 053 215	2 938 605	1 525 562	1 413 043
30 - 34	19 962 099	9 996 500	9 965 599	16 857 801	8 409 694	8 448 107	3 104 298	1 586 806	1 517 492
35 - 39	20 179 642	10 042 022	10 137 620	16 629 937	8 249 301	8 380 636	3 549 705	1 792 721	1 756 984
40 - 44	20 890 964	10 393 977	10 496 987	16 837 761	8 347 894	8 489 867	4 053 203	2 046 083	2 007 120
45 - 49	22 708 591	11 209 085	11 499 506	17 847 074	8 760 812	9 086 262	4 861 517	2 448 273	2 413 244
50 - 54	22 298 125	10 933 274	11 364 851	17 279 058	8 401 091	8 877 967	5 019 067	2 532 183	2 486 884
55 - 59	19 664 805	9 523 648	10 141 157	15 060 179	7 204 444	7 855 735	4 604 626	2 319 204	2 285 422
60 - 64	16 817 924	8 077 500	8 740 424	12 750 365	6 020 393	6 729 972	4 067 559	2 057 107	2 010 452
65 - 69	12 435 263	5 852 547	6 582 716	9 299 030	4 275 616	5 023 414	3 136 233	1 576 931	1 559 302
70 - 74	9 278 166	4 243 972	5 034 194	7 011 129	3 115 814	3 895 315	2 267 037	1 128 158	1 138 879
75 - 79	7 317 795	3 182 388	4 135 407	5 693 807	2 409 946	3 283 861	1 623 988	772 442	851 546
80 - 84	5 743 327	2 294 374	3 448 953	4 629 581	1 800 531	2 829 050	1 113 746	493 843	619 903
85 - 89	3 620 459	1 273 867	2 346 592	3 005 285	1 036 583	1 968 702	615 174	237 284	377 890
90 - 94	1 448 366	424 387	1 023 979	1 216 647	351 491	865 156	231 719	72 896	158 823
95 - 99	371 244	82 263	288 981	315 589	69 008	246 581	55 655	13 255	42 400
100 +	53 364	9 162	44 202	45 752	7 713	38 039	7 612	1 449	6 163
1 VII 2018 (ESDJ)[45]									
Total	327 167 434	161 128 679	166 038 755	...	...	...	...	...	...
0	3 848 208	1 968 505	1 879 703	...	...	...	...	...	...
1 - 4	15 962 067	8 163 697	7 798 370	...	...	...	...	...	...
5 - 9	20 195 642	10 315 990	9 879 652	...	...	...	...	...	...
10 - 14	20 879 527	10 658 840	10 220 687	...	...	...	...	...	...
15 - 19	21 097 221	10 774 908	10 322 313	...	...	...	...	...	...
20 - 24	21 873 579	11 201 547	10 672 032	...	...	...	...	...	...
25 - 29	23 561 756	12 018 838	11 542 918	...	...	...	...	...	...
30 - 34	22 136 018	11 191 871	10 944 147	...	...	...	...	...	...
35 - 39	21 563 587	10 790 190	10 773 397	...	...	...	...	...	...
40 - 44	19 714 301	9 797 410	9 916 891	...	...	...	...	...	...
45 - 49	20 747 135	10 263 995	10 483 140	...	...	...	...	...	...
50 - 54	20 884 564	10 277 207	10 607 357	...	...	...	...	...	...
55 - 59	21 940 985	10 669 327	11 271 658	...	...	...	...	...	...
60 - 64	20 331 651	9 729 536	10 602 115	...	...	...	...	...	...
65 - 69	17 086 893	8 034 813	9 052 080	...	...	...	...	...	...
70 - 74	13 405 423	6 211 272	7 194 151	...	...	...	...	...	...
75 - 79	9 267 066	4 144 674	5 122 392	...	...	...	...	...	...
80 - 84	6 127 308	2 590 366	3 536 942	...	...	...	...	...	...
85 - 89	3 898 995	1 496 255	2 402 740	...	...	...	...	...	...
90 - 94	1 958 772	646 642	1 312 130	...	...	...	...	...	...
95 - 99	592 809	162 814	429 995	...	...	...	...	...	...
100 +	93 927	19 982	73 945	...	...	...	...	...	...
United States Virgin Islands - Îles Vierges américaines[46]									
1 IV 2010 (CDJC)									
Total	106 405	50 854	55 551	...	...	...	...	...	...
0 - 4	7 500	3 736	3 764	...	...	...	...	...	...
5 - 9	7 150	3 694	3 456	...	...	...	...	...	...
10 - 14	7 484	3 849	3 635	...	...	...	...	...	...

7. Population by age, sex and urban/rural residence: latest available year, 2009 - 2018

Population selon l'âge, le sexe et la résidence, urbaine/rurale : dernière année disponible, 2009 - 2018 (continued - suite)

Continent, country or area, date, code[a] and age (in years) / Continent, pays ou zone, date, code[a] et âge (en années)	Total			Urban - Urbaine			Rural - Rurale		
	Both sexes Les deux sexes	Male Masculin	Female Féminin	Both sexes Les deux sexes	Male Masculin	Female Féminin	Both sexes Les deux sexes	Male Masculin	Female Féminin
AMERICA, NORTH - AMÉRIQUE DU NORD									
United States Virgin Islands - Îles Vierges américaines[46]									
1 IV 2010 (CDJC)									
15 - 19	7 560	3 765	3 795	...	...	...	...	...	...
20 - 24	5 894	2 707	3 187	...	...	...	...	...	...
25 - 29	5 969	2 695	3 274	...	...	...	...	...	...
30 - 34	6 137	2 825	3 312	...	...	...	...	...	...
35 - 39	6 675	3 133	3 542	...	...	...	...	...	...
40 - 44	7 450	3 506	3 944	...	...	...	...	...	...
45 - 49	7 743	3 680	4 063	...	...	...	...	...	...
50 - 54	7 900	3 800	4 100	...	...	...	...	...	...
55 - 59	7 192	3 341	3 851	...	...	...	...	...	...
60 - 64	7 367	3 510	3 857	...	...	...	...	...	...
65 - 69	5 853	2 883	2 970	...	...	...	...	...	...
70 - 74	3 717	1 739	1 978	...	...	...	...	...	...
75 - 79	2 328	1 043	1 285	...	...	...	...	...	...
80 - 84	1 332	568	764	...	...	...	...	...	...
85 +	1 154	380	774	...	...	...	...	...	...
AMERICA, SOUTH - AMÉRIQUE DU SUD									
Argentina - Argentine[29]									
1 VII 2018 (ESDF)									
Total	44 494 502	21 824 372	22 670 130	40 866 408	19 895 973	20 970 435	3 628 094	1 928 399	1 699 695
0 - 4	3 738 229	1 923 444	1 814 785	3 361 350	1 728 491	1 632 859	376 879	194 953	181 926
0	743 833	382 784	361 049	...	...	...	...	...	...
1 - 4	2 994 396	1 540 660	1 453 736	...	...	...	...	...	...
5 - 9	3 711 205	1 910 645	1 800 560	3 337 870	1 714 900	1 622 970	373 335	195 745	177 590
10 - 14	3 524 036	1 809 332	1 714 704	3 206 745	1 642 925	1 563 820	317 291	166 407	150 884
15 - 19	3 513 239	1 792 030	1 721 209	3 190 341	1 621 923	1 568 418	322 898	170 107	152 791
20 - 24	3 561 187	1 801 939	1 759 248	3 218 933	1 617 846	1 601 087	342 254	184 093	158 161
25 - 29	3 484 671	1 746 826	1 737 845	3 201 563	1 591 812	1 609 751	283 108	155 014	128 094
30 - 34	3 243 841	1 613 810	1 630 031	3 013 126	1 491 114	1 522 012	230 715	122 696	108 019
35 - 39	3 142 485	1 555 594	1 586 891	2 923 089	1 443 318	1 479 771	219 396	112 276	107 120
40 - 44	2 955 834	1 454 862	1 500 972	2 756 843	1 351 241	1 405 602	198 991	103 621	95 370
45 - 49	2 500 862	1 222 518	1 278 344	2 325 913	1 127 642	1 198 271	174 949	94 876	80 073
50 - 54	2 216 535	1 074 291	1 142 244	2 058 270	985 570	1 072 700	158 265	88 721	69 544
55 - 59	2 063 845	987 817	1 076 028	1 917 152	905 739	1 011 413	146 693	82 078	64 615
60 - 64	1 856 108	872 557	983 551	1 721 455	797 350	924 105	134 653	75 207	59 446
65 - 69	1 603 203	732 831	870 372	1 487 600	668 812	818 788	115 603	64 019	51 584
70 - 74	1 272 577	556 566	716 011	1 181 153	506 334	674 819	91 424	50 232	41 192
75 - 79	918 063	373 831	544 232	852 214	339 046	513 168	65 849	34 785	31 064
80 - 84	616 143	225 783	390 360	574 114	205 311	368 803	42 029	20 472	21 557
85 - 89	358 527	114 506	244 021	336 124	105 126	230 998	22 403	9 380	13 023
90 - 94	160 912	43 354	117 558	152 060	40 317	111 743	8 852	3 037	5 815
95 - 99	45 274	10 408	34 866	43 183	9 820	33 363	2 091	588	1 503
100 +	7 726	1 428	6 298	7 310	1 336	5 974	416	92	324
Bolivia (Plurinational State of) - Bolivie (État plurinational de)									
1 VII 2018 (ESDF)									
Total	11 307 314	5 695 665	5 611 649	7 848 776	3 886 115	3 962 661	3 458 538	1 809 550	1 648 988
0	242 817	123 378	119 439	163 126	82 879	80 247	79 691	40 499	39 192
1 - 4	970 680	492 694	477 986	653 561	331 692	321 869	317 119	161 002	156 117
5 - 9	1 215 318	619 505	595 813	815 873	414 476	401 397	399 445	205 029	194 416
10 - 14	1 192 846	608 074	584 772	802 186	405 872	396 314	390 660	202 202	188 458
15 - 19	1 118 753	569 803	548 950	768 767	386 522	382 245	349 986	183 281	166 705
20 - 24	1 017 689	517 369	500 320	727 350	362 369	364 981	290 339	155 000	135 339
25 - 29	921 173	466 805	454 368	674 241	332 203	342 038	246 932	134 602	112 330
30 - 34	850 874	430 358	420 516	626 677	308 554	318 123	224 197	121 804	102 393
35 - 39	756 261	381 952	374 309	555 723	273 234	282 489	200 538	108 718	91 820
40 - 44	640 666	323 227	317 439	464 454	227 378	237 076	176 212	95 849	80 363

Continent, country or area, date, code[a] and age (in years) / Continent, pays ou zone, date, code[a] et âge (en années)	Total			Urban - Urbaine			Rural - Rurale		
	Both sexes Les deux sexes	Male Masculin	Female Féminin	Both sexes Les deux sexes	Male Masculin	Female Féminin	Both sexes Les deux sexes	Male Masculin	Female Féminin
AMERICA, SOUTH - AMÉRIQUE DU SUD									
Bolivia (Plurinational State of) - Bolivie (État plurinational de)									
1 VII 2018 (ESDF)									
45 - 49	533 651	268 147	265 504	378 208	184 273	193 935	155 443	83 874	71 569
50 - 54	445 386	222 941	222 445	311 279	151 754	159 525	134 107	71 187	62 920
55 - 59	371 199	184 757	186 442	251 957	122 320	129 637	119 242	62 437	56 805
60 - 64	307 531	151 663	155 868	200 358	96 107	104 251	107 173	55 556	51 617
65 - 69	242 748	118 217	124 531	155 953	73 940	82 013	86 795	44 277	42 518
70 - 74	187 424	89 890	97 534	120 048	55 877	64 171	67 376	34 013	33 363
75 - 79	128 824	59 684	69 140	81 746	36 919	44 827	47 078	22 765	24 313
80 - 84	85 120	36 962	48 158	52 286	22 298	29 988	32 834	14 664	18 170
85 - 89	50 504	20 458	30 046	29 450	11 843	17 607	21 054	8 615	12 439
90 - 94	21 799	8 011	13 788	12 304	4 581	7 723	9 495	3 430	6 065
95 +	6 051	1 770	4 281	3 229	1 024	2 205	2 822	746	2 076
Brazil - Brésil									
31 VII 2010 (CDJC)									
Total	190 755 799	93 406 990	97 348 809	160 925 804	77 710 179	83 215 625	29 829 995	15 696 811	14 133 184
0	2 713 244	1 378 532	1 334 712	2 246 034	1 141 784	1 104 250	467 210	236 748	230 462
1 - 4	11 082 914	5 638 455	5 444 459	9 055 114	4 603 340	4 451 774	2 027 800	1 035 115	992 685
5 - 9	14 969 375	7 624 144	7 345 231	12 135 285	6 169 531	5 965 754	2 834 090	1 454 613	1 379 477
10 - 14	17 166 761	8 725 413	8 441 348	13 956 987	7 062 057	6 894 930	3 209 774	1 663 356	1 546 418
15 - 19	16 990 872	8 558 868	8 432 004	14 039 001	6 998 102	7 040 899	2 951 871	1 560 766	1 391 105
20 - 24	17 245 192	8 630 229	8 614 963	14 706 068	7 276 963	7 429 105	2 539 124	1 353 266	1 185 858
25 - 29	17 104 414	8 460 995	8 643 419	14 772 957	7 225 732	7 547 225	2 331 457	1 235 263	1 096 194
30 - 34	15 744 512	7 717 658	8 026 854	13 611 921	6 586 877	7 025 044	2 132 591	1 130 781	1 001 810
35 - 39	13 888 579	6 766 664	7 121 915	11 975 407	5 750 498	6 224 909	1 913 172	1 016 166	897 006
40 - 44	13 009 364	6 320 568	6 688 796	11 187 429	5 344 982	5 842 447	1 821 935	975 586	846 349
45 - 49	11 833 352	5 692 014	6 141 338	10 181 394	4 806 322	5 375 072	1 651 958	885 692	766 266
50 - 54	10 140 402	4 834 995	5 305 407	8 708 339	4 074 679	4 633 660	1 432 063	760 316	671 747
55 - 59	8 276 221	3 902 344	4 373 877	7 025 474	3 238 531	3 786 943	1 250 747	663 813	586 934
60 - 64	6 509 120	3 041 035	3 468 085	5 474 944	2 479 882	2 995 062	1 034 176	561 153	473 023
65 - 69	4 840 810	2 224 065	2 616 745	4 040 016	1 792 798	2 247 218	800 794	431 267	369 527
70 - 74	3 741 636	1 667 372	2 074 264	3 142 173	1 349 329	1 792 844	599 463	318 043	281 420
75 - 79	2 563 447	1 090 517	1 472 930	2 174 038	889 908	1 284 130	389 409	200 609	188 800
80 - 84	1 666 972	668 623	998 349	1 423 603	546 865	876 738	243 369	121 758	121 611
85 - 89	819 483	310 759	508 724	695 385	251 112	444 273	124 098	59 647	64 451
90 - 94	326 558	114 964	211 594	273 348	90 960	182 388	53 210	24 004	29 206
95 - 99	98 335	31 529	66 806	81 121	24 365	56 756	17 214	7 164	10 050
100 +	24 236	7 247	16 989	19 766	5 562	14 204	4 470	1 685	2 785
1 VII 2018 (ESDJ)[47]									
Total	208 494 900	101 971 173	106 523 727	...	...	...	...	...	...
0 - 4	14 787 557	7 565 301	7 222 256	...	...	...	...	...	...
5 - 9	14 537 829	7 432 381	7 105 448	...	...	...	...	...	...
10 - 14	15 182 024	7 751 948	7 430 076	...	...	...	...	...	...
15 - 19	16 439 846	8 364 062	8 075 784	...	...	...	...	...	...
20 - 24	17 294 780	8 716 490	8 578 290	...	...	...	...	...	...
25 - 29	17 068 593	8 512 314	8 556 279	...	...	...	...	...	...
30 - 34	17 296 659	8 555 280	8 741 379	...	...	...	...	...	...
35 - 39	16 661 965	8 148 183	8 513 782	...	...	...	...	...	...
40 - 44	14 879 035	7 213 769	7 665 266	...	...	...	...	...	...
45 - 49	13 281 287	6 401 687	6 879 600	...	...	...	...	...	...
50 - 54	12 293 932	5 877 917	6 416 015	...	...	...	...	...	...
55 - 59	10 746 091	5 059 761	5 686 330	...	...	...	...	...	...
60 - 64	8 797 470	4 076 794	4 720 676	...	...	...	...	...	...
65 - 69	6 823 731	3 103 440	3 720 291	...	...	...	...	...	...
70 - 74	4 938 529	2 194 687	2 743 842	...	...	...	...	...	...
75 - 79	3 376 250	1 439 622	1 936 628	...	...	...	...	...	...
80 - 84	2 191 860	881 564	1 310 296	...	...	...	...	...	...
85 - 89	1 165 517	435 871	729 646	...	...	...	...	...	...
90 +	731 945	240 102	491 843	...	...	...	...	...	...

Continent, country or area, date, code[a] and age (in years) / Continent, pays ou zone, date, code[a] et âge (en années)	Total			Urban - Urbaine			Rural - Rurale		
	Both sexes Les deux sexes	Male Masculin	Female Féminin	Both sexes Les deux sexes	Male Masculin	Female Féminin	Both sexes Les deux sexes	Male Masculin	Female Féminin
AMERICA, SOUTH - AMÉRIQUE DU SUD									
Chile - Chili									
1 VII 2018 (ESDF)									
Total	18 552 218	9 180 864	9 371 354	16 225 850	7 965 073	8 260 777	2 326 368	1 215 791	1 110 577
0	247 753	126 109	121 644	217 075	110 600	106 475	30 678	15 509	15 169
1 - 4	998 427	508 091	490 336	879 347	447 929	431 418	119 080	60 162	58 918
5 - 9	1 252 119	637 831	614 288	1 128 031	574 926	553 105	124 088	62 905	61 183
10 - 14	1 195 487	610 043	585 444	1 070 437	546 527	523 910	125 050	63 516	61 534
15 - 19	1 257 468	641 382	616 086	1 096 374	559 274	537 100	161 094	82 108	78 986
20 - 24	1 390 097	709 408	680 689	1 204 647	614 151	590 496	185 450	95 257	90 193
25 - 29	1 523 006	771 361	751 645	1 316 913	664 985	651 928	206 093	106 376	99 717
30 - 34	1 468 381	739 938	728 443	1 294 159	646 012	648 147	174 222	93 926	80 296
35 - 39	1 303 206	653 654	649 552	1 159 672	576 267	583 405	143 534	77 387	66 147
40 - 44	1 245 854	621 522	624 332	1 103 502	546 692	556 810	142 352	74 830	67 522
45 - 49	1 246 428	618 504	627 924	1 090 749	536 944	553 805	155 679	81 560	74 119
50 - 54	1 250 820	616 646	634 174	1 086 585	528 032	558 553	164 235	88 614	75 621
55 - 59	1 154 484	564 829	589 655	1 006 087	483 157	522 930	148 397	81 672	66 725
60 - 64	935 093	452 676	482 417	814 062	385 732	428 330	121 031	66 944	54 087
65 - 69	717 953	340 190	377 763	622 330	288 496	333 834	95 623	51 694	43 929
70 - 74	547 662	249 253	298 409	468 549	207 644	260 905	79 113	41 609	37 504
75 - 79	384 109	165 026	219 083	323 556	134 144	189 412	60 553	30 882	29 671
80 +	433 871	154 401	279 470	343 775	113 561	230 214	90 096	40 840	49 256
Colombia - Colombie[48]									
1 VII 2018 (ESDJ)									
Total	49 834 240	24 605 796	25 228 444	38 295 351	18 509 148	19 786 203	11 538 889	6 096 648	5 442 241
0	880 465	450 741	429 724	623 675	318 974	304 701	256 790	131 767	125 023
1 - 4	3 478 893	1 780 309	1 698 584	2 487 171	1 271 535	1 215 636	991 722	508 774	482 948
5 - 9	4 280 527	2 189 328	2 091 199	3 112 152	1 587 657	1 524 495	1 168 375	601 671	566 704
10 - 14	4 252 711	2 173 872	2 078 839	3 149 270	1 597 713	1 551 557	1 103 441	576 159	527 282
15 - 19	4 279 637	2 184 400	2 095 237	3 220 312	1 616 364	1 603 948	1 059 325	568 036	491 289
20 - 24	4 299 104	2 194 912	2 104 192	3 288 409	1 651 035	1 637 374	1 010 695	543 877	466 818
25 - 29	4 138 652	2 110 684	2 027 968	3 208 030	1 610 378	1 597 652	930 622	500 306	430 316
30 - 34	3 750 017	1 873 924	1 876 093	2 954 823	1 449 975	1 504 848	795 194	423 949	371 245
35 - 39	3 369 633	1 639 402	1 730 231	2 697 142	1 282 817	1 414 325	672 491	356 585	315 906
40 - 44	3 027 900	1 463 783	1 564 117	2 414 953	1 139 242	1 275 711	612 947	324 541	288 406
45 - 49	2 834 721	1 354 753	1 479 968	2 253 280	1 045 945	1 207 335	581 441	308 808	272 633
50 - 54	2 804 044	1 331 190	1 472 854	2 242 948	1 030 276	1 212 672	561 096	300 914	260 182
55 - 59	2 466 980	1 163 904	1 303 076	1 970 112	896 151	1 073 961	496 868	267 753	229 115
60 - 64	1 954 304	912 157	1 042 147	1 547 153	692 002	855 151	407 151	220 155	186 996
65 - 69	1 477 875	683 495	794 380	1 158 208	512 254	645 954	319 667	171 241	148 426
70 - 74	1 061 933	480 229	581 704	822 806	354 881	467 925	239 127	125 348	113 779
75 - 79	722 987	313 226	409 761	556 967	227 758	329 209	166 020	85 468	80 552
80 +	753 857	305 487	448 370	587 940	224 191	363 749	165 917	81 296	84 621
Ecuador - Équateur[49]									
1 VII 2018 (ESDF)									
Total	17 023 408	8 427 261	8 596 147	10 857 208	5 318 564	5 538 644	6 166 200	3 108 697	3 057 503
0	332 505	169 994	162 511	199 180	102 349	96 831	133 325	67 645	65 680
1 - 4	1 333 643	681 637	652 006	800 334	409 892	390 442	533 309	271 745	261 564
5 - 9	1 686 099	861 847	824 252	1 011 314	517 010	494 304	674 785	344 837	329 948
10 - 14	1 667 361	852 613	814 748	1 012 748	516 434	496 314	654 613	336 179	318 434
15 - 19	1 588 668	809 815	778 853	999 464	505 921	493 543	589 204	303 894	285 310
20 - 24	1 475 955	745 908	730 047	964 026	482 775	481 251	511 929	263 133	248 796
25 - 29	1 354 586	676 519	678 067	902 390	446 927	455 463	452 196	229 592	222 604
30 - 34	1 249 445	615 017	634 428	834 807	407 335	427 472	414 638	207 682	206 956
35 - 39	1 148 564	555 764	592 800	767 615	367 110	400 505	380 949	188 654	192 295
40 - 44	1 029 261	492 203	537 058	692 316	326 102	366 214	336 945	166 101	170 844
45 - 49	906 723	432 867	473 856	612 670	287 904	324 766	294 053	144 963	149 090
50 - 54	794 899	379 847	415 052	533 167	251 004	282 163	261 732	128 843	132 889
55 - 59	679 880	324 722	355 158	446 702	209 761	236 941	233 178	114 961	118 217
60 - 64	554 533	264 069	290 464	352 057	164 048	188 009	202 476	100 021	102 455
65 - 69	432 109	203 979	228 130	263 355	120 744	142 611	168 754	83 235	85 519
70 - 74	322 359	149 607	172 752	190 421	84 966	105 455	131 938	64 641	67 297
75 - 79	223 937	101 738	122 199	130 449	56 563	73 886	93 488	45 175	48 313
80 - 84	137 431	61 699	75 732	80 397	34 414	45 983	57 034	27 285	29 749
85 - 89	69 831	31 399	38 432	41 675	17 869	23 806	28 156	13 530	14 626

Continent, country or area, date, code[a] and age (in years) / Continent, pays ou zone, date, code[a] et âge (en années)	Total			Urban - Urbaine			Rural - Rurale		
	Both sexes Les deux sexes	Male Masculin	Female Féminin	Both sexes Les deux sexes	Male Masculin	Female Féminin	Both sexes Les deux sexes	Male Masculin	Female Féminin
AMERICA, SOUTH - AMÉRIQUE DU SUD									
Ecuador - Équateur[49]									
1 VII 2018 (ESDF)									
90 - 94	27 599	12 451	15 148	17 010	7 287	9 723	10 589	5 164	5 425
95 - 99	7 704	3 423	4 281	4 904	2 058	2 846	2 800	1 365	1 435
100 +	316	143	173	207	91	116	109	52	57
Falkland Islands (Malvinas) - Îles Falkland (Malvinas)[50]									
15 IV 2012 (CDFC)									
Total	2 840	1 491	1 349	...	...	...	...	...	...
0 - 4	152	72	80	...	...	...	...	...	...
5 - 9	161	69	92	...	...	...	...	...	...
10 - 14	152	68	84	...	...	...	...	...	...
15 - 19	143	68	75	...	...	...	...	...	...
20 - 24	165	89	76	...	...	...	...	...	...
25 - 29	203	88	115	...	...	...	...	...	...
30 - 34	217	115	102	...	...	...	...	...	...
35 - 39	256	132	124	...	...	...	...	...	...
40 - 44	266	158	108	...	...	...	...	...	...
45 - 49	225	130	95	...	...	...	...	...	...
50 - 54	235	127	108	...	...	...	...	...	...
55 - 59	189	109	80	...	...	...	...	...	...
60 - 64	145	89	56	...	...	...	...	...	...
65 - 69	109	55	54	...	...	...	...	...	...
70 - 74	72	42	30	...	...	...	...	...	...
75 - 79	62	30	32	...	...	...	...	...	...
80 +	58	29	29	...	...	...	...	...	...
Unknown - Inconnu	30	21	9	...	...	...	...	...	...
French Guiana - Guyane française									
1 I 2015 (CDJC)									
Total	259 865	128 973	130 892	224 631	110 366	114 265	35 234	18 606	16 628
0	5 715	2 805	2 910	4 912	2 407	2 505	803	398	405
1 - 4	23 246	11 995	11 251	19 865	10 303	9 562	3 380	1 692	1 688
5 - 9	29 563	15 050	14 512	24 945	12 721	12 224	4 618	2 330	2 288
10 - 14	28 237	14 151	14 085	23 887	11 964	11 923	4 350	2 187	2 163
15 - 19	23 941	12 158	11 784	20 668	10 423	10 245	3 273	1 734	1 539
20 - 24	18 529	8 960	9 569	15 668	7 490	8 177	2 861	1 470	1 392
25 - 29	18 563	8 674	9 890	15 921	7 291	8 630	2 642	1 382	1 259
30 - 34	19 077	9 230	9 846	16 297	7 658	8 639	2 780	1 572	1 207
35 - 39	18 394	9 068	9 326	15 956	7 716	8 240	2 438	1 352	1 086
40 - 44	17 650	8 701	8 949	15 506	7 498	8 009	2 144	1 203	941
45 - 49	14 715	7 357	7 359	13 056	6 400	6 656	1 659	956	703
50 - 54	12 133	6 042	6 091	10 795	5 289	5 507	1 338	754	585
55 - 59	9 951	5 010	4 941	8 961	4 447	4 514	990	562	427
60 - 64	7 749	3 959	3 790	7 048	3 579	3 470	701	381	320
65 - 69	5 038	2 574	2 464	4 512	2 283	2 229	526	291	235
70 - 74	3 066	1 496	1 570	2 747	1 343	1 404	319	153	166
75 - 79	1 859	860	999	1 648	751	897	211	109	102
80 - 84	1 237	479	758	1 107	431	676	129	47	82
85 - 89	723	257	466	677	236	442	46	21	25
90 - 94	356	102	254	335	94	241	20	8	12
95 - 99	100	32	68	95	30	65	5	2	3
100 +	24	13	10	23	12	10	1	1	-
1 I 2018 (ESDJ)									
Total	281 612	139 842	141 770	...	...	...	...	...	...
0 - 4	32 001	16 398	15 603	...	...	...	...	...	...
5 - 9	30 143	15 492	14 651	...	...	...	...	...	...
10 - 14	30 060	15 186	14 874	...	...	...	...	...	...
15 - 19	26 783	13 385	13 398	...	...	...	...	...	...
20 - 24	19 255	9 396	9 859	...	...	...	...	...	...
25 - 29	19 051	9 075	9 976	...	...	...	...	...	...
30 - 34	19 820	9 244	10 576	...	...	...	...	...	...
35 - 39	20 500	9 917	10 583	...	...	...	...	...	...
40 - 44	18 306	9 071	9 235	...	...	...	...	...	...

Continent, country or area, date, code[a] and age (in years) / Continent, pays ou zone, date, code[a] et âge (en années)	Total			Urban - Urbaine			Rural - Rurale		
	Both sexes Les deux sexes	Male Masculin	Female Féminin	Both sexes Les deux sexes	Male Masculin	Female Féminin	Both sexes Les deux sexes	Male Masculin	Female Féminin
AMERICA, SOUTH - AMÉRIQUE DU SUD									
French Guiana - Guyane française									
1 I 2018 (ESDJ)									
45 - 49	17 379	8 724	8 655	...	...	...	...	...	...
50 - 54	13 323	6 766	6 557	...	...	...	...	...	...
55 - 59	11 002	5 443	5 559	...	...	...	...	...	...
60 - 64	9 012	4 672	4 340	...	...	...	...	...	...
65 - 69	6 208	3 123	3 085	...	...	...	...	...	...
70 - 74	4 019	2 055	1 964	...	...	...	...	...	...
75 - 79	2 046	910	1 136	...	...	...	...	...	...
80 - 84	1 330	544	786	...	...	...	...	...	...
85 - 89	789	283	506	...	...	...	...	...	...
90 - 94	378	95	283	...	...	...	...	...	...
95 +	207	63	144	...	...	...	...	...	...
Guyana									
15 IX 2012 (CDFC)									
Total	746 955	371 805	375 150	...	...	...	...	...	...
0 - 4	70 440	35 876	34 564	...	...	...	...	...	...
5 - 9	71 268	35 954	35 314	...	...	...	...	...	...
10 - 14	83 139	42 302	40 837	...	...	...	...	...	...
15 - 19	84 798	42 749	42 049	...	...	...	...	...	...
20 - 24	63 282	31 350	31 932	...	...	...	...	...	...
25 - 29	52 061	25 487	26 574	...	...	...	...	...	...
30 - 34	53 099	26 103	26 996	...	...	...	...	...	...
35 - 39	51 479	25 457	26 022	...	...	...	...	...	...
40 - 44	47 955	24 212	23 743	...	...	...	...	...	...
45 - 49	43 115	21 573	21 542	...	...	...	...	...	...
50 - 54	37 444	18 878	18 566	...	...	...	...	...	...
55 - 59	29 043	14 045	14 998	...	...	...	...	...	...
60 - 64	21 513	10 479	11 034	...	...	...	...	...	...
65 - 69	13 835	6 638	7 197	...	...	...	...	...	...
70 - 74	10 339	4 817	5 522	...	...	...	...	...	...
75 - 79	6 908	3 037	3 871	...	...	...	...	...	...
80 - 84	4 079	1 714	2 365	...	...	...	...	...	...
85 +	3 158	1 134	2 024	...	...	...	...	...	...
Paraguay[51]									
1 VII 2016 (ESDF)									
Total	6 854 536	3 457 365	3 397 170	4 174 834	2 041 139	2 133 695	2 679 702	1 416 226	1 263 476
0 - 4	702 082	358 151	343 930	398 012	203 198	194 814	304 070	154 954	149 116
0	141 537	72 268	69 269	...	...	...	...	...	...
1 - 4	560 544	285 883	274 661	...	...	...	...	...	...
5 - 9	691 901	352 576	339 325	390 221	196 151	194 070	301 680	156 425	145 255
10 - 14	683 516	347 937	335 579	390 252	193 879	196 374	293 263	154 058	139 205
15 - 19	672 867	342 993	329 874	405 622	200 837	204 785	267 245	142 156	125 089
20 - 24	641 263	326 861	314 403	409 703	202 663	207 041	231 560	124 198	107 362
25 - 29	600 414	304 844	295 570	395 319	194 698	200 621	205 095	110 146	94 949
30 - 34	534 718	269 735	264 982	348 434	170 244	178 190	186 283	99 491	86 792
35 - 39	437 936	218 332	219 604	279 314	134 520	144 794	158 622	83 812	74 809
40 - 44	381 358	190 079	191 279	239 963	115 207	124 756	141 396	74 872	66 523
45 - 49	339 976	169 955	170 021	211 545	101 587	109 958	128 431	68 368	60 063
50 - 54	295 002	147 946	147 056	181 799	87 310	94 489	113 203	60 636	52 567
55 - 59	253 974	128 857	125 118	154 665	74 768	79 897	99 309	54 088	45 221
60 - 64	206 424	104 679	101 745	124 312	59 641	64 671	82 112	45 038	37 074
65 - 69	148 797	74 454	74 343	88 717	41 583	47 134	60 080	32 871	27 209
70 - 74	105 964	51 654	54 309	62 824	28 359	34 464	43 140	23 295	19 845
75 - 79	72 546	33 577	38 969	42 954	18 111	24 843	29 593	15 466	14 127
80 +	85 799	34 734	51 065	51 178	18 384	32 794	34 621	16 350	18 271
Peru - Pérou									
30 VI 2018 (ESDF)									
Total	32 162 184	16 105 008	16 057 176	25 156 589	12 427 084	12 729 505	7 005 595	3 677 924	3 327 671
0 - 4	2 817 164	1 438 133	1 379 031	2 019 234	1 034 545	984 689	797 930	403 588	394 342
0	561 564	286 966	274 598	...	...	...	...	...	...
1 - 4	2 255 600	1 151 167	1 104 433	...	...	...	...	...	...
5 - 9	2 871 130	1 463 817	1 407 313	2 084 165	1 061 211	1 022 954	786 965	402 606	384 359

7. Population by age, sex and urban/rural residence: latest available year, 2009 - 2018
Population selon l'âge, le sexe et la résidence, urbaine/rurale : dernière année disponible, 2009 - 2018 (continued - suite)

Continent, country or area, date, code[a] and age (in years) / Continent, pays ou zone, date, code[a] et âge (en années)	Total			Urban - Urbaine			Rural - Rurale		
	Both sexes Les deux sexes	Male Masculin	Female Féminin	Both sexes Les deux sexes	Male Masculin	Female Féminin	Both sexes Les deux sexes	Male Masculin	Female Féminin
AMERICA, SOUTH - AMÉRIQUE DU SUD									
Peru - Pérou									
30 VI 2018 (ESDF)									
10 - 14	2 913 831	1 484 041	1 429 790	2 145 319	1 086 105	1 059 214	768 512	397 936	370 576
15 - 19	2 886 398	1 466 914	1 419 484	2 203 356	1 106 376	1 096 980	683 042	360 538	322 504
20 - 24	2 839 502	1 438 445	1 401 057	2 275 786	1 135 369	1 140 417	563 716	303 076	260 640
25 - 29	2 738 402	1 383 393	1 355 009	2 207 175	1 095 905	1 111 270	531 227	287 488	243 739
30 - 34	2 528 404	1 273 217	1 255 187	2 010 384	991 862	1 018 522	518 020	281 355	236 665
35 - 39	2 317 407	1 164 344	1 153 063	1 874 116	919 732	954 384	443 291	244 612	198 679
40 - 44	2 122 547	1 063 630	1 058 917	1 729 525	844 325	885 200	393 022	219 305	173 717
45 - 49	1 843 174	919 522	923 652	1 504 937	733 833	771 104	338 237	185 689	152 548
50 - 54	1 598 842	792 702	806 140	1 325 780	647 643	678 137	273 062	145 059	128 003
55 - 59	1 339 831	657 818	682 013	1 107 375	537 269	570 106	232 456	120 549	111 907
60 - 64	1 067 857	517 390	550 467	859 788	412 712	447 076	208 069	104 678	103 391
65 - 69	827 092	394 420	432 672	657 507	311 240	346 267	169 585	83 180	86 405
70 - 74	603 971	281 419	322 552	475 123	219 768	255 355	128 848	61 651	67 197
75 - 79	426 984	191 745	235 239	335 663	148 497	187 166	91 321	43 248	48 073
80 +	419 648	174 058	245 590	341 356	140 692	200 664	78 292	33 366	44 926
Suriname									
1 VII 2017 (ESDJ)									
Total	583 200	290 800	292 400	386 500	190 700	195 800	196 700	100 100	96 600
0	9 785	5 012	4 773	6 471	3 304	3 167	3 314	1 708	1 606
1 - 4	44 015	22 388	21 627	26 329	13 496	12 833	17 686	8 892	8 794
5 - 9	49 800	25 700	24 100	29 600	15 300	14 300	20 200	10 400	9 800
10 - 14	49 300	25 300	24 000	30 500	15 600	14 900	18 800	9 700	9 100
15 - 19	48 400	24 700	23 700	31 000	15 700	15 300	17 400	9 000	8 400
20 - 24	46 900	23 700	23 200	30 900	15 500	15 400	16 000	8 200	7 800
25 - 29	45 300	22 700	22 600	31 000	15 400	15 600	14 300	7 300	7 000
30 - 34	43 300	21 600	21 700	29 900	14 800	15 100	13 400	6 800	6 600
35 - 39	41 100	20 500	20 600	28 400	14 000	14 400	12 700	6 500	6 200
40 - 44	38 500	19 200	19 300	26 600	13 100	13 500	11 900	6 100	5 800
45 - 49	36 900	18 500	18 400	25 200	12 400	12 800	11 700	6 100	5 600
50 - 54	32 900	16 300	16 600	22 600	11 000	11 600	10 300	5 300	5 000
55 - 59	28 300	13 800	14 500	19 500	9 300	10 200	8 800	4 500	4 300
60 - 64	22 900	11 000	11 900	16 000	7 500	8 500	6 900	3 500	3 400
65 - 69	17 100	8 000	9 100	12 000	5 500	6 500	5 100	2 500	2 600
70 - 74	12 400	5 600	6 800	8 800	3 900	4 900	3 600	1 700	1 900
75 - 79	8 100	3 500	4 600	5 800	2 500	3 300	2 300	1 000	1 300
80 +	8 200	3 300	4 900	5 900	2 400	3 500	2 300	900	1 400
Uruguay[2]									
1 VII 2018 (ESDJ)									
Total	3 505 985	1 697 985	1 808 000	3 341 003	1 606 843	1 734 160	164 982	91 142	73 840
0	45 410	23 243	22 168	43 652	22 340	21 312	1 758	902	856
1 - 4	182 986	93 647	89 339	175 607	89 843	85 763	7 379	3 804	3 575
5 - 9	233 033	119 148	113 885	223 038	113 951	109 087	9 995	5 197	4 798
10 - 14	242 769	124 083	118 685	231 554	118 257	113 297	11 215	5 826	5 388
15 - 19	259 930	132 725	127 205	249 057	126 865	122 193	10 873	5 860	5 013
20 - 24	271 801	137 980	133 821	261 249	132 144	129 105	10 553	5 836	4 716
25 - 29	254 975	128 502	126 473	244 506	122 603	121 903	10 468	5 899	4 570
30 - 34	243 113	121 941	121 172	232 406	115 926	116 480	10 707	6 015	4 692
35 - 39	238 542	118 006	120 536	227 140	111 609	115 531	11 402	6 397	5 005
40 - 44	238 326	117 416	120 910	226 426	110 721	115 705	11 900	6 695	5 205
45 - 49	215 789	105 152	110 636	204 501	98 810	105 691	11 288	6 342	4 946
50 - 54	201 938	96 974	104 964	191 121	90 819	100 302	10 817	6 155	4 662
55 - 59	199 083	94 770	104 313	188 360	88 598	99 762	10 723	6 172	4 551
60 - 64	177 921	83 066	94 855	168 065	77 451	90 615	9 856	5 616	4 240
65 - 69	146 069	65 921	80 149	137 481	60 949	76 531	8 588	4 971	3 617
70 - 74	121 377	52 140	69 237	114 550	48 215	66 334	6 827	3 925	2 902
75 - 79	94 928	37 975	56 954	90 029	35 221	54 808	4 899	2 754	2 146
80 - 84	69 163	24 787	44 376	66 005	23 150	42 855	3 157	1 637	1 521
85 - 89	44 506	14 009	30 497	42 779	13 220	29 558	1 728	789	939
90 +	24 326	6 500	17 826	23 477	6 149	17 328	849	351	498

223

Continent, country or area, date, code[a] and age (in years) Continent, pays ou zone, date, code[a] et âge (en années)	Total			Urban - Urbaine			Rural - Rurale		
	Both sexes Les deux sexes	Male Masculin	Female Féminin	Both sexes Les deux sexes	Male Masculin	Female Féminin	Both sexes Les deux sexes	Male Masculin	Female Féminin
AMERICA, SOUTH - **AMÉRIQUE DU SUD**									
Venezuela (Bolivarian Republic of) - Venezuela (République bolivarienne du)									
1 IX 2011 (CDJC)									
Total	27 227 930	13 549 752	13 678 178	24 180 964[52]	11 900 242[52]	12 280 722[52]	3 046 966[52]	1 649 510[52]	1 397 456[52]
0 - 4	2 437 631	1 254 208	1 183 423	2 130 561[52]	1 095 625[52]	1 034 936[52]	307 070[52]	158 583[52]	148 487[52]
5 - 9	2 402 364	1 236 217	1 166 147	2 083 248[52]	1 071 223[52]	1 012 025[52]	319 116[52]	164 994[52]	154 122[52]
10 - 14	2 516 779	1 298 191	1 218 588	2 179 907[52]	1 121 671[52]	1 058 236[52]	336 872[52]	176 520[52]	160 352[52]
15 - 19	2 641 320	1 336 159	1 305 161	2 317 888[52]	1 164 992[52]	1 152 896[52]	323 432[52]	171 167[52]	152 265[52]
20 - 24	2 560 649	1 280 125	1 280 524	2 289 728[52]	1 134 290[52]	1 155 438[52]	270 921[52]	145 835[52]	125 086[52]
25 - 29	2 344 332	1 159 400	1 184 932	2 104 335[52]	1 030 636[52]	1 073 699[52]	239 997[52]	128 764[52]	111 233[52]
30 - 34	2 219 741	1 105 617	1 114 124	1 994 628[52]	982 139[52]	1 012 489[52]	225 113[52]	123 478[52]	101 635[52]
35 - 39	1 905 253	942 311	962 942	1 708 084[52]	833 596[52]	874 488[52]	197 169[52]	108 715[52]	88 454[52]
40 - 44	1 755 490	873 509	881 981	1 578 118[52]	772 872[52]	805 246[52]	177 372[52]	100 637[52]	76 735[52]
45 - 49	1 528 781	747 704	781 077	1 377 721[52]	662 225[52]	715 496[52]	151 060[52]	85 479[52]	65 581[52]
50 - 54	1 337 934	651 255	686 679	1 208 133[52]	576 212[52]	631 921[52]	129 801[52]	75 043[52]	54 758[52]
55 - 59	1 108 799	530 935	577 864	1 002 491[52]	469 613[52]	532 878[52]	106 308[52]	61 322[52]	44 986[52]
60 - 64	848 358	407 656	440 702	763 622[52]	358 620[52]	405 002[52]	84 736[52]	49 036[52]	35 700[52]
65 - 69	568 688	267 691	300 997	507 772[52]	232 506[52]	275 266[52]	60 916[52]	35 185[52]	25 731[52]
70 - 74	410 455	189 285	221 170	364 425[52]	163 019[52]	201 406[52]	46 030[52]	26 266[52]	19 764[52]
75 - 79	292 992	130 126	162 866	259 357[52]	111 084[52]	148 273[52]	33 635[52]	19 042[52]	14 593[52]
80 - 84	188 895	78 996	109 899	168 413[52]	68 078[52]	100 335[52]	20 482[52]	10 918[52]	9 564[52]
85 - 89	104 141	40 560	63 581	93 151[52]	34 885[52]	58 266[52]	10 990[52]	5 675[52]	5 315[52]
90 - 94	40 370	14 875	25 495	36 160[52]	12 804[52]	23 356[52]	4 210[52]	2 071[52]	2 139[52]
95 +	14 958	4 932	10 026	13 222[52]	4 152[52]	9 070[52]	1 736[52]	780[52]	956[52]
1 VII 2018 (ESDF)									
Total	31 670 952	15 889 454	15 781 498	...	...	...	...	...	...
0	536 903	277 551	259 352	...	...	...	...	...	...
1 - 4	2 167 533	1 119 318	1 048 215	...	...	...	...	...	...
5 - 9	2 758 868	1 423 711	1 335 157	...	...	...	...	...	...
10 - 14	2 794 362	1 441 237	1 353 125	...	...	...	...	...	...
15 - 19	2 760 145	1 420 286	1 339 859	...	...	...	...	...	...
20 - 24	2 665 973	1 364 024	1 301 949	...	...	...	...	...	...
25 - 29	2 600 870	1 319 081	1 281 789	...	...	...	...	...	...
30 - 34	2 547 526	1 281 478	1 266 048	...	...	...	...	...	...
35 - 39	2 306 063	1 153 371	1 152 692	...	...	...	...	...	...
40 - 44	2 052 051	1 021 262	1 030 789	...	...	...	...	...	...
45 - 49	1 887 164	934 875	952 289	...	...	...	...	...	...
50 - 54	1 750 548	862 590	887 958	...	...	...	...	...	...
55 - 59	1 476 551	721 885	754 666	...	...	...	...	...	...
60 - 64	1 134 185	548 694	585 491	...	...	...	...	...	...
65 - 69	820 532	390 219	430 313	...	...	...	...	...	...
70 - 74	581 614	270 037	311 577	...	...	...	...	...	...
75 - 79	384 576	172 550	212 026	...	...	...	...	...	...
80 - 84	232 025	97 731	134 294	...	...	...	...	...	...
85 - 89	124 779	46 358	78 421	...	...	...	...	...	...
90 - 94	59 283	17 364	41 919	...	...	...	...	...	...
95 - 99	23 557	4 822	18 735	...	...	...	...	...	...
100 +	5 844	1 010	4 834	...	...	...	...	...	...
ASIA - ASIE									
Afghanistan[53]									
1 VII 2017 (ESDF)									
Total	28 224 323	14 438 456	13 785 867	7 148 224	3 631 353	3 516 871	21 076 099	10 807 104	10 268 995
0 - 4	4 808 437	2 428 976	2 379 461	1 015 897	520 969	494 928	3 792 540	1 908 007	1 884 533
5 - 9	4 539 772	2 360 084	2 179 688	985 757	506 032	479 725	3 554 015	1 854 052	1 699 963
10 - 14	3 970 838	2 126 274	1 844 564	1 039 616	551 669	487 947	2 931 221	1 574 605	1 356 617
15 - 19	3 208 826	1 628 746	1 580 080	952 546	469 972	482 574	2 256 281	1 158 774	1 097 506
20 - 24	2 509 764	1 252 034	1 257 729	738 398	377 352	361 046	1 771 366	874 682	896 684
25 - 29	1 942 657	952 973	989 685	491 787	240 181	251 605	1 450 870	712 791	738 079

Continent, country or area, date, code[a] and age (in years) / Continent, pays ou zone, date, code[a] et âge (en années)	Total			Urban - Urbaine			Rural - Rurale		
	Both sexes Les deux sexes	Male Masculin	Female Féminin	Both sexes Les deux sexes	Male Masculin	Female Féminin	Both sexes Les deux sexes	Male Masculin	Female Féminin
ASIA - ASIE									
Afghanistan[53]									
1 VII 2017 (ESDF)									
30 - 34	1 349 144	682 575	666 569	332 073	164 557	167 516	1 017 072	518 019	499 053
35 - 39	1 217 040	566 658	650 382	328 050	151 690	176 360	888 990	414 968	474 022
40 - 44	1 059 371	520 509	538 862	274 716	132 425	142 291	784 655	388 084	396 571
45 - 49	928 922	446 228	482 695	244 178	125 988	118 190	684 745	320 240	364 504
50 - 54	890 307	431 148	459 159	231 440	99 341	132 099	658 866	331 807	327 059
55 - 59	521 418	274 507	246 911	144 671	76 050	68 621	376 747	198 457	178 290
60 - 64	542 981	303 005	239 977	144 642	81 143	63 499	398 340	221 862	176 478
65 +	734 845	464 740	270 105	224 454	133 985	90 469	510 391	330 755	179 636
1 VII 2018 (ESDF)									
Total	30 075 018	15 312 423	14 762 595	...	...	...	...	...	...
0	1 011 598	503 980	507 619	...	...	...	...	...	...
1 - 4	4 142 244	2 103 609	2 038 635	...	...	...	...	...	...
5 - 9	4 929 495	2 564 900	2 364 595	...	...	...	...	...	...
10 - 14	4 188 398	2 202 487	1 985 911	...	...	...	...	...	...
15 - 19	3 297 037	1 687 205	1 609 832	...	...	...	...	...	...
20 - 24	2 620 528	1 271 939	1 348 589	...	...	...	...	...	...
25 - 29	2 255 741	1 075 012	1 180 729	...	...	...	...	...	...
30 - 34	1 482 848	752 696	730 153	...	...	...	...	...	...
35 - 39	1 374 813	687 002	687 811	...	...	...	...	...	...
40 - 44	1 101 839	540 701	561 138	...	...	...	...	...	...
45 - 49	986 968	472 668	514 300	...	...	...	...	...	...
50 - 54	778 372	379 709	398 663	...	...	...	...	...	...
55 - 59	569 052	292 561	276 491	...	...	...	...	...	...
60 - 64	519 797	277 788	242 009	...	...	...	...	...	...
65 - 69	343 047	210 123	132 924	...	...	...	...	...	...
70 - 74	237 365	143 242	94 123	...	...	...	...	...	...
75 - 79	109 808	68 225	41 583	...	...	...	...	...	...
80 - 84	77 533	46 948	30 585	...	...	...	...	...	...
85 +	48 534	31 629	16 905	...	...	...	...	...	...
Armenia - Arménie									
1 VII 2017 (ESDJ)									
Total	2 979 442	1 413 485	1 565 957	1 898 630	881 506	1 017 124	1 080 812	531 979	548 833
0	38 858	20 416	18 442	25 378	13 239	12 139	13 480	7 177	6 303
1 - 4	166 765	88 467	78 298	107 776	56 747	51 029	58 989	31 720	27 269
5 - 9	208 784	111 171	97 613	128 837	68 047	60 790	79 947	43 124	36 823
10 - 14	183 327	98 117	85 210	113 002	59 799	53 203	70 325	38 318	32 007
15 - 19	168 094	89 049	79 045	100 515	52 934	47 581	67 579	36 115	31 464
20 - 24	203 760	101 256	102 504	118 494	58 505	59 989	85 266	42 751	42 515
25 - 29	269 048	128 729	140 319	162 742	75 689	87 053	106 306	53 040	53 266
30 - 34	261 422	124 226	137 196	165 883	76 082	89 801	95 539	48 144	47 395
35 - 39	218 766	104 081	114 685	146 421	68 746	77 675	72 345	35 335	37 010
40 - 44	180 332	83 680	96 652	120 324	55 741	64 583	60 008	27 939	32 069
45 - 49	165 562	75 102	90 460	104 437	46 355	58 082	61 125	28 747	32 378
50 - 54	188 146	84 026	104 120	113 093	47 802	65 291	75 053	36 224	38 829
55 - 59	218 211	97 597	120 614	139 083	59 074	80 009	79 128	38 523	40 605
60 - 64	168 266	73 343	94 923	116 095	48 784	67 311	52 171	24 559	27 612
65 - 69	118 593	49 619	68 974	87 182	36 016	51 166	31 411	13 603	17 808
70 - 74	58 821	23 521	35 300	43 791	17 580	26 211	15 030	5 941	9 089
75 - 79	81 442	31 086	50 356	54 576	21 241	33 335	26 866	9 845	17 021
80 - 84	52 838	19 675	33 163	33 919	12 708	21 211	18 919	6 967	11 952
85 +	28 407	10 324	18 083	17 082	6 417	10 665	11 325	3 907	7 418
1 I 2018 (ESDJ)									
Total	2 972 732	1 408 199	1 564 533	...	...	...	...	...	...
0	37 431	19 577	17 854	...	...	...	...	...	...
1 - 4	165 888	87 851	78 037	...	...	...	...	...	...
5 - 9	209 942	111 816	98 126	...	...	...	...	...	...
10 - 14	186 396	99 762	86 634	...	...	...	...	...	...
15 - 19	165 236	87 587	77 649	...	...	...	...	...	...
20 - 24	195 883	97 796	98 087	...	...	...	...	...	...
25 - 29	264 677	126 140	138 537	...	...	...	...	...	...
30 - 34	262 742	124 735	138 007	...	...	...	...	...	...
35 - 39	222 377	105 642	116 735	...	...	...	...	...	...
40 - 44	181 367	84 155	97 212	...	...	...	...	...	...

7. Population by age, sex and urban/rural residence: latest available year, 2009 - 2018
Population selon l'âge, le sexe et la résidence, urbaine/rurale : dernière année disponible, 2009 - 2018 (continued - suite)

Continent, country or area, date, code[a] and age (in years) / Continent, pays ou zone, date, code[a] et âge (en années)	Total			Urban - Urbaine			Rural - Rurale		
	Both sexes Les deux sexes	Male Masculin	Female Féminin	Both sexes Les deux sexes	Male Masculin	Female Féminin	Both sexes Les deux sexes	Male Masculin	Female Féminin
ASIA - ASIE									
Armenia - Arménie									
1 I 2018 (ESDJ)									
45 - 49	165 304	74 908	90 396	...	...	...	...	...	...
50 - 54	181 926	80 873	101 053	...	...	...	...	...	...
55 - 59	217 266	96 688	120 578	...	...	...	...	...	...
60 - 64	171 704	74 801	96 903	...	...	...	...	...	...
65 - 69	122 057	51 065	70 992	...	...	...	...	...	...
70 - 74	61 759	24 521	37 238	...	...	...	...	...	...
75 - 79	77 487	29 615	47 872	...	...	...	...	...	...
80 - 84	53 956	19 893	34 063	...	...	...	...	...	...
85 +	29 334	10 774	18 560	...	...	...	...	...	...
Azerbaijan - Azerbaïdjan									
1 VII 2017 (ESDJ)									
Total	9 854 033	4 914 618	4 939 415	5 218 399	2 581 575	2 636 824	4 635 634	2 333 043	2 302 591
0	151 753	80 747	71 006	73 217	38 732	34 485	78 536	42 015	36 521
1 - 4	668 581	357 068	311 513	325 368	172 456	152 912	343 213	184 612	158 601
5 - 9	785 534	422 332	363 202	388 291	207 895	180 396	397 243	214 437	182 806
10 - 14	621 121	331 100	290 021	316 247	168 316	147 931	304 874	162 784	142 090
15 - 19	658 242	348 818	309 424	327 537	174 644	152 893	330 705	174 174	156 531
20 - 24	821 013	426 006	395 007	409 293	213 429	195 864	411 720	212 577	199 143
25 - 29	938 063	470 012	468 051	491 512	244 377	247 135	446 551	225 635	220 916
30 - 34	882 689	434 311	448 378	485 060	235 660	249 400	397 629	198 651	198 978
35 - 39	748 332	372 328	376 004	419 420	207 588	211 832	328 912	164 740	164 172
40 - 44	625 442	305 011	320 431	338 354	162 529	175 825	287 088	142 482	144 606
45 - 49	642 795	307 548	335 247	341 985	159 986	181 999	300 810	147 562	153 248
50 - 54	653 353	308 762	344 591	351 046	162 254	188 792	302 307	146 508	155 799
55 - 59	620 593	295 236	325 357	351 929	167 506	184 423	268 664	127 730	140 934
60 - 64	402 173	187 023	215 150	236 921	110 269	126 652	165 252	76 754	88 498
65 - 69	252 309	113 089	139 220	154 773	70 091	84 682	97 536	42 998	54 538
70 - 74	112 326	47 736	64 590	69 729	29 740	39 989	42 597	17 996	24 601
75 - 79	135 884	54 921	80 963	73 899	30 222	43 677	61 985	24 699	37 286
80 - 84	87 155	34 492	52 663	42 257	16 839	25 418	44 898	17 653	27 245
85 - 89	34 662	13 803	20 859	16 306	6 832	9 474	18 356	6 971	11 385
90 - 94	8 324	3 133	5 191	3 831	1 609	2 222	4 493	1 524	2 969
95 - 99	2 974	977	1 997	1 168	532	636	1 806	445	1 361
100 +	715	165	550	256	69	187	459	96	363
1 I 2018 (ESDJ)									
Total	9 898 085	4 938 027	4 960 058	...	...	...	...	...	...
0	144 041	76 584	67 457	...	...	...	...	...	...
1 - 4	661 151	352 747	308 404	...	...	...	...	...	...
5 - 9	809 184	435 140	374 044	...	...	...	...	...	...
10 - 14	619 933	330 569	289 364	...	...	...	...	...	...
15 - 19	652 947	346 315	306 632	...	...	...	...	...	...
20 - 24	799 835	416 062	383 773	...	...	...	...	...	...
25 - 29	934 198	469 579	464 619	...	...	...	...	...	...
30 - 34	895 263	440 773	454 490	...	...	...	...	...	...
35 - 39	763 744	379 614	384 130	...	...	...	...	...	...
40 - 44	629 011	307 907	321 104	...	...	...	...	...	...
45 - 49	639 572	305 985	333 587	...	...	...	...	...	...
50 - 54	649 344	306 752	342 592	...	...	...	...	...	...
55 - 59	632 358	300 244	332 114	...	...	...	...	...	...
60 - 64	419 422	195 291	224 131	...	...	...	...	...	...
65 - 69	262 285	117 693	144 592	...	...	...	...	...	...
70 - 74	118 094	50 215	67 879	...	...	...	...	...	...
75 - 79	129 834	52 341	77 493	...	...	...	...	...	...
80 - 84	88 778	35 052	53 726	...	...	...	...	...	...
85 - 89	36 884	14 724	22 160	...	...	...	...	...	...
90 - 94	8 265	3 165	5 100	...	...	...	...	...	...
95 - 99	3 193	1 092	2 101	...	...	...	...	...	...
100 +	749	183	566	...	...	...	...	...	...
Bahrain - Bahreïn									
1 VII 2018 (ESDJ)									
Total	1 503 091	946 864	556 227	...	...	...	...	...	...
0 - 4	106 724	54 501	52 223	...	...	...	...	...	...
5 - 9	100 991	51 506	49 485	...	...	...	...	...	...

Continent, country or area, date, code[a] and age (in years) / Continent, pays ou zone, date, code[a] et âge (en années)	Total			Urban - Urbaine			Rural - Rurale		
	Both sexes Les deux sexes	Male Masculin	Female Féminin	Both sexes Les deux sexes	Male Masculin	Female Féminin	Both sexes Les deux sexes	Male Masculin	Female Féminin
ASIA - ASIE									
Bahrain - Bahreïn									
1 VII 2018 (ESDJ)									
10 - 14	89 173	45 434	43 739	...	...	...	...	...	...
15 - 19	77 998	40 725	37 273	...	...	...	...	...	...
20 - 24	112 539	68 227	44 312	...	...	...	...	...	...
25 - 29	190 430	129 011	61 419	...	...	...	...	...	...
30 - 34	214 715	153 922	60 793	...	...	...	...	...	...
35 - 39	174 994	124 119	50 875	...	...	...	...	...	...
40 - 44	130 338	88 968	41 370	...	...	...	...	...	...
45 - 49	98 188	66 554	31 634	...	...	...	...	...	...
50 - 54	75 532	47 567	27 965	...	...	...	...	...	...
55 - 59	55 243	33 595	21 648	...	...	...	...	...	...
60 - 64	34 428	20 233	14 195	...	...	...	...	...	...
65 - 69	18 399	10 743	7 656	...	...	...	...	...	...
70 - 74	9 912	5 185	4 727	...	...	...	...	...	...
75 - 79	6 377	3 217	3 160	...	...	...	...	...	...
80 - 84	3 725	1 742	1 983	...	...	...	...	...	...
85 +	3 385	1 615	1 770	...	...	...	...	...	...
Bangladesh									
1 VII 2017 (ESDF)									
Total	162 700 000	81 400 000	81 300 000	49 216 750	24 623 500	24 593 250	113 483 250	56 776 500	56 706 750
0	2 436 891	1 208 026	1 228 865	737 160	365 428	371 732	1 699 732	842 598	857 133
1 - 4	11 327 160	5 664 698	5 662 463	3 426 466	1 713 571	1 712 895	7 900 694	3 951 127	3 949 568
5 - 9	16 052 703	8 030 259	8 022 444	4 855 943	2 429 153	2 426 789	11 196 760	5 601 105	5 595 655
10 - 14	17 810 565	8 876 905	8 933 659	5 387 696	2 685 264	2 702 432	12 422 869	6 191 641	6 231 227
15 - 19	15 477 914	7 406 791	8 071 124	4 682 069	2 240 554	2 441 515	10 795 845	5 166 236	5 629 609
20 - 24	14 896 950	7 752 164	7 144 786	4 506 327	2 345 030	2 161 298	10 390 622	5 407 134	4 983 488
25 - 29	14 840 165	7 729 130	7 111 034	4 489 150	2 338 062	2 151 088	10 351 015	5 391 069	4 959 947
30 - 34	13 508 777	6 925 428	6 583 349	4 086 405	2 094 942	1 991 463	9 422 372	4 830 486	4 591 886
35 - 39	12 056 662	6 042 214	6 014 448	3 647 140	1 827 770	1 819 370	8 409 522	4 214 444	4 195 077
40 - 44	9 809 464	4 823 256	4 986 207	2 967 363	1 459 035	1 508 328	6 842 101	3 364 221	3 477 880
45 - 49	8 272 231	3 929 632	4 342 600	2 502 350	1 188 714	1 313 636	5 769 881	2 740 918	3 028 963
50 - 54	7 861 997	3 970 624	3 891 373	2 378 254	1 201 114	1 177 140	5 483 743	2 769 510	2 714 233
55 - 59	5 574 823	2 754 269	2 820 554	1 686 384	833 166	853 218	3 888 439	1 921 103	1 967 337
60 - 64	4 576 797	2 241 804	2 334 993	1 384 481	678 146	706 335	3 192 316	1 563 659	1 628 657
65 - 69	3 423 913	1 706 046	1 717 867	1 035 734	516 079	519 655	2 388 179	1 189 967	1 198 212
70 - 74	2 197 280	1 058 503	1 138 775	664 677	320 197	344 480	1 532 602	738 306	794 296
75 - 79	1 141 089	542 655	598 433	345 179	164 153	181 026	795 909	378 502	417 407
80 - 84	734 610	369 969	364 642	222 220	111 916	110 304	512 391	258 053	254 338
85 - 89	329 421	167 221	162 200	99 650	50 584	49 066	229 771	116 637	113 135
90 - 94	192 178	101 764	90 414	58 134	30 784	27 350	134 044	70 980	63 064
95 +	178 410	98 641	79 769	53 969	29 839	24 130	124 441	68 802	55 639
Bhutan - Bhoutan									
30 V 2017 (CDFC)									
Total	727 145	380 453	346 692	274 316	143 313	131 003	452 829	237 140	215 689
0 - 4	57 474	29 176	28 298	21 453	11 059	10 394	36 021	18 117	17 904
5 - 9	62 991	32 035	30 956	22 567	11 429	11 138	40 424	20 606	19 818
10 - 14	68 952	34 656	34 296	24 285	12 129	12 156	44 667	22 527	22 140
15 - 19	68 286	34 679	33 607	30 378	15 058	15 320	37 908	19 621	18 287
20 - 24	75 415	41 075	34 340	35 689	18 941	16 748	39 726	22 134	17 592
25 - 29	79 280	42 802	36 478	35 586	18 698	16 888	43 694	24 104	19 590
30 - 34	65 180	35 059	30 121	27 753	14 698	13 055	37 427	20 361	17 066
35 - 39	55 549	29 689	25 860	22 460	12 039	10 421	33 089	17 650	15 439
40 - 44	41 495	22 274	19 221	14 868	8 387	6 481	26 627	13 887	12 740
45 - 49	35 533	18 865	16 668	11 938	6 810	5 128	23 595	12 055	11 540
50 - 54	29 317	15 456	13 861	8 334	4 706	3 628	20 983	10 750	10 233
55 - 59	23 898	12 379	11 519	5 494	2 895	2 599	18 404	9 484	8 920
60 - 64	20 711	10 498	10 213	4 321	2 150	2 171	16 390	8 348	8 042
65 - 69	14 654	7 585	7 069	2 998	1 481	1 517	11 656	6 104	5 552
70 - 74	11 468	5 876	5 592	2 401	1 069	1 332	9 067	4 807	4 260
75 - 79	7 871	3 965	3 906	1 715	802	913	6 156	3 163	2 993
80 - 84	5 397	2 651	2 746	1 172	542	630	4 225	2 109	2 116
85 +	3 674	1 733	1 941	904	420	484	2 770	1 313	1 457

7. Population by age, sex and urban/rural residence: latest available year, 2009 - 2018
Population selon l'âge, le sexe et la résidence, urbaine/rurale : dernière année disponible, 2009 - 2018 (continued - suite)

Continent, country or area, date, code[a] and age (in years) / Continent, pays ou zone, date, code[a] et âge (en années)	Total			Urban - Urbaine			Rural - Rurale		
	Both sexes Les deux sexes	Male Masculin	Female Féminin	Both sexes Les deux sexes	Male Masculin	Female Féminin	Both sexes Les deux sexes	Male Masculin	Female Féminin
ASIA - ASIE									
Brunei Darussalam - Brunéi Darussalam									
1 VII 2016 (ESDJ)[54]									
Total	417 256	214 104	203 152	312 448	160 061	152 387	104 808	54 043	50 765
0	3 878	2 075	1 803	2 945	1 582	1 363	933	493	440
1 - 4	24 549	12 789	11 760	18 534	9 661	8 873	6 015	3 128	2 887
5 - 9	30 426	15 673	14 753	23 168	11 918	11 250	7 258	3 755	3 503
10 - 14	34 306	17 663	16 643	25 904	13 378	12 526	8 402	4 285	4 117
15 - 19	36 417	18 949	17 468	27 115	14 167	12 948	9 302	4 782	4 520
20 - 24	39 027	20 544	18 483	28 741	15 067	13 674	10 286	5 477	4 809
25 - 29	39 812	21 416	18 396	29 722	15 861	13 861	10 090	5 555	4 535
30 - 34	36 895	19 313	17 582	27 970	14 506	13 464	8 925	4 807	4 118
35 - 39	34 492	17 815	16 677	26 642	13 749	12 893	7 850	4 066	3 784
40 - 44	31 164	15 743	15 421	23 783	11 945	11 838	7 381	3 798	3 583
45 - 49	27 701	13 682	14 019	20 748	10 264	10 484	6 953	3 418	3 535
50 - 54	23 160	11 651	11 509	17 466	8 819	8 647	5 694	2 832	2 862
55 - 59	19 239	9 462	9 777	14 213	7 049	7 164	5 026	2 413	2 613
60 - 64	14 591	7 068	7 523	10 457	5 061	5 396	4 134	2 007	2 127
65 - 69	8 958	4 257	4 701	6 337	3 053	3 284	2 621	1 204	1 417
70 - 74	5 095	2 537	2 558	3 564	1 735	1 829	1 531	802	729
75 - 79	3 780	1 737	2 043	2 625	1 142	1 483	1 155	595	560
80 - 84	2 206	974	1 232	1 491	637	854	715	337	378
85 - 89	1 015	498	517	679	314	365	336	184	152
90 - 94	396	184	212	254	105	149	142	79	63
95 - 99	124	64	60	75	40	35	49	24	25
100 +	25	10	15	15	8	7	10	2	8
1 VII 2018 (ESDJ)									
Total	442 400	233 400	209 000	...	...	...	...	...	...
0 - 4	30 100	15 000	15 100	...	...	...	...	...	...
5 - 9	30 100	15 600	14 500	...	...	...	...	...	...
10 - 14	31 400	16 500	14 900	...	...	...	...	...	...
15 - 19	37 700	19 300	18 400	...	...	...	...	...	...
20 - 24	41 400	22 200	19 200	...	...	...	...	...	...
25 - 29	42 800	23 900	18 900	...	...	...	...	...	...
30 - 34	41 800	23 100	18 700	...	...	...	...	...	...
35 - 39	38 600	21 100	17 500	...	...	...	...	...	...
40 - 44	35 100	18 800	16 300	...	...	...	...	...	...
45 - 49	31 500	16 500	15 000	...	...	...	...	...	...
50 - 54	25 500	13 200	12 300	...	...	...	...	...	...
55 - 59	21 000	10 200	10 800	...	...	...	...	...	...
60 - 64	15 200	7 900	7 300	...	...	...	...	...	...
65 - 69	9 600	5 200	4 400	...	...	...	...	...	...
70 - 74	4 700	2 300	2 400	...	...	...	...	...	...
75 - 79	3 400	1 400	2 000	...	...	...	...	...	...
80 - 84	1 600	800	800	...	...	...	...	...	...
85 +	900	400	500	...	...	...	...	...	...
Cambodia - Cambodge[55]									
1 VII 2015 (ESDF)									
Total	15 405 157	7 551 944	7 853 213	3 540 575	1 705 018	1 835 557	11 864 582	5 846 926	6 017 656
0	343 968	175 388	168 580	86 946	44 740	42 206	257 022	130 648	126 374
1 - 4	1 256 559	639 680	616 879	287 909	146 676	141 233	968 650	493 004	475 646
5 - 9	1 478 056	751 537	726 519	266 331	135 468	130 863	1 211 725	616 069	595 656
10 - 14	1 424 533	727 116	697 417	222 335	114 171	108 164	1 202 198	612 945	589 253
15 - 19	1 637 111	838 821	798 290	273 601	136 051	137 550	1 363 510	702 770	660 740
20 - 24	1 698 824	877 158	821 666	407 469	188 296	219 173	1 291 355	688 862	602 493
25 - 29	1 478 710	737 077	741 633	484 549	223 014	261 535	994 161	514 063	480 098
30 - 34	1 333 262	649 670	683 592	427 395	205 047	222 348	905 867	444 623	461 244
35 - 39	879 004	427 791	451 213	237 471	117 764	119 707	641 533	310 027	331 506
40 - 44	761 990	367 586	394 404	177 884	89 396	88 488	584 106	278 190	305 916
45 - 49	793 754	374 975	418 779	175 105	87 482	87 623	618 649	287 493	331 156
50 - 54	677 057	312 718	364 339	144 559	70 342	74 217	532 498	242 376	290 122
55 - 59	533 368	224 272	309 096	119 460	52 954	66 506	413 908	171 318	242 590
60 - 64	398 784	159 105	239 679	89 373	37 736	51 637	309 411	121 369	188 042
65 - 69	282 114	117 449	164 665	58 973	24 909	34 064	223 141	92 540	130 601
70 - 74	191 298	79 144	112 154	36 584	14 784	21 800	154 714	64 360	90 354

7. Population by age, sex and urban/rural residence: latest available year, 2009 - 2018
Population selon l'âge, le sexe et la résidence, urbaine/rurale : dernière année disponible, 2009 - 2018 (continued - suite)

Continent, country or area, date, code[a] and age (in years) / Continent, pays ou zone, date, code[a] et âge (en années)	Total			Urban - Urbaine			Rural - Rurale		
	Both sexes Les deux sexes	Male Masculin	Female Féminin	Both sexes Les deux sexes	Male Masculin	Female Féminin	Both sexes Les deux sexes	Male Masculin	Female Féminin
ASIA - ASIE									
Cambodia - Cambodge[55]									
1 VII 2015 (ESDF)									
75 - 79	126 227	50 567	75 660	23 103	8 844	14 259	103 124	41 723	61 401
80 +	110 538	41 890	68 648	21 528	7 344	14 184	89 010	34 546	54 464
China - Chine[57]									
1 XI 2010 (CDJC)[58]									
Total	1332810869	682 329 104	650 481 765	670 005 546	343 040 783	326 964 763	662 805 323	339 288 321	323 517 002
0 - 4	75 532 610	41 062 566	34 470 044	30 936 470	16 749 729	14 186 741	44 596 140	24 312 837	20 283 303
5 - 9	70 881 549	38 464 665	32 416 884	30 565 659	16 580 910	13 984 749	40 315 890	21 883 755	18 432 135
10 - 14	74 908 462	40 267 277	34 641 185	32 807 526	17 664 790	15 142 736	42 100 936	22 602 487	19 498 449
15 - 19	99 889 114	51 904 830	47 984 284	53 589 992	27 603 777	25 986 215	46 299 122	24 301 053	21 998 069
20 - 24	127 412 518	64 008 573	63 403 945	71 058 518	36 041 784	35 016 734	56 354 000	27 966 789	28 387 211
25 - 29	101 013 852	50 837 038	50 176 814	57 679 956	28 973 516	28 706 440	43 333 896	21 863 522	21 470 374
30 - 34	97 138 203	49 521 822	47 616 381	56 010 957	28 432 073	27 578 884	41 127 246	21 089 749	20 037 497
35 - 39	118 025 959	60 391 104	57 634 855	65 025 365	33 349 280	31 676 085	53 000 594	27 041 824	25 958 770
40 - 44	124 753 964	63 608 678	61 145 286	63 786 496	32 845 769	30 940 727	60 967 468	30 762 909	30 204 559
45 - 49	105 594 553	53 776 418	51 818 135	53 629 541	27 723 132	25 906 409	51 965 012	26 053 286	25 911 726
50 - 54	78 753 171	40 363 234	38 389 937	39 186 388	20 130 395	19 055 993	39 566 783	20 232 839	19 333 944
55 - 59	81 312 474	41 082 938	40 229 536	37 437 535	18 762 887	18 674 648	43 874 939	22 320 051	21 554 888
60 - 64	58 667 282	29 834 426	28 832 856	26 036 917	13 067 045	12 969 872	32 630 365	16 767 381	15 862 984
65 - 69	41 113 282	20 748 471	20 364 811	17 910 329	8 866 594	9 043 735	23 202 953	11 881 877	11 321 076
70 - 74	32 972 397	16 403 453	16 568 944	14 777 260	7 241 891	7 535 369	18 195 137	9 161 562	9 033 575
75 - 79	23 852 133	11 278 859	12 573 274	10 531 503	5 048 471	5 483 032	13 320 630	6 230 388	7 090 242
80 - 84	13 373 198	5 917 502	7 455 696	5 762 828	2 665 218	3 097 610	7 610 370	3 252 284	4 358 086
85 - 89	5 631 928	2 199 810	3 432 118	2 392 190	982 284	1 409 906	3 239 738	1 217 526	2 022 212
90 - 94	1 578 307	530 872	1 047 435	687 763	246 031	441 732	890 544	284 841	605 703
95 - 99	369 979	117 716	252 263	176 542	60 991	115 551	193 437	56 725	136 712
100 +	35 934	8 852	27 082	15 811	4 216	11 595	20 123	4 636	15 487
31 XII 2011 (ESDF)[59]									
Total	1347304706	690 634 118	656 670 588	...	...	...	...	...	...
0 - 4	76 270 588	41 467 059	34 803 529	...	...	...	...	...	...
5 - 9	72 092 941	39 108 235	32 984 706	...	...	...	...	...	...
10 - 14	73 507 059	39 657 647	33 849 412	...	...	...	...	...	...
15 - 19	94 574 118	49 489 412	45 084 706	...	...	...	...	...	...
20 - 24	127 725 882	64 991 765	62 732 941	...	...	...	...	...	...
25 - 29	105 010 588	52 912 941	52 096 471	...	...	...	...	...	...
30 - 34	96 644 706	49 303 529	47 341 176	...	...	...	...	...	...
35 - 39	113 994 118	58 317 647	55 676 471	...	...	...	...	...	...
40 - 44	126 342 353	64 477 647	61 864 706	...	...	...	...	...	...
45 - 49	118 650 588	60 510 588	58 140 000	...	...	...	...	...	...
50 - 54	73 181 176	37 436 471	35 744 706	...	...	...	...	...	...
55 - 59	84 314 118	42 603 529	41 709 412	...	...	...	...	...	...
60 - 64	62 009 412	31 397 647	30 611 765	...	...	...	...	...	...
65 - 69	42 416 471	21 251 765	21 164 706	...	...	...	...	...	...
70 - 74	33 912 941	16 934 118	16 978 824	...	...	...	...	...	...
75 - 79	24 910 588	11 716 471	13 195 294	...	...	...	...	...	...
80 - 84	14 075 294	6 263 529	7 811 765	...	...	...	...	...	...
85 - 89	5 642 353	2 182 353	3 460 000	...	...	...	...	...	...
90 - 94	1 690 588	524 706	1 165 882	...	...	...	...	...	...
95 +	341 176	85 882	254 118	...	...	...	...	...	...
China, Hong Kong SAR - Chine, Hong Kong RAS									
1 VII 2018 (ESDJ)									
Total	7 451 000	3 410 300	4 040 700	...	...	...	...	...	...
0	49 900	25 800	24 100	...	...	...	...	...	...
1 - 4	228 200	118 400	109 800	...	...	...	...	...	...
5 - 9	308 100	159 400	148 700	...	...	...	...	...	...
10 - 14	274 600	140 600	134 000	...	...	...	...	...	...
15 - 19	300 200	155 000	145 200	...	...	...	...	...	...
20 - 24	430 900	213 200	217 700	...	...	...	...	...	...
25 - 29	501 800	230 100	271 700	...	...	...	...	...	...
30 - 34	558 200	225 400	332 800	...	...	...	...	...	...
35 - 39	599 700	235 700	364 000	...	...	...	...	...	...
40 - 44	565 300	228 800	336 500	...	...	...	...	...	...
45 - 49	576 500	240 100	336 400	...	...	...	...	...	...

Continent, country or area, date, code[a] and age (in years) / Continent, pays ou zone, date, code[a] et âge (en années)	Total			Urban - Urbaine			Rural - Rurale		
	Both sexes Les deux sexes	Male Masculin	Female Féminin	Both sexes Les deux sexes	Male Masculin	Female Féminin	Both sexes Les deux sexes	Male Masculin	Female Féminin
ASIA - ASIE									
China, Hong Kong SAR - Chine, Hong Kong RAS									
1 VII 2018 (ESDJ)									
50 - 54	597 300	266 300	331 000	...	...	...	...	...	...
55 - 59	642 600	309 300	333 300	...	...	...	...	...	...
60 - 64	551 500	271 800	279 700	...	...	...	...	...	...
65 - 69	426 700	210 000	216 700	...	...	...	...	...	...
70 - 74	279 900	138 700	141 200	...	...	...	...	...	...
75 - 79	191 700	95 100	96 600	...	...	...	...	...	...
80 - 84	173 600	78 500	95 100	...	...	...	...	...	...
85 +	194 300	68 100	126 200	...	...	...	...	...	...
China, Macao SAR - Chine, Macao RAS[56]									
7 VIII 2016 (SSDJ)									
Total	650 834	314 018	336 816	...	...	...	...	...	...
0 - 4	30 999	16 318	14 681	...	...	...	...	...	...
5 - 9	25 932	13 391	12 541	...	...	...	...	...	...
10 - 14	20 916	10 672	10 244	...	...	...	...	...	...
15 - 19	32 689	15 762	16 927	...	...	...	...	...	...
20 - 24	52 773	25 613	27 160	...	...	...	...	...	...
25 - 29	71 139	35 421	35 718	...	...	...	...	...	...
30 - 34	63 877	31 900	31 977	...	...	...	...	...	...
35 - 39	50 042	24 570	25 472	...	...	...	...	...	...
40 - 44	51 495	23 797	27 698	...	...	...	...	...	...
45 - 49	50 630	22 077	28 553	...	...	...	...	...	...
50 - 54	53 376	23 451	29 925	...	...	...	...	...	...
55 - 59	49 272	24 205	25 067	...	...	...	...	...	...
60 - 64	38 311	18 674	19 637	...	...	...	...	...	...
65 - 69	26 349	13 599	12 750	...	...	...	...	...	...
70 - 74	12 127	6 045	6 082	...	...	...	...	...	...
75 - 79	7 918	3 858	4 060	...	...	...	...	...	...
80 - 84	6 358	2 535	3 823	...	...	...	...	...	...
85 +	6 631	2 130	4 501	...	...	...	...	...	...
Cyprus - Chypre[60]									
1 X 2011 (CDJC)									
Total	840 407	408 780	431 627	566 191	273 065	293 126	274 216	135 715	138 501
0 - 4	45 015	23 061	21 954	29 726	15 202	14 524	15 289	7 859	7 430
5 - 9	42 635	21 921	20 714	28 050	14 386	13 664	14 585	7 535	7 050
10 - 14	47 298	24 179	23 119	30 926	15 730	15 196	16 372	8 449	7 923
15 - 19	55 818	28 683	27 135	36 345	18 593	17 752	19 473	10 090	9 383
20 - 24	66 073	33 891	32 182	44 948	22 847	22 101	21 125	11 044	10 081
25 - 29	74 114	36 992	37 122	51 855	25 842	26 013	22 259	11 150	11 109
30 - 34	69 834	33 149	36 685	48 938	23 133	25 805	20 896	10 016	10 880
35 - 39	61 862	27 754	34 108	43 232	19 204	24 028	18 630	8 550	10 080
40 - 44	59 728	27 031	32 697	41 295	18 416	22 879	18 433	8 615	9 818
45 - 49	57 240	27 059	30 181	39 233	18 225	21 008	18 007	8 834	9 173
50 - 54	56 128	27 517	28 611	38 287	18 499	19 788	17 841	9 018	8 823
55 - 59	47 762	23 771	23 991	31 716	15 541	16 175	16 046	8 230	7 816
60 - 64	45 034	22 057	22 977	29 704	14 438	15 266	15 330	7 619	7 711
65 - 69	36 328	17 656	18 672	23 459	11 295	12 164	12 869	6 361	6 508
70 - 74	29 433	14 044	15 389	18 991	9 048	9 943	10 442	4 996	5 446
75 - 79	21 058	9 647	11 411	13 545	6 239	7 306	7 513	3 408	4 105
80 +	24 948	10 342	14 606	15 853	6 408	9 445	9 095	3 934	5 161
Unknown - Inconnu	99	26	73	88	19	69	11	7	4
1 I 2018 (ESDJ)									
Total	864 236	421 508	442 728	...	...	...	...	...	...
0	9 270	4 779	4 491	...	...	...	...	...	...
1 - 4	37 198	19 066	18 132	...	...	...	...	...	...
5 - 9	49 142	25 062	24 080	...	...	...	...	...	...
10 - 14	44 679	22 784	21 895	...	...	...	...	...	...
15 - 19	49 202	24 825	24 377	...	...	...	...	...	...
20 - 24	65 146	31 476	33 670	...	...	...	...	...	...
25 - 29	73 854	36 660	37 194	...	...	...	...	...	...
30 - 34	70 458	33 884	36 574	...	...	...	...	...	...
35 - 39	64 199	31 050	33 149	...	...	...	...	...	...

Continent, country or area, date, code[a] and age (in years) / Continent, pays ou zone, date, code[a] et âge (en années)	Total			Urban - Urbaine			Rural - Rurale		
	Both sexes Les deux sexes	Male Masculin	Female Féminin	Both sexes Les deux sexes	Male Masculin	Female Féminin	Both sexes Les deux sexes	Male Masculin	Female Féminin
ASIA - ASIE									
Cyprus - Chypre[60]									
1 I 2018 (ESDJ)									
40 - 44	55 215	26 299	28 916	...	...	...	...	...	...
45 - 49	53 431	25 911	27 520	...	...	...	...	...	...
50 - 54	54 170	26 586	27 584	...	...	...	...	...	...
55 - 59	54 081	26 633	27 448	...	...	...	...	...	...
60 - 64	46 971	23 133	23 838	...	...	...	...	...	...
65 - 69	45 330	22 063	23 267	...	...	...	...	...	...
70 - 74	34 465	16 205	18 260	...	...	...	...	...	...
75 - 79	26 950	12 488	14 462	...	...	...	...	...	...
80 - 84	17 651	7 596	10 055	...	...	...	...	...	...
85 - 89	9 213	3 657	5 556	...	...	...	...	...	...
90 - 94	2 996	1 125	1 871	...	...	...	...	...	...
95 - 99	522	193	329	...	...	...	...	...	...
100 +	93	33	60	...	...	...	...	...	...
Georgia - Géorgie									
5 XI 2014 (CDJC)									
Total	3 713 804	1 772 864	1 940 940	2 122 623	980 985	1 141 638	1 591 181	791 879	799 302
0 - 4	255 089	132 700	122 389	152 766	78 799	73 967	102 323	53 901	48 422
5 - 9	230 024	121 245	108 779	139 301	72 526	66 775	90 723	48 719	42 004
10 - 14	206 216	109 481	96 735	119 287	62 645	56 642	86 929	46 836	40 093
15 - 19	226 022	118 877	107 145	130 446	66 924	63 522	95 576	51 953	43 623
20 - 24	266 125	135 305	130 820	162 336	79 100	83 236	103 789	56 205	47 584
25 - 29	278 662	139 945	138 717	168 601	80 608	87 993	110 061	59 337	50 724
30 - 34	262 060	129 921	132 139	160 622	76 264	84 358	101 438	53 657	47 781
35 - 39	248 549	121 943	126 606	150 707	71 177	79 530	97 842	50 766	47 076
40 - 44	243 281	118 318	124 963	143 846	67 326	76 520	99 435	50 992	48 443
45 - 49	239 407	114 036	125 371	133 670	60 443	73 227	105 737	53 593	52 144
50 - 54	271 386	126 710	144 676	150 014	66 843	83 171	121 372	59 867	61 505
55 - 59	245 391	111 641	133 750	133 348	57 828	75 520	112 043	53 813	58 230
60 - 64	211 385	92 412	118 973	114 908	47 738	67 170	96 477	44 674	51 803
65 - 69	155 702	64 889	90 813	84 433	33 489	50 944	71 269	31 400	39 869
70 - 74	123 605	48 483	75 122	61 257	22 399	38 858	62 348	26 084	36 264
75 - 79	135 764	49 895	85 869	64 993	21 828	43 165	70 771	28 067	42 704
80 - 84	71 675	25 100	46 575	32 119	10 106	22 013	39 556	14 994	24 562
85 - 89	34 508	10 166	24 342	15 957	4 154	11 803	18 551	6 012	12 539
90 - 94	7 495	1 620	5 875	3 473	712	2 761	4 022	908	3 114
95 - 99	1 171	163	1 008	456	69	387	715	94	621
100 +	287	14	273	83	7	76	204	7	197
1 I 2018 (ESDJ)[61]									
Total	3 729 633	1 791 559	1 938 074	...	...	...	...	...	...
0	53 208	27 615	25 593	...	...	...	...	...	...
1 - 4	224 997	116 247	108 750	...	...	...	...	...	...
5 - 9	255 985	133 711	122 274	...	...	...	...	...	...
10 - 14	210 749	111 649	99 100	...	...	...	...	...	...
15 - 19	208 580	110 419	98 161	...	...	...	...	...	...
20 - 24	224 685	117 237	107 448	...	...	...	...	...	...
25 - 29	273 295	137 657	135 638	...	...	...	...	...	...
30 - 34	273 052	136 928	136 124	...	...	...	...	...	...
35 - 39	251 654	124 592	127 062	...	...	...	...	...	...
40 - 44	242 098	119 665	122 433	...	...	...	...	...	...
45 - 49	235 510	114 670	120 840	...	...	...	...	...	...
50 - 54	244 772	116 533	128 239	...	...	...	...	...	...
55 - 59	261 602	120 456	141 146	...	...	...	...	...	...
60 - 64	223 233	98 302	124 931	...	...	...	...	...	...
65 - 69	187 462	78 040	109 422	...	...	...	...	...	...
70 - 74	108 753	42 649	66 104	...	...	...	...	...	...
75 - 79	126 133	45 148	80 985	...	...	...	...	...	...
80 - 84	79 530	27 115	52 415	...	...	...	...	...	...
85 - 89	34 396	10 667	23 729	...	...	...	...	...	...
90 - 94	8 880	2 095	6 785	...	...	...	...	...	...
95 - 99	1 054	159	895	...	...	...	...	...	...
100 +	5	5	-	...	...	...	...	...	...

Continent, country or area, date, code[a] and age (in years) Continent, pays ou zone, date, code[a] et âge (en annèes)	Total			Urban - Urbaine			Rural - Rurale		
	Both sexes Les deux sexes	Male Masculin	Female Féminin	Both sexes Les deux sexes	Male Masculin	Female Féminin	Both sexes Les deux sexes	Male Masculin	Female Féminin

ASIA - ASIE

India - Inde[62]
9 II 2011 (CDFC)

Total	1210854977	623 270 258	587 584 719	377 106 125	195 489 200	181 616 925	833 748 852	427 781 058	405 967 794
0 - 4	112 806 778	58 632 074	54 174 704	29 820 118	15 595 697	14 224 421	82 986 660	43 036 377	39 950 283
5 - 9	126 928 126	66 300 466	60 627 660	33 120 514	17 475 207	15 645 307	93 807 612	48 825 259	44 982 353
10 - 14	132 709 212	69 418 835	63 290 377	35 904 718	18 930 677	16 974 041	96 804 494	50 488 158	46 316 336
15 - 19	120 526 449	63 982 396	56 544 053	36 623 977	19 411 839	17 212 138	83 902 472	44 570 557	39 331 915
20 - 24	111 424 222	57 584 693	53 839 529	37 589 176	19 446 031	18 143 145	73 835 046	38 138 662	35 696 384
25 - 29	101 413 965	51 344 208	50 069 757	35 345 695	17 968 219	17 377 476	66 068 270	33 375 989	32 692 281
30 - 34	88 594 951	44 660 674	43 934 277	30 683 172	15 726 482	14 956 690	57 911 779	28 934 192	28 977 587
35 - 39	85 140 684	42 919 381	42 221 303	29 077 977	14 793 820	14 284 157	56 062 707	28 125 561	27 937 146
40 - 44	72 438 112	37 545 386	34 892 726	24 857 104	12 980 151	11 876 953	47 581 008	24 565 235	23 015 773
45 - 49	62 318 327	32 138 114	30 180 213	21 630 099	11 273 844	10 356 255	40 688 228	20 864 270	19 823 958
50 - 54	49 069 254	25 843 266	23 225 988	17 037 466	9 053 719	7 983 747	32 031 788	16 789 547	15 242 241
55 - 59	39 146 055	19 456 012	19 690 043	13 284 541	6 919 483	6 365 058	25 861 514	12 536 529	13 324 985
60 - 64	37 663 707	18 701 749	18 961 958	11 372 462	5 770 157	5 602 305	26 291 245	12 931 592	13 359 653
65 - 69	26 454 983	12 944 326	13 510 657	7 538 713	3 736 015	3 802 698	18 916 270	9 208 311	9 707 959
70 - 74	19 208 842	9 651 499	9 557 343	5 401 242	2 673 320	2 727 922	13 807 600	6 978 179	6 829 421
75 - 79	9 232 503	4 490 603	4 741 900	2 848 786	1 377 179	1 471 607	6 383 717	3 113 424	3 270 293
80 - 84	6 220 229	2 927 040	3 293 189	1 800 347	807 610	992 737	4 419 882	2 119 430	2 300 452
85 - 89	2 383 167	1 120 106	1 263 061	785 179	349 809	435 370	1 597 988	770 297	827 691
90 - 94	1 446 534	652 465	794 069	422 547	180 500	242 047	1 023 987	471 965	552 022
95 - 99	633 297	294 759	338 538	187 628	84 120	103 508	445 669	210 639	235 030
100 +	605 778	289 325	316 453	198 314	95 860	102 454	407 464	193 465	213 999
Unknown - Inconnu	4 489 802	2 372 881	2 116 921	1 576 350	839 461	736 889	2 913 452	1 533 420	1 380 032

Indonesia - Indonésie[63]
1 VII 2018 (ESDJ)

Total	264 161 642	132 682 955	131 478 687	145 541 658	73 058 747	72 482 911	118 619 984	59 624 208	58 995 776
0 - 4	21 990 073	11 164 008	10 826 065	11 893 438	6 036 276	5 857 162	10 096 635	5 127 732	4 968 903
0	4 404 825	2 228 827	2 175 998	...	...	...	...	...	...
1 - 4	17 585 248	8 935 181	8 650 067	...	...	...	...	...	...
5 - 9	22 043 588	11 249 711	10 793 877	11 796 055	6 019 422	5 776 633	10 247 533	5 230 289	5 017 244
10 - 14	22 226 122	11 286 379	10 939 743	11 810 838	5 987 161	5 823 677	10 415 284	5 299 218	5 116 066
15 - 19	22 133 908	11 177 544	10 956 364	12 325 228	6 160 995	6 164 233	9 808 680	5 016 549	4 792 131
20 - 24	21 967 406	11 079 836	10 887 570	12 824 260	6 454 864	6 369 396	9 143 146	4 624 972	4 518 174
25 - 29	21 647 315	10 954 324	10 692 991	12 377 458	6 267 881	6 109 577	9 269 857	4 686 443	4 583 414
30 - 34	21 221 547	10 727 662	10 493 885	12 042 650	6 091 212	5 951 438	9 178 897	4 636 450	4 542 447
35 - 39	20 436 506	10 293 833	10 142 673	11 487 830	5 784 238	5 703 592	8 948 676	4 509 595	4 439 081
40 - 44	19 123 692	9 633 564	9 490 128	10 685 039	5 385 708	5 299 331	8 438 653	4 247 856	4 190 797
45 - 49	17 504 493	8 811 523	8 692 970	9 648 466	4 859 836	4 788 630	7 856 027	3 951 687	3 904 340
50 - 54	15 089 998	7 558 920	7 531 078	8 246 721	4 139 242	4 107 479	6 843 277	3 419 678	3 423 599
55 - 59	12 468 016	6 235 824	6 232 192	6 748 096	3 379 391	3 368 705	5 719 920	2 856 433	2 863 487
60 - 64	9 712 230	4 845 358	4 866 872	5 110 944	2 552 596	2 558 348	4 601 286	2 292 762	2 308 524
65 - 69	7 035 508	3 440 273	3 595 235	3 671 852	1 796 680	1 875 172	3 363 656	1 643 593	1 720 063
70 - 74	4 723 878	2 198 395	2 525 483	2 427 423	1 129 066	1 298 357	2 296 455	1 069 329	1 227 126
75 +	4 837 362	2 025 801	2 811 561	2 445 360	1 014 179	1 431 181	2 392 002	1 011 622	1 380 380

Iran (Islamic Republic of) - Iran (République islamique d')[64]
1 VII 2018 (ESDJ)

Total	82 083 918	41 538 139	40 545 779	61 329 440	31 030 645	30 298 795	20 754 478	10 507 494	10 246 984
0 - 4	7 316 828	3 750 695	3 566 133	5 213 821	2 678 920	2 534 901	2 103 007	1 071 775	1 031 232
5 - 9	6 820 958	3 499 772	3 321 186	4 884 070	2 514 075	2 369 995	1 936 888	985 697	951 191
10 - 14	5 939 991	3 041 369	2 898 622	4 276 749	2 196 376	2 080 373	1 663 242	844 993	818 249
15 - 19	5 432 976	2 776 809	2 656 167	3 972 371	2 022 466	1 949 905	1 460 605	754 343	706 262
20 - 24	5 855 580	2 972 197	2 883 383	4 240 903	2 109 543	2 131 360	1 614 677	862 654	752 023
25 - 29	7 514 732	3 797 617	3 717 115	5 627 990	2 801 277	2 826 713	1 886 742	996 340	890 402
30 - 34	8 681 214	4 379 494	4 301 720	6 732 317	3 379 493	3 352 824	1 948 897	1 000 001	948 896
35 - 39	7 758 690	3 926 042	3 832 648	5 999 544	3 034 298	2 965 246	1 759 146	891 744	867 402
40 - 44	6 014 486	3 062 261	2 952 225	4 607 415	2 353 776	2 253 639	1 407 071	708 485	698 586
45 - 49	5 052 773	2 570 346	2 482 427	3 927 426	2 012 550	1 914 876	1 125 347	557 796	567 551
50 - 54	4 239 745	2 138 470	2 101 275	3 319 558	1 691 332	1 628 226	920 187	447 138	473 049
55 - 59	3 523 536	1 756 315	1 767 221	2 712 599	1 369 629	1 342 970	810 937	386 686	424 251
60 - 64	2 816 536	1 388 788	1 427 748	2 133 645	1 075 600	1 058 045	682 891	313 188	369 703
65 - 69	1 938 803	923 600	1 015 203	1 433 554	699 536	734 018	505 249	224 064	281 185

Continent, country or area, date, code[a] and age (in years) / Continent, pays ou zone, date, code[a] et âge (en années)	Total			Urban - Urbaine			Rural - Rurale		
	Both sexes Les deux sexes	Male Masculin	Female Féminin	Both sexes Les deux sexes	Male Masculin	Female Féminin	Both sexes Les deux sexes	Male Masculin	Female Féminin
ASIA - ASIE									
Iran (Islamic Republic of) - Iran (République islamique d')[64]									
1 VII 2018 (ESDJ)									
70 - 74	1 264 958	594 822	670 136	920 848	438 874	481 974	344 110	155 948	188 162
75 - 79	847 337	414 691	432 646	599 783	292 290	307 493	247 554	122 401	125 153
80 +	1 064 775	544 851	519 924	726 847	360 610	366 237	337 928	184 241	153 687
Iraq									
1 VII 2015 (ESDF)									
Total	36 658 503	18 520 532	18 137 971	25 631 821	12 935 587	12 696 234	11 026 682	5 584 945	5 441 737
0	1 137 967	584 535	553 432	752 979	386 080	366 899	384 988	198 455	186 533
1 - 4	4 331 718	2 225 935	2 105 783	2 876 835	1 475 521	1 401 314	1 454 883	750 414	704 469
5 - 9	4 910 887	2 527 175	2 383 712	3 286 086	1 687 351	1 598 735	1 624 801	839 824	784 977
10 - 14	4 359 943	2 246 489	2 113 454	2 947 957	1 515 198	1 432 759	1 411 986	731 291	680 695
15 - 19	3 848 199	1 978 743	1 869 456	2 637 780	1 353 470	1 284 310	1 210 419	625 273	585 146
20 - 24	3 328 277	1 703 854	1 624 423	2 331 929	1 192 710	1 139 219	996 348	511 144	485 204
25 - 29	2 895 690	1 471 180	1 424 510	2 057 867	1 045 789	1 012 078	837 823	425 391	412 432
30 - 34	2 486 941	1 245 726	1 241 215	1 791 620	899 685	891 935	695 321	346 041	349 280
35 - 39	2 133 553	1 058 276	1 075 277	1 551 758	772 320	779 438	581 795	285 956	295 839
40 - 44	1 807 120	887 149	919 971	1 322 951	651 530	671 421	484 169	235 619	248 550
45 - 49	1 494 733	727 670	767 063	1 104 497	539 556	564 941	390 236	188 114	202 122
50 - 54	1 171 634	564 478	607 156	880 319	425 836	454 483	291 315	138 642	152 673
55 - 59	915 225	438 062	477 163	694 340	333 828	360 512	220 885	104 234	116 651
60 - 64	675 377	321 617	353 760	515 990	246 884	269 106	159 387	74 733	84 654
65 - 69	480 527	228 559	251 968	369 196	176 457	192 739	111 331	52 102	59 229
70 - 74	304 637	145 516	159 121	235 201	112 862	122 339	69 436	32 654	36 782
75 - 79	147 670	72 473	75 197	113 997	56 096	57 901	33 673	16 377	17 296
80 +	228 407	93 096	135 311	160 521	64 415	96 106	67 886	28 681	39 205
Israel - Israël[65]									
1 VII 2017 (ESDJ)									
Total	8 713 268	4 321 810	4 391 458	7 950 920	3 933 949	4 016 970	762 348	387 861	374 487
0	181 906	93 485	88 421	165 750	85 196	80 554	16 157	8 290	7 867
1 - 4	710 187	365 055	345 132	643 278	330 634	312 645	66 909	34 422	32 487
5 - 9	826 792	423 352	403 440	742 857	380 032	362 825	83 935	43 320	40 615
10 - 14	744 096	381 346	362 749	670 286	343 073	327 213	73 809	38 273	35 536
15 - 19	683 777	349 991	333 786	615 119	313 596	301 524	68 658	36 395	32 262
20 - 24	625 193	318 700	306 493	572 422	290 773	281 650	52 771	27 927	24 843
25 - 29	602 944	304 440	298 505	557 279	280 846	276 433	45 665	23 593	22 072
30 - 34	590 291	295 298	294 993	544 020	272 419	271 601	46 271	22 879	23 391
35 - 39	562 444	279 248	283 196	513 247	255 348	257 900	49 197	23 900	25 297
40 - 44	544 818	270 230	274 588	493 540	245 008	248 532	51 278	25 222	26 056
45 - 49	473 319	233 796	239 523	429 837	211 832	218 005	43 481	21 964	21 518
50 - 54	409 652	201 118	208 534	375 354	183 407	191 947	34 298	17 712	16 586
55 - 59	389 790	187 328	202 462	358 721	171 625	187 095	31 069	15 703	15 366
60 - 64	369 933	175 635	194 297	341 104	160 930	180 174	28 829	14 705	14 123
65 - 69	341 378	159 965	181 413	316 324	147 045	169 279	25 054	12 919	12 134
70 - 74	234 577	108 335	126 242	217 551	99 932	117 619	17 026	8 403	8 623
75 - 79	169 908	74 328	95 580	159 098	69 116	89 982	10 810	5 211	5 598
80 - 84	128 172	53 524	74 648	119 738	49 797	69 942	8 433	3 727	4 706
85 - 89	76 710	29 632	47 078	71 429	27 563	43 866	5 280	2 069	3 212
90 - 94	35 718	12 438	23 280	33 155	11 502	21 653	2 563	936	1 627
95 - 99	8 603	3 235	5 368	7 969	3 011	4 958	635	224	410
100 +	3 061	1 329	1 731	2 839	1 264	1 575	222	65	157
Japan - Japon[66]									
1 X 2015 (CDJC)									
Total	127 094 745	61 841 738	65 253 007	116 137 232	56 532 149	59 605 083	10 957 513	5 309 589	5 647 924
0 - 4	4 987 706	2 550 921	2 436 785	4 585 047	2 344 645	2 240 402	402 659	206 276	196 383
5 - 9	5 299 787	2 714 591	2 585 196	4 842 315	2 480 103	2 362 212	457 472	234 488	222 984
10 - 14	5 599 317	2 868 024	2 731 293	5 098 044	2 611 161	2 486 883	501 273	256 863	244 410
15 - 19	6 008 388	3 085 416	2 922 972	5 512 237	2 829 307	2 682 930	496 151	256 109	240 042
20 - 24	5 968 127	3 046 392	2 921 735	5 557 062	2 834 296	2 722 766	411 065	212 096	198 969
25 - 29	6 409 612	3 255 717	3 153 895	5 947 621	3 016 085	2 931 536	461 991	239 632	222 359
30 - 34	7 290 878	3 684 747	3 606 131	6 748 938	3 407 192	3 341 746	541 940	277 555	264 385
35 - 39	8 316 157	4 204 202	4 111 955	7 682 014	3 879 376	3 802 638	634 143	324 826	309 317
40 - 44	9 732 218	4 914 018	4 818 200	9 002 172	4 540 962	4 461 210	730 046	373 056	356 990

Continent, country or area, date, code[a] and age (in years) / Continent, pays ou zone, date, code[a] et âge (en années)	Total			Urban - Urbaine			Rural - Rurale		
	Both sexes Les deux sexes	Male Masculin	Female Féminin	Both sexes Les deux sexes	Male Masculin	Female Féminin	Both sexes Les deux sexes	Male Masculin	Female Féminin
ASIA - ASIE									
Japan - Japon[66]									
1 X 2015 (CDJC)									
45 - 49	8 662 804	4 354 877	4 307 927	8 008 263	4 026 225	3 982 038	654 541	328 652	325 889
50 - 54	7 930 296	3 968 311	3 961 985	7 266 826	3 636 156	3 630 670	663 470	332 155	331 315
55 - 59	7 515 246	3 729 523	3 785 723	6 791 248	3 368 519	3 422 729	723 998	361 004	362 994
60 - 64	8 455 010	4 151 119	4 303 891	7 593 671	3 722 143	3 871 528	861 339	428 976	432 363
65 - 69	9 643 867	4 659 662	4 984 205	8 719 913	4 203 013	4 516 900	923 954	456 649	467 305
70 - 74	7 695 811	3 582 440	4 113 371	6 983 090	3 247 479	3 735 611	712 721	334 961	377 760
75 - 79	6 276 856	2 787 417	3 489 439	5 654 811	2 511 652	3 143 159	622 045	275 765	346 280
80 - 84	4 961 420	1 994 326	2 967 094	4 425 840	1 779 702	2 646 138	535 580	214 624	320 956
85 - 89	3 117 257	1 056 641	2 060 616	2 749 324	932 310	1 817 014	367 933	124 331	243 602
90 - 94	1 349 120	333 335	1 015 785	1 183 214	292 810	890 404	165 906	40 525	125 381
95 - 99	359 347	63 265	296 082	314 841	55 450	259 391	44 506	7 815	36 691
100 +	61 763	8 383	53 380	54 031	7 351	46 680	7 732	1 032	6 700
Unknown - Inconnu	1 453 758	828 411	625 347	1 416 710	806 212	610 498	37 048	22 199	14 849
1 VII 2018 (ESDJ)[67]									
Total	126 529 000	61 558 000	64 972 000	...	...	...	...	...	...
0 - 4	4 870 000	2 495 000	2 376 000	...	...	...	...	...	...
5 - 9	5 206 000	2 666 000	2 540 000	...	...	...	...	...	...
10 - 14	5 409 000	2 769 000	2 640 000	...	...	...	...	...	...
15 - 19	5 953 000	3 056 000	2 898 000	...	...	...	...	...	...
20 - 24	6 307 000	3 249 000	3 058 000	...	...	...	...	...	...
25 - 29	6 248 000	3 204 000	3 044 000	...	...	...	...	...	...
30 - 34	6 978 000	3 551 000	3 427 000	...	...	...	...	...	...
35 - 39	7 739 000	3 921 000	3 819 000	...	...	...	...	...	...
40 - 44	9 183 000	4 651 000	4 532 000	...	...	...	...	...	...
45 - 49	9 613 000	4 854 000	4 759 000	...	...	...	...	...	...
50 - 54	8 285 000	4 163 000	4 123 000	...	...	...	...	...	...
55 - 59	7 634 000	3 808 000	3 826 000	...	...	...	...	...	...
60 - 64	7 632 000	3 764 000	3 868 000	...	...	...	...	...	...
65 - 69	9 493 000	4 592 000	4 901 000	...	...	...	...	...	...
70 - 74	8 146 000	3 825 000	4 321 000	...	...	...	...	...	...
75 - 79	6 823 000	3 051 000	3 772 000	...	...	...	...	...	...
80 - 84	5 354 000	2 194 000	3 160 000	...	...	...	...	...	...
85 - 89	3 499 000	1 217 000	2 282 000	...	...	...	...	...	...
90 - 94	1 652 000	444 000	1 208 000	...	...	...	...	...	...
95 - 99	435 000	76 000	359 000	...	...	...	...	...	...
100 +	70 000	9 000	61 000	...	...	...	...	...	...
Jordan - Jordanie[68]									
30 XI 2015 (CDFC)									
Total	9 531 712	5 046 824	4 484 888	8 611 323	4 561 944	4 049 379	920 389	484 880	435 509
0	208 691	107 002	101 689	186 255	95 466	90 789	22 436	11 536	10 900
1 - 4	885 507	454 278	431 229	792 037	406 308	385 729	93 470	47 970	45 500
5 - 9	1 169 491	597 975	571 516	1 050 857	537 071	513 786	118 634	60 904	57 730
10 - 14	1 010 398	519 876	490 522	910 848	468 508	442 340	99 550	51 368	48 182
15 - 19	947 821	498 519	449 302	854 544	449 845	404 699	93 277	48 674	44 603
20 - 24	945 975	519 140	426 835	856 226	470 218	386 008	89 749	48 922	40 827
25 - 29	830 606	459 841	370 765	750 184	414 978	335 206	80 422	44 863	35 559
30 - 34	734 400	395 939	338 461	663 266	357 518	305 748	71 134	38 421	32 713
35 - 39	651 190	352 691	298 499	589 773	319 919	269 854	61 417	32 772	28 645
40 - 44	560 931	304 330	256 601	508 054	276 252	231 802	52 877	28 078	24 799
45 - 49	473 409	258 567	214 842	431 427	236 137	195 290	41 982	22 430	19 552
50 - 54	349 837	187 189	162 648	320 505	171 594	148 911	29 332	15 595	13 737
55 - 59	244 699	127 359	117 340	225 052	117 524	107 528	19 647	9 835	9 812
60 - 64	167 078	86 254	80 824	152 320	78 409	73 911	14 758	7 845	6 913
65 - 69	135 653	67 492	68 161	124 292	62 013	62 279	11 361	5 479	5 882
70 - 74	99 792	52 668	47 124	91 281	48 326	42 955	8 511	4 342	4 169
75 - 79	64 187	32 428	31 759	58 154	29 476	28 678	6 033	2 952	3 081
80 +	52 047	25 276	26 771	46 248	22 382	23 866	5 799	2 894	2 905
80 - 84	30 957	15 324	15 633	...	...	...	...	...	...
85 - 89	13 738	6 387	7 351	...	...	...	...	...	...
90 - 94	4 035	1 797	2 238	...	...	...	...	...	...
95 +	3 317	1 768	1 549	...	...	...	...	...	...

Continent, country or area, date, code[a] and age (in years) / Continent, pays ou zone, date, code[a] et âge (en années)	Total			Urban - Urbaine			Rural - Rurale		
	Both sexes Les deux sexes	Male Masculin	Female Féminin	Both sexes Les deux sexes	Male Masculin	Female Féminin	Both sexes Les deux sexes	Male Masculin	Female Féminin
ASIA - ASIE									
Jordan - Jordanie[68]									
31 XII 2018 (ESDF)[69]									
Total	10 309 000	5 458 000	4 851 000	...	...	...	...	...	...
0	225 710	115 720	109 990	...	...	...	...	...	...
1 - 4	957 720	491 290	466 430	...	...	...	...	...	...
5 - 9	1 264 870	646 690	618 180	...	...	...	...	...	...
10 - 14	1 092 790	562 230	530 560	...	...	...	...	...	...
15 - 19	1 025 110	539 130	485 980	...	...	...	...	...	...
20 - 24	1 023 120	561 440	461 680	...	...	...	...	...	...
25 - 29	898 340	497 310	401 030	...	...	...	...	...	...
30 - 34	794 290	428 200	366 090	...	...	...	...	...	...
35 - 39	704 290	381 430	322 860	...	...	...	...	...	...
40 - 44	606 670	329 120	277 550	...	...	...	...	...	...
45 - 49	512 010	279 630	232 380	...	...	...	...	...	...
50 - 54	378 370	202 440	175 930	...	...	...	...	...	...
55 - 59	264 650	137 740	126 910	...	...	...	...	...	...
60 - 64	180 700	93 280	87 420	...	...	...	...	...	...
65 - 69	146 720	72 990	73 730	...	...	...	...	...	...
70 - 74	107 930	56 960	50 970	...	...	...	...	...	...
75 - 79	69 420	35 070	34 350	...	...	...	...	...	...
80 - 84	33 480	16 570	16 910	...	...	...	...	...	...
85 - 89	14 860	6 910	7 950	...	...	...	...	...	...
90 - 94	4 360	1 940	2 420	...	...	...	...	...	...
95 +	3 590	1 910	1 680	...	...	...	...	...	...
Kazakhstan[70]									
1 VII 2018 (ESDF)									
Total	18 276 452	8 852 247	9 424 205	10 604 004	4 998 115	5 605 890	7 672 448	3 854 133	3 818 316
0	391 099	201 800	189 300	227 168	117 251	109 917	163 931	84 549	79 383
1 - 4	1 566 326	807 377	758 949	893 116	460 640	432 477	673 210	346 737	326 473
5 - 9	1 805 259	927 460	877 800	999 946	514 384	485 562	805 313	413 076	392 238
10 - 14	1 417 302	728 340	688 962	731 935	376 498	355 437	685 368	351 842	333 526
15 - 19	1 124 377	575 253	549 124	585 174	299 407	285 767	539 203	275 846	263 357
20 - 24	1 252 534	638 074	614 460	702 014	346 481	355 533	550 521	291 593	258 928
25 - 29	1 564 473	779 359	785 115	998 153	474 663	523 490	566 321	304 696	261 625
30 - 34	1 544 464	763 318	781 146	957 735	459 785	497 950	586 729	303 533	283 196
35 - 39	1 281 340	631 396	649 944	773 131	371 912	401 219	508 209	259 484	248 726
40 - 44	1 157 298	559 863	597 435	679 887	317 313	362 574	477 412	242 550	234 862
45 - 49	1 074 936	513 474	561 463	628 851	288 592	340 259	446 086	224 882	221 204
50 - 54	1 009 256	473 249	536 007	583 111	261 743	321 368	426 145	211 506	214 639
55 - 59	990 806	450 459	540 347	579 346	252 330	327 016	411 460	198 130	213 331
60 - 64	744 391	319 731	424 661	440 539	179 625	260 914	303 853	140 106	163 747
65 - 69	547 061	216 390	330 671	332 294	124 602	207 692	214 767	91 788	122 979
70 - 74	282 374	104 875	177 499	173 743	61 068	112 675	108 632	43 808	64 824
75 - 79	270 601	87 925	182 676	161 984	49 266	112 718	108 617	38 660	69 957
80 - 84	167 316	50 673	116 643	103 367	29 098	74 270	63 949	21 575	42 375
85 - 89	60 515	16 079	44 436	38 222	9 696	28 526	22 293	6 381	15 912
90 - 94	20 281	5 347	14 934	12 058	2 880	9 179	8 223	2 469	5 754
95 - 99	3 485	1 312	2 173	1 788	655	1 133	1 697	657	1 040
100 +	963	498	466	448	229	219	515	269	247
Kuwait - Koweït									
1 VII 2018 (ESDF)									
Total	4 124 606	2 548 919	1 575 687	...	...	...	...	...	...
0	26 597	13 712	12 885	...	...	...	...	...	...
1 - 4	274 476	147 990	126 486	...	...	...	...	...	...
5 - 9	315 330	175 931	139 399	...	...	...	...	...	...
10 - 14	268 106	148 635	119 471	...	...	...	...	...	...
15 - 19	226 324	124 331	101 993	...	...	...	...	...	...
20 - 24	215 380	119 213	96 167	...	...	...	...	...	...
25 - 29	228 809	125 241	103 568	...	...	...	...	...	...
30 - 34	419 655	250 494	169 161	...	...	...	...	...	...
35 - 39	515 653	344 009	171 644	...	...	...	...	...	...
40 - 44	510 408	343 463	166 945	...	...	...	...	...	...
45 - 49	408 115	276 464	131 651	...	...	...	...	...	...
50 - 54	281 362	190 277	91 085	...	...	...	...	...	...
55 - 59	188 652	128 618	60 034	...	...	...	...	...	...

Continent, country or area, date, code[a] and age (in years) / Continent, pays ou zone, date, code[a] et âge (en années)	Total			Urban - Urbaine			Rural - Rurale		
	Both sexes Les deux sexes	Male Masculin	Female Féminin	Both sexes Les deux sexes	Male Masculin	Female Féminin	Both sexes Les deux sexes	Male Masculin	Female Féminin
ASIA - ASIE									
Kuwait - Koweït									
1 VII 2018 (ESDF)									
60 - 64	118 040	81 334	36 706	...	...	...	...	...	...
65 - 69	64 038	42 268	21 770	...	...	...	...	...	...
70 - 74	32 052	19 088	12 964	...	...	...	...	...	...
75 - 79	16 795	9 509	7 286	...	...	...	...	...	...
80 +	14 814	8 342	6 472	...	...	...	...	...	...
Kyrgyzstan - Kirghizstan[24]									
1 VII 2017 (ESDJ)									
Total	6 198 465	3 072 164	3 126 301	2 097 487	996 210	1 101 277	4 100 978	2 075 954	2 025 024
0	153 674	78 878	74 796	50 790	26 021	24 769	102 884	52 857	50 027
1 - 4	624 235	321 049	303 186	207 427	106 993	100 434	416 808	214 056	202 752
5 - 9	673 907	344 573	329 334	217 396	111 126	106 270	456 511	233 447	223 064
10 - 14	543 470	276 917	266 553	157 585	79 774	77 811	385 885	197 143	188 742
15 - 19	497 079	253 073	244 006	139 125	70 665	68 460	357 954	182 408	175 546
20 - 24	556 096	283 536	272 560	162 667	80 353	82 314	393 429	203 183	190 246
25 - 29	580 904	292 693	288 211	227 567	105 940	121 627	353 337	186 753	166 584
30 - 34	502 049	251 984	250 065	186 909	87 950	98 959	315 140	164 034	151 106
35 - 39	391 950	196 453	195 497	143 343	67 797	75 546	248 607	128 656	119 951
40 - 44	340 627	167 218	173 409	121 854	55 533	66 321	218 773	111 685	107 088
45 - 49	319 033	154 326	164 707	117 362	52 751	64 611	201 671	101 575	100 096
50 - 54	291 181	138 139	153 042	103 823	46 607	57 216	187 358	91 532	95 826
55 - 59	264 854	123 125	141 729	94 203	41 445	52 758	170 651	81 680	88 971
60 - 64	178 026	79 396	98 630	63 155	26 243	36 912	114 871	53 153	61 718
65 - 69	117 727	49 495	68 232	44 195	17 150	27 045	73 532	32 345	41 187
70 - 74	49 872	20 066	29 806	19 795	7 161	12 634	30 077	12 905	17 172
75 - 79	55 296	20 911	34 385	20 717	6 905	13 812	34 579	14 006	20 573
80 - 84	32 500	11 258	21 242	11 394	3 408	7 986	21 106	7 850	13 256
85 - 89	17 356	5 815	11 541	5 597	1 574	4 023	11 759	4 241	7 518
90 - 94	6 687	2 619	4 068	2 027	649	1 378	4 660	1 970	2 690
95 - 99	1 596	505	1 091	434	129	305	1 162	376	786
100 +	346	135	211	122	36	86	224	99	125
1 VII 2018 (ESDJ)									
Total	6 323 115	3 135 726	3 187 390	...	...	...	...	...	...
0	160 074	82 146	77 929	...	...	...	...	...	...
1 - 4	625 058	321 541	303 517	...	...	...	...	...	...
5 - 9	705 801	361 283	344 518	...	...	...	...	...	...
10 - 14	562 234	286 350	275 884	...	...	...	...	...	...
15 - 19	495 112	252 181	242 931	...	...	...	...	...	...
20 - 24	543 550	277 358	266 192	...	...	...	...	...	...
25 - 29	577 359	292 189	285 170	...	...	...	...	...	...
30 - 34	527 707	264 279	263 428	...	...	...	...	...	...
35 - 39	406 825	204 211	202 615	...	...	...	...	...	...
40 - 44	346 142	170 593	175 550	...	...	...	...	...	...
45 - 49	321 559	155 547	166 013	...	...	...	...	...	...
50 - 54	292 637	139 186	153 452	...	...	...	...	...	...
55 - 59	273 116	127 070	146 046	...	...	...	...	...	...
60 - 64	191 387	85 697	105 690	...	...	...	...	...	...
65 - 69	125 649	52 865	72 784	...	...	...	...	...	...
70 - 74	58 873	23 450	35 423	...	...	...	...	...	...
75 - 79	48 692	18 465	30 227	...	...	...	...	...	...
80 - 84	34 956	12 078	22 879	...	...	...	...	...	...
85 +	26 389	9 243	17 147	...	...	...	...	...	...
Lao People's Democratic Republic - République démocratique populaire lao									
1 III 2015 (CDJC)									
Total	6 492 228	3 254 770	3 237 458	2 137 831	1 076 928	1 060 903	4 354 397	2 177 842	2 176 555
0	118 387	60 356	58 031	33 508	17 278	16 230	84 879	43 078	41 801
1 - 4	563 596	286 106	277 490	155 156	79 243	75 913	408 440	206 863	201 577
5 - 9	679 209	345 380	333 829	175 575	89 631	85 944	503 634	255 749	247 885
10 - 14	718 606	363 026	355 580	189 707	96 093	93 614	528 899	266 933	261 966
15 - 19	699 010	354 360	344 650	222 599	112 931	109 668	476 411	241 429	234 982
20 - 24	654 037	325 601	328 436	247 125	126 005	121 120	406 912	199 596	207 316
25 - 29	615 988	308 988	307 000	231 466	117 561	113 905	384 522	191 427	193 095

Continent, country or area, date, code[a] and age (in years) / Continent, pays ou zone, date, code[a] et âge (en années)	Total			Urban - Urbaine			Rural - Rurale		
	Both sexes Les deux sexes	Male Masculin	Female Féminin	Both sexes Les deux sexes	Male Masculin	Female Féminin	Both sexes Les deux sexes	Male Masculin	Female Féminin
ASIA - ASIE									
Lao People's Democratic Republic - République démocratique populaire lao									
1 III 2015 (CDJC)									
30 - 34	496 234	250 383	245 851	184 851	92 976	91 875	311 383	157 407	153 976
35 - 39	420 083	212 523	207 560	150 894	75 793	75 101	269 189	136 730	132 459
40 - 44	343 870	170 808	173 062	125 290	61 840	63 450	218 580	108 968	109 612
45 - 49	295 907	149 656	146 251	109 574	55 072	54 502	186 333	94 584	91 749
50 - 54	267 418	127 272	140 146	95 530	46 444	49 086	171 888	80 828	91 060
55 - 59	197 607	98 615	98 992	70 696	35 929	34 767	126 911	62 686	64 225
60 - 64	147 179	74 106	73 073	49 885	25 446	24 439	97 294	48 660	48 634
65 - 69	98 901	47 563	51 338	33 849	16 540	17 309	65 052	31 023	34 029
70 - 74	71 427	32 930	38 497	24 393	11 302	13 091	47 034	21 628	25 406
75 - 79	47 078	21 871	25 207	17 089	7 933	9 156	29 989	13 938	16 051
80 +	57 691	25 226	32 465	20 644	8 911	11 733	37 047	16 315	20 732
80 - 84	30 190	13 519	16 671	...	...	...	...	...	...
85 - 89	15 267	6 744	8 523	...	...	...	...	...	...
90 - 94	7 036	3 041	3 995	...	...	...	...	...	...
95 +	5 198	1 922	3 276	...	...	...	...	...	...
1 VII 2018 (ESDJ)[71]									
Total	7 012 994	3 513 775	3 499 219	...	...	...	...	...	...
0 - 4	786 169	399 720	386 449	...	...	...	...	...	...
5 - 9	771 352	389 721	381 631	...	...	...	...	...	...
10 - 14	719 488	364 365	355 123	...	...	...	...	...	...
15 - 19	698 190	352 918	345 272	...	...	...	...	...	...
20 - 24	681 057	342 247	338 810	...	...	...	...	...	...
25 - 29	631 666	316 656	315 010	...	...	...	...	...	...
30 - 34	557 769	279 823	277 946	...	...	...	...	...	...
35 - 39	472 207	237 697	234 510	...	...	...	...	...	...
40 - 44	387 487	194 728	192 759	...	...	...	...	...	...
45 - 49	327 812	163 379	164 433	...	...	...	...	...	...
50 - 54	277 272	136 023	141 249	...	...	...	...	...	...
55 - 59	226 841	110 914	115 927	...	...	...	...	...	...
60 - 64	172 018	83 765	88 254	...	...	...	...	...	...
65 - 69	118 892	58 000	60 892	...	...	...	...	...	...
70 - 74	79 424	37 460	41 964	...	...	...	...	...	...
75 - 79	52 642	23 740	28 901	...	...	...	...	...	...
80 +	52 708	22 619	30 089	...	...	...	...	...	...
Malaysia - Malaisie[72]									
1 VII 2018 (ESDJ)									
Total	32 384 982	16 721 618	15 663 364	24 496 667	12 603 976	11 892 691	7 888 315	4 117 642	3 770 673
0	512 886	264 334	248 552	381 177	196 886	184 291	131 709	67 448	64 261
1 - 4	2 082 681	1 074 143	1 008 538	1 542 024	797 120	744 904	540 657	277 023	263 634
5 - 9	2 559 928	1 324 461	1 235 467	1 894 792	981 765	913 027	665 136	342 696	322 440
10 - 14	2 549 551	1 308 765	1 240 786	1 895 653	972 444	923 209	653 898	336 321	317 577
15 - 19	2 871 099	1 488 663	1 382 436	2 069 406	1 071 934	997 472	801 693	416 729	384 964
20 - 24	3 232 126	1 703 803	1 528 323	2 354 975	1 240 887	1 114 088	877 151	462 916	414 235
25 - 29	3 281 344	1 756 374	1 524 970	2 487 845	1 311 502	1 176 343	793 499	444 872	348 627
30 - 34	2 868 456	1 505 779	1 362 677	2 270 659	1 170 371	1 100 288	597 797	335 408	262 389
35 - 39	2 438 370	1 273 897	1 164 473	1 944 898	1 001 748	943 150	493 472	272 149	221 323
40 - 44	1 950 880	1 011 983	938 897	1 554 636	800 868	753 768	396 244	211 115	185 129
45 - 49	1 768 938	890 500	878 438	1 391 121	697 880	693 241	377 817	192 620	185 197
50 - 54	1 619 801	813 697	806 104	1 258 666	632 487	626 179	361 135	181 210	179 925
55 - 59	1 418 501	724 590	693 911	1 088 059	562 098	525 961	330 442	162 492	167 950
60 - 64	1 131 519	565 912	565 607	850 027	429 216	420 811	281 492	136 696	144 796
65 - 69	843 519	416 288	427 231	623 212	309 554	313 658	220 307	106 734	113 573
70 - 74	573 089	276 327	296 762	416 163	201 369	214 794	156 926	74 958	81 968
75 - 79	338 024	159 193	178 831	237 711	113 222	124 489	100 313	45 971	54 342
80 - 84	197 469	91 392	106 077	137 963	64 476	73 487	59 506	26 916	32 590
85 +	146 801	71 517	75 284	97 680	48 149	49 531	49 121	23 368	25 753
Maldives[73]									
1 VII 2018 (ESDF)									
Total	512 038	319 663	192 375	210 248	129 334	80 914	301 790	190 329	111 461
0 - 4	38 453	20 096	18 357	14 922	7 767	7 156	23 531	12 329	11 201
0	7 890	4 125	3 765	...	...	...	...	...	...

7. Population by age, sex and urban/rural residence: latest available year, 2009 - 2018
Population selon l'âge, le sexe et la résidence, urbaine/rurale : dernière année disponible, 2009 - 2018 (continued - suite)

Continent, country or area, date, code[a] and age (in years) — Continent, pays ou zone, date, code[a] et âge (en années)	Total			Urban - Urbaine			Rural - Rurale		
	Both sexes Les deux sexes	Male Masculin	Female Féminin	Both sexes Les deux sexes	Male Masculin	Female Féminin	Both sexes Les deux sexes	Male Masculin	Female Féminin
ASIA - ASIE									
Maldives[73]									
1 VII 2018 (ESDF)									
1 - 4	30 569	15 975	14 593	...	...	...	...	...	...
5 - 9	36 606	19 139	17 467	12 866	6 699	6 167	23 740	12 439	11 301
10 - 14	29 978	15 434	14 544	10 251	5 258	4 993	19 727	10 177	9 551
15 - 19	30 202	16 981	13 220	10 048	5 626	4 422	20 154	11 355	8 799
20 - 24	60 421	42 928	17 493	28 013	19 107	8 906	32 408	23 821	8 587
25 - 29	79 313	57 577	21 736	35 448	25 082	10 366	43 865	32 495	11 370
30 - 34	67 075	45 531	21 544	28 640	18 729	9 911	38 435	26 802	11 633
35 - 39	47 701	31 212	16 489	20 757	13 028	7 729	26 944	18 184	8 760
40 - 44	33 466	21 481	11 985	14 621	9 084	5 537	18 845	12 397	6 448
45 - 49	25 955	15 489	10 466	11 130	6 580	4 551	14 825	8 910	5 916
50 - 54	19 526	10 967	8 559	8 020	4 426	3 594	11 506	6 541	4 966
55 - 59	15 639	8 295	7 343	6 091	3 201	2 890	9 548	5 094	4 453
60 - 64	10 165	5 371	4 794	3 738	1 904	1 833	6 427	3 467	2 960
65 - 69	5 580	2 933	2 646	2 161	1 131	1 030	3 419	1 802	1 617
70 - 74	4 282	2 138	2 144	1 471	691	779	2 811	1 446	1 365
75 - 79	3 865	1 958	1 907	1 140	547	593	2 725	1 411	1 314
80 +	3 812	2 132	1 680	932	474	458	2 880	1 659	1 222
Mongolia - Mongolie									
11 XI 2010 (CDJC)									
Total	2 647 545	1 313 968	1 333 577	1 798 147	872 989	925 158	849 398	440 979	408 419
0 - 4	288 497	146 516	141 981	188 882	95 671	93 211	99 615	50 845	48 770
5 - 9	216 214	110 117	106 097	133 740	68 119	65 621	82 474	41 998	40 476
10 - 14	236 865	120 064	116 801	143 846	72 244	71 602	93 019	47 820	45 199
15 - 19	257 645	130 560	127 085	188 334	92 124	96 210	69 311	38 436	30 875
20 - 24	292 183	147 472	144 711	221 784	107 751	114 033	70 399	39 721	30 678
25 - 29	247 983	124 490	123 493	171 685	83 922	87 763	76 298	40 568	35 730
30 - 34	222 522	111 976	110 546	149 461	73 525	75 936	73 061	38 451	34 610
35 - 39	202 383	100 819	101 564	136 034	66 149	69 885	66 349	34 670	31 679
40 - 44	179 267	88 273	90 994	120 105	57 388	62 717	59 162	30 885	28 277
45 - 49	158 756	77 475	81 281	108 736	51 528	57 208	50 020	25 947	24 073
50 - 54	122 082	58 009	64 073	83 084	38 547	44 537	38 998	19 462	19 536
55 - 59	71 989	33 384	38 605	49 342	22 373	26 969	22 647	11 011	11 636
60 - 64	49 453	22 106	27 347	34 724	15 234	19 490	14 729	6 872	7 857
65 - 69	38 232	17 262	20 970	26 004	11 578	14 426	12 228	5 684	6 544
70 - 74	29 332	13 081	16 251	19 556	8 594	10 962	9 776	4 487	5 289
75 - 79	18 617	7 252	11 365	12 384	4 742	7 642	6 233	2 510	3 723
80 - 84	9 166	3 258	5 908	6 234	2 225	4 009	2 932	1 033	1 899
85 - 89	4 415	1 378	3 037	2 948	945	2 003	1 467	433	1 034
90 - 94	1 459	383	1 076	962	274	688	497	109	388
95 - 99	402	80	322	251	47	204	151	33	118
100 +	83	13	70	51	9	42	32	4	28
1 VII 2018 (ESDF)									
Total	3 208 189	1 577 109	1 631 080	...	...	...	...	...	...
0	76 883	39 609	37 274	...	...	...	...	...	...
1 - 4	315 672	161 890	153 783	...	...	...	...	...	...
5 - 9	349 845	178 702	171 143	...	...	...	...	...	...
10 - 14	242 575	123 754	118 821	...	...	...	...	...	...
15 - 19	230 702	117 328	113 374	...	...	...	...	...	...
20 - 24	244 976	123 826	121 150	...	...	...	...	...	...
25 - 29	302 640	151 793	150 847	...	...	...	...	...	...
30 - 34	289 229	143 890	145 339	...	...	...	...	...	...
35 - 39	242 766	119 628	123 139	...	...	...	...	...	...
40 - 44	219 723	106 474	113 249	...	...	...	...	...	...
45 - 49	189 273	90 041	99 232	...	...	...	...	...	...
50 - 54	162 615	75 499	87 116	...	...	...	...	...	...
55 - 59	132 141	59 430	72 711	...	...	...	...	...	...
60 - 64	83 823	35 979	47 845	...	...	...	...	...	...
65 - 69	48 817	19 998	28 819	...	...	...	...	...	...
70 - 74	31 505	12 638	18 867	...	...	...	...	...	...
75 - 79	24 121	9 785	14 337	...	...	...	...	...	...
80 - 84	12 587	4 517	8 070	...	...	...	...	...	...
85 - 89	6 098	1 798	4 300	...	...	...	...	...	...
90 - 94	1 680	450	1 231	...	...	...	...	...	...

Continent, country or area, date, code[a] and age (in years) Continent, pays ou zone, date, code[a] et âge (en années)	Total			Urban - Urbaine			Rural - Rurale		
	Both sexes Les deux sexes	Male Masculin	Female Féminin	Both sexes Les deux sexes	Male Masculin	Female Féminin	Both sexes Les deux sexes	Male Masculin	Female Féminin
ASIA - ASIE									
Mongolia - Mongolie									
1 VII 2018 (ESDF)									
95 - 99	465	74	391	...	...	...	...	...	...
100 + ...	58	10	48	...	...	...	...	...	...
Myanmar[61]									
1 X 2018 (ESDF)									
Total..............................	53 862 731	25 847 922	28 014 809	15 970 715	7 580 078	8 390 637	37 892 016	18 267 844	19 624 172
0 - 4	4 995 684	2 529 304	2 466 380	1 244 948	631 524	613 424	3 750 736	1 897 780	1 852 956
0	1 014 911	515 082	499 829	...	...	...	...	...	...
1 - 4	3 980 773	2 014 222	1 966 551	...	...	...	...	...	...
5 - 9	4 771 067	2 410 096	2 360 971	1 162 664	589 462	573 202	3 608 403	1 820 634	1 787 769
10 - 14	5 119 782	2 603 363	2 516 419	1 234 044	633 807	600 237	3 885 738	1 969 556	1 916 182
15 - 19	4 980 889	2 514 149	2 466 740	1 472 027	753 240	718 787	3 508 862	1 760 909	1 747 953
20 - 24	4 564 415	2 237 638	2 326 777	1 615 066	802 875	812 191	2 949 349	1 434 763	1 514 586
25 - 29	4 249 011	2 025 258	2 223 753	1 492 016	718 148	773 868	2 756 995	1 307 110	1 449 885
30 - 34	4 086 530	1 945 075	2 141 455	1 305 671	625 146	680 525	2 780 859	1 319 929	1 460 930
35 - 39	3 828 510	1 825 517	2 002 993	1 195 362	568 757	626 605	2 633 148	1 256 760	1 376 388
40 - 44	3 502 366	1 650 865	1 851 501	1 059 024	490 300	568 724	2 443 342	1 160 565	1 282 777
45 - 49	3 218 226	1 493 283	1 724 943	991 986	446 222	545 764	2 226 240	1 047 061	1 179 179
50 - 54	2 864 782	1 312 913	1 551 869	877 155	383 410	493 745	1 987 627	929 503	1 058 124
55 - 59	2 441 861	1 102 256	1 339 605	733 386	311 420	421 966	1 708 475	790 836	917 639
60 - 64	1 897 856	838 030	1 059 826	571 711	236 105	335 606	1 326 145	601 925	724 220
65 - 69	1 383 129	595 076	788 053	412 738	166 210	246 528	970 391	428 866	541 525
70 - 74	863 757	353 491	510 266	269 398	103 866	165 532	594 359	249 625	344 734
75 - 79	526 963	205 089	321 874	157 770	58 940	98 830	369 193	146 149	223 044
80 - 84	347 457	130 729	216 728	106 116	38 018	68 098	241 341	92 711	148 630
85 - 89	159 720	56 262	103 458	49 065	16 357	32 708	110 655	39 905	70 750
90 + ...	60 726	19 528	41 198	20 568	6 271	14 297	40 158	13 257	26 901
Nepal - Népal									
22 VI 2011 (CDJC)									
Total..............................	26 494 504	12 849 041	13 645 463	4 523 820	2 306 049	2 217 771	21 970 684	10 542 992	11 427 692
0 - 4	2 567 963	1 314 957	1 253 006	327 100	172 598	154 502	2 240 863	1 142 359	1 098 504
5 - 9	3 204 859	1 635 176	1 569 683	431 121	227 618	203 503	2 773 738	1 407 558	1 366 180
10 - 14	3 475 424	1 764 630	1 710 794	507 618	266 722	240 896	2 967 806	1 497 908	1 469 898
15 - 19	2 931 980	1 443 191	1 488 789	520 714	273 601	247 113	2 411 266	1 169 590	1 241 676
20 - 24	2 358 071	1 043 981	1 314 090	520 546	260 529	260 017	1 837 525	783 452	1 054 073
25 - 29	2 079 354	917 243	1 162 111	452 256	220 230	232 026	1 627 098	697 013	930 085
30 - 34	1 735 305	770 577	964 728	372 219	181 542	190 677	1 363 086	589 035	774 051
35 - 39	1 604 319	740 200	864 119	324 965	161 347	163 618	1 279 354	578 853	700 501
40 - 44	1 386 121	660 290	725 831	263 008	136 600	126 408	1 123 113	523 690	599 423
45 - 49	1 172 959	575 101	597 858	205 833	106 627	99 206	967 126	468 474	498 652
50 - 54	1 005 476	505 864	499 612	165 685	86 471	79 214	839 791	419 393	420 398
55 - 59	818 263	412 892	405 371	123 667	63 841	59 826	694 596	349 051	345 545
60 - 64	756 827	368 451	388 376	105 862	52 258	53 604	650 965	316 193	334 772
65 - 69	554 449	277 782	276 667	76 074	37 256	38 818	478 375	240 526	237 849
70 - 74	395 153	199 610	195 543	55 001	26 400	28 601	340 152	173 210	166 942
75 - 79	235 135	117 358	117 777	35 764	16 538	19 226	199 371	100 820	98 551
80 - 84	128 777	62 787	65 990	21 053	9 435	11 618	107 724	53 352	54 372
85 - 89	52 526	25 810	26 716	9 857	4 350	5 507	42 669	21 460	21 209
90 - 94	20 335	8 940	11 395	3 788	1 474	2 314	16 547	7 466	9 081
95 + ...	11 208	4 201	7 007	1 689	612	1 077	9 519	3 589	5 930
1 VII 2016 (ESDJ)[20]									
Total..............................	28 431 494	13 784 009	14 647 486	...	...	...	...	...	...
0 - 4	2 950 167	1 525 630	1 424 537	...	...	...	...	...	...
5 - 9	2 674 278	1 368 495	1 305 783	...	...	...	...	...	...
10 - 14	3 062 865	1 564 080	1 498 784	...	...	...	...	...	...
15 - 19	3 317 315	1 680 525	1 636 790	...	...	...	...	...	...
20 - 24	3 021 919	1 476 611	1 545 309	...	...	...	...	...	...
25 - 29	2 340 931	1 033 222	1 307 709	...	...	...	...	...	...
30 - 34	1 998 816	860 512	1 138 303	...	...	...	...	...	...
35 - 39	1 740 784	771 970	968 815	...	...	...	...	...	...
40 - 44	1 521 989	691 192	830 797	...	...	...	...	...	...
45 - 49	1 334 086	632 128	701 958	...	...	...	...	...	...
50 - 54	1 140 179	552 834	587 346	...	...	...	...	...	...
55 - 59	930 950	462 675	468 275	...	...	...	...	...	...

Continent, country or area, date, code[a] and age (in years) / Continent, pays ou zone, date, code[a] et âge (en années)	Total			Urban - Urbaine			Rural - Rurale		
	Both sexes Les deux sexes	Male Masculin	Female Féminin	Both sexes Les deux sexes	Male Masculin	Female Féminin	Both sexes Les deux sexes	Male Masculin	Female Féminin
ASIA - ASIE									
Nepal - Népal									
1 VII 2016 (ESDJ)[20]									
60 - 64	770 098	382 738	387 360	...	...	...	...	...	...
65 - 69	627 821	303 255	324 567	...	...	...	...	...	...
70 - 74	482 949	231 131	251 818	...	...	...	...	...	...
75 - 79	339 914	162 123	177 791	...	...	...	...	...	...
80 +	176 432	84 889	91 543	...	...	...	...	...	...
Oman									
1 VII 2009 (ESDF)									
Total	3 173 917	1 971 115	1 202 802	2 314 865	1 457 197	857 668	859 049	513 917	345 132
0 - 4	272 144	139 614	132 530	184 595	94 803	89 792	87 549	44 811	42 738
5 - 9	245 026	124 776	120 250	162 307	82 954	79 353	82 718	41 821	40 897
10 - 14	254 610	129 964	124 646	168 924	86 326	82 598	85 685	43 638	42 047
15 - 19	284 826	145 215	139 611	194 123	99 854	94 269	90 703	45 361	45 342
20 - 24	387 448	238 483	148 965	285 594	176 341	109 253	101 854	62 142	39 712
25 - 29	475 403	327 686	147 717	362 531	249 782	112 749	112 871	77 904	34 967
30 - 34	367 536	247 107	120 429	288 055	192 969	95 086	79 481	54 138	25 343
35 - 39	272 100	192 483	79 617	212 145	150 865	61 280	59 955	41 618	18 337
40 - 44	207 202	149 090	58 112	161 282	117 670	43 612	45 920	31 420	14 500
45 - 49	145 430	103 908	41 522	111 077	81 065	30 012	34 353	22 843	11 510
50 - 54	113 587	83 057	30 530	84 975	63 752	21 223	28 612	19 305	9 307
55 - 59	59 890	40 488	19 402	42 674	29 489	13 185	17 216	10 999	6 217
60 - 64	39 730	23 538	16 192	26 050	15 494	10 556	13 680	8 044	5 636
65 - 69	20 811	11 811	9 000	13 363	7 537	5 826	7 448	4 274	3 174
70 - 74	14 933	7 721	7 212	9 224	4 703	4 521	5 709	3 018	2 691
75 - 79	6 817	3 303	3 514	4 201	1 981	2 220	2 616	1 322	1 294
80 +	6 424	2 871	3 553	3 745	1 612	2 133	2 679	1 259	1 420
1 VII 2018 (ESDF)[74]									
Total	4 601 706	2 990 103	1 611 603	...	...	...	...	...	...
0 - 4	427 694	218 395	209 299	...	...	...	...	...	...
5 - 9	355 102	180 672	174 430	...	...	...	...	...	...
10 - 14	264 407	134 694	129 713	...	...	...	...	...	...
15 - 19	234 801	119 694	115 107	...	...	...	...	...	...
20 - 24	364 363	225 661	138 702	...	...	...	...	...	...
25 - 29	669 140	490 457	178 683	...	...	...	...	...	...
30 - 34	695 429	514 534	180 895	...	...	...	...	...	...
35 - 39	525 194	382 391	142 803	...	...	...	...	...	...
40 - 44	354 931	252 277	102 654	...	...	...	...	...	...
45 - 49	242 073	177 233	64 840	...	...	...	...	...	...
50 - 54	161 997	114 406	47 591	...	...	...	...	...	...
55 - 59	114 656	75 567	39 089	...	...	...	...	...	...
60 - 64	72 416	44 079	28 337	...	...	...	...	...	...
65 - 69	41 643	21 480	20 163	...	...	...	...	...	...
70 - 74	28 237	13 938	14 299	...	...	...	...	...	...
75 - 79	22 228	10 825	11 403	...	...	...	...	...	...
80 +	27 395	13 800	13 595	...	...	...	...	...	...
Philippines									
1 VIII 2015 (CDJC)[75]									
Total	100 979 303	51 069 962	49 909 341	51 728 697	25 884 921	25 843 776	49 250 606	25 185 041	24 065 565
0	2 076 015	1 073 402	1 002 613	1 034 367	534 903	499 464	1 041 648	538 499	503 149
1 - 4	8 742 916	4 517 083	4 225 833	4 223 884	2 185 173	2 038 711	4 519 032	2 331 910	2 187 122
5 - 9	10 842 920	5 596 837	5 246 083	5 192 082	2 680 013	2 512 069	5 650 838	2 916 824	2 734 014
10 - 14	10 493 942	5 405 418	5 088 524	5 038 321	2 588 533	2 449 788	5 455 621	2 816 885	2 638 736
15 - 19	10 191 185	5 202 239	4 988 946	5 215 933	2 612 060	2 603 873	4 975 252	2 590 179	2 385 073
20 - 24	9 467 494	4 795 772	4 671 722	5 129 397	2 555 317	2 574 080	4 338 097	2 240 455	2 097 642
25 - 29	8 360 447	4 252 817	4 107 630	4 602 240	2 310 548	2 291 692	3 758 207	1 942 269	1 815 938
30 - 34	7 341 894	3 755 963	3 585 931	4 032 971	2 038 876	1 994 095	3 308 923	1 717 087	1 591 836
35 - 39	6 742 687	3 447 349	3 295 338	3 664 250	1 848 714	1 815 536	3 078 437	1 598 635	1 479 802
40 - 44	5 849 328	2 995 391	2 853 937	3 117 283	1 575 802	1 541 481	2 732 045	1 419 589	1 312 456
45 - 49	5 284 325	2 680 464	2 603 861	2 767 792	1 381 650	1 386 142	2 516 533	1 298 814	1 217 719
50 - 54	4 430 547	2 227 579	2 202 968	2 293 852	1 129 580	1 164 272	2 136 695	1 097 999	1 038 696
55 - 59	3 606 834	1 785 436	1 821 398	1 843 549	893 459	950 090	1 763 285	891 977	871 308
60 - 64	2 761 183	1 325 815	1 435 368	1 397 075	657 593	739 482	1 364 108	668 222	695 886
65 - 69	1 916 125	878 327	1 037 798	926 892	417 491	509 401	989 233	460 836	528 397
70 - 74	1 220 080	523 237	696 843	542 499	226 767	315 732	677 581	296 470	381 111

Continent, country or area, date, code[a] and age (in years) / Continent, pays ou zone, date, code[a] et âge (en années)	Total			Urban - Urbaine			Rural - Rurale		
	Both sexes Les deux sexes	Male Masculin	Female Féminin	Both sexes Les deux sexes	Male Masculin	Female Féminin	Both sexes Les deux sexes	Male Masculin	Female Féminin
ASIA - ASIE									
Philippines									
1 VIII 2015 (CDJC)[75]									
75 - 79	859 098	338 520	520 578	372 881	141 733	231 148	486 217	196 787	289 430
80 - 84	475 140	169 388	305 752	200 286	67 663	132 623	274 854	101 725	173 129
85 - 89	218 226	69 930	148 296	92 449	28 055	64 394	125 777	41 875	83 902
90 - 94	74 955	21 868	53 087	31 013	8 294	22 719	43 942	13 574	30 368
95 - 99	19 966	5 956	14 010	8 031	2 244	5 787	11 935	3 712	8 223
100 +	3 996	1 171	2 825	1 650	453	1 197	2 346	718	1 628
1 VII 2017 (ESDJ)[12]									
Total	104 921 400	52 927 400	51 994 000	...	...	...	...	...	...
0	2 313 698	1 195 048	1 118 650	...	...	...	...	...	...
1 - 4	9 087 958	4 665 382	4 422 576	...	...	...	...	...	...
5 - 9	10 902 400	5 582 800	5 319 600	...	...	...	...	...	...
10 - 14	10 421 300	5 358 600	5 062 700	...	...	...	...	...	...
15 - 19	10 180 000	5 241 700	4 938 300	...	...	...	...	...	...
20 - 24	9 811 900	5 013 600	4 798 300	...	...	...	...	...	...
25 - 29	8 806 400	4 472 200	4 334 200	...	...	...	...	...	...
30 - 34	7 692 100	3 886 300	3 805 800	...	...	...	...	...	...
35 - 39	6 907 000	3 492 800	3 414 200	...	...	...	...	...	...
40 - 44	6 176 800	3 126 800	3 049 800	...	...	...	...	...	...
45 - 49	5 526 000	2 789 300	2 736 700	...	...	...	...	...	...
50 - 54	4 787 400	2 400 000	2 387 400	...	...	...	...	...	...
55 - 59	3 944 100	1 950 800	1 993 300	...	...	...	...	...	...
60 - 64	3 029 000	1 464 600	1 564 400	...	...	...	...	...	...
65 - 69	2 170 000	1 006 600	1 163 400	...	...	...	...	...	...
70 - 74	1 410 800	613 400	797 400	...	...	...	...	...	...
75 - 79	908 300	365 200	543 100	...	...	...	...	...	...
80 +	846 500	302 300	544 200	...	...	...	...	...	...
Qatar									
1 VII 2018 (ESDF)									
Total	2 760 170	2 048 206	711 964	2 760 170	2 048 206	711 964	...	...	...
0	28 073	14 333	13 740	28 073	14 333	13 740	...	...	...
1 - 4	115 409	58 753	56 656	115 409	58 753	56 656	...	...	...
5 - 9	136 265	69 207	67 058	136 265	69 207	67 058	...	...	...
10 - 14	105 472	53 858	51 614	105 472	53 858	51 614	...	...	...
15 - 19	85 156	47 656	37 500	85 156	47 656	37 500	...	...	...
20 - 24	264 624	219 454	45 170	264 624	219 454	45 170	...	...	...
25 - 29	453 728	363 316	90 412	453 728	363 316	90 412	...	...	...
30 - 34	491 592	387 278	104 314	491 592	387 278	104 314	...	...	...
35 - 39	394 620	308 830	85 790	394 620	308 830	85 790	...	...	...
40 - 44	262 930	202 986	59 944	262 930	202 986	59 944	...	...	...
45 - 49	180 306	142 201	38 105	180 306	142 201	38 105	...	...	...
50 - 54	108 395	83 950	24 445	108 395	83 950	24 445	...	...	...
55 - 59	67 064	51 161	15 903	67 064	51 161	15 903	...	...	...
60 - 64	35 061	25 684	9 377	35 061	25 684	9 377	...	...	...
65 - 69	14 988	9 997	4 991	14 988	9 997	4 991	...	...	...
70 - 74	7 725	4 677	3 048	7 725	4 677	3 048	...	...	...
75 - 79	4 563	2 576	1 987	4 563	2 576	1 987	...	...	...
80 +	4 199	2 289	1 910	4 199	2 289	1 910	...	...	...
Republic of Korea - République de Corée									
1 XI 2015 (CDJC)									
Total	51 069 375	25 608 502	25 460 873	41 677 695	20 791 896	20 885 799	9 391 680	4 816 606	4 575 074
0	422 337	216 797	205 540	353 330	181 250	172 080	69 007	35 547	33 460
1 - 4	1 836 333	942 214	894 119	1 529 774	784 742	745 032	306 559	157 472	149 087
5 - 9	2 267 851	1 169 770	1 098 081	1 893 768	976 334	917 434	374 083	193 436	180 647
10 - 14	2 427 792	1 262 770	1 165 022	2 042 651	1 060 734	981 917	385 141	202 036	183 105
15 - 19	3 194 079	1 668 683	1 525 396	2 679 885	1 395 027	1 284 858	514 194	273 656	240 538
20 - 24	3 531 108	1 887 776	1 643 332	2 980 057	1 568 333	1 411 724	551 051	319 443	231 608
25 - 29	3 265 288	1 728 888	1 536 400	2 757 203	1 428 161	1 329 042	508 085	300 727	207 358
30 - 34	3 811 610	1 986 796	1 824 814	3 221 411	1 651 851	1 569 560	590 199	334 945	255 254
35 - 39	3 926 862	2 022 466	1 904 396	3 306 159	1 678 522	1 627 637	620 703	343 944	276 759
40 - 44	4 338 827	2 218 442	2 120 385	3 656 010	1 837 640	1 818 370	682 817	380 802	302 015
45 - 49	4 388 157	2 217 013	2 171 144	3 677 944	1 829 471	1 848 473	710 213	387 542	322 671
50 - 54	4 263 447	2 153 186	2 110 261	3 506 520	1 751 909	1 754 611	756 927	401 277	355 650

Continent, country or area, date, code[a] and age (in years) / Continent, pays ou zone, date, code[a] et âge (en années)	Total			Urban - Urbaine			Rural - Rurale		
	Both sexes Les deux sexes	Male Masculin	Female Féminin	Both sexes Les deux sexes	Male Masculin	Female Féminin	Both sexes Les deux sexes	Male Masculin	Female Féminin
ASIA - ASIE									
Republic of Korea - République de Corée									
1 XI 2015 (CDJC)									
55 - 59	3 956 849	1 969 232	1 987 617	3 182 242	1 572 740	1 609 502	774 607	396 492	378 115
60 - 64	2 821 457	1 379 694	1 441 763	2 210 398	1 077 319	1 133 079	611 059	302 375	308 684
65 - 69	2 144 023	1 028 129	1 115 894	1 629 723	778 383	851 340	514 300	249 746	264 554
70 - 74	1 770 741	793 855	976 886	1 273 733	578 485	695 248	497 008	215 370	281 638
75 - 79	1 362 669	553 178	809 491	913 754	375 959	537 795	448 915	177 219	271 696
80 - 84	814 222	276 627	537 595	523 437	179 372	344 065	290 785	97 255	193 530
85 - 89	372 987	98 855	274 132	240 935	63 626	177 309	132 052	35 229	96 823
90 - 94	124 723	28 759	95 964	80 613	18 467	62 146	44 110	10 292	33 818
95 - 99	24 796	4 923	19 873	16 059	3 271	12 788	8 737	1 652	7 085
100 +	3 217	449	2 768	2 089	300	1 789	1 128	149	979
1 VII 2018 (ESDJ)									
Total	51 606 633	25 863 502	25 743 131	...	...	...	...	...	...
0	345 555	177 432	168 123	...	...	...	...	...	...
1 - 4	1 686 457	864 114	822 343	...	...	...	...	...	...
5 - 9	2 289 635	1 177 422	1 112 213	...	...	...	...	...	...
10 - 14	2 267 741	1 172 820	1 094 921	...	...	...	...	...	...
15 - 19	2 817 245	1 469 053	1 348 192	...	...	...	...	...	...
20 - 24	3 496 564	1 856 658	1 639 906	...	...	...	...	...	...
25 - 29	3 497 380	1 868 308	1 629 072	...	...	...	...	...	...
30 - 34	3 366 501	1 766 587	1 599 914	...	...	...	...	...	...
35 - 39	4 100 582	2 116 733	1 983 849	...	...	...	...	...	...
40 - 44	3 955 767	2 023 646	1 932 121	...	...	...	...	...	...
45 - 49	4 556 757	2 311 564	2 245 193	...	...	...	...	...	...
50 - 54	4 123 542	2 076 615	2 046 927	...	...	...	...	...	...
55 - 59	4 339 919	2 163 953	2 175 966	...	...	...	...	...	...
60 - 64	3 390 828	1 669 024	1 721 804	...	...	...	...	...	...
65 - 69	2 358 389	1 133 201	1 225 188	...	...	...	...	...	...
70 - 74	1 796 287	826 425	969 862	...	...	...	...	...	...
75 - 79	1 580 370	664 618	915 752	...	...	...	...	...	...
80 - 84	988 370	355 962	632 408	...	...	...	...	...	...
85 - 89	459 474	128 560	330 914	...	...	...	...	...	...
90 - 94	148 457	32 990	115 467	...	...	...	...	...	...
95 - 99	36 841	7 260	29 581	...	...	...	...	...	...
100 +	3 972	557	3 415	...	...	...	...	...	...
Saudi Arabia - Arabie saoudite									
1 VII 2018 (ESDF)									
Total	33 413 660	19 240 956	14 172 704	...	...	...	...	...	...
0 - 4	2 788 931	1 421 387	1 367 544	...	...	...	...	...	...
5 - 9	2 895 637	1 474 952	1 420 685	...	...	...	...	...	...
10 - 14	2 536 312	1 290 059	1 246 253	...	...	...	...	...	...
15 - 19	2 312 755	1 180 718	1 132 037	...	...	...	...	...	...
20 - 24	2 576 498	1 372 725	1 203 773	...	...	...	...	...	...
25 - 29	3 189 330	1 761 010	1 428 320	...	...	...	...	...	...
30 - 34	3 230 441	1 898 027	1 332 414	...	...	...	...	...	...
35 - 39	3 605 004	2 257 350	1 347 654	...	...	...	...	...	...
40 - 44	3 223 846	2 054 536	1 169 310	...	...	...	...	...	...
45 - 49	2 393 995	1 580 928	813 067	...	...	...	...	...	...
50 - 54	1 670 297	1 141 779	528 518	...	...	...	...	...	...
55 - 59	1 153 898	764 508	389 390	...	...	...	...	...	...
60 - 64	760 864	475 084	285 780	...	...	...	...	...	...
65 - 69	424 301	230 773	193 528	...	...	...	...	...	...
70 - 74	282 190	147 374	134 816	...	...	...	...	...	...
75 - 79	168 907	89 516	79 391	...	...	...	...	...	...
80 +	200 454	100 230	100 224	...	...	...	...	...	...
Singapore - Singapour[76]									
30 VI 2018 (ESDJ)									
Total	3 994 283	1 955 838	2 038 445	...	...	...	...	...	...
0 - 4	185 528	94 916	90 612	...	...	...	...	...	...
5 - 9	199 066	101 636	97 430	...	...	...	...	...	...
10 - 14	206 530	105 026	101 504	...	...	...	...	...	...
15 - 19	226 520	116 102	110 418	...	...	...	...	...	...

Continent, country or area, date, code[a] and age (in years) Continent, pays ou zone, date, code[a] et âge (en années)	Total			Urban - Urbaine			Rural - Rurale		
	Both sexes Les deux sexes	Male Masculin	Female Féminin	Both sexes Les deux sexes	Male Masculin	Female Féminin	Both sexes Les deux sexes	Male Masculin	Female Féminin
ASIA - ASIE									
Singapore - Singapour[76]									
30 VI 2018 (ESDJ)									
20 - 24	255 516	129 956	125 560	...	...	...	...	...	...
25 - 29	291 631	143 758	147 873	...	...	...	...	...	...
30 - 34	281 397	133 775	147 622	...	...	...	...	...	...
35 - 39	303 720	143 661	160 059	...	...	...	...	...	...
40 - 44	303 640	145 974	157 666	...	...	...	...	...	...
45 - 49	307 838	149 811	158 027	...	...	...	...	...	...
50 - 54	308 965	153 908	155 057	...	...	...	...	...	...
55 - 59	304 390	152 528	151 862	...	...	...	...	...	...
60 - 64	271 688	134 928	136 760	...	...	...	...	...	...
65 - 69	212 101	103 758	108 343	...	...	...	...	...	...
70 - 74	135 546	64 029	71 517	...	...	...	...	...	...
75 - 79	93 327	41 288	52 039	...	...	...	...	...	...
80 - 84	57 103	23 779	33 324	...	...	...	...	...	...
85 +	49 777	17 005	32 772	...	...	...	...	...	...
Sri Lanka									
20 III 2012 (CDJC)									
Total	20 359 439	9 856 634	10 502 805	3 704 470	1 800 327	1 904 143	16 654 969	8 056 307	8 598 662
0 - 4	1 743 862	879 223	864 639	281 707	142 039	139 668	1 462 155	737 184	724 971
5 - 9	1 747 752	882 108	865 644	292 480	147 539	144 941	1 455 272	734 569	720 703
10 - 14	1 640 052	829 069	810 983	286 653	145 640	141 013	1 353 399	683 429	669 970
15 - 19	1 644 249	819 927	824 322	306 654	155 546	151 108	1 337 595	664 381	673 214
20 - 24	1 532 883	742 316	790 567	308 605	151 666	156 939	1 224 278	590 650	633 628
25 - 29	1 552 848	743 510	809 338	290 825	142 387	148 438	1 262 023	601 123	660 900
30 - 34	1 639 415	796 866	842 549	294 944	145 860	149 084	1 344 471	651 006	693 465
35 - 39	1 409 077	686 037	723 040	260 479	127 396	133 083	1 148 598	558 641	589 957
40 - 44	1 359 209	661 623	697 586	253 831	124 363	129 468	1 105 378	537 260	568 118
45 - 49	1 285 830	618 140	667 690	237 646	113 675	123 971	1 048 184	504 465	543 719
50 - 54	1 219 460	581 293	638 167	223 940	106 249	117 691	995 520	475 044	520 476
55 - 59	1 064 229	500 871	563 358	192 715	90 444	102 271	871 514	410 427	461 087
60 - 64	917 910	425 428	492 482	169 167	78 370	90 797	748 743	347 058	401 685
65 - 69	633 289	283 764	349 525	121 751	54 401	67 350	511 538	229 363	282 175
70 - 74	412 414	181 846	230 568	77 909	33 807	44 102	334 505	148 039	186 466
75 - 79	283 186	116 389	166 797	52 087	21 036	31 051	231 099	95 353	135 746
80 - 84	159 379	64 250	95 129	30 707	11 775	18 932	128 672	52 475	76 197
85 - 89	73 441	28 293	45 148	14 121	5 097	9 024	59 320	23 196	36 124
90 - 94	24 258	9 293	14 965	4 932	1 790	3 142	19 326	7 503	11 823
95 +	16 696	6 388	10 308	3 317	1 247	2 070	13 379	5 141	8 238
1 VII 2018* (ESDJ)									
Total	21 670 000	10 492 000	11 178 000	...	...	...	...	...	...
0 - 4	1 859 000	938 000	921 000	...	...	...	...	...	...
5 - 9	1 863 000	940 000	923 000	...	...	...	...	...	...
10 - 14	1 748 000	884 000	864 000	...	...	...	...	...	...
15 - 19	1 752 000	873 000	879 000	...	...	...	...	...	...
20 - 24	1 632 000	790 000	842 000	...	...	...	...	...	...
25 - 29	1 653 000	791 000	862 000	...	...	...	...	...	...
30 - 34	1 745 000	848 000	897 000	...	...	...	...	...	...
35 - 39	1 499 000	730 000	769 000	...	...	...	...	...	...
40 - 44	1 446 000	704 000	742 000	...	...	...	...	...	...
45 - 49	1 368 000	658 000	710 000	...	...	...	...	...	...
50 - 54	1 297 000	618 000	679 000	...	...	...	...	...	...
55 - 59	1 132 000	533 000	599 000	...	...	...	...	...	...
60 - 64	975 000	452 000	523 000	...	...	...	...	...	...
65 - 69	672 000	301 000	371 000	...	...	...	...	...	...
70 - 74	438 000	193 000	245 000	...	...	...	...	...	...
75 - 79	301 000	124 000	177 000	...	...	...	...	...	...
80 +	290 000	115 000	175 000	...	...	...	...	...	...
State of Palestine - État de Palestine									
1 VII 2018 (ESDF)									
Total	4 854 013	2 469 162	2 384 851	...	...	...	...	...	...
0	144 628	73 660	70 968	...	...	...	...	...	...
1 - 4	527 236	270 876	256 360	...	...	...	...	...	...
5 - 9	636 603	326 275	310 328	...	...	...	...	...	...

7. Population by age, sex and urban/rural residence: latest available year, 2009 - 2018
Population selon l'âge, le sexe et la résidence, urbaine/rurale : dernière année disponible, 2009 - 2018 (continued - suite)

Continent, country or area, date, code[a] and age (in years) / Continent, pays ou zone, date, code[a] et âge (en années)	Total			Urban - Urbaine			Rural - Rurale		
	Both sexes Les deux sexes	Male Masculin	Female Féminin	Both sexes Les deux sexes	Male Masculin	Female Féminin	Both sexes Les deux sexes	Male Masculin	Female Féminin
ASIA - ASIE									
State of Palestine - État de Palestine									
1 VII 2018 (ESDF)									
10 - 14	568 587	290 728	277 859	...	...	...	...	...	...
15 - 19	498 904	255 091	243 813	...	...	...	...	...	...
20 - 24	483 088	247 472	235 616	...	...	...	...	...	...
25 - 29	431 967	220 872	211 095	...	...	...	...	...	...
30 - 34	329 028	165 658	163 370	...	...	...	...	...	...
35 - 39	265 052	132 494	132 558	...	...	...	...	...	...
40 - 44	233 462	118 137	115 325	...	...	...	...	...	...
45 - 49	193 620	98 704	94 916	...	...	...	...	...	...
50 - 54	166 567	86 118	80 449	...	...	...	...	...	...
55 - 59	129 123	66 604	62 519	...	...	...	...	...	...
60 - 64	88 092	44 449	43 643	...	...	...	...	...	...
65 - 69	62 543	30 807	31 736	...	...	...	...	...	...
70 - 74	40 910	19 264	21 646	...	...	...	...	...	...
75 - 79	25 945	10 887	15 058	...	...	...	...	...	...
80 +	28 658	11 066	17 592	...	...	...	...	...	...
Syrian Arab Republic - République arabe syrienne[77]									
1 VII 2011 (ESDF)									
Total	21 124 000	10 794 000	10 330 000	11 297 000	5 795 000	5 502 000	9 827 000	4 999 000	4 828 000
0 - 4	2 775 000	1 428 000	1 347 000	1 384 000	713 000	671 000	1 391 000	715 000	676 000
5 - 9	2 654 000	1 384 000	1 270 000	1 357 000	719 000	638 000	1 297 000	665 000	632 000
10 - 14	2 430 000	1 232 000	1 198 000	1 270 000	637 000	633 000	1 160 000	595 000	565 000
15 - 19	2 279 000	1 191 000	1 088 000	1 193 000	626 000	567 000	1 086 000	565 000	521 000
20 - 24	1 979 000	1 035 000	944 000	1 045 000	545 000	500 000	934 000	490 000	444 000
25 - 29	1 737 000	864 000	873 000	937 000	475 000	462 000	800 000	389 000	411 000
30 - 34	1 371 000	674 000	697 000	733 000	359 000	374 000	638 000	315 000	323 000
35 - 39	1 229 000	601 000	628 000	694 000	336 000	358 000	535 000	265 000	270 000
40 - 44	1 096 000	545 000	551 000	644 000	325 000	319 000	452 000	220 000	232 000
45 - 49	870 000	437 000	433 000	536 000	272 000	264 000	334 000	165 000	169 000
50 - 54	792 000	387 000	405 000	458 000	232 000	226 000	334 000	155 000	179 000
55 - 59	573 000	293 000	280 000	322 000	168 000	154 000	251 000	125 000	126 000
60 - 64	481 000	254 000	227 000	260 000	139 000	121 000	221 000	115 000	106 000
65 +	858 000	469 000	389 000	464 000	249 000	215 000	394 000	220 000	174 000
Tajikistan - Tadjikistan									
1 VII 2017 (ESDF)									
Total	8 837 002	4 479 048	4 357 954	2 321 759	1 182 016	1 139 743	6 515 243	3 297 032	3 218 211
0	224 995	118 565	106 430	50 031	26 474	23 557	174 964	118 565	106 430
1 - 4	885 670	465 737	419 933	204 985	108 161	96 825	680 685	357 576	323 109
5 - 9	1 074 733	553 954	520 779	255 779	131 657	124 123	818 953	422 297	396 656
10 - 14	851 189	436 951	414 238	210 298	108 099	102 199	640 891	328 852	312 038
15 - 19	858 011	439 613	418 398	226 373	117 834	108 539	631 639	321 779	309 860
20 - 24	848 141	431 299	416 842	235 041	126 421	108 619	613 100	304 878	308 223
25 - 29	846 288	425 391	420 897	242 848	131 999	110 849	603 439	293 393	310 047
30 - 34	715 242	360 052	355 191	179 732	90 412	89 320	535 511	269 640	265 871
35 - 39	531 353	268 676	262 676	141 429	69 185	72 243	389 924	199 491	190 433
40 - 44	447 205	222 016	225 189	127 224	59 788	67 436	319 981	162 228	157 753
45 - 49	405 207	199 311	205 895	121 805	58 033	63 772	283 401	141 278	142 124
50 - 54	363 568	177 575	185 993	106 768	51 032	55 737	256 800	126 543	130 257
55 - 59	305 780	149 842	155 939	88 355	42 448	45 907	217 425	107 393	110 032
60 - 64	192 419	92 991	99 428	55 008	25 849	29 158	137 412	67 142	70 270
65 - 69	118 043	56 588	61 456	33 871	15 678	18 193	84 172	40 909	43 263
70 - 74	57 974	29 379	28 595	16 415	7 820	8 595	41 558	21 559	20 000
75 - 79	57 417	27 614	29 804	14 830	6 675	8 154	42 588	20 938	21 649
80 - 84	32 937	14 388	18 548	7 240	2 984	4 257	25 696	11 405	14 291
85 - 89	14 802	6 647	8 156	2 639	1 058	1 581	12 164	5 589	6 575
90 - 94	5 038	2 094	2 944	891	318	573	4 147	1 776	2 371
95 - 99	902	336	565	156	73	84	745	264	481
100 +	89	30	58	41	19	23	48	12	35
Thailand - Thaïlande									
1 VII 2017 (ESDJ)									
Total	65 521 660	31 807 391	33 714 269	32 257 097	15 626 525	16 630 572	33 264 563	16 180 866	17 083 697
0 - 4	3 661 555	1 872 247	1 789 308	1 792 273	916 261	876 012	1 869 282	955 986	913 295

Continent, country or area, date, codeᵃ and age (in years) / Continent, pays ou zone, date, codeᵃ et âge (en années)	Total			Urban - Urbaine			Rural - Rurale		
	Both sexes Les deux sexes	Male Masculin	Female Féminin	Both sexes Les deux sexes	Male Masculin	Female Féminin	Both sexes Les deux sexes	Male Masculin	Female Féminin
ASIA - ASIE									
Thailand - Thaïlande									
1 VII 2017 (ESDJ)									
0	721 683	369 306	352 378	...	...	...	...	...	...
1 - 4	2 939 871	1 502 941	1 436 930	...	...	...	...	...	...
5 - 9	3 760 113	1 923 678	1 836 435	1 757 747	899 422	858 325	2 002 366	1 024 256	978 110
10 - 14	4 071 457	2 079 375	1 992 082	1 842 247	943 055	899 193	2 229 210	1 136 320	1 092 890
15 - 19	4 416 067	2 244 537	2 171 529	2 022 351	1 027 332	995 019	2 393 716	1 217 206	1 176 510
20 - 24	4 584 174	2 311 801	2 272 373	2 195 601	1 107 445	1 088 156	2 388 573	1 204 355	1 184 218
25 - 29	4 395 408	2 198 898	2 196 511	2 355 102	1 165 928	1 189 174	2 040 307	1 032 970	1 007 337
30 - 34	4 383 056	2 168 363	2 214 693	2 375 033	1 159 442	1 215 590	2 008 023	1 008 920	999 103
35 - 39	4 861 798	2 371 586	2 490 211	2 607 031	1 268 687	1 338 344	2 254 767	1 102 900	1 151 867
40 - 44	5 148 705	2 486 553	2 662 152	2 640 455	1 278 511	1 361 944	2 508 250	1 208 042	1 300 208
45 - 49	5 352 661	2 561 963	2 790 698	2 688 918	1 290 530	1 398 388	2 663 743	1 271 433	1 392 310
50 - 54	5 173 034	2 456 951	2 716 083	2 526 279	1 200 024	1 326 254	2 646 756	1 256 927	1 389 829
55 - 59	4 487 810	2 115 271	2 372 538	2 180 384	1 026 584	1 153 800	2 307 426	1 088 687	1 218 739
60 - 64	3 704 169	1 728 447	1 975 722	1 765 250	819 775	945 474	1 938 920	908 672	1 030 248
65 - 69	2 726 809	1 254 515	1 472 293	1 286 193	588 071	698 122	1 440 616	666 444	774 172
70 - 74	1 914 155	858 054	1 056 101	886 843	394 210	492 633	1 027 312	463 844	563 468
75 - 79	1 346 901	579 113	767 789	625 254	266 341	358 914	721 647	312 772	408 875
80 - 84	897 021	361 369	535 653	413 590	166 331	247 258	483 432	195 037	288 394
85 - 89	458 484	173 302	285 182	212 460	79 776	132 685	246 024	93 526	152 498
90 - 94	144 430	50 880	93 551	68 041	23 872	44 169	76 389	27 007	49 382
95 +	...	...	...	16 046	4 927	11 118	17 806	5 561	12 245
95 - 99	29 621	9 336	20 285	...	...	...	...	...	...
100 +	4 231	1 153	3 078	...	...	...	...	...	...
Timor-Leste									
11 VII 2015 (CDFC)									
Total	1 183 643	601 112	582 531	349 208	179 565	169 643	834 435	421 547	412 888
0 - 4	150 306	77 896	72 410	42 573	22 175	20 398	107 733	55 721	52 012
5 - 9	156 082	80 377	75 705	39 146	20 223	18 923	116 936	60 154	56 782
10 - 14	156 269	80 721	75 548	40 216	20 641	19 575	116 053	60 080	55 973
15 - 19	136 872	69 839	67 033	45 935	22 768	23 167	90 937	47 071	43 866
20 - 24	107 003	52 759	54 244	44 782	22 580	22 202	62 221	30 179	32 042
25 - 29	92 950	45 486	47 464	36 500	18 251	18 249	56 450	27 235	29 215
30 - 34	72 395	35 934	36 461	26 538	13 671	12 867	45 857	22 263	23 594
35 - 39	48 890	24 245	24 645	16 651	8 768	7 883	32 239	15 477	16 762
40 - 44	55 876	29 097	26 779	16 492	9 183	7 309	39 384	19 914	19 470
45 - 49	47 318	25 044	22 274	11 964	6 691	5 273	35 354	18 353	17 001
50 - 54	35 437	18 661	16 776	8 576	4 784	3 792	26 861	13 877	12 984
55 - 59	27 303	14 436	12 867	5 998	3 328	2 670	21 305	11 108	10 197
60 - 64	28 380	13 864	14 516	5 248	2 560	2 688	23 132	11 304	11 828
65 - 69	31 038	14 611	16 427	3 630	1 685	1 945	27 408	12 926	14 482
70 - 74	18 153	8 949	9 204	2 277	1 067	1 210	15 876	7 882	7 994
75 - 79	9 961	4 862	5 099	1 298	598	700	8 663	4 264	4 399
80 - 84	5 197	2 399	2 798	699	301	398	4 498	2 098	2 400
85 +	4 213	1 932	2 281	685	291	394	3 528	1 641	1 887
1 VII 2018 (ESDF)²									
Total	1 261 407	642 639	618 768	...	...	...	...	...	...
0	32 989	17 058	15 931	...	...	...	...	...	...
1 - 4	131 734	68 984	62 750	...	...	...	...	...	...
5 - 9	161 209	84 950	76 259	...	...	...	...	...	...
10 - 14	157 103	82 088	75 015	...	...	...	...	...	...
15 - 19	147 544	75 602	71 942	...	...	...	...	...	...
20 - 24	121 216	60 513	60 703	...	...	...	...	...	...
25 - 29	97 016	46 777	50 239	...	...	...	...	...	...
30 - 34	83 062	40 344	42 718	...	...	...	...	...	...
35 - 39	58 922	28 909	30 013	...	...	...	...	...	...
40 - 44	48 193	24 228	23 965	...	...	...	...	...	...
45 - 49	52 864	27 718	25 146	...	...	...	...	...	...
50 - 54	40 945	21 620	19 325	...	...	...	...	...	...
55 - 59	32 093	16 674	15 419	...	...	...	...	...	...
60 - 64	29 295	14 583	14 712	...	...	...	...	...	...
65 - 69	24 205	11 764	12 441	...	...	...	...	...	...
70 - 74	18 575	9 187	9 388	...	...	...	...	...	...

Continent, country or area, date, code[a] and age (in years) / Continent, pays ou zone, date, code[a] et âge (en années)	Total			Urban - Urbaine			Rural - Rurale		
	Both sexes Les deux sexes	Male Masculin	Female Féminin	Both sexes Les deux sexes	Male Masculin	Female Féminin	Both sexes Les deux sexes	Male Masculin	Female Féminin
ASIA - ASIE									
Timor-Leste									
1 VII 2018 (ESDF)[2]									
75 - 79	13 241	6 452	6 789	...	...	...	...	...	...
80 + ...	11 201	5 188	6 013	...	...	...	...	...	...
Turkey - Turquie[78]									
31 XII 2017 (ESDJ)									
Total...............................	80 810 525	40 535 135	40 275 390	71 253 963	35 693 468	35 560 495	9 556 562	4 841 667	4 714 895
0	1 241 005	636 974	604 031	1 118 272	573 775	544 497	122 733	63 199	59 534
1 - 4	5 240 844	2 689 617	2 551 227	4 717 025	2 420 781	2 296 244	523 819	268 836	254 983
5 - 9	6 340 769	3 254 177	3 086 592	5 679 625	2 915 440	2 764 185	661 144	338 737	322 407
10 - 14	6 210 870	3 188 333	3 022 537	5 494 571	2 821 740	2 672 831	716 299	366 593	349 706
15 - 19	6 526 587	3 351 043	3 175 544	5 735 054	2 940 694	2 794 360	791 533	410 349	381 184
20 - 24	6 456 510	3 294 336	3 162 174	5 717 305	2 884 466	2 832 839	739 205	409 870	329 335
25 - 29	6 231 542	3 163 889	3 067 653	5 624 013	2 830 269	2 793 744	607 529	333 620	273 909
30 - 34	6 296 924	3 189 075	3 107 849	5 740 742	2 890 468	2 850 274	556 182	298 607	257 575
35 - 39	6 560 696	3 308 413	3 252 283	5 967 676	2 999 337	2 968 339	593 020	309 076	283 944
40 - 44	5 740 819	2 891 799	2 849 020	5 184 194	2 607 118	2 577 076	556 625	284 681	271 944
45 - 49	5 055 154	2 556 364	2 498 790	4 503 010	2 274 075	2 228 935	552 144	282 289	269 855
50 - 54	4 675 455	2 349 139	2 326 316	4 085 217	2 051 674	2 033 543	590 238	297 465	292 773
55 - 59	3 966 727	1 977 328	1 989 399	3 401 103	1 695 083	1 706 020	565 624	282 245	283 379
60 - 64	3 371 238	1 651 215	1 720 023	2 816 950	1 382 877	1 434 073	554 288	268 338	285 950
65 - 69	2 511 904	1 188 986	1 322 918	2 046 237	971 061	1 075 176	465 667	217 925	247 742
70 - 74	1 737 267	784 614	952 653	1 381 052	625 361	755 691	356 215	159 253	196 962
75 - 79	1 249 185	533 757	715 428	968 613	412 873	555 740	280 572	120 884	159 688
80 - 84	801 676	330 240	471 436	616 467	249 353	367 114	185 209	80 887	104 322
85 - 89	434 833	152 317	282 516	331 475	113 810	217 665	103 358	38 507	64 851
90 - 94	133 942	38 337	95 605	104 284	29 070	75 214	29 658	9 267	20 391
95 - 99	21 162	4 439	16 723	16 861	3 543	13 318	4 301	896	3 405
100 + ...	5 416	743	4 673	4 217	600	3 617	1 199	143	1 056
Uzbekistan - Ouzbékistan[70]									
1 VII 2017 (ESDJ)									
Total...............................	32 388 563	16 259 425	16 129 138	16 414 114	8 207 397	8 206 717	15 974 449	8 052 028	7 922 421
0	693 105	360 389	332 716	318 791	165 826	152 965	374 314	194 563	179 751
1 - 4	2 739 880	1 423 471	1 316 409	1 250 396	649 787	600 609	1 489 484	773 684	715 800
5 - 9	3 161 368	1 631 656	1 529 712	1 429 113	737 265	691 848	1 732 255	894 391	837 864
10 - 14	2 660 443	1 367 045	1 293 398	1 298 093	665 119	632 974	1 362 350	701 926	660 424
15 - 19	2 625 778	1 343 781	1 281 997	1 299 312	663 849	635 463	1 326 466	679 932	646 534
20 - 24	3 136 874	1 602 543	1 534 331	1 549 589	794 795	754 794	1 587 285	807 748	779 537
25 - 29	3 167 393	1 606 691	1 560 702	1 568 271	802 180	766 091	1 599 122	804 511	794 611
30 - 34	2 831 729	1 422 352	1 409 377	1 458 346	735 170	723 176	1 373 383	687 182	686 201
35 - 39	2 270 453	1 136 422	1 134 031	1 189 102	594 465	594 637	1 081 351	541 957	539 394
40 - 44	1 989 240	992 699	996 541	1 069 430	529 760	539 670	919 810	462 939	456 871
45 - 49	1 744 705	854 306	890 399	979 865	488 349	491 516	764 840	365 957	398 883
50 - 54	1 585 708	761 203	824 505	856 267	410 854	445 413	729 441	350 349	379 092
55 - 59	1 421 340	683 970	737 370	781 454	371 917	409 537	639 886	312 053	327 833
60 - 64	949 659	450 708	498 951	538 135	250 605	287 530	411 524	200 103	211 421
65 - 69	588 343	272 502	315 841	348 287	156 865	191 422	240 056	115 637	124 419
70 - 74	267 585	123 562	144 023	155 901	68 707	87 194	111 684	54 855	56 829
75 - 79	276 508	120 601	155 907	161 867	65 638	96 229	114 641	54 963	59 678
80 - 84	145 584	58 299	87 285	81 655	29 506	52 149	63 929	28 793	35 136
85 + ...	132 868	47 225	85 643	80 240	26 740	53 500	52 628	20 485	32 143
Viet Nam									
1 IV 2009 (CDJC)									
Total...............................	85 846 997	42 413 143	43 433 854	25 436 896	12 349 995	13 086 901	60 410 101	30 063 148	30 346 953
0 - 4	7 034 144	3 662 889	3 371 255	1 949 105	1 019 547	929 558	5 085 039	2 643 342	2 441 697
5 - 9	6 710 737	3 458 159	3 252 578	1 757 679	910 339	847 340	4 953 058	2 547 820	2 405 238
10 - 14	7 248 378	3 725 369	3 523 009	1 761 650	904 731	856 919	5 486 728	2 820 638	2 666 090
15 - 17	5 236 771	2 681 653	2 555 118	1 311 350	662 369	648 981	3 925 421	2 019 284	1 906 137
18 - 19	3 727 131	1 896 261	1 830 870	1 188 578	562 169	626 409	2 538 553	1 334 092	1 204 461
20 - 24	8 432 867	4 253 618	4 179 249	2 759 456	1 305 436	1 454 020	5 673 411	2 948 182	2 725 229
25 - 29	7 790 003	3 904 730	3 885 273	2 519 920	1 205 518	1 314 402	5 270 083	2 699 212	2 570 871
30 - 34	6 868 158	3 462 905	3 405 253	2 164 824	1 062 838	1 101 986	4 703 334	2 400 067	2 303 267
35 - 39	6 531 607	3 298 266	3 233 341	2 059 356	1 027 075	1 032 281	4 472 251	2 271 191	2 201 060
40 - 44	5 966 856	2 967 934	2 998 922	1 818 188	896 290	921 898	4 148 668	2 071 644	2 077 024
45 - 49	5 450 928	2 642 466	2 808 462	1 728 008	840 047	887 961	3 722 920	1 802 419	1 920 501

Continent, country or area, date, code[a] and age (in years) / Continent, pays ou zone, date, code[a] et âge (en années)	Total			Urban - Urbaine			Rural - Rurale		
	Both sexes Les deux sexes	Male Masculin	Female Féminin	Both sexes Les deux sexes	Male Masculin	Female Féminin	Both sexes Les deux sexes	Male Masculin	Female Féminin
ASIA - ASIE									
Viet Nam									
1 IV 2009 (CDJC)									
50 - 54	4 412 051	2 082 098	2 329 953	1 435 970	683 749	752 221	2 976 081	1 398 349	1 577 732
55 - 59	2 984 619	1 364 319	1 620 300	931 382	421 296	510 086	2 053 237	943 023	1 110 214
60 - 64	1 937 948	861 897	1 076 051	590 161	259 193	330 968	1 347 787	602 704	745 083
65 - 69	1 554 678	653 287	901 391	453 756	195 857	257 899	1 100 922	457 430	643 492
70 - 74	1 412 538	568 312	844 226	378 105	155 224	222 881	1 034 433	413 088	621 345
75 - 79	1 198 893	480 088	718 805	306 226	125 948	180 278	892 667	354 140	538 527
80 - 84	725 985	264 997	460 988	182 550	69 573	112 977	543 435	195 424	348 011
85 +	622 705	183 895	438 810	140 632	42 796	97 836	482 073	141 099	340 974
1 IV 2018* (ESDJ)[79]									
Total	94 417 348	46 486 128	47 931 220	33 571 556	...	...	60 845 792	...	...
0	1 397 410	745 650	651 760	422 902	...	...	974 509	...	...
1 - 4	5 846 778	3 072 198	2 774 581	1 876 915	...	...	3 969 864	...	...
5 - 9	7 761 592	4 095 707	3 665 885	2 575 892	...	...	5 185 700	...	...
10 - 14	7 439 505	3 837 698	3 601 807	2 489 712	...	...	4 949 792	...	...
15 - 19	6 115 360	3 115 354	3 000 007	2 032 450	...	...	4 082 910	...	...
20 - 24	6 064 029	3 096 263	2 967 765	2 182 857	...	...	3 881 172	...	...
25 - 29	7 202 132	3 683 225	3 518 908	2 615 965	...	...	4 586 167	...	...
30 - 34	7 284 351	3 649 148	3 635 203	2 677 922	...	...	4 606 429	...	...
35 - 39	7 085 512	3 462 095	3 623 417	2 668 237	...	...	4 417 276	...	...
40 - 44	6 730 960	3 327 100	3 403 860	2 457 959	...	...	4 273 000	...	...
45 - 49	6 729 011	3 351 379	3 377 631	2 465 951	...	...	4 263 059	...	...
50 - 54	6 300 347	3 035 915	3 264 432	2 290 912	...	...	4 009 435	...	...
55 - 59	5 684 766	2 650 434	3 034 332	2 180 360	...	...	3 504 406	...	...
60 - 64	4 398 002	2 008 929	2 389 073	1 693 167	...	...	2 704 836	...	...
65 - 69	2 942 129	1 271 559	1 670 571	1 103 710	...	...	1 838 419	...	...
70 - 74	1 790 324	769 103	1 021 220	659 006	...	...	1 131 318	...	...
75 - 79	1 399 862	549 315	850 547	494 703	...	...	905 159	...	...
80 +	2 245 278	765 057	1 480 221	682 937	...	...	1 562 340	...	...
Yemen - Yémen[2]									
1 VII 2017 (ESDJ)									
Total	28 170 408	14 334 126	13 836 282	...	...	...	...	...	...
0 - 4	4 331 851	2 213 674	2 118 177	...	...	...	...	...	...
5 - 9	3 893 155	1 992 122	1 901 034	...	...	...	...	...	...
10 - 14	3 213 221	1 639 285	1 573 936	...	...	...	...	...	...
15 - 19	2 981 060	1 529 732	1 451 328	...	...	...	...	...	...
20 - 24	2 907 826	1 509 363	1 398 464	...	...	...	...	...	...
25 - 29	2 627 986	1 367 680	1 260 306	...	...	...	...	...	...
30 - 34	2 074 340	1 063 494	1 010 846	...	...	...	...	...	...
35 - 39	1 589 008	799 595	789 413	...	...	...	...	...	...
40 - 44	1 165 508	577 738	587 770	...	...	...	...	...	...
45 - 49	854 059	415 599	438 461	...	...	...	...	...	...
50 - 54	714 875	343 155	371 721	...	...	...	...	...	...
55 - 59	586 832	279 808	307 024	...	...	...	...	...	...
60 - 64	425 188	206 651	218 537	...	...	...	...	...	...
65 - 69	299 382	148 672	150 710	...	...	...	...	...	...
70 - 74	213 416	105 257	108 159	...	...	...	...	...	...
75 - 79	141 596	69 010	72 586	...	...	...	...	...	...
80 +	151 104	73 292	77 812	...	...	...	...	...	...
EUROPE									
Åland Islands - Îles d'Åland[39]									
1 VII 2018 (ESDJ)									
Total	29 638	14 795	14 843	11 709	5 621	6 089	17 929	9 174	8 755
0	288	151	137	97	49	48	191	102	89
1 - 4	1 270	648	622	460	238	222	810	410	400
5 - 9	1 659	846	813	560	287	274	1 099	560	539
10 - 14	1 681	873	808	566	274	292	1 115	599	516
15 - 19	1 561	827	734	612	313	300	949	515	435
20 - 24	1 320	704	616	660	354	306	660	350	310
25 - 29	1 787	958	829	832	458	374	956	501	455
30 - 34	1 769	896	873	760	395	365	1 009	501	508

7. Population by age, sex and urban/rural residence: latest available year, 2009 - 2018
Population selon l'âge, le sexe et la résidence, urbaine/rurale : dernière année disponible, 2009 - 2018 (continued - suite)

Continent, country or area, date, code[a] and age (in years) / Continent, pays ou zone, date, code[a] et âge (en années)	Total			Urban - Urbaine			Rural - Rurale		
	Both sexes Les deux sexes	Male Masculin	Female Féminin	Both sexes Les deux sexes	Male Masculin	Female Féminin	Both sexes Les deux sexes	Male Masculin	Female Féminin
EUROPE									
Åland Islands - Îles d'Åland[39]									
1 VII 2018 (ESDJ)									
35 - 39	1 869	976	893	736	378	358	1 133	598	535
40 - 44	1 860	938	922	707	341	366	1 153	597	556
45 - 49	1 967	983	984	737	352	385	1 230	631	600
50 - 54	2 186	1 069	1 118	796	369	427	1 390	700	691
55 - 59	1 964	958	1 006	729	322	408	1 235	637	598
60 - 64	1 951	925	1 026	762	332	430	1 189	594	596
65 - 69	1 946	923	1 023	778	337	442	1 168	586	582
70 - 74	1 804	900	904	752	345	407	1 052	555	498
75 - 79	1 165	592	573	487	234	254	678	359	320
80 - 84	797	344	453	346	136	210	451	208	243
85 - 89	490	200	290	208	81	127	282	119	164
90 - 94	247	70	177	102	23	79	145	48	98
95 - 99	60	16	44	25	6	19	35	10	25
100 +	4	1	3	3	1	2	2	-	2
Albania - Albanie									
1 VII 2013 (ESDJ)[5]									
Total	2 897 364	1 458 648	1 438 716	1 633 617	798 615	835 002	1 263 747	660 033	603 714
0 - 4	173 349	90 068	83 281	75 341	39 381	35 960	98 008	50 687	47 321
0	35 445	18 414	17 031	...	...	...	...	...	...
1 - 4	137 903	71 653	66 250	...	...	...	...	...	...
5 - 9	171 833	90 701	81 132	100 478	52 421	48 057	71 355	38 280	33 075
10 - 14	220 582	114 164	106 418	117 500	60 576	56 924	103 082	53 587	49 494
15 - 19	261 669	132 810	128 859	134 718	67 303	67 414	126 952	65 507	61 445
20 - 24	235 615	126 936	108 680	153 986	75 706	78 280	81 630	51 230	30 400
25 - 29	209 075	112 236	96 839	136 959	65 999	70 960	72 116	46 237	25 879
30 - 34	187 077	92 149	94 928	95 098	44 074	51 024	91 979	48 075	43 904
35 - 39	173 587	82 445	91 142	89 169	40 432	48 737	84 418	42 013	42 405
40 - 44	189 099	89 772	99 327	106 471	50 381	56 091	82 627	39 391	43 236
45 - 49	197 020	95 657	101 363	113 719	55 342	58 377	83 301	40 315	42 986
50 - 54	209 575	104 084	105 490	121 293	60 655	60 638	88 282	43 430	44 852
55 - 59	184 593	92 037	92 556	105 093	51 906	53 188	79 500	40 131	39 369
60 - 64	141 532	71 276	70 256	83 065	40 768	42 296	58 467	30 508	27 960
65 - 69	106 945	54 278	52 666	60 973	29 333	31 640	45 971	24 945	21 026
70 - 74	102 875	49 827	53 048	55 109	26 020	29 089	47 766	23 807	23 959
75 - 79	71 589	35 241	36 348	41 911	19 956	21 955	29 678	15 285	14 393
80 - 84	38 203	16 977	21 226	25 030	11 374	13 656	13 174	5 603	7 570
85 +	23 147	7 992	15 155	17 705	6 988	10 717	5 443	1 004	4 438
1 I 2018 (ESDJ)									
Total	2 870 324	1 438 609	1 431 715	...	...	...	...	...	...
0	30 867	16 207	14 660	...	...	...	...	...	...
1 - 4	131 549	67 319	64 230	...	...	...	...	...	...
5 - 9	163 875	84 180	79 695	...	...	...	...	...	...
10 - 14	180 659	93 638	87 021	...	...	...	...	...	...
15 - 19	214 636	108 620	106 016	...	...	...	...	...	...
20 - 24	247 137	124 533	122 604	...	...	...	...	...	...
25 - 29	234 063	121 319	112 744	...	...	...	...	...	...
30 - 34	194 459	103 177	91 282	...	...	...	...	...	...
35 - 39	164 817	83 056	81 761	...	...	...	...	...	...
40 - 44	165 031	79 849	85 182	...	...	...	...	...	...
45 - 49	181 015	87 168	93 847	...	...	...	...	...	...
50 - 54	195 813	95 533	100 280	...	...	...	...	...	...
55 - 59	204 061	101 185	102 876	...	...	...	...	...	...
60 - 64	173 175	84 807	88 368	...	...	...	...	...	...
65 - 69	131 026	64 306	66 720	...	...	...	...	...	...
70 - 74	98 509	48 627	49 882	...	...	...	...	...	...
75 - 79	87 199	41 404	45 795	...	...	...	...	...	...
80 - 84	49 425	23 579	25 846	...	...	...	...	...	...
85 +	23 008	10 102	12 906	...	...	...	...	...	...
Andorra - Andorre[39]									
1 I 2018 (ESDJ)									
Total	74 794	38 031	36 763	...	...	...	...	...	...
0 - 4	2 825	1 417	1 408	...	...	...	...	...	...
5 - 9	3 985	2 002	1 983	...	...	...	...	...	...

Continent, country or area, date, code[a] and age (in years) / Continent, pays ou zone, date, code[a] et âge (en années)	Total			Urban - Urbaine			Rural - Rurale		
	Both sexes Les deux sexes	Male Masculin	Female Féminin	Both sexes Les deux sexes	Male Masculin	Female Féminin	Both sexes Les deux sexes	Male Masculin	Female Féminin
EUROPE									
Andorra - Andorre[39]									
1 I 2018 (ESDJ)									
10 - 14	3 877	2 056	1 821	...	...	...	...	...	...
15 - 19	4 048	2 073	1 975	...	...	...	...	...	...
20 - 24	3 853	2 094	1 759	...	...	...	...	...	...
25 - 29	4 460	2 272	2 188	...	...	...	...	...	...
30 - 34	5 090	2 574	2 516	...	...	...	...	...	...
35 - 39	6 242	3 091	3 151	...	...	...	...	...	...
40 - 44	7 061	3 548	3 513	...	...	...	...	...	...
45 - 49	6 976	3 555	3 421	...	...	...	...	...	...
50 - 54	6 580	3 416	3 164	...	...	...	...	...	...
55 - 59	5 600	2 891	2 709	...	...	...	...	...	...
60 - 64	4 211	2 217	1 994	...	...	...	...	...	...
65 - 69	3 258	1 693	1 565	...	...	...	...	...	...
70 - 74	2 540	1 335	1 205	...	...	...	...	...	...
75 - 79	1 630	757	873	...	...	...	...	...	...
80 - 84	1 199	535	664	...	...	...	...	...	...
85 +	1 359	505	854	...	...	...	...	...	...
Austria - Autriche									
31 X 2011 (CDJC)									
Total	8 401 940	4 093 938	4 308 002	5 643 239	2 713 930	2 929 309	2 758 701	1 380 008	1 378 693
0 - 4	394 706	202 637	192 069	267 743	137 645	130 098	126 963	64 992	61 971
5 - 9	406 027	207 779	198 248	268 770	137 636	131 134	137 257	70 143	67 114
10 - 14	426 957	218 499	208 458	276 347	141 429	134 918	150 610	77 070	73 540
15 - 19	488 818	251 251	237 567	313 792	160 620	153 172	175 026	90 631	84 395
20 - 24	527 675	267 651	260 024	364 267	181 574	182 693	163 408	86 077	77 331
25 - 29	552 783	277 236	275 547	390 454	193 719	196 735	162 329	83 517	78 812
30 - 34	538 307	270 267	268 040	375 886	187 248	188 638	162 421	83 019	79 402
35 - 39	564 817	280 207	284 610	383 183	187 902	195 281	181 634	92 305	89 329
40 - 44	675 242	338 455	336 787	453 188	224 449	228 739	222 054	114 006	108 048
45 - 49	710 388	358 163	352 225	470 749	234 757	235 992	239 639	123 406	116 233
50 - 54	626 162	312 890	313 272	409 191	200 993	208 198	216 971	111 897	105 074
55 - 59	517 280	253 019	264 261	339 245	161 747	177 498	178 035	91 272	86 763
60 - 64	480 665	231 598	249 067	322 367	151 726	170 641	158 298	79 872	78 426
65 - 69	402 829	189 221	213 608	283 946	130 760	153 186	118 883	58 461	60 422
70 - 74	410 314	187 956	222 358	273 352	123 395	149 957	136 962	64 561	72 401
75 - 79	262 203	110 870	151 333	165 864	68 812	97 052	96 339	42 058	54 281
80 - 84	218 133	83 066	135 067	142 903	52 895	90 008	75 230	30 171	45 059
85 - 89	141 772	40 153	101 619	99 777	27 332	72 445	41 995	12 821	29 174
90 - 94	46 362	10 997	35 365	34 057	7 767	26 290	12 305	3 230	9 075
95 - 99	9 388	1 836	7 552	7 274	1 377	5 897	2 114	459	1 655
100 +	1 112	187	925	884	147	737	228	40	188
1 I 2018 (ESDJ)									
Total	8 822 267	4 338 518	4 483 749	...	...	...	...	...	...
0	86 460	44 609	41 851	...	...	...	...	...	...
1 - 4	345 548	178 101	167 447	...	...	...	...	...	...
5 - 9	418 903	215 722	203 181	...	...	...	...	...	...
10 - 14	422 091	216 400	205 691	...	...	...	...	...	...
15 - 19	446 497	232 261	214 236	...	...	...	...	...	...
20 - 24	543 335	279 722	263 613	...	...	...	...	...	...
25 - 29	603 826	309 000	294 826	...	...	...	...	...	...
30 - 34	598 813	303 752	295 061	...	...	...	...	...	...
35 - 39	588 265	296 654	291 611	...	...	...	...	...	...
40 - 44	571 243	284 470	286 773	...	...	...	...	...	...
45 - 49	666 736	332 581	334 155	...	...	...	...	...	...
50 - 54	715 390	359 280	356 110	...	...	...	...	...	...
55 - 59	644 612	321 042	323 570	...	...	...	...	...	...
60 - 64	523 556	253 644	269 912	...	...	...	...	...	...
65 - 69	448 191	211 851	236 340	...	...	...	...	...	...
70 - 74	380 051	173 824	206 227	...	...	...	...	...	...
75 - 79	383 384	168 992	214 392	...	...	...	...	...	...
80 - 84	210 513	85 112	125 401	...	...	...	...	...	...
85 - 89	144 461	51 017	93 444	...	...	...	...	...	...
90 - 94	64 880	17 464	47 416	...	...	...	...	...	...
95 - 99	14 493	2 873	11 620	...	...	...	...	...	...

7. Population by age, sex and urban/rural residence: latest available year, 2009 - 2018
Population selon l'âge, le sexe et la résidence, urbaine/rurale : dernière année disponible, 2009 - 2018 (continued - suite)

Continent, country or area, date, codeᵃ and age (in years) Continent, pays ou zone, date, codeᵃ et âge (en années)	Total			Urban - Urbaine			Rural - Rurale		
	Both sexes Les deux sexes	Male Masculin	Female Féminin	Both sexes Les deux sexes	Male Masculin	Female Féminin	Both sexes Les deux sexes	Male Masculin	Female Féminin
EUROPE									
Austria - Autriche									
1 I 2018 (ESDJ)									
100 - 104	958	145	813	...	...	...	...	...	...
105 - 109	60	2	58	...	...	...	...	...	...
110 +	1	-	1	...	...	...	...	...	...
Belarus - Bélarus									
1 I 2018 (ESDJ)									
Total	9 491 823	4 421 534	5 070 289	7 412 118	3 417 894	3 994 224	2 079 705	1 003 640	1 076 065
0	102 883	52 863	50 020	79 600	40 788	38 812	23 283	12 075	11 208
1 - 4	477 666	246 238	231 428	375 550	193 466	182 084	102 116	52 772	49 344
5 - 9	552 896	284 645	268 251	437 233	224 841	212 392	115 663	59 804	55 859
10 - 14	461 491	236 838	224 653	359 711	184 737	174 974	101 780	52 101	49 679
15 - 19	453 268	232 987	220 281	374 921	190 668	184 253	78 347	42 319	36 028
20 - 24	512 640	263 427	249 213	431 424	216 013	215 411	81 216	47 414	33 802
25 - 29	713 641	365 053	348 588	624 954	311 400	313 554	88 687	53 653	35 034
30 - 34	781 838	397 622	384 216	657 903	328 385	329 518	123 935	69 237	54 698
35 - 39	700 453	349 879	350 574	580 271	285 878	294 393	120 182	64 001	56 181
40 - 44	654 091	318 786	335 305	516 299	248 187	268 112	137 792	70 599	67 193
45 - 49	637 421	303 200	334 221	480 034	222 219	257 815	157 387	80 981	76 406
50 - 54	661 130	308 180	352 950	491 194	220 265	270 929	169 936	87 915	82 021
55 - 59	741 293	335 591	405 702	555 536	239 626	315 910	185 757	95 965	89 792
60 - 64	621 451	263 836	357 615	469 599	190 785	278 814	151 852	73 051	78 801
65 - 69	499 210	195 226	303 984	376 541	142 596	233 945	122 669	52 630	70 039
70 - 74	273 350	97 352	175 998	195 799	69 753	126 046	77 551	27 599	49 952
75 - 79	287 101	84 804	202 297	188 093	56 476	131 617	99 008	28 328	70 680
80 - 84	204 091	52 459	151 632	121 652	32 077	89 575	82 439	20 382	62 057
85 - 89	112 479	24 493	87 986	64 118	13 953	50 165	48 361	10 540	37 821
90 - 94	36 538	6 917	29 621	25 323	4 794	20 529	11 215	2 123	9 092
95 - 99	5 783	985	4 798	5 288	839	4 449	495	146	349
100 +	1 109	153	956	1 075	148	927	34	5	29
Belgium - Belgique									
1 I 2011 (CDJC)									
Total	11 000 638	5 401 718	5 598 920	10 842 520	5 322 172	5 520 348	158 118	79 546	78 572
0 - 4	645 512	330 184	315 328	636 217	325 336	310 881	9 295	4 848	4 447
5 - 9	607 325	310 560	296 765	597 723	305 654	292 069	9 602	4 906	4 696
10 - 14	614 460	313 738	300 722	604 574	308 723	295 851	9 886	5 015	4 871
15 - 19	649 018	331 790	317 228	638 725	326 452	312 273	10 293	5 338	4 955
20 - 24	684 093	344 647	339 446	674 173	339 520	334 653	9 920	5 127	4 793
25 - 29	700 373	351 045	349 328	691 593	346 539	345 054	8 780	4 506	4 274
30 - 34	722 936	364 728	358 208	713 667	360 044	353 623	9 269	4 684	4 585
35 - 39	741 204	375 815	365 389	730 809	370 490	360 319	10 395	5 325	5 070
40 - 44	789 895	401 530	388 365	778 159	395 446	382 713	11 736	6 084	5 652
45 - 49	828 167	418 827	409 340	816 018	412 531	403 487	12 149	6 296	5 853
50 - 54	781 240	391 809	389 431	770 016	385 999	384 017	11 224	5 810	5 414
55 - 59	702 331	349 489	352 842	692 496	344 347	348 149	9 835	5 142	4 693
60 - 64	650 904	320 714	330 190	641 771	316 010	325 761	9 133	4 704	4 429
65 - 69	480 199	230 217	249 982	473 668	226 987	246 681	6 531	3 230	3 301
70 - 74	448 374	205 382	242 992	441 884	202 344	239 540	6 490	3 038	3 452
75 - 79	401 594	171 538	230 056	395 900	168 962	226 938	5 694	2 576	3 118
80 - 84	304 788	115 591	189 197	300 342	113 821	186 521	4 446	1 770	2 676
85 - 89	180 495	57 963	122 532	177 932	57 048	120 884	2 563	915	1 648
90 - 94	52 708	13 541	39 167	52 007	13 341	38 666	701	200	501
95 - 99	13 392	2 412	10 980	13 233	2 381	10 852	159	31	128
100 +	1 630	198	1 432	1 613	197	1 416	17	1	16
1 I 2018 (ESDJ)									
Total	11 398 589	5 614 218	5 784 371	...	...	...	...	...	...
0	119 571	61 089	58 482	...	...	...	...	...	...
1 - 4	503 291	257 777	245 514	...	...	...	...	...	...
5 - 9	669 250	342 448	326 802	...	...	...	...	...	...
10 - 14	641 830	328 281	313 549	...	...	...	...	...	...
15 - 19	630 153	323 197	306 956	...	...	...	...	...	...
20 - 24	673 462	342 874	330 588	...	...	...	...	...	...
25 - 29	744 939	373 749	371 190	...	...	...	...	...	...
30 - 34	728 549	364 545	364 004	...	...	...	...	...	...
35 - 39	751 232	376 960	374 272	...	...	...	...	...	...

Continent, country or area, date, code[a] and age (in years) Continent, pays ou zone, date, code[a] et âge (en années)	Total			Urban - Urbaine			Rural - Rurale		
	Both sexes Les deux sexes	Male Masculin	Female Féminin	Both sexes Les deux sexes	Male Masculin	Female Féminin	Both sexes Les deux sexes	Male Masculin	Female Féminin
EUROPE									
Belgium - Belgique									
1 I 2018 (ESDJ)									
40 - 44	730 309	368 851	361 458	...	...	...	...	...	...
45 - 49	783 682	396 214	387 468	...	...	...	...	...	...
50 - 54	811 908	410 783	401 125	...	...	...	...	...	...
55 - 59	782 337	390 754	391 583	...	...	...	...	...	...
60 - 64	697 421	343 290	354 131	...	...	...	...	...	...
65 - 69	612 577	296 815	315 762	...	...	...	...	...	...
70 - 74	509 719	239 355	270 364	...	...	...	...	...	...
75 - 79	371 582	164 260	207 322	...	...	...	...	...	...
80 - 84	315 977	129 001	186 976	...	...	...	...	...	...
85 - 89	212 387	74 638	137 749	...	...	...	...	...	...
90 - 94	87 415	24 826	62 589	...	...	...	...	...	...
95 - 99	19 392	4 313	15 079	...	...	...	...	...	...
100 - 104	1 510	190	1 320	...	...	...	...	...	...
105 - 109	95	8	87	...	...	...	...	...	...
110 +	1	-	1	...	...	...	...	...	...
Bosnia and Herzegovina - Bosnie-Herzégovine									
30 IX 2013 (CDJC)									
Total	3 531 159	1 732 270	1 798 889	...	...	...	...	...	...
0 - 4	174 064	89 442	84 622	...	...	...	...	...	...
5 - 9	176 980	90 881	86 099	...	...	...	...	...	...
10 - 14	192 675	98 653	94 022	...	...	...	...	...	...
15 - 19	242 742	124 900	117 842	...	...	...	...	...	...
20 - 24	228 056	116 883	111 173	...	...	...	...	...	...
25 - 29	252 318	129 248	123 070	...	...	...	...	...	...
30 - 34	252 633	128 593	124 040	...	...	...	...	...	...
35 - 39	249 266	126 145	123 121	...	...	...	...	...	...
40 - 44	241 138	121 595	119 543	...	...	...	...	...	...
45 - 49	260 928	130 087	130 841	...	...	...	...	...	...
50 - 54	276 575	136 153	140 422	...	...	...	...	...	...
55 - 59	258 537	125 576	132 961	...	...	...	...	...	...
60 - 64	223 251	104 970	118 281	...	...	...	...	...	...
65 - 69	153 569	69 066	84 503	...	...	...	...	...	...
70 - 74	140 455	59 854	80 601	...	...	...	...	...	...
75 - 79	117 267	47 403	69 864	...	...	...	...	...	...
80 - 84	62 636	23 769	38 867	...	...	...	...	...	...
85 +	28 069	9 052	19 017	...	...	...	...	...	...
Bulgaria - Bulgarie									
1 I 2018 (ESDJ)									
Total	7 050 034	3 422 409	3 627 625	5 181 755	2 494 068	2 687 687	1 868 279	928 341	939 938
0	63 792	32 708	31 084	48 021	24 679	23 342	15 771	8 029	7 742
1 - 4	263 959	135 510	128 449	200 247	102 565	97 682	63 712	32 945	30 767
5 - 9	349 423	179 623	169 800	264 276	135 981	128 295	85 147	43 642	41 505
10 - 14	327 202	168 426	158 776	240 456	123 637	116 819	86 746	44 789	41 957
15 - 19	313 032	160 986	152 046	229 438	117 642	111 796	83 594	43 344	40 250
20 - 24	325 198	167 828	157 370	243 389	124 456	118 933	81 809	43 372	38 437
25 - 29	445 237	229 275	215 962	344 508	174 557	169 951	100 729	54 718	46 011
30 - 34	479 767	247 873	231 894	374 997	190 586	184 411	104 770	57 287	47 483
35 - 39	499 654	259 105	240 549	389 209	198 989	190 220	110 445	60 116	50 329
40 - 44	548 897	281 901	266 996	427 853	216 795	211 058	121 044	65 106	55 938
45 - 49	518 543	265 873	252 670	391 895	197 537	194 358	126 648	68 336	58 312
50 - 54	462 785	232 763	230 022	341 613	167 882	173 731	121 172	64 881	56 291
55 - 59	483 089	236 464	246 625	353 453	168 486	184 967	129 636	67 978	61 658
60 - 64	487 548	227 799	259 749	352 312	160 770	191 542	135 236	67 029	68 207
65 - 69	479 638	210 746	268 892	335 261	145 183	190 078	144 377	65 563	78 814
70 - 74	388 263	160 541	227 722	257 404	105 678	151 726	130 859	54 863	75 996
75 - 79	275 717	106 393	169 324	173 046	65 613	107 433	102 671	40 780	61 891
80 - 84	202 086	72 708	129 378	126 403	44 037	82 366	75 683	28 671	47 012
85 - 89	101 920	35 174	66 746	65 461	21 973	43 488	36 459	13 201	23 258
90 - 94	29 861	9 408	20 453	19 662	6 161	13 501	10 199	3 247	6 952
95 - 99	4 215	1 247	2 968	2 718	820	1 898	1 497	427	1 070
100 +	208	58	150	133	41	92	75	17	58
100 - 104	195	55	140	...	...	...	...	...	...

Continent, country or area, date, code[a] and age (in years) / Continent, pays ou zone, date, code[a] et âge (en années)	Total			Urban - Urbaine			Rural - Rurale		
	Both sexes Les deux sexes	Male Masculin	Female Féminin	Both sexes Les deux sexes	Male Masculin	Female Féminin	Both sexes Les deux sexes	Male Masculin	Female Féminin
EUROPE									
Bulgaria - Bulgarie									
1 I 2018 (ESDJ)									
105 - 109	13	3	10	...	...	...	...	...	...
110 +	-	-	-	...	...	...	...	...	...
Croatia - Croatie									
1 IV 2011 (CDJC)									
Total	4 284 889	2 066 335	2 218 554	2 368 506	1 121 328	1 247 178	1 916 383	945 007	971 376
0 - 4	212 709	109 251	103 458	116 367	59 768	56 599	96 342	49 483	46 859
5 - 9	204 317	104 841	99 476	108 481	55 715	52 766	95 836	49 126	46 710
10 - 14	235 402	120 633	114 769	124 241	63 763	60 478	111 161	56 870	54 291
15 - 19	244 177	124 918	119 259	130 369	66 506	63 863	113 808	58 412	55 396
20 - 24	261 658	133 455	128 203	142 681	72 037	70 644	118 977	61 418	57 559
25 - 29	289 066	147 416	141 650	164 754	82 466	82 288	124 312	64 950	59 362
30 - 34	294 619	149 998	144 621	173 166	86 363	86 803	121 453	63 635	57 818
35 - 39	284 754	143 984	140 770	165 450	81 745	83 705	119 304	62 239	57 065
40 - 44	286 933	143 603	143 330	161 295	78 845	82 450	125 638	64 758	60 880
45 - 49	307 561	152 446	155 115	167 593	80 182	87 411	139 968	72 264	67 704
50 - 54	320 502	157 981	162 521	174 963	81 945	93 018	145 539	76 036	69 503
55 - 59	311 818	153 750	158 068	174 376	81 746	92 630	137 442	72 004	65 438
60 - 64	272 740	127 851	144 889	154 706	69 577	85 129	118 034	58 274	59 760
65 - 69	202 002	89 364	112 638	114 109	49 018	65 091	87 893	40 346	47 547
70 - 74	212 401	88 912	123 489	113 737	47 978	65 759	98 664	40 934	57 730
75 - 79	175 526	66 456	109 070	91 966	35 801	56 165	83 560	30 655	52 905
80 - 84	108 104	35 999	72 105	56 658	19 022	37 636	51 446	16 977	34 469
85 - 89	47 641	12 415	35 226	26 213	7 045	19 168	21 428	5 370	16 058
90 - 94	10 758	2 580	8 178	6 081	1 517	4 564	4 677	1 063	3 614
95 - 99	2 003	446	1 557	1 181	270	911	822	176	646
100 +	198	36	162	119	19	100	79	17	62
1 I 2018 (ESDJ)									
Total	4 105 493	1 981 799	2 123 694	...	...	...	...	...	...
0	36 470	18 786	17 684	...	...	...	...	...	...
1 - 4	151 461	77 939	73 522	...	...	...	...	...	...
5 - 9	207 127	106 450	100 677	...	...	...	...	...	...
10 - 14	199 335	102 480	96 855	...	...	...	...	...	...
15 - 19	213 583	109 428	104 155	...	...	...	...	...	...
20 - 24	241 994	123 870	118 124	...	...	...	...	...	...
25 - 29	244 211	124 709	119 502	...	...	...	...	...	...
30 - 34	268 395	136 081	132 314	...	...	...	...	...	...
35 - 39	284 436	144 400	140 036	...	...	...	...	...	...
40 - 44	274 764	138 585	136 179	...	...	...	...	...	...
45 - 49	268 827	134 270	134 557	...	...	...	...	...	...
50 - 54	290 149	142 937	147 212	...	...	...	...	...	...
55 - 59	300 862	145 672	155 190	...	...	...	...	...	...
60 - 64	298 518	143 284	155 234	...	...	...	...	...	...
65 - 69	256 892	117 954	138 938	...	...	...	...	...	...
70 - 74	183 678	77 783	105 895	...	...	...	...	...	...
75 - 79	171 524	67 710	103 814	...	...	...	...	...	...
80 - 84	127 663	45 033	82 630	...	...	...	...	...	...
85 - 89	64 308	19 366	44 942	...	...	...	...	...	...
90 - 94	18 295	4 467	13 828	...	...	...	...	...	...
95 - 99	2 864	575	2 289	...	...	...	...	...	...
100 - 104	126	20	106	...	...	...	...	...	...
105 - 109	11	-	11	...	...	...	...	...	...
110 +	-	-	-	...	...	...	...	...	...
Czechia - Tchéquie									
1 I 2018 (ESDJ)									
Total	10 610 055	5 219 791	5 390 264	7 753 337	3 778 892	3 974 445	2 856 718	1 440 899	1 415 819
0	114 213	58 549	55 664	83 483	42 723	40 760	30 730	15 826	14 904
1 - 4	446 550	229 048	217 502	324 660	166 611	158 049	121 890	62 437	59 453
5 - 9	585 156	299 585	285 571	421 962	215 991	205 971	163 194	83 594	79 600
10 - 14	524 758	269 362	255 396	374 132	191 873	182 259	150 626	77 489	73 137
15 - 19	462 200	237 506	224 694	327 629	167 903	159 726	134 571	69 603	64 968
20 - 24	525 198	268 693	256 505	375 961	191 096	184 865	149 237	77 597	71 640
25 - 29	677 564	346 641	330 923	500 884	254 916	245 968	176 680	91 725	84 955
30 - 34	724 445	373 532	350 913	541 770	279 347	262 423	182 675	94 185	88 490

252

Continent, country or area, date, code[a] and age (in years) / Continent, pays ou zone, date, code[a] et âge (en années)	Total			Urban - Urbaine			Rural - Rurale		
	Both sexes Les deux sexes	Male Masculin	Female Féminin	Both sexes Les deux sexes	Male Masculin	Female Féminin	Both sexes Les deux sexes	Male Masculin	Female Féminin
EUROPE									
Czechia - Tchéquie									
1 I 2018 (ESDJ)									
35 - 39	817 364	421 221	396 143	598 863	307 657	291 206	218 501	113 564	104 937
40 - 44	934 896	480 288	454 608	676 286	344 129	332 157	258 610	136 159	122 451
45 - 49	741 070	379 907	361 163	537 308	271 776	265 532	203 762	108 131	95 631
50 - 54	700 067	355 788	344 279	512 267	256 611	255 656	187 800	99 177	88 623
55 - 59	617 823	308 389	309 434	449 376	220 946	228 430	168 447	87 443	81 004
60 - 64	698 568	336 853	361 715	507 616	240 613	267 003	190 952	96 240	94 712
65 - 69	684 548	317 104	367 444	499 058	226 717	272 341	185 490	90 387	95 103
70 - 74	569 661	248 936	320 725	426 697	182 561	244 136	142 964	66 375	76 589
75 - 79	358 552	145 902	212 650	271 154	109 336	161 818	87 398	36 566	50 832
80 - 84	226 588	82 491	144 097	170 794	62 068	108 726	55 794	20 423	35 371
85 - 89	141 839	45 232	96 607	107 999	34 575	73 424	33 840	10 657	23 183
90 - 94	49 852	12 853	36 999	38 358	9 965	28 393	11 494	2 888	8 606
95 - 99	8 485	1 749	6 736	6 585	1 355	5 230	1 900	394	1 506
100 +	658	162	496	495	123	372	163	39	124
100 - 104	530	114	416	...	...	...	...	...	...
105 - 109	128	48	80	...	...	...	...	...	...
110 +	-	-	-	...	...	...	...	...	...
Denmark - Danemark[80]									
1 VII 2018 (ESDJ)									
Total	5 789 957	2 881 620	2 908 337	...	...	...	...	...	...
0	62 327	31 900	30 427	...	...	...	...	...	...
1 - 4	240 336	123 467	116 869	...	...	...	...	...	...
5 - 9	318 609	163 474	155 135	...	...	...	...	...	...
10 - 14	338 216	173 267	164 949	...	...	...	...	...	...
15 - 19	344 054	176 135	167 919	...	...	...	...	...	...
20 - 24	387 147	198 102	189 045	...	...	...	...	...	...
25 - 29	391 149	199 468	191 681	...	...	...	...	...	...
30 - 34	342 891	175 092	167 799	...	...	...	...	...	...
35 - 39	335 028	169 102	165 926	...	...	...	...	...	...
40 - 44	375 371	188 121	187 250	...	...	...	...	...	...
45 - 49	390 385	196 354	194 031	...	...	...	...	...	...
50 - 54	424 108	213 989	210 119	...	...	...	...	...	...
55 - 59	371 594	185 850	185 744	...	...	...	...	...	...
60 - 64	341 937	169 301	172 636	...	...	...	...	...	...
65 - 69	321 932	157 184	164 748	...	...	...	...	...	...
70 - 74	327 607	158 166	169 441	...	...	...	...	...	...
75 - 79	217 254	100 799	116 455	...	...	...	...	...	...
80 - 84	139 375	60 424	78 951	...	...	...	...	...	...
85 - 89	76 235	29 047	47 188	...	...	...	...	...	...
90 - 94	34 384	10 257	24 127	...	...	...	...	...	...
95 - 99	8 936	1 975	6 961	...	...	...	...	...	...
100 +	1 082	146	936	...	...	...	...	...	...
Estonia - Estonie									
1 I 2018 (ESDJ)									
Total	1 319 133	621 084	698 049	914 850[81]	416 987[81]	497 863[81]	402 912[81]	203 465[81]	199 447[81]
0	14 075	7 375	6 700	10 265[81]	5 363[81]	4 902[81]	3 808[81]	2 011[81]	1 797[81]
1 - 4	55 961	28 728	27 233	40 901[81]	20 949[81]	19 952[81]	14 988[81]	7 743[81]	7 245[81]
5 - 9	75 839	38 921	36 918	54 445[81]	27 826[81]	26 619[81]	21 391[81]	11 095[81]	10 296[81]
10 - 14	69 351	35 660	33 691	48 763[81]	24 957[81]	23 806[81]	20 585[81]	10 701[81]	9 884[81]
15 - 19	60 173	30 908	29 265	40 230[81]	20 526[81]	19 704[81]	19 927[81]	10 374[81]	9 553[81]
20 - 24	66 593	34 129	32 464	45 671[81]	22 651[81]	23 020[81]	20 885[81]	11 459[81]	9 426[81]
25 - 29	93 383	48 834	44 549	66 060[81]	33 099[81]	32 961[81]	27 290[81]	15 715[81]	11 575[81]
30 - 34	97 528	50 784	46 744	71 953[81]	35 893[81]	36 060[81]	25 504[81]	14 837[81]	10 667[81]
35 - 39	90 787	46 742	44 045	66 526[81]	32 952[81]	33 574[81]	24 164[81]	13 725[81]	10 439[81]
40 - 44	90 476	46 228	44 248	63 898[81]	31 296[81]	32 602[81]	26 460[81]	14 847[81]	11 613[81]
45 - 49	90 222	45 169	45 053	60 839[81]	29 117[81]	31 722[81]	29 262[81]	15 982[81]	13 280[81]
50 - 54	82 941	40 263	42 678	54 455[81]	25 269[81]	29 186[81]	28 375[81]	14 935[81]	13 440[81]
55 - 59	89 278	41 770	47 508	58 931[81]	26 026[81]	32 905[81]	30 232[81]	15 692[81]	14 540[81]
60 - 64	84 144	37 181	46 963	56 956[81]	23 736[81]	33 220[81]	27 090[81]	13 409[81]	13 681[81]
65 - 69	76 931	31 388	45 543	52 344[81]	20 172[81]	32 172[81]	24 427[81]	11 158[81]	13 269[81]
70 - 74	54 277	20 531	33 746	36 009[81]	12 890[81]	23 119[81]	18 165[81]	7 614[81]	10 551[81]
75 - 79	54 895	18 058	36 837	37 355[81]	11 828[81]	25 527[81]	17 450[81]	6 212[81]	11 238[81]

7. Population by age, sex and urban/rural residence: latest available year, 2009 - 2018
Population selon l'âge, le sexe et la résidence, urbaine/rurale : dernière année disponible, 2009 - 2018 (continued - suite)

Continent, country or area, date, code[a] and age (in years) / Continent, pays ou zone, date, code[a] et âge (en années)	Total			Urban - Urbaine			Rural - Rurale		
	Both sexes Les deux sexes	Male Masculin	Female Féminin	Both sexes Les deux sexes	Male Masculin	Female Féminin	Both sexes Les deux sexes	Male Masculin	Female Féminin
EUROPE									
Estonia - Estonie									
1 I 2018 (ESDJ)									
80 - 84	38 735	10 992	27 743	26 340[81]	7 374[81]	18 966[81]	12 332[81]	3 606[81]	8 726[81]
85 - 89	23 377	5 616	17 761	15 974[81]	3 811[81]	12 163[81]	7 361[81]	1 797[81]	5 564[81]
90 - 94	8 609	1 590	7 019	5 922[81]	1 106[81]	4 816[81]	2 672[81]	482[81]	2 190[81]
95 - 99	1 449	209	1 240	939[81]	140[81]	799[81]	509[81]	69[81]	440[81]
100 +	109	8	101	74[81]	6[81]	68[81]	35[81]	2[81]	33[81]
100 - 104	104	8	96	...	...	...	...	...	...
105 - 109	5	-	5	...	...	...	...	...	...
110 +	-	-	-	...	...	...	...	...	...
Faeroe Islands - Îles Féroé									
1 VII 2018 (ESDJ)									
Total	51 040	26 352	24 688	19 600	9 873	9 727	31 440	16 479	14 961
0	683	326	357	257	119	138	426	207	219
1 - 4	2 836	1 400	1 436	1 126	553	573	1 710	847	863
5 - 9	3 459	1 810	1 649	1 323	675	648	2 136	1 135	1 001
10 - 14	3 703	1 870	1 833	1 397	678	719	2 306	1 192	1 114
15 - 19	3 585	1 863	1 722	1 414	730	684	2 171	1 133	1 038
20 - 24	3 045	1 672	1 373	1 169	616	553	1 876	1 056	820
25 - 29	2 970	1 628	1 342	1 149	620	529	1 821	1 008	813
30 - 34	2 912	1 565	1 347	1 110	569	541	1 802	996	806
35 - 39	3 026	1 565	1 461	1 190	612	578	1 836	953	883
40 - 44	3 179	1 704	1 475	1 237	663	574	1 942	1 041	901
45 - 49	3 247	1 702	1 545	1 265	626	639	1 982	1 076	906
50 - 54	3 490	1 859	1 631	1 516	794	722	1 974	1 065	909
55 - 59	3 192	1 628	1 564	1 233	635	598	1 959	993	966
60 - 64	2 870	1 458	1 412	1 075	521	554	1 795	937	858
65 - 69	2 733	1 403	1 330	1 028	515	513	1 705	888	817
70 - 74	2 217	1 179	1 038	770	389	381	1 447	790	657
75 - 79	1 674	826	848	591	275	316	1 083	551	532
80 - 84	1 066	484	582	351	153	198	715	331	384
85 - 89	758	304	454	248	93	155	510	211	299
90 - 94	328	90	238	122	31	91	206	59	147
95 - 99	58	15	43	25	6	19	33	9	24
100 +	9	1	8	4	-	4	5	1	4
Finland - Finlande[39]									
1 VII 2017 (ESDJ)[82]									
Total	5 478 862	2 701 086	2 777 777	3 904 835	1 907 533	1 997 303	1 574 027	793 553	780 474
0	51 580	26 258	25 323	38 114	19 422	18 692	13 466	6 836	6 631
1 - 4	229 902	117 709	112 194	166 234	85 156	81 078	63 668	32 553	31 116
5 - 9	307 848	157 298	150 551	216 747	110 655	106 092	91 101	46 643	44 459
10 - 14	298 161	152 325	145 836	205 801	105 230	100 572	92 360	47 096	45 264
15 - 19	295 784	151 870	143 914	207 929	105 097	102 832	87 855	46 773	41 082
20 - 24	330 016	169 169	160 847	270 598	135 532	135 067	59 418	33 638	25 780
25 - 29	349 307	179 431	169 876	284 519	145 237	139 282	64 788	34 194	30 594
30 - 34	352 679	181 964	170 715	274 822	141 839	132 983	77 857	40 125	37 733
35 - 39	346 741	178 577	168 164	261 772	134 830	126 942	84 969	43 747	41 222
40 - 44	326 906	167 906	159 000	240 378	123 373	117 005	86 528	44 534	41 995
45 - 49	331 826	168 138	163 689	237 399	119 653	117 746	94 428	48 485	45 943
50 - 54	369 122	185 580	183 542	257 374	127 829	129 545	111 749	57 752	53 997
55 - 59	363 167	180 278	182 890	245 202	119 474	125 728	117 965	60 804	57 162
60 - 64	367 465	179 346	188 119	242 346	114 701	127 645	125 119	64 645	60 474
65 - 69	370 677	178 341	192 336	243 504	113 101	130 403	127 173	65 240	61 933
70 - 74	289 516	134 910	154 606	193 128	87 200	105 929	96 388	47 711	48 678
75 - 79	208 300	90 686	117 614	135 915	57 500	78 415	72 386	33 186	39 200
80 - 84	146 115	57 824	88 291	92 980	35 534	57 446	53 135	22 290	30 846
85 - 89	95 655	31 759	63 896	60 089	19 200	40 889	35 566	12 559	23 007
90 - 94	39 128	10 086	29 043	24 357	5 994	18 363	14 772	4 092	10 680
95 - 99	8 141	1 503	6 638	5 075	902	4 173	3 067	601	2 466
100 +	831	132	699	557	77	480	274	55	219
1 I 2018 (ESDJ)									
Total	5 513 130	2 719 131	2 793 999	...	...	...	...	...	...
0	50 588	25 816	24 772	...	...	...	...	...	...
1 - 4	227 922	116 643	111 279	...	...	...	...	...	...
5 - 9	310 064	158 343	151 721	...	...	...	...	...	...

Continent, country or area, date, code[a] and age (in years) / Continent, pays ou zone, date, code[a] et âge (en années)	Total			Urban - Urbaine			Rural - Rurale		
	Both sexes Les deux sexes	Male Masculin	Female Féminin	Both sexes Les deux sexes	Male Masculin	Female Féminin	Both sexes Les deux sexes	Male Masculin	Female Féminin
EUROPE									
Finland - Finlande[39]									
1 I 2018 (ESDJ)									
10 - 14	301 850	154 230	147 620	...	...	...	...	...	...
15 - 19	296 055	152 215	143 840	...	...	...	...	...	...
20 - 24	327 752	168 014	159 738	...	...	...	...	...	...
25 - 29	354 325	182 223	172 102	...	...	...	...	...	...
30 - 34	352 269	181 676	170 593	...	...	...	...	...	...
35 - 39	350 498	180 761	169 737	...	...	...	...	...	...
40 - 44	332 814	170 871	161 943	...	...	...	...	...	...
45 - 49	327 889	166 331	161 558	...	...	...	...	...	...
50 - 54	369 756	185 887	183 869	...	...	...	...	...	...
55 - 59	364 798	181 216	183 582	...	...	...	...	...	...
60 - 64	367 232	179 220	188 012	...	...	...	...	...	...
65 - 69	370 001	178 082	191 919	...	...	...	...	...	...
70 - 74	307 517	143 498	164 019	...	...	...	...	...	...
75 - 79	207 063	90 458	116 605	...	...	...	...	...	...
80 - 84	148 572	59 117	89 455	...	...	...	...	...	...
85 - 89	96 791	32 397	64 394	...	...	...	...	...	...
90 - 94	40 012	10 445	29 567	...	...	...	...	...	...
95 - 99	8 508	1 557	6 951	...	...	...	...	...	...
100 - 104	818	127	691	...	...	...	...	...	...
105 - 109	36	4	32	...	...	...	...	...	...
110 +	-	-	-	...	...	...	...	...	...
France									
1 I 2015 (CDJC)									
Total	64 300 821	31 138 550	33 162 271	49 781 175	23 891 441	25 889 734	14 519 646	7 247 109	7 272 537
0 - 4	3 779 312	1 932 140	1 847 172	2 943 961	1 505 149	1 438 812	835 351	426 991	408 360
5 - 9	3 974 070	2 031 848	1 942 222	3 018 642	1 542 952	1 475 690	955 429	488 896	466 533
10 - 14	3 958 786	2 024 518	1 934 267	2 993 243	1 530 322	1 462 921	965 543	494 196	471 346
15 - 19	3 889 075	1 996 718	1 892 357	3 107 020	1 586 257	1 520 763	782 055	410 461	371 594
20 - 24	3 716 644	1 877 169	1 839 475	3 186 247	1 592 313	1 593 934	530 397	284 856	245 541
25 - 29	3 816 224	1 882 618	1 933 606	3 154 967	1 554 787	1 600 180	661 257	327 831	333 426
30 - 34	3 991 417	1 960 633	2 030 784	3 154 039	1 548 166	1 605 872	837 378	412 467	424 911
35 - 39	3 988 088	1 973 599	2 014 489	3 082 418	1 523 069	1 559 349	905 670	450 530	455 140
40 - 44	4 341 471	2 155 883	2 185 588	3 298 789	1 626 585	1 672 204	1 042 682	529 298	513 384
45 - 49	4 361 803	2 155 308	2 206 495	3 307 842	1 613 857	1 693 985	1 053 962	541 451	512 510
50 - 54	4 307 213	2 111 783	2 195 431	3 264 358	1 577 384	1 686 973	1 042 856	534 398	508 457
55 - 59	4 113 250	1 992 506	2 120 744	3 093 196	1 474 501	1 618 695	1 020 054	518 005	502 049
60 - 64	3 990 376	1 912 839	2 077 537	2 969 500	1 393 394	1 576 105	1 020 877	519 445	501 432
65 - 69	3 605 489	1 713 389	1 892 099	2 700 040	1 255 492	1 444 548	905 449	457 897	447 551
70 - 74	2 458 426	1 138 687	1 319 739	1 879 526	854 092	1 025 434	578 900	284 595	294 305
75 - 79	2 167 384	938 443	1 228 941	1 657 310	703 262	954 049	510 074	235 181	274 893
80 - 84	1 865 044	731 105	1 133 939	1 432 760	549 227	883 533	432 284	181 878	250 406
85 - 89	1 249 877	420 854	829 023	963 811	315 642	648 168	286 066	105 212	180 855
90 - 94	589 014	161 109	427 905	462 115	123 242	338 872	126 899	37 866	89 033
95 - 99	114 657	23 412	91 245	92 480	18 509	73 971	22 177	4 903	17 274
100 +	23 202	3 989	19 212	18 913	3 237	15 676	4 289	752	3 536
1 VII 2018* (ESDJ)[83]									
Total	64 768 552	31 343 809	33 424 743	...	...	...	...	...	...
0 - 4	3 588 449	1 831 330	1 757 120	...	...	...	...	...	...
5 - 9	3 952 065	2 021 574	1 930 491	...	...	...	...	...	...
10 - 14	3 986 006	2 038 372	1 947 634	...	...	...	...	...	...
15 - 19	3 964 077	2 032 963	1 931 114	...	...	...	...	...	...
20 - 24	3 615 809	1 829 038	1 786 772	...	...	...	...	...	...
25 - 29	3 714 952	1 839 633	1 875 319	...	...	...	...	...	...
30 - 34	3 927 986	1 918 394	2 009 592	...	...	...	...	...	...
35 - 39	4 098 094	2 006 607	2 091 488	...	...	...	...	...	...
40 - 44	4 020 158	1 989 736	2 030 422	...	...	...	...	...	...
45 - 49	4 406 984	2 182 420	2 224 564	...	...	...	...	...	...
50 - 54	4 339 114	2 132 289	2 206 825	...	...	...	...	...	...
55 - 59	4 186 282	2 030 963	2 155 319	...	...	...	...	...	...
60 - 64	3 963 968	1 890 955	2 073 013	...	...	...	...	...	...
65 - 69	3 847 700	1 816 359	2 031 341	...	...	...	...	...	...
70 - 74	3 088 685	1 431 432	1 657 254	...	...	...	...	...	...
75 - 79	2 115 333	937 679	1 177 655	...	...	...	...	...	...

Continent, country or area, date, code[a] and age (in years) / Continent, pays ou zone, date, code[a] et âge (en années)	Total			Urban - Urbaine			Rural - Rurale		
	Both sexes Les deux sexes	Male Masculin	Female Féminin	Both sexes Les deux sexes	Male Masculin	Female Féminin	Both sexes Les deux sexes	Male Masculin	Female Féminin
EUROPE									
France									
1 VII 2018* (ESDJ)[83]									
80 - 84	1 827 475	738 754	1 088 721	...	...	...	...	...	...
85 - 89	1 313 063	458 742	854 321	...	...	...	...	...	...
90 - 94	625 146	176 930	448 217	...	...	...	...	...	...
95 +	187 212	39 646	147 567	...	...	...	...	...	...
Germany - Allemagne									
9 V 2011 (CDJC)									
Total	80 219 695	39 145 941	41 073 754	64 444 232	31 227 832	33 216 400	15 775 463	7 918 109	7 857 354
0 - 4	3 338 895	1 714 872	1 624 023	2 712 601	1 393 763	1 318 838	626 294	321 109	305 185
5 - 9	3 525 830	1 809 024	1 716 806	2 798 622	1 435 745	1 362 877	727 208	373 279	353 929
10 - 14	3 940 566	2 021 305	1 919 261	3 074 610	1 575 684	1 498 926	865 956	445 621	420 335
15 - 19	4 013 880	2 057 155	1 956 725	3 144 832	1 606 068	1 538 764	869 048	451 087	417 961
20 - 24	4 835 639	2 463 932	2 371 707	3 993 247	2 003 582	1 989 665	842 392	460 350	382 042
25 - 29	4 872 533	2 455 885	2 416 648	4 113 697	2 057 507	2 056 190	758 836	398 378	360 458
30 - 34	4 751 911	2 385 305	2 366 606	3 942 747	1 977 628	1 965 119	809 164	407 677	401 487
35 - 39	4 742 893	2 378 055	2 364 838	3 833 417	1 920 448	1 912 969	909 476	457 607	451 869
40 - 44	6 351 189	3 209 481	3 141 708	5 029 918	2 540 433	2 489 485	1 321 271	669 048	652 223
45 - 49	6 999 679	3 547 254	3 452 425	5 488 622	2 771 239	2 717 383	1 511 057	776 015	735 042
50 - 54	6 206 294	3 113 463	3 092 831	4 845 747	2 413 038	2 432 709	1 360 547	700 425	660 122
55 - 59	5 419 450	2 668 976	2 750 474	4 252 008	2 066 178	2 185 830	1 167 442	602 798	564 644
60 - 64	4 702 815	2 298 903	2 403 912	3 753 504	1 808 314	1 945 190	949 311	490 589	458 722
65 - 69	4 173 351	1 999 287	2 174 064	3 423 376	1 624 839	1 798 537	749 975	374 448	375 527
70 - 74	4 861 239	2 247 196	2 614 043	3 931 373	1 801 914	2 129 459	929 866	445 282	484 584
75 - 79	3 270 283	1 413 881	1 856 402	2 633 648	1 128 379	1 505 269	636 635	285 502	351 133
80 - 84	2 328 083	878 797	1 449 286	1 890 025	704 565	1 185 460	438 058	174 232	263 826
85 - 89	1 335 076	369 029	966 047	1 108 944	302 059	806 885	226 132	66 970	159 162
90 - 94	430 600	95 074	335 526	368 116	79 884	288 232	62 484	15 190	47 294
95 - 99	106 044	17 388	88 656	93 152	15 094	78 058	12 892	2 294	10 598
100 +	13 445	1 679	11 766	12 026	1 471	10 555	1 419	208	1 211
1 I 2018 (ESDJ)[4]									
Total	82 792 351	40 843 565	41 948 786	...	...	...	...	...	...
0	785 074	402 569	382 505	...	...	...	...	...	...
1 - 4	3 061 704	1 571 649	1 490 055	...	...	...	...	...	...
5 - 9	3 642 216	1 871 418	1 770 798	...	...	...	...	...	...
10 - 14	3 682 765	1 895 259	1 787 506	...	...	...	...	...	...
15 - 19	4 080 567	2 131 312	1 949 255	...	...	...	...	...	...
20 - 24	4 602 514	2 413 076	2 189 438	...	...	...	...	...	...
25 - 29	5 298 080	2 749 822	2 548 258	...	...	...	...	...	...
30 - 34	5 290 252	2 716 697	2 573 555	...	...	...	...	...	...
35 - 39	5 163 210	2 612 793	2 550 417	...	...	...	...	...	...
40 - 44	4 788 357	2 411 226	2 377 131	...	...	...	...	...	...
45 - 49	5 943 287	2 999 227	2 944 060	...	...	...	...	...	...
50 - 54	6 968 045	3 517 989	3 450 056	...	...	...	...	...	...
55 - 59	6 401 516	3 196 294	3 205 222	...	...	...	...	...	...
60 - 64	5 375 053	2 627 990	2 747 063	...	...	...	...	...	...
65 - 69	4 711 694	2 252 151	2 459 543	...	...	...	...	...	...
70 - 74	3 611 909	1 684 492	1 927 417	...	...	...	...	...	...
75 - 79	4 235 423	1 884 435	2 350 988	...	...	...	...	...	...
80 - 84	2 885 211	1 186 669	1 698 542	...	...	...	...	...	...
85 - 89	1 495 440	527 220	968 220	...	...	...	...	...	...
90 - 94	617 295	162 714	454 581	...	...	...	...	...	...
95 - 99	138 545	26 156	112 389	...	...	...	...	...	...
100 - 104	12 042	1 955	10 087	...	...	...	...	...	...
105 - 109	1 859	344	1 515	...	...	...	...	...	...
110 +	293	108	185	...	...	...	...	...	...
Gibraltar[84]									
12 XI 2012 (CDJC)									
Total	32 194	16 061	16 133	...	...	...	...	...	...
0 - 4	1 952	982	970	...	...	...	...	...	...
5 - 9	1 894	967	927	...	...	...	...	...	...
10 - 14	1 987	1 050	937	...	...	...	...	...	...
15 - 19	1 997	1 038	959	...	...	...	...	...	...
20 - 24	2 028	1 042	986	...	...	...	...	...	...
25 - 29	1 985	999	986	...	...	...	...	...	...

7. Population by age, sex and urban/rural residence: latest available year, 2009 - 2018
Population selon l'âge, le sexe et la résidence, urbaine/rurale : dernière année disponible, 2009 - 2018 (continued - suite)

Continent, country or area, date, code[a] and age (in years) / Continent, pays ou zone, date, code[a] et âge (en années)	Total			Urban - Urbaine			Rural - Rurale		
	Both sexes Les deux sexes	Male Masculin	Female Féminin	Both sexes Les deux sexes	Male Masculin	Female Féminin	Both sexes Les deux sexes	Male Masculin	Female Féminin
EUROPE									
Gibraltar[84]									
12 XI 2012 (CDJC)									
30 - 34	2 154	1 107	1 047						
35 - 39	2 217	1 080	1 137	...	...	...	...	...	...
40 - 44	2 198	1 076	1 122	...	...	...	...	...	...
45 - 49	2 384	1 203	1 181	...	...	...	...	...	...
50 - 54	2 158	1 072	1 086	...	...	...	...	...	...
55 - 59	2 041	1 054	987	...	...	...	...	...	...
60 - 64	1 954	1 034	920	...	...	...	...	...	...
65 - 69	1 655	853	802	...	...	...	...	...	...
70 - 74	1 176	563	613	...	...	...	...	...	...
75 - 79	1 021	456	565	...	...	...	...	...	...
80 - 84	732	297	435	...	...	...	...	...	...
85 - 89	437	141	296	...	...	...	...	...	...
90 - 94	180	37	143	...	...	...	...	...	...
95 - 99	39	10	29	...	...	...	...	...	...
100 +	5	-	5	...	...	...	...	...	...
Greece - Grèce									
9 V 2011 (CDFC)									
Total	10 816 286	5 303 223	5 513 063	8 285 259	4 022 889	4 262 370	2 531 027	1 280 334	1 250 693
0 - 4	537 243	274 788	262 455	431 611	220 917	210 694	105 632	53 871	51 761
5 - 9	512 596	262 432	250 164	405 436	207 479	197 957	107 160	54 953	52 207
10 - 14	519 429	265 787	253 642	406 962	208 070	198 892	112 467	57 717	54 750
15 - 19	553 276	286 386	266 890	440 869	226 682	214 187	112 407	59 704	52 703
20 - 24	627 097	325 127	301 970	510 067	259 795	250 272	117 030	65 332	51 698
25 - 29	723 771	371 617	352 154	583 506	295 880	287 626	140 265	75 737	64 528
30 - 34	822 475	417 861	404 614	666 145	334 794	331 351	156 330	83 067	73 263
35 - 39	812 829	409 681	403 148	651 826	323 821	328 005	161 003	85 860	75 143
40 - 44	832 666	414 026	418 640	663 331	323 632	339 699	169 335	90 394	78 941
45 - 49	748 429	367 086	381 343	590 034	283 391	306 643	158 395	83 695	74 700
50 - 54	731 486	355 552	375 934	565 986	268 882	297 104	165 500	86 670	78 830
55 - 59	660 368	321 466	338 902	501 507	240 725	260 782	158 861	80 741	78 120
60 - 64	625 769	301 589	324 180	459 249	219 165	240 084	166 520	82 424	84 096
65 - 69	508 276	241 832	266 444	356 701	167 557	189 144	151 575	74 275	77 300
70 - 74	542 165	246 264	295 901	363 133	162 560	200 573	179 032	83 704	95 328
75 - 79	475 077	209 983	265 094	309 622	134 691	174 931	165 455	75 292	90 163
80 - 84	352 373	146 455	205 918	229 214	91 916	137 298	123 159	54 539	68 620
85 - 89	159 841	60 933	98 908	104 058	37 922	66 136	55 783	23 011	32 772
90 - 94	53 445	18 760	34 685	34 608	11 513	23 095	18 837	7 247	11 590
95 - 99	15 187	4 948	10 239	9 822	3 081	6 741	5 365	1 867	3 498
100 +	2 488	650	1 838	1 572	416	1 156	916	234	682
1 I 2018 (ESDF)									
Total	10 741 165	5 210 040	5 531 125	...	...	...	...	...	...
0	89 570	46 067	43 503	...	...	...	...	...	...
1 - 4	380 720	195 573	185 147	...	...	...	...	...	...
5 - 9	541 885	277 694	264 191	...	...	...	...	...	...
10 - 14	534 492	274 869	259 623	...	...	...	...	...	...
15 - 19	541 581	279 124	262 457	...	...	...	...	...	...
20 - 24	547 434	281 582	265 852	...	...	...	...	...	...
25 - 29	583 759	294 716	289 043	...	...	...	...	...	...
30 - 34	632 976	316 745	316 231	...	...	...	...	...	...
35 - 39	785 829	392 610	393 219	...	...	...	...	...	...
40 - 44	802 440	397 112	405 328	...	...	...	...	...	...
45 - 49	816 889	397 859	419 030	...	...	...	...	...	...
50 - 54	764 422	366 681	397 741	...	...	...	...	...	...
55 - 59	719 441	338 999	380 442	...	...	...	...	...	...
60 - 64	659 565	311 872	347 693	...	...	...	...	...	...
65 - 69	608 739	286 552	322 187	...	...	...	...	...	...
70 - 74	539 234	248 313	290 921	...	...	...	...	...	...
75 - 79	451 318	199 271	252 047	...	...	...	...	...	...
80 - 84	391 088	162 958	228 130	...	...	...	...	...	...
85 - 89	232 766	95 309	137 457	...	...	...	...	...	...
90 - 94	87 427	33 999	53 428	...	...	...	...	...	...
95 - 99	21 319	9 047	12 272	...	...	...	...	...	...
100 +	8 271	3 088	5 183	...	...	...	...	...	...

Continent, country or area, date, code[a] and age (in years) / Continent, pays ou zone, date, code[a] et âge (en annèes)	Total			Urban - Urbaine			Rural - Rurale		
	Both sexes Les deux sexes	Male Masculin	Female Féminin	Both sexes Les deux sexes	Male Masculin	Female Féminin	Both sexes Les deux sexes	Male Masculin	Female Féminin
EUROPE									
Guernsey - Guernesey									
31 III 2018 (ESDJ)									
Total	62 307	30 858	31 449	...	...	...	...	...	...
0	547	275	272	...	...	...	...	...	...
1 - 4	2 414	1 241	1 173	...	...	...	...	...	...
5 - 9	3 304	1 706	1 598	...	...	...	...	...	...
10 - 14	3 114	1 629	1 485	...	...	...	...	...	...
15 - 19	3 260	1 692	1 568	...	...	...	...	...	...
20 - 24	3 646	1 872	1 774	...	...	...	...	...	...
25 - 29	3 986	2 038	1 948	...	...	...	...	...	...
30 - 34	3 798	1 951	1 847	...	...	...	...	...	...
35 - 39	3 852	1 983	1 869	...	...	...	...	...	...
40 - 44	3 857	1 878	1 979	...	...	...	...	...	...
45 - 49	4 771	2 349	2 422	...	...	...	...	...	...
50 - 54	4 948	2 381	2 567	...	...	...	...	...	...
55 - 59	4 673	2 311	2 362	...	...	...	...	...	...
60 - 64	3 848	1 949	1 899	...	...	...	...	...	...
65 - 69	3 575	1 716	1 859	...	...	...	...	...	...
70 - 74	3 228	1 568	1 660	...	...	...	...	...	...
75 - 79	2 128	1 005	1 123	...	...	...	...	...	...
80 - 84	1 704	745	959	...	...	...	...	...	...
85 - 89	1 044	394	650	...	...	...	...	...	...
90 - 94	471	147	324	...	...	...	...	...	...
95 - 99	123	27	96	...	...	...	...	...	...
100 +	16	1	15	...	...	...	...	...	...
Hungary - Hongrie									
1 VII 2017 (ESDJ)[85]									
Total	9 787 966	4 673 447	5 114 520	6 896 039	3 252 609	3 643 431	2 891 927	1 420 838	1 471 089
0	94 472	48 486	45 986	65 495	33 586	31 909	28 978	14 900	14 078
1 - 4	369 076	189 635	179 441	261 601	134 646	126 955	107 475	54 989	52 486
5 - 9	471 587	241 798	229 789	331 449	169 878	161 571	140 138	71 920	68 218
10 - 14	487 256	250 255	237 001	330 116	169 516	160 601	157 140	80 740	76 401
15 - 19	491 205	252 622	238 583	335 852	171 419	164 433	155 353	81 203	74 150
20 - 24	587 671	302 152	285 520	403 344	205 586	197 758	184 327	96 566	87 762
25 - 29	623 050	321 742	301 308	438 331	223 406	214 925	184 719	98 336	86 383
30 - 34	608 560	310 916	297 645	437 747	220 600	217 148	170 813	90 316	80 497
35 - 39	735 917	371 888	364 030	534 518	266 279	268 240	201 399	105 609	95 790
40 - 44	830 575	420 306	410 270	597 106	298 432	298 675	233 469	121 874	111 595
45 - 49	713 629	358 147	355 483	500 572	247 919	252 653	213 057	110 228	102 830
50 - 54	600 261	295 262	304 999	410 746	198 472	212 275	189 515	96 791	92 724
55 - 59	607 975	286 977	320 999	412 077	189 447	222 630	195 898	97 530	98 369
60 - 64	726 638	328 890	397 749	510 846	224 899	285 947	215 792	103 991	111 802
65 - 69	600 223	257 318	342 906	428 152	179 746	248 407	172 071	77 572	94 499
70 - 74	460 123	185 161	274 962	336 413	134 655	201 759	123 710	50 507	73 204
75 - 79	353 142	126 613	226 529	253 284	91 841	161 444	99 858	34 772	65 086
80 - 84	234 708	73 653	161 055	167 601	53 727	113 874	67 108	19 926	47 182
85 - 89	131 698	37 194	94 504	96 166	27 813	68 353	35 533	9 382	26 151
90 - 94	47 907	11 469	36 438	35 531	8 569	26 963	12 376	2 900	9 476
95 - 99	10 668	2 443	8 225	7 903	1 792	6 111	2 766	651	2 115
100 +	1 628	525	1 103	1 192	386	807	436	139	297
1 I 2018 (ESDJ)									
Total	9 778 371	4 671 602	5 106 769	...	...	...	...	...	...
0	94 086	48 272	45 814	...	...	...	...	...	...
1 - 4	371 270	190 636	180 634	...	...	...	...	...	...
5 - 9	468 472	240 436	228 036	...	...	...	...	...	...
10 - 14	488 088	250 647	237 441	...	...	...	...	...	...
15 - 19	489 340	251 512	237 828	...	...	...	...	...	...
20 - 24	578 682	297 716	280 966	...	...	...	...	...	...
25 - 29	625 537	323 196	302 341	...	...	...	...	...	...
30 - 34	606 811	310 577	296 234	...	...	...	...	...	...
35 - 39	716 695	362 588	354 107	...	...	...	...	...	...
40 - 44	841 842	426 192	415 650	...	...	...	...	...	...
45 - 49	716 419	359 950	356 469	...	...	...	...	...	...
50 - 54	611 378	301 229	310 149	...	...	...	...	...	...
55 - 59	595 884	281 779	314 105	...	...	...	...	...	...

7. Population by age, sex and urban/rural residence: latest available year, 2009 - 2018
Population selon l'âge, le sexe et la résidence, urbaine/rurale : dernière année disponible, 2009 - 2018 (continued - suite)

Continent, country or area, date, code[a] and age (in years) / Continent, pays ou zone, date, code[a] et âge (en années)	Total Both sexes Les deux sexes	Total Male Masculin	Total Female Féminin	Urban - Urbaine Both sexes Les deux sexes	Urban - Urbaine Male Masculin	Urban - Urbaine Female Féminin	Rural - Rurale Both sexes Les deux sexes	Rural - Rurale Male Masculin	Rural - Rurale Female Féminin
EUROPE									
Hungary - Hongrie									
1 I 2018 (ESDJ)									
60 - 64	721 902	327 001	394 901	...	...	...	...	...	...
65 - 69	602 578	258 224	344 354	...	...	...	...	...	...
70 - 74	463 073	186 801	276 272	...	...	...	...	...	...
75 - 79	358 383	129 257	229 126	...	...	...	...	...	...
80 - 84	234 296	73 400	160 896	...	...	...	...	...	...
85 - 89	132 701	37 571	95 130	...	...	...	...	...	...
90 - 94	47 854	11 504	36 350	...	...	...	...	...	...
95 - 99	11 405	2 569	8 836	...	...	...	...	...	...
100 - 104	1 295	371	924	...	...	...	...	...	...
105 - 109	334	139	195	...	...	...	...	...	...
110 +	46	35	11	...	...	...	...	...	...
Iceland - Islande									
1 VII 2017 (ESDJ)[86]									
Total	343 400	174 317	169 083	321 288	162 440	158 848	22 112	11 877	10 235
0	4 071	2 087	1 984	3 864	1 971	1 893	207	116	91
1 - 4	17 314	8 768	8 546	16 429	8 339	8 090	885	429	456
5 - 9	23 721	12 198	11 523	22 552	11 573	10 980	1 169	626	543
10 - 14	22 007	11 230	10 777	20 775	10 603	10 173	1 232	628	604
15 - 19	21 934	11 112	10 823	20 513	10 384	10 129	1 421	728	694
20 - 24	25 454	13 170	12 284	23 714	12 310	11 404	1 740	860	880
25 - 29	26 816	14 190	12 627	25 046	13 193	11 853	1 770	997	774
30 - 34	23 951	12 558	11 393	22 658	11 819	10 839	1 293	739	555
35 - 39	23 887	12 418	11 469	22 680	11 760	10 920	1 207	658	549
40 - 44	22 460	11 582	10 878	21 242	10 919	10 323	1 218	663	555
45 - 49	21 075	10 753	10 322	19 702	10 003	9 700	1 373	750	623
50 - 54	22 152	11 016	11 137	20 470	10 126	10 344	1 682	890	793
55 - 59	21 346	10 761	10 585	19 634	9 821	9 813	1 712	940	772
60 - 64	19 004	9 586	9 419	17 477	8 726	8 751	1 528	860	668
65 - 69	15 797	7 973	7 824	14 573	7 311	7 263	1 224	663	562
70 - 74	12 070	5 998	6 072	11 116	5 457	5 660	954	542	413
75 - 79	8 019	3 825	4 195	7 404	3 488	3 916	616	337	279
80 - 84	6 105	2 737	3 369	5 647	2 498	3 149	459	239	220
85 - 89	4 152	1 694	2 459	3 859	1 540	2 319	294	154	140
90 - 94	1 665	552	1 113	1 570	508	1 062	96	45	51
95 - 99	362	102	261	328	83	245	35	19	16
100 +	42	14	29	39	13	27	3	1	2
1 I 2018 (ESDJ)									
Total	348 450	177 600	170 850	...	...	...	...	...	...
0	4 093	2 121	1 972	...	...	...	...	...	...
1 - 4	17 179	8 698	8 481	...	...	...	...	...	...
5 - 9	23 835	12 250	11 585	...	...	...	...	...	...
10 - 14	22 300	11 404	10 896	...	...	...	...	...	...
15 - 19	21 925	11 089	10 836	...	...	...	...	...	...
20 - 24	25 721	13 331	12 390	...	...	...	...	...	...
25 - 29	27 931	14 884	13 047	...	...	...	...	...	...
30 - 34	24 560	13 006	11 554	...	...	...	...	...	...
35 - 39	24 595	12 930	11 665	...	...	...	...	...	...
40 - 44	22 622	11 747	10 875	...	...	...	...	...	...
45 - 49	21 602	11 119	10 483	...	...	...	...	...	...
50 - 54	22 221	11 076	11 145	...	...	...	...	...	...
55 - 59	21 532	10 852	10 680	...	...	...	...	...	...
60 - 64	19 351	9 769	9 582	...	...	...	...	...	...
65 - 69	16 027	8 081	7 946	...	...	...	...	...	...
70 - 74	12 366	6 170	6 196	...	...	...	...	...	...
75 - 79	8 209	3 914	4 295	...	...	...	...	...	...
80 - 84	6 086	2 740	3 346	...	...	...	...	...	...
85 - 89	4 188	1 726	2 462	...	...	...	...	...	...
90 - 94	1 694	571	1 123	...	...	...	...	...	...
95 - 99	368	109	259	...	...	...	...	...	...
100 - 104	42	13	29	...	...	...	...	...	...
105 - 109	3	-	3	...	...	...	...	...	...
110 +	-	-	-	...	...	...	...	...	...

Continent, country or area, date, code[a] and age (in years) / Continent, pays ou zone, date, code[a] et âge (en années)	Total			Urban - Urbaine			Rural - Rurale		
	Both sexes Les deux sexes	Male Masculin	Female Féminin	Both sexes Les deux sexes	Male Masculin	Female Féminin	Both sexes Les deux sexes	Male Masculin	Female Féminin
EUROPE									
Ireland - Irlande									
10 IV 2011 (CDFC)									
Total	4 588 252	2 272 699	2 315 553	2 846 882	1 389 160	1 457 722	1 741 370	883 539	857 831
0 - 4	356 329	182 076	174 253	224 004	114 284	109 720	132 325	67 792	64 533
5 - 9	320 770	164 037	156 733	188 818	96 160	92 658	131 952	67 877	64 075
10 - 14	302 491	155 076	147 415	172 930	88 433	84 497	129 561	66 643	62 918
15 - 19	283 019	144 262	138 757	170 523	86 129	84 394	112 496	58 133	54 363
20 - 24	297 231	146 636	150 595	208 146	100 226	107 920	89 085	46 410	42 675
25 - 29	361 122	173 714	187 408	266 457	126 362	140 095	94 665	47 352	47 313
30 - 34	393 945	194 774	199 171	278 935	137 689	141 246	115 010	57 085	57 925
35 - 39	364 261	182 237	182 024	233 417	116 912	116 505	130 844	65 325	65 519
40 - 44	330 812	166 330	164 482	198 432	99 162	99 270	132 380	67 168	65 212
45 - 49	305 185	151 516	153 669	178 630	87 087	91 543	126 555	64 429	62 126
50 - 54	274 386	136 737	137 649	158 031	77 106	80 925	116 355	59 631	56 724
55 - 59	244 522	122 121	122 401	137 973	66 919	71 054	106 549	55 202	51 347
60 - 64	218 786	109 869	108 917	122 606	59 521	63 085	96 180	50 348	45 832
65 - 69	173 638	86 298	87 340	97 999	46 741	51 258	75 639	39 557	36 082
70 - 74	131 190	63 476	67 714	76 683	35 378	41 305	54 507	28 098	26 409
75 - 79	102 036	46 631	55 405	59 519	25 708	33 811	42 517	20 923	21 594
80 - 84	70 113	28 423	41 690	40 585	15 449	25 136	29 528	12 974	16 554
85 - 89	39 887	13 591	26 296	22 742	7 303	15 439	17 145	6 288	10 857
90 - 94	14 877	4 155	10 722	8 363	2 200	6 163	6 514	1 955	4 559
95 - 99	3 263	682	2 581	1 884	360	1 524	1 379	322	1 057
100 +	389	58	331	205	31	174	184	27	157
1 I 2018 (ESDF)[85]									
Total	4 830 392	2 392 223	2 438 169	...	...	...	...	...	...
0	62 179	31 890	30 289	...	...	...	...	...	...
1 - 4	257 689	131 868	125 821	...	...	...	...	...	...
5 - 9	357 069	182 116	174 953	...	...	...	...	...	...
10 - 14	329 511	168 916	160 595	...	...	...	...	...	...
15 - 19	313 291	159 558	153 733	...	...	...	...	...	...
20 - 24	285 136	145 176	139 960	...	...	...	...	...	...
25 - 29	289 887	144 229	145 658	...	...	...	...	...	...
30 - 34	337 951	161 910	176 041	...	...	...	...	...	...
35 - 39	395 840	192 309	203 531	...	...	...	...	...	...
40 - 44	367 138	181 935	185 203	...	...	...	...	...	...
45 - 49	338 570	169 000	169 570	...	...	...	...	...	...
50 - 54	305 197	151 211	153 986	...	...	...	...	...	...
55 - 59	277 508	137 528	139 980	...	...	...	...	...	...
60 - 64	244 778	121 490	123 288	...	...	...	...	...	...
65 - 69	214 718	106 432	108 286	...	...	...	...	...	...
70 - 74	175 461	86 211	89 250	...	...	...	...	...	...
75 - 79	120 484	57 023	63 461	...	...	...	...	...	...
80 - 84	84 888	37 339	47 549	...	...	...	...	...	...
85 - 89	47 785	18 567	29 218	...	...	...	...	...	...
90 - 94	18 908	5 910	12 998	...	...	...	...	...	...
95 - 99	5 572	1 420	4 152	...	...	...	...	...	...
100 - 104	767	174	593	...	...	...	...	...	...
105 - 109	64	11	53	...	...	...	...	...	...
110 +	1	-	1	...	...	...	...	...	...
Isle of Man - Île de Man									
24 IV 2016 (CDJC)									
Total	83 314	41 269	42 045	...	...	...	...	...	...
0 - 4	4 144	2 186	1 958	...	...	...	...	...	...
5 - 9	4 733	2 436	2 297	...	...	...	...	...	...
10 - 14	4 469	2 346	2 123	...	...	...	...	...	...
15 - 19	4 789	2 506	2 283	...	...	...	...	...	...
20 - 24	4 422	2 252	2 170	...	...	...	...	...	...
25 - 29	4 326	2 131	2 195	...	...	...	...	...	...
30 - 34	4 506	2 148	2 358	...	...	...	...	...	...
35 - 39	4 873	2 371	2 502	...	...	...	...	...	...
40 - 44	5 612	2 715	2 897	...	...	...	...	...	...
45 - 49	6 497	3 255	3 242	...	...	...	...	...	...
50 - 54	6 681	3 359	3 322	...	...	...	...	...	...
55 - 59	5 887	2 889	2 998	...	...	...	...	...	...

7. Population by age, sex and urban/rural residence: latest available year, 2009 - 2018
Population selon l'âge, le sexe et la résidence, urbaine/rurale : dernière année disponible, 2009 - 2018 (continued - suite)

Continent, country or area, date, code[a] and age (in years) Continent, pays ou zone, date, code[a] et âge (en années)	Total			Urban - Urbaine			Rural - Rurale		
	Both sexes Les deux sexes	Male Masculin	Female Féminin	Both sexes Les deux sexes	Male Masculin	Female Féminin	Both sexes Les deux sexes	Male Masculin	Female Féminin
EUROPE									
Isle of Man - Île de Man									
24 IV 2016 (CDJC)									
60 - 64	5 170	2 612	2 558	...	...	...	...	...	...
65 - 69	5 441	2 715	2 726	...	...	...	...	...	...
70 - 74	4 212	2 074	2 138	...	...	...	...	...	...
75 - 79	3 155	1 529	1 626	...	...	...	...	...	...
80 - 84	2 129	958	1 171	...	...	...	...	...	...
85 - 89	1 380	522	858	...	...	...	...	...	...
90 - 94	675	202	473	...	...	...	...	...	...
95 - 99	188	53	135	...	...	...	...	...	...
100 +	25	10	15	...	...	...	...	...	...
Italy - Italie									
1 I 2018 (ESDJ)									
Total	60 483 973	29 427 607	31 056 366	...	...	...	...	...	...
0	456 192	234 739	221 453	...	...	...	...	...	...
1 - 4	1 975 467	1 015 180	960 287	...	...	...	...	...	...
5 - 9	2 783 704	1 432 161	1 351 543	...	...	...	...	...	...
10 - 14	2 864 813	1 475 522	1 389 291	...	...	...	...	...	...
15 - 19	2 898 079	1 504 897	1 393 182	...	...	...	...	...	...
20 - 24	2 986 520	1 557 238	1 429 282	...	...	...	...	...	...
25 - 29	3 248 924	1 661 411	1 587 513	...	...	...	...	...	...
30 - 34	3 394 701	1 712 078	1 682 623	...	...	...	...	...	...
35 - 39	3 813 383	1 911 532	1 901 851	...	...	...	...	...	...
40 - 44	4 559 730	2 272 240	2 287 490	...	...	...	...	...	...
45 - 49	4 867 528	2 410 831	2 456 697	...	...	...	...	...	...
50 - 54	4 913 444	2 418 760	2 494 684	...	...	...	...	...	...
55 - 59	4 299 302	2 088 029	2 211 273	...	...	...	...	...	...
60 - 64	3 777 823	1 817 151	1 960 672	...	...	...	...	...	...
65 - 69	3 557 141	1 694 005	1 863 136	...	...	...	...	...	...
70 - 74	3 099 710	1 445 309	1 654 401	...	...	...	...	...	...
75 - 79	2 780 512	1 235 415	1 545 097	...	...	...	...	...	...
80 - 84	2 108 835	864 324	1 244 511	...	...	...	...	...	...
85 - 89	1 352 274	477 962	874 312	...	...	...	...	...	...
90 - 94	589 247	165 598	423 649	...	...	...	...	...	...
95 - 99	140 997	30 668	110 329	...	...	...	...	...	...
100 - 104	14 585	2 422	12 163	...	...	...	...	...	...
105 - 109	1 045	132	913	...	...	...	...	...	...
110 +	17	3	14	...	...	...	...	...	...
Jersey									
1 I 2018 (ESDJ)									
Total	106 800	53 061	53 739	...	...	...	...	...	...
0 - 4	5 405	2 712	2 693	...	...	...	...	...	...
5 - 9	5 861	2 946	2 915	...	...	...	...	...	...
10 - 14	5 742	2 861	2 881	...	...	...	...	...	...
15 - 19	5 717	2 923	2 794	...	...	...	...	...	...
20 - 24	6 133	3 144	2 989	...	...	...	...	...	...
25 - 29	6 942	3 464	3 478	...	...	...	...	...	...
30 - 34	7 267	3 741	3 526	...	...	...	...	...	...
35 - 39	7 749	3 929	3 820	...	...	...	...	...	...
40 - 44	7 523	3 849	3 674	...	...	...	...	...	...
45 - 49	7 915	3 995	3 920	...	...	...	...	...	...
50 - 54	8 586	4 317	4 269	...	...	...	...	...	...
55 - 59	7 559	3 766	3 793	...	...	...	...	...	...
60 - 64	6 340	3 093	3 247	...	...	...	...	...	...
65 - 69	5 363	2 619	2 744	...	...	...	...	...	...
70 - 74	4 623	2 222	2 401	...	...	...	...	...	...
75 - 79	3 161	1 465	1 696	...	...	...	...	...	...
80 - 84	2 537	1 147	1 390	...	...	...	...	...	...
85 - 89	1 491	585	906	...	...	...	...	...	...
Latvia - Lettonie									
1 I 2018 (ESDJ)									
Total	1 934 379	889 641	1 044 738	1 324 704	591 954	732 750	609 675	297 687	311 988
0	20 660	10 719	9 941	14 485	7 559	6 926	6 175	3 160	3 015
1 - 4	87 065	45 079	41 986	60 354	31 258	29 096	26 711	13 821	12 890
5 - 9	99 799	51 395	48 404	68 340	35 239	33 101	31 459	16 156	15 303

261

Continent, country or area, date, code[a] and age (in years) / Continent, pays ou zone, date, code[a] et âge (en années)	Total			Urban - Urbaine			Rural - Rurale		
	Both sexes Les deux sexes	Male Masculin	Female Féminin	Both sexes Les deux sexes	Male Masculin	Female Féminin	Both sexes Les deux sexes	Male Masculin	Female Féminin
EUROPE									
Latvia - Lettonie									
1 I 2018 (ESDJ)									
10 - 14	97 767	50 173	47 594	65 277	33 373	31 904	32 490	16 800	15 690
15 - 19	86 834	44 343	42 491	56 385	28 524	27 861	30 449	15 819	14 630
20 - 24	92 989	48 018	44 971	59 814	30 383	29 431	33 175	17 635	15 540
25 - 29	131 714	67 891	63 823	89 462	44 635	44 827	42 252	23 256	18 996
30 - 34	139 806	71 537	68 269	99 546	49 523	50 023	40 260	22 014	18 246
35 - 39	125 015	62 924	62 091	88 663	43 568	45 095	36 352	19 356	16 996
40 - 44	128 938	63 491	65 447	89 040	42 715	46 325	39 898	20 776	19 122
45 - 49	133 208	64 411	68 797	89 833	42 067	47 766	43 375	22 344	21 031
50 - 54	131 885	62 193	69 692	87 224	39 459	47 765	44 661	22 734	21 927
55 - 59	143 946	65 401	78 545	96 488	41 598	54 890	47 458	23 803	23 655
60 - 64	125 897	54 198	71 699	87 306	35 552	51 754	38 591	18 646	19 945
65 - 69	111 555	44 025	67 530	78 723	29 289	49 434	32 832	14 736	18 096
70 - 74	84 730	30 195	54 535	58 988	20 179	38 809	25 742	10 016	15 726
75 - 79	88 289	27 829	60 460	61 326	18 845	42 481	26 963	8 984	17 979
80 - 84	58 111	15 902	42 209	40 593	11 012	29 581	17 518	4 890	12 628
85 - 89	32 717	7 653	25 064	23 175	5 449	17 726	9 542	2 204	7 338
90 - 94	11 548	1 991	9 557	8 328	1 520	6 808	3 220	471	2 749
95 - 99	1 769	251	1 518	1 259	191	1 068	510	60	450
100 +	137	22	115	95	16	79	42	6	36
105 - 109	12	-	12	...	...	...	...	...	...
110 +	-	-	-	...	...	...	...	...	...
Liechtenstein									
1 I 2018 (ESDJ)									
Total	38 114	18 890	19 224	...	...	...	...	...	...
0	341	175	166	...	...	...	...	...	...
1 - 4	1 471	797	674	...	...	...	...	...	...
5 - 9	1 891	1 003	888	...	...	...	...	...	...
10 - 14	1 898	968	930	...	...	...	...	...	...
15 - 19	2 036	1 008	1 028	...	...	...	...	...	...
20 - 24	2 262	1 156	1 106	...	...	...	...	...	...
25 - 29	2 284	1 176	1 108	...	...	...	...	...	...
30 - 34	2 341	1 120	1 221	...	...	...	...	...	...
35 - 39	2 492	1 266	1 226	...	...	...	...	...	...
40 - 44	2 650	1 325	1 325	...	...	...	...	...	...
45 - 49	3 126	1 555	1 571	...	...	...	...	...	...
50 - 54	3 196	1 558	1 638	...	...	...	...	...	...
55 - 59	2 986	1 480	1 506	...	...	...	...	...	...
60 - 64	2 475	1 237	1 238	...	...	...	...	...	...
65 - 69	2 165	1 063	1 102	...	...	...	...	...	...
70 - 74	1 799	896	903	...	...	...	...	...	...
75 - 79	1 290	576	714	...	...	...	...	...	...
80 - 84	782	329	453	...	...	...	...	...	...
85 - 89	398	146	252	...	...	...	...	...	...
90 - 94	187	45	142	...	...	...	...	...	...
95 - 99	41	10	31	...	...	...	...	...	...
100 - 104	2	-	2	...	...	...	...	...	...
105 - 109	1	1	-	...	...	...	...	...	...
110 +	-	-	-	...	...	...	...	...	...
Lithuania - Lituanie[85]									
1 VII 2017 (ESDJ)									
Total	2 828 403	1 304 740	1 523 663	1 897 895	848 512	1 049 383	930 508	456 228	474 280
0	29 584	15 273	14 311	20 563	10 633	9 930	9 021	4 640	4 381
1 - 4	120 151	61 576	58 575	83 417	42 831	40 586	36 734	18 745	17 989
5 - 9	143 249	73 539	69 710	99 207	50 887	48 320	44 042	22 652	21 390
10 - 14	128 795	65 887	62 908	83 004	42 527	40 477	45 791	23 360	22 431
15 - 19	148 376	76 378	71 998	91 429	46 758	44 671	56 947	29 620	27 327
20 - 24	174 177	89 369	84 808	108 233	54 592	53 641	65 944	34 777	31 167
25 - 29	191 062	98 882	92 180	132 946	65 022	67 924	58 116	33 860	24 256
30 - 34	181 094	92 555	88 539	136 217	66 620	69 597	44 877	25 935	18 942
35 - 39	165 930	83 296	82 634	118 551	58 049	60 502	47 379	25 247	22 132
40 - 44	182 717	88 936	93 781	123 277	58 348	64 929	59 440	30 588	28 852
45 - 49	202 985	97 258	105 727	131 254	60 616	70 638	71 731	36 642	35 089
50 - 54	209 587	98 901	110 686	134 912	60 288	74 624	74 675	38 613	36 062

7. Population by age, sex and urban/rural residence: latest available year, 2009 - 2018
Population selon l'âge, le sexe et la résidence, urbaine/rurale : dernière année disponible, 2009 - 2018 (continued - suite)

Continent, country or area, date, code[a] and age (in years) / Continent, pays ou zone, date, code[a] et âge (en années)	Total			Urban - Urbaine			Rural - Rurale		
	Both sexes Les deux sexes	Male Masculin	Female Féminin	Both sexes Les deux sexes	Male Masculin	Female Féminin	Both sexes Les deux sexes	Male Masculin	Female Féminin
EUROPE									
Lithuania - Lituanie[85]									
1 VII 2017 (ESDJ)									
55 - 59	223 914	101 800	122 114	148 899	63 816	85 083	75 015	37 984	37 031
60 - 64	175 784	75 612	100 172	118 722	48 074	70 648	57 062	27 538	29 524
65 - 69	153 180	60 687	92 493	103 847	38 666	65 181	49 333	22 021	27 312
70 - 74	121 822	43 738	78 084	81 283	27 889	53 394	40 539	15 849	24 690
75 - 79	118 786	38 969	79 817	78 984	25 307	53 677	39 802	13 662	26 140
80 - 84	88 216	25 477	62 739	57 149	16 403	40 746	31 067	9 074	21 993
85 - 89	49 702	12 815	36 887	32 525	8 577	23 948	17 177	4 238	12 939
90 - 94	16 457	3 292	13 165	11 246	2 259	8 987	5 211	1 033	4 178
95 - 99	2 559	431	2 128	1 977	295	1 682	582	136	446
100 +	276	69	207	253	55	198	23	14	9
1 I 2018 (ESDJ)									
Total	2 808 901	1 297 293	1 511 608	...	...	...	...	...	...
0	28 760	14 808	13 952	...	...	...	...	...	...
1 - 4	120 039	61 616	58 423	...	...	...	...	...	...
5 - 9	144 244	74 030	70 214	...	...	...	...	...	...
10 - 14	128 394	65 635	62 759	...	...	...	...	...	...
15 - 19	143 700	74 011	69 689	...	...	...	...	...	...
20 - 24	165 798	85 213	80 585	...	...	...	...	...	...
25 - 29	188 743	97 923	90 820	...	...	...	...	...	...
30 - 34	182 390	93 561	88 829	...	...	...	...	...	...
35 - 39	164 220	82 909	81 311	...	...	...	...	...	...
40 - 44	179 678	87 904	91 774	...	...	...	...	...	...
45 - 49	201 483	96 924	104 559	...	...	...	...	...	...
50 - 54	206 585	97 542	109 043	...	...	...	...	...	...
55 - 59	224 693	102 362	122 331	...	...	...	...	...	...
60 - 64	178 377	77 003	101 374	...	...	...	...	...	...
65 - 69	155 137	61 570	93 567	...	...	...	...	...	...
70 - 74	119 484	42 981	76 503	...	...	...	...	...	...
75 - 79	118 653	38 920	79 733	...	...	...	...	...	...
80 - 84	88 358	25 462	62 896	...	...	...	...	...	...
85 - 89	50 390	12 962	37 428	...	...	...	...	...	...
90 - 94	16 818	3 445	13 373	...	...	...	...	...	...
95 - 99	2 693	450	2 243	...	...	...	...	...	...
100 - 104	210	47	163	...	...	...	...	...	...
105 - 109	44	10	34	...	...	...	...	...	...
110 +	10	5	5	...	...	...	...	...	...
Luxembourg									
1 I 2018 (ESDJ)									
Total	602 005	302 580	299 425	...	...	...	...	...	...
0	6 163	3 162	3 001	...	...	...	...	...	...
1 - 4	26 094	13 332	12 762	...	...	...	...	...	...
5 - 9	32 784	16 861	15 923	...	...	...	...	...	...
10 - 14	32 081	16 570	15 511	...	...	...	...	...	...
15 - 19	33 113	16 999	16 114	...	...	...	...	...	...
20 - 24	37 836	19 403	18 433	...	...	...	...	...	...
25 - 29	44 724	22 830	21 894	...	...	...	...	...	...
30 - 34	46 272	23 245	23 027	...	...	...	...	...	...
35 - 39	47 119	23 677	23 442	...	...	...	...	...	...
40 - 44	45 255	23 010	22 245	...	...	...	...	...	...
45 - 49	46 202	23 782	22 420	...	...	...	...	...	...
50 - 54	46 090	24 102	21 988	...	...	...	...	...	...
55 - 59	39 734	20 514	19 220	...	...	...	...	...	...
60 - 64	32 330	16 280	16 050	...	...	...	...	...	...
65 - 69	26 147	13 035	13 112	...	...	...	...	...	...
70 - 74	20 228	9 855	10 373	...	...	...	...	...	...
75 - 79	16 077	7 113	8 964	...	...	...	...	...	...
80 - 84	12 002	4 967	7 035	...	...	...	...	...	...
85 - 89	8 017	2 924	5 093	...	...	...	...	...	...
90 - 94	3 051	788	2 263	...	...	...	...	...	...
95 - 99	610	120	490	...	...	...	...	...	...
100 - 104	70	10	60	...	...	...	...	...	...
105 - 109	5	-	5	...	...	...	...	...	...
110 +	1	1	-	...	...	...	...	...	...

7. Population by age, sex and urban/rural residence: latest available year, 2009 - 2018
Population selon l'âge, le sexe et la résidence, urbaine/rurale : dernière année disponible, 2009 - 2018 (continued - suite)

Continent, country or area, date, code[a] and age (in years) / Continent, pays ou zone, date, code[a] et âge (en années)	Total			Urban - Urbaine			Rural - Rurale		
	Both sexes Les deux sexes	Male Masculin	Female Féminin	Both sexes Les deux sexes	Male Masculin	Female Féminin	Both sexes Les deux sexes	Male Masculin	Female Féminin
EUROPE									
Malta - Malte									
20 XI 2011 (CDFC)									
Total	417 432	207 625	209 807	400 557	199 151	201 406	16 875	8 474	8 401
0 - 4	20 061	10 347	9 714	19 247	9 926	9 321	814	421	393
5 - 9	19 419	9 971	9 448	18 602	9 562	9 040	817	409	408
10 - 14	22 248	11 355	10 893	21 218	10 854	10 364	1 030	501	529
15 - 19	26 182	13 509	12 673	25 026	12 907	12 119	1 156	602	554
20 - 24	29 450	15 062	14 388	28 269	14 475	13 794	1 181	587	594
25 - 29	30 320	15 722	14 598	29 154	15 110	14 044	1 166	612	554
30 - 34	30 194	15 641	14 553	29 141	15 074	14 067	1 053	567	486
35 - 39	28 799	14 757	14 042	27 712	14 202	13 510	1 087	555	532
40 - 44	25 236	12 840	12 396	24 151	12 293	11 858	1 085	547	538
45 - 49	26 895	13 574	13 321	25 716	12 972	12 744	1 179	602	577
50 - 54	30 596	15 292	15 304	29 293	14 628	14 665	1 303	664	639
55 - 59	29 246	14 655	14 591	28 127	14 052	14 075	1 119	603	516
60 - 64	30 595	15 130	15 465	29 452	14 551	14 901	1 143	579	564
65 - 69	23 728	11 429	12 299	22 791	10 986	11 805	937	443	494
70 - 74	16 205	7 389	8 816	15 572	7 106	8 466	633	283	350
75 - 79	13 287	5 579	7 708	12 749	5 332	7 417	538	247	291
80 - 84	8 494	3 181	5 313	8 121	3 036	5 085	373	145	228
85 - 89	4 567	1 622	2 945	4 371	1 546	2 825	196	76	120
90 - 94	1 583	480	1 103	1 532	455	1 077	51	25	26
95 - 99	296	82	214	284	77	207	12	5	7
100 +	31	8	23	29	7	22	2	1	1
1 I 2018 (ESDJ)[87]									
Total	475 701	240 599	235 102	...	...	...	...	...	...
0	4 456	2 280	2 176	...	...	...	...	...	...
1 - 4	18 515	9 666	8 849	...	...	...	...	...	...
5 - 9	22 487	11 516	10 971	...	...	...	...	...	...
10 - 14	20 771	10 698	10 073	...	...	...	...	...	...
15 - 19	22 678	11 609	11 069	...	...	...	...	...	...
20 - 24	31 126	16 456	14 670	...	...	...	...	...	...
25 - 29	40 105	20 878	19 227	...	...	...	...	...	...
30 - 34	38 538	20 490	18 048	...	...	...	...	...	...
35 - 39	36 589	19 229	17 360	...	...	...	...	...	...
40 - 44	33 246	17 364	15 882	...	...	...	...	...	...
45 - 49	28 589	14 856	13 733	...	...	...	...	...	...
50 - 54	27 787	14 175	13 612	...	...	...	...	...	...
55 - 59	31 264	15 685	15 579	...	...	...	...	...	...
60 - 64	30 033	15 091	14 942	...	...	...	...	...	...
65 - 69	29 302	14 404	14 898	...	...	...	...	...	...
70 - 74	26 329	12 514	13 815	...	...	...	...	...	...
75 - 79	13 947	6 214	7 733	...	...	...	...	...	...
80 - 84	11 248	4 618	6 630	...	...	...	...	...	...
85 - 89	5 907	2 030	3 877	...	...	...	...	...	...
90 - 94	2 248	702	1 546	...	...	...	...	...	...
95 - 99	472	111	361	...	...	...	...	...	...
100 - 104	52	7	45	...	...	...	...	...	...
105 - 109	12	6	6	...	...	...	...	...	...
110 +	-	-	-	...	...	...	...	...	...
Monaco[88]									
7 VI 2016 (CDJC)									
Total	37 308	18 240	19 068	...	...	...	...	...	...
0 - 16	5 560	2 814	2 746	...	...	...	...	...	...
17 - 24	2 678	1 377	1 302	...	...	...	...	...	...
25 - 34	3 563	1 786	1 777	...	...	...	...	...	...
35 - 44	4 409	2 091	2 318	...	...	...	...	...	...
45 - 54	6 042	3 032	3 010	...	...	...	...	...	...
55 - 64	5 396	2 726	2 670	...	...	...	...	...	...
65 - 74	4 968	2 414	2 553	...	...	...	...	...	...
75 +	4 692	2 001	2 691	...	...	...	...	...	...
Montenegro - Monténégro									
1 IV 2011 (CDJC)									
Total	620 029	306 236	313 793	399 264	193 691	205 573	220 765	112 545	108 220
0 - 4	38 950	20 361	18 589	25 277	13 247	12 030	13 673	7 114	6 559

7. Population by age, sex and urban/rural residence: latest available year, 2009 - 2018
Population selon l'âge, le sexe et la résidence, urbaine/rurale : dernière année disponible, 2009 - 2018 (continued - suite)

Continent, country or area, date, code[a] and age (in years) / Continent, pays ou zone, date, code[a] et âge (en années)	Total			Urban - Urbaine			Rural - Rurale		
	Both sexes Les deux sexes	Male Masculin	Female Féminin	Both sexes Les deux sexes	Male Masculin	Female Féminin	Both sexes Les deux sexes	Male Masculin	Female Féminin
EUROPE									
Montenegro - Monténégro									
1 IV 2011 (CDJC)									
5 - 9	38 430	20 016	18 414	24 781	12 973	11 808	13 649	7 043	6 606
10 - 14	41 371	21 389	19 982	26 526	13 698	12 828	14 845	7 691	7 154
15 - 19	44 093	22 815	21 278	28 376	14 654	13 722	15 717	8 161	7 556
20 - 24	42 816	22 084	20 732	28 218	14 347	13 871	14 598	7 737	6 861
25 - 29	45 793	23 299	22 494	31 083	15 290	15 793	14 710	8 009	6 701
30 - 34	44 495	22 188	22 307	30 133	14 495	15 638	14 362	7 693	6 669
35 - 39	41 879	20 523	21 356	27 869	13 311	14 558	14 010	7 212	6 798
40 - 44	40 496	20 136	20 360	26 265	12 539	13 726	14 231	7 597	6 634
45 - 49	43 089	21 401	21 688	28 332	13 444	14 888	14 757	7 957	6 800
50 - 54	43 613	21 817	21 796	28 705	13 851	14 854	14 908	7 966	6 942
55 - 59	41 223	20 509	20 714	27 021	13 143	13 878	14 202	7 366	6 836
60 - 64	34 196	15 941	18 255	21 738	9 981	11 757	12 458	5 960	6 498
65 - 69	22 121	9 774	12 347	12 692	5 522	7 170	9 429	4 252	5 177
70 - 74	25 141	10 909	14 232	14 441	6 116	8 325	10 700	4 793	5 907
75 - 79	17 184	7 251	9 933	9 665	4 041	5 624	7 519	3 210	4 309
80 - 84	10 021	4 050	5 971	5 375	2 112	3 263	4 646	1 938	2 708
85 - 89	3 739	1 324	2 415	2 038	699	1 339	1 701	625	1 076
90 - 94	885	283	602	453	130	323	432	153	279
95 - 99	202	61	141	103	30	73	99	31	68
100 +	44	13	31	23	7	16	21	6	15
Unknown - Inconnu	248	92	156	150	61	89	98	31	67
1 I 2018 (ESDJ)									
Total	622 359	307 741	314 618	...	...	...	...	...	...
0	7 513	3 915	3 598	...	...	...	...	...	...
1 - 4	29 916	15 504	14 412	...	...	...	...	...	...
5 - 9	37 729	19 659	18 070	...	...	...	...	...	...
10 - 14	37 272	19 471	17 801	...	...	...	...	...	...
15 - 19	40 901	21 180	19 721	...	...	...	...	...	...
20 - 24	40 372	20 847	19 525	...	...	...	...	...	...
25 - 29	40 003	20 662	19 341	...	...	...	...	...	...
30 - 34	46 132	23 551	22 581	...	...	...	...	...	...
35 - 39	44 649	22 404	22 245	...	...	...	...	...	...
40 - 44	42 123	20 641	21 482	...	...	...	...	...	...
45 - 49	40 032	19 712	20 320	...	...	...	...	...	...
50 - 54	41 237	20 374	20 863	...	...	...	...	...	...
55 - 59	42 085	20 582	21 503	...	...	...	...	...	...
60 - 64	40 430	19 749	20 681	...	...	...	...	...	...
65 - 69	33 880	15 534	18 346	...	...	...	...	...	...
70 - 74	19 879	8 526	11 353	...	...	...	...	...	...
75 - 79	18 608	7 652	10 956	...	...	...	...	...	...
80 - 84	12 155	4 831	7 324	...	...	...	...	...	...
85 - 89	5 438	2 186	3 252	...	...	...	...	...	...
90 - 94	1 557	612	945	...	...	...	...	...	...
95 - 99	435	145	290	...	...	...	...	...	...
100 - 104	10	3	7	...	...	...	...	...	...
105 - 109	3	1	2	...	...	...	...	...	...
110 +	-	-	-	...	...	...	...	...	...
Netherlands - Pays-Bas									
1 I 2011 (CDJC)									
Total	16 655 799	8 243 482	8 412 317	11 124 721	5 478 213	5 646 508	5 531 078	2 765 269	2 765 809
0 - 4	923 106	472 308	450 798	633 381	323 854	309 527	289 725	148 454	141 271
0	184 007	93 892	90 115	...	...	...	...	...	...
1 - 4	739 099	378 416	360 683	...	...	...	...	...	...
5 - 9	985 229	503 882	481 347	640 541	327 757	312 784	344 688	176 125	168 563
10 - 14	998 740	510 974	487 766	633 115	323 581	309 534	365 625	187 393	178 232
15 - 19	1 006 744	514 830	491 914	658 458	333 676	324 782	348 286	181 154	167 132
20 - 24	1 034 729	522 667	512 062	757 280	373 366	383 914	277 449	149 301	128 148
25 - 29	1 001 538	504 117	497 421	749 880	373 340	376 540	251 658	130 777	120 881
30 - 34	1 004 764	503 323	501 441	736 350	368 630	367 720	268 414	134 693	133 721
35 - 39	1 121 568	560 289	561 279	779 994	391 390	388 604	341 574	168 899	172 675
40 - 44	1 295 925	653 664	642 261	861 292	436 235	425 057	434 633	217 429	217 204
45 - 49	1 298 292	655 302	642 990	850 566	428 796	421 770	447 726	226 506	221 220
50 - 54	1 196 319	601 040	595 279	776 285	388 221	388 064	420 034	212 819	207 215

Continent, country or area, date, code[a] and age (in years) / Continent, pays ou zone, date, code[a] et âge (en années)	Total			Urban - Urbaine			Rural - Rurale		
	Both sexes Les deux sexes	Male Masculin	Female Féminin	Both sexes Les deux sexes	Male Masculin	Female Féminin	Both sexes Les deux sexes	Male Masculin	Female Féminin
EUROPE									
Netherlands - Pays-Bas									
1 I 2011 (CDJC)									
55 - 59	1 090 247	546 952	543 295	700 036	348 502	351 534	390 211	198 450	191 761
60 - 64	1 103 652	553 446	550 206	700 926	349 188	351 738	402 726	204 258	198 468
65 - 69	790 560	390 725	399 835	488 433	238 792	249 641	302 127	151 933	150 194
70 - 74	637 518	302 542	334 976	401 165	187 850	213 315	236 353	114 692	121 661
75 - 79	499 321	219 108	280 213	316 949	136 949	180 000	182 372	82 159	100 213
80 - 84	360 828	139 348	221 480	234 884	89 412	145 472	125 944	49 936	76 008
85 - 89	212 056	66 949	145 107	141 532	44 184	97 348	70 524	22 765	47 759
90 - 94	76 191	18 812	57 379	51 102	12 438	38 664	25 089	6 374	18 715
95 +	18 472	3 204	15 268	12 552	2 052	10 500	5 920	1 152	4 768
1 I 2018 (ESDJ)									
Total	17 181 084	8 527 041	8 654 043	...	...	...	...	...	...
0	169 566	87 001	82 565	...	...	...	...	...	...
1 - 4	698 533	358 019	340 514	...	...	...	...	...	...
5 - 9	928 066	475 503	452 563	...	...	...	...	...	...
10 - 14	966 459	494 511	471 948	...	...	...	...	...	...
15 - 19	1 048 032	536 852	511 180	...	...	...	...	...	...
20 - 24	1 068 781	542 817	525 964	...	...	...	...	...	...
25 - 29	1 106 157	560 319	545 838	...	...	...	...	...	...
30 - 34	1 052 789	530 554	522 235	...	...	...	...	...	...
35 - 39	1 025 356	512 925	512 431	...	...	...	...	...	...
40 - 44	1 038 312	516 723	521 589	...	...	...	...	...	...
45 - 49	1 268 823	634 188	634 635	...	...	...	...	...	...
50 - 54	1 279 846	644 223	635 623	...	...	...	...	...	...
55 - 59	1 211 510	606 130	605 380	...	...	...	...	...	...
60 - 64	1 079 738	537 540	542 198	...	...	...	...	...	...
65 - 69	999 537	495 875	503 662	...	...	...	...	...	...
70 - 74	871 925	424 486	447 439	...	...	...	...	...	...
75 - 79	588 740	273 902	314 838	...	...	...	...	...	...
80 - 84	408 255	172 825	235 430	...	...	...	...	...	...
85 - 89	246 487	88 775	157 712	...	...	...	...	...	...
90 - 94	99 410	28 774	70 636	...	...	...	...	...	...
95 - 99	22 582	4 776	17 806	...	...	...	...	...	...
100 - 104	2 085	312	1 773	...	...	...	...	...	...
105 - 109	93	11	82	...	...	...	...	...	...
110 +	2	-	2	...	...	...	...	...	...
North Macedonia - Macédoine du Nord									
1 I 2018 (ESDJ)									
Total	2 075 301	1 039 283	1 036 018	...	...	...	...	...	...
0	21 572	11 071	10 501	...	...	...	...	...	...
1 - 4	91 784	47 536	44 248	...	...	...	...	...	...
5 - 9	115 847	59 995	55 852	...	...	...	...	...	...
10 - 14	112 780	58 098	54 682	...	...	...	...	...	...
15 - 19	122 021	62 968	59 053	...	...	...	...	...	...
20 - 24	141 251	72 690	68 561	...	...	...	...	...	...
25 - 29	158 524	81 371	77 153	...	...	...	...	...	...
30 - 34	163 732	83 734	79 998	...	...	...	...	...	...
35 - 39	160 228	82 353	77 875	...	...	...	...	...	...
40 - 44	151 303	76 885	74 418	...	...	...	...	...	...
45 - 49	144 798	72 860	71 938	...	...	...	...	...	...
50 - 54	144 560	72 708	71 852	...	...	...	...	...	...
55 - 59	136 613	68 306	68 307	...	...	...	...	...	...
60 - 64	126 839	62 594	64 245	...	...	...	...	...	...
65 - 69	106 419	49 685	56 734	...	...	...	...	...	...
70 - 74	71 737	32 215	39 522	...	...	...	...	...	...
75 - 79	53 783	23 477	30 306	...	...	...	...	...	...
80 - 84	34 651	14 528	20 123	...	...	...	...	...	...
85 - 89	12 850	4 910	7 940	...	...	...	...	...	...
90 - 94	2 712	961	1 751	...	...	...	...	...	...
95 +	1 104	305	799	...	...	...	...	...	...
Unknown - Inconnu	193	33	160	...	...	...	...	...	...

Continent, country or area, date, code[a] and age (in years) / Continent, pays ou zone, date, code[a] et âge (en années)	Total			Urban - Urbaine			Rural - Rurale		
	Both sexes Les deux sexes	Male Masculin	Female Féminin	Both sexes Les deux sexes	Male Masculin	Female Féminin	Both sexes Les deux sexes	Male Masculin	Female Féminin
EUROPE									
Norway - Norvège									
19 XI 2011 (CDJC)[89]									
Total	4 979 955	2 495 777	2 484 178	3 951 427[81]	1 959 424[81]	1 992 003[81]	1 011 071[81]	524 519[81]	486 552[81]
0 - 4	310 523	159 582	150 941	252 348[81]	129 655[81]	122 693[81]	57 552[81]	29 590[81]	27 962[81]
5 - 9	300 625	153 598	147 027	239 702[81]	122 174[81]	117 528[81]	60 262[81]	31 070[81]	29 192[81]
10 - 14	312 618	160 122	152 496	245 562[81]	125 764[81]	119 798[81]	66 422[81]	34 008[81]	32 414[81]
15 - 19	324 682	167 701	156 981	254 774[81]	131 385[81]	123 389[81]	69 376[81]	36 049[81]	33 327[81]
20 - 24	329 537	167 828	161 709	268 150[81]	135 424[81]	132 726[81]	60 351[81]	31 776[81]	28 575[81]
25 - 29	321 171	163 754	157 417	268 356[81]	135 940[81]	132 416[81]	51 166[81]	26 654[81]	24 512[81]
30 - 34	325 241	166 578	158 663	269 924[81]	137 478[81]	132 446[81]	53 565[81]	27 843[81]	25 722[81]
35 - 39	352 008	180 904	171 104	286 185[81]	146 143[81]	140 042[81]	64 091[81]	33 501[81]	30 590[81]
40 - 44	373 191	191 483	181 708	297 629[81]	151 231[81]	146 398[81]	73 666[81]	38 863[81]	34 803[81]
45 - 49	350 537	180 834	169 703	275 817[81]	140 624[81]	135 193[81]	73 001[81]	38 909[81]	34 092[81]
50 - 54	322 729	165 233	157 496	250 381[81]	126 209[81]	124 172[81]	70 881[81]	37 897[81]	32 984[81]
55 - 59	304 335	154 029	150 306	233 724[81]	116 035[81]	117 689[81]	69 504[81]	37 194[81]	32 310[81]
60 - 64	286 319	144 699	141 620	218 480[81]	108 289[81]	110 191[81]	67 016[81]	35 823[81]	31 193[81]
65 - 69	247 451	122 740	124 711	188 932[81]	91 896[81]	97 036[81]	57 895[81]	30 414[81]	27 481[81]
70 - 74	166 680	78 850	87 830	126 640[81]	58 122[81]	68 518[81]	39 687[81]	20 517[81]	19 170[81]
75 - 79	130 209	58 013	72 196	99 673[81]	42 842[81]	56 831[81]	30 271[81]	15 028[81]	15 243[81]
80 - 84	108 243	44 024	64 219	84 440[81]	32 980[81]	51 460[81]	23 582[81]	10 955[81]	12 627[81]
85 - 89	74 057	25 608	48 449	58 579[81]	19 436[81]	39 143[81]	15 272[81]	6 085[81]	9 187[81]
90 - 94	32 243	8 769	23 474	25 938[81]	6 706[81]	19 232[81]	6 185[81]	2 017[81]	4 168[81]
95 - 99	6 825	1 310	5 515	5 593[81]	1 001[81]	4 592[81]	1 199[81]	300[81]	899[81]
100 +	731	118	613	600[81]	90[81]	510[81]	127[81]	26[81]	101[81]
1 I 2018 (ESDJ)[85]									
Total	5 295 619	2 668 371	2 627 248	...	...	...	...	...	...
0	56 965	29 337	27 628	...	...	...	...	...	...
1 - 4	242 614	124 580	118 034	...	...	...	...	...	...
5 - 9	323 672	166 196	157 476	...	...	...	...	...	...
10 - 14	315 683	161 596	154 087	...	...	...	...	...	...
15 - 19	321 959	166 175	155 784	...	...	...	...	...	...
20 - 24	342 370	176 979	165 391	...	...	...	...	...	...
25 - 29	371 575	189 553	182 022	...	...	...	...	...	...
30 - 34	358 391	183 675	174 716	...	...	...	...	...	...
35 - 39	349 993	180 314	169 679	...	...	...	...	...	...
40 - 44	354 394	182 198	172 196	...	...	...	...	...	...
45 - 49	380 674	195 200	185 474	...	...	...	...	...	...
50 - 54	358 543	184 083	174 460	...	...	...	...	...	...
55 - 59	322 182	164 396	157 786	...	...	...	...	...	...
60 - 64	300 179	150 564	149 615	...	...	...	...	...	...
65 - 69	272 143	136 101	136 042	...	...	...	...	...	...
70 - 74	246 071	120 283	125 788	...	...	...	...	...	...
75 - 79	155 459	72 089	83 370	...	...	...	...	...	...
80 - 84	105 747	45 210	60 537	...	...	...	...	...	...
85 - 89	72 313	27 055	45 258	...	...	...	...	...	...
90 - 94	34 417	10 594	23 823	...	...	...	...	...	...
95 - 99	9 248	2 019	7 229	...	...	...	...	...	...
100 +	1 027	174	853	...	...	...	...	...	...
Poland - Pologne[85]									
1 VII 2017 (ESDJ)									
Total	37 962 318	18 373 411	19 588 907	22 859 045	10 839 076	12 019 969	15 103 273	7 534 335	7 568 938
0	389 523	199 755	189 768	229 544	117 807	111 737	159 979	81 948	78 031
1 - 4	1 498 005	769 482	728 523	875 282	449 595	425 687	622 723	319 887	302 836
5 - 9	2 054 186	1 054 100	1 000 086	1 170 244	600 624	569 620	883 942	453 476	430 466
10 - 14	1 815 494	931 414	884 080	995 011	510 396	484 615	820 483	421 018	399 465
15 - 19	1 872 049	959 415	912 634	998 847	510 285	488 562	873 202	449 130	424 072
20 - 24	2 242 687	1 143 000	1 099 687	1 187 711	603 184	584 527	1 054 976	539 816	515 160
25 - 29	2 697 391	1 375 647	1 321 744	1 559 992	782 383	777 609	1 137 399	593 264	544 135
30 - 34	3 096 636	1 577 179	1 519 457	1 923 299	966 904	956 395	1 173 337	610 275	563 062
35 - 39	3 035 635	1 540 525	1 495 110	1 892 333	949 564	942 769	1 143 302	590 961	552 341
40 - 44	2 812 713	1 421 590	1 391 123	1 703 964	850 135	853 829	1 108 749	571 455	537 294
45 - 49	2 360 826	1 185 127	1 175 699	1 380 832	680 249	700 583	979 994	504 878	475 116
50 - 54	2 294 431	1 137 011	1 157 420	1 342 554	643 431	699 123	951 877	493 580	458 297
55 - 59	2 649 941	1 280 068	1 369 873	1 626 306	751 520	874 786	1 023 635	528 548	495 087

7. Population by age, sex and urban/rural residence: latest available year, 2009 - 2018
Population selon l'âge, le sexe et la résidence, urbaine/rurale : dernière année disponible, 2009 - 2018 (continued - suite)

Continent, country or area, date, code[a] and age (in years) Continent, pays ou zone, date, code[a] et âge (en années)	Total			Urban - Urbaine			Rural - Rurale		
	Both sexes Les deux sexes	Male Masculin	Female Féminin	Both sexes Les deux sexes	Male Masculin	Female Féminin	Both sexes Les deux sexes	Male Masculin	Female Féminin
EUROPE									
Poland - Pologne[85]									
1 VII 2017 (ESDJ)									
60 - 64	2 738 438	1 280 348	1 458 090	1 784 883	798 373	986 510	953 555	481 975	471 580
65 - 69	2 310 842	1 029 578	1 281 264	1 540 776	663 581	877 195	770 066	365 997	404 069
70 - 74	1 370 538	572 603	797 935	914 689	376 289	538 400	455 849	196 314	259 535
75 - 79	1 099 602	414 744	684 858	711 685	265 043	446 642	387 917	149 701	238 216
80 - 84	868 477	292 450	576 027	553 370	186 685	366 685	315 107	105 765	209 342
85 - 89	527 371	155 817	371 554	326 245	98 978	227 267	201 126	56 839	144 287
90 - 94	189 064	45 305	143 759	117 190	28 786	88 404	71 874	16 519	55 355
95 - 99	33 228	7 164	26 064	20 689	4 515	16 174	12 539	2 649	9 890
100 +	5 241	1 089	4 152	3 599	749	2 850	1 642	340	1 302
1 I 2018 (ESDJ)									
Total	37 976 687	18 380 299	19 596 388	...	...	...	...	...	...
0	394 398	202 398	192 000	...	...	...	...	...	...
1 - 4	1 502 984	771 889	731 095	...	...	...	...	...	...
5 - 9	2 046 161	1 050 390	995 771	...	...	...	...	...	...
10 - 14	1 843 246	945 376	897 870	...	...	...	...	...	...
15 - 19	1 850 599	948 612	901 987	...	...	...	...	...	...
20 - 24	2 194 530	1 118 599	1 075 931	...	...	...	...	...	...
25 - 29	2 664 508	1 358 655	1 305 853	...	...	...	...	...	...
30 - 34	3 061 736	1 559 745	1 501 991	...	...	...	...	...	...
35 - 39	3 061 457	1 554 123	1 507 334	...	...	...	...	...	...
40 - 44	2 849 028	1 440 130	1 408 898	...	...	...	...	...	...
45 - 49	2 392 061	1 200 621	1 191 440	...	...	...	...	...	...
50 - 54	2 277 147	1 129 057	1 148 090	...	...	...	...	...	...
55 - 59	2 589 297	1 252 331	1 336 966	...	...	...	...	...	...
60 - 64	2 752 175	1 287 505	1 464 670	...	...	...	...	...	...
65 - 69	2 343 022	1 044 978	1 298 044	...	...	...	...	...	...
70 - 74	1 434 021	600 701	833 320	...	...	...	...	...	...
75 - 79	1 082 638	408 931	673 707	...	...	...	...	...	...
80 - 84	869 716	293 207	576 509	...	...	...	...	...	...
85 - 89	533 203	157 485	375 718	...	...	...	...	...	...
90 - 94	193 051	46 623	146 428	...	...	...	...	...	...
95 - 99	36 425	7 820	28 605	...	...	...	...	...	...
100 +	5 284	1 123	4 161	...	...	...	...	...	...
Portugal									
21 III 2011 (CDJC)									
Total	10 562 178	5 046 600	5 515 578	6 438 593	3 047 968	3 390 625	4 123 585	1 998 632	2 124 953
0 - 4	482 647	246 396	236 251	316 068	161 365	154 703	166 579	85 031	81 548
5 - 9	525 087	268 965	256 122	329 692	168 925	160 767	195 395	100 040	95 355
10 - 14	564 595	288 638	275 957	344 809	176 287	168 522	219 786	112 351	107 435
15 - 19	565 250	288 525	276 725	342 328	174 252	168 076	222 922	114 273	108 649
20 - 24	582 065	293 023	289 042	358 412	178 982	179 430	223 653	114 041	109 612
25 - 29	656 076	324 848	331 228	425 629	208 104	217 525	230 447	116 744	113 703
30 - 34	773 567	378 734	394 833	508 225	247 125	261 100	265 342	131 609	133 733
35 - 39	824 683	402 307	422 376	529 287	255 858	273 429	295 396	146 449	148 947
40 - 44	773 098	374 962	398 136	478 840	228 255	250 585	294 258	146 707	147 551
45 - 49	770 294	370 989	399 305	466 564	219 783	246 781	303 730	151 206	152 524
50 - 54	722 360	346 248	376 112	435 982	203 867	232 115	286 378	142 381	143 997
55 - 59	677 651	322 095	355 556	410 020	190 860	219 160	267 631	131 235	136 396
60 - 64	634 741	298 546	336 195	382 547	177 485	205 062	252 194	121 061	131 133
65 - 69	551 701	253 004	298 697	319 398	146 189	173 209	232 303	106 815	125 488
70 - 74	496 438	220 461	275 977	273 513	119 844	153 669	222 925	100 617	122 308
75 - 79	429 706	180 131	249 575	231 208	94 394	136 814	198 498	85 737	112 761
80 - 84	297 888	113 325	184 563	159 578	57 948	101 630	138 310	55 377	82 933
85 - 89	164 356	55 635	108 721	88 444	28 423	60 021	75 912	27 212	48 700
90 - 94	53 847	15 679	38 168	29 038	7 847	21 191	24 809	7 832	16 977
95 - 99	14 602	3 816	10 786	8 158	2 029	6 129	6 444	1 787	4 657
100 +	1 526	273	1 253	853	146	707	673	127	546
1 I 2018 (ESDJ)									
Total	10 291 027	4 867 692	5 423 335	...	...	...	...	...	...
0	86 256	44 062	42 194	...	...	...	...	...	...
1 - 4	339 306	173 803	165 503	...	...	...	...	...	...
5 - 9	482 612	246 716	235 896	...	...	...	...	...	...
10 - 14	515 722	263 569	252 153	...	...	...	...	...	...

Continent, country or area, date, code[a] and age (in years) Continent, pays ou zone, date, code[a] et âge (en années)	Total			Urban - Urbaine			Rural - Rurale		
	Both sexes Les deux sexes	Male Masculin	Female Féminin	Both sexes Les deux sexes	Male Masculin	Female Féminin	Both sexes Les deux sexes	Male Masculin	Female Féminin
EUROPE									
Portugal									
1 I 2018 (ESDJ)									
15 - 19	555 911	284 302	271 609	...	...	...	...	...	...
20 - 24	537 290	272 265	265 025	...	...	...	...	...	...
25 - 29	549 467	274 790	274 677	...	...	...	...	...	...
30 - 34	591 800	289 672	302 128	...	...	...	...	...	...
35 - 39	704 918	337 482	367 436	...	...	...	...	...	...
40 - 44	812 053	387 741	424 312	...	...	...	...	...	...
45 - 49	767 109	365 910	401 199	...	...	...	...	...	...
50 - 54	753 649	356 250	397 399	...	...	...	...	...	...
55 - 59	722 561	340 474	382 087	...	...	...	...	...	...
60 - 64	659 099	307 055	352 044	...	...	...	...	...	...
65 - 69	619 886	285 246	334 640	...	...	...	...	...	...
70 - 74	521 503	228 953	292 550	...	...	...	...	...	...
75 - 79	424 997	178 645	246 352	...	...	...	...	...	...
80 - 84	349 350	135 091	214 259	...	...	...	...	...	...
85 - 89	206 414	70 742	135 672	...	...	...	...	...	...
90 - 94	72 504	19 744	52 760	...	...	...	...	...	...
95 - 99	14 352	3 512	10 840	...	...	...	...	...	...
100 +	4 268	1 668	2 600	...	...	...	...	...	...
Republic of Moldova - République de Moldova									
12 V 2014 (CDFC)[90]									
Total	2 804 801	1 352 099	1 452 702	950 994	446 386	504 608	1 853 807	905 713	948 094
0	34 742	17 769	16 973	11 564	5 908	5 656	23 178	11 861	11 317
1 - 4	137 250	70 542	66 708	45 992	23 671	22 321	91 258	46 871	44 387
5 - 9	160 684	82 455	78 229	51 998	26 779	25 219	108 686	55 676	53 010
10 - 14	150 027	77 275	72 752	42 183	21 853	20 330	107 844	55 422	52 422
15 - 19	183 692	93 727	89 965	57 768	29 495	28 273	125 924	64 232	61 692
20 - 24	231 153	118 376	112 777	77 320	37 799	39 521	153 833	80 577	73 256
25 - 29	251 465	129 771	121 694	90 050	44 660	45 390	161 415	85 111	76 304
30 - 34	214 870	109 201	105 669	80 739	40 112	40 627	134 131	69 089	65 042
35 - 39	190 795	95 575	95 220	68 490	33 899	34 591	122 305	61 676	60 629
40 - 44	176 906	87 451	89 455	60 280	28 942	31 338	116 626	58 509	58 117
45 - 49	173 564	84 288	89 276	56 962	25 991	30 971	116 602	58 297	58 305
50 - 54	208 674	98 512	110 162	70 891	31 525	39 366	137 783	66 987	70 796
55 - 59	203 825	93 612	110 213	71 363	30 767	40 596	132 462	62 845	69 617
60 - 64	181 690	79 681	102 009	66 059	27 851	38 208	115 631	51 830	63 801
65 - 69	95 407	39 652	55 755	35 591	14 688	20 903	59 816	24 964	34 852
70 - 74	85 270	32 645	52 625	26 949	10 612	16 337	58 321	22 033	36 288
75 - 79	65 096	22 757	42 339	20 154	6 884	13 270	44 942	15 873	29 069
80 - 84	37 980	12 543	25 437	10 243	3 261	6 982	27 737	9 282	18 455
85 - 89	16 502	4 801	11 701	4 893	1 334	3 559	11 609	3 467	8 142
90 - 94	4 277	1 148	3 129	1 228	270	958	3 049	878	2 171
95 - 99	574	158	416	170	38	132	404	120	284
100 +	358	160	198	107	47	60	251	113	138
1 VII 2018 (ESDJ)[91]									
Total	2 706 049	1 291 242	1 414 807	...	...	...	...	...	...
0	35 104	18 091	17 013	...	...	...	...	...	...
1 - 4	148 338	76 301	72 037	...	...	...	...	...	...
5 - 9	170 506	87 343	83 163	...	...	...	...	...	...
10 - 14	154 419	79 238	75 180	...	...	...	...	...	...
15 - 19	142 072	73 085	68 988	...	...	...	...	...	...
20 - 24	165 584	82 963	82 620	...	...	...	...	...	...
25 - 29	204 018	101 138	102 880	...	...	...	...	...	...
30 - 34	223 407	111 552	111 855	...	...	...	...	...	...
35 - 39	192 657	95 083	97 574	...	...	...	...	...	...
40 - 44	174 885	86 132	88 751	...	...	...	...	...	...
45 - 49	166 413	81 548	84 867	...	...	...	...	...	...
50 - 54	171 141	82 284	88 857	...	...	...	...	...	...
55 - 59	205 566	95 568	110 000	...	...	...	...	...	...
60 - 64	187 145	82 578	104 567	...	...	...	...	...	...
65 - 69	164 029	67 974	96 056	...	...	...	...	...	...
70 - 74	71 370	27 336	44 034	...	...	...	...	...	...
75 - 79	66 261	23 321	42 940	...	...	...	...	...	...

Continent, country or area, date, code[a] and age (in years) / Continent, pays ou zone, date, code[a] et âge (en années)	Total			Urban - Urbaine			Rural - Rurale		
	Both sexes Les deux sexes	Male Masculin	Female Féminin	Both sexes Les deux sexes	Male Masculin	Female Féminin	Both sexes Les deux sexes	Male Masculin	Female Féminin
EUROPE									
Republic of Moldova - République de Moldova									
1 VII 2018 (ESDJ)[91]									
80 - 84	40 645	13 001	27 644	...	...	...	...	...	...
85 +	22 487	6 706	15 781	...	...	...	...	...	...
Romania - Roumanie									
1 VII 2017 (ESDF)									
Total	19 591 668	9 579 992	10 011 676	10 519 506	5 021 154	5 498 352	9 072 162	4 558 838	4 513 324
0	198 868	101 946	96 922	109 442	56 295	53 147	89 426	45 651	43 775
1 - 4	782 603	402 237	380 366	426 169	219 304	206 865	356 434	182 933	173 501
5 - 9	1 021 919	525 490	496 429	525 659	270 869	254 790	496 260	254 621	241 639
10 - 14	1 051 976	540 299	511 677	504 576	258 747	245 829	547 400	281 552	265 848
15 - 19	1 064 153	546 831	517 322	478 133	243 456	234 677	586 020	303 375	282 645
20 - 24	1 037 326	530 315	507 011	508 756	251 362	257 394	528 570	278 953	249 617
25 - 29	1 250 201	653 665	596 536	740 334	367 845	372 489	509 867	285 820	224 047
30 - 34	1 303 965	677 298	626 667	780 204	395 458	384 746	523 761	281 840	241 921
35 - 39	1 470 353	751 131	719 222	850 552	426 105	424 447	619 801	325 026	294 775
40 - 44	1 528 525	783 095	745 430	833 901	414 331	419 570	694 624	368 764	325 860
45 - 49	1 665 481	854 891	810 590	918 642	446 482	472 160	746 839	408 409	338 430
50 - 54	1 119 473	568 683	550 790	637 175	302 890	334 285	482 298	265 793	216 505
55 - 59	1 218 433	593 574	624 859	713 002	327 890	385 112	505 431	265 684	239 747
60 - 64	1 353 953	628 178	725 775	797 782	361 912	435 870	556 171	266 266	289 905
65 - 69	1 165 868	516 372	649 496	625 962	275 958	350 004	539 906	240 414	299 492
70 - 74	781 901	328 371	453 530	373 928	154 961	218 967	407 973	173 410	234 563
75 - 79	700 904	269 495	431 409	316 330	119 699	196 631	384 574	149 796	234 778
80 - 84	509 213	184 112	325 101	219 624	76 909	142 715	289 589	107 203	182 386
85 - 89	260 289	89 495	170 794	112 234	36 548	75 686	148 055	52 947	95 108
90 - 94	85 938	28 276	57 662	37 777	11 591	26 186	48 161	16 685	31 476
95 - 99	18 440	5 656	12 784	8 382	2 313	6 069	10 058	3 343	6 715
100 +	1 886	582	1 304	942	229	713	944	353	591
1 I 2018 (ESDF)									
Total	19 530 631	9 553 249	9 977 382	...	...	...	...	...	...
0	199 634	102 426	97 208	...	...	...	...	...	...
1 - 4	791 733	406 719	385 014	...	...	...	...	...	...
5 - 9	1 007 808	518 409	489 399	...	...	...	...	...	...
10 - 14	1 053 304	541 153	512 151	...	...	...	...	...	...
15 - 19	1 053 067	540 482	512 585	...	...	...	...	...	...
20 - 24	1 026 719	524 285	502 434	...	...	...	...	...	...
25 - 29	1 208 369	633 267	575 102	...	...	...	...	...	...
30 - 34	1 315 282	684 044	631 238	...	...	...	...	...	...
35 - 39	1 440 567	737 386	703 181	...	...	...	...	...	...
40 - 44	1 538 621	788 247	750 374	...	...	...	...	...	...
45 - 49	1 611 389	827 251	784 138	...	...	...	...	...	...
50 - 54	1 201 162	611 299	589 863	...	...	...	...	...	...
55 - 59	1 181 828	577 647	604 181	...	...	...	...	...	...
60 - 64	1 350 887	627 282	723 605	...	...	...	...	...	...
65 - 69	1 187 748	525 592	662 156	...	...	...	...	...	...
70 - 74	790 424	332 889	457 535	...	...	...	...	...	...
75 - 79	687 970	264 824	423 146	...	...	...	...	...	...
80 - 84	510 128	183 615	326 513	...	...	...	...	...	...
85 - 89	266 178	91 315	174 863	...	...	...	...	...	...
90 - 94	86 516	28 475	58 041	...	...	...	...	...	...
95 - 99	19 320	6 030	13 290	...	...	...	...	...	...
100 +	1 977	612	1 365	...	...	...	...	...	...
Russian Federation - Fédération de Russie									
1 VII 2012 (ESDJ)									
Total	143 201 730	66 264 910	76 936 820	105 930 122	48 419 208	57 510 914	37 271 608	17 845 702	19 425 906
0	1 837 406	944 299	893 107	1 299 253	668 312	630 941	538 153	275 987	262 166
1 - 4	6 695 802	3 433 227	3 262 575	4 714 200	2 419 141	2 295 059	1 981 602	1 014 086	967 516
5 - 9	7 350 838	3 762 806	3 588 032	5 189 787	2 657 166	2 532 621	2 161 051	1 105 640	1 055 411
10 - 14	6 628 125	3 396 364	3 231 761	4 584 611	2 348 219	2 236 392	2 043 514	1 048 145	995 369
15 - 19	7 391 866	3 776 026	3 615 840	5 367 803	2 718 897	2 648 906	2 024 063	1 057 129	966 934
20 - 24	11 223 730	5 708 187	5 515 543	8 636 085	4 330 536	4 305 549	2 587 645	1 377 651	1 209 994
25 - 29	12 442 007	6 262 379	6 179 628	9 541 009	4 744 648	4 796 361	2 900 998	1 517 731	1 383 267

Continent, country or area, date, code[a] and age (in years) / Continent, pays ou zone, date, code[a] et âge (en années)	Total			Urban - Urbaine			Rural - Rurale		
	Both sexes Les deux sexes	Male Masculin	Female Féminin	Both sexes Les deux sexes	Male Masculin	Female Féminin	Both sexes Les deux sexes	Male Masculin	Female Féminin
EUROPE									
Russian Federation - Fédération de Russie									
1 VII 2012 (ESDJ)									
30 - 34	11 231 149	5 583 513	5 647 636	8 675 785	4 272 864	4 402 921	2 555 364	1 310 649	1 244 715
35 - 39	10 419 383	5 087 565	5 331 818	7 966 185	3 854 320	4 111 865	2 453 198	1 233 245	1 219 953
40 - 44	9 451 487	4 589 504	4 861 983	7 068 002	3 394 309	3 673 693	2 383 485	1 195 195	1 188 290
45 - 49	9 784 092	4 632 279	5 151 813	7 108 256	3 298 718	3 809 538	2 675 836	1 333 561	1 342 275
50 - 54	11 498 441	5 279 364	6 219 077	8 339 186	3 721 713	4 617 473	3 159 255	1 557 651	1 601 604
55 - 59	10 298 414	4 480 855	5 817 559	7 573 444	3 197 844	4 375 600	2 724 970	1 283 011	1 441 959
60 - 64	8 534 857	3 523 990	5 010 867	6 428 296	2 585 856	3 842 440	2 106 561	938 134	1 168 427
65 - 69	4 174 510	1 602 839	2 571 671	3 204 644	1 214 486	1 990 158	969 866	388 353	581 513
70 - 74	5 965 072	1 989 724	3 975 348	4 331 090	1 428 165	2 902 925	1 633 982	561 559	1 072 423
75 - 79	3 888 860	1 179 476	2 709 384	2 762 682	822 673	1 940 009	1 126 178	356 803	769 375
80 - 84	2 795 954	722 151	2 073 803	1 965 242	501 515	1 463 727	830 712	220 636	610 076
85 - 89	1 261 655	253 028	1 008 627	927 939	193 530	734 409	333 716	59 498	274 218
90 - 94	266 163	46 736	219 427	200 155	37 401	162 754	66 008	9 335	56 673
95 - 99	52 622	8 634	43 988	39 307	7 154	32 153	13 315	1 480	11 835
100 +	9 297	1 964	7 333	7 161	1 741	5 420	2 136	223	1 913
San Marino - Saint-Marin[39]									
1 VII 2018 (ESDJ)									
Total	34 536	16 835	17 701	...	...	...	...	...	...
0	245	128	117	...	...	...	...	...	...
1 - 4	1 161	605	556	...	...	...	...	...	...
5 - 9	1 728	887	841	...	...	...	...	...	...
10 - 14	1 689	872	817	...	...	...	...	...	...
15 - 19	1 744	930	814	...	...	...	...	...	...
20 - 24	1 660	856	804	...	...	...	...	...	...
25 - 29	1 638	828	810	...	...	...	...	...	...
30 - 34	1 820	885	935	...	...	...	...	...	...
35 - 39	2 215	1 055	1 160	...	...	...	...	...	...
40 - 44	2 848	1 362	1 486	...	...	...	...	...	...
45 - 49	3 121	1 526	1 595	...	...	...	...	...	...
50 - 54	3 165	1 505	1 660	...	...	...	...	...	...
55 - 59	2 701	1 335	1 366	...	...	...	...	...	...
60 - 64	2 101	998	1 103	...	...	...	...	...	...
65 - 69	1 843	905	938	...	...	...	...	...	...
70 - 74	1 625	782	843	...	...	...	...	...	...
75 - 79	1 252	579	673	...	...	...	...	...	...
80 - 84	959	426	533	...	...	...	...	...	...
85 - 89	653	258	395	...	...	...	...	...	...
90 - 94	279	92	187	...	...	...	...	...	...
95 - 99	76	20	56	...	...	...	...	...	...
100 +	13	1	12	...	...	...	...	...	...
Serbia - Serbie[92]									
1 VII 2017 (ESDJ)									
Total	7 020 858	3 419 815	3 601 043	4 256 129	2 027 177	2 228 952	2 764 729	1 392 638	1 372 091
0	64 478	33 206	31 272	43 873	22 667	21 206	20 605	10 539	10 066
1 - 4	261 984	135 098	126 886	180 522	93 033	87 489	81 462	42 065	39 397
5 - 9	331 621	171 044	160 577	212 930	109 890	103 040	118 691	61 154	57 537
10 - 14	350 643	180 137	170 506	209 705	107 523	102 182	140 938	72 614	68 324
15 - 19	350 625	180 260	170 365	206 171	105 841	100 330	144 454	74 419	70 035
20 - 24	399 041	205 454	193 587	236 585	120 201	116 384	162 456	85 253	77 203
25 - 29	437 129	223 615	213 514	271 482	134 688	136 794	165 647	88 927	76 720
30 - 34	478 955	244 115	234 840	310 947	153 265	157 682	168 008	90 850	77 158
35 - 39	493 414	250 597	242 817	324 811	160 619	164 192	168 603	89 978	78 625
40 - 44	496 393	249 664	246 729	315 145	154 345	160 800	181 248	95 319	85 929
45 - 49	467 401	232 209	235 192	284 694	137 508	147 186	182 707	94 701	88 006
50 - 54	468 651	229 275	239 376	278 480	131 283	147 197	190 171	97 992	92 179
55 - 59	496 133	238 816	257 317	292 357	134 445	157 912	203 776	104 371	99 405
60 - 64	545 866	258 265	287 601	318 342	144 009	174 333	227 524	114 256	113 268
65 - 69	492 375	225 114	267 261	287 560	125 711	161 849	204 815	99 403	105 412
70 - 74	304 276	132 765	171 511	171 374	72 399	98 975	132 902	60 366	72 536
75 - 79	270 107	111 611	158 496	146 977	58 822	88 155	123 130	52 789	70 341
80 - 84	191 784	75 078	116 706	102 443	39 571	62 872	89 341	35 507	53 834
85 - 89	89 040	32 939	56 101	45 076	15 854	29 222	43 964	17 085	26 879

Continent, country or area, date, code[a] and age (in years) Continent, pays ou zone, date, code[a] et âge (en années)	Total			Urban - Urbaine			Rural - Rurale		
	Both sexes Les deux sexes	Male Masculin	Female Féminin	Both sexes Les deux sexes	Male Masculin	Female Féminin	Both sexes Les deux sexes	Male Masculin	Female Féminin

EUROPE

Serbia - Serbie[92]
1 VII 2017 (ESDJ)

90 - 94	25 144	8 622	16 522	13 577	4 529	9 048	11 567	4 093	7 474
95 - 99	5 248	1 737	3 511	2 792	887	1 905	2 456	850	1 606
100 +	550	194	356	286	87	199	264	107	157

1 I 2018 (ESDJ)

Total	7 001 444	3 410 592	3 590 852	...	...	...	...	...	...
0	64 589	33 145	31 444	...	...	...	...	...	...
1 - 4	260 746	134 571	126 175	...	...	...	...	...	...
5 - 9	331 954	171 168	160 786	...	...	...	...	...	...
10 - 14	347 702	178 658	169 044	...	...	...	...	...	...
15 - 19	350 059	179 969	170 090	...	...	...	...	...	...
20 - 24	394 065	202 958	191 107	...	...	...	...	...	...
25 - 29	432 088	220 978	211 110	...	...	...	...	...	...
30 - 34	476 277	242 860	233 417	...	...	...	...	...	...
35 - 39	491 598	249 716	241 882	...	...	...	...	...	...
40 - 44	498 638	251 221	247 417	...	...	...	...	...	...
45 - 49	467 615	232 402	235 213	...	...	...	...	...	...
50 - 54	465 658	227 959	237 699	...	...	...	...	...	...
55 - 59	492 903	237 262	255 641	...	...	...	...	...	...
60 - 64	532 976	251 886	281 090	...	...	...	...	...	...
65 - 69	501 502	229 292	272 210	...	...	...	...	...	...
70 - 74	313 542	137 151	176 391	...	...	...	...	...	...
75 - 79	265 053	109 578	155 475	...	...	...	...	...	...
80 - 84	191 339	75 001	116 338	...	...	...	...	...	...
85 - 89	90 733	33 615	57 118	...	...	...	...	...	...
90 - 94	26 000	9 052	16 948	...	...	...	...	...	...
95 - 99	5 755	1 911	3 844	...	...	...	...	...	...
100 +	652	239	413	...	...	...	...	...	...

Slovakia - Slovaquie
1 VII 2017 (ESDJ)

Total	5 439 232	2 654 099	2 785 133	2 921 207	1 404 749	1 516 458	2 518 025	1 249 351	1 268 675
0	58 506	29 973	28 534	30 223	15 460	14 762	28 283	14 513	13 771
1 - 4	227 770	116 797	110 973	116 901	59 851	57 051	110 869	56 946	53 923
5 - 9	292 142	149 643	142 499	146 201	74 761	71 440	145 942	74 882	71 060
10 - 14	266 547	136 925	129 623	129 077	66 361	62 717	137 470	70 564	66 906
15 - 19	273 869	140 487	133 382	129 329	66 366	62 963	144 540	74 121	70 419
20 - 24	325 268	166 537	158 732	158 974	81 198	77 776	166 295	85 339	80 956
25 - 29	392 891	200 286	192 606	210 499	106 680	103 819	182 393	93 606	88 787
30 - 34	429 555	220 134	209 421	240 442	122 555	117 887	189 113	97 579	91 534
35 - 39	450 804	232 067	218 737	251 022	128 712	122 311	199 782	103 355	96 427
40 - 44	440 118	225 476	214 642	238 407	120 459	117 949	201 711	105 017	96 694
45 - 49	360 910	182 386	178 524	191 984	94 172	97 812	168 926	88 214	80 712
50 - 54	361 765	179 803	181 962	197 100	93 797	103 304	164 665	86 007	78 659
55 - 59	362 571	176 776	185 795	205 194	95 845	109 349	157 377	80 931	76 446
60 - 64	366 762	171 994	194 768	213 656	97 125	116 532	153 106	74 870	78 236
65 - 69	303 877	135 251	168 627	175 596	76 542	99 054	128 282	58 709	69 573
70 - 74	202 093	82 020	120 073	114 163	46 006	68 158	87 930	36 015	51 915
75 - 79	148 717	54 245	94 472	79 980	29 576	50 404	68 737	24 669	44 068
80 - 84	97 315	31 607	65 708	51 484	17 300	34 184	45 832	14 308	31 524
85 - 89	54 252	15 605	38 647	28 467	8 573	19 894	25 785	7 032	18 753
90 - 94	18 747	4 714	14 033	9 894	2 614	7 280	8 853	2 100	6 753
95 - 99	3 805	1 025	2 781	2 014	582	1 433	1 791	443	1 348
100 +	953	354	600	604	219	385	349	135	215

1 I 2018 (ESDJ)

Total	5 443 120	2 656 514	2 786 606	...	...	...	...	...	...
0	58 735	30 137	28 598	...	...	...	...	...	...
1 - 4	229 211	117 405	111 806	...	...	...	...	...	...
5 - 9	293 398	150 374	143 024	...	...	...	...	...	...
10 - 14	268 357	137 891	130 466	...	...	...	...	...	...
15 - 19	269 983	138 410	131 573	...	...	...	...	...	...
20 - 24	317 782	162 797	154 985	...	...	...	...	...	...
25 - 29	388 875	198 363	190 512	...	...	...	...	...	...
30 - 34	426 491	218 193	208 298	...	...	...	...	...	...
35 - 39	448 320	230 894	217 426	...	...	...	...	...	...

7. Population by age, sex and urban/rural residence: latest available year, 2009 - 2018
Population selon l'âge, le sexe et la résidence, urbaine/rurale : dernière année disponible, 2009 - 2018 (continued - suite)

Continent, country or area, date, code[a] and age (in years) / Continent, pays ou zone, date, code[a] et âge (en années)	Total			Urban - Urbaine			Rural - Rurale		
	Both sexes Les deux sexes	Male Masculin	Female Féminin	Both sexes Les deux sexes	Male Masculin	Female Féminin	Both sexes Les deux sexes	Male Masculin	Female Féminin
EUROPE									
Slovakia - Slovaquie									
1 I 2018 (ESDJ)									
40 - 44	445 774	228 727	217 047	...	...	...	...	...	...
45 - 49	365 979	185 074	180 905	...	...	...	...	...	...
50 - 54	359 661	178 886	180 775	...	...	...	...	...	...
55 - 59	358 744	175 069	183 675	...	...	...	...	...	...
60 - 64	366 955	172 407	194 548	...	...	...	...	...	...
65 - 69	310 141	138 343	171 798	...	...	...	...	...	...
70 - 74	207 429	84 586	122 843	...	...	...	...	...	...
75 - 79	151 077	55 276	95 801	...	...	...	...	...	...
80 - 84	97 143	31 593	65 550	...	...	...	...	...	...
85 - 89	55 074	15 881	39 193	...	...	...	...	...	...
90 - 94	18 891	4 722	14 169	...	...	...	...	...	...
95 - 99	4 086	1 106	2 980	...	...	...	...	...	...
100 +	1 014	380	634	...	...	...	...	...	...
Slovenia - Slovénie									
1 VII 2017 (ESDJ)									
Total	2 066 161	1 025 973	1 040 188	1 141 453	561 337	580 116	924 708	464 636	460 072
0	20 230	10 397	9 833	11 066	5 641	5 425	9 164	4 756	4 408
1 - 4	84 411	43 410	41 001	46 577	23 843	22 734	37 834	19 567	18 267
5 - 9	110 822	57 050	53 772	60 943	31 402	29 541	49 879	25 648	24 231
10 - 14	94 223	48 408	45 815	50 779	26 205	24 574	43 444	22 203	21 241
15 - 19	92 875	48 074	44 801	49 460	25 707	23 753	43 415	22 367	21 048
20 - 24	101 880	52 496	49 384	60 019	29 972	30 047	41 861	22 524	19 337
25 - 29	120 713	62 660	58 053	66 712	34 259	32 453	54 001	28 401	25 600
30 - 34	139 091	72 723	66 368	78 035	40 721	37 314	61 056	32 002	29 054
35 - 39	156 318	82 397	73 921	88 158	46 293	41 865	68 160	36 104	32 056
40 - 44	153 308	80 000	73 308	84 950	44 179	40 771	68 358	35 821	32 537
45 - 49	145 866	75 223	70 643	79 118	40 431	38 687	66 748	34 792	31 956
50 - 54	155 103	78 618	76 485	83 927	42 111	41 816	71 176	36 507	34 669
55 - 59	148 609	74 783	73 826	79 999	39 644	40 355	68 610	35 139	33 471
60 - 64	147 083	73 577	73 506	80 440	39 247	41 193	66 643	34 330	32 313
65 - 69	123 777	59 943	63 834	68 651	32 309	36 342	55 126	27 634	27 492
70 - 74	87 383	39 379	48 004	49 042	21 528	27 514	38 341	17 851	20 490
75 - 79	77 709	32 646	45 063	43 505	18 215	25 290	34 204	14 431	19 773
80 - 84	57 714	21 012	36 702	32 196	11 975	20 221	25 518	9 037	16 481
85 - 89	34 092	10 033	24 059	19 258	5 773	13 485	14 834	4 260	10 574
90 - 94	12 553	2 681	9 872	7 195	1 608	5 587	5 358	1 073	4 285
95 - 99	2 211	429	1 782	1 311	250	1 061	900	179	721
100 +	190	34	156	112	24	88	78	10	68
1 I 2018 (ESDJ)									
Total	2 066 880	1 027 041	1 039 839	...	...	...	...	...	...
0	20 224	10 476	9 748	...	...	...	...	...	...
1 - 4	83 287	42 707	40 580	...	...	...	...	...	...
5 - 9	111 564	57 462	54 102	...	...	...	...	...	...
10 - 14	95 602	49 138	46 464	...	...	...	...	...	...
15 - 19	93 057	48 170	44 887	...	...	...	...	...	...
20 - 24	101 073	52 221	48 852	...	...	...	...	...	...
25 - 29	117 900	61 380	56 520	...	...	...	...	...	...
30 - 34	137 904	72 091	65 813	...	...	...	...	...	...
35 - 39	155 455	82 025	73 430	...	...	...	...	...	...
40 - 44	153 903	80 411	73 492	...	...	...	...	...	...
45 - 49	145 715	75 406	70 309	...	...	...	...	...	...
50 - 54	154 888	78 329	76 559	...	...	...	...	...	...
55 - 59	148 581	75 018	73 563	...	...	...	...	...	...
60 - 64	146 465	72 939	73 526	...	...	...	...	...	...
65 - 69	126 209	61 251	64 958	...	...	...	...	...	...
70 - 74	88 217	39 922	48 295	...	...	...	...	...	...
75 - 79	78 583	33 139	45 444	...	...	...	...	...	...
80 - 84	57 858	21 321	36 537	...	...	...	...	...	...
85 - 89	34 773	10 267	24 506	...	...	...	...	...	...
90 - 94	13 039	2 882	10 157	...	...	...	...	...	...
95 - 99	2 396	453	1 943	...	...	...	...	...	...
100 +	187	33	154	...	...	...	...	...	...

Continent, country or area, date, code[a] and age (in years) / Continent, pays ou zone, date, code[a] et âge (en années)	Total			Urban - Urbaine			Rural - Rurale		
	Both sexes Les deux sexes	Male Masculin	Female Féminin	Both sexes Les deux sexes	Male Masculin	Female Féminin	Both sexes Les deux sexes	Male Masculin	Female Féminin
EUROPE									
Spain - Espagne[86]									
1 I 2018 (ESDJ)									
Total	46 658 447	22 881 882	23 776 565	...	...	...	...	...	...
0	392 563	202 087	190 476	...	...	...	...	...	...
1 - 4	1 713 663	882 314	831 349	...	...	...	...	...	...
5 - 9	2 423 973	1 250 866	1 173 107	...	...	...	...	...	...
10 - 14	2 448 365	1 261 152	1 187 213	...	...	...	...	...	...
15 - 19	2 263 846	1 167 453	1 096 393	...	...	...	...	...	...
20 - 24	2 261 480	1 153 467	1 108 013	...	...	...	...	...	...
25 - 29	2 512 344	1 264 328	1 248 016	...	...	...	...	...	...
30 - 34	2 853 411	1 420 073	1 433 338	...	...	...	...	...	...
35 - 39	3 577 708	1 795 555	1 782 153	...	...	...	...	...	...
40 - 44	3 972 626	2 014 901	1 957 725	...	...	...	...	...	...
45 - 49	3 767 855	1 902 769	1 865 086	...	...	...	...	...	...
50 - 54	3 592 109	1 791 837	1 800 272	...	...	...	...	...	...
55 - 59	3 205 171	1 578 213	1 626 958	...	...	...	...	...	...
60 - 64	2 713 839	1 316 834	1 397 005	...	...	...	...	...	...
65 - 69	2 406 131	1 147 212	1 258 919	...	...	...	...	...	...
70 - 74	2 126 644	983 119	1 143 525	...	...	...	...	...	...
75 - 79	1 538 604	679 146	859 458	...	...	...	...	...	...
80 - 84	1 422 641	576 201	846 440	...	...	...	...	...	...
85 - 89	953 320	345 121	608 199	...	...	...	...	...	...
90 - 94	401 175	122 286	278 889	...	...	...	...	...	...
95 - 99	99 751	24 994	74 757	...	...	...	...	...	...
100 +	11 228	1 954	9 274	...	...	...	...	...	...
Sweden - Suède[93]									
1 I 2018 (ESDJ)									
Total	10 120 242	5 082 662	5 037 580	...	...	...	...	...	...
0	116 614	59 899	56 715	...	...	...	...	...	...
1 - 4	485 430	249 946	235 484	...	...	...	...	...	...
5 - 9	612 180	314 886	297 294	...	...	...	...	...	...
10 - 14	580 453	298 557	281 896	...	...	...	...	...	...
15 - 19	544 838	286 062	258 776	...	...	...	...	...	...
20 - 24	616 919	319 535	297 384	...	...	...	...	...	...
25 - 29	734 003	377 368	356 635	...	...	...	...	...	...
30 - 34	662 493	340 535	321 958	...	...	...	...	...	...
35 - 39	628 193	321 544	306 649	...	...	...	...	...	...
40 - 44	641 675	326 651	315 024	...	...	...	...	...	...
45 - 49	656 677	332 859	323 818	...	...	...	...	...	...
50 - 54	683 300	347 535	335 765	...	...	...	...	...	...
55 - 59	586 614	295 905	290 709	...	...	...	...	...	...
60 - 64	564 707	282 290	282 417	...	...	...	...	...	...
65 - 69	560 392	276 584	283 808	...	...	...	...	...	...
70 - 74	556 484	272 290	284 194	...	...	...	...	...	...
75 - 79	376 600	178 446	198 154	...	...	...	...	...	...
80 - 84	252 121	110 252	141 869	...	...	...	...	...	...
85 - 89	163 165	62 448	100 717	...	...	...	...	...	...
90 - 94	75 720	23 928	51 792	...	...	...	...	...	...
95 - 99	19 580	4 790	14 790	...	...	...	...	...	...
100 +	2 084	352	1 732	...	...	...	...	...	...
Switzerland - Suisse[94]									
1 I 2018 (ESDJ)									
Total	8 484 130	4 206 434	4 277 696	7 191 266	3 554 201	3 637 065	1 292 864	652 233	640 631
0	85 611	43 971	41 640	73 309	37 647	35 662	12 302	6 324	5 978
1 - 4	348 132	178 922	169 210	295 930	151 998	143 932	52 202	26 924	25 278
5 - 9	426 484	219 276	207 208	359 822	184 904	174 918	66 662	34 372	32 290
10 - 14	408 828	209 592	199 236	343 526	176 214	167 312	65 302	33 378	31 924
15 - 19	431 439	223 310	208 129	361 169	186 957	174 212	70 270	36 353	33 917
20 - 24	488 709	251 439	237 270	411 823	210 963	200 860	76 886	40 476	36 410
25 - 29	572 817	290 366	282 451	494 137	249 198	244 939	78 680	41 168	37 512
30 - 34	598 895	302 605	296 290	520 126	262 221	257 905	78 769	40 384	38 385
35 - 39	600 727	303 314	297 413	519 323	261 991	257 332	81 404	41 323	40 081
40 - 44	582 171	292 806	289 365	500 449	251 172	249 277	81 722	41 634	40 088
45 - 49	633 596	318 687	314 909	536 900	269 825	267 075	96 696	48 862	47 834
50 - 54	673 096	340 498	332 598	567 256	286 120	281 136	105 840	54 378	51 462

7. Population by age, sex and urban/rural residence: latest available year, 2009 - 2018
Population selon l'âge, le sexe et la résidence, urbaine/rurale : dernière année disponible, 2009 - 2018 (continued - suite)

Continent, country or area, date, code[a] and age (in years) / Continent, pays ou zone, date, code[a] et âge (en années)	Total			Urban - Urbaine			Rural - Rurale		
	Both sexes Les deux sexes	Male Masculin	Female Féminin	Both sexes Les deux sexes	Male Masculin	Female Féminin	Both sexes Les deux sexes	Male Masculin	Female Féminin
EUROPE									
Switzerland - Suisse[94]									
1 I 2018 (ESDJ)									
55 - 59	591 887	298 232	293 655	494 194	248 532	245 662	97 693	49 700	47 993
60 - 64	491 373	244 430	246 943	408 478	201 762	206 716	82 895	42 668	40 227
65 - 69	429 492	207 401	222 091	357 592	170 599	186 993	71 900	36 802	35 098
70 - 74	392 361	186 071	206 290	330 007	155 087	174 920	62 354	30 984	31 370
75 - 79	294 176	132 535	161 641	248 929	111 329	137 600	45 247	21 206	24 041
80 - 84	217 197	90 418	126 779	184 121	76 353	107 768	33 076	14 065	19 011
85 - 89	139 897	50 799	89 098	118 439	42 849	75 590	21 458	7 950	13 508
90 - 94	61 287	18 089	43 198	52 057	15 328	36 729	9 230	2 761	6 469
95 - 99	14 445	3 416	11 029	12 389	2 928	9 461	2 056	488	1 568
100 +	1 510	257	1 253	1 290	224	1 066	220	33	187
Ukraine[95]									
1 I 2018 (ESDJ)									
Total	42 216 766	19 558 180	22 658 586	29 132 191	13 363 808	15 768 383	13 084 575	6 194 372	6 890 203
0	361 789	186 249	175 540	235 742	121 339	114 403	126 047	64 910	61 137
1 - 4	1 736 184	895 177	841 007	1 134 412	585 051	549 361	601 772	310 126	291 646
5 - 9	2 379 971	1 226 979	1 152 992	1 582 271	816 423	765 848	797 700	410 556	387 144
10 - 14	2 052 546	1 054 198	998 348	1 375 263	706 849	668 414	677 283	347 349	329 934
15 - 19	1 840 643	945 967	894 676	1 196 422	612 234	584 188	644 221	333 733	310 488
20 - 24	2 313 510	1 189 370	1 124 140	1 528 992	785 843	743 149	784 518	403 527	380 991
25 - 29	3 055 950	1 562 602	1 493 348	2 060 712	1 042 147	1 018 565	995 238	520 455	474 783
30 - 34	3 635 922	1 842 797	1 793 125	2 660 663	1 326 740	1 333 923	975 259	516 057	459 202
35 - 39	3 249 517	1 623 318	1 626 199	2 400 600	1 189 693	1 210 907	848 917	433 625	415 292
40 - 44	3 047 046	1 485 621	1 561 425	2 169 142	1 046 073	1 123 069	877 904	439 548	438 356
45 - 49	2 887 430	1 381 886	1 505 544	1 995 610	936 247	1 059 363	891 820	445 639	446 181
50 - 54	2 823 735	1 302 639	1 521 096	1 941 376	868 106	1 073 270	882 359	434 533	447 826
55 - 59	3 152 778	1 395 204	1 757 574	2 218 879	951 370	1 267 509	933 899	443 834	490 065
60 - 64	2 712 475	1 128 895	1 583 580	1 938 417	783 597	1 154 820	774 058	345 298	428 760
65 - 69	2 364 521	918 219	1 446 302	1 701 783	648 712	1 053 071	662 738	269 507	393 231
70 - 74	1 336 574	465 668	870 906	922 790	322 843	599 947	413 784	142 825	270 959
75 - 79	1 588 273	489 788	1 098 485	1 036 925	324 706	712 219	551 348	165 082	386 266
80 - 84	963 116	281 666	681 450	608 719	181 779	426 940	354 397	99 887	254 510
85 - 89	491 782	126 308	365 474	292 362	78 778	213 584	199 420	47 530	151 890
90 - 94	180 512	42 855	137 657	104 410	26 558	77 852	76 102	16 297	59 805
95 - 99	33 969	10 040	23 929	20 104	6 646	13 458	13 865	3 394	10 471
100 +	8 523	2 734	5 789	6 597	2 074	4 523	1 926	660	1 266
United Kingdom of Great Britain and Northern Ireland - Royaume-Uni de Grande-Bretagne et d'Irlande du Nord[96]									
27 III 2011 (CDJC)									
Total	63 182 178	31 028 143	32 154 035	51 217 521	25 124 237	26 093 284	11 964 657	5 903 906	6 060 751
0 - 4	3 913 953	2 002 494	1 911 459	3 302 119	1 689 719	1 612 400	611 834	312 775	299 059
5 - 9	3 516 615	1 799 999	1 716 616	2 878 114	1 472 489	1 405 625	638 501	327 510	310 991
10 - 14	3 669 326	1 878 838	1 790 488	2 951 079	1 509 796	1 441 283	718 247	369 042	349 205
15 - 19	3 996 452	2 040 725	1 955 727	3 277 414	1 667 480	1 609 934	719 038	373 245	345 793
20 - 24	4 297 198	2 164 141	2 133 057	3 737 543	1 863 922	1 873 621	559 655	300 219	259 436
25 - 29	4 306 340	2 145 054	2 161 286	3 781 906	1 876 471	1 905 435	524 434	268 583	255 851
30 - 34	4 125 449	2 059 312	2 066 137	3 573 410	1 789 511	1 783 899	552 039	269 801	282 238
35 - 39	4 194 477	2 082 310	2 112 167	3 495 390	1 745 563	1 749 827	699 087	336 747	362 340
40 - 44	4 625 635	2 283 902	2 341 733	3 734 709	1 851 446	1 883 263	890 926	432 456	458 470
45 - 49	4 643 100	2 293 572	2 349 528	3 683 527	1 821 257	1 862 270	959 573	472 315	487 258
50 - 54	4 094 454	2 028 748	2 065 706	3 216 769	1 593 822	1 622 947	877 685	434 926	442 759
55 - 59	3 614 078	1 785 598	1 828 480	2 790 096	1 378 906	1 411 190	823 982	406 692	417 290
60 - 64	3 807 974	1 868 912	1 939 062	2 869 025	1 404 882	1 464 143	938 949	464 030	474 919
65 - 69	3 017 480	1 463 355	1 554 125	2 248 845	1 082 105	1 166 740	768 635	381 250	387 385
70 - 74	2 462 745	1 162 621	1 300 124	1 874 997	873 593	1 001 404	587 748	289 028	298 720
75 - 79	2 006 019	903 433	1 102 586	1 549 014	686 269	862 745	457 005	217 164	239 841
80 - 84	1 498 896	615 163	883 733	1 166 619	470 552	696 067	332 277	144 611	187 666
85 - 89	918 343	324 063	594 280	717 808	249 645	468 163	200 535	74 418	126 117
90 - 94	368 425	104 072	264 353	287 454	80 165	207 289	80 971	23 907	57 064
95 - 99	92 951	19 756	73 195	72 117	15 038	57 079	20 834	4 718	16 116
100 +	12 268	2 075	10 193	9 566	1 606	7 960	2 702	469	2 233

7. Population by age, sex and urban/rural residence: latest available year, 2009 - 2018
Population selon l'âge, le sexe et la résidence, urbaine/rurale : dernière année disponible, 2009 - 2018 (continued - suite)

Continent, country or area, date, code[a] and age (in years) / Continent, pays ou zone, date, code[a] et âge (en années)	Total			Urban - Urbaine			Rural - Rurale		
	Both sexes Les deux sexes	Male Masculin	Female Féminin	Both sexes Les deux sexes	Male Masculin	Female Féminin	Both sexes Les deux sexes	Male Masculin	Female Féminin

EUROPE

United Kingdom of Great Britain and Northern Ireland - Royaume-Uni de Grande-Bretagne et d'Irlande du Nord[96]
1 I 2018 (ESDJ)[85]

Total	66 273 576	32 709 956	33 563 620	...	...	...	...	...	...
0	768 431	393 790	374 641	...	...	...	...	...	...
1 - 4	3 180 323	1 630 588	1 549 735	...	...	...	...	...	...
5 - 9	4 127 134	2 112 519	2 014 615	...	...	...	...	...	...
10 - 14	3 795 661	1 944 627	1 851 034	...	...	...	...	...	...
15 - 19	3 678 852	1 888 733	1 790 119	...	...	...	...	...	...
20 - 24	4 194 671	2 153 737	2 040 934	...	...	...	...	...	...
25 - 29	4 544 698	2 301 315	2 243 383	...	...	...	...	...	...
30 - 34	4 448 043	2 219 685	2 228 358	...	...	...	...	...	...
35 - 39	4 328 081	2 148 457	2 179 624	...	...	...	...	...	...
40 - 44	4 025 390	1 996 585	2 028 805	...	...	...	...	...	...
45 - 49	4 541 513	2 239 582	2 301 931	...	...	...	...	...	...
50 - 54	4 671 514	2 299 522	2 371 992	...	...	...	...	...	...
55 - 59	4 240 050	2 090 524	2 149 526	...	...	...	...	...	...
60 - 64	3 637 148	1 782 067	1 855 081	...	...	...	...	...	...
65 - 69	3 438 188	1 665 214	1 772 974	...	...	...	...	...	...
70 - 74	3 182 572	1 522 470	1 660 102	...	...	...	...	...	...
75 - 79	2 210 116	1 018 015	1 192 101	...	...	...	...	...	...
80 - 84	1 657 805	723 134	934 671	...	...	...	...	...	...
85 - 89	1 021 503	398 605	622 898	...	...	...	...	...	...
90 - 94	446 840	148 066	298 774	...	...	...	...	...	...
95 - 99	120 574	30 218	90 356	...	...	...	...	...	...
100 +	14 469	2 503	11 966	...	...	...	...	...	...

OCEANIA - OCÉANIE

American Samoa - Samoas américaines[46]
1 IV 2010 (CDJC)

Total	55 519	28 164	27 355	...	...	...	...	...	...
0 - 4	6 611	3 417	3 194	...	...	...	...	...	...
5 - 9	6 535	3 470	3 065	...	...	...	...	...	...
10 - 14	6 279	3 214	3 065	...	...	...	...	...	...
15 - 19	6 296	3 218	3 078	...	...	...	...	...	...
20 - 24	3 891	1 944	1 947	...	...	...	...	...	...
25 - 29	3 324	1 670	1 654	...	...	...	...	...	...
30 - 34	3 510	1 726	1 784	...	...	...	...	...	...
35 - 39	3 609	1 845	1 764	...	...	...	...	...	...
40 - 44	3 600	1 793	1 807	...	...	...	...	...	...
45 - 49	3 389	1 673	1 716	...	...	...	...	...	...
50 - 54	2 679	1 335	1 344	...	...	...	...	...	...
55 - 59	2 049	1 011	1 038	...	...	...	...	...	...
60 - 64	1 480	755	725	...	...	...	...	...	...
65 - 69	960	500	460	...	...	...	...	...	...
70 - 74	654	321	333	...	...	...	...	...	...
75 - 79	337	155	182	...	...	...	...	...	...
80 - 84	206	76	130	...	...	...	...	...	...
85 +	110	41	69	...	...	...	...	...	...

Australia - Australie[97]
1 VII 2017 (ESDJ)

Total	24 597 528	12 201 837	12 395 691	21 314 066	10 531 804	10 782 262	3 283 462	1 670 033	1 613 429
0	303 227	155 753	147 474	268 656	138 037	130 619	34 571	17 716	16 855
1 - 4	1 272 155	653 201	618 954	1 115 568	572 411	543 157	156 587	80 790	75 797
5 - 9	1 586 875	814 037	772 838	1 371 107	703 210	667 897	215 768	110 827	104 941
10 - 14	1 473 039	757 113	715 926	1 259 659	647 513	612 146	213 380	109 600	103 780
15 - 19	1 482 595	760 063	722 532	1 288 207	659 228	628 979	194 388	100 835	93 553
20 - 24	1 720 279	879 098	841 181	1 562 619	795 532	767 087	157 660	83 566	74 094
25 - 29	1 849 008	924 969	924 039	1 679 993	838 502	841 491	169 015	86 467	82 548

Continent, country or area, date, code[a] and age (in years) / Continent, pays ou zone, date, code[a] et âge (en années)	Total Both sexes Les deux sexes	Total Male Masculin	Total Female Féminin	Urban - Urbaine Both sexes Les deux sexes	Urban - Urbaine Male Masculin	Urban - Urbaine Female Féminin	Rural - Rurale Both sexes Les deux sexes	Rural - Rurale Male Masculin	Rural - Rurale Female Féminin
OCEANIA - OCÉANIE									
Australia - Australie[97]									
1 VII 2017 (ESDJ)									
30 - 34	1 832 757	908 555	924 202	1 655 874	820 098	835 776	176 883	88 457	88 426
35 - 39	1 660 667	827 897	832 770	1 483 375	739 731	743 644	177 292	88 166	89 126
40 - 44	1 603 720	797 516	806 204	1 407 059	698 952	708 107	196 661	98 564	98 097
45 - 49	1 647 910	806 828	841 082	1 423 214	694 761	728 453	224 696	112 067	112 629
50 - 54	1 535 583	754 302	781 281	1 303 343	637 776	665 567	232 240	116 526	115 714
55 - 59	1 506 217	738 590	767 627	1 254 203	611 210	642 993	252 014	127 380	124 634
60 - 64	1 331 968	649 215	682 753	1 094 674	527 382	567 292	237 294	121 833	115 461
65 - 69	1 192 970	586 268	606 702	973 438	471 260	502 178	219 532	115 008	104 524
70 - 74	958 778	470 860	487 918	785 414	379 542	405 872	173 364	91 318	82 046
75 - 79	677 347	321 841	355 506	562 271	262 637	299 634	115 076	59 204	55 872
80 - 84	468 911	209 819	259 092	397 507	174 854	222 653	71 404	34 965	36 439
85 - 89	306 874	124 606	182 268	264 337	105 889	158 448	42 537	18 717	23 820
90 - 94	144 986	49 649	95 337	126 957	43 023	83 934	18 029	6 626	11 403
95 - 99	37 675	10 717	26 958	33 222	9 458	23 764	4 453	1 259	3 194
100 +	3 987	940	3 047	3 369	798	2 571	618	142	476
1 VII 2018 (ESDJ)									
Total	24 992 860	12 397 401	12 595 459	...	...	...	...	...	...
0	313 544	161 154	152 390	...	...	...	...	...	...
1 - 4	1 268 687	651 711	616 976	...	...	...	...	...	...
5 - 9	1 604 449	823 406	781 043	...	...	...	...	...	...
10 - 14	1 515 720	779 174	736 546	...	...	...	...	...	...
15 - 19	1 491 008	765 106	725 902	...	...	...	...	...	...
20 - 24	1 739 976	890 600	849 376	...	...	...	...	...	...
25 - 29	1 877 334	940 782	936 552	...	...	...	...	...	...
30 - 34	1 862 558	921 260	941 298	...	...	...	...	...	...
35 - 39	1 722 345	857 577	864 768	...	...	...	...	...	...
40 - 44	1 593 899	793 312	800 587	...	...	...	...	...	...
45 - 49	1 670 884	818 996	851 888	...	...	...	...	...	...
50 - 54	1 528 997	749 470	779 527	...	...	...	...	...	...
55 - 59	1 529 383	749 984	779 399	...	...	...	...	...	...
60 - 64	1 359 403	661 441	697 962	...	...	...	...	...	...
65 - 69	1 207 000	589 971	617 029	...	...	...	...	...	...
70 - 74	1 017 943	500 024	517 919	...	...	...	...	...	...
75 - 79	700 394	333 699	366 695	...	...	...	...	...	...
80 - 84	485 668	218 466	267 202	...	...	...	...	...	...
85 - 89	309 056	126 240	182 816	...	...	...	...	...	...
90 - 94	149 761	52 338	97 423	...	...	...	...	...	...
95 - 99	40 350	11 537	28 813	...	...	...	...	...	...
100 +	4 501	1 153	3 348	...	...	...	...	...	...
Cook Islands - Îles Cook[98]									
1 XII 2011 (CDFC)									
Total	17 794	8 815	8 979	...	...	...	...	...	...
0 - 4	1 584	806	778	...	...	...	...	...	...
5 - 9	1 539	768	771	...	...	...	...	...	...
10 - 14	1 504	794	710	...	...	...	...	...	...
15 - 19	1 495	768	727	...	...	...	...	...	...
20 - 24	1 273	611	662	...	...	...	...	...	...
25 - 29	1 263	590	673	...	...	...	...	...	...
30 - 34	1 122	534	588	...	...	...	...	...	...
35 - 39	1 179	543	636	...	...	...	...	...	...
40 - 44	1 252	605	647	...	...	...	...	...	...
45 - 49	1 282	636	646	...	...	...	...	...	...
50 - 54	1 059	534	525	...	...	...	...	...	...
55 - 59	863	430	433	...	...	...	...	...	...
60 - 64	749	394	355	...	...	...	...	...	...
65 - 69	649	333	316	...	...	...	...	...	...
70 - 74	496	251	245	...	...	...	...	...	...
75 - 79	285	130	155	...	...	...	...	...	...
80 +	200	88	112	...	...	...	...	...	...
Fiji - Fidji									
17 IX 2017 (CDFC)									
Total	884 887	448 595	436 292	494 252	245 928	248 324	390 635	202 667	187 968
0 - 4	91 897	47 195	44 702	47 904	24 614	23 290	43 993	22 581	21 412

7. Population by age, sex and urban/rural residence: latest available year, 2009 - 2018
Population selon l'âge, le sexe et la résidence, urbaine/rurale : dernière année disponible, 2009 - 2018 (continued - suite)

Continent, country or area, date, code[a] and age (in years) / Continent, pays ou zone, date, code[a] et âge (en années)	Total			Urban - Urbaine			Rural - Rurale		
	Both sexes Les deux sexes	Male Masculin	Female Féminin	Both sexes Les deux sexes	Male Masculin	Female Féminin	Both sexes Les deux sexes	Male Masculin	Female Féminin
OCEANIA - OCÉANIE									
Fiji - Fidji									
17 IX 2017 (CDFC)									
5 - 9	88 295	45 243	43 052	45 436	23 231	22 205	42 859	22 012	20 847
10 - 14	79 596	40 715	38 881	40 784	20 676	20 108	38 812	20 039	18 773
15 - 19	74 088	38 032	36 056	42 045	20 713	21 332	32 043	17 319	14 724
20 - 24	73 616	37 464	36 152	46 942	23 397	23 545	26 674	14 067	12 607
25 - 29	69 308	35 253	34 055	41 756	21 030	20 726	27 552	14 223	13 329
30 - 34	68 818	35 266	33 552	40 741	20 609	20 132	28 077	14 657	13 420
35 - 39	65 150	33 382	31 768	37 684	18 904	18 780	27 466	14 478	12 988
40 - 44	53 514	27 697	25 817	30 590	15 476	15 114	22 924	12 221	10 703
45 - 49	49 504	25 314	24 190	27 872	13 998	13 874	21 632	11 316	10 316
50 - 54	48 610	24 649	23 961	26 585	13 241	13 344	22 025	11 408	10 617
55 - 59	42 008	21 263	20 745	23 113	11 249	11 864	18 895	10 014	8 881
60 - 64	30 615	14 891	15 724	16 744	7 805	8 939	13 871	7 086	6 785
65 - 69	21 328	10 076	11 252	11 469	5 138	6 331	9 859	4 938	4 921
70 - 74	14 148	6 367	7 781	7 342	3 131	4 211	6 806	3 236	3 570
75 + ...	14 392	5 788	8 604	7 245	2 716	4 529	7 147	3 072	4 075
French Polynesia - Polynésie française[5]									
1 I 2015 (ESDF)									
Total..................................	271 796	138 447	133 349	...	...	...	...	...	...
0 - 4	21 691	10 938	10 753	...	...	...	...	...	...
5 - 9	21 973	11 252	10 721	...	...	...	...	...	...
10 - 14	22 896	11 732	11 164	...	...	...	...	...	...
15 - 19	22 653	11 795	10 858	...	...	...	...	...	...
20 - 24	22 850	11 623	11 227	...	...	...	...	...	...
25 - 29	21 204	10 534	10 670	...	...	...	...	...	...
30 - 34	20 789	10 380	10 409	...	...	...	...	...	...
35 - 39	19 482	9 864	9 618	...	...	...	...	...	...
40 - 44	20 216	10 302	9 914	...	...	...	...	...	...
45 - 49	19 623	10 189	9 434	...	...	...	...	...	...
50 - 54	16 540	8 602	7 938	...	...	...	...	...	...
55 - 59	13 167	6 942	6 225	...	...	...	...	...	...
60 - 64	9 849	5 079	4 770	...	...	...	...	...	...
65 - 69	7 193	3 653	3 540	...	...	...	...	...	...
70 - 74	5 309	2 699	2 610	...	...	...	...	...	...
75 - 79	3 346	1 565	1 781	...	...	...	...	...	...
80 + ...	3 015	1 298	1 717	...	...	...	...	...	...
Guam[46]									
1 VII 2018 (ESDJ)									
Total..................................	167 772	86 329	81 443	...	...	...	...	...	...
0	3 218	1 662	1 556	...	...	...	...	...	...
1 - 4	12 818	6 624	6 194	...	...	...	...	...	...
5 - 9	15 559	8 054	7 505	...	...	...	...	...	...
10 - 14	14 505	7 553	6 952	...	...	...	...	...	...
15 - 19	14 240	7 563	6 677	...	...	...	...	...	...
20 - 24	13 268	7 129	6 139	...	...	...	...	...	...
25 - 29	12 396	6 533	5 863	...	...	...	...	...	...
30 - 34	10 492	5 438	5 054	...	...	...	...	...	...
35 - 39	9 252	4 636	4 616	...	...	...	...	...	...
40 - 44	9 337	4 737	4 600	...	...	...	...	...	...
45 - 49	10 556	5 377	5 179	...	...	...	...	...	...
50 - 54	10 344	5 449	4 895	...	...	...	...	...	...
55 - 59	9 465	4 930	4 535	...	...	...	...	...	...
60 - 64	7 398	3 697	3 701	...	...	...	...	...	...
65 - 69	6 051	2 986	3 065	...	...	...	...	...	...
70 - 74	3 930	1 875	2 055	...	...	...	...	...	...
75 - 79	2 460	1 123	1 337	...	...	...	...	...	...
80 - 84	1 594	637	957	...	...	...	...	...	...
85 - 89	688	254	434	...	...	...	...	...	...
90 - 94	171	62	109	...	...	...	...	...	...
95 - 99	27	9	18	...	...	...	...	...	...
100 + ...	3	1	2	...	...	...	...	...	...

Continent, country or area, date, code[a] and age (in years) Continent, pays ou zone, date, code[a] et âge (en années)	Total			Urban - Urbaine			Rural - Rurale		
	Both sexes Les deux sexes	Male Masculin	Female Féminin	Both sexes Les deux sexes	Male Masculin	Female Féminin	Both sexes Les deux sexes	Male Masculin	Female Féminin
OCEANIA - OCÉANIE									
Kiribati									
7 XI 2015 (CDFC)									
Total	110 136	54 096	56 040	56 388	27 159	29 229	53 748	26 937	26 811
0 - 4	14 393	7 546	6 847	7 140	3 724	3 416	7 253	3 822	3 431
5 - 9	13 600	6 903	6 697	6 470	3 313	3 157	7 130	3 590	3 540
10 - 14	10 445	5 309	5 136	4 700	2 327	2 373	5 745	2 982	2 763
15 - 19	11 676	5 851	5 825	6 290	2 988	3 302	5 386	2 863	2 523
20 - 24	10 319	5 199	5 120	6 137	3 015	3 122	4 182	2 184	1 998
25 - 29	9 672	4 682	4 990	5 468	2 603	2 865	4 204	2 079	2 125
30 - 34	8 012	3 838	4 174	4 356	2 052	2 304	3 656	1 786	1 870
35 - 39	6 584	3 161	3 423	3 422	1 661	1 761	3 162	1 500	1 662
40 - 44	5 091	2 433	2 658	2 555	1 198	1 357	2 536	1 235	1 301
45 - 49	5 707	2 676	3 031	2 724	1 227	1 497	2 983	1 449	1 534
50 - 54	4 905	2 372	2 533	2 483	1 182	1 301	2 422	1 190	1 232
55 - 59	3 321	1 548	1 773	1 694	743	951	1 627	805	822
60 - 64	2 406	1 051	1 355	1 174	494	680	1 232	557	675
65 - 69	1 748	731	1 017	815	322	493	933	409	524
70 - 74	1 238	460	778	551	183	368	687	277	410
75 - 79	608	217	391	241	86	155	367	131	236
80 - 84	267	80	187	109	30	79	158	50	108
85 - 89	109	30	79	42	6	36	67	24	43
90 - 94	24	7	17	10	3	7	14	4	10
95 - 99	11	2	9	7	2	5	4	-	4
100 +	-	-	-	-	-	-	-	-	-
Marshall Islands - Îles Marshall									
3 IV 2011 (CDFC)									
Total	53 158	27 243	25 915	39 205	19 927	19 278	13 953	7 316	6 637
0 - 4	7 743	4 031	3 712	5 617	2 901	2 716	2 126	1 130	996
5 - 9	7 017	3 622	3 395	4 794	2 459	2 335	2 223	1 163	1 060
10 - 14	6 493	3 385	3 108	4 400	2 293	2 107	2 093	1 092	1 001
15 - 19	4 731	2 417	2 314	3 793	1 917	1 876	938	500	438
20 - 24	5 094	2 614	2 480	3 955	2 015	1 940	1 139	599	540
25 - 29	4 404	2 159	2 245	3 288	1 585	1 703	1 116	574	542
30 - 34	3 789	1 876	1 913	2 819	1 387	1 432	970	489	481
35 - 39	3 136	1 587	1 549	2 369	1 197	1 172	767	390	377
40 - 44	2 785	1 419	1 366	2 151	1 083	1 068	634	336	298
45 - 49	2 344	1 189	1 155	1 766	876	890	578	313	265
50 - 54	1 930	1 016	914	1 503	782	721	427	234	193
55 - 59	1 576	815	761	1 167	595	572	409	220	189
60 - 64	1 052	583	469	803	444	359	249	139	110
65 - 69	522	284	238	399	219	180	123	65	58
70 - 74	250	131	119	182	95	87	68	36	32
75 - 79	152	62	90	103	44	59	49	18	31
80 - 84	92	31	61	61	19	42	31	12	19
85 - 89	36	21	15	26	16	10	10	5	5
90 - 94	12	1	11	9	-	9	3	1	2
95 +	-	-	-	-	-	-	-	-	-
Micronesia (Federated States of) - Micronésie (États fédérés de)[99]									
1 VII 2018 (ESDJ)									
Total	104 286	52 925	51 361	...	...	...	...	...	...
0	2 546	1 317	1 229	...	...	...	...	...	...
1 - 4	9 696	4 911	4 785	...	...	...	...	...	...
5 - 9	12 106	6 224	5 882	...	...	...	...	...	...
10 - 14	12 863	6 608	6 255	...	...	...	...	...	...
15 - 19	12 156	6 326	5 831	...	...	...	...	...	...
20 - 24	9 492	4 975	4 518	...	...	...	...	...	...
25 - 29	7 755	3 897	3 858	...	...	...	...	...	...
30 - 34	6 683	3 445	3 239	...	...	...	...	...	...
35 - 39	6 030	2 969	3 061	...	...	...	...	...	...
40 - 44	5 661	2 757	2 904	...	...	...	...	...	...
45 - 49	5 264	2 679	2 585	...	...	...	...	...	...
50 - 54	4 689	2 334	2 355	...	...	...	...	...	...

Continent, country or area, date, code[a] and age (in years) / Continent, pays ou zone, date, code[a] et âge (en années)	Total			Urban - Urbaine			Rural - Rurale		
	Both sexes Les deux sexes	Male Masculin	Female Féminin	Both sexes Les deux sexes	Male Masculin	Female Féminin	Both sexes Les deux sexes	Male Masculin	Female Féminin
OCEANIA - OCÉANIE									
Micronesia (Federated States of) - Micronésie (États fédérés de)[99]									
1 VII 2018 (ESDJ)									
55 - 59	3 663	1 901	1 761	...	...	...	...	...	...
60 - 64	2 324	1 185	1 139	...	...	...	...	...	...
65 +	3 355	1 396	1 959	...	...	...	...	...	...
Nauru									
1 VII 2016 (ESDF)									
Total	11 014	5 547	5 467	...	...	...	...	...	...
0	321	164	157	...	...	...	...	...	...
1 - 4	1 324	675	649	...	...	...	...	...	...
5 - 9	1 579	854	725	...	...	...	...	...	...
10 - 14	1 142	562	579	...	...	...	...	...	...
15 - 19	1 012	525	488	...	...	...	...	...	...
20 - 24	836	434	402	...	...	...	...	...	...
25 - 29	930	461	468	...	...	...	...	...	...
30 - 34	900	444	457	...	...	...	...	...	...
35 - 39	723	377	346	...	...	...	...	...	...
40 - 44	562	277	285	...	...	...	...	...	...
45 - 49	443	220	223	...	...	...	...	...	...
50 - 54	452	212	240	...	...	...	...	...	...
55 - 59	343	152	190	...	...	...	...	...	...
60 - 64	242	110	131	...	...	...	...	...	...
65 - 69	127	50	77	...	...	...	...	...	...
70 - 74	40	15	25	...	...	...	...	...	...
75 +	39	15	24	...	...	...	...	...	...
New Caledonia - Nouvelle-Calédonie									
1 I 2017 (ESDF)									
Total	278 495	140 000	138 495	...	...	...	...	...	...
0 - 4	20 587	10 481	10 106	...	...	...	...	...	...
5 - 9	21 295	11 009	10 286	...	...	...	...	...	...
10 - 14	21 505	10 922	10 583	...	...	...	...	...	...
15 - 19	22 963	11 621	11 342	...	...	...	...	...	...
20 - 24	19 937	10 329	9 608	...	...	...	...	...	...
25 - 29	20 738	10 338	10 400	...	...	...	...	...	...
30 - 34	21 487	10 760	10 727	...	...	...	...	...	...
35 - 39	20 717	10 255	10 462	...	...	...	...	...	...
40 - 44	21 555	10 853	10 702	...	...	...	...	...	...
45 - 49	19 744	9 795	9 949	...	...	...	...	...	...
50 - 54	17 719	8 939	8 780	...	...	...	...	...	...
55 - 59	13 955	7 010	6 945	...	...	...	...	...	...
60 - 64	11 230	5 722	5 508	...	...	...	...	...	...
65 - 69	8 877	4 516	4 361	...	...	...	...	...	...
70 - 74	6 650	3 339	3 311	...	...	...	...	...	...
75 - 79	4 642	2 157	2 485	...	...	...	...	...	...
80 - 84	2 793	1 198	1 595	...	...	...	...	...	...
85 - 89	1 538	607	931	...	...	...	...	...	...
90 - 94	436	119	317	...	...	...	...	...	...
95 +	127	30	97	...	...	...	...	...	...
New Zealand - Nouvelle-Zélande[100]									
1 VII 2018 (ESDJ)									
Total	4 885 570	2 408 890	2 476 680	4 223 710	2 071 350	2 152 360	661 860	337 540	324 320
0	60 220	30 870	29 350	52 500	26 880	25 620	7 730	3 990	3 730
1 - 4	246 290	126 530	119 760	214 390	110 130	104 270	31 890	16 400	15 490
5 - 9	327 240	167 910	159 330	281 220	144 250	136 970	46 020	23 660	22 360
10 - 14	310 950	159 200	151 740	263 170	134 750	128 420	47 780	24 460	23 320
15 - 19	314 160	161 060	153 090	273 550	139 520	134 020	40 610	21 540	19 070
20 - 24	358 260	186 440	171 820	323 780	167 460	156 320	34 480	18 980	15 500
25 - 29	380 050	193 850	186 200	345 970	176 010	169 960	34 080	17 850	16 240
30 - 34	330 720	161 920	168 800	298 490	145 850	152 630	32 230	16 060	16 170
35 - 39	297 660	144 100	153 560	264 360	127 800	136 560	33 300	16 310	16 990
40 - 44	291 120	140 050	151 060	252 110	120 880	131 230	39 010	19 170	19 840

7. Population by age, sex and urban/rural residence: latest available year, 2009 - 2018
Population selon l'âge, le sexe et la résidence, urbaine/rurale : dernière année disponible, 2009 - 2018 (continued - suite)

Continent, country or area, date, code[a] and age (in years) / Continent, pays ou zone, date, code[a] et âge (en années)	Total			Urban - Urbaine			Rural - Rurale		
	Both sexes Les deux sexes	Male Masculin	Female Féminin	Both sexes Les deux sexes	Male Masculin	Female Féminin	Both sexes Les deux sexes	Male Masculin	Female Féminin
OCEANIA - OCÉANIE									
New Zealand - Nouvelle-Zélande[100]									
1 VII 2018 (ESDJ)									
45 - 49	324 420	155 190	169 230	275 290	131 160	144 130	49 130	24 020	25 110
50 - 54	312 930	150 970	161 960	261 360	125 580	135 780	51 570	25 390	26 190
55 - 59	312 600	150 880	161 710	257 510	123 400	134 110	55 090	27 480	27 610
60 - 64	272 010	131 400	140 610	222 290	106 130	116 170	49 720	25 280	24 440
65 - 69	237 180	115 320	121 850	194 770	93 350	101 420	42 410	21 970	20 430
70 - 74	195 330	94 430	100 890	163 380	77 580	85 800	31 940	16 850	15 090
75 - 79	138 330	65 030	73 310	119 400	55 030	64 370	18 930	9 990	8 940
80 - 84	89 370	40 270	49 100	79 910	35 330	44 580	9 460	4 940	4 520
85 - 89	55 710	22 970	32 750	51 150	20 610	30 540	4 570	2 360	2 210
90 +	31 020	10 500	20 520	29 110	9 660	19 450	1 910	840	1 070
Niue - Nioué[85]									
1 VII 2017* (ESDJ)									
Total	1 591	762	829	...	...	...	...	...	...
0 - 4	135	68	67	...	...	...	...	...	...
5 - 14	312	149	163	...	...	...	...	...	...
15 - 24	160	77	83	...	...	...	...	...	...
25 - 34	220	101	119	...	...	...	...	...	...
35 - 44	182	87	95	...	...	...	...	...	...
45 - 54	192	101	91	...	...	...	...	...	...
55 - 64	178	88	90	...	...	...	...	...	...
65 - 74	114	55	59	...	...	...	...	...	...
75 +	98	36	62	...	...	...	...	...	...
Norfolk Island - Île Norfolk									
9 VIII 2011 (CDFC)									
Total	2 302	1 082	1 220	...	...	...	...	...	...
0 - 4	106	53	53	...	...	...	...	...	...
5 - 9	123	63	60	...	...	...	...	...	...
10 - 14	132	69	63	...	...	...	...	...	...
15 - 19	73	35	38	...	...	...	...	...	...
20 - 24	41	20	21	...	...	...	...	...	...
25 - 29	60	19	41	...	...	...	...	...	...
30 - 34	100	48	52	...	...	...	...	...	...
35 - 39	127	56	71	...	...	...	...	...	...
40 - 44	146	64	82	...	...	...	...	...	...
45 - 49	167	81	86	...	...	...	...	...	...
50 - 54	180	86	94	...	...	...	...	...	...
55 - 59	232	103	129	...	...	...	...	...	...
60 - 64	262	120	142	...	...	...	...	...	...
65 - 69	205	99	106	...	...	...	...	...	...
70 - 74	142	70	72	...	...	...	...	...	...
75 - 79	96	49	47	...	...	...	...	...	...
80 - 84	58	24	34	...	...	...	...	...	...
85 +	52	23	29	...	...	...	...	...	...
Northern Mariana Islands - Îles Mariannes septentrionales									
1 VII 2011 (ESDF)									
Total	46 050	22 153	23 897	...	...	...	...	...	...
0 - 4	4 852	2 495	2 357	...	...	...	...	...	...
5 - 9	3 622	1 883	1 739	...	...	...	...	...	...
10 - 14	3 500	1 971	1 529	...	...	...	...	...	...
15 - 19	3 802	2 121	1 681	...	...	...	...	...	...
20 - 24	3 398	1 607	1 791	...	...	...	...	...	...
25 - 29	3 831	1 050	2 781	...	...	...	...	...	...
30 - 34	3 696	1 008	2 688	...	...	...	...	...	...
35 - 39	3 211	1 550	1 661	...	...	...	...	...	...
40 - 44	3 584	1 858	1 726	...	...	...	...	...	...
45 - 49	3 738	1 967	1 771	...	...	...	...	...	...
50 - 54	3 441	1 824	1 617	...	...	...	...	...	...
55 - 59	2 270	1 260	1 010	...	...	...	...	...	...
60 - 64	1 440	769	671	...	...	...	...	...	...
65 - 69	794	366	428	...	...	...	...	...	...

Continent, country or area, date, code[a] and age (in years) / Continent, pays ou zone, date, code[a] et âge (en années)	Total			Urban - Urbaine			Rural - Rurale		
	Both sexes Les deux sexes	Male Masculin	Female Féminin	Both sexes Les deux sexes	Male Masculin	Female Féminin	Both sexes Les deux sexes	Male Masculin	Female Féminin
OCEANIA - OCÉANIE									
Northern Mariana Islands - Îles Mariannes septentrionales									
1 VII 2011 (ESDF)									
70 - 74	416	248	168	...	...	...	...	...	...
75 - 79	239	101	138	...	...	...	...	...	...
80 - 84	147	54	93	...	...	...	...	...	...
85 - 89	53	17	36	...	...	...	...	...	...
90 - 94	14	3	11	...	...	...	...	...	...
95 - 99	1	1	-	...	...	...	...	...	...
100 +	1	-	1	...	...	...	...	...	...
Palau - Palaos									
13 IV 2015 (CDJC)									
Total	17 661	9 433	8 228	14 209	7 620	6 589	3 452	1 813	1 639
0 - 4	1 200	653	547	962	528	434	238	125	113
5 - 9	1 219	614	605	932	483	449	287	131	156
10 - 14	1 209	636	573	916	489	427	293	147	146
15 - 19	1 201	624	577	975	495	480	226	129	97
20 - 24	1 195	687	508	1 018	587	431	177	100	77
25 - 29	1 217	694	523	1 041	581	460	176	113	63
30 - 34	1 338	759	579	1 163	661	502	175	98	77
35 - 39	1 420	813	607	1 215	701	514	205	112	93
40 - 44	1 501	861	640	1 235	715	520	266	146	120
45 - 49	1 538	820	718	1 248	657	591	290	163	127
50 - 54	1 363	708	655	1 067	549	518	296	159	137
55 - 59	1 126	605	521	856	459	397	270	146	124
60 - 64	851	432	419	641	318	323	210	114	96
65 - 69	554	271	283	414	202	212	140	69	71
70 - 74	314	137	177	233	106	127	81	31	50
75 +	415	119	296	293	89	204	122	30	92
Papua New Guinea - Papouasie-Nouvelle-Guinée[101]									
1 VII 2016 (ESDF)									
Total	8 151 300	...	...	...	...	...	...	...	...
0 - 14	2 970 800	...	...	...	...	...	...	...	...
15 - 24	1 641 400	...	...	...	...	...	...	...	...
25 - 59	3 177 700	...	...	...	...	...	...	...	...
60 +	361 400	...	...	...	...	...	...	...	...
Pitcairn									
31 XII 2013 (CDJC)									
Total	49	23	26	...	...	...	...	...	...
0 - 17	8	3	5	...	...	...	...	...	...
18 - 40	7	4	3	...	...	...	...	...	...
41 - 64	24	13	11	...	...	...	...	...	...
65 +	10	3	7	...	...	...	...	...	...
Samoa									
7 XI 2016 (CDFC)									
Total	195 979	100 892	95 087	37 391	18 760	18 631	158 588	82 132	76 456
0	5 554	2 870	2 684	964	484	480	4 590	2 386	2 204
1 - 4	22 605	11 731	10 874	3 866	1 985	1 881	18 739	9 746	8 993
5 - 9	25 019	13 151	11 868	4 444	2 312	2 132	20 575	10 839	9 736
10 - 14	21 438	11 056	10 382	3 813	1 942	1 871	17 625	9 114	8 511
15 - 19	18 952	9 968	8 984	3 771	1 870	1 901	15 181	8 098	7 083
20 - 24	15 919	8 184	7 735	3 391	1 699	1 692	12 528	6 485	6 043
25 - 29	13 332	6 700	6 632	2 780	1 363	1 417	10 552	5 337	5 215
30 - 34	11 916	6 051	5 865	2 482	1 230	1 252	9 434	4 821	4 613
35 - 39	10 799	5 564	5 235	2 150	1 115	1 035	8 649	4 449	4 200
40 - 44	10 252	5 333	4 919	1 959	950	1 009	8 293	4 383	3 910
45 - 49	9 774	5 240	4 534	1 843	960	883	7 931	4 280	3 651
50 - 54	8 448	4 336	4 112	1 682	845	837	6 766	3 491	3 275
55 - 59	7 010	3 658	3 352	1 356	683	673	5 654	2 975	2 679
60 - 64	5 225	2 667	2 558	1 039	508	531	4 186	2 159	2 027
65 - 69	3 475	1 702	1 773	689	333	356	2 786	1 369	1 417
70 - 74	2 688	1 267	1 421	513	246	267	2 175	1 021	1 154

Continent, country or area, date, code[a] and age (in years) Continent, pays ou zone, date, code[a] et âge (en années)	Total			Urban - Urbaine			Rural - Rurale		
	Both sexes Les deux sexes	Male Masculin	Female Féminin	Both sexes Les deux sexes	Male Masculin	Female Féminin	Both sexes Les deux sexes	Male Masculin	Female Féminin
OCEANIA - OCÉANIE									
Samoa									
7 XI 2016 (CDFC)									
75 - 79	1 750	746	1 004	334	136	198	1 416	610	806
80 - 84	1 011	365	646	184	63	121	827	302	525
85 - 89	476	163	313	90	24	66	386	139	247
90 - 94	159	48	111	21	1	20	138	47	91
95 - 99	27	6	21	4	-	4	23	6	17
100 +	6	2	4	1	-	1	5	2	3
Unknown - Inconnu	144	84	60	15	11	4	129	73	56
Solomon Islands - Îles Salomon									
22 XI 2009 (CDFC)									
Total	515 870	264 455	251 415	102 030	53 596	48 434	413 840	210 859	202 981
0 - 4	76 227	39 728	36 499	12 500	6 573	5 927	63 727	33 155	30 572
5 - 9	71 126	36 974	34 152	11 328	5 853	5 475	59 798	31 121	28 677
10 - 14	61 931	32 562	29 369	10 354	5 382	4 972	51 577	27 180	24 397
15 - 19	51 212	26 189	25 023	10 995	5 525	5 470	40 217	20 664	19 553
20 - 24	45 419	22 399	23 020	12 344	6 360	5 984	33 075	16 039	17 036
25 - 29	42 674	20 794	21 880	11 160	5 696	5 464	31 514	15 098	16 416
30 - 34	37 592	18 807	18 785	8 817	4 568	4 249	28 775	14 239	14 536
35 - 39	33 151	17 010	16 141	7 447	4 000	3 447	25 704	13 010	12 694
40 - 44	23 638	12 070	11 568	5 161	2 808	2 353	18 477	9 262	9 215
45 - 49	19 713	10 189	9 524	4 064	2 265	1 799	15 649	7 924	7 725
50 - 54	14 339	7 498	6 841	2 818	1 650	1 168	11 521	5 848	5 673
55 - 59	11 787	6 111	5 676	2 011	1 198	813	9 776	4 913	4 863
60 - 64	8 916	4 535	4 381	1 272	726	546	7 644	3 809	3 835
65 - 69	7 021	3 693	3 328	822	466	356	6 199	3 227	2 972
70 - 74	4 698	2 402	2 296	478	259	219	4 220	2 143	2 077
75 - 79	3 374	1 784	1 590	279	160	119	3 095	1 624	1 471
80 - 84	1 525	800	725	102	58	44	1 423	742	681
85 - 89	894	512	382	58	34	24	836	478	358
90 - 94	301	170	131	8	4	4	293	166	127
95 +	332	228	104	12	11	1	320	217	103
1 VII 2018 (ESDF)[102]									
Total	666 557	340 521	326 036	...	...	...	...	...	...
0 - 4	82 563	42 655	39 908	...	...	...	...	...	...
5 - 9	81 965	42 134	39 831	...	...	...	...	...	...
10 - 14	79 847	41 077	38 769	...	...	...	...	...	...
15 - 19	71 605	36 936	34 670	...	...	...	...	...	...
20 - 24	58 974	30 516	28 458	...	...	...	...	...	...
25 - 29	51 579	26 664	24 915	...	...	...	...	...	...
30 - 34	48 491	24 988	23 503	...	...	...	...	...	...
35 - 39	42 314	21 397	20 917	...	...	...	...	...	...
40 - 44	37 106	18 302	18 804	...	...	...	...	...	...
45 - 49	31 329	15 550	15 779	...	...	...	...	...	...
50 - 54	22 890	11 486	11 404	...	...	...	...	...	...
55 - 59	18 288	9 187	9 100	...	...	...	...	...	...
60 - 64	13 009	6 587	6 422	...	...	...	...	...	...
65 - 69	10 367	5 110	5 257	...	...	...	...	...	...
70 - 74	7 227	3 483	3 744	...	...	...	...	...	...
75 - 79	4 886	2 430	2 455	...	...	...	...	...	...
80 +	4 117	2 020	2 098	...	...	...	...	...	...
Tokelau - Tokélaou									
18 X 2016 (CDFC)									
Total	1 285	652	633	...	...	...	...	...	...
0 - 4	139	74	65	...	...	...	...	...	...
5 - 9	150	75	75	...	...	...	...	...	...
10 - 14	137	72	65	...	...	...	...	...	...
15 - 19	116	63	53	...	...	...	...	...	...
20 - 24	93	54	39	...	...	...	...	...	...
25 - 29	86	39	47	...	...	...	...	...	...
30 - 34	79	36	43	...	...	...	...	...	...
35 - 39	62	35	27	...	...	...	...	...	...
40 - 44	75	35	40	...	...	...	...	...	...
45 - 49	81	41	40	...	...	...	...	...	...

Continent, country or area, date, code[a] and age (in years) / Continent, pays ou zone, date, code[a] et âge (en années)	Total Both sexes Les deux sexes	Total Male Masculin	Total Female Féminin	Urban - Urbaine Both sexes Les deux sexes	Urban - Urbaine Male Masculin	Urban - Urbaine Female Féminin	Rural - Rurale Both sexes Les deux sexes	Rural - Rurale Male Masculin	Rural - Rurale Female Féminin
OCEANIA - OCÉANIE									
Tokelau - Tokélaou									
18 X 2016 (CDFC)									
50 - 54	63	27	36	...	...	...	...	...	...
55 - 59	53	33	20	...	...	...	...	...	...
60 - 64	54	31	23	...	...	...	...	...	...
65 - 69	37	14	23	...	...	...	...	...	...
70 - 74	25	14	11	...	...	...	...	...	...
75 +	35	9	26	...	...	...	...	...	...
Tonga									
30 XI 2016 (CDJC)									
Total	100 651	50 255	50 396	23 221	11 529	11 692	77 430	38 726	38 704
0 - 4	12 499	6 440	6 059	2 648	1 357	1 291	9 851	5 083	4 768
5 - 9	12 153	6 417	5 736	2 557	1 351	1 206	9 596	5 066	4 530
10 - 14	11 882	6 139	5 743	2 518	1 244	1 274	9 364	4 895	4 469
15 - 19	10 502	5 449	5 053	2 374	1 246	1 128	8 128	4 203	3 925
20 - 24	8 234	4 106	4 128	2 070	1 029	1 041	6 164	3 077	3 087
25 - 29	6 629	3 162	3 467	1 762	888	874	4 867	2 274	2 593
30 - 34	6 521	2 994	3 527	1 641	790	851	4 880	2 204	2 676
35 - 39	5 645	2 704	2 941	1 368	641	727	4 277	2 063	2 214
40 - 44	5 189	2 473	2 716	1 209	577	632	3 980	1 896	2 084
45 - 49	5 181	2 600	2 581	1 220	605	615	3 961	1 995	1 966
50 - 54	4 150	2 129	2 021	1 012	519	493	3 138	1 610	1 528
55 - 59	3 254	1 571	1 683	803	369	434	2 451	1 202	1 249
60 - 64	2 696	1 297	1 399	628	301	327	2 068	996	1 072
65 - 69	2 030	968	1 062	474	215	259	1 556	753	803
70 - 74	1 601	735	866	345	154	191	1 256	581	675
75 - 79	1 250	575	675	269	121	148	981	454	527
80 - 84	725	315	410	175	70	105	550	245	305
85 - 89	358	127	231	78	23	55	280	104	176
90 - 94	99	25	74	27	5	22	72	20	52
95 +	12	6	6	2	1	1	10	5	5
Unknown - Inconnu	41	23	18	41	23	18	-	-	-
Tuvalu									
1 VII 2016 (ESDF)									
Total	11 153	...	...	...	...	...	...	...	...
0 - 4	1 345	...	...	...	...	...	...	...	...
5 - 9	1 102	...	...	...	...	...	...	...	...
10 - 14	1 041	...	...	...	...	...	...	...	...
15 - 19	1 177	...	...	...	...	...	...	...	...
20 - 24	1 068	...	...	...	...	...	...	...	...
25 - 29	960	...	...	...	...	...	...	...	...
30 - 34	670	...	...	...	...	...	...	...	...
35 - 39	430	...	...	...	...	...	...	...	...
40 - 44	485	...	...	...	...	...	...	...	...
45 - 49	638	...	...	...	...	...	...	...	...
50 - 54	693	...	...	...	...	...	...	...	...
55 - 59	605	...	...	...	...	...	...	...	...
60 - 64	387	...	...	...	...	...	...	...	...
65 - 69	187	...	...	...	...	...	...	...	...
70 - 74	172	...	...	...	...	...	...	...	...
75 - 79	114	...	...	...	...	...	...	...	...
80 +	79	...	...	...	...	...	...	...	...
Vanuatu									
16 XI 2009 (CDFC)									
Total	234 023	119 091	114 932	57 195	29 618	27 577	176 828	89 473	87 355
0 - 4	33 367	17 310	16 057	7 224	3 828	3 396	26 143	13 482	12 661
5 - 9	29 685	15 455	14 230	5 591	2 850	2 741	24 094	12 605	11 489
10 - 14	27 921	14 762	13 159	5 250	2 755	2 495	22 671	12 007	10 664
15 - 19	23 882	12 027	11 855	6 460	3 122	3 338	17 422	8 905	8 517
20 - 24	21 541	10 415	11 126	7 186	3 606	3 580	14 355	6 809	7 546
25 - 29	18 415	9 124	9 291	5 542	2 937	2 605	12 873	6 187	6 686
30 - 34	15 693	7 790	7 903	4 517	2 300	2 217	11 176	5 490	5 686
35 - 39	14 171	7 076	7 095	3 844	1 965	1 879	10 327	5 111	5 216
40 - 44	11 523	5 814	5 709	3 242	1 710	1 532	8 281	4 104	4 177
45 - 49	10 241	5 066	5 175	2 817	1 474	1 343	7 424	3 592	3 832

Continent, country or area, date, code[a] and age (in years) Continent, pays ou zone, date, code[a] et âge (en années)	Total			Urban - Urbaine			Rural - Rurale		
	Both sexes Les deux sexes	Male Masculin	Female Féminin	Both sexes Les deux sexes	Male Masculin	Female Féminin	Both sexes Les deux sexes	Male Masculin	Female Féminin
OCEANIA - OCÉANIE									
Vanuatu									
16 XI 2009 (CDFC)									
50 - 54	7 415	3 789	3 626	1 923	1 036	887	5 492	2 753	2 739
55 - 59	6 363	3 261	3 102	1 495	845	650	4 868	2 416	2 452
60 - 64	4 319	2 192	2 127	826	455	371	3 493	1 737	1 756
65 - 69	3 826	2 054	1 772	590	355	235	3 236	1 699	1 537
70 +	5 661	2 956	2 705	688	380	308	4 973	2 576	2 397
7 XI 2016 (CDFC)									
Total	272 459	138 265	134 194	...	...	...	...	...	...
0 - 4	38 936	20 172	18 764	...	...	...	...	...	...
5 - 9	37 148	19 276	17 872	...	...	...	...	...	...
10 - 14	29 846	15 560	14 286	...	...	...	...	...	...
15 - 19	25 902	13 207	12 695	...	...	...	...	...	...
20 - 24	24 862	11 738	13 124	...	...	...	...	...	...
25 - 29	23 031	10 986	12 045	...	...	...	...	...	...
30 - 34	18 067	8 909	9 158	...	...	...	...	...	...
35 - 39	16 233	8 148	8 085	...	...	...	...	...	...
40 - 44	13 251	6 726	6 525	...	...	...	...	...	...
45 - 49	11 833	6 125	5 708	...	...	...	...	...	...
50 - 54	9 329	4 756	4 573	...	...	...	...	...	...
55 - 59	7 227	3 792	3 435	...	...	...	...	...	...
60 - 64	5 357	2 832	2 525	...	...	...	...	...	...
65 - 69	4 010	2 089	1 921	...	...	...	...	...	...
70 +	7 225	3 838	3 387	...	...	...	...	...	...
Unknown - Inconnu	202	111	91	...	...	...	...	...	...
Wallis and Futuna Islands - Îles Wallis et Futuna									
22 VII 2013 (CDFC)									
Total	12 197	5 927	6 270	...	...	...	...	...	...
0 - 4	997	507	490	...	...	...	...	...	...
5 - 9	1 136	560	576	...	...	...	...	...	...
10 - 14	1 297	687	610	...	...	...	...	...	...
15 - 19	1 168	615	553	...	...	...	...	...	...
20 - 24	583	257	326	...	...	...	...	...	...
25 - 29	600	266	334	...	...	...	...	...	...
30 - 34	719	315	404	...	...	...	...	...	...
35 - 39	864	398	466	...	...	...	...	...	...
40 - 44	922	434	488	...	...	...	...	...	...
45 - 49	762	354	408	...	...	...	...	...	...
50 - 54	761	344	417	...	...	...	...	...	...
55 - 59	669	352	317	...	...	...	...	...	...
60 - 64	571	310	261	...	...	...	...	...	...
65 - 69	462	238	224	...	...	...	...	...	...
70 - 74	309	153	156	...	...	...	...	...	...
75 - 79	201	82	119	...	...	...	...	...	...
80 - 84	111	35	76	...	...	...	...	...	...
85 - 89	50	17	33	...	...	...	...	...	...
90 - 94	15	3	12	...	...	...	...	...	...
95 +	-	-	-	...	...	...	...	...	...

FOOTNOTES - NOTES

Italics: estimates which are less reliable. - Italiques : estimations moins sûres.

* Provisional. - Données provisoires.

[a] 'Code' indicates the source of data, as follows:
CDFC - Census, de facto, complete tabulation
CDFS - Census, de facto, sample tabulation
CDJC - Census, de jure, complete tabulation
CDJS - Census, de jure, sample tabulation
SSDF - Sample survey, de facto
SSDJ - Sample survey, de jure
ESDF - Estimates, de facto

ESDJ - Estimates, de jure

Le 'Code' indique la source des données, comme suit :
CDFC - Recensement, population de fait, tabulation complète
CDFS - Recensement, population de fait, tabulation par sondage
CDJC - Recensement, population de droit, tabulation complète
CDJS - Recensement, population de droit, tabulation par sondage
SSDF - Enquête par sondage, population de fait
SSDJ - Enquête par sondage, population de droit
ESDF - Estimations, population de fait
ESDJ - Estimations, population de droit

[1] Postcensal estimates. - Estimations post censitaires.
[2] Data refer to national projections. - Les données se réfèrent aux projections nationales.

7. Population by age, sex and urban/rural residence: latest available year 2005 - 2018

Población según la edad, el sexo y la residencia, urbana/rural : dernière année disponible, 2005 - 2018 (continued - suite)

3 Projections based on the 2013 Population Census. - Projections fondées sur le recensement de la population de 2013.

4 Data based on the 2011 Census. - Données fondées sur le recensement de 2011.

5 Unrevised data. - Les données n'ont pas été révisées.

6 Source: Population projections and estimates of priority targets for the various health programs and interventions, National Institute of Statistics (2016). - Source : Projections démographiques et estimations des cibles prioritaires des différents programmes et interventions de sante, Institut National de la Statistique (2016).

7 Projections based on the 2014 Population Census. - Projections fondées sur le recensement de la population de 2014.

8 Projections based on the 2000 quick population count results and 1995, 2002 and 2010 Eritrea Demographic and Health Surveys. - Projections fondées sur le dénombrement rapide de la population de 2000 et sur les enquêtes érythréennes de la démographie et de la santé de 1995, 2002 et 2010.

9 Data refer to national projections based on 2007 census. - Les données sont des projections nationales d'après les résultats du recensement de la population de 2007.

10 Estimates considering also the results of the 2007 Population Census. - Estimations en prenant en considération les résultats du recensement de la population de 2007.

11 Source: Integrated Household Survey (IHS) 2015/2016. - Source: Enquête intégrée auprès des ménages (IHS) 2015/2016.

12 Data based on the 2010 Population Census. - Les données sont fondées sur le recensement de la population de 2010.

13 Population in households only. Postcensal estimates. - Population dans les ménages seulement. Estimations post censitaires.

14 Post-censal estimates based on the 2009 Population Census. - Les estimations post-censitaire fondées sur le recensement de la population de 2009.

15 Data refer to Libyan nationals only. - Les données se raportent aux nationaux libyens seulement.

16 Projections considering also the results of the 2009 Population Census. - Projections en prenant en considération les résultats du recensement de la population de 2009.

17 Excludes the islands of St. Brandon and Agalega. - Non compris les îles St. Brandon et Agalega.

18 Based on the results of the 2011 Population Census. - Basé sur les résultats du recensement de la population de 2011.

19 Projections based on the results of national survey on population and health conducted between 2010 and 2011, and especially population and housing census 2014. - Des projections de la population fondées sur les résultats de l'enquête nationale de la population et de la santé réalisée entre 2010 et 2011 et, surtout, du recensement général de la population et de l'habitat de 2014.

20 Data refer to projections based on the 2011 Population Census. - Les données se réfèrent aux projections basées sur le recensement de la population de 2011.

21 Projections based on the 2012 Population and Housing Census. - Projections fondées sur le recensement 2012 de la population et des logements.

22 Data are projections based on the 2006 Population Census. - Projections fondées sur le recensement de la population de 2006.

23 Data are projections based on the 2008 Population and Housing Census. - Projection basée sur le recensement 2008 de la population et des logements.

24 Data refer to annual average population. - Les données correspondent à la population annuelle moyenne.

25 Data refer to total resident population, Saint Helenian and other nationalities. - Les données concernent la population résidente totale, originaire de Sainte-Hélène ou possédant une autre nationalité.

26 Projections based on the 2012 Population Census. - Projections fondées sur le recensement de la population de 2012.

27 The urban area is reconfigured by extending the urban agglomeration of Lomé to include all the prefecture of Golfe and the new prefecture of Agoènyvé. - L'espace urbaine a été reconstitué par l'extension de l'agglomération de Lomé à toute la préfecture du Golfe et à la nouvelle préfecture d'Agoènyvé.

28 Projections based on the 2002 Population Census. - Projections fondées sur le recensement de la population de 2002.

29 Projections based on the 2010 Population and Housing Census. - Projections fondées sur le recensement 2010 de la population et des logements.

30 Data for urban and rural do not add up to the total; reason for discrepancy not ascertained. Projections based on the 2012 Population Census. - La somme des données pour la résidence urbaine et rurale n'est pas égale au total; on ne sait pas comment s'explique la divergence. Projections fondées sur le recensement de la population de 2012.

31 Data refer to national projections. Projections based on the 2010 Population and Housing Census. - Les données se réfèrent aux projections nationales. Projections fondées sur le recensement 2010 de la population et des logements.

32 Data refers to resident population adjusted for the undercount of 18 per cent and including the institutional population. - Les données concernent la population résidente, y compris la population des institutions, et ont été ajustées pour tenir compte du sous-dénombrement estimé à 18 p. 100.

33 Bermuda is 100 per cent urban. - 100 pour cent de la population des Bermudes est urbaine.

34 Data refer to projections based on the 2016 Population Census. - Les données se réfèrent aux projections basées sur le recensement de la population de 2016.

35 To ensure confidentiality, the values, including totals are randomly rounded either up or down to a multiple of '5' or '10.' As a result, when these data are summed or grouped, the total value may not match the individual values since totals and sub-totals are independently rounded. Similarly, percentages, which are calculated on rounded data, may not necessarily add up to 100%. - À des fins de confidentialité, les chiffres, y compris les totaux, sont aléatoirement arrondis au multiple de 5 ou de 10 inférieur ou supérieur. Par conséquent, lorsque ces chiffres sont additionnés, le total peut ne pas correspondre à la somme des valeurs individuelles, dans la mesure où les totaux et les totaux partiels sont arrondis indépendamment. De même, la somme des pourcentages, qui sont calculés à partir des données arrondies, peut ne pas correspondre à 100 %.

36 Preliminary postcensal estimates. Adjusted for census net undercoverage (including adjustment for incompletely enumerated Indian reserves). - Estimations post censitaires préliminaires. Ajusté pour le sous-estimation du recensement (y compris les réservations en Inde incomplètement énumérées).

37 Based on the national household survey of 2018. - D'après l'enquête nationale auprès des ménages de 2018.

38 Estimates or projections based on the 2007 Population Census. - Estimations ou projections fondées sur le recensement de la population de 2007.

39 Population statistics are compiled from registers. - Les statistiques de la population sont compilées à partir des registres.

40 Excluding data for Saint Barthélémy and Saint Martin. - Non compris les données pour Saint Barthélémy et Saint Martin.

41 Projections produced by l'Institut Haïtien de Statistique et d'Informatique (IHSI) and the Latin American and Caribbean Demographic Centre (CELADE) - Population Division of ECLAC. - Les données sont projections produits par l'Institut Haïtien de Statistique et d'Informatique (IHSI) et le centre démographique de l'Amérique latine et les Caraïbes - Division de la population de la CEPALC.

42 Including an estimation of 1 334 585 persons corresponding to 448 195 housing units without information of the occupants. - Y compris une estimation de 1 334 585 personnes correspondant aux 448 195 unités d'habitation sans information sur les occupants.

43 The population projections of CONAPO (National Population Council). - Les projections démographiques de la CONAPO (Conseil national de la population).

44 Including armed forces stationed in the area. Postcensal estimates. - Y compris les militaires en garnison sur le territoire. Estimations post censitaires.

45 Excluding U.S. Armed Forces overseas and civilian U.S. citizens whose usual place of residence is outside the United States. Postcensal estimates. - Non compris les militaires américains à l'étranger et les civils américains dont le lieu de résidence habituel est en dehors des États-Unis. Estimations post censitaires.

46 Including armed forces stationed in the area. - Y compris les militaires en garnison sur le territoire.

47 Data include persons in remote areas, military personnel outside the country, merchant seamen at sea, civilian seasonal workers outside the country, and other civilians outside the country, and exclude nomads, foreign military, civilian aliens temporarily in the country, transients on ships and Indian jungle population. Data refer to national projections. - Y compris les personnes vivant dans des régions éloignées, le personel militaire en dehors du pays, les marins marchands, les ouvriers saisonniers en dehors du pays, et autres civils en dehors du pays, et non compris les nomades, les militaires étrangers, les étrangers civils temporairement dans le pays, les transiteurs sur des bateaux et les Indiens de la jungle. Les données se réfèrent aux projections nationales.

48 Data are revised projections taking into consideration also the results of the 2005 census. - Les données sont des projections révisées tenant compte également des résultats du recensement de 2005.

49 Excludes nomadic Indian tribes. Data based on the 2010 Population Census. - Non compris les tribus d'Indiens nomades. Les données sont fondées sur le recensement de la population de 2010.

50 A dispute exists between the governments of Argentina and the United Kingdom of Great Britain and Northern Ireland concerning sovereignty over the Falkland Islands (Malvinas). Excluding military personnel and their families, visitors and transients. - La souveraineté sur les îles Falkland (Malvinas) fait l'objet d'un différend entre le Gouvernement argentin et le Gouvernement du Royaume-Uni de Grande-Bretagne et d'Irlande du Nord. Non compris les militaires et leur familles, ni les visiteurs et transients.

51 Estimates or projections considering also the results of the 2012 Population Census. - Estimations ou projections en prennant en considération les résultats du recensement de la population de 2012.

52 For operational purposes, population centers with 2,500 and more inhabitants are considered as urban area and less than 2,500 are considered as rural area. - À des fins opérationnelles, les centres de population comptant 2 500 habitants ou plus sont considérés comme zones urbaines, ceux qui en comptent moins de 2 500 comme zones rurales.

53 Data refer to the settled population based on the 1979 Population Census and the latest household prelisting. The refugees of Afghanistan in Iran, Pakistan, and an estimated 1.5 million nomads, are not included. - Les données se rapportent à la population stationnaire sur la base du recensement de 1979 et du recensement préliminaire des logements le plus récent. Sont exclus les réfugiés d'Afghanistan en Iran et au Pakistan et les nomades estimés à 1,5 million.

54 Source: 2016 Population and Housing Census Update. - Source : Révision des chiffres du recensement de la population et des logements de 2016.

55 Excluding foreign diplomatic personnel and their dependants. Data based on the 2008 Population Census. - Non compris le personnel diplomatique étranger et les membres de leur famille les accompagnant. Données fondées sur le recensement de population de 2008.

56 Population by-census is conducted between two population censuses, adopting a sampling method to select 29,421 housing units in Macao for enumeration, with the unit of observation being the individuals residing in the selected housing units. - Aux fins du recensement partiel de la population, conduit entre deux recensements, la méthode d'échantillonnage adoptée a permis de sélectionner 29 421 unités d'habitation à Macao, l'unité d'observation étant les personnes qui y résident.

57 For statistical purposes, the data for China do not include those for the Hong Kong Special Administrative Region (Hong Kong SAR), Macao Special Administrative Region (Macao SAR) and Taiwan province of China. - Pour la présentation des statistiques, les données pour la Chine ne comprennent pas la Région Administrative Spéciale de Hong Kong (Hong Kong RAS), la Région Administrative Spéciale de Macao (Macao RAS) et Taïwan province de Chine.

58 Data exclude 2.3 million servicemen, 4.65 million persons with permanent resident status difficult to define, and 0.12 per cent undercount based on the post enumeration survey. - Les données ne comprennent pas 2,3 millions de militaires, 4,65 millions de personnes ayant le statut de résident permanent mais difficiles à définir, et des lacunes estimées à 0,12 pour cent sur la base de l'enquête de vérification du recensement.

59 Because of rounding, totals are not in all cases the sum of the respective components. Data have been adjusted on the basis of the Population Census of 2010. - Les chiffres étant arrondis, les totaux ne correspondent pas toujours rigoureusement à la somme des composants respectifs. Les données ont été ajustées à partir des résultats du recensement de la population de 2010.

60 Data refer to government controlled areas. - Les données se rapportent aux zones contrôlées par le Gouvernement.

61 Based on the results of the 2014 Population Census. - D'après les résultats du recensement de la population de 2014.

62 Includes data for the Indian-held part of Jammu and Kashmir, the final status of which has not yet been determined. - Y compris les données pour la partie du Jammu et du Cachemire occupée par l'Inde dont le statut définitif n'a pas encore été déterminé.

63 Data are based on the publication: "Indonesia Population Projection 2015-2045" - Les données sont basées sur la publication : << Indonesia Population Projection 2015-2045 >>

64 Data refer to the Iranian Year which begins on 21 March and ends on 20 March of the following year. - Les données concernent l'année iranienne, qui commence le 21 mars et se termine le 20 mars de l'année suivante.

65 Because of rounding, totals are not in all cases the sum of the respective components. Includes data for East Jerusalem and Israeli residents in certain other territories under occupation by Israeli military forces since June 1967. Data refer to Israeli citizens and permanent residents who are listed in the Population Register. - Les chiffres étant arrondis, les totaux ne correspondent pas toujours rigoureusement à la somme des composants respectifs. Y compris les données pour Jérusalem-Est et les résidents israéliens dans certains autres territoires occupés depuis 1967 par les forces armées israéliennes. Les données se rapportent aux citoyens israéliens et aux résidents permanents qui sont répertoriés dans le registre de la population.

66 Excluding diplomatic personnel outside the country and foreign military and civilian personnel and their dependants stationed in the area. - Non compris le personnel diplomatique hors du pays ni les militaires et agents civils étrangers en poste sur le territoire et les membres de leur famille les accompagnant.

67 Because of rounding, totals are not in all cases the sum of the respective components. Estimates based on the complete counts of the 2015 Population Census. - Les chiffres étant arrondis, les totaux ne correspondent pas toujours rigoureusement à la somme des composants respectifs. Estimations basées sur le dénombrement complet du recensement de la population de 2015.

68 Excluding data for Jordanian territory under occupation since June 1967 by Israeli military forces. - Non compris les données pour le territoire jordanien occupé depuis juin 1967 par les forces armées israéliennes.

69 Because of rounding, totals are not in all cases the sum of the respective components. - Les chiffres étant arrondis, les totaux ne correspondent pas toujours rigoureusement à la somme des composants respectifs.

70 Data refer to resident population. - Les données concernent la population résidente.

71 Because of rounding, totals are not in all cases the sum of the respective components. Estimates based on the results of 2015 population census. - Les chiffres étant arrondis, les totaux ne correspondent pas toujours rigoureusement à la somme des composants respectifs. Estimations fondées sur les résultats du recensement de la population de 2015.

72 Estimates based on the adjusted results of the Population and Housing Census of 2010. - Les estimations sont fondée sur les résultats ajustées du recensement de la population et de l'habitat de 2010.

73 Data refer to resident population which includes resident Maldivians and resident foreigners. Estimates based on the 2014 Population Census. - Les données concernent la population résidente, qui comprend les Maldiviens et les étrangers. Estimations fondées sur le recensement de la population de 2014.

74 Data refer to registered population data from Royal Oman Police. - Les données portent sur la population enregistrée par la police royale de l'Oman.

75 Excluding 2134 Filipinos in Philippine Embassies, Consulates and Missions Abroad. - Excepté 2134 Philippins travaillant dans les ambassades, les consulats et les missions des Philippines à l'étranger.

76 Data refer to resident population which comprises Singapore citizens and permanent residents. Data exclude residents who have been away from Singapore for a continuous period of 12 months or longer as at the reference date. - Les données se rapportent à la population résidente composé des citoyens de Singapour et des résidents permanents. Non compris les résidents hors de Singapour pour une période ininterrompue de 12 mois ou plus avant de la date de référence.

77 Including Palestinian refugees. - Y compris les réfugiés de Palestine.

78 Data based on Address Based Population Registration System. - Les données sont basées sur le registre national de la population basé sur l'adresse.

79 Data are adjusted according to the results of the 2009 census and 2014 intercensus. - Les données ont été ajustées à partir des résultats du recensement de la population de 2009 et des données intercensitaires de 2014.

80 Excluding Faeroe Islands and Greenland shown separately, if available. Population statistics are compiled from registers. - Non compris les Iles Féroé et le Groenland, qui font l'objet de rubriques distinctes, si disponible. Les statistiques de la population sont compilées à partir des registres.

81 The total number may include 'Unknown residence', but the categories urban and rural do not. - Le nombre total peut inclure les personnes dont la résidence n'est pas connue, à l'inverse des catégories de population urbaine et rurale.

82 Excluding Åland Islands. - Non compris les Îles d'Åland.

83 Excluding diplomatic personnel outside the country and including members of alien armed forces not living in military camps and foreign diplomatic personnel not living in embassies or consulates. Data refer to annual average population. - Non compris le personnel diplomatique hors du pays et y compris les militaires étrangers ne vivant pas dans des camps militaires et le personnel diplomatique étranger ne vivant pas dans les ambassades ou les consulats. Les données correspondent à la population annuelle moyenne.

84 Excluding military personnel, visitors and transients. - Non compris les militaires, ni les visiteurs et transients.

85 Data refer to usually resident population. - Les données concernent la population habituellement résidente.

86 Data refer to registered resident population. - Les données concernent la population enregistrée résidente.

87 Including civilian nationals temporarily outside the country. - Y compris les civils nationaux temporairement hors du pays.

88 Data refer to resident population only. - Pour la population résidante seulement.

89 Including residents temporarily outside the country. Population statistics are compiled from registers. - Y compris les résidents se trouvant temporairement hors du pays. Les statistiques de la population sont compilées à partir des registres.

90 Excludes non-residents present in country at time of census (visitors, foreigners temporarily residing in country, etc.). Tiraspol, Bender, Slobozia, Ribnita, Camenca Yrigoricpol/Grigoriopol are districts from Transnistria where the census was not conducted. - Exclue les non-résidents présents dans le pays au moment du recensement (visiteurs, étrangers résidant temporairement dans le pays, etc.). Tiraspol, Bender, Slobozia, Ribnita, Camenca, Yrigoricpol/Grigoriopol sont des districts de la Transnistrie où le recensement n'a pas eu lieu.

91 Excluding Transnistria and the municipality of Bender. Data refer to usual resident population based on the 2014 Census. Tiraspol, Bender, Slobozia, Ribnita, Camenca Yrigoricpol/Grigoriopol are districts from Transnistria where the

2014 census was not conducted. - Les données ne tiennent pas compte de l'information sur la Transnistria et la municipalité de Bender. Les données se rapportent à la population habituellement résidente et sont fondées sur le recensement de 2014. Tiraspol, Bender, Slobozia, Ribnita, Camenca, Yrigoricpol/Grigoriopol sont des districts de la Transnistrie où le recensement n'a pas eu lieu.

[92] Excludes data for Kosovo and Metohia. Based on the results of the 2011 Population Census. - Sans les données pour le Kosovo et Metohie. Basé sur les résultats du recencement de la population de 2011.

[93] Population statistics are compiled from registers. Data refer to registered resident population. - Les statistiques de la population sont compilées à partir des registres. Les données concernent la population enregistrée résidente.

[94] Data refer to legal resident population. - Les données concernent la population légalement résidente.

[95] The Government of Ukraine has informed the United Nations that it is not in a position to provide statistical data concerning the Autonomous Republic of Crimea and the city of Sevastopol. - Le gouvernement Ukrainien a informé l'ONU qu'il n'est pas en mesure de fournir des données statistiques concernant la République autonome de Crimée et la ville de Sébastopol.

[96] Excluding Channel Islands (Guernsey and Jersey) and Isle of Man, shown separately, if available. - Non compris les îles Anglo-Normandes (Guernesey et Jersey) et l'île de Man, qui font l'objet de rubriques distinctes, si disponible.

[97] Based on the results of the 2016 Population Census. - Basé sur les résultats du recencement de la population de 2016.

[98] Excluding Niue, shown separately, which is part of Cook Islands, but because of remoteness is administered separately. - Non compris Nioué, qui fait l'objet d'une rubrique distincte et qui fait partie des îles Cook, mais qui, en raison de son éloignement, est administrée séparément.

[99] Based on the 2010 Population and Housing Census and 2013/2014 Household Income and Expenditure Survey. - Données fondées sur les résultat du recensement de la population et de l'habitat de 2010, et ceux de l'enquête auprès des ménages sur des revenus et des dépenses de 2013/2014.

[100] Because of rounding, totals are not in all cases the sum of the respective components. Intercensal estimates. - Les chiffres étant arrondis, les totaux ne correspondent pas toujours rigoureusement à la somme des composants respectifs. Estimations inter-censitaires.

[101] Estimates are prepared by the Secretariat of the Pacific Community based on the last population and housing census. - Les estimations sont préparées par le Secrétariat de la Communauté du Pacifique à partir des résultats du dernier recensement de la population et de l'habitat.

[102] Projections based on adjusted 2009 census counts. - Projections fondées à partir des comptes rajustés du recensement de 2009.

Table 8 - Demographic Yearbook 2018

Table 8 presents population of capital cities and cities of 100 000 or more inhabitants for the latest available year between 1999 and 2018.

Description of variables: Since the way in which cities are delimited differs from one country or area to another, the table not only presents data for the so-called city proper, but also for the urban agglomeration, if available.

City proper is defined as a locality with legally fixed boundaries and an administratively recognized urban status, usually characterized by some form of local government.

Urban agglomeration has been defined as comprising the city or town proper and also the suburban fringe or densely settled territory lying outside of, but adjacent to, the city boundaries.

For some countries or areas, however, the data relate to entire administrative divisions known, for example, as shi or municipalities (municipios) which are composed of a populated centre and adjoining territory, some of which may contain other, often separate urban localities or may be distinctively rural in character. For this group of countries or areas the type of civil division is given in a footnote.

The surface area of the city or urban agglomeration is presented, when available.

City names are presented in the original language of the country or area in which the cities are located. In cases where the original names are not in the Roman alphabet, they have been romanized. Cities are listed in English alphabetical order.

Capital cities are shown in the table regardless of their population size. The names of the capital cities are printed in capital letters. The designation of any specific city as a capital city is as reported by the country or area.

The table also covers cities whose urban agglomeration's population exceeds 100 000; that is, while the urban agglomeration should have a population of 100 000 or more to be included in the table, the city proper may be of a smaller population size.

The reference date of each population figure appears in the left-most column of the table. Estimates based on results of sample surveys and city censuses or from other sources are explained by the 'code' also appearing in the left-most column of the table. The codes are explained at the end of the table.

Reliability of data: Specific information is generally not available on the reliability of the estimates of the population of cities or urban agglomerations presented in this table.

In the absence of such quality assessment, data from population censuses, sample surveys and city censuses are considered reliable and, therefore, set in Roman type. Other estimates are considered reliable if they are based on a complete census (or a sample survey), and have been adjusted by a continuous population register or adjusted on the basis of the calculated balance of births, deaths, and migration.

Limitations: Statistics on the population of capital cities and cities of 100 000 or more inhabitants are subject to the same qualifications as have been set forth for population statistics in general as discussed in section 3 of the Technical Notes.

International comparability of data on city population is limited by variations in national concepts and definitions. Although an effort is made to reduce the sources of non-comparability somewhat by presenting the data for both city proper and urban agglomeration, many serious problems of comparability remain.

Data presented in the "city proper" column for some countries represent an urban administrative area legally distinguished from surrounding rural territory, while for other countries these data represent a commune or an equally small administrative unit. In still other countries, the administrative units may be relatively extensive and thereby include considerable territories beyond the urban centre itself.

City data are also especially affected by whether the data refer to *de facto* or *de jure* population, as well as variations among countries in how each of these concepts is applied. With reference to the total population, the difference between the *de facto* and *de jure* population is discussed at length in section 3.1.1 of the Technical Notes.

Data on city populations based on intercensal estimates present additional problems: comparability is impaired by the different methods used in making the estimates, and by the loss of precision in applying to selected segments of the population methods best suited for the whole population. For example, it is far more difficult to apply the component method of estimating population growth to cities than it is to the entire country.

Births and deaths occurring in the cities do not all originate in the population present in or resident of that area. Therefore, the use of natural increase to estimate the probable size of the city population is a potential source of error. Internal migration is another component of population change that cannot be measured with accuracy in many areas. Because of these factors, estimates in this table may be less valuable in general and in particular limited for purposes of international comparison.

City data, even when set in Roman type, are often not as reliable as estimates for the total population of the country or area. Furthermore, because the sources of these data include censuses (national or city), surveys and estimates, the years to which they refer vary widely. In addition, because city boundaries may alter over time, comparisons covering different years should be carried out with caution.

Earlier data: Population of capital cities and cities with a population of 100 000 or more have been shown in previous issues of the *Demographic Yearbook*. For more information on specific topics and years for which data are reported, readers should consult the Historical Index.

290

Tableau 8 – *Annuaire démographique 2018*

Le tableau 8 présente les données les plus récentes disponibles pour la période 1999 – 2018 sur la population des capitales et des villes de 100 000 habitants ou plus.

Description des variables : étant donné que les villes ne sont pas délimitées de la même manière dans tous les pays ou zones, on s'est efforcé de donner, dans ce tableau, des chiffres correspondant non seulement aux villes proprement dites, mais aussi, le cas échéant, aux agglomérations urbaines.

On entend par villes proprement dites les localités qui ont des limites juridiquement définies et sont administrativement considérées comme villes, ce qui se caractérise généralement par l'existence d'une autorité locale.

L'agglomération urbaine comprend, par définition, la ville proprement dite ainsi que la proche banlieue, c'est-à-dire la zone fortement peuplée qui est extérieure, mais contiguë aux limites de la ville.

En outre, dans certains pays ou zones, les données se rapportent à des divisions administratives entières, connues par exemple sous le nom de shi ou de municipios, qui comportent une agglomération et le territoire avoisinant, lequel peut englober d'autres agglomérations urbaines tout à fait distinctes ou être à caractère essentiellement rural. Pour ce groupe de pays ou zones, le type de division administrative est indiqué en note.

On trouvera en plus la superficie des villes ou des agglomérations urbaines chaque fois que possible.

Les noms des villes sont indiqués dans la langue du pays ou zone où ces villes sont situées. Les noms de villes qui ne sont pas à l'origine libellés en caractères latins ont été romanisés. Les villes sont énumérées dans l'ordre alphabétique anglais.

Les capitales figurent dans le tableau quel que soit le chiffre de leur population et leur nom a été imprimé en lettres majuscules. Ne sont indiquées comme capitales que les villes ainsi désignées par le pays ou zone intéressé.

En ce qui concerne les autres villes, le tableau indique celles dont la population est égale ou supérieure à 100 000 habitants. Ce chiffre limite s'applique à l'agglomération urbaine et non à la ville proprement dite, dont la population peut être moindre.

La date à laquelle se réfère le chiffre correspondant, figure dans la colonne de gauche du tableau. Le 'code' aussi figurant dans la colonne de gauche du tableau, permet de savoir si les estimations sont fondées sur les résultats d'enquêtes par sondage ou de recensements municipaux ou sont tirées d'autres sources. Les codes utilisés sont expliqués à la fin du tableau.

Fiabilité des données : on ne possède généralement pas de renseignements précis sur la fiabilité des estimations de la population des villes ou agglomérations urbaines présentées dans ce tableau.

Les données provenant de recensements de la population, d'enquêtes par sondage ou de recensements municipaux sont jugées sûres et figurent par conséquent en caractères romains. D'autres estimations sont considérées comme sûres si elles sont fondées sur un recensement complet (ou une enquête par sondage) et ont été ajustées en fonction des données provenant d'un registre permanent de population ou en fonction de la balance, établie par le calcul des naissances, des décès et des migrations.

Insuffisance des données : les statistiques portant sur la population des capitales et des villes de 100 000 habitants ou plus appellent toutes les réserves qui ont été formulées à la section 3 des Notes techniques à propos des statistiques de la population en général.

La comparabilité internationale des données portant sur la population des villes est compromise par la diversité des définitions nationales. Bien que l'on se soit efforcé de réduire les facteurs de non-comparabilité en présentant à la fois dans le tableau les données relatives aux villes proprement dites et celles concernant les agglomérations urbaines, de graves problèmes de comparabilité n'en subsistent pas moins.

Pour certains pays, les données figurant dans la colonne intitulée « Ville proprement dite » correspondent à une zone administrative urbaine juridiquement distincte du territoire rural environnant, tandis que pour d'autres pays ces données correspondent à une commune ou petite unité administrative analogue. Pour d'autres encore, les unités administratives en cause peuvent être relativement étendues et englober par conséquent un vaste territoire au-delà du centre urbain lui-même.

L'emploi de données se rapportant tantôt à la population de fait, tantôt à la population de droit, ainsi que les différences de traitement de ces deux notions d'un pays à l'autre influent particulièrement sur les statistiques urbaines. En ce qui concerne la population totale, la différence entre population de fait et population de droit est expliquée en détail à la section 3.1.1 des Notes techniques.

Les statistiques relatives à la population urbaine qui sont fondées sur des estimations intercensitaires posent encore plus de problèmes que les données issues de recensement. Leur comparabilité est compromise par la diversité des méthodes employées pour établir les estimations, et par l'imprécision qui résulte de l'application de certaines méthodes qui sont conçues pour être appliquées à l'ensemble de la population. La méthode des composantes, par exemple, est beaucoup plus difficile à appliquer en vue de l'estimation de l'accroissement de la population lorsqu'il s'agit de villes que lorsqu'il s'agit d'un pays tout entier.

Les naissances et décès qui surviennent dans les villes ne correspondent pas tous à la population présente ou résidente. En conséquence, des erreurs peuvent se produire si l'on établit pour les villes des estimations fondées sur l'accroissement naturel de la population. Les migrations intérieures constituent un second élément d'estimation que, dans bien des régions, on ne peut pas toujours mesurer avec exactitude. Pour ces raisons, les estimations présentées dans ce tableau risquent dans l'ensemble d'être peu fiables et leur valeur est particulièrement limitée du point de vue des comparaisons internationales.

Même lorsqu'elles figurent en caractères romains, il arrive souvent que les statistiques urbaines ne soient pas aussi fiables que les estimations concernant la population totale de la zone ou du pays considéré. De surcroît, comme ces statistiques proviennent aussi bien de recensements (nationaux ou municipaux) que d'enquêtes ou d'estimations, les années auxquelles elles se rapportent sont extrêmement variables. Enfin, comme les limites urbaines varient parfois d'une époque à une autre, il y a lieu d'être prudent lorsque l'on compare des données se rapportant à des années différentes.

Données publiées antérieurement : des statistiques concernant la population des capitales et des villes de 100 000 habitants ou plus ont été présentées dans des éditions antérieures de l'*Annuaire démographique*. Pour plus de précisions concernant les années et les sujets pour lesquels des données ont été publiées, se reporter à l'index historique.

Continent, country or area, date, code[a] and city / Continent, pays ou zone, date, code[a] et ville	City proper - Ville proprement dite				Urban agglomeration - Agglomération urbaine			
	Population			Surface area - Superficie (km²)	Population			Surface area - Superficie (km²)
	Both sexes - Les deux sexes	Male - Masculin	Female - Féminin		Both sexes - Les deux sexes	Male - Masculin	Female - Féminin	
AFRICA - AFRIQUE								
Algeria - Algérie								
16 IV 2008 (CDJC)								
Adrar	200 834	...	...	...	...	...	...	...
Ain Defla	450 280	...	...	...	...	...	...	...
Ain Temouchent	299 341	...	...	...	...	...	...	...
ALGIERS (EL DJAZAIR)	2 712 944	...	...	...	...	...	...	...
Annaba	442 230	...	...	...	...	...	...	...
Batna	768 444	...	...	...	...	...	...	...
Béchar	236 213	...	...	...	...	...	...	...
Bejaïa	559 981	...	...	...	...	...	...	...
Beskra (Biskra)	563 245	...	...	...	...	...	...	...
Bordj Bou Arreridj	422 986	...	...	...	...	...	...	...
Bouira	372 196	...	...	...	...	...	...	...
Boumerdes	459 250	...	...	...	...	...	...	...
Chlef	521 070	...	...	...	...	...	...	...
El Bayadh	192 958	...	...	...	...	...	...	...
El Boulaïda (Blida)	719 515	...	...	...	...	...	...	...
El Djelfa	825 411	...	...	...	...	...	...	...
El Oued	495 573	...	...	...	...	...	...	...
El Tarf	230 157	...	...	...	...	...	...	...
Ghardaïa	355 701	...	...	...	...	...	...	...
Ghilizane (Relizane)	432 386	...	...	...	...	...	...	...
Guelma	363 716	...	...	...	...	...	...	...
Jijel	391 096	...	...	...	...	...	...	...
Khenchela	288 849	...	...	...	...	...	...	...
Laghouat	371 204	...	...	...	...	...	...	...
Lemdiyya (Médéa)	519 383	...	...	...	...	...	...	...
Mestghanem (Mostaganem)	338 143	...	...	...	...	...	...	...
Mila	440 735	...	...	...	...	...	...	...
Mouaskar (Mascara)	513 432	...	...	...	...	...	...	...
M'Sila	666 848	...	...	...	...	...	...	...
Naama	160 381	...	...	...	...	...	...	...
Oum El Bouaghi	467 997	...	...	...	...	...	...	...
Qacentina (Constantine)	717 646	...	...	...	...	...	...	...
Saïda	248 939	...	...	...	...	...	...	...
Sidi-bel-Abbès	517 836	...	...	...	...	...	...	...
Skikda	543 402	...	...	...	...	...	...	...
Souq Ahras	308 319	...	...	...	...	...	...	...
Stif (Sétif)	856 457	...	...	...	...	...	...	...
Tamanrasset	136 822	...	...	...	...	...	...	...
Tbessa (Tébessa)	515 786	...	...	...	...	...	...	...
Tihert (Tiaret)	637 991	...	...	...	...	...	...	...
Tilimsen (Tlemcen)	672 490	...	...	...	...	...	...	...
Tipaza	343 838	...	...	...	...	...	...	...
Tissemsilt	193 011	...	...	...	...	...	...	...
Tizi Ouzou	585 775	...	...	...	...	...	...	...
Wahran (Oran)	1 165 687	...	...	...	...	...	...	...
Wargla (Ouargla)	473 543	...	...	...	...	...	...	...
Angola[1]								
1 VII 2018 (ESDF)								
Benguela	...	...	...	...	623 777[2]	298 548[2]	325 229[2]	2137
Cabinda	...	...	...	...	699 053[2]	346 539[2]	352 514[2]	2260
Cazengo	...	...	...	...	192 036[2]	93 416[2]	98 620[2]	2046
Cuanhama	...	...	...	...	424 306[2]	198 823[2]	225 483[2]	23575
Cuito	...	...	...	...	512 706[2]	246 705[2]	266 001[2]	4692
Dande	...	...	...	...	267 879[2]	134 206[2]	133 672[2]	6075
Huambo	...	...	...	...	815 685[2]	393 548[2]	422 136[2]	2813
LUANDA	...	...	...	...	2 487 444[2]	1 206 033[2]	1 281 411[2]	118
Lubango	...	...	...	...	876 339[2]	424 076[2]	452 263[2]	2786
Lucapa	...	...	...	...	173 862[2]	92 986[2]	80 877[2]	19887
Luena	...	...	...	...	283 387[2]	138 817[2]	144 570[2]	41763
Malanje	...	...	...	...	569 474[2]	276 747[2]	292 727[2]	2838
M'banza-Kongo	...	...	...	...	205 272[2]	102 728[2]	102 544[2]	7091
Menongue	...	...	...	...	513 374[2]	249 789[2]	263 584[2]	23323

	City proper - Ville proprement dite				Urban agglomeration - Agglomération urbaine			
Continent, country or area, date, code[a] and city	Population			Surface area - Superficie (km²)	Population			Surface area - Superficie (km²)
Continent, pays ou zone, date, code[a] et ville	Both sexes - Les deux sexes	Male - Masculin	Female - Féminin		Both sexes - Les deux sexes	Male - Masculin	Female - Féminin	
AFRICA - AFRIQUE								
Angola[1]								
1 VII 2018 (ESDF)								
Namibe	...	...	...	...	335 892[2]	164 812[2]	171 079[2]	9110
Saurimo	...	...	...	...	501 904[2]	247 906[2]	253 999[2]	16977
Sumbe	...	...	...	...	313 894[2]	150 291[2]	163 603[2]	4058
Uíge	...	...	...	...	581 835[2]	286 741[2]	295 095[2]	1105
Benin - Bénin								
11 V 2013 (CDFC)								
Cotonou	679 012	325 872	353 140	...	...	...	...	...
Parakou	255 478	127 328	128 150	...	...	...	...	...
PORTO-NOVO	264 320	126 016	138 304	...	...	...	...	...
Botswana								
1 VII 2017 (ESDJ)								
Francistown	110 077[3]	...	...	199	...	...	...	...
GABORONE	264 311[3]	...	...	198	...	...	...	...
Burkina Faso								
9 XII 2006 (CDFC)								
Banfora	75 917	38 399	37 518	...	109 824	54 581	55 243	...
Bobo Dioulasso	489 967	244 136	245 831	...	554 042	275 703	278 339	...
Dori	21 078	10 431	10 647	...	106 808	52 992	53 816	...
Fada N'gourma	41 785	21 220	20 565	...	124 577	62 193	62 384	...
Gorom-Gorom	8 882	4 509	4 373	...	106 346	53 129	53 217	...
Kaya	54 365	26 989	27 376	...	117 122	56 209	60 913	...
Koudougou	88 184	42 803	45 381	...	138 209	64 362	73 847	...
OUAGADOUGOU	1 475 223	745 289	729 934	...	1 475 223	745 289	729 934	...
Ouahigouya	73 153	36 370	36 783	...	125 030	61 002	64 028	...
Solenzo	16 850	8 557	8 293	...	121 819	59 892	61 927	...
Tenkodogo	44 491	21 476	23 015	...	124 985	58 003	66 982	...
Burundi								
16 VIII 2008 (CDJC)								
BUJUMBURA	497 169	274 979	222 190	...	...	...	...	...
Cabo Verde[4]								
1 VII 2011 (ESDF)								
PRAIA	...	...	...	...	133 863	65 412	68 451	...
Cameroon - Cameroun[5]								
1 VII 2016 (ESDJ)								
Douala	2 948 464	1 488 593	1 459 871	...	...	...	...	...
YAOUNDE	2 873 567	1 450 087	1 423 480	...	...	...	...	...
Côte d'Ivoire								
15 V 2014 (CDJC)								
Abengourou	100 910	51 153	49 757	...	...	...	...	...
Abidjan	4 395 243	2 180 526	2 214 717	...	...	...	...	...
Anyama	103 297	52 169	51 128	...	...	...	...	...
Bouake	536 719	273 502	263 217	...	...	...	...	...
Daloa	245 360	128 922	116 438	...	...	...	...	...
Divo	105 397	54 614	50 783	...	...	...	...	...
Gagnoa	160 465	82 615	77 850	...	...	...	...	...
Korhogo	243 048	126 493	116 555	...	...	...	...	...
Man	148 945	77 005	71 940	...	...	...	...	...
San Pédro	164 944	85 168	79 776	...	...	...	...	...
Soubre	101 196	53 799	47 397	...	...	...	...	...
YAMOUSSOUKRO	212 670	107 871	104 799	...	...	...	...	...
Djibouti								
29 V 2009 (CDFC)								
DJIBOUTI	475 322		...	...				
Egypt - Égypte[6]								
18 IV 2017 (CDFC)								
Alexandria	...	...	...	...	5 163 750	2 654 824	2 508 926	...
CAIRO	...	...	...	...	9 539 673	4 960 625	4 579 048	...
Port Said	...	...	...	...	749 371	385 129	364 242	...
Suez	...	...	...	...	728 180	374 399	353 781	...
Equatorial Guinea - Guinée équatoriale								
1 VII 2001 (ESDF)								
MALABO	...	...	...	...	211 276	106 923	104 353	...

8. Population of capital cities and cities of 100 000 or more inhabitants: latest available year, 1999 - 2018
Population des capitales et des villes de 100 000 habitants ou plus : dernière année disponible, 1999 - 2018 (continued - suite)

Continent, country or area, date, code[a] and city / Continent, pays ou zone, date, code[a] et ville	City proper - Ville proprement dite				Urban agglomeration - Agglomération urbaine			
	Population			Surface area - Superficie (km²)	Population			Surface area - Superficie (km²)
	Both sexes - Les deux sexes	Male - Masculin	Female - Féminin		Both sexes - Les deux sexes	Male - Masculin	Female - Féminin	
AFRICA - AFRIQUE								
Eritrea - Érythrée								
1 VII 2018 (ESDF)								
ASMARA	501 203	230 080	271 123	59	...	...	...	
Ethiopia - Éthiopie								
1 VII 2017 (ESDF)								
ADDIS ABABA	4 215 965	2 097 591	2 118 375	...	...	...	...	
Awassa	241 825	120 317	121 509	...	...	...	...	
Bahir Dar	239 192	119 006	120 186	...	...	...	...	
Debre Zeit	153 782	76 512	77 270	...	...	...	...	
Dessie	184 817	91 953	92 864	...	...	...	...	
Dire Dawa	358 914	178 572	180 342	...	...	...	...	
Gondar	318 625	158 527	160 098	...	...	...	...	
Harar	152 920	76 083	76 837	...	...	...	...	
Jimma	186 148	92 615	93 533	...	...	...	...	
Mekele	471 545	234 610	236 935	...	...	...	...	
Nazareth	338 890	168 610	170 280	...	...	...	...	
Gabon								
22 V 2013 (CDFC)								
Franceville	...	...	...	...	110 568	63 518	47 050	...
LIBREVILLE	...	...	...	...	703 939	360 012	343 927	...
Port-Gentil	...	...	...	...	136 462	69 978	66 484	...
Ghana								
26 IX 2010 (CDFC)								
ACCRA	1 594 419	763 870	830 549	...	...	...	...	...
Ashiaman	190 972	93 727	97 245	...	...	...	...	...
Koforidua	122 300	59 056	63 244	...	...	...	...	...
Kumasi	1 730 249	826 479	903 770	...	...	...	...	...
Madina	111 926	54 271	57 655	...	...	...	...	...
Obuasi	168 641	81 015	87 626	...	...	...	...	...
Tamale	223 252	111 109	112 143	...	...	...	...	...
Tema	292 773	139 958	152 815	...	...	...	...	...
Guinea - Guinée[7]								
15 III 2014 (CDJC)								
Boke	185 548	94 132	91 416	...	...	...	...	
CONAKRY	1 659 785	832 734	827 051	...	1 879 695	942 184	937 511	
Coyah	216 928	103 627	113 301	...	...	...	...	
Dubreka	157 017	79 041	77 976	...	...	...	...	
Kankan	190 722	96 574	94 148	...	...	...	...	
Kindia	138 695	67 746	70 949	...	...	...	...	
Nzérékoré	195 027	97 286	97 741	...	...	...	...	
Siguiri	127 492	65 562	61 930	...	...	...	...	
Guinea-Bissau - Guinée-Bissau								
15 III 2009 (CDFC)								
BISSAU	387 909	...	...	...	...	...	...	
Kenya								
1 VII 2010 (ESDF)								
Eldoret	247 500	...	...	...	312 351[8]	...	...	...
Garissa	109 224	...	...	...	115 744[8]	...	...	...
Kangundo	13 119	...	...	...	205 603[8]	...	...	...
Karuri	107 754	...	...	...	115 731[8]	...	...	...
Kikuyu	200 285	...	...	...	264 714[8]	...	...	...
Kisumu	254 016	...	...	...	383 444[8]	...	...	...
Machakos	40 819	...	...	...	109 648[8]	...	...	...
Mavoko/AthiRiver	108 924	...	...	...	135 571[8]	...	...	...
Mombasa	905 627	...	...	...	925 137[8]	...	...	...
NAIROBI	3 109 861	1 590 658	1 519 203	695	...	...	...	...
Nakuru	343 395	...	...	...	367 183[8]	...	...	...
Ngong	103 927	...	...	...	107 042[8]	...	...	...
Ruiru	238 329	...	...	...	240 226[8]	...	...	...
Thika	136 386	...	...	...	151 225[8]	...	...	...
Lesotho[9]								
10 IV 2016 (CDJC)								
MASERU	330 760	...	...	...	...	...	...	

8. Population of capital cities and cities of 100 000 or more inhabitants: latest available year, 1999 - 2018
Population des capitales et des villes de 100 000 habitants ou plus : dernière année disponible, 1999 - 2018 (continued - suite)

Continent, country or area, date, code[a] and city / Continent, pays ou zone, date, code[a] et ville	City proper - Ville proprement dite				Urban agglomeration - Agglomération urbaine			
	Population			Surface area - Superficie (km²)	Population			Surface area - Superficie (km²)
	Both sexes - Les deux sexes	Male - Masculin	Female - Féminin		Both sexes - Les deux sexes	Male - Masculin	Female - Féminin	

AFRICA - AFRIQUE

Liberia - Libéria[10]								
21 III 2008 (CDFC)								
MONROVIA	...	...	...	...	970 824	476 473	494 351	
Madagascar[11]								
1 VII 2018 (ESDF)								
ANTANANARIVO	...	...	...		1 521 898	...	...	
Antsirabe	...	...	...		279 382	...	...	
Antsiranana	...	...	...		134 742	...	...	
Fianarantsoa	...	...	...		222 961	...	...	
Mahajanga	...	...	...		258 471	...	...	
Toamasina	...	...	...		321 778	...	...	
Toliara	...	...	...		183 588	...	...	
Malawi								
3 IX 2018 (CDJC)								
Blantyre City	800 264	401 172	399 092		...	...	...	
LILONGWE	989 318	497 201	492 117		...	...	...	
Mzuzu City	221 272	108 848	112 424		...	...	...	
Zomba City	105 013	51 619	53 394		...	...	...	
Mali								
1 IV 2009 (CDFC)								
BAMAKO[12]	...	...	...	...	1 810 366	907 643	902 723	
Kayes	...	...	...	...	149 129	76 470	72 659	
Koutiala	...	...	...	...	141 444	70 905	70 539	
Mopti	...	...	...	...	120 786	60 080	60 706	
Ségou	...	...	...	...	133 501	66 819	66 682	
Sikasso	...	...	...	...	226 618	114 171	112 447	
Mauritania - Mauritanie[13]								
24 III 2013 (CDJC)								
Nouadhibou	118 167	67 275	50 892		...	...	...	
NOUAKCHOTT	958 399	494 885	463 514		...	...	...	
Mauritius - Maurice[14]								
1 VII 2018 (ESDJ)								
Beau Bassin - Rose Hill	104 086	51 625	52 461	21	...	...	...	
PORT LOUIS	147 448	73 689	73 759	61	...	...	...	
Vacoas - Phoenix	106 022	51 201	54 821	106	...	...	...	
Morocco - Maroc								
1 VII 2014 (ESDF)								
Agadir	505 765	...	...	...	598 484	...	...	...
Al Hoceima	137 024	...	...	...	399 586	...	...	...
Azilal	100 327	...	...	...	553 121	...	...	...
Béni-Mellal	325 405	...	...	...	549 559	...	...	...
Benslimane	113 341	...	...	...	232 509	...	...	...
Berkane	182 203	...	...	...	288 807	...	...	...
Berrechid	272 356	...	...	...	482 119	...	...	...
Casablanca (Dar-el-Beida)	3 352 399	...	...	...	3 352 399	...	...	...
Chtouka-Ait Baha	111 522	...	...	...	369 706	...	...	...
El Hajeb	121 226	...	...	...	246 461	...	...	...
El Kelâa des Sraghna	152 900	...	...	...	536 191	...	...	...
El-Jadida	311 038	...	...	...	784 432	...	...	...
Errachidia	193 748	...	...	...	418 069	...	...	...
Essaouira	106 319	...	...	...	450 569	...	...	...
Fès	1 126 551	...	...	...	1 146 967	...	...	...
Fquih Ben Salah	204 732	...	...	...	502 021	...	...	...
Guelmim	138 788	...	...	...	187 428	...	...	...
Inezgane ait Melloul	511 209	...	...	...	538 786	...	...	...
Kénitra	604 206	...	...	...	1 058 359	...	...	...
Khemisset	279 890	...	...	...	541 868	...	...	...
Khénifra	228 509	...	...	...	370 952	...	...	...
Khouribga	376 829	...	...	...	541 365	...	...	...
Laayoune	234 870	...	...	...	237 384	...	...	...
Larache	264 802	...	...	...	496 264	...	...	...
Marrakech	978 045	...	...	...	1 325 571	...	...	...
M'Diq-Fnideq	196 586	...	...	...	208 337	...	...	...
Médiouna	119 054	...	...	...	171 684	...	...	...
Meknès	685 408	...	...	...	833 456	...	...	...

Continent, country or area, date, code[a] and city / Continent, pays ou zone, date, code[a] et ville	City proper - Ville proprement dite				Urban agglomeration - Agglomération urbaine			
	Population			Surface area - Superficie (km²)	Population			Surface area - Superficie (km²)
	Both sexes - Les deux sexes	Male - Masculin	Female - Féminin		Both sexes - Les deux sexes	Male - Masculin	Female - Féminin	
AFRICA - AFRIQUE								
Morocco - Maroc								
1 VII 2014 (ESDF)								
Midelt	124 684	...	...	...	288 757	...	...	...
Mohammedia	288 131	...	...	...	403 087	...	...	...
Nador	390 913	...	...	...	564 354	...	...	...
Nouaceur	271 052	...	...	...	331 651	...	...	...
Ouarzazate	113 230	...	...	...	297 018	...	...	...
Oued Ed-Dahab	105 193	...	...	...	125 747	...	...	...
Oujda	504 480	...	...	...	550 406	...	...	...
RABAT	578 644	...	...	...	578 644	...	...	...
Rehamna	102 715	...	...	...	314 605	...	...	...
Safi	345 595	...	...	...	691 128	...	...	...
Salé	912 957	...	...	...	979 228	...	...	...
Sefrou	154 973	...	...	...	286 009	...	...	...
Settat	215 665	...	...	...	633 500	...	...	...
Sidi Kacem	168 302	...	...	...	521 694	...	...	...
Sidi Slimane	130 576	...	...	...	319 528	...	...	...
Skhirate-Témara	512 867	...	...	...	570 855	...	...	...
Tanger	998 972	...	...	...	1 059 562	...	...	...
Taourirt	149 604	...	...	...	232 712	...	...	...
Taroudannt	247 428	...	...	...	837 797	...	...	...
Taza	207 719	...	...	...	528 917	...	...	...
Tétouan	396 806	...	...	...	549 062	...	...	...
Youssoufia	100 617	...	...	...	251 692	...	...	...
Mozambique								
1 VII 2015 (ESDF)								
Beira	460 904	231 684	229 220	633	...	...	...	...
Chimoio	314 751	158 700	156 051	174	...	...	...	...
Lichinga	214 614	108 147	106 467	290	...	...	...	...
MAPUTO	1 241 702	597 109	644 593	300	...	...	...	...
Matola	927 123	447 365	479 759	375	...	...	...	...
Maxixe	127 372	57 145	70 227	282	...	...	...	...
Nacala	241 066	118 325	122 741	340	...	...	...	...
Nampula	622 423	313 343	309 080	320	...	...	...	...
Pemba	199 457	99 447	100 010	194	...	...	...	...
Quelimane	241 077	121 599	119 478	117	...	...	...	...
Tete	213 406	107 128	106 278	286	...	...	...	...
Xai-Xai	128 946	59 452	69 494	135	...	...	...	...
Namibia - Namibie								
28 VIII 2011 (CDFC)								
WINDHOEK	325 858	160 730	165 128	5133	...	...	...	...
Niger								
10 XII 2012 (CDJC)								
Maradi	267 249	137 051	130 198	...	...	...	...	...
NIAMEY	1 026 848	511 166	515 682	...	...	...	...	...
Tahoua	149 498	74 096	75 402	...	...	...	...	...
Zinder	322 935	162 705	160 230	...	...	...	...	...
Republic of South Sudan - République de Soudan du Sud								
21 IV 2008 (CDFC)								
JUBA	230 195	129 427	100 768	56	...	...	...	...
Malakal	114 528	60 440	54 088	25	...	...	...	...
Wau	118 331	63 777	54 554	75	...	...	...	...
Reunion - Réunion								
1 I 2015 (CDJC)								
SAINT-DENIS	146 985	68 447	78 538	...	179 925	84 554	95 371	...
Saint-Paul	105 967	52 163	53 804	...	173 967	85 212	88 755	...
Rwanda								
15 VIII 2012 (CDJC)								
KIGALI	859 332	451 673	407 659	...	...	...	...	...
Saint Helena ex. dep. - Sainte-Hélène sans dép.								
7 II 2016 (CDJC)								
JAMESTOWN	657[15]	341[15]	316[15]	6	...	...	...	...

Continent, country or area, date, code[a] and city / Continent, pays ou zone, date, code[a] et ville	City proper - Ville proprement dite				Urban agglomeration - Agglomération urbaine			
	Population			Surface area - Superficie (km²)	Population			Surface area - Superficie (km²)
	Both sexes - Les deux sexes	Male - Masculin	Female - Féminin		Both sexes - Les deux sexes	Male - Masculin	Female - Féminin	
AFRICA - AFRIQUE								
Sao Tome and Principe - Sao Tomé-et-Principe								
25 VIII 2001 (CDJC)								
SAO TOME	...	...	...	...	49 957	24 003	25 954	...
Senegal - Sénégal[16]								
31 XII 2011 (ESDJ)								
DAKAR	1 056 009	526 299	529 710	...	...	...	...	...
Diourbel	279 667	136 961	142 706	...	...	...	...	...
Guediawaye	317 464	157 992	159 472	...	...	...	...	...
Kaolack	410 577	199 057	211 520	...	...	...	...	...
Mbour	605 346	307 461	297 885	...	...	...	...	...
Pikine	941 245	472 868	468 377	...	...	...	...	...
Rufisque	333 032	167 942	165 090	...	...	...	...	...
Saint Louis	277 245	136 957	140 289	...	...	...	...	...
Thiès	618 436	304 087	314 349	...	...	...	...	...
Ziguinchor	337 295	167 048	170 247	...	...	...	...	...
Seychelles[17]								
26 VIII 2010 (CDFC)								
VICTORIA	...	...	...	...	26 450	...	...	...
Sierra Leone								
5 XII 2015 (CDFC)								
Bo	174 369	83 998	90 371	...	...	...	...	...
FREETOWN	1 055 964	528 207	527 757	...	...	...	...	...
Kenema	200 443	97 818	102 625	...	...	...	...	...
Makeni	124 634	61 494	63 140	...	...	...	...	...
Somalia - Somalie								
1 VII 2001 (ESDF)								
MOGADISHU	1 212 000	...	...	...	...	...	...	...
South Africa - Afrique du Sud								
10 X 2011 (CDFC)								
CAPE TOWN[18]	433 688	209 082	224 607	...	...	...	...	...
Durban	595 061	288 871	306 189	...	...	...	...	...
Johannesburg	957 441	484 293	473 148	...	...	...	...	...
PRETORIA[18]	741 651	359 139	382 512	...	...	...	...	...
Togo[4]								
1 VII 2015 (ESDF)								
Kara	104 400							
LOME	...	...	...	...	1 788 600	...	...	...
Sokode	101 900							
Tunisia - Tunisie[19]								
23 IV 2014 (CDFC)								
Monastir	...	...	...	...	548 828	274 215	274 613	...
TUNIS	...	...	...	...	1 056 247	528 145	528 102	...
Uganda - Ouganda								
27 VIII 2014 (CDFC)								
Gulu[20]	...	...	...	...	149 802	...	...	...
Hoima[20]	...	...	...	...	100 126	...	...	...
KAMPALA	1 507 114	...	...	...	...	...	...	...
Kasese[20]	...	...	...	...	101 557	...	...	...
Kira[20]	...	...	...	...	317 428	...	...	...
Lugazi[20]	...	...	...	...	114 163	...	...	...
Makindye Ssabagabo[20]	...	...	...	...	282 664	...	...	...
Masaka[20]	...	...	...	...	103 293	...	...	...
Mbarara[20]	...	...	...	...	195 160	...	...	...
Mukono[20]	...	...	...	...	162 744	...	...	...
Nansana[20]	...	...	...	...	365 857	...	...	...
United Republic of Tanzania - République Unie de Tanzanie								
1 VII 2018 (ESDF)								
Arusha[21]	1 000 923	481 431	519 492	...	...	...	...	...
Dar es Salaam	5 147 070	2 512 614	2 634 456	1393	...	...	...	...
DODOMA[21]	506 943	247 621	259 322	...	...	...	...	...
Mbeya[21]	471 971	225 384	246 587	...	...	...	...	...
Tanga[21]	326 515	156 419	170 096	...	...	...	...	...

Continent, country or area, date, code[a] and city / Continent, pays ou zone, date, code[a] et ville	City proper - Ville proprement dite				Urban agglomeration - Agglomération urbaine			
	Population			Surface area - Superficie (km²)	Population			Surface area - Superficie (km²)
	Both sexes - Les deux sexes	Male - Masculin	Female - Féminin		Both sexes - Les deux sexes	Male - Masculin	Female - Féminin	
AFRICA - AFRIQUE								
Western Sahara - Sahara occidental[22]								
1 VII 1999 (ESDF)								
EL AAIUN	169 000	...	...	...	...	...	...	...
Zambia - Zambie								
16 X 2010 (CDJC)								
Chingola	216 626	108 464	108 162	...	...	...	...	...
Chipata	455 783	224 934	230 849	...	...	...	...	...
Kabwe	202 360	98 781	103 579	...	...	...	...	...
Kasama	231 824	114 208	117 616	...	...	...	...	...
Kitwe	517 543	256 740	260 803	...	...	...	...	...
Livingstone	139 509	68 763	70 746	...	...	...	...	...
Luanshya	156 059	77 368	78 691	...	...	...	...	...
LUSAKA	1 747 152	860 424	886 728	...	...	...	...	...
Mufulira	162 889	81 355	81 534	...	...	...	...	...
Ndola	451 246	223 020	228 226	...	...	...	...	...
Zimbabwe								
17 VIII 2012 (CDFC)								
Bulawayo	653 337	303 346	349 991	...	...	...	...	...
Chitungwiza	356 840	168 600	188 240	...	...	...	...	...
HARARE	1 485 231	716 595	768 636	...	...	...	...	...
Mutare	262 124	125 850	136 274	...	...	...	...	...
AMERICA, NORTH - AMÉRIQUE DU NORD								
Anguilla								
11 V 2011 (CDFC)								
THE VALLEY	2 812	...	...	...	...	...	...	...
Aruba								
29 IX 2010 (CDJC)								
ORANJESTAD	28 295	13 139	15 156	...	...	...	...	...
Bahamas								
1 VII 2016* (ESDF)								
NASSAU	266 100	128 100	138 000	...	...	...	...	...
Belize								
1 VII 2018 (ESDJ)								
BELMOPAN	23 038	...	...	...	...	...	...	...
Bermuda - Bermudes[23]								
20 V 2016 (CDJC)								
HAMILTON	854	480	374	...	...	...	...	...
Canada[24]								
1 VII 2018* (ESDJ)								
Abbotsford	153 745	77 171	76 574	...	...	...	...	...
Abbotsford-Mission	...	...	...	...	196 007	98 950	97 057	...
Ajax	126 924	62 105	64 819	...	...	...	...	...
Barrie	147 685	72 591	75 094	...	210 800	104 922	105 878	...
Belleville	53 971	26 160	27 811	...	109 932	54 409	55 523	...
Brampton	656 977	328 751	328 226	...	...	...	...	...
Brantford	104 231	51 052	53 179	...	147 548	72 923	74 625	...
Burlington	189 204	91 527	97 677	...	...	...	...	...
Burnaby	248 071	122 439	125 632	...	...	...	...	...
Calgary	1 311 833	656 759	655 074	...	1 486 050	744 427	741 623	...
Cambridge	136 945	68 196	68 749	...	...	...	...	...
Chatham-Kent	105 445	52 138	53 307	...	105 877	52 370	53 507	...
Chilliwack	91 346	45 902	45 444	...	110 600	55 696	54 904	...
Coquitlam	149 391	73 792	75 599	...	...	...	...	...
Delta	108 724	53 691	55 033	...	...	...	...	...
Edmonton	1 004 947	500 833	504 114	...	1 420 916	712 995	707 921	...
Gatineau	282 596	138 860	143 736	...	...	...	...	...
Greater Sudbury / Grand Sudbury	168 141	83 343	84 798	...	171 471	85 103	86 368	...
Guelph	140 683	69 167	71 516	...	162 612	80 319	82 293	...
Halifax	430 230	210 681	219 549	...	430 512	210 812	219 700	...
Hamilton	567 979	281 061	286 918	...	786 641	387 089	399 552	...
Kamloops	97 842	48 826	49 016	...	112 361	56 155	56 206	...
Kelowna	138 513	67 895	70 618	...	212 311	104 595	107 716	...

8. Population of capital cities and cities of 100 000 or more inhabitants: latest available year, 1999 - 2018
Population des capitales et des villes de 100 000 habitants ou plus : dernière année disponible, 1999 - 2018 (continued - suite)

Continent, country or area, date, code[a] and city / Continent, pays ou zone, date, code[a] et ville	City proper - Ville proprement dite				Urban agglomeration - Agglomération urbaine			
	Population			Surface area - Superficie (km²)	Population			Surface area - Superficie (km²)
	Both sexes - Les deux sexes	Male - Masculin	Female - Féminin		Both sexes - Les deux sexes	Male - Masculin	Female - Féminin	
AMERICA, NORTH - AMÉRIQUE DU NORD								
Canada[24]								
1 VII 2018* (ESDJ)								
Kingston	132 943	64 945	67 998	...	173 450	85 698	87 752	
Kitchener	254 740	127 087	127 653		...	...	...	
Kitchener-Cambridge-Waterloo	...	...	...	...	567 740	284 208	283 532	
Langley	128 487	63 156	65 331		...	...	...	
Laval	432 858	213 184	219 674		...	...	...	
Lethbridge	98 960	48 835	50 125		124 553	62 166	62 387	
Lévis V	146 080	72 386	73 694		...	...	...	
London	414 959	203 184	211 775		532 984	261 900	271 084	
Longueuil	243 921	120 314	123 607		...	...	...	
Markham	336 445	165 247	171 198		...	...	...	
Milton	120 558	60 127	60 431		...	...	...	
Mississauga	747 651	369 246	378 405		...	...	...	
Moncton	75 613	37 013	38 600		152 604	75 586	77 018	
Montréal	1 784 420	883 439	900 981		4 255 541	2 105 983	2 149 558	
Nanaimo	97 826	47 745	50 081		112 881	57 449	57 449	
Oakville	206 452	100 574	105 878		...	...	...	
Oshawa	169 509	83 704	85 805		405 631	200 443	205 188	
OTTAWA	1 007 501	513 146	494 355		...	...	...	
Ottawa - Gatineau	...	...	...		1 414 399	696 194	718 205	
Peterborough	86 538	41 373	45 165		131 283	63 842	67 441	
Québec	542 602	266 819	275 783		817 408	405 226	412 182	
Red Deer	104 493	51 819	52 674		...	...	...	
Regina	233 170	116 741	116 429		257 337	129 389	127 948	
Richmond	209 838	101 079	108 759		...	...	...	
Richmond Hill	199 496	97 681	101 815		...	...	...	
Saanich	121 032	59 399	61 633		...	...	...	
Saguenay	146 436	73 443	72 993		162 057	81 736	80 321	
Saint John	70 455	34 030	36 425		130 107	63 560	66 547	
Saskatoon	268 188	133 353	134 835		322 568	161 700	160 868	
Sherbrooke	166 863	82 373	84 490		218 797	108 357	110 440	
St. Catharines	139 168	67 377	71 791		...	...	...	
St. Catharines-Niagara	...	...	...		429 036	210 460	218 576	
St. John's	110 999	54 202	56 797		212 501	104 528	107 973	
Surrey	568 158	283 405	284 753		...	...	...	
Terrebonne	115 484	57 786	57 698		...	...	...	
Thunder Bay	112 014	55 299	56 715		126 481	62 780	63 701	
Toronto	2 956 024	1 439 904	1 516 120		6 341 935	3 228 527	3 113 408	
Trois-Rivières	136 954	67 013	69 941		159 078	78 251	80 827	
Vancouver	676 593	333 764	342 829		2 650 005	1 304 380	1 345 625	
Vaughan	318 279	156 102	162 177		...	...	...	
Victoria	92 292	44 365	47 927		395 523	193 309	202 214	
Waterloo	115 921	58 809	57 112		...	...	...	
Whitby	135 345	66 644	68 701		...	...	...	
Windsor	229 787	114 887	114 900		349 718	174 092	175 626	
Winnipeg	753 674	372 567	381 107		832 186	413 212	418 974	
Cayman Islands - Îles Caïmanes[25]								
10 X 2010 (CDJC)								
GEORGE TOWN	28 089	14 253	13 836		...	...	...	
Costa Rica[26]								
1 VII 2018 (ESDJ)								
Alajuela	306 206	155 321	150 885		...	...	...	
Cartago	161 727	81 211	80 516		...	...	...	
Desamparados	240 671	120 030	120 641		...	...	...	
Goicoechea	136 112	67 156	68 956		...	...	...	
Heredia	140 131	68 971	71 160		...	...	...	
La Unión	110 194	55 325	54 869		...	...	...	
Pérez Zeledón	142 789	71 229	71 560		...	...	...	
Pococí	146 482	76 003	70 479		...	...	...	
Puntarenas	136 328	69 830	66 498		...	...	...	
San Carlos	194 207	99 648	94 559		...	...	...	
SAN JOSÉ	342 188	169 415	172 773		...	...	...	

8. Population of capital cities and cities of 100 000 or more inhabitants: latest available year, 1999 - 2018
Population des capitales et des villes de 100 000 habitants ou plus : dernière année disponible, 1999 - 2018 (continued - suite)

Continent, country or area, date, code[a] and city / Continent, pays ou zone, date, code[a] et ville	City proper - Ville proprement dite				Urban agglomeration - Agglomération urbaine			
	Population			Surface area - Superficie (km²)	Population			Surface area - Superficie (km²)
	Both sexes - Les deux sexes	Male - Masculin	Female - Féminin		Both sexes - Les deux sexes	Male - Masculin	Female - Féminin	
AMERICA, NORTH - AMÉRIQUE DU NORD								
Cuba								
1 VII 2018 (ESDJ)								
Bayamo	159 797	...	...	...	...	...	...	...
Camagüey	307 527	...	...	...	...	...	...	...
Ciego de Ávila	120 153	...	...	...	...	...	...	...
Cienfuegos	151 287	...	...	...	...	...	...	...
Guantánamo	215 847	...	...	...	...	...	...	...
Holguín	296 199	...	...	...	...	...	...	...
LA HABANA	2 130 517	...	...	...	...	...	...	...
Las Tunas	171 631	...	...	...	...	...	...	...
Matanzas	141 909	...	...	...	...	...	...	...
Pinar del Río	144 102	...	...	...	...	...	...	...
Sancti Spíritus	108 883	...	...	...	...	...	...	...
Santa Clara	216 498	...	...	...	...	...	...	...
Santiago de Cuba	433 540	...	...	...	...	...	...	...
Dominican Republic - République dominicaine[4]								
1 VII 2018 (ESDJ)								
Bajos de Haina	136 157	67 034	69 123	...	...	...	...	...
Baní	166 522	82 432	84 090	...	...	...	...	...
Boca Chica	167 784	83 011	84 773	...	...	...	...	...
Bonao	131 036	65 827	65 209	...	...	...	...	...
Higüey	311 001	160 335	150 666	...	...	...	...	...
La Romana	152 344	73 740	78 604	...	...	...	...	...
La Vega	257 145	129 761	127 384	...	...	...	...	...
Los Alcarrizos	322 256	160 348	161 908	...	...	...	...	...
Moca	184 611	93 411	91 200	...	...	...	...	...
Puerto Plata	163 663	81 627	82 036	...	...	...	...	...
San Cristóbal	255 184	126 138	129 046	...	...	...	...	...
San Francisco de Macoris	193 244	96 403	96 841	...	...	...	...	...
San Juan de la Maguana	127 548	67 224	60 324	...	...	...	...	...
San Pedro de Macorís	203 461	98 378	105 083	...	...	...	...	...
Santiago de los Caballeros	739 631	360 557	379 074	...	...	...	...	...
SANTO DOMINGO	1 029 607	489 728	539 879	...	1 029 607	489 728	539 879	...
Santo Domingo East - Santo Domingo Este	1 121 121	539 625	581 496	...	...	...	...	...
Santo Domingo North - Santo Domingo Norte	625 430	310 303	315 127	...	...	...	...	...
Santo Domingo West - Santo Domingo Oeste	429 260	207 989	221 271	...	...	...	...	...
El Salvador								
1 VII 2017 (ESDJ)								
Ahuachapán	129 750	61 829	67 921	244.8	...	...	...	...
Apopa	185 073	84 297	100 776	51.8	...	...	...	...
Ciudad Delgado	128 012	59 141	68 871	33.4	...	...	...	...
Ilopango	135 703	61 394	74 309	34.6	...	...	...	...
Mejicanos	144 872	65 747	79 125	22.1	...	...	...	...
San Martin	103 245	47 568	55 677	55.8	...	...	...	...
San Miguel	265 921	123 506	142 415	594	...	...	...	...
SAN SALVADOR	238 244	108 919	129 325	72.3	...	...	...	...
Santa Ana	272 554	129 805	142 749	400.1	...	...	...	...
Santa Tecla	138 695	62 884	75 811	112.2	...	...	...	...
Soyapango	283 223	128 956	154 267	29.7	...	...	...	...
Greenland - Groenland[27]								
1 VII 2018 (ESDJ)								
NUUK (GODTHAB)	17 798	9 379	8 419	...	...	...	...	...
Grenada - Grenade								
12 V 2011 (CDFC)								
ST. GEORGE'S	...	...	...	...	38 251	19 124	19 127	...
Guadeloupe								
8 III 1999 (CDJC)								
BASSE-TERRE	12 377	5 687	6 690	...	44 747	21 252	23 495	...
Pointe-à-Pitre	...	...	...	...	171 773	...	...	...
Guatemala								
24 XI 2002 (CDJC)								
CUIDAD DE GUATEMALA	942 348	444 429	497 919	...	...	...	...	...

8. Population of capital cities and cities of 100 000 or more inhabitants: latest available year, 1999 - 2018
Population des capitales et des villes de 100 000 habitants ou plus : dernière année disponible, 1999 - 2018 (continued - suite)

Continent, country or area, date, code[a] and city / Continent, pays ou zone, date, code[a] et ville	City proper - Ville proprement dite				Urban agglomeration - Agglomération urbaine			
	Population			Surface area - Superficie (km²)	Population			Surface area - Superficie (km²)
	Both sexes - Les deux sexes	Male - Masculin	Female - Féminin		Both sexes - Les deux sexes	Male - Masculin	Female - Féminin	
AMERICA, NORTH - AMÉRIQUE DU NORD								
Haiti - Haïti								
1 VII 1999 (ESDJ)								
Cap-Haitien	113 555	50 064	63 491	10	...	...	...	...
Carrefour	336 222	146 838	189 384	23	...	...	...	...
Delmas	284 079	124 774	159 305	26	...	...	...	...
PORT-AU-PRINCE	990 558	436 170	554 388	21	...	...	...	...
Honduras								
10 VIII 2013 (CDFC)								
Catacamas	117 493	57 796	59 697	...	...	...	...	...
Choloma	231 669	111 124	120 545	...	...	...	...	...
Choluteca	152 519	73 637	78 882	...	...	...	...	...
Comayagua	144 785	69 290	75 495	...	...	...	...	...
Danlí	195 916	97 441	98 474	...	...	...	...	...
El Progreso	188 366	89 734	98 633	...	...	...	...	...
Juticalpa	124 828	59 944	64 885	...	...	...	...	...
La Ceiba	197 267	93 209	104 058	...	...	...	...	...
Olanchito	104 609	50 858	53 750	...	...	...	...	...
Puerto Cortés	122 426	59 113	63 313	...	...	...	...	...
San Pedro Sula	719 064	343 111	375 953	...	...	...	...	...
TEGUCIGALPA	1 157 509	544 099	613 410	...	...	...	...	...
Villanueva	149 977	72 504	77 474	...	...	...	...	...
Jamaica - Jamaïque								
4 IV 2011 (CDJC)								
KINGSTON[28]	...	...	...	...	592 291	285 509	306 782	149
Montego Bay	...	...	...	...	111 037	53 601	57 436	76.7
Portmore	...	...	...	...	182 800	85 380	97 420	182.1
Spanish Town	...	...	...	...	149 479	72 885	76 594	64.6
Martinique								
1 I 2015 (CDJC)								
FORT-DE-FRANCE	82 502	36 647	45 855	...	123 369	55 149	68 220	...
Mexico - Mexique[4]								
1 VII 2018 (ESDJ)								
Acapulco	...	...	...	...	935 273	450 674	484 599	...
Acayucan	...	...	...	...	122 233	58 831	63 402	...
Aguascalientes	...	...	...	...	1 056 561	513 692	542 869	...
Apatzingán de la Constitución	...	...	...	...	102 668	...	...	...
Campeche	...	...	...	...	298 741	144 761	153 980	...
Cancún	...	...	...	...	869 665	438 425	431 240	...
Cárdenas	...	...	...	...	106 341	...	...	...
Celaya	...	...	...	...	748 825	357 790	391 035	...
Chetumal	...	...	...	...	258 539	128 157	130 381	...
Chihuahua	...	...	...	...	979 563	474 852	504 710	...
Chilpacingo de los Bravo	...	...	...	...	321 081	153 276	167 805	...
Ciudad Acuña	...	...	...	...	147 888	...	...	...
Ciudad Del Carmen	...	...	...	...	194 484	...	...	...
Ciudad Guzmán	...	...	...	...	105 539	...	...	...
Ciudad Lázaro Cárdenas	...	...	...	...	145 394	...	...	...
Ciudad Obregón	...	...	...	...	347 857	...	...	...
Ciudad Valles	...	...	...	...	135 938	...	...	...
Ciudad Victoria	...	...	...	...	365 089	177 720	187 369	...
Coatzacoalcos	...	...	...	...	379 805	184 135	195 670	...
Colima-Villa de Álvarez	...	...	...	...	388 618	188 810	199 808	...
Comitán de Domínguez	...	...	...	...	114 136	...	...	...
Córdoba	...	...	...	...	341 041	161 527	179 514	...
Cuauhtemoc	...	...	...	...	134 525	...	...	...
Cuautla	...	...	...	...	491 750	237 210	254 540	...
Cuernavaca	...	...	...	...	1 032 278	495 869	536 409	...
Culiacán Rosales	...	...	...	...	966 609	471 964	494 645	...
Delicias	...	...	...	...	206 090	101 034	105 056	...
Ensenada	...	...	...	...	542 896	272 046	270 850	...
Fresnillo	...	...	...	...	136 448	...	...	...
Guadalajara	...	...	...	...	5 060 750	2 474 500	2 586 251	...
Guanajuato	...	...	...	...	187 490	89 790	97 700	...
Guaymas	...	...	...	...	231 206	115 076	116 130	...
Hermosillo	...	...	...	...	907 233	451 792	455 442	...

8. Population of capital cities and cities of 100 000 or more inhabitants: latest available year, 1999 - 2018
Population des capitales et des villes de 100 000 habitants ou plus : dernière année disponible, 1999 - 2018 (continued - suite)

Continent, country or area, date, code[a] and city / Continent, pays ou zone, date, code[a] et ville	City proper - Ville proprement dite				Urban agglomeration - Agglomération urbaine			
	Population			Surface area - Superficie (km²)	Population			Surface area - Superficie (km²)
	Both sexes - Les deux sexes	Male - Masculin	Female - Féminin		Both sexes - Les deux sexes	Male - Masculin	Female - Féminin	

AMERICA, NORTH - AMÉRIQUE DU NORD

Mexico - Mexique[4]
1 VII 2018 (ESDJ)

Heroica Nogales	...	...	...	...	256 387	128 644	127 743	...
Hidalgo del Parral	...	...	...	...	124 395	59 970	64 425	...
Iguala de la Independencia	...	...	...	...	122 790	...	...	...
Irapuato	...	...	...	...	420 702	...	...	...
Juárez	...	...	...	...	1 462 133	721 450	740 683	...
La Laguna	...	...	...	...	1 417 538	694 648	722 890	...
La Paz	...	...	...	...	313 204	156 237	156 967	...
La Piedad-Pénjamo	...	...	...	...	266 495	126 345	140 150	...
Lagos de Moreno	...	...	...	...	109 186	...	...	...
León	...	...	...	...	1 757 811	851 520	906 292	...
Los Mochis	...	...	...	...	294 684	...	...	...
Manzanillo	...	...	...	...	165 809	...	...	...
Matamoros	...	...	...	...	542 609	268 068	274 541	...
Mazatlán	...	...	...	...	492 420	241 214	251 206	...
Mérida	...	...	...	...	1 196 520	583 179	613 341	...
Mexicali	...	...	...	...	1 065 882	535 044	530 839	...
MEXICO, CIUDAD DE	...	...	...	...	21 800 320	10 550 177	11 250 142	...
Minatitlán	...	...	...	...	387 131	186 999	200 132	...
Monclova-Frontera	...	...	...	...	374 058	185 520	188 538	...
Monterrey	...	...	...	...	4 834 971	2 401 433	2 433 538	...
Morelia	...	...	...	...	908 203	433 134	475 069	...
Moroleón Uriangato - Moroleón-Uriangato	...	...	...	...	115 793	54 866	60 927	...
Navojoa	...	...	...	...	130 446	...	...	...
Nuevo Laredo	...	...	...	...	428 927	211 931	216 995	...
Oaxaca	...	...	...	...	683 128	321 071	362 057	...
Ocotlán	...	...	...	...	179 113	87 702	91 411	...
Orizaba	...	...	...	...	463 767	220 275	243 492	...
Pachuca	...	...	...	...	594 972	284 036	310 936	...
Piedras Negras	...	...	...	...	197 488	98 913	98 575	...
Playa del Carmen	...	...	...	...	214 734	...	...	...
Poza Rica	...	...	...	...	548 859	264 819	284 040	...
Puebla-Tlaxcala	...	...	...	...	3 046 766	1 459 887	1 586 878	...
Puerto Vallarta	...	...	...	...	469 204	234 997	234 207	...
Querétaro	...	...	...	...	1 337 686	648 702	688 984	...
Reynosa-Río Bravo	...	...	...	...	843 968	418 611	425 356	...
Rioverde-Ciudad Fernández	...	...	...	...	146 908	71 669	75 240	...
Salamanca	...	...	...	...	173 831	...	...	...
Saltillo	...	...	...	...	935 663	463 629	472 034	...
San Cristóbal de las Casas	...	...	...	...	179 648	...	...	...
San Francisco del Rincón	...	...	...	...	200 318	97 502	102 816	...
San José del Cabo	...	...	...	...	105 369	...	...	...
San Juan Bautista Tuxtepec	...	...	...	...	114 259	...	...	...
San Juan del Río	...	...	...	...	157 552	...	...	...
San Luis Potosí-Soledad de Graciano Sánchez	...	...	...	...	1 188 221	572 625	615 596	...
San Luis Río Colorado	...	...	...	...	182 121	...	...	...
Tampico	...	...	...	...	955 119	463 507	491 612	...
Tapachula de Cordova y Ordoñez	...	...	...	...	369 198	177 585	191 613	...
Tecomán	...	...	...	...	164 541	82 301	82 240	...
Tehuacán	...	...	...	...	329 094	155 552	173 543	...
Tehuantepec	...	...	...	...	180 296	86 835	93 461	...
Tepatitlán De Morelos	...	...	...	...	103 284	...	...	...
Tepic	...	...	...	...	512 386	248 821	263 565	...
Teziutlán	...	...	...	...	135 074	64 140	70 934	...
Tianguistenco	...	...	...	...	188 474	91 657	96 817	...
Tijuana	...	...	...	...	2 024 994	1 012 792	1 012 202	...
Tlaxcala	...	...	...	...	568 140	273 042	295 098	...
Toluca	...	...	...	...	2 386 157	1 165 288	1 220 869	...
Tula	...	...	...	...	227 415	110 541	116 873	...
Tulancingo	...	...	...	...	272 228	129 071	143 157	...
Túxpan de Rodríguez Cano	...	...	...	...	118 894	...	...	...
Tuxtla Gutiérrez	...	...	...	...	853 518	410 616	442 902	...
Uruapan	...	...	...	...	301 766	...	...	...
Veracruz	...	...	...	...	906 976	431 333	475 643	...

Continent, country or area, date, code[a] and city	City proper - Ville proprement dite				Urban agglomeration - Agglomération urbaine			
	Population			Surface area - Superficie (km²)	Population			Surface area - Superficie (km²)
Continent, pays ou zone, date, code[a] et ville	Both sexes - Les deux sexes	Male - Masculin	Female - Féminin		Both sexes - Les deux sexes	Male - Masculin	Female - Féminin	
AMERICA, NORTH - AMÉRIQUE DU NORD								
Mexico - Mexique[4]								
1 VII 2018 (ESDJ)								
Victoria de Durango	...	...	...	...	660 663	319 622	341 041	...
Villahermosa	...	...	...	...	851 925	415 126	436 800	...
Xalapa	...	...	...	...	787 443	373 471	413 972	...
Zacatecas-Guadalupe	...	...	...	...	377 668	181 167	196 500	...
Zamora-Jacona	...	...	...	...	266 904	128 356	138 548	...
Nicaragua								
1 VII 2009 (ESDJ)								
Chinandega	...	...	...	...	*106 635*	...	...	...
León	...	...	...	...	*156 049*	...	...	...
MANAGUA	...	...	...	...	*985 143*	...	...	...
Masaya	...	...	...	...	*110 491*	...	...	...
Tipitapa	...	...	...	...	*105 773*	...	...	...
Panama								
1 VII 2018 (ESDF)								
CIUDAD DE PANAMÁ	481 993[29]	229 593[29]	252 400[29]	98	1 107 085[29]	541 645[29]	565 440[29]	288
San Miguelito	370 009[29]	180 925[29]	189 084[29]	50	...	...	...	...
Puerto Rico - Porto Rico								
1 VII 2017 (ESDJ)								
Bayamón	179 565[30]	84 586[30]	94 979[30]	71	...	...	...	...
Caguas	129 604[30]	60 042[30]	69 562[30]	94	...	...	...	...
Carolina	154 489[30]	70 385[30]	84 104[30]	73	...	...	...	...
Ponce	140 859[30]	67 705[30]	73 154[30]	184	...	...	...	...
SAN JUAN	337 288[30]	153 757[30]	183 531[30]	77	...	...	...	...
Saint Lucia - Sainte-Lucie[7]								
10 V 2010 (CDJC)								
CASTRIES	4 173	2 044	2 129		...	...	...	...
Saint Pierre and Miquelon - Saint Pierre-et-Miquelon								
1 I 2015 (CDJC)								
SAINT-PIERRE	5 415	2 639	2 776	...	...	...	...	...
Trinidad and Tobago - Trinité-et-Tobago								
9 I 2011 (CDJC)								
PORT-OF-SPAIN	37 074	18 008	19 066	12	...	...	...	...
Turks and Caicos Islands - Îles Turques et Caïques								
25 I 2012 (CDJC)								
GRAND TURK	4 831	2 325	2 506	...	...	...	...	...
United States of America - États-Unis d'Amérique[31]								
1 VII 2016 (ESDJ)								
Abilene (TX)	122 225[32]	...	...	276.3[33]	...	...	...	...
Akron (OH)	197 633[32]	...	...	160.7[33]	...	...	...	...
Albuquerque (NM)	559 277[32]	...	...	487.4[33]	...	...	...	...
Alexandria (VA)	155 810[32]	...	...	39[33]	...	...	...	...
Allentown (PA)	120 443[32]	...	...	45.4[33]	...	...	...	...
Amarillo (TX)	199 582[32]	...	...	262.5[33]	...	...	...	...
Anaheim (CA)	351 043[32]	...	...	129.4[33]	...	...	...	...
Anchorage (AK)	298 192[32]	...	...	4420.1[33]	...	...	...	...
Ann Arbor (MI)	120 782[32]	...	...	72.7[33]	...	...	...	...
Antioch (CA)	110 898[32]	...	...	76.2[33]	...	...	...	...
Arlington (TX)	392 772[32]	...	...	248.2[33]	...	...	...	...
Arvada (CO)	117 453[32]	...	...	100[33]	...	...	...	...
Athens (GA)	123 371[32]	...	...	301.4[33]	...	...	...	...
Atlanta (GA)	472 522[32]	...	...	345.7[33]	...	...	...	...
Augusta (GA)	197 081[32]	...	...	783.4[33]	...	...	...	...
Aurora (CO)	361 710[32]	...	...	397.6[33]	...	...	...	...
Aurora (IL)	201 110[32]	...	...	116.3[33]	...	...	...	...
Austin (TX)	947 890[32]	...	...	810[33]	...	...	...	...
Bakersfield (CA)	376 380[32]	...	...	385.4[33]	...	...	...	...
Baltimore (MD)	614 664[32]	...	...	209.6[33]	...	...	...	...
Baton Rouge (LA)	227 715[32]	...	...	222.5[33]	...	...	...	...
Beaumont (TX)	118 299[32]	...	...	212.8[33]	...	...	...	...
Bellevue (WA)	141 400[32]	...	...	86.7[33]	...	...	...	...

8. Population of capital cities and cities of 100 000 or more inhabitants: latest available year, 1999 - 2018
Population des capitales et des villes de 100 000 habitants ou plus : dernière année disponible, 1999 - 2018 (continued - suite)

Continent, country or area, date, code[a] and city Continent, pays ou zone, date, code[a] et ville	City proper - Ville proprement dite				Urban agglomeration - Agglomération urbaine			
	Population			Surface area - Superficie (km²)	Population			Surface area - Superficie (km²)
	Both sexes - Les deux sexes	Male - Masculin	Female - Féminin		Both sexes - Les deux sexes	Male - Masculin	Female - Féminin	
AMERICA, NORTH - AMÉRIQUE DU NORD								
United States of America - États-Unis d'Amérique[31]								
1 VII 2016 (ESDJ)								
Berkeley (CA)	121 240[32]	...	...	27.1[33]	...	...	...	...
Billings (MT)	110 323[32]	...	...	113.2[33]	...	...	...	...
Birmingham (AL)	212 157[32]	...	...	378.4[33]	...	...	...	...
Boise City (ID)	223 154[32]	...	...	212.6[33]	...	...	...	...
Boston (MA)	673 184[32]	...	...	125.2[33]	...	...	...	...
Boulder (CO)	108 090[32]	...	...	64.3[33]	...	...	...	...
Bridgeport (CT)	145 936[32]	...	...	41.6[33]	...	...	...	...
Broken Arrow (OK)	107 403[32]	...	...	159.9[33]	...	...	...	...
Brownsville (TX)	183 823[32]	...	...	343.1[33]	...	...	...	...
Buffalo (NY)	256 902[32]	...	...	104.6[33]	...	...	...	...
Burbank (CA)	104 447[32]	...	...	44.9[33]	...	...	...	...
Cambridge (MA)	110 651[32]	...	...	16.6[33]	...	...	...	...
Cape Coral (FL)	179 804[32]	...	...	273.5[33]	...	...	...	...
Carlsbad (CA)	113 952[32]	...	...	97.7[33]	...	...	...	...
Carrollton (TX)	133 351[32]	...	...	94[33]	...	...	...	...
Cary (NC)	162 320[32]	...	...	146.3[33]	...	...	...	...
Cedar Rapids (IA)	131 127[32]	...	...	183.3[33]	...	...	...	...
Centennial (CO)	109 932[32]	...	...	76.5[33]	...	...	...	...
Chandler (AZ)	247 477[32]	...	...	168.2[33]	...	...	...	...
Charleston (SC)	134 385[32]	...	...	282.4[33]	...	...	...	...
Charlotte (NC)	842 051[32]	...	...	790.9[33]	...	...	...	...
Chattanooga (TN)	177 571[32]	...	...	370.6[33]	...	...	...	...
Chesapeake (VA)	237 940[32]	...	...	876.7[33]	...	...	...	...
Chicago (IL)	2 704 958[32]	...	...	588.8[33]	...	...	...	...
Chula Vista (CA)	267 172[32]	...	...	128.5[33]	...	...	...	...
Cincinnati (OH)	298 800[32]	...	...	200.4[33]	...	...	...	...
Clarksville (TN)	150 287[32]	...	...	254.5[33]	...	...	...	...
Clearwater (FL)	114 361[32]	...	...	67[33]	...	...	...	...
Cleveland (OH)	385 809[32]	...	...	201.3[33]	...	...	...	...
Clovis (CA)	106 583[32]	...	...	62.7[33]	...	...	...	...
College Station (TX)	112 141[32]	...	...	132.1[33]	...	...	...	...
Colorado Springs (CO)	465 101[32]	...	...	506.7[33]	...	...	...	...
Columbia (MO)	120 612[32]	...	...	168.3[33]	...	...	...	...
Columbia (SC)	134 309[32]	...	...	345.8[33]	...	...	...	...
Columbus (GA)	197 485[32]	...	...	560.5[33]	...	...	...	...
Columbus (OH)	860 090[32]	...	...	565.8[33]	...	...	...	...
Concord (CA)	128 726[32]	...	...	79.1[33]	...	...	...	...
Coral Springs (FL)	130 059[32]	...	...	61.6[33]	...	...	...	...
Corona (CA)	166 785[32]	...	...	102.2[33]	...	...	...	...
Corpus Christi (TX)	325 733[32]	...	...	452.1[33]	...	...	...	...
Costa Mesa (CA)	112 822[32]	...	...	40.7[33]	...	...	...	...
Dallas (TX)	1 317 929[32]	...	...	882.9[33]	...	...	...	...
Daly City (CA)	106 472[32]	...	...	19.8[33]	...	...	...	...
Davenport (IA)	102 612[32]	...	...	162.9[33]	...	...	...	...
Davie (FL)	101 871[32]	...	...	90.4[33]	...	...	...	...
Dayton (OH)	140 489[32]	...	...	144.2[33]	...	...	...	...
Denton (TX)	133 808[32]	...	...	241.9[33]	...	...	...	...
Denver (CO)	693 060[32]	...	...	397.1[33]	...	...	...	...
Des Moines (IA)	215 472[32]	...	...	230.3[33]	...	...	...	...
Detroit (MI)	672 795[32]	...	...	359.4[33]	...	...	...	...
Downey (CA)	113 267[32]	...	...	32.1[33]	...	...	...	...
Durham (NC)	263 016[32]	...	...	284.3[33]	...	...	...	...
El Cajon (CA)	103 768[32]	...	...	37.5[33]	...	...	...	...
El Monte (CA)	115 807[32]	...	...	24.8[33]	...	...	...	...
El Paso (TX)	683 080[32]	...	...	665[33]	...	...	...	...
Elgin (IL)	112 123[32]	...	...	97[33]	...	...	...	...
Elizabeth (NJ)	128 640[32]	...	...	31.9[33]	...	...	...	...
Elk Grove (CA)	169 743[32]	...	...	109.3[33]	...	...	...	...
Escondido (CA)	151 613[32]	...	...	96[33]	...	...	...	...

Continent, country or area, date, code[a] and city Continent, pays ou zone, date, code[a] et ville	City proper - Ville proprement dite				Urban agglomeration - Agglomération urbaine			
	Population			Surface area - Superficie (km²)	Population			Surface area - Superficie (km²)
	Both sexes - Les deux sexes	Male - Masculin	Female - Féminin		Both sexes - Les deux sexes	Male - Masculin	Female - Féminin	

AMERICA, NORTH - AMÉRIQUE DU NORD

United States of America - États-Unis d'Amérique[31]
1 VII 2016 (ESDJ)

Eugene (OR)	166 575[32]	...	...	114.3[33]	...	...	...	...
Evansville (IN)	119 477[32]	...	...	122.6[33]	...	...	...	...
Everett (WA)	109 043[32]	...	...	86.1[33]	...	...	...	...
Fairfield (CA)	114 756[32]	...	...	106[33]	...	...	...	...
Fargo (ND)	120 762[32]	...	...	127.7[33]	...	...	...	...
Fayetteville (NC)	204 759[32]	...	...	382.7[33]	...	...	...	...
Fontana (CA)	209 665[32]	...	...	111.4[33]	...	...	...	...
Fort Collins (CO)	164 207[32]	...	...	144.6[33]	...	...	...	...
Fort Lauderdale (FL)	178 752[32]	...	...	89.7[33]	...	...	...	...
Fort Wayne (IN)	264 488[32]	...	...	286.5[33]	...	...	...	...
Fort Worth (TX)	854 113[32]	...	...	888.1[33]	...	...	...	...
Fremont (CA)	233 136[32]	...	...	200.6[33]	...	...	...	...
Fresno (CA)	522 053[32]	...	...	296.3[33]	...	...	...	...
Frisco (TX)	163 656[32]	...	...	175.3[33]	...	...	...	...
Fullerton (CA)	140 721[32]	...	...	58.1[33]	...	...	...	...
Gainesville (FL)	131 591[32]	...	...	161.4[33]	...	...	...	...
Garden Grove (CA)	174 858[32]	...	...	46.5[33]	...	...	...	...
Garland (TX)	234 943[32]	...	...	147.7[33]	...	...	...	...
Gilbert (AZ)	237 133[32]	...	...	176.1[33]	...	...	...	...
Glendale (AZ)	245 895[32]	...	...	153[33]	...	...	...	...
Glendale (CA)	200 831[32]	...	...	78.8[33]	...	...	...	...
Grand Prairie (TX)	190 682[32]	...	...	187.2[33]	...	...	...	...
Grand Rapids (MI)	196 445[32]	...	...	115.1[33]	...	...	...	...
Greeley (CO)	103 990[32]	...	...	123.9[33]	...	...	...	...
Green Bay (WI)	105 139[32]	...	...	117.7[33]	...	...	...	...
Greensboro (NC)	287 027[32]	...	...	332.3[33]	...	...	...	...
Gresham (OR)	111 523[32]	...	...	60.3[33]	...	...	...	...
Hampton (VA)	135 410[32]	...	...	133.3[33]	...	...	...	...
Hartford (CT)	123 243[32]	...	...	45[33]	...	...	...	...
Hayward (CA)	158 937[32]	...	...	117.9[33]	...	...	...	...
Henderson (NV)	292 969[32]	...	...	271.2[33]	...	...	...	...
Hialeah (FL)	236 387[32]	...	...	55.6[33]	...	...	...	...
High Point City (NC)	111 223[32]	...	...	143[33]	...	...	...	...
Hillsboro (OR)	105 164[32]	...	...	64.7[33]	...	...	...	...
Hollywood (FL)	151 998[32]	...	...	70.6[33]	...	...	...	...
Houston (TX)	2 303 482[32]	...	...	1651.2[33]	...	...	...	...
Huntington Beach (CA)	200 652[32]	...	...	69.8[33]	...	...	...	...
Huntsville (AL)	193 079[32]	...	...	552.6[33]	...	...	...	...
Independence (MO)	117 030[32]	...	...	201.6[33]	...	...	...	...
Indianapolis (IN)	855 164[32]	...	...	936.3[33]	...	...	...	...
Inglewood (CA)	110 654[32]	...	...	23.5[33]	...	...	...	...
Irvine (CA)	266 122[32]	...	...	169.9[33]	...	...	...	...
Irving (TX)	238 289[32]	...	...	173.6[33]	...	...	...	...
Jackson (MS)	169 148[32]	...	...	287.6[33]	...	...	...	...
Jacksonville (FL)	880 619[32]	...	...	1935.9[33]	...	...	...	...
Jersey City (NJ)	264 152[32]	...	...	38.3[33]	...	...	...	...
Joliet (IL)	148 262[32]	...	...	166.9[33]	...	...	...	...
Jurupa Valley (CA)	103 541[32]	...	...	111.2[33]	...	...	...	...
Kansas City (KS)	151 709[32]	...	...	323.3[33]	...	...	...	...
Kansas City (MO)	481 420[32]	...	...	815.8[33]	...	...	...	...
Kent (WA)	127 514[32]	...	...	87.4[33]	...	...	...	...
Killeen (TX)	143 400[32]	...	...	138.7[33]	...	...	...	...
Knoxville (TN)	186 239[32]	...	...	255.2[33]	...	...	...	...
Lafayette (LA)	127 626[32]	...	...	139.4[33]	...	...	...	...
Lakeland (FL)	106 420[32]	...	...	170.7[33]	...	...	...	...
Lakewood (CO)	154 393[32]	...	...	111[33]	...	...	...	...
Lancaster (CA)	160 106[32]	...	...	244.2[33]	...	...	...	...
Lansing (MI)	116 020[32]	...	...	101.3[33]	...	...	...	...
Laredo (TX)	257 156[32]	...	...	261.9[33]	...	...	...	...

8. Population of capital cities and cities of 100 000 or more inhabitants: latest available year, 1999 - 2018
Population des capitales et des villes de 100 000 habitants ou plus : dernière année disponible, 1999 - 2018 (continued - suite)

Continent, country or area, date, code[a] and city / Continent, pays ou zone, date, code[a] et ville	City proper - Ville proprement dite				Urban agglomeration - Agglomération urbaine			
	Population			Surface area - Superficie (km²)	Population			Surface area - Superficie (km²)
	Both sexes - Les deux sexes	Male - Masculin	Female - Féminin		Both sexes - Les deux sexes	Male - Masculin	Female - Féminin	

AMERICA, NORTH - AMÉRIQUE DU NORD

United States of America - États-Unis d'Amérique[31]
1 VII 2016 (ESDJ)

Las Cruces (NM)	101 759[32]	...	...	199.3[33]	...	...	...	...
Las Vegas (NV)	632 912[32]	...	...	348[33]	...	...	...	...
League City (TX)	102 010[32]	...	...	132.6[33]	...	...	...	...
Lewisville (TX)	104 659[32]	...	...	95[33]	...	...	...	...
Lexington-Fayette (KY)	318 449[32]	...	...	734.6[33]	...	...	...	...
Lincoln (NE)	280 364[32]	...	...	238.6[33]	...	...	...	...
Little Rock (AR)	198 541[32]	...	...	307.4[33]	...	...	...	...
Long Beach (CA)	470 130[32]	...	...	130.3[33]	...	...	...	...
Los Angeles (CA)	3 976 322[32]	...	...	1214[33]	...	...	...	...
Louisville (KY)	616 261[32]	...	...	841.7[33]	...	...	...	...
Lowell (MA)	110 558[32]	...	...	35.2[33]	...	...	...	...
Lubbock (TX)	252 506[32]	...	...	322.8[33]	...	...	...	...
Macon-Bibb (GA)	152 555[32]	...	...	645.6[33]	...	...	...	...
Madison (WI)	252 551[32]	...	...	199.3[33]	...	...	...	...
Manchester (NH)	110 506[32]	...	...	85.6[33]	...	...	...	...
McAllen (TX)	142 212[32]	...	...	151.1[33]	...	...	...	...
McKinney City (TX)	172 298[32]	...	...	163.1[33]	...	...	...	...
Memphis (TN)	652 717[32]	...	...	822[33]	...	...	...	...
Mesa (AZ)	484 587[32]	...	...	357.1[33]	...	...	...	...
Mesquite (TX)	143 736[32]	...	...	122.3[33]	...	...	...	...
Miami (FL)	453 579[32]	...	...	93.2[33]	...	...	...	...
Miami Gardens (FL)	113 058[32]	...	...	47.2[33]	...	...	...	...
Midland City (TX)	134 610[32]	...	...	192.6[33]	...	...	...	...
Milwaukee (WI)	595 047[32]	...	...	249.1[33]	...	...	...	...
Minneapolis (MN)	413 651[32]	...	...	139.9[33]	...	...	...	...
Miramar (FL)	138 449[32]	...	...	76.1[33]	...	...	...	...
Mobile (AL)	192 904[32]	...	...	361[33]	...	...	...	...
Modesto (CA)	212 175[32]	...	...	111.3[33]	...	...	...	...
Montgomery (AL)	200 022[32]	...	...	414[33]	...	...	...	...
Moreno Valley (CA)	205 499[32]	...	...	132.8[33]	...	...	...	...
Murfreesboro (TN)	131 947[32]	...	...	144.7[33]	...	...	...	...
Murrieta (CA)	111 674[32]	...	...	87[33]	...	...	...	...
Naperville (IL)	147 122[32]	...	...	100.2[33]	...	...	...	...
Nashville-Davidson (TN)	660 388[32]	...	...	1232.7[33]	...	...	...	...
New Haven (CT)	129 934[32]	...	...	48.4[33]	...	...	...	...
New Orleans (LA)	391 495[32]	...	...	438.8[33]	...	...	...	...
New York (NY)	8 537 673[32]	...	...	780.8[33]	...	...	...	...
Newark (NJ)	281 764[32]	...	...	62.5[33]	...	...	...	...
Newport News (VA)	181 825[32]	...	...	178.9[33]	...	...	...	...
Norfolk (VA)	245 115[32]	...	...	138[33]	...	...	...	...
Norman (OK)	122 180[32]	...	...	463[33]	...	...	...	...
North Charleston (SC)	109 298[32]	...	...	190.8[33]	...	...	...	...
North Las Vegas (NV)	238 702[32]	...	...	253.9[33]	...	...	...	...
Norwalk (CA)	106 178[32]	...	...	25.1[33]	...	...	...	...
Oakland (CA)	420 005[32]	...	...	144.8[33]	...	...	...	...
Oceanside (CA)	175 464[32]	...	...	106.8[33]	...	...	...	...
Odessa (TX)	117 871[32]	...	...	117[33]	...	...	...	...
Oklahoma City (OK)	638 367[32]	...	...	1570.3[33]	...	...	...	...
Olathe (KS)	135 473[32]	...	...	157.6[33]	...	...	...	...
Omaha (NE)	446 970[32]	...	...	345[33]	...	...	...	...
Ontario (CA)	173 212[32]	...	...	129.3[33]	...	...	...	...
Orange (CA)	140 504[32]	...	...	65.7[33]	...	...	...	...
Orlando (FL)	277 173[32]	...	...	272.5[33]	...	...	...	...
Overland Park (KS)	188 966[32]	...	...	194.6[33]	...	...	...	...
Oxnard (CA)	207 906[32]	...	...	69.7[33]	...	...	...	...
Palm Bay City (FL)	110 104[32]	...	...	170.2[33]	...	...	...	...
Palmdale (CA)	157 356[32]	...	...	274.5[33]	...	...	...	...
Pasadena (CA)	142 059[32]	...	...	59.5[33]	...	...	...	...
Pasadena (TX)	153 351[32]	...	...	112.6[33]	...	...	...	...

Continent, country or area, date, code[a] and city / Continent, pays ou zone, date, code[a] et ville	City proper - Ville proprement dite				Urban agglomeration - Agglomération urbaine			
	Population			Surface area - Superficie (km²)	Population			Surface area - Superficie (km²)
	Both sexes - Les deux sexes	Male - Masculin	Female - Féminin		Both sexes - Les deux sexes	Male - Masculin	Female - Féminin	

AMERICA, NORTH - AMÉRIQUE DU NORD

United States of America - États-Unis d'Amérique[31]
1 VII 2016 (ESDJ)

Continent, country or area, date, code[a] and city	Both sexes	Male	Female	Surface area	Both sexes	Male	Female	Surface area
Paterson (NJ)	147 000[32]	...	...	21.8[33]	...	...	...	
Pearland (TX)	113 570[32]	...	...	120[33]	...	...	...	
Pembroke Pines (FL)	168 587[32]	...	...	85.5[33]	...	...	...	
Peoria (AZ)	164 173[32]	...	...	455[33]	...	...	...	
Peoria (IL)	114 265[32]	...	...	124.9[33]	...	...	...	
Philadelphia (PA)	1 567 872[32]	...	...	347.5[33]	...	...	...	
Phoenix (AZ)	1 615 017[32]	...	...	1340.7[33]	...	...	...	
Pittsburgh (PA)	303 625[32]	...	...	143.4[33]	...	...	...	
Plano (TX)	286 057[32]	...	...	185.6[33]	...	...	...	
Pomona (CA)	152 494[32]	...	...	59.4[33]	...	...	...	
Pompano Beach (FL)	109 393[32]	...	...	62.3[33]	...	...	...	
Port St. Lucie (FL)	185 132[32]	...	...	307.9[33]	...	...	...	
Portland (OR)	639 863[32]	...	...	345.7[33]	...	...	...	
Providence (RI)	179 219[32]	...	...	47.7[33]	...	...	...	
Provo (UT)	116 868[32]	...	...	107.9[33]	...	...	...	
Pueblo (CO)	110 291[32]	...	...	138.8[33]	...	...	...	
Raleigh (NC)	458 880[32]	...	...	375.7[33]	...	...	...	
Rancho Cucamonga (CA)	176 534[32]	...	...	103.6[33]	...	...	...	
Reno (NV)	245 255[32]	...	...	277.9[33]	...	...	...	
Renton (WA)	100 953[32]	...	...	60.7[33]	...	...	...	
Rialto (CA)	103 314[32]	...	...	57.8[33]	...	...	...	
Richardson (TX)	113 347[32]	...	...	74[33]	...	...	...	
Richmond (CA)	109 813[32]	...	...	77.8[33]	...	...	...	
Richmond (VA)	223 170[32]	...	...	154.9[33]	...	...	...	
Riverside (CA)	324 722[32]	...	...	210.4[33]	...	...	...	
Rochester (MN)	114 011[32]	...	...	141.3[33]	...	...	...	
Rochester (NY)	208 880[32]	...	...	92.7[33]	...	...	...	
Rockford (IL)	147 651[32]	...	...	164.4[33]	...	...	...	
Roseville (CA)	132 671[32]	...	...	111.3[33]	...	...	...	
Round Rock (TX)	120 892[32]	...	...	92.1[33]	...	...	...	
Sacramento (CA)	495 234[32]	...	...	253.6[33]	...	...	...	
Salem (OR)	167 419[32]	...	...	125.8[33]	...	...	...	
Salinas (CA)	157 218[32]	...	...	61.2[33]	...	...	...	
Salt Lake City (UT)	193 744[32]	...	...	288[33]	...	...	...	
San Angelo (TX)	100 702[32]	...	...	155.3[33]	...	...	...	
San Antonio (TX)	1 492 510[32]	...	...	1194[33]	...	...	...	
San Bernardino (CA)	216 239[32]	...	...	159.3[33]	...	...	...	
San Buenaventura (CA)	109 592[32]	...	...	56.5[33]	...	...	...	
San Diego (CA)	1 406 630[32]	...	...	842.3[33]	...	...	...	
San Francisco (CA)	870 887[32]	...	...	121.5[33]	...	...	...	
San Jose (CA)	1 025 350[32]	...	...	459.7[33]	...	...	...	
San Mateo (CA)	103 959[32]	...	...	31.4[33]	...	...	...	
Sandy Springs (GA)	105 703[32]	...	...	97.5[33]	...	...	...	
Santa Ana (CA)	334 217[32]	...	...	70.3[33]	...	...	...	
Santa Clara (CA)	125 948[32]	...	...	47.7[33]	...	...	...	
Santa Clarita (CA)	181 972[32]	...	...	136.6[33]	...	...	...	
Santa Maria (CA)	106 290[32]	...	...	59[33]	...	...	...	
Santa Rosa (CA)	175 155[32]	...	...	106.9[33]	...	...	...	
Savannah (GA)	146 763[32]	...	...	268.3[33]	...	...	...	
Scottsdale (AZ)	246 645[32]	...	...	476.4[33]	...	...	...	
Seattle (WA)	704 352[32]	...	...	217.1[33]	...	...	...	
Shreveport (LA)	194 920[32]	...	...	277.5[33]	...	...	...	
Simi Valley (CA)	126 327[32]	...	...	107.4[33]	...	...	...	
Sioux Falls (SD)	174 360[32]	...	...	195.3[33]	...	...	...	
South Bend (IN)	101 735[32]	...	...	107.2[33]	...	...	...	
Spokane (WA)	215 973[32]	...	...	178[33]	...	...	...	
Springfield (IL)	115 715[32]	...	...	155.6[33]	...	...	...	
Springfield (MA)	154 074[32]	...	...	82.5[33]	...	...	...	
Springfield (MO)	167 319[32]	...	...	213.2[33]	...	...	...	

8. Population of capital cities and cities of 100 000 or more inhabitants: latest available year, 1999 - 2018
Population des capitales et des villes de 100 000 habitants ou plus : dernière année disponible, 1999 - 2018 (continued - suite)

Continent, country or area, date, code[a] and city / Continent, pays ou zone, date, code[a] et ville	City proper - Ville proprement dite				Urban agglomeration - Agglomération urbaine			
	Population			Surface area - Superficie (km²)	Population			Surface area - Superficie (km²)
	Both sexes - Les deux sexes	Male - Masculin	Female - Féminin		Both sexes - Les deux sexes	Male - Masculin	Female - Féminin	
AMERICA, NORTH - AMÉRIQUE DU NORD								
United States of America - États-Unis d'Amérique[31]								
1 VII 2016 (ESDJ)								
St. Louis (MO)	311 404[32]	...	...	160.5[33]	...	...	...	...
St. Paul (MN)	302 398[32]	...	...	134.6[33]	...	...	...	...
St. Petersburg (FL)	260 999[32]	...	...	159.9[33]	...	...	...	...
Stamford (CT)	129 113[32]	...	...	97.4[33]	...	...	...	...
Sterling Heights (MI)	132 427[32]	...	...	94.6[33]	...	...	...	...
Stockton (CA)	307 072[32]	...	...	159.7[33]	...	...	...	...
Sunnyvale (CA)	152 771[32]	...	...	56.9[33]	...	...	...	...
Surprise (AZ)	132 677[32]	...	...	279.3[33]	...	...	...	...
Syracuse (NY)	143 378[32]	...	...	64.9[33]	...	...	...	...
Tacoma (WA)	211 277[32]	...	...	128.8[33]	...	...	...	...
Tallahassee (FL)	190 894[32]	...	...	260.1[33]	...	...	...	...
Tampa (FL)	377 165[32]	...	...	293.7[33]	...	...	...	...
Temecula (CA)	113 054[32]	...	...	96.5[33]	...	...	...	...
Tempe (AZ)	182 498[32]	...	...	103.5[33]	...	...	...	...
Thornton (CO)	136 703[32]	...	...	92.5[33]	...	...	...	...
Thousand Oaks (CA)	128 888[32]	...	...	142.9[33]	...	...	...	...
Toledo (OH)	278 508[32]	...	...	209.1[33]	...	...	...	...
Topeka (KS)	126 808[32]	...	...	159.2[33]	...	...	...	...
Torrance (CA)	147 195[32]	...	...	53[33]	...	...	...	...
Tucson (AZ)	530 706[32]	...	...	597.8[33]	...	...	...	...
Tulsa (OK)	403 090[32]	...	...	509.8[33]	...	...	...	...
Tyler (TX)	104 798[32]	...	...	146.7[33]	...	...	...	...
Urban Honolulu (HI)	351 792[32]	...	...	156.8[33]	...	...	...	...
Vallejo (CA)	121 299[32]	...	...	79.4[33]	...	...	...	...
Vancouver (WA)	174 826[32]	...	...	121.6[33]	...	...	...	...
Victorville City (CA)	122 265[32]	...	...	189.9[33]	...	...	...	...
Virginia Beach (VA)	452 602[32]	...	...	633.8[33]	...	...	...	...
Visalia (CA)	131 074[32]	...	...	97.1[33]	...	...	...	...
Vista (CA)	101 659[32]	...	...	48.4[33]	...	...	...	...
Waco (TX)	134 432[32]	...	...	230.6[33]	...	...	...	...
Warren (MI)	135 125[32]	...	...	89.1[33]	...	...	...	...
WASHINGTON (DC)	681 170[32]	...	...	158.4[33]	...	...	...	...
Waterbury (CT)	108 272[32]	...	...	73.9[33]	...	...	...	...
West Covina (CA)	107 847[32]	...	...	41.5[33]	...	...	...	...
West Jordan (UT)	113 699[32]	...	...	83.7[33]	...	...	...	...
West Palm Beach (FL)	108 161[32]	...	...	142.8[33]	...	...	...	...
West Valley City (UT)	136 574[32]	...	...	91.9[33]	...	...	...	...
Westminster (CO)	113 875[32]	...	...	82.2[33]	...	...	...	...
Wichita (KS)	389 902[32]	...	...	415.4[33]	...	...	...	...
Wichita Falls (TX)	104 724[32]	...	...	187[33]	...	...	...	...
Wilmington (NC)	117 525[32]	...	...	133.7[33]	...	...	...	...
Winston-Salem (NC)	242 203[32]	...	...	343.2[33]	...	...	...	...
Worcester (MA)	184 508[32]	...	...	96.8[33]	...	...	...	...
Yonkers (NY)	200 807[32]	...	...	46.7[33]	...	...	...	...
United States Virgin Islands - Îles Vierges américaines[34]								
1 IV 2010 (CDJC)								
CHARLOTTE AMALIE	10 354	...	...	...	...	...	...	...
AMERICA, SOUTH - AMÉRIQUE DU SUD								
Argentina - Argentine[35]								
1 VII 2016 (ESDF)								
Bahía Blanca-Cerri	...	...	...	...	308 922	148 808	160 114	...
Bariloche	...	...	...	...	158 989	80 341	78 648	...
BUENOS AIRES	...	...	...	...	13 879 707	6 732 655	7 147 052	...
Catamarca	...	...	...	...	213 186	103 592	109 594	...
Comodoro Rivadavia-Rada Tilly	...	...	...	...	218 596	111 629	106 967	...
Concordia	...	...	...	...	161 990	79 065	82 925	...

8. Population of capital cities and cities of 100 000 or more inhabitants: latest available year, 1999 - 2018
Population des capitales et des villes de 100 000 habitants ou plus : dernière année disponible, 1999 - 2018 (continued - suite)

Continent, country or area, date, code[a] and city Continent, pays ou zone, date, code[a] et ville	City proper - Ville proprement dite				Urban agglomeration - Agglomération urbaine			
	Population			Surface area - Superficie (km²)	Population			Surface area - Superficie (km²)
	Both sexes - Les deux sexes	Male - Masculin	Female - Féminin		Both sexes - Les deux sexes	Male - Masculin	Female - Féminin	
AMERICA, SOUTH - AMÉRIQUE DU SUD								
Argentina - Argentine[35]								
1 VII 2016 (ESDF)								
Córdoba	...	...	...	...	1 525 490	731 552	793 938	...
Corrientes	...	...	...	...	386 379	185 631	200 748	...
Formosa	...	...	...	...	260 788	126 622	134 166	...
La Plata	...	...	...	...	843 851	409 347	434 504	...
La Rioja	...	...	...	...	207 085	101 956	105 129	...
Mar del Plata-Batán	...	...	...	...	641 065	308 438	332 627	...
Mendoza	...	...	...	...	1 094 209	533 737	560 472	...
Neuquén-Plottier	...	...	...	...	314 478	155 618	158 860	...
Paraná	...	...	...	...	276 125	132 139	143 986	...
Posadas	...	...	...	...	358 832	172 792	186 040	...
Rawson-Trelew-Playa Unión	...	...	...	...	139 698	68 235	71 463	...
Resistencia	...	...	...	...	412 445	198 970	213 475	...
Río Cuarto	...	...	...	...	173 807	83 516	90 291	...
Rio Gallegos	...	...	...	...	112 455	56 849	55 606	...
Rosario	...	...	...	...	1 444 436	701 272	743 164	...
Salta	...	...	...	...	634 644	306 877	327 767	...
San Juan	...	...	...	...	520 430	251 730	268 700	...
San Luis - El Chorrillo	...	...	...	...	221 410	108 478	112 932	...
San Nicolás-Villa Constitución	...	...	...	...	190 447	93 127	97 320	...
San Salvador de Jujuy-Palpalá	...	...	...	...	341 634	165 159	176 475	...
Santa Fé	...	...	...	...	534 341	256 803	277 538	...
Santa Rosa-Toay	...	...	...	...	127 055	61 725	65 330	...
Santiago del Estero-La Banda	...	...	...	...	410 083	198 119	211 964	...
Tucumán-Tafí Viejo	...	...	...	...	873 873	420 897	452 976	...
Ushuaia-Río Grande	...	...	...	...	139 989	72 112	67 877	...
Bolivia (Plurinational State of) - Bolivie (État plurinational de)								
1 VII 2010 (ESDF)								
Cochabamba	618 376	294 711	323 666	...	...	...	...	...
El Alto	953 253	463 069	490 184	...	...	...	...	...
LA PAZ	835 361	397 608	437 753	...	...	...	...	...
Oruro	216 724	104 294	112 430	...	...	...	...	...
Potosí	154 693	74 591	80 103	...	...	...	...	...
Sacaba	155 668	75 113	80 555	...	...	...	...	...
Santa Cruz	1 616 063	785 941	830 122	...	...	...	...	...
SUCRE	284 032	137 943	146 090	...	...	...	...	...
Tarija	194 313	94 231	100 082	...	...	...	...	...
Yacuiba	112 096	55 346	56 750	...	...	...	...	...
Brazil - Brésil[36]								
1 VII 2016 (ESDJ)								
Abaeteluba	151 934	...	...	...	...	...	...	...
Açailândia	110 543	...	...	...	...	...	...	...
Aguas Lindas de Goiás	191 499	...	...	...	...	...	...	...
Alagoinhas	155 362	...	...	...	...	...	...	...
Almirante Tamandaré	114 129	...	...	...	...	...	...	...
Altamira	109 938	...	...	...	...	...	...	...
Alvorada	207 392	...	...	...	...	...	...	...
Americana	231 621	...	...	...	...	...	...	...
Ananindeua	510 834	...	...	...	...	...	...	...
Anápolis	370 875	...	...	...	...	...	...	...
Angra dos Reis	191 504	...	...	...	...	...	...	...
Aparecida de Goiania	532 135	...	...	...	...	...	...	...
Apucarana	131 571	...	...	...	...	...	...	...
Aracaju	641 523	...	...	...	...	...	...	...
Araçatuba	193 828	...	...	...	...	...	...	...
Araguaina	173 112	...	...	...	...	...	...	...
Araguario	116 871	...	...	...	...	...	...	...
Arapiraca	232 671	...	...	...	...	...	...	...
Arapongas	116 960	...	...	...	...	...	...	...
Araraquara	228 664	...	...	...	...	...	...	...
Araras	130 102	...	...	...	...	...	...	...
Araruama	124 940	...	...	...	...	...	...	...
Araucária	135 459	...	...	...	...	...	...	...

Continent, country or area, date, code[a] and city / Continent, pays ou zone, date, code[a] et ville	City proper - Ville proprement dite				Urban agglomeration - Agglomération urbaine			
	Population			Surface area - Superficie (km²)	Population			Surface area - Superficie (km²)
	Both sexes - Les deux sexes	Male - Masculin	Female - Féminin		Both sexes - Les deux sexes	Male - Masculin	Female - Féminin	

AMERICA, SOUTH - AMÉRIQUE DU SUD

Brazil - Brésil[36]
1 VII 2016 (ESDJ)

Araxá	103 287	...	...	...	...	...	...	...
Ariquemes	105 896	...	...	...	...	...	...	...
Assis	102 268	...	...	...	...	...	...	...
Atibaia	138 449	...	...	...	...	...	...	...
Bacabal	103 020	...	...	...	...	...	...	...
Bagé	121 986	...	...	...	...	...	...	...
Balneário Camboriú	131 727	...	...	...	...	...	...	...
Barbacena	135 829	...	...	...	...	...	...	...
Barcarena	118 537	...	...	...	...	...	...	...
Barra Mansa	180 126	...	...	...	...	...	...	...
Barreiras	155 519	...	...	...	...	...	...	...
Barretos	119 948	...	...	...	...	...	...	...
Barueri	264 935	...	...	...	...	...	...	...
Bauru	369 368	...	...	...	...	...	...	...
Belém	1 446 042	...	...	...	...	...	...	...
Belford Roxo	494 141	...	...	...	...	...	...	...
Belo Horizonte	2 513 451	...	...	...	...	...	...	...
Bento Gonçalves	114 203	...	...	...	...	...	...	...
Betim	422 354	...	...	...	...	...	...	...
Birigui	119 536	...	...	...	...	...	...	...
Blumenou	343 715	...	...	...	...	...	...	...
Boa Vista	326 419	...	...	...	...	...	...	...
Botucatu	141 032	...	...	...	...	...	...	...
Bragança	122 881	...	...	...	...	...	...	...
Bragança Paulista	162 435	...	...	...	...	...	...	...
BRASILIA	2 977 216	...	...	...	...	...	...	...
Brusque	125 810	...	...	...	...	...	...	...
Cabo de Santo Agostinho	202 636	...	...	...	...	...	...	...
Cabo Frio	212 289	...	...	...	...	...	...	...
Cachoeirinha	126 666	...	...	...	...	...	...	...
Cachoeiro de Itapemirim	210 325	...	...	...	...	...	...	...
Camacari	292 074	...	...	...	...	...	...	...
Camaragibe	155 228	...	...	...	...	...	...	...
Cambé	104 592	...	...	...	...	...	...	...
Cametá	132 515	...	...	...	...	...	...	...
Campina Grande	407 754	...	...	...	...	...	...	...
Campinas	1 173 370	...	...	...	...	...	...	...
Campo Grande	863 982	...	...	...	...	...	...	...
Campo Largo	125 719	...	...	...	...	...	...	...
Campos dos Goytacazes	487 186	...	...	...	...	...	...	...
Canoas	342 634	...	...	...	...	...	...	...
Caraguatatuba	115 071	...	...	...	...	...	...	...
Carapicuíba	394 465	...	...	...	...	...	...	...
Cariacica	384 621	...	...	...	...	...	...	...
Caruaru	351 686	...	...	...	...	...	...	...
Cascavel	316 226	...	...	...	...	...	...	...
Castanhal	192 571	...	...	...	...	...	...	...
Catalão	100 590	...	...	...	...	...	...	...
Catanduva	120 092	...	...	...	...	...	...	...
Caucaia	358 164	...	...	...	...	...	...	...
Caxias	161 926	...	...	...	...	...	...	...
Caxias do Sul	479 236	...	...	...	...	...	...	...
Chapecó	209 553	...	...	...	...	...	...	...
Codo	120 548	...	...	...	...	...	...	...
Colatina	123 598	...	...	...	...	...	...	...
Colombo	234 941	...	...	...	...	...	...	...
Conselheiro Lafaiete	126 420	...	...	...	...	...	...	...
Contagem	653 800	...	...	...	...	...	...	...
Coronel Fabriciano	109 857	...	...	...	...	...	...	...
Corumbá	109 294	...	...	...	...	...	...	...
Cotia	233 696	...	...	...	...	...	...	...
Crato	129 662	...	...	...	...	...	...	...
Criciúma	209 153	...	...	...	...	...	...	...

Continent, country or area, date, codeª and city Continent, pays ou zone, date, codeª et ville	City proper - Ville proprement dite				Urban agglomeration - Agglomération urbaine			
	Population			Surface area - Superficie (km²)	Population			Surface area - Superficie (km²)
	Both sexes - Les deux sexes	Male - Masculin	Female - Féminin		Both sexes - Les deux sexes	Male - Masculin	Female - Féminin	

AMERICA, SOUTH - AMÉRIQUE DU SUD

Brazil - Brésil[36]
  1 VII 2016 (ESDJ)

Cubatao	127 887	...	...	...	...	...	...	...
Cuiabá	585 367	...	...	...	...	...	...	...
Curitiba	1 893 997	...	...	...	...	...	...	...
Diadema	415 180	...	...	...	...	...	...	...
Divinópolis	232 945	...	...	...	...	...	...	...
Dourados	215 486	...	...	...	...	...	...	...
Duque de Caxias	886 917	...	...	...	...	...	...	...
Embu	264 448	...	...	...	...	...	...	...
Erechim	102 906	...	...	...	...	...	...	...
Eunápolis	114 275	...	...	...	...	...	...	...
Feira de Santana	622 639	...	...	...	...	...	...	...
Ferraz de Vasconcelos	186 808	...	...	...	...	...	...	...
Florianópolis	477 798	...	...	...	...	...	...	...
Formosa	114 036	...	...	...	...	...	...	...
Fortaleza	2 609 716	...	...	...	...	...	...	...
Foz do Iguaçu	263 915	...	...	...	...	...	...	...
Franca	344 704	...	...	...	...	...	...	...
Francisco Morato	169 942	...	...	...	...	...	...	...
Franco da Rocha	147 650	...	...	...	...	...	...	...
Garanhuns	137 810	...	...	...	...	...	...	...
Goiânia	1 448 639	...	...	...	...	...	...	...
Governador Valadares	279 665	...	...	...	...	...	...	...
Gravatai	273 742	...	...	...	...	...	...	...
Guarapari	121 506	...	...	...	...	...	...	...
Guarapuava	179 256	...	...	...	...	...	...	...
Guaratinguetá	119 753	...	...	...	...	...	...	...
Guarujá	313 421	...	...	...	...	...	...	...
Guarulhos	1 337 087	...	...	...	...	...	...	...
Hortolandia	219 039	...	...	...	...	...	...	...
Ibirité	175 721	...	...	...	...	...	...	...
Igarassu	113 956	...	...	...	...	...	...	...
Iguatu	102 013	...	...	...	...	...	...	...
Ilhéus	178 210	...	...	...	...	...	...	...
Imperatriz	253 873	...	...	...	...	...	...	...
Indaiatuba	235 367	...	...	...	...	...	...	...
Ipatinga	259 324	...	...	...	...	...	...	...
Itabiraí	118 481	...	...	...	...	...	...	...
Itaboraí	230 786	...	...	...	...	...	...	...
Itabuna	220 386	...	...	...	...	...	...	...
Itaguaí	120 855	...	...	...	...	...	...	...
Itajaí	208 958	...	...	...	...	...	...	...
Itapecerica da Serra	169 103	...	...	...	...	...	...	...
Itapetininga	158 561	...	...	...	...	...	...	...
Itapevi	226 488	...	...	...	...	...	...	...
Itapipoca	126 234	...	...	...	...	...	...	...
Itaquaquecetuba	356 774	...	...	...	...	...	...	...
Itatiba	114 912	...	...	...	...	...	...	...
Itu	168 643	...	...	...	...	...	...	...
Ituiutaba	103 945	...	...	...	...	...	...	...
Itumbiara	101 544	...	...	...	...	...	...	...
Jaboatao dos Guarapes	691 125	...	...	...	...	...	...	...
Jacareí	228 214	...	...	...	...	...	...	...
Jandira	120 177	...	...	...	...	...	...	...
Japeri	100 562	...	...	...	...	...	...	...
Jaraguá do Sul	167 300	...	...	...	...	...	...	...
Jaú	144 828	...	...	...	...	...	...	...
Jequié	161 880	...	...	...	...	...	...	...
Ji-Paraná	131 560	...	...	...	...	...	...	...
Joao Pessoa	801 718	...	...	...	...	...	...	...
Joinville	569 645	...	...	...	...	...	...	...
Juazeiro	220 253	...	...	...	...	...	...	...
Juàzeiro do Norte	268 248	...	...	...	...	...	...	...
Juiz de Fora	559 636	...	...	...	...	...	...	...

Continent, country or area, date, code[a] and city	City proper - Ville proprement dite				Urban agglomeration - Agglomération urbaine			
	Population			Surface area - Superficie (km²)	Population			Surface area - Superficie (km²)
Continent, pays ou zone, date, code[a] et ville	Both sexes - Les deux sexes	Male - Masculin	Female - Féminin		Both sexes - Les deux sexes	Male - Masculin	Female - Féminin	

AMERICA, SOUTH - AMÉRIQUE DU SUD

Brazil - Brésil[36]
1 VII 2016 (ESDJ)

Jundiaí	405 740	...	...	...	...	...	...	...
Lagarto	103 188	...	...	...	...	...	...	...
Lages	158 620	...	...	...	...	...	...	...
Lauro de Freitas	194 641	...	...	...	...	...	...	...
Lavras	101 208	...	...	...	...	...	...	...
Leme	100 296	...	...	...	...	...	...	...
Limeira	298 701	...	...	...	...	...	...	...
Linhares	166 491	...	...	...	...	...	...	...
Londrina	553 393	...	...	...	...	...	...	...
Luziânia	196 864	...	...	...	...	...	...	...
Macae	239 471	...	...	...	...	...	...	...
Macapá	465 495	...	...	...	...	...	...	...
Maceió	1 021 709	...	...	...	...	...	...	...
Magé	236 319	...	...	...	...	...	...	...
Manaus	2 094 391	...	...	...	...	...	...	...
Maraba	266 932	...	...	...	...	...	...	...
Maracanau	223 188	...	...	...	...	...	...	...
Maranguape	125 058	...	...	...	...	...	...	...
Maricá	149 876	...	...	...	...	...	...	...
Marília	233 639	...	...	...	...	...	...	...
Maringá	403 063	...	...	...	...	...	...	...
Marituba	125 435	...	...	...	...	...	...	...
Mauá	457 696	...	...	...	...	...	...	...
Mesquita	171 020	...	...	...	...	...	...	...
Moji das Cruzes	429 321	...	...	...	...	...	...	...
Moji-Guaçu	148 327	...	...	...	...	...	...	...
Montes Claros	398 288	...	...	...	...	...	...	...
Mossoró	291 937	...	...	...	...	...	...	...
Muriaé	107 916	...	...	...	...	...	...	...
Natal	877 662	...	...	...	...	...	...	...
Nilópolis	158 319	...	...	...	...	...	...	...
Niterói	497 883	...	...	...	...	...	...	...
Nossa Senhora do Socorro	179 661	...	...	...	...	...	...	...
Nova Friburgo	185 102	...	...	...	...	...	...	...
Nova Iguaçu	797 435	...	...	...	...	...	...	...
Novo Gama	108 410	...	...	...	...	...	...	...
Nôvo Hamburgo	249 113	...	...	...	...	...	...	...
Olinda	390 144	...	...	...	...	...	...	...
Osasco	696 382	...	...	...	...	...	...	...
Ourinhos	111 056	...	...	...	...	...	...	...
Paço do Lumiar	119 915	...	...	...	...	...	...	...
Palhoça	161 395	...	...	...	...	...	...	...
Palmas	279 856	...	...	...	...	...	...	...
Paragominas	108 547	...	...	...	...	...	...	...
Paranaguá	151 829	...	...	...	...	...	...	...
Parauapebas	196 259	...	...	...	...	...	...	...
Parintins	112 716	...	...	...	...	...	...	...
Parnaíba	150 201	...	...	...	...	...	...	...
Parnamirim	248 623	...	...	...	...	...	...	...
Passo Fundo	197 798	...	...	...	...	...	...	...
Passos	113 807	...	...	...	...	...	...	...
Patos	107 067	...	...	...	...	...	...	...
Patos de Minas	149 856	...	...	...	...	...	...	...
Paulínia	100 128	...	...	...	...	...	...	...
Paulista	325 590	...	...	...	...	...	...	...
Paulo Afonso	119 930	...	...	...	...	...	...	...
Pelotas	343 651	...	...	...	...	...	...	...
Petrolina	337 683	...	...	...	...	...	...	...
Petrópolis	298 158	...	...	...	...	...	...	...
Pindamonhangaba	162 327	...	...	...	...	...	...	...
Pinhais	128 256	...	...	...	...	...	...	...
Piracicaba	394 419	...	...	...	...	...	...	...
Piraquara	106 132	...	...	...	...	...	...	...

Continent, country or area, date, code[a] and city / Continent, pays ou zone, date, code[a] et ville	City proper - Ville proprement dite				Urban agglomeration - Agglomération urbaine			
	Population			Surface area - Superficie (km²)	Population			Surface area - Superficie (km²)
	Both sexes - Les deux sexes	Male - Masculin	Female - Féminin		Both sexes - Les deux sexes	Male - Masculin	Female - Féminin	

AMERICA, SOUTH - AMÉRIQUE DU SUD

Brazil - Brésil[36]
  1 VII 2016 (ESDJ)

Poà	114 650	...	...	...	...	...	...	...
Poços de Caldas	164 912	...	...	...	...	...	...	...
Ponta Grossa	341 130	...	...	...	...	...	...	...
Porto Alegre	1 481 019	...	...	...	...	...	...	...
Porto Seguro	147 444	...	...	...	...	...	...	...
Porto Velho	511 219	...	...	...	...	...	...	...
Pouso Alegre	145 535	...	...	...	...	...	...	...
Praia Grande	304 705	...	...	...	...	...	...	...
Presidente Prudente	223 749	...	...	...	...	...	...	...
Queimados	144 525	...	...	...	...	...	...	...
Recife	1 625 583	...	...	...	...	...	...	...
Resende	126 084	...	...	...	...	...	...	...
Ribeirao das Neves	325 846	...	...	...	...	...	...	...
Ribeirao Pires	121 130	...	...	...	...	...	...	...
Ribeirao Prêto	674 405	...	...	...	...	...	...	...
Rio Branco	377 057	...	...	...	...	...	...	...
Rio Claro	201 473	...	...	...	...	...	...	...
Rio das Ostras	136 626	...	...	...	...	...	...	...
Rio de Janeiro	6 498 837	...	...	...	...	...	...	...
Rio Grande	208 641	...	...	...	...	...	...	...
Rio Verde	212 237	...	...	...	...	...	...	...
Rondonópolis	218 899	...	...	...	...	...	...	...
Sabára	135 196	...	...	...	...	...	...	...
Salto	115 193	...	...	...	...	...	...	...
Salvador	2 938 092	...	...	...	...	...	...	...
Santa Bárbara D'Oeste	191 024	...	...	...	...	...	...	...
Santa Cruz do Capibaribe	103 660	...	...	...	...	...	...	...
Santa Cruz do Sul	126 775	...	...	...	...	...	...	...
Santa Luzia (Minas Gerais)	217 610	...	...	...	...	...	...	...
Santa Maria	277 309	...	...	...	...	...	...	...
Santa Rita	135 915	...	...	...	...	...	...	...
Santana	113 854	...	...	...	...	...	...	...
Santana de Parnaíba	129 261	...	...	...	...	...	...	...
Santarém	294 447	...	...	...	...	...	...	...
Santo André	712 749	...	...	...	...	...	...	...
Santo Antônio de Jesus	102 469	...	...	...	...	...	...	...
Santos	434 359	...	...	...	...	...	...	...
Sao Bernardo do Campo	822 242	...	...	...	...	...	...	...
Sao Caetano do Sul	158 825	...	...	...	...	...	...	...
Sao Carlo	243 765	...	...	...	...	...	...	...
São Félix do Xingu	120 580	...	...	...	...	...	...	...
Sao Gonçalo	1 044 058	...	...	...	...	...	...	...
Sao Joao de Meriti	460 541	...	...	...	...	...	...	...
Sao José	236 029	...	...	...	...	...	...	...
Sao José de Ribamar	176 008	...	...	...	...	...	...	...
Sao José do Rio Prêto	446 649	...	...	...	...	...	...	...
Sao José dos Campos	695 992	...	...	...	...	...	...	...
Sao José dos Pinhais	302 759	...	...	...	...	...	...	...
Sao Leopoldo	229 678	...	...	...	...	...	...	...
São Lourenço da Mata	111 197	...	...	...	...	...	...	...
Sao Luís	1 082 935	...	...	...	...	...	...	...
São Mateus	126 437	...	...	...	...	...	...	...
Sao Paulo	12 038 175	...	...	...	...	...	...	...
Sao Vicente	357 989	...	...	...	...	...	...	...
Sapucaia do Sul	138 933	...	...	...	...	...	...	...
Senador Canedo	102 947	...	...	...	...	...	...	...
Serra	494 109	...	...	...	...	...	...	...
Sertaozinho	121 412	...	...	...	...	...	...	...
Sete Lagoas	234 221	...	...	...	...	...	...	...
Simoes Filho	134 674	...	...	...	...	...	...	...
Sinop	132 934	...	...	...	...	...	...	...
Sobral	203 682	...	...	...	...	...	...	...
Sorocaba	652 481	...	...	...	...	...	...	...

Continent, country or area, date, codeᵃ and city / Continent, pays ou zone, date, codeᵃ et ville	City proper - Ville proprement dite				Urban agglomeration - Agglomération urbaine			
	Population			Surface area - Superficie (km²)	Population			Surface area - Superficie (km²)
	Both sexes - Les deux sexes	Male - Masculin	Female - Féminin		Both sexes - Les deux sexes	Male - Masculin	Female - Féminin	
AMERICA, SOUTH - AMÉRIQUE DU SUD								
Brazil - Brésil[36]								
1 VII 2016 (ESDJ)								
Sumaré	269 522	...	...	...	...	...	...	
Susano	288 056	...	...	...	...	...	...	...
Taboao da Serra	275 948	...	...	...	...	...	...	
Tailândia	100 300	...	...	...	...	...	...	
Tatuí	117 823	...	...	...	...	...	...	
Taubaté	305 174	...	...	...	...	...	...	
Teixeira de Freitas	159 813	...	...	...	...	...	...	
Teófilo Otoni	141 502	...	...	...	...	...	...	
Teresina	847 430	...	...	...	...	...	...	
Teresópolis	174 587	...	...	...	...	...	...	
Timon	166 295	...	...	...	...	...	...	
Toledo	133 824	...	...	...	...	...	...	
Três Lagoas	115 561	...	...	...	...	...	...	
Trindade	119 385	...	...	...	...	...	...	
Tubarão	103 674	...	...	...	...	...	...	
Tucuruí	108 885	...	...	...	...	...	...	
Ubá	112 186	...	...	...	...	...	...	
Uberaba	325 279	...	...	...	...	...	...	
Uberlândia	669 672	...	...	...	...	...	...	
Umuarama	109 132	...	...	...	...	...	...	
Uruguaiana	129 720	...	...	...	...	...	...	
Valinhos	122 163	...	...	...	...	...	...	
Valparaíso de Goiás	156 419	...	...	...	...	...	...	
Varginha	133 384	...	...	...	...	...	...	
Varzea Grande	271 339	...	...	...	...	...	...	
Varzea Paulista	117 772	...	...	...	...	...	...	
Vespasiano	120 510	...	...	...	...	...	...	
Viamao	252 872	...	...	...	...	...	...	
Vila Velha	479 664	...	...	...	...	...	...	
Vitória	359 555	...	...	...	...	...	...	
Vitória da Conquista	346 069	...	...	...	...	...	...	
Vitória de Santo Antao	136 706	...	...	...	...	...	...	
Volta Redonda	263 659	...	...	...	...	...	...	
Votorantim	118 858	...	...	...	...	...	...	
Chile - Chili								
1 VII 2017 (ESDF)								
Alto Hospicio	124 877	63 281	61 596	17[37]	...	...	...	...
Antofagasta	388 545	205 983	182 562	44[37]	...	...	...	...
Arica	229 689	114 441	115 248	42[37]	...	...	...	...
Calama	180 283	91 633	88 650	18[37]	...	...	...	...
Chiguallante	101 244	48 160	53 084	34[37]	...	...	...	...
Chillán	159 476	75 030	84 446	33[37]	...	...	...	...
Concepción	220 746	104 151	116 595	56[37]	...	...	...	...
Copiapó	175 162	88 912	86 250	48[37]	...	...	...	...
Coquimbo	216 623	105 602	111 021	42[37]	...	...	...	...
Coronel	109 709	51 462	58 247	25[37]	...	...	...	...
Curicó	102 710	49 371	53 339	21[37]	...	...	...	...
Hualpén	108 803	50 733	58 070	11.9[37]	...	...	...	...
Iquique	196 562	98 599	97 963	22[37]	...	...	...	...
La Serena	205 635	100 151	105 484	66[37]	...	...	...	...
Los Ángeles	128 933	61 836	67 097	27[37]	...	...	...	...
Osorno	139 550	66 890	72 660	32[37]	...	...	...	...
Puente Alto	625 551	308 490	317 061	64[37]	...	...	...	...
Puerto Montt	213 119	106 266	106 853	40[37]	...	...	...	...
Punta Arenas	124 169	61 603	62 566	39[37]	...	...	...	...
Quilpué	172 049	83 317	88 732	38[37]	...	...	...	...
Rancagua	225 563	112 119	113 444	50[37]	...	...	...	...
San Bernardo	296 583	147 549	149 034	52[37]	...	...	...	...
San Pedro de la Paz	139 174	64 934	74 240	49[37]	...	...	...	...
SANTIAGO	5 613 962[38]	2 723 688[38]	2 890 274[38]	843[37]	...	...	...	...
Talca	203 873	97 557	106 316	46[37]	...	...	...	...

8. Population of capital cities and cities of 100 000 or more inhabitants: latest available year, 1999 - 2018
Population des capitales et des villes de 100 000 habitants ou plus : dernière année disponible, 1999 - 2018 (continued - suite)

Continent, country or area, date, code[a] and city / Continent, pays ou zone, date, code[a] et ville	City proper - Ville proprement dite				Urban agglomeration - Agglomération urbaine			
	Population			Surface area - Superficie (km²)	Population			Surface area - Superficie (km²)
	Both sexes - Les deux sexes	Male - Masculin	Female - Féminin		Both sexes - Les deux sexes	Male - Masculin	Female - Féminin	
AMERICA, SOUTH - AMÉRIQUE DU SUD								
Chile - Chili								
1 VII 2017 (ESDF)								
Temuco	221 375	105 706	115 669	46[37]	...	...	...	...
Valdivia	143 207	69 519	73 688	42[37]	...	...	...	...
Valparaíso	295 113	147 418	147 695	47[37]	...	...	...	...
Villa Alemana	144 417	70 578	73 839	31[37]	...	...	...	...
Viña del Mar	326 759	157 481	169 278	87[37]	...	...	...	...
Colombia - Colombie								
1 VII 2018 (ESDJ)								
Apartadó[39]	195 068	98 521	96 547	...	...	...	...	...
Armenia (Quindio)[39]	301 224[39]	145 458[39]	155 766[39]	115[40]	...	...	...	...
Barrancabermeja[39]	191 495	94 616	96 879	...	...	...	...	...
Barranquilla[39]	1 232 462	598 372	634 090	...	...	...	...	...
Bello[39]	482 287	233 257	249 030	...	...	...	...	...
BOGOTÁ, D.C.[39]	8 181 047	3 963 853	4 217 194	...	...	...	...	...
Bucaramanga[39]	528 610	254 705	273 905	...	...	...	...	...
Buenaventura[39]	424 047	206 210	217 837	...	...	...	...	...
Cali[39]	2 445 405	1 168 899	1 276 506	...	...	...	...	...
Cartagena[39]	1 036 134	501 471	534 663	...	...	...	...	...
Cartago[39]	134 308	64 655	69 653	...	...	...	...	...
Caucasia[39]	120 479	58 386	62 093	...	...	...	...	...
Chía[39]	135 752	65 336	70 416	...	...	...	...	...
Ciénaga (Magdalena)[39]	105 206	52 630	52 576	...	...	...	...	...
Cúcuta[39]	668 838	323 452	345 386	...	...	...	...	...
Dosquebradas[39]	204 739	100 089	104 650	...	...	...	...	...
Duitama[39]	113 954	52 154	61 800	...	...	...	...	...
Envigado[39]	238 221	114 641	123 580	...	...	...	...	...
Facatativá[39]	139 364	69 653	69 711	...	...	...	...	...
Florencia[39]	181 493	89 243	92 250	...	...	...	...	...
Floridablanca[39]	267 124	127 375	139 749	...	...	...	...	...
Fusagasugá[39]	142 426	70 542	71 884	...	...	...	...	...
Girardot[39]	106 818	50 413	56 405	...	...	...	...	...
Girón[39]	195 499	97 678	97 821	...	...	...	...	...
Gudalajara de Buga[39]	114 562	56 131	58 431	...	...	...	...	...
Ibagué[39]	569 336	276 386	292 950	...	...	...	...	...
Ipiales[39]	148 297	73 210	75 087	...	...	...	...	...
Itagüí[39]	276 916	135 186	141 730	...	...	...	...	...
Jamundí[39]	127 228	61 776	65 452	...	...	...	...	...
Lorica[39]	120 558	60 213	60 345	...	...	...	...	...
Magangué[39]	123 955	62 730	61 225	...	...	...	...	...
Maicao[39]	164 424	80 874	83 550	...	...	...	...	...
Malambo[39]	127 202	64 870	62 332	...	...	...	...	...
Manaure[39]	116 248	57 242	59 006	...	...	...	...	...
Manizales[39]	400 136	190 819	209 317	...	...	...	...	...
Medellín[39]	2 529 403	1 190 358	1 339 045	...	...	...	...	...
Montería[39]	460 082	223 233	236 849	...	...	...	...	...
Neiva[39]	347 438	166 181	181 257	...	...	...	...	...
Ocaña	100 461[39]	49 605[39]	50 856[39]	463[40]	...	...	...	...
Palmira[39]	310 594	149 816	160 778	...	...	...	...	...
Pasto[39]	455 678	220 492	235 186	...	...	...	...	...
Pereira[39]	476 636	225 372	251 264	...	...	...	...	...
Piedecuesta[39]	159 760	77 602	82 158	...	...	...	...	...
Pitalito[39]	133 205	66 111	67 094	...	...	...	...	...
Popayán[39]	284 737	138 214	146 523	...	...	...	...	...
Quibdo[39]	116 178	58 414	57 764	...	...	...	...	...
Riohacha[39]	286 973	141 424	145 549	...	...	...	...	...
Rionegro (Antioquia)[39]	126 193	62 703	63 490	...	...	...	...	...
Sabanalarga	101 339[39]	51 625[39]	49 714[39]	399[40]	...	...	...	...
San Andrés de Tumaco[39]	212 692	106 016	106 676	...	...	...	...	...
Santa Marta[39]	507 455	248 330	259 125	...	...	...	...	...
Sincelejo[39]	286 749	141 147	145 602	...	...	...	...	...
Soacha[39]	544 997	269 163	275 834	...	...	...	...	...
Sogamoso[39]	111 799	53 010	58 789	...	...	...	...	...

8. Population of capital cities and cities of 100 000 or more inhabitants: latest available year, 1999 - 2018
Population des capitales et des villes de 100 000 habitants ou plus : dernière année disponible, 1999 - 2018 (continued - suite)

Continent, country or area, date, code[a] and city / Continent, pays ou zone, date, code[a] et ville	City proper - Ville proprement dite				Urban agglomeration - Agglomération urbaine			
	Population			Surface area - Superficie (km²)	Population			Surface area - Superficie (km²)
	Both sexes - Les deux sexes	Male - Masculin	Female - Féminin		Both sexes - Les deux sexes	Male - Masculin	Female - Féminin	
AMERICA, SOUTH - AMÉRIQUE DU SUD								
Colombia - Colombie								
1 VII 2018 (ESDJ)								
Soledad[39]	666 247	329 863	336 384	...	...	...	...	...
Tierralta[39]	107 302	54 400	52 902	...	...	...	...	...
Tuluá[39]	219 148	105 247	113 901	...	...	...	...	...
Tunja[39]	199 221	95 601	103 620	...	...	...	...	...
Turbo[39]	172 314	87 186	85 128	...	...	...	...	...
Uribia[39]	192 721	94 438	98 283	...	...	...	...	...
Valledupar[39]	483 286	236 135	247 151	...	...	...	...	...
Villavicencio[39]	516 831	250 971	265 860	...	...	...	...	...
Yopal[39]	149 426	74 753	74 673	...	...	...	...	...
Yumbo[39]	125 663	63 069	62 594	...	...	...	...	...
Zipaquirá[39]	128 426	63 264	65 162	...	...	...	...	...
Ecuador - Équateur[29]								
1 VII 2018 (ESDF)								
Ambato	178 203	...	...	...	...	...	...	...
Babahoyo	102 531	...	...	...	...	...	...	...
Cuenca	396 990	...	...	...	...	...	...	...
Durán	294 734	...	...	...	...	...	...	...
Esmeraldas	196 666	...	...	...	...	...	...	...
Guayaquil	2 581 884	...	...	...	...	...	...	...
Ibarra	159 591	...	...	...	...	...	...	...
La Libertad	114 123	...	...	...	...	...	...	...
Loja	226 824	...	...	...	...	...	...	...
Machala	266 255	...	...	...	...	...	...	...
Manta	250 489	...	...	...	...	...	...	...
Milagro	154 204	...	...	...	...	...	...	...
Portoviejo	237 982	...	...	...	...	...	...	...
Quevedo	181 373	...	...	...	...	...	...	...
QUITO	1 805 522	...	...	...	...	...	...	...
Riobamba	168 514	...	...	...	...	...	...	...
Santo Domingo de los Colorados	335 123	...	...	...	...	...	...	...
Falkland Islands (Malvinas) - Îles Falkland (Malvinas)[41]								
15 IV 2012 (CDFC)								
STANLEY	2 108	1 055	1 053	...	...	...	...	...
French Guiana - Guyane française								
1 I 2015 (CDJC)								
CAYENNE	57 614	26 666	30 948	...	114 017	54 462	59 555	...
Guyana								
15 IX 2012 (CDFC)								
GEORGETOWN	24 849	...	...	...	118 368	...	...	...
Paraguay								
1 VII 2014 (ESDF)								
ASUNCIÓN[42]	512 919	236 790	276 129	117	2 887 087	1 402 891	1 484 196	2582
Capiatá	257 116	127 676	129 440	87.7	...	...	...	...
Ciudad del Este	317 525	159 726	157 799	149	...	...	...	...
Fernando de la Mora	200 112	95 174	104 937	21	...	...	...	...
Lambaré	210 725	101 019	109 706	26.8	...	...	...	...
Luque	358 265	175 663	182 602	152.5	...	...	...	...
San Lorenzo	354 283	171 242	183 042	54.2	...	...	...	...
Peru - Pérou								
30 VI 2018 (ESDF)								
Arequipa	893 491	429 534	463 957	...	...	...	...	...
Ayacucho	190 861	94 254	96 607	...	...	...	...	...
Cajamarca	248 222	122 101	126 121	...	...	...	...	...
Chiclayo	617 089	293 991	323 098	...	...	...	...	...
Chimbote	380 011	191 689	188 322	...	...	...	...	...
Chincha Alta	185 054	92 784	92 270	...	...	...	...	...
Cuzco	448 124	217 973	230 151	...	...	...	...	...
Huancayo	375 857	178 123	197 734	...	...	...	...	...
Huánuco	181 318	86 297	95 021	...	...	...	...	...
Huaral	102 811	50 641	52 170	...	...	...	...	...
Huaraz	136 628	67 152	69 476	...	...	...	...	...
Ica	251 573	124 069	127 504	...	...	...	...	...

8. Population of capital cities and cities of 100 000 or more inhabitants: latest available year, 1999 - 2018
Population des capitales et des villes de 100 000 habitants ou plus : dernière année disponible, 1999 - 2018 (continued - suite)

Continent, country or area, date, code[a] and city / Continent, pays ou zone, date, code[a] et ville	City proper - Ville proprement dite				Urban agglomeration - Agglomération urbaine			
	Population			Surface area - Superficie (km²)	Population			Surface area - Superficie (km²)
	Both sexes - Les deux sexes	Male - Masculin	Female - Féminin		Both sexes - Les deux sexes	Male - Masculin	Female - Féminin	
AMERICA, SOUTH - AMÉRIQUE DU SUD								
Peru - Pérou								
30 VI 2018 (ESDF)								
Iquitos	450 799	227 401	223 398	...	...	...	...	...
Jaen	100 551	49 999	50 552	...	...	...	...	...
Juliaca	294 921	143 315	151 606	...	...	...	...	...
LIMA[43]	10 350 721	5 026 529	5 324 192	...	...	...	...	...
Paita	104 367	51 908	52 459	...	...	...	...	...
Pisco	105 394	53 747	51 647	...	...	...	...	...
Piura	458 262	222 570	235 692	...	...	...	...	...
Pucallpa	211 708	110 628	101 080	...	...	...	...	...
Puno	147 385	71 407	75 978	...	...	...	...	...
Sullana	206 213	100 741	105 472	...	...	...	...	...
Tacna	306 021	155 738	150 283	...	...	...	...	...
Tarapoto	153 613	79 932	73 681	...	...	...	...	...
Trujillo	833 379	404 885	428 494	...	...	...	...	...
Tumbes	115 141	62 636	52 505	...	...	...	...	...
Suriname								
13 VIII 2012 (CDJC)								
PARAMARIBO	240 924	119 439	121 485	182	...	...	...	...
Wanica	118 222	57 776	60 446	443	...	...	...	...
Uruguay[44]								
1 VII 2018 (ESDJ)								
MONTEVIDEO	1 381 946	650 588	731 358	...	...	...	...	...
Venezuela (Bolivarian Republic of) - Venezuela (République bolivarienne du)								
1 VII 2015 (ESDF)								
Anaco(F) (Capital)	140 496	...	...	...	...	...	...	...
Barinas	389 578	...	...	...	...	...	...	...
Barquisimeto	881 127	...	...	...	...	...	...	...
Baruta	358 221	...	...	...	...	...	...	...
Cabimas	293 365	...	...	...	...	...	...	...
Cagua	118 290	...	...	...	...	...	...	...
CARACAS	2 082 130	...	...	...	...	...	...	...
Carora	111 963	...	...	...	...	...	...	...
Carúpano	156 380	...	...	...	...	...	...	...
Ciudad Bolívar	407 452	...	...	...	...	...	...	...
Ciudad Guayana	877 547	...	...	...	...	...	...	...
Ciudad Ojeda	216 489	...	...	...	...	...	...	...
Cua	143 164	...	...	...	...	...	...	...
Cumaná	358 138	...	...	...	...	...	...	...
El Tigre	203 403	...	...	...	...	...	...	...
Guacara	192 536	...	...	...	...	...	...	...
Guanare	160 234	...	...	...	...	...	...	...
Guarenas	247 131	...	...	...	...	...	...	...
Guatire	177 794	...	...	...	...	...	...	...
Los Guayos	173 878	...	...	...	...	...	...	...
Los Teques	216 358	...	...	...	...	...	...	...
Maracaibo	1 653 215	...	...	...	...	...	...	...
Maracay	419 052	...	...	...	...	...	...	...
Maturín	571 276	...	...	...	...	...	...	...
Mérida	248 410	...	...	...	...	...	...	...
Naguanagua	161 658	...	...	...	...	...	...	...
Ocumare Del Tuy	197 952	...	...	...	...	...	...	...
Petare	434 320	...	...	...	...	...	...	...
Pozuelos (F) (Capital)	144 045	...	...	...	...	...	...	...
Puerto Cabello	193 025	...	...	...	...	...	...	...
Punto Fijo	272 239	...	...	...	...	...	...	...
San Cristóbal	282 830	...	...	...	...	...	...	...
San Fernando de Apure	217 590	...	...	...	...	...	...	...
San Francisco	106 763	...	...	...	...	...	...	...
Santa Lucía	133 543	...	...	...	...	...	...	...
Táriba	132 657	...	...	...	...	...	...	...
Tocuyito	186 755	...	...	...	...	...	...	...
Turmero	238 570	...	...	...	...	...	...	...

8. Population of capital cities and cities of 100 000 or more inhabitants: latest available year, 1999 - 2018
Population des capitales et des villes de 100 000 habitants ou plus : dernière année disponible, 1999 - 2018 (continued - suite)

Continent, country or area, date, code[a] and city / Continent, pays ou zone, date, code[a] et ville	City proper - Ville proprement dite				Urban agglomeration - Agglomération urbaine			
	Population			Surface area - Superficie (km²)	Population			Surface area - Superficie (km²)
	Both sexes - Les deux sexes	Male - Masculin	Female - Féminin		Both sexes - Les deux sexes	Male - Masculin	Female - Féminin	
AMERICA, SOUTH - AMÉRIQUE DU SUD								
Venezuela (Bolivarian Republic of) - Venezuela (République bolivarienne du)								
1 VII 2015 (ESDF)								
Valencia	888 109	...	...	...	...	...	...	...
Valera	161 771	...	...	...	...	...	...	...
ASIA - ASIE								
Afghanistan								
1 VII 2016 (ESDF)								
Baghalan Center (Puli Khumry)	110 902	56 839	54 063	...	...	...	...	...
Balkh Center (Mazar- Sharif)	415 053	212 918	202 135	...	...	...	...	...
Herat Center	491 967	249 865	242 102	...	...	...	...	...
KABUL CENTER	3 817 241	1 975 705	1 841 536	...	...	...	...	...
Kandhar Center (Kndhar)	448 262	230 744	217 518	...	...	...	...	...
Kunduz Center	162 168	83 384	78 784	...	...	...	...	...
Nngarhar Center (Jlal Abad)	232 901	119 901	113 000	...	...	...	...	...
Armenia - Arménie								
1 VII 2017 (ESDJ)								
Gyumri (Leninakan)	115 231	52 891	62 340	...	...	...	...	...
YEREVAN	1 076 716	497 362	579 354	223	...	...	...	...
Azerbaijan - Azerbaïdjan								
1 VII 2017 (ESDJ)								
BAKU	2 254 175	1 120 553	1 133 622	2150	...	...	...	...
Ganja	331 986	161 956	170 030	110	...	...	...	...
Sumgayit	340 091	167 703	172 388	80	...	...	...	...
Bahrain - Bahreïn								
1 VII 2006 (ESDF)								
MANAMA	176 909	113 503	63 406	30	...	...	...	...
Bangladesh								
15 III 2011 (CDFC)								
Barisal	339 308	174 980	164 328	...	...	...	...	...
Chittagong	2 591 681	1 367 282	1 224 399	...	...	...	...	...
Comilla	296 010	153 523	142 487	...	...	...	...	...
DHAKA	8 906 035	4 931 802	3 974 233	...	...	...	...	...
Khulna	664 728	346 069	318 659	...	...	...	...	...
Mymensingh	389 918	200 053	189 865	...	...	...	...	...
Narayanganj	286 330	148 214	138 116	...	...	...	...	...
Rajshahi	449 756	232 974	216 782	...	...	...	...	...
Saidpur	133 433	68 884	64 549	...	...	...	...	...
Bhutan - Bhoutan								
30 V 2017 (CDFC)								
THIMPHU	114 551	58 996	55 555	26.1	...	...	...	...
Brunei Darussalam - Brunéi Darussalam								
21 VIII 2001 (CDFC)								
BANDAR SERI BEGAWAN	27 285	13 639	13 646	100.4	...	...	...	...
Cambodia - Cambodge[45]								
1 VII 2011 (ESDF)								
Bat Dambang	1 126 345	558 945	567 400	...	...	...	...	...
PHNOM PENH	1 570 791	738 159	832 631	...	...	...	...	...
Seam Reab	999 703	493 184	506 519	...	...	...	...	...
China - Chine[46]								
1 VII 2016 (ESDF)								
BEIJING (PEKING)	...	...	...	...	18 796 000	...	...	...
China, Hong Kong SAR - Chine, Hong Kong RAS								
1 VII 2018 (ESDJ)								
HONG KONG SAR	7 451 000	3 410 300	4 040 700	...	...	...	...	...
China, Macao SAR - Chine, Macao RAS[47]								
7 VIII 2016 (SSDJ)								
MACAO	650 834	314 018	336 816	...	...	...	...	...
Cyprus - Chypre								
1 I 2017 (ESDJ)								
LEFKOSIA[48]	...	...	...	...	244 200	...	...	...
Lemesos[49]	...	...	...	...	182 600	...	...	...

8. Population of capital cities and cities of 100 000 or more inhabitants: latest available year, 1999 - 2018
Population des capitales et des villes de 100 000 habitants ou plus : dernière année disponible, 1999 - 2018 (continued - suite)

Continent, country or area, date, code[a] and city Continent, pays ou zone, date, code[a] et ville	City proper - Ville proprement dite				Urban agglomeration - Agglomération urbaine			
	Population			Surface area - Superficie (km²)	Population			Surface area - Superficie (km²)
	Both sexes - Les deux sexes	Male - Masculin	Female - Féminin		Both sexes - Les deux sexes	Male - Masculin	Female - Féminin	

ASIA - ASIE

Democratic People's Republic of Korea - République populaire démocratique de Corée
1 X 2008 (CDJC)

Anju	167 646	79 187	88 459	...	...	...	...	...
Chongjin	614 892	292 741	322 151	...	...	...	...	...
Haeju	241 599	116 594	125 005	...	...	...	...	...
Hamhung	614 198	292 058	322 140	...	...	...	...	...
Huichon	136 093	64 547	71 546	...	...	...	...	...
Hyesan	174 015	82 604	91 411	...	...	...	...	...
Jongju	102 659	48 423	54 236	...	...	...	...	...
Kaechon	262 389	124 222	138 167	...	...	...	...	...
Kaesong	192 578	90 653	101 925	...	...	...	...	...
Kanggye	251 971	120 305	131 666	...	...	...	...	...
Kim Chaek	155 284	73 133	82 151	...	...	...	...	...
Kusong	155 181	73 677	81 504	...	...	...	...	...
Nampho	310 864	150 091	160 773	...	...	...	...	...
Phyongsong	236 583	115 817	120 766	...	...	...	...	...
PYONGYANG	2 581 076	1 233 765	1 347 311	...	...	...	...	...
Rason	158 337	74 777	83 560	...	...	...	...	...
Sariwon	271 434	130 181	141 253	...	...	...	...	...
Sinpho	130 951	63 207	67 744	...	...	...	...	...
Sinuiju	334 031	158 139	175 892	...	...	...	...	...
Sunchon	250 738	119 727	131 011	...	...	...	...	...
Tanchon	240 873	113 221	127 652	...	...	...	...	...
Tokchon	210 571	99 655	110 916	...	...	...	...	...
Wonsan	328 467	155 903	172 564	...	...	...	...	...

Georgia - Géorgie
1 VII 2016 (ESDJ)

Batumi	155 000	...	...	...	...	...	...	...
Kutaisi	147 500	...	...	...	...	...	...	...
Rustavi	126 200	...	...	...	...	...	...	...
TBILISI	1 113 800	...	...	...	...	...	...	...

India - Inde
9 II 2011 (CDFC)

Abohar	...	...	...	...	145 302	76 984	68 318	...
Achalpur	...	...	...	...	112 311	58 108	54 203	...
Adilabad	...	...	...	...	117 167	59 448	57 719	...
Adityapur	...	...	...	...	174 355	91 664	82 691	...
Adoni	...	...	...	...	184 625	91 736	92 889	...
Agartala	...	...	...	...	400 004	200 132	199 872	...
Agra	...	...	...	...	1 585 704	845 902	739 802	...
Ahmadabad	...	...	...	...	5 633 927	2 968 460	2 665 467	...
Ahmadnagar	...	...	...	...	350 859	178 899	171 960	...
Aizawl	...	...	...	...	293 416	144 913	148 503	...
Ajmer	...	...	...	...	542 321	278 545	263 776	...
Akbarpur	...	...	...	...	111 447	57 330	54 117	...
Akola	...	...	...	...	425 817	217 393	208 424	...
Alandur	...	...	...	...	164 430	82 332	82 098	...
Alappuzha	...	...	...	...	240 991	116 439	124 552	...
Aligarh	...	...	...	...	874 408	461 772	412 636	...
Allahabad	...	...	...	...	1 168 385	630 577	537 808	...
Alwar	...	...	...	...	322 568	170 530	152 038	...
Ambala	...	...	...	...	195 153	102 607	92 546	...
Ambala Sadar	...	...	...	...	104 974	54 680	50 294	...
Ambarnath	...	...	...	...	253 475	132 582	120 893	...
Ambattur	...	...	...	...	466 205	234 923	231 282	...
Ambikapur	...	...	...	...	121 071	62 776	58 295	...
Ambur	...	...	...	...	114 608	56 382	58 226	...
Amravati	...	...	...	...	647 057	329 992	317 065	...
Amreli	...	...	...	...	117 967	59 902	58 065	...
Amritsar	...	...	...	...	1 159 227	615 417	543 810	...
Amroha	...	...	...	...	198 471	103 097	95 374	...
Anand	...	...	...	...	209 410	108 403	101 007	...
Anantapur	...	...	...	...	267 161	133 919	133 242	...
Anantnag	...	...	...	...	150 592	77 712	72 880	...

Continent, country or area, date, code[a] and city / Continent, pays ou zone, date, code[a] et ville	City proper - Ville proprement dite				Urban agglomeration - Agglomération urbaine			
	Population			Surface area - Superficie (km²)	Population			Surface area - Superficie (km²)
	Both sexes - Les deux sexes	Male - Masculin	Female - Féminin		Both sexes - Les deux sexes	Male - Masculin	Female - Féminin	
ASIA - ASIE								
India - Inde								
9 II 2011 (CDFC)								
Arrah	...	...	...	...	261 430	138 804	122 626	...
Asansol	...	...	...	...	563 917	292 387	271 530	...
Ashoknagar Kalyangarh	...	...	...	...	121 592	61 236	60 356	...
Aurangabad (Bihar)	...	...	...	...	102 244	53 542	48 702	...
Aurangabad (Maharashtra)	...	...	...	...	1 175 116	609 206	565 910	...
Avadi	...	...	...	...	345 996	175 658	170 338	...
Azamgarh	...	...	...	...	110 983	57 878	53 105	...
Badlapur	...	...	...	...	174 226	90 365	83 861	...
Bagaha	...	...	...	...	112 634	59 614	53 020	...
Bagalkot	...	...	...	...	111 933	56 378	55 555	...
Bahadurgarh	...	...	...	...	170 767	91 721	79 046	...
Baharampur	...	...	...	...	195 223	100 247	94 976	...
Bahraich	...	...	...	...	186 223	97 653	88 570	...
Baidyabati	...	...	...	...	121 110	62 485	58 625	...
Baleshwar Town	...	...	...	...	144 373	73 721	70 652	...
Ballia	...	...	...	...	104 424	55 459	48 965	...
Bally (Census Town)	...	...	...	...	113 377	58 530	54 847	...
Bally (Municipality)	...	...	...	...	293 373	156 911	136 462	...
Balurghat	...	...	...	...	153 279	76 730	76 549	...
Banda	...	...	...	...	160 473	85 370	75 103	...
Bankura	...	...	...	...	137 386	69 843	67 543	...
Bansberia	...	...	...	...	103 920	53 760	50 160	...
Banswara	...	...	...	...	101 017	51 585	49 432	...
Baran	...	...	...	...	117 992	61 071	56 921	...
Baranagar	...	...	...	...	245 213	126 187	119 026	...
Barasat	...	...	...	...	278 435	140 822	137 613	...
Baraut	...	...	...	...	103 764	55 013	48 751	...
Barddhaman	...	...	...	...	314 265	159 936	154 329	...
Bareilly	...	...	...	...	904 797	477 515	427 282	...
Baripada Town	...	...	...	...	116 849	60 489	56 360	...
Barnala	...	...	...	...	116 449	62 554	53 895	...
Barrackpur	...	...	...	...	152 783	78 349	74 434	...
Barshi	...	...	...	...	118 722	60 801	57 921	...
Basirhat	...	...	...	...	125 254	63 223	62 031	...
Basti	...	...	...	...	114 657	60 095	54 562	...
Batala	...	...	...	...	158 621	83 655	74 966	...
Bathinda	...	...	...	...	285 788	151 524	134 264	...
Beawar	...	...	...	...	151 152	77 616	73 536	...
Begusarai	...	...	...	...	252 008	133 722	118 286	...
Belgaum	...	...	...	...	490 045	246 537	243 508	...
Bellary	...	...	...	...	410 445	206 149	204 296	...
Bettiah	...	...	...	...	132 209	69 529	62 680	...
Betul	...	...	...	...	103 330	52 823	50 507	...
Bhadrak	...	...	...	...	121 338	62 335	59 003	...
Bhadravati	...	...	...	...	151 102	75 009	76 093	...
Bhadreswar	...	...	...	...	101 477	53 330	48 147	...
Bhagalpur	...	...	...	...	400 146	212 813	187 333	...
Bhalswa Jahangir Pur	...	...	...	...	197 148	106 388	90 760	...
Bharatpur	...	...	...	...	252 838	134 040	118 798	...
Bharuch	...	...	...	...	169 007	86 810	82 197	...
Bhatpara	...	...	...	...	386 019	204 539	181 480	...
Bhavnagar	...	...	...	...	605 882	315 429	290 453	...
Bhilai Nagar	...	...	...	...	627 734	323 479	304 255	...
Bhilwara	...	...	...	...	359 483	187 081	172 402	...
Bhimavaram	...	...	...	...	146 961	72 441	74 520	...
Bhind	...	...	...	...	197 585	105 352	92 233	...
Bhiwadi	...	...	...	...	104 921	59 712	45 209	...
Bhiwandi	...	...	...	...	709 665	415 339	294 326	...
Bhiwani	...	...	...	...	196 057	104 026	92 031	...
Bhopal	...	...	...	...	1 798 218	936 168	862 050	...
Bhubaneswar Town	...	...	...	...	885 363	468 043	417 320	...
Bhuj	...	...	...	...	148 834	78 813	70 021	...
Bhusawal	...	...	...	...	187 421	96 147	91 274	...

8. Population of capital cities and cities of 100 000 or more inhabitants: latest available year, 1999 - 2018
Population des capitales et des villes de 100 000 habitants ou plus : dernière année disponible, 1999 - 2018 (continued - suite)

Continent, country or area, date, code[a] and city / Continent, pays ou zone, date, code[a] et ville	City proper - Ville proprement dite				Urban agglomeration - Agglomération urbaine			
	Population			Surface area - Superficie (km²)	Population			Surface area - Superficie (km²)
	Both sexes - Les deux sexes	Male - Masculin	Female - Féminin		Both sexes - Les deux sexes	Male - Masculin	Female - Féminin	

ASIA - ASIE

India - Inde
9 II 2011 (CDFC)

Bid	...	...	...	...	146 709	75 566	71 143	...
Bidar	...	...	...	...	216 020	111 470	104 550	...
Bidhan Nagar	...	...	...	...	215 514	109 014	106 500	...
Biharsharif	...	...	...	...	297 268	155 216	142 052	...
Bijapur	...	...	...	...	327 427	165 177	162 250	...
Bikaner	...	...	...	...	644 406	338 442	305 964	...
Bilaspur	...	...	...	...	365 579	188 342	177 237	...
Bokaro Steel City	...	...	...	...	414 820	219 646	195 174	...
Bongaon	...	...	...	...	108 864	55 382	53 482	...
Botad	...	...	...	...	130 327	67 675	62 652	...
Brahmapur	...	...	...	...	356 598	185 754	170 844	...
Bruhat Bengaluru Mahanagara Palike (BBMP)	...	...	...	...	8 495 492	4 420 006	4 075 486	...
Budaun	...	...	...	...	159 285	83 176	76 109	...
Bulandshahar	...	...	...	...	230 024	120 275	109 749	...
Bundi	...	...	...	...	104 919	54 485	50 434	...
Burari	...	...	...	...	146 190	78 103	68 087	...
Burhanpur	...	...	...	...	210 886	108 187	102 699	...
Buxar	...	...	...	...	102 861	54 277	48 584	...
Champdani	...	...	...	...	111 251	59 350	51 901	...
Chandannagar	...	...	...	...	166 867	84 009	82 858	...
Chandausi	...	...	...	...	114 383	60 256	54 127	...
Chandigarh	...	...	...	...	970 602	531 051	439 551	...
Chandrapur	...	...	...	...	320 379	164 085	156 294	...
Chapra	...	...	...	...	202 352	106 501	95 851	...
Chas	...	...	...	...	141 640	74 727	66 913	...
Chennai	...	...	...	...	4 646 732	2 335 844	2 310 888	...
Chhatarpur	...	...	...	...	142 128	75 070	67 058	...
Chhindwara	...	...	...	...	175 052	89 396	85 656	...
Chikmagalur	...	...	...	...	118 401	58 702	59 699	...
Chilakaluripet	...	...	...	...	101 398	50 207	51 191	...
Chitradurga	...	...	...	...	145 853	73 020	72 833	...
Chittaurgarh	...	...	...	...	116 406	60 068	56 338	...
Chittoor	...	...	...	...	160 722	80 060	80 662	...
Churu	...	...	...	...	120 157	61 774	58 383	...
Coimbatore	...	...	...	...	1 050 721	526 163	524 558	...
Cuddalore	...	...	...	...	173 636	85 700	87 936	...
Cuttack	...	...	...	...	610 189	316 242	293 947	...
Dabgram	...	...	...	...	119 040	61 078	57 962	...
Dallo Pura	...	...	...	...	154 791	81 262	73 529	...
Damoh	...	...	...	...	139 561	72 869	66 692	...
Darbhanga	...	...	...	...	296 039	155 637	140 402	...
Darjiling	...	...	...	...	118 805	59 187	59 618	...
Datia	...	...	...	...	100 284	52 772	47 512	...
Davanagere	...	...	...	...	434 971	219 776	215 195	...
Deesa	...	...	...	...	111 160	58 657	52 503	...
Dehradun	...	...	...	...	574 840	301 207	273 633	...
Dehri	...	...	...	...	137 231	72 372	64 859	...
Delhi Cantonment	...	...	...	...	110 351	63 757	46 594	...
Delhi Municipal Corporation (DMC)	...	...	...	...	11 034 555	5 882 117	5 152 438	...
Deoghar	...	...	...	...	203 123	107 997	95 126	...
Deoli	...	...	...	...	169 122	90 914	78 208	...
Deoria	...	...	...	...	129 479	67 462	62 017	...
Dewas	...	...	...	...	289 550	150 081	139 469	...
Dhamtari	...	...	...	...	101 677	50 807	50 870	...
Dhanbad	...	...	...	...	1 162 472	614 722	547 750	...
Dharmavaram	...	...	...	...	121 874	62 250	59 624	...
Dhaulpur	...	...	...	...	133 075	71 298	61 777	...
Dhule	...	...	...	...	375 559	193 446	182 113	...
Dibrugarh	...	...	...	...	145 488	75 318	70 170	...
Dimapur	...	...	...	...	122 834	64 300	58 534	...
Dinapur Nizamat	...	...	...	...	182 429	96 875	85 554	...
Dindigul	...	...	...	...	207 327	103 027	104 300	...
Dohad	...	...	...	...	118 846	60 515	58 331	...

Continent, country or area, date, code[a] and city / Continent, pays ou zone, date, code[a] et ville	City proper - Ville proprement dite				Urban agglomeration - Agglomération urbaine			
	Population			Surface area - Superficie (km²)	Population			Surface area - Superficie (km²)
	Both sexes - Les deux sexes	Male - Masculin	Female - Féminin		Both sexes - Les deux sexes	Male - Masculin	Female - Féminin	
ASIA - ASIE								
India - Inde								
9 II 2011 (CDFC)								
Dum Dum	...	...	...	...	114 786	58 566	56 220	...
Durg	...	...	...	...	268 806	136 641	132 165	...
Durgapur	...	...	...	...	566 517	294 255	272 262	...
Eluru	...	...	...	...	218 020	107 511	110 509	...
English Bazar	...	...	...	...	205 521	106 824	98 697	...
Erode	...	...	...	...	157 101	78 222	78 879	...
Etah	...	...	...	...	118 517	62 590	55 927	...
Etawah	...	...	...	...	256 838	135 439	121 399	...
Faizabad	...	...	...	...	165 228	85 620	79 608	...
Faridabad	...	...	...	...	1 414 050	754 542	659 508	...
Farrukhabad-cum-Fatehgarh	...	...	...	...	276 581	145 641	130 940	...
Fatehpur	...	...	...	...	193 193	101 263	91 930	...
Firozabad	...	...	...	...	604 214	319 415	284 799	...
Firozpur	...	...	...	...	110 313	58 451	51 862	...
Gadag-Betigeri	...	...	...	...	172 612	85 920	86 692	...
Gandhidham	...	...	...	...	247 992	131 484	116 508	...
Gandhinagar	...	...	...	...	292 797	153 443	139 354	...
Gangánagar	...	...	...	...	237 780	127 840	109 940	...
Gangapur City	...	...	...	...	119 090	62 829	56 261	...
Gangawati	...	...	...	...	114 642	57 230	57 412	...
Gangtok	...	...	...	...	100 286	52 459	47 827	...
Gaya	...	...	...	...	474 093	250 037	224 056	...
Ghaziabad	...	...	...	...	1 648 643	874 607	774 036	...
Ghazipur	...	...	...	...	121 020	63 513	57 507	...
Giridih	...	...	...	...	114 533	59 966	54 567	...
Godhra	...	...	...	...	143 644	74 230	69 414	...
Gokal Pur	...	...	...	...	121 870	64 857	57 013	...
Gonda	...	...	...	...	114 046	59 948	54 098	...
Gondal	...	...	...	...	112 197	58 300	53 897	...
Gondiya	...	...	...	...	132 813	66 500	66 313	...
Gorakhpur	...	...	...	...	673 446	353 907	319 539	...
Greater Hyderabad Municipal Corporation (GHMC)	...	...	...	...	6 993 262	3 576 640	3 416 622	...
Greater Mumbai	...	...	...	...	12 442 373	6 715 931	5 726 442	...
Greater Noida	...	...	...	...	102 054	55 540	46 514	...
Greater Visakhapatnam Municipal Corporation (GVMC)	...	...	...	...	1 728 128	873 599	854 529	...
Gudivada	...	...	...	...	118 167	59 062	59 105	...
Gulbarga	...	...	...	...	543 147	276 552	266 595	...
Guna	...	...	...	...	180 935	94 464	86 471	...
Guntakal	...	...	...	...	126 270	62 851	63 419	...
Guntur	...	...	...	...	670 073	331 435	338 638	...
Gurgaon	...	...	...	...	886 519	480 042	406 477	...
Guwahati	...	...	...	...	962 334	498 450	463 884	...
Gwalior	...	...	...	...	1 054 420	561 165	493 255	...
Habra	...	...	...	...	147 221	74 592	72 629	...
Hajipur	...	...	...	...	147 688	78 047	69 641	...
Haldia	...	...	...	...	200 827	104 841	95 986	...
Haldwani-cum-Kathgodam	...	...	...	...	201 461	105 580	95 881	...
Halisahar	...	...	...	...	124 939	65 467	59 472	...
Hanumangarh	...	...	...	...	150 958	79 709	71 249	...
Haora	...	...	...	...	1 077 075	561 220	515 855	...
Hapur	...	...	...	...	262 983	139 525	123 458	...
Hardoi	...	...	...	...	197 029	103 619	93 410	...
Hardwar	...	...	...	...	231 338	123 455	107 883	...
Hassan	...	...	...	...	155 006	77 051	77 955	...
Hastsal	...	...	...	...	176 877	94 833	82 044	...
Hathras	...	...	...	...	143 020	76 054	66 966	...
Hazaribag	...	...	...	...	142 489	74 132	68 357	...
Hindaun	...	...	...	...	105 452	55 834	49 618	...
Hindupur	...	...	...	...	151 677	76 370	75 307	...
Hinganghat	...	...	...	...	101 805	52 577	49 228	...
Hisar	...	...	...	...	307 024	166 494	140 530	...

8. Population of capital cities and cities of 100 000 or more inhabitants: latest available year, 1999 - 2018
Population des capitales et des villes de 100 000 habitants ou plus : dernière année disponible, 1999 - 2018 (continued - suite)

Continent, country or area, date, code[a] and city / Continent, pays ou zone, date, code[a] et ville	City proper - Ville proprement dite				Urban agglomeration - Agglomération urbaine			
	Population			Surface area - Superficie (km²)	Population			Surface area - Superficie (km²)
	Both sexes - Les deux sexes	Male - Masculin	Female - Féminin		Both sexes - Les deux sexes	Male - Masculin	Female - Féminin	
ASIA - ASIE								
India - Inde								
9 II 2011 (CDFC)								
Hoshangabad	...	...	...	...	117 988	61 716	56 272	...
Hoshiarpur	...	...	...	...	168 653	88 304	80 349	...
Hospet	...	...	...	...	206 167	102 668	103 499	...
Hosur	...	...	...	...	116 821	59 351	57 470	...
Hubli-Dharwad	...	...	...	...	943 788	474 518	469 270	...
Hugli-Chinsurah	...	...	...	...	179 931	90 217	89 714	...
Ichalkaranji	...	...	...	...	287 353	149 164	138 189	...
Imphal	...	...	...	...	277 196	135 059	142 137	...
Indore	...	...	...	...	1 994 397	1 035 912	958 485	...
Jabalpur	...	...	...	...	1 081 677	559 361	522 316	...
Jagadhri	...	...	...	...	124 894	67 685	57 209	...
Jagdalpur	...	...	...	...	125 463	63 989	61 474	...
Jagtial	...	...	...	...	103 930	51 828	52 102	...
Jaipur	...	...	...	...	3 046 163	1 603 125	1 443 038	...
Jalandhar	...	...	...	...	868 929	460 811	408 118	...
Jalgaon	...	...	...	...	460 228	240 590	219 638	...
Jalna	...	...	...	...	285 577	147 092	138 485	...
Jalpaiguri	...	...	...	...	107 341	53 708	53 633	...
Jamalpur	...	...	...	...	105 434	56 072	49 362	...
Jammu	...	...	...	...	576 198	303 689	272 509	...
Jamnagar	...	...	...	...	600 943	313 214	287 729	...
Jamshedpur	...	...	...	...	677 350	353 212	324 138	...
Jamuria	...	...	...	...	149 220	77 379	71 841	...
Jaunpur	...	...	...	...	180 362	93 718	86 644	...
Jehanabad	...	...	...	...	103 202	54 710	48 492	...
Jetpur Navagadh	...	...	...	...	118 302	62 174	56 128	...
Jhansi	...	...	...	...	505 693	265 449	240 244	...
Jhunjhunun	...	...	...	...	118 473	61 548	56 925	...
Jind	...	...	...	...	167 592	89 253	78 339	...
Jodhpur	...	...	...	...	1 056 191	555 371	500 820	...
Jorhat	...	...	...	...	126 736	65 489	61 247	...
Junagadh	...	...	...	...	319 462	163 413	156 049	...
Kadapa	...	...	...	...	344 893	173 314	171 579	...
Kaithal	...	...	...	...	144 915	76 794	68 121	...
Kakinada	...	...	...	...	384 182	188 308	195 874	...
Kalol	...	...	...	...	134 426	70 995	63 431	...
Kalyan Dombivali	...	...	...	...	1 247 327	649 626	597 701	...
Kalyani	...	...	...	...	100 575	50 727	49 848	...
Kamarhati	...	...	...	...	330 211	170 293	159 918	...
Kancheepuram	...	...	...	...	164 384	81 992	82 392	...
Kanchrapara	...	...	...	...	129 576	65 436	64 140	...
Kanhangad	...	...	...	...	125 564	58 564	67 000	...
Kanpur	...	...	...	...	2 768 057	1 490 547	1 277 510	...
Kanpur (Cantonment Board)	...	...	...	...	108 534	58 550	49 984	...
Karaikkudi	...	...	...	...	106 714	53 348	53 366	...
Karawal Nagar	...	...	...	...	224 281	119 951	104 330	...
Karimnagar	...	...	...	...	289 821	146 145	143 676	...
Karnal	...	...	...	...	302 140	159 653	142 487	...
Kasganj	...	...	...	...	101 277	53 552	47 725	...
Kashipur	...	...	...	...	121 623	63 609	58 014	...
Katihar	...	...	...	...	240 838	127 240	113 598	...
Khammam	...	...	...	...	196 283	96 898	99 385	...
Khandwa	...	...	...	...	200 738	102 901	97 837	...
Khanna	...	...	...	...	128 137	67 801	60 336	...
Kharagpur	...	...	...	...	207 604	106 559	101 045	...
Khardaha	...	...	...	...	108 496	54 879	53 617	...
Khargone	...	...	...	...	116 150	59 752	56 398	...
Khora	...	...	...	...	190 005	102 574	87 431	...
Khurja	...	...	...	...	121 207	63 825	57 382	...
Kirari Suleman Nagar	...	...	...	...	283 211	152 348	130 863	...
Kishanganj	...	...	...	...	105 782	55 143	50 639	...
Kishangarh	...	...	...	...	154 886	80 024	74 862	...
Kochi	...	...	...	...	633 553	312 358	321 195	...

Continent, country or area, date, code[a] and city / Continent, pays ou zone, date, code[a] et ville	City proper - Ville proprement dite				Urban agglomeration - Agglomération urbaine			
	Population			Surface area - Superficie (km²)	Population			Surface area - Superficie (km²)
	Both sexes - Les deux sexes	Male - Masculin	Female - Féminin		Both sexes - Les deux sexes	Male - Masculin	Female - Féminin	

ASIA - ASIE

India - Inde
9 II 2011 (CDFC)

Kolar	...	...	...	...	138 462	69 910	68 552	...
Kolhapur	...	...	...	...	549 236	280 366	268 870	...
Kolkata (Calcutta)	...	...	...	...	4 496 694	2 356 766	2 139 928	...
Kollam	...	...	...	...	367 107	177 072	190 035	...
Korba	...	...	...	...	365 253	189 772	175 481	...
Kota	...	...	...	...	1 001 694	528 601	473 093	...
Kozhikode	...	...	...	...	550 440	262 939	287 501	...
Krishnanagar	...	...	...	...	153 062	77 146	75 916	...
Kulti	...	...	...	...	313 809	163 193	150 616	...
Kumbakonam	...	...	...	...	140 156	69 340	70 816	...
Kurichi	...	...	...	...	123 667	61 815	61 852	...
Kurnool	...	...	...	...	457 633	228 148	229 485	...
Lakhimpur	...	...	...	...	151 993	80 523	71 470	...
Lalitpur	...	...	...	...	133 305	69 529	63 776	...
Latur	...	...	...	...	382 940	197 737	185 203	...
Loni	...	...	...	...	516 082	275 025	241 057	...
Lucknow	...	...	...	...	2 817 105	1 460 970	1 356 135	...
Ludhiana	...	...	...	...	1 618 879	874 908	743 971	...
Machilipatnam	...	...	...	...	169 892	83 594	86 298	...
Madanapalle	...	...	...	...	180 180	90 700	89 480	...
Madavaram	...	...	...	...	119 105	59 887	59 218	...
Madhyamgram	...	...	...	...	196 127	98 864	97 263	...
Madurai	...	...	...	...	1 017 865	509 302	508 563	...
Mahbubnagar	...	...	...	...	190 400	96 142	94 258	...
Mahesana	...	...	...	...	190 753	100 558	90 195	...
Maheshtala	...	...	...	...	448 317	229 693	218 624	...
Mainpuri	...	...	...	...	136 557	71 274	65 283	...
Malappuram	...	...	...	...	101 386	48 957	52 429	...
Malegaon	...	...	...	...	481 228	244 080	237 148	...
Malerkotla	...	...	...	...	135 424	71 376	64 048	...
Mandoli	...	...	...	...	120 417	64 159	56 258	...
Mandsaur	...	...	...	...	141 667	72 488	69 179	...
Mandya	...	...	...	...	137 358	68 662	68 696	...
Mangalagiri	...	...	...	...	107 197	53 301	53 896	...
Mangalore	...	...	...	...	499 487	247 903	251 584	...
Mango	...	...	...	...	223 805	115 970	107 835	...
Mathura	...	...	...	...	349 909	185 983	163 926	...
Maunath Bhanjan	...	...	...	...	278 745	142 967	135 778	...
Medinipur	...	...	...	...	169 264	84 977	84 287	...
Meerut	...	...	...	...	1 305 429	688 118	617 311	...
Mira Bhayandar	...	...	...	...	809 378	429 260	380 118	...
Miryalaguda	...	...	...	...	104 918	52 565	52 353	...
Mirzapur-cum-Vindhyachal	...	...	...	...	234 871	125 601	109 270	...
Modinagar	...	...	...	...	130 325	69 268	61 057	...
Moga	...	...	...	...	163 397	86 604	76 793	...
Moradabad	...	...	...	...	887 871	464 580	423 291	...
Morena	...	...	...	...	200 482	108 390	92 092	...
Morvi	...	...	...	...	210 451	109 451	101 000	...
Motihari	...	...	...	...	126 158	67 861	58 297	...
Mughalsarai	...	...	...	...	109 650	57 682	51 968	...
Muktsar	...	...	...	...	116 747	61 725	55 022	...
Munger	...	...	...	...	213 303	113 291	100 012	...
Murwara (Katni)	...	...	...	...	221 883	115 348	106 535	...
Mustafabad	...	...	...	...	127 167	66 889	60 278	...
Muzaffarnagar	...	...	...	...	392 768	206 782	185 986	...
Muzaffarpur	...	...	...	...	354 462	187 564	166 898	...
Mysore	...	...	...	...	920 550	461 042	459 508	...
Nabadwip	...	...	...	...	125 543	65 415	60 128	...
Nadiad	...	...	...	...	225 071	115 903	109 168	...
Nagaon	...	...	...	...	121 628	61 642	59 986	...
Nagapattinam	...	...	...	...	102 905	50 793	52 112	...
Nagaur	...	...	...	...	105 218	54 126	51 092	...
Nagda	...	...	...	...	100 039	51 373	48 666	...

Continent, country or area, date, code[a] and city	City proper - Ville proprement dite				Urban agglomeration - Agglomération urbaine			
	Population			Surface area - Superficie (km²)	Population			Surface area - Superficie (km²)
Continent, pays ou zone, date, code[a] et ville	Both sexes - Les deux sexes	Male - Masculin	Female - Féminin		Both sexes - Les deux sexes	Male - Masculin	Female - Féminin	

ASIA - ASIE

India - Inde
9 II 2011 (CDFC)

Nagercoil	...	...	...	...	224 849	109 938	114 911	...
Nagpur	...	...	...	...	2 405 665	1 225 405	1 180 260	...
Naihati	...	...	...	...	217 900	109 849	108 051	...
Nalgonda	...	...	...	...	154 326	77 320	77 006	...
Nanded Waghala	...	...	...	...	550 439	285 433	265 006	...
Nandurbar	...	...	...	...	111 037	57 412	53 625	...
Nandyal	...	...	...	...	211 424	105 826	105 598	...
Nangloi Jat	...	...	...	...	205 596	110 056	95 540	...
Narasaraopet	...	...	...	...	117 489	59 424	58 065	...
Nashik	...	...	...	...	1 486 053	782 517	703 536	...
Navi Mumbai (New Bombay)	...	...	...	...	1 120 547	610 060	510 487	...
Navi Mumbai Panvel Raigad	...	...	...	...	195 373	107 342	88 031	...
Navsari	...	...	...	...	171 109	88 486	82 623	...
Neemuch	...	...	...	...	128 561	67 890	60 671	...
Nellore	...	...	...	...	547 621	278 787	268 834	...
New Delhi Municipal Council (NDMC)	...	...	...	...	257 803	140 234	117 569	...
Neyveli	...	...	...	...	105 731	53 409	52 322	...
Nizamabad	...	...	...	...	311 152	154 929	156 223	...
Noida	...	...	...	...	637 272	349 397	287 875	...
North Barrackpur	...	...	...	...	132 806	66 924	65 882	...
North Dum Dum	...	...	...	...	249 142	126 279	122 863	...
Ongole	...	...	...	...	208 344	104 646	103 698	...
Orai	...	...	...	...	190 575	101 306	89 269	...
Osmanabad	...	...	...	...	111 825	57 824	54 001	...
Ozhukarai	...	...	...	...	300 104	148 464	151 640	...
Palakkad	...	...	...	...	130 955	63 833	67 122	...
Palanpur	...	...	...	...	141 592	74 088	67 504	...
Pali	...	...	...	...	230 075	119 924	110 151	...
Pallavaram	...	...	...	...	233 984	117 405	116 579	...
Palwal	...	...	...	...	131 926	69 997	61 929	...
Panchkula	...	...	...	...	211 355	111 731	99 624	...
Panihati	...	...	...	...	377 347	189 446	187 901	...
Panipat	...	...	...	...	295 970	158 063	137 907	...
Panvel	...	...	...	...	180 020	92 484	87 536	...
Parbhani	...	...	...	...	307 170	156 520	150 650	...
Patan	...	...	...	...	133 737	69 898	63 839	...
Pathankot	...	...	...	...	156 306	82 045	74 261	...
Patiala	...	...	...	...	446 246	236 198	210 048	...
Patna	...	...	...	...	1 684 297	893 445	790 852	...
Pilibhit	...	...	...	...	127 988	67 614	60 374	...
Pimpri Chinchwad	...	...	...	...	1 727 692	942 533	785 159	...
Pithampur	...	...	...	...	126 200	70 250	55 950	...
Porbandar	...	...	...	...	152 760	78 604	74 156	...
Port Blair	...	...	...	...	108 058	57 761	50 297	...
Proddatur	...	...	...	...	163 970	81 874	82 096	...
Puducherry	...	...	...	...	244 377	119 430	124 947	...
Pudukkottai	...	...	...	...	117 630	58 737	58 893	...
Pune	...	...	...	...	3 124 458	1 603 675	1 520 783	...
Puri	...	...	...	...	200 564	104 086	96 478	...
Purnia	...	...	...	...	282 248	148 077	134 171	...
Puruliya	...	...	...	...	121 067	62 351	58 716	...
Rae Bareli	...	...	...	...	191 316	99 903	91 413	...
Raichur	...	...	...	...	234 073	117 657	116 416	...
Raiganj	...	...	...	...	183 612	96 388	87 224	...
Raigarh	...	...	...	...	150 019	76 865	73 154	...
Raipur	...	...	...	...	1 027 264	527 365	499 899	...
Rajahmundry	...	...	...	...	376 333	185 970	190 363	...
Rajapalayam	...	...	...	...	130 442	64 765	65 677	...
Rajarhat Gopalpur	...	...	...	...	402 844	203 911	198 933	...
Rajkot	...	...	...	...	1 323 363	693 473	629 890	...
Rajnandgaon	...	...	...	...	163 114	81 929	81 185	...
Rajpur Sonarpur	...	...	...	...	424 368	215 405	208 963	...
Ramagundam	...	...	...	...	242 979	123 430	119 549	...

Continent, country or area, date, code[a] and city	City proper - Ville proprement dite				Urban agglomeration - Agglomération urbaine			
	Population			Surface area - Superficie (km²)	Population			Surface area - Superficie (km²)
Continent, pays ou zone, date, code[a] et ville	Both sexes - Les deux sexes	Male - Masculin	Female - Féminin		Both sexes - Les deux sexes	Male - Masculin	Female - Féminin	
ASIA - ASIE								
India - Inde								
9 II 2011 (CDFC)								
Rampur	...	...	...	...	325 313	169 681	155 632	...
Ranchi	...	...	...	...	1 073 427	558 872	514 555	...
Ranibennur	...	...	...	...	106 406	54 040	52 366	...
Raniganj	...	...	...	...	129 441	67 578	61 863	...
Ratlam	...	...	...	...	264 914	134 915	129 999	...
Raurkela Industrial Township	...	...	...	...	216 410	112 897	103 513	...
Raurkela Town	...	...	...	...	320 040	169 095	150 945	...
Rewa	...	...	...	...	235 654	124 012	111 642	...
Rewari	...	...	...	...	143 021	75 764	67 257	...
Rishra	...	...	...	...	124 577	66 606	57 971	...
Robertson Pet	...	...	...	...	162 230	80 375	81 855	...
Rohtak	...	...	...	...	374 292	198 237	176 055	...
Roorkee	...	...	...	...	118 200	63 434	54 766	...
Rudrapur	...	...	...	...	154 554	81 340	73 214	...
S.A.S. Nagar	...	...	...	...	166 864	87 380	79 484	...
Sagar	...	...	...	...	274 556	143 425	131 131	...
Saharanpur	...	...	...	...	705 478	371 740	333 738	...
Saharsa	...	...	...	...	156 540	83 291	73 249	...
Salem	...	...	...	...	829 267	417 317	411 950	...
Sambalpur	...	...	...	...	189 366	97 460	91 906	...
Sambhal	...	...	...	...	220 813	115 767	105 046	...
Sangli-Miraj Kupwad	...	...	...	...	502 793	253 640	249 153	...
Santipur	...	...	...	...	151 777	77 011	74 766	...
Sasaram	...	...	...	...	147 408	77 599	69 809	...
Satara	...	...	...	...	120 195	61 129	59 066	...
Satna	...	...	...	...	282 977	149 415	133 562	...
Sawai Madhopur	...	...	...	...	121 106	63 014	58 092	...
Secunderabad	...	...	...	...	217 910	113 577	104 333	...
Sehore	...	...	...	...	109 118	56 335	52 783	...
Seoni	...	...	...	...	102 343	52 352	49 991	...
Serampore	...	...	...	...	181 842	93 694	88 148	...
Shahjahanpur	...	...	...	...	329 736	173 006	156 730	...
Shamli	...	...	...	...	107 266	57 187	50 079	...
Shikohabad	...	...	...	...	107 404	56 794	50 610	...
Shillong	...	...	...	...	143 229	70 135	73 094	...
Shimla	...	...	...	...	169 578	93 152	76 426	...
Shimoga	...	...	...	...	322 650	162 018	160 632	...
Shivpuri	...	...	...	...	179 977	95 132	84 845	...
Sikar	...	...	...	...	244 497	126 837	117 660	...
Silchar	...	...	...	...	178 865	89 961	88 904	...
Siliguri	...	...	...	...	513 264	263 702	249 562	...
Singrauli	...	...	...	...	220 257	116 867	103 390	...
Sirsa	...	...	...	...	182 534	96 175	86 359	...
Sitapur	...	...	...	...	177 234	92 696	84 538	...
Siwan	...	...	...	...	135 066	70 756	64 310	...
Solapur	...	...	...	...	951 558	481 064	470 494	...
Sonipat	...	...	...	...	289 333	154 407	134 926	...
South Dum Dum	...	...	...	...	403 316	202 214	201 102	...
Srikakulam	...	...	...	...	137 944	68 457	69 487	...
Srinagar	...	...	...	...	1 206 419	631 830	574 589	...
Sujangarh	...	...	...	...	101 523	51 906	49 617	...
Sultan Pur Majra	...	...	...	...	181 554	95 687	85 867	...
Sultanpur	...	...	...	...	107 640	56 420	51 220	...
Surat	...	...	...	...	4 501 610	2 565 803	1 935 807	...
Surendranagar Dudhrej	...	...	...	...	177 851	92 675	85 176	...
Suryapet	...	...	...	...	106 805	52 773	54 032	...
Tadepalligudem	...	...	...	...	104 032	51 438	52 594	...
Tadpatri	...	...	...	...	108 171	54 015	54 156	...
Tambaram	...	...	...	...	174 787	89 060	85 727	...
Tenali	...	...	...	...	164 937	81 427	83 510	...
Thane	...	...	...	...	1 841 488	975 399	866 089	...
Thanesar	...	...	...	...	155 152	83 994	71 158	...
Thanjavur	...	...	...	...	222 943	109 199	113 744	...

8. Population of capital cities and cities of 100 000 or more inhabitants: latest available year, 1999 - 2018
Population des capitales et des villes de 100 000 habitants ou plus : dernière année disponible, 1999 - 2018 (continued - suite)

Continent, country or area, date, code[a] and city / Continent, pays ou zone, date, code[a] et ville	City proper - Ville proprement dite				Urban agglomeration - Agglomération urbaine			
	Population			Surface area - Superficie (km²)	Population			Surface area - Superficie (km²)
	Both sexes - Les deux sexes	Male - Masculin	Female - Féminin		Both sexes - Les deux sexes	Male - Masculin	Female - Féminin	
ASIA - ASIE								
India - Inde								
9 II 2011 (CDFC)								
Thiruvananthapuram	...	...	...	...	788 271	384 004	404 267	...
Thoothukkudi	...	...	...	...	237 830	118 298	119 532	...
Thrissur	...	...	...	...	315 957	152 296	163 661	...
Tinsukia	...	...	...	...	116 322	62 303	54 019	...
Tiruchirappalli	...	...	...	...	847 387	418 400	428 987	...
Tirunelveli	...	...	...	...	473 637	233 659	239 978	...
Tirupati	...	...	...	...	295 323	150 125	145 198	...
Tiruppur	...	...	...	...	444 352	227 311	217 041	...
Tiruvannamalai	...	...	...	...	145 278	72 406	72 872	...
Tiruvottiyur	...	...	...	...	249 446	125 300	124 146	...
Titagarh	...	...	...	...	116 541	62 735	53 806	...
Tonk	...	...	...	...	165 294	84 806	80 488	...
Tumkur	...	...	...	...	302 143	152 925	149 218	...
Udaipur	...	...	...	...	451 100	233 959	217 141	...
Udgir	...	...	...	...	103 550	54 013	49 537	...
Udupi	...	...	...	...	144 960	71 614	73 346	...
Ujjain	...	...	...	...	515 215	264 871	250 344	...
Ulhasnagar	...	...	...	...	506 098	269 048	237 050	...
Uluberia	...	...	...	...	235 345	120 741	114 604	...
Unnao	...	...	...	...	177 658	93 021	84 637	...
Uttarpara Kotrung	...	...	...	...	159 147	81 410	77 737	...
Vadodara	...	...	...	...	1 752 371	912 721	839 650	...
Valsad	...	...	...	...	139 764	71 400	68 364	...
Vapi	...	...	...	...	163 630	94 105	69 525	...
Varanasi	...	...	...	...	1 198 491	635 140	563 351	...
Vasai-Virar City	...	...	...	...	1 222 390	648 172	574 218	...
Vellore	...	...	...	...	185 803	91 342	94 461	...
Veraval	...	...	...	...	171 121	87 009	84 112	...
Vidisha	...	...	...	...	155 951	81 488	74 463	...
Vijayawada	...	...	...	...	1 143 232	574 794	568 438	...
Vizianagaram	...	...	...	...	228 720	112 290	116 430	...
Warangal	...	...	...	...	704 570	353 309	351 261	...
Wardha	...	...	...	...	106 444	53 697	52 747	...
Yamunanagar	...	...	...	...	217 071	115 663	101 408	...
Yavatmal	...	...	...	...	116 551	58 549	58 002	...
Indonesia - Indonésie								
1 VII 2018 (ESDJ)								
Ambon	431 092	215 223	215 869	359.5	...	...	...	...
Balikpapan	624 033	318 535	305 498	512	...	...	...	...
Banda Aceh	264 054	136 169	127 885	61	...	...	...	...
Bandar Lampung	1 033 601	518 960	514 641	296	...	...	...	...
Bandjarmasin	692 288	344 564	347 724	73	...	...	...	...
Bandung	2 525 220	1 275 030	1 250 190	168	...	...	...	...
Batam	1 347 762	688 198	659 564	960	...	...	...	...
Bengkulu	354 079	177 231	176 848	145	...	...	...	...
Binjai	274 063	136 793	137 270	59	...	...	...	...
Bitung	193 883	98 202	95 681	304	...	...	...	...
Blitar	503 718	253 076	250 642	33	...	...	...	...
Bogor	5 162 044	2 644 661	2 517 383	112	...	...	...	...
Cirebon (Tjirebon)	1 891 957	967 609	924 348	40	...	...	...	...
Denpasar	938 188	478 816	459 372	128	...	...	...	...
Gorontalo	138 590	67 236	71 354	66	...	...	...	...
JAKARTA[50]	10 428 001	5 212 569	5 215 432	662	...	...	...	...
Jambi	585 392	292 509	292 883	205	...	...	...	...
Kediri	800 716	403 055	397 661	63	...	...	...	...
Madiun	237 668	117 818	119 850	34	...	...	...	...
Magelang	413 946	207 123	206 823	18	...	...	...	...
Makasar (Ujung Pandang)	1 502 459	744 057	758 402	176	...	...	...	...
Malang	1 382 786	695 308	687 478	145	...	...	...	...
Manado	427 409	213 250	214 159	158	...	...	...	...
Mataram	483 908	240 914	242 994	61	...	...	...	...
Medan	2 269 588	1 121 730	1 147 858	265	...	...	...	...
Mojokerto	598 783	300 406	298 377	16	...	...	...	...

8. Population of capital cities and cities of 100 000 or more inhabitants: latest available year, 1999 - 2018
Population des capitales et des villes de 100 000 habitants ou plus : dernière année disponible, 1999 - 2018 (continued - suite)

Continent, country or area, date, code[a] and city / Continent, pays ou zone, date, code[a] et ville	City proper - Ville proprement dite				Urban agglomeration - Agglomération urbaine			
	Population			Surface area - Superficie (km²)	Population			Surface area - Superficie (km²)
	Both sexes - Les deux sexes	Male - Masculin	Female - Féminin		Both sexes - Les deux sexes	Male - Masculin	Female - Féminin	
ASIA - ASIE								
Indonesia - Indonésie								
1 VII 2018 (ESDJ)								
Padang	941 136	470 051	471 085	695	...	...	...	...
Pakalongan	498 568	248 731	249 837	45	...	...	...	...
Pakanbaru	1 090 735	556 689	534 046	632	...	...	...	...
Palangkaraya	265 154	134 411	130 743	2400	...	...	...	...
Palembang	1 649 298	823 359	825 939	364	...	...	...	...
Pangkal Pinang	201 207	102 142	99 065	119	...	...	...	...
Pare Pare	142 391	69 925	72 466	99	...	...	...	...
Pasuruan	799 137	399 425	399 712	35	...	...	...	...
Pematang Siantar	254 010	123 897	130 113	56	...	...	...	...
Probolinggo	458 338	225 066	233 272	57	...	...	...	...
Salatiga	190 872	93 423	97 449	53	...	...	...	...
Samarinda	831 608	424 424	407 184	717	...	...	...	...
Semarang	459 358	222 781	236 577	374	...	...	...	...
Sukabumi	1 301 873	658 536	643 337	49	...	...	...	...
Surabaya	2 885 245	1 425 085	1 460 160	351	...	...	...	...
Surakarta	515 865	251 014	264 851	44	...	...	...	...
Tangerang	3 050 758	1 563 442	1 487 316	154	...	...	...	...
Tanjung Balai	174 049	87 794	86 255	108	...	...	...	...
Tebing Tinggi	163 292	80 763	82 529	31	...	...	...	...
Tegal	895 902	445 229	450 673	34	...	...	...	...
Yogyakarta	427 801	208 222	219 579	33	...	...	...	...
Iran (Islamic Republic of) - Iran (République islamique d')								
24 IX 2016 (CDJC)								
Abadan	231 476	115 745	115 731	...	...	...	...	...
Ahar	100 641	50 386	50 255	...	...	...	...	...
Ahwaz	1 184 788	596 774	588 014	...	...	...	...	...
Amol	237 528	118 706	118 822	...	...	...	...	...
Andimeshk	135 116	68 218	66 898	...	...	...	...	...
Andisheh	116 062	58 717	57 345	...	...	...	...	...
Arak	520 944	263 143	257 801	...	...	...	...	...
Ardabil	529 374	269 387	259 987	...	...	...	...	...
Babol	250 217	124 863	125 354	...	...	...	...	...
Bam	127 396	65 128	62 268	...	...	...	...	...
Bandar-e-Abbas	526 648	269 033	257 615	...	...	...	...	...
Bandar-e-Anzali	118 564	58 802	59 762	...	...	...	...	...
Bandar-e-Mahshahr	162 797	81 717	81 080	...	...	...	...	...
Baneh	110 218	55 609	54 609	...	...	...	...	...
Behbahan	122 604	62 124	60 480	...	...	...	...	...
Birjand	203 636	102 399	101 237	...	...	...	...	...
Bojnurd	228 931	114 441	114 490	...	...	...	...	...
Borazjan	110 567	55 675	54 892	...	...	...	...	...
Borujerd	234 997	117 255	117 742	...	...	...	...	...
Bukand	193 501	97 659	95 842	...	...	...	...	...
Bushehr	223 504	115 260	108 244	...	...	...	...	...
Chabahar	106 739	54 657	52 082	...	...	...	...	...
Dezful	264 709	135 925	128 784	...	...	...	...	...
Dorud	121 638	61 395	60 243	...	...	...	...	...
Esfahan	1 961 260	989 168	972 092	...	...	...	...	...
Fardis	181 174	90 573	90 601	...	...	...	...	...
Fasa	110 825	55 650	55 175	...	...	...	...	...
Golestan (Soltanabad)	239 556	123 923	115 633	...	...	...	...	...
Gonbad-e-Kavus	151 910	75 899	76 011	...	...	...	...	...
Gorgan	350 676	174 797	175 879	...	...	...	...	...
Hamadan	554 406	276 455	277 951	...	...	...	...	...
Ilam	194 030	98 276	95 754	...	...	...	...	...
Iranshahr	113 750	58 143	55 607	...	...	...	...	...
Islam Shahr (Qasemabad)	448 129	227 808	220 321	...	...	...	...	...
Izeh	119 399	59 665	59 734	...	...	...	...	...
Jahrom	141 634	73 641	67 993	...	...	...	...	...
Jiroft	130 429	66 874	63 555	...	...	...	...	...
Kamal Shahr	141 669	72 661	69 008	...	...	...	...	...
Karaj	1 592 492	802 398	790 094	...	...	...	...	...

8. Population of capital cities and cities of 100 000 or more inhabitants: latest available year, 1999 - 2018
Population des capitales et des villes de 100 000 habitants ou plus : dernière année disponible, 1999 - 2018 (continued - suite)

Continent, country or area, date, code[a] and city / Continent, pays ou zone, date, code[a] et ville	City proper - Ville proprement dite				Urban agglomeration - Agglomération urbaine			
	Population			Surface area - Superficie (km²)	Population			Surface area - Superficie (km²)
	Both sexes - Les deux sexes	Male - Masculin	Female - Féminin		Both sexes - Les deux sexes	Male - Masculin	Female - Féminin	

ASIA - ASIE

Iran (Islamic Republic of) - Iran (République islamique d')
24 IX 2016 (CDJC)

Kashan	304 487	154 100	150 387	...	...	...	...	...
Kashmar	102 282	51 616	50 666	...	...	...	...	...
Kerman	537 718	272 715	265 003	...	...	...	...	...
Kermanshah	946 651	474 073	472 578	...	...	...	...	...
Khomeini shahr	247 128	127 450	119 678	...	...	...	...	...
Khoramabad	373 416	186 481	186 935	...	...	...	...	...
Khoramshahr	133 097	66 113	66 984	...	...	...	...	...
Khoy	198 845	99 712	99 133	...	...	...	...	...
Lahijan	101 073	50 123	50 950	...	...	...	...	...
Mahabad	168 393	84 271	84 122	...	...	...	...	...
Malard	281 027	143 278	137 749	...	...	...	...	...
Malayer	170 237	85 487	84 750	...	...	...	...	...
Marand	130 825	66 671	64 154	...	...	...	...	...
Maraqeh	175 255	87 868	87 387	...	...	...	...	...
Marivan	136 654	69 679	66 975	...	...	...	...	...
Marvadsht	148 858	76 363	72 495	...	...	...	...	...
Mashhad	3 001 184	1 503 824	1 497 360	...	...	...	...	...
Masjed Soleyman	100 497	51 019	49 478	...	...	...	...	...
Miandoab	134 425	68 679	65 746	...	...	...	...	...
Mohammad Shahr	119 418	60 988	58 430	...	...	...	...	...
Najafabad	235 281	118 710	116 571	...	...	...	...	...
Nasim Shahr	200 393	103 371	97 022	...	...	...	...	...
Nazar Abad	119 512	61 074	58 438	...	...	...	...	...
Neyshabur	264 375	132 273	132 102	...	...	...	...	...
Orumiyeh	736 224	369 043	367 181	...	...	...	...	...
Pakdasht	236 319	120 459	115 860	...	...	...	...	...
Qaem shahr	204 953	101 999	102 954	...	...	...	...	...
Qarchak	231 075	118 260	112 815	...	...	...	...	...
Qazvin	402 748	203 702	199 046	...	...	...	...	...
Qods	309 605	158 567	151 038	...	...	...	...	...
Qom	1 201 158	609 541	591 617	...	...	...	...	...
Quchan	101 604	51 501	50 103	...	...	...	...	...
Rafsanjan	161 909	83 607	78 302	...	...	...	...	...
Rasht	679 995	336 313	343 682	...	...	...	...	...
Robatkarim	105 393	53 647	51 746	...	...	...	...	...
Sabzewar	243 700	121 667	122 033	...	...	...	...	...
Sanandaj	412 767	208 059	204 708	...	...	...	...	...
Saqez	165 258	82 984	82 274	...	...	...	...	...
Sari	309 820	153 823	155 997	...	...	...	...	...
Saveh	220 762	112 742	108 020	...	...	...	...	...
Semnan	185 129	94 411	90 718	...	...	...	...	...
Shahinshahr	173 329	86 008	87 321	...	...	...	...	...
Shahr-e-Kord	190 441	94 789	95 652	...	...	...	...	...
Shahreza	134 952	68 191	66 761	...	...	...	...	...
Shahriar	309 607	156 085	153 522	...	...	...	...	...
Shahrud	150 129	75 656	74 473	...	...	...	...	...
Shiraz	1 565 572	785 450	780 122	...	...	...	...	...
Shoshtar	101 878	51 762	50 116	...	...	...	...	...
Sirjan	199 704	102 656	97 048	...	...	...	...	...
Tabriz	1 558 693	786 661	772 032	...	...	...	...	...
TEHRAN	8 693 706	4 324 155	4 369 551	...	...	...	...	...
Torbat-e-heydariyeh	140 019	71 603	68 416	...	...	...	...	...
Torbatejam	100 449	50 772	49 677	...	...	...	...	...
Varamin	225 628	114 215	111 413	...	...	...	...	...
Yasooj	134 532	68 427	66 105	...	...	...	...	...
Yazd	529 673	269 732	259 941	...	...	...	...	...
Zabol	134 950	67 691	67 259	...	...	...	...	...
Zahedan	587 730	299 550	288 180	...	...	...	...	...
Zanjan	430 871	217 406	213 465	...	...	...	...	...

8. Population of capital cities and cities of 100 000 or more inhabitants: latest available year, 1999 - 2018

Population des capitales et des villes de 100 000 habitants ou plus : dernière année disponible, 1999 - 2018 (continued - suite)

Continent, country or area, date, code[a] and city Continent, pays ou zone, date, code[a] et ville	City proper - Ville proprement dite				Urban agglomeration - Agglomération urbaine			
	Population			Surface area - Superficie (km²)	Population			Surface area - Superficie (km²)
	Both sexes - Les deux sexes	Male - Masculin	Female - Féminin		Both sexes - Les deux sexes	Male - Masculin	Female - Féminin	
ASIA - ASIE								
Iraq								
1 VII 2015 (ESDF)								
Abi Gharaq Nahia	108 630	55 009	53 621	191	...	...	...	...
Abna'a Al-Rafidain Nahia	153 712	77 827	75 885	...	...	...	...	...
Abu Al-Khaseeb Qadha Center	215 247	108 228	107 019	1152	...	...	...	...
Abu-Gharib Qadha Center	149 858	76 274	73 584	431	...	...	...	...
Al-Adhamia Qadha Center	286 036	144 825	141 211	29	...	...	...	...
Al-Amara Qadha Center	541 034	270 426	270 608	2862	...	...	...	...
Al-Amirya Nahia	101 119	51 899	49 220	2532	...	...	...	...
Al-Basrah Qadha Center	1 225 793	616 525	609 268	1085	...	...	...	...
Al-Dair Nahia	101 882	50 969	50 913	825	...	...	...	...
Al-Dijail Qadha Center	105 345	53 240	52 105	1286	...	...	...	...
Al-Diwaniya Qadha Center	421 571	212 293	209 278	319	...	...	...	...
Al-Fahama Nahia	619 474	313 651	305 823	90	...	...	...	...
Al-Falluja Qadha Center	321 106	165 111	155 995	478	...	...	...	...
Al-Forat Nahia	379 668	192 233	187 435	...	...	...	...	...
Al-Garma Nahia	129 783	66 577	63 206	1038	...	...	...	...
Al-Gharraf Nahia	118 081	59 318	58 763	623	...	...	...	...
Al-Habbaniya Nahia	133 202	68 366	64 836	714	...	...	...	...
Al-Hamza Qadha Center	128 472	64 739	63 733	600	...	...	...	...
Al-Hartha Nahia	156 391	78 509	77 882	...	...	...	...	...
Al-Hassainya Nahia	147 103	74 383	72 720	334	...	...	...	...
Al-Hawiga Qadha Center	115 910	58 508	57 402	1903	...	...	...	...
Al-Hilla Qadha Center	559 834	282 142	277 692	161	...	...	...	...
Al-Hindiya Qadha Center	113 021	57 001	56 020	134	...	...	...	...
Al-Hur Nahia	231 635	116 740	114 895	...	...	...	...	...
Al-Iskandaria Nahia	159 516	80 514	79 002	283	...	...	...	...
Al-Jisr Nahia	159 306	81 464	77 842	153	...	...	...	...
Al-Kadimiya Qadha Center	420 968	213 144	207 824	32	...	...	...	...
Al-Kaim Qadha Center	104 989	53 971	51 018	6460	...	...	...	...
Al-Karkh Qadha Center	113 397	57 415	55 982	...	...	...	...	...
Al-Karrada Al-Sharqia Nahia	318 615	161 321	157 294	49	...	...	...	...
Al-Khalis Qadha Center	139 713	70 624	69 089	1109	...	...	...	...
Al-Kifl Nahia	140 182	71 029	69 153	526	...	...	...	...
Al-Kufa Qadha Center	232 670	116 667	116 003	129	...	...	...	...
Al-Kut Qadha Center	436 673	220 490	216 183	2540	...	...	...	...
Al-Madhatiya Nahia	135 941	68 724	67 217	498	...	...	...	...
Al-Mahawil Qadha Center	116 899	59 181	57 718	608	...	...	...	...
Al-Mamoon Nahia	985 798	499 128	486 670	82	...	...	...	...
Al-Mansour Nahia	434 839	220 167	214 672	119	...	...	...	...
Al-Mashroo Nahia	127 344	64 449	62 895	834	...	...	...	...
Al-Mejar Al-Kabir Qadha Center	108 979	54 373	54 606	506	...	...	...	...
Al-Mosal Qadha Center	1 384 260	708 546	675 714	1783	...	...	...	...
Al-Mounawara Nahia	287 799	145 718	142 081	...	...	...	...	...
Al-Muqdadya Qadha Center	157 593	79 612	77 981	768	...	...	...	...
Al-Najaf Qadha Center	746 180	372 423	373 757	1133	...	...	...	...
Al-Nasir & Al-Salam Nahia	160 606	82 184	78 422	262	...	...	...	...
Al-Nasiriya Qadha Center	537 544	269 480	268 064	1277	...	...	...	...
Al-Noamaniya Qadha Center	111 647	56 363	55 284	946	...	...	...	...
Al-Qasim Nahia	159 420	80 545	78 875	528	...	...	...	...
Al-Qayarra Nahia	129 811	66 129	63 682	686	...	...	...	...
Al-Qurna Qadha Center	136 677	68 704	67 973	1248	...	...	...	...
Al-Ramadi Qadha Center	419 053	215 292	203 761	7829	...	...	...	...
Al-Rifaai Qadha Center	155 478	78 087	77 391	1345	...	...	...	...
Al-Rumaitha Qadha Center	118 011	59 581	58 430	106	...	...	...	...
Al-Rusafa Qadha Center	118 018	59 755	58 263	...	...	...	...	...
Al-Samawa Qadha Center	288 948	145 984	142 964	941	...	...	...	...
Al-Shamal Nahia	158 475	81 035	77 440	...	...	...	...	...
Al-Shattra Qadha Center	239 680	120 266	119 414	384	...	...	...	...
Al-Shirqat Qadha Center	208 586	105 453	103 133	1515	...	...	...	...
Al-Sideeq Al-Akbar Nahia	172 057	87 116	84 941	...	...	...	...	...
Al-Suwaira Qadha Center	142 924	72 148	70 776	1345	...	...	...	...
Al-Taji Nahia	164 894	84 470	80 424	388	...	...	...	...
Al-Wihda Nahia	204 585	104 438	100 147	890	...	...	...	...
Al-Yousifya Nahia	131 507	67 600	63 907	486	...	...	...	...

8. Population of capital cities and cities of 100 000 or more inhabitants: latest available year, 1999 - 2018
Population des capitales et des villes de 100 000 habitants ou plus : dernière année disponible, 1999 - 2018 (continued - suite)

Continent, country or area, date, code[a] and city / Continent, pays ou zone, date, code[a] et ville	City proper - Ville proprement dite				Urban agglomeration - Agglomération urbaine			
	Population			Surface area - Superficie (km²)	Population			Surface area - Superficie (km²)
	Both sexes - Les deux sexes	Male - Masculin	Female - Féminin		Both sexes - Les deux sexes	Male - Masculin	Female - Féminin	
ASIA - ASIE								
Iraq								
1 VII 2015 (ESDF)								
Al-Zohour Nahia	209 918	106 332	103 586	...	...	...	...	...
Al-Zubair Qadha Center	378 758	190 200	188 558	1134	...	...	...	...
Arbil Qadha Center	787 997	398 450	389 547	2790	...	...	...	...
BAGHDAD	1 211 934[51]	613 625[51]	598 309[51]	111	...	...	...	...
Bakrago Nahia	101 892	51 077	50 815	...	...	...	...	...
Baquba Qadha Center	276 029	138 681	137 348	580	...	...	...	...
Bashiqa Nahia	140 258	71 487	68 771	497	...	...	...	...
Beni Saad Nahia	127 268	64 496	62 772	497	...	...	...	...
Beygee Qadha Center	175 395	88 596	86 799	1188	...	...	...	...
Duhouk Qadha Center	328 113	164 245	163 868	577	...	...	...	...
Kalar Qadha Center	144 235	72 047	72 188	2201	...	...	...	...
Kerbela Qadha Center	514 356	259 193	255 163	2397	...	...	...	...
Kirkuk Qadha Center	938 336	471 419	466 917	1956	...	...	...	...
Mahmudiya Qadha Center	154 741	78 846	75 895	68	...	...	...	...
Qalat Siker Nahia	100 315	50 373	49 942	614	...	...	...	...
Saddat Al-Hindin Nahia	116 247	58 839	57 408	388	...	...	...	...
Sader /1 Qadha Center	130 153	65 899	64 254	...	...	...	...	...
Samarra Qadha Center	203 011	102 444	100 567	4504	...	...	...	...
Shat Al-Arab Qadha Center	136 043	68 413	67 630	1516	...	...	...	...
Sulaimania Qadha Center	651 173	325 147	326 026	3404	...	...	...	...
Suq AL-Shoyolh Qadha Center	126 652	63 493	63 159	285	...	...	...	...
Telafar Qadha Center	206 835	105 780	101 055	3206	...	...	...	...
That Al Salasil Nahia	277 494	140 647	136 847	147	...	...	...	...
Tikrit Qadha Center	182 464	92 119	90 345	991	...	...	...	...
Tooz-Khormato Qadha Center	117 458	59 233	58 225	1253	...	...	...	...
Zummar Nahia	128 017	65 210	62 807	1247	...	...	...	...
Israel - Israël								
1 VII 2017 (ESDJ)								
Ashdod	222 237	108 358	113 879	46	...	...	...	...
Ashqelon	136 199	66 339	69 860	45	...	...	...	...
Bat Yam	128 779	61 267	67 512	8	...	...	...	...
Be'er Sheva	206 680	100 994	105 687	117	...	...	...	...
Bene Beraq	191 369	97 805	93 564	7	...	...	...	...
Bet Shemesh	112 066	56 069	55 998	38	...	...	...	...
Haifa	280 339	134 802	145 537	65	...	...	...	...
Holon	191 731	92 541	99 190	19	...	...	...	...
JERUSALEM[52]	891 977	444 195	447 782	126	...	...	...	...
Netanya	212 468	103 389	109 079	31	...	...	...	...
Petah Tiqwa	238 263	116 670	121 593	36	...	...	...	...
Ramat Gan	154 976	74 106	80 870	16	...	...	...	...
Rehovot	137 053	66 937	70 115	24	...	...	...	...
Rishon Leziyyon	248 591	121 866	126 725	59	...	...	...	...
Tel Aviv-Yafo	441 379	218 658	222 721	52	...	...	...	...
Japan - Japon								
1 X 2015 (CDJC)								
Abiko	131 606[53]	64 614[53]	66 992[53]	43.2[54]	...	...	...	...
Ageo	225 196[53]	112 157[53]	113 039[53]	45.5[54]	...	...	...	...
Aizuwakamatsu	124 062[53]	59 200[53]	64 862[53]	383[54]	...	...	...	...
Akashi	293 409[53]	141 801[53]	151 608[53]	49.4[54]	...	...	...	...
Akishima	111 539[53]	55 394[53]	56 145[53]	17.3[54]	...	...	...	...
Akita	315 814[53]	148 851[53]	166 963[53]	906.1[54]	...	...	...	...
Amagasaki	452 563[53]	219 059[53]	233 504[53]	50.7[54]	...	...	...	...
Anjo	184 140[53]	94 073[53]	90 067[53]	86.1[54]	...	...	...	...
Aomori	287 648[53]	133 560[53]	154 088[53]	824.6[54]	...	...	...	...
Asahikawa	339 605[53]	156 402[53]	183 203[53]	747.7[54]	...	...	...	...
Asaka	136 299[53]	69 971[53]	66 328[53]	18.3[54]	...	...	...	...
Ashikaga	149 452[53]	73 161[53]	76 291[53]	177.8[54]	...	...	...	...
Atsugi	225 714[53]	116 658[53]	109 056[53]	93.8[54]	...	...	...	...
Beppu	122 138[53]	55 482[53]	66 656[53]	125.3[54]	...	...	...	...
Chiba	971 882[53]	482 840[53]	489 042[53]	271.8[54]	...	...	...	...
Chigasaki	239 348[53]	116 894[53]	122 454[53]	35.7[54]	...	...	...	...
Chikusei	104 573[53]	51 663[53]	52 910[53]	205.3[54]	...	...	...	...

8. Population of capital cities and cities of 100 000 or more inhabitants: latest available year, 1999 - 2018
Population des capitales et des villes de 100 000 habitants ou plus : dernière année disponible, 1999 - 2018 (continued - suite)

Continent, country or area, date, code[a] and city / Continent, pays ou zone, date, code[a] et ville	City proper - Ville proprement dite				Urban agglomeration - Agglomération urbaine			
	Population			Surface area - Superficie (km²)	Population			Surface area - Superficie (km²)
	Both sexes - Les deux sexes	Male - Masculin	Female - Féminin		Both sexes - Les deux sexes	Male - Masculin	Female - Féminin	
ASIA - ASIE								
Japan - Japon								
1 X 2015 (CDJC)								
Chikushino	101 081[53]	47 995[53]	53 086[53]	87.7[54]	...	...	...	...
Chofu	229 061[53]	111 921[53]	117 140[53]	21.6[54]	...	...	...	...
Daito	123 217[53]	60 302[53]	62 915[53]	18.3[54]	...	...	...	...
Ebetsu	120 636[53]	57 391[53]	63 245[53]	187.4[54]	...	...	...	...
Ebina	130 190[53]	65 620[53]	64 570[53]	26.6[54]	...	...	...	...
Fuchu	260 274[53]	132 172[53]	128 102[53]	29.4[54]	...	...	...	...
Fuji	248 399[53]	121 901[53]	126 498[53]	245[54]	...	...	...	...
Fujieda	143 605[53]	70 049[53]	73 556[53]	194.1[54]	...	...	...	...
Fujimi	108 102[53]	53 312[53]	54 790[53]	19.8[54]	...	...	...	...
Fujimino	110 970[53]	54 910[53]	56 060[53]	14.6[54]	...	...	...	...
Fujinomiya	130 770[53]	64 281[53]	66 489[53]	389.1[54]	...	...	...	...
Fujisawa	423 894[53]	210 032[53]	213 862[53]	69.6[54]	...	...	...	...
Fukaya	143 811[53]	71 594[53]	72 217[53]	138.4[54]	...	...	...	...
Fukui	265 904[53]	128 892[53]	137 012[53]	536.4[54]	...	...	...	...
Fukuoka	1 538 681[53]	726 666[53]	812 015[53]	343.4[54]	...	...	...	...
Fukushima	294 247[53]	144 690[53]	149 557[53]	767.7[54]	...	...	...	...
Fukuyama	464 811[53]	225 414[53]	239 397[53]	518.1[54]	...	...	...	...
Funabashi	622 890[53]	311 358[53]	311 532[53]	85.6[54]	...	...	...	...
Gifu	406 735[53]	193 760[53]	212 975[53]	203.6[54]	...	...	...	...
Habikino	112 683[53]	53 243[53]	59 440[53]	26.5[54]	...	...	...	...
Hachinohe	231 257[53]	110 493[53]	120 764[53]	305.5[54]	...	...	...	...
Hachioji	577 513[53]	291 238[53]	286 275[53]	186.4[54]	...	...	...	...
Hadano	167 378[53]	85 552[53]	81 826[53]	103.8[54]	...	...	...	...
Hakodate	265 979[53]	120 376[53]	145 603[53]	677.9[54]	...	...	...	...
Hakusan	109 287[53]	53 085[53]	56 202[53]	754.9[54]	...	...	...	...
Hamamatsu	797 980[53]	395 509[53]	402 471[53]	1558.1[54]	...	...	...	...
Handa	116 908[53]	58 444[53]	58 464[53]	47.4[54]	...	...	...	...
Hatsukaichi	114 906[53]	54 654[53]	60 252[53]	489.5[54]	...	...	...	...
Higashihiroshima	192 907[53]	97 962[53]	94 945[53]	635.2[54]	...	...	...	...
Higashikurume	116 632[53]	56 738[53]	59 894[53]	12.9[54]	...	...	...	...
Higashimurayama	149 956[53]	73 314[53]	76 642[53]	17.1[54]	...	...	...	...
Higashiomi	114 180[53]	56 601[53]	57 579[53]	388.4[54]	...	...	...	...
Higashiosaka	502 784[53]	246 053[53]	256 731[53]	61.8[54]	...	...	...	...
Hikone	113 679[53]	56 090[53]	57 589[53]	196.9[54]	...	...	...	...
Himeji	535 664[53]	258 724[53]	276 940[53]	534.5[54]	...	...	...	...
Hino	186 283[53]	93 349[53]	92 934[53]	27.6[54]	...	...	...	...
Hirakata	404 152[53]	192 816[53]	211 336[53]	65.1[54]	...	...	...	...
Hiratsuka	258 227[53]	129 456[53]	128 771[53]	67.8[54]	...	...	...	...
Hirosaki	177 411[53]	81 367[53]	96 044[53]	524.2[54]	...	...	...	...
Hiroshima	1 194 034[53]	576 850[53]	617 184[53]	906.5[54]	...	...	...	...
Hitachi	185 054[53]	92 595[53]	92 459[53]	225.7[54]	...	...	...	...
Hitachinaka	155 689[53]	78 270[53]	77 419[53]	99.9[54]	...	...	...	...
Hofu	115 942[53]	55 910[53]	60 032[53]	189.4[54]	...	...	...	...
Ibaraki	280 033[53]	135 705[53]	144 328[53]	76.5[54]	...	...	...	...
Ichihara	274 656[53]	141 134[53]	133 522[53]	368.2[54]	...	...	...	...
Ichikawa	481 732[53]	242 652[53]	239 080[53]	57.5[54]	...	...	...	...
Ichinomiya	380 868[53]	185 869[53]	194 999[53]	113.8[54]	...	...	...	...
Ichinoseki	121 583[53]	58 804[53]	62 779[53]	1256.4[54]	...	...	...	...
Iida	101 581[53]	48 443[53]	53 138[53]	658.7[54]	...	...	...	...
Iizuka	129 146[53]	61 249[53]	67 897[53]	214.1[54]	...	...	...	...
Ikeda	103 069[53]	49 372[53]	53 697[53]	22.1[54]	...	...	...	...
Ikoma	118 233[53]	55 972[53]	62 261[53]	53.2[54]	...	...	...	...
Imabari	158 114[53]	74 336[53]	83 778[53]	419.1[54]	...	...	...	...
Inazawa	136 867[53]	67 500[53]	69 367[53]	79.4[54]	...	...	...	...
Iruma	148 390[53]	73 408[53]	74 982[53]	44.7[54]	...	...	...	...
Isahaya	138 078[53]	65 029[53]	73 049[53]	341.8[54]	...	...	...	...
Ise	127 817[53]	60 467[53]	67 350[53]	208.4[54]	...	...	...	...
Isehara	101 514[53]	51 429[53]	50 085[53]	55.6[54]	...	...	...	...
Isesaki	208 814[53]	104 234[53]	104 580[53]	139.4[54]	...	...	...	...

8. Population of capital cities and cities of 100 000 or more inhabitants: latest available year, 1999 - 2018
Population des capitales et des villes de 100 000 habitants ou plus : dernière année disponible, 1999 - 2018 (continued - suite)

Continent, country or area, date, code[a] and city / Continent, pays ou zone, date, code[a] et ville	City proper - Ville proprement dite				Urban agglomeration - Agglomération urbaine			
	Population			Surface area - Superficie (km²)	Population			Surface area - Superficie (km²)
	Both sexes - Les deux sexes	Male - Masculin	Female - Féminin		Both sexes - Les deux sexes	Male - Masculin	Female - Féminin	

ASIA - ASIE

Japan - Japon
1 X 2015 (CDJC)

Ishinomaki	147 214[53]	71 826[53]	75 388[53]	554.6[54]	...	...	...	...
Itami	196 883[53]	95 641[53]	101 242[53]	25[54]	...	...	...	...
Iwaki	350 237[53]	172 829[53]	177 408[53]	1232[54]	...	...	...	...
Iwakuni	136 757[53]	64 455[53]	72 302[53]	873.7[54]	...	...	...	...
Iwata	167 210[53]	84 130[53]	83 080[53]	163.5[54]	...	...	...	...
Izumi (Osaka)	186 109[53]	89 868[53]	96 241[53]	85[54]	...	...	...	...
Izumisano	100 966[53]	48 506[53]	52 460[53]	56.5[54]	...	...	...	...
Izumo	171 938[53]	82 707[53]	89 231[53]	624.4[54]	...	...	...	...
Joetsu	196 987[53]	95 990[53]	100 997[53]	973.8[54]	...	...	...	...
Kadoma	123 576[53]	60 620[53]	62 956[53]	12.3[54]	...	...	...	...
Kagoshima	599 814[53]	279 108[53]	320 706[53]	547.6[54]	...	...	...	...
Kakamigahara	144 690[53]	71 167[53]	73 523[53]	87.8[54]	...	...	...	...
Kakegawa	114 602[53]	57 126[53]	57 476[53]	265.7[54]	...	...	...	...
Kakogawa	267 435[53]	131 170[53]	136 265[53]	138.5[54]	...	...	...	...
Kamagaya	108 917[53]	53 490[53]	55 427[53]	21.1[54]	...	...	...	...
Kamakura	173 019[53]	81 664[53]	91 355[53]	39.7[54]	...	...	...	...
Kanazawa	465 699[53]	226 007[53]	239 692[53]	468.6[54]	...	...	...	...
Kanoya	103 608[53]	49 555[53]	54 053[53]	448.2[54]	...	...	...	...
Karatsu	122 785[53]	57 547[53]	65 238[53]	487.6[54]	...	...	...	...
Kariya	149 765[53]	78 456[53]	71 309[53]	50.4[54]	...	...	...	...
Kashihara	124 111[53]	58 888[53]	65 223[53]	39.6[54]	...	...	...	...
Kashiwa	413 954[53]	205 971[53]	207 983[53]	114.7[54]	...	...	...	...
Kasuga	110 743[53]	53 284[53]	57 459[53]	14.2[54]	...	...	...	...
Kasugai	306 508[53]	151 955[53]	154 553[53]	92.8[54]	...	...	...	...
Kasukabe	232 709[53]	114 813[53]	117 896[53]	66[54]	...	...	...	...
Kawachinagano	106 987[53]	50 182[53]	56 805[53]	109.6[54]	...	...	...	...
Kawagoe	350 745[53]	175 559[53]	175 186[53]	109.1[54]	...	...	...	...
Kawaguchi	578 112[53]	292 067[53]	286 045[53]	62[54]	...	...	...	...
Kawanishi	156 375[53]	73 882[53]	82 493[53]	53.4[54]	...	...	...	...
Kawasaki	1 475 213[53]	749 038[53]	726 175[53]	143[54]	...	...	...	...
Kazo	112 229[53]	55 828[53]	56 401[53]	133.3[54]	...	...	...	...
Kirishima	125 857[53]	59 966[53]	65 891[53]	603.2[54]	...	...	...	...
Kiryu	114 714[53]	55 327[53]	59 387[53]	274.5[54]	...	...	...	...
Kisarazu	134 141[53]	67 450[53]	66 691[53]	139[54]	...	...	...	...
Kishiwada	194 911[53]	93 160[53]	101 751[53]	72.7[54]	...	...	...	...
Kitakyushu	961 286[53]	452 682[53]	508 604[53]	492[54]	...	...	...	...
Kitami	121 226[53]	58 020[53]	63 206[53]	1427.4[54]	...	...	...	...
Kobe	1 537 272[53]	726 700[53]	810 572[53]	557[54]	...	...	...	...
Kochi	337 190[53]	157 002[53]	180 188[53]	309[54]	...	...	...	...
Kodaira	190 005[53]	93 777[53]	96 228[53]	20.5[54]	...	...	...	...
Kofu	193 125[53]	94 448[53]	98 677[53]	212.5[54]	...	...	...	...
Koga	140 946[53]	70 354[53]	70 592[53]	123.6[54]	...	...	...	...
Koganei	121 396[53]	60 168[53]	61 228[53]	11.3[54]	...	...	...	...
Kokubunji	122 742[53]	60 274[53]	62 468[53]	11.5[54]	...	...	...	...
Komaki	149 462[53]	75 430[53]	74 032[53]	62.8[54]	...	...	...	...
Komatsu	106 919[53]	51 844[53]	55 075[53]	371.1[54]	...	...	...	...
Konosu	118 072[53]	58 346[53]	59 726[53]	67.4[54]	...	...	...	...
Koriyama	335 444[53]	167 096[53]	168 348[53]	757.2[54]	...	...	...	...
Koshigaya	337 498[53]	167 023[53]	170 475[53]	60.2[54]	...	...	...	...
Kuki	152 311[53]	75 993[53]	76 318[53]	82.4[54]	...	...	...	...
Kumagaya	198 742[53]	99 169[53]	99 573[53]	159.8[54]	...	...	...	...
Kumamoto	740 822[53]	348 470[53]	392 352[53]	390.3[54]	...	...	...	...
Kurashiki	477 118[53]	230 081[53]	247 037[53]	355.6[54]	...	...	...	...
Kure	228 552[53]	110 173[53]	118 379[53]	352.8[54]	...	...	...	...
Kurume	304 552[53]	144 971[53]	159 581[53]	230[54]	...	...	...	...
Kusatsu	137 247[53]	70 129[53]	67 118[53]	67.8[54]	...	...	...	...
Kushiro	174 742[53]	82 185[53]	92 557[53]	1362.9[54]	...	...	...	...
Kuwana	140 303[53]	68 740[53]	71 563[53]	136.7[54]	...	...	...	...
Kyoto	1 475 183[53]	699 748[53]	775 435[53]	827.8[54]	...	...	...	...

Continent, country or area, date, code[a] and city / Continent, pays ou zone, date, code[a] et ville	City proper - Ville proprement dite				Urban agglomeration - Agglomération urbaine			
	Population			Surface area - Superficie (km²)	Population			Surface area - Superficie (km²)
	Both sexes - Les deux sexes	Male - Masculin	Female - Féminin		Both sexes - Les deux sexes	Male - Masculin	Female - Féminin	
ASIA - ASIE								
Japan - Japon								
1 X 2015 (CDJC)								
Machida	432 348[53]	212 312[53]	220 036[53]	71.8[54]	...	...	...	...
Maebashi	336 154[53]	164 136[53]	172 018[53]	311.6[54]	...	...	...	...
Marugame	110 010[53]	53 183[53]	56 827[53]	111.8[54]	...	...	...	...
Matsubara	120 750[53]	58 096[53]	62 654[53]	16.7[54]	...	...	...	...
Matsudo	483 480[53]	240 928[53]	242 552[53]	61.4[54]	...	...	...	...
Matsue	206 230[53]	99 565[53]	106 665[53]	573[54]	...	...	...	...
Matsumoto	243 293[53]	119 479[53]	123 814[53]	978.5[54]	...	...	...	...
Matsusaka	163 863[53]	78 548[53]	85 315[53]	623.7[54]	...	...	...	...
Matsuyama	514 865[53]	241 656[53]	273 209[53]	429.4[54]	...	...	...	...
Minoh	133 411[53]	63 938[53]	69 473[53]	47.9[54]	...	...	...	...
Misato	136 521[53]	68 950[53]	67 571[53]	30.1[54]	...	...	...	...
Mishima	110 046[53]	53 836[53]	56 210[53]	62[54]	...	...	...	...
Mitaka	186 936[53]	90 641[53]	96 295[53]	16.4[54]	...	...	...	...
Mito	270 783[53]	132 799[53]	137 984[53]	217.3[54]	...	...	...	...
Miyakonojo	165 029[53]	77 521[53]	87 508[53]	653.4[54]	...	...	...	...
Miyazaki	401 138[53]	188 177[53]	212 961[53]	643.7[54]	...	...	...	...
Moriguchi	143 042[53]	68 987[53]	74 055[53]	12.7[54]	...	...	...	...
Morioka	297 631[53]	141 089[53]	156 542[53]	886.5[54]	...	...	...	...
Musashino	144 730[53]	69 475[53]	75 255[53]	11[54]	...	...	...	...
Nagahama	118 193[53]	57 703[53]	60 490[53]	681[54]	...	...	...	...
Nagano	377 598[53]	182 843[53]	194 755[53]	834.8[54]	...	...	...	...
Nagaoka	275 133[53]	134 198[53]	140 935[53]	891.1[54]	...	...	...	...
Nagareyama	174 373[53]	86 249[53]	88 124[53]	35.3[54]	...	...	...	...
Nagasaki	429 508[53]	198 716[53]	230 792[53]	405.9[54]	...	...	...	...
Nagoya	2 295 638[53]	1 133 640[53]	1 161 998[53]	326.5[54]	...	...	...	...
Naha	319 435[53]	154 685[53]	164 750[53]	39.6[54]	...	...	...	...
Nara	360 310[53]	167 899[53]	192 411[53]	276.9[54]	...	...	...	...
Narashino	167 909[53]	84 323[53]	83 586[53]	21[54]	...	...	...	...
Narita	131 190[53]	65 928[53]	65 262[53]	213.8[54]	...	...	...	...
Nasushiobara	117 146[53]	58 148[53]	58 998[53]	592.7[54]	...	...	...	...
Neyagawa	237 518[53]	115 131[53]	122 387[53]	24.7[54]	...	...	...	...
Niigata	810 157[53]	389 512[53]	420 645[53]	726.5[54]	...	...	...	...
Niihama	119 903[53]	57 551[53]	62 352[53]	234.5[54]	...	...	...	...
Niiza	162 122[53]	80 627[53]	81 495[53]	22.8[54]	...	...	...	...
Nishinomiya	487 850[53]	228 354[53]	259 496[53]	100[54]	...	...	...	...
Nishio	167 990[53]	84 669[53]	83 321[53]	161.2[54]	...	...	...	...
Nishitokyo	200 012[53]	97 830[53]	102 182[53]	15.8[54]	...	...	...	...
Nobeoka	125 159[53]	58 993[53]	66 166[53]	868[54]	...	...	...	...
Noda	153 583[53]	76 541[53]	77 042[53]	103.6[54]	...	...	...	...
Numazu	195 633[53]	95 980[53]	99 653[53]	187[54]	...	...	...	...
Obihiro	169 327[53]	80 994[53]	88 333[53]	619.3[54]	...	...	...	...
Odawara	194 086[53]	94 697[53]	99 389[53]	113.8[54]	...	...	...	...
Ogaki	159 879[53]	77 430[53]	82 449[53]	206.6[54]	...	...	...	...
Oita	478 146[53]	229 844[53]	248 302[53]	502.4[54]	...	...	...	...
Okayama	719 474[53]	345 913[53]	373 561[53]	790[54]	...	...	...	...
Okazaki	381 051[53]	192 771[53]	188 280[53]	387.2[54]	...	...	...	...
Okinawa	139 279[53]	67 522[53]	71 757[53]	49.7[54]	...	...	...	...
Ome	137 381[53]	68 677[53]	68 704[53]	103.3[54]	...	...	...	...
Omuta	117 360[53]	53 859[53]	63 501[53]	81.5[54]	...	...	...	...
Onomichi	138 626[53]	66 292[53]	72 334[53]	285.1[54]	...	...	...	...
Osaka	2 691 185[53]	1 302 562[53]	1 388 623[53]	225.2[54]	...	...	...	...
Osaki	133 391[53]	65 120[53]	68 271[53]	796.8[54]	...	...	...	...
Oshu	119 422[53]	57 377[53]	62 045[53]	993.3[54]	...	...	...	...
Ota	219 807[53]	111 610[53]	108 197[53]	175.5[54]	...	...	...	...
Otaru	121 924[53]	54 985[53]	66 939[53]	243.8[54]	...	...	...	...
Otsu	340 973[53]	164 799[53]	176 174[53]	464.5[54]	...	...	...	...
Oyama	166 760[53]	84 100[53]	82 660[53]	171.8[54]	...	...	...	...
Saga	236 372[53]	111 453[53]	124 919[53]	431.8[54]	...	...	...	...
Sagamihara	720 780[53]	361 060[53]	359 720[53]	328.7[54]	...	...	...	...

335

Continent, country or area, date, code[a] and city Continent, pays ou zone, date, code[a] et ville	City proper - Ville proprement dite				Urban agglomeration - Agglomération urbaine			
	Population			Surface area - Superficie (km²)	Population			Surface area - Superficie (km²)
	Both sexes - Les deux sexes	Male - Masculin	Female - Féminin		Both sexes - Les deux sexes	Male - Masculin	Female - Féminin	
ASIA - ASIE								
Japan - Japon								
1 X 2015 (CDJC)								
Saijo	108 174[53]	51 807[53]	56 367[53]	510[54]	...	...	...	...
Saitama	1 263 979[53]	627 238[53]	636 741[53]	217.4[54]	...	...	...	...
Sakado	101 679[53]	51 307[53]	50 372[53]	41[54]	...	...	...	...
Sakai	839 310[53]	402 379[53]	436 931[53]	209.7[54]	...	...	...	...
Sakata	106 244[53]	50 293[53]	55 951[53]	603[54]	...	...	...	...
Sakura	172 739[53]	84 434[53]	88 305[53]	103.7[54]	...	...	...	...
Sanda	112 691[53]	54 184[53]	58 507[53]	210.3[54]	...	...	...	...
Sano	118 919[53]	58 507[53]	60 412[53]	356[54]	...	...	...	...
Sapporo	1 952 356[53]	910 614[53]	1 041 742[53]	1121.3[54]	...	...	...	...
Sasebo	255 439[53]	120 198[53]	135 241[53]	426.1[54]	...	...	...	...
Sayama	152 405[53]	76 580[53]	75 825[53]	49[54]	...	...	...	...
Sendai	1 082 159[53]	527 170[53]	554 989[53]	786.3[54]	...	...	...	...
Seto	129 046[53]	63 189[53]	65 857[53]	111.4[54]	...	...	...	...
Shimonoseki	268 517[53]	124 722[53]	143 795[53]	715.9[54]	...	...	...	...
Shizuoka	704 989[53]	343 338[53]	361 651[53]	1411.9[54]	...	...	...	...
Shunan	144 842[53]	69 819[53]	75 023[53]	656.3[54]	...	...	...	...
Soka	247 034[53]	125 225[53]	121 809[53]	27.5[54]	...	...	...	...
Suita	374 468[53]	180 669[53]	193 799[53]	36.1[54]	...	...	...	...
Suzuka	196 403[53]	97 500[53]	98 903[53]	194.5[54]	...	...	...	...
Tachikawa	176 295[53]	86 978[53]	89 317[53]	24.4[54]	...	...	...	...
Tajimi	110 441[53]	53 378[53]	57 063[53]	91.3[54]	...	...	...	...
Takamatsu	420 748[53]	205 049[53]	215 699[53]	375.4[54]	...	...	...	...
Takaoka	172 125[53]	82 802[53]	89 323[53]	209.6[54]	...	...	...	...
Takarazuka	224 903[53]	104 215[53]	120 688[53]	101.8[54]	...	...	...	...
Takasaki	370 884[53]	181 601[53]	189 283[53]	459.2[54]	...	...	...	...
Takatsuki	351 829[53]	168 057[53]	183 772[53]	105.3[54]	...	...	...	...
Tama	146 631[53]	71 762[53]	74 869[53]	21[54]	...	...	...	...
Tochigi	159 211[53]	78 209[53]	81 002[53]	331.5[54]	...	...	...	...
Toda	136 150[53]	69 674[53]	66 476[53]	18.2[54]	...	...	...	...
Tokai	111 944[53]	58 170[53]	53 774[53]	43.4[54]	...	...	...	...
Tokorozawa	340 386[53]	168 205[53]	172 181[53]	72.1[54]	...	...	...	...
Tokushima	258 554[53]	123 014[53]	135 540[53]	191.3[54]	...	...	...	...
TOKYO	9 272 740[55]	4 567 247[55]	4 705 493[55]	626.7[54]	...	...	...	...
Tomakomai	172 737[53]	84 605[53]	88 132[53]	561.6[54]	...	...	...	...
Tondabayashi	113 984[53]	53 693[53]	60 291[53]	39.7[54]	...	...	...	...
Toride	106 570[53]	52 489[53]	54 081[53]	69.9[54]	...	...	...	...
Tottori	193 717[53]	94 151[53]	99 566[53]	765.3[54]	...	...	...	...
Toyama	418 686[53]	203 427[53]	215 259[53]	1241.8[54]	...	...	...	...
Toyohashi	374 765[53]	187 801[53]	186 964[53]	261.9[54]	...	...	...	...
Toyokawa	182 436[53]	90 869[53]	91 567[53]	161.1[54]	...	...	...	...
Toyonaka	395 479[53]	187 319[53]	208 160[53]	36.4[54]	...	...	...	...
Toyota	422 542[53]	222 169[53]	200 373[53]	918.3[54]	...	...	...	...
Tsu	279 886[53]	135 718[53]	144 168[53]	711.1[54]	...	...	...	...
Tsuchiura	140 804[53]	70 101[53]	70 703[53]	122.9[54]	...	...	...	...
Tsukuba	226 963[53]	114 774[53]	112 189[53]	283.7[54]	...	...	...	...
Tsuruoka	129 652[53]	61 761[53]	67 891[53]	1311.5[54]	...	...	...	...
Tsuyama	103 746[53]	49 561[53]	54 185[53]	506.3[54]	...	...	...	...
Ube	169 429[53]	81 133[53]	88 296[53]	286.7[54]	...	...	...	...
Ueda	156 827[53]	76 776[53]	80 051[53]	552[54]	...	...	...	...
Uji	184 678[53]	89 014[53]	95 664[53]	67.5[54]	...	...	...	...
Urasoe	114 232[53]	55 471[53]	58 761[53]	19.5[54]	...	...	...	...
Urayasu	164 024[53]	81 057[53]	82 967[53]	17.3[54]	...	...	...	...
Uruma	118 898[53]	59 409[53]	59 489[53]	87[54]	...	...	...	...
Utsunomiya	518 594[53]	258 960[53]	259 634[53]	416.9[54]	...	...	...	...
Wakayama	364 154[53]	171 215[53]	192 939[53]	208.8[54]	...	...	...	...
Yachiyo	193 152[53]	95 224[53]	97 928[53]	51.4[54]	...	...	...	...
Yaizu	139 462[53]	68 168[53]	71 294[53]	70.3[54]	...	...	...	...
Yamagata	253 832[53]	121 575[53]	132 257[53]	381.3[54]	...	...	...	...
Yamaguchi	197 422[53]	94 245[53]	103 177[53]	1023.2[54]	...	...	...	...

8. Population of capital cities and cities of 100 000 or more inhabitants: latest available year, 1999 - 2018
Population des capitales et des villes de 100 000 habitants ou plus : dernière année disponible, 1999 - 2018 (continued - suite)

Continent, country or area, date, code[a] and city / Continent, pays ou zone, date, code[a] et ville	City proper - Ville proprement dite				Urban agglomeration - Agglomération urbaine			
	Population			Surface area - Superficie (km²)	Population			Surface area - Superficie (km²)
	Both sexes - Les deux sexes	Male - Masculin	Female - Féminin		Both sexes - Les deux sexes	Male - Masculin	Female - Féminin	
ASIA - ASIE								
Japan - Japon								
1 X 2015 (CDJC)								
Yamato	232 922[53]	116 714[53]	116 208[53]	27.1[54]				
Yao	268 800[53]	128 284[53]	140 516[53]	41.7[54]	...	...	...	...
Yatsushiro	127 472[53]	59 221[53]	68 251[53]	681.4[54]	...	...	...	...
Yokkaichi	311 031[53]	154 674[53]	156 357[53]	206.4[54]	...	...	...	...
Yokohama	3 724 844[53]	1 855 985[53]	1 868 859[53]	437.5[54]	...	...	...	...
Yokosuka	406 586[53]	202 775[53]	203 811[53]	100.8[54]	...	...	...	...
Yonago	149 313[53]	70 628[53]	78 685[53]	132.4[54]	...	...	...	...
Zama	128 737[53]	64 478[53]	64 259[53]	17.6[54]	...	...	...	...
Jordan - Jordanie								
31 XII 2018 (ESDF)								
AMMAN	3 728 346	1 989 375	1 738 971	...	...	...	...	...
Aqaba	160 265	92 006	68 259	...	...	...	...	...
Irbid	542 884	283 401	259 483	...	...	...	...	...
Madaba	113 771	60 689	53 082	...	...	...	...	...
Mafraq	114 490	59 900	54 590	...	...	...	...	...
Mukhayyam Al-Za'tary	122 152	60 816	61 336	...	...	...	...	...
Ramtha	168 134	87 719	80 415	...	...	...	...	...
Russiefa	510 391	272 134	238 257	...	...	...	...	...
Salt	107 874	56 263	51 611	...	...	...	...	...
Zarqa	685 941	358 769	327 172	...	...	...	...	...
Kazakhstan[56]								
1 VII 2018 (ESDF)								
Aktau	182 415	87 925	94 491	...	...	...	...	...
Aktobe	482 523	227 949	254 574	...	...	...	...	...
Almaty	1 828 325	834 930	993 395	...	...	...	...	...
ASTANA	1 054 481	506 784	547 697	...	...	...	...	...
Atirau	267 762	128 170	139 593	...	...	...	...	...
Ekibastuz	143 348	68 500	74 849	...	...	...	...	...
Karaganda	499 467	229 582	269 885	...	...	...	...	...
Koktshetau	148 053	68 613	79 441	...	...	...	...	...
Kustanai	241 342	108 612	132 730	...	...	...	...	...
Kyzylorda	271 069	132 160	138 909	...	...	...	...	...
Pavlodar	344 343	156 273	188 071	...	...	...	...	...
Petropavlovsk (Severo- Kazakhstanskaya oblast)	218 494	98 452	120 042	...	...	...	...	...
Rudni	129 507	60 838	68 669	...	...	...	...	...
Semipalatinsk	326 273	152 028	174 245	...	...	...	...	...
Shimkent	980 628	471 516	509 113	...	...	...	...	...
Taldykorgan	145 288	67 537	77 752	...	...	...	...	...
Taraz	356 808	167 923	188 885	...	...	...	...	...
Temirtau	186 110	86 834	99 276	...	...	...	...	...
Turkestan	163 143	81 801	81 342	...	...	...	...	...
Uralsk	301 330	139 702	161 629	...	...	...	...	...
Ust-Kamenogorsk	330 352	149 324	181 029	...	...	...	...	...
Kuwait - Koweït								
1 VII 2010 (ESDF)								
Farwanyiah	101 867	68 326	33 541		...	...	...	...
Hawalli	127 982	84 506	43 477	...	...	...	...	...
Jaleeb Al-Shuykh	219 629	180 786	38 843	...	...	...	...	...
Salmiya	177 009	103 119	73 890	...	...	...	...	...
South Kheetan	113 426	104 655	8 770	...	...	...	...	...
Kyrgyzstan - Kirghizstan[57]								
1 VII 2017 (ESDJ)								
BISHKEK	976 734	456 400	520 334	...	991 257	463 566	527 691	...
Osh	256 763	123 228	133 535	...	285 372	137 889	147 483	...
Lao People's Democratic Republic - République démocratique populaire lao[58]								
1 VII 2014 (ESDJ)								
VIENTIANE	...	...	...	...	828 494	414 217	414 277	...
Lebanon - Liban[59]								
1 X 2011 (SSDF)								
BEIRUT	...	...	...	...	363 033	179 737	183 296	...

Continent, country or area, date, code[a] and city / Continent, pays ou zone, date, code[a] et ville	City proper - Ville proprement dite				Urban agglomeration - Agglomération urbaine			
	Population			Surface area - Superficie (km²)	Population			Surface area - Superficie (km²)
	Both sexes - Les deux sexes	Male - Masculin	Female - Féminin		Both sexes - Les deux sexes	Male - Masculin	Female - Féminin	

ASIA - ASIE

Malaysia - Malaisie[60]
1 VII 2018 (ESDJ)

Alor Setar	134 611	...	...	...	...	...	...	
Bintulu Townland	138 829	...	...	...	...	...	...	
Georgetown	224 256	...	...	...	...	...	...	
Kajang dan Sungai Chua	113 053	...	...	...	...	...	...	
Klang	292 134	...	...	...	...	...	...	
Kota Kinabalu	248 893	...	...	...	...	...	...	
KUALA LUMPUR	1 824 323	...	...	...	...	...	...	
Kuala Terengganu	241 583	...	...	...	...	...	...	
Kuantan	412 022	...	...	...	...	...	...	
Kuching "Bandaraya Kuching Utara dan Selatan"	155 675	...	...	...	...	...	...	
Majlis Perbandaran Ipoh	483 299	...	...	...	...	...	...	
MB Johor Bahru (Johor Bahru)	510 788	...	...	...	...	...	...	
Miri Townland	153 663	...	...	...	...	...	...	
MP Kota Bharu	325 913	...	...	...	...	...	...	
Petaling Jaya	215 152	...	...	...	...	...	...	
Sandakan	199 648	...	...	...	...	...	...	
Selayang Baru	183 759	...	...	...	...	...	...	
Seremban	378 429	...	...	...	...	...	...	
Shah Alam	192 055	...	...	...	...	...	...	
Sibu "Majlis Perbandaran Sibu"	190 384	...	...	...	...	...	...	
Subang Jaya	208 353	...	...	...	...	...	...	
Sungai Petani	199 141	...	...	...	...	...	...	
Taiping	241 470	...	...	...	...	...	...	
Tawau	145 022	...	...	...	...	...	...	

Maldives
1 VII 2018 (ESDF)

| MALÉ | 210 248[61] | 129 334[61] | 80 914[61] | 2 | ... | ... | ... | |

Mongolia - Mongolie
1 VII 2018 (ESDF)

Bayan-Olgii	103 847	51 922	51 925	45.7	...	...	...	
Darkhan-Uul	104 999	51 621	53 378	3.3	...	...	...	
Hovsgol	132 763	65 985	66 778	100.6	...	...	...	
Orkhon	104 992	51 464	53 528	1	...	...	...	
Ovorhangay	116 105	57 824	58 281	62.9	...	...	...	
Selenge	110 504	55 974	54 530	41.2	...	...	...	
ULAANBAATAR	1 477 174	710 744	766 430	4.7	...	...	...	

Myanmar
29 III 2014 (CDFC)

Bago	...	...	...	...	491 434	235 529	255 905	
Dawei	...	...	...	...	125 605	60 044	65 561	
Hpa-an	...	...	...	...	421 575	203 910	217 665	
Loikaw	...	...	...	...	128 401	63 109	65 292	
Magway	...	...	...	...	289 247	135 103	154 144	
Mandalay	...	...	...	...	1 225 546	598 429	627 117	
Mawlamyine	...	...	...	...	289 388	139 026	150 362	
Monywa	...	...	...	...	372 095	171 951	200 144	
Myitkyina	...	...	...	...	306 949	148 485	158 464	
NAY PYI TAW[62]	...	...	...	...	1 160 242	565 155	595 087	
Pathein	...	...	...	...	287 071	137 663	149 408	
Sittway	...	...	...	...	147 899	70 470	77 429	
Taunggyi	...	...	...	...	381 639	185 954	195 685	
Yangon	...	...	...	...	5 211 431	2 466 918	2 744 513	

Nepal - Népal
22 VI 2011 (CDJC)

Bharatpur	143 836	71 175	72 661	...	...	...	...	
Bhimdutta	104 599	51 087	53 512	...	...	...	...	
Biratnagar	201 125	101 949	99 176	...	...	...	...	
Birgunj	135 904	72 580	63 324	...	...	...	...	
Butwal	118 462	58 808	59 654	...	...	...	...	
Dhangadhi	101 970	51 439	50 531	...	...	...	...	
Dharan	116 181	54 599	61 582	...	...	...	...	
KATHMANDU	975 453	511 841	463 612	...	...	...	...	

Continent, country or area, date, code[a] and city / Continent, pays ou zone, date, code[a] et ville	City proper - Ville proprement dite				Urban agglomeration - Agglomération urbaine			
	Population			Surface area - Superficie (km²)	Population			Surface area - Superficie (km²)
	Both sexes - Les deux sexes	Male - Masculin	Female - Féminin		Both sexes - Les deux sexes	Male - Masculin	Female - Féminin	
ASIA - ASIE								
Nepal - Népal								
22 VI 2011 (CDJC)								
Lalitpur	220 802	113 781	107 021	...	...	...	...	...
Pokhara	255 465	126 238	129 227	...	...	...	...	...
Oman								
1 VII 2018 (ESDF)								
Al Buraymi	107 679[63]	72 002[63]	35 677[63]	1223	...	...	...	...
Al Mudaybi	118 164[63]	73 633[63]	44 531[63]	12108	...	...	...	...
Al Rustaq	122 985[63]	70 142[63]	52 843[63]	2262	...	...	...	...
As Seeb	406 771[63]	249 253[63]	157 518[63]	489	...	...	...	...
As Suwayq	181 448[63]	110 185[63]	71 263[63]	1007	...	...	...	...
Barka	151 158[63]	95 623[63]	55 535[63]	698	...	...	...	...
Bawshar	372 405[63]	291 470[63]	80 935[63]	340	...	...	...	...
Ibri	171 555[63]	104 320[63]	67 235[63]	32697	...	...	...	...
Jaalan Bani Bu Ali	103 599[63]	64 215[63]	39 384[63]	2977	...	...	...	...
MUSCAT	315 443[63]	235 404[63]	80 039[63]	274	...	...	...	...
Mutrah	226 219[63]	170 038[63]	56 181[63]	90	...	...	...	...
Nizwa	127 180[63]	76 232[63]	50 948[63]	4489	...	...	...	...
Saham	150 416[63]	90 394[63]	60 022[63]	1495	...	...	...	...
Salalah	368 159[63]	263 737[63]	104 422[63]	4943	...	...	...	...
Sohar	237 632[63]	159 012[63]	78 620[63]	2025	...	...	...	...
Sur	121 061[63]	75 188[63]	45 873[63]	1908	...	...	...	...
Pakistan								
15 III 2017* (CDFC)								
Faisalabad (Lyallpur)	3 203 846	...	...	...	...	...	...	...
Gujranwala	2 027 001	...	...	...	...	...	...	...
Hyderabad	1 732 693	...	...	...	...	...	...	...
ISLAMABAD	1 014 825	...	...	...	...	...	...	...
Karachi	14 910 352	...	...	...	...	...	...	...
Lahore	11 126 285	...	...	...	...	...	...	...
Multan	1 871 843	...	...	...	...	...	...	...
Peshawar	1 970 042	...	...	...	...	...	...	...
Quetta	1 001 205	...	...	...	...	...	...	...
Rawalpindi	2 098 231	...	...	...	...	...	...	...
Philippines								
1 VIII 2015 (CDJC)								
Angeles	411 634	...	...	...	...	...	...	...
Bacolod	561 875	...	...	...	...	...	...	...
Baguio	345 366	...	...	...	...	...	...	...
Butuan	337 063	...	...	...	...	...	...	...
Cagayan de Oro	675 950	...	...	...	...	...	...	...
Caloocan	1 583 978	...	...	...	...	...	...	...
Cebu	922 611	...	...	...	...	...	...	...
Cotabato	299 438	...	...	...	...	...	...	...
Davao	1 632 991	...	...	...	...	...	...	...
General Santos	594 446	...	...	...	...	...	...	...
Iligan	342 618	...	...	...	...	...	...	...
Iloilo	447 992	...	...	...	...	...	...	...
Isabela	112 788	...	...	...	...	...	...	...
Lapu-Lapu	408 112	...	...	...	...	...	...	...
Las Piñas	588 894	...	...	...	...	...	...	...
Lucena City	266 248	...	...	...	...	...	...	...
Makati	582 602	...	...	...	...	...	...	...
Malabon	365 525	...	...	...	...	...	...	...
Mandaluyong	386 276	...	...	...	...	...	...	...
Mandaue	362 654	...	...	...	...	...	...	...
MANILA	1 780 148	...	...	...	...	...	...	...
Marikina	450 741	...	...	...	...	...	...	...
Muntinlupa	504 509	...	...	...	...	...	...	...
Navotas	249 463	...	...	...	...	...	...	...
Olongapo	233 040	...	...	...	...	...	...	...
Paranaque	665 822	...	...	...	...	...	...	...
Pasay	416 522	...	...	...	...	...	...	...
Pasig	755 300	...	...	...	...	...	...	...

8. Population of capital cities and cities of 100 000 or more inhabitants: latest available year, 1999 - 2018
Population des capitales et des villes de 100 000 habitants ou plus : dernière année disponible, 1999 - 2018 (continued - suite)

Continent, country or area, date, code[a] and city / Continent, pays ou zone, date, code[a] et ville	City proper - Ville proprement dite				Urban agglomeration - Agglomération urbaine			
	Population			Surface area - Superficie (km²)	Population			Surface area - Superficie (km²)
	Both sexes - Les deux sexes	Male - Masculin	Female - Féminin		Both sexes - Les deux sexes	Male - Masculin	Female - Féminin	
ASIA - ASIE								
Philippines								
1 VIII 2015 (CDJC)								
Puerto Princesa	255 116				...	...	...	...
Quezon City	2 936 116				...	...	...	...
San Juan	122 180				...	...	...	...
Tacloban	242 089	...			...	...	...	...
Taguig	804 915				...	...	...	...
Valenzuela	620 422				...	...	...	...
Zamboanga	861 799				...	...	...	...
Qatar								
20 IV 2015 (CDFC)								
Al-Khoor	202 031	181 000	21 031		...	...	...	...
Al-Rayyan	605 712	406 783	198 929		...	...	...	...
Al-Wakrah	299 037	248 103	50 934		...	...	...	...
DOHA	956 457	706 430	250 027		...	...	...	...
Republic of Korea - République de Corée								
1 VII 2017 (ESDJ)								
Busan (Pusan)	3 428 923	1 688 567	1 740 356	769.9[64]	...	...	...	...
Daegu (Taegu)	2 465 268	1 226 252	1 239 016	883.6[64]	...	...	...	...
Daejeon (Taejon)	1 531 256	768 766	762 490	539.3[64]	...	...	...	...
Gwangju (Kwangchu)	1 500 977	748 034	752 943	501.2[64]	...	...	...	...
Incheon	2 923 047	1 470 976	1 452 071	1062.6[64]	...	...	...	...
Jeju (Cheju)	634 161	320 174	313 987	1849.1[64]	...	...	...	...
Sejong	275 594	138 558	137 036	464.9[64]	...	...	...	...
SEOUL	9 776 305	4 785 234	4 991 071	605.2[64]	...	...	...	...
Ulsan	1 165 646	605 925	559 721	1060.8[64]	...	...	...	...
Saudi Arabia - Arabie saoudite								
27 IV 2010 (CDFC)								
Abha	236 157	136 118	100 039		...	...	...	...
Ad-Dammam	903 312	546 924	356 388		...	...	...	...
Al-Hawiyah	148 151	78 735	69 416		...	...	...	...
Al-Hufuf	660 788	361 672	299 116		...	...	...	...
Al-Jubayl	337 778	237 912	99 866		...	...	...	...
Al-Khubar	219 679	131 646	88 033		...	...	...	...
Al-Madinah	1 100 093	608 720	491 373		...	...	...	...
Al-Qatif	118 327	66 504	51 823		...	...	...	...
Al-Qurrayyat	116 162	63 412	52 750		...	...	...	...
Al-Seeh	234 607	131 391	103 216		...	...	...	...
Ar'ar	167 057	90 771	76 286		...	...	...	...
Ath-Thuqbah	238 066	149 691	88 375		...	...	...	...
At-Ta'if	579 970	306 682	273 288		...	...	...	...
Buraydah	467 410	268 604	198 806		...	...	...	...
Dhahran	120 521	68 746	51 775		...	...	...	...
Hafar al-Batin	271 642	148 396	123 246		...	...	...	...
Ha'il	310 897	170 882	140 015		...	...	...	...
Jiddah	3 430 697	1 996 716	1 433 981		...	...	...	...
Jizan	127 743	76 987	50 756		...	...	...	...
Khamis Mushayt	430 828	245 756	185 072		...	...	...	...
Makkah	1 534 731	861 737	672 994		...	...	...	...
Najran (Aba as-Suud)	298 288	166 143	132 145		...	...	...	...
RIYADH	5 188 286	3 059 287	2 128 999		...	...	...	...
Sekaka	150 257	84 881	65 376		...	...	...	...
Tabuk	512 629	281 672	230 957		...	...	...	...
Unayzah	152 895	86 385	66 510		...	...	...	...
Yanbu al-Bahr	233 236	140 897	92 339		...	...	...	...
Singapore - Singapour								
30 VI 2018 (ESDJ)								
SINGAPORE	5 638 676[65]	...	...	722.5[66]	...	...	...	...
Sri Lanka[67]								
17 VII 2001 (CDFC)								
COLOMBO	647 100	346 366	300 734		...	...	...	...
Dehiwala-Mount Lavinia	210 546	105 522	105 024		...	...	...	...
Kandy	109 343	54 288	55 055		...	...	...	...
Moratuwa	177 563	87 313	90 250		...	...	...	...

8. Population of capital cities and cities of 100 000 or more inhabitants: latest available year, 1999 - 2018
Population des capitales et des villes de 100 000 habitants ou plus : dernière année disponible, 1999 - 2018 (continued - suite)

Continent, country or area, date, code[a] and city / Continent, pays ou zone, date, code[a] et ville	City proper - Ville proprement dite				Urban agglomeration - Agglomération urbaine			
	Population			Surface area - Superficie (km²)	Population			Surface area - Superficie (km²)
	Both sexes - Les deux sexes	Male - Masculin	Female - Féminin		Both sexes - Les deux sexes	Male - Masculin	Female - Féminin	
ASIA - ASIE								
Sri Lanka[67]								
17 VII 2001 (CDFC)								
Negombo	121 701	60 947	60 754	...	...	...	...	...
Sri Jayawardanapura Kotte	116 366	59 993	56 373	...	...	...	...	...
State of Palestine - État de Palestine								
1 VII 2018 (ESDF)								
EAST JERUSALEM - JÉRUSALEM-EST[68]	278 552	...	...	...	...	...	...	...
Gaza	583 447	...	...	...	...	...	...	...
Hebron	199 319	...	...	...	...	...	...	...
Jabalya	170 646	...	...	...	...	...	...	...
Khan Yunis	202 682	...	...	...	...	...	...	...
Nablus	155 545	...	...	...	...	...	...	...
Rafah	169 851	...	...	...	...	...	...	...
Syrian Arab Republic - République arabe syrienne								
1 VII 2008 (ESDF)								
Aleppo	4 450 000	2 292 000	2 158 000	...	...	...	...	...
Al-Hasakeh	1 392 000	701 000	691 000	...	...	...	...	...
Al-Raqqah	865 000	456 000	409 000	...	...	...	...	...
Al-Sweida	349 000	171 000	178 000	...	...	...	...	...
DAMASCUS	1 680 000	857 000	823 000	...	...	...	...	...
Damasus rural	2 529 000	1 302 000	1 227 000	...	...	...	...	...
Deir El-Zor	1 111 000	563 000	548 000	...	...	...	...	...
Dra'a	930 000	472 000	458 000	...	...	...	...	...
Hama	1 508 000	768 000	740 000	...	...	...	...	...
Homs	1 667 000	852 000	815 000	...	...	...	...	...
Idleb	1 376 000	704 000	672 000	...	...	...	...	...
Lattakia	951 000	480 000	471 000	...	...	...	...	...
Tartous	756 000	383 000	373 000	...	...	...	...	...
Tajikistan - Tadjikistan								
1 VII 2017 (ESDF)								
DUSHANBE	823 787	430 622	393 165	...	...	...	...	...
Khujand	176 710	...	...	...	...	...	...	...
Thailand - Thaïlande								
1 IX 2010 (CDJC)								
Ang Thong	...	...	...	...	109 207	51 540	57 667	...
BANGKOK	...	...	...	...	8 305 218	4 032 586	4 272 632	1569
Buri Ram	...	...	...	...	375 999	181 546	194 453	...
Chachoengsao	...	...	...	...	206 250	101 475	104 775	...
Chai Nat	...	...	...	...	205 456	97 373	108 083	...
Chaiyaphum	...	...	...	...	205 112	99 280	105 832	...
Chanthaburi	...	...	...	...	243 126	118 221	124 905	...
Chiang Mai	...	...	...	...	967 020	466 145	500 875	...
Chiang Rai	...	...	...	...	455 732	220 391	235 341	...
Chon Buri	...	...	...	...	1 158 989	575 208	583 781	...
Chumphon	...	...	...	...	147 912	75 339	72 573	...
Kalasin	...	...	...	...	428 940	208 863	220 077	...
Kamphaeng Phet	...	...	...	...	211 774	101 456	110 318	...
Kanchanaburi	...	...	...	...	292 521	143 986	148 535	...
Khon Kaen	...	...	...	...	703 123	339 011	364 112	...
Lampang	...	...	...	...	372 463	180 360	192 103	...
Lamphun	...	...	...	...	262 832	126 662	136 170	...
Loei	...	...	...	...	164 180	81 302	82 878	...
Lop Buri	...	...	...	...	235 827	118 964	116 863	...
Maha Sarakham	...	...	...	...	153 740	72 143	81 597	...
Mukdahan	...	...	...	...	180 600	89 190	91 410	...
Nakhon Pathom	...	...	...	...	339 736	166 150	173 586	...
Nakhon Phanom	...	...	...	...	123 720	59 683	64 037	...
Nakhon Ratchasima	...	...	...	...	653 075	316 329	336 746	...
Nakhon Sawan	...	...	...	...	225 903	107 298	118 605	...
Nakhon Si Thammarat	...	...	...	...	265 606	127 460	138 146	...
Narathiwat	...	...	...	...	133 718	64 616	69 102	...
Nong Bua Lam Phu	...	...	...	...	203 142	98 164	104 978	...
Nong Khai	...	...	...	...	232 798	113 989	118 809	...
Nonthaburi	...	...	...	...	797 739	383 826	413 913	...
Pathum Thani	...	...	...	...	757 175	358 679	398 496	...

Continent, country or area, date, code[a] and city / Continent, pays ou zone, date, code[a] et ville	City proper - Ville proprement dite				Urban agglomeration - Agglomération urbaine			
	Population			Surface area - Superficie (km²)	Population			Surface area - Superficie (km²)
	Both sexes - Les deux sexes	Male - Masculin	Female - Féminin		Both sexes - Les deux sexes	Male - Masculin	Female - Féminin	
ASIA - ASIE								
Thailand - Thaïlande								
1 IX 2010 (CDJC)								
Pattani	...	...	...	...	104 617	51 305	53 312	...
Phatthalung	...	...	...	...	244 783	117 039	127 744	...
Phayao	...	...	...	...	221 062	106 657	114 405	...
Phetchabun	...	...	...	...	172 275	82 257	90 018	...
Phetchaburi	...	...	...	...	175 675	83 735	91 940	...
Phichit	...	...	...	...	131 283	62 446	68 837	...
Phitsanulok	...	...	...	...	201 466	93 098	108 368	...
Phra Nakhon Si Ayutthaya	...	...	...	...	365 736	173 280	192 456	...
Phrae	...	...	...	...	156 099	75 175	80 924	...
Phuket	...	...	...	...	358 159	175 144	183 015	...
Prachuap Khiri Khan	...	...	...	...	177 011	87 525	89 486	...
Ranong	...	...	...	...	123 596	62 090	61 506	...
Ratchaburi	...	...	...	...	317 886	149 460	168 426	...
Rayong	...	...	...	...	445 939	224 068	221 871	...
Roi Et	...	...	...	...	365 113	176 648	188 465	...
Sa Kaeo	...	...	...	...	135 536	66 447	69 089	...
Sakon Nakhon	...	...	...	...	315 788	153 785	162 003	...
Samut Prakan	...	...	...	...	1 082 993	527 487	555 506	...
Samut Sakhon	...	...	...	...	479 186	237 778	241 408	...
Saraburi	...	...	...	...	239 281	114 885	124 396	...
Si Sa Ket	...	...	...	...	160 508	77 363	83 145	...
Songkhla	...	...	...	...	800 970	382 828	418 142	...
Sukhothai	...	...	...	...	166 782	79 139	87 643	...
Suphan Buri	...	...	...	...	228 496	108 666	119 830	...
Surat Thani	...	...	...	...	410 984	198 909	212 075	...
Surin	...	...	...	...	153 159	73 082	80 077	...
Tak	...	...	...	...	146 769	70 754	76 015	...
Trat	...	...	...	...	110 398	52 309	58 089	...
Ubon Ratchathani	...	...	...	...	411 954	198 655	213 299	...
Udon Thani	...	...	...	...	483 057	232 326	250 731	...
Uttaradit	...	...	...	...	151 047	72 244	78 803	...
Yala	...	...	...	...	119 744	58 041	61 703	...
Yasothon	...	...	...	...	127 173	63 885	63 288	...
Timor-Leste[69]								
11 VII 2015 (CDFC)								
DILI	222 323	114 792	107 531	...	...	...	...	...
Turkey - Turquie[70]								
31 XII 2017 (ESDJ)								
Adana	...	...	...	...	2 216 475	1 108 939	1 107 536	...
Adıyaman	251 893	126 353	125 540	...	...	...	...	...
Afyonkarahisar	229 810	113 175	116 635	...	...	...	...	...
Ağrı	117 431	60 409	57 022	...	...	...	...	...
Aksaray	220 459	109 444	111 015	...	...	...	...	...
Amasya	109 240	55 196	54 044	...	...	...	...	...
ANKARA	...	...	...	...	5 445 026	2 702 492	2 742 534	...
Antalya	...	...	...	...	2 364 396	1 192 582	1 171 814	...
Aydın	...	...	...	...	1 080 839	539 726	541 113	...
Balıkesir	...	...	...	...	1 204 824	602 275	602 549	...
Batman	411 251	206 665	204 586	...	...	...	...	...
Bingöl	117 014	58 948	58 066	...	...	...	...	...
Bolu	168 187	83 068	85 119	...	...	...	...	...
Bursa	...	...	...	...	2 936 803	1 470 341	1 466 462	...
Çanakkale	132 854	66 518	66 336	...	...	...	...	...
Cizre	118 953	60 759	58 194	...	...	...	...	...
Çorum	265 171	131 284	133 887	...	...	...	...	...
Denizli	...	...	...	...	1 018 735	507 543	511 192	...
Diyarbakir	...	...	...	...	1 699 901	857 070	842 831	...
Düzce	169 111	83 496	85 615	...	...	...	...	...
Edirne	166 494	83 120	83 374	...	...	...	...	...
Elazığ	381 794	190 069	191 725	...	...	...	...	...
Ereğli	118 030	58 193	59 837	...	...	...	...	...
Erzurum	...	...	...	...	760 476	379 227	381 249	...
Eskişehir	...	...	...	...	860 620	429 078	431 542	...

Continent, country or area, date, code[a] and city Continent, pays ou zone, date, code[a] et ville	City proper - Ville proprement dite				Urban agglomeration - Agglomération urbaine			
	Population			Surface area - Superficie (km²)	Population			Surface area - Superficie (km²)
	Both sexes - Les deux sexes	Male - Masculin	Female - Féminin		Both sexes - Les deux sexes	Male - Masculin	Female - Féminin	
ASIA - ASIE								
Turkey - Turquie[70]								
31 XII 2017 (ESDJ)								
Gaziantep	...	...	...	...	2 005 515	1 012 992	992 523	...
Giresun	112 415	55 186	57 229	...	...	...	...	...
Hatay	...	...	...	...	1 575 226	790 209	785 017	...
Isparta	230 011	117 159	112 852	...	...	...	...	...
İstanbul	...	...	...	...	15 029 231	7 529 491	7 499 740	...
İzmir	...	...	...	...	4 279 677	2 133 548	2 146 129	...
Kahramanmaraş	...	...	...	...	1 127 623	572 111	555 512	...
Karabük	119 548	59 053	60 495	...	...	...	...	...
Karaman	158 566	78 856	79 710	...	...	...	...	...
Kastamonu	116 737	57 250	59 487	...	...	...	...	...
Kayseri	...	...	...	...	1 376 722	689 595	687 127	...
Kırıkkale	194 828	96 518	98 310	...	...	...	...	...
Kırşehir	137 290	68 719	68 571	...	...	...	...	...
Kocaeli	...	...	...	...	1 883 270	953 145	930 125	...
Konya	...	...	...	...	2 180 149	1 081 718	1 098 431	...
Kütahya	244 544	121 244	123 300	...	...	...	...	...
Lüleburgaz	117 075	59 396	57 679	...	...	...	...	...
Malatya	...	...	...	...	786 676	391 869	394 807	...
Manisa	...	...	...	...	1 413 041	710 378	702 663	...
Mardin	...	...	...	...	809 719	406 320	403 399	...
Mersin	...	...	...	...	1 793 931	895 374	898 557	...
Muğla	...	...	...	...	938 751	478 950	459 801	...
Nevşehir	106 738	51 806	54 932	...	...	...	...	...
Niğde	141 010	72 387	68 623	...	...	...	...	...
Ordu	...	...	...	...	742 341	371 061	371 280	...
Osmaniye	233 242	116 828	116 414	...	...	...	...	...
Rize	117 664	57 501	60 163	...	...	...	...	...
Sakarya	...	...	...	...	990 214	496 488	493 726	...
Samsun	...	...	...	...	1 312 990	649 524	663 466	...
Şanlıurfa	...	...	...	...	1 985 753	999 299	986 454	...
Siirt	148 906	77 206	71 700	...	...	...	...	...
Sivas	344 185	171 546	172 639	...	...	...	...	...
Tekirdağ	...	...	...	...	1 005 463	516 496	488 967	...
Tokat	152 314	75 263	77 051	...	...	...	...	...
Trabzon	...	...	...	...	786 326	388 713	397 613	...
Uşak	211 187	106 915	104 272	...	...	...	...	...
Van	...	...	...	...	1 106 891	563 824	543 067	...
Yalova	119 605	59 017	60 588	...	...	...	...	...
Zonguldak	108 424	52 800	55 624	...	...	...	...	...
United Arab Emirates - Émirats arabes unis								
1 VII 2002 (ESDF)								
ABU DHABI	527 000	359 000	168 000	...	...	...	...	...
Ajman	205 000	122 000	83 000	...	...	...	...	...
Al-Ayn	328 000	215 000	113 000	...	...	...	...	...
Al-Sharjah	488 000	317 000	171 000	...	...	...	...	...
Dubai	1 089 000	759 000	330 000	...	...	...	...	...
Uzbekistan - Ouzbékistan[56]								
1 I 2018 (ESDJ)								
Almalyk	...	...	...	...	127 468	61 758	65 710	...
Andizhan	427 447	214 310	213 137	...	...	...	...	...
Angren	...	...	...	...	183 563	91 401	92 162	...
Bukhara	276 433	137 022	139 411	...	...	...	...	...
Chirchik	...	...	...	...	154 584	75 937	78 647	...
Fergana	278 510	137 888	140 622	...	...	...	...	...
Jizzax	171 734	85 882	85 852	...	...	...	...	...
Karshi	267 561	133 496	134 065	...	...	...	...	...
Kokand	...	...	...	...	245 509	119 985	125 524	...
Margilan	...	...	...	...	201 669	101 337	100 332	...
Namangan	600 209	308 226	291 983	...	...	...	...	...
Navoi	135 548	68 774	66 774	...	...	...	...	...
Nukus	310 945	153 178	157 767	...	...	...	...	...
Samarkand	529 633	255 987	273 646	...	...	...	...	...
Shahrisabz	...	...	...	...	134 531	68 090	66 441	...

8. Population of capital cities and cities of 100 000 or more inhabitants: latest available year, 1999 - 2018
Population des capitales et des villes de 100 000 habitants ou plus : dernière année disponible, 1999 - 2018 (continued - suite)

Continent, country or area, date, code[a] and city / Continent, pays ou zone, date, code[a] et ville	City proper - Ville proprement dite				Urban agglomeration - Agglomération urbaine			
	Population			Surface area - Superficie (km²)	Population			Surface area - Superficie (km²)
	Both sexes - Les deux sexes	Male - Masculin	Female - Féminin		Both sexes - Les deux sexes	Male - Masculin	Female - Féminin	
ASIA - ASIE								
Uzbekistan - Ouzbékistan[56]								
1 I 2018 (ESDJ)								
TASHKENT	2 464 933	1 202 495	1 262 438	...	...	...	...	...
Termez	143 790	70 634	73 156	...	...	...	...	...
Urgentch	140 180	70 541	69 639	...	...	...	...	...
Yemen - Yémen								
1 VII 2009* (ESDF)								
Adan	*684 322*	...	...	...	*684 322*	...	...	...
SANA'A	*1 976 286*	...	...	...	*2 022 867*	...	...	...
EUROPE								
Åland Islands - Îles d'Åland								
1 VII 2018 (ESDJ)								
MARIEHAMN	11 709[27]	5 621[27]	6 089[27]	12	...	...	...	...
Albania - Albanie								
1 X 2011 (CDJC)								
Durrës	113 249	56 511	56 738	...	...	...	...	...
TIRANA	418 495	203 239	215 256	...	...	...	...	...
Andorra - Andorre[27]								
1 VII 2011 (ESDJ)								
ANDORRA LA VELLA	...	...	...	...	22 205	11 056	11 149	...
Austria - Autriche								
1 I 2018 (ESDJ)								
Graz	286 292	140 952	145 340	...	...	...	...	...
Innsbruck	132 493	64 794	67 699	...	...	...	...	...
Klagenfurt	100 369	47 528	52 841	...	...	...	...	...
Linz	204 846	99 289	105 557	...	...	...	...	...
Salzburg	153 377	73 567	79 810	...	...	...	...	...
WIEN	1 888 776	920 765	968 011	...	...	...	...	...
Belarus - Bélarus								
1 I 2018 (ESDJ)								
Baranovichi	179 166	81 256	97 910	85	...	...	...	...
Bobruisk	217 546	101 477	116 069	96	...	...	...	...
Borisov	143 051	67 061	75 990	46	...	...	...	...
Brest	347 576	160 790	186 786	146	...	...	...	...
Gomel	...	...	...	...	535 693	244 234	291 459	140
Grodno	370 919	168 336	202 583	142	...	...	...	...
Lida	101 616	47 496	54 120	...	...	...	...	...
MINSK	1 982 444	902 211	1 080 233	348	...	...	...	...
Mogilev	381 353	175 151	206 202	119	...	...	...	...
Mozir	111 733	52 974	58 759	44	...	...	...	...
Novopolotsk	...	...	...	...	107 479	51 228	56 251	48
Orsha	115 052	52 982	62 070	...	...	...	...	...
Pinsk	137 961	63 424	74 537	47	...	...	...	...
Soligorsk	106 627	49 882	56 745	15	...	...	...	...
Vitebsk	...	...	...	...	377 932	167 506	210 426	145
Belgium - Belgique								
1 I 2011 (CDJC)								
Anderlecht	108 940	53 707	55 233	18	...	...	...	...
Antwerpen (Anvers)	498 473	247 192	251 281	205	718 730	354 576	364 154	394
Brugge	117 260	56 952	60 308	138	117 260	56 952	60 308	138
BRUXELLES (BRUSSEL)	174 383	90 317	84 066	33	1 550 299[71]	754 208[71]	796 091[71]	573[71]
Charleroi	204 150	99 221	104 929	102	291 806	141 106	150 700	199
Gent (Gand)	248 358	122 457	125 901	156	280 151	137 980	142 171	207
Liège (Luik)	195 965	96 509	99 456	69	491 767	238 134	253 633	367
Namur	110 175	53 019	57 156	176	110 175	53 019	57 156	176
Schaerbeek	127 525	63 020	64 505	8	...	...	...	...
Bulgaria - Bulgarie								
1 I 2018 (ESDJ)								
Burgas	202 694	96 488	106 206	...	...	...	...	...
Plovdiv	345 213	164 094	181 119	...	...	...	...	...
Ruse	144 125	69 966	74 159	...	...	...	...	...
SOFIA	1 238 438	592 089	646 349	...	...	...	...	...

8. Population of capital cities and cities of 100 000 or more inhabitants: latest available year, 1999 - 2018
Population des capitales et des villes de 100 000 habitants ou plus : dernière année disponible, 1999 - 2018 (continued - suite)

Continent, country or area, date, code[a] and city / Continent, pays ou zone, date, code[a] et ville	City proper - Ville proprement dite				Urban agglomeration - Agglomération urbaine			
	Population			Surface area - Superficie (km²)	Population			Surface area - Superficie (km²)
	Both sexes - Les deux sexes	Male - Masculin	Female - Féminin		Both sexes - Les deux sexes	Male - Masculin	Female - Féminin	
EUROPE								
Bulgaria - Bulgarie								
1 I 2018 (ESDJ)								
Stara Zagora	136 307	65 319	70 988	...	...	...	...	...
Varna	335 854	162 365	173 489	...	...	...	...	...
Croatia - Croatie								
1 IV 2011 (CDJC)								
Osijek	108 048	50 357	57 691	174	...	...	...	...
Rijeka	128 624	60 951	67 673	43	...	...	...	...
Split	178 102	84 477	93 625	79	...	...	...	...
ZAGREB	790 017	369 339	420 678	641	...	...	...	...
Czechia - Tchéquie								
1 I 2018 (ESDJ)								
Brno	379 527	183 300	196 227	225.7[33]	...	...	...	...
Liberec	103 979	50 329	53 650	105.1[33]	...	...	...	...
Olomouc	100 494	47 615	52 879	100.9[33]	...	...	...	...
Ostrava	290 450	140 768	149 682	204.8[33]	...	...	...	...
Plzen	170 936	82 988	87 948	133.3[33]	...	...	...	...
PRAHA	1 294 513	629 550	664 963	485.2[33]	...	...	...	...
Denmark - Danemark[72]								
1 VII 2018 (ESDJ)								
Ålborg	213 271[27]	107 482[27]	105 789[27]	1137.4	...	...	...	...
Århus	341 497[27]	168 169[27]	173 328[27]	467.9	...	...	...	...
Esbjerg	116 061[27]	58 200[27]	57 861[27]	795.1	...	...	...	...
Frederiksberg	103 914[27]	49 144[27]	54 770[27]	8.7	...	...	...	...
KOBENHAVN	616 098[27]	304 652[27]	311 446[27]	86.6	...	...	...	...
Odense	202 663[27]	100 245[27]	102 418[27]	305.6	...	...	...	...
Vejle	114 464[27]	57 269[27]	57 195[27]	1058.4	...	...	...	...
Estonia - Estonie								
1 I 2018 (ESDJ)								
TALLINN	430 805	194 273	236 532	...	...	...	...	...
Faeroe Islands - Îles Féroé								
1 VII 2018 (ESDJ)								
TÓRSHAVN	13 262	6 621	6 641	6[73]	19 600	9 873	9 727	15[74]
Finland - Finlande[75]								
1 VII 2017 (ESDJ)								
Espoo	276 814[27]	137 395[27]	139 419[27]	312	...	...	...	...
HELSINKI	639 227[27]	303 124[27]	336 103[27]	214	...	...	...	...
Jyvaskyla	139 519[27]	68 614[27]	70 906[27]	1171	...	...	...	...
Kuopio	117 975[27]	57 462[27]	60 513[27]	3241	...	...	...	...
Lahti	119 513[27]	57 588[27]	61 925[27]	459	...	...	...	...
Oulu	201 168[27]	100 381[27]	100 788[27]	2971	...	...	...	...
Tampere	230 064[27]	111 579[27]	118 485[27]	525	...	...	...	...
Turku	188 637[27]	90 017[27]	98 620[27]	246	...	...	...	...
Vantaa	221 184[27]	109 521[27]	111 664[27]	238	...	...	...	...
France								
1 I 2015 (CDJC)								
Aix-en-Provence[76]	142 668	67 070	75 598	...	...	...	...	...
Amiens	132 874[76]	63 049[76]	69 825[76]	...	162 637	77 405	85 232	...
Angers	151 520[76]	70 013[76]	81 507[76]	...	225 978	105 860	120 118	...
Argenteuil[76]	110 388	54 149	56 239	...	...	...	...	...
Besançon	116 676[76]	54 726[76]	61 950[76]	...	135 448	63 794	71 654	...
Bordeaux	249 712[76]	117 403[76]	132 309[76]	...	904 359	431 444	472 915	...
Boulogne-Billancourt[76]	117 931	55 415	62 516	...	...	...	...	...
Brest	139 163[76]	68 320[76]	70 843[76]	...	200 530	98 235	102 295	...
Caen	106 260[76]	50 047[76]	56 213[76]	...	198 639	94 037	104 602	...
Clermont-Ferrand	141 398[76]	67 196[76]	74 202[76]	...	265 892	125 811	140 081	...
Dijon	155 114[76]	72 985[76]	82 129[76]	...	243 244	114 786	128 458	...
Grenoble	160 649[76]	77 519[76]	83 130[76]	...	512 591	249 141	263 450	...
Le Havre	172 366[76]	81 082[76]	91 284[76]	...	237 578	112 535	125 043	...
Le Mans	143 325[76]	66 870[76]	76 455[76]	...	210 018	99 384	110 634	...
Lille	232 741[76]	112 619[76]	120 122[76]	...	1 039 397	498 466	540 931	...
Limoges	133 627[76]	62 060[76]	71 567[76]	...	183 347	85 799	97 548	...
Lyon	513 275[76]	240 623[76]	272 652[76]	...	1 639 558	785 665	853 893	...

8. Population of capital cities and cities of 100 000 or more inhabitants: latest available year, 1999 - 2018
Population des capitales et des villes de 100 000 habitants ou plus : dernière année disponible, 1999 - 2018 (continued - suite)

Continent, country or area, date, code[a] and city / Continent, pays ou zone, date, code[a] et ville	City proper - Ville proprement dite				Urban agglomeration - Agglomération urbaine			
	Population			Surface area - Superficie (km²)	Population			Surface area - Superficie (km²)
	Both sexes - Les deux sexes	Male - Masculin	Female - Féminin		Both sexes - Les deux sexes	Male - Masculin	Female - Féminin	
EUROPE								
France								
1 I 2015 (CDJC)								
Marseille	861 635[76]	408 487[76]	453 148[76]	...	1 585 498[77]	756 867[77]	828 631[77]	...
Metz	117 492[76]	57 390[76]	60 102[76]	...	285 268	138 242	147 026	...
Montpellier	277 639[76]	130 109[76]	147 530[76]	...	428 909	203 366	225 543	...
Montreuil[76]	106 691	52 788	53 903	...	...	...	...	...
Mulhouse	110 370[76]	54 011[76]	56 359[76]	...	246 511	119 610	126 901	...
Nancy	105 162[76]	50 411[76]	54 751[76]	...	285 659	136 682	148 977	...
Nantes	303 382[76]	144 654[76]	158 728[76]	...	633 690	303 454	330 236	...
Nice	342 522[76]	160 123[76]	182 399[76]	...	943 354	445 620	497 734	...
Nîmes	150 672[76]	71 659[76]	79 013[76]	...	184 750	87 991	96 759	...
Orléans	114 644[76]	54 387[76]	60 257[76]	...	278 131	134 130	144 001	...
PARIS	2 206 488[76]	1 038 493[76]	1 167 995[76]	...	10 706 072[78]	5 158 244[78]	5 547 828[78]	...
Perpignan	121 934[76]	57 150[76]	64 784[76]	...	200 971	94 613	106 358	...
Reims	184 076[76]	86 890[76]	97 186[76]	...	212 949	100 629	112 320	...
Rennes	215 366[76]	101 905[76]	113 461[76]	...	330 871	158 754	172 117	...
Rouen	110 169[76]	52 690[76]	57 479[76]	...	467 133	221 315	245 818	...
Saint-Denis[76]	111 103	56 501	54 602	...	...	...	...	...
Saint-Étienne	171 057[76]	81 077[76]	89 980[76]	...	373 130	177 568	195 562	...
Strasbourg	277 270[76]	131 692[76]	145 578[76]	...	461 101	219 722	241 379	...
Toulon	167 479[76]	79 436[76]	88 043[76]	...	569 793	271 171	298 622	...
Toulouse	471 941[76]	228 540[76]	243 401[76]	...	948 433	461 054	487 379	...
Tours	136 252[76]	62 843[76]	73 409[76]	...	353 042	166 391	186 651	...
Villeurbanne[76]	148 665	72 291	76 374	...	...	...	...	...
Germany - Allemagne								
1 I 2018 (ESDJ)								
Aachen	246 272[3]	128 064[3]	118 208[3]	161	...	...	...	...
Augsburg	292 851[3]	143 867[3]	148 984[3]	147	...	...	...	...
Bergisch Gladbach	111 627[3]	53 477[3]	58 150[3]	83	...	...	...	...
BERLIN	3 613 495[3]	1 776 267[3]	1 837 228[3]	891	...	...	...	...
Bielefeld	332 552[3]	160 267[3]	172 285[3]	259	...	...	...	...
Bochum	365 529[3]	178 122[3]	187 407[3]	146	...	...	...	...
Bonn	325 490[3]	155 605[3]	169 885[3]	141	...	...	...	...
Bottrop	117 364[3]	57 116[3]	60 248[3]	101	...	...	...	...
Braunschweig	248 023[3]	122 721[3]	125 302[3]	193	...	...	...	...
Bremen	568 006[3]	280 484[3]	287 522[3]	318	...	...	...	...
Bremerhaven	113 026[3]	56 181[3]	56 845[3]	102	...	...	...	...
Chemnitz	246 855[3]	121 771[3]	125 084[3]	221	...	...	...	...
Cottbus	101 036[3]	49 792[3]	51 244[3]	166	...	...	...	...
Darmstadt	158 254[3]	80 565[3]	77 689[3]	122	...	...	...	...
Dortmund	586 600[3]	288 076[3]	298 524[3]	281	...	...	...	...
Dresden	551 072[3]	274 513[3]	276 559[3]	328	...	...	...	...
Duisburg	498 110[3]	246 183[3]	251 927[3]	233	...	...	...	...
Düsseldorf	617 280[3]	298 330[3]	318 950[3]	217	...	...	...	...
Erfurt	212 988[3]	103 683[3]	109 305[3]	270	...	...	...	...
Erlangen	110 998[3]	55 200[3]	55 798[3]	77	...	...	...	...
Essen	583 393[3]	283 206[3]	300 187[3]	210	...	...	...	...
Frankfurt am Main	746 878[3]	368 721[3]	378 157[3]	248	...	...	...	...
Freiburg im Breisgau	229 636[3]	109 537[3]	120 099[3]	153	...	...	...	...
Fürth	126 526[3]	61 962[3]	64 564[3]	63	...	...	...	...
Gelsenkirchen	260 305[3]	129 548[3]	130 757[3]	105	...	...	...	...
Göttingen	119 529[3]	58 238[3]	61 291[3]	117	...	...	...	...
Hagen	187 730[3]	91 443[3]	96 287[3]	160	...	...	...	...
Halle (Saale)	239 173[3]	115 771[3]	123 402[3]	135	...	...	...	...
Hamburg	1 830 584[3]	897 207[3]	933 377[3]	755	...	...	...	...
Hamm	179 185[3]	88 012[3]	91 173[3]	226	...	...	...	...
Hannover	535 061[3]	261 192[3]	273 869[3]	204	...	...	...	...
Heidelberg	160 601[3]	77 319[3]	83 282[3]	109	...	...	...	...
Heilbronn	125 113[3]	63 068[3]	62 045[3]	100	...	...	...	...
Herne	156 490[3]	76 665[3]	79 825[3]	51	...	...	...	...
Hildesheim	101 744[3]	48 413[3]	53 331[3]	92	...	...	...	...
Ingolstadt	135 244[3]	68 292[3]	66 952[3]	133	...	...	...	...

8. Population of capital cities and cities of 100 000 or more inhabitants: latest available year, 1999 - 2018
Population des capitales et des villes de 100 000 habitants ou plus : dernière année disponible, 1999 - 2018 (continued - suite)

Continent, country or area, date, code[a] and city / Continent, pays ou zone, date, code[a] et ville	City proper - Ville proprement dite				Urban agglomeration - Agglomération urbaine			
	Population			Surface area - Superficie (km²)	Population			Surface area - Superficie (km²)
	Both sexes - Les deux sexes	Male - Masculin	Female - Féminin		Both sexes - Les deux sexes	Male - Masculin	Female - Féminin	
EUROPE								
Germany - Allemagne								
1 I 2018 (ESDJ)								
Jena	111 099[3]	55 472[3]	55 627[3]	115	...	...	...	...
Karlsruhe	311 919[3]	159 659[3]	152 260[3]	173	...	...	...	...
Kassel	200 736[3]	98 371[3]	102 365[3]	107	...	...	...	...
Kiel	247 943[3]	120 809[3]	127 134[3]	119	...	...	...	...
Koblenz	113 844[3]	55 372[3]	58 472[3]	105	...	...	...	...
Köln	1 080 394[3]	526 965[3]	553 429[3]	405	...	...	...	...
Krefeld	226 699[3]	110 467[3]	116 232[3]	138	...	...	...	...
Leipzig	581 980[3]	285 777[3]	296 203[3]	298	...	...	...	...
Leverkusen	163 577[3]	79 675[3]	83 902[3]	79	...	...	...	...
Lübeck	216 318[3]	103 884[3]	112 434[3]	214	...	...	...	...
Ludwigshafen am Rhein	168 497[3]	83 893[3]	84 604[3]	77	...	...	...	...
Magdeburg	238 478[3]	117 677[3]	120 801[3]	201	...	...	...	...
Mainz	215 110[3]	104 564[3]	110 546[3]	98	...	...	...	...
Mannheim	307 997[3]	153 663[3]	154 334[3]	145	...	...	...	...
Moers	103 949[3]	50 468[3]	53 481[3]	68	...	...	...	...
Mönchengladbach	262 188[3]	128 925[3]	133 263[3]	170	...	...	...	...
Mülheim an der Ruhr	171 265[3]	82 616[3]	88 649[3]	91	...	...	...	...
München	1 456 039[3]	708 422[3]	747 617[3]	311	...	...	...	...
Münster (Westf.)	313 559[3]	150 360[3]	163 199[3]	303	...	...	...	...
Neuss	153 810[3]	74 499[3]	79 311[3]	100	...	...	...	...
Nürnberg	515 201[3]	250 702[3]	264 499[3]	186	...	...	...	...
Oberhausen	211 422[3]	103 851[3]	107 571[3]	77	...	...	...	...
Offenbach am Main	126 658[3]	62 566[3]	64 092[3]	45	...	...	...	...
Oldenburg (Oldenburg)	167 081[3]	79 833[3]	87 248[3]	103	...	...	...	...
Osnabrück	164 374[3]	79 505[3]	84 869[3]	120	...	...	...	...
Paderborn	149 075[3]	74 117[3]	74 958[3]	180	...	...	...	...
Pforzheim	124 289[3]	61 032[3]	63 257[3]	98	...	...	...	...
Potsdam	175 710[3]	85 046[3]	90 664[3]	188	...	...	...	...
Recklinghausen	113 360[3]	55 218[3]	58 142[3]	67	...	...	...	...
Regensburg	150 894[3]	73 121[3]	77 773[3]	81	...	...	...	...
Remscheid	110 584[3]	54 482[3]	56 102[3]	75	...	...	...	...
Reutlingen	115 762[3]	57 266[3]	58 496[3]	87	...	...	...	...
Rostock	208 409[3]	102 700[3]	105 709[3]	181	...	...	...	...
Saarbrücken	180 966[3]	89 755[3]	91 211[3]	168	...	...	...	...
Salzgitter	104 548[3]	51 990[3]	52 558[3]	224	...	...	...	...
Siegen	102 337[3]	50 074[3]	52 263[3]	115	...	...	...	...
Solingen	158 803[3]	77 157[3]	81 646[3]	90	...	...	...	...
Stuttgart	632 743[3]	316 126[3]	316 617[3]	207	...	...	...	...
Trier	110 013[3]	54 181[3]	55 832[3]	117	...	...	...	...
Ulm	125 596[3]	62 321[3]	63 275[3]	119	...	...	...	...
Wiesbaden	278 654[3]	133 148[3]	145 506[3]	204	...	...	...	...
Wolfsburg	123 914[3]	61 559[3]	62 355[3]	205	...	...	...	...
Wuppertal	353 590[3]	173 025[3]	180 565[3]	168	...	...	...	...
Würzburg	126 635[3]	60 447[3]	66 188[3]	88	...	...	...	...
Gibraltar								
31 XII 2016 (ESDF)								
GIBRALTAR	34 003[79]	17 093[79]	16 910[79]	6	...	...	...	...
Greece - Grèce								
9 V 2011 (CDFC)								
ATHINAI	664 046	315 210	348 836	...	...	...	...	...
Calithèa	100 641	46 782	53 859	...	...	...	...	...
Iraclion	140 730	68 024	72 706	...	...	...	...	...
Larissa	144 651	70 797	73 854	...	...	...	...	...
Patral	167 446	81 114	86 332	...	...	...	...	...
Pésterion	139 981	68 563	71 418	...	...	...	...	...
Pireas	163 688	78 200	85 488	...	...	...	...	...
Thessaloniki	315 196	143 813	171 383	...	...	...	...	...
Guernsey - Guernesey								
31 III 2015 (CDJC)								
ST. PETER PORT	18 599	...	...	...	...	...	...	...

8. Population of capital cities and cities of 100 000 or more inhabitants: latest available year, 1999 - 2018
Population des capitales et des villes de 100 000 habitants ou plus : dernière année disponible, 1999 - 2018 (continued - suite)

Continent, country or area, date, code[a] and city / Continent, pays ou zone, date, code[a] et ville	City proper - Ville proprement dite				Urban agglomeration - Agglomération urbaine			
	Population			Surface area - Superficie (km²)	Population			Surface area - Superficie (km²)
	Both sexes - Les deux sexes	Male - Masculin	Female - Féminin		Both sexes - Les deux sexes	Male - Masculin	Female - Féminin	
EUROPE								
Holy See - Saint-Siège[80]								
21 VI 2012 (ESDF)								
VATICAN CITY	451	...	...	...	...	...	...	...
Hungary - Hongrie								
1 VII 2017 (ESDJ)								
BUDAPEST	1 751 219[81]	813 904[81]	937 316[81]	525.1	2 595 024[81]	1 220 741[81]	1 374 284[81]	2538.4
Debrecen	202 098[81]	94 452[81]	107 646[81]	461.7	265 861[81]	125 973[81]	139 889[81]	1081.8
Györ	129 698[81]	61 409[81]	68 289[81]	174.6	233 797[81]	113 415[81]	120 382[81]	1607
Kecskemét	110 726[81]	51 942[81]	58 784[81]	322.6	132 518[81]	62 737[81]	69 781[81]	666.1
Miskolc	156 414[81]	72 592[81]	83 822[81]	236.7	246 373[81]	116 163[81]	130 210[81]	982.3
Nyiregyhaza	117 405[81]	54 649[81]	62 756[81]	274.5	147 467[81]	69 389[81]	78 078[81]	554.2
Pécs	144 432[81]	66 182[81]	78 250[81]	162.8	179 882[81]	83 627[81]	96 255[81]	671.3
Szeged	161 130[81]	74 108[81]	87 022[81]	281	204 062[81]	95 354[81]	108 708[81]	804.5
Iceland - Islande								
1 VII 2017 (ESDJ)								
REYKJAVIK	124 644[82]	62 634[82]	62 010[82]	274	219 681[82]	110 333[82]	109 349[82]	1044[83]
Ireland - Irlande								
1 IV 2016 (ESDJ)								
Cork	124 391	61 255	63 136	...	...	...	...	...
DUBLIN	544 107	267 319	276 788	...	...	...	...	...
Isle of Man - Île de Man								
23 IV 2006 (CDJC)								
DOUGLAS	26 218	13 000	13 218	...	...	...	...	...
Italy - Italie								
1 VII 2017 (ESDJ)								
Ancona	100 810	48 235	52 575	...	...	...	...	...
Bari	323 784	155 569	168 216	...	...	...	...	...
Bergamo	120 605	56 845	63 761	...	...	...	...	...
Bologna	388 814	183 451	205 364	...	...	...	...	...
Bolzano	107 134	51 406	55 728	...	...	...	...	...
Brescia	196 708	92 896	103 812	...	...	...	...	...
Cagliari	154 095	71 922	82 173	...	...	...	...	...
Catania	312 508	150 391	162 117	...	...	...	...	...
Ferrara	132 144	62 160	69 984	...	...	...	...	...
Firenze	381 603	179 092	202 512	...	...	...	...	...
Foggia	151 549	73 191	78 358	...	...	...	...	...
Forli	117 905	56 684	61 221	...	...	...	...	...
Genova	581 849	274 528	307 321	...	...	...	...	...
Giugliano in Campania	124 100	61 529	62 571	...	...	...	...	...
Latina	126 311	61 259	65 052	...	...	...	...	...
Livorno	158 644	76 056	82 588	...	...	...	...	...
Messina	235 628	112 892	122 736	...	...	...	...	...
Milano	1 358 871	650 603	708 269	...	...	...	...	...
Modena	185 000	88 488	96 512	...	...	...	...	...
Monza	123 277	59 116	64 161	...	...	...	...	...
Napoli	968 165	462 665	505 500	...	...	...	...	...
Novara	104 234	50 218	54 016	...	...	...	...	...
Padova	210 135	98 832	111 303	...	...	...	...	...
Palermo	671 070	320 718	350 353	...	...	...	...	...
Parma	195 052	93 310	101 742	...	...	...	...	...
Perugia	166 180	79 251	86 929	...	...	...	...	...
Pescara	119 819	56 058	63 761	...	...	...	...	...
Piacenza	102 719	48 948	53 771	...	...	...	...	...
Prato	192 897	93 417	99 481	...	...	...	...	...
Ravenna	159 086	77 175	81 912	...	...	...	...	...
Reggio di Calabria	181 999	87 200	94 799	...	...	...	...	...
Reggio nell'Emilia	171 718	83 627	88 091	...	...	...	...	...
Rimini	149 156	71 378	77 778	...	...	...	...	...
ROMA	2 873 147	1 362 624	1 510 524	...	...	...	...	...
Salerno	134 410	62 759	71 651	...	...	...	...	...
Sassari	127 151	61 121	66 030	...	...	...	...	...
Siracusa	121 818	59 623	62 195	...	...	...	...	...
Taranto	198 922	94 899	104 024	...	...	...	...	...
Terni	111 322	52 435	58 888	...	...	...	...	...
Torino	884 680	421 658	463 023	...	...	...	...	...

8. Population of capital cities and cities of 100 000 or more inhabitants: latest available year, 1999 - 2018
Population des capitales et des villes de 100 000 habitants ou plus : dernière année disponible, 1999 - 2018 (continued - suite)

Continent, country or area, date, code[a] and city / Continent, pays ou zone, date, code[a] et ville	City proper - Ville proprement dite				Urban agglomeration - Agglomération urbaine			
	Population			Surface area - Superficie (km²)	Population			Surface area - Superficie (km²)
	Both sexes - Les deux sexes	Male - Masculin	Female - Féminin		Both sexes - Les deux sexes	Male - Masculin	Female - Féminin	
EUROPE								
Italy - Italie								
1 VII 2017 (ESDJ)								
Trento	117 707	56 530	61 177	...	...	...	...	...
Trieste	204 286	97 522	106 764	...	...	...	...	...
Venezia	261 613	124 029	137 585	...	...	...	...	...
Verona	257 314	121 698	135 617	...	...	...	...	...
Vicenza	111 909	52 899	59 010	...	...	...	...	...
Jersey								
11 III 2001 (CDJC)								
ST. HELIER	28 310	13 669	14 641	8.6	...	...	...	...
Latvia - Lettonie								
1 I 2018 (ESDJ)								
RIGA	637 971	283 579	354 392	304	...	...	...	...
Liechtenstein								
1 VII 2018 (ESDJ)								
VADUZ	5 605	2 739	2 866	17	...	...	...	...
Lithuania - Lituanie								
1 VII 2017 (ESDJ)								
Kaunas	290 527	127 266	163 261	157	...	...	...	...
Klaipeda	150 109	67 465	82 644	98	...	...	...	...
Shauliai	100 895	45 129	55 766	81	...	...	...	...
VILNIUS	546 382	245 380	301 002	401	...	...	...	...
Luxembourg								
1 I 2018 (ESDJ)								
LUXEMBOURG-VILLE	116 323	59 544	56 779	51	...	...	...	...
Malta - Malte								
1 VII 2017 (ESDJ)								
VALLETTA	5 735[84]	2 836[84]	2 899[84]	1	...	...	...	...
Monaco								
9 VI 2008 (CDJC)								
MONACO	31 109	15 076[85]	15 914[85]	...	...	...	...	...
Montenegro - Monténégro								
1 IV 2011 (CDJC)								
PODGORICA	185 937	90 614	95 323	1441	...	...	...	...
Netherlands - Pays-Bas								
1 I 2015 (ESDJ)								
Alkmaar	107 106	52 973	54 133	...	...	...	...	...
Almere	196 932	97 666	99 266	...	...	...	...	...
Alphen aan den	107 396	53 321	54 075	...	...	...	...	...
Amersfoort	152 481	74 967	77 514	...	...	...	...	...
AMSTERDAM	821 752	404 881	416 871	...	...	...	...	...
Apeldoorn	158 099	78 163	79 936	...	...	...	...	...
Arnhem	152 293	75 872	76 421	...	...	...	...	...
Breda	180 937	88 620	92 317	...	...	...	...	...
Delft	101 030	54 035	46 995	...	...	...	...	...
Dordrecht	118 899	58 646	60 253	...	...	...	...	...
Ede	111 575	54 790	56 785	...	...	...	...	...
Eindhoven	223 209	114 034	109 175	...	...	...	...	...
Emmen	107 775	53 399	54 376	...	...	...	...	...
Enschede	158 553	80 411	78 142	...	...	...	...	...
Groningen	200 336	99 657	100 679	...	...	...	...	...
Haarlem	156 645	76 481	80 164	...	...	...	...	...
Haarlemmermeer	144 152	71 642	72 510	...	...	...	...	...
Leeuwarden	107 691	53 264	54 427	...	...	...	...	...
Leiden	121 562	59 084	62 478	...	...	...	...	...
Maastricht	122 397	58 799	63 598	...	...	...	...	...
Nijmegen	170 681	81 934	88 747	...	...	...	...	...
Rotterdam	623 652	307 001	316 651	...	...	...	...	...
s-Gravenhage	514 861	254 187	260 674	...	...	...	...	...
s-Hertogenbosch	150 889	74 424	76 465	...	...	...	...	...
Tilburg	211 648	105 179	106 469	...	...	...	...	...
Utrecht	334 176	162 556	171 620	...	...	...	...	...
Venlo	100 536	49 978	50 558	...	...	...	...	...
Westland	104 302	51 937	52 365	...	...	...	...	...
Zaanstad	151 418	74 778	76 640	...	...	...	...	...

8. Population of capital cities and cities of 100 000 or more inhabitants: latest available year, 1999 - 2018
Population des capitales et des villes de 100 000 habitants ou plus : dernière année disponible, 1999 - 2018 (continued - suite)

Continent, country or area, date, code[a] and city / Continent, pays ou zone, date, code[a] et ville	City proper - Ville proprement dite				Urban agglomeration - Agglomération urbaine			
	Population			Surface area - Superficie (km²)	Population			Surface area - Superficie (km²)
	Both sexes - Les deux sexes	Male - Masculin	Female - Féminin		Both sexes - Les deux sexes	Male - Masculin	Female - Féminin	
EUROPE								
Netherlands - Pays-Bas								
1 I 2015 (ESDJ)								
Zoetermeer	124 025	60 554	63 471	...	...	...	...	...
Zwolle	123 861	60 759	63 102	...	...	...	...	...
North Macedonia - Macédoine du Nord								
1 VII 2016 (ESDJ)								
SKOPJE	546 824	267 738	279 086	...	...	...	...	...
Norway - Norvège								
1 I 2014 (ESDJ)								
OSLO	634 293	316 114	318 179	426	...	...	...	...
Poland - Pologne[86]								
1 VII 2017 (ESDJ)								
Bialystok	294 362[81]	138 234[81]	156 128[81]	102[40]	...	...	...	...
Bielsko-Biala	170 005[81]	80 283[81]	89 722[81]	125[40]	...	...	...	...
Bydgoszcz	352 870[81]	166 186[81]	186 684[81]	176[40]	...	...	...	...
Bytom	167 359[81]	79 823[81]	87 536[81]	69[40]	...	...	...	...
Chorzów	108 205[81]	51 382[81]	56 823[81]	33[40]	...	...	...	...
Czestochowa	223 373[81]	104 819[81]	118 554[81]	160[40]	...	...	...	...
Dabrowa Górnicza	120 478[81]	57 741[81]	62 737[81]	189[40]	...	...	...	...
Elblag	118 925[81]	56 801[81]	62 124[81]	80[40]	...	...	...	...
Gdansk	463 352[81]	220 029[81]	243 323[81]	262[40]	...	...	...	...
Gdynia	243 910[81]	115 200[81]	128 710[81]	135[40]	...	...	...	...
Gliwice	180 193[81]	86 712[81]	93 481[81]	134[40]	...	...	...	...
Gorzów Wielkopolski	122 299[81]	58 052[81]	64 247[81]	86[40]	...	...	...	...
Kalisz	100 812[81]	46 876[81]	53 936[81]	69[40]	...	...	...	...
Katowice	301 202[81]	144 027[81]	157 175[81]	165[40]	...	...	...	...
Kielce	195 655[81]	92 056[81]	103 599[81]	110[40]	...	...	...	...
Koszalin	105 989[81]	49 864[81]	56 125[81]	98[40]	...	...	...	...
Kraków	759 104[81]	354 667[81]	404 437[81]	327[40]	...	...	...	...
Lódz	692 284[81]	315 581[81]	376 703[81]	293[40]	...	...	...	...
Lublin	341 794[81]	157 525[81]	184 269[81]	147[40]	...	...	...	...
Olsztyn	173 693[81]	81 005[81]	92 688[81]	88[40]	...	...	...	...
Opole	127 084[81]	60 059[81]	67 025[81]	149[40]	...	...	...	...
Plock	119 840[81]	56 581[81]	63 259[81]	88[40]	...	...	...	...
Poznan	538 439[81]	251 515[81]	286 924[81]	262[40]	...	...	...	...
Radom	212 765[81]	100 980[81]	111 785[81]	112[40]	...	...	...	...
Ruda Slaska	137 546[81]	66 521[81]	71 025[81]	78[40]	...	...	...	...
Rybnik	137 436[81]	67 049[81]	70 387[81]	148[40]	...	...	...	...
Rzeszów	186 391[81]	88 270[81]	98 121[81]	120[40]	...	...	...	...
Sosnowiec	203 001[81]	96 035[81]	106 966[81]	91[40]	...	...	...	...
Szczecin	401 940[81]	191 243[81]	210 697[81]	301[40]	...	...	...	...
Tarnów	106 709[81]	50 282[81]	56 427[81]	72[40]	...	...	...	...
Torun	199 490[81]	92 705[81]	106 785[81]	116[40]	...	...	...	...
Tychy	126 661[81]	61 053[81]	65 608[81]	82[40]	...	...	...	...
Walbrzych	112 720[81]	53 132[81]	59 588[81]	85[40]	...	...	...	...
WARSZAWA	1 754 511[81]	806 730[81]	947 781[81]	517[40]	...	...	...	...
Wloclawek	110 563[81]	51 999[81]	58 564[81]	84[40]	...	...	...	...
Wroclaw	634 873[81]	297 251[81]	337 622[81]	293[40]	...	...	...	...
Zabrze	172 909[81]	83 411[81]	89 498[81]	80[40]	...	...	...	...
Zielona Góra	139 818[81]	66 649[81]	73 169[81]	277[40]	...	...	...	...
Portugal								
1 VII 2017 (ESDJ)								
Amadora	179 056	83 342	95 714	...	...	...	...	...
LISBOA	505 526	231 436	274 091	...	...	...	...	...
Porto	214 353	96 470	117 884	...	...	...	...	...
Republic of Moldova - République de Moldova[87]								
12 V 2014 (CDFC)								
CHIŞINĂU (KISHINEV)	339 079	157 341	181 738	...	...	...	...	...
Romania - Roumanie								
1 VII 2017 (ESDF)								
BUCURESTI	1 826 830	847 906	978 924	240	...	...	...	...

Continent, country or area, date, code[a] and city	City proper - Ville proprement dite				Urban agglomeration - Agglomération urbaine			
	Population			Surface area - Superficie (km²)	Population			Surface area - Superficie (km²)
Continent, pays ou zone, date, code[a] et ville	Both sexes - Les deux sexes	Male - Masculin	Female - Féminin		Both sexes - Les deux sexes	Male - Masculin	Female - Féminin	

EUROPE

Russian Federation - Fédération de Russie
1 VII 2012 (ESDJ)

Abakan	168 655	77 052	91 603	...	...	...	...	...
Achinsk	107 943	48 069	59 874	...	109 229	...	...	...
Almetievsk	148 384	69 433	78 951	...	...	...	...	...
Anapa	...	...	...	...	156 928	...	...	...
Angarsk	231 944	105 405	126 539	...	...	...	...	...
Arkhangelsk	350 258	156 523	193 735	...	357 264	...	...	...
Armavir	190 831	87 524	103 307	...	209 742	...	...	...
Artem (Primorskiy Krai)	102 605	49 147	53 458	...	112 102	...	...	...
Arzamas	105 506	47 208	58 298	...	...	...	...	...
Astrakhan	526 363	241 489	284 874	...	...	...	...	...
Balakovo	196 918	88 075	108 843	...	...	...	...	...
Balashikha	228 567	112 191	116 376	...	238 284	...	...	...
Barnaul	625 679	279 300	346 379	...	686 306	...	...	...
Bataisk	115 016	54 477	60 539	...	...	...	...	...
Belgorod	369 815	167 120	202 695	...	...	...	...	...
Belovo	...	...	...	...	132 144	...	...	...
Berezniki	153 806	68 365	85 441	...	...	...	...	...
Biisk	206 327	91 943	114 384	...	215 780	...	...	...
Blagoveshchensk (Amurskaya oblast)	216 691	97 135	119 556	...	222 065	...	...	...
Bor	...	...	...	...	122 201	...	...	...
Bratsk	242 604	109 596	133 008	...	...	...	...	...
Bryansk	411 798	183 540	228 258	...	430 987	...	...	...
Cheboksary	462 669	206 721	255 948	...	473 189	...	...	...
Chelyabinsk	1 149 829	514 456	635 373	...	...	...	...	...
Cherepovets	315 186	142 977	172 209	...	...	...	...	...
Cherkessk	126 884	55 588	71 296	...	...	...	...	...
Chita	329 391	152 092	177 299	...	329 868	...	...	...
Derbent	119 647	57 527	62 120	...	...	...	...	...
Dimitrovgrad	120 750	55 838	64 912	...	...	...	...	...
Domodedovo	...	...	...	...	142 743	...	...	...
Dzerzhinsk (Nizhegorodskaya oblast)	238 327	105 346	132 981	...	248 649	...	...	...
Ekaterinburg	1 386 909	621 499	765 410	...	1 420 285	...	...	...
Elektrostal	156 136	71 093	85 043	...	...	...	...	...
Elets	107 347	48 757	58 590	...	...	...	...	...
Elista	104 177	47 317	56 860	...	108 753	...	...	...
Engels	210 190	95 953	114 237	...	211 825	...	...	...
Esentuky	101 851	45 327	56 524	...	...	...	...	...
Groznyi	276 524	136 615	139 909	...	...	...	...	...
Hasaviurt	133 188	63 867	69 321	...	...	...	...	...
Irkutsk	601 993	269 003	332 990	...	...	...	...	...
Ivanovo	408 952	180 083	228 869	...	...	...	...	...
Izhevsk	631 182	281 708	349 474	...	...	...	...	...
Kaliningrad (Kaliningradskaya oblast)	437 456	200 849	236 607	...	...	...	...	...
Kaluga	328 871	146 008	182 863	...	344 766	...	...	...
Kamensk-Uralsky	172 639	77 327	95 312	...	174 493	...	...	...
Kamyshin	117 352	53 822	63 530	...	...	...	...	...
Kaspiysk	102 421	49 393	53 028	...	...	...	...	...
Kazan	1 168 745	520 694	648 051	...	...	...	...	...
Kemerovo	538 188	240 431	297 757	...	...	...	...	...
Khabarovsk	589 596	273 949	315 647	...	...	...	...	...
Khimki	218 275	99 122	119 153	...	...	...	...	...
Kirov	480 594	211 205	269 389	...	505 346	...	...	...
Kiselevsk	...	...	...	...	101 180	...	...	...
Kislovodsk	129 313	58 854	70 459	...	136 142	...	...	...
Kolomna	144 838	66 469	78 369	...	...	...	...	...
Komsomolsk-na-Amure	259 081	120 197	138 884	...	...	...	...	...
Kopeysk	139 161	66 142	73 019	...	141 291	...	...	...
Korolev (Moskovskaya oblast)	186 460	84 232	102 228	...	...	...	...	...
Kostroma	270 366	120 622	149 744	...	...	...	...	...
Kovrov	...	...	...	...	346 922	154 144	192 778	...
Krasnodar	773 970	350 519	423 451	...	861 181	...	...	...
Krasnogorsk	125 198	56 432	68 766	...	125 787	...	...	...
Krasnoyarsk	1 006 856	456 171	550 685	...	1 007 654	...	...	...

Continent, country or area, date, code[a] and city / Continent, pays ou zone, date, code[a] et ville	City proper - Ville proprement dite				Urban agglomeration - Agglomération urbaine			
	Population			Surface area - Superficie (km²)	Population			Surface area - Superficie (km²)
	Both sexes - Les deux sexes	Male - Masculin	Female - Féminin		Both sexes - Les deux sexes	Male - Masculin	Female - Féminin	

EUROPE

Russian Federation - Fédération de Russie
1 VII 2012 (ESDJ)

Kurgan	326 729	146 140	180 589	...	...	...	...	...
Kursk	425 950	189 025	236 925	...	...	...	...	...
Kyzyl	112 659	52 137	60 522	...	...	...	...	...
Leninsk-Kuznetsky	100 073	45 651	54 422	...	102 285	...	...	...
Lipetsk	508 585	230 178	278 407	...	...	...	...	...
Lyubertsy	178 884	80 564	98 320	...	...	...	...	...
Magadan	95 263	45 084	50 179	...	101 933	...	...	...
Magnitogorsk	410 733	186 534	224 199	...	...	...	...	...
Maikop	144 579	64 512	80 067	...	167 281	...	...	...
Makhachkala	575 243	271 687	303 556	...	701 753	...	...	...
Mezhdurechensk	100 278	46 498	53 780	...	102 465	...	...	...
Miass	150 806	67 824	82 982	...	166 205	...	...	...
MOSKVA	11 918 057	5 495 477	6 422 580	...	...	...	...	...
Murmansk	303 754	139 944	163 810	...	...	...	...	...
Murom	113 330	50 293	63 037	...	122 545	...	...	...
Mytishchi	176 825	80 425	96 400	...	185 204	...	...	...
Naberezhnye Tchelny	517 831	237 620	280 211	...	...	...	...	...
Nakhodka	158 649	75 081	83 568	...	159 633	...	...	...
Naltchik	239 230	106 648	132 582	...	265 051	...	...	...
Nazran	100 574	44 126	56 448	...	...	...	...	...
Neftekamsk	123 202	57 271	65 931	...	135 013	...	...	...
Nefteyugansk	125 528	61 635	63 893	...	...	...	...	...
Nevinnomyssk	117 949	53 611	64 338	...	...	...	...	...
Nizhnekamsk	235 179	111 262	123 917	...	235 279	...	...	...
Nizhnevartovsk	261 011	125 937	135 074	...	...	...	...	...
Nizhny Novgorod	1 257 260	552 285	704 975	...	1 266 231	...	...	...
Nizhny Tagil	358 651	162 731	195 920	...	362 185	...	...	...
Noginsk	101 779	45 741	56 038	...	103 843	...	...	...
Norilsk	177 506	89 198	88 308	...	178 363	...	...	...
Novocheboksarsk	...	...	...	...	124 288	...	...	...
Novocherkassk	171 081	81 921	89 160	...	...	...	...	...
Novokuybishevsk	107 244	48 418	58 826	...	109 521	...	...	...
Novokuznetsk	549 383	247 386	301 997	...	...	...	...	...
Novomoskovsk (Tulskaya oblast)	129 555	57 961	71 594	...	141 893	...	...	...
Novorossiysk	248 857	117 707	131 150	...	305 421	...	...	...
Novoshakhtinsk	110 243	50 410	59 833	...	...	...	...	...
Novosibirsk	1 511 369	694 959	816 410	...	...	...	...	...
Novotroitsk	...	...	...	...	103 061	...	...	...
Novy Urengoy	114 332	59 841	54 491	...	...	...	...	...
Noyabrsk	108 662	53 237	55 425	...	...	...	...	...
Obninsk	105 722	48 323	57 399	...	...	...	...	...
Odintsovo	137 706	63 405	74 301	...	143 848	...	...	...
Oktyabrsky	111 109	51 956	59 153	...	...	...	...	...
Omsk	1 158 627	526 757	631 870	...	...	...	...	...
Orekhovo-Zuevo	121 341	53 443	67 898	...	...	...	...	...
Orel	318 642	139 662	178 980	...	...	...	...	...
Orenburg	555 420	252 906	302 514	...	571 041	...	...	...
Orsk	237 194	106 127	131 067	...	241 327	...	...	...
Penza	519 948	234 270	285 678	...	...	...	...	...
Perm	1 007 272	444 386	562 886	...	1 007 285	...	...	...
Pervouralsk	125 421	56 144	69 277	...	149 796	...	...	...
Petropavlovsk-Kamchatsky	180 702	88 743	91 959	...	...	...	...	...
Petrozavodsk	267 102	118 638	148 464	...	...	...	...	...
Podolsk	200 059	89 931	110 128	...	...	...	...	...
Prokopyevsk	206 023	91 944	114 079	...	...	...	...	...
Pskov	205 062	92 439	112 623	...	...	...	...	...
Pushkino	104 020	46 649	57 371	...	...	...	...	...
Pyatigorsk	144 603	64 578	80 025	...	212 968	...	...	...
Rostov-na-Donu	1 100 091	501 068	599 023	...	...	...	...	...
Rubtsovsk	146 075	69 084	76 991	...	...	...	...	...
Ryazan	526 919	237 791	289 128	...	...	...	...	...
Rybinsk	197 359	87 921	109 438	...	...	...	...	...
Salavat	155 174	72 449	82 725	...	...	...	...	...

8. Population of capital cities and cities of 100 000 or more inhabitants: latest available year, 1999 - 2018
Population des capitales et des villes de 100 000 habitants ou plus : dernière année disponible, 1999 - 2018 (continued - suite)

Continent, country or area, date, code[a] and city / Continent, pays ou zone, date, code[a] et ville	City proper - Ville proprement dite				Urban agglomeration - Agglomération urbaine			
	Population			Surface area - Superficie (km²)	Population			Surface area - Superficie (km²)
	Both sexes - Les deux sexes	Male - Masculin	Female - Féminin		Both sexes - Les deux sexes	Male - Masculin	Female - Féminin	
EUROPE								
Russian Federation - Fédération de Russie								
1 VII 2012 (ESDJ)								
Samara (Samarskaya oblast)	1 170 381	522 660	647 721	...	1 170 485	...	...	...
Saransk	298 103	132 543	165 560	...	326 473	...	...	...
Sarapyul	100 362	44 678	55 684	...	...	...	...	...
Saratov	838 321	373 676	464 645	...	...	...	...	...
Sergiev Posad	109 076	48 786	60 290	...	...	...	...	...
Serov	...	...	...	...	115 858	...	...	...
Serpukhov	126 729	57 494	69 235	...	107 904	...	...	...
Severodvinsk	189 313	87 781	101 532	...	190 513	...	...	...
Seversk	109 630	50 705	58 925	...	116 340	...	...	...
Shakhty	238 031	107 544	130 487	...	...	...	...	...
Shchelkovo	111 406	50 812	60 594	...	113 726	...	...	...
Smolensk	330 451	147 446	183 005	...	...	...	...	...
Sochi	364 171	164 632	199 539	...	441 407	...	...	...
St. Petersburg	4 990 602	2 247 375	2 743 227	...	...	...	...	...
Stary Oskol	220 719	100 902	119 817	...	256 790	...	...	...
Stavropol	408 361	187 593	220 768	...	408 560	...	...	...
Sterlitamak	275 087	125 443	149 644	...	...	...	...	...
Surgut	321 062	153 832	167 230	...	...	...	...	...
Syktivkar	239 341	107 945	131 396	...	255 283	...	...	...
Syzran	177 404	79 804	97 600	...	178 205	...	...	...
Taganrog	255 671	114 508	141 163	...	...	...	...	...
Tambov	281 348	126 427	154 921	...	...	...	...	...
Tobolsk	...	...	...	...	101 955	...	...	...
Tolyatti	719 363	331 248	388 115	...	...	...	...	...
Tomsk	543 596	252 173	291 423	...	565 000	...	...	...
Tula	496 656	220 675	275 981	...	...	...	...	...
Tver	407 896	180 459	227 437	...	...	...	...	...
Tyumen	621 918	288 291	333 627	...	644 799	...	...	...
Ufa	1 075 007	484 893	590 114	...	1 084 420	...	...	...
Uhta	99 680	47 563	52 117	...	121 479	...	...	...
Ulan-Ude	413 850	191 732	222 118	...	...	...	...	...
Ulyanovsk	614 878	278 103	336 775	...	637 637	...	...	...
Ussurlisk	163 465	79 562	83 903	...	189 502	...	...	...
Velikiy Novgorod	219 941	95 446	124 495	...	...	...	...	...
Vladikavkaz (Osetinskaya ASSR)	309 173	139 818	169 355	...	327 448	...	...	...
Vladimir	346 922	154 144	192 778	...	349 525	...	...	...
Vladivostok	598 927	282 260	316 667	...	624 281	...	...	...
Volgodonsk	170 189	78 251	91 938	...	...	...	...	...
Volgograd	1 018 762	460 095	558 667	...	...	...	...	...
Vologda	305 397	135 292	170 105	...	313 679	...	...	...
Volzhsky	320 761	148 339	172 422	...	327 460	...	...	...
Voronezh	997 447	447 484	549 963	...	...	...	...	...
Yakutsk	282 419	132 612	149 807	...	298 926	...	...	...
Yaroslavl	597 161	262 042	335 119	...	...	...	...	...
Yoshkar-Ola	254 987	114 331	140 656	...	265 626	...	...	...
Yuzhno-Sakhalinsk	188 242	89 200	99 042	...	195 104	...	...	...
Zheleznodorozhny	138 814	62 719	76 095	...	...	...	...	...
Zhukovsky	106 555	49 027	57 528	...	...	...	...	...
Zlatoust	172 972	78 071	94 901	...	175 178	...	...	...
San Marino - Saint-Marin								
1 VII 2018 (ESDJ)								
SAN MARINO	4 127	2 008	2 119	...	...	...	...	...
Serbia - Serbie								
1 VII 2017 (ESDJ)								
BEOGRAD (BELGRADE)	1 378 682[88]	642 546[88]	736 136[88]	716	1 687 132[89]	796 627[89]	890 505[89]	3232[19]
Čačak	71 883[88]	34 242[88]	37 641[88]	35	111 075[89]	53 917[89]	57 158[89]	636[19]
Kragujevac	150 623[88]	72 510[88]	78 113[88]	83	177 977[89]	86 349[89]	91 628[89]	834[19]
Kraljevo	66 688[88]	32 144[88]	34 544[88]	42	119 585[89]	58 737[89]	60 848[89]	1529[19]
Kruševac	57 213[88]	27 173[88]	30 040[88]	11	122 437[89]	59 862[89]	62 575[89]	853[19]
Leskovac	63 618[88]	30 808[88]	32 810[88]	64	136 888[89]	68 102[89]	68 786[89]	1024[19]
Niš	185 853[88]	88 795[88]	97 058[88]	49	256 825[89]	124 584[89]	132 241[89]	596[19]
Novi Pazar	72 372[88]	35 727[88]	36 645[88]	15	105 490[89]	52 517[89]	52 973[89]	742[19]
Novi Sad	291 706[88]	136 637[88]	155 069[88]	164	356 126[89]	168 693[89]	187 433[89]	699[19]

8. Population of capital cities and cities of 100 000 or more inhabitants: latest available year, 1999 - 2018
Population des capitales et des villes de 100 000 habitants ou plus : dernière année disponible, 1999 - 2018 (continued - suite)

Continent, country or area, date, code[a] and city / Continent, pays ou zone, date, code[a] et ville	City proper - Ville proprement dite				Urban agglomeration - Agglomération urbaine			
	Population			Surface area - Superficie (km²)	Population			Surface area - Superficie (km²)
	Both sexes - Les deux sexes	Male - Masculin	Female - Féminin		Both sexes - Les deux sexes	Male - Masculin	Female - Féminin	
EUROPE								
Serbia - Serbie								
1 VII 2017 (ESDJ)								
Pancevo	89 024[88]	42 752[88]	46 272[88]	263	120 361[89]	58 594[89]	61 767[89]	755[19]
Šabac	52 929[88]	24 791[88]	28 138[88]	31	111 709[89]	54 567[89]	57 142[89]	797[19]
Smederevo	62 593[88]	30 259[88]	32 334[88]	42	104 125[89]	51 360[89]	52 765[89]	484[19]
Subotica	103 694[88]	49 344[88]	54 350[88]	205	137 753[89]	66 216[89]	71 537[89]	1007[19]
Zrenjanin	73 945[88]	35 183[88]	38 762[88]	193	117 735[89]	57 256[89]	60 479[89]	1325[19]
Slovakia - Slovaquie								
1 VII 2017 (ESDJ)								
BRATISLAVA	427 744	200 853	226 891	368[64]	...	...	...	
Kosice	239 119	114 648	124 471	244[64]	...	...	...	
Slovenia - Slovénie								
1 VII 2017 (ESDJ)								
LJUBLJANA	279 650	134 856	144 794	164	281 494	135 788	145 706	171
Maribor	94 248	46 052	48 196	41	107 834	52 775	55 059	99
Spain - Espagne[36]								
1 VII 2017 (ESDJ)								
A Coruña	244 474	113 474	131 000	...	...	...	...	...
Albacete	172 933	84 560	88 373	...	...	...	...	...
Alcalá de Henares	194 030	94 618	99 412	...	...	...	...	...
Alcobendas	115 450	55 409	60 041	...	...	...	...	...
Alcorcón	168 821	81 492	87 329	...	...	...	...	...
Algeciras	121 273	59 808	61 465	...	...	...	...	...
Alicante/Alacant	330 782	160 328	170 454	...	...	...	...	...
Almería	196 120	95 498	100 622	...	...	...	...	...
Badajoz	150 536	72 995	77 541	...	...	...	...	...
Badalona	216 794	106 654	110 140	...	...	...	...	...
Barakaldo	100 374	48 534	51 840	...	...	...	...	...
Barcelona	1 620 576	766 293	854 283	...	...	...	...	...
Bilbao	345 465	162 751	182 714	...	...	...	...	...
Burgos	175 772	83 653	92 119	...	...	...	...	...
Cádiz	117 513	55 649	61 864	...	...	...	...	...
Cartagena	214 060	106 844	107 216	...	...	...	...	...
Castellón de la Plana/Castelló de la Plana	170 193	82 349	87 844	...	...	...	...	...
Córdoba	325 812	156 469	169 343	...	...	...	...	...
Donostia/San Sebastián	186 517	87 702	98 815	...	...	...	...	...
Dos Hermanas	132 859	65 430	67 429	...	...	...	...	...
Elche/Elx	229 650	113 838	115 812	...	...	...	...	...
Fuenlabrada	194 127	95 835	98 292	...	...	...	...	...
Getafe	179 517	87 878	91 639	...	...	...	...	...
Gijón	272 104	128 281	143 823	...	...	...	...	...
Granada	232 489	107 629	124 860	...	...	...	...	...
Huelva	144 686	69 568	75 118	...	...	...	...	...
Jaén	113 847	54 740	59 107	...	...	...	...	...
Jerez de la Frontera	212 897	104 137	108 760	...	...	...	...	...
Las Palmas de Gran Canaria	378 083	182 957	195 126	...	...	...	...	...
Leganés	188 072	91 401	96 671	...	...	...	...	...
León	125 044	56 679	68 365	...	...	...	...	...
L'Hospitalet de Llobregat	259 208	125 254	133 954	...	...	...	...	...
Lleida	137 591	67 962	69 629	...	...	...	...	...
Logroño	151 046	71 793	79 253	...	...	...	...	...
MADRID	3 203 157	1 490 395	1 712 762	...	...	...	...	...
Málaga	570 014	274 004	296 010	...	...	...	...	...
Marbella	141 317	68 100	73 217	...	...	...	...	...
Mataró	126 557	62 731	63 826	...	...	...	...	...
Móstoles	206 842	100 900	105 942	...	...	...	...	...
Murcia	445 212	217 529	227 683	...	...	...	...	...
Ourense	105 570	48 039	57 531	...	...	...	...	...
Oviedo	220 160	101 976	118 184	...	...	...	...	...
Palma de Mallorca	408 076	198 742	209 334	...	...	...	...	...
Pamplona/Iruña	198 102	93 756	104 346	...	...	...	...	...
Parla	127 077	63 236	63 841	...	...	...	...	...
Reus	103 300	49 917	53 383	...	...	...	...	...
Sabadell	210 832	102 540	108 292	...	...	...	...	...
Salamanca	144 207	65 490	78 717	...	...	...	...	...

8. Population of capital cities and cities of 100 000 or more inhabitants: latest available year, 1999 - 2018
Population des capitales et des villes de 100 000 habitants ou plus : dernière année disponible, 1999 - 2018 (continued - suite)

Continent, country or area, date, code[a] and city / Continent, pays ou zone, date, code[a] et ville	City proper - Ville proprement dite				Urban agglomeration - Agglomération urbaine			
	Population			Surface area - Superficie (km²)	Population			Surface area - Superficie (km²)
	Both sexes - Les deux sexes	Male - Masculin	Female - Féminin		Both sexes - Les deux sexes	Male - Masculin	Female - Féminin	
EUROPE								
Spain - Espagne[36]								
1 VII 2017 (ESDJ)								
San Cristóbal de La Laguna	154 602	74 951	79 651	...	...	...	...	...
Santa Coloma de Gramenet	118 209	58 650	59 559	...	...	...	...	...
Santa Cruz de Tenerife	204 274	97 569	106 705	...	...	...	...	...
Santander	171 997	79 381	92 616	...	...	...	...	...
Sevilla	689 072	327 048	362 024	...	...	...	...	...
Tarragona	131 903	64 111	67 792	...	...	...	...	...
Telde	102 214	50 365	51 849	...	...	...	...	...
Terrassa	217 481	107 048	110 433	...	...	...	...	...
Torrejón de Ardoz	128 871	63 512	65 359	...	...	...	...	...
Valencia	789 610	375 979	413 631	...	...	...	...	...
Valladolid	299 290	140 637	158 653	...	...	...	...	...
Vigo	293 314	138 923	154 391	...	...	...	...	...
Vitoria-Gasteiz	248 076	120 929	127 147	...	...	...	...	...
Zaragoza	665 909	318 798	347 111	...	...	...	...	...
Sweden - Suède								
1 VII 2007 (ESDJ)								
Göteborg	491 630	242 916	248 714	449	...	...	...	...
Helsingborg	124 188	60 672	63 516	346	...	...	...	...
Jönköping	122 952	60 462	62 490	1485	...	...	...	...
Linköping	139 474	70 239	69 235	1431	...	...	...	...
Malmö	278 523	135 997	142 526	154	...	...	...	...
Norrköping	126 072	62 323	63 749	1491	...	...	...	...
Orebro	129 703	63 123	66 581	1371	...	...	...	...
STOCKHOLM	789 024	384 243	404 781	187	...	...	...	...
Umeå	111 503	55 549	55 955	2316	...	...	...	...
Uppsala	186 364	91 149	95 215	2465	...	...	...	...
Västerås	133 324	66 056	67 269	956	...	...	...	...
Switzerland - Suisse								
31 XII 2017 (ESDJ)								
Baden-Brugg	30 304	15 238	15 066	19.5	110 693[90]	55 195[90]	55 498[90]	91.6[90]
Bâle	171 513	83 195	88 318	23.9	547 761[90]	267 670[90]	280 091[90]	695.9[90]
BERNE	133 798	64 518	69 280	51.6	418 225[90]	203 529[90]	214 696[90]	780.6[90]
Fribourg	38 521	19 135	19 386	9.3	108 809[90]	54 273[90]	54 536[90]	229[90]
Genève	200 548	96 497	104 051	15.9	592 060[90]	287 733[90]	304 327[90]	536.5[90]
Lausanne	138 905	67 048	71 857	41.4	420 757[90]	206 644[90]	214 113[90]	772.6[90]
Lugano	63 494	30 663	32 831	76	151 207[90]	73 494[90]	77 713[90]	303.9[90]
Luzern	81 401	39 191	42 210	29.1	229 407[90]	112 895[90]	116 512[90]	290.5[90]
Olten-Zofingen	29 950	14 793	15 157	22.6	100 866[90]	50 426[90]	50 440[90]	155.9[90]
St. Gallen	75 522	37 021	38 501	39.4	166 762[90]	82 505[90]	84 257[90]	318.6[90]
Winterthur	110 912	54 445	56 467	68.1	141 619[90]	69 803[90]	71 816[90]	148.5[90]
Zug	30 205	15 261	14 944	21.6	130 668[90]	66 092[90]	64 576[90]	225.8[90]
Zürich	409 241	204 001	205 240	87.9	1 369 041[90]	682 461[90]	686 580[90]	1305.1[90]
Ukraine								
1 I 2018 (ESDJ)								
Alchevsk	107 542	49 388	58 154	...	...	...	...	...
Berdyansk	111 955	49 467	62 488	...	114 999	50 916	64 083	...
Bila Tserkva	205 247	94 552	110 695	...	...	...	...	...
Cherkasy	275 469	125 816	149 653	...	276 363	126 286	150 077	...
Chernihiv	283 579	130 070	153 509	...	...	...	...	...
Chernivtsi	261 924	120 154	141 770	...	...	...	...	...
Dnepropetrovsk	990 381	448 624	541 757	...	992 812	449 811	543 001	...
Dniprodzerzhynsk	234 516	105 482	129 034	...	241 432	108 600	132 832	...
Donets'k	910 252	402 964	507 288	...	926 086	410 162	515 924	...
Enakievo (Yenakievo)	78 867	34 982	43 885	...	106 873	47 580	59 293	...
Gorlivka	243 536	109 276	134 260	...	260 223	116 767	143 456	...
Ivano-Frankivsk	232 502	108 571	123 931	...	254 696	118 538	136 158	...
Kharkiv	1 430 515	661 485	769 030	...	...	...	...	...
Kherson	287 826	129 252	158 574	...	324 888	146 606	178 282	...
Khmelnitsky (Hmilnyk)	265 583	122 358	143 225	...	...	...	...	...
Kirovograd	225 489	102 466	123 023	...	233 509	106 112	127 397	...
Kramatorsk	155 155	69 162	85 993	...	188 096	84 508	103 588	...
Krasny Lutch	80 602	37 365	43 237	...	120 539	56 080	64 459	...

Continent, country or area, date, code[a] and city / Continent, pays ou zone, date, code[a] et ville	City proper - Ville proprement dite				Urban agglomeration - Agglomération urbaine			
	Population			Surface area - Superficie (km²)	Population			Surface area - Superficie (km²)
	Both sexes - Les deux sexes	Male - Masculin	Female - Féminin		Both sexes - Les deux sexes	Male - Masculin	Female - Féminin	

EUROPE

Ukraine
  1 I 2018 (ESDJ)

Krementchug	220 271	99 788	120 483	...	...	...	...	...
Krivoy Rog	628 181	282 312	345 869	...	630 941	283 708	347 233	...
KYIV	2 893 215	1 338 208	1 555 007	...	...	...	...	...
Lugansk	403 254	179 899	223 355	...	429 077	192 140	236 937	...
Luts'k	213 422	96 046	117 376	...	...	...	...	...
Lviv	720 105	336 316	383 789	...	750 044	350 357	399 687	...
Lysychansk	97 935	44 135	53 800	...	112 489	50 742	61 747	...
Makijivka	343 102	154 621	188 481	...	380 789	172 086	208 703	...
Mariupol	441 098	200 308	240 790	...	462 319	210 216	252 103	...
Melitopol	153 839	69 496	84 343	...	...	...	...	...
Nikolaev	481 760	218 915	262 845	...	...	...	...	...
Nikopol	114 156	50 748	63 408	...	...	...	...	...
Odessa	993 831	465 195	528 636	...	...	...	...	...
Pavlograd	107 127	48 998	58 129	...	...	...	...	...
Poltava	282 523	130 579	151 944	...	...	...	...	...
Rivne	243 152	111 490	131 662	...	...	...	...	...
Sievierodonetsk	104 828	46 578	58 250	...	115 013	51 434	63 579	...
Slovyansk	109 374	47 524	61 850	...	112 479	48 958	63 521	...
Sumy	263 681	118 921	144 760	...	266 550	120 314	146 236	...
Ternopil	217 171	100 200	116 971	...	...	...	...	...
Uzhhorod	112 436	52 377	60 059	...	...	...	...	...
Vinnitsa	370 017	169 260	200 757	...	...	...	...	...
Zaporozhye	741 496	334 920	406 576	...	...	...	...	...
Zhytomyr	265 679	122 455	143 224	...	...	...	...	...

United Kingdom of Great Britain and Northern Ireland - Royaume-Uni de Grande-Bretagne et d'Irlande du Nord[91]
  27 III 2011 (CDJC)

Aberdeen	207 932	102 858	105 078	...	...	...	...	...
Belfast	280 211	134 693	145 518	...	...	...	...	...
Birmingham	1 085 810	534 038	551 772	...	...	...	...	...
Bolton	194 189	95 924	98 265	...	...	...	...	...
Bournemouth	187 503	93 390	94 113	...	...	...	...	...
Bradford	349 561	173 024	176 537	...	...	...	...	...
Brighton and Hove	229 700	115 245	114 455	...	...	...	...	...
Bristol	535 907	265 968	269 939	...	...	...	...	...
Cardiff	335 145	164 427	170 718	...	...	...	...	...
Coventry	325 949	162 069	163 880	...	...	...	...	...
Derby	255 394	126 402	128 992	...	...	...	...	...
Edinburgh	482 005	234 608	247 397	...	...	...	...	...
Glasgow[92]	1 209 143	580 857	628 286	...	...	...	...	...
Kingston-upon-Hull	284 321	141 905	142 416	...	...	...	...	...
Leeds	474 632	233 488	241 144	...	...	...	...	...
Leicester	443 760	218 722	225 038	...	...	...	...	...
Liverpool	552 267	271 342	280 925	...	...	...	...	...
LONDON[93]	8 135 667	4 015 297	4 120 370	...	...	...	...	...
Luton	211 228	105 905	105 323	...	...	...	...	...
Manchester	510 746	256 984	253 762	...	...	...	...	...
Newcastle-upon-Tyne	268 064	134 375	133 689	...	...	...	...	...
Northampton	215 173	105 617	109 556	...	...	...	...	...
Nottingham	289 301	145 855	143 446	...	...	...	...	...
Plymouth	234 982	116 444	118 538	...	...	...	...	...
Portsmouth	238 137	119 369	118 768	...	...	...	...	...
Reading	218 705	109 236	109 469	...	...	...	...	...
Sheffield	518 090	255 755	262 335	...	...	...	...	...
Southampton	253 651	127 630	126 021	...	...	...	...	...
Stoke-on-Trent	270 726	134 642	136 084	...	...	...	...	...
Wolverhampton	210 319	104 047	106 272	...	...	...	...	...

8. Population of capital cities and cities of 100 000 or more inhabitants: latest available year, 1999 - 2018
Population des capitales et des villes de 100 000 habitants ou plus : dernière année disponible, 1999 - 2018 (continued - suite)

Continent, country or area, date, code[a] and city / Continent, pays ou zone, date, code[a] et ville	City proper - Ville proprement dite				Urban agglomeration - Agglomération urbaine			
	Population			Surface area - Superficie (km²)	Population			Surface area - Superficie (km²)
	Both sexes - Les deux sexes	Male - Masculin	Female - Féminin		Both sexes - Les deux sexes	Male - Masculin	Female - Féminin	
OCEANIA - OCÉANIE								
American Samoa - Samoas américaines[34]								
1 IV 2010 (CDJC)								
PAGO PAGO	3 656	...	...	...	...	...	...	...
Australia - Australie								
1 VII 2017 (ESDJ)								
Adelaide	24 193[94]	12 289[94]	11 904[94]	15.6	1 315 522[95]	646 403[95]	669 119[95]	2246.2
Ballarat	105 438[94]	51 154[94]	54 284[94]	739	...	...	...	...
Brisbane	1 209 322[94]	598 640[94]	610 682[94]	1342.7	2 331 913[95]	1 153 356[95]	1 178 557[95]	5326.7
Cairns	163 814[94]	80 869[94]	82 945[94]	1689.3	...	...	...	...
CANBERRA	411 667[94]	203 786[94]	207 881[94]	2358.2	411 667[95]	203 786[95]	207 881[95]	2358.2
Canberra-Queanbeyan	470 438[94]	233 427[94]	237 011[94]	7677.1	...	...	...	...
Central Coast	339 196[94]	165 783[94]	173 413[94]	1681.1	...	...	...	...
Darwin	85 914[94]	44 207[94]	41 707[94]	111.3	134 802[95]	70 830[95]	63 972[95]	374.4
Geelong	245 751[94]	120 362[94]	125 389[94]	1248	261 208[95]	127 972[95]	133 236[95]	1329
Gold Coast	591 356[94]	288 512[94]	302 844[94]	1333.7	606 291[95]	295 866[95]	310 425[95]	1857.9
Gold Coast-Tweed Heads	686 213[94]	334 437[94]	351 776[94]	2641.4	...	...	...	...
Greater Adelaide	...	...	...	...	1 334 167[95]	655 847[95]	678 320[95]	3259.8
Greater Brisbane	...	...	...	...	2 413 457[95]	1 194 981[95]	1 218 476[95]	15842
Greater Darwin	...	...	...	...	148 884[95]	78 495[95]	70 389[95]	3163.9
Greater Hobart	...	...	...	...	229 088[95]	114 067[95]	115 021[95]	1695.4
Greater Melbourne	...	...	...	...	4 843 781[95]	2 393 605[95]	2 450 176[95]	9992.5
Greater Perth	...	...	...	...	2 039 041[95]	1 015 914[95]	1 023 127[95]	6416.2
Greater Sydney	...	...	...	...	5 132 355[95]	2 548 906[95]	2 583 449[95]	12368.2
Hobart	52 785[94]	26 378[94]	26 407[94]	77.9	210 338[95]	104 540[95]	105 798[95]	1149.3
Melbourne	158 923[94]	77 918[94]	81 005[94]	37.4	4 670 461[95]	2 307 720[95]	2 362 741[95]	6189.1
Newcastle	162 358[94]	80 645[94]	81 713[94]	186.8	171 145[95]	84 943[95]	86 202[95]	224.9
Newcastle-Maitland	243 347[94]	120 327[94]	123 020[94]	578.3	480 422[95]	236 813[95]	243 609[95]	1179.1
Perth	27 340[94]	14 333[94]	13 007[94]	13.7	2 000 767[95]	995 407[95]	1 005 360[95]	3531.9
Sunshine Coast	311 211[94]	150 631[94]	160 580[94]	2253.9	...	...	...	...
Sydney	232 926[94]	120 965[94]	111 961[94]	26.7	4 741 249[95]	2 357 126[95]	2 384 123[95]	4196.3
Toowoomba	166 045[94]	81 106[94]	84 939[94]	12957.2	...	...	...	...
Townsville	192 988[94]	96 784[94]	96 204[94]	3730.8	...	...	...	...
Wollongong	...	...	...	...	298 431[95]	147 654[95]	150 777[95]	572.3
Cook Islands - Îles Cook[96]								
1 XII 2016* (CDFC)								
RAROTONGA	13 044	6 372	6 672	...	...	...	...	...
Fiji - Fidji								
16 IX 2007 (CDFC)								
SUVA	74 481	37 032	37 449	...	...	...	...	...
French Polynesia - Polynésie française								
22 VIII 2012 (CDFC)								
PAPEETE	25 763	12 971	12 792	...	...	...	...	...
Guam								
1 VII 2010 (ESDJ)								
AGANA	1 051	625	426	3	...	...	...	...
Kiribati								
7 XI 2015 (CDFC)								
TARAWA	...	...	...	...	63 017	30 416	32 601	...
Marshall Islands - Îles Marshall								
3 IV 2011 (CDFC)								
MAJURO	27 797	...	...	...	...	...	...	...
Micronesia (Federated States of) - Micronésie (États fédérés de)								
1 IV 2000 (CDJC)								
PALIKIR	6 227	...	...	...	...	...	...	...
New Caledonia - Nouvelle-Calédonie								
26 VIII 2014 (CDFC)								
NOUMEA	99 926	49 218	50 708	...	...	...	...	...
New Zealand - Nouvelle-Zélande[97]								
1 VII 2018 (ESDJ)								
Auckland	1 695 900	837 600	858 300	...	...	...	...	...
Christchurch	388 500	195 000	193 500	...	...	...	...	...
Dunedin	130 700	63 300	67 400	...	404 600	203 100	201 500	...

8. Population of capital cities and cities of 100 000 or more inhabitants: latest available year, 1999 - 2018
Population des capitales et des villes de 100 000 habitants ou plus : dernière année disponible, 1999 - 2018 (continued - suite)

Continent, country or area, date, code[a] and city	City proper - Ville proprement dite				Urban agglomeration - Agglomération urbaine			
	Population			Surface area - Superficie (km²)	Population			Surface area - Superficie (km²)
Continent, pays ou zone, date, code[a] et ville	Both sexes - Les deux sexes	Male - Masculin	Female - Féminin		Both sexes - Les deux sexes	Male - Masculin	Female - Féminin	
OCEANIA - OCÉANIE								
New Zealand - Nouvelle-Zélande[97]								
1 VII 2018 (ESDJ)								
Hamilton	169 300	82 200	87 100	...	241 200	117 400	123 900	...
Lower Hutt	105 900	51 900	54 000	...	...	...	...	...
Napier-Hastings	...	...	...	...	134 500	64 500	70 000	...
Tauranga	135 000	64 700	70 300	...	141 600	67 900	73 700	...
WELLINGTON.............	216 300	106 400	109 900	...	418 500	205 400	213 100	...
Niue - Nioué								
11 IX 2011 (CDFC)								
ALOFI	639	311	328	...	...	...	...	...
Northern Mariana Islands - Îles Mariannes septentrionales								
1 IV 2010 (CDFC)								
GARAPAN	3 983	1 953	2 030	...	...	...	...	...
Palau - Palaos								
13 IV 2015 (CDJC)								
KOROR	...	...	...	...	11 754	...	...	...
Papua New Guinea - Papouasie-Nouvelle-Guinée								
10 VII 2011 (CDFC)								
PORT MORESBY...........	364 125	194 834	169 291	...	...	...	...	...
Pitcairn								
31 XII 2013 (CDJC)								
ADAMSTOWN	49	23	26	...	...	...	...	...
Samoa								
7 XI 2016 (CDFC)								
APIA	37 391	18 760	18 631	...	...	...	...	...
Solomon Islands - Îles Salomon								
22 XI 2009 (CDFC)								
HONIARA	64 609	...	...	...	80 082	...	...	...
Tonga								
30 XI 2016 (CDJC)								
NUKU'ALOFA...............	...	...	...	...	35 184	17 490	17 694	...
Tuvalu								
4 XI 2012 (CDFC)								
FUNAFUTI	6 152	...	...	...	...	...	...	...
Vanuatu								
16 XI 2009 (CDFC)								
PORT VILA..................	44 039	...	...	...	...	...	...	...
Wallis and Futuna Islands - Îles Wallis et Futuna								
21 VII 2008 (CDFC)								
META-UTU	1 126	...	...	...	...	...	...	...

FOOTNOTES - NOTES

The capital city of each country is shown in capital letters. Figures in italics are estimates of questionnable reliability. For definition of city proper and urban agglomeration, method of evaluation and limitations of data see Technical Notes for this table. - Le nom de la capitale de chaque pays est imprimé en majuscules. Les chiffres en italique sont des estimations dont la fiabilité n'est pas assurée. Pour la définition de la ville proprement dite et de l'agglomération urbaine, et pour les méthodes d'évaluation et les insuffisances de données, voir les notes techniques pour ce tableau.

Italics: estimates which are less reliable. - Italiques : estimations moins sûres.

* Provisional. - Données provisoires.

[a] 'Code' indicates the source of data, as follows:
CDFC - Census, de facto, complete tabulation
CDFS - Census, de facto, sample tabulation
CDJC - Census, de jure, complete tabulation
CDJS - Census, de jure, sample tabulation
SSDF - Sample survey, de facto
SSDJ - Sample survey, de jure

ESDF - Estimates, de facto
ESDJ - Estimates, de jure

Le 'Code' indique la source des données, comme suit :
CDFC - Recensement, population de fait, tabulation complète
CDFS - Recensement, population de fait, tabulation par sondage
CDJC - Recensement, population de droit, tabulation complète
CDJS - Recensement, population de droit, tabulation par sondage
SSDF - Enquête par sondage, population de fait
SSDJ - Enquête par sondage, population de droit
ESDF - Estimations, population de fait
ESDJ - Estimations, population de droit

[1] Data refer to provincial capitals. - Les données se rapportent aux capitales des provinces.
[2] Postcensal estimates. - Estimations post censitaires.
[3] Data based on the 2011 Census. - Données fondées sur le recensement de 2011.
[4] Data refer to national projections. - Les données se réfèrent aux projections nationales.
[5] Source: Population projections and estimates of priority targets for the various health programs and interventions, National Institute of Statistics (2016). -

Source : Projections démographiques et estimations des cibles prioritaires des différents programmes et interventions de sante, Institut National de la Statistique (2016).

[6] Data refer to Total Urban Governorates. - Les données concernent les gouvernorats entièrement urbaines.

[7] Population in households only. - Population dans les ménages seulement.

[8] Data refer to the city proper plus the peri-urban area. - Les données concernent la population de la ville proprement dite et de la zone périurbaine.

[9] Data refer to Maseru Urban Centre. - Les données concernent le centre urbain de Maseru.

[10] Data refer to Greater Monrovia. - Les données concernent la région métropolitaine de Monrovia.

[11] Data refer to projections based on the 1993 Population Census. - Les données se réfèrent aux projections basées sur le recensement de la population de 1993.

[12] Data refer to District de Bamako. - Les données concernent le district de Bamako.

[13] Including nomadic population. - Y compris la population nomade.

[14] Excludes the islands of St. Brandon and Agalega. - Non compris les îles St. Brandon et Agalega.

[15] Data refer to total resident population, Saint Helenian and other nationalities. - Les données concernent la population résidente totale, originaire de Sainte-Hélène ou possédant une autre nationalité.

[16] Projections based on the 2002 Population Census. - Projections fondées sur le recensement de la population de 2002.

[17] Data refer to Greater Victoria. - Les données concernent la région métropolitaine de Victoria.

[18] Bloemfontein is the judicial capital, Cape Town is the legislative capital and Pretoria is the administrative capital. - Bloemfontein est la capitale judiciaire, Le Cap est la capitale législative et Pretoria est la capitale administrative.

[19] Data for urban agglomeration refer to communes which are administrative divisions. - Les données pour l'agglomération urbaine se rapportent aux communes qui sont des divisions administrative.

[20] Data for urban agglomeration refer to urban center (municipality). - Les données de l'agglomération urbaine se rapportent au centre urbain (commune).

[21] Data refer to the City Council. - Les données se rapportent au conseil municipal.

[22] Comprising the Northern Region (former Saguia el Hamra) and Southern Region (former Rio de Oro). - Comprend la région septentrionale (ancien Saguia-el-Hamra) et la région méridionale (ancien Rio de Oro).

[23] Bermuda is 100 per cent urban. - 100 pour cent de la population des Bermudes est urbaine.

[24] Preliminary postcensal estimates. Adjusted for census net undercoverage (including adjustment for incompletely enumerated Indian reserves). The "City proper" uses the geographic definition of Census Subdivision (CSD): Census subdivision (CSD) is the general term for municipalities (as determined by provincial/territorial legislation) or areas treated as municipal equivalents for statistical purposes. The "Urban Agglomeration" uses the geographic definition of Census Metropolitan Area\Census Agglomeration (CMA\CA). - Estimations post censitaires préliminaires. Ajusté pour le sous-estimation du recensement (y compris les réservations en Inde incomplètement énumérées). La ville est délimitée selon la définition géographique de la subdivision pour le recensement, qui est le terme générique utilisé pour désigner les municipalités (telles que définies par la législation provinciale ou territorial) et les zones considérées comme telles à des fins statistiques. L'agglomération urbaine correspond à la définition géographique de la région métropolitaine ou de l'agglomération pour le recensement.

[25] Excluding the institutional population. - Non compris la population dans les institutions.

[26] Data refers to "cantons" rather than to cities. Data are based on population estimates and projections. - Les données concernent les « cantons », et non les villes. Les données sont fondées sur des estimations et des projections démographiques.

[27] Population statistics are compiled from registers. - Les statistiques de la population sont compilées à partir de registres.

[28] Data refer to Kingston Metropolitan Area. - Données pour la zone métropolitaine de Kingston.

[29] Data based on the 2010 Population Census. - Les données sont fondées sur le recensement de la population de 2010.

[30] Including armed forces stationed in the area. Postcensal estimates. - Y compris les militaires en garnison sur le territoire. Estimations post censitaires.

[31] City refers to a type of incorporated place in 49 states and the District of Columbia, that has an elected government and provides a range of government functions and services. Also included among the cities on this list is Urban Honolulu, Hawaii Census Designated Place (CDP), for which the Census Bureau reports data under agreement with the State of Hawaii (instead of the combined city and county of Honolulu). - Par ville, on entend un lieu doté de la personnalité morale dans 49 États et dans le district de Columbia, qui a un gouvernement élu et fournit tout un ensemble de fonctions et de services publics. Sont également inclus Honolulu, lieu chargé du recensement pour Hawaii, pour lequel le Census Bureau établit les données en accord avec l'État de Hawaii (au lieu de la ville et du comté d'Honolulu).

[32] Excluding U.S. Armed Forces overseas and civilian U.S. citizens whose usual place of residence is outside the United States. - Non compris les militaires américains à l'étranger et les civils américains dont le lieu de résidence habituel est en dehors des États-Unis.

[33] Excluding inland water. - Exception faite des eaux intérieures.

[34] Including armed forces stationed in the area. - Y compris les militaires en garnison sur le territoire.

[35] Projections based on the 2010 Population and Housing Census. - Projections fondées sur le recensement 2010 de la population et des logements.

[36] Data refer to municipalities, which may contain an urban centre as well as rural areas. - Pour municipios qui peuvent comprendre un centre urbain et aussi une zone rurale.

[37] Excluding interior waters. - Eaux intérieures non comprises.

[38] Data exclude the population of the cities of Puente Alto and San Bernardo. - Les données ne comprennent pas la population des villes de Puente Alto et de San Bernardo.

[39] Data are revised projections taking into consideration also the results of the 2005 census. - Les données sont des projections révisées tenant compte également des résultats du recensement de 2005.

[40] Surface area includes interior waters. - La superficie comprend les eaux intérieures.

[41] Data excludes "temporary visitors". - Données n'incluant pas les « visiteurs temporaires ».

[42] The Metropolitan Area of Asunción is made up of Asunción and the 19 Central Department districts. - La zone métropolitaine d'Asunción est composée d'Asunción et de 19 districts du Département central.

[43] Data refer to the Province of Lima and the Constitutional Province of Callao. - Les données concernent la province de Lima et la province constitutionnelle de Callao.

[44] Data refer to national projections. Data refer to the department of Montevideo. - Les données se réfèrent aux projections nationales. Les données concernent le département de Montevideo.

[45] Excluding foreign diplomatic personnel and their dependants. Data based on the 2008 Population Census. - Non compris le personnel diplomatique étranger et les membres de leur famille les accompagnant. Données fondées sur le recensement de population de 2008.

[46] Data refer only to the population in urban areas of Beijing. - Les données ne concernent que la population des zones urbaines de Beijing.

[47] Population by-census is conducted between two population censuses, adopting a sampling method to select 29,421 housing units in Macao for enumeration, with the unit of observation being the individuals residing in the selected housing units. - Aux fins du recensement partiel de la population, conduit entre deux recensements, la méthode d'échantillonnage adoptée a permis de sélectionner 29 421 unités d'habitation à Macao, l'unité d'observation étant les personnes qui y résident.

[48] The urban agglomeration of Lefkosia is composed of Lefkosia municipality, Agios Dometios, Egkomi, Strovolos, Aglangia, Lakatameia, Anthoupoli, Latsia and Geri. - L'agglomération urbaine de Lefkosia est composée de la municipalité de Lefkosia et Agios Dometios, Egkomi, Strovolos, Aglangia, Lakatameia, Anthoupoli, Latsia et Geri.

[49] The urban agglomeration of Lemesos is composed of Lemesos municipality, Mesa Geitonia, Agios Athanasios, Germasogeia, Pano Polemidia, Ypsonas and Kato Polemidia. - L'agglomération de Lemesos comprend la municipalité du même nom, ainsi que Mesa Geitonia, Agios Athanasios, Germasogeia, Pano Polemidia, Ypsonas et Kato Polemidia.

[50] Including Kep. Seribu, North Jakarta, East Jakarta, South Jakarta, West Jakarta and Central Jakarta. - Y compris les îles Seribu, Jakarta-Nord, Jakarta-Est, Jakarta-Sud, Jakarta-Ouest et Jakarta-Centre.

[51] Data refer to "Baghdad Al-Jedeeda Nahia" - Les données concernent le district Al-Jadeeda de Bagdad (Baghdad Al-Jedeeda Nahiya).

[52] Designation and data provided by Israel. The position of the United Nations on the question of Jerusalem is contained in General Assembly resolution 181 (II) and subsequent resolutions of the General Assembly and the Security Council concerning this question. Including East Jerusalem. - Appelation de données fournies par Israel. La position des Nations Unies concernant la question de Jérusalem est décrite dans la resolution 181 (II) de l'Assemblée générale et résolutions ultérieures de l'Assemblée générale et du Conseil de sécurité sur cette question. Y compris Jérusalem-Est.

[53] Excluding diplomatic personnel outside the country and foreign military and civilian personnel and their dependants stationed in the area. - Non compris le personnel diplomatique hors du pays ni les militaires et agents civils étrangers en poste sur le territoire et les membres de leur famille les accompagnant.

54 Land areas are based on the "Municipalities Area Statistics of Japan, 2015" published by the Geospatial Information Authority of Japan, Ministry of Land, Infrastructure, Transport and Tourism. - Les zones terrestres sont déterminées selon les statistiques relatives aux municipalités du Japon en 2015, publiées par l'Autorité japonaise d'information géospatiale du Ministère de l'aménagement foncier, des infrastructures, des transports et du tourisme.

55 Excluding diplomatic personnel outside the country and foreign military and civilian personnel and their dependants stationed in the area. Data for Tokyo refer to 23 ku (wards) of Tokyo. - Non compris le personnel diplomatique hors du pays ni les militaires et agents civils étrangers en poste sur le territoire et les membres de leur famille les accompagnant. Données relatives à Tokyo concernant 23 ku (arrondissements de la ville).

56 Data refer to resident population. - Les données concernent la population résidente.

57 Data refer to annual average population. - Les données correspondent à la population annuelle moyenne.

58 Based on the results of the 2005 Population and Housing Census. - Données fondées sur les résultats du recensement de la population et de l'habitat de 2005.

59 Source: Living conditions of household survey, October 2011 to September 2012. - Source: Enquête sur les conditions de vie des ménages, octobre 2011 à septembre 2012.

60 Estimates based on the adjusted results of the Population and Housing Census of 2010. - Les estimations sont fondée sur les résultats ajustées du recensement de la population et de l'habitat de 2010.

61 Data refer to resident population which includes resident Maldivians and resident foreigners. - Les données concernent la population résidente, qui comprend les Maldiviens et les étrangers.

62 Including population from all eight townships. - Y compris la population des huit municipalités.

63 Data refer to registered population data from Royal Oman Police. - Les données portent sur la population enregistrée par la police royale de l'Oman.

64 Land area includes inland water. - La zone terrestre comprend les eaux intérieures.

65 Data refer to total population, which comprises Singapore residents and non-residents. Data exclude residents who have been away from Singapore for a continuous period of 12 months or longer as at the reference date. - Les données se rapportent à la population totale composé des résidents de Singapour et les non résidents. Non compris les résidents hors de Singapour pour une période ininterrompue de 12 mois ou plus avant de la date de référence.

66 The land area of Singapore comprises the mainland and other islands. - La superficie terrestre de Singapour comprend l'île principale et les autres îles.

67 The Population and Housing Census 2001 did not cover the whole area of the country due to the security problems; data refer to the 18 districts for which the census was completed only (in three districts it was not possible to conduct the census at all and in four districts it was partially conducted). - Le recensement de la population et du logement de 2001 n'a pas été réalisé sur la superficie totale du pays à cause de problèmes de sécurité; les données ne concernent que les 18 districts entièrement recensés (3 districts n'ont pas été recensés du tout, et 4 ont été recensés en partie).

68 Designation and data provided by the State of Palestine. The position of the United Nations on the question of Jerusalem is contained in General Assembly resolution 181 (II) and subsequent resolutions of the General Assembly and the Security Council concerning this question. - Appellation de données fournies par l'État de Palestine. La position des Nations Unies concernant la question de Jérusalem est décrite dans la résolution 181 (II) de l'Assemblée générale et résolutions ultérieures de l'Assemblée générale et du Conseil de sécurité sur cette question.

69 Data refer to urban area of municipality of Dili. - Les données se réfèrent à la zone urbaine de la municipalité de Dili.

70 Data based on Address Based Population Registration System. - Les données sont basées sur le registre national de la population basé sur l'adresse.

71 Data include Anderlecht and Schaerbeek. - Les données comprennent Anderlecht et Schaerbeek.

72 Excluding Faeroe Islands and Greenland shown separately, if available. - Non compris les Iles Féroé et le Groenland, qui font l'objet de rubriques distinctes, si disponible.

73 Land area refers to built over area. - Partie du territoire désigne une zone bâtie.

74 Urban Agglomeration refers to Tórshavn, Hoyvík, Argir and Hvítanes. Land area refers to built over area. - Agglomération urbaine fait référence à Tórshavn, Hoyvík, Argir et Hvítanes. Partie du territoire désigne une zone bâtie.

75 Excluding Åland Islands. - Non compris les Îles d'Åland.

76 City proper refers to commune or municipality. - La ville proprement dite se rapporte à la commune ou à la municipalité.

77 The city of Aix-en-Provence is part of the urban agglomeration of Marseille. - La ville d'Aix-en-Provence fait partie de l'agglomération urbaine de Marseille.

78 The communes of Argenteuil, Boulogne-Billancourt and Montreuil are parts of the urban agglomeration of Paris. - Les communes de Argenteuil, Boulogne-Billancourt et Montreuil font partie de l'agglomération urbaine de Paris.

79 Excluding military personnel, visitors and transients. - Non compris les militaires, ni les visiteurs et transients.

80 Data refer to the Vatican City State. - Les données se rapportent à l'Etat de la Cité du Vatican.

81 Data refer to usually resident population. - Les données concernent la population habituellement résidente.

82 Data refer to registered resident population. - Les données concernent la population enregistrée résidente.

83 The urban agglomeration of the capital area includes the following communes: Bessastaðahreppur, Garðabær, Hafnarfjörður, Kjósarhreppur, Kópavogur, Mosfellsbær ,Reykjavík, Seltjarnarnes. - L'agglomération urbaine de la capitale comprend les communes suivantes : Bessastaðahreppur, Garðabær, Hafnarfjörður, Kjósarhreppur, Kópavogur, Mosfellsbær ,Reykjavík, Seltjarnarnes.

84 Including civilian nationals temporarily outside the country. - Y compris les civils nationaux temporairement hors du pays.

85 Figures for male and female population do not add up to the figure for total population, because they exclude 119 persons of unknown sex. - Les chiffres relatifs à la population masculine et féminine ne correspondent pas au chiffre de la population totale, parce que l'on en a exclu 119 personnes de sexe inconnu.

86 City is defined as an administratively separated area entitled to civil (municipal) rights. - Une ville est définie comme une zone administrativement distincte dotée de droits municipaux.

87 Excludes non-residents present in country at time of census (visitors, foreigners temporarily residing in country, etc.). - Exclue les non-résidents présents dans le pays au moment du recensement (visiteurs, étrangers résidant temporairement dans le pays, etc.).

88 Excludes data for Kosovo and Metohia. - Sans les données pour le Kosovo et Metohia.

89 Excludes data for Kosovo and Metohia. Data for urban agglomeration refer to communes which are administrative divisions. - Sans les données pour le Kosovo et Metohia. Les données pour l'agglomération urbaine se rapportent aux communes qui sont des divisions administrative.

90 From 2014, urban refers to urban centers and areas under the influence of urban centers. - A partir de 2014, le territoire inclut l'espace des centres urbains ainsi que l'espace sous influence des centres urbains.

91 Excluding Channel Islands (Guernsey and Jersey) and Isle of Man, shown separately, if available. - Non compris les îles Anglo-Normandes (Guernesey et Jersey) et l'île de Man, qui font l'objet de rubriques distinctes, si disponible.

92 Data refer to Greater Glasgow. - Les données concernent la région métropolitaine de Glasgow.

93 Data refer to Greater London. - Les données concernent la région métropolitaine de London.

94 City proper areas are based on 2017 Local Government Areas (LGAs): Gold Coast-Tweed and Newcastle-Maitland consist of two LGAs; Canberra is the Australian Capital Territory (ACT) Greater Capital City Statistical Area (GCCSA) and is unincorporated (no local government); and Canberra-Queanbeyan is the ACT GCCSA and Queanbeyan-Palerang Regional (LGA). - Les zones urbaines sont définies sur la base des zones d'administration locale de 2017. Ainsi, Gold Coast-Tweed et Newcastle-Maitland se composent de deux zones d'administration locale ; Canberra, grande capitale régionale du Territoire de la capitale australienne, ne dépend d'aucun gouvernement local ; et Canberra-Queanbeyan, grande capitale régionale du Territoire de la capitale australienne, relève du gouvernement local de Queanbeyan-Palerang.

95 Urban Agglomeration areas are based the 2016 edition of the Australian Statistical Geography Standard: Gold Coast is a Statistical Area Level 4 (SA4); Newcastle and Wollongong are SA3s; Greater Adelaide, Brisbane, Darwin, Hobart, Melbourne and Perth are GCCSAs; and all other areas are Significant Urban Areas (SUAs). - Les zones d'agglomération urbaine sont définies sur la base de la Norme géographique australienne de statistique de 2016. Ainsi, Gold Coast est une zone de statistiques de niveau 4 ; Newcastle et Wollongong sont des zones de statistiques de niveau 3 ; Greater Adelaide, Brisbane, Darwin, Hobart, Melbourne et Perth sont des grandes capitales régionales ; et toutes les autres zones sont des zones urbaines importantes.

96 Excluding Niue, shown separately, which is part of Cook Islands, but because of remoteness is administered separately. - Non compris Nioué, qui fait l'objet d'une rubrique distincte et qui fait partie des îles Cook, mais qui, en raison de son éloignement, est administrée séparément.

97 Because of rounding, totals are not in all cases the sum of the respective components. Intercensal estimates. 1. Land area excludes inlet, inland water and oceanic areas. 2. A city is a territorial authority which is a distinct entity, is predominantly urban in character, has a minimum population of 50,000 and is a major centre of activity within its parent region. 3. Urban agglomerations refer to

main urban areas that are centres with populations of 30,000 or more. Since 2011 Auckland includes Manukau city, North Shore city, and Waktakere city and Wellington urban area includes Lower Hutt. Napier-Hastings consist of two separate territorial authorities. Napier is a city, while Hastings is a district based on the New Zealand Standard Areas Classification. - Les chiffres étant arrondis, les totaux ne correspondent pas toujours rigoureusement à la somme des composants respectifs. Estimations inter-censitaires. 1. La superficie terrestre exclut les cours d'eau, les eaux intérieures et les zones océaniques. 2. Par « ville », on entend une autorité territoriale qui est une entité distincte, de caractère essentiellement urbain, dont la population s'élève à au moins 50 000 personnes et qui représente l'un des principaux centres d'activité de la région dans laquelle elle se trouve. 3. Par « agglomérations urbaines », on entend les grandes zones urbaines dont la population s'élève à au moins 30 000 personnes. Depuis 2011, Auckland comprend Manukau City, North Shore City et Waktakere city, tandis que la zone urbaine de Wellington comprend Lower Hutt. Napier-Hastings se compose de deux autorités territoriales distinctes. Ainsi, selon les règles de classification des territoires néo-zélandais, Napier est une ville et Hastings est un district.

Table 9 - *Demographic Yearbook 2018*

Table 9 presents live births and crude birth rates by urban/rural residence for as many years as possible between 2014 and 2018.

Description of variables: Live birth is defined as the complete expulsion or extraction from its mother of a product of conception, irrespective of the duration of pregnancy, which after such separation, breathes or shows any other evidence of life such as beating of the heart, pulsation of the umbilical cord, or definite movements of voluntary muscles, whether or not the umbilical cord has been cut or the placenta is attached; each product of such a birth is considered live-born[1].

Statistics on the number of live births are obtained from civil registers unless otherwise noted. For those countries or areas where civil registration statistics on live births are considered reliable the birth rates shown have been calculated on the basis of registered live births.

For certain countries, there is a discrepancy between the total number of live births shown in this table and those shown in subsequent tables for the same year. Usually this discrepancy arises because the total number of live births occurring in a given year is revised but not the remaining tabulations.

Rate computation: Crude birth rates are the annual number of live births per 1 000 mid-year population.

Rates by urban/rural residence are the annual number of live births, in the appropriate urban or rural category, per 1 000 corresponding mid-year population. Rates are calculated only for data considered complete, that is, coded with a "C" and for estimates and live births statistics for the 12 month period prior to the census date, coded with a "|". These rates are calculated by the Statistics Division of the United Nations based on the appropriate reference population (for example: total population, nationals only, etc.) if known and available. If the reference population is not known or unavailable, the total population is used to calculate the rates. Therefore, if the population that is used to calculate the rates is different from the correct reference population, the rates presented might under- or overstate the true situation in a country or area.

Rates presented in this table are limited to those countries or areas having a minimum number of 30 live births in a given year.

Reliability of data: Each country or area has been asked to indicate the estimated completeness of the live births recorded in its civil register. These national assessments are indicated by the quality codes "C" and "U" that appear in the first column of this table.

"C" indicates that the data are estimated to be virtually complete, that is, representing at least 90 per cent of the live births occurring each year, whereas "U" indicates that data are estimated to be incomplete, that is, representing less than 90 per cent of the live births occurring each year. A third code "..." indicates that no information was provided regarding completeness.

Data from civil registers that are reported as incomplete or of unknown completeness (coded "U" or "...") are considered unreliable. They appear in italics in this table and rates are not calculated for these data.

These quality codes apply only to data from civil registers. If data from other sources are presented, the symbol "|" is shown instead of the quality code. For more information about the quality of vital statistics data in general, and the information available on the basis of the completeness estimates in particular, see section 4.2 of the Technical Notes.

Limitations: Statistics on live births are subject to the same qualifications as have been set forth for vital statistics in general and birth statistics in particular as discussed in section 4 of the Technical Notes.

The reliability of data, an indication of which is described above, is an important factor in considering the limitations. In addition, some live births are tabulated by date of registration and not by date of occurrence; these have been indicated by a plus sign "+". Whenever the lag between the date of occurrence and date of registration is prolonged and, therefore, a large proportion of the live birth registrations are delayed, birth statistics for any given year may be seriously affected.

Another factor that limits international comparability is the practice of some countries or areas not to include in live birth statistics infants who were born alive but died before the registration of the birth or within the first 24 hours of life, thus underestimating the total number of life births. Statistics of this type are footnoted.

In addition, it should be noted that rates are affected also by the quality and limitations of the population estimates that are used in their computation. The problems of under-enumeration or over-enumeration and, to some extent, the differences in definition of total population have been discussed in section 3 of the Technical Notes dealing with population data in general, and specific information pertaining to individual countries or areas is given in the footnotes to table 3.

The rates estimated from the results of sample surveys are subject to possibilities of considerable error as a result of omissions in reporting of births, or as a result of erroneous reporting of births that occurred outside the reference period. However, rates estimated from sample surveys have the advantage of the availability of a built-in and strictly corresponding population base.

It should be emphasized that crude birth rates - like crude death, marriage and divorce rates - may be seriously affected by the age-sex structure of the populations to which they relate. Nevertheless, they do provide a simple measure of the level of and changes in fertility.

The urban/rural classification of birth may refer to the residence of mother or the place of delivery, according to the national practice and it is provided by each country or area. In addition, the comparability of data by urban/rural residence is affected by the national definition of urban and rural used in tabulating these data. It is assumed, in the absence of specific information to the contrary, that the definitions of urban and rural used in connection with the national population census were also used in the compilation of the vital statistics for each country or area. However, it cannot be ruled out that, for a given country or area, different definitions of urban and rural are used for the vital statistics data and the population census data respectively. When known, the definitions of urban used in national population census are presented at the end of the technical notes to table 6. As discussed in detail in the technical notes to table 6, these definitions vary considerably from one area or country to another. Urban/rural differentials in vital rates may also be affected by whether the vital events have been tabulated in terms of place of occurrence or place of usual residence. This problem is discussed in more detail in section 4.1.4.1 of the Technical notes.

Earlier data: Live births have been shown in each issue of the *Demographic Yearbook*. Information on the years and specific topics covered is presented in the Historical Index.

NOTES

[1] *Principles and Recommendations for a Vital Statistics System Revision 3*, Sales No. E.13.XVII.10, United Nations, New York, 2014.

Tableau 9 – *Annuaire démographique 2018*

Le tableau 9 présente des données sur les naissances vivantes et les taux bruts de natalité selon le lieu de résidence (zone urbaine ou rurale) pour le plus grand nombre d'années possible entre 2014 et 2018.

Description des variables : La naissance vivante est l'expulsion ou l'extraction complète du corps de la mère, indépendamment de la durée de gestation, d'un produit de la conception qui, après cette séparation, respire ou manifeste tout autre signe de vie, tel que battement de cœur, pulsation du cordon ombilical ou contraction effective d'un muscle soumis à l'action de la volonté, que le cordon ombilical ait été coupé ou non et que le placenta soit ou non demeuré attaché ; tout produit d'une telle naissance est considéré comme « enfant né vivant »[1].

Sauf indication contraire, les statistiques relatives au nombre de naissances vivantes sont établies sur la base des registres de l'état civil. Pour les pays ou zones où les statistiques obtenues auprès des services de l'état civil sont jugées sûres, les taux de natalité indiqués ont été calculés par la Division de statistique de l'ONU d'après les naissances vivantes enregistrées.

Pour quelques pays il y a une discordance entre le nombre total des naissances présenté dans ce tableau et ceux présentés après pour la même année. Habituellement ces différences apparaissent lorsque le nombre total des naissances pour une certaine année a été révisé alors que les autres tabulations ne l'ont pas été.

Calcul des taux : Les taux bruts de natalité représentent le nombre annuel de naissances vivantes pour 1 000 habitants au milieu de l'année.

Les taux selon le lieu de résidence (zone urbaine ou rurale) représentent le nombre annuel de naissances vivantes, classées selon la catégorie urbaine ou rurale appropriée pour 1 000 habitants au milieu de l'année. Les taux ont été calculés seulement pour les données considérées complètes, c'est-à-dire celles associées au code « C », ainsi que pour les estimations et les statistiques des naissances vivantes dans la periode des douze mois précédante la date de recensement associées au code « | ». Ces taux sont calculés par la division de statistique des Nations Unies sur la base de la population de référence adéquate (par exemple : population totale, nationaux seulement, etc.) si connue et disponible. Si la population de référence n'est pas connue ou n'est pas disponible, la population totale est utilisée pour calculer les taux. Par conséquent, si la population utilisée pour calculer les taux est différente de la population de référence adéquate, les taux présentés sont susceptibles de sous ou sur estimer la situation réelle d'un pays ou d'un territoire.

Les taux présentés dans ce tableau se rapportent seulement aux pays ou zones où l'on a enregistré un nombre minimal de 30 naissances vivantes au cours d'une année donnée.

Fiabilité des données : Il a été demandé à chaque pays ou zone d'indiquer le degré estimatif de complétude des données sur les naissances vivantes figurant dans ses registres d'état civil. Ces évaluations nationales sont signalées par les codes de qualité "C" et "U" qui apparaissent dans la deuxième colonne du tableau.

La lettre "C" indique que les données sont jugées à peu près complètes, c'est-à-dire qu'elles représentent au moins 90 p. 100 des naissances vivantes survenues chaque année ; la lettre "U" signifie que les données sont jugées incomplètes, c'est-à-dire qu'elles représentent moins de 90 p. 100 des naissances vivantes survenues chaque année. Un troisième code, "...", indique qu'aucun renseignement n'a été communiqué quant à la complétude des données.

Les données provenant des registres de l'état civil qui sont déclarées incomplètes ou dont le degré de complétude n'est pas connu (code "U" ou "...") sont jugées douteuses. Elles apparaissent en italique dans le tableau. Les taux pour ces données ne sont pas calculés.

Les codes de qualité ne s'appliquent qu'aux données provenant des registres de l'état civil. Si l'on présente des données autres que celles de l'état civil, le signe "|" est utilisé à la place du code de qualité. Pour plus de précisions sur la qualité des données reposant sur les statistiques de l'état civil en général et les estimations de complétude en particulier, voir la section 4.2 des Notes techniques.

Insuffisance des données : Les statistiques concernant les naissances vivantes appellent toutes les réserves qui ont été formulées à propos des statistiques de l'état civil en général et des statistiques des naissances en particulier (voir la section 4 des Notes techniques).

La fiabilité des données, au sujet de laquelle des indications ont été fournies plus haut, est un facteur important. Il faut également tenir compte du fait que, dans certains cas, les données relatives aux naissances vivantes sont exploitées selon la date de l'enregistrement et non selon la date de l'événement ; ces cas ont été signalés par le signe '+'. Chaque fois que le décalage entre l'événement et son enregistrement est grand et qu'une forte proportion des naissances vivantes fait l'objet d'un enregistrement tardif, les statistiques des naissances vivantes pour une année donnée peuvent être considérablement faussées.

Un autre facteur qui nuit à la comparabilité internationale est la pratique de certains pays ou zones qui consiste à ne pas inclure dans les statistiques des naissances vivantes les enfants nés vivants mais décédés avant l'enregistrement de leur naissance ou dans les 24 heures qui ont suivi la naissance, pratique qui conduit à sous-estimer le nombre total de naissances vivantes. Lorsque ce facteur a joué, cela a été signalé en note à la fin du tableau.

La qualité et les limitations des estimations concernant la population ont également une incidence sur le calcul des taux. Les problèmes liés au sur-dénombrement ou au sous-dénombrement et, dans une certaine mesure, aux différences dans la définition de la population totale ont été abordés à la section 3 des Notes techniques relative aux données sur la population en général et des précisions sur certains pays ou zones sont données dans les notes se rapportant au tableau 3.

Les taux estimatifs fondés sur les résultats d'enquêtes par sondage comportent des possibilités d'erreurs considérables dues soit à des omissions dans les déclarations, soit au fait que l'on a déclaré à tort des naissances survenues en réalité hors de la période considérée. Toutefois, les taux estimatifs fondés sur les résultats d'enquêtes par sondage présentent un gros avantage : le chiffre de population utilisé comme base est, par définition, rigoureusement correspondant.

Il faut souligner que les taux bruts de natalité, de même que les taux bruts de mortalité, de nuptialité et de divortialité, peuvent varier très sensiblement selon la structure par âge et par sexe de la population à laquelle ils se rapportent. Ils offrent néanmoins un moyen simple de mesurer le niveau et l'évolution de la natalité.

La classification des naissances selon le lieu de résidence (zone urbaine ou rurale) peut se rapporter au lieu de résidence de la mère ou au lieu d'occurrence et correspond à celle indiquée par chaque pays ou zone. En outre, la comparabilité des données selon le lieu de résidence (zone urbaine ou rurale) peut être limitée par les définitions nationales des termes « urbain » et « rural » utilisées pour la mise en tableaux de ces données. En l'absence d'indications contraires, on a supposé que les mêmes définitions avaient servi pour le recensement national de la population et pour l'établissement des statistiques de l'état civil pour chaque pays ou zone. Toutefois, il n'est pas exclu que, pour une zone ou un pays donné, des définitions différentes aient été retenues. Les définitions du terme « urbain » utilisées pour les recensements nationaux de population ont été présentées à la fin des notes techniques du tableau 6 lorsqu'elles étaient connues. Comme on l'a précisé dans les notes techniques relatives au tableau 6, ces définitions varient considérablement d'un pays ou d'une zone à l'autre. La différence entre ces taux pour les zones urbaines et rurales pourra aussi être faussée selon que les faits d'état civil auront été classés d'après le lieu de l'événement ou le lieu de résidence habituel. Ce problème est examiné plus en détail à la section 4.1.4.1 des Notes techniques.

Données publiées antérieurement : Les différentes éditions de l'*Annuaire démographique* contiennent des données sur les naissances vivantes. Pour plus de précisions concernant les années et les sujets pour lesquels des données ont été publiées, se reporter à l'index historique.

NOTES
[1] *Principes et recommandations pour un système de statistique de l'état civil, troisième révision*, numéro de vente : E.13.XVII.10, publication des Nations Unies, New York, 2014.

9. Live births and crude birth rates, by urban/rural residence: 2014 - 2018
Naissances vivantes et taux bruts de natalité selon la résidence, urbaine/rurale : 2014 - 2018

Continent, country or area, and urban/rural residence / Continent, pays ou zone et résidence, urbaine/rurale	Code[a]	Number - Nombre					Rate - Taux				
		2014	2015	2016	2017	2018	2014	2015	2016	2017	2018
AFRICA - AFRIQUE											
Algeria - Algérie[1]											
Total	C	1 014 248	1 040 285	1 066 823	...	...	25.9	26.0	26.1	...	...
Angola[2]											
Total	|	1 152 490	...	...	...	...	44.5	...	...	...	...
Urban - Urbaine	|	670 605	...	...	...	...	41.3	...	...	...	...
Rural - Rurale	|	481 884	...	...	...	...	49.9	...	...	...	...
Botswana[3]											
Total	U	41 741	46 765	49 984	...	...	...	...	...	...	...
Total	C	...	...	...	43 290	...	...	...	...	19.1	...
Burundi[4]											
Total	+U	253 698	266 820	...	...	...	...	...	...	...	...
Congo[5]											
Total	+U	111 360	...	...	...	...	...	...	...	...	...
Urban - Urbaine	+U	84 849	...	...	...	...	...	...	...	...	...
Rural - Rurale	+U	26 511	...	...	...	...	...	...	...	...	...
Côte d'Ivoire											
Total	+U	631 804	626 783	659 247	619 181	635 924	...	...	...	...	...
Egypt - Égypte											
Total	+C	2 720 495	2 685 276	2 600 173	2 557 440	...	31.3	30.2	28.6	26.9	...
Urban - Urbaine	+C	1 228 275	1 224 729	1 241 469	1 292 661	...	33.1	32.2	31.9	32.0	...
Rural - Rurale[6]	+C	1 492 220	1 460 547	1 358 704	1 264 779	...	30.0	28.7	26.1	23.1	...
Guinea - Guinée[6]											
Total	|	440 340	...	...	...	...	41.5	...	...	...	...
Urban - Urbaine	|	132 995	...	...	...	...	36.1	...	...	...	...
Rural - Rurale	|	307 345	...	...	...	...	44.4	...	...	...	...
Kenya											
Total	+U	954 254	950 224	948 351	923 487	1 148 352	...	...	...	...	...
Lesotho											
Total	+U	...	10 800	9 655	9 463	...	...	...	...	...	...
Malawi[7]											
Total	|	...	...	...	...	576 525	...	...	...	...	32.8
Urban - Urbaine	|	...	...	...	...	84 639	...	...	...	...	30.1
Rural - Rurale	|	...	...	...	...	491 886	...	...	...	...	33.4
Mauritius - Maurice[8]											
Total	+C	13 283	12 640	12 948	13 385	12 980	10.5	10.0	10.2	10.6	10.3
Urban - Urbaine	+C	5 158	5 150	5 302	5 303	5 362	10.0	10.0	10.3	10.3	10.4
Rural - Rurale	+C	8 125	7 490	7 646	8 082	7 618	10.9	10.1	10.2	10.8	10.1
Mayotte											
Total	C	7 306	8 997	9 496	9 762	...	32.0	38.3	38.9	38.2	...
Mozambique[9]											
Total	U	794 718	...	...	...	...	...	...	...	...	...
Reunion - Réunion[10]											
Total	C	14 095	14 011	13 742	13 708	...	16.6	16.4	16.0	15.9	...
Urban - Urbaine	C	...	...	13 225	...	...	...	...	...	...	...
Rural - Rurale	C	...	...	483	...	...	...	...	...	...	...
Saint Helena ex. dep. - Sainte-Hélène sans dép.											
Total	C	48	40	35	36	26	10.9	8.9	7.5	7.9	...
Sao Tome and Principe - Sao Tomé-et-Principe											
Total	C	4 939	5 022	5 105	5 190	...	26.6	26.5	26.4	26.3	...
Seychelles											
Total	+C	1 557	1 592	1 645	1 651	1 650	17.0	17.0	17.4	17.2	17.1
South Africa - Afrique du Sud											
Total	U	1 019 495	966 162	...	...	...	...	...	...	...	...
Total	C	...	...	906 375	913 499	...	...	...	16.2	16.1	...
Tunisia - Tunisie											
Total	C	225 887	222 534	219 441	209 236	...	20.5	20.0	19.4	18.3	...
AMERICA, NORTH - AMÉRIQUE DU NORD											
Anguilla											
Total	+C	151	165	135	145	...	10.6	11.2	9.0	...	...

9. Live births and crude birth rates, by urban/rural residence: 2014 - 2018
Naissances vivantes et taux bruts de natalité selon la résidence, urbaine/rurale : 2014 - 2018 (continued - suite)

Continent, country or area, and urban/rural residence — Continent, pays ou zone et résidence, urbaine/rurale	Code[a]	Number - Nombre					Rate - Taux				
		2014	2015	2016	2017	2018	2014	2015	2016	2017	2018
AMERICA, NORTH - AMÉRIQUE DU NORD											
Antigua and Barbuda - Antigua-et-Barbuda											
Total	+C	1 100	1 159	1 063	1 108	1 015	12.3	12.8	11.5	11.8	10.7
Aruba											
Total	C	1 376	1 244	1 259	1 202	*1 028	12.8	11.4	11.4	10.8	*9.2
Bahamas											
Total	+U	*4 365	*4 253	*4 093	*4 017	...	...	...	...	...	...
Barbados - Barbade											
Total	+C	2 902	...	...	...	...	10.5	...	...	...	...
Belize											
Total	U	7 319	7 459	7 226	7 252	7 775	...	...	...	...	...
Urban - Urbaine[11]	U	2 952	3 075	2 863	...	...	...	...	...	...	...
Rural - Rurale[11]	U	4 339	4 353	4 301	...	...	...	...	...	...	...
Bermuda - Bermudes[12]											
Total	C	574	583	591	576	527	9.3	9.4	9.3	9.0	8.2
British Virgin Islands - Îles Vierges britanniques											
Total	C	280	266	269	248	...	...	9.1	...	...	...
Canada[13]											
Total	C	384 100	382 392	383 102	376 291	...	10.8	10.7	10.6	10.3	...
Cayman Islands - Îles Caïmanes											
Total	C	711	649	660	625	640	12.5	11.0	10.8	9.9	9.7
Costa Rica											
Total	C	71 793[14]	71 819	70 004	68 816	*68 479	15.0	14.9	14.3	13.9	*13.7
Urban - Urbaine	C	41 631[14]	49 744	48 392	47 273	*46 647	12.0	14.2	13.6	13.2	*12.8
Rural - Rurale	C	30 162[14]	22 075	21 612	21 543	*21 832	23.2	16.7	16.2	15.9	*15.9
Cuba											
Total	C	122 643	125 064	116 872	114 971	*116 333	10.9	11.1	10.4	10.2	*10.4
Urban - Urbaine	C	96 930	99 434	93 565	93 370	...	11.2	11.5	10.8	10.8	...
Rural - Rurale	C	25 713	25 630	23 307	21 601	...	9.9	9.9	9.0	8.3	...
Curaçao											
Total	C	1 963	1 877	1 789	1 548	1 727	12.6	11.9	11.2	9.7	10.8
Dominica - Dominique											
Total	+C	858	...	...	...	...	12.0	...	...	...	...
Dominican Republic - République dominicaine											
Total	U	165 783	161 622	152 370	148 061	...	...	...	...	...	...
Urban - Urbaine[15]	U	132 817	124 566	...	...	...	...	...	...	...	...
Rural - Rurale[15]	U	22 725	19 766	...	...	...	...	...	...	...	...
El Salvador[16]											
Total	C	108 903	109 617	...	...	...	17.2	17.0	...	...	...
Urban - Urbaine	C	62 372	...	...	...	...	...	...	...	...	...
Rural - Rurale	C	46 531	...	...	...	...	...	...	...	...	...
Greenland - Groenland											
Total	C	805	854	830	853	819	14.3	15.2	14.8	15.2	14.6
Urban - Urbaine	C	703	719	699	734	699	14.6	14.9	14.4	15.1	14.4
Rural - Rurale	C	102	135	131	119	120	12.7	17.2	16.9	15.6	16.1
Grenada - Grenade											
Total	+C	1 750	1 694	1 577	1 398	...	16.0	15.4	14.2	12.5	...
Guadeloupe[10]											
Total	C	5 683	5 368	5 276	4 626	...	14.2	13.5	13.4	11.8	...
Guatemala											
Total	C	386 195	391 425	390 382	381 664	...	24.4	24.2	23.6	22.5	...
Jamaica - Jamaïque											
Total	C	36 996	37 900	36 160	34 169	*33 092	13.6	13.9	13.3	12.5	*12.1
Martinique[10]											
Total	C	4 367	3 972	3 782	3 640	...	11.4	10.5	10.0	9.8	...
Urban - Urbaine	C	...	...	...	3 080	...	...	...	...	...	...
Rural - Rurale	C	...	...	...	560	...	...	...	...	...	...
Mexico - Mexique											
Total	C	2 129 825[17]	2 096 274[17]	2 028 358[17]	*2 234 039	...	17.8	17.3	16.5	*18.0	...
Urban - Urbaine[18]	C	1 563 395	1 540 464	1 476 247	...	...	18.0	17.6	16.6	...	...
Rural - Rurale[18]	C	464 897	442 539	440 219	...	...	14.1	13.3	13.1	...	...
Montserrat											
Total	C	50	48	46	...	...	10.0	9.6	9.1	...	...

Continent, country or area, and urban/rural residence / Continent, pays ou zone et résidence, urbaine/rurale	Code[a]	Number - Nombre					Rate - Taux				
		2014	2015	2016	2017	2018	2014	2015	2016	2017	2018
AMERICA, NORTH - AMÉRIQUE DU NORD											
Nicaragua											
Total	+U	...	...	137 772	...	...	...	...	...	...	...
Urban - Urbaine	+U	...	...	71 668	...	...	...	...	...	...	...
Rural - Rurale	+U	...	...	66 104	...	...	...	...	...	...	...
Panama											
Total	C	75 183	*75 901	*75 184	*76 166	*74 518	19.2	*19.1	*18.6	*18.6	*17.9
Urban - Urbaine	C	49 006	*48 960	*47 818	*47 837	...	18.5	*18.1	*17.2	*16.9	...
Rural - Rurale	C	26 177	*26 941	*27 366	*28 329	...	20.6	*21.3	*21.6	*22.5	...
Puerto Rico - Porto Rico											
Total	C	34 503	31 241	28 344	24 395	21 467	9.8	9.0	8.3	7.3	6.7
Urban - Urbaine	C	19 014[15]	18 995	18 210	16 368	13 929	...	...	...	...	...
Rural - Rurale	C	15 469[15]	12 246	10 134	8 027	7 538	...	...	...	...	...
Saint Kitts and Nevis - Saint-Kitts-et-Nevis											
Total	+C	641	...	...	...	...	...	...	...	...	...
Saint Lucia - Sainte-Lucie											
Total	+C	2 026	...	...	...	...	11.7	...	...	...	...
Saint Pierre and Miquelon - Saint-Pierre-et-Miquelon											
Total	C	61	...	...	30	...	...	...	...	...	...
Saint Vincent and the Grenadines - Saint-Vincent-et-les Grenadines											
Total	C	1 841	1 813	1 729	*1 540	...	16.7	16.4	15.7	*13.9	...
Saint-Barthélemy											
Total	C	96	...	...	72	...	10.0	...	...	...	...
Saint-Martin (French part) - Saint-Martin (partie française)											
Total	C	693	...	...	500	...	19.6	...	...	14.0	...
Sint Maarten (Dutch part) - Saint-Martin (partie néerlandaise)											
Total	+C	532	500	458	363	...	14.3	13.1	11.6	9.0	...
Trinidad and Tobago - Trinité-et-Tobago											
Total	C	*18 729	*18 062	...	...	...	*13.9	*13.4	...	...	...
Turks and Caicos Islands - Îles Turques et Caïques											
Total	C	437	437	518	555	*454	12.4	11.9	13.7	13.9	*11.0
United States of America - États-Unis d'Amérique											
Total	C	3 988 076	3 978 497	...	...	...	12.5	12.4	...	...	...
AMERICA, SOUTH - AMÉRIQUE DU SUD											
Argentina - Argentine											
Total	C	777 012	770 040	728 035	704 609	...	18.2	17.9	16.7	16.0	...
Bolivia (Plurinational State of) - Bolivie (État plurinational de)											
Total	U	153 016	...	...	...	...	...	...	...	...	...
Total	+U	...	277 498	...	...	...	...	...	...	...	...
Brazil - Brésil											
Total[19]	U	2 913 121	...	...	...	...	...	...	...	...	...
Total	C	...	3 058 783	2 903 933	2 962 815	...	...	15.0	14.1	14.3	...
Chile - Chili											
Total	C	250 997	244 670	231 749	*219 186	...	14.1	13.6	12.7	*11.9	...
Urban - Urbaine	C	228 458	222 438	211 920	...	...	14.7	14.1	13.3	...	...
Rural - Rurale	C	22 539	22 232	19 829	...	...	10.0	9.8	8.6	...	...
Colombia - Colombie											
Total	U	669 137	660 999	647 521	656 704	...	...	...	...	...	...
Urban - Urbaine[15]	U	530 841	526 365	514 829	515 706	...	...	...	...	...	...
Rural - Rurale[15]	U	137 856	134 215	132 183	139 651	...	...	...	...	...	...

Continent, country or area, and urban/rural residence / Continent, pays ou zone et résidence, urbaine/rurale	Co-de[a]	Number - Nombre					Rate - Taux				
		2014	2015	2016	2017	2018	2014	2015	2016	2017	2018
AMERICA, SOUTH - AMÉRIQUE DU SUD											
Ecuador - Équateur[20]											
Total	U	278 460	283 313	272 090	*288 123	...	...	...	...	...	...
Urban - Urbaine	U	222 212	222 575	212 673	*270 322	...	...	...	...	...	...
Rural - Rurale	U	56 248	60 738	59 417	*17 801	...	...	...	...	...	...
French Guiana - Guyane française[10]											
Total	C	6 591	6 806	7 270	8 057	...	26.1	26.7	27.7	29.4	...
Paraguay											
Total	+U	116 592	132 241	128 117	129 903	123 187	...	...	...	...	...
Peru - Pérou											
Total	+U	492 008[21]	529 029[21]	522 269[21]	*511 867[21]	*494 034[22]	...	...	...	...	...
Urban - Urbaine[21]	+U	...	384 757	...	...	...	...	...	...	...	...
Rural - Rurale[21]	+U	...	144 272	...	...	...	...	...	...	...	...
Suriname											
Total	C	10 407	10 148	9 910	9 785	...	18.6	17.9	17.2	16.8	...
Urban - Urbaine	C	6 898	6 683	6 561	6 471	...	...	...	...	16.7	...
Rural - Rurale	C	3 509	3 465	3 349	3 314	...	...	...	...	16.8	...
Uruguay											
Total	C	48 368	48 926	47 058	43 036	...	14.0	14.1	13.5	12.3	...
Venezuela (Bolivarian Republic of) - Venezuela (République bolivarienne du)											
Total	U	597 773	600 875	642 644	579 349	...	...	...	...	...	...
ASIA - ASIE											
Armenia - Arménie											
Total	C	43 031	41 763	40 592	37 700	...	14.3	13.9	13.6	12.7	...
Urban - Urbaine	C	...	27 124	26 474	24 611	...	...	14.2	13.9	13.0	...
Rural - Rurale	C	...	14 639	14 118	13 089	...	...	13.4	13.0	12.1	...
Azerbaijan - Azerbaïdjan[23]											
Total	+C	170 503	166 210	159 464	144 041	...	17.9	17.2	16.3	14.6	...
Urban - Urbaine	+C	81 822	81 149	76 954	69 479	...	16.1	15.8	14.9	13.3	...
Rural - Rurale	+C	88 681	85 061	82 510	74 562	...	19.9	18.8	18.0	16.1	...
Bahrain - Bahreïn[24]											
Total	C	20 931	20 983	20 714	20 581	...	15.9	15.3	14.5	13.7	...
Bangladesh											
Total	U	2 963 520	2 987 320	3 006 960	3 009 950	...	...	...	...	...	...
Urban - Urbaine	U	758 692	754 215	763 301	791 637	...	...	...	...	...	...
Rural - Rurale	U	2 204 828	2 233 105	2 243 659	2 218 313	...	...	...	...	...	...
Bhutan - Bhoutan[2]											
Total	I	...	...	...	11 239	...	...	...	...	15.5	...
Brunei Darussalam - Brunéi Darussalam											
Total	+C	6 891	6 699	6 437	6 452	...	16.9	16.2	15.4	15.0	...
China - Chine[25]											
Total	I	16 870 000	16 550 000	17 860 000	17 230 000	15 230 000	12.4	12.1	13.0	12.4	10.9
China, Hong Kong SAR - Chine, Hong Kong RAS											
Total	C	62 305	59 878	60 856	56 548	53 716	8.6	8.2	8.3	7.7	7.2
China, Macao SAR - Chine, Macao RAS											
Total	C	7 360	7 055	7 146	6 529	*5 925	11.8	11.0	11.1	10.0	*8.9
Cyprus - Chypre[26]											
Total	C	9 258	9 170	9 455	9 229	...	10.9	10.8	11.1	10.7	...
Georgia - Géorgie											
Total	C	60 635	59 249	56 569	53 293	*51 138	16.3	15.9	15.2	14.3	*13.7
Urban - Urbaine	C	...	33 898	32 227	...	...	...	15.9	15.1	...	...
Rural - Rurale	C	...	25 351	24 342	...	...	...	15.9	15.3	...	...
India - Inde[27]											
Total	I	...	...	...	...	...	21.0	20.8	20.4	20.2	...
Urban - Urbaine	I	...	...	...	...	...	17.4	17.3	17.0	16.8	...
Rural - Rurale	I	...	...	...	...	...	22.7	22.4	22.1	21.8	...

Continent, country or area, and urban/rural residence — Continent, pays ou zone et résidence, urbaine/rurale	Code[a]	Number - Nombre					Rate - Taux				
		2014	2015	2016	2017	2018	2014	2015	2016	2017	2018
ASIA - ASIE											
Iran (Islamic Republic of) - Iran (République islamique d')[28]											
Total	+C	1 534 362	1 570 219	1 528 053	1 487 913	*1 388 249	19.7	19.9	19.1	18.4	*16.9
Urban - Urbaine	+C	1 178 921	1 208 142	1 176 032	1 143 558	...	20.9	21.1	19.9	19.0	...
Rural - Rurale	+C	355 441	362 077	352 021	344 355	...	16.6	16.9	16.9	16.6	...
Israel - Israël[29]											
Total	C	176 427	178 723	181 405	183 648	*184 135	21.5	21.3	21.2	21.1	*20.7
Urban - Urbaine	C	160 223	162 225	164 561	167 264	...	21.4	21.2	21.1	21.0	...
Rural - Rurale	C	16 204	16 498	16 844	16 384	...	22.7	22.4	22.5	21.5	...
Japan - Japon[30]											
Total	C	1 003 539[15]	1 005 677[15]	976 978[15]	946 065[15]	*918 397	7.9	7.9	7.7	7.5	*7.3
Urban - Urbaine[31]	C	926 229	928 962	902 855	875 127	...	...	...	...	...	...
Rural - Rurale[31]	C	77 245	76 662	74 058	70 887	...	...	...	...	...	...
Jordan - Jordanie[32]											
Total	C	188 902	198 018	197 789	211 441	...	21.5	20.7	20.2	21.0	...
Kazakhstan											
Total	C	399 309	398 458	400 694	390 262	397 799	23.1	22.7	22.5	21.6	21.8
Urban - Urbaine	C	222 821	225 808	229 731	226 847	235 014	23.1	22.7	22.6	21.9	22.2
Rural - Rurale	C	176 488	172 650	170 963	163 415	162 785	23.1	22.7	22.3	21.2	21.2
Kuwait - Koweït											
Total	C	61 313	59 271	58 797	59 172	...	16.3	14.9	14.4	14.7	...
Kyrgyzstan - Kirghizstan											
Total	C	161 813	163 452	158 160	153 620	171 149	27.7	27.4	26.0	24.8	27.1
Urban - Urbaine	C	55 463	52 477	51 610	52 829	...	28.2	26.1	25.2	25.2	...
Rural - Rurale	C	106 350	110 975	106 550	100 791	...	27.5	28.1	26.5	24.6	...
Lebanon - Liban											
Total	C	104 872	...	...	...	...	...	...	...	...	...
Malaysia - Malaisie											
Total	C	528 612	521 136	508 203	508 685	...	17.2	16.7	16.1	15.9	...
Urban - Urbaine	C	357 848	350 677	342 253	337 792	...	15.8	15.1	14.5	14.0	...
Rural - Rurale	C	170 764	170 459	165 950	170 893	...	21.1	21.3	20.9	21.5	...
Maldives[33]											
Total	C	7 245	6 986	6 756	6 723	...	21.2	20.3	19.3	18.8	...
Urban - Urbaine	C	2 378[34]	2 404[15]	2 431[15]	875[15]	...	...	18.0	17.6	6.1	...
Rural - Rurale	C	4 521[34]	4 211[15]	3 996[15]	5 008[15]	...	...	20.0	18.8	23.4	...
Mongolia - Mongolie											
Total	+C	82 839	82 130	79 920	75 321	78 444	28.0	27.1	25.9	23.9	24.5
Urban - Urbaine	+C	56 148	60 861	55 161	51 912	52 487	28.2	29.8	26.0	24.3	24.2
Rural - Rurale	+C	26 691	21 269	24 759	23 409	25 957	27.5	21.6	25.6	23.2	25.1
Myanmar[35]											
Total	+U	736 369	739 152	765 844	...	...	...	...	...	...	...
Urban - Urbaine	+U	227 119	233 206	250 564	...	...	...	...	...	...	...
Rural - Rurale	+U	509 250	505 946	515 280	...	...	...	...	...	...	...
Oman											
Total[36]	U	82 981	86 286	88 346	...	...	...	...	...	...	...
Total	C	...	...	...	90 371	89 071	...	...	...	19.8	19.4
Philippines											
Total	C	1 748 857	1 744 767	1 731 289	1 700 618	...	17.5	17.2	16.8	16.2	...
Qatar											
Total	C	25 443	26 622	26 816	27 906	*25 513	11.5	10.9	10.2	10.2	*9.2
Urban - Urbaine	C	25 443	26 622	26 816	...	...	11.5	10.9	10.2	...	...
Republic of Korea - République de Corée[37]											
Total	C	435 435	438 420	406 243	357 771	...	8.6	8.6	7.9	7.0	...
Urban - Urbaine	C	364 615[15]	367 143	338 973	296 550	...	8.8	8.8	8.2	7.1	...
Rural - Rurale	C	70 818[15]	71 277	67 270	61 221	...	7.5	7.5	7.1	6.4	...
Saudi Arabia - Arabie saoudite[38]											
Total	I	514 325[39]	449 149[39]	447 040[39]	488 130	...	17.0	14.5	14.1	15.0	...
Singapore - Singapour											
Total	C	42 232	42 185	41 251	39 615	...	10.9	10.8	10.5	10.0	...
Sri Lanka											
Total	+C	349 744	336 097	*331 073	*326 052	*328 112	16.8	16.0	*15.6	*15.2	*15.1
Urban - Urbaine	+C	245 469	236 537	...	...	...	...	...	...	...	...
Rural - Rurale[40]	+C	104 275	99 560	...	...	...	...	...	...	...	...

Continent, country or area, and urban/rural residence / Continent, pays ou zone et résidence, urbaine/rurale	Code[a]	Number - Nombre					Rate - Taux				
		2014	2015	2016	2017	2018	2014	2015	2016	2017	2018
ASIA - ASIE											
State of Palestine - État de Palestine[41]											
Total	U	128 073	133 185	138 238	140 441		...	...	...	...	...
Tajikistan - Tadjikistan[42]											
Total	U	229 460	237 541	230 044	224 057		...	...	...	...	...
Urban - Urbaine	U	54 878	53 034	51 042	51 561		...	...	...	...	...
Rural - Rurale	U	174 582	184 507	179 002	172 496		...	...	...	...	...
Thailand - Thaïlande											
Total	+U	776 370	738 930	666 207	656 570		...	...	...	...	...
Timor-Leste[43]											
Total	I	...	36 202	...	...	...	...	30.2	...	...	...
Turkey - Turquie											
Total	C	1 349 467	1 334 465	1 311 895	1 291 055	*1 248 847	17.4	16.9	16.4	16.1	*15.4
United Arab Emirates - Émirats arabes unis											
Total[44]	...	95 860	97 328	98 299	...		...	...	...	...	...
Total	C	...	...	...	97 738		...	...	...	10.5	...
Uzbekistan - Ouzbékistan											
Total	+C	718 036	734 141	726 170	715 519	*768 520	23.3	23.5	22.8	22.1	*23.5
Urban - Urbaine	+C	326 231	325 660	332 035	325 152	...	20.8	20.5	20.6	19.8	...
Rural - Rurale	+C	391 805	408 481	394 135	390 367	...	25.9	26.5	25.1	24.4	...
Yemen - Yémen[45]											
Total	U	476 570	...	575 556	645 833		...	...	...	...	...
EUROPE											
Åland Islands - Îles d'Åland											
Total	C	282	275	293	279	*280	9.8	9.5	10.1	9.5	*9.4
Urban - Urbaine	C	98	97	112	109	...	8.6	8.5	9.7	9.4	...
Rural - Rurale	C	184	178	181	170	...	10.6	10.2	10.3	9.6	...
Albania - Albanie											
Total	C	35 760	32 715	31 733	30 869	28 934	12.4	11.4	11.0	10.7	10.1
Andorra - Andorre											
Total	C	639	659	634	588	543	9.1	9.3	8.8	8.0	7.3
Austria - Autriche											
Total	C	81 722	84 381[46]	87 675[46]	87 633[46]	*85 535[46]	9.6	9.8	10.0	10.0	*9.7
Belarus - Bélarus											
Total	C	118 534	119 028	117 779	102 556	...	12.5	12.5	12.4	10.8	...
Urban - Urbaine	C	91 704	91 870	91 005	78 852	...	12.6	12.5	12.3	10.6	...
Rural - Rurale	C	26 830	27 158	26 774	23 704	...	12.3	12.7	12.7	11.3	...
Belgium - Belgique[47]											
Total	C	125 014	122 274	121 896	119 690	*118 319	11.1	10.8	10.8	10.5	*10.4
Urban - Urbaine	C	123 346	120 591	...	...	...	...	...	...	...	...
Rural - Rurale	C	1 668	1 683	...	...	...	...	...	...	...	...
Bosnia and Herzegovina - Bosnie-Herzégovine											
Total	C	29 247	28 906	29 276	29 158	...	8.3	8.2	8.3	8.3	...
Bulgaria - Bulgarie											
Total	C	67 585	65 950	64 984	63 955	...	9.4	9.2	9.1	9.0	...
Urban - Urbaine	C	50 704	49 486	48 733	48 005	...	9.6	9.4	9.3	9.0	...
Rural - Rurale	C	16 881	16 464	16 251	15 950	...	8.7	8.5	8.5	8.5	...
Croatia - Croatie											
Total	C	39 566	37 503	37 537	36 556	*36 945	9.3	8.9	9.0	8.9	*9.0
Urban - Urbaine	C	22 894	21 802	21 645	21 156	...	...	...	...	...	...
Rural - Rurale	C	16 672	15 701	15 892	15 400	...	...	...	...	...	...
Czechia - Tchéquie											
Total	C	109 860	110 764	112 663	114 405	*114 036	10.4	10.5	10.7	10.8	*10.7
Urban - Urbaine	C	80 841	81 413	82 912	83 980	...	10.5	10.6	10.7	10.8	...
Rural - Rurale	C	29 019	29 351	29 751	30 425	...	10.2	10.3	10.5	10.7	...
Denmark - Danemark[48]											
Total	C	56 870	58 205	61 614	61 397	...	10.1	10.3	10.8	10.7	...
Estonia - Estonie											
Total	C	13 551	13 907	14 053	13 784	*14 270	10.3	10.6	10.7	10.5	*10.8
Urban - Urbaine	C	9 452	9 553[15]	9 566	10 049[15]	...	10.5	10.6	10.6	10.5	...
Rural - Rurale	C	4 099	4 353[15]	4 487	3 731[15]	...	9.8	10.5	10.8	9.2	...

Continent, country or area, and urban/rural residence / Continent, pays ou zone et résidence, urbaine/rurale	Code[a]	Number - Nombre					Rate - Taux				
		2014	2015	2016	2017	2018	2014	2015	2016	2017	2018
EUROPE											
Faeroe Islands - Îles Féroé											
Total	C	636	605	675	656	684	13.1	12.4	13.6	13.1	13.4
Urban - Urbaine	C	265	227	...	247	268	14.4	12.2	...	12.8	13.7
Rural - Rurale	C	371	378	...	409	416	12.3	12.5	...	13.2	13.2
Finland - Finlande											
Total	C	56 950[49]	55 197[49]	52 521[49]	50 042[49]	*47 307	10.5	10.1	9.6	9.1	*8.6
Urban - Urbaine[49]	C	41 103	40 711	38 853	37 193	...	10.9	10.6	10.0	9.5	...
Rural - Rurale[49]	C	15 847	14 486	13 668	12 849	...	9.5	9.0	8.6	8.2	...
France											
Total	C	806 101	760 421	744 697	730 242	719 737	12.6	11.8	11.5	11.3	11.1
Urban - Urbaine	C	647 448	611 062[50]	601 770[50]	591 457[50]	...	...	...	...	...	...
Rural - Rurale	C	158 653	147 304[50]	140 951[50]	136 626[50]	...	...	...	...	...	...
Germany - Allemagne											
Total	C	714 927	737 575	792 137	784 901	*787 523	8.8	9.0	9.6	9.5	*9.5
Gibraltar[51]											
Total	+C	488	492	424	...	...	14.7	14.7	12.5	...	...
Greece - Grèce											
Total	C	92 149	91 847	92 898	88 553	86 440	8.5	8.5	8.6	8.2	8.0
Urban - Urbaine	C	62 785	63 283	64 223	...	...	...	...	...	...	...
Rural - Rurale	C	29 364	28 564	28 675	...	...	...	...	...	...	...
Guernsey - Guernesey											
Total	C	628	580	595	571	543	10.1	9.3	9.6	9.2	8.7
Hungary - Hongrie											
Total	C	93 281[52]	92 135[52]	95 361[52]	94 646[52]	*89 522	9.5	9.4	9.7	9.7	*9.2
Urban - Urbaine[53]	C	65 095	63 961	65 866	64 894	...	9.4	9.2	9.5	9.4	...
Rural - Rurale[53]	C	28 166	28 153	29 495	29 707	...	9.7	9.7	10.2	10.3	...
Iceland - Islande											
Total	C	4 375	4 129	4 034	4 071	4 228	13.4	12.5	12.0	11.9	12.1
Urban - Urbaine	C	4 164	3 924	3 617	3 860	...	13.6	12.7	11.5	12.0	...
Rural - Rurale	C	211	205	169	211	...	10.2	10.0	9.8	9.5	...
Ireland - Irlande											
Total	+C	67 285	65 537	63 836	61 824	*61 016	14.4	13.9	13.4	12.9	*12.6
Isle of Man - Île de Man											
Total	+C	805	785	758	753	717	9.3	9.0	8.9	9.0	...
Italy - Italie											
Total	C	502 596	485 780	473 438	458 151	...	8.3	8.0	7.8	7.6	...
Jersey[17]											
Total	+C	985	1 021	1 020	954	942	9.8	9.9	9.8	9.0	8.8
Latvia - Lettonie											
Total	C	21 746	21 979	21 968	20 828	19 314	10.9	11.1	11.2	10.7	10.0
Urban - Urbaine	C	15 094	15 099	15 154	14 507	...	11.2	11.2	11.3	...	...
Rural - Rurale	C	6 652	6 880	6 814	6 321	...	10.4	10.9	10.9	...	...
Liechtenstein											
Total	C	372	325	378	338	...	10.0	8.7	10.0	8.9	...
Lithuania - Lituanie											
Total	C	30 369	31 475	30 623	28 696	*28 517	10.4	10.8	10.7	10.1	*10.2
Urban - Urbaine	C	20 989	21 589	21 256	19 851	...	10.7	11.1	11.0	10.5	...
Rural - Rurale	C	9 380	9 886	9 367	8 845	...	9.7	10.4	10.0	9.5	...
Luxembourg											
Total	C	6 070	6 115	6 050	6 174	6 274	10.9	10.7	10.4	10.4	10.4
Malta - Malte											
Total	C	4 191	4 325	4 476	4 319	4 444	9.6	9.7	9.8	9.2	9.3
Monaco[54]											
Total	C	974	1 067	938	958	983	26.4	28.4	24.6	25.5	25.7
Montenegro - Monténégro											
Total	C	7 529	7 386	7 569	7 432	7 264	12.1	11.9	12.2	11.9	11.7
Netherlands - Pays-Bas[55]											
Total	C	175 181	170 510	172 520	169 836	168 525	10.4	10.1	10.1	9.9	9.8
North Macedonia - Macédoine du Nord											
Total	C	23 596	23 075	23 002	21 754	21 333	11.4	11.1	11.1	10.5	10.3
Urban - Urbaine	C	13 764	13 357	13 536	12 841	...	...	...	...	...	...
Rural - Rurale	C	9 832	9 718	9 466	8 913	...	...	...	...	...	...
Norway - Norvège											
Total	C	58 976	58 815	58 890	56 633	55 120	11.5	11.3	11.3	10.7	10.4

9. Live births and crude birth rates, by urban/rural residence: 2014 - 2018
Naissances vivantes et taux bruts de natalité selon la résidence, urbaine/rurale : 2014 - 2018 (continued - suite)

Continent, country or area, and urban/rural residence / Continent, pays ou zone et résidence, urbaine/rurale	Co-de[a]	Number - Nombre					Rate - Taux				
		2014	2015	2016	2017	2018	2014	2015	2016	2017	2018
EUROPE											
Poland - Pologne											
Total	C	375 160	369 308	382 257	401 982	388 178	9.9	9.7	10.1	10.6	10.2
Urban - Urbaine	C	217 699	217 391	226 296	236 143	228 714	9.5	9.5	9.9	10.3	...
Rural - Rurale	C	157 461	151 917	155 961	165 839	159 464	10.5	10.1	10.3	11.0	...
Portugal[17]											
Total	C	82 367	85 500	87 126	86 154	87 020	7.9	8.3	8.4	8.4	8.5
Republic of Moldova - République de Moldova[56]											
Total	C	38 616	38 610	37 394	34 060	32 606	13.5	13.6	13.3	12.4	12.0
Urban - Urbaine	C	14 060	13 555	13 359	12 392	11 998	...	...	...	...	...
Rural - Rurale	C	24 556	25 055	24 035	21 668	20 608	...	...	...	...	...
Romania - Roumanie											
Total	C	198 740	197 491	200 009	202 151	*186 450	10.0	10.0	10.1	10.3	*9.5
Urban - Urbaine	C	109 093	108 744	...	111 637	...	10.2	10.2	...	10.6	...
Rural - Rurale	C	89 647	88 747	...	90 514	...	9.8	9.7	...	10.0	...
San Marino - Saint-Marin											
Total	C	296	269	262	228	235	8.8	8.0	7.7	6.6	6.8
Serbia - Serbie[57]											
Total	+C	66 461	65 657	64 734	64 894	*63 543	9.3	9.3	9.2	9.2	*9.1
Urban - Urbaine	+C	46 036	45 640	44 794	43 783	...	10.8	10.7	10.5	10.3	...
Rural - Rurale	+C	20 425	20 017	19 940	21 111	...	7.1	7.1	7.1	7.6	...
Slovakia - Slovaquie											
Total	C	55 033	55 602	57 557	57 969	...	10.2	10.3	10.6	10.7	...
Urban - Urbaine	C	28 379	29 082	29 719	29 810	...	9.7	10.0	10.2	10.2	...
Rural - Rurale	C	26 654	26 520	27 838	28 159	...	10.7	10.6	11.1	11.2	...
Slovenia - Slovénie											
Total	C	21 165	20 641	20 345	20 241	19 585	10.3	10.0	9.9	9.8	9.5
Urban - Urbaine	C	10 707	10 871	10 765	11 023	...	10.2	9.8	9.7	9.7	...
Rural - Rurale	C	10 458	9 770	9 580	9 218	...	10.3	10.2	10.0	10.0	...
Spain - Espagne											
Total	C	426 076	418 432	408 734	391 265	*367 374	9.2	9.0	8.8	8.4	*7.9
Sweden - Suède											
Total	C	114 907	114 870	117 425	115 416	*115 832	11.9	11.7	11.8	11.5	*11.4
Switzerland - Suisse											
Total	C	85 287	86 559	87 883	87 381	87 851	10.4	10.5	10.5	10.3	10.4
Urban - Urbaine	C	64 109[58]	74 039	75 327	74 978	...	10.6	10.6	10.6	...	...
Rural - Rurale[59]	C	21 178[58]	12 520	12 556	12 403	...	9.8	9.7	9.7	...	...
Ukraine[59]											
Total	+C	465 882	411 781	397 037	363 987	*335 874	10.8	9.6	9.3	8.6	*7.9
Urban - Urbaine	+C	304 190	266 082	258 688	237 874	...	...	9.0	8.8	8.1	...
Rural - Rurale	+C	161 692	145 699	138 349	126 113	...	...	11.0	10.5	9.7	...
United Kingdom of Great Britain and Northern Ireland - Royaume-Uni de Grande-Bretagne et d'Irlande du Nord[60]											
Total	C	775 908	776 746	774 386	754 754	...	12.0	11.9	11.8	11.4	...
OCEANIA - OCÉANIE											
American Samoa - Samoa américaines											
Total	C	1 084	1 096	1 013	1 001	...	17.5	18.0	16.8	16.6	...
Australia - Australie											
Total	C	299 697	305 377	311 104	309 142	...	12.8	12.8	12.9	12.6	...
Urban - Urbaine[61]	C	204 990	208 466	215 561	214 142	...	10.1	10.1	10.3	10.0	...
Rural - Rurale[61]	C	93 175	94 562	93 466	92 995	...	28.8	29.1	28.6	28.3	...
Cook Islands - Îles Cook[62]											
Total	+C	204	*205	...	...	...	11.0	*11.0	...	...	...
Fiji - Fidji											
Total	+C	18 251	...	...	...	...	21.1	...	...	...	...
French Polynesia - Polynésie française											
Total	C	4 151	3 888	3 969	3 820	...	15.3	14.2	14.5	13.9	...
Guam[63]											
Total	C	3 396	3 367	3 433	3 292	3 175	21.1	20.8	21.1	20.1	18.9

9. Live births and crude birth rates, by urban/rural residence: 2014 - 2018
Naissances vivantes et taux bruts de natalité selon la résidence, urbaine/rurale : 2014 - 2018 (continued - suite)

Continent, country or area, and urban/rural residence / Continent, pays ou zone et résidence, urbaine/rurale	Code[a]	Number - Nombre					Rate - Taux				
		2014	2015	2016	2017	2018	2014	2015	2016	2017	2018
OCEANIA - OCÉANIE											
Nauru											
Total	C	...	360	358	304	...	...	31.9	32.5	...	...
New Caledonia - Nouvelle-Calédonie											
Total	C	4 370	4 191	4 271	4 059	...	16.3	15.4	15.6	14.6	...
New Zealand - Nouvelle-Zélande[64]											
Total	+C	57 243	61 038	59 427[65]	59 610[65]	58 020[65]	12.7	13.3	12.7	12.4	11.9
Urban - Urbaine[15]	+C	50 355	53 205	51 849[65]	51 876[65]	...	13.0	13.4	12.8	12.5	...
Rural - Rurale[15]	+C	6 873	7 827	7 572[65]	7 728[65]	...	11.0	12.3	11.9	11.9	...
Niue - Nioué											
Total	C	20	26	27	...	...	...	...	...	...	...
Northern Mariana Islands - Îles Mariannes septentrionales[66]											
Total	U	*1 057*	...	...	...	...	...	...	...	...	...
Palau - Palaos											
Total	C	241	242	213	221	256	13.7	13.7	12.0	12.4	14.0
Samoa[67]											
Total	+U	*8 521*	*8 206*	*9 378*	*9 277*	*13 234*[68]					
Tuvalu											
Total	+U	*261*	*208*	*210*	...	...					
Vanuatu											
Total	+U	*6 774*									

FOOTNOTES - NOTES

Italics: data from civil registers which are incomplete or of unknown completeness. - Italiques : données incomplètes ou dont le degré d'exactitude n'est pas connu, provenant des registres de l'état civil.

* Provisional. - Données provisoires.

[a] 'Code' indicates the source of data, as follows:
C - Civil registration, estimated over 90% complete
U - Civil registration, estimated less than 90% complete
| - Other source, estimated reliable
+ - Data tabulated by date of registration rather than occurence
... - Information not available

Le 'Code' indique la source des données, comme suit :
C - Registres de l'état civil considérés complets à 90 p. 100 au moins
U - Registres de l'état civil qui ne sont pas considérés complets à 90 p. 100 au moins
| - Autre source, considérée pas douteuses
+ - Données exploitées selon la date de l'enregistrement et non la date de l'événement
... - Information pas disponible

[1] Excluding live-born infants who died before their birth was registered. Data refer to Algerian population only. - Non compris les enfants nés vivants décédés avant l'enregistrement de leur naissance. Les données ne concernent que la population algérienne.
[2] Data refer to the 12 months preceding the census in May. - Les données se rapportent aux 12 mois précédant le recensement de mai.
[3] Source: Vital Statistics Report. - Source: Vital Statistics Report.
[4] Data refer only to events recorded in hospitals and health centres. - Ces données ne concernent que les faits d'état civil enregistrés dans les hôpitaux et les centres de santé uniquement.
[5] Urban area here is composed of six communes: Brazzaville, Pointe-Noire, Dolisie, N'kayi, Mossendjo and Ouesso. The data on rural area are the result of the difference between total and urban area. - Le milieu urbain ici est constitué des six communes: Brazzaville, Pointe-Noire, Dolisie, N'kayi, Mossendjo et Ouesso. Les informations sur la zone rurale ont été déduites en celles de l'ensemble et du milieu urbain.

[6] Adjusted number of births in households referring to the 12 months preceding the census in March. - Le nombre ajusté de naissances vivantes des ménages ordinaires se rapportent aux 12 mois précédant le recensement de mars.
[7] Data refer to the 12 months preceding the census in September. - Les données se rapportent aux 12 mois précédant le recensement de septembre.
[8] Excludes the islands of St. Brandon and Agalega. - Non compris les îles St. Brandon et Agalega.
[9] Source: Ministry of Health, National Directorate of Planning and Cooperation. - Source : Ministère de la santé, Direction nationale de la planification et de la coopération.
[10] Excluding live-born infants who died before their birth was registered. - Non compris les enfants nés vivants décédés avant l'enregistrement de leur naissance.
[11] Unrevised data. - Les données n'ont pas été révisées.
[12] Bermuda is 100 per cent urban. Excluding non-residents and foreign service personnel and their dependants. - 100 pour cent de la population des Bermudes est urbaine. À l'exclusion des non-résidents et du personnel diplomatique et de leurs charges de famille.
[13] Including Canadian residents temporarily in the United States, but excluding United States residents temporarily in Canada. - Y compris les résidents canadiens se trouvant temporairement aux Etats-Unis, mais ne comprenant pas les résidents des Etats-Unis se trouvant temporairement au Canada.
[14] Definition of urban and rural distribution changed from the year 2014. - La définition de la répartition urbaine et rurale a changé depuis 2014.
[15] The total number may include 'Unknown residence', but the categories urban and rural do not. - Le nombre total peut inclure les personnes dont la résidence n'est pas connue, à l'inverse des catégories de population urbaine et rurale.
[16] Excluding children born in the country of non-resident mothers. - Exceptés les enfants nés dans le pays des mères non-résidentes.
[17] Data refer to births to resident mothers. - Ces données concernent les enfants nés de mères résidentes.
[18] Data refer to births to resident mothers. The total number may include 'Unknown residence', but the categories urban and rural do not. - Ces données concernent les enfants nés de mères résidentes. Le nombre total peut inclure les personnes dont la résidence n'est pas connue, à l'inverse des catégories de population urbaine et rurale.
[19] Including births abroad and births of unknown residence of mother. - Y compris les naissances à l'étranger et les naissances pour lesquelles le lieu de résidence de la mère est inconnu.
[20] Excludes nomadic Indian tribes. - Non compris les tribus d'Indiens nomades.

21 Source: Reports of the Ministry of Health. - Source : Rapports du Ministère de la Santé.

22 Data extracted from online system representing only 86.8 per cent of estimated births. - Données extraites du système en ligne, qui ne représentent que 86,8 % du nombre total estimé de naissances.

23 Excluding infants born alive of less than 28 weeks' gestation, of less than 1 000 g in weight and 35 cm in length, who die within seven days of birth. - Non compris les enfants nés vivants après moins de 28 semaines de gestations, pesant moins de 1 000 g, mesurant moins de 35 cm et décédés dans les sept jours qui ont suivi leur naissance.

24 Sources: Births and Deaths National Registration System database, and medical records of government hospitals. - Les sources: Les bases de données des << Births and Deaths National Registration System >> et les dossiers médicaux des hôpitaux du gouvernement.

25 For statistical purposes, the data for China do not include those for the Hong Kong Special Administrative Region (Hong Kong SAR), Macao Special Administrative Region (Macao SAR) and Taiwan province of China. Data have been estimated on the basis of the annual National Sample Survey on Population Changes. - Pour la présentation des statistiques, les données pour la Chine ne comprennent pas la Région Administrative Spéciale de Hong Kong (Hong Kong RAS), la Région Administrative Spéciale de Macao (Macao RAS) et Taïwan province de Chine. Les données ont été estimées sur la base de l'enquête annuelle "National Sample Survey on Population Changes".

26 Data refer to government controlled areas. - Les données se rapportent aux zones contrôlées par le Gouvernement.

27 Includes data for the Indian-held part of Jammu and Kashmir, the final status of which has not yet been determined. Rates were obtained by the Sample Registration System of India, which is a large demographic survey. - Y compris les données pour la partie du Jammu et du Cachemire occupée par l'Inde dont le statut définitif n'a pas encore été déterminé. Les taux ont été obtenus par le Système de l'enregistrement par échantillon de l'Inde qui est une large enquête démographique.

28 Data refer to the Iranian Year which begins on 21 March and ends on 20 March of the following year. - Les données concernent l'année iranienne, qui commence le 21 mars et se termine le 20 mars de l'année suivante.

29 Includes data for East Jerusalem and Israeli residents in certain other territories under occupation by Israeli military forces since June 1967. - Y compris les données pour Jérusalem-Est et les résidents israéliens dans certains autres territoires occupés depuis 1967 par les forces armées israéliennes.

30 Data refer to Japanese nationals in Japan only. - Les données se raportent aux nationaux japonais au Japon seulement.

31 The total number may include 'Unknown residence', but the categories urban and rural do not. Urban and rural distribution refers to the residence of the child. - Le nombre total peut inclure les personnes dont la résidence n'est pas connue, à l'inverse des catégories de population urbaine et rurale. La répartition urbain/rural se réfère au domicile de l'enfant.

32 Excluding data for Jordanian territory under occupation since June 1967 by Israeli military forces. Excluding foreigners, including registered Palestinian refugees. - Non compris les données pour le territoire jordanien occupé depuis juin 1967 par les forces armées israéliennes. Non compris les étrangers, mais y compris les réfugiés de Palestine enregistrés.

33 Data do not include foreigners. - Les données sur les etrangers ne sont pas inclus.

34 Excluding births occurred abroad. - Hormis les naissances intervenues à l'étranger.

35 Data are from Vital Registration System (VRS). - Les données proviennent du système d'enregistrement des faits d'état civil.

36 Data from Births and Deaths Notification System (Ministry of Health and all health care providers). - Les données proviennent du système de notification des naissances et des décès (Ministère de la santé et tous prestataires de soins de santé).

37 Data refer to residence of child. Excluding alien armed forces, civilian aliens employed by armed forces, and foreign diplomatic personnel and their dependants. - Les données correspondent à la résidence de l'enfant. Non compris les militaires étrangers, les civils étrangers employés par les forces armées ni le personnel diplomatique étranger et les membres de leur famille les accompagnant.

38 Survey based estimates. - Estimations basées sur des enquêtes.

39 Data refer to Saudi Arabian nationals only. - Les données ne concernent que les ressortissants saoudiens.

40 Data for rural areas include data of estate sectors consisting of all plantations which are 20 acres or more in extent and with ten or more resident labourers. - Les données pour les zones rurales comprennent celles pour les domaines, dont l'ensemble des plantations de plus de 10 hectares comptant au moins 10 travailleurs résidents.

41 Source: Palestinian Central Bureau of Statistics, Population Register, updated version 2018. Data exclude Jerusalem ID holders. - Source: Bureau central de statistique palestinien, registre de la population, version actualisée jusqu'au 2018. Les données ne tiennent pas compte des détenteurs de carte d'identité de Jérusalem.

42 Excluding infants born alive of less than 28 weeks' gestation, of less than 1 000 g in weight and 35 cm in length, who die within seven days of birth. Data have been adjusted for under-registration. - Non compris les enfants nés vivants après moins de 28 semaines de gestations, pesant moins de 1 000 g, mesurant moins de 35 cm et décédés dans les sept jours qui ont suivi leur naissance. Y compris un ajustement pour sous-enregistrement.

43 Data refer to the 12 months preceding the census in July. - Les données se rapportent aux 12 mois précédant le recensement de juillet.

44 The registration of births and deaths is conducted by the Ministry of Health. An estimate of completeness is not provided. - L'enregistrement des naissances et des décès est mené par le Ministère de la Santé. Le degré estimatif de complétude n'est pas fourni.

45 Including Non-Yemeni births. - Y compris les naissances non-yéménites.

46 Including births occurring abroad of mothers with residence in Austria. - Y compris les naissances survenues à l'étranger des mères avec résidence en Autriche.

47 Including armed forces stationed outside the country, but excluding alien armed forces stationed in the area. - Y compris les militaires nationaux hors du pays, mais non compris les militaires étrangers en garnison sur le territoire.

48 Excluding Faeroe Islands and Greenland shown separately, if available. - Non compris les Îles Féroé et le Groenland, qui font l'objet de rubriques distinctes, si disponible.

49 Excluding Åland Islands. - Non compris les Îles d'Åland.

50 Data for urban and rural exclude events corresponding to nationals residing outside the country, which may be included in the total. - Les données relatives à les categories urbaine et rurale n'englobent pas les faits d'état civil qui concernent les nationaux se trouvant à l'étranger, lesquels faits peuvent être inclus au total.

51 Including live births by military personnel and their dependants. - Y compris les naissances vivantes parmi les membres du personnel militaire et leurs personnes à charge.

52 Data include the live births of women with Hungarian usual residence regardless of whether the live birth occurred in Hungary or in a foreign country, and do not include the live births of women with foreign country usual residence. Data include the live births of women with unknown residence and homeless. - Les données concernent les enfants nés vivants de femmes dont la résidence habituelle est en Hongrie, que la naissance vivante ait eu lieu en Hongrie ou dans un pays étranger, et ne comprennent pas les enfants nés vivants de femmes dont la résidence habituelle est dans un pays étranger. Les données incluent les enfants nés vivants de femmes dont la résidence n'est pas connue et de femmes sans domicile fixe.

53 Data include the live births of women with Hungarian usual residence regardless of whether the live birth occurred in Hungary or in a foreign country, and do not include the live births of women with foreign country usual residence. - Les données concernent les enfants nés vivants de femmes dont la résidence habituelle est en Hongrie, que la naissance vivante ait eu lieu en Hongrie ou dans un pays étranger, et ne comprennent pas les enfants nés vivants de femmes dont la résidence habituelle est dans un pays étranger.

54 Source: City Hall, Civil Status Registry Office, resident and non-resident births. - Source : La mairie, Bureau de l'État Civil, toutes les naissances.

55 Including residents outside the country if listed in a Netherlands population register. - Englobe les résidents se trouvant à l'étranger à condition qu'ils soient inscrits sur le registre de population des Pays-Bas.

56 Excluding Transnistria and the municipality of Bender. - Les données ne tiennent pas compte de l'information sur la Transnistria et la municipalité de Bender.

57 Excludes data for Kosovo and Metohia. - Sans les données pour le Kosovo et Metohie.

58 From 2014, urban refers to urban centers and areas under the influence of urban centers. - A partir de 2014, le territoire urbain inclut l'espace des centres urbains ainsi que l'espace sous influence des centres urbains.

59 The Government of Ukraine has informed the United Nations that it is not in a position to provide statistical data concerning the Autonomous Republic of Crimea and the city of Sevastopol. Data refer to births with weight 500g and more (if weight is unknown - with length 25 centimeters and more, or with gestation during 22 weeks or more). - Le gouvernement Ukrainien a informé l'ONU qu'il n'est pas en mesure de fournir des données statistiques concernant la République autonome de Crimée et la ville de Sébastopol. Données concernant les nouveau-nés de 500 grammes ou plus (si le poids est inconnu – de 25 centimètres de long ou plus, ou après une grossesse de 22 semaines ou plus).

60 Excluding Channel Islands (Guernsey and Jersey) and Isle of Man, shown separately, if available. Data tabulated by date of occurrence for England and Wales, and by date of registration for Northern Ireland and Scotland. - Non

compris les îles Anglo-Normandes (Guernesey et Jersey) et l'île de Man, qui font l'objet de rubriques distinctes, si disponible. Données exploitées selon la date de l'événement pour l'Angleterre et le pays de Galles, et selon la date de l'enregistrement pour l'Irlande du Nord et l'Ecosse.

[61] Data for urban and rural figures do not add up to the total because they exclude the events occurred in Migratory, Special Purpose and Other Territories. Urban refers to Greater Capital City Statistical Areas, and rural refers to other areas within the state or territory. - La somme des chiffres des catégories « en zone urbaine » et « en zone rurale » ne correspond pas au total du fait qu'en sont exclus les événements qui ont eu lieu dans les territoires de migration, les territoires à destination spéciale et autres territoires. Urbain renvoie aux zones statistiques de la capitale métropolitaine, et rural aux autres zones de l'État ou territoire.

[62] Excluding Niue, shown separately, which is part of Cook Islands, but because of remoteness is administered separately. - Non compris Nioué, qui fait l'objet d'une rubrique distincte et qui fait partie des îles Cook, mais qui, en raison de son éloignement, est administrée séparément.

[63] Including United States military personnel, their dependants and contract employees. - Y compris les militaires des Etats-Unis, les membres de leur famille les accompagnant et les agents contractuels des Etats-Unis.

[64] Random rounding to base 3 is applied in this table as a confidentiality measure. - Les chiffres sont arrondis à la base 3 de manière aléatoire, pour des raisons de confidentialité.

[65] Data refers to births registered in the country to mothers resident in the country. - Les données se rapportent aux naissances enregistrées dans le pays pour lesquelles la mère réside dans le pays.

[66] Source: Commonwealth Health Center - Vital Statistics Office - Source : Centre de Santé du Commonwealth - Bureau des statistiques d'État civil.

[67] Source: Births, Deaths, and Marriages Registration Division, Samoa Bureau of Statistics. - Source : Division de l'enregistrement des naissances, des décès et des mariages du Bureau de statistique du Samoa.

[68] The huge increase in 2018 is due to late registrations of all unregistered persons regardless of their age conducted mid-February to June. - La forte augmentation constatée en 2018 s'explique par l'organisation, de la mi-février au mois de juin, d'une campagne de déclaration tardive pour toutes les personnes qui n'étaient pas encore déclarées, quel que soit leur âge.

Table 10 - *Demographic Yearbook 2018*

Table 10 presents live births by age of mother and sex of the child, general fertility rate, and age-specific fertility rates for the latest available year between 2009 and 2018.

Description of variables: Age is defined as age at last birthday, that is, the difference between the date of birth and the date of the occurrence of the event, expressed in completed solar years. The age classification used in this table is the following: under 15 years, 5-year age groups through 45-49 years, and 50 years and over. A different classification may appear as provided by the reporting country or area.

Rate computation: Age-specific fertility rates are the annual number of births to women in each age group per 1 000 female population in the same age group. These rates are calculated by the Statistics Division of the United Nations.

Since relatively few births occur to women below 15 or above 50 years of age, age-specific fertility rates for women under 20 years of age and for those 45 years of age or over are computed on the female population aged 15-19 and 45-49, respectively. Similarly, the rate for women of "All ages" is based on all live births irrespective of age of mother and is computed on the female population aged 15-49 years. This rate for "All ages" is known as the general fertility rate. The age-specific fertility rates for age groups of women below 15 or 50 and above years of age are not calculated.

Births to mothers of unknown age are distributed proportionately across the age groups, by the Statistics Division of the United Nations, in accordance with the distribution of births by age of mother prior to the calculation of the rates.

The population used in computing the rates is the estimated or enumerated distribution of females by age. First priority was given to the estimated population and second priority to the enumerated population, i.e. to census returns of the year to which the births referred.

Rates presented in this table are limited to those for countries or areas having at least a total of 100 live births in a given year.

Reliability of data: Data from civil registers of live births which are reported as incomplete (less than 90 per cent completeness) or of unknown completeness are considered unreliable and are set in *italics* rather than in roman type. Rates are not computed if the data on live births from civil registers are reported as incomplete (less than 90 per cent completeness) or of unknown completeness. Table 9 and the technical notes for that table provide more detailed information on the completeness of live-birth registration. For more information about the quality of vital statistics data in general, see section 4.2 of the Technical Notes.

Limitations: Statistics on live births by age of mother are subject to the same qualifications as have been set forth for vital statistics in general and birth statistics in particular as discussed in section 4 of the Technical Notes. These include differences in the completeness of registration, the method used to determine age of mother and the quality of the reported information relating to age of mother.

The reliability of the data described above, is an important factor in considering the limitations. In addition, some live births are tabulated by date of registration and not by date of occurrence; these are indicated in the table by a plus sign "+". Whenever the lag between the date of occurrence and date of registration is prolonged and, therefore, a large proportion of the live birth registrations are delayed, birth statistics for any given year may be seriously affected. For example, the age of the mother will almost always refer to the date of registration rather than to the date of birth of the child. Hence, in those countries or areas where registration of births is delayed, possibly for years, statistics on births by age of mother should be used with caution.

Another factor which limits international comparability is the practice of some countries or areas of not including in live birth statistics infants who were born alive but died before the registration of the birth or within the first 24 hours of life, thus underestimating the total number of live births. Statistics of this type are footnoted.

Because these statistics are classified according to age, they are subject to the limitations with respect to accuracy of age reporting similar to those already discussed in connection with section 3.1.3 of the Technical Notes. The factors influencing the accuracy of reporting may be somewhat dissimilar in vital statistics (because of the differences in the method of taking a census and registering a birth) but, in general, the same errors can be observed. The absence of frequencies in the unknown age group does not necessarily indicate completely accurate reporting and tabulation of the age item. It is often an indication that the unknowns have been eliminated by assigning ages to them before tabulation, or by proportionate distribution after tabulation.

On the other hand, large frequencies in the unknown age category may indicate that a large proportion of the births are born outside of wedlock, the records for which tend to be incomplete so far as characteristics of the parents are concerned.

Another limitation of age reporting may result from calculating age of mother at birth of child (or at time of registration) from year of birth rather than from day, month and year of birth. Information on this factor is given in footnotes when known.

In few countries, data by age refer to deliveries rather than to live births causing under-enumeration in the event of a multiple birth. This practice leads to lack of strict comparability, both among countries or areas relying on this practice and between data shown in this table and table 9.

Rates shown in this table are subject to the same limitations that affect the corresponding statistics on live births. In cases of rates based on births tabulated by date of registration and not by date of occurrence; the effect of including delayed registration on the distribution of births by age of mother may be noted in the age-specific fertility rates for women at older ages. In some cases, high age-specific rates for women aged 45 years and over may reflect age of mother at registration of birth and not fertility at these older ages.

Earlier data: Live births and live-birth rates by age of mother (i.e. age-specific fertility rates), have been shown for the latest available year in each issue of the Yearbook. Information on the years and specific topics covered is presented in the Historical Index.

Tableau 10 – *Annuaire démographique 2018*

Le tableau 10 présente les données les plus récentes disponibles pour la période 2009 - 2018 sur les naissances vivantes selon l'âge de la mère et le sexe de l'enfant, le taux de fécondité et les taux de fécondité par âge.

Description des variables : l'âge désigne l'âge au dernier anniversaire, c'est-à-dire la différence entre la date de naissance et la date de l'événement exprimée en années solaires révolues. La classification par âge utilisée dans ce tableau comprend les catégories suivantes : moins de 15 ans, groupes quinquennaux jusqu'à 45-49 ans, 50 ans et plus, et âge inconnu. Des groupes d'âge différents sont parfois utilisés lorsque les pays ou territoires ont fourni les données dans une autre classification.

Les taux de fécondité par âge représentent le nombre annuel de naissances vivantes intervenues dans un groupe d'âge donné pour 1 000 femmes du groupe d'âge. Ces taux ont été calculés par la Division de statistique de l'ONU.

Étant donné que le nombre de naissances parmi les femmes de moins de 15 ans ou de plus de 50 ans est relativement peu élevé, les taux de fécondité par âge parmi les femmes âgées de moins de 20 ans et celles de 45 ans et plus ont été calculés sur la base des populations féminines âgées de 15 à 19 ans et de 45 à 49 ans, respectivement. De même, le taux pour les femmes de « tous âges » est fondé sur la totalité des naissances vivantes, indépendamment de l'âge de la mère et ce chiffre est rapporté à l'effectif de la population féminine âgée de 15 à 49 ans. Ce taux « tous âges » est le taux global de fécondité ou simplement taux de fécondité. Les taux de fécondité parmi les femmes âgées de moins de 15 ans ou celles de 50 ans et plus n'ont pas été calculés.

Les naissances pour lesquelles l'âge de la mère était inconnu ont été réparties par la Division de statistique de l'ONU, avant le calcul des taux, suivant les proportions observées pour celles où l'âge de la mère était connu.

Les chiffres de population utilisés pour le calcul des taux proviennent de dénombrements ou de répartitions estimatives de la population féminine selon l'âge. On a utilisé de préférence les estimations de la population; à défaut, on s'est contenté des données censitaires se rapportant à l'année des naissances.

Les taux présentés dans ce tableau ne concernent que les pays ou zones où l'on a enregistré un total d'au moins 100 naissances vivantes dans une année donnée.

Fiabilité des données : les données sur les naissances vivantes provenant des registres de l'état civil qui sont déclarées incomplètes (degré de complétude inférieur à 90 p. 100) ou dont le degré de complétude n'est pas connu, sont jugées douteuses et apparaissent en italique et non en caractères romains. On a choisi de ne pas faire figurer des taux calculés à partir de données sur les naissances vivantes issues de registres de l'état civil qui sont déclarées incomplètes (degré de complétude inférieur à 90 p. 100) ou dont le degré de complétude n'est pas connu. Le tableau 9 et les notes techniques qui s'y rapportent présentent des renseignements plus détaillés sur le degré de complétude de l'enregistrement des naissances vivantes. Pour plus de précisions sur la qualité des statistiques de l'état civil en général, voir la section 4.2 des Notes techniques.

Insuffisance des données : les statistiques relatives aux naissances vivantes selon l'âge de la mère appellent toutes les réserves qui ont été formulées à propos des statistiques de l'état civil en général et des statistiques de naissances en particulier (voir la section 4 des Notes techniques). Ceci inclut les différences de complétude d'enregistrement des faits d'état civil, de méthode pour déterminer l'âge de la mère et de qualité d'information concernant l'âge de la mère.

La fiabilité des données, au sujet de laquelle des indications ont été données plus haut, est un facteur important. Il faut également tenir compte du fait que, dans certains cas, les données relatives aux naissances vivantes sont exploitées selon la date de l'enregistrement et non la date de l'événement ; ces cas ont été signalés dans le tableau par le signe '+'. Chaque fois que le décalage entre l'événement et son enregistrement est grand et qu'une forte proportion des naissances vivantes fait l'objet d'un enregistrement tardif, les statistiques des naissances vivantes pour une année donnée peuvent être considérablement faussées. Par exemple, l'âge de la mère représente presque toujours son âge à la date de l'enregistrement et non à la date de la naissance de l'enfant. Ainsi, dans les pays ou zones où l'enregistrement des naissances est tardif, le retard atteignant parfois plusieurs années, il faut utiliser avec prudence les statistiques concernant les naissances selon l'âge de la mère.

Un autre facteur qui nuit à la comparabilité internationale est la pratique de certains pays ou zones qui consiste à ne pas inclure dans les statistiques des naissances vivantes les enfants nés vivants mais décédés avant l'enregistrement de leur naissance ou dans les 24 heures qui ont suivi la naissance, pratique qui conduit à sous-estimer le nombre total de naissances vivantes. Quand pareil facteur a joué, cela a été signalé en note à la fin du tableau.

Étant donné que les statistiques du tableau 10 sont classées selon l'âge, elles appellent les mêmes réserves concernant l'exactitude des déclarations d'âge que celles formulées à la section 3.1.3 des Notes techniques. Dans le cas des statistiques de l'état civil, les facteurs qui interviennent à cet égard sont parfois différents, étant donné que le recensement de la population et l'enregistrement des naissances se font par des méthodes différentes, mais, d'une manière générale, les erreurs observées seront les mêmes. Si aucun nombre ne figure dans la rangée réservée aux âges inconnus, cela ne signifie pas nécessairement que les déclarations d'âge et l'exploitation des données par âge ont été tout à fait exactes. C'est souvent une indication que l'on a attribué un âge aux personnes d'âge inconnu avant l'exploitation des données ou qu'elles ont été réparties proportionnellement entre les différents groupes après cette opération.

À l'inverse, lorsque le nombre des personnes d'âge inconnu est important, cela peut signifier que la proportion de naissances parmi les mères célibataires est élevée, étant donné qu'en pareil cas l'acte de naissance ne contient pas tous les renseignements concernant les parents.

Les déclarations par âge peuvent comporter des distorsions, du fait que l'âge de la mère au moment de la naissance d'un enfant (ou de la déclaration de naissance) est donné par année de naissance et non par date exacte (jour, mois et année).

Dans quelques pays, la classification par âges se réfère aux accouchements, et non aux naissances vivantes, ce qui conduit à un sous-dénombrement en cas de naissances gémellaires. Cette pratique nuit à la comparabilité des données, à la fois entre pays ou zones qui recourent à cette méthode et entre les données présentées dans le tableau 10 et celles du tableau 9.

Les taux présentés dans ce tableau sont sujets aux mêmes limitations qui affectent les statistiques correspondantes de naissances vivantes. Dans le cas des taux basés sur des naissances par date d'enregistrement et non par date d'occurrence, l'effet peut être visible sur les taux de fécondité par âge des femmes aux âges plus élevés. Dans certains cas, les taux de fécondité des femmes de plus de 45 ans peuvent refléter l'âge de la mère à l'enregistrement plus que la fécondité à ces âges.

Données publiées antérieurement : les différentes éditions de l'*Annuaire démographique* regroupent les dernières statistiques dont on disposait à l'époque sur les naissances vivantes selon l'âge de la mère et les taux des naissances vivantes selon l'âge de la mère (taux de fécondité par âge). Pour plus de précisions concernant les années pour lesquels des données ont été publiées, se reporter à l'index historique.

10. Live births by age of mother and sex of child, general and age-specific fertility rates: latest available year, 2009 - 2018
Naissances vivantes selon l'âge de la mère et le sexe de l'enfant, taux de fécondité et taux de fécondité par âge : dernière année disponible, 2009 - 2018

Continent, country or area, year, code[a] and age of mother (in years) / Continent, pays ou zone, année, code[a] et âge de la mère (en années)	Total	Male Masculin	Female Féminin	Rate Taux
AFRICA - AFRIQUE				
Botswana[1]				
2017 (C)				
Total	43 290	21 940	21 350	62.2
10 - 14	18	9	9	..
15 - 19	3 597	1 810	1 787	31.4
20 - 24	11 334	5 828	5 506	96.1
25 - 29	10 883	5 451	5 432	94.8
30 - 34	9 535	4 789	4 746	80.3
35 - 39	5 849	3 020	2 829	61.1
40 - 44	1 713	869	844	23.0
45 - 49	117	48	69	2.1
50 +	8	6	2	..
Unknown - Inconnu	236	110	126	..
Congo				
2014 (+U)				
Total	111 360	56 565	54 795	...
0 - 14	687	338	349	...
15 - 19	17 013	8 672	8 341	...
20 - 24	27 445	14 025	13 420	...
25 - 29	27 607	14 099	13 508	...
30 - 34	20 583	10 316	10 267	...
35 - 39	12 659	6 443	6 216	...
40 - 44	4 369	2 172	2 197	...
45 - 49	695	345	350	...
50 +	302	155	147	..
Côte d'Ivoire[2]				
2014 (I)				
Total	841 081	426 128	414 953	154.0
0 - 14	3 653	1 875	1 778	..
15 - 19	77 375	39 411	37 964	74.5
20 - 24	192 965	97 499	95 466	178.1
25 - 29	221 215	112 113	109 102	210.1
30 - 34	183 792	92 806	90 986	213.2
35 - 39	105 637	53 532	52 105	171.7
40 - 44	40 638	20 721	19 917	91.0
45 +	15 806	8 171	7 635	43.7
Egypt - Égypte				
2012 (+C)				
Total	2 629 769	1 343 402	1 286 367	121.1
0 - 19	71 275	36 022	35 253	23.8
20 - 24	1 298 851	665 452	633 399	403.8
25 - 29	399 915	201 967	197 948	127.5
30 - 34	223 307	111 754	111 553	86.0
35 - 39	83 362	41 121	42 241	41.3
40 - 44	21 510	11 229	10 281	12.2
45 +	3 802	2 233	1 569	2.3
Unknown - Inconnu	527 747	273 624	254 123	..
Ghana[3]				
2010 (I)				
Total	623 700	306 159	317 541	98.1
0 - 14	917	381	536	..
15 - 19	40 307	19 067	21 240	31.0
20 - 24	126 417	61 277	65 140	103.4
25 - 29	167 306	82 741	84 565	151.1
30 - 34	130 724	64 600	66 124	147.1
35 - 39	92 751	46 285	46 466	124.6
40 - 44	41 898	20 783	21 115	68.3
45 - 49	14 742	7 071	7 671	30.4
50 +	8 638	3 954	4 684	..
Guinea - Guinée[4]				
2014 (I)				
Total	416 607	204 309	212 298	161.9
0 - 14	3 494	1 728	1 766	..
15 - 19	62 085	30 684	31 401	105.6
20 - 24	96 498	47 687	48 811	194.3

Continent, country or area, year, code[a] and age of mother (in years) / Continent, pays ou zone, année, code[a] et âge de la mère (en années)	Total	Male Masculin	Female Féminin	Rate Taux
AFRICA - AFRIQUE				
Guinea - Guinée[4]				
2014 (I)				
25 - 29	101 210	49 832	51 378	227.6
30 - 34	72 323	35 456	36 867	204.4
35 - 39	44 261	21 594	22 667	155.4
40 - 44	21 347	10 144	11 203	90.0
45 - 49	9 266	4 348	4 918	54.9
50 +	6 123	2 839	3 284	..
Kenya				
2009 (U)				
Total	691 312	354 154	337 158	...
0 - 14	3 877	2 019	1 858	...
15 - 19	89 664	45 562	44 102	...
20 - 24	221 828	113 572	108 256	...
25 - 29	174 571	89 674	84 897	...
30 - 34	103 940	53 395	50 545	...
35 - 39	49 527	25 424	24 103	...
40 - 44	13 231	6 713	6 518	...
45 - 49	2 165	1 097	1 068	...
50 +	823	423	400	...
Unknown - Inconnu	31 686	16 275	15 411	...
2018 (+U)				
Total	1 148 352	...	...	...
10 - 14	4 214	...	...	...
15 - 19	135 113	...	...	...
20 - 24	332 533	...	...	...
25 - 29	303 898	...	...	...
30 - 34	213 056	...	...	...
35 - 39	102 232	...	...	...
40 - 44	27 702	...	...	...
45 - 49	4 354	...	...	...
50 +	747	...	...	...
Unknown - Inconnu	24 503	...	...	..
Lesotho				
2017 (+U)				
Total	9 463	...	...	...
10 - 14	15	...	...	...
15 - 19	901	...	...	...
20 - 24	2 181	...	...	...
25 - 29	2 621	...	...	...
30 - 34	2 171	...	...	...
35 - 39	1 224	...	...	...
40 - 44	320	...	...	...
45 - 49	30	...	...	...
Libya - Libye[5]				
2009 (+U)				
Total	134 682	...	...	...
0 - 19	733	...	...	...
20 - 24	7 067	...	...	...
25 - 29	17 792	...	...	...
30 - 34	18 491	...	...	...
35 - 39	9 801	...	...	...
40 - 44	3 334	...	...	...
45 +	409	...	...	...
Unknown - Inconnu	77 055	...	...	...
Malawi[3]				
2018 (I)				
Total	576 525	...	...	135.1
15 - 19	104 087	...	...	100.9
20 - 24	177 544	...	...	203.1
25 - 29	120 735	...	...	186.7
30 - 34	93 091	...	...	157.6
35 - 39	57 215	...	...	114.2
40 - 44	19 252	...	...	53.1
45 - 49	4 601	...	...	17.6

10. Live births by age of mother and sex of child, general and age-specific fertility rates: latest available year, 2009 - 2018
Naissances vivantes selon l'âge de la mère et le sexe de l'enfant, taux de fécondité et taux de fécondité par âge : dernière année disponible, 2009 - 2018 (continued - suite)

Continent, country or area, year, code[a] and age of mother (in years) / Continent, pays ou zone, année, code[a] et âge de la mère (en années)	Total	Male Masculin	Female Féminin	Rate Taux
AFRICA - AFRIQUE				
Mali[6]				
2009 (I)				
Total	666 216	324 862	341 354	208.9
12 - 14	34 953	17 432	17 521	..
15 - 19	97 788	47 793	49 995	124.8
20 - 24	138 189	67 575	70 614	225.7
25 - 29	140 359	68 914	71 445	256.8
30 - 34	108 467	52 837	55 630	253.5
35 - 39	74 059	35 667	38 392	226.6
40 - 44	45 402	21 748	23 654	164.9
45 +	26 999	12 896	14 103	124.3
Mauritania - Mauritanie[7]				
2013 (I)				
Total	114 420	...	...	137.6
15 - 19	14 258	...	...	77.0
20 - 24	34 153	...	...	216.2
25 - 29	31 533	...	...	232.3
30 - 34	20 082	...	...	176.6
35 - 39	10 479	...	...	109.9
40 - 44	3 421	...	...	43.2
45 - 49	493	...	...	7.6
Mauritius - Maurice[8]				
2018 (+C)				
Total	12 980	6 711	6 269	40.7
10 - 14	29	14	15	..
15 - 19	1 117	573	544	23.4
20 - 24	2 627	1 377	1 250	54.9
25 - 29	3 991	2 094	1 897	84.3
30 - 34	3 138	1 607	1 531	75.9
35 - 39	1 629	823	806	33.7
40 - 44	361	178	183	8.1
45 - 49	14	7	7	♦0.4
50 +	2	1	1	..
Unknown - Inconnu	72	37	35	..
Mayotte				
2017 (C)				
Total	9 762	...	...	148.9
0 - 14	56	...	...	..
15 - 19	1 047	...	...	79.4
20 - 24	2 342	...	...	245.3
25 - 29	2 468	...	...	242.7
30 - 34	2 097	...	...	204.3
35 - 39	1 304	...	...	138.3
40 - 44	418	...	...	55.4
45 - 49	30	...	...	♦5.5
50 +	-	...	...	..
Unknown - Inconnu	...	...	...	..
Namibia - Namibie[9]				
2011 (I)				
Total	61 523	30 560	30 963	110.8
0 - 14	873	443	430	..
15 - 19	7 593	3 723	3 870	62.5
20 - 24	16 655	8 235	8 420	152.3
25 - 29	14 296	7 109	7 187	157.7
30 - 34	11 017	5 632	5 385	145.3
35 - 39	7 237	3 531	3 706	113.0
40 - 44	2 982	1 451	1 531	58.4
45 +	870	436	434	20.2
Reunion - Réunion[10]				
2017 (C)				
Total	13 708	...	...	65.7
0 - 14	21	...	...	..
15 - 19	1 006	...	...	29.9
20 - 24	2 950	...	...	114.6
25 - 29	3 836	...	...	142.0
AFRICA - AFRIQUE				
Reunion - Réunion[10]				
2017 (C)				
30 - 34	3 259	...	...	115.1
35 - 39	1 986	...	...	66.5
40 - 44	610	...	...	19.5
45 - 49	37	...	...	1.1
50 +	3	...	...	..
Unknown - Inconnu	-	...	...	..
Saint Helena ex. dep. - Sainte-Hélène sans dép.				
2018 (C)				
Total	26	11	15	...
10 - 14	-	-	-	...
15 - 19	1	1	-	..
20 - 24	5	2	3	..
25 - 29	4	1	3	..
30 - 34	8	3	5	..
35 - 39	4	2	2	..
40 - 44	2	-	2	..
45 - 49	-	-	-	..
50 +	-	-	-	..
Unknown - Inconnu	2	2	-	..
Seychelles				
2015 (+C)				
Total	1 592	814	778	66.2
0 - 14	5	3	2	..
15 - 19	187	89	98	69.9
20 - 24	420	211	209	136.0
25 - 29	406	209	197	130.7
30 - 34	325	176	149	78.7
35 - 39	189	99	90	50.0
40 - 44	56	25	31	15.3
45 - 49	4	2	2	♦1.1
50 +	-	-	-	..
2018 (+C)				
Total	1 650	...	...	..
0 - 14	5	...	...	..
15 - 19	212	...	...	..
20 - 24	412	...	...	..
25 - 29	404	...	...	..
30 - 34	322	...	...	..
35 - 39	206	...	...	..
40 - 44	87	...	...	..
45 +	2	...	...	..
South Africa - Afrique du Sud[11]				
2017 (C)				
Total	897 750	452 686	445 064	58.2
10 - 14	1 302	664	638	..
15 - 19	97 143	49 159	47 984	41.4
20 - 24	228 936	116 088	112 848	89.9
25 - 29	235 466	118 682	116 784	86.8
30 - 34	191 418	96 292	95 126	75.4
35 - 39	102 565	51 276	51 289	50.5
40 - 44	30 318	15 168	15 150	18.3
45 - 49	2 122	1 070	1 052	1.5
50 +	155	71	84	..
Unknown - Inconnu	8 325	4 216	4 109	..
Tunisia - Tunisie				
2016 (C)				
Total	219 441	...	...	72.6
15 - 19	1 948	...	...	8.4
20 - 24	18 400	...	...	70.0
25 - 29	39 120	...	...	137.9
30 - 34	40 213	...	...	134.1

Continent, country or area, year, code[a] and age of mother (in years) / Continent, pays ou zone, année, code[a] et âge de la mère (en années)	Number - Nombre Total	Male Masculin	Female Féminin	Rate Taux
AFRICA - AFRIQUE				
Tunisia - Tunisie				
2016 (C)				
35 - 39	23 442	...	...	86.6
40 - 44	6 277	...	...	27.7
45 +	345	...	...	1.6
Unknown - Inconnu	89 697	...	...	
Zambia - Zambie[12]				
2010 (I)				
Total	442 998	224 756	218 242	141.4
12 - 14	921	470	451	..
15 - 19	58 999	29 701	29 298	75.4
20 - 24	128 270	65 048	63 222	200.0
25 - 29	114 701	58 366	56 335	205.1
30 - 34	74 066	37 666	36 400	178.4
35 - 39	45 452	23 072	22 380	139.5
40 - 44	16 150	8 181	7 969	72.5
45 - 49	4 439	2 252	2 187	23.7
AMERICA, NORTH - AMÉRIQUE DU NORD				
Antigua and Barbuda - Antigua-et-Barbuda				
2018 (+C)				
Total	1 015	...	...	38.9
10 - 14	1	...	...	..
15 - 19	100	...	...	27.6
20 - 24	272	...	...	70.8
25 - 29	252	...	...	67.7
30 - 34	223	...	...	60.1
35 - 39	138	...	...	37.4
40 - 44	28	...	...	+7.4
45 +	1	...	...	+0.3
Aruba				
2017 (C)				
Total	1 202	642	560	45.6
10 - 14	1	1	-	..
15 - 19	94	50	44	26.1
20 - 24	300	154	146	93.7
25 - 29	338	180	158	104.0
30 - 34	274	143	131	76.3
35 - 39	156	94	62	39.4
40 - 44	35	19	16	8.6
45 - 49	4	1	3	+0.8
Bahamas				
2012 (+U)				
Total	4 469	2 279	2 187	...
0 - 14	4	2	2	..
15 - 19	497	261	236	...
20 - 24	1 028	524	504	...
25 - 29	1 123	580	543	...
30 - 34	972	496	476	...
35 - 39	632	318	314	...
40 - 44	193	91	102	...
45 - 49	15	5	10	...
50 +	1	1	-	..
Unknown - Inconnu	1	1	-	...
Belize[13]				
2016 (U)				
Total	7 200	3 615	3 585	...
0 - 14	20	11	9	...
15 - 19	1 337	653	684	...
20 - 24	2 323	1 171	1 152	...
25 - 29	1 780	924	856	...
30 - 34	1 054	524	530	...

Continent, country or area, year, code[a] and age of mother (in years) / Continent, pays ou zone, année, code[a] et âge de la mère (en années)	Number - Nombre Total	Male Masculin	Female Féminin	Rate Taux
AMERICA, NORTH - AMÉRIQUE DU NORD				
Belize[13]				
2016 (U)				
35 - 39	543	260	283	...
40 - 44	129	65	64	...
45 - 49	14	7	7	...
50 +	-	-	-	...
Unknown - Inconnu	-	-	-	...
Bermuda - Bermudes[14]				
2017 (C)				
Total	576	289	287	42.5
10 - 14	-	-	-	..
15 - 19	5	1	4	+3.5
20 - 24	45	26	19	28.9
25 - 29	106	64	42	55.5
30 - 34	201	94	107	97.1
35 - 39	169	76	93	80.5
40 - 44	48	26	22	22.5
45 - 49	2	2	-	+0.9
50 +	-	-	-	..
British Virgin Islands - Îles Vierges britanniques				
2017 (C)				
Total	248	...	...	...
13 - 19	16	...	...	...
20 - 24	35	...	...	...
25 - 29	51	...	...	...
30 - 34	86	...	...	...
35 - 39	32	...	...	...
40 +	20	...	...	...
Unknown - Inconnu	8	...	...	...
Canada[15]				
2009 (C)				
Total	380 863	195 445	185 418	46.1
0 - 14	104	52	52	..
15 - 19	15 534	7 997	7 537	14.1
20 - 24	57 778	29 564	28 214	51.5
25 - 29	116 878	60 099	56 779	101.3
30 - 34	120 734	62 132	58 602	107.4
35 - 39	57 733	29 493	28 240	50.7
40 - 44	11 364	5 720	5 644	9.3
45 - 49	605	316	289	0.4
Unknown - Inconnu[16]	133	72	61	..
2017 (C)				
Total	376 291	...	...	45.5
10 - 14	65	...	...	..
15 - 19	7 793	...	...	7.7
20 - 24	42 521	...	...	36.9
25 - 29	106 329	...	...	87.0
30 - 34	134 319	...	...	107.6
35 - 39	70 415	...	...	56.9
40 - 44	13 879	...	...	11.7
45 - 49	914	...	...	0.8
Unknown - Inconnu[16]	56	...	...	..
Cayman Islands - Îles Caïmanes				
2018 (C)				
Total	640	...	...	...
10 - 14	-	...	...	...
15 - 19	25	...	...	...
20 - 24	85	...	...	...
25 - 29	154	...	...	...
30 - 34	183	...	...	...
35 - 39	146	...	...	...
40 - 44	47	...	...	...

10. Live births by age of mother and sex of child, general and age-specific fertility rates: latest available year, 2009 - 2018
Naissances vivantes selon l'âge de la mère et le sexe de l'enfant, taux de fécondité et taux de fécondité par âge : dernière année disponible, 2009 - 2018 (continued - suite)

Continent, country or area, year, code[a] and age of mother (in years) — Continent, pays ou zone, année, code[a] et âge de la mère (en années)	Total	Male Masculin	Female Féminin	Rate Taux
AMERICA, NORTH - AMÉRIQUE DU NORD				
Costa Rica				
2018* (C)				
Total	68 479	34 868	33 611	52.1
10 - 14	258	133	125	..
15 - 19	9 273	4 778	4 495	47.9
20 - 24	18 116	9 239	8 877	87.8
25 - 29	18 023	9 118	8 905	92.7
30 - 34	13 987	7 099	6 888	69.6
35 - 39	7 185	3 686	3 499	37.7
40 - 44	1 521	753	768	8.9
45 - 49	84	44	40	0.5
50 +	2	2	-	..
Unknown - Inconnu	30	16	14	..
Cuba				
2017 (C)				
Total	114 971	59 698	55 273	43.0
10 - 14	409	202	207	..
15 - 19	17 287	8 989	8 298	50.8
20 - 24	32 554	16 964	15 590	95.8
25 - 29	34 429	17 811	16 618	87.2
30 - 34	20 261	10 564	9 697	56.6
35 - 39	7 688	3 997	3 691	25.2
40 - 44	2 144	1 067	1 077	5.0
45 - 49	139	75	64	0.3
50 +	37	19	18	..
Unknown - Inconnu	23	10	13	..
Curaçao				
2016 (C)				
Total	1 789	901	888	47.8
0 - 14	4	2	2	..
15 - 19	113	64	49	22.9
20 - 24	417	202	215	91.6
25 - 29	465	233	232	98.2
30 - 34	421	211	210	82.8
35 - 39	255	136	119	49.9
40 - 44	65	33	32	11.2
45 - 49	6	2	4	♦0.9
50 +	-	-	-	..
Unknown - Inconnu	43	18	25	..
2018 (C)				
Total	1 727	...	...	..
0 - 19	117	...	...	..
20 - 24	353	...	...	..
25 - 29	466	...	...	..
30 - 34	442	...	...	..
35 - 39	236	...	...	..
40 +	73	...	...	..
Unknown - Inconnu	40	...	...	..
Dominican Republic - République dominicaine				
2017 (U)				
Total	148 061	75 105	72 956	...
10 - 14	658	359	299	...
15 - 19	23 762	12 025	11 737	...
20 - 24	44 489	22 580	21 909	...
25 - 29	39 143	19 932	19 211	...
30 - 34	24 310	12 360	11 950	...
35 - 39	10 910	5 430	5 480	...
40 - 44	2 230	1 120	1 110	...
45 - 49	109	53	56	...
50 +	9	6	3	...
Unknown - Inconnu	2 441	1 240	1 201	..

Continent, country or area, year, code[a] and age of mother (in years) — Continent, pays ou zone, année, code[a] et âge de la mère (en années)	Total	Male Masculin	Female Féminin	Rate Taux
AMERICA, NORTH - AMÉRIQUE DU NORD				
El Salvador[17]				
2015 (C)				
Total	109 617	56 757	52 860	58.9
0 - 14	923	466	457	..
15 - 19	23 452	12 226	11 226	67.2
20 - 24	32 224	16 716	15 508	94.1
25 - 29	24 090	12 451	11 639	82.7
30 - 34	17 103	8 802	8 301	68.5
35 - 39	8 891	4 564	4 327	39.2
40 - 44	2 333	1 205	1 128	11.1
45 - 49	171	96	75	0.9
50 +	45	17	28	..
Unknown - Inconnu	385	214	171	..
Greenland - Groenland				
2018 (C)				
Total	819	432	387	63.3
10 - 14	1	1	-	..
15 - 19	68	37	31	37.2
20 - 24	219	114	105	104.4
25 - 29	253	121	132	111.2
30 - 34	182	105	77	87.3
35 - 39	78	46	32	44.7
40 - 44	18	8	10	♦13.5
45 - 49	-	-	-	-
50 +	-	-	-	..
Grenada - Grenade				
2014 (+C)				
Total	1 750	900	850	62.8
10 - 14	4	1	3	..
15 - 19	169	91	78	35.9
20 - 24	481	252	229	101.2
25 - 29	500	257	243	103.1
30 - 34	351	179	172	88.9
35 - 39	166	85	81	52.3
40 - 44	50	24	26	16.8
45 - 49	5	2	3	♦1.6
Unknown - Inconnu	24	9	15	..
Guadeloupe[10]				
2017 (C)				
Total	4 626	...	...	47.9
10 - 14	9	...	...	..
15 - 19	237	...	...	16.1
20 - 24	805	...	...	78.3
25 - 29	1 223	...	...	107.7
30 - 34	1 191	...	...	99.4
35 - 39	794	...	...	60.7
40 - 44	333	...	...	19.6
45 - 49	31	...	...	1.7
50 +	3	...	...	..
Guatemala				
2011 (C)				
Total	373 692	189 724	183 968	102.4
0 - 14	2 841	1 426	1 415	..
15 - 19	75 175	38 415	36 760	92.4
20 - 24	108 949	55 558	53 391	157.0
25 - 29	85 914	43 599	42 315	142.0
30 - 34	58 050	29 264	28 786	113.4
35 - 39	30 892	15 540	15 352	73.8
40 - 44	10 220	5 136	5 084	30.5
45 - 49	1 176	573	603	4.4
50 +	290	127	163	..
Unknown - Inconnu	185	86	99	..
2016 (C)				
Total	390 382	...	...	92.4
10 - 14	2 138	...	...	..

10. Live births by age of mother and sex of child, general and age-specific fertility rates: latest available year, 2009 - 2018
Naissances vivantes selon l'âge de la mère et le sexe de l'enfant, taux de fécondité et taux de fécondité par âge : dernière année disponible, 2009 - 2018 (continued - suite)

Continent, country or area, year, code[a] and age of mother (in years) / Continent, pays ou zone, année, code[a] et âge de la mère (en années)	Number - Nombre			Rate Taux
	Total	Male Masculin	Female Féminin	
AMERICA, NORTH - AMÉRIQUE DU NORD				
Guatemala				
2016 (C)				
15 - 19	71 903	...	...	79.9
20 - 24	118 747	...	...	148.0
25 - 29	91 918	...	...	135.2
30 - 34	61 247	...	...	102.6
35 - 39	33 894	...	...	67.4
40 - 44	9 687	...	...	23.5
45 - 49	682	...	...	2.1
50 +	65	...	...	..
Unknown - Inconnu	101	...	...	..
Honduras				
2012 (+U)				
Total	196 119	...	...	..
0 - 14	1 571	...	...	..
15 - 19	41 882	...	...	..
20 - 24	56 501	...	...	..
25 - 29	43 429	...	...	..
30 - 34	28 675	...	...	..
35 - 39	14 730	...	...	..
40 - 44	4 791	...	...	..
45 - 49	575	...	...	..
50 +	471	...	...	..
Unknown - Inconnu	3 494	...	...	..
Jamaica - Jamaïque[18]				
2011 (|)				
Total	49 676	23 949[19]	23 339[19]	66.0
15 - 19	6 167	3 034[19]	2 884[19]	50.5
20 - 24	13 977	6 852[19]	6 451[19]	129.9
25 - 29	12 348	5 923[19]	5 900[19]	108.7
30 - 34	8 746	4 182[19]	4 145[19]	73.9
35 - 39	6 001	2 816[19]	2 875[19]	48.9
40 - 44	2 109	1 014[19]	956[19]	21.2
45 - 49	328	128[19]	128[19]	4.8
Martinique[10]				
2017 (C)				
Total	3 640	...	...	46.5
10 - 14	3	...	...	..
15 - 19	213	...	...	18.6
20 - 24	666	...	...	79.5
25 - 29	926	...	...	98.9
30 - 34	987	...	...	99.0
35 - 39	630	...	...	61.3
40 - 44	199	...	...	15.7
45 - 49	16	...	...	♦1.0
50 +	-	...	...	
Mexico - Mexique[20]				
2016 (C)				
Total	2 028 358	1 032 107[19]	996 234[19]	60.3
10 - 14	6 531	3 332[19]	3 199[19]	..
15 - 19	341 688	174 771[19]	166 915[19]	62.2
20 - 24	606 757	309 257[19]	297 496[19]	112.1
25 - 29	510 603	258 816[19]	251 781[19]	100.1
30 - 34	347 242	176 371[19]	170 869[19]	72.2
35 - 39	167 475	85 047[19]	82 427[19]	36.2
40 - 44	40 787	20 747[19]	20 039[19]	9.5
45 - 49	2 831	1 430[19]	1 401[19]	0.7
50 +	278	124[19]	154[19]	..
Unknown - Inconnu	4 166	2 212[19]	1 953[19]	..
Montserrat				
2016 (C)				
Total	46	23	23	...
0 - 14	-	-	-	..
15 - 19	2	-	2	..
AMERICA, NORTH - AMÉRIQUE DU NORD				
Montserrat				
2016 (C)				
20 - 24	10	5	5	...
25 - 29	11	7	4	...
30 - 34	11	6	5	...
35 - 39	8	4	4	...
40 - 44	4	1	3	...
45 - 49	-	-	-	..
50 +	-	-	-	..
Nicaragua				
2010 (+U)				
Total	132 165	68 726	63 439	...
0 - 14	1 539	793	746	...
15 - 19	33 963	17 752	16 211	...
20 - 24	38 897	20 181	18 716	...
25 - 29	30 273	15 790	14 483	...
30 - 34	17 301	8 942	8 359	...
35 - 39	8 010	4 156	3 854	...
40 - 44	1 943	992	951	...
45 - 49	209	105	104	...
50 +	30	15	15	..
Panama				
2017* (C)				
Total	76 166	39 413	36 753	72.2
10 - 14	517	299	218	..
15 - 19	13 056	6 869	6 187	75.3
20 - 24	21 673	11 125	10 548	132.3
25 - 29	18 495	9 556	8 939	118.3
30 - 34	13 467	6 907	6 560	89.1
35 - 39	6 998	3 640	3 358	48.4
40 - 44	1 810	950	860	13.1
45 - 49	133	64	69	1.0
50 +	10	3	7	..
Unknown - Inconnu	7		7	..
Puerto Rico - Porto Rico				
2018 (C)				
Total	21 467	10 991	10 476	...
10 - 14	13	8	5	...
15 - 19	1 934	1 010	924	...
20 - 24	6 715	3 402	3 313	...
25 - 29	6 153	3 141	3 012	...
30 - 34	4 001	2 067	1 934	...
35 - 39	2 151	1 104	1 047	...
40 - 44	472	243	229	...
45 - 49	25	14	11	...
50 +	3	2	1	..
Saint Lucia - Sainte-Lucie				
2014 (+C)				
Total	2 026	...	...	42.3
10 - 14	6	...	...	..
15 - 19	295	...	...	40.3
20 - 24	536	...	...	70.7
25 - 29	481	...	...	66.7
30 - 34	391	...	...	57.0
35 - 39	245	...	...	38.7
40 - 44	64	...	...	10.1
45 +	8	...	...	♦1.3
Saint Pierre and Miquelon - Saint Pierre-et-Miquelon				
2014 (C)				
Total	61	30	31	...
10 - 14	5	3	2	..
15 - 19	25	12	13	...
20 - 24	17	11	6	...
25 - 29	11	3	8	...

10. Live births by age of mother and sex of child, general and age-specific fertility rates: latest available year, 2009 - 2018
Naissances vivantes selon l'âge de la mère et le sexe de l'enfant, taux de fécondité et taux de fécondité par âge : dernière année disponible, 2009 - 2018 (continued - suite)

Continent, country or area, year, code[a] and age of mother (in years) / Continent, pays ou zone, année, code[a] et âge de la mère (en années)	Total	Male Masculin	Female Féminin	Rate Taux
AMERICA, NORTH - AMÉRIQUE DU NORD				
Saint Pierre and Miquelon - Saint Pierre-et-Miquelon				
2014 (C)				
30 - 34	2	1	1	..
35 - 39	1	-	1	..
40 - 44	-	-	-	..
45 - 49	-	-	-	..
50 +	-	-	-	..
Saint Vincent and the Grenadines - Saint-Vincent-et-les Grenadines				
2017* (C)				
Total	1 540	742	798	55.1
10 - 14	11	5	6	..
15 - 19	241	109	132	49.5
20 - 24	395	193	202	92.6
25 - 29	363	177	186	88.5
30 - 34	276	126	150	69.2
35 - 39	192	104	88	51.6
40 - 44	54	27	27	15.9
45 - 49	8	1	7	♦2.2
Unknown - Inconnu	-	-	-	..
Saint-Barthélemy				
2014 (C)				
Total	96	59	37	..
10 - 14	-	-	-	..
15 - 19	-	-	-	..
20 - 24	10	7	3	..
25 - 29	30	18	12	..
30 - 34	31	19	12	..
35 - 39	18	10	8	..
40 - 44	7	5	2	..
45 - 49	-	-	-	..
50 +	-	-	-	..
Saint-Martin (French part) - Saint-Martin (partie française)				
2014 (C)				
Total	693	370	323	88.6
10 - 14	-	-	-	..
15 - 19	55	33	22	52.9
20 - 24	134	79	55	131.1
25 - 29	195	100	95	181.4
30 - 34	175	81	94	155.3
35 - 39	117	67	50	106.5
40 - 44	15	9	6	♦12.2
45 - 49	2	1	1	♦1.6
50 +	-	-	-	..
Trinidad and Tobago - Trinité-et-Tobago				
2009 (C)				
Total	17 949	9 067	8 882	...
0 - 14	24	10	14	..
15 - 19	1 961	961	1 000	...
20 - 24	5 029	2 620	2 409	...
25 - 29	5 258	2 606	2 652	...
30 - 34	3 422	1 715	1 707	...
35 - 39	1 763	910	853	...
40 - 44	432	218	214	...
45 - 49	31	13	18	...
50 +	3	1	2	..
Unknown - Inconnu	26	13	13	..
AMERICA, NORTH - AMÉRIQUE DU NORD				
Turks and Caicos Islands - Îles Turques et Caïques				
2016 (C)				
Total	518	272	246	44.7
0 - 14	-	-	-	..
15 - 19	31	17	14	27.3
20 - 24	79	47	32	58.8
25 - 29	117	55	62	73.6
30 - 34	141	77	64	77.5
35 - 39	116	54	62	57.4
40 - 44	26	19	7	♦13.9
45 - 49	-	-	-	..
50 +	-	-	-	..
Unknown - Inconnu	8	3	5	..
2018* (C)				
Total	454	...	...	..
0 - 14	1	...	...	..
15 - 19	22	...	...	..
20 - 24	68	...	...	..
25 - 29	98	...	...	..
30 - 34	134	...	...	..
35 - 39	107	...	...	..
40 - 44	24	...	...	..
45 - 49	-	...	...	..
50 +	-	...	...	..
Unknown - Inconnu	-	...	...	..
United States of America - États-Unis d'Amérique				
2015 (C)				
Total	3 978 497	2 036 161	1 942 336	53.7
0 - 14	2 500	1 265	1 235	..
15 - 19	229 715	118 021	111 694	22.3
20 - 24	850 509	435 461	415 048	76.8
25 - 29	1 152 311	589 719	562 592	104.3
30 - 34	1 094 693	560 429	534 264	101.5
35 - 39	527 996	269 784	258 212	51.8
40 - 44	111 848	56 922	54 926	11.0
45 - 49	8 171	4 172	3 999	0.8
50 +	754	388	366	..
Unknown - Inconnu	-	-	-	..
AMERICA, SOUTH - AMÉRIQUE DU SUD				
Argentina - Argentine				
2017 (C)				
Total	704 609	357 467[19]	342 673[19]	63.4
0 - 14	2 493	1 249[19]	1 236[19]	..
15 - 19	91 586	46 321[19]	44 780[19]	54.2
20 - 24	169 299	85 996[19]	82 303[19]	97.9
25 - 29	165 665	84 302[19]	80 508[19]	98.5
30 - 34	142 831	72 403[19]	69 667[19]	90.5
35 - 39	92 677	47 215[19]	44 942[19]	59.6
40 +	25 471	12 826[19]	12 523[19]	9.6
Unknown - Inconnu	14 587	7 155[19]	6 714[19]	..
Brazil - Brésil				
2017 (+C)				
Total	2 874 466	1 473 166[19]	1 400 998[19]	50.9
10 - 14	19 156	9 923[19]	9 227[19]	..
15 - 19	437 603	224 840[19]	212 705[19]	52.1
20 - 24	715 776	367 504[19]	348 205[19]	85.4
25 - 29	686 420	351 382[19]	334 982[19]	81.5
30 - 34	586 037	299 955[19]	286 027[19]	67.0
35 - 39	334 720	171 042[19]	163 640[19]	40.1

10. Live births by age of mother and sex of child, general and age-specific fertility rates: latest available year, 2009 - 2018
Naissances vivantes selon l'âge de la mère et le sexe de l'enfant, taux de fécondité et taux de fécondité par âge : dernière année disponible, 2009 - 2018 (continued - suite)

Continent, country or area, year, code[a] and age of mother (in years) / Continent, pays ou zone, année, code[a] et âge de la mère (en années)	Number - Nombre			Rate Taux
	Total	Male Masculin	Female Féminin	
AMERICA, SOUTH - AMÉRIQUE DU SUD				
Brazil - Brésil				
2017 (+C)				
40 - 44	77 923	39 742[19]	38 177[19]	10.6
45 - 49	4 525	2 290[19]	2 235[19]	0.7
50 +	364	191[19]	173[19]	..
Unknown - Inconnu	11 942	6 297[19]	5 627[19]	
Chile - Chili				
2017* (C)				
Total	219 186	111 660[19]	107 501[19]	46.9
10 - 14	476	...	...	..
15 - 19	16 823	...	...	26.9
20 - 24	45 006	...	...	65.1
25 - 29	59 403	...	...	78.9
30 - 34	53 919	...	...	75.9
35 - 39	33 573	...	...	52.8
40 - 44	9 105	...	...	14.6
45 - 49	545	...	...	0.9
50 +	34	...	...	..
Unknown - Inconnu	302	...	...	..
Colombia - Colombie				
2017 (U)				
Total	656 704	336 576[19]	320 035[19]	...
10 - 14	5 883	3 065[19]	2 817[19]	..
15 - 19	128 634	66 315[19]	62 299[19]	...
20 - 24	190 092	97 116[19]	92 954[19]	...
25 - 29	154 921	79 371[19]	75 530[19]	...
30 - 34	105 381	54 244[19]	51 123[19]	...
35 - 39	57 095	28 988[19]	28 098[19]	...
40 - 44	13 444	6 869[19]	6 568[19]	...
45 - 49	1 027	486[19]	541[19]	...
50 +	146	86[19]	60[19]	..
Unknown - Inconnu	81	36[19]	45[19]	..
Ecuador - Équateur[21]				
2017* (U)				
Total	288 123	147 783	140 340	...
10 - 14	2 247	1 182	1 065	..
15 - 19	54 051	27 861	26 190	...
20 - 24	77 725	39 964	37 761	...
25 - 29	67 801	34 722	33 079	...
30 - 34	50 139	25 519	24 620	...
35 - 39	26 854	13 778	13 076	...
40 - 44	6 951	3 563	3 388	...
45 - 49	488	249	239	...
50 +	12	5	7	..
Unknown - Inconnu	1 855	940	915	..
French Guiana - Guyane française[10]				
2017 (C)				
Total	8 057	...	...	114.8
10 - 14	52	...	...	..
15 - 19	1 015	...	...	79.7
20 - 24	1 706	...	...	178.3
25 - 29	1 988	...	...	201.8
30 - 34	1 818	...	...	171.2
35 - 39	1 117	...	...	111.6
40 - 44	332	...	...	35.7
45 - 49	28	...	...	♦3.5
50 +	1	...	...	
Guyana[3]				
2012 (|)				
Total	13 023	...	...	65.5
15 - 19	2 082	...	...	49.5
20 - 24	3 939	...	...	123.4
25 - 29	2 918	...	...	109.8

Continent, country or area, year, code[a] and age of mother (in years) / Continent, pays ou zone, année, code[a] et âge de la mère (en années)	Number - Nombre			Rate Taux
	Total	Male Masculin	Female Féminin	
AMERICA, SOUTH - AMÉRIQUE DU SUD				
Guyana[3]				
2012 (|)				
30 - 34	2 304	...	...	85.3
35 - 39	1 347	...	...	51.8
40 - 44	397	...	...	16.7
45 - 49	36	...	...	1.7
Paraguay[11]				
2016 (+U)				
Total	122 336	...	...	...
10 - 14	215	...	...	..
15 - 19	15 391	...	...	...
20 - 24	32 373	...	...	...
25 - 29	30 646	...	...	...
30 - 34	22 502	...	...	...
35 - 39	11 900	...	...	...
40 - 44	3 863	...	...	...
45 - 49	776	...	...	...
50 +	253	...	...	...
Unknown - Inconnu	4 417	...	...	...
Peru - Pérou[22]				
2017* (+U)				
Total	511 867	261 367	250 500	...
10 - 14	1 453	747	706	..
15 - 19	61 285	31 305	29 980	...
20 - 24	124 865	64 206	60 659	...
25 - 29	121 992	62 078	59 914	...
30 - 34	104 704	53 392	51 312	...
35 - 39	70 016	35 785	34 231	...
40 - 44	25 453	12 822	12 631	...
45 - 49	1 993	984	1 009	..
50 +	106	48	58	..
Unknown - Inconnu	-	-	-	..
Suriname				
2017 (C)				
Total	9 785	5 012	4 773	65.5
10 - 14	45	...	...	..
15 - 19	1 368	...	...	57.7
20 - 24	2 390	...	...	103.0
25 - 29	2 516	...	...	111.3
30 - 34	2 064	...	...	95.1
35 - 39	1 113	...	...	54.0
40 - 44	266	...	...	13.8
45 - 49	23	...	...	♦1.3
50 +	-	...	...	..
Uruguay				
2016 (C)				
Total	47 058	24 247[19]	22 806[19]	55.1
10 - 14	120	57[19]	63[19]	..
15 - 19	6 578	3 409[19]	3 168[19]	50.3
20 - 24	11 267	5 755[19]	5 511[19]	85.7
25 - 29	10 764	5 532[19]	5 229[19]	86.3
30 - 34	10 294	5 346[19]	4 948[19]	86.2
35 - 39	6 368	3 266[19]	3 102[19]	51.7
40 - 44	1 568	821[19]	747[19]	13.5
45 - 49	90	56[19]	34[19]	0.8
50 +	3	2[19]	1[19]	..
Unknown - Inconnu	6	3[19]	3[19]	..
Venezuela (Bolivarian Republic of) - Venezuela (République bolivarienne du)				
2017 (U)				
Total	579 349	298 705	280 644	...
10 - 14	4 275	2 213	2 062	..
15 - 19	107 018	55 351	51 667	...
20 - 24	166 164	85 845	80 319	...

10. Live births by age of mother and sex of child, general and age-specific fertility rates: latest available year, 2009 - 2018
Naissances vivantes selon l'âge de la mère et le sexe de l'enfant, taux de fécondité et taux de fécondité par âge : dernière année disponible, 2009 - 2018 (continued - suite)

Continent, country or area, year, code[a] and age of mother (in years) — Continent, pays ou zone, année, code[a] et âge de la mère (en années)	Total	Male Masculin	Female Féminin	Rate Taux
AMERICA, SOUTH - AMÉRIQUE DU SUD				
Venezuela (Bolivarian Republic of) - Venezuela (République bolivarienne du)				
2017 (U)				
25 - 29	140 277	72 002	68 275	...
30 - 34	94 664	48 667	45 997	...
35 - 39	48 719	25 195	23 524	...
40 - 44	12 698	6 442	6 256	...
45 - 49	1 248	669	579	...
50 +	293	154	139	...
Unknown - Inconnu	3 993	2 167	1 826	...
ASIA - ASIE				
Armenia - Arménie				
2017 (C)				
Total	37 700	19 731	17 969	49.5
0 - 14	2	2	-	..
15 - 19	1 665	885	780	21.1
20 - 24	11 323	5 799	5 524	110.5
25 - 29	13 626	7 105	6 521	97.1
30 - 34	7 700	4 161	3 539	56.1
35 - 39	2 884	1 532	1 352	25.1
40 - 44	458	227	231	4.7
45 - 49	38	18	20	0.4
50 +	4	2	2	..
Azerbaijan - Azerbaïdjan[23]				
2017 (+C)				
Total	144 041	76 584	67 457	54.3
0 - 14	-	-	-	
15 - 19	14 129	7 275	6 854	45.7
20 - 24	55 506	28 880	26 626	140.5
25 - 29	45 857	24 754	21 103	98.0
30 - 34	20 406	11 210	9 196	45.5
35 - 39	6 737	3 742	2 995	17.9
40 - 44	1 299	668	631	4.1
45 - 49	94	46	48	0.3
50 +	13	9	4	
Bahrain - Bahreïn[24]				
2014 (C)				
Total	20 931	10 785	10 146	69.3
0 - 14	-	-	-	
15 - 19	521	281	240	14.7
20 - 24	4 370	2 254	2 116	100.5
25 - 29	6 572	3 340	3 232	115.3
30 - 34	5 497	2 868	2 629	102.1
35 - 39	3 084	1 586	1 498	67.2
40 - 44	781	404	377	22.4
45 - 49	93	45	48	2.9
50 +	9	5	4	..
Unknown - Inconnu	4	2	2	..
2017 (C)				
Total	20 581	...	...	63.3
10 - 14	1	...	...	..
15 - 19	495	...	...	13.4
20 - 24	4 092	...	...	94.0
25 - 29	6 502	...	...	106.2
30 - 34	5 554	...	...	93.3
35 - 39	3 002	...	...	59.0
40 - 44	859	...	...	20.9
45 - 49	70	...	...	2.2
50 +	5	...	...	..
Unknown - Inconnu	1	...	...	..
ASIA - ASIE				
Bangladesh				
2010 (U)				
Total	2 868 494	1 451 664	1 416 831	...
15 - 19	404 570	209 615	194 955	...
20 - 24	1 055 194	527 993	527 201	...
25 - 29	762 338	383 627	378 710	...
30 - 34	389 547	199 767	189 780	...
35 - 39	192 438	97 826	94 613	...
40 - 44	49 380	25 206	24 174	...
45 +	15 027	7 630	7 397	...
Brunei Darussalam - Brunéi Darussalam				
2016 (+C)				
Total	6 437	3 382	3 055	54.5
10 - 14	3	1	2	..
15 - 19	170	101	69	9.7
20 - 24	920	495	425	49.8
25 - 29	2 101	1 109	992	114.2
30 - 34	1 896	973	923	107.8
35 - 39	1 064	558	506	63.8
40 - 44	269	142	127	17.4
45 - 49	12	3	9	◆0.9
50 +	2	-	2	..
Unknown - Inconnu	-	-	-	
2017 (+C)				
Total	6 452	...	...	53.6
10 - 14	2	...	...	..
15 - 19	164	...	...	9.4
20 - 24	880	...	...	48.4
25 - 29	2 015	...	...	106.6
30 - 34	2 031	...	...	111.6
35 - 39	1 068	...	...	61.7
40 - 44	271	...	...	17.3
45 - 49	20	...	...	◆1.4
50 +	-	...	...	
Unknown - Inconnu	1	...	...	
China, Hong Kong SAR - Chine, Hong Kong RAS				
2018 (C)				
Total	53 716	27 895[19]	25 820[19]	26.8
10 - 14	1	1	-	..
15 - 19	302	134	168	2.1
20 - 24	3 036	1 592	1 444	13.9
25 - 29	11 547	5 942	5 605	42.5
30 - 34	21 241	11 038[19]	10 202[19]	63.8
35 - 39	14 402	7 552	6 850	39.6
40 - 44	2 959	1 513	1 446	8.8
45 - 49	212	113	99	0.6
50 +	16	10	6	..
Unknown - Inconnu	-	-	-	
China, Macao SAR - Chine, Macao RAS				
2017 (C)				
Total	6 529	3 382	3 147	...
0 - 24	611	302	309	...
25 - 29	2 455	1 288	1 167	...
30 - 34	2 317	1 168	1 149	...
35 - 39	903	489	414	...
40 +	243	135	108	...
Cyprus - Chypre[25]				
2017 (C)				
Total	9 229	4 765	4 464	41.8
0 - 14	-	-	-	
15 - 19	161	77	84	6.5
20 - 24	870	454	416	25.9

10. Live births by age of mother and sex of child, general and age-specific fertility rates: latest available year, 2009 - 2018
Naissances vivantes selon l'âge de la mère et le sexe de l'enfant, taux de fécondité et taux de fécondité par âge : dernière année disponible, 2009 - 2018 (continued - suite)

Continent, country or area, year, code[a] and age of mother (in years) — Continent, pays ou zone, année, code[a] et âge de la mère (en années)	Total	Male Masculin	Female Féminin	Rate Taux
ASIA - ASIE				
Cyprus - Chypre[25]				
2017 (C)				
25 - 29	2 539	1 323	1 216	69.4
30 - 34	3 548	1 827	1 721	98.2
35 - 39	1 730	898	832	52.3
40 - 44	337	164	173	11.6
45 - 49	39	22	17	1.4
50 +	5	-	5	..
Unknown - Inconnu	-	-	-	..
Georgia - Géorgie				
2017 (C)				
Total	53 293	27 658	25 635	62.5
0 - 14	10	6	4	..
15 - 19	3 604	1 837	1 767	36.2
20 - 24	13 834	7 188	6 646	126.1
25 - 29	17 350	8 992	8 358	126.6
30 - 34	11 496	6 014	5 482	84.5
35 - 39	5 581	2 884	2 697	44.1
40 - 44	1 285	670	615	10.5
45 - 49	112	54	58	0.9
50 +	21	13	8	..
Unknown - Inconnu	-	-	-	..
Indonesia - Indonésie[26]				
2010 (I)				
Total	6 028 921	...	...	92.5
0 - 14	1 054	...	...	..
15 - 19	344 318	...	...	33.5
20 - 24	1 435 265	...	...	143.5
25 - 29	1 787 802	...	...	167.4
30 - 34	1 352 605	...	...	136.9
35 - 39	776 985	...	...	84.8
40 - 44	254 427	...	...	31.0
45 - 49	57 924	...	...	8.3
50 +	18 541	...	...	..
Iran (Islamic Republic of) - Iran (République islamique d')[27]				
2017 (+C)				
Total	1 450 271	747 368	702 903	63.7
10 - 14	1 534	797	737	..
15 - 19	88 361	45 452	42 909	33.5
20 - 24	284 754	146 614	138 140	95.3
25 - 29	429 377	221 567	207 810	110.7
30 - 34	391 739	201 539	190 200	91.6
35 - 39	197 447	101 538	95 909	54.5
40 - 44	44 506	23 109	21 397	15.9
45 - 49	3 195	1 696	1 499	1.3
50 +	315	178	137	..
Unknown - Inconnu	9 043	4 878	4 165	..
Israel - Israël[28]				
2017 (C)				
Total	183 648	94 310	89 338	90.4
10 - 14	-	-	-	..
15 - 19	3 059	1 639	1 420	9.2
20 - 24	32 143	16 501	15 642	105.0
25 - 29	53 108	27 340	25 768	178.1
30 - 34	54 655	28 152	26 503	185.5
35 - 39	31 035	15 726	15 309	109.7
40 - 44	8 553	4 422	4 131	31.2
45 - 49	773	370	403	3.2
50 +	84	40	44	..
Unknown - Inconnu	238	120	118	..

Continent, country or area, year, code[a] and age of mother (in years) — Continent, pays ou zone, année, code[a] et âge de la mère (en années)	Total	Male Masculin	Female Féminin	Rate Taux
ASIA - ASIE				
Japan - Japon[29]				
2017 (C)				
Total	946 065	484 449	461 616	36.6
10 - 14	37	15	22	..
15 - 19	9 861	5 004	4 857	3.4
20 - 24	79 264	40 527	38 737	26.2
25 - 29	240 933	123 639	117 294	78.1
30 - 34	345 419	176 837	168 582	98.0
35 - 39	216 938	110 849	106 089	55.4
40 - 44	52 101	26 827	25 274	11.1
45 - 49	1 450	724	726	0.3
50 +	62	27	35	..
Unknown - Inconnu	-	-	-	..
Kazakhstan				
2018 (C)				
Total	397 799	205 224	192 575	87.6
10 - 14	15	8	7	..
15 - 19	13 126	6 762	6 364	23.9
20 - 24	101 075	52 349	48 726	164.5
25 - 29	129 241	66 562	62 679	164.6
30 - 34	96 002	49 680	46 322	122.9
35 - 39	46 719	23 898	22 821	71.9
40 - 44	11 106	5 690	5 416	18.6
45 - 49	471	246	225	0.8
50 +	38	24	14	..
Unknown - Inconnu	6	5	1	..
Kuwait - Koweït				
2017 (C)				
Total	59 172	30 333	28 839	61.0
15 - 19	592	308	284	6.4
20 - 24	7 854	4 004	3 850	91.6
25 - 29	16 974	8 684	8 290	157.1
30 - 34	16 229	8 255	7 974	98.1
35 - 39	9 291	4 823	4 468	58.8
40 - 44	2 553	1 321	1 232	16.3
45 +	236	133	103	2.1
Unknown - Inconnu	5 443	2 805	2 638	..
Kyrgyzstan - Kirghizstan				
2017 (C)				
Total	153 620	78 967	74 653	96.7
10 - 14	2	-	2	..
15 - 19	8 261	4 196	4 065	33.9
20 - 24	51 059	26 260	24 799	187.5
25 - 29	47 515	24 406	23 109	165.0
30 - 34	29 613	15 196	14 417	118.5
35 - 39	13 587	7 044	6 543	69.5
40 - 44	3 270	1 698	1 572	18.9
45 - 49	195	106	89	1.2
50 +	8	4	4	..
Unknown - Inconnu	110	57	53	..
Malaysia - Malaisie				
2017 (C)				
Total	508 685	262 575	246 110	58.5
0 - 14	176	83	93	..
15 - 19	12 572	6 533	6 039	9.1
20 - 24	70 608	36 350	34 258	45.9
25 - 29	163 195	84 183	79 012	108.2
30 - 34	159 064	82 291	76 773	118.0
35 - 39	81 728	42 145	39 583	73.8
40 - 44	19 506	10 021	9 485	20.9
45 - 49	1 283	679	604	1.5
50 +	53	23	30	..
Unknown - Inconnu	500	267	233	..

10. Live births by age of mother and sex of child, general and age-specific fertility rates: latest available year, 2009 - 2018
Naissances vivantes selon l'âge de la mère et le sexe de l'enfant, taux de fécondité et taux de fécondité par âge : dernière année disponible, 2009 - 2018 (continued - suite)

Continent, country or area, year, code[a] and age of mother (in years) / Continent, pays ou zone, année, code[a] et âge de la mère (en années)	Total	Male Masculin	Female Féminin	Rate Taux
ASIA - ASIE				
Maldives[30]				
2017 (C)				
Total	6 723	3 403	3 320	67.4
10 - 14	1	1	-	..
15 - 19	119	65	54	9.1
20 - 24	1 382	712	670	85.2
25 - 29	2 321	1 163	1 158	124.0
30 - 34	1 823	882	941	100.2
35 - 39	829	455	374	61.0
40 - 44	230	116	114	22.0
45 - 49	13	8	5	♦1.4
50 +	2	1	1	..
Unknown - Inconnu	3	-	3	..
Mongolia - Mongolie				
2018 (+C)				
Total	78 444	40 260	38 184	90.5
10 - 14	57	30	27	..
15 - 19	3 484	1 814	1 670	30.7
20 - 24	18 147	9 342	8 805	149.8
25 - 29	24 451	12 568	11 883	162.1
30 - 34	19 076	9 762	9 314	131.3
35 - 39	10 473	5 377	5 096	85.1
40 - 44	2 636	1 308	1 328	23.3
45 - 49	119	58	61	1.2
50 +	1	1	-	..
Myanmar[31]				
2016 (+U)				
Total	765 844	396 053	369 791	...
10 - 14	87	46	41	..
15 - 19	43 206	23 281	19 925	...
20 - 24	186 098	95 726	90 372	...
25 - 29	214 606	110 567	104 039	...
30 - 34	170 095	87 838	82 257	...
35 - 39	98 410	50 926	47 484	...
40 - 44	27 825	14 460	13 365	...
45 - 49	3 050	1 582	1 468	...
50 +	67	35	32	...
Unknown - Inconnu	22 400	11 592	10 808	...
Oman				
2018 (C)				
Total	89 071	45 125	43 946	96.4
15 - 19	1 369	682	687	11.9
20 - 24	12 803	6 495	6 308	92.3
25 - 29	27 094	13 776	13 318	151.6
30 - 34	25 651	12 947	12 704	141.8
35 - 39	16 249	8 230	8 019	113.8
40 - 44	5 443	2 762	2 681	53.0
45 - 49	417	210	207	6.4
50 +	47	25	22	..
Philippines				
2017 (C)				
Total	1 700 618	887 972	812 646	62.8
10 - 14	2 077	1 128	949	..
15 - 19	194 401	101 698	92 703	39.5
20 - 24	471 356	246 831	224 525	98.5
25 - 29	442 757	230 875	211 882	102.4
30 - 34	321 538	167 759	153 779	84.7
35 - 39	194 338	101 086	93 252	57.1
40 - 44	63 350	32 960	30 390	20.8
45 - 49	6 147	3 204	2 943	2.3
50 +	328	159	169	..
Unknown - Inconnu	4 326	2 272	2 054	..
ASIA - ASIE				
Qatar				
2017 (C)				
Total	27 906	14 289	13 617	64.1
15 - 19	353	188	165	9.8
20 - 24	3 726	1 897	1 829	79.2
25 - 29	8 687	4 526	4 161	93.6
30 - 34	8 993	4 557	4 436	94.1
35 - 39	4 742	2 402	2 340	62.1
40 - 44	1 298	659	639	24.7
45 - 49	93	54	39	2.7
50 +	14	6	8	..
Republic of Korea - République de Corée[32]				
2017 (C)				
Total	357 771	184 308	173 463	28.6
0 - 14	6	3	3	..
15 - 19	1 520	761	759	1.1
20 - 24	15 768	8 202	7 566	9.6
25 - 29	74 026	38 155	35 871	47.0
30 - 34	161 045	83 021	78 024	96.7
35 - 39	92 645	47 692	44 953	47.2
40 - 44	12 202	6 246	5 956	6.1
45 - 49	373	203	170	0.2
50 +	9	5	4	..
Unknown - Inconnu	177	20	157	..
Saudi Arabia - Arabie saoudite[33]				
2017 (I)				
Total	488 130	254 511	233 619	59.3
15 - 19	10 679	5 299	5 380	9.6
20 - 24	80 426	39 573	40 853	68.0
25 - 29	155 776	82 107	73 669	111.6
30 - 34	126 583	61 190	65 393	97.2
35 - 39	84 258	49 267	34 991	64.1
40 - 44	20 430	11 607	8 823	17.9
45 - 49	9 069	5 454	3 615	11.4
50 +	909	14	895	..
Singapore - Singapour				
2017 (C)				
Total	39 615	20 408	19 207	39.2
10 - 14	8	4	4	..
15 - 19	302	163	139	2.7
20 - 24	2 011	1 016	995	15.8
25 - 29	10 216	5 326	4 890	69.1
30 - 34	16 214	8 267	7 947	110.3
35 - 39	9 063	4 715	4 348	57.3
40 - 44	1 707	871	836	10.6
45 - 49	88	44	44	0.6
50 +	6	2	4	..
Unknown - Inconnu	-	-	-	..
Sri Lanka				
2015 (+C)				
Total	336 097	172 049	164 048	60.9
10 - 14	38	24	14	..
15 - 19	13 568	6 998	6 570	16.0
20 - 24	64 173	32 928	31 245	78.8
25 - 29	101 615	52 054	49 561	121.8
30 - 34	98 371	50 326	48 045	113.3
35 - 39	46 912	23 947	22 965	63.0
40 - 44	10 336	5 230	5 106	14.4
45 - 49	1 042	520	522	1.5
50 +	42	22	20	..

10. Live births by age of mother and sex of child, general and age-specific fertility rates: latest available year, 2009 - 2018
Naissances vivantes selon l'âge de la mère et le sexe de l'enfant, taux de fécondité et taux de fécondité par âge : dernière année disponible, 2009 - 2018 (continued - suite)

Continent, country or area, year, code[a] and age of mother (in years) / Continent, pays ou zone, année, code[a] et âge de la mère (en années)	Total	Male Masculin	Female Féminin	Rate Taux
ASIA - ASIE				
Tajikistan - Tadjikistan[34]				
2017 (U)				
Total	224 057	...	...	...
10 - 14	-	...	...	..
15 - 19	12 909	...	...	...
20 - 24	94 079	...	...	...
25 - 29	68 115	...	...	...
30 - 34	34 296	...	...	...
35 - 39	11 864	...	...	...
40 - 44	2 296	...	...	...
45 - 49	126	...	...	...
50 +	1	...	...	...
Unknown - Inconnu	371	...	...	...
Thailand - Thaïlande				
2017 (+U)				
Total	656 570	338 520	318 050	...
10 - 14	2 559	1 339	1 220	..
15 - 19	82 019	42 461	39 558	...
20 - 24	153 712	79 268	74 444	...
25 - 29	167 423	86 142	81 281	...
30 - 34	146 251	75 761	70 490	...
35 - 39	83 345	42 622	40 723	...
40 - 44	19 619	10 099	9 520	...
45 - 49	1 079	555	524	...
50 +	45	30	15	..
Unknown - Inconnu	518	243	275	..
Turkey - Turquie				
2017 (C)				
Total	1 291 055	662 928	628 127	61.1
0 - 14	227	123	104	..
15 - 19	69 003	35 424	33 579	21.9
20 - 24	301 196	154 812	146 384	96.0
25 - 29	401 814	206 372	195 442	132.0
30 - 34	308 176	158 036	150 140	99.9
35 - 39	165 264	84 816	80 448	51.2
40 - 44	33 115	17 045	16 070	11.7
45 - 49	2 342	1 185	1 157	0.9
50 +	377	201	176	..
Unknown - Inconnu	9 541	4 914	4 627	..
United Arab Emirates - Émirats arabes unis				
2017 (C)				
Total	97 738	50 121[19]	47 612[19]	...
10 - 14	-	-[19]	-[19]	..
15 - 19	944	500[19]	444[19]	...
20 - 24	10 788	5 488[19]	5 300[19]	...
25 - 29	26 788	13 647[19]	13 141[19]	...
30 - 34	32 444	16 672[19]	15 772[19]	...
35 - 39	19 959	10 360[19]	9 599[19]	...
40 - 44	5 930	2 998[19]	2 931[19]	...
45 - 49	812	421[19]	388[19]	...
50 +	73	35[19]	37[19]	..
Unknown - Inconnu	5	-[19]	-[19]	..
Uzbekistan - Ouzbékistan				
2017 (+C)				
Total	715 519	372 414	343 105	81.2
10 - 14	-	-	-	..
15 - 19	24 371	12 520	11 851	19.0
20 - 24	280 466	144 516	135 950	182.8
25 - 29	248 400	129 197	119 203	159.2
30 - 34	122 382	64 863	57 519	86.8
35 - 39	34 894	18 659	16 235	30.8
40 - 44	4 729	2 496	2 233	4.7
45 - 49	252	148	104	0.3
50 +	25	15	10	..

Continent, country or area, year, code[a] and age of mother (in years) / Continent, pays ou zone, année, code[a] et âge de la mère (en années)	Total	Male Masculin	Female Féminin	Rate Taux
EUROPE				
Åland Islands - Îles d'Åland				
2017 (C)				
Total	279	142	137	47.5
10 - 14	-	-	-	..
15 - 19	2	1	1	+2.7
20 - 24	29	20	9	+45.0
25 - 29	93	44	49	113.0
30 - 34	88	44	44	102.2
35 - 39	60	31	29	68.9
40 - 44	7	2	5	+7.6
45 - 49	-	-	-	..
50 +	-	-	-	..
Albania - Albanie				
2017 (C)				
Total	30 869	16 208	14 661	44.6
0 - 14	19	9	10	..
15 - 19	1 710	867	843	16.0
20 - 24	8 262	4 291	3 971	67.1
25 - 29	10 981	5 706	5 275	100.0
30 - 34	6 904	3 674	3 230	76.9
35 - 39	2 494	1 392	1 102	30.6
40 - 44	426	230	196	5.0
45 - 49	32	19	13	0.3
50 +	9	4	5	..
Unknown - Inconnu	32	16	16	..
Andorra - Andorre				
2015 (C)				
Total	659	336	323	...
0 - 14	1	1	-	..
15 - 19	5	4	1	...
20 - 24	32	15	17	...
25 - 29	123	58	65	...
30 - 34	253	140	113	...
35 - 39	198	89	109	...
40 - 44	40	26	14	...
45 - 49	5	2	3	...
50 +	1	-	1	...
Unknown - Inconnu	1	1	-	..
2018 (C)				
Total	543	...	...	29.3
15 - 19	5	...	...	+2.5
20 - 24	23	...	...	+13.1
25 - 29	108	...	...	49.4
30 - 34	181	...	...	71.9
35 - 39	160	...	...	50.8
40 - 44	55	...	...	15.7
45 +	11	...	...	+3.2
Austria - Autriche[35]				
2017 (C)				
Total	87 633	45 253	42 380	44.1
0 - 14	10	4	6	..
15 - 19	1 465	753	712	6.8
20 - 24	10 760	5 505	5 255	40.5
25 - 29	26 134	13 560	12 574	89.0
30 - 34	29 782	15 420	14 362	100.9
35 - 39	16 048	8 253	7 795	55.8
40 - 44	3 216	1 657	1 559	11.1
45 - 49	202	94	108	0.6
50 +	16	7	9	..
Belarus - Bélarus				
2017 (C)				
Total	102 556	...	...	45.9
0 - 14	11	...	...	..
15 - 19	2 945	...	...	13.4
20 - 24	20 271	...	...	78.2

10. Live births by age of mother and sex of child, general and age-specific fertility rates: latest available year, 2009 - 2018
Naissances vivantes selon l'âge de la mère et le sexe de l'enfant, taux de fécondité et taux de fécondité par âge : dernière année disponible, 2009 - 2018 (continued - suite)

Continent, country or area, year, code[a] and age of mother (in years) / Continent, pays ou zone, année, code[a] et âge de la mère (en années)	Total	Male Masculin	Female Féminin	Rate Taux
EUROPE				
Belarus - Bélarus				
2017 (C)				
25 - 29	35 630	...	...	100.7
30 - 34	29 191	...	...	76.3
35 - 39	12 141	...	...	34.8
40 - 44	2 266	...	...	6.7
45 - 49	73	...	...	0.2
50 +	4	...	...	..
Unknown - Inconnu	24	...	...	
Belgium - Belgique[36]				
2017 (C)				
Total	119 690	61 179	58 511	47.9
0 - 14	17	9	8	..
15 - 19	1 799	924	875	5.9
20 - 24	12 540	6 514	6 026	38.1
25 - 29	39 519	20 165	19 354	107.9
30 - 34	41 364	21 061	20 303	114.8
35 - 39	18 985	9 680	9 305	51.4
40 - 44	4 076	2 112	1 964	11.3
45 - 49	267	136	131	0.7
50 +	22	12	10	..
Unknown - Inconnu	1 101	566	535	..
Bosnia and Herzegovina - Bosnie-Herzégovine				
2010 (C)				
Total	33 528	17 277	16 251	35.2
12 - 14	8	6	2	..
15 - 19	1 792	950	842	13.5
20 - 24	8 293	4 282	4 011	59.4
25 - 29	11 690	5 949	5 741	86.2
30 - 34	7 985	4 144	3 841	66.8
35 - 39	3 027	1 560	1 467	24.3
40 - 44	557	287	270	3.9
45 - 49	30	14	16	0.2
50 +	1	-	1	..
Unknown - Inconnu	145	85	60	..
Bulgaria - Bulgarie				
2017 (C)				
Total	63 955	32 787	31 168	41.8
0 - 14	269	128	141	..
15 - 19	5 769	3 001	2 768	38.2
20 - 24	11 690	5 971	5 719	71.5
25 - 29	19 565	10 092	9 473	88.6
30 - 34	16 586	8 479	8 107	71.5
35 - 39	7 986	4 060	3 926	32.7
40 - 44	1 874	949	925	7.1
45 - 49	190	95	95	0.8
50 +	25	11	14	..
Unknown - Inconnu	1	1	-	..
Croatia - Croatie				
2017 (C)				
Total	36 556	18 845	17 711	40.9
0 - 14	7	3	4	..
15 - 19	990	524	466	9.3
20 - 24	4 807	2 446	2 361	40.6
25 - 29	10 347	5 328	5 019	85.1
30 - 34	12 482	6 468	6 014	93.0
35 - 39	6 609	3 426	3 183	46.9
40 - 44	1 251	620	631	9.2
45 - 49	61	30	31	0.4
50 +	1	-	1	..
Unknown - Inconnu	1	-	1	..

Continent, country or area, year, code[a] and age of mother (in years) / Continent, pays ou zone, année, code[a] et âge de la mère (en années)	Total	Male Masculin	Female Féminin	Rate Taux
EUROPE				
Czechia - Tchéquie				
2017 (C)				
Total	114 405	58 671	55 734	48.0
0 - 14	9	8	1	..
15 - 19	2 644	1 349	1 295	11.8
20 - 24	13 382	6 859	6 523	50.8
25 - 29	34 530	17 661	16 869	103.7
30 - 34	39 442	20 196	19 246	111.9
35 - 39	20 125	10 386	9 739	49.8
40 - 44	4 086	2 115	1 971	9.1
45 - 49	180	93	87	0.5
50 +	7	4	3	..
Denmark - Danemark[37]				
2017 (C)				
Total	61 397	31 467	29 930	48.6
0 - 14	3	1	2	..
15 - 19	471	251	220	2.8
20 - 24	6 575	3 408	3 167	34.6
25 - 29	20 806	10 640	10 166	111.8
30 - 34	20 881	10 701	10 180	127.8
35 - 39	10 198	5 226	4 972	60.2
40 - 44	2 314	1 169	1 145	12.1
45 - 49	142	69	73	0.7
50 +	7	2	5	..
Estonia - Estonie				
2017 (C)				
Total	13 784	7 191	6 593	48.0
0 - 14	1	1	-	..
15 - 19	293	158	135	10.1
20 - 24	1 604	826	778	48.0
25 - 29	4 438	2 326	2 112	98.0
30 - 34	4 418	2 278	2 140	95.2
35 - 39	2 337	1 227	1 110	53.2
40 - 44	652	356	296	14.7
45 - 49	39	17	22	0.9
50 +	2	2	-	..
Faeroe Islands - Îles Féroé				
2018 (C)				
Total	684	346	338	66.6
10 - 14	-	-	-	..
15 - 19	13	6	7	♦7.6
20 - 24	105	44	61	76.6
25 - 29	218	125	93	162.7
30 - 34	228	113	115	169.5
35 - 39	95	45	50	65.1
40 - 44	22	10	12	♦14.9
45 - 49	2	2	-	♦1.3
50 +	-	-	-	..
Unknown - Inconnu	1	1	-	..
Finland - Finlande				
2017 (C)				
Total	50 321	25 674	24 647	44.3
0 - 14	-	-	-	..
15 - 19	704	378	326	4.9
20 - 24	6 363	3 212	3 151	39.6
25 - 29	14 733	7 496	7 237	86.7
30 - 34	17 120	8 779	8 341	100.3
35 - 39	9 124	4 653	4 471	54.3
40 - 44	2 132	1 083	1 049	13.4
45 - 49	131	66	65	0.8
50 +	14	7	7	..
France				
2014 (C)				
Total	806 101	411 604	394 497	57.1
10 - 14	134	66	68	..

Continent, country or area, year, code[a] and age of mother (in years) / Continent, pays ou zone, année, code[a] et âge de la mère (en années)	Number - Nombre			Rate Taux
	Total	Male Masculin	Female Féminin	

EUROPE

France
2014 (C)

Continent, country or area	Total	Male	Female	Rate
15 - 19	15 977	8 153	7 824	8.6
20 - 24	103 146	52 889	50 257	55.9
25 - 29	255 898	130 683	125 215	131.6
30 - 34	267 500	136 400	131 100	131.1
35 - 39	128 988	65 989	62 999	65.0
40 - 44	32 280	16 303	15 977	14.5
45 - 49	2 059	1 070	989	0.9
50 +	119	51	68	..

2018 (C)

	Total	Male	Female	Rate
Total	719 737	...	...	51.6
0 - 19	8 869	...	...	4.6
20 - 24	71 872	...	...	40.2
25 - 29	200 722	...	...	107.0
30 - 34	254 936	...	...	126.9
35 - 39	143 921	...	...	68.8
40 - 44	36 493	...	...	18.0
45 - 49	2 752	...	...	1.2
50 +	172	...	...	..

Germany - Allemagne
2017 (C)

	Total	Male	Female	Rate
Total	784 901	402 517	382 384	45.6
0 - 14	123	61	62	..
15 - 19	15 807	8 136	7 671	8.0
20 - 24	80 159	40 959	39 200	36.7
25 - 29	219 119	112 414	106 705	85.5
30 - 34	279 884	143 610	136 274	109.4
35 - 39	157 100	80 512	76 588	62.3
40 - 44	30 282	15 580	14 702	12.7
45 - 49	1 694	865	829	0.6
50 +	147	75	72	..
Unknown - Inconnu	586	305	281	..

Gibraltar[38]
2016 (+C)

	Total	Male	Female	Rate
Total	424	201	223	...
0 - 19	6	3	3	...
20 - 24	53	23	30	...
25 - 29	120	57	63	...
30 - 34	128	61	67	...
35 - 39	92	45	47	...
40 +	25	12	13	...

Greece - Grèce
2017 (C)

	Total	Male	Female	Rate
Total	88 553	45 686	42 867	37.1
0 - 14	75	43	32	..
15 - 19	2 279	1 176	1 103	8.7
20 - 24	7 344	3 750	3 594	27.3
25 - 29	19 107	9 813	9 294	65.4
30 - 34	31 236	16 147	15 089	93.6
35 - 39	22 184	11 522	10 662	55.6
40 - 44	5 385	2 758	2 627	13.2
45 - 49	795	406	389	1.9
50 +	148	71	77	..
Unknown - Inconnu	-	-	-	..

2018 (C)

	Total	Male	Female	Rate
Total	86 440	...	...	36.8
0 - 14	105	...	...	..
15 - 19	2 226	...	...	8.5
20 - 24	7 225	...	...	27.2
25 - 29	18 316	...	...	63.4
30 - 34	29 781	...	...	94.2
35 - 39	22 140	...	...	56.3
40 - 44	5 614	...	...	13.9
45 - 49	920	...	...	2.2

EUROPE

Greece - Grèce
2018 (C)

	Total	Male	Female	Rate
50 +	113	...	...	..
Unknown - Inconnu	-	...	...	..

Hungary - Hongrie[39]
2017 (C)

	Total	Male	Female	Rate
Total	94 646	48 591	46 055	42.0
0 - 14	67	36	31	..
15 - 19	5 480	2 853	2 627	23.0
20 - 24	13 406	6 933	6 473	47.0
25 - 29	24 352	12 415	11 937	80.8
30 - 34	28 378	14 564	13 814	95.3
35 - 39	18 176	9 315	8 861	49.9
40 - 44	4 606	2 366	2 240	11.2
45 - 49	173	103	70	0.5
50 +	8	6	2	..
Unknown - Inconnu	-	-	-	..

Iceland - Islande
2017 (C)

	Total	Male	Female	Rate
Total	4 071	2 112	1 959	51.0
0 - 14	-	-	-	..
15 - 19	65	33	32	6.0
20 - 24	601	323	278	48.9
25 - 29	1 363	704	659	107.9
30 - 34	1 221	622	599	107.2
35 - 39	659	341	318	57.5
40 - 44	148	82	66	13.6
45 - 49	12	5	7	♦1.2
50 +	2	2	-	..
Unknown - Inconnu	-	-	-	..

Ireland - Irlande
2017 (+C)

	Total	Male	Female	Rate
Total	61 824	31 779	30 045	52.9
0 - 14	4	3	1	..
15 - 19	1 034	528	506	6.9
20 - 24	5 115	2 686	2 429	37.7
25 - 29	10 781	5 570	5 211	72.2
30 - 34	21 653	11 055	10 598	118.0
35 - 39	18 944	9 766	9 178	94.1
40 - 44	3 971	2 006	1 965	21.8
45 - 49	306	159	147	1.8
50 +	16	6	10	..
Unknown - Inconnu	-	-	-	..

Isle of Man - Île de Man[6]
2016 (I)

	Total	Male	Female	Rate
Total	731	...	...	41.4
10 - 14	1	...	...	..
15 - 19	23	...	...	♦10.1
20 - 24	111	...	...	51.2
25 - 29	178	...	...	81.1
30 - 34	238	...	...	100.9
35 - 39	146	...	...	58.4
40 - 44	33	...	...	11.4
45 - 49	1	...	...	♦0.3
50 +	-	...	...	..

Italy - Italie
2017 (C)

	Total	Male	Female	Rate
Total	458 151	235 733	222 418	35.7
0 - 14	6	4	2	..
15 - 19	6 045	3 098	2 947	4.3
20 - 24	38 179	19 501	18 678	26.5
25 - 29	103 110	53 107	50 003	64.8
30 - 34	153 618	79 464	74 154	90.3
35 - 39	116 945	60 159	56 786	60.5
40 - 44	36 474	18 597	17 877	15.7

Continent, country or area, year, code[a] and age of mother (in years) / Continent, pays ou zone, année, code[a] et âge de la mère (en années)	Total	Male Masculin	Female Féminin	Rate Taux
EUROPE				
Italy - Italie				
2017 (C)				
45 - 49	3 410	1 618	1 792	1.4
50 +	364	185	179	..
Latvia - Lettonie				
2017 (C)				
Total	20 828	10 797	10 031	49.0
0 - 14	7	2	5	..
15 - 19	621	314	307	14.8
20 - 24	2 967	1 469	1 498	59.6
25 - 29	6 699	3 525	3 174	100.4
30 - 34	6 269	3 269	3 000	92.5
35 - 39	3 320	1 734	1 586	53.2
40 - 44	895	459	436	13.4
45 - 49	45	23	22	0.6
50 +	1	1	-	..
Unknown - Inconnu	4	1	3	..
Liechtenstein				
2017 (C)				
Total	338	176	162	39.3
0 - 14	-	-	-	..
15 - 19	1	1	-	♦1.0
20 - 24	30	14	16	♦27.3
25 - 29	85	39	46	76.4
30 - 34	132	70	62	111.5
35 - 39	74	40	34	61.2
40 - 44	14	10	4	♦10.4
45 - 49	2	2	-	♦1.2
50 +	-	-	-	..
Unknown - Inconnu	-	-	-	..
Lithuania - Lituanie				
2017 (C)				
Total	28 696	14 775	13 921	46.3
0 - 14	4	2	2	..
15 - 19	875	436	439	12.2
20 - 24	3 992	2 029	1 963	47.1
25 - 29	10 082	5 222	4 860	109.4
30 - 34	9 136	4 749	4 387	103.2
35 - 39	3 724	1 893	1 831	45.1
40 - 44	841	424	417	9.0
45 - 49	33	15	18	0.3
50 +	-	-	-	..
Unknown - Inconnu	9	5	4	..
Luxembourg				
2017 (C)				
Total	6 174	3 171	3 003	42.5
0 - 14	-	-	-	..
15 - 19	68	41	27	4.2
20 - 24	443	226	217	24.5
25 - 29	1 442	712	730	68.3
30 - 34	2 408	1 248	1 160	106.6
35 - 39	1 436	744	692	62.7
40 - 44	339	179	160	15.6
45 - 49	23	13	10	♦1.0
50 +	1	-	1	..
Unknown - Inconnu	14	8	6	..
Malta - Malte				
2017 (C)				
Total	4 319	2 215	2 104	40.1
0 - 14	1	-	1	..
15 - 19	137	65	72	12.2
20 - 24	470	235	235	32.1
25 - 29	1 260	635	625	68.0
30 - 34	1 558	802	756	88.6
35 - 39	758	408	350	45.0

Continent, country or area, year, code[a] and age of mother (in years) / Continent, pays ou zone, année, code[a] et âge de la mère (en années)	Total	Male Masculin	Female Féminin	Rate Taux
EUROPE				
Malta - Malte				
2017 (C)				
40 - 44	129	69	60	8.3
45 - 49	6	1	5	♦0.4
50 +	-	-	-	..
Unknown - Inconnu	-	-	-	..
Montenegro - Monténégro				
2017 (C)				
Total	7 432	3 873	3 559	51.0
0 - 14	2	-	2	..
15 - 19	195	114	81	10.0
20 - 24	1 207	629	578	62.4
25 - 29	2 260	1 188	1 072	115.7
30 - 34	2 202	1 118	1 084	99.3
35 - 39	1 138	615	523	52.6
40 - 44	244	123	121	11.7
45 - 49	30	13	17	1.5
50 +	1	-	1	..
Unknown - Inconnu	153	73	80	..
2018 (C)				
Total	7 264	...	...	50.0
15 - 19	187	...	...	9.6
20 - 24	1 114	...	...	57.9
25 - 29	2 280	...	...	119.7
30 - 34	2 223	...	...	100.0
35 - 39	1 093	...	...	49.9
40 - 44	234	...	...	11.1
45 - 49	21	...	...	♦1.0
50 +	1	...	...	..
Unknown - Inconnu	111	...	...	..
Netherlands - Pays-Bas[40]				
2017 (C)				
Total	169 836	87 159	82 677	45.1
0 - 14	-	-	-	..
15 - 19	1 410	707	703	2.8
20 - 24	13 809	7 080	6 729	26.4
25 - 29	51 473	26 483	24 990	95.7
30 - 34	66 095	33 969	32 126	129.0
35 - 39	31 183	15 971	15 212	61.2
40 - 44	5 515	2 771	2 744	10.2
45 - 49	317	157	160	0.5
50 +	34	21	13	..
North Macedonia - Macédoine du Nord				
2017 (C)				
Total	21 754	11 160	10 594	42.6
0 - 14	20	11	9	..
15 - 19	945	500	445	15.8
20 - 24	4 218	2 131	2 087	60.4
25 - 29	7 549	3 922	3 627	97.4
30 - 34	6 031	3 027	3 004	75.4
35 - 39	2 520	1 317	1 203	32.6
40 - 44	433	235	198	5.8
45 - 49	23	11	12	♦0.3
50 +	3	1	2	..
Unknown - Inconnu	12	5	7	..
2018 (C)				
Total	21 333	...	...	41.9
10 - 14	19	...	...	..
15 - 19	909	...	...	15.4
20 - 24	3 991	...	...	58.2
25 - 29	7 281	...	...	94.4
30 - 34	6 055	...	...	75.7
35 - 39	2 603	...	...	33.4
40 - 44	447	...	...	6.0

10. Live births by age of mother and sex of child, general and age-specific fertility rates: latest available year, 2009 - 2018
Naissances vivantes selon l'âge de la mère et le sexe de l'enfant, taux de fécondité et taux de fécondité par âge : dernière année disponible, 2009 - 2018 (continued - suite)

Continent, country or area, year, code[a] and age of mother (in years) — Continent, pays ou zone, année, code[a] et âge de la mère (en années)	Total	Male Masculin	Female Féminin	Rate Taux
EUROPE				
North Macedonia - Macédoine du Nord				
2018 (C)				
45 - 49	26	...	...	♦0.4
50 +	2	...	...	..
Unknown - Inconnu	-	...	...	..
Norway - Norvège				
2017 (C)				
Total	56 633	29 173	27 460	47.0
0 - 14	-	-	-	..
15 - 19	467	247	220	3.0
20 - 24	5 741	2 967	2 774	34.7
25 - 29	18 682	9 590	9 092	103.0
30 - 34	20 057	10 374	9 683	115.6
35 - 39	9 515	4 891	4 624	56.5
40 - 44	2 025	1 036	989	11.6
45 - 49	133	63	70	0.7
50 +	13	5	8	..
Poland - Pologne				
2017 (C)				
Total	401 982	206 410	195 572	45.1
0 - 14	44	26	18	..
15 - 19	10 032	5 146	4 886	11.0
20 - 24	55 928	28 691	27 237	50.9
25 - 29	132 464	67 893	64 571	100.2
30 - 34	134 904	69 426	65 478	88.8
35 - 39	57 563	29 639	27 924	38.5
40 - 44	10 642	5 391	5 251	7.6
45 - 49	397	195	202	0.3
50 +	8	3	5	..
Unknown - Inconnu	-	-	-	..
Portugal[20]				
2017 (C)				
Total	86 154	44 072	42 082	37.2
0 - 14	42	22	20	..
15 - 19	2 131	1 095	1 036	7.8
20 - 24	8 764	4 422	4 342	33.0
25 - 29	18 914	9 627	9 287	68.8
30 - 34	28 668	14 681	13 987	93.0
35 - 39	21 626	11 197	10 429	57.8
40 - 44	5 712	2 889	2 823	13.5
45 - 49	277	132	145	0.7
50 +	20	7	13	..
Unknown - Inconnu	-	-	-	..
Republic of Moldova - République de Moldova[41]				
2018 (C)				
Total	32 606	16 864	15 742	51.1
10 - 14	6	4	2	..
15 - 19	2 190	1 129	1 061	31.7
20 - 24	8 219	4 231	3 988	99.5
25 - 29	10 316	5 417	4 899	100.3
30 - 34	8 000	4 097	3 903	71.5
35 - 39	3 246	1 667	1 579	33.3
40 - 44	601	306	295	6.8
45 - 49	27	13	14	♦0.3
50 +	1	-	1	..
Unknown - Inconnu	-	-	-	..
Romania - Roumanie				
2017 (C)				
Total	202 151	103 825	98 326	44.7
0 - 14	742	365	377	..
15 - 19	18 938	9 689	9 249	36.6
20 - 24	37 101	19 042	18 059	73.2
25 - 29	62 405	32 005	30 400	104.6

Continent, country or area, year, code[a] and age of mother (in years) — Continent, pays ou zone, année, code[a] et âge de la mère (en années)	Total	Male Masculin	Female Féminin	Rate Taux
EUROPE				
Romania - Roumanie				
2017 (C)				
30 - 34	52 101	26 959	25 142	83.1
35 - 39	25 356	12 918	12 438	35.3
40 - 44	5 198	2 693	2 505	7.0
45 - 49	302	149	153	0.4
50 +	8	5	3	..
Unknown - Inconnu	-	-	-	..
Russian Federation - Fédération de Russie[23]				
2011 (C)				
Total	1 796 629	923 804	872 825	48.3
12 - 14	351	174	177	..
15 - 19	103 533	53 162	50 371	25.2
20 - 24	510 184	262 085	248 099	85.1
25 - 29	603 791	311 250	292 541	101.2
30 - 34	379 884	195 518	184 366	68.6
35 - 39	165 364	84 832	80 532	31.8
40 - 44	30 221	15 168	15 053	6.3
45 - 49	1 481	680	801	0.3
50 +	138	65	73	..
Unknown - Inconnu	1 682	870	812	..
San Marino - Saint-Marin				
2017 (C)				
Total	228	121	107	29.5
0 - 14	-	-	-	..
15 - 19	1	-	1	♦1.2
20 - 24	8	5	3	♦10.9
25 - 29	50	28	22	61.6
30 - 34	76	38	38	79.1
35 - 39	64	33	31	51.6
40 - 44	25	13	12	♦16.1
45 - 49	3	3	-	♦1.9
50 +	1	1	-	..
Unknown - Inconnu	-	-	-	..
Serbia - Serbie[42]				
2017 (+C)				
Total	64 894	33 321	31 573	42.2
0 - 14	44	21	23	..
15 - 19	2 580	1 319	1 261	15.2
20 - 24	11 124	5 675	5 449	57.6
25 - 29	19 605	9 989	9 616	92.0
30 - 34	19 506	10 192	9 314	83.2
35 - 39	9 704	4 937	4 767	40.0
40 - 44	2 048	1 053	995	8.3
45 - 49	151	73	78	0.6
50 +	15	6	9	..
Unknown - Inconnu	117	56	61	..
Slovakia - Slovaquie				
2017 (C)				
Total	57 969	29 773	28 196	44.4
10 - 14	43	21	22	..
15 - 19	3 555	1 832	1 723	26.7
20 - 24	8 860	4 576	4 284	55.8
25 - 29	17 269	8 823	8 446	89.7
30 - 34	18 085	9 229	8 856	86.4
35 - 39	8 535	4 474	4 061	39.0
40 - 44	1 579	793	786	7.4
45 - 49	43	25	18	0.2
50 +	-	-	-	..
Unknown - Inconnu	-	-	-	..
Slovenia - Slovénie				
2017 (C)				
Total	20 241	10 483	9 758	46.4
0 - 14	2	2	-	..

Continent, country or area, year, code[a] and age of mother (in years) / Continent, pays ou zone, année, code[a] et âge de la mère (en années)	Total	Male Masculin	Female Féminin	Rate Taux
EUROPE				
Slovenia - Slovénie				
2017 (C)				
15 - 19	181	87	94	4.0
20 - 24	2 104	1 115	989	42.6
25 - 29	6 471	3 379	3 092	111.5
30 - 34	7 309	3 757	3 552	110.1
35 - 39	3 442	1 786	1 656	46.6
40 - 44	696	341	355	9.5
45 - 49	34	15	19	0.5
50 +	2	1	1	..
Unknown - Inconnu	-	-	-	..
Spain - Espagne				
2017 (C)				
Total	391 265	201 442	189 823	37.2
0 - 14	113	61	52	..
15 - 19	7 644	3 898	3 746	7.0
20 - 24	27 862	14 337	13 525	25.2
25 - 29	68 440	35 244	33 196	54.9
30 - 34	132 442	68 124	64 318	90.9
35 - 39	119 192	61 420	57 772	65.8
40 - 44	32 766	16 895	15 871	16.8
45 - 49	2 645	1 379	1 266	1.4
50 +	161	84	77	..
Unknown - Inconnu	-	-	-	..
Sweden - Suède				
2017 (C)				
Total	115 416	59 256	56 160	53.1
0 - 14	4	3	1	..
15 - 19	1 109	581	528	4.3
20 - 24	12 441	6 436	6 005	41.0
25 - 29	37 178	19 012	18 166	105.8
30 - 34	39 039	20 008	19 031	123.4
35 - 39	20 522	10 624	9 898	67.5
40 - 44	4 772	2 400	2 372	15.1
45 - 49	320	172	148	1.0
50 +	30	19	11	..
Unknown - Inconnu	1	1	-	..
Switzerland - Suisse				
2017 (C)				
Total	87 381	44 873	42 508	45.3
0 - 14	1	1	-	..
15 - 19	503	262	241	2.4
20 - 24	6 179	3 264	2 915	25.8
25 - 29	22 052	11 323	10 729	78.4
30 - 34	33 543	17 236	16 307	113.5
35 - 39	20 446	10 392	10 054	69.4
40 - 44	4 309	2 214	2 095	14.9
45 - 49	323	167	156	1.0
50 +	25	14	11	..
Unknown - Inconnu	-	-	-	..
Ukraine[43]				
2017 (+C)				
Total	363 987	...	...	36.2
0 - 14	157	...	...	..
15 - 19	18 616	...	...	20.6
20 - 24	85 744	...	...	74.2
25 - 29	119 038	...	...	77.8
30 - 34	91 477	...	...	51.2
35 - 39	39 072	...	...	24.3
40 - 44	8 360	...	...	5.3
45 - 49	683	...	...	0.5
50 +	179	...	...	..
Unknown - Inconnu	661	...	...	..
EUROPE				
United Kingdom of Great Britain and Northern Ireland - Royaume-Uni de Grande-Bretagne et d'Irlande du Nord[44]				
2017 (C)				
Total	754 754	387 030	367 724	50.9
0 - 14	84	50	34	..
15 - 19	22 792	11 848	10 944	12.6
20 - 24	108 052	55 778	52 274	52.6
25 - 29	210 730	108 153	102 577	94.0
30 - 34	241 621	123 448	118 173	108.8
35 - 39	139 244	71 279	67 965	64.7
40 - 44	29 667	15 147	14 520	14.5
45 - 49	2 315	1 200	1 115	1.0
50 +	248	126	122	..
Unknown - Inconnu	1	1	-	..
OCEANIA - OCÉANIE				
American Samoa - Samoas américaines				
2017 (C)				
Total	1 001	471	530	...
10 - 14	...	...	...	...
15 - 19	95	...	...	...
20 - 24	292	...	...	...
25 - 29	272	...	...	...
30 - 34	173	...	...	...
35 - 39	121	...	...	...
40 - 44	45	...	...	...
45 - 49	3	...	...	...
50 +	-	...	...	...
Australia - Australie				
2017 (C)				
Total	309 142	159 221	149 921	52.5
10 - 14	66	33	33	..
15 - 19	7 335	3 745	3 590	10.2
20 - 24	36 117	18 587	17 530	42.9
25 - 29	82 656	42 528	40 128	89.5
30 - 34	109 925	56 656	53 269	119.0
35 - 39	59 512	30 702	28 810	71.5
40 - 44	12 414	6 420	5 994	15.4
45 - 49	904	444	460	1.1
50 +	118	54	64	..
Unknown - Inconnu	95	52	43	..
Cook Islands - Îles Cook[45]				
2015* (+C)				
Total	205	...	...	...
0 - 19	24	...	...	...
20 - 24	63	...	...	...
25 - 29	47	...	...	...
30 - 34	38	...	...	...
35 - 39	21	...	...	...
40 - 44	12	...	...	...
45 +	-	...	...	...
French Polynesia - Polynésie française[13]				
2014 (C)				
Total	4 161	...	...	...
15 - 19	454	...	...	...
20 - 24	1 079	...	...	...
25 - 29	1 075	...	...	...
30 - 34	888	...	...	...

10. Live births by age of mother and sex of child, general and age-specific fertility rates: latest available year, 2009 - 2018
Naissances vivantes selon l'âge de la mère et le sexe de l'enfant, taux de fécondité et taux de fécondité par âge : dernière année disponible, 2009 - 2018 (continued - suite)

Continent, country or area, year, code[a] and age of mother (in years) / Continent, pays ou zone, année, code[a] et âge de la mère (en années)	Number - Nombre			Rate Taux
	Total	Male Masculin	Female Féminin	
OCEANIA - OCÉANIE				
French Polynesia - Polynésie française[13]				
2014 (C)				
35 - 39	485	...	...	
40 - 44	166	...	...	
45 +	14	...	...	
Guam[46]				
2018 (C)				
Total	3 175	1 655	1 520	83.3
10 - 14	3	2	1	
15 - 19	234	143	91	35.1
20 - 24	833	441	392	135.7
25 - 29	927	479	448	158.2
30 - 34	692	346	346	137.0
35 - 39	388	200	188	84.1
40 - 44	90	42	48	19.6
45 - 49	7	2	5	◆1.4
50 +	1	-	-	..
Unknown - Inconnu	1	-	1	..
Nauru				
2011 (C)				
Total	370	190	180	...
15 - 19	40	22	18	...
20 - 24	126	69	57	...
25 - 29	111	57	54	...
30 - 34	55	22	33	...
35 - 39	33	17	16	...
40 - 44	5	3	2	...
45 - 49	-	-	-	...
New Caledonia - Nouvelle-Calédonie				
2015 (C)				
Total	4 191	...	...	...
0 - 19	197	...	...	...
20 - 24	888	...	...	...
25 - 29	1 148	...	...	...
30 - 34	1 046	...	...	...
35 - 39	671	...	...	...
40 - 44	233	...	...	...
45 - 49	6	...	...	...
50 +	2	...	...	...
New Zealand - Nouvelle-Zélande[47]				
2017 (+C)				
Total	59 610	30 588	29 022	52.5
10 - 14	18	12	3	..
15 - 19	2 301	1 200	1 098	14.9
20 - 24	9 387	4 818	4 569	55.2
25 - 29	16 734	8 574	8 163	93.7
30 - 34	18 795	9 567	9 225	117.0
35 - 39	9 933	5 154	4 779	66.8
40 - 44	2 292	1 185	1 107	14.9
45 +	150	78	72	0.9
Unknown - Inconnu	45	24	18	..
2018 (+C)				
Total	58 020	...	...	50.3
10 - 14	15	...	...	..
15 - 19	2 061	...	...	13.5
20 - 24	8 688	...	...	50.6
25 - 29	16 227	...	...	87.1
30 - 34	18 708	...	...	110.8

Continent, country or area, year, code[a] and age of mother (in years) / Continent, pays ou zone, année, code[a] et âge de la mère (en années)	Number - Nombre			Rate Taux
	Total	Male Masculin	Female Féminin	
OCEANIA - OCÉANIE				
New Zealand - Nouvelle-Zélande[47]				
2018 (+C)				
35 - 39	10 023	...	...	65.3
40 - 44	2 145	...	...	14.2
45 +	153	...	...	0.9
Niue - Nioué[48]				
2009 (C)				
Total	31	...	...	...
0 - 14	-	...	...	..
15 - 19	1	...	...	...
20 - 24	9	...	...	...
25 - 29	12	...	...	...
30 - 34	6	...	...	...
35 - 39	1	...	...	...
40 - 44	1	...	...	...
45 +	1	...	...	...
Palau - Palaos				
2018 (C)				
Total	256	125	131	...
15 - 19	32	18	14	...
20 - 24	48	23	25	...
25 - 29	74	37	37	...
30 - 34	53	27	26	...
35 - 39	39	14	25	...
40 - 44	9	5	4	...
45 - 49	1	1	-	...
Samoa[49]				
2016 (I)				
Total	4 835	2 556	2 279	110.1
10 - 14	-	-	-	..
15 - 19	282	143	139	31.4
20 - 24	1 290	672	618	166.8
25 - 29	1 321	705	616	199.2
30 - 34	965	501	464	164.5
35 - 39	634	349	285	121.1
40 - 44	277	150	127	56.3
45 - 49	66	36	30	14.6
Tokelau - Tokélaou[50]				
2011 (I)				
Total	16	...	...	...
0 - 14	-	...	...	..
15 - 19	1	...	...	...
20 - 24	6	...	...	...
25 - 29	4	...	...	...
30 - 34	4	...	...	...
35 - 39	1	...	...	...
Tuvalu				
2016 (+U)				
Total	210	...	...	...
10 - 14	-	...	...	..
15 - 19	14	...	...	...
20 - 24	67	...	...	...
25 - 29	55	...	...	...
30 - 34	44	...	...	...
35 - 39	23	...	...	...
40 - 44	7	...	...	...
45 - 49	-	...	...	...

FOOTNOTES - NOTES

♦ Rates based on 30 or fewer births. - Taux basés sur 30 naissances ou moins.

* Provisional. - Données provisoires.

a 'Code' indicates the source of data, as follows:
  C - Civil registration, estimated over 90% complete
  U - Civil registration, estimated less than 90% complete
  | - Other source, estimated reliable
  + - Data tabulated by date of registration rather than occurrence
  ... Information not available

Le 'Code' indique la source des données, comme suit :
  C - Registres de l'état civil considérés complets à 90 p. 100 au moins
  U - Registres de l'état civil qui ne sont pas considérés complets à 90 p. 100 au moins
  | - Autre source, considérée fiable
  + - Données exploitées selon la date de l'enregistrement et non la date de l'événement
  ... Information non disponible

[1] Source: Vital Statistics Report. - Source: Vital Statistics Report.
[2] Data refer to the 12 months preceding the census in May. - Les données se rapportent aux 12 mois précédant le recensement de mai.
[3] Data refer to the 12 months preceding the census in September. - Les données se rapportent aux 12 mois précédant le recensement de septembre.
[4] Unadjusted number of births in households referring to the 12 months preceding the census in March. - Le nombre non ajusté de naissances vivantes des ménages ordinaires se rapportent aux 12 mois précédant le recensement de mars.
[5] Data refer to Libyan nationals only. - Les données se raportent aux nationaux libyens seulement.
[6] Data refer to the 12 months preceding the census in April. - Les données se rapportent aux douze mois précédant le recensement d'avril.
[7] Data refer to the 12 months preceding the census in March. Including nomadic population. - Les données se rapportent aux 12 mois précédant le recensement de mars. Y compris la population nomade.
[8] Excludes the islands of St. Brandon and Agalega. - Non compris les îles St. Brandon et Agalega.
[9] Data refer to the 12 months preceding the census in August. - Les données se rapportent aux 12 mois précédant le recensement d'août.
[10] Excluding live-born infants who died before their birth was registered. - Non compris les enfants nés vivants décédés avant l'enregistrement de leur naissance.
[11] Reason for discrepancy between these figures and corresponding figures shown elsewhere not ascertained. - On ne sait pas comment s'explique la divergence entre ces chiffres et les chiffres correspondants indiqués ailleurs.
[12] Data refer to the 12 months preceding the census in October. - Les données se rapportent aux 12 mois précédant le recensement de octobre.
[13] Unrevised data. - Les données n'ont pas été révisées.
[14] Excluding non-residents and foreign service personnel and their dependants. - À l'exclusion des non-résidents et du personnel diplomatique et de leurs charges de famille.
[15] Including Canadian residents temporarily in the United States, but excluding United States residents temporarily in Canada. - Y compris les résidents canadiens se trouvant temporairement aux Etats-Unis, mais ne comprenant pas les résidents des Etats-Unis se trouvant temporairement au Canada.
[16] For confidentiality reasons, live births to mothers aged 50 and over and the adopted children with no information on their birth mother are included in 'age of mother Unknown'. - Pour des raisons de confidentialité, on a classé dans la catégorie « âge de la mère Inconnu» les naissances vivantes concernant des femmes âgées de plus de 50 ans et les enfants adoptés nés de mères sur lesquelles on ne dispose pas d'information.
[17] Excluding children born in the country of non-resident mothers. - Exceptés les enfants nés dans le pays des mères non-résidentes.
[18] Data refer to period from 1 January 2010 to 3 April 2011. Data refer to population in private households. - Les données concernent la période du 1 janvier 2010 au 3 avril 2011. Les données portent sur la population des ménages privés.
[19] Figures for male and female may not add up to the total, since they do not include the category "Unknown". - La somme des chiffres indiqués pour les sexes masculin et féminin peut n'être pas égale au total parce qu'elle n'inclut pas la catégorie " inconnue ".
[20] Data refer to births to resident mothers. - Ces données concernent les enfants nés de mères résidentes.

[21] Excludes nomadic Indian tribes. - Non compris les tribus d'Indiens nomades.
[22] Source: Reports of the Ministry of Health. - Source : Rapports du Ministère de la Santé.
[23] Excluding infants born alive of less than 28 weeks' gestation, of less than 1 000 g in weight and 35 cm in length, who die within seven days of birth. - Non compris les enfants nés vivants après moins de 28 semaines de gestations, pesant moins de 1 000 g, mesurant moins de 35 cm et décédés dans les sept jours qui ont suivi leur naissance.
[24] Sources: Births and Deaths National Registration System database, and medical records of government hospitals. - Les sources: Les bases de données des << Births and Deaths National Registration System >> et les dossiers médicaux des hôpitaux du gouvernement.
[25] Data refer to government controlled areas. - Les données se rapportent aux zones contrôlées par le Gouvernement.
[26] Data are from 1 January 2009 to 1 May 2010. - Les données vont du 1er janvier 2009 au 1er mai 2010.
[27] Data refer to current birth data; excluding delayed birth registrations. Data refer to the Iranian Year which begins on 21 March and ends on 20 March of the following year. - Les données se rapportent aux naissances actuelles; les déclarations tardives des naissances ne sont pas compris. Les données concernent l'année iranienne, qui commence le 21 mars et se termine le 20 mars de l'année suivante.
[28] Includes data for East Jerusalem and Israeli residents in certain other territories under occupation by Israeli military forces since June 1967. - Y compris les données pour Jérusalem-Est et les résidents israéliens dans certains autres territoires occupés depuis 1967 par les forces armées israéliennes.
[29] Data refer to Japanese nationals in Japan only. - Les données se raportent aux nationaux japonais au Japon seulement.
[30] Data do not include foreigners. - Les données sur les etrangers ne sont pas inclus.
[31] Data are from Vital Registration System (VRS). - Les données proviennent du système d'enregistrement des faits d'état civil.
[32] Excluding alien armed forces, civilian aliens employed by armed forces, and foreign diplomatic personnel and their dependants. - Non compris les militaires étrangers, les civils étrangers employés par les forces armées ni le personnel diplomatique étranger et les membres de leur famille les accompagnant.
[33] Survey based estimates. - Estimations basées sur des enquêtes.
[34] Excluding infants born alive of less than 28 weeks' gestation, of less than 1 000 g in weight and 35 cm in length, who die within seven days of birth. Data have been adjusted for under-registration. - Non compris les enfants nés vivants après moins de 28 semaines de gestations, pesant moins de 1 000 g, mesurant moins de 35 cm et décédés dans les sept jours qui ont suivi leur naissance. Y compris un ajustement pour sous-enregistrement.
[35] Including births occurring abroad of mothers with residence in Austria. - Y compris les naissances survenues à l'étranger des mères avec résidence en Autriche.
[36] Including armed forces stationed outside the country, but excluding alien armed forces stationed in the area. - Y compris les militaires nationaux hors du pays, mais non compris les militaires étrangers en garnison sur le territoire.
[37] Excluding Faeroe Islands and Greenland shown separately, if available. - Non compris les Iles Féroé et le Groenland, qui font l'objet de rubriques distinctes, si disponible.
[38] Including live births by military personnel and their dependants. - Y compris les naissances vivantes parmi les membres du personnel militaire et leurs personnes à charge.
[39] Data include the live births of women with Hungarian usual residence regardless of whether the live birth occurred in Hungary or in a foreign country, and do not include the live births of women with foreign country usual residence. - Les données concernent les enfants nés vivants de femmes dont la résidence habituelle est en Hongrie, que la naissance vivante ait eu lieu en Hongrie ou dans un pays étranger, et ne comprennent pas les enfants nés vivants de femmes dont la résidence habituelle est dans un pays étranger.
[40] Including residents outside the country if listed in a Netherlands population register. - Englobe les résidents se trouvant à l'étranger à condition qu'ils soient inscrits sur le registre de population des Pays-Bas.
[41] Excluding Transnistria and the municipality of Bender. - Les données ne tiennent pas compte de l'information sur la Transnistria et la municipalité de Bender.
[42] Excludes data for Kosovo and Metohia. - Sans les données pour le Kosovo et Metohie.
[43] Data refer to births with weight 500g and more (if weight is unknown - with length 25 centimeters and more, or with gestation during 22 weeks or more). The Government of Ukraine has informed the United Nations that it is not in a position to provide statistical data concerning the Autonomous Republic of Crimea and the city of Sevastopol. - Données concernant les nouveau-nés de 500 grammes ou plus (si le poids est inconnu – de 25 centimètres de long ou plus, ou après une grossesse de 22 semaines ou plus). Le gouvernement Ukrainien a informé l'ONU

qu'il n'est pas en mesure de fournir des données statistiques concernant la République autonome de Crimée et la ville de Sébastopol.

[44] Excluding Channel Islands (Guernsey and Jersey) and Isle of Man, shown separately, if available. Data tabulated by date of occurrence for England and Wales, and by date of registration for Northern Ireland and Scotland. - Non compris les îles Anglo-Normandes (Guernesey et Jersey) et l'île de Man, qui font l'objet de rubriques distinctes, si disponible. Données exploitées selon la date de l'événement pour l'Angleterre et le pays de Galles, et selon la date de l'enregistrement pour l'Irlande du Nord et l'Ecosse.

[45] Excluding Niue, shown separately, which is part of Cook Islands, but because of remoteness is administered separately. - Non compris Nioué, qui fait l'objet d'une rubrique distincte et qui fait partie des îles Cook, mais qui, en raison de son éloignement, est administrée séparément.

[46] Including United States military personnel, their dependants and contract employees. - Y compris les militaires des Etats-Unis, les membres de leur famille les accompagnant et les agents contractuels des Etats-Unis.

[47] Random rounding to base 3 is applied in this table as a confidentiality measure. Data refers to births registered in the country to mothers resident in the country. - Les chiffres sont arrondis à la base 3 de manière aléatoire, pour des raisons de confidentialité. Les données se rapportent aux naissances enregistrées dans le pays pour lesquelles la mère réside dans le pays.

[48] Includes children born in New Zealand to women resident in Niue who chose to travel to New Zealand to give birth. - Y compris les enfants nés en Nouvelle-Zélande de femmes résidant à Nioué qui ont choisi de se rendre en Nouvelle-Zélande pour accoucher.

[49] Data refer to the 12 months preceding the census in November. The question on live births was not asked to females fifty years of age or more. - Données se rapportant aux 12 mois précédant le recensement de novembre. La question sur les naissances vivantes n'était pas posée aux femmes âgées cinquante ans ou plus.

[50] Data refer to usually resident population present on census night. Data refer to the 12 months preceding the census in October. - Les données concernent la population habituellement résidente présente la nuit du recensement. Les données se rapportent aux 12 mois précédant le recensement de octobre.

Table 11 - *Demographic Yearbook 2018*

Table 11 presents live births by age of father and live birth rates by age of father for the latest available year between 2009 and 2018.

Description of variables: Age is defined as age at last birthday, that is, the difference between the date of birth and the date of the occurrence of the event, expressed in completed solar years. The age classification used in this table is the following: under 20 years, 5-year age groups through 60-64 years, 65 years and over, and age unknown. A different classification may appear as provided by reporting country or area.

Rate computation: Live-birth rates specific to age of father are the annual number of births to a man in each age group per 1 000 male population in the same age group. These rates are calculated by the Statistics Division of the United Nations.

Since relatively few births occur to men below 15 or above 59 years of age, birth rates for men under 20 years of age and for those 55 years of age or over are computed on the male population aged 15-19 and 55-59, respectively. Similarly, the rate for men of "All ages" is based on all live births irrespective of age of father, and it is computed on the male population aged 15-59 years.

Births to fathers of unknown age are distributed proportionally across the age groups, by the Statistics Division of the United Nations, in accordance with the distribution of births by age of father prior to the calculation of the rates.

The population used in computing the rates is the estimated or enumerated distribution of males by age. First priority is given to the estimated population and second priority to the enumerated population, i.e. to census returns of the year to which the births refer.

Rates presented in this table are limited to those for countries or areas having at least a total of 100 live births in a given year.

Reliability of data: Data from civil registers of live births which are reported as incomplete (less than 90 per cent completeness) or of unknown completeness are considered unreliable and are set in *italics* rather than in roman type. Rates are not computed if the data on live births from civil registers are reported as incomplete (less than 90 per cent completeness) or of unknown completeness. Table 9 and the technical notes for that table provide more detailed information on the completeness of birth registration. For more information about the quality of vital statistics data in general, see section 4.2 of the Technical Notes.

Limitations: Statistics on live births by age of father are subject to the same qualifications as have been set forth for vital statistics in general and birth statistics in particular as discussed in section 4 of the Technical Notes. These include differences in the completeness of registration, the method used to determine age of father and the quality of the reported information relating to age of father.

The reliability of the data described above, is an important factor in considering the limitations. In addition, some live births are tabulated by date of registration and not by date of occurrence; these are indicated in the table by a plus sign "+". Whenever the lag between the date of occurrence and date of registration is prolonged and, therefore, a large proportion of the live-birth registrations are delayed, birth statistics for any given year may be seriously affected. For example, the age of the father will almost always refer to the date of registration rather than to the date of birth of the child. Hence, in those countries or areas where registration of births is delayed, possibly for years, statistics on births by age of father should be used with caution.

Another factor which limits international comparability is the practice of some countries or areas of not including in live birth statistics infants who were born alive but died before the registration of the birth or within the first 24 hours of life, thus underestimating the total number of live births. Statistics of this type are footnoted.

Because these statistics are classified according to age, they are subject to the limitations with respect to accuracy of age reporting similar to those already discussed in connection with section 3.1.3 of the Technical Notes. The factors influencing the accuracy of reporting may be somewhat dissimilar in vital statistics (because of the differences in the method of taking a census and registering a birth) but, in general, the same errors can be observed. The absence of frequencies in the unknown age group does not necessarily indicate completely accurate reporting and tabulation of the age item. It is often an indication that the unknowns have been eliminated by assigning ages to them before tabulation, or by proportionate distribution after tabulation.

On the other hand, large frequencies in the unknown age category may indicate that a large proportion of the births are born outside of wedlock, the records for which tend to be incomplete so far as characteristics of the parents are concerned.

Another limitation of age reporting may result from calculating age of father at birth of child (or at time of registration) from year of birth rather than from day, month and year of birth. Information on this factor is given in footnotes when known.

In few countries, data by age refer to deliveries rather than to live births causing under-enumeration in the event of a multiple birth. This practice leads to lack of strict comparability, both among countries or areas relying on this practice and between data shown in this table and table 9.

Rates shown in this table are subject to the same limitations that affect the corresponding statistics on live births. In cases of rates based on births tabulated by date of registration and not by date of occurrence; the effect of including delayed registration on the distribution of births by age of father may be noted in the age-specific fertility rates for men at older ages. In some cases, high age-specific rates for men aged 55 years and over may reflect age of father at registration of birth and not fertility at these older ages.

Earlier data: Live births and live birth rates by age of father have been shown in previous issues of the *Demographic Yearbook*. Information on the specific years is presented in the Historical Index.

401

Tableau 11 – *Annuaire démographique 2018*

Le tableau 11 présente les données les plus récentes disponibles pour la période 2009 - 2018 sur les naissances vivantes selon l'âge du père et les taux des naissances vivantes selon l'âge du père.

Description des variables : l'âge désigne l'âge au dernier anniversaire, c'est-à-dire la différence entre la date de naissance et la date de l'événement exprimée en années solaires révolues. La classification par âge utilisée dans ce tableau comprend les catégories suivantes : moins de 20 ans, groupes quinquennaux jusqu'à 60-64 ans, 65 ans et plus, et âge inconnu. Des groupes d'âge différents sont parfois utilisés lorsque les pays ou territoires ont fourni les données dans une autre classification.

Les taux de natalité selon l'âge du père représentent le nombre annuel de naissances vivantes intervenues dans un groupe d'âge donné pour 1 000 hommes du groupe d'âge. Ces taux ont été calculés par la Division de statistique de l'ONU.

Étant donné que le nombre de naissances parmi les hommes de moins de 15 ans ou de plus de 59 ans est relativement peu élevé, les taux de natalité parmi les hommes âgées de moins de 20 ans et celles de 55 ans et plus ont été calculés sur la base des populations masculines âgées de 15 à 19 ans et de 55 à 59 ans, respectivement. De même, le taux pour les hommes de « tous âges » est fondé sur la totalité des naissances vivantes, indépendamment de l'âge du père et ce chiffre est rapporté à l'effectif de la population masculine âgée de 15 à 59 ans.

Les naissances pour lesquelles l'âge du père était inconnu ont été réparties par la Division de statistique de l'ONU, avant le calcul des taux, suivant les proportions observées pour celles où l'âge du père était connu.

Les chiffres de population utilisés pour le calcul des taux proviennent de dénombrements ou de répartitions estimatives de la population masculine selon l'âge. On a utilisé de préférence les estimations de la population; à défaut, on s'est contenté des données censitaires se rapportant à l'année des naissances.

Les taux présentés dans ce tableau ne concernent que les pays ou zones où l'on a enregistré un total d'au moins 100 naissances vivantes dans une année donnée.

Fiabilité des données : les données sur les naissances vivantes provenant des registres de l'état civil qui sont déclarées incomplètes (degré de complétude inférieur à 90 p. 100) ou dont le degré de complétude n'est pas connu sont jugées douteuses et apparaissent en italique et non en caractères romains. On a choisi de ne pas faire figurer dans le tableau 11 des taux calculés à partir de données sur les naissances vivantes issues de registres de l'état civil qui sont déclarées incomplètes (degré de complétude inférieur à 90 p. 100) ou dont le degré de complétude n'est pas connu. Le tableau 9 et les notes techniques qui s'y rapportent présentent des renseignements plus détaillés sur le degré de complétude de l'enregistrement des naissances vivantes. Pour plus de précisions sur la qualité des statistiques de l'état civil en général, voir la section 4.2 des Notes techniques.

Insuffisance des données : les statistiques relatives aux naissances vivantes selon l'âge du père appellent toutes les réserves qui ont été formulées à propos des statistiques de l'état civil en général et des statistiques de naissances en particulier (voir la section 4 des Notes techniques). Ceci inclut les différences de complétude d'enregistrement des faits d'état civil, de méthode pour déterminer l'âge du père et de qualité d'information concernant l'âge du père.

La fiabilité des données, au sujet de laquelle des indications ont été données plus haut, est un facteur important. Il faut également tenir compte du fait que, dans certains cas, les données relatives aux naissances vivantes sont exploitées selon la date de l'enregistrement et non la date de l'événement ; ces cas ont été signalés dans le tableau par le signe '+'. Chaque fois que le décalage entre l'événement et son enregistrement est grand et qu'une forte proportion des naissances vivantes fait l'objet d'un enregistrement tardif, les statistiques des naissances vivantes pour une année donnée peuvent être considérablement faussées. Par exemple, l'âge du père représente presque toujours son âge à la date de l'enregistrement et non à la date de la naissance de l'enfant. Ainsi, dans les pays ou zones où l'enregistrement des naissances est tardif, le retard atteignant parfois plusieurs années, il faut utiliser avec prudence les statistiques concernant les naissances selon l'âge du père.

Un autre facteur qui nuit à la comparabilité internationale est la pratique de certains pays ou zones qui consiste à ne pas inclure dans les statistiques des naissances vivantes les enfants nés vivants mais

402

décédés avant l'enregistrement de leur naissance ou dans les 24 heures qui ont suivi la naissance, pratique qui conduit à sous-estimer le nombre total de naissances vivantes. Quand pareil facteur a joué, cela a été signalé en note à la fin du tableau.

Étant donné que les statistiques du tableau 11 sont classées selon l'âge, elles appellent les mêmes réserves concernant l'exactitude des déclarations d'âge que celles formulées à la section 3.1.3 des Notes techniques. Dans le cas des statistiques de l'état civil, les facteurs qui interviennent à cet égard sont parfois différents, étant donné que le recensement de la population et l'enregistrement des naissances se font par des méthodes différentes, mais, d'une manière générale, les erreurs observées seront les mêmes. Si aucun nombre ne figure dans la rangée réservée aux âges inconnus, cela ne signifie pas nécessairement que les déclarations d'âge et l'exploitation des données par âge ont été tout à fait exactes. C'est souvent une indication que l'on a attribué un âge aux personnes d'âge inconnu avant l'exploitation des données ou qu'elles ont été réparties proportionnellement entre les différents groupes après cette opération.

À l'inverse, lorsque le nombre des personnes d'âge inconnu est important, cela peut signifier que la proportion de naissances parmi les parents célibataires est élevée, étant donné qu'en pareil cas l'acte de naissance ne contient pas tous les renseignements concernant les parents.

Les déclarations par âge peuvent comporter des distorsions, du fait que l'âge du père au moment de la naissance d'un enfant (ou de la déclaration de naissance) est donné par année de naissance et non par date exacte (jour, mois et année).

Dans quelques pays, la classification par âges se réfère aux accouchements, et non aux naissances vivantes, ce qui conduit à un sous-dénombrement en cas de naissances gémellaires. Cette pratique nuit à la comparabilité des données, à la fois entre pays ou zones qui recourent à cette méthode et entre les données présentées dans le tableau 11 et celles du tableau 9.

Les taux présentés dans ce tableau, sont sujets aux mêmes limitations qui affectent les statistiques correspondantes de naissances vivantes. Dans le cas des taux basés sur des naissances par date d'enregistrement et non par date d'occurrence, l'effet peut être visible sur les taux de fécondité par âge des hommes aux âges plus élevés. Dans certains cas, les taux de fécondité des hommes de plus de 55 ans peuvent refléter l'âge du père à l'enregistrement plus que la fécondité à ces âges.

Données publiées antérieurement : Les données sur les naissances vivantes selon l'âge du père et les taux des naissances vivantes selon l'âge du père ont été publié antérieurement dans l'*Annuaire démographique*. Pour plus de précisions concernant les années pour lesquels des données ont été publiées, se reporter à l'index historique.

11. Live births and live birth rates by age of father: latest available year, 2009 - 2018
Naissances vivantes et taux de natalité selon l'âge du père : dernière année disponible, 2009 - 2018

Continent, country or area, year, code[a] and age of father (in years) / Continent, pays ou zone, année, code[a] et âge du père (en années)	Number - Nombre, Both sexes Les deux sexes	Rate Taux
AFRICA - AFRIQUE		
Egypt - Égypte		
2012 (+C)		
Total	2 629 769	101.6
0 - 19	4 700	1.2
20 - 24	119 826	28.3
25 - 29	1 489 063	364.7
30 - 34	502 329	150.1
35 - 39	288 404	111.4
40 - 44	134 381	59.4
45 - 49	60 206	29.0
50 - 54	19 391	10.6
55 - 59	6 333	4.2
60 +	5 136	...
Mauritius - Maurice[1]		
2018 (+C)		
Total	12 980	31.2
0 - 19	1 146	23.3
20 - 24	2 627	54.0
25 - 29	3 991	82.1
30 - 34	3 138	74.5
35 - 39	1 629	32.8
40 - 44	361	7.9
45 - 49	14	♦0.3
50 - 54	2	...
55 - 59	-	
60 - 64	-	
65 +	-	
Unknown - Inconnu	72	
Saint Helena ex. dep. - Sainte-Hélène sans dép.		
2018 (C)		
Total	26	...
0 - 19	-	
20 - 24	3	...
25 - 29	8	...
30 - 34	3	...
35 - 39	6	...
40 - 44	2	...
45 - 49	1	...
50 - 54	-	
55 - 59	-	
60 - 64	-	..
65 +	-	..
Unknown - Inconnu	3	..
South Africa - Afrique du Sud[2]		
2016 (U)		
Total	876 435	...
0 - 19	4 502	...
20 - 24	35 319	...
25 - 29	72 871	...
30 - 34	93 538	...
35 - 39	69 193	...
40 - 44	41 377	...
45 - 49	17 105	...
50 - 54	6 369	...
55 - 59	2 340	...
60 - 64	844	..
Unknown - Inconnu	532 977	..
AMERICA, NORTH - AMÉRIQUE DU NORD		
Bahamas[3]		
2014* (+U)		
Total	4 196	...
0 - 19	63	...
20 - 24	576	...
25 - 29	742	...

Continent, country or area, year, code[a] and age of father (in years) / Continent, pays ou zone, année, code[a] et âge du père (en années)	Number - Nombre, Both sexes Les deux sexes	Rate Taux
AMERICA, NORTH - AMÉRIQUE DU NORD		
Bahamas[3]		
2014* (+U)		
30 - 34	815	...
35 - 39	659	...
40 - 44	388	...
45 - 49	167	...
50 - 54	60	...
55 - 59	23	...
60 - 64	5	..
65 +	6	..
Unknown - Inconnu	692	..
Canada[4]		
2017 (C)		
Total	376 291	33.8
0 - 19	2 764	2.7
20 - 24	21 834	18.3
25 - 29	72 476	58.8
30 - 34	122 875	101.5
35 - 39	87 938	75.5
40 - 44	35 348	31.8
45 - 49	11 745	10.2
50 - 54	3 456	2.7
55 - 59	1 003	0.8
60 - 64	266	..
65 +	114	..
Unknown - Inconnu	16 472	..
Costa Rica		
2018* (C)		
Total	68 479	44.7
0 - 19	965	7.1
20 - 24	5 520	41.0
25 - 29	9 186	76.4
30 - 34	9 630	85.2
35 - 39	6 547	63.2
40 - 44	3 039	32.3
45 - 49	1 214	14.4
50 - 54	514	5.4
55 - 59	217	2.5
60 - 64	84	..
65 +	6 236	..
Unknown - Inconnu	25 327	..
Cuba		
2017 (C)		
Total	114 971	31.9
0 - 19	2 825	8.9
20 - 24	17 269	54.0
25 - 29	29 287	79.1
30 - 34	22 805	68.9
35 - 39	12 279	44.2
40 - 44	9 026	23.7
45 - 49	4 949	11.4
50 - 54	2 037	4.7
55 - 59	549	1.8
60 - 64	154	..
65 +	93	..
Unknown - Inconnu	13 698	..
Dominican Republic - République dominicaine		
2017 (U)		
Total	148 061	...
0 - 19	3 112	...
20 - 24	24 672	...
25 - 29	34 653	...
30 - 34	28 952	...
35 - 39	19 392	...
40 - 44	9 842	...
45 - 49	4 860	...
50 - 54	2 343	...

Continent, country or area, year, code[a] and age of father (in years) / Continent, pays ou zone, année, code[a] et âge du père (en années)	Number - Nombre / Both sexes Les deux sexes	Rate Taux
AMERICA, NORTH - AMÉRIQUE DU NORD		
Dominican Republic - République dominicaine		
2017 (U)		
55 - 59	942	...
60 - 64	424	..
65 +	228	..
Unknown - Inconnu	18 641	..
El Salvador[5]		
2014 (C)		
Total	108 903	62.6
0 - 19	6 884	22.6
20 - 24	22 522	84.4
25 - 29	22 722	115.0
30 - 34	18 048	114.4
35 - 39	12 219	84.6
40 - 44	6 345	47.2
45 - 49	2 957	25.3
50 - 54	1 360	13.7
55 - 59	666	7.9
60 - 64	309	..
65 +	199	..
Unknown - Inconnu	14 672	..
Guatemala		
2016 (C)		
Total	390 382	91.0
0 - 19	19 482	24.6
20 - 24	86 609	125.7
25 - 29	86 999	155.4
30 - 34	65 396	140.6
35 - 39	42 972	117.5
40 - 44	21 537	76.4
45 - 49	8 592	38.5
50 +	6 438	19.1
Unknown - Inconnu	52 357	..
Mexico - Mexique[6]		
2016 (C)		
Total	2 028 358	55.1
0 - 19	123 479	24.0
20 - 24	453 316	93.3
25 - 29	482 689	110.6
30 - 34	386 151	97.2
35 - 39	231 847	61.7
40 - 44	108 479	30.8
45 - 49	40 033	12.7
50 - 54	15 321	5.8
55 - 59	6 294	2.9
60 - 64	2 493	..
65 +	1 435	..
Unknown - Inconnu	176 821	..
Panama		
2017* (C)		
Total	76 166	59.8
0 - 19	2 720	21.7
20 - 24	11 024	93.9
25 - 29	12 835	115.8
30 - 34	11 477	107.5
35 - 39	7 677	75.2
40 - 44	4 100	42.3
45 - 49	1 925	21.8
50 - 54	729	9.7
55 - 59	273	4.4
60 - 64	127	..
65 +	72	..
Unknown - Inconnu	23 207	..
Puerto Rico - Porto Rico		
2018 (C)		
Total	21 467	...
0 - 19	765	...

Continent, country or area, year, code[a] and age of father (in years) / Continent, pays ou zone, année, code[a] et âge du père (en années)	Number - Nombre / Both sexes Les deux sexes	Rate Taux
AMERICA, NORTH - AMÉRIQUE DU NORD		
Puerto Rico - Porto Rico		
2018 (C)		
20 - 24	4 439	...
25 - 29	5 690	...
30 - 34	4 357	...
35 - 39	2 906	...
40 - 44	1 357	...
45 - 49	495	...
50 - 54	189	...
55 - 59	68	...
60 - 64	18	..
65 +	6	..
Unknown - Inconnu	1 177	..
Trinidad and Tobago - Trinité-et-Tobago		
2009 (C)		
Total	17 949	...
0 - 19	389	...
20 - 24	3 027	...
25 - 29	4 916	...
30 - 34	4 149	...
35 - 39	2 682	...
40 - 44	1 416	...
45 - 49	730	...
50 - 54	259	...
55 - 59	73	...
60 +	51	..
Unknown - Inconnu	257	..
United States of America - États-Unis d'Amérique		
2015 (C)		
Total	3 978 497	41.1
0 - 19	78 966	8.3
20 - 24	477 664	46.6
25 - 29	866 460	86.4
30 - 34	1 031 310	107.7
35 - 39	648 051	72.5
40 - 44	263 377	29.9
45 - 49	89 921	9.9
50 - 54	29 105	3.0
55 +	12 911	1.4
Unknown - Inconnu	480 732	..
AMERICA, SOUTH - AMÉRIQUE DU SUD		
Chile - Chili		
2016 (C)		
Total	231 749	39.4
0 - 19	8 816	14.5
20 - 24	33 617	50.3
25 - 29	51 003	72.8
30 - 34	52 206	81.2
35 - 39	37 021	64.4
40 - 44	18 804	33.2
45 - 49	6 638	11.7
50 +	3 506	3.4
Unknown - Inconnu	20 138	..
Colombia - Colombie		
2017 (U)		
Total	656 704	...
0 - 19	39 747	...
20 - 24	146 434	...
25 - 29	164 892	...
30 - 34	134 505	...
35 - 39	85 259	...
40 - 44	39 602	...
45 - 49	16 265	...
50 - 54	7 147	...

Continent, country or area, year, code[a] and age of father (in years) / Continent, pays ou zone, année, code[a] et âge du père (en années)	Number - Nombre Both sexes Les deux sexes	Rate Taux
AMERICA, SOUTH - AMÉRIQUE DU SUD		
Colombia - Colombie		
2017 (U)		
55 - 59	2 236	...
60 - 64	867	..
65 +	368	..
Unknown - Inconnu	19 382	..
Ecuador - Équateur		
2011 (+U)		
Total	229 780	...
0 - 19	4 219	...
20 - 24	16 514	...
25 - 29	17 040	...
30 - 34	14 115	...
35 - 39	8 339	...
40 - 44	4 405	...
45 - 49	1 864	...
50 - 54	719	...
55 - 59	274	...
60 - 64	104	...
65 +	94	...
Unknown - Inconnu	162 093	..
Uruguay		
2017 (C)		
Total	43 036	41.1
0 - 19	882	9.8
20 - 24	4 447	48.7
25 - 29	5 985	70.4
30 - 34	7 309	90.9
35 - 39	5 724	72.2
40 - 44	2 802	36.4
45 - 49	987	14.3
50 - 54	344	5.3
55 - 59	156	2.5
60 - 64	46	..
65 +	21	..
Unknown - Inconnu	14 333	..
Venezuela (Bolivarian Republic of) - Venezuela (République bolivarienne du)		
2017 (U)		
Total	579 319	...
0 - 19	26 717	...
20 - 24	99 854	...
25 - 29	114 790	...
30 - 34	96 967	...
35 - 39	63 612	...
40 - 44	33 254	...
45 - 49	16 443	...
50 - 54	7 164	...
55 - 59	2 913	...
60 - 64	1 181	...
65 +	613	...
Unknown - Inconnu	115 811	..
ASIA - ASIE		
Azerbaijan - Azerbaïdjan[7]		
2017 (+C)		
Total	137 716	42.1
0 - 19	243	0.7
20 - 24	16 979	39.9
25 - 29	54 934	116.9
30 - 34	40 262	92.7
35 - 39	16 815	45.2
40 - 44	5 877	19.3
45 - 49	1 896	6.2

Continent, country or area, year, code[a] and age of father (in years) / Continent, pays ou zone, année, code[a] et âge du père (en années)	Number - Nombre Both sexes Les deux sexes	Rate Taux
ASIA - ASIE		
Azerbaijan - Azerbaïdjan[7]		
2017 (+C)		
50 - 54	485	1.6
55 +	225	0.8
Bahrain - Bahreïn[8]		
2017 (C)		
Total	20 581	27.0
15 - 19	27	♦0.7
20 - 24	1 309	20.0
25 - 29	4 807	32.4
30 - 34	5 921	37.9
35 - 39	4 511	38.0
40 - 44	2 476	28.5
45 - 49	989	15.0
50 - 54	343	7.5
55 - 59	116	3.5
60 - 64	56	..
65 +	18	..
Unknown - Inconnu	8	..
Brunei Darussalam - Brunéi Darussalam		
2016 (+C)		
Total	6 437	43.3
0 - 19	22	♦1.2
20 - 24	352	18.3
25 - 29	1 595	79.6
30 - 34	1 940	107.3
35 - 39	1 274	76.4
40 - 44	559	37.9
45 - 49	188	14.7
50 - 54	52	4.8
55 +	42	4.7
Unknown - Inconnu	413	..
China, Hong Kong SAR - Chine, Hong Kong RAS		
2018 (C)		
Total	53 716	25.5
0 - 19	75	0.5
20 - 24	1 472	7.0
25 - 29	7 281	32.1
30 - 34	17 026	76.7
35 - 39	15 923	68.6
40 - 44	7 014	31.1
45 - 49	2 600	11.0
50 - 54	901	3.4
55 - 59	431	1.4
60 - 64	159	..
65 +	51	..
Unknown - Inconnu	783	..
China, Macao SAR - Chine, Macao RAS		
2017 (C)		
Total	6 529	...
0 - 24	213	...
25 - 29	1 724	...
30 - 34	2 338	...
35 - 39	1 229	...
40 - 44	532	...
45 +	427	...
Unknown - Inconnu	66	..
Cyprus - Chypre[9]		
2016 (C)		
Total	9 455	36.5
0 - 19	30	1.2
20 - 24	348	10.8
25 - 29	1 731	49.6
30 - 34	3 400	106.2
35 - 39	2 472	86.6
40 - 44	889	35.4
45 - 49	308	12.2

11. Live births and live birth rates by age of father: latest available year, 2009 - 2018
Naissances vivantes et taux de natalité selon l'âge du père : dernière année disponible, 2009 - 2018 (continued - suite)

Continent, country or area, year, code[a] and age of father (in years) Continent, pays ou zone, année, code[a] et âge du père (en années)	Number - Nombre Both sexes Les deux sexes	Rate Taux	Continent, country or area, year, code[a] and age of father (in years) Continent, pays ou zone, année, code[a] et âge du père (en années)	Number - Nombre Both sexes Les deux sexes	Rate Taux
ASIA - ASIE			**ASIA - ASIE**		
Cyprus - Chypre[9]			Kyrgyzstan - Kirghizstan		
2016 (C)			2016 (C)		
50 +	139	2.7	25 - 29	49 641	189.4
Unknown - Inconnu	138	..	30 - 34	37 790	176.0
Georgia - Géorgie			35 - 39	21 462	125.6
2016 (C)			40 - 44	10 116	68.4
Total	56 569	51.1	45 - 49	3 018	22.0
0 - 19	569	5.1	50 - 54	713	5.7
20 - 24	8 640	72.2	55 - 59	215	2.0
25 - 29	16 650	121.9	60 - 64	47	..
30 - 34	14 105	107.3	65 +	26	..
35 - 39	8 738	72.8	Unknown - Inconnu	15 928	..
40 - 44	4 421	38.0	Malaysia - Malaisie		
45 - 49	1 529	13.7	2017 (C)		
50 - 54	394	3.3	Total	508 685	46.0
55 +	154	1.3	0 - 19	2 072	1.5
Unknown - Inconnu	1 369	..	20 - 24	29 824	18.2
Israel - Israël[10]			25 - 29	123 467	74.3
2017 (C)			30 - 34	159 247	111.1
Total	183 648	75.3	35 - 39	101 979	86.7
0 - 19	403	1.2	40 - 44	45 986	48.0
20 - 24	15 304	49.5	45 - 49	16 613	19.7
25 - 29	40 909	138.5	50 - 54	5 375	6.9
30 - 34	55 474	193.7	55 - 59	1 907	2.8
35 - 39	40 562	149.8	60 - 64	580	..
40 - 44	18 591	70.9	65 +	245	..
45 - 49	4 980	22.0	Unknown - Inconnu	21 390	..
50 - 54	1 271	6.5	Maldives[12]		
55 - 59	412	2.3	2017 (C)		
60 - 64	137	..	Total	6 723	58.2
65 +	79	..	0 - 19	1	♦0.1
Unknown - Inconnu	5 526	..	20 - 24	321	19.3
Japan - Japon[11]			25 - 29	1 851	97.8
2017 (C)			30 - 34	2 023	115.5
Total	924 968	26.8	35 - 39	1 282	97.2
0 - 19	3 579	1.2	40 - 44	697	68.5
20 - 24	50 493	15.8	45 - 49	329	36.1
25 - 29	185 751	57.4	50 - 54	91	11.3
30 - 34	310 646	85.3	55 - 59	30	4.4
35 - 39	231 186	57.5	60 - 64	8	..
40 - 44	105 836	22.0	65 +	4	..
45 - 49	29 266	6.2	Unknown - Inconnu	86	..
50 - 54	6 019	1.5	Mongolia - Mongolie		
55 - 59	1 559	0.4	2018 (+C)		
60 - 64	436	..	Total	78 444	79.4
65 +	194	..	0 - 19	791	7.6
Unknown - Inconnu	3	..	20 - 24	11 280	102.2
Kazakhstan			25 - 29	21 858	161.5
2018 (C)			30 - 34	19 322	150.6
Total	397 799	73.9	35 - 39	10 946	102.6
0 - 19	1 284	2.4	40 - 44	4 441	46.8
20 - 24	41 049	69.3	45 - 49	1 059	13.2
25 - 29	118 035	163.2	50 +	232	1.9
30 - 34	108 253	152.9	Unknown - Inconnu	8 515	..
35 - 39	61 584	105.1	Oman		
40 - 44	28 553	55.0	2017 (C)		
45 - 49	7 947	16.7	Total	90 371	38.1
50 - 54	1 708	3.9	0 - 19	40	0.3
55 - 59	482	1.2	20 - 24	3 737	15.0
60 - 64	131	..	25 - 29	20 505	39.7
65 +	37	..	30 - 34	26 538	54.9
Unknown - Inconnu	28 736	..	35 - 39	19 274	55.6
Kyrgyzstan - Kirghizstan			40 - 44	9 893	43.7
2016 (C)			45 - 49	3 808	23.8
Total	158 160	86.0	50 - 54	1 407	13.8
0 - 19	413	1.8	55 - 59	643	9.2
20 - 24	18 791	72.3	60 - 64	253	..

11. Live births and live birth rates by age of father: latest available year, 2009 - 2018
Naissances vivantes et taux de natalité selon l'âge du père : dernière année disponible, 2009 - 2018 (continued - suite)

Continent, country or area, year, code[a] and age of father (in years) / Continent, pays ou zone, année, code[a] et âge du père (en années)	Number - Nombre Both sexes Les deux sexes	Rate Taux
ASIA - ASIE		
Oman		
2017 (C)		
65 +	274	..
Unknown - Inconnu	3 999	..
Philippines		
2017 (C)		
Total	1 700 618	52.5
0 - 19	52 342	10.9
20 - 24	317 520	69.0
25 - 29	416 168	101.4
30 - 34	346 451	97.1
35 - 39	233 730	72.9
40 - 44	118 109	41.2
45 - 49	49 611	19.4
50 - 54	16 893	7.7
55 - 59	6 152	3.4
60 - 64	2 530	..
65 +	1 493	..
Unknown - Inconnu	139 619	..
Qatar		
2016 (C)		
Total	26 816	15.3
0 - 19	8	♦0.1
20 - 24	845	3.7
25 - 29	4 613	12.3
30 - 34	8 528	24.4
35 - 39	7 038	26.9
40 - 44	3 559	18.0
45 - 49	1 403	10.1
50 +	822	5.8
Republic of Korea - République de Corée[13]		
2017 (C)		
Total	357 771	20.2
0 - 19	316	0.2
20 - 24	5 327	2.9
25 - 29	35 206	19.9
30 - 34	134 872	74.7
35 - 39	129 431	62.6
40 - 44	38 723	18.8
45 - 49	8 394	3.7
50 - 54	1 408	0.7
55 - 59	319	0.2
60 - 64	56	..
65 +	14	..
Unknown - Inconnu	3 705	..
Singapore - Singapour		
2017 (C)		
Total	39 615	31.1
0 - 19	84	0.7
20 - 24	835	6.4
25 - 29	5 989	42.5
30 - 34	13 758	105.1
35 - 39	11 677	82.7
40 - 44	4 732	31.8
45 - 49	1 431	9.8
50 - 54	469	3.0
55 - 59	141	0.9
60 - 64	42	..
65 +	10	..
Unknown - Inconnu	447	..
Tajikistan - Tadjikistan[14]		
2017 (U)		
Total	224 057	...
0 - 19	404	...
20 - 24	37 120	...
25 - 29	87 552	...
30 - 34	54 556	...

Continent, country or area, year, code[a] and age of father (in years) / Continent, pays ou zone, année, code[a] et âge du père (en années)	Number - Nombre Both sexes Les deux sexes	Rate Taux
ASIA - ASIE		
Tajikistan - Tadjikistan[14]		
2017 (U)		
35 - 39	23 226	...
40 - 44	8 326	...
45 - 49	2 581	...
50 - 54	716	...
55 - 59	370	...
60 - 64	187	...
65 +	92	...
Unknown - Inconnu	8 927	..
Turkey - Turquie		
2017 (C)		
Total	1 291 055	49.5
0 - 19	6 424	1.9
20 - 24	107 107	32.9
25 - 29	359 528	114.9
30 - 34	392 527	124.4
35 - 39	269 245	82.3
40 - 44	103 423	36.2
45 - 49	28 383	11.2
50 - 54	7 323	3.2
55 - 59	1 878	1.0
60 - 64	783	..
65 +	437	..
Unknown - Inconnu	13 997	..
Uzbekistan - Ouzbékistan[15]		
2017 (+C)		
Total	654 605	62.9
0 - 19	830	0.6
20 - 24	80 089	50.0
25 - 29	284 186	176.9
30 - 34	194 440	136.7
35 - 39	71 290	62.7
40 - 44	18 041	18.2
45 - 49	3 878	4.5
50 - 54	1 061	1.4
55 - 59	467	0.7
60 - 64	200	..
65 +	123	..
EUROPE		
Åland Islands - Îles d'Åland		
2012 (C)		
Total	292	35.4
0 - 19	-	-
20 - 24	20	♦25.1
25 - 29	57	76.1
30 - 34	83	100.3
35 - 39	77	87.8
40 - 44	25	♦27.3
45 - 49	10	♦10.2
50 - 54	2	♦2.2
55 - 59	1	♦1.1
60 - 64	-	..
65 +	-	..
Unknown - Inconnu	17	..
Albania - Albanie		
2017 (C)		
Total	30 869	33.9
0 - 19	64	0.6
20 - 24	1 379	11.0
25 - 29	7 781	64.8
30 - 34	10 972	109.2
35 - 39	6 489	79.9
40 - 44	2 607	33.0

Continent, country or area, year, code[a] and age of father (in years) / Continent, pays ou zone, année, code[a] et âge du père (en années)	Number - Nombre — Both sexes Les deux sexes	Rate Taux	Continent, country or area, year, code[a] and age of father (in years) / Continent, pays ou zone, année, code[a] et âge du père (en années)	Number - Nombre — Both sexes Les deux sexes	Rate Taux
EUROPE			**EUROPE**		
Albania - Albanie			**Bosnia and Herzegovina - Bosnie-Herzégovine**		
2017 (C)			2010 (C)		
45 - 49	808	9.3	Total	33 528	28.0
50 - 54	182	1.9	0 - 19	99	0.7
55 - 59	33	0.3	20 - 24	3 174	23.3
60 - 64	20	..	25 - 29	9 300	75.0
65 +	9	..	30 - 34	10 238	90.1
Unknown - Inconnu	525	..	35 - 39	5 624	49.2
Andorra - Andorre			40 - 44	2 203	16.5
2015 (C)			45 - 49	672	4.8
Total	659	...	50 - 54	150	1.2
0 - 19	3	...	55 - 59	29	0.3
20 - 24	18	...	60 - 64	9	..
25 - 29	70	...	65 +	4	..
30 - 34	203	...	Unknown - Inconnu	2 026	..
35 - 39	202	...	**Bulgaria - Bulgarie**		
40 - 44	104	...	2017 (C)		
45 - 49	23	...	Total	63 955	30.5
50 - 54	11	...	0 - 19	726	5.2
55 - 59	4	...	20 - 24	4 930	32.4
60 - 64	3	...	25 - 29	13 438	65.7
65 +	-	..	30 - 34	17 594	81.0
Unknown - Inconnu	18	..	35 - 39	11 925	52.1
Austria - Autriche[16]			40 - 44	5 258	21.5
2017 (C)			45 - 49	1 396	6.1
Total	50 868	18.7	50 - 54	405	2.0
0 - 19	32	0.1	55 - 59	118	0.6
20 - 24	1 966	7.0	60 - 64	26	..
25 - 29	9 770	31.8	65 +	14	..
30 - 34	16 979	56.0	Unknown - Inconnu	8 125	..
35 - 39	13 571	46.3	**Croatia - Croatie**		
40 - 44	5 731	20.0	2017 (C)		
45 - 49	1 942	5.8	Total	36 556	30.2
50 - 54	631	1.8	0 - 19	243	2.2
55 - 59	164	0.5	20 - 24	2 109	17.3
60 - 64	52	..	25 - 29	7 266	58.3
65 +	30	..	30 - 34	12 316	90.5
Belarus - Bélarus[15]			35 - 39	9 100	63.7
2017 (C)			40 - 44	3 589	26.3
Total	89 038	30.8	45 - 49	994	7.5
0 - 19	509	2.2	50 - 54	279	2.0
20 - 24	9 440	34.5	55 - 59	73	0.5
25 - 29	28 977	77.9	60 - 64	16	..
30 - 34	28 523	72.2	65 +	7	..
35 - 39	14 559	42.0	Unknown - Inconnu	564	..
40 - 44	5 085	16.0	**Czechia - Tchéquie**		
45 - 49	1 409	4.7	2017 (C)		
50 - 54	381	1.2	Total	114 405	36.0
55 +	155	0.5	0 - 19	402	1.8
Belgium - Belgique			20 - 24	5 852	22.9
2014 (C)			25 - 29	21 252	65.7
Total	125 014	37.3	30 - 34	34 853	100.2
0 - 19	532	1.7	35 - 39	26 873	67.5
20 - 24	6 420	18.9	40 - 44	12 261	27.8
25 - 29	27 224	79.5	45 - 49	3 134	9.1
30 - 34	41 459	116.9	50 - 54	1 020	3.1
35 - 39	25 524	72.7	55 - 59	317	1.1
40 - 44	11 502	30.7	60 - 64	131	..
45 - 49	4 559	11.7	65 +	62	..
50 - 54	1 602	4.1	Unknown - Inconnu	8 248	..
55 - 59	502	1.4	**Denmark - Danemark[17]**		
60 - 64	153	..	2017 (C)		
65 +	64	..	Total	61 397	36.2
Unknown - Inconnu	5 473	..	0 - 19	77	0.5
			20 - 24	2 799	15.2
			25 - 29	14 243	79.4
			30 - 34	19 967	126.5

11. Live births and live birth rates by age of father: latest available year, 2009 - 2018
Naissances vivantes et taux de natalité selon l'âge du père : dernière année disponible, 2009 - 2018 (continued - suite)

Continent, country or area, year, code[a] and age of father (in years) Continent, pays ou zone, année, code[a] et âge du père (en années)	Number - Nombre Both sexes Les deux sexes	Rate Taux
EUROPE		
Denmark - Danemark[17]		
2017 (C)		
35 - 39	12 509	78.8
40 - 44	5 009	28.3
45 - 49	1 516	8.3
50 - 54	475	2.4
55 - 59	126	0.7
60 - 64	42	..
65 +	12	..
Unknown - Inconnu	4 622	..
Estonia - Estonie		
2017 (C)		
Total	13 784	35.8
0 - 19	60	2.1
20 - 24	745	22.4
25 - 29	3 221	68.4
30 - 34	4 178	88.2
35 - 39	2 827	64.1
40 - 44	1 292	29.6
45 - 49	529	12.6
50 - 54	136	3.5
55 - 59	55	1.4
60 - 64	10	..
65 +	6	..
Unknown - Inconnu	725	..
Faeroe Islands - Îles Féroé		
2018 (C)		
Total	684	45.0
0 - 19	4	♦2.3
20 - 24	39	25.2
25 - 29	155	103.0
30 - 34	203	140.4
35 - 39	137	94.7
40 - 44	63	40.0
45 - 49	20	♦12.7
50 - 54	10	♦5.8
55 - 59	1	♦0.7
60 - 64	-	..
65 +	-	..
Unknown - Inconnu	52	..
Finland - Finlande[18]		
2017 (C)		
Total	50 042	32.0
0 - 19	245	1.7
20 - 24	3 410	21.0
25 - 29	10 878	63.1
30 - 34	15 813	90.5
35 - 39	11 063	64.5
40 - 44	4 497	27.9
45 - 49	1 452	9.0
50 - 54	485	2.7
55 - 59	157	0.9
60 - 64	37	..
65 +	13	..
Unknown - Inconnu	1 992	..
France		
2017 (C)		
Total	730 242	40.0
0 - 19	2 343	1.2
20 - 24	34 195	18.7
25 - 29	148 087	78.1
30 - 34	239 631	121.4
35 - 39	177 992	87.3
40 - 44	81 022	39.2
45 - 49	31 338	14.3
50 - 54	10 741	4.9
55 - 59	3 555	1.7

Continent, country or area, year, code[a] and age of father (in years) Continent, pays ou zone, année, code[a] et âge du père (en années)	Number - Nombre Both sexes Les deux sexes	Rate Taux
EUROPE		
France		
2017 (C)		
60 - 64	1 201	..
65 +	137	..
Germany - Allemagne		
2015 (C)		
Total	737 575	29.9
0 - 19	2 243	1.1
20 - 24	32 100	14.4
25 - 29	131 482	51.6
30 - 34	225 083	92.2
35 - 39	175 580	76.6
40 - 44	80 879	33.7
45 - 49	30 309	9.7
50 - 54	8 600	2.6
55 - 59	2 256	0.8
60 - 64	625	..
65 +	303	..
Unknown - Inconnu	48 115	..
Greece - Grèce		
2016 (C)		
Total	92 898	30.0
0 - 19	188	0.7
20 - 24	1 747	6.6
25 - 29	9 517	34.5
30 - 34	27 011	83.0
35 - 39	28 680	76.3
40 - 44	13 689	36.6
45 - 49	4 651	12.4
50 - 54	1 123	3.4
55 - 59	322	1.0
60 - 64	94	..
65 +	16	..
Unknown - Inconnu	5 860	..
Hungary - Hongrie[19]		
2017 (C)		
Total	94 646	32.4
0 - 19	1 033	4.7
20 - 24	5 888	22.6
25 - 29	14 300	51.5
30 - 34	23 169	86.3
35 - 39	21 696	67.5
40 - 44	11 423	31.5
45 - 49	3 080	10.0
50 - 54	751	2.9
55 - 59	253	1.0
60 - 64	108	..
65 +	43	..
Unknown - Inconnu	12 902	..
Iceland - Islande		
2017 (C)		
Total	4 071	37.9
0 - 19	29	♦2.7
20 - 24	338	26.3
25 - 29	1 071	77.2
30 - 34	1 193	97.2
35 - 39	836	68.9
40 - 44	351	31.0
45 - 49	110	10.5
50 - 54	34	3.2
55 - 59	10	♦1.0
60 - 64	3	..
65 +	4	..
Unknown - Inconnu	92	..

11. Live births and live birth rates by age of father: latest available year, 2009 - 2018
Naissances vivantes et taux de natalité selon l'âge du père : dernière année disponible, 2009 - 2018 (continued - suite)

Continent, country or area, year, code[a] and age of father (in years) / Continent, pays ou zone, année, code[a] et âge du père (en années)	Number - Nombre / Both sexes Les deux sexes	Rate Taux	Continent, country or area, year, code[a] and age of father (in years) / Continent, pays ou zone, année, code[a] et âge du père (en années)	Number - Nombre / Both sexes Les deux sexes	Rate Taux
EUROPE			**EUROPE**		
Italy - Italie			Malta - Malte		
2017 (C)			2017 (C)		
Total	458 151	26.1	35 - 39	1 073	59.8
0 - 19	1 168	0.8	40 - 44	391	24.1
20 - 24	12 614	8.8	45 - 49	116	8.3
25 - 29	54 021	35.2	50 - 54	34	2.5
30 - 34	118 352	74.1	55 - 59	12	♦0.8
35 - 39	127 129	70.8	60 - 64	2	..
40 - 44	75 344	35.4	65 +	2	..
45 - 49	25 445	11.4	Unknown - Inconnu	144	..
50 - 54	7 139	3.2	Montenegro - Monténégro		
55 - 59	1 872	1.0	2009 (C)		
60 - 64	547	..	Total	8 642	43.2
65 +	235	..	0 - 19	32	1.5
Unknown - Inconnu	34 285	..	20 - 24	616	27.3
Latvia - Lettonie			25 - 29	2 011	90.0
2017 (C)			30 - 34	2 268	113.7
Total	20 828	37.2	35 - 39	1 574	85.9
0 - 19	125	2.9	40 - 44	800	43.7
20 - 24	1 498	29.2	45 - 49	287	14.9
25 - 29	5 340	78.0	50 - 54	89	4.6
30 - 34	6 423	93.2	55 - 59	23	♦1.3
35 - 39	3 971	65.3	60 - 64	1	..
40 - 44	1 847	29.2	65 +	6	..
45 - 49	718	11.5	Unknown - Inconnu	935	..
50 - 54	215	3.5	Netherlands - Pays-Bas[20]		
55 - 59	73	1.1	2014 (C)		
60 - 64	31	..	Total	175 181	34.8
65 +	6	..	0 - 19	333	0.7
Unknown - Inconnu	581	..	20 - 24	6 226	12.1
Lithuania - Lituanie			25 - 29	33 346	66.4
2017 (C)			30 - 34	60 729	125.6
Total	28 696	34.7	35 - 39	41 980	87.5
0 - 19	148	2.0	40 - 44	17 247	30.0
20 - 24	1 859	21.6	45 - 49	5 280	8.5
25 - 29	7 560	79.3	50 - 54	1 495	2.5
30 - 34	10 014	112.2	55 - 59	403	0.7
35 - 39	5 279	65.7	60 - 64	97	..
40 - 44	1 967	22.9	65 +	56	..
45 - 49	599	6.4	Unknown - Inconnu	7 989	..
50 - 54	176	1.8	North Macedonia - Macédoine du Nord		
55 - 59	51	0.5	2018 (C)		
60 - 64	13	..	Total	21 333	31.7
65 +	3	..	0 - 19	127	2.1
Unknown - Inconnu	1 027	..	20 - 29	7 063	48.0
Luxembourg			30 - 39	11 312	71.3
2017 (C)			40 - 49	1 784	12.5
Total	6 174	31.9	50 +	106	0.8
0 - 19	18	♦1.1	Unknown - Inconnu	941	..
20 - 24	236	12.8	Norway - Norvège		
25 - 29	950	44.3	2012 (C)		
30 - 34	1 906	85.8	Total	60 255	38.8
35 - 39	1 748	77.5	0 - 19	271	1.7
40 - 44	756	34.3	20 - 24	3 931	23.9
45 - 49	267	11.5	25 - 29	13 332	83.2
50 - 54	93	4.0	30 - 34	19 068	116.9
55 - 59	31	1.6	35 - 39	13 188	76.5
60 - 64	7	..	40 - 44	5 590	30.1
65 +	2	..	45 - 49	1 822	10.3
Unknown - Inconnu	160	..	50 - 54	524	3.3
Malta - Malte			55 - 59	176	1.2
2017 (C)			60 - 64	47	..
Total	4 319	29.3	65 +	9	..
0 - 19	34	3.0	Unknown - Inconnu	2 297	..
20 - 24	213	13.6			
25 - 29	814	42.1			
30 - 34	1 484	77.8			

Continent, country or area, year, code[a] and age of father (in years) / Continent, pays ou zone, année, code[a] et âge du père (en années)	Number - Nombre — Both sexes Les deux sexes	Rate Taux
EUROPE		
Poland - Pologne		
2017 (C)		
Total	401 982	34.6
0 - 19	1 493	1.6
20 - 24	26 406	23.8
25 - 29	99 545	74.4
30 - 34	142 884	93.2
35 - 39	82 676	55.2
40 - 44	28 505	20.6
45 - 49	6 731	5.8
50 - 54	1 845	1.7
55 - 59	590	0.5
60 - 64	204	..
65 +	64	..
Unknown - Inconnu	11 039	..
Portugal[6]		
2017 (C)		
Total	86 154	29.5
0 - 19	794	2.8
20 - 24	5 120	19.1
25 - 29	14 172	52.3
30 - 34	25 388	87.6
35 - 39	23 630	69.9
40 - 44	11 164	29.3
45 - 49	3 104	8.7
50 - 54	882	2.5
55 - 59	313	0.9
60 - 64	88	..
65 +	34	..
Unknown - Inconnu	1 465	..
Republic of Moldova - République de Moldova[21]		
2018 (C)		
Total	32 606	40.3
0 - 19	170	2.5
20 - 24	3 634	47.5
25 - 29	9 526	102.0
30 - 34	9 303	90.3
35 - 39	4 887	55.7
40 - 44	1 853	23.3
45 - 49	527	7.0
50 +	198	1.2
Unknown - Inconnu	2 508	..
Romania - Roumanie		
2017 (C)		
Total	202 151	33.9
0 - 19	3 143	6.1
20 - 24	16 924	34.0
25 - 29	47 953	78.1
30 - 34	60 003	94.4
35 - 39	40 121	56.9
40 - 44	15 965	21.7
45 - 49	4 457	5.6
50 - 54	849	1.6
55 - 59	263	0.5
60 - 64	93	..
65 +	35	..
Unknown - Inconnu	12 345	..
Russian Federation - Fédération de Russie[22]		
2012 (C)		
Total	1 902 084	41.9
0 - 19	12 731	3.9
20 - 24	256 939	51.4
25 - 29	564 777	103.0
30 - 34	431 851	88.4
35 - 39	245 613	55.2
40 - 44	102 880	25.6
45 - 49	33 963	8.4
EUROPE		
Russian Federation - Fédération de Russie[22]		
2012 (C)		
50 - 54	11 671	2.5
55 - 59	3 196	0.8
60 +	1 203	..
Unknown - Inconnu	237 260	..
San Marino - Saint-Marin		
2017 (C)		
Total	228	22.4
0 - 19	-	-
20 - 24	4	♦5.1
25 - 29	17	♦21.8
30 - 34	64	72.2
35 - 39	73	67.7
40 - 44	44	32.2
45 - 49	16	♦10.9
50 - 54	2	♦1.4
55 - 59	1	♦0.8
60 - 64	-	..
65 +	-	..
Unknown - Inconnu	7	..
Serbia - Serbie[23]		
2017 (+C)		
Total	64 894	31.6
0 - 19	386	2.3
20 - 24	4 309	22.1
25 - 29	13 923	65.6
30 - 34	20 592	88.9
35 - 39	14 538	61.1
40 - 44	5 623	23.7
45 - 49	1 619	7.3
50 - 54	409	1.9
55 - 59	128	0.6
60 - 64	40	..
65 +	19	..
Unknown - Inconnu	3 308	..
Slovakia - Slovaquie		
2017 (C)		
Total	57 969	33.6
0 - 19	449	3.7
20 - 24	3 546	24.7
25 - 29	10 561	61.2
30 - 34	17 031	89.8
35 - 39	12 162	60.8
40 - 44	4 735	24.4
45 - 49	1 068	6.8
50 - 54	269	1.7
55 - 59	88	0.6
60 - 64	15	..
65 +	8	..
Unknown - Inconnu	8 037	..
Slovenia - Slovénie		
2017 (C)		
Total	20 241	32.3
0 - 19	59	1.2
20 - 24	876	16.9
25 - 29	4 387	71.1
30 - 34	7 106	99.2
35 - 39	5 027	61.9
40 - 44	1 854	23.5
45 - 49	446	6.0
50 - 54	134	1.7
55 - 59	43	0.6
60 - 64	8	..
65 +	2	..
Unknown - Inconnu	299	..

Continent, country or area, year, code[a] and age of father (in years) / Continent, pays ou zone, année, code[a] et âge du père (en années)	Number - Nombre — Both sexes Les deux sexes	Rate Taux
EUROPE		
Spain - Espagne		
2017 (C)		
Total	391 265	27.8
0 - 19	2 010	1.8
20 - 24	12 376	11.1
25 - 29	41 691	34.1
30 - 34	105 004	75.0
35 - 39	129 475	72.9
40 - 44	64 027	32.8
45 - 49	18 134	9.9
50 - 54	4 545	2.6
55 - 59	1 190	0.8
60 - 64	367	..
65 +	139	..
Unknown - Inconnu	12 307	..
Sweden - Suède		
2012 (C)		
Total	113 177	40.2
0 - 19	443	1.5
20 - 24	7 043	21.2
25 - 29	23 661	77.8
30 - 34	36 139	122.1
35 - 39	26 932	86.6
40 - 44	11 433	35.6
45 - 49	4 023	12.0
50 - 54	1 169	4.0
55 - 59	404	1.4
60 - 64	116	..
65 +	52	..
Unknown - Inconnu	1 762	..
Switzerland - Suisse[15]		
2017 (C)		
Total	65 357	25.0
0 - 19	3	-
20 - 24	970	3.8
25 - 29	8 931	30.9
30 - 34	22 018	72.9
35 - 39	20 125	66.9
40 - 44	8 849	30.1
45 - 49	3 046	9.5
50 - 54	987	2.9
55 - 59	285	1.0
60 - 64	98	..
65 +	45	..
Unknown - Inconnu	-	..
Ukraine[24]		
2017 (+C)		
Total	363 987	28.4
0 - 19	2 271	2.7
20 - 24	39 307	36.4
25 - 29	100 369	71.0
30 - 34	96 216	59.3
35 - 39	51 522	36.4
40 - 44	21 653	16.5
45 - 49	6 819	5.6
50 - 54	1 977	1.7
55 - 59	950	0.8
Unknown - Inconnu	42 903	..
United Kingdom of Great Britain and Northern Ireland - Royaume-Uni de Grande-Bretagne et d'Irlande du Nord[25]		
2017 (C)		
Total	754 754	39.1
0 - 19	8 106	4.5

Continent, country or area, year, code[a] and age of father (in years) / Continent, pays ou zone, année, code[a] et âge du père (en années)	Number - Nombre — Both sexes Les deux sexes	Rate Taux
EUROPE		
United Kingdom of Great Britain and Northern Ireland - Royaume-Uni de Grande-Bretagne et d'Irlande du Nord[25]		
2017 (C)		
20 - 24	59 908	29.2
25 - 29	155 358	71.4
30 - 34	220 563	105.1
35 - 39	165 366	82.0
40 - 44	70 283	36.7
45 - 49	25 346	11.9
50 - 54	7 808	3.6
55 - 59	2 390	1.2
60 - 64	673	..
65 +	316	..
Unknown - Inconnu	38 637	..
OCEANIA - OCÉANIE		
Australia - Australie		
2017 (C)		
Total	309 142	41.8
0 - 19	2 927	4.0
20 - 24	20 819	24.6
25 - 29	58 262	65.3
30 - 34	101 069	115.4
35 - 39	72 732	91.1
40 - 44	28 607	37.2
45 - 49	9 446	12.1
50 - 54	2 800	3.9
55 - 59	937	1.3
60 - 64	315	..
65 +	148	..
Unknown - Inconnu[26]	11 080	..
New Caledonia - Nouvelle-Calédonie		
2015 (C)		
Total	4 191	...
0 - 19	49	...
20 - 24	433	...
25 - 29	798	...
30 - 34	968	...
35 - 39	728	...
40 - 44	436	...
45 - 49	131	...
50 - 54	43	...
55 - 59	13	...
60 +	4	...
Unknown - Inconnu	588	...
New Zealand - Nouvelle-Zélande[27]		
2017 (+C)		
Total	59 610	42.1
0 - 19	1 209	7.8
20 - 24	6 201	35.2
25 - 29	12 741	73.4
30 - 34	17 295	118.9
35 - 39	11 694	89.4
40 - 44	4 944	36.8
45 - 49	1 704	11.6
50 - 54	522	3.6
55 - 59	174	1.2
60 - 64	51	..
65 +	24	..
Unknown - Inconnu	3 057	..

FOOTNOTES - NOTES

♦ Rates based on 30 or fewer births. - Taux basés sur 30 naissances ou moins.

˙ Provisional. - Données provisoires.

ª 'Code' indicates the source of data, as follows:
C - Civil registration, estimated over 90% complete
U - Civil registration, estimated less than 90% complete
| - Other source, estimated reliable
+ - Data tabulated by date of registration rather than occurrence
... Information not available

Le 'Code' indique la source des données, comme suit :
C - Registres de l'état civil considérés complets à 90 p. 100 au moins
U - Registres de l'état civil qui ne sont pas considérés complets à 90 p. 100 au moins
| - Autre source, considérée fiable
+ - Données exploitées selon la date de l'enregistrement et non la date de l'événement
... Information non disponible

[1] Excludes the islands of St. Brandon and Agalega. - Non compris les îles St. Brandon et Agalega.

[2] Reason for discrepancy between these figures and corresponding figures shown elsewhere not ascertained. - On ne sait pas comment s'explique la divergence entre ces chiffres et les chiffres correspondants indiqués ailleurs.

[3] Unrevised data. - Les données n'ont pas été révisées.

[4] Including Canadian residents temporarily in the United States, but excluding United States residents temporarily in Canada. - Y compris les résidents canadiens se trouvant temporairement aux Etats-Unis, mais ne comprenant pas les résidents des Etats-Unis se trouvant temporairement au Canada.

[5] Excluding children born in the country of non-resident mothers. - Exceptés les enfants nés dans le pays de mères non-résidentes.

[6] Data refer to births to resident mothers. - Ces données concernent les enfants nés de mères résidentes.

[7] Excluding newborns registered by application of mothers. Excluding infants born alive of less than 28 weeks' gestation, of less than 1 000 g in weight and 35 cm in length, who die within seven days of birth. - Exception faite des nouveau-nés qui ont été enregistrés à la demande des mères. Non compris les enfants nés vivants après moins de 28 semaines de gestations, pesant moins de 1 000 g, mesurant moins de 35 cm et décédés dans les sept jours qui ont suivi leur naissance.

[8] Sources: Births and Deaths National Registration System database, and medical records of government hospitals. - Les sources: Les bases de données des << Births and Deaths National Registration System >> et les dossiers médicaux des hôpitaux du gouvernement.

[9] Data refer to government controlled areas. - Les données se rapportent aux zones contrôlées par le Gouvernement.

[10] Includes data for East Jerusalem and Israeli residents in certain other territories under occupation by Israeli military forces since June 1967. - Y compris les données pour Jérusalem-Est et les résidents israéliens dans certains autres territoires occupés depuis 1967 par les forces armées israéliennes.

[11] Data refer to Japanese nationals in Japan only. Data refer to live births in wedlock only. - Les données se raportent aux nationaux japonais au Japon seulement. Les données ne concernent que les naissances vivantes de parents mariés.

[12] Data do not include foreigners. - Les données sur les etrangers ne sont pas inclus.

[13] Excluding alien armed forces, civilian aliens employed by armed forces, and foreign diplomatic personnel and their dependants. - Non compris les militaires étrangers, les civils étrangers employés par les forces armées ni le personnel diplomatique étranger et les membres de leur famille les accompagnant.

[14] Data have been adjusted for under-registration. Excluding infants born alive of less than 28 weeks' gestation, of less than 1 000 g in weight and 35 cm in length, who die within seven days of birth. - Y compris un ajustement pour sous-enregistrement. Non compris les enfants nés vivants après moins de 28 semaines de gestations, pesant moins de 1 000 g, mesurant moins de 35 cm et décédés dans les sept jours qui ont suivi leur naissance.

[15] Data refer to live births in wedlock only. - Les données ne concernent que les naissances vivantes de parents mariés.

[16] Data refer to live births in wedlock only. Including births occurring abroad of mothers with residence in Austria. - Les données ne concernent que les naissances vivantes de parents mariés. Y compris les naissances survenues à l'étranger des mères avec résidence en Autriche.

[17] Excluding Faeroe Islands and Greenland shown separately, if available. - Non compris les Iles Féroé et le Groenland, qui font l'objet de rubriques distinctes, si disponible.

[18] Excluding Åland Islands. - Non compris les Îles d'Åland.

[19] Data include the live births of women with Hungarian usual residence regardless of whether the live birth occurred in Hungary or in a foreign country, and do not include the live births of women with foreign country usual residence. Data include the live births of women with unknown residence and homeless. - Les données concernent les enfants nés vivants de femmes dont la résidence habituelle est en Hongrie, que la naissance vivante ait eu lieu en Hongrie ou dans un pays étranger, et ne comprennent pas les enfants nés vivants de femmes dont la résidence habituelle est dans un pays étranger. Les données incluent les enfants nés vivants de femmes dont la résidence n'est pas connue et de femmes sans domicile fixe.

[20] Including residents outside the country if listed in a Netherlands population register. - Englobe les résidents se trouvant à l'étranger à condition qu'ils soient inscrits sur le registre de population des Pays-Bas.

[21] Excluding Transnistria and the municipality of Bender. - Les données ne tiennent pas compte de l'information sur la Transnistria et la municipalité de Bender.

[22] Excluding infants born alive of less than 28 weeks' gestation, of less than 1 000 g in weight and 35 cm in length, who die within seven days of birth. - Non compris les enfants nés vivants après moins de 28 semaines de gestations, pesant moins de 1 000 g, mesurant moins de 35 cm et décédés dans les sept jours qui ont suivi leur naissance.

[23] Excludes data for Kosovo and Metohia. - Sans les données pour le Kosovo et Metohie.

[24] The Government of Ukraine has informed the United Nations that it is not in a position to provide statistical data concerning the Autonomous Republic of Crimea and the city of Sevastopol. Data refer to births with weight 500g and more (if weight is unknown - with length 25 centimeters and more, or with gestation during 22 weeks or more). - Le gouvernement Ukrainien a informé l'ONU qu'il n'est pas en mesure de fournir des données statistiques concernant la République autonome de Crimée et la ville de Sébastopol. Données concernant les nouveau-nés de 500 grammes ou plus (si le poids est inconnu – de 25 centimètres de long ou plus, ou après une grossesse de 22 semaines ou plus).

[25] Excluding Channel Islands (Guernsey and Jersey) and Isle of Man, shown separately, if available. Data tabulated by date of occurrence for England and Wales, and by date of registration for Northern Ireland and Scotland. - Non compris les îles Anglo-Normandes (Guernesey et Jersey) et l'île de Man, qui font l'objet de rubriques distinctes, si disponible. Données exploitées selon la date de l'événement pour l'Angleterre et le pays de Galles, et selon la date de l'enregistrement pour l'Irlande du Nord et l'Ecosse.

[26] Data includes births born in wedlock for which age of father is unknown and births born out of wedlock not acknowledged by the father for which therefore age of father is unknown. - Les données se rapportent aux enfants légitimes pour lesquels l'âge du père n'est pas connu et hors mariage non reconnues par le père et pour lesquelles l'âge du père n'est par conséquent pas connu.

[27] Random rounding to base 3 is applied in this table as a confidentiality measure. Data refers to births registered in the country to mothers resident in the country. - Les chiffres sont arrondis à la base 3 de manière aléatoire, pour des raisons de confidentialité. Les données se rapportent aux naissances enregistrées dans le pays pour lesquelles la mère réside dans le pays.

Table 12 - *Demographic Yearbook 2018*

Table 12 presents late foetal deaths and late foetal-death ratios by urban/rural residence for as many years as possible between 2014 and 2018.

Description of variables: Late foetal deaths are foetal deaths[1] of 28 or more completed weeks of gestation. Foetal deaths of unknown gestational age are included with those 28 or more weeks.

Statistics on the number of late foetal deaths are obtained from civil registers unless otherwise noted.

The urban/rural classification of late foetal deaths is as provided by each country or area; it is presumed to be based on the national census definitions of urban population that have been set forth at the end of the technical notes for table 6.

Ratio computation: Late foetal-death ratios are the annual number of late foetal deaths per 1 000 live births (as shown in table 9) in the same year. The live-birth base was adopted because it is assumed to be more comparable from one country or area to another than the sum of live births and foetal deaths.

Ratios by urban/rural residence are the annual number of late foetal deaths, in the appropriate urban or rural category, per 1 000 corresponding live births (as shown in table 9). These ratios are calculated by the United Nations Statistics Division.

Ratios presented in this table are limited to those for countries or areas and urban/rural areas having at least a total of 30 late foetal deaths in a given year.

Reliability of data: Each country or area is asked to indicate the estimated completeness of the late foetal deaths recorded in its civil register. These national assessments are indicated by the quality codes "C", "U" and "..." that appear in the first column of this table.

"C" indicates that the data are estimated to be virtually complete, that is, representing at least 90 per cent of the late foetal deaths occurring each year, while "U" indicates that data are estimated to be incomplete, that is, representing less than 90 per cent of the late foetal deaths occurring each year. The code "..." indicates that no information was provided regarding completeness.

Data from civil registers which are reported as incomplete or of unknown completeness (coded "U" or "...") are considered unreliable. They appear in italics in this table. Ratios are not computed for data so coded.

For more information about the quality of vital statistics data in general, see section 4.2 of the Technical Notes.

Limitations: Statistics on late foetal deaths are subject to the same qualifications as have been set forth for vital statistics in general and foetal-death statistics in particular as discussed in section 4 of the Technical Notes.

The reliability of the data is a very important factor. Of all vital statistics, the registration of foetal deaths is probably the most incomplete.

Variation in the definition of foetal deaths, and in particular late foetal deaths, also limits international comparability. The criterion of 28 or more completed weeks of gestation to distinguish late foetal deaths is not universally used; some countries or areas use different durations of gestation or other criteria such as size of the foetus. In addition, the difficulty of accurately determining gestational age further reduces comparability. However, to promote comparability, late foetal deaths shown in this table are restricted to those of at least 28 or more completed weeks of gestation. Wherever this is not possible, a footnote is provided.

Late foetal-death ratios are subject to the limitations of the data on live births with which they have been calculated. These have been set forth in the technical notes for table 9.

It must be pointed out that when late foetal deaths and live births are both under registered, the resulting ratios may be of reasonable magnitude. For the countries or areas where live-birth registration is poorest, the late foetal-death ratios may be the largest, effectively masking the completeness of the base data. For this reason, possible variations in birth-registration completeness as well as the reported completeness of late foetal deaths must always be borne in mind in evaluating late foetal-death ratios.

Finally, it may be noted that the counting of live-born infants as late foetal deaths, because they died before the registration of the birth or within the first 24 hours of life, has the effect of inflating the late foetal-death ratios unduly by decreasing the birth denominator and increasing the foetal-death numerator. This factor should not be overlooked in using data from this table.

The comparability of data by urban/rural residence is affected by the national definitions of urban and rural used in tabulating these data. It is assumed, in the absence of specific information to the contrary, that the definitions of urban and rural used in connection with the national population census were also used in the compilation of the vital statistics for each country or area. However, it cannot be excluded that, for a given country or area, different definitions of urban and rural are used for the vital statistics data and the population census data respectively. When known, the definitions of urban used in national population censuses are presented at the end of the technical notes for table 6. As discussed in detail in the technical notes for table 6, these definitions vary considerably from one country or area to another.

Urban/rural differentials in late foetal death ratios may also be affected by whether the late foetal deaths and live births have been tabulated in terms of place of occurrence or place of usual residence. This problem is discussed in more detail in section 4.1.4.1 of the Introduction.

Earlier data: Late foetal deaths and late foetal-death ratios have been shown in each issue of the Demographic Yearbook beginning with the 1951 issue. A special topic CD on natality published in 2001 presents the data for all available years from 1990 to 1998. For more information on specific topics, and years for which data are reported, readers should consult the Historical Index.

NOTES

[1] For definition, see section 4.1.1 of the Introduction.

Tableau 12 – *Annuaire démographique 2018*

Le tableau 12 présente des données sur les morts fœtales tardives et les rapports de mortinatalité selon le lieu de résidence (zone urbaine ou rurale) pour le plus grand nombre d'années possible entre 2014 et 2018.

Description des variables : Par mort fœtale tardive, on entend le décès d'un fœtus[1] survenu après 28 semaines complètes de gestation au moins. Les morts fœtales pour lesquelles la durée de la période de gestation n'est pas connue sont comprises dans cette catégorie.

Sauf indication contraire, les statistiques du nombre de morts fœtales tardives sont établies sur la base des registres de l'état civil.

La classification des morts fœtales tardives selon le lieu de résidence (zone urbaine ou rurale) est celle qui a été communiquée par chaque pays ou zone ; on part du principe qu'elle repose sur les définitions de la population urbaine utilisées pour les recensements nationaux, telles qu'elles sont reproduites à la fin des notes techniques du tableau 6.

Calcul des rapports : les rapports de mortinatalité représentent le nombre annuel de morts fœtales tardives pour 1 000 naissances vivantes (telles qu'elles sont présentées au tableau 9) survenues pendant la même année. On a pris pour base de calcul les naissances vivantes parce que l'on pense qu'elles sont plus facilement comparables d'un pays ou d'une zone à l'autre que la somme des naissances vivantes et des morts fœtales.

Les rapports selon le lieu de résidence (zone urbaine ou rurale) représentent le nombre annuel de morts fœtales tardives, classées selon la catégorie urbaine ou rurale appropriée pour 1 000 naissances vivantes (telles qu'elles sont présentées au tableau 9) survenues parmi la population correspondante. Ces rapports ont été calculés par la Division des statistiques de l'Organisation des Nations Unies.

Les rapports présentés dans le tableau 12 ne concernent que les pays ou zones où l'on a enregistré un total d'au moins 30 morts fœtales tardives pendant une année donnée.

Fiabilité des données : il a été demandé à chaque pays ou zone d'indiquer le degré estimatif de complétude des données sur les morts fœtales tardives figurant dans ses registres d'état civil. Ces évaluations nationales sont signalées par les codes de qualité "C", "U" et "..." qui apparaissent dans la deuxième colonne du tableau.

La lettre "C" indique que les données sont jugées à peu près complètes, c'est-à-dire qu'elles représentent au moins 90 p. 100 des morts fœtales tardives survenues chaque année ; la lettre "U" signifie que les données sont jugées incomplètes, c'est-à-dire qu'elles représentent moins de 90 p.100 des morts fœtales tardives survenues chaque année. Le code "..." indique qu'aucun renseignement n'a été communiqué quant à la complétude des données.

Les données provenant des registres de l'état civil qui sont déclarées incomplètes ou dont le degré de complétude n'est pas connu (code "U" ou "...") sont jugées douteuses. Elles apparaissent en italique dans le tableau ; les rapports, dans ces cas, n'ont pas été calculés.

Pour plus de précisions sur la qualité des données reposant sur les statistiques de l'état civil en général, voir la section 4.2 des Notes techniques.

Insuffisance des données : les statistiques des morts fœtales tardives appellent toutes les réserves qui ont été formulées à propos des statistiques de l'état civil en général et des statistiques concernant les morts fœtales en particulier (voir la section 4 des Notes techniques).

La fiabilité des données est un facteur très important. Les statistiques concernant les morts fœtales sont probablement les moins complètes de toutes les statistiques de l'état civil.

L'hétérogénéité des définitions de la mort fœtale et, en particulier, de la mort fœtale tardive nuit aussi à la comparabilité internationale des données. Le critère des 28 semaines complètes de gestation au moins n'est pas universellement utilisé ; certains pays ou zones retiennent des critères différents pour la durée de la période de gestation ou d'autres critères tels que la taille du fœtus. De surcroît, la comparabilité est rendue malaisée par le fait qu'il est difficile d'établir avec précision l'âge gestationnel. Pour faciliter les comparaisons, les morts fœtales tardives considérées ici sont exclusivement celles qui sont survenues au terme de 28 semaines de gestation au moins. Les exceptions sont signalées en note.

Les rapports de mortinatalité appellent en outre toutes les réserves qui ont été formulées à propos des statistiques des naissances vivantes qui ont servi à leur calcul (voir à ce sujet les notes techniques relatives au tableau 9).

En ce qui concerne le calcul des rapports, il convient de noter que, si l'enregistrement des morts fœtales tardives et celui des naissances vivantes sont loin d'être exhaustifs, les rapports de mortinatalité peuvent être raisonnables. C'est parfois pour les pays ou zones où l'enregistrement des naissances vivantes laisse le plus à désirer que les rapports de mortinatalité sont les plus élevés, ce qui masque le caractère incomplet des données de base. Aussi, pour porter un jugement sur la qualité des rapports de mortinatalité, il ne faut jamais oublier que la complétude de l'enregistrement des naissances comme celle de l'enregistrement des morts fœtales tardives peuvent varier sensiblement.

Enfin, on notera que l'inclusion parmi les morts fœtales tardives des décès d'enfants nés vivants qui sont décédés avant l'enregistrement de leur naissance ou dans les 24 heures qui ont suivi la naissance conduit à des rapports de mortinatalité exagérés parce que le dénominateur (nombre de naissances) se trouve alors diminué et le numérateur (morts fœtales) augmenté. Il importe de ne pas négliger ce facteur lorsque l'on utilise les données du tableau 12.

La comparabilité des données selon le lieu de résidence (zone urbaine ou rurale) peut être limitée par les définitions nationales des termes « urbain » et « rural » utilisées pour la mise en tableaux de ces données. En l'absence d'indications contraires, on a supposé que les mêmes définitions avaient servi pour le recensement national de la population et pour l'établissement des statistiques de l'état civil pour chaque pays ou zone. Toutefois, il n'est pas exclu que, pour une zone ou un pays donné, des définitions différentes aient été retenues. Les définitions du terme « urbain » utilisées pour les recensements nationaux de population ont été présentées à la fin des notes techniques du tableau 6 lorsqu'elles étaient connues. Comme on l'a précisé dans les notes techniques relatives au tableau 6, ces définitions varient considérablement d'un pays ou d'une zone à l'autre.

La différence entre les rapports de mortinatalité pour les zones urbaines et rurales pourra aussi être faussée selon que les morts fœtales tardives et les naissances vivantes auront été classées d'après le lieu de l'événement ou le lieu de résidence habituel. Ce problème est examiné plus en détail à la section 4.1.4.1 des Notes techniques.

Données publiées antérieurement : les éditions de l'*Annuaire démographique* parues à partir de 1951 contiennent des statistiques concernant les morts fœtales tardives et les rapports de mortinatalité. Un CD-ROM sur la natalité paru en 2001 présente les données pour toutes les années disponibles de 1990 à 1998. Pour plus de précisions concernant les années et les sujets pour lesquels des données ont été publiées, se reporter à l'index.

NOTE

[1] Pour la définition, voir la section 4.1.1 de l'Introduction.

Continent, country or area, and urban/rural residence / Continent, pays ou zone et résidence, urbaine/rurale	Code[a]	Number - Nombre					Ratio - Rapport				
		2014	2015	2016	2017	2018	2014	2015	2016	2017	2018
AFRICA - AFRIQUE											
Algeria - Algérie											
Total	+U	15 077	14 620	14 236	...	...	...	...	...	...	...
Botswana[1]											
Total	+U	...	...	496	371	...	...	...	...	...	...
Mauritius - Maurice[2]											
Total	+C	138	125	127	135	130	10.4	9.9	9.8	10.1	10.0
Urban - Urbaine	+C	54	54	52	53	57	10.5	10.5	9.8	10.0	10.6
Rural - Rurale	+C	84	71	75	82	73	10.3	9.5	9.8	10.1	9.6
South Africa - Afrique du Sud											
Total	...	15 157	14 341	11 961	...	...	...	...	...	...	...
Tunisia - Tunisie											
Total	U	2 411	2 268	2 475	2 463	...	...	...	...	...	...
AMERICA, NORTH - AMÉRIQUE DU NORD											
Belize											
Total	U	66	55	54	...	...	...	...	...	...	...
Urban - Urbaine	U	24	24	21	...	...	...	...	...	...	...
Rural - Rurale	U	42	31	33	...	...	...	...	...	...	...
Bermuda - Bermudes[3]											
Total	C	1	2	4[4]	-[4]	4[4]	...	...	...	...	...
British Virgin Islands - Îles Vierges britanniques											
Total	C	3	1	2	2	...	...	...	...	...	...
Canada[5]											
Total	C	1 140	1 078	1 068	1 073	...	3.0	2.8	2.8	2.9	...
Costa Rica											
Total	C	319	326	314	276	*316	4.4	4.5	4.5	4.0	*4.6
Urban - Urbaine	C	176	208	198	164	*202	4.2	4.2	4.1	3.5	*4.3
Rural - Rurale	C	143	118	116	112	*114	4.7	5.3	5.4	5.2	*5.2
Cuba[6]											
Total	C	1 135	1 190	1 251	1 312	...	9.3	9.5	10.7	11.4	...
Dominican Republic - République dominicaine											
Total	U	1 604	2 133	2 062	2 153	2 234	...	...	...	...	...
Guatemala[7]											
Total	C	3 236	3 121	3 161	3 033	...	8.4	8.0	8.1	7.9	...
Mexico - Mexique[8]											
Total	+U	9 755	9 685	9 068	8 968	...	...	...	...	...	...
Urban - Urbaine[9]	+U	7 287	7 005	6 623	6 257	...	...	...	...	...	...
Rural - Rurale[9]	+U	2 325	2 407	2 151	1 947	...	...	...	...	...	...
Montserrat											
Total	C	2	1	-	...	...	...	...	...	...	...
Panama											
Total	U	423	*436	*373	*419	...	...	...	...	...	...
Puerto Rico - Porto Rico[7]											
Total	C	417	358	311	257	241	12.1	11.5	11.0	10.5	11.2
Urban - Urbaine	C	239[9]	205[9]	165	146	140	12.6	10.8	9.1	8.9	10.1
Rural - Rurale	C	151[9]	130[9]	146	111	101	9.8	10.6	14.4	13.8	13.4
United States of America - États-Unis d'Amérique											
Total	C	11 311	11 354	...	...	...	2.8	2.9	...	...	...
AMERICA, SOUTH - AMÉRIQUE DU SUD											
Argentina - Argentine											
Total	C	4 043	3 785	3 782	3 604	...	5.2	4.9	5.2	5.1	...
Brazil - Brésil											
Total	U	14 853	16 851	16 224	16 413	...	...	...	...	...	...
Chile - Chili[10]											
Total	C	1 254	1 185	1 114	...	...	5.0	4.8	4.8	...	...
Urban - Urbaine	C	1 126	1 067	1 011	...	...	4.9	4.8	4.8	...	...
Rural - Rurale	C	128	118	103	...	...	5.7	5.3	5.2	...	...

12. Late foetal deaths and late foetal death ratios, by urban/rural residence: 2014 - 2018
Morts foetales tardives et rapports de mortinatalité, selon la résidence, urbaine/rurale : 2014 - 2018 (continued - suite)

Continent, country or area, and urban/rural residence / Continent, pays ou zone et résidence, urbaine/rurale	Code[a]	Number - Nombre					Ratio - Rapport				
		2014	2015	2016	2017	2018	2014	2015	2016	2017	2018
AMERICA, SOUTH - AMÉRIQUE DU SUD											
Colombia - Colombie											
Total	U	5 591	5 935	5 728	5 939	...	...	...	...	...	...
Urban - Urbaine[9]	U	4 160	4 477	4 327	4 362	...	...	...	...	...	...
Rural - Rurale[9]	U	1 387	1 406	1 354	1 486	...	...	...	...	...	...
Ecuador - Équateur[11]											
Total	...	932	1 028	1 001	1 063	...	...	...	...	...	...
Urban - Urbaine	...	771	849	822	881	...	...	...	...	...	...
Rural - Rurale	...	161	179	179	182	...	...	...	...	...	...
Uruguay											
Total	C	229	199	183	197	...	4.7	4.1	3.9	4.6	...
Venezuela (Bolivarian Republic of) - Venezuela (République bolivarienne du)											
Total	U	2 895	2 483	3 028	2 202	...	...	...	...	...	...
ASIA - ASIE											
Armenia - Arménie											
Total	C	746	796	699	634	...	17.3	19.1	17.2	16.8	...
Urban - Urbaine	C	...	509	431	408	...	...	18.8	16.3	16.6	...
Rural - Rurale	C	...	287	268	226	...	...	19.6	19.0	17.3	...
Azerbaijan - Azerbaïdjan											
Total	+C	764	904	920	1 158	...	4.5	5.4	5.8	8.0	...
Bahrain - Bahreïn[12]											
Total	...	132	...	...	...	...	...	...	...	...	...
China, Hong Kong SAR - Chine, Hong Kong RAS											
Total	...	167	150	180	139	124	...	...	...	...	...
China, Macao SAR - Chine, Macao RAS											
Total	C	12	6	11	12	...	...	...	...	...	...
Georgia - Géorgie											
Total	C	640	589	558	506	...	10.6	9.9	9.9	9.5	...
Urban - Urbaine	C	336	321	310	...	...	...	9.5	9.6	...	...
Rural - Rurale	C	304	268	248	...	...	...	10.6	10.2	...	...
Israel - Israël[13]											
Total	C	601	561	...	...	...	3.4	3.1	...	...	...
Urban - Urbaine[9]	C	537	511	...	...	...	3.4	3.1	...	...	...
Rural - Rurale[9]	C	57	42	...	...	...	3.5	2.5	...	...	...
Japan - Japon[14]											
Total	C	1 790	1 830	1 699	1 616	...	1.8	1.8	1.7	1.7	...
Urban - Urbaine	C	1 657	1 695	1 584	1 499	...	1.8	1.8	1.8	1.7	...
Rural - Rurale	C	131	134	114	117	...	1.7	1.7	1.5	1.7	...
Kazakhstan											
Total	C	2 507	2 344	2 382	2 321	2 257	6.3	5.9	5.9	5.9	5.7
Urban - Urbaine	C	1 325	1 268	1 251	1 247	1 236	5.9	5.6	5.4	5.5	5.3
Rural - Rurale	C	1 182	1 076	1 131	1 074	1 021	6.7	6.2	6.6	6.6	6.3
Kuwait - Koweït											
Total	C	433	405	220	234	...	7.1	6.8	3.7	4.0	...
Kyrgyzstan - Kirghizstan											
Total	C	1 555	1 484	*1 423	1 387	...	9.6	9.1	*9.0	9.0	...
Urban - Urbaine[15]	C	1 147	1 080	*1 006	1 039	...	20.7	20.6	*19.5	19.7	...
Rural - Rurale[15]	C	408	404	*417	348	...	3.8	3.6	*3.9	3.5	...
Malaysia - Malaisie											
Total	C	2 277	2 325	...	...	...	4.3	4.5	...	...	...
Urban - Urbaine	C	1 484	1 507	...	...	...	4.1	4.3	...	...	...
Rural - Rurale	C	793	818	...	...	...	4.6	4.8	...	...	...
Maldives[7]											
Total	...	37	47	41	34	...	...	...	...	...	...
Urban - Urbaine	...	27	12	16	2[9]	...	...	...	...	...	...
Rural - Rurale	...	10	35	25	31[9]	...	...	...	...	...	...
Mongolia - Mongolie											
Total	+C	...	557	484	451	...	...	6.8	6.1	6.0	...

Continent, country or area, and urban/rural residence / Continent, pays ou zone et résidence, urbaine/rurale	Code[a]	Number - Nombre					Ratio - Rapport				
		2014	2015	2016	2017	2018	2014	2015	2016	2017	2018
ASIA - ASIE											
Myanmar[16]											
Total	+U	5 687	5 382	5 328	...	...	...	...	...	...	...
Urban - Urbaine	+U	2 332	2 644	2 634	...	...	...	...	...	...	...
Rural - Rurale	+U	3 355	2 738	2 694	...	...	...	...	...	...	...
Oman											
Total[17]	U	335	...	403	...	...	...	...	...	...	...
Total	C	...	...	...	266	206	...	...	...	2.9	2.3
Philippines											
Total	...	4 148	4 151	4 468	...	...	...	...	...	...	...
Republic of Korea - République de Corée[18]											
Total	C	897	836	709	606	...	2.1	1.9	1.7	1.7	...
Urban - Urbaine[9]	C	611	695	556	466	...	1.7	1.9	1.6	1.6	...
Rural - Rurale[9]	C	135	119	117	112	...	1.9	1.7	1.7	1.8	...
Singapore - Singapour											
Total	+C	86	90	89	99	...	2.0	2.1	2.2	2.5	...
Sri Lanka											
Total	+U	708	715	959	1 039	...	...	...	...	...	...
Tajikistan - Tadjikistan											
Total	U	2 265	2 346	2 326	2 061	...	...	...	...	...	...
Urban - Urbaine	U	951	1 701	1 819	1 635	...	...	...	...	...	...
Rural - Rurale	U	1 314	645	507	426	...	...	...	...	...	...
United Arab Emirates - Émirats arabes unis											
Total	...	465	492	475	413	...	...	...	...	...	...
Uzbekistan - Ouzbékistan											
Total	+C	5 768	6 636	6 471	6 488	...	8.0	9.0	8.9	9.1	...
Urban - Urbaine	+C	3 383	3 653	3 444	3 313	...	10.4	11.2	10.4	10.2	...
Rural - Rurale	+C	2 385	2 983	3 027	3 175	...	6.1	7.3	7.7	8.1	...
EUROPE											
Åland Islands - Îles d'Åland											
Total	C	-	-	1	-	...	...	...	...	...	...
Urban - Urbaine	C	-	-	...	-	...	...	...	...	...	...
Rural - Rurale	C	-	-	...	-	...	...	...	...	...	...
Albania - Albanie											
Total	C	...	...	61	...	...	...	...	1.9	...	...
Andorra - Andorre											
Total	C	-	1	...	...	...	...	...	...	...	...
Austria - Autriche[7]											
Total	C	273	281	290	294	...	3.3	3.3	3.3	3.4	...
Belarus - Bélarus											
Total	C	256	271	282	202	...	2.2	2.3	2.4	2.0	...
Urban - Urbaine	C	196	192	207	151	...	2.1	2.1	2.3	1.9	...
Rural - Rurale	C	60	79	75	51	...	2.2	2.9	2.8	2.2	...
Belgium - Belgique											
Total	C	596	...	542	...	...	4.8	...	4.4	...	...
Urban - Urbaine	C	588	...	...	...	...	4.8	...	...	...	...
Rural - Rurale	C	8	...	...	...	...	...	...	...	...	...
Bulgaria - Bulgarie[7]											
Total	C	498	420	462	404	379	7.4	6.4	7.1	6.3	...
Urban - Urbaine	C	338	284	333	290	...	6.7	5.7	6.8	6.0	...
Rural - Rurale	C	160	136	129	114	...	9.5	8.3	7.9	7.1	...
Croatia - Croatie[19]											
Total	C	150	163	169	149	...	3.8	4.3	4.5	4.1	...
Urban - Urbaine	C	77	91	97	84	...	3.4	4.2	4.5	4.0	...
Rural - Rurale	C	73	72	72	65	...	4.4	4.6	4.5	4.2	...
Czechia - Tchéquie[20]											
Total	C	296	296	296	295	383	2.7	2.7	2.6	2.6	3.4
Urban - Urbaine	C	210	224	215	220	...	2.6	2.8	2.6	2.6	...
Rural - Rurale	C	86	72	81	75	...	3.0	2.5	2.7	2.5	...
Denmark - Danemark[21]											
Total	C	234	...	237	246	...	4.1	...	3.8	4.0	...

12. Late foetal deaths and late foetal death ratios, by urban/rural residence: 2014 - 2018
Morts foetales tardives et rapports de mortinatalité, selon la résidence, urbaine/rurale : 2014 - 2018 (continued - suite)

Continent, country or area, and urban/rural residence	Code[a]	Number - Nombre					Ratio - Rapport				
Continent, pays ou zone et résidence, urbaine/rurale		2014	2015	2016	2017	2018	2014	2015	2016	2017	2018
EUROPE											
Estonia - Estonie											
Total	C	38	19	38	36	...	2.8	...	2.7	2.6	...
Urban - Urbaine	C	28	14	30	30	...	...	...	3.1	3.0	...
Rural - Rurale	C	10	5	8	6	...	...	...	...	...	...
Faeroe Islands - Îles Féroé											
Total	C	-	3	2	1	...	...	...	...	...	...
Urban - Urbaine	C	-	...	...	...	...	...	...	...	...	...
Rural - Rurale	C	-	...	...	...	...	...	...	...	...	...
Finland - Finlande[22]											
Total	C	115	115	116	96	...	2.0	2.1	2.2	1.9	...
Urban - Urbaine	C	83	77	86	79	...	2.0	1.9	2.2	2.1	...
Rural - Rurale	C	32	38	30	17	...	2.0	2.6	2.2	...	...
Germany - Allemagne											
Total	C	2 597	2 787	2 914	3 003	3 030	3.6	3.8	3.7	3.8	3.8
Greece - Grèce											
Total	C	296	272	283	316	335	3.2	3.0	3.0	3.6	3.9
Urban - Urbaine	C	200	182	182	...	...	3.2	2.9	2.8	...	...
Rural - Rurale	C	96	90	101	...	...	3.3	3.2	3.5	...	...
Hungary - Hongrie[23]											
Total	C	421	408	410	435	...	4.5	4.4	4.3	4.6	...
Urban - Urbaine[24]	C	274	265	250	272	...	4.2	4.1	3.8	4.2	...
Rural - Rurale[24]	C	143	138	156	161	...	5.1	4.9	5.3	5.4	...
Iceland - Islande											
Total	C	11	8	10	7	5	...	...	...	...	...
Urban - Urbaine	C	11	8	9	6	...	...	...	...	...	...
Rural - Rurale	C	-	-	1	1	...	...	...	...	...	...
Ireland - Irlande[25]											
Total	C	164	194	173	...	...	2.4	3.0	2.7	...	...
Italy - Italie											
Total	C	1 364	1 305	1 308	1 265	...	2.7	2.7	2.8	2.8	...
Latvia - Lettonie											
Total	C	83	72	88	70	...	3.8	3.3	4.0	3.4	...
Lithuania - Lituanie[19]											
Total	C	139	126	130	102	115	4.6	4.0	4.2	3.6	4.0
Urban - Urbaine	C	96	88	86	65	...	4.6	4.1	4.0	3.3	...
Rural - Rurale	C	43	38	44	37	...	4.6	3.8	4.7	4.2	...
Luxembourg											
Total	C	30	50	36	37	...	4.9	8.2	6.0	6.0	...
Malta - Malte[19]											
Total	C	26	...	...	...	...	...	...	...	...	...
Netherlands - Pays-Bas[26]											
Total	C	487	500	493	482	...	2.8	2.9	2.9	2.8	...
North Macedonia - Macédoine du Nord											
Total	C	171	185	197	192	...	7.2	8.0	8.6	8.8	...
Urban - Urbaine	C	106	110	116	110	...	7.7	8.2	8.6	8.6	...
Rural - Rurale	C	65	75	81	82	...	6.6	7.7	8.6	9.2	...
Norway - Norvège											
Total	C	217	174	183	139	...	3.7	3.0	3.1	2.5	...
Poland - Pologne											
Total	C	928	...	...	...	...	2.5	...	...	...	...
Portugal[27]											
Total	C	214	216	214	182	...	2.6	2.5	2.5	2.1	...
Romania - Roumanie[7]											
Total	C	782	735	732	697	...	3.9	3.7	3.7	3.4	...
Urban - Urbaine	C	373	340	...	347	...	3.4	3.1	...	3.1	...
Rural - Rurale	C	409	395	...	350	...	4.6	4.5	...	3.9	...
San Marino - Saint-Marin											
Total	C	-	-	2	-	-	...	...	...	...	...
Serbia - Serbie[28]											
Total	+C	348	388	377	349	...	5.2	5.9	5.8	5.4	...
Urban - Urbaine	+C	242	261	258	250	...	5.3	5.7	5.8	5.7	...
Rural - Rurale	+C	106	127	119	99	...	5.2	6.3	6.0	4.7	...
Slovakia - Slovaquie[29]											
Total	C	166	184	160	159	...	3.0	3.3	2.8	2.7	...
Urban - Urbaine	C	76	85	74	71	...	2.7	2.9	2.5	2.4	...
Rural - Rurale	C	90	99	86	88	...	3.4	3.7	3.1	3.1	...

Continent, country or area, and urban/rural residence / Continent, pays ou zone et résidence, urbaine/rurale	Code[a]	Number - Nombre					Ratio - Rapport				
		2014	2015	2016	2017	2018	2014	2015	2016	2017	2018
EUROPE											
Slovenia - Slovénie											
Total	C	47	55	67	55	...	2.2	2.7	3.3	2.7	...
Spain - Espagne											
Total	C	1 320	1 287	1 295[7]	1 246[7]	...	3.1	3.1	3.2	3.2	...
Sweden - Suède											
Total	C	456	429	414	399	...	4.0	3.7	3.5	3.5	...
Switzerland - Suisse[7]											
Total	C	368	357	371	362	...	4.3	4.1	4.2	4.1	...
Urban - Urbaine	C	262[30]	314	317	305	...	4.1	4.2	4.2	4.1	...
Rural - Rurale	C	106[30]	43	54	57	...	5.0	3.4	4.3	4.6	...
Ukraine[31]											
Total	+C	3 656	3 318	2 244	2 136	...	7.8	8.1	5.7	5.9	...
Urban - Urbaine	+C	2 316	2 035	1 387	1 326	...	7.6	7.6	5.4	5.6	...
Rural - Rurale	+C	1 340	1 283	857	810	...	8.3	8.8	6.2	6.4	...
United Kingdom of Great Britain and Northern Ireland - Royaume-Uni de Grande-Bretagne et d'Irlande du Nord[32]											
Total	C	3 563	3 434	3 377[33]	3 157	...	4.6	4.4	4.4	4.2	...
OCEANIA - OCÉANIE											
Australia - Australie[34]											
Total	C	293	330	334	343	...	1.0	1.1	1.1	1.1	...
Urban - Urbaine[35]	C	171	198	231	215	...	0.8	0.9	1.1	1.0	...
Rural - Rurale[35]	C	103	111	90	102	...	1.1	1.2	1.0	1.1	...
Guam											
Total	C	36[7]	45[7]	44[36]	43[36]	51[36]	10.6	13.4	12.8	13.1	16.1
New Zealand - Nouvelle-Zélande[37]											
Total	+C	147	117	144	141	...	2.6	1.9	2.4	2.4	...
Urban - Urbaine	+C	123	105	123	117	...	2.4	2.0	2.4	2.4	...
Rural - Rurale	+C	21	12	21	21	...	2.4	2.0	2.4	2.3	...
Palau - Palaos[38]											
Total	C	3	4	7	2	3	...	...	...	...	...

FOOTNOTES - NOTES

Italics: data from civil registers which are incomplete or of unknown completeness. - Italiques : données incomplètes ou dont le degré d'exactitude n'est pas connu, provenant des registres de l'état civil.

* Provisional. - Données provisoires.

a 'Code' indicates the source of data, as follows:
C - Civil registration, estimated over 90% complete
U - Civil registration, estimated less than 90% complete
| - Other source, estimated reliable
+ - Data tabulated by date of registration rather than occurence
... - Information not available

Le 'Code' indique la source des données, comme suit :
C - Registres de l'état civil considérés complets à 90 p. 100 au moins
U - Registres de l'état civil qui ne sont pas considérés complets à 90 p. 100 au moins
| - Autre source, considérée pas douteuses
+ - Données exploitées selon la date de l'enregistrement et non la date de l'événement
... - Information pas disponible

1 Source: Statistics Botswana. - Source: Statistics Botswana.
2 Excludes the islands of St. Brandon and Agalega. - Non compris les îles St. Brandon et Agalega.

3 Bermuda is 100 per cent urban. - 100 pour cent de la population des Bermudes est urbaine.
4 Source: Bermuda Hospitals Board (BHB). - Source : Conseil des hôpitaux des Bermudes.
5 Including Canadian residents temporarily in the United States, but excluding United States residents temporarily in Canada. - Y compris les résidents canadiens se trouvant temporairement aux Etats-Unis, mais ne comprenant pas les résidents des Etats-Unis se trouvant temporairement au Canada.
6 Late foetal death is indicated by the fact that the foetus is at least 500 g or more in weight. - Les décès foetaux tardifs sont caractérisés par le fait que le foetus pèse au moins 500 g.
7 Data refer to total foetal deaths. - Y compris toutes les morts foetales.
8 Data refer to resident population only. - Pour la population résidante seulement.
9 The total number may include 'Unknown residence', but the categories urban and rural do not. - Le nombre total peut inclure les personnes dont la résidence n'est pas connue, à l'inverse des catégories de population urbaine et rurale.
10 Late foetal death is indicated by the fact that the foetus is at least 22 completed weeks of gestational age. - Les décès intra-utérins tardifs sont définis comme survenant après 22 semaines au moins de gestation.
11 Excludes nomadic Indian tribes. - Non compris les tribus d'Indiens nomades.
12 Sources: Births and Deaths National Registration System database, and medical records of government hospitals. - Les sources: Les bases de données des << Births and Deaths National Registration System >> et les dossiers médicaux des hôpitaux du gouvernement.
13 Includes data for East Jerusalem and Israeli residents in certain other territories under occupation by Israeli military forces since June 1967. - Y

423

compris les données pour Jérusalem-Est et les résidents israéliens dans certains autres territoires occupés depuis 1967 par les forces armées israéliennes.

[14] Data refer to Japanese nationals in Japan only. The total number may include 'Unknown residence', but the categories urban and rural do not. Data exclude unknown duration of pregnancy. - Les données se raportent aux nationaux japonais au Japon seulement. Le nombre total peut inclure les personnes dont la résidence n'est pas connue, à l'inverse des catégories de population urbaine et rurale. Exception faite des grossesses dont la durée n'est pas connue.

[15] Urban and rural figures refer to the late foetal deaths collected based on the location of the medical facilities, regardless of the mothers' permanent residence location. - Les chiffres urbains et ruraux concernent les décès tardifs du fœtus recueillis sur la base de l'emplacement des établissements médicaux, indépendamment du lieu de résidence permanente des mères.

[16] Data are from Vital Registration System (VRS). - Les données proviennent du système d'enregistrement des faits d'état civil.

[17] Data from Births and Deaths Notification System (Ministry of Health and all health care providers). - Les données proviennent du système de notification des naissances et des décès (Ministère de la santé et tous prestataires de soins de santé).

[18] Excluding alien armed forces, civilian aliens employed by armed forces, and foreign diplomatic personnel and their dependants. - Non compris les militaires étrangers, les civils étrangers employés par les forces armées ni le personnel diplomatique étranger et les membres de leur famille les accompagnant.

[19] Late foetal death is defined as an infant born without any signs of life, weighing at least 500 g, after duration of pregnancy of at least 22 weeks. - On dit qu'il y a mort intra-utérine tardive lorsqu'un enfant pesant au minimum 500 g naît sans donner aucun signe de vie au terme d'une grossesse qui a duré au moins 22 semaines.

[20] Since 1 April 2012, a stillborn child is defined in guidelines for filling in a death certificate as a child fully expelled or removed out of the mother's body, not showing any sign of life and whose birth weight is 500 g or more. If the weight is not possible to determine then duration of pregnancy must be 22 weeks or more. If the duration of pregnancy is not possible to determine, the foetus length must be 25 cm or more. - Depuis le 1er avril 2012, un enfant mort-né est défini dans les directives relatives à l'établissement du certificat de décès comme un enfant complètement expulsé par la mère ou retiré de son corps, ne montrant aucun signe de vie et ayant atteint un poids de 500 g. S'il est impossible d'en déterminer le poids, la durée de gestation doit être au moins de 22 semaines. S'il est impossible de déterminer la durée de gestation, la longueur du fœtus doit être au moins de 25 cm.

[21] Excluding Faeroe Islands and Greenland shown separately, if available. - Non compris les Îles Féroé et le Groenland, qui font l'objet de rubriques distinctes, si disponible.

[22] Excluding Åland Islands. - Non compris les Îles d'Åland.

[23] Late foetal death is indicated by the fact that the foetus is at least 24 completed weeks of gestation (it was 28 weeks until 1996) and does not show any sign of life after the separation from its mother; the foetus has to be 30 cm or more in length or 500 g or more in weight if its gestational age cannot be determined. - Pour qu'il y ait mort foetale tardive, il faut que le décès d'un foetus survienne après 24 semaines complètes de gestation au moins (28 semaines jusqu'en 1996), que le foetus n'ait pas donné signe de vie après avoir été séparé de la mère, qu'il mesure 30 cm au moins ou pèse 500 g si la durée de la période de gestation n'est pas connue.

[24] The urban and rural categories do not include the data of foreigners, persons of unknown residence and the homeless, whereas the total category includes them. - Les chiffres portant sur la population urbaine et rurale n' incluent pas les données relatives aux étrangers, aux personnes dont la résidence n'est pas connue et aux personnes sans domicile fixe, à l'inverse, le total les inclut.

[25] Data refer to events registered within one year of occurrence. - Les données portent sur des événements enregistrés dans l'année pendant laquelle ils sont survenus.

[26] Including residents outside the country if listed in a Netherlands population register. - Englobe les résidents se trouvant à l'étranger à condition qu'ils soient inscrits sur le registre de population des Pays-Bas.

[27] Data refer to usually resident population. - Les données concernent la population habituellement résidente.

[28] Excludes data for Kosovo and Metohia. Data refer to total foetal deaths. - Sans les données pour le Kosovo et Metohie. Y compris toutes les morts foetales.

[29] Including foetal deaths of at least 1 000 g in weight or 28 weeks of gestation. - Y compris les morts de fœtus pesant au moins 1 000 g ou après 28 semaines de gestation.

[30] From 2014, urban refers to urban centers and areas under the influence of urban centers. - A partir de 2014, le territoire urbain inclut l'espace des centres urbains ainsi que l'espace sous influence des centres urbains.

[31] The Government of Ukraine has informed the United Nations that it is not in a position to provide statistical data concerning the Autonomous Republic of Crimea and the city of Sevastopol. - Le gouvernement Ukrainien a informé l'ONU qu'il n'est pas en mesure de fournir des données statistiques concernant la République autonome de Crimée et la ville de Sébastopol.

[32] Excluding Channel Islands (Guernsey and Jersey) and Isle of Man, shown separately, if available. - Non compris les Îles Anglo-Normandes (Guernesey et Jersey) et l'île de Man, qui font l'objet de rubriques distinctes, si disponible.

[33] From 2016 onwards late foetal deaths to non-UK residents are excluded. Late foetal deaths that occurred in one of the constituent countries of UK to a resident of another constituent country of UK are also excluded. - À partir de 2016, les données ne tiennent plus compte des cas de mortalité fœtale tardive qui concernent des personnes ne résidant pas au Royaume-Uni. Sont également exclus les cas de mortalité fœtale tardive survenus dans l'un des pays constitutifs du Royaume-Uni et qui concernent un résident d'un autre de ces pays.

[34] Late foetal deaths include deaths of foetuses of 28 weeks or more of gestation and with a birth weight of at least 400 grams. Data exclude foetal deaths for which the period of gestation and birthweight was not stated on the Medical Certificate of Cause of Perinatal Death. - La mortalité foetale tardive recouvre les décès de foetus de 28 semaines ou plus pesant au moins 400 grammes à la naissance. Les données ne tiennent pas compte des décès intra-utérins pour lesquels la période de gestation et le poids à la naissance n'étaient pas indiqués sur le certificat médical faisant état de la cause du décès périnatal.

[35] Data for urban and rural figures do not add up to the total because they exclude the events occurred in Migratory, Special Purpose and Other Territories. Urban refers to Greater Capital City Statistical Areas, and rural refers to other areas within the state or territory. - La somme des chiffres des catégories « en zone urbaine » et « en zone rurale » ne correspond pas au total du fait qu'en sont exclus les événements qui ont eu lieu dans les territoires de migration, les territoires à destination spéciale et autres territoires. Urbain renvoie aux zones statistiques de la capitale métropolitaine, et rural aux autres zones de l'État ou territoire.

[36] Including United States military personnel, their dependants and contract employees. - Y compris les militaires des Etats-Unis, les membres de leur famille les accompagnant et les agents contractuels des Etats-Unis.

[37] The total number may include 'Unknown residence', but the categories urban and rural do not. Data refer to resident population only. Random rounding to base 3 is applied in this table as a confidentiality measure. - Le nombre total peut inclure les personnes dont la résidence n'est pas connue, à l'inverse des catégories de population urbaine et rurale. Pour la population résidante seulement. Les chiffres sont arrondis à la base 3 de manière aléatoire, pour des raisons de confidentialité.

[38] Data includes abortions. - Les données comprennnent les avortement.

Table 13 - *Demographic Yearbook 2018*

Table 13 presents legally induced abortions for as many years as available between 2009 and 2018.

Description of variables: There are two major categories of abortion: spontaneous and induced. Induced abortions are those initiated by deliberate action undertaken with the intention of terminating pregnancy; all other abortions are considered spontaneous.

The induction of abortion is subject to governmental regulation in most, if not all, countries or areas. This regulation varies from complete prohibition in some countries or areas to abortion on request, with services provided by governmental health authorities, in others. More generally, governments have attempted to define the conditions under which a pregnancy may lawfully be terminated and have established procedures for authorizing abortion in individual cases.

Information on abortion policies is collected by the United Nations Population Division and published in the *Abortion Policies and Reproductive Health around the World*[1].

Reliability of data: Unlike data on live births and foetal deaths, which are generally collected through systems of vital registration, data on abortion are collected from a variety of sources. Because of this, the quality specification on the completeness of civil registers, which is presented for other tables, does not appear here.

Limitations: With regard to the collection of information on abortions, a variety of sources are used, but hospital records are the most common source of information. This implies that most cases that have no contact with hospitals are missed. Data from other sources are probably also incomplete. The data in the present table are limited to legally induced abortions, which, by their nature, might be assumed to be more complete than data on all induced abortions.

Earlier data: Legally induced abortions have been shown previously in all issues of the *Demographic Yearbook* since the twenty-third issue. For more information on specific topics and years for which data are reported, readers should consult the Historical Index.

NOTES

[1] United Nations, Department of Economic and Social Affairs, Population Division (2014). *Abortion Policies and Reproductive Health around the World* (United Nations publication, Sales No. E.14.XIII.11).

Tableau 13 – *Annuaire démographique 2018*

Le tableau 13 présente les données disponibles, relatives aux avortements provoqués légalement, entre 2009 et 2018.

Description des variables : l'avortement peut être spontané ou provoqué. L'avortement provoqué est celui qui résulte de manœuvres délibérées, entreprises afin d'interrompre la grossesse ; tous les autres avortements sont considérés comme spontanés.

L'interruption délibérée de la grossesse fait l'objet d'une réglementation officielle dans la plupart des pays ou zones, sinon dans tous. Cette réglementation va de l'interdiction totale à l'autorisation de l'avortement sur demande, pratiqué par des services de santé publique. Le plus souvent, les gouvernements se sont efforcés de définir les circonstances dans lesquelles la grossesse peut être interrompue licitement et de fixer une procédure d'autorisation.

La Division de la population des Nations Unies collecte des informations sur les politiques en matière d'avortement et les publient dans *Abortion Policies and Reproductive Health around the World*[1].

Fiabilité des données : à la différence des données sur les naissances vivantes et les morts fœtales, qui proviennent généralement des registres d'état civil, les données sur l'avortement sont tirées de sources diverses. Aussi ne trouve-t-on pas ici une évaluation de la qualité des données semblable à celle qui indique, pour les autres tableaux, le degré d'exhaustivité des données de l'état civil.

Insuffisance des données : en ce qui concerne les renseignements sur l'avortement, un grand nombre de sources sont utilisées, les relevés hospitaliers restant cependant la source la plus commune. Il s'ensuit que la plupart des cas qui ne passent pas par les hôpitaux sont ignorés. Il faut aussi tenir compte du fait que les données provenant d'autres sources sont probablement incomplètes. Les données du tableau 13 se limitent aux avortements provoqués pour raisons légales dont on peut supposer, en raison de leur nature même, que les statistiques sont plus complètes que les données concernant l'ensemble des avortements provoqués.

Données publiées antérieurement : des statistiques concernant les avortements provoqués pour raisons légales sont publiées dans *l'Annuaire démographique* depuis la vingt-troisième édition. Pour plus de précisions concernant les années et les sujets pour lesquels des données ont été publiées, se reporter à l'index historique.

NOTES

[1] United Nations, Department of Economic and Social Affairs, Population Division (2014). *Abortion Policies and Reproductive Health around the World* (United Nations publication, Sales No. E.14.XIII.11).

13. Legally induced abortions: 2009 - 2018
Avortements provoqués légalement : 2009 - 2018

Continent and country or area / Continent et pays ou zone	Number - Nombre									
	2009	**2010**	**2011**	**2012**	**2013**	**2014**	**2015**	**2016**	**2017**	**2018**
AFRICA - AFRIQUE										
Burundi[1]	6 329	6 272	3 547	3 630	3 152	...	...	...	...	...
Reunion - Réunion	4 402	4 349	4 508	4 280	...					
Seychelles	471	556	579	533	515	549	478	509	521	473
AMERICA, NORTH - AMÉRIQUE DU NORD										
Bermuda - Bermudes[2]	290	275	268	271	270	239	227	226	231	183
Costa Rica[3]	7 848	7 697	7 882	7 405	7 283	*7 137	...	...	...	...
Cuba	84 724	71 398	83 943	83 682	84 373	85 782	91 500	85 445	83 904	...
Dominican Republic - République dominicaine	22 393	20 946	24 210	26 303	24 605	26 699	21 600	21 266	19 413	14 835
Greenland - Groenland	799	858	743	784	875	864	864	855	883	...
Mexico - Mexique[4]	867	*986	1 041	294	271	301	411	394	489	...
AMERICA, SOUTH - AMÉRIQUE DU SUD										
Colombia - Colombie	69	82	120	212	633	876	3 002	1 588[5]	577[5]	...
Ecuador - Équateur[6]	40 201	42 541	42 574	41 712	40 256	35 719	31 302	30 410	30 331	...
Paraguay	...	...	...	4 353						
ASIA - ASIE										
Armenia - Arménie	13 797	...	...	...	...	11 892	11 104	10 448	10 006	...
Azerbaijan - Azerbaïdjan	24 554[7]	26 799[7]	27 787[7]	31 037	27 892	27 220	27 452	34 569	37 599	...
Bahrain - Bahreïn[8]	2 394	2 525	2 452	2 463	...	...	...	...	...	...
China, Hong Kong SAR - Chine, Hong Kong RAS	12 028	11 231	11 864	11 298	10 653	10 359	9 890	9 481	8 780	8 518
Georgia - Géorgie	24 311	25 585	30 590	39 225	37 018	33 469	33 377	29 641	24 937	...
Israel - Israël[9]	19 849	19 575	18 974	18 822	18 263	18 646	18 510	18 032	...	...
Japan - Japon	226 878	212 694[10]	202 106	196 639	186 253	181 905	176 388	168 015	164 621	...
Kazakhstan	113 320	106 074	95 288	95 654	84 265	83 709	81 440	78 857	80 328	...
Kyrgyzstan - Kirghizstan[11]	22 088	21 675	23 728	23 547	21 673	24 456	22 084	20 783	19 486	19 176
Mongolia - Mongolie	12 602	12 492	17 504	18 473	15 628	18 145	18 168	18 316	17 530	15 822
Singapore - Singapour	12 318	12 082	11 940	10 624	9 282	8 515	7 942	7 217	6 815	...
Tajikistan - Tadjikistan	19 470	19 510	17 503	16 618	15 984	17 347	16 864	14 957	13 963	...
Uzbekistan - Ouzbékistan	45 968	40 651	38 809	37 634	38 546	41 352	40 201	42 417	42 433	...
EUROPE										
Åland Islands - Îles d'Åland	68	70	73	60	70	66	69	76	74	...
Albania - Albanie	8 139	6 919	7 042	6 755	6 442	5 572	5 619	1 206	1 000	...
Belarus - Bélarus	35 967	33 262	32 031	28 628	31 206	29 797	29 217	27 467	25 249	...
Belgium - Belgique	18 870	19 095	19 578	...	...	...	...	...	...	...
Bulgaria - Bulgarie	33 733	31 548	31 716	29 992	29 505	28 145	27 782	26 412	24 287	...
Croatia - Croatie	4 450	4 043	4 347	3 571	3 161	3 020	3 002	2 520	2 416	...
Czechia - Tchéquie	24 636	23 998	24 055	23 032	22 714	21 893	20 403	20 406	19 415	18 298
Denmark - Danemark[12]	16 664	16 596	16 085	16 220	15 986	15 440	15 325	...	...	...
Estonia - Estonie[13]	7 542	7 068	6 668	6 056	5 777	6 901	4 889	6 248	3 997	...
Faeroe Islands - Îles Féroé	51	33	33	34	23	30	21	26	...	...
Finland - Finlande[14]	10 437	10 231	10 622	10 177	10 060	9 714	9 372	9 311	9 258	...
France[15]	208 662	211 248	206 888	205 300	214 649	210 703	204 139	200 330	...	...
Germany - Allemagne	110 694	110 431	108 867	106 815	102 802	99 715	99 237	98 721	101 209	...
Hungary - Hongrie	43 181	40 449	38 443	36 118	34 891	32 663	31 176	30 439	28 496	26 941
Iceland - Islande	981	977	970	980	963	951	921	1 021	...	...
Italy - Italie[16]	114 793[16]	112 463[17]	110 041[17]	103 191[18]	100 342[19]	95 400[20]	87 369[21]	84 874	80 497	...
Jersey	220	200	200	200	190	160	190	180	170	190
Latvia - Lettonie	8 881	7 443	7 089	6 197	5 557	5 318	4 802	4 366	3 917	3 636
Lithuania - Lituanie	8 024	6 989	6 205	6 033	5 353	5 231	4 735	4 502	4 294	3 590
Montenegro - Monténégro	...	...	...	...	...	943	980	763	637	...
North Macedonia - Macédoine du Nord	5 648	5 078	5 324	5 387	4 983	4 738	4 587	4 251	4 236	...

Continent and country or area Continent et pays ou zone	Number - Nombre									
	2009	**2010**	**2011**	**2012**	**2013**	**2014**	**2015**	**2016**	**2017**	**2018**
EUROPE										
Norway - Norvège	15 774	15 735	15 343	...	...	...	...	...	...	...
Poland - Pologne[22]	538	644	669	752	745	970	1 040	1 098	1 057	...
Portugal	19 848	20 137	20 480	19 156	18 281	16 762	16 652	*15 959	*15 492	...
Republic of Moldova - République de Moldova	14 634	14 785	15 710	14 838	...	...	...	...	...	...
Romania - Roumanie	116 060	101 915	103 386	87 975	86 432	78 371	70 885	63 518	56 238	...
Russian Federation - Fédération de Russie	1 292 389	1 186 108	1 124 880	1 063 982	1 012 399	...	...	...	...	...
Serbia - Serbie[23]	18 215	17 466	15 963	15 301	13 650	12 923	12 242	11 093	10 378	...
Slovakia - Slovaquie	13 240	12 582	11 789	11 214	11 105	10 582	10 058	9 390	9 083	...
Slovenia - Slovénie	4 653	4 328	4 263	4 106	4 011	4 060	3 682	3 736	3 529	...
Spain - Espagne	111 482	113 031	118 359	112 390	...	94 796	94 188	...	94 123	...
Sweden - Suède	37 524	37 693	37 750	37 366	...	36 629	38 071	38 177	36 616	...
Switzerland - Suisse[24]	10 187	10 650	10 715	10 531	10 177	10 016	10 088	10 102	9 863	...
Ukraine	194 845	176 774	169 131	153 147	147 736	116 104[25]	106 357[25]	101 121[25]	94 665[25]	...
United Kingdom of Great Britain and Northern Ireland - Royaume-Uni de Grande-Bretagne et d'Irlande du Nord[26]	208 854	209 048	208 636	203 419[27]	...	...	...	197 659	...	...
OCEANIA - OCÉANIE										
Guam[28]	266	269	295	275	213	209	263	289	239	102
New Zealand - Nouvelle-Zélande	17 550	16 630	15 863	14 745	14 073	13 137	13 155	12 823	13 285	...

FOOTNOTES - NOTES

Italics: estimates which are less reliable. - Italiques : estimations moins sûres.

* Provisional. - Données provisoires.

[1] Data refer only to events recorded in hospitals and health centres. - Ces données ne concernent que les faits d'état civil enregistrés dans les hôpitaux et les centres de santé uniquement.

[2] Source: Bermuda Hospitals Board (BHB). - Source : Conseil des hôpitaux des Bermudes.

[3] Excluding abortions performed in private hospitals. - Non comprises les interruptions volontaires de grossesse effectuées dans des hôpitaux privés.

[4] Data refer to 'Therapeutic Abortions'. According to Mexican law, only induced abortions, prescribed by medical reasons or induced because of pregnancy coming from sexual aggression, are considered as legal; data refer only to the former. Refers to residence of the mother. To calculate the total number of abortions, only foetal deaths of less than 20 weeks of gestation were considered. Excluding abortions in the country by women with usual residence outside of the country. - Les données se rapportent aux « interruptions volontaires de grossesse pour des motifs thérapeutiques ». D'après la loi mexicaine, seuls sont considérés légaux les avortements déclenchés pour des raisons médicales ou parce que la grossesse est le résultat d'une agression sexuelle; les données se réfèrent seulement à la première. Correspond à la résidence de la mère. Seuls les morts fœtales survenues à moins de 20 semaines de gestation ont été prises en compte aux fins du calcul du nombre total d'avortements. Hors avortements dans le pays par des femmes avec résidence habituelle en dehors du pays.

[5] Affected by underreporting since, by law, legally induced abortions are not reported directly to the civil registry. - Font l'objet d'une sous-déclaration, toutes les interruptions volontaires de grossesse pratiquées légalement n'étant pas déclarées dans la mesure où la loi n'impose pas de les inscrire directement au registre civil.

[6] Data refer to abortions registered in hospitals due to pregnancy complications. - Les données renvoient aux avortements enregistrés dans les hôpitaux du fait des complications de la grossesse.

[7] Data are from the Ministry of Health only before expansion to include data form other sources. - Les données proviennent du Ministère de la santé uniquement, avant inclusion de données provenant d'autres sources.

[8] Data refer to spontaneous abortions and miscarriages. - Données se rapportant aux avortements spontanés et fausses couches.

[9] Includes data for East Jerusalem and Israeli residents in certain other territories under occupation by Israeli military forces since June 1967. Data refer to applications to commissions for termination of pregnancy and not to authorizations. - Y compris les données pour Jérusalem-Est et les résidents israéliens dans certains autres territoires occupés depuis 1967 par les forces armées israéliennes. Les données relatives aux avortements provoqués légalement se rapportent aux demandes d'autorisation et non aux autorisations elles-mêmes.

[10] Excluding data of cities and towns in the jurisdiction of Sousou Public Health and Welfare Office of Fukushima Prefecture due to the impact of the Great East Japan Earthquake. - Ne sont pas incluses les données relatives aux agglomérations relevant du bureau de la santé publique et des services sociaux de Sousou dans la préfecture de Fukushima, en raison des conséquences du grand séisme dans l'est du Japon.

[11] Based on administrative reporting of the Ministry of Health. - Les données reposent sur les rapports administratifs du Ministère de la santé.

[12] Excluding Faeroe Islands and Greenland shown separately, if available. - Non compris les Îles Féroé et le Groenland, qui font l'objet de rubriques distinctes, si disponible.

[13] Data refer to resident population only. - Pour la population résidante seulement.

[14] Excluding Åland Islands. - Non compris les Îles d'Åland.

[15] Data refer to women between 15 and 49 years of age. - Le total se rapporte uniquement aux femmes dont l'âge est compris entre 15 et 49 ans.

[16] Data are incomplete for Abruzzo, Campania, Basilicata, Sicilia and Sardegna regions. - Données incomplètes pour les régions des Abruzzes, de Campanie, de Basilicate, de Sicile et de Sardaigne.

[17] Data are incomplete for Umbria, Campania and Sicilia regions. - Les données sont incomplètes pour l'Ombrie, la Campanie et la Sicile.

[18] Data are incomplete for Umbria, Abruzzo, Campania, Puglia and Sicilia regions. - Les données sont incomplètes pour les régions d'Ombrie, des Abruzzes, de Campanie, des Pouilles et de Sicile.

[19] Data are incomplete for Liguria, Campania, Puglia and Sardegna regions. - Les données sont incomplètes pour les régions suivantes : Ligurie, Campanie, Pouilles et Sardaigne.

[20] Data are incomplete for Lombardia, Marche, Campania, Basilicata, Sicilia and Sardegna regions. - Les données sont incomplètes pour les régions suivantes : Lombardie, Marches, Campanie, Basilicate, Sicile et Sardaigne.

[21] Data are incomplete for Sicilia and Sardegna regions. - Les données sont incomplètes pour les régions suivantes : Sicile et Sardaigne.

22 Based on hospital and polyclinic records. - D'après les registres des hôpitaux et des polycliniques.

23 Excludes data for Kosovo and Metohia. - Sans les données pour le Kosovo et Metohie.

24 Data refer to termination of pregnancy for women who are Switzerland residents. - Les données portent sur les interruptions de grossesse pratiquées sur des femmes qui résident en Suisse.

25 The Government of Ukraine has informed the United Nations that it is not in a position to provide statistical data concerning the Autonomous Republic of Crimea and the city of Sevastopol. - Le gouvernement Ukrainien a informé l'ONU qu'il n'est pas en mesure de fournir des données statistiques concernant la République autonome de Crimée et la ville de Sébastopol.

26 Excluding Northern Ireland. Excluding Channel Islands (Guernsey and Jersey) and Isle of Man, shown separately, if available. - Non compris l'Irlande du Nord. Non compris les îles Anglo-Normandes (Guernesey et Jersey) et l'île de Man, qui font l'objet de rubriques distinctes, si disponible.

27 Including provisional data for Scotland. - Y compris les données provisoires pour l'Écosse.

28 Including United States military personnel, their dependants and contract employees. - Y compris les militaires des Etats-Unis, les membres de leur famille les accompagnant et les agents contractuels des Etats-Unis.

Table 14 - *Demographic Yearbook 2018*

Table 14 presents legally induced abortions by age and number of previous live births of women for the latest available year between 2009 and 2018.

Description of variables: Age is defined as age at last birthday, that is, the difference between the date of birth and the date of the occurrence of the event, expressed in complete solar years. The age classification used in this table is the following: under 15 years, 5-year age groups through 45-49 years and 50 years and over.

Except where otherwise indicated, eight categories are used in classifying the number of previous live births: 0 through 5, 6 or more live births, and, if required, number of live births unknown.

Information on abortion policies is collected by the United Nations Population Division and published in the *Abortion Policies and Reproductive Health around the World*[1].

Reliability of data: Unlike data on live births and foetal deaths, which are generally collected through systems of vital registration, data on abortion are collected from a variety of sources. Because of this, the quality specification on the completeness of civil registers, which is presented for other tables, does not appear here.

Limitations: With regard to the collection of information on abortions, a variety of sources are used, but hospital records are the most common source of information. This implies that most cases that have no contact with hospitals are missed. Data from other sources are probably also incomplete. The data in the present table are limited to legally induced abortions, which, by their nature, might be assumed to be more complete than data on all induced abortions.

In addition, deficiencies in the reporting of age and number of previous live births of the woman, differences in the method used for obtaining the age of the woman, and the proportion of abortions for which age or previous live births of the woman are unknown must all be taken into account in using these data.

Earlier data: Legally induced abortions by age and previous live births of women have been shown previously in most issues of the *Demographic Yearbook* since the twenty-third issue. For more information on specific topics and years for which data are reported, readers should consult the Historical Index.

NOTES

[1] United Nations, Department of Economic and Social Affairs, Population Division (2014). *Abortion Policies and Reproductive Health around the World* (United Nations publication, Sales No. E.14.XIII.11).

Tableau 14 – *Annuaire démographique 2018*

Le tableau 14 présente les données les plus récentes disponibles entre 2009 et 2018 sur les avortements provoqués pour des raisons légales, selon l'âge de la mère et le nombre de naissances vivantes précédentes.

Description des variables : L'âge considéré est l'âge au dernier anniversaire, c'est-à-dire la différence entre la date de naissance et la date de l'avortement, exprimée en années solaires révolues. La classification par âge utilisée dans le tableau 14 est la suivante : moins de 15 ans, groupes quinquennaux jusqu'à 45-49 ans, 50 ans et plus, et âge inconnu.

Sauf indication contraire, les naissances vivantes antérieures sont classées dans les huit catégories suivantes: 0 à 5 naissances vivantes, 6 naissances vivantes ou plus et, le cas échéant, nombre de naissances vivantes inconnu.

La Division de la population des Nations Unies collecte des informations sur les politiques en matière d'avortement et les publient dans *Abortion Policies and Reproductive Health around the World*[1].

Fiabilité des données : à la différence des données sur les naissances vivantes et les morts fœtales, qui proviennent généralement des registres d'état civil, les données sur l'avortement sont tirées de sources diverses. Aussi ne trouve-t-on pas ici une évaluation de la qualité des données semblable à celle qui indique, pour les autres tableaux, le degré d'exhaustivité des données de l'état civil.

Insuffisance des données : en ce qui concerne les renseignements sur l'avortement, un grand nombre de sources sont utilisées, les relevés hospitaliers restant cependant la source la plus commune. Il s'ensuit que la plupart des cas qui ne passent pas par les hôpitaux sont ignorés. Il faut aussi tenir compte du fait que les données provenant d'autres sources sont probablement incomplètes. Les données du tableau 14 se limitent aux avortements provoqués pour raisons légales dont on peut supposer, en raison de leur nature même, que les statistiques sont plus complètes que les données concernant l'ensemble des avortements provoqués.

En outre, on doit tenir compte, lorsque l'on utilise ces données, des erreurs de déclaration de l'âge de la mère et du nombre des naissances vivantes précédentes, de l'hétérogénéité des méthodes de calcul de l'âge de la mère et de la proportion d'avortements pour lesquels l'âge de la mère ou le nombre des naissances vivantes ne sont pas connus.

Données publiées antérieurement : Depuis la vingt-troisième édition, la plupart des éditions de l'*Annuaire démographique* contiennent des statistiques concernant les avortements provoqués pour raisons légales, selon l'âge de la mère et le nombre de naissances vivantes antérieures. Pour plus de précisions concernant les années et les sujets pour lesquels des données ont été publiées, se reporter à l'index historique.

NOTES

[1] United Nations, Department of Economic and Social Affairs, Population Division (2014). *Abortion Policies and Reproductive Health around the World* (United Nations publication, Sales No. E.14.XIII.11).

14. Legally induced abortions by age and number of previous live births of women: latest available year, 2009 - 2018
Avortments provoqués légalement selon l'âge de la femme et selon le nombre des naissances vivantes précédentes : dernière année disponible, 2009 - 2018

Continent, country or area, year and age / Continent, pays ou zone, année et âge	Number of previous live births / Nombre des naissances vivantes précédentes								
	Total	0	1	2	3	4	5	6+	Unknown - Inconnu
AFRICA - AFRIQUE									
Seychelles									
2018									
Total	473	...	...	...	...	...	...	...	...
10 - 14	6	...	...	...	...	...	...	...	...
15 - 19	73	...	...	...	...	...	...	...	...
20 - 24	77	...	...	...	...	...	...	...	...
25 - 29	100	...	...	...	...	...	...	...	...
30 - 34	107	...	...	...	...	...	...	...	...
35 - 39	70	...	...	...	...	...	...	...	...
40 - 44	34	...	...	...	...	...	...	...	...
45 - 49	6	...	...	...	...	...	...	...	...
AMERICA, NORTH - AMÉRIQUE DU NORD									
Bermuda - Bermudes[1]									
2018									
Total	183	...	...	...	...	...	...	...	183
0 - 14	-	...	...	...	...	...	...	...	-
15 - 19	9	...	...	...	...	...	...	...	9
20 - 24	42	...	...	...	...	...	...	...	42
25 - 29	59	...	...	...	...	...	...	...	59
30 - 34	30	...	...	...	...	...	...	...	30
35 - 39	32	...	...	...	...	...	...	...	32
40 - 44	10	...	...	...	...	...	...	...	10
45 - 49	1	...	...	...	...	...	...	...	1
50 +	-	...	...	...	...	...	...	...	-
Unknown - Inconnu	-	...	...	...	...	...	...	...	-
Costa Rica[2]									
2009									
Total	7 848	...	...	...	...	...	...	...	...
10 - 14	68	...	...	...	...	...	...	...	...
15 - 19	1 275	...	...	...	...	...	...	...	...
20 - 44	6 437	...	...	...	...	...	...	...	...
45 +	68	...	...	...	...	...	...	...	...
Cuba									
2017									
Total	83 904	...	...	...	...	...	...	...	...
12 - 14	1 512	...	...	...	...	...	...	...	...
15 - 19	19 474	...	...	...	...	...	...	...	...
20 - 34	54 629	...	...	...	...	...	...	...	...
35 - 49	8 289	...	...	...	...	...	...	...	...
Mexico - Mexique[3]									
2017									
Total	489	172	155	75	36	10	2	2	37
0 - 14	4	3	-	-	-	-	-	-	1
15 - 19	58	38	12	-	-	-	-	-	8
20 - 24	120	58	35	12	5	1	-	-	9
25 - 29	116	37	42	22	5	1	-	-	9
30 - 34	97	24	35	21	10	2	1	-	4
35 - 39	69	9	22	17	12	3	1	2	3
40 - 44	18	2	7	3	4	2	-	-	-
45 - 49	1	-	-	-	-	-	-	-	1
50 +	-	-	-	-	-	-	-	-	-
Unknown - Inconnu	6	1	2	-	-	1	-	-	2
AMERICA, SOUTH - AMÉRIQUE DU SUD									
Colombia - Colombie[4]									
2017									
Total	577	217	172	74	25	12	6	3	68
0 - 14	25	22	3	-	-	-	-	-	-
15 - 19	91	62	18	4	-	-	-	-	7
20 - 24	145	59	41	19	2	3	-	-	21
25 - 29	115	37	29	17	7	1	1	-	23
30 - 34	83	20	34	9	6	4	2	1	7
35 - 39	73	13	34	11	6	3	2	1	3

14. Legally induced abortions by age and number of previous live births of women: latest available year, 2009 - 2018
Avortments provoqués légalement selon l'âge de la femme et selon le nombre des naissances vivantes précédentes :
dernière année disponible, 2009 - 2018 (continued - suite)

Continent, country or area, year and age / Continent, pays ou zone, année et âge	Total	Number of previous live births / Nombre des naissances vivantes précédentes							Unknown - Inconnu
		0	1	2	3	4	5	6+	
AMERICA, SOUTH - AMÉRIQUE DU SUD									
Colombia - Colombie[4]									
2017									
40 - 44	36	4	11	13	3	1	1	1	2
45 - 49	4	-	2	1	1	-	-	-	-
50 +	-	-	-	-	-	-	-	-	-
Unknown - Inconnu	5	-	-	-	-	-	-	-	5
Ecuador - Équateur[5]									
2017									
Total	30 331	...	...	...	...	...	...	...	...
0 - 14	281	...	...	...	...	...	...	...	...
15 - 19	4 327	...	...	...	...	...	...	...	...
20 - 24	7 013	...	...	...	...	...	...	...	...
25 - 29	6 836	...	...	...	...	...	...	...	...
30 - 34	5 512	...	...	...	...	...	...	...	...
35 - 39	4 182	...	...	...	...	...	...	...	...
40 - 44	1 880	...	...	...	...	...	...	...	...
45 - 49	272	...	...	...	...	...	...	...	...
50 +	28	...	...	...	...	...	...	...	...
ASIA - ASIE									
Armenia - Arménie									
2017									
Total	10 006	...	...	...	...	...	...	...	...
0 - 14	-	...	...	...	...	...	...	...	...
15 - 29	387	...	...	...	...	...	...	...	...
30 - 44	7 455	...	...	...	...	...	...	...	...
45 +	2 164	...	...	...	...	...	...	...	...
Azerbaijan - Azerbaïdjan									
2016									
Total	34 569	...	...	...	...	...	...	...	...
0 - 14	-	...	...	...	...	...	...	...	...
15 - 19	1 261	...	...	...	...	...	...	...	...
20 - 24	7 773	...	...	...	...	...	...	...	...
25 - 29	11 289	...	...	...	...	...	...	...	...
30 - 34	8 930	...	...	...	...	...	...	...	...
35 - 39	5 267	...	...	...	...	...	...	...	...
40 +	49	...	...	...	...	...	...	...	...
China, Hong Kong SAR - Chine, Hong Kong RAS									
2018									
Total	8 518	4 278	1 774	1 985	391	71	14	5	...
0 - 14	10	10	-	-	-	-	-	-	...
15 - 19	469	449	19	1	-	-	-	-	...
20 - 24	1 523	1 311	146	58	8	-	-	-	...
25 - 29	1 756	1 165	335	201	41	11	3	-	...
30 - 34	1 985	797	503	561	107	14	2	1	...
35 - 39	1 837	404	513	734	150	30	4	2	...
40 - 44	841	132	228	380	80	15	4	2	...
45 - 49	94	10	30	48	5	1	-	-	...
50 +	3	-	-	2	-	-	1	-	...
Georgia - Géorgie									
2017									
Total	24 937	...	...	...	...	...	...	...	...
0 - 14	1	...	...	...	...	...	...	...	...
15 - 19	596	...	...	...	...	...	...	...	...
20 - 24	4 064	...	...	...	...	...	...	...	...
25 - 29	6 993	...	...	...	...	...	...	...	...
30 - 34	6 625	...	...	...	...	...	...	...	...
35 - 39	4 637	...	...	...	...	...	...	...	...
40 - 44	1 826	...	...	...	...	...	...	...	...
45 - 49	177	...	...	...	...	...	...	...	...
50 +	18	...	...	...	...	...	...	...	...
Unknown - Inconnu	-	...	...	...	...	...	...	...	...

14. Legally induced abortions by age and number of previous live births of women: latest available year, 2009 - 2018
Avortments provoqués légalement selon l'âge de la femme et selon le nombre des naissances vivantes précédentes : dernière année disponible, 2009 - 2018 (continued - suite)

| Continent, country or area, year and age
Continent, pays ou zone, année et âge | Total | Number of previous live births
Nombre des naissances vivantes précédentes | | | | | | | | |
		0	1	2	3	4	5	6+	Unknown - Inconnu
ASIA - ASIE										
Israel - Israël[6]										
2016										
Total	18 032	7 174	2 557	3 575	2 886	1 127	384	329	...
0 - 14	36	36	-	-	-	-	-	-	...
15 - 19	1 596	1 515	62	15	3	1	-	-	...
20 - 24	3 254	2 535	422	229	50	12	5	1	...
25 - 29	3 715	1 761	740	666	388	117	32	11	...
30 - 34	3 857	847	718	1 102	768	285	87	50	...
35 - 39	3 472	326	417	1 046	1 026	406	128	123	...
40 - 44	1 888	131	178	468	587	273	120	131	...
45 - 49	201	21	17	47	63	30	11	12	...
50 +	13	2	3	2	1	3	1	1	...
Japan - Japon										
2017										
Total	164 621	...	...	...	...	...	...	...	...
0 - 14	218	...	...	...	...	...	...	...	...
15 - 19	13 910	...	...	...	...	...	...	...	...
20 - 24	39 270	...	...	...	...	...	...	...	...
25 - 29	32 222	...	...	...	...	...	...	...	...
30 - 34	33 082	...	...	...	...	...	...	...	...
35 - 39	29 641	...	...	...	...	...	...	...	...
40 - 44	14 876	...	...	...	...	...	...	...	...
45 - 49	1 363	...	...	...	...	...	...	...	...
50 +	11	...	...	...	...	...	...	...	...
Unknown - Inconnu	28	...	...	...	...	...	...	...	...
Kyrgyzstan - Kirghizstan[7]										
2018										
Total	19 176	...	...	...	...	...	...	...	...
0 - 19	1 476	...	...	...	...	...	...	...	...
20 - 24	4 463	...	...	...	...	...	...	...	...
25 - 29	5 301	...	...	...	...	...	...	...	...
30 - 34	4 137	...	...	...	...	...	...	...	...
35 +	3 799	...	...	...	...	...	...	...	...
Mongolia - Mongolie										
2017										
Total	17 530	...	...	...	...	...	...	...	...
0 - 19	921	...	...	...	...	...	...	...	...
20 - 24	2 950	...	...	...	...	...	...	...	...
25 - 29	4 918	...	...	...	...	...	...	...	...
30 - 34	4 408	...	...	...	...	...	...	...	...
35 - 39	2 815	...	...	...	...	...	...	...	...
40 - 44	1 375	...	...	...	...	...	...	...	...
45 - 49	139	...	...	...	...	...	...	...	...
50 +	4	...	...	...	...	...	...	...	...
Singapore - Singapour										
2017										
Total	6 815	2 990	1 344	1 700	537	^244	...	...	...
0 - 24	1 357	1 133	142	63	13	^6	...	...	...
25 - 29	1 627	1 007	308	213	62	^37	...	...	...
30 - 34	1 674	543	433	498	132	^68	...	...	...
35 - 39	1 492	243	330	630	213	^76	...	...	...
40 - 44	605	58	119	267	108	^53	...	...	...
45 +	60	6	12	29	9	^4	...	...	...
Unknown - Inconnu	-	-	-	-	-	^-	...	...	...
Tajikistan - Tadjikistan										
2017										
Total	13 963	...	...	...	...	...	...	...	...
0 - 14	...	...	...	...	...	...	...	...	...
15 - 17	8	...	...	...	...	...	...	...	...
18 - 19	1 068	...	...	...	...	...	...	...	...
20 - 34	10 085	...	...	...	...	...	...	...	...
35 +	2 802	...	...	...	...	...	...	...	...
Uzbekistan - Ouzbékistan										
2017										
Total	42 433	5 992	9 657	12 809	7 906	4 543	1 367	159	...
0 - 14	2	2	-	-	-	-	-	-	...
15 - 19	1 928	832	640	211	67	106	65	7	...
20 - 24	11 269	2 648	2 763	3 688	1 693	407	68	2	...
25 - 29	15 623	1 978	3 510	4 987	2 571	1 943	602	32	...

14. Legally induced abortions by age and number of previous live births of women: latest available year, 2009 - 2018
Avortments provoqués légalement selon l'âge de la femme et selon le nombre des naissances vivantes précédentes :
dernière année disponible, 2009 - 2018 (continued - suite)

Continent, country or area, year and age / Continent, pays ou zone, année et âge	Total	Number of previous live births / Nombre des naissances vivantes précédentes							Unknown - Inconnu
		0	1	2	3	4	5	6+	
ASIA - ASIE									
Uzbekistan - Ouzbékistan									
2017									
30 - 34	8 339	397	1 936	2 596	2 074	1 088	219	29	...
35 - 39	4 231	104	726	1 084	1 253	723	271	70	...
40 - 44	918	26	74	177	235	262	139	5	...
45 +	123	5	8	66	13	14	3	14	...
EUROPE									
Åland Islands - Îles d'Åland									
2012									
Total	60	31	12	10	5	-	2	-	...
0 - 14	-	-	-	-	-	-	-	-	...
15 - 19	9	9	-	-	-	-	-	-	...
20 - 24	15	11	3	1	-	-	-	-	...
25 - 29	17	6	4	4	1	-	2	-	...
30 - 34	7	2	1	3	1	-	-	-	...
35 - 39	7	1	3	1	2	-	-	-	...
40 - 44	5	2	1	1	1	-	-	-	...
45 - 49	-	-	-	-	-	-	-	-	...
50 +	-	-	-	-	-	-	-	-	...
2017									
Total	74	...	...	...	...	...	...	...	...
0 - 14	-	...	...	...	...	...	...	...	...
15 - 19	12	...	...	...	...	...	...	...	...
20 - 24	21	...	...	...	...	...	...	...	...
25 - 29	16	...	...	...	...	...	...	...	...
30 - 34	9	...	...	...	...	...	...	...	...
35 - 39	14	...	...	...	...	...	...	...	...
40 - 44	2	...	...	...	...	...	...	...	...
45 - 49	-	...	...	...	...	...	...	...	...
50 +	-	...	...	...	...	...	...	...	...
Albania - Albanie									
2017									
Total	1 000	267	204	329	134	49	14	3	...
0 - 14	-	-	-	-	-	-	-	-	...
15 - 19	36	28	6	1	1	-	-	-	...
20 - 24	145	97	26	19	2	1	-	-	...
25 - 29	243	85	67	70	17	2	1	1	...
30 - 34	241	30	54	100	42	11	3	1	...
35 - 39	212	18	36	90	44	19	4	1	...
40 - 44	96	5	12	35	24	15	5	-	...
45 - 49	23	3	2	12	4	1	1	-	...
50 +	2	1	-	1	-	-	-	-	...
Unknown - Inconnu	2	-	1	1	-	-	-	-	...
Belarus - Bélarus									
2017									
Total	25 249	...	...	...	...	...	...	...	...
0 - 14	8	...	...	...	...	...	...	...	...
15 - 19	847	...	...	...	...	...	...	...	...
20 - 24	3 651	...	...	...	...	...	...	...	...
25 - 29	6 299	...	...	...	...	...	...	...	...
30 - 34	7 776	...	...	...	...	...	...	...	...
35 - 39	4 636	...	...	...	...	...	...	...	...
40 - 44	1 818	...	...	...	...	...	...	...	...
45 +	214	...	...	...	...	...	...	...	...
Belgium - Belgique									
2011									
Total	19 578	9 145	4 266	3 698	1 636	581	174	78	...
0 - 14	87	86	1	-	-	-	-	-	...
15 - 19	2 575	2 339	207	28	1	-	-	-	...
20 - 24	5 027	3 430	1 070	425	87	12	3	-	...
25 - 29	4 688	1 992	1 249	983	332	104	20	8	...
30 - 34	3 745	863	997	1 131	512	176	46	20	...
35 - 39	2 454	349	538	796	483	184	70	34	...
40 - 44	923	78	188	308	207	99	30	13	...

14. Legally induced abortions by age and number of previous live births of women: latest available year, 2009 - 2018
Avortments provoqués légalement selon l'âge de la femme et selon le nombre des naissances vivantes précédentes : dernière année disponible, 2009 - 2018 (continued - suite)

Continent, country or area, year and age Continent, pays ou zone, année et âge	Total	Number of previous live births Nombre des naissances vivantes précédentes							
		0	1	2	3	4	5	6+	Unknown - Inconnu
EUROPE									
Belgium - Belgique									
2011									
45 - 49	78	7	16	27	14	6	5	3	...
50 +	1	1	-	-	-	-	-	-	...
Bulgaria - Bulgarie									
2017									
Total	24 287	...	...	...	...	...	...	...	...
0 - 14	115	...	...	...	...	...	...	...	...
15 - 19	2 057	...	...	...	...	...	...	...	...
20 - 24	4 589	...	...	...	...	...	...	...	...
25 - 29	6 119	...	...	...	...	...	...	...	...
30 - 34	5 640	...	...	...	...	...	...	...	...
35 - 39	4 229	...	...	...	...	...	...	...	...
40 - 44	1 431	...	...	...	...	...	...	...	...
45 - 49	99	...	...	...	...	...	...	...	...
50 +	8	...	...	...	...	...	...	...	...
Croatia - Croatie									
2017									
Total	2 416	782	482	678	301	78	29	16	50
0 - 14	2	2	-	-	-	-	-	-	-
15 - 19	155	133	14	3	-	-	-	-	5
20 - 24	420	282	74	33	13	6	-	-	12
25 - 29	458	166	107	106	46	8	6	3	16
30 - 34	602	114	133	213	92	26	10	7	7
35 - 39	550	66	111	230	99	22	8	6	8
40 - 44	219	19	42	88	49	16	3	-	2
45 - 49	8	-	1	5	2	-	-	-	-
50 +	2	-	-	-	-	-	2	-	-
Czechia - Tchéquie									
2017									
Total	19 415	5 706	5 068	6 042	1 818	508	155	118	...
0 - 14	34	34	-	-	-	-	-	-	...
15 - 19	1 222	1 004	174	39	5	-	-	-	...
20 - 24	3 298	1 774	972	404	120	23	5	-	...
25 - 29	4 240	1 542	1 234	998	308	111	38	9	...
30 - 34	4 137	756	1 281	1 479	412	114	58	37	...
35 - 39	4 006	426	948	1 875	539	146	31	41	...
40 - 44	2 265	161	430	1 135	395	93	21	30	...
45 - 49	207	9	28	108	38	21	2	1	...
50 +	6	-	1	4	1	-	-	-	...
Denmark - Danemark[8]									
2014									
Total	15 097	...	...	...	...	...	...	...	...
0 - 19	2 051	...	...	...	...	...	...	...	...
20 - 24	4 023	...	...	...	...	...	...	...	...
25 - 29	3 324	...	...	...	...	...	...	...	...
30 - 34	2 609	...	...	...	...	...	...	...	...
35 - 39	2 045	...	...	...	...	...	...	...	...
40 - 44	967	...	...	...	...	...	...	...	...
45 +	78	...	...	...	...	...	...	...	...
Estonia - Estonie[9]									
2017									
Total	3 997	1 150	1 153	1 141	408	99	27	15	4
0 - 14	7	7	-	-	-	-	-	-	-
15 - 19	306	259	40	7	-	-	-	-	-
20 - 24	745	426	214	89	10	5	-	-	1
25 - 29	947	281	376	223	52	11	3	1	-
30 - 34	902	116	275	346	117	34	8	5	1
35 - 39	752	40	174	345	150	28	8	5	2
40 - 44	305	19	70	119	68	19	6	4	-
45 - 49	33	2	4	12	11	2	2	-	-
50 +	-	-	-	-	-	-	-	-	-
Faeroe Islands - Îles Féroé									
2016									
Total	26	...	...	...	...	...	...	...	...
0 - 14	-	...	...	...	...	...	...	...	...
15 - 19	3	...	...	...	...	...	...	...	...
20 - 24	6	...	...	...	...	...	...	...	...
25 - 29	7	...	...	...	...	...	...	...	...

14. Legally induced abortions by age and number of previous live births of women: latest available year, 2009 - 2018
Avortments provoqués légalement selon l'âge de la femme et selon le nombre des naissances vivantes précédentes :
dernière année disponible, 2009 - 2018 (continued - suite)

Continent, country or area, year and age Continent, pays ou zone, année et âge	Total	Number of previous live births Nombre des naissances vivantes précédentes							Unknown - Inconnu
		0	1	2	3	4	5	6+	
EUROPE									
Faeroe Islands - Îles Féroé									
2016									
30 - 34	3	...	...	...	...	...	...	...	...
35 - 39	6	...	...	...	...	...	...	...	...
40 - 44	-	...	...	...	...	...	...	...	...
45 - 49	1	...	...	...	...	...	...	...	...
50 + ...	-	...	...	...	...	...	...	...	...
Finland - Finlande									
2017									
Total	9 332	4 139	1 753	1 820	824	273	82	48	393
0 - 14	22	21	-	-	-	-	-	-	1
15 - 19	1 065	944	56	-	-	-	-	-	65
20 - 24	2 358	1 560	427	190	29	-	-	-	152
25 - 29	2 193	937	513	436	164	48	4	1	90
30 - 34	1 825	405	404	574	262	104	21	11	44
35 - 39	1 303	197	251	434	246	86	38	19	32
40 - 44	516	68	91	173	111	31	17	17	8
45 - 49	50	7	11	13	12	4	2	-	1
50 + ...	-	-	-	-	-	-	-	-	-
France[10]									
2009									
Total[11]	208 290	...	...	...	...	...	...	...	...
15 - 19	29 004	...	...	...	...	...	...	...	...
20 - 24	52 360	...	...	...	...	...	...	...	...
25 - 29	46 237								
30 - 34	36 351	...	...	...	...	...	...	...	...
35 - 39	30 125	...	...	...	...	...	...	...	...
40 - 44	12 805	...	...	...	...	...	...	...	...
45 - 49	1 408	...	...	...	...	...	...	...	...
Germany - Allemagne									
2017									
Total	101 209	39 627	24 036	24 069	8 995	2 906	^1 576	...	...
0 - 14	280	280	-	-	-	-	^-	...	...
15 - 19	7 633	6 795	708	125	5	-	^-	...	...
20 - 24	19 942	12 802	4 431	2 054	519	96	^40	...	...
25 - 29	24 859	10 202	6 785	5 388	1 815	473	^196	...	...
30 - 34	23 127	5 729	6 080	7 193	2 714	954	^457	...	...
35 - 39	17 643	2 809	4 322	6 379	2 646	916	^571	...	...
40 - 44	7 018	936	1 557	2 657	1 175	422	^271	...	...
45 - 49	691	73	151	266	119	44	^38	...	...
50 + ...	16	1	2	7	2	1	^3	...	...
Hungary - Hongrie									
2013									
Total	34 891	9 707	8 781	8 536	4 632	1 821	808	606	-
0 - 14	168	165	3	-	-	-	-	-	-
15 - 19	4 423	3 395	869	132	25	2	-	-	-
20 - 24	7 335	3 135	2 182	1 309	542	134	28	5	-
25 - 29	6 935	1 622	1 902	1 692	1 007	450	173	89	-
30 - 34	6 839	837	1 737	2 032	1 229	520	277	207	-
35 - 39	6 624	451	1 528	2 331	1 325	521	240	228	-
40 - 44	2 406	94	526	976	470	184	86	70	-
45 - 49	160	8	34	63	34	10	4	7	-
50 + ...	1	-	-	1	-	-	-	-	-
Unknown - Inconnu	-	-	-	-	-	-	-	-	-
2014									
Total	32 663	...	...	...	...	...	...	...	...
0 - 14	161	...	...	...	...	...	...	...	...
15 - 19	4 245	...	...	...	...	...	...	...	...
20 - 24	7 109	...	...	...	...	...	...	...	...
25 - 29	6 562	...	...	...	...	...	...	...	...
30 - 34	6 035	...	...	...	...	...	...	...	...
35 - 39	6 066	...	...	...	...	...	...	...	...
40 - 44	2 325	...	...	...	...	...	...	...	...
45 - 49	157	...	...	...	...	...	...	...	...
50 + ...	3	...	...	...	...	...	...	...	...
Unknown - Inconnu	-	...	...	...	...	...	...	...	...

14. Legally induced abortions by age and number of previous live births of women: latest available year, 2009 - 2018
Avortments provoqués légalement selon l'âge de la femme et selon le nombre des naissances vivantes précédentes : dernière année disponible, 2009 - 2018 (continued - suite)

Continent, country or area, year and age — Continent, pays ou zone, année et âge	Number of previous live births — Nombre des naissances vivantes précédentes								
	Total	0	1	2	3	4	5	6+	Unknown - Inconnu
EUROPE									
Iceland - Islande									
2011									
Total	969	415	249	186	83	29	5	2	-
0 - 14	2	2	-	-	-	-	-	-	-
15 - 19	174	155	16	3	-	-	-	-	-
20 - 24	289	182	84	21	2	-	-	-	-
25 - 29	187	46	73	52	10	6	-	-	-
30 - 34	169	25	40	56	36	11	1	-	-
35 - 39	109	5	29	45	20	9	1	-	-
40 - 44	35	-	7	8	12	3	3	2	-
45 - 49	4	-	-	1	3	-	-	-	-
50 +	-	-	-	-	-	-	-	-	-
Unknown - Inconnu	-	-	-	-	-	-	-	-	-
Italy - Italie									
2016									
Total	84 874	32 598	19 733	21 772	6 907	1 450	352	148	1 914
0 - 14	165	156	-	-	-	-	-	-	9
15 - 19	6 275	5 415	486	73	11	5	-	-	285
20 - 24	14 675	9 882	2 960	1 136	225	26	3	7	436
25 - 29	17 314	7 436	4 510	3 709	984	186	37	24	428
30 - 34	18 188	4 937	4 857	5 689	1 852	391	79	34	349
35 - 39	17 724	3 103	4 433	6 875	2 343	499	151	60	260
40 - 44	9 562	1 513	2 248	3 910	1 360	308	72	21	130
45 - 49	911	136	225	367	127	34	10	1	11
50 +	30	10	6	8	3	1	-	1	1
Unknown - Inconnu	30	10	8	5	2	-	-	-	5
Latvia - Lettonie									
2017									
Total	3 917	...	...	...	...	...	...	...	...
0 - 14	8	...	...	...	...	...	...	...	...
15 - 19	183	...	...	...	...	...	...	...	...
20 - 24	617	...	...	...	...	...	...	...	...
25 - 29	982	...	...	...	...	...	...	...	...
30 - 34	938	...	...	...	...	...	...	...	...
35 - 39	744	...	...	...	...	...	...	...	...
40 - 44	416	...	...	...	...	...	...	...	...
45 - 49	29	...	...	...	...	...	...	...	...
50 +	-	...	...	...	...	...	...	...	...
Unknown - Inconnu	-	...	...	...	...	...	...	...	...
Lithuania - Lituanie									
2017									
Total	4 294	-	-	-	-	-	-	-	4 294
0 - 14	1	-	-	-	-	-	-	-	1
15 - 19	226	-	-	-	-	-	-	-	226
20 - 24	736	-	-	-	-	-	-	-	736
25 - 29	992	-	-	-	-	-	-	-	992
30 - 34	987	-	-	-	-	-	-	-	987
35 - 39	889	-	-	-	-	-	-	-	889
40 - 44	401	-	-	-	-	-	-	-	401
45 - 49	62	-	-	-	-	-	-	-	62
50 +	...	-	-	-	-	-	-	-	...
Unknown - Inconnu	-	-	-	-	-	-	-	-	...
Poland - Pologne[12]									
2017									
Total	1 057	...	...	...	...	...	...	...	...
0 - 19	18	...	...	...	...	...	...	...	...
20 - 24	18	...	...	...	...	...	...	...	...
25 - 29	81	...	...	...	...	...	...	...	...
30 - 34	226	...	...	...	...	...	...	...	...
35 - 39	287	...	...	...	...	...	...	...	...
40 +	427	...	...	...	...	...	...	...	...
Portugal									
2017*									
Total	15 492	6 757	4 417	3 187	856	203	48	24	-
0 - 14	46	46	-	-	-	-	-	-	-
15 - 19	1 438	1 328	100	9	1	-	-	-	-
20 - 24	3 563	2 410	887	233	30	1	1	1	-
25 - 29	3 469	1 559	1 139	598	147	21	5	-	-
30 - 34	2 937	783	1 008	834	232	60	13	7	-

14. Legally induced abortions by age and number of previous live births of women: latest available year, 2009 - 2018
Avortements provoqués légalement selon l'âge de la femme et selon le nombre des naissances vivantes précédentes : dernière année disponible, 2009 - 2018 (continued - suite)

Continent, country or area, year and age / Continent, pays ou zone, année et âge	Total	Number of previous live births / Nombre des naissances vivantes précédentes								Unknown - Inconnu
		0	1	2	3	4	5	6+	

EUROPE

Portugal
2017*

35 - 39	2 608	451	854	936	267	76	15	9	-
40 - 44	1 277	142	391	528	159	39	13	5	-
45 - 49	118	19	31	40	19	6	1	2	-
50 +	-	-	-	-	-	-	-	-	-
Unknown - Inconnu	36	19	7	9	1	-	-	-	-

Republic of Moldova - République de Moldova
2012

Total	14 838	...	...	...	...	...	...	...	...
0 - 14	9	...	...	...	...	...	...	...	...
15 - 19	1 383	...	...	...	...	...	...	...	...
Unknown - Inconnu	13 446	...	...	...	...	...	...	...	...

Romania - Roumanie
2017

Total	56 238	...	...	...	...	...	...	...	...
0 - 14	289	...	...	...	...	...	...	...	...
15 - 19	5 267	...	...	...	...	...	...	...	...
20 - 24	10 493	...	...	...	...	...	...	...	...
25 - 29	13 114	...	...	...	...	...	...	...	...
30 - 34	12 349	...	...	...	...	...	...	...	...
35 - 39	9 911	...	...	...	...	...	...	...	...
40 - 44	4 398	...	...	...	...	...	...	...	...
45 - 49	399	...	...	...	...	...	...	...	...
50 +	18	...	...	...	...	...	...	...	...
Unknown - Inconnu	-	...	...	...	...	...	...	...	...

Russian Federation - Fédération de Russie
2013

Total	1 012 399	...	...	...	...	...	...	...	...
0 - 14	474	...	...	...	...	...	...	...	...
15 - 19	47 732	...	...	...	...	...	...	...	...
20 - 24	203 802	...	...	...	...	...	...	...	...
25 - 29	285 859	...	...	...	...	...	...	...	...
30 - 34	242 437	...	...	...	...	...	...	...	...
35 - 39	165 856	...	...	...	...	...	...	...	...
40 - 44	61 059	...	...	...	...	...	...	...	...
45 - 49	5 029	...	...	...	...	...	...	...	...
50 +	151	...	...	...	...	...	...	...	...

Serbia - Serbie[13]
2017

Total	10 378	2 951	2 022	3 630	1 260	344	103	68	...
0 - 14	4	4	-	-	-	-	-	-	...
15 - 19	390	321	40	20	7	2	-	-	...
20 - 24	1 392	853	261	188	64	26	-	-	...
25 - 29	2 090	739	455	597	193	74	25	7	...
30 - 34	2 588	500	539	1 032	353	99	43	22	...
35 - 39	2 570	356	480	1 174	407	99	29	25	...
40 - 44	1 232	160	228	564	218	42	6	14	...
45 - 49	106	16	18	53	17	2	-	-	...
50 +	6	2	1	2	1	-	-	-	...

Slovakia - Slovaquie
2017

Total	9 082	2 798	2 695	2 331	794	214	104	146	-
0 - 14	13	13	-	-	-	-	-	-	-
15 - 19	571	445	102	19	4	1	-	-	-
20 - 24	1 410	729	393	215	62	8	1	2	-
25 - 29	2 009	748	606	398	157	57	26	17	-
30 - 34	2 229	510	768	618	196	51	39	47	-
35 - 39	1 901	278	574	697	223	63	26	40	-
40 - 44	883	68	241	359	135	30	11	39	-
45 - 49	64	6	10	25	17	4	1	1	-
50 +	2	1	1	-	-	-	-	-	-
Unknown - Inconnu	-	-	-	-	-	-	-	-	-

Slovenia - Slovénie
2017

Total	3 529	1 145	787	1 096	330	51	21	13	86
0 - 14	1	1	-	-	-	-	-	-	-
15 - 19	176	157	11	1	1	-	-	-	6

14. Legally induced abortions by age and number of previous live births of women: latest available year, 2009 - 2018
Avortments provoqués légalement selon l'âge de la femme et selon le nombre des naissances vivantes précédentes : dernière année disponible, 2009 - 2018 (continued - suite)

Continent, country or area, year and age / Continent, pays ou zone, année et âge	Total	Number of previous live births — Nombre des naissances vivantes précédentes							
		0	1	2	3	4	5	6+	Unknown - Inconnu
EUROPE									
Slovenia - Slovénie									
2017									
20 - 24	566	410	78	36	9	2	1	-	30
25 - 29	667	284	177	149	31	4	3	4	15
30 - 34	861	168	234	341	79	14	6	2	17
35 - 39	822	94	206	363	117	21	7	3	11
40 - 44	401	29	78	183	89	9	4	4	5
45 - 49	34	2	3	23	4	1	-	-	-
50 +	1	-	-	-	-	-	-	-	1
Unknown - Inconnu	-	-	-	-	-	-	-	-	-
Spain - Espagne									
2017									
Total	94 123	43 130	24 352	18 966	5 502	^1 562	...	...	611
0 - 14	345	345	-	-	-	^_	...	...	
15 - 19	9 410	8 389	875	132	13	^1	...	...	
20 - 24	19 667	13 583	4 411	1 373	246	^51	...	...	3
25 - 29	20 381	9 841	5 839	3 502	925	^216	...	...	58
30 - 34	19 551	6 126	5 896	5 338	1 611	^422	...	...	158
35 - 39	17 037	3 612	5 050	5 792	1 781	^562	...	...	240
40 - 44	7 145	1 166	2 125	2 593	855	^278	...	...	128
45 - 49	587	68	156	236	71	^32	...	...	24
Sweden - Suède[14]									
2010									
Total	37 693	19 435	6 240	7 203	2 993	814	264	137	607
0 - 14	191	178	4	1	-	-	-	-	8
15 - 19	6 199	5 826	214	14	2	-	-	-	143
20 - 24	10 068	7 708	1 587	480	76	5	2	2	208
25 - 29	7 495	3 558	1 838	1 476	385	79	28	10	121
30 - 34	6 124	1 424	1 336	2 113	884	208	77	18	64
35 - 39	5 073	572	862	2 073	1 053	318	88	62	45
40 - 44	2 248	137	353	948	524	174	58	39	15
45 - 49	238	11	33	85	66	27	10	4	2
50 +	56	20	13	13	3	3	1	2	1
Unknown - Inconnu	1	1	-	-	-	-	-	-	-
Switzerland - Suisse[15]									
2017									
Total	9 863	1 902	758	811	252	88	...	...	6 052
0 - 14	4	2	-	-	-	-	...	...	2
15 - 19	686	267	13	3	-	-	...	...	403
20 - 24	1 891	597	98	28	2	1	...	...	1 165
25 - 29	2 288	537	185	135	35	8	...	...	1 388
30 - 34	2 287	289	237	257	73	22	...	...	1 409
35 - 39	1 800	154	157	239	77	38	...	...	1 135
40 - 44	790	41	59	133	51	18	...	...	488
45 - 49	98	7	5	15	13	1	...	...	57
50 +	5	-	2	1	-	-	...	...	2
Unknown - Inconnu	14	8	2	-	1	-	...	...	3
Ukraine[16]									
2017									
Total	94 665	...	...	...	...	...	...	...	...
0 - 14	39	...	...	...	...	...	...	...	...
15 - 19	4 221	...	...	...	...	...	...	...	...
20 - 34	68 707	...	...	...	...	...	...	...	...
35 +	21 698	...	...	...	...	...	...	...	...
United Kingdom of Great Britain and Northern Ireland - Royaume-Uni de Grande-Bretagne et d'Irlande du Nord[17]									
2016									
Total	197 659	...	...	...	...	...	...	...	...
0 - 14	492	...	...	...	...	...	...	...	...
15 - 19	25 761	...	...	...	...	...	...	...	...
20 - 24	53 834	...	...	...	...	...	...	...	...
25 - 29	49 248	...	...	...	...	...	...	...	...
30 - 34	36 146	...	...	...	...	...	...	...	...
35 - 39	23 219	...	...	...	...	...	...	...	...
40 - 44	8 181	...	...	...	...	...	...	...	...
45 - 49	749	...	...	...	...	...	...	...	...

14. Legally induced abortions by age and number of previous live births of women: latest available year, 2009 - 2018
Avortments provoqués légalement selon l'âge de la femme et selon le nombre des naissances vivantes précédentes :
dernière année disponible, 2009 - 2018 (continued - suite)

Continent, country or area, year and age — Continent, pays ou zone, année et âge	Number of previous live births — Nombre des naissances vivantes précédentes								
	Total	0	1	2	3	4	5	6+	Unknown - Inconnu
EUROPE									
United Kingdom of Great Britain and Northern Ireland - Royaume-Uni de Grande-Bretagne et d'Irlande du Nord[17]									
2016									
50 +	29	...	...	...	...	...	...	...	...
Unknown - Inconnu	-	...	...	...	...	...	...	...	...
OCEANIA - OCÉANIE									
Guam									
2015									
Total	263	...	...	...	...	...	...	...	...
0 - 14	-	...	...	...	...	...	...	...	...
15 - 19	20	...	...	...	...	...	...	...	...
20 - 24	89	...	...	...	...	...	...	...	...
25 - 29	60	...	...	...	...	...	...	...	...
30 - 34	52	...	...	...	...	...	...	...	...
35 - 39	27	...	...	...	...	...	...	...	...
40 - 44	12	...	...	...	...	...	...	...	...
45 - 49	2	...	...	...	...	...	...	...	...
50 +	-	...	...	...	...	...	...	...	...
Unknown - Inconnu	1	...	...	...	...	...	...	...	...
New Zealand - Nouvelle-Zélande									
2015									
Total	13 155	5 665	2 715	2 728	1 264	473	193	117	...
0 - 14	32	32	-	-	-	-	-	-	...
15 - 19	1 635	1 393	208	31	3	-	-	-	...
20 - 24	3 777	2 257	891	470	129	27	3	-	...
25 - 29	3 256	1 183	764	744	376	129	44	16	...
30 - 34	2 309	521	483	712	344	149	63	37	...
35 - 39	1 483	210	261	510	280	117	60	45	...
40 - 44	598	59	94	238	121	48	21	17	...
45 +	65	10	14	23	11	3	2	2	...
2017									
Total	13 285	5 656	2 706	^4 923	...	...	...	...	...
0 - 14	30	...	...	...	...	...	...	...	...
15 - 19	1 414	...	...	...	...	...	...	...	...
20 - 24	3 599	...	...	...	...	...	...	...	...
25 - 29	3 632	...	...	...	...	...	...	...	...
30 - 34	2 419	...	...	...	...	...	...	...	...
35 - 39	1 562	...	...	...	...	...	...	...	...
40 - 44	584	...	...	...	...	...	...	...	...
45 +	45	...	...	...	...	...	...	...	...

FOOTNOTES - NOTES

Italics: estimates which are less reliable. - Italiques : estimations moins sûres.

* Provisional. - Données provisoires.

^ Indicates an open-ended group, for example 4+. - indique un groupe d'âge ouvert, par exemple 4 ou plus.

[1] Source: Bermuda Hospitals Board (BHB). - Source : Conseil des hôpitaux des Bermudes.

[2] Excluding abortions performed in private hospitals. - Non comprises les interruptions volontaires de grossesse effectuées dans des hôpitaux privés.

[3] Refers to residence of the mother. To calculate the total number of abortions, only foetal deaths of less than 20 weeks of gestation were considered. Data refer to 'Therapeutic Abortions'. According to Mexican law, only induced abortions, prescribed by medical reasons or induced because of pregnancy coming from sexual aggression, are considered as legal; data refer only to the former. Excluding abortions in the country by women with usual residence outside of the country. - Correspond à la résidence de la mère. Seuls les morts fœtales survenues à moins de 20 semaines de gestation ont été prises en compte aux fins du calcul du nombre total d'avortements. Les données se rapportent aux « interruptions volontaires de grossesse pour des motifs thérapeutiques ». D'après la loi mexicaine, seuls sont considérés légaux les avortements déclenchés pour des raisons médicales ou parce que la grossesse est le résultat d'une agression sexuelle; les données se réfèrent seulement à la première. Hors avortements dans le pays par des femmes avec résidence habituelle en dehors du pays.

[4] Affected by underreporting since, by law, legally induced abortions are not reported directly to the civil registry. - Font l'objet d'une sous-déclaration, toutes les interruptions volontaires de grossesse pratiquées légalement n'étant pas déclarées dans la mesure où la loi n'impose pas de les inscrire directement au registre civil.

[5] Data refer to abortions registered in hospitals due to pregnancy complications. - Les données renvoient aux avortements enregistrés dans les hôpitaux du fait des complications de la grossesse.

[6] Data refer to applications to commissions for termination of pregnancy and not to authorizations. Includes data for East Jerusalem and Israeli residents in certain other territories under occupation by Israeli military forces since June 1967. - Les données relatives aux avortements provoqués légalement se rapportent aux demandes d'autorisation et non aux autorisations elles-mêmes. Y compris les données pour Jérusalem-Est et les résidents israéliens dans certains autres territoires occupés depuis 1967 par les forces armées israéliennes.

[7] Based on administrative reporting of the Ministry of Health. - Les données reposent sur les rapports administratifs du Ministère de la santé.

[8] Excluding Faeroe Islands and Greenland shown separately, if available. Unrevised data. - Non compris les Îles Féroé et le Groenland, qui font l'objet de rubriques distinctes, si disponible. Les données n'ont pas été révisées.

[9] Data refer to resident population only. - Pour la population résidante seulement.

[10] Unrevised data. - Les données n'ont pas été révisées.

[11] Data refer to women between 15 and 49 years of age. - Le total se rapporte uniquement aux femmes dont l'âge est compris entre 15 et 49 ans.

[12] Based on hospital and polyclinic records. - D'après les registres des hôpitaux et des polycliniques.

[13] Excludes data for Kosovo and Metohia. - Sans les données pour le Kosovo et Metohie.

[14] Data refer to abortions by previous deliveries of mother rather than previous live births of mother. - Avortements selon les accouchements précédents de la mère plutôt que selon les naissances vivantes de la mère.

[15] Data refer to termination of pregnancy for women who are Switzerland residents. - Les données portent sur les interruptions de grossesse pratiquées sur des femmes qui résident en Suisse.

[16] The Government of Ukraine has informed the United Nations that it is not in a position to provide statistical data concerning the Autonomous Republic of Crimea and the city of Sevastopol. - Le gouvernement Ukrainien a informé l'ONU qu'il n'est pas en mesure de fournir des données statistiques concernant la République autonome de Crimée et la ville de Sébastopol.

[17] Excluding Channel Islands (Guernsey and Jersey) and Isle of Man, shown separately, if available. Excluding Northern Ireland. - Non compris les Îles Anglo-Normandes (Guernesey et Jersey) et l'île de Man, qui font l'objet de rubriques distinctes, si disponible. Non compris l'Irlande du Nord.

442

Table 15 - *Demographic Yearbook 2018*

Table 15 presents infant deaths and infant mortality rates by urban/rural residence for as many years as possible between 2014 and 2018.

Description of variables: Infant deaths are deaths of live-born infants under one year of age.

Statistics on the number of infant deaths are obtained from civil registers unless otherwise noted. Infant mortality rates are, in most instances, calculated from data on registered infant deaths and registered live births for a country or area where civil registration is considered reliable (that is, with an estimated completeness of 90 per cent or more).

The urban/rural classification of infant deaths is that provided by each reporting country or area; it is presumed to be based on the national census definitions of urban population that have been set forth at the end of the technical notes of table 6.

Rate computation: Infant mortality rates are the annual number of deaths of infants under one year of age per 1 000 live births (as shown in table 9) in the same year.

Rates by urban/rural residence are the annual number of infant deaths, in the appropriate urban or rural category, per 1 000 corresponding live births (as shown in table 9). These rates have been calculated by the United Nations Statistics Division.

Rates presented in this table have been limited to those countries or areas having at least a total of 30 infant deaths in a given year and for which the quality code is represented by a "C" or a symbol "|".

Reliability of data: Each country or area has been asked to indicate the estimated completeness of the infant deaths recorded in its civil register. These national assessments are indicated by the quality codes "C", "U" and "|" that appear in the first column of this table.

"C" indicates that the data are estimated to be virtually complete, that is, representing at least 90 per cent of the infant deaths occurring each year, while "U" indicates that data are estimated to be incomplete that is, representing less than 90 per cent of the infant deaths occurring each year. The code "|" indicates that the source of data is not civil registration, but it is still considered reliable. The code "..." indicates that no information was provided regarding completeness.

Data from civil registers that are reported as incomplete or of unknown completeness (coded "U" or "...") are considered unreliable. They appear in italics in this table; rates are not computed for data so coded.

Limitations: Statistics on infant deaths are subject to the same qualifications as have been set forth for vital statistics and particularly for death statistics discussed in section 4 of the Technical Notes.

The reliability of the data, an indication of which is described above, is an important factor in considering the limitations. In addition, some infant deaths are tabulated by date of registration and not by date of occurrence; these have been indicated by a plus sign "+". Whenever the lag between the date of occurrence and date of registration is prolonged and, therefore, a large proportion of the infant-death registrations are delayed, infant-death statistics for any given year may be seriously affected.

Another factor that limits international comparability is the practice of some countries or areas not to include in infant-death statistics infants who were born alive but died before the registration of the birth or within the first 24 hours of life, thus underestimating the total number of infant deaths. Statistics of this type are footnoted.

The method of reckoning age at death for infants may also introduce non-comparability. If year alone, rather than completed minutes, hours, days and months elapsed since birth, is used to calculate age at time of death, many of the infants who died during the eleventh month of life and some of those who died at younger ages will be classified as having completed one year of age and thus be excluded. The effect would be to underestimate the number of infant deaths. Information on this factor is given in footnotes when known. Reckoning of infant age is further discussed in the technical notes for table 16.

In addition, infant mortality rates are subject to the limitations of the data on live births that have been used as denominators for these rates. These have been set forth in the technical notes for table 9.

Because the two components of the infant mortality rate, infant deaths in the numerator and live births in the denominator, are both obtained from systems of civil registration, the limitations which affect live birth statistics are very similar to those which have been mentioned above in connection with the infant death statistics. It is important to consider the reliability of the data (the completeness of registration) and the method of tabulation (by date of occurrence or by date of registration) of live birth statistics as well as infant death statistics, both of which are used to calculate infant mortality rates. The quality code and use of italics to indicate unreliable data presented in this table refer only to infant deaths. Similarly, the indication of the basis of tabulation (the use of the symbol "+" to indicate data tabulated by date of registration) presented in this table also refers only to infant deaths. Table 9 provides the corresponding information for live births.

If the registration of infant deaths is more complete than the registration of live births, then infant mortality rates would be biased upwards. If, however, the registration of live births is more complete than registration of infant deaths, infant mortality rates would be biased downwards.

Infant mortality rates may be seriously affected by the practice of some countries or areas of not considering infants that were born alive but died before the registration of the birth or within the first 24 hours of life as live birth and subsequently infant death. Although this practice results in both the number of infant deaths in the numerator and the number of live births in the denominator being underestimated, its impact is greater on the numerator of the infant mortality rate. As a result, this practice causes infant mortality rates to be biased downwards.

Infant mortality rates will also be underestimated if the method of reckoning age at death results in an underestimation of the number of infant deaths. This point has been discussed above.

Because of all these factors care should be taken in comparing infant mortality rates.

With respect to the method of calculating infant mortality rates used in this table, it should be noted that no adjustment was made to take account of the fact that a proportion of the infant deaths that occur during a given year are deaths of infants that were born during the preceding year and hence are not taken from the universe of births used to compute the rates. However, unless the number of live births or infant deaths is changing rapidly, the error involved is insignificant.

The comparability of data by urban/rural residence is affected by the national definitions of urban and rural used in tabulating these data. It is assumed, in the absence of specific information to the contrary, that the definitions of urban and rural used in connection with the national population census were also used in the compilation of the vital statistics for each country or area. However, it cannot be denied that, for some countries or areas, different definitions of urban and rural may be used for the vital statistics data and the population census data respectively. When known, the definitions of urban used in national population censuses are presented at the end of the technical notes for table 6. As discussed in detail in the technical notes for table 6, these definitions vary considerably from one country or area to another.

Urban/rural differentials in infant mortality rates may also be affected by whether the infant deaths and live births have been tabulated in terms of place of occurrence or place of usual residence. This problem is discussed in more detail in section 4.1.4.1 of the Technical Notes.

Earlier data: Infant deaths and infant mortality rates have been shown in previous issues of the *Demographic Yearbook*. For more information on specific topics and years for which data are reported, readers should consult the Historical Index.

Tableau 15 – *Annuaire démographique 2018*

Le tableau 15 présente des données sur les décès d'enfants de moins d'un an et les taux de mortalité infantile selon le lieu de résidence (zone urbaine ou rurale) pour le plus grand nombre d'années possible entre 2014 et 2018.

Description des variables : les chiffres se rapportent aux décès d'enfants de moins d'un an.

Sauf indication contraire, les statistiques concernant le nombre de décès d'enfants de moins d'un an sont établies à partir des registres de l'état civil. Dans la plupart des cas, les taux de mortalité infantile sont calculés à partir des données relatives aux décès enregistrés d'enfants de moins d'un an et aux naissances vivantes enregistrées dans un pays ou une zone lorsque les registres de l'état civil sont jugés fiables (exhaustivité estimée à 90 p. 100 ou plus).

La classification des décès d'enfants de moins d'un an selon le lieu de résidence (zone urbaine ou rurale) est celle qui a été communiquée par chaque pays ou zone ; on part du principe qu'elle repose sur les définitions de la population urbaine utilisées pour les recensements nationaux, telles qu'elles sont reproduites à la fin des notes techniques du tableau 6.

Calcul des taux : Les taux de mortalité infantile représentent le nombre annuel de décès d'enfants de moins d'un an pour 1 000 naissances vivantes (présentées dans le tableau 9) survenues pendant la même année.

Les taux selon le lieu de résidence (zone urbaine ou rurale) représentent le nombre annuel de décès d'enfants de moins d'un an, classés selon la catégorie urbaine ou rurale appropriée pour 1 000 naissances vivantes survenues parmi la population correspondante (présentées dans le tableau 9). Ces taux ont été calculés par la Division des statistiques de l'Organisation des Nations Unies.

Les taux présentés dans ce tableau se rapportent seulement aux pays ou zones où l'on a enregistré au moins un total de 30 décès d'enfants de moins d'un an au cours d'une année donnée et pour lesquels le code de qualité est soit "C" ou "|".

Fiabilité des données : il a été demandé à chaque pays ou zone d'indiquer le degré estimatif de complétude des données sur les décès d'enfants de moins d'un an figurant dans ses registres d'état civil. Ces évaluations nationales sont signalées par les codes de qualité "C", "U" et "|" qui apparaissent dans la deuxième colonne du tableau.

La lettre "C" indique que les données sont jugées à peu près complètes, c'est-à-dire qu'elles représentent au moins 90 p. 100 des décès d'enfants de moins d'un an survenus chaque année ; la lettre "U" signifie que les données sont jugées incomplètes, c'est-à-dire qu'elles représentent moins de 90 p.100 des décès d'enfants de moins d'un an survenus chaque année. Le symbole 'I' indique que la source des données n'est pas un registre de l'état civil, mais est quand même considérée fiable. Le code "..." dénote qu'aucun renseignement n'a été communiqué quant à la complétude des données.

Les données provenant des registres de l'état civil qui sont déclarées incomplètes ou dont le degré de complétude n'est pas connu (code "U" ou "...") sont jugées douteuses. Elles apparaissent en italique dans le tableau ; les taux, dans ces cas là, n'ont pas été calculés.

Insuffisance des données : les statistiques des décès d'enfants de moins d'un an appellent toutes les réserves qui ont été formulées à propos des statistiques de l'état civil en général et des statistiques concernant les décès en particulier (voir la section 4 des notes techniques).

La fiabilité des données, au sujet de laquelle des indications ont été fournies plus haut, est un facteur important. Il faut également tenir compte du fait que, dans certains cas, les données relatives aux décès d'enfants de moins d'un an sont exploitées selon la date de l'enregistrement et non la date de l'événement ; ces cas ont été signalés par le signe "+". Chaque fois que le décalage entre l'événement et son enregistrement est grand et qu'une forte proportion des décès d'enfants de moins d'un an fait l'objet d'un enregistrement tardif, les statistiques des décès d'enfants de moins d'un an pour une année donnée peuvent être considérablement faussées.

Un autre facteur qui nuit à la comparabilité internationale est la pratique de certains pays ou zones qui consiste à ne pas inclure dans les statistiques des décès d'enfants de moins d'un an les enfants nés vivants mais décédés avant l'enregistrement de leur naissance ou dans les 24 heures qui ont suivi la naissance, pratique qui conduit à sous-estimer le nombre total de décès d'enfants de moins d'un an. Quand pareil facteur a joué, cela a été signalé en note.

Les méthodes appliquées pour calculer l'âge au moment du décès peuvent également nuire à la comparabilité des données. Si l'on utilise à cet effet l'année seulement, et non pas les minutes, heures, jours et mois qui se sont écoulés depuis la naissance, de nombreux enfants décédés au cours du onzième mois qui a suivi leur naissance et certains enfants décédés encore plus jeunes seront classés comme décédés à un an révolu et donc exclus des données. Cette pratique conduit à sous-estimer le nombre de décès d'enfants de moins d'un an. Les renseignements dont on dispose sur ce facteur apparaissent en note à la fin du tableau. La question du calcul de l'âge au moment du décès est examinée plus en détail dans les notes techniques se rapportant au tableau 16.

Les taux de mortalité infantile appellent en outre toutes les réserves qui ont été formulées à propos des statistiques des naissances vivantes qui ont servi à leur calcul (voir à ce sujet les notes techniques relatives au tableau 9).

Les deux composantes du taux de mortalité infantile - décès d'enfants de moins d'un an au numérateur et naissances vivantes au dénominateur - étant obtenues à partir des registres de l'état civil, les statistiques des naissances vivantes appellent des réserves presque identiques à celles qui ont été formulées plus haut à propos des statistiques des décès d'enfants de moins d'un an. Il importe de prendre en considération la fiabilité des données (complétude de l'enregistrement) et le mode d'exploitation (selon la date de l'événement ou selon la date de l'enregistrement) dans le cas des statistiques des naissances vivantes tout comme dans le cas de celles des décès d'enfants de moins d'un an, puisque les unes et les autres servent au calcul des taux de mortalité infantile. Dans le tableau 15, le code de qualité et l'emploi de caractères italiques pour signaler les données moins sûres ne concernent que les décès d'enfants de moins d'un an. L'indication du mode d'exploitation des données (emploi du signe "+" pour signaler les données exploitées selon la date de l'enregistrement) ne porte là aussi que sur les décès d'enfants de moins d'un an. Le tableau 9 contient les renseignements correspondants pour les naissances vivantes.

Si l'enregistrement des décès d'enfants de moins d'un an est plus complet que l'enregistrement des naissances vivantes, les taux de mortalité infantile seront entachés d'une erreur par excès. En revanche, si l'enregistrement des naissances vivantes est plus complet que l'enregistrement des décès d'enfants de moins d'un an, les taux de mortalité infantile seront entachés d'une erreur par défaut.

Les taux de mortalité infantile peuvent être gravement faussés par la pratique de certains pays ou zones qui consiste à ne pas classer dans les naissances vivantes et ensuite dans les décès d'enfants de moins d'un an les enfants nés vivants mais décédés soit avant l'enregistrement de leur naissance, soit dans les 24 heures qui ont suivi la naissance. Cette pratique conduit à sous-estimer aussi bien le nombre des décès d'enfants de moins d'un an, qui constitue le numérateur, que le nombre des naissances vivantes, qui constitue le dénominateur, mais c'est pour le numérateur du taux de mortalité infantile que la distorsion est la plus marquée. Ce système a pour effet d'introduire une erreur par défaut dans les taux de mortalité infantile.

Les taux de mortalité infantile seront également sous-estimés si la méthode utilisée pour calculer l'âge au moment du décès conduit à sous-estimer le nombre de décès d'enfants de moins d'un an. Cette question a été examinée plus haut.

Tous ces facteurs sont importants et il faut donc en tenir compte lorsque l'on compare les taux de mortalité infantile.

En ce qui concerne la méthode de calcul des taux de mortalité infantile utilisée dans le tableau, il convient de noter qu'il n'a pas été tenu compte du fait qu'une partie des décès survenus pendant une année donnée sont des décès d'enfants nés l'année précédente et ne correspondent donc pas à l'ensemble des naissances utilisé pour le calcul des taux. Toutefois, l'erreur n'est pas grave, à moins que le nombre des naissances vivantes ou des décès d'enfants de moins d'un an ne varie rapidement.

La comparabilité des données selon le lieu de résidence (zone urbaine ou rurale) peut être limitée par les définitions nationales des termes « urbain » et « rural » utilisées pour la mise en tableaux de ces données. En l'absence d'indications contraires, on a supposé que les mêmes définitions avaient servi pour le recensement national de la population et pour l'établissement des statistiques de l'état civil pour chaque pays ou zone. Toutefois, il n'est pas exclu que, pour une zone ou un pays donné, des définitions différentes aient été retenues. Les définitions du terme « urbain » utilisées pour les recensements nationaux de population ont été présentées à la fin des notes techniques du tableau 6 lorsqu'elles étaient connues. Comme on l'a précisé dans les notes techniques relatives au tableau 6, ces définitions varient considérablement d'un pays ou d'une zone à l'autre.

La différence entre les taux de mortalité infantile pour les zones urbaines et rurales pourra aussi être faussée selon que les décès d'enfants de moins d'un an et les naissances vivantes auront été classés d'après le lieu de l'événement ou le lieu de résidence habituel. Ce problème est examiné plus en détail à la section 4.1.4.1 des Notes techniques.

Données publiées antérieurement : des statistiques concernant les décès d'enfants de moins d'un an et les taux de mortalité infantile ont déjà été présentées dans des éditions antérieures de l'*Annuaire démographique*. Pour plus de précisions concernant les années et les sujets pour lesquels des données ont été publiées, se reporter à l'index historique.

15. Infant deaths and infant mortality rates, by urban/rural residence: 2014 - 2018
Décès d'enfants de moins d'un an et taux de mortalité infantile, selon la résidence, urbaine/rurale : 2014 - 2018

Continent, country or area, and urban/rural residence / Continent, pays ou zone et résidence, urbaine/rurale	Code[a]	Number - Nombre					Rate - Taux				
		2014	2015	2016	2017	2018	2014	2015	2016	2017	2018
AFRICA - AFRIQUE											
Algeria - Algérie[1]											
Total	U	22 282	23 150	22 271	...		...			...	...
Angola[2]											
Total	I	45 627	...	...	...	...	39.6	...	...	...	...
Urban - Urbaine	I	22 825	...	...	...	...	34.0	...	...	...	...
Rural - Rurale	I	22 801	...	...	...	...	47.3	...	...	...	...
Botswana[3]											
Total	U	1 045	1 012	1 041	985	...	...	...	...	...	...
Congo[4]											
Total	+U	2 240	...	...	...	...	...	...	...	...	...
Urban - Urbaine	+U	2 212	...	...	...	...	...	...	...	...	...
Rural - Rurale	+U	28	...	...	...	...	...	...	...	...	...
Côte d'Ivoire[2]											
Total	I	44 530	...	...	...	...	70.5	...	...	...	...
Egypt - Égypte											
Total	C	39 679	42 050	39 301	38 685	...	14.6	15.7	15.1	15.1	...
Urban - Urbaine	C	23 952	25 528	24 370	24 674	...	19.5	20.8	19.6	19.1	...
Rural - Rurale	C	15 727	16 522	14 931	14 011	...	10.5	11.3	11.0	11.1	...
Guinea - Guinée[5]											
Total	I	33 762	...	...	...	...	76.7	...	...	...	...
Urban - Urbaine	I	9 105	...	...	...	...	68.5	...	...	...	...
Rural - Rurale	I	24 657	...	...	...	...	80.2	...	...	...	...
Kenya											
Total	+U	22 986	23 123	21 475	19 895	20 350	...	...	...	...	...
Lesotho											
Total	+U	...	218	17	158	...	...	...	...	...	...
Mauritius - Maurice[6]											
Total	+C	194	173	154	164	181	14.6	13.7	11.9	12.3	13.9
Urban - Urbaine	+C	72	81	57	57	74	14.0	15.7	10.8	10.7	13.8
Rural - Rurale	+C	122	92	97	107	107	15.0	12.3	12.7	13.2	14.0
Mayotte											
Total	C	70	71	96	86	...	9.6	7.9	10.1	8.8	...
Reunion - Réunion											
Total	C	94	93	98	87	...	6.7	6.6	7.1	6.3	...
Urban - Urbaine	C	...	...	...	80	...	...	...	...	6.0	...
Rural - Rurale	C	...	...	...	7	...	...	...	...	...	...
Saint Helena ex. dep. - Sainte-Hélène sans dép.											
Total	C	1	1	1	-	-	...	...	...	...	...
Seychelles											
Total	+C	17	17		18		...	...	...	...	...
South Africa - Afrique du Sud											
Total	U	26 785	24 994	20 649	...	...	...	...	...	...	...
AMERICA, NORTH - AMÉRIQUE DU NORD											
Antigua and Barbuda - Antigua-et-Barbuda											
Total	+C	13	10	13	...	...	...	...	...	...	...
Aruba											
Total	+C	5	6	5	6	...	...	...	...	...	...
Bahamas											
Total	+C	*85	*82	*70	*72	...	*19.5	*19.3	*17.1	*17.9	...
Belize											
Total	U	91	127	100	104	98	...	...	...	...	...
Urban - Urbaine	U	30	58	44[7]	...	...	...	...	...	...	...
Rural - Rurale	U	61	69	59[7]	...	...	...	...	...	...	...
Bermuda - Bermudes[8]											
Total	C	2	2	2	-	...	...	...	...	...	...
British Virgin Islands - Îles Vierges britanniques											
Total	C	5	4	4	7	...	...	...	...	...	...
Canada[9]											
Total	C	1 794	1 737	1 742	1 700	...	4.7	4.5	4.5	4.5	...

Continent, country or area, and urban/rural residence / Continent, pays ou zone et résidence, urbaine/rurale	Code[a]	Number - Nombre					Rate - Taux				
		2014	2015	2016	2017	2018	2014	2015	2016	2017	2018
AMERICA, NORTH - AMÉRIQUE DU NORD											
Costa Rica											
Total	C	575	557	555	548	*573	8.0	7.8	7.9	8.0	*8.4
Urban - Urbaine	C	362	404	422	381	*401	8.7	8.1	8.7	8.1	*8.6
Rural - Rurale	C	213	153	133	167	*172	7.1	6.9	6.2	7.8	*7.9
Cuba											
Total	C	514	535	497	465	*461	4.2	4.3	4.3	4.0	*4.0
Urban - Urbaine	C	413	429	419	399	...	4.3	4.3	4.5	4.3	...
Rural - Rurale	C	101	106	78	66	...	3.9	4.1	3.3	3.1	...
Curaçao											
Total	C	24	20	20	16	14	...	...	...	...	...
Dominican Republic - République dominicaine											
Total	U	848	935	810	674	...	...	...	...	...	...
Urban - Urbaine[10]	U	714	779	706	106	...	...	...	...	...	...
Rural - Rurale[10]	U	55	35	52	-	...	...	...	...	...	...
El Salvador[11]											
Total	C	876	...	...	...	...	8.0	...	...	...	...
Urban - Urbaine	C	569	...	...	...	...	9.1	...	...	...	...
Rural - Rurale	C	307	...	...	...	...	6.6	...	...	...	...
Greenland - Groenland											
Total	C	6	9	6	6	5	...	...	...	...	...
Urban - Urbaine	C	5	9	6	6		...	...	...	...	...
Rural - Rurale	C	1	-	-	-		...	...	...	...	...
Grenada - Grenade											
Total	+C	33	28	31	34	...	18.9	...	19.7	24.3	...
Guadeloupe[12]											
Total	C	41	43	41	40	...	7.2	8.0	7.8	8.6	...
Guatemala											
Total	C	7 342	8 202	8 366	7 626	...	19.0	21.0	21.4	20.0	...
Martinique											
Total	C	...	...	...	40	...	...	...	...	11.0	...
Urban - Urbaine	C	...	...	...	36	...	...	...	...	...	...
Rural - Rurale	C	...	...	...	4	...	...	...	...	11.7	...
Mexico - Mexique[13]											
Total	+C	26 385	26 045	24 722	25 180	...	12.4	12.4	12.2	11.3	...
Urban - Urbaine[10]	+C	19 987	19 753	18 766	19 114	...	12.8	12.8	12.7	...	...
Rural - Rurale[10]	+C	5 870	5 832	5 593	5 766	...	12.6	13.2	12.7	...	...
Montserrat											
Total	C	-	3	-	...	...	...	...	...	...	...
Panama											
Total	C	1 036	935	*1 046	*1 063	...	13.8	12.3	*13.9	*14.0	...
Urban - Urbaine	C	585	543	*556	*589	...	11.9	11.1	*11.6	*12.3	...
Rural - Rurale	C	451	392	*490	*474	...	17.2	14.6	*17.9	*16.7	...
Puerto Rico - Porto Rico											
Total	C	242	222	222	172	142	7.0	7.1	7.8	7.1	6.6
Urban - Urbaine	C	141	124	122	100	83	7.4	6.5	6.7	6.1	6.0
Rural - Rurale	C	101	98	100	72	59	6.5	8.0	9.9	9.0	7.8
Saint Lucia - Sainte-Lucie											
Total	+C	29	...	...	...	...	...	...	...	...	...
Saint Pierre and Miquelon - Saint Pierre-et-Miquelon											
Total	C	-	...	...	-	...	...	...	...	...	...
Saint Vincent and the Grenadines - Saint-Vincent-et-les Grenadines											
Total	C	29	26	25	...	...	...	...	...	...	...
Saint-Barthélemy											
Total	C	...	...	...	-	...	...	...	...	...	...
Saint-Martin (French part) - Saint-Martin (partie française)											
Total	C	5	...	...	5	...	...	...	...	...	...
Turks and Caicos Islands - Îles Turques et Caïques											
Total	C	1	1	...	3	*-	...	...	...	...	...

15. Infant deaths and infant mortality rates, by urban/rural residence: 2014 - 2018
Décès d'enfants de moins d'un an et taux de mortalité infantile, selon la résidence, urbaine/rurale : 2014 - 2018 (continued - suite)

Continent, country or area, and urban/rural residence / Continent, pays ou zone et résidence, urbaine/rurale	Co-de[a]	Number - Nombre					Rate - Taux				
		2014	2015	2016	2017	2018	2014	2015	2016	2017	2018
AMERICA, NORTH - AMÉRIQUE DU NORD											
United States of America - États-Unis d'Amérique											
Total	C	23 215	23 455	...	...	...	5.8	5.9	...		
AMERICA, SOUTH - AMÉRIQUE DU SUD											
Argentina - Argentine											
Total	C	8 202	7 445	7 093	6 579	...	10.6	9.7	9.7	9.3	
Brazil - Brésil											
Total[14]	U	31 679	...	...	...	...	...	...	...	...	
Total	+C	...	31 238	30 541	30 636	...	...	10.2	10.5	10.3	
Chile - Chili											
Total	C	1 825	1 683	1 629	*1 559	...	7.3	6.9	7.0	*7.1	
Urban - Urbaine	C	1 604	1 506	1 471	...	...	7.0	6.8	6.9	...	
Rural - Rurale	C	221	177	158	...	...	9.8	8.0	8.0	...	
Colombia - Colombie											
Total	U	7 589	7 244	7 220	7 044	...	...	...	...	...	
Urban - Urbaine[10]	U	5 642	5 384	5 365	5 246	...	...	...	...	...	
Rural - Rurale[10]	U	1 873	1 799	1 800	1 713	...	...	...	...	...	
Ecuador - Équateur[15]											
Total	U	2 862	3 011	3 078	3 252	...	...	...	...	...	
Urban - Urbaine	U	2 335	2 503	2 505	2 667	...	...	...	...	...	
Rural - Rurale	U	527	508	573	585	...	...	...	...	...	
Paraguay											
Total	+U	468	...	485	...	490	...	...	...	...	
Peru - Pérou[16]											
Total	+U	4 243	3 852	3 756	*5 224	...	...	...	...	...	
Suriname											
Total	C	163	149	170	199	...	15.7	14.7	17.2	20.3	
Urban - Urbaine	C	117	101	131	146	...	17.0	15.1	20.0	22.6	
Rural - Rurale	C	46	48	39	53	...	13.1	13.9	11.6	16.0	
Uruguay											
Total	C	376	367	376	280	...	7.8	7.5	8.0	6.5	
Venezuela (Bolivarian Republic of) - Venezuela (République bolivarienne du)											
Total	C	8 396	9 276	11 783	11 671	...	14.0	15.4	18.3	20.1	
ASIA - ASIE											
Armenia - Arménie[17]											
Total	C	376	370	352	311	...	8.7	8.9	8.7	8.2	
Urban - Urbaine	C	...	233	201	178	...	...	8.6	7.6	7.2	
Rural - Rurale	C	...	137	151	133	...	...	9.4	10.7	10.2	
Azerbaijan - Azerbaïdjan[17]											
Total	+C	1 655	2 033	1 666	1 700	...	9.7	12.2	10.4	11.8	
Urban - Urbaine	+C	1 324	1 602	1 380	1 363	...	16.2	19.7	17.9	19.6	
Rural - Rurale	+C	331	431	286	337	...	3.7	5.1	3.5	4.5	
Bahrain - Bahreïn[18]											
Total	C	218	156	109	133	...	10.4	7.4	5.3	6.5	
Bangladesh											
Total	U	88 906	86 632	84 195	72 239	...	...	...	...	...	
Urban - Urbaine	U	19 726	21 118	21 373	17 416	...	...	...	...	...	
Rural - Rurale	U	69 180	65 514	62 822	54 823	...	...	...	...	...	
Brunei Darussalam - Brunéi Darussalam											
Total	+C	51	58	52	60	...	7.4	8.7	8.1	9.3	
China, Hong Kong SAR - Chine, Hong Kong RAS											
Total	C	103	85	109	97	80	1.7	1.4	1.8	1.7	1.5

Continent, country or area, and urban/rural residence / Continent, pays ou zone et résidence, urbaine/rurale	Co-de[a]	Number - Nombre					Rate - Taux				
		2014	2015	2016	2017	2018	2014	2015	2016	2017	2018
ASIA - ASIE											
China, Macao SAR - Chine, Macao RAS											
Total	C	15	11	...	...	...	...	...	...	...	...
Total[19]	I	...	...	12	...	...	...	...	...	...	...
Cyprus - Chypre[20]											
Total	C	19	25	25	...	...	...	...	...	...	...
Georgia - Géorgie[17]											
Total	C	578	507	507	512	...	9.5	8.6	9.0	9.6	...
Urban - Urbaine	C	...	259	253	...	...	...	7.6	7.9	...	...
Rural - Rurale	C	...	248	254	...	...	...	9.8	10.4	...	...
India - Inde[21]											
Total	I	...	...	...	...	...	39.0	37.0	34.0	33.0	...
Urban - Urbaine	I	...	...	...	...	...	26.0	25.0	23.0	23.0	...
Rural - Rurale	I	...	...	...	...	...	43.0	41.0	38.0	37.0	...
Iran (Islamic Republic of) - Iran (République islamique d')[22]											
Total	+C	7 430	...	8 261	8 304	...	4.8	...	5.4	5.6	...
Urban - Urbaine	+C	5 590	...	6 115	6 296	...	4.7	...	5.2	5.5	...
Rural - Rurale	+C	1 840	...	2 146	2 008	...	5.2	...	6.1	5.8	...
Israel - Israël[23]											
Total	C	548	563	570	564	543	3.1	3.2	3.1	3.1	2.9
Urban - Urbaine[10]	C	494	496	491	509	477	3.1	3.1	3.0	3.0	...
Rural - Rurale[10]	C	53	63	78	55	66	3.3	3.8	4.6	3.4	...
Japan - Japon[24]											
Total	C	2 080	1 916	1 928	1 761	...	2.1	1.9	2.0	1.9	...
Urban - Urbaine	C	1 891	1 754	1 768	1 636	...	2.0	1.9	2.0	1.9	...
Rural - Rurale	C	187	161	158	122	...	2.4	2.1	2.1	1.7	...
Kazakhstan											
Total	C	3 907	3 751	3 438	3 109	3 184	9.8	9.4	8.6	8.0	8.0
Urban - Urbaine	C	2 222	2 177	1 936	1 700	1 846	10.0	9.6	8.4	7.5	7.9
Rural - Rurale	C	1 685	1 574	1 502	1 409	1 338	9.5	9.1	8.8	8.6	8.2
Kuwait - Koweït											
Total	C	456	456	448	413	...	7.4	7.7	7.6	7.0	...
Kyrgyzstan - Kirghizstan											
Total	C	3 268	2 945	2 621	2 401	...	20.2	18.0	16.6	15.6	...
Urban - Urbaine	C	2 099	1 853	1 586	1 586	...	37.8	35.3	30.7	30.0	...
Rural - Rurale	C	1 169	1 092	1 035	815	...	11.0	9.8	9.7	8.1	...
Malaysia - Malaisie											
Total	C	3 543	3 582	3 390	3 496	...	6.7	6.9	6.7	6.9	...
Urban - Urbaine	C	2 313	2 301	2 186	2 288	...	6.5	6.6	6.4	6.8	...
Rural - Rurale	C	1 230	1 281	1 204	1 208	...	7.2	7.5	7.3	7.1	...
Maldives[25]											
Total	C	59	63	53	64	...	8.1	9.0	7.8	9.5	...
Urban - Urbaine	C	15[26]	8[10]	35[10]	6[10]	...	...	...	14.4	...	...
Rural - Rurale	C	33[26]	17[10]	14[10]	55[10]	...	7.3	...	...	11.0	...
Mongolia - Mongolie											
Total	+C	1 251	1 234	1 315	1 009	1 037	15.1	15.0	16.5	13.4	13.2
Urban - Urbaine	+C	...	...	...	...	809	...	...	...	...	15.4
Rural - Rurale	+C	...	...	...	...	228	...	...	...	...	8.8
Myanmar[27]											
Total	+U	9 386	9 849	9 476	...	...	...	...	...	...	...
Urban - Urbaine	+U	5 806	6 256	4 819	...	...	...	...	...	...	...
Rural - Rurale	+U	3 580	3 593	4 657	...	...	...	...	...	...	...
Oman											
Total[28]	U	645	818	816	...	...	...	...	...	...	...
Total	C	...	...	...	850	762	...	...	...	9.4	8.6
Philippines											
Total	C	21 572	20 750	21 874	...	...	12.3	11.9	12.6	...	...
Qatar											
Total	C	168	197	161	151	...	6.6	7.4	6.0	5.4	...
Urban - Urbaine	C	168	197	161	...	...	6.6	7.4	6.0	...	...
Republic of Korea - République de Corée[29]											
Total	C	1 305	1 190	1 154	1 000	...	3.0	2.7	2.8	2.8	...
Urban - Urbaine	C	1 063	1 010	945	821	...	2.9	2.8	2.8	2.8	...
Rural - Rurale	C	242	180	209	179	...	3.4	2.5	3.1	2.9	...

15. Infant deaths and infant mortality rates, by urban/rural residence: 2014 - 2018
Décès d'enfants de moins d'un an et taux de mortalité infantile, selon la résidence, urbaine/rurale : 2014 - 2018 (continued - suite)

Continent, country or area, and urban/rural residence / Continent, pays ou zone et résidence, urbaine/rurale	Code[a]	Number - Nombre					Rate - Taux				
		2014	2015	2016	2017	2018	2014	2015	2016	2017	2018
ASIA - ASIE											
Saudi Arabia - Arabie saoudite[30]											
Total	I	...	...	5 084[31]	6 608	...	...	...	11.4	13.5	...
Singapore - Singapour											
Total	+C	83	84	101	94	...	2.0	2.0	2.4	2.4	...
Sri Lanka											
Total	+C	2 662	*2 845	...	...	...	7.6	*8.5	...	...	...
Urban - Urbaine	+C	2 318	...	...	...	...	9.4	...	...	...	...
Rural - Rurale[32]	+C	344	...	...	...	...	3.3	...	...	...	...
State of Palestine - État de Palestine[33]											
Total	U	800	871	880	821		...	...	...	...	...
Tajikistan - Tadjikistan[17]											
Total	U	3 273	3 082	2 725	2 405		...	...	...	...	...
Urban - Urbaine	U	1 515	1 617	1 479	1 362		...	...	...	...	...
Rural - Rurale	U	1 758	1 465	1 246	1 043		...	...	...	...	...
Thailand - Thaïlande											
Total	+U	4 615	4 221	4 233	3 861		...	...	...	...	...
Turkey - Turquie[34]											
Total	C	14 951	13 666	13 006	11 849		11.1	10.2	9.9	9.2	...
United Arab Emirates - Émirats arabes unis											
Total[35]	...	652	640	597	...	...	...	...	...	...	...
Total	C	...	...	...	607		...	...	...	6.2	...
Uzbekistan - Ouzbékistan[17]											
Total	+C	7 688	8 320	7 764	8 235	...	10.7	11.3	10.7	11.5	...
Urban - Urbaine	+C	4 312	4 494	4 235	4 473	...	13.2	13.8	12.8	13.8	...
Rural - Rurale	+C	3 376	3 826	3 529	3 762	...	8.6	9.4	9.0	9.6	...
EUROPE											
Åland Islands - Îles d'Åland											
Total	C	-	-	1	-	-	...	...	...	...	...
Urban - Urbaine	C	-	-	-	-	-	...	...	...	...	...
Rural - Rurale	C	-	-	1	-	-	...	...	...	...	...
Albania - Albanie											
Total	C	281	233	277	248	...	7.9	7.1	8.7	8.0	...
Andorra - Andorre											
Total	C	2	-	...	...	...	...	...	...	...	...
Austria - Autriche											
Total	C	249	259	269	256	231	3.0	3.1	3.1	2.9	2.7
Belarus - Bélarus											
Total	C	409	352	373	332	...	3.5	3.0	3.2	3.2	...
Urban - Urbaine	C	291	254	288	225	...	3.2	2.8	3.2	2.9	...
Rural - Rurale	C	118	98	85	107	...	4.4	3.6	3.2	4.5	...
Belgium - Belgique[36]											
Total	C	423	400	387	429	...	3.4	3.3	3.2	3.6	...
Urban - Urbaine	C	420	396	...	...	...	3.4	3.3	...	...	...
Rural - Rurale	C	3	4	...	...	...	...	...	...	...	...
Bosnia and Herzegovina - Bosnie-Herzégovine											
Total	C	140	174	152	183	...	4.8	6.0	5.2	6.3	...
Bulgaria - Bulgarie											
Total	C	517	434	423	408	358	7.6	6.6	6.5	6.4	...
Urban - Urbaine	C	340	255	285	257	...	6.7	5.2	5.8	5.4	...
Rural - Rurale	C	177	179	138	151	...	10.5	10.9	8.5	9.5	...
Croatia - Croatie											
Total	C	199	154	161	148	...	5.0	4.1	4.3	4.0	...
Urban - Urbaine	C	101	91	82	99	...	4.4	4.2	3.8	4.7	...
Rural - Rurale	C	98	63	79	49	...	5.9	4.0	5.0	3.2	...
Czechia - Tchéquie											
Total	C	263	272	317	304	...	2.4	2.5	2.8	2.7	...
Urban - Urbaine	C	197	193	231	225	...	2.4	2.4	2.8	2.7	...
Rural - Rurale	C	66	79	86	79	...	2.3	2.7	2.9	2.6	...
Denmark - Danemark[37]											
Total	C	229	216	194	231	226	4.0	3.7	3.1	3.8	...

15. Infant deaths and infant mortality rates, by urban/rural residence: 2014 - 2018

Décès d'enfants de moins d'un an et taux de mortalité infantile, selon la résidence, urbaine/rurale : 2014 - 2018 (continued - suite)

Continent, country or area, and urban/rural residence — Continent, pays ou zone et résidence, urbaine/rurale	Code[a]	Number - Nombre					Rate - Taux				
		2014	2015	2016	2017	2018	2014	2015	2016	2017	2018
EUROPE											
Estonia - Estonie											
Total	C	36	35	33	32	...	2.7	2.5	2.3	2.3	...
Urban - Urbaine	C	24	24	24	23	...	...	...	...	...	...
Rural - Rurale	C	12	11	9	9	...	...	...	...	...	...
Faeroe Islands - Îles Féroé											
Total	C	4	-	3	6	-	...	...	...	...	...
Urban - Urbaine	C	1	-	1	2	-	...	...	...	...	...
Rural - Rurale	C	3	-	2	4	-	...	...	...	...	...
Finland - Finlande[38]											
Total	C	124	97	99	102	101	2.2	1.8	1.9	2.0	2.1
Urban - Urbaine	C	93	66	72	73	...	2.3	1.6	1.9	2.0	...
Rural - Rurale	C	31	31	27	29	...	2.0	2.1	...	...	...
France											
Total	C	2 598	2 655	2 577	2 639	...	3.2	3.5	3.5	3.6	...
Urban - Urbaine[39]	C	2 138	2 219	2 165	2 211	...	3.3	3.6	3.6	3.7	...
Rural - Rurale[39]	C	441	408	386	406	...	2.8	2.8	2.7	3.0	...
Germany - Allemagne											
Total	C	2 284	2 405	2 700	2 571	2 505	3.2	3.3	3.4	3.3	3.2
Greece - Grèce											
Total	C	346	364	387	306	300	3.8	4.0	4.2	3.5	3.5
Urban - Urbaine	C	242	254	254	...	...	3.9	4.0	4.0	...	...
Rural - Rurale	C	104	110	133	...	...	3.5	3.9	4.6	...	...
Hungary - Hongrie[40]											
Total	C	418	383	368	328	304	4.5	4.2	3.9	3.5	3.4
Urban - Urbaine[41]	C	274	242	231	182	...	4.2	3.8	3.5	2.8	...
Rural - Rurale[41]	C	144	140	136	145	...	5.1	5.0	4.6	4.9	...
Iceland - Islande											
Total	C	9	9	3	11	7	...	...	...	...	...
Urban - Urbaine	C	9	8	3	11	...	...	...	...	...	...
Rural - Rurale	C	-	1	-	-	...	...	...	...	...	...
Ireland - Irlande											
Total	+C	224	225	208	174	187	3.3	3.4	3.3	2.8	3.1
Isle of Man - Île de Man[42]											
Total	I	...	...	2	...	...	...	...	...	...	...
Italy - Italie											
Total	C	1 523	1 398	1 427	1 251	...	3.0	2.9	3.0	2.7	...
Latvia - Lettonie											
Total	C	83	90	81	86	...	3.8	4.1	3.7	4.1	...
Urban - Urbaine	C	53	59	53	64	...	3.5	3.9	3.5	4.4	...
Rural - Rurale	C	30	31	28	22	...	4.5	4.5	...	...	...
Liechtenstein											
Total	C	1	2	1	-	...	...	...	...	...	...
Lithuania - Lituanie											
Total	C	118	132	139	85	96	3.9	4.2	4.5	3.0	3.4
Urban - Urbaine	C	69	92	96	59	...	3.3	4.3	4.5	3.0	...
Rural - Rurale	C	49	40	43	26	...	5.2	4.0	4.6	...	...
Luxembourg											
Total	C	17	17	23	20	27	...	...	...	...	...
Malta - Malte											
Total	C	21	25	33	30	25	...	...	7.4	6.9	...
Montenegro - Monténégro											
Total	C	37	16	26	10	12	4.9	...	...	...	...
Netherlands - Pays-Bas[43]											
Total	C	630	561	597	607	...	3.6	3.3	3.5	3.6	...
North Macedonia - Macédoine du Nord											
Total	C	233	198	273	201	122	9.9	8.6	11.9	9.2	5.7
Urban - Urbaine	C	144	116	153	102	...	10.5	8.7	11.3	7.9	...
Rural - Rurale	C	89	82	120	99	...	9.1	8.4	12.7	11.1	...
Norway - Norvège[44]											
Total	C	139	133	128	130	129	2.4	2.3	2.2	2.3	2.3
Poland - Pologne											
Total	C	1 583	1 476	1 522	1 604	1 494	4.2	4.0	4.0	4.0	3.8
Urban - Urbaine	C	885	859	876	931	823	4.1	4.0	3.9	3.9	3.6
Rural - Rurale	C	698	617	646	673	671	4.4	4.1	4.1	4.1	4.2
Portugal[45]											
Total	C	236	250	282	229	...	2.9	2.9	3.2	2.7	...

15. Infant deaths and infant mortality rates, by urban/rural residence: 2014 - 2018
Décès d'enfants de moins d'un an et taux de mortalité infantile, selon la résidence, urbaine/rurale : 2014 - 2018 (continued - suite)

Continent, country or area, and urban/rural residence / Continent, pays ou zone et résidence, urbaine/rurale	Code[a]	Number - Nombre					Rate - Taux				
		2014	2015	2016	2017	2018	2014	2015	2016	2017	2018
EUROPE											
Republic of Moldova - République de Moldova[46]											
Total	C	372	375	353	330	326	9.6	9.7	9.4	9.7	10.0
Urban - Urbaine	C	...	141	131	107	120	...	10.4	9.8	8.6	10.0
Rural - Rurale	C	...	234	222	223	206	...	9.3	9.2	10.3	10.0
Romania - Roumanie											
Total	C	1 632	1 500	1 398	1 364	...	8.2	7.6	7.0	6.7	...
Urban - Urbaine	C	651	648	...	587	...	6.0	6.0	...	5.3	...
Rural - Rurale	C	981	852	...	777	...	10.9	9.6	...	8.6	...
San Marino - Saint-Marin											
Total	C	1	-	1	-	1	...	...	...	...	...
Serbia - Serbie[47]											
Total	+C	381	346	348	305	...	5.7	5.3	5.4	4.7	...
Urban - Urbaine	+C	268	258	265	212	...	5.8	5.7	5.9	4.8	...
Rural - Rurale	+C	113	88	83	93	...	5.5	4.4	4.2	4.4	...
Slovakia - Slovaquie											
Total	C	318	285	311	263	288	5.8	5.1	5.4	4.5	...
Urban - Urbaine	C	160	117	133	107	...	5.6	4.0	4.5	3.6	...
Rural - Rurale	C	158	168	178	156	...	5.9	6.3	6.4	5.5	...
Slovenia - Slovénie											
Total	C	39	33	41	42	33	1.8	1.6	2.0	2.1	1.7
Urban - Urbaine	C	19	17	15	26	...	...	...	...	...	...
Rural - Rurale	C	20	16	26	16	...	...	...	...	...	...
Spain - Espagne											
Total	C	1 202	1 117	1 097	1 064	...	2.8	2.7	2.7	2.7	...
Sweden - Suède											
Total	C	251	282	292	278	...	2.2	2.5	2.5	2.4	...
Switzerland - Suisse											
Total	C	331	340	316	310	...	3.9	3.9	3.6	3.5	...
Urban - Urbaine	C	256[48]	282	279	268	...	4.0	3.8	3.7	3.6	...
Rural - Rurale	C	75[48]	58	37	42	...	3.5	4.6	2.9	3.4	...
Ukraine[49]											
Total	+C	3 656	3 318	2 955	2 786	2 397	7.8	8.1	7.4	7.7	7.1
Urban - Urbaine	+C	2 316	2 035	1 788	1 666	...	7.6	7.6	6.9	7.0	...
Rural - Rurale	+C	1 340	1 283	1 167	1 120	...	8.3	8.8	8.4	8.9	...
United Kingdom of Great Britain and Northern Ireland - Royaume-Uni de Grande-Bretagne et d'Irlande du Nord[50]											
Total	+C	2 990	3 004	2 976	2 947	...	3.9	3.9	3.8	3.9	...
OCEANIA - OCÉANIE											
American Samoa - Samoas américaines											
Total	C	9	11	14	14	...	...	...	...	...	...
Australia - Australie											
Total	C	1 012	991	970	1 019	...	3.4	3.2	3.1	3.3	...
Urban - Urbaine[51]	C	617	606	630	655	...	3.0	2.9	2.9	3.1	...
Rural - Rurale[51]	C	380	361	326	355	...	4.1	3.8	3.5	3.8	...
Cook Islands - Îles Cook[52]											
Total	+C	-	-	...	...	...	...	...	...	...	...
Fiji - Fidji											
Total	+C	141	...	...	...	...	7.7	...	...	...	...
French Polynesia - Polynésie française											
Total	C	27	24	21	29	...	...	...	...	...	...
Guam[53]											
Total	C	28	47	37	28	37	...	14.0	10.8	...	11.7
New Caledonia - Nouvelle-Calédonie											
Total	C	23	25	16	20	...	...	...	...	...	...

Continent, country or area, and urban/rural residence / Continent, pays ou zone et résidence, urbaine/rurale	Code[a]	Number - Nombre					Rate - Taux				
		2014	2015	2016	2017	2018	2014	2015	2016	2017	2018
OCEANIA - OCÉANIE											
New Zealand - Nouvelle-Zélande[54]											
Total	+C	327	249	213[55]	228[55]	222[55]	5.7	4.1	3.6	3.8	3.8
Urban - Urbaine[10]	+C	288	216	189[55]	198[55]	...	5.7	4.1	3.6	3.8	...
Rural - Rurale[10]	+C	24	30	18[55]	27[55]	...	...	...	3.8	...	...
Northern Mariana Islands - Îles Mariannes septentrionales[56]											
Total	U	7	...	...	...	...	...	...	...	...	...
Palau - Palaos											
Total	C	3	4	-	5	3	...	...	...	...	...
Vanuatu											
Total	+U	*86*	...	...	...	...	...	...	...	...	...

FOOTNOTES - NOTES

Italics: data from civil registers which are incomplete or of unknown completeness. - *Italiques : données incomplètes ou dont le degré d'exactitude n'est pas connu, provenant des registres de l'état civil.*

* Provisional. - *Données provisoires.*

a 'Code' indicates the source of data, as follows:
C - Civil registration, estimated over 90% complete
U - Civil registration, estimated less than 90% complete
| - Other source, estimated reliable
+ - Data tabulated by date of registration rather than occurence
... - Information not available

Le 'Code' indique la source des données, comme suit :
C - *Registres de l'état civil considérés complets à 90 p. 100 au moins*
U - *Registres de l'état civil qui ne sont pas considérés complets à 90 p. 100 au moins*
| - *Autre source, considérée pas douteuses*
+ - *Données exploitées selon la date de l'enregistrement et non la date de l'événement*
... - *Information pas disponible*

[1] Excluding live-born infants who died before their birth was registered. Data refer to Algerian population only. - *Non compris les enfants nés vivants décédés avant l'enregistrement de leur naissance. Les données ne concernent que la population algérienne.*
[2] Data refer to the 12 months preceding the census in May. - *Les données se rapportent aux 12 mois précédant le recensement de mai.*
[3] Source: Vital Statistics Report. - *Source: Vital Statistics Report.*
[4] Urban area here is composed of six communes: Brazzaville, Pointe-Noire, Dolisie, N'kayi, Mossendjo and Ouesso. The data on rural area are the result of the difference between total and urban area. - *Le milieu urbain ici est constitué des six communes: Brazzaville, Pointe-Noire, Dolisie, N'kayi, Mossendjo et Ouesso. Les informations sur la zone rurale ont été déduites en celles de l'ensemble et du milieu urbain.*
[5] Adjusted number of infant deaths in households referring to the 12 months preceding the census in March. - *Le nombre ajusté de décès d'enfants des ménages ordinaires se rapportent aux 12 mois précédant le recensement de mars.*
[6] Excludes the islands of St. Brandon and Agalega. - *Non compris les îles St. Brandon et Agalega.*
[7] Unrevised data. - *Les données n'ont pas été révisées.*
[8] Bermuda is 100 per cent urban. - *100 pour cent de la population des Bermudes est urbaine.*
[9] Including Canadian residents temporarily in the United States, but excluding United States residents temporarily in Canada. - *Y compris les résidents canadiens se trouvant temporairement aux Etats-Unis, mais ne comprenant pas les résidents des Etats-Unis se trouvant temporairement au Canada.*

[10] The total number may include 'Unknown residence', but the categories urban and rural do not. - *Le nombre total peut inclure les personnes dont la résidence n'est pas connue, à l'inverse des catégories de population urbaine et rurale.*
[11] Excluding infant deaths to mothers living abroad. - *Exception faite des décès d'enfants en bas âge survenus lorsque la mère résidait à l'étranger.*
[12] Excluding live-born infants who died before their birth was registered. - *Non compris les enfants nés vivants décédés avant l'enregistrement de leur naissance.*
[13] Data refer to resident population only. - *Pour la population résidante seulement.*
[14] Including deaths abroad and deaths of unknown residence of mother. - *Y compris décès à l'étranger et décès de nourrissons nés de mères dont le lieu de résidence n'est pas connu.*
[15] Excludes nomadic Indian tribes. - *Non compris les tribus d'Indiens nomades.*
[16] Source: Reports of the Ministry of Health. - *Source : Rapports du Ministère de la Santé.*
[17] Excluding infants born alive of less than 28 weeks' gestation, of less than 1 000 g in weight and 35 cm in length, who die within seven days of birth. - *Non compris les enfants nés vivants après moins de 28 semaines de gestations, pesant moins de 1 000 g, mesurant moins de 35 cm et décédés dans les sept jours qui ont suivi leur naissance.*
[18] Deaths include deaths among some visitors. Sources: Births and Deaths National Registration System database, and medical records of government hospitals. - *Les décès comprennent des décès parmi certains visiteurs. Les sources: Les bases de données des << Births and Deaths National Registration System >> et les dossiers médicaux des hôpitaux du gouvernement.*
[19] Data refer to the 12 months preceding the census in August. - *Les données se rapportent aux 12 mois précédant le recensement d'août.*
[20] Data refer to government controlled areas. - *Les données se rapportent aux zones contrôlées par le Gouvernement.*
[21] Rates were obtained by the Sample Registration System of India, which is a large demographic survey. Includes data for the Indian-held part of Jammu and Kashmir, the final status of which has not yet been determined. - *Les taux ont été obtenus par le Système de l'enregistrement par échantillon de l'Inde qui est une large enquête démographique. Y compris les données pour la partie du Jammu et du Cachemire occupée par l'Inde dont le statut définitif n'a pas encore été déterminé.*
[22] Data refer to the Iranian Year which begins on 21 March and ends on 20 March of the following year. - *Les données concernent l'année iranienne, qui commence le 21 mars et se termine le 20 mars de l'année suivante.*
[23] Including deaths abroad of Israeli residents who were out of the country for less than a year. Includes data for East Jerusalem and Israeli residents in certain other territories under occupation by Israeli military forces since June 1967. - *Y compris les décès à l'étranger de résidents israéliens qui ont quitté le pays depuis moins d'un an. Y compris les données pour Jérusalem-Est et les résidents israéliens dans certains autres territoires occupés depuis 1967 par les forces armées israéliennes.*
[24] Data refer to Japanese nationals in Japan only. The total number may include 'Unknown residence', but the categories urban and rural do not. - *Les données se raportent aux nationaux japonais au Japon seulement. Le nombre total peut inclure les personnes dont la résidence n'est pas connue, à l'inverse des catégories de population urbaine et rurale.*

15. Infant deaths and infant mortality rates, by internitural residence: 2014 - 2016

Décès d'enfants de moins d'un an et taux de mortalité infantile, par zone résiden — internitural residence 2014 - 2016 (continued,
suite)

25 Data do not include foreigners. - Les données sur les etrangers ne sont pas inclus.

26 Excluding deaths occurred abroad. - Hormis les décès à l'étranger.

27 Data are from Vital Registration System (VRS). - Les données proviennent du système d'enregistrement des faits d'état civil.

28 Data from Births and Deaths Notification System (Ministry of Health and all health care providers). - Les données proviennent du système de notification des naissances et des décès (Ministère de la santé et tous prestataires de soins de santé).

29 Excluding alien armed forces, civilian aliens employed by armed forces, and foreign diplomatic personnel and their dependants. - Non compris les militaires étrangers, les civils étrangers employés par les forces armées ni le personnel diplomatique étranger et les membres de leur famille les accompagnant.

30 Survey based estimates. - Estimations basées sur des enquêtes.

31 Data refer to Saudi Arabian nationals only. - Les données ne concernent que les ressortissants saoudiens.

32 Data for rural areas include data of estate sectors consisting of all plantations which are 20 acres or more in extent and with ten or more resident labourers. - Les données pour les zones rurales comprennent celles pour les domaines, dont l'ensemble des plantations de plus de 10 hectares comptant au moins 10 travailleurs résidents.

33 Source: Palestinian Central Bureau of Statistics, Population Register, updated version 2018. Data exclude Jerusalem ID holders. - Source: Bureau central de statistique palestinien, registre de la population, version actualisée jusqu'au 2018. Les données ne tiennent pas compte des détenteurs de carte d'identité de Jérusalem.

34 Data from MERNIS (Central Population Administrative System). - Données de MERNIS (Système central de données démographiques).

35 The registration of births and deaths is conducted by the Ministry of Health. An estimate of completeness is not provided. - L'enregistrement des naissances et des décès est mené par le Ministère de la Santé. Le degré estimatif de complétude n'est pas fourni.

36 Including armed forces stationed outside the country, but excluding alien armed forces stationed in the area. - Y compris les militaires nationaux hors du pays, mais non compris les militaires étrangers en garnison sur le territoire.

37 Excluding Faeroe Islands and Greenland shown separately, if available. - Non compris les Iles Féroé et le Groenland, qui font l'objet de rubriques distinctes, si disponible.

38 Excluding Åland Islands. - Non compris les Îles d'Åland.

39 Data for urban and rural exclude events corresponding to nationals residing outside the country, which may be included in the total. - Les données relatives à les categories urbaine et rurale n'englobent pas les faits d'état civil qui concernent les nationaux se trouvant à l'étranger, lesquels faits peuvent être inclus au total.

40 Data include the deceased infants with Hungarian usual residence regardless of whether the death occurred in Hungary or in a foreign country, and do not include the deceased infants with foreign country usual residence. - Les données comprennent les nourrissons décédés alors que leur résidence habituelle était en Hongrie, que le décès ait eu lieu en Hongrie ou dans un pays étranger, et ne comprennent pas les nourrissons décédés dont la residence habituelle était dans un pays étranger.

41 The urban and rural categories do not include the data of foreigners, persons of unknown residence and the homeless, whereas the total category includes them. - Les chiffres portant sur la population urbaine et rurale n' incluent pas les données relatives aux étrangers, aux personnes dont la résidence n'est pas connue et aux personnes sans domicile fixe, à l'inverse, le total les inclut.

42 Data refer to the 12 months preceding the census in April. - Les données se rapportent aux douze mois précédant le recensement d'avril.

43 Including residents outside the country if listed in a Netherlands population register. - Englobe les résidents se trouvant à l'étranger à condition qu'ils soient inscrits sur le registre de population des Pays-Bas.

44 Including residents temporarily outside the country. - Y compris les résidents se trouvant temporairement hors du pays.

45 Data refer to usually resident population. - Les données concernent la population habituellement résidente.

46 Excluding Transnistria and the municipality of Bender. - Les données ne tiennent pas compte de l'information sur la Transnistria et la municipalité de Bender.

47 Excludes data for Kosovo and Metohia. - Sans les données pour le Kosovo et Metohie.

48 From 2014, urban refers to urban centers and areas under the influence of urban centers. - A partir de 2014, le territoire urbain inclut l'espace des centres urbains ainsi que l'espace sous influence des centres urbains.

49 The Government of Ukraine has informed the United Nations that it is not in a position to provide statistical data concerning the Autonomous Republic of Crimea and the city of Sevastopol. Data includes deaths resulting from births with weight 500 g and more (if weight is unknown - with length 25 cm and more, or with gestation during 22 weeks or more). - Le gouvernement Ukrainien a

informé l'ONU qu'il n'est pas en mesure de fournir des données statistiques concernant la République autonome de Crimée et la ville de Sébastopol. Y compris les décès de nouveau-nés de 500 g ou plus (si le poids est inconnu – de 25 cm de long ou plus, ou après une grossesse de 22 semaines ou plus).

50 Excluding Channel Islands (Guernsey and Jersey) and Isle of Man, shown separately, if available. - Non compris les îles Anglo-Normandes (Guernesey et Jersey) et l'Île de Man, qui font l'objet de rubriques distinctes, si disponible.

51 Urban refers to Greater Capital City Statistical Areas, and rural refers to other areas within the state or territory. Data for urban and rural figures do not add up to the total because they exclude the events occurred in Migratory, Special Purpose and Other Territories. - Urbain renvoie aux zones statistiques de la capitale métropolitaine, et rural aux autres zones de l'État ou territoire. La somme des chiffres des catégories « en zone urbaine » et « en zone rurale » ne correspond pas au total du fait qu'en sont exclus les événements qui ont eu lieu dans les territoires de migration, les territoires à destination spéciale et autres territoires.

52 Excluding Niue, shown separately, which is part of Cook Islands, but because of remoteness is administered separately. - Non compris Nioué, qui fait l'objet d'une rubrique distincte et qui fait partie des îles Cook, mais qui, en raison de son éloignement, est administrée séparément.

53 Including United States military personnel, their dependants and contract employees. - Y compris les militaires des Etats-Unis, les membres de leur famille les accompagnant et les agents contractuels des Etats-Unis.

54 Random rounding to base 3 is applied in this table as a confidentiality measure. - Les chiffres sont arrondis à la base 3 de manière aléatoire, pour des raisons de confidentialité.

55 Data refer to deaths of residents only. - Les données renvoient aux décès de résidents uniquement.

56 Source: U.S. National Center for Health Statistics, National Vital Statistics Reports (NVSR). - Source : US National Center for Health Statistics, National Vital Statistics Reports (NVSR).

Table 16 - *Demographic Yearbook 2018*

Table 16 presents infant deaths and infant mortality rates by age and sex for latest available year between 2009 and 2018.

Description of variables: Age is defined as hours, days and months of life completed, based on the difference between the hour, day, month and year of birth and the hour, day, month and year of death. The age classification used in this table is as follows: Main categories are "under 1 day", "1-6 days", "7-27 days" and "28 days – 11 months". Additional subcategories are shown within "7-27 days" and "28 days to 11 months" wherever available.

Rate computation: Infant mortality rates by age and sex are the annual number of infant deaths that occurred in a specific age-sex group per 1 000 live births of the corresponding sex. These rates have been calculated by the United Nations Statistics Division. The denominator for all these rates, regardless of age of infant at death, is the total number of live births by sex.

Infant deaths of unknown age are included only in the rate for under one year of age. Infant deaths of unknown sex are included in the rate for the total and, hence, these rates, should agree with the infant mortality rates shown in table 15. Discrepancies are explained in footnotes.

Rates presented in this table have been limited to those countries or areas having at least a total of 100 deaths in a given year. Moreover, rates specific for individual sub-categories based on 30 or fewer infant deaths are identified by the symbol "♦".

Reliability of data: Data from civil registers of infant deaths which are reported as incomplete (less than 90 percent completeness) or of unknown completeness are considered unreliable and are set in italics rather than in roman type. Rates on these data are not computed. Table 15 and its technical notes provide more detailed information on the completeness of infant death registration. For more information about the quality of vital statistics, and the information available on their completeness, see section 4.2 of the Technical Notes.

Limitations: Statistics on infant deaths by age and sex are subject to the same qualifications as have been set forth for vital statistics and particularly for death statistics discussed in section 4 of the Technical Notes.

The reliability of the data, an indication of which is described above, is an important factor in considering the limitations. In addition, some infant deaths are tabulated by date of registration and not by date of occurrence; these have been indicated by a plus sign "+". Whenever the lag between the date of occurrence and date of registration is prolonged and, therefore, a large proportion of the infant-death registrations are delayed, infant-death statistics for any given year may be seriously affected.

Another factor that limits international comparability is the practice of some countries or areas of not including in infant-death statistics infants who were born alive but died before the registration of the birth or within the first 24 hours of life, thus underestimating the total number of infant deaths. Statistics of this type are footnoted. In this table, this practice may contribute to the lack of comparability among deaths under one year, under 28 days, under one week and under one day.

Variation in the method of reckoning age at the time of death may also introduce non-comparability. Although it is to some degree a limiting factor throughout the age span, it is an especially important consideration with respect to deaths at ages under one day, under one week (early neonatal deaths) and under 28 days (neonatal deaths). As noted above, the recommended method of reckoning infant age at death is to calculate duration of life in minutes, hours and days, as appropriate. This gives age in completed units of time. In some countries or areas, however, infant age is calculated to the nearest day only, that is, age at death for an infant is the difference between the day, month and year of birth and the day, month and year of death. The result of this procedure is to classify as deaths at age one day, many deaths of infants that occurred before the infants had completed 24 hours of life. The under-one-day class is thus understated while the frequency in the 1-6-day age group is inflated.

A special limitation on comparability of neonatal (under 28 days) deaths is the variation in the classification of infant age used. Some countries or areas continue to report infant age in calendar, rather than lunar month (4-week or 28-day) periods. This failure to tabulate infant deaths under 4 weeks of age in terms of completed days introduces another source of variation between countries or areas. Deaths

457

classified as occurring under one month usually connote deaths within any one calendar month; these frequencies are not strictly comparable with those referring to deaths within 4 weeks or 27 completed days.

In addition, infant mortality rates by age and sex are subject to the limitations of the data on live births with which they have been calculated. These have been set forth in the technical notes for table 9. These limitations have also been discussed in the technical notes for table 15.

In addition, it should be noted that infant mortality rates by age are affected by the problems related to the practice of excluding infants who were born alive but died before the registration of the birth or within the first 24 hours of life from both infant-death and live-birth statistics and the problems related to the reckoning of infant age at death. These factors, which have been described above, may affect certain age groups more than others. In so far as the numbers of infant deaths for the various age groups are underestimated or overestimated, the corresponding rates for the various age groups will also be underestimated or overestimated. The youngest age groups are more likely to be underestimated than other age groups; the youngest age group (under one day) is likely to be the most seriously affected.

Earlier data: Infant deaths and infant mortality rates by age and sex have been shown in previous issues of the *Demographic Yearbook*. For information on specific years covered, readers should consult the Historical Index.

Tableau 16 – *Annuaire démographique 2018*

Le tableau 16 présente les données les plus récentes disponible, entre 2009 et 2018, sur les décès d'enfants de moins d'un an et les taux de mortalité infantile selon l'âge et le sexe.

Description des variables : l'âge est exprimé en heures, jours et mois révolus et est calculé en retranchant la date de la naissance (heure, jour, mois et année) de celle du décès (heure, jour, mois et année). Les tranches d'âge utilisées dans ce tableau se présentent comme suit : les catégories principales sont « moins d'un jour », « 1-6 jours », « 7-27 jours » et « 28 jours à 11 mois ». Des sous-catégories additionnelles pour « 7-27 jours » et « 28 jours à 11 mois » sont présentées lorsque disponibles.

Calcul des taux : les taux de mortalité infantile selon l'âge et le sexe représentent le nombre annuel de décès d'enfants de moins d'un an intervenu dans un groupe d'âge donné parmi la population de sexe masculin ou féminin pour 1 000 naissances vivantes survenues parmi la population du même sexe. Ces taux ont été calculés par la Division de statistique du Département des affaires économiques et sociales de l'Organisation des Nations Unies. Le dénominateur de tous ces taux, quel que soit l'âge de l'enfant au moment du décès, est le nombre total de naissances vivantes selon le sexe.

Il n'est tenu compte des décès d'enfants d'âge « inconnu » que pour le calcul du taux relatif à l'ensemble des décès de moins d'un an. Étant donné que les décès d'enfants de sexe inconnu sont compris dans le numérateur des taux concernant le total, les chiffres obtenus devraient concorder avec les taux de mortalité infantile du tableau 15. Les divergences sont expliquées en note.

Les taux présentés dans le tableau 16 ne concernent que les pays ou zones où l'on a enregistré un total d'au moins 100 décès au cours d'une année donnée. Les taux relatifs à des sous-catégories qui sont fondées sur un nombre égal ou inférieur à 30 décès d'enfants âgés de moins d'un an sont signalés par le signe "♦".

Fiabilité des données : les données relatives aux décès d'enfants de moins d'un an provenant de registres de l'état civil qui sont déclarées incomplètes (degré de complétude inférieur à 90 p.100) ou dont le degré de complétude n'est pas connu sont jugées douteuses et apparaissent en italique et non en caractères romains. Les taux à partir de ces données n'ont pas été calculés. Le tableau 15 et les notes techniques se rapportant à ce tableau comportent des renseignements plus détaillés sur le degré de complétude de l'enregistrement des décès d'enfants de moins d'un an. Pour plus de précisions sur la qualité des données reposant sur les statistiques de l'état civil en général et les estimations de complétude en particulier, voir la section 4.2 des Notes techniques.

Insuffisance des données : les statistiques des décès d'enfants de moins d'un an selon l'âge et le sexe appellent toutes les réserves qui ont été formulées à propos des statistiques de l'état civil en général et des statistiques concernant les décès en particulier (voir la section 4 des Notes techniques).

La fiabilité des données, au sujet de laquelle des indications ont été fournies plus haut, est un facteur important. Il faut également tenir compte du fait que, dans certains cas, les données relatives aux décès d'enfants de moins d'un an sont exploitées selon la date de l'enregistrement et non la date de l'événement ; ces cas ont été signalés par le signe "+". Chaque fois que le décalage entre l'événement et son enregistrement est grand et qu'une forte proportion des décès d'enfants de moins d'un an fait l'objet d'un enregistrement tardif, les statistiques des décès d'enfants de moins d'un an pour une année donnée peuvent être considérablement faussées.

Un autre facteur qui nuit à la comparabilité internationale est la pratique de certains pays ou zones qui consiste à ne pas inclure dans les statistiques des décès d'enfants de moins d'un an les enfants nés vivants mais décédés soit avant l'enregistrement de leur naissance, soit dans les 24 heures qui ont suivi la naissance, pratique qui conduit à sous-estimer le nombre total de décès d'enfants de moins d'un an. Quand pareil facteur a joué, cela a été signalé en note. Dans le tableau 16 en particulier, ce système peut limiter la comparabilité des données concernant les décès d'enfants de moins d'un an, de moins de 28 jours, de moins d'une semaine et de moins d'un jour.

Le manque d'uniformité des méthodes suivies pour calculer l'âge au moment du décès nuit également à la comparabilité des données. Ce facteur influe dans une certaine mesure sur les données relatives à la mortalité à tous les âges, mais il a des répercussions particulièrement marquées sur les statistiques des décès de moins d'un jour et de moins d'une semaine (mortalité néo-natale précoce) et de moins de 28 jours (mortalité néo-natale). Comme on l'a dit, l'âge d'un enfant de moins d'un an à son décès est calculé, selon la méthode recommandée, en évaluant la durée de vie en minutes, heures et jours, selon le cas. L'âge est ainsi exprimé en unités de temps révolues. Toutefois, dans certains pays ou zones, l'âge de ces enfants est ramené au jour le plus proche en retranchant la date de la naissance (jour, mois et année) de celle du décès (jour, mois et année). Il s'ensuit que de nombreux décès survenus dans les vingt-quatre heures qui suivent la naissance sont classés comme décès d'un jour. Dans ces conditions, les données concernant les décès de moins d'un jour sont entachées d'une erreur par défaut et celles qui se rapportent aux décès de 1 à 6 jours d'une erreur par excès.

La comparabilité des données relatives à la mortalité néo-natale (moins de 28 jours) est influencée par un facteur spécial : l'hétérogénéité de la classification par âge utilisée pour les enfants de moins d'un an. Dans un certain nombre de pays ou zones, on continue d'utiliser le mois civil au lieu du mois lunaire (4 semaines ou 28 jours).

Lorsque les données relatives aux décès de moins de 4 semaines ne sont pas exploitées sur la base de l'âge en jours révolus, il existe une nouvelle cause de non-comparabilité internationale. Les décès de moins d'un mois sont généralement ceux qui se produisent au cours d'un mois civil ; les taux calculés sur la base de ces données ne sont pas strictement comparables à ceux qui sont établis à partir des données concernant les décès survenus dans les 4 semaines ou 27 jours révolus qui suivent la naissance.

Les taux de mortalité infantile selon l'âge et le sexe appellent en outre toutes les réserves qui ont été formulées à propos des statistiques des naissances vivantes qui ont servi à leur calcul (voir à ce sujet les notes techniques relatives au tableau 9). Ces insuffisances ont également été examinées dans les notes techniques relatives au tableau 15.

Il convient de signaler aussi que les taux de mortalité infantile selon l'âge peuvent être gravement faussés par la pratique qui consiste à ne pas classer dans les naissances vivantes et ensuite dans les décès d'enfants de moins d'un an les enfants nés vivants mais décédés soit avant l'enregistrement de leur naissance, soit dans les 24 heures qui ont suivi la naissance, et par les problèmes que pose le calcul de l'âge de l'enfant au moment du décès. Ces facteurs, qui ont été décrits plus haut, peuvent fausser les statistiques concernant certains groupes d'âge plus que d'autres. Si le nombre des décès d'enfants de moins d'un an pour chaque groupe d'âge est sous-estimé ou surestimé, les taux correspondants pour chacun de ces groupes d'âge seront eux aussi sous-estimés ou surestimés. Les risques de sous-estimation sont plus grands pour les groupes les plus jeunes ; c'est pour le groupe d'âge le plus jeune de tous (moins d'un jour) que les données risquent de comporter les plus grosses erreurs.

Données publiées antérieurement : des statistiques des décès d'enfants de moins d'un an et des taux de mortalité infantile selon l'âge et le sexe ont déjà été présentées dans des éditions antérieures de l'*Annuaire démographique*. Pour plus de précisions concernant les années pour lesquelles ces données ont été publiées, se reporter à l'index historique.

Continent, country or area, year, code[a] and age Continent, pays ou zone, année, code[a] et âge	Number - Nombre			Rate - Taux		
	Both sexes Les deux sexes	Male Masculin	Female Féminin	Both sexes Les deux sexes	Male Masculin	Female Féminin
AFRICA - AFRIQUE						
Botswana[1]						
2017 (U)						
Total	985	539	446	...	...	...
Less than 1 day - Moins de 1 jour	102	59	43	...	...	...
1 - 6 days - 1 - 6 jours	324	180	144	...	...	...
7 - 27 days - 7 - 27 jours	193	103	90	...	...	...
7 - 13 days - 7 - 13 jours	99	51	48	...	...	...
14 - 20 days - 14 - 20 jours	57	29	28	...	...	...
21 - 27 days - 21 - 27 jours	37	23	14	...	...	...
28 days - 11 months - 28 jours - 11 mois	366	197	169	...	...	...
28 days - less than 2 months - 28 jours - moins de 2 mois	83	53	30	...	...	...
2 months - 2 mois	50	27	23	...	...	...
3 months - 3 mois	36	17	19	...	...	...
4 months - 4 mois	30	13	17	...	...	...
5 months - 5 mois	29	18	11	...	...	...
6 months - 6 mois	26	11	15	...	...	...
7 months - 7 mois	19	9	10	...	...	...
8 months - 8 mois	23	12	11	...	...	...
9 months - 9 mois	24	12	12	...	...	...
10 months - 10 mois	22	12	10	...	...	...
11 months - 11 mois	24	13	11	...	...	...
Egypt - Égypte						
2017 (C)						
Total	38 685	...	...	15.1	...	...
1 - 6 days - 1 - 6 jours	7 454	...	...	2.9	...	...
7 - 27 days - 7 - 27 jours	10 325	...	...	4.0	...	...
7 - 13 days - 7 - 13 jours	5 165	...	...	2.0	...	...
14 - 20 days - 14 - 20 jours	3 222	...	...	1.3	...	...
21 - 27 days - 21 - 27 jours	1 938	...	...	0.8	...	...
28 days - 11 months - 28 jours - 11 mois	20 906	...	...	8.2	...	...
28 days - less than 2 months - 28 jours - moins de 2 mois	5 334	...	...	2.1	...	...
2 months - 2 mois	3 644	...	...	1.4	...	...
3 months - 3 mois	2 580	...	...	1.0	...	...
4 months - 4 mois	2 153	...	...	0.8	...	...
5 months - 5 mois	1 698	...	...	0.7	...	...
6 months - 6 mois	1 424	...	...	0.6	...	...
7 months - 7 mois	1 138	...	...	0.4	...	...
8 months - 8 mois	965	...	...	0.4	...	...
9 months - 9 mois	767	...	...	0.3	...	...
10 months - 10 mois	671	...	...	0.3	...	...
11 months - 11 mois	532	...	...	0.2	...	...
Mauritius - Maurice[2]						
2018 (+C)						
Total	181	93	88	13.9	13.9	14.0
Less than 1 day - Moins de 1 jour	17	7	10	♦1.3	♦1.0	♦1.6
1 - 6 days - 1 - 6 jours	72	38	34	5.5	5.7	5.4
7 - 27 days - 7 - 27 jours	46	27	19	3.5	♦4.0	♦3.0
7 - 13 days - 7 - 13 jours	21	12	9	♦1.6	♦1.8	♦1.4
14 - 20 days - 14 - 20 jours	11	8	3	♦0.8	♦1.2	♦0.5
21 - 27 days - 21 - 27 jours	14	7	7	♦1.1	♦1.0	♦1.1
28 days - 11 months - 28 jours - 11 mois	46	21	25	3.5	♦3.1	♦4.0
28 days - less than 2 months - 28 jours - moins de 2 mois	16	9	7	♦1.2	♦1.3	♦1.1
2 months - 2 mois	10	7	3	♦0.8	♦1.0	♦0.5
3 months - 3 mois	4	1	3	♦0.3	♦0.1	♦0.5
4 months - 4 mois	3	1	2	♦0.2	♦0.1	♦0.3
5 months - 5 mois	2	1	1	♦0.2	♦0.1	♦0.2
6 months - 6 mois	1	-	1	♦0.1	-	♦0.2
7 months - 7 mois	2	-	2	♦0.2	-	♦0.3
8 months - 8 mois	5	1	4	♦0.4	♦0.1	♦0.6
9 months - 9 mois	1	-	1	♦0.1	-	♦0.2
10 months - 10 mois	2	1	1	♦0.2	♦0.1	♦0.2
11 months - 11 mois	-	-	-			
Saint Helena ex. dep. - Sainte-Hélène sans dép.						
2018 (C)						
Total	-	-	-	...	...	...
Less than 1 day - Moins de 1 jour	-	-	-	...	...	...
1 - 6 days - 1 - 6 jours	-	-	-	...	...	...

Continent, country or area, year, code[a] and age / Continent, pays ou zone, année, code[a] et âge	Number - Nombre			Rate - Taux		
	Both sexes Les deux sexes	Male Masculin	Female Féminin	Both sexes Les deux sexes	Male Masculin	Female Féminin
AFRICA - AFRIQUE						
Saint Helena ex. dep. - Sainte-Hélène sans dép.						
2018 (C)						
7 - 27 days - 7 - 27 jours	-	-	-	...	...	...
7 - 13 days - 7 - 13 jours	-	-	-	...	...	...
14 - 20 days - 14 - 20 jours	-	-	-	...	...	...
21 - 27 days - 21 - 27 jours	-	-	-	...	...	...
28 days - 11 months - 28 jours - 11 mois	-	-	-	...	...	...
28 days - less than 2 months - 28 jours - moins de 2 mois	-	-	-	...	...	...
2 months - 2 mois	-	-	-	...	...	...
3 months - 3 mois	-	-	-	...	...	...
4 months - 4 mois	-	-	-	...	...	...
5 months - 5 mois	-	-	-	...	...	...
6 months - 6 mois	-	-	-	...	...	...
7 months - 7 mois	-	-	-	...	...	...
8 months - 8 mois	-	-	-	...	...	...
9 months - 9 mois	-	-	-	...	...	...
10 months - 10 mois	-	-	-	...	...	...
11 months - 11 mois	-	-	-	...	...	...
South Africa - Afrique du Sud						
2016 (U)						
Total	20 649	10 963[3]	9 284[3]	...	...	...
Less than 1 day - Moins de 1 jour	2 363	1 265[3]	978[3]	...	...	...
1 - 6 days - 1 - 6 jours	4 109	2 266[3]	1 735[3]	...	...	...
7 - 27 days - 7 - 27 jours	2 709	1 401[3]	1 249[3]	...	...	...
7 - 13 days - 7 - 13 jours	1 315	666[3]	624[3]	...	...	...
14 - 20 days - 14 - 20 jours	769	406[3]	342[3]	...	...	...
21 - 27 days - 21 - 27 jours	625	329[3]	283[3]	...	...	...
28 days - 11 months - 28 jours - 11 mois	11 468	6 031[3]	5 322[3]	...	...	...
28 days - less than 2 months - 28 jours - moins de 2 mois	2 403	1 269[3]	1 104[3]	...	...	...
2 months - 2 mois	1 701	887[3]	792[3]	...	...	...
3 months - 3 mois	1 512	746[3]	754[3]	...	...	...
4 months - 4 mois	1 107	594[3]	501[3]	...	...	...
5 months - 5 mois	875	476[3]	393[3]	...	...	...
6 months - 6 mois	821	438[3]	376[3]	...	...	...
7 months - 7 mois	732	398[3]	328[3]	...	...	...
8 months - 8 mois	650	343[3]	303[3]	...	...	...
9 months - 9 mois	615	323[3]	288[3]	...	...	...
10 months - 10 mois	546	279[3]	258[3]	...	...	...
11 months - 11 mois	506	278[3]	225[3]	...	...	...
AMERICA, NORTH - AMÉRIQUE DU NORD						
Aruba						
2017 (+C)						
Total	6	4	2	...	...	...
Less than 1 day - Moins de 1 jour	3	1	2	...	...	...
1 - 6 days - 1 - 6 jours	1	1	-	...	...	...
7 - 27 days - 7 - 27 jours	-	-	-	...	...	...
7 - 13 days - 7 - 13 jours	-	-	-	...	...	...
14 - 20 days - 14 - 20 jours	-	-	-	...	...	...
21 - 27 days - 21 - 27 jours	-	-	-	...	...	...
28 days - 11 months - 28 jours - 11 mois	2	2	-	...	...	...
28 days - less than 2 months - 28 jours - moins de 2 mois	-	-	-	...	...	...
2 months - 2 mois	-	-	-	...	...	...
3 months - 3 mois	2	2	-	...	...	...
4 months - 4 mois	-	-	-	...	...	...
5 months - 5 mois	-	-	-	...	...	...
6 months - 6 mois	-	-	-	...	...	...
7 months - 7 mois	-	-	-	...	...	...
8 months - 8 mois	-	-	-	...	...	...
9 months - 9 mois	-	-	-	...	...	...
10 months - 10 mois	-	-	-	...	...	...
11 months - 11 mois	-	-	-	...	...	...

16. Infant deaths and infant mortality rates by age and sex: latest available year, 2009 - 2018
Décès d'enfants de moins d'un an et taux de mortalité infantile selon l'âge et le sexe : dernière année disponible, 2009 - 2018 (continued - suite)

Continent, country or area, year, code[a] and age / Continent, pays ou zone, année, code[a] et âge	Number - Nombre			Rate - Taux		
	Both sexes Les deux sexes	Male Masculin	Female Féminin	Both sexes Les deux sexes	Male Masculin	Female Féminin
AMERICA, NORTH - AMÉRIQUE DU NORD						
Bahamas						
2012 (+C)						
Total..................	57	26	31	...	...	...
Less than 1 day - Moins de 1 jour	-	-	-	...	...	...
1 - 6 days - 1 - 6 jours	18	10	8	...	...	...
7 - 27 days - 7 - 27 jours	19	8	11	...	...	...
7 - 13 days - 7 - 13 jours	16	6	10	...	...	...
14 - 20 days - 14 - 20 jours	2	1	1	...	...	...
21 - 27 days - 21 - 27 jours	1	1	-	...	...	...
28 days - 11 months - 28 jours - 11 mois..........	20	8	12	...	...	...
28 days - less than 2 months - 28 jours - moins de 2 mois	9	5	4	...	...	...
2 months - 2 mois..........	3	1	2	...	...	...
3 months - 3 mois..........	2	1	1	...	...	...
4 months - 4 mois..........	3	-	3	...	...	...
5 months - 5 mois..........	-	-	-	...	...	...
6 months - 6 mois..........	-	-	-	...	...	...
7 months - 7 mois..........	1	-	1	...	...	...
8 months - 8 mois..........	1	1	-	...	...	...
9 months - 9 mois..........	1	-	1	...	...	...
10 months - 10 mois..........	-	-	-	...	...	...
11 months - 11 mois..........	-	-	-	...	...	...
Belize[4]						
2016 (U)						
Total..................	103	61	42	...	...	...
Less than 1 day - Moins de 1 jour	29	14	15	...	...	...
1 - 6 days - 1 - 6 jours	36	26	10	...	...	...
7 - 27 days - 7 - 27 jours	15	8	7	...	...	...
7 - 13 days - 7 - 13 jours	2	1	1	...	...	...
14 - 20 days - 14 - 20 jours	5	2	3	...	...	...
21 - 27 days - 21 - 27 jours	8	5	3	...	...	...
28 days - 11 months - 28 jours - 11 mois..........	23	13	10	...	...	...
28 days - less than 2 months - 28 jours - moins de 2 mois	1	-	1	...	...	...
2 months - 2 mois..........	4	2	2	...	...	...
3 months - 3 mois..........	7	4	3	...	...	...
4 months - 4 mois..........	3	3	-	...	...	...
5 months - 5 mois..........	2	1	1	...	...	...
6 months - 6 mois..........	2	1	1	...	...	...
7 months - 7 mois..........	1	1	-	...	...	...
8 months - 8 mois..........	-	-	-	...	...	...
9 months - 9 mois..........	3	1	2	...	...	...
10 months - 10 mois..........	-	-	-	...	...	...
11 months - 11 mois..........	-	-	-	...	...	...
Bermuda - Bermudes						
2017 (C)						
Total..................	-	-	-	...	...	...
Less than 1 day - Moins de 1 jour	-	-	-	...	...	...
1 - 6 days - 1 - 6 jours	-	-	-	...	...	...
7 - 27 days - 7 - 27 jours	-	-	-	...	...	...
7 - 13 days - 7 - 13 jours	-	-	-	...	...	...
14 - 20 days - 14 - 20 jours	-	-	-	...	...	...
21 - 27 days - 21 - 27 jours	-	-	-	...	...	...
28 days - 11 months - 28 jours - 11 mois..........	-	-	-	...	...	...
28 days - less than 2 months - 28 jours - moins de 2 mois	-	-	-	...	...	...
2 months - 2 mois..........	-	-	-	...	...	...
3 months - 3 mois..........	-	-	-	...	...	...
4 months - 4 mois..........	-	-	-	...	...	...
5 months - 5 mois..........	-	-	-	...	...	...
6 months - 6 mois..........	-	-	-	...	...	...
7 months - 7 mois..........	-	-	-	...	...	...
8 months - 8 mois..........	-	-	-	...	...	...
9 months - 9 mois..........	-	-	-	...	...	...
10 months - 10 mois..........	-	-	-	...	...	...
11 months - 11 mois..........	-	-	-	...	...	...
Canada[5]						
2015 (C)						
Total..................	1 737	937	800	4.5	4.8	4.3
Less than 1 day - Moins de 1 jour	950	499	451	2.5	2.5	2.4
1 - 6 days - 1 - 6 jours	203	119	84	0.5	0.6	0.5

Continent, country or area, year, code[a] and age / Continent, pays ou zone, année, code[a] et âge	Number - Nombre			Rate - Taux		
	Both sexes Les deux sexes	Male Masculin	Female Féminin	Both sexes Les deux sexes	Male Masculin	Female Féminin

AMERICA, NORTH - AMÉRIQUE DU NORD

Canada[5]						
2015 (C)						
7 - 27 days - 7 - 27 jours	200	103	97	0.5	0.5	0.5
7 - 13 days - 7 - 13 jours	94	55	39	0.2	0.3	0.2
14 - 20 days - 14 - 20 jours	55	28	27	0.1	◆0.1	◆0.1
21 - 27 days - 21 - 27 jours	51	20	31	0.1	◆0.1	0.2
28 days - 11 months - 28 jours - 11 mois	454	259	195	1.2	1.3	1.0
28 days - less than 2 months - 28 jours - moins de 2 mois	185	109	76	0.5	0.6	0.4
2 months - 2 mois	70	43	27	0.2	0.2	◆0.1
3 months - 3 mois	59	37	22	0.2	0.2	◆0.1
4 months - 4 mois	27	15	12	◆0.1	◆0.1	◆0.1
5 months - 5 mois	33	16	17	0.1	◆0.1	◆0.1
6 months - 6 mois	25	10	15	◆0.1	◆0.1	◆0.1
7 months - 7 mois	15	8	7	-	-	-
8 months - 8 mois	17	8	9	-	-	-
9 months - 9 mois	8	6	2	-	-	-
10 months - 10 mois	8	5	3	-	-	-
11 months - 11 mois	7	2	5	-	-	-
Costa Rica						
2018* (C)						
Total	573	309	264	8.4	8.9	7.9
Less than 1 day - Moins de 1 jour	170	90	80	2.5	2.6	2.4
1 - 6 days - 1 - 6 jours	163	90	73	2.4	2.6	2.2
7 - 27 days - 7 - 27 jours	103	55	48	1.5	1.6	1.4
7 - 13 days - 7 - 13 jours	71	42	29	1.0	1.2	◆0.9
14 - 20 days - 14 - 20 jours	22	11	11	◆0.3	◆0.3	◆0.3
21 - 27 days - 21 - 27 jours	10	2	8	◆0.1	◆0.1	◆0.2
28 days - 11 months - 28 jours - 11 mois	137	74	63	2.0	2.1	1.9
28 days - less than 2 months - 28 jours - moins de 2 mois	53	28	25	0.8	0.8	◆0.7
2 months - 2 mois	26	17	9	◆0.4	◆0.5	◆0.3
3 months - 3 mois	9	4	5	◆0.1	◆0.1	◆0.1
4 months - 4 mois	14	7	7	◆0.2	◆0.2	◆0.2
5 months - 5 mois	11	2	9	◆0.2	◆0.1	◆0.3
6 months - 6 mois	1	1		-	-	-
7 months - 7 mois	10	7	3	◆0.1	◆0.2	◆0.1
8 months - 8 mois	4	3	1	◆0.1	◆0.1	-
9 months - 9 mois	3	1	2	-	-	◆0.1
10 months - 10 mois	4	3	1	◆0.1	◆0.1	-
11 months - 11 mois	2	1	1	-	-	-
Cuba						
2017 (C)						
Total	465	256	209	4.0	◆4.3	3.8
Less than 1 day - Moins de 1 jour	46	27	19	0.4	◆0.5	◆0.3
1 - 6 days - 1 - 6 jours	100	54	46	0.9	0.9	0.8
7 - 27 days - 7 - 27 jours	95	60	35	0.8	1.0	0.6
7 - 13 days - 7 - 13 jours	50	31	19	0.4	0.5	◆0.3
14 - 20 days - 14 - 20 jours	25	16	9	◆0.2	◆0.3	◆0.2
21 - 27 days - 21 - 27 jours	20	13	7	◆0.2	◆0.2	◆0.1
28 days - 11 months - 28 jours - 11 mois	224	115	109	1.9	1.9	2.0
28 days - less than 2 months - 28 jours - moins de 2 mois	67	33	34	0.6	0.6	0.6
2 months - 2 mois	50	30	20	0.4	0.5	0.4
3 months - 3 mois	19	9	10	◆0.2	◆0.2	◆0.2
4 months - 4 mois	22	11	11	◆0.2	◆0.2	◆0.1
5 months - 5 mois	17	11	6	◆0.1	◆0.2	◆0.1
6 months - 6 mois	11	5	6	◆0.1	◆0.1	◆0.1
7 months - 7 mois	9	3	6	◆0.1	◆0.1	◆0.1
8 months - 8 mois	5	3	2	-	◆0.1	-
9 months - 9 mois	9	3	6	◆0.1	◆0.1	◆0.1
10 months - 10 mois	8	2	6	◆0.1	-	◆0.1
11 months - 11 mois	7	5	2	◆0.1	◆0.1	-
Curaçao						
2016 (C)						
Total	20	11	9	...	...	...
Less than 1 day - Moins de 1 jour	7	3	4	...	...	...
1 - 6 days - 1 - 6 jours	3	1	2	...	...	...
7 - 27 days - 7 - 27 jours	7	5	2	...	...	...
7 - 13 days - 7 - 13 jours	6	4	2	...	...	...
14 - 20 days - 14 - 20 jours	1	1	-	...	...	...

Continent, country or area, year, code[a] and age Continent, pays ou zone, année, code[a] et âge	Number - Nombre			Rate - Taux		
	Both sexes Les deux sexes	Male Masculin	Female Féminin	Both sexes Les deux sexes	Male Masculin	Female Féminin
AMERICA, NORTH - AMÉRIQUE DU NORD						
Curaçao						
2016 (C)						
21 - 27 days - 21 - 27 jours	-	-	-	...	...	...
28 days - 11 months - 28 jours - 11 mois...........	39	20	19	...	...	...
28 days - less than 2 months - 28 jours - moins de 2 mois	1	-	1	...	...	...
2 months - 2 mois	18	9	9	...	...	...
3 months - 3 mois	20	11	9	...	...	...
4 months - 4 mois	-	-	-	...	...	...
5 months - 5 mois	-	-	-	...	...	...
6 months - 6 mois	-	-	-	...	...	...
7 months - 7 mois	-	-	-	...	...	...
8 months - 8 mois	-	-	-	...	...	...
9 months - 9 mois	-	-	-	...	...	...
10 months - 10 mois	-	-	-	...	...	...
11 months - 11 mois	-	-	-	...	...	...
Dominican Republic - République dominicaine						
2017 (U)						
Total............	674	372	302	...	...	...
Less than 1 day - Moins de 1 jour	95	53	42	...	...	...
1 - 6 days - 1 - 6 jours	239	134	105	...	...	...
7 - 27 days - 7 - 27 jours	144	82	62	...	...	...
7 - 13 days - 7 - 13 jours	85	54	31	...	...	...
14 - 20 days - 14 - 20 jours	36	18	18	...	...	...
21 - 27 days - 21 - 27 jours	23	10	13	...	...	...
28 days - 11 months - 28 jours - 11 mois............	196	103	93	...	...	...
28 days - less than 2 months - 28 jours - moins de 2 mois	61	28	33	...	...	...
2 months - 2 mois	21	16	5	...	...	...
3 months - 3 mois	26	11	15	...	...	...
4 months - 4 mois	23	14	9	...	...	...
5 months - 5 mois	14	8	6	...	...	...
6 months - 6 mois	11	7	4	...	...	...
7 months - 7 mois	10	4	6	...	...	...
8 months - 8 mois	10	5	5	...	...	...
9 months - 9 mois	8	4	4	...	...	...
10 months - 10 mois	6	3	3	...	...	...
11 months - 11 mois	6	3	3	...	...	...
El Salvador[6]						
2014 (C)						
Total............	876	491	385	8.0	8.8	7.3
Less than 1 day - Moins de 1 jour	158	90	68	1.5	1.6	1.3
1 - 6 days - 1 - 6 jours	163	91	72	1.5	1.6	1.4
7 - 27 days - 7 - 27 jours	141	78	63	1.3	1.4	1.2
7 - 13 days - 7 - 13 jours	65	32	33	0.6	0.6	0.6
14 - 20 days - 14 - 20 jours	42	24	18	0.4	♦0.4	♦0.3
21 - 27 days - 21 - 27 jours	34	22	12	0.3	♦0.4	♦0.2
28 days - 11 months - 28 jours - 11 mois............	414	232	182	3.8	4.1	3.4
28 days - less than 2 months - 28 jours - moins de 2 mois	97	49	48	0.9	0.9	0.9
2 months - 2 mois	56	33	23	0.5	0.6	♦0.4
3 months - 3 mois	44	28	16	0.4	♦0.5	♦0.3
4 months - 4 mois	35	23	12	0.3	♦0.4	♦0.2
5 months - 5 mois	26	16	10	♦0.2	♦0.3	♦0.2
6 months - 6 mois	38	27	11	0.3	♦0.5	♦0.2
7 months - 7 mois	28	13	15	♦0.3	♦0.2	♦0.3
8 months - 8 mois	20	10	10	♦0.2	♦0.2	♦0.2
9 months - 9 mois	21	9	12	♦0.2	♦0.2	♦0.2
10 months - 10 mois	21	9	12	♦0.2	♦0.2	♦0.2
11 months - 11 mois	28	15	13	♦0.3	♦0.3	♦0.2
Grenada - Grenade						
2014 (+C)						
Total............	33	21	12			
Less than 1 day - Moins de 1 jour	18	11	7	...	...	...
1 - 6 days - 1 - 6 jours	6	4	2	...	...	...
7 - 27 days - 7 - 27 jours	3	1	2	...	...	...
28 days - 11 months - 28 jours - 11 mois............	6	5	1	...	...	...
28 days - 3 months - 28 jours - 3 mois............	2	1	1	...	...	...
4 - 6 months - 4 - 6 mois	1	1	-	...	...	...
7 - 11 months - 7 - 11 mois	3	3	-	...	...	...

Continent, country or area, year, code[a] and age / Continent, pays ou zone, année, code[a] et âge	Number - Nombre			Rate - Taux		
	Both sexes Les deux sexes	Male Masculin	Female Féminin	Both sexes Les deux sexes	Male Masculin	Female Féminin
AMERICA, NORTH - AMÉRIQUE DU NORD						
Guatemala						
2016 (C)						
Total	8 366	4 750	3 616	21.4	23.9	18.8
Less than 1 day - Moins de 1 jour	421	221	200	1.1	1.1	1.0
1 - 6 days - 1 - 6 jours	2 217	1 304	913	5.7	6.6	4.8
7 - 27 days - 7 - 27 jours	1 486	847	639	3.8	4.3	3.3
7 - 13 days - 7 - 13 jours	768	439	329	2.0	2.2	1.7
14 - 27 days - 14 - 27 jours	718	408	310	1.8	2.1	1.6
28 days - 11 months - 28 jours - 11 mois	4 242	2 378	1 864	10.9	12.0	9.7
28 days - less than 2 months - 28 jours - moins de 2 mois	1 665	935	730	4.3	4.7	3.8
2 - 11 months - 2 - 11 mois	2 577	1 443	1 134	6.6	7.3	5.9
Mexico - Mexique[7]						
2017 (+C)						
Total	25 180	14 051	11 043	11.3	...	...
Less than 1 day - Moins de 1 jour	4 625	2 515	2 053	2.1	...	...
1 - 6 days - 1 - 6 jours	6 154	3 574	2 566	2.8	...	...
7 - 27 days - 7 - 27 jours	4 977	2 773	2 194	2.2	...	...
7 - 13 days - 7 - 13 jours	2 673	1 506	1 161	1.2	...	...
14 - 20 days - 14 - 20 jours	1 356	741	612	0.6	...	...
21 - 27 days - 21 - 27 jours	948	526	421	0.4	...	...
28 days - 11 months - 28 jours - 11 mois	9 423	5 188	4 230	4.2	...	...
28 days - less than 2 months - 28 jours - moins de 2 mois	2 830	1 611	1 217	1.3	...	...
2 months - 2 mois	1 641	951	688	0.7	...	...
3 months - 3 mois	1 156	654	502	0.5	...	...
4 months - 4 mois	869	465	403	0.4	...	...
5 months - 5 mois	663	346	317	0.3	...	...
6 months - 6 mois	511	268	243	0.2	...	...
7 months - 7 mois	443	225	218	0.2	...	...
8 months - 8 mois	393	194	199	0.2	...	...
9 months - 9 mois	346	174	172	0.2	...	...
10 months - 10 mois	324	178	146	0.1	...	...
11 months - 11 mois	247	122	125	0.1	...	...
Unknown - Inconnu	1	1	-	-	...	...
Montserrat						
2016 (C)						
Total	-	-	-	...	...	...
Less than 1 day - Moins de 1 jour	-	-	-	...	...	...
1 - 6 days - 1 - 6 jours	-	-	-	...	...	...
7 - 27 days - 7 - 27 jours	-	-	-	...	...	...
28 days - 11 months - 28 jours - 11 mois	-	-	-	...	...	...
Panama						
2017* (C)						
Total	1 063	590	473	14.0	15.0	12.9
Less than 1 day - Moins de 1 jour	128	67	61	1.7	1.7	1.7
1 - 6 days - 1 - 6 jours	283	160	123	3.7	4.1	3.3
7 - 27 days - 7 - 27 jours	172	99	73	2.3	2.5	2.0
7 - 13 days - 7 - 13 jours	79	43	36	1.0	1.1	1.0
14 - 20 days - 14 - 20 jours	52	33	19	0.7	0.8	♦0.5
21 - 27 days - 21 - 27 jours	41	23	18	0.5	♦0.6	♦0.5
28 days - 11 months - 28 jours - 11 mois	480	264	216	6.3	6.7	5.9
28 days - less than 2 months - 28 jours - moins de 2 mois	159	81	78	2.1	2.1	2.1
2 months - 2 mois	78	46	32	1.0	1.2	0.9
3 months - 3 mois	52	31	21	0.7	0.8	♦0.6
4 months - 4 mois	33	19	14	0.4	♦0.5	♦0.4
5 months - 5 mois	24	10	14	♦0.3	♦0.3	♦0.4
6 months - 6 mois	34	18	16	0.4	♦0.5	♦0.4
7 months - 7 mois	17	10	7	♦0.2	♦0.3	♦0.2
8 months - 8 mois	25	16	9	♦0.3	♦0.4	♦0.2
9 months - 9 mois	14	8	6	♦0.2	♦0.2	♦0.2
10 months - 10 mois	21	12	9	♦0.3	♦0.3	♦0.2
11 months - 11 mois	23	13	10	♦0.3	♦0.3	♦0.3
Puerto Rico - Porto Rico						
2018 (C)						
Total	142	82	60	6.6	7.5	5.7
Less than 1 day - Moins de 1 jour	27	12	15	♦1.3	♦1.1	♦1.4
1 - 6 days - 1 - 6 jours	38	26	12	1.8	♦2.4	♦1.1
7 - 27 days - 7 - 27 jours	25	14	11	♦1.2	♦1.3	♦1.1
7 - 13 days - 7 - 13 jours	14	7	7	♦0.7	♦0.6	♦0.7

16. Infant deaths and infant mortality rates by age and sex: latest available year, 2009 - 2018
Décès d'enfants de moins d'un an et taux de mortalité infantile selon l'âge et le sexe : dernière année disponible, 2009 - 2018 (continued - suite)

Continent, country or area, year, code[a] and age / Continent, pays ou zone, année, code[a] et âge	Number - Nombre			Rate - Taux		
	Both sexes Les deux sexes	Male Masculin	Female Féminin	Both sexes Les deux sexes	Male Masculin	Female Féminin
AMERICA, NORTH - AMÉRIQUE DU NORD						
Puerto Rico - Porto Rico						
2018 (C)						
14 - 20 days - 14 - 20 jours	6	3	3	◆0.3	◆0.3	◆0.3
21 - 27 days - 21 - 27 jours	5	4	1	◆0.2	◆0.4	◆0.1
28 days - 11 months - 28 jours - 11 mois	52	30	22	2.4	2.7	◆2.1
28 days - less than 2 months - 28 jours - moins de 2 mois	18	12	6	◆0.8	◆1.1	◆0.6
2 months - 2 mois	9	6	3	◆0.4	◆0.5	◆0.3
3 months - 3 mois	5	3	2	◆0.2	◆0.3	◆0.2
4 months - 4 mois	6	3	3	◆0.3	◆0.3	◆0.3
5 months - 5 mois	4	2	2	◆0.2	◆0.3	◆0.2
6 months - 6 mois	3	3	-	◆0.1	◆0.3	-
7 months - 7 mois	3	-	3	◆0.1	-	◆0.3
8 months - 8 mois	2	1	1	◆0.1	◆0.1	◆0.1
9 months - 9 mois	-	-	-	-	-	-
10 months - 10 mois	1	-	1	-	-	◆0.1
11 months - 11 mois	1	-	1	-	-	◆0.1
Saint Vincent and the Grenadines - Saint-Vincent-et-les Grenadines						
2016 (C)						
Total	25	11	14	...	...	...
Less than 1 day - Moins de 1 jour	4	2	2	...	...	...
1 - 6 days - 1 - 6 jours	11	5	6	...	...	...
7 - 27 days - 7 - 27 jours	4	2	2	...	...	...
28 days - 11 months - 28 jours - 11 mois	6	2	4	...	...	...
28 days - 6 months - 28 jours - 6 mois	4	1	3	...	...	...
7 - 11 months - 7 - 11 mois	2	1	1	...	...	...
Trinidad and Tobago - Trinité-et-Tobago						
2012* (C)						
Total	213	103	110	11.4	10.9	11.9
Less than 1 day - Moins de 1 jour	43	16	27	2.3	◆1.7	◆2.9
1 - 6 days - 1 - 6 jours	60	29	31	3.2	◆3.1	3.3
7 - 27 days - 7 - 27 jours	37	19	18	2.0	◆2.0	◆1.9
7 - 13 days - 7 - 13 jours	18	10	8	◆1.0	◆1.1	◆0.9
14 - 20 days - 14 - 20 jours	13	7	6	◆0.7	◆0.7	◆0.6
21 - 27 days - 21 - 27 jours	6	2	4	◆0.3	◆0.2	◆0.4
28 days - 11 months - 28 jours - 11 mois	73	39	34	3.9	4.1	3.7
28 days - less than 2 months - 28 jours - moins de 2 mois	36	16	20	1.9	◆1.7	◆2.2
2 - 11 months - 2 - 11 mois	37	23	14	2.0	◆2.4	◆1.5
United States of America - États-Unis d'Amérique						
2015 (C)						
Total	23 455	13 008	10 447	5.9	6.4	5.4
Less than 1 day - Moins de 1 jour	9 479	5 226	4 253	2.4	2.6	2.2
1 - 6 days - 1 - 6 jours	3 088	1 733	1 355	0.8	0.9	0.7
7 - 27 days - 7 - 27 jours	3 085	1 632	1 453	0.8	0.8	0.7
7 - 13 days - 7 - 13 jours	1 442	765	677	0.4	0.4	0.3
14 - 20 days - 14 - 20 jours	950	500	450	0.2	0.2	0.2
21 - 27 days - 21 - 27 jours	693	367	326	0.2	0.2	0.2
28 days - 11 months - 28 jours - 11 mois	7 803	4 417	3 386	2.0	2.2	1.7
28 days - less than 2 months - 28 jours - moins de 2 mois	2 050	1 105	945	0.5	0.5	0.5
2 months - 2 mois	1 462	838	624	0.4	0.4	0.3
3 months - 3 mois	1 144	681	463	0.3	0.3	0.2
4 months - 4 mois	826	489	337	0.2	0.2	0.2
5 months - 5 mois	623	371	252	0.2	0.2	0.1
6 months - 6 mois	460	252	208	0.1	0.1	0.1
7 months - 7 mois	344	210	134	0.1	0.1	0.1
8 months - 8 mois	286	159	127	0.1	0.1	0.1
9 months - 9 mois	239	123	116	0.1	0.1	0.1
10 months - 10 mois	184	98	86	-	-	-
11 months - 11 mois	185	91	94	-	-	-
AMERICA, SOUTH - AMÉRIQUE DU SUD						
Brazil - Brésil						
2017 (+C)						
Total	30 636	16 597[3]	13 682[3]	10.3	10.9	9.5
Less than 1 day - Moins de 1 jour	6 678	3 609[3]	2 948[3]	2.3	2.4	2.0
1 - 6 days - 1 - 6 jours	9 168	5 105[3]	3 982[3]	3.1	3.4	2.8

16. Infant deaths and infant mortality rates by age and sex: latest available year, 2009 - 2018
Décès d'enfants de moins d'un an et taux de mortalité infantile selon l'âge et le sexe : dernière année disponible, 2009 - 2018 (continued - suite)

Continent, country or area, year, code[a] and age / Continent, pays ou zone, année, code[a] et âge	Number - Nombre			Rate - Taux		
	Both sexes Les deux sexes	Male Masculin	Female Féminin	Both sexes Les deux sexes	Male Masculin	Female Féminin
AMERICA, SOUTH - AMÉRIQUE DU SUD						
Brazil - Brésil						
2017 (+C)						
7 - 27 days - 7 - 27 jours	5 359	2 875[3]	2 453[3]	1.8	1.9	1.7
7 - 13 days - 7 - 13 jours	2 847	1 499[3]	1 332[3]	1.0	1.0	0.9
14 - 20 days - 14 - 20 jours	1 518	826[3]	684[3]	0.5	0.5	0.5
21 - 27 days - 21 - 27 jours	994	550[3]	437[3]	0.3	0.4	0.3
28 days - 11 months - 28 jours - 11 mois	9 431	5 008[3]	4 299[3]	3.2	3.3	3.0
28 days - less than 2 months - 28 jours - moins de 2 mois	3 045	1 648[3]	1 372[3]	1.0	1.1	1.0
2 months - 2 mois	1 520	852[3]	655[3]	0.5	0.6	0.5
3 months - 3 mois	1 053	542[3]	498[3]	0.4	0.4	0.3
4 months - 4 mois	799	422[3]	363[3]	0.3	0.3	0.3
5 months - 5 mois	661	342[3]	305[3]	0.2	0.2	0.2
6 months - 6 mois	548	271[3]	268[3]	0.2	0.2	0.2
7 months - 7 mois	451	243[3]	202[3]	0.2	0.2	0.1
8 months - 8 mois	388	208[3]	174[3]	0.1	0.1	0.1
9 months - 9 mois	388	189[3]	191[3]	0.1	0.1	0.1
10 months - 10 mois	316	161[3]	143[3]	0.1	0.1	0.1
11 months - 11 mois	262	130[3]	128[3]	0.1	0.1	0.1
Chile - Chili						
2016 (C)						
Total	1 629	873[8]	730[8]	7.0	7.4	6.4
Less than 1 day - Moins de 1 jour	641	343[8]	276[8]	2.8	2.9	2.4
1 - 6 days - 1 - 6 jours	315	170[8]	144[8]	1.4	1.4	1.3
7 - 27 days - 7 - 27 jours	257	145[8]	109[8]	1.1	1.2	1.0
7 - 13 days - 7 - 13 jours	121	64[8]	56[8]	0.5	0.5	0.5
14 - 20 days - 14 - 20 jours	90	50[8]	39[8]	0.4	0.4	0.3
21 - 27 days - 21 - 27 jours	46	31[8]	14[8]	0.2	0.3	♦0.1
28 days - 11 months - 28 jours - 11 mois	416	215[8]	201[8]	1.8	1.8	1.8
28 days - less than 2 months - 28 jours - moins de 2 mois	128	72[8]	56[8]	0.6	0.6	0.5
2 months - 2 mois	62	33[8]	29[8]	0.3	0.3	♦0.3
3 months - 3 mois	47	16[8]	31[8]	0.2	♦0.1	0.3
4 months - 4 mois	42	25[8]	17[8]	0.2	♦0.2	♦0.1
5 months - 5 mois	41	23[8]	18[8]	0.2	♦0.2	♦0.2
6 months - 6 mois	19	11[8]	8[8]	♦0.1	♦0.1	♦0.1
7 months - 7 mois	16	10[8]	6[8]	♦0.1	♦0.1	♦0.1
8 months - 8 mois	25	9[8]	16[8]	♦0.1	♦0.1	♦0.1
9 months - 9 mois	15	6[8]	9[8]	♦0.1	♦0.1	♦0.1
10 months - 10 mois	9	4[8]	5[8]	-	-	-
11 months - 11 mois	12	6[8]	6[8]	♦0.1	♦0.1	♦0.1
Colombia - Colombie						
2017 (U)						
Total	7 044	3 986[8]	3 050[8]	...	...	...
Less than 1 day - Moins de 1 jour	1 385	800[8]	580[8]	...	...	...
1 - 6 days - 1 - 6 jours	1 728	1 048[8]	678[8]	...	...	...
7 - 27 days - 7 - 27 jours	1 415	784[8]	631[8]	...	...	...
7 - 13 days - 7 - 13 jours	740	417[8]	323[8]	...	...	...
14 - 20 days - 14 - 20 jours	416	224[8]	192[8]	...	...	...
21 - 27 days - 21 - 27 jours	259	143[8]	116[8]	...	...	...
28 days - 11 months - 28 jours - 11 mois	2 516	1 354[8]	1 161[8]	...	...	...
28 days - less than 2 months - 28 jours - moins de 2 mois	641	341[8]	299[8]	...	...	...
2 months - 2 mois	440	239[8]	201[8]	...	...	...
3 months - 3 mois	323	173[8]	150[8]	...	...	...
4 months - 4 mois	231	110[8]	121[8]	...	...	...
5 months - 5 mois	182	103[8]	79[8]	...	...	...
6 months - 6 mois	157	80[8]	77[8]	...	...	...
7 months - 7 mois	151	90[8]	61[8]	...	...	...
8 months - 8 mois	129	74[8]	55[8]	...	...	...
9 months - 9 mois	102	57[8]	45[8]	...	...	...
10 months - 10 mois	86	56[8]	30[8]	...	...	...
11 months - 11 mois	74	31[8]	43[8]	...	...	...
Unknown - Inconnu	8	5[8]	3[8]	...	...	...

16. Infant deaths and infant mortality rates by age and sex: latest available year, 2009 - 2018
Décès d'enfants de moins d'un an et taux de mortalité infantile selon l'âge et le sexe : dernière année disponible, 2009 - 2018 (continued - suite)

Continent, country or area, year, code[a] and age / Continent, pays ou zone, année, code[a] et âge	Number - Nombre			Rate - Taux		
	Both sexes Les deux sexes	Male Masculin	Female Féminin	Both sexes Les deux sexes	Male Masculin	Female Féminin
AMERICA, SOUTH - AMÉRIQUE DU SUD						
Ecuador - Équateur[9]						
2017 (U)						
Total	3 252	1 792	1 460	...	...	...
Less than 1 day - Moins de 1 jour	384	206	178	...	...	...
1 - 6 days - 1 - 6 jours	875	514	361	...	...	...
7 - 27 days - 7 - 27 jours	600	346	254	...	...	...
7 - 13 days - 7 - 13 jours	304	176	128	...	...	...
14 - 20 days - 14 - 20 jours	167	91	76	...	...	...
21 - 27 days - 21 - 27 jours	129	79	50	...	...	...
28 days - 11 months - 28 jours - 11 mois	1 393	726	667	...	...	...
28 days - less than 2 months - 28 jours - moins de 2 mois	538	298	240	...	...	...
2 months - 2 mois	207	104	103	...	...	...
3 months - 3 mois	142	71	71	...	...	...
4 months - 4 mois	113	47	66	...	...	...
5 months - 5 mois	82	39	43	...	...	...
6 months - 6 mois	76	42	34	...	...	...
7 months - 7 mois	55	32	23	...	...	...
8 months - 8 mois	65	36	29	...	...	...
9 months - 9 mois	44	18	26	...	...	...
10 months - 10 mois	33	18	15	...	...	...
11 months - 11 mois	38	21	17	...	...	...
Peru - Pérou[10]						
2017* (+U)						
Total	5 224	2 773[8]	2 182[8]	...	...	...
Less than 1 day - Moins de 1 jour	1 050	607	443	...	...	...
1 - 6 days - 1 - 6 jours	1 145	656	489	...	...	...
7 - 27 days - 7 - 27 jours	851	480	371	...	...	...
7 - 13 days - 7 - 13 jours	416	244	172	...	...	...
14 - 20 days - 14 - 20 jours	237	123	114	...	...	...
21 - 27 days - 21 - 27 jours	198	113	85	...	...	...
28 days - 11 months - 28 jours - 11 mois	1 909	1 030	879	...	...	...
28 days - less than 2 months - 28 jours - moins de 2 mois	574	302	272	...	...	...
2 months - 2 mois	336	187	149	...	...	...
3 months - 3 mois	223	121	102	...	...	...
4 months - 4 mois	184	100	84	...	...	...
5 months - 5 mois	130	74	56	...	...	...
6 months - 6 mois	112	64	48	...	...	...
7 months - 7 mois	91	51	40	...	...	...
8 months - 8 mois	64	32	32	...	...	...
9 months - 9 mois	65	35	30	...	...	...
10 months - 10 mois	70	31	39	...	...	...
11 months - 11 mois	60	33	27	...	...	...
Unknown - Inconnu	269	_[8]	_[8]	...	...	...
Uruguay						
2017 (C)						
Total	280	152[3]	127[3]	6.5	6.9	6.1
Less than 1 day - Moins de 1 jour	46	21	25	1.1	◆0.9	◆1.2
1 - 6 days - 1 - 6 jours	82	48[3]	33[3]	1.9	2.2	1.6
7 - 27 days - 7 - 27 jours	59	35	24	1.4	1.6	◆1.1
7 - 13 days - 7 - 13 jours	29	20	9	◆0.7	◆0.9	◆0.4
14 - 20 days - 14 - 20 jours	16	12	4	◆0.4	◆0.5	◆0.2
21 - 27 days - 21 - 27 jours	14	3	11	◆0.3	◆0.1	◆0.5
28 days - 11 months - 28 jours - 11 mois	93	48	45	2.2	2.2	2.2
28 days - less than 2 months - 28 jours - moins de 2 mois	25	12	13	◆0.6	◆0.5	◆0.6
2 months - 2 mois	16	9	7	◆0.4	◆0.4	◆0.3
3 months - 3 mois	10	5	5	◆0.2	◆0.2	◆0.2
4 months - 4 mois	10	5	5	◆0.2	◆0.2	◆0.2
5 months - 5 mois	5	4	1	◆0.1	◆0.2	-
6 months - 6 mois	6	5	1	◆0.1	◆0.2	-
7 months - 7 mois	3	3	-	◆0.1	◆0.1	-
8 months - 8 mois	3	1	2	◆0.1	-	◆0.1
9 months - 9 mois	5	-	5	◆0.1	-	◆0.2
10 months - 10 mois	5	2	3	◆0.1	◆0.1	◆0.1
11 months - 11 mois	5	2	3	◆0.1	◆0.1	◆0.1
Venezuela (Bolivarian Republic of) - Venezuela (République bolivarienne du)						
2017 (C)						
Total	11 671	6 626	5 045	...		

16. Infant deaths and infant mortality rates by age and sex: latest available year, 2009 - 2018
Décès d'enfants de moins d'un an et taux de mortalité infantile selon l'âge et le sexe : dernière année disponible, 2009 - 2018 (continued - suite)

Continent, country or area, year, code[a] and age / Continent, pays ou zone, année, code[a] et âge	Number - Nombre			Rate - Taux		
	Both sexes Les deux sexes	Male Masculin	Female Féminin	Both sexes Les deux sexes	Male Masculin	Female Féminin
ASIA - ASIE						
Armenia - Arménie[11]						
2017 (C)						
Total	311	174	137	8.2	8.8	7.6
Less than 1 day - Moins de 1 jour	29	17	12	♦0.8	♦0.9	♦0.7
1 - 6 days - 1 - 6 jours	128	74	54	3.4	3.8	3.0
7 - 27 days - 7 - 27 jours	78	44	34	2.1	2.2	1.9
7 - 13 days - 7 - 13 jours	41	28	13	1.1	♦1.4	♦0.7
14 - 20 days - 14 - 20 jours	25	10	15	♦0.7	♦0.5	♦0.8
21 - 27 days - 21 - 27 jours	12	6	6	♦0.3	♦0.3	♦0.3
28 days - 11 months - 28 jours - 11 mois	76	39	37	2.0	2.0	2.1
28 days - less than 2 months - 28 jours - moins de 2 mois	22	13	9	♦0.6	♦0.7	♦0.5
2 months - 2 mois	9	3	6	♦0.2	♦0.2	♦0.3
3 months - 3 mois	10	5	5	♦0.3	♦0.3	♦0.3
4 months - 4 mois	14	7	7	♦0.4	♦0.4	♦0.4
5 months - 5 mois	5	5	-	♦0.1	♦0.3	-
6 months - 6 mois	6	3	3	♦0.2	♦0.2	♦0.2
7 months - 7 mois	3	3	-	♦0.1	♦0.2	-
8 months - 8 mois	2	-	2	♦0.1	-	♦0.1
9 months - 9 mois	1	-	1	-	-	♦0.1
10 months - 10 mois	1	-	1	-	-	♦0.1
11 months - 11 mois	3	-	3	♦0.1	-	♦0.2
Azerbaijan - Azerbaïdjan[11]						
2017 (+C)						
Total	1 700	993	707	11.8	13.0	10.5
Less than 1 day - Moins de 1 jour	250	132	118	1.7	1.7	1.7
1 - 6 days - 1 - 6 jours	519	302	217	3.6	3.9	3.2
7 - 27 days - 7 - 27 jours	184	110	74	1.3	1.4	1.1
7 - 13 days - 7 - 13 jours	113	76	37	0.8	1.0	0.5
14 - 20 days - 14 - 20 jours	49	24	25	0.3	♦0.3	♦0.4
21 - 27 days - 21 - 27 jours	22	10	12	♦0.2	♦0.1	♦0.2
28 days - 11 months - 28 jours - 11 mois	747	449	298	5.2	5.9	4.4
28 days - less than 2 months - 28 jours - moins de 2 mois	105	66	39	0.7	0.9	0.6
2 months - 2 mois	93	62	31	0.6	0.8	0.5
3 months - 3 mois	81	54	27	0.6	0.7	♦0.4
4 months - 4 mois	71	62	9	0.5	0.8	♦0.1
5 months - 5 mois	81	38	43	0.6	0.5	0.6
6 months - 6 mois	74	43	31	0.5	0.6	0.5
7 months - 7 mois	52	30	22	0.4	0.4	♦0.3
8 months - 8 mois	76	40	36	0.5	0.5	0.5
9 months - 9 mois	47	19	28	0.3	♦0.2	♦0.4
10 months - 10 mois	37	19	18	0.3	♦0.2	♦0.3
11 months - 11 mois	30	16	14	0.2	♦0.2	♦0.2
Bahrain - Bahreïn[12]						
2014 (C)						
Total	218	113	105	10.4	10.5	10.3
Less than 1 day - Moins de 1 jour	25	12	13	♦1.2	♦1.1	♦1.3
1 - 6 days - 1 - 6 jours	55	34	21	2.6	3.2	♦2.1
7 - 27 days - 7 - 27 jours	23	15	8	♦1.1	♦1.4	♦0.8
7 - 13 days - 7 - 13 jours	8	6	2	♦0.4	♦0.6	♦0.2
14 - 20 days - 14 - 20 jours	7	4	3	♦0.3	♦0.4	♦0.3
21 - 27 days - 21 - 27 jours	8	5	3	♦0.4	♦0.5	♦0.3
28 days - 11 months - 28 jours - 11 mois	80	36	44	3.8	3.3	4.3
28 days - less than 2 months - 28 jours - moins de 2 mois	34	11	23	1.6	♦1.0	♦2.3
2 months - 2 mois	12	5	7	♦0.6	♦0.5	♦0.7
3 months - 3 mois	6	4	2	♦0.3	♦0.4	♦0.2
4 months - 4 mois	8	5	3	♦0.4	♦0.5	♦0.3
5 months - 5 mois	8	5	3	♦0.4	♦0.5	♦0.3
6 months - 6 mois	5	1	4	♦0.2	♦0.1	♦0.4
7 months - 7 mois	3	2	1	♦0.1	♦0.2	♦0.1
8 months - 8 mois	1	1	-	-	♦0.1	-
9 months - 9 mois	1	1	-	-	♦0.1	-
10 months - 10 mois	1	-	1	-	-	♦0.1
11 months - 11 mois	1	1	-	-	♦0.1	-
Unknown - Inconnu	35	16	19	1.7	♦1.5	♦1.9
Bangladesh						
2010 (U)						
Total	*104 591*	*55 178*	*49 413*	...	...	...
1 - 6 days - 1 - 6 jours	*56 108*	*30 276*	*25 832*	...	...	...

16. Infant deaths and infant mortality rates by age and sex: latest available year, 2009 - 2018
Décès d'enfants de moins d'un an et taux de mortalité infantile selon l'âge et le sexe : dernière année disponible, 2009 - 2018 (continued - suite)

Continent, country or area, year, code[a] and age / Continent, pays ou zone, année, code[a] et âge	Number - Nombre			Rate - Taux		
	Both sexes Les deux sexes	Male Masculin	Female Féminin	Both sexes Les deux sexes	Male Masculin	Female Féminin
ASIA - ASIE						
Bangladesh						
2010 (U)						
7 - 27 days - 7 - 27 jours	17 576	9 234	8 342	...	...	...
7 - 13 days - 7 - 13 jours	8 488	4 491	3 997	...	...	...
14 - 20 days - 14 - 20 jours	4 845	2 546	2 299	...	...	...
21 - 27 days - 21 - 27 jours	4 243	2 197	2 046	...	...	...
28 days - 11 months - 28 jours - 11 mois	30 907	15 668	15 239	...	...	...
28 days - less than 2 months - 28 jours - moins de 2 mois	7 377	3 906	3 471	...	...	...
2 months - 2 mois	5 234	2 674	2 560	...	...	...
3 months - 3 mois	4 381	2 248	2 133	...	...	...
4 months - 4 mois	2 628	1 333	1 295	...	...	...
5 months - 5 mois	1 188	606	582	...	...	...
6 months - 6 mois	2 123	1 050	1 073	...	...	...
7 months - 7 mois	1 361	669	692	...	...	...
8 months - 8 mois	1 905	918	987	...	...	...
9 months - 9 mois	1 420	696	724	...	...	...
10 months - 10 mois	1 188	566	622	...	...	...
11 months - 11 mois	2 102	1 002	1 100	...	...	...
China, Hong Kong SAR - Chine, Hong Kong RAS						
2018 (C)						
Total	80	41[3]	38[3]	...	...	...
Less than 1 day - Moins de 1 jour	11	6	5	...	...	...
1 - 6 days - 1 - 6 jours	22	10	12	...	...	...
7 - 27 days - 7 - 27 jours	18	10	8	...	...	...
7 - 13 days - 7 - 13 jours	9	4	5	...	...	...
14 - 20 days - 14 - 20 jours	7	6	1	...	...	...
21 - 27 days - 21 - 27 jours	2	-	2	...	...	...
28 days - 11 months - 28 jours - 11 mois	28	15	13	...	...	...
28 days - less than 2 months - 28 jours - moins de 2 mois	4	1	3	...	...	...
2 months - 2 mois	7	4	3	...	...	...
3 months - 3 mois	7	4	3	...	...	...
4 months - 4 mois	3	1	2	...	...	...
5 months - 5 mois	-	-	-	...	...	...
6 months - 6 mois	1	1	-	...	...	...
7 months - 7 mois	2	1	1	...	...	...
8 months - 8 mois	3	3	-	...	...	...
9 months - 9 mois	1	-	1	...	...	...
10 months - 10 mois	-	-	-	...	...	...
11 months - 11 mois	-	-	-	...	...	...
Unknown - Inconnu	1	_[3]	_[3]	...	...	...
China, Macao SAR - Chine, Macao RAS						
2010 (C)						
Total	15	7	8	...	...	...
Less than 1 day - Moins de 1 jour	7	3	4	...	...	...
1 - 6 days - 1 - 6 jours	4	2	2	...	...	...
7 - 27 days - 7 - 27 jours	2	1	1	...	...	...
7 - 13 days - 7 - 13 jours	-	-	-	...	...	...
14 - 20 days - 14 - 20 jours	1	-	1	...	...	...
21 - 27 days - 21 - 27 jours	1	1	-	...	...	...
28 days - 11 months - 28 jours - 11 mois	2	1	1	...	...	...
28 days - less than 2 months - 28 jours - moins de 2 mois	1	-	1	...	...	...
2 months - 2 mois	-	-	-	...	...	...
3 months - 3 mois	-	-	-	...	...	...
4 months - 4 mois	1	1	-	...	...	...
5 months - 5 mois	-	-	-	...	...	...
6 months - 6 mois	-	-	-	...	...	...
7 months - 7 mois	-	-	-	...	...	...
8 months - 8 mois	-	-	-	...	...	...
9 months - 9 mois	-	-	-	...	...	...
10 months - 10 mois	-	-	-	...	...	...
11 months - 11 mois	-	-	-	...	...	...
Cyprus - Chypre[13]						
2011 (C)						
Total	30	18	12	...	...	...
Less than 1 day - Moins de 1 jour	10	6	4	...	...	...
1 - 6 days - 1 - 6 jours	8	4	4	...	...	...
7 - 27 days - 7 - 27 jours	3	2	1	...	...	...
28 days - 11 months - 28 jours - 11 mois	9	6	3	...	...	...

16. Infant deaths and infant mortality rates by age and sex: latest available year, 2009 - 2018

Décès d'enfants de moins d'un an et taux de mortalité infantile selon l'âge et le sexe : dernière année disponible, 2009 - 2018 (continued - suite)

Continent, country or area, year, code[a] and age / Continent, pays ou zone, année, code[a] et âge	Number - Nombre			Rate - Taux		
	Both sexes Les deux sexes	Male Masculin	Female Féminin	Both sexes Les deux sexes	Male Masculin	Female Féminin
ASIA - ASIE						
Georgia - Géorgie[11]						
2017 (C)						
Total	512	278	234	9.6	10.1	9.1
Less than 1 day - Moins de 1 jour	62	33	29	1.2	1.2	♦1.1
1 - 6 days - 1 - 6 jours	176	99	77	3.3	3.6	3.0
7 - 27 days - 7 - 27 jours	124	69	55	2.3	2.5	2.1
28 days - 11 months - 28 jours - 11 mois	150	77	73	2.8	2.8	2.8
Israel - Israël[14]						
2018 (C)						
Total	543	278[3]	264[3]	2.9	...	...
Less than 1 day - Moins de 1 jour	133	64[3]	68[3]	0.7	...	...
1 - 6 days - 1 - 6 jours	121	66[3]	55[3]	0.7	...	...
7 - 27 days - 7 - 27 jours	104	54[3]	50[3]	0.6	...	...
7 - 13 days - 7 - 13 jours	60	30[3]	30[3]	0.3	...	...
14 - 20 days - 14 - 20 jours	25	16[3]	9[3]	♦0.1	...	...
21 - 27 days - 21 - 27 jours	19	8[3]	11[3]	♦0.1	...	...
28 days - 11 months - 28 jours - 11 mois	185	94[3]	91[3]	1.0	...	...
28 days - less than 2 months - 28 jours - moins de 2 mois	57	26[3]	31[3]	0.3	...	...
2 months - 2 mois	28	19[3]	9[3]	♦0.2	...	...
3 months - 3 mois	14	5[3]	9[3]	♦0.1	...	...
4 months - 4 mois	20	11[3]	9[3]	♦0.1	...	...
5 months - 5 mois	13	6[3]	7[3]	♦0.1	...	...
6 months - 6 mois	17	7[3]	10[3]	♦0.1	...	...
7 months - 7 mois	5	4[3]	1[3]	-	...	...
8 months - 8 mois	7	2[3]	5[3]	-	...	...
9 months - 9 mois	8	1[3]	7[3]	-	...	...
10 months - 10 mois	7	5[3]	2[3]	-	...	...
11 months - 11 mois	9	8[3]	1[3]	-	...	...
Japan - Japon[15]						
2017 (C)						
Total	1 761	929	832	1.9	1.9	1.8
Less than 1 day - Moins de 1 jour	447	247	200	0.5	0.5	0.4
1 - 6 days - 1 - 6 jours	178	100	78	0.2	0.2	0.2
7 - 27 days - 7 - 27 jours	207	113	94	0.2	0.2	0.2
7 - 13 days - 7 - 13 jours	80	49	31	0.1	0.1	0.1
14 - 20 days - 14 - 20 jours	74	37	37	0.1	0.1	0.1
21 - 27 days - 21 - 27 jours	53	27	26	0.1	♦0.1	♦0.1
28 days - 11 months - 28 jours - 11 mois	929	469	460	1.0	1.0	1.0
28 days - less than 2 months - 28 jours - moins de 2 mois	200	102	98	0.2	0.2	0.2
2 months - 2 mois	119	63	56	0.1	0.1	0.1
3 months - 3 mois	104	58	46	0.1	0.1	0.1
4 months - 4 mois	107	44	63	0.1	0.1	0.1
5 months - 5 mois	83	46	37	0.1	0.1	0.1
6 months - 6 mois	67	29	38	0.1	♦0.1	0.1
7 months - 7 mois	65	31	34	0.1	0.1	0.1
8 months - 8 mois	60	35	25	0.1	0.1	♦0.1
9 months - 9 mois	53	28	25	0.1	♦0.1	♦0.1
10 months - 10 mois	41	22	19	-	-	-
11 months - 11 mois	30	11	19	-	-	-
Kazakhstan						
2018 (C)						
Total	3 184	1 892	1 292	8.0	9.2	6.7
Less than 1 day - Moins de 1 jour	168	88	80	0.4	0.4	0.4
1 - 6 days - 1 - 6 jours	878	540	338	2.2	2.6	1.8
7 - 27 days - 7 - 27 jours	775	464	311	1.9	2.3	1.6
7 - 13 days - 7 - 13 jours	378	233	145	1.0	1.1	0.8
14 - 20 days - 14 - 20 jours	229	137	92	0.6	0.7	0.5
21 - 27 days - 21 - 27 jours	168	94	74	0.4	0.5	0.4
28 days - 11 months - 28 jours - 11 mois	1 363	800	563	3.4	3.9	2.9
28 days - less than 2 months - 28 jours - moins de 2 mois	466	291	175	1.2	1.4	0.9
2 months - 2 mois	197	115	82	0.5	0.6	0.4
3 months - 3 mois	150	78	72	0.4	0.4	0.4
4 months - 4 mois	111	70	41	0.3	0.3	0.2
5 months - 5 mois	95	53	42	0.2	0.3	0.2
6 months - 6 mois	82	54	28	0.2	0.3	♦0.1
7 months - 7 mois	62	30	32	0.2	0.1	0.2
8 months - 8 mois	60	35	25	0.2	0.2	♦0.1

16. Infant deaths and infant mortality rates by age and sex: latest available year, 2009 - 2018

Décès d'enfants de moins d'un an et taux de mortalité infantile selon l'âge et le sexe : dernière année disponible, 2009 - 2018 (continued - suite)

Continent, country or area, year, code[a] and age / Continent, pays ou zone, année, code[a] et âge	Number - Nombre			Rate - Taux		
	Both sexes Les deux sexes	Male Masculin	Female Féminin	Both sexes Les deux sexes	Male Masculin	Female Féminin
ASIA - ASIE						
Kazakhstan						
2018 (C)						
9 months - 9 mois	54	27	27	0.1	♦0.1	♦0.1
10 months - 10 mois	47	32	15	0.1	0.2	♦0.1
11 months - 11 mois	39	15	24	0.1	♦0.1	♦0.1
Kuwait - Koweït						
2017 (C)						
Total	413	254	159	7.0	8.4	5.5
Less than 1 day - Moins de 1 jour	106	65	41	1.8	2.1	1.4
1 - 6 days - 1 - 6 jours	70	48	22	1.2	1.6	♦0.8
7 - 27 days - 7 - 27 jours	105	61	44	1.8	2.0	1.5
7 - 13 days - 7 - 13 jours	41	24	17	0.7	♦0.8	♦0.6
14 - 20 days - 14 - 20 jours	43	23	20	0.7	♦0.8	♦0.7
21 - 27 days - 21 - 27 jours	21	14	7	♦0.4	♦0.5	♦0.2
28 days - 11 months - 28 jours - 11 mois	132	80	52	2.2	2.6	1.8
28 days - less than 2 months - 28 jours - moins de 2 mois	42	28	14	0.7	♦0.9	♦0.5
2 months - 2 mois	19	7	12	♦0.3	♦0.2	♦0.4
3 months - 3 mois	10	5	5	♦0.2	♦0.2	♦0.2
4 months - 4 mois	12	7	5	♦0.2	♦0.2	♦0.2
5 months - 5 mois	9	6	3	♦0.2	♦0.2	♦0.1
6 months - 6 mois	10	5	5	♦0.2	♦0.2	♦0.2
7 months - 7 mois	8	4	4	♦0.1	♦0.1	♦0.1
8 months - 8 mois	4	3	1	♦0.1	♦0.1	-
9 months - 9 mois	6	6	-	♦0.1	♦0.2	-
10 months - 10 mois	5	4	1	♦0.1	♦0.1	♦0.1
11 months - 11 mois	7	5	2	♦0.1	♦0.2	♦0.1
Kyrgyzstan - Kirghizstan						
2017 (C)						
Total	2 401	1 340	1 061	15.6	17.0	14.2
Less than 1 day - Moins de 1 jour	558	320	238	3.6	4.1	3.2
1 - 6 days - 1 - 6 jours	992	567	425	6.5	7.2	5.7
7 - 27 days - 7 - 27 jours	262	147	115	1.7	1.9	1.5
7 - 13 days - 7 - 13 jours	167	97	70	1.1	1.2	0.9
14 - 20 days - 14 - 20 jours	63	32	31	0.4	0.4	0.4
21 - 27 days - 21 - 27 jours	32	18	14	0.2	♦0.2	♦0.2
28 days - 11 months - 28 jours - 11 mois	589	306	283	3.8	3.9	3.8
28 days - less than 2 months - 28 jours - moins de 2 mois	143	66	77	0.9	0.8	1.0
2 months - 2 mois	68	36	32	0.4	0.5	0.4
3 months - 3 mois	66	40	26	0.4	0.5	♦0.3
4 months - 4 mois	55	30	25	0.4	0.4	♦0.3
5 months - 5 mois	63	32	31	0.4	0.4	0.4
6 months - 6 mois	35	15	20	0.2	♦0.2	♦0.3
7 months - 7 mois	49	19	30	0.3	♦0.2	0.4
8 months - 8 mois	33	19	14	0.2	♦0.2	♦0.2
9 months - 9 mois	27	16	11	♦0.2	♦0.2	♦0.1
10 months - 10 mois	27	17	10	♦0.2	♦0.2	♦0.1
11 months - 11 mois	23	16	7	♦0.1	♦0.2	♦0.1
Maldives[16]						
2017 (C)						
Total	64	42	22	...	...	...
Less than 1 day - Moins de 1 jour	17	13	4	...	...	...
1 - 6 days - 1 - 6 jours	28	16	12	...	...	...
7 - 27 days - 7 - 27 jours	6	3	3	...	...	...
7 - 13 days - 7 - 13 jours	3	1	2	...	...	...
14 - 20 days - 14 - 20 jours	3	2	1	...	...	...
21 - 27 days - 21 - 27 jours	-	-	-	...	...	...
28 days - 11 months - 28 jours - 11 mois	13	10	3	...	...	...
28 days - less than 2 months - 28 jours - moins de 2 mois	5	4	1	...	...	...
2 months - 2 mois	3	2	1	...	...	...
3 months - 3 mois	2	1	1	...	...	...
4 months - 4 mois	1	1	-	...	...	...
5 months - 5 mois	-	-	-	...	...	...
6 months - 6 mois	2	2	-	...	...	...
7 months - 7 mois	-	-	-	...	...	...
8 months - 8 mois	-	-	-	...	...	...
9 months - 9 mois	-	-	-	...	...	...
10 months - 10 mois	-	-	-	...	...	...
11 months - 11 mois	-	-	-	...	...	...

16. Infant deaths and infant mortality rates by age and sex: latest available year, 2009 - 2018
Décès d'enfants de moins d'un an et taux de mortalité infantile selon l'âge et le sexe : dernière année disponible, 2009 - 2018 (continued - suite)

Continent, country or area, year, code[a] and age Continent, pays ou zone, année, code[a] et âge	Number - Nombre			Rate - Taux		
	Both sexes Les deux sexes	Male Masculin	Female Féminin	Both sexes Les deux sexes	Male Masculin	Female Féminin
ASIA - ASIE						
Mongolia - Mongolie						
2017 (+C)						
Total..	1 009	572	437	13.4	14.7	12.0
1 - 6 days - 1 - 6 jours	475	282	193	6.3	7.2	5.3
7 - 27 days - 7 - 27 jours	172	94	78	2.3	2.4	2.1
28 days - 11 months - 28 jours - 11 mois..........	362	196	166	4.8	5.0	4.6
Myanmar[17]						
2016 (+U)						
Total..	9 476	5 334	4 142	...	...	...
Less than 1 day - Moins de 1 jour	243	127	116	...	...	...
1 - 6 days - 1 - 6 jours	4 242	2 459	1 783	...	...	...
7 - 27 days - 7 - 27 jours	1 646	939	707	...	...	...
7 - 13 days - 7 - 13 jours	854	504	350	...	...	...
14 - 20 days - 14 - 20 jours	459	240	219	...	...	...
21 - 27 days - 21 - 27 jours	333	195	138	...	...	...
28 days - 11 months - 28 jours - 11 mois..........	3 019	1 620	1 399	...	...	...
28 days - less than 2 months - 28 jours - moins de 2 mois	898	500	398	...	...	...
2 months - 2 mois	510	270	240	...	...	...
3 months - 3 mois	315	165	150	...	...	...
4 months - 4 mois	260	129	131	...	...	...
5 months - 5 mois	201	99	102	...	...	...
6 months - 6 mois	206	117	89	...	...	...
7 months - 7 mois	117	61	56	...	...	...
8 months - 8 mois	150	72	78	...	...	...
9 months - 9 mois	124	78	46	...	...	...
10 months - 10 mois	130	72	58	...	...	...
11 months - 11 mois	108	57	51	...	...	...
Unknown - Inconnu	326	189	137	...	...	...
Oman						
2017 (C)						
Total..	850	450	400	9.4	9.7	9.1
Less than 1 day - Moins de 1 jour	250	130	120	2.8	2.8	2.7
1 - 6 days - 1 - 6 jours	184	96	88	2.0	2.1	2.0
7 - 27 days - 7 - 27 jours	126	71	55	1.4	1.5	1.2
7 - 13 days - 7 - 13 jours	56	29	27	0.6	♦0.6	♦0.6
14 - 20 days - 14 - 20 jours	34	17	17	0.4	♦0.4	♦0.4
21 - 27 days - 21 - 27 jours	36	25	11	0.4	♦0.5	♦0.2
28 days - 11 months - 28 jours - 11 mois..........	290	153	137	3.2	3.3	3.1
28 days - less than 2 months - 28 jours - moins de 2 mois	59	37	22	0.7	0.8	♦0.5
2 months - 2 mois	38	18	20	0.4	♦0.4	♦0.5
3 months - 3 mois	33	16	17	0.4	♦0.3	♦0.4
4 months - 4 mois	33	16	17	0.4	♦0.3	♦0.4
5 months - 5 mois	27	12	15	♦0.3	♦0.3	♦0.3
6 months - 6 mois	20	13	7	♦0.2	♦0.3	♦0.2
7 months - 7 mois	20	10	10	♦0.2	♦0.2	♦0.2
8 months - 8 mois	15	7	8	♦0.2	♦0.2	♦0.2
9 months - 9 mois	12	5	7	♦0.1	♦0.1	♦0.2
10 months - 10 mois	17	8	9	♦0.2	♦0.2	♦0.2
11 months - 11 mois	16	11	5	♦0.2	♦0.2	♦0.1
Philippines						
2016 (C)						
Total..	21 874	12 566	9 308	12.6	13.9	11.2
Less than 1 day - Moins de 1 jour	2 964	1 651	1 313	1.7	1.8	1.6
1 - 6 days - 1 - 6 jours	5 836	3 520	2 316	3.4	3.9	2.8
7 - 27 days - 7 - 27 jours	2 773	1 626	1 147	1.6	1.8	1.4
7 - 13 days - 7 - 13 jours	1 416	822	594	0.8	0.9	0.7
14 - 20 days - 14 - 20 jours	742	452	290	0.4	0.5	0.4
21 - 27 days - 21 - 27 jours	615	352	263	0.4	0.4	0.3
28 days - 11 months - 28 jours - 11 mois..........	10 301	5 769	4 532	5.9	6.4	5.5
28 days - less than 2 months - 28 jours - moins de 2 mois	2 396	1 377	1 019	1.4	1.5	1.2
2 months - 2 mois	1 284	731	553	0.7	0.8	0.7
3 months - 3 mois	1 074	608	466	0.6	0.7	0.6
4 months - 4 mois	952	523	429	0.5	0.6	0.5
5 months - 5 mois	899	499	400	0.5	0.6	0.5
6 months - 6 mois	794	447	347	0.5	0.5	0.4
7 months - 7 mois	690	392	298	0.4	0.4	0.4
8 months - 8 mois	656	369	287	0.4	0.4	0.3
9 months - 9 mois	566	306	260	0.3	0.3	0.3

16. Infant deaths and infant mortality rates by age and sex: latest available year, 2009 - 2018

Décès d'enfants de moins d'un an et taux de mortalité infantile selon l'âge et le sexe : dernière année disponible, 2009 - 2018 (continued - suite)

Continent, country or area, year, code[a] and age Continent, pays ou zone, année, code[a] et âge	Number - Nombre			Rate - Taux		
	Both sexes Les deux sexes	Male Masculin	Female Féminin	Both sexes Les deux sexes	Male Masculin	Female Féminin
ASIA - ASIE						
Philippines						
2016 (C)						
10 months - 10 mois	499	265	234	0.3	0.3	0.3
11 months - 11 mois	491	252	239	0.3	0.3	0.3
Qatar						
2017 (C)						
Total	151	83	68	5.4	5.8	5.0
Less than 1 day - Moins de 1 jour	-	-	-	-	-	-
1 - 6 days - 1 - 6 jours	79	48	31	2.8	3.4	2.3
7 - 27 days - 7 - 27 jours	28	15	13	◆1.0	◆1.0	◆1.0
7 - 13 days - 7 - 13 jours	13	6	7	◆0.5	◆0.4	◆0.5
14 - 20 days - 14 - 20 jours	9	7	2	◆0.3	◆0.5	◆0.1
21 - 27 days - 21 - 27 jours	6	2	4	◆0.2	◆0.1	◆0.3
28 days - 11 months - 28 jours - 11 mois	44	20	24	1.6	◆1.4	◆1.8
28 days - less than 2 months - 28 jours - moins de 2 mois	10	5	5	◆0.4	◆0.3	◆0.4
2 months - 2 mois	11	6	5	◆0.4	◆0.4	◆0.4
3 months - 3 mois	6	2	4	◆0.2	◆0.1	◆0.3
4 months - 4 mois	3	1	2	◆0.1	◆0.1	◆0.1
5 months - 5 mois	1	-	1	-	-	◆0.1
6 months - 6 mois	6	3	3	◆0.2	◆0.2	◆0.2
7 months - 7 mois	2	-	2	◆0.1	-	◆0.1
8 months - 8 mois	2	1	1	◆0.1	◆0.1	◆0.1
9 months - 9 mois	1	1	-	-	◆0.1	-
10 months - 10 mois	2	1	1	◆0.1	◆0.1	◆0.1
11 months - 11 mois	-	-	-	-	-	-
Republic of Korea - République de Corée[18]						
2017 (C)						
Total	1 000	569	431	2.8	3.1	2.5
Less than 1 day - Moins de 1 jour	145	77	68	0.4	0.4	0.4
1 - 6 days - 1 - 6 jours	202	125	77	0.6	0.7	0.4
7 - 27 days - 7 - 27 jours	199	104	95	0.6	0.6	0.5
7 - 13 days - 7 - 13 jours	87	43	44	0.2	0.2	0.3
14 - 20 days - 14 - 20 jours	72	42	30	0.2	0.2	0.2
21 - 27 days - 21 - 27 jours	40	19	21	0.1	◆0.1	0.1
28 days - 11 months - 28 jours - 11 mois	454	263	191	1.3	1.4	1.1
28 days - less than 2 months - 28 jours - moins de 2 mois	119	61	58	0.3	0.3	0.3
2 months - 2 mois	61	41	20	0.2	0.2	◆0.1
3 months - 3 mois	55	30	25	0.2	0.2	◆0.1
4 months - 4 mois	58	37	21	0.2	0.2	◆0.1
5 months - 5 mois	46	25	21	0.1	◆0.1	◆0.1
6 months - 6 mois	22	13	9	◆0.1	◆0.1	◆0.1
7 months - 7 mois	30	21	9	0.1	◆0.1	◆0.1
8 months - 8 mois	18	7	11	◆0.1	-	◆0.1
9 months - 9 mois	21	14	7	◆0.1	◆0.1	-
10 months - 10 mois	16	11	5	-	◆0.1	-
11 months - 11 mois	8	3	5	-	-	-
Singapore - Singapour						
2017 (+C)						
Total	94	44	50	...	...	...
Less than 1 day - Moins de 1 jour	15	6	9	...	...	...
1 - 6 days - 1 - 6 jours	20	9	11	...	...	...
7 - 27 days - 7 - 27 jours	13	4	9	...	...	...
7 - 13 days - 7 - 13 jours	6	1	5	...	...	...
14 - 20 days - 14 - 20 jours	3	2	1	...	...	...
21 - 27 days - 21 - 27 jours	4	1	3	...	...	...
28 days - 11 months - 28 jours - 11 mois	46	25	21	...	...	...
28 days - less than 2 months - 28 jours - moins de 2 mois	12	6	6	...	...	...
2 months - 2 mois	6	5	1	...	...	...
3 months - 3 mois	8	5	3	...	...	...
4 months - 4 mois	2	-	2	...	...	...
5 months - 5 mois	3	2	1	...	...	...
6 months - 6 mois	5	2	3	...	...	...
7 months - 7 mois	5	2	3	...	...	...
8 months - 8 mois	-	-	-	...	...	...
9 months - 9 mois	4	3	1	...	...	...
10 months - 10 mois	-	-	-	...	...	...
11 months - 11 mois	1	-	1	...	...	...

16. Infant deaths and infant mortality rates by age and sex: latest available year, 2009 - 2018
Décès d'enfants de moins d'un an et taux de mortalité infantile selon l'âge et le sexe : dernière année disponible, 2009 - 2018 (continued - suite)

Continent, country or area, year, code[a] and age / Continent, pays ou zone, année, code[a] et âge	Number - Nombre			Rate - Taux		
	Both sexes Les deux sexes	Male Masculin	Female Féminin	Both sexes Les deux sexes	Male Masculin	Female Féminin
ASIA - ASIE						
Sri Lanka						
2014 (+C)						
Total	2 662	1 505	1 157	7.6	8.4	6.8
1 - 6 days - 1 - 6 jours	1 291	735	556	3.7	4.1	3.3
7 - 27 days - 7 - 27 jours	587	333	254	1.7	1.9	1.5
28 days - 11 months - 28 jours - 11 mois	784	437	347	2.2	2.4	2.0
28 days - 2 months - 28 jours - 2 mois	328	199	129	0.9	1.1	0.8
3 - 5 months - 3 - 5 mois	246	125	121	0.7	0.7	0.7
6 - 8 months - 6 - 8 mois	128	66	62	0.4	0.4	0.4
9 - 11 months - 9 - 11 mois	82	47	35	0.2	0.3	0.2
Tajikistan - Tadjikistan[11]						
2017 (U)						
Total	2 405	1 384	1 021	...	...	...
Less than 1 day - Moins de 1 jour	539	313	226	...	...	...
1 - 6 days - 1 - 6 jours	875	536	339	...	...	...
7 - 27 days - 7 - 27 jours	212	108	104	...	...	...
7 - 13 days - 7 - 13 jours	136	66	70	...	...	...
14 - 20 days - 14 - 20 jours	48	27	21	...	...	...
21 - 27 days - 21 - 27 jours	28	15	13	...	...	...
28 days - 11 months - 28 jours - 11 mois	779	427	352	...	...	...
28 days - less than 2 months - 28 jours - moins de 2 mois	16	10	6	...	...	...
2 - 11 months - 2 - 11 mois	763	417	346	...	...	...
Thailand - Thaïlande						
2016 (+U)						
Total	4 233	2 360	1 873	...	...	...
Less than 1 day - Moins de 1 jour	340	168	172	...	...	...
1 - 6 days - 1 - 6 jours	1 171	666	505	...	...	...
7 - 27 days - 7 - 27 jours	1 384	789	595	...	...	...
7 - 13 days - 7 - 13 jours	450	274	176	...	...	...
14 - 20 days - 14 - 20 jours	238	134	104	...	...	...
21 - 27 days - 21 - 27 jours	165	93	72	...	...	...
28 days - 11 months - 28 jours - 11 mois	1 869	1 035	844	...	...	...
28 days - less than 2 months - 28 jours - moins de 2 mois	531	288	243	...	...	...
2 months - 2 mois	303	172	131	...	...	...
3 months - 3 mois	239	126	113	...	...	...
4 months - 4 mois	179	96	83	...	...	...
5 months - 5 mois	126	75	51	...	...	...
6 months - 6 mois	98	53	45	...	...	...
7 months - 7 mois	87	59	38	...	...	...
8 months - 8 mois	90	50	40	...	...	...
9 months - 9 mois	78	42	36	...	...	...
10 months - 10 mois	74	34	40	...	...	...
11 months - 11 mois	64	40	24	...	...	...
Turkey - Turquie[19]						
2017 (C)						
Total	11 849	6 450	5 399	9.2	9.7	8.6
Less than 1 day - Moins de 1 jour	1 567	840	727	1.2	1.3	1.2
1 - 6 days - 1 - 6 jours	3 512	2 019	1 493	2.7	3.0	2.4
7 - 27 days - 7 - 27 jours	2 431	1 298	1 133	1.9	2.0	1.8
7 - 13 days - 7 - 13 jours	1 259	700	559	1.0	1.1	0.9
14 - 20 days - 14 - 20 jours	713	375	338	0.6	0.6	0.5
21 - 27 days - 21 - 27 jours	459	223	236	0.4	0.3	0.4
28 days - 11 months - 28 jours - 11 mois	4 972	2 645	2 327	3.9	4.0	3.7
28 days - less than 2 months - 28 jours - moins de 2 mois	1 977	1 085	892	1.5	1.6	1.4
2 months - 2 mois	633	352	281	0.5	0.5	0.4
3 months - 3 mois	489	252	237	0.4	0.4	0.4
4 months - 4 mois	419	206	213	0.3	0.3	0.3
5 months - 5 mois	355	194	161	0.3	0.3	0.3
6 months - 6 mois	262	132	130	0.2	0.2	0.2
7 months - 7 mois	236	122	114	0.2	0.2	0.2
8 months - 8 mois	190	103	87	0.1	0.2	0.1
9 months - 9 mois	151	80	71	0.1	0.1	0.1
10 months - 10 mois	141	68	73	0.1	0.1	0.1
11 months - 11 mois	119	51	68	0.1	0.1	0.1
United Arab Emirates - Émirats arabes unis						
2017 (C)						
Total	607	329[8]	276[8]	6.2	6.6	5.8
Less than 1 day - Moins de 1 jour	125	70[8]	53[8]	1.3	1.4	1.1

Décès d'enfants de moins d'un an et taux de mortalité infantile selon l'âge et le sexe : dernière année disponible, 2009 - 2018 (continued - suite)

Continent, country or area, year, code[a] and age Continent, pays ou zone, année, code[a] et âge	Number - Nombre			Rate - Taux		
	Both sexes Les deux sexes	Male Masculin	Female Féminin	Both sexes Les deux sexes	Male Masculin	Female Féminin
ASIA - ASIE						
United Arab Emirates - Émirats arabes unis						
2017 (C)						
1 - 6 days - 1 - 6 jours	154	87[8]	67[8]	1.6	1.7	1.4
7 - 27 days - 7 - 27 jours	111	58[8]	53[8]	1.1	1.2	1.1
Uzbekistan - Ouzbékistan[11]						
2017 (+C)						
Total	8 235	4 799	3 436	11.5	12.9	10.0
Less than 1 day - Moins de 1 jour	1 013	594	419	1.4	1.6	1.2
1 - 6 days - 1 - 6 jours	3 190	1 898	1 292	4.5	5.1	3.8
7 - 27 days - 7 - 27 jours	1 364	820	544	1.9	2.2	1.6
7 - 13 days - 7 - 13 jours	862	528	334	1.2	1.4	1.0
14 - 20 days - 14 - 20 jours	292	178	114	0.4	0.5	0.3
21 - 27 days - 21 - 27 jours	210	114	96	0.3	0.3	0.3
28 days - 11 months - 28 jours - 11 mois	2 668	1 487	1 181	3.7	4.0	3.4
28 days - less than 2 months - 28 jours - moins de 2 mois	600	351	249	0.8	0.9	0.7
2 months - 2 mois	345	200	145	0.5	0.5	0.4
3 months - 3 mois	305	168	137	0.4	0.5	0.4
4 months - 4 mois	261	149	112	0.4	0.4	0.3
5 months - 5 mois	226	122	104	0.3	0.3	0.3
6 months - 6 mois	218	120	98	0.3	0.3	0.3
7 months - 7 mois	181	90	91	0.3	0.2	0.3
8 months - 8 mois	138	65	73	0.2	0.2	0.2
9 months - 9 mois	166	86	80	0.2	0.2	0.2
10 months - 10 mois	112	65	47	0.2	0.2	0.1
11 months - 11 mois	116	71	45	0.2	0.2	0.1
EUROPE						
Åland Islands - Îles d'Åland						
2017 (C)						
Total						
Less than 1 day - Moins de 1 jour	-	-	-	...	...	...
1 - 6 days - 1 - 6 jours	-	-	-	...	...	...
7 - 27 days - 7 - 27 jours	-	-	-	...	...	...
7 - 13 days - 7 - 13 jours	-	-	-	...	...	...
14 - 20 days - 14 - 20 jours	-	-	-	...	...	...
21 - 27 days - 21 - 27 jours	-	-	-	...	...	...
28 days - 11 months - 28 jours - 11 mois	-	-	-	...	...	...
28 days - less than 2 months - 28 jours - moins de 2 mois	-	-	-	...	...	...
2 - 11 months - 2 - 11 mois	-	-	-	...	...	...
Albania - Albanie						
2017 (C)						
Total	248	130	118	8.0	8.0	8.0
Less than 1 day - Moins de 1 jour	97	47	50	3.1	2.9	3.4
1 - 6 days - 1 - 6 jours	57	32	25	1.8	2.0	♦1.7
7 - 27 days - 7 - 27 jours	40	23	17	1.3	♦1.4	♦1.2
7 - 13 days - 7 - 13 jours	26	14	12	♦0.8	♦0.9	♦0.8
14 - 20 days - 14 - 20 jours	9	6	3	♦0.3	♦0.4	♦0.2
21 - 27 days - 21 - 27 jours	5	3	2	♦0.2	♦0.2	♦0.1
28 days - 11 months - 28 jours - 11 mois	54	28	26	1.7	♦1.7	♦1.8
28 days - less than 2 months - 28 jours - moins de 2 mois	18	7	11	♦0.6	♦0.4	♦0.8
2 months - 2 mois	6	5	1	♦0.2	♦0.3	♦0.1
3 months - 3 mois	4	3	1	♦0.1	♦0.2	♦0.1
4 months - 4 mois	6	5	1	♦0.2	♦0.3	♦0.1
5 months - 5 mois	7	2	5	♦0.2	♦0.1	♦0.3
6 months - 6 mois	2	-	2	♦0.1	-	♦0.1
7 months - 7 mois	1	-	1		-	♦0.1
8 months - 8 mois	3	1	2	♦0.1	♦0.1	♦0.1
9 months - 9 mois	1	1	-	-	♦0.1	-
10 months - 10 mois	3	3	-	♦0.1	♦0.2	-
11 months - 11 mois	3	1	2	♦0.1	♦0.1	♦0.1
Andorra - Andorre						
2009 (C)						
Total	1	-	1	...	...	...
Less than 1 day - Moins de 1 jour	-	-	-	...	...	...
1 - 6 days - 1 - 6 jours	1	-	1	...	...	...

Continent, country or area, year, code[a] and age Continent, pays ou zone, année, code[a] et âge	Number - Nombre			Rate - Taux		
	Both sexes Les deux sexes	Male Masculin	Female Féminin	Both sexes Les deux sexes	Male Masculin	Female Féminin
EUROPE						
Andorra - Andorre						
2009 (C)						
7 - 27 days - 7 - 27 jours	-	-	-	...	...	...
28 days - 11 months - 28 jours - 11 mois	-	-	-	...	...	...
Austria - Autriche						
2017 (C)						
Total	256	136	120	2.9	3.0	2.8
Less than 1 day - Moins de 1 jour	100	57	43	1.1	1.3	1.0
1 - 6 days - 1 - 6 jours	37	24	13	0.4	+0.5	+0.3
7 - 27 days - 7 - 27 jours	42	19	23	0.5	+0.4	+0.5
7 - 13 days - 7 - 13 jours	15	6	9	+0.2	+0.1	+0.2
14 - 20 days - 14 - 20 jours	13	7	6	+0.1	+0.2	+0.1
21 - 27 days - 21 - 27 jours	14	6	8	+0.2	+0.1	+0.2
28 days - 11 months - 28 jours - 11 mois	74	34	40	0.8	0.8	0.9
28 days - less than 2 months - 28 jours - moins de 2 mois	26	9	17	+0.3	+0.2	+0.4
2 months - 2 mois	3	1	2	-	-	-
3 months - 3 mois	11	5	6	+0.1	+0.1	+0.1
4 months - 4 mois	3	-	3	-	-	+0.1
5 months - 5 mois	8	7	1	+0.1	+0.2	-
6 months - 6 mois	4	2	2	-	-	-
7 months - 7 mois	7	4	3	+0.1	+0.1	-
8 months - 8 mois	2	2	-	-	-	-
9 months - 9 mois	4	3	1	-	+0.1	-
10 months - 10 mois	4	1	3	-	-	+0.1
11 months - 11 mois	2	-	2	-	-	-
Unknown - Inconnu	3	2	1	-	-	-
Belarus - Bélarus						
2017 (C)						
Total	332	181	151	3.2	3.4	3.0
Less than 1 day - Moins de 1 jour	30	18	12	0.3	+0.3	+0.2
1 - 6 days - 1 - 6 jours	65	32	33	0.6	0.6	0.7
7 - 27 days - 7 - 27 jours	66	38	28	0.6	0.7	+0.6
7 - 13 days - 7 - 13 jours	25	13	12	+0.2	+0.2	+0.2
14 - 20 days - 14 - 20 jours	25	13	12	+0.2	+0.2	+0.2
21 - 27 days - 21 - 27 jours	16	12	4	+0.2	+0.2	+0.1
28 days - 11 months - 28 jours - 11 mois	171	93	78	1.7	1.8	1.6
28 days - less than 2 months - 28 jours - moins de 2 mois	59	27	32	0.6	+0.5	0.6
2 months - 2 mois	28	18	10	+0.3	+0.3	+0.2
3 months - 3 mois	14	6	8	+0.1	+0.1	+0.2
4 months - 4 mois	12	7	5	+0.1	+0.1	+0.1
5 months - 5 mois	10	10	-	+0.1	+0.2	-
6 months - 6 mois	16	10	6	+0.2	+0.2	+0.1
7 months - 7 mois	8	4	4	+0.1	+0.1	+0.1
8 months - 8 mois	10	5	5	+0.1	+0.1	+0.1
9 months - 9 mois	5	1	4	-	-	+0.1
10 months - 10 mois	4	3	1	-	+0.1	-
11 months - 11 mois	5	2	3	-	-	+0.1
Belgium - Belgique[20]						
2014 (C)						
Total	423	247	176	3.4	3.8	2.9
Less than 1 day - Moins de 1 jour	115	61	54	0.9	1.0	0.9
1 - 6 days - 1 - 6 jours	91	58	33	0.7	0.9	0.5
7 - 27 days - 7 - 27 jours	79	39	40	0.6	0.6	0.7
7 - 13 days - 7 - 13 jours	40	21	19	0.3	+0.3	+0.3
14 - 20 days - 14 - 20 jours	25	11	14	+0.2	+0.2	+0.2
21 - 27 days - 21 - 27 jours	14	7	7	+0.1	+0.1	+0.1
28 days - 11 months - 28 jours - 11 mois	138	89	49	1.1	1.4	0.8
28 days - less than 2 months - 28 jours - moins de 2 mois	42	25	17	0.3	+0.4	+0.3
2 months - 2 mois	23	17	6	+0.2	+0.3	+0.1
3 months - 3 mois	13	9	4	+0.1	+0.1	+0.1
4 months - 4 mois	15	12	3	+0.1	+0.2	-
5 months - 5 mois	11	7	4	+0.1	+0.1	+0.1
6 months - 6 mois	8	3	5	+0.1	-	+0.1
7 months - 7 mois	9	8	1	+0.1	+0.1	-
8 months - 8 mois	7	4	3	+0.1	+0.1	-
9 months - 9 mois	2	2	-	-	-	-
10 months - 10 mois	5	1	4	-	-	+0.1
11 months - 11 mois	3	1	2	-	-	-

Continent, country or area, year, code[a] and age Continent, pays ou zone, année, code[a] et âge	Number - Nombre			Rate - Taux		
	Both sexes Les deux sexes	Male Masculin	Female Féminin	Both sexes Les deux sexes	Male Masculin	Female Féminin
EUROPE						
Bosnia and Herzegovina - Bosnie-Herzégovine						
2010 (C)						
Total	216	125	91	6.4	7.2	5.6
Less than 1 day - Moins de 1 jour	74	43	31	2.2	2.5	1.9
1 - 6 days - 1 - 6 jours	89	56	33	2.7	3.2	2.0
7 - 27 days - 7 - 27 jours	19	13	6	♦0.6	♦0.8	♦0.4
7 - 13 days - 7 - 13 jours	10	6	4	♦0.3	♦0.3	♦0.2
14 - 20 days - 14 - 20 jours	6	6	-	♦0.2	♦0.3	-
21 - 27 days - 21 - 27 jours	3	1	2	♦0.1	♦0.1	♦0.1
28 days - 11 months - 28 jours - 11 mois	34	13	21	1.0	♦0.8	♦1.3
28 days - less than 2 months - 28 jours - moins de 2 mois	5	2	3	♦0.1	♦0.1	♦0.2
2 months - 2 mois	10	6	4	♦0.3	♦0.3	♦0.2
3 months - 3 mois	1	-	1	-	-	♦0.1
4 months - 4 mois	5	2	3	♦0.1	♦0.1	♦0.2
5 months - 5 mois	3	1	2	♦0.1	♦0.1	♦0.1
6 months - 6 mois	3	1	2	♦0.1	♦0.1	♦0.1
7 months - 7 mois	-	-	-	-	-	-
8 months - 8 mois	1	-	1	-	-	♦0.1
9 months - 9 mois	4	-	4	♦0.1	-	♦0.2
10 months - 10 mois	1	1	-	-	♦0.1	-
11 months - 11 mois	1	-	1	-	-	♦0.1
Bulgaria - Bulgarie						
2017 (C)						
Total	408	227	181	6.4	6.9	5.8
Less than 1 day - Moins de 1 jour	63	35	28	1.0	1.1	♦0.9
1 - 6 days - 1 - 6 jours	104	59	45	1.6	1.8	1.4
7 - 27 days - 7 - 27 jours	76	43	33	1.2	1.3	1.1
7 - 13 days - 7 - 13 jours	30	15	15	0.5	♦0.5	♦0.5
14 - 20 days - 14 - 20 jours	29	15	14	♦0.5	♦0.5	♦0.4
21 - 27 days - 21 - 27 jours	17	13	4	♦0.3	♦0.4	♦0.1
28 days - 11 months - 28 jours - 11 mois	165	90	75	2.6	2.7	2.4
28 days - less than 2 months - 28 jours - moins de 2 mois	43	27	16	0.7	♦0.8	♦0.5
2 months - 2 mois	24	14	10	♦0.4	♦0.4	♦0.3
3 months - 3 mois	23	10	13	♦0.4	♦0.3	♦0.4
4 months - 4 mois	21	12	9	♦0.3	♦0.4	♦0.3
5 months - 5 mois	12	9	3	♦0.2	♦0.3	♦0.1
6 months - 6 mois	7	3	4	♦0.1	♦0.1	♦0.1
7 months - 7 mois	6	3	3	♦0.1	♦0.1	♦0.1
8 months - 8 mois	9	5	4	♦0.1	♦0.2	♦0.1
9 months - 9 mois	11	4	7	♦0.2	♦0.1	♦0.2
10 months - 10 mois	4	2	2	♦0.1	♦0.1	♦0.1
11 months - 11 mois	5	1	4	♦0.1	-	♦0.1
Croatia - Croatie						
2017 (C)						
Total	148	89	59	4.0	4.7	3.3
Less than 1 day - Moins de 1 jour	34	20	14	0.9	♦1.1	♦0.8
1 - 6 days - 1 - 6 jours	38	26	12	1.0	♦1.4	♦0.7
7 - 27 days - 7 - 27 jours	25	13	12	♦0.7	♦0.7	♦0.7
7 - 13 days - 7 - 13 jours	12	8	4	♦0.3	♦0.4	♦0.2
14 - 20 days - 14 - 20 jours	6	2	4	♦0.2	♦0.1	♦0.2
21 - 27 days - 21 - 27 jours	7	3	4	♦0.2	♦0.2	♦0.2
28 days - 11 months - 28 jours - 11 mois	51	30	21	1.4	1.6	♦1.2
28 days - less than 2 months - 28 jours - moins de 2 mois	20	10	10	♦0.5	♦0.5	♦0.6
2 months - 2 mois	9	8	1	♦0.2	♦0.4	♦0.1
3 months - 3 mois	3	1	2	♦0.1	♦0.1	♦0.1
4 months - 4 mois	5	1	4	♦0.1	♦0.1	♦0.2
5 months - 5 mois	1	-	1	-	-	♦0.1
6 months - 6 mois	4	3	1	♦0.1	♦0.2	♦0.1
7 months - 7 mois	3	2	1	♦0.1	♦0.1	♦0.1
8 months - 8 mois	1	1	-	-	♦0.1	-
9 months - 9 mois	-	-	-	-	-	-
10 months - 10 mois	2	2	-	♦0.1	♦0.1	-
11 months - 11 mois	3	2	1	♦0.1	♦0.1	♦0.1
Czechia - Tchéquie						
2017 (C)						
Total	304	183	121	2.7	3.1	2.2
Less than 1 day - Moins de 1 jour	62	33	29	0.5	0.6	♦0.5
1 - 6 days - 1 - 6 jours	75	46	29	0.7	0.8	♦0.5

Continent, country or area, year, code[a] and age / Continent, pays ou zone, année, code[a] et âge	Number - Nombre			Rate - Taux		
	Both sexes Les deux sexes	Male Masculin	Female Féminin	Both sexes Les deux sexes	Male Masculin	Female Féminin
EUROPE						
Czechia - Tchéquie						
2017 (C)						
7 - 27 days - 7 - 27 jours	66	39	27	0.6	0.7	◆0.5
7 - 13 days - 7 - 13 jours	27	14	13	◆0.2	◆0.2	◆0.2
14 - 20 days - 14 - 20 jours	22	14	8	◆0.2	◆0.2	◆0.1
21 - 27 days - 21 - 27 jours	17	11	6	◆0.1	◆0.2	◆0.1
28 days - 11 months - 28 jours - 11 mois	101	65	36	0.9	1.1	0.6
28 days - less than 2 months - 28 jours - moins de 2 mois	33	22	11	0.3	◆0.4	◆0.2
2 months - 2 mois	21	14	7	◆0.2	◆0.2	◆0.1
3 months - 3 mois	8	5	3	◆0.1	◆0.1	◆0.1
4 months - 4 mois	12	7	5	◆0.1	◆0.1	◆0.1
5 months - 5 mois	3	3	-	-	◆0.1	-
6 months - 6 mois	9	6	3	◆0.1	◆0.1	◆0.1
7 months - 7 mois	2	2	-	-	-	-
8 months - 8 mois	4	2	2	-	-	-
9 months - 9 mois	1	-	1	-	-	-
10 months - 10 mois	5	2	3	-	-	◆0.1
11 months - 11 mois	3	2	1	-	-	-
Denmark - Danemark[21]						
2017 (C)						
Total	231	133	98	3.8	4.2	3.3
Less than 1 day - Moins de 1 jour	126	72	54	2.1	2.3	1.8
1 - 6 days - 1 - 6 jours	41	23	18	0.7	◆0.7	◆0.6
7 - 27 days - 7 - 27 jours	25	14	11	◆0.4	◆0.4	◆0.4
7 - 13 days - 7 - 13 jours	12	5	7	◆0.2	◆0.2	◆0.2
14 - 20 days - 14 - 20 jours	7	6	1	◆0.1	◆0.2	-
21 - 27 days - 21 - 27 jours	6	3	3	◆0.1	◆0.1	◆0.1
28 days - 11 months - 28 jours - 11 mois	39	24	15	0.6	◆0.8	◆0.5
28 days - less than 2 months - 28 jours - moins de 2 mois	13	5	8	◆0.2	◆0.2	◆0.3
2 months - 2 mois	2	-	2	-	-	◆0.1
3 months - 3 mois	4	4	-	◆0.1	◆0.1	-
4 months - 4 mois	7	6	1	◆0.1	◆0.2	-
5 months - 5 mois	6	5	1	◆0.1	◆0.2	-
6 months - 6 mois	-	-	-	-	-	-
7 months - 7 mois	2	1	1	-	-	-
8 months - 8 mois	4	2	2	◆0.1	◆0.1	◆0.1
9 months - 9 mois	1	1	-	-	-	-
10 months - 10 mois	-	-	-	-	-	-
11 months - 11 mois	-	-	-	-	-	-
Estonia - Estonie						
2017 (C)						
Total	32	20	12	...	...	...
Less than 1 day - Moins de 1 jour	9	5	4	...	...	...
1 - 6 days - 1 - 6 jours	6	5	1	...	...	...
7 - 27 days - 7 - 27 jours	4	3	1	...	...	...
7 - 13 days - 7 - 13 jours	4	3	1	...	...	...
14 - 20 days - 14 - 20 jours	-	-	-	...	...	...
21 - 27 days - 21 - 27 jours	-	-	-	...	...	...
28 days - 11 months - 28 jours - 11 mois	13	7	6	...	...	...
28 days - less than 2 months - 28 jours - moins de 2 mois	2	2	-	...	...	...
2 months - 2 mois	2	2	-	...	...	...
3 months - 3 mois	-	-	-	...	...	...
4 months - 4 mois	1	-	1	...	...	...
5 months - 5 mois	1	-	1	...	...	...
6 months - 6 mois	-	-	-	...	...	...
7 months - 7 mois	-	-	-	...	...	...
8 months - 8 mois	-	-	-	...	...	...
9 months - 9 mois	2	2	-	...	...	...
10 months - 10 mois	4	1	3	...	...	...
11 months - 11 mois	1	-	1	...	...	...
Faeroe Islands - Îles Féroé						
2018 (C)						
Total	-	-	-	...	...	...
Less than 1 day - Moins de 1 jour	-	-	-	...	...	...
1 - 6 days - 1 - 6 jours	-	-	-	...	...	...
7 - 27 days - 7 - 27 jours	-	-	-	...	...	...
7 - 13 days - 7 - 13 jours	-	-	-	...	...	...
14 - 20 days - 14 - 20 jours	-	-	-	...	...	...

16. Infant deaths and infant mortality rates by age and sex: latest available year, 2009 - 2018
Décès d'enfants de moins d'un an et taux de mortalité infantile selon l'âge et le sexe : dernière année disponible, 2009 - 2018 (continued - suite)

Continent, country or area, year, code[a] and age Continent, pays ou zone, année, code[a] et âge	Number - Nombre			Rate - Taux		
	Both sexes Les deux sexes	Male Masculin	Female Féminin	Both sexes Les deux sexes	Male Masculin	Female Féminin
EUROPE						
Faeroe Islands - Îles Féroé						
2018 (C)						
21 - 27 days - 21 - 27 jours	-	-	-	...	...	...
28 days - 11 months - 28 jours - 11 mois...............	-	-	-	...	...	...
28 days - less than 2 months - 28 jours - moins de 2 mois	-	-	-	...	...	...
2 - 11 months - 2 - 11 mois...............	-	-	-	...	...	...
Finland - Finlande[22]						
2017 (C)						
Total................	102	55	47	2.0	2.2	1.9
Less than 1 day - Moins de 1 jour	25	11	14	♦0.5	♦0.4	♦0.6
1 - 6 days - 1 - 6 jours	26	17	9	♦0.5	♦0.7	♦0.4
7 - 27 days - 7 - 27 jours	19	11	8	♦0.4	♦0.4	♦0.3
7 - 13 days - 7 - 13 jours	2	1	1	-	-	-
14 - 20 days - 14 - 20 jours	8	5	3	♦0.2	♦0.2	♦0.1
21 - 27 days - 21 - 27 jours	9	5	4	♦0.2	♦0.2	♦0.2
28 days - 11 months - 28 jours - 11 mois...............	32	16	16	0.6	♦0.6	♦0.7
28 days - less than 2 months - 28 jours - moins de 2 mois	8	2	6	♦0.2	♦0.1	♦0.2
2 months - 2 mois...............	8	4	4	♦0.2	♦0.2	♦0.2
3 months - 3 mois...............	3	2	1	♦0.1	♦0.1	-
4 months - 4 mois...............	4	2	2	♦0.1	♦0.1	♦0.1
5 months - 5 mois...............	2	1	1	-	-	-
6 months - 6 mois...............	1	1	-	-	-	-
7 months - 7 mois...............	2	1	1	-	-	-
8 months - 8 mois...............	1	1	-	-	-	-
9 months - 9 mois...............	1	1	-	-	-	-
10 months - 10 mois...............	1	1	-	-	-	-
11 months - 11 mois...............	1	-	1	-	-	-
France						
2017 (C)						
Total................	2 639	1 444	1 195	3.6	3.9	3.4
Less than 1 day - Moins de 1 jour	711	389	322	1.0	1.0	0.9
1 - 6 days - 1 - 6 jours	643	372	271	0.9	1.0	0.8
7 - 27 days - 7 - 27 jours	581	306	275	0.8	0.8	0.8
7 - 13 days - 7 - 13 jours	319	166	153	0.4	0.4	0.4
14 - 20 days - 14 - 20 jours	152	82	70	0.2	0.2	0.2
21 - 27 days - 21 - 27 jours	110	58	52	0.2	0.2	0.1
28 days - 11 months - 28 jours - 11 mois...............	704	377	327	1.0	1.0	0.9
28 days - less than 2 months - 28 jours - moins de 2 mois	240	129	111	0.3	0.3	0.3
2 months - 2 mois...............	103	56	47	0.1	0.1	0.1
3 months - 3 mois...............	84	43	41	0.1	0.1	0.1
4 months - 4 mois...............	63	35	28	0.1	0.1	♦0.1
5 months - 5 mois...............	48	31	17	0.1	0.1	-
6 months - 6 mois...............	39	21	18	0.1	♦0.1	♦0.1
7 months - 7 mois...............	35	20	15	-	♦0.1	-
8 months - 8 mois...............	28	16	12	-	-	-
9 months - 9 mois...............	24	11	13	-	-	-
10 months - 10 mois...............	24	9	15	-	-	-
11 months - 11 mois...............	16	6	10	-	-	-
Germany - Allemagne						
2017 (C)						
Total................	2 571	1 420	1 151	3.3	3.5	3.0
Less than 1 day - Moins de 1 jour	897	510	387	1.1	1.3	1.0
1 - 6 days - 1 - 6 jours	514	301	213	0.7	0.7	0.6
7 - 27 days - 7 - 27 jours	380	209	171	0.5	0.5	0.4
28 days - 11 months - 28 jours - 11 mois...............	780	400	380	1.0	1.0	1.0
Greece - Grèce						
2017 (C)						
Total................	306	161	145	3.5	3.5	3.4
Less than 1 day - Moins de 1 jour	58	29	29	0.7	♦0.6	♦0.7
1 - 6 days - 1 - 6 jours	82	43	39	0.9	0.9	0.9
7 - 27 days - 7 - 27 jours	68	35	33	0.8	0.8	0.8
28 days - 11 months - 28 jours - 11 mois...............	96	53	43	1.1	1.2	1.0
Unknown - Inconnu	2	1	1	-	-	-
Hungary - Hongrie[23]						
2017 (C)						
Total................	328	190	138	3.5	3.9	3.0
Less than 1 day - Moins de 1 jour	48	25	23	0.5	♦0.5	♦0.5
1 - 6 days - 1 - 6 jours	83	49	34	0.9	1.0	0.7

Continent, country or area, year, code[a] and age Continent, pays ou zone, année, code[a] et âge	Number - Nombre			Rate - Taux		
	Both sexes Les deux sexes	Male Masculin	Female Féminin	Both sexes Les deux sexes	Male Masculin	Female Féminin
EUROPE						
Hungary - Hongrie[23]						
2017 (C)						
7 - 27 days - 7 - 27 jours	74	45	29	0.8	0.9	♦0.6
7 - 13 days - 7 - 13 jours	38	22	16	0.4	♦0.5	♦0.3
14 - 20 days - 14 - 20 jours	24	13	11	♦0.3	♦0.3	♦0.2
21 - 27 days - 21 - 27 jours	12	10	2	♦0.1	♦0.2	-
28 days - 11 months - 28 jours - 11 mois	123	71	52	1.3	1.5	1.1
28 days - less than 2 months - 28 jours - moins de 2 mois	41	26	15	0.4	0.5	♦0.3
2 months - 2 mois	22	15	7	♦0.2	♦0.3	♦0.2
3 months - 3 mois	18	11	7	♦0.2	♦0.2	♦0.2
4 months - 4 mois	7	2	5	♦0.1	-	♦0.1
5 months - 5 mois	5	2	3	♦0.1	-	♦0.1
6 months - 6 mois	7	2	5	♦0.1	-	♦0.1
7 months - 7 mois	6	3	3	♦0.1	♦0.1	♦0.1
8 months - 8 mois	5	1	4	♦0.1	-	♦0.1
9 months - 9 mois	4	2	2	-	-	-
10 months - 10 mois	1	1	-	-	-	-
11 months - 11 mois	7	6	1	♦0.1	♦0.1	-
Iceland - Islande						
2017 (C)						
Total	11	5	6	...	...	...
Less than 1 day - Moins de 1 jour	3	-	3	...	...	...
1 - 6 days - 1 - 6 jours	4	3	1	...	...	...
7 - 27 days - 7 - 27 jours	2	2	-	...	...	...
7 - 13 days - 7 - 13 jours	1	1	-	...	...	...
14 - 20 days - 14 - 20 jours	-	-	-	...	...	...
21 - 27 days - 21 - 27 jours	1	1	-	...	...	...
28 days - 11 months - 28 jours - 11 mois	2	-	2	...	...	...
28 days - less than 2 months - 28 jours - moins de 2 mois	1	-	1	...	...	...
2 months - 2 mois	1	-	1	...	...	...
3 months - 3 mois	-	-	-	...	...	...
4 months - 4 mois	-	-	-	...	...	...
5 months - 5 mois	-	-	-	...	...	...
6 months - 6 mois	-	-	-	...	...	...
7 months - 7 mois	-	-	-	...	...	...
8 months - 8 mois	-	-	-	...	...	...
9 months - 9 mois	-	-	-	...	...	...
10 months - 10 mois	-	-	-	...	...	...
11 months - 11 mois	-	-	-	...	...	...
Ireland - Irlande						
2011 (+C)						
Total	262	150	112	3.5	4.0	3.1
Less than 1 day - Moins de 1 jour	88	43	45	1.2	1.1	1.2
1 - 6 days - 1 - 6 jours	59	38	21	0.8	1.0	♦0.6
7 - 27 days - 7 - 27 jours	41	30	11	0.6	0.8	♦0.3
7 - 13 days - 7 - 13 jours	18	13	5	♦0.2	♦0.3	♦0.1
14 - 20 days - 14 - 20 jours	17	13	4	♦0.2	♦0.3	♦0.1
21 - 27 days - 21 - 27 jours	6	4	2	♦0.1	♦0.1	♦0.1
28 days - 11 months - 28 jours - 11 mois	74	39	35	1.0	1.0	1.0
28 days - less than 2 months - 28 jours - moins de 2 mois	20	12	8	♦0.3	♦0.3	♦0.2
2 months - 2 mois	17	7	10	♦0.2	♦0.2	♦0.3
3 months - 3 mois	11	4	7	♦0.1	♦0.1	♦0.2
4 months - 4 mois	5	5	-	♦0.1	♦0.1	-
5 months - 5 mois	6	3	3	♦0.1	♦0.1	♦0.1
6 months - 6 mois	3	1	2	-	-	♦0.1
7 months - 7 mois	2	1	1	-	-	-
8 months - 8 mois	1	-	1	-	-	-
9 months - 9 mois	4	3	1	♦0.1	♦0.1	-
10 months - 10 mois	4	2	2	♦0.1	♦0.1	♦0.1
11 months - 11 mois	1	1	-	-	-	-
Italy - Italie						
2013 (C)						
Total	1 493	864	629	2.9	3.3	2.5
Less than 1 day - Moins de 1 jour	268	153	115	0.5	0.6	0.5
1 - 6 days - 1 - 6 jours	447	279	168	0.9	1.1	0.7
7 - 27 days - 7 - 27 jours	311	175	136	0.6	0.7	0.5
7 - 13 days - 7 - 13 jours	151	87	64	0.3	0.3	0.3
14 - 20 days - 14 - 20 jours	92	47	45	0.2	0.2	0.2

16. Infant deaths and infant mortality rates by age and sex: latest available year, 2009 - 2018
Décès d'enfants de moins d'un an et taux de mortalité infantile selon l'âge et le sexe : dernière année disponible, 2009 - 2018 (continued - suite)

Continent, country or area, year, code[a] and age Continent, pays ou zone, année, code[a] et âge	Number - Nombre			Rate - Taux		
	Both sexes Les deux sexes	Male Masculin	Female Féminin	Both sexes Les deux sexes	Male Masculin	Female Féminin
EUROPE						
Italy - Italie						
2013 (C)						
21 - 27 days - 21 - 27 jours	68	41	27	0.1	0.2	♦0.1
28 days - 11 months - 28 jours - 11 mois	467	257	210	0.9	1.0	0.8
28 days - less than 2 months - 28 jours - moins de 2 mois	149	90	59	0.3	0.3	0.2
2 months - 2 mois	69	31	38	0.1	0.1	0.2
3 months - 3 mois	50	20	30	0.1	♦0.1	0.1
4 months - 4 mois	44	26	18	0.1	0.1	0.1
5 months - 5 mois	35	21	14	0.1	♦0.1	♦0.1
6 months - 6 mois	33	21	12	0.1	♦0.1	-
7 months - 7 mois	27	10	17	♦0.1	-	♦0.1
8 months - 8 mois	20	16	4	-	♦0.1	-
9 months - 9 mois	18	11	7	-	-	-
10 months - 10 mois	13	6	7	-	-	-
11 months - 11 mois	9	5	4	-	-	-
Latvia - Lettonie						
2017 (C)						
Total	86	50	36	...	...	...
Less than 1 day - Moins de 1 jour	32	21	11	...	...	...
1 - 6 days - 1 - 6 jours	18	10	8	...	...	...
7 - 27 days - 7 - 27 jours	16	12	4	...	...	...
7 - 13 days - 7 - 13 jours	8	5	3	...	...	...
14 - 20 days - 14 - 20 jours	6	6	-	...	...	...
21 - 27 days - 21 - 27 jours	2	1	1	...	...	...
28 days - 11 months - 28 jours - 11 mois	20	7	13	...	...	...
28 days - less than 2 months - 28 jours - moins de 2 mois	8	2	6	...	...	...
2 months - 2 mois	1	-	1	...	...	...
3 months - 3 mois	3	-	3	...	...	...
4 months - 4 mois	3	1	2	...	...	...
5 months - 5 mois	3	2	1	...	...	...
6 months - 6 mois	-	-	-	...	...	...
7 months - 7 mois	1	1	-	...	...	...
8 months - 8 mois	-	-	-	...	...	...
9 months - 9 mois	1	1	-	...	...	...
10 months - 10 mois	-	-	-	...	...	...
11 months - 11 mois	-	-	-	...	...	...
Liechtenstein						
2015 (C)						
Total	2	2	-	...	...	...
1 - 6 days - 1 - 6 jours	2	2	-	...	...	...
Lithuania - Lituanie						
2017 (C)						
Total	85	45	40	...	...	...
Less than 1 day - Moins de 1 jour	21	10	11	...	...	...
1 - 6 days - 1 - 6 jours	18	7	11	...	...	...
7 - 27 days - 7 - 27 jours	11	6	5	...	...	...
7 - 13 days - 7 - 13 jours	6	4	2	...	...	...
14 - 20 days - 14 - 20 jours	4	2	2	...	...	...
21 - 27 days - 21 - 27 jours	1	-	1	...	...	...
28 days - 11 months - 28 jours - 11 mois	35	22	13	...	...	...
28 days - less than 2 months - 28 jours - moins de 2 mois	11	6	5	...	...	...
2 months - 2 mois	5	4	1	...	...	...
3 months - 3 mois	7	4	3	...	...	...
4 months - 4 mois	3	1	2	...	...	...
5 months - 5 mois	4	4	-	...	...	...
6 months - 6 mois	2	1	1	...	...	...
7 months - 7 mois	1	-	1	...	...	...
8 months - 8 mois	-	-	-	...	...	...
9 months - 9 mois	-	-	-	...	...	...
10 months - 10 mois	2	2	-	...	...	...
11 months - 11 mois	-	-	-	...	...	...
Luxembourg						
2017 (C)						
Total	20	15	5	...	...	...
Less than 1 day - Moins de 1 jour	8	7	1	...	...	...
1 - 6 days - 1 - 6 jours	5	3	2	...	...	...
7 - 27 days - 7 - 27 jours	-	-	-	...	...	...
7 - 13 days - 7 - 13 jours	-	-	-	...	...	...

Continent, country or area, year, code[a] and age / Continent, pays ou zone, année, code[a] et âge	Number - Nombre			Rate - Taux		
	Both sexes Les deux sexes	Male Masculin	Female Féminin	Both sexes Les deux sexes	Male Masculin	Female Féminin
EUROPE						
Luxembourg						
2017 (C)						
14 - 20 days - 14 - 20 jours	-	-	-	...	...	...
21 - 27 days - 21 - 27 jours	-	-	-	...	...	...
28 days - 11 months - 28 jours - 11 mois	7	5	2	...	...	...
28 days - less than 2 months - 28 jours - moins de 2 mois	1	1	-	...	...	...
2 months - 2 mois	1	1	-	...	...	...
3 months - 3 mois	1	1	-	...	...	...
4 months - 4 mois	1	1	-	...	...	...
5 months - 5 mois	2	1	1	...	...	...
6 months - 6 mois	-	-	-	...	...	...
7 months - 7 mois	-	-	-	...	...	...
8 months - 8 mois	-	-	-	...	...	...
9 months - 9 mois	1	-	1	...	...	...
10 months - 10 mois	-	-	-	...	...	...
11 months - 11 mois	-	-	-	...	...	...
Malta - Malte						
2016 (C)						
Total	33	20	13	...	...	...
Less than 1 day - Moins de 1 jour	9	6	3	...	...	...
1 - 6 days - 1 - 6 jours	12	4	8	...	...	...
7 - 27 days - 7 - 27 jours	3	2	1	...	...	...
7 - 13 days - 7 - 13 jours	3	2	1	...	...	...
14 - 20 days - 14 - 20 jours	-	-	-	...	...	...
21 - 27 days - 21 - 27 jours	-	-	-	...	...	...
28 days - 11 months - 28 jours - 11 mois	9	8	-	...	...	...
28 days - less than 2 months - 28 jours - moins de 2 mois	6	6	-	...	...	...
2 months - 2 mois	1	1	-	...	...	...
3 months - 3 mois	-	-	-	...	...	...
4 months - 4 mois	1	-	1	...	...	...
5 months - 5 mois	1	1	-	...	...	...
6 months - 6 mois	-	-	-	...	...	...
7 months - 7 mois	-	-	-	...	...	...
8 months - 8 mois	-	-	-	...	...	...
9 months - 9 mois	-	-	-	...	...	...
10 months - 10 mois	-	-	-	...	...	...
11 months - 11 mois	-	-	-	...	...	...
Montenegro - Monténégro						
2017 (C)						
Total	10	5	5	...	...	...
Less than 1 day - Moins de 1 jour	2	1	1	...	...	...
1 - 6 days - 1 - 6 jours	2	1	1	...	...	...
7 - 27 days - 7 - 27 jours	1	1	-	...	...	...
28 days - 11 months - 28 jours - 11 mois	5	2	3	...	...	...
Netherlands - Pays-Bas[24]						
2017 (C)						
Total	607	347	260	3.6	4.0	3.1
Less than 1 day - Moins de 1 jour	205	101	104	1.2	1.2	1.3
1 - 6 days - 1 - 6 jours	136	88	48	0.8	1.0	0.6
7 - 27 days - 7 - 27 jours	118	68	50	0.7	0.8	0.6
28 days - 11 months - 28 jours - 11 mois	148	90	58	0.9	1.0	0.7
North Macedonia - Macédoine du Nord						
2018 (C)						
Total	122	...	...	5.7	...	...
Less than 1 day - Moins de 1 jour	23	...	...	♦1.1	...	...
1 - 6 days - 1 - 6 jours	50	...	...	2.3	...	...
7 - 27 days - 7 - 27 jours	14	...	...	♦0.7	...	...
28 days - 11 months - 28 jours - 11 mois	35	...	...	1.6	...	...
28 days - less than 2 months - 28 jours - moins de 2 mois	12	...	...	♦0.6	...	...
Norway - Norvège[25]						
2017 (C)						
Total	130	67	63	2.3	2.3	2.3
Less than 1 day - Moins de 1 jour	34	20	14	0.6	♦0.7	♦0.5
1 - 6 days - 1 - 6 jours	38	16	22	0.7	♦0.5	♦0.8
7 - 27 days - 7 - 27 jours	21	13	8	♦0.4	♦0.4	♦0.3
28 days - 11 months - 28 jours - 11 mois	37	18	19	0.7	♦0.6	♦0.7

16. Infant deaths and infant mortality rates by age and sex: latest available year, 2009 - 2018
Décès d'enfants de moins d'un an et taux de mortalité infantile selon l'âge et le sexe : dernière année disponible, 2009 - 2018 (continued - suite)

Continent, country or area, year, code[a] and age / Continent, pays ou zone, année, code[a] et âge	Number - Nombre Both sexes Les deux sexes	Male Masculin	Female Féminin	Rate - Taux Both sexes Les deux sexes	Male Masculin	Female Féminin
EUROPE						
Poland - Pologne						
2017 (C)						
Total	1 604	908	696	4.0	4.4	3.6
Less than 1 day - Moins de 1 jour	498	280	218	1.2	1.4	1.1
1 - 6 days - 1 - 6 jours	358	211	147	0.9	1.0	0.8
7 - 27 days - 7 - 27 jours	280	149	131	0.7	0.7	0.7
7 - 13 days - 7 - 13 jours	135	72	63	0.3	0.3	0.3
14 - 20 days - 14 - 20 jours	90	49	41	0.2	0.2	0.2
21 - 27 days - 21 - 27 jours	55	28	27	0.1	◆0.1	◆0.1
28 days - 11 months - 28 jours - 11 mois	468	268	200	1.2	1.3	1.0
28 days - less than 2 months - 28 jours - moins de 2 mois	138	82	56	0.3	0.4	0.3
2 months - 2 mois	85	51	34	0.2	0.2	0.2
3 months - 3 mois	67	32	35	0.2	0.2	0.2
4 months - 4 mois	30	17	13	0.1	◆0.1	◆0.1
5 months - 5 mois	31	20	11	0.1	◆0.1	◆0.1
6 months - 6 mois	29	19	10	◆0.1	◆0.1	◆0.1
7 months - 7 mois	27	16	11	◆0.1	◆0.1	◆0.1
8 months - 8 mois	10	3	7	-	-	-
9 months - 9 mois	13	7	6	-	-	-
10 months - 10 mois	15	9	6	-	-	-
11 months - 11 mois	23	12	11	◆0.1	◆0.1	◆0.1
Portugal[26]						
2017 (C)						
Total	229	134	95	2.7	3.0	2.3
Less than 1 day - Moins de 1 jour	41	19	22	0.5	◆0.4	◆0.5
1 - 6 days - 1 - 6 jours	60	31	29	0.7	0.7	0.7
7 - 27 days - 7 - 27 jours	54	38	16	0.6	0.9	◆0.4
7 - 13 days - 7 - 13 jours	31	24	7	0.4	◆0.5	◆0.2
14 - 20 days - 14 - 20 jours	15	9	6	◆0.2	◆0.2	◆0.1
21 - 27 days - 21 - 27 jours	8	5	3	◆0.1	◆0.1	◆0.1
28 days - 11 months - 28 jours - 11 mois	74	46	28	0.9	1.0	◆0.7
28 days - less than 2 months - 28 jours - moins de 2 mois	24	13	11	◆0.3	◆0.3	◆0.3
2 months - 2 mois	9	5	4	◆0.1	◆0.1	◆0.1
3 months - 3 mois	7	7	-	◆0.1	◆0.2	-
4 months - 4 mois	8	6	2	◆0.1	◆0.1	-
5 months - 5 mois	3	2	1	-	-	-
6 months - 6 mois	3	1	2	-	-	-
7 months - 7 mois	8	6	2	◆0.1	◆0.1	-
8 months - 8 mois	5	3	2	◆0.1	◆0.1	-
9 months - 9 mois	1	1	-	-	-	-
10 months - 10 mois	3	2	1	-	-	-
11 months - 11 mois	3	-	3	-	-	◆0.1
Republic of Moldova - République de Moldova[27]						
2016 (C)						
Total	353	204	149	9.4	10.6	8.2
Less than 1 day - Moins de 1 jour	75	41	34	2.0	2.1	1.9
1 - 6 days - 1 - 6 jours	94	59	35	2.5	3.1	1.9
7 - 27 days - 7 - 27 jours	73	42	31	2.0	2.2	1.7
28 days - 11 months - 28 jours - 11 mois	111	62	49	3.0	3.2	2.7
Romania - Roumanie						
2017 (C)						
Total	1 364	779	585	6.7	7.5	5.9
Less than 1 day - Moins de 1 jour	137	72	65	0.7	0.7	0.7
1 - 6 days - 1 - 6 jours	351	200	151	1.7	1.9	1.5
7 - 27 days - 7 - 27 jours	270	156	114	1.3	1.5	1.2
7 - 13 days - 7 - 13 jours	129	72	57	0.6	0.7	0.6
14 - 20 days - 14 - 20 jours	81	50	31	0.4	0.5	0.3
21 - 27 days - 21 - 27 jours	60	34	26	0.3	0.3	◆0.3
28 days - 11 months - 28 jours - 11 mois	606	351	255	3.0	3.4	2.6
28 days - less than 2 months - 28 jours - moins de 2 mois	189	113	76	0.9	1.1	0.8
2 months - 2 mois	93	52	41	0.5	0.5	0.4
3 months - 3 mois	77	50	27	0.4	0.5	◆0.3
4 months - 4 mois	60	35	25	0.3	0.3	◆0.3
5 months - 5 mois	55	31	24	0.3	0.3	◆0.2
6 months - 6 mois	42	18	24	0.2	◆0.2	◆0.2
7 months - 7 mois	20	12	8	◆0.1	◆0.1	◆0.1
8 months - 8 mois	20	10	10	◆0.1	◆0.1	◆0.1
9 months - 9 mois	20	11	9	◆0.1	◆0.1	◆0.1

485

Continent, country or area, year, code[a] and age / Continent, pays ou zone, année, code[a] et âge	Number - Nombre			Rate - Taux		
	Both sexes Les deux sexes	Male Masculin	Female Féminin	Both sexes Les deux sexes	Male Masculin	Female Féminin
EUROPE						
Romania - Roumanie						
2017 (C)						
10 months - 10 mois	17	10	7	♦0.1	♦0.1	♦0.1
11 months - 11 mois	13	9	4	♦0.1	♦0.1	-
Russian Federation - Fédération de Russie[11]						
2012 (C)						
Total	16 306	9 219	7 087	8.6	9.4	7.7
Less than 1 day - Moins de 1 jour	1 897	1 009	888	1.0	1.0	1.0
1 - 6 days - 1 - 6 jours	5 072	2 961	2 111	2.7	3.0	2.3
7 - 27 days - 7 - 27 jours	3 438	1 958	1 480	1.8	2.0	1.6
7 - 13 days - 7 - 13 jours	1 798	1 020	778	0.9	1.0	0.8
14 - 20 days - 14 - 20 jours	952	560	392	0.5	0.6	0.4
21 - 27 days - 21 - 27 jours	688	378	310	0.4	0.4	0.3
28 days - 11 months - 28 jours - 11 mois	5 898	3 290	2 608	3.1	3.4	2.8
28 days - less than 2 months - 28 jours - moins de 2 mois	2 063	1 166	897	1.1	1.2	1.0
2 months - 2 mois	942	525	417	0.5	0.5	0.5
3 months - 3 mois	691	372	319	0.4	0.4	0.3
4 months - 4 mois	562	333	229	0.3	0.3	0.2
5 months - 5 mois	417	221	196	0.2	0.2	0.2
6 months - 6 mois	334	184	150	0.2	0.2	0.2
7 months - 7 mois	252	139	113	0.1	0.1	0.1
8 months - 8 mois	219	127	92	0.1	0.1	0.1
9 months - 9 mois	172	86	86	0.1	0.1	0.1
10 months - 10 mois	134	74	60	0.1	0.1	0.1
11 months - 11 mois	112	63	49	0.1	0.1	0.1
Unknown - Inconnu	1	1	-	-	-	-
San Marino - Saint-Marin						
2014 (C)						
Total	1	1	-	...	...	...
Less than 1 day - Moins de 1 jour	-	-	-	...	...	...
1 - 6 days - 1 - 6 jours	-	-	-	...	...	...
7 - 27 days - 7 - 27 jours	-	-	-	...	...	...
28 days - 11 months - 28 jours - 11 mois	1	1	-	...	...	...
Serbia - Serbie[28]						
2017 (+C)						
Total	305	176	129	4.7	5.3	4.1
Less than 1 day - Moins de 1 jour	93	40	53	1.4	1.2	1.7
1 - 6 days - 1 - 6 jours	68	44	24	1.0	1.3	♦0.8
7 - 27 days - 7 - 27 jours	47	29	18	0.7	♦0.9	♦0.6
7 - 13 days - 7 - 13 jours	17	11	6	♦0.3	♦0.3	♦0.2
14 - 20 days - 14 - 20 jours	19	11	8	♦0.3	♦0.3	♦0.3
21 - 27 days - 21 - 27 jours	11	7	4	♦0.2	♦0.2	♦0.1
28 days - 11 months - 28 jours - 11 mois	97	63	34	1.5	1.9	1.1
28 days - less than 2 months - 28 jours - moins de 2 mois	36	22	14	0.6	♦0.7	♦0.4
2 months - 2 mois	15	9	6	♦0.2	♦0.3	♦0.2
3 months - 3 mois	12	10	2	♦0.2	♦0.3	♦0.1
4 months - 4 mois	7	5	2	♦0.1	♦0.2	♦0.1
5 months - 5 mois	4	3	1	♦0.1	♦0.1	-
6 months - 6 mois	6	4	2	♦0.1	♦0.1	♦0.1
7 months - 7 mois	2	1	1	-	-	-
8 months - 8 mois	4	3	1	♦0.1	♦0.1	-
9 months - 9 mois	3	1	2	-	-	♦0.1
10 months - 10 mois	5	3	2	♦0.1	♦0.1	♦0.1
11 months - 11 mois	3	2	1	-	♦0.1	-
Slovakia - Slovaquie						
2017 (C)						
Total	263	155	108	4.5	5.2	3.8
Less than 1 day - Moins de 1 jour	62	37	25	1.1	1.2	♦0.9
1 - 6 days - 1 - 6 jours	40	25	15	0.7	♦0.8	♦0.5
7 - 27 days - 7 - 27 jours	50	30	20	0.9	1.0	♦0.7
7 - 13 days - 7 - 13 jours	30	17	13	0.5	♦0.6	♦0.5
14 - 20 days - 14 - 20 jours	13	8	5	♦0.2	♦0.3	♦0.2
21 - 27 days - 21 - 27 jours	7	5	2	♦0.1	♦0.2	♦0.1
28 days - 11 months - 28 jours - 11 mois	111	63	48	1.9	2.1	1.7
28 days - less than 2 months - 28 jours - moins de 2 mois	34	17	17	0.6	♦0.6	♦0.6
2 months - 2 mois	22	14	8	0.4	♦0.5	♦0.3
3 months - 3 mois	10	6	4	♦0.2	♦0.2	♦0.1
4 months - 4 mois	12	7	5	♦0.2	♦0.2	♦0.2

Continent, country or area, year, code[a] and age / Continent, pays ou zone, année, code[a] et âge	Number - Nombre			Rate - Taux		
	Both sexes Les deux sexes	Male Masculin	Female Féminin	Both sexes Les deux sexes	Male Masculin	Female Féminin
EUROPE						
Slovakia - Slovaquie						
2017 (C)						
5 months - 5 mois	9	6	3	♦0.2	♦0.2	♦0.1
6 months - 6 mois	6	3	3	♦0.1	♦0.1	♦0.1
7 months - 7 mois	4	2	2	♦0.1	♦0.1	♦0.1
8 months - 8 mois	7	4	3	♦0.1	♦0.1	♦0.1
9 months - 9 mois	1	-	1	-	-	-
10 months - 10 mois	5	3	2	♦0.1	♦0.1	♦0.1
11 months - 11 mois	1	1	-	-	-	-
Slovenia - Slovénie						
2017 (C)						
Total	42	21	21	...	...	...
Less than 1 day - Moins de 1 jour	10	3	7	...	...	...
1 - 6 days - 1 - 6 jours	8	6	2	...	...	...
7 - 27 days - 7 - 27 jours	9	5	4	...	...	...
7 - 13 days - 7 - 13 jours	3	3	-	...	...	...
14 - 20 days - 14 - 20 jours	2	2	-	...	...	...
21 - 27 days - 21 - 27 jours	4	-	4	...	...	...
28 days - 11 months - 28 jours - 11 mois	15	7	8	...	...	...
28 days - less than 2 months - 28 jours - moins de 2 mois	7	2	5	...	...	...
2 months - 2 mois	2	2	-	...	...	...
3 months - 3 mois	-	-	-	...	...	...
4 months - 4 mois	2	1	1	...	...	...
5 months - 5 mois	-	-	-	...	...	...
6 months - 6 mois	1	-	1	...	...	...
7 months - 7 mois	2	2	-	...	...	...
8 months - 8 mois	-	-	-	...	...	...
9 months - 9 mois	-	-	-	...	...	...
10 months - 10 mois	-	-	-	...	...	...
11 months - 11 mois	1	-	1	...	...	...
Spain - Espagne						
2017 (C)						
Total	1 064	601	463	2.7	3.0	2.4
Less than 1 day - Moins de 1 jour	208	109	99	0.5	0.5	0.5
1 - 6 days - 1 - 6 jours	275	159	116	0.7	0.8	0.6
7 - 27 days - 7 - 27 jours	245	140	105	0.6	0.7	0.6
7 - 13 days - 7 - 13 jours	136	89	47	0.3	0.4	0.2
14 - 20 days - 14 - 20 jours	70	34	36	0.2	0.2	0.2
21 - 27 days - 21 - 27 jours	39	17	22	0.1	♦0.1	♦0.1
28 days - 11 months - 28 jours - 11 mois	336	193	143	0.9	1.0	0.8
28 days - less than 2 months - 28 jours - moins de 2 mois	94	58	36	0.2	0.3	0.2
2 months - 2 mois	47	29	18	0.1	♦0.1	♦0.1
3 months - 3 mois	53	30	23	0.1	0.1	♦0.1
4 months - 4 mois	28	13	15	♦0.1	♦0.1	♦0.1
5 months - 5 mois	25	13	12	♦0.1	♦0.1	♦0.1
6 months - 6 mois	17	13	4	-	♦0.1	-
7 months - 7 mois	15	10	5	-	-	-
8 months - 8 mois	28	11	17	♦0.1	♦0.1	♦0.1
9 months - 9 mois	12	6	6	-	-	-
10 months - 10 mois	11	8	3	-	-	-
11 months - 11 mois	6	2	4	-	-	-
Sweden - Suède						
2017 (C)						
Total	278	146	132	2.4	2.5	2.4
Less than 1 day - Moins de 1 jour	64	31	33	0.6	0.5	0.6
1 - 6 days - 1 - 6 jours	64	39	25	0.6	0.7	♦0.4
7 - 27 days - 7 - 27 jours	62	30	32	0.5	0.5	0.6
28 days - 11 months - 28 jours - 11 mois	87	45	42	0.8	0.8	0.7
Unknown - Inconnu	1	1	-	-	-	-
Switzerland - Suisse						
2017 (C)						
Total	310	178	132	3.5	4.0	3.1
Less than 1 day - Moins de 1 jour	167	95	72	1.9	2.1	1.7
1 - 6 days - 1 - 6 jours	40	20	20	0.5	♦0.4	♦0.5
7 - 27 days - 7 - 27 jours	36	25	11	0.4	♦0.6	♦0.3
7 - 13 days - 7 - 13 jours	13	10	3	♦0.1	♦0.2	♦0.1
14 - 20 days - 14 - 20 jours	12	8	4	♦0.1	♦0.2	♦0.1
21 - 27 days - 21 - 27 jours	11	7	4	♦0.1	♦0.2	♦0.1

16. Infant deaths and infant mortality rates by age and sex: latest available year, 2009 - 2018
Décès d'enfants de moins d'un an et taux de mortalité infantile selon l'âge et le sexe : dernière année disponible, 2009 - 2018 (continued - suite)

Continent, country or area, year, code[a] and age / Continent, pays ou zone, année, code[a] et âge	Number - Nombre			Rate - Taux		
	Both sexes Les deux sexes	Male Masculin	Female Féminin	Both sexes Les deux sexes	Male Masculin	Female Féminin
EUROPE						
Switzerland - Suisse						
2017 (C)						
28 days - 11 months - 28 jours - 11 mois	67	38	29	0.8	0.8	♦0.7
28 days - less than 2 months - 28 jours - moins de 2 mois	16	8	8	♦0.2	♦0.2	♦0.2
2 months - 2 mois	10	8	2	♦0.1	♦0.2	♦0.1
3 months - 3 mois	9	6	3	♦0.1	♦0.1	♦0.1
4 months - 4 mois	7	4	3	♦0.1	♦0.1	♦0.1
5 months - 5 mois	3	1	2	-	-	-
6 months - 6 mois	6	5	1	♦0.1	♦0.1	-
7 months - 7 mois	3	1	2	-	-	-
8 months - 8 mois	5	1	4	♦0.1	-	♦0.1
9 months - 9 mois	2	-	2	-	-	-
10 months - 10 mois	4	2	2	-	-	-
11 months - 11 mois	2	2	-	-	-	-
Ukraine[29]						
2017 (+C)						
Total	2 786	1 608	1 178	7.7	8.6	6.7
Less than 1 day - Moins de 1 jour	455	247	208	1.3	1.3	1.2
1 - 6 days - 1 - 6 jours	764	463	301	2.1	2.5	1.7
7 - 27 days - 7 - 27 jours	579	338	241	1.6	1.8	1.4
7 - 13 days - 7 - 13 jours	313	181	132	0.9	1.0	0.7
14 - 20 days - 14 - 20 jours	154	95	59	0.4	0.5	0.3
21 - 27 days - 21 - 27 jours	112	62	50	0.3	0.3	0.3
28 days - 11 months - 28 jours - 11 mois	988	560	428	2.7	3.0	2.4
28 days - less than 2 months - 28 jours - moins de 2 mois	296	161	135	0.8	0.9	0.8
2 months - 2 mois	152	90	62	0.4	0.5	0.4
3 months - 3 mois	117	66	51	0.3	0.4	0.3
4 months - 4 mois	105	65	40	0.3	0.3	0.2
5 months - 5 mois	66	34	32	0.2	0.2	0.2
6 months - 6 mois	64	32	32	0.2	0.2	0.2
7 months - 7 mois	52	28	24	0.1	♦0.1	♦0.1
8 months - 8 mois	32	20	12	0.1	♦0.1	♦0.1
9 months - 9 mois	34	20	14	0.1	♦0.1	♦0.1
10 months - 10 mois	33	20	13	0.1	♦0.1	♦0.1
11 months - 11 mois	37	24	13	0.1	♦0.1	♦0.1
United Kingdom of Great Britain and Northern Ireland - Royaume-Uni de Grande-Bretagne et d'Irlande du Nord[30]						
2017 (+C)						
Total	2 947	1 651	1 296	3.9	4.3	3.5
Less than 1 day - Moins de 1 jour	1 076	616	460	1.4	1.6	1.3
1 - 6 days - 1 - 6 jours	562	329	233	0.7	0.9	0.6
7 - 27 days - 7 - 27 jours	482	271	211	0.6	0.7	0.6
7 - 13 days - 7 - 13 jours	255	152	103	0.3	0.4	0.3
14 - 20 days - 14 - 20 jours	128	68	60	0.2	0.2	0.2
21 - 27 days - 21 - 27 jours	99	51	48	0.1	0.1	0.1
28 days - 11 months - 28 jours - 11 mois	827	435	392	1.1	1.1	1.1
28 days - less than 2 months - 28 jours - moins de 2 mois	287	160	127	0.4	0.4	0.3
2 months - 2 mois	147	68	79	0.2	0.2	0.2
3 months - 3 mois	87	53	34	0.1	0.1	0.1
4 months - 4 mois	65	36	29	0.1	0.1	♦0.1
5 months - 5 mois	60	32	28	0.1	0.1	♦0.1
6 months - 6 mois	31	20	11	-	♦0.1	-
7 months - 7 mois	42	19	23	0.1	-	♦0.1
8 months - 8 mois	32	10	22	-	-	♦0.1
9 months - 9 mois	23	9	14	-	-	-
10 months - 10 mois	23	10	13	-	-	-
11 months - 11 mois	30	18	12	-	-	-
OCEANIA - OCÉANIE						
Australia - Australie						
2017 (C)						
Total	1 019	562	457	3.3	3.5	3.0
Less than 1 day - Moins de 1 jour	466	266	200	1.5	1.7	1.3
1 - 6 days - 1 - 6 jours	160	87	73	0.5	0.5	0.5
7 - 27 days - 7 - 27 jours	118	69	49	0.4	0.4	0.3
7 - 13 days - 7 - 13 jours	61	41	20	0.2	0.3	♦0.1

16. Infant deaths and infant mortality rates by age and sex: latest available year, 2009 - 2018
Décès d'enfants de moins d'un an et taux de mortalité infantile selon l'âge et le sexe : dernière année disponible, 2009 - 2018 (continued - suite)

Continent, country or area, year, code[a] and age / Continent, pays ou zone, année, code[a] et âge	Number - Nombre			Rate - Taux		
	Both sexes Les deux sexes	Male Masculin	Female Féminin	Both sexes Les deux sexes	Male Masculin	Female Féminin
OCEANIA - OCÉANIE						
Australia - Australie						
2017 (C)						
14 - 20 days - 14 - 20 jours	36	19	17	0.1	♦0.1	♦0.1
21 - 27 days - 21 - 27 jours	21	9	12	♦0.1	♦0.1	♦0.1
28 days - 11 months - 28 jours - 11 mois	275	140	135	0.9	0.9	0.9
28 days - less than 2 months - 28 jours - moins de 2 mois	79	40	39	0.3	0.3	0.3
2 months - 2 mois	63	37	26	0.2	♦0.2	♦0.2
3 months - 3 mois	34	18	16	0.1	♦0.1	♦0.1
4 months - 4 mois	24	10	14	♦0.1	♦0.1	♦0.1
5 months - 5 mois	12	7	5	-	-	-
6 months - 6 mois	15	3	12	-	-	♦0.1
7 months - 7 mois	15	7	8	-	-	♦0.1
8 months - 8 mois	10	5	5	-	-	-
9 months - 9 mois	8	5	3	-	-	-
10 months - 10 mois	10	6	4	-	-	-
11 months - 11 mois	5	2	3	-	-	-
Guam[31]						
2015 (C)						
Total	47	23	24	...	...	...
Less than 1 day - Moins de 1 jour	10	4	6	...	...	...
1 - 6 days - 1 - 6 jours	16	9	7	...	...	...
7 - 27 days - 7 - 27 jours	7	1	6	...	...	...
7 - 13 days - 7 - 13 jours	2	-	2	...	...	...
14 - 20 days - 14 - 20 jours	4	1	3	...	...	...
21 - 27 days - 21 - 27 jours	1	-	1	...	...	...
28 days - 11 months - 28 jours - 11 mois	14	9	5	...	...	...
28 days - less than 2 months - 28 jours - moins de 2 mois	2	2	-	...	...	...
2 months - 2 mois	3	3	-	...	...	...
3 months - 3 mois	3	-	3	...	...	...
4 months - 4 mois	-	-	-	...	...	...
5 months - 5 mois	-	-	-	...	...	...
6 months - 6 mois	2	1	1	...	...	...
7 months - 7 mois	-	-	-	...	...	...
8 months - 8 mois	2	2	-	...	...	...
9 months - 9 mois	1	-	1	...	...	...
10 months - 10 mois	1	-	1	...	...	...
11 months - 11 mois	-	-	-	...	...	...
New Caledonia - Nouvelle-Calédonie						
2015 (C)						
Total	25	18	7	...	...	...
Less than 1 day - Moins de 1 jour	4	3	1	...	...	...
1 - 6 days - 1 - 6 jours	5	4	1	...	...	...
7 - 27 days - 7 - 27 jours	7	5	2	...	...	...
7 - 13 days - 7 - 13 jours	5	4	1	...	...	...
14 - 20 days - 14 - 20 jours	2	1	1	...	...	...
21 - 27 days - 21 - 27 jours	-	-	-	...	...	...
28 days - 11 months - 28 jours - 11 mois	9	6	3	...	...	...
28 days - less than 2 months - 28 jours - moins de 2 mois	3	1	2	...	...	...
2 - 11 months - 2 - 11 mois	6	5	1	...	...	...
New Zealand - Nouvelle-Zélande[32]						
2017 (+C)						
Total	228	123	108	3.8	4.0	3.7
Less than 1 day - Moins de 1 jour	81	45	36	1.4	1.5	1.2
1 - 6 days - 1 - 6 jours	33	15	18	0.6	♦0.5	♦0.6
7 - 27 days - 7 - 27 jours	33	18	15	0.6	♦0.6	♦0.5
7 - 13 days - 7 - 13 jours	12	3	6	♦0.2	♦0.1	♦0.2
14 - 20 days - 14 - 20 jours	9	6	3	♦0.2	♦0.2	♦0.1
21 - 27 days - 21 - 27 jours	9	6	3	♦0.2	♦0.2	♦0.1
28 days - 11 months - 28 jours - 11 mois	81	36	36	1.4	1.2	1.2
28 days - less than 2 months - 28 jours - moins de 2 mois	15	9	6	♦0.3	♦0.1	♦0.3
2 months - 2 mois	15	9	6	♦0.3	♦0.3	♦0.2
3 months - 3 mois	9	3	6	♦0.3	♦0.1	♦0.1
4 months - 4 mois	12	6	6	♦0.2	♦0.2	♦0.2
5 months - 5 mois	12	6	3	♦0.2	♦0.2	♦0.1
6 months - 6 mois	6	-	6	♦0.1	-	♦0.1
7 months - 7 mois	-	-	-	-	-	-
8 months - 8 mois	3	3	-	♦0.1	♦0.1	-
9 months - 9 mois	3	3	3	♦0.1	♦0.1	♦0.1

16. Infant deaths and infant mortality rates by age and sex: latest available year, 2009 - 2018
Décès d'enfants de moins d'un an et taux de mortalité infantile selon l'âge et le sexe : dernière année disponible, 2009 - 2018 (continued - suite)

Continent, country or area, year, code[a] and age / Continent, pays ou zone, année, code[a] et âge	Number - Nombre			Rate - Taux		
	Both sexes Les deux sexes	Male Masculin	Female Féminin	Both sexes Les deux sexes	Male Masculin	Female Féminin
OCEANIA - OCÉANIE						
New Zealand - Nouvelle-Zélande[32]						
2017 (+C)						
10 months - 10 mois	3	3	3	♦0.1	♦0.1	♦0.1
11 months - 11 mois	3	-	-	♦0.1	-	-

FOOTNOTES - NOTES

Italics: data from civil registers which are incomplete or of unknown completeness. - Italiques : données incomplètes ou dont le degré d'exactitude n'est pas connu, provenant des registres de l'état civil.

♦ Rates based on 30 or fewer infant deaths. - Taux basés sur 30 décès d'enfants ou moins.

* Provisional. - Données provisoires.

[a] 'Code' indicates the source of data, as follows:
C - Civil registration, estimated over 90% complete
U - Civil registration, estimated less than 90% complete
| - Other source, estimated reliable
+ - Data tabulated by date of registration rather than occurence
... - Information not available

Le 'Code' indique la source des données, comme suit :
C - Registres de l'état civil considérés complets à 90 p. 100 au moins
U - Registres de l'état civil qui ne sont pas considérés complets à 90 p. 100 au moins
| - Autre source, considérée pas douteuses
+ - Données exploitées selon la date de l'enregistrement et non la date de l'événement
... - Information pas disponible

[1] Source: Statistics Botswana. - Source: Statistics Botswana.
[2] Excludes the islands of St. Brandon and Agalega. - Non compris les îles St. Brandon et Agalega.
[3] Data for male and female categories may exclude infant deaths of unknown sex. - Les données pour les catégories hommes et femmes peuvent exclure décès d'enfant de sexe inconnu.
[4] Unrevised data. - Les données n'ont pas été révisées.
[5] Including Canadian residents temporarily in the United States, but excluding United States residents temporarily in Canada. - Y compris les résidents canadiens se trouvant temporairement aux Etats-Unis, mais ne comprenant pas les résidents des Etats-Unis se trouvant temporairement au Canada.
[6] Excluding infant deaths to mothers living abroad. - Exception faite des décès d'enfants en bas âge survenus lorsque la mère résidait à l'étranger.
[7] Data refer to resident population only. Data for male and female categories may exclude infant deaths of unknown sex. - Pour la population résidante seulement. Les données pour les catégories hommes et femmes peuvent exclure décès d'enfant de sexe inconnu.
[8] Figures for male and female may not add up to the total, since they do not include the category "Unknown". - La somme des chiffres indiqués pour les sexes masculin et féminin peut n'être pas égale au total parce qu'elle n'inclut pas la catégorie " inconnue ".
[9] Excludes nomadic Indian tribes. - Non compris les tribus d'Indiens nomades.
[10] Source: Reports of the Ministry of Health. - Source : Rapports du Ministère de la Santé.
[11] Excluding infants born alive of less than 28 weeks' gestation, of less than 1 000 g in weight and 35 cm in length, who die within seven days of birth. - Non compris les enfants nés vivants après moins de 28 semaines de gestations, pesant moins de 1 000 g, mesurant moins de 35 cm et décédés dans les sept jours qui ont suivi leur naissance.
[12] Deaths include deaths among some visitors. Sources: Births and Deaths National Registration System database, and medical records of government hospitals. - Les décès comprennent des décès parmi certains visiteurs. Les sources: Les bases de données des << Births and Deaths National Registration System >> et les dossiers médicaux des hôpitaux du gouvernement.

[13] Data refer to government controlled areas. - Les données se rapportent aux zones contrôlées par le Gouvernement.
[14] Includes data for East Jerusalem and Israeli residents in certain other territories under occupation by Israeli military forces since June 1967. Including deaths abroad of Israeli residents who were out of the country for less than a year. - Y compris les données pour Jérusalem-Est et les résidents israéliens dans certains autres territoires occupés depuis 1967 par les forces armées israéliennes. Y compris les décès à l'étranger de résidents israéliens qui ont quitté le pays depuis moins d'un an.
[15] Data refer to Japanese nationals in Japan only. - Les données se raportent aux nationaux japonais au Japon seulement.
[16] Data do not include foreigners. - Les données sur les etrangers ne sont pas inclus.
[17] Data are from Vital Registration System (VRS). - Les données proviennent du système d'enregistrement des faits d'état civil.
[18] Excluding alien armed forces, civilian aliens employed by armed forces, and foreign diplomatic personnel and their dependants. - Non compris les militaires étrangers, les civils étrangers employés par les forces armées ni le personnel diplomatique étranger et les membres de leur famille les accompagnant.
[19] Data from MERNIS (Central Population Administrative System). - Données de MERNIS (Système central de données démographiques).
[20] Including armed forces stationed outside the country, but excluding alien armed forces stationed in the area. - Y compris les militaires nationaux hors du pays, mais non compris les militaires étrangers en garnison sur le territoire.
[21] Excluding Faeroe Islands and Greenland shown separately, if available. - Non compris les Iles Féroé et le Groenland, qui font l'objet de rubriques distinctes, si disponible.
[22] Excluding Åland Islands. - Non compris les Îles d'Åland.
[23] Data include the deceased infants with Hungarian usual residence regardless of whether the death occurred in Hungary or in a foreign country, and do not include the deceased infants with foreign country usual residence. - Les données comprennent les nourrissons décédés alors que leur résidence habituelle était en Hongrie, que le décès ait eu lieu en Hongrie ou dans un pays étranger, et ne comprennent pas les nourrissons décédés dont la residence habituelle était dans un pays étranger.
[24] Including residents outside the country if listed in a Netherlands population register. - Englobe les résidents se trouvant à l'étranger à condition qu'ils soient inscrits sur le registre de population des Pays-Bas.
[25] Including residents temporarily outside the country. - Y compris les résidents se trouvant temporairement hors du pays.
[26] Data refer to usually resident population. - Les données concernent la population habituellement résidente.
[27] Excluding Transnistria and the municipality of Bender. - Les données ne tiennent pas compte de l'information sur la Transnistria et la municipalité de Bender.
[28] Excludes data for Kosovo and Metohia. - Sans les données pour le Kosovo et Metohie.
[29] Data includes deaths resulting from births with weight 500 g and more (if weight is unknown - with length 25 cm and more, or with gestation during 22 weeks or more). The Government of Ukraine has informed the United Nations that it is not in a position to provide statistical data concerning the Autonomous Republic of Crimea and the city of Sevastopol. - Y compris les décès de nouveau-nés de 500 g ou plus (si le poids est inconnu – de 25 cm de long ou plus, ou après une grossesse de 22 semaines ou plus). Le gouvernement Ukrainien a informé l'ONU qu'il n'est pas en mesure de fournir des données statistiques concernant la République autonome de Crimée et la ville de Sébastopol.
[30] Excluding Channel Islands (Guernsey and Jersey) and Isle of Man, shown separately, if available. - Non compris les îles Anglo-Normandes (Guernesey et Jersey) et l'île de Man, qui font l'objet de rubriques distinctes, si disponible.

Table 17 - *Demographic Yearbook 2018*

Table 17 presents maternal deaths and maternal mortality ratios for as many years available between 2007 and 2016.

Description of variables: Maternal deaths are defined for the purposes of the *Demographic Yearbook* as those caused by deliveries and complications of pregnancy, childbirth and the puerperium, within 42 days of termination of pregnancy. They are usually defined as deaths coded "38-41" for ICD-9 Basic Tabulation List or as deaths coded "A34", "O00-O95", "O98-O99" for ICD-10, respectively[1]. However, data for ICD-10 shown in this table include deaths due to "O96" and "O97" which refer to deaths from any obstetric cause occurring more than 42 days but less than one year after delivery and death from sequelae of direct obstetric causes occurring one year or more after delivery.

For further information on the definition of maternal mortality from the tenth revisions of the *International Statistical Classification of Diseases and Related Health Problems*[2], see also section 4.3 of the Technical Notes.

Statistics on maternal death presented in this table are provided by the World Health Organisation. They are limited to countries or areas that meet the criterion that cause-of-death statistics are either classified by or convertible to the ninth or tenth revisions mentioned above. Data that are classified by the tenth revision are set in bold in the table.

Ratios computation: Maternal mortality ratios are the annual number of maternal deaths per 100 000 live births (table 9) in the same year. These ratios have been calculated by the United Nations Statistics Division. If maternal mortality data are considered incomplete, or if live birth data for the year are not available, no ratio has been calculated. Ratios based on 30 or fewer maternal deaths are identified by the symbol "♦".

Reliability of data: Countries and areas that have incomplete (less than 90 per cent completeness) or of unknown completeness of cause of deaths data coverage are considered to provide unreliable data, which are set in *italics* rather than in roman type. Ratios on these data are not computed. Information on completeness is normally provided by the World Health Organisation. When this is not the case, information on completeness is set to coincide with that of table 18. The reliability of data for the completeness of cause of death provided by the World Health Organisation[3] may differ from the reliability of data for the total number of reported deaths. Therefore, there are cases when the quality code in table 18 does not correspond with the typeface used in this table.

Territorial composition, as set in Section 2.2 of "Technical Notes on the Statistical Tables", including or excluding certain population of a country, refers only to the denominator.

Limitations: Statistics on maternal deaths are subject to the same qualifications that have been set forth for vital statistics in general and death statistics in particular as discussed in section 4 of the Technical Notes. The reliability of the data, an indication of which is described above, is an important factor in considering the limitations. In addition, maternal-death statistics are subject to all the qualifications relating to cause-of-death statistics. These have been set forth in section 4 of the Technical Notes.

Maternal mortality ratios are subject to the limitations of the data on live births with which they have been calculated. These have been set forth in the technical notes for table 9. Specific information pertaining to individual countries or areas is given in the footnotes to table 9.

The calculation of the maternal mortality ratios based on the total number of live births approximates the risk of dying from complications of pregnancy, childbirth or puerperium. Ideally this rate should be based on the number of women exposed to the risk of pregnancy, in other words, the number of women conceiving. Since it is impossible to know how many women have conceived, the total number of live births is used in calculating this rate.

Earlier data: Maternal deaths and maternal mortality ratios have been shown in previous issues of the *Demographic Yearbook*. For information on specific years covered, the reader should consult the Index.

It should however be noted that in issues prior to 1975, maternal mortality rates were calculated using the female population rather than live births for the denominators. Therefore, maternal mortality ratios published since 1975 are not comparable to the earlier maternal death rates.

NOTES

[1] Except for Belarus, Russian Federation, Seychelles, Turkmenistan and Ukraine, where A34 and O95 are excluded.
[2] *International Statistical Classification of Diseases and Related Health Problems*, Tenth Revision, Volume 2, World Health Organization, Geneva, 1992. The publication is available online at: http://www.who.int/classifications/icd/en/
[3] For more information on specific method used for countries, see "Mathers CD, Bernard C, Iburg KM, Inoue M, Ma Fat D, Shibuya K et al. *Global burden of disease in 2002: data sources, methods and results*. Geneva, World Health Organization, 2003 (GPE Discussion Paper No. 54).

Tableau 17 – *Annuaire démographique 2018*

Le tableau 17 présente des statistiques et des taux de mortalité liée à la maternité pour les années disponibles entre 2007 et 2016.

Description des variables : aux fins de l'*Annuaire démographique*, les décès liés à la maternité sont ceux entraînés par l'accouchement ou les complications de la grossesse, de l'accouchement et des suites de couches dans un délai de 42 jours après la terminaison de la grossesse. Ils sont généralement associés aux codes 38 à 41 dans le cas de la liste de base pour la mise en tableaux de la CIM-9 et aux codes A34, O00 à O95 et O98 et O99 dans le cas de la CIM-10[1]. Les statistiques associées à des codes correspondant à la CIM-10 englobent des décès de type O96 et O97, qui désignent les décès liés à des causes obstétriques se produisant après 42 jours mais moins d'un an après l'accouchement et les décès entraînés par les séquelles de complications obstétriques directes qui se produisent un an ou plus après l'accouchement.

Pour plus de précisions concernant les définitions de la mortalité liée à la maternité dans la dixième révision de la *Classification statistique internationale des maladies et des problèmes de santé connexes*[2], se reporter également à la section 4.3 des Notes techniques.

Les statistiques de mortalité liée à la maternité présentées dans le tableau 17 émanent de l'Organisation mondiale de la santé. Elles ne se rapportent qu'aux pays ou zones qui répondent aux critères selon lesquels les statistiques relatives à la cause des décès sont conformes à la liste de la neuvième ou de la dixième révision de la CIM ou peuvent être aisément comparées aux catégories de cette liste. Les données conformes à la dixième révision sont indiquées en gras dans le tableau.

Calcul des taux : les taux de mortalité maternelle représentent le nombre annuel de décès dus à la maternité pour 100 000 naissances vivantes (données du tableau 9) de la même année. Ces taux ont été calculés par la Division de statistique du Département des affaires économiques et sociales de l'Organisation des Nations Unies. Si les données des décès dus à la maternité sont incomplètes ou si les naissances vivantes pour l'année ne sont pas disponibles, les taux ne sont pas calculés. Les taux fondés sur 30 décès liés à la maternité ou moins sont signalés par le signe "♦".

Fiabilité des données : les statistiques relatives aux pays et aux zones pour lesquels la couverture des données concernant les causes de décès est incomplète (mois de 90 pour cent) ou dont le degré de complétude n'est pas connue sont jugés douteuses et apparaissent en *italique* et non en caractères romains. Les taux correspondant ne sont pas calculés. L'information sur la complétude est normalement fournie par l'Organisation Mondiale de la Santé. Si ce n'est pas le cas, l'information sur la complétude est reprise de tableau 18. La fiabilité des données relatives aux causes de décès fournie par l'Organisation Mondiale de la Santé[3] peut différer de la fiabilité des données relatives au nombre de décès enregistrés. En conséquence, il peut apparaitre de différences entre les codes de fiabilité du tableau 18 et du présent tableau.

La composition territoriale est définie dans la Section 2.2 des "Notes Techniques sur les tableaux statistiques". L'inclusion ou l'exclusion de certaines populations d'un pays ne concerne que le dénominateur.

Insuffisance des données : les statistiques de la mortalité liée à la maternité appellent toutes les réserves qui ont été formulées à propos des statistiques de l'état civil en général et des statistiques relatives à la mortalité en particulier (voir la section 4 des Notes techniques). La fiabilité des données, au sujet de laquelle des indications ont été fournies plus haut, est un facteur important. En outre, les statistiques de la mortalité liée à la maternité appellent les mêmes réserves que celles exposées à la section 4 des Notes techniques en ce qui concerne les statistiques des causes de décès.

Les taux de mortalité maternelle appellent également toutes les réserves formulées à propos des statistiques des naissances vivantes qui ont servi à leur calcul (voir à ce sujet les notes techniques relatives au tableau 9). Des précisions sur certains pays ou zones sont données dans les notes se rapportant au tableau 9.

En prenant le nombre total des naissances vivantes comme base pour le calcul des taux de mortalité maternelle, on obtient une mesure approximative de la probabilité de décès dus aux complications de la grossesse, de l'accouchement et des suites de couches. Idéalement, ces taux devraient être calculés sur la base du nombre de femmes exposées aux risques liés à la grossesse, c'est-à-dire sur la base du nombre de femmes qui conçoivent. Étant donné qu'il est impossible de connaître le nombre de femmes ayant conçu, c'est le nombre total de naissances vivantes que l'on utilise pour calculer ces taux.

Données publiées antérieurement : des statistiques concernant les décès liés à la maternité (nombre de décès et taux) ont déjà été présentées dans des éditions antérieures de l'*Annuaire démographique*. Pour plus de précisions concernant les années pour lesquelles ces données ont été publiées, se reporter à l'index.

Il faut souligner que, avant 1975, les taux de mortalité maternelle étaient calculés sur la base de la population féminine et non sur celle du nombre de naissances vivantes. Ils ne sont donc pas comparables à ceux qui figurent dans les éditions de l'*Annuaire démographique* parues après 1975.

NOTES

[1] Sauf pour Bélarus, Fédération de Russie, Seychelles, Turkménistan et Ukraine où A34 et O95 sont exclus.
[2] *Classification statistique internationale des maladies et des problèmes de santé connexes*, dixième révision, volume 2. Genève, Organisation mondiale de la santé, 1992.
[3] Pour plus d'information sur les méthodes spécifiques utilisées pour les pays, voir "Mathers CD, Bernard C, Iburg KM, Inoue M, Ma Fat D, Shibuya K et al. *Global burden of disease in 2002: data sources, methods and results*. Geneva, World Health Organization, 2003 (GPE Discussion Paper No. 54).

17. Maternal deaths and maternal mortality ratios: 2007 - 2016
Mortalité liée à la maternité, nombre de décès et taux : 2007 - 2016

Continent and country or area — Continent et pays ou zone	Code[a]	2007	2008	2009	2010	2011	2012	2013	2014	2015	2016
AFRICA - AFRIQUE											
Cabo Verde											
Number - Nombre	C					5	1				...
Egypt - Égypte											
Number - Nombre	C	567	449	579	519	550	531	503	497	410	...
Rate - Taux	C	29.1	21.9	26.1	23.0	22.5	20.2	19.2	18.3	15.3	...
Mauritius - Maurice											
Number - Nombre	+C	6	6	10	4	5	9	9	7	4	6
Rate - Taux	+C	♦35.2	♦36.6	♦65.2	♦26.7	♦34.0	♦62.1	♦66.7	♦52.7	♦31.6	♦46.3
Mayotte											
Number - Nombre	C	...	...	...	...	-	1	1	2		...
Rate - Taux	C	...	...	...	...	...	...	...	♦27.4	...	...
Morocco - Maroc											
Number - Nombre	U	...	74	...	65	98	93	62	77	...	...
Reunion - Réunion											
Number - Nombre	...	...	2	1	...	5	2	2	2	...	...
Seychelles											
Number - Nombre	+C	-	1	1	2	-	-	-	-	3	...
Rate - Taux	+C	-	♦64.7	♦63.3	♦133.0	-	-	-	-	♦188.4	...
South Africa - Afrique du Sud											
Number - Nombre	C	1 762	1 808	1 880	1 658	1 260	1 050	946	1 027	942	...
Rate - Taux	C	163.8	163.4	178.2	161.3	121.6	101.5	92.8	100.7	97.5	...
Tunisia - Tunisie											
Number - Nombre	U	...	...	...	...	...	...	28	...	...	...
AMERICA, NORTH - AMÉRIQUE DU NORD											
Anguilla											
Number - Nombre	...	...	...	1	-	1	-	-	-	-	-
Antigua and Barbuda - Antigua-et-Barbuda											
Number - Nombre	+U	1	-	-	...	...	1	-	-	-	...
Aruba											
Number - Nombre	...	...	-	-	-	2	-	-	-		
Bahamas											
Number - Nombre	...	...	...	3[1]	7[1]	5[1]	-[1]	3[2]	3[2]	...	...	...
Rate - Taux	...	...	...	♦54.7	♦130.9	♦99.0	-	...	...	...	...
Barbados - Barbade											
Number - Nombre	...	...	...	2[3]	-[3]	-[3]	2[3]	1[4]	1[4]	...	...
Rate - Taux	...	...	...	♦56.4	-	-	♦60.9	...	...	...	...
Belize											
Number - Nombre	...	2[3]	2[3]	4[3]	4[3]	-[3]	2[4]	-[4]	-[4]	-[4]	...
Rate - Taux	...	♦28.4	♦28.1	♦53.9	♦55.3	...	...	...	...	...	...
Bermuda - Bermudes											
Number - Nombre		-	-	-	-	-	-	-	-	-	...
British Virgin Islands - Îles Vierges britanniques											
Number - Nombre	...	...	-	-	...	...	...	...	...	...	...
Canada											
Number - Nombre	C	24	34	29	24	18	22	23	...	...	...
Rate - Taux	C	♦6.5	9.0	♦7.6	♦6.4	♦4.8	♦5.8	♦6.0	...	...	...
Cayman Islands - Îles Caïmanes											
Number - Nombre	...	...	-	-	-	...	...	-	...	...	...
Costa Rica											
Number - Nombre	...	10[2]	20[2]	10[1]	14[1]	17[1]	22[2]	10[2]	21[2]	...	...
Rate - Taux	...	...	...	♦13.3	♦19.7	♦23.1	...	...	...	...	...
Cuba											
Number - Nombre	C	42	57	66	61	61	55	56	50	58	...
Rate - Taux	C	37.3	46.5	50.8	47.8	45.8	43.8	44.5	40.8	46.4	...
Dominica - Dominique											
Number - Nombre	+C	-	1	-	2	-	-	-	-	-	...
Rate - Taux	+C	-	♦103.7	-	♦214.4	-	-	-	-	...	...
Dominican Republic - République dominicaine											
Number - Nombre	U	...	...	56	37	188	177	215	...	...	...

17. Maternal deaths and maternal mortality ratios: 2007 - 2016
Mortalité liée à la maternité, nombre de décès et taux : 2007 - 2016 (continued - suite)

Continent and country or area / Continent et pays ou zone	Code[a]	2007	2008	2009	2010	2011	2012	2013	2014	2015	2016
AMERICA, NORTH - AMÉRIQUE DU NORD											
El Salvador											
Number - Nombre	...	17[2]	18[2]	14[2]	19[2]	16[2]	17[1]	39[1]	52[1]	...	
Rate - Taux	...	...	...	...	...	...	◆15.3	35.6	47.7	...	
Grenada - Grenade											
Number - Nombre	...	-[4]	-[3]	-[3]	-[3]	-[3]	2[3]	1[3]	-[3]	-[3]	2[3]
Rate - Taux	...	...	-	-	-	-	◆120.4	◆54.4	-	-	◆126.8
Guadeloupe											
Number - Nombre	...	...	2	1	1	-	4	1	-	...	...
Guatemala											
Number - Nombre	...	310[4]	328[4]	346[4]	355[3]	315[3]	356[3]	318[3]	291[3]	298[3]	
Rate - Taux	...	...	...	...	98.1	84.3	91.6	82.1	75.4	76.1	
Honduras											
Number - Nombre	+U	...	...	...	28	47	31	37	...	...	...
Jamaica - Jamaïque											
Number - Nombre	...	...	...	...	28	28	...	...	...	...	...
Martinique											
Number - Nombre	...	...	1	2	-	2	1	3	-	...	...
Mexico - Mexique											
Number - Nombre	+C	1 122	1 135	1 230	1 030	1 027	1 036	969	995	905	...
Rate - Taux	+C	51.3	50.6	54.6	47.5	45.4	47.3	44.7	46.7	43.2	
Montserrat											
Number - Nombre	...	...	-	-	-	-	-	-	-	-	...
Nicaragua											
Number - Nombre	+U	...	69	78	80	71	72	71	53	59	...
Panama											
Number - Nombre	+C	40[1]	41[1]	29[1]	41[1]	59[1]	49	41	44	40	...
Rate - Taux	+C	59.4	59.6	◆42.4	60.3	80.5	64.9	55.6	58.5	52.7	
Puerto Rico - Porto Rico											
Number - Nombre	...	...	6	10	6	5	1	2	3	15	
Saint Kitts and Nevis - Saint-Kitts-et-Nevis											
Number - Nombre	+U	-	1	-	-	1	1	...	-	-	...
Saint Lucia - Sainte-Lucie											
Number - Nombre	...	...	1[3]	...	3[4]	1[4]	1[3]	1[3]	2[3]	...	...
Rate - Taux	...	...	◆45.2	...	...	...	◆49.9	◆46.0	◆98.7	...	...
Saint Pierre and Miquelon - Saint Pierre-et-Miquelon											
Number - Nombre	...	...	-	-	-	...	...	...	...	...	...
Saint Vincent and the Grenadines - Saint-Vincent-et-les Grenadines											
Number - Nombre	...	-	2[1]	-[1]	2[1]	1[1]	-[1]	2[1]	1[1]	-[1]	...
Rate - Taux	...	...	◆105.2	-	◆112.1	◆58.0	-	◆115.1	◆54.3	-	...
Trinidad and Tobago - Trinité-et-Tobago											
Number - Nombre	U	...	11	...	...	...	...	...	...	...	...
Turks and Caicos Islands - Îles Turques et Caïques											
Number - Nombre	...	...	-	1	...	...	...	-	-	...	...
United States of America - États-Unis d'Amérique											
Number - Nombre	C	766	795	962	825	931	990	1 138	1 123	1 140	...
Rate - Taux	C	17.7	18.7	23.3	20.6	23.5	25.0	28.9	28.2	28.7	
United States Virgin Islands - Îles Vierges américaines											
Number - Nombre	...	...	...	-	-	-	...	...	...	-	...
AMERICA, SOUTH - AMÉRIQUE DU SUD											
Argentina - Argentine											
Number - Nombre	+C	332	319	422	331	318	280	274	307	333	...
Rate - Taux	+C	47.4	42.8	56.6	43.8	42.0	37.9	36.3	39.5	43.2	...

17. Maternal deaths and maternal mortality ratios: 2007 - 2016
Mortalité liée à la maternité, nombre de décès et taux : 2007 - 2016 (continued - suite)

Continent and country or area Continent et pays ou zone	Co-de[a]	2007	2008	2009	2010	2011	2012	2013	2014	2015	2016
AMERICA, SOUTH - AMÉRIQUE DU SUD											
Brazil - Brésil											
Number - Nombre	...	1 613[4]	1 641[3]	1 884[3]	1 728[3]	1 680[3]	1 647[3]	1 788[3]	1 889[3]	1 896[3]	
Rate - Taux	...	...	58.8	68.4	62.6	59.5	58.2	63.1	64.8	62.0	
Chile - Chili											
Number - Nombre	C	42	36	43	46	46	54	52	56	56	
Rate - Taux	C	17.5	14.6	17.0	18.4	18.6	22.2	21.5	22.3	22.9	
Colombia - Colombie											
Number - Nombre	...	503[3]	433[3]	496[3]	474[3]	459[3]	452[4]	381[4]	491[4]	476[4]	
Rate - Taux	...	70.9	60.5	70.9	72.4	69.0	...	...	...	...	
Ecuador - Équateur											
Number - Nombre	U	176	162	208	202	239	202	158	169	183	
French Guiana - Guyane française											
Number - Nombre	...	...	4	1	3	-	2	1	3	...	
Guyana											
Number - Nombre	...	...	16[4]	9[4]	20[4]	14[4]	14[3]	9[3]	...	...	
Paraguay											
Number - Nombre	+U	...	117	128	100	94	91	100	71	...	
Peru - Pérou											
Number - Nombre	+U	155	192	163	137	148	126	97	112	110	
Suriname											
Number - Nombre	...	...	9[3]	11[3]	6[3]	7[3]	2[4]	11[4]	7[4]	...	
Rate - Taux	...	...	♦89.1	♦112.3	♦61.8	♦72.1	...	...	...	...	
Uruguay											
Number - Nombre	C	...	6	11	2	...	5	9	9	11	
Rate - Taux	C	...	♦12.7	♦23.3	♦4.2	...	♦10.4	♦18.5	♦18.6	♦22.5	
Venezuela (Bolivarian Republic of) - Venezuela (République bolivarienne du)											
Number - Nombre	...	332[3]	377[3]	434[3]	412[3]	436[3]	416[4]	410[4]	...	...	
Rate - Taux	...	54.0	64.8	73.1	69.7	70.9	...	...	...	...	
ASIA - ASIE											
Armenia - Arménie											
Number - Nombre	...	...	16[4]	12[4]	4[4]	6[4]	5[3]	9[3]	8[3]	7[3]	14[3]
Rate - Taux	...	...	...	...	...	...	♦11.8	♦21.5	♦18.6	♦16.8	♦34.5
Azerbaijan - Azerbaïdjan											
Number - Nombre	C	30	...	...	...	...	...	...	...	...	
Rate - Taux	C	♦19.7	...	...	...	...	...	...	...	...	
Bahrain - Bahreïn											
Number - Nombre	...	3[3]	3[3]	3[4]	1[4]	2[4]	2[3]	4[3]	2[3]	...	
Rate - Taux	...	♦18.7	♦17.6	...	...	...	♦10.5	♦20.0	♦9.6	...	
Brunei Darussalam - Brunéi Darussalam											
Number - Nombre	...	1[1]	-[1]	1[1]	1[2]	-[2]	3[1]	1[1]	-[1]	2[1]	
Rate - Taux	...	♦15.8	-	♦15.1	...	...	♦43.4	♦15.0	-	♦29.9	
China, Hong Kong SAR - Chine, Hong Kong RAS											
Number - Nombre	...	1	2	2	1	1	2	-	2	1	
Cyprus - Chypre											
Number - Nombre	U	-	1	-	1	-	...	1	2	-	
Georgia - Géorgie											
Number - Nombre	C	2	...	32	13	21	12	16	18	19	
Rate - Taux	C	♦4.1	...	50.5	♦20.8	♦36.2	♦21.0	♦27.6	♦29.7	♦32.1	
Iran (Islamic Republic of) - Iran (République islamique d')											
Number - Nombre	U	...	...	...	...	...	...	113	104	111	
Iraq											
Number - Nombre	U	...	62	...	...	...	...	...	...	...	
Israel - Israël											
Number - Nombre	C	7	8	5	7	2	9	14	10	7	
Rate - Taux	C	♦4.6	♦5.1	♦3.1	♦4.2	♦1.2	♦5.3	♦8.2	♦5.7	♦3.9	
Japan - Japon											
Number - Nombre	C	39	41	61	49	43	50	41	33	44	...
Rate - Taux	C	3.6	3.8	5.7	4.6	4.1	4.8	4.0	3.3	4.4	...

Continent and country or area / Continent et pays ou zone	Code[a]	2007	2008	2009	2010	2011	2012	2013	2014	2015	2016
ASIA - ASIE											
Jordan - Jordanie											
Number - Nombre	U	...	25	26	46	34	44	...	...	...	
Kazakhstan											
Number - Nombre	...	107[4]	86[3]	94[3]	65[3]	48[3]	41[4]	41[4]	37[4]	35[4]	...
Rate - Taux	...	...	24.1	26.4	17.7	12.9	...	...	...	...	
Kuwait - Koweït											
Number - Nombre	...	.[3]	5[3]	7[3]	3[3]	6[3]	1[4]	4[4]	7[4]	...	
Rate - Taux	...	-	♦9.2	♦12.4	♦5.2	♦10.3	...	...	...	...	
Kyrgyzstan - Kirghizstan											
Number - Nombre	...	64[4]	70[3]	86[3]	75[3]	81[3]	76[3]	56[3]	81[3]	63[3]	
Rate - Taux	...	...	55.0	63.5	51.3	54.1	49.1	36.0	50.1	38.5	
Malaysia - Malaisie											
Number - Nombre	U	...	133	...	...	...	122	108	119	...	
Maldives											
Number - Nombre	...	2[1]	4[2]	...	7[2]	4[2]	...	...	...	...	
Rate - Taux	...	♦30.4	...								
Mongolia - Mongolie											
Number - Nombre	U	...	...	...	...	...	...	...	...	...	38
Oman											
Number - Nombre	U	...	...	3	6	...	...	...	-		
Philippines											
Number - Nombre	U	...	1 731	...	1 718	1 465	...	...	...		
Qatar											
Number - Nombre	...	5[3]	2[3]	4[3]	2[4]	1[4]	1[4]	.[4]	1[4]	3[4]	.[4]
Rate - Taux	...	♦31.9	♦11.6	♦21.8	...						
Republic of Korea - République de Corée											
Number - Nombre	C	...	39	48	75	85	56	51	48	42	...
Rate - Taux	C	...	8.4	10.8	16.0	18.0	11.6	11.7	11.0	9.6	
Saudi Arabia - Arabie saoudite											
Number - Nombre	U	...	...	54	...	...	45	...	...	...	...
Singapore - Singapour											
Number - Nombre	+U		2	-	1	2	1	-	-	3	
Syrian Arab Republic - République arabe syrienne											
Number - Nombre	+C	...	...	...	23	...	...	...	...	...	
Rate - Taux	+C	...	...	...	♦2.6	...	...	...	...	...	
Tajikistan - Tadjikistan											
Number - Nombre	U	...	...	...	...	...	...	...	...	...	18
Thailand - Thaïlande											
Number - Nombre	+U	...	...	...	78	71	141	166	166	167	177
Turkey - Turquie											
Number - Nombre	+U	...	...	37	46	58	55	302	273	220	
Turkmenistan - Turkménistan											
Number - Nombre	U	...	...	...	...	...	7	9	4	5	
United Arab Emirates - Émirats arabes unis											
Number - Nombre	+U	...	1	2	4	...	...	...	...	...	
Uzbekistan - Ouzbékistan											
Number - Nombre	C	...	...	...	...	...	103	120	131	...	
Rate - Taux	C	...	...	...	...	...	16.5	17.7	18.2	...	
EUROPE											
Andorra - Andorre											
Number - Nombre	C	...	...	...	...	...	-	-	-	-	...
Austria - Autriche											
Number - Nombre	C	3	2	2	1	2	1	1	7	4	5
Rate - Taux	C	♦3.9	♦2.6	♦2.6	♦1.3	♦2.6	♦1.3	♦1.3	♦8.6	♦4.7	♦5.7
Belarus - Bélarus											
Number - Nombre	C	7	3	1	1	1	...	-	1	...	
Rate - Taux	C	♦6.8	♦2.8	♦0.9	♦0.9	♦0.9	...	-	♦0.8	...	
Belgium - Belgique											
Number - Nombre	C	...	7	6	8	9	5	3	6	4	...
Rate - Taux	C	...	♦5.5	♦4.7	♦6.1	♦7.0	♦3.9	♦2.4	♦4.8	♦3.3	
Bosnia and Herzegovina - Bosnie-Herzégovine											
Number - Nombre		...	...	...	...	2[4]	...	...	.[3]	...	...

17. Maternal deaths and maternal mortality ratios: 2007 - 2016
Mortalité liée à la maternité, nombre de décès et taux : 2007 - 2016 (continued - suite)

Continent and country or area / Continent et pays ou zone	Code[a]	2007	2008	2009	2010	2011	2012	2013	2014	2015	2016
EUROPE											
Bulgaria - Bulgarie											
Number - Nombre	C	8	5	4	6	2	3	8	5	...	...
Rate - Taux	C	♦10.6	♦6.4	♦4.9	♦7.9	♦2.8	♦4.3	♦12.0	♦7.4	...	
Croatia - Croatie											
Number - Nombre	C	6	3	6	4	4	3	2	1	1	1
Rate - Taux	C	♦14.3	♦6.9	♦13.5	♦9.2	♦9.7	♦7.2	♦5.0	♦2.5	♦2.7	♦2.7
Czechia - Tchéquie											
Number - Nombre	C	3	7	3	3	2	6	1	4	2	1
Rate - Taux	C	♦2.6	♦5.9	♦2.5	♦2.6	♦1.8	♦5.5	♦0.9	♦3.6	♦1.8	♦0.9
Denmark - Danemark											
Number - Nombre	C	...	4	4	-	2	-	1	3		
Rate - Taux	C	...	♦6.2	♦6.4	-	♦3.4	-	♦1.8	♦5.3		
Estonia - Estonie											
Number - Nombre	C	-	-	-	1	1	1	1	-	-	
Rate - Taux	C	-	-	-	♦6.3	♦6.8	♦7.1	♦7.4	-	-	
Finland - Finlande											
Number - Nombre	C	1	5	1	3	-	2	1	3	2	
Rate - Taux	C	♦1.7	♦8.4	♦1.7	♦4.9	-	♦3.4	♦1.7	♦5.3	♦3.6	
France											
Number - Nombre	C	60	52	75	68	45	44	38	37	...	
Rate - Taux	C	7.6	6.5	9.5	8.5	5.7	5.6	4.9	4.6	...	
Germany - Allemagne											
Number - Nombre	C	28	36	35	37	32	31	29	29	24	...
Rate - Taux	C	♦4.1	5.3	5.3	5.5	4.8	4.6	♦4.3	♦4.1	♦3.3	
Greece - Grèce											
Number - Nombre	C	2	-	4	6	4	1	-	4	5	
Rate - Taux	C	♦1.8	-	♦3.4	♦5.2	♦3.8	♦1.0	-	♦4.3	♦5.4	
Hungary - Hongrie											
Number - Nombre	C	8	17	18	14	9	9	13	6	5	11
Rate - Taux	C	♦8.2	♦17.1	♦18.7	♦15.5	♦10.2	♦10.0	♦14.5	♦6.4	♦5.4	♦11.5
Iceland - Islande											
Number - Nombre	C	-	-	-	...	...	-	-	-		
Ireland - Irlande											
Number - Nombre	+C	1	3	3	3	2	2	3	1		
Rate - Taux	+C	♦1.4	♦4.0	♦4.0	♦4.0	♦2.7	♦2.8	♦4.4	♦1.5		
Italy - Italie											
Number - Nombre	C	13	13	19	16	14	11	14	6	16	
Rate - Taux	C	♦2.3	♦2.3	♦3.3	♦2.8	♦2.6	♦2.1	♦2.7	♦1.2	♦3.3	
Latvia - Lettonie											
Number - Nombre	+C	6	2	7	4	-	4	2	2	12	
Rate - Taux	+C	♦25.0	♦8.2	♦31.8	♦20.2	-	♦20.1	♦9.7	♦9.2	♦54.6	
Lithuania - Lituanie											
Number - Nombre	+C	2	3	-	2	2	3	2	1	3	2
Rate - Taux	+C	♦6.7	♦9.5	-	♦6.5	♦6.6	♦9.8	♦6.7	♦3.3	♦9.5	♦6.5
Luxembourg											
Number - Nombre	+C	1	1	-	1	-	1	1	-		
Rate - Taux	+C	♦18.3	♦17.9	-	♦17.0	-	♦16.6	♦16.4	-		
Malta - Malte											
Number - Nombre	+C	-	1	-	1	-	-	-	-		
Rate - Taux	+C	-	♦24.9	-	♦25.7	-	-	-	-		
Montenegro - Monténégro											
Number - Nombre	C	1	-	-	...	...	...	...	...	...	
Rate - Taux	C	♦12.8	-	-	...	...	...	...	...	...	
Netherlands - Pays-Bas											
Number - Nombre	+C	9	8	9	4	3	6	5	5	6	6
Rate - Taux	+C	♦5.0	♦4.3	♦4.9	♦2.2	♦1.7	♦3.4	♦2.9	♦2.9	♦3.5	♦3.5
North Macedonia - Macédoine du Nord											
Number - Nombre	...		-	.[3]	1[3]	2[3]	...	1[3]	1[3]	...	...
Rate - Taux	...		...	-	♦4.2	♦8.2	...	♦4.2	♦4.3	...	...
Norway - Norvège											
Number - Nombre	+C	4	3	1	3	3	-	2	2	-	
Rate - Taux	+C	♦6.8	♦5.0	♦1.6	♦4.9	♦5.0	-	♦3.4	♦3.4	-	
Poland - Pologne											
Number - Nombre	C	11	19	8	9	9	4	7	8	6	
Rate - Taux	C	♦2.8	♦4.6	♦1.9	♦2.2	♦2.3	♦1.0	♦1.9	♦2.1	♦1.6	
Portugal											
Number - Nombre	+C	5	4	7	8	5	4	5	6		
Rate - Taux	+C	♦4.9	♦3.8	♦7.0	♦7.9	♦5.2	♦4.5	♦6.0	♦7.3	...	...

Continent and country or area / Continent et pays ou zone	Code[a]	2007	2008	2009	2010	2011	2012	2013	2014	2015	2016
EUROPE											
Republic of Moldova - République de Moldova											
Number - Nombre	...	7[1]	17[1]	7[1]	18[1]	6[1]	12[2]	6[2]	7[2]	12[2]	7[2]
Rate - Taux	...	♦18.4	♦43.6	♦17.2	♦44.5	♦15.3	...	...	...	...	...
Romania - Roumanie											
Number - Nombre	+C	33	30	47	51	50	23	27	24	27	17
Rate - Taux	+C	15.4	♦13.5	21.1	24.0	25.5	♦11.4	♦14.8	♦12.1	♦13.7	♦8.5
Russian Federation - Fédération de Russie											
Number - Nombre	+C	356	359	388	298	291	221	216	...	...	...
Rate - Taux	+C	22.1	20.9	22.0	16.7	16.2	11.6	11.4	...	...	...
San Marino - Saint-Marin											
Number - Nombre	+C	...	...	...	...	...	-	-	-	-	
Serbia - Serbie											
Number - Nombre	...	.2	4[2]	6[2]	12[1]	7[1]	10[1]	9[1]	8[1]	8[1]	...
Rate - Taux	...	...	...	...	♦17.6	♦10.7	♦14.9	♦13.7	♦12.0	♦12.2	...
Slovakia - Slovaquie											
Number - Nombre	C	-	2	6	-	...	3	1	2	...	
Rate - Taux	C	-	♦3.5	♦9.8	-	...	♦5.4	♦1.8	♦3.6	...	
Slovenia - Slovénie											
Number - Nombre	C	3	2	1	-	...	1	1	2	1	
Rate - Taux	C	♦15.1	♦9.2	♦4.6	-	...	♦4.6	♦4.7	♦9.4	♦4.8	
Spain - Espagne											
Number - Nombre	C	13	24	17	20	14	10	18	9	15	...
Rate - Taux	C	♦2.6	♦4.6	♦3.4	♦4.1	♦3.0	♦2.2	♦4.2	♦2.1	♦3.6	...
Sweden - Suède											
Number - Nombre	C	2	6	6	3	1	5	7	4	1	3
Rate - Taux	C	♦1.9	♦5.5	♦5.4	♦2.6	♦0.9	♦4.4	♦6.2	♦3.5	♦0.9	♦2.6
Switzerland - Suisse											
Number - Nombre	C	1	8	3	3	3	7	2	5	6	...
Rate - Taux	C	♦1.3	♦10.4	♦3.8	♦3.7	♦3.7	♦8.5	♦2.4	♦5.9	♦6.9	...
Ukraine											
Number - Nombre	+C	...	79	129	116	85	66	...	69	60	...
Rate - Taux	+C	...	15.5	25.2	23.3	16.9	12.7	...	14.8	14.6	...
United Kingdom of Great Britain and Northern Ireland - Royaume-Uni de Grande-Bretagne et d'Irlande du Nord											
Number - Nombre	+C	56	49	74	40	53	51	50	52	35	...
Rate - Taux	+C	7.3	6.2	9.4	5.0	6.6	6.3	6.4	6.7	4.5	...
OCEANIA - OCÉANIE											
Australia - Australie											
Number - Nombre	C	...	6	9	12	12	16	6	12	8	...
Rate - Taux	C	...	♦2.0	♦3.0	♦4.0	♦4.0	♦5.2	♦1.9	♦4.0	♦2.6	...
Fiji - Fidji											
Number - Nombre	+C	...	...	5	...	4	8	...	...	...	...
Rate - Taux	+C	...	...	♦27.5	...	♦20.5	♦43.4	...	...	...	...
New Zealand - Nouvelle-Zélande											
Number - Nombre	+C	13	7	11	6	7	7	10	...	...	...
Rate - Taux	+C	♦20.3	♦10.9	♦17.6	♦9.4	♦11.4	♦11.4	♦17.0	...	...	...

FOOTNOTES - NOTES

Data in bold refer to maternal deaths based on ICD-10 Classification, otherwise data refer to maternal deaths based on ICD-9 Classification. - Les données en typographie gras se rapportent aux décès maternelles basées sur la classification CIM-10, autrement les données se rapportent aux décès maternelles basées sur la classification CIM-9.

Italics: data from civil registers which are incomplete or of unknown completeness. - Italiques : données incomplètes ou dont le degré d'exactitude n'est pas connu, provenant des registres de l'état civil.

* Provisional. - Données provisoires.

♦ Rates based on 30 or fewer deaths. - Taux basés sur 30 décès ou moins.

[a] 'Code' indicates the source of data, as follows:
C - Civil registration, estimated over 90% complete
U - Civil registration, estimated less than 90% complete
| - Other source, estimated reliable
+ - Data tabulated by date of registration rather than occurence
... - Information not available

Le 'Code' indique la source des données, comme suit :

C - Registres de l'état civil considérés complets à 90 p. 100 au moins
U - Registres de l'état civil qui ne sont pas considérés complets à 90 p. 100 au moins
| - Autre source, considérée pas douteuses
+ - Données exploitées selon la date de l'enregistrement et non la date de l'événement
... - Information pas disponible

[1] The code is +C. - Le code est +C.
[2] The code is +U. - Le code est +U.
[3] The code is C. - Le code est C.
[4] The code is U. - Le code est U.

Table 18 - *Demographic Yearbook 2018*

Table 18 presents deaths and crude death rates by urban/rural residence for as many years as possible between 2014 and 2018.

Description of variables: Death is defined as the permanent disappearance of all evidence of life at any time after live birth has taken place (post-natal cessation of vital functions without capability of resuscitation).

Statistics on the number of deaths are obtained from civil registers unless otherwise noted. For those countries or areas where civil registration statistics on deaths are considered reliable (estimated completeness of 90 per cent or more), the death rates shown have been calculated on the basis of registered deaths.

The urban/rural classification of deaths is that provided by each country or area; it is presumed to be based on the national census definitions of urban population that have been set forth at the end of the technical notes for table 6.

For certain countries, there is a discrepancy between the total number of deaths shown in this table and those shown in subsequent tables for the same year. Usually this discrepancy arises because the total number of deaths occurring in a given year is revised although the remaining tabulations are not.

Rate computation: Crude death rates are the annual number of deaths per 1 000 mid-year population.

Rates by urban/rural residence are the annual number of deaths, in the appropriate urban or rural category, per 1 000 corresponding mid-year population. These rates are calculated by the United Nations Statistics Division based on the appropriate reference population (for example: total population, nationals only etc.) if known and available. If the reference population is not known or unavailable, the total population is used to calculate the rates. Therefore, if the population that is used to calculate the rates is different from the correct reference population, the rates presented might under- or overstate the true situation in a country or area.

Rates presented in this table are limited to those countries or areas with a minimum number of 30 deaths in a given year.

Reliability of data: Each country or area has been asked to indicate the estimated completeness of the deaths recorded in its civil register. These national assessments are indicated by the quality codes "C", "U" and "|" that appear in the first column of this table. "C" indicates that the data are estimated to be virtually complete, that is, representing at least 90 per cent of the deaths occurring each year, while "U" indicates that data are estimated to be incomplete that is, representing less than 90 per cent of the deaths occurring each year. The code "|" indicates that the source of data is different than civil registration and is explained by a footnote. The code "..." indicates that no information was provided regarding completeness or no assessment has been done in the country.

Data from civil registers that are reported as incomplete or of unknown completeness (code "U" or "...") are considered unreliable. They appear in italics in this table; rates based on these data are not computed.

Limitations: Statistics on deaths are subject to the same qualifications as have been set forth for vital statistics and particularly for death statistics discussed in section 4 of the Introduction.

The reliability of the data, an indication of which is described above, is an important factor in considering the limitations. In addition, some deaths are tabulated by date of registration and not by date of occurrence; these have been indicated with a plus sign "+". Whenever the lag between the date of occurrence and date of registration is prolonged and, therefore, a large proportion of the death registrations are delayed, death statistics for any given year may be seriously affected. However, delays in the registration of deaths are less common and shorter than in the registration of live births.

International comparability in mortality statistics may also be affected by the exclusion of deaths of infants who were born alive but died before the registration of the birth or within the first 24 hours of life. Statistics of this type are footnoted.

In addition, it should be noted that rates are affected also by the quality and limitations of the population estimates that are used in their computation. The problems of under-enumeration or over-enumeration and, to some extent, the differences in definition of total population have been discussed in section 3 of the Introduction, dealing generally with population data. Specific information pertaining to individual countries or areas is given in the footnotes to table 3.

It should be emphasized that crude death rates -- like other crude rates, such as of birth, marriage and divorce -- may be seriously affected by the age-sex structure of the populations to which they relate. Nevertheless, they do provide a simple measure of the level and changes in mortality.

The comparability of data by urban/rural residence is affected by the national definitions of urban and rural used in tabulating these data. It is assumed, in the absence of specific information to the contrary, that the definitions of urban and rural used in connection with the national population census were also used in the compilation of the vital statistics for each country or area. However, it cannot be excluded that, for a given country or area, different definitions of urban and rural are used for the vital statistics data and the population census data respectively. When known, the definitions of urban used in national population censuses are presented at the end of the technical notes for table 6. As discussed in detail in the technical notes for table 6, these definitions vary considerably from one country or area to another.

Earlier data: Deaths and crude death rates have been presented in each issue of the *Demographic Yearbook*. For information on specific years covered, the reader should consult the Historical Index.

504

Tableau 18 – *Annuaire démographique 2018*

Le tableau 18 présente le nombre des décès et les taux bruts de mortalité selon le lieu de résidence (zone urbaine ou rurale) pour le plus grand nombre d'années possible entre 2014 et 2018.

Description des variables : Le décès est défini comme la disparition permanente de tout signe de vie à un moment quelconque postérieur à la naissance vivante (cessation des fonctions vitales après la naissance sans possibilité de réanimation).

Sauf indication contraire, les statistiques relatives au nombre de décès sont établies sur la base des registres d'état civil. Pour les pays ou zones où les données concernant l'enregistrement des décès par les services de l'état civil sont jugées sûres (complétude estimée à 90 p. 100 ou plus), les taux de mortalité ont été calculés d'après les décès enregistrés.

La répartition des décès entre zones urbaines et zones rurales est celle qui a été communiquée par chaque pays ou zone ; on part du principe qu'elle repose sur les définitions de la population urbaine utilisées pour les recensements nationaux, qui sont reproduites à la fin des notes techniques du tableau 6.

Pour quelques pays il y a une discordance entre le nombre total des décès présenté dans ce tableau et ceux présentés après pour la même année. Habituellement ces différences apparaissent lorsque le nombre total des décès pour une certaine année a été révisé alors que les autres tabulations ne l'ont pas été.

Calcul des taux : Les taux bruts de mortalité représentent le nombre annuel de décès pour 1 000 habitants en milieu d'année.

Les taux selon le lieu de résidence (zone urbaine ou rurale) représentent le nombre annuel de décès, classés selon la catégorie urbaine ou rurale appropriée, pour 1 000 habitants en milieu d'année. Ces taux sont calculés par la division de statistique des Nations Unies sur la base de la population de référence adéquate (par exemple : population totale, nationaux seulement, etc.) si connue et disponible. Si la population de référence n'est pas connue ou n'est pas disponible, la population totale est utilisée pour calculer les taux. Par conséquent, si la population utilisée pour calculer les taux est différente de la population de référence adéquate, les taux présentés sont susceptibles de sous ou sur estimer la situation réelle d'un pays ou d'un territoire.

Les taux présentés dans ce tableau se rapportent seulement aux pays ou zones où l'on a enregistré un nombre minimal de 30 décès au cours d'une année donnée.

Fiabilité des données : Il a été demandé à chaque pays ou zone d'indiquer le degré estimatif de complétude des données sur les décès d'enfants de moins d'un an figurant dans ses registres d'état civil. Ces évaluations nationales sont signalées par les codes de qualité "C", "U" et "|" qui apparaissent dans la deuxième colonne du tableau.

La lettre "C" indique que les données sont jugées à peu près complètes, c'est-à-dire qu'elles représentent au moins 90 p. 100 des décès survenus chaque année ; la lettre "U" signifie que les données sont jugées incomplètes, c'est-à-dire qu'elles représentent moins de 90 p.100 des décès survenus chaque année. Le symbole "|" indique que la source des données n'est pas un registre de l'état civil ; le symbole, dans ce cas, est accompagné par une note explicative. Le code "..." dénote qu'aucun renseignement n'a été communiqué quant à la complétude des données.

Les données provenant des registres de l'état civil qui sont déclarées incomplètes ou dont le degré de complétude n'est pas connu (code "U" ou "...") sont jugées douteuses. Elles apparaissent en italique dans le présent tableau et les taux correspondants n'ont pas été calculés.

Insuffisance des données : Les statistiques relatives à la mortalité appellent les mêmes réserves que celles qui ont été formulées à propos des statistiques de l'état civil en général et des statistiques relatives aux décès en particulier (voir la section 4 des Notes techniques).

La fiabilité des données, au sujet de laquelle des indications ont été fournies plus haut, est un facteur important. Il faut également tenir compte du fait que, dans certains cas, les décès sont classés par date d'enregistrement et non par date d'occurrence ; ces cas ont été signalés par le signe "+". Chaque fois que le décalage entre le décès et son enregistrement est grand et qu'une forte proportion des décès fait l'objet d'un enregistrement tardif, les statistiques relatives aux décès survenus pendant l'année peuvent être considérablement faussées.

En règle générale, toutefois, les décès sont enregistrés beaucoup plus rapidement que les naissances vivantes, et les retards prolongés sont rares.

Un autre facteur qui nuit à la comparabilité internationale est la pratique qui consiste à ne pas inclure dans les statistiques de la mortalité les enfants nés vivants mais décédés avant l'enregistrement de leur naissance ou dans les 24 heures qui ont suivi la naissance. Quand pareil facteur a joué, cela a été signalé en note à la fin du tableau.

Il convient de noter par ailleurs que l'exactitude des taux dépend également de la qualité et des limitations des estimations de la population qui sont utilisées pour leur calcul. Le problème des erreurs par excès ou par défaut commises lors du dénombrement et, dans une certaine mesure, le problème de l'hétérogénéité des définitions de la population totale ont été examinés à la section 3 des Notes techniques, relative à la population en général ; des indications concernant certains pays ou zones sont données en note à la fin du tableau 3.

Il faut souligner que les taux bruts de mortalité, de même que les taux bruts de natalité, de nuptialité et de divortialité, peuvent varier très sensiblement selon la composition par âge et par sexe de la population à laquelle ils se rapportent. Ils offrent néanmoins un moyen simple de mesurer le niveau et l'évolution de la mortalité.

La comparabilité des données selon le lieu de résidence (zone urbaine ou rurale) peut être limitée par les définitions nationales des termes « urbain » et « rural » utilisées pour le classement de ces données. En l'absence d'indications contraires, on a supposé que les mêmes définitions avaient servi pour le recensement national de la population et pour l'établissement des statistiques de l'état civil pour chaque pays ou zone. Toutefois, il n'est pas exclu que, pour une zone ou un pays donné, des définitions différentes aient été retenues. Les définitions du terme « urbain » utilisées pour les recensements nationaux de population ont été présentées à la fin du tableau 6 lorsqu'elles étaient connues. Comme on l'a précisé dans les notes techniques relatives au tableau 6, ces définitions varient considérablement d'un pays ou d'une zone à l'autre.

Données publiées antérieurement : les différentes éditions de l'*Annuaire démographique* contiennent des statistiques des décès et des taux bruts de mortalité. Pour plus de précisions concernant les années pour lesquelles ces données ont été publiées, se reporter à l'index historique.

18. Deaths and crude death rates, by urban/rural residence: 2014 - 2018
Décès et taux bruts de mortalité, selon la résidence, urbaine/rurale : 2014 - 2018

Continent, country or area, and urban/rural residence — Continent, pays ou zone et résidence, urbaine/rurale	Code[a]	Number - Nombre					Rate - Taux				
		2014	2015	2016	2017	2018	2014	2015	2016	2017	2018
AFRICA - AFRIQUE											
Algeria - Algérie[1]											
Total	U	173 781	182 570	180 404	...	...	...	...	...	...	...
Angola[2]											
Total	I	239 252	...	...	...	...	9.2	...	...	...	...
Urban - Urbaine	I	135 698	...	...	...	...	8.4	...	...	...	...
Rural - Rurale	I	103 553	...	...	...	...	10.7	...	...	...	...
Botswana[3]											
Total	U	12 177	13 030	12 825	12 386		...	...	...	...	
Congo											
Total	+U	13 413	...	...	...		...	...	...	...	
Côte d'Ivoire[4]											
Total	+U	45 023	47 065	45 995	44 813	46 385	...	...	...	...	...
Urban - Urbaine	+U	...	...	37 487	37 965	40 520	...	...	...	...	...
Rural - Rurale	+U	...	...	8 508	6 848	5 865	...	...	...	...	...
Egypt - Égypte											
Total	C	531 864	573 879	556 148	547 208	...	6.1	6.5	6.1	5.7	...
Urban - Urbaine	C	299 490	324 422	319 409	319 980	...	8.1	8.5	8.2	7.9	...
Rural - Rurale	C	232 374	249 457	236 739	227 228	...	4.7	4.9	4.5	4.1	...
Guinea - Guinée[5]											
Total	I	119 969	...	...	...	...	11.3	...	...	...	...
Urban - Urbaine	I	32 394	...	...	...	...	8.8	...	...	...	...
Rural - Rurale	I	87 575	...	...	...	...	12.7	...	...	...	...
Kenya											
Total	+U	198 611	200 205	189 930	190 877	192 019	...	...	...	...	...
Lesotho											
Total	+U	...	17 929	13 768	13 671	...	...	...	...	...	...
Malawi[6]											
Total	I	...	...	...	...	110 776	...	...	...	...	...
Urban - Urbaine	I	...	...	...	...	13 595	...	...	...	...	6.3
Rural - Rurale	I	...	...	...	...	97 181	...	...	...	...	4.8
Mauritius - Maurice[7]											6.6
Total	+C	9 682	9 747	10 174	10 140	10 787	7.7	7.7	8.1	8.0	8.5
Urban - Urbaine	+C	4 203	4 454	4 658	4 560	4 891	8.1	8.6	9.0	8.9	9.5
Rural - Rurale	+C	5 479	5 293	5 516	5 580	5 896	7.4	7.1	7.4	7.4	7.8
Mayotte											
Total	C	590	636	705	735	...	2.6	2.7	2.9	2.9	...
Reunion - Réunion											
Total	C	4 355	4 531	4 689	4 673	...	5.1	5.3	5.5	5.4	...
Urban - Urbaine	C	...	...	...	4 458	...	...	...	...	...	...
Rural - Rurale	C	...	...	...	215	...	...	...	...	...	...
Saint Helena ex. dep. - Sainte-Hélène sans dép.											
Total	C	61	55	45	58	52	13.9	12.3	9.7	12.7	11.3
Sao Tome and Principe - Sao Tomé-et-Principe											
Total	C	1 243	1 226	1 212	1 202	...	6.7	6.5	6.3	6.1	...
Seychelles											
Total	+C	725	703	747	748	818	7.9	7.5	7.9	7.8	8.5
South Africa - Afrique du Sud											
Total	U	476 891	473 266	456 612	...	...	...	...	...	...	...
Tunisia - Tunisie											
Total	U	62 785	65 743	62 601	67 447	...	...	...	...	...	...
AMERICA, NORTH - AMÉRIQUE DU NORD											
Anguilla[8]											
Total	+C	59	61	*83	...	...	4.1	4.1	*5.5	...	...
Antigua and Barbuda - Antigua-et-Barbuda											
Total	+C	590	527	542	599	581	6.6	5.8	5.9	6.4	6.1
Aruba											
Total	C	643	679	781	707	*717	6.0	6.2	7.1	6.4	*6.4
Bahamas											
Total	+C	*2 132	*2 243	*2 288	*2 372	...	*5.9	*6.1	*6.1	*6.3	...

18. Deaths and crude death rates, by urban/rural residence: 2014 - 2018
Décès et taux bruts de mortalité, selon la résidence, urbaine/rurale : 2014 - 2018 (continued - suite)

Continent, country or area, and urban/rural residence — Continent, pays ou zone et résidence, urbaine/rurale	Code[a]	Number - Nombre					Rate - Taux				
		2014	2015	2016	2017	2018	2014	2015	2016	2017	2018
AMERICA, NORTH - AMÉRIQUE DU NORD											
Barbados - Barbade											
Total	+C	2 580	...	...	...	...	9.3	...	...	...	...
Belize											
Total	U	1 620	1 772	1 805	1 872	1 886	...	...	...	...	...
Urban - Urbaine	U	906	910	958[9]	...	...	...	...	...	...	...
Rural - Rurale	U	714	862	838[9]	...	...	...	...	...	...	...
Bermuda - Bermudes[10]											
Total	C	480	478	492	481	...	7.8	7.7	7.7	7.5	...
British Virgin Islands - Îles Vierges britanniques											
Total	C	111	136	120	155	...	...	4.7	...	...	...
Canada[11]											
Total	C	258 821	264 333	267 213	276 689	...	7.3	7.4	7.4	7.6	...
Cayman Islands - Îles Caïmanes[12]											
Total	C	163	170	193	216	214	2.9	2.9	3.2	3.4	3.3
Costa Rica											
Total	C	20 553	21 039	22 603	23 251	*23 786	4.3	4.4	4.6	4.7	*4.8
Urban - Urbaine	C	14 481[13]	17 103	17 988	17 879	*18 031	4.2	4.9	5.1	5.0	*5.0
Rural - Rurale	C	6 072[13]	3 936	4 615	5 372	*5 755	4.7	3.2	3.0	4.0	*4.2
Cuba											
Total	C	96 330	99 691	99 388	106 949	*106 201	8.6	8.9	8.8	9.5	*9.5
Urban - Urbaine	C	81 866	84 365	84 574	89 855	...	9.5	9.8	9.8	10.4	...
Rural - Rurale	C	14 464	15 326	14 814	17 094	...	5.6	5.9	5.7	6.6	...
Curaçao											
Total	C	1 370	1 398	1 482	1 420	1 399	8.8	8.8	9.3	8.9	8.8
Dominica - Dominique											
Total	+C	590	...	...	...	...	8.2	...	...	...	...
Dominican Republic - République dominicaine											
Total	U	40 697	41 234	43 382	41 152	...	...	...	...	...	...
Urban - Urbaine[14]	U	32 686	33 222	35 000	...	...	...	...	...	...	...
Rural - Rurale[14]	U	7 364	7 107	6 953	...	...	...	...	...	...	...
El Salvador											
Total	C	37 461	...	...	...	...	5.9	...	...	...	...
Urban - Urbaine	C	24 617	...	...	...	...	...	...	...	...	...
Rural - Rurale	C	12 844	...	...	...	...	...	...	...	...	...
Greenland - Groenland											
Total	C	461	472	487	499	487	8.2	8.4	8.7	8.9	8.7
Urban - Urbaine	C	388	407	408	428	421	8.0	8.4	8.4	8.8	8.7
Rural - Rurale	C	73	65	79	71	66	9.1	8.3	10.2	9.3	8.9
Grenada - Grenade											
Total	+C	958	869	898	885	...	8.8	7.9	8.1	7.9	...
Guadeloupe[15]											
Total	C	3 451	3 052	3 383	3 273	...	8.6	7.7	8.6	8.3	...
Guatemala											
Total	C	77 807	80 876	82 565	81 726	...	4.9	5.0	5.0	4.8	...
Jamaica - Jamaïque											
Total	U	18 320	19 249	19 761	18 879	18 859	...	...	...	...	...
Martinique[15]											
Total	C	3 319	3 058	3 284	3 217	...	8.7	8.1	8.7	8.7	...
Urban - Urbaine	C	...	...	...	2 631	...	...	...	...	...	...
Rural - Rurale	C	...	...	...	586	...	...	...	...	...	...
Mexico - Mexique[16]											
Total	+C	632 587	654 593	684 437	693 848	...	5.3	5.4	5.6	5.6	...
Urban - Urbaine[14]	+C	482 499	496 737	520 912	535 703	...	5.6	5.7	5.9	6.0	...
Rural - Rurale[14]	+C	140 144	147 354	153 699	152 136	...	4.3	4.4	4.6	4.5	...
Montserrat											
Total	C	32	49	43	...	...	6.4	9.8	8.5	...	...
Nicaragua											
Total	+U	...	...	23 205	...	...	...	...	...	...	...
Urban - Urbaine	+U	...	...	15 198	...	...	...	...	...	...	...
Rural - Rurale	+U	...	...	8 007	...	...	...	...	...	...	...
Panama											
Total	C	18 171	18 182	*18 882	*19 482	*18 478	4.6	4.6	*4.7	*4.8	*4.4
Urban - Urbaine	C	12 379	12 265	*12 617	*12 974	...	4.7	4.5	*4.6	*4.6	...
Rural - Rurale	C	5 792	5 917	*6 265	*6 508	...	4.6	4.7	*5.0	*5.2	...

Continent, country or area, and urban/rural residence / Continent, pays ou zone et résidence, urbaine/rurale	Co-de[a]	Number - Nombre					Rate - Taux				
		2014	2015	2016	2017	2018	2014	2015	2016	2017	2018

AMERICA, NORTH - AMÉRIQUE DU NORD

Puerto Rico - Porto Rico											
Total	C	30 333	28 409	29 649	31 140	29 060	8.6	8.2	8.7	9.3	9.1
Urban - Urbaine	C	16 952[14]	14 824[14]	15 038[14]	16 236	15 393	...	...	...	...	...
Rural - Rurale	C	13 155[14]	13 099[14]	14 019[14]	14 904	13 667	...	...	...	...	...
Saint Kitts and Nevis - Saint-Kitts-et-Nevis											
Total	+C	411	...	...	...	...	...	...	...	...	...
Saint Lucia - Sainte-Lucie											
Total	+C	1 358	...	...	...	...	7.9	...	...	...	...
Saint Pierre and Miquelon - Saint-Pierre-et-Miquelon											
Total	C	50	...	...	65	...	...	...	...	...	...
Saint Vincent and the Grenadines - Saint-Vincent-et-les Grenadines											
Total	C	1 006	885	930	...	...	9.1	8.0	8.4	...	...
Saint-Barthélemy											
Total	C	53	...	...	40	...	5.5	...	...	...	...
Saint-Martin (French part) - Saint-Martin (partie française)											
Total	C	161	...	...	152	...	4.5	...	...	4.3	...
Sint Maarten (Dutch part) - Saint-Martin (partie néerlandaise)											
Total	+C	169	197	160	172	...	4.6	5.2	4.1	4.2	...
Trinidad and Tobago - Trinité-et-Tobago											
Total	C	*11 461	*11 240	...	...	...	*8.5	*8.3	...	...	...
Turks and Caicos Islands - Îles Turques et Caïques[17]											
Total	C	76	97	89	122	*103	2.2	2.6	2.3	3.1	*2.5
United States of America - États-Unis d'Amérique											
Total	C	2 626 418	2 712 630	...	...	...	8.2	8.5	...	...	...

AMERICA, SOUTH - AMÉRIQUE DU SUD

Argentina - Argentine											
Total	C	325 539	333 407	352 992	341 688	...	7.6	7.7	8.1	7.8	...
Brazil - Brésil[18]											
Total	+C	1 194 164	1 231 400	1 274 630	1 277 579	...	5.9	6.0	6.2	6.2	...
Chile - Chili											
Total	C	101 960	103 327	104 026	*106 344	...	5.7	5.7	5.7	*5.8	...
Urban - Urbaine	C	88 055	89 935	90 010	...	...	5.7	5.7	5.7	...	...
Rural - Rurale	C	13 905	13 392	14 016	...	...	6.2	5.9	6.1	...	...
Colombia - Colombie											
Total	U	210 051	219 472	223 078	227 624	...	...	...	...	...	...
Urban - Urbaine[14]	U	168 236	177 609	179 379	183 065	...	...	...	...	...	...
Rural - Rurale[14]	U	39 128	39 828	41 536	41 752	...	...	...	...	...	...
Ecuador - Équateur[19]											
Total	U	63 788	65 391	68 304	69 247	...	...	...	...	...	...
Urban - Urbaine	U	49 380	50 239	52 752	53 285	...	...	...	...	...	...
Rural - Rurale	U	14 408	15 152	15 552	15 962	...	...	...	...	...	...
French Guiana - Guyane française[15]											
Total	C	786	834	901	964	...	3.1	3.3	3.4	3.5	...
Guyana											
Total	+C	5 268	4 922	5 109	4 909	...	7.1	6.6	6.9	6.6	...
Paraguay											
Total	+U	22 625	24 885	27 243	26 404	29 139	...	...	...	...	...
Urban - Urbaine[20]	+U	15 940	...	...	...	...	...	...	...	...	...
Rural - Rurale[20]	+U	6 579	...	...	...	...	...	...	...	...	...
Peru - Pérou[21]											
Total	+U	96 460	96 240	97 241	*121 024	...	...	...	...	...	...

Continent, country or area, and urban/rural residence / Continent, pays ou zone et résidence, urbaine/rurale	Co-de[a]	Number - Nombre					Rate - Taux				
		2014	2015	2016	2017	2018	2014	2015	2016	2017	2018
AMERICA, SOUTH - AMÉRIQUE DU SUD											
Suriname											
Total	C	3 738	3 663	3 591	3 508	...	6.7	6.5	6.2	6.0	...
Urban - Urbaine	C	2 519	2 536	2 489	2 404	...	...	...	...	6.2	...
Rural - Rurale	C	1 219	1 127	1 102	1 104	...	...	...	...	5.6	...
Uruguay											
Total	C	32 122	32 967	34 273	33 173	...	9.3	9.5	9.8	9.5	...
Venezuela (Bolivarian Republic of) - Venezuela (République bolivarienne du)											
Total	C	159 239	163 712	188 725	190 236	...	5.3	5.4	6.1	6.1	...
ASIA - ASIE											
Armenia - Arménie[22]											
Total	C	27 714	27 878	28 226	27 157	...	9.2	9.3	9.4	9.1	...
Urban - Urbaine	C	...	17 743	18 257	17 418	...	...	9.3	9.6	9.2	...
Rural - Rurale	C	...	10 135	9 969	9 739	...	...	9.3	9.2	9.0	...
Azerbaijan - Azerbaïdjan[22]											
Total	+C	55 648	54 697	56 648	57 109	...	5.8	5.7	5.8	5.8	...
Urban - Urbaine	+C	29 988	29 628	31 385	31 222	...	5.9	5.8	6.1	6.0	...
Rural - Rurale	+C	25 660	25 069	25 263	25 887	...	5.7	5.5	5.5	5.6	...
Bahrain - Bahreïn[23]											
Total	C	2 805	2 787	2 858	2 902	...	2.1	2.0	2.0	1.9	...
Bangladesh											
Total	U	815 360	810 390	820 080	829 770	...	...	...	...	...	...
Urban - Urbaine	U	180 851	210 266	199 122	206 514	...	...	...	...	...	...
Rural - Rurale	U	634 509	600 124	620 958	623 256	...	...	...	...	...	...
Bhutan - Bhoutan[2]											
Total	I	...	...	...	4 894	...	...	...	...	6.7	...
Brunei Darussalam - Brunéi Darussalam											
Total	+C	1 470	1 547	1 632	1 696	...	3.6	3.8	3.9	3.9	...
China - Chine[24]											
Total	I	9 770 000	9 750 000	9 770 000	9 860 000	9 930 000	7.2	7.1	7.1	7.1	7.1
China, Hong Kong SAR - Chine, Hong Kong RAS											
Total	C	45 087	46 108	46 905	46 829	47 400	6.2	6.3	6.4	6.3	6.4
China, Macao SAR - Chine, Macao RAS											
Total	C	1 939	2 002	2 248	2 120	*2 069	3.1	3.1	3.5	3.2	*3.1
Cyprus - Chypre[25]											
Total	C	5 424	5 859	5 471	5 996	...	6.4	6.9	6.4	7.0	...
Georgia - Géorgie[22]											
Total	C	49 087	49 121	50 771	47 822	*46 524	13.2	13.2	13.7	12.8	*12.5
Urban - Urbaine	C	...	26 139	26 788	...	...	...	12.3	12.6	...	...
Rural - Rurale	C	...	22 982	23 983	...	...	...	14.4	15.1	...	...
India - Inde[26]											
Total	I	...	...	...	...	...	6.7	6.5	6.4	6.3	...
Urban - Urbaine	I	...	...	...	...	...	5.5	5.4	5.4	5.3	...
Rural - Rurale	I	...	...	...	...	...	7.3	7.1	6.9	6.9	...
Iran (Islamic Republic of) - Iran (République islamique d')[27]											
Total	+C	446 333	374 827	369 751	376 678	*376 839	5.7	4.8	4.6	4.6	*4.6
Urban - Urbaine	+C	302 184	280 765	274 870[14]	278 448	...	5.4	4.9	4.6	4.6	...
Rural - Rurale	+C	144 149	94 062	94 788[14]	98 230	...	6.7	4.4	4.6	4.7	...
Israel - Israël[28]											
Total	C	42 457	44 507	44 244	44 867	44 434	5.2	5.3	5.2	5.1	5.0
Urban - Urbaine[14]	C	39 912	41 775	41 560	42 160	41 791	5.3	5.5	5.3	5.3	...
Rural - Rurale[14]	C	2 533	2 723	2 677	2 705	2 641	3.6	3.7	3.6	3.5	...
Japan - Japon[29]											
Total	C	1 273 004[14]	1 290 444[14]	1 307 748[14]	1 340 397[14]	*1 362 482	10.0	10.1	10.3	10.6	*10.8
Urban - Urbaine[14]	C	1 130 587	1 147 467	1 162 734	1 194 280	...	...	...	...	...	...
Rural - Rurale[14]	C	141 084	141 799	143 801	144 963	...	...	...	...	...	...

Continent, country or area, and urban/rural residence / Continent, pays ou zone et résidence, urbaine/rurale	Code[a]	Number - Nombre					Rate - Taux				
		2014	2015	2016	2017	2018	2014	2015	2016	2017	2018
ASIA - ASIE											
Jordan - Jordanie[30]											
Total	U	25 782	26 640	27 608	27 516	...	...	...	...	...	...
Kazakhstan											
Total	U	132 287	130 811	131 231	129 009	130 448	...	...	...	...	...
Urban - Urbaine	U	77 803	77 319	78 001	76 522	79 172	...	...	...	...	...
Rural - Rurale	U	54 484	53 492	53 230	52 487	51 276	...	...	...	...	...
Kuwait - Koweït											
Total	C	6 031	6 481	6 338	6 679	...	1.6	1.6	1.6	1.7	...
Kyrgyzstan - Kirghizstan											
Total	C	35 564	34 808	33 475	33 166	32 989	6.1	5.8	5.5	5.4	5.2
Urban - Urbaine	C	12 802	12 294	11 664	11 647	...	6.5	6.1	5.7	5.6	...
Rural - Rurale	C	22 762	22 514	21 811	21 519	...	5.9	5.7	5.4	5.2	...
Lebanon - Liban											
Total	C	27 020	...	...	...	...	...	...	...	...	...
Malaysia - Malaisie											
Total	C	150 318	155 786	162 201	168 168	...	4.9	5.0	5.1	5.3	...
Urban - Urbaine	C	97 989	101 309	104 817	108 772	...	4.3	4.4	4.4	4.5	...
Rural - Rurale	C	52 329	54 477	57 384	59 396	...	6.5	6.8	7.2	7.5	...
Maldives[31]											
Total	C	1 143	1 130	1 226	1 241	...	3.3	3.3	3.5	3.5	...
Urban - Urbaine	C	546[32]	260[14]	263[14]	207[14]	...	...	1.9	1.9	1.4	...
Rural - Rurale	C	492[32]	744[14]	846[14]	1 015[14]	...	...	3.5	4.0	4.7	...
Mongolia - Mongolie											
Total	+C	16 521	17 620	17 763	17 357	17 864	5.6	5.8	5.8	5.5	5.6
Urban - Urbaine	+C	11 406	11 753	11 182	11 425	11 575	5.7	5.8	5.3	5.3	5.3
Rural - Rurale	+C	5 115	5 867	6 581	5 932	6 289	5.3	6.0	6.8	5.9	6.1
Myanmar[33]											
Total	+U	213 085	225 526	213 187	...	...	...	...	...	...	...
Urban - Urbaine	+U	96 697	102 923	88 606	...	...	...	...	...	...	...
Rural - Rurale	+U	116 388	122 603	124 581	...	...	...	...	...	...	...
Oman											
Total	U	7 819[34]	8 167[34]	8 196[34]	8 861	8 979	...	...	...	...	...
Philippines											
Total	C	551 716	560 605	582 183	*579 262	...	5.5	5.5	5.6	*5.5	...
Qatar											
Total	C	2 366	2 317	2 347	2 294	*2 320	1.1	1.0	0.9	0.8	*0.8
Urban - Urbaine	C	2 366	2 317	2 347	2 294	*2 320	1.1	1.0	0.9	0.8	*0.8
Republic of Korea - République de Corée[35]											
Total	C	267 692	275 895	280 827	285 534	...	5.3	5.4	5.5	5.6	...
Urban - Urbaine	C	184 631[14]	189 851[14]	193 664[14]	196 654	...	4.5	4.6	4.7	4.7	...
Rural - Rurale	C	83 055[14]	86 038[14]	87 162[14]	88 880	...	8.9	9.1	9.1	9.2	...
Saudi Arabia - Arabie saoudite[36]											
Total	I	...	69 206[37]	58 097[37]	58 915[38]	...	...	2.2	1.8	1.8	...
Singapore - Singapour											
Total	+C	19 393	19 862	20 017	20 905	...	5.0	5.1	5.1	5.3	...
Sri Lanka											
Total	+C	128 185	*131 614	*130 765	*139 822	*139 498	6.2	*6.3	*6.2	*6.5	*6.4
Urban - Urbaine	+C	55 211	...	...	...	...	...	...	...	...	...
Rural - Rurale[39]	+C	72 974	...	...	...	...	...	...	...	...	...
State of Palestine - État de Palestine[40]											
Total	U	13 390	12 075	12 202	11 778	...	...	...	...	...	...
Tajikistan - Tadjikistan[22]											
Total	U	32 879	33 563	34 134	32 027	...	...	...	...	...	...
Urban - Urbaine	U	9 830	9 959	9 944	9 516	...	...	...	...	...	...
Rural - Rurale	U	23 049	23 604	24 190	22 511	...	...	...	...	...	...
Thailand - Thaïlande											
Total	+U	435 624	445 964	469 085	458 010	...	...	...	...	...	...
Timor-Leste[41]											
Total	I	...	9 209	...	...	...	...	7.7	...	...	...
Turkey - Turquie[42]											
Total	C	391 091	405 365	422 726	425 781	*426 106	5.0	5.1	5.3	5.3	*5.2

Continent, country or area, and urban/rural residence / Continent, pays ou zone et résidence, urbaine/rurale	Code[a]	Number - Nombre					Rate - Taux				
		2014	2015	2016	2017	2018	2014	2015	2016	2017	2018
ASIA - ASIE											
United Arab Emirates - Émirats arabes unis											
Total[43]	...	8 265	8 755	8 988	...	...	...	...	...	...	...
Total	C	...	...	...	8 826	...	...	...	...	0.9	...
Uzbekistan - Ouzbékistan[22]											
Total	+C	149 761	152 035	154 791	160 723	*154 913	4.9	4.9	4.9	5.0	*4.7
Urban - Urbaine	+C	81 991	81 094	81 736	84 969	...	5.2	5.1	5.1	5.2	...
Rural - Rurale	+C	67 770	70 941	73 055	75 754	...	4.5	4.6	4.6	4.7	...
Yemen - Yémen[44]											
Total	U	32 140	...	25 927	31 999	...	...	...	...	...	...
EUROPE											
Åland Islands - Îles d'Åland											
Total	C	251	285	297	235	272	8.7	9.8	10.2	8.0	9.2
Urban - Urbaine	C	104	114	120	96	...	9.1	9.9	10.4	8.3	...
Rural - Rurale	C	147	171	177	139	...	8.5	9.8	10.1	7.8	...
Albania - Albanie											
Total	C	20 656	22 418	21 388	22 232	21 804	7.1	7.8	7.4	7.7	7.6
Andorra - Andorre											
Total	C	276	282	310	323	335	3.9	4.0	4.3	4.4	4.5
Austria - Autriche[45]											
Total	C	78 252	83 073	80 669	83 270	83 975	9.2	9.6	9.2	9.5	9.5
Belarus - Bélarus											
Total	C	121 542	120 026	119 379	119 311	...	12.8	12.6	12.6	12.6	...
Urban - Urbaine	C	74 236	73 563	73 599	73 972	...	10.2	10.0	10.0	10.0	...
Rural - Rurale	C	47 306	46 463	45 780	45 339	...	21.8	21.7	21.6	21.7	...
Belgium - Belgique[46]											
Total	C	104 755	110 541	108 097	109 666	110 645	9.3	9.8	9.5	9.6	9.7
Urban - Urbaine	C	103 223	108 942	...	...	...	...	...	...	...	...
Rural - Rurale	C	1 532	1 599	...	...	...	...	...	...	...	...
Bosnia and Herzegovina - Bosnie-Herzégovine											
Total	C	34 824	37 070	35 530	36 336	...	9.9	10.5	10.1	10.4	...
Bulgaria - Bulgarie											
Total	C	108 952	110 117	107 580	109 791	108 526	15.1	15.3	15.1	15.5	15.4
Urban - Urbaine	C	67 008	67 749	67 192	68 418	...	12.7	12.9	12.9	13.2	...
Rural - Rurale	C	41 944	42 368	40 388	41 373	...	21.6	21.9	21.1	22.0	...
Croatia - Croatie											
Total	C	50 839	54 205	51 542	53 477	*52 706	12.0	12.9	12.3	13.0	*12.8
Urban - Urbaine	C	26 230	28 365	27 000	28 311	...	...	...	...	...	...
Rural - Rurale	C	24 609	25 840	24 542	25 166	...	...	...	...	...	...
Czechia - Tchéquie											
Total	C	105 665	111 173	107 750	111 443	*112 920	10.0	10.5	10.2	10.5	*10.6
Urban - Urbaine	C	77 826	81 854	79 384	82 135	...	10.1	10.6	10.3	10.6	...
Rural - Rurale	C	27 839	29 319	28 366	29 308	...	9.8	10.3	10.0	10.3	...
Denmark - Danemark[47]											
Total	C	51 340	52 555	52 824	53 261	55 232	9.1	9.3	9.2	9.2	9.5
Estonia - Estonie											
Total	C	15 484	15 243	15 392	15 543	15 751	11.8	11.6	11.7	11.8	11.9
Urban - Urbaine	C	10 464	10 491[14]	10 539[14]	10 030[14]	...	11.7	11.7	11.7	11.0	...
Rural - Rurale	C	5 020	4 744[14]	4 836[14]	5 503[14]	...	12.0	11.4	11.7	13.6	...
Faeroe Islands - Îles Féroé											
Total	C	394	377	379	447	392	8.1	7.7	7.7	8.9	7.7
Urban - Urbaine	C	131	102	122	159	144	7.1	5.5	6.4	8.3	7.3
Rural - Rurale	C	263	275	257	288	248	8.7	9.1	8.4	9.3	7.9
Finland - Finlande[48]											
Total	C	51 935	52 207	53 626	53 487	54 255	9.6	9.6	9.8	9.8	9.8
Urban - Urbaine	C	32 260	32 941	33 949	33 748	...	8.6	8.6	8.7	8.6	...
Rural - Rurale	C	19 675	19 266	19 677	19 739	...	11.8	12.0	12.4	12.5	...
France											
Total	C	545 021	581 770	581 073	593 606	*595 500	8.5	9.0	9.0	9.2	*9.2
Urban - Urbaine	C	414 263	441 398[49]	441 334[49]	451 637[49]	...	...	...	...	...	...
Rural - Rurale	C	130 758	138 220[49]	137 674[49]	139 881[49]	...	...	...	...	...	...

Continent, country or area, and urban/rural residence / Continent, pays ou zone et résidence, urbaine/rurale	Code[a]	Number - Nombre					Rate - Taux				
		2014	2015	2016	2017	2018	2014	2015	2016	2017	2018
EUROPE											
Germany - Allemagne											
Total	C	868 356	925 200	910 902	932 272	954 874	10.7	11.3	11.1	11.3	11.5
Gibraltar[50]											
Total	+C	248	235	249	...	...	7.5	7.0	7.3	...	...
Greece - Grèce											
Total	C	113 740	121 183	118 785	124 501	120 297	10.4	11.2	11.0	11.6	11.2
Urban - Urbaine	C	63 724	67 843	67 121	...	...	...	...	...	...	...
Rural - Rurale	C	50 016	53 340	51 664	...	...	...	...	...	...	...
Guernsey - Guernesey											
Total	C	526	557	536	586	575	8.4	9.0	8.6	9.4	9.2
Hungary - Hongrie[51]											
Total	C	126 294	131 575	127 098	131 877	131 045	12.8	13.4	13.0	13.5	13.4
Urban - Urbaine[52]	C	85 796	89 692	86 815	89 822	...	12.3	12.9	12.6	13.0	...
Rural - Rurale[52]	C	40 331	41 717	40 130	41 911	...	13.8	14.4	13.8	14.5	...
Iceland - Islande											
Total	C	2 049	2 178	2 309	2 238	2 254	6.3	6.6	6.9	6.5	6.5
Urban - Urbaine	C	1 936	2 009	2 038	2 070	...	6.3	6.5	6.5	6.4	...
Rural - Rurale	C	113	169	183	168	...	5.4	8.1	8.6	7.6	...
Ireland - Irlande											
Total	+C	29 188	30 064	30 390	30 317	*31 116	6.3	6.4	6.4	6.3	*6.4
Isle of Man - Île de Man											
Total	+C	787	...	852	837	903	9.1	...	10.0	10.0	...
Italy - Italie											
Total	C	598 364	647 571	615 261	649 061	...	9.8	10.7	10.1	10.7	...
Jersey											
Total	+C	704	762	831	803	...	7.0	7.4	8.0	7.6	...
Latvia - Lettonie											
Total	C	28 466	28 478	28 580	28 757	28 820	14.3	14.4	14.6	14.8	14.9
Urban - Urbaine	C	18 847	18 884	18 877	19 134	...	13.9	14.0	14.1	...	...
Rural - Rurale	C	9 619	9 594	9 701	9 623	...	15.0	15.2	15.6	...	...
Liechtenstein											
Total	C	268	252	271	249	...	7.2	6.7	7.2	6.6	...
Lithuania - Lituanie											
Total	C	40 252	41 776	41 106	40 142	39 574	13.7	14.4	14.3	14.2	14.2
Urban - Urbaine	C	24 823	25 850	25 817	24 941	...	12.6	13.2	13.4	13.1	...
Rural - Rurale	C	15 429	15 926	15 289	15 201	...	16.0	16.7	16.2	16.3	...
Luxembourg											
Total	C	3 841	3 983	3 967	4 263	4 318	6.9	7.0	6.8	7.1	7.2
Malta - Malte											
Total	C	3 270	3 442	3 342	3 571	3 688	7.5	7.7	7.3	7.6	7.8
Monaco[53]											
Total	C	524	595	503[54]	490	528	14.2	15.8	13.2	13.0	13.8
Montenegro - Monténégro											
Total	C	6 014	6 329	6 464	6 523	6 504	9.7	10.2	10.4	10.5	10.5
Netherlands - Pays-Bas[55]											
Total	C	139 223	147 134	148 997	150 214	153 363	8.3	8.7	8.7	8.8	8.9
North Macedonia - Macédoine du Nord											
Total	C	19 718	20 461	20 417	20 318	19 727	9.5	9.9	9.9	9.8	9.5
Urban - Urbaine	C	11 944	12 462	12 438	12 426	...	...	...	...	...	...
Rural - Rurale	C	7 774	7 999	7 983	7 892	...	...	...	...	...	...
Norway - Norvège[56]											
Total	C	40 369	40 676	40 726	40 774	40 840	7.9	7.8	7.8	7.7	7.7
Poland - Pologne											
Total	C	376 467	394 921	388 009	402 852	414 200	9.9	10.4	10.2	10.6	10.9
Urban - Urbaine	C	229 697	242 067	236 749	247 346	255 280	10.0	10.6	10.4	10.8	...
Rural - Rurale	C	146 770	152 854	151 260	155 506	158 920	9.7	10.1	10.0	10.3	...
Portugal[57]											
Total	C	104 843	108 539	110 573	109 758	113 000	10.1	10.5	10.7	10.7	11.0
Republic of Moldova - République de Moldova[58]											
Total	C	39 494	39 906	38 489	36 768	37 200	13.8	14.1	13.7	13.3	13.7
Urban - Urbaine	C	...	...	12 766	12 473	12 866	...	...	...	...	...
Rural - Rurale	C	...	...	25 723	24 295	24 334	...	...	...	...	...

Continent, country or area, and urban/rural residence / Continent, pays ou zone et résidence, urbaine/rurale	Co-de[a]	Number - Nombre					Rate - Taux				
		2014	2015	2016	2017	2018	2014	2015	2016	2017	2018
EUROPE											
Romania - Roumanie											
Total	C	254 965	261 294	257 215	261 402	*262 987	12.8	13.2	13.1	13.3	*13.5
Urban - Urbaine	C	118 040	121 616	...	123 079	...	11.0	11.4	...	11.7	...
Rural - Rurale	C	136 925	139 678	...	138 323	...	14.9	15.3	...	15.2	...
San Marino - Saint-Marin											
Total	C	252	235	253	278	244	7.5	6.9	7.4	8.1	7.1
Serbia - Serbie[59]											
Total	+C	101 247	103 678	100 834	103 722	*103 091	14.2	14.6	14.3	14.8	*14.7
Urban - Urbaine	+C	53 932	56 161	54 902	56 387	...	12.6	13.2	12.9	13.2	...
Rural - Rurale	+C	47 315	47 517	45 932	47 335	...	16.5	16.8	16.4	17.1	...
Slovakia - Slovaquie											
Total	C	51 346	53 826	52 351	53 914	54 293	9.5	9.9	9.6	9.9	10.0
Urban - Urbaine	C	26 198	27 254	27 070	27 666	...	9.0	9.3	9.3	9.5	...
Rural - Rurale	C	25 148	26 572	25 281	26 248	...	10.1	10.6	10.1	10.4	...
Slovenia - Slovénie											
Total	C	18 886	19 834	19 689	20 509	20 485	9.2	9.6	9.5	9.9	9.9
Urban - Urbaine	C	9 103	10 098	9 890	10 753	...	8.7	9.1	8.9	9.4	...
Rural - Rurale	C	9 783	9 736	9 799	9 756	...	9.7	10.2	10.2	10.6	...
Spain - Espagne											
Total	C	393 734	420 408	408 231	422 037	*423 636	8.5	9.1	8.8	9.1	*9.1
Sweden - Suède											
Total		88 976	90 907	90 982	91 972	*92 185	9.2	9.3	9.2	9.1	*9.1
Switzerland - Suisse											
Total	C	63 938	67 606	64 964	66 971	67 088	7.8	8.2	7.8	7.9	7.9
Urban - Urbaine	C	47 089[60]	56 647	54 293	56 155	...	7.8	8.1	7.7	...	...
Rural - Rurale	C	16 849[60]	10 959	10 671	10 816	...	7.8	8.5	8.2	...	...
Ukraine[61]											
Total	+C	632 296	594 796	583 631	574 123	*587 665	14.7	13.9	13.7	13.5	*13.9
Urban - Urbaine	+C	391 739	358 749	354 634	350 549	...	...	12.1	12.0	11.9	...
Rural - Rurale	+C	240 557	236 047	228 997	223 574	...	...	17.9	17.4	17.1	...
United Kingdom of Great Britain and Northern Ireland - Royaume-Uni de Grande-Bretagne et d'Irlande du Nord[62]											
Total	+C	568 840	601 272	595 655	605 748	...	8.8	9.2	9.1	9.2	...
OCEANIA - OCÉANIE											
American Samoa - Samoas américaines											
Total	C	259	314	280	310	...	4.2	5.2	4.7	5.1	...
Australia - Australie											
Total	C	153 580	159 052	158 504	160 909	158 493	6.5	6.7	6.6	6.5	6.3
Urban - Urbaine[63]	C	91 129	94 156	93 337	95 223	...	4.5	4.6	4.5	4.5	...
Rural - Rurale[63]	C	61 892	64 388	64 638	65 170	...	19.1	19.8	19.8	19.8	...
Cook Islands - Îles Cook[64]											
Total	+C	113	*102	...	...	...	6.1	*5.5	...	...	...
Fiji - Fidji											
Total	+C	5 801	...	...	...	...	6.7	...	...	...	...
French Polynesia - Polynésie française											
Total	C	1 441	1 405	1 390	1 581	...	5.3	5.1	5.1	5.7	...
Guam[65]											
Total	C	952	1 009	1 022	1 008	1 056	5.9	6.2	6.3	6.2	6.3
Nauru											
Total	C	...	90	100	94	...	...	8.0	9.1	...	...
New Caledonia - Nouvelle-Calédonie											
Total	C	1 406	1 465	1 569	1 529	...	5.2	5.4	5.7	5.5	...
New Zealand - Nouvelle-Zélande[66]											
Total	+C	31 065	31 608	31 179[67]	33 339[67]	33 222[67]	6.9	6.9	6.6	7.0	6.8
Urban - Urbaine[14]	+C	27 930	28 455	27 912[67]	29 913[67]	...	7.2	7.2	6.9	7.2	...
Rural - Rurale[14]	+C	3 099	3 132	3 246[67]	3 411[67]	...	5.0	4.9	5.1	5.3	...

Continent, country or area, and urban/rural residence / Continent, pays ou zone et résidence, urbaine/rurale	Code[a]	Number - Nombre					Rate - Taux				
		2014	2015	2016	2017	2018	2014	2015	2016	2017	2018
OCEANIA - OCÉANIE											
Niue - Nioué											
Total	C	5	16	7							
Norfolk Island - Île Norfolk[68]											
Total	+C	13	11	...							
Northern Mariana Islands - Îles Mariannes septentrionales[69]											
Total	U	220	...	...							
Palau - Palaos											
Total	C	167	136	175	183	143	9.5	7.7	9.9	10.3	7.8
Samoa[70]											
Total	+U	882	*1 112*	*2 020*	*1 037*	*1 114*	...	...	...	...	...
Tuvalu											
Total	+U	85	66	90			...	...	...	...	...
Vanuatu											
Total	+U	614	...	...			...	...	...	...	...

FOOTNOTES - NOTES

Italics: data from civil registers which are incomplete or of unknown completeness. - Italiques : données incomplètes ou dont le degré d'exactitude n'est pas connu, provenant des registres de l'état civil.

* Provisional. - Données provisoires.

a 'Code' indicates the source of data, as follows:
C - Civil registration, estimated over 90% complete
U - Civil registration, estimated less than 90% complete
| - Other source, estimated reliable
+ - Data tabulated by date of registration rather than occurence
... - Information not available

Le 'Code' indique la source des données, comme suit :
C - Registres de l'état civil considérés complets à 90 p. 100 au moins
U - Registres de l'état civil qui ne sont pas considérés complets à 90 p. 100 au moins
| - Autre source, considérée pas douteuses
+ - Données exploitées selon la date de l'enregistrement et non la date de l'événement
... - Information pas disponible

[1] Excluding live-born infants who died before their birth was registered. Data refer to Algerian population only. - Non compris les enfants nés vivants décédés avant l'enregistrement de leur naissance. Les données ne concernent que la population algérienne.
[2] Data refer to the 12 months preceding the census in May. - Les données se rapportent aux 12 mois précédant le recensement de mai.
[3] Source: Vital Statistics Report. - Source: Vital Statistics Report.
[4] The rate of registration of deaths is less than 20 per cent at the national level. - Le taux d'enregistrement des décès est inférieur à 20 p. 100 au niveau national.
[5] Adjusted number of deaths in households referring to the 12 months preceding the census in March. - Le nombre ajusté de décès des ménages ordinaires se rapportent aux 12 mois précédant le recensement de mars.
[6] Data refer to the 12 months preceding the census in September. - Les données se rapportent aux 12 mois précédant le recensement de septembre.
[7] Excludes the islands of St. Brandon and Agalega. - Non compris les îles St. Brandon et Agalega.
[8] Excluding visitors. - Ne comprend pas les visiteurs.
[9] Unrevised data. - Les données n'ont pas été révisées.
[10] Excluding non-residents and foreign service personnel and their dependants. Bermuda is 100 per cent urban. - À l'exclusion des non-résidents et du personnel diplomatique et de leurs charges de famille. 100 pour cent de la population des Bermudes est urbaine.
[11] Including Canadian residents temporarily in the United States, but excluding United States residents temporarily in Canada. - Y compris les résidents

canadiens se trouvant temporairement aux Etats-Unis, mais ne comprenant pas les résidents des Etats-Unis se trouvant temporairement au Canada.
[12] Including resident deaths outside of the islands but buried in the islands. - Y compris les décès de résidents hors des îles mais inhumés dans les îles.
[13] Definition of urban and rural distribution changed from the year 2014. - La définition de la répartition urbaine et rurale a changé depuis 2014.
[14] The total number may include 'Unknown residence', but the categories urban and rural do not. - Le nombre total peut inclure les personnes dont la résidence n'est pas connue, à l'inverse des catégories de population urbaine et rurale.
[15] Excluding live-born infants who died before their birth was registered. - Non compris les enfants nés vivants décédés avant l'enregistrement de leur naissance.
[16] Data refer to resident population only. - Pour la population résidante seulement.
[17] Excluding deaths of persons living abroad. - Exception faite des personnes décédées à l'étranger.
[18] Including deaths abroad and deaths of unknown place of residence. - Y compris décès à l'étranger et décès dont le lieu de résidence n'est pas connu.
[19] Excludes nomadic Indian tribes. - Non compris les tribus d'Indiens nomades.
[20] Data for urban and rural exclude deaths of unknown residence. - Les données pur la résidence urbaine et rurale non comprent pas les décès dont on ignore la résidence.
[21] Source: Reports of the Ministry of Health. - Source : Rapports du Ministère de la Santé.
[22] Excluding infants born alive of less than 28 weeks' gestation, of less than 1 000 g in weight and 35 cm in length, who die within seven days of birth. - Non compris les enfants nés vivants après moins de 28 semaines de gestations, pesant moins de 1 000 g, mesurant moins de 35 cm et décédés dans les sept jours qui ont suivi leur naissance.
[23] Sources: Births and Deaths National Registration System database, and medical records of government hospitals. - Les sources: Les bases de données des << Births and Deaths National Registration System >> et les dossiers médicaux des hôpitaux du gouvernement.
[24] For statistical purposes, the data for China do not include those for the Hong Kong Special Administrative Region (Hong Kong SAR), Macao Special Administrative Region (Macao SAR) and Taiwan province of China. Data have been estimated on the basis of the annual National Sample Survey on Population Changes. - Pour la présentation des statistiques, les données pour la Chine ne comprennent pas la Région Administrative Spéciale de Hong Kong (Hong Kong RAS), la Région Administrative Spéciale de Macao (Macao RAS) et Taïwan province de Chine. Les données ont été estimées sur la base de l'enquête annuelle "National Sample Survey on Population Changes".
[25] Data refer to government controlled areas. Data refer to deaths of residents only. - Les données se rapportent aux zones contrôlées par le Gouvernement. Les données renvoient aux décès de résidents uniquement.
[26] Rates were obtained by the Sample Registration System of India, which is a large demographic survey. Includes data for the Indian-held part of Jammu and Kashmir, the final status of which has not yet been determined. - Les taux ont été obtenus par le Système de l'enregistrement par échantillon de l'Inde qui est une

large enquête démographique. Y compris les données pour la partie du Jammu et du Cachemire occupée par l'Inde dont le statut définitif n'a pas encore été déterminé.

[27] Data refer to the Iranian Year which begins on 21 March and ends on 20 March of the following year. - Les données concernent l'année iranienne, qui commence le 21 mars et se termine le 20 mars de l'année suivante.

[28] Including deaths abroad of Israeli residents who were out of the country for less than a year. Includes data for East Jerusalem and Israeli residents in certain other territories under occupation by Israeli military forces since June 1967. - Y compris les décès à l'étranger de résidents israéliens qui ont quitté le pays depuis moins d'un an. Y compris les données pour Jérusalem-Est et les résidents israéliens dans certains autres territoires occupés depuis 1967 par les forces armées israéliennes.

[29] Data refer to Japanese nationals in Japan only. - Les données se raportent aux nationaux japonais au Japon seulement.

[30] Excluding data for Jordanian territory under occupation since June 1967 by Israeli military forces. Excluding foreigners, including registered Palestinian refugees. - Non compris les données pour le territoire jordanien occupé depuis juin 1967 par les forces armées israéliennes. Non compris les étrangers, mais y compris les réfugiés de Palestine enregistrés.

[31] Data do not include foreigners. - Les données sur les etrangers ne sont pas inclus.

[32] Excluding deaths occurred abroad. Data by the place of occurrence of death, not by the residence of deceased. - Hormis les décès à l'étranger. Données classées selon le lieu du décès, et non selon le lieu de résidence de la personne décédée.

[33] Data are from Vital Registration System (VRS). - Les données proviennent du système d'enregistrement des faits d'état civil.

[34] Data from Births and Deaths Notification System (Ministry of Health and all health care providers). - Les données proviennent du système de notification des naissances et des décès (Ministère de la santé et tous prestataires de soins de santé).

[35] Excluding alien armed forces, civilian aliens employed by armed forces, and foreign diplomatic personnel and their dependants. - Non compris les militaires étrangers, les civils étrangers employés par les forces armées ni le personnel diplomatique étranger et les membres de leur famille les accompagnant.

[36] Data refer to Saudi Arabian nationals only. - Les données ne concernent que les ressortissants saoudiens.

[37] Based on 2010 population census and 2016 demographic survey. - D'après le recensement de la population de 2010 et l'enquête démographique de 2016.

[38] Survey based estimates. - Estimations basées sur des enquêtes.

[39] Data for rural areas include data of estate sectors consisting of all plantations which are 20 acres or more in extent and with ten or more resident labourers. - Les données pour les zones rurales comprennent celles pour les domaines, dont l'ensemble des plantations de plus de 10 hectares comptant au moins 10 travailleurs résidents.

[40] Source: Palestinian Central Bureau of Statistics, Population Register, updated version 2018. Data exclude Jerusalem ID holders. - Source: Bureau central de statistique palestinien, registre de la population, version actualisée jusqu'au 2018. Les données ne tiennent pas compte des détenteurs de carte d'identité de Jérusalem.

[41] Data refer to the 12 months preceding the census in July. - Les données se rapportent aux 12 mois précédant le recensement de juillet.

[42] Data from MERNIS (Central Population Administrative System). - Données de MERNIS (Système central de données démographiques).

[43] The registration of births and deaths is conducted by the Ministry of Health. An estimate of completeness is not provided. - L'enregistrement des naissances et des décès est mené par le Ministère de la Santé. Le degré estimatif de complétude n'est pas fourni.

[44] Including Non-Yemeni deaths. - Y compris les décès non-yéménites.

[45] Including deaths of nationals abroad. - Y compris les décès des nationaux survenus à l'étranger.

[46] Including armed forces stationed outside the country, but excluding alien armed forces stationed in the area. - Y compris les militaires nationaux hors du pays, mais non compris les militaires étrangers en garnison sur le territoire.

[47] Excluding Faeroe Islands and Greenland shown separately, if available. - Non compris les Iles Féroé et le Groenland, qui font l'objet de rubriques distinctes, si disponible.

[48] Excluding Åland Islands. - Non compris les Îles d'Åland.

[49] Data for urban and rural exclude events corresponding to nationals residing outside the country, which may be included in the total. - Les données relatives à les categories urbaine et rurale n'englobent pas les faits d'état civil qui concernent les nationaux se trouvant à l'étranger, lesquels faits peuvent être inclus au total.

[50] Excluding armed forces. - Non compris les militaires en garnison.

[51] Data include the deceased persons with Hungarian usual residence regardless of whether the death occurred in Hungary or in a foreign country, and do not include the deceased persons with foreign country usual residence. - Les

données comprennent tous les décès survenus alors que leur résidence habituelle était en Hongrie, que le décès ait eu lieu en Hongrie ou dans un pays étranger, et ne comprennent pas les décès des personnes dont la residence habituelle était dans un pays étranger.

[52] The urban and rural categories do not include the data of foreigners, persons of unknown residence and the homeless, whereas the total category includes them. - Les chiffres portant sur la population urbaine et rurale n' incluent pas les données relatives aux étrangers, aux personnes dont la résidence n'est pas connue et aux personnes sans domicile fixe, à l'inverse, le total les inclut.

[53] Source: City Hall, Civil Status Registry Office, resident and non-resident deaths. - Source : La mairie, Bureau de l'État Civil, toutes les décès.

[54] Including still births. - Les données comprennent les mortinaissances.

[55] Including residents outside the country if listed in a Netherlands population register. - Englobe les résidents se trouvant à l'étranger à condition qu'ils soient inscrits sur le registre de population des Pays-Bas.

[56] Including residents temporarily outside the country. - Y compris les résidents se trouvant temporairement hors du pays.

[57] Data refer to usually resident population. - Les données concernent la population habituellement résidente.

[58] Excluding Transnistria and the municipality of Bender. - Les données ne tiennent pas compte de l'information sur la Transnistria et la municipalité de Bender.

[59] Excludes data for Kosovo and Metohia. - Sans les données pour le Kosovo et Metohie.

[60] From 2014, urban refers to urban centers and areas under the influence of urban centers. - A partir de 2014, le territoire urbain inclut l'espace des centres urbains ainsi que l'espace sous influence des centres urbains.

[61] The Government of Ukraine has informed the United Nations that it is not in a position to provide statistical data concerning the Autonomous Republic of Crimea and the city of Sevastopol. Data includes deaths resulting from births with weight 500 g and more (if weight is unknown - with length 25 cm and more, or with gestation during 22 weeks or more). - Le gouvernement Ukrainien a informé l'ONU qu'il n'est pas en mesure de fournir des données statistiques concernant la République autonome de Crimée et la ville de Sébastopol. Y compris les décès de nouveau-nés de 500 g ou plus (si le poids est inconnu – de 25 cm de long ou plus, ou après une grossesse de 22 semaines ou plus).

[62] Excluding Channel Islands (Guernsey and Jersey) and Isle of Man, shown separately, if available. - Non compris les îles Anglo-Normandes (Guernesey et Jersey) et l'île de Man, qui font l'objet de rubriques distinctes, si disponible.

[63] Urban refers to Greater Capital City Statistical Areas, and rural refers to other areas within the state or territory. Data for urban and rural figures do not add up to the total because they exclude the events occurred in Migratory, Special Purpose and Other Territories. - Urbain renvoie aux zones statistiques de la capitale métropolitaine, et rural aux autres zones de l'État ou territoire. La somme des chiffres des catégories « en zone urbaine » et « en zone rurale » ne correspond pas au total du fait qu'en sont exclus les événements qui ont eu lieu dans les territoires de migration, les territoires à destination spéciale et autres territoires.

[64] Excluding Niue, shown separately, which is part of Cook Islands, but because of remoteness is administered separately. - Non compris Nioué, qui fait l'objet d'une rubrique distincte et qui fait partie des îles Cook, mais qui, en raison de son éloignement, est administrée séparément.

[65] Including United States military personnel, their dependants and contract employees. - Y compris les militaires des Etats-Unis, les membres de leur famille les accompagnant et les agents contractuels des Etats-Unis.

[66] Random rounding to base 3 is applied in this table as a confidentiality measure. - Les chiffres sont arrondis à la base 3 de manière aléatoire, pour des raisons de confidentialité.

[67] Data refer to deaths of residents only. - Les données renvoient aux décès de résidents uniquement.

[68] Data cover the period from 1 July of the previous year to 30 June of the present year. - Pour la période allant du 1er juillet de l'année précédente au 30 juin de l'année en cours.

[69] Source: Commonwealth Health Center - Vital Statistics Office - Source : Centre de Santé du Commonwealth - Bureau des statistiques d'État civil

[70] Source: Births, Deaths, and Marriages Registration Division, Samoa Bureau of Statistics. - Source : Division de l'enregistrement des naissances, des décès et des mariages du Bureau de statistique du Samoa.

Table 19 - *Demographic Yearbook 2018*

Table 19 presents deaths by age and sex and age-specific death rates by sex for the latest available year between 2009 and 2018.

Description of variables: Age is defined as age at last birthday, that is, the difference between the date of birth and the date of the occurrence of the event, expressed in completed solar years. The age classification used in this table is the following: under 1 year, 1-4 years, 5-year age groups through 95-99 years, and 100 years or over.

Rate computation: Age-specific death rates by sex are the annual number of deaths in each age-sex group per 1 000 population in the same age-sex group. These rates are calculated by the United Nations Statistics Division.

Deaths at unknown age and the population of unknown age are excluded from age-specific rate calculations but are part of the death rate for all ages combined.

Death rates for infants under one year of age in this table differ from the infant mortality rates shown elsewhere, because the latter are computed per 1 000 live births rather than per 1 000 population.

The population used in computing the rates is the estimated or the enumerated population by age and sex reported to United Nations Statistics Division. First priority is given to an estimate and second priority to census returns of the year to which the deaths refer.

Rates presented in this table have been limited to those countries or areas having at least a total of 100 deaths in a given year. Moreover, rates specific for individual sub-categories that are based on 30 or fewer deaths are identified by the symbol "♦".

Reliability of data: Data from civil registers of deaths that are reported as incomplete (less than 90 per cent completeness) or of unknown completeness are considered unreliable and are set in italics rather than in roman type. Table 18 and the technical notes for that table provide more detailed information on the completeness of death registration. For more information about the quality of vital statistics data in general and the information available on the basis of the completeness estimates in particular, see section 4.2 of the Introduction.

Rates are not computed if data from civil registers of deaths are reported as incomplete (less than 90 per cent completeness) or of unknown completeness, and therefore deemed unreliable.

Limitations: Statistics on deaths by age and sex are subject to the same qualifications as are set forth for vital statistics and particularly for death statistics discussed in section 4 of the Introduction.

The reliability of the data is an important factor in considering the limitations. In addition, some deaths are tabulated by date of registration and not by date of occurrence; these have been indicated by a plus sign "+". Whenever the lag between the date of occurrence and date of registration is prolonged and, therefore, a large proportion of the death registrations are delayed, death statistics for any given year may be seriously affected. However, delays in the registration of deaths are less common and shorter than in the registration of live births.

International comparability in mortality statistics may also be affected by the exclusion of deaths of infants who were born alive but died before the registration of the birth or within the first 24 hours of life. Statistics of this type are footnoted.

Because these statistics are classified according to age, they are subject to the limitations with respect to accuracy of age reporting similar to those already discussed in connection with section 3.1.3 of the Introduction. The factors influencing the accuracy of reporting may be somewhat dissimilar in vital statistics (because of the differences in the method of taking a census and registering a death) but, in general, the same errors can be observed.

The absence of data in the unknown age group does not necessarily indicate completely accurate reporting and tabulation of the age item. It is often an indication that the unknowns have been eliminated by assigning ages to them before tabulation, or by proportionate distribution after tabulation.

International comparability of statistics on deaths by age is also affected by the use of different methods to determine age at death. If age is obtained from an item that simply requests age at death in completed years or is derived from information on year of birth and death rather than from information on complete date (day, month and year) of birth and death, the number of deaths classified in the under-one-year age group will tend to be reduced and the number of deaths in the next age group will tend to be somewhat increased. A similar bias may affect other age groups but its impact is usually negligible. Information on this factor is given in the footnotes when known.

Limitations of rates: Rates shown in this table are subject to the same limitations that affect the corresponding data and are set forth in the technical notes for table 18. These include differences in the completeness of registration, the treatment of infants who were born alive but died before the registration of their birth or within the first 24 hours of life, the method used to determine age at death and the quality of the reported information relating to age at death. In addition, some rates are based on deaths tabulated by date of registration and not by date of occurrence; these have been indicated with a plus sign "+".

The problem of obtaining precise correspondence between deaths (numerator) and population (denominator) as regards the inclusion or exclusion of armed forces, refugees, displaced persons and other special groups is particularly difficult where age-specific death rates are concerned. Even when deaths and population do correspond conceptually, comparability of the rates may be affected by abnormal conditions such as absence from the country or area of large numbers of young men in the military forces or working abroad as temporary workers. Death rates may appear high in the younger ages, simply because a large section of the able-bodied members of the age group, whose death rates under normal conditions might be less than the average for persons of their age, is not included. Therefore, care should be exercised in using these rates for comparative purposes.

Also, in a number of cases the rates shown here for all ages combined differ from crude death rates shown elsewhere, because in this table they are computed on the population for which an appropriate age-sex distribution was available, while the crude death rates shown elsewhere may utilize a different total population. The population by age and sex might refer to a census date within the year rather than to the mid-point, or it might be more or less inclusive as regards ethnic groups, armed forces and so forth. In a few instances, the difference is attributable to the fact that the rates in this table were computed on the mean population whereas the corresponding rates in other tables were computed on an estimate for 1 July.

Earlier data: Age-specific deaths and death rates by sex have been shown for the latest available year in each issue of the *Demographic Yearbook* since the 1955 issue. For information on specific years covered, the reader should consult the Historical Index.

Tableau 19 – *Annuaire démographique 2018*

Le tableau 19 présente les données disponibles les plus récentes, entre 2009 et 2018, sur les décès et les taux de mortalité selon l'âge et le sexe.

Description des variables : L'âge considéré est l'âge au dernier anniversaire, c'est-à-dire la différence entre la date de naissance et la date du décès, exprimée en années solaires révolues. La classification par âge est la suivante : moins d'un an, 1 à 4 ans, groupes quinquennaux jusqu'à 95-99 ans et 100 ans et plus.

Calcul des taux : les taux de mortalité selon l'âge et le sexe représentent le nombre annuel de décès survenus pour chaque sexe et chaque groupe d'âge pour 1 000 personnes du même groupe. Ces taux ont été calculés par la Division de statistique de l'ONU.

On n'a pas tenu compte des décès à un âge inconnu ni de la population d'âge inconnu, sauf dans les taux de mortalité pour tous les âges combinés.

Il convient de noter que, dans ce tableau, les taux de mortalité des groupes de moins d'un an sont différents des taux de mortalité infantile qui figurent dans d'autres tableaux, ces derniers ayant été établis pour 1 000 naissances vivantes et non pour 1 000 habitants.

Les chiffres de population utilisés pour le calcul des taux proviennent de dénombrements ou de répartitions estimatives de la population selon l'âge et le sexe. On a utilisé de préférence les estimations de la population; à défaut, on s'est contenté des données censitaires se rapportant à l'année des décès.

Les taux présentés dans ce tableau ne se rapportent qu'aux pays ou zones où l'on a enregistré un total d'au moins 100 décès pendant l'année. Les taux relatifs à des sous-catégories, qui sont fondés sur 30 décès ou moins, sont signalés par le signe "♦".

Fiabilité des données : Les données sur les décès issues des registres d'état civil qui sont déclarées incomplètes (degré d'exhaustivité inférieur à 90 p.100) ou dont le degré d'exhaustivité n'est pas connu sont jugées douteuses et apparaissent en italique et non en caractères romains. Le tableau 18 et les notes techniques s'y rapportant présentent des renseignements plus détaillés sur le degré d'exhaustivité de l'enregistrement des décès. Pour plus de précisions sur la qualité des statistiques de l'état civil en général et le degré de complétude en particulier, voir la section 4.2 de l'Introduction.

On a choisi de ne pas faire figurer dans le tableau 19 des taux calculés à partir de données sur les décès issues de registres d'état civil qui sont déclarées incomplètes (degré d'exhaustivité inférieur à 90 p. 100) ou dont le degré d'exhaustivité n'est pas connu.

Insuffisance des données : Les statistiques des décès selon l'âge et le sexe appellent les mêmes réserves que les statistiques de l'état civil en général et les statistiques relatives à la mortalité en particulier (voir la section 4 des Notes techniques).

La fiabilité des données est un facteur important. Il faut également tenir compte du fait que, dans certains cas, les données relatives aux décès sont classées par date d'enregistrement et non par date d'occurrence ; ces cas ont été signalés par le signe "+". Chaque fois que le décalage entre le décès et son enregistrement est grand et qu'une forte proportion des décès fait l'objet d'un enregistrement tardif, les statistiques des décès de l'année peuvent être considérablement faussées. En règle générale, toutefois, les décès sont enregistrés beaucoup plus rapidement que les naissances vivantes, et les retards prolongés sont rares.

Un autre facteur qui nuit à la comparabilité internationale est la pratique de certains pays ou zones qui consiste à ne pas inclure dans les statistiques des décès les enfants nés vivants mais décédés avant l'enregistrement de leur naissance ou dans les 24 heures qui ont suivi la naissance, pratique qui conduit à sous-évaluer le nombre de décès à moins d'un an. Quand pareil facteur a joué, cela a été signalé en note à la fin du tableau.

Étant donné que les statistiques relatives à la mortalité sont classées selon l'âge, elles appellent les mêmes réserves concernant l'exactitude des déclarations d'âge que celles qui ont été formulées à la section 3.1.3 des Notes techniques. Dans le cas des données d'état civil, les facteurs qui interviennent à cet égard sont parfois un peu différents, du fait que le recensement et l'enregistrement des décès se font par des méthodes différentes, mais, d'une manière générale, les erreurs observées sont les mêmes.

Si aucun nombre ne figure dans la rangée réservée aux âges inconnus, cela ne signifie pas nécessairement que les déclarations d'âge et le classement par âge sont tout à fait exacts. C'est souvent une indication que l'on a attribué un âge aux personnes d'âge inconnu avant l'exploitation des données ou qu'elles ont été réparties proportionnellement entre les différents groupes après cette opération.

Le manque d'uniformité des méthodes suivies pour obtenir l'âge au moment du décès nuit également à la comparabilité internationale des données. Si l'âge est connu, soit d'après la réponse à une simple question sur l'âge du décès en années révolues, soit d'après l'année de la naissance et l'année du décès, et non d'après des renseignements concernant la date exacte (jour, mois et année) de la naissance et du décès, le nombre de décès classés dans la catégorie « moins d'un an » sera entaché d'une erreur par défaut et le chiffre figurant dans la catégorie suivante d'une erreur par excès.

Les données pour les autres groupes d'âge pourront être entachées d'une distorsion analogue, mais les répercussions seront généralement négligeables. Les imperfections, lorsqu'elles étaient connues, ont été signalées en note à la fin du tableau.

Insuffisance des taux : les taux présentés dans le tableau 19 appellent les mêmes réserves que celles formulées à propos des fréquences correspondantes (voir à ce sujet les notes techniques se rapportant au tableau 18). Leurs imperfections tiennent notamment aux différences d'exhaustivité de l'enregistrement, au classement des enfants nés vivants mais décédés avant l'enregistrement de leur naissance ou dans les 24 heures qui ont suivi la naissance, à la méthode utilisée pour obtenir l'âge au moment du décès, et à la qualité des déclarations concernant l'âge au moment du décès. En outre, dans certains cas, les données relatives aux décès sont classées par date d'enregistrement et non par date de l'événement ; ces cas ont été signalés par le signe "+".

S'agissant des taux de mortalité par âge, il est particulièrement difficile d'établir une correspondance exacte entre les décès (numérateur) et la population (dénominateur) du fait de l'inclusion ou de l'exclusion des militaires, des réfugiés, des personnes déplacées et d'autres groupes spéciaux. Il convient d'ajouter que, même lorsque population et décès correspondent, la comparabilité des taux peut être compromise par des conditions anormales telles que l'absence du pays ou de la zone d'un grand nombre de jeunes gens qui sont sous les drapeaux ou qui travaillent à l'étranger comme travailleurs temporaires. Il arrive ainsi que les taux de mortalité paraissent élevés parmi les groupes les plus jeunes simplement parce que l'on en a exclu un grand nombre d'individus en bonne santé pour lesquels le taux de mortalité pourrait être, dans des conditions normales, inférieur à la moyenne observée pour les personnes du même âge. Par conséquent, il importe d'être prudent quand on les utilise ces taux de mortalité dans des comparaisons.

De même, les taux indiqués pour tous les âges combinés diffèrent dans plusieurs cas des taux bruts de mortalité qui figurent dans d'autres tableaux, parce qu'ils se rapportent à une population pour laquelle on disposait d'une répartition par âge et par sexe appropriée, tandis que les taux bruts de mortalité indiqués ailleurs peuvent avoir été calculés sur la base d'un chiffre de population totale différent. Ainsi, il est possible que les chiffres de population par âge et par sexe proviennent d'un recensement effectué dans le courant de l'année et non au milieu de l'année, et qu'ils se différencient des autres chiffres de population en excluant ou en incluant certains groupes ethniques, les militaires, etc. Quelquefois, la différence tient à ce que les taux du tableau 19 ont été calculés sur la base de la population moyenne, alors que les taux correspondants des autres tableaux reposent sur une estimation au 1er juillet.

Données publiées antérieurement : Les éditions de l'*Annuaire démographique* parues depuis 1955 présentent les statistiques les plus récentes dont on disposait à l'époque sur les décès selon l'âge et le sexe et sur les taux de mortalité selon l'âge et le sexe. Pour plus de précisions concernant les années pour lesquelles ces données ont été publiées, se reporter à l'index historique.

19. Deaths by age and sex and age-specific death rates by sex: latest available year, 2009 - 2018
Décès et taux de mortalité selon l'âge et le sexe : dernière année disponible, 2009 - 2018

Continent, country or area, date, code[a] and age (in years) / Continent, pays ou zone, date, code[a] et âge (en années)	Number - Nombre			Rate - Taux		
	Both sexes Les deux sexes	Male Masculin	Female Féminin	Both sexes Les deux sexes	Male Masculin	Female Féminin
AFRICA - AFRIQUE						
Algeria - Algérie[1]						
2016 (U)						
Total	180 404	92 981	87 423			
0	22 271	12 157	10 114	...	...	...
1 - 4	2 986	1 581	1 406	...	...	...
5 - 9	1 458	795	664	...	...	...
10 - 14	1 066	570	495	...	...	...
15 - 19	1 610	1 008	601	...	...	...
20 - 24	2 440	1 630	810	...	...	...
25 - 29	2 741	1 710	1 031	...	...	...
30 - 34	3 362	1 892	1 470	...	...	...
35 - 39	3 685	1 957	1 728	...	...	...
40 - 44	4 206	2 134	2 071	...	...	...
45 - 49	5 321	2 711	2 611	...	...	...
50 - 54	6 817	3 651	3 166	...	...	...
55 - 59	8 144	4 457	3 687	...	...	...
60 - 64	11 005	6 279	4 726	...	...	...
65 - 69	11 794	6 649	5 145	...	...	...
70 - 74	12 746	6 905	5 841	...	...	...
75 - 79	18 197	9 162	9 035	...	...	...
80 - 84	22 572	10 897	11 675	...	...	...
85 +	37 984	16 836	21 147	...	...	...
Botswana[2]						
2017 (U)						
Total	12 386	6 601	5 785			
0	985	539	446	...	...	...
1 - 4	221	113	108	...	...	...
5 - 9	93	54	39	...	...	...
10 - 14	83	45	38	...	...	...
15 - 19	175	110	65	...	...	...
20 - 24	327	185	142	...	...	...
25 - 29	454	256	198	...	...	...
30 - 34	633	346	287	...	...	...
35 - 39	740	406	334	...	...	...
40 - 44	756	422	334	...	...	...
45 - 49	690	394	296	...	...	...
50 - 54	676	401	275	...	...	...
55 - 59	748	429	319	...	...	...
60 - 64	748	452	296	...	...	...
65 - 69	754	467	287	...	...	...
70 - 74	679	379	300	...	...	...
75 - 79	851	487	364	...	...	...
80 - 84	774	378	396	...	...	...
85 - 89	915	380	535	...	...	...
90 - 94	574	187	387	...	...	...
95 - 99	326	106	220	...	...	...
100 +	156	48	108	...	...	...
Unknown - Inconnu	28	17	11	...	...	..
Congo						
2014 (+U)						
Total	13 413	7 106	6 307			
0	2 240	1 241	999	...	...	...
1 - 4	1 072	542	530	...	...	...
5 - 14	582	325	257	...	...	...
15 - 59	5 352	2 873	2 479	...	...	...
60 +	4 165	2 123	2 042	...	...	...
Egypt - Égypte						
2017 (C)						
Total	547 208	300 898	246 310	5.7	6.1	5.3
0	38 685	20 964	17 721	14.9	15.6	14.0
1 - 4	11 184	6 046	5 138	1.1	1.1	1.0
5 - 9	4 599	2 720	1 879	0.4	0.5	0.4
10 - 14	3 788	2 448	1 340	0.4	0.5	0.3
15 - 19	6 292	4 305	1 987	0.7	0.9	0.5
20 - 24	6 565	4 637	1 928	0.8	1.1	0.5
25 - 29	7 201	4 862	2 339	0.9	1.2	0.6
30 - 34	8 695	5 646	3 049	1.2	1.5	0.8

19. Deaths by age and sex and age-specific death rates by sex: latest available year, 2009 - 2018
Décès et taux de mortalité selon l'âge et le sexe : dernière année disponible, 2009 - 2018 (continued - suite)

Continent, country or area, date, code[a] and age (in years) / Continent, pays ou zone, date, code[a] et âge (en années)	Number - Nombre			Rate - Taux		
	Both sexes Les deux sexes	Male Masculin	Female Féminin	Both sexes Les deux sexes	Male Masculin	Female Féminin
AFRICA - AFRIQUE						
Egypt - Égypte						
2017 (C)						
35 - 39	10 005	6 393	3 612	1.5	1.9	1.1
40 - 44	12 343	7 758	4 585	2.4	2.9	1.8
45 - 49	17 557	11 229	6 328	4.0	4.9	3.0
50 - 54	32 080	20 586	11 494	8.0	10.0	5.9
55 - 59	45 493	28 810	16 683	13.9	16.7	10.7
60 - 64	59 405	36 007	23 398	22.3	25.3	18.9
65 - 69	67 018	37 985	29 033	38.8	40.1	37.2
70 - 74	61 623	32 111	29 512	60.4	60.2	60.6
75 +	154 675	68 391	86 284	166.2	142.8	191.1
75 - 79	56 925	27 754	29 171	...	...	...
80 - 84	47 982	21 385	26 597	...	...	...
85 +	49 768	19 252	30 516	...	...	...
Ghana[3]						
2010 (|)						
Total	163 534	84 214	79 320	6.6	7.0	6.3
0	28 068	15 807	12 261	38.4	42.7	34.0
1 - 4	17 868	9 424	8 444	6.7	6.9	6.4
5 - 9	6 275	3 437	2 838	2.0	2.2	1.8
10 - 14	3 641	1 587	2 054	1.2	1.1	1.4
15 - 19	4 399	1 752	2 647	1.7	1.3	2.0
20 - 24	5 467	2 117	3 350	2.4	1.9	2.7
25 - 29	6 325	2 516	3 809	3.1	2.7	3.4
30 - 34	8 218	3 397	4 821	4.9	4.3	5.4
35 - 39	8 215	3 579	4 636	5.8	5.3	6.2
40 - 44	8 855	4 141	4 714	7.5	7.2	7.7
45 - 49	7 573	3 715	3 858	8.1	8.2	8.0
50 - 54	8 577	4 376	4 201	10.3	11.1	9.6
55 - 59	5 656	3 564	2 092	10.8	13.8	7.9
60 - 64	7 159	4 418	2 741	15.0	19.5	11.0
65 - 69	5 670	3 360	2 310	19.3	24.7	14.7
70 - 74	8 443	5 096	3 347	24.0	34.1	16.6
75 - 79	6 197	3 599	2 598	30.1	40.4	22.2
80 - 84	6 543	3 346	3 197	41.1	53.7	33.1
85 - 89	4 436	2 166	2 270	53.4	65.8	45.3
90 - 94	3 650	1 797	1 853	71.5	94.6	57.8
95 +	2 299	1 020	1 279	99.3	116.6	88.9
Guinea - Guinée[4]						
2014 (|)						
Total	129 896	70 815	59 081	12.3	13.9	10.9
0	36 556	20 751	15 805	112.1	125.9	97.9
1 - 4	21 083	11 308	9 775	14.7	15.6	13.7
5 - 9	5 661	3 128	2 533	3.3	3.6	3.0
10 - 14	3 237	1 821	1 416	2.6	2.9	2.3
15 - 19	3 585	1 630	1 955	3.2	3.1	3.3
20 - 24	3 775	1 806	1 969	4.2	4.4	4.0
25 - 29	4 350	1 934	2 416	5.6	5.7	5.4
30 - 34	4 366	2 077	2 289	6.9	7.5	6.5
35 - 39	3 909	1 986	1 923	7.6	8.7	6.8
40 - 44	4 168	2 226	1 942	9.5	11.1	8.2
45 - 49	3 567	2 063	1 504	10.9	12.9	8.9
50 - 54	4 461	2 562	1 899	15.0	17.5	12.5
55 - 59	2 963	1 857	1 106	14.0	16.2	11.4
60 - 64	4 659	2 695	1 964	22.8	25.6	19.8
65 - 69	3 490	2 070	1 420	27.4	30.4	23.9
70 - 74	5 181	2 884	2 297	44.4	50.7	38.8
75 - 79	3 461	2 029	1 432	54.2	59.8	47.9
80 - 84	4 300	2 248	2 052	84.3	91.1	78.0
85 - 89	2 350	1 297	1 053	113.4	120.2	106.0
90 - 94	1 673	929	744	142.4	165.0	121.6
95 +	3 101	1 514	1 587	259.3	264.8	254.2
95 - 99	1 886	963	923	...	...	...
100 +	1 215	551	664	...	...	...

19. Deaths by age and sex and age-specific death rates by sex: latest available year, 2009 - 2018
Décès et taux de mortalité selon l'âge et le sexe : dernière année disponible, 2009 - 2018 (continued - suite)

Continent, country or area, date, code[a] and age (in years) Continent, pays ou zone, date, code[a] et âge (en annèes)	Number - Nombre			Rate - Taux		
	Both sexes Les deux sexes	Male Masculin	Female Féminin	Both sexes Les deux sexes	Male Masculin	Female Féminin
AFRICA - AFRIQUE						
Kenya						
2018 (+U)						
Total	192 019	106 318	85 701	...	...	...
0	20 350	10 598	9 752	...	...	...
1 - 4	8 238	4 558	3 680	...	...	...
5 - 14	7 303	3 958	3 345	...	...	...
15 - 24	12 333	7 017	5 316	...	...	...
25 - 34	20 409	11 383	9 026	...	...	...
35 - 44	23 249	13 671	9 578	...	...	...
45 - 54	21 306	12 518	8 788	...	...	...
55 - 74	39 505	23 020	16 485	...	...	...
75 +	39 326	19 595	19 731	...	...	...
Lesotho						
2017 (+U)						
Total	13 671	7 096	6 575	...	...	...
0 - 4	276	139	137	...	...	...
5 - 9	82	40	42	...	...	...
10 - 14	94	56	38	...	...	...
15 - 19	197	108	89	...	...	...
20 - 24	360	218	142	...	...	...
25 - 29	666	352	314	...	...	...
30 - 34	1 007	548	459	...	...	...
35 - 39	1 067	606	461	...	...	...
40 - 44	955	527	428	...	...	...
45 - 49	771	430	341	...	...	...
50 - 54	786	447	339	...	...	...
55 - 59	929	539	390	...	...	...
60 - 64	981	588	393	...	...	...
65 - 69	949	581	368	...	...	...
70 - 74	919	504	415	...	...	...
75 +	3 632	1 413	2 219	...	...	...
Malawi[3]						
2018 (|)						
Total	110 776	61 881	48 895	6.3	7.3	5.4
0	12 586	6 787	5 799	24.1	26.2	22.0
1 - 4	11 362	6 037	5 325	5.6	6.0	5.2
5 - 9	4 902	2 594	2 308	1.9	2.0	1.7
10 - 14	3 249	1 745	1 504	1.3	1.4	1.2
15 - 19	3 596	1 930	1 666	1.8	1.9	1.6
20 - 24	4 614	2 608	2 006	2.8	3.4	2.3
25 - 29	5 267	3 124	2 143	4.3	5.4	3.3
30 - 34	6 010	3 588	2 422	5.4	6.9	4.1
35 - 39	6 790	4 087	2 703	7.0	8.7	5.4
40 - 44	5 849	3 657	2 192	8.0	10.0	6.0
45 - 49	5 554	3 537	2 017	10.4	12.9	7.7
50 - 54	5 032	3 043	1 989	13.0	16.2	10.0
55 - 59	4 321	2 586	1 735	14.1	18.0	10.7
60 - 64	4 394	2 611	1 783	18.7	24.2	14.0
65 - 69	4 477	2 568	1 909	18.6	23.8	14.4
70 - 74	4 835	2 756	2 079	33.4	43.2	25.7
75 - 79	5 054	2 717	2 337	40.5	52.7	32.0
80 - 84	4 465	2 121	2 344	70.1	87.9	59.3
85 - 89	3 825	1 796	2 029	69.9	86.6	59.7
90 - 94	1 938	876	1 062	128.1	167.0	107.4
Mali[5]						
2009 (|)						
Total	62 371	34 387	27 984	4.3	4.8	3.8
0 - 4	29 336	16 098	13 238	11.2	12.1	10.2
5 - 9	3 486	1 933	1 553	1.5	1.6	1.3
10 - 14	1 598	914	684	0.9	1.0	0.8
15 - 19	1 638	777	861	1.1	1.1	1.1
20 - 24	1 570	712	858	1.4	1.3	1.4
25 - 29	1 618	752	866	1.6	1.7	1.6
30 - 34	1 729	839	890	2.1	2.2	2.1
35 - 39	1 604	798	806	2.5	2.5	2.5
40 - 44	1 547	858	689	2.8	3.2	2.5
45 - 49	1 462	890	572	3.3	3.9	2.6

Continent, country or area, date, code[a] and age (in years)	Number - Nombre			Rate - Taux		
Continent, pays ou zone, date, code[a] et âge (en années)	Both sexes Les deux sexes	Male Masculin	Female Féminin	Both sexes Les deux sexes	Male Masculin	Female Féminin

AFRICA - AFRIQUE

Mali[5]
2009 (|)

50 - 54	1 527	884	643	4.0	4.7	3.3
55 - 59	1 544	954	590	5.5	6.4	4.4
60 - 64	1 960	1 201	759	7.8	9.4	6.1
65 - 69	1 958	1 152	806	11.8	13.0	10.5
70 - 74	2 093	1 198	895	15.7	17.8	13.5
75 - 79	1 891	1 113	778	24.5	27.2	21.5
80 +	3 372	1 836	1 536	39.4	43.7	35.2
Unknown - Inconnu	2 438	1 478	960	..	..	..

Mauritius - Maurice[6]
2018 (+C)

Total	10 787	5 939	4 848	8.5	9.5	7.6
0	181	93	88	13.9	14.0	13.9
1 - 4	33	18	15	0.6	♦0.7	♦0.6
5 - 9	10	7	3	♦0.1	♦0.2	♦0.1
10 - 14	19	10	9	♦0.2	♦0.2	♦0.2
15 - 19	67	46	21	0.7	0.9	♦0.4
20 - 24	91	66	25	0.9	1.3	♦0.5
25 - 29	117	80	37	1.2	1.6	0.8
30 - 34	105	71	34	1.3	1.7	0.8
35 - 39	241	174	67	2.4	3.5	1.4
40 - 44	323	216	107	3.5	4.7	2.4
45 - 49	440	298	142	5.4	7.3	3.5
50 - 54	660	448	212	7.0	9.6	4.5
55 - 59	859	565	294	9.9	13.4	6.7
60 - 64	1 040	640	400	14.4	18.4	10.6
65 - 69	1 353	841	512	23.0	30.9	16.3
70 - 74	1 212	675	537	33.8	43.4	26.5
75 - 79	1 103	566	537	53.2	67.1	43.7
80 - 84	1 124	494	630	80.2	93.6	72.1
85 +	1 809	631	1 178	175.2	197.7	165.1
85 - 89	862	346	516	...	...	...
90 - 94	694	226	468	...	...	...
95 - 99	204	48	156	...	...	...
100 +	49	11	38	...	...	...

Mayotte
2017 (C)

Total	735	366	369	2.9	3.0	2.8
0 - 4	115	54	61	2.9	2.7	3.1
0	86	39	47	10.6	9.4	11.8
5 - 9	9	8	1	♦0.2	♦0.4	♦0.1
10 - 14	13	7	6	♦0.4	♦0.4	♦0.3
15 - 19	3	3	-	♦0.1	♦0.2	-
20 - 24	14	7	7	♦0.8	♦1.0	♦0.7
25 - 29	13	6	7	♦0.8	♦0.9	♦0.7
30 - 34	19	12	7	♦1.1	♦1.7	♦0.7
35 - 39	28	10	18	♦1.7	♦1.3	♦1.9
40 - 44	27	13	14	♦1.9	♦1.9	♦1.9
45 - 49	32	18	14	2.8	♦3.0	♦2.6
50 - 54	46	19	27	6.2	♦5.0	♦7.4
55 - 59	49	22	27	8.1	♦7.0	♦9.3
60 - 64	45	24	21	10.7	♦10.8	♦10.6
65 - 69	48	26	22	16.7	♦16.9	♦16.4
70 - 74	68	33	35	41.8	42.0	41.7
75 - 79	63	31	32	54.9	56.6	53.3
80 - 84	66	36	30	103.8	114.3	♦93.5
85 - 89	44	20	24	135.8	♦139.9	♦132.6
90 - 94	20	11	9	♦172.4	♦196.4	♦150.0
95 +	13	6	7	♦112.1	♦120.0	♦106.1
95 - 99	11	5	6	...	...	...
100 +	2	1	1	...	...	...

Namibia - Namibie[7]
2011 (|)

Total	22 668	12 491	10 177	10.7	12.2	9.3
0	2 685	1 411	1 274	41.9	44.1	39.6
1 - 4	1 346	719	627	6.1	6.5	5.7

Continent, country or area, date, code[a] and age (in years) Continent, pays ou zone, date, code[a] et âge (en années)	Number - Nombre			Rate - Taux		
	Both sexes Les deux sexes	Male Masculin	Female Féminin	Both sexes Les deux sexes	Male Masculin	Female Féminin
AFRICA - AFRIQUE						
Namibia - Namibie[7]						
2011 (I)						
5 - 9	447	255	192	1.9	2.1	1.6
10 - 14	384	212	172	1.6	1.7	1.4
15 - 19	577	298	279	2.4	2.5	2.3
20 - 24	918	537	381	4.3	5.1	3.5
25 - 29	1 233	645	588	7.0	7.4	6.5
30 - 34	1 591	890	701	10.7	12.1	9.2
35 - 39	1 487	873	614	11.9	14.3	9.6
40 - 44	1 323	807	516	13.5	17.2	10.1
45 - 49	1 140	698	442	14.2	18.6	10.3
50 - 54	917	535	382	14.9	19.5	11.2
55 - 59	891	562	329	18.6	26.1	12.5
60 - 64	994	584	410	24.4	31.7	18.3
65 - 69	766	424	342	24.6	32.3	19.0
70 - 74	739	424	315	30.7	41.3	22.8
75 - 79	682	382	300	39.5	54.5	29.3
80 - 84	792	402	390	55.3	76.2	43.1
85 - 89	638	282	356	68.6	90.2	57.6
90 - 94	549	234	315	80.6	98.4	71.1
95 +	1 003	403	600	178.7	228.6	155.8
Unknown - Inconnu	1 566	914	652	..	..	..
Niger						
2011 (+U)						
Total	6 761	...	...	...	...	...
0	236	...	...	...	...	...
1 - 4	329	...	...	...	...	...
5 - 9	120	...	...	...	...	...
10 - 14	81	...	...	...	...	...
15 - 19	147	...	...	...	...	...
20 - 24	242	...	...	...	...	...
25 - 29	319	...	...	...	...	...
30 - 34	378	...	...	...	...	...
35 - 39	414	...	...	...	...	...
40 - 44	470	...	...	...	...	...
45 - 49	485	...	...	...	...	...
50 - 54	495	...	...	...	...	...
55 - 59	443	...	...	...	...	...
60 - 64	541	...	...	...	...	...
65 - 69	443	...	...	...	...	...
70 - 74	517	...	...	...	...	...
75 - 79	347	...	...	...	...	...
80 - 84	298	...	...	...	...	...
85 - 89	112	...	...	...	...	...
90 - 94	90	...	...	...	...	...
95 - 99	26	...	...	...	...	...
100 +	53	...	...	...	...	...
Unknown - Inconnu	175	...	...	..	..	..
Reunion - Réunion						
2017 (C)						
Total	4 673	2 521	2 152	5.4	6.1	4.8
0 - 4	101	52	49	1.6	1.7	1.6
0	87	43	44	7.2	7.0	7.4
5 - 9	12	6	6	♦0.2	♦0.2	♦0.2
10 - 14	3	2	1	-	♦0.1	-
15 - 19	20	12	8	♦0.3	♦0.3	♦0.2
20 - 24	22	16	6	♦0.4	♦0.6	♦0.2
25 - 29	48	38	10	1.0	1.6	♦0.4
30 - 34	39	28	11	0.8	♦1.2	♦0.4
35 - 39	73	53	20	1.3	2.2	♦0.7
40 - 44	87	65	22	1.5	2.4	♦0.7
45 - 49	152	91	61	2.4	3.0	1.9
50 - 54	198	136	62	3.0	4.3	1.9
55 - 59	284	194	90	5.2	7.4	3.2
60 - 64	360	234	126	7.8	10.6	5.2
65 - 69	410	260	150	12.1	16.2	8.4
70 - 74	447	288	159	19.0	26.3	12.6

19. Deaths by age and sex and age-specific death rates by sex: latest available year, 2009 - 2018
Décès et taux de mortalité selon l'âge et le sexe : dernière année disponible, 2009 - 2018 (continued - suite)

Continent, country or area, date, code[a] and age (in years) / Continent, pays ou zone, date, code[a] et âge (en années)	Number - Nombre			Rate - Taux		
	Both sexes Les deux sexes	Male Masculin	Female Féminin	Both sexes Les deux sexes	Male Masculin	Female Féminin
AFRICA - AFRIQUE						
Reunion - Réunion						
2017 (C)						
75 - 79	546	304	242	30.7	39.8	23.8
80 - 84	613	307	306	51.1	67.8	41.1
85 - 89	610	260	350	98.4	125.2	84.8
90 - 94	425	130	295	158.5	169.7	154.0
95 +	223	45	178	267.4	277.8	264.9
95 - 99	171	40	131	...	...	...
100 +	52	5	47	...	...	...
Saint Helena ex. dep. - Sainte-Hélène sans dép.						
2018 (C)						
Total	52	32	20	...	...	...
0	-	-	-	...	...	...
1 - 4	-	-	-	...	...	...
5 - 9	-	-	-	...	...	...
10 - 14	-	-	-	...	...	...
15 - 19	-	-	-	...	...	...
20 - 24	-	-	-	...	...	...
25 - 29	-	-	-	...	...	...
30 - 34	-	-	-	...	...	...
35 - 39	-	-	-	...	...	...
40 - 44	-	-	-	...	...	...
45 - 49	1	-	1	...	...	...
50 - 54	3	1	2	...	...	...
55 - 59	3	3	-	...	...	...
60 - 64	2	2	-	...	...	...
65 - 69	10	7	3	...	...	...
70 - 74	5	4	1	...	...	...
75 - 79	12	7	5	...	...	...
80 - 84	6	5	1	...	...	...
85 - 89	4	2	2	...	...	...
90 - 94	3	1	2	...	...	...
95 - 99	2	-	2	...	...	...
100 +	1	-	1	...	...	...
Sao Tome and Principe - Sao Tomé-et-Principe[8]						
2012 (I)						
Total	1 287	735	552	7.2	8.3	6.1
0	132	82	50	23.1	27.8	18.0
1 - 4	69	41	29	3.1	3.7	♦2.6
5 - 9	18	5	13	♦0.7	♦0.4	♦1.0
10 - 14	29	20	10	♦1.4	♦1.9	♦0.9
15 - 19	29	23	6	♦1.6	♦2.5	♦0.7
20 - 24	54	36	18	3.4	4.5	♦2.3
25 - 29	39	26	13	2.6	♦3.5	♦1.7
30 - 34	41	31	10	3.3	5.0	♦1.6
35 - 39	61	41	20	6.3	8.4	♦4.1
40 - 44	51	34	17	6.5	8.6	♦4.4
45 - 49	49	24	25	7.8	♦7.9	♦7.7
50 - 54	77	44	33	14.4	16.9	12.0
55 - 59	52	21	31	13.6	♦11.6	15.4
60 - 64	86	59	27	32.3	44.1	♦20.4
65 - 69	60	33	27	31.2	35.9	♦26.8
70 - 74	102	60	42	54.3	70.6	40.9
75 - 79	103	51	52	73.0	83.7	64.8
80 +	234	104	130	170.1	198.1	152.8
Seychelles						
2018 (+C)						
Total	818	470	348	...	...	...
0	31	12	19	...	...	...
1 - 4	3	1	2	...	...	...
5 - 9	5	4	1	...	...	...
10 - 14	1	1	-	...	...	...
15 - 19	5	3	2	...	...	...
20 - 24	14	13	1	...	...	...
25 - 29	15	11	4	...	...	...
30 - 34	29	19	10	...	...	...
35 - 39	17	10	7	...	...	...

19. Deaths by age and sex and age-specific death rates by sex: latest available year, 2009 - 2018
Décès et taux de mortalité selon l'âge et le sexe : dernière année disponible, 2009 - 2018 (continued - suite)

Continent, country or area, date, code[a] and age (in years) / Continent, pays ou zone, date, code[a] et âge (en annèes)	Number - Nombre			Rate - Taux		
	Both sexes Les deux sexes	Male Masculin	Female Féminin	Both sexes Les deux sexes	Male Masculin	Female Féminin
AFRICA - AFRIQUE						
Seychelles						
2018 (+C)						
40 - 44	26	16	10	...	...	...
45 - 49	46	32	14	...	...	...
50 - 54	51	36	15	...	...	...
55 - 59	60	47	13	...	...	...
60 - 64	67	45	22	...	...	...
65 - 69	60	39	21	...	...	...
70 - 74	71	38	33	...	...	...
75 - 79	83	50	33	...	...	...
80 - 84	103	47	56	...	...	...
85 +	131	46	85	...	...	...
Sierra Leone[9]						
2013 (+U)						
Total	19 403	9 982	9 421	...	...	...
0	2 276	1 151	1 125	...	...	...
1 - 4	2 413	1 168	1 245	...	...	...
5 - 14	2 904	1 447	1 457	...	...	...
15 +	11 810	6 216	5 594	...	...	...
South Africa - Afrique du Sud						
2016 (U)						
Total	456 612	240 001[10]	214 988[10]	...	...	...
0	20 649	10 963[10]	9 284[10]	...	...	...
1 - 4	7 008	3 686[10]	3 281[10]	...	...	...
5 - 9	2 965	1 672[10]	1 287[10]	...	...	...
10 - 14	3 083	1 781[10]	1 298[10]	...	...	...
15 - 19	6 821	4 019[10]	2 781[10]	...	...	...
20 - 24	13 708	8 272[10]	5 375[10]	...	...	...
25 - 29	22 209	12 851[10]	9 238[10]	...	...	...
30 - 34	28 519	16 597[10]	11 769[10]	...	...	...
35 - 39	28 244	16 535[10]	11 558[10]	...	...	...
40 - 44	29 290	17 270[10]	11 898[10]	...	...	...
45 - 49	28 635	16 890[10]	11 656[10]	...	...	...
50 - 54	31 618	18 470[10]	13 093[10]	...	...	...
55 - 59	33 917	19 796[10]	14 055[10]	...	...	...
60 - 64	36 372	20 689[10]	15 633[10]	...	...	...
65 - 69	35 684	19 486[10]	16 168[10]	...	...	...
70 - 74	31 418	15 753[10]	15 632[10]	...	...	...
75 - 79	32 210	14 361[10]	17 829[10]	...	...	...
80 - 84	25 323	9 280[10]	16 031[10]	...	...	...
85 - 89	21 280	6 736[10]	14 525[10]	...	...	...
90 - 94	10 508	2 975[10]	7 527[10]	...	...	...
95 - 99	5 114	1 211[10]	3 897[10]	...	...	...
100 +	1 325	304[10]	1 018[10]	...	...	...
Unknown - Inconnu	712	404[10]	155[10]	..	..	..
Zambia - Zambie[11]						
2010 (I)						
Total	164 385	87 693	76 692	12.6	13.6	11.6
0	35 103	18 953	16 150	79.7	86.1	73.2
1 - 4	28 943	15 297	13 646	16.0	17.0	15.0
5 - 9	8 405	4 519	3 886	4.4	4.7	4.0
10 - 14	4 836	2 550	2 286	2.7	2.9	2.6
15 - 19	5 856	2 821	3 035	3.8	3.8	3.9
20 - 24	7 967	3 746	4 221	6.7	6.8	6.6
25 - 29	10 471	5 112	5 359	9.9	10.3	9.6
30 - 34	11 305	5 986	5 319	13.5	14.1	12.8
35 - 39	9 972	5 698	4 274	14.6	16.0	13.1
40 - 44	7 336	4 334	3 002	15.5	17.3	13.5
45 - 49	6 021	3 603	2 418	16.0	19.1	12.9
50 - 54	4 770	2 687	2 083	16.7	19.4	14.3
55 - 59	3 546	2 056	1 490	18.3	21.3	15.3
60 - 64	3 929	2 146	1 783	23.3	27.4	19.8
65 - 69	3 363	1 732	1 631	27.4	30.5	24.7
70 - 74	4 084	2 138	1 946	43.8	48.7	39.4
75 +	8 478	4 315	4 163	65.1	67.1	63.2

Continent, country or area, date, code[a] and age (in years) / Continent, pays ou zone, date, code[a] et âge (en années)	Number - Nombre			Rate - Taux		
	Both sexes Les deux sexes	Male Masculin	Female Féminin	Both sexes Les deux sexes	Male Masculin	Female Féminin
AMERICA, NORTH - AMÉRIQUE DU NORD						
Anguilla[12]						
2013 (+C)[13]						
Total	72	43	29	...	...	...
0	3	2	1	...	...	...
1 - 4	-	-	-	...	...	...
5 - 9	-	-	-	...	...	...
10 - 14	-	-	-	...	...	...
15 - 19	2	2	-	...	...	...
20 - 24	1	1	-	...	...	...
25 - 29	2	2	-	...	...	...
30 - 34	-	-	-	...	...	...
35 - 39	2	1	1	...	...	...
40 - 44	-	-	-	...	...	...
45 - 49	1	1	-	...	...	...
50 - 54	5	3	2	...	...	...
55 - 59	5	3	2	...	...	...
60 - 64	3	3	-	...	...	...
65 - 69	7	3	4	...	...	...
70 - 74	4	3	1	...	...	...
75 - 79	9	5	4	...	...	...
80 - 84	8	5	3	...	...	...
85 +	20	9	11	...	...	...
2015 (+C)						
Total	61	...	...	...	...	...
0 - 4	5	...	...	...	...	...
5 - 14	-	...	...	...	...	...
15 - 29	3	...	...	...	...	...
30 - 44	5	...	...	...	...	...
45 - 59	8	...	...	...	...	...
60 - 64	-	...	...	...	...	...
65 - 69	1	...	...	...	...	...
70 - 74	6	...	...	...	...	...
75 - 79	8	...	...	...	...	...
80 - 84	8	...	...	...	...	...
85 +	15	...	...	...	...	...
Antigua and Barbuda - Antigua-et-Barbuda						
2016 (+C)						
Total	542	...	...	5.9	...	...
0	13	...	...	...	...	...
1 - 4	2	...	...	...	...	...
5 - 9	1	...	...	♦0.1	...	...
10 - 14	2	...	...	♦0.3	...	...
15 - 19	4	...	...	♦0.5	...	...
20 - 24	7	...	...	♦0.9	...	...
25 - 29	9	...	...	♦1.3	...	...
30 - 34	6	...	...	♦0.9	...	...
35 - 39	14	...	...	♦2.1	...	...
40 - 44	14	...	...	♦2.0	...	...
45 - 49	14	...	...	♦2.1	...	...
50 - 54	30	...	...	♦4.8	...	...
55 - 59	43	...	...	8.5	...	...
60 - 64	39	...	...	10.9	...	...
65 - 69	48	...	...	17.2	...	...
70 - 74	59	...	...	29.3	...	...
75 - 79	46	...	...	37.2	...	...
80 - 84	67	...	...	84.3	...	...
85 +	124	...	...	131.8	...	...
Aruba						
2017 (C)						
Total	707	353	354	6.4	6.7	6.1
0	6	4	2	♦4.8	♦6.1	♦3.4
1 - 4	-	-	-	-	-	-
5 - 9	2	2	-	♦0.3	♦0.6	-
10 - 14	-	-	-	-	-	-
15 - 19	1	-	1	♦0.1	-	♦0.3
20 - 24	3	2	1	♦0.5	♦0.6	♦0.3
25 - 29	3	3	-	♦0.5	♦0.9	-

Continent, country or area, date, code[a] and age (in years) / Continent, pays ou zone, date, code[a] et âge (en années)	Number - Nombre			Rate - Taux		
	Both sexes Les deux sexes	Male Masculin	Female Féminin	Both sexes Les deux sexes	Male Masculin	Female Féminin
AMERICA, NORTH - AMÉRIQUE DU NORD						
Aruba						
2017 (C)						
30 - 34	4	2	2	◆0.6	◆0.6	◆0.6
35 - 39	6	2	4	◆0.8	◆0.6	◆1.0
40 - 44	11	5	6	◆1.5	◆1.4	◆1.5
45 - 49	19	11	8	◆2.2	◆2.8	◆1.7
50 - 54	19	14	5	◆2.1	◆3.3	◆1.0
55 - 59	47	24	23	5.3	◆5.9	◆4.9
60 - 64	66	32	34	9.2	9.8	8.6
65 - 69	69	40	29	12.8	16.4	◆9.8
70 - 74	75	45	30	20.0	27.8	◆14.0
75 - 79	106	49	57	40.5	43.9	37.9
80 - 84	112	55	57	69.2	94.1	55.1
85 - 89	96	44	52	115.4	143.1	99.1
90 - 94	39	14	25	155.1	◆203.4	◆136.9
95 - 99	17	5	12	◆222.7	◆220.6	◆223.6
100 +	6	-	6	◆411.9	-	◆530.3
Bahamas						
2012 (+C)						
Total	1 995	1 094	901	5.5	6.2	4.9
0	57	26	31	8.6	◆7.6	9.7
1 - 4	18	10	8	◆0.7	◆0.8	◆0.7
5 - 9	9	5	4	◆0.3	◆0.3	◆0.3
10 - 14	8	6	2	◆0.3	◆0.4	◆0.1
15 - 19	27	17	10	◆0.9	◆1.1	◆0.6
20 - 24	57	42	15	1.9	2.9	◆1.0
25 - 29	49	42	7	1.8	3.2	◆0.5
30 - 34	72	52	20	2.8	4.1	◆1.5
35 - 39	84	47	37	3.1	3.5	2.6
40 - 44	100	58	42	3.6	4.4	2.9
45 - 49	130	72	58	4.9	5.6	4.2
50 - 54	159	84	75	6.8	7.5	6.2
55 - 59	147	94	53	8.5	11.4	5.9
60 - 64	149	83	66	12.2	14.5	10.2
65 - 69	147	87	60	16.1	21.0	12.1
70 - 74	183	96	87	27.6	32.9	23.5
75 - 79	176	93	83	43.0	54.4	34.9
80 - 84	170	81	89	98.0	154.6	74.0
85 - 89	116	61	55	143.7	279.8	91.5
90 +	137	38	99	259.0	351.9	222.0
90 - 94	90	30	60	...	...	...
95 - 99	36	6	30	...	...	...
100 +	11	2	9	...	...	...
Belize						
2018 (U)						
Total	1 886	1 092	794	...	...	...
0	98	54	44	...	...	...
1 - 4	17	10	7	...	...	...
5 - 9	9	5	4	...	...	...
10 - 14	20	12	8	...	...	...
15 - 19	28	18	10	...	...	...
20 - 24	58	45	13	...	...	...
25 - 29	78	58	20	...	...	...
30 - 34	63	40	23	...	...	...
35 - 39	87	54	33	...	...	...
40 - 44	78	47	31	...	...	...
45 - 49	102	60	42	...	...	...
50 - 54	97	51	46	...	...	...
55 - 59	126	73	53	...	...	...
60 - 64	163	88	75	...	...	...
65 +	862	477	385	...	...	...
Bermuda - Bermudes[14]						
2017 (C)						
Total	481	244	237	7.8	8.3	7.4
1 - 4	-	-	-	-	-	-
5 - 9	-	-	-	-	-	-
10 - 14	-	-	-	-	-	-

Continent, country or area, date, code[a] and age (in years) / Continent, pays ou zone, date, code[a] et âge (en années)	Number - Nombre			Rate - Taux		
	Both sexes Les deux sexes	Male Masculin	Female Féminin	Both sexes Les deux sexes	Male Masculin	Female Féminin
AMERICA, NORTH - AMÉRIQUE DU NORD						
Bermuda - Bermudes[14]						
2017 (C)						
15 - 19	-	-	-	-	-	-
20 - 24	5	4	1	♦1.7	♦2.8	♦0.6
25 - 29	3	2	1	♦0.8	♦1.2	♦0.5
30 - 34	6	6	-	♦1.5	♦3.1	-
35 - 39	3	2	1	♦0.7	♦0.9	♦0.5
40 - 44	5	2	3	♦1.2	♦0.9	♦1.4
45 - 49	11	7	4	♦2.3	♦3.0	♦1.7
50 - 54	15	6	9	♦2.8	♦2.3	♦3.4
55 - 59	27	19	8	♦5.2	♦8.0	♦2.8
60 - 64	39	31	8	8.8	15.2	♦3.3
65 - 69	40	27	13	11.2	♦16.4	♦6.8
70 - 74	40	20	20	14.0	♦15.4	♦12.8
75 - 79	52	25	27	26.9	♦30.1	♦24.5
80 - 84	57	35	22	40.0	61.5	♦25.7
85 +	178	58	120	154.0	165.2	149.1
85 - 89	83	36	47	...	...	...
90 - 94	67	20	47	...	...	...
95 - 99	24	2	22	...	...	...
100 +	4	-	4	...	...	...
British Virgin Islands - Îles Vierges britanniques						
2017 (C)						
Total	155	102	53	...	...	...
0 - 4	1	1	-	...	...	...
5 - 9	-	-	-	...	...	...
10 - 14	1	-	1	...	...	...
15 - 19	2	2	-	...	...	...
20 - 24	4	3	1	...	...	...
25 - 29	3	2	1	...	...	...
30 - 34	5	5	-	...	...	...
35 - 39	4	2	2	...	...	...
40 - 44	7	5	2	...	...	...
45 - 49	7	4	3	...	...	...
50 - 54	9	7	2	...	...	...
55 - 59	13	11	2	...	...	...
60 - 64	11	6	5	...	...	...
65 - 69	20	15	5	...	...	...
70 - 74	12	9	3	...	...	...
75 - 79	15	11	4	...	...	...
80 - 84	9	2	7	...	...	...
85 +	24	10	14	...	...	...
Unknown - Inconnu	1	1	-	...	...	...
Canada[15]						
2017 (C)						
Total	276 689	141 098	135 591	7.6	7.8	7.4
0 - 4	1 948	1 080	868	1.0	1.1	0.9
5 - 9	165	84	81	0.1	0.1	0.1
10 - 14	198	108	90	0.1	0.1	0.1
15 - 19	732	487	245	0.4	0.5	0.2
20 - 24	1 369	977	392	0.6	0.8	0.3
25 - 29	1 786	1 270	516	0.7	1.0	0.4
30 - 34	2 083	1 450	633	0.8	1.1	0.5
35 - 39	2 351	1 578	773	1.0	1.3	0.6
40 - 44	2 833	1 776	1 057	1.2	1.5	0.9
45 - 49	4 525	2 761	1 764	1.9	2.3	1.5
50 - 54	7 785	4 718	3 067	2.9	3.5	2.3
55 - 59	12 460	7 463	4 997	4.6	5.6	3.7
60 - 64	17 263	10 357	6 906	7.2	8.8	5.7
65 - 69	21 971	13 094	8 877	11.0	13.5	8.7
70 - 74	27 413	15 947	11 466	17.9	21.7	14.4
75 - 79	30 633	17 101	13 532	29.0	34.9	23.8
80 - 84	38 157	20 176	17 981	50.8	61.3	42.6
85 - 89	44 967	21 276	23 691	91.1	110.2	78.8
90 - 94	37 413	14 006	23 407	162.5	192.5	148.7
95 - 99	16 970	4 692	12 278	261.4	301.8	248.7
100 +	3 667	697	2 970	398.7	438.6	390.4

Continent, country or area, date, code[a] and age (in years) Continent, pays ou zone, date, code[a] et âge (en années)	Number - Nombre			Rate - Taux		
	Both sexes Les deux sexes	Male Masculin	Female Féminin	Both sexes Les deux sexes	Male Masculin	Female Féminin
AMERICA, NORTH - AMÉRIQUE DU NORD						
Cayman Islands - Îles Caïmanes[16]						
2018 (C)						
Total	214	120	94	...	...	...
0 - 14	6	2	4	...	...	...
15 - 19	1	-	1	...	...	...
20 - 24	-	-	-	...	...	...
25 - 29	5	4	1	...	...	...
30 - 34	3	2	1	...	...	...
35 - 39	3	3	-	...	...	...
40 - 49	18	11	7	...	...	...
50 - 59	24	12	12	...	...	...
60 - 69	48	31	17	...	...	...
70 - 79	34	23	11	...	...	...
80 - 89	43	22	21	...	...	...
90 +	29	10	19	...	...	...
Costa Rica						
2018* (C)						
Total	23 786	13 605	10 181	4.8	5.6	4.0
0	573	309	264	...	...	...
1 - 4	73	50	23	...	...	...
5 - 9	57	33	24	0.2	0.2	♦0.1
10 - 14	67	45	22	0.2	0.2	♦0.1
15 - 19	254	192	62	0.6	0.9	0.3
20 - 24	426	343	83	1.0	1.6	0.4
25 - 29	496	362	134	1.3	1.9	0.7
30 - 34	514	373	141	1.4	2.1	0.7
35 - 39	529	364	165	1.5	2.2	0.9
40 - 44	602	391	211	1.9	2.6	1.2
45 - 49	755	470	285	2.6	3.5	1.8
50 - 54	1 104	704	400	3.5	4.7	2.4
55 - 59	1 419	899	520	4.9	6.6	3.4
60 - 64	1 769	1 157	612	7.1	10.1	4.6
65 - 69	1 940	1 193	747	9.8	13.0	7.0
70 - 74	2 145	1 234	911	15.9	21.8	11.7
75 - 79	2 501	1 410	1 091	26.3	29.4	23.1
80 - 84	2 741	1 429	1 312	43.3	50.4	37.5
85 - 89	2 756	1 352	1 404	87.8	103.9	76.4
90 - 94	1 962	867	1 095	113.0	119.0	108.7
95 +	1 092	422	670	176.1	203.2	162.4
95 - 99	846	327	519	...	...	...
100 +	246	95	151	...	...	...
Unknown - Inconnu	11	6	5	..	..	..
Cuba						
2017 (C)						
Total	106 949	58 283	48 666	9.5	10.4	8.6
0	465	256	209	4.0	4.3	3.8
1 - 4	162	94	68	0.3	0.4	0.3
5 - 9	84	58	26	0.1	0.2	♦0.1
10 - 14	128	73	55	0.2	0.2	0.2
15 - 19	280	181	99	0.4	0.5	0.3
20 - 24	374	254	120	0.5	0.7	0.4
25 - 29	556	379	177	0.7	0.9	0.4
30 - 34	687	475	212	0.9	1.3	0.6
35 - 39	726	459	267	1.2	1.5	0.9
40 - 44	1 532	991	541	1.8	2.3	1.3
45 - 49	2 765	1 760	1 005	2.8	3.6	2.0
50 - 54	4 790	3 092	1 698	4.7	6.2	3.3
55 - 59	5 876	3 696	2 180	8.2	10.6	5.9
60 - 64	7 492	4 517	2 975	12.6	15.9	9.6
65 - 69	10 158	5 947	4 211	19.4	23.7	15.4
70 - 74	12 855	7 387	5 468	30.2	37.0	24.1
75 - 79	14 503	8 055	6 448	46.4	55.6	38.4
80 - 84	14 779	7 647	7 132	75.4	86.7	66.1
85 +	28 698	12 928	15 770	157.9	169.6	149.5
85 - 89	13 652	6 581	7 071	...	...	...
90 - 94	9 395	4 164	5 231	...	...	...
95 - 99	4 347	1 689	2 658	...	...	...

Continent, country or area, date, code[a] and age (in years) Continent, pays ou zone, date, code[a] et âge (en années)	Number - Nombre			Rate - Taux		
	Both sexes Les deux sexes	Male Masculin	Female Féminin	Both sexes Les deux sexes	Male Masculin	Female Féminin
AMERICA, NORTH - AMÉRIQUE DU NORD						
Cuba						
2017 (C)						
100 +	1 304	494	810	...	...	...
Unknown - Inconnu	39	34	5	..	..	..
Curaçao						
2018 (C)						
Total	1 399	720	679	...	...	...
0	14	...	...	...	...	...
1 - 19	6	...	...	...	...	...
20 - 24	9	...	...	...	...	...
25 - 29	10	...	...	...	...	...
30 - 34	13	...	...	...	...	...
35 - 39	11	...	...	...	...	...
40 - 44	14	...	...	...	...	...
45 - 49	36	...	...	...	...	...
50 - 54	43	...	...	...	...	...
55 - 59	88	...	...	...	...	...
60 - 64	123	...	...	...	...	...
65 - 69	117	...	...	...	...	...
70 - 74	175	...	...	...	...	...
75 - 79	178	...	...	...	...	...
80 - 84	222	...	...	...	...	...
85 - 89	177	...	...	...	...	...
90 - 94	107	...	...	...	...	...
95 - 99	39	...	...	...	...	...
100 +	17	...	...	...	...	...
Dominican Republic - République dominicaine						
2017 (U)						
Total	41 152	23 887	17 253	...	...	...
0	674	368	299	...	...	...
1 - 4	145	81	64	...	...	...
5 - 9	128	73	55	...	...	...
10 - 14	149	97	52	...	...	...
15 - 19	551	402	149	...	...	...
20 - 24	1 030	813	217	...	...	...
25 - 29	957	715	242	...	...	...
30 - 34	994	680	314	...	...	...
35 - 39	1 108	702	406	...	...	...
40 - 44	1 406	904	502	...	...	...
45 - 49	1 779	1 150	629	...	...	...
50 - 54	2 178	1 379	799	...	...	...
55 - 59	2 580	1 638	942	...	...	...
60 - 64	3 175	1 936	1 239	...	...	...
65 - 69	3 695	2 234	1 461	...	...	...
70 - 74	3 835	2 321	1 514	...	...	...
75 - 79	4 196	2 335	1 861	...	...	...
80 - 84	4 426	2 256	2 170	...	...	...
85 - 89	3 930	1 932	1 998	...	...	...
90 - 94	2 280	992	1 288	...	...	...
95 +	1 478	616	862	...	...	...
Unknown - Inconnu	458	263	190	..	...	...
El Salvador						
2014 (C)						
Total	37 461	21 326	16 135	5.9	7.2	4.8
0	876	491	385	7.0	7.7	6.3
1 - 4	240	131	109	0.5	0.5	0.5
5 - 9	125	66	59	0.2	0.2	0.2
10 - 14	250	160	90	0.4	0.5	0.3
15 - 19	983	813	170	1.4	2.3	0.5
20 - 24	1 139	926	213	1.8	3.0	0.6
25 - 29	1 047	869	178	2.1	3.8	0.6
30 - 34	1 249	1 015	234	2.9	5.6	1.0
35 - 39	1 348	1 061	287	3.5	6.4	1.3
40 - 44	1 313	942	371	3.6	6.1	1.8
45 - 49	1 492	985	507	4.7	7.3	2.8
50 - 54	1 669	1 022	647	6.3	8.9	4.2
55 - 59	1 991	1 129	862	8.9	11.6	6.8

Continent, country or area, date, code[a] and age (in years) / Continent, pays ou zone, date, code[a] et âge (en années)	Number - Nombre			Rate - Taux		
	Both sexes Les deux sexes	Male Masculin	Female Féminin	Both sexes Les deux sexes	Male Masculin	Female Féminin
AMERICA, NORTH - AMÉRIQUE DU NORD						
El Salvador						
2014 (C)						
60 - 64	2 302	1 275	1 027	12.1	15.4	9.6
65 - 69	2 678	1 398	1 280	17.1	20.4	14.6
70 - 74	3 107	1 644	1 463	24.7	29.7	20.8
75 - 79	3 687	1 826	1 861	38.6	44.0	34.4
80 +	11 965	5 573	6 392	109.6	120.9	101.3
80 - 84	4 057	1 977	2 080	...	...	...
85 - 89	3 853	1 851	2 002	...	...	...
90 - 94	2 642	1 186	1 456	...	...	...
95 +	1 413	559	854	...	...	...
Greenland - Groenland						
2018 (C)						
Total	487	275	212	8.7	9.3	8.0
0	6	3	3	♦7.4	♦7.1	♦7.8
1 - 4	1	-	1	♦0.3	-	♦0.6
5 - 9	-	-	-	-	-	-
10 - 14	-	-	-	-	-	-
15 - 19	15	9	6	♦4.1	♦4.8	♦3.3
20 - 24	8	5	3	♦1.9	♦2.3	♦1.4
25 - 29	11	10	1	♦2.4	♦4.2	♦0.4
30 - 34	7	6	1	♦1.6	♦2.8	♦0.5
35 - 39	6	3	3	♦1.6	♦1.6	♦1.7
40 - 44	8	4	4	♦2.7	♦2.5	♦3.0
45 - 49	7	7	-	♦2.0	♦3.7	-
50 - 54	26	15	11	♦5.1	♦5.4	♦4.6
55 - 59	43	31	12	9.8	12.9	♦6.1
60 - 64	51	30	21	16.0	♦16.6	♦15.2
65 - 69	66	39	27	34.3	35.6	♦32.6
70 - 74	59	38	21	44.3	49.0	♦37.8
75 - 79	78	42	36	93.0	102.4	83.9
80 - 84	52	21	31	140.2	♦128.8	149.0
85 - 89	30	9	21	♦192.3	♦163.6	♦207.9
90 - 94	10	2	8	♦294.1	♦181.8	♦347.8
95 +	3	1	...	♦1000.0	♦333.3	...
95 - 99	3	1	2	...	...	...
100 +	-	-	-	...	...	...
Grenada - Grenade						
2014 (+C)						
Total	958	514	444	8.8	9.3	8.2
0 - 4	35	23	12	4.1	♦5.2	♦2.9
0	33	21	12	...	...	...
1 - 4	2	2	-	...	...	...
5 - 9	1	-	1	♦0.1	-	♦0.3
10 - 14	5	3	2	♦0.7	♦0.8	♦0.5
15 - 19	4	3	1	♦0.4	♦0.6	♦0.2
20 - 24	14	8	6	♦1.4	♦1.6	♦1.2
25 - 29	12	8	4	♦1.2	♦1.6	♦0.8
30 - 34	16	10	6	♦2.0	♦2.4	♦1.5
35 - 39	17	8	9	♦2.6	♦2.4	♦2.8
40 - 44	19	11	8	♦3.0	♦3.3	♦2.7
45 - 49	25	16	9	♦3.9	♦4.9	♦2.9
50 - 54	58	39	19	8.7	11.4	♦5.9
55 - 59	57	32	25	9.8	10.7	♦9.0
60 - 64	64	43	21	15.1	19.8	♦10.2
65 - 69	64	39	25	19.8	24.4	♦15.3
70 +	567	271	296	67.2	75.0	61.3
70 - 74	85	50	35	...	...	...
75 - 79	114	67	47	...	...	...
80 - 84	127	59	68	...	...	...
85 - 89	122	58	64	...	...	...
90 - 94	71	22	49	...	...	...
95 - 99	32	12	20	...	...	...
100 +	16	3	13	...	...	...

19. Deaths by age and sex and age-specific death rates by sex: latest available year, 2009 - 2018
Décès et taux de mortalité selon l'âge et le sexe : dernière année disponible, 2009 - 2018 (continued - suite)

Continent, country or area, date, code[a] and age (in years) Continent, pays ou zone, date, code[a] et âge (en années)	Number - Nombre			Rate - Taux		
	Both sexes Les deux sexes	Male Masculin	Female Féminin	Both sexes Les deux sexes	Male Masculin	Female Féminin
AMERICA, NORTH - AMÉRIQUE DU NORD						
Guadeloupe[17]						
2017 (C)						
Total	3 273	1 695	1 578	7.6	8.6	6.8
0 - 4	49	33	16	2.0	2.7	♦1.4
0	40	25	15	8.9	♦10.9	♦6.9
5 - 9	2	1	1	♦0.1	♦0.1	♦0.1
10 - 14	3	3	-	♦0.1	♦0.2	-
15 - 19	16	13	3	♦0.5	♦0.9	♦0.2
20 - 24	21	16	5	♦1.0	♦1.5	♦0.5
25 - 29	25	18	7	♦1.2	♦2.0	♦0.6
30 - 34	20	15	5	♦1.0	♦1.7	♦0.4
35 - 39	16	12	4	♦0.7	♦1.3	♦0.3
40 - 44	57	38	19	1.9	3.0	♦1.1
45 - 49	67	38	29	2.1	2.7	♦1.6
50 - 54	131	84	47	3.8	5.3	2.5
55 - 59	162	91	71	5.2	6.2	4.3
60 - 64	181	116	65	6.5	9.1	4.4
65 - 69	262	162	100	10.8	14.6	7.6
70 - 74	290	172	118	16.1	21.1	12.0
75 - 79	398	238	160	29.9	41.2	21.3
80 - 84	482	234	248	46.5	55.7	40.2
85 - 89	380	166	214	62.0	79.9	52.9
90 - 94	427	168	259	136.2	167.2	121.7
95 - 99	223	65	158	238.2	213.1	250.4
100 +	61	12	49	381.3	♦375.0	382.8
Guatemala						
2017 (C)						
Total	81 726	45 726	36 000	4.8	5.5	4.2
0	7 626	4 408	3 218	...	...	...
1 - 4	2 296	1 207	1 089	...	...	...
5 - 9	696	360	336	0.3	0.3	0.3
10 - 14	765	424	341	0.4	0.4	0.3
15 - 19	2 427	1 712	715	1.3	1.8	0.8
20 - 24	2 992	2 261	731	1.8	2.8	0.9
25 - 29	2 725	2 013	712	2.0	3.0	1.0
30 - 34	2 629	1 865	764	2.2	3.4	1.2
35 - 39	2 913	1 994	919	3.0	4.5	1.8
40 - 44	2 956	1 909	1 047	3.8	5.6	2.4
45 - 49	3 225	1 963	1 262	5.3	7.3	3.7
50 - 54	3 699	2 080	1 619	7.5	9.5	5.9
55 - 59	4 487	2 368	2 119	11.3	13.2	9.8
60 - 64	5 063	2 594	2 469	14.8	16.3	13.5
65 +	36 875	18 368	18 507	46.5	50.1	43.5
65 - 69	5 756	2 984	2 772	...	...	...
70 - 74	5 936	3 052	2 884	...	...	...
75 - 79	6 426	3 288	3 138	...	...	...
80 - 84	6 820	3 433	3 387	...	...	...
85 - 89	6 603	3 185	3 418	...	...	...
90 - 94	3 816	1 742	2 074	...	...	...
95 +	1 518	684	834	...	...	...
Unknown - Inconnu	352	200	152	..	..	..
Jamaica - Jamaïque[18]						
2011 (I)						
Total	21 001	10 061[10]	8 618[10]	7.8	7.6	6.3
0 - 4	361	187[10]	163[10]	1.6	1.7	1.5
5 - 9	118	53[10]	61[10]	0.5	0.4	0.5
10 - 14	128	74[10]	54[10]	0.5	0.5	0.4
15 - 19	382	288[10]	90[10]	1.5	2.3	0.7
20 - 24	521	423[10]	92[10]	2.5	4.2	0.9
25 - 29	515	367[10]	136[10]	2.4	3.6	1.2
30 - 34	451	304[10]	134[10]	2.0	2.9	1.1
35 - 39	557	319[10]	224[10]	2.4	3.0	1.8
40 - 44	609	329[10]	268[10]	3.1	3.3	2.7
45 - 49	631	324[10]	299[10]	4.7	4.8	4.4
50 - 54	749	418[10]	320[10]	6.4	6.8	5.7
55 - 59	702	367[10]	319[10]	8.1	8.1	7.8

Continent, country or area, date, code[a] and age (in years) / Continent, pays ou zone, date, code[a] et âge (en années)	Number - Nombre			Rate - Taux		
	Both sexes Les deux sexes	Male Masculin	Female Féminin	Both sexes Les deux sexes	Male Masculin	Female Féminin
AMERICA, NORTH - AMÉRIQUE DU NORD						
Jamaica - Jamaïque[18]						
2011 (I)						
60 - 64	1 003	501[10]	482[10]	14.6	14.9	13.7
65 - 69	1 031	554[10]	448[10]	15.7	17.5	13.2
70 - 74	1 343	700[10]	610[10]	22.4	24.6	19.3
75 +	9 932	4 853[10]	4 918[10]	94.6	115.9	77.9
75 - 79	1 567	805[10]	722[10]	...	...	...
80 - 84	1 721	876[10]	806[10]	...	...	...
85 - 89	3 057	1 259[10]	1 798[10]	...	...	...
90 +	3 505	1 913[10]	1 592[10]	...	...	...
Unknown - Inconnu	1 968	-[10]	-[10]	..	..	..
Martinique[17]						
2017 (C)						
Total	3 217	1 660	1 557	8.7	9.7	7.8
0 - 4	41	24	17	2.3	◆2.7	◆1.9
0	40	23	17	12.2	◆13.9	◆10.5
5 - 9	4	4	-	◆0.2	◆0.4	-
10 - 14	4	2	2	◆0.2	◆0.2	◆0.2
15 - 19	15	10	5	◆0.6	◆0.8	◆0.4
20 - 24	10	7	3	◆0.6	◆0.8	◆0.4
25 - 29	14	9	5	◆0.8	◆1.1	◆0.5
30 - 34	19	14	5	◆1.1	◆1.9	◆0.5
35 - 39	12	6	6	◆0.7	◆0.8	◆0.6
40 - 44	39	20	19	1.8	◆2.1	◆1.5
45 - 49	62	37	25	2.2	2.9	◆1.6
50 - 54	100	61	39	3.0	4.1	2.1
55 - 59	146	99	47	4.8	7.0	2.9
60 - 64	184	126	58	7.0	10.4	4.1
65 - 69	233	147	86	10.5	14.6	7.1
70 - 74	282	168	114	16.3	21.2	12.2
75 - 79	321	186	135	23.4	30.8	17.6
80 - 84	490	245	245	46.4	55.3	40.0
85 - 89	510	241	269	80.4	100.1	68.4
90 - 94	428	173	255	138.5	186.2	118.0
95 +	303	81	222	193.2	231.4	182.3
95 - 99	221	65	156	...	...	...
100 +	82	16	66	...	...	...
Mexico - Mexique[19]						
2017 (+C)						
Total	693 848	387 050[10]	306 675[10]	5.6	6.4	4.8
0	25 180	14 051[10]	11 043[10]	11.4	12.4	10.2
1 - 4	4 886	2 624[10]	2 260[10]	0.6	0.6	0.5
5 - 9	2 554	1 388[10]	1 166[10]	0.2	0.2	0.2
10 - 14	3 372	1 918[10]	1 454[10]	0.3	0.3	0.3
15 - 19	9 211	6 749[10]	2 462[10]	0.8	1.2	0.4
20 - 24	14 348	11 169[10]	3 179[10]	1.3	2.1	0.6
25 - 29	15 759	12 204[10]	3 555[10]	1.6	2.5	0.7
30 - 34	16 548	12 609[10]	3 938[10]	1.8	2.9	0.8
35 - 39	18 973	13 737[10]	5 236[10]	2.2	3.3	1.1
40 - 44	24 188	16 644[10]	7 543[10]	2.9	4.3	1.7
45 - 49	29 298	18 936[10]	10 362[10]	3.9	5.4	2.6
50 - 54	36 758	22 565[10]	14 193[10]	5.8	7.5	4.2
55 - 59	45 883	27 078[10]	18 805[10]	8.8	11.1	6.8
60 - 64	53 502	30 281[10]	23 218[10]	12.9	15.6	10.6
65 - 69	58 332	32 353[10]	25 978[10]	18.9	22.4	15.8
70 - 74	64 100	34 712[10]	29 387[10]	28.6	33.5	24.3
75 - 79	69 897	36 435[10]	33 462[10]	44.8	51.4	39.2
80 - 84	73 131	35 995[10]	37 135[10]	72.6	80.3	66.4
85 - 89	64 077	29 192[10]	34 885[10]	112.8	119.3	107.8
90 - 94	41 629	17 646[10]	23 983[10]	164.6	169.4	161.2
95 - 99	17 087	6 595[10]	10 491[10]	204.6	201.8	206.5
100 +	4 283	1 485[10]	2 798[10]	207.0	193.9	214.6
Unknown - Inconnu	852	684[10]	142[10]	..	..	..

19. Deaths by age and sex and age-specific death rates by sex: latest available year, 2009 - 2018
Décès et taux de mortalité selon l'âge et le sexe : dernière année disponible, 2009 - 2018 (continued - suite)

Continent, country or area, date, code[a] and age (in years) Continent, pays ou zone, date, code[a] et âge (en années)	Number - Nombre			Rate - Taux		
	Both sexes Les deux sexes	Male Masculin	Female Féminin	Both sexes Les deux sexes	Male Masculin	Female Féminin
AMERICA, NORTH - AMÉRIQUE DU NORD						
Montserrat						
2016 (C)						
Total	43	26	17	...	...	...
0	-	-	-	...	...	...
1 - 4	-	-	-	...	...	...
5 - 9	-	-	-	...	...	...
10 - 14	-	-	-	...	...	...
15 - 19	-	-	-	...	...	...
20 - 24	1	-	1	...	...	...
25 - 29	1	1	-	...	...	...
30 - 34	-	-	-	...	...	...
35 - 39	-	-	-	...	...	...
40 - 44	-	-	-	...	...	...
45 - 49	-	-	-	...	...	...
50 - 54	1	-	1	...	...	...
55 - 59	-	-	-	...	...	...
60 - 64	3	2	1	...	...	...
65 - 69	7	4	3	...	...	...
70 - 74	7	7	-	...	...	...
75 - 79	1	1	-	...	...	...
80 - 84	8	3	5	...	...	...
85 - 89	5	4	1	...	...	...
90 +	9	4	5	...	...	...
Nicaragua						
2010 (+U)						
Total	19 944	11 416	8 528	...	...	...
0	1 891	1 077	814	...	...	...
1 - 4	252	155	97	...	...	...
5 - 9	155	86	69	...	...	...
10 - 14	182	95	87	...	...	...
15 - 19	458	313	145	...	...	...
20 - 24	564	428	136	...	...	...
25 - 29	672	514	158	...	...	...
30 - 34	615	458	157	...	...	...
35 - 39	697	491	206	...	...	...
40 - 44	758	495	263	...	...	...
45 - 49	843	540	303	...	...	...
50 - 54	997	594	403	...	...	...
55 - 59	1 166	693	473	...	...	...
60 - 64	1 258	704	554	...	...	...
65 - 69	1 385	787	598	...	...	...
70 - 74	1 584	863	721	...	...	...
75 - 79	1 740	931	809	...	...	...
80 +	4 727	2 192	2 535	...	...	...
Panama						
2017* (C)						
Total	19 482	11 096	8 386	4.8	5.4	4.1
0	1 063	590	473	14.3	15.5	13.0
1 - 4	263	141	122	0.9	0.9	0.8
5 - 9	104	53	51	0.3	0.3	0.3
10 - 14	113	74	39	0.3	0.4	0.2
15 - 19	241	183	58	0.7	1.0	0.3
20 - 24	378	288	90	1.1	1.7	0.5
25 - 29	423	313	110	1.3	2.0	0.7
30 - 34	392	273	119	1.3	1.8	0.8
35 - 39	378	231	147	1.3	1.6	1.0
40 - 44	470	282	188	1.7	2.0	1.4
45 - 49	685	416	269	2.7	3.3	2.1
50 - 54	802	488	314	3.7	4.5	2.9
55 - 59	990	606	384	5.4	6.7	4.1
60 - 64	1 184	745	439	8.3	10.7	6.0
65 - 69	1 463	879	584	13.4	16.7	10.3
70 - 74	1 764	1 054	710	21.4	27.0	16.3
75 - 79	1 984	1 159	825	33.5	42.2	26.0
80 - 84	2 113	1 169	944	54.3	66.5	44.2
85 - 89	2 090	1 068	1 022	93.3	109.1	81.0
90 - 94	1 515	664	851	143.6	149.7	139.1

Continent, country or area, date, code[a] and age (in years)	Number - Nombre			Rate - Taux		
Continent, pays ou zone, date, code[a] et âge (en années)	Both sexes Les deux sexes	Male Masculin	Female Féminin	Both sexes Les deux sexes	Male Masculin	Female Féminin
AMERICA, NORTH - AMÉRIQUE DU NORD						
Panama						
2017* (C)						
95 - 99	785	311	474	214.3	210.0	217.2
100 +	251	88	163	361.2	322.3	386.3
Unknown - Inconnu	31	21	10	..	..	..
Puerto Rico - Porto Rico						
2018 (C)						
Total	29 060	15 885	13 175	...	...	...
0	142	82	60	...	...	...
1 - 4	22	13	9	...	...	...
5 - 9	8	4	4	...	...	...
10 - 14	24	9	15	...	...	...
15 - 19	88	70	18	...	...	...
20 - 24	264	224	40	...	...	...
25 - 29	274	246	28	...	...	...
30 - 34	330	251	79	...	...	...
35 - 39	383	287	96	...	...	...
40 - 44	514	377	137	...	...	...
45 - 49	638	437	201	...	...	...
50 - 54	950	616	334	...	...	...
55 - 59	1 361	917	444	...	...	...
60 - 64	1 856	1 201	655	...	...	...
65 - 69	2 517	1 537	980	...	...	...
70 - 74	3 179	1 856	1 323	...	...	...
75 - 79	3 693	2 058	1 635	...	...	...
80 - 84	4 095	2 111	1 984	...	...	...
85 - 89	4 041	1 814	2 227	...	...	...
90 - 94	2 937	1 186	1 751	...	...	...
95 - 99	1 361	484	877	...	...	...
100 +	374	97	277	...	...	...
Unknown - Inconnu	9	8	1	..	..	..
Saint Pierre and Miquelon - Saint Pierre-et-Miquelon						
2014 (C)						
Total	50	21	29	...	...	...
0	-	-	-	...	...	...
1 - 4	-	-	-	...	...	...
5 - 9	-	-	-	...	...	...
10 - 14	-	-	-	...	...	...
15 - 19	-	-	-	...	...	...
20 - 24	-	-	-	...	...	...
25 - 29	-	-	-	...	...	...
30 - 34	-	-	-	...	...	...
35 - 39	-	-	-	...	...	...
40 - 44	2	1	1	...	...	...
45 - 49	-	-	-	...	...	...
50 - 54	-	-	-	...	...	...
55 - 59	3	2	1	...	...	...
60 - 64	5	4	1	...	...	...
65 - 69	7	4	3	...	...	...
70 - 74	4	3	1	...	...	...
75 - 79	3	1	2	...	...	...
80 - 84	7	3	4	...	...	...
85 - 89	3	1	2	...	...	...
90 - 94	9	2	7	...	...	...
95 - 99	5	-	5	...	...	...
100 +	2	-	2	...	...	...
Saint Vincent and the Grenadines - Saint-Vincent-et-les Grenadines						
2016 (C)						
Total	930	507	423	8.4	9.0	7.9
0	25	11	14	♦15.8	♦13.8	♦17.9
1 - 4	2	2	-	♦0.3	♦0.6	-
5 - 9	3	2	1	♦0.3	♦0.5	♦0.2
10 - 14	3	3	-	♦0.3	♦0.6	-
15 - 19	10	8	2	♦1.0	♦1.6	♦0.4
20 - 24	12	7	5	♦1.4	♦1.6	♦1.2
25 - 29	16	11	5	♦1.9	♦2.6	♦1.2

19. Deaths by age and sex and age-specific death rates by sex: latest available year, 2009 - 2018
Décès et taux de mortalité selon l'âge et le sexe : dernière année disponible, 2009 - 2018 (continued - suite)

Continent, country or area, date, code[a] and age (in years) / Continent, pays ou zone, date, code[a] et âge (en années)	Number - Nombre			Rate - Taux		
	Both sexes Les deux sexes	Male Masculin	Female Féminin	Both sexes Les deux sexes	Male Masculin	Female Féminin
AMERICA, NORTH - AMÉRIQUE DU NORD						
Saint Vincent and the Grenadines - Saint-Vincent-et-les Grenadines						
2016 (C)						
30 - 34	21	15	6	◆2.6	◆3.8	◆1.5
35 - 39	21	12	9	◆2.8	◆3.1	◆2.4
40 - 44	29	20	9	◆4.0	◆5.2	◆2.7
45 - 49	29	17	12	◆3.8	◆4.3	◆3.3
50 - 54	62	36	26	9.4	10.3	◆8.3
55 - 59	81	52	29	15.9	19.3	◆12.1
60 - 64	75	45	30	19.4	22.4	◆16.2
65 - 69	88	59	29	30.6	39.7	◆20.9
70 - 74	75	40	35	29.3	30.6	27.9
75 - 79	99	47	52	49.5	47.9	51.1
80 - 84	95	44	51	65.2	65.1	65.3
85 +	183	75	108	152.2	153.4	151.4
Unknown - Inconnu	1	1	-	-	..	..
Saint-Barthélemy						
2014 (C)						
Total	53	30	23	...	...	...
0	-	-	-	...	...	...
1 - 4	-	-	-	...	...	...
5 - 9	-	-	-	...	...	...
10 - 14	-	-	-	...	...	...
15 - 19	-	-	-	...	...	...
20 - 24	1	1	-	...	...	...
25 - 29	-	-	-	...	...	...
30 - 34	-	-	-	...	...	...
35 - 39	1	1	-	...	...	...
40 - 44	1	-	1	...	...	...
45 - 49	1	1	-	...	...	...
50 - 54	5	2	3	...	...	...
55 - 59	4	3	1	...	...	...
60 - 64	3	2	1	...	...	...
65 - 69	6	4	2	...	...	...
70 - 74	4	2	2	...	...	...
75 - 79	9	6	3	...	...	...
80 - 84	5	2	3	...	...	...
85 - 89	4	2	2	...	...	...
90 - 94	6	2	4	...	...	...
95 - 99	3	2	1	...	...	...
100 +	-	-	-	...	...	...
Saint-Martin (French part) - Saint-Martin (partie française)						
2014 (C)						
Total	161	97	64	4.5	5.7	3.5
0	5	3	2	...	...	...
1 - 4	-	-	-			
5 - 9	2	2	-	◆0.9	◆1.8	-
10 - 14	1	1	-	◆0.5	◆0.9	-
15 - 19	4	4	-	◆1.9	◆3.7	-
20 - 24	3	2	1	◆1.5	◆1.9	◆1.0
25 - 29	1	1	-	◆0.5	◆1.0	-
30 - 34	4	1	3	◆1.8	◆0.9	◆2.7
35 - 39	4	4	-	◆1.8	◆3.7	-
40 - 44	6	6	-	◆2.5	◆4.9	-
45 - 49	11	6	5	◆4.6	◆5.0	◆4.1
50 - 54	13	7	6	◆5.5	◆6.0	◆4.9
55 - 59	13	8	5	◆5.8	◆7.3	◆4.3
60 - 64	15	10	5	◆6.8	◆9.5	◆4.4
65 - 69	12	9	3	◆6.2	◆9.8	◆3.0
70 - 74	6	4	2	◆4.6	◆6.7	◆2.9
75 - 79	19	10	9	◆15.9	◆19.5	◆13.3
80 - 84	14	5	9	◆13.9	◆12.7	◆14.6
85 - 89	14	9	5	◆21.2	◆40.7	◆11.4
90 - 94	11	4	7	◆35.5	◆47.6	◆31.0
95 - 99	2	1	1	◆39.2	◆90.9	◆25.0
100 +	1	-	1	◆90.9	-	◆100.0

19. Deaths by age and sex and age-specific death rates by sex: latest available year, 2009 - 2018
Décès et taux de mortalité selon l'âge et le sexe : dernière année disponible, 2009 - 2018 (continued - suite)

Continent, country or area, date, code[a] and age (in years) / Continent, pays ou zone, date, code[a] et âge (en années)	Number - Nombre			Rate - Taux		
	Both sexes Les deux sexes	Male Masculin	Female Féminin	Both sexes Les deux sexes	Male Masculin	Female Féminin
AMERICA, NORTH - AMÉRIQUE DU NORD						
Trinidad and Tobago - Trinité-et-Tobago						
2011* (C)						
Total	9 435	5 441	3 994	7.1	8.2	6.0
0	252	150	102	15.0	17.4	12.5
1 - 4	33	20	13	0.4	◆0.5	◆0.3
5 - 9	22	12	10	◆0.2	◆0.3	◆0.2
10 - 14	26	13	13	◆0.3	◆0.3	◆0.3
15 - 19	93	70	23	0.9	1.4	◆0.5
20 - 24	183	153	30	1.6	2.7	◆0.5
25 - 29	230	163	67	1.9	2.6	1.1
30 - 34	229	163	66	2.2	3.0	1.3
35 - 39	232	139	93	2.5	3.0	2.0
40 - 44	281	173	108	3.3	4.0	2.5
45 - 49	443	273	170	4.6	5.6	3.6
50 - 54	607	382	225	7.0	8.7	5.2
55 - 59	737	456	281	10.1	12.4	7.7
60 - 64	841	524	317	14.3	17.7	10.9
65 - 69	948	572	376	21.2	26.5	16.3
70 - 74	988	586	402	32.6	41.3	25.0
75 - 79	939	518	421	45.3	55.8	36.7
80 - 84	868	426	442	68.5	79.5	60.4
85 +	1 475	642	833	138.3	159.8	125.3
Unknown - Inconnu	8	6	2	..	..	..
Turks and Caicos Islands - Îles Turques et Caïques[20]						
2018* (C)						
Total	103	60	43	...	...	...
0	-	-	-	...	...	...
1 - 4	-	-	-	...	...	...
5 - 9	-	-	-	...	...	...
10 - 14	-	-	-	...	...	...
15 - 19	2	1	1	...	...	...
20 - 24	4	2	2	...	...	...
25 - 29	9	9	-	...	...	...
30 - 34	4	3	1	...	...	...
35 - 39	2	2	-	...	...	...
40 - 44	9	5	4	...	...	...
45 - 49	11	8	3	...	...	...
50 - 54	7	2	5	...	...	...
55 - 59	4	3	1	...	...	...
60 - 64	6	1	5	...	...	...
65 - 69	6	3	3	...	...	...
70 - 74	8	6	2	...	...	...
75 - 79	11	8	3	...	...	...
80 - 84	7	3	4	...	...	...
85 +	13	4	9	...	...	...
United States of America - États-Unis d'Amérique						
2015 (C)						
Total	2 712 630	1 373 404	1 339 226	8.4	8.7	8.2
0	23 455	13 008	10 447	5.9	6.4	5.4
1 - 4	3 965	2 281	1 684	0.2	0.3	0.2
5 - 9	2 402	1 377	1 025	0.1	0.1	0.1
10 - 14	3 009	1 776	1 233	0.1	0.2	0.1
15 - 19	10 186	7 187	2 999	0.5	0.7	0.3
20 - 24	20 308	15 159	5 149	0.9	1.3	0.5
25 - 29	23 898	17 173	6 725	1.1	1.5	0.6
30 - 34	27 619	18 608	9 011	1.3	1.7	0.8
35 - 39	31 417	20 190	11 227	1.5	2.0	1.1
40 - 44	41 671	25 480	16 191	2.1	2.5	1.6
45 - 49	64 377	38 807	25 570	3.1	3.8	2.4
50 - 54	110 117	66 740	43 377	4.9	6.1	3.8
55 - 59	159 589	97 172	62 417	7.3	9.2	5.6
60 - 64	198 196	120 454	77 742	10.4	13.2	7.8
65 - 69	235 482	137 630	97 852	14.7	18.1	11.6
70 - 74	259 534	144 717	114 817	22.6	27.3	18.6
75 - 79	290 405	153 719	136 686	35.7	42.6	30.3
80 - 84	347 161	170 127	177 034	59.9	70.5	52.3
85 - 89	390 747	168 932	221 815	101.1	117.1	91.6

19. Deaths by age and sex and age-specific death rates by sex: latest available year, 2009 - 2018
Décès et taux de mortalité selon l'âge et le sexe : dernière année disponible, 2009 - 2018 (continued - suite)

Continent, country or area, date, code[a] and age (in years) / Continent, pays ou zone, date, code[a] et âge (en années)	Number - Nombre			Rate - Taux		
	Both sexes Les deux sexes	Male Masculin	Female Féminin	Both sexes Les deux sexes	Male Masculin	Female Féminin
AMERICA, NORTH - AMÉRIQUE DU NORD						
United States of America - États-Unis d'Amérique						
2015 (C)						
90 - 94	313 796	112 676	201 120	169.5	191.3	159.4
95 - 99	127 628	35 157	92 471	257.9	274.7	252.0
100 +	27 530	4 939	22 591	357.7	327.3	365.0
Unknown - Inconnu	138	95	43	..	..	..
AMERICA, SOUTH - AMÉRIQUE DU SUD						
Argentina - Argentine						
2017 (C)						
Total	341 688	174 221[10]	166 731[10]	7.8	8.1	7.4
0	6 579	3 629[10]	2 938[10]	8.8	9.4	8.1
1 - 4	1 194	651[10]	539[10]	0.4	0.4	0.4
5 - 9	725	410[10]	315[10]	0.2	0.2	0.2
10 - 14	837	476[10]	361[10]	0.2	0.3	0.2
15 - 19	2 457	1 710[10]	741[10]	0.7	1.0	0.4
20 - 24	3 559	2 682[10]	871[10]	1.0	1.5	0.5
25 - 29	3 360	2 371[10]	979[10]	1.0	1.4	0.6
30 - 34	3 550	2 357[10]	1 187[10]	1.1	1.5	0.7
35 - 39	4 586	2 883[10]	1 691[10]	1.5	1.9	1.1
40 - 44	5 706	3 474[10]	2 226[10]	2.0	2.5	1.5
45 - 49	7 603	4 605[10]	2 981[10]	3.1	3.9	2.4
50 - 54	10 751	6 669[10]	4 060[10]	4.9	6.3	3.6
55 - 59	16 067	9 918[10]	6 126[10]	7.9	10.2	5.8
60 - 64	23 476	14 474[10]	8 953[10]	12.8	16.8	9.2
65 - 69	30 902	18 977[10]	11 869[10]	19.6	26.4	13.9
70 - 74	36 869	21 656[10]	15 142[10]	29.9	40.2	21.8
75 - 79	41 320	22 355[10]	18 898[10]	46.2	61.6	35.6
80 - 84	46 478	21 789[10]	24 597[10]	76.6	98.2	63.9
85 +	93 729	32 102[10]	61 438[10]	168.4	195.2	156.7
Unknown - Inconnu	1 940	1 033[10]	819[10]	..	..	..
Bolivia (Plurinational State of) - Bolivie (État plurinational de)[21]						
2012 (|)						
Total	127 050	59 027	68 023	12.6	11.8	13.5
0	5 363	2 406	2 957	26.6	23.4	29.9
1 - 4	6 695	3 085	3 610	7.5	6.8	8.3
5 - 9	2 531	1 183	1 348	2.5	2.3	2.8
10 - 14	1 961	827	1 134	1.8	1.5	2.1
15 - 19	3 699	1 460	2 239	3.3	2.6	4.1
20 - 24	4 767	1 618	3 149	4.9	3.3	6.5
25 - 29	4 089	1 393	2 696	5.0	3.4	6.6
30 - 34	4 323	1 556	2 767	5.7	4.2	7.3
35 - 39	4 670	1 868	2 802	7.4	6.0	8.7
40 - 44	4 597	1 849	2 748	8.4	6.8	10.0
45 - 49	5 769	2 483	3 286	12.5	10.9	14.0
50 - 54	6 298	2 849	3 449	15.6	14.3	16.9
55 - 59	6 851	2 946	3 905	21.1	18.5	23.7
60 - 64	9 105	4 256	4 849	32.5	31.7	33.3
65 - 69	9 801	4 792	5 009	47.9	48.8	47.1
70 - 74	9 701	4 649	5 052	63.6	64.7	62.7
75 - 79	9 798	4 756	5 042	98.7	105.7	92.9
80 - 84	11 190	5 952	5 238	138.0	172.7	112.3
85 - 89	8 493	4 674	3 819	224.0	294.3	173.3
90 - 94	3 927	2 332	1 595	267.8	388.9	184.0
95 +	3 422	2 093	1 329	415.6	633.3	269.6
Brazil - Brésil						
2017 (+C)						
Total	1 277 579[22]	714 528[10]	562 577[10]	6.2	7.0	5.3
0	30 636[22]	16 753[10]	13 779[10]	10.9	11.7	10.1
1 - 4	5 516[22]	3 004[10]	2 508[10]	0.5	0.5	0.4
5 - 9	3 062[22]	1 795[10]	1 267[10]	0.2	0.2	0.2
10 - 14	4 388[22]	2 687[10]	1 701[10]	0.3	0.3	0.2

Continent, country or area, date, code[a] and age (in years) Continent, pays ou zone, date, code[a] et âge (en années)	Number - Nombre			Rate - Taux		
	Both sexes Les deux sexes	Male Masculin	Female Féminin	Both sexes Les deux sexes	Male Masculin	Female Féminin
AMERICA, SOUTH - AMÉRIQUE DU SUD						
Brazil - Brésil						
2017 (+C)						
15 - 19	20 082[22]	16 529[10]	3 546[10]	1.2	1.9	0.4
20 - 24	27 498[22]	23 105[10]	4 386[10]	1.6	2.7	0.5
25 - 29	25 585[22]	20 397[10]	5 182[10]	1.5	2.4	0.6
30 - 34	28 339[22]	20 987[10]	7 346[10]	1.6	2.4	0.8
35 - 39	33 317[22]	23 039[10]	10 271[10]	2.0	2.8	1.2
40 - 44	38 192[22]	25 286[10]	12 903[10]	2.6	3.5	1.8
45 - 49	48 759[22]	31 139[10]	17 617[10]	3.7	4.9	2.6
50 - 54	66 216[22]	41 845[10]	24 366[10]	5.5	7.2	3.9
55 - 59	84 208[22]	52 132[10]	32 065[10]	8.1	10.4	5.9
60 - 64	103 303[22]	62 634[10]	40 657[10]	12.3	15.9	9.1
65 - 69	116 441[22]	68 697[10]	47 734[10]	18.2	23.5	13.8
70 - 74	125 124[22]	70 133[10]	54 979[10]	28.0	35.5	22.0
75 - 79	136 631[22]	71 852[10]	64 763[10]	44.3	55.5	36.2
80 - 84	137 690[22]	65 906[10]	71 767[10]	70.4	85.2	60.8
85 - 89	122 817[22]	52 132[10]	70 670[10]	117.1	134.2	107.0
90 +	116 311[22]	41 918[10]	74 363[10]	188.7	211.3	177.9
90 - 94	76 538[22]	29 058[10]	47 469[10]	...	...	...
95 - 99	30 338[22]	10 062[10]	20 266[10]	...	...	...
100 +	9 435[22]	2 798[10]	6 628[10]	...	...	...
Unknown - Inconnu	3 464[22]	2 558[10]	707[10]	..	..	..
Chile - Chili						
2016 (C)						
Total	104 026	54 761[10]	49 239[10]	5.7	6.1	5.4
0	1 629	873[10]	730[10]	6.5	6.9	6.0
1 - 4	250	124[10]	126[10]	0.3	0.2	0.3
5 - 9	165	88[10]	77[10]	0.1	0.1	0.1
10 - 14	195	103[10]	92[10]	0.2	0.2	0.1
15 - 19	568	387[10]	181[10]	0.4	0.6	0.2
20 - 24	910	668[10]	242[10]	0.6	0.9	0.3
25 - 29	1 038	802[10]	236[10]	0.7	1.0	0.3
30 - 34	1 165	851[10]	314[10]	0.8	1.2	0.5
35 - 39	1 414	1 009[10]	405[10]	1.1	1.6	0.6
40 - 44	2 060	1 402[10]	658[10]	1.7	2.3	1.1
45 - 49	2 777	1 779[10]	998[10]	2.2	2.9	1.6
50 - 54	4 382	2 780[10]	1 602[10]	3.5	4.6	2.6
55 - 59	5 674	3 500[10]	2 174[10]	5.2	6.6	3.9
60 - 64	7 186	4 391[10]	2 795[10]	8.4	10.6	6.3
65 - 69	8 973	5 422[10]	3 551[10]	13.5	17.3	10.1
70 - 74	11 086	6 344[10]	4 742[10]	21.8	27.6	17.0
75 - 79	12 550	6 832[10]	5 718[10]	35.3	45.2	28.0
80 +	42 004	17 406[10]	24 598[10]	104.8	123.7	94.6
80 - 84	13 955	6 887[10]	7 068[10]	...	...	...
85 - 89	14 531	6 205[10]	8 326[10]	...	...	...
90 - 94	9 048	3 130[10]	5 918[10]	...	...	...
95 - 99	3 580	1 033[10]	2 547[10]	...	...	...
100 +	890	151[10]	739[10]	...	...	...
Colombia - Colombie						
2017 (U)						
Total	227 624	125 450[10]	102 119[10]	...	...	...
0	7 044	3 986[10]	3 050[10]	...	...	...
1 - 4	1 504	871[10]	633[10]	...	...	...
5 - 9	866	506[10]	359[10]	...	...	...
10 - 14	1 103	638[10]	465[10]	...	...	...
15 - 19	3 765	2 921[10]	842[10]	...	...	...
20 - 24	5 653	4 573[10]	1 079[10]	...	...	...
25 - 29	5 548	4 339[10]	1 208[10]	...	...	...
30 - 34	5 223	3 873[10]	1 349[10]	...	...	...
35 - 39	5 231	3 541[10]	1 688[10]	...	...	...
40 - 44	5 308	3 334[10]	1 968[10]	...	...	...
45 - 49	6 804	4 064[10]	2 739[10]	...	...	...
50 - 54	9 208	5 408[10]	3 793[10]	...	...	...
55 - 59	12 042	6 975[10]	5 067[10]	...	...	...

Continent, country or area, date, code[a] and age (in years) / Continent, pays ou zone, date, code[a] et âge (en années)	Number - Nombre			Rate - Taux		
	Both sexes / Les deux sexes	Male / Masculin	Female / Féminin	Both sexes / Les deux sexes	Male / Masculin	Female / Féminin

AMERICA, SOUTH - AMÉRIQUE DU SUD

Colombia - Colombie
2017 (U)

60 - 64	15 253	8 835[10]	6 415[10]	...	...	...
65 - 69	17 891	10 293[10]	7 597[10]	...	...	...
70 - 74	20 565	11 565[10]	8 996[10]	...	...	...
75 - 79	25 714	13 869[10]	11 844[10]	...	...	...
80 - 84	28 107	13 964[10]	14 142[10]	...	...	...
85 - 89	26 293	12 066[10]	14 227[10]	...	...	...
90 - 94	16 378	6 852[10]	9 526[10]	...	...	...
95 - 99	6 551	2 421[10]	4 127[10]	...	...	...
100 +	1 547	541[10]	1 000[10]	...	...	...
Unknown - Inconnu	26	15[10]	5[10]	...	...	...

Ecuador - Équateur[23]
2017 (U)

Total	69 247	37 997	31 250	...	...	...
0	3 252	1 792	1 460	...	...	...
1 - 4	711	404	307	...	...	...
5 - 9	415	231	184	...	...	...
10 - 14	507	286	221	...	...	...
15 - 19	1 079	722	357	...	...	...
20 - 24	1 560	1 176	384	...	...	...
25 - 29	1 578	1 197	381	...	...	...
30 - 34	1 569	1 101	468	...	...	...
35 - 39	1 689	1 153	536	...	...	...
40 - 44	1 736	1 084	652	...	...	...
45 - 49	2 153	1 291	862	...	...	...
50 - 54	2 765	1 615	1 150	...	...	...
55 - 59	3 548	2 042	1 506	...	...	...
60 - 64	4 328	2 488	1 840	...	...	...
65 - 69	5 029	2 858	2 171	...	...	...
70 - 74	5 846	3 220	2 626	...	...	...
75 - 79	6 700	3 643	3 057	...	...	...
80 - 84	7 602	3 918	3 684	...	...	...
85 - 89	7 834	3 801	4 033	...	...	...
90 - 94	5 812	2 601	3 211	...	...	...
95 - 99	2 721	1 063	1 658	...	...	...
100 +	811	309	502	...	...	...
Unknown - Inconnu	2	2	...	...	...	...

French Guiana - Guyane française[17]
2017 (C)

Total	964	546	418	3.5	4.0	3.0
0	84	48	36	13.2	14.8	11.5
1 - 4	11	5	6	♦0.4	♦0.4	♦0.5
5 - 9	-	-	-	-	-	-
10 - 14	7	2	5	♦0.2	♦0.1	♦0.3
15 - 19	15	8	7	♦0.6	♦0.6	♦0.5
20 - 24	10	7	3	♦0.5	♦0.8	♦0.3
25 - 29	21	13	8	♦1.1	♦1.5	♦0.8
30 - 34	13	9	4	♦0.7	♦1.0	♦0.4
35 - 39	34	20	14	1.7	♦2.1	♦1.4
40 - 44	41	25	16	2.2	♦2.8	♦1.7
45 - 49	48	27	21	2.9	♦3.2	♦2.6
50 - 54	48	36	12	3.7	5.5	♦1.8
55 - 59	64	44	20	6.0	8.3	♦3.8
60 - 64	78	42	36	9.0	9.4	8.5
65 - 69	84	49	35	14.5	16.8	12.1
70 - 74	85	54	31	23.1	28.9	17.1
75 - 79	78	52	26	40.3	58.6	♦24.8
80 - 84	75	37	38	57.2	71.0	48.1
85 - 89	81	39	42	101.8	130.4	84.5
90 - 94	57	22	35	158.8	♦258.8	127.7
95 - 99	24	5	19	♦164.4	♦151.5	♦168.1
100 +	5	2	3	♦108.7	♦90.9	♦125.0
Unknown - Inconnu	1	-	1	..	..	..

Continent, country or area, date, codeᵃ and age (in years) / Continent, pays ou zone, date, codeᵃ et âge (en années)	Number - Nombre			Rate - Taux		
	Both sexes Les deux sexes	Male Masculin	Female Féminin	Both sexes Les deux sexes	Male Masculin	Female Féminin
AMERICA, SOUTH - AMÉRIQUE DU SUD						
Paraguay						
2018 (+U)						
Total	29 139	16 575[10]	12 513[10]	...	...	...
0	490	283[10]	205[10]	...	...	...
1 - 4	166	99[10]	67[10]	...	...	...
5 - 9	119	66[10]	53[10]	...	...	...
10 - 14	147	83[10]	63[10]	...	...	...
15 - 19	414	285[10]	128[10]	...	...	...
20 - 24	586	446[10]	138[10]	...	...	...
25 - 29	564	411[10]	153[10]	...	...	...
30 - 34	547	363[10]	183[10]	...	...	...
35 - 39	661	431[10]	228[10]	...	...	...
40 - 44	749	464[10]	285[10]	...	...	...
45 - 49	1 022	655[10]	366[10]	...	...	...
50 - 54	1 416	900[10]	514[10]	...	...	...
55 - 59	1 918	1 249[10]	668[10]	...	...	...
60 - 64	2 315	1 477[10]	834[10]	...	...	...
65 - 69	2 635	1 596[10]	1 037[10]	...	...	...
70 - 74	2 926	1 726[10]	1 195[10]	...	...	...
75 - 79	3 214	1 781[10]	1 426[10]	...	...	...
80 - 84	3 119	1 601[10]	1 509[10]	...	...	...
85 +	6 062	2 621[10]	3 434[10]	...	...	...
Unknown - Inconnu	69	38[10]	27[10]	..	..	...
Peru - Pérou[24]						
2017* (+U)						
Total	121 024	63 579[10]	56 737[10]	...	...	...
0	5 274	2 926	2 348	...	...	...
1 - 4	1 276	716	560	...	...	...
5 - 9	721	417	304	...	...	...
10 - 14	703	375	328	...	...	...
15 - 19	1 294	786	508	...	...	...
20 - 24	1 922	1 287	635	...	...	...
25 - 29	1 962	1 357	605	...	...	...
30 - 34	2 196	1 463	733	...	...	...
35 - 39	2 562	1 622	940	...	...	...
40 - 44	3 143	1 871	1 272	...	...	...
45 - 49	3 801	2 139	1 662	...	...	...
50 - 54	4 823	2 708	2 115	...	...	...
55 - 59	5 816	3 258	2 558	...	...	...
60 - 64	7 185	3 964	3 221	...	...	...
65 - 69	8 762	4 636	4 126	...	...	...
70 - 74	11 089	5 921	5 168	...	...	...
75 - 79	13 082	6 946	6 136	...	...	...
80 - 84	15 729	8 042	7 687	...	...	...
85 - 89	14 777	7 119	7 658	...	...	...
90 - 94	9 694	4 271	5 423	...	...	...
95 - 99	3 673	1 462	2 211	...	...	...
100 +	832	293	539	...	...	...
Unknown - Inconnu	708	_[10]	_[10]	..	..	..
Suriname						
2017 (C)						
Total	3 508	1 941	1 567	6.0	6.7	5.4
0	199	122	77	20.3	24.3	16.1
1 - 4	29	13	16	♦0.7	♦0.6	♦0.7
5 - 9	24	14	10	♦0.5	♦0.5	♦0.4
10 - 14	14	4	10	♦0.3	♦0.2	♦0.4
15 - 19	32	17	15	0.7	♦0.7	♦0.6
20 - 24	65	44	21	1.4	1.9	♦0.9
25 - 29	66	41	25	1.5	1.8	♦1.1
30 - 34	80	48	32	1.8	2.2	1.5
35 - 39	108	61	47	2.6	3.0	2.3
40 - 44	104	62	42	2.7	3.2	2.2
45 - 49	157	99	58	4.3	5.4	3.2
50 - 54	224	148	76	6.8	9.1	4.6
55 - 59	314	195	119	11.1	14.1	8.2
60 - 64	300	180	120	13.1	16.4	10.1

Continent, country or area, date, code[a] and age (in years) Continent, pays ou zone, date, code[a] et âge (en années)	Number - Nombre			Rate - Taux		
	Both sexes Les deux sexes	Male Masculin	Female Féminin	Both sexes Les deux sexes	Male Masculin	Female Féminin
AMERICA, SOUTH - AMÉRIQUE DU SUD						
Suriname						
2017 (C)						
65 - 69	319	183	136	18.7	22.9	14.9
70 - 74	334	176	158	26.9	31.4	23.2
75 - 79	349	187	162	43.1	53.4	35.2
80 +	790	347	443	96.3	105.2	90.4
80 - 84	321	162	159	...	...	...
85 - 89	280	114	166	...	...	...
90 - 94	133	49	84	...	...	...
95 - 99	43	16	27	...	...	...
100 +	13	6	7	...	...	...
Uruguay						
2016 (C)						
Total	34 273	17 212[10]	17 050[10]	9.8	10.2	9.5
0	376	219[10]	156[10]	8.2	9.4	7.0
1 - 4	52	34[10]	18[10]	0.3	0.4	♦0.2
5 - 9	33	18[10]	15[10]	0.1	♦0.1	♦0.1
10 - 14	36	24[10]	12[10]	0.1	♦0.2	♦0.1
15 - 19	169	129[10]	40[10]	0.6	0.9	0.3
20 - 24	268	200[10]	68[10]	1.0	1.5	0.5
25 - 29	246	196[10]	50[10]	1.0	1.5	0.4
30 - 34	276	193[10]	83[10]	1.2	1.6	0.7
35 - 39	347	210[10]	137[10]	1.4	1.8	1.1
40 - 44	446	287[10]	159[10]	1.9	2.5	1.4
45 - 49	591	366[10]	225[10]	2.8	3.6	2.1
50 - 54	1 039	688[10]	351[10]	5.1	7.0	3.3
55 - 59	1 506	930[10]	576[10]	7.7	10.0	5.6
60 - 64	2 268	1 425[10]	842[10]	13.4	18.1	9.3
65 - 69	2 764	1 789[10]	975[10]	19.5	28.0	12.5
70 - 74	3 527	2 100[10]	1 427[10]	29.9	41.5	21.2
75 - 79	4 291	2 301[10]	1 990[10]	45.9	62.0	35.3
80 - 84	5 244	2 467[10]	2 776[10]	74.9	98.6	61.7
85 - 89	5 429	2 086[10]	3 340[10]	125.4	153.3	112.5
90 +	5 082	1 438[10]	3 644[10]	225.5	242.1	219.6
90 - 94	3 498	1 090[10]	2 408[10]	...	...	...
95 - 99	1 584	348[10]	1 236[10]	...	...	...
Unknown - Inconnu	283	112[10]	166[10]	..	..	..
Venezuela (Bolivarian Republic of) - Venezuela (République bolivarienne du)						
2017 (C)						
Total	190 236	113 648	76 588	6.1	7.2	4.9
0	13 873	7 875	5 998	25.7	28.3	23.0
1 - 4	1 957	1 040	917	0.9	0.9	0.9
5 - 9	909	518	391	0.3	0.4	0.3
10 - 14	1 170	742	428	0.4	0.5	0.3
15 - 19	4 612	3 769	843	1.7	2.7	0.6
20 - 24	7 957	6 879	1 078	3.0	5.1	0.8
25 - 29	7 168	5 924	1 244	2.8	4.5	1.0
30 - 34	6 068	4 669	1 399	2.4	3.7	1.1
35 - 39	5 832	4 090	1 742	2.6	3.6	1.5
40 - 44	5 716	3 726	1 990	2.8	3.7	2.0
45 - 49	6 790	4 178	2 612	3.6	4.5	2.8
50 - 54	8 859	5 538	3 321	5.2	6.6	3.8
55 - 59	11 711	7 163	4 548	8.2	10.3	6.3
60 - 64	14 295	8 709	5 586	13.2	16.6	10.0
65 - 69	16 026	9 719	6 307	20.4	26.1	15.3
70 - 74	16 026	9 503	6 523	28.8	36.7	21.9
75 - 79	16 755	9 318	7 437	45.4	56.2	36.6
80 - 84	16 708	8 552	8 156	75.0	90.9	63.3
85 - 89	14 648	6 815	7 833	121.5	152.4	103.3
90 - 94	9 023	3 534	5 489	157.2	209.9	135.3
95 - 99	3 287	1 123	2 164	145.1	236.6	120.8
100 +	846	264	582	152.3	260.9	128.1

Continent, country or area, date, code[a] and age (in years) Continent, pays ou zone, date, code[a] et âge (en années)	Number - Nombre			Rate - Taux		
	Both sexes Les deux sexes	Male Masculin	Female Féminin	Both sexes Les deux sexes	Male Masculin	Female Féminin

ASIA - ASIE

Armenia - Arménie[25]
2017 (C)

Total	27 157	13 841	13 316	9.1	9.8	8.5
0	311	174	137	8.0	8.5	7.4
1 - 4	54	37	17	0.3	0.4	♦0.2
5 - 9	36	19	17	0.2	♦0.2	♦0.2
10 - 14	27	17	10	♦0.1	♦0.2	♦0.1
15 - 19	86	68	18	0.5	0.8	♦0.2
20 - 24	91	62	29	0.4	0.6	♦0.3
25 - 29	150	106	44	0.6	0.8	0.3
30 - 34	180	127	53	0.7	1.0	0.4
35 - 39	233	166	67	1.1	1.6	0.6
40 - 44	333	243	90	1.8	2.9	0.9
45 - 49	524	373	151	3.2	5.0	1.7
50 - 54	1 127	801	326	6.0	9.5	3.1
55 - 59	1 939	1 335	604	8.9	13.7	5.0
60 - 64	2 399	1 549	850	14.3	21.1	9.0
65 - 69	2 619	1 582	1 037	22.1	31.9	15.0
70 - 74	1 897	1 040	857	32.3	44.2	24.3
75 - 79	4 850	2 309	2 541	59.6	74.3	50.5
80 - 84	4 809	2 024	2 785	91.0	102.9	84.0
85 +	5 492	1 809	3 683	193.3	175.2	203.7
85 - 89	3 882	1 373	2 509	...	...	...
90 - 94	1 354	378	976	...	...	...
95 - 99	203	42	161	...	...	...
100 +	53	16	37	...	...	...

Azerbaijan - Azerbaïdjan[25]
2017 (+C)

Total	57 109	30 429	26 680	5.8	6.2	5.4
0	1 700	993	707	11.2	12.3	10.0
1 - 4	358	212	146	0.5	0.6	0.5
5 - 9	224	135	89	0.3	0.3	0.2
10 - 14	183	112	71	0.3	0.3	0.2
15 - 19	309	213	96	0.5	0.6	0.3
20 - 24	457	292	165	0.6	0.7	0.4
25 - 29	615	419	196	0.7	0.9	0.4
30 - 34	735	489	246	0.8	1.1	0.5
35 - 39	937	621	316	1.3	1.7	0.8
40 - 44	1 206	855	351	1.9	2.8	1.1
45 - 49	2 038	1 452	586	3.2	4.7	1.7
50 - 54	3 519	2 368	1 151	5.4	7.7	3.3
55 - 59	5 267	3 487	1 780	8.5	11.8	5.5
60 - 64	5 784	3 627	2 157	14.4	19.4	10.0
65 - 69	5 786	3 333	2 453	22.9	29.5	17.6
70 - 74	3 792	2 002	1 790	33.8	41.9	27.7
75 - 79	8 407	3 928	4 479	61.9	71.5	55.3
80 - 84	8 677	3 598	5 079	99.6	104.3	96.4
85 - 89	5 162	1 879	3 283	148.9	136.1	157.4
90 - 94	1 435	336	1 099	172.4	107.2	211.7
95 - 99	364	65	299	122.4	66.5	149.7
100 +	154	13	141	215.4	♦78.8	256.4

Bahrain - Bahreïn[26]
2017 (C)

Total	2 902	1 783	1 119	1.9	1.9	2.0
0	133	69	64	...	...	...
1 - 4	29	17	12	...	...	...
5 - 9	14	7	7	♦0.1	♦0.1	♦0.1
10 - 14	20	9	11	♦0.2	♦0.2	♦0.3
15 - 19	34	25	9	0.4	♦0.6	♦0.2
20 - 24	52	39	13	0.5	0.6	♦0.3
25 - 29	88	71	17	0.4	0.5	♦0.3
30 - 34	109	91	18	0.5	0.6	♦0.3
35 - 39	112	87	25	0.7	0.7	♦0.5
40 - 44	158	113	45	1.2	1.3	1.1
45 - 49	146	106	40	1.5	1.6	1.2
50 - 54	171	114	57	2.3	2.5	2.1
55 - 59	245	148	97	4.5	4.5	4.6

19. Deaths by age and sex and age-specific death rates by sex: latest available year, 2009 - 2018
Décès et taux de mortalité selon l'âge et le sexe : dernière année disponible, 2009 - 2018 (continued - suite)

Continent, country or area, date, code[a] and age (in years) / Continent, pays ou zone, date, code[a] et âge (en années)	Number - Nombre			Rate - Taux		
	Both sexes Les deux sexes	Male Masculin	Female Féminin	Both sexes Les deux sexes	Male Masculin	Female Féminin
ASIA - ASIE						
Bahrain - Bahreïn[26]						
2017 (C)						
60 - 64	259	164	95	8.2	8.8	7.4
65 - 69	259	171	88	15.3	17.5	12.3
70 - 74	202	112	90	22.6	24.2	21.0
75 +	871	440	431	70.5	75.0	66.4
Brunei Darussalam - Brunéi Darussalam						
2016 (+C)						
Total	1 632	890	742	3.9	4.2	3.7
0	52	25	27	13.4	♦12.0	♦15.0
1 - 4	13	9	4	♦0.5	♦0.7	♦0.3
5 - 9	9	6	3	♦0.3	♦0.4	♦0.2
10 - 14	8	6	2	♦0.2	♦0.3	♦0.1
15 - 19	10	6	4	♦0.3	♦0.3	♦0.2
20 - 24	19	15	4	♦0.5	♦0.7	♦0.2
25 - 29	33	18	15	0.8	♦0.8	♦0.8
30 - 34	39	25	14	1.1	♦1.3	♦0.8
35 - 39	57	38	19	1.7	2.1	♦1.1
40 - 44	72	45	27	2.3	2.9	♦1.8
45 - 49	100	60	40	3.6	4.4	2.9
50 - 54	125	85	40	5.4	7.3	3.5
55 - 59	149	85	64	7.7	9.0	6.5
60 - 64	137	68	69	9.4	9.6	9.2
65 - 69	137	74	63	15.3	17.4	13.4
70 - 74	153	77	76	30.0	30.4	29.7
75 - 79	157	76	81	41.5	43.8	39.6
80 - 84	180	86	94	81.6	88.3	76.3
85 - 89	113	58	55	111.3	116.5	106.4
90 - 94	48	23	25	121.2	♦125.0	♦117.9
95 - 99	19	5	14	♦153.2	♦78.1	♦233.3
100 +	2	-	2	♦80.0	-	♦133.3
2017 (+C)						
Total	1 696	...	...	3.9	...	...
0	60	...	...	...	...	...
1 - 4	13	...	...	...	...	...
5 - 9	8	...	...	♦0.3	...	...
10 - 14	7	...	...	♦0.2	...	...
15 - 19	9	...	...	♦0.2	...	...
20 - 24	24	...	...	♦0.6	...	...
25 - 29	32	...	...	0.8	...	...
30 - 34	31	...	...	0.8	...	...
35 - 39	54	...	...	1.5	...	...
40 - 44	69	...	...	2.1	...	...
45 - 49	80	...	...	2.7	...	...
50 - 54	112	...	...	4.5	...	...
55 - 59	148	...	...	7.3	...	...
60 - 64	139	...	...	9.5	...	...
65 - 69	155	...	...	16.0	...	...
70 - 74	141	...	...	29.4	...	...
75 - 79	218	...	...	62.3	...	...
80 - 84	188	...	...	104.4	...	...
85 +	208	...	...	160.0	...	...
85 - 89	125	...	...	...	...	...
90 - 94	62	...	...	...	...	...
95 - 99	15	...	...	...	...	...
100 +	6	...	...	...	...	...
China - Chine[27]						
2010 (¦)						
Total	7 421 990	4 293 783	3 128 207	5.6	6.3	4.8
0	60 217	32 026	28 191	4.4	4.3	4.5
1 - 4	39 591	23 119	16 472	0.6	0.7	0.6
5 - 9	21 183	13 621	7 562	0.3	0.4	0.2
10 - 14	23 088	15 243	7 845	0.3	0.4	0.2
15 - 19	40 469	28 088	12 381	0.4	0.5	0.3
20 - 24	62 552	43 738	18 814	0.5	0.7	0.3
25 - 29	60 661	42 497	18 164	0.6	0.8	0.4
30 - 34	79 960	55 804	24 156	0.8	1.1	0.5

Continent, country or area, date, code[a] and age (in years)	Number - Nombre			Rate - Taux		
Continent, pays ou zone, date, code[a] et âge (en années)	Both sexes Les deux sexes	Male Masculin	Female Féminin	Both sexes Les deux sexes	Male Masculin	Female Féminin
ASIA - ASIE						
China - Chine[27]						
2010 (I)						
35 - 39	140 531	98 382	42 149	1.2	1.6	0.7
40 - 44	216 353	149 111	67 242	1.7	2.3	1.1
45 - 49	262 531	179 446	83 085	2.5	3.3	1.6
50 - 54	337 397	226 888	110 509	4.3	5.6	2.9
55 - 59	494 339	324 817	169 522	6.1	7.9	4.2
60 - 64	586 160	377 069	209 091	10.0	12.6	7.3
65 - 69	695 662	435 007	260 655	16.9	21.0	12.8
70 - 74	999 653	599 394	400 259	30.3	36.5	24.2
75 - 79	1 162 694	657 140	505 554	48.7	58.3	40.2
80 - 84	1 081 704	553 704	528 000	80.9	93.6	70.8
85 - 89	686 462	306 678	379 784	121.9	139.4	110.7
90 - 94	279 569	104 048	175 521	177.1	196.0	167.6
95 - 99	74 729	23 292	51 437	202.0	197.9	203.9
100 +	16 485	4 671	11 814	458.8	527.7	436.2
China, Hong Kong SAR - Chine, Hong Kong RAS						
2018 (C)						
Total	47 400	26 418[10]	20 981[10]	6.4	7.7	5.2
0	80	41[10]	38[10]	1.6	1.6	1.6
1 - 4	26	11	15	◆0.1	◆0.1	◆0.1
5 - 9	24	12	12	◆0.1	◆0.1	◆0.1
10 - 14	26	16	10	◆0.1	◆0.1	◆0.1
15 - 19	53	32	21	0.2	0.2	◆0.1
20 - 24	109	75	34	0.3	0.4	0.2
25 - 29	149	102	47	0.3	0.4	0.2
30 - 34	208	119	89	0.4	0.5	0.3
35 - 39	291	168	123	0.5	0.7	0.3
40 - 44	566	329	237	1.0	1.4	0.7
45 - 49	806	451	355	1.4	1.9	1.1
50 - 54	1 436	840	596	2.4	3.2	1.8
55 - 59	2 298	1 441	857	3.6	4.7	2.6
60 - 64	3 133	2 101	1 032	5.7	7.7	3.7
65 - 69	3 738	2 555	1 183	8.8	12.2	5.5
70 - 74	3 910	2 683	1 227	14.0	19.3	8.7
75 - 79	4 722	3 229	1 493	24.6	34.0	15.5
80 - 84	7 361	4 338	3 023	42.4	55.3	31.8
85 +	18 413	7 839	10 574	94.8	115.1	83.8
Unknown - Inconnu	51	36	15	..	..	..
China, Macao SAR - Chine, Macao RAS						
2017 (C)						
Total	2 120	1 252	868	...	...	...
0 - 19	25	12	13	...	...	...
20 - 24	16	13	3	...	...	...
25 - 29	12	8	4	...	...	...
30 - 34	20	17	3	...	...	...
35 - 39	19	14	5	...	...	...
40 - 44	34	26	8	...	...	...
45 - 49	49	31	18	...	...	...
50 - 54	94	69	25	...	...	...
55 - 59	153	107	46	...	...	...
60 - 64	225	147	78	...	...	...
65 - 69	235	176	59	...	...	...
70 - 74	188	135	53	...	...	...
75 - 79	166	119	47	...	...	...
80 - 84	247	137	110	...	...	...
85 +	637	241	396	...	...	...
Cyprus - Chypre[28]						
2017 (C)						
Total	5 996	3 158	2 838	7.0	7.5	6.4
0	12	6	6	◆1.3	◆1.3	◆1.3
1 - 4	7	3	4	◆0.2	◆0.2	◆0.2
5 - 9	7	1	6	◆0.1	-	◆0.3
10 - 14	4	3	1	◆0.1	◆0.1	-
15 - 19	6	5	1	◆0.1	◆0.2	-
20 - 24	24	19	5	◆0.4	◆0.6	◆0.1
25 - 29	15	10	5	◆0.2	◆0.3	◆0.1

19. Deaths by age and sex and age-specific death rates by sex: latest available year, 2009 - 2018
Décès et taux de mortalité selon l'âge et le sexe : dernière année disponible, 2009 - 2018 (continued - suite)

Continent, country or area, date, code[a] and age (in years) Continent, pays ou zone, date, code[a] et âge (en années)	Number - Nombre			Rate - Taux		
	Both sexes Les deux sexes	Male Masculin	Female Féminin	Both sexes Les deux sexes	Male Masculin	Female Féminin
ASIA - ASIE						
Cyprus - Chypre[28]						
2017 (C)						
30 - 34	24	13	11	◆0.3	◆0.4	◆0.3
35 - 39	34	25	9	0.5	◆0.8	◆0.3
40 - 44	52	34	18	0.9	1.3	◆0.6
45 - 49	76	55	21	1.4	2.1	◆0.8
50 - 54	133	75	58	2.4	2.8	2.1
55 - 59	196	126	70	3.7	4.8	2.6
60 - 64	322	221	101	6.9	9.6	4.3
65 - 69	431	285	146	9.6	13.0	6.3
70 - 74	574	377	197	17.1	23.8	11.1
75 - 79	730	428	302	27.4	34.7	21.2
80 - 84	1 053	547	506	61.0	73.9	51.2
85 - 89	1 214	517	697	133.5	144.7	126.2
90 - 94	780	296	484	262.0	267.9	259.9
95 - 99	258	95	163	556.6	508.0	589.5
100 +	44	17	27	543.2	◆404.8	◆692.3
Georgia - Géorgie[25]						
2017 (C)						
Total	47 822	24 423	23 399	12.8	13.7	12.1
0	512	278	234	9.4	9.9	8.8
1 - 4	82	49	33	0.4	0.4	0.3
5 - 9	55	34	21	0.2	0.3	◆0.2
10 - 14	57	37	20	0.3	0.3	◆0.2
15 - 19	103	67	36	0.5	0.6	0.4
20 - 24	202	162	40	0.9	1.4	0.4
25 - 29	298	238	60	1.1	1.7	0.4
30 - 34	315	234	81	1.2	1.7	0.6
35 - 39	521	415	106	2.1	3.3	0.8
40 - 44	809	620	189	3.3	5.2	1.5
45 - 49	1 159	865	294	4.9	7.5	2.4
50 - 54	1 814	1 343	471	7.3	11.4	3.6
55 - 59	2 899	2 105	794	11.2	17.6	5.7
60 - 64	3 439	2 315	1 124	15.5	23.7	9.0
65 - 69	4 346	2 795	1 551	23.6	36.5	14.4
70 - 74	3 702	2 119	1 583	35.5	52.0	24.9
75 - 79	8 541	4 054	4 487	64.8	85.6	53.1
80 - 84	8 558	3 523	5 035	111.1	132.9	99.7
85 +	10 410	3 170	7 240	233.3	247.4	227.6
85 - 89	6 833	2 331	4 502	...	...	...
90 - 94	2 872	724	2 148	...	...	...
95 - 99	571	98	473	...	...	...
100 +	134	17	117	...	...	...
Indonesia - Indonésie[29]						
2010 (I)						
Total	1 236 154	687 976	548 178	5.2	5.8	4.6
0	106 846	61 546	45 300	24.3	27.2	21.2
1 - 4	37 689	20 958	16 731	2.1	2.2	1.9
5 - 9	19 409	10 807	8 602	0.8	0.9	0.8
10 - 14	15 382	9 029	6 353	0.7	0.8	0.6
15 - 19	23 642	14 948	8 694	1.1	1.4	0.8
20 - 24	27 089	16 020	11 069	1.4	1.6	1.1
25 - 29	31 020	17 855	13 165	1.5	1.7	1.2
30 - 34	31 290	17 168	14 122	1.6	1.7	1.4
35 - 39	38 257	20 382	17 875	2.1	2.2	1.9
40 - 44	49 757	26 901	22 856	3.0	3.2	2.8
45 - 49	65 139	36 351	28 788	4.6	5.2	4.1
50 - 54	89 078	51 820	37 258	7.7	8.8	6.5
55 - 59	86 308	53 355	32 953	10.2	12.1	8.1
60 - 64	105 991	62 663	43 328	17.5	21.4	13.8
65 - 69	107 730	62 508	45 222	23.0	28.1	18.3
70 - 74	138 235	76 159	62 076	40.0	49.7	32.2
75 - 79	92 062	49 343	42 719	46.5	58.6	37.6
80 - 84	86 057	42 547	43 510	75.3	88.4	65.8
85 +	85 173	37 616	47 557	119.4	133.2	110.3

19. Deaths by age and sex and age-specific death rates by sex: latest available year, 2009 - 2018
Décès et taux de mortalité selon l'âge et le sexe : dernière année disponible, 2009 - 2018 (continued - suite)

Continent, country or area, date, code[a] and age (in years) / Continent, pays ou zone, date, code[a] et âge (en années)	Number - Nombre			Rate - Taux		
	Both sexes Les deux sexes	Male Masculin	Female Féminin	Both sexes Les deux sexes	Male Masculin	Female Féminin
ASIA - ASIE						
Iran (Islamic Republic of) - Iran (République islamique d')[30]						
2017 (+U)						
Total	353 855	200 985	152 870	...	...	...
0	8 304	4 515	3 789	...	...	...
1 - 4	3 638	1 935	1 703	...	...	...
5 - 9	2 392	1 329	1 063	...	...	...
10 - 14	2 219	1 256	963	...	...	...
15 - 19	4 364	3 060	1 304	...	...	...
20 - 24	5 766	4 223	1 543	...	...	...
25 - 29	7 520	5 253	2 267	...	...	...
30 - 34	8 959	5 774	3 185	...	...	...
35 - 39	8 781	5 887	2 894	...	...	...
40 - 44	8 956	6 068	2 888	...	...	...
45 - 49	11 346	7 559	3 787	...	...	...
50 - 54	14 142	9 287	4 855	...	...	...
55 - 59	20 321	13 204	7 117	...	...	...
60 - 64	25 028	15 490	9 538	...	...	...
65 - 69	27 338	15 447	11 891	...	...	...
70 - 74	30 272	16 242	14 030	...	...	...
75 +	160 390	82 250	78 140	...	...	...
Unknown - Inconnu	4 119	2 206	1 913	..	..	...
Israel - Israël[31]						
2018 (C)						
Total	44 434	22 364[10]	22 069[10]	...	...	...
0	543	278[10]	264[10]	...	...	...
1 - 4	116	62	54	...	...	...
5 - 9	67	45	22	...	...	...
10 - 14	64	37	27	...	...	...
15 - 19	156	119	37	...	...	...
20 - 24	204	162	42	...	...	...
25 - 29	220	158	62	...	...	...
30 - 34	244	163	81	...	...	...
35 - 39	322	199	123	...	...	...
40 - 44	511	337	174	...	...	...
45 - 49	688	435	253	...	...	...
50 - 54	1 070	689	381	...	...	...
55 - 59	1 556	996	560	...	...	...
60 - 64	2 310	1 429	881	...	...	...
65 - 69	3 491	2 104	1 387	...	...	...
70 - 74	4 207	2 472	1 735	...	...	...
75 - 79	4 675	2 539	2 136	...	...	...
80 - 84	6 951	3 382	3 569	...	...	...
85 - 89	7 678	3 290	4 388	...	...	...
90 - 94	6 389	2 409	3 980	...	...	...
95 - 99	2 488	898	1 590	...	...	...
100 +	473	154	319	...	...	...
Unknown - Inconnu	11	7	4	..	..	..
Japan - Japon[32]						
2017 (C)						
Total	1 340 397	690 683	649 714	10.6	11.2	10.0
0	1 761	929	832	...	...	...
1 - 4	693	367	326	...	...	...
5 - 9	351	209	142	0.1	0.1	0.1
10 - 14	437	276	161	0.1	0.1	0.1
15 - 19	1 161	810	351	0.2	0.3	0.1
20 - 24	2 024	1 468	556	0.3	0.5	0.2
25 - 29	2 276	1 547	729	0.4	0.5	0.2
30 - 34	3 254	2 154	1 100	0.5	0.6	0.3
35 - 39	4 749	3 074	1 675	0.6	0.8	0.4
40 - 44	8 817	5 503	3 314	0.9	1.1	0.7
45 - 49	14 019	8 942	5 077	1.5	1.9	1.1
50 - 54	19 060	12 345	6 715	2.4	3.0	1.7
55 - 59	27 527	18 506	9 021	3.6	4.9	2.4
60 - 64	44 904	31 103	13 801	5.7	8.0	3.5
65 - 69	92 433	64 245	28 188	9.2	13.2	5.4
70 - 74	109 141	74 272	34 869	14.4	20.9	8.6

Continent, country or area, date, code[a] and age (in years) Continent, pays ou zone, date, code[a] et âge (en années)	Number - Nombre			Rate - Taux		
	Both sexes Les deux sexes	Male Masculin	Female Féminin	Both sexes Les deux sexes	Male Masculin	Female Féminin
ASIA - ASIE						
Japan - Japon[32]						
2017 (C)						
75 - 79	155 804	99 591	56 213	23.3	33.4	15.2
80 - 84	226 168	129 904	96 264	43.0	60.7	30.8
85 - 89	270 070	129 775	140 295	80.3	111.9	63.7
90 - 94	223 386	78 355	145 031	142.9	191.1	125.8
95 - 99	104 089	22 846	81 243	258.3	326.4	244.0
100 +	27 804	4 087	23 717	408.9	454.1	402.0
Unknown - Inconnu	469	375	94	..	..	..
Kazakhstan						
2018 (U)						
Total	130 448	70 338	60 110	...	...	...
0	3 184	1 892	1 292	...	...	...
1 - 4	837	496	341	...	...	...
5 - 9	482	308	174	...	...	...
10 - 14	411	272	139	...	...	...
15 - 19	688	470	218	...	...	...
20 - 24	1 104	810	294	...	...	...
25 - 29	1 780	1 310	470	...	...	...
30 - 34	2 580	1 916	664	...	...	...
35 - 39	3 437	2 439	998	...	...	...
40 - 44	4 413	3 157	1 256	...	...	...
45 - 49	5 717	3 922	1 795	...	...	...
50 - 54	7 488	5 159	2 329	...	...	...
55 - 59	11 185	7 501	3 684	...	...	...
60 - 64	12 849	8 306	4 543	...	...	...
65 - 69	14 501	8 800	5 701	...	...	...
70 - 74	10 370	5 608	4 762	...	...	...
75 - 79	16 555	7 412	9 143	...	...	...
80 - 84	16 215	6 227	9 988	...	...	...
85 - 89	9 983	2 900	7 083	...	...	...
90 - 94	5 440	1 194	4 246	...	...	...
95 - 99	1 025	190	835	...	...	...
100 +	182	28	154	...	...	...
Unknown - Inconnu	22	21	1	..	..	..
Kuwait - Koweït						
2017 (C)						
Total	6 679	4 309	2 370	1.7	1.8	1.5
0	413	254	159	7.2	8.5	5.8
1 - 4	71	44	27	0.3	0.3	♦0.2
5 - 9	73	36	37	0.2	0.2	0.3
10 - 14	52	34	18	0.2	0.2	♦0.2
15 - 19	90	76	14	0.4	0.6	♦0.1
20 - 24	182	149	33	0.9	1.3	0.3
25 - 29	217	176	41	0.8	1.3	0.3
30 - 34	241	179	62	0.5	0.7	0.3
35 - 39	275	211	64	0.5	0.6	0.4
40 - 44	356	283	73	0.7	0.9	0.4
45 - 49	396	320	76	1.1	1.3	0.6
50 - 54	504	360	144	2.0	2.1	1.6
55 - 59	464	362	102	2.7	3.2	1.8
60 - 64	546	363	183	5.2	5.2	5.3
65 - 69	516	286	230	9.4	8.2	11.5
70 - 74	549	266	283	19.5	16.6	23.4
75 - 79	588	305	283	38.1	35.0	42.2
80 +	930	455	475	70.2	63.5	78.2
80 - 84	463	229	234	...	...	...
85 - 89	285	142	143	...	...	...
90 - 94	131	64	67	...	...	...
95 +	51	20	31	...	...	...
Unknown - Inconnu	216	150	66	..	..	..
Kyrgyzstan - Kirghizstan						
2017 (C)						
Total	33 166	18 632	14 534	5.4	6.1	4.6
0	2 401	1 340	1 061	15.6	17.0	14.2
1 - 4	459	275	184	0.7	0.9	0.6
5 - 9	202	138	64	0.3	0.4	0.2

Continent, country or area, date, code[a] and age (in years) / Continent, pays ou zone, date, code[a] et âge (en années)	Number - Nombre			Rate - Taux		
	Both sexes Les deux sexes	Male Masculin	Female Féminin	Both sexes Les deux sexes	Male Masculin	Female Féminin
ASIA - ASIE						
Kyrgyzstan - Kirghizstan						
2017 (C)						
10 - 14	196	128	68	0.4	0.5	0.3
15 - 19	282	182	100	0.6	0.7	0.4
20 - 24	433	295	138	0.8	1.0	0.5
25 - 29	579	401	178	1.0	1.4	0.6
30 - 34	796	567	229	1.6	2.3	0.9
35 - 39	931	654	277	2.4	3.3	1.4
40 - 44	1 234	865	369	3.6	5.2	2.1
45 - 49	1 618	1 125	493	5.1	7.3	3.0
50 - 54	2 141	1 492	649	7.4	10.8	4.2
55 - 59	2 863	1 915	948	10.8	15.6	6.7
60 - 64	3 066	1 934	1 132	17.2	24.4	11.5
65 - 69	3 005	1 720	1 285	25.5	34.8	18.8
70 - 74	1 793	989	804	36.0	49.3	27.0
75 - 79	3 735	1 761	1 974	67.5	84.2	57.4
80 - 84	3 352	1 464	1 888	103.1	130.0	88.9
85 - 89	2 744	997	1 747	158.1	171.5	151.4
90 - 94	1 023	329	694	153.0	125.6	170.6
95 - 99	238	53	185	149.1	105.0	169.6
100 +	73	6	67	211.0	♦44.4	317.5
Unknown - Inconnu	2	2	-	..	..	..
Malaysia - Malaisie						
2017 (C)						
Total	168 168	96 522	71 646	5.2	5.8	4.6
0	3 496	1 939	1 557	6.8	7.3	6.2
1 - 4	799	453	346	0.4	0.4	0.3
5 - 9	618	354	264	0.2	0.3	0.2
10 - 14	774	505	269	0.3	0.4	0.2
15 - 19	1 860	1 433	427	0.6	1.0	0.3
20 - 24	2 318	1 745	573	0.7	1.0	0.4
25 - 29	2 465	1 758	707	0.8	1.0	0.5
30 - 34	3 156	2 201	955	1.1	1.5	0.7
35 - 39	3 855	2 637	1 218	1.6	2.1	1.1
40 - 44	5 250	3 595	1 655	2.7	3.6	1.8
45 - 49	7 427	4 883	2 544	4.2	5.5	2.9
50 - 54	10 579	6 849	3 730	6.6	8.4	4.7
55 - 59	14 275	9 031	5 244	10.3	12.8	7.7
60 - 64	16 907	10 510	6 397	15.6	19.3	11.8
65 - 69	18 532	11 230	7 302	22.7	27.9	17.7
70 - 74	19 001	11 117	7 884	36.0	43.5	28.9
75 - 79	20 151	10 775	9 376	60.2	68.2	53.0
80 +	36 698	15 507	21 191	113.3	101.6	123.8
80 - 84	18 106	8 431	9 675	...	...	...
85 - 89	11 479	4 632	6 847	...	...	...
90 - 94	5 100	1 801	3 299	...	...	...
95 +	2 013	643	1 370	...	...	...
Unknown - Inconnu	7	-	7	..	..	..
Maldives[33]						
2017 (C)						
Total	1 241	750	491	3.5	4.1	2.8
0	64	42	22	8.2	10.3	♦5.8
1 - 4	8	5	3	♦0.3	♦0.3	♦0.2
5 - 9	8	2	6	♦0.2	♦0.1	♦0.4
10 - 14	5	2	3	♦0.2	♦0.1	♦0.4
15 - 19	13	9	4	♦0.5	♦0.7	♦0.3
20 - 24	16	10	6	♦0.5	♦0.6	♦0.4
25 - 29	29	18	11	♦0.8	♦0.9	♦0.6
30 - 34	25	18	7	♦0.7	♦1.0	♦0.4
35 - 39	20	16	4	♦0.7	♦1.2	♦0.3
40 - 44	18	10	8	♦0.9	♦1.0	♦0.8
45 - 49	31	24	7	1.7	♦2.6	♦0.7
50 - 54	36	21	15	2.2	♦2.6	♦1.9
55 - 59	76	47	29	5.6	6.8	♦4.4
60 - 64	79	51	28	8.7	10.8	♦6.4
65 - 69	72	48	24	14.5	18.6	♦10.1
70 - 74	148	82	66	33.4	37.3	29.6

19. Deaths by age and sex and age-specific death rates by sex: latest available year, 2009 - 2018
Décès et taux de mortalité selon l'âge et le sexe : dernière année disponible, 2009 - 2018 (continued - suite)

Continent, country or area, date, code[a] and age (in years) / Continent, pays ou zone, date, code[a] et âge (en années)	Number - Nombre			Rate - Taux		
	Both sexes Les deux sexes	Male Masculin	Female Féminin	Both sexes Les deux sexes	Male Masculin	Female Féminin
ASIA - ASIE						
Maldives[33]						
2017 (C)						
75 - 79	246	130	116	60.8	63.4	58.1
80 +	347	215	132	101.2	111.6	87.9
80 - 84	186	118	68	...	...	...
85 - 89	98	57	41	...	...	...
90 - 94	43	28	15	...	...	...
95 - 99	13	8	5	...	...	...
100 +	7	4	3	...	...	...
Mongolia - Mongolie						
2018 (+C)						
Total	17 864	10 782	7 082	5.6	6.8	4.3
0	1 037	602	435	13.5	15.2	11.7
1 - 4	241	139	102	0.8	0.9	0.7
5 - 9	54	33	21	0.2	0.2	◆0.1
10 - 14	30	18	12	◆0.1	◆0.1	◆0.1
15 - 19	147	100	47	0.6	0.9	0.4
20 - 24	227	159	68	0.9	1.3	0.6
25 - 29	364	259	105	1.2	1.7	0.7
30 - 34	563	414	149	1.9	2.9	1.0
35 - 39	719	534	185	3.0	4.5	1.5
40 - 44	975	690	285	4.4	6.5	2.5
45 - 49	1 385	1 000	385	7.3	11.1	3.9
50 - 54	1 641	1 169	472	10.1	15.5	5.4
55 - 59	1 924	1 306	618	14.6	22.0	8.5
60 - 64	1 739	1 123	616	20.7	31.2	12.9
65 - 69	1 438	859	579	29.5	43.0	20.1
70 - 74	1 255	702	553	39.8	55.5	29.3
75 - 79	1 463	736	727	60.7	75.2	50.7
80 - 84	1 195	497	698	94.9	110.0	86.5
85 - 89	911	310	601	149.4	172.5	139.8
90 - 94	359	100	259	213.7	222.5	210.5
95 - 99	148	29	119	318.6	◆391.9	304.7
100 +	49	3	46	844.8	◆300.0	958.3
Myanmar[34]						
2016 (+U)						
Total	213 187	123 828	89 359	...	...	...
0	9 475	5 334	4 141	...	...	...
1 - 4	1 891	975	916	...	...	...
5 - 9	1 417	796	621	...	...	...
10 - 14	1 606	917	689	...	...	...
15 - 19	2 743	1 793	950	...	...	...
20 - 24	4 134	2 795	1 339	...	...	...
25 - 29	5 500	3 976	1 524	...	...	...
30 - 34	8 332	6 358	1 974	...	...	...
35 - 39	10 512	8 147	2 365	...	...	...
40 - 44	11 597	8 779	2 818	...	...	...
45 - 49	13 390	9 564	3 826	...	...	...
50 - 54	14 304	9 577	4 727	...	...	...
55 - 59	15 711	9 894	5 817	...	...	...
60 - 64	17 064	9 912	7 152	...	...	...
65 - 69	18 494	10 065	8 429	...	...	...
70 - 74	17 235	8 895	8 340	...	...	...
75 - 79	19 081	9 277	9 804	...	...	...
80 - 84	17 922	7 906	10 016	...	...	...
85 +	22 300	8 525	13 775	...	...	...
Unknown - Inconnu	479	343	136	..	..	..
Oman						
2018 (U)						
Total	8 979	5 599	3 380	...	...	...
0	762	399	363	...	...	...
1 - 4	223	122	101	...	...	...
5 - 9	92	49	43	...	...	...
10 - 14	80	52	28	...	...	...
15 - 19	122	94	28	...	...	...
20 - 24	199	153	46	...	...	...
25 - 29	314	233	81	...	...	...

Continent, country or area, date, code[a] and age (in years) / Continent, pays ou zone, date, code[a] et âge (en années)	Number - Nombre			Rate - Taux		
	Both sexes Les deux sexes	Male Masculin	Female Féminin	Both sexes Les deux sexes	Male Masculin	Female Féminin
ASIA - ASIE						
Oman						
2018 (U)						
30 - 34	387	294	93	...	...	...
35 - 39	376	279	97	...	...	...
40 - 44	411	330	81	...	...	...
45 - 49	396	308	88	...	...	...
50 - 54	438	321	117	...	...	...
55 - 59	498	362	136	...	...	...
60 - 64	676	427	249	...	...	...
65 +	4 005	2 176	1 829	...	...	...
Philippines						
2016 (C)						
Total	582 183	334 678	247 505	5.6	6.4	4.8
0 - 4	31 004	17 471	13 533	2.7	3.0	2.4
0	21 874	12 566	9 308	...	...	...
1 - 4	9 130	4 905	4 225	...	...	...
5 - 9	5 395	2 944	2 451	0.5	0.5	0.5
10 - 14	4 637	2 708	1 929	0.4	0.5	0.4
15 - 19	7 922	5 121	2 801	0.8	1.0	0.6
20 - 24	11 583	8 043	3 540	1.2	1.6	0.7
25 - 29	13 641	9 765	3 876	1.6	2.2	0.9
30 - 34	15 659	10 957	4 702	2.1	2.9	1.3
35 - 39	19 439	13 190	6 249	2.9	3.8	1.9
40 - 44	23 348	15 500	7 848	3.9	5.1	2.6
45 - 49	31 066	20 549	10 517	5.7	7.5	3.9
50 - 54	38 786	25 329	13 457	8.3	10.8	5.8
55 - 59	45 860	29 879	15 981	12.0	15.8	8.3
60 - 64	53 206	34 113	19 093	18.4	24.4	12.8
65 - 69	57 687	35 595	22 092	27.8	37.1	19.8
70 - 74	55 132	31 660	23 472	41.5	55.0	31.1
75 - 79	56 419	29 107	27 312	63.4	81.5	51.3
80 +	111 110	42 548	68 562	137.0	146.8	131.6
80 - 84	50 596	22 055	28 541	...	...	...
85 - 89	34 942	12 913	22 029	...	...	...
90 - 94	18 077	5 453	12 624	...	...	...
95 +	7 495	2 127	5 368	...	...	...
95 - 99	7 495	2 127	5 368	...	...	...
Unknown - Inconnu	289	199	90	..	..	..
Qatar						
2017 (C)						
Total	2 294	1 669	625	0.8	0.8	0.9
0	151	83	68	5.5	5.9	5.0
1 - 4	35	20	15	0.3	♦0.3	♦0.3
5 - 9	17	10	7	♦0.1	♦0.2	♦0.1
10 - 14	15	11	4	♦0.1	♦0.2	♦0.1
15 - 19	40	38	2	0.4	0.7	♦0.1
20 - 24	86	81	5	0.3	0.3	♦0.1
25 - 29	147	137	10	0.3	0.4	♦0.1
30 - 34	138	129	9	0.3	0.4	♦0.1
35 - 39	156	140	16	0.4	0.5	♦0.2
40 - 44	144	122	22	0.6	0.6	♦0.4
45 - 49	147	119	28	0.8	0.8	♦0.8
50 - 54	160	120	40	1.4	1.3	1.7
55 - 59	199	157	42	2.7	2.7	2.7
60 - 64	165	118	47	4.8	4.7	5.1
65 - 69	180	107	73	11.6	9.9	15.5
70 - 74	131	82	49	17.6	18.4	16.4
75 - 79	133	73	60	35.2	34.1	36.6
80 +	247	122	125	67.8	65.3	70.4
80 - 84	108	59	49	...	...	...
85 - 89	77	36	41	...	...	...
90 - 94	45	15	30	...	...	...
95 +	17	12	5	...	...	...
Unknown - Inconnu	3	-	3	..	..	..

Continent, country or area, date, code[a] and age (in years) / Continent, pays ou zone, date, code[a] et âge (en années)	Number - Nombre			Rate - Taux		
	Both sexes Les deux sexes	Male Masculin	Female Féminin	Both sexes Les deux sexes	Male Masculin	Female Féminin
ASIA - ASIE						
Republic of Korea - République de Corée[35]						
2017 (C)						
Total..........	285 534	154 328	131 206	5.6	6.0	5.1
0	1 000	569	431	2.6	2.9	2.3
1 - 4	261	139	122	0.1	0.2	0.1
5 - 9	210	134	76	0.1	0.1	0.1
10 - 14	197	115	82	0.1	0.1	0.1
15 - 19	626	424	202	0.2	0.3	0.1
20 - 24	1 087	750	337	0.3	0.4	0.2
25 - 29	1 384	953	431	0.4	0.5	0.3
30 - 34	1 849	1 153	696	0.5	0.6	0.4
35 - 39	3 062	1 983	1 079	0.8	0.9	0.5
40 - 44	4 680	3 089	1 591	1.1	1.5	0.8
45 - 49	8 022	5 647	2 375	1.8	2.5	1.1
50 - 54	11 260	8 296	2 964	2.7	3.9	1.4
55 - 59	16 431	12 359	4 072	3.9	5.9	1.9
60 - 64	17 721	13 059	4 662	5.6	8.4	2.9
65 - 69	19 942	14 172	5 770	8.7	12.9	4.9
70 - 74	26 828	17 571	9 257	15.3	22.0	9.7
75 - 79	43 132	25 446	17 686	28.9	41.0	20.2
80 - 84	50 618	24 679	25 939	54.4	75.1	43.1
85 - 89	42 481	15 111	27 370	99.9	130.3	88.5
90 - 94	24 706	6 634	18 072	178.9	214.7	168.6
95 - 99	8 329	1 777	6 552	268.4	282.6	264.8
100 +	1 667	252	1 415	431.1	464.9	425.6
Unknown - Inconnu	41	16	25	..	..	..
Saudi Arabia - Arabie saoudite[36]						
2016 (|)						
Total..........	58 097	35 497	22 600	1.8	1.9	1.7
0 - 4	5 084	2 273	2 811	1.9	1.7	2.1
5 - 9	1 033	577	456	0.4	0.4	0.3
10 - 14	2 125	1 206	919	0.9	1.0	0.8
15 - 19	1 487	1 368	119	0.7	1.2	0.1
20 - 24	4 859	3 146	1 713	2.0	2.4	1.5
25 - 29	3 926	2 673	1 253	1.3	1.6	0.9
30 - 34	2 106	1 582	524	0.7	0.9	0.4
35 - 39	3 232	2 207	1 025	1.0	1.0	0.8
40 - 44	2 714	2 027	687	0.9	1.0	0.6
45 - 49	2 629	1 233	1 396	1.2	0.8	1.8
50 - 54	3 031	2 571	460	1.9	2.4	0.9
55 - 59	3 901	2 404	1 497	3.6	3.3	4.0
60 - 64	2 895	1 844	1 051	4.0	4.1	3.8
65 - 69	2 547	1 181	1 366	6.3	5.4	7.4
70 - 74	4 186	2 922	1 264	15.5	20.7	9.8
75 - 79	1 846	709	1 137	11.5	8.3	14.9
80 +	10 496	5 574	4 922	54.6	58.1	51.1
80 - 84	4 678	1 900	2 778	...	...	...
85 +	5 818	3 674	2 144	...	...	...
Singapore - Singapour						
2017 (+C)						
Total..........	20 905	11 363	9 542	5.3	5.8	4.7
0 - 4	116	54	62	0.6	0.6	0.7
0	94	44	50	...	...	...
1 - 4	22	10	12	...	...	...
5 - 9	13	8	5	♦0.1	♦0.1	♦0.1
10 - 14	25	12	13	♦0.1	♦0.1	♦0.1
15 - 19	55	37	18	0.2	0.3	♦0.2
20 - 24	94	67	27	0.4	0.5	♦0.2
25 - 29	139	99	40	0.5	0.7	0.3
30 - 34	148	100	48	0.5	0.8	0.3
35 - 39	205	135	70	0.7	0.9	0.4
40 - 44	325	222	103	1.0	1.5	0.6
45 - 49	492	304	188	1.6	2.1	1.2
50 - 54	869	541	328	2.8	3.5	2.1
55 - 59	1 232	759	473	4.1	5.0	3.1
60 - 64	1 739	1 116	623	6.6	8.5	4.7
65 - 69	2 121	1 346	775	10.4	13.5	7.4

Continent, country or area, date, code[a] and age (in years) Continent, pays ou zone, date, code[a] et âge (en années)	Number - Nombre			Rate - Taux		
	Both sexes Les deux sexes	Male Masculin	Female Féminin	Both sexes Les deux sexes	Male Masculin	Female Féminin
ASIA - ASIE						
Singapore - Singapour						
2017 (+C)						
70 - 74	2 139	1 365	774	17.9	24.2	12.3
75 - 79	2 764	1 567	1 197	30.1	38.7	23.3
80 - 84	3 013	1 511	1 502	55.4	67.5	47.0
85 +	5 416	2 120	3 296	115.4	133.0	106.3
85 - 89	2 843	1 249	1 594	...	...	...
90 - 94	1 682	641	1 041	...	...	...
95 - 99	702	190	512	...	...	...
100 +	189	40	149	...	...	...
Sri Lanka						
2014 (+C)						
Total	128 185	72 634	55 551	6.2	7.2	5.2
0	2 662	1 505	1 157	...	...	...
1 - 4	533	302	231	...	...	...
5 - 9	384	219	165	0.2	0.2	0.2
10 - 14	406	231	175	0.2	0.3	0.2
15 - 19	903	611	292	0.5	0.7	0.3
20 - 24	1 185	837	348	0.8	1.1	0.4
25 - 29	1 232	869	363	0.8	1.1	0.4
30 - 34	1 617	1 118	499	1.0	1.4	0.6
35 - 39	1 943	1 321	622	1.4	1.9	0.8
40 - 44	2 604	1 805	799	1.9	2.7	1.1
45 - 49	4 271	2 996	1 275	3.3	4.7	1.9
50 - 54	6 617	4 481	2 136	5.3	7.6	3.3
55 - 59	8 599	5 800	2 799	7.9	11.4	4.9
60 - 64	11 743	7 616	4 127	12.5	17.5	8.2
65 - 69	14 024	8 651	5 373	21.7	29.8	15.1
70 - 74	15 975	9 097	6 878	37.9	48.9	29.3
75 - 79	15 993	8 382	7 611	55.3	70.4	44.8
80 +	37 443	16 760	20 683	134.2	152.4	122.4
80 - 84	16 638	7 790	8 848	...	...	...
85 +	20 805	8 970	11 835	...	...	...
Unknown - Inconnu	51	33	18	..	..	..
State of Palestine - État de Palestine[37]						
2017 (U)						
Total	11 778	6 197	5 581			
0	821	454	367	...	...	...
1 - 4	248	128	120	...	...	...
5 - 9	139	74	65	...	...	...
10 - 14	111	78	33	...	...	...
15 - 19	164	116	48	...	...	...
20 - 24	191	137	54	...	...	...
25 - 29	189	125	64	...	...	...
30 - 34	170	114	56	...	...	...
35 - 39	199	108	91	...	...	...
40 - 44	226	147	79	...	...	...
45 - 49	375	229	146	...	...	...
50 - 54	563	353	210	...	...	...
55 - 59	780	471	309	...	...	...
60 - 64	884	553	331	...	...	...
65 - 69	1 027	593	434	...	...	...
70 - 74	1 284	644	640	...	...	...
75 - 79	1 176	517	659	...	...	...
80 - 84	1 279	561	718	...	...	...
85 - 89	1 068	447	621	...	...	...
90 - 94	572	228	344	...	...	...
95 - 99	222	87	135	...	...	...
100 +	90	33	57	...	...	...
Tajikistan - Tadjikistan[25]						
2017 (U)						
Total	32 027	17 894	14 133			
0	2 405	1 384	1 021	...	...	...
1 - 4	610	335	275	...	...	...
5 - 9	230	128	102	...	...	...
10 - 14	186	120	66	...	...	...
15 - 19	268	161	107	...	...	...

19. Deaths by age and sex and age-specific death rates by sex: latest available year, 2009 - 2018
Décès et taux de mortalité selon l'âge et le sexe : dernière année disponible, 2009 - 2018 (continued - suite)

Continent, country or area, date, code[a] and age (in years) / Continent, pays ou zone, date, code[a] et âge (en années)	Number - Nombre			Rate - Taux		
	Both sexes Les deux sexes	Male Masculin	Female Féminin	Both sexes Les deux sexes	Male Masculin	Female Féminin
ASIA - ASIE						
Tajikistan - Tadjikistan[25]						
2017 (U)						
20 - 24	363	231	132	...	...	...
25 - 29	561	336	225	...	...	...
30 - 34	670	415	255	...	...	...
35 - 39	704	435	269	...	...	...
40 - 44	952	602	350	...	...	...
45 - 49	1 219	671	548	...	...	...
50 - 54	1 732	1 004	728	...	...	...
55 - 59	2 599	1 550	1 049	...	...	...
60 - 64	2 870	1 605	1 265	...	...	...
65 - 69	3 024	1 723	1 301	...	...	...
70 - 74	2 433	1 427	1 006	...	...	...
75 - 79	4 025	2 264	1 761	...	...	...
80 - 84	3 599	1 848	1 751	...	...	...
85 - 89	2 381	1 169	1 212	...	...	...
90 - 94	882	395	487	...	...	...
95 - 99	247	74	173	...	...	...
100 +	10	4	6	...	...	...
Unknown - Inconnu	57	13	44	..	..	..
Thailand - Thaïlande						
2017 (+U)						
Total	458 010	260 701	197 309	...	...	...
0	3 861	2 115	1 746	...	...	...
1 - 4	1 491	864	627	...	...	...
5 - 9	1 151	682	469	...	...	...
10 - 14	1 834	1 211	623	...	...	...
15 - 19	4 713	3 674	1 039	...	...	...
20 - 24	5 667	4 390	1 277	...	...	...
25 - 29	6 141	4 665	1 476	...	...	...
30 - 34	8 078	6 037	2 041	...	...	...
35 - 39	12 464	9 182	3 282	...	...	...
40 - 44	17 700	13 060	4 640	...	...	...
45 - 49	23 888	16 722	7 166	...	...	...
50 - 54	29 991	20 275	9 716	...	...	...
55 - 59	35 146	23 267	11 879	...	...	...
60 - 64	38 964	24 242	14 722	...	...	...
65 - 69	43 026	25 312	17 714	...	...	...
70 - 74	43 436	24 130	19 306	...	...	...
75 - 79	51 711	26 772	24 939	...	...	...
80 - 84	54 305	25 038	29 267	...	...	...
85 - 89	43 216	18 094	25 122	...	...	...
90 - 94	22 424	8 085	14 339	...	...	...
95 - 99	7 063	2 382	4 681	...	...	...
100 +	1 731	498	1 233	...	...	...
Unknown - Inconnu	9	4	5	..	..	..
Turkey - Turquie[38]						
2017 (C)						
Total	425 781	233 113	192 668	5.3	5.8	4.8
0	11 849	6 450	5 399	9.5	10.1	8.9
1 - 4	2 590	1 369	1 221	0.5	0.5	0.5
5 - 9	1 309	786	523	0.2	0.2	0.2
10 - 14	1 369	849	520	0.2	0.3	0.2
15 - 19	2 939	2 137	802	0.5	0.6	0.3
20 - 24	3 315	2 519	796	0.5	0.8	0.3
25 - 29	3 385	2 557	828	0.5	0.8	0.3
30 - 34	3 771	2 614	1 157	0.6	0.8	0.4
35 - 39	5 123	3 321	1 802	0.8	1.0	0.6
40 - 44	6 904	4 533	2 371	1.2	1.6	0.8
45 - 49	9 962	6 670	3 292	2.0	2.6	1.3
50 - 54	16 206	11 000	5 206	3.5	4.7	2.2
55 - 59	22 622	15 685	6 937	5.7	7.9	3.5
60 - 64	32 661	22 243	10 418	9.7	13.5	6.1
65 - 69	39 660	25 485	14 175	15.8	21.4	10.7
70 - 74	46 451	27 592	18 859	26.7	35.2	19.8
75 - 79	58 503	31 045	27 458	46.8	58.2	38.4
80 - 84	66 404	32 614	33 790	82.8	98.8	71.7

Continent, country or area, date, code[a] and age (in years) Continent, pays ou zone, date, code[a] et âge (en années)	Number - Nombre			Rate - Taux		
	Both sexes Les deux sexes	Male Masculin	Female Féminin	Both sexes Les deux sexes	Male Masculin	Female Féminin
ASIA - ASIE						
Turkey - Turquie[38]						
2017 (C)						
85 - 89	56 869	22 887	33 982	130.8	150.3	120.3
90 - 94	27 150	9 112	18 038	202.7	237.7	188.7
95 - 99	5 474	1 455	4 019	258.7	327.8	240.3
100 +	1 265	190	1 075	233.6	255.7	230.0
United Arab Emirates - Émirats arabes unis						
2017 (C)						
Total	8 826	6 168[10]	2 654[10]			
0	607	329[10]	274[10]	...	...	...
1 - 4	138	73[10]	65[10]	...	...	...
5 - 9	62	31[10]	33[10]	...	...	...
10 - 14	75	37[10]	38[10]	...	...	...
15 - 19	122	102[10]	19[10]	...	...	...
20 - 24	327	277[10]	47[10]	...	...	...
25 - 29	428	359[10]	73[10]	...	...	...
30 - 34	493	412[10]	78[10]	...	...	...
35 - 39	530	438[10]	94[10]	...	...	...
40 - 44	583	483[10]	99[10]	...	...	...
45 - 49	616	497[10]	121[10]	...	...	...
50 - 54	656	516[10]	137[10]	...	...	...
55 - 59	676	532[10]	142[10]	...	...	...
60 - 64	640	477[10]	167[10]	...	...	...
65 - 69	517	337[10]	178[10]	...	...	...
70 - 74	591	351[10]	239[10]	...	...	...
75 - 79	556	309[10]	248[10]	...	...	...
80 - 84	488	290[10]	251[10]	...	...	...
85 +	693	297[10]	346[10]	...	...	...
Unknown - Inconnu	26	21[10]	5[10]	..	..	..
Uzbekistan - Ouzbékistan[25]						
2017 (+C)						
Total	160 723	87 716	73 007	5.0	5.4	4.5
0	8 235	4 799	3 436	11.9	13.3	10.3
1 - 4	2 777	1 556	1 221	1.0	1.1	0.9
5 - 9	1 052	657	395	0.3	0.4	0.3
10 - 14	1 005	637	368	0.4	0.5	0.3
15 - 19	1 728	978	750	0.7	0.7	0.6
20 - 24	2 407	1 404	1 003	0.8	0.9	0.7
25 - 29	2 791	1 759	1 032	0.9	1.1	0.7
30 - 34	3 362	2 088	1 274	1.2	1.5	0.9
35 - 39	3 933	2 516	1 417	1.7	2.2	1.2
40 - 44	5 080	3 265	1 815	2.6	3.3	1.8
45 - 49	6 698	4 204	2 494	3.8	4.9	2.8
50 - 54	9 777	6 098	3 679	6.2	8.0	4.5
55 - 59	14 504	9 021	5 483	10.2	13.2	7.4
60 - 64	15 823	9 416	6 407	16.7	20.9	12.8
65 - 69	16 170	8 937	7 233	27.5	32.8	22.9
70 - 74	11 309	6 144	5 165	42.3	49.7	35.9
75 - 79	20 139	10 021	10 118	72.8	83.1	64.9
80 - 84	16 388	7 602	8 786	112.6	130.4	100.7
85 +	17 545	6 614	10 931	132.0	140.1	127.6
EUROPE						
Åland Islands - Îles d'Åland						
2017 (C)						
Total	235	115	120	8.0	7.9	8.2
0	-	-	-	-	-	-
1 - 4	1	1	-	♦0.8	♦1.6	-
5 - 9	-	-	-	-	-	-
10 - 14	-	-	-	-	-	-
15 - 19	-	-	-	-	-	-
20 - 24	1	1	-	♦0.7	♦1.4	-
25 - 29	-	-	-	-	-	-
30 - 34	2	1	1	♦1.2	♦1.1	♦1.2

19. Deaths by age and sex and age-specific death rates by sex: latest available year, 2009 - 2018
Décès et taux de mortalité selon l'âge et le sexe : dernière année disponible, 2009 - 2018 (continued - suite)

Continent, country or area, date, code[a] and age (in years) / Continent, pays ou zone, date, code[a] et âge (en années)	Number - Nombre			Rate - Taux		
	Both sexes Les deux sexes	Male Masculin	Female Féminin	Both sexes Les deux sexes	Male Masculin	Female Féminin
EUROPE						
Åland Islands - Îles d'Åland						
2017 (C)						
35 - 39	-	-	-	-	-	-
40 - 44	2	1	1	♦1.1	♦1.1	♦1.1
45 - 49	3	2	1	♦1.5	♦2.0	♦1.0
50 - 54	11	8	3	♦5.2	♦6.4	♦1.0
55 - 59	7	6	1	♦3.6	♦6.4	♦1.0
60 - 64	11	4	7	♦5.5	♦4.2	♦6.7
65 - 69	15	11	4	♦7.8	♦11.8	♦4.0
70 - 74	26	14	12	♦15.3	♦16.5	♦14.1
75 - 79	23	13	10	♦20.9	♦23.5	♦18.2
80 - 84	36	18	18	46.0	♦53.7	♦40.3
85 - 89	37	18	19	78.6	♦93.3	♦68.3
90 - 94	43	15	28	182.2	♦241.9	♦160.9
95 - 99	15	1	14	♦267.9	♦100.0	♦304.3
100 +	2	1	1	♦500.0	♦666.7	♦400.0
Albania - Albanie						
2017 (C)						
Total	22 232	11 610	10 622	7.7	8.0	7.4
0	248	130	118	7.9	8.0	7.9
1 - 4	36	20	16	0.3	♦0.3	♦0.2
5 - 9	30	16	14	♦0.2	♦0.2	♦0.2
10 - 14	45	26	19	0.2	♦0.3	♦0.2
15 - 19	76	48	28	0.3	0.4	♦0.3
20 - 24	109	68	41	0.4	0.5	0.3
25 - 29	105	79	26	0.5	0.6	♦0.2
30 - 34	112	81	31	0.6	0.8	0.3
35 - 39	165	110	55	1.0	1.3	0.7
40 - 44	218	138	80	1.3	1.7	0.9
45 - 49	392	253	139	2.1	2.9	1.5
50 - 54	646	429	217	3.3	4.4	2.2
55 - 59	1 015	709	306	5.0	7.1	3.0
60 - 64	1 302	847	455	7.7	10.2	5.3
65 - 69	1 679	1 057	622	13.0	16.6	9.5
70 - 74	2 255	1 335	920	23.1	27.6	18.6
75 - 79	3 719	1 971	1 748	43.4	48.2	39.0
80 - 84	4 427	2 247	2 180	91.9	98.2	86.2
85 +	5 653	2 046	3 607	249.6	211.9	277.6
85 - 89	3 325	1 390	1 935	...	...	...
90 - 94	1 533	467	1 066	...	...	...
95 - 99	609	162	447	...	...	...
100 +	186	27	159	...	...	...
Andorra - Andorre						
2018 (C)						
Total	335	178	157	4.5	4.7	4.3
0 - 9	-	-	-	-	-	-
10 - 19	2	1	1	♦0.3	♦0.2	♦0.3
20 - 29	2	1	1	♦0.2	♦0.2	♦0.3
30 - 39	5	3	2	♦0.4	♦0.5	♦0.4
40 - 49	19	12	7	♦1.4	♦1.7	♦1.0
50 - 59	31	18	13	2.5	♦2.9	♦2.2
60 - 69	47	32	15	6.3	8.2	♦4.2
70 - 79	64	44	20	15.3	21.0	♦9.6
80 - 89	100	48	52	...	...	...
90 +	65	19	46	...	...	...
Austria - Autriche[39]						
2017 (C)						
Total	83 270	39 902	43 368	9.5	9.2	9.7
0	256	136	120	3.0	3.0	2.9
1 - 4	58	37	21	0.2	0.2	♦0.1
5 - 9	26	15	11	♦0.1	♦0.1	♦0.1
10 - 14	40	22	18	0.1	♦0.1	♦0.1
15 - 19	125	87	38	0.3	0.4	0.2
20 - 24	174	134	40	0.3	0.5	0.2
25 - 29	245	178	67	0.4	0.6	0.2
30 - 34	275	184	91	0.5	0.6	0.3
35 - 39	389	260	129	0.7	0.9	0.4

19. Deaths by age and sex and age-specific death rates by sex: latest available year, 2009 - 2018
Décès et taux de mortalité selon l'âge et le sexe : dernière année disponible, 2009 - 2018 (continued - suite)

Continent, country or area, date, code[a] and age (in years) / Continent, pays ou zone, date, code[a] et âge (en années)	Number - Nombre			Rate - Taux		
	Both sexes Les deux sexes	Male Masculin	Female Féminin	Both sexes Les deux sexes	Male Masculin	Female Féminin
EUROPE						
Austria - Autriche[39]						
2017 (C)						
40 - 44	589	374	215	1.0	1.3	0.7
45 - 49	1 117	720	397	1.7	2.1	1.2
50 - 54	2 049	1 305	744	2.9	3.6	2.1
55 - 59	3 052	2 030	1 022	4.8	6.4	3.2
60 - 64	4 009	2 553	1 456	7.8	10.3	5.5
65 - 69	5 601	3 509	2 092	12.4	16.5	8.8
70 - 74	7 469	4 556	2 913	19.9	26.5	14.3
75 - 79	11 070	6 293	4 777	29.5	38.0	22.7
80 - 84	11 944	5 885	6 059	56.7	69.6	48.1
85 - 89	16 211	6 717	9 494	112.5	132.9	101.5
90 - 94	13 341	3 810	9 531	205.4	224.3	198.7
95 - 99	4 664	1 010	3 654	338.7	372.1	330.5
100 +	566	87	479	522.4	554.1	517.0
Belarus - Bélarus						
2017 (C)						
Total	119 311	59 266	60 045	12.6	13.4	11.8
0	332	181	151	3.0	3.2	2.8
1 - 4	89	53	36	0.2	0.2	0.2
5 - 9	78	46	32	0.1	0.2	0.1
10 - 14	67	34	33	0.1	0.1	0.1
15 - 19	160	114	46	0.4	0.5	0.2
20 - 24	314	230	84	0.6	0.8	0.3
25 - 29	617	464	153	0.9	1.2	0.4
30 - 34	1 027	797	230	1.3	2.0	0.6
35 - 39	1 576	1 172	404	2.3	3.4	1.2
40 - 44	2 280	1 690	590	3.5	5.3	1.8
45 - 49	3 316	2 448	868	5.2	8.1	2.6
50 - 54	5 053	3 740	1 313	7.5	11.9	3.6
55 - 59	8 424	6 181	2 243	11.4	18.4	5.5
60 - 64	10 784	7 642	3 142	17.6	29.5	8.9
65 - 69	12 186	7 953	4 233	24.8	41.3	14.2
70 - 74	9 698	5 503	4 195	36.9	59.3	24.7
75 - 79	16 905	7 703	9 202	56.5	86.9	43.7
80 - 84	18 632	6 591	12 041	92.9	128.6	80.7
85 - 89	17 483	4 790	12 693	156.5	194.5	145.7
90 - 94	8 501	1 634	6 867	238.3	247.3	236.3
95 - 99	1 579	262	1 317	302.7	297.4	303.8
100 +	210	38	172	207.1	261.2	198.0
Belgium - Belgique[40]						
2017 (C)						
Total	109 666	53 825	55 841	9.6	9.6	9.7
0	429	241	188	3.6	3.9	3.2
1 - 4	84	51	33	0.2	0.2	0.1
5 - 9	60	36	24	0.1	0.1	♦0.1
10 - 14	67	43	24	0.1	0.1	♦0.1
15 - 19	150	97	53	0.2	0.3	0.2
20 - 24	264	191	73	0.4	0.6	0.2
25 - 29	323	234	89	0.4	0.6	0.2
30 - 34	425	280	145	0.6	0.8	0.4
35 - 39	630	410	220	0.8	1.1	0.6
40 - 44	893	589	304	1.2	1.6	0.8
45 - 49	1 544	936	608	2.0	2.4	1.6
50 - 54	2 462	1 495	967	3.0	3.6	2.4
55 - 59	3 927	2 486	1 441	5.0	6.4	3.7
60 - 64	5 764	3 597	2 167	8.3	10.6	6.2
65 - 69	7 728	4 884	2 844	12.7	16.5	9.0
70 - 74	9 482	5 693	3 789	19.2	24.6	14.4
75 - 79	11 929	6 821	5 108	31.8	41.2	24.4
80 - 84	17 647	8 988	8 659	55.8	70.0	46.1
85 - 89	22 361	9 467	12 894	106.7	129.2	94.6
90 - 94	16 865	5 654	11 211	195.1	231.7	180.7
95 - 99	5 809	1 480	4 329	316.4	365.7	302.5
100 +	823	152	671	489.6	669.6	461.5

19. Deaths by age and sex and age-specific death rates by sex: latest available year, 2009 - 2018
Décès et taux de mortalité selon l'âge et le sexe : dernière année disponible, 2009 - 2018 (continued - suite)

Continent, country or area, date, code[a] and age (in years) / Continent, pays ou zone, date, code[a] et âge (en années)	Number - Nombre			Rate - Taux		
	Both sexes Les deux sexes	Male Masculin	Female Féminin	Both sexes Les deux sexes	Male Masculin	Female Féminin
EUROPE						
Bosnia and Herzegovina - Bosnie-Herzégovine						
2010 (C)						
Total	35 118	17 900	17 218	9.1	9.5	8.8
0 - 4	252	143	109	1.5	1.7	1.3
0	216	125	91	6.5	7.3	5.6
1 - 4	36	18	18	0.3	♦0.3	♦0.3
5 - 9	28	19	9	♦0.1	♦0.2	♦0.1
10 - 14	27	14	13	♦0.1	♦0.1	♦0.1
15 - 19	84	58	26	0.3	0.4	♦0.2
20 - 24	120	92	28	0.4	0.6	♦0.2
25 - 29	165	130	35	0.6	1.0	0.3
30 - 34	160	109	51	0.7	0.9	0.4
35 - 39	254	180	74	1.0	1.5	0.5
40 - 44	432	265	167	1.5	1.9	1.2
45 - 49	844	553	291	2.7	3.7	1.9
50 - 54	1 465	980	485	5.5	7.2	3.7
55 - 59	2 141	1 429	712	9.2	13.6	5.6
60 - 64	2 610	1 647	963	14.3	19.1	10.0
65 - 69	3 390	2 032	1 358	16.8	22.6	12.1
70 - 74	6 045	3 199	2 846	32.8	38.8	27.9
75 - 79	6 948	3 344	3 604	57.7	66.1	51.6
80 - 84	6 006	2 440	3 566	125.3	124.5	125.9
85 +	4 119	1 254	2 865	164.3	175.6	159.9
85 - 89	3 105	966	2 139	...	...	...
90 - 94	737	210	527	...	...	...
95 - 99	245	69	176	...	...	...
100 +	32	9	23	...	...	...
Unknown - Inconnu	28	12	16	..	..	..
Bulgaria - Bulgarie						
2017 (C)						
Total	109 791	56 781	53 010	15.5	16.5	14.6
0	408	227	181	6.4	6.9	5.8
1 - 4	91	54	37	0.3	0.4	0.3
5 - 9	46	36	10	0.1	0.2	♦0.1
10 - 14	56	36	20	0.2	0.2	♦0.1
15 - 19	140	100	40	0.4	0.6	0.3
20 - 24	191	134	57	0.6	0.8	0.3
25 - 29	320	232	88	0.7	1.0	0.4
30 - 34	447	320	127	0.9	1.3	0.5
35 - 39	729	505	224	1.4	1.9	0.9
40 - 44	1 395	941	454	2.6	3.4	1.7
45 - 49	2 223	1 540	683	4.3	5.8	2.7
50 - 54	3 395	2 384	1 011	7.3	10.2	4.4
55 - 59	5 430	3 725	1 705	11.2	15.7	6.9
60 - 64	8 074	5 462	2 612	16.5	23.9	10.0
65 - 69	11 496	7 458	4 038	23.9	35.3	15.0
70 - 74	13 195	7 641	5 554	34.5	48.2	24.8
75 - 79	15 154	7 608	7 546	55.2	71.7	44.7
80 - 84	20 017	8 566	11 451	97.9	116.0	87.7
85 - 89	16 850	6 461	10 389	169.1	187.5	159.3
90 - 94	8 350	2 807	5 543	280.8	298.6	272.5
95 - 99	1 660	509	1 151	415.8	428.8	410.3
100 +	124	35	89	536.8	534.4	537.8
Croatia - Croatie						
2017 (C)						
Total	53 477	25 861	27 616	13.0	13.0	12.9
0	148	89	59	4.0	4.7	3.2
1 - 4	35	21	14	0.2	♦0.3	♦0.2
5 - 9	30	14	16	♦0.1	♦0.1	♦0.2
10 - 14	20	10	10	♦0.1	♦0.1	♦0.1
15 - 19	58	45	13	0.3	0.4	♦0.1
20 - 24	107	86	21	0.4	0.7	♦0.2
25 - 29	118	84	34	0.5	0.7	0.3
30 - 34	146	106	40	0.5	0.8	0.3
35 - 39	259	180	79	0.9	1.2	0.6
40 - 44	381	256	125	1.4	1.8	0.9
45 - 49	686	473	213	2.5	3.5	1.6

19. Deaths by age and sex and age-specific death rates by sex: latest available year, 2009 - 2018
Décès et taux de mortalité selon l'âge et le sexe : dernière année disponible, 2009 - 2018 (continued - suite)

Continent, country or area, date, code[a] and age (in years) Continent, pays ou zone, date, code[a] et âge (en années)	Number - Nombre			Rate - Taux		
	Both sexes Les deux sexes	Male Masculin	Female Féminin	Both sexes Les deux sexes	Male Masculin	Female Féminin
EUROPE						
Croatia - Croatie						
2017 (C)						
50 - 54	1 339	917	422	4.6	6.4	2.8
55 - 59	2 246	1 562	684	7.4	10.7	4.4
60 - 64	3 598	2 479	1 119	12.0	17.2	7.2
65 - 69	4 691	3 080	1 611	18.5	26.6	11.7
70 - 74	5 035	2 972	2 063	27.6	38.5	19.7
75 - 79	8 193	4 175	4 018	47.3	61.3	38.3
80 - 84	10 871	4 525	6 346	85.8	102.0	77.1
85 - 89	9 602	3 318	6 284	153.4	175.6	143.8
90 - 94	4 660	1 204	3 456	259.9	280.6	253.4
95 - 99	1 151	242	909	419.9	434.5	416.2
100 +	103	23	80	660.3	◆821.4	625.0
Czechia - Tchéquie						
2017 (C)						
Total	111 443	56 442	55 001	10.5	10.8	10.2
0	304	183	121	2.7	3.1	2.2
1 - 4	67	38	29	0.2	0.2	◆0.1
5 - 9	53	33	20	0.1	0.1	◆0.1
10 - 14	41	25	16	0.1	◆0.1	◆0.1
15 - 19	130	87	43	0.3	0.4	0.2
20 - 24	260	198	62	0.5	0.7	0.2
25 - 29	338	273	65	0.5	0.8	0.2
30 - 34	501	361	140	0.7	1.0	0.4
35 - 39	684	475	209	0.8	1.1	0.5
40 - 44	1 239	847	392	1.3	1.8	0.9
45 - 49	1 656	1 116	540	2.3	3.0	1.5
50 - 54	2 751	1 901	850	3.9	5.4	2.5
55 - 59	4 095	2 794	1 301	6.6	9.0	4.2
60 - 64	7 827	5 314	2 513	11.1	15.6	6.9
65 - 69	11 772	7 583	4 189	17.1	23.8	11.3
70 - 74	14 693	8 822	5 871	26.7	36.7	18.9
75 - 79	14 346	7 685	6 661	41.1	54.2	32.1
80 - 84	16 865	7 645	9 220	74.0	92.3	63.5
85 - 89	18 875	6 937	11 938	134.6	156.1	124.6
90 - 94	11 863	3 455	8 408	240.0	273.2	228.6
95 - 99	2 810	632	2 178	357.1	390.1	348.5
100 +	273	38	235	403.5	231.7	458.5
Denmark - Danemark[41]						
2017 (C)						
Total	53 261	26 870	26 391	9.2	9.4	9.1
0	231	133	98	3.7	4.2	3.3
1 - 4	36	23	13	0.2	◆0.2	◆0.1
5 - 9	15	9	6	-	◆0.1	-
10 - 14	20	14	6	◆0.1	◆0.1	-
15 - 19	71	46	25	0.2	0.3	◆0.1
20 - 24	119	92	27	0.3	0.5	◆0.1
25 - 29	128	88	40	0.3	0.5	0.2
30 - 34	140	101	39	0.4	0.6	0.2
35 - 39	218	133	85	0.6	0.8	0.5
40 - 44	370	226	144	1.0	1.2	0.8
45 - 49	711	453	258	1.8	2.3	1.3
50 - 54	1 294	785	509	3.1	3.7	2.4
55 - 59	1 915	1 194	721	5.2	6.5	3.9
60 - 64	2 917	1 810	1 107	8.6	10.7	6.4
65 - 69	4 223	2 557	1 666	12.9	16.0	10.0
70 - 74	6 628	3 920	2 708	20.7	25.4	16.3
75 - 79	6 993	3 871	3 122	34.0	40.7	28.2
80 - 84	8 341	4 288	4 053	62.6	74.9	53.4
85 - 89	8 597	3 859	4 738	113.8	135.4	100.8
90 - 94	6 862	2 467	4 395	199.5	243.1	181.3
95 - 99	2 842	707	2 135	317.9	365.2	304.8
100 +	590	94	496	538.8	626.7	524.9
Estonia - Estonie						
2017 (C)						
Total	15 543	7 325	8 218	11.8	11.8	11.8
0	32	20	12	2.3	◆2.7	◆1.8

Continent, country or area, date, code[a] and age (in years) Continent, pays ou zone, date, code[a] et âge (en années)	Number - Nombre			Rate - Taux		
	Both sexes Les deux sexes	Male Masculin	Female Féminin	Both sexes Les deux sexes	Male Masculin	Female Féminin
EUROPE						
Estonia - Estonie						
2017 (C)						
1 - 4	10	5	5	♦0.2	♦0.2	♦0.2
5 - 9	6	4	2	♦0.1	♦0.1	♦0.1
10 - 14	11	4	7	♦0.2	♦0.1	♦0.2
15 - 19	22	15	7	♦0.4	♦0.5	♦0.2
20 - 24	39	27	12	0.6	♦0.8	♦0.4
25 - 29	74	61	13	0.8	1.2	♦0.3
30 - 34	108	84	24	1.1	1.7	♦0.5
35 - 39	127	105	22	1.4	2.3	♦0.5
40 - 44	198	152	46	2.2	3.3	1.0
45 - 49	272	196	76	3.1	4.4	1.7
50 - 54	430	305	125	5.1	7.5	2.9
55 - 59	688	496	192	7.7	11.9	4.0
60 - 64	1 091	746	345	13.0	20.2	7.4
65 - 69	1 384	915	469	18.1	29.4	10.4
70 - 74	1 395	847	548	26.1	42.0	16.4
75 - 79	2 184	1 100	1 084	39.2	60.4	28.9
80 - 84	2 558	995	1 563	67.4	92.8	57.4
85 - 89	2 821	824	1 997	122.0	148.7	113.6
90 - 94	1 637	359	1 278	197.3	237.4	188.4
95 - 99	378	57	321	286.3	309.8	282.4
100 +	78	8	70	666.7	♦727.3	660.4
Faeroe Islands - Îles Féroé						
2018 (C)						
Total	392	218	174	7.7	8.3	7.0
0	-	-	-	-	-	-
1 - 4	-	-	-	-	-	-
5 - 9	-	-	-	-	-	-
10 - 14	1	1	-	♦0.3	♦0.5	-
15 - 19	1	1	-	♦0.3	♦0.5	-
20 - 24	-	-	-	-	-	-
25 - 29	1	1	-	♦0.3	♦0.6	-
30 - 34	-	-	-	-	-	-
35 - 39	-	-	-	-	-	-
40 - 44	4	1	3	♦1.3	♦0.6	♦2.0
45 - 49	5	3	2	♦1.5	♦1.8	♦1.3
50 - 54	4	3	1	♦1.1	♦1.6	♦0.6
55 - 59	12	9	3	♦3.8	♦5.5	♦1.9
60 - 64	24	14	10	♦8.4	♦9.6	♦7.1
65 - 69	32	26	6	11.7	♦18.5	♦4.5
70 - 74	39	26	13	17.6	♦22.1	♦12.5
75 - 79	46	27	19	27.5	♦32.7	♦22.4
80 - 84	68	39	29	63.8	80.6	♦49.8
85 - 89	62	35	27	81.8	115.1	♦59.5
90 - 94	51	20	31	155.5	♦222.2	130.3
95 - 99	33	10	23	569.0	♦666.7	♦534.9
100 +	9	2	7	♦1000.0	♦2000.0	♦875.0
Finland - Finlande						
2017 (C)						
Total	53 722	26 895	26 827	9.8	10.0	9.7
0	102	55	47	2.0	2.1	1.9
1 - 4	34	18	16	0.1	♦0.2	♦0.1
5 - 9	24	11	13	♦0.1	♦0.1	♦0.1
10 - 14	23	12	11	♦0.1	♦0.1	♦0.1
15 - 19	111	78	33	0.4	0.5	0.2
20 - 24	184	130	54	0.6	0.8	0.3
25 - 29	205	158	47	0.6	0.9	0.3
30 - 34	255	186	69	0.7	1.0	0.4
35 - 39	290	202	88	0.8	1.1	0.5
40 - 44	431	302	129	1.3	1.8	0.8
45 - 49	594	402	192	1.8	2.4	1.2
50 - 54	1 178	778	400	3.2	4.2	2.2
55 - 59	1 742	1 141	601	4.8	6.3	3.3
60 - 64	2 956	1 993	963	8.0	11.1	5.1
65 - 69	4 551	2 948	1 603	12.3	16.5	8.3
70 - 74	5 331	3 344	1 987	18.4	24.8	12.9

Continent, country or area, date, code[a] and age (in years) Continent, pays ou zone, date, code[a] et âge (en années)	Number - Nombre			Rate - Taux		
	Both sexes Les deux sexes	Male Masculin	Female Féminin	Both sexes Les deux sexes	Male Masculin	Female Féminin
EUROPE						
Finland - Finlande						
2017 (C)						
75 - 79	6 466	3 707	2 759	31.0	40.9	23.5
80 - 84	8 301	4 207	4 094	56.8	72.8	46.4
85 - 89	10 235	4 248	5 987	107.0	133.8	93.7
90 - 94	7 648	2 345	5 303	195.5	232.5	182.6
95 - 99	2 650	558	2 092	325.5	371.3	315.2
100 +	411	72	339	494.9	547.5	485.0
France						
2014 (C)						
Total	545 021	274 346	270 675	8.5	8.8	8.2
0	9 243	1 369	7 874	...	...	...
1 - 4	2 570	1 433	1 137	...	...	...
5 - 9	475	263	212	...	...	...
10 - 14	315	179	136	...	...	...
15 - 19	322	186	136	0.1	0.1	0.1
20 - 24	874	608	266	0.2	0.3	0.1
25 - 29	1 433	1 084	349	0.4	0.6	0.2
30 - 34	1 891	1 375	516	0.5	0.7	0.3
35 - 39	2 397	1 724	673	0.6	0.9	0.3
40 - 44	3 391	2 261	1 130	0.8	1.0	0.5
45 - 49	5 937	3 813	2 124	1.4	1.8	1.0
50 - 54	9 927	6 439	3 488	2.3	3.1	1.6
55 - 59	15 506	10 139	5 367	3.8	5.1	2.5
60 - 64	22 794	15 313	7 481	5.7	8.0	3.6
65 - 69	31 694	21 512	10 182	9.0	12.9	5.5
70 - 74	37 507	25 054	12 453	15.9	23.0	9.8
75 - 79	36 818	23 518	13 300	16.9	25.0	10.8
80 - 84	54 549	32 006	22 543	29.4	44.4	19.9
85 - 89	84 954	44 085	40 869	70.2	108.6	50.9
90 - 94	106 248	45 822	60 426	186.5	295.2	145.8
95 - 99	91 920	30 570	61 350	1010.5	1639.8	848.3
100 +	24 256	5 593	18 663	1068.9	1659.9	965.8
Germany - Allemagne						
2017 (C)						
Total	932 272	457 761	474 511	11.3	11.2	11.3
0	2 571	1 420	1 151	3.3	3.5	3.0
1 - 4	439	235	204	0.1	0.2	0.1
5 - 9	266	138	128	0.1	0.1	0.1
10 - 14	302	158	144	0.1	0.1	0.1
15 - 19	904	609	295	0.2	0.3	0.1
20 - 24	1 417	1 007	410	0.3	0.4	0.2
25 - 29	1 833	1 277	556	0.3	0.5	0.2
30 - 34	2 714	1 832	882	0.5	0.7	0.3
35 - 39	3 752	2 494	1 258	0.7	1.0	0.5
40 - 44	5 314	3 427	1 887	1.1	1.4	0.8
45 - 49	11 750	7 474	4 276	1.9	2.4	1.4
50 - 54	22 885	14 750	8 135	3.3	4.2	2.4
55 - 59	35 073	22 802	12 271	5.6	7.2	3.9
60 - 64	47 691	30 743	16 948	9.0	11.8	6.2
65 - 69	62 729	39 834	22 895	13.5	17.9	9.5
70 - 74	75 585	45 747	29 838	20.8	27.0	15.4
75 - 79	139 236	80 098	59 138	32.4	42.0	24.8
80 - 84	165 341	83 620	81 721	59.3	73.2	49.6
85 - 89	173 944	72 676	101 268	116.2	138.8	104.1
90 - 94	127 857	37 286	90 571	209.0	237.3	199.2
95 - 99	44 672	9 288	35 384	335.2	371.9	326.8
100 +	5 997	846	5 151	407.9	350.0	419.3
Greece - Grèce						
2018 (C)						
Total	120 297	61 387	58 910	11.2	11.8	10.7
0	300	169	131	3.3	3.7	3.0
1 - 4	51	28	23	0.1	♦0.1	♦0.1
5 - 9	42	20	22	0.1	♦0.1	♦0.1
10 - 14	58	41	17	0.1	0.1	♦0.1
15 - 19	125	92	33	0.2	0.3	0.1
20 - 24	219	167	52	0.4	0.6	0.2

19. Deaths by age and sex and age-specific death rates by sex: latest available year, 2009 - 2018
Décès et taux de mortalité selon l'âge et le sexe : dernière année disponible, 2009 - 2018 (continued - suite)

Continent, country or area, date, code[a] and age (in years) / Continent, pays ou zone, date, code[a] et âge (en années)	Number - Nombre			Rate - Taux		
	Both sexes Les deux sexes	Male Masculin	Female Féminin	Both sexes Les deux sexes	Male Masculin	Female Féminin
EUROPE						
Greece - Grèce						
2018 (C)						
25 - 29	216	157	59	0.4	0.5	0.2
30 - 34	355	254	101	0.6	0.8	0.3
35 - 39	626	452	174	0.8	1.2	0.4
40 - 44	899	618	281	1.1	1.6	0.7
45 - 49	1 508	973	535	1.8	2.4	1.3
50 - 54	2 531	1 697	834	3.3	4.6	2.1
55 - 59	3 811	2 633	1 178	5.3	7.8	3.1
60 - 64	5 328	3 639	1 689	8.1	11.7	4.9
65 - 69	6 854	4 627	2 227	11.3	16.1	6.9
70 - 74	10 166	6 434	3 732	18.9	25.9	12.8
75 - 79	13 090	7 542	5 548	29.0	37.8	22.0
80 - 84	22 688	11 315	11 373	58.0	69.4	49.9
85 +	51 311	20 511	30 800	146.7	145.0	147.8
Unknown - Inconnu	19	18	1	..	..	..
Hungary - Hongrie[42]						
2017 (C)						
Total	131 877	64 171	67 706	13.5	13.7	13.2
0	328	190	138	3.5	3.9	3.0
1 - 4	73	35	38	0.2	0.2	0.2
5 - 9	60	29	31	0.1	♦0.1	0.1
10 - 14	71	44	27	0.1	0.2	♦0.1
15 - 19	135	96	39	0.3	0.4	0.2
20 - 24	214	165	49	0.4	0.5	0.2
25 - 29	311	238	73	0.5	0.7	0.2
30 - 34	478	327	151	0.8	1.1	0.5
35 - 39	828	533	295	1.1	1.4	0.8
40 - 44	1 363	907	456	1.6	2.2	1.1
45 - 49	2 621	1 767	854	3.7	4.9	2.4
50 - 54	4 094	2 772	1 322	6.8	9.4	4.3
55 - 59	7 022	4 708	2 314	11.5	16.4	7.2
60 - 64	12 656	8 295	4 361	17.4	25.2	11.0
65 - 69	14 317	8 835	5 482	23.9	34.3	16.0
70 - 74	15 056	8 590	6 466	32.7	46.4	23.5
75 - 79	17 901	8 655	9 246	50.7	68.4	40.8
80 - 84	20 416	8 014	12 402	87.0	108.8	77.0
85 - 89	19 565	6 312	13 253	148.6	169.7	140.2
90 - 94	11 076	2 883	8 193	231.2	251.4	224.8
95 - 99	2 947	695	2 252	276.2	284.5	273.8
100 +	345	81	264	212.0	154.4	239.3
Iceland - Islande						
2017 (C)						
Total	2 238	1 124	1 114	6.5	6.4	6.6
0	11	5	6	♦2.7	♦2.4	♦3.0
1 - 4	3	-	3	♦0.2	-	♦0.4
5 - 9	2	-	2	♦0.1	-	♦0.2
10 - 14	3	3	-	♦0.1	♦0.3	-
15 - 19	5	3	2	♦0.2	♦0.3	♦0.2
20 - 24	10	8	2	♦0.4	♦0.6	♦0.2
25 - 29	12	10	2	♦0.4	♦0.7	♦0.2
30 - 34	22	17	5	♦0.9	♦1.4	♦0.4
35 - 39	23	18	5	♦1.0	♦1.4	♦0.4
40 - 44	14	11	3	♦0.6	♦0.9	♦0.3
45 - 49	27	18	9	♦1.3	♦1.7	♦0.9
50 - 54	55	38	17	2.5	3.4	♦1.5
55 - 59	84	57	27	3.9	5.3	♦2.6
60 - 64	96	53	43	5.1	5.5	4.6
65 - 69	141	88	53	8.9	11.0	6.8
70 - 74	202	122	80	16.7	20.3	13.2
75 - 79	250	128	122	31.2	33.5	29.1
80 - 84	390	205	185	63.9	74.9	54.9
85 - 89	436	189	247	105.0	111.6	100.5
90 - 94	308	113	195	185.0	204.7	175.2
95 - 99	128	32	96	353.6	315.3	368.5
100 +	16	6	10	♦381.0	♦444.4	♦350.9

19. Deaths by age and sex and age-specific death rates by sex: latest available year, 2009 - 2018
Décès et taux de mortalité selon l'âge et le sexe : dernière année disponible, 2009 - 2018 (continued - suite)

Continent, country or area, date, code[a] and age (in years) / Continent, pays ou zone, date, code[a] et âge (en années)	Number - Nombre			Rate - Taux		
	Both sexes Les deux sexes	Male Masculin	Female Féminin	Both sexes Les deux sexes	Male Masculin	Female Féminin
EUROPE						
Ireland - Irlande						
2017 (+C)						
Total	30 317	15 425	14 892	6.3	6.5	6.2
0	187	90	97	3.0	2.8	3.1
1 - 4	28	17	11	◆0.1	◆0.1	◆0.1
5 - 9	27	12	15	◆0.1	◆0.1	◆0.1
10 - 14	18	10	8	◆0.1	◆0.1	◆0.1
15 - 19	56	36	20	0.2	0.2	◆0.1
20 - 24	87	64	23	0.3	0.5	◆0.2
25 - 29	125	91	34	0.4	0.6	0.2
30 - 34	186	123	63	0.5	0.7	0.3
35 - 39	238	153	85	0.6	0.8	0.4
40 - 44	373	230	143	1.0	1.3	0.8
45 - 49	514	314	200	1.6	1.9	1.2
50 - 54	804	501	303	2.7	3.4	2.0
55 - 59	1 115	694	421	4.1	5.1	3.1
60 - 64	1 589	927	662	6.6	7.7	5.5
65 - 69	2 241	1 367	874	10.6	13.1	8.3
70 - 74	3 109	1 843	1 266	18.6	22.4	14.9
75 - 79	3 949	2 293	1 656	33.9	41.9	26.9
80 - 84	5 011	2 637	2 374	60.7	73.2	51.0
85 - 89	5 251	2 354	2 897	114.1	135.2	101.3
90 - 94	3 807	1 272	2 535	207.0	230.1	197.0
95 - 99	1 367	353	1 014	279.4	283.8	277.9
100 +	235	44	191	380.9	360.7	385.9
Isle of Man - Île de Man[5]						
2016 (I)						
Total	870	437	433	10.4	10.6	10.3
0	2	-	2	◆2.5	-	◆5.3
1 - 4	1	1	-	◆0.3	◆0.6	-
5 - 9	-	-	-	-	-	-
10 - 14	3	2	1	◆0.7	◆0.9	◆0.5
15 - 19	1	1	-	◆0.2	◆0.4	-
20 - 24	3	2	1	◆0.7	◆0.9	◆0.5
25 - 29	3	3	-	◆0.7	◆1.4	-
30 - 34	5	3	2	◆1.1	◆1.4	◆0.8
35 - 39	5	4	1	◆1.0	◆1.7	◆0.4
40 - 44	8	6	2	◆1.4	◆2.2	◆0.7
45 - 49	11	7	4	◆1.7	◆2.2	◆1.2
50 - 54	22	15	7	◆3.3	◆4.5	◆2.1
55 - 59	28	16	12	◆4.8	◆5.5	◆4.0
60 - 64	36	23	13	7.0	◆8.8	◆5.1
65 - 69	60	38	22	11.0	14.0	◆8.1
70 - 74	85	50	35	20.2	24.1	16.4
75 - 79	126	78	48	39.9	51.0	29.5
80 - 84	128	64	64	60.1	66.8	54.7
85 - 89	153	67	86	110.9	128.4	100.2
90 - 94	118	38	80	174.8	188.1	169.1
95 - 99	58	15	43	308.5	◆283.0	318.5
100 +	14	4	10	◆560.0	◆400.0	◆666.7
Italy - Italie						
2017 (C)						
Total	649 061	309 505	339 556	10.7	10.5	10.9
0	1 251	670	581	2.7	2.8	2.6
1 - 4	232	132	100	0.1	0.1	0.1
5 - 9	192	99	93	0.1	0.1	0.1
10 - 14	261	159	102	0.1	0.1	0.1
15 - 19	561	404	157	0.2	0.3	0.1
20 - 24	872	629	243	0.3	0.4	0.2
25 - 29	1 001	721	280	0.3	0.4	0.2
30 - 34	1 324	893	431	0.4	0.5	0.3
35 - 39	2 055	1 283	772	0.5	0.7	0.4
40 - 44	4 084	2 560	1 524	0.9	1.1	0.7
45 - 49	7 167	4 406	2 761	1.5	1.8	1.1
50 - 54	11 480	7 071	4 409	2.4	2.9	1.8
55 - 59	16 282	10 126	6 156	3.8	4.9	2.8
60 - 64	23 211	14 603	8 608	6.2	8.1	4.4

565

19. Deaths by age and sex and age-specific death rates by sex: latest available year, 2009 - 2018
Décès et taux de mortalité selon l'âge et le sexe : dernière année disponible, 2009 - 2018 (continued - suite)

Continent, country or area, date, code[a] and age (in years) / Continent, pays ou zone, date, code[a] et âge (en années)	Number - Nombre			Rate - Taux		
	Both sexes Les deux sexes	Male Masculin	Female Féminin	Both sexes Les deux sexes	Male Masculin	Female Féminin
EUROPE						
Italy - Italie						
2017 (C)						
65 - 69	35 704	22 289	13 415	10.0	13.0	7.1
70 - 74	49 737	30 357	19 380	16.4	21.5	11.9
75 - 79	79 492	45 679	33 813	28.5	36.9	21.8
80 - 84	112 299	57 645	54 654	53.7	67.6	44.2
85 - 89	140 863	60 474	80 389	104.7	128.0	92.1
90 - 94	112 295	37 506	74 789	192.4	230.2	177.8
95 - 99	40 901	10 416	30 485	304.6	356.6	290.2
100 +	7 797	1 383	6 414	468.6	505.9	461.3
Latvia - Lettonie						
2018 (C)						
Total	28 820	13 546	15 274	14.9	15.2	14.6
0 - 4	75	41	34	0.7	0.7	0.7
5 - 9	15	10	5	♦0.2	♦0.2	♦0.1
10 - 14	16	11	5	♦0.2	♦0.2	♦0.1
15 - 19	45	35	10	0.5	0.8	♦0.2
20 - 24	68	44	24	0.7	0.9	♦0.5
25 - 29	120	101	19	0.9	1.5	♦0.3
30 - 34	245	192	53	1.8	2.7	0.8
35 - 39	285	215	70	2.3	3.4	1.1
40 - 44	491	359	132	3.8	5.7	2.0
45 - 49	660	476	184	5.0	7.4	2.7
50 - 54	1 040	741	299	7.9	11.9	4.3
55 - 59	1 605	1 141	464	11.2	17.4	5.9
60 - 64	2 050	1 372	678	16.3	25.3	9.5
65 - 69	2 636	1 636	1 000	23.6	37.2	14.8
70 - 74	2 751	1 540	1 211	32.5	51.0	22.2
75 - 79	4 105	1 977	2 128	46.5	71.0	35.2
80 - 84	4 668	1 737	2 931	80.3	109.2	69.4
85 +	7 053	1 646	5 407	152.8	166.0	149.1
Liechtenstein						
2017 (C)						
Total	249	127	122	6.6	6.8	6.4
0	-	-	-	-	-	-
1 - 4	-	-	-	-	-	-
5 - 9	-	-	-	-	-	-
10 - 14	1	1	-	♦0.5	♦1.0	-
15 - 19	-	-	-	-	-	-
20 - 24	1	1	-	♦0.5	♦0.9	-
25 - 29	1	1	-	♦0.4	♦0.9	-
30 - 34	1	-	1	♦0.4	-	♦0.8
35 - 39	-	-	-	-	-	-
40 - 44	3	3	-	♦1.1	♦2.3	-
45 - 49	8	7	1	♦2.5	♦4.4	♦0.6
50 - 54	7	4	3	♦2.2	♦2.6	♦1.9
55 - 59	8	5	3	♦2.7	♦3.5	♦2.0
60 - 64	17	8	9	♦7.0	♦6.6	♦7.3
65 - 69	31	22	9	14.2	♦20.2	♦8.2
70 - 74	23	15	8	♦12.9	♦17.1	♦8.9
75 - 79	31	21	10	25.1	♦37.6	♦14.8
80 - 84	40	16	24	53.1	♦53.0	♦53.2
85 - 89	31	12	19	80.7	♦84.5	♦78.5
90 - 94	33	7	26	180.3	♦175.0	♦181.8
95 - 99	11	3	8	♦261.9	♦250.0	♦266.7
100 +	2	1	1	♦500.0	♦500.0	♦500.0
Lithuania - Lituanie						
2017 (C)						
Total	40 142	19 286	20 856	14.2	14.8	13.7
0	85	45	40	2.9	2.9	2.8
1 - 4	22	15	7	♦0.2	♦0.2	♦0.1
5 - 9	24	17	7	♦0.2	♦0.2	♦0.1
10 - 14	21	14	7	♦0.2	♦0.2	♦0.1
15 - 19	65	51	14	0.4	0.7	♦0.2
20 - 24	111	79	32	0.6	0.9	0.4
25 - 29	201	159	42	1.1	1.6	0.5
30 - 34	294	229	65	1.6	2.5	0.7

Continent, country or area, date, code[a] and age (in years) Continent, pays ou zone, date, code[a] et âge (en années)	Number - Nombre			Rate - Taux		
	Both sexes Les deux sexes	Male Masculin	Female Féminin	Both sexes Les deux sexes	Male Masculin	Female Féminin
EUROPE						
Lithuania - Lituanie						
2017 (C)						
35 - 39	406	295	111	2.4	3.5	1.3
40 - 44	655	492	163	3.6	5.5	1.7
45 - 49	1 003	717	286	4.9	7.4	2.7
50 - 54	1 433	1 030	403	6.8	10.4	3.6
55 - 59	2 213	1 569	644	9.9	15.4	5.3
60 - 64	2 600	1 824	776	14.8	24.1	7.7
65 - 69	3 287	2 115	1 172	21.5	34.9	12.7
70 - 74	3 706	2 115	1 591	30.4	48.4	20.4
75 - 79	5 325	2 651	2 674	44.8	68.0	33.5
80 - 84	6 706	2 640	4 066	76.0	103.6	64.8
85 - 89	6 917	2 152	4 765	139.2	167.9	129.2
90 - 94	3 940	872	3 068	239.4	264.9	233.0
95 - 99	970	167	803	379.1	387.5	377.3
100 +	158	38	120	572.5	550.7	579.7
Luxembourg						
2017 (C)						
Total	4 263	2 131	2 132	7.2	7.2	7.3
0	20	15	5	✦3.3	✦4.8	✦1.7
1 - 4	6	3	3	✦0.2	✦0.2	✦0.2
5 - 9	2	1	1	✦0.1	✦0.1	✦0.1
10 - 14	1	-	1	-	-	✦0.1
15 - 19	9	7	2	✦0.3	✦0.4	✦0.1
20 - 24	12	10	2	✦0.3	✦0.5	✦0.1
25 - 29	17	9	8	✦0.4	✦0.4	✦0.4
30 - 34	11	9	2	✦0.2	✦0.4	✦0.1
35 - 39	31	20	11	0.7	✦0.9	✦0.5
40 - 44	37	22	15	0.8	✦1.0	✦0.7
45 - 49	94	56	38	2.0	2.3	1.7
50 - 54	119	77	42	2.6	3.3	2.0
55 - 59	147	92	55	3.8	4.6	3.0
60 - 64	226	144	82	7.2	9.1	5.2
65 - 69	380	252	128	14.9	19.7	10.0
70 - 74	422	259	163	21.6	27.4	16.2
75 - 79	517	276	241	32.6	39.6	27.1
80 - 84	620	304	316	52.5	63.0	45.2
85 - 89	855	353	502	108.2	125.2	98.7
90 - 94	538	167	371	190.8	244.2	173.8
95 - 99	164	53	111	288.7	384.1	258.1
100 +	35	2	33	473.0	✦250.0	500.0
Malta - Malte						
2018 (C)						
Total	3 688	1 876	1 812	7.8	7.8	7.7
0	25	16	9	✦5.6	✦7.0	✦4.1
1 - 4	4	3	1	✦0.2	✦0.3	✦0.1
5 - 9	2	-	2	✦0.1	-	✦0.2
10 - 14	-	-	-	-	-	-
15 - 19	1	1	-	-	✦0.1	-
20 - 24	7	5	2	✦0.2	✦0.3	✦0.1
25 - 34	35	24	11	0.4	✦0.6	✦0.3
35 - 44	59	33	26	0.8	0.9	✦0.8
45 - 54	113	73	40	2.0	2.5	1.5
55 - 64	328	196	132	5.4	6.4	4.3
65 - 74	739	473	266	13.3	17.6	9.3
75 +	2 375	1 052	1 323	70.1	76.9	65.5
Montenegro - Monténégro						
2018 (C)						
Total	6 504	3 353	3 151	10.5	10.9	10.0
0	12	8	4	✦1.6	✦2.0	✦1.1
1 - 4	9	4	5	✦0.3	✦0.3	✦0.3
5 - 9	1	1	-	-	✦0.1	-
10 - 14	7	5	2	✦0.2	✦0.3	✦0.1
15 - 19	8	8	-	✦0.2	✦0.4	-
20 - 24	19	13	6	✦0.5	✦0.6	✦0.3
25 - 29	17	11	6	✦0.4	✦0.5	✦0.3
30 - 34	31	21	10	0.7	✦0.9	✦0.4

19. Deaths by age and sex and age-specific death rates by sex: latest available year, 2009 - 2018
Décès et taux de mortalité selon l'âge et le sexe : dernière année disponible, 2009 - 2018 (continued - suite)

Continent, country or area, date, code[a] and age (in years) / Continent, pays ou zone, date, code[a] et âge (en années)	Number - Nombre			Rate - Taux		
	Both sexes / Les deux sexes	Male / Masculin	Female / Féminin	Both sexes / Les deux sexes	Male / Masculin	Female / Féminin
EUROPE						
Montenegro - Monténégro						
2018 (C)						
35 - 39	38	27	11	0.9	♦1.2	♦0.5
40 - 44	79	52	27	1.9	2.5	♦1.3
45 - 49	136	85	51	3.4	4.3	2.5
50 - 54	187	118	69	4.5	5.8	3.3
55 - 59	376	247	129	8.9	12.0	6.0
60 - 64	522	340	182	12.9	17.2	8.8
65 - 69	718	459	259	21.2	29.5	14.1
70 - 74	656	380	276	33.0	44.6	24.3
75 - 79	1 042	505	537	56.0	66.0	49.0
80 - 84	1 223	514	709	100.6	106.4	96.8
85 +	1 423	555	868	191.2	188.3	193.1
Netherlands - Pays-Bas[43]						
2017 (C)						
Total	150 214	72 661	77 553	8.8	8.6	9.0
0	607	347	260	3.5	3.9	3.1
1 - 4	87	46	41	0.1	0.1	0.1
5 - 9	79	46	33	0.1	0.1	0.1
10 - 14	99	62	37	0.1	0.1	0.1
15 - 19	228	156	72	0.2	0.3	0.1
20 - 24	304	214	90	0.3	0.4	0.2
25 - 29	358	260	98	0.3	0.5	0.2
30 - 34	444	271	173	0.4	0.5	0.3
35 - 39	632	376	256	0.6	0.7	0.5
40 - 44	1 021	592	429	1.0	1.1	0.8
45 - 49	2 042	1 165	877	1.6	1.8	1.4
50 - 54	3 393	1 941	1 452	2.6	3.0	2.3
55 - 59	5 345	3 014	2 331	4.5	5.1	3.9
60 - 64	7 971	4 607	3 364	7.5	8.7	6.3
65 - 69	11 544	6 850	4 694	11.4	13.6	9.2
70 - 74	15 537	9 173	6 364	19.2	23.3	15.3
75 - 79	18 484	10 456	8 028	32.3	39.6	26.1
80 - 84	24 358	12 521	11 837	60.6	74.5	50.6
85 - 89	28 041	11 925	16 116	116.9	140.2	104.2
90 - 94	20 770	6 629	14 141	210.9	240.2	199.5
95 - 99	7 671	1 826	5 845	354.3	403.4	341.3
100 +	1 199	184	1 015	538.9	575.0	532.8
North Macedonia - Macédoine du Nord						
2018 (C)						
Total	19 727	10 339	9 388	9.5	9.9	9.1
0	122	71	51	5.7	6.4	4.9
1 - 4	14	11	3	♦0.2	♦0.2	♦0.1
5 - 9	13	6	7	♦0.1	♦0.1	♦0.1
10 - 14	22	15	7	♦0.2	♦0.3	♦0.1
15 - 24	70	54	16	0.3	0.4	♦0.1
25 - 34	166	114	52	0.5	0.7	0.3
35 - 44	372	244	128	1.2	1.5	0.8
45 - 54	1 000	656	344	3.5	4.5	2.4
55 - 64	2 716	1 736	980	10.3	13.3	7.4
65 - 74	4 610	2 656	1 954	25.9	32.4	20.3
75 - 84	6 877	3 243	3 634	77.8	85.3	72.1
85 +	3 745	1 533	2 212	224.7	248.2	210.9
Norway - Norvège[44]						
2017 (C)						
Total	40 774	19 649	21 125	7.7	7.4	8.1
0	130	67	63	2.2	2.2	2.2
1 - 4	33	21	12	0.1	♦0.2	♦0.1
5 - 9	20	9	11	♦0.1	♦0.1	♦0.1
10 - 14	26	12	14	♦0.1	♦0.1	♦0.1
15 - 19	75	51	24	0.2	0.3	♦0.2
20 - 24	141	116	25	0.4	0.7	♦0.2
25 - 29	151	103	48	0.4	0.5	0.3
30 - 34	167	118	49	0.5	0.6	0.3
35 - 39	204	128	76	0.6	0.7	0.5
40 - 44	296	178	118	0.8	1.0	0.7
45 - 49	516	302	214	1.4	1.6	1.2

Continent, country or area, date, code[a] and age (in years) Continent, pays ou zone, date, code[a] et âge (en annèes)	Number - Nombre			Rate - Taux		
	Both sexes Les deux sexes	Male Masculin	Female Féminin	Both sexes Les deux sexes	Male Masculin	Female Féminin
EUROPE						
Norway - Norvège[44]						
2017 (C)						
50 - 54	820	492	328	2.3	2.7	1.9
55 - 59	1 233	765	468	3.8	4.7	3.0
60 - 64	1 824	1 109	715	6.1	7.4	4.8
65 - 69	2 897	1 741	1 156	10.6	12.8	8.5
70 - 74	4 091	2 305	1 786	17.1	19.8	14.6
75 - 79	4 518	2 515	2 003	29.7	35.8	24.5
80 - 84	5 844	3 052	2 792	55.6	68.2	46.2
85 - 89	7 640	3 368	4 272	106.1	125.8	94.4
90 - 94	6 717	2 377	4 340	194.3	225.6	180.5
95 - 99	2 979	747	2 232	327.8	381.6	313.0
100 +	452	73	379	458.4	450.6	460.0
Poland - Pologne						
2017 (C)						
Total	402 852	207 671	195 181	10.6	11.3	10.0
0	1 604	908	696	4.1	4.5	3.7
1 - 4	241	140	101	0.2	0.2	0.1
5 - 9	178	97	81	0.1	0.1	0.1
10 - 14	209	116	93	0.1	0.1	0.1
15 - 19	661	461	200	0.4	0.5	0.2
20 - 24	1 251	989	262	0.6	0.9	0.2
25 - 29	1 836	1 480	356	0.7	1.1	0.3
30 - 34	2 847	2 247	600	0.9	1.4	0.4
35 - 39	4 019	3 048	971	1.3	2.0	0.6
40 - 44	5 795	4 302	1 493	2.1	3.0	1.1
45 - 49	8 173	5 971	2 202	3.5	5.0	1.9
50 - 54	12 829	9 282	3 547	5.6	8.2	3.1
55 - 59	23 897	16 785	7 112	9.0	13.1	5.2
60 - 64	36 727	24 971	11 756	13.4	19.5	8.1
65 - 69	44 898	28 778	16 120	19.4	28.0	12.6
70 - 74	37 264	21 986	15 278	27.2	38.4	19.1
75 - 79	45 552	24 055	21 497	41.4	58.0	31.4
80 - 84	59 982	26 561	33 421	69.1	90.8	58.0
85 - 89	64 164	22 713	41 451	121.7	145.8	111.6
90 - 94	39 146	10 264	28 882	207.1	226.6	200.9
95 - 99	10 087	2 251	7 836	303.6	314.2	300.6
100 +	1 492	266	1 226	284.7	244.3	295.3
Portugal[45]						
2017 (C)						
Total	109 758	55 088	54 670	10.7	11.3	10.1
0	229	134	95	2.6	3.0	2.2
1 - 4	52	31	21	0.2	0.2	✦0.1
5 - 9	45	26	19	0.1	✦0.1	✦0.1
10 - 14	47	29	18	0.1	✦0.1	✦0.1
15 - 19	117	88	29	0.2	0.3	✦0.1
20 - 24	195	124	71	0.4	0.5	0.3
25 - 29	240	171	69	0.4	0.6	0.3
30 - 34	307	207	100	0.5	0.7	0.3
35 - 39	577	370	207	0.8	1.1	0.6
40 - 44	1 084	692	392	1.3	1.8	0.9
45 - 49	1 710	1 136	574	2.2	3.1	1.4
50 - 54	2 878	1 948	930	3.8	5.4	2.3
55 - 59	3 884	2 754	1 130	5.4	8.1	3.0
60 - 64	5 111	3 512	1 599	7.8	11.5	4.6
65 - 69	6 836	4 489	2 347	11.1	15.9	7.1
70 - 74	9 032	5 555	3 477	17.5	24.5	12.0
75 - 79	13 066	7 379	5 687	30.7	41.3	23.0
80 - 84	19 656	9 900	9 756	56.4	73.5	45.7
85 - 89	22 215	9 382	12 833	110.2	136.4	96.6
90 - 94	16 131	5 485	10 646	228.7	283.8	207.9
95 - 99	5 369	1 480	3 889	355.2	383.5	345.6
100 +	977	196	781	228.5	120.4	295.1
Republic of Moldova - République de Moldova[46]						
2018 (C)						
Total	37 200	19 720	17 480	13.7	15.3	12.4
0	326	195	131	9.3	10.8	7.7

19. Deaths by age and sex and age-specific death rates by sex: latest available year, 2009 - 2018
Décès et taux de mortalité selon l'âge et le sexe : dernière année disponible, 2009 - 2018 (continued - suite)

Continent, country or area, date, code[a] and age (in years) / Continent, pays ou zone, date, code[a] et âge (en années)	Number - Nombre			Rate - Taux		
	Both sexes Les deux sexes	Male Masculin	Female Féminin	Both sexes Les deux sexes	Male Masculin	Female Féminin
EUROPE						
Republic of Moldova - République de Moldova[46]						
2018 (C)						
1 - 4	59	31	28	0.4	0.4	♦0.4
5 - 9	44	28	16	0.3	♦0.3	♦0.2
10 - 14	44	25	19	0.3	♦0.3	♦0.3
15 - 19	95	68	27	0.7	0.9	♦0.4
20 - 24	130	102	28	0.8	1.2	♦0.3
25 - 29	227	177	50	1.1	1.8	0.5
30 - 34	410	318	92	1.8	2.9	0.8
35 - 39	584	445	139	3.0	4.7	1.4
40 - 44	876	639	237	5.0	7.4	2.7
45 - 49	1 173	858	315	7.0	10.5	3.7
50 - 54	1 718	1 231	487	10.0	15.0	5.5
55 - 59	3 011	2 048	963	14.6	21.4	8.8
60 - 64	4 256	2 883	1 373	22.7	34.9	13.1
65 - 69	5 299	3 124	2 175	32.3	46.0	22.6
70 - 74	3 223	1 658	1 565	45.2	60.7	35.5
75 - 79	5 121	2 277	2 844	77.3	97.6	66.2
80 - 84	5 049	1 916	3 133	124.2	147.4	113.3
85 +	5 536	1 682	3 854	246.2	250.8	244.2
85 - 89	3 628	1 151	2 477	...	...	...
90 - 94	1 537	424	1 113	...	...	...
95 - 99	348	98	250	...	...	...
100 +	23	9	14	...	...	...
Unknown - Inconnu	19	15	4	..	..	..
Romania - Roumanie						
2017 (C)						
Total	261 402	136 154	125 248	13.3	14.2	12.5
0	1 364	779	585	6.9	7.6	6.0
1 - 4	275	143	132	0.4	0.4	0.3
5 - 9	155	94	61	0.2	0.2	0.1
10 - 14	215	130	85	0.2	0.2	0.2
15 - 19	486	356	130	0.5	0.7	0.3
20 - 24	564	425	139	0.5	0.8	0.3
25 - 29	906	654	252	0.7	1.0	0.4
30 - 34	1 177	824	353	0.9	1.2	0.6
35 - 39	1 983	1 380	603	1.3	1.8	0.8
40 - 44	3 560	2 543	1 017	2.3	3.2	1.4
45 - 49	7 384	5 371	2 013	4.4	6.3	2.5
50 - 54	7 734	5 613	2 121	6.9	9.9	3.9
55 - 59	14 041	9 974	4 067	11.5	16.8	6.5
60 - 64	21 982	15 041	6 941	16.2	23.9	9.6
65 - 69	26 066	16 684	9 382	22.4	32.3	14.4
70 - 74	25 698	14 794	10 904	32.9	45.1	24.0
75 - 79	38 390	19 097	19 293	54.8	70.9	44.7
80 - 84	46 678	19 921	26 757	91.7	108.2	82.3
85 - 89	39 260	14 759	24 501	150.8	164.9	143.5
90 - 94	19 118	6 294	12 824	222.5	222.6	222.4
95 - 99	3 948	1 163	2 785	214.1	205.6	217.9
100 +	418	115	303	221.6	197.6	232.4
Russian Federation - Fédération de Russie[25]						
2011 (C)						
Total	1 925 720	997 494	928 226	13.5	15.1	12.1
0 - 4	16 465	9 472	6 993	2.1	2.3	1.8
0	13 168	7 572	5 596	8.0	9.0	7.0
1 - 4	3 297	1 900	1 397	0.5	0.6	0.5
5 - 9	1 972	1 160	812	0.3	0.3	0.2
10 - 14	2 006	1 249	757	0.3	0.4	0.2
15 - 19	6 656	4 634	2 022	0.8	1.1	0.5
20 - 24	18 666	14 374	4 292	1.5	2.3	0.7
25 - 29	32 160	24 684	7 476	2.7	4.1	1.3
30 - 34	45 452	34 853	10 599	4.1	6.4	1.9
35 - 39	50 630	38 270	12 360	5.0	7.7	2.4
40 - 44	55 007	40 708	14 299	6.0	9.1	3.0
45 - 49	81 813	60 225	21 588	7.7	12.0	3.8
50 - 54	124 961	89 971	34 990	10.9	17.1	5.6
55 - 59	156 587	108 205	48 382	15.6	24.9	8.5

Continent, country or area, date, code[a] and age (in years) / Continent, pays ou zone, date, code[a] et âge (en années)	Number - Nombre			Rate - Taux		
	Both sexes Les deux sexes	Male Masculin	Female Féminin	Both sexes Les deux sexes	Male Masculin	Female Féminin
EUROPE						
Russian Federation - Fédération de Russie[25]						
2011 (C)						
60 - 64	177 990	118 728	59 262	22.7	36.6	12.9
65 - 69	111 156	66 246	44 910	27.8	44.4	17.9
70 - 74	263 633	136 875	126 758	40.8	62.8	29.6
75 - 79	232 616	99 250	133 366	65.5	92.9	53.7
80 - 84	290 314	94 614	195 700	101.1	129.8	91.4
85 - 89	172 178	35 533	136 645	166.8	187.8	162.0
90 - 94	56 714	9 585	47 129	244.6	241.3	245.3
95 - 99	18 647	2 652	15 995	320.7	294.4	325.5
100 +	2 562	320	2 242	352.6	294.4	380.8
Unknown - Inconnu	7 536	5 887	1 649	..	..	..
San Marino - Saint-Marin						
2017 (C)						
Total	278	125	153	8.1	7.5	8.7
0	-	-	-	-	-	-
1 - 4	1	-	1	♦0.8	-	♦1.7
5 - 9	-	-	-	-	-	-
10 - 14	-	-	-	-	-	-
15 - 19	-	-	-	-	-	-
20 - 24	-	-	-	-	-	-
25 - 29	-	-	-	-	-	-
30 - 34	-	-	-	-	-	-
35 - 39	1	1	-	♦0.4	♦0.9	-
40 - 44	1	-	1	♦0.3	-	♦0.6
45 - 49	7	4	3	♦2.2	♦2.6	♦1.9
50 - 54	5	4	1	♦1.6	♦2.7	♦0.6
55 - 59	12	5	7	♦4.8	♦4.1	♦5.6
60 - 64	6	5	1	♦2.9	♦5.1	♦0.9
65 - 69	15	10	5	♦8.2	♦11.4	♦5.3
70 - 74	18	12	6	♦11.8	♦16.3	♦7.6
75 - 79	32	19	13	26.0	♦32.5	♦20.2
80 - 84	46	23	23	50.1	♦56.8	♦44.8
85 - 89	56	19	37	86.7	♦82.6	88.9
90 - 94	53	18	35	202.3	♦222.2	193.4
95 - 99	22	5	17	♦293.3	♦294.1	♦293.1
100 +	3	-	3	♦375.0	...	♦375.0
Serbia - Serbie[47]						
2017 (+C)						
Total	103 722	51 756	51 966	14.8	15.1	14.4
0	305	176	129	4.7	5.3	4.1
1 - 4	70	36	34	0.3	0.3	0.3
5 - 9	30	16	14	♦0.1	♦0.1	♦0.1
10 - 14	61	38	23	0.2	0.2	♦0.1
15 - 19	106	75	31	0.3	0.4	0.2
20 - 24	161	127	34	0.4	0.6	0.2
25 - 29	239	177	62	0.5	0.8	0.3
30 - 34	382	283	99	0.8	1.2	0.4
35 - 39	596	384	212	1.2	1.5	0.9
40 - 44	924	595	329	1.9	2.4	1.3
45 - 49	1 533	975	558	3.3	4.2	2.4
50 - 54	2 792	1 774	1 018	6.0	7.7	4.3
55 - 59	4 846	3 192	1 654	9.8	13.4	6.4
60 - 64	8 401	5 350	3 051	15.4	20.7	10.6
65 - 69	11 344	7 072	4 272	23.0	31.4	16.0
70 - 74	10 564	5 820	4 744	34.7	43.8	27.7
75 - 79	16 342	7 915	8 427	60.5	70.9	53.2
80 - 84	21 118	9 061	12 057	110.1	120.7	103.3
85 - 89	16 423	6 246	10 177	184.4	189.6	181.4
90 - 94	6 319	2 100	4 219	251.3	243.6	255.4
95 - 99	1 097	326	771	209.0	187.7	219.6
100 +	69	18	51	125.5	♦92.8	143.3
Slovakia - Slovaquie						
2017 (C)						
Total	53 914	27 489	26 425	9.9	10.4	9.5
0	263	155	108	4.5	5.2	3.8
1 - 4	58	36	22	0.3	0.3	♦0.2

571

19. Deaths by age and sex and age-specific death rates by sex: latest available year, 2009 - 2018
Décès et taux de mortalité selon l'âge et le sexe : dernière année disponible, 2009 - 2018 (continued - suite)

Continent, country or area, date, code[a] and age (in years) / Continent, pays ou zone, date, code[a] et âge (en années)	Number - Nombre			Rate - Taux		
	Both sexes Les deux sexes	Male Masculin	Female Féminin	Both sexes Les deux sexes	Male Masculin	Female Féminin
EUROPE						
Slovakia - Slovaquie						
2017 (C)						
5 - 9	34	18	16	0.1	♦0.1	♦0.1
10 - 14	33	22	11	0.1	♦0.2	♦0.1
15 - 19	107	76	31	0.4	0.5	0.2
20 - 24	153	122	31	0.5	0.7	0.2
25 - 29	231	157	74	0.6	0.8	0.4
30 - 34	322	235	87	0.7	1.1	0.4
35 - 39	486	338	148	1.1	1.5	0.7
40 - 44	792	567	225	1.8	2.5	1.0
45 - 49	1 102	756	346	3.1	4.1	1.9
50 - 54	2 038	1 440	598	5.6	8.0	3.3
55 - 59	3 075	2 126	949	8.5	12.0	5.1
60 - 64	4 987	3 433	1 554	13.6	20.0	8.0
65 - 69	5 768	3 743	2 025	19.0	27.7	12.0
70 - 74	5 924	3 466	2 458	29.3	42.3	20.5
75 - 79	6 915	3 437	3 478	46.5	63.4	36.8
80 - 84	8 090	3 258	4 832	83.1	103.1	73.5
85 - 89	7 973	2 616	5 357	147.0	167.6	138.6
90 - 94	4 440	1 221	3 219	236.8	259.0	229.4
95 - 99	1 033	250	783	271.5	244.0	281.6
100 +	90	17	73	94.4	♦48.1	121.8
Slovenia - Slovénie						
2017 (C)						
Total	20 509	10 136	10 373	9.9	9.9	10.0
0	42	21	21	2.1	♦2.0	♦2.1
1 - 4	5	2	3	♦0.1	-	♦0.1
5 - 9	7	3	4	♦0.1	♦0.1	♦0.1
10 - 14	8	4	4	♦0.1	♦0.1	♦0.1
15 - 19	21	13	8	♦0.2	♦0.3	♦0.2
20 - 24	43	27	16	0.4	♦0.5	♦0.3
25 - 29	55	45	10	0.5	0.7	♦0.2
30 - 34	73	58	15	0.5	0.8	♦0.2
35 - 39	96	65	31	0.6	0.8	0.4
40 - 44	150	99	51	1.0	1.2	0.7
45 - 49	265	173	92	1.8	2.3	1.3
50 - 54	533	369	164	3.4	4.7	2.1
55 - 59	863	579	284	5.8	7.7	3.8
60 - 64	1 378	940	438	9.4	12.8	6.0
65 - 69	1 645	1 092	553	13.3	18.2	8.7
70 - 74	1 782	1 127	655	20.4	28.6	13.6
75 - 79	2 603	1 476	1 127	33.5	45.2	25.0
80 - 84	3 626	1 733	1 893	62.8	82.5	51.6
85 - 89	3 927	1 481	2 446	115.2	147.6	101.7
90 - 94	2 572	668	1 904	204.9	249.2	192.9
95 - 99	718	146	572	324.7	340.3	321.0
100 +	97	15	82	510.5	♦441.2	525.6
Spain - Espagne						
2017 (C)						
Total	422 037	212 526	209 511	9.1	9.3	8.8
0	1 064	601	463	2.7	3.0	2.4
1 - 4	213	127	86	0.1	0.1	0.1
5 - 9	169	89	80	0.1	0.1	0.1
10 - 14	198	103	95	0.1	0.1	0.1
15 - 19	384	251	133	0.2	0.2	0.1
20 - 24	569	391	178	0.3	0.3	0.2
25 - 29	767	533	234	0.3	0.4	0.2
30 - 34	1 088	753	335	0.4	0.5	0.2
35 - 39	2 027	1 299	728	0.6	0.7	0.4
40 - 44	3 422	2 174	1 248	0.9	1.1	0.6
45 - 49	5 967	3 838	2 129	1.6	2.0	1.1
50 - 54	9 954	6 587	3 367	2.8	3.7	1.9
55 - 59	14 234	9 572	4 662	4.5	6.1	2.9
60 - 64	17 935	12 207	5 728	6.7	9.4	4.2
65 - 69	24 173	16 581	7 592	10.1	14.6	6.1
70 - 74	32 671	21 493	11 178	15.6	22.2	9.9
75 - 79	40 463	24 417	16 046	26.4	36.1	18.7

19. Deaths by age and sex and age-specific death rates by sex: latest available year, 2009 - 2018
Décès et taux de mortalité selon l'âge et le sexe : dernière année disponible, 2009 - 2018 (continued - suite)

Continent, country or area, date, code[a] and age (in years) Continent, pays ou zone, date, code[a] et âge (en années)	Number - Nombre			Rate - Taux		
	Both sexes Les deux sexes	Male Masculin	Female Féminin	Both sexes Les deux sexes	Male Masculin	Female Féminin
EUROPE						
Spain - Espagne						
2017 (C)						
80 - 84	72 430	38 248	34 182	50.5	66.0	40.0
85 - 89	91 166	40 301	50 865	97.7	119.6	85.3
90 - 94	70 865	24 784	46 081	179.6	206.8	167.8
95 - 99	26 972	7 189	19 783	280.6	298.1	274.7
100 +	5 306	988	4 318	411.9	390.2	417.3
Sweden - Suède						
2017 (C)						
Total	91 972	44 856	47 116	9.1	8.9	9.4
0	278	146	132	2.4	2.4	2.3
1 - 4	49	24	25	0.1	♦0.1	♦0.1
5 - 9	38	19	19	0.1	♦0.1	♦0.1
10 - 14	51	29	22	0.1	♦0.1	♦0.1
15 - 19	129	88	41	0.2	0.3	0.2
20 - 24	268	205	63	0.4	0.6	0.2
25 - 29	400	302	98	0.6	0.8	0.3
30 - 34	358	241	117	0.5	0.7	0.4
35 - 39	401	279	122	0.6	0.9	0.4
40 - 44	578	374	204	0.9	1.1	0.6
45 - 49	906	534	372	1.4	1.6	1.1
50 - 54	1 495	893	602	2.2	2.6	1.8
55 - 59	2 139	1 288	851	3.7	4.4	2.9
60 - 64	3 646	2 186	1 460	6.5	7.8	5.2
65 - 69	5 926	3 474	2 452	10.5	12.4	8.5
70 - 74	9 432	5 437	3 995	17.2	20.3	14.3
75 - 79	10 982	6 163	4 819	29.9	35.6	24.9
80 - 84	14 124	7 279	6 845	56.6	67.0	48.5
85 - 89	17 864	8 085	9 779	109.6	130.5	96.8
90 - 94	15 217	5 723	9 494	201.2	239.5	183.5
95 - 99	6 665	1 887	4 778	340.5	394.7	322.9
100 +	1 026	200	826	504.8	584.8	488.6
Switzerland - Suisse						
2017 (C)						
Total	66 971	32 406	34 565	7.9	7.7	8.1
0	310	178	132	3.6	4.0	3.2
1 - 4	48	30	18	0.1	♦0.2	♦0.1
5 - 9	25	14	11	♦0.1	♦0.1	♦0.1
10 - 14	31	15	16	0.1	♦0.1	♦0.1
15 - 19	92	64	28	0.2	0.3	♦0.1
20 - 24	143	112	31	0.3	0.4	0.1
25 - 29	188	128	60	0.3	0.4	0.2
30 - 34	222	156	66	0.4	0.5	0.2
35 - 39	329	201	128	0.6	0.7	0.4
40 - 44	440	285	155	0.8	1.0	0.5
45 - 49	854	538	316	1.3	1.7	1.0
50 - 54	1 492	965	527	2.2	2.8	1.6
55 - 59	2 128	1 341	787	3.6	4.6	2.7
60 - 64	2 773	1 804	969	5.7	7.5	4.0
65 - 69	4 040	2 504	1 536	9.4	12.1	6.9
70 - 74	5 852	3 522	2 330	15.1	19.1	11.4
75 - 79	7 261	4 117	3 144	25.2	31.8	19.8
80 - 84	10 571	5 339	5 232	48.9	59.7	41.3
85 - 89	13 566	5 831	7 735	98.2	117.2	87.5
90 - 94	11 324	3 894	7 430	186.9	218.7	173.7
95 - 99	4 491	1 207	3 284	319.3	363.1	305.7
100 +	791	161	630	517.7	619.2	496.8
Ukraine[48]						
2017 (+C)						
Total	574 123	281 784	292 339	13.6	14.4	12.9
0	2 786	1 608	1 178	7.4	8.2	6.4
1 - 4	598	357	241	0.3	0.4	0.3
5 - 9	391	214	177	0.2	0.2	0.2
10 - 14	402	254	148	0.2	0.2	0.2
15 - 19	890	633	257	0.5	0.7	0.3
20 - 24	1 908	1 492	416	0.8	1.2	0.4
25 - 29	4 071	3 091	980	1.3	1.9	0.6

19. Deaths by age and sex and age-specific death rates by sex: latest available year, 2009 - 2018
Décès et taux de mortalité selon l'âge et le sexe : dernière année disponible, 2009 - 2018 (continued - suite)

Continent, country or area, date, code[a] and age (in years) / Continent, pays ou zone, date, code[a] et âge (en années)	Number - Nombre			Rate - Taux		
	Both sexes Les deux sexes	Male Masculin	Female Féminin	Both sexes Les deux sexes	Male Masculin	Female Féminin
EUROPE						
Ukraine[48]						
2017 (+C)						
30 - 34	7 460	5 679	1 781	2.1	3.1	1.0
35 - 39	10 358	7 706	2 652	3.2	4.8	1.6
40 - 44	13 614	10 018	3 596	4.5	6.7	2.3
45 - 49	17 043	12 408	4 635	6.0	9.1	3.1
50 - 54	23 962	17 277	6 685	8.3	13.1	4.3
55 - 59	36 678	25 946	10 732	11.6	18.6	6.1
60 - 64	46 399	31 156	15 243	17.2	27.8	9.7
65 - 69	58 382	35 464	22 918	25.2	39.4	16.2
70 - 74	49 917	26 199	23 718	37.9	57.4	27.5
75 - 79	99 211	43 174	56 037	59.4	83.4	48.6
80 - 84	82 511	29 856	52 655	91.7	113.2	82.8
85 - 89	73 757	20 398	53 359	147.4	159.0	143.3
90 - 94	36 507	7 556	28 951	211.5	188.0	218.7
95 - 99	6 549	1 127	5 422	203.3	119.4	238.1
100 +	729	171	558	94.9	71.2	105.7
United Kingdom of Great Britain and Northern Ireland - Royaume-Uni de Grande-Bretagne et d'Irlande du Nord[49]						
2017 (+C)						
Total	605 748	297 999	307 749	9.2	9.1	9.2
0	2 947	1 651	1 296	3.8	4.2	3.5
1 - 4	433	247	186	0.1	0.2	0.1
5 - 9	301	171	130	0.1	0.1	0.1
10 - 14	317	178	139	0.1	0.1	0.1
15 - 19	870	579	291	0.2	0.3	0.2
20 - 24	1 407	1 005	402	0.3	0.5	0.2
25 - 29	1 984	1 395	589	0.4	0.6	0.3
30 - 34	2 782	1 812	970	0.6	0.8	0.4
35 - 39	4 125	2 597	1 528	1.0	1.2	0.7
40 - 44	5 862	3 623	2 239	1.4	1.8	1.1
45 - 49	9 846	6 048	3 798	2.2	2.7	1.6
50 - 54	14 818	8 747	6 071	3.2	3.8	2.6
55 - 59	20 013	12 013	8 000	4.8	5.8	3.8
60 - 64	27 755	16 495	11 260	7.7	9.4	6.1
65 - 69	42 015	24 743	17 272	12.0	14.6	9.6
70 - 74	59 330	34 313	25 017	19.3	23.3	15.6
75 - 79	74 125	40 707	33 418	33.9	40.4	28.3
80 - 84	97 550	49 940	47 610	59.5	70.1	51.4
85 - 89	110 516	49 262	61 254	109.2	125.5	98.9
90 - 94	85 338	31 323	54 015	191.4	214.4	180.2
95 - 99	36 868	10 047	26 821	315.0	346.8	304.6
100 +	6 546	1 103	5 443	445.4	444.9	445.5
OCEANIA - OCÉANIE						
American Samoa - Samoas américaines						
2017 (C)						
Total	310	176	134	...	...	...
0	14	5	9	...	...	...
1 - 4	1	1	-	...	...	...
5 - 9	2	1	1	...	...	...
10 - 14	1	1	-	...	...	...
15 - 19	3	3	-	...	...	...
20 - 24	6	6	-	...	...	...
25 - 29	4	3	1	...	...	...
30 - 34	5	4	1	...	...	...
35 - 39	7	3	4	...	...	...
40 - 44	7	3	4	...	...	...
45 - 49	19	14	5	...	...	...
50 - 54	25	12	13	...	...	...
55 - 59	22	17	5	...	...	...
60 - 64	31	20	11	...	...	...
65 - 69	34	18	16	...	...	...
70 - 74	36	21	15	...	...	...

19. Deaths by age and sex and age-specific death rates by sex: latest available year, 2009 - 2018
Décès et taux de mortalité selon l'âge et le sexe : dernière année disponible, 2009 - 2018 (continued - suite)

Continent, country or area, date, code[a] and age (in years) Continent, pays ou zone, date, code[a] et âge (en années)	Number - Nombre			Rate - Taux		
	Both sexes Les deux sexes	Male Masculin	Female Féminin	Both sexes Les deux sexes	Male Masculin	Female Féminin
OCEANIA - OCÉANIE						
American Samoa - Samoas américaines						
2017 (C)						
75 - 79	37	22	15			
80 - 84	23	12	11	...	...	...
85 +	33	10	23	...	...	...
Australia - Australie						
2017 (C)						
Total	160 909	82 858	78 051	6.5	6.8	6.3
0	1 019	562	457	3.4	3.6	3.1
1 - 4	190	103	87	0.1	0.2	0.1
5 - 9	123	66	57	0.1	0.1	0.1
10 - 14	140	87	53	0.1	0.1	0.1
15 - 19	443	291	152	0.3	0.4	0.2
20 - 24	679	506	173	0.4	0.6	0.2
25 - 29	842	601	241	0.5	0.6	0.3
30 - 34	1 089	748	341	0.6	0.8	0.4
35 - 39	1 395	919	476	0.8	1.1	0.6
40 - 44	1 958	1 246	712	1.2	1.6	0.9
45 - 49	2 980	1 856	1 124	1.8	2.3	1.3
50 - 54	4 008	2 398	1 610	2.6	3.2	2.1
55 - 59	5 865	3 603	2 262	3.9	4.9	2.9
60 - 64	7 806	4 834	2 972	5.9	7.4	4.4
65 - 69	11 007	6 768	4 239	9.2	11.5	7.0
70 - 74	14 535	8 793	5 742	15.2	18.7	11.8
75 - 79	18 017	10 440	7 577	26.6	32.4	21.3
80 - 84	23 029	12 340	10 689	49.1	58.8	41.3
85 - 89	29 184	13 879	15 305	95.1	111.4	84.0
90 - 94	24 683	9 514	15 169	170.2	191.6	159.1
95 - 99	9 954	2 920	7 034	264.2	272.5	260.9
100 +	1 958	381	1 577	491.1	405.3	517.6
Unknown - Inconnu	5	3	2	..	..	..
Cook Islands - Îles Cook[50]						
2009 (+C)						
Total	67	37	30			
0	2	1	1	...	...	...
1 - 4	1	1	-	...	...	...
5 - 9	-	-	-	...	...	...
10 - 14	-	-	-	...	...	...
15 - 19	3	2	1	...	...	...
20 - 24	3	3	-	...	...	...
25 - 29	1	1	-	...	...	...
30 - 34	2	1	1	...	...	...
35 - 39	4	3	1	...	...	...
40 - 44	-	-	-	...	...	...
45 - 49	2	1	1	...	...	...
50 - 54	3	1	2	...	...	...
55 - 59	1	1	-	...	...	...
60 - 64	6	3	3	...	...	...
65 - 69	8	4	4	...	...	...
70 - 74	9	1	8	...	...	...
75 - 79	8	5	3	...	...	...
80 +	14	9	5	...	...	...
Guam[51]						
2018 (C)						
Total	1 056	638	418	6.3	7.4	5.1
0	37	16	21	11.5	♦9.6	♦13.5
1 - 4	6	4	2	♦0.5	♦0.6	♦0.3
5 - 9	2	2	-	♦0.1	♦0.2	-
10 - 14	2	1	1	♦0.1	♦0.1	♦0.1
15 - 19	10	9	1	♦0.7	♦1.2	♦0.1
20 - 24	23	20	3	♦1.7	♦2.8	♦0.5
25 - 29	25	16	9	♦2.0	♦2.4	♦1.5
30 - 34	19	16	3	♦1.8	♦2.9	♦0.6
35 - 39	40	31	9	4.3	6.7	♦1.9
40 - 44	36	28	8	3.9	♦5.9	♦1.7
45 - 49	50	30	20	4.7	♦5.6	♦3.9
50 - 54	81	56	25	7.8	10.3	♦5.1

19. Deaths by age and sex and age-specific death rates by sex: latest available year, 2009 - 2018
Décès et taux de mortalité selon l'âge et le sexe : dernière année disponible, 2009 - 2018 (continued - suite)

Continent, country or area, date, code[a] and age (in years) / Continent, pays ou zone, date, code[a] et âge (en années)	Number - Nombre			Rate - Taux		
	Both sexes Les deux sexes	Male Masculin	Female Féminin	Both sexes Les deux sexes	Male Masculin	Female Féminin
OCEANIA - OCÉANIE						
Guam[51]						
2018 (C)						
55 - 59	101	63	38	10.7	12.8	8.4
60 - 64	106	68	38	14.3	18.4	10.3
65 - 69	107	61	46	17.7	20.4	15.0
70 - 74	105	65	40	26.7	34.7	19.5
75 - 79	84	48	36	34.1	42.7	26.9
80 - 84	92	41	51	57.7	64.4	53.3
85 - 89	55	30	25	79.9	♦118.1	♦57.6
90 - 94	59	25	34	345.0	♦403.2	311.9
95 - 99	15	7	8	♦555.6	♦777.8	♦444.4
100 +	1	1	-	♦333.3	♦1000.0	-
Kiribati[52]						
2011 (U)						
Total	481	279	202	...	...	...
0 - 4	132	75	57	...	...	...
5 - 19	14	10	4	...	...	...
20 - 29	34	24	10	...	...	...
30 - 39	28	15	13	...	...	...
40 - 49	60	37	23	...	...	...
50 - 59	74	42	32	...	...	...
60 - 69	54	34	20	...	...	...
70 +	85	42	43	...	...	...
Nauru						
2011 (C)						
Total	75	41	34	...	...	...
0	10	5	5	...	...	...
1 - 4	1	1	-	...	...	...
5 - 9	-	-	-	...	...	...
10 - 14	1	1	-	...	...	...
15 - 19	-	-	-	...	...	...
20 - 24	2	2	-	...	...	...
25 - 29	5	1	4	...	...	...
30 - 34	4	1	3	...	...	...
35 - 39	2	1	1	...	...	...
40 - 44	2	2	-	...	...	...
45 - 49	6	3	3	...	...	...
50 - 54	15	7	8	...	...	...
55 - 59	9	7	2	...	...	...
60 - 64	6	2	4	...	...	...
65 - 69	4	2	2	...	...	...
70 +	8	6	2	...	...	...
New Caledonia - Nouvelle-Calédonie						
2015 (C)						
Total	1 465	853	612	...	...	...
0	25	18	7	...	...	...
1 - 4	7	4	3	...	...	...
5 - 9	2	-	2	...	...	...
10 - 14	6	4	2	...	...	...
15 - 19	19	13	6	...	...	...
20 - 24	26	22	4	...	...	...
25 - 29	19	17	2	...	...	...
30 - 34	32	23	9	...	...	...
35 - 39	24	21	3	...	...	...
40 - 44	58	45	13	...	...	...
45 - 49	58	41	17	...	...	...
50 - 54	77	48	29	...	...	...
55 - 59	83	46	37	...	...	...
60 - 64	120	76	44	...	...	...
65 - 69	144	95	49	...	...	...
70 - 74	154	91	63	...	...	...
75 - 79	177	94	83	...	...	...
80 - 84	167	83	84	...	...	...
85 - 89	144	66	78	...	...	...
90 - 94	76	29	47	...	...	...
95 +	47	17	30	...	...	...

Continent, country or area, date, code[a] and age (in years)	Number - Nombre			Rate - Taux		
Continent, pays ou zone, date, code[a] et âge (en années)	Both sexes Les deux sexes	Male Masculin	Female Féminin	Both sexes Les deux sexes	Male Masculin	Female Féminin
OCEANIA - OCÉANIE						
New Zealand - Nouvelle-Zélande[53]						
2018 (+C)						
Total	33 222	16 983	16 239	6.8	7.1	6.6
0	222	117	105	3.7	3.8	3.6
1 - 4	54	27	27	0.2	♦0.2	♦0.2
5 - 9	30	15	12	♦0.1	♦0.1	♦0.1
10 - 14	45	21	24	0.1	♦0.1	♦0.2
15 - 19	141	96	42	0.4	0.6	0.3
20 - 24	195	138	54	0.5	0.7	0.3
25 - 29	207	135	69	0.5	0.7	0.4
30 - 34	228	147	81	0.7	0.9	0.5
35 - 39	261	147	111	0.9	1.0	0.7
40 - 44	366	225	144	1.3	1.6	1.0
45 - 49	573	336	240	1.8	2.2	1.4
50 - 54	936	540	396	3.0	3.6	2.4
55 - 59	1 446	858	585	4.6	5.7	3.6
60 - 64	1 830	1 080	753	6.7	8.2	5.4
65 - 69	2 406	1 386	1 017	10.1	12.0	8.3
70 - 74	3 198	1 845	1 356	16.4	19.5	13.4
75 - 79	3 999	2 247	1 752	28.9	34.6	23.9
80 - 84	4 875	2 610	2 265	54.5	64.8	46.1
85 - 89	5 634	2 673	2 961	101.1	116.4	90.4
90 +	6 582	2 343	4 242	212.2	223.1	206.7
90 - 94	4 593	1 809	2 784	...	...	...
95 - 99	1 680	486	1 197	...	...	...
100 +	309	48	261	...	...	...
Niue - Nioué[54]						
2009 (C)						
Total	12	6	6	...	...	...
0	-	-	-	...	...	...
1 - 4	-	-	-	...	...	...
5 - 9	-	-	-	...	...	...
10 - 14	-	-	-	...	...	...
15 - 19	-	-	-	...	...	...
20 - 24	-	-	-	...	...	...
25 - 29	-	-	-	...	...	...
30 - 34	-	-	-	...	...	...
35 - 39	-	-	-	...	...	...
40 - 44	-	-	-	...	...	...
45 - 49	-	-	-	...	...	...
50 - 54	-	-	-	...	...	...
55 - 59	2	2	-	...	...	...
60 - 64	-	-	-	...	...	...
65 - 69	-	-	-	...	...	...
70 - 74	1	-	1	...	...	...
75 - 79	1	1	-	...	...	...
80 +	8	3	5	...	...	...
Palau - Palaos						
2018 (C)						
Total	143	79	64	...	...	...
0	3	1	2	...	...	...
1 - 14	-	-	-	...	...	...
15 - 24	3	2	1	...	...	...
25 - 44	11	7	4	...	...	...
45 - 64	43	33	10	...	...	...
65 +	83	36	47	...	...	...
Samoa[21]						
2016 (|)						
Total	853	446	407	4.4	4.4	4.3
0	69	32	37	12.4	11.1	13.8
1 - 4	26	14	12	♦1.2	♦1.2	♦1.1
5 - 9	9	4	5	♦0.4	♦0.3	♦0.4
10 - 14	4	2	2	♦0.2	♦0.2	♦0.2
15 - 19	16	8	7	♦0.8	♦0.8	♦0.8
20 - 24	17	9	8	♦1.1	♦1.1	♦1.0
25 - 29	10	4	6	♦0.8	♦0.6	♦0.9
30 - 34	25	16	10	♦2.1	♦2.6	♦1.7

Continent, country or area, date, code[a] and age (in years) / Continent, pays ou zone, date, code[a] et âge (en années)	Number - Nombre			Rate - Taux		
	Both sexes Les deux sexes	Male Masculin	Female Féminin	Both sexes Les deux sexes	Male Masculin	Female Féminin
OCEANIA - OCÉANIE						
Samoa[21]						
2016 (|)						
35 - 39	16	7	10	♦1.5	♦1.3	♦1.9
40 - 44	27	14	13	♦2.6	♦2.6	♦2.6
45 - 49	37	16	21	3.8	♦3.1	♦4.6
50 - 54	67	40	28	7.9	9.2	♦6.8
55 - 59	80	52	27	11.4	14.2	♦8.1
60 - 64	78	50	27	14.9	18.7	♦10.6
65 - 69	67	37	30	19.3	21.7	♦16.9
70 - 74	60	29	32	22.3	♦22.9	22.5
75 - 79	79	40	39	45.1	53.6	38.8
80 - 84	58	29	29	57.4	♦79.5	♦44.9
85 - 89	43	17	26	90.3	♦104.3	♦83.1
90 - 94	32	9	23	201.3	♦187.5	♦207.2
95 - 99	8	2	6	♦296.3	♦333.3	♦285.7
100 +	2	2	-	♦333.3	♦1000.0	...
Unknown - Inconnu	22	14	8	..	..	..
Tuvalu						
2016 (+U)						
Total	90	45	45	...	...	...
0 - 4	9	4	5	...	...	...
5 - 9	-	-	-	...	...	...
10 - 14	-	-	-	...	...	...
15 - 19	-	-	-	...	...	...
20 - 24	-	-	-	...	...	...
25 - 29	4	3	1	...	...	...
30 - 34	1	-	1	...	...	...
35 - 39	-	-	-	...	...	...
40 - 44	4	-	4	...	...	...
45 - 49	2	1	1	...	...	...
50 - 54	5	4	1	...	...	...
55 - 59	12	8	4	...	...	...
60 - 64	9	6	3	...	...	...
65 - 69	9	3	6	...	...	...
70 - 74	8	3	5	...	...	...
75 - 79	17	8	9	...	...	...
80 +	10	5	5	...	...	...
Vanuatu						
2014 (+U)						
Total	614	370[10]	234[10]	...	...	...
0 - 4	133	56[10]	68[10]	...	...	...
5 - 9	3	1	2	...	...	...
10 - 14	4	2	2	...	...	...
15 - 19	9	6	3	...	...	...
20 - 24	11	7	4	...	...	...
25 - 29	9	7	2	...	...	...
30 - 34	15	11	4	...	...	...
35 - 39	17	10	7	...	...	...
40 - 44	37	25	12	...	...	...
45 - 49	51	34	17	...	...	...
50 - 54	53	37	16	...	...	...
55 - 59	38	26	12	...	...	...
60 - 64	62	39	23	...	...	...
65 - 69	25	16	9	...	...	...
70 - 74	41	25	16	...	...	...
75 - 79	26	22	4	...	...	...
80 +	42	26[10]	15[10]	...	...	...
Unknown - Inconnu	38	20	18	..	..	..

FOOTNOTES - NOTES

♦ Rates based on 30 or fewer deaths. - Taux basés sur 30 décès ou moins.

Italics: estimates which are less reliable. - Italiques : estimations moins sûres.

* Provisional. - Données provisoires.

[a] 'Code' indicates the source of data, as follows:
C - Civil registration, estimated over 90% complete
U - Civil registration, estimated less than 90% complete
\| - Other source, estimated reliable
+ - Data tabulated by date of registration rather than occurence
... - Information not available

Le 'Code' indique la source des données, comme suit :

C - Registres de l'état civil considérés complets à 90 p. 100 au moins

U - Registres de l'état civil qui ne sont pas considérés complets à 90 p. 100 au moins

| - Autre source, considérée pas douteuses

+ - Données exploitées selon la date de l'enregistrement et non la date de l'événement

... - Information pas disponible

[1] Excluding live-born infants who died before their birth was registered. Data refer to Algerian population only. - Non compris les enfants nés vivants décédés avant l'enregistrement de leur naissance. Les données ne concernent que la population algérienne.

[2] Source: Vital Statistics Report. - Source: Vital Statistics Report.

[3] Data refer to the 12 months preceding the census in September. - Les données se rapportent aux 12 mois précédant le recensement de septembre.

[4] Unadjusted number of deaths in households referring to the 12 months preceding the census in March. - Le nombre non ajusté de décès des ménages ordinaires se rapportent aux 12 mois précédant le recensement de mars.

[5] Data refer to the 12 months preceding the census in April. - Les données se rapportent aux douze mois précédant le recensement d'avril.

[6] Excludes the islands of St. Brandon and Agalega. - Non compris les îles St. Brandon et Agalega.

[7] Data refer to the 12 months preceding the census in August. - Les données se rapportent aux 12 mois précédant le recensement d'août.

[8] Data refer to the 12 months preceding the census in May. - Les données se rapportent aux 12 mois précédant le recensement de mai.

[9] Source: National Office of Births and Deaths. - Source : Le bureau national des naissances et des décès.

[10] Figures for male and female may not add up to the total, since they do not include the category "Unknown". - La somme des chiffres indiqués pour les sexes masculin et féminin peut n'être pas égale au total parce qu'elle n'inclut pas la catégorie " inconnue ".

[11] Data refer to the 12 months preceding the census in October. - Les données se rapportent aux 12 mois précédant le recensement de octobre.

[12] Excluding visitors. - Ne comprend pas les visiteurs.

[13] Unrevised data. - Les données n'ont pas été révisées.

[14] Excluding non-residents and foreign service personnel and their dependants. Bermuda is 100 per cent urban. - À l'exclusion des non-résidents et du personnel diplomatique et de leurs charges de famille. 100 pour cent de la population des Bermudes est urbaine.

[15] Including Canadian residents temporarily in the United States, but excluding United States residents temporarily in Canada. - Y compris les résidents canadiens se trouvant temporairement aux Etats-Unis, mais ne comprenant pas les résidents des Etats-Unis se trouvant temporairement au Canada.

[16] Including resident deaths outside of the islands but buried in the islands. - Y compris les décès de résidents hors des îles mais inhumés dans les îles.

[17] Excluding live-born infants who died before their birth was registered. - Non compris les enfants nés vivants décédés avant l'enregistrement de leur naissance.

[18] Data refer to population in private households. Data refer to period from 1 January 2010 to 3 April 2011. - Les données portent sur la population des ménages privés. Les données concernent la période du 1 janvier 2010 au 3 avril 2011.

[19] Data refer to resident population only. - Pour la population résidante seulement.

[20] Excluding deaths of persons living abroad. - Exception faite des personnes décédées à l'étranger.

[21] Data refer to the 12 months preceding the census in November. - Données se rapportant aux 12 mois précédant le recensement de novembre.

[22] Including deaths abroad and deaths of unknown place of residence. - Y compris décès à l'étranger et décès dont le lieu de résidence n'est pas connu.

[23] Excludes nomadic Indian tribes. - Non compris les tribus d'Indiens nomades.

[24] Source: Reports of the Ministry of Health. - Source : Rapports du Ministère de la Santé.

[25] Excluding infants born alive of less than 28 weeks' gestation, of less than 1 000 g in weight and 35 cm in length, who die within seven days of birth. - Non compris les enfants nés vivants après moins de 28 semaines de gestations, pesant moins de 1 000 g, mesurant moins de 35 cm et décédés dans les sept jours qui ont suivi leur naissance.

[26] Sources: Births and Deaths National Registration System database, and medical records of government hospitals. - Les sources: Les bases de données des << Births and Deaths National Registration System >> et les dossiers médicaux des hôpitaux du gouvernement.

[27] For statistical purposes, the data for China do not include those for the Hong Kong Special Administrative Region (Hong Kong SAR), Macao Special Administrative Region (Macao SAR) and Taiwan province of China. Data refer to the 12 months preceding the census in November. - Pour la présentation des statistiques, les données pour la Chine ne comprennent pas la Région Administrative Spéciale de Hong Kong (Hong Kong RAS), la Région Administrative Spéciale de Macao (Macao RAS) et Taïwan province de Chine. Données se rapportant aux 12 mois précédant le recensement de novembre.

[28] Data refer to government controlled areas. Data refer to deaths of residents only. - Les données se rapportent aux zones contrôlées par le Gouvernement. Les données renvoient aux décès de résidents uniquement.

[29] Data are from 1 January 2009 to 1 May 2010. - Les données vont du 1er janvier 2009 au 1er mai 2010.

[30] Data refer to the Iranian Year which begins on 21 March and ends on 20 March of the following year. Data refer to current deaths; excluding delayed registrations. - Les données concernent l'année iranienne, qui commence le 21 mars et se termine le 20 mars de l'année suivante. Les données se rapportent aux décès actuels; les déclarations tardives des décès ne sont pas compris.

[31] Includes data for East Jerusalem and Israeli residents in certain other territories under occupation by Israeli military forces since June 1967. Including deaths abroad of Israeli residents who were out of the country for less than a year. - Y compris les données pour Jérusalem-Est et les résidents israéliens dans certains autres territoires occupés depuis 1967 par les forces armées israéliennes. Y compris les décès à l'étranger de résidents israéliens qui ont quitté le pays depuis moins d'un an.

[32] Data refer to Japanese nationals in Japan only. - Les données se raportent aux nationaux japonais au Japon seulement.

[33] Data do not include foreigners. - Les données sur les etrangers ne sont pas inclus.

[34] Data are from Vital Registration System (VRS). - Les données proviennent du système d'enregistrement des faits d'état civil.

[35] Excluding alien armed forces, civilian aliens employed by armed forces, and foreign diplomatic personnel and their dependants. - Non compris les militaires étrangers, les civils étrangers employés par les forces armées ni le personnel diplomatique étranger et les membres de leur famille les accompagnant.

[36] Data refer to Saudi Arabian nationals only. Based on 2010 population census and 2016 demographic survey. - Les données ne concernent que les ressortissants saoudiens. D'après le recensement de la population de 2010 et l'enquête démographique de 2016.

[37] Source: Palestinian Central Bureau of Statistics, Population Register, updated version 2018. Data exclude Jerusalem ID holders. - Source: Bureau central de statistique palestinien, registre de la population, version actualisée jusqu'au 2018. Les données ne tiennent pas compte des détenteurs de carte d'identité de Jérusalem.

[38] Data from MERNIS (Central Population Administrative System). - Données de MERNIS (Système central de données démographiques).

[39] Including deaths of nationals abroad. - Y compris les décès des nationaux survenus à l'étranger.

[40] Including armed forces stationed outside the country, but excluding alien armed forces stationed in the area. - Y compris les militaires nationaux hors du pays, mais non compris les militaires étrangers en garnison sur le territoire.

[41] Excluding Faeroe Islands and Greenland shown separately, if available. - Non compris les Iles Féroé et le Groenland, qui font l'objet de rubriques distinctes, si disponible.

[42] Data include the deceased persons with Hungarian usual residence regardless of whether the death occurred in Hungary or in a foreign country, and do not include the deceased persons with foreign country usual residence. - Les données comprennent tous les décès survenus alors que leur résidence habituelle était en Hongrie, que le décès ait eu lieu en Hongrie ou dans un pays étranger, et ne comprennent pas les décès des personnes dont la residence habituelle était dans un pays étranger.

[43] Including residents outside the country if listed in a Netherlands population register. - Englobe les résidents se trouvant à l'étranger à condition qu'ils soient inscrits sur le registre de population des Pays-Bas.

[44] Including residents temporarily outside the country. - Y compris les résidents se trouvant temporairement hors du pays.

[45] Data refer to usually resident population. - Les données concernent la population habituellement résidente.

[46] Excluding Transnistria and the municipality of Bender. - Les données ne tiennent pas compte de l'information sur la Transnistria et la municipalité de Bender.

[47] Excludes data for Kosovo and Metohia. - Sans les données pour le Kosovo et Metohie.

[48] Data includes deaths resulting from births with weight 500 g and more (if weight is unknown - with length 25 cm and more, or with gestation during 22 weeks or more). The Government of Ukraine has informed the United Nations that it is not in a position to provide statistical data concerning the Autonomous

Republic of Crimea and the city of Sevastopol. - Y compris les décès de nouveau-nés de 500 g ou plus (si le poids est inconnu – de 25 cm de long ou plus, ou après une grossesse de 22 semaines ou plus). Le gouvernement Ukrainien a informé l'ONU qu'il n'est pas en mesure de fournir des données statistiques concernant la République autonome de Crimée et la ville de Sébastopol.

[49] Excluding Channel Islands (Guernsey and Jersey) and Isle of Man, shown separately, if available. - Non compris les îles Anglo-Normandes (Guernesey et Jersey) et l'île de Man, qui font l'objet de rubriques distinctes, si disponible.

[50] Excluding Niue, shown separately, which is part of Cook Islands, but because of remoteness is administered separately. Unrevised data. - Non compris Nioué, qui fait l'objet d'une rubrique distincte et qui fait partie des îles Cook, mais qui, en raison de son éloignement, est administrée séparément. Les données n'ont pas été révisées.

[51] Including United States military personnel, their dependants and contract employees. - Y compris les militaires des Etats-Unis, les membres de leur famille les accompagnant et les agents contractuels des Etats-Unis.

[52] Excluding deaths of unknown age or sex. - Les données ne comprennent pas les décès d'âge ou de sexe inconnus.

[53] Data refer to deaths of residents only. Random rounding to base 3 is applied in this table as a confidentiality measure. - Les données renvoient aux décès de résidents uniquement. Les chiffres sont arrondis à la base 3 de manière aléatoire, pour des raisons de confidentialité.

[54] Includes deaths occurred in New Zealand but buried in Niue and deaths occurred in Niue but buried elsewhere. - Y compris les personnes décédées en Nouvelle-Zélande qui sont enterrées à Nioué et les personnes décédées à Nioué qui sont enterrées ailleurs.

Table 20 - *Demographic Yearbook 2018*

Table 20 presents the life tables' probabilities of dying in the five year interval following specified ages ($_5q_x$), for each sex, for the latest available year between 2004 and 2018. The probabilities are multiplied by a thousand, that is, the values presented in the table are $1000*_5q_x$.

Male and female probabilities of dying are shown separately for selected ages beginning at birth and proceeding at every fifth age thereafter up to age 100.

The values presented in the table are derived by the United Nations Statistics Division from the official complete life tables reported by the countries or areas.

Data are shown with one decimal regardless of the number of digits provided in the original computation.

The life table is a statistical device for summarizing the mortality experience of a population, from which the probability of dying, survivorship and expectation of life can be calculated. It is based on the assumption that the theoretical cohort is subject, throughout its existence, to the age-specific mortality rates observed at a particular time. Thus, levels of mortality prevailing at the time a life table is constructed are assumed to remain unchanged into the future until all members of the cohort have died.

Reliability of data: The values shown in this table are derived from official complete life tables. It is assumed that, if necessary, the basic data (population and deaths classified by age and sex) have been adjusted for deficiencies before their use in constructing the complete life tables.

Limitations: The life tables' probabilities of dying are subject to the same qualifications as have been set forth for population statistics in general and death statistics in particular, as discussed in sections 3 and 4, respectively, of the Technical Notes. They must be interpreted strictly using the underlying assumption that surviving cohorts are subjected to the same age-specific mortality rates of the period to which the life table refers.

Earlier data: The life tables' probabilities of dying at specified ages, for each sex, have been shown in previous issues of the *Demographic Yearbook*. For information on specific years covered, the reader should consult the Historical Index.

Tableau 20 – *Annuaire démographique 2018*

Le tableau 20 donne les probabilités de décès dans l'intervalle de cinq ans que suit l'âge spécifié ($_5q_x$), pour chaque sexe, pour la dernière année disponible entre 2004 et 2018. Les probabilités sont multipliées par mille, c'est-à-dire que les valeurs indiquées dans le tableau sont égales à 1000*$_5q_x$.

Les probabilités de décès sont indiquées séparément pour les hommes et les femmes pour différents âges, depuis la naissance puis tous les cinq ans jusqu'à 100 ans.

Les chiffres indiqués dans ce tableau ont été calculés par la Division de statistique de l'Organisation des Nations Unies à partir des tables de mortalité complètes communiquées par les pays ou zones.

Les données sont arrondies à la première décimale, indépendamment du nombre de décimales qui figurent dans le calcul initial.

La table de mortalité est un moyen statistique que s'utilise pour donner un aperçu complet de la mortalité d'une population incluant les probabilités de décès et l'espérance de vie à chaque âge. Les tables de mortalité reposent sur l'hypothèse que chaque cohorte théoriquement distinguée connaît, pendant toute son existence, les taux de mortalité par âge observé à un moment donné. Les taux de mortalité correspondant à l'époque à laquelle sont calculées les tables de mortalité sont ainsi censés demeurer inchangées dans l'avenir jusqu'au décès de tous les membres de la cohorte.

Fiabilité des donnés : Les chiffres indiqués dans ce tableau ont été calculés à partir des tables officielles de mortalité complètes. En ce qui concerne les chiffres extraits de tables officielles de mortalité, on part du principe que les données de base (effectif de la population et nombre de décès selon l'âge et le sexe) ont été ajustées, en tant que de besoin, avant de servir à l'établissement de la table de mortalité.

Insuffisance des données : Les probabilités de décès appellent les mêmes réserves que celles qui ont été formulées à propos des statistiques de la population en général et des statistiques de mortalité en particulier (voir les sections 3 et 4 des Notes techniques). Lorsque l'on interprète les données, il ne faut jamais perdre de vue que, par hypothèse, les cohortes de survivants sont soumises, pour chaque âge, aux conditions de mortalité de la période visée par la table de mortalité.

Données publiées antérieurement : Les probabilités de décès pour chaque sexe figuraient déjà dans des éditions antérieures de *l'Annuaire démographique*. Pour plus de précisions concernant les années pour lesquelles ces données ont été publiées, se reporter à l'index historique.

20. Probability of dying in the five year interval following specified age (5qx), by sex, latest available year: 2004 - 2018
Probabilité de décès dans l'intervalle de cinq ans qui suit un âge donné (5qx), par sexe, dernière année disponible : 2004 - 2018

Continent, country or area and date / Continent, pays ou zone et date	0	5	10	15	20	25	30	35	40	45	50	55	60	65	70	75	80	85	90	95	100
AFRICA - AFRIQUE																					
Republic of South Sudan - République de Soudan du Sud 2010																					
Male - Hommes	130.6	14.1	10.8	18.5	25.6	27.0	28.8	33.1	40.1	51.8	70.0	98.7	143.7	213.2	316.6	457.7	624.2	785.1	907.0	...	...
Female - Femmes	111.9	13.7	10.7	18.4	25.9	27.8	30.2	35.2	43.3	56.8	78.0	111.6	164.6	245.8	362.8	513.5	678.3	826.7	931.7	...	...
AMERICA, NORTH - AMÉRIQUE DU NORD																					
Canada 2014 - 2016																					
Male - Hommes	5.5	0.4	0.6	2.0	3.7	4.2	4.7	5.3	7.5	11.5	17.6	27.2	42.6	67.5	107.7	172.6	275.1	429.2	630.1	812.2	918.3
Female - Femmes	4.9	0.4	0.5	1.1	1.5	1.8	2.3	3.0	4.8	7.7	11.6	17.7	27.5	44.0	71.7	119.0	199.5	332.7	529.3	744.5	887.7
Costa Rica 2018																					
Male - Hommes	8.2	0.7	1.2	3.3	5.7	6.7	7.5	8.7	11.3	15.9	22.7	33.6	51.2	80.5	123.5	193.9	289.5	417.1	581.0	755.8	*1000
Female - Femmes	6.7	0.5	0.8	1.4	1.5	1.7	2.4	3.4	5.0	7.9	12.0	19.4	30.9	50.6	81.1	135.2	228.6	361.9	529.8	718.1	*1000
Cuba 2011 - 2013																					
Male - Hommes	6.0	1.0	1.3	2.4	3.5	4.5	5.7	7.3	10.5	17.5	29.3	44.9	67.2	100.5	148.8	223.2	334.7	477.3	602.9	645.4	*1000
Female - Femmes	5.6	0.9	0.9	1.4	1.9	2.4	3.0	4.1	6.5	11.0	18.7	29.3	44.6	67.0	104.8	168.7	270.2	421.1	577.7	655.4	*1000
Curaçao 2016																					
Male - Hommes	9.6	0.4	0.5	2.1	5.8	7.2	7.2	8.9	11.0	15.4	28.1	49.3	69.2	103.7	158.6	226.0	359.1	525.1	701.4	841.0	...
Female - Femmes	14.6	0.3	0.2	0.7	1.8	2.5	2.9	3.9	6.2	8.9	12.1	19.1	33.3	53.2	83.1	148.5	257.1	388.1	571.7	776.1	...
Dominican Republic - République dominicaine 2010 - 2015																					
Male - Hommes	33.8	1.5	2.2	6.6	12.0	13.8	15.2	17.5	21.3	28.4	42.9	61.1	86.0	127.0	178.3	282.0	*1000	...	...	...	...
Female - Femmes	25.6	1.4	1.5	2.8	4.8	6.6	8.4	10.7	14.3	19.4	30.9	45.6	64.3	98.8	145.1	253.9	*1000	...	...	...	...
Greenland - Groenland 2009 - 2013																					
Male - Hommes	15.4	0.5	2.8	15.7	22.9	16.2	14.3	13.6	18.4	25.9	35.9	72.3	87.1	167.8	303.9	470.3	648.6	758.8	...	...	...
Female - Femmes	7.0	0.5	2.7	10.3	8.0	2.5	6.9	10.8	9.1	20.1	26.0	50.6	83.8	147.4	209.0	326.2	565.3	731.9	970.6	...	...
Jamaica - Jamaïque 2006																					
Male - Hommes	31.7	2.8	2.5	4.5	6.5	6.5	7.0	9.4	14.5	23.2	37.5	60.5	96.9	153.2	236.8	353.8	502.7	667.6	817.2	921.8	*1000
Female - Femmes	18.0	1.3	1.1	1.7	2.6	3.4	4.3	5.9	8.7	13.9	22.8	38.0	63.2	104.5	169.8	268.2	405.3	574.1	747.0	883.6	*1000
Martinique 2007																					
Male - Hommes	11.6	1.0	1.1	4.2	8.8	7.5	8.8	8.5	10.4	13.5	26.7	28.9	42.2	87.6	122.7	202.9	325.3	532.7	663.7	834.4	*1000
Female - Femmes	7.8	0.4	0.7	0.6	2.1	2.9	4.6	4.1	4.8	5.3	11.3	14.8	28.6	45.6	76.8	135.3	216.7	362.2	508.4	810.4	*1000
Mexico - Mexique 2005																					
Male - Hommes	21.6	1.7	2.2	4.3	7.4	9.9	12.0	15.1	20.3	28.7	41.3	59.9	86.6	124.3	176.5	246.8	337.7	448.7	574.2	702.2	*1000
Female - Femmes	17.4	1.3	1.2	1.8	2.4	3.1	4.3	6.4	9.9	15.4	23.9	37.2	57.5	88.4	134.4	201.1	293.6	414.1	557.1	705.8	*1000
Panama[1] 2017																					
Male - Hommes	21.1	1.9	2.4	6.9	12.4	13.9	12.8	12.3	14.1	18.7	26.8	39.5	58.6	86.8	127.8	185.7	265.3	369.3	496.0	635.5	*1000
Female - Femmes	15.9	1.2	1.4	2.3	3.3	4.2	5.1	6.3	8.1	11.0	15.8	23.6	36.2	56.5	88.6	138.4	212.9	318.8	457.5	617.8	*1000
Puerto Rico - Porto Rico 2016 - 2018																					
Male - Hommes	7.9	0.4	0.4	3.4	10.1	11.4	13.9	15.1	17.4	22.5	32.2	47.2	62.3	88.5	118.5	177.5	263.6	*1000	...	...	...
Female - Femmes	6.8	0.5	0.5	0.9	1.7	2.1	3.6	4.7	6.8	9.7	14.4	21.2	29.8	45.2	70.4	114.5	194.0	*1000	...	...	...
United States of America - États-Unis d'Amérique 2014																					
Male - Hommes	7.4	0.6	0.8	3.1	6.1	7.0	7.9	9.3	12.2	18.8	29.8	45.1	63.7	86.6	130.0	198.4	311.2	481.1	670.9	828.2	*1000
Female - Femmes	6.2	0.5	0.6	1.3	2.2	2.9	3.8	5.4	7.9	12.1	18.9	27.3	38.4	56.6	89.8	145.1	239.4	390.6	588.0	774.4	*1000

583

20. Probability of dying in the five year interval following specified age (5qx), by sex, latest available year: 2004 - 2018
Probabilité de décès dans l'intervalle de cinq ans qui suit un âge donné (5qx), par sexe, dernière année disponible : 2004 - 2018 (continued - suite)

Continent, country or area and date / Continent, pays ou zone et date	0	5	10	15	20	25	30	35	40	45	50	55	60	65	70	75	80	85	90	95	100
AMERICA, SOUTH - AMÉRIQUE DU SUD																					
Argentina - Argentine 2008 - 2010																					
Male - Hommes	15.8	1.3	1.8	5.3	7.5	7.9	8.1	10.0	14.5	22.1	37.3	59.5	89.5	133.8	194.0	289.6	431.2	568.1	692.6	804.3	*1000
Female - Femmes	13.0	1.0	1.2	2.2	2.6	3.1	4.0	5.7	8.4	13.2	20.4	31.0	45.5	68.2	105.9	175.1	309.8	460.7	614.6	762.3	*1000
Bolivia (Plurinational State of) - Bolivie (État plurinational de)[2] 2016 - 2017																					
Male - Hommes	44.2	5.3	4.1	8.9	13.6	14.2	16.1	18.9	24.3	30.8	41.6	57.2	83.1	117.2	167.4	233.2	329.5	416.5	609.4	*1000	...
Female - Femmes	34.5	3.5	2.4	4.7	5.3	5.9	7.4	9.9	14.4	20.0	27.8	39.3	57.6	84.3	119.8	165.8	236.7	317.6	487.2	*1000	...
Brazil - Brésil 2015																					
Male - Hommes	17.4	1.5	1.9	8.2	12.5	12.6	13.5	15.7	20.2	28.1	40.3	56.8	79.0	114.1	168.7	246.7	*1000		...	...	...
Female - Femmes	14.7	1.1	1.2	2.2	2.8	3.5	4.7	6.4	9.6	14.8	21.7	31.6	46.7	71.9	112.3	173.9	*1000		...	...	...
Chile - Chili 2018 - 2019																					
Male - Hommes	8.2	0.7	0.9	3.0	4.6	5.3	6.4	8.0	11.1	15.8	23.6	35.0	53.5	84.1	128.6	198.5	308.1	443.2	591.6	747.7	*1000
Female - Femmes	7.1	0.6	0.8	1.3	1.6	1.7	2.3	3.5	5.3	8.4	12.6	19.2	30.3	49.5	78.6	128.8	219.3	351.8	503.3	659.1	*1000
Ecuador - Équateur[3] 2018																					
Male - Hommes	20.7	0.9	1.0	3.2	4.5	6.2	8.9	10.3	12.8	19.2	28.7	41.4	67.3	102.7	161.8	251.6	380.6	549.2	722.5	854.0	*1000
Female - Femmes	17.9	0.9	1.0	1.8	2.2	2.8	3.2	4.1	5.6	8.4	13.5	20.0	31.6	52.4	94.4	173.2	309.4	492.6	691.8	846.0	*1000
French Guiana - Guyane française 2007																					
Male - Hommes	16.3	1.5	2.1	4.9	7.7	8.1	10.0	14.0	17.2	29.4	16.0	32.3	52.4	79.5	135.5	261.3	306.7	474.0	733.7	...	...
Female - Femmes	15.1	1.9	1.3	1.4	1.2	3.0	4.6	4.2	11.9	11.0	10.4	11.6	26.7	85.4	77.4	203.8	253.1	321.1	434.3	...	...
Uruguay 2004																					
Male - Hommes	20.0	1.3	1.3	3.5	5.8	6.8	7.2	9.0	12.8	21.2	36.4	62.2	95.4	145.2	204.6	305.7	430.5	610.5	776.7	862.5	*1000
Female - Femmes	15.5	1.0	1.1	1.6	1.9	2.7	3.8	5.2	7.9	12.5	19.4	30.5	41.2	63.4	97.2	177.7	292.9	472.0	654.3	820.5	*1000
ASIA - ASIE																					
Armenia - Arménie 2016 - 2017																					
Male - Hommes	11.3	1.1	0.9	4.9	5.1	4.5	5.2	7.7	14.8	24.9	48.2	66.2	99.7	139.2	210.1	325.0	416.0	594.3	804.6	871.0	...
Female - Femmes	8.7	0.9	0.8	1.1	1.7	1.5	2.1	2.9	5.2	9.1	15.6	24.8	41.5	66.8	122.7	227.6	349.4	605.2	961.5	979.0	...
Azerbaijan - Azerbaïdjan 2017																					
Male - Hommes	14.6	1.6	1.7	3.0	3.4	4.4	5.6	8.4	14.0	23.3	37.6	57.9	94.5	139.1	193.7	300.4	415.8	500.4	395.1	285.6	...
Female - Femmes	11.8	1.2	1.2	1.5	2.1	2.1	2.8	4.2	5.5	8.7	16.5	27.2	50.0	85.7	132.3	239.9	394.4	558.1	643.5	531.7	...
China, Hong Kong SAR - Chine, Hong Kong RAS 2018																					
Male - Hommes	1.9	0.4	0.6	1.0	1.7	2.2	2.6	3.8	6.7	9.7	15.1	23.4	37.8	59.0	94.8	156.8	245.5	358.2	501.0	664.1	*1000
Female - Femmes	2.0	0.4	0.4	0.7	0.8	0.9	1.2	1.8	3.4	5.4	8.8	12.8	18.2	27.1	43.1	75.7	148.5	267.6	438.5	642.6	*1000
China, Macao SAR - Chine, Macao RAS 2002 - 2005																					
Male - Hommes	7.2	0.6	0.4	1.7	3.9	5.4	6.2	7.6	9.0	13.6	17.8	25.8	43.1	72.1	128.9	239.9	369.5	574.4	841.2	991.4	*1000
Female - Femmes	5.2	0.4	0.2	0.9	1.5	1.9	2.3	3.8	4.7	5.9	7.4	10.9	19.3	33.3	70.4	186.2	317.0	485.2	717.3	923.7	*1000
Israel - Israël[4] 2013 - 2017																					
Male - Hommes	4.2	0.5	0.7	1.6	2.6	2.7	2.9	3.8	6.0	10.2	17.0	26.8	41.5	66.0	108.3	178.9	288.3	438.0	609.6	767.3	*1000
Female - Femmes	3.6	0.4	0.5	0.7	0.9	1.1	1.5	2.2	3.6	6.0	9.6	14.9	23.3	38.7	68.8	125.9	227.0	383.9	581.2	768.6	*1000
Japan - Japon[5] 2015																					
Male - Hommes	2.9	0.5	0.5	1.3	2.5	2.7	3.2	4.1	6.2	10.0	16.2	25.7	41.2	65.8	100.6	160.7	278.5	450.1	652.9	810.7	...
Female - Femmes	2.5	0.4	0.4	0.7	1.0	1.3	1.7	2.4	3.7	5.8	8.9	12.3	18.0	27.3	43.9	77.2	150.4	286.0	501.4	728.1	...

20. Probability of dying in the five year interval following specified age (5qx), by sex, latest available year: 2004 - 2018
Probabilité de décès dans l'intervalle de cinq ans qui suit un âge donné (5qx), par sexe, dernière année disponible : 2004 - 2018 (continued - suite)

Continent, country or area and date / Continent, pays ou zone et date	0	5	10	15	20	25	30	35	40	45	50	55	60	65	70	75	80	85	90	95	100

Age (in years) - Age (en années)

ASIA - ASIE

Kazakhstan
2018

	0	5	10	15	20	25	30	35	40	45	50	55	60	65	70	75	80	85	90	95	100
Male - Hommes	11.6	1.7	1.9	4.1	6.3	8.4	12.6	19.2	27.9	37.5	53.0	80.5	123.6	186.9	240.3	342.4	471.7	613.4	766.5	844.2	...
Female - Femmes	8.5	1.0	1.0	2.0	2.4	3.0	4.3	7.7	10.5	15.9	21.5	33.7	52.6	83.6	130.9	218.6	366.1	534.5	745.2	858.2	...

Kyrgyzstan - Kirghizstan
2016

	0	5	10	15	20	25	30	35	40	45	50	55	60	65	70	75	80	85	90	95	100
Male - Hommes	20.9	1.9	2.3	3.2	5.1	7.3	10.9	18.5	26.6	35.7	49.8	75.6	119.3	169.1	365.1	542.3	677.0	734.3	813.7	880.6	*1000
Female - Femmes	18.4	0.9	1.4	2.5	2.8	3.1	4.5	7.3	11.1	14.0	20.8	36.0	60.4	92.0	162.1	277.6	469.6	596.6	685.9	794.8	*1000

Qatar
2006

	0	5	10	15	20	25	30	35	40	45	50	55	60	65	70	75	80	85	90	95	100
Male - Hommes	10.2	0.8	1.8	9.4	8.9	6.5	5.6	6.6	7.1	9.0	16.1	22.1	42.2	88.0	167.5	248.6	376.7	*1000	...	...	...
Female - Femmes	9.0	1.3	0.9	2.2	1.4	2.4	1.2	1.8	3.8	6.7	9.8	22.1	76.0	120.2	253.6	354.1	348.3	*1000	...	...	...

Republic of Korea - République de Corée
2017

	0	5	10	15	20	25	30	35	40	45	50	55	60	65	70	75	80	85	90	95	100
Male - Hommes	3.6	0.5	0.5	1.3	2.0	2.8	3.4	4.8	7.4	12.4	19.6	29.2	41.8	63.5	104.1	190.6	324.5	497.3	679.8	832.3	*1000
Female - Femmes	3.0	0.3	0.4	0.7	1.0	1.4	2.1	2.8	3.9	5.4	7.3	9.8	14.6	24.6	46.7	97.8	201.4	373.1	584.6	778.1	*1000

Singapore - Singapour[6]
2018

	0	5	10	15	20	25	30	35	40	45	50	55	60	65	70	75	80	85	90	95	100
Male - Hommes	2.7	0.3	0.5	1.3	1.7	1.8	2.3	3.2	5.3	9.1	15.2	25.0	40.9	64.6	109.3	174.1	280.9	433.1	616.0	793.6	*1000
Female - Femmes	2.7	0.4	0.4	0.5	0.7	0.8	1.3	1.8	2.8	5.4	9.4	14.5	22.4	34.7	59.0	111.2	203.7	339.1	516.6	708.2	*1000

Turkey - Turquie
2015 - 2017

	0	5	10	15	20	25	30	35	40	45	50	55	60	65	70	75	80	85	90	95	100
Male - Hommes	12.8	1.3	1.5	3.3	4.2	4.2	4.2	5.2	8.0	13.7	24.2	41.8	68.2	106.9	169.1	262.7	393.0	569.0	726.3	811.6	*1000
Female - Femmes	11.4	0.9	0.9	1.3	1.3	1.5	1.8	2.8	4.4	7.1	11.4	18.7	31.7	55.0	101.7	184.0	306.8	474.7	636.5	721.2	*1000

EUROPE

Austria - Autriche
2017

	0	5	10	15	20	25	30	35	40	45	50	55	60	65	70	75	80	85	90	95	100
Male - Hommes	3.5	0.2	0.5	1.8	2.7	3.2	3.3	4.7	6.8	10.8	18.1	32.5	50.1	78.4	123.9	175.0	298.3	498.5	707.9	880.5	...
Female - Femmes	3.1	0.3	0.4	0.9	0.8	1.2	1.6	2.4	3.6	5.8	10.6	16.2	27.0	42.7	69.2	109.3	216.1	407.9	652.4	835.3	...

Belarus - Bélarus
2017

	0	5	10	15	20	25	30	35	40	45	50	55	60	65	70	75	80	85	90	95	100
Male - Hommes	3.9	0.8	0.8	2.3	4.2	6.2	10.2	16.8	26.4	39.5	57.7	88.1	139.0	188.0	257.4	359.3	485.0	627.6	769.8	887.4	...
Female - Femmes	3.3	0.7	0.7	1.1	1.5	2.1	3.1	5.7	8.8	12.9	18.2	27.2	44.0	68.1	113.7	202.6	340.2	529.0	741.7	911.5	...

Belgium - Belgique[7]
2015

	0	5	10	15	20	25	30	35	40	45	50	55	60	65	70	75	80	85	90	95	100
Male - Hommes	4.2	0.5	0.4	1.4	3.2	3.0	4.0	5.4	7.7	12.4	20.1	35.5	55.2	81.7	122.3	193.8	315.6	506.2	717.7	872.7	*1000
Female - Femmes	3.6	0.4	0.5	0.8	1.1	1.3	2.0	2.8	4.9	8.3	12.6	21.3	33.1	44.8	71.3	119.0	222.4	406.4	643.5	832.8	*1000

Bulgaria - Bulgarie
2015 - 2017

	0	5	10	15	20	25	30	35	40	45	50	55	60	65	70	75	80	85	90	95	100
Male - Hommes	9.0	0.9	1.2	3.1	4.5	4.9	6.5	10.3	16.1	28.7	49.5	77.7	114.9	161.4	214.0	304.5	446.3	617.4	788.7	867.9	...
Female - Femmes	6.2	0.5	0.7	1.5	1.5	2.2	3.0	4.4	8.1	14.0	21.5	33.4	48.6	71.2	115.0	205.1	361.2	564.5	759.5	859.5	...

Czechia - Tchéquie
2017

	0	5	10	15	20	25	30	35	40	45	50	55	60	65	70	75	80	85	90	95	100
Male - Hommes	3.9	0.5	0.5	1.8	3.5	4.0	4.7	5.6	8.8	15.2	26.6	43.5	75.0	112.8	169.6	245.6	375.2	555.4	746.2	885.6	...
Female - Femmes	2.8	0.3	0.4	0.9	1.1	1.1	1.8	2.7	4.3	7.6	12.3	20.6	34.0	54.9	90.6	155.3	279.7	470.9	693.4	865.5	...

Denmark - Danemark[8]
2016 - 2017

	0	5	10	15	20	25	30	35	40	45	50	55	60	65	70	75	80	85	90	95	100
Male - Hommes	4.6	0.5	0.4	1.3	2.0	2.1	3.2	4.4	6.0	10.7	18.6	34.7	52.8	77.7	122.2	189.6	323.2	508.0	731.9	865.0	...
Female - Femmes	3.6	0.3	0.2	0.9	0.9	1.2	1.4	2.3	4.2	7.3	13.2	21.0	33.8	50.0	79.1	134.7	243.8	399.2	616.5	798.6	...

Estonia - Estonie
2017

	0	5	10	15	20	25	30	35	40	45	50	55	60	65	70	75	80	85	90	95	100
Male - Hommes	3.4	0.5	0.6	2.4	3.8	6.1	8.4	11.3	16.3	21.9	36.8	58.1	96.5	138.1	190.8	263.1	379.0	536.4	725.1	828.7	*1000
Female - Femmes	2.2	0.3	1.1	1.2	1.8	1.4	2.6	2.5	5.2	8.5	14.3	19.9	36.1	50.6	80.0	135.0	255.3	444.4	629.1	777.5	*1000

Faeroe Islands - Îles Féroé
2017 - 2018

	0	5	10	15	20	25	30	35	40	45	50	55	60	65	70	75	80	85	90	95	100
Male - Hommes	6.4	0.0	2.4	0.0	0.0	0.0	0.0	0.0	5.9	6.4	10.4	31.3	53.1	84.6	94.0	186.7	344.4	442.5	641.6	...	...
Female - Femmes	11.0	0.0	0.0	0.0	0.0	0.0	0.0	0.0	6.9	3.2	6.6	12.4	35.9	28.7	48.4	113.2	187.7	254.7	518.2	970.3	...

20. Probability of dying in the five year interval following specified age (5qx), by sex, latest available year: 2004 - 2018
Probabilité de décès dans l'intervalle de cinq ans qui suit un âge donné (5qx), par sexe, dernière année disponible : 2004 - 2018 (continued - suite)

Continent, country or area and date / Continent, pays ou zone et date	0	5	10	15	20	25	30	35	40	45	50	55	60	65	70	75	80	85	90	95	100
EUROPE																					
Finland - Finlande[9]																					
2017																					
Male - Hommes	2.7	0.4	0.4	2.6	3.8	4.4	5.1	5.7	9.0	11.7	20.5	31.1	54.0	78.9	118.7	187.0	310.9	503.8	711.7	861.7	...
Female - Femmes	2.5	0.4	0.4	1.1	1.7	1.4	2.0	2.6	4.1	5.8	10.7	16.3	25.1	40.6	63.4	111.7	209.9	382.8	614.4	823.5	...
France																					
2014 - 2016																					
Male - Hommes	4.5	0.4	0.5	1.7	2.9	3.6	4.4	5.9	9.0	14.9	23.5	38.2	55.4	74.0	104.2	159.5	268.8	447.6	660.4	832.5	...
Female - Femmes	3.8	0.3	0.4	0.8	1.1	1.3	1.7	2.8	4.6	7.8	12.1	17.8	24.8	34.2	52.4	88.6	169.0	326.2	553.1	771.3	...
Germany - Allemagne																					
2013 - 2015																					
Male - Hommes	4.2	0.4	0.4	1.5	2.3	2.6	3.5	4.8	7.4	12.9	22.9	38.2	59.2	85.8	126.1	198.4	334.8	518.8	724.9	868.7	...
Female - Femmes	3.6	0.3	0.4	0.8	1.0	1.1	1.7	2.6	4.2	7.3	12.7	20.1	30.7	46.9	70.1	123.7	238.9	426.5	657.8	828.6	...
Greece - Grèce																					
2016																					
Male - Hommes	5.8	0.6	0.6	1.7	2.8	3.3	4.0	5.4	7.9	13.8	24.1	38.4	57.2	81.6	120.3	190.8	315.9	463.9	611.3	767.4	...
Female - Femmes	3.9	0.4	0.5	0.8	0.9	1.1	1.8	2.7	4.3	6.8	10.4	16.0	23.5	38.3	67.2	133.7	269.8	437.9	591.9	753.6	...
Hungary - Hongrie																					
2017																					
Male - Hommes	4.7	0.5	0.9	1.8	2.8	3.7	5.2	6.9	11.2	23.4	46.2	78.3	118.2	159.4	208.2	295.2	422.7	628.3	861.8	985.1	...
Female - Femmes	4.0	0.7	0.5	0.8	0.9	1.2	2.4	3.7	5.9	11.4	21.6	35.4	52.4	75.9	112.3	190.6	321.4	551.9	834.4	984.8	...
Iceland - Islande																					
2016 - 2017																					
Male - Hommes	2.4	0.0	0.9	2.4	2.2	3.7	6.1	6.9	4.9	8.4	13.1	24.1	29.1	56.6	106.8	159.4	310.9	502.1	722.5	815.6	...
Female - Femmes	2.9	0.7	0.0	0.4	1.4	0.8	1.7	1.7	1.6	4.6	8.6	14.9	24.8	38.8	75.8	138.3	228.5	397.3	637.6	811.6	...
Ireland - Irlande																					
2005 - 2007																					
Male - Hommes	4.9	0.6	0.8	3.6	5.4	4.7	5.1	5.7	8.6	13.3	21.1	33.3	54.5	88.7	148.8	247.0	395.4	567.3	730.3	919.0	...
Female - Femmes	4.5	0.4	0.7	1.6	1.5	1.6	2.0	3.0	5.2	9.2	13.6	21.3	33.8	53.6	90.1	153.4	284.4	460.5	643.4	800.7	...
Italy - Italie																					
2017																					
Male - Hommes	3.6	0.4	0.5	1.4	2.1	2.2	2.7	3.7	5.7	9.3	14.7	24.2	39.7	64.0	102.4	170.4	292.3	484.8	706.0	841.6	...
Female - Femmes	3.2	0.3	0.4	0.6	0.8	1.0	1.3	2.2	3.4	5.7	8.9	13.9	21.8	35.3	59.2	103.6	201.1	377.8	609.7	781.9	...
Latvia - Lettonie																					
2006																					
Male - Hommes	10.5	1.4	1.6	3.0	6.2	11.3	18.6	28.3	40.6	56.3	76.6	104.3	143.2	199.8	282.1	397.7	547.0	712.6	...	...	...
Female - Femmes	12.7	1.3	1.2	1.5	2.2	3.2	4.8	7.3	11.2	17.3	26.7	41.0	63.0	96.1	145.1	215.5	312.2	436.5	...	...	...
Lithuania - Lituanie																					
2017																					
Male - Hommes	3.9	1.2	1.1	3.0	4.5	8.0	12.4	17.6	27.0	36.6	50.1	75.0	114.0	161.3	214.6	291.5	410.3	582.7	761.1	894.4	*1000
Female - Femmes	3.3	0.5	0.6	0.8	1.5	2.3	3.6	6.4	9.0	13.4	17.9	25.7	38.8	61.2	97.1	155.5	283.0	488.1	717.6	868.3	*1000
Luxembourg																					
2015 - 2017																					
Male - Hommes	3.2	0.4	0.1	1.7	2.2	1.8	2.3	3.2	6.0	9.9	16.8	27.8	44.7	78.9	117.9	178.4	293.5	485.4	725.7	*1000	...
Female - Femmes	1.8	0.0	0.5	0.3	0.5	0.9	0.8	2.0	4.7	6.3	9.0	14.4	25.8	43.4	76.2	113.0	206.8	383.4	595.1	*1000	...
Malta - Malte																					
2012																					
Male - Hommes	5.6	0.5	0.4	0.4	2.3	2.2	5.4	4.8	6.1	12.6	14.8	26.8	46.3	77.4	112.0	220.3	378.6	640.6	887.5	975.9	*1000
Female - Femmes	6.0	0.6	0.9	0.8	0.0	2.0	2.7	1.8	5.6	4.5	11.8	13.5	27.6	41.3	67.7	130.5	273.1	474.9	737.6	853.6	*1000
Netherlands - Pays-Bas																					
2009																					
Male - Hommes	4.8	0.5	0.6	1.4	2.3	2.4	3.0	4.1	6.6	10.7	18.7	30.3	49.9	79.1	132.1	225.2	363.5	539.8	738.0	...	...
Female - Femmes	4.1	0.4	0.5	0.8	1.0	1.3	1.7	2.9	5.0	8.9	15.0	21.5	32.5	47.8	76.4	136.1	249.6	428.5	644.7	...	...
North Macedonia - Macédoine du Nord																					
2016																					
Male - Hommes	11.2	0.9	1.1	1.8	2.7	2.9	3.5	5.3	10.4	16.6	31.0	53.3	86.1	129.3	195.6	306.8	482.5	694.9	885.7	...	...
Female - Femmes	10.7	0.6	0.8	1.1	0.9	1.5	2.1	3.4	5.2	9.2	16.5	28.0	47.2	79.2	136.2	257.5	444.1	658.5	808.7	...	...
Norway - Norvège																					
2018																					
Male - Hommes	2.6	0.3	0.5	1.3	2.9	3.1	3.6	4.6	5.4	7.8	12.9	22.5	36.4	58.7	95.7	167.7	288.9	478.9	677.5	858.5	...
Female - Femmes	2.4	0.2	0.5	0.8	0.7	1.2	1.3	2.2	3.4	5.5	8.8	15.4	24.5	40.5	65.0	117.1	210.6	373.1	608.6	814.9	...
Poland - Pologne																					
2018																					
Male - Hommes	4.9	0.5	0.7	2.4	4.4	5.3	7.0	10.0	15.8	24.6	38.8	61.9	93.8	134.3	180.7	254.8	369.1	501.3	642.5	778.5	...
Female - Femmes	4.1	0.4	0.6	1.1	1.3	1.4	1.9	3.1	5.1	8.9	14.7	25.6	40.8	61.4	94.0	147.1	260.3	417.2	588.6	758.0	...

20. Probability of dying in the five year interval following specified age (5qx), by sex, latest available year: 2004 - 2018
Probabilité de décès dans l'intervalle de cinq ans qui suit un âge donné (5qx), par sexe, dernière année disponible :
2004 - 2018 (continued - suite)

Continent, country or area and date / Continent, pays ou zone et date	Age (in years) - Age (en années)																				
	0	5	10	15	20	25	30	35	40	45	50	55	60	65	70	75	80	85	90	95	100
EUROPE																					
Portugal 2015 - 2017																					
Male - Hommes	4.3	0.5	0.5	1.5	2.4	2.9	3.2	5.0	9.3	16.2	26.6	40.4	56.2	78.1	118.5	193.3	333.6	624.5	854.1	968.1	...
Female - Femmes	3.1	0.4	0.4	0.7	1.0	1.0	1.4	2.7	4.5	7.0	10.8	14.9	22.6	34.4	60.4	111.0	228.9	519.6	791.1	948.8	...
Republic of Moldova - République de Moldova 2012																					
Male - Hommes	12.2	1.4	2.0	4.4	5.6	7.1	11.3	19.8	30.9	50.0	71.2	102.2	157.9	176.7	292.1	388.4	503.1	558.6	*1000	...	...
Female - Femmes	12.1	1.1	1.2	1.6	1.8	2.4	3.6	8.1	10.6	16.1	26.8	44.1	78.0	103.1	191.4	289.0	418.9	550.8	*1000	...	...
Romania - Roumanie 2015 - 2017																					
Male - Hommes	9.4	0.9	1.3	2.7	3.6	4.1	4.8	7.9	14.5	26.1	45.6	74.3	106.3	146.4	203.1	295.8	425.0	574.2	716.6	835.5	...
Female - Femmes	7.6	0.7	0.8	1.2	1.2	1.6	2.0	3.4	6.2	10.2	17.6	28.0	45.0	70.2	115.1	197.9	343.6	523.0	700.8	844.7	...
Russian Federation - Fédération de Russie 2012																					
Male - Hommes	11.6	1.7	1.8	5.4	11.6	19.0	30.3	36.8	42.1	56.4	77.9	110.6	155.6	193.8	273.2	361.6	481.9	577.2	694.9	771.0	*1000
Female - Femmes	9.5	1.1	1.2	2.5	3.4	5.6	9.0	11.6	14.3	18.9	26.2	39.5	57.7	84.1	137.1	230.5	372.9	543.1	716.4	825.0	*1000
San Marino - Saint-Marin 2017																					
Male - Hommes	2.5	0.0	0.0	1.9	2.7	1.9	0.5	2.4	3.2	4.1	11.1	20.6	29.4	49.1	76.1	153.8	285.3	430.4	655.9	933.0	...
Female - Femmes	2.7	0.0	0.0	1.3	0.0	0.0	0.5	0.8	3.7	5.0	6.2	11.3	14.0	27.7	45.6	74.0	170.1	341.0	564.7	821.0	...
Serbia - Serbie[10] 2010 - 2012																					
Male - Hommes	8.1	0.5	0.9	2.4	3.7	4.7	6.4	8.2	13.3	25.5	44.0	69.0	101.6	148.5	216.4	334.2	492.1	676.0	856.4	973.0	...
Female - Femmes	6.5	0.6	0.9	1.1	1.5	2.0	2.6	4.3	7.4	12.8	21.1	33.3	50.4	82.2	147.2	265.6	432.9	632.3	840.3	975.2	...
Slovakia - Slovaquie 2017																					
Male - Hommes	6.4	0.6	0.8	2.6	3.8	3.9	5.3	7.2	12.6	20.9	38.6	59.0	94.8	131.0	193.0	275.3	409.9	563.4	731.5	879.9	...
Female - Femmes	4.5	0.5	0.4	1.1	1.0	1.8	2.2	3.3	5.3	9.7	16.1	25.0	39.3	59.3	97.5	171.3	313.6	537.2	800.2	966.0	...
Slovenia - Slovénie 2017																					
Male - Hommes	2.2	0.3	0.4	1.3	2.6	3.6	3.9	3.9	6.2	11.4	23.2	38.0	62.4	88.5	134.2	205.5	345.6	540.7	738.5	914.4	...
Female - Femmes	2.4	0.4	0.5	0.9	1.6	0.9	1.1	2.1	3.5	6.5	10.7	19.1	29.5	42.8	66.3	118.8	231.6	411.4	643.3	827.4	...
Spain - Espagne 2017																					
Male - Hommes	3.5	0.4	0.4	1.1	1.7	2.1	2.6	3.5	5.4	10.1	18.5	30.2	46.1	70.3	105.9	167.5	282.9	460.8	658.3	775.7	*1000
Female - Femmes	2.8	0.3	0.4	0.6	0.8	0.9	1.1	2.0	3.2	5.7	9.4	14.4	20.7	29.9	48.9	90.2	182.5	354.9	579.9	757.4	*1000
Sweden - Suède 2012																					
Male - Hommes	3.5	0.4	0.5	1.4	3.2	3.6	3.2	3.8	5.4	9.2	15.2	25.0	40.8	65.6	109.3	186.3	322.6	519.0	727.6	886.1	...
Female - Femmes	2.7	0.3	0.5	0.9	1.1	1.1	1.6	2.8	3.4	6.4	11.0	16.2	26.3	45.6	71.4	126.8	229.8	416.2	644.1	827.2	...
Switzerland - Suisse 2017																					
Male - Hommes	4.7	0.3	0.3	1.3	2.3	2.0	2.5	3.4	4.9	8.0	14.1	23.3	36.6	57.6	92.5	152.1	261.2	457.6	696.1	855.0	...
Female - Femmes	3.5	0.3	0.3	0.4	0.6	0.9	1.3	1.8	2.8	4.7	8.1	13.2	20.6	32.7	55.0	98.9	188.0	359.9	606.4	815.6	...
Ukraine[11] 2017																					
Male - Hommes	10.0	1.0	1.4	3.6	6.4	10.2	16.6	25.5	35.8	48.0	67.8	97.2	142.0	194.1	269.7	370.4	492.4	608.2	711.8	802.9	...
Female - Femmes	7.8	0.8	0.8	1.5	1.9	3.3	5.4	8.8	12.3	16.7	23.2	33.0	51.9	85.1	141.2	235.8	388.7	563.4	750.7	901.0	...
United Kingdom of Great Britain and Northern Ireland - Royaume-Uni de Grande-Bretagne et d'Irlande du Nord[12] 2015 - 2017																					
Male - Hommes	4.9	0.4	0.5	1.5	2.5	3.2	4.3	6.0	9.1	13.1	18.9	29.3	46.9	71.1	113.8	186.8	306.2	483.7	681.3	837.9	...
Female - Femmes	4.0	0.3	0.4	0.8	1.1	1.4	2.3	3.5	5.4	8.3	12.8	19.6	30.9	47.3	77.9	133.5	234.9	403.8	613.3	794.5	...

20. Probability of dying in the five year interval following specified age (5qx), by sex, latest available year: 2004 - 2018
Probabilité de décès dans l'intervalle de cinq ans qui suit un âge donné (5qx), par sexe, dernière année disponible : 2004 - 2018 (continued - suite)

Continent, country or area and date / Continent, pays ou zone et date	0	5	10	15	20	25	30	35	40	45	50	55	60	65	70	75	80	85	90	95	100
OCEANIA - OCÉANIE																					
Australia - Australie																					
2015 - 2017																					
Male - Hommes	4.1	0.4	0.6	2.0	3.0	3.5	4.4	5.8	8.3	12.0	17.4	26.3	39.2	59.3	95.8	159.2	271.9	448.3	650.3	793.0	...
Female - Femmes	3.6	0.3	0.5	1.0	1.2	1.4	2.1	3.1	4.7	7.2	10.8	15.8	22.9	36.1	60.5	106.2	195.8	355.6	581.1	769.8	...
New Zealand - Nouvelle-Zélande																					
2012 - 2014																					
Male - Hommes	5.9	0.7	0.9	3.2	4.1	4.0	4.2	5.6	7.6	11.6	17.6	26.2	40.3	65.4	108.3	176.2	298.2	485.4	667.7	822.5	*1000
Female - Femmes	4.9	0.5	0.7	1.5	1.6	1.5	2.3	3.2	5.1	8.0	12.5	17.9	28.2	43.2	71.4	126.3	219.4	391.0	615.3	807.3	*1000

FOOTNOTES - NOTES

* Open-ended group (e.g. 80 years or over). - Groupe d'âge ouvert (par exemple, 80 ans ou plus).

[1] Excluding Indian jungle population. - Non compris les Indiens de la jungle.

[2] Data refer to the 12 months from 30 June 2016 to 30 June 2017. - Les données font référence aux douze mois de 30 juin 2016 à 30 juin 2017.

[3] Data based on the 2010 Population Census. Excludes nomadic Indian tribes. - Les données sont fondées sur le recensement de la population de 2010. Non compris les tribus d'Indiens nomades.

[4] Includes data for East Jerusalem and Israeli residents in certain other territories under occupation by Israeli military forces since June 1967. - Y compris les données pour Jérusalem-Est et les résidents israéliens dans certains autres territoires occupés depuis 1967 par les forces armées israéliennes.

[5] Data refer to Japanese nationals in Japan only. - Les données se raportent aux nationaux japonais au Japon seulement.

[6] Provisional data. Data refer to resident population which comprises Singapore citizens and permanent residents. - Données provisoires. Les données se rapportent à la population résidente composé des citoyens de Singapour et des résidents permanents.

[7] Provisional data. - Données provisoires.

[8] Excluding Faeroe Islands and Greenland shown separately, if available. - Non compris les Iles Féroé et le Groenland, qui font l'objet de rubriques distinctes, si disponible.

[9] Excluding Åland Islands. - Non compris les Îles d'Åland.

[10] Excludes data for Kosovo and Metohia. - Sans les données pour le Kosovo et Metohie.

[11] The Government of Ukraine has informed the United Nations that it is not in a position to provide statistical data concerning the Autonomous Republic of Crimea and the city of Sevastopol. - Le gouvernement Ukrainien a informé l'ONU qu'il n'est pas en mesure de fournir des données statistiques concernant la République autonome de Crimée et la ville de Sébastopol.

[12] Excluding Channel Islands (Guernsey and Jersey) and Isle of Man, shown separately, if available. - Non compris les îles Anglo-Normandes (Guernesey et Jersey) et l'île de Man, qui font l'objet de rubriques distinctes, si disponible.

Table 21 - *Demographic Yearbook 2018*

Table 21 presents life expectancy at specified ages for each sex, for the latest available year between 1999 and 2018.

Description of variables: Life expectancy at age x, e_x, is defined as the average number of years of life remaining to persons who have reached age *x* if they continue to be subject to the mortality conditions of the period indicated in the life table.

Male and female life expectancy values are shown separately at selected ages beginning at birth and proceeding at every fifth age thereafter up to age 100.

The table shows life expectancy derived from a complete or abridged life table as reported by the country or area.

Data are shown with one decimal regardless of the number of digits provided in the original computation.

The life table is a statistical device for summarizing the mortality experience of a population, from which the probability of dying, survivorship and life expectancy can be calculated. It is based on the assumption that the theoretical cohort is subject, throughout its existence, to the age-specific mortality rates observed at a particular time period. Thus, levels of mortality prevailing at the time a life table is constructed are assumed to remain unchanged into the future until all members of the cohort have died.

Reliability of data: The values shown in this table come from official life tables. It is assumed that, if necessary, the basic data (population and deaths classified by age and sex) have been adjusted for deficiencies before their use in constructing the life tables.

Limitations: Life expectancy values are subject to the same qualifications as have been set forth for population statistics in general and death statistics in particular, as discussed in sections 3 and 4, respectively, of the Technical Notes. They must be interpreted strictly using the underlying assumption that surviving cohorts are subjected to the same age-specific mortality rates of the period to which the life table refers.

Earlier data: Life expectancy values at specified ages for each sex have been shown in previous issues of the *Demographic Yearbook*. For information on specific years covered, the reader should consult the Historical Index.

Tableau 21 – *Annuaire démographique 2018*

Le tableau 21 présente les espérances de vie à des âges déterminés, pour chaque sexe, pour la dernière année disponible entre 1999 et 2018.

Description des variables : L'espérance de vie à l'âge x, e_x, se définit comme le nombre moyen d'années restant à vivre aux hommes et aux femmes qui ont atteint l'âge x, à supposer qu'ils continuent de connaître les mêmes conditions de mortalité observées pendant la période sur laquelle porte la table de mortalité.

Les chiffres sont présentés séparément pour chaque sexe à partir de la naissance et puis tous les cinq ans jusqu'à 100 ans.

Dans le tableau figurent les espérances de vie calculées selon les tables de mortalité complètes ou abrégées communiquées par les pays et les zones.

Les données sont arrondies à la première décimale, indépendamment du nombre de décimales qui figurent dans le calcul initial.

La table de mortalité est un moyen statistique que s'utilise pour donner un aperçu complet de la mortalité d'une population incluant les probabilités de décès et l'espérance de vie à chaque âge. Les tables de mortalité reposent sur l'hypothèse que chaque cohorte théoriquement distinguée connaît, pendant toute son existence, les taux de mortalité par âge observé à un moment donné. Les taux de mortalité correspondant à l'époque à laquelle sont calculées les tables de mortalité sont ainsi censés demeurer inchangées dans l'avenir jusqu'au décès de tous les membres de la cohorte.

Fiabilité des donnés : Les chiffres figurant dans ce tableau proviennent de tables officielles de mortalité. En ce qui concerne les chiffres extraits de tables officielles de mortalité, on part du principe les données de base (effectif de la population et nombre de décès selon l'âge et le sexe) ont été ajustées, en tant que de besoin, avant de servir à l'établissement de la table de mortalité.

Insuffisance des données : les espérances de vie appellent les mêmes réserves que celles qui ont été formulées à propos des statistiques de la population en général et des statistiques de mortalité en particulier (voir les sections 3 et 4 des Notes techniques). Lorsque l'on interprète les données, il ne faut jamais perdre de vue que, par hypothèse, les cohortes de survivants sont soumises, pour chaque âge, aux conditions de mortalité de la période visée par la table de mortalité.

Données publiées antérieurement : les espérances de vie à des âges déterminés pour chaque sexe figuraient déjà dans des éditions antérieures de *l'Annuaire démographique*. Pour plus de précisions concernant les années pour lesquelles ces données ont été publiées, se reporter à l'index historique.

21. Life expectancy at specified ages for each sex: latest available year, 1999 - 2018
Espérance de vie à un âge donné pour chaque sexe : dernière année disponible, 1999 - 2018

Continent, country or area and date / Continent, pays ou zone et date	0	5	10	15	20	25	30	35	40	45	50	55	60	65	70	75	80	85	90	95	100
AFRICA - AFRIQUE																					
Algeria - Algérie[1]																					
2016																					
Male - Hommes	77.1	74.2	69.3	64.4	59.6	54.9	50.1	45.4	40.7	36.0	31.4	27.0	22.7	18.8	15.1	11.7	8.8	6.5	...	...	...
Female - Femmes	78.2	75.1	70.2	65.3	60.5	55.6	50.7	45.9	41.2	36.5	31.9	27.4	23.0	18.9	14.9	11.2	7.9	5.3	...	...	...
2017																					
Male - Hommes	76.9	...	...	...	...	...	...	...	...	...	...	...	...	...	...	...	...	...	...	...	...
Female - Femmes	78.2	...	...	...	...	...	...	...	...	...	...	...	...	...	...	...	...	...	...	...	...
Angola																					
2018																					
Male - Hommes	60.6	...	...	...	...	...	...	...	...	...	...	...	...	...	...	...	...	...	...	...	...
Female - Femmes	63.4	...	...	...	...	...	...	...	...	...	...	...	...	...	...	...	...	...	...	...	...
Benin - Bénin[2]																					
2002																					
Male - Hommes	57.2	63.4	59.1	54.7	50.2	45.9	41.8	37.8	33.8	30.0	26.2	22.7	19.4	16.2	13.2	10.6	8.1	5.5	3.8	...	...
Female - Femmes	61.3	65.4	61.2	56.7	52.3	48.1	43.9	39.9	36.0	32.1	28.3	24.6	21.2	18.0	14.2	10.8	7.7	4.8	2.9	...	...
Botswana[3]																					
2016																					
Male - Hommes	64.9	62.0	57.4	52.6	48.1	43.9	40.3	37.3	34.4	31.7	28.4	24.9	21.3	17.7	14.1	10.4	6.7	...	...	...	...
Female - Femmes	65.9	62.8	58.1	53.3	48.6	44.1	39.8	36.0	32.5	29.2	25.7	22.3	19.0	15.6	12.4	9.1	5.8	...	...	...	...
Burkina Faso[4]																					
2006																					
Male - Hommes	55.8	60.0	55.9	51.3	46.9	42.8	38.6	34.5	30.5	26.6	22.8	19.3	16.0	12.9	10.3	8.1	6.2	4.8	...	...	...
Female - Femmes	57.5	61.6	57.6	53.1	48.6	44.4	40.2	36.1	32.0	28.0	24.1	20.3	16.8	13.5	10.7	8.4	6.4	4.9	...	...	...
Burundi																					
2008																					
Male - Hommes	46.0	49.7	46.5	42.5	39.0	35.8	32.4	28.9	25.4	21.9	18.6	15.3	12.3	9.5	7.2	5.2	3.8	...	...	...	...
Female - Femmes	51.8	55.4	52.1	47.9	44.0	40.3	36.7	33.0	29.2	25.4	21.5	17.8	14.2	11.0	8.3	6.0	4.4	...	...	...	...
2017																					
Male - Hommes	56.9	...	...	...	...	...	...	...	...	...	...	...	...	...	...	...	...	...	...	...	...
Female - Femmes	61.3	...	...	...	...	...	...	...	...	...	...	...	...	...	...	...	...	...	...	...	...
Cabo Verde																					
2010[5]																					
Male - Hommes	69.7	66.3	61.4	56.6	51.9	47.3	42.8	38.5	34.4	30.6	26.8	23.3	20.1	17.0	14.2	11.6	9.4	...	...	...	...
Female - Femmes	79.2	75.4	70.5	65.6	60.7	55.9	51.1	46.3	41.7	37.1	32.6	28.3	24.2	20.3	16.6	13.4	10.8	...	...	...	...
2018[6]																					
Male - Hommes	72.6	...	...	...	...	...	...	...	...	...	...	...	...	...	...	...	...	...	...	...	...
Female - Femmes	80.4	...	...	...	...	...	...	...	...	...	...	...	...	...	...	...	...	...	...	...	...
Congo																					
2007																					
Male - Hommes	50.1	...	...	...	...	...	...	...	...	...	...	...	...	...	...	...	...	...	...	...	...
Female - Femmes	53.3	...	...	...	...	...	...	...	...	...	...	...	...	...	...	...	...	...	...	...	...
Côte d'Ivoire																					
2016																					
Male - Hommes	54.9	...	...	...	...	...	...	...	...	...	...	...	...	...	...	...	...	...	...	...	...
Female - Femmes	57.5	...	...	...	...	...	...	...	...	...	...	...	...	...	...	...	...	...	...	...	...
Djibouti[7]																					
2002																					
Male - Hommes	51.8	...	...	...	...	...	...	...	...	...	...	...	...	...	...	...	...	...	...	...	...
Female - Femmes	54.1	...	...	...	...	...	...	...	...	...	...	...	...	...	...	...	...	...	...	...	...
Egypt - Égypte																					
2016																					
Male - Hommes	70.5	67.0	62.1	57.2	52.4	47.5	42.7	37.9	33.1	28.5	24.1	20.1	16.3	12.8	9.5	6.6	3.6	...	...	...	...
Female - Femmes	73.3	69.6	64.7	59.7	54.8	49.9	44.9	40.0	35.1	30.3	25.6	21.1	16.9	12.9	9.3	6.0	2.4	...	...	...	...
2018																					
Male - Hommes	71.2	...	...	...	...	...	...	...	...	...	...	...	...	...	...	...	...	...	...	...	...
Female - Femmes	74.0	...	...	...	...	...	...	...	...	...	...	...	...	...	...	...	...	...	...	...	...
Equatorial Guinea - Guinée équatoriale																					
2001																					
Male - Hommes	58.4	...	...	...	...	...	...	...	...	...	...	...	...	...	...	...	...	...	...	...	...
Female - Femmes	59.6	...	...	...	...	...	...	...	...	...	...	...	...	...	...	...	...	...	...	...	...
Eswatini																					
2007																					
Male - Hommes	42.2	44.9	40.5	36.0	31.5	27.5	24.9	23.3	22.1	20.9	19.1	17.4	15.4	13.6	10.9	8.9	...	...	...	...	...
Female - Femmes	43.1	48.2	43.9	39.3	35.0	32.3	30.9	30.3	29.5	27.6	25.1	22.7	19.5	16.8	13.5	10.5	...	...	...	...	...

591

Continent, country or area and date / Continent, pays ou zone et date	0	5	10	15	20	25	30	35	40	45	50	55	60	65	70	75	80	85	90	95	100
AFRICA - AFRIQUE																					
2018[8]																					
Male - Hommes	44.1	...	...	...	...	...	...	...	...	...	...	...	...	...	...	...	...	...	...	...	...
Female - Femmes	48.1	...	...	...	...	...	...	...	...	...	...	...	...	...	...	...	...	...	...	...	...
Ghana[9]																					
2010																					
Male - Hommes	59.4	60.9	57.0	52.5	48.3	44.2	40.2	36.1	32.0	27.9	24.0	20.2	16.6	13.3	10.4	7.9	5.9	...	...	...	...
Female - Femmes	64.4	64.9	60.7	56.1	51.7	47.3	43.0	38.7	34.4	30.2	26.1	22.1	18.2	14.6	11.4	8.7	6.5	...	...	...	...
Guinea - Guinée																					
2014[10]																					
Male - Hommes	57.4	62.5	58.3	53.9	49.5	45.3	41.2	37.2	33.3	29.6	25.9	22.3	18.7	15.1	11.8	8.4	5.0	...	...	...	...
Female - Femmes	60.4	65.5	61.1	56.6	52.3	48.0	43.9	39.9	35.8	31.8	27.8	23.9	19.8	16.1	12.3	8.8	5.0	...	...	...	...
2017																					
Male - Hommes	58.4	...	...	...	...	...	...	...	...	...	...	...	...	...	...	...	...	...	...	...	...
Female - Femmes	61.4	...	...	...	...	...	...	...	...	...	...	...	...	...	...	...	...	...	...	...	...
Guinea-Bissau - Guinée-Bissau																					
2008 - 2009																					
Male - Hommes	49.2	49.8	45.3	41.0	36.8	32.8	29.3	26.2	23.3	20.7	18.0	15.5	13.1	11.2	9.4	8.0	6.8	...	...	...	...
Female - Femmes	51.2	50.1	45.7	41.5	37.8	34.4	31.3	28.4	25.6	22.9	20.0	17.4	14.9	12.8	10.6	8.8	7.1	...	...	...	...
2014																					
Male - Hommes	51.2	...	...	...	...	...	...	...	...	...	...	...	...	...	...	...	...	...	...	...	...
Female - Femmes	53.6	...	...	...	...	...	...	...	...	...	...	...	...	...	...	...	...	...	...	...	...
Kenya[2]																					
2009																					
Male - Hommes	57.8	58.1	53.9	49.7	45.3	41.0	36.9	33.3	30.2	27.1	23.9	20.4	16.7	13.2	10.0	7.0	4.0	...	...	...	...
Female - Femmes	60.7	60.1	55.8	51.4	46.9	42.6	38.7	35.7	33.0	29.8	26.2	22.3	18.3	14.5	11.0	7.7	4.7	...	...	...	...
Lesotho[11]																					
2006																					
Male - Hommes	39.8	40.4	36.0	31.5	27.2	23.6	20.9	19.2	18.2	17.3	16.4	14.9	13.2	11.3	9.4	7.4	5.3	2.9	...	...	...
Female - Femmes	42.9	42.7	38.4	33.8	29.6	26.3	24.2	23.2	22.8	22.3	21.5	20.2	18.6	16.7	14.5	12.1	9.6	7.4	...	...	...
2016																					
Male - Hommes	51.7	...	...	...	...	...	...	...	...	...	...	...	...	...	...	...	...	...	...	...	...
Female - Femmes	59.6	...	...	...	...	...	...	...	...	...	...	...	...	...	...	...	...	...	...	...	...
Madagascar[12]																					
2018																					
Male - Hommes	63.3	...	...	...	...	...	...	...	...	...	...	...	...	...	...	...	...	...	...	...	...
Female - Femmes	65.2	...	...	...	...	...	...	...	...	...	...	...	...	...	...	...	...	...	...	...	...
Malawi																					
2008																					
Male - Hommes	47.4	...	...	...	...	...	...	...	...	...	...	...	...	...	...	...	...	...	...	...	...
Female - Femmes	50.6	...	...	...	...	...	...	...	...	...	...	...	...	...	...	...	...	...	...	...	...
Mauritania - Mauritanie																					
2013																					
Male - Hommes	58.3	61.5	57.5	53.0	48.7	44.6	40.5	36.4	32.2	28.2	24.2	20.4	16.8	13.5	10.5	8.0	6.0	...	...	...	...
Female - Femmes	61.8	63.8	59.8	55.3	50.9	46.6	42.4	38.1	33.9	29.8	25.6	21.7	17.8	14.3	11.2	8.5	6.4	...	...	...	...
Mauritius - Maurice[13]																					
2016 - 2018																					
Male - Hommes	71.3	67.3	62.4	57.5	52.7	48.0	43.4	38.8	34.4	30.1	26.0	22.2	18.6	15.2	12.2	9.5	7.3	5.2	...	...	...
Female - Femmes	77.7	73.7	68.8	63.9	59.0	54.1	49.3	44.5	39.8	35.2	30.8	26.4	22.2	18.3	14.7	11.5	8.7	6.3	...	...	...
Mayotte																					
2015																					
Male - Hommes	75.3	...	...	...	56.7	...	...	...	37.8	...	...	...	20.5	...	...	...	...	...	...	...	...
Female - Femmes	77.2	...	...	...	58.4	...	...	...	39.0	...	...	...	20.9	...	...	...	...	...	...	...	...
2017																					
Male - Hommes	75.4	...	...	...	...	...	...	...	...	...	...	...	...	...	...	...	...	...	...	...	...
Female - Femmes	76.0	...	...	...	...	...	...	...	...	...	...	...	...	...	...	...	...	...	...	...	...
Morocco - Maroc																					
2013																					
Male - Hommes	72.4	...	...	...	...	...	...	...	...	...	...	...	...	...	...	...	...	...	...	...	...
Female - Femmes	75.1	...	...	...	...	...	...	...	...	...	...	...	...	...	...	...	...	...	...	...	...
Mozambique																					
2014																					
Male - Hommes	50.2	54.0	50.0	45.6	41.6	37.7	33.9	30.1	26.5	22.9	19.6	16.4	13.5	10.9	8.7	6.8	5.0	...	...	...	...
Female - Femmes	55.4	59.0	54.8	50.3	46.1	42.1	38.1	34.1	30.2	26.3	22.5	19.0	15.7	12.7	10.0	7.7	5.8	...	...	...	...

Continent, country or area and date / Continent, pays ou zone et date	0	5	10	15	20	25	30	35	40	45	50	55	60	65	70	75	80	85	90	95	100
AFRICA - AFRIQUE																					
2016																					
Male - Hommes	52.0	...	...	...	...	...	...	...	...	...	...	...	...	...	...	...	...	...	...	...	...
Female - Femmes	56.2	...	...	...	...	...	...	...	...	...	...	...	...	...	...	...	...	...	...	...	...
Namibia - Namibie																					
2011																					
Male - Hommes	53.3	52.4	48.0	43.4	39.0	35.1	31.5	28.6	25.8	23.2	20.6	17.7	15.1	12.6	9.8	7.4	5.6	...	...	...	...
Female - Femmes	60.5	59.6	55.1	50.5	46.1	42.0	38.4	35.2	32.0	28.7	25.2	21.6	17.9	14.5	11.3	8.6	6.5	...	...	...	...
Republic of South Sudan - République de Soudan du Sud																					
2010																					
Male - Hommes	54.4	57.4	53.2	48.8	44.6	40.7	36.8	32.8	28.9	25.0	21.2	17.6	14.2	11.2	8.5	6.3	4.5	3.2	2.2	1.5	...
Female - Femmes	54.5	56.2	51.9	47.5	43.3	39.4	35.4	31.5	27.5	23.7	19.9	16.4	13.1	10.2	7.7	5.6	4.1	2.9	2.0	1.4	...
Reunion - Réunion																					
2015																					
Male - Hommes	77.1	...	...	...	58.1	...	...	...	39.3	...	...	...	21.8	...	...	...					
Female - Femmes	83.6	...	...	...	64.3	...	...	...	44.8	...	...	...	26.2	...	...	...					
2017																					
Male - Hommes	78.1	...	...	...	...	...	...	...	...	...	...	...	...	...	...	...	...	...	...	...	...
Female - Femmes	84.5	...	...	...	...	...	...	...	...	...	...	...	...	...	...	...	...	...	...	...	...
Rwanda																					
2002																					
Male - Hommes	48.4	58.4	54.4	49.9	45.6	41.6	37.5	33.5	29.4	25.4	21.6	17.9	14.5	11.4	8.6	6.3	4.6	...	...	...	...
Female - Femmes	53.8	63.1	58.8	54.3	49.9	45.7	41.4	37.2	32.9	28.7	24.5	20.4	16.5	12.9	9.8	7.1	5.1	...	...	...	...
2017																					
Male - Hommes	64.6	...	...	...	...	...	...	...	...	...	...	...	...	...	...	...	...	...	...	...	...
Female - Femmes	68.4	...	...	...	...	...	...	...	...	...	...	...	...	...	...	...	...	...	...	...	...
Saint Helena ex. dep. - Sainte-Hélène sans dép.[14]																					
2003 - 2012																					
Male - Hommes	72.0	68.1	63.4	...	53.9	...	44.2	...	35.5	...	27.1	...	19.3	...	12.5	...	7.2	...	...	...	...
Female - Femmes	79.7	75.3	70.3	...	60.3	...	51.0	...	41.8	...	32.0	...	23.0	...	15.5	...	8.6	...	...	...	...
2009 - 2018																					
Male - Hommes	74.3	...	...	...	...	...	...	...	...	...	...	...	...	...	...	...	...	...	...	...	...
Female - Femmes	80.4	...	...	...	...	...	...	...	...	...	...	...	...	...	...	...	...	...	...	...	...
Sao Tome and Principe - Sao Tomé-et-Principe																					
2011 - 2012																					
Male - Hommes	62.1	59.5	54.6	50.1	45.8	41.6	37.5	33.4	29.6	25.8	22.1	18.4	15.2	12.0	9.8	7.4	5.0	...	...	...	...
Female - Femmes	68.7	65.9	61.2	56.5	51.8	47.1	42.5	38.0	33.5	29.3	25.3	21.7	18.2	14.9	11.8	9.0	6.6	...	...	...	...
2017																					
Male - Hommes	64.0	...	...	...	...	...	...	...	...	...	...	...	...	...	...	...	...	...	...	...	...
Female - Femmes	70.5	...	...	...	...	...	...	...	...	...	...	...	...	...	...	...	...	...	...	...	...
Senegal - Sénégal[15]																					
2013																					
Male - Hommes	63.2	...	...	...	...	...	...	...	...	...	...	...	...	...	...	...	...	...	...	...	...
Female - Femmes	66.5	...	...	...	...	...	...	...	...	...	...	...	...	...	...	...	...	...	...	...	...
Seychelles																					
2007																					
Male - Hommes	68.9	65.0	60.2	55.3	50.5	45.9	41.6	37.0	32.7	28.7	24.4	20.9	17.1	14.1	11.0	9.0	7.4	...	...	...	...
Female - Femmes	77.7	73.3	68.5	63.5	58.5	53.7	48.9	44.3	39.5	35.3	31.0	26.4	22.2	18.5	15.1	12.1	9.2	...	...	...	...
2018																					
Male - Hommes	68.5	...	...	...	...	...	...	...	...	...	...	...	...	...	...	...	...	...	...	...	...
Female - Femmes	77.4	...	...	...	...	...	...	...	...	...	...	...	...	...	...	...	...	...	...	...	...
Sierra Leone[16]																					
2015																					
Male - Hommes	48.3	50.2	46.4	42.4	38.5	34.8	31.5	28.3	25.4	22.5	19.8	17.0	14.7	12.3	10.4	8.5	7.1	5.7	4.8	3.6	1.7
Female - Femmes	50.8	52.2	48.3	44.2	40.4	36.9	33.8	30.8	27.7	25.1	22.3	19.9	16.9	14.9	12.1	10.3	8.0	6.7	5.2	3.8	1.6
South Africa - Afrique du Sud																					
2014																					
Male - Hommes	59.1	...	...	...	...	...	...	...	...	...	...	...	...	...	...	...	...	...	...	...	...
Female - Femmes	63.1	...	...	...	...	...	...	...	...	...	...	...	...	...	...	...	...	...	...	...	...

21. Life expectancy at specified ages for each sex: latest available year, 1999 - 2018
Espérance de vie à un âge donné pour chaque sexe : dernière année disponible, 1999 - 2018 (continued - suite)

Continent, country or area and date / Continent, pays ou zone et date	0	5	10	15	20	25	30	35	40	45	50	55	60	65	70	75	80	85	90	95	100
AFRICA - AFRIQUE																					
Sudan - Soudan																					
2008																					
Male - Hommes	58.1	...	...	...	...	...	...	...	...	...	...	...	...	...	...	...	...	...	...	...	...
Female - Femmes	61.4	...	...	...	...	...	...	...	...	...	...	...	...	...	...	...	...	...	...	...	...
Tunisia - Tunisie																					
2016																					
Male - Hommes	74.5	...	...	...	...	...	...	...	...	...	...	...	...	...	...	...	...	...	...	...	...
Female - Femmes	78.1	...	...	...	...	...	...	...	...	...	...	...	...	...	...	...	...	...	...	...	...
Uganda - Ouganda																					
2002[17]																					
Male - Hommes	48.8	53.0	49.2	44.8	40.5	36.6	33.6	31.0	28.4	25.8	23.2	20.4	17.2	14.4	11.6	9.2	6.7	4.1	...	...	...
Female - Femmes	52.0	56.0	52.1	47.6	43.3	39.6	36.7	34.2	31.5	28.6	25.6	22.3	18.9	15.7	12.6	9.9	7.0	4.2	...	...	...
2014[18]																					
Male - Hommes	62.2	...	...	...	...	...	...	...	...	...	...	...	...	...	...	...	...	...	...	...	...
Female - Femmes	64.2	...	...	...	...	...	...	...	...	...	...	...	...	...	...	...	...	...	...	...	...
Zimbabwe																					
2001 - 2002																					
Male - Hommes	45.8	44.2	40.0	35.4	30.9	26.8	23.8	22.1	21.8	21.3	20.4	19.2	17.7	15.7	13.7	11.4	9.5	7.5	6.2	5.2	...
Female - Femmes	50.3	48.6	44.2	39.7	35.3	32.1	30.4	30.1	30.2	29.0	27.6	25.3	22.9	20.2	17.6	14.8	12.2	9.9	8.1	7.3	...
2012																					
Male - Hommes	57.4	...	...	...	...	...	...	...	...	...	...	...	...	...	...	...	...	...	...	...	...
Female - Femmes	64.0	...	...	...	...	...	...	...	...	...	...	...	...	...	...	...	...	...	...	...	...
AMERICA, NORTH - AMÉRIQUE DU NORD																					
Anguilla																					
2000 - 2002																					
Male - Hommes	76.5	72.1	67.1	62.1	57.3	53.1	48.4	43.7	39.4	34.7	30.2	25.4	21.1	16.5	12.7	10.0	8.0	6.9	...	...	...
Female - Femmes	81.1	76.4	71.4	66.4	61.4	57.1	52.7	47.7	42.7	38.3	33.5	28.7	24.0	19.4	15.3	10.8	8.3	7.6	...	...	...
Antigua and Barbuda - Antigua-et-Barbuda																					
2017																					
Male - Hommes	74.4	...	...	...	...	...	...	...	...	...	...	...	...	...	...	...	...	...	...	...	...
Female - Femmes	80.5	...	...	...	...	...	...	...	...	...	...	...	...	...	...	...	...	...	...	...	...
Aruba																					
2010 - 2011																					
Male - Hommes	73.9	69.4	64.4	59.5	54.6	50.0	45.4	40.8	36.3	31.7	27.3	23.1	19.1	15.3	12.3	9.4	7.3	5.0	3.5	2.7	...
Female - Femmes	79.8	76.2	71.2	66.2	61.3	56.4	51.5	46.6	42.0	37.3	32.6	27.9	23.8	19.7	16.0	12.5	9.5	6.8	5.0	3.8	...
Bahamas																					
1999 - 2001																					
Male - Hommes	69.9	...	...	...	...	...	...	...	...	...	...	...	...	...	...	...	...	...	...	...	...
Female - Femmes	76.4	...	...	...	...	...	...	...	...	...	...	...	...	...	...	...	...	...	...	...	...
Bermuda - Bermudes																					
2018																					
Male - Hommes	79.5	74.8	69.8	64.8	59.9	55.3	50.8	46.1	41.4	36.7	32.0	27.6	23.5	19.7	16.0	12.6	9.5	6.5	...	...	...
Female - Femmes	85.7	80.9	76.0	71.1	66.1	61.2	56.3	51.4	46.5	41.6	36.9	32.2	27.7	23.2	18.9	15.0	11.4	8.2	...	...	...
British Virgin Islands - Îles Vierges britanniques																					
2004																					
Male - Hommes	69.9	...	...	...	...	...	...	...	...	...	...	...	...	...	...	...	...	...	...	...	...
Female - Femmes	78.5	...	...	...	...	...	...	...	...	...	...	...	...	...	...	...	...	...	...	...	...
Canada																					
2014 - 2016																					
Male - Hommes	79.9	75.4	70.4	65.4	60.6	55.8	51.0	46.2	41.5	36.8	32.1	27.7	23.4	19.3	15.5	12.1	9.0	6.5	4.4	3.0	2.1
Female - Femmes	84.0	79.4	74.5	69.5	64.6	59.7	54.8	49.9	45.0	40.2	35.5	30.9	26.4	22.1	18.0	14.2	10.7	7.7	5.3	3.5	2.4
Cayman Islands - Îles Caïmanes[19]																					
2010																					
Male - Hommes	79.8	75.5	70.5	65.6	61.1	56.8	52.2	47.4	42.5	37.6	32.9	28.3	23.9	19.6	15.2	11.6	8.9	6.2	5.0	3.6	2.5
Female - Femmes	84.7	80.1	75.1	70.1	65.1	60.3	55.3	50.4	45.4	40.5	35.7	30.8	26.1	21.5	17.0	13.2	9.8	7.2	4.9	3.8	2.5

21. Life expectancy at specified ages for each sex: latest available year, 1999 - 2018
Espérance de vie à un âge donné pour chaque sexe : dernière année disponible, 1999 - 2018 (continued - suite)

Continent, country or area and date / Continent, pays ou zone et date	0	5	10	15	20	25	30	35	40	45	50	55	60	65	70	75	80	85	90	95	100

AMERICA, NORTH - AMÉRIQUE DU NORD

	0	5	10	15	20	25	30	35	40	45	50	55	60	65	70	75	80	85	90	95	100
Costa Rica 2018																					
Male - Hommes	77.8	73.4	68.5	63.6	58.8	54.1	49.4	44.8	40.2	35.6	31.1	26.8	22.6	18.7	15.1	11.9	9.1	6.8	4.8	3.3	...
Female - Femmes	82.9	78.4	73.5	68.5	63.6	58.7	53.8	49.0	44.1	39.3	34.6	30.0	25.5	21.3	17.3	13.5	10.2	7.5	5.3	3.6	...
Cuba 2011 - 2013																					
Male - Hommes	76.5	72.0	67.0	62.1	57.3	52.5	47.7	42.9	38.2	33.6	29.2	25.0	21.0	17.3	14.0	11.0	8.4	6.3	4.9	3.8	2.0
Female - Femmes	80.4	75.9	71.0	66.0	61.1	56.2	51.4	46.5	41.7	36.9	32.3	27.9	23.6	19.6	15.8	12.4	9.4	6.9	5.1	3.8	2.1
Curaçao 2016																					
Male - Hommes	74.9	71.1	66.2	61.2	56.3	51.6	47.0	42.3	37.7	33.0	28.5	24.3	20.4	16.7	13.3	10.4	7.6	5.5	3.9	2.8	2.4
Female - Femmes	81.0	77.7	72.7	67.7	62.8	57.9	53.0	48.2	43.3	38.6	33.9	29.3	24.8	20.6	16.6	12.8	9.6	7.0	4.9	3.3	2.2
2015 - 2017																					
Male - Hommes	74.7	...	...	...	...	...	...	...	...	...	...	...	...	...	...	...	...	...	...	...	...
Female - Femmes	81.5	...	...	...	...	...	...	...	...	...	...	...	...	...	...	...	...	...	...	...	...
Dominica - Dominique 2008																					
Male - Hommes	73.8	...	...	...	...	...	...	...	...	...	...	...	...	...	...	...	...	...	...	...	...
Female - Femmes	78.2	...	...	...	...	...	...	...	...	...	...	...	...	...	...	...	...	...	...	...	...
Dominican Republic - République dominicaine 2010 - 2015																					
Male - Hommes	70.0	67.5	62.6	57.7	53.0	48.7	44.3	40.0	35.6	31.3	27.2	23.3	19.6	16.2	13.2	10.5	8.6	...	...	...	...
Female - Femmes	74.8	71.8	66.9	62.0	57.1	52.4	47.7	43.1	38.5	34.1	29.7	25.5	21.6	17.9	14.6	11.7	9.7	...	...	...	...
El Salvador[20] 2000 - 2005																					
Male - Hommes	65.4	62.6	57.8	52.9	48.7	45.0	41.5	37.8	34.1	30.4	26.8	23.3	20.0	16.7	13.8	11.1	9.0	...	...	...	...
Female - Femmes	74.9	72.0	67.1	62.3	57.5	52.9	48.2	43.6	39.0	34.6	30.3	26.1	22.1	18.4	15.0	12.0	9.6	...	...	...	...
Greenland - Groenland 2017 - 2018																					
Male - Hommes	69.4	65.1	60.3	55.3	51.6	47.2	43.0	38.4	33.7	29.2	24.5	20.2	16.2	12.7	9.9	7.4	5.8	4.1	4.0	1.5	...
Female - Femmes	72.5	68.0	63.2	58.3	53.8	49.0	44.4	39.7	35.0	30.6	25.7	21.2	16.8	13.1	10.3	7.5	5.4	3.9	2.7	1.4	...
Guadeloupe 2015																					
Male - Hommes	77.0	...	...	...	58.2	...	...	...	40.4	...	...	...	23.5	...	...	...	...	...	...	...	...
Female - Femmes	84.8	...	...	...	65.6	...	...	...	46.1	...	...	...	27.4	...	...	...	...	...	...	...	...
Guatemala 1995 - 2000																					
Male - Hommes	61.4	60.6	56.0	51.2	46.8	42.7	38.8	34.9	31.2	27.4	23.7	20.1	16.8	13.6	10.7	8.2	6.1	...	...	...	...
Female - Femmes	67.2	66.2	62.6	56.9	52.3	47.7	43.3	38.9	34.6	30.4	26.3	22.3	18.6	15.2	12.0	9.2	6.9	...	...	...	...
2010 - 2015																					
Male - Hommes	67.9	...	...	...	...	...	...	...	...	...	...	...	...	...	...	...	...	...	...	...	...
Female - Femmes	75.0	...	...	...	...	...	...	...	...	...	...	...	...	...	...	...	...	...	...	...	...
Jamaica - Jamaïque 2011																					
Male - Hommes	70.4	67.0	62.1	57.2	52.7	48.7	44.7	40.6	36.6	32.4	28.3	24.2	20.3	16.4	12.8	9.5	6.5	...	...	...	...
Female - Femmes	78.0	74.3	69.5	64.6	59.7	54.8	50.0	45.3	40.6	36.0	31.5	27.1	22.9	18.7	14.7	11.0	7.6	...	...	...	...
Martinique 2015																					
Male - Hommes	79.4	...	...	...	60.1	...	...	...	41.7	...	...	...	24.1	...	...	...	...	...	...	...	...
Female - Femmes	84.7	...	...	...	65.4	...	...	...	45.9	...	...	...	27.4	...	...	...	...	...	...	...	...
Mexico - Mexique 2008																					
Male - Hommes	72.8	69.2	64.3	59.4	54.7	50.0	45.5	40.9	36.5	32.1	27.9	23.9	20.2	16.8	13.7	11.0	8.7	6.6	4.9	3.5	2.6
Female - Femmes	77.5	73.8	68.9	63.9	59.0	54.2	49.3	44.5	39.7	35.1	30.6	26.2	22.1	18.3	14.8	11.7	9.0	6.8	4.9	3.5	2.6
2018																					
Male - Hommes	72.2	...	...	...	...	...	...	...	...	...	...	...	...	...	...	...	...	...	...	...	...
Female - Femmes	77.9	...	...	...	...	...	...	...	...	...	...	...	...	...	...	...	...	...	...	...	...
Nicaragua 2005 - 2010																					
Male - Hommes	63.4	61.1	56.5	51.8	47.9	44.2	40.5	36.5	32.5	28.6	24.9	21.3	17.7	14.6	11.6	9.0	6.5	...	...	...	...
Female - Femmes	68.9	66.2	61.4	56.7	52.1	47.6	43.0	38.5	34.1	29.8	25.7	21.9	18.1	14.9	11.8	9.3	6.9	...	...	...	...

Continent, country or area and date / Continent, pays ou zone et date	0	5	10	15	20	25	30	35	40	45	50	55	60	65	70	75	80	85	90	95	100

AMERICA, NORTH - AMÉRIQUE DU NORD

Panama[21]
2017
| Male - Hommes | 75.2 | 71.8 | 66.9 | 62.1 | 57.5 | 53.2 | 48.9 | 44.5 | 40.0 | 35.5 | 31.2 | 26.9 | 22.9 | 19.2 | 15.8 | 12.7 | 10.0 | 7.7 | 5.8 | 4.2 | 2.5 |
| Female - Femmes | 81.2 | 77.5 | 72.6 | 67.7 | 62.9 | 58.1 | 53.3 | 48.6 | 43.8 | 39.2 | 34.6 | 30.1 | 25.8 | 21.6 | 17.8 | 14.2 | 11.1 | 8.4 | 6.2 | 4.3 | 2.5 |

Puerto Rico - Porto Rico
2016 - 2018
| Male - Hommes | 76.5 | 72.1 | 67.2 | 62.2 | 57.4 | 52.9 | 48.5 | 44.2 | 39.8 | 35.5 | 31.2 | 27.2 | 23.4 | 19.8 | 16.5 | 13.3 | 10.6 | 8.5 | ... | ... | ... |
| Female - Femmes | 84.7 | 80.3 | 75.4 | 70.4 | 65.4 | 60.6 | 55.7 | 50.9 | 46.1 | 41.4 | 36.8 | 32.3 | 27.9 | 23.7 | 19.7 | 16.0 | 12.7 | 10.1 | ... | ... | ... |

Saint Lucia - Sainte-Lucie
2005
| Male - Hommes | 69.9 | 66.4 | 61.5 | 56.6 | 52.0 | 47.4 | 43.1 | 38.6 | 34.3 | 30.1 | 25.9 | 21.7 | 17.9 | 14.7 | 11.8 | 9.0 | 7.2 | 5.2 | ... | ... | ... |
| Female - Femmes | 75.7 | 72.2 | 67.3 | 62.4 | 57.5 | 52.6 | 47.8 | 43.2 | 38.4 | 33.8 | 29.2 | 25.0 | 20.8 | 17.2 | 13.8 | 10.4 | 7.7 | 4.8 | ... | ... | ... |
2012
| Male - Hommes | 75.3 | ... | ... | ... | ... | ... | ... | ... | ... | ... | ... | ... | ... | ... | ... | ... | ... | ... | ... | ... | ... |
| Female - Femmes | 82.5 | ... | ... | ... | ... | ... | ... | ... | ... | ... | ... | ... | ... | ... | ... | ... | ... | ... | ... | ... | ... |

Saint Vincent and the Grenadines - Saint-Vincent-et-les Grenadines
2016
| Male - Hommes | 71.0 | 66.8 | 62.1 | 57.3 | 52.8 | 48.3 | 43.8 | 39.5 | 35.1 | 30.9 | 26.5 | 22.7 | 19.6 | 16.7 | 14.7 | 11.7 | 9.0 | 6.5 | ... | ... | ... |
| Female - Femmes | 75.2 | 71.1 | 66.3 | 61.4 | 56.5 | 51.8 | 47.1 | 42.5 | 38.0 | 33.5 | 29.0 | 25.1 | 21.4 | 17.9 | 14.7 | 11.5 | 9.2 | 6.6 | ... | ... | ... |

Sint Maarten (Dutch part) - Saint-Martin (partie néerlandaise)
2015 - 2017
| Male - Hommes | 74.0 | 70.1 | 65.3 | 60.4 | 55.6 | 51.1 | 46.8 | 42.1 | 37.5 | 32.7 | 28.2 | 24.0 | 20.0 | 16.4 | 12.6 | 9.6 | 6.8 | 4.2 | 4.8 | ... | ... |
| Female - Femmes | 82.8 | 79.2 | 74.2 | 69.2 | 64.2 | 59.5 | 54.5 | 49.6 | 44.8 | 40.0 | 35.2 | 30.5 | 26.1 | 21.8 | 17.6 | 14.3 | 11.3 | 8.1 | 6.8 | ... | ... |

Trinidad and Tobago - Trinité-et-Tobago[2]
2011
| Male - Hommes | 71.4 | 67.6 | 62.7 | 57.8 | 53.2 | 49.0 | 44.7 | 40.4 | 36.0 | 31.7 | 27.5 | 23.5 | 19.6 | 16.2 | 12.9 | 10.2 | 7.9 | 6.0 | ... | ... | ... |
| Female - Femmes | 77.8 | 74.1 | 69.2 | 64.2 | 59.4 | 54.6 | 49.9 | 45.3 | 40.6 | 36.2 | 31.7 | 27.5 | 23.3 | 19.4 | 15.9 | 12.6 | 9.7 | 7.6 | ... | ... | ... |

Turks and Caicos Islands - Îles Turques et Caïques
2001
| Male - Hommes | 79.0 | 75.3 | 70.3 | 65.3 | 60.3 | 55.8 | 50.8 | 46.0 | 41.2 | 37.1 | 33.0 | 28.4 | 24.3 | 20.8 | 17.5 | 12.5 | 7.5 | 4.1 | ... | ... | ... |
| Female - Femmes | 77.4 | 72.5 | 67.5 | 62.5 | 57.5 | 52.9 | 48.2 | 43.4 | 38.6 | 33.8 | 29.6 | 25.0 | 20.0 | 17.0 | 13.2 | 11.7 | 10.3 | 8.8 | ... | ... | ... |
2012
| Male - Hommes | 75.8 | ... | ... | ... | ... | ... | ... | ... | ... | ... | ... | ... | ... | ... | ... | ... | ... | ... | ... | ... | ... |
| Female - Femmes | 77.8 | ... | ... | ... | ... | ... | ... | ... | ... | ... | ... | ... | ... | ... | ... | ... | ... | ... | ... | ... | ... |

United States of America - États-Unis d'Amérique
2014
| Male - Hommes | 76.4 | 72.0 | 67.0 | 62.1 | 57.3 | 52.6 | 48.0 | 43.3 | 38.7 | 34.2 | 29.8 | 25.6 | 21.7 | 18.0 | 14.4 | 11.2 | 8.3 | 5.9 | 4.1 | 2.9 | 2.1 |
| Female - Femmes | 81.2 | 76.7 | 71.7 | 66.8 | 61.9 | 57.0 | 52.1 | 47.3 | 42.6 | 37.9 | 33.3 | 28.9 | 24.7 | 20.5 | 16.6 | 13.0 | 9.7 | 7.0 | 4.8 | 3.3 | 2.3 |
2015
| Male - Hommes | 76.3 | ... | ... | ... | ... | ... | ... | ... | ... | ... | ... | ... | ... | ... | ... | ... | ... | ... | ... | ... | ... |
| Female - Femmes | 81.2 | ... | ... | ... | ... | ... | ... | ... | ... | ... | ... | ... | ... | ... | ... | ... | ... | ... | ... | ... | ... |

AMERICA, SOUTH - AMÉRIQUE DU SUD

Argentina - Argentine
2008 - 2010
| Male - Hommes | 72.1 | 68.2 | 63.3 | 58.4 | 53.7 | 49.1 | 44.5 | 39.8 | 35.2 | 30.7 | 26.3 | 22.2 | 18.5 | 15.0 | 11.9 | 9.2 | 6.9 | 5.2 | 4.0 | 3.1 | 2.6 |
| Female - Femmes | 78.8 | 74.8 | 69.9 | 65.0 | 60.1 | 55.3 | 50.5 | 45.6 | 40.9 | 36.2 | 31.7 | 27.3 | 23.1 | 19.0 | 15.2 | 11.7 | 8.6 | 6.3 | 4.7 | 3.5 | 2.9 |
2015[6]
| Male - Hommes | 73.7 | ... | ... | ... | ... | ... | ... | ... | ... | ... | ... | ... | ... | ... | ... | ... | ... | ... | ... | ... | ... |
| Female - Femmes | 80.3 | ... | ... | ... | ... | ... | ... | ... | ... | ... | ... | ... | ... | ... | ... | ... | ... | ... | ... | ... | ... |

Continent, country or area and date / Continent, pays ou zone et date	0	5	10	15	20	25	30	35	40	45	50	55	60	65	70	75	80	85	90	95	100
AMERICA, SOUTH - AMÉRIQUE DU SUD																					
Bolivia (Plurinational State of) - Bolivie (État plurinational de)[22]																					
2016 - 2017																					
Male - Hommes	69.1	67.3	62.6	57.9	53.4	49.1	44.7	40.4	36.2	32.0	27.9	24.0	20.3	16.9	13.8	11.1	8.7	6.8	4.9	3.7	...
Female - Femmes	75.9	73.6	68.9	64.0	59.3	54.6	50.0	45.3	40.7	36.3	32.0	27.8	23.8	20.1	16.8	13.7	10.9	8.5	6.3	4.8	...
Brazil - Brésil																					
2015																					
Male - Hommes	71.9	68.2	63.3	58.4	53.9	49.5	45.1	40.7	36.3	32.0	27.9	23.9	20.2	16.7	13.5	10.7	8.4	...	...	...	...
Female - Femmes	79.1	75.3	70.4	65.4	60.6	55.7	50.9	46.2	41.4	36.8	32.3	28.0	23.8	19.8	16.2	12.9	10.1	...	...	...	...
Chile - Chili																					
2018 - 2019																					
Male - Hommes	77.7	73.3	68.3	63.4	58.6	53.8	49.1	44.4	39.7	35.2	30.7	26.4	22.2	18.3	14.8	11.6	8.8	6.6	4.9	3.6	2.9
Female - Femmes	83.2	78.8	73.9	68.9	64.0	59.1	54.2	49.3	44.5	39.7	35.0	30.4	26.0	21.7	17.7	14.0	10.7	7.9	5.9	4.4	3.7
Colombia - Colombie																					
2010 - 2015																					
Male - Hommes	72.1	68.9	64.0	59.1	54.5	50.1	45.7	41.3	36.8	32.3	27.9	23.7	19.7	16.0	12.7	9.8	7.4	...	...	...	...
Female - Femmes	78.5	74.9	70.0	65.1	60.2	55.4	50.6	45.8	41.0	36.3	31.7	27.2	22.9	18.8	15.0	11.6	8.7	...	...	...	...
2015 - 2020																					
Male - Hommes	73.1	...	...	...	...	...	...	...	...	...	...	...	...	...	...	...	...	...	...	...	...
Female - Femmes	79.4	...	...	...	...	...	...	...	...	...	...	...	...	...	...	...	...	...	...	...	...
Ecuador - Équateur[23]																					
2018																					
Male - Hommes	74.1	70.7	65.7	60.8	56.0	51.2	46.5	41.9	37.3	32.8	28.4	24.1	20.0	16.3	12.9	9.8	7.3	5.2	3.6	2.4	0.5
Female - Femmes	79.7	76.2	71.3	66.3	61.4	56.6	51.7	46.9	42.1	37.3	32.6	28.0	23.5	19.2	15.1	11.4	8.2	5.7	3.8	2.5	0.5
French Guiana - Guyane française																					
2015																					
Male - Hommes	76.4	...	...	...	58.0	...	...	...	39.5	...	...	...	22.0	...	...	...	...	...	...	...	...
Female - Femmes	82.0	...	...	...	63.0	...	...	...	43.6	...	...	...	25.3	...	...	...	...	...	...	...	...
Paraguay																					
2018																					
Male - Hommes	71.4	...	...	...	...	...	...	...	...	...	...	...	...	...	...	...	...	...	...	...	...
Female - Femmes	77.2	...	...	...	...	...	...	...	...	...	...	...	...	...	...	...	...	...	...	...	...
Peru - Pérou																					
2010 - 2015																					
Male - Hommes	71.5	69.0	64.3	59.4	54.7	50.0	45.5	40.9	36.4	32.0	27.7	23.6	19.8	16.2	13.0	10.1	7.7	...	...	...	...
Female - Femmes	76.8	73.8	69.0	64.1	59.3	54.5	49.7	45.0	40.3	35.7	31.2	26.9	22.7	18.7	15.0	11.7	8.8	...	...	...	...
Suriname																					
2013 - 2015																					
Male - Hommes	70.1	66.5	61.6	56.8	52.1	47.5	42.9	38.5	34.1	29.9	25.9	22.2	18.5	14.9	11.7	8.6	5.9	4.0	...	...	...
Female - Femmes	75.3	71.5	66.6	61.7	57.0	52.2	47.6	42.9	38.4	33.8	29.4	25.2	21.1	17.1	13.3	9.8	6.6	4.3	...	...	...
Uruguay																					
2010																					
Male - Hommes	72.8	68.5	63.6	58.7	54.0	49.4	44.8	40.2	35.6	31.0	26.6	22.4	18.6	15.1	12.0	9.3	7.0	5.2	4.0	...	...
Female - Femmes	80.0	75.6	70.7	65.8	60.9	56.1	51.2	46.4	41.6	36.9	32.3	27.9	23.6	19.5	15.6	12.0	8.9	6.4	4.5	...	...
2016																					
Male - Hommes	73.8	...	...	...	...	...	...	...	...	...	...	...	...	...	...	...	...	...	...	...	...
Female - Femmes	80.6	...	...	...	...	...	...	...	...	...	...	...	...	...	...	...	...	...	...	...	...
Venezuela (Bolivarian Republic of) - Venezuela (République bolivarienne du)																					
1995 - 2000																					
Male - Hommes	68.6	66.6	61.8	56.9	52.3	47.8	43.3	38.8	34.3	29.9	25.6	21.6	17.9	14.5	11.4	8.6	5.9	...	...	...	...
Female - Femmes	74.5	72.1	67.2	62.3	57.5	52.6	47.8	43.1	38.4	33.7	29.2	24.9	20.8	16.9	13.3	9.9	6.9	...	...	...	...
2018[24]																					
Male - Hommes	72.6	...	...	...	...	...	...	...	...	...	...	...	...	...	...	...	...	...	...	...	...
Female - Femmes	78.7	...	...	...	...	...	...	...	...	...	...	...	...	...	...	...	...	...	...	...	...

Continent, country or area and date / Continent, pays ou zone et date	Age (in years) - Age (en années)																				
	0	5	10	15	20	25	30	35	40	45	50	55	60	65	70	75	80	85	90	95	100
ASIA - ASIE																					
Afghanistan																					
2004																					
Male - Hommes	45.0	...	...	...	...	...	...	...	...	...	...	...	...	...	...	...	...	...	...	...	...
Female - Femmes	44.0	...	...	...	...	...	...	...	...	...	...	...	...	...	...	...	...	...	...	...	...
Armenia - Arménie																					
2016 - 2017																					
Male - Hommes	71.9	67.8	62.8	57.9	53.2	48.4	43.6	38.9	34.1	29.6	25.3	21.4	17.8	14.5	11.4	8.7	6.7	4.7	3.1	2.8	0.7
Female - Femmes	78.7	74.4	69.4	64.5	59.6	54.7	49.7	44.8	40.0	35.1	30.4	25.9	21.5	17.3	13.3	9.8	6.9	4.3	1.9	1.5	0.6
Azerbaijan - Azerbaïdjan																					
2017																					
Male - Hommes	73.1	69.1	64.2	59.3	54.5	49.7	44.9	40.1	35.4	30.9	26.6	22.5	18.7	15.4	12.5	9.9	8.0	7.0	6.8	4.9	1.0
Female - Femmes	77.8	73.7	68.8	63.8	58.9	54.1	49.2	44.3	39.5	34.7	30.0	25.4	21.0	17.0	13.4	10.0	7.3	5.5	4.4	3.8	0.9
Bahrain - Bahreïn																					
2001																					
Male - Hommes	73.2	69.3	64.4	59.5	54.7	49.9	45.2	40.4	35.6	30.9	26.4	22.0	17.8	14.1	11.3	9.5	...	...	...	...	...
Female - Femmes	76.2	72.0	67.1	62.1	57.2	52.3	47.4	42.5	37.7	32.9	28.2	23.7	19.6	15.9	12.9	10.9	...	...	...	...	...
2010 - 2015																					
Male - Hommes	75.8	...	...	...	...	...	...	...	...	...	...	...	...	...	...	...	...	...	...	...	...
Female - Femmes	77.4	...	...	...	...	...	...	...	...	...	...	...	...	...	...	...	...	...	...	...	...
Bangladesh																					
2017																					
Male - Hommes	70.6	71.7	68.3	63.5	58.7	54.2	49.4	44.7	39.9	35.2	30.6	26.2	22.3	18.5	15.2	11.9	9.5	7.1	...	...	...
Female - Femmes	73.5	74.6	71.1	66.3	61.4	56.8	52.0	47.1	42.4	37.7	33.1	28.8	24.6	20.4	16.7	13.1	10.2	6.9	...	...	...
Bhutan - Bhoutan																					
2005																					
Male - Hommes	65.7	...	...	...	...	...	...	...	...	...	...	...	...	...	...	...	...	...	...	...	...
Female - Femmes	66.9	...	...	...	...	...	...	...	...	...	...	...	...	...	...	...	...	...	...	...	...
Brunei Darussalam - Brunéi Darussalam																					
2017																					
Male - Hommes	76.3	...	...	...	...	...	...	...	...	...	...	...	...	...	...	...	...	...	...	...	...
Female - Femmes	78.3	...	...	...	...	...	...	...	...	...	...	...	...	...	...	...	...	...	...	...	...
China - Chine[25]																					
2010																					
Male - Hommes	66.8	...	...	...	...	...	...	...	...	...	...	...	...	...	...	...	...	...	...	...	...
Female - Femmes	70.5	...	...	...	...	...	...	...	...	...	...	...	...	...	...	...	...	...	...	...	...
China, Hong Kong SAR - Chine, Hong Kong RAS																					
2018																					
Male - Hommes	82.3	77.4	72.5	67.5	62.6	57.7	52.8	47.9	43.1	38.4	33.7	29.2	24.8	20.7	16.8	13.3	10.3	7.8	5.8	4.2	2.9
Female - Femmes	87.7	82.8	77.9	72.9	67.9	63.0	58.1	53.1	48.2	43.4	38.6	33.9	29.3	24.8	20.4	16.2	12.3	9.0	6.3	4.3	2.9
China, Macao SAR - Chine, Macao RAS																					
2012 - 2015																					
Male - Hommes	79.9	75.2	70.3	65.3	60.4	55.6	50.7	45.9	41.2	36.6	32.0	27.6	23.4	19.3	15.5	12.1	9.2	7.3	...	...	...
Female - Femmes	86.3	81.5	76.5	71.6	66.6	61.8	56.8	51.9	47.1	42.2	37.5	32.9	28.3	23.8	19.4	15.5	12.2	9.6	...	...	...
2015 - 2018																					
Male - Hommes	80.6	...	...	...	...	...	...	...	...	...	...	...	...	...	...	...	...	...	...	...	...
Female - Femmes	86.6	...	...	...	...	...	...	...	...	...	...	...	...	...	...	...	...	...	...	...	...
Cyprus - Chypre[26]																					
2013																					
Male - Hommes	80.0	75.1	70.2	65.3	60.4	55.5	50.7	45.8	41.0	36.3	31.6	27.0	22.6	18.5	14.7	11.2	8.2	5.9	...	...	...
Female - Femmes	84.8	79.8	74.9	69.9	64.9	60.0	55.0	50.1	45.2	40.3	35.4	30.6	25.9	21.4	17.2	13.1	9.5	6.6	...	...	...
2017																					
Male - Hommes	80.0	...	...	...	...	...	...	...	...	...	...	...	...	...	...	...	...	...	...	...	...
Female - Femmes	84.1	...	...	...	...	...	...	...	...	...	...	...	...	...	...	...	...	...	...	...	...
Democratic People's Republic of Korea - République populaire démocratique de Corée																					
2008																					
Male - Hommes	65.6	...	...	...	...	...	...	...	...	...	...	...	...	...	...	...	...	...	...	...	...
Female - Femmes	72.7	...	...	...	...	...	...	...	...	...	...	...	...	...	...	...	...	...	...	...	...

21. Life expectancy at specified ages for each sex: latest available year, 1999 - 2018
Espérance de vie à un âge donné pour chaque sexe : dernière année disponible, 1999 - 2018 (continued - suite)

Continent, country or area and date / Continent, pays ou zone et date	0	5	10	15	20	25	30	35	40	45	50	55	60	65	70	75	80	85	90	95	100
ASIA - ASIE																					
Georgia - Géorgie																					
2016																					
Male - Hommes	68.2	64.1	59.1	54.2	49.4	44.7	40.1	35.6	31.2	27.0	23.0	19.4	16.0	12.9	10.1	7.6	5.5	3.7	...	...	...
Female - Femmes	77.1	72.8	67.9	62.9	58.0	53.2	48.3	43.5	38.7	33.9	29.3	24.8	20.6	16.5	12.7	9.3	6.5	4.4	...	...	...
India - Inde[27]																					
2012 - 2016																					
Male - Hommes	67.4	65.5	60.8	56.0	51.2	46.6	42.0	37.5	33.1	28.8	24.7	20.8	17.3	14.0	11.0	8.4	6.1	4.5	...	...	...
Female - Femmes	70.2	68.9	64.1	59.3	54.6	49.9	45.2	40.6	35.9	31.4	26.9	22.9	18.9	15.3	12.1	9.3	6.7	4.8	...	...	...
Indonesia - Indonésie																					
2018																					
Male - Hommes	69.3	...	...	...	...	...	...	...	...	...	...	...	...	...	...	...	...	...	...	...	...
Female - Femmes	73.2	...	...	...	...	...	...	...	...	...	...	...	...	...	...	...	...	...	...	...	...
Iran (Islamic Republic of) - Iran (République islamique d')[28]																					
2016																					
Male - Hommes	72.5	...	...	...	...	...	...	...	...	...	...	...	...	...	...	...	...	...	...	...	...
Female - Femmes	75.5	...	...	...	...	...	...	...	...	...	...	...	...	...	...	...	...	...	...	...	...
Israel - Israël[29]																					
2013 - 2017																					
Male - Hommes	80.4	75.7	70.8	65.8	60.9	56.1	51.2	46.4	41.5	36.8	32.1	27.6	23.3	19.2	15.4	11.9	8.9	6.5	4.7	3.3	2.4
Female - Femmes	84.2	79.5	74.5	69.5	64.6	59.6	54.7	49.8	44.9	40.0	35.3	30.6	26.0	21.6	17.3	13.4	9.9	7.1	4.9	3.3	2.3
Japan - Japon[30]																					
2017																					
Male - Hommes	81.1	76.3	71.3	66.4	61.5	56.6	51.7	46.9	42.1	37.3	32.6	28.1	23.7	19.6	15.7	12.2	9.0	6.3	4.3	2.8	1.8
Female - Femmes	87.3	82.5	77.5	72.5	67.6	62.6	57.7	52.8	47.9	43.1	38.3	33.6	29.0	24.4	20.0	15.8	11.8	8.4	5.6	3.6	2.4
Jordan - Jordanie[31]																					
2012																					
Male - Hommes	72.7	69.1	64.2	59.3	54.4	49.6	44.8	40.0	35.2	30.5	26.0	21.7	17.8	14.2	10.9	8.2	6.0	...	...	...	...
Female - Femmes	76.7	73.1	68.1	63.2	58.2	53.3	48.4	43.6	38.7	33.9	29.3	24.7	20.3	16.2	12.4	9.2	6.8	...	...	...	...
2017																					
Male - Hommes	72.4	...	...	...	...	...	...	...	...	...	...	...	...	...	...	...	...	...	...	...	...
Female - Femmes	74.6	...	...	...	...	...	...	...	...	...	...	...	...	...	...	...	...	...	...	...	...	...
Kazakhstan																					
2018																					
Male - Hommes	68.8	64.6	59.7	54.8	50.0	45.3	40.7	36.2	31.8	27.6	23.6	19.8	16.3	13.2	10.7	8.3	6.2	4.7	3.3	2.5	0.8
Female - Femmes	77.2	72.9	68.0	63.1	58.2	53.3	48.5	43.7	39.0	34.4	29.9	25.5	21.3	17.3	13.6	10.3	7.4	5.3	3.5	2.4	0.8
Kuwait - Koweït																					
2017																					
Male - Hommes	79.7	...	...	...	...	...	...	...	...	...	...	...	...	...	...	...	...	...	...	...	...
Female - Femmes	82.7	...	...	...	...	...	...	...	...	...	...	...	...	...	...	...	...	...	...	...	...	...
Kyrgyzstan - Kirghizstan																					
2018																					
Male - Hommes	67.4	63.8	58.9	54.0	49.1	44.4	39.6	34.9	30.5	26.2	22.1	18.1	14.3	10.7	7.4	5.2	4.1	3.1	2.5	2.1	1.8
Female - Femmes	75.6	71.8	66.9	62.0	57.1	52.3	47.4	42.6	37.8	33.2	28.6	24.2	19.9	15.9	12.1	8.6	6.3	4.7	3.5	2.6	1.9
Lao People's Democratic Republic - République démocratique populaire lao[32]																					
2018																					
Male - Hommes	64.0	...	...	...	...	...	...	...	...	...	...	...	...	...	...	...	...	...	...	...	...
Female - Femmes	68.0	...	...	...	...	...	...	...	...	...	...	...	...	...	...	...	...	...	...	...	...	...
Malaysia - Malaisie																					
2018																					
Male - Hommes	72.7	68.3	63.4	58.5	53.8	49.0	44.3	39.6	34.9	30.5	26.3	22.3	18.5	15.0	11.7	8.7	6.2	...	...	...	...
Female - Femmes	77.6	73.1	68.2	63.3	58.4	53.5	48.6	43.8	39.0	34.3	29.7	25.4	21.2	17.2	13.5	10.0	7.1	...	...	...	...
Maldives																					
2015																					
Male - Hommes	73.1	69.0	64.0	59.1	54.3	49.4	44.6	39.7	34.8	29.9	25.2	20.7	16.2	11.9	7.9	4.7	...	...	...	...	...
Female - Femmes	74.6	70.3	65.4	60.5	55.6	50.7	45.7	40.7	35.8	31.0	26.1	21.4	16.7	12.2	7.8	4.4	...	...	...	...	...
2016																					
Male - Hommes	73.0	...	...	...	...	...	...	...	...	...	...	...	...	...	...	...	...	...	...	...	...
Female - Femmes	74.7	...	...	...	...	...	...	...	...	...	...	...	...	...	...	...	...	...	...	...	...	...

21. Life expectancy at specified ages for each sex: latest available year, 1999 - 2018
Espérance de vie à un âge donné pour chaque sexe : dernière année disponible, 1999 - 2018 (continued - suite)

Continent, country or area and date / Continent, pays ou zone et date	0	5	10	15	20	25	30	35	40	45	50	55	60	65	70	75	80	85	90	95	100
ASIA - ASIE																					
Mongolia - Mongolie 2018																					
Male - Hommes	66.1	62.6	57.8	53.0	48.3	43.7	39.2	34.8	30.7	26.7	23.2	20.0	17.1	14.6	12.4	...	...	...			
Female - Femmes	75.8	72.2	67.3	62.4	57.6	52.8	48.0	43.3	38.7	34.1	29.8	25.8	21.9	18.4	15.3	...	...	...			
Myanmar[33] 2016																					
Male - Hommes	60.3	60.0	55.4	50.8	46.1	41.7	37.5	33.6	30.0	26.5	23.1	19.6	16.4	13.2	10.4	7.8	5.6	4.2	...	...	
Female - Femmes	69.8	69.1	64.5	59.7	54.9	50.2	45.6	40.9	36.4	31.9	27.6	23.3	19.3	15.6	12.2	9.1	6.4	4.8	...	...	
Nepal - Népal 2011																					
Male - Hommes	65.5	...	...	...	...	...	...	...	...	...	...	...	...	...	...	...	...	...	...	...	...
Female - Femmes	67.9	...	...	...	...	...	...	...	...	...	...	...	...	...	...	...	...	...	...	...	...
Oman 2013																					
Male - Hommes	74.8	70.9	66.0	61.1	56.4	51.8	47.1	42.4	37.6	33.0	28.5	24.3	20.4	16.9	13.6	10.4	...	...	...		
Female - Femmes	78.5	74.3	69.4	64.4	59.5	54.6	49.7	44.8	39.9	35.1	30.5	25.9	21.6	17.5	13.8	10.2	...	...	...		
2018[34]																					
Male - Hommes	75.0	...	...	...	...	...	...	...	...	...	...	...	...	...	...	...	...	...	...	...	...
Female - Femmes	79.1	...	...	...	...	...	...	...	...	...	...	...	...	...	...	...	...	...	...	...	...
Pakistan[35] 2007																					
Male - Hommes	63.6	65.3	60.7	55.9	51.3	46.7	42.2	37.7	33.3	29.0	25.0	21.3	18.1	15.2	12.7	10.8	9.2	7.3	...		
Female - Femmes	67.6	68.6	64.1	59.5	54.9	50.3	45.7	41.1	36.5	32.1	27.7	23.5	19.6	16.2	13.4	10.9	8.6	6.1	...		
Philippines[6] 2010																					
Male - Hommes	66.9	...	...	...	...	...	...	...	...	...	...	...	...	...	...	...	...	...	...	...	...
Female - Femmes	73.0	...	...	...	...	...	...	...	...	...	...	...	...	...	...	...	...	...	...	...	...
Qatar 2015																					
Male - Hommes	77.5	73.1	68.2	63.3	58.9	54.5	49.8	45.1	40.4	35.6	31.2	26.9	22.9	22.3	18.6	15.2	12.3	...			
Female - Femmes	82.1	77.8	72.8	67.9	62.9	57.9	53.1	48.2	43.3	38.5	33.8	29.3	25.0	21.3	18.2	16.5	14.9	...			
2017																					
Male - Hommes	79.0	...	...	...	...	...	...	...	...	...	...	...	...	...	...	...	...	...	...	...	...
Female - Femmes	82.5	...	...	...	...	...	...	...	...	...	...	...	...	...	...	...	...	...	...	...	...
Republic of Korea - République de Corée 2017																					
Male - Hommes	79.7	75.0	70.0	65.0	60.1	55.2	50.4	45.5	40.8	36.0	31.5	27.0	22.8	18.6	14.7	11.1	8.1	5.8	4.0	2.8	2.0
Female - Femmes	85.7	81.0	76.0	71.0	66.1	61.1	56.2	51.3	46.5	41.6	36.8	32.1	27.4	22.8	18.3	14.0	10.2	7.1	4.8	3.3	2.3
Saudi Arabia - Arabie saoudite[36] 2018																					
Male - Hommes	73.7	...	...	...	...	...	...	...	...	...	...	...	...	...	...	...	...	...	...	...	...
Female - Femmes	76.4	...	...	...	...	...	...	...	...	...	...	...	...	...	...	...	...	...	...	...	...
Singapore - Singapour[37] 2018																					
Male - Hommes	81.0	76.2	71.2	66.3	61.3	56.4	51.5	46.6	41.8	37.0	32.3	27.8	23.4	19.3	15.4	12.0	9.0	6.5	4.6	3.1	2.1
Female - Femmes	85.4	80.6	75.6	70.7	65.7	60.8	55.8	50.9	46.0	41.1	36.3	31.6	27.0	22.6	18.3	14.3	10.7	7.8	5.5	3.8	2.6
Sri Lanka 2000 - 2002																					
Male - Hommes	68.8	65.0	60.2	55.3	50.6	46.2	41.9	37.6	33.2	29.0	24.9	21.1	17.6	14.5	11.6	9.2	7.2	5.5	4.2	...	...
Female - Femmes	77.2	73.3	68.4	63.5	58.6	53.9	49.1	44.3	39.5	34.8	30.2	25.7	21.5	17.5	13.9	10.7	8.0	5.8	4.1	...	...
State of Palestine - État de Palestine 2001																					
Male - Hommes	70.5	67.5	62.7	57.8	53.1	48.4	43.6	38.9	34.2	29.6	25.2	21.1	17.2	13.8	10.7	8.1	6.1	...	...	...	
Female - Femmes	73.6	70.3	65.5	60.5	55.7	50.9	46.1	41.3	36.6	32.0	27.5	23.2	19.0	15.2	11.7	8.8	6.4	...	...	...	
2017																					
Male - Hommes	72.8	...	...	...	...	...	...	...	...	...	...	...	...	...	...	...	...	...	...	...	...
Female - Femmes	75.1	...	...	...	...	...	...	...	...	...	...	...	...	...	...	...	...	...	...	...	...
Tajikistan - Tadjikistan 2008																					
Male - Hommes	69.7	67.9	63.0	58.1	53.3	48.5	43.7	39.1	34.6	30.1	25.7	21.6	17.9	14.7	12.2	10.4	9.2	...	...	...	
Female - Femmes	74.8	72.5	67.6	62.7	57.8	52.9	48.1	43.4	38.6	33.9	29.4	25.0	21.0	17.5	14.7	12.5	11.1	...	...	...	

Continent, country or area and date / Continent, pays ou zone et date	0	5	10	15	20	25	30	35	40	45	50	55	60	65	70	75	80	85	90	95	100
ASIA - ASIE																					
2017																					
Male - Hommes	73.0	...	...	...	...	...	...	...	...	...	...	...	...	...	...	...	...	...	...	...	...
Female - Femmes	76.9	...	...	...	...	...	...	...	...	...	...	...	...	...	...	...	...	...	...	...	...
Thailand - Thaïlande																					
2018																					
Male - Hommes	72.2	...	...	...	...	...	...	...	...	...	...	...	...	...	...	...	...	...	...	...	...
Female - Femmes	78.9	...	...	...	...	...	...	...	...	...	...	...	...	...	...	...	...	...	...	...	...
Timor-Leste[3]																					
2018																					
Male - Hommes	66.3	...	...	...	...	...	...	...	...	...	...	...	...	...	...	...	...	...	...	...	...
Female - Femmes	68.8	...	...	...	...	...	...	...	...	...	...	...	...	...	...	...	...	...	...	...	...
Turkey - Turquie																					
2015 - 2017																					
Male - Hommes	75.3	71.3	66.4	61.5	56.7	51.9	47.1	42.3	37.5	32.8	28.2	23.8	19.7	16.0	12.6	9.6	7.1	5.1	3.8	3.1	3.3
Female - Femmes	80.8	76.7	71.8	66.8	61.9	57.0	52.1	47.2	42.3	37.5	32.7	28.1	23.5	19.2	15.2	11.6	8.6	6.3	4.7	4.0	4.3
United Arab Emirates - Émirats arabes unis																					
2006																					
Male - Hommes	76.7	72.5	67.6	62.7	57.9	53.1	48.3	43.5	38.7	33.9	29.3	24.8	20.7	16.9	13.8	11.3	10.2	...	...	...	...
Female - Femmes	78.8	74.5	69.5	64.6	59.7	54.8	49.8	44.9	40.0	35.2	30.4	25.8	21.6	18.0	15.4	14.0	14.5	...	...	...	...
Uzbekistan - Ouzbékistan																					
2017																					
Male - Hommes	71.3	67.6	62.7	57.9	53.1	48.3	43.5	38.8	34.2	29.8	25.4	21.4	17.7	14.3	11.5	9.0	7.4	7.1	...	...	...
Female - Femmes	76.1	72.1	67.2	62.3	57.5	52.7	47.8	43.0	38.3	33.6	29.1	24.7	20.5	16.7	13.4	10.6	8.7	7.8	...	...	...
Viet Nam																					
2018																					
Male - Hommes	70.9	67.9	63.1	58.2	53.5	48.7	44.0	39.3	34.6	30.1	25.9	21.9	18.3	15.1	12.3	10.1	8.3	...	...	...	...
Female - Femmes	76.2	72.3	67.4	62.5	57.6	52.7	47.8	43.0	38.3	33.6	29.1	24.8	20.7	16.9	13.7	11.0	8.9	...	...	...	...
Yemen - Yémen																					
2004																					
Male - Hommes	60.2	...	...	...	...	...	...	...	...	...	...	...	...	...	...	...	...	...	...	...	...
Female - Femmes	62.0	...	...	...	...	...	...	...	...	...	...	...	...	...	...	...	...	...	...	...	...
EUROPE																					
Åland Islands - Îles d'Åland																					
2017																					
Male - Hommes	81.2	76.7	71.7	66.7	61.7	57.2	52.2	47.5	42.5	37.7	33.0	29.2	25.1	20.6	16.7	13.0	9.3	6.6	4.1	3.7	1.0
Female - Femmes	85.9	80.9	75.9	70.9	65.9	60.9	55.9	51.2	46.2	41.4	36.6	32.1	27.2	23.1	18.5	14.7	10.8	7.7	4.8	3.4	2.5
Albania - Albanie																					
2017																					
Male - Hommes	77.1	72.8	67.9	62.9	58.1	53.2	48.4	43.6	38.8	34.2	29.6	25.2	21.0	17.0	13.3	9.9	6.9	4.7	...	...	...
Female - Femmes	80.0	75.7	70.8	65.9	61.0	56.0	51.1	46.2	41.3	36.5	31.8	27.1	22.5	18.0	13.8	9.9	6.4	3.6	...	...	...
Austria - Autriche																					
2017																					
Male - Hommes	79.3	74.5	69.5	64.6	59.7	54.8	50.0	45.2	40.4	35.6	31.0	26.5	22.3	18.3	14.7	11.4	8.2	5.6	3.8	2.5	1.7
Female - Femmes	83.9	79.2	74.2	69.2	64.3	59.3	54.4	49.5	44.6	39.7	35.0	30.3	25.8	21.4	17.2	13.3	9.6	6.5	4.2	2.8	1.9
Belarus - Bélarus																					
2017																					
Male - Hommes	69.3	64.5	59.6	54.6	49.8	45.0	40.2	35.6	31.2	26.9	22.9	19.2	15.8	12.9	10.3	8.0	6.1	4.5	3.3	2.4	1.6
Female - Femmes	79.2	74.4	69.5	64.5	59.6	54.7	49.8	45.0	40.2	35.5	31.0	26.5	22.2	18.0	14.2	10.6	7.7	5.3	3.5	2.2	1.3
Belgium - Belgique																					
2018																					
Male - Hommes	79.2	74.6	69.6	64.6	59.7	54.9	50.0	45.2	40.4	35.7	31.1	26.6	22.4	18.4	14.7	11.3	8.3	5.8	3.9	2.5	1.6
Female - Femmes	83.7	79.0	74.0	69.1	64.1	59.2	54.2	49.3	44.5	39.7	35.0	30.3	25.9	21.6	17.5	13.6	10.0	6.9	4.5	3.0	2.0
Bosnia and Herzegovina - Bosnie-Herzégovine																					
2003																					
Male - Hommes	71.3	...	...	...	...	...	...	...	...	...	...	...	...	...	...	...	...	...	...	...	...
Female - Femmes	76.7	...	...	...	...	...	...	...	...	...	...	...	...	...	...	...	...	...	...	...	...

21. Life expectancy at specified ages for each sex: latest available year, 1999 - 2018
Espérance de vie à un âge donné pour chaque sexe : dernière année disponible, 1999 - 2018 (continued - suite)

Continent, country or area and date / Continent, pays ou zone et date	0	5	10	15	20	25	30	35	40	45	50	55	60	65	70	75	80	85	90	95	100

EUROPE

Bulgaria - Bulgarie
2015 - 2017
| Male - Hommes | 71.3 | 66.9 | 62.0 | 57.0 | 52.2 | 47.4 | 42.6 | 37.9 | 33.3 | 28.8 | 24.5 | 20.7 | 17.2 | 14.1 | 11.3 | 8.7 | 6.4 | 4.5 | 3.1 | 2.2 | 0.5 |
| Female - Femmes | 78.4 | 73.9 | 68.9 | 64.0 | 59.1 | 54.1 | 49.3 | 44.4 | 39.6 | 34.9 | 30.3 | 25.9 | 21.8 | 17.7 | 13.9 | 10.3 | 7.3 | 5.0 | 3.3 | 2.2 | 0.5 |

Croatia - Croatie
2017
| Male - Hommes | 74.9 | 70.4 | 65.4 | 60.4 | 55.6 | 50.7 | 45.9 | 41.1 | 36.3 | 31.6 | 27.1 | 22.9 | 19.0 | 15.5 | 12.3 | 9.4 | 6.9 | 5.0 | ... | ... | ... |
| Female - Femmes | 81.0 | 76.3 | 71.4 | 66.4 | 61.4 | 56.5 | 51.6 | 46.6 | 41.8 | 36.9 | 32.2 | 27.6 | 23.2 | 18.9 | 14.9 | 11.2 | 8.0 | 5.6 | ... | ... | ... |

Czechia - Tchéquie
2017
| Male - Hommes | 76.0 | 71.3 | 66.3 | 61.4 | 56.5 | 51.7 | 46.9 | 42.1 | 37.3 | 32.6 | 28.1 | 23.7 | 19.7 | 16.1 | 12.8 | 9.9 | 7.3 | 5.1 | 3.5 | 2.4 | 1.8 |
| Female - Femmes | 81.8 | 77.1 | 72.1 | 67.1 | 62.2 | 57.2 | 52.3 | 47.4 | 42.5 | 37.7 | 33.0 | 28.3 | 23.9 | 19.6 | 15.6 | 11.9 | 8.6 | 5.9 | 3.9 | 2.6 | 1.8 |

Denmark - Danemark[38]
2016 - 2017
| Male - Hommes | 79.0 | 74.3 | 69.4 | 64.4 | 59.5 | 54.6 | 49.7 | 44.8 | 40.0 | 35.3 | 30.6 | 26.1 | 22.0 | 18.1 | 14.4 | 11.0 | 8.0 | 5.5 | 3.7 | 2.6 | ... |
| Female - Femmes | 82.9 | 78.2 | 73.2 | 68.2 | 63.3 | 58.3 | 53.4 | 48.5 | 43.6 | 38.7 | 34.0 | 29.4 | 25.0 | 20.8 | 16.7 | 12.9 | 9.5 | 6.8 | 4.6 | 3.1 | ... |

Estonia - Estonie
2017
| Male - Hommes | 73.7 | 68.9 | 63.9 | 59.0 | 54.1 | 49.3 | 44.6 | 40.0 | 35.4 | 30.9 | 26.6 | 22.5 | 18.7 | 15.4 | 12.4 | 9.8 | 7.4 | 5.3 | 3.8 | 2.8 | 1.4 |
| Female - Femmes | 82.3 | 77.5 | 72.5 | 67.6 | 62.7 | 57.8 | 52.9 | 48.0 | 43.1 | 38.3 | 33.6 | 29.1 | 24.6 | 20.4 | 16.4 | 12.6 | 9.1 | 6.4 | 4.4 | 3.0 | 1.5 |

Faeroe Islands - Îles Féroé
2017 - 2018
| Male - Hommes | 80.1 | 75.6 | 70.6 | 65.8 | 60.8 | 55.8 | 50.8 | 45.8 | 40.8 | 36.0 | 31.2 | 26.6 | 22.3 | 18.5 | 14.9 | 11.2 | 8.2 | 6.3 | 4.3 | 2.6 | 2.1 |
| Female - Femmes | 84.8 | 80.7 | 75.7 | 70.7 | 65.7 | 60.7 | 55.7 | 50.7 | 45.7 | 41.1 | 36.2 | 31.4 | 26.7 | 22.6 | 18.2 | 14.0 | 10.5 | 7.4 | 4.3 | 1.4 | 0.8 |

Finland - Finlande[39]
2017
| Male - Hommes | 78.7 | 73.9 | 68.9 | 64.0 | 59.1 | 54.3 | 49.6 | 44.8 | 40.0 | 35.4 | 30.8 | 26.3 | 22.1 | 18.2 | 14.6 | 11.2 | 8.1 | 5.6 | 3.8 | 2.6 | 1.8 |
| Female - Femmes | 84.2 | 79.4 | 74.4 | 69.5 | 64.5 | 59.6 | 54.7 | 49.8 | 45.0 | 40.1 | 35.3 | 30.7 | 26.2 | 21.8 | 17.6 | 13.6 | 9.9 | 6.9 | 4.5 | 2.9 | 1.8 |

France
2014 - 2016
| Male - Hommes | 79.2 | 74.6 | 69.6 | 64.6 | 59.7 | 54.9 | 50.1 | 45.3 | 40.6 | 35.9 | 31.4 | 27.1 | 23.1 | 19.3 | 15.6 | 12.1 | 8.9 | 6.2 | 4.2 | 2.9 | 2.4 |
| Female - Femmes | 85.3 | 80.6 | 75.6 | 70.7 | 65.7 | 60.8 | 55.9 | 51.0 | 46.1 | 41.3 | 36.6 | 32.0 | 27.5 | 23.2 | 18.9 | 14.8 | 11.0 | 7.7 | 5.1 | 3.3 | 2.3 |

Germany - Allemagne
2017
| Male - Hommes | 78.7 | 74.0 | 69.1 | 64.1 | 59.2 | 54.3 | 49.4 | 44.6 | 39.8 | 35.0 | 30.4 | 26.0 | 21.9 | 18.1 | 14.5 | 11.2 | 8.3 | 5.9 | ... | ... | ... |
| Female - Femmes | 83.4 | 78.7 | 73.7 | 68.7 | 63.8 | 58.9 | 53.9 | 49.0 | 44.1 | 39.3 | 34.5 | 29.9 | 25.5 | 21.2 | 17.1 | 13.2 | 9.6 | 6.7 | ... | ... | ... |

Gibraltar
2001
| Male - Hommes | 78.5 | 73.5 | 68.5 | 63.5 | 58.5 | 53.5 | ... | 43.5 | .... | 33.9 | ... | 25.8 | ... | 17.9 | ... | 11.3 | ... | ... | ... | ... | ... |
| Female - Femmes | 83.3 | 79.5 | 75.0 | 70.0 | 65.0 | 60.0 | ... | 50.3 | ... | 40.3 | ... | 30.3 | ... | 20.6 | ... | 13.7 | ... | ... | ... | ... | ... |

Greece - Grèce
2017
| Male - Hommes | 78.8 | 74.1 | 69.1 | 64.2 | 59.3 | 54.5 | 49.7 | 44.8 | 40.1 | 35.3 | 30.8 | 26.5 | 22.4 | 18.6 | 15.0 | 11.8 | 8.8 | 6.6 | ... | ... | ... |
| Female - Femmes | 83.9 | 79.2 | 74.2 | 69.3 | 64.3 | 59.4 | 54.4 | 49.5 | 44.6 | 39.8 | 35.0 | 30.3 | 25.8 | 21.4 | 17.1 | 13.1 | 9.4 | 6.4 | ... | ... | ... |

Hungary - Hongrie
2017
| Male - Hommes | 72.4 | 67.7 | 62.8 | 57.8 | 52.9 | 48.1 | 43.2 | 38.5 | 33.7 | 29.1 | 24.7 | 20.7 | 17.3 | 14.2 | 11.5 | 8.8 | 6.4 | 4.3 | 2.7 | 1.5 | 0.6 |
| Female - Femmes | 79.0 | 74.3 | 69.4 | 64.4 | 59.4 | 54.5 | 49.6 | 44.7 | 39.8 | 35.0 | 30.4 | 26.0 | 21.9 | 18.0 | 14.2 | 10.7 | 7.6 | 4.9 | 2.9 | 1.5 | 0.6 |

Iceland - Islande
2016 - 2017
| Male - Hommes | 80.6 | 75.8 | 70.8 | 65.8 | 61.0 | 56.1 | 51.3 | 46.6 | 41.9 | 37.1 | 32.4 | 27.8 | 23.4 | 19.0 | 15.0 | 11.5 | 8.2 | 5.6 | 3.8 | 2.9 | 1.5 |
| Female - Femmes | 83.9 | 79.2 | 74.2 | 69.2 | 64.3 | 59.4 | 54.4 | 49.5 | 44.6 | 39.6 | 34.8 | 30.1 | 25.5 | 21.1 | 16.8 | 13.0 | 9.6 | 6.7 | 4.4 | 2.8 | 1.5 |

Ireland - Irlande
2017
| Male - Hommes | 80.4 | 75.7 | 70.7 | 65.7 | 60.8 | 55.9 | 51.1 | 46.3 | 41.5 | 36.7 | 32.0 | 27.5 | 23.2 | 19.0 | 15.1 | 11.5 | 8.6 | 6.3 | ... | ... | ... |
| Female - Femmes | 84.0 | 79.3 | 74.3 | 69.3 | 64.4 | 59.4 | 54.5 | 49.6 | 44.7 | 39.8 | 35.1 | 30.4 | 25.8 | 21.4 | 17.2 | 13.3 | 9.9 | 7.0 | ... | ... | ... |

Italy - Italie
2017
| Male - Hommes | 80.6 | 75.9 | 70.9 | 65.9 | 61.0 | 56.2 | 51.3 | 46.4 | 41.6 | 36.8 | 32.1 | 27.6 | 23.2 | 19.0 | 15.1 | 11.6 | 8.4 | 5.8 | 3.9 | 2.7 | 1.9 |
| Female - Femmes | 84.9 | 80.2 | 75.2 | 70.2 | 65.3 | 60.3 | 55.4 | 50.5 | 45.6 | 40.7 | 35.9 | 31.2 | 26.6 | 22.2 | 17.9 | 13.8 | 10.1 | 7.0 | 4.7 | 3.2 | 2.1 |

Latvia - Lettonie
2017
| Male - Hommes | 69.8 | 65.2 | 60.2 | 55.3 | 50.5 | 45.8 | 41.1 | 36.7 | 32.3 | 28.1 | 24.1 | 20.4 | 17.0 | 14.0 | 11.3 | 8.9 | 6.8 | 4.9 | 3.5 | 2.5 | ... |
| Female - Femmes | 79.6 | 74.9 | 69.9 | 65.0 | 60.1 | 55.2 | 50.3 | 45.5 | 40.8 | 36.1 | 31.6 | 27.2 | 22.9 | 18.8 | 15.1 | 11.6 | 8.4 | 5.8 | 3.9 | 2.9 | ... |

Continent, country or area and date / Continent, pays ou zone et date	Age (in years) - Age (en années)																				
	0	5	10	15	20	25	30	35	40	45	50	55	60	65	70	75	80	85	90	95	100
EUROPE																					
Lithuania - Lituanie																					
2017																					
Male - Hommes	70.7	66.0	61.1	56.1	51.3	46.5	41.8	37.3	33.0	28.8	24.8	21.0	17.4	14.4	11.6	9.1	6.8	4.9	3.4	2.4	1.8
Female - Femmes	80.4	75.6	70.7	65.7	60.8	55.9	51.0	46.2	41.4	36.8	32.3	27.8	23.5	19.3	15.4	11.7	8.4	5.7	3.7	2.5	1.7
Luxembourg																					
2015 - 2017																					
Male - Hommes	79.9	75.2	70.2	65.2	60.3	55.4	50.5	45.7	40.8	36.0	31.4	26.8	22.5	18.5	14.8	11.4	8.4	5.8	3.8	3.1	...
Female - Femmes	84.4	79.5	74.5	69.6	64.6	59.6	54.7	49.7	44.8	40.0	35.2	30.5	26.0	21.6	17.4	13.6	10.0	6.9	4.6	2.8	...
Malta - Malte																					
2017																					
Male - Hommes	80.2	75.9	70.9	65.9	61.0	56.2	51.3	46.5	41.6	36.9	32.1	27.5	23.1	19.0	15.2	11.6	8.5	5.9	...	...	...
Female - Femmes	84.6	80.0	75.0	70.1	65.1	60.2	55.2	50.2	45.3	40.5	35.7	31.1	26.6	22.2	17.9	13.9	10.2	7.3	...	...	...
Netherlands - Pays-Bas																					
2017																					
Male - Hommes	80.2	75.6	70.6	65.6	60.7	55.8	51.0	46.1	41.2	36.5	31.8	27.2	22.8	18.7	14.9	11.4	8.2	5.8	...	...	...
Female - Femmes	83.4	78.7	73.7	68.8	63.8	58.9	53.9	49.0	44.1	39.3	34.5	29.9	25.4	21.2	17.0	13.2	9.6	6.6	...	...	...
North Macedonia - Macédoine du Nord																					
2016																					
Male - Hommes	73.7	69.5	64.5	59.6	54.7	49.9	45.0	40.1	35.3	30.7	26.2	21.9	18.0	14.4	11.2	8.3	5.8	3.9	2.5	2.4	...
Female - Femmes	77.5	73.4	68.4	63.5	58.5	53.6	48.6	43.7	38.9	34.1	29.4	24.8	20.4	16.3	12.5	9.0	6.3	4.3	3.0	2.7	...
Norway - Norvège																					
2018																					
Male - Hommes	81.0	76.2	71.2	66.3	61.4	56.5	51.7	46.9	42.1	37.3	32.6	28.0	23.5	19.3	15.4	11.7	8.5	5.9	4.0	2.6	1.8
Female - Femmes	84.5	79.7	74.7	69.7	64.8	59.8	54.9	50.0	45.1	40.2	35.4	30.7	26.2	21.8	17.6	13.6	10.0	7.0	4.6	3.0	2.1
Poland - Pologne																					
2018																					
Male - Hommes	73.9	69.2	64.2	59.3	54.4	49.7	44.9	40.2	35.6	31.1	26.8	22.8	19.1	15.8	12.9	10.2	7.8	5.9	4.4	3.3	2.4
Female - Femmes	81.7	77.0	72.0	67.1	62.2	57.2	52.3	47.4	42.6	37.8	33.1	28.5	24.2	20.1	16.3	12.7	9.4	6.8	4.8	3.4	2.4
Portugal																					
2015 - 2017																					
Male - Hommes	77.7	73.1	68.1	63.1	58.2	53.4	48.5	43.7	38.9	34.2	29.7	25.5	21.4	17.6	13.8	10.3	7.2	4.4	2.7	1.7	1.1
Female - Femmes	83.4	78.7	73.7	68.7	63.8	58.8	53.9	49.0	44.1	39.3	34.5	29.9	25.3	20.8	16.5	12.3	8.5	5.3	3.2	1.9	1.2
2018																					
Male - Hommes	77.8	...	...	...	...	...	...	...	...	...	...	...	...	...	...	...	...	...	...	...	...
Female - Femmes	83.4	...	...	...	...	...	...	...	...	...	...	...	...	...	...	...	...	...	...	...	...
Republic of Moldova - République de Moldova[40]																					
2012																					
Male - Hommes	67.2	63.1	58.1	53.3	48.5	43.7	39.0	34.5	30.1	26.0	22.2	18.7	15.5	13.0	10.2	8.4	7.1	6.9	7.8	...	...
Female - Femmes	75.0	70.9	66.0	61.0	56.1	51.2	46.4	41.5	36.8	32.2	27.7	23.4	19.3	15.7	12.2	9.5	7.4	5.9	5.3	...	...
2017																					
Male - Hommes	69.4	...	...	...	...	...	...	...	...	...	...	...	...	...	...	...	...	...	...	...	...
Female - Femmes	77.0	...	...	...	...	...	...	...	...	...	...	...	...	...	...	...	...	...	...	...	...
Romania - Roumanie																					
2015 - 2017																					
Male - Hommes	72.3	67.9	63.0	58.1	53.2	48.4	43.6	38.8	34.1	29.5	25.3	21.3	17.8	14.7	11.7	9.1	6.8	5.0	3.7	2.6	0.8
Female - Femmes	79.2	74.8	69.9	64.9	60.0	55.1	50.2	45.3	40.4	35.6	31.0	26.5	22.2	18.1	14.3	10.8	7.8	5.5	3.8	2.6	0.8
Russian Federation - Fédération de Russie																					
2012																					
Male - Hommes	64.6	60.3	55.4	50.5	45.8	41.3	37.0	33.1	29.3	25.4	21.8	18.4	15.4	12.8	10.2	8.1	6.4	5.1	4.0	3.0	1.4
Female - Femmes	75.9	71.6	66.7	61.7	56.9	52.1	47.3	42.8	38.2	33.7	29.3	25.1	21.0	17.1	13.4	10.2	7.4	5.3	3.8	2.8	1.8
San Marino - Saint-Marin																					
2017																					
Male - Hommes	82.7	77.9	72.9	67.9	63.0	58.2	53.3	48.3	43.4	38.5	33.7	29.0	24.6	20.2	16.1	12.2	8.9	6.4	4.2	2.2	...
Female - Femmes	86.8	82.0	77.0	72.0	67.1	62.1	57.1	52.2	47.2	42.4	37.6	32.8	28.1	23.5	19.1	14.8	10.8	7.4	4.8	2.7	...
Serbia - Serbie[41]																					
2017																					
Male - Hommes	73.0	68.4	63.4	58.5	53.6	48.8	44.0	39.2	34.5	29.9	25.5	21.4	17.7	14.3	11.4	8.5	6.2	4.3	...	...	...
Female - Femmes	77.9	73.3	68.3	63.4	58.4	53.5	48.5	43.6	38.8	34.0	29.4	25.0	20.7	16.7	12.9	9.5	6.6	4.5	...	...	...

21. Life expectancy at specified ages for each sex: latest available year, 1999 - 2018
Espérance de vie à un âge donné pour chaque sexe : dernière année disponible, 1999 - 2018 (continued - suite)

Continent, pays ou zone et date	0	5	10	15	20	25	30	35	40	45	50	55	60	65	70	75	80	85	90	95	100
EUROPE																					
Slovakia - Slovaquie																					
2017																					
Male - Hommes	73.8	69.2	64.3	59.3	54.5	49.7	44.8	40.1	35.3	30.7	26.3	22.3	18.5	15.2	12.1	9.4	7.0	5.1	3.6	2.5	1.6
Female - Femmes	80.3	75.7	70.7	65.8	60.8	55.9	51.0	46.1	41.2	36.5	31.8	27.3	22.9	18.7	14.7	11.0	7.7	5.1	3.1	1.8	1.0
2018																					
Male - Hommes	73.7	...	...	...	...	...	...	...	...	...	...	...	...	...	...	...	...	...	...	...	...
Female - Femmes	80.4	...	...	...	...	...	...	...	...	...	...	...	...	...	...	...	...	...	...	...	...
Slovenia - Slovénie																					
2017																					
Male - Hommes	78.1	73.2	68.2	63.3	58.4	53.5	48.7	43.9	39.0	34.2	29.6	25.3	21.1	17.4	13.8	10.5	7.6	5.3	3.6	2.6	2.0
Female - Femmes	83.7	78.9	73.9	68.9	64.0	59.1	54.1	49.2	44.3	39.4	34.7	30.0	25.6	21.2	17.1	13.1	9.5	6.6	4.3	2.8	2.1
2018																					
Male - Hommes	78.3	...	...	...	...	...	...	...	...	...	...	...	...	...	...	...	...	...	...	...	...
Female - Femmes	84.0	...	...	...	...	...	...	...	...	...	...	...	...	...	...	...	...	...	...	...	...
Spain - Espagne																					
2017																					
Male - Hommes	80.4	75.7	70.7	65.7	60.8	55.9	51.0	46.1	41.3	36.5	31.8	27.4	23.1	19.1	15.4	11.9	8.7	6.1	4.2	3.0	1.8
Female - Femmes	85.7	81.0	76.0	71.0	66.1	61.1	56.2	51.2	46.3	41.5	36.7	32.0	27.4	23.0	18.6	14.4	10.6	7.3	4.9	3.3	2.1
Sweden - Suède																					
2017																					
Male - Hommes	80.8	76.0	71.0	66.0	61.1	56.3	51.5	46.7	41.9	37.1	32.4	27.8	23.4	19.2	15.2	11.6	8.4	5.7	...	...	...
Female - Femmes	84.1	79.4	74.4	69.4	64.5	59.5	54.6	49.7	44.8	39.9	35.1	30.4	25.9	21.5	17.3	13.4	9.8	6.8	...	...	...
Switzerland - Suisse																					
2017																					
Male - Hommes	81.4	76.8	71.8	66.8	61.9	57.0	52.1	47.3	42.4	37.6	32.9	28.3	23.9	19.7	15.8	12.1	8.8	6.0	3.9	2.6	1.8
Female - Femmes	85.4	80.7	75.7	70.8	65.8	60.8	55.9	50.9	46.0	41.2	36.3	31.6	27.0	22.5	18.2	14.1	10.3	7.1	4.6	3.0	2.1
2018																					
Male - Hommes	81.7	...	...	...	...	...	...	...	...	...	...	...	...	...	...	...	...	...	...	...	...
Female - Femmes	85.4	...	...	...	...	...	...	...	...	...	...	...	...	...	...	...	...	...	...	...	...
Ukraine [42]																					
2017																					
Male - Hommes	67.0	62.7	57.7	52.8	48.0	43.3	38.7	34.3	30.2	26.2	22.4	18.8	15.5	12.7	10.1	7.9	6.2	4.8	3.8	3.0	2.1
Female - Femmes	76.8	72.4	67.4	62.5	57.6	52.7	47.9	43.1	38.5	33.9	29.4	25.1	20.8	16.8	13.2	9.9	7.1	5.0	3.4	2.3	1.5
United Kingdom of Great Britain and Northern Ireland - Royaume-Uni de Grande-Bretagne et d'Irlande du Nord [43]																					
2015 - 2017																					
Male - Hommes	79.2	74.6	69.6	64.6	59.7	54.9	50.0	45.2	40.5	35.9	31.3	26.8	22.6	18.6	14.8	11.3	8.3	5.9	4.0	2.8	2.1
Female - Femmes	82.9	78.2	73.2	68.2	63.3	58.4	53.4	48.6	43.7	38.9	34.3	29.7	25.2	20.9	16.8	13.0	9.6	6.7	4.6	3.1	2.2
OCEANIA - OCÉANIE																					
American Samoa - Samoas américaines																					
2011																					
Male - Hommes	71.1	66.8	61.9	57.0	52.2	47.4	42.6	38.0	33.5	29.1	25.3	21.4	18.0	14.6	11.7	9.6	...	...	...	...	...
Female - Femmes	77.8	73.3	68.3	63.4	58.5	53.6	48.9	44.4	39.6	35.0	30.6	26.5	22.8	19.2	16.1	13.8	...	...	...	...	...
Australia - Australie																					
2015 - 2017																					
Male - Hommes	80.5	75.8	70.8	65.9	61.0	56.2	51.4	46.6	41.8	37.2	32.6	28.1	23.8	19.7	15.7	12.1	8.9	6.3	4.3	3.1	2.1
Female - Femmes	84.6	79.9	75.0	70.0	65.1	60.1	55.2	50.3	45.5	40.7	36.0	31.3	26.8	22.3	18.1	14.1	10.4	7.3	4.9	3.3	2.3
Cook Islands - Îles Cook [44]																					
2006																					
Male - Hommes	69.5	66.0	61.3	56.5	52.0	47.4	42.8	38.1	33.6	29.1	24.8	20.9	17.5	14.3	11.4	9.0	7.3	...	...	...	...
Female - Femmes	76.2	72.4	67.4	62.4	57.4	52.7	48.0	43.2	38.4	33.6	29.1	24.7	20.4	16.4	12.6	9.5	6.9	...	...	...	...
Fiji - Fidji																					
2013																					
Male - Hommes	66.3	62.1	57.2	52.4	47.6	42.9	38.2	33.5	29.0	24.8	20.8	17.1	13.6	10.2	7.0	4.6	...	...	...	...	...
Female - Femmes	70.4	66.2	61.3	56.5	51.6	46.8	42.0	37.3	32.7	28.3	24.0	20.0	16.3	12.6	9.2	6.4	...	...	...	...	...

21. Life expectancy at specified ages for each sex: latest available year, 1999 - 2018
Espérance de vie à un âge donné pour chaque sexe : dernière année disponible, 1999 - 2018 (continued - suite)

Continent, country or area and date / Continent, pays ou zone et date	0	5	10	15	20	25	30	35	40	45	50	55	60	65	70	75	80	85	90	95	100
OCEANIA - OCÉANIE																					
French Polynesia - Polynésie française																					
2012																					
Male - Hommes	73.3	69.6	64.6	59.8	55.0	50.3	45.7	41.0	36.2	31.6	27.1	22.7	18.3	14.8	11.4	8.5	6.5	4.7	...	...	...
Female - Femmes	78.2	73.8	68.8	63.9	59.1	54.1	49.3	44.5	39.7	35.0	30.4	26.1	22.0	17.9	14.2	10.6	7.6	5.0	...	...	...
2017																					
Male - Hommes	74.0	...	...	...	...	...	...	...	...	...	...	...	...	...	...	...	...	...	...	...	...
Female - Femmes	77.7	...	...	...	...	...	...	...	...	...	...	...	...	...	...	...	...	...	...	...	...
Guam																					
2017																					
Male - Hommes	73.6	...	...	...	...	...	...	...	...	...	...	...	...	...	...	...	...	...	...	...	...
Female - Femmes	78.6	...	...	...	...	...	...	...	...	...	...	...	...	...	...	...	...	...	...	...	...
Kiribati																					
2005																					
Male - Hommes	58.9	58.2	53.6	48.9	44.4	40.0	35.6	31.3	27.1	23.1	19.4	16.0	13.0	10.4	8.3	6.6	5.3	4.2	...	...	...
Female - Femmes	63.1	62.6	57.9	53.1	48.6	44.1	39.7	35.4	31.2	27.1	23.2	19.5	16.1	13.1	10.4	8.1	6.2	4.7	...	...	...
Marshall Islands - Îles Marshall																					
2004																					
Male - Hommes	67.0	...	...	...	...	...	...	...	...	...	...	...	...	...	...	...	...	...	...	...	...
Female - Femmes	70.6	...	...	...	...	...	...	...	...	...	...	...	...	...	...	...	...	...	...	...	...
Micronesia (Federated States of) - Micronésie (États fédérés de)																					
2000																					
Male - Hommes	66.5	...	...	...	...	...	...	...	...	...	...	...	...	...	...	...	...	...	...	...	...
Female - Femmes	67.5	...	...	...	...	...	...	...	...	...	...	...	...	...	...	...	...	...	...	...	...
Nauru[45]																					
2011																					
Male - Hommes	56.8	...	...	...	...	...	...	...	...	...	...	...	...	...	...	...	...	...	...	...	...
Female - Femmes	62.7	...	...	...	...	...	...	...	...	...	...	...	...	...	...	...	...	...	...	...	...
New Caledonia - Nouvelle-Calédonie																					
2017																					
Male - Hommes	75.1	70.1	65.2	60.2	55.2	50.3	45.5	40.6	35.8	31.1	26.5	...	21.9	...	13.4	...	6.2	...			
Female - Femmes	80.1	75.1	70.2	65.2	60.3	55.3	50.4	45.5	40.6	35.7	30.9	...	26.2	...	17.0	...	8.6	...			
New Zealand - Nouvelle-Zélande																					
2016 - 2018																					
Male - Hommes	80.2	75.5	70.6	65.6	60.8	56.0	51.2	46.4	41.7	37.0	32.4	27.9	23.7	19.6	15.6	12.0	8.8	6.3	4.5	...	...
Female - Femmes	83.6	79.0	74.0	69.0	64.1	59.3	54.4	49.5	44.7	39.8	35.1	30.5	26.1	21.7	17.5	13.6	10.1	7.1	4.9	...	...
Niue - Nioué																					
2007 - 2011																					
Male - Hommes	70.1	...	...	...	...	...	...	...	...	...	...	...	...	...	...	...	...	...	...	...	...
Female - Femmes	76.3	...	...	...	...	...	...	...	...	...	...	...	...	...	...	...	...	...	...	...	...
Northern Mariana Islands - Îles Mariannes septentrionales																					
2009																					
Male - Hommes	74.5	...	...	...	...	...	...	...	...	...	...	...	...	...	...	...	...	...	...	...	...
Female - Femmes	79.9	...	...	...	...	...	...	...	...	...	...	...	...	...	...	...	...	...	...	...	...
Palau - Palaos																					
2005																					
Male - Hommes	66.3	...	...	...	...	...	...	...	...	...	...	...	...	...	...	...	...	...	...	...	...
Female - Femmes	72.1	...	...	...	...	...	...	...	...	...	...	...	...	...	...	...	...	...	...	...	...
Papua New Guinea - Papouasie-Nouvelle-Guinée																					
2000																					
Male - Hommes	53.7	54.1	50.2	45.7	41.6	37.7	33.7	29.8	25.9	22.1	18.5	15.0	11.9	9.2	6.9	5.0	3.6	2.6	1.7	0.6	...
Female - Femmes	54.8	54.7	50.8	46.3	42.1	38.1	34.1	30.1	26.2	22.3	18.6	15.2	12.0	9.2	6.8	5.0	3.6	2.5	1.6	0.6	...
Samoa																					
2006																					
Male - Hommes	71.5	...	...	...	...	...	...	...	...	...	...	...	...	...	...	...	...	...	...	...	...
Female - Femmes	74.2	...	...	...	...	...	...	...	...	...	...	...	...	...	...	...	...	...	...	...	...

21. Life expectancy at specified ages for each sex: latest available year, 1999 - 2018
Espérance de vie à un âge donné pour chaque sexe : dernière année disponible, 1999 - 2018 (continued - suite)

Continent, country or area and date / Continent, pays ou zone et date	0	5	10	15	20	25	30	35	40	45	50	55	60	65	70	75	80	85	90	95	100
OCEANIA - OCÉANIE																					
Solomon Islands - Îles Salomon																					
2009																					
Male - Hommes	66.2	...	...	...	...	...	...	...	...	...	...	...	...	...	...	...	...	...	...	...	...
Female - Femmes	73.1	...	...	...	...	...	...	...	...	...	...	...	...	...	...	...	...	...	...	...	...
Tonga																					
2006																					
Male - Hommes	67.3	64.1	59.3	54.5	49.9	45.4	40.7	36.2	31.6	27.2	23.4	19.4	15.9	13.0	9.4	6.3	4.0	...	...	...	...
Female - Femmes	73.0	69.3	64.6	59.8	55.0	50.1	45.2	40.4	35.7	31.3	27.1	23.0	19.0	15.3	11.6	8.6	6.1	...	...	...	...
2010																					
Male - Hommes	65.0																				
Female - Femmes	69.0																				
Tuvalu																					
1997 - 2002																					
Male - Hommes	61.7	59.5	54.8	50.0	45.2	40.6	35.9	32.1	28.0	24.1	20.0	17.1	13.7	10.8	9.0	6.9	5.4	...	...	...	...
Female - Femmes	65.1	62.6	57.7	53.7	50.0	45.3	40.9	36.6	32.2	28.1	23.8	20.3	16.9	13.2	10.6	7.9	6.4	...	...	...	...
Vanuatu[46]																					
2009																					
Male - Hommes	69.6	66.4	61.6	56.8	52.1	47.5	42.8	38.1	33.5	29.0	24.7	20.6	16.8	13.4	10.4	7.9	6.0	...	...	...	...
Female - Femmes	72.7	69.3	64.5	59.5	54.7	49.9	45.1	40.3	35.5	30.8	26.3	22.0	18.0	14.4	11.2	8.5	6.4	...	...	...	...
Wallis and Futuna Islands - Îles Wallis et Futuna																					
2003																					
Male - Hommes	73.1	...	...	...	...	...	...	...	...	...	...	...	...	...	...	...	...	...	...	...	...
Female - Femmes	75.5	...	...	...	...	...	...	...	...	...	...	...	...	...	...	...	...	...	...	...	...

FOOTNOTES - NOTES

[1] Data refer to Algerian population only. - Les données ne concernent que la population algérienne.

[2] Based on the results of the Population Census. - D'après les résultats du recensement de la population.

[3] Data refer to national projections. - Les données se réfèrent aux projections nationales.

[4] Based on the results of the 2006 Population and Housing Census. - Données fondées sur les résultats du recensement de la population et de l'habitat de 2006.

[5] Data refer to the 12 months preceding the census in June. - Les données se rapportent aux 12 mois précédant le recensement de juin.

[6] Projections based on the 2010 Population and Housing Census. - Projections fondées sur le recensement 2010 de la population et des logements.

[7] Source: Department of Statistics and Demographic Studies (DISED); 2002 EDAM-IS2 and 2002 EDSF/PAPFAM surveys - Source : Direction de la Statistique et des Etudes Démographiques (DISED); 2002 Enquête Djiboutienne auprès des Ménages (EDAM-IS2) et 2002 Enquête Djiboutienne sur la Sante de la Famille (EDSF/PAPFAM - 2002)

[8] Data refer to projections based on the 2007 Population Census. - Les données se réfèrent aux projections basées sur le recensement de la population de 2007.

[9] Based on the results of the 2010 Population Census. - D'après le résultats du recensement de la population de 2010.

[10] Based on underlying data of the Population and Housing Census 2014. - Données fondées sur le recensement de la population de 2014.

[11] Data refer to the 12 months preceding the census in April. - Les données se rapportent aux douze mois précédant le recensement d'avril.

[12] Data refer to projections based on the 1993 Population Census. - Les données se réfèrent aux projections basées sur le recensement de la population de 1993.

[13] Excludes the islands of St. Brandon and Agalega. - Non compris les îles St. Brandon et Agalega.

[14] Data refer to Saint Helenian resident population. - Pour la population résidante de Sainte-Hélène.

[15] Data refer to the 12 months preceding the census in November. - Données se rapportant aux 12 mois précédant le recensement de novembre.

[16] Data refer to the 12 months preceding the census in December. - Les données se rapportent aux 12 mois précédant le recensement de décembre.

[17] Based on underlying data of the 2002 Population Census. - Données fondées sur le recensement de la population de 2002.

[18] Based on the results of the 2014 Population Census. Provisional data. - D'après les résultats du recensement de la population de 2014. Données provisoires.

[19] Data are based on a small number of deaths. - Les données sont basées sur un nombre limité de décès.

[20] Data refer to projections based on the 1992 Population Census. - Les données se réfèrent aux projections basées sur le recensement de la population de 1992.

[21] Excluding Indian jungle population. - Non compris les Indiens de la jungle.

[22] Data refer to the 12 months from 30 June 2016 to 30 June 2017. - Les données font référence aux douze mois de 30 juin 2016 à 30 juin 2017.

[23] Data based on the 2010 Population Census. Excludes nomadic Indian tribes. - Les données sont fondées sur le recensement de la population de 2010. Non compris les tribus d'Indiens nomades.

[24] Based on the results of the 2011 Population Census. - Basé sur les résultats du recencement de la population de 2011.

[25] For statistical purposes, the data for China do not include those for the Hong Kong Special Administrative Region (Hong Kong SAR), Macao Special Administrative Region (Macao SAR) and Taiwan province of China. - Pour la présentation des statistiques, les données pour la Chine ne comprennent pas la Région Administrative Spéciale de Hong Kong (Hong Kong RAS), la Région Administrative Spéciale de Macao (Macao RAS) et Taïwan province de Chine.

[26] Data refer to government controlled areas. - Les données se rapportent aux zones contrôlées par le Gouvernement.

[27] Includes data for the Indian-held part of Jammu and Kashmir, the final status of which has not yet been determined. - Y compris les données pour la partie du Jammu et du Cachemire occupée par l'Inde dont le statut définitif n'a pas encore été déterminé.

[28] Data refer to the Iranian Year which begins on 21 March and ends on 20 March of the following year. - Les données concernent l'année iranienne, qui commence le 21 mars et se termine le 20 mars de l'année suivante.

[29] Includes data for East Jerusalem and Israeli residents in certain other territories under occupation by Israeli military forces since June 1967. - Y compris les données pour Jérusalem-Est et les résidents israéliens dans certains autres territoires occupés depuis 1967 par les forces armées israéliennes.

[30] Data refer to Japanese nationals in Japan only. - Les données se raportent aux nationaux japonais au Japon seulement.

[31] Excluding data for Jordanian territory under occupation since June 1967 by Israeli military forces. Excluding foreigners, including registered Palestinian refugees. - Non compris les données pour le territoire jordanien occupé depuis juin 1967 par les forces armées israéliennes. Non compris les étrangers, mais y compris les réfugiés de Palestine enregistrés.

[32] Based on underlying data of the 2015 census. - Données fondées sur celles extraites du recensement de 2015.

[33] Based on Vital Registration System (VRS). - Système d'enregistrement des faits d'état civil.

[34] Data refer to Omani citizen only. - Les données concernent les citoyens d'Oman uniquement.

[35] Based on the results of the Pakistan Demographic Survey. Excluding data for the Pakistan-held part of Jammu and Kashmir, the final status of which has not yet been determined. - Données extraites de l'enquête démographique effectuée par le Pakistan. Non compris les données concernant la partie du Jammu et Cachemire occupée par le Pakistan dont le statut définitif n'a pas été déterminé.

[36] Data refer to Saudi Arabian nationals only. - Les données ne concernent que les ressortissants saoudiens.

[37] Data refer to resident population which comprises Singapore citizens and permanent residents. Provisional data. - Les données se rapportent à la population résidente composé des citoyens de Singapour et des résidents permanents. Données provisoires.

[38] Excluding Faeroe Islands and Greenland shown separately, if available. - Non compris les Iles Féroé et le Groenland, qui font l'objet de rubriques distinctes, si disponible.

[39] Excluding Åland Islands. - Non compris les Îles d'Åland.

[40] Excluding Transnistria and the municipality of Bender. - Les données ne tiennent pas compte de l'information sur la Transnistria et la municipalité de Bender.

[41] Excludes data for Kosovo and Metohia. - Sans les données pour le Kosovo et Metohie.

[42] The Government of Ukraine has informed the United Nations that it is not in a position to provide statistical data concerning the Autonomous Republic of Crimea and the city of Sevastopol. - Le gouvernement Ukrainien a informé l'ONU qu'il n'est pas en mesure de fournir des données statistiques concernant la République autonome de Crimée et la ville de Sébastopol.

[43] Excluding Channel Islands (Guernsey and Jersey) and Isle of Man, shown separately, if available. - Non compris les îles Anglo-Normandes (Guernesey et Jersey) et l'île de Man, qui font l'objet de rubriques distinctes, si disponible.

[44] Excluding Niue, shown separately, which is part of Cook Islands, but because of remoteness is administered separately. - Non compris Nioué, qui fait l'objet d'une rubrique distincte et qui fait partie des îles Cook, mais qui, en raison de son éloignement, est administrée séparément.

[45] Data refer to the 12 months preceding the census in October. - Les données se rapportent aux 12 mois précédant le recensement de octobre.

[46] Based on underlying data of the 2009 census. - Données fondées sur celles extraites du recensement de 2009.

Table 22 - *Demographic Yearbook 2018*

Table 22 presents the number of marriages and crude marriage rates by urban/rural residence for every year with available data between 2014 and 2018.

Description of variables: Marriage is defined as the act, ceremony or process by which the legal relationship of spouses is constituted. The legality of the union may be established by civil, religious or other means as recognized by the laws of each country[1].

Marriage statistics in this table, therefore, include both first marriages and remarriages after divorce, widowhood or annulment. They do not, unless otherwise noted, include resumption of marriage ties after legal separation. These statistics refer to the number of marriages performed, and not to the number of persons marrying.

Statistics shown are obtained from civil registers of marriage. Exceptions, such as data from church registers, are identified in footnotes.

The urban/rural classification of marriages is that provided by each country or area; it is presumed to be based on the national census definitions of urban population which have been set forth at the end of the notes for table 6.

For certain countries, there is a discrepancy between the total number of marriages shown in this table and those shown in subsequent tables for the same year. Usually this discrepancy arises because the total number of marriages occurring in a given year is revised although the remaining tabulations are not.

Rate computation: Crude marriage rates are the annual number of marriages per 1 000 mid-year population. Rates by urban/rural residence are the annual number of marriages, in the appropriate urban or rural category, per 1 000 corresponding mid-year population. Rates presented in this table have been limited to those for countries or areas having at least a total of 30 marriages in a given year. These rates are calculated by the United Nations Statistics Division based on the appropriate reference population (for example: total population, nationals only, etc.) if known and available. If the reference population is not known or unavailable the total population is used to calculate the rates. Therefore, if the population that is used to calculate the rates is different from the correct reference population, the rates presented might under- or overstate the true situation in a country or area.

Reliability of data: Each country or area has been asked to indicate the estimated completeness of the number of marriages recorded in its civil register. These national assessments are indicated by the quality codes "C" and "U" that appear in the first column of this table.

"C" indicates that the data are estimated to be virtually complete, that is, representing at least 90 per cent of the marriages occurring each year, while "U" indicates that data are estimated to be incomplete, that is representing less than 90 per cent of the marriages occurring each year. The code "..." indicates that no information was provided regarding completeness.

Data from civil registers which are reported as incomplete or of unknown completeness (coded "U" or "...") are considered unreliable. They appear in italics in this table; rates are not computed for these data.

These quality codes apply only to data from civil registers. For more information about the quality of vital statistics data in general, see section 4.2 of the Technical Notes.

Limitations: Statistics on marriages are subject to the same qualifications that have been set forth for vital statistics in general and marriage statistics in particular as discussed in section 4 of the Technical Notes.

The fact that marriage is a legal event, unlike birth and death that are biological events, has implications for international comparability of data. Marriage has been defined, for statistical purposes, in terms of the laws of individual countries or areas. These laws vary throughout the world. In addition, comparability is further limited because some countries or areas compile statistics only for civil marriages although religious marriages may also be legally recognized; in other countries or areas, the only available records are church registers and, therefore, the statistics may not reflect marriages that are civil marriages only.

Because in many countries or areas marriage is a civil legal contract which, to establish its legality, must be celebrated before a civil officer, it follows that for these countries or areas registration would tend to be almost automatic at the time of, or immediately following, the marriage ceremony. This factor should be kept in mind when considering the reliability of data, described above. For this reason the practice of tabulating data by date of registration does not generally pose serious problems of comparability as it does in the case of birth and death statistics.

As indicators of family formation, the statistics on the number of marriages presented in this table are bound to be deficient to the extent that they do not include either customary unions, which are not registered even though they are considered legal and binding under customary law, or consensual unions (also known as extra-legal or de facto unions). In general, lower marriage rates over a period of years are an indication of higher incidence of customary or consensual unions.

In addition, rates are affected also by the quality and limitations of the population estimates that are used in their computation. The problems of under-enumeration or over-enumeration and, to some extent, the differences in definition of total population have been discussed in section 3 of the Technical Notes dealing with population data in general, and specific information pertaining to individual countries or areas is given in the footnotes to table 3.

Strict correspondence between the numerator of the rate and the denominator is not always obtained; for example, marriages among civilian and military segments of the population may be related to civilian population. The effect of this may be to increase the rates, but, in most cases, this effect is negligible.

It should be emphasized that crude marriage rates like crude birth, death and divorce rates, may be seriously affected by the age-sex-marital structure of the population to which they relate. Crude marriage rates do, however, provide a simple measure of the level and changes in marriage.

The comparability of data by urban/rural residence is affected by the national definitions of urban and rural used in tabulating these data. It is assumed, in the absence of specific information to the contrary, that the definitions of urban and rural used in connection with the national population census were also used in the compilation of the vital statistics for each country or area. However, it cannot be excluded that, for a given country or area, different definitions of urban and rural are used for the vital statistics data and the population census data respectively. When known, the definitions of urban in national population censuses are presented at the end of the technical notes for table 6. As discussed in detail in the notes, these definitions vary considerably from one country or area to another.

In addition to problems of comparability, marriage rates classified by urban/rural residence are also subject to certain special types of bias. If, when calculating marriage rates, different definitions of urban are used in connection with the vital events and the population data, and if this results in a net difference between the numerator and denominator of the rate in the population at risk, then the marriage rates would be biased. Urban/rural differentials in marriage rates may also be affected by whether the vital events have been tabulated in terms of place of occurrence or place of usual residence. This problem is discussed in more detail in section 4.1.4.1 of the Technical Notes.

Earlier data: Marriages and crude marriage rates have been shown in each issue of the *Demographic Yearbook*. For more information on specific topics, and years for which data are reported, readers should consult the Historical Index.

NOTES

[1] *Principles and Recommendations for a Vital Statistics System Revision 3*, Sales No. E.13.XVII.10, United Nations, New York, 2014.

Tableau 22 – *Annuaire démographique 2018*

Le tableau 22 présente des données sur les mariages et les taux bruts de nuptialité selon le lieu de résidence (zone urbaine ou rurale) pour les années où l'information est disponible entre 2014 et 2018.

Description des variables : le mariage désigne l'acte, la cérémonie ou la procédure qui établit un rapport légal entre les époux. L'union peut être rendue légale par une procédure civile ou religieuse, ou par toute autre procédure, conformément à la législation du pays[1].

Les statistiques de la nuptialité présentées dans ce tableau comprennent donc les premiers mariages et les remariages faisant suite à un divorce, un veuvage ou une annulation. Toutefois, sauf indication contraire, elles ne comprennent pas les unions reconstituées après une séparation légale. Ces statistiques se rapportent au nombre de mariages célébrés, non au nombre de personnes qui se marient.

Les statistiques présentées reposent sur l'enregistrement des mariages par les services de l'état civil. Les exceptions (données provenant des registres des églises, par exemple) font l'objet d'une note à la fin du tableau.

La classification des mariages selon le lieu de résidence (zone urbaine ou rurale) est celle qui a été communiquée par chaque pays ou zone ; on part du principe qu'elle repose sur les définitions de la population urbaine utilisées pour les recensements nationaux telles qu'elles sont reproduites à la fin des notes se rapportant au tableau 6.

Pour quelques pays il y a une discordance entre le nombre total de mariages présenté dans ce tableau et ceux présentés après pour la même année. Habituellement ces différences apparaissent lorsque le nombre total des mariages pour une certaine année a été révisé alors que les autres tabulations ne l'ont pas été.

Calcul des taux : les taux bruts de nuptialité représentent le nombre annuel de mariages pour 1 000 habitants au milieu de l'année. Les taux selon le lieu de résidence (zone urbaine ou rurale) représentent le nombre annuel de mariages, classés selon la catégorie urbaine ou rurale appropriée, pour 1 000 habitants au milieu de l'année. Les taux de ce tableau ne se rapportent qu'aux pays ou zones où l'on a enregistré un total d'au moins 30 mariages pendant une année donnée. Ces taux sont calculés par la division de statistique des Nations Unies sur la base de la population de référence adéquate (par exemple : population totale, nationaux seulement, etc.) si connue et disponible. Si la population de référence n'est pas connue ou n'est pas disponible, la population totale est utilisée pour calculer les taux. Par conséquent, si la population utilisée pour calculer les taux est différente de la population de référence adéquate, les taux présentés sont susceptibles de sous ou sur estimer la situation réelle d'un pays ou d'un territoire.

Fiabilité des données : il a été demandé à chaque pays ou zone d'indiquer le degré estimatif de complétude des données sur les mariages figurant dans ses registres d'état civil. Ces évaluations nationales sont signalées par les codes de qualité "C" et "U" qui apparaissent dans la deuxième colonne du tableau.

La lettre "C" indique que les données sont jugées à peu près complètes, c'est-à-dire qu'elles représentent au moins 90 p. 100 des mariages survenus chaque année ; la lettre "U" signale que les données sont jugées incomplètes, c'est-à-dire qu'elles représentent moins de 90 p. 100 des mariages survenus chaque année. Le code "..." indique qu'aucun renseignement n'a été communiqué quant à la complétude des données.

Les données issues des registres de l'état civil qui sont déclarées incomplètes ou dont le degré de complétude n'est pas connu (code "U" ou "...") sont jugées douteuses. Elles apparaissent en italique dans le tableau et les taux correspondants n'ont pas été calculés.

Les codes de qualité ne s'appliquent qu'aux données provenant des registres de l'état civil. Pour plus de précisions sur la qualité des données reposant sur les statistiques de l'état civil en général, voir la section 4.2 des Notes techniques.

Insuffisance des données : les statistiques relatives aux mariages appellent les mêmes réserves que celles qui ont été formulées à propos des statistiques de l'état civil en général et des statistiques concernant la nuptialité en particulier (voir la section 4 des Notes techniques).

Le fait que le mariage soit un acte juridique, à la différence de la naissance et du décès, qui sont des faits biologiques, a des répercussions sur la comparabilité internationale des données. Aux fins de la statistique, le mariage est défini par la législation de chaque pays ou zone. Cette législation varie d'un pays à l'autre. La comparabilité est limitée en outre du fait que certains pays ou zones ne réunissent des statistiques que pour les mariages civils, bien que les mariages religieux y soient également reconnus par la loi ; dans d'autres, les seuls relevés disponibles sont les registres des églises et, en conséquence, les statistiques peuvent ne pas rendre compte des mariages exclusivement civils.

Étant donné que, dans de nombreux pays ou zones, le mariage est un contrat juridique civil qui, pour être légal, doit être conclu devant un officier d'état civil, il s'ensuit que dans ces pays ou zones l'enregistrement se fait à peu près systématiquement au moment de la cérémonie ou immédiatement après. Il faut tenir compte de cet élément lorsque l'on évalue la fiabilité des données, dont il est question plus haut. C'est pourquoi la pratique consistant à exploiter les données selon la date de l'enregistrement ne pose généralement pas les graves problèmes de comparabilité auxquels on se heurte dans le cas des statistiques concernant les naissances et les décès.

Les statistiques relatives au nombre des mariages présentées dans ce tableau donnent une idée forcément trompeuse de la formation des familles, dans la mesure où elles ne tiennent compte ni des mariages coutumiers, qui ne sont pas enregistrés bien qu'ils soient considérés comme légaux et créateurs d'obligations en vertu du droit coutumier, ni des unions consensuelles (appelées également unions non légalisées ou unions de fait). En général, une diminution du taux de nuptialité pendant un certain nombre d'années indique une augmentation des mariages coutumiers ou des unions consensuelles.

L'exactitude des taux dépend également de la qualité et des insuffisances des estimations de population qui sont utilisées pour leur calcul. Le problème des erreurs par excès ou par défaut commises lors du dénombrement et, dans une certaine mesure, le problème de l'hétérogénéité des définitions de la population totale ont été examinés à la section 3 des Notes techniques relative à la population en général ; des indications concernant les différents pays ou zones sont données en note à la fin du tableau 3.

Il n'a pas toujours été possible d'obtenir une correspondance rigoureuse entre le numérateur et le dénominateur pour le calcul des taux. Par exemple, les mariages parmi la population civile et les militaires sont parfois rapportés à la population civile. Cela peut avoir pour effet d'accroître les taux, mais, dans la plupart des cas, il est probable que la différence sera négligeable.

Il faut souligner que les taux bruts de nuptialité, de même que les taux bruts de natalité, de mortalité et de divortialité, peuvent varier sensiblement selon la structure par âge et par sexe de la population à laquelle ils se rapportent. Les taux bruts de nuptialité offrent néanmoins un moyen simple de mesurer la fréquence et l'évolution des mariages.

La comparabilité des données selon le lieu de résidence (zone urbaine ou rurale) peut être limitée par les définitions nationales des termes « urbain » et « rural » utilisées pour le classement de ces données. En l'absence d'indications contraires, on a supposé que les mêmes définitions avaient servi pour le recensement national de la population et pour l'établissement des statistiques de l'état civil pour chaque pays ou zone. Toutefois, il n'est pas exclu que, pour une zone ou un pays donné, des définitions différentes aient été retenues. Les définitions du terme « urbain » utilisées pour les recensements nationaux de population ont été présentées à la fin des notes techniques du tableau 6 lorsqu'elles étaient connues. Comme on l'a précisé dans les notes techniques relatives au tableau 6, ces définitions varient considérablement d'un pays ou d'une zone à l'autre.

Outre les problèmes de comparabilité, les taux de nuptialité classés selon le lieu de résidence (zone urbaine ou rurale) sont également sujets à des distorsions particulières. Si l'on utilise des définitions différentes du terme « urbain » pour classer les faits d'état civil et les données relatives à la population lors du calcul des taux et qu'il en résulte une différence nette entre le numérateur et le dénominateur pour le taux de la population exposée au risque, les taux de nuptialité s'en trouveront faussés. La différence entre ces taux pour les zones urbaines et rurales pourra aussi être faussée selon que les faits d'état civil auront été classés d'après le lieu où ils se sont produits ou d'après le lieu de résidence habituel. Ce problème est examiné plus en détail à la section 4.1.4.1 des Notes techniques.

Données publiées antérieurement : les différentes éditions de *l'Annuaire démographique* regroupent des données sur le nombre des mariages. Pour plus de précisions concernant les années et les sujets pour lesquels des données ont été publiées, se reporter à l'index historique.

NOTE

[1] *Principes et recommandations pour un système de statistique de l'état civil, troisième révision,* numéro de vente : E.13.XVII.10, publication des Nations Unies, New York, 2014.

Continent, country or area, and urban/rural residence / Continent, pays ou zone et résidence, urbaine/rurale	Code[a]	Number - Nombre					Rate - Taux				
		2014	2015	2016	2017	2018	2014	2015	2016	2017	2018
AFRICA - AFRIQUE											
Algeria - Algérie[1]											
Total	...	386 422	369 074	356 600	...	...	...	...	...	...	...
Botswana[2]											
Total	+U	5 591	6 677	6 051	6 203	...	...	...	...	...	...
Congo											
Total	+U	3 625	...	...	...	...	...	...	...	...	...
Urban - Urbaine	+U	3 257	...	...	...	...	...	...	...	...	...
Rural - Rurale	+U	368	...	...	...	...	...	...	...	...	...
Côte d'Ivoire											
Total	+U	...	25 689	26 678	26 316	30 554	...	...	...	...	...
Urban - Urbaine	+U	...	23 750	25 189	...	28 221	...	...	...	...	...
Rural - Rurale	+U	...	1 939	1 489	...	2 333	...	...	...	...	...
Egypt - Égypte											
Total	+C	953 137	969 399[3]	938 526[3]	912 606	...	11.0	10.9	10.3	9.6	...
Urban - Urbaine	+C	384 799	409 906[3]	370 411[3]	356 634	...	10.4	10.8	9.5	8.8	...
Rural - Rurale	+C	568 338	559 493[3]	568 115[3]	555 972	...	11.4	11.0	10.9	10.2	...
Lesotho											
Total	+U	2 576	2 660	2 640	...	...	...	...	...	...	...
Mauritius - Maurice[4]											
Total	+C	9 959	9 709	10 042	9 757	10 034	7.9	7.7	7.9	7.7	7.9
Urban - Urbaine	+C	3 216	3 194	3 224	3 186	3 326	6.2	6.2	6.2	6.2	6.5
Rural - Rurale	+C	6 743	6 515	6 818	6 571	6 708	9.1	8.7	9.1	8.8	8.9
Mayotte											
Total	C	467	346	346	...	...	2.0	1.5	1.4	...	...
Reunion - Réunion											
Total	C	2 771	2 827	2 882	2 866	...	3.3	3.3	3.4	3.3	...
Urban - Urbaine	C	...	...	...	2 782	...	...	...	...	...	...
Rural - Rurale	C	...	...	...	84	...	...	...	...	...	...
Saint Helena ex. dep. - Sainte-Hélène sans dép.											
Total	C	13	9	9	18	10	...	...	...	...	...
Sao Tome and Principe - Sao Tomé-et-Principe											
Total	C	270	305	302	215	...	1.5	1.6	1.6	1.1	...
Seychelles[5]											
Total	+C	1 655	1 845	2 147	2 821	3 131	18.1	19.7	22.7	29.4	32.4
South Africa - Afrique du Sud											
Total	...	150 852	138 627	139 512	135 458	...	...	...	...	...	...
Sudan - Soudan											
Total	U	...	158 051	...	...	...	...	...	...	...	...
Tunisia - Tunisie											
Total	...	110 830	108 453	98 125	95 336	...	...	...	...	...	...
AMERICA, NORTH - AMÉRIQUE DU NORD											
Anguilla[6]											
Total	C	64	40	64	64	...	4.5	2.7	4.2	...	...
Aruba											
Total	C	617	696	639	537	...	5.7	6.4	5.8	4.8	...
Bahamas[7]											
Total	+C	*3 964	*3 829	*3 950	*3 574	...	*10.9	*10.4	*10.6	*9.5	...
Barbados - Barbade											
Total	+C	1 855	...	...	...	...	6.7	...	...	...	...
Bermuda - Bermudes[8]											
Total	C	477	509	450	430	...	7.7	8.2	7.1	6.7	...
British Virgin Islands - Îles Vierges britanniques											
Total	C	250	236	229	177	...	...	8.1	...	...	...
Cayman Islands - Îles Caïmanes[9]											
Total	+C	452	468	493	513	516	7.9	7.9	8.1	8.1	7.8
Costa Rica[10]											
Total	C	25 909	26 512	26 718	25 501	*23 604	5.4	5.5	5.5	5.2	*4.7
Urban - Urbaine	C	17 905	21 258	21 565	20 129	*18 695	5.2	6.1	6.1	5.6	*5.1
Rural - Rurale	C	8 004	5 254	5 153	5 372	*4 909	6.1	4.0	3.9	4.0	*3.6

22. Marriages and crude marriage rates, by urban/rural residence: 2014 - 2018
Mariages et taux bruts de nuptialité, selon la résidence, urbaine/rurale : 2014 - 2018 (continued - suite)

Continent, country or area, and urban/rural residence / Continent, pays ou zone et résidence, urbaine/rurale	Code[a]	Number - Nombre					Rate - Taux				
		2014	2015	2016	2017	2018	2014	2015	2016	2017	2018
AMERICA, NORTH - AMÉRIQUE DU NORD											
Cuba[11]											
Total	C	63 954	61 902	61 903	53 684	*58 070	5.7	5.5	5.5	4.8	*5.2
Urban - Urbaine	C	58 137	57 600	57 596	49 874	...	6.7	6.7	6.7	5.8	...
Rural - Rurale	C	5 817	4 302	4 307	3 810	...	2.2	1.7	1.7	1.5	...
Curaçao[12]											
Total	C	696	703	695	729	...	4.5	4.4	4.4	4.6	...
Dominican Republic - République dominicaine											
Total	+C	47 235	50 158	52 896	49 625	...	4.8	5.0	5.3	4.9	...
Grenada - Grenade											
Total	+C	618	669	635	629	...	5.7	6.1	5.7	5.6	...
Guadeloupe											
Total	C	1 198	1 172	1 185	1 104	...	3.0	3.0	3.0	2.8	...
Guatemala											
Total	C	79 496	79 177	69 613	71 597	...	5.0	4.9	4.2	4.2	...
Jamaica - Jamaïque											
Total	+C	18 699	18 373	17 609	17 411	...	6.9	6.7	6.5	6.4	...
Martinique											
Total	C	968	1 017	1 067	1 034	...	2.5	2.7	2.8	2.8	...
Urban - Urbaine	C	...	...	...	877	...	...	...	...	...	...
Rural - Rurale	C	...	...	...	157	...	...	...	...	...	...
Mexico - Mexique[13]											
Total	+C	577 713	558 022	543 749	528 678	501 298	4.8	4.6	4.4	4.3	4.0
Urban - Urbaine[14]	+C	420 856	416 507	411 481	405 427	...	4.8	4.7	4.6	4.5	...
Rural - Rurale[14]	+C	119 600	108 675	100 862	104 059	...	3.6	3.3	3.0	3.1	...
Montserrat											
Total	C	14	14	10	...	...	...	...	...	...	...
Nicaragua											
Total	+U	31 145	26 628	22 097	...	...	...	...	...	...	...
Panama[10]											
Total	C	12 869	*14 341	*14 233	*13 360	...	3.3	*3.6	*3.5	*3.3	...
Urban - Urbaine	C	10 443	*11 824	*11 730	*10 863	...	4.0	*4.4	*4.2	*3.8	...
Rural - Rurale	C	2 426	*2 517	*2 503	*2 497	...	1.9	*2.0	*2.0	*2.0	...
Puerto Rico - Porto Rico											
Total	C	16 702	17 002	15 907	12 793	13 895	4.7	4.9	4.7	3.8	4.3
Saint Pierre and Miquelon - Saint Pierre-et-Miquelon											
Total	C	...	...	...	8	...	...	...	...	...	...
Saint Vincent and the Grenadines - Saint-Vincent-et-les Grenadines											
Total	C	526	574	...	...	...	4.8	5.2	...	...	...
Saint-Barthélemy											
Total	C	...	...	...	26	...	...	...	...	...	...
Saint-Martin (French part) - Saint-Martin (partie française)											
Total	C	...	...	...	88	...	...	...	...	2.5	...
Sint Maarten (Dutch part) - Saint-Martin (partie néerlandaise)											
Total	+C	251	251	306	158	...	6.8	6.6	7.8	3.9	...
Turks and Caicos Islands - Îles Turques et Caïques											
Total	C	...	474	621	295	...	...	12.9	16.4	7.4	...
United States of America - États-Unis d'Amérique											
Total	C	2 140 272[15]	2 221 579	...	...	...	6.7	6.9	...	...	...
AMERICA, SOUTH - AMÉRIQUE DU SUD											
Argentina - Argentine											
Total	C	119 266	118 809	119 334	127 378	...	2.8	2.8	2.7	2.9	...

Continent, country or area, and urban/rural residence / Continent, pays ou zone et résidence, urbaine/rurale	Co-de[a]	Number - Nombre					Rate - Taux				
		2014	2015	2016	2017	2018	2014	2015	2016	2017	2018
AMERICA, SOUTH - AMÉRIQUE DU SUD											
Bolivia (Plurinational State of) - Bolivie (État plurinational de)											
Total	+U	60 105	39 942	...	...	...	...	...	...	...	...
Brazil - Brésil											
Total	+U	1 106 440[13]	1 137 348[13]	1 095 535[13]	1 064 489	...	...	...	...	...	...
Chile - Chili											
Total	+C	64 868	61 744	62 464	*61 320	...	3.6	3.4	3.4	*3.3	...
Urban - Urbaine[16]	+C	59 858	56 984	57 413	...	...	3.8	3.6	3.6	...	...
Rural - Rurale[16]	+C	5 010	4 760	5 051	...	...	2.2	2.1	2.2	...	...
Ecuador - Équateur[17]											
Total	U	60 328	60 636	57 738	60 353	...	...	...	...	...	...
Urban - Urbaine[16]	U	50 434	50 425	47 322	48 946	...	...	...	...	...	...
Rural - Rurale[16]	U	9 894	10 211	10 416	11 407	...	...	...	...	...	...
French Guiana - Guyane française											
Total	C	573	590	631	...	...	2.3	2.3	2.4	...	...
Guyana[18]											
Total	C	4 679	4 744	4 445	3 990	4 008	6.3	6.4	6.0	5.4	...
Paraguay											
Total	U	19 527	19 504	19 440	19 760	19 660	...	...	...	...	...
Peru - Pérou[19]											
Total	+C	95 770	86 191	94 094	90 806	*79 740	3.1	2.8	3.0	2.9	*2.5
Suriname											
Total	C	2 143	2 010	2 125	1 996	...	3.8	3.5	3.7	3.4	...
Uruguay											
Total	C	10 226	9 501	9 820	...	...	3.0	2.7	2.8	...	...
Venezuela (Bolivarian Republic of) - Venezuela (République bolivarienne du)											
Total	C	94 519	91 688	84 349	82 213	...	3.1	3.0	2.7	2.6	...
ASIA - ASIE											
Armenia - Arménie											
Total	+C	18 912	17 603	16 294	15 214	...	6.3	5.9	5.4	5.1	...
Urban - Urbaine	+C	...	11 836	11 113	10 469	...	...	6.2	5.8	5.5	...
Rural - Rurale	+C	...	5 767	5 181	4 745	...	...	5.3	4.8	4.4	...
Azerbaijan - Azerbaïdjan											
Total	+C	84 912	68 773	66 771	62 923	...	8.9	7.1	6.8	6.4	...
Urban - Urbaine	+C	43 608	36 623	36 739	33 047	...	8.6	7.1	7.1	6.3	...
Rural - Rurale	+C	41 304	32 150	30 032	29 876	...	9.3	7.1	6.6	6.4	...
Bahrain - Bahreïn											
Total	...	7 673	6 953	7 019	6 691	6 039	...	...	...	...	...
Bangladesh											
Total	...	1 946 376	2 020 095	2 263 889	2 327 608	...	...	...	...	...	...
Brunei Darussalam - Brunéi Darussalam											
Total	+C	2 992	2 750	2 532	2 540	...	7.3	6.7	6.1	5.9	...
China, Hong Kong SAR - Chine, Hong Kong RAS											
Total	C	56 454	51 609	50 008	51 817	49 331	7.8	7.1	6.8	7.0	6.6
China, Macao SAR - Chine, Macao RAS											
Total	+C	4 085	3 719	3 891	3 883	3 842	6.6	5.8	6.0	5.9	5.8
Cyprus - Chypre[20]											
Total	C	5 378	6 092	6 375	5 882	...	6.3	7.2	7.5	6.8	...
Georgia - Géorgie											
Total	C	31 526	29 157	25 101	23 684	23 202	8.5	7.8	6.7	6.4	6.2
Urban - Urbaine[16]	C	18 363	17 127	14 961	...	...	...	8.1	7.0	...	...
Rural - Rurale[16]	C	13 163	12 030	10 140	...	...	...	7.6	6.4	...	...
Indonesia - Indonésie											
Total	U	2 110 776	1 958 394	...	...	...	...	...	...	...	...

22. Marriages and crude marriage rates, by urban/rural residence: 2014 - 2018
Mariages et taux bruts de nuptialité, selon la résidence, urbaine/rurale : 2014 - 2018 (continued - suite)

Continent, country or area, and urban/rural residence / Continent, pays ou zone et résidence, urbaine/rurale	Co-de[a]	Number - Nombre					Rate - Taux				
		2014	2015	2016	2017	2018	2014	2015	2016	2017	2018
ASIA - ASIE											
Iran (Islamic Republic of) - Iran (République islamique d')[21]											
Total	+C	724 324	685 352	668 303	608 956	...	9.3	8.7	8.3	7.5	...
Urban - Urbaine	+C	...	562 671	588 460	539 421	...	...	9.8	9.9	8.9	...
Rural - Rurale	+C	...	122 681	79 843	69 535	...	...	5.7	3.8	3.3	...
Israel - Israël[22]											
Total	C	50 797	53 579	52 809	...	...	6.2	6.4	6.2	...	...
Urban - Urbaine[23]	C	45 729	48 236	47 651	...	...	6.1	6.3	6.1	...	...
Rural - Rurale[23]	C	3 715	3 936	3 828	...	...	5.2	5.3	5.1	...	...
Japan - Japon[24]											
Total	+C	643 749	635 156	620 531	606 866	...	5.1	5.0	4.9	4.8	...
Urban - Urbaine[16]	+C	598 792	590 947	578 265	566 338	...	...	...	...	...	...
Rural - Rurale[16]	+C	44 957	44 209	42 266	40 528	...	...	...	...	...	...
Jordan - Jordanie[25]											
Total	+C	81 209	81 373	81 343	77 700	70 734	9.2	8.5	8.3	7.7	6.9
Kazakhstan											
Total	+C	159 328	148 769	141 702	141 791	137 797	9.2	8.5	8.0	7.9	7.5
Urban - Urbaine	+C	105 172	98 927	94 672	96 865	95 964	10.9	10.0	9.3	9.4	9.0
Rural - Rurale	+C	54 156	49 842	47 030	44 926	41 833	7.1	6.6	6.1	5.8	5.5
Kuwait - Koweït											
Total	C	15 086	15 412	14 693	13 932	14 400	4.0	3.9	3.6	3.5	3.5
Kyrgyzstan - Kirghizstan											
Total	C	54 942	52 043	47 837	43 350	49 579	9.4	8.7	7.9	7.0	7.8
Urban - Urbaine	C	17 150	15 875	15 990	16 274	...	8.7	7.9	7.8	7.8	...
Rural - Rurale	C	37 792	36 168	31 847	27 076	...	9.8	9.2	7.9	6.6	...
Lebanon - Liban											
Total	C	41 049	...	...	...	...	...	...	...	...	...
Malaysia - Malaisie											
Total	+C	...	...	*200 274	*190 532	...	...	...	*6.3	*5.9	...
Maldives											
Total	...	...	5 763	5 488	5 237	5 290	...	...	...	...	...
Urban - Urbaine	...	...	2 610	2 527	...	...	...	...	...	...	...
Rural - Rurale	...	...	3 153	2 961	...	...	...	...	...	...	...
Mongolia - Mongolie											
Total	+C	17 332	17 586	16 778	20 470	21 020	5.8	5.8	5.4	6.5	6.6
Urban - Urbaine	+C	12 075	12 506	11 915	14 617	15 332	6.1	6.1	5.6	6.8	7.1
Rural - Rurale	+C	5 257	5 080	4 863	5 853	5 688	5.4	5.2	5.0	5.8	5.5
Oman											
Total	U	28 152	25 659	24 014	22 284	20 005	...	...	...	...	...
Philippines											
Total	U	429 723	439 424	419 268	434 932	...	...	...	...	...	...
Qatar											
Total	C	3 674	3 724	3 830	3 718	3 758	1.7	1.5	1.5	1.4	1.4
Urban - Urbaine	C	3 674	3 724	3 830	3 718	3 758	1.7	1.5	1.5	1.4	1.4
Republic of Korea - République de Corée[26]											
Total	+C	305 507	302 828	281 635	264 455	257 622	6.0	5.9	5.5	5.2	5.0
Urban - Urbaine[23]	+C	248 965	247 486	229 747	214 584	208 646	6.0	6.0	5.5	5.2	5.0
Rural - Rurale[23]	+C	48 818	48 638	46 792	44 756	43 693	5.2	5.1	4.9	4.7	4.5
Singapore - Singapour[27]											
Total	+C	28 407	28 322	27 971	28 212	27 007	7.3	7.3	7.1	7.1	6.8
Sri Lanka											
Total	+C	177 792	*175 939	*173 990	*169 365	*170 027	8.6	*8.4	*8.2	*7.9	*7.8
State of Palestine - État de Palestine											
Total	C	43 732	50 438	49 930	47 218	...	...	9.9	11.1	10.8	10.0
Tajikistan - Tadjikistan											
Total	+C	95 537	76 956	72 499	78 638	...	11.6	9.1	8.4	8.9	...
Urban - Urbaine	+C	25 757	19 810	18 378	20 184	...	11.7	8.9	8.1	8.7	...
Rural - Rurale	+C	69 780	57 146	54 121	58 454	...	11.5	9.2	8.5	9.0	...
Thailand - Thaïlande											
Total	U	296 258	304 392	307 746	297 501	...	...	...	...	...	...
Turkey - Turquie[28]											
Total	C	599 704	602 982	594 493	569 459	...	7.7	7.7	7.4	7.1	...

Continent, country or area, and urban/rural residence / Continent, pays ou zone et résidence, urbaine/rurale	Code[a]	Number - Nombre					Rate - Taux				
		2014	2015	2016	2017	2018	2014	2015	2016	2017	2018
ASIA - ASIE											
United Arab Emirates - Émirats arabes unis											
Total	...	16 917	16 248	...	15 150	...	...	...	...	...	...
Uzbekistan - Ouzbékistan											
Total	+C	296 055	287 582	275 048	306 197	311 379	9.6	9.2	8.6	9.5	9.5
Urban - Urbaine	+C	136 707	131 216	125 820	138 681	145 756	8.7	8.3	7.8	8.4	8.8
Rural - Rurale	+C	159 348	156 366	149 228	167 516	165 623	10.5	10.1	9.5	10.5	10.3
EUROPE											
Åland Islands - Îles d'Åland											
Total	C	115	118	123	112	*115	4.0	4.1	4.2	3.8	*3.9
Urban - Urbaine	C	53	49	49	48	*44	4.6	4.3	4.3	4.1	*3.8
Rural - Rurale	C	62	69	74	64	*71	3.6	3.9	4.2	3.6	*4.0
Albania - Albanie											
Total	C	23 769	24 997	22 562	22 641	23 104	8.2	8.7	7.8	7.9	8.0
Andorra - Andorre											
Total	C	271	285	295	320	293	3.9	4.0	4.1	4.4	3.9
Austria - Autriche											
Total	C	37 458[29]	44 502[30]	44 890[30]	44 981[30]	46 468[30]	4.4	5.2	5.1	5.1	5.3
Belarus - Bélarus											
Total	C	83 942	82 030	64 536	66 215	*60 714	8.9	8.6	6.8	7.0	*6.4
Urban - Urbaine	C	69 649	68 305	53 819	55 372	...	9.5	9.3	7.3	7.5	...
Rural - Rurale	C	14 293	13 725	10 717	10 843	...	6.6	6.4	5.1	5.2	...
Belgium - Belgique[31]											
Total	C	39 879	40 049	44 725	44 329	...	3.6	3.5	3.9	3.9	...
Urban - Urbaine	C	39 332	39 500	...	...	...	...	...	...	...	...
Rural - Rurale	C	547	549	...	...	...	...	...	...	...	...
Bosnia and Herzegovina - Bosnie-Herzégovine											
Total	C	18 409	19 680	19 233	19 617	...	5.2	5.6	5.5	5.6	...
Bulgaria - Bulgarie[32]											
Total	C	24 596	27 720	26 803	28 593	28 961	3.4	3.9	3.8	4.0	4.1
Urban - Urbaine	C	18 756	20 795	19 977	21 536	21 463	3.6	4.0	3.8	4.1	4.1
Rural - Rurale	C	5 840	6 925	6 826	7 057	7 498	3.0	3.6	3.6	3.7	4.0
Croatia - Croatie[10]											
Total	C	19 501	19 834	20 467	20 310	...	4.6	4.7	4.9	4.9	...
Urban - Urbaine	C	10 924	10 937	11 287	11 231	...	...	...	...	...	...
Rural - Rurale	C	8 577	8 897	9 180	9 079	...	...	...	...	...	...
Czechia - Tchéquie[10]											
Total	C	45 575	48 191	50 768	52 567	*54 470	4.3	4.6	4.8	5.0	*5.1
Urban - Urbaine	C	33 356	35 192	37 207	38 240	...	4.3	4.6	4.8	4.9	...
Rural - Rurale	C	12 219	12 999	13 561	14 327	...	4.3	4.6	4.8	5.0	...
Denmark - Danemark[33]											
Total	C	28 331	28 853	30 767	31 777	32 525	5.0	5.1	5.4	5.5	5.6
Estonia - Estonie											
Total	C	6 220	6 815	6 360	6 447	6 573	4.7	5.2	4.8	4.9	5.0
Urban - Urbaine[34]	C	4 232	4 660	4 214	4 493	...	4.7	5.2	4.7	4.9	...
Rural - Rurale[34]	C	1 496	1 733	1 748	1 548	...	3.6	4.2	4.2	3.8	...
Faeroe Islands - Îles Féroé											
Total	C	250	268	268	275	285	5.2	5.5	5.4	5.5	5.6
Finland - Finlande[35]											
Total	C	24 347	24 590	24 341	23 731	...	4.5	4.5	4.5	4.3	...
Urban - Urbaine	C	18 485	18 838	18 676	18 470	...	4.9	4.9	4.8	4.7	...
Rural - Rurale	C	5 862	5 752	5 665	5 261	...	3.5	3.6	3.6	3.3	...
France[13]											
Total	C	235 315	230 364	226 614	227 758	*229 000	3.7	3.6	3.5	3.5	*3.5
Urban - Urbaine[36]	C	182 905	179 606	177 747	...	...	...	...	...	...	...
Rural - Rurale[36]	C	49 824	48 118	46 219	...	...	...	...	...	...	...
Germany - Allemagne											
Total	C	385 952	400 115	410 426	407 466	*416 615	4.8	4.9	5.0	4.9	*5.0
Gibraltar[9]											
Total	+C	204	195	199	...	...	6.2	5.8	5.9	...	...

Continent, country or area, and urban/rural residence / Continent, pays ou zone et résidence, urbaine/rurale	Code[a]	Number - Nombre					Rate - Taux				
		2014	2015	2016	2017	2018	2014	2015	2016	2017	2018
EUROPE											
Greece - Grèce											
Total	C	53 105	53 672	49 632	50 138	47 428	4.9	5.0	4.6	4.7	4.4
Urban - Urbaine	C	37 743	37 870	35 268	...	...	...	...	...	...	...
Rural - Rurale	C	15 362	15 802	14 364	...	...	...	...	...	...	...
Hungary - Hongrie[11]											
Total	C	38 780	46 137	51 805	50 572	50 828	3.9	4.7	5.3	5.2	5.2
Urban - Urbaine[37]	C	28 854	33 144	36 422	35 416	...	4.2	4.8	5.3	5.1	...
Rural - Rurale[37]	C	9 538	12 492	14 810	14 528	...	3.3	4.3	5.1	5.0	...
Ireland - Irlande											
Total	+C	22 045	22 116[13]	22 626[13]	22 021[13]	21 053[13]	4.7	4.7	4.8	4.6	4.4
Isle of Man - Île de Man											
Total	+C	197	199	240	247	...	2.3	2.3	2.8	2.9	...
Italy - Italie											
Total	C	189 765	194 377	203 258	191 287	...	3.1	3.2	3.4	3.2	...
Latvia - Lettonie[10]											
Total	C	12 515	13 617	13 002	13 150	13 058	6.3	6.9	6.6	6.8	6.8
Liechtenstein[10]											
Total	C	208	205	198	229	...	5.6	5.5	5.3	6.0	...
Lithuania - Lituanie											
Total	C	22 142	21 987	21 347	21 186	19 734	7.6	7.6	7.4	7.5	7.1
Urban - Urbaine	C	15 250	15 219	14 914	14 684	13 530	7.7	7.8	7.7	7.7	...
Rural - Rurale	C	6 892	6 768	6 433	6 502	6 204	7.2	7.1	6.8	7.0	...
Luxembourg[9]											
Total	C	1 657	2 052[13]	1 884[13]	1 908[13]	1 956[13]	3.0	3.6	3.2	3.2	3.2
Malta - Malte											
Total	C	2 871	3 002	3 034	2 934	...	6.6	6.7	6.7	6.3	...
Monaco											
Total	C	222	213	193	206	182	6.0	5.7	5.1	5.5	4.8
Montenegro - Monténégro											
Total	C	3 527	3 837	3 178	3 272	3 321	5.7	6.2	5.1	5.3	5.3
Netherlands - Pays-Bas[38]											
Total	C	65 333	64 308	65 249	64 402	64 315	3.9	3.8	3.8	3.8	3.7
North Macedonia - Macédoine du Nord											
Total	C	13 813	14 186	13 199	13 781	13 494	6.7	6.9	6.4	6.6	6.5
Urban - Urbaine	C	7 782	8 168	7 328	8 868	...	...	...	...	...	...
Rural - Rurale	C	6 031	6 018	5 871	4 913	...	...	...	...	...	...
Norway - Norvège[13]											
Total	C	23 462	23 227	23 672	23 134	21 704	4.6	4.5	4.5	4.4	4.1
Poland - Pologne											
Total	C	188 488	188 832	193 455	192 576	192 443	5.0	5.0	5.1	5.1	5.1
Urban - Urbaine	C	110 030	111 246	114 612	114 338	114 841	4.8	4.9	5.0	5.0	...
Rural - Rurale	C	78 458	77 586	78 843	78 238	77 602	5.2	5.2	5.2	5.2	...
Portugal[39]											
Total	C	31 478	32 393	32 399	33 634	34 637	3.0	3.1	3.1	3.3	3.4
Republic of Moldova - République de Moldova											
Total	C	25 624	24 709	21 992	20 924	20 399	9.0	8.7	7.8	7.6	7.5
Urban - Urbaine	C	13 376	12 919	11 233	10 980	10 799	...	...	...	...	...
Rural - Rurale	C	12 248	11 790	10 759	9 944	9 600	...	...	...	...	...
Romania - Roumanie											
Total	C	118 075	125 454	133 183	142 613	143 292	5.9	6.3	6.8	7.3	7.3
Urban - Urbaine	C	76 833	80 975	84 226	91 212	91 960	7.2	7.6	8.0	8.7	...
Rural - Rurale	C	41 242	44 479	48 957	51 401	51 332	4.5	4.9	5.4	5.7	...
San Marino - Saint-Marin[40]											
Total	C	187	182	181	159[41]	151[41]	5.6	5.4	5.3	4.6	4.4
Serbia - Serbie[42]											
Total	+C	36 429	36 949[43]	35 921[43]	36 047[43]	36 321[43]	5.1	5.2	5.1	5.1	5.2
Urban - Urbaine	+C	23 718	24 521[43]	23 554[43]	23 757[43]	...	5.6	5.7	5.5	5.6	...
Rural - Rurale	+C	12 711	12 428[43]	12 367[43]	12 290[43]	...	4.4	4.4	4.4	4.4	...
Slovakia - Slovaquie[10]											
Total	C	26 737	28 775	29 897	31 309	31 177	4.9	5.3	5.5	5.8	5.7
Urban - Urbaine	C	15 280	16 443	16 793	17 588	17 196	5.2	5.6	5.7	6.0	...
Rural - Rurale	C	11 457	12 332	13 104	13 721	13 981	4.6	4.9	5.2	5.4	...

Continent, country or area, and urban/rural residence / Continent, pays ou zone et résidence, urbaine/rurale	Code[a]	Number - Nombre					Rate - Taux				
		2014	2015	2016	2017	2018	2014	2015	2016	2017	2018
EUROPE											
Slovenia - Slovénie[44]											
Total	C	6 571	6 449	6 667	6 481	7 256	3.2	3.1	3.2	3.1	3.5
Urban - Urbaine	C	3 365	3 418	3 665	3 630	...	3.2	3.1	3.3	3.2	...
Rural - Rurale	C	3 206	3 031	3 002	2 851	...	3.2	3.2	3.1	3.1	...
Spain - Espagne											
Total	C	160 256	166 651	173 049	171 320	*163 430	3.4	3.6	3.7	3.7	*3.5
Sweden - Suède[13]											
Total	C	53 051	52 314	53 817	52 497	50 796	5.5	5.3	5.4	5.2	5.0
Switzerland - Suisse[45]											
Total	C	41 891	41 437	41 646	40 599	40 716	5.1	5.0	5.0	4.8	4.8
Urban - Urbaine	C	32 019[46]	35 758	35 995	35 208	...	5.3	5.1	5.1	...	...
Rural - Rurale	C	9 872[46]	5 679	5 651	5 391	...	4.6	4.4	4.4	...	...
Ukraine[47]											
Total	+C	294 962	299 038	229 453	249 522	...	6.9	7.0	5.4	5.9	...
Urban - Urbaine	+C	224 539	222 747	172 663	191 826	...	...	7.5	5.8	6.5	...
Rural - Rurale	+C	70 423	76 291	56 790	57 696	...	...	5.8	4.3	4.4	...
United Kingdom of Great Britain and Northern Ireland - Royaume-Uni de Grande-Bretagne et d'Irlande du Nord[48]											
Total	C	289 841	283 559	...	...	...	4.5	4.4	...	...	...
OCEANIA - OCÉANIE											
American Samoa - Samoas américaines											
Total	C	217	264	253	228	...	3.5	4.3	4.2	3.8	...
Australia - Australie											
Total	+C	121 197	113 595	118 401	112 954	...	5.2	4.8	4.9	4.6	...
Cook Islands - Îles Cook[49]											
Total	+C	746	720	...	...	...	40.1	38.5	...	...	...
Fiji - Fidji											
Total	+C	8 501	...	...	...	...	9.8	...	...	...	...
French Polynesia - Polynésie française											
Total	C	1 480	1 456	1 487	1 254	...	5.5	5.3	5.4	4.5	...
Guam[50]											
Total	C	1 463	1 348[13]	1 185[13]	1 244[13]	1 251[13]	9.1	8.3	7.3	7.6	7.5
New Caledonia - Nouvelle-Calédonie											
Total	C	971	983[13]	894[13]	...	...	3.6	3.6	3.3	...	...
New Zealand - Nouvelle-Zélande[51]											
Total	+C	20 125	19 947[52]	20 235[52]	*20 685[52]	20 949[52]	4.5	4.3	4.3	*4.3	4.3
Norfolk Island - Île Norfolk[53]											
Total	+C	15	24	...	...	...	...	...	...	...	...
Samoa											
Total	U	...	865	...	...	2 861[54]	...	...	...	...	...

FOOTNOTES - NOTES

Italics: data from civil registers which are incomplete or of unknown completeness. - Italiques : données incomplètes ou dont le degré d'exactitude n'est pas connu, provenant des registres de l'état civil.

* Provisional. - Données provisoires.

[a] 'Code' indicates the source of data, as follows:
C - Civil registration, estimated over 90% complete
U - Civil registration, estimated less than 90% complete
| - Other source, estimated reliable
+ - Data tabulated by date of registration rather than occurence
... - Information not available

Le 'Code' indique la source des données, comme suit :
C - Registres de l'état civil considérés complets à 90 p. 100 au moins
U - Registres de l'état civil qui ne sont pas considérés complets à 90 p. 100 au moins
| - Autre source, considérée pas douteuse
+ - Données exploitées selon la date de l'enregistrement et non la date de l'événement
... - Information pas disponible

[1] Data refer to Algerian population only. - Les données ne concernent que la population algérienne.
[2] Source: Vital Statistics Report. - Source: Vital Statistics Report.
[3] Including marriages resumed after 'revocable divorce' (among Moslem population), which approximates legal separation. - Y compris les unions

reconstituées après un 'divorce révocable' (parmi la population musulmane), qui est à peu près l'équivalent d'une séparation légale.

[4] Excludes the islands of St. Brandon and Agalega. - Non compris les îles St. Brandon et Agalega.

[5] Including visitors. - Y compris les visiteurs.

[6] Excluding visitors. - Ne comprend pas les visiteurs.

[7] Including non-residents. - Y compris les non-résidents.

[8] Bermuda is 100 per cent urban. - 100 pour cent de la population des Bermudes est urbaine.

[9] Data refer to marriages where one or both partners are residents. - Les données portent sur les mariages pour lesquels l'un des deux partenaires ou les deux sont résidents.

[10] Data refer to marriages by residence of the groom. - Les données concernent les mariages selon la résidence du marié.

[11] Marriages registered by residence of bride. - Les mariages sont enregistrés selon le lieu de résidence de la mariée.

[12] Data refers to the number of marriages of which at least one of the partners is a resident of Curacao. - Les données concernent le nombre de mariages dont au moins l'un des partenaires est un résident de Curaçao.

[13] Including same sex marriages. - Y compris les mariages entre personnes du même sexe.

[14] The total number may include 'Unknown residence', but the categories urban and rural do not. Urban and rural distribution refers to the usual residence of the bride. - Le nombre total peut inclure les personnes dont la résidence n'est pas connue, à l'inverse des catégories de population urbaine et rurale. La répartition entre résidence urbaine et résidence rurale fait référence au lieu de résidence habituel de la mariée.

[15] Excluding data for Georgia, one of the states of the United States of America. - À l'exclusion des données pour la Géorgie, l'un des États des États-Unis d'Amérique.

[16] Urban and rural residence refers to the place of usual residence of groom. - Le lieu de résidence (zone urbaine ou zone rurale) correspond au lieu de résidence habituel du marié.

[17] Excludes nomadic Indian tribes. - Non compris les tribus d'Indiens nomades.

[18] Excluding Amerindians. - Non compris les Amérindiens.

[19] Data are compiled from the National Registers of Identification and Civil Status (RENIEC). - Les données sont rédigées à partir des Registres Nationaux d'Identification et d'État Civil (RENIEC).

[20] Data refer to government controlled areas. Data refer to marriages of residents only. - Les données se rapportent aux zones contrôlées par le Gouvernement. Les données ne portent que sur les mariages de résidents.

[21] Data refer to the Iranian Year which begins on 21 March and ends on 20 March of the following year. - Les données concernent l'année iranienne, qui commence le 21 mars et se termine le 20 mars de l'année suivante.

[22] Includes data for East Jerusalem and Israeli residents in certain other territories under occupation by Israeli military forces since June 1967. - Y compris les données pour Jérusalem-Est et les résidents israéliens dans certains autres territoires occupés depuis 1967 par les forces armées israéliennes.

[23] The total number may include 'Unknown residence', but the categories urban and rural do not. Urban and rural residence refers to the place of usual residence of groom. - Le nombre total peut inclure les personnes dont la résidence n'est pas connue, à l'inverse des catégories de population urbaine et rurale. Le lieu de résidence (zone urbaine ou zone rurale) correspond au lieu de résidence habituel du marié.

[24] Data refer to Japanese nationals in Japan only. - Les données se raportent aux nationaux japonais au Japon seulement.

[25] Excluding data for Jordanian territory under occupation since June 1967 by Israeli military forces. Excluding foreigners, including registered Palestinian refugees. - Non compris les données pour le territoire jordanien occupé depuis juin 1967 par les forces armées israéliennes. Non compris les étrangers, mais y compris les réfugiés de Palestine enregistrés.

[26] Excluding alien armed forces, civilian aliens employed by armed forces, and foreign diplomatic personnel and their dependants. - Non compris les militaires étrangers, les civils étrangers employés par les forces armées ni le personnel diplomatique étranger et les membres de leur famille les accompagnant.

[27] Excluding marriages previously officiated outside Singapore or under religious and customary rites. Data comprise civil marriages registered under the Women's Charter and Muslim marriages registered under the Administration of Muslim Law Act. - Ne comprend pas les mariages prononcés ailleurs qu'à Singapour ni les mariages religieux ou coutumiers. Les données comprennent les mariages civils enregistrés en vertu de la Charte des droits de la femme, ainsi que les mariages musulmans enregistrés en vertu de la loi sur l'administration du droit islamique.

[28] Data from MERNIS (Central Population Administrative System). - Données de MERNIS (Système central de données démographiques).

[29] Excluding marriages of aliens temporarily in the area. - Non compris les mariages d'étrangers temporairement dans la région.

[30] Excluding marriages of aliens temporarily in the area, but including marriages abroad of persons with residence in Austria. - Non compris les mariages d'étrangers temporairement dans la région, mais y compris des mariages à l'étranger de personnes ayant leur résidence en Autriche.

[31] Including armed forces stationed outside the country and alien armed forces in the area, if the marriage is performed by local authority. Including same sex marriages. - Y compris les militaires nationaux hors du pays et les militaires étrangers en garnison sur le territoire, si le mariage a été célébré par l'autorité locale. Y compris les mariages entre personnes du même sexe.

[32] Including nationals outside the country, but excluding foreigners in the country. - Y compris les nationaux à l'étranger, mais non compris les étrangers sur le territoire.

[33] Excluding Faeroe Islands and Greenland shown separately, if available. - Non compris les Iles Féroé et le Groenland, qui font l'objet de rubriques distinctes, si disponible.

[34] The difference between 'Total' and the sum of urban and rural is due to the unknown place of residence of grooms and to grooms living outside the country. Urban and rural residence refers to the place of usual residence of groom. - La différence entre le « Total » et la somme des chiffres urbains et ruraux s'explique par le fait que la résidence du marié n'est pas toujours connue ou est située à l'étranger. Le lieu de résidence (zone urbaine ou zone rurale) correspond au lieu de résidence habituel du marié.

[35] Urban and rural distribution refers to the usual residence of the bride. Excluding Åland Islands. - La répartition entre résidence urbaine et résidence rurale fait référence au lieu de résidence habituel de la mariée. Non compris les Îles d'Åland.

[36] Data for urban and rural exclude events corresponding to nationals residing outside the country, which may be included in the total. - Les données relatives à les categories urbaine et rurale n'englobent pas les faits d'état civil qui concernent les nationaux se trouvant à l'étranger, lesquels faits peuvent être inclus au total.

[37] The urban and rural categories do not include the data of foreigners, persons of unknown residence and the homeless, whereas the total category includes them. - Les chiffres portant sur la population urbaine et rurale n' incluent pas les données relatives aux étrangers, aux personnes dont la résidence n'est pas connue et aux personnes sans domicile fixe, à l'inverse, le total les inclut.

[38] Marriages of couples of which at least one partner is recorded in a Dutch municipal register, irrespective of the country where the marriage was performed. Including same sex marriages. Data exclude registered partnerships. - Correspond aux mariages pour lesquels au moins l'un des partenaires est inscrit sur un registre municipal néerlandais, quel que soit le pays dans lequel le mariage est célébré. Y compris les mariages entre personnes du même sexe. Les données ne comprennent pas les partenariats d'un pacte civil enregistrés.

[39] Marriages registered by place of occurrence of marriage. Including same sex marriages. - Mariages enregistrés en fonction du lieu de l'événement. Y compris les mariages entre personnes du même sexe.

[40] Includes civil and religious marriages as well as not specified. - Englobe les mariages civils et religieux et ceux pour lesquels rien n'a été indiqué.

[41] If either the groom or the bride (or both) is (are) resident in San Marino, their marriage is included in these data, independently of the place of occurrence of marriage. - Si l'un ou les deux époux résident à Saint-Marin, leur mariage est compris dans ces données, quel que soit le lieu où a été conclu le mariage.

[42] Excludes data for Kosovo and Metohia. - Sans les données pour le Kosovo et Metohia.

[43] Residence refers to residence of groom. - La catégorie « résidence » correspond au lieu de résidence du jeune marié.

[44] Data refer to residence of groom or bride before marriage. - Données relatives au lieu de résidence du marié ou de la mariée avant le mariage.

[45] Data based on the residence of groom if he has permanent address in the country, otherwise, based on the residence of bride. If neither partner is a permanent resident, the marriage is not included in the official statistics. - Les données sont fondées sur la résidence du marié si celui-ci a une adresse permanente dans le pays, sinon elles sont fondées sur la résidence de la mariée. Si aucun des deux partenaires n'est un résident permanent, le mariage n'apparaît pas dans les statistiques officielles.

[46] From 2014, urban refers to urban centers and areas under the influence of urban centers. - A partir de 2014, le territoire urbain inclut l'espace des centres urbains ainsi que l'espace sous influence des centres urbains.

[47] The Government of Ukraine has informed the United Nations that it is not in a position to provide statistical data concerning the Autonomous Republic of Crimea and the city of Sevastopol. - Le gouvernement Ukrainien a informé l'ONU qu'il n'est pas en mesure de fournir des données statistiques concernant la République autonome de Crimée et la ville de Sébastopol.

[48] Excluding Channel Islands (Guernsey and Jersey) and Isle of Man, shown separately, if available. Data tabulated by date of occurrence for England and Wales, and by date of registration for Northern Ireland and Scotland. - Non compris les îles Anglo-Normandes (Guernesey et Jersey) et l'île de Man, qui font l'objet de rubriques distinctes, si disponible. Données exploitées selon la date de

l'événement pour l'Angleterre et le pays de Galles, et selon la date de l'enregistrement pour l'Irlande du Nord et l'Ecosse.

[49] Including non-residents. Excluding Niue, shown separately, which is part of Cook Islands, but because of remoteness is administered separately. - Y compris les non-résidents. Non compris Nioué, qui fait l'objet d'une rubrique distincte et qui fait partie des îles Cook, mais qui, en raison de son éloignement, est administrée séparément.

[50] Including United States military personnel, their dependants and contract employees. - Y compris les militaires des Etats-Unis, les membres de leur famille les accompagnant et les agents contractuels des Etats-Unis.

[51] Including same sex marriages. Data refer to marriages and civil unions by residence of 'partner 2'. - Y compris les mariages entre personnes du même sexe. Les données concernent les mariages et les unions civiles selon la résidence du « partenaire 2 ».

[52] Data have been randomly rounded. - Ces données ont été arrondies de façon aléatoire.

[53] Data cover the period from 1 July of the previous year to 30 June of the present year. - Pour la période allant du 1er juillet de l'année précédente au 30 juin de l'année en cours.

[54] Source: Births, Deaths, and Marriages Registration Division, Samoa Bureau of Statistics. - Source : Division de l'enregistrement des naissances, des décès et des mariages du Bureau de statistique du Samoa.

Table 23 - *Demographic Yearbook 2018*

Table 23 presents the marriages cross-classified by age of groom and age of bride for the latest available year between 2009 and 2018.

Description of variables: Marriage is defined as the act, ceremony or process by which the legal relationship of spouses is constituted. The legality of the union may be established by civil, religious or other means as recognized by the laws of each country[1].

Marriage statistics in this table, therefore, include both first marriages and remarriages after divorce, widowhood or annulment. They do not, unless otherwise noted, include resumption of marriage ties after legal separation. These statistics refer to the number of marriages performed, and not to the number of persons marrying.

Age is defined as age at last birthday, that is, the difference between the date of birth and the date of the occurrence of the event, expressed in completed solar years. The age classification used for brides in this table is the following: under 15 years, 5-year age groups through 90-94, and 95 years and over, depending on the availability of data. Age classification for grooms is restricted to: under 15 years, 5-year age groups from 15 to 59, and 60 years and over.

In an effort to provide interpretation of these statistics, countries or areas providing data on marriages by age of groom and bride have been requested to specify "the minimum legal age at which marriage can take place with and without parental consent". This information is presented in the table 23-1 below.

Reliability of data: Data from civil registers of marriages that are reported as incomplete (less than 90 per cent completeness) or of unknown completeness are considered unreliable and are set in *italics* rather than in roman type. Table 23 and the technical notes for that table provide more detailed information on the completeness of marriage registration. For more information about the quality of vital statistics data in general, see Section 4.2 of the Technical Notes.

Limitations: Statistics on marriages by age of groom and age of bride are subject to the same qualifications as have been set forth for vital statistics in general and marriage statistics in particular as discussed in Section 4 of the Technical Notes.

The fact that marriage is a legal event, unlike birth and death that are biological events, has implications for international comparability of data. Marriage has been defined, for statistical purposes, in terms of the laws of individual countries or areas. These laws vary throughout the world. In addition, comparability is further limited because some countries or areas compile statistics only for civil marriages although religious marriages may also be legally recognized; in other countries or areas, the only available records are church registers and, therefore, the statistics may not reflect marriages that are civil marriages only.

Because in many countries or areas marriage is a civil legal contract which, to establish its legality, must be celebrated before a civil officer, it follows that for these countries or areas registration would tend to be almost automatic at the time of, or immediately following, the marriage ceremony. This factor should be kept in mind when considering the reliability of data, described above.

Because these statistics are classified according to age, they are subject to the limitations with respect to accuracy of age reporting similar to those already discussed in connection with Section 3.1.3 of the Technical Notes. It is probable that biases are less pronounced in marriage statistics, because information is obtained from the persons concerned and since marriage is a legal act, the participants are likely to give correct information. However, in some countries or areas, there appears to be a concentration of marriages at the legal minimum age for marriage and at the age at which valid marriage may be contracted without parental consent, indicating perhaps an overstatement in some cases to comply with the law.

Aside from the possibility of age misreporting, it should be noted that marriage patterns at younger ages, that is, for ages up to 24 years, are influenced to a large extent by laws regarding the minimum age for marriage.

Factors that may influence age reporting, particularly at older ages include an inclination to understate the age of the bride in order that it may be equal to or less than that of the groom.

The absence of data in the unknown age group does not necessarily indicate completely accurate reporting and tabulation of the age item. It is sometimes an indication that the unknowns have been eliminated by assigning ages to them before tabulation, or by proportionate distribution after tabulation.

Another age-reporting factor that must be kept in mind in using these data is the variation that may result from calculating age at marriage from year of birth rather than from day, month and year of birth. Information on this factor is given in footnotes when known.

Earlier data: Marriages by age of groom and age of bride have been shown for the latest available year in most issues of the *Demographic Yearbook*. Data cross-classified by age of groom and bride have been presented in previous issues featuring marriage and divorce statistics. For information on the specific topics and the years covered, readers should consult the Historical Index.

23-1 Minimum legal age at which marriage can take place

Country or area	With parental consent		Without parental consent	
	Groom	Bride	Groom	Bride
Africa				
Andorra	14	14	16	16
Botswana	18	18	21	21
Burkina Faso[2]	18	15	20	17
Burundi[5]			21	18
Cameroon[3]	18	15	21	18
Congo	16-17	16-17	18	18
Egypt	18	18		
Eswatini	18	18	21	21
Ghana			18	18
Guinea	18	18	21	21
Liberia	16	16	21	18
Libya[4]	18	18		
Malawi[5]			18	18
Mauritius	16	16	18	18
Morocco[5]			18	18
Namibia	18	18	21	21
Saint Helena ex. Dep.	16	16	21	21
Senegal	Under 18	Under 18	18	18
Seychelles	16	16	18	18
Sierra Leone[5]			18	18
South Africa[6]	Under 21	Under 21	21	21
Tunisia	15	15	18	18
Uganda[5, 7]			18	18
Zimbabwe	16	16	18	18
America, North				
Anguilla	16	16	18	18
Aruba[8]	16	16	18	18
Bermuda	16	16	18	18
Canada[9]	16	16	18	18

Country or area	With parental consent		Without parental consent	
	Groom	Bride	Groom	Bride
Cayman Islands	16	16	18	18
Costa Rica	15	15	18	18
Cuba	16	14	18	16
Curaçao	16	16	18	18
Dominican Republic	16	15	18	18
El Salvador	Under 18	Under 18	18	18
Greenland[5]			18	18
Jamaica	16	16	18	18
Mexico[10]	Under 18	Under 18	18	18
Montserrat[11]	16	16	18	18
Nicaragua	16	16	21	21
Panama			18	18
Puerto Rico	17	17	21	21
Saint Helena	16	16	21	21
Saint Vincent and the Grenadines			18	18
Trinidad and Tobago[12]	Under 18	Under 18	18	18
America, South				
Argentina	18	16	21	21
Bolivia (Plurinational State of)[13]	16	14	18	18
Brazil	16	16	18	18
Chile	16	16	18	18
Colombia	14	14	18	18
Ecuador			18	18
Suriname	17	15	21	21
Uruguay	16	16	18	18
Venezuela (Bolivarian Republic of)	16	14	18	18
Asia				
Armenia			18	17
Azerbaijan	18	17		
Bahrain			15	
Cambodia			18	18
China, Hong Kong SAR	16	16	21	21
China, Macao SAR	16	16	18	18
Cyprus	16	16	18	18
Georgia	16	16	18	18
Indonesia			19	16
Iran (Islamic Republic of)	18	15		
Israel[5]			18	18

Country or area	With parental consent		Without parental consent	
	Groom	Bride	Groom	Bride
Japan	18	16	20	20
Jordan	18	18		
Kazakhstan	16	16	18	18
Kyrgyzstan[5]			16	16
Malaysia[14]	18	16 and 18	18 and 21	18 and 21
Mongolia			18	18
Nepal	18	18	20	20
Oman[5]			18	18
Philippines	18	18	21	21
Republic of Korea	18	18	19	19
Singapore[15]	Under 21	Under 21	21	21
State of Palestine[16]		14.5	15.5	
Tajikistan	17	17	18	18
Turkey	16	16	18	18
Uzbekistan	18	17		
Europe				
Åland Islands[19]			18	18
Albania	Under 18	Under 18	18	18
Austria[17]	16	16	18	18
Belarus	15	15	18	18
Belgium[5]			18	18
Bosnia and Herzegovina			18	18
Bulgaria	16	16	18	18
Croatia	16	16	18	18
Czechia[18]	16	16	18	18
Denmark	15	15	18	18
Estonia	15	15	18	18
Faeroe Islands[5]			18	18
Finland[19]			18	18
France[5]			18	18
Germany[20]	16	16	18	18
Gibraltar	16	16	18	18
Greece[21]			18	18
Hungary	16	16	18	18
Iceland	No limit	No limit	18	18
Ireland[5, 22]			18	18
Isle of Man	16	16	18	18
Italy	16	16	18	18
Jersey	16	16	18	18
Latvia	16	16	18	18

Country or area	With parental consent		Without parental consent	
	Groom	Bride	Groom	Bride
Liechtenstein[17]			18	18
Lithuania[23]	15	15	18	18
Luxembourg			18	18
Malta			16	16
Montenegro	16	16	18	18
Netherlands	16	16	18	18
North Macedonia	16	16	18	18
Norway	16	16	18	18
Poland[24]			18	18
Portugal	16	16	18	18
Republic of Moldova			18	16
Romania[25]	16	16	18	18
Russian Federation	16	16	18	18
San Marino[26]	16	14	18	18
Serbia[27]	16	16	18	18
Slovakia			16	16
Slovenia	15	15	18	18
Spain	16	16	18	18
Sweden[28]			18	18
Switzerland			18	18
Ukraine[17]	16	16	18	18
United Kingdom of Great Britain and Northern Ireland	16	16	18	18
Oceania				
Australia[29]	16	16	18	18
Cook Islands	16	16	21	21
Guam[30]	17	17	18	18
New Caledonia			18	18
New Zealand	16	16	18	18

NOTES

[1] *Principles and Recommendations for a Vital Statistics System Revision 3,* Sales No. E.13.XVII.10, United Nations, New York, 2014.

[2] In addition, an age waiver may be granted by a civil court for a serious reason from 15 years for women and 18 years for men.

[3] Marriages can be exceptionally authorised by the President of the Republic for brides who are at least 13 years old without parental consent.

[4] According to the Islamic law, marriage requires parental consent. Consent of the bride herself, as well as the guardian's consent are fundamental in the marriage contract. Young men usually choose the consent of the parents. Minimum age at marriage is usually 18 years. According to the law, marriage is not restricted to individuals over the age of 18 years.

[5] The minimum legal age at which marriage can take place is the same with or without parental consent.

[6] Marriages under the age of 18 can be performed with parental consent or with judicial permission if parental consent has been unreasonably refused. Additionally, boys under the age of 18 and girls under the age of 16 may also be required to seek the consent of the Minister of Home Affairs.

[7] As reported by Uganda Bureau of Statistics, marriages with or without parental consent may occur much earlier than 18 years of age.

[8] The legal minimum marriage age is 18, with two exceptions: if the persons concerned are older than 16 and the woman is pregnant or has given birth or the Minister of Security and Justice grants a dispensation based on their request.

[9] Marriage is under provincial and territory legislations. Without parental consent, the minimum legal age at which marriage can take place is 18 years of age in all provinces and territories in Canada except in British Columbia, Newfoundland and Labrador, Nova Scotia, Nunavut, and Yukon where the minimum legal age is 19 years. With parental consent, the minimum legal age is 16 years in all provinces except in Northwest Territories, Nunavut, and Yukon. With parental consent, in Northwest Territories and Yukon, the minimum legal age is 15 years whereas in Nunavut, the minimum legal age is 18 years.

[10] Each of the 31 Federal States and the Federal District has its own civil code for marriage. Marriages under 18 require parental consent. Additionally, in the Federal District and in the states of Guanajuato, Morelos, Puebla and San Luis Potosí the minimum age with parental consent is 16 for both bride and groom and in the states of Michoacán, Nayarit, Sinaloa and Sonora the minimum age with parental consent is 14 for the bride and 16 for the groom.

[11] Consent can be given by a guardian or a person who has custody of the child wishing to marry. Also, the Governor has discretion to permit persons as young as 15 years and 1 day old to marry, if he thinks that getting married is in the best interest of the persons who are intending to marry and the persons in this instance must have also received the necessary consent.

[12] With parental consent, age for marriage is 14 years for males and 12 years for females in a civil marriage; 16 years for males and 12 years for females in a Muslim marriage; 18 years for males and 14 years for females in a Hindu marriage; and 18 years for males and 16 for females in Orisa marriage.

[13] Grooms younger than 16 and brides younger than 14 need court authorization.

[14] For marriage with parental consent, it is 18 years of age for males whereas it is 18 years of age for non-Muslim females and 16 years of age for Muslim females. Without parental consent, it is 21 years of age for non-Muslims and 18 years of age for Muslims.

[15] Specified minimum legal marriage age refers to marriages contracted under the Women's Charter. For Muslim marriages under the Administration of Muslim Law Act, no marriage shall be solemnised when either party is below the age of 18 years. Notwithstanding that, Muslim women below the age of 18 years who have attained the age of puberty may be married under the Administration of the Muslim Law Act.

[16] The legal marriage age for females is 14 years, 6 months and 22 days. There must be parental consent (father or brother if the father is dead). The legal marriage age for males is 15 years, 6 months and 21 days. Parental consent is not required.

[17] Persons less than 18 years old need a decision of the court.

[18] The court may, for important reasons, allow the marriage of a minor over 16 years.

[19] Persons less than 18 years old need the permission of the Ministry of Justice.

[20] Marriage at 16-17 years of age requires that the other spouse be an adult (18 years or older) and an exemption from the requirement of majority by a competent family court.

[21] Under some conditions (e.g. pregnancy) the marriage can take place without age restrictions.

[22] An exemption on the minimum age can be granted by court order if granting of such an exemption is in the best interests of the parties to the intended marriage and good reasons for the application can be demonstrated.

[23] In addition to parental consent, persons less than 18 years old need judicial approval. In case of pregnancy, marriage can be allowed below 15 years of age.

[24] Females can marry at the age of 16 or 17 years with parental and court consent.

[25] Marriage for persons under 18 years requires parental consent, a medical certificate and the agreement by the local family court.

[26] The heads of the State of San Marino can allow marriages of males of 14 years and older and females of 12 years and older.

[27] Marriage is not allowed for persons below the age of 18; only the court may, for good cause, permit marriage to a minor who has attained the age of 16 years of age, and attained physical and mental maturity to exercise the rights and responsibilities of marriage. Parental consent is not required.

[28] With parental consent, no limit but authorities must approve; without parental consent, 18 years of age for Swedish citizens.

29 Persons 16 or 17 years old need the court approval.

30 Under 18, both a court order and parent or legal guardian consent are needed.

Tableau 23 – *Annuaire démographique 2018*

Le tableau 23présente des statistiques concernant les mariages classés selon l'âge de l'époux et selon l'âge de l'épouse pour les années où les données sont disponibles entre 2009 et 2018.

Description des variables : le mariage désigne l'acte, la cérémonie ou la procédure qui établit un rapport légal entre les époux. L'union peut être rendue légale par une procédure civile ou religieuse, ou par toute autre procédure, conformément à la législation du pays[1].

Les statistiques de la nuptialité présentées dans ce tableau comprennent donc les premiers mariages et les remariages faisant suite à un divorce, un veuvage ou une annulation. Toutefois, sauf indication contraire, elles ne comprennent pas les unions reconstituées après une séparation légale. Ces statistiques se rapportent au nombre de mariages célébrés, non au nombre de personnes qui se marient.

L'âge désigne l'âge au dernier anniversaire, c'est-à-dire la différence entre la date de naissance et la date de l'événement, exprimée en années solaires révolues. Le classement par âge pour l'épouse utilisé dans ce tableau comprend les groupes suivants : moins de 15 ans, groupes quinquennaux jusqu'à 90-94 ans, et 95 ans et plus, selon la disponibilité des données. Le classement par âge pour l'époux est : moins de 15 ans, groupes quinquennal de 15 jusqu' à 59 ans et 60 ans et plus.

Dans un effort de fournir l'interprétation de ces statistiques, les pays ou les zones fournissant des données sur les mariages par l'âge de l'épouse et de par l'âge de l'époux ont été demandés d'indiquer « l'âge légal minimum avec auquel le mariage peut avoir lieu avec et sans consentement parental ». Cette information est présentée dans le tableau 24-1 ci-dessous.

Fiabilité des données : les données sur les mariages issues des registres de l'état civil qui sont déclarées incomplètes (degré de complétude inférieur à 90 p. 100) ou dont le degré de complétude n'est pas connu sont jugées douteuses et apparaissent en italique et non en caractères romains. Le tableau 23 et les notes techniques s'y rapportant présentent des renseignements plus détaillés sur le degré de complétude de l'enregistrement des mariages. Pour plus de précisions sur la qualité des données reposant sur les statistiques de l'état civil en général, voir la section 4.2 des notes techniques.

Insuffisance des données : les statistiques des mariages selon l'âge de l'époux et selon l'âge de l'épouse appellent les mêmes réserves que celles formulées à propos des statistiques de l'état civil en général et des statistiques de la nuptialité en particulier (voir la section 4 des Notes techniques).

Le fait que le mariage soit un acte juridique, à la différence de la naissance et du décès, qui sont des faits biologiques, a des répercussions sur la comparabilité internationale des données. Aux fins de la statistique, le mariage est défini par la législation de chaque pays ou zone. Cette législation varie d'un pays à l'autre. La comparabilité est limitée en outre du fait que certains pays et zones ne réunissent des statistiques que pour les mariages civils, bien que les mariages religieux y soient également reconnus par la loi ; dans d'autres, les seuls relevés disponibles sont les registres des églises et, en conséquence, les statistiques peuvent ne pas rendre compte des mariages exclusivement civils.

Le mariage étant, dans de nombreux pays ou zones, un contrat juridique civil qui, pour être légal, doit être conclu devant un officier d'état civil, il s'ensuit que, dans ces pays ou zones, l'enregistrement se fait à peu près systématiquement au moment de la cérémonie ou immédiatement après. Il faut tenir compte de cet élément lorsque l'on évalue la fiabilité des données, dont il est question plus haut.

Étant donné que ces statistiques sont classées selon l'âge, elles appellent les mêmes réserves concernant l'exactitude des déclarations d'âge que celles dont il a déjà été question à la section 3.1.3 des Notes techniques. Il est probable que les statistiques de la nuptialité sont moins faussées par ce genre d'erreur, car les renseignements sont donnés par les intéressés eux-mêmes, et, comme le mariage est un acte juridique, il y a toutes chances que leurs déclarations soient exactes. Toutefois, dans certains pays ou zones, il semble y avoir une concentration de mariages à l'âge minimal légal de nubilité ainsi qu'à l'âge auquel le mariage peut être valablement contracté sans le consentement des parents, ce qui peut indiquer que certains déclarants se vieillissent pour se conformer à la loi.

Outre la possibilité d'erreurs dans les déclarations d'âge, il convient de noter que la législation fixant l'âge minimal de nubilité influe notablement sur les caractéristiques de la nuptialité pour les premiers âges, c'est-à-dire jusqu'à 24 ans.

Parmi les facteurs pouvant exercer une influence sur les déclarations d'âge, en particulier celles qui sont faites par des personnes plus âgées, il faut citer la tendance à diminuer l'âge de l'épouse de façon qu'il soit égal ou inférieur à celui de l'époux.

Si aucun nombre ne figure dans la rangée réservée aux âges inconnus, cela ne signifie pas nécessairement que les déclarations d'âge et l'exploitation des données par âge aient été tout à fait exactes. C'est parfois une indication que l'on a attribué un âge aux personnes d'âge inconnu avant l'exploitation des données ou qu'elles ont été réparties proportionnellement entre les différents groupes après cette opération.

Il importe de ne pas oublier non plus, lorsque l'on utilisera ces données, que l'on calcule parfois l'âge des conjoints au moment du mariage sur la base de l'année de naissance seulement et non d'après la date exacte (jour, mois et année) de naissance. Des renseignements à ce sujet sont donnés en note chaque fois que possible.

Donnés publiées antérieurement : on trouve dans la plupart des éditions de l'*Annuaire démographique* des statistiques concernant les mariages selon l'âge de l'époux et selon l'âge de l'épouse qui ont été établies à partir des données les plus récentes dont on disposait à l'époque. Des données croisant l'âge des époux ont été présentées dans des éditions antérieurs, plus particulièrement consacrées aux statistiques de la nuptialité et de la divortialité. Pour plus de précisions concernant les années et les sujets pour lesquels des données ont été publiées, se reporter à l'index historique.

23-1 L'âge légal minimum auquel le mariage peut avoir lieu

Pays ou zone	Avec consentement parental		Sans consentement parental	
	Epoux	Epouse	Epoux	Epouse
Afrique				
Afrique du Sud[2]	Moins de 21	Moins de 21	21	21
Andorre	14	14	16	16
Botswana	18	18	21	21
Burkina Faso[3]	18	15	20	17
Burundi[6]			21	18
Cameroun[4]	18	15	21	18
Congo	16-17	16-17	18	18
Egypte	18	18		
Eswatini	18	18	21	21
Ghana			18	18
Guinée	18	18	21	21
Libéria	16	16	21	21
Libye[5]	18	18		
Malawi[6]			18	18
Maurice	16	16	18	18
Maroc[6]			18	18
Namibie	18	18	21	21
Ouganda[6, 7]			18	18
Sainte-Hélène sans dép.	16	16	21	21
Sénégal	Moins de 18	Moins de 18	18	18
Seychelles	16	16	18	18
Sierra Leone[6]			18	18
Tunisie	15	15	18	18

Pays ou zone	Avec consentement parental		Sans consentement parental	
	Epoux	Epouse	Epoux	Epouse
Zimbabwe	16	16	18	18
Amérique du Nord				
Anguilla	16	16	18	18
Aruba[8]	16	16	18	18
Bermudes	16	16	18	18
Canada[9]	16	16	18	18
Costa Rica	15	15	18	18
Cuba	16	14	18	16
Curaçao	16	16	18	18
El Salvador	Moins de 18	Moins de 18	18	18
Groenland[6]			18	18
Îles Caïmanes	16	16	18	18
Jamaïque	16	16	18	18
Mexique[10]	Moins de 18	Moins de 18	18	18
Montserrat[11]	16	16	18	18
Nicaragua	16	16	21	21
Panama			18	18
Porto Rico	17	17	21	21
République dominicaine	16	15	18	18
Sainte-Hélène	16	16	21	21
Saint-Vincent-et-les Grenadines			18	18
Trinité-et-Tobago[12]	Moins de 18	Moins de 18	18	18
Amérique du Sud				
Argentine	18	16	21	21
Bolivie (État plurinational de)[13]	16	14	18	18
Brésil	16	16	18	18
Chili	16	16	18	18
Colombie	14	14	18	18
Equateur			18	18
Suriname	17	15	21	21
Uruguay	16	16	18	18
Venezuela (République bolivarienne du)	16	14	18	18
Asie				
Arménie			18	17
Azerbaïdjan	18	17		
Bahreïn			15	

Pays ou zone	Avec consentement parental		Sans consentement parental	
	Epoux	Epouse	Epoux	Epouse
Cambodge			18	18
Chine, Hong Kong RAS	16	16	21	21
Chine, Macao RAS	16	16	18	18
Chypre	16	16	18	18
État de Palestine[14]		14.5	15.5	
Géorgie	16	16	18	18
Indonésie			19	16
Iran (République islamique d')	18	15		
Israël[6]			18	18
Japon	18	16	20	20
Jordanie	18	18		
Kazakhstan	16	16	18	18
Kirghizistan[6]			16	16
Malaisie[15]	18	16 et 18	18 et 21	18 et 21
Mongolie			18	18
Népal	18	18	20	20
Oman[6]			18	18
Ouzbékistan	18	17		
Philippines	18	18	21	21
République de Corée	18	18	19	19
Singapour[16]	Moins de 21	Moins de 21	21	21
Tadjikistan	17	17	18	18
Turquie	16	16	18	18
Europe				
Albanie	Moins de 18	Moins de 18	18	18
Allemagne[17]	16	16	18	18
Autriche[18]	16	16	18	18
Bélarus	15	15	18	18
Belgique**Error! Bookmark not defined.**			18	18
Bosnie-Herzégovine			18	18
Bulgarie	16	16	18	18
Croatie	16	16	18	18
Danemark	15	15	18	18
Espagne	16	16	18	18
Estonie	15	15	18	18
Fédération de Russie	16	16	18	18
Finlande[19]			18	18

Pays ou zone	Avec consentement parental		Sans consentement parental	
	Epoux	Epouse	Epoux	Epouse
France[6]			18	18
Gibraltar	16	16	18	18
Grèce[20]			18	18
Hongrie	16	16	18	18
Île de Man	16	16	18	18
Îles d'Åland[19]			18	18
Îles Féroé[6]			18	18
Irlande[6, 21]			18	18
Islande	Pas de limites	Pas de limites	18	18
Italie	16	16	18	18
Jersey	16	16	18	18
Lettonie	16	16	18	18
Liechtenstein[18]			18	18
Lituanie[22]	15	15	18	18
Luxembourg			18	18
Macédoine du Nord	16	16	18	18
Malte			16	16
Monténégro	16	16	18	18
Norvège	16	16	18	18
Pays-Bas	16	16	18	18
Pologne[23]			18	18
Portugal	16	16	18	18
République de Moldova			18	16
Roumanie[24]	16	16	18	18
Royaume-Uni de Grande-Bretagne et d'Irlande du Nord	16	16	18	18
San Marino[25]	16	14	18	18
Serbie[26]	16	16	18	18
Slovaquie			16	16
Slovénie	15	15	18	18
Suède[27]			18	18
Suisse			18	18
Tchéquie[28]	16	16	18	18
Ukraine[18]	16	16	18	18
Océanie				
Australie[29]	16	16	18	18
Guam[30]	17	17	18	18
Îles Cook	16	16	21	21
Nouvelle-Calédonie			18	18

Pays ou zone	Avec consentement parental		Sans consentement parental	
	Epoux	Epouse	Epoux	Epouse
Nouvelle-Zélande	16	16	18	18

NOTES

[1] *Principes et recommandations pour un système de statistique de l'état civil, troisième révision,* numéro de vente : E.13.XVII.10, publication des Nations Unies, New York, 2014.

[2] Il est possible de se marier avant 18 ans avec consentement parental, ou autorisation judiciaire si le consentement parental a été refusé sans motif raisonnable. De plus, les garçons âgés de moins de 18 ans et les filles âgées de moins de 16 ans peuvent être également tenus de demander le consentement du Ministère de l'intérieur.

[3] De plus, une dispense d'âge peut être accordée par un tribunal civil pour motif grave à partir de 15 ans pour les femmes et de 18 ans pour les hommes.

[4] Par ailleurs, à défaut d'avoir l'âge requis pour se marier avec l'aval des parents, la jeune fille peut exceptionnellement être autorisée par le Président de la République à se marier à 13 ans.

[5] Conformément à la loi islamique, le mariage requiert le consentement parental. Le consentement de la mariée, elle-même ainsi que le consentement du tuteur sont fondamentaux dans le contrat de mariage. Les jeunes hommes choisissent habituellement le consentement des parents. L'âge minimum du mariage est généralement 18 ans. Conformément à la loi, le mariage n'est pas limité aux individus âgés de plus de 18 ans.

[6] L'âge minimum légal du mariage est le même avec ou sans le consentement parental.

[7] Tel que le signale l'"Uganda Bureau of Statistics", les mariages avec ou sans le consentement parental peuvent se produire beaucoup plus tôt que 18 ans.

[8] L'âge minimum légal du mariage est 18 ans, avec deux exceptions : si les personnes en cause ont plus de 16 ans et la femme est enceinte ou a accouché, ou si le Ministre de la sécurité et de la justice leur a accordé une dispense sur leur demande.

[9] Le mariage est en vertu des législations provinciales et territoriales. Sans le consentement des parents, l'âge minimum légal du mariage est de 18 ans dans toutes les provinces et territoires du Canada sauf en Colombie-Britannique, Terre-Neuve-et-Labrador, la Nouvelle-Écosse, du Nunavut et du Yukon, où l'âge minimum légal est de 19 ans. Avec le consentement des parents, l'âge minimum légal est de 16 ans dans toutes les provinces sauf dans les Territoires du Nord-Ouest, Nunavut et Yukon. Avec le consentement des parents, dans les Territoires du Nord-Ouest et le Yukon l'âge minimum légal est de 15 ans alors que dans le Nunavut, l'âge minimum légal est de 18 ans.

[10] Chacun des 31 Etats fédéraux et du District fédéral a son propre code civil pour le mariage. Avant 18 ans, il faut le consentement parental pour pouvoir se marier. De plus, dans le District fédéral et les États de Guanajuato, Morelos, Puebla et San Luis Potosí l'âge minimum, avec consentement parental, est de 16 ans pour le fiancé et la fiancée, et dans les États de Michoacán, Nayarit, Sinaloa et Sonora, l'âge minimum avec consentement parental est de 14 ans pour la fiancée et 16 ans pour le fiancé.

[11] Le consentement peut être donné par un tuteur ou une personne qui a la garde de l'enfant qui souhaitent se marier. En outre, le gouverneur a la faculté de permettre aux personnes âgées d'au moins 15 ans et 1 jour de se marier, s'il pense que le mariage est dans le meilleur intérêt des personnes qui ont l'intention de s'unir et que les personnes concernées aient également reçu le consentement nécessaire.

[12] Avec l'âge du le consentement parental, l'âge minimum du mariage pour se marier est de 14 ans pour les hommes et de 12 ans pour les femmes pour un mariage civil ; de 16 ans pour les hommes et de 12 ans pour les femmes pour un mariage musulman ; de 18 ans pour les hommes et de 14 ans pour les femmes pour un mariage hindou, et de18 ans pour les hommes et de 16 pour les femmes pour un mariage orisa.

[13] Il est nécessaire d'avoir une autorisation judiciaire pour se marier avant 16 ans pour les hommes et avant 14 ans pour les femmes.

[14] L'âge légal du mariage pour les femmes est de 14 ans, 6 mois et 22 jours. Le consentement parental (du père ou du frère si le père est mort) est requis. L'âge légal du mariage pour les hommes est de 15 ans, 6 mois et 21 jours. Le consentement parental n'est pas nécessaire.

[15] Pour le mariage avec le consentement parental, il est de 18 ans pour les hommes alors qu'il est de 18 ans pour les femmes non-musulmanes et il est de 16 ans pour les femmes musulmanes. Sans le consentement parental, il est de 21 ans pour les non-musulmans et de 18 ans pour les musulmans.

[16] L'âge minimum légal du mariage spécifié correspond à des mariages contractés en vertu de la Charte des femmes. Pour les mariages musulmans sous l'administration de la « Loi sur le Droit Musulman », aucun mariage ne doit être célébré lorsque l'une des parties est en dessous de l'âge de 18 ans. Néanmoins, les femmes musulmanes en dessous de l'âge de 18 ans qui ont atteint l'âge de la puberté peuvent être mariées dans le cadre de l'administration de la « Loi sur le Droit Musulman ».

[17] Le mariage à 16-17 ans exige que l'autre conjoint soit un adulte (18 ans ou plus) ainsi qu'une exemption de l'obligation de la majorité par un juge aux affaires familiales.

[18] Les personnes âgées de moins de 18 ans doivent obtenir l'autorisation de la justice.

[19] Les personnes âgées de moins de 18 ans doivent obtenir l'autorisation du ministère de la justice.

[20] Dans certaines conditions (par exemple la grossesse), le mariage peut avoir lieu sans restriction d'âge.

[21] Une exemption sur l'âge minimum peut être accordée par ordonnance du tribunal si l'octroi d'une telle exemption est dans le meilleur intérêt des parties ayant l'intention de se marier et si la demande est appuyée par de bonnes raisons.

[22] En plus du consentement parental, les personnes de moins de 18 ans doivent obtenir l'approbation judiciaire. En cas de grossesse, le mariage peut être autorisé en dessous de 15 ans.

[23] Les femmes peuvent se marier à l'âge de 16 ou 17 ans avec les autorisations des parents et du tribunal.

[24] Le mariage avant 18 ans exige le consentement parental, un certificat médical et l'autorisation du tribunal local de famille.

[25] Les chefs de l'État de Saint-Marin peuvent autoriser le mariage d'hommes de 14 ans et plus et de femmes de 12 ans et plus.

[26] Il n'est pas permis de se marier avant 18 ans ; seul le tribunal peut, pour un motif valable, y autoriser une personne mineure ayant atteint l'âge de 16 ans et parvenue à la maturité physique et mentale voulue pour exercer les droits et les responsabilités du mariage. Le consentement parental n'est pas requis.

[27] Avec le consentement des parents, aucune limite mais les autorités doivent approuver. Sans le consentement parental, l'âge minimum légal du mariage est de 18 ans pour les citoyens suédois.

[28] Il est possible de se marier de 16 ans par autorisation judiciaire pour des raisons importantes.

[29] Les personnes âgées 16 ou 17 ans doivent obtenir l'autorisation du tribunal.

[30] Le mariage avant 18 ans exige le consentement parental ou de personne qui a la garde de mineur, et l'autorisation du tribunal.

23. Marriages by age of groom and by age of bride: latest available year, 2009 - 2018
Mariages selon l'âge de l'époux et selon l'âge de l'épouse : dernière année disponible, 2009 - 2018

Continent, country or area, year, code[a] and age of bride / Continent, pays ou zone, date, code[a] et âge de l'épouse	Total	__	__	__	Age of groom - - âge de l'époux	__	__	__	__	__	__	__	Unknown Inconnu
		0-14	15-19	20-24	25-29	30-34	35-39	40-44	45-49	50-54	55-59	60+	
AFRICA - AFRIQUE													
Botswana[1,2]													
2017 (+U)													
Total	6 203	-	-	41	547	1 297	1 401	1 018	603	429	320	547	...
0 - 14	-	-	-	-	-	-	-	-	-	-	-	-	...
15 - 19	7	-	-	3	3	-	1	-	-	-	-	-	...
20 - 24	374	-	-	26	138	128	47	22	7	4	1	1	...
25 - 29	1 380	-	-	8	320	553	314	122	40	11	5	7	...
30 - 34	1 611	-	-	1	69	500	595	286	97	38	15	8	...
35 - 39	1 190	-	-	1	10	99	378	379	193	82	42	15	...
40 - 44	600	-	-	-	2	17	49	163	162	116	56	35	...
45 - 49	384	-	-	-	1	6	12	41	80	106	84	54	...
50 - 54	263	-	-	-	3	3	4	3	18	61	79	92	...
55 - 59	157	-	-	-	-	-	-	-	4	9	33	111	...
60 - 64	114	-	-	-	-	-	1	-	2	1	3	107	...
65 +	123	-	-	-	-	-	1	-	1	2	-	117	...
Congo													
2014 (+U)													
Total	3 625	...	5	32	275	581	647	512	427	1 146[s]	...	...	...
15 - 19	58	...	...	...	...	...	...	...	...	...	...	...	...
20 - 24	352	...	...	...	...	...	...	...	...	...	...	...	...
25 - 29	677	...	...	...	...	...	...	...	...	...	...	...	...
30 - 34	690	...	...	...	...	...	...	...	...	...	...	...	...
35 - 39	593	...	...	...	...	...	...	...	...	...	...	...	...
40 - 44	482	...	...	...	...	...	...	...	...	...	...	...	...
45 - 49	389	...	...	...	...	...	...	...	...	...	...	...	...
50 +	384	...	...	...	...	...	...	...	...	...	...	...	...
Egypt - Égypte													
2017 (+C)													
Total	912 606	11 898	168 833	380 721	191 823	63 605	30 354	19 854	14 851	11 035	7 302	12 330	...
0 - 14	270 030	7 319	85 729	129 287	41 233	4 958	785	289	163	97	49	121	...
15 - 19	343 095	3 485	72 733	175 825	72 642	13 020	2 806	1 056	643	401	196	288	...
20 - 24	146 595	738	7 721	63 589	48 305	15 988	5 207	2 330	1 228	735	370	384	...
25 - 29	68 241	198	1 561	8 620	22 751	17 646	8 038	4 026	2 436	1 425	836	704	...
30 - 34	36 485	66	491	1 976	4 842	8 909	7 908	5 021	3 169	1 958	1 091	1 054	...
35 - 39	20 915	21	202	586	1 231	2 143	4 222	4 529	3 142	2 162	1 293	1 384	...
40 - 44	11 455	33	126	288	411	602	946	1 958	2 557	1 839	1 233	1 462	...
45 - 49	6 585	6	80	169	163	186	299	454	1 173	1 616	1 115	1 324	...
50 - 54	2 916	4	28	71	56	52	70	119	243	636	714	923	...
55 - 59	1 352	6	15	43	35	29	27	22	56	111	332	676	...
60 - 64	508	3	12	16	12	5	10	17	13	22	53	345	...
65 - 69	222	3	6	6	4	3	3	5	-	11	9	172	...
70 - 74	624	4	55	118	76	37	22	19	23	16	6	248	...
75 +	3 583	12	74	127	62	27	11	9	5	6	5	3 245	...
Lesotho													
2013 (+U)													
Total	4 552	...	11	370	1 402	1 133	635	325	225	175	99	162	15
15 - 19	188	...	9	101	56	15	7	-	-	-	-	-	-
20 - 24	1 230	...	2	235	673	237	55	10	6	8	2	1	1
25 - 29	1 502	...	-	28	611	597	165	55	21	11	7	7	-
30 - 34	792	...	-	6	51	246	289	109	49	24	9	9	-
35 - 39	370	...	-	-	3	28	103	106	65	34	19	11	1
40 - 44	173	...	-	-	1	1	8	38	57	39	14	15	-
45 - 49	116	...	-	-	-	2	2	6	24	50	22	10	-
50 - 54	40	...	-	-	-	-	1	-	2	8	17	12	-
55 - 59	23	...	-	-	-	-	-	-	-	1	-	7	15
60 - 64	11	...	-	-	-	-	-	-	-	-	1	2	8
65 +	91	...	-	-	6	7	3	1	-	-	-	74	-
Unknown - Inconnu	16	...	-	-	1	-	2	-	-	-	-	-	13
2016 (+U)													
Total	2 640	...	6	149	666	689	473	290	131	236[s]	...	...	...
15 - 19	53	...	...	...	...	...	...	...	...	...	...	...	...
20 - 24	571	...	...	...	...	...	...	...	...	...	...	...	...
25 - 29	840	...	...	...	...	...	...	...	...	...	...	...	...
30 - 34	595	...	...	...	...	...	...	...	...	...	...	...	...
35 - 39	297	...	...	...	...	...	...	...	...	...	...	...	...
40 - 44	144	...	...	...	...	...	...	...	...	...	...	...	...

Continent, country or area, year, code[a] and age of bride / Continent, pays ou zone, date, code[a] et âge de l'épouse	Total	0-14	15-19	20-24	25-29	30-34	35-39	40-44	45-49	50-54	55-59	60+	Unknown Inconnu
AFRICA - AFRIQUE													
Lesotho													
2016													
45 - 49	68	...	...	...	...	...	...	...	...	...	...	...	...
50 +	72	...	...	...	...	...	...	...	...	...	...	...	...
Mauritius - Maurice[3]													
2018 (+C)													
Total	10 034	-	119	978	3 157	2 337	1 376	784	468	351	255	209	...
0 - 14	-	-	-	-	-	-	-	-	-	-	-	-	...
15 - 19	590	-	84	298	151	34	15	4	2	2	-	-	...
20 - 24	2 157	-	33	510	1 045	400	127	31	6	2	2	1	...
25 - 29	3 457	-	2	135	1 687	1 085	393	103	27	12	9	4	...
30 - 34	1 550	-	-	19	223	622	414	169	62	26	9	6	...
35 - 39	983	-	-	9	35	153	322	261	118	51	20	14	...
40 - 44	511	-	-	5	11	27	77	145	129	61	42	14	...
45 - 49	323	-	-	1	3	13	20	49	76	89	47	25	...
50 - 54	250	-	-	-	1	1	6	18	37	78	67	42	...
55 - 59	135	-	-	-	-	-	1	-	1	10	22	46	55
60 - 64	50	-	-	1	1	-	2	2	1	7	11	25	...
65 - 69	19	-	-	-	-	1	-	1	-	1	-	16	...
70 - 74	8	-	-	-	-	-	-	-	-	-	2	6	...
75 +	1	-	-	-	-	-	-	-	-	-	-	1	...
Saint Helena ex. dep. - Sainte-Hélène sans dép.													
2018 (C)													
Total	10	-	-	1	1	4	1	-	1	1	-	1	...
0 - 14	-	-	-	-	-	-	-	-	-	-	-	-	...
15 - 19	-	-	-	-	-	-	-	-	-	-	-	-	...
20 - 24	-	-	-	-	-	-	-	-	-	-	-	-	...
25 - 29	3	-	-	1	1	1	-	-	-	-	-	-	...
30 - 34	1	-	-	-	-	1	-	-	-	-	-	-	...
35 - 39	2	-	-	-	-	2	-	-	-	-	-	-	...
40 - 44	-	-	-	-	-	-	-	-	-	-	-	-	...
45 - 49	-	-	-	-	-	-	-	-	-	-	-	-	...
50 - 54	1	-	-	-	-	-	1	-	-	-	-	-	...
55 - 59	2	-	-	-	-	-	-	-	-	1	1	-	...
60 - 64	1	-	-	-	-	-	-	-	-	-	-	1	...
65 - 69	-	-	-	-	-	-	-	-	-	-	-	-	...
70 - 74	-	-	-	-	-	-	-	-	-	-	-	-	...
75 +	-	-	-	-	-	-	-	-	-	-	-	-	...
Seychelles[4]													
2018 (+C)													
Total	3 131	...	1	90	609	825	621	357	247	198	183[t]	...	...
15 - 19	11	...	-	4	6	-	-	1	-	-	-[t]	...	...
20 - 24	187	...	-	40	82	39	11	6	3	3	3[t]	...	...
25 - 29	833	...	1	24	330	279	123	41	17	13	5[t]	...	...
30 - 34	939	...	-	10	139	369	250	96	44	17	14[t]	...	...
35 - 39	541	...	-	5	32	103	174	112	60	30	25[t]	...	...
40 - 44	258	...	-	1	13	21	44	65	55	27	32[t]	...	...
45 - 49	177	...	-	5	2	4	12	28	43	53	30[t]	...	...
50 - 54	120	...	-	-	3	5	4	6	20	51	31[t]	...	...
55 +	65	...	-	1	2	5	3	2	5	4	43[t]	...	...
South Africa - Afrique du Sud													
2017 (...)													
Total	135 458	...	81	5 022	23 165	29 976	24 941	18 492	12 714	8 347	5 476	7 244	...
15 - 19	886	...	34	423	279	97	31	9	9	2	1	1	...
20 - 24	14 155	...	32	3 286	6 702	2 761	895	269	123	58	17	12	...
25 - 29	35 237	...	10	1 002	13 062	13 199	5 245	1 769	624	191	75	60	...
30 - 34	31 619	...	5	221	2 447	11 061	10 540	4 659	1 680	602	267	137	...
35 - 39	20 708	...	-	69	488	2 223	6 434	6 555	3 001	1 176	451	311	...
40 - 44	13 388	...	-	15	129	493	1 340	3 985	4 080	1 944	880	522	...
45 - 49	8 688	...	-	6	52	103	356	962	2 479	2 430	1 333	967	...
50 - 54	5 088	...	-	-	5	32	83	216	573	1 476	1 390	1 313	...
55 - 59	2 910	...	-	-	-	5	12	53	116	370	802	1 552	...
60 - 64	1 538	...	-	-	1	1	4	12	21	80	211	1 208	...
65 - 69	723	...	-	-	-	1	1	2	5	11	37	666	...
70 +	518	...	-	-	-	-	-	1	3	7	12	495	...

Continent, country or area, year, code[a] and age of bride / Continent, pays ou zone, date, code[a] et âge de l'épouse	Total	_	_	_	_	Age of groom - - âge de l'époux	_	_	_	_	_	_	Unknown Inconnu
		0-14	15-19	20-24	25-29	30-34	35-39	40-44	45-49	50-54	55-59	60+	

AFRICA - AFRIQUE

Tunisia - Tunisie
2017 (...)

	Total	0-14	15-19	20-24	25-29	30-34	35-39	40-44	45-49	50-54	55-59	60+	Unknown
Total	95 336	...	236[f]	4 258	23 220	32 204	17 803	7 518	3 403	2 177	1 439	3 078	...
0 - 19	5 001	...	...	...	...	...	...	...	...	...	...	...	...
20 - 24	23 486	...	...	...	...	...	...	...	...	...	...	...	...
25 - 29	32 524	...	...	...	...	...	...	...	...	...	...	...	...
30 - 34	17 227	...	...	...	...	...	...	...	...	...	...	...	...
35 - 39	8 196	...	...	...	...	...	...	...	...	...	...	...	...
40 - 44	4 326	...	...	...	...	...	...	...	...	...	...	...	...
45 - 49	2 381	...	...	...	...	...	...	...	...	...	...	...	...
50 +	2 195	...	...	...	...	...	...	...	...	...	...	...	...

AMERICA, NORTH - AMÉRIQUE DU NORD

Anguilla[5]
2013 (C)

	Total	0-14	15-19	20-24	25-29	30-34	35-39	40-44	45-49	50-54	55-59	60+	Unknown
Total	42	4	9	9	4	4	4	1	-	1	...	...	6
0 - 14	5	2	2	-	-	-	1	-	-	-	...	...	-
15 - 19	12	1	5	3	3	-	-	-	-	-	...	...	-
20 - 24	9	-	1	5	1	1	1	-	-	-	...	...	-
25 - 29	5	1	1	1	-	2	-	-	-	-	...	...	-
30 - 34	3	-	-	-	-	-	2	1	-	-	...	...	-
35 - 39	2	-	-	-	-	1	-	-	-	1	...	...	-
40 - 44	-	-	-	-	-	-	-	-	-	-	...	...	-
45 - 49	-	-	-	-	-	-	-	-	-	-	...	...	-
50 - 54	-	-	-	-	-	-	-	-	-	-	...	...	-
Unknown - Inconnu	6	-	-	-	-	-	-	-	-	-	...	...	6

Aruba
2017 (C)

	Total	0-14	15-19	20-24	25-29	30-34	35-39	40-44	45-49	50-54	55-59	60+	Unknown
Total	537	-	11	58	126	100	72	50	52	32	16	19	1
0 - 14	-	-	-	-	-	-	-	-	-	-	-	-	-
15 - 19	3	-	1	2	-	-	-	-	-	-	-	-	-
20 - 24	45	-	6	19	9	6	2	3	-	-	-	-	-
25 - 29	94	-	3	23	47	11	7	3	-	-	-	-	-
30 - 34	80	-	1	6	33	24	9	3	1	3	-	-	-
35 - 39	85	-	-	4	18	30	20	6	5	1	-	-	1
40 - 44	71	-	-	2	9	13	21	12	12	1	-	1	-
45 - 49	54	-	-	1	7	9	7	7	15	6	1	1	-
50 - 54	48	-	-	1	2	4	4	10	13	9	3	2	-
55 - 59	21	-	-	-	1	1	-	3	5	7	4	-	-
60 - 64	21	-	-	-	-	2	2	3	1	2	5	6	-
65 - 69	10	-	-	-	-	-	-	-	-	3	2	5	-
70 - 74	4	-	-	-	-	-	-	-	-	-	1	3	-
75 +	1	-	-	-	-	-	-	-	-	-	-	1	-

Bahamas
2013 (+C)

	Total	0-14	15-19	20-24	25-29	30-34	35-39	40-44	45-49	50-54	55-59	60+	Unknown
Total	2 122	...	...	...	104	472	498	325	223	163	106	226	5
25 - 29	171	...	...	...	24	64	39	16	3	5	-	20	-
30 - 34	543	...	...	...	27	202	161	62	42	13	12	24	-
35 - 39	391	...	...	...	9	61	131	87	48	24	12	18	1
40 - 44	249	...	...	...	5	21	53	70	50	28	9	13	-
45 - 49	219	...	...	...	5	24	33	28	38	44	23	24	-
50 - 54	192	...	...	...	6	21	28	26	22	38	21	30	-
55 - 59	133	...	...	...	6	17	20	17	9	6	18	39	1
60 +	216	...	...	...	22	62	33	17	10	4	11	56	1
Unknown - Inconnu	8	...	...	...	-	-	-	2	1	1	-	2	2

Bermuda - Bermudes
2017 (C)

	Total	0-14	15-19	20-24	25-29	30-34	35-39	40-44	45-49	50-54	55-59	60+	Unknown
Total	430	-	-	8	62	106	67	55	35	38	29	30	...
0 - 14	-	-	-	-	-	-	-	-	-	-	-	-	...
15 - 19	-	-	-	-	-	-	-	-	-	-	-	-	...
20 - 24	18	-	-	5	8	4	-	-	1	-	-	-	...
25 - 29	103	-	-	2	42	38	13	5	2	1	-	-	...
30 - 34	107	-	-	1	10	50	23	17	3	2	1	-	...
35 - 39	66	-	-	-	2	12	21	15	8	2	4	2	...

23. Marriages by age of groom and by age of bride: latest available year, 2009 - 2018
Mariages selon l'âge de l'époux et selon l'âge de l'épouse : dernière année disponible, 2009 - 2018 (continued - suite)

Continent, country or area, year, code[a] and age of bride / Continent, pays ou zone, date, code[a] et âge de l'épouse	Total	0-14	15-19	20-24	25-29	30-34	35-39	40-44	45-49	50-54	55-59	60+	Unknown Inconnu
AMERICA, NORTH - AMÉRIQUE DU NORD													
Bermuda - Bermudes													
2017													
40 - 44	48	-	-	-	-	1	9	15	12	7	3	1	...
45 - 49	26	-	-	-	-	1	1	1	7	12	3	1	...
50 - 54	18	-	-	-	-	-	-	1	1	9	6	1	...
55 - 59	23	-	-	-	-	-	-	1	1	3	10	8	...
60 - 64	15	-	-	-	-	-	-	-	-	2	2	11	...
65 - 69	5	-	-	-	-	-	-	-	-	-	-	5	...
70 - 74	1	-	-	-	-	-	-	-	-	-	-	1	...
75 +	-	-	-	-	-	-	-	-	-	-	-	-	...
Costa Rica[6]													
2018* (C)													
Total	23 604	-	181	2 481	5 309	5 145	3 300	2 196	1 551	1 155	855	1 399	32
0 - 14	-												
15 - 19	870	-	97	447	208	73	25	11	5	1	1	2	-
20 - 24	3 977	-	63	1 329	1 565	639	209	87	42	22	9	11	1
25 - 29	6 091	-	13	491	2 448	1 917	721	255	136	51	32	22	5
30 - 34	4 659	-	4	132	735	1 736	1 090	499	245	102	62	50	4
35 - 39	2 898	-	2	54	222	522	842	619	301	169	86	80	1
40 - 44	1 807	-	1	17	85	171	266	470	351	217	129	98	2
45 - 49	1 193	-	-	3	24	59	100	166	281	250	146	160	4
50 - 54	859	-	-	2	10	10	34	56	117	218	183	228	1
55 - 59	564	-	-	1	2	5	7	19	47	87	134	262	-
60 - 64	342	-	-	-	2	2	2	8	15	25	51	237	-
65 - 69	160	-	-	-	2	2	-	2	5	8	14	127	-
70 - 74	77	-	1	-	-	-	-	1	3	3	4	65	-
75 +	56	-	-	-	-	-	1	1	-	-	1	54	-
Unknown - Inconnu	51	-	5	6	9	3	3	3	2	3	3	-	14
Cuba[7]													
2017 (C)													
Total	53 684	-	880	5 241	9 472	8 167	5 600	5 890	5 606	4 903	2 825	5 099	1
0 - 14	45	-	14	17	7	4	2	-	-	1	-	-	-
15 - 19	3 495	-	527	1 440	887	363	118	50	45	34	14	17	-
20 - 24	8 182	-	206	2 258	2 973	1 361	561	343	208	145	54	73	-
25 - 29	10 378	-	76	904	3 373	2 782	1 262	918	497	302	128	136	-
30 - 34	7 509	-	22	295	1 185	1 984	1 550	1 118	699	344	151	161	-
35 - 39	4 643	-	11	136	425	741	894	1 014	713	426	150	133	-
40 - 44	5 121	-	6	71	255	426	611	1 154	1 222	841	271	264	-
45 - 49	5 050	-	6	48	153	246	347	769	1 224	1 185	579	493	-
50 - 54	4 184	-	4	35	93	138	151	317	681	1 083	746	936	-
55 - 59	2 217	-	1	17	44	52	49	118	188	354	488	906	-
60 - 64	1 370	-	1	10	38	36	30	44	66	124	145	876	-
65 - 69	759	-	-	3	13	11	12	16	29	34	57	584	-
70 - 74	438	-	5	2	14	11	9	16	14	14	24	329	-
75 +	293	-	1	5	12	12	4	13	20	16	18	191	1
Curaçao[8]													
2016 (C)													
Total	695	-	1	35	104	108	116	73	70	63	55	59	11
0 - 14	-												
15 - 19	9	-	1	5	1	-	1	1	-	-	-	-	-
20 - 24	82	-	-	20	36	9	9	5	3	-	-	-	-
25 - 29	141	-	-	9	46	35	33	8	6	2	2	-	-
30 - 34	133	-	-	1	18	50	23	16	16	2	4	3	-
35 - 39	75	-	-	-	2	9	26	15	10	8	3	2	-
40 - 44	70	-	-	-	1	3	12	21	13	13	5	2	-
45 - 49	57	-	-	-	-	2	9	5	14	13	8	6	-
50 - 54	60	-	-	-	-	-	1	1	8	19	21	10	-
55 - 59	31	-	-	-	-	-	-	2	1	3	10	15	-
60 - 64	11	-	-	-	-	-	-	-	-	2	1	8	-
65 - 69	10	-	-	-	-	-	-	-	-	1	1	8	-
70 - 74	3	-	-	-	-	-	-	-	-	-	-	3	-
75 +	2	-	-	-	-	-	-	-	-	-	-	2	-
Unknown - Inconnu	11	-	-	-	-	-	-	-	-	-	-	-	11

Continent, country or area, year, code[a] and age of bride / Continent, pays ou zone, date, code[a] et âge de l'épouse	Total	0-14	15-19	20-24	25-29	30-34	35-39	40-44	45-49	50-54	55-59	60+	Unknown Inconnu
AMERICA, NORTH - AMÉRIQUE DU NORD													
Dominican Republic - République dominicaine													
2017 (+C)													
Total	49 625	-	374	5 966	10 069	7 856	6 426	5 038	4 333	3 464	2 287	3 490	322
0 - 14	-	-	-	-	-	-	-	-	-	-	-	-	-
15 - 19	2 271	-	167	1 173	569	163	87	38	26	24	9	13	2
20 - 24	9 750	-	136	3 093	3 676	1 472	636	303	159	120	83	65	7
25 - 29	10 503	-	42	1 048	3 686	2 769	1 365	628	407	259	144	138	17
30 - 34	7 351	-	16	316	1 077	1 887	1 755	985	565	366	171	205	8
35 - 39	6 014	-	3	163	556	834	1 395	1 324	788	456	243	246	6
40 - 44	4 612	-	3	84	240	346	618	954	1 030	609	340	381	7
45 - 49	3 618	-	1	47	146	211	316	456	795	777	405	459	5
50 - 54	2 471	-	2	22	65	101	142	202	365	553	476	541	2
55 - 59	1 330	-	1	7	23	49	67	88	107	174	261	551	2
60 - 64	786	-	-	5	9	9	23	40	49	79	88	483	1
65 - 69	356	-	-	1	1	5	8	11	20	25	47	237	1
70 - 74	147	-	-	-	1	3	2	2	6	9	14	110	-
75 +	71	-	-	-	-	1	1	3	4	1	1	58	2
Unknown - Inconnu	345	-	3	7	20	6	11	4	12	12	5	3	262
El Salvador[9]													
2012 (...)													
Total	29 267	-	1 098	6 586	6 762	5 101	3 026	2 078	1 528	989	671	1 294	134
0 - 14	37	-	10	16	6	3	2	-	-	-	-	-	-
15 - 19	3 670	-	544	1 856	787	250	113	53	25	12	5	9	16
20 - 24	8 329	-	414	3 407	2 652	1 113	374	176	90	37	12	19	35
25 - 29	6 227	-	80	933	2 304	1 713	647	264	153	70	27	23	13
30 - 34	4 049	-	16	230	704	1 360	902	414	223	82	47	53	18
35 - 39	2 433	-	14	69	179	436	654	509	272	134	74	84	8
40 - 44	1 604	-	4	25	58	118	208	410	348	175	107	149	2
45 - 49	1 144	-	2	6	18	54	80	174	290	234	125	157	4
50 - 54	633	-	-	3	6	15	16	43	84	162	140	164	-
55 - 59	403	-	1	1	1	6	5	10	23	61	89	206	-
60 - 64	242	-	1	-	1	2	2	10	10	12	26	177	1
65 +	279	-	2	1	-	2	3	3	3	7	13	245	-
Unknown - Inconnu	217	-	10	39	46	29	20	12	7	3	6	8	37
Grenada - Grenade													
2014 (+C)													
Total	618	...	33	119	128	114	65	48	50	34	26		1
15 - 19	3	...	3	-	-	-	-	-	-	-	-	-	-
20 - 24	82	...	18	32	23	6	2	-	1	-	-	-	-
25 - 29	150	...	8	63	46	18	5	3	4	1	2		-
30 - 34	135	...	3	17	39	40	20	6	5	4	1		-
35 - 39	87	...	1	6	12	31	18	8	5	5	1		-
40 - 44	59	...	-	1	5	12	15	16	7	2	1		-
45 - 49	42	...	-	-	2	5	3	9	13	7	3		-
50 - 54	31	...	-	-	-	1	2	5	14	7	2		-
55 - 59	11	...	-	-	-	1	-	-	-	4	6		-
60 - 64	8	...	-	-	1	-	-	-	1	2	4		-
65 +	9	...	-	-	-	-	-	1	-	2	6		-
Unknown - Inconnu	1	...	-	-	-	-	-	-	-	-	-		1
Guatemala													
2016 (C)													
Total	69 613	...	3 770	22 309	17 775	9 964	5 310	3 047	2 002	1 483	1 170	2 775	8
15 - 19	10 278	...	1 955	6 003	1 714	391	128	35	29	10	6	6	1
20 - 24	25 405	...	1 567	12 810	7 847	2 188	616	202	87	39	23	25	1
25 - 29	14 915	...	188	2 798	6 294	3 787	1 151	354	162	78	39	62	2
30 - 34	7 674	...	44	556	1 491	2 705	1 687	637	269	124	72	89	-
35 - 39	4 196	...	12	107	327	696	1 288	952	396	182	99	137	-
40 - 44	2 273	...	-	21	69	145	321	594	530	272	135	185	1
45 - 49	1 513	...	-	10	20	34	84	201	367	390	180	226	1
50 - 54	1 089	...	2	3	9	9	23	55	123	279	282	304	-
55 - 59	868	...	-	-	2	6	7	14	31	69	239	499	1
60 - 64	602	...	-	-	1	1	4	-	8	26	66	496	-
65 +	792	...	-	-	-	1	-	3	-	14	29	745	-
Unknown - Inconnu	8	...	2	1	1	1	1	-	-	-	-	1	1

Continent, pays ou zone, date, code[a] et âge de l'épouse	Total	0-14	15-19	20-24	25-29	30-34	35-39	40-44	45-49	50-54	55-59	60+	Unknown Inconnu
AMERICA, NORTH - AMÉRIQUE DU NORD													
Mexico - Mexique[10]													
2017 (+C)													
Total	528 678	-	21 110	126 106	142 133	90 757	49 809	30 847	20 256	14 050	11 250	21 704	656
0 - 14	33	-	15	14	2	1	-		1			-	-
15 - 19	58 114	-	13 231	32 384	9 161	2 192	662	260	116	45	24	23	16
20 - 24	150 151	-	6 784	71 846	50 424	14 363	4 133	1 508	599	232	120	109	33
25 - 29	135 036	-	852	17 392	64 739	34 983	10 860	3 615	1 417	571	285	296	26
30 - 34	74 135	-	161	3 261	13 749	29 333	16 308	6 497	2 598	1 117	576	518	17
35 - 39	39 835	-	44	835	2 958	7 267	12 478	8 612	3 842	1 795	1 003	995	6
40 - 44	25 206	-	10	215	778	1 852	3 812	7 075	5 279	2 779	1 600	1 798	8
45 - 49	17 281	-	5	87	198	554	1 114	2 387	4 484	3 610	2 175	2 664	3
50 - 54	11 721	-	1	19	53	138	294	634	1 406	2 778	2 807	3 589	2
55 - 59	7 621	-		7	18	31	91	158	352	785	1 886	4 293	-
60 - 64	4 645	-		2	6	8	21	54	115	234	532	3 672	1
65 - 69	2 274	-		8	1	5	8	13	22	63	173	1 979	2
70 - 74	1 186	-			1	3	6	8	8	26	44	1 090	
75 +	714	-		1	2	2	2	4	3	12	17	668	3
Unknown - Inconnu	726		7	35	43	25	20	22	14	3	8	10	539
Montserrat													
2016 (C)													
Total	10	-	-	1	3	2	1	-	-	-	2	1	...
0 - 14	-												...
15 - 19	-												...
20 - 24	2			1	1	-							...
25 - 29	2				1	-					1	-	...
30 - 34	3			1	1	1							...
35 - 39	1					1							...
40 - 44	-												...
45 - 49	-												...
50 - 54	-												...
55 - 59	-												...
60 - 64	2										1	1	...
65 - 69	-												...
70 - 74	-												...
75 +	-												...
Panama[6]													
2017* (C)													
Total	13 360	-	87	1 384	2 729	2 380	1 804	2 325	1 195	718	247	491	...
0 - 14	-												...
15 - 19	388	-	39	190	90	34	10	9	4	-	-	12	...
20 - 24	2 165	-	38	772	787	292	120	68	11	4	-	73	...
25 - 29	3 030	-	4	270	1 256	852	333	205	37	9	3	61	...
30 - 34	2 212	-	5	64	332	739	558	350	88	14	4	58	...
35 - 39	1 560	-	-	25	101	231	457	537	141	24	8	36	...
40 - 44	1 958	-	-	9	51	115	216	881	434	163	40	49	...
45 - 49	955	-	-	1	6	15	22	136	374	306	69	26	...
50 - 54	302	-	-	-	1	1	1	7	51	168	70	3	...
55 - 59	59	-	-	-	-	-	1	-	-	11	47	-	...
60 +	731	-	1	53	105	101	86	132	55	19	6	173	...
Puerto Rico - Porto Rico													
2018 (C)													
Total	13 895	-	193	1 855	2 874	2 059	1 645	1 402	1 136	938	659	1 134	...
0 - 14	-												...
15 - 19	265	-	81	141	34	8	1	-	-	-	-	-	...
20 - 24	2 045	-	91	1 111	601	165	48	18	7	2	2	-	...
25 - 29	2 922	-	15	454	1 496	588	215	91	40	18	3	2	...
30 - 34	2 056	-	4	101	500	768	403	169	62	29	11	9	...
35 - 39	1 667	-	-	33	162	323	532	329	163	79	26	20	...
40 - 44	1 365	-	2	11	51	129	263	398	250	150	63	48	...
45 - 49	1 135	-	-	3	20	52	122	244	305	216	90	83	...
50 - 54	850	-	-	1	5	21	37	88	171	225	171	131	...
55 - 59	630	-	-	-	3	2	19	35	77	120	146	228	...
60 - 64	481	-	-	-	1	-	3	24	40	66	83	263	...
65 - 69	241	-	-	-	-	1	2	2	13	18	36	169	...
70 - 74	146	-	-	-	-	1	-	1	5	9	23	107	...
75 +	92	-	-	-	-	1	-	3	3	6	5	74	...

23. Marriages by age of groom and by age of bride: latest available year, 2009 - 2018
Mariages selon l'âge de l'époux et selon l'âge de l'épouse : dernière année disponible, 2009 - 2018 (continued - suite)

Continent, pays ou zone, date, code[a] et âge de l'épouse	Total	0-14	15-19	20-24	25-29	30-34	35-39	40-44	45-49	50-54	55-59	60+	Unknown Inconnu
AMERICA, NORTH - AMÉRIQUE DU NORD													
Saint Vincent and the Grenadines - Saint-Vincent-et-les Grenadines[11]													
2015 (C)													
Total	572	-	-	26	83	113	84	76	48	60	32	50	...
0 - 14	-	-	-	-	-	-	-	-	-	-	-	-	...
15 - 19	5	-	-	1	-	1	1	1	-	-	-	1	...
20 - 24	60	-	-	14	27	11	5	2	1	-	-	-	...
25 - 29	130	-	-	10	39	42	27	8	2	1	-	1	...
30 - 34	98	-	-	-	6	37	23	17	6	7	1	1	...
35 - 39	91	-	-	1	7	10	21	26	10	10	5	1	...
40 - 44	68	-	-	-	2	8	3	15	15	15	6	4	...
45 - 49	51	-	-	-	-	3	3	3	12	15	3	12	...
50 - 54	31	-	-	-	1	1	1	3	1	8	10	6	...
55 - 59	17	-	-	-	-	-	-	-	-	3	4	10	...
60 - 64	15	-	-	-	-	-	-	2	1	1	2	9	...
65 - 69	3	-	-	-	-	-	-	-	-	-	-	3	...
70 - 74	3	-	-	-	-	-	-	-	-	-	1	2	...
75 +	-	-	-	-	-	-	-	-	-	-	-	-	...
Trinidad and Tobago - Trinité-et-Tobago													
2013* (C)													
Total	8 017	-	86	826	2 111	1 787	1 091	699	502	377	231	305	2
0 - 14	5	-	2	2	1	-	-	-	-	-	-	-	-
15 - 19	374	-	48	180	91	39	10	4	2	-	-	-	-
20 - 24	1 432	-	24	389	627	233	80	43	21	8	5	2	-
25 - 29	2 406	-	7	179	1 028	760	243	106	43	27	9	3	1
30 - 34	1 526	-	5	46	244	531	385	160	80	39	19	16	1
35 - 39	889	-	-	22	76	142	243	192	102	61	28	23	-
40 - 44	545	-	-	4	29	54	83	119	120	74	35	27	-
45 - 49	363	-	-	1	10	20	26	54	90	83	35	44	-
50 - 54	217	-	-	-	3	5	12	18	30	53	50	46	-
55 - 59	150	-	-	1	-	2	8	3	10	25	32	69	-
60 - 64	61	-	-	-	1	1	1	-	1	6	11	40	-
65 +	47	-	-	1	-	-	-	-	3	1	7	35	-
Unknown - Inconnu	2	-	-	1	1	-	-	-	-	-	-	-	-
AMERICA, SOUTH - AMÉRIQUE DU SUD													
Bolivia (Plurinational State of) - Bolivie (État plurinational de)													
2012* (U)													
Total	34 542	...	...	...	...	...	...	...	...	...	1 864[t]	...	11
15 - 24	11 851	...	...	...	...	...	...	...	...	...	...	...	...
25 - 34	16 113	...	...	...	...	...	...	...	...	...	...	...	...
35 - 44	3 944	...	...	...	...	...	...	...	...	...	...	...	...
45 - 54	1 335	...	...	...	...	...	...	...	...	...	...	...	...
55 +	1 247	...	...	...	...	...	...	...	...	...	...	...	...
Unknown - Inconnu	52	...	...	...	...	...	...	...	...	...	...	...	...
Brazil - Brésil													
2017 (+U)													
Total	1064489	8	25 373	181 714	248 167	210 566	142 883	87 932	58 988	41 247	26 871	40 474	266
0 - 14	209	4	104	68	18	7	4	1	3	-	-	-	-
15 - 19	97 883	4	16 421	53 647	19 184	5 700	1 897	607	247	112	30	32	2
20 - 24	231 097	-	6 827	90 142	86 094	31 593	10 817	3 500	1 242	504	194	179	5
25 - 29	242 917	-	1 370	26 248	96 818	74 599	28 400	9 371	3 555	1 491	607	454	4
30 - 34	182 136	-	422	7 664	31 981	64 797	46 067	18 081	7 381	3 269	1 373	1 091	10
35 - 39	121 654	-	155	2 714	9 976	23 380	35 997	25 826	12 671	6 145	2 620	2 170	-
40 - 44	73 661	-	49	817	2 809	7 124	12 996	18 472	15 161	8 333	4 111	3 786	3
45 - 49	49 572	-	17	280	849	2 382	4 557	8 007	11 591	10 224	5 845	5 818	2
50 - 54	31 828	-	4	87	302	709	1 546	2 811	4 870	7 248	6 373	7 875	3
55 - 59	16 923	-	-	25	85	175	417	824	1 600	2 664	3 694	7 439	-
60 - 64	8 974	-	3	7	24	60	118	286	437	880	1 375	5 783	1

Continent, country or area, year, code[a] and age of bride / Continent, pays ou zone, date, code[a] et âge de l'épouse	Total	0-14	15-19	20-24	25-29	30-34	35-39	40-44	45-49	50-54	55-59	60+	Unknown Inconnu
AMERICA, SOUTH - AMÉRIQUE DU SUD													
Brazil - Brésil													
2017													
65 +	7 356	-	1	9	16	33	60	140	229	375	649	5 844	-
Unknown - Inconnu	279		6	11	7	7	6	1	2	-	3		236
Chile - Chili													
2016 (+C)													
Total	62 464	-	349	5 741	14 963	13 908	8 289	5 450	3 804	3 076	2 336	4 548	...
0 - 14	-												
15 - 19	1 217	-	176	666	270	77	17	8	-	3	-	-	...
20 - 24	8 796	-	124	3 416	3 685	1 082	309	106	39	24	5	6	...
25 - 29	17 161	-	33	1 323	8 423	5 208	1 487	439	141	64	25	18	...
30 - 34	12 785	-	16	249	1 997	5 670	3 016	1 141	425	182	56	33	...
35 - 39	7 056	-	-	56	437	1 352	2 381	1 611	693	300	130	96	...
40 - 44	4 703	-	-	25	100	374	764	1 363	1 043	551	282	201	...
45 - 49	3 481	-	-	6	41	110	238	526	866	763	448	483	...
50 - 54	2 925	-	-	-	8	28	60	192	430	722	668	817	...
55 - 59	1 960	-	-	-	2	5	11	54	117	330	433	1 008	...
60 - 64	1 229	-	-	-	-	1	4	4	36	102	211	871	...
65 - 69	606	-	-	-	-	-	2	4	13	27	57	503	...
70 - 74	322	-	-	-	-	-	-	1	-	6	13	302	...
75 +	223	-	-	-	-	1	-	1	1	2	8	210	...
Ecuador - Équateur[12]													
2017 (U)													
Total	60 353	-	1 636	12 326	16 240	11 371	6 771	3 807	2 469	1 792	1 320	2 621	-
0 - 14	-												
15 - 19	5 247	-	975	2 891	1 014	248	82	17	8	6	3	3	-
20 - 24	16 467	-	585	7 303	5 964	1 799	566	168	53	15	6	8	-
25 - 29	15 864	-	62	1 711	7 245	4 679	1 474	445	146	50	26	26	-
30 - 34	8 895	-	9	300	1 559	3 424	2 238	820	307	127	58	53	-
35 - 39	5 164	-	4	81	340	917	1 696	1 160	522	231	111	102	-
40 - 44	3 071	-	1	26	69	228	518	797	672	373	198	189	-
45 - 49	2 074	-	-	7	29	60	134	286	517	496	278	267	-
50 - 54	1 404	-	-	6	13	14	48	82	177	345	326	393	-
55 - 59	904	-	-	1	6	2	9	25	46	101	211	503	-
60 - 64	577	-	-	-	1	-	3	4	15	34	73	447	-
65 - 69	325	-	-	-	-	-	3	1	5	10	18	288	-
70 - 74	206	-	-	-	-	-	-	1	-	2	8	195	-
75 +	155	-	-	-	-	-	-	1	1	2	4	147	-
Unknown - Inconnu												-	-
Paraguay													
2018 (U)													
Total	19 660	-	455	3 424	5 352	4 132	2 528	1 313	824	570	376	677	9
0 - 14	-												
15 - 19	2 041	-	301	1 027	473	155	50	23	7	2	2	1	-
20 - 24	4 621	-	118	1 749	1 838	622	198	57	16	13	3	7	-
25 - 29	5 306	-	28	483	2 299	1 638	559	165	64	32	20	18	-
30 - 34	3 196	-	6	108	536	1 187	810	285	129	71	31	32	1
35 - 39	1 923	-	2	30	142	371	617	402	181	83	44	51	-
40 - 44	976	-	-	12	37	98	195	225	198	98	63	50	-
45 - 49	621	-	-	10	14	36	65	97	143	128	53	75	-
50 - 54	374	-	-	3	6	14	16	29	55	94	76	81	-
55 - 59	244	-	-	-	2	6	6	15	16	28	60	111	-
60 - 64	147	-	-	-	1	1	6	8	6	11	10	104	-
65 - 69	95	-	-	1	-	-	2	4	5	5	8	70	-
70 - 74	62	-	-	-	-	-	1	3	2	2	6	48	-
75 +	31	-	-	-	-	-	1	-	2	1	-	27	-
Unknown - Inconnu	23	-	-	1	4	4	-	-	-	2	-	2	8
Peru - Pérou[13,14]													
2017 (+C)													
Total	77 520	2	745	8 248	17 494	17 558	12 352	7 528	4 743	3 182	2 032	3 635	1
0 - 14	7	1	2	1	2	-	1	-	-	-	-	-	-
15 - 19	2 907	-	491	1 493	659	170	56	24	11	3	-	-	-
20 - 24	13 084	1	218	4 914	5 188	1 889	603	157	72	24	14	4	-
25 - 29	20 400	-	27	1 479	8 794	6 646	2 364	719	228	85	34	24	-
30 - 34	16 473	-	5	265	2 278	6 767	4 603	1 608	551	225	99	72	-
35 - 39	9 935	-	2	74	455	1 663	3 603	2 470	966	417	160	125	-

23. Marriages by age of groom and by age of bride: latest available year, 2009 - 2018
Mariages selon l'âge de l'époux et selon l'âge de l'épouse : dernière année disponible, 2009 - 2018 (continued - suite)

Continent, pays ou zone, date, code[a] et âge de l'épouse	Total	Age of groom - - âge de l'époux 0-14	15-19	20-24	25-29	30-34	35-39	40-44	45-49	50-54	55-59	60+	Unknown Inconnu
AMERICA, SOUTH - AMÉRIQUE DU SUD													
Peru - Pérou[13,14]													
2017													
40 - 44	5 770	-	-	19	92	343	888	1 875	1 425	650	245	233	
45 - 49	3 670	-	-	2	19	67	199	535	1 109	920	437	382	
50 - 54	2 240	-	-	1	6	13	26	118	291	661	554	570	
55 - 59	1 310	-	-	1	-	-	6	15	75	144	360	709	
60 - 64	823	-	-	-	-	-	1	4	11	45	95	667	
65 - 69	495	-	-	-	-	-	1	1	3	6	27	457	
70 - 74	244	-	-	-	-	-	1	2	1	1	6	233	
75 +	162	-	-	-	-	-	-	-	-	1	1	159	1
Venezuela (Bolivarian Republic of) - Venezuela (République bolivarienne du)													
2016 (C)													
Total	84 349	2	1 718	15 084	22 936	16 410	10 357	6 625	4 328	2 720	1 791	2 378	...
0 - 14	72	-	25	33	8	2	3	-	1	-	-	-	...
15 - 19	6 605	1	1 040	3 454	1 403	433	158	53	27	17	9	10	...
20 - 24	20 630	-	459	8 472	7 872	2 441	825	309	157	46	25	24	...
25 - 29	22 412	1	114	2 333	10 214	6 150	2 204	803	352	134	55	52	...
30 - 34	13 919	-	44	533	2 475	5 155	3 193	1 447	603	261	115	93	...
35 - 39	8 483	-	21	154	648	1 538	2 657	1 805	927	418	171	144	...
40 - 44	5 044	-	7	49	200	464	895	1 425	1 000	537	253	214	...
45 - 49	3 227	-	4	24	71	152	295	514	848	629	380	310	...
50 - 54	1 855	-	2	9	20	39	86	192	291	448	389	379	...
55 - 59	1 035	-	1	8	10	16	18	47	77	160	252	446	...
60 - 64	606	-	6	6	5	5	8	17	31	49	104	381	...
65 - 69	252	-	1	-	3	2	4	8	7	11	30	179	...
70 - 74	120	-	-	-	4	5	1	3	1	6	5	90	...
75 +	89	-	-	2	3	10	5	4	1	5	3	56	...
ASIA - ASIE													
Armenia - Arménie													
2017 (+C)													
Total	15 214	...	43	2 233	5 795	3 664	1 597	864	380	242	139	257	...
15 - 19	814	...	24	344	381	60	3	-	2	-	-	-	...
20 - 24	5 574	...	19	1 633	2 853	967	90	9	2	1	-	-	...
25 - 29	4 693	...	-	226	2 251	1 700	426	68	15	6	-	-	...
30 - 34	2 022	...	-	20	239	798	672	228	46	13	5	1	...
35 - 39	1 056	...	-	5	49	105	343	375	129	37	10	3	...
40 - 44	443	...	-	4	11	20	46	154	116	65	17	10	...
45 - 49	230	...	-	-	8	8	14	22	55	67	24	32	...
50 - 54	125	...	-	-	2	4	-	5	10	39	37	28	...
55 - 59	117	...	-	1	-	1	1	1	1	12	37	63	...
60 +	140	...	-	-	1	1	2	2	4	2	9	119	...
Azerbaijan - Azerbaïdjan													
2017 (+C)													
Total	62 923	...	279	15 259	28 472	10 930	3 442	1 695	1 029	658	494	665	...
15 - 19	14 020	...	175	5 335	7 094	1 318	86	9	2	-	1	-	...
20 - 24	27 678	...	96	8 506	14 141	4 257	576	79	14	6	2	1	...
25 - 29	12 377	...	6	1 231	6 325	3 465	1 008	256	65	15	3	3	...
30 - 34	4 240	...	2	142	743	1 515	1 008	544	202	57	21	6	...
35 - 39	1 996	...	-	33	127	294	587	469	303	120	36	27	...
40 - 44	1 028	...	-	8	29	59	134	246	244	163	90	55	...
45 - 49	691	...	-	2	11	15	29	64	153	169	147	101	...
50 - 54	425	...	-	1	2	4	9	22	36	93	110	148	...
55 - 59	283	...	-	1	-	3	3	6	7	29	67	167	...
60 +	185	...	-	-	-	2	-	3	6	17		157	...
Bahrain - Bahreïn													
2018 (...)													
Total	6 039	...	127	1 619	2 289	941	378	227	155	303[s]	...	...	...
0 - 14	6	...	2	4	-	-	-	-	-	-[s]	...	...	...
15 - 19	897	...	107	534	209	30	5	7	2	3[s]	...	...	...
20 - 24	2 440	...	15	948	1 225	194	24	15	6	13[s]	...	...	...
25 - 29	1 456	...	2	109	732	444	93	29	18	29[s]	...	...	...

23. Marriages by age of groom and by age of bride: latest available year, 2009 - 2018
Mariages selon l'âge de l'époux et selon l'âge de l'épouse : dernière année disponible, 2009 - 2018 (continued - suite)

Continent, country or area, year, code[a] and age of bride / Continent, pays ou zone, date, code[a] et âge de l'épouse	Total	0-14	15-19	20-24	25-29	30-34	35-39	40-44	45-49	50-54	55-59	60+	Unknown Inconnu
ASIA - ASIE													
Bahrain - Bahreïn													
2018													
30 - 34	580	...	1	16	83	212	149	51	32	36[s]	...	...	...
35 - 39	296	...	-	4	26	43	83	75	30	35[s]	...	...	...
40 - 44	173	...	-	4	5	16	18	37	41	52[s]	...	...	...
45 - 49	99	...	-	-	6	2	4	7	21	59[s]	...	...	...
50 +	92	...	-	-	3	-	2	6	5	76[s]	...	...	...
Brunei Darussalam - Brunéi Darussalam													
2016 (+C)													
Total	2 532	-	39	401	1 078	519	241	102	49	33	28	42	...
0 - 14	-	...	...	...	...	...	...	...	...	...	...	...	...
15 - 19	146	...	...	...	...	...	...	...	...	...	...	...	...
20 - 24	624	...	...	...	...	...	...	...	...	...	...	...	...
25 - 29	1 063	...	...	...	...	...	...	...	...	...	...	...	...
30 - 34	379	...	...	...	...	...	...	...	...	...	...	...	...
35 - 39	151	...	...	...	...	...	...	...	...	...	...	...	...
40 - 44	89	...	...	...	...	...	...	...	...	...	...	...	...
45 - 49	37	...	...	...	...	...	...	...	...	...	...	...	...
50 - 54	19	...	...	...	...	...	...	...	...	...	...	...	...
55 - 59	13	...	...	...	...	...	...	...	...	...	...	...	...
60 - 64	6	...	...	...	...	...	...	...	...	...	...	...	...
65 - 69	3	...	...	...	...	...	...	...	...	...	...	...	...
70 +	2	...	...	...	...	...	...	...	...	...	...	...	...
China, Hong Kong SAR - Chine, Hong Kong RAS													
2018 (C)													
Total	49 331	-	86	2 582	11 193	13 539	7 481	4 211	3 148	2 292	1 984	2 815	...
0 - 14	-	-	-	-	-	-	-	-	-	-	-	-	...
15 - 19	309	-	38	159	81	21	6	1	1	1	1	-	...
20 - 24	4 639	-	37	1 710	1 810	688	235	66	45	23	16	9	...
25 - 29	15 560	-	9	528	7 236	5 329	1 501	489	217	110	79	62	...
30 - 34	12 904	-	2	111	1 680	6 166	2 903	1 013	441	255	197	136	...
35 - 39	6 346	-	-	46	251	992	2 124	1 256	724	395	291	267	...
40 - 44	3 666	-	-	16	82	219	495	880	737	455	370	412	...
45 - 49	2 849	-	-	8	34	87	157	371	685	520	408	579	...
50 - 54	1 673	-	-	2	15	26	45	110	215	406	338	516	...
55 - 59	823	-	-	2	4	7	10	20	62	108	218	392	...
60 - 64	342	-	-	-	-	3	3	2	17	12	55	250	...
65 - 69	123	-	-	-	-	1	2	1	2	6	8	103	...
70 - 74	51	-	-	-	-	-	-	-	1	1	2	47	...
75 +	46	-	-	-	-	-	-	2	1	-	1	42	...
China, Macao SAR - Chine, Macao RAS													
2009 (+C)													
Total	3 035	-	18	608	1 023	697	286	157	98	68	39	41	...
0 - 14	-	-	-	-	-	-	-	-	-	-	-	-	...
15 - 19	66	-	5	40	17	3	1	-	-	-	-	-	...
20 - 24	993	-	12	445	353	125	36	14	5	3	-	-	...
25 - 29	1 166	-	1	109	575	313	94	42	13	11	7	1	...
30 - 34	444	-	-	10	62	212	83	33	25	12	5	2	...
35 - 39	195	-	-	4	9	30	62	41	26	8	8	7	...
40 - 44	72	-	-	-	5	8	9	17	12	9	6	6	...
45 - 49	58	-	-	-	1	4	1	7	16	14	8	7	...
50 - 54	20	-	-	-	1	2	-	3	1	9	2	2	...
55 - 59	11	-	-	-	-	-	-	-	1	2	2	8	...
60 - 64	4	-	-	-	-	-	-	-	-	1	1	2	...
65 - 69	1	-	-	-	-	-	-	-	-	-	1	-	...
70 +	5	-	-	-	-	-	-	-	-	-	-	5	...
2015 (+C)													
Total	3 719	...	...	418[g]	...	...	...	...	392[r]	...	...	...	...
0 - 24	861	...	...	...	...	...	...	...	...	...	...	...	...
25 - 34	2 317	...	...	...	...	...	...	...	...	...	...	...	...
35 - 44	348	...	...	...	...	...	...	...	...	...	...	...	...
45 +	193	...	...	...	...	...	...	...	...	...	...	...	...

Continent, country or area, year, code[a] and age of bride / Continent, pays ou zone, date, code[a] et âge de l'épouse	Total	0-14	15-19	20-24	25-29	30-34	35-39	40-44	45-49	50-54	55-59	60+	Unknown Inconnu
ASIA - ASIE													
Cyprus - Chypre[15,16]													
2016 (C)													
Total	6 375	-	59	687	1 952	1 933	792	322	199	142	106	164	19
0 - 14	-	-	-	-	-	-	-	-	-	-	-	-	-
15 - 19	168	-	15	87	48	12	5	1	-	-	-	-	-
20 - 24	838	-	20	298	371	111	31	5	1	1	-	-	-
25 - 29	2 376	-	13	150	1 147	822	188	29	13	8	3	3	-
30 - 34	1 651	-	7	74	287	791	322	88	36	29	9	8	-
35 - 39	692	-	3	47	67	153	186	125	55	23	13	20	-
40 - 44	310	-	-	24	24	31	41	58	47	34	22	29	-
45 - 49	153	-	-	3	7	7	14	14	34	27	21	26	-
50 - 54	78	-	-	2	1	3	3	2	8	14	22	23	-
55 - 59	46	-	1	-	-	-	1	-	4	6	11	23	-
60 +	41	-	-	1	-	2	-	-	1	-	5	32	-
Unknown - Inconnu	22	...	-	1	-	1	1	-	-	-	-	-	19
Georgia - Géorgie													
2016 (C)													
Total	25 101	...	458[h]	5 695	7 174	4 533	2 919	1 848	1 040	592	386	456	...
16 - 19	2 545	...	...	...	...	...	...	...	...	...	...	...	...
20 - 24	7 978	...	...	...	...	...	...	...	...	...	...	...	...
25 - 29	6 096	...	...	...	...	...	...	...	...	...	...	...	...
30 - 34	3 514	...	...	...	...	...	...	...	...	...	...	...	...
35 - 39	2 204	...	...	...	...	...	...	...	...	...	...	...	...
40 - 44	1 237	...	...	...	...	...	...	...	...	...	...	...	...
45 - 49	673	...	...	...	...	...	...	...	...	...	...	...	...
50 - 54	423	...	...	...	...	...	...	...	...	...	...	...	...
55 - 59	234	...	...	...	...	...	...	...	...	...	...	...	...
60 +	197	...	...	...	...	...	...	...	...	...	...	...	...
Iran (Islamic Republic of) - Iran (République islamique d')[17]													
2017 (+C)													
Total	608 956	417	24 404	171 010	217 108	111 719	39 392	15 564	8 950	5 639	4 452	10 299	2
0 - 14	35 551	181	5 472	19 749	8 902	1 006	140	51	33	11	3	1	2
15 - 19	170 925	168	15 379	83 090	60 190	10 503	1 105	271	107	53	20	39	-
20 - 24	166 332	39	2 883	54 544	77 712	26 228	3 730	703	270	117	48	58	-
25 - 29	120 447	14	477	10 923	55 236	40 398	9 952	2 098	752	288	138	171	-
30 - 34	63 610	5	146	2 124	12 235	26 290	14 287	4 769	1 971	818	449	516	-
35 - 39	28 328	-	32	469	2 310	6 106	8 135	5 059	2 849	1 409	873	1 086	-
40 - 44	11 859	-	14	89	420	969	1 712	2 061	2 043	1 519	1 118	1 914	-
45 - 49	5 931	-	1	20	87	185	289	467	756	1 002	938	2 186	-
50 - 54	2 860	-	-	2	12	25	34	73	143	317	550	1 704	-
55 - 59	1 677	-	-	-	3	5	6	7	23	83	258	1 292	-
60 - 64	803	-	-	-	1	2	2	4	3	17	50	724	-
65 - 69	391	-	-	-	-	-	-	1	-	4	6	380	-
70 - 74	147	-	-	-	-	2	-	-	-	-	-	145	-
75 +	85	-	-	-	-	-	-	-	-	1	1	83	-
Unknown - Inconnu	10	10	-	-	-	-	-	-	-	-	-	-	-
Israel - Israël[18]													
2016 (C)													
Total	52 809	...	2 021	13 140	19 078	10 106	3 433	1 492	770	516	337	620	1 296
15 - 19	6 681	...	1 374	3 468	1 303	212	17	2	3	1	-	-	301
20 - 24	19 198	...	590	8 758	7 360	1 668	245	42	12	4	-	1	518
25 - 29	16 251	...	4	611	9 333	4 915	891	191	44	9	3	-	250
30 - 34	5 604	...	1	47	789	2 784	1 332	396	101	31	7	5	111
35 - 39	1 970	...	-	8	66	307	733	496	191	65	28	17	59
40 - 44	887	...	-	1	6	45	112	251	225	125	57	42	23
45 - 49	487	...	-	2	3	5	10	38	136	140	58	79	16
50 - 54	335	...	-	-	-	3	3	6	27	99	101	87	9
55 - 59	204	...	-	-	-	1	-	3	3	13	58	122	4
60 - 64	121	...	-	-	-	-	-	-	2	6	109		4
65 - 69	81	...	-	-	-	-	-	-	-	1	79		1
70 - 74	31	...	-	-	-	-	-	-	-	2	29		-
75 +	15	...	-	-	-	-	-	-	-	-	15		-
Unknown - Inconnu	944	...	52	245	218	166	90	67	28	27	16	35	-

Continent, country or area, year, code[a] and age of bride / Continent, pays ou zone, date, code[a] et âge de l'épouse	Total	0-14	15-19	20-24	25-29	30-34	35-39	40-44	45-49	50-54	55-59	60+	Unknown Inconnu
ASIA - ASIE													
Japan - Japon[19]													
2017 (+C)													
Total	480 257	-	4 504	51 393	152 059	114 415	68 962	41 143	21 471	10 568	6 237	9 504	1
0 - 14	-	-	-	-	-	-	-	-	-	-	-	-	-
15 - 19	8 142	-	3 320	3 252	873	345	161	83	53	21	22	12	-
20 - 24	75 098	-	1 066	35 531	24 282	8 533	3 442	1 361	480	197	107	99	-
25 - 29	177 820	-	81	10 050	103 398	43 440	14 168	4 456	1 438	428	188	173	-
30 - 34	108 285	-	26	1 923	19 308	49 240	24 379	9 058	2 901	863	330	257	-
35 - 39	56 766	-	5	503	3 434	10 559	21 267	13 559	5 068	1 420	549	402	-
40 - 44	26 594	-	4	109	607	1 887	4 424	9 836	5 952	2 244	917	614	-
45 - 49	12 849	-	-	18	123	345	903	2 226	4 330	2 666	1 256	982	-
50 - 54	6 799	-	2	6	27	55	196	447	1 035	2 227	1 429	1 375	-
55 - 59	3 426	-	-	1	3	8	19	99	181	402	1 157	1 556	-
60 - 64	1 816	-	-	-	3	2	2	14	24	72	207	1 492	-
65 - 69	1 416	-	-	-	1	1	1	3	8	23	65	1 314	-
70 - 74	712	-	-	-	-	-	-	-	1	5	8	698	-
75 +	533	-	-	-	-	-	-	1	-	-	2	530	-
Unknown - Inconnu	1	-	-	-	-	-	-	-	-	-	-	-	1
Jordan - Jordanie[20]													
2010 (+C)													
Total	62 107	...	16 151	25 559	12 760	4 002	1 795	1 151	437	252[s]	...	...	...
18 - 19	1 262	...	1 017	191	40	11	1	2	-	-[s]	...	...	...
20 - 24	14 272	...	6 768	6 453	835	139	42	20	7	8[s]	...	...	...
25 - 29	25 434	...	6 276	12 608	5 720	633	120	45	16	16[s]	...	...	...
30 - 34	11 523	...	1 603	4 782	3 679	1 153	197	70	25	14[s]	...	...	...
35 - 39	4 064	...	299	1 043	1 434	819	350	92	19	8[s]	...	...	...
40 - 44	2 365	...	99	321	681	647	358	217	35	7[s]	...	...	...
45 - 49	1 139	...	35	81	220	283	249	196	57	18[s]	...	...	...
50 - 54	639	...	14	37	73	152	169	121	53	20[s]	...	...	...
55 - 59	425	...	12	18	35	80	95	107	56	22[s]	...	...	...
60 - 64	318	...	11	7	21	40	66	97	39	37[s]	...	...	...
65 +	666	...	17	18	22	45	148	184	130	102[s]	...	...	...
Kazakhstan													
2018 (+C)													
Total	137 797	-	2 146	40 161	49 429	21 847	10 370	5 768	3 213	2 013	1 360	1 490	-
0 - 14	-	-	-	-	-	-	-	-	-	-	-	-	-
15 - 19	15 219	-	1 547	8 960	4 016	602	74	10	6	1	-	3	-
20 - 24	60 170	-	525	27 653	26 134	4 938	733	141	25	14	2	5	-
25 - 29	30 498	-	63	3 005	16 069	8 464	2 161	532	143	43	15	3	-
30 - 34	14 859	-	8	438	2 653	6 145	3 733	1 317	390	110	41	24	-
35 - 39	7 841	-	2	82	464	1 360	2 796	1 985	732	284	95	41	-
40 - 44	4 127	-	1	18	76	270	703	1 356	961	459	202	81	-
45 - 49	2 354	-	-	3	11	57	152	339	756	556	301	179	-
50 - 54	1 207	-	-	1	3	10	13	74	149	416	315	226	-
55 - 59	780	-	-	-	1	1	4	11	37	99	288	339	-
60 - 64	426	-	-	1	1	-	1	3	13	25	83	299	-
65 - 69	208	-	-	-	-	-	-	-	1	6	18	183	-
70 - 74	67	-	-	-	1	-	-	-	-	-	-	66	-
75 +	41	-	-	-	-	-	-	-	-	-	-	41	-
Kuwait - Koweït													
2017 (C)													
Total	13 932	-	189	3 426	4 761	2 371	1 266	728	1 191[r]	...	...	...	...
0 - 14	-	-	-	-	-	-	-	-	-[r]	...	...	...	...
15 - 19	1 829	-	127	1 194	424	64	9	4	7[r]	...	...	...	...
20 - 24	4 946	-	55	1 914	2 345	497	87	26	22[r]	...	...	...	...
25 - 29	3 469	-	6	275	1 656	1 004	348	101	79[r]	...	...	...	...
30 - 34	1 687	-	-	28	240	577	423	210	209[r]	...	...	...	...
35 - 39	996	-	1	7	52	161	279	214	282[r]	...	...	...	...
40 - 44	539	-	-	4	26	44	78	116	271[r]	...	...	...	...
45 +	466	-	-	4	18	24	42	57	321[r]	...	...	...	...
Kyrgyzstan - Kirghizstan													
2017 (C)													
Total	43 350	-	408	13 240	17 746	5 913	2 526	1 506	891	456	317	347	...
0 - 14	-	-	-	-	-	-	-	-	-	-	-	-	...
15 - 19	8 283	-	314	4 987	2 774	186	17	4	-	1	-	-	...

Continent, country or area, year, code[a] and age of bride / Continent, pays ou zone, date, code[a] et âge de l'épouse	Total	0-14	15-19	20-24	25-29	30-34	35-39	40-44	45-49	50-54	55-59	60+	Unknown Inconnu
ASIA - ASIE													
Kyrgyzstan - Kirghizstan													
2017													
20 - 24	20 416	-	87	7 745	10 636	1 700	201	30	11	3	3	-	...
25 - 29	7 888	-	6	449	3 929	2 567	676	201	41	11	3	5	...
30 - 34	3 296	-	1	52	346	1 274	996	428	144	32	16	7	...
35 - 39	1 686	-	-	6	44	155	542	530	274	87	30	18	...
40 - 44	897	-	-	1	16	27	82	264	286	128	61	32	...
45 - 49	400	-	-	-	-	2	11	34	105	120	73	55	...
50 - 54	225	-	-	-	1	2	1	12	20	60	68	61	...
55 - 59	154	-	-	-	-	-	-	1	9	11	52	81	...
60 - 64	63	-	-	-	-	-	-	1	1	2	10	49	...
65 - 69	22	-	-	-	-	-	-	1	-	1	-	20	...
70 - 74	9	-	-	-	-	-	-	-	-	-	1	8	...
75 +	11	-	-	-	-	-	-	-	-	-	-	11	...
Mongolia - Mongolie													
2018 (+C)													
Total	21 020	...	188[j]	4 730	8 018	4 057	1 626	940	703	758[s]	...	...	...
18 - 19	602	...	...	...	...	...	...	...	...	...	...	...	...
20 - 24	6 408	...	...	...	...	...	...	...	...	...	...	...	...
25 - 29	7 534	...	...	...	...	...	...	...	...	...	...	...	...
30 - 34	3 073	...	...	...	...	...	...	...	...	...	...	...	...
35 - 39	1 422	...	...	...	...	...	...	...	...	...	...	...	...
40 - 44	870	...	...	...	...	...	...	...	...	...	...	...	...
45 - 49	579	...	...	...	...	...	...	...	...	...	...	...	...
50 +	532	...	...	...	...	...	...	...	...	...	...	...	...
Philippines[21]													
2017 (U)													
Total	434 264	8	7 595	94 040	157 297	95 020	39 813	16 431	8 728	5 359	3 838	6 120	15
0 - 14	51	3	17	22	6	3	-	-	-	-	-	-	-
15 - 19	32 318	4	4 198	18 384	7 124	1 748	449	187	77	49	47	51	-
20 - 24	137 424	1	2 941	59 239	55 016	14 171	3 595	1 137	604	284	180	256	-
25 - 29	148 451	-	343	13 960	78 031	40 449	10 338	2 777	1 090	610	386	464	3
30 - 34	68 137	-	63	1 900	14 131	31 305	13 739	3 922	1 458	666	442	510	1
35 - 39	25 348	-	25	408	2 345	5 876	8 980	4 313	1 679	759	442	520	1
40 - 44	10 118	-	6	95	464	1 074	1 989	2 896	1 745	807	464	578	-
45 - 49	5 520	-	1	27	138	286	531	872	1 417	1 039	529	680	-
50 - 54	3 269	-	-	5	33	81	136	236	463	775	674	866	-
55 - 59	1 798	-	-	-	7	22	40	53	149	255	466	806	-
60 - 64	1 014	-	-	-	-	4	14	25	37	81	144	709	-
65 - 69	504	-	-	-	-	-	2	11	5	26	58	402	-
70 - 74	183	-	-	-	-	-	-	2	3	6	4	167	1
75 +	114	-	-	-	-	-	-	-	-	-	2	109	1
Unknown - Inconnu	15	-	1	-	2	1	-	-	1	-	-	2	8
Qatar													
2017 (C)													
Total	3 718	...	40[f]	888	1 370	703	314	158	105	74	29	36	1
0 - 19	462	...	24[f]	259	154	23	-	1	-	1	-	-	-
20 - 24	1 387	...	13[f]	542	641	159	23	4	-	-	1	3	1
25 - 29	971	...	3[f]	70	451	299	90	29	16	7	4	2	-
30 - 34	477	...	-[f]	13	89	166	103	52	35	11	4	4	-
35 - 39	226	...	-[f]	4	27	41	68	42	18	16	7	3	-
40 - 44	109	...	-[f]	-	7	9	20	20	23	16	4	10	-
45 - 49	54	...	-[f]	-	1	5	7	7	10	15	3	6	-
50 - 54	22	...	-[f]	-	-	1	3	3	2	6	3	4	-
55 - 59	9	...	-[f]	-	-	-	-	-	1	2	3	3	-
60 +	1	...	-[f]	-	-	-	-	-	-	-	-	1	-
Republic of Korea - République de Corée[22]													
2018 (+C)													
Total	257 622	-	467	6 779	55 212	92 844	48 875	20 013	12 700	8 149	6 457	6 126	...
0 - 14	-	-	-	-	-	-	-	-	-	-	-	-	...
15 - 19	2 666	-	306	559	265	244	531	516	220	22	3	-	...
20 - 24	18 632	-	141	4 319	7 064	3 456	1 724	1 134	638	123	24	9	...
25 - 29	90 434	-	12	1 597	39 254	39 468	7 521	1 479	757	234	83	29	...
30 - 34	77 094	-	6	250	7 803	44 168	20 496	2 949	943	324	110	45	...

23. Marriages by age of groom and by age of bride: latest available year, 2009 - 2018
Mariages selon l'âge de l'époux et selon l'âge de l'épouse : dernière année disponible, 2009 - 2018 (continued - suite)

Continent, pays ou zone, date, code[a] et âge de l'épouse	Total	0-14	15-19	20-24	25-29	30-34	35-39	40-44	45-49	50-54	55-59	60+	Unknown Inconnu
ASIA - ASIE													
Republic of Korea - République de Corée[22]													
2018													
35 - 39	31 559	-	2	42	705	4 935	16 064	7 255	1 819	468	196	73	...
40 - 44	12 403	-	-	9	84	476	2 080	5 082	3 165	1 022	366	119	...
45 - 49	9 434	-	-	1	30	87	392	1 297	3 808	2 507	988	324	...
50 - 54	7 003	-	-	2	7	10	56	253	1 077	2 599	2 264	735	...
55 - 59	4 793	-	-	-	-	-	7	44	245	716	1 966	1 815	...
60 - 64	2 141	-	-	-	-	-	4	4	28	115	401	1 589	...
65 - 69	816	-	-	-	-	-	-	-	-	16	47	753	...
70 - 74	383	-	-	-	-	-	-	-	-	2	8	373	...
75 +	264	-	-	-	-	-	-	-	-	1	1	262	...
Singapore - Singapour[23,24]													
2017 (+C)													
Total	28 212	-	58	1 376	10 494	8 102	3 623	1 925	1 047	690	464	433	...
0 - 14	-	-	-	-	-	-	-	-	-	-	-	-	...
15 - 19	204	-	38	104	34	15	6	3	2	1	1	-	...
20 - 24	3 259	-	16	855	1 667	436	160	67	30	16	7	5	...
25 - 29	13 361	-	3	346	7 636	3 979	875	319	130	45	20	8	...
30 - 34	6 490	-	1	54	967	3 115	1 455	507	196	110	62	23	...
35 - 39	2 595	-	-	10	147	434	910	587	280	93	71	63	...
40 - 44	1 145	-	-	3	27	98	168	342	207	171	77	52	...
45 - 49	623	-	-	3	9	21	42	82	152	138	95	81	...
50 - 54	295	-	-	-	4	3	4	11	39	94	71	69	...
55 - 59	144	-	-	1	3	-	3	6	10	15	47	59	...
60 +	96	-	-	-	-	1	-	1	1	7	13	73	...
Sri Lanka													
2014 (+C)													
Total	177 792	-b	...	...	...	...	...	...	...	...	...	...	...
0 - 15	90	-b	...	...	...	...	...	...	...	...	...	...	...
16 - 20	44 451	-b	...	...	...	...	...	...	...	...	...	...	...
21 - 25	63 336	-b	...	...	...	...	...	...	...	...	...	...	...
26 - 30	42 964	-b	...	...	...	...	...	...	...	...	...	...	...
31 - 35	14 842	-b	...	...	...	...	...	...	...	...	...	...	...
36 - 40	6 022	-b	...	...	...	...	...	...	...	...	...	...	...
41 - 45	3 081	-b	...	...	...	...	...	...	...	...	...	...	...
46 - 50	1 535	-b	...	...	...	...	...	...	...	...	...	...	...
51 - 55	786	-b	...	...	...	...	...	...	...	...	...	...	...
56 - 60	418	-b	...	...	...	...	...	...	...	...	...	...	...
61 - 65	177	-b	...	...	...	...	...	...	...	...	...	...	...
66 - 70	68	-b	...	...	...	...	...	...	...	...	...	...	...
71 - 75	18	-b	...	...	...	...	...	...	...	...	...	...	...
76 +	4	-b	...	...	...	...	...	...	...	...	...	...	...
State of Palestine - État de Palestine													
2017 (C)													
Total	47 218	...	2 527	18 534	17 247	4 674	1 471	870	555	402	326	612	...
12 - 14	761	...	217	427	111	6	-	-	-	-	-	-	...
15 - 19	18 761	...	2 066	10 449	5 528	633	56	20	8	-	-	1	...
20 - 24	18 984	...	229	7 234	8 933	2 042	352	106	47	20	12	9	...
25 - 29	5 487	...	11	378	2 446	1 513	618	289	124	57	21	30	...
30 - 34	1 607	...	2	31	179	381	299	254	185	127	80	69	...
35 - 39	826	...	2	7	32	79	106	139	118	108	91	144	...
40 - 44	442	...	-	5	12	12	36	49	50	43	71	164	...
45 - 49	201	...	-	1	2	4	2	10	19	32	36	95	...
50 - 54	88	...	-	-	4	1	1	1	4	13	8	56	...
55 - 59	48	...	-	2	-	2	1	2	-	1	7	33	...
60 - 64	10	...	-	-	-	1	-	-	-	1	-	8	...
65 +	3	...	-	-	-	-	-	-	-	-	-	3	...
Tajikistan - Tadjikistan													
2017 (+C)													
Total	78 638	-	2 274	39 639	25 734	5 120	2 262	1 568	933	457	294	269	88
0 - 14	-	-	-	-	-	-	-	-	-	-	-	-	
15 - 19	34 438	-	2 029	23 068	9 136	183	-	-	-	-	-	-	22
20 - 24	30 941	-	243	16 092	12 927	1 608	42	-	-	-	-	-	29

23. Marriages by age of groom and by age of bride: latest available year, 2009 - 2018
Mariages selon l'âge de l'époux et selon l'âge de l'épouse : dernière année disponible, 2009 - 2018 (continued - suite)

Continent, country or area, year, code[a] and age of bride / Continent, pays ou zone, date, code[a] et âge de l'épouse	Total	____	____	____	____	Age of groom - - âge de l'époux	____	____	____	____	____	____	Unknown Inconnu
		0-14	15-19	20-24	25-29	30-34	35-39	40-44	45-49	50-54	55-59	60+	
ASIA - ASIE													
Tajikistan - Tadjikistan													
2017													
25 - 29	6 704	-	-	438	3 454	2 132	562	99	10	-	-	-	9
30 - 34	3 269	-	-	-	180	1 149	1 177	478	170	79	28	4	4
35 - 39	1 807	-	-	-	-	41	475	709	309	142	86	45	-
40 - 44	860	-	-	-	-	-	3	278	328	111	68	72	-
45 - 49	309	-	-	-	-	-	-	2	114	91	57	44	1
50 - 54	114	-	-	-	-	-	-	-	-	33	36	45	-
55 - 59	54	-	-	-	-	-	-	-	-	-	18	36	-
60 - 64	17	-	-	-	-	-	-	-	-	-	-	17	-
65 - 69	4	-	-	-	-	-	-	-	-	-	-	4	-
70 - 74	1	-	-	-	-	-	-	-	-	-	-	1	-
75 +	1	-	-	-	-	-	-	-	-	-	-	1	-
Unknown - Inconnu	119	-	2	41	37	7	3	2	2	1	1	-	23
Turkey - Turquie[25]													
2017 (C)													
Total	569 459	-[b]	9 867[h]	135 927	227 475	101 409	42 108	19 440	11 196	7 756	5 289	8 992	...
0 - 15	-	-[b]	-[h]	-	-	-	-	-	-	-	-	-	...
16 - 19	89 852	-[b]	7 418[h]	45 189	30 627	5 649	798	125	35	5	4	2	...
20 - 24	200 225	-[b]	2 087[h]	74 314	94 963	23 979	3 998	659	133	56	15	21	...
25 - 29	152 574	-[b]	204[h]	13 216	85 982	40 328	10 026	2 010	548	162	54	44	...
30 - 34	51 801	-[b]	34[h]	1 300	9 957	21 548	12 677	4 165	1 341	484	177	118	...
35 - 39	27 118	-[b]	16[h]	313	1 801	5 283	9 002	6 024	2 692	1 154	473	360	...
40 - 44	14 256	-[b]	1[h]	71	343	995	2 423	3 851	3 145	1 807	861	759	...
45 - 49	7 922	-[b]	-[h]	8	77	157	457	890	1 860	1 988	1 191	1 294	...
50 - 54	4 589	-[b]	-[h]	4	11	28	74	142	363	1 167	1 206	1 594	...
55 - 59	2 525	-[b]	1[h]	-	1	4	7	24	64	204	661	1 559	...
60 - 64	1 439	-[b]	-[h]	-	-	1	4	6	15	38	125	1 250	...
65 - 69	678	-[b]	-[h]	1	1	2	-	4	3	10	24	633	...
70 - 74	262	-[b]	-[h]	-	-	-	-	1	2	3	3	253	...
75 +	146	-[b]	-[h]	-	-	-	-	-	-	3	1	142	...
Unknown - Inconnu	16 072	-[b]	106[h]	1 511	3 712	3 435	2 642	1 539	995	675	494	963	...
Uzbekistan - Ouzbékistan													
2017 (+C)													
Total	306 197	-	2 649	108 881	146 378	26 314	8 985	5 183	3 067	1 921	1 414	1 405	...
0 - 14	-												
15 - 19	66 016	-	1 990	36 320	26 657	960	62	16	8	2	-	1	...
20 - 24	171 521	-	624	69 637	92 210	8 207	641	137	42	10	6	7	...
25 - 29	43 202	-	33	2 724	25 957	10 995	2 454	632	256	94	30	27	...
30 - 34	14 333	-	1	167	1 378	5 585	3 922	1 763	794	382	204	137	...
35 - 39	6 047	-	-	27	139	471	1 726	1 805	894	478	310	197	...
40 - 44	2 549	-	1	3	30	69	145	724	684	412	268	213	...
45 - 49	1 216	-	-	-	4	20	23	76	324	306	233	230	...
50 - 54	731	-	-	3	1	4	9	24	52	191	216	231	...
55 - 59	366	-	-	-	-	2	3	2	7	35	127	190	...
60 - 64	122	-	-	-	-	-	-	2	6	9	16	89	...
65 - 69	67	-	-	-	1	1	-	1	-	1	1	62	...
70 - 74	13	-	-	-	-	-	-	-	-	1	-	12	...
75 +	14	-	-	-	1	-	-	1	-	-	3	9	...
EUROPE													
Åland Islands - Îles d'Åland													
2017 (C)													
Total	112	-	-	-	15	31	16	9	11	11	11	8	...
0 - 14	-												
15 - 19	-												
20 - 24	3	-	-	-	2	1	-	-	-	-	-	-	...
25 - 29	20	-	-	-	8	7	4	-	1	-	-	-	...
30 - 34	32	-	-	-	3	17	6	4	1	-	1	-	...
35 - 39	8	-	-	-	1	4	2	-	1	-	-	-	...
40 - 44	12	-	-	-	1	2	2	3	3	-	-	1	...
45 - 49	17	-	-	-	-	1	2	4	6	3	1		...
50 - 54	10	-	-	-	-	-	1	-	1	5	2	1	...

23. Marriages by age of groom and by age of bride: latest available year, 2009 - 2018
Mariages selon l'âge de l'époux et selon l'âge de l'épouse : dernière année disponible, 2009 - 2018 (continued - suite)

Continent, country or area, year, code[a] and age of bride / Continent, pays ou zone, date, code[a] et âge de l'épouse	Total	Age of groom - âge de l'époux 0-14	15-19	20-24	25-29	30-34	35-39	40-44	45-49	50-54	55-59	60+	Unknown Inconnu
EUROPE													
Åland Islands - Îles d'Åland													
2017													
55 - 59	4	-	-	-	-	-	-	-	-	-	4	-	...
60 - 64	5	-	-	-	-	-	-	-	-	-	1	4	...
65 - 69	-	-	-	-	-	-	-	-	-	-	-	-	...
70 - 74	1	-	-	-	-	-	-	-	-	-	-	1	...
75 +	-	-	-	-	-	-	-	-	-	-	-	1	...
Albania - Albanie													
2017 (C)													
Total	22 641	-	120	3 251	9 205	6 171	2 131	853	430	238	119	123	...
0 - 14	-	-	-	-	-	-	-	-	-	-	-	-	...
15 - 19	3 856	-	77	1 079	2 035	599	54	11	1	-	-	-	...
20 - 24	8 836	-	31	1 802	4 183	2 354	401	51	14	-	-	-	...
25 - 29	6 011	-	7	243	2 574	2 173	758	199	44	8	3	2	...
30 - 34	2 181	-	2	53	266	868	612	251	94	25	7	3	...
35 - 39	889	-	1	27	72	120	237	214	142	55	16	5	...
40 - 44	401	-	1	13	36	33	45	87	79	75	22	10	...
45 - 49	237	-	1	18	17	12	13	30	40	50	37	19	...
50 - 54	119	-	-	9	13	7	8	6	10	17	20	29	...
55 - 59	59	-	-	3	7	4	2	2	3	6	11	21	...
60 - 64	34	-	-	1	2	1	1	2	2	2	3	20	...
65 - 69	4	-	-	2	-	-	-	-	-	-	-	2	...
70 - 74	4	-	-	-	-	-	-	-	-	-	-	4	...
75 +	10	-	-	1	-	-	-	-	1	-	-	8	...
2018 (C)													
Total	23 104	...	165	3 399	9 057	6 422	2 250	879	446	486	...	...	...
0 - 19	3 656	...	...	...	...	...	...	...	...	...	...	...	...
20 - 24	8 734	...	...	...	...	...	...	...	...	...	...	...	...
25 - 29	6 219	...	...	...	...	...	...	...	...	...	...	...	...
30 - 34	2 343	...	...	...	...	...	...	...	...	...	...	...	...
35 - 39	1 029	...	...	...	...	...	...	...	...	...	...	...	...
40 - 44	530	...	...	...	...	...	...	...	...	...	...	...	...
45 - 49	299	...	...	...	...	...	...	...	...	...	...	...	...
50 +	294	...	...	...	...	...	...	...	...	...	...	...	...
Andorra - Andorre													
2016 (C)													
Total	295	-		18	50	58	62	41	29	20	10	7	...
0 - 14	-	-	-	-	-	-	-	-	-	-	-	-	...
15 - 19	3	-	-	3	-	-	-	-	-	-	-	-	...
20 - 24	30	-	-	11	15	1	2	1	-	-	-	-	...
25 - 29	48	-	-	3	20	17	6	1	1	-	-	-	...
30 - 34	66	-	-	-	10	25	22	3	5	1	-	-	...
35 - 39	63	-	-	1	5	10	23	17	4	2	-	1	...
40 - 44	40	-	-	-	-	3	7	14	8	7	1	-	...
45 - 49	19	-	-	-	-	1	1	4	4	3	5	1	...
50 - 54	17	-	-	-	-	1	1	-	7	5	2	1	...
55 - 59	7	-	-	-	-	-	-	1	-	1	2	3	...
60 - 64	2	-	-	-	-	-	-	-	-	1	-	1	...
65 - 69	-	-	-	-	-	-	-	-	-	1	-	1	...
70 - 74	-	-	-	-	-	-	-	-	-	-	-	-	...
75 +	-	-	-	-	-	-	-	-	-	-	-	-	...
Austria - Autriche[26]													
2017 (C)													
Total	44 981	-	122	2 994	8 809	10 522	7 098	4 350	3 567	3 056	2 105	2 358	...
0 - 14	-	-	-	-	-	-	-	-	-	-	-	-	...
15 - 19	567	-	57	334	139	22	11	2	1	-	1	-	...
20 - 24	5 259	-	47	2 006	2 302	646	155	61	24	7	3	8	...
25 - 29	11 368	-	9	494	4 901	4 270	1 165	327	115	50	20	17	...
30 - 34	10 209	-	5	106	1 144	4 456	2 973	918	367	155	48	37	...
35 - 39	6 007	-	1	37	228	883	2 228	1 453	688	312	106	71	...
40 - 44	3 482	-	1	8	52	166	408	1 100	967	471	196	113	...
45 - 49	3 066	-	1	7	22	50	104	346	891	883	475	287	...
50 - 54	2 583	-	1	2	14	20	42	117	409	817	658	503	...
55 - 59	1 431	-	-	-	7	8	7	23	78	283	462	563	...
60 - 64	586	-	-	-	-	-	4	2	22	63	107	388	...
65 - 69	269	-	-	-	-	1	1	1	3	13	23	227	...

Continent, country or area, year, code[a] and age of bride / Continent, pays ou zone, date, code[a] et âge de l'épouse	Total	0-14	15-19	20-24	25-29	30-34	35-39	40-44	45-49	50-54	55-59	60+	Unknown Inconnu
EUROPE													
Austria - Autriche[26]													
2017													
70 - 74	100	-	-	-	-	-	-	-	1	2	5	92	...
75 +	54	-	-	-	-	-	-	-	1	-	1	52	...
Belarus - Bélarus													
2017 (C)													
Total	66 215	71[d]	843[j]	15 131	21 338	11 761	6 047	3 640	2 617	1 795	1 475	1 497	...
0 - 17	492	50[d]	143[j]	220	55	19	2	2	1	-	-	-	...
18 - 19	3 476	11[d]	406[j]	2 121	765	136	20	9	5	1	2	-	...
20 - 24	22 109	9[d]	241[j]	10 302	9 271	1 831	342	77	23	5	7	1	...
25 - 29	17 167	1[d]	41[j]	2 073	8 712	4 695	1 175	319	99	36	9	7	...
30 - 34	9 449	-[d]	10[j]	335	1 991	3 686	2 170	809	293	99	38	18	...
35 - 39	5 138	-[d]	1[j]	64	440	1 079	1 630	1 087	545	179	82	31	...
40 - 44	2 993	-[d]	1[j]	13	80	232	548	899	714	317	118	71	...
45 - 49	2 072	-[d]	-[j]	-	18	69	125	294	671	514	281	100	...
50 - 54	1 384	-[d]	-[j]	2	5	12	27	113	205	432	419	169	...
55 - 59	992	-[d]	-[j]	1	1	2	7	25	48	172	393	343	...
60 +	943	-[d]	-[j]	-	-	-	1	6	13	40	126	757	...
Belgium - Belgique[27,28]													
2015 (C)													
Total	40 049	-	69	2 350	9 971	8 521	5 515	3 966	3 101	2 588	1 809	2 159	...
0 - 14	-	-	-	-	-	-	-	-	-	-	-	-	...
15 - 19	398	-	34	200	126	27	6	2	3	-	-	-	...
20 - 24	5 029	-	31	1 592	2 483	656	169	50	30	7	8	3	...
25 - 29	11 749	-	2	467	6 197	3 717	897	285	111	47	18	8	...
30 - 34	7 535	-	1	70	888	3 265	2 041	786	287	122	54	21	...
35 - 39	4 901	-	1	10	190	638	1 769	1 307	569	270	94	53	...
40 - 44	3 333	-	-	6	47	155	460	1 062	892	437	187	87	...
45 - 49	2 619	-	-	4	28	43	127	349	801	714	332	221	...
50 - 54	2 166	-	-	1	6	12	31	94	315	721	542	444	...
55 - 59	1 265	-	-	-	4	2	11	23	79	226	422	498	...
60 - 64	610	-	-	-	2	4	3	3	12	35	123	428	...
65 - 69	278	-	-	-	-	1	1	5	-	8	25	238	...
70 - 74	103	-	-	-	-	-	-	-	1	1	3	98	...
75 +	63	-	-	-	-	1	-	-	1	-	1	60	...
Bosnia and Herzegovina - Bosnie-Herzégovine													
2012 (C)													
Total	18 235	-	147	3 617	6 959	3 922	1 571	739	438	259	185	398	...
0 - 14	-	-	-	-	-	-	-	-	-	-	-	-	...
15 - 19	1 885	-	91	1 028	606	122	27	6	2	1	-	2	...
20 - 24	6 191	-	48	2 130	2 958	844	160	36	7	5	2	1	...
25 - 29	5 764	-	8	403	2 936	1 833	431	113	26	10	2	2	...
30 - 34	2 228	-	-	42	405	941	581	172	66	14	2	5	...
35 - 39	871	-	-	10	35	150	292	240	92	34	14	4	...
40 - 44	437	-	-	1	9	20	56	117	122	60	19	33	...
45 - 49	349	-	-	2	6	6	13	41	85	76	52	68	...
50 - 54	237	-	-	-	2	4	6	10	30	39	52	94	...
55 - 59	136	-	-	-	-	-	2	3	6	17	34	74	...
60 - 64	78	-	-	-	-	2	1	1	-	1	7	66	...
65 - 69	27	-	-	-	-	-	-	-	1	2	1	23	...
70 - 74	18	-	-	-	-	-	-	-	1	-	-	17	...
75 +	9	-	-	-	-	-	-	-	-	-	-	9	...
Unknown - Inconnu	5	-	-	1	2	-	2	-	-	-	-	-	...
Bulgaria - Bulgarie[29]													
2017 (C)													
Total	28 593	-	367	3 289	8 448	7 106	3 860	2 421	1 327	696	456	623	...
0 - 14	-	-	-	-	-	-	-	-	-	-	-	-	...
15 - 19	1 854	-	285	1 003	438	104	15	5	2	1	1	-	...
20 - 24	6 046	-	74	1 746	2 917	1 044	195	50	13	5	1	1	...
25 - 29	9 261	-	4	437	4 271	3 321	930	217	55	15	7	4	...
30 - 34	5 061	-	1	75	663	2 156	1 453	509	139	40	19	6	...
35 - 39	2 698	-	1	20	114	379	969	819	268	79	36	13	...
40 - 44	1 713	-	2	7	34	80	217	657	459	146	66	45	...
45 - 49	928	-	-	1	9	18	61	140	295	223	121	60	...

23. Marriages by age of groom and by age of bride: latest available year, 2009 - 2018
Mariages selon l'âge de l'époux et selon l'âge de l'épouse : dernière année disponible, 2009 - 2018 (continued - suite)

Continent, country or area, year, code[a] and age of bride / Continent, pays ou zone, date, code[a] et âge de l'épouse	Total	0-14	15-19	20-24	25-29	30-34	35-39	40-44	45-49	50-54	55-59	60+	Unknown Inconnu
EUROPE													
Bulgaria - Bulgarie[29]													
2017													
50 - 54	471	-	-	-	1	3	14	22	74	139	109	109	...
55 - 59	265	-	-	-	1	1	6	1	19	39	73	125	...
60 - 64	154	-	-	-	-	-	-	1	2	6	18	127	...
65 - 69	81	-	-	-	-	-	-	-	1	2	4	74	...
70 - 74	39	-	-	-	-	-	-	-	-	1	1	37	...
75 +	22	-	-	-	-	-	-	-	-	-	-	22	...
Croatia - Croatie[6]													
2017 (C)													
Total	20 310	-	117	1 955	6 569	5 890	2 649	1 237	595	424	304	570	...
0 - 14	-	-	-	-	-	-	-	-	-	-	-	-	...
15 - 19	601	-	74	324	150	34	11	6	1	1	-	-	...
20 - 24	4 206	-	35	1 187	2 038	731	155	46	7	5	2	-	...
25 - 29	7 555	-	7	379	3 562	2 723	665	162	35	13	4	5	...
30 - 34	4 180	-	1	57	703	1 953	993	334	93	34	8	4	...
35 - 39	1 734	-	-	8	96	378	633	400	147	44	15	13	...
40 - 44	747	-	-	-	14	58	159	206	156	82	42	30	...
45 - 49	462	-	-	-	3	10	30	65	109	124	60	61	...
50 - 54	316	-	-	-	2	2	2	11	38	80	79	102	...
55 - 59	231	-	-	-	-	1	-	6	7	29	59	129	...
60 - 64	139	-	-	-	-	-	-	-	2	9	21	107	...
65 - 69	91	-	-	-	-	-	-	-	-	2	9	80	...
70 - 74	30	-	-	-	-	-	-	-	-	-	3	27	...
75 +	15	-	-	-	-	-	-	-	-	1	2	12	...
Unknown - Inconnu	3	-	-	-	1	-	1	1	-	-	-	-	...
Czechia - Tchéquie													
2017 (C)													
Total	52 567	-	73	2 878	13 233	13 867	8 628	5 385	2 863	2 139	1 319	2 182	...
0 - 14	-	-	-	-	-	-	-	-	-	-	-	-	...
15 - 19	372	-	31	192	93	33	15	7	-	1	-	-	...
20 - 24	6 282	-	25	1 707	2 969	1 060	342	119	38	17	2	3	...
25 - 29	18 112	-	11	752	8 102	6 332	2 012	652	150	67	19	15	...
30 - 34	12 008	-	3	153	1 656	5 113	3 235	1 285	367	124	47	25	...
35 - 39	6 060	-	2	52	303	1 017	2 160	1 566	561	263	77	59	...
40 - 44	3 835	-	-	14	85	247	664	1 267	793	455	169	141	...
45 - 49	2 266	-	-	5	19	54	160	367	668	540	249	204	...
50 - 54	1 654	-	1	2	2	9	34	99	221	490	397	399	...
55 - 59	918	-	-	1	2	-	5	22	53	130	251	454	...
60 - 64	574	-	-	-	2	-	1	1	12	40	84	434	...
65 - 69	320	-	-	-	-	1	-	-	-	7	21	291	...
70 - 74	112	-	-	-	-	-	-	1	-	4	1	107	...
75 +	54	-	-	-	-	1	-	-	-	1	2	50	...
Denmark - Danemark[30]													
2017 (C)													
Total	31 777	-	32	1 355	6 760	7 200	4 631	3 014	2 263	2 203	1 531	2 095	693
0 - 14	-	-	-	-	-	-	-	-	-	-	-	-	-
15 - 19	158	-	18	72	29	11	5	1	-	-	-	-	22
20 - 24	2 771	-	11	902	1 288	312	85	32	10	2	3	2	124
25 - 29	8 656	-	1	271	4 334	2 862	664	192	81	28	12	7	204
30 - 34	6 566	-	-	27	761	3 128	1 748	517	162	77	15	9	122
35 - 39	3 799	-	-	10	106	526	1 522	1 015	337	133	41	30	79
40 - 44	2 380	-	-	3	30	92	350	802	613	304	95	36	55
45 - 49	1 809	-	1	1	4	20	62	214	613	587	201	72	34
50 - 54	1 787	-	-	-	-	2	10	57	243	698	494	253	30
55 - 59	1 066	-	-	-	-	1	2	10	44	156	402	437	14
60 - 64	673	-	-	-	-	-	2	-	4	31	102	532	2
65 - 69	324	-	-	-	-	1	-	-	1	4	17	297	2
70 - 74	217	-	-	-	-	-	-	-	1	6	208	297	4
75 +	113	-	-	-	-	-	-	-	1	-	3	108	1
Unknown - Inconnu	1 458	-	1	69	208	245	181	174	154	182	140	104	-
Estonia - Estonie													
2017 (C)													
Total	6 447	-	23	431	1 458	1 579	1 026	639	452	275	205	205	154
0 - 14	-	-	-	-	-	-	-	-	-	-	-	-	-
15 - 19	103	-	12	58	22	6	2	-	1	-	-	-	2

23. Marriages by age of groom and by age of bride: latest available year, 2009 - 2018
Mariages selon l'âge de l'époux et selon l'âge de l'épouse : dernière année disponible, 2009 - 2018 (continued - suite)

Continent, pays ou zone, date, code[a] et âge de l'épouse	Total	0-14	15-19	20-24	25-29	30-34	35-39	40-44	45-49	50-54	55-59	60+	Unknown Inconnu
EUROPE													
Estonia - Estonie													
2017													
20 - 24	824	-	9	254	358	136	23	10	2	1	-	-	31
25 - 29	1 897	-	1	82	850	644	198	50	18	11	4	1	38
30 - 34	1 401	-	-	22	165	570	377	149	58	18	5	2	35
35 - 39	882	-	-	8	36	162	298	229	94	19	12	3	21
40 - 44	501	-	-	1	13	34	77	137	136	50	28	13	12
45 - 49	321	-	-	-	4	8	29	40	93	77	42	22	6
50 - 54	209	-	-	-	1	2	5	13	34	76	49	24	3
55 - 59	124	-	-	-	-	-	-	1	7	15	49	49	3
60 - 64	64	-	-	-	-	1	1	1	3	6	11	41	1
65 - 69	25	-	-	-	-	-	-	-	-	-	2	23	
70 - 74	10	-	-	-	-	-	-	-	-	-	1	9	
75 +	14	-	-	-	-	-	-	-	-	-	-	14	
Unknown - Inconnu	72	-	1	6	9	17	16	9	6	2	2	4	-
Faeroe Islands - Îles Féroé[11]													
2018 (C)													
Total	230	-	-	20	35	55	36	30	21	14	10	9	...
0 - 14	-												
15 - 19	4	-	-	3	1	-	-	-	-	-	-	-	...
20 - 24	30	-	-	15	12	3	-	-	-	-	-	-	...
25 - 29	48	-	-	2	17	22	5	2	-	-	-	-	...
30 - 34	55	-	-	-	3	26	18	5	2	1	-	-	...
35 - 39	37	-	-	-	1	4	7	10	10	2	2	1	...
40 - 44	23	-	-	-	1	-	5	9	6	1	-	1	...
45 - 49	13	-	-	-	-	-	1	2	3	5	1	1	...
50 - 54	12	-	-	-	-	-	-	2	-	4	5	1	...
55 - 59	3	-	-	-	-	-	-	-	-	1	2	-	...
60 - 64	1	-	-	-	-	-	-	-	-	-	-	1	...
65 - 69	2	-	-	-	-	-	-	-	-	-	-	2	...
70 - 74	1	-	-	-	-	-	-	-	-	-	-	1	...
75 +	1	-	-	-	-	-	-	-	-	-	-	1	...
Finland - Finlande[31]													
2017 (C)													
Total	23 731	-	154	1 835	5 223	5 434	3 350	2 084	2 346	1 222	925	1 158	...
0 - 14	-												...
15 - 19	393	-	91	230	54	12	3	-	1	2	-	-	...
20 - 24	2 664	-	55	1 141	1 061	286	82	20	11	5	3	-	...
25 - 29	6 350	-	5	294	3 215	2 111	510	131	55	21	5	3	...
30 - 34	4 869	-	-	90	635	2 307	1 243	402	134	44	7	7	...
35 - 39	2 908	-	2	38	164	524	1 097	631	299	103	26	24	...
40 - 44	1 948	-	-	19	46	121	289	606	603	167	63	34	...
45 - 49	2 163	-	1	13	28	44	84	227	991	416	246	113	...
50 - 54	979	-	-	3	16	18	28	46	185	327	247	109	...
55 - 59	660	-	-	7	3	7	10	14	51	101	218	249	...
60 - 64	415	-	-	-	1	1	2	4	12	30	93	272	...
65 - 69	202	-	-	-	3	1	1	3	6	13	175	...
70 - 74	114	-	-	-	-	-	1	1	1	4	108	...
75 +	66	-	-	-	-	-	-	-	1	1	64	...
France[32]													
2016 (C)													
Total	219 549	-	166	9 004	46 926	52 709	33 649	22 808	16 263	13 868	10 339	13 817	...
0 - 14	-												...
15 - 19	1 366	-	77	623	467	144	42	9	1	2	-	1	...
20 - 24	19 743	-	66	6 083	9 710	2 798	695	228	90	38	16	19	...
25 - 29	57 737	-	17	1 818	29 958	19 397	4 537	1 224	458	191	84	53	...
30 - 34	48 860	-	2	317	5 381	24 038	12 962	3 843	1 435	552	210	120	...
35 - 39	29 564	-	3	111	927	4 647	11 525	7 650	2 860	1 132	435	274	...
40 - 44	19 963	-	-	34	304	1 104	2 823	7 051	4 809	2 350	949	539	...
45 - 49	14 373	-	-	14	115	383	770	2 054	4 379	3 817	1 708	1 133	...
50 - 54	12 179	-	-	3	47	137	207	559	1 729	4 011	3 190	2 296	...
55 - 59	7 843	-	-	1	10	39	60	150	366	1 333	2 631	3 253	...
60 - 64	4 415	-	1	-	4	12	20	32	111	339	836	3 060	...
65 +	3 506	-	-	-	3	10	8	8	25	103	280	3 069	...

23. Marriages by age of groom and by age of bride: latest available year, 2009 - 2018
Mariages selon l'âge de l'époux et selon l'âge de l'épouse : dernière année disponible, 2009 - 2018 (continued - suite)

Continent, country or area, year, code[a] and age of bride / Continent, pays ou zone, date, code[a] et âge de l'épouse	Total	0-14	15-19	20-24	25-29	30-34	35-39	40-44	45-49	50-54	55-59	60+	Unknown Inconnu
EUROPE													
Germany - Allemagne													
2015 (C)													
Total	400 115	-	660	20 450	88 623	99 432	58 243	34 353	31 943	27 698	17 978	20 735	...
0 - 14	-	-	-	-	-	-	-	-	-	-	-	-	...
15 - 19	3 551	-	353	1 986	917	194	51	18	19	9	3	1	...
20 - 24	42 750	-	252	13 264	21 255	5 760	1 445	425	205	86	38	20	...
25 - 29	115 844	-	41	4 214	53 466	42 240	11 137	2 888	1 234	424	124	76	...
30 - 34	92 114	-	10	722	10 777	42 625	25 272	8 070	3 016	1 075	360	187	...
35 - 39	45 351	-	3	156	1 656	7 102	16 286	11 562	5 576	2 031	628	351	...
40 - 44	25 477	-	1	65	333	1 090	2 940	7 438	7 807	3 801	1 290	712	...
45 - 49	26 968	-	-	26	147	276	805	2 786	9 129	8 399	3 449	1 951	...
50 - 54	23 812	-	-	11	46	105	244	910	3 835	8 584	6 121	3 956	...
55 - 59	13 259	-	-	6	21	26	45	198	868	2 571	4 449	5 075	...
60 - 64	6 493	-	-	-	3	8	15	46	210	573	1 198	4 440	...
65 - 69	2 558	-	-	-	2	5	-	7	32	122	244	2 146	...
70 - 74	1 155	-	-	-	-	-	2	2	8	16	44	1 083	...
75 +	783	-	-	-	-	1	1	3	4	7	30	737	...
Greece - Grèce													
2016 (C)													
Total	49 632	...	176	1 648	9 428	16 906	11 115	4 995	2 482	1 151	750	981	...
0 - 14	9	...	5	4	-	-	-	-	-	-	-	-	...
15 - 19	781	...	139	339	193	79	21	7	-	1	1	1	...
20 - 24	4 867	...	27	897	2 131	1 266	405	99	31	5	3	3	...
25 - 29	15 158	...	5	319	5 301	6 387	2 369	594	137	31	9	6	...
30 - 34	15 990	...	-	77	1 526	7 576	4 742	1 483	415	116	33	22	...
35 - 39	7 378	...	-	10	238	1 384	2 907	1 764	750	201	79	45	...
40 - 44	2 654	...	-	1	31	178	565	794	621	266	117	81	...
45 - 49	1 349	...	-	1	8	30	84	204	398	286	186	152	...
50 - 54	717	...	-	-	-	6	14	40	100	181	178	198	...
55 - 59	425	...	-	-	-	-	4	8	21	51	118	223	...
60 - 64	180	...	-	-	-	-	3	1	7	12	20	137	...
65 - 69	81	...	-	-	-	-	1	1	1	-	4	74	...
70 - 74	27	...	-	-	-	-	-	-	1	1	1	24	...
75 +	16	...	-	-	-	-	-	-	-	-	1	15	...
Hungary - Hongrie[7]													
2017 (C)													
Total	50 572	-	325	3 223	11 764	12 599	8 690	5 500	2 981	1 804	1 326	2 360	-
0 - 14	-	-	-	-	-	-	-	-	-	-	-	-	-
15 - 19	1 120	-	226	565	223	63	26	7	7	3	-	-	-
20 - 24	6 647	-	72	1 878	2 982	1 120	411	123	45	8	6	2	-
25 - 29	15 777	-	17	591	6 726	5 548	2 012	630	169	44	18	22	-
30 - 34	10 810	-	4	124	1 416	4 501	3 107	1 195	320	94	27	22	-
35 - 39	6 170	-	4	39	307	1 028	2 225	1 635	599	179	78	76	-
40 - 44	3 925	-	1	21	80	269	694	1 366	898	360	136	100	-
45 - 49	2 360	-	1	4	21	53	172	412	672	537	288	200	-
50 - 54	1 471	-	-	-	9	13	33	103	195	410	347	361	-
55 - 59	1 002	-	-	1	-	2	7	19	55	112	300	506	-
60 - 64	728	-	-	-	-	1	2	8	17	44	97	559	-
65 - 69	365	-	-	-	-	-	1	1	4	11	23	325	-
70 - 74	139	-	-	-	-	1	-	1	-	1	4	132	-
75 +	58	-	-	-	-	-	-	-	-	1	2	55	-
Unknown - Inconnu	-	-	-	-	-	-	-	-	-	-	-	-	-
Iceland - Islande[33,34]													
2011 (C)													
Total	1 458	-	3	77	302	334	272	161	111	74	64	55	5
0 - 14	-	-	-	-	-	-	-	-	-	-	-	-	-
15 - 19	6	-	-	2	4	-	-	-	-	-	-	-	-
20 - 24	152	-	3	52	69	21	1	3	1	1	-	-	1
25 - 29	371	-	-	19	173	115	44	9	5	3	1	1	1
30 - 34	350	-	-	3	43	157	104	25	9	3	4	1	1
35 - 39	243	-	-	1	7	33	101	62	22	9	6	1	1
40 - 44	113	-	-	-	3	6	14	44	28	11	3	4	-
45 - 49	94	-	-	-	1	-	6	15	36	24	7	4	1
50 - 54	68	-	-	-	-	1	1	2	9	18	25	12	-
55 - 59	30	-	-	-	-	-	1	-	1	4	15	9	-
60 - 64	18	-	-	-	-	-	-	-	-	1	2	14	-

Continent, country or area, year, code[a] and age of bride / Continent, pays ou zone, date, code[a] et âge de l'épouse	Total	0-14	15-19	20-24	25-29	30-34	35-39	40-44	45-49	50-54	55-59	60+	Unknown Inconnu
EUROPE													
Iceland - Islande[33,34]													
2011													
65 - 69	7	-	-	-	-	-	-	-	-	-	1	6	-
70 - 74	2	-	-	-	-	-	-	-	-	-	-	2	-
75 +	1	-	-	-	-	-	-	-	-	-	-	1	-
Unknown - Inconnu	3	-	-	-	-	2	1	-	-	-	-	-	-
Ireland - Irlande													
2012 (+C)													
Total	20 713	...	102	516	4 523	8 245	3 896	1 585	766	452	258	370	...
15 - 19	237	...	80	91	43	17	5	-	-	-	1	-	...
20 - 24	968	...	22	258	457	168	40	13	7	3	-	-	...
25 - 29	6 485	...	-	136	2 944	2 670	578	110	33	10	-	4	...
30 - 34	8 016	...	-	25	930	4 640	1 858	419	102	28	11	3	...
35 - 39	2 827	...	-	5	120	673	1 149	588	200	67	15	10	...
40 - 44	995	...	-	1	20	54	228	331	198	99	40	24	...
45 - 49	542	...	-	-	8	18	29	97	157	120	71	42	...
50 - 54	340	...	-	-	-	3	6	21	53	97	81	79	...
55 - 59	168	...	-	-	1	2	2	4	12	25	33	89	...
60 - 64	89	...	-	-	-	-	1	2	2	3	6	75	...
65 - 69	26	...	-	-	-	-	-	-	1	-	-	25	...
70 - 74	17	...	-	-	-	-	-	-	1	-	-	16	...
75 +	3	...	-	-	-	-	-	-	-	-	-	3	...
Italy - Italie													
2017 (C)													
Total	191 287	...	178	5 458	33 351	53 560	35 885	21 825	13 745	9 979	6 773	10 533	...
15 - 19	1 294	...	87	650	399	108	31	12	2	2	-	3	...
20 - 24	13 970	...	66	3 129	6 956	2 684	734	226	96	29	27	23	...
25 - 29	51 667	...	17	1 294	20 104	21 179	6 445	1 759	520	194	81	74	...
30 - 34	51 991	...	4	237	4 769	24 230	15 207	5 019	1 575	608	181	161	...
35 - 39	27 534	...	2	87	783	4 244	10 191	7 231	2 999	1 203	477	317	...
40 - 44	17 155	...	1	30	203	790	2 525	5 506	4 170	2 244	929	757	...
45 - 49	11 248	...	1	21	90	217	570	1 632	3 040	2 687	1 567	1 423	...
50 - 54	7 844	...	-	6	37	73	146	353	1 050	2 160	1 906	2 113	...
55 - 59	4 634	...	-	3	5	27	23	68	237	686	1 186	2 399	...
60 - 64	2 284	...	-	1	4	6	6	12	48	132	333	1 742	...
65 - 69	954	...	-	-	1	1	5	5	6	22	68	846	...
70 - 74	434	...	-	-	-	-	2	1	1	9	12	409	...
75 +	278	...	-	-	-	1	-	1	1	3	6	266	...
Latvia - Lettonie[6]													
2017 (C)													
Total	13 150	-	46	802	3 393	3 173	1 823	1 275	894	611	465	668	-
0 - 14	-	-	-	-	-	-	-	-	-	-	-	-	-
15 - 19	159	-	26	80	38	14	1	-	-	-	-	-	-
20 - 24	1 669	-	16	524	822	232	49	18	4	3	1	-	-
25 - 29	3 950	-	2	158	1 981	1 352	329	85	29	10	4	-	-
30 - 34	2 804	-	1	30	439	1 203	722	271	91	27	13	7	-
35 - 39	1 476	-	-	8	86	278	484	372	163	48	29	8	-
40 - 44	1 017	-	-	2	19	78	185	332	235	105	43	18	-
45 - 49	774	-	1	-	5	14	41	147	260	177	84	45	-
50 - 54	501	-	-	-	2	2	9	35	74	159	133	87	-
55 - 59	358	-	-	-	1	-	2	12	32	56	120	135	-
60 - 64	206	-	-	-	-	-	-	1	2	17	29	157	-
65 - 69	132	-	-	-	-	-	1	-	3	8	9	111	-
70 - 74	59	-	-	-	-	-	-	1	1	1	-	56	-
75 +	45	-	-	-	-	-	-	1	-	-	-	44	-
Unknown - Inconnu	-	-	-	-	-	-	-	-	-	-	-	-	-
Liechtenstein[6]													
2017 (C)													
Total	229	-	-	7	45	58	35	30	20	19	5	10	...
Lithuania - Lituanie													
2017 (C)													
Total	21 186	-	92	2 114	7 149	5 109	2 375	1 454	1 027	744	518	604	-
0 - 14	-	-	-	-	-	-	-	-	-	-	-	-	-
15 - 19	418	-	52	226	105	28	5	1	1	-	-	-	-
20 - 24	4 162	-	27	1 372	2 095	501	110	38	12	5	1	1	-
25 - 29	7 750	-	9	444	4 210	2 408	499	127	36	9	4	4	-

Continent, country or area, year, code[a] and age of bride / Continent, pays ou zone, date, code[a] et âge de l'épouse	Total	Age of groom - - âge de l'époux											Unknown Inconnu
		0-14	15-19	20-24	25-29	30-34	35-39	40-44	45-49	50-54	55-59	60+	
EUROPE													
Lithuania - Lituanie													
2017													
30 - 34	3 840	-	4	56	606	1 729	927	344	110	49	5	10	-
35 - 39	1 768	-	-	11	107	339	583	423	202	59	31	13	-
40 - 44	1 134	-	-	5	22	82	192	343	278	138	49	25	-
45 - 49	871	-	-	-	4	17	49	128	264	228	125	56	-
50 - 54	521	-	-	-	-	3	8	39	95	158	130	88	-
55 - 59	384	-	-	-	-	2	2	10	24	82	130	134	-
60 - 64	193	-	-	-	-	-	-	1	5	15	39	133	-
65 - 69	79	-	-	-	-	-	-	-	-	1	3	75	-
70 - 74	41	-	-	-	-	-	-	-	-	-	1	40	-
75 +	25	-	-	-	-	-	-	-	-	-	-	25	-
Unknown - Inconnu	-												-
Luxembourg[10,35]													
2017 (C)													
Total	1 908	-	6	100	375	453	315	214	157	128	88	72	-
0 - 14	-	-	-	-	-	-	-	-	-	-	-	-	-
15 - 19	15	-	1	7	7	-	-	-	-	-	-	-	-
20 - 24	183	-	3	62	85	20	9	3	1	-	-	-	-
25 - 29	504	-	2	21	210	191	50	14	7	8	-	1	-
30 - 34	456	-	-	5	53	179	122	56	19	11	7	4	-
35 - 39	266	-	-	1	16	48	95	57	25	15	7	2	-
40 - 44	195	-	-	4	2	10	32	55	36	33	15	8	-
45 - 49	117	-	-	-	2	2	7	20	39	19	18	10	-
50 - 54	93	-	-	-	-	2	-	6	24	35	17	9	-
55 - 59	56	-	-	-	-	-	-	3	6	6	21	20	-
60 - 64	15	-	-	-	-	1	-	-	-	1	2	11	-
65 - 69	-	-	-	-	-	-	-	-	-	-	-	-	-
70 - 74	7	-	-	-	-	-	-	-	-	-	1	6	-
75 +	1	-	-	-	-	-	-	-	-	-	-	1	-
Unknown - Inconnu	-	-	-	-	-	-	-	-	-	-	-	-	-
Malta - Malte													
2016 (C)													
Total	3 034	...	3[h]	134	925	907	447	197	156	103	65	96	1
16 - 19	9	...	1[h]	4	3	1	-	-	-	-	-	-	-
20 - 24	362	...	2[h]	76	200	64	14	3	2	-	-	1	-
25 - 29	1 177	...	-[h]	42	603	396	106	20	7	2	-	1	-
30 - 34	725	...	-[h]	8	91	372	178	46	23	5	-	2	-
35 - 39	327	...	-[h]	2	24	62	112	75	31	9	6	5	1
40 - 44	152	...	-[h]	1	2	8	24	36	45	22	9	5	-
45 - 49	116	...	-[h]	1	1	2	8	12	36	29	13	14	-
50 - 54	85	...	-[h]	-	1	-	5	4	11	26	21	17	-
55 - 59	43	...	-[h]	-	-	-	-	-	1	8	14	20	-
60 - 64	18	...	-[h]	-	-	-	-	-	-	1	2	15	-
65 +	17	...	-[h]	-	-	1	-	-	-	-	-	16	-
Unknown - Inconnu	3	...	-[h]	-	-	1	-	1	-	1	-	-	-
Montenegro - Monténégro													
2009 (C)													
Total	3 829	...	26	619	1 371	876	425	232	131	66	31	52	...
0 - 14	-	...	-	-	-	-	-	-	-	-	-	-	...
15 - 19	376	...	15	172	131	41	11	4	1	-	-	1	...
20 - 24	1 268	...	9	358	600	217	53	22	6	2	1	-	...
25 - 29	1 243	...	1	75	549	406	151	47	12	1	1	-	...
30 - 34	517	...	-	8	81	176	135	79	33	5	-	-	...
35 - 39	203	...	-	3	8	32	60	47	33	16	2	2	...
40 - 44	96	...	-	2	1	2	15	25	31	10	7	3	...
45 - 49	55	...	1	1	-	1	-	7	12	15	7	11	...
50 - 54	34	...	-	-	1	1	-	1	1	15	6	9	...
55 - 59	22	...	-	-	-	-	-	-	2	1	5	14	...
60 - 64	8	...	-	-	-	-	-	-	-	1	2	5	...
65 - 69	7	...	-	-	-	-	-	-	-	-	2	5	...
70 - 74	-	...	-	-	-	-	-	-	-	-	-	7	...
75 +		...	-	-	-	-	-	-	-	-	-	-	...

Continent, country or area, year, code[a] and age of bride — Continent, pays ou zone, date, code[a] et âge de l'épouse	Total	Age of groom - - âge de l'époux											Unknown Inconnu
		0-14	15-19	20-24	25-29	30-34	35-39	40-44	45-49	50-54	55-59	60+	

EUROPE

Netherlands - Pays-Bas[10,36]
2014 (C)

	Total	0-14	15-19	20-24	25-29	30-34	35-39	40-44	45-49	50-54	55-59	60+	Unknown
Total	75 696	...	93	5 415	18 406	18 053	10 388	7 078	5 065	4 156	2 989	4 053	...
15 - 19	707	...	53	359	202	57	17	12	4	2	1		...
20 - 24	11 835	...	30	4 051	5 752	1 433	345	130	62	21	3	8	...
25 - 29	22 426	...	7	856	10 426	8 207	1 966	609	201	95	36	23	...
30 - 34	15 494	...	3	105	1 726	7 034	4 306	1 512	478	202	73	55	...
35 - 39	7 942	...	-	24	214	1 050	2 925	2 245	929	329	136	90	...
40 - 44	5 397	...	-	9	53	205	641	1 840	1 499	730	259	161	...
45 - 49	4 147	...	-	8	26	54	137	529	1 325	1 229	503	336	...
50 - 54	3 524	...	-	3	7	8	42	162	427	1 163	1 036	676	...
55 - 59	2 113	...	-	-	-	3	8	31	107	302	702	960	...
60 - 64	1 153	...	-	-	-	2	1	5	27	60	189	869	...
65 - 69	569	...	-	-	-	-	-	2	4	18	44	501	...
70 - 74	251	...	-	-	-	-	-	1	1	4	5	240	...
75 +	138	...	-	-	-	-	-	-	1	1	2	134	...

North Macedonia - Macédoine du Nord
2018 (C)

	Total	0-14	15-19	20-24	25-29	30-34	35-39	40-44	45-49	50-54	55-59	60+	Unknown
Total	13 494	...	165[f]	2 522	4 999	3 150	1 263	571	351	222	251[t]	...	...
0 - 19	1 038	...	129[f]	595	262	40	7	4	-	-	1[t]	...	...
20 - 24	4 371	...	34[f]	1 669	2 060	517	72	12	6	1	-[t]	...	...
25 - 29	4 446	...	2[f]	218	2 364	1 493	292	55	15	5	2[t]	...	...
30 - 34	1 859	...	-[f]	31	264	934	478	112	31	3	6[t]	...	...
35 - 39	831	...	-[f]	6	40	126	344	207	64	33	11[t]	...	...
40 - 44	437	...	-[f]	2	6	29	56	150	128	38	28[t]	...	...
45 - 49	241	...	-[f]	1	3	9	11	25	85	67	40[t]	...	...
50 - 54	144	...	-[f]	-	-	2	3	3	20	57	59[t]	...	...
55 +	127	...	-[f]	-	-	-	-	3	2	18	104[t]	...	...

Norway - Norvège
2012 (C)

	Total	0-14	15-19	20-24	25-29	30-34	35-39	40-44	45-49	50-54	55-59	60+	Unknown
Total	24 077	-	38	1 503	5 000	5 362	3 852	2 786	1 989	1 440	1 018	1 089	...
0 - 14	-	-	-	-	-	-	-	-	-	-	-	-	...
15 - 19	352	-	19	164	105	35	14	10	3	1	-	1	...
20 - 24	3 246	-	15	1 069	1 372	457	164	79	51	21	7	11	...
25 - 29	6 632	-	3	226	2 933	2 215	721	289	140	61	25	19	...
30 - 34	5 312	-	-	29	486	2 197	1 503	614	245	129	64	45	...
35 - 39	3 099	-	1	13	82	386	1 128	840	352	154	79	64	...
40 - 44	2 083	-	-	1	19	55	259	718	553	270	128	80	...
45 - 49	1 463	-	-	1	2	10	51	180	477	416	201	125	...
50 - 54	981	-	-	-	1	4	9	48	137	301	291	190	...
55 - 59	505	-	-	-	-	1	2	6	24	74	177	221	...
60 - 64	231	-	-	-	-	1	1	2	5	13	37	172	...
65 - 69	129	-	-	-	-	-	-	-	2	-	8	119	...
70 - 74	28	-	-	-	-	-	-	-	-	-	1	27	...
75 +	15	-	-	-	-	-	-	-	-	-	-	15	...
Unknown - Inconnu	1	-	-	-	-	1	-	-	-	-	-	-	...

Poland - Pologne
2017 (C)

	Total	0-14	15-19	20-24	25-29	30-34	35-39	40-44	45-49	50-54	55-59	60+	Unknown
Total	192 576	-	420	22 465	77 056	46 236	19 460	9 496	5 268	3 682	2 891	5 602	...
0 - 14	-	-	-	-	-	-	-	-	-	-	-	-	...
15 - 19	2 677	-	253	1 642	623	116	31	9	-	1	-	2	...
20 - 24	47 407	-	138	16 596	24 702	4 940	771	185	49	17	5	4	...
25 - 29	77 540	-	19	3 761	45 843	22 268	4 381	900	222	89	37	20	...
30 - 34	31 794	-	6	365	4 999	15 577	7 621	2 262	623	207	85	49	...
35 - 39	13 206	-	3	81	685	2 663	4 961	2 975	1 094	451	171	122	...
40 - 44	7 186	-	1	12	155	534	1 343	2 293	1 567	730	336	215	...
45 - 49	4 370	-	-	4	40	124	285	653	1 182	1 015	590	477	...
50 - 54	2 916	-	-	-	4	12	51	157	399	773	743	777	...
55 - 59	2 223	-	-	3	3	-	11	43	91	256	611	1 205	...
60 - 64	1 697	-	-	1	2	1	3	13	26	96	225	1 330	...
65 - 69	975	-	-	-	-	-	1	4	9	36	63	862	...
70 - 74	379	-	-	-	-	-	1	1	3	6	19	349	...
75 +	206	-	-	-	-	1	-	1	3	5	6	190	...

23. Marriages by age of groom and by age of bride: latest available year, 2009 - 2018
Mariages selon l'âge de l'époux et selon l'âge de l'épouse : dernière année disponible, 2009 - 2018 (continued - suite)

Continent, country or area, year, code[a] and age of bride / Continent, pays ou zone, date, code[a] et âge de l'épouse	Total	\[Age of groom – âge de l'époux\] 0-14	15-19	20-24	25-29	30-34	35-39	40-44	45-49	50-54	55-59	60+	Unknown Inconnu
EUROPE													
Portugal[10,37,38]													
2017 (C)													
Total	33 634	-	118	1 846	7 522	8 622	5 368	3 379	2 098	1 574	1 110	1 997	...
0 - 14	-	-	-	-	-	-	-	-	-	-	-	-	...
15 - 19	350	-	89	164	67	16	8	5	1	-	-	-	...
20 - 24	3 287	-	20	1 092	1 521	423	141	55	22	8	4	1	...
25 - 29	9 500	-	7	474	4 627	3 211	808	231	78	35	19	10	...
30 - 34	7 967	-	-	84	1 062	3 797	2 051	628	208	79	35	23	...
35 - 39	4 555	-	2	22	183	897	1 663	1 055	439	170	74	50	...
40 - 44	2 861	-	-	10	43	206	508	934	604	318	137	101	...
45 - 49	1 865	-	-	-	14	50	145	331	479	443	211	192	...
50 - 54	1 349	-	-	-	2	14	29	112	196	356	309	331	...
55 - 59	869	-	-	-	1	6	9	18	46	119	257	413	...
60 - 64	548	-	-	-	2	1	4	8	20	39	43	431	...
65 - 69	287	-	-	-	-	1	2	-	3	5	15	261	...
70 - 74	122	-	-	-	-	-	-	-	2	2	3	115	...
75 +	74	-	-	-	-	-	-	2	-	-	3	69	...
Republic of Moldova - République de Moldova													
2012[39] (C)													
Total	18 565	-	308	7 229	7 959	2 219	583	143	61	37	12	13	1
0 - 14	-	-	-	-	-	-	-	-	-	-	-	-	-
15 - 19	2 706	-	189	1 743	675	83	11	3	1	1	-	-	-
20 - 24	10 091	-	108	4 720	4 452	710	92	5	2	-	2	-	-
25 - 29	4 470	-	9	714	2 535	975	188	39	7	2	-	1	-
30 - 34	938	-	1	41	274	384	191	33	9	4	1	-	-
35 - 39	241	-	-	8	19	64	79	44	17	9	-	1	-
40 - 44	66	-	-	3	4	1	20	17	15	5	1	-	-
45 - 49	25	-	1	-	-	1	1	1	9	10	1	1	-
50 - 54	11	-	-	-	-	-	1	1	1	2	3	3	-
55 - 59	10	-	-	-	-	-	-	-	-	3	3	4	-
60 - 64	5	-	-	-	-	1	-	-	-	1	1	2	-
65 - 69	-	-	-	-	-	-	-	-	-	-	-	-	-
70 - 74	1	-	-	-	-	-	-	-	-	-	-	1	-
75 +	-	-	-	-	-	-	-	-	-	-	-	-	-
Unknown - Inconnu	1	-	-	-	-	-	-	-	-	-	-	-	1
2018 (C)													
Total	20 399	...	107[f]	3 932	7 740	4 211	1 729	1 643[n]	...	702[o]	...	335	...
0 - 19	1 408	...	...	...	...	...	...	...	...	...	...	...	...
20 - 24	7 452	...	...	...	...	...	...	...	...	...	...	...	...
25 - 29	5 644	...	...	...	...	...	...	...	...	...	...	...	...
30 - 34	2 678	...	...	...	...	...	...	...	...	...	...	...	...
35 - 39	1 300	...	...	...	...	...	...	...	...	...	...	...	...
40 - 49	1 238	...	...	...	...	...	...	...	...	...	...	...	...
50 - 59	511	...	...	...	...	...	...	...	...	...	...	...	...
60 +	168	...	...	...	...	...	...	...	...	...	...	...	...
Romania - Roumanie													
2017 (C)													
Total	142 613	-	700	14 794	48 600	35 541	18 122	9 865	6 418	3 272	2 254	3 047	...
0 - 14	-	-	-	-	-	-	-	-	-	-	-	-	...
15 - 19	7 745	-	451	3 571	2 803	725	150	32	12	-	-	1	...
20 - 24	34 964	-	219	8 723	18 412	6 069	1 234	239	52	11	4	1	...
25 - 29	45 984	-	16	2 098	22 539	15 600	4 305	1 033	286	61	26	20	...
30 - 34	23 768	-	9	313	4 017	10 340	6 204	2 044	598	141	65	37	...
35 - 39	12 368	-	2	66	652	2 193	4 587	3 046	1 226	373	119	104	...
40 - 44	7 335	-	2	17	134	485	1 269	2 509	1 886	608	252	173	...
45 - 49	5 240	-	-	4	31	114	309	794	1 863	1 142	543	440	...
50 - 54	2 416	-	1	1	7	7	52	136	384	754	590	484	...
55 - 59	1 459	-	-	1	2	5	9	25	90	140	515	672	...
60 - 64	793	-	-	-	3	1	2	5	15	34	104	629	...
65 - 69	373	-	-	-	-	2	1	2	5	6	33	324	...
70 - 74	105	-	-	-	-	-	-	-	1	-	2	102	...
75 +	63	-	-	-	-	-	-	-	-	2	1	60	...

Continent, country or area, year, code[a] and age of bride / Continent, pays ou zone, date, code[a] et âge de l'épouse	Total	0-14	15-19	20-24	25-29	30-34	35-39	40-44	45-49	50-54	55-59	60+	Unknown Inconnu
EUROPE													
Russian Federation - Fédération de Russie													
2012[40] (C)													
Total	1213598	...	15 848	312 104	402 995	191 131	105 357	63 778	43 196	34 745	21 315	23 078	51
15 - 19	81 342	...	9 599	50 495	18 055	2 523	468	130	38	20	7	6	1
20 - 24	425 562	...	5 186	200 558	173 664	35 196	7 918	2 062	620	221	80	54	3
25 - 29	337 474	...	802	50 809	166 737	80 206	26 188	8 444	2 758	1 022	326	182	-
30 - 34	154 765	...	189	8 034	34 743	52 674	34 829	15 241	5 645	2 339	749	318	4
35 - 39	83 803	...	50	1 683	7 769	15 610	25 204	18 450	9 030	4 074	1 366	564	3
40 - 44	45 822	...	17	377	1 571	3 745	7 817	13 055	10 391	5 807	2 044	996	2
45 - 49	31 345	...	1	94	327	880	2 159	4 456	9 684	8 528	3 435	1 778	3
50 - 54	25 096	...	1	37	89	230	606	1 487	3 793	9 098	6 198	3 553	4
55 - 59	14 880	...	1	7	22	46	121	360	985	2 837	5 299	5 202	10
60 +	13 481	...	2	8	16	20	47	91	252	798	1 811	10 424	12
Unknown - Inconnu	28	...	-	2	2	1	-	2	-	1	-	1	19
San Marino - Saint-Marin[41]													
2016 (C)													
Total	181	-	-	3	35	49	38	16	6	3	1	4	26
0 - 14	-												
15 - 19	-												
20 - 24	9	-	-	2	5	1	-	-	-	-	-	-	1
25 - 29	57	-	-	1	23	22	6	3	-	-	-	-	2
30 - 34	44	-	-	-	6	15	15	3	1	-	-	1	3
35 - 39	30	-	-	-	-	7	13	3	2	-	-	-	5
40 - 44	13	-	-	-	1	2	-	2	2	1	-	-	5
45 - 49	4	-	-	-	-	-	-	1	-	1	-	1	1
50 - 54	5	-	-	-	-	-	-	-	-	-	-	-	5
55 - 59	-												
60 - 64	-												
65 - 69	1	-	-	-	-	-	-	-	-	-	-	1	-
70 - 74	-												
75 +	-												
Unknown - Inconnu	18	-	-	-	-	2	4	4	1	1	1	1	4
Serbia - Serbie[42,43]													
2017 (+C)													
Total	36 047	-	209	3 624	10 782	9 784	4 888	2 465	1 431	889	651	1 254	70
0 - 14	-												
15 - 19	1 349	-	125	667	399	99	44	10	4	-	-	-	1
20 - 24	7 595	-	71	2 207	3 483	1 360	326	81	33	9	9	11	5
25 - 29	11 993	-	8	595	5 518	4 248	1 206	270	80	31	16	10	11
30 - 34	7 138	-	-	107	1 115	3 294	1 757	610	160	52	19	15	9
35 - 39	3 243	-	3	21	176	587	1 193	769	311	115	32	32	4
40 - 44	1 773	-	2	9	51	121	251	555	425	180	92	84	3
45 - 49	1 075	-	-	8	10	32	68	116	298	250	138	148	7
50 - 54	767	-	-	-	6	7	18	35	78	164	185	273	1
55 - 59	466	-	-	-	-	3	5	11	25	51	114	256	1
60 - 64	265	-	-	1	-	1	-	-	8	17	30	208	-
65 - 69	147	-	-	1	-	-	1	2	3	8	8	124	-
70 - 74	64	-	-	-	1	-	1	-	1	2	4	55	1
75 +	45	-	-	-	1	-	-	1	2	2	3	36	-
Unknown - Inconnu	127	-	-	8	23	31	19	5	3	8	1	2	27
Slovakia - Slovaquie[6]													
2017 (C)													
Total	31 309	-	428	2 502	9 071	8 806	4 900	2 352	1 163	785	508	794	...
0 - 14	-												
15 - 19	963	-	345	471	106	24	8	6	-	2	1	-	...
20 - 24	5 012	-	75	1 468	2 382	798	218	50	12	7	-	2	...
25 - 29	11 454	-	6	456	5 440	4 068	1 139	263	57	16	7	2	...
30 - 34	7 076	-	2	70	939	3 166	1 971	631	190	72	19	16	...
35 - 39	3 162	-	-	26	151	603	1 178	748	257	123	48	28	...
40 - 44	1 595	-	-	8	39	113	304	494	329	168	93	47	...
45 - 49	792	-	-	2	10	26	60	122	221	186	83	82	...
50 - 54	572	-	-	1	1	4	15	30	73	160	132	156	...
55 - 59	317	-	-	-	2	4	2	6	19	34	90	160	...
60 - 64	237	-	-	-	1	-	3	-	4	14	27	188	...
65 - 69	88	-	-	-	-	-	-	2	1	3	8	74	...

23. Marriages by age of groom and by age of bride: latest available year, 2009 - 2018
Mariages selon l'âge de l'époux et selon l'âge de l'épouse : dernière année disponible, 2009 - 2018 (continued - suite)

Continent, country or area, year, code[a] and age of bride / Continent, pays ou zone, date, code[a] et âge de l'épouse	Total	0-14	15-19	20-24	25-29	30-34	35-39	40-44	45-49	50-54	55-59	60+	Unknown Inconnu
EUROPE													
Slovakia - Slovaquie[6]													
2017													
70 - 74	31	-	-	-	-	-	2	-	-	-	-	29	...
75 +	10	-	-	-	-	-	-	-	-	-	-	10	...
Slovenia - Slovénie[44]													
2017 (C)													
Total	6 481	-	20	382	1 575	1 856	1 192	645	318	214	98	181	...
0 - 14	-	-	-	-	-	-	-	-	-	-	-	-	...
15 - 19	75	-	11	35	20	5	1	2	-	-	-	1	...
20 - 24	764	-	6	240	363	121	25	6	1	2	-	-	...
25 - 29	2 029	-	2	82	954	737	192	48	10	2	1	1	...
30 - 34	1 682	-	1	19	195	784	487	140	37	12	5	2	...
35 - 39	935	-	-	3	32	172	377	239	72	27	8	5	...
40 - 44	442	-	-	2	9	28	87	163	91	40	14	8	...
45 - 49	229	-	-	1	1	5	15	37	74	64	15	17	...
50 - 54	166	-	-	-	-	2	5	8	27	52	32	40	...
55 - 59	70	-	-	-	-	-	1	1	5	11	13	39	...
60 - 64	52	-	-	-	-	1	2	1	1	4	7	36	...
65 - 69	22	-	-	-	-	1	-	-	-	-	2	19	...
70 - 74	11	-	-	1	-	-	-	-	-	-	1	9	...
75 +	4	-	-	-	-	-	-	-	-	-	-	4	...
Spain - Espagne[11]													
2017 (C)													
Total	166 730	-	136	2 800	21 159	46 407	38 097	23 686	12 907	8 460	5 500	7 578	...
0 - 14	-	-	-	-	-	-	-	-	-	-	-	-	...
15 - 19	692	-	58	288	213	87	33	8	4	1	-	-	...
20 - 24	6 380	-	48	1 433	2 948	1 260	425	162	54	29	12	9	...
25 - 29	34 099	-	18	757	12 941	14 721	4 099	1 022	320	122	53	46	...
30 - 34	48 832	-	10	208	4 044	24 341	14 795	3 864	997	318	144	111	...
35 - 39	32 441	-	-	76	754	4 849	14 401	8 416	2 497	860	341	247	...
40 - 44	19 515	-	2	24	182	861	3 538	7 686	4 224	1 750	698	550	...
45 - 49	10 986	-	-	7	53	207	620	2 005	3 448	2 538	1 177	931	...
50 - 54	6 938	-	-	5	18	55	135	417	1 081	2 078	1 598	1 551	...
55 - 59	3 973	-	-	2	5	16	37	85	229	623	1 152	1 824	...
60 - 64	1 761	-	-	-	-	7	10	15	38	106	264	1 321	...
65 - 69	702	-	-	-	-	1	3	4	12	27	51	604	...
70 - 74	275	-	-	-	1	-	-	2	1	7	8	256	...
75 +	136	-	-	-	-	2	1	-	2	1	2	128	...
Sweden - Suède													
2012 (C)													
Total	50 044	-	69	1 803	7 703	10 419	8 284	5 587	4 328	2 880	2 142	2 688	4 141
0 - 14	-	-	-	-	-	-	-	-	-	-	-	-	-
15 - 19	668	-	33	130	81	26	7	1	1	-	-	1	388
20 - 24	4 680	-	27	1 194	1 729	551	164	63	30	7	4	2	909
25 - 29	11 233	-	5	378	4 640	3 898	1 046	288	123	41	15	12	787
30 - 34	10 932	-	2	71	1 004	4 783	3 106	858	319	104	37	30	618
35 - 39	7 543	-	1	12	183	930	3 005	1 924	666	218	81	54	469
40 - 44	5 154	-	1	10	43	175	732	1 768	1 317	434	192	87	395
45 - 49	3 922	-	-	5	19	42	178	525	1 383	905	407	180	278
50 - 54	2 665	-	-	2	2	7	36	127	395	863	690	383	160
55 - 59	1 595	-	-	1	2	6	5	28	75	242	526	647	63
60 - 64	934	-	-	-	-	1	5	4	16	58	150	657	43
65 - 69	468	-	-	-	-	-	-	1	2	8	36	396	25
70 - 74	160	-	-	-	-	-	-	-	-	-	4	153	3
75 +	90	-	-	-	-	-	-	-	1	-	-	86	3
Switzerland - Suisse[45]													
2017 (C)													
Total	40 599	-	49	2 189	8 686	11 454	7 019	3 563	2 427	1 920	1 398	1 894	...
0 - 14	-	-	-	-	-	-	-	-	-	-	-	-	...
15 - 19	361	-	27	198	99	23	11	1	2	-	-	-	...
20 - 24	4 536	-	13	1 444	2 114	647	201	57	31	13	11	5	...
25 - 29	11 241	-	7	401	4 910	4 164	1 190	295	160	70	26	18	...
30 - 34	11 172	-	1	80	1 212	5 296	3 054	914	366	136	58	55	...
35 - 39	5 538	-	-	35	228	1 043	1 997	1 211	528	278	131	87	...
40 - 44	2 719	-	1	16	70	172	405	778	607	348	189	133	...
45 - 49	1 845	-	-	11	27	57	113	212	462	446	273	244	...

Continent, pays ou zone, date, code[a] et âge de l'épouse	Total	| Age of groom - - âge de l'époux											Unknown Inconnu
		0-14	15-19	20-24	25-29	30-34	35-39	40-44	45-49	50-54	55-59	60+	

EUROPE

Switzerland - Suisse[45]
2017

Âge de l'épouse	Total	0-14	15-19	20-24	25-29	30-34	35-39	40-44	45-49	50-54	55-59	60+	Unknown Inconnu
50 - 54	1 607	-	-	2	19	34	33	71	200	457	377	414	...
55 - 59	845	-	-	2	4	8	12	14	49	127	240	389	...
60 - 64	443	-	-	-	1	6	3	9	14	35	80	295	...
65 - 69	135	-	-	-	1	2	-	1	7	5	8	111	...
70 - 74	86	-	-	-	1	2	-	-	1	2	4	76	...
75 +	71	-	-	-	-	-	-	-	-	3	1	67	...

Ukraine[46]
2017 (+C)

Âge de l'épouse	Total	0-14	15-19	20-24	25-29	30-34	35-39	40-44	45-49	50-54	55-59	60+	Unknown Inconnu
Total	249 522	-	3 789	56 884	78 608	45 607	22 588	14 412	9 638	6 731	4 941	6 324	...
0 - 14	8	-	4	4	-	-	-	-	-	-	-	-	...
15 - 19	20 728	-	2 168	12 144	5 205	938	181	51	26	10	3	2	...
20 - 24	82 691	-	1 312	35 807	34 284	8 793	1 735	487	171	63	28	11	...
25 - 29	63 072	-	220	7 128	30 287	17 879	5 259	1 529	486	165	80	39	...
30 - 34	34 565	-	37	1 296	6 995	13 115	7 823	3 372	1 223	455	173	76	...
35 - 39	18 038	-	30	350	1 367	3 664	5 213	4 161	1 962	810	335	146	...
40 - 44	11 273	-	10	87	338	935	1 778	3 210	2 650	1 337	592	336	...
45 - 49	7 427	-	4	45	85	201	469	1 191	2 122	1 766	984	560	...
50 - 54	4 918	-	4	15	28	61	97	304	726	1 473	1 270	940	...
55 - 59	3 222	-	-	6	13	16	24	78	218	480	1 084	1 303	...
60 +	3 580	-	-	2	6	5	9	29	54	172	392	2 911	...

United Kingdom of Great Britain and Northern Ireland - Royaume-Uni de Grande-Bretagne et d'Irlande du Nord[47,48]
2015 (C)

Âge de l'épouse	Total	0-14	15-19	20-24	25-29	30-34	35-39	40-44	45-49	50-54	55-59	60+	Unknown Inconnu
Total	283 559	-	641	15 591	68 340	69 010	39 069	26 215	21 607	17 079	11 057	14 920	30
0 - 14	-	-	-	-	-	-	-	-	-	-	-	-	-
15 - 19	1 768	-	423	899	332	77	21	9	3	2	1	1	-
20 - 24	27 833	-	170	10 300	12 785	3 279	800	269	125	55	24	26	-
25 - 29	83 717	-	38	3 412	43 842	26 748	6 646	1 875	739	271	91	53	2
30 - 34	64 435	-	4	692	9 223	30 902	15 431	5 160	1 977	690	245	110	1
35 - 39	32 355	-	3	196	1 598	6 098	11 433	7 764	3 340	1 270	420	233	-
40 - 44	22 008	-	1	56	370	1 355	3 413	7 156	5 606	2 637	934	480	-
45 - 49	19 234	-	-	25	119	394	952	2 922	6 512	4 998	2 151	1 161	-
50 - 54	14 622	-	-	7	50	114	284	826	2 526	5 039	3 431	2 345	-
55 - 59	8 495	-	1	3	13	28	68	188	593	1 583	2 755	3 263	-
60 - 64	4 377	-	1	-	2	4	13	30	139	400	743	3 045	-
65 - 69	2 661	-	-	-	3	4	5	7	39	97	208	2 298	-
70 - 74	1 243	-	-	-	-	2	1	3	2	27	40	1 168	-
75 +	774	-	-	-	1	1	-	5	6	10	14	737	-
Unknown - Inconnu	37	-	-	-	3	4	2	1	-	-	-	-	27

OCEANIA - OCÉANIE

Australia - Australie[49]
2017 (+C)

Âge de l'épouse	Total	0-14	15-19	20-24	25-29	30-34	35-39	40-44	45-49	50-54	55-59	60+	Unknown Inconnu
Total	112 954	-	346	9 879	32 808	28 746	14 183	8 082	6 117	4 584	3 512	4 701	-
0 - 14	-	-	-	-	-	-	-	-	-	-	-	-	-
15 - 19	1 174	-	160	639	273	78	17	-	5	-	-	-	-
20 - 24	16 225	-	143	6 906	6 846	1 616	377	144	82	54	26	31	-
25 - 29	38 514	-	28	1 931	21 046	11 561	2 617	709	340	141	72	66	-
30 - 34	25 947	-	4	296	3 890	12 774	5 913	1 820	653	294	161	141	-
35 - 39	11 285	-	3	79	572	2 207	4 008	2 489	1 086	478	214	145	-
40 - 44	6 507	-	-	22	137	369	937	2 019	1 640	754	347	290	-
45 - 49	5 155	-	-	13	34	95	213	692	1 655	1 298	712	444	-
50 - 54	3 579	-	-	3	5	31	68	158	502	1 141	982	683	-
55 - 59	2 214	-	-	-	3	-	21	38	124	329	764	941	-
60 - 64	1 183	-	-	-	-	-	9	11	24	70	178	897	-
65 - 69	655	-	-	-	-	-	4	-	6	14	37	588	-
70 - 74	306	-	-	-	-	-	-	-	-	7	17	293	-
75 +	204	-	-	-	-	-	-	-	-	-	3	200	-
Unknown - Inconnu	-	-	-	-	-	-	-	-	-	-	-	-	-

23. Marriages by age of groom and by age of bride: latest available year, 2009 - 2018
Mariages selon l'âge de l'époux et selon l'âge de l'épouse : dernière année disponible, 2009 - 2018 (continued - suite)

Continent, country or area, year, code[a] and age of bride / Continent, pays ou zone, date, code[a] et âge de l'épouse	Total	0-14	15-19	20-24	25-29	30-34	35-39	40-44	45-49	50-54	55-59	60+	Unknown Inconnu
OCEANIA - OCÉANIE													
New Caledonia - Nouvelle-Calédonie													
2010 (C)													
Total	908	...	2[f]	62	149	200	171	169[n]	...	90[o]	...	65	-
0 - 19	13	...	1[f]	6	2	2	1	1[n]	...	-[o]	...	-	-
20 - 24	118	...	-[f]	36	51	18	10	2[n]	...	1[o]	...	-	-
25 - 29	194	...	1[f]	16	77	63	20	13[n]	...	3[o]	...	1	-
30 - 34	205	...	-[f]	4	14	94	62	27[n]	...	4[o]	...	-	-
35 - 39	139	...	-[f]	-	3	19	55	52[n]	...	7[o]	...	3	-
40 - 49	150	...	-[f]	-	2	4	22	65[n]	...	41[o]	...	16	-
50 - 59	59	...	-[f]	-	-	-	1	9[n]	...	30[o]	...	19	-
60 +	30	...	-[f]	-	-	-	-	-[n]	...	4[o]	...	26	-
New Zealand - Nouvelle-Zélande[10,50,51]													
2016 (+C)													
Total	20 235	-	60	1 590	5 085	4 728	2 649	1 611	1 365	1 053	822	1 266	...
0 - 14	-	-	-	-	-	-	-	-	-	-	-	-	...
15 - 19	339	-	57	213	45	12	6	-	-	-	-	-	...
20 - 24	3 459	-	-	1 380	1 605	351	84	24	12	3	3	-	...
25 - 29	6 642	-	-	-	3 438	2 433	516	147	66	24	12	15	...
30 - 34	3 912	-	-	-	-	1 935	1 359	369	162	48	21	15	...
35 - 39	1 758	-	-	-	-	-	684	666	267	84	30	21	...
40 - 44	1 281	-	-	-	-	-	-	405	522	201	87	66	...
45 - 49	1 071	-	-	-	-	-	-	-	327	429	195	117	...
50 - 54	798	-	-	-	-	-	-	-	-	264	330	207	...
55 - 59	477	-	-	-	-	-	-	-	-	-	153	327	...
60 - 64	243	-	-	-	-	-	-	-	-	-	-	246	...
65 - 69	144	-	-	-	-	-	-	-	-	-	-	144	...
70 - 74	69	-	-	-	-	-	-	-	-	-	-	69	...
75 +	51	-	-	-	-	-	-	-	-	-	-	51	...
Niue - Nioué													
2009 (C)													
Total	12	...	-	2	3	4	-	1	1	-	1	-	-
15 - 19	-	...	...	...	...	...	...	...	...	...	...	...	-
20 - 24	-	...	...	...	...	...	...	...	...	...	...	...	-
25 - 29	3	...	...	...	...	...	...	...	...	...	...	...	-
30 - 34	4	...	...	...	...	...	...	...	...	...	...	...	-
35 - 39	3	...	...	...	...	...	...	...	...	...	...	...	-
40 - 44	-	...	...	...	...	...	...	...	...	...	...	...	-
45 - 49	1	...	...	...	...	...	...	...	...	...	...	...	-
50 - 54	1	...	...	...	...	...	...	...	...	...	...	...	-
55 - 59	-	...	...	...	...	...	...	...	...	...	...	...	-
60 - 64	-	...	...	...	...	...	...	...	...	...	...	...	-
65 +	-	...	...	...	...	...	...	...	...	...	...	...	-

FOOTNOTES - NOTES

Italics: data from civil registers which are incomplete or of unknown completeness. - Italiques : données incomplètes ou dont le degré d'exactitude n'est pas connu, provenant des registres de l'état civil.

* Provisional. - Données provisoires.

[a] 'Code' indicates the source of data, as follows:
C - Civil registration, estimated over 90% complete
U - Civil registration, estimated less than 90% complete
| - Other source, estimated reliable
+ - Data tabulated by date of registration rather than occurence
... - Information not available

Le 'Code' indique la source des données, comme suit :
C - Registres de l'état civil considérés complèts à 90 p. 100 au moins
U - Registres de l'état civil qui ne sont pas considérés complèts à 90 p. 100 au moins
| - Autre source, considérée pas douteuses

+ - Données exploitées selon la date de l'enregistrement et non la date de l'événement
... - Information pas disponible

[b] Refers to 0-15 years of age. - Données se raportent au groupe d'âges 0-15.
[c] Refers to 0-16 years of age. - Données se raportent au groupe d'âges 0-16.
[d] Refers to 0-17 years of age. - Données se raportent au groupe d'âges 0-17.
[e] Refers to 0-18 years of age. - Données se raportent au groupe d'âges 0-18.
[f] Refers to 0-19 years of age. - Données se raportent au groupe d'âges 0-19.
[g] Refers to 0-24 years of age. - Données se raportent au groupe d'âges 0-24.
[h] Refers to 16-19 years of age. - Données se raportent au groupe d'âges 16-19.
[i] Refers to 17-19 years of age. - Données se raportent au groupe d'âges 17-19.
[j] Refers to 18-19 years of age. - Données se raportent au groupe d'âges 18-19.
[k] Refers to 19-24 years of age. - Données se raportent au groupe d'âges 19-24.
[l] Refers to 20-29 years of age. - Données se raportent au groupe d'âges 20-29.
[m] Refers to 30-39 years of age. - Données se raportent au groupe d'âges 30-39.
[n] Refers to 40-49 years of age. - Données se raportent au groupe d'âges 40-49.
[o] Refers to 50-59 years of age. - Données se raportent au groupe d'âges 50-59.
[p] Refers to 35+ years of age. - Données se raportent au groupe d'âges 35+.
[q] Refers to 40+ years of age. - Données se raportent au groupe d'âges 40+.

r Refers to 45+ years of age. - Données se raportent au groupe d'âges 45+.

s Refers to 50+ years of age. - Données se raportent au groupe d'âges 50+.

t Refers to 55+ years of age. - Données se raportent au groupe d'âges 55+.

1 Source: Vital Statistics Report. - Source: Vital Statistics Report.

2 Since 2010, the average age at first marriage has increased by four years, due in part to the initiative of encouraging long cohabiting couples to get married. - Depuis 2010, l'âge moyen au premier mariage a augmenté de quatre ans, en partie grâce à l'initiative d'encourager les couples cohabitant depuis longtemps au mariage.

3 Excludes the islands of St. Brandon and Agalega. - Non compris les îles St. Brandon et Agalega.

4 Including visitors. - Y compris les visiteurs.

5 Excluding visitors. - Ne comprend pas les visiteurs.

6 Data refer to marriages by residence of the groom. - Les données concernent les mariages selon la résidence du marié.

7 Marriages registered by residence of bride. - Les mariages sont enregistrés selon le lieu de résidence de la mariée.

8 Data refers to the number of marriages of which at least one of the partners is a resident of Curacao. - Les données concernent le nombre de mariages dont au moins l'un des partenaires est un résident de Curaçao.

9 Including marriages where bride/groom are non-residents. - Y compris les mariages pour lesquels le marié et la mariée sont des non-résidents.

10 Including same sex marriages. - Y compris les mariages entre personnes du même sexe.

11 As reported by the country. Reasons for discrepancy with other tables not ascertained. - Comme indiqué par le pays. L'on ne connaît pas la raison des écarts avec d'autres tableaux.

12 Excludes nomadic Indian tribes. - Non compris les tribus d'Indiens nomades.

13 Data are compiled from the National Registers of Identification and Civil Status (RENIEC). - Les données sont rédigées à partir des Registres Nationaux d'Identification et d'État Civil (RENIEC).

14 Data extracted from online system representing only 86.0% of the total marriages. - Données extraites du système en ligne, qui ne représentent que 86,0 % du nombre total de mariages.

15 Data refer to marriages of residents only. - Les données ne portent que sur les mariages de résidents.

16 Data refer to government controlled areas. - Les données se rapportent aux zones contrôlées par le Gouvernement.

17 Data refer to the Iranian Year which begins on 21 March and ends on 20 March of the following year. - Les données concernent l'année iranienne, qui commence le 21 mars et se termine le 20 mars de l'année suivante.

18 Includes data for East Jerusalem and Israeli residents in certain other territories under occupation by Israeli military forces since June 1967. - Y compris les données pour Jérusalem-Est et les résidents israéliens dans certains autres territoires occupés depuis 1967 par les forces armées israéliennes.

19 Data refer to Japanese nationals in Japan only; and to grooms and brides whose marriages occurred and were registered in the same year. - Les données se raportent aux nationaux japonais au Japon seulement; et aux époux et épouses dont le mariage a été célébré et enregistré la même année.

20 Excluding data for Jordanian territory under occupation since June 1967 by Israeli military forces. Excluding foreigners, including registered Palestinian refugees. - Non compris les données pour le territoire jordanien occupé depuis juin 1967 par les forces armées israéliennes. Non compris les étrangers, mais y compris les réfugiés de Palestine enregistrés.

21 Excluding marriages by groom and bride that are under "Married" status. - Sauf mariages entre personnes qui ont le statut de « marié(e) ».

22 Excluding alien armed forces, civilian aliens employed by armed forces, and foreign diplomatic personnel and their dependants. - Non compris les militaires étrangers, les civils étrangers employés par les forces armées ni le personnel diplomatique étranger et les membres de leur famille les accompagnant.

23 Data comprise civil marriages registered under the Women's Charter and Muslim marriages registered under the Administration of Muslim Law Act. - Les données comprennent les mariages civils enregistrés en vertu de la Charte des droits de la femme, ainsi que les mariages musulmans enregistrés en vertu de la loi sur l'administration du droit islamique.

24 Excluding marriages previously officiated outside Singapore or under religious and customary rites. - Ne comprend pas les mariages prononcés ailleurs qu'à Singapour ni les mariages religieux ou coutumiers.

25 Data from MERNIS (Central Population Administrative System). - Données de MERNIS (Système central de données démographiques).

26 Excluding marriages of aliens temporarily in the area, but including marriages abroad of persons with residence in Austria. - Non compris les mariages d'étrangers temporairement dans la région, mais y compris des mariages à l'étranger de personnes ayant leur résidence en Autriche.

27 Since 2003, marriage between persons of the same sex is authorized in Belgium, but the sex of spouses is not revealed. In this table, husband is used for first spouse, whereas wife is used for second spouse. - Depuis 2003, le mariage entre personnes de même sexe est autorisé en Belgique, mais le sexe des conjoints n'est pas indiqué. Dans ce tableau, la mention "époux" est utilisée pour le premier conjoint et la mention "épouse" pour le second conjoint.

28 Including armed forces stationed outside the country and alien armed forces in the area, if the marriage is performed by local authority. - Y compris les militaires nationaux hors du pays et les militaires étrangers en garnison sur le territoire, si le mariage a été célébré par l'autorité locale.

29 Including nationals outside the country, but excluding foreigners in the country. - Y compris les nationaux à l'étranger, mais non compris les étrangers sur le territoire.

30 Excluding Faeroe Islands and Greenland shown separately, if available. - Non compris les Iles Féroé et le Groenland, qui font l'objet de rubriques distinctes, si disponible.

31 Excluding Åland Islands. - Non compris les Îles d'Åland.

32 Data refer to marriages between persons of different sex. - Les données se rapportent aux mariages entre personnes de sexe différent.

33 Data for residence abroad are excluded. - Les données relatives aux résidents à l'étranger sont exclues.

34 Data refer to common residence after marriage. - Données se rapportant à la résidence commune après le mariage.

35 Data refer to marriages where one or both partners are residents. - Les données portent sur les mariages pour lesquels l'un des deux partenaires ou les deux sont résidents.

36 Marriages of couples of which at least one partner is recorded in a Dutch municipal register, irrespective of the country where the marriage was performed. - Correspond aux mariages pour lesquels au moins l'un des partenaires est inscrit sur un registre municipal néerlandais, quel que soit le pays dans lequel le mariage est célébré.

37 Marriages registered by place of occurrence of marriage. - Mariages enregistrés en fonction du lieu de l'événement.

38 Groom refers to the man for opposite sex marriages, and to spouse 1 as specified in the Civil Register for same sex marriages. Bride refers to the woman for opposite sex marriages, and to spouse 2 as specified in the Civil Register for same sex marriages. - Marié se réfère à l'homme en cas de mariage entre personnes de sexe différent et à l'époux 1 inscrit sur le Registre d'état civil en cas de mariage entre personnes du même sexe. Mariée se réfère à la femme en cas de mariage entre personnes de sexe différent et à l'époux 2 inscrit sur le Registre d'état civil en cas de mariage entre personnes du même sexe.

39 Data refer to first marriages only. - Données se rapportent aux premiers mariages seulement.

40 Data refer to population 15 years of age or more. - Les données concernent la population âgée de 15 ans ou plus.

41 Includes civil and religious marriages as well as not specified. - Englobe les mariages civils et religieux et ceux pour lesquels rien n'a été indiqué.

42 Excludes data for Kosovo and Metohia. - Sans les données pour le Kosovo et Metohia.

43 Residence refers to residence of groom. - La catégorie « résidence » correspond au lieu de résidence du jeune marié.

44 Data refer to residence of groom or bride before marriage. - Données relatives au lieu de résidence du marié ou de la mariée avant le mariage.

45 Data based on the residence of groom if he has permanent address in the country, otherwise, based on the residence of bride. If neither partner is a permanent resident, the marriage is not included in the official statistics. - Les données sont fondées sur la résidence du marié si celui-ci a une adresse permanente dans le pays, sinon elles sont fondées sur la résidence de la mariée. Si aucun des deux partenaires n'est un résident permanent, le mariage n'apparaît pas dans les statistiques officielles.

46 The Government of Ukraine has informed the United Nations that it is not in a position to provide statistical data concerning the Autonomous Republic of Crimea and the city of Sevastopol. - Le gouvernement Ukrainien a informé l'ONU qu'il n'est pas en mesure de fournir des données statistiques concernant la République autonome de Crimée et la ville de Sébastopol.

47 Data tabulated by date of occurrence for England and Wales, and by date of registration for Northern Ireland and Scotland. - Données exploitées selon la date de l'événement pour l'Angleterre et le pays de Galles, et selon la date de l'enregistrement pour l'Irlande du Nord et l'Ecosse.

48 Excluding Channel Islands (Guernsey and Jersey) and Isle of Man, shown separately, if available. - Non compris les îles Anglo-Normandes (Guernesey et Jersey) et l'île de Man, qui font l'objet de rubriques distinctes, si disponible.

49 Data for certain cells suppressed by national statistical office for confidentiality reasons. - Les données pour certaines cases ont été supprimées par le bureau national de statistiques pour des raisons de confidentialité.

50 Data refer to marriages and civil unions by residence of 'partner 2'. - Les données concernent les mariages et les unions civiles selon la résidence du « partenaire 2 ».

51 Data have been randomly rounded. - Ces données ont été arrondies de façon aléatoire.

Table 24 - *Demographic Yearbook 2018*

Table 24 presents the number of divorces and crude divorce rates for as many years as possible between 2014 and 2018.

Description of variables: Divorce is defined as a final legal dissolution of a marriage, that is, the separation of husband and wife which confers on the parties the right to remarriage under civil, religious and/or other provisions, according to the laws of each country[1].

Unless otherwise noted, divorce statistics exclude legal separations that do not allow remarriage. These statistics refer to the number of divorces granted, and not to the number of persons divorcing.

Divorce statistics are obtained from court records and/or civil registers according to national practice. The actual compilation of these statistics may be the responsibility of the civil registrar, the national statistical office or other government offices.

The urban/rural classification of divorces is that provided by each country or area; it is presumed to be based on the national census definitions of urban population, which have been set forth at the end of the technical notes for table 6.

Rate computation: Crude divorce rates by urban/rural residence are the annual number of divorces per 1 000 mid-year population. Rates presented in this table have been limited to those countries or areas having at least a total of 30 divorces in a given year. These rates are calculated by the United Nations Statistics Division based on the appropriate reference population (for example: total population, nationals only etc.) if known and available. If the reference population is not known or unavailable, the total population is used to calculate the rates. Therefore, if the population that is used to calculate the rates is different from the correct reference population, the rates presented might under- or overstate the true situation in a country or area.

Reliability of data: Each country or area has been asked to indicate the estimated completeness of the divorces recorded in its civil register. These national assessments are indicated by the quality codes "C" and "U" that appear in the first column of this table.

"C" indicates that the data are estimated to be virtually complete, that is, representing at least 90 per cent of the divorces that occur each year, while "U" indicates that data are estimated to be incomplete, that is, representing less than 90 per cent of the divorces occurring each year. The code "..." indicates that no information was provided regarding completeness.

Data from civil registers that are reported as incomplete or of unknown completeness (coded "U" or "...") are considered unreliable. They appear in *italics* in this table and the rates were not computed on data so coded. These quality codes apply only to data from civil registers. For more information about the quality of vital statistics data in general, see section 4.2 of the Technical Notes.

Limitations: Statistics on divorces are subject to the same qualifications as have been set forth for vital statistics in general and divorce statistics in particular as discussed in section 4 of the Technical Notes.

Divorce, like marriage, is a legal event, and this has implications for international comparability of data. Divorce has been defined, for statistical purposes, in terms of the laws of individual countries or areas. The laws pertaining to divorce vary considerably from one country or area to another. This variation in the legal provision for divorce also affects the incidence of divorce, which is relatively low in countries or areas where divorce decrees are difficult to obtain.

Since divorces are granted by courts and statistics on divorce refer to the actual divorce decree, effective as of the date of the decree, marked year-to-year fluctuations may reflect court delays and clearances rather than trends in the incidence of divorce. The comparability of divorce statistics may also be affected by tabulation procedures. In some countries or areas annulments and/or legal separations may be included. This practice is more common for countries or areas in which the number of divorces is small. Information on this practice is given in the footnotes when known.

The registration of a divorce in many countries or areas is the responsibility solely of the court or the authority which granted it. Since the registration recording such cases is part of the records of the court proceedings, divorces are likely to be registered soon after the decree is granted. For this reason the practice of tabulating data by date of registration does not generally pose serious problems of comparability as it does in the case of birth and death statistics.

As noted briefly above, the incidence of divorce is affected by the relative ease or difficulty of obtaining a divorce according to the laws of individual countries or areas. The incidence of divorce is also affected by the ability of individuals to meet financial and other costs of the court procedures. Connected with this aspect is the influence of certain religious faiths on the incidence of divorce. For all these reasons, divorce statistics are not strictly comparable as measures of family dissolution by legal means. Furthermore, family dissolution by other than legal means, such as separation, is not measured in statistics for divorce.

For certain countries or areas there is or was no legal provision for divorce in the sense used here, and therefore no data for these countries or areas appear in this table.

In addition, it should be noted that rates are affected also by the quality and limitations of the population estimates that are used in their computation. The problems of under-enumeration or over-enumeration, and to some extent, the differences in definition of total population, have been discussed in section 3 of the Technical Notes dealing with population data in general, and specific information pertaining to individual countries or areas is given in the footnotes to table 3.

As will be seen from the footnotes, strict correspondence between the numerator of the rate and the denominator is not always obtained; for example, divorces among civilian plus military segments of the population may be related to civilian population only. The effect of this may be to increase the rates but, in most cases, the effect is negligible.

As mentioned above, data for some countries or areas may include annulments and/or legal separations. This practice affects the comparability of the crude divorce rates. For example, inclusion of annulments in the numerator of the rates produces a negligible effect on the rates, but inclusion of legal separations may have a measurable effect on the level.

It should be emphasized that crude divorce rates like crude birth, death and marriage rates may be seriously affected by age-sex structure of the populations to which they relate. Like crude marriage rates, they are also affected by the existing distribution of the population by marital status. Nevertheless, crude divorce rates provide a simple measure of the level and changes in divorces.

The comparability of data by urban/rural residence is affected by the national definitions of urban and rural used in tabulating these data. It is assumed, in the absence of specific information to the contrary, that the definitions of urban and rural used in connection with the national population census were also used in the compilation of the vital statistics for each country or area. However, it cannot be excluded that, for a given country or area, different definitions of urban and rural are used for the vital statistics data and the population census data respectively. When known, the definitions of urban in national population censuses are presented at the end of the technical notes for table 6. As discussed in detail in the notes, these definitions vary considerably from one country or area to another.

In addition to problems of comparability, divorce rates classified by urban/rural residence are also subject to certain special types of bias. If, when calculating divorce rates, different definitions of urban are used in connection with the vital events and the population data, and if this results in a net difference between the numerator and denominator of the rate in the population at risk, then the divorce rates would be biased. Urban/rural differentials in divorce rates may also be affected by whether the vital events have been tabulated in terms of place of occurrence or place of usual residence. This problem is discussed in more detail in section 4.1.4.1 of the Technical Notes.

Earlier data: Divorces have been shown in previous issues of the *Demographic Yearbook*. The earliest data, which were for 1935, appeared in the 1951 issue. For more information on specific topics and years for which data are reported, readers should consult the Historical Index.

NOTES

[1] For definition, please see section 4.1.1 of the Technical Notes.

Tableau 24 – *Annuaire démographique 2018*

Le tableau 24 présente des statistiques concernant les divorces et les taux bruts de divortialité, pour le plus grand nombre d'années possible entre 2014 et 2018.

Description des variables : le divorce est la dissolution légale et définitive des liens du mariage, c'est-à-dire la séparation de l'époux et de l'épouse qui confère aux parties le droit de se remarier civilement ou religieusement, ou selon toute autre procédure, conformément à la législation du pays[1].

Sauf indication contraire, les statistiques de la divortialité n'englobent pas les séparations légales qui excluent un remariage. Ces statistiques se rapportent aux jugements de divorce prononcés, non aux personnes divorcées.

Les statistiques de la divortialité proviennent, selon la pratique suivie par chaque pays, des actes des tribunaux et/ou des registres de l'état civil. L'officier d'état civil, les services nationaux de statistique ou d'autres services gouvernementaux peuvent être chargés d'établir ces statistiques.

La classification des divorces selon le lieu de résidence (zone urbaine ou rurale) est celle qui a été communiquée par chaque pays ou zone ; on part du principe qu'elle repose sur les définitions de la population urbaine utilisées pour les recensements nationaux, qui sont reproduites à la fin des notes techniques du tableau 6.

Calcul des taux : les taux bruts de divortialité selon le lieu de résidence (zone urbaine ou rurale) représentent le nombre annuel de divorces enregistrés pour 1 000 habitants au milieu de l'année. Les taux de ce tableau ne se rapportent qu'aux pays ou zones où l'on a enregistré un total d'au moins 30 divorces pendant une année donnée. Ces taux sont calculés par la division de statistique des Nations Unies sur la base de la population de référence adéquate (par exemple : population totale, nationaux seulement, etc.) si connue et disponible. Si la population de référence n'est pas connue ou n'est pas disponible, la population totale est utilisée pour calculer les taux. Par conséquent, si la population utilisée pour calculer les taux est différente de la population de référence adéquate, les taux présentés sont susceptibles de sous ou sur estimer la situation réelle d'un pays ou d'un territoire.

Fiabilité des données : il a été demandé à chaque pays ou zone d'indiquer le degré estimatif de complétude des données sur les divorces figurant dans ses registres d'état civil. Ces évaluations nationales sont désignées par les codes de qualité "C" et "U" qui apparaissent dans la deuxième colonne du tableau.

La lettre "C" indique que les données sont jugées à peu près complètes, c'est-à-dire qu'elles représentent au moins 90 p. 100 des divorces survenus chaque année ; la lettre "U" signale que les données sont jugées incomplètes, c'est-à-dire qu'elles représentent moins de 90 p. 100 des divorces survenus chaque année. Le code "..." indique qu'aucun renseignement n'a été communiqué quant à la complétude des données.

Les données issues des registres de l'état civil qui sont déclarées incomplètes ou dont le degré de complétude n'est pas connu (code "U" ou "...") sont jugées douteuses. Elles apparaissent en italique dans le tableau et les taux correspondants n'ont pas été calculés. Les codes de qualité ne s'appliquent qu'aux données extraites des registres de l'état civil. Pour plus de précisions sur la qualité des données reposant sur les statistiques de l'état civil en général, voir la section 4.2 des notes techniques.

Insuffisance des données : les statistiques des divorces appellent les mêmes réserves que celles formulées à propos des statistiques de l'état civil en général et des statistiques de divortialité en particulier (voir la section 4 des notes techniques).

Le divorce est, comme le mariage, un acte juridique, et ce fait influe sur la comparabilité internationale des données. Aux fins de la statistique, le divorce est défini par la législation de chaque pays ou zone. La législation sur le divorce varie considérablement d'un pays ou d'une zone à l'autre, ce qui influe aussi sur la fréquence des divorces, laquelle est relativement faible dans les pays ou zones où le jugement de divorce est difficile à obtenir.

Du fait que les divorces sont prononcés par les tribunaux et que les statistiques de la divortialité se rapportent aux jugements de divorce proprement dits, qui prennent effet à la date où ces jugements sont rendus, il se peut que des fluctuations annuelles accusées traduisent le rythme plus ou moins rapide auquel les affaires sont jugées plutôt que l'évolution de la fréquence des divorces. Les méthodes d'exploitation des données peuvent aussi influer sur la comparabilité des statistiques de la divortialité. Dans certains pays ou zones, ces statistiques peuvent comprendre les annulations et/ou les séparations légales. C'est notamment le cas dans les pays ou zones où les divorces sont peu nombreux. Lorsqu'ils sont connus, des renseignements à ce propos sont donnés en note à la fin du tableau.

Étant donné que dans de nombreux pays ou zones, le tribunal ou l'autorité qui a prononcé le divorce est seul habilité à enregistrer cet acte, et, comme l'acte d'enregistrement figure alors sur les registres du tribunal, l'enregistrement suit généralement de peu le jugement. C'est pourquoi la pratique consistant à exploiter les données selon la date de l'enregistrement ne pose généralement pas les graves problèmes de comparabilité auxquels on se heurte dans le cas des statistiques des naissances et des décès.

Comme on l'a brièvement mentionné ci-dessus, la fréquence des divorces est fonction notamment de la facilité relative avec laquelle la législation de chaque pays ou zone permet d'obtenir le divorce. Elle dépend également de la capacité des intéressés à supporter les frais de procédure. Il faut aussi citer l'influence de certaines religions sur la fréquence des divorces. Pour toutes ces raisons, les statistiques de divortialité ne sont pas rigoureusement comparables et ne permettent pas de mesurer exactement la fréquence des dissolutions légales des mariages. De plus, elles ne rendent pas compte des cas de dissolution extrajudiciaire du mariage, comme la séparation.

Dans certains pays ou zones, il n'existe ou il n'existait pas de législation sur le divorce selon l'acception retenue aux fins de ce tableau, si bien que l'on ne dispose pas de données les concernant.

De surcroît, il convient de noter que l'exactitude des taux dépend également de la qualité et des insuffisances des estimations de population qui sont utilisées pour leur calcul. Le problème des erreurs par excès ou par défaut commises lors du dénombrement et, dans une certaine mesure, le problème de l'hétérogénéité des définitions de la population totale ont été examinés à la section 3 des notes techniques, relative à la population en général ; des explications concernant les différents pays ou zones sont données en note à la fin du tableau 3.

Comme on le verra dans les notes, il n'a pas toujours été possible d'obtenir une correspondance rigoureuse entre le numérateur et le dénominateur pour le calcul des taux. Par exemple, les divorces parmi la population civile et les militaires sont parfois rapportés à la population civile seulement. Cela peut avoir pour effet d'accroître les taux, mais, dans la plupart des cas, il est probable que la différence sera négligeable.

Comme indiqué plus haut, les données concernant certains pays ou zones peuvent comprendre les annulations et/ou les séparations légales. Cette pratique influe sur la comparabilité des taux bruts de divortialité. Par exemple, l'inclusion des annulations dans le numérateur a une influence négligeable, mais l'inclusion des séparations légales peut avoir un effet appréciable.

Il faut souligner que les taux bruts de divortialité, de même que les taux bruts de natalité, de mortalité et de nuptialité, peuvent varier sensiblement selon la structure par âge et par sexe. Comme les taux bruts de nuptialité, ils peuvent également varier en raison de la répartition de la population selon l'état matrimonial. Les taux bruts de divortialité offrent néanmoins un moyen simple de mesurer la fréquence et l'évolution des divorces.

La comparabilité des données selon le lieu de résidence (zone urbaine ou rurale) peut être limitée par les définitions nationales des termes « urbain » et « rural » utilisées pour la mise en tableaux de ces données. En l'absence d'indications contraires, on a supposé que les mêmes définitions avaient servi pour le recensement national de la population et pour l'établissement des statistiques de l'état civil pour chaque pays ou zone. Toutefois, il n'est pas exclu que, pour une zone ou un pays donné, des définitions différentes aient été retenues. Les définitions du terme « urbain » utilisées pour les recensements nationaux de population ont été présentées à la fin des notes techniques du tableau 6 lorsqu'elles étaient connues. Comme on l'a précisé dans les notes techniques relatives au tableau 6, ces définitions varient considérablement d'un pays ou d'une zone à l'autre.

Outre les problèmes de comparabilité, les taux de divortialité classés selon le lieu de résidence (zone urbaine ou rurale) sont également sujets à des distorsions particulières. Si l'on utilise des définitions différentes du terme « urbain » pour classer les faits d'état civil et les données relatives à la population lors du calcul des taux et qu'il en résulte une différence nette entre le numérateur et le dénominateur pour le taux de la population exposée au risque, les taux de divortialité s'en trouveront faussés. La différence entre ces taux pour les zones urbaines et rurales pourra aussi être faussée selon que les faits d'état civil auront été classés d'après le lieu de l'événement ou d'après le lieu de résidence habituel. Ce problème est examiné plus en détail à la section 4.1.4.1 des notes techniques.

Données publiées antérieurement : des statistiques concernant les divorces ont déjà été présentées dans des éditions antérieures de l'*Annuaire démographique*. Les plus anciennes, qui portaient sur 1935, ont été publiées dans l'édition de 1951. Pour plus de précisions concernant les années et les sujets pour lesquels des données ont été publiées, se reporter à l'index historique.

NOTE

[1] Pour la définition, voir la section 4.1.1 des Notes techniques.

24. Divorces and crude divorce rates by urban/rural residence: 2014 - 2018
Divorces et taux bruts de divortialité selon la résidence, urbaine/rurale : 2014 - 2018

Continent, country or area, and urban/rural residence — Continent, pays ou zone et résidence, urbaine/rurale	Code[a]	Number - Nombre					Rate - Taux				
		2014	2015	2016	2017	2018	2014	2015	2016	2017	2018
AFRICA - AFRIQUE											
Algeria - Algérie[1]											
Total	+U	60 844	59 909	62 128	...	...	...	...	...	...	...
Côte d'Ivoire											
Total	+U	...	...	1 285	1 317	1 431	...	...	...	...	...
Egypt - Égypte[2]											
Total	+C	180 344	199 867	192 079	198 269	...	2.1	2.2	2.1	2.1	...
Urban - Urbaine	+C	97 953	114 780	105 200	108 224	...	2.6	3.0	2.7	2.7	...
Rural - Rurale	+C	82 391	85 087	86 879	90 045	...	1.7	1.7	1.7	1.6	...
Lesotho											
Total	+U	...	...	169	197	...	...	...	...	...	...
Urban - Urbaine	+U	...	...	82	...	...	...	...	...	...	...
Rural - Rurale	+U	...	...	87	...	...	...	...	...	...	...
Mauritius - Maurice[3]											
Total	+C	2 262	2 161	1 910	1 996	2 425	1.8	1.7	1.5	1.6	1.9
Mayotte											
Total	C	155	139	...	...	...	0.7	0.6	...	...	...
Reunion - Réunion											
Total	C	1 420	1 561	...	...	...	1.7	1.8	...	...	...
Saint Helena ex. dep. - Sainte-Hélène sans dép.											
Total	C	4	3	-	-	...	...	...	...	...	...
Seychelles											
Total	+C	158	149	185	207	166	1.7	1.6	2.0	2.2	1.7
South Africa - Afrique du Sud											
Total	...	24 689	25 260	25 326	25 390	...	...	...	...	...	...
Sudan - Soudan											
Total	U	...	43 926	...	...	...	...	...	...	...	...
Tunisia - Tunisie											
Total	...	14 527	14 982	15 632	16 452	...	...	...	...	...	...
AMERICA, NORTH - AMÉRIQUE DU NORD											
Aruba											
Total	C	468	366	382	378	...	4.3	3.4	3.5	3.4	...
Barbados - Barbade											
Total	+C	443	...	...	...	...	1.6	...	...	...	...
Bermuda - Bermudes[4]											
Total	C	104	116	120	173	...	1.7	1.9	1.9	2.7	...
British Virgin Islands - Îles Vierges britanniques											
Total	C	75	71	68	49	...	...	2.4	...	...	...
Costa Rica											
Total	+C	10 864	10 111	13 155	12 661	...	2.3	2.1	2.7	2.6	...
Total	C	...	...	...	...	*11 003	...	...	...	...	*2.2
Cuba											
Total	C	32 934	33 174	31 598	32 183	*30 433	2.9	3.0	2.8	2.9	*2.7
Urban - Urbaine[5]	C	30 817	30 990	29 309	29 951	...	3.6	3.6	3.4	3.5	...
Rural - Rurale[5]	C	2 030	2 081	2 125	2 043	...	0.8	0.8	0.8	0.8	...
Curaçao											
Total	C	344	375	365	415	...	2.2	2.4	2.3	2.6	...
Dominica - Dominique											
Total	+C	80	...	...	...	...	1.1	...	...	...	...
Dominican Republic - République dominicaine											
Total	+C	19 370	20 352	21 873	24 218	...	2.0	2.0	2.2	2.4	...
Grenada - Grenade											
Total	+C	195	221	203	...	...	1.8	2.0	1.8	...	...
Guadeloupe											
Total	C	729	659	...	...	...	1.8	1.7	...	...	...
Guatemala											
Total	C	5 575	5 726	5 665	5 808	...	0.4	0.4	0.3	0.3	...
Jamaica - Jamaïque											
Total	+C	1 744	1 734	2 146	2 882	3 402	0.6	0.6	0.8	1.1	1.2
Martinique											
Total	C	414	369	...	...	...	1.1	1.0	...	...	...

24. Divorces and crude divorce rates by urban/rural residence: 2014 - 2018
Divorces et taux bruts de divortialité selon la résidence, urbaine/rurale : 2014 - 2018 (continued - suite)

Continent, country or area, and urban/rural residence / Continent, pays ou zone et résidence, urbaine/rurale	Code[a]	Number - Nombre					Rate - Taux				
		2014	2015	2016	2017	2018	2014	2015	2016	2017	2018
AMERICA, NORTH - AMÉRIQUE DU NORD											
Mexico - Mexique[6]											
Total	+C	113 478	123 883	139 807	147 581	...	0.9	1.0	1.1	1.2	...
Urban - Urbaine[7]	+C	101 093	108 804	119 819	122 052	...	1.2	1.2	1.4	1.4	...
Rural - Rurale[7]	+C	5 786	6 305	6 725	7 793	...	0.2	0.2	0.2	0.2	...
Nicaragua											
Total	+U	7 069	7 461	6 363	...						
Panama											
Total	C	4 336	*4 479	*4 360	*4 470	...	1.1	*1.1	*1.1	*1.1	...
Urban - Urbaine	C	3 781	*3 806	*3 730	*3 778	...	1.4	*1.4	*1.3	*1.3	...
Rural - Rurale	C	555	*673	*630	*692	...	0.4	*0.5	*0.5	*0.5	...
Puerto Rico - Porto Rico											
Total	C	11 776	11 877	10 998	8 515	9 644	3.3	3.4	3.2	2.6	3.0
Saint Lucia - Sainte-Lucie											
Total	+C	*55	...	...	...	...	*0.3	...			
Saint Vincent and the Grenadines - Saint-Vincent-et-les Grenadines											
Total	C	39	...	...	...		0.4	...			
Sint Maarten (Dutch part) - Saint-Martin (partie néerlandaise)											
Total	+C	108	117	89	91		2.9	3.1	2.3	2.2	
Turks and Caicos Islands - Îles Turques et Caïques											
Total	C	31	47	36	18	...	0.9	1.3	0.9	...	...
United States of America - États-Unis d'Amérique[8]											
Total	C	813 862	800 909	...	...	...	2.6	2.5	...	...	...
AMERICA, SOUTH - AMÉRIQUE DU SUD											
Brazil - Brésil											
Total	...	341 181	328 960	344 526	295 108		...	...	...	...	...
Ecuador - Équateur[9]											
Total	U	24 771	25 692	25 648	28 771		...	...	...	...	...
Urban - Urbaine[10]	U	22 854	24 021	23 180	25 685		...	...	...	...	...
Rural - Rurale[10]	U	1 917	1 671	2 468	3 086		...	...	...	...	...
French Guiana - Guyane française											
Total	C	251	209	...	...	...	1.0	0.8			
Peru - Pérou[11]											
Total	+C	13 598	13 757	*15 109	15 931	...	0.4	0.4	*0.5	0.5	
Suriname[12]											
Total	C	778	733	636	855		1.4	1.3	1.1	1.5	...
Venezuela (Bolivarian Republic of) - Venezuela (République bolivarienne du)											
Total	C	26 127	24 126	21 966	22 673	...	0.9	0.8	0.7	0.7	...
ASIA - ASIE											
Armenia - Arménie											
Total	+C	4 496	3 670	3 648	3 940	...	1.5	1.2	1.2	1.3	...
Urban - Urbaine	+C	...	2 801	2 923	3 130	...	...	1.5	1.5	1.6	...
Rural - Rurale	+C	...	869	725	810	...	...	0.8	0.7	0.7	...
Azerbaijan - Azerbaïdjan											
Total	+C	12 088	12 764	13 114	14 514	...	1.3	1.3	1.3	1.5	...
Urban - Urbaine	+C	8 190	8 658	9 173	9 780	...	1.6	1.7	1.8	1.9	...
Rural - Rurale	+C	3 898	4 106	3 941	4 734	...	0.9	0.9	0.9	1.0	...
Bahrain - Bahreïn											
Total	...	1 795	1 745	1 749	1 890	1 929	...	...	...	...	...

Continent, country or area, and urban/rural residence / Continent, pays ou zone et résidence, urbaine/rurale	Code[a]	Number - Nombre					Rate - Taux				
		2014	2015	2016	2017	2018	2014	2015	2016	2017	2018
ASIA - ASIE											
Brunei Darussalam - Brunéi Darussalam											
Total	+C	522	545	566	632	...	1.3	1.3	1.4	1.5	...
China, Hong Kong SAR - Chine, Hong Kong RAS											
Total	...	20 019	20 075	17 196	19 394	20 321	...	...	...	...	...
China, Macao SAR - Chine, Macao RAS											
Total	+C	1 308	1 168	1 245	1 479	1 544	2.1	1.8	1.9	2.3	2.3
Cyprus - Chypre[13]											
Total	C	1 884	1 807	1 948	1 932	...	2.2	2.1	2.3	2.2	...
Georgia - Géorgie											
Total	C	9 119	9 112	9 539	10 222	10 288	2.4	2.5	2.6	2.7	2.8
Urban - Urbaine	C	6 253	6 320	6 565	...	...	...	3.0	3.1	...	...
Rural - Rurale	C	2 866	2 792	2 974	...	...	...	1.8	1.9	...	...
Indonesia - Indonésie											
Total	U	344 237	347 256	...	...	...	...	...	...	...	...
Iran (Islamic Republic of) - Iran (République islamique d')[14]											
Total	+C	163 569	163 765	174 392	174 578	...	2.1	2.1	2.2	2.2	...
Urban - Urbaine	+C	...	146 714	162 668	163 466	...	...	2.6	2.7	2.7	...
Rural - Rurale	+C	...	17 051	11 724	11 112	...	...	0.8	0.6	0.5	...
Israel - Israël[15]											
Total	C	14 430	14 487	14 819	...	...	1.8	1.7	1.7	...	...
Urban - Urbaine[16]	C	13 166	13 095	13 385	...	...	1.8	1.7	1.7	...	...
Rural - Rurale[16]	C	929	1 070	1 042	...	...	1.3	1.5	1.4	...	...
Japan - Japon[17]											
Total	+C	222 107	226 215	216 798	212 262	...	1.7	1.8	1.7	1.7	...
Urban - Urbaine	+C	204 352	208 181	199 561	195 520	...	...	...	...	...	...
Rural - Rurale	+C	17 755	18 034	17 237	16 742	...	...	...	...	...	...
Jordan - Jordanie[18]											
Total	+C	20 911	22 070	21 969	21 210	...	2.4	2.3	2.2	2.1	...
Kazakhstan											
Total	+C	52 673	53 293	51 993	54 626	54 797	3.0	3.0	2.9	3.0	3.0
Urban - Urbaine	+C	39 433	39 846	38 716	40 774	41 122	4.1	4.0	3.8	3.9	3.9
Rural - Rurale	+C	13 240	13 447	13 277	13 852	13 675	1.7	1.8	1.7	1.8	1.8
Kuwait - Koweït											
Total	C	7 327	7 201	7 223	7 433	7 869	1.9	1.8	1.8	1.8	1.9
Kyrgyzstan - Kirghizstan											
Total	C	9 235	8 588	9 102	9 588	10 434	1.6	1.4	1.5	1.5	1.7
Urban - Urbaine	C	5 324	4 797	5 297	5 302	...	2.7	2.4	2.6	2.5	...
Rural - Rurale	C	3 911	3 791	3 805	4 286	...	1.0	1.0	0.9	1.0	...
Lebanon - Liban											
Total	+C	7 206	...	...	...	...	...	...	...	...	...
Maldives											
Total	...	...	3 358	3 417	...	...	...	...	...	...	...
Urban - Urbaine	...	...	1 455	1 496	...	...	...	...	...	...	...
Rural - Rurale	...	...	1 903	1 921	...	...	...	...	...	...	...
Mongolia - Mongolie											
Total	+C	3 750	3 873	4 003	3 945	4 201	1.3	1.3	1.3	1.3	1.3
Urban - Urbaine	+C	3 333	3 455	3 501	3 384	3 615	1.7	1.7	1.6	1.6	1.7
Rural - Rurale	+C	417	418	502	561	586	0.4	0.4	0.5	0.6	0.6
Oman											
Total	U	3 622	3 619	3 736	3 867	3 662	...	...	...	...	...
Qatar											
Total	C	1 315	1 307	1 151	1 206	...	0.6	0.5	0.4	0.4	...
Urban - Urbaine	C	1 315	1 307	1 151	1 206	...	0.6	0.5	0.4	0.4	...
Republic of Korea - République de Corée[19]											
Total	+C	115 510	109 153	107 328	106 032	108 684	2.3	2.1	2.1	2.1	2.1
Urban - Urbaine[16]	+C	89 689	84 958	83 872	82 470	84 098	2.2	2.0	2.0	2.0	2.0
Rural - Rurale[16]	+C	22 596	21 384	21 504	21 744	22 692	2.4	2.3	2.3	2.3	2.3
Singapore - Singapour											
Total	+C	6 861	7 117	7 207	7 207	6 990	1.8	1.8	1.8	1.8	1.8

24. Divorces and crude divorce rates by urban/rural residence: 2014 - 2018
Divorces et taux bruts de divortialité selon la résidence, urbaine/rurale : 2014 - 2018 (continued - suite)

Continent, country or area, and urban/rural residence / Continent, pays ou zone et résidence, urbaine/rurale	Code[a]	Number - Nombre					Rate - Taux				
		2014	2015	2016	2017	2018	2014	2015	2016	2017	2018
ASIA - ASIE											
State of Palestine - État de Palestine											
Total	C	7 603	8 179	8 510	8 568	...	1.7	1.8	1.8	1.8	...
Tajikistan - Tadjikistan											
Total	+C	9 037	8 346	8 845	10 053	...	1.1	1.0	1.0	1.1	...
Urban - Urbaine	+C	3 279	3 366	3 557	3 870	...	1.5	1.5	1.6	1.7	...
Rural - Rurale	+C	5 758	4 980	5 288	6 183	...	0.9	0.8	0.8	0.9	...
Thailand - Thaïlande											
Total	...	111 810	117 880	118 539	121 617	...	...	...	...	...	...
Turkey - Turquie[20]											
Total	C	130 913	131 830	126 164	128 411	...	1.7	1.7	1.6	1.6	...
United Arab Emirates - Émirats arabes unis											
Total	...	4 809	4 913	...	4 403	...	...	...	...	...	...
Uzbekistan - Ouzbékistan											
Total	+C	28 811	29 647	29 340	31 929	...	0.9	0.9	0.9	1.0	...
Urban - Urbaine	+C	19 634	19 480	18 605	19 618	...	1.3	1.2	1.2	1.2	...
Rural - Rurale	+C	9 177	10 167	10 735	12 311	...	0.6	0.7	0.7	0.8	...
EUROPE											
Åland Islands - Îles d'Åland											
Total	C	50	77	62	44	*55	1.7	2.7	2.1	1.5	*1.9
Urban - Urbaine	C	20	44	35	29	*31	...	3.8	3.0	...	*2.6
Rural - Rurale	C	30	33	27	15	*24	1.7	1.9	...	...	...
Albania - Albanie											
Total	C	4 240	3 761	4 345	4 508	...	1.5	1.3	1.5	1.6	...
Austria - Autriche											
Total	C	16 647[21]	16 351[21]	15 919[21]	16 180[21]	16 304[22]	1.9	1.9	1.8	1.8	1.8
Belarus - Bélarus											
Total	C	34 864	32 984	32 628	32 006	*33 152	3.7	3.5	3.4	3.4	*3.5
Urban - Urbaine	C	30 436	28 419	28 326	27 977	...	4.2	3.9	3.8	3.8	...
Rural - Rurale	C	4 428	4 565	4 302	4 029	...	2.0	2.1	2.0	1.9	...
Belgium - Belgique[23]											
Total	C	24 310	24 414	23 583	23 068	...	2.2	2.2	2.1	2.0	...
Urban - Urbaine	C	24 029	24 132	...	...	...	...	...	...	...	...
Rural - Rurale	C	281	282	...	...	...	...	...	...	...	...
Bosnia and Herzegovina - Bosnie-Herzégovine											
Total	C	1 655	1 997	1 797	1 961	...	0.5	0.6	0.5	0.6	...
Bulgaria - Bulgarie[24]											
Total	C	10 584	10 483	10 603	10 411	10 596	1.5	1.5	1.5	1.5	1.5
Urban - Urbaine	C	8 680	8 629	8 603	8 438	8 517	1.6	1.6	1.6	1.6	1.6
Rural - Rurale	C	1 904	1 854	2 000	1 973	2 079	1.0	1.0	1.0	1.0	1.1
Croatia - Croatie											
Total	C	6 570	6 010	7 036	6 265	...	1.6	1.4	1.7	1.5	...
Urban - Urbaine	C	4 585	4 170	4 955	4 408	...	...	...	...	...	...
Rural - Rurale	C	1 985	1 840	2 081	1 857	...	...	...	...	...	...
Czechia - Tchéquie											
Total	C	26 764	26 083	24 996	25 755	*24 122	2.5	2.5	2.4	2.4	*2.3
Urban - Urbaine	C	20 676	19 646	18 569	19 060	...	2.7	2.6	2.4	2.5	...
Rural - Rurale	C	6 088	6 437	6 427	6 695	...	2.2	2.3	2.3	2.4	...
Denmark - Danemark[25]											
Total	C	19 435	16 343	17 222	15 265	15 034	3.4	2.9	3.0	2.6	2.6
Estonia - Estonie											
Total	C	3 218	3 382	3 262	3 323	3 199	2.4	2.6	2.5	2.5	2.4
Urban - Urbaine[26]	C	2 197	2 226	2 143	2 283	...	2.4	2.5	2.4	2.5	...
Rural - Rurale[26]	C	836	985	908	863	...	2.0	2.4	2.2	2.1	...
Faeroe Islands - Îles Féroé											
Total	C	83	78	52	65	80	1.7	1.6	1.1	1.3	1.6
Finland - Finlande[27]											
Total	C	13 632	13 862	13 479	13 188	...	2.5	2.5	2.5	2.4	...
Urban - Urbaine	C	10 229	10 521	10 254	10 013	...	2.7	2.7	2.6	2.6	...
Rural - Rurale	C	3 403	3 341	3 225	3 175	...	2.0	2.1	2.0	2.0	...
France											
Total	C	120 568	120 731	124 768	...	...	1.9	1.9	1.9	...	...

24. Divorces and crude divorce rates by urban/rural residence: 2014 - 2018
Divorces et taux bruts de divortialité selon la résidence, urbaine/rurale : 2014 - 2018 (continued - suite)

Continent, country or area, and urban/rural residence / Continent, pays ou zone et résidence, urbaine/rurale	Code[a]	Number - Nombre					Rate - Taux				
		2014	2015	2016	2017	2018	2014	2015	2016	2017	2018
EUROPE											
Germany - Allemagne											
Total	C	166 199	163 335	162 397	153 501	148 066	2.1	2.0	2.0	1.9	1.8
Gibraltar											
Total	+C	72	61	85	...	...	2.2	1.8	2.5	...	...
Greece - Grèce											
Total	C	14 427	15 600	11 013	19 190	...	1.3	1.4	1.0	1.8	...
Hungary - Hongrie[12]											
Total	C	19 576	20 315	19 552	18 495	16 952	2.0	2.1	2.0	1.9	1.7
Urban - Urbaine[28]	C	14 801	15 168	14 741	13 737	...	2.1	2.2	2.1	2.0	...
Rural - Rurale[28]	C	4 536	4 893	4 540	4 426	...	1.6	1.7	1.6	1.5	...
Ireland - Irlande											
Total	+C	2 629	3 289	3 255	3 412	...	0.6	0.7	0.7	0.7	...
Italy - Italie											
Total	C	52 355	82 469	99 071	91 629	...	0.9	1.4	1.6	1.5	...
Latvia - Lettonie											
Total	C	6 271	5 151	6 061	5 943	5 697	3.1	2.6	3.1	3.1	2.9
Liechtenstein[29]											
Total	C	82	98	81	90	...	2.2	2.6	2.1	2.4	...
Lithuania - Lituanie											
Total	C	9 806	9 371	8 879	8 518	8 640	3.3	3.2	3.1	3.0	3.1
Urban - Urbaine	C	6 831	6 394	6 037	5 897	...	3.5	3.3	3.1	3.1	...
Rural - Rurale	C	2 975	2 977	2 842	2 621	...	3.1	3.1	3.0	2.8	...
Luxembourg											
Total	C	1 453	1 345	1 241	1 192	1 230	2.6	2.4	2.1	2.0	2.0
Malta - Malte											
Total	C	323	372	371	312	...	0.7	0.8	0.8	0.7	...
Monaco											
Total	C	86	74	89	69	78[30]	2.3	2.0	2.3	1.8	2.0
Montenegro - Monténégro											
Total	C	584	577	703	765	849	0.9	0.9	1.1	1.2	1.4
Netherlands - Pays-Bas[6]											
Total	C	35 409[31]	34 232[31]	33 414[32]	32 768[32]	...	2.1	2.0	2.0	1.9	...
North Macedonia - Macédoine du Nord											
Total	C	2 210	2 200	1 985	1 994	1 620	1.1	1.1	1.0	1.0	0.8
Urban - Urbaine	C	1 472	1 420	1 315	1 309	...	...	...	...	...	...
Rural - Rurale	C	738	780	670	685	...	...	...	...	...	...
Norway - Norvège[6]											
Total	C	9 918	9 793	9 944	10 567	...	1.9	1.9	1.9	2.0	...
Poland - Pologne											
Total	C	65 761	67 296	63 497	65 257	62 843	1.7	1.8	1.7	1.7	1.7
Urban - Urbaine[33]	C	48 490	48 896	45 904	46 840	45 153	2.1	2.1	2.0	2.0	...
Rural - Rurale[33]	C	16 632	17 587	16 690	17 472	16 654	1.1	1.2	1.1	1.2	...
Portugal[34]											
Total	C	21 988	23 377	22 649	21 577	...	2.1	2.3	2.2	2.1	...
Republic of Moldova - République de Moldova											
Total	C	11 130	11 199	10 605	9 312	10 721	3.9	4.0	3.8	3.4	4.0
Urban - Urbaine	C	7 834	10 915	10 112	8 954	10 338	...	...	...	...	...
Rural - Rurale	C	3 296	284	493	358	383	...	...	...	...	...
Romania - Roumanie											
Total	C	27 188	31 527	30 497	31 147	...	1.4	1.6	1.5	1.6	...
Urban - Urbaine	C	18 692	21 496	20 485	20 625	...	1.7	2.0	1.9	2.0	...
Rural - Rurale	C	8 496	10 031	10 012	10 522	...	0.9	1.1	1.1	1.2	...
San Marino - Saint-Marin											
Total	C	51	65	83	90	...	1.5	1.9	2.4	2.6	...
Serbia - Serbie[35]											
Total	+C	7 614	9 381[12]	9 046[12]	9 262[12]	9 995[12]	1.1	1.3	1.3	1.3	1.4
Urban - Urbaine	+C	5 322	6 833[12]	6 532[12]	6 714[12]	...	1.2	1.6	1.5	1.6	...
Rural - Rurale	+C	2 292	2 548[12]	2 514[12]	2 548[12]	...	0.8	0.9	0.9	0.9	...
Slovakia - Slovaquie											
Total	C	10 514	9 786	9 286	9 618	...	1.9	1.8	1.7	1.8	...
Urban - Urbaine	C	6 490	5 945	5 664	5 824	...	2.2	2.0	1.9	2.0	...
Rural - Rurale	C	4 024	3 841	3 622	3 794	...	1.6	1.5	1.4	1.5	...

Continent, country or area, and urban/rural residence / Continent, pays ou zone et résidence, urbaine/rurale	Code[a]	Number - Nombre					Rate - Taux				
		2014	2015	2016	2017	2018	2014	2015	2016	2017	2018
EUROPE											
Slovenia - Slovénie											
Total	C	2 469	2 432	2 531	2 387	2 347	1.2	1.2	1.2	1.2	1.1
Urban - Urbaine	C	1 399	1 484	1 545	1 483	...	1.3	1.3	1.4	1.3	...
Rural - Rurale	C	1 070	948	986	904	...	1.1	1.0	1.0	1.0	...
Spain - Espagne											
Total	C	100 746	96 562	96 824	97 960	*95 254	2.2	2.1	2.1	2.1	*2.0
Sweden - Suède[6]											
Total	C	26 143	24 876	24 258	24 210	24 958	2.7	2.5	2.4	2.4	2.5
Switzerland - Suisse											
Total	C	16 737	16 982	17 028	15 906	16 542	2.0	2.1	2.0	1.9	1.9
Urban - Urbaine	C	14 397[36]	...	14 638	13 729	...	2.4	...	2.1	...	...
Rural - Rurale	C	2 340[36]	...	2 390	2 177	...	1.1	...	1.8	...	...
Ukraine[37]											
Total	+C	130 673	129 373	129 997	128 734	...	3.0	3.0	3.0	3.0	...
United Kingdom of Great Britain and Northern Ireland - Royaume-Uni de Grande-Bretagne et d'Irlande du Nord[38]											
Total	C	122 656	112 412	118 158	...	...	1.9	1.7	1.8	...	...
OCEANIA - OCÉANIE											
American Samoa - Samoas américaines											
Total	C	63	43	80	89	...	1.0	0.7	1.3	1.5	...
Australia - Australie											
Total	+C	46 498	48 517	46 604	49 032	...	2.0	2.0	1.9	2.0	...
Guam[39]											
Total	C	739	657	647	683	572	4.6	4.1	4.0	4.2	3.4
New Zealand - Nouvelle-Zélande											
Total	+C	8 171	8 523[40]	8 169[40]	8 001[40]	7 455[40]	1.8	1.9	1.7	1.7	1.5

FOOTNOTES - NOTES

Italics: data from civil registers which are incomplete or of unknown completeness. - Italiques : données incomplètes ou dont le degré d'exactitude n'est pas connu, provenant des registres de l'état civil.

* Provisional. - Données provisoires.

[a] 'Code' indicates the source of data, as follows:
C - Civil registration, estimated over 90% complete
U - Civil registration, estimated less than 90% complete
| - Other source, estimated reliable
+ - Data tabulated by date of registration rather than occurence
... - Information not available

Le 'Code' indique la source des données, comme suit :
C - Registres de l'état civil considérés complèts à 90 p. 100 au moins
U - Registres de l'état civil qui ne sont pas considérés complèts à 90 p. 100 au moins
| - Autre source, considérée pas douteuses
+ - Données exploitées selon la date de l'enregistrement et non la date de l'événement
... - Information pas disponible

[1] Data refer to Algerian population only. - Les données ne concernent que la population algérienne.
[2] Including 'revocable divorces' (among Muslim population), which approximate legal separations. - Y compris les 'divorces révocables' (parmi la population musulmane), qui sont plus ou moins l'équivalent des séparations légales.
[3] Excludes the islands of St. Brandon and Agalega. - Non compris les îles St. Brandon et Agalega.

[4] Bermuda is 100 per cent urban. - 100 pour cent de la population des Bermudes est urbaine.
[5] The sum of urban and rural doesn't correspond to the total because of unknown residence of divorces of foreigner spouses. - La somme des zones urbaines et rurales ne correspond pas au total en raison de la résidence inconnue des divorces des conjoints étrangers.
[6] Including same sex divorces. - Y compris les divorces entre conjoints du même sexe.
[7] The total number may include 'Unknown residence', but the categories urban and rural do not. - Le nombre total peut inclure les personnes dont la résidence n'est pas connue, à l'inverse des catégories de population urbaine et rurale.
[8] Excluding data for California, Georgia, Hawaii, Indiana, and Minnesota. - À l'exclusion des données pour la Californie, la Géorgie, Hawaï, l'Indiana et le Minnesota.
[9] Excludes nomadic Indian tribes. - Non compris les tribus d'Indiens nomades.
[10] Urban and rural residence refers to the place of usual residence of husband. - Le lieu de résidence (zone urbaine ou zone rurale) correspond au lieu de résidence habituel du mari.
[11] Data are compiled from the National Registers of Identification and Civil Status (RENIEC). - Les données sont rédigées à partir des Registres Nationaux d'Identification et d'État Civil (RENIEC).
[12] Including annulments. - Y compris les annulations.
[13] Data refer to government controlled areas. - Les données se rapportent aux zones contrôlées par le Gouvernement.
[14] Data refer to the Iranian Year which begins on 21 March and ends on 20 March of the following year. - Les données concernent l'année iranienne, qui commence le 21 mars et se termine le 20 mars de l'année suivante.
[15] Includes data for East Jerusalem and Israeli residents in certain other territories under occupation by Israeli military forces since June 1967. - Y compris les données pour Jérusalem-Est et les résidents israéliens dans certains autres territoires occupés depuis 1967 par les forces armées israéliennes.

¹⁶ The total number may include 'Unknown residence', but the categories urban and rural do not. Urban and rural residence refers to the place of usual residence of husband. - Le nombre total peut inclure les personnes dont la résidence n'est pas connue, à l'inverse des catégories de population urbaine et rurale. Le lieu de résidence (zone urbaine ou zone rurale) correspond au lieu de résidence habituel du mari.

¹⁷ Data refer to Japanese nationals in Japan only. - Les données se raportent aux nationaux japonais au Japon seulement.

¹⁸ Excluding data for Jordanian territory under occupation since June 1967 by Israeli military forces. Excluding foreigners, including registered Palestinian refugees. - Non compris les données pour le territoire jordanien occupé depuis juin 1967 par les forces armées israéliennes. Non compris les étrangers, mais y compris les réfugiés de Palestine enregistrés.

¹⁹ Excluding alien armed forces, civilian aliens employed by armed forces, and foreign diplomatic personnel and their dependants. - Non compris les militaires étrangers, les civils étrangers employés par les forces armées ni le personnel diplomatique étranger et les membres de leur famille les accompagnant.

²⁰ Data from MERNIS (Central Population Administrative System). - Données de MERNIS (Système central de données démographiques).

²¹ Excluding divorces of aliens temporarily in the area. - Non compris les divorces d'étrangers temporairement dans la région.

²² Excluding divorces of aliens temporarily in the area, but including divorces abroad of persons with residence in Austria. - Non compris les divorces d'étrangers temporairement dans la région, mais y compris des divorces à l'étranger de personnes ayant leur résidence en Autriche.

²³ Including divorces among armed forces stationed outside the country and alien armed forces in the area. - Y compris les divorces de militaires nationaux hors du pays et les militaires étrangers en garnison sur le territoire.

²⁴ Including nationals outside the country, but excluding foreigners in the country. Including annulments. - Y compris les nationaux à l'étranger, mais non compris les étrangers sur le territoire. Y compris les annulations.

²⁵ Excluding Faeroe Islands and Greenland shown separately, if available. - Non compris les Îles Féroé et le Groenland, qui font l'objet de rubriques distinctes, si disponible.

²⁶ Urban and rural residence refers to the place of usual residence of husband. The difference between 'Total' and the sum of urban and rural is due to the unknown place of residence of husbands and to husbands living outside the country. - Le lieu de résidence (zone urbaine ou zone rurale) correspond au lieu de résidence habituel du mari. La différence entre le « Total » et la somme des chiffres urbains et ruraux s'explique par le fait que la résidence du mari n'est pas toujours connue ou est située à l'étranger.

²⁷ Excluding Åland Islands. Including annulments. - Non compris les Îles d'Åland. Y compris les annulations.

²⁸ The urban and rural categories do not include the data of foreigners, persons of unknown residence and the homeless, whereas the total category includes them. - Les chiffres portant sur la population urbaine et rurale n' incluent pas les données relatives aux étrangers, aux personnes dont la résidence n'est pas connue et aux personnes sans domicile fixe, à l'inverse, le total les inclut.

²⁹ Data refer to divorces by residence of the husband. - Les données concernent les divorces selon la résidence du mari.

³⁰ Data include separated. - Y compris les séparés.

³¹ Based on the general office for civil registration. - Données provenant des services généraux d'état civil.

³² Including residents outside the country if listed in a Netherlands population register. - Englobe les résidents se trouvant à l'étranger à condition qu'ils soient inscrits sur le registre de population des Pays-Bas.

³³ Data for urban and rural exclude divorces if both persons live abroad. - Les données pour les zones urbaines et rurales excluent le divorce si les deux personnes vivent à l'étranger.

³⁴ Data refer to resident spouses only. - Les données concernent uniquement les conjoints résidents.

³⁵ Excludes data for Kosovo and Metohia. - Sans les données pour le Kosovo et Metohie.

³⁶ From 2014, urban refers to urban centers and areas under the influence of urban centers. - A partir de 2014, le territoire urbain inclut l'espace des centres urbains ainsi que l'espace sous influence des centres urbains.

³⁷ The Government of Ukraine has informed the United Nations that it is not in a position to provide statistical data concerning the Autonomous Republic of Crimea and the city of Sevastopol. - Le gouvernement Ukrainien a informé l'ONU qu'il n'est pas en mesure de fournir des données statistiques concernant la République autonome de Crimée et la ville de Sébastopol.

³⁸ Excluding Channel Islands (Guernsey and Jersey) and Isle of Man, shown separately, if available. Including annulments. Data tabulated by date of occurrence for England and Wales, and by date of registration for Northern Ireland and Scotland. - Non compris les îles Anglo-Normandes (Guernesey et Jersey) et l'île de Man, qui font l'objet de rubriques distinctes, si disponible. Y compris les annulations. Données exploitées selon la date de l'événement pour l'Angleterre et le pays de Galles, et selon la date de l'enregistrement pour l'Irlande du Nord et l'Ecosse.

³⁹ Including United States military personnel, their dependants and contract employees. - Y compris les militaires des Etats-Unis, les membres de leur famille les accompagnant et les agents contractuels des Etats-Unis.

⁴⁰ Data have been randomly rounded. - Ces données ont été arrondies de façon aléatoire.

Table 25 - *Demographic Yearbook 2018*

Table 25 presents the number of divorces according to the duration of marriage and the percentage distribution for the latest available year between 2009 and 2018.

Description of variables: Divorces are the final legal dissolutions of a marriage, which confer on the parties the right to remarry as defined by the laws of each country or area. Unless otherwise noted, divorce statistics exclude legal separations which do not allow remarriage. These statistics refer to the number of divorces granted, and not to the number of persons divorcing.

Duration of marriage is defined as the interval of time between the day, month and year of marriage and the day, month and year of divorce in completed years. This definition refers to the "legal" duration rather than the "effective" duration; having been calculated until the day, month and year of the actual divorce decree rather than until the separation date or the date when the couple ceased to live as man and wife.

The duration of marriage classification used in this table to the extent possible, is the following: under one year, single years of duration through 9 years, 10-14 years, 15-19 years, 20 years and over and duration unknown, when appropriate.

Reliability of data: Data from civil registers of divorces which are reported as incomplete (less than 90 per cent completeness) or of unknown completeness are considered unreliable and are set in italics rather than in roman type. For more information about the quality of vital statistics data in general, see section 4.2 of the Technical Notes.

Limitations: Statistics on divorces by duration of marriage are subject to the same qualifications which have been set forth for vital statistics in general and divorce statistics in particular as discussed in section 4 of the Technical Notes.

Earlier data: Divorces by duration by marriage, cross-classified by age of husband and by age of wife have been shown previously in issues of the *Demographic Yearbook* featuring marriage and divorce. For information on years covered, readers should consult the Historical Index.

Tableau 25 – *Annuaire démographique 2018*

Le tableau 25 indique le nombre de divorces selon la durée du mariage et la répartition des pourcentages, pour la dernière année disponible entre 2009 et 2018.

Description des variables : le divorce est la dissolution définitive des liens du mariage qui confère aux parties le droit de se remarier, telle qu'elle est définie par la législation de chaque pays ou zone. Sauf indication contraire, les statistiques de la divortialité n'englobent pas les séparations légales qui excluent le remariage. Ces statistiques se rapportent aux jugements de divorce prononcés, non aux personnes divorcées.

La durée du mariage correspond à l'intervalle du temps qui s'est écoulé entre la date exacte (jour, mois et année) du mariage et la date exacte (jour, mois et année) du divorce exprimé en années révolues. Cette définition est celle de la durée "légale" du mariage et non de sa durée "effective", puisque la durée est calculée jusqu'à la date (jour, mois et année) du jugement de divorce et non jusqu'à la date de la séparation ou la date à laquelle le couple a cessé de vivre comme mari et femme.

Le classement selon la durée du mariage utilisé dans ce tableau dans la mesure du possible comprend les catégories suivantes : moins d'un an, une catégorie par an jusqu'à 9 ans inclus, 10-14 ans, 15-19 ans, 20 ans et plus et, le cas échéant, une catégorie pour la durée du mariage inconnue.

Fiabilité des données : les données sur les divorces provenant des registres de l'état civil qui sont déclarées incomplètes (degré de complétude inférieur à 90 pour cent) ou dont le degré de complétude n'est pas connu, sont jugées douteuses et apparaissent en italique et non en caractères romains. Pour plus de précisions sur la qualité des données reposant sur les statistiques de l'état civil en general, voir la section 4.2 des Notes techniques.

Insuffisance des données : les statistiques des divorces selon la durée du mariage, appellent toutes les réserves qui ont été formulées à propos des statistiques de l'état civil en general et des statistiques des divorces en particulier (voir les explications figurant à la section 4 des Notes techniques).

Données publiées antérieurement : les statistiques des divorces selon la durée du mariage, classées selon l'âge de l'époux, d'une part, et selon l'âge de l'épouse, d'autre part, ont été présentées dans des éditions antérieures de *l'Annuaire démographique* qui avaient comme sujet spécial la nuptialité et la divortialité. Pour plus de précisions concernant les années pour lesquelles ces données ont été publiées, on se reportera à l'index historique.

679

25. Divorces and percentage distribution by duration of marriage, latest available year: 2009 - 2018
Divorces et répartition des pourcentages selon la durée du mariage, dernière année disponible: 2009 - 2018

Continent, country or area, year, code and duration of marriage (in years) / Continent, pays ou zone, année, code et durée du mariage (en années)	Number of divorces / Nombre de divorces	Per cent / Pour cent
AFRICA - AFRIQUE		
Egypt - Égypte[1]		
2017 (+C)		
Total	198 269	100.0
Less than 1 - Moins de 1	29 663	15.0
1	21 070	10.6
2	13 959	7.0
3	10 847	5.5
4	8 750	4.4
5	7 227	3.6
6	6 182	3.1
7	5 435	2.7
8	4 048	2.0
9	4 122	2.1
10 - 14	14 148	7.1
15 - 19	8 213	4.1
20 +	13 341	6.7
Not stated - Inconnu	51 264	25.9
Lesotho		
2017 (+U)		
Total	197	100.0
Less than 5 - Moins de 5	37	18.8
5 - 9	71	36.0
10 - 14	42	21.3
15 - 19	18	9.1
20 +	29	14.7
Mauritius - Maurice[2]		
2018 (+C)		
Total	2 425	100.0
Less than 1 - Moins de 1	7	0.3
1	67	2.8
2	106	4.4
3	137	5.6
4	137	5.6
5	119	4.9
6	129	5.3
7	140	5.8
8	130	5.4
9	120	4.9
10 - 14	526	21.7
15 - 19	342	14.1
20 +	465	19.2
Seychelles		
2018 (+C)		
Total	166	100.0
Less than 1 - Moins de 1	4	2.4
1	-	0.0
2	5	3.0
3	12	7.2
4	9	5.4
5	10	6.0
6	12	7.2
7	10	6.0
8	9	5.4
9	10	6.0
10 - 14	36	21.7
15 - 19	28	16.9
20 +	21	12.7
South Africa - Afrique du Sud		
2017 (...)		
Total	25 390	100.0
Less than 1 - Moins de 1	63	0.2
1	658	2.6
2	1 044	4.1
3	1 283	5.1
4	1 376	5.4
5	1 429	5.6
6	1 420	5.6
7	1 413	5.6

Continent, country or area, year, code and duration of marriage (in years) / Continent, pays ou zone, année, code et durée du mariage (en années)	Number of divorces / Nombre de divorces	Per cent / Pour cent
AFRICA - AFRIQUE		
South Africa - Afrique du Sud		
2017 (...)		
8	1 378	5.4
9	1 266	5.0
10 - 14	4 985	19.6
15 - 19	3 236	12.7
20 +	4 787	18.9
Not stated - Inconnu	1 052	4.1
AMERICA, NORTH - AMÉRIQUE DU NORD		
Aruba		
2017 (C)		
Total	378	100.0
Less than 1 - Moins de 1	1	0.3
1	13	3.4
2	30	7.9
3	21	5.6
4	17	4.5
5	21	5.6
6	29	7.7
7	15	4.0
8	24	6.3
9	16	4.2
10 - 14	69	18.3
15 - 19	42	11.1
20 +	74	19.6
Not stated - Inconnu	6	1.6
Bermuda - Bermudes		
2017 (C)		
Total	173	100.0
Less than 1 - Moins de 1	-	0.0
1	1	0.6
2	5	2.9
3	8	4.6
4	11	6.4
5	4	2.3
6	7	4.0
7	11	6.4
8	8	4.6
9	7	4.0
10 - 14	49	28.3
15 - 19	32	18.5
20 +	30	17.3
Cuba		
2017 (C)		
Total	32 183	100.0
Less than 1 - Moins de 1	2 661	8.3
1	2 939	9.1
2	2 790	8.7
3	2 260	7.0
4	1 876	5.8
5	1 602	5.0
6	1 422	4.4
7	1 235	3.8
8	1 205	3.7
9	1 050	3.3
10 - 14	3 246	10.1
15 - 19	2 382	7.4
20 - 24	7 515	23.4
Not stated - Inconnu	-	0.0
Curaçao		
2016 (C)		
Total	365	100.0
Less than 1 - Moins de 1	3	0.8
1	12	3.3

Continent, country or area, year, code and duration of marriage (in years) / Continent, pays ou zone, année, code et durée du mariage (en années)	Number of divorces / Nombre de divorces	Per cent / Pour cent
AMERICA, NORTH - AMÉRIQUE DU NORD		
Curaçao		
2016 (C)		
2	17	4.7
3	23	6.3
4	22	6.0
5	25	6.8
6	28	7.7
7	21	5.8
8	26	7.1
9	13	3.6
10 - 14	53	14.5
15 - 19	44	12.1
20 +	75	20.5
Not stated - Inconnu	3	0.8
Dominican Republic - République dominicaine		
2016 (+C)		
Total	21 750	100.0
Less than 1 - Moins de 1	8	0.0
1	266	1.2
2	470	2.2
3	554	2.5
4	435	2.0
5	481	2.2
6	429	2.0
7	374	1.7
8	346	1.6
9	327	1.5
10 - 14	1 097	5.0
15 - 19	854	3.9
20 +	1 187	5.5
Not stated - Inconnu	14 922	68.6
El Salvador		
2012 (...)		
Total	7 138	100.0
Less than 1 - Moins de 1	77	1.1
1	161	2.3
2	239	3.3
3	271	3.8
4	320	4.5
5	302	4.2
6	296	4.1
7	293	4.1
8	300	4.2
9	311	4.4
10 - 14	1 508	21.1
15 - 19	1 138	15.9
20 +	1 705	23.9
Not stated - Inconnu	217	3.0
Grenada - Grenade[3]		
2014 (+C)		
Total	119	100.0
1	4	3.4
2	7	5.9
3	5	4.2
4	8	6.7
5 - 9	43	36.1
10 - 14	18	15.1
15 - 19	17	14.3
20 +	14	11.8
Not stated - Inconnu	3	2.5
Jamaica - Jamaïque		
2018 (+C)		
Total	3 402	100.0
Less than 5 - Moins de 5	266	7.8
5 - 9	779	22.9
10 - 14	778	22.9

Continent, country or area, year, code and duration of marriage (in years) / Continent, pays ou zone, année, code et durée du mariage (en années)	Number of divorces / Nombre de divorces	Per cent / Pour cent
AMERICA, NORTH - AMÉRIQUE DU NORD		
Jamaica - Jamaïque		
2018 (+C)		
15 - 19	756	22.2
20 +	823	24.2
Mexico - Mexique[4]		
2017 (+C)		
Total	147 581	100.0
Less than 1 - Moins de 1	1 663	1.1
1	5 503	3.7
2	6 315	4.3
3	6 622	4.5
4	6 768	4.6
5	6 641	4.5
6	5 981	4.1
7	5 546	3.8
8	5 565	3.8
9	5 401	3.7
10 - 14	23 160	15.7
15 - 19	21 799	14.8
20 +	45 320	30.7
Not stated - Inconnu	1 297	0.9
Panama		
2017* (C)		
Total	4 470	100.0
Less than 5 - Moins de 5	711	15.9
5 - 9	1 181	26.4
10 - 14	682	15.3
15 - 19	575	12.9
20 +	1 321	29.6
Trinidad and Tobago - Trinité-et-Tobago		
2009 (C)		
Total	2 629	100.0
Less than 1 - Moins de 1	-	0.0
1	40	1.5
2	78	3.0
3	100	3.8
4	126	4.8
5	127	4.8
6	137	5.2
7	124	4.7
8	122	4.6
9	135	5.1
10 - 14	512	19.5
15 - 19	369	14.0
20 +	752	28.6
Not stated - Inconnu	7	0.3
AMERICA, SOUTH - AMÉRIQUE DU SUD		
Brazil - Brésil		
2017 (...)		
Total	295 108	100.0
Less than 3 - Moins de 3	34 081	11.5
3	15 792	5.4
4	15 136	5.1
5	14 753	5.0
6	13 606	4.6
7	12 482	4.2
8	12 050	4.1
9	11 658	4.0
10 - 14	45 574	15.4
15 - 19	33 888	11.5
20 +	78 062	26.5
Not stated - Inconnu	8 026	2.7

Continent, country or area, year, code and duration of marriage (in years) / Continent, pays ou zone, année, code et durée du mariage (en années)	Number of divorces / Nombre de divorces	Per cent / Pour cent
AMERICA, SOUTH - AMÉRIQUE DU SUD		
Chile - Chili		
2010 (C)		
Total	1 558	100.0
Less than 1 - Moins de 1	11	0.7
1	17	1.1
2	36	2.3
3	35	2.2
4	36	2.3
5	32	2.1
6	28	1.8
7	39	2.5
8	38	2.4
9	47	3.0
10 - 14	270	17.3
15 - 19	211	13.5
20 +	610	39.2
Not stated - Inconnu	148	9.5
Ecuador - Équateur[5]		
2017 (U)		
Total	28 771	100.0
Less than 1 - Moins de 1	433	1.5
1	761	2.6
2	1 066	3.7
3	1 114	3.9
4	1 186	4.1
5	1 315	4.6
6	1 354	4.7
7	1 355	4.7
8	1 349	4.7
9	1 290	4.5
10 - 14	4 910	17.1
15 - 19	4 145	14.4
20 +	8 493	29.5
Not stated - Inconnu	-	0.0
Suriname[6]		
2017 (C)		
Total	855	100.0
Less than 1 - Moins de 1	9	1.1
1 - 3	149	17.4
4 - 6	160	18.7
7 - 9	152	17.8
10 - 12	89	10.4
13 - 15	79	9.2
16 - 18	53	6.2
19 - 21	51	6.0
22 - 24	28	3.3
25 - 27	29	3.4
28 - 30	18	2.1
31 - 33	12	1.4
34 - 36	9	1.1
37+	17	2.0
Venezuela (Bolivarian Republic of) - Venezuela (République bolivarienne du)[7]		
2017 (C)		
Total	22 669	100.0
Less than 1 - Moins de 1	222	1.0
1	442	1.9
2	717	3.2
3	889	3.9
4	1 102	4.9
5	1 412	6.2
6	1 324	5.8
7	1 329	5.9
8	1 201	5.3
9	1 103	4.9
10 - 14	3 960	17.5
15 - 19	3 379	14.9

Continent, country or area, year, code and duration of marriage (in years) / Continent, pays ou zone, année, code et durée du mariage (en années)	Number of divorces / Nombre de divorces	Per cent / Pour cent
AMERICA, SOUTH - AMÉRIQUE DU SUD		
Venezuela (Bolivarian Republic of) - Venezuela (République bolivarienne du)[7]		
2017 (C)		
20 +	5 534	24.4
Not stated - Inconnu	55	0.2
ASIA - ASIE		
Armenia - Arménie		
2017 (+C)		
Total	3 940	100.0
Less than 1 - Moins de 1	248	6.3
1	195	4.9
2	336	8.5
3	273	6.9
4	218	5.5
5 - 9	793	20.1
10 - 14	630	16.0
15 - 19	357	9.1
20 +	890	22.6
Not stated - Inconnu	-	0.0
Azerbaijan - Azerbaïdjan		
2017 (+C)		
Total	14 514	100.0
Less than 1 - Moins de 1	316	2.2
1	860	5.9
2	1 096	7.6
3	1 277	8.8
4	1 114	7.7
5	965	6.6
6	943	6.5
7	788	5.4
8	743	5.1
9	700	4.8
10 - 14	2 681	18.5
15 - 19	991	6.8
20 +	2 040	14.1
Bahrain - Bahreïn		
2018 (...)		
Total	1 929	100.0
Less than 1 - Moins de 1	384	19.9
1 - 2	367	19.0
3 - 4	252	13.1
5 - 6	189	9.8
7 - 9	184	9.5
10 - 14	216	11.2
15 - 19	149	7.7
20 +	182	9.4
Not stated - Inconnu	6	0.3
Brunei Darussalam - Brunéi Darussalam		
2016 (+C)		
Total	566	100.0
Less than 1 - Moins de 1	5	0.9
1	27	4.8
2	31	5.5
3	37	6.5
4	39	6.9
5	33	5.8
6	40	7.1
7	43	7.6
8	39	6.9
9	23	4.1
10 - 14	93	16.4
15 - 19	73	12.9
20 +	83	14.7

25. Divorces and percentage distribution by duration of marriage, latest available year: 2009 - 2018
Divorces et répartition des pourcentages selon la durée du mariage, dernière année disponible: 2009 - 2018 (continued - suite)

Continent, country or area, year, code and duration of marriage (in years) — Continent, pays ou zone, année, code et durée du mariage (en années)	Number of divorces — Nombre de divorces	Per cent — Pour cent
ASIA - ASIE		
China, Macao SAR - Chine, Macao RAS		
2018 (+C)		
Total	1 544	100.0
Less than 5 - Moins de 5	292	18.9
5 - 9	503	32.6
10 - 14	347	22.5
15 - 19	128	8.3
20 +	274	17.7
Cyprus - Chypre[8]		
2017 (C)		
Total	1 931	100.0
Less than 1 - Moins de 1	50	2.6
1	109	5.6
2	59	3.1
3	105	5.4
4	108	5.6
5	122	6.3
6	100	5.2
7	129	6.7
8	81	4.2
9	122	6.3
10 - 14	357	18.5
15 - 19	229	11.9
20 +	360	18.6
Georgia - Géorgie		
2017 (C)		
Total	10 222	100.0
Less than 1 - Moins de 1	922	9.0
1	607	5.9
2	635	6.2
3	599	5.9
4	568	5.6
5	530	5.2
6	531	5.2
7	520	5.1
8	496	4.9
9	424	4.1
10 - 14	1 207	11.8
15 - 19	754	7.4
20 +	2 386	23.3
Not stated - Inconnu	43	0.4
Iran (Islamic Republic of) - Iran (République islamique d')[9]		
2017 (+C)		
Total	174 578	100.0
Less than 1 - Moins de 1	17 078	9.8
1	16 958	9.7
2	14 512	8.3
3	12 939	7.4
4	11 264	6.5
5 - 9	40 531	23.2
10 - 14	25 516	14.6
15 +	35 780	20.5
Israel - Israël[10]		
2016 (C)		
Total	14 819	100.0
Less than 1 - Moins de 1	809	5.5
1	948	6.4
2	865	5.8
3	779	5.3
4	677	4.6
5	700	4.7
6	586	4.0
7	557	3.8
8	572	3.9
9	456	3.1
10 - 14	2 122	14.3
ASIA - ASIE		
Israel - Israël[10]		
2016 (C)		
15 - 19	1 613	10.9
20 +	2 815	19.0
Not stated - Inconnu	1 320	8.9
Japan - Japon[11]		
2017 (+C)		
Total	212 262	100.0
Less than 1 - Moins de 1	12 895	6.1
1	15 282	7.2
2	14 310	6.7
3	12 783	6.0
4	11 221	5.3
5 - 9	42 334	19.9
10 - 14	28 223	13.3
15 - 19	22 951	10.8
20 +	38 286	18.0
Not stated - Inconnu	13 977	6.6
Kazakhstan		
2018 (+C)		
Total	54 797	100.0
Less than 1 - Moins de 1	2 919	5.3
1	4 084	7.5
2	4 385	8.0
3	4 361	8.0
4	4 161	7.6
5	3 837	7.0
6	3 449	6.3
7	2 809	5.1
8	2 483	4.5
9	2 258	4.1
10 - 14	8 416	15.4
15 - 19	3 952	7.2
20 +	7 683	14.0
Not stated - Inconnu	-	0.0
Kuwait - Koweït		
2018 (C)		
Total	7 869	100.0
Less than 1 - Moins de 1	1 452	18.5
1	1 055	13.4
2	738	9.4
3	628	8.0
4	496	6.3
5 - 9	1 517	19.3
10 - 14	874	11.1
15 - 19	436	5.5
20 +	673	8.6
Kyrgyzstan - Kirghizstan		
2017 (C)		
Total	9 588	100.0
Less than 1 - Moins de 1	247	2.6
1	523	5.5
2	660	6.9
3	651	6.8
4	712	7.4
5	702	7.3
6	679	7.1
7	562	5.9
8	533	5.6
9	455	4.7
10 - 14	1 605	16.7
15 - 19	811	8.5
20 +	1 448	15.1
Mongolia - Mongolie		
2018 (+C)		
Total	4 201	100.0
Less than 1 - Moins de 1	21	0.5

Continent, country or area, year, code and duration of marriage (in years) / Continent, pays ou zone, année, code et durée du mariage (en années)	Number of divorces / Nombre de divorces	Per cent / Pour cent
ASIA - ASIE		
Mongolia - Mongolie		
2018 (+C)		
1 - 3	280	6.7
4 - 6	519	12.4
7 - 9	773	18.4
10 - 14	1 310	31.2
15 - 19	499	11.9
20 +	799	19.0
Qatar		
2017 (C)		
Total	1 206	100.0
Less than 1 - Moins de 1	466	38.6
1	147	12.2
2	106	8.8
3	66	5.5
4	61	5.1
5 - 9	168	13.9
10 - 14	89	7.4
15 - 19	42	3.5
20 +	55	4.6
Not stated - Inconnu	6	0.5
Republic of Korea - République de Corée[12]		
2018 (+C)		
Total	108 684	100.0
Less than 1 - Moins de 1	3 778	3.5
1	4 912	4.5
2	4 981	4.6
3	4 860	4.5
4	4 678	4.3
5	4 411	4.1
6	4 121	3.8
7	3 886	3.6
8	4 050	3.7
9	3 595	3.3
10 - 14	15 540	14.3
15 - 19	13 545	12.5
20 +	36 327	33.4
Not stated - Inconnu	-	0.0
Singapore - Singapour		
2018 (+C)		
Total	6 990	100.0
Less than 5 - Moins de 5	1 374	19.7
5 - 9	2 047	29.3
10 - 14	1 269	18.2
15 - 19	833	11.9
20 +	1 467	21.0
State of Palestine - État de Palestine		
2017 (C)		
Total	8 568	100.0
Less than 1 - Moins de 1	3 974	46.4
1	1 349	15.7
2	604	7.0
3	361	4.2
4	359	4.2
5	256	3.0
6	209	2.4
7	155	1.8
8	145	1.7
9	118	1.4
10 - 14	451	5.3
15 - 19	221	2.6
20 +	366	4.3
Tajikistan - Tadjikistan		
2017 (+C)		
Total	10 053	100.0
Less than 1 - Moins de 1	717	7.1
1	709	7.1
2	880	8.8

Continent, country or area, year, code and duration of marriage (in years) / Continent, pays ou zone, année, code et durée du mariage (en années)	Number of divorces / Nombre de divorces	Per cent / Pour cent
ASIA - ASIE		
Tajikistan - Tadjikistan		
2017 (+C)		
3	979	9.7
4	883	8.8
5	718	7.1
6	693	6.9
7	604	6.0
8	523	5.2
9	473	4.7
10 - 14	954	9.5
15 - 19	407	4.0
20 +	998	9.9
Not stated - Inconnu	515	5.1
Turkey - Turquie[13]		
2017 (C)		
Total	128 411	100.0
Less than 1 - Moins de 1	4 074	3.2
1	13 124	10.2
2	9 664	7.5
3	8 420	6.6
4	7 664	6.0
5	6 775	5.3
6	5 932	4.6
7	5 402	4.2
8	5 262	4.1
9	5 170	4.0
10 - 14	20 370	15.9
15 - 19	14 693	11.4
20 +	21 722	16.9
Not stated - Inconnu	139	0.1
Uzbekistan - Ouzbékistan		
2017 (+C)		
Total	31 929	100.0
Less than 1 - Moins de 1	1 130	3.5
1	2 227	7.0
2	2 660	8.3
3	2 933	9.2
4	2 742	8.6
5	2 367	7.4
6	2 230	7.0
7	1 934	6.1
8	1 507	4.7
9	1 387	4.3
10 - 14	4 060	12.7
15 - 19	2 658	8.3
20 +	4 094	12.8
EUROPE		
Austria - Autriche[14]		
2017 (C)		
Total	16 180	100.0
Less than 1 - Moins de 1	268	1.7
1	760	4.7
2	983	6.1
3	1 032	6.4
4	945	5.8
5	865	5.3
6	809	5.0
7	732	4.5
8	669	4.1
9	644	4.0
10 - 14	2 648	16.4
15 - 19	2 084	12.9
20 +	3 741	23.1

25. Divorces and percentage distribution by duration of marriage, latest available year: 2009 - 2018
Divorces et répartition des pourcentages selon la durée du mariage, dernière année disponible: 2009 - 2018 (continued - suite)

Continent, country or area, year, code and duration of marriage (in years) Continent, pays ou zone, année, code et durée du mariage (en années)	Number of divorces Nombre de divorces	Per cent Pour cent
EUROPE		
Belarus - Bélarus		
2017 (C)		
Total	32 006	100.0
Less than 1 - Moins de 1	990	3.1
1	2 458	7.7
2	2 920	9.1
3	2 815	8.8
4	2 488	7.8
5 - 9	8 633	27.0
10 - 14	4 580	14.3
15 - 19	2 804	8.8
20 +	4 318	13.5
Belgium - Belgique[15]		
2017 (C)		
Total	23 068	100.0
Less than 1 - Moins de 1	143	0.6
1	629	2.7
2	944	4.1
3	995	4.3
4	1 098	4.8
5	1 144	5.0
6	1 178	5.1
7	1 228	5.3
8	1 123	4.9
9	1 088	4.7
10 - 14	4 026	17.5
15 - 19	2 832	12.3
20 +	6 640	28.8
Bosnia and Herzegovina - **Bosnie-Herzégovine**		
2010 (C)		
Total	1 676	100.0
Less than 1 - Moins de 1	100	6.0
1	139	8.3
2	121	7.2
3	133	7.9
4	131	7.8
5	94	5.6
6	71	4.2
7	72	4.3
8	64	3.8
9	46	2.7
10 - 14	244	14.6
15 - 19	139	8.3
20 +	322	19.2
Bulgaria - Bulgarie[16]		
2017 (C)		
Total	10 411	100.0
Less than 1 - Moins de 1	161	1.5
1	378	3.6
2	387	3.7
3	413	4.0
4	380	3.6
5	395	3.8
6	369	3.5
7	354	3.4
8	379	3.6
9	379	3.6
10 - 14	1 747	16.8
15 - 19	1 425	13.7
20 +	3 644	35.0
Croatia - Croatie		
2017 (C)		
Total	6 265	100.0
Less than 1 - Moins de 1	99	1.6
1	172	2.7
2	245	3.9

Continent, country or area, year, code and duration of marriage (in years) Continent, pays ou zone, année, code et durée du mariage (en années)	Number of divorces Nombre de divorces	Per cent Pour cent
EUROPE		
Croatia - Croatie		
2017 (C)		
3	272	4.3
4	280	4.5
5	284	4.5
6	283	4.5
7	246	3.9
8	283	4.5
9	286	4.6
10 - 14	1 124	17.9
15 - 19	877	14.0
20 +	1 814	29.0
Czechia - Tchéquie		
2017 (C)		
Total	25 755	100.0
Less than 1 - Moins de 1	230	0.9
1	858	3.3
2	1 010	3.9
3	1 096	4.3
4	1 106	4.3
5	1 130	4.4
6	1 162	4.5
7	1 097	4.3
8	1 140	4.4
9	1 194	4.6
10 - 14	4 613	17.9
15 - 19	3 582	13.9
20 +	7 424	28.8
Not stated - Inconnu	113	0.4
Denmark - Danemark[17]		
2017 (C)		
Total	15 265	100.0
Less than 1 - Moins de 1	551	3.6
1	790	5.2
2	787	5.2
3	781	5.1
4	681	4.5
5	700	4.6
6	708	4.6
7	733	4.8
8	740	4.8
9	745	4.9
10 - 14	2 842	18.6
15 - 19	2 158	14.1
20 +	2 899	19.0
Not stated - Inconnu	150	1.0
Estonia - Estonie		
2016 (C)		
Total	3 262	100.0
Less than 1 - Moins de 1	80	2.5
1	198	6.1
2	175	5.4
3	204	6.3
4	175	5.4
5	142	4.4
6	140	4.3
7	143	4.4
8	159	4.9
9	150	4.6
10 - 14	406	12.4
15 - 19	255	7.8
20 +	824	25.3
Not stated - Inconnu	211	6.5
Faeroe Islands - Îles Féroé[18]		
2018 (C)		
Total	61	100.0
Less than 1 - Moins de 1	-	0.0

25. Divorces and percentage distribution by duration of marriage, latest available year: 2009 - 2018
Divorces et répartition des pourcentages selon la durée du mariage, dernière année disponible: 2009 - 2018 (continued - suite)

Continent, country or area, year, code and duration of marriage (in years) / Continent, pays ou zone, année, code et durée du mariage (en années)	Number of divorces / Nombre de divorces	Per cent / Pour cent
EUROPE		
Faeroe Islands - Îles Féroé[18]		
2018 (C)		
1	3	4.9
2	3	4.9
3	3	4.9
4	5	8.2
5	2	3.3
6	4	6.6
7	1	1.6
8	1	1.6
9	4	6.6
10 - 14	9	14.8
15 - 19	10	16.4
20 +	16	26.2
Finland - Finlande		
2017 (C)		
Total	13 485	100.0
Less than 1 - Moins de 1	109	0.8
1	600	4.4
2	860	6.4
3	838	6.2
4	883	6.5
5	848	6.3
6	861	6.4
7	769	5.7
8	726	5.4
9	643	4.8
10 - 14	2 355	17.5
15 - 19	1 511	11.2
20 +	2 476	18.4
Not stated - Inconnu	6	0.0
France		
2011 (C)		
Total	129 802	100.0
Less than 1 - Moins de 1	158	0.1
1	1 468	1.1
2	3 489	2.7
3	5 045	3.9
4	6 173	4.8
5	6 788	5.2
6	6 914	5.3
7	6 488	5.0
8	6 088	4.7
9	5 573	4.3
10 - 14	25 093	19.3
15 - 19	17 840	13.7
20 +	38 685	29.8
Germany - Allemagne		
2017 (C)		
Total	153 501	100.0
Less than 1 - Moins de 1	30	0.0
1	955	0.6
2	5 132	3.3
3	6 555	4.3
4	5 719	3.7
5	7 789	5.1
6	7 876	5.1
7	7 698	5.0
8	7 352	4.8
9	6 877	4.5
10 - 14	28 997	18.9
15 - 19	23 094	15.0
20 +	45 427	29.6
Greece - Grèce		
2016 (C)		
Total	11 013	100.0
Less than 1 - Moins de 1	17	0.2
1	206	1.9

Continent, country or area, year, code and duration of marriage (in years) / Continent, pays ou zone, année, code et durée du mariage (en années)	Number of divorces / Nombre de divorces	Per cent / Pour cent
EUROPE		
Greece - Grèce		
2016 (C)		
2	347	3.2
3	384	3.5
4	450	4.1
5	572	5.2
6	541	4.9
7	561	5.1
8	501	4.5
9	488	4.4
10 - 14	2 056	18.7
15 - 19	1 688	15.3
20 +	3 185	28.9
Not stated - Inconnu	17	0.2
Hungary - Hongrie		
2017 (C)		
Total	18 495	100.0
Less than 1 - Moins de 1	221	1.2
1	751	4.1
2	806	4.4
3	796	4.3
4	719	3.9
5	764	4.1
6	666	3.6
7	622	3.4
8	686	3.7
9	699	3.8
10 - 14	3 352	18.1
15 - 19	2 629	14.2
20 +	5 784	31.3
Not stated - Inconnu	-	0.0
Iceland - Islande[19]		
2011 (C)		
Total	516	100.0
Less than 1 - Moins de 1	6	1.2
1	16	3.1
2	20	3.9
3	37	7.2
4	36	7.0
5	38	7.4
6	28	5.4
7	20	3.9
8	33	6.4
9	16	3.1
10 - 14	101	19.6
15 - 19	63	12.2
20 +	100	19.4
Italy - Italie		
2016 (C)		
Total	99 071	100.0
Less than 1 - Moins de 1	6	0.0
1	156	0.2
2	708	0.7
3	1 245	1.3
4	2 017	2.0
5	2 407	2.4
6	2 939	3.0
7	3 632	3.7
8	4 014	4.1
9	4 020	4.1
10 - 14	18 450	18.6
15 - 19	16 785	16.9
20 +	42 692	43.1
Latvia - Lettonie		
2017 (C)		
Total	5 943	100.0
Less than 1 - Moins de 1	34	0.6
1	215	3.6

Continent, country or area, year, code and duration of marriage (in years) / Continent, pays ou zone, année, code et durée du mariage (en années)	Number of divorces / Nombre de divorces	Per cent / Pour cent
EUROPE		
Latvia - Lettonie		
2017 (C)		
2	346	5.8
3	349	5.9
4	384	6.5
5	351	5.9
6	302	5.1
7	229	3.9
8	222	3.7
9	279	4.7
10 - 14	1 093	18.4
15 - 19	541	9.1
20 +	1 598	26.9
Not stated - Inconnu	-	0.0
Liechtenstein[20]		
2012* (C)		
Total	87	100.0
Less than 1 - Moins de 1	-	0.0
1	7	8.0
2	4	4.6
3	2	2.3
4	4	4.6
5	9	10.3
6	7	8.0
7	7	8.0
8	5	5.7
9	3	3.4
10 - 14	10	11.5
15 - 19	14	16.1
20 +	15	17.2
Lithuania - Lituanie		
2017 (C)		
Total	8 518	100.0
Less than 1 - Moins de 1	49	0.6
1	271	3.2
2	514	6.0
3	520	6.1
4	511	6.0
5	474	5.6
6	363	4.3
7	310	3.6
8	377	4.4
9	421	4.9
10 - 14	1 405	16.5
15 - 19	821	9.6
20 +	2 482	29.1
Not stated - Inconnu	-	0.0
Luxembourg		
2017 (C)		
Total	1 192	100.0
Less than 1 - Moins de 1	7	0.6
1	31	2.6
2	36	3.0
3	56	4.7
4	57	4.8
5	60	5.0
6	51	4.3
7	67	5.6
8	66	5.5
9	49	4.1
10 - 14	221	18.5
15 - 19	187	15.7
20 +	304	25.5
Not stated - Inconnu	-	0.0
Malta - Malte		
2016 (C)		
Total	371	100.0
Less than 1 - Moins de 1	-	0.0
EUROPE		
Malta - Malte		
2016 (C)		
1	-	0.0
2	-	0.0
3	-	0.0
4	-	0.0
5	-	0.0
6	-	0.0
7	-	0.0
8	-	0.0
9	-	0.0
10 - 14	-	0.0
15 - 19	-	0.0
20 +	-	0.0
Montenegro - Monténégro		
2017 (C)		
Total	765	100.0
Less than 1 - Moins de 1	38	5.0
1	50	6.5
2	57	7.5
3	47	6.1
4	43	5.6
5	45	5.9
6	31	4.1
7	40	5.2
8	35	4.6
9	44	5.8
10 - 14	110	14.4
15 - 19	84	11.0
20 +	141	18.4
Not stated - Inconnu	-	0.0
Netherlands - Pays-Bas[21]		
2017 (C)		
Total	32 768	100.0
Less than 1 - Moins de 1	391	1.2
1	1 096	3.3
2	1 243	3.8
3	1 364	4.2
4	1 534	4.7
5	1 510	4.6
6	1 506	4.6
7	1 458	4.4
8	1 395	4.3
9	1 334	4.1
10 - 14	5 676	17.3
15 - 19	4 922	15.0
20 +	9 339	28.5
North Macedonia - Macédoine du Nord		
2018 (C)		
Total	1 620	100.0
Less than 1 - Moins de 1	104	6.4
1	122	7.5
2	139	8.6
3	115	7.1
4	81	5.0
5 - 9	322	19.9
10 - 14	236	14.6
15 - 19	185	11.4
20 +	316	19.5
Norway - Norvège[4]		
2017 (C)		
Total	10 567	100.0
Less than 1 - Moins de 1	14	0.1
1	213	2.0
2	414	3.9
3	565	5.3
4	628	5.9

25. Divorces and percentage distribution by duration of marriage, latest available year: 2009 - 2018
Divorces et répartition des pourcentages selon la durée du mariage, dernière année disponible: 2009 - 2018 (continued - suite)

Continent, country or area, year, code and duration of marriage (in years) / Continent, pays ou zone, année, code et durée du mariage (en années)	Number of divorces / Nombre de divorces	Per cent / Pour cent
EUROPE		
Norway - Norvège[4]		
2017 (C)		
5	597	5.6
6	644	6.1
7	551	5.2
8	585	5.5
9	520	4.9
10 - 14	2 013	19.0
15 - 19	1 435	13.6
20 +	2 095	19.8
Not stated - Inconnu	293	2.8
Poland - Pologne		
2017 (C)		
Total	65 257	100.0
Less than 1 - Moins de 1	339	0.5
1	1 691	2.6
2	2 357	3.6
3	2 702	4.1
4	3 007	4.6
5	2 963	4.5
6	3 202	4.9
7	3 419	5.2
8	3 576	5.5
9	3 183	4.9
10 - 14	11 095	17.0
15 - 19	9 300	14.3
20 +	18 423	28.2
Not stated - Inconnu	-	0.0
Portugal[22]		
2017 (C)		
Total	21 577	100.0
Less than 1 - Moins de 1	347	1.6
1	558	2.6
2	644	3.0
3	649	3.0
4	734	3.4
5	704	3.3
6	703	3.3
7	716	3.3
8	748	3.5
9	733	3.4
10 - 14	3 373	15.6
15 - 19	3 536	16.4
20 +	8 132	37.7
Not stated - Inconnu	-	0.0
Republic of Moldova - République de Moldova		
2018 (C)		
Total	10 721	100.0
Less than 1 - Moins de 1	235	2.2
1	505	4.7
2	660	6.2
3	692	6.5
4	668	6.2
5 - 9	2 638	24.6
10 - 14	1 999	18.6
15 - 19	1 007	9.4
20 +	2 317	21.6
Not stated - Inconnu	-	0.0
Romania - Roumanie		
2017 (C)		
Total	31 147	100.0
Less than 1 - Moins de 1	673	2.2
1	1 328	4.3
2	1 533	4.9
3	1 371	4.4
4	1 389	4.5
EUROPE		
Romania - Roumanie		
2017 (C)		
5	1 325	4.3
6	1 266	4.1
7	1 415	4.5
8	1 498	4.8
9	1 605	5.2
10 - 14	5 723	18.4
15 - 19	3 998	12.8
20 +	8 023	25.8
Not stated - Inconnu	-	0.0
Russian Federation - Fédération de Russie		
2011 (C)		
Total	669 376	100.0
Less than 1 - Moins de 1	33 567	5.0
1	50 768	7.6
2	58 099	8.7
3	57 871	8.6
4	50 042	7.5
5 - 9	165 467	24.7
10 - 14	82 645	12.3
15 - 19	60 911	9.1
20 +	109 624	16.4
Not stated - Inconnu	382	0.1
San Marino - Saint-Marin		
2014 (C)		
Total	51	100.0
Less than 1 - Moins de 1	-	0.0
1	-	0.0
2	-	0.0
3	1	2.0
4	3	5.9
5	2	3.9
6	3	5.9
7	3	5.9
8	1	2.0
9	3	5.9
10 - 14	7	13.7
15 - 19	9	17.6
20 +	19	37.3
Serbia - Serbie[23]		
2017 (+C)		
Total	9 262	100.0
Less than 1 - Moins de 1	368	4.0
1	545	5.9
2	552	6.0
3	546	5.9
4	451	4.9
5	397	4.3
6	412	4.4
7	375	4.0
8	343	3.7
9	339	3.7
10 - 14	1 401	15.1
15 - 19	1 197	12.9
20 +	2 336	25.2
Not stated - Inconnu	-	0.0
Slovakia - Slovaquie		
2017 (C)		
Total	9 618	100.0
Less than 1 - Moins de 1	62	0.6
1	246	2.6
2	360	3.7
3	398	4.1
4	368	3.8
5	387	4.0
6	373	3.9
7	360	3.7

25. Divorces and percentage distribution by duration of marriage, latest available year: 2009 - 2018
Divorces et répartition des pourcentages selon la durée du mariage, dernière année disponible: 2009 - 2018 (continued - suite)

Continent, country or area, year, code and duration of marriage (in years) Continent, pays ou zone, année, code et durée du mariage (en années)	Number of divorces Nombre de divorces	Per cent Pour cent
EUROPE		
Slovakia - Slovaquie		
2017 (C)		
8	409	4.3
9	377	3.9
10 - 14	1 687	17.5
15 - 19	1 396	14.5
20 + ...	3 195	33.2
Not stated - Inconnu	-	0.0
Slovenia - Slovénie		
2017 (C)		
Total	2 387	100.0
Less than 1 - Moins de 1	40	1.7
1	88	3.7
2	94	3.9
3	106	4.4
4	96	4.0
5	117	4.9
6	109	4.6
7	81	3.4
8	99	4.1
9	83	3.5
10 - 14	358	15.0
15 - 19	317	13.3
20 + ...	799	33.5
Not stated - Inconnu	-	0.0
Spain - Espagne		
2017 (C)		
Total	97 960	100.0
Less than 1 - Moins de 1	849	0.9
1	2 452	2.5
2	3 058	3.1
3	3 560	3.6
4	3 933	4.0
5	4 135	4.2
6	4 073	4.2
7	4 050	4.1
8	4 204	4.3
9	4 102	4.2
10 - 14	17 234	17.6
15 - 19	14 144	14.4
20 + ...	32 166	32.8
Sweden - Suède[4]		
2017 (C)		
Total	24 210	100.0
Less than 1 - Moins de 1	460	1.9
1	1 209	5.0
2	1 654	6.8
3	1 808	7.5
4	2 026	8.4
5	1 612	6.7
6	1 423	5.9
7	1 326	5.5
8	1 161	4.8
9	1 052	4.3
10 - 14	3 947	16.3
15 - 19	2 466	10.2
20 + ...	3 776	15.6
Not stated - Inconnu	290	1.2
Switzerland - Suisse		
2017 (C)		
Total	15 906	100.0
Less than 1 - Moins de 1	136	0.9
1	389	2.4
2	471	3.0
3	596	3.7
4	645	4.1
5	791	5.0
6	837	5.3

Continent, country or area, year, code and duration of marriage (in years) Continent, pays ou zone, année, code et durée du mariage (en années)	Number of divorces Nombre de divorces	Per cent Pour cent
EUROPE		
Switzerland - Suisse		
2017 (C)		
7	863	5.4
8	733	4.6
9	706	4.4
10 - 14	2 928	18.4
15 - 19	2 235	14.1
20 + ...	4 576	28.8
Not stated - Inconnu	-	0.0
Ukraine[24]		
2010 (+C)		
Total	126 068	100.0
Less than 1 - Moins de 1	3 957	3.1
1	8 423	6.7
2	12 437	9.9
3	10 291	8.2
4	8 780	7.0
5 - 9	29 912	23.7
10 - 14	17 542	13.9
15 - 19	13 370	10.6
20 + ...	21 356	16.9
United Kingdom of Great Britain and Northern Ireland - Royaume-Uni de Grande-Bretagne et d'Irlande du Nord[25]		
2016 (C)		
Total	118 505	100.0
Less than 1 - Moins de 1	63	0.1
1	1 723	1.5
2	3 611	3.0
3	5 439	4.6
4	6 650	5.6
5	6 689	5.6
6	6 396	5.4
7	6 030	5.1
8	5 734	4.8
9	5 462	4.6
10 - 14	23 582	19.9
15 - 19	16 240	13.7
20 + ...	30 886	26.1
OCEANIA - OCÉANIE		
Australia - Australie		
2017 (+C)		
Total	49 032	100.0
Less than 1 - Moins de 1	-	0.0
1	501	1.0
2	1 982	4.0
3	2 509	5.1
4	3 120	6.4
5	3 145	6.4
6	2 782	5.7
7	2 415	4.9
8	2 332	4.8
9	2 077	4.2
10 - 14	8 361	17.1
15 - 19	6 355	13.0
20 + ...	13 452	27.4
Not stated - Inconnu	1	0.0
New Zealand - Nouvelle-Zélande[26]		
2016 (+C)		
Total	8 169	100.0
Less than 5 - Moins de 5	906	11.1
5	399	4.9
6	387	4.7
7	372	4.6

25. Divorces and percentage distribution by duration of marriage, latest available year: 2009 - 2018
Divorces et répartition des pourcentages selon la durée du mariage, dernière année disponible: 2009 - 2018 (continued - suite)

Continent, country or area, year, code and duration of marriage (in years) Continent, pays ou zone, année, code et durée du mariage (en années)	Number of divorces Nombre de divorces	Per cent Pour cent
OCEANIA - OCÉANIE		
New Zealand - Nouvelle-Zélande[26]		
2016 (+C)		
8	411	5.0
9	369	4.5
10 - 14	1 518	18.6
15 - 19	1 239	15.2
20 + ...	2 571	31.5
Samoa		
2009 (U)		
Total...	48	*100.0*
Less than 1 - Moins de 1	-	*0.0*
1	-	*0.0*
2	-	*0.0*

Continent, country or area, year, code and duration of marriage (in years) Continent, pays ou zone, année, code et durée du mariage (en années)	Number of divorces Nombre de divorces	Per cent Pour cent
OCEANIA - OCÉANIE		
Samoa		
2009 (U)		
3	2	*4.2*
4	-	*0.0*
5	1	*2.1*
6	2	*4.2*
7	3	*6.3*
8	2	*4.2*
9	2	*4.2*
10 - 14	4	*8.3*
15 - 19	10	*20.8*
20 + ...	7	*14.6*
Not stated - Inconnu	15	*31.3*

FOOTNOTES - NOTES

Italics: estimates which are less reliable. - Italiques: estimations moins sûres.

* Provisional. - Données provisoires.

'Code' indicates the source of data, as follows:
C - Civil registration, estimated over 90% complete
U - Civil registration, estimated less than 90% complete
| - Other source, estimated reliable
+ - Data tabulated by date of registration rather than occurence.
... - Information not available

Le 'Code' indique la source des données, comme suit:
C - Registres de l'état civil considérés complets à 90 p. 100 au moins.
U - Registres de l'état civil qui ne sont pas considérés complets à 90 p. 100 au moins.
| - Autre source, considérée pas douteuses.
+ - Données exploitées selon la date de l'enregistrement et non la date de l'événement.
... - Information non disponible.

[1] Including 'revocable divorces' (among Muslim population), which approximate legal separations. - Y compris les 'divorces révocables' (parmi la population musulmane), qui sont plus au moins l'équivalent des séparations légales.
[2] Excludes the islands of St. Brandon and Agalega. - Non compris les îles St. Brandon et Agalega.
[3] Unrevised data. - Les données n'ont pas été révisées.
[4] Including same sex divorces. - Y compris les divorces entre conjoints du même sexe.
[5] Excludes nomadic Indian tribes. - Non compris les tribus d'Indiens nomades.
[6] Including annulments. - Y compris les annulations.
[7] Reason for discrepancy between these figures and corresponding figures shown elsewhere not ascertained. - On ne sait pas comment s'explique la divergence entre ces chiffres et les chiffres correspondants indiqués ailleurs.
[8] Data refer to government controlled areas. The total number of divorce does not include divorces for which the date of marriage was not stated. - Les données se rapportent aux zones contrôlées par le Gouvernement.
[9] Data refer to the Iranian Year which begins on 21 March and ends on 20 March of the following year. - Les données concernent l'année iranienne, qui commence le 21 mars et se termine le 20 mars de l'année suivante.
[10] Includes data for East Jerusalem and Israeli residents in certain other territories under occupation by Israeli military forces since June 1967. - Y compris les données pour Jérusalem-Est et les résidents israéliens dans certains autres territoires occupés depuis 1967 par les forces armées israéliennes.
[11] Data refer to Japanese nationals in Japan only. - Les données se raportent aux nationaux japonais au Japon seulement.

[12] Excluding alien armed forces, civilian aliens employed by armed forces, and foreign diplomatic personnel and their dependants. - Non compris les militaires étrangers, les civils étrangers employés par les forces armées ni le personnel diplomatique étranger et les membres de leur famille les accompagnant.
[13] Data from MERNIS (Central Population Administrative System). - Données de MERNIS (Système central de données démographiques).
[14] Excluding divorces of aliens temporarily in the area. - Non compris les divorces d'étrangers temporairement dans la région.
[15] Including divorces among armed forces stationed outside the country and alien armed forces in the area. - Y compris les divorces de militaires nationaux hors du pays et les militaires étrangers en garnison sur le territoire.
[16] Including annulments. Including nationals outside the country, but excluding foreigners in the country. - Y compris les annulations. Y compris les nationaux à l'étranger, mais non compris les étrangers sur le territoire.
[17] Excluding Faeroe Islands and Greenland shown separately, if available. - Non compris les îles Féroé et le Groenland, qui font l'objet de rubriques distinctes, si disponible.
[18] As reported by the country. Reasons for discrepancy with other tables not ascertained. - Comme indiqué par le pays. L'on ne connaît pas la raison des écarts avec d'autres tableaux.
[19] Data refer to common residence before divorce. - Données se rapportant à la résidence commune avant le divorce.
[20] Data refer to divorces by residence of the husband. - Les données concernent les divorces selon la résidence du mari.
[21] Including residents outside the country if listed in a Netherlands population register. - Englobe les résidents se trouvant à l'étranger à condition qu'ils soient inscrits sur le registre de population des Pays-Bas.
[22] Data refer to resident spouses only. - Les données concernent uniquement les conjoints résidents.
[23] Including annulments. Excludes data for Kosovo and Metohia. - Y compris les annulations. Sans les données pour le Kosovo et Metohie.
[24] Data are given according to the state of civil registration (under the Law of Ukraine "On state registration of acts of civil status" from 1 July 2010). - Les données sont fournies selon l'état de l'état civil (en vertu de la loi ukrainienne du 1er juillet 2010 sur l'enregistrement des actes de l'état civil).
[25] Data tabulated by date of occurrence for England and Wales, and by date of registration for Northern Ireland and Scotland. Excluding Channel Islands (Guernsey and Jersey) and Isle of Man, shown separately, if available. - Données exploitées selon la date de l'événement pour l'Angleterre et le pays de Galles, et selon la date de l'enregistrement pour l'Irlande du Nord et l'Ecosse. Non compris les îles Anglo-Normandes (Guernesey et Jersey) et l'île de Man, qui font l'objet de rubriques distinctes, si disponible.
[26] Data have been randomly rounded. - Ces données ont été arrondies de façon aléatoire.

Continent and country or area — Continent et pays ou zone	Population estimates (in thousands) - Estimations de population (en milliers)									
	2009	2010	2011	2012	2013	2014	2015	2016	2017	2018
AFRICA - AFRIQUE										
Algeria - Algérie	35 334	35 977	36 661	37 384	38 140	38 924	39 728	40 551	41 389	42 228
Angola	22 514	23 356	24 221	25 108	26 016	26 942	27 884	28 842	29 817	30 810
Benin - Bénin	8 945	9 199	9 461	9 729	10 005	10 287	10 576	10 872	11 175	11 485
Botswana	1 953	1 987	2 015	2 040	2 063	2 089	2 121	2 160	2 205	2 254
Burkina Faso	15 141	15 605	16 082	16 571	17 073	17 586	18 111	18 646	19 193	19 751
Burundi	8 398	8 676	8 958	9 246	9 540	9 844	10 160	10 488	10 827	11 175
Cabo Verde	487	493	499	505	512	518	525	531	537	544
Cameroon - Cameroun	19 790	20 341	20 906	21 485	22 077	22 682	23 298	23 927	24 566	25 216
Central African Republic - République centrafricaine	4 338	4 387	4 419	4 436	4 448	4 464	4 493	4 538	4 596	4 666
Chad - Tchad	11 560	11 952	12 361	12 785	13 220	13 664	14 111	14 562	15 017	15 478
Comoros - Comores	673	690	707	724	742	759	777	796	814	832
Congo	4 145	4 274	4 395	4 510	4 623	4 737	4 856	4 981	5 111	5 244
Côte d'Ivoire	20 059	20 533	21 029	21 547	22 088	22 648	23 226	23 823	24 437	25 069
Democratic Republic of the Congo - République démocratique du Congo	62 449	64 564	66 755	69 021	71 359	73 767	76 245	78 789	81 399	84 068
Djibouti	828	840	854	868	883	899	914	929	944	959
Egypt - Égypte	81 135	82 761	84 529	86 422	88 405	90 425	92 443	94 447	96 443	98 424
Equatorial Guinea - Guinée équatoriale	902	944	987	1 031	1 076	1 122	1 169	1 215	1 262	1 309
Eritrea - Érythrée	3 120	3 170	3 214	3 250	3 281	3 311	3 343	3 377	3 413	3 453
Eswatini	1 057	1 065	1 072	1 079	1 087	1 095	1 104	1 114	1 125	1 136
Ethiopia - Éthiopie	85 234	87 640	90 140	92 727	95 386	98 094	100 835	103 603	106 400	109 224
Gabon	1 569	1 624	1 685	1 750	1 817	1 884	1 948	2 008	2 065	2 119
Gambia - Gambie	1 740	1 793	1 848	1 905	1 964	2 024	2 086	2 149	2 214	2 280
Ghana	24 171	24 780	25 388	25 996	26 608	27 224	27 849	28 482	29 121	29 767
Guinea - Guinée	9 964	10 192	10 420	10 652	10 893	11 151	11 432	11 738	12 068	12 414
Guinea-Bissau - Guinée-Bissau	1 484	1 523	1 563	1 605	1 648	1 692	1 737	1 782	1 828	1 874
Kenya	40 902	42 031	43 178	44 343	45 520	46 700	47 878	49 052	50 221	51 393
Lesotho	1 990	1 996	2 004	2 015	2 029	2 043	2 059	2 075	2 092	2 108
Liberia - Libéria	3 754	3 891	4 017	4 136	4 248	4 360	4 472	4 587	4 702	4 819
Libya - Libye	6 134	6 198	6 247	6 286	6 320	6 362	6 418	6 492	6 581	6 679
Madagascar	20 569	21 152	21 744	22 347	22 961	23 590	24 234	24 894	25 571	26 262
Malawi	14 128	14 540	14 962	15 396	15 839	16 290	16 745	17 205	17 670	18 143
Mali	14 581	15 049	15 515	15 979	16 450	16 934	17 439	17 965	18 512	19 078
Mauritania - Mauritanie	3 393	3 494	3 599	3 707	3 817	3 931	4 046	4 164	4 283	4 403
Mauritius - Maurice[1]	1 244	1 248	1 251	1 253	1 255	1 257	1 259	1 262	1 264	1 267
Mayotte	202	209	215	221	227	234	240	246	253	260
Morocco - Maroc	31 929	32 343	32 782	33 242	33 716	34 192	34 664	35 126	35 581	36 029
Mozambique	22 895	23 532	24 188	24 863	25 561	26 286	27 042	27 830	28 649	29 496
Namibia - Namibie	2 081	2 119	2 157	2 195	2 234	2 273	2 315	2 358	2 403	2 448
Niger	15 843	16 464	17 115	17 795	18 504	19 240	20 002	20 789	21 602	22 443
Nigeria - Nigéria	154 325	158 503	162 805	167 229	171 766	176 405	181 137	185 960	190 873	195 875
Republic of South Sudan - République de Soudan du Sud	9 142	9 508	9 831	10 114	10 355	10 555	10 716	10 833	10 911	10 976
Reunion - Réunion	824	831	837	844	851	857	863	870	876	883
Rwanda	9 783	10 039	10 293	10 550	10 812	11 084	11 369	11 669	11 981	12 302
Sao Tome and Principe - Sao Tomé-et-Principe	176	180	185	188	192	196	199	203	207	211
Senegal - Sénégal	12 335	12 678	13 034	13 402	13 782	14 175	14 578	14 994	15 419	15 854
Seychelles	91	91	92	93	93	94	95	96	96	97
Sierra Leone	6 273	6 416	6 563	6 713	6 864	7 017	7 172	7 329	7 488	7 650
Somalia - Somalie	11 718	12 044	12 376	12 715	13 064	13 424	13 797	14 186	14 589	15 008
South Africa - Afrique du Sud	50 477	51 217	52 004	52 833	53 687	54 544	55 386	56 208	57 010	57 793
Sudan - Soudan	33 784	34 545	35 350	36 194	37 073	37 978	38 903	39 847	40 813	41 802
Togo	6 251	6 422	6 596	6 774	6 955	7 138	7 323	7 510	7 698	7 889
Tunisia - Tunisie	10 526	10 635	10 742	10 847	10 953	11 063	11 180	11 304	11 433	11 565
Uganda - Ouganda	31 411	32 428	33 477	34 559	35 695	36 912	38 225	39 649	41 167	42 729
United Republic of Tanzania - République Unie de Tanzanie[2]	43 074	44 347	45 674	47 053	48 483	49 961	51 483	53 049	54 660	56 313
Western Sahara - Sahara occidental	474	480	488	496	505	515	526	539	553	567
Zambia - Zambie	13 215	13 606	14 023	14 465	14 927	15 400	15 879	16 363	16 854	17 352
Zimbabwe	12 527	12 698	12 894	13 115	13 350	13 587	13 815	14 030	14 237	14 439
AMERICA, NORTH - AMÉRIQUE DU NORD										
Anguilla	13	13	14	14	14	14	14	14	15	15
Antigua and Barbuda - Antigua-et-Barbuda	87	88	89	90	92	93	94	95	95	96
Aruba	101	102	102	103	103	104	104	105	105	106
Bahamas	350	355	360	364	367	371	374	378	382	386
Barbados - Barbade	281	282	283	284	284	285	285	286	286	287

Continent and country or area Continent et pays ou zone	Population estimates (in thousands) - Estimations de population (en milliers)									
	2009	**2010**	**2011**	**2012**	**2013**	**2014**	**2015**	**2016**	**2017**	**2018**

AMERICA, NORTH - AMÉRIQUE DU NORD

Belize..	315	322	330	338	346	353	361	368	376	383
Bermuda - Bermudes	66	65	65	65	64	64	64	63	63	63
Bonaire, Saba and Sint Eustatius - Bonaire, Saba et Saint-Eustache	20	21	22	23	24	24	25	25	25	26
British Virgin Islands - Îles Vierges britanniques	27	28	28	29	29	29	29	29	30	30
Canada	33 746	34 148	34 539	34 922	35 297	35 664	36 027	36 383	36 732	37 075
Cayman Islands - Îles Caïmanes	55	57	58	59	60	61	62	63	63	64
Costa Rica	4 521	4 577	4 633	4 688	4 742	4 795	4 848	4 899	4 950	4 999
Cuba	11 227	11 226	11 237	11 257	11 283	11 307	11 325	11 335	11 339	11 338
Curaçao	145	149	152	155	157	158	160	161	162	163
Dominica - Dominique	71	71	71	71	71	71	71	71	71	72
Dominican Republic - République dominicaine..................	9 577	9 695	9 813	9 931	10 048	10 165	10 282	10 398	10 513	10 627
El Salvador	6 158	6 184	6 211	6 238	6 266	6 295	6 325	6 356	6 388	6 421
Greenland - Groenland.......................	57	57	57	56	56	56	56	56	56	57
Grenada - Grenade	106	106	107	107	108	109	110	110	111	111
Guadeloupe	405	406	406	404	403	401	400	400	400	400
Guatemala	14 316	14 630	14 949	15 271	15 596	15 923	16 252	16 583	16 915	17 248
Haiti - Haïti	9 798	9 949	10 100	10 251	10 401	10 549	10 696	10 840	10 982	11 123
Honduras	8 151	8 317	8 481	8 641	8 799	8 956	9 113	9 271	9 429	9 588
Jamaica - Jamaïque	2 796	2 810	2 826	2 842	2 859	2 875	2 891	2 906	2 921	2 935
Martinique...	397	395	392	388	385	381	378	377	376	376
Mexico - Mexique	112 464	114 093	115 695	117 274	118 827	120 355	121 858	123 333	124 777	126 191
Montserrat	5	5	5	5	5	5	5	5	5	5
Nicaragua	5 746	5 824	5 903	5 983	6 062	6 143	6 223	6 304	6 385	6 466
Panama	3 579	3 643	3 706	3 771	3 835	3 901	3 968	4 037	4 107	4 177
Puerto Rico - Porto Rico....................	3 597	3 580	3 560	3 537	3 504	3 454	3 382	3 283	3 164	3 040
Saint Kitts and Nevis - Saint-Kitts-et-Nevis	49	49	49	49	50	50	51	52	52	52
Saint Lucia - Sainte-Lucie	172	174	176	177	178	178	179	180	181	182
Saint Pierre and Miquelon - Saint Pierre-et-Miquelon	6	6	6	6	6	6	6	6	6	6
Saint Vincent and the Grenadines - Saint-Vincent-et-les Grenadines	108	108	108	108	109	109	109	109	110	110
Sint Maarten (Dutch part) - Saint-Martin (partie néerlandaise)............	34	34	35	36	38	39	40	41	41	42
Trinidad and Tobago - Trinité-et-Tobago	1 321	1 328	1 336	1 345	1 354	1 362	1 370	1 378	1 384	1 390
Turks and Caicos Islands - Îles Turques et Caïques...........	32	33	33	34	35	35	36	37	37	38
United States of America - États-Unis d'Amérique..............	306 308	309 011	311 584	314 044	316 401	318 673	320 878	323 016	325 085	327 096
United States Virgin Islands - Îles Vierges américaines......	106	106	106	106	105	105	105	105	105	105

AMERICA, SOUTH - AMÉRIQUE DU SUD

Argentina - Argentine	40 483	40 896	41 320	41 755	42 196	42 638	43 075	43 508	43 937	44 361
Bolivia (Plurinational State of) - Bolivie (État plurinational de)	9 885	10 049	10 213	10 378	10 542	10 707	10 870	11 032	11 193	11 353
Brazil - Brésil	193 887	195 714	197 515	199 287	201 036	202 764	204 472	206 163	207 834	209 469
Chile - Chili	16 886	17 063	17 234	17 400	17 572	17 759	17 969	18 209	18 470	18 729
Colombia - Colombie	44 750	45 223	45 663	46 076	46 495	46 968	47 521	48 175	48 910	49 661
Ecuador - Équateur	14 774	15 011	15 244	15 474	15 707	15 952	16 212	16 491	16 785	17 084
Falkland Islands (Malvinas) - Îles Falkland (Malvinas)........	3	3	3	3	3	3	3	3	3	3
French Guiana - Guyane française	228	233	238	244	249	255	261	268	275	283
Guyana...	748	749	752	755	759	763	767	771	775	779
Paraguay	6 164	6 248	6 334	6 422	6 510	6 600	6 689	6 778	6 867	6 956
Peru - Pérou	28 793	29 028	29 264	29 507	29 774	30 090	30 471	30 926	31 444	31 989
Suriname	523	529	535	541	547	553	559	565	571	576
Uruguay	3 350	3 359	3 369	3 379	3 389	3 400	3 412	3 424	3 437	3 449
Venezuela (Bolivarian Republic of) - Venezuela (République bolivarienne du)	28 031	28 440	28 888	29 361	29 781	30 043	30 082	29 851	29 402	28 887

ASIA - ASIE

Afghanistan	28 395	29 186	30 117	31 161	32 270	33 371	34 414	35 383	36 296	37 172
Armenia - Arménie	2 888	2 877	2 877	2 884	2 898	2 912	2 926	2 936	2 945	2 952
Azerbaijan - Azerbaïdjan[3]	8 924	9 032	9 146	9 265	9 385	9 506	9 623	9 736	9 845	9 950
Bahrain - Bahreïn	1 185	1 241	1 278	1 300	1 315	1 336	1 372	1 426	1 494	1 569
Bangladesh	145 925	147 575	149 273	151 006	152 761	154 517	156 256	157 977	159 685	161 377
Bhutan - Bhoutan	678	686	693	702	710	719	728	737	746	754
Brunei Darussalam - Brunéi Darussalam	384	389	394	399	404	410	415	420	424	429

Continent and country or area / Continent et pays ou zone	Population estimates (in thousands) - Estimations de population (en milliers)									
	2009	2010	2011	2012	2013	2014	2015	2016	2017	2018
ASIA - ASIE										
Cambodia - Cambodge	14 094	14 312	14 541	14 780	15 026	15 275	15 521	15 766	16 009	16 250
China - Chine[4]	1 361 169	1 368 811	1 376 498	1 384 206	1 391 883	1 399 454	1 406 848	1 414 049	1 421 022	1 427 648
China, Hong Kong SAR - Chine, Hong Kong RAS	6 925	6 966	7 007	7 047	7 089	7 135	7 186	7 244	7 306	7 372
China, Macao SAR - Chine, Macao RAS	526	538	551	564	577	590	602	613	623	632
Cyprus - Chypre[5]	1 098	1 113	1 125	1 135	1 144	1 152	1 161	1 170	1 180	1 189
Democratic People's Republic of Korea - République populaire démocratique de Corée	24 428	24 549	24 673	24 801	24 930	25 058	25 184	25 308	25 430	25 550
Georgia - Géorgie[6]	4 119	4 099	4 081	4 064	4 049	4 035	4 024	4 015	4 009	4 003
India - Inde	1 217 726	1 234 281	1 250 288	1 265 780	1 280 842	1 295 601	1 310 152	1 324 517	1 338 677	1 352 642
Indonesia - Indonésie	238 621	241 834	245 116	248 452	251 805	255 128	258 383	261 556	264 651	267 671
Iran (Islamic Republic of) - Iran (République islamique d')	72 925	73 763	74 635	75 540	76 482	77 466	78 492	79 564	80 674	81 800
Iraq	28 973	29 742	30 725	31 890	33 157	34 412	35 572	36 611	37 553	38 434
Israel - Israël	7 190	7 346	7 487	7 615	7 735	7 854	7 978	8 109	8 244	8 382
Japan - Japon	128 555	128 542	128 499	128 424	128 314	128 169	127 985	127 763	127 503	127 202
Jordan - Jordanie	6 893	7 262	7 663	8 090	8 519	8 919	9 267	9 554	9 786	9 965
Kazakhstan	16 043	16 252	16 491	16 752	17 026	17 303	17 572	17 831	18 080	18 320
Kuwait - Koweït	2 821	2 992	3 168	3 349	3 526	3 691	3 836	3 957	4 056	4 137
Kyrgyzstan - Kirghizstan	5 335	5 422	5 518	5 622	5 731	5 845	5 959	6 074	6 190	6 304
Lao People's Democratic Republic - République démocratique populaire lao	6 149	6 249	6 348	6 445	6 541	6 640	6 741	6 846	6 953	7 061
Lebanon - Liban	4 813	4 953	5 202	5 538	5 913	6 261	6 533	6 714	6 819	6 859
Malaysia - Malaisie[7]	27 735	28 208	28 651	29 068	29 469	29 867	30 271	30 685	31 105	31 528
Maldives	353	366	380	397	416	435	455	476	496	516
Mongolia - Mongolie	2 674	2 720	2 770	2 825	2 882	2 940	2 998	3 056	3 114	3 170
Myanmar	50 250	50 601	50 991	51 414	51 852	52 281	52 681	53 045	53 383	53 708
Nepal - Népal	26 884	27 013	27 041	26 989	26 917	26 906	27 015	27 263	27 633	28 096
Oman	2 876	3 041	3 251	3 498	3 765	4 027	4 267	4 479	4 666	4 829
Pakistan	175 526	179 425	183 340	187 280	191 261	195 305	199 427	203 631	207 906	212 228
Philippines	92 414	93 967	95 570	97 213	98 872	100 513	102 113	103 664	105 173	106 651
Qatar	1 655	1 856	2 036	2 196	2 337	2 459	2 566	2 654	2 725	2 782
Republic of Korea - République de Corée	49 347	49 546	49 786	50 061	50 346	50 608	50 823	50 983	51 096	51 172
Saudi Arabia - Arabie saoudite	26 630	27 421	28 268	29 155	30 052	30 917	31 718	32 443	33 101	33 703
Singapore - Singapour	4 967	5 131	5 264	5 369	5 454	5 526	5 592	5 654	5 708	5 758
Sri Lanka	20 124	20 262	20 398	20 533	20 663	20 789	20 908	21 021	21 128	21 229
State of Palestine - État de Palestine[8]	3 958	4 056	4 150	4 242	4 334	4 429	4 529	4 636	4 747	4 863
Syrian Arab Republic - République arabe syrienne	21 206	21 363	21 082	20 439	19 578	18 711	17 997	17 466	17 096	16 945
Tajikistan - Tadjikistan	7 365	7 527	7 698	7 875	8 060	8 253	8 454	8 664	8 880	9 101
Thailand - Thaïlande	66 867	67 195	67 518	67 836	68 145	68 439	68 715	68 971	69 210	69 428
Timor-Leste	1 074	1 094	1 113	1 133	1 153	1 174	1 196	1 219	1 243	1 268
Turkey - Turquie	71 321	72 327	73 443	74 651	75 925	77 229	78 529	79 828	81 116	82 340
Turkmenistan - Turkménistan	5 008	5 087	5 174	5 268	5 366	5 466	5 565	5 662	5 758	5 851
United Arab Emirates - Émirats arabes unis	7 917	8 550	8 947	9 142	9 198	9 214	9 263	9 361	9 487	9 631
Uzbekistan - Ouzbékistan	28 065	28 516	28 977	29 449	29 933	30 426	30 930	31 442	31 960	32 476
Viet Nam	87 092	87 968	88 871	89 802	90 753	91 714	92 677	93 640	94 601	95 546
Yemen - Yémen	22 516	23 155	23 808	24 473	25 147	25 823	26 498	27 168	27 835	28 499
EUROPE										
Albania - Albanie	2 973	2 948	2 929	2 914	2 904	2 896	2 891	2 886	2 884	2 883
Andorra - Andorre	84	84	84	82	81	79	78	77	77	77
Austria - Autriche	8 373	8 410	8 454	8 502	8 556	8 615	8 679	8 747	8 820	8 891
Belarus - Bélarus	9 433	9 421	9 415	9 417	9 424	9 432	9 439	9 446	9 450	9 453
Belgium - Belgique	10 860	10 939	11 014	11 085	11 154	11 221	11 288	11 354	11 420	11 482
Bosnia and Herzegovina - Bosnie-Herzégovine	3 736	3 705	3 661	3 605	3 543	3 482	3 429	3 386	3 352	3 324
Bulgaria - Bulgarie	7 474	7 425	7 379	7 334	7 290	7 246	7 200	7 152	7 102	7 052
Croatia - Croatie	4 341	4 328	4 313	4 296	4 277	4 256	4 233	4 209	4 183	4 156
Czechia - Tchéquie	10 488	10 537	10 567	10 581	10 587	10 591	10 601	10 619	10 641	10 666
Denmark - Danemark	5 526	5 555	5 583	5 611	5 638	5 664	5 689	5 711	5 732	5 752
Estonia - Estonie	1 336	1 332	1 328	1 323	1 319	1 316	1 315	1 317	1 319	1 323
Faeroe Islands - Îles Féroé	48	48	48	48	48	48	48	48	48	48
Finland - Finlande[9]	5 342	5 366	5 390	5 415	5 439	5 461	5 481	5 498	5 511	5 523
France	62 543	62 880	63 222	63 564	63 894	64 194	64 453	64 668	64 843	64 991
Germany - Allemagne	80 900	80 827	80 856	80 973	81 174	81 450	81 787	82 194	82 658	83 124
Gibraltar	34	34	34	34	34	34	34	34	34	34
Greece - Grèce	10 959	10 888	10 829	10 781	10 741	10 701	10 660	10 615	10 569	10 522
Holy See - Saint-Siège	1	1	1	1	1	1	1	1	1	1
Hungary - Hongrie	9 959	9 927	9 896	9 864	9 834	9 805	9 778	9 753	9 730	9 708

Continent and country or area Continent et pays ou zone	Population estimates (in thousands) - Estimations de population (en milliers)									
	2009	**2010**	**2011**	**2012**	**2013**	**2014**	**2015**	**2016**	**2017**	**2018**

EUROPE

Iceland - Islande	316	320	323	326	327	329	330	332	334	337
Ireland - Irlande	4 495	4 554	4 591	4 608	4 615	4 627	4 652	4 696	4 753	4 819
Isle of Man - Île de Man	84	85	85	85	84	83	83	83	84	84
Italy - Italie	59 106	59 325	59 589	59 879	60 167	60 410	60 578	60 663	60 674	60 627
Latvia - Lettonie	2 145	2 119	2 094	2 069	2 045	2 021	1 998	1 974	1 951	1 928
Liechtenstein	36	36	36	37	37	37	37	38	38	38
Lithuania - Lituanie	3 167	3 124	3 083	3 046	3 009	2 971	2 932	2 890	2 845	2 801
Luxembourg	497	508	519	531	543	555	567	579	592	604
Malta - Malte	412	414	418	422	426	430	434	436	438	439
Monaco	35	36	36	36	37	37	38	38	38	39
Montenegro - Monténégro	623	624	625	626	626	627	627	627	628	628
Netherlands - Pays-Bas	16 626	16 683	16 738	16 792	16 844	16 893	16 938	16 981	17 021	17 060
North Macedonia - Macédoine du Nord	2 069	2 071	2 072	2 074	2 076	2 078	2 079	2 081	2 082	2 083
Norway - Norvège[10]	4 827	4 886	4 948	5 014	5 079	5 142	5 200	5 251	5 296	5 338
Poland - Pologne	38 352	38 330	38 287	38 227	38 158	38 091	38 034	37 989	37 953	37 922
Portugal	10 604	10 596	10 569	10 526	10 473	10 418	10 368	10 326	10 289	10 256
Republic of Moldova - République de Moldova[11]	4 098	4 086	4 079	4 076	4 075	4 073	4 071	4 066	4 060	4 052
Romania - Roumanie	20 638	20 472	20 337	20 227	20 133	20 036	19 925	19 796	19 654	19 506
Russian Federation - Fédération de Russie	143 327	143 479	143 703	143 994	144 325	144 665	144 985	145 275	145 530	145 734
San Marino - Saint-Marin	31	31	32	32	33	33	33	34	34	34
Serbia - Serbie[12]	9 023	8 991	8 964	8 940	8 919	8 898	8 877	8 854	8 830	8 803
Slovakia - Slovaquie	5 401	5 404	5 409	5 415	5 422	5 429	5 436	5 442	5 448	5 453
Slovenia - Slovénie	2 034	2 043	2 051	2 058	2 063	2 067	2 071	2 074	2 076	2 078
Spain - Espagne[13]	46 584	46 931	47 084	47 063	46 931	46 778	46 672	46 634	46 647	46 693
Sweden - Suède	9 313	9 390	9 467	9 543	9 618	9 692	9 765	9 836	9 905	9 972
Switzerland - Suisse	7 714	7 809	7 907	8 008	8 109	8 206	8 297	8 380	8 456	8 526
Ukraine[14]	45 971	45 792	45 620	45 454	45 287	45 112	44 922	44 714	44 488	44 246
United Kingdom of Great Britain and Northern Ireland - Royaume-Uni de Grande-Bretagne et d'Irlande du Nord	62 829	63 460	64 022	64 525	64 984	65 423	65 860	66 298	66 727	67 142

OCEANIA - OCÉANIE

American Samoa - Samoas américaines	57	56	56	56	56	56	56	56	56	55
Australia - Australie[15]	21 751	22 155	22 538	22 904	23 255	23 596	23 932	24 263	24 585	24 898
Cook Islands - Îles Cook	19	18	18	18	18	18	18	18	18	18
Fiji - Fidji	854	860	863	865	866	866	869	872	877	883
French Polynesia - Polynésie française	265	266	268	269	270	272	273	275	276	278
Guam	159	159	160	160	160	161	162	163	164	166
Kiribati	101	103	105	106	108	109	111	113	114	116
Marshall Islands - Îles Marshall	56	56	57	57	57	57	57	58	58	58
Micronesia (Federated States of) - Micronésie (États fédérés de)	103	103	103	105	106	107	109	110	111	113
Nauru	10	10	10	10	10	10	10	10	11	11
New Caledonia - Nouvelle-Calédonie	250	254	257	261	264	268	271	274	277	280
New Zealand - Nouvelle-Zélande	4 323	4 370	4 419	4 468	4 519	4 568	4 615	4 659	4 702	4 743
Niue - Nioué	2	2	2	2	2	2	2	2	2	2
Northern Mariana Islands - Îles Mariannes septentrionales	54	54	54	54	55	55	56	56	57	57
Palau - Palaos	18	18	18	18	18	18	18	18	18	18
Papua New Guinea - Papouasie-Nouvelle-Guinée	7 145	7 311	7 472	7 631	7 788	7 947	8 108	8 272	8 438	8 606
Samoa	185	186	187	189	191	192	194	195	195	196
Solomon Islands - Îles Salomon	515	528	542	556	571	587	603	619	636	653
Tokelau - Tokélaou	1	1	1	1	1	1	1	1	1	1
Tonga	104	104	104	103	102	101	101	101	102	103
Tuvalu	10	11	11	11	11	11	11	11	11	12
Vanuatu	230	236	243	250	257	264	271	278	285	293
Wallis and Futuna Islands - Îles Wallis et Futuna	13	13	12	12	12	12	12	12	12	12

SOURCE

United Nations, Department of Economic and Social Affairs, Population Division (2019). 2019 Revision of World Population Prospects - Organisation des Nations Unies, Département des affaires économiques et sociales, Division de la population (2019). Perspectives de la population mondiale : La révision de 2019

FOOTNOTES - NOTES

[1] Including Agalega, Rodrigues and Saint Brandon. - Y compris Agalega, Rodrigues et Saint Brandon.

[2] Including Zanzibar. - Y compris le Zanzibar.

[3] Including Nagorno-Karabakh. - Y compris le Haut-Karabakh.

[4] For statistical purposes, the data for China do not include Hong Kong and Macao Special Administrative Regions (SAR) of China. - A des fins statistiques, les données pour la Chine ne comprennent pas les Régions Administratives Spéciales (SAR) de Hong Kong et Macao.

[5] Refers to the whole country. - Les données se rapportent au pays en entier.

[6] Including Abkhazia and South Ossetia. - Y compris l'Abkhazie et l'Ossétie du Sud.

[7] Including Sabah and Sarawak. - Y compris le Sabah et le Sarawak.

[8] Including East Jerusalem. - Y compris Jérusalem-Est.

[9] Including Åland Islands. - Y compris les îles Åland.

[10] Including Svalbard and Jan Mayen Islands. - Y compris Svalbard et l'île Jan Mayen.

[11] Including Transnistria. - Y compris la Transnistrie.

[12] Including Kosovo. - Y compris le Kosovo.

[13] Including Canary Islands, Ceuta and Melilla. - Y compris les îles Canaries, Ceuta et Melilla.

[14] Including Crimea. - Y compris la Crimée.

[15] Including Christmas Island, Cocos (Keeling) Islands and Norfolk Island. - Y compris les îles Christmas, Cocos (Keeling) et Norfolk.

Annex II: Vital statistics summary, United Nations estimates: 2015-2020
Annexe II: Aperçu des statistiques de l'état civil, estimations des Nations Unies : 2015-2020

Continent and country or area / Continent et pays ou zone	Crude birth rate - Taux bruts de natalité	Crude death rate - Taux bruts de mortalité	Infant mortality rate - Décès d'enfants de moins d'un an	Life expectancy at birth - Espérance de vie à la naissance		Total fertility rate - Indice synthétique de fécondité	Natural increase - Accroissement naturel
				Male - Masculin	Female - Féminin		
AFRICA - AFRIQUE							
Algeria - Algérie	24.7	4.7	21.2	75.4	77.8	3.05	20.0
Angola	40.9	8.3	61.5	57.8	63.4	5.55	32.6
Benin - Bénin	36.4	9.0	61.1	59.8	62.8	4.87	27.4
Botswana	25.1	5.8	30.2	66.0	71.9	2.89	19.3
Burkina Faso	38.2	8.3	54.2	60.1	61.6	5.23	29.9
Burundi	39.3	8.0	42.4	59.2	62.8	5.45	31.2
Cabo Verde	19.7	5.6	16.9	69.2	75.9	2.29	14.0
Cameroon - Cameroun	35.6	9.4	61.2	57.5	60.0	4.60	26.3
Central African Republic - République centrafricaine	35.4	12.4	81.9	50.5	54.9	4.75	23.0
Chad - Tchad	42.4	12.2	74.5	52.4	55.2	5.80	30.2
Comoros - Comores	32.1	7.3	53.1	62.3	65.8	4.24	24.8
Congo	33.1	6.8	35.3	62.7	65.6	4.45	26.3
Côte d'Ivoire	35.9	10.2	60.4	56.1	58.6	4.68	25.7
Democratic Republic of the Congo - République démocratique du Congo	41.4	9.6	64.9	58.7	61.7	5.96	31.8
Djibouti	21.7	7.1	33.4	64.6	68.7	2.76	14.6
Egypt - Égypte	26.5	5.8	15.6	69.5	74.1	3.33	20.7
Equatorial Guinea - Guinée équatoriale	33.5	9.4	66.1	57.3	59.4	4.55	24.0
Eritrea - Érythrée	30.6	7.2	34.7	63.6	68.0	4.10	23.4
Eswatini	26.7	9.4	41.4	55.2	63.9	3.03	17.3
Ethiopia - Éthiopie	32.6	6.7	37.0	64.1	67.9	4.30	25.9
Gabon	32.0	6.9	35.3	64.0	68.2	4.00	25.1
Gambia - Gambie	38.8	8.0	44.8	60.2	63.0	5.25	30.8
Ghana	29.6	7.3	35.6	62.6	64.7	3.89	22.2
Guinea - Guinée	36.6	8.5	51.6	60.3	61.5	4.74	28.0
Guinea-Bissau - Guinée-Bissau	35.4	9.7	57.1	55.8	59.7	4.51	25.7
Kenya	28.9	5.5	36.3	63.8	68.5	3.52	23.4
Lesotho	27.0	14.3	62.3	50.4	56.8	3.16	12.7
Liberia - Libéria	33.2	7.6	54.1	62.2	65.0	4.35	25.6
Libya - Libye	19.0	5.1	10.5	69.9	75.7	2.25	13.9
Madagascar	32.8	6.1	29.0	64.9	68.1	4.11	26.7
Malawi	34.3	6.8	41.3	60.3	66.6	4.25	27.5
Mali	41.8	9.8	65.8	58.0	59.5	5.92	32.0
Mauritania - Mauritanie	33.9	7.3	53.4	63.0	66.2	4.59	26.6
Mauritius - Maurice[1]	10.2	8.3	11.2	71.4	78.3	1.39	1.9
Mayotte	28.3	2.7	4.2	76.0	82.9	3.73	25.6
Morocco - Maroc	19.1	5.1	19.9	75.1	77.5	2.42	14.0
Mozambique	37.7	8.6	53.9	57.0	62.9	4.89	29.1
Namibia - Namibie	28.8	8.2	33.4	60.0	65.8	3.42	20.6
Niger	46.3	8.4	46.3	60.7	63.0	6.95	37.9
Nigeria - Nigéria	38.1	12.0	62.1	53.3	55.1	5.42	26.1
Republic of South Sudan - République de Soudan du Sud ...	35.2	10.6	64.4	56.0	58.9	4.74	24.6
Reunion - Réunion	14.9	6.2	2.7	77.3	83.8	2.27	8.7
Rwanda	32.1	5.3	29.2	66.3	70.5	4.10	26.8
Sao Tome and Principe - Sao Tomé-et-Principe	31.8	4.9	26.4	67.7	72.5	4.35	26.9
Senegal - Sénégal	34.7	5.8	32.7	65.3	69.4	4.65	28.9
Seychelles	16.8	7.8	10.9	69.8	77.3	2.46	9.0
Sierra Leone	33.7	11.9	80.8	53.2	54.9	4.32	21.8
Somalia - Somalie	41.9	10.9	69.3	55.3	58.7	6.12	30.9
South Africa - Afrique du Sud	20.7	9.5	27.2	60.2	67.1	2.41	11.1
Sudan - Soudan	32.4	7.2	42.9	63.1	66.8	4.43	25.1
Togo	33.3	8.6	49.7	59.7	61.4	4.35	24.8
Tunisia - Tunisie	17.7	6.3	12.7	74.4	78.5	2.20	11.5
Uganda - Ouganda	38.4	6.7	46.1	60.4	65.0	5.01	31.8
United Republic of Tanzania - République Unie de Tanzanie[2]	36.9	6.5	41.2	63.0	66.6	4.92	30.4
Western Sahara - Sahara occidental	20.3	4.9	28.8	68.2	71.9	2.42	15.4
Zambia - Zambie	36.3	6.6	45.6	60.3	66.2	4.66	29.7
Zimbabwe	30.8	8.1	38.7	59.2	62.2	3.63	22.8
AMERICA, NORTH - AMÉRIQUE DU NORD							
Antigua and Barbuda - Antigua-et-Barbuda	15.5	6.3	5.2	75.7	77.9	2.00	9.1
Aruba	11.7	9.0	13.6	73.6	78.4	1.90	2.7
Bahamas	14.0	6.7	5.9	71.5	75.9	1.76	7.3
Barbados - Barbade	10.7	9.0	10.0	77.6	80.4	1.62	1.7

Continent and country or area / Continent et pays ou zone	Crude birth rate - Taux bruts de natalité	Crude death rate - Taux bruts de mortalité	Infant mortality rate - Décès d'enfants de moins d'un an	Life expectancy at birth - Espérance de vie à la naissance Male - Masculin	Female - Féminin	Total fertility rate - Indice synthétique de fécondité	Natural increase - Accroissement naturel
AMERICA, NORTH - AMÉRIQUE DU NORD							
Belize	20.9	4.7	12.8	71.4	77.6	2.32	16.2
Canada	10.5	7.7	4.5	80.2	84.3	1.53	2.7
Costa Rica	14.1	5.0	7.3	77.4	82.7	1.76	9.1
Cuba	10.2	8.9	4.5	76.7	80.7	1.62	1.3
Curaçao	10.8	8.8	9.1	75.5	81.4	1.76	2.1
Dominican Republic - République dominicaine	19.7	6.1	25.9	70.7	77.1	2.36	13.6
El Salvador	18.4	7.0	14.6	68.1	77.5	2.05	11.4
Grenada - Grenade	16.6	9.5	15.0	70.1	75.0	2.07	7.1
Guadeloupe	11.7	8.2	4.6	78.1	85.2	2.17	3.5
Guatemala	24.8	4.8	20.7	71.0	76.8	2.90	20.0
Haiti - Haïti	24.5	8.6	54.3	61.4	65.7	2.96	16.0
Honduras	21.8	4.4	15.0	72.7	77.3	2.49	17.4
Jamaica - Jamaïque	16.2	7.6	11.8	72.8	75.9	1.99	8.7
Martinique	9.9	9.1	5.6	78.9	85.4	1.88	0.8
Mexico - Mexique	17.7	6.0	13.5	72.1	77.8	2.14	11.8
Nicaragua	20.9	5.1	16.8	70.6	77.7	2.42	15.8
Panama	19.1	5.1	14.1	75.1	81.5	2.47	14.0
Puerto Rico - Porto Rico	7.4	9.3	5.5	76.2	83.3	1.22	-2.0
Saint Lucia - Sainte-Lucie	12.1	7.1	12.5	74.7	77.4	1.44	5.0
Saint Vincent and the Grenadines - Saint-Vincent-et-les Grenadines	14.3	9.2	14.6	70.1	74.9	1.90	5.1
Trinidad and Tobago - Trinité-et-Tobago	13.1	8.3	22.0	70.7	76.0	1.73	4.8
United States of America - États-Unis d'Amérique	12.0	8.7	5.8	76.3	81.3	1.78	3.3
United States Virgin Islands - Îles Vierges américaines	11.8	8.5	8.2	77.7	82.9	2.05	3.3
AMERICA, SOUTH - AMÉRIQUE DU SUD							
Argentina - Argentine	17.1	7.6	10.2	73.0	79.8	2.27	9.5
Bolivia (Plurinational State of) - Bolivie (État plurinational de)	21.9	6.8	29.7	68.3	74.1	2.75	15.1
Brazil - Brésil	14.1	6.4	13.0	71.9	79.3	1.74	7.7
Chile - Chili	12.5	6.1	6.7	77.4	82.3	1.65	6.3
Colombia - Colombie	15.0	5.5	12.6	74.2	79.8	1.82	9.5
Ecuador - Équateur	19.9	5.1	13.6	74.0	79.6	2.44	14.8
French Guiana - Guyane française	25.6	2.9	8.7	76.7	83.0	3.36	22.6
Guyana	20.1	7.4	26.8	66.7	72.9	2.47	12.6
Paraguay	20.7	5.5	19.0	72.1	76.2	2.45	15.2
Peru - Pérou	18.1	5.5	12.8	73.7	79.2	2.27	12.6
Suriname	18.7	7.3	17.5	68.3	74.9	2.43	11.3
Uruguay	13.9	9.5	8.7	73.9	81.3	1.98	4.5
Venezuela (Bolivarian Republic of) - Venezuela (République bolivarienne du)	18.0	7.0	25.7	68.4	76.1	2.28	11.1
ASIA - ASIE							
Afghanistan	32.9	6.5	51.7	62.9	65.8	4.56	26.3
Armenia - Arménie	14.2	9.9	10.8	71.1	78.3	1.76	4.3
Azerbaijan - Azerbaïdjan[3]	17.1	6.8	20.8	70.3	75.3	2.08	10.3
Bahrain - Bahreïn	14.2	2.4	6.0	76.3	78.2	2.00	11.8
Bangladesh	18.4	5.5	26.8	70.5	74.1	2.05	12.8
Bhutan - Bhoutan	17.5	6.3	24.1	71.0	71.6	2.00	11.2
Brunei Darussalam - Brunéi Darussalam	15.0	4.4	7.9	74.5	76.9	1.85	10.6
Cambodia - Cambodge	22.7	6.0	23.7	67.2	71.5	2.52	16.7
China - Chine[4]	11.9	7.1	9.9	74.5	79.0	1.69	4.8
China, Hong Kong SAR - Chine, Hong Kong RAS	11.1	6.6	1.3	81.8	87.5	1.33	4.5
China, Macao SAR - Chine, Macao RAS	11.0	3.9	2.6	81.1	87.0	1.20	7.1
Cyprus - Chypre[5]	10.6	7.0	3.5	78.7	82.8	1.34	3.6
Democratic People's Republic of Korea - République populaire démocratique de Corée	13.9	9.1	13.9	68.3	75.4	1.91	4.9
Georgia - Géorgie[6]	13.6	12.8	9.4	69.1	77.9	2.06	0.7
India - Inde	18.0	7.2	32.0	68.1	70.5	2.24	10.8
Indonesia - Indonésie	18.2	6.4	18.9	69.3	73.6	2.32	11.8
Iran (Islamic Republic of) - Iran (République islamique d')	19.1	4.9	12.8	75.3	77.6	2.15	14.2
Iraq	29.1	4.8	24.1	68.3	72.4	3.68	24.3
Israel - Israël	20.4	5.3	2.7	81.0	84.3	3.04	15.1

Annex II: Vital statistics summary, United Nations estimates: 2015-2020
Annexe II: Aperçu des statistiques de l'état civil, estimations des Nations Unies : 2015-2020 (continued - suite)

Continent and country or area / Continent et pays ou zone	Crude birth rate - Taux bruts de natalité	Crude death rate - Taux bruts de mortalité	Infant mortality rate - Décès d'enfants de moins d'un an	Life expectancy at birth - Espérance de vie à la naissance		Total fertility rate - Indice synthétique de fécondité	Natural increase - Accroissement naturel
				Male - Masculin	Female - Féminin		
ASIA - ASIE							
Japan - Japon....................	7.5	10.4	1.8	81.3	87.5	1.37	-2.9
Jordan - Jordanie	22.0	3.9	14.6	72.7	76.1	2.77	18.2
Kazakhstan....................	21.4	7.1	7.7	68.8	77.4	2.76	14.2
Kuwait - Koweït	14.4	2.7	7.1	74.6	76.4	2.10	11.7
Kyrgyzstan - Kirghizstan	24.8	6.1	15.5	67.2	75.4	3.00	18.7
Lao People's Democratic Republic - République démocratique populaire lao	23.8	6.5	38.8	65.7	69.2	2.70	17.3
Lebanon - Liban	17.6	4.3	9.4	77.0	80.8	2.09	13.3
Malaysia - Malaisie[7]	16.8	5.1	5.9	74.0	78.1	2.01	11.8
Maldives	14.4	2.8	6.8	77.1	80.4	1.88	11.6
Mongolia - Mongolie	24.4	6.3	18.1	65.5	73.8	2.90	18.1
Myanmar	17.7	8.2	38.4	63.7	69.8	2.17	9.5
Nepal - Népal	20.0	6.4	27.9	68.8	71.7	1.93	13.6
Oman	19.6	2.4	7.3	75.8	80.1	2.93	17.2
Pakistan....................	28.5	7.0	61.3	66.1	68.0	3.55	21.5
Philippines	20.6	5.8	19.7	67.1	75.3	2.58	14.7
Qatar	9.7	1.2	6.3	78.9	81.8	1.88	8.5
Republic of Korea - République de Corée	7.4	5.9	2.1	79.6	85.7	1.11	1.5
Saudi Arabia - Arabie saoudite	18.0	3.5	6.3	73.7	76.5	2.34	14.6
Singapore - Singapour	8.8	4.4	1.6	81.3	85.5	1.21	4.3
Sri Lanka	16.0	6.6	7.6	73.3	80.1	2.21	9.4
State of Palestine - État de Palestine[8]	29.4	3.5	17.5	72.2	75.5	3.67	26.0
Syrian Arab Republic - République arabe syrienne	24.0	5.5	15.5	65.9	77.7	2.84	18.5
Tajikistan - Tadjikistan	31.2	4.9	29.3	68.6	73.1	3.61	26.3
Thailand - Thaïlande	10.5	7.6	7.8	73.1	80.6	1.54	2.9
Timor-Leste	29.7	6.0	37.3	67.2	71.3	4.10	23.7
Turkey - Turquie	16.2	5.4	8.9	74.3	80.2	2.08	10.8
Turkmenistan - Turkménistan	24.0	7.1	43.3	64.5	71.5	2.79	16.9
United Arab Emirates - Émirats arabes unis	10.4	1.5	5.5	77.1	79.1	1.42	8.9
Uzbekistan - Ouzbékistan	21.8	5.8	20.8	69.4	73.6	2.43	16.0
Viet Nam	16.9	6.3	16.7	71.2	79.4	2.06	10.7
Yemen - Yémen	30.7	6.0	43.2	64.4	67.7	3.84	24.7
EUROPE							
Albania - Albanie	11.8	7.8	8.0	76.7	80.1	1.62	4.0
Austria - Autriche	9.9	9.9	3.2	78.9	83.8	1.53	0.1
Belarus - Bélarus	11.8	12.6	3.0	69.3	79.3	1.71	-0.7
Belgium - Belgique	10.9	9.8	2.8	79.0	83.7	1.72	1.1
Bosnia and Herzegovina - Bosnie-Herzégovine.........	8.2	10.6	6.0	74.7	79.7	1.27	-2.4
Bulgaria - Bulgarie	9.0	15.4	6.3	71.3	78.5	1.56	-6.4
Croatia - Croatie	8.9	13.1	4.0	75.0	81.4	1.45	-4.2
Czechia - Tchéquie	10.5	10.5	2.3	76.5	81.8	1.64	0.0
Denmark - Danemark	10.7	9.7	3.1	78.7	82.7	1.76	1.0
Estonia - Estonie	10.4	11.6	2.0	74.0	82.5	1.59	-1.3
Finland - Finlande[9]	9.4	9.7	1.7	78.8	84.5	1.53	-0.4
France	11.2	9.3	3.0	79.4	85.4	1.85	2.0
Germany - Allemagne	9.4	11.2	3.2	78.7	83.6	1.59	-1.7
Greece - Grèce	7.8	10.8	2.8	79.5	84.5	1.30	-3.0
Hungary - Hongrie	9.5	12.5	4.1	73.0	80.1	1.49	-3.0
Iceland - Islande	12.1	6.7	1.3	81.2	84.3	1.77	5.4
Ireland - Irlande	13.0	6.0	2.7	80.4	83.7	1.84	7.0
Italy - Italie	7.6	10.5	2.6	81.0	85.4	1.33	-2.8
Latvia - Lettonie	10.8	14.6	3.3	69.9	79.8	1.72	-3.8
Lithuania - Lituanie	10.3	13.6	4.0	70.0	81.1	1.67	-3.2
Luxembourg	10.7	7.1	2.9	79.8	84.2	1.45	3.5
Malta - Malte	9.8	8.2	5.0	80.4	84.1	1.45	1.6
Montenegro - Monténégro	11.8	10.7	2.8	74.2	79.1	1.75	1.1
Netherlands - Pays-Bas	10.1	8.7	2.5	80.3	83.8	1.66	1.4
North Macedonia - Macédoine du Nord	10.9	10.0	10.7	73.6	77.7	1.50	0.9
Norway - Norvège[10]	11.1	8.0	2.1	80.2	84.2	1.68	3.1
Poland - Pologne	9.9	10.1	3.3	74.5	82.4	1.42	-0.2
Portugal	7.8	10.6	3.0	78.7	84.6	1.29	-2.8
Republic of Moldova - République de Moldova[11]	10.2	11.6	12.4	67.4	75.9	1.26	-1.5
Romania - Roumanie	9.8	13.0	6.7	72.4	79.3	1.62	-3.2
Russian Federation - Fédération de Russie.........	12.8	12.7	5.8	66.8	77.5	1.82	0.1

Continent and country or area Continent et pays ou zone	Crude birth rate - Taux bruts de natalité	Crude death rate - Taux bruts de mortalité	Infant mortality rate - Décès d'enfants de moins d'un an	Life expectancy at birth - Espérance de vie à la naissance		Total fertility rate - Indice synthétique de fécondité	Natural increase - Accroissement naturel
				Male - Masculin	Female - Féminin		
EUROPE							
Serbia - Serbie[12]	9.6	13.2	4.9	73.2	78.4	1.46	-3.6
Slovakia - Slovaquie	10.5	9.9	4.8	73.7	80.8	1.50	0.6
Slovenia - Slovénie	9.7	9.9	1.9	78.3	83.9	1.60	-0.2
Spain - Espagne[13]	8.5	9.0	2.3	80.6	86.1	1.33	-0.5
Sweden - Suède	11.9	9.2	2.0	80.8	84.4	1.85	2.7
Switzerland - Suisse	10.3	8.0	3.4	81.6	85.4	1.54	2.3
Ukraine[14]	9.6	15.2	7.2	66.8	76.6	1.44	-5.6
United Kingdom of Great Britain and Northern Ireland - Royaume-Uni de Grande-Bretagne et d'Irlande du Nord	11.5	9.4	3.8	79.4	82.9	1.75	2.2
OCEANIA - OCÉANIE							
Australia - Australie[15]	12.9	6.6	3.1	81.2	85.2	1.83	6.3
Fiji - Fidji	21.5	8.1	20.3	65.6	69.1	2.79	13.3
French Polynesia - Polynésie française	14.8	5.6	6.7	75.3	79.7	1.95	9.2
Guam	16.6	5.2	8.7	76.5	83.3	2.32	11.4
Kiribati	28.1	6.3	43.0	63.9	72.0	3.58	21.7
Micronesia (Federated States of) - Micronésie (États fédérés de)	22.9	6.6	23.5	66.1	69.4	3.08	16.3
New Caledonia - Nouvelle-Calédonie	14.3	5.7	11.5	74.7	80.2	1.97	8.6
New Zealand - Nouvelle-Zélande	12.6	7.0	3.8	80.3	83.8	1.90	5.7
Papua New Guinea - Papouasie-Nouvelle-Guinée	27.2	7.5	41.9	62.9	65.5	3.59	19.8
Samoa	24.5	5.2	13.4	71.1	75.2	3.90	19.3
Solomon Islands - Îles Salomon	32.7	4.3	15.5	71.1	74.6	4.44	28.5
Tonga	24.5	7.2	12.5	68.8	72.7	3.58	17.3
Vanuatu	29.8	5.3	22.4	68.8	71.9	3.80	24.5

SOURCE

United Nations, Department of Economic and Social Affairs, Population Division (2019). 2019 Revision of World Population Prospects - Organisation des Nations Unies, Département des affaires économiques et sociales, Division de la population (2019). Perspectives de la population mondiale : La révision de 2019

FOOTNOTES - NOTES

[1] Including Agalega, Rodrigues and Saint Brandon. - Y compris Agalega, Rodrigues et Saint Brandon.
[2] Including Zanzibar. - Y compris le Zanzibar.
[3] Including Nagorno-Karabakh. - Y compris le Haut-Karabakh.
[4] For statistical purposes, the data for China do not include Hong Kong and Macao Special Administrative Regions (SAR) of China. - A des fins statistiques, les données pour la Chine ne comprennent pas les Régions Administratives Spéciales (SAR) de Hong Kong et Macao.
[5] Refers to the whole country. - Les données se rapportent au pays en entier.
[6] Including Abkhazia and South Ossetia. - Y compris l'Abkhazie et l'Ossétie du Sud.
[7] Including Sabah and Sarawak. - Y compris le Sabah et le Sarawak.
[8] Including East Jerusalem. - Y compris Jérusalem-Est.
[9] Including Åland Islands. - Y compris les îles Åland.
[10] Including Svalbard and Jan Mayen Islands. - Y compris Svalbard et l'île Jan Mayen.
[11] Including Transnistria. - Y compris la Transnistrie.
[12] Including Kosovo. - Y compris le Kosovo.
[13] Including Canary Islands, Ceuta and Melilla. - Y compris les îles Canaries, Ceuta et Melilla.
[14] Including Crimea. - Y compris la Crimée.
[15] Including Christmas Island, Cocos (Keeling) Islands and Norfolk Island. - Y compris les îles Christmas, Cocos (Keeling) et Norfolk.

Historical index
(See notes at end of index)

Subject-matter	Year of issue	Time coverage	Subject-matter	Year of issue	Time coverage
A			**Ageing**	*see "Population ageing"*	
Abortions, Legal	1971	Latest			
	1972	1964-72	**Annulments**	1958	1948-57
	1973	1965-73		1968	1958-67
	1974	1965-74		1976	1966-75
	1975	1965-74			
	1976	1966-75	**Annulment rates**................	1958	1948-57
	1977	1967-76		1968	1958-67
	1978	1968-77		1976	1966-75
	1979	1969-78			
	1980	1971-79	**B**		
	1981	1972-80			
	1982	1973-81	**Bibliography**	1948	1930-48
	1983	1974-82		1949-50	1930-50
	1984	1975-83		1951-1952	1930-51[i]
	1985	1976-84		1953	1900-53
	1986	1977-85		1954	1900-54[i]
	1987	1978-86		1955	1900-55[i]
	1988	1979-87			
	1989	1980-88	**Births**	1948	1932-47
	1990	1981-89		1949-50	1934-49
	1991	1982-90		1951	1935-50
	1992	1983-91		1952	1936-51
	1993	1984-92		1953	1950-52
	1994	1985-93		1954	1938-53
	1995	1986-94		1955	1946-54
	1996	1987-95		1956	1947-55
	1997	1988-96		1957	1948-56
	1998	1989-97		1958	1948-57
	1999	1990-98		1959	1949-58
	2000	1991-99		1960	1950-59
	2001	1993-01		1961	1952-61
	2002	1993-02		1962	1953-62
	2003	1994-03		1963	1954-63
	2004	1995-04		1964	1960-64
	2005	1996-05		1965	1946-65
	2006	1997-06		1966	1957-66
	2007	1998-07		1967	1963-67
	2008	1999-08		1968	1964-68
	2009-2010	2001-10		1969	1950-69
	2011	2002-11		1970	1966-70
	2012	2003-12		1971	1967-71
	2013	2004-13		1972	1968-72
	2014	2005-14		1973	1969-73
	2015	2006-15		1974	1970-74
	2016	2007-16		1975	1956-75
	2017	2008-17		1976	1972-76
	2018	2009-18		1977	1973-77
				1978	1974-78
Abortions, Legal	1971-1975	Latest		1978HS[ii]	1948-78
by age of woman and	1977-1981	Latest		1979	1975-79
number of previous live	1983-2018	Latest		1980	1976-80
births of woman				1981	1962-81

Historical index
(See notes at end of index)

Subject-matter	Year of issue	Time coverage
	1982	1978-82
	1983	1979-83
	1984	1980-84
	1985	1981-85
	1986	1967-86
	1987	1983-87
	1988	1984-88
	1989	1985-89
	1990	1986-90
	1991	1987-91
	1992	1983-92
	1993	1989-93
	1994	1990-94
	1995	1991-95
	1996	1992-96
	1997	1993-97
	1997HS[III]	1948-97
	1998	1994-98
	1999	1995-99
	1999CD[iv]	1980-99
	2000	1996-00
	2001	1997-01
	2002	1998-02
	2003	1999-03
	2004	2000-04
	2005	2001-05
	2006	2002-06
	2007	2003-07
	2008	2004-08
	2009-2010	2006-10
	2011	2007-11
	2012	2008-12
	2013	2009-13
	2014	2010-14
	2015	2011-15
	2016	2012-16
	2017	2013-17
	2018	2014-18
Births		
by age of father	1949-50	1942-49
	1954	1936-53
	1959	1949-58
	1965	1955-64
	1969	1963-68
	1975	1966-74
	1981	1972-80
	1999CD[iv]	1990-98
	2007-2018	Latest
Births		
by age of mother	1948	1936-47
	1949-50	1936-49
	1954	1936-53
	1955-1956	Latest
	1958	Latest

Subject-matter	Year of issue	Time coverage
	1959	1949-58
	1960-1964	Latest
	1965	1955-64
	1966-1968	Latest
	1969	1963-68
	1970-1974	Latest
	1975	1966-74
	1976-1978	Latest
	1978HS[II]	1948-77
	1979-1980	Latest
	1981	1972-80
	1982-1985	Latest
	1986	1977-85
	1987-1991	Latest
	1992	1983-92
	1993-1997	Latest
	1997HS[III]	1948-96
	1998-99	Latest
	1999CD[iv]	1990-98
	2000-2018	Latest
Births		
by age of mother and birth order	1949-50	1936-47
	1954	Latest
	1959	1949-58
	1965	1955-64
	1969	1963-68
	1975	1966-74
	1981	1972-80
	1986	1977-85
	1999CD[iv]	1990-98
Births		
by age of mother and sex of child	1965-1968	Latest
	1969	1963-68
	1970-1974	Latest
	1975	1966-74
	1976-1978	Latest
	1978HS[II]	1948-77
	1979-1980	Latest
	1981	1972-80
	1982-1985	Latest
	1986	1977-85
	1987-1991	Latest
	1992	1983-92
	1993-1997	Latest
	1997HS[III]	1948-96
	1998-99	Latest
	1999CD[iv]	1990-98
	2000-2018	Latest
Births		
by age of mother and urban/rural residence	*see "Births by urban/rural residence and age of mother"*	

Subject-matter	Year of issue	Time coverage	Subject-matter	Year of issue	Time coverage
Births	1948	1936-47		1975	Latest
by birth order	1949-50	1936-49		1981	1972-80
	1954	1936-53		1986	1977-85
	1955	Latest		1999CD[iv]	1990-98
	1959	1949-58			
	1965	1955-64	**Births**	1965	Latest
	1969	1963-68	by urban/rural	1967	Latest
	1975	1966-74	residence	1968	1964-68
	1981	1972-80		1969	1964-68
	1986	1977-85		1970	1966-70
	1999CD[iv]	1990-98		1971	1967-71
				1972	1968-72
Births	1975	Latest		1973	1969-73
by birth weight	1981	1972-80		1974	1970-74
	1986	1977-85		1975	1956-75
	1999CD[iv]	1990-98		1976	1972-76
				1977	1973-77
Births	1975	Latest		1978	1974-78
by gestational age	1981	1972-80		1979	1975-79
	1986	1977-85		1980	1976-80
	1999CD[iv]	1990-98		1981	1962-81
				1982	1978-82
Births	1959	1949-58		1983	1979-83
by legitimacy status	1965	1955-64		1984	1980-84
	1969	1963-68		1985	1981-85
	1975	1966-74		1986	1967-86
	1981	1972-80		1987	1983-87
	1986	1977-85		1988	1984-88
	1999CD[iv]	1990-98		1989	1985-89
				1990	1986-90
Births	2002	1980-02		1991	1987-91
by month of birth				1992	1983-92
				1993	1989-93
Births	1965	Latest		1994	1990-94
by occupation of father	1969	Latest		1995	1991-95
				1996	1992-96
Births	1959	1949-58		1997	1993-97
by sex of child	1965	1955-64		1998	1994-98
	1967-1968	Latest		1999	1995-99
	1969	1963-68		1999CD[iv]	1980-99
	1970-1974	Latest		2000	1996-00
	1975	1956-75		2001	1997-01
	1976-1980	Latest		2002	1998-02
	1981	1962-81		2003	1999-03
	1982-1985	Latest		2004	2000-04
	1986	1967-86		2005	2001-05
	1987-1991	Latest		2006	2002-06
	1992	1983-92		2007	2003-07
	1993-1999	Latest		2008	2004-08
	1999CD[iv]	1990-98		2009-2010	2006-10
	2000-2018	Latest		2011	2007-11
				2012	2008-12
Births	1965	Latest		2013	2009-13
by plurality	1969	Latest		2014	2010-14

Historical index
(See notes at end of index)

Subject-matter	Year of issue	Time coverage	Subject-matter	Year of issue	Time coverage
	2015	2011-15	Births	1948	1936-47
	2016	2012-16	legitimate, by duration	1949-50	1936-49
	2017	2013-17	of marriage	1954	1936-53
	2018	2014-18		1959	1949-58
				1965	1955-64
Births	1965	Latest		1969	1963-68
by urban/rural	1969-1974	Latest		1975	1966-74
residence and age of	1975	1966-74		1981	1972-80
mother	1976-1980	Latest		1986	1977-85
	1981	1972-80		1999CD[iv]	1990-98
	1982-1985	Latest			
	1986	1977-85	Birth rates	1948	1932-47
	1987-1991	Latest		1949-50	1932-49
	1992	1983-92		1951	1905-30[v]
	1993-1997	Latest			1930-50
	1997HS[III]	1948-96		1952	1920-34[v]
	1998-1999	Latest			1934-51
	1999CD[iv]	1990-98		1953	1920-39[v]
	2000-2006	Latest			1940-52
				1954	1920-39[v]
Births	1959	1949-58			1939-53
illegitimate	1965	1955-64		1955	1920-34[v]
	1969	1963-68			1946-54
	1975	1966-74		1956	1947-55
	1981	1972-80		1957	1948-56
	1986	1977-85		1958	1948-57
	1999CD[iv]	1990-98		1959	1920-54[v]
					1953-58
Births	1948	1936-47		1960	1950-59
legitimate	1949-50	1936-49		1961	1945-59[v]
	1954	1936-53			1952-61
	1959	1949-58		1962	1945-54[v]
	1965	1955-64			1952-62
	1969	1963-68		1963	1945-59[v]
	1975	1966-74			1954-63
	1981	1972-80		1964	1960-64
	1986	1977-85		1965	1920-64[v]
	1999CD[iv]	1990-98			1950-65
				1966	1950-64[v]
Births	1959	1949-58			1957-66
legitimate, by age of	1965	1955-64		1967	1963-67
father	1969	1963-68		1968	1964-68
	1975	1966-74		1969	1925-69[v]
	1981	1972-80			1954-69
	1986	1977-85		1970	1966-70
				1971	1967-71
Births	1954	1936-53		1972	1968-72
legitimate, by age of	1959	1949-58		1973	1969-73
mother	1965	1955-64		1974	1970-74
	1969	1963-68		1975	1956-75
	1975	1966-74		1976	1972-76
	1981	1972-80		1977	1973-77
	1986	1977-85		1978	1974-78
				1978HS[II]	1948-78

Subject-matter	Year of issue	Time coverage	Subject-matter	Year of issue	Time coverage
	1979	1975-79	by age of mother	1949-50	1936-49
	1980	1976-80		1951	1936-50
	1981	1962-81		1952	1936-50
	1982	1978-82		1953	1936-52
	1983	1979-83		1954	1936-53
	1984	1980-84		1955-1956	Latest
	1985	1981-85		1959	1949-58
	1986	1967-86		1965	1955-64
	1987	1983-87		1969	1963-68
	1988	1984-88		1975	1966-74
	1989	1985-89		1976-1978	Latest
	1990	1986-90		1978HS[ii]	1948-77
	1991	1987-91		1979-1980	Latest
	1992	1983-92		1981	1972-80
	1993	1989-93		1982-1985	Latest
	1994	1990-94		1986	1977-85
	1995	1991-95		1987-1991	Latest
	1996	1992-96		1992	1983-92
	1997	1993-97		1993-1997	Latest
	1997HS[iii]	1948-97		1997HS[iii]	1948-96
	1998	1994-98		1998-1999	Latest
	1999	1995-99		1999CD[iv]	1990-98
	1999CD[iv]	1985-99		2000-2018	Latest
	2000	1996-00			
	2001	1997-01	**Birth rates**	1954	1948&51
	2002	1998-02	by age of mother and	1959	1949-58
	2003	1999-03	birth order	1965	1955-64
	2004	2000-04		1969	1963-68
	2005	2001-05		1975	1966-74
	2006	2002-06		1981	1972-80
	2007	2003-07		1986	1977-85
	2008	2004-08		1999CD[iv]	1990-98
	2009-2010	2006-10			
	2011	2007-11	**Birth rates**		*see "Birth rates by*
	2012	2008-12	by age of mother and		*urban/rural residence and*
	2013	2009-13	urban/rural residence		*age of mother"*
	2014	2010-14			
	2015	2011-15	**Birth rates**	1951	1936-49
	2016	2012-16	by birth order	1952	1936-50
	2017	2013-17		1953	1936-52
	2018	2014-18		1954	1936-53
				1955	Latest
Birth rates	1949-50	1942-49		1959	1949-58
by age of father	1954	1936-53		1965	1955-64
	1959	1949-58		1969	1963-68
	1965	1955-64		1975	1966-74
	1969	1963-68		1981	1972-80
	1975	1966-74		1986	1977-85
	1981	1972-80		1999CD[iv]	1990-98
	1986	1977-85			
	1999CD[iv]	1990-98	**Birth rates**	1965	Latest
	2007-2018	Latest	by urban/rural	1967	Latest
			residence	1968	1964-68
Birth rates	1948	1936-47		1969	1964-68

Historical index
(See notes at end of index)

Subject-matter	Year of issue	Time coverage	Subject-matter	Year of issue	Time coverage
	1970	1966-70		1981	1972-80
	1971	1967-71		1982-1985	Latest
	1972	1968-72		1986	1977-85
	1973	1969-73		1987-1991	Latest
	1974	1970-74		1992	1983-92
	1975	1956-75		1993-1997	Latest
	1976	1972-76		1997HS[iii]	1948-96
	1977	1973-77		1998-1999	Latest
	1978	1974-78		1999CD[iv]	1990-98
	1979	1975-79		2000-2006	Latest
	1980	1976-80			
	1981	1962-81	**Birth rates**	1949-50	1947
	1982	1978-82	estimated (for	1956-1977	Latest
	1983	1979-83	continents)	1978-1979	1970-75
	1984	1980-84		1980-1983	1975-80
	1985	1981-85		1984-1986	1980-85
	1986	1967-86		1987-1992	1985-90
	1987	1983-87		1993-1997	1990-95
	1988	1984-88		1998-2000	1995-00
	1989	1985-89		2001-2005	2000-05
	1990	1986-90		2006-2010	2005-10
	1991	1987-91		2011-2015	2010-15
	1992	1983-92		2016-2018	2015-20
	1993	1989-93			
	1994	1990-94	**Birth rates**	1964-1977	Latest
	1995	1991-95	estimated (for macro	1978-1979	1970-75
	1996	1992-96	regions)	1980-1983	1975-80
	1997	1993-97		1984-1986	1980-85
	1998	1994-98		1987-1992	1985-90
	1999	1995-99		1993-1997	1990-95
	1999CD[iv]	1985-99		1998-2000	1995-00
	2000	1996-00		2001-2005	2000-05
	2001	1997-01		2006-2010	2005-10
	2002	1998-02		2011-2015	2010-15
	2003	1999-03		2016-2018	2015-20
	2004	2000-04			
	2005	2001-05	**Birth rates**	1949/1950	1947
	2006	2002-06	estimated (for regions)	1956-1977	Latest
	2007	2003-07		1978-1979	1970-75
	2008	2004-08		1980-1983	1975-80
	2009-2010	2006-10		1984-1986	1980-85
	2011	2007-11		1987-1992	1985-90
	2012	2008-12		1993-1997	1990-95
	2013	2009-13		1998-2000	1995-00
	2014	2010-14		2001-2005	2000-05
	2015	2011-15		2006-2010	2005-10
	2016	2012-16		2011-2015	2010-15
	2017	2013-17		2016-2018	2015-20
	2018	2014-18			
			Birth rates	1949-50	1947
Birth rates	1965	Latest	estimated (for the	1956-1977	Latest
by urban/rural	1969	Latest	world)	1978-1979	1970-75
residence and age of	1975	1966-74		1980-1983	1975-80
mother	1976-1980	Latest		1984-1986	1980-85

Subject-matter	Year of issue	Time coverage
	1987-1992	1985-90
	1993-1997	1990-95
	1998-2000	1995-00
	2001-2005	2000-05
	2006-2010	2005-10
	2011-2015	2010-15
	2016-2018	2015-20
Birth rates .... illegitimate	1959	1949-58
Birth rates .... legitimate	1954	1936-53
	1959	1949-58
	1965	Latest
	1969	Latest
	1975	Latest
	1981	Latest
	1986	Latest
Birth rates .... legitimate by age of father	1959	1949-58
	1965	Latest
	1969	Latest
	1975	Latest
	1981	Latest
	1986	Latest
Birth rates .... legitimate by age of mother	1954	1936-53
	1959	1949-58
	1965	Latest
	1969	Latest
	1975	Latest
	1981	Latest
	1986	Latest
Birth rates .... legitimate by duration of marriage	1959	1950-57
	1965	Latest
	1969	Latest
	1975	Latest
Birth ratios .... fertility	1949/1950	Latest
	1954	Latest
	1959	1949-58
	1965	1955-65
	1969	1963-68
	1975	1965-74
	1978HS[ii]	1948-77
	1981	1972-80
	1986	1977-85
	1997HS[iii]	1948-96
	1999CD[iv]	1980-99
Birth ratios .... illegitimate	1959	1949-58
	1965	1955-64
	1969	1963-68

Subject-matter	Year of issue	Time coverage
	1975	1965-74
	1981	1972-80
	1986	1977-85
C		
Child-woman ratios	1949-50	1900-50
	1954	1900-52
	1955	1945-54
	1959	1935-59
	1963	1955-63
	1965	1945-65
	1969	Latest
	1975	1966-74
	1978HS[ii]	1948-77
	1981	1962-80
	1986	1967-85
	1997HS[iii]	1948-96
	1999CD[iv]	1980-99
Child-woman ratios .... by urban/rural residence	1965	Latest
	1969	Latest
Children .... born alive, by age of mother	1949-50	Latest
	1954	1930-53
	1955	1945-54
	1959	1949-58
	1963	1955-63
	1965	1955-65
	1969	Latest
	1971	1962-71
	1973	1965-73
	1975	1965-74
	1978HS[ii]	1948-77
	1981	1972-80
	1986	1977-85
	1997HS[iii]	1948-96
Children .... born alive, by age of mother and urban/rural residence	1971	1962-71
	1973	1965-73
	1975	1965-74
	1981	1972-80
	1986	1977-85
	1997HS[iii]	1948-96
Children .... involved in divorces	1958	1949-57
	1968	1958-67
	1976	1966-75
	1982	1972-81
	1990	1980-89
Children .... living, by age of mother	1949-50	Latest
	1954	1930-53

Subject-matter	Year of issue	Time coverage
	1955	1945-54
	1959	1949-58
	1963	1955-63
	1965	1955-65
	1968	1955-67
	1969	Latest
	1971	1962-71
	1973	1965-73
	1975	1965-74
	1978HS[II]	1948-77
	1981	1972-80
	1986	1977-85
	1997HS[III]	1948-96
Children	1971	1962-71
living, by age of mother	1973	1965-73
and urban/rural	1975	1965-74
residence	1981	1972-80
	1986	1977-85
	1997HS[III]	1948-96
Cities	see "Population of cities"	

D

Deaths	1948	1932-47
	1949-50	1934-49
	1951	1935-50
	1952	1936-51
	1953	1950-52
	1954	1946-53
	1955	1946-54
	1956	1947-55
	1957	1940-56
	1958	1948-57
	1959	1949-58
	1960	1950-59
	1961	1952-61
	1962	1953-62
	1963	1954-63
	1964	1960-64
	1966	1947-66
	1967	1963-67
	1968	1964-68
	1969	1965-69
	1970	1966-70
	1971	1967-71
	1972	1968-72
	1973	1969-73
	1974	1965-74
	1975	1971-75
	1976	1972-76
	1977	1973-77
	1978	1974-78

Subject-matter	Year of issue	Time coverage
	1978HS[II]	1948-78
	1979	1975-79
	1980	1971-80
	1981	1977-81
	1982	1978-82
	1983	1979-83
	1984	1980-84
	1985	1976-85
	1986	1982-86
	1987	1983-87
	1988	1984-88
	1989	1985-89
	1990	1986-90
	1991	1987-91
	1992	1983-92
	1993	1989-93
	1994	1990-94
	1995	1991-95
	1996	1987-96
	1997	1993-97
	1997HS[III]	1948-97
	1998	1994-98
	1999	1995-99
	2000	1996-00
	2001	1997-01
	2002	1998-02
	2003	1999-03
	2004	2000-04
	2005	2001-05
	2006	2002-06
	2007	2003-07
	2008	2004-08
	2009-2010	2006-10
	2011	2007-11
	2012	2008-12
	2013	2009-13
	2014	2010-14
	2015	2011-15
	2016	2012-16
	2017	2013-17
	2018	2014-18
Deaths	1948	1936-47
by age and sex	1951	1936-50
	1955-1956	Latest
	1957	1948-56
	1958-1960	Latest
	1961	1955-60
	1962-1965	Latest
	1966	1961-65
	1967-1973	Latest
	1974	1965-73
	1975-1979	Latest
	1978HS[II]	1948-77

Subject-matter	Year of issue	Time coverage	Subject-matter	Year of issue	Time coverage
	1980	1971-79			
	1981-1984	Latest	**Deaths**	1951	Latest
	1985	1976-84	by cause, age and sex	1952	Latest
	1986-1991	Latest		1957	Latest
	1992	1983-92		1961	Latest
	1993-1995	Latest		1967	Latest
	1996	1987-95		1974	Latest
	1997	Latest		1980	Latest
	1997HS[iii]	1948-96		1985	Latest
	1998-2018	Latest		1991PA[vii]	1960-90
				1996	Latest
Deaths	1967-1973	Latest			
by age and sex and	1974	1965-73	**Deaths**	1967	Latest
urban/rural residence	1975-1979	Latest	by cause, age and sex		
	1980	1971-79	and urban/rural		
	1981-1984	Latest	residence		
	1985	1976-84			
	1986-1991	Latest	**Deaths**	1967	Latest
	1992	1983-92	by cause and sex	1974	Latest
	1993-1995	Latest		1980	Latest
	1996	1987-95		1985	Latest
	1997	Latest		1991PA[vii]	1960-90
	1997HS[iii]	1948-96		1996	Latest
	1998-2006	Latest		2006	2002-06
				2008	2004-08
Deaths	1951	1947-50		2011	2006-10
by cause	1952	1947-51[vi]		2013	2008-12
	1953	Latest		2015	2010-14
	1954	1945-53		2017	2012-16
	1955-1956	Latest			
	1957	1952-56	**Deaths**	1958	Latest
	1958-1960	Latest	by marital status, age	1961	Latest
	1961	1955-60	and sex	1967	Latest
	1962-1965	Latest		1974	Latest
	1966	1960-65		1980	Latest
	1967-1973	Latest		1985	Latest
	1974	1965-73		1991PA[vii]	1950-90
	1975-1979	Latest		1996	Latest
	1980	1971-79		2003	Latest
	1981-1984	Latest			
	1985	1976-84	**Deaths**	1951	1946-50
	1986-1991	Latest	by month	1967	1962-66
	1991PA[vii]	1960-90		1974	1965-73
	1992-1995	Latest		1980	1971-79
	1996	1987-95		1985	1976-84
	1997-2000	Latest		2001	1985-00
	2002	1995-02		2005	2001-05
	2004	1995-04			
	2006	2002-06	**Deaths**	1957	Latest
	2008	2004-08	by occupation and age,	1961	1957-60
	2011	2006-10	males	1967	1962-66
	2013	2008-12			
	2015	2010-14	**Deaths**	1957	Latest
	2017	2012-16		1974	1965-73

Historical index
(See notes at end of index)

Subject-matter	Year of issue	Time coverage	Subject-matter	Year of issue	Time coverage
by type of certification and cause (numbers)	1980	1971-79		2012	2008-12
	1985	1976-84		2013	2009-13
				2014	2010-14
Deaths	1957	Latest		2015	2011-15
by type of certification and cause (percent)	1961	1955-60		2016	2012-16
	1966	1960-65		2017	2013-17
	1974	1965-73		2018	2014-18
	1980	1971-79			
	1985	1976-84	**Deaths**		
			of infants (see infant deaths)		
Deaths	1967	Latest			
by urban/rural residence	1968	1964-68	**Death rates**	1948	1932-47
	1969	1965-69		1949-50	1932-49
	1970	1966-70		1951	1905-30^v
	1971	1967-71			1930-50
	1972	1968-72		1952	1920-34^v
	1973	1969-73			1934-51
	1974	1965-74		1953	1920-39^v
	1975	1971-75			1940-52
	1976	1972-76		1954	1920-39^v
	1977	1973-77			1946-53
	1978	1974-78		1955	1920-34^v
	1979	1975-79			1946-54
	1980	1971-80		1956	1947-55
	1981	1977-81		1957	1930-56
	1982	1978-82		1958	1948-57
	1983	1979-83		1959	1949-58
	1984	1980-84		1960	1950-59
	1985	1976-85		1961	1945-59^v
	1986	1982-86			1952-61
	1987	1983-87		1962	1945-54^v
	1988	1984-88			1952-62
	1989	1985-89		1963	1945-59^v
	1990	1986-90			1954-63
	1991	1987-91		1964	1960-64
	1992	1983-92		1965	1961-65
	1993	1989-93		1966	1920-64^v
	1994	1990-94			1951-66
	1995	1991-95		1967	1963-67
	1996	1987-96		1968	1964-68
	1997	1993-97		1969	1965-69
	1998	1994-98		1970	1966-70
	1999	1995-99		1971	1967-71
	2000	1996-00		1972	1968-72
	2001	1997-01		1973	1969-73
	2002	1998-02		1974	1965-74
	2003	1999-03		1975	1971-75
	2004	2000-04		1976	1972-76
	2006	2002-06		1977	1973-77
	2007	2003-07		1978	1974-78
	2008	2004-08		1978HS^{ii}	1948-78
	2009-2010	2006-10		1979	1975-79
	2011	2007-11		1980	1971-80

Subject-matter	Year of issue	Time coverage
	1981	1977-81
	1982	1978-82
	1983	1979-83
	1984	1980-84
	1985	1976-85
	1986	1982-86
	1987	1983-87
	1988	1984-88
	1989	1985-89
	1990	1986-90
	1991	1987-91
	1992	1983-92
	1993	1989-93
	1994	1990-94
	1995	1991-95
	1996	1987-96
	1997	1993-97
	1997HS[iii]	1948-97
	1998	1994-98
	1999	1995-99
	2000	1996-00
	2001	1997-01
	2002	1998-02
	2003	1999-03
	2004	2000-04
	2005	2001-05
	2006	2002-06
	2007	2003-07
	2008	2004-08
	2009-2010	2006-10
	2011	2007-11
	2012	2008-12
	2013	2009-13
	2014	2010-14
	2015	2011-15
	2016	2012-16
	2017	2013-17
	2018	2014-18
Death rates	1948	1935-47
by age and sex	1949-50	1936-49
	1951	1936-50
	1952	1936-51
	1953	1940-52
	1954	1946-53
	1955-1956	Latest
	1957	1948-56
	1961	1952-60
	1966	1950-65
	1972	Latest
	1974	1965-73
	1975-1979	Latest
	1978HS[ii]	1948-77
	1980	1971-79

Subject-matter	Year of issue	Time coverage
	1981-1984	Latest
	1985	1976-84
	1986-1991	Latest
	1991PA[vii]	1950-1990
	1992	1983-1992
	1993-1995	Latest
	1996	1987-95
	1997	Latest
	1997HS[iii]	1948-96
	1998-2018	Latest
Death rates	1967	Latest
by age, sex and	1972	Latest
urban/rural residence	1974	1965-73
	1975-1979	Latest
	1980	1971-79
	1981-1984	Latest
	1985	1976-84
	1986-1991	Latest
	1991PA[vii]	1950-1990
	1992	1983-1992
	1993-1995	Latest
	1996	1987-95
	1997	Latest
	1997HS[iii]	1948-96
	1998-2006	Latest
Death rates	1951	1947-49
by cause	1952	1947-51[vi]
	1953	1947-52
	1954	1945-53
	1955-1956	Latest
	1957	1952-56
	1958-1960	Latest
	1961	1955-60
	1962-1965	Latest
	1966	1960-65
	1967-1973	Latest
	1974	1965-73
	1975-1979	Latest
	1980	1971-79
	1981-1984	Latest
	1985	1976-84
	1986-1991	Latest
	1991PA[vii]	1960-90
	1992-1995	Latest
	1996	1987-95
	1997-2000	Latest
	2002	1995-02
	2004	1995-04
	2006	2002-06
	2008	2004-08
	2011	2006-10
	2013	2008-12

Subject-matter	Year of issue	Time coverage	Subject-matter	Year of issue	Time coverage
	2015	2010-14		1986	1982-86
	2017	2012-16		1987	1983-87
				1988	1984-88
Death rates....................	1957	Latest		1989	1985-89
by cause, age and sex	1961	Latest		1990	1986-90
	1991PA[vii]	1960-90		1991	1987-91
				1992	1983-92
Death rates....................	1967	Latest		1993	1989-93
by cause and sex	1974	Latest		1994	1990-94
	1980	Latest		1995	1991-95
	1985	Latest		1996	1987-96
	1996	Latest		1997	1993-97
	2006	2002-06		1998	1994-98
	2008	2004-08		1999	1995-99
	2011	2006-10		1987	1983-87
	2013	2008-12		1988	1984-88
	2015	2010-14		1989	1985-89
	2017	2012-16		1990	1986-90
				1991	1987-91
Death rates....................	1961	Latest		1992	1983-92
by marital status, age	1967	Latest		1993	1989-93
and sex	1974	Latest		1994	1990-94
	1980	Latest		1995	1991-95
	1985	Latest		1996	1987-96
	1996	Latest		1997	1993-97
	2003	Latest		1998	1994-98
				1999	1995-99
Death rates....................	1957	Latest		2000	1996-00
by occupation, age and sex				2001	1997-01
				2002	1998-02
				2003	1999-03
Death rates....................	1961	Latest		2004	2000-04
by occupation and age, males	1967	Latest		2005	2001-05
				2006	2002-06
				2007	2003-07
Death rates....................	1967	Latest		2008	2004-08
by urban/rural residence	1968	1964-68		2009-2010	2006-10
	1969	1965-69		2011	2007-11
	1970	1966-70		2012	2008-12
	1971	1967-71		2013	2009-13
	1972	1968-72		2014	2010-14
	1973	1969-73		2015	2011-15
	1974	1965-74		2016	2012-16
	1975	1971-75		2017	2013-17
	1976	1972-76		2018	2014-18
	1977	1973-77			
	1978	1974-78	**Death rates**	1949-50	1947
	1979	1975-79	estimated (for continents)	1956-1977	Latest
	1980	1971-80		1978-1979	1970-75
	1981	1977-81		1980-1983	1975-80
	1982	1978-82		1984-1986	1980-85
	1983	1979-83		1984-1986	1980-85
	1984	1980-84		1987-1992	1985-90
	1985	1976-85		1993-1997	1990-95

Subject-matter	Year of issue	Time coverage
	1998-2000	1995-00
	2001-2005	2000-05
	2006-2010	2005-10
	2011-2015	2010-15
	2016-2018	2015-20
Death rates............................	1964-1977	Latest
estimated (for macro regions)	1978-1979	1970-75
	1980-1983	1975-80
	1984-1986	1980-85
	1987-1992	1985-90
	1993-1997	1990-95
	1998-2000	1995-00
	2001-2005	2000-05
	2006-2010	2005-10
	2011-2015	2010-15
	2016-2018	2015-20
Death rates............................	1949-50	1947
estimated (for regions)	1956-1977	Latest
	1978-1979	1970-75
	1980-1983	1975-80
	1984-1986	1980-85
	1987-1992	1985-90
	1993-1997	1990-95
	1998-2000	1995-00
	2001-2005	2000-05
	2006-2010	2005-10
	2011-2015	2010-15
	2016-2018	2015-20
Death rates............................	1949-50	1947
estimated (for the world)	1956-1977	Latest
	1978-1979	1970-75
	1980-1983	1975-80
	1984-1986	1980-85
	1987-1992	1985-90
	1993-1997	1990-95
	1998-2000	1995-00
	2001-2005	2000-05
	2006-2010	2005-10
	2011-2015	2010-15
	2016-2018	2015-20
Death rates............................		
of infants (see infant deaths)		
Density of population.........	1949-50	1920-49
of continents	1951-1999	Latest
	2000	2000
	2001	2001
	2002	2002
	2003	2003

Subject-matter	Year of issue	Time coverage
	2004	2004
	2005	2005
	2006	2006
	2007	2007
	2008	2008
	2009-2010	2010
	2011	2011
	2012	2012
	2013	2013
	2014	2014
	2015	2015
	2016	2016
	2017	2017
	2018	2018
Density of population.........	1948-1999	Latest
of countries	2000	2000
	2001	2001
	2002	2002
	2003	2003
	2004	2004
	2005	2005
	2006	2006
	2007	2007
	2008	2008
	2009-2010	2010
	2011	2011
	2012	2012
	2013	2013
	2014	2014
	2015	2015
	2016	2016
	2017	2017
	2018	2018
Density of population.........	1964-1999	Latest
of major areas	2000	2000
	2001	2001
	2002	2002
	2003	2003
	2004	2004
	2005	2005
	2006	2006
	2007	2007
	2008	2008
	2009-2010	2010
	2011	2011
	2012	2012
	2013	2013
	2014	2014
	2015	2015
	2016	2016
	2017	2017
	2018	2018

Subject-matter	Year of issue	Time coverage	Subject-matter	Year of issue	Time coverage
Density of population.........	1949-50	1920-49		1960	1950-59
of regions	1952-1999	Latest		1961	1952-61
	2000	2000		1962	1953-62
	2001	2001		1963	1954-63
	2002	2002		1964	1960-64
	2003	2003		1965	1961-65
	2004	2004		1966	1962-66
	2005	2005		1967	1963-67
	2006	2006		1968	1949-68
	2007	2007		1969	1965-69
	2008	2008		1970	1966-70
	2009-2010	2010		1971	1967-71
	2011	2011		1972	1968-72
	2012	2012		1973	1969-73
	2013	2013		1974	1970-74
	2014	2014		1975	1971-75
	2015	2015		1976	1957-76
	2016	2016		1977	1973-77
	2017	2017		1978	1974-78
	2018	2018		1979	1975-79
				1980	1976-80
				1981	1977-81
				1982	1963-82
Density of population.........	1949-50	1920-49		1983	1979-83
of the world	1952-1999	Latest		1984	1980-84
	2000	2000		1985	1981-85
	2001	2001		1986	1982-86
	2002	2002		1987	1983-87
	2003	2003		1988	1984-88
	2004	2004		1989	1985-89
	2005	2005		1990	1971-90
	2006	2006		1991	1987-91
	2007	2007		1992	1988-92
	2008	2008		1993	1989-93
	2009-2010	2010		1994	1990-94
	2011	2011		1995	1991-95
	2012	2012		1996	1992-96
	2013	2013		1997	1993-97
	2014	2014		1998	1994-98
	2015	2015		1999	1995-99
	2016	2016		2000	1996-00
	2017	2017		2001	1997-01
	2018	2018		2002	1998-02
				2003	1999-03
Disability	see "Population disabled"			2004	2000-04
				2005	2001-05
Divorces	1951	1935-50		2006	2002-06
	1952	1936-51		2007	2003-07
	1953	1950-52		2008	2004-08
	1954	1946-53		2009-2010	2006-10
	1955	1946-54		2011	2007-11
	1956	1947-55		2012	2008-12
	1957	1948-56		2013	2009-13
	1958	1940-57		2014	2010-14
	1959	1949-58			

Subject-matter	Year of issue	Time coverage	Subject-matter	Year of issue	Time coverage
	2015	2011-15		2008	2004-08
	2016	2012-16		2009-2010	2006-10
	2017	2013-17		2011	2007-11
	2018	2014-18		2012	2008-12
				2013	2009-13
Divorces	1968	1958-67		2014	2010-14
by age of husband	1976	1966-75		2015	2011-15
	1982	1972-81		2016	2012-16
	1987	1975-86		2017	2013-17
	1990	1980-89		2018	2014-18
Divorces	1968	1958-67	**Divorce, percentage distribution**	2007	Latest
by age of wife	1976	1966-75	by duration of marriage	2009-2010	Latest
	1982	1972-81		2012	Latest
	1987	1975-86		2014	Latest
	1990	1980-89		2016	Latest
				2018	Latest
Divorces	1958	1946-57			
by age of wife classified	1968	Latest	**Divorce, percentage distribution**	2007	Latest
by age of husband	1976	Latest	by number of children involved		
	1982	Latest			
	1990	Latest			
			Divorce rates	1952	1935-51
Divorces	1958	1948-57		1953	1936-52
by duration of marriage	1968	1958-67		1954	1946-53
	1976	1966-75		1955	1946-54
	1982	1972-81		1956	1947-55
	1990	1980-89		1957	1948-56
	2007	Latest		1958	1930-57
	2009-2010	Latest		1959	1949-58
	2012	Latest		1960	1950-59
	2014	Latest		1961	1952-61
	2016	Latest		1962	1953-62
	2018	Latest		1963	1954-63
				1964	1960-64
Divorces	1958	1946-57		1965	1961-65
by duration of marriage	1968	Latest		1966	1962-66
and age of husband,	1976	Latest		1967	1963-67
wife	1982	Latest		1968	1920-64[v]
	1990	Latest			1953-68
				1969	1965-69
Divorces	1958	1948-57		1970	1966-70
by number of children	1968	1958-67		1971	1967-71
involved	1976	1966-75		1972	1968-72
	1982	1972-81		1973	1969-73
	1990	1980-89		1974	1970-74
	2007	Latest		1975	1971-75
				1976	1957-76
Divorces	2002	1998-02		1977	1973-77
by urban/rural	2003	1999-03		1978	1974-78
residence	2004	2000-04		1979	1975-79
	2005	2001-05		1980	1976-80
	2006	2002-06			
	2007	2003-07			

Historical index
(See notes at end of index)

Subject-matter	Year of issue	Time coverage
	1969	1965-69
	1970	1966-70
	1971	1967-71
	1972	1968-72
	1973	1969-73
	1974	1970-74
	1975	1971-75
	1976	1957-76
	1977	1973-77
	1978	1974-78
	1979	1975-79
	1980	1976-80
	1969	1965-69
	1970	1966-70
	1971	1967-71
	1972	1968-72
	1973	1969-73
	1974	1970-74
	1975	1971-75
	1976	1957-76
	1977	1973-77
	1978	1974-78
	1979	1975-79
	1980	1976-80
	1981	1977-81
	1982	1963-82
	1983	1979-83
	1984	1980-84
	1985	1981-85
	1986	1982-86
	1987	1983-87
	1988	1984-88
	1989	1985-89
	1990	1971-90
	1991	1987-91
	1992	1988-92
	1993	1989-93
	1994	1990-94
	1995	1991-95
	1996	1992-96
	1997	1993-97
	1998	1994-98
	1999	1995-99
	2000	1996-00
	2001	1997-01
	2002	1998-02
	2003	1999-03
	2004	2000-04
	2005	2001-05
	2006	2002-06
	2007	2003-07
	2008	2004-08
	2009-2010	2006-10
	2011	2007-11

Subject-matter	Year of issue	Time coverage
	2012	2008-12
	2013	2009-13
	2014	2010-14
	2015	2011-15
	2016	2012-16
	2017	2013-17
	2018	2014-18
Divorce rates	1968	Latest
by age of husband	1976	Latest
	1982	Latest
	1987	1975-86
	1990	Latest
Divorce rates	1968	Latest
by age of wife	1976	Latest
	1982	Latest
	1987	1975-86
	1990	Latest
Divorce rates	1953	1935-52
for married couples	1954	1935-53
	1958	1935-56
	1968	1935-67
	1976	1966-75
	1978HS[II]	1948-77
	1982	1972-81
	1990	1980-89
Divorce rates	2002	1998-02
by urban/rural residence	2003	1999-03
	2004	2000-04
	2005	2001-05
	2006	2002-06
	2007	2003-07
	2008	2004-08
	2009-2010	2006-10
	2011	2007-11
	2012	2008-12
	2013	2009-13
	2014	2010-14
	2015	2011-15
	2016	2012-16
	2017	2013-17
	2018	2014-18

E

Subject-matter		
Economically active population	see "Population, economically active"	
Economically inactive population	see "Population, economically inactive"	

715

Subject-matter	Year of issue	Time coverage	Subject-matter	Year of issue	Time coverage
				2014	2010-14
Emigrants..........................		see "Migration (international)"		2015	2011-15
				2016	2012-16
				2017	2013-17
Ethnic composition		see "Population by ethnic composition and sex"		2018	2014-18
			Fertility ratios	1949-50	1900-50
Expectation of life		see "Life tables"		1954	1900-52
				1955	1945-54
F				1959	1935-59
				1963	1955-63
Fertility rates......................	1948	1936-47		1965	1955-65
general	1949-50	1936-49		1969	Latest
	1951	1936-50		1975	1966-74
	1952	1936-50		1978HS[ii]	1948-77
	1953	1936-52		1981	1962-80
	1954	1936-53		1986	1967-85
	1955-1956	Latest		1997HS[iii]	1948-96
	1959	1949-58		1999CD[iv]	1980-99
	1960-1964	Latest			
	1965	1955-64	Foetal deaths	1957	1950-56
	1966-1974	Latest	by period of gestation	1959	1949-58
	1975	1966-74		1961	1952-60
	1976-1978	Latest		1965	5-Latest
	1978HS[ii]	1948-77		1966	1956-65
	1979-1980	Latest		1967-1968	Latest
	1981	1962-80		1969	1963-68
	1982-1985	Latest		1974	1965-73
	1986	1977-85		1975	1966-74
	1987-1991	Latest		1980	1971-79
	1992	1983-92		1981	1972-80
	1993-1997	Latest		1985	1976-84
	1997HS[iii]	1948-96		1986	1977-85
	1998-2018	Latest		1996	1987-95
				1999CD[iv]	1990-98
Fertility rates......................	1986	1967-85			
total	1987-1997	Latest	Foetal deaths, late..............	1951	1935-50
	1997HS[iii]	1948-96		1952	1936-51
	1998	1995-98		1953	1936-52
	1999	1996-99		1954	1938-53
	1999CD[iv]	1980-99		1955	1946-54
	2000	1995-00		1956	1947-55
	2001	1997-01		1957	1948-56
	2002	1998-02		1958	1948-57
	2003	1999-03		1959	1949-58
	2004	2000-04		1960	1950-59
	2005	2001-05		1961	1952-60
	2006	2002-06		1962	1953-61
	2007	2003-07		1963	1953-62
	2008	2004-08		1964	1959-63
	2009-2010	2006-10		1965	1955-64
	2011	2007-11		1966	1947-65
	2012	2008-12		1967	1962-66
	2013	2009-13		1968	1963-67

Subject-matter	Year of issue	Time coverage	Subject-matter	Year of issue	Time coverage
	1969	1959-68		1969	1963-68
	1970	1965-69		1975	1966-74
	1971	1966-70		1981	1972-80
	1972	1967-71		1986	1977-85
	1973	1968-72		1999CD[iv]	1990-98
	1974	1965-73			
	1975	1966-74	**Foetal deaths, late**	1954	Latest
	1976	1971-75	by age of mother and	1959	1949-58
	1977	1972-76	birth order	1965	3-Latest
	1978	1973-77		1969	1963-68
	1979	1974-78		1975	1966-74
	1980	1971-79		1981	1972-80
	1981	1972-80		1986	1977-85
	1982	1977-81		1999CD[iv]	1990-98
	1983	1978-82			
	1984	1979-83	**Foetal deaths, late**	1957	1950-56
	1985	1975-84	by period of gestation	1959	1949-58
	1986	1977-85		1961	1952-60
	1987	1982-86		1965	5-Latest
	1988	1983-87		1966	1956-65
	1989	1984-88		1967-1968	Latest
	1990	1985-89		1969	1963-68
	1991	1986-90		1974	1965-73
	1992	1987-91		1975	1966-74
	1993	1988-92		1980	1971-79
	1994	1989-93		1981	1972-80
	1995	1990-94		1985	1976-84
	1996	1987-95		1986	1977-85
	1997	1992-96		1996	1987-95
	1998	1993-97			
	1999	1994-98	**Foetal deaths, late**	1961	1952-60
	1999CD[iv]	1990-98	by sex	1965	5 Latest
	2000	1995-99		1969	1963-68
	2001	1997-01		1975	1966-74
	2002	1998-02		1981	1972-80
	2003	1999-03		1986	1977-85
	2004	2000-04			
	2005	2001-05	**Foetal deaths, late**	1971	1966-70
	2006	2002-06	by urban/rural	1972	1967-71
	2007	2003-07	residence	1973	1968-72
	2008	2004-08		1974	1965-73
	2009-2010	2006-10		1975	1966-74
	2011	2007-11		1976	1971-75
	2012	2008-12		1977	1972-76
	2013	2009-13		1978	1973-77
	2014	2010-14		1979	1974-78
	2015	2011-15		1980	1971-79
	2016	2012-16		1981	1972-80
	2017	2013-17		1982	1977-81
	2018	2014-18		1983	1978-82
				1984	1979-83
Foetal deaths, late	1954	1936-53		1985	1975-84
by age of mother	1959	1949-58		1986	1977-85
	1965	1955-64		1987	1982-86

Subject-matter	Year of issue	Time coverage	Subject-matter	Year of issue	Time coverage
	1988	1983-87	legitimate by age of mother	1965	1955-64
	1989	1984-88		1969	1963-68
	1990	1985-89		1975	1966-74
	1991	1986-90		1981	1972-80
	1992	1987-91		1986	1977-85
	1993	1988-92			
	1994	1989-93	Foetal death ratios	1957	1950-56
	1995	1990-94	by period of gestation	1959	1949-58
	1996	1987-95		1961	1952-60
	1997	1992-96		1965	5-Latest
	1998	1993-97		1966	1956-65
	1999	1994-98		1967-1968	Latest
	1999CD[iv]	1990-98		1969	1963-68
	2000	1995-99		1974	1965-73
	2001	1997-01		1975	1966-74
	2002	1998-02		1980	1971-79
	2003	1999-03		1981	1972-80
	2004	2000-04		1985	1976-84
	2005	2001-05		1986	1977-85
	2006	2002-06		1996	1987-95
	2007	2003-07		1999CD[iv]	1990-98
	2008	2004-08			
	2009-2010	2006-10	Foetal death ratios, late	1951	1935-50
	2011	2007-11		1952	1935-51
	2012	2008-12		1953	1936-52
	2013	2009-13		1954	1938-53
	2014	2010-14		1955	1946-54
	2015	2011-15		1956	1947-55
	2016	2012-16		1957	1948-56
	2017	2013-17		1958	1948-57
	2018	2014-18		1959	1920-54[v]
					1953-58
Foetal deaths, late	1961	1952-60		1960	1950-59
illegitimate	1965	5-Latest		1961	1945-49[v]
	1969	1963-68			1952-60
	1975	1966-74		1962	1945-54[v]
	1981	1972-80			1952-61
	1986	1977-85		1963	1945-59[v]
					1953-62
Foetal deaths, late	1961	1952-60		1964	1959-63
illegitimate, percent	1965	5-Latest		1965	1950-64[v]
	1969	1963-68			1955-64
	1975	1966-74		1966	1950-64[v]
	1981	1972-80			1956-65
	1986	1977-85		1967	1962-66
				1968	1963-67
Foetal deaths, late	1959	1949-58		1969	1950-64[v]
legitimate	1965	1955-64			1959-68
	1969	1963-68		1970	1965-69
	1975	1966-74		1971	1966-70
	1981	1972-80		1972	1967-71
	1986	1977-85		1973	1968-72
				1974	1965-73
Foetal deaths, late	1959	1949-58		1975	1966-74

Subject-matter	Year of issue	Time coverage
	1976	1971-75
	1977	1972-76
	1978	1973-77
	1979	1974-78
	1980	1971-79
	1981	1972-80
	1982	1977-81
	1983	1978-82
	1984	1979-83
	1985	1975-84
	1986	1977-85
	1987	1982-86
	1988	1983-87
	1989	1984-88
	1990	1985-89
	1991	1986-90
	1992	1987-91
	1993	1988-92
	1994	1989-93
	1995	1990-94
	1996	1987-95
	1997	1992-96
	1998	1993-97
	1999	1994-98
	1999CD[iv]	1990-98
	2000	1995-99
	2001	1997-01
	2002	1998-02
	2003	1999-03
	2004	2000-04
	2005	2001-05
	2006	2002-06
	2007	2003-07
	2008	2004-08
	2009-2010	2006-10
	2011	2007-11
	2012	2008-12
	2013	2009-13
	2014	2010-14
	2015	2011-15
	2016	2012-16
	2017	2013-17
	2018	2014-18
Foetal death ratios, late ..... by age of mother	1954	1936-53
	1959	1949-58
	1965	1955-64
	1969	1963-68
	1975	1966-74
	1981	1972-80
	1986	1977-85
	1996	1987-95
	1999CD[iv]	1990-98

Subject-matter	Year of issue	Time coverage
Foetal death ratios, late ..... by age of mother and birth order	1954	Latest
	1959	1949-58
	1965	3-Latest
	1969	1963-68
	1975	1966-74
	1981	1972-80
	1986	1977-85
	1999CD[iv]	1990-98
Foetal death ratios, late ..... by period of gestation	1957	1950-56
	1959	1949-58
	1961	1952-60
	1965	5-Latest
	1966	1956-65
	1967-1968	Latest
	1969	1963-68
	1974	1965-73
	1975	1966-74
	1980	1971-79
	1981	1972-80
	1985	1976-84
	1986	1977-85
Foetal death ratios, late ..... by urban/rural residence	1971	1966-70
	1972	1967-71
	1973	1968-72
	1974	1965-73
	1975	1966-74
	1976	1971-75
	1977	1972-76
	1978	1973-77
	1979	1974-78
	1980	1971-79
	1981	1972-80
	1982	1977-81
	1983	1978-82
	1984	1979-83
	1985	1975-84
	1986	1977-85
	1987	1982-86
	1988	1983-87
	1989	1984-88
	1990	1985-89
	1991	1986-90
	1992	1987-91
	1993	1988-92
	1994	1989-93
	1995	1990-94
	1996	1987-95
	1997	1992-96
	1998	1993-97
	1999	1994-98
	1999CD[iv]	1990-98
	2000	1995-99

Subject-matter	Year of issue	Time coverage	Subject-matter	Year of issue	Time coverage
	2001	1997-01		1976	Latest
	2002	1998-02		1982	Latest
	2003	1999-03		1987	1975-86
	2004	2000-04		1990	1980-89
	2005	2001-05		1995	1985-95
	2006	2002-06			
	2007	2003-07	**Households**	1962	1955-62
	2008	2004-08	average size of	1963	1955-63[vi]
	2009-2010	2006-10		1968	Latest
	2011	2007-11		1971	1962-71
	2012	2008-12		1973	1965-73[vi]
	2013	2009-13		1976	Latest
	2014	2010-14		1982	Latest
	2015	2011-15		1987	1975-86
	2016	2012-16		1990	1980-89
	2017	2013-17			
	2018	2014-18	**Households**	1987	1975-86
Foetal death ratios, late	1961	1952-60	by age, sex of householder, size and urban/rural residence	1995	1985-95
illegitimate	1965	5-Latest			
Foetal death ratios, late	1959	1949-58	**Households**	1987	1975-86
legitimate	1965	1955-64	by type of household and urban/rural residence	1995	1988-95
	1969	1963-68			
	1975	1966-74			
	1981	1972-80	**Households**	1987	1975-86
	1986	1977-85	by marital status of householder and urban/rural residence	1995	1985-95
Foetal death ratios, late	1959	1949-58			
legitimate by age of mother	1965	1955-64	**Households**	1987	1975-86
	1969	1963-68	by relationship to householder and urban/rural residence	1995	1985-95
	1975	1966-74			
	1981	1972-80			
	1986	1977-85	**Households**	1955	1945-54
			by size	1962	1955-62
G				1963	1955-63[vi]
Gestational age of foetal deaths		see "Foetal deaths by period of gestation"		1971	1962-71
				1973	1965-73[vi]
				1976	Latest
Gross reproduction rates		see "Reproduction rates"		1982	Latest
				1987	1975-86
H				1990	1980-89
				1995	1985-95
Homeless		see "Population, homeless by age and sex"			
			Households	1991PA[vii]	Latest
			by size and number of persons 60+		
Households	1955	1945-54			
	1962	1955-62	**Households**	1968	Latest
	1963	1955-63[vi]	by size and urban/rural residence	1971	1962-71
	1968	Latest		1973	1965-73[vi]
	1971	1962-71		1976	Latest
	1973	1965-73[vi]			

Historical index
(See notes at end of index)

Subject-matter	Year of issue	Time coverage
	1982	Latest
	1987	1975-86
	1990	1980-89
	1995	1985-95
Households .... headship rates by age and sex of householder and urban/rural residence	1987	1975-86
	1995	1985-95
Households .... number of family nuclei by size of	1973	1965-73
	1976	Latest
	1982	Latest
	1987	1975-86
	1990	1980-90
Households .... population by relationship to householder	1987	1975-86
	1991PA[vii]	Latest
Households .... by sex and persons 60+	1991PA[vii]	Latest
Households .... population in each type of	1955	1945-54
	1962	1955-62
	1963	1955-63[vi]
	1968	Latest
	1971	1962-71
	1973	1965-73[vi]
	1976	Latest
	1982	Latest
	1987	1975-86
	1990	1980-89
	1995	1985-95
Illegitimacy rates and ratios .... of births	1959	1949-58
	1965	1955-64
	1969	1963-68
	1975	1966-74
	1981	1972-80
	1986	1977-85
	1999CD[iv]	1990-98
Illegitimacy rates and ratios .... of foetal deaths, late	1961	1952-60
	1965	5-Latest
	1969	1963-68
	1975	1966-74
	1981	1972-80

Subject-matter	Year of issue	Time coverage
	1986	1977-85
Illegitimate .... birth(s)	1959	1949-58
	1965	1955-64
	1969	1963-68
	1975	1966-74
	1981	1972-80
	1986	1977-85
	1999CD[iv]	1990-98
	see also "Births"	
Illegitimate .... foetal death(s), late	1961	1952-60
	1965	5-Latest
	1969	1963-68
	1975	1966-74
	1981	1972-80
	1986	1977-85
	see also "Foetal deaths, late"	
Illiteracy rates	*see "Population, illiteracy rates "*	
Immigrants	*see "Migration ((international)"*	
Infant deaths	1948	1932-47
	1949-50	1934-49
	1951	1935-50
	1952	1936-51
	1953	1950-52
	1954	1946-53
	1955	1946-54
	1956	1947-55
	1957	1948-56
	1958	1948-57
	1959	1949-58
	1960	1950-59
	1961	1952-61
	1962	1953-62
	1963	1954-63
	1964	1960-64
	1965	1961-65
	1966	1947-66
	1967	1963-67
	1968	1964-68
	1969	1965-69
	1970	1966-70
	1971	1967-71
	1972	1968-72
	1973	1969-73
	1974	1965-74
	1975	1971-75
	1976	1972-76

Subject-matter	Year of issue	Time coverage	Subject-matter	Year of issue	Time coverage
	1977	1973-77		1981-1984	Latest
	1978	1974-78		1985	1976-84
	1978HS[ii]	1948-78		1986-1991	Latest
	1979	1975-79		1992	1983-92
	1980	1971-80		1993-1995	Latest
	1981	1977-81		1996	1987-95
	1982	1978-82		1997-2004	Latest
	1983	1979-83		2005	1996-05
	1984	1980-84		2006-2018	Latest
	1985	1976-85			
	1986	1982-86	Infant deaths.....................	1967-1973	Latest
	1987	1983-87	by age and sex and	1974	1965-73
	1988	1984-88	urban/rural residence	1975-1979	Latest
	1989	1985-89		1980	1971-79
	1990	1986-90		1981-1984	Latest
	1991	1987-91		1985	1976-84
	1992	1983-92		1986-1991	Latest
	1993	1989-93		1992	1983-92
	1994	1990-94		1993-1995	Latest
	1995	1991-95		1996	1987-95
	1996	1987-96		1997-1999	Latest
	1997	1993-97			
	1997HS[iii]	1948-97	Infant deaths.....................	1967	1962-66
	1998	1994-98	by month	1974	1965-73
	1999	1995-99		1980	1971-79
	2000	1996-00		1985	1976-84
	2001	1997-01			
	2002	1998-02	Infant deaths.....................	1967	Latest
	2003	1999-03	by urban/rural	1968	1964-68
	2004	2000-04	residence	1969	1965-69
	2005	2001-05		1970	1966-70
	2006	2002-06		1971	1967-71
	2007	2003-07		1972	1968-72
	2008	2004-08		1973	1969-73
	2009-2010	2006-10		1974	1965-74
	2011	2007-11		1975	1971-75
	2012	2008-12		1976	1972-76
	2013	2009-13		1977	1973-77
	2014	2010-14		1978	1974-78
	2015	2011-15		1979	1975-79
	2016	2012-16		1980	1971-80
	2017	2013-17		1981	1977-81
	2018	2014-18		1982	1978-82
				1983	1979-83
Infant deaths.....................	1948	1936-47		1984	1980-84
by age and sex	1951	1936-49		1985	1976-85
	1957	1948-56		1986	1982-86
	1961	1952-60		1987	1983-87
	1962-1965	Latest		1988	1984-88
	1966	1956-65		1989	1985-89
	1967-1973	Latest		1990	1986-90
	1974	1965-73		1991	1987-91
	1975-1979	Latest		1992	1983-92
	1980	1971-79		1993	1989-93

Historical index
(See notes at end of index)

Subject-matter	Year of issue	Time coverage
	1994	1990-94
	1995	1991-95
	1996	1987-96
	1997	1993-97
	1998	1994-98
	1999	1995-99
	2000	1996-00
	2001	1997-01
	2002	1998-02
	2003	1999-03
	2004	2000-04
	2005	2001-05
	2006	2002-06
	2007	2003-07
	2008	2004-08
	2009-2010	2006-10
	2011	2007-11
	2012	2008-12
	2013	2009-13
	2014	2010-14
	2015	2011-15
	2016	2012-16
	2017	2013-17
	2018	2014-18
Infant mortality rates	1948	1932-47
	1949-50	1932-49
	1951	1930-50
	1952	1920-34[v]
		1934-51
	1953	1920-39[v]
		1940-52
	1954	1920-39[v]
		1946-53
	1955	1920-34[v]
		1946-54
	1956	1947-55
	1957	1948-56
	1958	1948-57
	1959	1949-58
	1960	1950-59
	1961	1945-59[v]
		1952-61
	1962	1945-54[v]
		1952-62
	1963	1945-59[v]
	1963	1954-63
	1964	1960-64
	1965	1961-65
	1966	1920-64[v]
		1951-66
	1967	1963-67
	1968	1964-68
	1969	1965-69

Subject-matter	Year of issue	Time coverage
	1970	1966-70
	1971	1967-71
	1972	1968-72
	1973	1969-73
	1974	1965-74
	1975	1971-75
	1976	1972-76
	1977	1973-77
	1978	1974-78
	1978HS[II]	1948-78
	1979	1975-79
	1980	1971-80
	1981	1977-81
	1982	1978-82
	1983	1979-83
	1984	1980-84
	1985	1976-85
	1986	1982-86
	1987	1983-87
	1988	1984-88
	1989	1985-89
	1990	1986-90
	1991	1987-91
	1992	1983-92
	1993	1989-93
	1994	1990-94
	1995	1991-95
	1996	1987-96
	1997	1993-97
	1997HS[III]	1948-97
	1998	1994-98
	1999	1995-99
	2000	1996-00
	2001	1997-01
	2002	1998-02
	2003	1999-03
	2004	2000-04
	2005	2001-05
	2006	2002-06
	2007	2003-07
	2008	2004-08
	2009-2010	2006-10
	2011	2007-11
	2012	2008-12
	2013	2009-13
	2014	2010-14
	2015	2011-15
	2016	2012-16
	2017	2013-17
	2018	2014-18
Infant mortality rates	1948	1936-47
by age and sex	1951	1936-49
	1957	1948-56

Subject-matter	Year of issue	Time coverage	Subject-matter	Year of issue	Time coverage
	1961	1952-60		1994	1990-94
	1966	1956-65		1995	1991-95
	1967	1962-66		1996	1987-96
	1971-1973	Latest		1997	1993-97
	1974	1965-73		1998	1994-98
	1975-1979	Latest		1999	1995-99
	1980	1971-79		2000	1996-00
	1981-1984	Latest		2001	1997-01
	1985	1976-84		2002	1998-02
	1986-1991	Latest		2003	1999-03
	1992	1983-92		2004	2000-04
	1993-1995	Latest		2005	2001-05
	1996	1987-95		2006	2002-06
	1997-2018	Latest		2007	2003-07
				2008	2004-08
Infant mortality rates	1971-1973	Latest		2009-2010	2006-10
by age and sex and	1974	1965-73		2011	2007-11
urban/rural residence	1975-1979	Latest		2012	2008-12
	1980	1971-79		2013	2009-13
	1981-1984	Latest		2014	2010-14
	1985	1976-84		2015	2011-15
	1986-1991	Latest		2016	2012-16
	1992	1983-92		2017	2013-17
	1993-1995	Latest		2018	2014-18
	1996	1987-95			
	1997-1999	Latest	**Intercensal rates of**	1948	1900-48
			population increase	1949-50	1900-50
Infant mortality rates	1967	Latest		1951	1900-51
by urban/rural	1968	1964-68		1952	1850-1952
residence	1969	1965-69		1953	1850-1953
	1970	1966-70		1955	1850-1954
	1971	1967-71		1960	1900-61
	1972	1968-72		1962	1900-62
	1973	1969-73		1964	1955-64
	1974	1965-74		1970	1900-70
	1975	1971-75		1978HS[ii]	1948-78
	1976	1972-76		1997HS[iii]	1948-97
	1977	1973-77			
	1978	1974-78	**International migration**	see "Migration"	
	1979	1975-79			
	1980	1971-80	**L**		
	1981	1977-81			
	1982	1978-82	**Late foetal deaths**	see "Foetal deaths, late"	
	1983	1979-83			
	1984	1980-84	**Life tables**	1959-1973	Latest
	1985	1976-85	life expectancy at birth,	1974	2 latest
	1986	1982-86	by sex	1975-1978	Latest
	1987	1983-87		1978HS[ii]	1948-77
	1988	1984-88		1979	Latest
	1989	1985-89		1980	2 latest
	1990	1986-90		1981-1984	Latest
	1991	1987-91		1985	2 latest
	1992	1983-92		1986-1991	Latest
	1993	1989-93		1991PA[vii]	1950-90

Subject-matter	Year of issue	Time coverage
	1992-1995	Latest
	1996	2 latest
	1997	Latest
	1997HS[iii]	1948-96
	1998	1995-98
	1999	1995-99
	2000	1995-00
	2001	1997-01
	2002	1998-02
	2003	1999-03
	2004	2000-04
	2005	2001-05
	2006	2002-06
	2007	2003-07
	2008	2004-08
	2009-10	2006-10
	2011	2007-11
	2012	2008-12
	2013	2009-13
	2014	2010-14
	2015	2011-15
	2016	2012-16
	2017	2013-17
	2018	2014-18
Life tables.......................... life expectancy at specified ages, by sex	1948	1891-1945
	1951	1891-1950
	1952	1891-1951[vi]
	1953	1891-1952
	1954	1891-1953[vi]
	1955-1956	Latest
	1957	1900-56
	1958-1960	Latest
	1961	1940-60
	1962-1964	Latest
	1966	2 latest
	1967	1900-66
	1968-1973	Latest
	1974	2 latest
	1975-1978	Latest
	1978HS[ii]	1948-77
	1979	Latest
	1980	2 latest
	1981-1984	Latest
	1985	2 latest
	1986-1991	Latest
	1991PA[vii]	1950-90
	1992-1995	Latest
	1996	2 latest
	1997	Latest
	1997HS[iii]	1948-96
	1998-2018	Latest

Subject-matter	Year of issue	Time coverage
Life tables.......................... probabilities of dying at specified ages, by sex	1948	1891-1945
	1951	1891-1950
	1952	1891-1951[vi]
	1953	1891-1952
	1954	1891-1953[vi]
	1957	1900-56
	1961	1940-60
	1966	2 latest
	1974	2 latest
	1980	2 latest
	1985	2 latest
	1996	2 latest
	2008-2018	Latest
Life tables.......................... survivors at specified ages, by sex	1948	1891-1945
	1951	1891-1950
	1952	1891-1951[vi]
	1953	1891-1952
	1954	1891-1953[vi]
	1957	1900-56
	1961	1940-60
	1966	2 latest
	1974	2 latest
	1980	2 latest
	1985	2 latest
	1996	2 latest
Literacy..............................		*see "Population by literacy"*
Localities............................		*see "Population in localities"*

M

Subject-matter	Year of issue	Time coverage
Major civil divisions............		*see "Population by major civil divisions"*
Marriages............................	1948	1932-47
	1949-50	1934-49
	1951	1935-50
	1952	1936-51
	1953	1950-52
	1954	1946-53
	1955	1946-54
	1956	1947-55
	1957	1948-56
	1958	1940-57
	1959	1949-58
	1960	1950-59
	1961	1952-61
	1962	1953-62
	1963	1954-63
	1964	1960-64

Subject-matter	Year of issue	Time coverage	Subject-matter	Year of issue	Time coverage
	1965	1956-65	**Marriages**	1948	1936-47
	1966	1962-66	by age of bride	1949-50	1936-49
	1967	1963-67		1958	1948-57
	1968	1949-68		1959-1967	Latest
	1969	1965-69		1968	1958-67
	1970	1966-70		1969-1975	Latest
	1971	1967-71		1976	1966-75
	1972	1968-72		1977-1981	Latest
	1973	1969-73		1982	1972-81
	1974	1970-74		1983-1986	Latest
	1975	1971-75		1987	1975-86
	1976	1957-76		1988-1989	Latest
	1977	1973-77		1990	1980-1989
	1978	1974-78		1991-1997	Latest
	1979	1975-79		1998	1993-97
	1980	1976-80		1999	1994-98
	1981	1977-81		2000	1995-99
	1982	1963-82		2001	1997-01
	1983	1979-83		2002	1998-02
	1984	1980-84		2003	1999-03
	1985	1981-85		2004	2000-04
	1986	1982-86		2005	2001-05
	1987	1983-87		2006-2018	Latest
	1988	1984-88			
	1989	1985-89	**Marriages**	1958	1948-57
	1990	1971-90	by age of bride and age	1968	Latest
	1991	1987-91	of groom	1976	Latest
	1992	1988-92		1982	Latest
	1993	1989-93		1990	Latest
	1994	1990-94		2006-2018	Latest
	1995	1991-95			
	1996	1992-96	**Marriages**	1958	1948-57
	1997	1993-97	by age of bride and	1968	Latest
	1998	1994-98	previous marital status	1976	Latest
	1999	1995-99		1982	Latest
	2000	1996-00		1990	Latest
	2001	1997-01			
	2002	1998-02	**Marriages**	1948	1936-47
	2003	1999-03	by age of groom	1949-50	1936-49
	2004	2000-04		1958	1948-57
	2005	2001-05		1959-1967	Latest
	2006	2002-06		1968	1958-67
	2007	2003-07		1969-1975	Latest
	2008	2004-08		1976	1966-75
	2009-2010	2006-10		1977-1981	Latest
	2011	2007-11		1982	1972-81
	2012	2008-12		1983-1986	Latest
	2013	2009-13		1987	1975-86
	2014	2010-14		1988-1989	Latest
	2015	2011-15		1990	1980-1989
	2016	2012-16		1990-1997	Latest
	2017	2013-17		1998	1993-97
	2018	2014-18		1999	1994-98
				2000	1995-99

Subject-matter	Year of issue	Time coverage	Subject-matter	Year of issue	Time coverage
	2001	1997-01		1987	1983-87
	2002	1998-02		1988	1984-88
	2003	1999-03		1989	1985-89
	2004	2000-04		1990	1971-90
	2005	2001-05		1991	1987-91
	2006-2018	Latest		1992	1988-92
				1993	1989-93
Marriages	1958	1948-57		1994	1990-94
by age of groom and	1968	Latest		1995	1991-95
previous marital status	1976	Latest		1996	1992-96
	1982	Latest		1997	1993-97
	1990	Latest		1998	1994-98
				1999	1995-99
Marriages	1968	1963-67		2000	1996-00
by month				2001	1997-01
				2002	1998-02
Marriages	1958	1946-57		2003	1999-03
by previous marital	1968	Latest		2004	2000-04
status of bride and age	1976	Latest		2005	2001-05
	1982	Latest		2006	2002-06
	1990	Latest		2007	2003-07
				2008	2004-08
Marriages	1949-50	Latest		2009-2010	2006-10
by previous marital	1958	1948-57		2011	2007-11
status of bride and	1968	1958-67		2012	2008-12
groom	1976	1966-75		2013	2009-13
	1982	1972-81		2014	2010-14
	1990	1980-89		2015	2011-15
				2016	2012-16
Marriages	1958	1946-57		2017	2013-17
by previous marital	1968	Latest		2018	2014-18
status of groom and	1976	Latest			
age	1982	Latest	**Marriage, first**	1976	Latest
	1990	Latest	by detailed age of	1982	1972-81
			groom and bride	1990	1980-89
Marriages	1968	Latest			
by urban/rural	1969	1965-69	**Marriage rates**	1948	1932-47
residence	1970	1966-70		1949-50	1932-49
	1971	1967-71		1951	1930-50
	1972	1968-72		1952	1920-34[v]
	1973	1969-73			1934-51
	1974	1970-74		1953	1920-39[v]
	1975	1971-75			1940-52
	1976	1957-76		1954	1920-39[v]
	1977	1973-77			1946-53
	1978	1974-78		1955	1920-34[v]
	1979	1975-79			1946-54
	1980	1976-80		1956	1947-55
	1981	1977-81		1957	1948-56
	1982	1963-82		1958	1930-57
	1983	1979-83		1959	1949-58
	1984	1980-84		1960	1950-59
	1985	1981-85		1961	1952-61
	1986	1982-86		1962	1953-62

Subject-matter	Year of issue	Time coverage	Subject-matter	Year of issue	Time coverage
	1963	1954-63		2017	2013-17
	1964	1960-64		2018	2014-18
	1965	1956-65			
	1966	1962-66	Marriage rates	1948	1936-46
	1967	1963-67	by age and sex	1949-50	1936-49
	1968	1920-64ᵛ		1953	1936-51
		1953-68		1954	1936-52
	1969	1965-69		1958	1935-56
	1970	1966-70		1968	1955-67
	1971	1967-71		1976	1966-75
	1972	1968-72		1982	1972-81
	1973	1969-73		1987	1975-86
	1974	1970-74		1990	1980-89
	1975	1971-75			
	1976	1957-76	Marriage rates	1958	1935-56
	1977	1973-77	by sex among	1968	1935-67
	1978	1974-78	marriageable	1976	1966-75
	1979	1975-79	population	1982	1972-81
	1980	1976-80		1990	1980-89
	1981	1977-81			
	1982	1963-82	Marriage rates	1968	Latest
	1983	1979-83	by urban/rural	1969	1965-69
	1984	1980-84	residence	1970	1966-70
	1985	1981-85		1971	1967-71
	1986	1982-86		1972	1968-72
	1987	1983-87		1973	1969-73
	1988	1984-88		1974	1970-74
	1989	1985-89		1975	1971-75
	1990	1971-90		1976	1957-76
	1991	1987-91		1977	1973-77
	1992	1988-92		1978	1974-78
	1993	1989-93		1979	1975-79
	1994	1990-94		1980	1976-80
	1995	1991-95		1981	1977-81
	1996	1992-96		1982	1963-82
	1997	1993-97		1983	1979-83
	1998	1994-98		1984	1980-84
	1999	1995-99		1985	1981-85
	2000	1996-00		1986	1982-86
	2001	1997-01		1987	1983-87
	2002	1998-02		1988	1984-88
	2003	1999-03		1989	1985-89
	2004	2000-04		1990	1971-90
	2005	2001-05		1991	1987-91
	2006	2002-06		1992	1988-92
	2007	2003-07		1993	1989-93
	2008	2004-08		1994	1990-94
	2009-2010	2006-10		1995	1991-95
	2011	2007-11		1996	1992-96
	2012	2008-12		1997	1993-97
	2013	2009-13		1998	1994-98
	2014	2010-14		1999	1995-99
	2015	2011-15		2000	1996-00
	2016	2012-16		2001	1997-01

Historical index
(See notes at end of index)

Subject-matter	Year of issue	Time coverage	Subject-matter	Year of issue	Time coverage
	2002	1998-02		1997	1987-96
	2003	1999-03		1998	1988-97
	2004	2000-04		1999	1989-98
	2005	2001-05		2000	1991-00
	2006	2002-06		2001	1991-00
	2007	2003-07		2002	1995-02
	2008	2004-08		2003	1995-02
	2009-2010	2006-10		2004	1995-04
	2011	2007-11		2005	1995-04
	2012	2008-12		2006	1997-06
	2013	2009-13		2007	1997-06
	2014	2010-14		2008	1999-08
	2015	2011-15		2009-2010	1999-08
	2016	2012-16		2011-2012	2001-10
	2017	2013-17		2013-2014	2003-12
	2018	2014-18		2015-2016	2005-14
				2017-2018	2007-16
Marriage rates, first............	1982	1972-81			
by detailed age of groom and bride	1990	1980-89	**Maternal deaths**	1951	Latest
			by age	1952	Latest[vi]
				1957	Latest
Married population by age and sex........................	*see "Population by marital status"*			1961	Latest
				1967	Latest
				1974	Latest
Maternal deaths................	1951	1947-50		1980	Latest
	1952	1947-51		1985	Latest
	1953	Latest			
	1954	1945-53	**Maternal mortality rates**	1951	1947-50
	1955-1956	Latest		1952	1947-51
	1957	1952-56		1953	Latest
	1958-1960	Latest		1954	1945-53
	1961	1955-60		1955-1956	Latest
	1962-1965	Latest		1957	1952-62
	1966	1960-65		1958-1960	Latest
	1967-1973	Latest		1961	1955-60
	1974	1965-73		1962-1965	Latest
	1975-1979	Latest		1966	1960-65
	1980	1971-79		1967-1973	Latest
	1981	1972-80		1974	1965-73
	1982	1972-81		1975	1966-74
	1983	1973-82		1976	1966-75
	1984	1974-83		1977	1967-76
	1985	1975-84		1978	1968-77
	1986	1976-85		1979	1969-78
	1987	1977-86		1980	1971-79
	1988	1978-87		1981	1972-80
	1989	1979-88		1982	1972-81
	1990	1980-89		1983	1973-82
	1991	1981-90		1984	1974-83
	1992	1982-91		1985	1975-84
	1993	1983-92		1986	1976-85
	1994	1984-93		1987	1977-86
	1995	1985-94		1988	1978-87
	1996	1986-95		1989	1979-88

Subject-matter	Year of issue	Time coverage	Subject-matter	Year of issue	Time coverage
	1990	1980-89		1976	1969-75
	1991	1981-90		1977	1967-76
	1992	1982-91		1985	1975-84
	1993	1983-92		1989	1979-88
	1994	1984-93		1996	1986-95
	1995	1985-94			
	1996	1986-95	Migration (international) ...	1949-50	1945-49
	1997	1987-96	departures, by major	1951	1946-50
	1998	1988-97	categories	1952	1947-51
	1999	1989-98		1954	1948-53
	2000	1991-00		1957	1951-56
	2001	1991-00		1959	1953-58
	2002	1995-02		1962	1956-61
	2003	1995-02		1966	1960-65
	2004	1995-04		1968	1966-67
	2006	1997-06		1977	1967-76
	2007	1997-06		1985	1975-84
	2008	1999-08		1989	1979-88
	2009-2010	1999-08		1996	1986-95
	2011-2012	2001-10			
	2013-2014	2003-12	Migration (international) ...	1948	1945-47
	2015-2016	2005-14	emigrants (long term)	1949-50	1946-48
	2017-2018	2007-16	by age and sex	1951	1948-50
				1952	1949-51
Migration (international) ...	1970	1963-69		1954	1950-53
arrivals	1972	1965-71		1957	1953-56
	1974	1967-73		1959	1955-58
	1976	1969-75		1962	1958-61
	1977	1967-76		1966	1960-65
	1985	1975-84		1970	1962-69
	1989	1979-88		1977	1967-76
	1996	1986-95		1989	1975-88
Migration (international) ...	1949-50	1945-49	Migration (international) ...	1948	1945-47
arrivals, by major	1951	1946-50	emigrants (long term)	1949-50	1945-48
categories	1952	1947-51	by country or area of	1951	1948-50
	1954	1948-53	intended residence	1952	1949-51
	1957	1951-56		1954	1950-53
	1959	1953-58		1957	1953-56
	1962	1956-61		1959	1956-58
	1966	1960-65		1977	1958-76
	1968	1966-67		1989	1975-88
	1977	1967-76			
	1985	1975-84	Migration (international) ...	1948	1945-47
	1989	1979-88	immigrants (long term)	1949-50	1946-48
	1996	1986-95	by age and sex	1951	1948-50
				1952	1949-51
Migration (international) ...	1948	1936-47		1954	1950-53
continental and	1977	1967-76		1957	1953-56
inter-continental				1959	1955-58
				1962	1958-61
Migration (international) ...	1970	1963-69		1966	1960-65
departures	1972	1965-71		1970	1962-69
	1974	1967-73		1977	1967-76

Subject-matter	Year of issue	Time coverage	Subject-matter	Year of issue	Time coverage
	1989	1975-88		2003	1999-03
				2004	2000-04
Migration (international) ...	1948	1945-47		2005	2001-05
immigrants (long term)	1949-50	1945-48		2006	2002-06
by country or area of	1951	1948-50		2007	2003-07
last residence	1952	1949-51		2008	2004-08
	1954	1950-53		2009-2010	2006-10
	1957	1953-56		2011	2007-11
	1959	1956-58		2012	2008-12
	1977	1958-76		2013	2009-13
	1989	1975-88		2014	2010-14
	1948	1945-47		2015	2011-15
	1949-50	1945-48		2016	2012-16
				2017	2013-17
Migration (international) ...	1952	1947-51		2018	2014-18
refugees repatriated by					
the International			**Neonatal deaths**	1948	1936-47
Refugee Organization,			by sex	1951	1936-50
by country or area of				1957	1948-56
destination				1961	1952-60
				1963-1965	Latest
Migration (international) ...	1952	1947-51		1966	1961-65
refugees resettled by				1967	1962-66
the International				2000-2018	Latest
Refugee Organization,					
by country or area of			**Neonatal deaths**	1968-1973	Latest
destination			by sex and urban/rural	1974	1965-73
			residence	1975-1979	Latest
Mortality		see "Deaths", "Death		1980	1971-79
		rates", "Foetal deaths",		1981-1984	Latest
		"Foetal death ratios",		1985	1976-84
		"Infant deaths", "Infant		1986-1991	Latest
		mortality rates", "Life		1992	1983-92
		tables", "Maternal deaths",		1993-1995	Latest
		"Maternal mortality rates",		1996	1987-95
		"Neonatal deaths",		1997	Latest
		"Neonatal mortality rates",		1997HS[III]	1948-96
		"Perinatal deaths",		1998-1999	Latest
		"Perinatal death ratios",			
		"Post-neonatal deaths" and	**Neonatal mortality rates**	1948	1936-47
		"Post-neonatal mortality	by sex	1951	1936-50
		rates"		1957	1948-56
				1961	1952-60
				1966	1956-65
N				1967	1962-66
				2000-2018	Latest
Natality................................		see "Births" and "Birth			
		rates"	**Neonatal mortality rates**	1971-1973	Latest
			by sex and urban/rural	1974	1965-73
Natural increase rate	1958-1978	Latest	residence	1975-1979	Latest
	1978HS[ii]	1948-78		1980	1971-79
	1979-1997	Latest		1981-1984	Latest
	1998	1995-98		1985	1976-84
	1999	1996-99		1986-1991	Latest
	2000	1995-00			
	2001	1997-01			
	2002	1998-02			

Subject-matter	Year of issue	Time coverage		Subject-matter	Year of issue	Time coverage
	1992	1983-92			1970	1950-70
	1993-1995	Latest			1971	1962-71
	1996	1987-95			1972	Latest
	1997	Latest			1973	1965-73
	1997HS[iii]	1948-96			1974-1978	Latest
	1998-1999	Latest			1978HS[ii]	1948-77
					1979-1991	Latest
Net reproduction rates.......	*see "Reproduction rates"*				1991PA[vii]	1950-90
					1992-1997	Latest
Nuptiality	*see "Marriages"*				1997HS[iii]	1948-97
					1998-2018	Latest
P				**Population**...........................	1948	1945 & Latest
Perinatal deaths.................	1961	1952-60		by age groups and sex	1949-50	Latest[vi]
	1966	1956-65		(estimated)	1951-1959	Latest
	1971	1966-70			1960	1940-60
	1974	1965-73			1961-1969	Latest
	1980	1971-79			1970	1950-70
	1985	1976-84			1971-1997	Latest
	1996	1987-95			1997HS[iii]	1948-97
					1998-2018	Latest
Perinatal deaths.................	1971	1966-70		**Population**...........................	1948	1945 & Latest
by urban/rural	1974	1965-73		by age groups and sex	1949-50	Latest[vi]
residence	1980	1971-79		(percentage	1951-1952	Latest
	1985	1976-84		distribution)		
	1996	1987-95				
Perinatal death ratios........	1961	1952-60		**Population**...........................	1956	1945-55
	1966	1956-65		by country or area of	1963	1955-63
	1971	1966-70		birth and sex	1964	1955-64[vi]
	1974	1965-73			1971	1962-71
	1980	1971-79			1973	1965-73[vi]
	1985	1976-84			*see also "Population,*	
	1996	1987-95			*foreign born"*	
Perinatal death ratios........	1971	1966-70		**Population**...........................	1977	Latest
by urban/rural	1974	1965-73		by country or area of	1983	1974-83
residence	1980	1971-79		birth and sex and age	1989	1980-88[vi]
	1985	1976-84			*see also "Population,*	
	1996	1987-95			*foreign born"*	
Population...........................	1991PA[vii]	1950-90		**Population**...........................	1956	1945-55
ageing, selected				by citizenship	1963	1955-63
indicators					1964	1955-64[vi]
					1971	1962-71
					1973	1965-73[vi]
Population...........................	1948-1952	Latest				
by age groups and sex	1953	1950-52		**Population**...........................	1977	Latest
(enumerated)	1954-1959	Latest[vi]		by citizenship, sex and	1983	1974-83
	1960	1940-60		age	1989	Latest
	1961	Latest				
	1962	1955-62				
	1963	1955-63		**Population**...........................	1956	1945-55
	1964	1955-64[vi]		by ethnic composition	1963	1955-63
	1965-1969	Latest		and sex	1964	1955-64[vi]

Subject-matter	Year of issue	Time coverage
	1971	1962-71
	1973	1965-73[vi]
	1979	1970-79[vi]
	1983	1974-83
	1988	1980-88[vi]
	1993	1985-93
Population............ by type of household, number and size	1955	1945-54
	1962	1955-62
	1963	1955-63[vi]
	1968	Latest
	1971	1962-71
	1973	1965-73[vi]
	1976	Latest
	1982	Latest
	1987	1975-86
	1990	1980-89
	1995	1985-95

see also "Households"

Subject-matter	Year of issue	Time coverage
Population............ by language and sex	1956	1945-55
	1963	1955-63
	1964	1955-64[vi]
	1971	1962-71
	1973	1965-73[vi]
	1979	1970-79[vi]
	1983	1974-83
	1988	1980-88[vi]
	1993	1985-93

Subject-matter	Year of issue	Time coverage
Population............ by level of education, age and sex	1956	1945-55
	1963	1955-63
	1964	1955-64[vi]
	1971	1962-71
	1973	1965-73[vi]
	1979	1970-79[vi]
	1983	1974-83
	1988	1980-88[vi]
	1993	1985-93

Subject-matter	Year of issue	Time coverage
Population............ by literacy, age and sex	1948	Latest
	1955	1945-54
	1963	1955-63
	1964	1955-64[vi]
	1971	1962-71

see also "Population, illiterate"

Subject-matter	Year of issue	Time coverage
Population............ by literacy, age, sex and urban/rural residence	1973	1965-73[vi]
	1979	1970-79[vi]
	1983	1974-83
	1988	1980-88[vi]
	1993	1985-93

Subject-matter	Year of issue	Time coverage
Population............ by localities of 100 000+ inhabitants	1948	Latest
	1952	Latest
	1955	1945-54
	1960	1920-61
	1962	1955-62
	1963	1955-63[vi]
	1970	1950-70
	1971	1962-71
	1973	1965-73[vi]
	1979	1970-79[vi]
	1983	1974-83
	1988	1980-88[vi]
	1993	1985-93

see also "Population of cities of 100 000+ inhabitants"

Subject-matter	Year of issue	Time coverage
Population............ by localities of 20 000+ inhabitants	1948	Latest
	1952	Latest
	1955	1945-54
	1960	1920-61
	1962	1955-62
	1963	1955-63[vi]
	1970	1950-70
	1971	1962-71
	1973	1965-73[vi]
	1979	1970-79[vi]
	1983	1974-83
	1988	1980-88[vi]
	1993	1985-93

Subject-matter	Year of issue	Time coverage
Population............ by locality size-classes and sex	1948	Latest
	1952	Latest
	1955	1945-54
	1962	1955-62
	1963	1955-63[vi]
	1971	1962-71
	1973	1965-73[vi]
	1979	1970-79[vi]
	1983	1974-83
	1988	1980-88[vi]
	1993	1985-93

Subject-matter	Year of issue	Time coverage
Population............ by major civil divisions	1952	Latest
	1955	1945-54
	1962	1955-62
	1963	1955-63[vi]
	1971	1962-71
	1973	1965-73[vi]
	1979	1970-79[vi]
	1983	1974-83
	1988	1980-88[vi]
	1993	1985-93

Subject-matter	Year of issue	Time coverage
Population	1948	Latest
by marital status, age	1949/50	1926-48
and sex	1955	1945-54
	1958	1945-57
	1962	1955-62[vi]
	1963	1955-63[vi]
	1965	1955-65
	1968	1955-67
	1971	1962-71
	1973	1965-73[vi]
	1976	1966-75
	1978HS[ii]	1948-77
	1982	1972-81
	1987	1975-86
	1990	1980-89
	1997HS[iii]	1948-96

see also "Population, married" and "Population, single"

Subject-matter	Year of issue	Time coverage
Population	1991PA[vii]	Latest
for persons 60+ and urban/rural		
Population	1948	Latest
for persons 60+ and urban/rural (percentage distribution)		
Population	1956	1945-55
by religion and sex	1963	1955-63
	1964	1955-64[vi]
	1971	1962-71
	1973	1965-73[vi]
	1979	1970-79[vi]
	1983	1974-83
	1988	1980-88[vi]
	1993	1985-93
Population	1956	1945-55
by school attendance, age and sex	1963	1955-63
	1964	1955-64[vi]
	1971	1962-71
	1973	1965-73[vi]
	1979	1970-79
	1983	1974-83
	1988	1980-88[vi]
	1993	1985-93
Population	1948-1952	Latest
by sex (enumerated)	1953	1950-52
	1954-1959	Latest
	1960	1900-61

Subject-matter	Year of issue	Time coverage
	1961	Latest
	1962	1900-62
	1963	1955-63
	1964	1955-64
	1965-1969	Latest
	1970	1950-70
	1971	1962-71
	1972	Latest
	1973	1965-73
	1974-1978	Latest
	1978HS[ii]	1948-78
	1979-1982	Latest
	1983	1974-83
	1984-1997	Latest
	1997HS[iii]	1948-97
	1998-2018	Latest
Population	1948	1945 & latest
by sex (estimated)	1949-50-1959	Latest
	1960	1940-60
	1961-1969	Latest
	1970	1950-70
	1971	1962-71
	1972	Latest
	1973	1965-73
	1974-1997	Latest
	1997HS[iii]	1948-97
	1998-1999	Latest
	2000	1991-00
	2001	1992-01
	2002	1993-02
	2003	1994-03
	2004	1995-04
	2005	1996-05
	2006	1997-06
	2007	1998-07
	2008	1999-08
	2009-2010	2001-10
	2011	2002-11
	2012	2003-12
	2013	2004-13
	2014	2005-14
	2015	2006-15
	2016	2007-16
	2017	2008-17
	2018	2009-18
Population	1955	1945-54
by single years of age and sex	1962	1955-62
	1963	1955-63[vi]
	1971	1962-71
	1973	1965-73[vi]
	1979	1970-79[vi]
	1983	1974-83

Subject-matter	Year of issue	Time coverage
	1988	1980-88[vi]
	1993	1985-93
Population........................ cities		*see "Population of cities"*
Population........................ civil division		*see "Population by major civil divisions"*
Population........................ density		*see "Density of population"*
Population........................ disabled	1991PA[vii]	Latest
Population........................ economically active:	1945	1945-54
	1956	1945-55
- by age and sex	1964	1955-64
	1972	1962-72
- by age and sex and urban/rural residence	1973	1965-73[vi]
	1979	1970-79[vi]
	1984	1974-84
	1988	1980-88[vi]
	1994	1985-94
- by age and sex (per cent)	1949-50	1930-48
	1954	Latest
	1955	1945-54
	1956	1945-55
	1964	1955-64
	1972	1962-72
- by age and sex, and urban/rural residence (per cent)	1973	1965-73[vi]
	1979	1970-79[vi]
	1984	1974-84
	1988	1980-88[vi]
	1994	1985-94
- by industry, age and sex	1956	1945-55
	1964	1955-64
	1972	1962-72
- by industry, age, sex and urban/rural residence	1973	1965-74[vi]
	1979	1970-79[vi]
	1984	1974-84
	1988	1980-88[vi]
	1994	1985-94
- by industry, status in employment and sex	1948	Latest
	1949-50	Latest
	1955	1945-54
	1964	1955-64
	1972	1962-72

Subject-matter	Year of issue	Time coverage
- by industry, status in employment and sex and urban/rural residence	1973	1965-73[vi]
	1979	1970-79[vi]
	1984	1974-84
	1988	1980-88[vi]
	1994	1985-94
- by living arrangements, age, sex and urban/rural residence	1987	1975-86
	1995	1985-95
- by occupation, age and sex	1956	1945-55
	1964	1955-64
	1972	1962-72
- by occupation, age, sex, and urban/rural residence	1973	1965-73[vi]
	1979	1970-79[vi]
	1984	1974-84
	1988	1980-88[vi]
	1994	1985-94
- by occupation, status in employment and sex	1956	1945-55
	1964	1955-64
	1972	1962-72
- by occupation, status in employment and sex and urban/rural residence	1973	1965-73[vi]
	1979	1970-7vi[vi]
	1984	1974-84
	1988	1980-88[vi]
	1994	1985-94
- by sex	1948	Latest
	1949-50	1926-48
	1955	1945-54
	1956	1945-55
	1960	1920-60
	1963	1955-63
	1964	1955-64
	1970	1950-70
	1972	1962-72
	1973	1965-73[vi]
	1979	1970-79[vi]
	1984	1974-84
	1994	1985-94
- by status in employment, age and sex	1956	1945-55
	1964	1955-64
	1972	1962-72
- by status in employment, age and sex and	1973	1965-73[vi]
	1979	1970-79[vi]
	1984	1974-84

Subject-matter	Year of issue	Time coverage	Subject-matter	Year of issue	Time coverage
urban/rural residence	1988	1980-88[vi]		1963	1955-63
	1994	1985-94		1965	1955-65
				1969	Latest
- female, by marital status and age	1956	1945-55		1971	1962-71
	1964	1955-64		1973	1965-73[vi]
	1968	Latest		1975	1965-74
	1972	1962-72		1978HS[ii]	1948-77
				1981	1972-80
- female, by marital status and age and urban/rural residence	1973	1965-73[vi]		1986	1977-85
	1979	1970-79[vi]		1997HS[iii]	1948-96
	1984	1974-84			
	1988	1980-88[vi]	**Population........................**	1949-50	Latest
	1994	1985-94	female, by number of children living and age	1954	1930-53
				1955	1945-54
- foreign-born by occupation, age and sex	1984	1974-84		1959	1949-58
	1988	1980-88[vi]		1963	1955-63
	1994	1985-94		1965	1955-65
				1968-1969	Latest
- foreign-born, by occupation and sex	1977	Latest		1971	1962-71
		see also "Population, foreign-born by occupation, age and sex"		1973	1965-73[vi]
				1975	1965-74
				1978HS[ii]	1948-77
				1981	1972-80
- unemployed, by age and sex	1949-50	1946-49		1986	1977-85
				1997HS[iii]	1948-96
Population........................	1956	1945-54	**Population........................**	1987	1975-86
economically inactive by sub-groups and sex	1964	1955-64	female, in households, by age, sex of householder, size and relationship to householder and urban/rural residence	1995	1991-95
	1972	1962-72			
	1973	1965-73[vi]			
	1979	1970-79[vi]			
	1984	1974-84[vi]			
	1988	1980-88[vi]			
	1994	1985-94	**Population........................**	1987	1875-86
			institutional, by age, sex and urban/rural residence	1995	1991-95
Population........................	1991PA[vii]	1950-90			
elderly, by economic, characteristics and urban/rural residence					
			Population........................	1957	1953-56
			growth rates (annual average for countries or areas)	1958	1953-57
Population........................	1991PA[vii]	1950-90		1959	1953-58
elderly, by socio-demographic characteristics and urban/rural residence				1960	1953-59
				1961	1953-60
				1962	1958-61
				1963	1958-62
Population........................	1968	Latest		1964	1958-63
female, by age and duration of marriage				1965	1958-64
				1966	1958-66
				1967	1963-67
				1968	1963-68
Population........................	1949-50	Latest		1969	1963-69
female, by number of children born alive and age	1954	1930-53		1970	1963-70
	1955	1945-54		1971	1963-71
	1959	1949-58			

Historical index
(See notes at end of index)

Subject-matter	Year of issue	Time coverage		Subject-matter	Year of issue	Time coverage
	1972	1963-72				1960-62
	1973	1970-73			1964	1958-63
	1974	1970-74				1960-63
	1975	1970-75			1965	1958-64
	1976	1970-76				1960-64
	1977	1970-77			1966	1958-66
	1978	1975-78				1960-66
	1979	1975-79			1967	1960-67
	1980	1975-80				1963-67
	1981	1975-81			1968	1960-68
	1982	1975-82				1963-68
	1983	1980-83			1969	1960-69
	1984	1980-84				1963-69
	1985	1980-85			1970	1963-70
	1986	1980-86				1965-70
	1987	1980-87			1971	1963-71
	1988	1985-88				1965-71
	1989	1985-89			1972	1963-72
	1990	1985-90				1965-72
	1991	1985-91			1973	1965-73
	1992	1985-92				1970-73
	1993	1990-93			1974	1965-74
	1994	1990-94				1970-74
	1995	1990-95			1975	1965-75
	1996	1990-96				1970-75
	1997	1990-97			1976	1965-76
	1998	1993-98				1970-76
	1999	1995-99			1977	1965-77
	2000	1995-00				1970-77
	2001	1995-01			1978-1979	1970-75
	2002	1995-02			1980-1983	1975-80
	2003	2000-03			1984-1986	1980-85
	2004	2000-04			1987-1992	1985-90
	2005	2000-05			1993-1997	1990-95
	2006	2000-06			1998-2000	1995-00
	2007	2005-07			2001-2005	2000-05
	2008	2005-08			2006-2010	2005-10
	2009-2010	2005-10			2011-2015	2010-15
	2011	2005-11			2016-2018	2015-20
	2012	2005-12				
	2013	2010-13		**Population**.......................... homeless by age and sex	1991PA[vii]	Latest
	2014	2010-14				
	2015	2010-15				
	2016	2010-16		**Population**.......................... illiteracy rates by sex	1948	Latest
	2017	2010-17			1955	1945-54
	2018	2010-18			1960	1920-60
					1963	1955-63[vi]
Population.......................... growth rates (annual average for the world, macro-regions (continents) and regions)	1957	1950-56			1964	1955-64[vi]
	1958	1950-57			1970	1950-70
	1959	1950-58				
	1960	1950-59		**Population**..........................	1973	1965-73
	1961	1950-60			1979	1970-79[vi]
	1962	1950-61			1983	1974-83
	1963	1958-62				

Subject-matter	Year of issue	Time coverage
illiteracy rates by sex	1988	1980-88[vi]
and urban/rural	1993	1985-93
residence		
Population	1948	Latest
illiterate, by sex	1955	1945-54
	1960	1920-60
	1963	1955-63
	1964	1955-64
	1970	1950-70
Population	1948	Latest
illiterate, by sex and	1955	1945-54
age	1963	1955-63
	1964	1955-64[vi]
	1970	1950-70
Population	1973	1965-73
illiterate, by sex and	1979	1970-79[vi]
age and urban/rural	1983	1974-83
residence	1988	1980-88[vi]
	1993	1985-93
Population	1973	1965-73
illiterate, by sex and	1979	1970-79[vi]
urban/rural residence	1983	1974-83
	1988	1980-88[vi]
	1993	1985-93
Population	1991PA[vii]	Latest
in collective living		
quarters and homeless		
Population	see "Population by type of household" and "Households"	
in households		
Population	see "Population by localities" and "Population by locality size-classes"	
in localities		
Population	see "Population growth rates"	
increase rates		
Population	1955	1945-54
literacy rates by sex	see also "Population illiteracy rates"	
Population	1955	1945-54
literacy rates by sex and age		
Population	1948	Latest
literate, by sex and age	1955	1945-54
	1963	1955-63

Subject-matter	Year of issue	Time coverage
	1964	1955-64[vi]
	1971	1962-71
	see also "Population, illiterate"	
Population	1971	1962-71
literate, by sex and age	1973	1965-73[vi]
by urban/rural	1979	1970-74[vi]
residence	1983	1974-83
	1988	1980-88[vi]
	1993	1985-93
	1987	1975-86
Population	1991PA[vii]	1950-90
living arrangements	1995	1985-95
Population	see "Population by localities"	
localities		
Population	see "Population by major civil divisions"	
major civil divisions		
Population	1954	1926-52
married by age and sex	1960	1920-60
(numbers and percent)	1970	1950-70
	see also "Population by marital status"	
Population	1968	Latest
married female by		
percentage and		
duration of marriage		
Population	1976	1966-75
ever married	1978HS[ii]	1948-77
proportion by sex,	1982	1972-81
selected ages	1990	1980-89
Population	1972	1962-72
not economically active		
Population	1973	1965-73[vi]
not economically active	1979	1970-79[vi]
by urban/rural	1984	1974-84
residence	1988	1980-88[vi]
	1994	1985-94
Population	1952	Latest
of cities (capital city)	1955	1945-54
	1957	Latest
	1960	1939-61
	1962	1955-62
	1963	1955-63
	1964-1969	Latest

Subject-matter	Year of issue	Time coverage		Subject-matter	Year of issue	Time coverage
	1970	1950-70			1964	1955-64
	1971	1962-71			1965	1946-65
	1972	Latest			1966	1947-66
	1973	1965-73			1967	1958-67
	1974-2018	Latest			1968	1959-68
					1969	1960-69
Population..........................	1952	Latest			1970	1950-70
of cities of 100 000+	1955	1945-54			1971	1962-71
inhabitants	1957	Latest			1972	1963-72
	1960	1939-61			1973	1964-73
	1962	1955-62			1974	1965-74
	1963	1955-63			1975	1966-75
	1964-1969	Latest			1976	1967-76
	1970	1950-70			1977	1968-77
	1971	1962-71			1978	1969-78
	1972	Latest			1978HS[ii]	1948-78
	1973	1965-73			1979	1970-79
	1974-2018	Latest			1980	1971-80
					1981	1972-81
Population..........................	*see "Population of major*				1982	1973-82
of continents	*regions"*				1983	1974-83
					1984	1975-84
Population..........................	1948	1900-48			1985	1976-85
of countries or areas	1949-50	1900-50			1986	1977-86
(totals, enumerated)	1951	1900-51			1987	1978-87
	1952	1850-1952			1988	1979-88
	1953	1850-1953			1989	1980-89
	1954	Latest			1990	1981-90
	1955	1850-1954			1991	1982-91
	1956-1961	Latest			1992	1983-92
	1962	1900-62			1993	1984-93
	1963	Latest			1994	1985-94
	1964	1955-64			1995	1986-95
	1965-1978	Latest			1996	1987-96
	1978HS[ii]	1948-78			1997	1988-97
	1979-1997	Latest			1997HS[iii]	1948-97
	1997HS[iii]	1948-97			1998	1989-98
	1998-2018	Latest			1999	1990-99
					2000	1991-00
Population..........................	1948	1932-47			2001	1992-01
of countries or areas	1949-50	1932-49			2002	1993-02
(totals, estimated)	1951	1930-50			2003	1994-03
	1952	1920-51			2004	1995-04
	1953	1920-53			2005	1996-05
	1954	1920-54			2006	1997-06
	1955	1920-55			2007	1998-07
	1956	1920-56			2008	1999-08
	1957	1940-57			2009-2010	2001-10
	1958	1939-58			2011	2002-11
	1959	1940-59			2012	2003-12
	1960	1920-60			2013	2004-13
	1961	1941-61			2014	2005-14
	1962	1942-62			2015	2006-15
	1963	1943-63			2016	2007-16

Subject-matter	Year of issue	Time coverage	Subject-matter	Year of issue	Time coverage
	2017	2008-17		2002	1950-02
	2018	2009-18		2003	1950-03
				2004	1950-04
Population........................	1949-50	1920-49		2005	1950-05
- of major regions	1951	1950		2006	1950-06
	1952	1920-51		2007	1950-07
	1953	1920-52		2008	1950-08
	1954	1920-53		2009-2010	1950-10
	1955	1920-54		2011	1960-11
	1956	1920-55		2012	1960-12
	1957	1920-56		2013	1960-13
	1958	1920-57		2014	1960-14
	1959	1920-58		2015	1960-15
	1960	1920-59		2016	1960-16
	1961	1920-60		2017	1960-17
	1962	1920-61		2018	1960-18
	1963	1930-62			
	1964	1930-63	Population........................	1949-50	1920-49
	1965	1930-65	- of regions	1952	1920-51
	1966	1930-66		1953	1920-52
	1967	1930-67		1954	1920-53
	1968	1930-68		1955	1920-54
	1969	1930-69		1956	1920-55
	1970	1950-70		1957	1920-56
	1971	1950-71		1958	1920-57
	1972	1950-72		1959	1920-58
	1973	1950-73		1960	1920-59
	1974	1950-74		1961	1920-60
	1975	1950-75		1962	1920-61
	1976	1950-76		1963	1930-62
	1977	1950-77		1964	1930-63
	1978	1950-78		1965	1930-65
	1979	1950-79		1966	1930-66
	1980	1950-80		1967	1930-67
	1981	1950-81		1968	1930-68
	1982	1950-82		1969	1930-69
	1983	1950-83		1970	1950-70
	1984	1950-84		1971	1950-71
	1985	1950-85		1972	1950-72
	1986	1950-86		1973	1950-73
	1987	1950-87		1974	1950-74
	1988	1950-88		1975	1950-75
	1989	1950-89		1976	1950-76
	1990	1950-90		1977	1950-77
	1991	1950-91		1978	1950-78
	1992	1950-92		1979	1950-79
	1993	1950-93		1980	1950-80
	1994	1950-94		1981	1950-81
	1995	1950-95		1982	1950-82
	1996	1950-96		1983	1950-83
	1997	1950-97		1984	1950-84
	1998-1999	1950-00		1985	1950-85
	2000	1950-00		1986	1950-86
	2001	1950-01		1987	1950-87

Subject-matter	Year of issue	Time coverage	Subject-matter	Year of issue	Time coverage
	1988	1950-88		1974	1950-74
	1989	1950-89		1975	1950-75
	1990	1950-90		1976	1950-76
	1991	1950-91		1977	1950-77
	1992	1950-92		1978	1950-78
	1993	1950-93		1979	1950-79
	1994	1950-94		1980	1950-80
	1995	1950-95		1981	1950-81
	1996	1950-96		1982	1950-82
	1997	1950-97		1983	1950-83
	1998-1999	1950-00		1984	1950-84
	2000	1950-00		1985	1950-85
	2001	1950-01		1986	1950-86
	2002	1950-02		1987	1950-87
	2003	1950-03		1988	1950-88
	2004	1950-04		1989	1950-89
	2005	1950-05		1990	1950-90
	2006	1950-06		1991	1950-91
	2007	1950-07		1992	1950-92
	2008	1950-08		1993	1950-93
	2009-2010	1950-10		1994	1950-94
	2011	1960-11		1995	1950-95
	2012	1960-12		1996	1950-96
	2013	1960-13		1997	1950-97
	2014	1960-14		1998-1999	1950-00
	2015	1960-15		2000	1950-00
	2016	1960-16		2001	1950-01
	2017	1960-17		2002	1950-02
	2018	1960-18		2003	1950-03
				2004	1950-04
				2005	1950-05
				2006	1950-06
				2007	1950-07
				2008	1950-08
				2009-2010	1950-10
				2011	1960-11
				2012	1960-12
				2013	1960-13
				2014	1960-14
				2015	1960-15
				2016	1960-16
				2017	1960-17
Population...........................	1949-50	1920-49		2018	1960-18
- of the world	1951	1950			
	1952	1920-51	Population...........................	see "Population by	
	1953	1920-52	rural residence	urban/rural residence"	
	1954	1920-53			
	1955	1920-54			
	1956	1920-55			
	1957	1920-56	Population...........................	1960	1920-60
	1958	1920-57	single, by age and sex	1970	1950-70
	1959	1920-58	(numbers)		
	1960	1920-59		see also "Population by	
	1961	1920-60		marital status"	
	1962	1920-61			
	1963	1930-62			
	1964	1930-63	Population...........................	1949-50	1926-48
	1965	1930-65	single, by age and sex	1960	1920-60
	1966	1930-66	(percent)	1970	1950-70
	1967	1930-67			
	1968	1930-68			
	1969	1930-69			
	1970	1950-70			
	1971	1950-71			
	1972	1950-72			
	1973	1950-73			

Subject-matter	Year of issue	Time coverage	Subject-matter	Year of issue	Time coverage
				1967	Latest
Population..........................	1968	1964-68		1970	1950-70
urban/rural residence:	1969	1965-69		1971	1962-71
	1970	1950-70		1972	Latest
	1971	1962-71		1973	1965-73
	1972	1968-72		1974-1978	Latest
	1973	1965-73		1978HS[ii]	1948-77
	1974	1966-74		1979-1996	Latest
	1975	1967-75		1979-1997	Latest
	1976	1967-76		1997HS[iii]	1948-96
	1977	1968-77		1998-2018	Latest
	1978	1969-78			
	1979	1970-79	- by age and sex	1963	Latest
	1980	1971-80	(estimated)	1967	Latest
	1981	1972-81		1970	1950-70
	1982	1973-82		1971-1997	Latest
	1983	1974-83		1997HS[iii]	1948-96
	1984	1975-84		1998-2018	Latest
	1985	1976-85			
	1986	1977-86	- by country or area	1971	1962-71
	1987	1978-87	of birth and sex	1973	1965-73[vi]
	1988	1979-88			
	1989	1980-89	- by country or area	1977	Latest
	1990	1981-90	of birth and sex and		
	1991	1982-91	age		
	1992	1983-92			
	1993	1984-93	- by citizenship and	1971	1962-71
	1994	1985-94	sex	1973	1965-73[vi]
	1995	1986-95			
	1996	1987-96	- by citizenship and	1977	Latest
	1997	1988-97	sex and age	1983	1974-83
	1998	1989-98		1989	1980-88
	1999	1990-99			
	2000	1991-00	- by ethnic	1971	Latest
	2001	1992-01	composition and	1973	1965-73[vi]
	2002	1993-02	sex	1979	1970-79[vi]
	2003	1994-03		1983	1974-83
	2004	1995-04		1988	1980-88[vi]
	2005	1996-05		1993	1985-93
	2006	1997-06			
	2007	1998-07	- by households,	1968	Latest
	2008	1999-08	number and size	1971	1962-71
	2009-2010	2001-10		1973	1965-73[vi]
	2011	2002-11		1976	Latest
	2012	2003-12		1982	Latest
	2013	2004-13		1987	1975-86
	2014	2005-14		1990	1980-89
	2015	2006-15		1995	1985-95
	2016	2007-16			
	2017	2008-17		*see also "Households"*	
	2018	2009-18			
			- by language and	1971	1962-71
- by age and sex	1963	1955-63	sex	1973	1965-73[vi]
(enumerated)	1964	1955-64[vi]		1979	1970-79[vi]

Subject-matter	Year of issue	Time coverage	Subject-matter	Year of issue	Time coverage
	1983	1974-83		1974	1966-74
	1988	1980-88[vi]		1975	1967-75
	1993	1985-93		1976	1967-76
				1977	1968-77
- by level of education, age and sex	1971	1962-71		1978	1969-78
	1973	1965-73[vi]		1979	1970-79
	1979	1970-79[vi]		1980	1971-80
	1983	1974-83		1981	1972-81
	1988	1980-88[vi]		1982	1973-82
	1993	1985-93		1983	1974-83
				1984	1975-84
- by literacy, age and sex	1971	1962-71		1985	1976-85
	1973	1965-73[vi]		1986	1977-86
	1979	1970-79[vi]		1987	1978-87
	1983	1974-83		1988	1979-88
	1988	1980-88[vi]		1989	1980-89
	1993	1985-93		1990	1981-90
				1991	1982-91
- by major civil divisions	1971	1962-71		1992	1983-92
	1973	1965-73[vi]		1993	1984-93
	1979	1970-79[vi]		1994	1985-94
	1983	1974-83		1995	1986-95
	1988	1980-88[vi]		1996	1987-96
	1993	1985-93		1997	1988-97
				1998	1989-98
- by marital status, age and sex	1971	1962-71		1999	1990-99
	1973	1965-73[vi]		2000	1991-00
				2001	1992-01
- by religion and sex	1971	1962-71		2002	1993-02
	1973	1965-73[vi]		2003	1994-03
	1979	1970-79[vi]		2004	1995-04
	1983	1974-83		2005	1996-05
	1988	1980-88[vi]		2006	1997-06
	1993	1985-93		2007	1998-07
				2008	1999-08
- by school attendance, age and sex	1971	1962-71		2009-2010	2001-10
	1973	1965-73[vi]		2011	2002-11
	1979	1970-79[vi]		2012	2003-12
	1983	1974-83		2013	2004-13
	1988	1980-88[vi]		2014	2005-14
	1993	1985-93		2015	2006-15
				2016	2007-16
- by sex (numbers)	1948	Latest		2017	2008-17
	1952	1900-51		2018	2009-18
	1955	1945-54			
	1960	1920-60	- by sex (percent)	1948	Latest
	1962	1955-62		1952	1900-51
	1963	1955-63		1955	1945-54
	1964	1955-64[vi]		1960	1920-60
	1967	Latest		1962	1955-62
	1970	1950-70		1970	1950-70
	1971	1962-71		1971	1962-71
	1972	Latest		1973	1965-73
	1973	1965-73		1974	1966-74

Subject-matter	Year of issue	Time coverage	Subject-matter	Year of issue	Time coverage
	1975	1967-75		1981	1972-80
	1976	1967-76		1986	1977-85
	1977	1968-77		1997HS[iii]	1948-96
	1978	1969-78			
	1979	1970-79	- female, by number	1971	1962-71
	1980	1971-80	of children living	1973	1965-73[vi]
	1981	1972-81	and age	1975	1965-74
	1982	1973-82		1978HS[ii]	1948-77
	1983	1974-83		1981	1972-80
	1984	1975-84		1986	1977-85
	1985	1976-85		1997HS[iii]	1948-96
	1986	1977-86			
	1987	1978-87	Post-neonatal deaths	1948	1936-47
	1988	1979-88	by sex	1951	1936-50
	1989	1980-89		1957	1948-56
	1990	1981-90		1961	1952-60
	1991	1982-91		1963-1965	Latest
	1992	1983-92		1966	1961-65
	1993	1984-93		1967	1962-66
	1994	1985-94		1968-1973	Latest
	1995	1986-95		1974	1965-73
	1996	1987-96		1975-1979	Latest
	1997	1988-97		1980	1971-79
	1998	1989-98		1981-1984	Latest
	1999	1990-99		1985	1976-84
	2000	1991-00		1986-1991	Latest
	2001	1992-01		1992	1983-92
	2002	1993-02		1993-1995	Latest
	2003	1994-03		1996	1987-95
	2004	1995-04		1997	Latest
	2005	1996-05		1997HS[ii]	1948-96
	2006	1997-06		1998-2018	Latest
	2007	1998-07			
	2008	1999-08	Post-neonatal deaths	1971-1973	Latest
	2009-2010	2001-10	by urban/rural	1974	1965-73
	2011	2002-11	residence	1975-1979	Latest
	2012	2003-12		1980	1971-79
	2013	2004-13		1981-1984	Latest
	2014	2005-14		1985	1976-84
	2015	2006-15		1986-1991	Latest
	2016	2007-16		1992	1983-92
	2017	2008-17		1993-1995	Latest
	2018	2009-18		1996	1987-95
- by single years of	1971	1962-71		1997	Latest
age and sex	1973	1965-73[vi]		1997HS[ii]	1948-96
	1979	1970-79[vi]		1998-1999	Latest
	1983	1974-83			
	1993	1985-93	Post-neonatal mortality		
			rates	1948	1936-47
- female, by number	1971	1962-71	by sex	1951	1936-50
of children born	1973	1965-73[vi]		1957	1948-56
alive and age	1975	1965-74		1961	1952-60
	1978HS[ii]	1948-77		1966	1956-65
				1967	1962-66

Subject-matter	Year of issue	Time coverage
	1968-1973	Latest
	1974	1965-73
	1975-1979	Latest
	1980	1971-79
	1981-1984	Latest
	1985	1976-84
	1986-1991	Latest
	1992	1983-92
	1993-1995	Latest
	1996	1987-95
	1997	Latest
	1997HS [ii]	1948-96
	1998-2018	Latest
Post-neonatal mortality rates	1971-1973	Latest
by urban/rural residence	1974	1965-73
	1975-1979	Latest
	1980	1971-79
	1981-1984	Latest
	1985	1976-84
	1986-1991	Latest
	1992	1983-92
	1993-1995	Latest
	1996	1987-95
	1997	Latest
	1997HS [ii]	1948-96
	1998-1999	Latest

R

Subject-matter	Year of issue	Time coverage
Rates		*see "Annulments", "Births", "Deaths", "Divorces", "Fertility", "Illiteracy", "Infant Mortality", "Intercensal", "Life Tables", "Literacy", "Marriages", "Maternal mortality", "Natural increase", "Neo natal mortality", "Population growth", "Post neo natal mortality" and "Reproduction"*
Ratios		*see "Births", "Child-woman", "Fertility", "Foetal deaths" and "Perinatal mortality"*
Refugees, by country or area of destination repatriated by the International Refugee Organization	1952	1947-51

Subject-matter	Year of issue	Time coverage
Refugees, by country or area of destination resettled by the International Refugee Organization	1952	1947-51
Religion		*see "Population by religion"*
Reproduction rates, gross and net	1948	1920-47
	1949-50	1900-48
	1954	1920-53
	1965	1930-64
	1969	1963-68
	1975	1966-74
	1978HS [ii]	1948-77
	1981	1962-80
	1986	1967-85
	1997HS [iii]	1948-96
	1999CD [iv]	1980-99
Rural/urban births		*see "Births"*
Rural/urban population		*see "Population, urban/rural residence"*

S

Subject-matter	Year of issue	Time coverage
Sex		*see appropriate subject entry, e.g., "Births", "Death rates", "Migration", "Population", etc.*
Size of (living) family female population by age	1949-50	Latest
	1954	1930-53
	1955	1945-54
	1959	1949-58
	1963	1955-63
	1965	1955-65
	1968	1955-67
	1969	Latest
	1971	1962-71
	1973	1965-73 [vi]
	1975	1965-74
	1978HS [ii]	1948-77
	1981	1972-80
	1986	1977-85
	1997HS [iii]	1948-96
		see also "Children"

Historical index
(See notes at end of index)

Subject-matter	Year of issue	Time coverage	Subject-matter	Year of issue	Time coverage
Special text	*see separate listing in Appendix to this Index*			2002	2002
				2003	2003
				2004	2004
Special topic	*see "Topic of each Demographic Yearbook"*			2005	2005
				2006	2006
				2007	2007
Still births	*see "Foetal deaths, late"*			2008	2008
				2009-2010	2010
Surface area	1949-50-1999	Latest		2011	2011
of continents	2000	2000		2012	2012
	2001	2001		2013	2013
	2002	2002		2014	2014
	2003	2003		2015	2015
	2004	2004		2016	2016
	2005	2005		2017	2017
	2006	2006		2018	2018
	2007	2007			
	2008	2008	**Surface area**	1949-50-1999	Latest
	2009-2010	2010	of the world	2000	2000
	2011	2011		2001	2001
	2012	2012		2002	2002
	2013	2013		2003	2003
	2014	2014		2004	2004
	2015	2015		2005	2005
	2016	2016		2006	2006
	2017	2017		2007	2007
	2018	2018		2008	2008
				2009-2010	2010
				2011	2011
				2012	2012
				2013	2013
Surface area	1948-2018	Latest		2014	2014
of countries or areas				2015	2015
				2016	2016
				2017	2017
Surface area	1964-1999	Latest		2018	2018
of macro-regions	2000	2000			
	2001	2001	**Survivors**	*see "Life tables"*	
	2002	2002			
	2003	2003			
	2004	2004			
	2005	2005			
	2006	2006	**T**		
	2007	2007			
	2008	2008	**Text**	*see separate listing in Appendix to this Index*	
	2009-2010	2010			
	2011	2011			
	2012	2012			
	2013	2013	**Topic of each**		
	2014	2014	**Demographic Yearbook**		
	2015	2015	- Divorce	*see Topic "Marriage and Divorce" below*	
	2016	2016			
	2017	2017			
	2018	2018	- General demography	1948	1900-48
				1953	1950-53
Surface area	1952-1999	Latest	- Historical supplement	1978HS[ii]	1948-78
of regions	2000	2000		1997HS[iii]	1948-97
	2001	2001			

Historical index
(See notes at end of index)

Subject-matter	Year of issue	Time coverage		Subject-matter	Year of issue	Time coverage
					1971	1962-71
- Marriage and Divorce	1958	1930-57			1973	1965-73[vi]
	1968	1920-68			1979	1970-79[vi]
	1976	1957-76			1983	1974-83
	1982	1963-82			1988	1980-88[vi]
	1990	1971-90			1993	1985-93
- Migration (international)	1977	1958-76		· Ethnic characteristics	1956	1945-55
	1989	1975-88			1963	1955-63
					1964	1955-64[vi]
- Mortality	1951	1905-50			1971	1962-71
	1957	1930-56			1973	1965-73[vi]
	1961	1945-61			1979	1970-79[vi]
	1966	1920-66			1983	1974-83
	1967	1900-67			1988	1980-88[vi]
	1974	1965-74			1993	1985-93
	1980	1971-80				
	1985	1976-85		· Fertility characteristics	1940/50	1900-50
	1992	1983-92			1954	1900-53
	1996	1987-96			1955	1945-54
					1959	1935-59
- Natality	1949-50	1932-49			1963	1955-63
	1954	1920-53			1965	1955-65
	1959	1920-58			1969	Latest
	1965	1920-65			1971	1962-71
	1969	1925-69			1973	1965-73[vi]
	1975	1956-75			1975	1965-75
	1981	1962-81			1981	1972-81
	1986	1967-86			1986	1977-86
	1992	1983-92			1992	1983-92
	1999CD[iv]	1980-99				
- Nuptiality	*see Topic "Marriage and Divorce" above*			· Geographic characteristics	1952	1900-51
					1955	1945-54
- Population Ageing and the Situation of Elderly Persons	1991PA[vii]	1950-90			1962	1955-62
					1964	1955-64[vi]
					1971	1962-71
					1973	1965-73[vi]
- Population Census:					1979	1970-79[vi]
· Economic characteristics	1956	1945-55			1983	1974-83
	1964	1955-64			1988	1980-88[vi]
	1972	1962-72			1993	1985-93
	1973	1965-73[vi]				
	1979	1970-79[vi]		· Household characteristics	1955	1945-54
	1984	1974-84			1962	1955-62
	1988	1980-88[vi]			1963	1955-63[vi]
	1994	1985-94			1971	1962-71
	2014[viii]	1995-2014			1973	1965-73[vi]
					1976	1966-75
· Educational characteristics	1955	1945-54			1983	1974-83
	1956	1945-55			1987	1975-86
	1963	1955-63			1995	1985-95
	1964	1955-64[vi]			2013[viii]	1995-2013

Subject-matter	Year of issue	Time coverage
· Personal characteristics	1955	1945-54
	1962	1955-62
	1971	1962-71
	1973	1965-73[vi]
	1979	1970-79[vi]
	1983	1974-83
	1988	1980-88[vi]
	1993	1985-93
- Population trends	1960	1920-60
	1970	1950-70

Subject-matter	Year of issue	Time coverage
U		
Urban/rural births		see "Births"
Urban/rural deaths............		see "Deaths"
Urban/rural infant deaths .		see "Infant deaths"
Urban/rural population		see "Population, urban/rural residence"
Urban/rural population by average size of households		see "Households"

APPENDIX

Special text of each Demographic Yearbook

Divorce:

'Uses of Marriage and Divorce Statistics', 1958.

Marriage:

'Uses of Marriage and Divorce Statistics', 1958.

Households:

'Concepts and definitions of households, householder and institutional population', 1987.

Migration:

'Statistics of International Migration', 1977.

Mortality:

'Recent Mortality Trends', 1951.
'Development of Statistics of Causes of Death', 1951.
'Factors in Declining Mortality', 1957.
'Notes on Methods of Evaluating the Reliability of Conventional Mortality Statistics', 1961.
'Recent Trends of Mortality', 1966.
'Mortality Trends among Elderly Persons', 1991PA[vii].

Natality:

'Graphic Presentation of Trends in Fertility', 1959.
'Recent Trends in Birth Rates', 1965.
'Recent Changes in World Fertility', 1969.

Population

'World Population Trends, 1920-1949', 1949-50.
'Urban Trends and Characteristics', 1952.
'Background to the 1950 Censuses of Population', 1955.
'The World Demographic Situation', 1956.
'How Well Do We Know the Present Size and Trend of the World's Population?', 1960.
'Notes on Availability of National Population Census Data and Methods of Estimating their Reliability', 1962.
'Availability and Adequacy of Selected Data Obtained from Population Censuses Taken 1955-1963', 1963.
'Availability of Selected Population Census Statistics: 1955-1964', 1964.
'Statistical Concepts and Definitions of Urban and Rural Population', 1967.
'Statistical Concepts and Definitions of Household', 1968.
'How Well Do We Know the Present Size and Trend of the World's Population?', 1970.
'United Nations Recommendations on Topics to be Investigated in a Population Census
Compared with Country Practice in National Censuses taken 1965-1971', 1971.
'Statistical Definitions of Urban Population and their Use in Applied Demography', 1972.
'Dates of National Population and Housing Census carried out during the decade 1965-1974', 1974.
'Dates of National Population and/or Housing Censuses taken or anticipated during the decade 1975-1984', 1979.
'Dates of National Population and/or Housing Censuses taken during the decade 1965-1974 and
taken or anticipated during the decade 1975-1984', 1983.
'Dates of National Population and/or Housing Censuses taken during the decade 1975-1984 and taken or
anticipated during the decade 1985-1994', 1988 and 1993.
'Statistics Concerning the Economically Active Population: An Overview', 1984.
'Disability', 1991PA[vii].
'Population Ageing', 1991PA[vii].
'Special Needs for the Study of Population Ageing and Elderly Persons', 1991PA[vii].

Historical index

GENERAL NOTES

This cumulative index covers the contents of each of the 69 issues of the Demographic Yearbook. 'Year of issue' stands for the particular issue in which the indicated subject-matter appears. Unless otherwise specified, 'Time coverage' designates the years for which annual statistics are shown in the Demographic Yearbook referred to in 'Year of issue' column. 'Latest' or '2 latest' indicates that data are for latest available year(s) only.

---

[i] Only titles not available for preceding bibliography.
[ii] Historical Supplement to the 30th DYB published in a separate volume in year 1979.
[iii] Historical Supplement to the 49th DYB published in a separate volume (CD-ROM) in year 2000.
[iv] Supplement to the 51st DYB focusing on natality published in a separate volume (CD-ROM) in year 2002.
[v] Five year average rates.
[vi] Only data not available for preceding issue.
[vii] Population ageing published in separate volume.
[viii] Tables published online.

Index historique
(Voir notes à la fin de l'index)

Sujet	Année de l'édition	Période considérée
A		
Accroissement intercensitaire de la population, taux d'	1948	1900-48
	1949-50	1900-50
	1951	1900-51
	1952	1850-1952
	1953	1850-1953
	1955	1850-1954
	1960	1900-61
	1962	1900-62
	1964	1955-64
	1970	1900-70
	1978 SR [I]	1948-78
	1997 SR [II]	1948-97
Accroissement naturel, taux d'	1958-1978	Dernière
	1978 SR [I]	1948-78
	1979-1997	Dernière
	1997 SR [II]	1948-97
	1998	1995-98
	1999	1996-99
	2000	1995-00
	2001	1997-01
	2002	1998-02
	2003	1999-03
	2004	2000-04
	2005	2001-05
	2006	2002-06
	2007	2003-07
	2008	2004-08
	2009-2010	2006-10
	2011	2007-11
	2012	2008-12
	2013	2009-13
	2014	2010-14
	2015	2011-15
	2016	2012-16
	2017	2013-17
	2018	2014-18
Activité économique	*voir: Population active*	
Age	*voir la rubrique appropriée par sujet, p.ex. Immigrants: Mortalité, taux de: Naissances: Population: etc.*	
Analphabètes	*voir: Population*	

Sujet	Année de l'édition	Période considérée
Alphabétisme selon le sexe, taux d'	1948	Dernière
	1955	1945-54
	1960	1920-60
	1963	1955-63
	1964	1955-64 [III]
	1970	1950-70
	1971	1962-71
	1973	1965-73
	1979	1970-79 [III]
	1983	1974-83
	1988	1980-88 [III]
	1993	1985-93 [III]
Alphabétisme selon le sexe et l'âge, taux d'	1948	Dernière
	1955	1945-54
	1971	1962-71
	1973	1965-73 [III]
	1979	1970-79 [III]
	1983	1974-83
	1988	1980-88 [III]
Alphabètes	*voir: Population*	
Annulations	1958	1948-57
	1968	1958-67
	1976	1966-75
Annulations, taux	1958	1948-57
	1968	1958-67
	1976	1966-75
Avortements, légaux	1971	Dernière
	1972	1964-72
	1973	1965-73
	1974	1965-74
	1975	1965-74
	1976	1965-75
	1977	1967-76
	1978	1968-77
	1979	1969-78
	1980	1971-79
	1981	1972-80
	1982	1973-81
	1983	1974-82
	1984	1975-83
	1985	1976-84
	1986	1977-85
	1987	1978-86
	1988	1979-87
	1989	1980-88
	1990	1981-89

Index historique
(Voir notes à la fin de l'index)

Sujet	Année de l'édition	Période considérée	Sujet	Année de l'édition	Période considérée
	1992	1983-91		1952	1936-51
	1993	1984-92		1953	1950-52
	1994	1985-93		1954	1946-53
	1995	1986-94		1955	1946-54
	1996	1987-95		1956	1947-55
	1997	1988-96		1957	1940-56
	1998	1989-97		1958	1948-57
	1999	1990-98		1959	1949-58
	2000	1991-99		1960	1950-59
	2001	1993-01		1961	1952-61
	2002	1993-02		1962	1953-62
	2003	1994-03		1963	1954-63
	2004	1995-04		1964	1960-64
	2005	1996-05		1965	1961-65
	2006	1997-06		1966	1947-66
	2007	1998-07		1967	1963-67
	2008	1999-08		1968	1964-68
	2009-2010	2001-10		1969	1965-69
	2011	2002-11		1970	1966-70
	2012	2003-12		1971	1967-71
	2013	2004-13		1972	1968-72
	2014	2005-14		1973	1969-73
	2015	2006-15		1974	1965-74
	2016	2007-16		1975	1971-75
	2017	2008-17		1976	1972-76
	2018	2009-18		1977	1973-77
				1978	1974-78
Avortements, légaux	1971-1975	Dernière		1978SR [i]	1948-78
selon l'âge de la mère	1977-1981	Dernière		1979	1975-79
et le nombre des	1983-2018	Dernière		1980	1971-80
naissances vivantes				1981	1977-81
antérieures de la mère				1982	1978-82
				1983	1979-83
				1984	1980-84
B				1985	1976-85
Bibliographie	1948	1930-48		1986	1982-86
	1949-50	1930-50		1987	1983-87
	1951-1952	1930-51 [iv]		1988	1984-88
	1953	1900-53		1989	1985-89
	1954	1900-54 [iv]		1990	1986-90
	1955	1900-55 [iv]		1991	1987-91
				1992	1983-92
C				1993	1989-93
				1994	1990-94
Cause de décès	voir: *Décès*, selon la cause			1995	1991-95
				1996	1987-96
Chômeurs	voir: *Population*			1997	1993-97
				1997SR [ii]	1948-97
Composition ethnique	voir: *Population*			1998	1994-98
				1999	1995-99
Décès	1948	1932-47		2000	1996-00
	1949-50	1934-49		2001	1997-01
	1951	1935-50			

Sujet	Année de l'édition	Période considérée	Sujet	Année de l'édition	Période considérée
	2002	1998-02		1996	1987-95
	2003	1999-03		1997	Dernière
	2004	2000-04		1997SR [II]	1948-96
	2005	2001-05		1998-2006	Dernière
	2006	2002-06			
	2007	2003-07	**Décès**...........................	1951	1947-50
	2008	2004-08	selon la cause	1952	1947-51 [III]
	2009-2010	2006-10		1953	Dernière
	2011	2007-11		1954	1945-53
	2012	2008-12		1955-1956	Dernière
	2013	2009-13		1957	1952-56
	2014	2010-14		1958-1960	Dernière
	2015	2011-15		1961	1955-60
	2016	2012-16		1962-1965	Dernière
	2017	2013-17		1966	1960-65
	2018	2014-18		1967-1973	Dernière
				1974	1965-73
Décès...........................		*voir: Mortalité infantile*		1975-1979	Dernière
d'enfants de moins d'un an				1980	1971-79
				1981-1984	Dernière
				1985	1976-84
Décès...........................	1948	1936-47		1986-1995	Dernière
selon l'âge et le sexe	1951	1936-50		1996	1987-95
	1955-1956	Dernière		1997-2000	Dernière
	1957	1948-56		2002	1995-02
	1958-1960	Dernière		2004	1995-04
	1961	1955-60		2006	2002-06
	1962-1965	Dernière		2008	2004-08
	1966	1961-65		2011	2006-10
	1967-1973	Dernière		2013	2008-12
	1974	1965-73		2015	2010-14
	1975-1979	Dernière		2017	2012-16
	1978 SR [I]	1948-77			
	1980	1971-79	**Décès**...........................	1951	Dernière
	1981-1984	Dernière	selon la cause, l'âge et	1952	Dernière [III]
	1985	1976-84	le sexe	1957	Dernière
	1986-1991	Dernière		1961	Dernière
	1992	1983-92		1967	Dernière
	1993-1995	Dernière		1974	Dernière
	1996	1987-95		1980	Dernière
	1997	Dernière		1985	Dernière
	1997SR [II]	1948-96		1991 VP [V]	1960-90
	1998-2018	Dernière		1996	Dernière
Décès...........................	1967-1973	Dernière	**Décès**...........................	1967	Dernière
selon l'âge et le sexe et la résidence (urbaine/rurale)	1974	1965-73	selon la cause, l'âge et le sexe et la résidence (urbaine/rurale)		
	1975-1979	Dernière			
	1980	1971-79			
	1981-1984	Dernière			
	1985	1976-84	**Décès**...........................	1967	Dernière
	1986-1991	Dernière	selon la cause et le sexe	1974	Dernière
	1992	1983-92		1980	Dernière
	1993-1995	Dernière		1985	Dernière

Index historique
(Voir notes à la fin de l'index)

Sujet	Année de l'édition	Période considérée
	1991VP [v]	1960-90
	1996	Dernière
	2006	2002-06
	2008	2004-08
	2011	2006-10
	2013	2008-12
	2015	2010-14
	2017	2012-16
Décès............... selon la résidence (urbaine/rurale)	1967	Dernière
	1968	1964-68
	1969	1965-69
	1970	1966-70
	1971	1967-71
	1972	1968-72
	1973	1969-73
	1974	1965-74
	1975	1971-75
	1976	1972-76
	1977	1973-77
	1978	1974-78
	1979	1975-79
	1980	1971-80
	1981	1977-81
	1982	1978-82
	1983	1979-83
	1984	1980-84
	1985	1976-85
	1986	1982-86
	1987	1983-87
	1988	1984-88
	1989	1985-89
	1990	1986-90
	1991	1987-91
	1992	1983-92
	1993	1989-93
	1994	1990-94
	1995	1991-95
	1996	1987-96
	1997	1993-97
	1998	1994-98
	1999	1995-99
	2001	1997-01
	2002	1998-02
	2003	1999-03
	2004	2000-04
	2005	2001-05
	2006	2002-06
	2007	2003-07
	2008	2004-08
	2009-2010	2006-10
	2011	2007-11
	2012	2008-12

Sujet	Année de l'édition	Période considérée
	2013	2009-13
	2014	2010-14
	2015	2011-15
	2016	2012-16
	2017	2013-17
	2018	2014-18
Décès............ selon l'état matrimonial, l'âge et le sexe	1958	Dernière
	1961	Dernière
	1967	Dernière
	1974	Dernière
	1980	Dernière
	1985	Dernière
	1991 VP [v]	1950-90
	1996	Dernière
	2003	Dernière
Décès............ selon le mois	1951	1946-50
	1967	1962-66
	1974	1965-73
	1980	1971-79
	1985	1976-84
	2001	1985-00
	2005	2001-05
Décès............ selon la profession et l'âge (sexe masculin)	1957	Dernière
	1961	1957-60
	1967	1962-66
Décès............ selon le type de certification et la cause (nombres)	1957	Dernière
	1974	1965-73
	1980	1971-79
	1985	1976-84
Décès............ selon le type de certification et la cause (pourcentage)	1957	Dernière
	1961	1955-60
	1966	1960-65
	1974	1965-73
	1980	1971-79
	1985	1976-84
Décès, taux de	1948	1932-47
	1949-50	1932-49
	1951	1905-30 [vi]
		1930-50
	1952	1920-34 [vi]
		1934-51
	1953	1920-39 [vi]
		1940-52
	1954	1920-39 [vi]
		1946-53
	1955	1920-34 [vi]
		1946-54

Index historique
(Voir notes à la fin de l'index)

Sujet	Année de l'édition	Période considérée
	1956	1947-55
	1957	1930-56
	1958	1948-57
	1959	1949-58
	1960	1950-59
	1961	1945-59 vi
		1952-61
	1962	1945-54 vi
		1952-62
	1963	1945-59 vi
		1954-63
	1964	1960-64
	1965	1961-65
	1966	1920-64 vi
		1951-66
	1967	1963-67
	1968	1964-68
	1969	1965-69
	1970	1966-70
	1971	1967-71
	1972	1968-72
	1973	1969-73
	1974	1965-74
	1975	1971-75
	1976	1972-76
	1977	1973-77
	1978	1974-78
	1978SR I	1948-78
	1979	1975-79
	1980	1971-80
	1981	1977-81
	1982	1978-82
	1983	1979-83
	1984	1980-84
	1985	1976-85
	1986	1982-86
	1987	1983-87
	1988	1984-88
	1989	1985-89
	1990	1986-90
	1991	1987-91
	1992	1983-92
	1993	1989-93
	1994	1990-94
	1995	1991-95
	1996	1987-96
	1997	1993-97
	1997SR II	1948-97
	1998	1994-98
	1999	1995-99
	2000	1996-00
	2001	1997-01

Sujet	Année de l'édition	Période considérée
	2002	1998-02
	2003	1999-03
	2004	2000-04
	2005	2001-05
	2006	2002-06
	2007	2003-07
	2008	2004-08
	2009-2010	2006-10
	2011	2007-11
	2012	2008-12
	2013	2009-13
	2014	2010-14
	2015	2011-15
	2016	2012-16
	2017	2013-17
	2018	2014-18

Décès, taux de .... *voir: Mortalités infantile*
d'enfants de moins
d'un an

Décès, taux de		
estimatifs, pour les continents	1949-50	1947
	1956-1977	Dernière
	1978-1979	1970-75
	1980-1983	1975-80
	1984-1986	1980-85
	1987-1992	1985-90
	1993-1997	1990-95
	1998-2000	1995-00
	2001-2005	2000-05
	2006-2010	2005-10
	2011-2015	2010-15
	2016-2018	2015-20

Décès, taux de		
estimatifs, pour les grandes régions (continentales)	1964-1977	Dernière
	1978-1979	1970-75
	1980-1983	1975-80
	1984-1986	1980-85
	1987-1992	1985-90
	1993-1997	1990-95
	1998-2000	1995-00
	2001-2005	2000-05
	2006-2010	2005-10
	2011-2015	2010-15
	2016-2018	2015-20

Décès, taux de		
estimatifs, pour les régions	1949-50	1947
	1956-1977	Dernière
	1978-1979	1970-75
	1980-1983	1975-80
	1984-1986	1980-85
	1987-1992	1985-90
	1993-1997	1990-95

Sujet	Année de l'édition	Période considérée
	1998-2000	1995-00
	2001-2005	2000-05
	2006-2010	2005-10
	2011-2015	2010-15
	2016-2018	2015-20
Décès, taux de .... estimatifs, pour l'ensemble du monde	1949-50	1947
	1956-1977	Dernière
	1978-1979	1970-75
	1980-1983	1975-80
	1984-1986	1980-85
	1987-1992	1985-90
	1993-1997	1990-95
	1998-2000	1995-00
	2001-2005	2000-05
	2006-2010	2005-10
	2011-2015	2010-15
	2016-2018	2015-20
Décès, taux de .... selon l'âge et le sexe	1948	1935-47
	1949-50	1936-49
	1951	1936-50
	1952	1936-51
	1953	1940-52
	1954	1946-53
	1955-1956	Dernière
	1957	1948-56
	1961	1952-60
	1966	1950-65
	1967	Dernière
	1972	Dernière
	1974	1965-73
	1975-1978	Dernière
	1978SR [i]	1948-77
	1979	Dernière
	1980	1971-79
	1981-1984	Dernière
	1985	1976-84
	1986-1991	Dernière
	1991 VP [v]	1950-90
	1992	1983-92
	1993-1995	Dernière
	1996	1987-95
	1997	Dernière
	1997SR [ii]	1948-96
	1998-2018	Dernière
Décès, taux de .... selon l'âge, le sexe et la résidence (urbaine/rurale)	1967	Dernière
	1972	Dernière
	1974	1965-73
	1975-1978	Dernière
	1979	Dernière
	1980	1971-79

Sujet	Année de l'édition	Période considérée
	1981-1984	Dernière
	1985	1976-84
	1986-1991	Dernière
	1991 VP [v]	1950-90
	1992	1983-92
	1993-1995	Dernière
	1996	1987-95
	1997	Dernière
	1997SR [ii]	1948-96
	1998-2006	Dernière
Décès, taux de .... selon la cause	1951	1947-49
	1952	1947-51
	1953	1947-52
	1954	1945-53
	1955-1956	Dernière
	1957	1952-56
	1958-1960	Dernière
	1961	1955-60
	1962-1965	Dernière
	1966	1960-65
	1967-1973	Dernière
	1974	1965-73
	1975-1979	Dernière
	1980	1971-79 [vi]
	1981-1984	Dernière
	1985	1976-84
	1986-1995	Dernière
	1996	1987-95
	1997-2000	Dernière
	2002	1985-02
	2004	1995-04
	2006	2002-06
	2008	2004-08
	2011	2006-10
	2013	2008-12
	2015	2010-14
	2017	2012-16
Décès, taux de .... selon la cause, l'âge et le sexe	1957	Dernière
	1961	Dernière
	1991 VP [v]	1960-90
Décès, taux de .... selon la cause et le sexe	1967	Dernière
	1974	Dernière
	1980	Dernière
	1985	Dernière
	1991 VP [v]	1960-90
	1996	Dernière
	2006	2002-06
	2008	2004-08
	2011	2006-10

Sujet	Année de l'édition	Période considérée	Sujet	Année de l'édition	Période considérée
	2013	2008-12		2000	1996-00
	2015	2010-14		2001	1997-01
	2017	2012-16		2002	1998-02
				2003	1999-03
Décès, taux de	1961	Dernière		2004	2000-04
selon l'état	1967	Dernière		2005	2001-05
matrimonial, l'âge et le	1974	Dernière		2006	2002-06
sexe	1980	Dernière		2007	2003-07
	1985	Dernière		2008	2004-08
	1996	Dernière		2009-2010	2006-10
	2003	Dernière		2011	2007-11
				2012	2008-12
Décès, taux de	1957	Dernière		2013	2009-13
selon la profession,				2014	2010-14
l'âge et le sexe				2015	2011-15
				2016	2012-16
Décès, taux de	1961	Dernière		2017	2013-17
selon la profession et	1967	Dernière		2018	2014-18
l'âge (sexe masculin)					
			Densité de population	1949-50	1920-49
Décès, taux de	1967	Dernière	des continents	1951-1999	Dernière
selon la résidence	1968	1964-68		2001	2001
(urbaine/rurale)	1969	1965-69		2002	2002
	1970	1966-70		2003	2003
	1971	1967-71		2004	2004
	1972	1968-72		2005	2005
	1973	1969-73		2006	2006
	1974	1965-74		2007	2007
	1975	1971-75		2008	2008
	1976	1972-76		2009-2010	2010
	1977	1973-77		2011	2011
	1978	1974-78		2012	2012
	1979	1975-79		2013	2013
	1980	1971-80		2014	2014
	1981	1977-81		2015	2015
	1982	1978-82		2016	2016
	1983	1979-83		2017	2017
	1984	1980-84		2018	2018
	1985	1976-85			
	1986	1982-86	**Densité de population**	1964-1999	Dernière
	1987	1983-87	des grandes régions	2000	2000
	1988	1984-88	(continentales)	2001	2001
	1989	1985-89		2002	2002
	1990	1986-90		2003	2003
	1991	1987-91		2004	2004
	1992	1983-92		2005	2005
	1993	1989-93		2006	2006
	1994	1990-94		2007	2007
	1995	1991-95		2008	2008
	1996	1987-96		2009-2010	2010
	1997	1993-97		2011	2011
	1998	1994-98		2012	2012
	1999	1995-99		2013	2013

Sujet	Année de l'édition	Période considérée	Sujet	Année de l'édition	Période considérée
	2014	2014		2004	2004
	2015	2015		2005	2005
	2016	2016		2006	2006
	2017	2017		2007	2007
	2018	2018		2008	2008
				2009-2010	2010
Densité de population	1948-1999	Dernière		2011	2011
des pays ou zones	2000	2000		2012	2012
	2001	2001		2013	2013
	2002	2002		2014	2014
	2003	2003		2015	2015
	2004	2004		2016	2016
	2005	2005		2017	2017
	2006	2006		2018	2018
	2007	2007			
	2008	2008	**Dimension de la famille**		
	2009-2010	2010	**vivante**	1949-1950	Dernière
	2011	2011	selon l'âge des femmes	1954	1930-53
	2012	2012		1955	1945-54
	2013	2013		1959	1949-58
	2014	2014		1963	1955-63
	2015	2015		1965	1955-65
	2016	2016		1968	1955-67
	2017	2017		1969	Dernière
	2018	2018		1971	1962-71
				1973	1965-73 [iii]
				1975	1965-74
Densité de population	1949-50	1920-49		1978SR [i]	1948-77
des régions	1952-1999	Dernière		1981	1972-80
	2000	2000		1986	1977-85
	2001	2001		1997SR [ii]	1948-96
	2002	2002			
	2003	2003		*voir également: Enfants*	
	2004	2004			
	2005	2005	**Divorces**	1951	1935-50
	2006	2006		1952	1936-51
	2007	2007		1953	1950-52
	2008	2008		1954	1946-53
	2009-2010	2010		1955	1946-54
	2011	2011		1956	1947-55
	2012	2012		1957	1948-56
	2013	2013		1958	1940-57
	2014	2014		1959	1949-58
	2015	2015		1960	1950-59
	2016	2016		1961	1952-61
	2017	2017		1962	1953-62
	2018	2018		1963	1954-63
				1964	1960-64
Densité de population	1949-50	1920-49		1965	1961-65
du monde	1952-1999	Dernière		1966	1962-66
	2000	2000		1967	1963-67
	2001	2001		1968	1949-68
	2002	2002		1969	1965-69
	2003	2003			

Sujet	Année de l'édition	Période considérée	Sujet	Année de l'édition	Période considérée
	1970	1966-70		2006	2002-06
	1971	1967-71		2007	2003-07
	1972	1968-72		2008	2004-08
	1973	1969-73		2009-2010	2006-10
	1974	1970-74		2011	2007-11
	1975	1971-75		2012	2008-12
	1976	1957-76		2013	2009-13
	1977	1973-77		2014	2010-14
	1962	1953-62		2015	2011-15
	1963	1954-63		2016	2012-16
	1964	1960-64		2017	2013-17
	1965	1961-65		2018	2014-18
	1966	1962-66			
	1967	1963-67	Divorces	1968	1958-67
	1968	1949-68	selon l'âge de l'épouse	1976	1966-75
	1969	1965-69		1982	1972-81
	1970	1966-70		1987	1975-86
	1971	1967-71		1990	1980-89
	1972	1968-72			
	1973	1969-73	Divorces	1958	1946-57
	1974	1970-74	selon l'âge de l'épouse,	1968	Dernière
	1975	1971-75	classés par âge de	1976	Dernière
	1976	1957-76	l'époux	1982	Dernière
	1977	1973-77		1990	Dernière
	1978	1974-78			
	1979	1975-79	Divorces	1968	1958-67
	1980	1976-80	selon l'âge de l'époux	1976	1966-75
	1981	1977-81		1982	1972-81
	1982	1963-82		1987	1975-86
	1983	1979-83		1990	1980-89
	1984	1980-84			
	1985	1981-85	Divorces	1958	1948-57
	1986	1982-86	selon la durée du	1968	1958-67
	1987	1983-87	mariage	1976	1966-75
	1988	1984-88		1982	1972-81
	1989	1985-89		1990	1980-89
	1990	1971-90		2007	Dernière
	1991	1987-91		2009-2010	Dernière
	1992	1988-92		2012	Dernière
	1993	1989-93		2014	Dernière
	1994	1990-94		2016	Dernière
	1995	1991-95			
	1996	1992-96	Divorces	1958	1946-57
	1997	1993-97	selon la durée du	1968	Dernière
	1998	1994-98	mariage, classés selon	1976	Dernière
	1999	1995-99	l'âge de l'épouse et	1982	Dernière
	2000	1996-00	selon l'âge de l'époux	1990	Dernière
	2001	1997-01			
	2002	1998-02	Divorces	1958	1948-57
	2003	1999-03	selon le nombre	1968	1958-67
	2004	2000-04	d'enfants	1976	1966-75
	2005	2001-05		1982	1972-81
				2007	Dernière

Sujet	Année de l'édition	Période considérée	Sujet	Année de l'édition	Période considérée
Divorces	2002	1998-02		1973	1969-73
selon la résidence	2003	1999-03		1974	1970-74
(urbaine/rurale)	2004	2000-04		1975	1971-75
	2005	2001-05		1976	1957-76
	2006	2002-06		1977	1973-77
	2007	2003-07		1978	1974-78
	2008	2004-08		1979	1975-79
	2009-2010	2006-10		1980	1976-80
	2011	2007-11		1981	1977-81
	2012	2008-12		1982	1963-82
	2013	2009-13		1983	1979-83
	2014	2010-14		1984	1980-84
	2015	2011-15		1985	1981-85
	2016	2012-16		1986	1982-86
	2017	2013-17		1987	1983-87
	2018	2014-18		1988	1984-88
				1989	1985-89
				1990	1971-90
Divortialité, répartition des				1991	1987-91
pourcentages	2007	Dernière		1992	1988-92
selon la durée du	2009-2010	Dernière		1993	1989-93
mariage	2012	Dernière		1994	1990-94
	2014	Dernière		1995	1991-95
	2016	Dernière		1996	1992-96
	2018	Dernière		1997	1993-97
				1998	1994-98
				1999	1995-99
Divortialité, répartition des				2000	1996-00
pourcentages	2007	Dernière		2001	1997-01
selon le nombre				2002	1998-02
d'enfants				2003	1999-03
				2004	2000-04
Divortialité, taux de	1952	1935-51		2005	2001-05
	1953	1936-52		2006	2002-06
	1954	1946-53		2007	2003-07
	1955	1946-54		2008	2004-08
	1956	1947-55		2009-2010	2006-10
	1957	1948-56		2011	2007-11
	1958	1930-57		2012	2008-12
	1959	1949-58		2013	2009-13
	1960	1950-59		2014	2010-14
	1961	1952-61		2015	2011-15
	1962	1953-62		2016	2012-16
	1963	1954-63		2017	2013-17
	1964	1960-64		2018	2014-18
	1965	1961-65			
	1966	1962-66			
	1967	1963-67	**Divortialité, taux de**	1953	1935-52
	1968	1920-64 [vi]	pour la population	1954	1935-53
		1953-68	mariée	1958	1935-56
	1969	1965-69		1968	1935-67
	1970	1966-70		1976	1966-75
	1971	1967-71		1978SR [i]	1948-77
	1972	1968-72		1982	1972-81

Sujet	Année de l'édition	Période considérée
	1990	1980-89
Divortialité, taux de............	1968	Dernière
selon l'âge de l'épouse	1976	Dernière
	1982	Dernière
	1987	1975-86
	1990	Dernière
Divortialité, taux de............	1968	Dernière
selon l'âge de l'époux	1976	Dernière
	1982	Dernière
	1987	1975-86
	1990	Dernière
Divortialité, taux de............	2002	1998-02
selon la résidence (urbaine/rurale)	2003	1999-03
	2004	2000-04
	2005	2001-05
	2006	2002-06
	2007	2003-07
	2008	2004-08
	2009-2010	2006-10
	2011	2007-11
	2012	2008-12
	2013	2009-13
	2014	2010-14
	2015	2011-15
	2016	2012-16
	2017	2013-17
Durée du mariage..............	*voir: Divorces selon la durée du mariage*	

E

Sujet	Année de l'édition	Période considérée
Emigrants..........................	*voir: Migration internationale*	
Enfants, nombre................	1958	1948-57
dont il est tenu compte dans les divorces	1968	1958-67
	1976	1966-75
	1982	1972-81
	1990	1980-89
Enfants, nombre................	1949-50	Dernière
mis au monde, selon l'âge de la mère	1954	1930-53
	1955	1945-54
	1959	1949-58
	1963	1955-63
	1965	1955-65
	1969	Dernière
	1971	1962-71
	1973	1965-73 [iii]
	1975	1965-74

Sujet	Année de l'édition	Période considérée
	1978SR [i]	1948-77
	1981	1972-80
	1986	1977-85
	1997SR [ii]	1948-96
Enfants, nombre..............	1971	1962-71
mis au monde, selon l'âge de la mère et la résidence (urbaine/rurale)	1973	1965-73 [iii]
	1975	1965-74
	1981	1972-80
	1986	1977-85
	1997SR [ii]	1948-96
Enfants, nombre..............	1949-50	Dernière
nés vivants, selon l'âge de la mère	1954	1930-53
	1955	1945-54
	1959	1949-58
	1963	1955-63
	1965	1955-65
	1968	1955-67
	1969	Dernière
	1971	1962-71
	1973	1965-73 [iii]
	1975	1965-74
	1978SR [i]	1948-77
	1981	1972-80
	1986	1977-85
	1997SR [ii]	1948-96
Enfants, nombre	1971	1962-71
nés vivants, selon l'âge de la mère et la résidence (urbaine/rurale)	1973	1965-73 [iii]
	1975	1965-74
	1981	1972-80
	1986	1977-85
	1997SR [ii]	1948-96
Espérance de vie................	*voir: Mortalité, tables de*	
Etat matrimonial................	*voir la rubrique appropriée par sujet, p.ex., Décès, Population, etc.*	

F

Sujet	Année de l'édition	Période considérée
Fécondité, indice synthétique de...................	1986	1967-1985
	1987-1997	Dernière
	1997SR [ii]	1948-96
	1998	1995-98
	1999	1996-99
	1999CD [vii]	1980-99
	2000	1995-00
	2001	1997-01
	2002	1998-02
	2003	1999-03
	2004	2000-04

Sujet	Année de l'édition	Période considérée
	2005	2001-05
	2006	2002-06
	2007	2003-07
	2008	2004-08
	2009-2010	2006-10
	2011	2007-11
	2012	2008-12
	2013	2009-13
	2014	2010-14
	2015	2011-15
	2016	2012-16
	2017	2013-17
	2018	2014-18
Fécondité proportionnelle..	1949-50	1900-50
	1954	1900-52
	1955	1945-54
	1959	1935-59
	1963	1955-63
	1965	1955-65
	1969	Dernière
	1975	1966-74
	1978SR [i]	1948-77
	1981	1962-80
	1986	1967-85
	1997SR [ii]	1948-96
	1999CD [vii]	1980-99
Fécondité, taux global de...	1948	1936-47
	1949-50	1936-49
	1951	1936-50
	1952	1936-50
	1953	1936-52
	1954	1936-53
	1955-1956	Dernière
	1959	1949-58
	1960-1964	Dernière
	1965	1955-64
	1966-1974	Dernière
	1975	1966-74
	1976-1978	Dernière
	1978SR [i]	1948-77
	1979-1980	Dernière
	1981	1962-80
	1982-1985	Dernière
	1986	1977-85
	1987-1991	Dernière
	1992	1983-92
	1993-1997	Dernière
	1997SR [ii]	1948-96
	1998-2018	Dernière

I

Sujet	Année de l'édition	Période considérée
Illégitime	1961	1952-60
morts fœtales tardives	1965	5-Dernières
	1969	1963-68
	1975	1966-74
	1981	1972-80
	1986	1977-85
	voir également: morts fœtales tardives	
Illégitime	1961	1952-60
morts fœtales tardives, rapports de	1965	5-Dernières
	1969	1963-68
	1975	1966-74
	1981	1972-80
	1986	1977-85
Illégitime	1959	1949-58
naissances	1965	1955-64
	1969	1963-68
	1975	1966-74
	1981	1972-80
	1986	1977-85
	1999CD [vii]	1990-98
	voir également: Naissances	
Illégitime	1959	1949-58
naissances, rapports de	1965	1955-64
	1969	1963-68
	1975	1966-74
	1981	1972-80
	1986	1977-85
	1999CD [vii]	1990-98
Immigrants	*voir: Migration international*	
Instruction, degré d'	*voir: Population*	

L

Sujet	Année de l'édition	Période considérée
Langue et sexe	*voir: Population*	
Localités	*voir: Population, selon l'importance des localités*	

M

Sujet	Année de l'édition	Période considérée
Mariages	1948	1932-47
	1949-50	1934-49
	1951	1935-50
	1952	1936-51
	1953	1950-52

Sujet	Année de l'édition	Période considérée	Sujet	Année de l'édition	Période considérée
	1954	1946-53		2006	2002-06
	1955	1946-54		2007	2003-07
	1956	1947-55		2008	2004-08
	1957	1948-56		2009-2010	2006-10
	1958	1940-57		2011	2007-11
	1959	1949-58		2012	2008-12
	1960	1950-59		2013	2009-13
	1961	1952-61		2014	2010-14
	1962	1953-62		2015	2011-15
	1963	1954-63		2016	2012-16
	1964	1960-64		2017	2013-17
	1965	1956-65		2018	2014-18
	1966	1962-66			
	1967	1963-67	**Mariages**	1948	1936-47
	1968	1949-68	selon l'âge de l'épouse	1949-50	1936-49
	1969	1965-69		1958	1948-57
	1970	1966-70		1959-1967	Dernière
	1971	1967-71		1968	1958-67
	1972	1968-72		1969-1975	Dernière
	1973	1969-73		1976	1966-75
	1974	1970-74		1977-1981	Dernière
	1975	1971-75		1982	1972-81
	1976	1957-76		1983-1986	Dernière
	1977	1973-77		1987	1975-86
	1978	1974-78		1988-1989	Dernière
	1979	1975-79		1990	1980-89
	1980	1976-80		1991-1997	Dernière
	1981	1977-81		1998	1993-97
	1982	1963-82		1999	1994-98
	1983	1979-83		2000	1995-99
	1984	1980-84		2001	1997-01
	1985	1981-85		2002	1998-02
	1986	1982-86		2003	1999-03
	1987	1983-87		2004	2000-04
	1988	1984-88		2005	2001-05
	1989	1985-89		2006-2018	Dernière
	1990	1971-90			
	1991	1987-91	**Mariages**	1958	1948-57
	1992	1988-92	selon l'âge de l'épouse	1968	Dernière
	1993	1989-93	et l'âge de l'époux	1976	Dernière
	1994	1990-94		1982	Dernière
	1995	1991-95		1990	Dernière
	1996	1992-96		2006-2018	Dernière
	1997	1993-97			
	1998	1994-98	**Mariages**	1958	1948-57
	1999	1995-99	selon l'âge de l'épouse	1968	Dernière
	2000	1996-00	et l'état matrimonial	1976	Dernière
	2001	1997-01	antérieur	1982	Dernière
	2002	1998-02		1990	Dernière
	2003	1999-03			
	2004	2000-04	**Mariages**	1948	1936-47
	2005	2001-05	selon l'âge de l'époux	1949-50	1936-49
				1958	1948-57

Sujet	Année de l'édition	Période considérée	Sujet	Année de l'édition	Période considérée
	1959-1967	Dernière	Mariages	1949-50	Dernière
	1968	1958-67	selon l'état matrimonial	1958	1948-57
	1969-1975	Dernière	antérieur de l'époux et	1968	1958-67
	1976	1966-75	l'état matrimonial	1976	1966-75
	1977-1981	Dernière	antérieur de l'épouse	1982	1972-81
	1982	1972-81		1990	1980-89
	1983-1986	Dernière			
	1987	1975-86	Mariages	1968	Dernière
	1988-1989	Dernière	selon la résidence	1969	1965-69
	1990	1980-89	(urbaine/rurale)	1970	1966-70
	1991-1997	Dernière		1971	1967-71
	1998	1993-97		1972	1968-72
	1999	1994-98		1973	1969-73
	2000	1995-99		1974	1970-74
	2001	1997-01		1975	1971-75
	2002	1998-02		1976	1957-76
	2003	1999-03		1977	1973-77
	2004	2000-04		1978	1974-78
	2005	2001-05		1979	1975-79
	2006-2018	Dernière		1980	1976-80
				1981	1977-81
Mariages	1958	1948-57		1982	1963-82
selon l'âge de l'époux	1968	Dernière		1983	1979-83
et l'âge de l'épouse	1976	Dernière		1984	1980-84
	1982	Dernière		1985	1981-85
	1990	Dernière		1986	1982-86
	2006-2018	Dernière		1987	1983-87
				1988	1984-88
Mariages	1958	1946-57		1989	1985-89
selon l'âge de l'époux	1968	Dernière		1990	1971-90
et l'état matrimonial	1976	Dernière		1991	1987-91
antérieur	1982	Dernière		1992	1988-92
	1990	Dernière		1993	1989-93
				1994	1990-94
Mariages	1958	1946-57		1995	1991-95
selon l'état matrimonial	1968	Dernière		1996	1992-96
antérieur de l'épouse et	1976	Dernière		1997	1993-97
l'âge	1982	Dernière		1998	1994-98
	1990	Dernière		1999	1995-99
				2000	1996-00
Mariages	1949-50	Dernière		2001	1997-01
selon l'état matrimonial	1958	1948-57		2002	1998-02
antérieur de l'épouse et	1968	1958-67		2003	1999-03
l'état matrimonial	1976	1966-75		2004	2000-04
antérieur de l'époux	1982	1972-81		2005	2001-05
	1990	1980-89		2006	2002-06
				2007	2003-07
Mariages	1958	1946-57		2008	2004-08
selon l'état matrimonial	1968	Dernière		2009-2010	2006-10
antérieur de l'époux et	1976	Dernière		2011	2007-11
l'âge	1982	Dernière		2012	2008-12
	1990	Dernière		2013	2009-13
				2014	2010-14

Sujet	Année de l'édition	Période considérée
	2015	2011-15
	2016	2012-16
	2017	2013-17
	2018	2014-18
Mariages	1968	1963-67
selon le mois		
Mariages, premiers	1976	Dernière
classification détaillé	1982	1972-81
selon l'âge de l'épouse	1990	1980-89
et de l'époux		
Mariages, taux de	*voir: Nuptialité, taux de*	
Ménages	1955	1945-54
	1962	1955-62
	1963	1955-63 [iii]
	1968	Dernière
	1971	1962-71
	1973	1965-73 [iii]
	1976	Dernière
	1982	Dernière
	1987	1975-86
	1990	1980-89
	1995	1985-95
Ménages	1962	1955-62
dimension moyenne	1963	1955-63 [iii]
des	1968	Dernière
	1971	1962-71
	1973	1965-73 [iii]
	1976	Dernière
	1982	Dernière
	1987	1975-86
	1990	1980-89
	1995	1985-95
Ménages	1987	1975-86
selon le lien avec le	1995	1985-95
chef de ménage et la		
résidence		
urbaine/rurale		
Ménages	1973	1965-73
nombre de noyaux	1976	Dernière
familiaux, selon la	1982	Dernière
dimension des	1987	1975-86
	1990	1980-89
Ménages	1955	1945-54
population dans	1962	1955-62
chaque dimension des	1963	1955-63 [iii]
	1968	Dernière

Sujet	Année de l'édition	Période considérée
	1971	1962-71
	1973	1965-73
	1976	Dernière
	1982	Dernière
	1987	1975-86
	1990	1980-89
	1995	1985-95
Ménages	1991 VP [v]	Dernière
selon la dimension et		
personnes 60+		
Ménages	1955	1945-54
population dans	1962	1955-62
chaque catégorie de	1963	1955-63 [iii]
	1968	Dernière
	1971	1962-71
	1973	1965-73 [iii]
	1976	Dernière
	1982	Dernière
	1987	1975-86
	1990	1980-89
	1995	1985-95
Ménages	1987	1975-86
répartition des chefs,	1995	1985-95
âge, sexe et résidence		
urbaine/rurale		
Ménages	1955	1945-54
selon la dimension et la	1962	1955-62
résidence	1963	1955-63 [iii]
(urbaine/rurale	1971	1962-71
	1973	1965-73 [iii]
	1976	Dernière
	1982	Dernière
	1987	1975-86
	1990	1980-89
	1995	1985-95
Ménages	1991 VP [v]	Dernière
selon le sexe et		
personnes 60+		
Ménages	1987	1976-86
selon l'âge et le sexe du	1995	1985-95
chef de ménage, la		
dimension et la		
résidence		
urbaine/rurale		
Ménages	1987	1975-86
selon la situation	1995	1985-95
matrimoniale et la		

Sujet	Année de l'édition	Période considérée	Sujet	Année de l'édition	Période considérée
résidence urbaine/rurale				1959	1953-58
				1962	1956-61
				1966	1960-65
Ménages....................	1987	1975-86		1968	1966-67
selon le type de famille et la résidence urbaine/rurale	1995	1985-95		1977	1967-76
				1985	1975-84
				1989	1979-88
				1996	1986-95
Ménages....................	1987	1975-86			
selon le type et la résidence urbaine/rurale	1995	1985-95	**Migration internationale** .... immigrants (à long terme) selon l'âge et le sexe	1948	1945-47
				1949-50	1946-48
				1951	1948-50
				1952	1949-51
Migration internationale .... continentale et intercontinentale	1948	1936-47		1954	1950-53
	1977	1967-76		1957	1953-56
				1959	1955-58
				1962	1958-61
Migration internationale .... émigrants (à long terme) selon l'âge et le sexe	1948	1945-47		1966	1960-65
	1949-50	1946-48		1970	1962-69
	1951	1948-50		1977	1967-76
	1952	1949-51		1989	1975-88
	1954	1950-53			
	1957	1953-56	**Migration internationale** .... immigrants (à long terme) selon le pays ou zone de dernière résidence	1948	1945-47
	1959	1955-58		1949-50	1945-48
	1962	1958-61		1951	1948-50
	1966	1960-65		1952	1949-51
	1970	1962-69		1954	1950-53
	1977	1967-76		1957	1953-56
	1989	1975-88		1959	1956-58
				1977	1958-76
Migration internationale	1948	1945-47		1989	1975-88
	1949-50	1945-48			
	1951	1948-50	**Migration internationale** .... réfugiés rapatriés par l'Organisation internationale pour les réfugiés, selon le pays ou zone de destination	1952	1947-51
	1952	1949-51			
	1954	1950-53			
	1957	1953-56			
	1959	1956-58			
	1977	1958-76			
	1989	1975-88			
			Migration internationale .... réfugiés réinstallés par l'Organisation Internationale pour les Réfugiés, selon le pays ou zone de destination	1952	1947-51
Migration internationale .... entrées	1970	1963-69			
	1972	1965-71			
	1974	1967-73			
	1976	1969-75			
	1977	1967-76	**Migration internationale** .... sorties	1970	1963-69
	1985	1975-84		1972	1965-71
	1989	1979-88		1974	1967-73
	1996	1986-95		1976	1969-75
				1977	1967-76
Migration internationale .... entrées, par catégories principales	1949-50	1945-49		1985	1975-84
	1951	1946-50		1989	1979-88
	1952	1947-51		1996	1986-95
	1954	1948-53			
	1957	1951-56			

Sujet	Année de l'édition	Période considérée	Sujet	Année de l'édition	Période considérée
Migration internationale	1949-50	1945-49		1955	1946-54
sorties par catégories	1951	1946-50		1956	1947-55
principales	1952	1947-51		1957	1948-56
	1954	1948-53		1958	1948-57
	1957	1951-56		1959	1920-54 [vi]
	1959	1953-58			1953-58
	1962	1956-61		1960	1950-59
	1966	1960-65		1961	1945-49 [vi]
	1968	1966-67			1952-60
	1977	1967-76		1962	1945-54 [vi]
	1985	1975-84			1952-61
	1989	1979-88		1963	1945-59 [vi]
	1996	1986-95			1953-62
				1964	1959-63
Mortalité	*voir: Décès; Décès, taux de;*			1965	1950-64 [vi]
	Enfants de moins d'un an,				1955-64
	décès d'; Mortalité fœtale,			1966	1950-64 [vi]
	rapports de; Mortalité				1956-65
	infantile, taux de; Mortalité			1967	1962-66
	maternelle, taux de; Mortalité			1968	1963-67
	néonatale, taux de; Mortalité			1969	1950-64 [vi]
	périnatale; Mortalité post-			1969	1959-68
	néonatale, taux de; Mortalité,			1970	1965-69
	tables de; Mortalité, taux de			1971	1966-70
	Morts fœtales; Morts			1972	1967-71
	néonatales; Morts post-			1973	1968-72
	néonatales			1974	1965-73
				1975	1966-74
Mortalité fœtale.................	*voir: Morts fœtales*			1976	1971-75
				1977	1972-76
Mortalité fœtale, rapports				1978	1973-77
de...	1957	1950-56		1979	1974-78
selon la période de	1959	1949-58		1980	1971-79
gestation	1961	1952-60		1981	1972-80
	1965	5-Dernières		1982	1977-81
	1966	1956-65		1983	1978-82
	1967-1968	Dernière		1984	1979-83
	1969	1963-68		1985	1975-84
	1974	1965-73		1986	1977-85
	1975	1966-74		1987	1982-86
	1980	1971-79		1988	1983-87
	1981	1972-80		1989	1984-88
	1985	1976-84		1964	1959-63
	1986	1977-85		1990	1985-89
	1996	1987-95		1991	1986-90
	1999CD [vii]	1990-98		1992	1987-91
				1993	1988-92
Mortalité fœtale tardive	*voir: Morts fœtales tardive*			1994	1989-93
				1995	1990-94
Mortalité fœtale tardive,				1996	1987-95
rapports de.........................	1951	1935-50		1997	1992-96
	1952	1935-51		1998	1993-97
	1953	1936-52			
	1954	1938-53			

Sujet	Année de l'édition	Période considérée
	1999	1994-98
	1999CD [vii]	1990-98
	2000	1995-99
	2001	1997-01
	2002	1998-02
	2003	1999-03
	2004	2000-04
	2005	2001-05
	2006	2002-06
	2007	2003-07
	2008	2004-08
	2009-2010	2006-10
	2011	2007-11
	2012	2008-12
	2013	2009-13
	2014	2010-14
	2015	2011-15
	2016	2012-16
	2017	2013-17
	2018	2014-18
Mortalité fœtale tardive, rapports de	1961	1952-60
illégitimes	1965	5-Dernières
Mortalité fœtale tardive, rapports de	1959	1949-58
légitimes	1965	1955-64
	1969	1963-68
	1975	1966-74
	1981	1972-80
	1986	1977-85
Mortalité fœtale tardive, rapports de	1959	1949-58
légitimes selon l'âge de la mère	1965	1955-64
	1969	1963-68
	1975	1966-74
	1981	1972-80
	1986	1977-85
Mortalité fœtale tardive, rapports de	1954	1936-53
selon l'âge de la mère	1959	1949-58
	1965	1955-64
	1969	1963-68
	1975	1966-74
	1981	1972-80
	1986	1977-85
	1999CD [vii]	1990-98

Sujet	Année de l'édition	Période considérée
Mortalité fœtale tardive, rapports de	1954	Dernière
selon l'âge de la mère	1959	1949-58
et le rang de naissance	1965	3-Dernières
	1969	1963-68
	1975	1966-74
	1981	1972-80
	1986	1977-85
	1999CD [vii]	1990-98
Mortalité fœtale tardive, rapports de	1957	1950-56
selon la période de gestation	1959	1949-58
	1961	1952-60
	1965	5-Dernières
	1966	1956-65
	1967-1968	Dernière
	1969	1963-68
	1974	1965-73
	1975	1966-74
	1980	1971-79
	1981	1972-80
	1985	1976-84
	1986	1977-85
	1996	1987-95
Mortalité fœtale tardive, rapports de	1971	1966-70
selon la résidence (urbaine/rurale)	1972	1967-71
	1973	1968-72
	1974	1965-73
	1975	1966-74
	1976	1971-75
	1977	1972-76
	1978	1973-77
	1979	1974-78
	1980	1971-79
	1981	1972-80
	1982	1977-81
	1983	1978-82
	1984	1979-83
	1985	1975-84
	1986	1977-85
	1987	1982-86
	1988	1983-87
	1989	1984-88
	1990	1985-89
	1991	1986-90
	1992	1987-91
	1993	1988-92
	1994	1989-93
	1995	1990-94
	1996	1987-95

Sujet	Année de l'édition	Période considérée	Sujet	Année de l'édition	Période considérée
	1997	1992-96		1978	1974-78
	1998	1993-97		1978SR [I]	1948-78
	1999	1994-98		1979	1975-79
	1999CD [vii]	1990-98		1980	1971-80
	2000	1995-99		1981	1977-81
	2001	1997-01		1982	1978-82
	2002	1998-02		1983	1979-83
	2003	1999-03		1984	1980-84
	2004	2000-04		1985	1976-85
	2005	2001-05		1986	1982-86
	2006	2002-06		1987	1983-87
	2007	2003-07		1988	1984-88
	2008	2004-08		1989	1985-89
	2009-2010	2006-10		1990	1986-90
	2011	2007-11		1991	1987-91
	2012	2008-12		1992	1983-92
	2013	2009-13		1993	1989-93
	2014	2010-14		1994	1990-94
	2015	2011-15		1995	1991-95
	2016	2012-16		1996	1987-96
	2017	2013-17		1997	1993-97
	2018	2014-18		1997SR [II]	1948-97
				1998	1994-98
Mortalité infantile				1999	1995-99
(nombres)	1948	1932-47		2000	1996-00
	1949-50	1934-49		2001	1997-01
	1951	1935-50		2002	1998-02
	1952	1936-51		2003	1999-03
	1953	1950-52		2004	2000-04
	1954	1946-53		2005	2001-05
	1955	1946-54		2006	2002-06
	1956	1947-55		2007	2003-07
	1957	1948-56		2008	2004-08
	1958	1948-57		2009-2010	2006-10
	1959	1949-58		2011	2007-11
	1960	1950-59		2012	2008-12
	1961	1952-61		2013	2009-13
	1962	1953-62		2014	2010-14
	1963	1954-63		2015	2011-15
	1964	1960-64		2016	2012-16
	1965	1961-65		2017	2013-17
	1966	1947-66		2018	2014-18
	1967	1963-67				
	1968	1964-68	**Mortalité infantile**		
	1969	1965-69	**(nombres)**	1948	1936-47
	1970	1966-70	selon l'âge et le sexe	1951	1936-49
	1971	1967-71		1957	1948-56
	1972	1968-72		1961	1952-60
	1973	1969-73		1962-1965	Dernière
	1974	1965-74		1966	1956-65
	1975	1971-75		1967-1973	Dernière
	1976	1972-76		1974	1965-73
	1977	1973-77		1975-1979	Dernière

Sujet	Année de l'édition	Période considérée
	1980	1971-79
	1981-1984	Dernière
	1985	1976-84
	1986-1991	Dernière
	1992	1983-92
	1993-1995	Dernière
	1996	1987-95
	1997-2004	Dernière
	2005	1996-05
	2006-2018	Dernière
Mortalité infantile (nombres).......... selon l'âge et le sexe et la résidence (urbaine/rurale)	1968-1973	Dernière
	1974	1965-73
	1975-1979	Dernière
	1980	1971-79
	1981-1984	Dernière
	1985	1976-84
	1986-1991	Dernière
	1992	1983-92
	1993-1995	Dernière
	1996	1987-95
	1997-1999	Dernière
Mortalité infantile (nombres).......... selon la résidence (urbaine/rurale)	1967	Dernière
	1968	1964-68
	1969	1965-69
	1970	1966-70
	1971	1967-71
	1972	1968-72
	1973	1969-73
	1974	1965-74
	1975	1971-75
	1976	1972-76
	1977	1973-77
	1978	1974-78
	1979	1975-79
	1980	1971-80
	1981	1977-81
	1982	1978-82
	1983	1979-83
	1984	1980-84
	1985	1976-85
	1986	1982-86
	1987	1983-87
	1988	1984-88
	1989	1985-89
	1990	1986-90
	1991	1987-91
	1992	1983-92
	1993	1989-93
	1994	1990-94

Sujet	Année de l'édition	Période considérée
	1995	1991-95
	1996	1987-96
	1997	1993-97
	1998	1994-98
	1999	1995-99
	2000	1996-00
	2001	1997-01
	2002	1998-02
	2003	1999-03
	2004	2000-04
	2005	2001-05
	2006	2002-06
	2007	2003-07
	2008	2004-08
	2009-2010	2006-10
	2011	2007-11
	2012	2008-12
	2013	2009-13
	2014	2010-14
	2015	2011-15
	2016	2012-16
	2017	2013-17
	2018	2014-18
Mortalité infantile (nombres).......... selon le mois	1967	1962-66
	1974	1965-73
	1980	1971-79
	1985	1976-84
Mortalité infantile, taux de	1948	1932-47
	1949-50	1932-49
	1951	1930-50
	1952	1920-34 [vi]
		1934-51
	1953	1920-39 [vi]
		1940-52
	1954	1920-39 [vi]
		1946-53
	1955	1920-34 [vi]
		1946-54
	1956	1947-55
	1957	1948-56
	1958	1948-57
	1959	1949-58
	1960	1950-59
	1961	1945-59 [vi]
		1952-61
	1962	1945-59 [vi]
		1952-62
	1963	1945-59 [vi]
		1954-63
	1964	1960-64

Sujet	Année de l'édition	Période considérée	Sujet	Année de l'édition	Période considérée
	1965	1961-65		2015	2011-15
	1966	1920-64 [vi]		2016	2012-16
		1951-66		2017	2013-17
	1967	1963-67		2018	2014-18
	1968	1964-68			
	1969	1965-69	**Mortalité infantile, taux de**	1948	1936-47
	1970	1966-70	selon l'âge et le sexe	1951	1936-49
	1971	1967-71		1957	1948-56
	1972	1968-72		1961	1952-60
	1973	1969-73		1966	1956-65
	1974	1965-74		1967	1962-66
	1975	1971-75		1971-1973	Dernière
	1976	1972-76		1974	1965-73
	1977	1973-77		1975-1979	Dernière
	1978	1974-78		1980	1971-79
	1978SR [I]	1948-78		1981-1984	Dernière
	1979	1975-79		1985	1976-84
	1980	1971-80		1986-1991	Dernière
	1981	1977-81		1992	1983-92
	1982	1978-82		1993-1995	Dernière
	1983	1979-83		1996	1987-95
	1984	1980-84		1997-2018	Dernière
	1985	1976-85			
	1986	1982-86	**Mortalité infantile, taux de**	1971-1973	Dernière
	1987	1983-87	selon l'âge et le sexe et	1974	1965-73
	1988	1984-88	la résidence	1975-1979	Dernière
	1989	1985-89	(urbaine/rurale)	1980	1971-79
	1990	1986-90		1981-1984	Dernière
	1991	1987-91		1985	1976-84
	1992	1983-92		1986-1991	Dernière
	1993	1989-93		1992	1983-92
	1994	1990-94		1993-1995	Dernière
	1995	1991-95		1996	1987-95
	1996	1987-96		1997-1999	Dernière
	1997	1993-97			
	1997SR [II]	1948-97	**Mortalité infantile, taux de**	1967	Dernière
	1998	1994-98	selon la résidence	1968	1964-68
	1999	1995-99	(urbaine/rurale)	1969	1965-69
	2000	1996-00		1970	1966-70
	2001	1997-01		1971	1967-71
	2002	1998-02		1972	1968-72
	2003	1999-03		1973	1969-73
	2004	2000-04		1974	1965-74
	2005	2001-05		1975	1971-75
	2006	2002-06		1976	1972-76
	2007	2003-07		1977	1973-77
	2008	2004-08		1978	1974-78
	2009-2010	2006-10		1979	1975-79
	2011	2007-11		1980	1971-80
	2012	2008-12		1981	1977-81
	2013	2009-13		1982	1978-82
	2014	2010-14		1983	1979-83
				1984	1980-84

Sujet	Année de l'édition	Période considérée	Sujet	Année de l'édition	Période considérée
	1985	1976-85		1985	1975-84
	1986	1982-86		1986	1976-85
	1987	1983-87		1987	1977-86
	1988	1984-88		1988	1978-87
	1989	1985-89		1989	1979-88
	1990	1986-90		1990	1980-89
	1991	1987-91		1991	1981-90
	1992	1983-92		1992	1982-91
	1993	1989-93		1993	1983-92
	1994	1990-94		1994	1984-93
	1995	1991-95		1995	1985-94
	1996	1987-96		1996	1986-95
	1997	1993-97		1997	1987-96
	1998	1994-98		1998	1988-97
	1999	1995-99		1999	1989-98
	2000	1996-00		2000	1991-00
	2001	1997-01		2001	1991-00
	2002	1998-02		2002	1995-02
	2003	1999-03		2003	1995-02
	2004	2000-04		2004	1995-04
	2005	2001-05		2005	1995-04
	2006	2002-06		2006	1997-06
	2007	2003-07		2007	1997-06
	2008	2004-08		2008	1999-08
	2009-2010	2006-10		2009-2010	1999-08
	2011	2007-11		2011-2012	2001-10
	2012	2008-12		2013-2014	2003-12
	2013	2009-13		2015-2016	2005-14
	2014	2010-14		2017-2018	2007-16
	2015	2011-15			
	2016	2012-16	**Mortalité maternelle**		
	2017	2013-17	**(nombres)**............................	1951	Dernière
	2018	2014-18	selon l'âge	1952	Dernière
				1957	Dernière
Mortalité maternelle				1961	Dernière
(nombres)............................	1951	1947-50		1967	Dernière
	1952	1947-51		1974	Dernière
	1953	Dernière		1980	Dernière
	1954	1945-53		1985	Dernière
	1955-1956	Dernière			
	1957	1952-56	**Mortalité maternelle, taux**		
	1958-1960	Dernière	**de**............................	1951	1947-50
	1961	1955-60		1952	1947-51
	1962-1965	Dernière		1953	Dernière
	1966	1960-65		1954	1945-53
	1967-1973	Dernière		1955-1956	Dernière
	1974	1965-73		1957	1952-56
	1975-1979	Dernière		1958-1960	Dernière
	1980	1971-79		1961	1955-60
	1981	1972-80		1962-1965	Dernière
	1982	1972-81		1966	1960-65
	1983	1973-82		1967-1973	Dernière
	1984	1974-83		1974	1965-73

Sujet	Année de l'édition	Période considérée	Sujet	Année de l'édition	Période considérée
	1975	1966-74	**Mortalité néonatale**............	1968-1973	Dernière
	1976	1966-75	selon le sexe et la	1974	1965-73
	1977	1967-76	résidence	1975-1979	Dernière
	1978	1968-77	(urbaine/rurale)	1980	1971-79
	1979	1969-78		1981-1984	Dernière
	1980	1971-79		1985	1976-84
	1981	1972-80		1986-1991	Dernière
	1982	1972-81		1992	1983-92
	1983	1973-82		1993-1995	Dernière
	1984	1974-83		1996	1987-95
	1985	1975-84		1997	Dernière
	1986	1976-85		1997SR [II]	1948-96
	1987	1977-86		1998-1999	Dernière
	1988	1978-87			
	1989	1979-88	**Mortalité néonatale, taux de**............	1948	1936-47
	1990	1980-89	selon le sexe	1951	1936-50
	1991	1981-90		1957	1948-56
	1992	1982-91		1961	1952-60
	1993	1983-92		1966	1956-65
	1994	1984-93		1967	1962-66
	1995	1985-94		2000-2018	Dernière
	1996	1986-95			
	1997	1987-96	**Mortalité néonatale, taux de**............	1968	Dernière
	1998	1988-97	selon le sexe et la	1971-1973	Dernière
	1999	1989-98	résidence	1974	1965-73
	2000	1991-00	(urbaine/rurale)	1975-1979	Dernière
	2001	1991-00		1980	1971-79
	2002	1995-02		1981-1984	Dernière
	2003	1995-02		1985	1976-84
	2004	1995-04		1986-1991	Dernière
	2005	1995-04		1992	1983-92
	2006	1997-06		1993-1995	Dernière
	2007	1997-06		1996	1987-95
	2008	1999-08		1997	Dernière
	2009-2010	1999-08		1997SR [II]	1948-96
	2011-2012	2001-10		1998-1999	Dernière
	2013-2014	2003-12			
	2015-2016	2005-14	**Mortalité périnatale (nombres)**............	1961	1952-60
	2017-2018	2007-16		1966	1956-65
				1971	1966-70
Mortalité maternelle, taux de............	1957	Dernière		1974	1965-73
selon l'âge	1961	Dernière		1980	1971-79
				1985	1976-84
Mortalité néonatale...........	1948	1936-47		1996	1987-95
selon le sexe (nombres)	1951	1936-50			
	1957	1948-56	**Mortalité périnatale (nombres)**............	1971	1966-70
	1961	1952-60	selon la résidence	1974	1965-73
	1963-1965	Dernière	(urbaine/rurale)	1980	1971-79
	1966	1961-65		1985	1976-84
	1967	1962-66			
	2000-2018	Dernière			

Sujet	Année de l'édition	Période considérée	Sujet	Année de l'édition	Période considérée
	1996	1987-95		1998-1999	Dernière
Mortalité périnatale, rapports de......................	1961	1952-60	**Mortalité post-néonatale, taux de**	1948	1936-47
	1966	1956-65	selon le sexe	1951	1936-50
	1971	1966-70		1957	1948-56
	1974	1965-73		1961	1952-60
	1980	1971-79		1966	1956-65
	1985	1976-84		1967	1962-66
	1996	1987-95		1968-1973	Dernière
				1974	1965-73
Mortalité périnatale, rapports de........................	1971	1966-70		1975-1979	Dernière
selon la résidence	1974	1965-73		1980	1971-79
(urbaine/rurale)	1980	1971-79		1981-1984	Dernière
	1985	1976-84		1985	1976-84
	1996	1987-95		1986-1991	Dernière
				1992	1983-92
Mortalité post-néonatale (nombres)......................	1948	1936-47		1993-1995	Dernière
selon le sexe	1951	1936-50		1996	1987-95
	1957	1948-56		1997	Dernière
	1961	1952-60		1997SR [ii]	1948-96
	1963-1965	Dernière		1998-2018	Dernière
	1966	1961-65			
	1967	1962-66	**Mortalité post-néonatale, taux de**	1971-1973	Dernière
	1968-1973	Dernière	selon la résidence	1974	1965-73
	1974	1965-73	(urbaine/rurale)	1975-1979	Dernière
	1975-1979	Dernière		1980	1971-79
	1980	1971-79		1981-1984	Dernière
	1981-1984	Dernière		1985	1976-84
	1985	1976-84		1986-1991	Dernière
	1986-1991	Dernière		1992	1983-92
	1992	1983-92		1993-1995	Dernière
	1993-1995	Dernière		1996	1987-95
	1996	1987-95		1997	Dernière
	1997	Dernière		1997SR [ii]	1948-96
	1997SR [ii]	1948-96		1998-1999	Dernière
	1998-2018	Dernière			
			Mortalité, tables de	1959-1973	Dernière
Mortalité post-néonatale (nombres)......................	1971-1973	Dernière	espérance de vie à la	1974	2-Dernière
selon la résidence	1974	1965-73	naissance selon le sexe	1975-1978	Dernière
(urbaine/rurale)	1975-1979	Dernière		1978SR [i]	1948-77
	1980	1971-79		1979	Dernière
	1981-1984	Dernière		1980	2-Dernières
	1985	1976-84		1981-1984	Dernière
	1986-1991	Dernière		1985	2-Dernières
	1992	1983-92		1986-1991	Dernière
	1993-1995	Dernière		1991 VP [v]	1950-90
	1996	1987-95		1992-1995	Dernière
	1997	Dernière		1996	2-Dernières
	1997SR [ii]	1948-96		1997	Dernière
				1997SR [ii]	1948-1996
				1998	1995-98

Sujet	Année de l'édition	Période considérée
	1999	1995-99
	2000	1995-00
	2001	1997-01
	2002	1998-02
	2003	1999-03
	2004	2000-04
	2005	2001-05
	2006	2002-06
	2007	2003-07
	2008	2004-08
	2009-10	2006-10
	2011	2007-11
	2012	2008-12
	2013	2009-13
	2014	2010-14
	2015	2011-15
	2016	2012-16
	2017	2013-17
	2018	2014-18
Mortalité, tables de .... espérance de vie à un âge donné selon le sexe	1948	1891-1945
	1951	1891-1950
	1952	1891-1951 [iii]
	1953	1891-1952
	1954	1891-1953 [iii]
	1955-1956	Dernière
	1957	1900-56
	1958-1960	Dernière
	1961	1940-60
	1962-64	Dernière
	1966	2-Dernières
	1967	1900-66
	1968-1973	Dernière
	1974	2-Dernières
	1975-1978	Dernière
	1978HS [i]	1948-77
	1979	Dernière
	1980	2-Dernières
	1981-1984	Dernière
	1985	2-Dernières
	1986-1991	Dernière
	1991 VP [v]	1950-90
	1992-1994	Dernière
	1996	2-Dernières
	1997	Dernière
	1997SR [ii]	1948-96
	1998-2018	Dernière
Mortalité, tables de .... probabilité de décès à un âge donné selon le sexe	1948	1891-1945
	1951	1891-1950
	1952	1891-1951 [iii]
	1953	1891-1952
	1954	1891-1953 [iii]

Sujet	Année de l'édition	Période considérée
	1957	1900-56
	1961	1940-60
	1966	2-Dernières
	1974	2-Dernières
	1980	2-Dernières
	1985	2-Dernières
	1996	2-Dernières
	2008-2018	Dernière
Mortalité, tables de .... survivants à un âge donné selon le sexe	1948	1891-1945
	1951	1891-1950
	1952	1891-1951 [iii]
	1953	1891-1952
	1954	1891-1953 [iii]
	1957	1900-56
	1961	1940-60
	1966	2-Dernières
	1974	2-Dernières
	1980	2-Dernières
	1985	2-Dernières
	1996	2-Dernières
Mort-nés		voir: Morts fœtales tardive
Morts fœtales .... selon la période de gestation	1957	1950-56
	1959	1949-58
	1961	1952-60
	1965	5-Dernières
	1966	1956-65
	1967-1968	Dernière
	1969	1963-68
	1974	1965-73
	1975	1966-74
	1980	1971-79
	1981	1972-80
	1985	1976-84
	1986	1977-85
	1996	1987-95
	1999CD [vii]	1990-98
Morts fœtales tardives	1951	1935-50
	1952	1936-51
	1953	1936-52
	1954	1938-53
	1955	1946-54
	1956	1947-55
	1957	1948-56
	1958	1948-57
	1959	1949-58
	1960	1950-59
	1961	1952-60
	1962	1953-61
	1963	1953-62

Sujet	Année de l'édition	Période considérée	Sujet	Année de l'édition	Période considérée
	1964	1959-63		2016	2012-16
	1965	1955-64		2017	2013-17
	1966	1947-65		2018	2014-18
	1967	1962-66			
	1968	1963-67	Morts fœtales tardives	1961	1952-60
	1969	1959-68	illégitimes	1965	5-Dernières
	1970	1965-69		1969	1963-68
	1971	1966-70		1975	1966-74
	1972	1967-71		1981	1972-80
	1973	1968-72		1986	1977-85
	1974	1965-73			
	1975	1966-74	Morts fœtales tardives	1961	1952-60
	1976	1971-75	illégitimes, en	1965	5-Dernières
	1977	1972-76	pourcentage	1969	1963-68
	1978	1973-77		1975	1966-74
	1979	1974-78		1981	1972-80
	1980	1971-79		1986	1977-85
	1981	1972-80			
	1982	1977-81	Morts fœtales tardives	1959	1949-58
	1983	1978-82	légitimes	1965	1955-64
	1984	1979-83		1969	1963-68
	1985	1975-84		1975	1966-74
	1986	1977-85		1981	1972-80
	1987	1982-86		1986	1977-85
	1988	1983-87			
	1989	1984-88	Morts fœtales tardives	1959	1949-58
	1990	1985-89	légitimes selon l'âge de	1965	1955-64
	1991	1986-90	la mère	1969	1963-68
	1992	1987-91		1975	1966-74
	1993	1988-92		1981	1972-80
	1994	1989-93		1986	1977-85
	1995	1990-94			
	1996	1987-95	Morts fœtales tardives	1954	1936-53
	1997	1992-96	selon l'âge de la mère	1959	1949-58
	1998	1993-97		1965	1955-64
	1999	1994-98		1969	1963-68
	1999CD [vii]	1990-98		1975	1966-74
	2000	1995-99		1981	1972-80
	2001	1997-01		1986	1977-85
	2002	1998-02		1999CD [vii]	1990-98
	2003	1999-03			
	2004	2000-04	Morts fœtales tardives	1954	Dernière
	2005	2001-05	selon l'âge de la mère	1959	1949-58
	2006	2002-06	et le rang de naissance	1965	3-Dernières
	2007	2003-07		1969	1963-68
	2008	2004-08		1975	1966-74
	2009-2010	2006-10		1981	1972-80
	2011	2007-11		1986	1977-85
	2012	2008-12		1999CD [vii]	1990-98
	2013	2009-13			
	2014	2010-14	Morts fœtales tardives	1957	1950-56
	2015	2011-15	selon la période de	1959	1949-58
			gestation	1961	1952-60

Sujet	Année de l'édition	Période considérée	Sujet	Année de l'édition	Période considérée
	1965	5-Dernières		2012	2008-12
	1966	1956-65		2013	2009-13
	1967-1968	Dernière		2014	2010-14
	1969	1963-68		2015	2011-15
	1974	1965-73		2016	2012-16
	1975	1966-74		2017	2013-17
	1980	1971-79		2018	2014-18
	1981	1972-80			
	1985	1976-84	Morts fœtales tardives.......	1961	1952-60
	1986	1977-85	selon le sexe	1965	5-Dernières
	1996	1987-95		1969	1963-68
				1975	1966-74
Morts fœtales tardives.......	1971	1966-70		1981	1972-80
selon la résidence	1972	1967-71		1986	1977-85
(urbaine/rurale)	1973	1968-72			
	1974	1965-73	Mortinatalité, rapports de..	voir: Mortalité fœtale tardive	
	1975	1966-74			
	1976	1971-75	Morts néonatales, selon le		
	1977	1972-76	sexe	voir: Mortalité post-néonatale	
	1978	1973-77			
	1979	1974-78	Morts post-néonatales,		
	1980	1971-79	selon le sexe	voir: Mortalité post-néonatale	
	1981	1972-80			
	1982	1977-81	# N		
	1983	1978-82			
	1984	1979-83	Naissances	1948	1932-47
	1985	1975-84		1949-50	1934-49
	1986	1977-85		1951	1935-50
	1987	1982-86		1952	1936-51
	1988	1983-87		1953	1950-52
	1989	1984-88		1954	1938-53
	1990	1985-89		1955	1946-54
	1991	1986-90		1956	1947-55
	1992	1987-91		1957	1948-56
	1993	1988-92		1958	1948-57
	1994	1989-93		1959	1949-58
	1995	1990-94		1960	1950-59
	1996	1987-95		1961	1952-61
	1997	1992-96		1962	1953-62
	1998	1993-97		1963	1954-63
	1999	1994-98		1964	1960-64
	1999CD [vii]	1990-98		1965	1946-65
	2000	1995-99		1966	1957-66
	2001	1997-01		1967	1963-67
	2002	1998-02		1968	1964-68
	2003	1999-03		1969	1950-69
	2004	2000-04		1970	1966-70
	2005	2001-05		1971	1967-71
	2006	2002-06		1972	1968-72
	2007	2003-07		1973	1969-73
	2008	2004-08		1974	1970-74
	2009-2010	2006-10		1975	1956-75
	2011	2007-11		1976	1972-76

Sujet	Année de l'édition	Période considérée	Sujet	Année de l'édition	Période considérée
	1977	1973-77	**Naissances**	1948	1936-47
	1978	1974-78	légitimes	1949-50	1936-49
	1978SR [i]	1948-78		1954	1936-53
	1979	1975-79		1959	1949-58
	1980	1976-80		1965	1955-64
	1981	1962-81		1969	1963-68
	1982	1978-82		1975	1966-74
	1983	1979-83		1981	1972-80
	1984	1980-84		1986	1977-85
	1985	1981-85		1999CD [vii]	1990-98
	1986	1967-86			
	1987	1983-87	**Naissances**	1954	1936-53
	1988	1984-88	légitimes selon l'âge de	1959	1949-58
	1989	1985-89	la mère	1965	1955-64
	1990	1986-90		1969	1963-68
	1991	1987-91		1975	1966-74
	1992	1983-92		1981	1972-80
	1993	1989-93		1986	1977-85
	1994	1990-94			
	1995	1991-95	**Naissances**	1959	1949-58
	1996	1992-96	légitimes selon l'âge du	1965	1955-64
	1997	1993-97	père	1969	1963-68
	1997SR [ii]	1948-97		1975	1966-74
	1998	1994-98		1981	1972-80
	1999	1995-99		1986	1977-85
	1999CD [vii]	1980-99			
	2000	1996-00	**Naissances**	1948	1936-47
	2001	1997-01	légitimes selon la durée	1949-50	1936-49
	2002	1998-02	du mariage	1954	1936-53
	2003	1999-03		1959	1949-58
	2004	2000-04		1965	1955-64
	2005	2001-05		1969	1963-68
	2006	2002-06		1975	1966-74
	2007	2003-07		1981	1972-80
	2008	2004-08		1986	1977-85
	2009-2010	2006-10		1999CD [vii]	1990-98
	2011	2007-11			
	2012	2008-12	**Naissances**	1948	1936-47
	2013	2009-13	selon l'âge de la mère	1949-50	1936-49
	2014	2010-14		1954	1936-53
	2015	2011-15		1955-1956	Dernière
	2016	2012-16		1958	Dernière
	2017	2013-17		1959	1949-58
	2018	2014-18		1960-1964	Dernière
				1965	1955-64
				1966-1968	Dernière
Naissances	1959	1949-58		1969	1963-68
illégitimes	1965	1955-64		1970-1974	Dernière
	1969	1963-68		1975	1966-74
	1975	1966-74		1976-1978	Dernière
	1981	1972-80		1978SR [i]	1948-77
	1986	1977-85		1979-1980	Dernière
	1999CD [vii]	1990-98		1981	1972-80

Index historique
(Voir notes à la fin de l'index)

Sujet	Année de l'édition	Période considérée	Sujet	Année de l'édition	Période considérée
	1982-1985	Dernière			
	1986	1977-85	**Naissances**	1975	Dernière
	1987-1991	Dernière	selon la durée de	1981	1972-80
	1992	1983-92	gestation	1986	1977-85
	1993-1997	Dernière		1999CD [vii]	1990-98
	1997SR [ii]	1948-96'			
	1998-1999	Dernière	**Naissances**	2002	1980-02
	1999CD [vii]	1990-98	selon le mois		
	2000-2018	Dernière			
			Naissances	1965	Dernière
Naissances	1949-50	1936-47	selon la profession du	1969	Dernière
selon l'âge de la mère	1954	Dernière	père		
et le rang de naissance	1959	1949-58			
	1965	1955-64	**Naissances**	1965	Dernière
	1969	1963-68	selon la résidence	1967	Dernière
	1975	1966-74	(urbaine/rurale)	1968	1964-68
	1981	1972-80		1969	1964-68
	1986	1977-85		1970	1966-70
	1999CD [vii]	1990-98		1971	1967-71
				1972	1968-72
Naissances	*voir: selon la résidence*			1973	1969-73
selon l'âge de la mère	*(urbaine/rurale), ci-dessous*			1974	1970-74
et la résidence				1975	1956-75
(urbaine/rurale)				1976	1972-76
				1977	1973-77
Naissances	1965-1968	Dernière		1978	1974-78
selon l'âge de la mère	1969	1963-68		1979	1975-79
et le sexe	1970-1974	Dernière		1980	1976-80
	1975	1966-74		1981	1962-81
	1976-1978	Dernière		1982	1978-82
	1978SR [i]	1948-77		1983	1979-83
	1979-1980	Dernière		1984	1980-84
	1981	1972-80		1985	1981-85
	1982-1985	Dernière		1986	1967-86
	1986	1977-85		1987	1983-87
	1987-1991	Dernière		1988	1984-88
	1992	1983-92		1989	1985-89
	1993-1997	Dernière		1990	1986-90
	1997SR [ii]	1948-96		1991	1987-91
	1998-1999	Dernière		1992	1983-92
	1999CD [vii]	1990-98		1993	1989-93
	2000-2018	Dernière		1994	1990-94
				1995	1991-95
Naissances	1949-50	1942-49		1996	1992-96
selon l'âge du père	1954	1936-53		1997	1993-97
	1959	1949-58		1998	1994-98
	1965	1955-64		1999	1995-99
	1969	1963-68		1999CD [vii]	1980-99
	1975	1966-74		2000	1996-00
	1981	1972-80		2001	1997-01
	1986	1977-85		2002	1998-02
	1999CD [vii]	1990-98		2003	1999-03
	2007-2018	Dernière		2004	2000-04

779

Sujet	Année de l'édition	Période considérée
	2005	2001-05
	2006	2002-06
	2007	2003-07
	2008	2004-08
	2009-2010	2006-10
	2011	2007-11
	2012	2008-12
	2013	2009-13
	2014	2010-14
	2015	2011-15
	2016	2012-16
	2017	2013-17
	2018	2014-18
Naissances	1965	Dernière
selon la résidence	1969-1974	Dernière
(urbaine/rurale) et l'âge	1975	1966-74
de la mère	1976-1980	Dernière
	1981	1972-80
	1982-1985	Dernière
	1986	1977-85
	1987-1991	Dernière
	1992	1983-92
	1993-1997	Dernière
	1997SR [ii]	1948-96
	1998-1999	Dernière
	1999CD [vii]	1990-98
	2000-2006	Dernière
Naissances	1975	Dernière
selon le poids à la	1981	1972-80
naissance	1986	1977-85
	1999CD [vii]	1990-98
Naissances	1948	1936-47
selon le rang de	1949-50	1936-49
naissance	1954	1936-53
	1955	Dernière
	1959	1949-58
	1965	1955-64
	1969	1963-68
	1975	1966-74
	1981	1972-80
	1986	1977-85
	1999CD [vii]	1990-98
Naissances	1959	1949-58
selon le sexe	1965	1955-64
	1967-1968	Dernière
	1969	1963-68
	1970-1974	Dernière
	1975	1956-75
	1976-1980	Dernière

Sujet	Année de l'édition	Période considérée
	1981	1962-81
	1982-1985	Dernière
	1986	1967-86
	1987-1991	Dernière
	1992	1983-92
	1993-1997	Dernière
	1997SR [ii]	1948-96
	1998-1999	Dernière
	1999CD [vii]	1980-1999
	2000-2018	Dernière
Naissances	1965	Dernière
selon les naissances	1969	Dernière
multiples	1975	Dernière
	1981	1972-80
	1986	1977-85
	1999CD [vii]	1990-98
Natalité proportionnelle	1949-50	Dernière
fécondité	1954	Dernière
	1959	1949-58
	1965	1955-65
	1969	1963-68
	1975	1965-74
	1978SR [i]	1948-77
	1981	1972-80
	1986	1977-85
	1997SR [ii]	1948-1996
	1999CD [vii]	1980-99
Natalité proportionnelle	1959	1949-58
illégitime	1965	1955-65
	1969	1963-68
	1975	1965-74
	1981	1972-80
	1986	1977-85
Natalité, taux de	1948	1932-47
	1949-50	1932-49
	1951	1905-30 [vi]
		1930-50
	1952	1920-34 [vi]
		1934-51
	1953	1920-39 [vi]
		1940-52
	1954	1920-39 [vi]
		1939-53
	1955	1920-34 [vi]
		1946-54
	1956	1947-55
	1957	1948-56
	1958	1948-57
	1959	1920-54 [vi]

Sujet	Année de l'édition	Période considérée	Sujet	Année de l'édition	Période considérée
		1953-58		2002	1998-02
	1960	1950-59		2003	1999-03
	1961	1945-59 [vi]		2004	2000-04
		1952-61		2005	2001-05
	1962	1945-54 [vi]		2006	2002-06
		1952-62		2007	2003-07
	1963	1945-59 [vi]		2008	2004-08
		1954-63		2009-2010	2006-10
	1964	1960-64		2011	2007-11
	1965	1920-64 [vi]		2012	2008-12
		1950-65		2013	2009-13
	1966	1950-64 [vi]		2014	2010-14
		1957-66		2015	2011-15
	1967	1963-67		2016	2012-16
	1968	1964-68		2017	2013-17
	1969	1925-69 [vi]		2018	2014-18
		1954-69			
	1970	1966-70	Natalité, taux de	1949-50	1947
	1971	1967-71	estimatifs, pour les	1956-1977	Dernière
	1972	1968-72	continents	1978-1979	1970-75
	1973	1969-73		1980-1986	1975-80
	1974	1970-74		1987-1992	1985-90
	1975	1956-75		1993-1997	1990-95
	1976	1972-76		1998-2000	1995-00
	1977	1973-77		2001-2005	2000-05
	1978	1974-78		2006-2010	2005-10
	1978SR [i]	1948-78		2011-2015	2010-15
	1979	1975-79		20162018	2015-20
	1980	1976-80			
	1981	1962-81	Natalité, taux de	1964-1977	Dernière
	1982	1978-82	estimatifs, pour les	1978-1979	1970-75
	1983	1979-83	grandes régions	1980-1983	1975-80
	1984	1980-84		1984-1986	1980-85
	1985	1981-85		1987-1992	1985-90
	1986	1967-86		1993-1997	1990-95
	1987	1983-87		1998-2000	1995-00
	1988	1984-88		2001-2005	2000-05
	1989	1985-89		2006-2010	2005-10
	1990	1986-90		2011-2015	2010-15
	1991	1987-91		2016-2018	2015-20
	1992	1983-92			
	1993	1989-93	Natalité, taux de	1949-50	1947
	1994	1990-94	estimatifs, pour les	1956-1977	Dernière
	1995	1991-95	régions	1978-1979	1970-75
	1996	1992-96		1980-1983	1975-80
	1997	1993-97		1984-1986	1980-85
	1997SR [ii]	1948-97		1987-1992	1985-90
	1998	1994-98		1993-1997	1990-95
	1999	1995-99		1998-2000	1995-00
	1999CD [vii]	1985-99		2001-2005	2000-05
	2000	1996-00		2006-2010	2005-10
	2001	1997-01		2011-2015	2010-15
				2016-2018	2015-20

Sujet	Année de l'édition	Période considérée	Sujet	Année de l'édition	Période considérée
				1959	1949-58
Natalité, taux de	1949-50	1947		1965	1955-64
estimatifs, pour le	1956-1977	Dernière		1969	1963-68
monde				1975	1966-74
	1978-1979	1970-75		1976-1978	Dernière
	1980-1983	1975-80		1978SR [i]	1948-77
	1984-1986	1980-85		1979-1980	Dernière
	1987-1992	1985-90		1981	1972-80
	1993-1997	1990-95		1982-1985	Dernière
	1998-2000	1995-00		1986	1977-85
	2001-2005	2000-05		1987-1991	Dernière
	2006-2010	2005-10		1992	1983-92
	2011-2015	2010-15		1993-1997	Dernière
	2016-2018	2015-20		1975SR [ii]	1948-96
				1998-1999	Dernière
Natalité, taux de	1959	1949-58		1999CD [vii]	1990-98
illégitimes				2000-2018	Dernière
Natalité, taux de	1954	1936-53	**Natalité, taux de**	1954	1948, 1951
légitimes	1959	1949-58	selon l'âge de la mère	1959	1949-58
	1965	Dernière	et le rang de naissance	1965	1955-64
	1969	Dernière		1969	1963-68
	1975	Dernière		1975	1966-74
	1981	Dernière		1981	1972-80
	1986	Dernière		1986	1977-85
				1999CD [vii]	1990-98
Natalité, taux de	1954	1936-53			
légitimes selon l'âge de	1959	1949-58	**Natalité, taux de**	*voir: (urbaine/rurale), ci-*	
la mère	1965	Dernière	selon l'âge de la mère	*dessous*	
	1969	Dernière	et la résidence		
	1975	Dernière	(urbaine/rurale)		
	1981	Dernière			
	1986	Dernière	**Natalité, taux de**	1949-50	1942-49
			selon l'âge du père	1954	1936-53
Natalité, taux de	1959	1949-58		1959	1949-58
légitimes selon l'âge du	1965	Dernière		1965	1955-64
père	1969	Dernière		1969	1963-68
	1975	Dernière		1975	1966-74
	1981	Dernière		1981	1972-80
	1986	Dernière		1986	1977-85
				1999CD [vii]	1990-98
Natalité, taux de	1959	1950-57		2007-2018	Dernière
légitimes selon la durée	1965	Dernière			
du mariage	1969	Dernière	**Natalité, taux de**	*voir: légitimes selon la durée*	
	1975	Dernière	selon la durée du	*du mariage*	
			mariage		
Natalité, taux de	1948	1936-47			
selon l'âge de la mère	1949-50	1936-49	**Natalité, taux de**	1951	1936-49
	1951	1936-50	selon le rang de	1952	1936-50
	1952	1936-50	naissance	1953	1936-52
	1953	1936-52		1954	1936-53
	1954	1936-53		1955	Dernière
	1955-1956	Dernière		1959	1949-58

Index historique
(Voir notes à la fin de l'index)

Sujet	Année de l'édition	Période considérée	Sujet	Année de l'édition	Période considérée
	1965	1955-64		2012	2008-12
	1969	1963-68		2013	2009-13
	1975	1966-74		2014	2010-14
	1981	1972-80		2015	2011-15
	1986	1977-85		2016	2012-16
	1999CD [vii]	1990-98		2017	2013-17
				2018	2014-18
Natalité, taux de	1965	Dernière			
selon la résidence	1967	Dernière	**Natalité, taux de**	1965	Dernière
(urbaine/rurale)	1968	1964-68	selon la résidence	1969	Dernière
	1969	1964-68	(urbaine/rurale) et l'âge	1975	1966-74
	1970	1966-70	de la mère	1976-1980	Dernière
	1971	1967-71		1981	1972-80
	1972	1968-72		1982-1985	Dernière
	1973	1969-73		1986	1977-85
	1974	1970-74		1987-1991	Dernière
	1975	1956-75		1992	1983-92
	1976	1972-76		1993-1997	Dernière
	1977	1973-77		1997SR [ll]	1948-96
	1978	1974-78		1998-1999	Dernière
	1979	1975-79		1999CD [vii]	1990-98
	1980	1976-80		2000-2006	Dernière
	1981	1962-81			
	1982	1978-82	**Nationalité**		voir: Population
	1983	1979-83			
	1984	1980-84	**Nuptialité**		voir: Mariages
	1985	1981-85			
	1986	1967-86	**Nuptialité, taux de**	1948	1932-47
	1987	1983-87		1949-50	1932-49
	1988	1984-88		1951	1930-50
	1989	1985-89		1952	1920-34 [vi]
	1990	1986-90			1934-51
	1991	1987-91		1953	1920-39 [vi]
	1992	1983-92			1940-52
	1993	1989-93		1954	1920-39 [vi]
	1994	1990-94			1946-53
	1995	1991-95		1955	1920-34 [vi]
	1996	1992-96			1946-54
	1997	1993-97		1956	1947-55
	1998	1994-98		1957	1948-56
	1999	1995-99		1958	1930-57
	1999CD [vii]	1985-99		1959	1949-58
	2000	1996-00		1960	1950-59
	2001	1997-01		1961	1952-61
	2002	1998-02		1962	1953-62
	2003	1999-03		1963	1954-63
	2004	2000-04		1964	1960-64
	2005	2001-05		1965	1956-65
	2006	2002-06		1966	1962-66
	2007	2003-07		1967	1963-67
	2008	2004-08		1968	1953-68
	2009-2010	2006-10		1969	1965-69
	2011	2007-11		1970	1966-70

Sujet	Année de l'édition	Période considérée	Sujet	Année de l'édition	Période considérée
	1971	1967-71		1995	1991-95
	1972	1968-72		1996	1992-96
	1973	1969-73		1997	1993-97
	1974	1970-74		1998	1994-98
	1975	1971-75		1999	1995-99
	1976	1957-76		2000	1996-00
	1977	1973-77		2001	1997-01
	1978	1974-78		2002	1998-02
	1979	1975-79		2003	1999-03
	1980	1976-80		2004	2000-04
	1981	1977-81		2005	2001-05
	1982	1963-82		2006	2002-06
	1983	1979-83		2007	2003-07
	1984	1980-84		2008	2004-08
	1985	1981-85		2009-2010	2006-10
	1986	1982-86		2011	2007-11
	1987	1983-87		2012	2008-12
	1988	1984-88		2013	2009-13
	1989	1985-89		2014	2010-14
	1990	1971-90		2015	2011-15
	1991	1987-91		2016	2012-16
	1992	1988-92		2017	2013-17
	1993	1989-93		2018	2014-18
	1994	1990-94			
	1995	1991-95	**Nuptialité, taux de**	1948	1936-46
	1996	1992-96	selon l'âge et le sexe	1949-50	1936-49
	1997	1993-97		1953	1936-51
	1998	1994-98		1954	1936-52
	1999	1995-99		1958	1935-56
	1972	1968-72		1968	1955-67
	1973	1969-73		1976	1966-75
	1974	1970-74		1982	1972-81
	1975	1971-75		1987	1975-86
	1976	1957-76		1990	1980-89
	1977	1973-77			
	1978	1974-78	**Nuptialité, taux de**	1968	Dernière
	1979	1975-79	selon la résidence	1969	1965-69
	1980	1976-80	(urbaine/rurale)	1970	1966-70
	1981	1977-81		1971	1967-71
	1982	1963-82		1972	1968-72
	1983	1979-83		1973	1969-73
	1984	1980-84		1974	1970-74
	1985	1981-85		1975	1971-75
	1986	1982-86		1976	1957-76
	1987	1983-87		1977	1973-77
	1988	1984-88		1978	1974-78
	1989	1985-89		1979	1975-79
	1990	1971-90		1980	1976-80
	1991	1987-91		1981	1977-81
	1992	1988-92		1982	1963-82
	1993	1989-93		1983	1979-83
	1994	1990-94		1984	1980-84
				1985	1981-85

Index historique
(Voir notes à la fin de l'index)

Sujet	Année de l'édition	Période considérée
	1986	1982-86
	1987	1983-87
	1988	1984-88
	1989	1985-89
	1990	1971-90
	1991	1987-91
	1992	1988-92
	1993	1989-93
	1994	1990-94
	1995	1991-95
	1996	1992-96
	1997	1993-97
	1998	1994-98
	1999	1995-99
	2000	1996-00
	2001	1997-01
	2002	1998-02
	2003	1999-03
	2004	2000-04
	2005	2001-05
	2006	2002-06
	2007	2003-07
	2008	2004-08
	2009-2010	2006-10
	2011	2007-11
	2012	2008-12
	2013	2009-13
	2014	2010-14
	2015	2011-15
	2016	2012-16
	2017	2013-17
	2018	2014-18
Nuptialité, taux de	1958	1935-56
selon le sexe et la	1968	1935-67
population mariable	1976	1966-75
	1982	1972-81
	1990	1980-89
Nuptialité au premier mariage, taux de, classification détaillée selon l'âge de l'épouse et de l'époux	1982	1972-81
	1990	1980-89

P

Sujet	Année de l'édition	Période considérée
Population	1957	1953-56
accroissement, taux d'	1958	1953-57
(annuels moyens pour	1959	1953-58
les pays ou zones)	1960	1953-59
	1961	1953-60

Sujet	Année de l'édition	Période considérée
	1962	1958-61
	1963	1958-62
	1964	1958-63
	1965	1958-64
	1966	1958-66
	1967	1963-67
	1968	1963-68
	1969	1963-69
	1970	1963-70
	1971	1963-71
	1972	1963-72
	1973	1970-73
	1974	1970-74
	1975	1970-75
	1976	1970-76
	1977	1970-77
	1978	1975-78
	1979	1975-79
	1980	1975-80
	1981	1975-81
	1982	1975-82
	1983	1980-83
	1984	1980-84
	1985	1980-85
	1986	1980-86
	1987	1980-87
	1988	1985-88
	1989	1985-89
	1990	1985-90
	1991	1985-91
	1992	1985-92
	1993	1990-93
	1994	1990-94
	1995	1990-95
	1996	1990-96
	1997	1990-97
	1998	1993-98
	1999	1995-99
	2000	1995-00
	2001	1995-01
	2002	1995-02
	2003	2000-03
	2004	2000-04
	2005	2000-05
	2006	2000-06
	2007	2005-07
	2008	2005-08
	2009-2010	2005-10
	2011	2005-11
	2012	2005-12
	2013	2010-13
	2014	2010-14

Sujet	Année de l'édition	Période considérée
	2015	2010-15
	2016	2010-16
	2017	2010-17
	2018	2010-18
Population.......................	1957	1950-56
accroissement, taux d'	1958	1950-57
(annuels moyens pour	1959	1950-58
le monde, les grandes	1960	1950-59
régions (continentes) et	1961	1950-60
les régions	1962	1950-61
géographiques)	1963	1958-62
		1960-62
	1964	1958-63
		1960-63
	1965	1958-64
		1960-64
	1966	1958-66
		1960-66
	1967	1960-67
		1963-67
	1968	1960-68
		1963-68
	1969	1960-69
		1963-69
	1970	1963-70
		1965-70
	1971	1963-71
		1965-71
	1972	1963-72
		1965-72
	1973	1965-73
		1970-73
	1974	1965-74
		1970-74
	1975	1965-75
		1970-75
	1976	1965-76
		1970-76
	1977	1965-77
		1970-77
	1978-1979	1970-75
	1980-1983	1975-80
	1984-1986	1980-85
	1987-1992	1985-90
	1993-1997	1990-95
	1998-2000	1995-00
	2001-2005	2000-05
	2006-2010	2005-10
	2011-2015	2010-15
	2016-2018	2015-20

Sujet	Année de l'édition	Période considérée
Population.......................	1956	1945-55
active:	1967	1955-64
-féminin, selon l'état	1968	Dernière
matrimonial et l'âge	1972	1962-77
-féminin, selon l'état	1973	1965-73
matrimonial et l'âge	1979	1970-79
et la résidence	1984	1974-84
(urbaine/rurale)	1988	1980-88 [iii]
	1994	1985-94
-née à l'étranger	1984	1974-84
selon la profession,	1989	1980-88
l'âge et le sexe	1994	1985-94
-née à l'étranger	1977	Dernière
selon la profession,		
l'âge et le sexe		
-selon l'âge et le	1955	1945-54
sexe	1956	1945-55
	1964	1955-64
	1972	1962-72
-selon l'âge et le	1973	1965-73 [iii]
sexe et la résidence	1979	1970-79 [iii]
(urbaine/rurale)	1984	1974-84
	1988	1980-88 [iii]
	1994	1985-94
-selon l'âge et le	1948	Dernière
sexe en	1949-50	1930-48
pourcentage	1955	1945-54
	1956	1945-55
	1964	1955-64
	1972	1962-72
-selon l'âge et le	1973	1965-73 [iii]
sexe et la résidence	1979	1970-79 [iii]
(urbaine/ rurale) en	1984	1974-84
pourcentage	1988	1980-88 [iii]
	1994	1985-94
-selon la branche	1956	1945-55
d'activité	1964	1955-64
économique, le	1972	1962-72
sexe, et l'âge		
-selon la branche	1973	1965-73 [iii]
d'activité	1979	1970-79 [iii]
économique, le	1984	1974-84
sexe, et l'âge et la	1988	1980-88 [iii]
résidence		
(urbaine/rurale)		

Sujet	Année de l'édition	Période considérée
-selon la branche d'activité économique la situation dans la profession et le sexe	1948	Dernière
	1949-50	Dernière
	1955	1945-54
	1964	1955-64
	1972	1962-72
-selon la branche d'activité économique la situation dans la profession et le sexe et la résidence (urbaine/rurale)	1973	1965-73 [iii]
	1979	1970-79
	1984	1974-84
	1988	1980-88 [iii]
	1994	1985-94
-selon la profession, la l'âge et le sexe	1956	1945-55
	1964	1955-64
	1972	1962-72
-selon la profession, l'âge et le sexe et la résidence (urbaine/rurale)	1973	1965-73 [iii]
	1979	1970-79 [iii]
	1984	1974-84
	1988	1980-88 [iii]
	1994	1985-84
-selon la profession, la situation dans la profession et le sexe	1956	1945-55
	1964	1955-64
	1972	1962-72
-selon la profession, la situation dans la profession et le sexe et la résidence (urbaine/rurale)	1973	1965-73 [iii]
	1979	1970-79 [iii]
	1984	1974-84
	1988	1980-88 [iii]
	1994	1985-94
-selon le sexe	1948	Dernière
	1949-50	1926-48
	1955	1945-54
	1956	1945-55
	1960	1920-60
	1963	1955-63
	1964	1955-64
	1970	1950-70
	1972	1962-72
	1973	1965-73 [iii]
	1979	1970-79 [iii]
	1984	1974-84
	1988	1980-88 [iii]
	1994	1985-94
-chômeurs selon l'âge et le sexe	1949-50	1946-49
Population	1948	Dernière
	1955	1945-54

Sujet	Année de l'édition	Période considérée
alphabète selon l'âge et le sexe	1963	1955-63
	1964	1955-64 [iii]
	1971	1962-71
	voir également: analphabète, ci-dessous	
Population alphabète selon l'âge et le sexe et la résidence (urbaine/rurale)	1973	1965-73 [iii]
	1979	1970-79 [iii]
	1983	1974-84
	1988	1980-88 [iii]
	1993	1985-93
Population alphabétisme selon le sexe, taux d'	1955	1945-54
	voir également: analphabétisme, taux d', ci-dessous	
Population alphabétisme selon le sexe et l'âge, taux d'	1955	1945-54
Population analphabète selon le sexe	1948	Dernière
	1955	1945-54
	1960	1920-60
	1963	1955-63
	1964	1955-64 [iii]
	1970	1950-70
Population analphabète selon le sexe et la résidence (urbaine/rurale)	1973	1965-73
	1979	1970-79 [iii]
	1983	1974-83
	1988	1980-88 [iii]
Population analphabète selon le sexe et l'âge	1948	Dernière
	1955	1945-54
	1963	1955-63
	1964	1955-64 [iii]
	1970	1950-70
Population analphabète selon le sexe et l'âge et la résidence (urbaine/rurale)	1973	1965-73
	1979	1970-79 [iii]
	1983	1974-83
	1988	1980-88 [iii]
	1993	1985-93 [iii]
Population analphabète selon le sexe, taux d'......	1948	Dernière
	1955	1945-54
	1960	1920-60
	1963	1955-63
	1964	1955-64 [iii]
	1970	1950-70

Sujet	Année de l'édition	Période considérée	Sujet	Année de l'édition	Période considérée
Population	1973	1965-73		1954	1920-53
analphabète selon le	1979	1970-79 [iii]		1955	1920-54
sexe, taux d'...... et la	1983	1974-83		1956	1920-55
résidence	1988	1980-88 [iii]		1957	1920-56
(urbaine/rurale)	1993	1985-93 [iii]		1958	1920-57
				1959	1920-58
Population	1948	Dernière		1960	1920-59
analphabète selon le	1955	1945-54		1961	1920-60
sexe et l'âge, taux d'......	1960	1920-60		1962	1920-61
	1963	1955-63 [iii]		1963	1930-62
	1964	1955-64 [iii]		1964	1930-63
	1970	1950-70		1965	1930-65
				1966	1930-66
Population	1973	1965-73		1967	1930-67
analphabète selon le	1979	1970-79 [iii]		1968	1930-68
sexe et l'âge, taux d'......	1983	1974-83		1969	1930-69
et la résidence	1988	1980-88 [iii]		1970	1950-70
(urbaine/rurale)	1993	1985-93 [iii]		1971	1950-71
				1972	1950-72
Population	1960	1920-60		1973	1950-73
célibataire selon l'âge	1970	1950-70		1974	1950-74
et le sexe (nombres)		*voir également: selon l'état*		1975	1950-75
		matrimonial, ci-dessous		1976	1950-76
				1977	1950-77
Population	1949-50	1926-48		1978	1950-78
célibataire selon l'âge	1960	1920-60		1979	1950-79
et le sexe	1970	1950-70		1980	1950-80
(pourcentages)				1981	1950-81
				1982	1950-82
Population		*voir: selon l'importance*		1983	1950-83
dans les localités		*des localités, ci-dessous*		1984	1950-84
				1985	1950-85
Population	1987	1975-86		1986	1950-86
des collectivités, âge et	1995	1985-95		1987	1950-87
sexe et résidence				1988	1950-88
urbaine/rurale				1989	1950-89
				1990	1950-90
Population	1955	1945-54		1991	1950-91
dans les ménages selon	1962	1955-62		1992	1950-92
le type et la dimension	1963	1955-63 [iii]		1993	1950-93
des ménages privés				1994	1950-94
		voir également: Ménages		1995	1950-95
				1996	1950-96
Population	1991VP [v]	Dernière		1997	1950-97
dans les logements				1998-2000	1950-00
collectifs et sans abri				2001	1950-01
				2002	1950-02
Population	1991VP [v]	Dernière		2003	1950-03
Sans abri selon le sexe				2004	1950-04
et l'âge				2005	1950-05
				2006	1950-06
Population	1949-50	1920-49		2007	1950-07
des grandes régions	1951	1950			
(continentales)	1952	1920-51			
	1953	1920-52			

Index historique
(Voir notes à la fin de l'index)

Sujet	Année de l'édition	Période considérée	Sujet	Année de l'édition	Période considérée
	2008	1950-08		1974	1965-74
	2009-2010	1950-10		1975	1966-75
	2011	1960-11		1976	1967-76
	2012	1960-12		1977	1968-77
	2013	1960-13		1978	1969-78
	2014	1960-14		1978SR [I]	1948-78
	2015	1960-15		1979	1970-79
	2016	1960-16		1980	1971-80
	2017	1960-17		1981	1972-81
	2018	1960-18		1982	1973-82
				1983	1974-83
Population..........................	1948	1900-48		1984	1975-84
des pays ou zones	1949-50	1900-50		1985	1976-85
(total, dénombrée)	1951	1900-51		1986	1977-86
	1952	1850-1952		1987	1978-87
	1953	1850-1953		1988	1979-88
	1954	Dernière		1989	1980-89
	1955	1850-1954		1990	1981-90
	1956-1961	Dernière		1991	1982-91
	1962	1900-62		1992	1983-92
	1963	Dernière		1993	1984-93
	1964	1955-64		1994	1985-94
	1965-1978	Dernière		1995	1986-95
	1978SR [I]	1948-78		1996	1987-96
	1979-1997	Dernière		1997	1988-97
	1979SR [II]	1948-78		1997SR [II]	1948-97
	1998-2018	Dernière		1998	1989-98
				1999	1990-99
Population..........................	1948	1932-47		2000	1991-00
des pays ou zones	1949-50	1932-49		2001	1992-01
(total, estimée)	1951	1930-50		2002	1993-02
	1952	1920-51		2003	1994-03
	1953	1920-53		2004	1995-04
	1954	1920-54		2005	1996-05
	1955	1920-55		2006	1997-06
	1956	1920-56		2007	1998-07
	1957	1940-57		2008	1999-08
	1958	1939-58		2009-2010	2001-10
	1959	1940-59		2011	2002-11
	1960	1920-60		2012	2003-12
	1961	1941-61		2013	2004-13
	1962	1942-62		2014	2005-14
	1963	1943-63		2015	2006-15
	1964	1955-64		2016	2007-16
	1965	1946-65		2017	2008-17
	1966	1947-66		2018	2009-18
	1967	1958-67			
	1968	1959-68	**Population**..........................	1952	Dernière
	1969	1960-69	des principales	1955	1945-54
	1970	1950-70	divisions	1962	1955-62
	1971	1962-71	administratives	1963	1955-63 [III]
	1972	1963-72		1971	1962-71
	1973	1964-73		1973	1965-73 [III]

789

Sujet	Année de l'édition	Période considérée
	1979	1970-79 [iii]
	1983	1974-83
	1988	1980-88 [iii]
	1993	1985-93
Population	1949-50	1920-49
des régions	1952	1920-51
	1953	1920-52
	1954	1920-53
	1955	1920-54
	1956	1920-55
	1957	1920-56
	1958	1920-57
	1959	1920-58
	1960	1920-59
	1961	1920-60
	1962	1920-61
	1963	1930-62
	1964	1930-63
	1965	1930-65
	1966	1930-66
	1967	1930-67
	1968	1930-68
	1969	1930-69
	1970	1950-70
	1971	1950-71
	1972	1950-72
	1973	1950-73
	1974	1950-74
	1975	1950-75
	1976	1950-76
	1977	1950-77
	1978	1950-78
	1979	1950-79
	1980	1950-80
	1981	1950-81
	1982	1950-82
	1983	1950-83
	1984	1950-84
	1985	1950-85
	1986	1950-86
	1987	1950-87
	1988	1950-88
	1989	1950-89
	1990	1950-90
	1991	1950-91
	1992	1950-92
	1993	1950-93
	1994	1950-94
	1995	1950-95
	1996	1950-96
	1997	1950-97

Sujet	Année de l'édition	Période considérée
	1998-2000	1950-00
	2001	1950-01
	2002	1950-02
	2003	1950-03
	2004	1950-04
	2005	1950-05
	2006	1950-06
	2007	1950-07
	2008	1950-08
	2009-2010	1950-10
	2011	1960-11
	2012	1960-12
	2013	1960-13
	2014	1960-14
	2015	1960-15
	2016	1960-16
	2017	1960-17
	2018	1960-18
Population	1952	Dernière
des villes (capitale)	1955	1945-54
	1957	Dernière
	1960	1939-61
	1962	1955-62
	1963	1955-63
	1964-1969	Dernière
	1970	1950-70
	1971	1962-71
	1972	Dernière
	1973	1965-73
	1974-2018	Dernière
Population	1952	Dernière
des villes (de 100 000	1955	1945-54
habitants et plus)	1957	Dernière
	1960	1939-61
	1962	1955-62
	1963	1955-63
	1964-1969	Dernière
	1970	1950-70
	1971	1962-71
	1972	Dernière
	1973	1965-73
	1974-2018	Dernière
Population	1949-50	1920-49
du monde	1951	1950
	1952	1920-51
	1953	1920-52
	1954	1920-53
	1955	1920-54
	1956	1920-55
	1957	1920-56

Index historique
(Voir notes à la fin de l'index)

Sujet	Année de l'édition	Période considérée	Sujet	Année de l'édition	Période considérée
	1958	1920-57		2013	1960-13
	1959	1920-58		2014	1960-14
	1960	1920-59		2015	1960-15
	1961	1920-60		2016	1960-16
	1962	1920-61		2017	1960-17
	1963	1930-62		2018	1960-18
	1964	1930-63			
	1965	1930-65	Population	1987	1975-86
	1966	1930-66	effectifs des ménages,	1995	1950-95
	1967	1930-67	âge, sexe et résidence		
	1968	1930-68	urbaine/rurale		
	1969	1930-69			
	1970	1950-70	Population	1968	Dernière
	1971	1950-71	féminine, selon l'âge et		
	1972	1950-72	selon l'âge et la durée		
	1973	1950-73	du mariage		
	1974	1950-74			
	1975	1950-75	Population	1949-50	Dernière
	1976	1950-76	féminine, selon le	1954	1930-53
	1977	1950-77	nombre total d'enfants	1955	1945-54
	1978	1950-78	nés vivants et l'âge	1959	1949-58
	1979	1950-79		1963	1955-63
	1980	1950-80		1965	1955-65
	1981	1950-81		1969	Dernière
	1982	1950-82		1971	1962-71
	1983	1950-83		1973	1965-73 [iii]
	1984	1950-84		1975	1965-74
	1985	1950-85		1978SR [i]	1948-77
	1986	1950-86		1981	1972-80
	1987	1950-87		1986	1977-85
	1988	1950-88		1997SR [ii]	1948-96
	1989	1950-89			
	1990	1950-90	Population	1949-50	Dernière
	1991	1950-91	féminine, selon le	1954	1930-53
	1992	1950-92	nombre total d'enfants	1955	1945-54
	1993	1950-93	vivants et l'âge	1959	1949-58
	1994	1950-94		1963	1955-63
	1995	1950-95		1965	1955-65
	1996	1950-96		1968-1969	Dernière
	1997	1950-97		1971	1962-71
	1998-2000	1950-00		1973	1965-73 [iii]
	2001	1950-01		1975	1965-74
	2002	1950-02		1978SR [i]	1948-77
	2003	1950-03		1981	1972-80
	2004	1950-04		1986	1977-85
	2005	1950-05		1997SR [ii]	1948-96
	2006	1950-06			
	2007	1950-07	Population	1968	Dernière
	2008	1950-08	féminine mariée: selon		
	2009-2010	1950-10	l'âge actuel et la durée		
	2011	1960-11	du présent mariage		
	2012	1960-12	Population	1956	1945-55
				1963	1955-63

Sujet	Année de l'édition	Période considérée
fréquentant l'école selon l'âge et le sexe	1964	1955-64 [iii]
	1971	1962-71
	1973	1965-73 [iii]
	1979	1970-79
	1983	1974-83
	1988	1980-88 [iii]
	1993	1985-93 [iii]
Population.......................... inactive par sous-groupes, âge et sexe	1956	1945-55
	1964	1955-64
	1972	1962-72
	1973	1965-73 [iii]
	1979	1970-79 [iii]
	1984	1974-84
	1988	1980-88 [iii]
	1994	1985-94
Population.......................... mariée selon l'âge et le sexe (nombres et pourcentages)	1954	1926-52
	1960	1920-60
	1970	1950-70
	voir également: Population selon l'état matrimonial	
Population.......................... par année d'âge et par sexe	1955	1945-54
	1962	1955-62
	1963	1955-63 [iii]
	1971	1962-71
	1973	1965-73 [iii]
	1979	1970-79 [iii]
	1983	1974-83
	1988	1980-88 [iii]
	1993	1985-93
Population.......................... par groupes d'âge et par sexe (dénombrée)	1948-1952	Dernière
	1953	1950-52
	1954-1959	Dernière
	1960	1940-60
	1961	Dernière
	1962	1955-62
	1963	1955-63
	1964	1955-64 [iii]
	1965-1969	Dernière
	1970	1950-70
	1971	1962-71
	1972	Dernière
	1973	1965-73
	1974-1978	Dernière
	1978SR [i]	1948-77
	1979-1991	Dernière
	1991 VP [v]	1950-90
	1992-1997	Dernière
	1997SR [ii]	1948-97
	1998-2018	Dernière
Population.......................... par groupes d'âge et par sexe (estimée)	1948	1945 et der'
	1949-50	Dernière
	1951-1954	Dernière
	1955-1959	Dernière
	1960	1940-60
	1961-1969	Dernière
	1970	1950-70
	1971-1997	Dernière
	1997SR [ii]	1948-97
	1998-2018	Dernière
Population.......................... par groupes d'âge et par sexe (pourcentage)	1948	1945 et der'
	1949-50	Dernière
	1951-1952	Dernière
Population.......................... par ménages, nombres et dimension moyenne selon la résidence (urbaine/rurale)	1955	1945-54
	1962	1955-62
	1963	1955-63 [iii]
	1968	Dernière
	1971	1962-71
	1973	1965-72 [iii]
	1976	1ernière
	1982	Dernière
	1987	1975-86
	1990	1980-89
	1995	1985-95
	voir aussi: Ménages	
Population.......................... personnes âgées selon caractéristique socio-démographique	1991VP [v]	1950-90
Population.......................... selon caractéristique économique	1991VP [v]	1950-90
Population.......................... personnes atteintes d'incapacités	1991VP [v]	Dernière
Population.......................... rurale	*voir: urbaine/rurale (résidence), ci-dessous*	
Population.......................... selon la composition ethnique et le sexe	1956	1945-55
	1963	1955-63
	1964	1955-64 [iii]
	1971	1962-71
	1973	1965-73 [iii]
	1979	1970-79 [iii]
	1983	1974-83

Sujet	Année de l'édition	Période considérée
	1988	1980-88 [iii]
	1993	1985-93
Population selon l'état matrimonial, l'âge et le sexe	1948	Dernière
	1949-50	1926-48
	1955	1945-54
	1958	1945-57
	1962	1955-62
	1963	1955-63 [iii]
	1965	1955-65
	1968	1955-67
	1971	1962-71
	1973	1965-73 [iii]
	1976	1966-75
	1978 SR [i]	1948-77
	1982	1972-81
	1987	1975-86
	1990	1980-89
	1997SR [ii]	1948-96

voir également: Population mariée et célibataire

Sujet	Année de l'édition	Période considérée
Population selon le type de ménage et la résidence urbaine/rurale	1987	1975-86
	1995	1985-95
Population selon l'importance des localités de 100 000 habitants et plus	1948	Dernière
	1952	Dernière
	1955	1945-54
	1960	1920-61
	1962	1955-62
	1963	1955-63 [iii]
	1970	1950-70
	1971	1962-71
	1973	1965-73 [iii]
	1979	1970-79 [iii]
	1983	1974-83
	1988	1980-88 [iii]
	1993	1985-93
Population selon l'importance des localités de 20 000 habitants et plus	1948	Dernière
	1952	Dernière
	1955	1945-54
	1960	1920-61
	1962	1955-62
	1963	1955-63 [iii]
	1970	1950-70
	1971	1962-71
	1973	1965-73 [iii]
	1979	1970-79 [iii]
	1983	1974-83
	1988	1980-88 [iii]

Sujet	Année de l'édition	Période considérée
	1993	1985-93
Population selon l'importance des localités et le sexe	1948	Dernière
	1952	Dernière
	1955	1945-54
	1962	1955-62
	1963	1955-63 [iii]
	1971	1962-71
	1973	1965-73 [iii]
	1979	1970-79 [iii]
	1983	1974-83
	1988	1980-88 [iii]
	1993	1985-93
Population selon la langue et le sexe	1956	1945-55
	1963	1955-63
	1964	1955-64 [iii]
	1971	1962-71
	1973	1965-73 [iii]
	1979	1970-79 [iii]
	1983	1974-83
	1988	1980-88 [iii]
	1993	1985-93
Population selon le niveau d'instruction, l'âge et le sexe	1956	1945-55
	1963	1955-63
	1964	1955-64 [iii]
	1971	1962-71
	1973	1965-73 [iii]
	1979	1970-79 [iii]
	1983	1974-83
	1988	1980-88 [iii]
	1993	1985-93
Population selon le pays ou zone de naissance et le sexe	1956	1945-55
	1963	1955-63
	1964	1955-64 [iii]
	1971	1962-71
	1973	1965-73 [iii]
Population selon le pays ou zone de naissance et le sexe et l'âge	1977	Dernière
	1983	1974-83
	1989	1980-88
Population selon la nationalité juridique	1956	1945-55
	1963	1955-63
	1964	1955-64 [iii]
	1971	1962-71
	1973	1965-73 [iii]
Population	1977	Dernière
	1983	1974-83

Sujet	Année de l'édition	Période considérée	Sujet	Année de l'édition	Période considérée
selon la nationalité juridique et le sexe et l'âge	1989	1980-88			
			Population......................		voir: des principales divisions administratives, ci-dessus
Population....................	1948-1952	Dernière	selon les principales divisions administratives		
selon le sexe (dénombrée):	1953	1950-52			
	1954-1959	Dernière	Population......................	1956	1945-55
	1960	1900-61	selon la religion et le	1963	1955-63
	1961	Dernière	sexe	1964	1955-64 [iii]
	1962	1900-62		1971	1962-71
	1963	1955-63		1973	1965-73 [iii]
	1964	1955-64		1979	1970-79 [iii]
	1965-1969	Dernière		1983	1974-83
	1970	1950-70		1988	1980-88 [iii]
	1971	1962-71		1993	1985-93
	1972	Dernière			
	1973	1965-73	Population......................	1968	1964-68
	1974-1978	Dernière	selon la résidence	1969	1965-69
	1978SR [i]	1948-78	(urbaine/rurale)	1970	1950-70
	1979-1982	Dernière		1971	1962-71
	1983	1974-83		1972	1968-72
	1984-1991	Dernière		1973	1965-73
	1991 VP [v]	1950-90		1974	1966-74
	1992-1997	Dernière		1975	1967-75
	1997SR [ii]	1948-97		1976	1967-76
	1998-2018	Dernière		1977	1968-77
				1978	1969-78
-selon le sexe (estimée)	1948-1949-50	1945 et der'		1979	1970-79
	1951-1954	Dernière [iii]		1980	1971-80
	1955-1959	Dernière		1981	1972-81
	1960	1940-60		1982	1973-82
	1961-1969	Dernière		1983	1974-83
	1970	1950-70		1984	1975-84
	1971	1962-71		1985	1976-85
	1972	Dernière		1986	1977-86
	1973	1965-73		1987	1978-87
	1974-1997	Dernière		1988	1979-88
	1997SR [ii]	1948-97		1989	1980-89
	1998-2004	Dernière		1990	1981-90
	2005	1996-05		1991	1982-91
	2006	1997-06		1992	1983-92
	2007	1998-07		1993	1984-93
	2008	1999-08		1994	1985-94
	2009-2010	2001-10		1995	1986-95
	2011	2002-11		1996	1987-96
	2012	2003-12		1997	1988-97
	2013	2004-13		1998	1989-98
	2014	2005-14		1999	1990-99
	2015	2006-15		2000	1991-00
	2016	2007-16		2001	1992-01
	2017	2008-17		2002	1993-02
	2018	2009-18		2003	1994-03
				2004	1995-04

Sujet	Année de l'édition	Période considérée	Sujet	Année de l'édition	Période considérée
	2005	1996-05			
	2006	1997-06	-selon l'âge et le	1963	Dernière
	2007	1998-07	sexe: estimée	1967	Dernière
	2008	1999-08		1970	1950-70
	2009-2010	2001-10		1971-1997	Dernière
	2011	2002-11		1997SR [II]	1948-97
	2012	2003-12		1998-2018	Dernière
	2013	2004-13			
	2014	2005-14	-selon	1971	1962-71
	2015	2006-15	l'alphabétisme,	1973	1965-73 [III]
	2016	2007-16	l'âge et le sexe	1979	1970-79 [III]
	2017	2008-17		1983	1974-83
	2018	2009-18		1988	1980-88 [III]
				1993	1985-93
Population..........................	1948-1952	Dernière			
selon la résidence	1953	1950-52	-selon la	1971	1962-71
(urbaine/rurale) et :	1954-1959	Dernière	composition	1973	1965-73 [III]
-féminine: selon le	1971	1962-71	ethnique et le sexe	1979	1970-79 [III]
nombre total	1973	1965-73 [III]		1983	1974-83
d'enfants nés	1975	1965-74		1988	1980-88 [III]
vivants et l'âge	1978SR [I]	1948-77		1993	1985-93
	1981	1972-80			
	1986	1977-85	-selon l'état	1971	1962-71
	1997SR [II]	1948-96	matrimonial, l'âge	1973	1965-73 [III]
			et le sexe		
-féminine: selon le	1971	1962-71			
nombre total	1973	1965-73 [III]	-selon la langue et	1971	1962-71
d'enfants vivants et	1975	1965-74	le sexe	1973	1965-73 [III]
l'âge	1978SR [I]	1948-77		1979	1970-79 [III]
	1981	1972-80		1983	1974-83
	1986	1977-85		1988	1980-88 [III]
	1997SR [II]	1948-96		1993	1985-93
-fréquentant l'école	1971	1962-71	-selon la nationalité	1971	1962-71
selon l'âge et le	1973	1965-73 [III]	juridique et le sexe	1973	1965-73 [III]
sexe	1979	1970-79 [III]			
	1983	1974-83	-selon la nationalité	1977	Dernière
	1988	1980-88 [III]	juridique et le sexe	1983	1974-83
	1993	1985-93	et l'âge	1989	1980-88
-selon l'âge et le	1963	1955-63	-selon le niveau	1971	1962-71
sexe: dénombrée	1964	1955-64 [III]	d'instruction, l'âge	1973	1965-73 [III]
	1967	Dernière	et le sexe	1979	1970-79 [III]
	1970	1950-70		1983	1974-83
	1971	1962-71		1988	1980-88 [III]
	1972	Dernière		1993	1985-93
	1973	1965-73			
	1974-78	Dernière	-selon le pays ou	1971	1962-71
	1978SR [I]	1948-77	zone de naissance	1973	1965-73 [III]
	1979-91	Dernière	et le sexe		
	1991VP [V]	1950-90			
	1992-97	Dernière	-selon le pays ou	1977	Dernière
	1997SR [II]	1948-97	zone de naissance	1983	1974-83
	1998-2018	Dernière	et le sexe et l'âge	1989	1980-88

Sujet	Année de l'édition	Période considérée	Sujet	Année de l'édition	Période considérée
-selon les	1971	1962-71		2000	1991-00
principales divisions	1973	1965-73 [iii]		2001	1992-01
administratives	1979	1970-79 [iii]		2002	1993-02
	1983	1974-83		2003	1994-03
	1988	1980-88 [iii]		2004	1995-04
	1993	1985-93		2005	1996-05
				2006	1997-06
				2007	1998-07
-selon la religion et	1971	1962-71		2008	1999-08
le sexe	1973	1965-73 [iii]		2009-2010	2001-10
	1979	1970-79 [iii]		2011	2002-11
	1983	1974-83		2012	2003-12
	1988	1980-88 [iii]		2013	2004-13
	1993	1985-93		2014	2005-14
				2015	2006-15
-selon le sexe	1948	Dernière		2016	2007-16
(nombres)	1952	1900-51		2017	2008-17
	1955	1945-54		2018	2009-18
	1960	1920-60			
	1962	1955-62	-selon le sexe	1948	Dernière
	1963	1955-63	(pourcentage)	1952	1900-51
	1964	1955-64 [iii]		1955	1945-54
	1967	Dernière		1960	1920-60
	1970	1950-70		1962	1955-62
	1971	1962-71		1970	1950-70
	1972	Dernière		1971	1962-71
	1973	1965-73		1973	1965-73
	1974	1966-74		1974	1966-74
	1975	1967-75		1975	1967-75
	1976	1967-76		1976	1967-76
	1977	1968-77		1977	1968-77
	1978	1969-78		1978	1969-78
	1979	1970-79		1979	1970-79
	1980	1971-80		1980	1971-80
	1981	1972-81		1981	1972-81
	1982	1973-82		1982	1973-82
	1983	1974-83		1983	1974-83
	1984	1975-84		1984	1975-84
	1985	1976-85		1985	1976-85
	1986	1977-86		1986	1977-86
	1987	1978-87		1987	1978-87
	1988	1979-88		1988	1979-88
	1989	1980-89		1989	1980-89
	1990	1981-90		1990	1981-90
	1991	1982-91		1991	1982-91
	1992	1983-92		1992	1983-92
	1993	1984-93		1993	1984-93
	1994	1985-94		1994	1985-94
	1995	1986-95		1995	1986-95
	1996	1987-96		1996	1987-96
	1997	1988-97		1997	1988-97
	1998	1989-98		1998	1989-98
	1999	1990-99		1999	1990-99

Sujet	Année de l'édition	Période considérée	Sujet	Année de l'édition	Période considérée
	2000	1991-00	**Réfugiés selon le pays ou zone de destination**...........	1952	1947-51
	2001	1992-01	rapatriés par l'Organisation Internationale pour les réfugiés		
	2002	1993-02			
	2003	1994-03			
	2004	1995-04			
	2005	1996-05			
	2006	1997-06	**Réfugiés selon le pays ou zone de destination**...........	1952	1947-51
	2007	1998-07	réinstallés par l'Organisation Internationale pour les réfugiés		
	2008	1999-08			
	2009-2010	2001-10			
	2011	2002-11			
	2012	2003-12			
	2013	2004-13	**Religion**	*voir: Population, selon la religion et le sexe*	
	2014	2005-14			
	2015	2006-15			
	2016	2007-16	**Reproduction, taux bruts et nets de**	1948	1920-47
	2017	2008-17		1949-50	1900-48
	2018	2009-18		1954	1920-53
				1965	1930-64
				1969	1963-68
Population........................ Vieillissement indicateurs divers	1991 VP [v]	1950-90		1975	1966-74
				1978SR [i]	1948-77
				1981	1962-80
Population........................ Villes	*voir: des villes, ci-dessus*			1986	1967-85
				1997SR [ii]	1948-96
R				1999CD [vii]	1980-99
Rapports..............................	*voir: Fécondité proportionnelle; Mortalité fœtale (tardive), rapports de; Mortalité périnatale, rapports de; Natalité proportionnelle; Rapports enfants-femmes*		**S**		
			Sans abri	*voir : Population, sans abri selon le sexe et l'âge*	
Rapports enfants-femmes..	1949-50	1900-50	**Sexe**...................................	*voir: la rubrique appropriée par sujet, p. ex., Immigrants; Mortalité, taux de; Naissance; Population, etc.*	
	1954	1900-52			
	1955	1945-54			
	1959	1935-59			
	1963	1955-63	**Situation dans la profession**	*voir: Population active*	
	1965	1945-65			
	1969	Dernière			
	1975	1966-74	**Sujet spécial des divers Annuaires démographiques**................		
	1978SR [i]	1948-77			
	1981	1962-80	-Démographie générale	1948	1900-48
	1986	1967-85		1953	1850-1953
	1997SR [ii]	1948-96			
	1999CD [vii]	1980-1999	-Divorce	*voir: Mariage et divorce, ci-dessous*	
Rapports enfants-femmes.. -dans les zones (urbaines/rurales)	1965	Dernière			
	1969	Dernière	-Mariage et Divorce	1958	1930-57
				1968	1920-68
				1976	1957-76
				1982	1963-82

Sujet	Année de l'édition	Période considérée	Sujet	Année de l'édition	Période considérée
	1990	1971-90		1964	1955-64 [iii]
				1971	1962-71
-Migration (Internationale)	1977	1958-76		1973	1965-73 [iii]
	1989	1975-88		1979	1970-79 [iii]
				1983	1974-83
-Mortalité	1951	1905-50		1988	1980-88 [iii]
	1957	1930-56		1993	1985-93
	1961	1945-61			
	1966	1920-66	· Caractéristiques individuelles	1955	1945-54
	1967	1900-67		1962	1955-62
	1974	1965-74		1971	1962-71
	1980	1971-80		1973	1965-73 [iii]
	1985	1976-85		1979	1970-79 [iii]
	1992	1983-92		1983	1974-83
	1996	1987-96		1988	1980-88 [iii]
				1993	1985-93
-Natalité	1949-50	1932-49	· Caractéristiques relatives à l'éducation	1955	1945-54
	1954	1920-53		1956	1945-55
	1959	1920-58			
	1965	1920-65		1963	1955-63 [iii]
	1969	1925-69		1964	1955-64
	1975	1956-75		1971	1962-71
	1981	1962-81		1973	1965-73 [iii]
	1986	1967-86		1979	1970-79
	1992	1983-92		1983	1974-83
	1999CD [vii]	1980-99		1988	1980-88
				1993	1985-93
-Nuptialité	voir: Mariage et Divorce, ci-dessus		· Caractéristiques relatives aux ménages	1955	1945-54
				1962	1955-62
-Recensements de population:				1963	1955-63 [iii]
· Caractéristiques économiques	1956	1945-55		1971	1962-71
	1964	1955-64		1973	1965-73 [iii]
	1972	1962-72		1976	1966-75
	1973	1965-73 [iii]		1983	1974-83
	1979	1970-79 [iii]		1987	1975-86
	1984	1974-84		1995	1985-95
	1988	1980-88 [iii]		2013 [viii]	1995-2013
	1994	1985-94			
	2014 [viii]	1995-2014	· Caractéristiques relatives à la fécondité	1949-50	1900-50
				1954	1900-53
· Caractéristiques ethniques	1956	1945-55		1955	1945-54
	1963	1955-63		1959	1935-59
	1964	1955-64		1963	1955-63
	1971	1962-71		1965	1955-65
	1973	1965-73 [iii]		1969	Dernière
	1979	1970-79 [iii]		1971	1962-71
	1983	1974-83		1973	1965-73 [iii]
	1988	1980-88 [iii]		1975	1965-75
	1993	1985-93		1981	1972-81
· Caractéristiques géographiques	1952	1900-51		1986	1977-86
	1955	1945-54		1992	1983-92
	1962	1955-62			

Sujet	Année de l'édition	Période considérée
	1999CD [vii]	1980-99
-Evolution de la population	1960	1920-60
	1970	1950-70
-Supplément historique	1978SR [i]	1948-78
	1997SR [ii]	1948-97
-Vieillissement de la population et situation des personnes âgées	1991VP [v]	1950-90
Superficie .... des continents	1949-50-1999	Dernière
	2000	2000
	2001	2001
	2002	2002
	2003	2003
	2004	2004
	2005	2005
	2006	2006
	2007	2007
	2008	2008
	2009-2010	2010
	2011	2011
	2012	2012
	2013	2013
	2014	2014
	2015	2015
	2016	2016
	2017	2017
	2018	2018
Superficie .... des grandes régions (continentales)	1964-1999	Dernière
	2000	2000
	2001	2001
	2002	2002
	2003	2003
	2004	2004
	2005	2005
	2006	2006
	2007	2007
	2008	2008
	2009-2010	2010
	2011	2011
	2012	2012
	2013	2013
	2014	2014
	2015	2015
	2016	2016
	2017	2017
	2018	2018
Superficie .... des pays ou zones	1948-2018	Dernière

Sujet	Année de l'édition	Période considérée
Superficie .... des régions	1952-1999	Dernière
	2000	2000
	2001	2001
	2002	2002
	2003	2003
	2004	2004
	2005	2005
	2006	2006
	2007	2007
	2008	2008
	2009-2010	2010
	2011	2011
	2012	2012
	2013	2013
	2014	2014
	2015	2015
	2016	2016
	2017	2017
	2018	2018
Superficie .... du monde	1949-50-1999	Dernière
	2000	2000
	2001	2001
	2004	2004
	2005	2005
	2006	2006
	2007	2007
	2008	2008
	2009-2010	2010
	2011	2011
	2012	2012
	2013	2013
	2014	2014
	2015	2015
	2016	2016
	2017	2017
	2018	2018
Survivants	*voir: Mortalité, tables de*	

T

Tables de mortalité	*voir: Mortalité, tables de*	

Index historique
(Voir notes à la fin de l'index)

Sujet	Année de l'édition	Période considérée
Taux............................		voir: Accroissement intercensitaire de la population; Accroissement naturel; Alphabétisme; Analphabétisme; Annulation; Divortialité; Fécondité Intercensitaire; Mortalité Infantile, Mortalité maternelle; Mortalité néonatale; Mortalité post-néonatale; Mortalité, tables de; Mortalité; Natalité; Nuptialité; Reproduction; taux bruts et nets de
Taux bruts de reproduction		voir: Reproduction
Taux nets de reproduction.		voir: Reproduction
Texte spécial		voir liste détaillée dans l'Appendice de cet index

Sujet	Année de l'édition	Période considérée
U		
Urbaine/rurale (décès)		voir: Décès
Urbaine/rurale (ménages: dimension moyenne des) ..		voir: Ménages
Urbaine/rurale (mortalité infantile)		voir: Mortalité infantile
Urbaine/rurale (naissances)		voir: Naissances
Urbaine/rurale(population)		voir: Population selon la résidence (urbaine/rurale)
V		
Vieillissement		voir: Population
Villes...............................		voir: Population

APPENDICE

Texte spécial de chaque Annuaire démographique

Divorce:

"Application des statistiques de la nuptialité et de la divortialité", 1958.

Mariage:

"Application des statistiques de la nuptialité et de la divortialité", 1958.

Ménages:

"Concepts et définitions des ménages, du chef de ménage et de la population des collectivités", 1987.

Migration:

"'Statistiques des migrations internationales",1977.

Mortalité:

"Tendances récentes de la mortalité", 1951.
"Développement des statistiques des causes de décès",1951.
"Les facteurs du fléchissement de la mortalité",1957.
"Notes sur les méthodes d'évaluation de la fiabilité des statistiques classiques de la mortalité",1961.
"Mortalité: Tendances récentes",1966.
"Tendances de la mortalité chez les personnes âgées",1991VP [v].

Natalité:

"Présentation graphiques des tendances de la fécondité",1959.

"Taux de natalité: Tendances récentes",1965.

Population:

"Tendances démo-graphiques mondiales,1920-1949",1949-50.
"Mouvements d'urbanisation et ses caractéristiques",1952.
"Les recensements de population de 1950",1955.
"Situation démographique mondiale",1956.
"Ce que nous savons de l'état et de l'évolution de la population mondiale",1960.
"Notes sur les statistiques disponibles des recensements nationaux de population et méthodes d'évaluation de leur exactitude",1962.
"Disponibilité et qualité de certaines données statistiques fondées sur les recensements de population effectués entre 1955 et 1963",1963.
"Disponibilité de certaines statistiques fondées sur les recensements de population: 1955-1964",1964.

"Définitions et concepts statistiques de la population urbaine et de la population rurale",1967.
"Application des statistiques de la nuptialité et de la divortialité",1958.
"Ce que nous savons de l'état et de l'évolution de la population mondiale",1970.
"Recommandations de l'Organisation des Nations Unies quant aux sujets sur lesquels doit porter un recensement de population, en regard de la pratique adoptée par les différents pays dans les recensements nationaux effectués de 1965 à 1971",1971.
"Les définitions statistiques de la population urbaine et leurs usages en démographie appliquée",1972.

"Evolution récente de la fécondité dans le monde",1969.
"Dates des recensements nationaux de la population et de l'habitation effectués au cours de la décennie 1965-1974", 1974.

"Dates des recensements nationaux de la population et de l'habitation effectués ou prévus, au cours de la décennie 1975-1984",1979.

"Dates des recensements nationaux de la population et/ou de l'habitation effectués au cours de la décennie 1965-1974 et effectués ou prévus au cours de la décennie1975-1984",1983.

"Définitions et concepts statistiques du ménage",1968.

"Dates des recensements nationaux de la population et/ou de l'habitation effectués au cours de la décennie 1975-1984 et effectués ou prévus au cours de la décennie1985-1994", 1988, 1993.

"Statistiques concernant la population active: un aperçu",1984.

"'Etude du vieillissement et de la situation des personnes âgées: Besoins particuliers",1991VP [v].

"Les incapacités", 1991VP [v].

"Le vieillissement", 1991VP [v].

Notes générales

Cet index alphabétique donne la liste des sujets traités dans chacune de 69 éditions de l'Annuaire démographique. La colonne "Année de l'édition" indique l'édition spécifique dans laquelle le sujet a été traité. Sauf indication contraire, la colonne "Période considérée" désigne les années pour lesquelles les statistiques annuelles apparaissant dans l'Annuaire démographique sont indiquées sous la colonne "Année de l'édition". La rubrique "Dernière" ou " 2-Dernières" indique que les données représentent la ou les dernières années disponibles seulement.

---

[i] Le Supplément rétrospectif du 30ème Annuaire Démographique fait l'objet d'un tirage spécial publié en 1979.

[ii] Le Supplément rétrospectif du 49ème Annuaire Démographique fait l'objet d'un tirage spécial (CD-ROM) publié en 2000.

[iii] Données non disponibles dans l'édition précédente seulement.

[iv] Titres non disponibles dans la bibliographie précédente seulement.

[v] Vieillissement de la population.

[vi] Taux moyens pour 5 ans.

[vii] Le Supplément du 51 Annuaire Démographique, ayant comme suject la natalité, fait l'objet d'un tirage spécial (CD-ROM) publié en 2002.

[viii] Les tableaux sont publiés en ligne.

SUPPLEMENTAL INDEX OF DATASETS PUBLISHED ONLINE[1]

In recent years, additionally to publishing annually the United Nations *Demographic Yearbook*, several demographic and social datasets are published online via the UNdata portal. UNdata portal is an internet based data service maintained by the Statistics Division of the Department of Economic and Social Affairs of the United Nations. Below is an alphabetical order list of datasets published online as of October 2019 . These datasets can be accessed at http://data.un.org/Explorer.aspx?d=POP.

- City population by sex, city and city type
- Deaths by age, sex and urban/rural residence
- Deaths by cause of death, age and sex
- Deaths by month of death
- Deaths by sex and urban/rural residence
- Divorces by urban/rural residence
- Economically active foreign-born population by occupation, age, sex and urban/rural residence
- Employed population by age, sex and industry
- Employed population by age, sex and marital status
- Employed population by occupation, age and sex
- Employed population by status in employment, age and sex
- Employed population by status in employment, industry and sex
- Employed population by status in employment, occupation and sex
- Female population by age, number of children ever born and urban/rural residence
- Female population by age, number of children living and urban/rural residence
- Foreign population (non-citizens) 15 years of age or over by country of citizenship, educational attainment and sex
- Foreign population (non-citizens) by country of citizenship, age and sex
- Foreign-born population 15 years of age or over by country/area of birth, educational attainment and sex
- Foreign-born population by country/area of birth, age and sex
- Households by age and sex of reference person and by size of household
- Households by broad types of living quarters/number of roofless by urban/rural location
- Households by broad types of living quarters/number of roofless for selected cities
- Households by type of household and sex and marital status of head of household or other reference member
- Households by type of household, age and sex of head of household or other reference member
- Households in housing units by type of housing unit and availability of communication technology devices/access to Internet for selected cities
- Households in housing units by type of housing unit and tenure of household for selected cities
- Households in housing units by type of housing unit and urban/rural residence
- Households in housing units by type of housing unit for selected cities
- Households in housing units by type of housing unit, availability of communication technology devices/access to Internet by urban/rural location
- Households in housing units by type of housing unit, tenure of household and urban/rural residence
- Infant deaths by sex and urban/rural residence
- Inflows by purpose of staying abroad and sex
- Inflows by reason for admission and sex
- Legally induced abortions by urban/rural residence of woman
- Live births by age of mother and sex of child
- Live births by birth order and age of mother
- Live births by birth order and sex of child
- Live births by birth weight and sex of child
- Live births by gestational age
- Live births by month of birth
- Live births by plurality
- Live births by sex and urban/rural residence
- Live births in wedlock by duration of marriage
- Living quarters by broad types and urban/rural location
- Living quarters by broad types for selected cities

---

[1] This supplemental index is available only in English.

- Marriages by urban/rural residence
- Marriages cross-classified by previous marital status of husband and wife
- Native and foreign-born population by age, sex and urban/rural residence
- Number of departing international migrants by citizenship status, age and sex
- Number of emigrating citizens by future country of usual residence and sex
- Number of incoming foreign migrants by country of citizenship and sex
- Number of incoming international migrants by previous country of usual residence and sex
- Number of incoming migrants by citizenship status, age and sex
- Occupants of housing units by type of housing unit and number of rooms for selected cities
- Occupants of housing units by type of housing unit and urban/rural residence
- Occupants of housing units by type of housing unit for selected cities
- Occupants of housing units by type of housing unit, number of rooms and urban/rural residence
- Occupied housing units by type of housing unit and availability of kitchen for selected cities
- Occupied housing units by type of housing unit and construction material of outer walls for selected cities
- Occupied housing units by type of housing unit and main source of drinking water for selected cities
- Occupied housing units by type of housing unit and main type of fuel used for cooking for selected cities
- Occupied housing units by type of housing unit and main type of solid waste disposal for selected cities
- Occupied housing units by type of housing unit and number of rooms for selected cities
- Occupied housing units by type of housing unit and type of bathing facilities for selected cities
- Occupied housing units by type of housing unit and type of lighting for selected cities
- Occupied housing units by type of housing unit and type of toilet for selected cities
- Occupied housing units by type of housing unit and type of water supply system for selected cities
- Occupied housing units by type of housing unit and urban/rural location
- Occupied housing units by type of housing unit for selected cities
- Occupied housing units by type of housing unit, availability of kitchen and urban/rural location
- Occupied housing units by type of housing unit, construction material of outer walls and urban/rural residence
- Occupied housing units by type of housing unit, main source of drinking water and urban/rural location
- Occupied housing units by type of housing unit, main type of fuel used for cooking and urban/rural location
- Occupied housing units by type of housing unit, main type of solid waste disposal and urban/rural location
- Occupied housing units by type of housing unit, number of rooms and urban/rural location
- Occupied housing units by type of housing unit, type of bathing facilities and urban/rural location
- Occupied housing units by type of housing unit, type of lighting and urban/rural location
- Occupied housing units by type of housing unit, type of toilet and urban/rural location
- Occupied housing units by type of housing unit, type of water supply system and urban/rural location
- Outflows by purpose of going abroad and sex
- Outflows by status at time of departure and sex
- Population 15 years of age and over, by educational attainment, age and sex
- Population 5 to 24 years of age by school attendance, sex and urban/rural residence
- Population by activity status, age, sex and urban/rural residence
- Population by age, sex and urban/rural residence
- Population by broad types of living quarters/number of roofless and sex for selected cities
- Population by broad types of living quarters/number of roofless, sex and urban/rural residence
- Population by citizenship status, age and sex
- Population by language, sex and urban/rural residence
- Population by literacy, age, sex and urban/rural residence
- Population by marital status, age, sex and urban/rural residence
- Population by national and/or ethnic group, sex and urban/rural residence
- Population by religion, sex and urban/rural residence
- Population by sex and urban/rural residence
- Population by type of living quarters, age and sex
- Population in collective living quarters by type of living quarters and sex for selected cities
- Population in collective living quarters by type of living quarters, sex and urban/rural residence
- Population in households by relation to head of household or other reference member and by age and sex
- Population in households by type of household, age and sex
- Population in households by type of household, age and sex of head of household or other reference member
- Population not economically active by functional category, age, sex and urban/rural residence